Handbook of Terrorist and Insurgent Groups

Handbook of Terrorist and Insurgent Groups: A Global Survey of Threats, Tactics, and Characteristics examines the most current and significant terrorist and insurgent groups around the world. The purpose is to create a descriptive mosaic of what is a pointedly global security challenge.

The volume brings together conceptual approaches to terrorism, insurgency, and cyberterrorism with substantive and empirical analyses of individual groups, organisations, and networks. By doing so, not only does the coverage highlight the past, present, and future orientations of the most prominent groups, but it also examines and illustrates their key characteristics and how they operate, including key leaders and ideologues. Highlighting specific, individual groups, the chapters collectively present a robust and comprehensive outlook on the current geography of terrorism and insurgency groups operating in the world today.

This comprehensive volume brings the collective expertise and knowledge of more than 50 academics, intelligence and security officials, and professionals together, all of whom are considered subject experts in their respective areas of research and practice. The volume is based on both desk-based and fieldwork conducted by experts in these areas, incorporating analyses of secondary literature but also the use of primary data including first-hand interviews on the various groups' regions of operation, their tactics, and how their ideologies motivate their actions.

Handbook of Terrorist and Insurgent Groups
A Global Survey of Threats, Tactics, and Characteristics

Edited by
Scott N. Romaniuk
Animesh Roul
Amparo Pamela Fabe
János Besenyő

CRC Press
Taylor & Francis Group
Boca Raton London New York

CRC Press is an imprint of the
Taylor & Francis Group, an **informa** business

First edition published 2024
by CRC Press
2385 NW Executive Center Drive, Suite 320, Boca Raton FL 33431

and by CRC Press
4 Park Square, Milton Park, Abingdon, Oxon, OX14 4RN

CRC Press is an imprint of Taylor & Francis Group, LLC

ISBN: 978-1-138-38773-7 (hbk)
ISBN: 978-1-032-71490-5 (pbk)
ISBN: 978-0-429-42606-3 (ebk)

DOI: 10.4324/9780429426063

Typeset in Berling
by MPS Limited, Dehradun

CONTENTS

ABOUT THE EDITORS

Scott N. Romaniuk is a research fellow at the Centre for Contemporary Asia Studies, Corvinus Institute for Advanced Studies (CIAS), Corvinus University of Budapest. He was previously a Newton International Fellow of The British Academy and a visiting fellow at the International Centre for Policing and Security at the University of South Wales. Prior to that, he was a non-resident fellow at the Taiwan Centre for Security Studies, a non-resident visiting fellow at the Centre for Studies of South & South-East Asian Societies at Kazi Nazrul University, and a postdoctoral research fellow at the University of Alberta's China Institute. He holds a PhD in International Studies from the University of Trento. His research lies at the intersection of international relations (IR), geopolitics, and critical security studies, with regional foci on the Middle East, Africa, and the Indo-Pacific. His current work examines, in part, the regulation of emerging technologies, their role in great power politics and rivalries, and their implications for regional and global security architectures. He is the lead editor of the forthcoming Routledge Handbook of Artificial Intelligence and National Security; Money Laundering and Terrorism Financing through Hawala Money Transfer Operators (Palgrave Macmillan); China and Counter-Terrorism: Dimensions of Internal-External Security (Edinburgh University Press); and co-editor of The Palgrave Handbook of Geopolitics and Security in the Indo-Pacific (Springer). He can be reached at scott.romaniuk@uni-corvinus.hu. ORCID: https://orcid.org/0000-0001-5081-2515.

Animesh Roul is the executive director of the New Delhi-based policy research group Society for the Study of Peace and Conflict. He specializes in counterterrorism, radical Islam, terror financing, and armed conflict and violence in South Asia. Roul has written extensively on these subject areas, being published in edited books, journals, and policy magazines. He co-authored a book on India's indigenous terror group Indian Mujahideen (Springer, 2013). He is regularly cited in the *Washington Post*, *Reuters*, the *Wall Street Journal*, and *Hindustan Times*, among periodicals, and regularly contributes to The Jamestown Foundation's *Terrorism Monitor* and *Militant Leadership Monitor*.

Amparo Pamela Fabe is a Professor of Financial Terrorism and Transnational Organized Crime at the Philippine Public Safety College and the National Police College. Professor Fabe helped write Republic Act 11479, known as the Philippine's Anti-Terrorism Act of 2020, particularly the section on penalizing the material support for terrorism. She is a Visiting Fellow at the International Center for Policing and Security at the University of South Wales and a Fellow of the Daniel K. Inouye Asia-Pacific Center for Security Studies. She completed the WayOut Certification Training for the European Union Integrated Exit Program for Prison and Probation Program of the University of Toulouse Jean-Jaureas and the Postgraduate Program in Hate Crime/Hate Speech at the United Nations Interregional Crime and Justice Center, Rome, Italy. Professor Fabe is the Philippine National Police Representative to the Secretariat and to the ASEAN Senior Officials' Meeting on Transnational Crime (SOMTC). She is a Preventing/Countering Violent Extremism specialist of the Armed Forces of the Philippines. Fabe is a member of the United Nations Cryptocurrencies Working Group for Southeast Asia and a member of the United Nations Office of Drugs and Crime Contact Group on Sulu and Celebes Sea. Her affiliations include the American Chamber Overseas Security Advisory Council (East Asia and the Pacific), and the International Corrections and Prison Association.

János Besenyő is a Professor at the Óbuda University, Donát Bánki Faculty of Mechanical and Safety Engineering (Hungary) and head of the Africa Research Institute. Between 1987 and 2018, he served as a professional soldier and served in several peace operations in Africa and Afghanistan. He received a PhD in military science from Zrínyi Miklós National Defense University (Hungary) and he received a habilitated doctorate at Eötvös Loránd University (Hungary). In 2014, he established the Scientific Research Centre of the Hungarian Defence Forces General Staff and was its first leader from 2014 to 2018. His most recent publication is *Conflict and Peace in Western Sahara The Role of the UN's Peacekeeping Mission (MINURSO)*.

CONTRIBUTORS

Gizem Gönay Akbaş
Business Analyst
Turkey

Gordon Alley-Young
Kingsborough Community College - City University of New York
USA

Ferdinand Arslanian
University of St Andrews
UK

Fathima Azmiya Badurdeen
Technical University of Mombasa
Kenya

Matthew Bamber
Graduate Institute of International and Development Studies
Switzerland

Abdul Basit
S. Rajaratnam School of International Studies
Singapore

Piyali Basu
Women's Christian College
India

Nell Bennett
Macquarie University
Australia

János Besenyő
Óbuda University
Hungary

Sanchita Bhattacharya
Institute for Conflict Management
India

Jeroen J. J. Van den Bosch
Adam Mickiewicz University
Poland

Srinjoy Bose
University of New South Wales
Australia

Tobias Burgers
Fulbright University Vietnam
Vietnam

Pascal Carlucci
Radban Academy
UAE

Renny Castañeda
American University in the Emirates
UAE

Kalliopi Chainoglou
University of Macedonia
Greece

Sarah Clifford
University of Alberta
Canada

Nathaniel D. Danjibo
University of Ibadan
Nigeria

Biplab Debnath
Tripura University
India

Jorge Eduardo Delgado
University of Oxford
UK

Glen M. E. Duerr
Cedarville University
USA

Elif Merve Dumankaya
Bilkent University
Turkey

Marios P. Efthymiopoulos
Neapolis University Pafos
Cyprus

Nail Elhan
Hitit University
Turkey

Tyler Evans
American University in the Emirates
UAE

Mariam Farida
Macquarie University
Australia

Diana Flórez
King's College London
UK

Francis Grice
McDaniel College
USA

Suzette A. Haughton
The University of the West Indies
Mona Campus
Jamaica

tavis d. jules
Loyola University Chicago
USA

Tamer Kaşıkcı
Eskisehir Osmangazi University
Turkey

Filiz Katman
Istanbul Aydin University
Turkey

Serdar Kaya
Simon Fraser University
Canada

János Kemény
University of Public Service
Hungary

Attila Máté Kovács
Óbuda University
Hungary

Alok Kumar
Shri Lal Bahadur Shastri National Sanskrit University
India

Kleanthis Kyriakidis
American University in the Emirates
UAE

Wangchu Lama
Sikkim University
India

Olivier Lewis
Rabdan Academy
UAE

Paul Lushenko
U.S. Army War College
USA

Alexandra J. Macintire
McDaniel College
USA

Rohan Malhotra
Independent Researcher
India

Mary Manjikian
Regent University
USA

Péter Marton
Corvinus University of Budapest
Hungary

Scott McGallagher
University of Edinburgh
UK

Richard McNeil-Willson
Leiden University
Germany

Hikmet Mengüaslan
Aydın Adnan Menderes University
Turkey

Md Nurul Momen
University of Rajshahi
Bangladesh

Uddipan Mukherjee
Ministry of Defence
India

Ta-Mbi Nkongho
University of Buea
Cameroon

John Sunday Ojo
University of Portsmouth
UK

James Okolie-Osemene
University of Agriculture and Environmental Sciences
Nigeria

Adekunle Toyin Olawunmi
Chrisland University
Nigeria

David Andrew Omona
Uganda Christian University
Uganda

Anwar Ouassini
Delaware State University
USA

Nabil Ouassini
Prairie View A&M University
USA

Júlia Palik
Peace Research Institute Oslo (PRIO)
Norway

Sameer Patil
Observer Research Foundation (ORF)
India

Salvin Paul
Dr. B.R. Ambedkar University Delhi
India

Dennis F. Quilala
University of the Philippines Diliman
Philippines

Zia Ur Rehman
Freelance Journalist and Researcher
Pakistan

Tamanna Shah
Ohio University
USA

Gábor Sinkó
Óbuda University
Hungary

Donald Stoker
National Defense University
USA

S. S. Tabraz
Indian Institute of Technology
Madras
India

William A. Taylor
Angelo State University
USA

Joan Andrea Toledo
Indo-Pacific Alliance Corp.
Philippines

Arun Vishwanathan
Central University of Gujarat
India

Wendell C. Wallace
The University of the West Indies
St. Augustine
Trinidad and Tobago

Murat Yeşiltaş
Sakarya University
Turkey

Mustafa Yetim
Eskişehir Osmangazi University
Turkey

Fatma Yol
Bilkent University
Turkey

Noureddin Mahmoud Zaamout
University of Alberta
Canada

Farhan Zahid
National Police Academy in Islamabad
Pakistan

Michael G. Zekulin
The Australian National University
Australia

INTRODUCTION

The Contemporary Global Terrorism and Insurgency Landscape

Scott N. Romaniuk, Animesh Roul, Amparo Pamela Fabe, and János Besenyő

> *It is curious how a specific date—not a year, but a specific month and a specific day—have almost universally come to define a world historical crisis. ... In the case of the attacks on the World Trade Centre and the Pentagon, it is as if we instantly understood that the meaning of these 'events' were global, beyond locality, an out of geography experience. September 11 was a place we all shared.*
>
> Ken Booth and Tim Dunne (eds.), *Worlds in Collision: Terror and the Future of Global Order*, Palgrave Macmillan, 2002, p. 1.

TERROR TRANSFORMATIONS

The discourse on terrorism and insurgency has experienced a substantial shift since the tragic September 11, 2001, terrorist attacks on the United States (US), as Booth and Dunne accurately noted in the above quote. Even though terrorism and insurgency were present for many years prior to this important movement, non-state violent actors of all stripes, such as Islamist zealots, warlords, left-wing extremists, and anti-government resistance forces, continue to lead numerous terrorist and insurgent movements in the modern world. These groups present an enormous security challenge on a global scale. The most notable of them are transnational jihadist movements, which are under the control of a bicephalic Salafi-Takfiri monster that emerged from al-Qaeda, the original global militant Sunni Islamist network and the sinister architect of 9/11.

The landscape of global terrorism and insurgency has evolved into a multifaceted and interconnected phenomenon. Five main factors primarily influence the discourse surrounding terrorism and insurgency: i) typologies of terrorism; ii) terrorists' use of online digital platforms and online spaces; iii) dominance of jihadist organisations and jihadism globally; iv) the persistence of communist terrorist groups in India, Latin America, South America, and South and Southeast Asia; and v) terrorism financing.

The typology of terrorism serves as the primary focal point in discussions concerning terrorism and insurgency. The concept of typology has been described as "a purposive, planned selection, abstraction, combination and accentuation of a set of criteria with empirical references." Typologies can differ along several axes, including the relationship between a type and actual experience, the level of abstraction employed, the intended purpose of the type, the specific time period to which it pertains, the spatial extent it encompasses, and the functional requirements imposed upon it (McKinney, 1966). This volume thoroughly examines the different typologies of terrorism, opening with the conceptual framework as proposed by Donald Stoker. The focus of this volume revolves around acts of terrorism perpetrated by various terrorist organisations, including but not limited to the Islamic State (IS) (Ferdinand Arslanian, Scott N. Romaniuk, and Amparo Pamela Fabe), Jamaat-ul-Mujahideen (Md. Nurul Momen), Abu Sayyaf Group (Anwar Ouassini and Nabil Ouassini), Chechen group (Mary Manjikian), Jema'ah Islamiyah, Moro Islamic Liberation Front (Amparo Pamela Fabe and Scott N. Romaniuk), Euskadi Ta Askatasuna, or ETA (Neil Bennet). This volume also critically analyses the lone-wolf terrorist paradigm as discussed by tavis d. jules, Max Crumley-Effinger, and Scott McGallagher.

The use of digital platforms and online spaces by extremist groups is an integral component in the debate around terrorism and insurgency. According to the 2023 Report on Patterns of Online Terrorist Exploitation, terrorists persist in harnessing diverse, lesser-known digital venues to disseminate their ideological messaging. File-sharing is leveraged to the greatest extent in comparison to the quantity of content detected, while archiving platforms have the lowest level of efficiency in terms of content removal from their services. Wendell C. Wallace and Scott N. Romaniuk's chapter offers a stimulating analysis of the use of social media and the internet.

Thirdly, discussions surrounding terrorism and insurgency have been greatly influenced by the worldwide prevalence of jihadism and jihadist organisations. Jihadism progressed via a series of five distinct phases. The central figure of the initial phase was Sayyid Qutb, an advocate of "takfirism," which entailed the excommunication of fellow Muslims. The second stage involves cross-pollination, which refers to the blending of Salafism and Islamism promoted by the Muslim Brotherhood. Causation constitutes the third phase. The Soviet invasion of Afghanistan (1979–1989) and the

DOI: 10.4324/9780429426063-1

first Gulf War (1990–1991) introduced militant Salafist ideologies that define this period. The invasion of Iraq by the US marked the fifth phase, during which the objectives, strategies, and identities of jihadist organisations underwent gradual transformations.

Al-Qaeda and the Islamic State are the most widely recognised jihadist organisations. The long-term objectives of these two jihadist entities include the strict application of Sharia law and the reformation of society. Nonetheless, subtle distinctions exist regarding strategy, aim, and identity. While intimidating locals, ISIS focuses on issues that are distinct to Muslim communities. Additionally, members are recruited globally. A governmental structure, encompassing social services, taxation, administration, and humanitarian assistance, controls its domains. ISIS adheres to a zero-sum strategy, whereby individuals are either ISIS members or non-believers ("infidels"). Al-Qaeda seeks support from local communities for a strategic plan. The network establishes alliances with indigenous militias and strives to reduce unintended damage to others, thereby comparably enhancing its moral footing (United States Institute of Peace and Woodrow Wilson International Center for Scholars, 2021).

The presence of communist terrorist organisations in regions such as Latin America, South Asia, and Southeast Asia is the fourth major factor that dominates discussions concerning terrorism and insurgency. This volume places a special emphasis on the Communist Party of the Philippines-New People's Army-National Democratic Front (Amparo Pamela Fabe and Joan Andrea Toledo), the Revolutionary Armed Forces of Colombia-People's Army (Diana Flores and Olivier Lewis), the Maoist movements in India and Nepal (Uddipan Mukherjee), and the Sendero Luminoso (Suzette A. Haughton and Scott N. Romaniuk).

The fifth most prominent factor that permeates the discourse on terrorism and insurgency is the prevalence of terrorism finance among the various terrorist organisations, as determined by the rate at which they implement new financial mechanisms. Each chapter that focuses on a specific terrorist organisation dedicates a segment to the financing of terrorism. Terrorist organisations may employ the following methods to raise funds: i) using the internet to procure illicit commodities or raise funds; ii) soliciting donations for crowdfunding campaigns via social media and encrypted messaging platforms; and iii) transferring funds internationally among terrorist network participants via P2P value transfers.

CONTRIBUTION

To address the aforementioned established and emerging threats, as well as a number of lesser-known, localised insurgencies, this edited volume compiles the knowledge of an esteemed international panel of scholars, researchers, policymakers, and journalists. Their objective is to investigate the violent expressions of terrorist and insurgency movements that are afflicting various regions across the globe. The objective of this volume is to enhance comprehension of the preeminent concerns of our era through the implementation of both conceptual and regional methodologies. Through a thorough analysis of various networks and organisations, the distinguished authors present a comprehensive and robust perspective on the worldwide terrorism and insurgency landscape. Salient chapters of the book consist of the use of terrorism in war (Peter Marton), Correlations Between Terrorism, Fundamentalism, and Extremism (Salvin Paul, Alok Kumar, and Scott N. Romaniuk), Ta-Mbi Nkhongho and Molua Ewange's experiences assimilating from Boko Haram in Cameroon, and Epistemological Foundations of Terrorism (Salvin Paul, Sanchitta Bhattacharya, and Scott N. Romaniuk).

STRUCTURE OF THE BOOK

A variety of fundamental issues regarding this dynamic, multifaceted, and diverse subject are addressed in the conceptual section. The chapters that make up this section of the book investigate the foundational elements of insurgency and counterterrorism. These chapters include in-depth looks at foundational facets in the study of terrorism, such as Jeroen Bosch's "anatomy of terror" and "typology of insurgency." For instance, the chapter on the anatomy of terror reinterprets terror as a political concept. In addition to confronting other urgent matters, this section covers a variety of strategic and tactical topics, including religious terrorism, urban insurgency, hybrid threats, guerrilla warfare, and counterinsurgency architecture. The insightful observations made by Kleanthis Kyriakidis, Renny Castañeda, and Marios-Panagiotis Efthymiopoulos regarding Jihadi brides, indigenous terrorism (Michael G. Zekulin), and lone-wolf terrorism (tavis d. jules, Max Crumley-Effinger, and Scott McGallagher) are some of the most fascinating parts of this section. Since 2014, the rise of Islamic states throughout the Middle East and beyond has inextricably linked these concerns, and extremist brides in particular.

Scholars are currently debating whether women who participate in jihad are passive victims, active participants, or motivated by a desire for adventure or religious conviction. Similar to this, a series of incidents in both the US and Europe have prompted extensive analysis of the concept of the lone-wolf terrorist, which refers to an individual acting independently and motivated by personal motivations. Ted Kaczynski and Anders Breivik are notable examples of lone-wolf terrorists include individuals such as Ted Kaczynski and Anders Breivik. The chapter on home-grown terrorism critically analyses the topic, elucidating its transformation and progression over time.

Before initiating a region-wide exploration, the second section of the book has three critical chapters that look at the convergence of terrorism with cyberspace, commonly known as cyberterrorism. Each terrorist or insurgent group in the world exploits the internet and social media, posing a unique challenge before the international community, particularly tech giants, struggles to control the tsunami of digital propaganda, facilitation, and inciting acts of terrorism across the globe. For example, one of the chapters primarily discusses how terrorist and extremist groups use the internet and social media tools for radicalization and recruitment (Wendell Wallace and Scott N. Romaniuk).

Subsequently, the volume adopts a more systematic approach in the regional and case studies section, which comprises a sequence of comprehensive and targeted chapters examining terrorist and insurgency activities across all inhabited continents: Asia, Europe, Africa, and the Americas. This section purposefully organises over fifty chapters to provide comprehensive information on the most relevant and notoriously violent groups worldwide. The principal aim of these chapters is to furnish a comprehensive synopsis of terrorist and insurgency movements, emphasising the determinants influencing the formation of such groups or movements, organisational attributes, leadership configurations, violent endeavours, and potential future trajectories.

Africa

Over an extended period, the African continent has experienced myriad forms of insurgencies and terrorist attacks, particularly in North, Central, and Eastern Africa. The metrics show an upward trend, and terror groups' geographical influence is also growing across the regions. This section presents chapters that delve into prominent terrorist organisations associated with al-Qaeda and Islamic State groups. These include al-Qaeda in Islamic Maghreb (AQIM), al-Shabaab, Boko Haram, Ansar al-Din (AAD), and the Lord's Resistance Army (LRA) (Andrew David Omona and Scott N. Romaniuk). The collection of chapters exhibits the geographical spread and dominance of these groups, as well as their growing power in the absence of concerted international or regional counter-terrorism efforts. A vivid illustration of this can be seen in the case of Ansar al-Din (William Taylor), an organisation now operating in Mali with aspirations to extend its influence in Mauritania and the Ivory Coast. It is worth noting that Ansar al-Din has strong ties with AQIM (tavis d. jules and Scott N. Romaniuk) and is an integral member of the broader al-Qaeda "coalition" operating in Africa.

This section additionally provides clarification on the Movement for the Liberation of Azawad (MNLA) (Adekunle Olawunmi), a northern Mali-based al-Qaeda splinter (breakaway) group that has exploited the political instability in Mali to its advantage since 2012. The regional segment would have been incomplete if the two primary deadliest terrorist groups on the African continent, namely Boko Haram (Nathaniel Danjibo and Scott N. Romaniuk) and al-Shabaab (James Osemene and Scott N. Romaniuk), were not discussed. These groups are responsible for the highest number of fatalities and widespread sectarian and anti-government unrest in Nigeria, Somalia, and Kenya. Furthermore, their sphere of influence has extended to adjacent countries, including Chad, Niger, and Cameroon, among others. The chapters within this section provide insight into the historical underpinnings of these jihadist insurgencies, examining their ideological origins and potential future challenges.

The subsequent section of the book delves into an analysis of the most notable and historically significant far-left insurgency movements in the Americas. This part comprises chapters that examine a range of distinct groups, primarily focusing on anti-state guerrilla activities with the objective of attaining power and supplanting the governance of the putative "new democracy" in Colombia, Peru, and Mexico. Prominent chapters within the context of armed resistance movements in Latin America include the Revolutionary Armed Forces of Colombia (FARC) (Olivier Lewis and Diana Florez), the National Liberation Army (Jorge E. Delgado), and the Zapatista Army of National Liberation (tavis d. jules and Scott N. Romaniuk). This part also examines the Shining Path insurgency movement and its effects on the Peruvian state, as well as the counterinsurgency measures implemented to suppress and manage this movement (Suzette A. Haughton and Scott N. Romaniuk). This group of chapters provides a detailed examination of the economic and socio-political determinants seen in Latin American nations, which ultimately gave rise to the emergence of Marxist-Leninist guerrilla organisations.

Europe

The collection of chapters in this part highlights the historical impact of non-religious insurgencies and anti-establishment movements on many European nations, including Greece, Turkey, Spain, and Ireland, including the Irish Republican Army (IRA) (Sarah Clifford), the Fighting People's Revolutionary Powers (Kalliopi Chainoglou), and Euskadi Ta Askatasuna (ETA) (Nell Bennet).

The Middle East

Frequently characterised as the cradle of Islamic terrorism, the Middle East has a long history of experiencing terrorism and insurgency activities. The chapters in this section provide an in-depth examination of various terrorist and insurgency activities originating from the region, encompassing both Shia and Sunni-led groups. The volume is enriched by the inclusion of several prominent chapters, namely al-Qaeda in the Arabian Peninsula (Rohan Malhotra), Hay'at Tahrir al-Sham and Jabhat al-Nusra

(Serdar Kaya), Hezbollah (Mariam Farida), Hamas (Filiz Katman), and IS.

Central Asia

Since the 1980s, terrorism and insurgencies have been a common occurrence in Central Asia. Many terrorist groups and offshoots draw their ideological and operational inspiration from the conflict-stricken regions of Afghanistan and Pakistan, where these areas serve as their bases of operation, recruitment hubs, or training sites. This part comprises chapters that go into many major factions, including the Afghan Taliban (Nabil Ouassini and Anwar Ouassini), al-Qaeda Central (Abdul Basit), its influential South Asian branch al-Qaeda in the Indian Subcontinent (AQIS) in Pakistan (Farhan Zahid), and the Haqqani Network (Fatma Yol, Gizem Gönay Akbaş, and Elif Merve Dumankaya). This section also analyses the IS-Khorasan Province (ISKP), which is considered the most resilient branch of the Islamic State (IS) (Animesh Roul and Scott N. Romaniuk) and the Islamic Movement of Uzbekistan (IMU) (Rohan Malhotra). These organisations maintain operational headquarters in Afghanistan and the surrounding nations and have been involved in acts of terrorism within the region for years.

South Asia

For several decades, the stability of states in South Asia has been under threat from a multitude of active terrorist and rebel groups, numbering over a hundred. A considerable number of non-state armed groups exhibit a tendency to instigate or sustain acts of violence, targeting not just the state but frequently extending their aggression towards civilian populations and individuals of foreign nationality. Within this collection, the portion dedicated to South Asia includes chapters that discuss the highly diversified and dynamic terrorist landscape of this region. These chapters focus on several influential and active movements that operate inside Pakistan, Nepal, Sri Lanka, Bangladesh, and India. Groups of significance include Lashkar-e-Taiba Pakistan (Arun Vishwanathan and Sameer Patil), Jamaatul Mujahideen Bangladesh (Nurul Momen), Jaish-e-Muhamad (Sanchita Bhattacharjee), and Tehreek-e-Taliban Pakistan (TTP) (Zia Ur Rehman).

These chapters carefully examine the genesis and evolution of these groups, their links to international jihadist organisations, their ideological goals, and their operational capacities, in addition to the states' counter-terrorism tactics used against them. The Liberation Tigers of Tamil Eelam (LTTE) of Sri Lanka (Fathima Azmiya), the United Liberation Front of Assam (ULFA) (Piyali Basu), and the Nepalese Maoist Movement (Uddipan Mukherjee) are just a few of the section's distinctive chapters that change the focus of the story to non-religious separatist and far-left violence in the region.

Southeast Asia

Both indigenous and international factors have a role in the origins of terrorism and insurgency in Southeast Asia. These include regional ambitions against autocratic or oppressive rulers, administrations, and armed forces, in addition to the impact of the Ummatic global vision and the Caliphate worldview on the Muslim populace. Particularly over the past several decades, jihadist movements like the Islamic State and al-Qaeda have impacted Southeast Asian nations. This regional component consists of chapters covering organizations active in Indonesia, Thailand, the Philippines, and Myanmar. Southeast Asia continues to be a hotbed of violence and extremism, as demonstrated by the chapters on the al-Qaeda-affiliated Jema'ah Islamiyah in Indonesia (Scott N. Romaniuk and Amparo Pamela Fabe), the Arakan Rohingya Salvation Army (Scott N. Romaniuk and Animesh Roul), the Abu Sayyaf Group (Anwar Ouassini and Nabil Ouassini), and the Ethnic Armed Insurgent Groups in Myanmar (Biplab Debnath).

References

Booth, K. & Dunne, T. (eds.). (2002). Worlds in Collision: Terror and the Future of Global Order. London: Palgrave Macmillan.

McKinney, J.C. (1966). *Constructive typology and social theory*. New York: Appleton-Century-Crofts.

United States Institute of Peace and Woodrow Wilson International Center for Scholars. (2021). *The Jihadi threat: ISIS Al-Qaeda and beyond*. Washington, DC.

PART I

CONCEPTS AND THEORIES

1

CONCEPTUALISING INSURGENCY

Olivier Lewis and Scott N. Romaniuk

ON THE POLITICS OF CONCEPTUALISATION

When reading a text, we are often tempted to skip definitions and jump straight to cases. Conceptualisation can, at times, be a dry and pedantic academic exercise. The reality, however, is that terms matter. Wording and connotations can cause emotional reactions and significantly affect events. Likewise, categorising an event, process, or entity within a wider grouping can positively or negatively impact those concerned. In everyday life, the psychological and material effects of labelling are confirmed by the phenomenon of political correctness, i.e., efforts to avoid offence in speech. In academia, the importance of language was most famously supported by the post-structuralist movement, whose members (logically) questioned such a term and its application to specific people. Placing an individual, group, event, or process "in a box" is an eminently political act.

The definition of a political act is, thus, an über-political act, for it attempts to circumscribe what can be recognised as political (see Kochi, 2009; Crelinsten, 2013). Political and apolitical distinctions can be consequential, both in terms of legality and legitimacy. In some cases, being politically active can provide rights and prestige, in contrast to criminal activity, for example. In other cases, being apolitical provides authority and gravitas. Debates about technical and scientific expertise and knowledge centre on such dichotomies. Such good-versus-bad distinctions are often simple, but they are not always generalisable. They are often particular to regional value systems (or "cultures"). Altruism is often valued more than selfishness, but not always. Objectivity is often placed above subjectivity and bias, but not always. The tragedies of playwrights in ancient Greece often dramatised the clash of incompatible value systems (e.g., Antigone) (see Cowley, 2001). In a similar vein, Max Weber later argued that the value spheres of religion, politics, science, economics, and love were incommensurable (Weber, 2004). The fascist jurist Carl Schmitt made similar remarks when discussing politics as a friend/enemy distinction and his infamous "partisan":

> The intensely political character of the partisan is crucial since he has to be distinguished from the common thief and criminal, whose motives aim at private enrichment. This conceptual criterion of his political character possesses—in its exact inversion—the very same structure as the case of pirates in maritime law, whose concept is based on the unpolitical character of his bad deed which aim at private theft and profit. The pirate is possessed of what jurisprudence knows as animus furandi [felonious intent] (see Schmitt, 2007).

The point is simply that labelling something as (a)political has import. Terms matter.

Conceptual work also has the potential to be political in the sense of liberating thought (see Dewey, 1923; Freire, 1970). The objective of this chapter is not to provide a definitive definition or formal typology of insurgencies but rather, following the work of Ariel Merari (1993), to outline the core characteristics that distinguish insurgencies from other types of political violence. By reviewing the ontology of insurgencies and similar types of political violence, the aim is to help the reader question others' labels and categorisations.

CONCEPTUALISATION METHODS AND TRADE-OFFS

Conceptualisation, the effort to align terms with definitions and referents (see Gerring, 1999), can be done via two methods, one analytic and one synthetic (Goertz, 2012). The analytic method, which primarily uses logic to form the concept, has the benefit of reducing bias and facilitating the identification of potential cases that do not yet exist. Bias is avoided because meaning, not cases, is the foundation of the conceptualisation (on conceptualisation as a check on bias, see Schmid and Jongman, 2005). Mental shortcuts (such as availability heuristics, confirmation bias, and anchoring)

DOI: 10.4324/9780429426063-3

might be of great use in daily life, but they can easily sabotage efforts to produce valid concepts. Because of its greater breadth, the analytical method can lead to strange conceptualisations (see Gerring, 1999). The synthetic method, on the other hand, because it is based on familiar examples, tends to result in familiar definitions, similar to those used in vernacular speech. Simplifying, we can say that the analytical method favours *deductive reasoning* and the synthetic method favours *inductive reasoning*.

The rich presentation of instances in each chapter can be applied to this chapter, even if it is based on the analytic technique and was prepared with the large number and variety of cases offered in this manuscript in mind. The ultimate result is an investigation of the ontological boundaries of what characterises an insurgency and what sets an insurgency apart from other forms of political violence, rather than a formal conceptualisation. After all, one of the fundamental purposes of concepts is to make distinctions. What follows cannot be taken as being infallible because notions are inherently flawed and subject to constant debate. However, it is hoped that this will encourage readers to approach the remainder of the book and next works with a critical eye, challenging ideas and their applications, and always considering who stands to gain from such conceptual structures.

Don't Essentialise the Insurgent!

The conservative commentator William F. Buckley is known for summarising Eric Voegelin's *The New Science of Politics* with the slogan "Don't immanentize the eschaton!" (Voegelin, 1987; Goldberg, 2002). Simply put, the call was for far-left ideologues to cease trying to create heaven on earth. Voegelin and Buckley argued that dividing the world between good and evil and acting on those premises leads to radicalism and the justification of all sorts of violence (of course, the same might be said of *far-right* "immentisations of eschatons", especially today). Regarding the conceptualisation of insurgency, we could make a similar call, namely "Don't essentialise the insurgent!", where essentialisation refers to the assertion that things have certain immutable essences. Those familiar with philosophy and psychology will know that essentialism is often the foundation of prejudice and stereotypical thinking (see Morton et al., 2009). In concept development, essentialism is to be found in actor- and organisation-based typologies (see De la Calle and Sánchez-Cuenca, 2011; Asal et al., 2012). Definitions of "insurgents" and "terrorists" therefore can easily lay the foundation for hasty and sweeping generalisations that are often employed in government definitions of terrorist and insurgent threats, subsequently informing counter-terror and counter-insurgent policies and practises (see Schmid and Jongman, 2005: 43–50). However, even the most well-established models for conducting unconventional warfare, that is, warfare against terrorists, guerrillas, and insurgents, are simply models from which increasingly messy realities depart. In terms of both actions and identities, people are never just one thing (e.g., insurgents) (see Tilly, 2004: 4). Instead, definitions and typologies ought to be based on means and ends. This chapter, therefore, will seek to conceptualise not insurgents as actors but rather insurgency as an end.

Avoiding essentialism, however, need not mean ignoring the legal status or the social position of those who commit acts of violence. Politics (including political violence) is often conflictual and therefore often leads to the formation of opposing groups and organisations (protagonists against antagonists) (Mouffe, 2005; Schmitt, 2008). Here is not the place to cover the history of the law of war, but it must be said that, like terrorism, the term "insurgency" is generally applied to acts by non-state actors (NSAs), i.e., actors who are not formally part of a state or, at least, who are not following a state's chain of command (a.k.a. non-state armed groups or violent non-state actors [VNSAs]) (Williams, 2008). The statelessness of these political actors might explain, for example, the habitual conflation of terrorists and "freedom fighters" (Merari, 1993: 226; see Ganor, 2002; Khalil, 2013; Lewis, 2015). While insurgents can be lawful combatants, state actors are rarely called "insurgents". But even this simple state/non-state distinction must be made with caution, as many *de jure* states can be considered "failing" or even "failed" states, and many insurgencies result in the creation of *de facto* and occasionally even *de jure* states (Johnston, 2008). Similarly, as seen in Afghanistan, a government and its armed forces can lose *de facto* and *de jure* sovereignty and become, in effect, an insurgent group (see Farrell and Giustozzi, 2013; see also Ouassini and Ouassini in this volume).

More broadly, we see that the term insurgency can only be understood within a broader historical context, namely a state-based world order with established or recognised governments. The Cambridge Dictionary, for example, defines an insurgent as "someone who is fighting against the government in their own country", and an insurgency as "an occasion when a group of people attempt to take control of their country by force" (Cambridge University Press, 2008). So, although the term "insurgency" clearly has an oppositional connotation ("against", "take control"), it is also historically contingent on the existence of states ("government", "country"). Few would categorise military coups and revolutions in ancient Athens or rebellions and revolts in late-mediaeval Flanders as insurgencies.

Part of the problem here lies in the classification of "terrorist" and "insurgent". To be sure, the term "terrorist" carries a considerable degree of pejorative cargo; it is a term that would typically breed grotesque resentment, particularly among Western audiences, for its intimately violent and destructive character. In nearly every terrorist act, civilians are a key ingredient, producing a natural revulsion towards such a tactic. Insurgents and guerrillas, however, regularly use terrorist tactics to drive their causes; they are essentially natural components of the insurgent movement, just as violence is a natural part of counter-terror and counter-insurgent operations conducted by any state.

Though we tend to look at insurgents and guerrillas through a different lens, bequeathing the latter two with greater legitimacy than the former, their relationship with elements embedded within their cause frame both has a strident difference from that of terrorists. Often, insurgents and guerrillas relate to supposedly noble causes, suffused with such terms as "liberty", "liberation", "freedom", "independence", and so on. This language can serve a strong purpose for insurgents and guerrillas by establishing an identity very different from that of their terrorist counterparts. Governments equally so. Perhaps the most important component to be unearthed from any definitional discussion about terrorists, insurgents, and guerrillas is the degree to which each is ascribed legitimacy. As Ünal (2016: n.p.) states, "[t]he bottom line for definitional disputes about these terms is the degree of legitimacy or lack thereof and the end goal of the ontology of a violent uprising, which is highly subjective and ideological due to the self-proclamation of righteousness". Jules and Romaniuk illustrate this point in their chapter on the Ejército Zapatista de Liberación Nacional (Zapatista Army of National Liberation, EZLN). The composition of the group is complex and has experienced significant changes over the years. Its within-state identity does not always harmonise with labels applied to the EZLN beyond the state. Thus, the group carries several labels: on the one hand, it is depicted as a violent terrorist group with a vested interest in killing, while more just labels depict the group as a critical player in the movement for justice and democracy for Mexico's poor and suppressed indigenous peoples. They have been and continue to be seen as the voices of the voiceless.

The term "insurgency" refers to modern international humanitarian law, which attempts to control modern conflict, in addition to this oppositional aspect, as was stated. The status of combatants, especially those who are fighting against the government's soldiers, is in dispute here. Without getting into the specifics of the law, it is safe to conclude that the term "insurgent" frequently implies a sense of illegality, which explains the term's frequent associations with phrases like "illegal combatant" or "unprivileged combatant". This is thus because the main purpose of international humanitarian law is to manage war between states, not armed conflict (within a state) between the armed forces of a government and rebels.

On Subversive Political Violence

The illegal and illegitimate nature of an insurgency, at least from a government's perspective, helps one understand why the term "insurgency" is generally employed in relation to colonial and civil wars. Carl Schmitt, for example, clearly defines "partisans" by their irregularity, placing them in both inter-state wars and civil and colonial wars (2007: 2). The prototypical "partisan" war for him was "the Spanish Guerrilla War of 1808" (the Peninsular War). Napoleon's troops were in effect occupying Spain, and thus the war can be interpreted as one of "national liberation", although it can be noted that British forces also participated in the hostilities. Schmitt goes as far as calling the Spanish guerrillero "a first, typical case of the irregular cannon fodder of international political conflict" (2007: 4–5). As mentioned previously, insurgents and partisans are, in this sense, part of a wider class, generally referred to as "non-state armed actors" or "violent non-state actors", which can include rebels but also militias, paramilitary forces, mercenaries, and corporations (see Gutiérrez Sanín, 2008; Williams, 2008).

The dialectical twist that Schmitt explores to great effect is to be found in the irregular combatants who, *unlike their government's forces*, fight to counter the occupying foreign forces. Schmitt, the committed fascist, even mentions as examples the resistance fighters of World War Two in "Poland, the Balkans, France, Albania, and Greece". So, although insurgencies are generally defined as attempts to subvert established governments, the government being subverted may very well be seen, in the eyes of the insurgent, not as established but rather as alien. Another example that Schmitt uses is Tolstoy's *War and Peace*, where Russian peasants attack French troops. For insurgents, it is often the occupying government that is subversive, destroying what was established. This tension helps explain ongoing legal debates surrounding the question of occupation and the administration of foreign territories (e.g., Palestine) (ICRC, 2020).

ON MULTIPOLAR CONFLICTS

Insurgencies are often understood as part of colonial conflicts and civil wars, i.e., rebellions by minorities (Tarrow, 2007). Moreover, insurgencies are often understood as relating to "internal wars" and not inter-state wars (on state-state, state-civilian, and civilian-civilian political violence, see Merari, 1993). Regarding civil war, grievance and greed best explain the onset of insurgencies (Collier and Hoeffler, 1998; Fearon and Laitin, 2003). But no matter the veracity of the intra-state/inter-state dichotomy and the reasons for strife, most scholars agree that one colonial or civil war can encompass many insurgencies, many civilian groupings, and many diasporas (Tarrow, 2007; on the role of diaspora, see Roul's chapter on the Rohingya in this volume). One of the most common features of insurgent groups is their tendency to both splinter and merge (see Ouassini and Ouassini in this volume). In this organisational shuffle, political objectives are often abandoned. Some groups and troops will defect to join opposing governmental forces, while others will splinter in order to better "spoil" the peace.[1] Intriguingly, although newcomers (i.e., foreign fighters and transnational insurgents) generally bring much-needed material resources, the strange ideas and tactics they bring with them can trigger not only a loss of popular support but also a loss of *organisational cohesion* (Bakke, 2014). Paraphrasing Virgil, we could say, "Fear the foreign fighters, especially when they bear gifts".

Equally, an ostentatiously "domestic" fight can easily overflow, especially when "external" actors provide refuge, finance, arms, and other resources (Collier & Sambanis, 2005) (see also Stoker's insurgency chapter in this volume). In other words, when studying insurgencies, the risk of methodological nationalism is great. Just as social movements and terrorism are rarely binary and rarely purely domestic (see Asal et al., 2012; Tarrow and Tilly, 2007) (see also Zekulin's chapter in this volume), insurgencies and civil wars are often *transnational* phenomena (see Arielli and Collins, 2012, 2013; Bakke, 2014; Tamm, 2016a, 2016b). "The armed partisan remains always dependent on the collaboration with a regular organization [...]" (Schmitt, 2007: 12). Again, examples of sanctuary and "external" (state and non-state) support are visible in both pre-existing publications (Hashim, 2011) and this volume (e.g., Grice and Macintire on Tibetan insurgencies; Roul on the Islamic State-Khorasan Province). In fact, with the "return" of geopolitics, some scholars have focused on insurgents as the agents of states, notably in the form of "proxy wars" (e.g., Mumford, 2013; Rauta, 2016). Although this resembles recent debates about "state-sponsored" terrorism (e.g., Byman and Kreps, 2010), it also has interesting parallels to wider discussions concerning covert action and "hybrid" warfare (Cormac and Aldrich, 2018; Murray and Mansoor, 2012). One of the most fascinating aspects of foreign patrons (external sponsors) is their ability to divide and rule over competing rebel leaders (Tamm, 2016b). Adapting our Aeneidian phrase, we could say, "Fear both the foreign fighters and the state sponsors, especially when they bear gifts".

MEANS VS. ENDS

Although coups are virtually never presented as a form of insurgency (for an exception, see Merari, 1993), the similarities are striking. Schmitt's fascination with General Raoul Salan and his putsch in Algiers is a case in point (Schmitt, 2007). Like an insurgency, a coup involves an effort to remove an established and recognised government from power via subversion and often violence. One difference between the two might be the fact that a coup involves treasonous military officers, but insurgencies also often involve treasonous military officers. Instead, one could say that the major differences between coups and insurgencies are speed and casualties. Although not always made explicit, insurgencies are generally thought to be a part of protracted and relatively deadly conflicts (i.e., civil or colonial wars); coups are not. If an insurgency results in a rapid and relatively bloodless victory, can it not be called a coup? We should also note, however, that as a form of political violence, coups are defined more by their means (speed as a tactic) than by their ends (revolt).

Often, insurgencies are associated with guerrilla warfare. This is because insurgents often try to use the asymmetric nature of their combat to their advantage.[2] Just as terrorism is considered the tool of the weak, insurgency is often considered the tool of the few. Terrorism and insurgency, in other words, connote an "underdog" status. This helps understand the romanticisation of Cuban-Argentinian Marxist revolutionary Ernesto "Che" Guevara by generations of youths, notably the plethora of Che gifts and merchandise in the form of shirts, hats, military wear, and accessories for men and women that can be found online in just a few clicks. Another, more ethical example of "Davids" fighting against the odds might be the month-long insurgency of the Warsaw Ghetto in 1943. The snipers who survived and continued fighting were called the "rubble resistance" (Kurzman, 1993: 336; see Asal et al., 2012).

The association of insurgencies with guerrilla warfare might also be due to the telluric nature of many insurgencies, which are concealed in rural or urban terrain. As just mentioned, insurgencies, by definition, are conducted against an occupying force or an established government (e.g., the American War of Independence, the American Civil War) (Keithly, 2001; Sutherland, 2009; see Asal et al., 2012). The degree of *de facto* territorial control can affect which tactics the parties might employ (Asal et al., 2012; Kalyvas, 2006). Patrick Johnston (2008), for example, has focused on insurgency as a quest for territorial (and thus population) control (see Mampilly and Stewart, 2020). De la Calle and Sánchez-Cuenca (2011) develop an actor-based definition of insurgents as those who control territory (e.g., camps, roadblocks). And while Stathis Kalyvas concentrates on degrees of territorial control in civil wars, Weinstein argues that one of the determinants of indiscriminate violence by "rebel groups" is simply *access to resources* (Kalyvas, 2006; Tarrow, 2007; Weinstein, 2006).

Pace de la Calle and Sanchez-Cuenca note that although insurgents often employ guerrilla warfare, they also often employ terrorism, sabotage, propaganda, and even conventional war (Merari, 1993: 243). What distinguishes the concept of insurgency from the concepts of terrorism, guerrilla warfare, coups, etc. is a reference to ends (i.e., goals), namely the quest for *land* and *governance* (Khalil, 2013; Lewis, 2015; Merari, 1993) (see also Stoker's insurgency chapter in this volume).

- Whether legitimate or not, and no matter the tactics employed, colonial and civil wars are generally also *for* Schmitt, who, for example, clearly distinguishes "partisan" warfare from irregular *maritime* warfare

(Schmitt, 2007: 14). Terrain is not just the means but also the ends. In this sense, insurgency is quite different from issue-specific forms of political violence (e.g., environmentalists, anti-abortionists, and animal rights activists).

- Insurgencies are a type of revolt, a type of resistance – hence the widespread use of the term "rebel" instead of "insurgent". As seen with some Communist and Islamist insurgencies, the reengineering of the entire world order might be the end, but such an insurgency remains against an established, recognised form of (global) governance (Ojakangas, 2007; Slomp, 2009).

For Kalyvas (2006), the difference between private Hobbesian violence and public Schmittian violence is key to understanding the causes of violence during civil wars. Indeed, although "insurgency" is an ends-based concept, it does not preclude the simultaneous existence of more base motives by some participants in the hostilities, be they members of a rebel group or not. In fact, just as motives can vary *within* a terrorist organisation (Crenshaw, 1987), reasons and ends can vary between associated insurgents, ranging from the opportunistic to the committed (Tarrow, 2007; Weinstein, 2006). In fact, as seen with the so-called "foreign fighters", some members are simply attracted by the lifestyle of power and "primitive gratification", seek to fill a void or escape the routine, or merely want to rebel against parental authority (Cronin, 2015; Gutiérrez Sanín, 2008: 23) (see also Zekulin's chapter in this volume).

Notes

1 Such reorganisations are covered in both past academic literature (e.g., Bakke et al., 2012; Tamm, 2016a, 2016b) and this manuscript (e.g., Fabe and Romaniuk on the Moro Islamic Liberation Front; Momen on the Jamaat-ul-Mujahideen Bangladesh; Taylor on Ansar al-Dine; Zaamout on the Syrian Muslim Brotherhood; Zahid on Al-Qaeda in the Indian Subcontinent; Yetim and Kasikci on the Izz as-Din al-Qassam Brigades).

2 Although an insurgency can take place in the streets and in the hills, it can also take place in the deserts and in the fields.

References

Arielli, N., & Collins, B. (2012). *Transnational soldiers: Foreign military enlistment in the modern era*. Springer.

Arielli, N., & Collins, B. (2013). Conclusions: Jihadists, diasporas and professional contractors—the resurgence of non-state recruitment since the 1980s. In *Transnational soldiers*. (pp. 250–256). Springer.

Asal, I., De la Calle, L., Findley, M., & Young, J. (2012). Killing civilians or holding territory? How to think about terrorism. *International Studies Review, 14*, 475–497.

Bakke, K.M. (2014). Help wanted? The mixed record of foreign fighters in domestic insurgencies. *International Security, 38*(4), 150–187.

Bakke, K.M., Cunningham, K.G., & Seymour, L.J. (2012). A plague of initials: Fragmentation, cohesion, and infighting in civil wars. *Perspectives on Politics, 10*(2), 265–283.

Byman, D., & Kreps, S.E. (2010). Agents of destruction? Applying principal-agent analysis to state-sponsored terrorism. *International Studies Perspectives, 11*(1), 1–18.

Cambridge University Press. (2008). *Cambridge academic content dictionary reference book with CD-ROM*. Cambridge University Press.

Collier, P., & Hoeffler, A. (1998). On economic causes of civil war. *Oxford Economic Papers, 50*(4), 563–573.

Collier, P., & Sambanis, N. (2005). *Understanding civil war (Volume 1: Africa) evidence and analysis*. The World Bank.

Cormac, R., & Aldrich, R.J. (2018). Grey is the new black: Covert action and implausible deniability. *International Affairs, 94*(3), 477–494.

Cowley, C. (2001). Moral dilemmas in Greek tragedies: A discussion of Aeschylus's Agamemnon and Sophokles's Antigone. *Classical World, 94*(4), 339–355.

Crelinsten, R. (2013). *Counterterrorism*. Wiley.

Crenshaw, M. (1987). Theories of terrorism: Instrumental and organizational approaches. *The Journal of Strategic Studies, 10*(4), 13–31.

Cronin, A.K. (2015). ISIS is not a terrorist group: Why counterterrorism won't stop the latest jihadist threat. *Foreign Affairs, 94*, 87.

De la Calle, L., & Sánchez-Cuenca, I. (2011). What we talk about when we talk about terrorism. *Politics & Society, 39*(3), 451–472.

Dewey, J. (1923). *Democracy and education: An introduction to the philosophy of education*. Macmillan.

Farrell, T., & Giustozzi, A. (2013). The Taliban at war: Inside the Helmand insurgency, 2004–2012. *International Affairs, 89*(4), 845–871.

Fearon, J.D., & Laitin, D.D. (2003). Ethnicity, insurgency, and civil war. *American Political Science Review, 97*(1), 75–90.

Freire, P. (1970). *Pedagogy of the oppressed*. Continuum.

Ganor, B. (2002). Defining terrorism: Is one man's terrorist another man's freedom fighter? *Police Practice and Research, 3*(4), 287–304. doi:10.1080/1561426022000032060

Gerring, J. (1999). What makes a concept good? A criterial framework for understanding concept formation in the social sciences. *Polity, 31*(3), 357–393. doi:10.2307/3235246

Goertz, G. (2012). *Social science concepts: A user's guide*. Princeton University Press.

Goldberg, J. (2002, January 16). Immanent corrections. *National Review, 54*(2), 42–44.

Gutiérrez Sanín, F. (2008). Telling the difference: Guerrillas and paramilitaries in the Colombian war. *Politics & Society, 36*(1), 3–34.

Hashim, A.S. (2011). *Insurgency and counter-insurgency in Iraq*. Cornell University Press.

ICRC. (2020). Occupation. Retrieved from https://www.icrc.org/en/war-and-law/contemporary-challenges-for-ihl/occupation

Johnston, P. (2008). The geography of insurgent organization and its consequences for civil wars: Evidence from Liberia and Sierra Leone. *Security Studies, 17*(1), 107–137.

Kalyvas, S.N. (2006). *The logic of violence in civil war*. Cambridge University Press.

Keithly, D. (2001). Poor, nasty and brutish: Guerrilla operations in Americas first civil war. *Civil Wars, 4*(3), 35–69.

Khalil, J. (2013). Know your enemy: On the futility of distinguishing between terrorists and insurgents. *Studies in Conflict & Terrorism, 36*(5), 419–430.

Kochi, T. (2009). *The other's war: Recognition and the violence of ethics*. Routledge.

Kurzman, D. (1993). *The Bravest Battle: The twenty-eight days of the Warsaw Ghetto uprising*. Da Capo Press.

Lewis, O. (2015). Conceptualizing counterterrorism. In S.N. Romaniuk & S.T. Webb (Eds.), *Insurgency and counterinsurgency in modern war* (pp. 1–16). Taylor & Francis.

Mampilly, Z., & Stewart, M.A. (2020). A typology of rebel political institutional arrangements. *Journal of Conflict Resolution, 64*(3), 534–562.

Merari, A. (1993). Terrorism as a strategy of insurgency. *Terrorism and Political Violence, 5*(4), 213–251.

Morton, T.A., Hornsey, M.J., & Postmes, T. (2009). Shifting ground: The variable use of essentialism in contexts of inclusion and exclusion. *British Journal of Social Psychology, 48*(1), 35–59.

Mouffe, C. (2005). *On the political*. Psychology Press.

Mumford, A. (2013). Proxy warfare and the future of conflict. *The RUSI Journal, 158*(2), 40–46.

Murray, W., & Mansoor, P.R. (2012). *Hybrid warfare: Fighting complex opponents from the ancient world to the present*. Cambridge University Press.

Ojakangas, M. (2007). A terrifying world without an exterior. In L. Odysseos & F. Petito (Eds.), *The international political thought of Carl Schmitt: Terror, liberal war and the crisis of global order*.

Rauta, V. (2016). Proxy agents, auxiliary forces, and sovereign defection: Assessing the outcomes of using non-state actors in civil conflicts. *Southeast European and Black Sea Studies, 16*(1), 91–111.

Schmid, A.P., & Jongman, A.J. (2005). *Political terrorism: A new guide to actors, authors, concepts, data bases, theories, and literature*. Transaction Publishers.

Schmitt, C. (2007). *Theory of the Partisan: Intermediate commentary on the concept of the political*. Telos Press Pub.

Schmitt, C. (2008). *The concept of the political: Expanded edition*. University of Chicago Press.

Slomp, G. (2009). *Carl Schmitt and the politics of hostility, violence and terror*. Palgrave Macmillan.

Sutherland, D.E. (2009). *A savage conflict: The decisive role of Guerrillas in the American civil war*. Univ of North Carolina Press.

Tamm, H. (2016a). The origins of transnational alliances: Rulers, rebels, and political survival in the Congo wars. *International Security, 41*(1), 147–181.

Tamm, H. (2016b). Rebel leaders, internal rivals, and external resources: How state sponsors affect insurgent cohesion. *International Studies Quarterly, 60*(4), 599–610.

Tarrow, S. (2007). Inside insurgencies: Politics and violence in an age of civil war. *Perspectives on Politics, 5*(3), 587–600.

Tarrow, S., & Tilly, C. (2007). Contentious politics and social movements. In R. Goodin & C. Tilly (Eds.), *The Oxford handbook of comparative politics* (pp. 746–777). Oxford University Press.

Tilly, C. (2004). Terror, terrorism, terrorists. *Sociological Theory, 22*(1), 5–13.

Ünal, M. C. (2016). Terrorism versus insurgency: a conceptual analysis. *Crime, Law and Social Change, 66*(1), 21–57.

Voegelin, E. (1987). *The new science of politics: An introduction*. University of Chicago Press.

Weber, M. (2004). *The vocation lectures*. Hackett Pub.

Weinstein, J.M. (2006). *Inside rebellion: The politics of insurgent violence*. Cambridge University Press.

Williams, P. (2008). Violent non-state actors and national and international security. *International Relations and Security Network, 25*, 1–21.

2

THE ARCHITECTURE OF COUNTERINSURGENCY

From Classical to Quantum and Beyond

Uddipan Mukherjee

INTRODUCTION

A couple of days before being eliminated, holed up inside the Golden Temple complex with a few hundred of his men and boys and confronted with thousands of soldiers of the Indian Army, on the third of June 1984, Khalistani insurgent leader Jarnail Singh Bhindranwale roared, "Sheep always outnumber the lions. But one lion can take care of a thousand sheep" (Kirpekar, 1984).

In a video posted in the Al Furquan media of the Islamic State [IS], the group's erstwhile leader Abu Bakr al-Baghdadi lauded the suicide bombers of the April 2019 church and hotel blasts in Sri Lanka: "Your brothers in Sri Lanka have healed the hearts of monotheists with their suicide bombings, which shook the beds of the crusaders during Easter to avenge your brothers in Baghouz" (Mukherjee, 2019).

Baghdadi, however, had to commit suicide in a nondescript village in Syria near the Turkish border barely six months later as counterinsurgent forces chased him (BBC, 2019). A frail heart patient, Charu Mazumdar, the chief ideologue of India's communist/Maoist insurgency, died of custodial interrogation on the 28th of July 1972 (Banerjee, 2016). Yet he spoke of "class annihilation" and the destruction of the bourgeoisie by an armed insurrection, to be operationalised through squad-level guerrilla warfare in the villages.

Be it the army, the police, or their combination, the braggadocio of the insurgents is tamed by a thoughtful philosophy of counterinsurgency (COIN), aided by planning, technology, leadership, and execution. Mazumdar's comrades were made to bite the dust by Operation Steeplechase (Pubby, 2009), a joint execution by the Indian Army, paramilitary, and police in July–August 1971, while it was Operation Geronimo, performed to precision by the American Navy SEALs on May 2, 2011, at Abottabad inside Pakistan, that sealed the fate of Osama bin Laden, almost ten years after the collapse of the twin towers.

The targeted elimination and killing of the top leadership of Al Qaeda and the Taliban fused pretty well with the COIN campaign (in the Afghan rural hinterlands) propounded under the doctrinal aegis of the meaty American Field Manual on COIN. The people-centric COIN approach was put to work in the tribal areas of Afghanistan because that model had yielded tangible results in Iraq, which aided the withdrawal of the combat troops from the region.

Nevertheless, whether the job is "winning hearts and minds" in the "classical COIN" paradigm or conducting drone and stealth operations to target insurgent leadership or camps, "intelligence" holds the key. Progress in technology notwithstanding, human intelligence [HUMINT] in COIN operations still stands in good stead, as was genuinely reflected in the elimination of former IS chief Baghdadi in October 2019. STRATFOR's Fred Burton concurs with the HUMINT school of thought as he asserts (Burton, 2011): "All this surface-level discussion (of sovereignty, etc.), however, largely ignores almost ten years of intelligence development in the hunt for bin Laden".

Humility becomes more pertinent in an environment where the insurgent leaders – the main targets for the counterinsurgency – start to shun "technology" and rely on human couriers. Osama, in his last years at Abbottabad, hardly used the internet. It was the human courier Abu Ahmed al-Kuwaiti who ultimately paved the way for nabbing Osama. And "an IS defector reportedly provided, via clandestine communication, a room-by-room description of the building in which Baghdadi was hiding, as well as the leader's personal items', wrote Eyal Tsir Cohen and Ellora Katz for the Brookings Institution (Cohen and Katz, 2019). Similarly, top Maoist leaders in India, their spokesperson Cherukuri Rajkumar (Chakravarti, 2018), and media-savvy politburo member Mallojula Koteswara Rao alias Kishenji (Hindustan Times, 2011) were eliminated by Indian security forces, specifically based on HUMINT.

Though it was the Spanish guerrillas in the modern world who harassed Napoleon to the extreme and made his COIN

DOI: 10.4324/9780429426063-4

campaign questionable, in order to trace the genesis of COIN, David Kilcullen cites the victory of the Ptolemies in Egypt over the Seleucids in 218 BCE, reflecting the logical inference that both insurgency and COIN existed since the formation of the state (Kilcullen, 2012). Furthermore, the US Army/Marine Corps COIN Field Manual (Army Field Manual, 2006) asserts that "insurgency and its tactics are as old as warfare itself".

The COIN philosophy at large – strategic, tactical, and operational – obviously traces its roots back much further than the modern era and far beyond the confines of American or West – European participation (Brady, 2017). Apart from their military component, COIN campaigns include attempts to wean away the local population by socio-politically discrediting the insurgents.

THE CLASSICAL COIN

Kilcullen rightly described the beginning of the "Classical COIN" philosophy as an outcome of RAND's April 1962 week-long symposium (Kilcullen, 2012). He argues that the conceptual framework of classical COIN was obtained through "lessons and insights from past insurgent conflicts" and "by studying contemporary wars of national liberation and drawing, by analogy, lessons for current and future COIN". A veteran of the Algerian insurgency, the French army officer David Galula was one of the chief proponents of classical COIN.

Along with discussing population-centric classical COIN, Galula, interestingly enough, points to a case of infiltration as an instrument of COIN. For instance, in Czarist Russia, the Okhrana succeeded in sneaking into the Bolshevik Party. Later, Lenin discovered that some of his most trusted companions had been in the pay of the Czar's police.

Nevertheless, reiterating the population-centric classical COIN, Galula lays down four laws of COIN (Galula, 1964):

- The support of the population is necessary for the counterinsurgent.
- The support of the population is gained through an active minority fighting the insurgency.
- Effective political action against the population must be preceded by military and police operations against the insurgents.
- The COIN operations require a large concentration of effort, resources, and personnel.

The Western-conceptual construct of "winning hearts and minds" focused on population-centric classical COIN received its 21st-century boost when Lt. General McChrystal, the commander of the US Forces in Afghanistan and the International Security Assistance Force (ISAF), finalised a 66-page report (Packer, 2009) on August 30, 2009. Stanley A. McChrystal was a former commander of the Joint Special Operations Command who ran all special operations in Iraq. He was associated with the capture of Saddam Hussein and the annihilation of Abu Musab al-Zarqawi, leader of Al Qaeda in Iraq.

The McChrystal report re-emphasised (Washington Post, 2009) the aspects of classical COIN. He advocated a troop surge in Afghanistan, over and above the 68,000 American troops already stationed there. However, he categorically pointed out in his report that a mere troop buildup was not a necessary and sufficient condition for "success" in Afghanistan.

He drew attention to a major lacuna of the coalition forces, that is, not extending support to the Afghan masses, fundamentally due to the inability of the ISAF forces to come out of their security cocoons. In his report (Mukherjee, 2009), McChrystal talked about an "integrated civilian-military COIN campaign". He appreciated that the Afghan masses needed a secure environment and a solid institutional framework providing them with justice and civil liberties, which were to be developed by a democratic government stripped of corruption. Moreover, the ISAF should also have a major role to play in this contentious issue by being physically and psychologically closer to the common Afghans.

21ST-CENTURY VARIANT OF CLASSICAL COIN: OBAMA-PETRAEUS-MCCHRYSTAL DOCTRINE

The sole purpose of the US's invasion of Afghanistan was to seize Osama bin Laden and destroy and dismantle Al Qaeda. The associated reason was to target the Taliban government since they were reluctant to hand over Osama and had provided sanctuary to him. The US forces bungled at the cave complex of Tora Bora in 2001, and since then Osama has remained out of reach, presumably in Pakistan, until his capture in Abottabad.

Soon after assuming the Presidency in January 2009, the first thing that Obama did was to inflate the number of US troops in Afghanistan by another 17,000 in order to support the situation on the ground. In the middle of the same year, Obama appointed Lt. Gen. Stanley McChrystal as commander of the NATO-ISAF forces in Afghanistan. At about the same time, the American president expressed his confidence in CENTCOM (Central Command) Chief David Petraeus.

The aim was to embark on a COIN drive so as to muster as much popular support as possible, which in the future would create a friendly political and military setting so as to have an honourable retreat from Afghanistan. The idea was not to let contemporary historians and political commentators term Afghanistan "Obama's Vietnam".

The McChrystal report, in fact, lifted "several pages" of the COIN Manual of the US Army bearing the signature of David Petraeus. McChrystal requested a troop "surge" to the tune of 40,000. After some dilly-dallying, in December 2009, Obama agreed upon the "surge", though restricting the amount to 30,000. The primary objective behind the "surge" was to employ the COIN strategy of "Clear, Hold, and Build" (CHB) so as to "clear" the chosen areas of the Taliban, and thereafter "hold" those areas for a considerable time period, and finally "build" infrastructure and institutions so that the incumbent Afghan government can permanently entrench itself. According to McChrystal, NATO-ISAF needed to have a better mix with the masses in order to win over the latter. NATO-ISAF was directed to reduce the collateral damage to a bare minimum.

The "surge" would destabilise the Taliban command structure for a reasonable time frame and impede the regrouping of Al Qaeda after the US withdrawal. In this context, it is worthwhile to mention that the suggested (Yi, 2018) force ratio is about 50:1 (one security person for 50 civilians, which includes militants) for a successful COIN campaign. However, even that may not guarantee "success", as was seen in Algeria's FLN insurgency. Interestingly, the Indian forces in Kashmir have reportedly resorted to a ratio of 30:1 and have been successful in quelling the insurgency fomented by cross-border terrorists (Baruah, 2019). In Afghanistan, another American aim was to train, develop, and increase the number of the local police and the Afghan National Army. The reason was simple. The US wanted to leave Afghanistan in secure hands. They did not want to repeat the Vietnam fiasco.

Nevertheless, it is not as if successful coins were a rarity in the classical paradigm of the 20th century (Amidror, 2010). The US Army succeeded twice in the Philippines, once from 1899 to 1902 and thereafter from 1946 to 1954. As if to prove that the Philippines was not an exceptional case, the British Army won a challenging COIN war in Malaya (present-day Malaysia) between 1952 and 1957. The British had also waged successful COIN campaigns during the 1930s in British Mandatory Palestine and later in the 1970s in Dhofar Province in Oman.

Nonetheless, "success" itself needs to be elaborated in COIN architecture. That is what distinguishes it from a conventional war. A total victory "eliminates the guerrilla groups and their demands from the political and global map" (Amidror, 2010). For instance, the defeat of communist guerrillas in Greece after the Second World War (WW II) falls into this category. Another outcome could be a temporary victory. However, a sufficient victory, in which the insurgency is not destroyed but is contained at a minimal level with constant efforts to prevent its re-emergence, is pragmatic enough. For example, the insurgency in Northern Ireland and the Basque separatist movement in Spain are examples of this typology (Amidror, 2010).

Kilcullen opines (Kilcullen, 2012) that the new 21st-century avatar of COIN emanating in Iraq and Afghanistan in a post-9/11 environment is the neo-classical variety because authors and practitioners of the classical age, Galula, Thompson, and other writers, still highly influence the reinvigorated COIN doctrine embodied in the US Army/Marine Corps Field Manual, FM 3-24, brought out in December 2006. "The COIN renaissance of 2005–6 can be considered a Neo-Classical Revival, resting on the application and updating of classical precepts for the new campaigns", writes Kilcullen (2012). However, Kilcullen's conceptual construct of "accelerated COIN" is what engages practitioners and theorists alike. He posits that the population-centric classical COIN operations across Iraq and Afghanistan could be "accelerated" by adding two layers:

1. Highly lethal counter-network targeting (primarily using special operations and air power, supported by an intensive intelligence effort) to destroy the network of terror cells.
2. Reconciliation and reintegration are needed to make peace with amenable insurgents.

The first layer of "highly lethal counter-network targeting" can include targeted killing (TK) missions, which have been conducted by the Israeli Defence Forces (IDF) against its Palestinian adversaries since the early 1950s. Since the outbreak of the second Palestinian intifada in October 2000, the IDF has eliminated cadres of Hamas, Islamic Jihad, and other Palestinian groups in the Gaza Strip and West Bank (Catignani, 2012). The TK, or "quantified/discrete" targeted operations, were implemented by air strikes and intelligence operations so as to eliminate terrorists even beyond Israeli borders.

THE QUANTUM COIN

Daniel Byman asserts (Byman, 2009) that "talking with insurgents is often a necessary first step towards defeating them or reaching an acceptable compromise". Nevertheless, Byman concludes on a far less optimistic note, as he says: "Talks with insurgents are politically costly, usually fail, and can often backfire" (Byman, 2009). He, however, believes that talks are "often necessary to end conflicts, transform an insurgent group into a legitimate political actor, or wean them away from violence" (Byman, 2009).

At the other end of the ideational spectrum, Stahl and Owen, while substantiating the policy adopted by Israel in its COIN operations, stress the elimination of the insurgent leaders as an effective instrument of state policy to counter the growth of rebellion (Stahl and Owen, 2010). They vouch for the TK of insurgent leaders. The authors counter-argue the somewhat cliché and prevalent belief that killing one leader will simply result in ten more ready to supplant the leadership. They seem to further the view that persistent application of TK would continue to deplete the insurgent groups in terms of their brains and, consequently, their morale.

Augmenting the TK strategy, the researchers also posit (Stahl and Owen, 2010): "The more time leaders spend underground (in fear of TK), the less time they have for conducting armed activity against the state". In this context, they put forward the instance of Hamas' leader Abdel Aziz al-Rantissi, who was forced to hide underground for four weeks – the very period for which he was the chief of the militant organisation.

For the Maoist insurgency in India, when the movement first erupted, the government adopted a two-pronged approach to wipe it out. First, through "Operation Steeplechase", the triumvirate of the army, paramilitary, and police formed three concentric circles (the army formed the outer circle and the police the inner circle to perform the combing operations) and destroyed the very nervous system of the insurgency. At the same time, the police penetrated deep into the organisational structure of the ultras by planting their "moles". In fact, with the aid of HUMINT, TK, and targeted incarceration (TI) of the insurgent leaders, the first phase of the movement declined.

After Charu Mazumdar's death in prison and the TK/TI of the top brass, the Maoist insurgents (then termed "Naxals") splintered into innumerable and inconsequential factions. In this connection, it must be mentioned that between 1997 and 2007, there were about 1,800 TK (encounter deaths, as per police parlance) conducted by the police in the South Indian state of Andhra Pradesh (Banaji, 2010). The insurgency in Andhra Pradesh has, however, reached its nadir due to the accelerated COIN implemented through the special forces (Greyhounds), along with the effective usage of the TK-TI strategy. Alarmingly, however, according to an opinion poll, 58% of the people who were interviewed in the erstwhile Maoist-affected regions in Andhra Pradesh averred that Maoism or Naxalism had been good for their area (TNN, 2010).

Interestingly, Stahl and Owen (2010) are optimistic that with enough TK, "there will come a point" in time when the insurgent group is forced to compromise, as was the case with Hamas in 2004. Furthermore, it must be mentioned that ideologically strong movements like the Maoist rebellion might not "bend" easily. For instance, the five-decade-old Filipino communist movement has yet to see a politically negotiated settlement, though the government has been "talking" to the ultras since 1985. On a positive note, though, even with intermittent hiccups, the FARC insurgents in Colombia are being disarmed and reintegrated into the mainstream (NPR, 2020).

Martha Crenshaw observes (Crenshaw, 1991) that insurgencies may decline because of three reasons: (1) physical defeat, (2) the decision of the group to abandon terrorist strategy, and (3) organisational disintegration.

It is true that development and governance are the keys to long-term tranquillity, but the "small war" must be won as a prerequisite. In this regard, quantum COIN is a viable option; quantised or discrete operations targeting insurgent leadership and important cadres, coupled with classical COIN operations, would accelerate the organisational disintegration leading to the physical defeat of the insurgent group. Here, it is perhaps pertinent to quote Luttwak, who says that there would probably be no harm if "war is given a chance" (Luttwak, 1999).

Though not exactly, a contextual reference with regard to successful Quantum COIN was in Sri Lanka, where "almost the entire senior leadership of the LTTE was eliminated" in Eelam War IV from April 2006 to May 2009 (Hashim, 2013).

Legal Aspects of Quantum COIN

In November 2000, Israel was the first state to proclaim that it operated a policy of TK against the Palestinian militants. Since September 11, 2001, however, the United States has consistently conducted TK operations against Al Qaeda and its associated members. Colonel Peter M. Cullen asserts (Cullen, 2007) that in spite of the genuine controversy surrounding this subject of TK, a carefully orchestrated policy with such a focused approach can be a legal, moral, and effective tool in the campaign against insurgency and terrorism. Case studies of TK in Afghanistan have also yielded encouraging results (Wilner, 2010).

Nils Melzer states that "the dramatic events of September 11, 2001, led the United States, and soon after also Pakistan and Russia, to openly induct the method of TK into their repertoire of COIN" (Melzer, 2008). From the juridical point of view, Melzer concludes that "the international *lex lata* [present scheme of law] provides a clear and satisfactory regulatory framework for state-sponsored targeted killings, which requires careful and coherent interpretation".

Returning to Cullen, he tersely states that the concept of TK is a new paradigm with which international law is yet to come to terms. Melzer, too, continually insists on devising a *lex ferenda* (what the law should be) so as to properly deal with the subject of TK. Blum and Heymann of the Harvard Law School opine (Blum and Heymann, 2010) that the rights of democratically elected governments to use deadly force against their citizens are constrained by both domestic criminal law and international human rights norms, which attempt to protect the individual's right to life and liberty.

A 2016 RAND study on TK affirms (Davis et al., 2016) that there is a lack of transparency and clarity in the US government's policies for drones and TK. The researchers make it clear that threats, including those from IS, "do not change the characteristics of warfare in such a way as to rule out applying international law". The authors suggest striking a balance in order to ensure operational flexibility as well as the protection of human rights. From Osama to Bagdadi and then Soleimani, the American position, however, seems to be (Gurmendi, 2020) "consistent in arguing that it is the need of self-defence against non-state actors that justifies their killing". In 2010, legal adviser to the US Department of State, Harold Koh, uttered (Gurmendi, 2020): "A state that is engaged in armed conflict or in legitimate self-defence is not required to provide targets with legal process before the state may use lethal force".

However, while attempting to theorise TK, Tovy nicely articulates that "targeted killings have become an effective operational tool, albeit a controversial one, within the complex of activities that a state carries out in the battle against terrorists or guerrilla fighters" (Tovy, 2009).

Tovy lists some credible COIN programmes in the post-WWII era to substantiate his arguments. Mainly, the author quotes the suppression of the communist insurgency in Malaya and the effectively implemented Phoenix programme against the Viet Cong communist guerrillas (Tovy, 2009). In both of these cases, especially in Phoenix, the counterinsurgents relied on targeting the leadership. Quite logically, Tovy consistently mentions in his article that the targeted approach in the Phoenix programme never actually meant "targeted killing". In fact, it denoted the TI of the top leaders and extracted credible ground intelligence [HUMINT] from them.

Boyden, Menard, and Ramirez raise suspicion about the efficacy of the TK paradigm. In a crisp thesis (Boyden et al., 2009), they propose a six-step methodology with an embedded, robust analytic framework for determining the effectiveness of TK. By analysing Israel's programme during the *Second Intifada*, they ultimately concluded that TK was not effective.

On the other hand, Patrick Johnston of the RAND Corporation presents a mathematical modelling of suitable case studies (Johnston, 2012), "which challenges the extant notion that high-value targeting is ineffective". Specifically, Johnston's results showed "that removing insurgent leaders increases governments' chances of defeating insurgencies, reduces insurgent attacks, and diminishes overall levels of violence". However, Johnston cautions us against blind adherence to the 100% efficacy of the targeted approach when he writes that "a variety of different empirical tests consistently demonstrated that governments were more likely to defeat insurgencies following the successful removal of top insurgent leaders, but this probability was consistently estimated at around 25 to 30 percent".

Classical-Quantum Coupling: The Indian Paradigm

It is a significant feature that Indian authors on COIN have hardly discussed the targeted approach as a tactical methodology against insurgents. It is nothing unnatural, though, in the Indian context, which culturally repudiates any form of "killing", even if it is for the establishment of law and order in the long run.

Furthermore, the constitutional provisions debar such an approach on the basis of the "principle of natural justice" and human rights. To clarify further, in India, a TK is invariably interpreted as an extra-judicial "assassination" where the accused is denied *audi alteram partem*, or the "right to be heard". Even any COIN operation that eventually leads to the elimination of a key leader, viz., Maoist spokesperson Azad or the dreaded Kishenji, is lambasted in unequivocal terms as "fake encounters" by the rights activists.

Such an overpowering intellectual matrix, combined with the existing cultural psyche, submerges the cognition of the targeted approach, which, in the maximum possible theoretical arguments, finally seeks shelter in the semantics of "murder" and "brutality". Against this backdrop, it is essential to point out that in the Indian case, the targeted approach must connote TI, compounded with the TK of the insurgent leadership, as and when the situation demands it. The latter, however, needs to be followed as a matter of practise. At the same time, there is no need to shun it altogether.

It may be remembered that the elimination of key Maoist leaders in the early 1970s actually derailed the erstwhile *Naxal* insurgency, forcing the movement to run out of steam. A repetition of that approach has already shown its effectiveness, as the intensity of the insurgency has exhibited a decreasing trend since 2009 (Mukherjee, 2018). Nevertheless, two paths may well be traversed. First, a national-level legislative debate is warranted to arrive at a law to accommodate TK. Second, objective research must be conducted in the theoretical sphere in order to test the hypothesis of the targeted approach in the Indian scenario.

It must, however, be construed that the tactical weaponry of targeted approaches as a measure of COIN is in no way a licence to kill. By fair calculations, it is a tactical doctrine within an overall ambit of strategy. Equivalently, it must be borne in mind that the insurgent too possesses no licence to kill.

CRAFTING A COIN ARCHITECTURE FOR INDIA'S MAOIST INSURGENCY

Choking the Financial Flow

Insofar as finances are concerned, the Maoist rebels generally depend on:

1. Revolutionary tax from the people in their (mostly rural) "liberated zones"
2. Extortion of the contractors, corporations, and companies in their "liberated zones"
3. Funds and grants generated in urban areas from sympathisers and frontal organisations
4. Dacoities
5. Arms smuggling/sales
6. Money laundering

In order to counter issues enumerated in 1 and 2 above, the geographical expanse of the "liberated zones" needs to shrink considerably. In that regard, the clear-hold-build strategy under the umbrella of the classical-quantum COIN paradigm is the perfect choice. The more the guerrillas are thrown out of their zones, the local people as well as the outsiders will feel assured and hence will stop financing the rebels and will not be coerced into supplying them with money and logistics.

The following should be emphasised:

- Espionage in frontal organisations
- TI of suspected leadership of frontal organisations
- Espionage on college or university campuses, especially for those with a history of rebellion
- Espionage in social media interactions of suspected or potential rebels in urban areas – on Facebook, Telegram, WhatsApp, and Twitter, as well as the Dark Net

Overall, multi-agency coordination by the security forces is important to nab the financial trails of the ultras. In fact, the government has a set of teams in this regard (ET Bureau, 2018) and ought to continue with this.

The bottom line is that to thwart the financial pipeline of the Maoists, multi-pronged action is required, both from a security perspective and from a purely financial angle.

Targeting Urban Ideologues

In addition to the prescription on stifling the financial flow of the insurgents, the security forces must have a very strong public relations wing in urban areas that ought to structure the anti-Maoist perception among youth through seminars in colleges, universities, and academic institutions. A vigorous pro-government ideological propaganda campaign on television, radio, social media, and the internet, among other platforms, is the order of the day.

Academic courses on "internal security" and COIN at graduate and post-graduate levels would enhance the culture of research on insurgency and COIN in the country. The academic discourses in the Humanities and Arts faculty, especially the disciplines of sociology and political science, are to be monitored so that seditious literature, sentiment, or thought is not encouraged in the classroom. It would do no harm to keep in mind that the COIN war is continually fought in the propaganda space.

Disarmament, Rehabilitation, and Reintegration

The present surrender and rehabilitation policy laid down by the Ministry of Home Affairs (MHA) of the Government of India is good enough on the policy front (MHA, 2009).

However, insofar as the financial implications are concerned, the following amendments are suggested:

- The overall grant amount needs to be enhanced to ₹5,00,000 for the surrendered Maoist cadres.
- The scheme needs to be tailored for each state or province, keeping in mind the specific requirements of the insurgent-affected states.
- The minimum amount to be granted for giving up any weapon needs to be ₹1,000.
- Vigorous advertisement of the rehabilitation schemes through print, digital, and social media is imperative. *Nukkad nataks* (street shows) and processions through Maoist-affected villages and blocks in the local dialects ought to emphasise the details of the rehabilitation schemes so as to make them more popular.
- Anti-Maoist concepts to be propagated in the schools in the Maoist-affected areas.

Strengthening the Role of the Police

Alice Hills writes (Hills, 2012) that there is no coherent or comprehensive orthodoxy regarding the police role in COIN. Fair and Ganguly remark on the fact that there has been a considerable lack of attention in academic circles on the role of the police in COIN operations (Fair and Ganguly, 2014). Moreover, bringing in the army to counter the Maoists is always fraught with politico-legal implications in a democratic set-up, let alone ethical considerations of the army "fighting against its own people". The introduction of the army militarises the conflict, and the insurgency gravitates towards further radicalisation. The Indian army has nonetheless done a remarkable job in the north-eastern insurgencies as well as in Kashmir. But it has the Armed Forces Special Powers Act (AFSPA) to smooth its functioning in those areas. However, on a positive note, the deployment of the army in the Maoist-affected areas, albeit for training purposes, can have the impact of deterrence on the rebels. Shanthie Mariet D'Souza, in fact, recommends (D'Souza, 2009) the introduction of the army to deal with Maoism. She argues that militant activities could best be resolved through police-military operations. She cites the examples of the Khalistani insurgency and the terrorism in Tripura, both of which were quelled through brute force.

In the north-eastern Indian state of Tripura, "there were 636 police personnel per 100,000 people", a figure far greater than the national average of 141 (Kumar, 2016). To defeat the insurgents, the Tripura police came out with a "concept and conduct of COIN operations" in August 2000 and formed Quick Reaction Teams at each company-level operation base. Small-unit operations by the Tripura police turned out to be hugely effective (Kumar, 2016). A similar operational paradigm was also successful in Sri Lanka in the Eelam War IV (Hashim, 2013). Specialised training for COIN operations, enhanced capacity for intelligence gathering, modernisation of the police force, and strictly adhering to standard operating procedures, among other factors, made the Tripura police COIN operations successful (Kumar, 2016).

In this backdrop, the following are suggested:

1. Every Maoist-affected state ought to raise Special Forces (trained in COIN operations) in the model of the Greyhounds of Andhra Pradesh.
2. In addition to the Special Forces specifically dedicated to anti-Maoist operations, a sizable chunk of the state police forces (of Maoist-affected states)

must also be trained in COIN operations for a period of one to two years.

3. More COIN schools are to be raised in the Maoist-affected states. Every affected state must have at least two COIN warfare schools. The services of expert faculty members and trainers from the Indian Army, paramilitary forces, Central Armed Police Force (CAPF), and state police need to be utilised. Foreign trainers and army and police officers with the requisite exposure and experience can be roped in. Officials from Israel and the USA could be a good choice. Conferences with officers of the stature of General Petraeus, McChrystal, John Nagl, and David Kilcullen would be beneficial.
4. The integrated command structure under MHA as the nodal authority needs to be continued and strengthened. Every Maoist-affected state must be made to realise the urgency of cooperating with MHA in COIN strategy and operations, irrespective of its political affiliation.
5. Intelligence sharing among states needs to be done in letter and spirit. This is significant since the insurgents hop from one state to another through jungles and rough terrain.
6. Every Maoist-affected state to earmark funds for COIN operations, in addition to the funding being received from MHA. In fact, the Government of India has done appreciable work in this sphere (PIB, 2019). The state governments need to align accordingly.
7. During any anti-Maoist operation, the state police contingent needs to be equitably distributed alongside the CAPFs. In fact, joint training of the CAPFs and state police forces could be commenced to instil better camaraderie and synergy.
8. MHA at the national level and state governments at the provincial level should introduce academic disciplines in colleges, universities, academic institutions, and think-tanks related to defence and strategic studies with specialisation in COIN, internal security, insurgency management, and the like. Degrees from the bachelor's level to the PhD level could be offered.
9. Security personnel can also be trained in weapon management, maintenance, tackling IEDs, and using UAVs, among other relevant topics, in the institutes and organisations under the MoD, viz., ordnance factories, DRDO, and defence PSUs.
10. Training security personnel in local dialects and languages is a pre-requisite so that they enhance the probability of gathering human intelligence as well as mingle with the local population much better in order to win their hearts and minds.

In addition, Joint Action Committees comprising the state police, CAPF, civil administration, civilian experts, and other branches of the government could be formed in each Maoist-affected district to look into the modalities of the COIN. However, it would be very challenging to rope in the judiciary for this venture. But the district civil administration can apprise the district judiciary from time to time of the developments of the COIN. In fact, prior intimation to the judicial authorities regarding the charge sheets being drafted could help in these cases so that the insurgents are denied easy bail.

Also, serious thought must be given to inducting selected "embedded journalists" with the security forces while embarking on a COIN operation. That would help in the proper dissemination of news in the local, national, and international arenas and naturally build the brand image of the COIN forces.

Explosives and Ammunition

The largest chunk of weapons accessible to the rebels is homemade and low-tech. In order to stem this flow of weapons, the rebels need to be continuously monitored, their base areas searched and combed, and the overall CHB doctrine of the COIN needs to be implemented.

However, access to explosives and ammunition from external sources could be denied through proper intelligence and coordination. Only a thorough synergy among the different security agencies can help the security forces track the connection between the rebels with:

1. Arms smugglers within and without Indian borders
2. North-East Insurgents
3. Trans-national terrorists

Any such connection needs to be monitored through multi-agency tracking and nipped in the bud. The National Investigation Agency (NIA) and state Special Task Forces (STFs) have done commendable work on this. They need to continue doing so, but with credible ground intelligence inputs.

Penetration into the Maoist Base Area

At present, the Maoists have established several *Janathana Sarkars*, or liberated zones, but their fundamental base is in the territorially inaccessible forests of Abujhmaad, in the central Indian state of Chattisgarh. To physically capture Abujhmaad, a holistic combination of the following is required:

1. UAVs, drones, and satellite imagery will be used for tracking down the Maoist presence in the jungles.
2. District or area-level police forces to induct from the local population or ethnicities. More recruitment needs to be done since in COIN operations, at least a 50:1 force ratio is required. In Sri Lanka, in Eelam War IV and in the Tripura COIN war, there was a definite surge in recruitment. As Kumar (2016) opines, "the shortage of troops cannot be compensated through firepower or technology", and "the deployment of local forces is especially helpful in COIN due to their better cultural and situational awareness".
3. Division among insurgent ranks is essential since that would deplete their strengths as well as leave them in disarray. This method was successfully implemented in Sri Lanka (Hashim, 2013) when Col. Karuna defected from the LTTE.

4. Air power can be used not only for the supply of logistics but also in offensive mode to reduce troop casualties, effect faster troop movement, and target the elimination of the insurgents.

Along with Abujhmaad, multiple streams of forces can be unleashed simultaneously in other Maoist zones. In fact, the operations can be worked out in major Maoist-affected districts in such a manner that the rebels do not get a breather and their supply lines are jeopardised. This amount of targeted and comprehensive attack will eventually wipe out the rebels' structure on the ground.

Ground-Level Governance

1. A Tribes Advisory Council (TAC) as per the Fifth Schedule of the Indian Constitution could be constituted in the Maoist-affected states.
2. Humane security personnel armed with an effective public relations and communication strategy are the need of the hour at ground zero.
3. *Gramme Sabhas* (village assemblies) could be the actual conduits of grievance redressal centres for the people so that they do not seek justice at the hands of the Maoists.
4. Local journalists need to be befriended by the state police so as to garner leverage in the war of information, propaganda, and perception. The security forces on the ground as well as in the national and international fora have to be imposed as a humane workforce dedicated to the development of the country, whereas the anti-people face of the Maoists needs to be projected in all quarters. A designated spokesperson for the security forces in the district ought to be appointed. It would be preferable if a civilian officer not directly related to the operations was made the spokesperson, because that would help bridge any trust deficit between the security forces and the local population and media houses.

Legal Procedure

The issue that warrants application of mind is to evolve legal procedures to provide immunity to security personnel w.r.t. TK of insurgents. An act in this domain needs to be formulated and put up for parliamentary approval. A new act, viz., the Police Forces Special Powers Act [PFSPA], is required in this direction since AFSPA cannot be implemented because, in Maoist-affected districts, state police, CAPFs, and Special Forces are being used and are likely to be used in the foreseeable future. Naturally, they need proper legal immunity to work in challenging conditions like the Army has under AFSPA.

Development Is Supreme

Government schemes abound in basic education, potable water, health facilities, and the like. However, for all the government schemes to be implemented properly, the CHB phase of the classical-quantum COIN needs to be completed. Without the area being cleared of insurgents, development cannot be initiated.

Non-governmental Organisations (NGOs) could be encouraged in Maoist-affected areas, but only after proper scrutiny and examination of their funding. The most important aspect here is the training of the local youth to make them employable. The government's schemes in this direction need to be implemented in mission mode. The more the tribals and the lower castes are made job-ready, the less likely they are to join the insurgency. In this process, the water would be denied to the "insurgent" fish, and the requisite transformation from a belligerent insurgent guerrilla base to mainstream society would take place.

A holistic combination of the classical-quantum COIN paradigm along with local specificities could work especially well for not only the Indian case but also for countering other protracted insurgencies (communist or otherwise) in Asia and beyond.

References

Amidror, Y. (2010, August 23). "Winning counterinsurgency war – The Israeli experience", Jerusalem Centre for Public Affairs, https://jcpa.org/wp-content/uploads/2011/11/Amidror-perspectives-2.pdf, accessed on 21 Sep 2020.

Army Field Manual 3-24: Counterinsurgency. (2006):12, https://www.hsdl.org/?abstract&did=468442, accessed on 20 Sep 2020.

Banaji, J. (2010, October 14). "The ironies of Indian Maoism", *International Socialism, 128*, 129–148.

Banerjee, R. (2016, July 03). "The man India loves to forget", The Week, https://www.theweek.in/theweek/cover/charu-majumdar-naxalbari.html, accessed on 20 Sep 2020.

Baruah, S.K. (2019, August 7). "Boxed inside Kashmir Valley with 1:30 security-civilian ratio", https://www.moneycontrol.com/news/india/boxed-inside-kashmir-valley-with-130-security-civilian-ratio-4303011.html, accessed on 21 Sep 2020.

BBC News. (2019, October 28), "Abu Bakr al-Baghdadi: IS leader 'dead after US raid' in Syria", https://www.bbc.com/news/world-us-canada-50200339, accessed on 20 Sep 2020.

Blum, G. and Heymann, P.B. (2010, June 28). Law and policy of targeted killing. *Harvard National Security Journal, 1*(145), 26, Harvard Law School.

Boyden, A.W., Menard, P.P. and Ramirez, R. (2009, December). "Making the case: What is the problem with targeted killing?", Naval Postgraduate School, https://apps.dtic.mil/sti/pdfs/ADA514257.pdf, accessed on 21 Sep 2020.

Brady, K.R. (2017, June 25). *Insurgency and counterinsurgency in the modern era: Forms, framings, and the future.* Department of War Studies, King's College London.

Burton, F. (2011, May 26). The Bin Laden Operation: Tapping Human intelligence. STRATFOR. https://worldview.stratfor.com/article/bin-laden-operation-tapping-human-intelligence

Byman, D. (2009, April). Talking with insurgents: A guide for the perplexed. *The Washington Quarterly*, pp. 125–137.

Catignani, S. (2012). Israeli counterinsurgency: The never-ending 'Whack-a-Mole'. In Paul B. Rich and Isabelle Duyvesteyn (Eds.), *The Routledge handbook of insurgency and counterinsurgency*. (pp. 263–275). London: Routledge.

Chakravarti, S. (2018, March 1). "Azad's death and India's lost opportunity for peace with maoists", Live Mint, https://www.livemint.com/Opinion/uAYynCLrBZ8Ttc786TbmzK/Azads-death-and-Indias-lost-opportunity-for-peace-with-Mao.html, accessed on 20 Sep 2020.

Cohen, E.T. and Katz, E. (2019, November 6). "What we can learn about US intelligence from the Baghdadi raid", Brookings, https://www.brookings.edu/blog/order-from-chaos/2019/11/06/what-we-can-learn-about-us-intelligence-from-the-baghdadi-raid/, accessed on 20 Sep 2020.

Crenshaw, M. (1991). How terrorism declines. *Terrorism and Political Violence*, *3*(1), 69–87.

Cullen, P.M. (2007, March 30). "The role of targeted killing in the campaign against terror", U.S. Army War College, https://apps.dtic.mil/sti/pdfs/ADA471529.pdf, accessed on 21 Sep 2020.

Davis, L.E., McNerney, M. and Greenberg, M.D. (2016). "Clarifying the rules for targeted killing", RAND Corporation, https://www.rand.org/content/dam/rand/pubs/research_reports/RR1600/RR1610/RAND_RR1610.pdf, accessed on 21 Sep 2020.

D'Souza, S.M. (2009, July). Countering the Naxalites: Is there a need to 'bring in' the army? *Journal of Defence Studies*, *3*(3), 125–132.

ET Bureau. (2018, July 11). "Government sets up teams to choke Naxal funding", https://economictimes.indiatimes.com/news/defence/govt-sets-up-teams-to-choke-naxal-funding/articleshow/64072449.cms?from=mdr, accessed on 21 Sep 2020.

Fair, C.C. and Ganguly, S. (2014). *Policing insurgencies*. Oxford University Press, ISBN 978-0-19-809488-3

Galula, D. (1964). "Counterinsurgency warfare: Theory and practice", Praeger Security International, https://pdfs.semanticscholar.org/f2d2/aedbdcab918cc7c2d837882aff7068db6d4f.pdf?_ga=2.202081169.1287526801.1600635672-773388636.1595170065, accessed on 21 Sep 2020.

Gurmendi, A. (2020, January 09). "Raising questions on targeted killings as first strikes in IACs", http://opiniojuris.org/2020/01/09/raising-questions-on-targeted-killings-as-first-strikes-in-iacs/, accessed on 21 Sep 2020.

Hashim, A.S. (2013). "When counterinsurgency wins, Sri Lanka's defeat of the Tamil Tigers", University of Pennsylvania Press, ISBN 978-93-82993-47-6.

Hills, A. (2012). Insurgency, counterinsurgency and policing. In P. B. Rich & I. Duyvesteyn (Eds.), The *Routledge Handbook of Insurgency and Counterinsurgency* (pp. 98-108). London: Routledge.

Hindustan Times. (2011, November 24). "Top maoist jeader Kishenji Hilled", https://web.archive.org/web/20111126182836/http://www.hindustantimes.com/India-news/NewDelhi/Bloody-end-for-Maoist-leader-Kishenji-CRPF-kills-him-in-Bengal/Article1-773485.aspx, accessed on 20 Sep 2020.

Johnston, P.B. (Spring 2012). Does decapitation work? Assessing the effectiveness of leadership targeting in counterinsurgency campaigns. *Quarterly Journal: International Security*, 79(36).

Kaur, A., Auroro, J. S., Singh, K., Kamath, M. V., Gupta, S., Kirpekar, S., Sethi, S., and Singh, T. (2020). *The Punjab Story*. New Delhi: Roli Books.

Kilcullen, D. (2012). Counterinsurgency: The state of a controversial art. In P. B. Rich & I. Duyvesteyn (Eds.), *The Routledge handbook of insurgency and counterinsurgency* (pp. 128–153). London: Routledge.

Kirpekar, S. (1984). *Operation Bluestar: An eyewitness account, the Punjab story*. ROLI BOOKS, p. 106.

Kumar, K. (2016). Police and counterinsurgency: The untold story of Tripura's coin campaign. Sage, ISBN 978-93-515-0747-5 (HB).

Luttwak, E.N. (1999, July/August). "Give War a Chance", Foreign Affairs.

Melzer, Nils. (2008). "Targeted killing in international law", Oxford University Press. ISBN 9780199533169

MHA (Ministry of Home Affairs). (2009, August 27). "Guidelines for surrender-cum-rehabilitation of Naxalites in the Naxal affected states", https://www.mha.gov.in/sites/default/files/surrrenderPolAendments070909_0.pdf, accessed on 21 Sep 2020.

Mukherjee, U. (2009, October 6). "The McChrystal report and India", IPCS, Article 2978, http://www.ipcs.org/comm_select.php?articleNo=2978, accessed on 21 Sep 2020.

Mukherjee, U. (2018, July). No need to talk: Answering the Maoist question. *Faultlines*, *22*, 41–62.

Mukherjee, U. (2019, May 17). "Fighting venom with venom: Is there a case for using Al Qaeda against ISIS?", Swarajya, https://swarajyamag.com/politics/fighting-venom-with-venom-is-there-a-case-for-using-al-qaeda-against-isis, accessed on 20 Sep 2020.

Npr. (2020, February 6). "Colombia's FARC rebels laid down their weapons, but a growing number are being killed", https://www.npr.org/2020/02/06/802764177/colombias-farc-rebels-laid-down-their-weapons-but-a-growing-number-are-being-kil, accessed on 21 Sep 2020.

Packer, G. (2009, September 23). "Reading the McChrystal Report", The New Yorker, https://www.newyorker.com/news/george-packer/reading-the-mcchrystal-report, accessed on 21 Sep 2020.

PIB Delhi. (2019, July 17). "Steady decline in casualties in Naxal attacks", PIB Delhi, https://pib.gov.in/PressReleaseIframePage.aspx?PRID=1579194, accessed on 21 Sep 2020.

Pubby, M. (2009, October 4). "Anti-Maoist operation has a '71 template", The Indian Express, http://archive.indianexpress.com/news/antimaoist-operation-has-a--71-template/528868/, accessed on 20 Sep 2020.

Stahl, A.E. and Owen, W.F. (Winter 2010). Targeted killings work. *Infinity Journal*, *1*(1), 10–13.

TNN. (2010, September 28). "58% in AP say Naxalism is good, finds TOI poll", https://timesofindia.indiatimes.com/india/58-in-AP-say-Naxalism-is-good-finds-TOI-poll/articleshow/6639631.cms, accessed on 17 September 2020.

Tovy, T. (2009). The theoretical aspect of targeted killings: The phoenix program as a case study. *Journal of Military and Strategic Studies*, *11*(4), 1–24

Washington Post. (2009, September 21). "COMISAF initial assessment (unclassified)", https://www.washingtonpost.com/wp-dyn/content/article/2009/09/21/AR2009092100110.html, accessed on 21 Sep 2020.

Wilner, A.S. (2010, March 9). Targeted killings in Afghanistan: Measuring coercion and deterrence.*Counterterrorism and Counterinsurgency, Studies in Conflict & Terrorism*, *33*(4), 307–329.

Yi, D.W. (2018). "Counterinsurgency force ratios: An investigation into military logic", School of Advanced Military Studies US Army Command and General Staff College, https://apps.dtic.mil/sti/pdfs/AD1071542.pdf, accessed on 21 Sep 2020.

3

A TYPOLOGY OF INSURGENCY AND COUNTERINSURGENCY[1]

Donald Stoker

INTRODUCTION

The literature on insurgency and counterinsurgency is voluminous, and this is certainly not the place to discuss it. Much of the writing on these topics is tactical and thus not directly related to our discussion, which concerns political and strategic matters. The literature suffers from an endemic lack of self-awareness on this point, too often failing to deal with the reality that tactical fixes usually cannot address the larger strategic challenges. This failure can lead to simplistic recommendations for addressing one of the most complicated military problems. Unfortunately, space requires us to risk making the same error.

THE FOUNDATION FOR ANALYSIS: THE POLITICAL AIM

As with all wars, we must begin the analysis by understanding the political aims sought. Insurrections are invariably classified as limited wars because the insurgents, tactically, fight using traditional guerrilla warfare methods with forces that are usually (but certainly not always) small, weak, and poorly armed, at least initially. This is a fallacious point upon which to base one's analysis, as it is the political aim that provides the clearest basis for this, not the size of the force or the means and methods of warfare. Insurrections can pursue limited or unlimited political aims, which depend on the situation at hand. Do the insurgents want the overthrow of the regime (an unlimited political aim) or do they want something else, say, for example, 13 colonies in an imperial backwater (Clausewitz, 1984; Corbett, 1988)? Mao Tse-Tung's Communists sought an unlimited political aim: the overthrow of the Chinese Nationalist regime. The insurgents may also have different aims against different opponents. The North Vietnamese sought not only the destruction of the South Vietnamese regime but also the ousting of the US from South Vietnam. In either case, the primacy of politics reigns supreme. This remains true even if the political aim is clothed in religious rhetoric.

As always, the value of the political aim is key (Clausewitz, 1984). If the insurgents want the overthrow of the regime, this implies a high value on the object for the insurgents as well as the leaders and supporters of the regime that is now protecting itself. It is the counterinsurgent who is fighting the war for a limited political purpose. Indeed, the counterinsurgent, or counterinsurrectionist (a term taken from historian Jeremy Black), is always seeking a limited political aim because it wishes to preserve the government and its control. Understandably, some will see this as counterintuitive (Black, 2016). The political aim of maintaining control should not be confused with the fact that the government might be forced to destroy the enemy to achieve its limited aim. Do not confuse the goal with the means and methods used.

If the aim of the insurgents is not regime change but the redress of some grievances, the regime is wise to try and settle this via negotiations, which have historically been one of the ways of ending an insurrection or insurgency and should not be baulked at except under very unusual circumstances. Sometimes the counterinsurgent surrenders to impatience here when they shouldn't, denies the legitimacy of any grievances, and fights when talking might be the answer. The counterinsurgent also sometimes wants to fight with the tools and methods they possess without incurring much in the way of political or social costs while failing to realise when they need to adjust to the situation at hand (Darling, 1974). The classic 1940 US Marine Corps *Small Wars Manual* offers excellent advice here: "The application of purely military measures may not, by itself, restore peace and orderly government because the fundamental causes of the conditions of unrest may be economic, political, or social" (USMC, 1987).

DOI: 10.4324/9780429426063-5

Negotiations can be even more useful if they can lead to quick achievement of the political aim desired, though one should be cautious about ceasing to apply military pressure during negotiations as this can be interpreted as weakness.

SETTING THE STAGE

Insurgent or insurrectionist groups can be broken into two types: patriotic partisan resistance movements and revolutionary movements. Patriotic partisan resistance groups usually begin spontaneously in the wake of an enemy invasion and then become more organised. The Free French Resistance against the Nazis during the Second World War is a famous example. Resistance doesn't end until the invaders are expelled or the insurgents are convinced they can't achieve their aims. Because they are usually directed at an invader, such movements can have a larger base of support than revolutionary movements because their appeal is broader (Mao, 2000). Carl von Clausewitz studied and planned such efforts and offers what he calls "Conditions Under Which a General Uprising Can Succeed":

- The war must be fought in the interior of the country.
- There cannot be a single decisive action.
- The theatre of operations must be fairly large.
- The national character must be suited to that type of war.
- The country must be rough and inaccessible because of mountains, forests, marshes, or the local methods of cultivation (Clausewitz, 1984: 480).

The second type of insurrectionist group – revolutionary movements – has ideological or religious foundations. In the modern era, they have most often been Marxist in character, though the Islamic State and other similar groups represent religiously driven cousins (Whiteside, 2016). Mao Tse-Tung's Communists are the most famous and among the most successful. These movements usually last until the enemy government is toppled or the rebels are killed.

What most term "terrorism" and "guerrilla warfare" are the primary violent tools insurgent groups use to get what they want. Terrorism is considered a tool of the weak, though it is conceptually flawed and restricting to view it that way. The North Vietnamese Communists commonly used terror against South Vietnam, but they were not weak in comparison to their South Vietnamese opponent. Some groups (such as the early Russian anarchists) went so far as to believe that terror alone would be enough to incite the masses and bring down the hated regime, though most realised this was unlikely (Neumann and Smith, 2005).

There are many definitions of terrorism, but one of the best is this: "terrorism is the intentional use of, or threat to use, violence against civilians or civilian targets in order to attain political aims" (Ganor, 2010). Terror is used to obtain a political objective, but the point is not the death and destruction it generates; this is the visual result that is part of an effort to attack the target's spirit while simultaneously creating fear, thus driving the target to make political changes (Neumann and Smith, 2005).

Terrorism is also often mistakenly called a tactic. One of the reasons for this is a failure to understand the differences between tactics and strategy. For the Algerian FLN (Front de libération nationale) members who launched the 1954 uprising against France, terrorism was a strategy, not a tactic. Terror against civilians was intended to provoke a heavy French reaction, which would drive people into the rebel camp (Horne, 2006; Porch, 2003). Terrorism was a plank of North Vietnam's strategy against South Vietnam. It helped undermine and destabilise the South Vietnamese government while driving people to support the Communist cause or face the murder of themselves or their families. Terror was a primary element of the Islamic State's warfighting strategy. The confusion here is that observers see the tactical application of violence in the form of car bombings or assassinations and then insist that terrorism is a tactic. This overlooks the concepts driving the tactical execution.

Terror also doesn't always work. During the Malayan Emergency (1948–1966), it drove people away from the insurgency (McCuen, 1966). Islamic State gained much through using terror, but this also helped bring the US, France, and other nations into the war against them. Also, the counterinsurgents must work to ensure that they are not blamed for enemy acts. This can be difficult. The Algerian insurrectionists successfully pinned one of their 1957 massacres on the French, and US forces in Iraq unfairly received the blame for a 2004 Baghdad bombing (Neumann and Smith, 2005).

Successful insurrectionist movements make great use of distraction and deception. They seek to draw the enemy to one thing while attacking another. Deception, manoeuvre, flexibility, and concealment of their true purpose – these are the attributes of successful guerrilla operations. Counterinsurgency theorist John J. McCuen argues that for the revolutionary to win, they must take Mao's advice and wage a "strategically protracted war" and 1) wear down the enemy's strength through the cumulative effects of combat, 2) get stronger by gaining the support of the people while establishing base areas and taking needed material from the enemy, and 3) obtain outside support, political and especially military (McCuen, 1966: 30).

The counterinsurgent always wants a quick war and is too often surprised by the reality that counterinsurgency takes a long time and is almost always protracted. Scholars differ on how long insurgencies last, as there are so many different variables involved in calculating this, most of which are very difficult to control. Six to 11 years is not unusual (Johnston and Urlacher, 2012; Stoker, 2007). Counterinsurgency expert Robert Thompson wrote: "If one tries to talk about speed in pacification, it must be remembered that it will take as long to get back to the preferred status quo ante as it took the other side to get to the new position" (Dougherty, 2012: 92–93).

There are many factors that contribute to the length of an insurgency – material and psychological – on both sides. Sometimes the counterinsurgent simply doesn't understand the task facing them. Theorist John McCuen wrote: "Winning a revolutionary war will take massive organisation, dedication, sacrifice, and time. The government must decide early if it is willing to pay the price. Half-measures lead only to protracted and costly defeats" (Singh, 1995: 141–142). Insurgency theorist David Galula believed that one of France's greatest problems in suppressing the rebellion in Algeria was "the political instability in France and the absence of a firm, continuing, clear-cut policy on the part of the various French governments all through the war." The counterinsurgent must have a clear aim that it keeps in sight and a coherent programme that impresses upon the opponent that the counterinsurgent is "acting according to a well-thought-out plan that leaves them no room for maneuvering."

Furthermore, Galula insists that the French, despite the experience of their wars in Indochina and Algeria, never possessed a coherent counterinsurgency doctrine (Galula, 2006: 177, 208, 268). Historian Jeffrey Record aptly observed that for the counterinsurgent, "the combination of a weaker political will and an inferior strategy can be a recipe for defeat" (Record, 2007: 67). The protracted nature of such conflicts can then have cross-generational effects by forcing many to engage in long-term conflict or through the creation of thousands of internally displaced people (IDPs) and refugees who seek refuge by the thousands, as observed in the case of more than 100,000 Saharawis forced to make their way across the desert from the Western Sahara to Algeria under fire and aerial bombardment (Besenyő, 2010).

A TYPOLOGY OF INSURGENCY AND COUNTERINSURGENCY

Critically, when there is an insurrection or insurgency, *both sides* must strive to control the following three key factors: 1) the support of the people, 2) the control of internal or external sanctuary by the insurgents, and 3) whether or not the insurgent has outside support. If the insurgents secure all three of these, this will likely mean victory for the rebels. If the counterinsurgent force controls these factors, it will probably win.

The Support of the People

Winning the support of the people is crucial for the results of the insurrection. They are "the key to the entire struggle," and their alienation from their rulers can be a source of insurrection (Taber, 2007: 22–23). This is not always the case, though, as groups such as the Chinese and North Vietnamese Communists worked to alienate the people from their regimes, but the people were still the key. Mao Tse-Tung wrote: "Because guerrilla warfare basically derives from the masses and is supported by them, it can neither exist nor flourish if it separates itself from their sympathies and cooperation" (Mao, 2000: 44). The challenge for both sides lies in determining how to win them to your camp while keeping them from the opponent, or at least ensuring their neutrality.

The issue of means in wars of this type is often a sticking point. One of the great mistakes of counterinsurgents is believing they can win cheaply and using minimal force to do so. One must always use a level of means *sufficient* to obtain the political aim. Sometimes a small force is the answer. The level and intensity of the insurgency will reveal this. But one of the most common errors made by counterinsurgents is not sending sufficient force quickly enough. McCuen writes: "The sooner the governing power reacts, the less will be the resources required and the shorter will be the period in which they have to be applied … Remember that the most serious – and the most common – error in counter-insurgency warfare is to do too little, too late" (Singh, 1995: 139). The *Small Wars Manual* advises that "when forced to resort to arms to carry out the object of the intervention, the operation must be pursued energetically and expeditiously in order to overcome the resistance as quickly as possible" (USMC, 1987: 13).

Unfortunately, this is often easier said than done, and sometimes it's not the whole answer. In an effort to quell the 1954 Algerian revolt, the French eventually put large numbers of troops on the ground. They mobilised reservists, extended the mandatory service time of conscripts, and committed elite units such as the paratroopers and the Foreign Legion, all to try to ensure they had sufficient forces to provide security as well as hunt down the insurgents. The French eventually destroyed the bulk of the insurgent force in Algeria, but this did not ultimately deliver victory. Numerous other factors, such as the existence of external sanctuary and support, supported the Algerian cause (Clayton, 1994; Porch, 2013).

When the insurgency began in Iraq in 2003 against the US and allied forces, the US had insufficient troops on the ground to exert control over Iraq and hunt down insurgents. Indeed, the US never got a handle on the situation in Iraq until it increased its own troop numbers, stood up large numbers of Iraqi police and army units, and armed anti-Al Qaeda Sunni tribesmen. Quickly dispatching larger numbers of troops earlier and with better military and civilian planning and leadership might have prevented some of these problems or at least made it possible to stabilise Iraq sooner (Gordon and Trainor, 2007; 2012). The US should have remembered the advice of its hard-won past experience. The *Small Wars*

Manual advised: "The occupying force must be strong enough to hold all of the strategic points of the country, protect its communications, and at the same time furnish an operating force sufficient to overcome the opposition wherever it appears" (USMC, 1987: 15).

Gaining an understanding of the depths of the insurgency is also critical. One reason the British initially suffered failure in Malaya was that the Communist insurgency had already metastasised. The British had supported it at the outset of the Japanese occupation during World War II. By the end of the war in 1945, it was well-developed and had deep roots in the countryside. By 1951, the insurgency had reached its peak strength of 10,000 active members but also had more than 100,000 supporters (Corum, 2006). Something similar occurred in South Vietnam. The famous soldier and writer Bernard Fall determined that in South Vietnam, evidence of Communist penetration could be seen in the assassination of village chieftains, the failure of the South to collect taxes in a district, and the success of the Viet Cong in taxing the area. Six months before the 1963 murder of South Vietnam's president, Ngo Dinh Diem, between March and May 1963, the Communists were collecting taxes in 42 of 45 South Vietnamese provinces (Fall, 2015). The insurgency had metastasised *before* the US escalation. This makes the counterinsurgent's job much more difficult, though not impossible. More time, effort, and sacrifice will inevitably be required.

Winning back a population under insurgent control can be difficult. In *Small Wars*, C.E. Callwell advises keeping the enemy under constant pressure, but this can only be done by first properly preparing. To do this, he essentially argues for a version of what the French called *quadrillage*. The theatre is divided into sections that include outposts for defence; these are supported by fast columns pursuing the insurgents. The size of the sections is based on the geography and terrain. These zones are further subdivided to systematically strip them of the food supplies needed by the enemy and methodically clear the guerrillas. Troops should be moved from less troublesome to more difficult zones, a decision made based upon local conditions. The concept dates at least to the French Revolutionaries' efforts to suppress the 1793 uprising in the Vendée (Callwell, 1996; Clayton, 1994; Porch, 2013).

There are many similar ideas that seek to restore government control and separate the insurgents from the people. One is population resettlement. This famously worked wonders in Malaysia, where the primary source of the insurgency's manpower – the ethnic Chinese minority – could be resettled in protected villages. The US and South Vietnam launched a similar plan known as the strategic hamlet programme. The results were mixed, partly because of South Vietnamese failures in the implementation of the programme and partly because the majority Buddhist South Vietnamese had ancestral ties to their land and resented being moved (Beckett, 1997; Lewy, 1980; Turley, 2009).

Totalitarian states also undertake clearing operations and remove populations sympathetic to or susceptible to insurgent influence, but democratic states generally intend to co-opt the people, while authoritarians usually punish them. Stalin's forced population removal of minorities that might prove disloyal, as well as his wholesale murder of the population in places like Ukraine, made it exceedingly difficult for an insurgency to emerge. Displacing the population by mass deportations or mass importation of sympathetic populations, such as the Chinese Communist practise of moving Han Chinese into Tibet, is another way of controlling the situation (Ucko, 2016). This, though, can produce resentments that create problems.

A related point is that one of the factors upon which the guerrillas can sometimes count is the self-restraint of the counterinsurgent when dealing with the civilian population. One cannot make a blanket statement here, but this is generally a behaviour rule among democratic states conducting counterinsurgency (Luttwak, 1987). This does not apply to totalitarian states. The Russians used military power to prevent the insurgents from establishing themselves among the population in Ukraine in the post-Second World War era and in Chechnya in 1999. In Chechnya, the Russian response convinced many Chechen leaders that it was impossible to resist. This allowed the Russians to co-opt them and shift the burden to local security forces. The Syrians acted similarly against the Muslim Brotherhood in the 1980s. Such brutality can have effects that are, to some, counterintuitive: "Paradoxically, collective punishment has at times turned the population against the rebels, who are blamed for the devastation." This has sometimes been the reaction of civilians in the Syrian Civil War, who blame the rebels for Assad bombing them (Ucko, 2016: 43). It is not so easy to predict the reaction of the population to violence in such circumstances. It seems to boil down to the harsh issue of who the people fear the most.

How counterinsurgents should use force is a critical issue and will directly affect the direction in which the population sways. Killing the leaders of insurgent groups often increases the chances of a government victory and reduces the level of insurgent violence. The government rarely suffers any negative effects as a result of this, and it's "likely to be more effective than capturing them." The more the group is dependent on the leader, the greater the effect. Killing insurgent leaders, though, does not guarantee success. This is particularly true if the group has a well-developed bureaucracy and popular support. Some studies have found that killing the leaders becomes less effective if the group has existed for more than 25 years (Johnston, 2012: 75; Jordan, 2014). As is so often the case, the result depends on the circumstances.

One issue is whether the counterinsurgents should concentrate on killing the insurgents or winning over the population through other means. The answer is usually both. But what is also critical is establishing the rule of law, which is especially important for underpinning the credibility of the counterinsurgent. Insurgents exploit the contradictions in governance, law, land ownership, minority rights, or whatever else gives them an edge.

Insurgency expert Otto Heilbrunn boils down the counterinsurgent's use of force:

> To sum up: security operations will produce dividends only if the police and members of the population co-operate; the terrorists' hold over the population is thus broken, and the security forces have a good chance to win the hearts and minds campaign. If this co-operation cannot be obtained, the security forces are unlikely to win. Military operations can only immobilise the terrorists, and their hold over the population will probably continue; while counter-terror can lead to the terrorists' arrest but strengthens the people's allegiance to the terrorists' cause (Heilbrunn, 1969: 56–57).

If one is a foreign state conducting counterinsurgency in another land, this adds another layer of difficulty, especially if the uprising is fuelled by nationalism (Howard, 1969). During the Algerian War, the French viewed themselves as protecting part of France, but the bulk of native Algerians saw them as an alien force.

The quality of governance can sway the people and is critical to consider, especially if one is conducting counterinsurgency in another state. If the host nation suffers from bad government, the counterinsurgency effort is less likely to succeed. This doesn't mean it can't, but one must assume the difficulty increases by an order of magnitude. American diplomat George F. Kennan wrote in February 1948: "You can help any government but one that does not know how to govern." One reason George Marshall refused to allow the post-Second World War US mission to China to expand and assume the same roles as the advisory mission to Greece – meaning allowing US advisors to give tactical and strategic advice – was because Marshall believed US advisors could exert influence over Greek leaders more readily than they could over China's head, Chiang Kai-Shek. Rightly or wrongly, many of Truman's advisors believed the Nationalists lost their civil war because of Chiang's "inability to govern" (Pach, 1991: 195). If the decision is made to provide assistance, it must be appropriate. When advising, it is wise to remember Lawrence of Arabia's Article 15: that it is better they "do it tolerably than that you do it perfectly" (Lawrence, 1917).

It is critically important to find the source of the problem. Is it internal to the government itself or external? Internal problems run to the obvious: weak, oppressive, or corrupt leaders are common, as are problems in the system itself. Sometimes the need for reform is obvious, but there is a general failure to address it. Here, it is important to determine whether the problems are self-generated and if the regime has a willingness to tackle them. Unfortunately, it is too often the case that governments simply fail to understand the conditions in their own countries. This can make them weak and susceptible to internal attacks (USMC, 1987). Addressing political, economic, and other grievances can be a useful tool for ending an insurgency, as rebel groups often exploit them. Doing so removes points around which insurrectionists can rally support.

What is sometimes forgotten here is that at least some of the governing problems may be external because the country is suffering from subversion or the effects of the insurgency. During the Vietnam War, there were obvious problems of corruption and incompetence in the South Vietnamese government that dramatically reduced its effectiveness. But the South's governance capability was seriously undermined by the Communist North's constant propaganda and extensive campaign of assassination and kidnapping against Southern officials. This drastically increases the problem of governance while discrediting the regime, which is the point of the activity as the insurgents establish a shadow government to replace the state's rulers. Counterinsurgency theorist Bernard Fall observed in regard to Vietnam: "When a country is being subverted, it is not being outfought; it is being out-administered" (Fall, 2015: 45–46).

The counterinsurgent should remember to treat prisoners well. If not, this can have negative effects on their relations with the people. Don't be afraid to treat them under the rules of the Geneva Convention if this is necessary to maintain internal or foreign support. One can certainly add the caveat that this does not mean recognition of the political legitimacy of the opponent, but that this is being done for administrative reasons and to demonstrate integrity to the international community. Exert public pressure upon the insurgents to do the same, though this will undoubtedly fail because the insurgents, especially smaller groups, usually lack the willingness or ability to act according to any international norms. Mao argued for the good treatment of prisoners as a way to win them to his cause. But the Communists also never shrank from using any form of violence they believed useful. Another option is to treat counterinsurgents as criminals. One then faces the problems of criminal prosecution and all that this entails. Sometimes, though, this might be the best solution. This will be determined by the circumstances. Don't be afraid to give amnesty to insurgents if this will end the war on acceptable terms and if you can bear the domestic and international political costs of doing so.

A harsh truth is that the counterinsurgent cannot fight as the insurgent does. Their aims are different, which dictates what each side can and must do to achieve its goals. The guerrilla often holds the initiative and often "has the freedom of his poverty" (Taber, 2007: 22). Robert Taber writes:

> By contrast, the purpose of the counter-revolutionary is negative and defensive. It is to restore order, to protect property, to preserve existing forms and interests by force of arms, *where persuasion has already failed*. His means may be political in so far as they involve the use of still more persuasion—the promise of social and economic reforms, bribes of a more localized sort, counter-propaganda of various kinds.

> But primarily the counter-insurgent's task must be *to destroy the revolution by destroying its promise*—that means by proving, militarily, that it cannot and will not succeed (Taber, 2007: 23).

One problem is that counterinsurgents become so concerned with tactical issues that they do not see the larger picture. Indeed, some examinations of counterinsurgency argue that counterinsurgency is largely a form of tactic (Porch, 2013).

Critically, both sides will try to win over the people through propaganda or information operations. This is an arena where the counterinsurgent is often weak. Galula criticised the French effort in Algeria by noting: "If there was a field in which we were definitely and infinitely more stupid than our opponents, it was propaganda" (Galula, 2006: 104). This same argument has been made regarding US information operations against the Islamic State (Ingram and Whiteside, 2019).

Controlling Sanctuary

For the insurgent, who is usually weaker than the regime he opposes, or, in the case of the North Vietnamese, weaker than the primary ally of its opponent, possession of sanctuary for its government and its military forces is a vital component for building towards success. For the counter-insurgent, removing insurgent sanctuary, both foreign and internal, is critical. One of the primary reasons the Afghan Taliban could continue its war against the US after 2002 was its possession of sanctuary in Pakistan.

The political objectives will, of course, affect sanctuaries as well as where the war will be fought (Hampton, 1957). This acts as a constraint upon military activity, particularly on the part of the counterinsurgent, who historically restricts where its military forces will fight by placing sanctuary countries off limits, or, as was the case with the British in the War for American Independence, simply lacks sufficient forces to control enough territory to effectively remove the sanctuary. One observer notes this post-Second World War truth: "The respect for sanctuary has been carried to an extraordinary extent in twentieth-century limited war" (McClintock, 1957: 200).

The loss of sanctuary can be fatal to insurgents. The post-Second World War Greek Communist insurgents lost bases and support from Yugoslavia's Tito after his 1948 rift with the Soviet Union. Moreover, the Greeks learned to do counterinsurgency, addressed economic issues, and had much US support (Black, 2016). During the Korean War (1950–1953), with UN help, South Korea isolated the battlespace and, in the anti-guerrilla operation Ratkiller, killed 20,000 insurgents and bandits by the end of January 1952 (Ridgway, 1967). Mao's "Long March" allowed him to construct a sanctuary in the Chinese hinterland, and though the Japanese invasion also contributed to the survival of Chinese Communism, the ability to create and preserve a safe base also proved instrumental. Sanctuaries in Tunisia and Morocco didn't prevent the French from essentially destroying the insurrectionist FLN forces inside Algeria, but they did permit the FLN to build an army as an international symbol of resistance. The Tamil Tiger rebels in Sri Lanka had no sanctuary and no external ally. When Sri Lankan forces penetrated the Tamil heartland and killed the rebel leader, the movement died.

One of the great benefits enjoyed consistently by the North Vietnamese Communist forces was sanctuary. As rebels against France, they had external sanctuary in China when needed, as well as internal sanctuary in many parts of what is now northern Vietnam. When the US began fighting the North Vietnamese conquest of South Vietnam, the Communist forces benefited from external sanctuary in North Vietnam, Laos, and Cambodia. This gave the North the ability to dictate the momentum of the war, the timing of their offensives, a relatively secure line of supply via Laos, and safe areas for refit and resupply in Cambodia (Herring, 2008: 739). The US's inability to control the battlespace under such constraints meant that it could not protect pacification efforts from North Vietnamese attacks, which was important for ensuring their success, especially against a deep-rooted insurgency (Daddis, 2014).

Controlling Outside Support

Something that most successful insurgencies have in common is external assistance (Record, 2007). Mao agreed (O'Connor, 1969). This can be material or diplomatic, with material usually but not always being more important. The insurgents generally strive to secure external assistance, and with good reason. They are almost always weak in comparison with their enemies, and external assistance can give them arms, money, critical diplomatic recognition, and many other things they need to succeed. The counter-insurgents must separate the insurgents from outside support. This can be as critical as separating the insurgents from the people, which also must be done.

Insurgent movements can win without outside support, but it's difficult. The Bolsheviks fought their way to success without external help, securing their victory in 1921. In their 1919–1921 war, the Irish Republican insurrectionists succeeded in gaining most of what they wanted from Britain without significant outside support. Mao Tse-Tung's Chinese Communists received outside support from the Soviet Union near the end of their struggle against the Nationalists, but this, arguably, sped up rather than determined their success. The possession of capable, resolute leaders, their ability to successfully appeal ideologically to the Chinese people, and the weaknesses of their opponent contributed greatly to the Communists' victory.

Without external support, defeat is the more likely result for the insurgents. The Confederacy failed to achieve its independence partially because Abraham Lincoln helped ensure Great Britain and France didn't join the war on the side of the rebel South. The Malaysian Communist insurgents (1954–1962) had no outside help and didn't succeed. The West Papuan Independence Movement against Indonesia has not succeeded despite many years of resistance; it has no outside support. The mid-nineteenth-century Taiping rebels had no foreign support, while the Chinese government received Anglo-French aid that helped it achieve victory. The 1967 Biafran revolt in Nigeria was quickly crushed because the Biafrans' sea links were cut. This made foreign aid impossible (Black, 2016). The American colonists triumphed over Great Britain, but the intervention of France and Spain – particularly the former – proved decisive. The Vietnamese Communists won against France in 1954. Chinese aid (and sanctuary) were critical. Soviet and Chinese support also greatly contributed to the North Vietnamese victory over the US and South Vietnam. The Algerian insurgents triumphed even after suffering the near destruction of their forces in Algeria because of international political support.

DEFINING VICTORY IN INSURGENCY AND COUNTERINSURGENCY

The aims being sought define victory. The political aims of the insurgents differ from those of the counterinsurgents. Usually, for the rebels, the control of their own state counts as a victory. This was certainly the view of the Algerians and Mao's Communists. For the counterinsurgent, it's not so simple. Galula points out that "counterinsurgency seldom ends with a ceasefire and a triumphal parade" (Galula, 2006: 244). In his view, victory had been achieved when the counterinsurgent could remove the bulk of its forces, "leaving the population to take care of itself with the help of a normal contingent of police and Army forces" (Galula, 2006: 168). The bottom line in counterinsurgency is: do the people support the government? If not, one should consider quitting.

CONCLUSION

The above has touched upon numerous very complex issues and is obviously only an introduction to the topic. A knowledge of history and a creative mind are among the most important things that political leaders and soldiers can bring to the construction of strategy, but the above presents a clear framework for critically analysing insurgency and counterinsurgency at the strategic level, not the tactical or operational level, that I believe is useful to civilian and military analysts and practitioners. Most importantly, it helps teach us how to *think* about insurgency and counter-insurgency in a clear manner. Finally, none of us should think ourselves beyond repeating the mistakes of our predecessors, especially when confronted with one of war's most frustrating problems.

Note

1 This originally appeared as Stoker (2019a). "A Typology of Insurgency and Counterinsurgency." *Infinity Journal*, 6(4), pp. 10–14. It is adapted from Stoker (2019b). *Why America Loses Wars: Limited War and U.S. Strategy From the Korean War to the Present*. Cambridge: Cambridge University Press.

References

Beckett, I. (1997). Robert Thompson and the British advisory mission to South Vietnam, 1961–1965. *Small Wars & Insurgencies*, *8*(3), 41–63.

Besenyő, J. (2010). Saharawi refugees in Algeria. *Academic and Applied Research in Military Science*, *9*(1), 67–78. http://real.mtak.hu/83783/1/Besenyo_saharawi_refugees_in_Algeria_u.pdf

Black, J. (2016). *Insurgency and counterinsurgency: A global history*. London: Rowan and Littlefield.

Callwell, C. (1996). *Small wars: Their principles and practice*. Lincoln, NE: University of Nebraska Press.

Clausewitz, Carl von. (1984). *On war*. M. Howard & P. Paret (Eds. & Trans.). Princeton, NJ: Princeton University Press.

Clayton, A. (1994). *The wars of French decolonization*. London: Routledge.

Corbett, J. (1988). *Some principles of maritime strategy*. Annapolis, MD: Naval Institute Press.

Corum, J. (2006). Building the Malayan army and police – Britain's experience during the Malayan emergency, 1948–1960. In K. Gott (Ed.), *Security assistance: US and International historical perspectives*. (pp. 292–313). Leavenworth, KS: Combat Studies Institute Press.

Daddis, G. (2014). *Westmoreland's war: Reassessing American strategy in Vietnam*. Oxford: Oxford University Press.

Darling, R. (1974). A new conceptual scheme for analyzing counterinsurgency. *Military Review*, *54*(6), 54–66.

Dougherty, K. (2012). *The United States military in limited war: Case studies in success and failure*. Jefferson, NC: McFarland.

Fall, B. (2015). The theory and practice of insurgency and counter-insurgency. *Military Review*, *95*(5), 40–48.

Galula, D. (2006). *Pacification in Algeria, 1956–1958*. Santa Monica, CA: Rand.

Ganor, B. (2010). "Defining terrorism—is one man's terrorist another man's freedom fighter?" *International Institute for Counterterrorism*, https://www.ict.org.il/Article/1123/Defining-Terrorism-Is-One-Mans-Terrorist-Another-Mans-Freedom-Fighter#gsc.tab=0.

Gordon, M. & Trainor, B. (2007). *Cobra II: The inside story of the invasion and occupation of Iraq*. New York, NY: Vintage.

Gordon M. & Trainor, B. (2012). *Endgame: The inside story of the conflict in the Gulf*. New York, NY: Pantheon.

Hampton, E. (1957). Unlimited confusion over limited war. *Air University Quarterly Review, 9*, 28–47.

Heilbrunn, O. (1969). When the counter-insurgents cannot win. *Royal United Services Institution Journal, 114*(653), 55–58.

Herring, G. (2008). *From colony to superpower: US foreign relations since 1776*. Oxford: Oxford University Press.

Horne, A. (2006). *A savage war of peace: Algeria, 1954–1962*. New York, NY: New York Review Books.

Howard, M. (1969). The classical strategists. *The Adelphi Papers, 9*(54), 18–32.

Ingram, H. & Whiteside, C. (2019). Outshouting the flea: Islamic state and modern asymmetric strategic communications. In A. Dew, M. Genest, & S.C.M. Payne (Eds.), *From quills to tweets: How America communicates war and revolution*. Washington, DC: Georgetown University Press.

Johnston, P. (2012). Does decapitation work? Assessing the effectiveness of leadership targeting in counterinsurgency campaigns. *International Security, 36*(4) (Spring 2012), 47–79.

Johnston, P. & Urlacher, B. (2012). "Explaining the duration of counterinsurgency campaigns," http://patrickjohnston.info/materials/duration.pdf.

Jordan, J. (2014). Attacking the leader, missing the mark: Why terrorist groups survive decapitation strikes. *International Security, 38*(4), 7–38.

Lawrence, T.E. (1917). "The 27 articles of T. E. Lawrence," *The Arab Bulletin*, https://wwi.lib.byu.edu/index.php/The_27_Articles_of_T.E._Lawrence.

Lewy, G. (1980). *America in Vietnam*. Oxford: Oxford University Press.

Luttwak, E. (1987). *Strategy: The logic of war and peace*. Cambridge, MA: Belknap Press of Harvard.

Mao Tse-Tung. (2000). *On guerrilla warfare*. S. Griffith II (Trans.). Urbana, IL: University of Illinois Press.

McClintock, R. (1957). *The meaning of limited war*. Boston, MA: Houghton, Mifflin.

McCuen, J. (1966). *The art of counter-revolutionary warfare: A psycho-politico-military strategy of counter-insurgency*. Harrisburg, PA: Stackpole.

Neumann, P. & Smith, M.L.R. (2005). Strategic terrorism: The framework and its fallacies. *Journal of Strategic Studies, 28*(4), 571–595.

O'Connor, G. (1969). Victory in modern war. *Journal of Peace Research, 6*(4), 367–384.

Pach, C. (1991). *Arming the free world: The origins of the United States military assistance program, 1945–1950*. Chapel Hill, NC: UNC Press.

Porch, D. (2003). *The French secret services: A history of French intelligence from the Dreyfus affair to the Gulf War*. New York, NY: Farrar, Straus, & Giroux.

Porch, D. (2013). *Counterinsurgency: Exposing the myths of the new way of war* . Cambridge: Cambridge University Press.

Record, J. (2007). *Beating Goliath: Why insurgencies win*. Washington, DC: Potomac Books.

Ridgway, M. (1967). *The Korean War*. New York, NY: Da Capo.

Singh, S. (1995). *Limited war: The challenge to US military strategy*. New Delhi: Lancers Books.

Stoker, D. (2007). "Insurgencies rarely win and Iraq won't be any different (maybe)." *Foreign Policy*, http://foreignpolicy.com/2007/01/15/insurgencies-rarely-win-and-iraq-wont-be-any-different-maybe/.

Stoker, D. (2019a). A typology of insurgency and counterinsurgency. *Infinity Journal, 6*(4), 10–14.

Stoker, D. (2019b). *Why America loses wars: Limited war and U.S. strategy from the Korean War to the present*. Cambridge: Cambridge University Press.

Taber, R. (2007). *The war of the flea: Guerrilla warfare theory and practice*. St. Albans, UK: Paladin.

Turley, W. (2009). *The second Indochina War: A concise political and military history* (2nd ed.). Lanham, MD: Rowan and Littlefield.

Ucko, E. (2016). "The people are revolting": An anatomy of authoritarian counterinsurgency. *Journal of Strategic Studies, 39*(1), 43–45.

USMC. (1987). *Small wars manual*. Washington, DC: USGPO.

Whiteside, C. (2016). The Islamic state and the return of revolutionary warfare. *Small Wars & Insurgencies, 27*(5), 743–776.

4

WESTERN COUNTERINSURGENCY THEORETICAL DEVELOPMENT IN THE 20TH AND 21ST CENTURIES

Scott N. Romaniuk and János Kemény

INTRODUCTION

Like any kind of armed warfare, counterinsurgency (COIN) contains a diverse body of theoretical and practical publications, ranging from brief papers on specialised subjects to big books on more broad themes. Although there have been many papers on the subject, theory development has been one of COIN's most underappreciated areas. There are many causes for this, including the Western militaries' emphasis on conventional conflicts and the emergence of nuclear conflict after the end of the Second World War, the political nature of COIN campaigns and the unfavourable political connotations of such conflicts, and the declining number of conflicts in which Western nations – the US and NATO members – have participated. As part of a deeper examination of COIN theory and application, this chapter analyses the challenges of historical theory development, the internationalisation of theory development, and the consequences of a changing international environment.

Our approach consists of two parts. This chapter begins by outlining some of the fundamental components that make up the triangle formed by politics, science, international relations (IR), and COIN theory. The second, and more crucial, point is that we refute the claim that COIN is only a set of tactics that expire at the operational level. While this claim is strongly ingrained into the existing COIN debate, our argument is that this popular interpretation and claim are false. Instead, COIN campaigns are strategy-driven endeavours, but in contrast to the traditional Western mindset – which we also see as a hangover from the Second World War – they are political in nature, employing violence as a key component of an array of further strategies intended to support political agents and their respective interests.

However, this defies more than one conventional value. Firstly, traditional civil-military relations in the United States and Western Europe are based on the depoliticisation of the armed forces. In such conflicts, company and battalion commanders become mayors, regional leaders, and power brokers, yielding significant political influence. Secondly, with the notable exceptions of the United States Marine Corps (USMC) and France's Légion étrangère (French Foreign Legion, FFL), it is difficult to identify a uniformed service in the Western world that embraces COIN (or small wars, or other alternative labels that may be applied) as part of its history and identity. This is in stark contrast to the traditional views of military leaders regarding what their armed services and military-combat capabilities are inherently about. The idea that "COIN battles" necessitate technologically advanced solutions for the troops is a key component of platform- and system-centric thinking. Third, there is a flood of historical baggage, or colonial history, and political restrictions on interventionism as a third aspect, which makes thorough discussions of the subject complicated and extremely difficult to navigate in a political context. Lastly, we pay attention to the arguments in favour of the modifications that have been and are continuously being made to contemporary militaries that make them less suitable for COIN tactics. Examples include the more high-tech approach, which limits the essential capabilities required to win wars and inhibits the Western view of doing so by using lots of armour, scores of drones, and high-tech platforms.

Five sections comprise this chapter. In the first section, we look at the persistent myths that serve as barriers to current COIN theory's advancement. Then, we focus on key flaws in the most recent iterations of COIN theory, underscoring a crucial change in the form of the actual transnationalisation of insurgencies. We emphasise three aspects in this section: *structural problems*, *political ramifications*, and *maintaining support*. The roles that doctrine can play are then taken into account as we place these features within that environment. We provide a general conclusion.

DOI: 10.4324/9780429426063-6

MISCONCEPTIONS AND CONSTRAINTS ON THEORETICAL DEVELOPMENT

The wars in Iraq and Afghanistan are somewhat out of the ordinary for COIN theory and practise because they were fought by the US as a "third party" (officially supporting the government and security apparatus of each country but in practise doing most of the fighting for an extended period of time), and other tasks, such as stability operations, support of foreign security forces (including the building of partner organisations from scratch), institution building, and so on, were therefore perceived as less important. This is a significant factor in the perception of counterinsurgency as "nation building" under a new label in public discourse during the Iraq War (Tierney, 2016: 2018). However, there were other issues that may arise from various operations, so that wasn't the only issue. Counter-narcotics and COIN operations in the early stages were frequently pursuing opposing goals and adversely affecting one another, as David Kilcullen (2009: 62–65) noted in the context of the Afghan conflict, even if they were pointing to a superficial or perceived success on some level of engagement but failing to bring the COIN orchestrator any closer to the further and desired objective.

Counterinsurgency also carries historical "baggage." It can be seen as a remnant of colonial times, which is true of the British and French experiences as well as, to a lesser extent, the US experience, such as the Banana Wars of the early 20th century and the US experience in the Philippines. This element turned into a political liability after the Second World War, especially after decolonisation. This, more crucially from a theoretical standpoint, demoted COIN to a position of lesser relevance, and over time, the institutional memory of such wars faded. The work of Andrew Birtle (2006: 132–136) on the evolution of the US Army's Counterinsurgency Doctrine between 1942 and 1976 provides a superb summary of the subject. Birtle, for instance, demonstrates how the US Army drew heavily from the wartime lessons learned by the German and Japanese militaries as well as its own experience aiding Allied COIN forces when developing its post-Second World War COIN strategy. The paradoxical history of the USMC after 1945 serves as a useful illustration of the latter. The "Small Wars Manual,"[1] the most significant doctrinal text based on experiences in Central America, was largely forgotten, only to be reintroduced to a broader readership during the Iraq War. The USMC kept the COIN mission as a key component of its institutional identity (Schlosser, 2010: 4–6, 9).

The administrative and policing aspects of counterinsurgency are typically more crucial in the long term than the military alone, though policy and law enforcement authorities tend to receive little attention as counterterrorist and counter-insurgent operatives and actors (see Fair and Ganguly, 2014). Policing frequently plays a more significant role in destroying the logistical and other supporting elements of an insurgent movement than military operations. Occasionally, this feature can be questioned, as the US found out during the Vietnam War. Additionally, to destroy an insurgent movement, the counterinsurgent side frequently needs to make high-level political decisions. Since non-military agencies, NGOs, IGOs, and other actors have various interests and opportunities working in such an operational environment, it can be challenging to prepare for this complex interagency component.

Coin campaigns exhibit further troubling features. These conflicts take place "among the people," which implies that the public is intimately involved. In this form of battle, legitimacy is something that most of the population grants to one side or the other through active or passive support, and the involvement of a third party may be difficult. This applies to both the use of force and the political aspects of the war. The Army Field Manual 3–24, *Counterinsurgency*, was instrumental in addressing the variegation in counterinsurgency approaches in the field as well as unfit conventional tactics that were largely ineffective because of their misalignment with the enemy US forces were facing in the battle. Cancian (2017: n.p.) writes:

> FM 3–24 frames insurgency as a contest between insurgents and governments over an undecided population, a contest whose outcome is principally determined by the relative capability of each side to govern people. The undecided civilian population, the manual's theory suggests, will support the side that they think can best provide services. Initially, the government's poor track record at providing basic and essential services—public safety, infrastructure, even trash collection—fosters either active or passive support of the insurgents.

The shift away from motorised and mechanised infantry, which typically play a key role in COIN operations (such as the ambushing and raiding of insurgent groups and their positions) and are better-suited for population control measures than other types of infantry, has indirectly been caused by modern militaries' focus on complex weapons platforms, which are expensive to develop, purchase, operate, and maintain.

As a picture of the plethora of advances that characterise the changing nature of conflict and COIN operations, the previously mentioned matters are critical new features to consider when analysing the progress of COIN theory, as well as the potential to conduct large-scale operations of this sort.

THE LIMITS OF CONTEMPORARY COIN THEORY DEVELOPMENT

The COIN battles in which the US and its close partners and allies have been involved for much of the 2000s and 2010s have been unusual for Western armed forces because the relevance of COIN theory and practise declined after decolonisation and the Vietnam War. The US Army's lexicon expanded to include new terms like "Military Operations Other Than War" (MOOTW), "Discreet Military Operations" (DMOs), and "Small-Footprint Approach/Interventions," but it still covered a much wider range of topics, such as "disaster relief," "counter-drug operations," "peacekeeping," "counterterrorism operations," and other fields (Lewis 2012: 384).

Since the COIN battles of the early Cold War era, the global landscape has changed significantly. Despite Colonel Roger Trinquier, a veteran of the French wars in Indochina and Algeria, lamenting in his book that it is getting harder to close sanctuaries in other nations as the international system changes, these difficulties received little attention. Because of the strength of multinational organisations and the complexity of global issues, Trinquier (1985: 101) stated that "this kind of involvement would lead to reactions throughout the entire world and surely to an unanticipated extension of the conflict." The National Liberation Front (Viet Cong) and the Taliban, for example, have both used cross-border spaces and tunnels as sanctuaries against their respective opponents. The Taliban, having regained control of Afghanistan after a prolonged conflict with the United States and its North Atlantic Treaty Organisation (NATO) allies, have provided a safe haven for terrorist groups, including the Tehrik-e Taliban Pakistan (TTP), to launch attacks against Pakistani security and military forces along the border and within the Pakistani state.

Today's COIN practitioners continue to have difficulties finding outside assistance and responding to other international and, more recently, transnational concerns. One such example is how diasporas, foreign organisations, and other actors can get up-to-date information on conflicts while supporting insurgent forces politically, ideologically, or occasionally materially, thanks to the opportunities provided by modern communications technology (Mackinlay, 2005: 36). This relates to the phenomenon of shifting, broadening identities, which is not particularly novel as, for instance, some currents of political Islam in the Islamic world aim to supplant nationalistic thought (most authors use the immediate aftermath of the 1973 Yom Kippur War as a starting point). This indicates that a major trend over the past few decades has been the transnationalisation of insurgencies in practise. One may say that this trend has existed since the start of the anti-Soviet phase of the war in Afghanistan and has become stronger in the 1990s and 2000s.

Transnationalisation is due to two important trends: first, the spread of technology (meaning the news cycle as well as the ability to communicate and "telework," for instance, on propaganda or other aspects); and second, the "widening" of identities in diasporas and other communities. On the counterinsurgent side, there were important changes to the structure of the armed forces (the most important of which was the elimination of organic logistics and sapper units, as well as the reduction of infantry in favour of armoured units), which made the use of allies and PMCs inevitable, making the battlefield even more complex than it otherwise would have been.

The evolution of insurgent groups has seen a significant shift. Unlike the experiences of the early Cold War era, post-Cold War insurgent groups are relatively loosely organised militarily, and many of them do not seek international recognition (which indeed has become an increasingly difficult task with the end of the Cold War).[2] Instead, they aim to win over the support of the groups. Because of this, finding a political solution is challenging because politics and the military continue to be closely intertwined. Many contemporary insurgent organisations reject the conventions of war and avoid them not only out of military necessity but also as a declaration that they do not seek legitimacy in the international arena.

Structural Issues

At the same time, the third-party counterinsurgent has structural challenges that the counterinsurgent side of colonial history did not (Simpson, 2010). The most obvious one is that an expeditionary conflict needs to continue to enjoy domestic political backing. With overseas military operations spanning years or decades, expeditionary campaigns and operations have a reputation for placing unreasonable expectations on the third-party counterinsurgent. The metrics of this part can be equally, if not even more, perplexing for the public because the duration cannot be known to government authorities (Mack, 1975).

Numerous conflicts lack immediate military solutions or are impossible for the military to quickly resolve. However, the political leadership, which makes the decision regarding the deployment of forces, must rely on the military's understanding of the conflict and translate this into agreeable political rhetoric that is both resilient and successful in winning over support for military involvement in the conflict. Since it might produce results that are at odds with the apolitical character of Western militaries, this is a challenging assignment that could badly sever civil-military ties. An exemplary example of this is General William Westmoreland's position as a vociferous advocate of the Vietnam War prior to 1968, whose most notable event was a presentation before the US Congress in April 1967 (Sorley, 2012: 147–148).

Political Effects

Even though the host country's government often depends on Western forces to function, the nature of COIN techniques has a substantial political impact on the host nation, and Western personnel frequently end up as local power brokers. This combination of issues also brings to the fore the dilemma of material support and political scheming, which can be a part of the political process between the host nation and third-party counterinsurgents. When and under what conditions how much help is given to a host nation with what kind of technical aid, whether it be military, economic, technological, or another type of direct material support, constitutes a very political decision. When a third party in a conflict chooses how much help it will offer to the supporting (or host) nation, the decision is always political and based on political rather than military decision-making. Accordingly, the amount of help given might either be above or far below what the nation being supported requests, depending on the political climate.[3]

Third-party support, whether direct or indirect, is part of a larger picture that also includes financial assistance, intelligence sharing and cooperation, military-related assistance (such as security assistance, FID, and direct military assistance), and international political assistance. All these fields have important ramifications for a third-party COIN conflict and are usually separate political decisions – and often essentially ad hoc decisions. What the supported nation requests, needs, can, and is able to use from the provided support and what the third party provides are separate and distinct.

During the early Cold War, some subjects were briefly discussed from the viewpoint of third-party conflict. In this context, Sir Robert Thompson's work merits mentioning. In his book, Defeating Communist Insurgencies, Thompson (1966: 160) makes reference to the issue of foreign economic and military aid and states the following:

> there are however, other aspects where the domestic policy of the supporting power may influence the degree and form of aid and even the internal policies of the threatened country when they are dependent on such aid. This is a difficult problem, particularly since it may affect the timing of particular lines of action.

He also lists concerns that could be problematic for an outside power supporting the host nation, such as taking on government roles for which it is not qualified, overemphasising crash-training and similar programmes without the real possibility of the host nation running these programmes on its own, overtaxing the host state's economy, and giving financial assistance to industries that do not benefit significant portions of the population. He emphasises the issue of the host government's capacity to receive aid and how this capacity may change because of military action (Thompson, 1966: 161–163). Regrettably, Thompson just briefly addresses these topics, but the issues he brings up are still relevant in the modern world.

Maintaining Support

Since demonstrating progress is essential for winning and maintaining political support in the domestic politics of the third-party nation(s) as well as the host nation, the use of metrics continues to be a concern. The political aspect is significant, even though it can be difficult to track the development of COIN engagements. No third party, especially one that is democratic, can commit to a prolonged engagement in such a conflict without a clear departure plan since the imperial ideology and dedication of former colonial countries have expired. If the host country has most of the populace's support and is capable of restraining and ultimately eliminating the threat, the exit strategy in these scenarios includes leaving a capable host nation partner behind and pushing forward on its own without a workable escape plan. In these situations, the exit strategy entails leaving a capable host nation partner behind and moving forward on its own if the host nation has most of the populace's support and can contain and ultimately defeat the insurgency that the third party was brought in to help with.

Conversely, monitoring political and military progress has been and will continue to be a delicate task. Using such metrics in third-party political discourse can also cause conflict between political and military elites because they are almost certain to have different viewpoints on the conflict(s) at hand. French misadventures in this sector were the subject of a 1966 article by Bernard Fall (1966: 3–6) that provided some insightful observations. Fall demonstrates how relying entirely on military-style indications for analysis may be deceiving and lead to major errors regarding the strength of an insurgent movement (see McNerney et al., 2018). During the course of guerrilla operations in the Western Sahara that would follow the Moroccan military's advance into the Western Sahara in November 1975, numerous miscalculations had been made about Sahrawis insurgents. For one, the Sahrawis made use of Algerian and Vietnamese models for the establishment of their armed resistance forces; however, the Sahrawis received material support from the Algerian government but also received local support from natives whose military capabilities had been substantially underestimated and snubbed (Besenyő, 2017). It was not just the military supplies that had been given to the insurgents; it was also the natives' knowledge of local lands and topographical features. As Besenyő (2017: 26) notes, "the critics of the capabilities of the natives did not take into account that the Sahrawis had lived in the area for centuries and were acclimatised to its peculiarities. Knowing all the caravan routes, passable paths, and water sources, they could use all the opportunities provided by the desert against the Moroccan troops."

Several of the conventional COIN best practises are either irrelevant or impractical in the current security environment. This is valid for some aspects of colonial-era approaches to population control and resource management. These include overt methods like the utilisation of strategically positioned hamlets as well as more covert ones like mass deportations and incarceration, which can occasionally cause regional imbalances and crises (see Busch, 2002). Many, if not most, of these methods would be counterproductive in today's strategic and information environment, not to mention that even in the decades that followed the end of the Second World War, the outcomes of their use varied widely, in no small part based on the strategic and local context. For example, the British used strategic hamlets effectively during the Malayan conflict, but the US and the Republic of Vietnam failed in their efforts to emulate the British model.

THE ROLE OF DOCTRINE

In recent decades, Western counterinsurgency (COIN) theory has revealed inherent flaws. Williamson (2011) notes that while there may be similarities between the processes of innovation and adaptation, they occur in distinct situations (see also, Murray, 2011). This observation is made in the context of traditional interstate combat. It is evident that the circumstances of armed conflict are not replicable in a nonviolent environment. It could be contended that during the period between the conclusion of the Vietnam War and the commencement of the Iraq War in 2003, there was limited scope for novelty in the context of COIN. Furthermore, given that Western countries did not engage in COIN operations with substantial conventional units, it seems that there was no opportunity for modification to take place.

Considering this, key turning points in the development of thinking about COIN campaigns included the adaptation of Field Manual 3–24 in 2006 and NATO AJP-3.4.4. The Army Doctrine Publication 1–01 (Department of the Army, 2019: 1–2) defines the role of doctrine as:

> Fundamental principles, with supporting tactics, techniques, procedures, and terms and symbols, used for the conduct of operations and as a guide for actions of operating forces, and elements of the institutional force that directly support operations in support of national objectives.

A particular armed force's doctrine is not its only source of information, and while a suitable adaptation process can result in desirable results, this often raises the cost of an organisation's knowledge acquisition relative to what it would have otherwise needed to pay. Additionally, throughout the Iraq and Afghan wars, some lessons learned from other types of warfare were partially translated (Ricks, 2006: 192).

We should emphasise that theoretical gaps are challenging to ignore and that some elements have received legitimate criticism from a variety of sources, considering this and the previously indicated factors. The absence of first-hand experience with the problem and the urgent need to develop a COIN philosophy led to the discovery of the following intriguing strategy: The experiences of Britain, France, and the US served as major sources of inspiration for FM 3–24, which was mostly based on insurgencies during the early Cold War period.

The model of the resistance and insurgency pyramid, which was formulated by the Special Operations Research Office (SORO), has been used as a model for many decades by both Western Special Operations Forces (SOF) and scholars who study resistance combat (for an unaltered rendition of the SORO pyramid, refer to Molnar et al., 1966: 29). According to Jeffrey Hasler (2017: 11), the principle of resistance, which was previously embraced by students and academics across all levels, should now be examined with a loyal yet critical opposition. According to Hasler (2017: 11).

> A great many things below the overt-clandestine "waterline" which purport to show a division between those activities which are "clandestine" and those which are "overt" are superficial, assume too narrow of a focus, suit only a specific example, or are arguably misleading or inarguably wrong.

While unconventional warfare (UW) is still a practical, affordable kind of indirect warfare, several of the classic UW's underlying assumptions have become less accurate over the past two decades, according to David Kilcullen's essay, "The Evolution of Unconventional Warfare" (2019: 61). The model still provides a useful framework for expanding our understanding of resistance warfare, but it needs to be updated as military forces engage in new forms of conflict and combat with insurgents in environments that are less familiar and less known than those that were previously known or understood. In other words, and in keeping with Kilkullen's approach to the ageing model, our newer, messier realities deviated from the static structures of earlier knowledge pertaining to various forms of irregular warfare.

The ability to translate theoretical knowledge – and doctrine in particular – into effective tactical, operational, and strategic engagement is not a given. Political aspects – including those at the local, national, and international levels – are significant on each level, but no theory or ideology can fully account for them, as we contend in this essay (see Watts et al., 2014). The fact that these military operations have expanded internationally, partly because of how labour-intensive they are, is another significant trend. Therefore, from a strategic standpoint, adhering to sound theoretical and practical approaches by a nation's fighting force in each theatre is insufficient, even though every allied fighting force must approach operations from this perspective. This is further complicated by the presence of private military and security firms (PMSCs) on contemporary battlefields.

CONCLUSION

Since the end of the Second World War, there has been a substantial shift in the political environment that currently governs COIN operations and campaigns involving Western forces. Since it is a politically challenging task and there is still room for development from a theoretical standpoint (i.e., from the perspective of political science and IR), third-party participation in intrastate conflicts in general is usually an underappreciated aspect of analysing counterinsurgencies and counterinsurgency engagements. Military doctrine is a fundamental starting point for analysis. However, as we have attempted to show, it becomes decoupled from political analysis, particularly at the strategic and lower levels, because it is deemed problematic for Western forces to actively participate in a host country's local (and occasionally national) politics. Others, on the other hand, consider COIN operations as deleterious to military readiness, in part because they require new attitudes, skills, and resources – an issue that is not entirely new (Galula, 2006: 62–63).

Military leaders as well as policymakers will benefit from the tactical and operational insights gained from the third-party COIN campaigns of the previous two decades. The costs (expenses on a political, economic, and human scale) of COIN operations appeared to be elusive, and the lessons were frequently bitter. However, given that conflicts fought by irregular forces appear to be the norm rather than the near-peer conflicts that Western militaries have traditionally supported, it is crucial to create the proper theoretical framework for COIN operations and keep the tactical and operational lessons learned at the forefront of military thinking. This problem has not necessarily been present in the past. David French (2006: 49–50) argues that the British army encountered a comparable circumstance during the interwar period. He claims that despite prioritising the prevention of war with near-pearls, the British army was compelled to deal with the exigency of colonial threats. While doing so, the British army lost crucial skills, which negatively impacted its performance in the opening phases of the War in Europe in 1939. It's also vital to remember that the British COIN experience was uneven and had conflicting outcomes after 1945. The British example highlights both the challenge of attaining the ideal balance and the importance of maintaining a balanced force structure.

Political science and IR theories can contribute to the conversation by advancing the knowledge of military and civilian leaders on academic perspectives and analytical methods for approaching a variety of contemporary conflicts, where Western militaries are engaged in combat with irregular actors who have material and structural advantages over powerful third-party actors with easy access to military resources. The wars in Iraq and Afghanistan present important opportunities and convincing justifications to advance our understanding of third-party conflicts.

Notes

1 While the "Small Wars Manual" is technologically obsolete, it covers crucial tactical and operational aspects in depth. To be sure, as with any historical document, it must be seen in context, as some of the reasoning and perspectives underlying it will almost certainly be unfamiliar to today's readers. The 1940 edition is freely available for research (Department of the Navy, 1940).

2 This is not always the case, though, as certain well-known and recent events involving ISIS and Daesh show that some organisations seek to increase their visibility and renown around the world.

3 The national will to fight, its definition and applicability, and the US experience in relation to various national wills to face invading and aggressor states are all comprehensively and remarkably assessed by McNerney et al. (2018).

References

Besenyő, J. (2017). Guerrilla operations in Western Sahara: The Polisario versus Morocco and Mauritania. *Connections: The Quarterly Journal*, *16*(3), 23–45.

Birtle, A.J. (2006). "U.S. army counterinsurgency and contingency operations doctrine 1942–1976." Washington, DC: Center of Military History United States Army. https://history.army.mil/html/books/us_army_counterinsurgency/CMH_70-98-1_US%20Army_Counterinsurgency_WQ.pdf

Busch, P. (2002). Killing the 'Vietcong': The British advisory mission and the strategic Hamlet programme. *Journal of Strategic Studies*, *25*(1), 135–162.

Cancian, M. (2017, February 21). "FM 3-24-2.0? Why US counterinsurgency doctrine needs and update." Modern War Institute, West Point, USA. https://mwi.usma.edu/fm-3-24-2-0-us-counterinsurgency-doctrine-needs-update/

Department of the Army. (2019, July 31). "Army doctrine publication No. 1-01 – Doctrine primer." https://armypubs.army.mil/epubs/DR_pubs/DR_a/pdf/web/ARN18138_ADP%201-01%20FINAL%20WEB.pdf

Department of the Navy. (1940). "Fleet marine force reference publication (FMFRP) 12–15, small wars manual." Washington, DC: Government Printing Office. https://www.marines.mil/Portals/1/Publications/FMFRP%2012-15%20%20Small%20Wars%20Manual.pdf

Fair, C.C. and Ganguly, S. (Eds.). (2014). *Policing insurgencies: Cops as counterinsurgents*. New Delhi: Oxford University Press.

Fall, B.B. (1966, April). "Insurgency indicators." *Military Review*, 3–11. http://cgsc.contentdm.oclc.org/utils/getfile/collection/p124201coll1/id/640/filename/641.pdf

French, D. (2006). Big wars and small wars between the war, 1919–39. In H. Strachan (Ed.), *Big wars and small wars: The British army and the lessons of war in the 20th century*. (pp. 36–53). Abingdon: Routledge.

Galula, D. (2006). *Counterinsurgency warfare: Theory and practice*. Westport: Praeger Security International.

Hasler, J. (2017). "The SORO resistance pyramid challenge: Critical observations and questions on a classic." https://www.soc.mil/SWCS/SWmag/archive/SW3003/SoroResistanceChallenged.pdf

Kilcullen, D. (2009). *The accidental Guerrilla: Fighting small wars in the midst of a1 big one*. London: C. Hurst & Company.

Kilcullen, D. (2019). The evolution of unconventional warfare. *Scandinavian Journal of Military Studies*, *2*(1), 61–71. 10.31374/sjms.35

Lewis, A. (2012). *The American culture of war: The history of U.S. military force from world war 2 to operation enduring freedom*. Abingdon: Routledge.

Mack, A. (1975, January). Why big nations lose small wars: The politics of asymmetric conflict. *World Politics*, *27*(2), 175–200.

Mackinlay, J. (2005). "Defeating complex insurgency, The Cornwallis Group." http://www.ismor.com/cornwallis/cornwallis_2005/CX_2005_03-MackinlayJ.pdf

McNerney, M.J., Connable, B., Zimmerman, S.R., Lander, N., Posard, M.N., Castillo, J.J., Madden, D., Blum, I., Frank, A., and Fernandes, B.J. (2018). *In Hyo Seol, Christopher Paul, and Andrew Parasiliti, national will to fight: Why some states keep fighting and others don't*. Santa Monica: RAND Corporation. https://www.rand.org/pubs/research_reports/RR2477.html. Also available in print form.

Molnar, A.R., Tinker, J.M., and LeNoir, J.D. (1966, September). "Human factors considerations of undergrounds in insurgencies." Department of the Army. https://apps.dtic.mil/dtic/tr/fulltext/u2/a592949.pdf

Murray, W. (2011). *Military adaptation in war: With fear of change*. Cambridge: Cambridge University Press.

Ricks, T.E. (2006). *Fiasco: The American military adventure in Iraq*. London: Penguin Books.

Schlosser, N.J. (2010). The marine corps' small wars manual: An old solution to a new challenge? *Fortitudine: Bulletin of the Marine Corps Historical Program*, *35*(1), 4–10. https://www.marines.mil/Portals/1/Publications/Fortitudine%20Vol%2035%20No%201%20z.pdf

Simpson, E.M. (2010). *The perils of third-party counterinsurgency campaigns*. Cambridge: Harvard University Press.

Sorley, L. (2012). *Westmoreland: The general who lost Vietnam*. Boston: Mariner Books.

Thompson, R.G.K. (1966). *Defeating communist insurgency: The lessons of Malaya and Vietnam*. New York and London: F. A. Praeger.

Tierney, D. (2016). The backlash against nation-building. *PRISM: The Journal of Complex Operations*, *5*(3), 13–28. https://cco.ndu.edu/Portals/96/Documents/prism/prism_5-3/The_Backlash_Against_Nation-Building.pdf?ver=Wb8kJiXH10HRqZJ7EUwqgg%3d%3d

Tierney, D. (2018). Avoiding nation-building: From Nixon to Trump. *Parameters*, *48*(1), 25–36.

Trinquier, R. (1985). *Modern warfare: A French view of counterinsurgency*. Combat Studies Institute. https://www.armyupress.army.mil/Portals/7/combat-studies-institute/csi-books/Modern-Warfare.pdf

Watts, S., Campbell, J.H., Johnston, P.B., Lalwani, S., and Brana, S.H. (2014). *Countering others' insurgencies: Understanding U.S. small-footprint interventions in local context*. Santa Barbara: RAND Corporation.

Williamson, M. (2011). *Military adaptation in war: With fear of change*. New York: Cambridge University Press.

5

TERRORISM[1]

Looking through the Definitional Kaleidoscope

Scott N. Romaniuk and Olivier Lewis

Whoever fights with monsters should see to it that he does not become one himself.

And when you stare for a long time into an abyss, the abyss stares back into you.

Nietzsche, 2002, p. 69

INTRODUCTION

Smashing into globally recognised icons of success and power while much of the Western world watched on television, the September 11, 2001 attacks (9/11) brought talent and funding not just to the militant Islamists of Al-Qaeda but also to terrorism studies and terrorism scholars, especially in North America and Europe. While non-state actors have killed, maimed, and intimidated innocent civilians throughout history, the images of people jumping from skyscrapers and the recordings of plane passengers making last calls to loved ones marked a generation of social scientists. But while scholars continue to invest their attention into this area of political violence, little has been achieved in terms of developing more innovative and profound conceptualisations and interpretations (for exceptions, see Coady, 1985, 2004; Primoratz, 1990, 1997, 2004a, 2004b, 2015; Crimmins and De Vriese, 2006). Most terrorism scholars work with specific cases in mind (e.g., 9/11), which anchor their conceptual efforts.

Conceptual methods are inductive and synthetic, sometimes even based on an unrepresentative sample of cases. The reasoning, consequently, is circular. The definitional debate, meanwhile, remains contested and loathed. While terrorism legislation is slowly being homogenised, or at least harmonised (Roach, 2011), across the world, academics tend to avoid the definitional debates, agreeing to disagree. Terrorism databases, therefore, increasingly allow the user to select conceptual preferences. Databases are designed to dodge most definitional decisions (see Asal et al., 2012).

This chapter seeks to outline the contentious landscape of terrorism studies, presenting to readers the most divisive issues. This is important for policymaking as a result of divergent definitions having the power to alter understandings and consequently possible responses to "terrorism." Of course, states, soldiers, and scholars are unlikely to ever agree on a single definition of terrorism, but this is the way it should be. Like all debates, the degree to which definitions can be publicly contested is an indicator of liberty writ large. In those areas of the world where terms and labels cannot be contested, academia and politics are not free. Indeed, while violence (especially physical violence) is a pervasive theme in nearly every definition of terrorism, what is often lost in abstraction are the larger *political* reconfigurations underway in each of the cases considered. Indeed, political violence can be both a cause and a symptom of larger societal conflicts. Perhaps the most critical issue in the debate on definitions of terrorism (especially when civil society is included in the analysis) is the degree to which the term has been misused by states.

The chapter is divided into six parts. The first presents a condensed version of a traditional history. This exercise is perforce perilous, not just due to its extreme brevity but also due to the difficulty of writing this history of a contested concept and the plethora of possible referents. The second and third parts are fairly conventional, for they provide brief reviews of academic and legal definitions of terrorism. Working from these three sections, the second half of the chapter presents the key contested aspects of terrorism definitions. The fourth section explains why conceptualisations of terrorism tend to focus on non-state actors, i.e., people who are apparently not officially employed by states and do not necessarily work in any state's interests. The fifth section reviews how wars of national liberation have been at the centre of definitional debates and why such wars are likely to remain relevant even after the demise of de jure empires and colonies. Rather than provide another review, the sixth and final section ends with the presentation of what

DOI: 10.4324/9780429426063-7

is arguably the core characteristic of all types of terrorism, namely the attempt to *intimidate* (for political ends via abnormal and abhorrent forms of violence). Whether one is studying armed rebels, militias, empires, or totalitarian regimes, communicative function is something that all types of terrorism have in common.

THE TRADITIONAL HISTORY OF TERRORISM

Political violence is by no means a unique challenge or problem for states in the 21st century. Physical and psychological violence have always been used to oppose and challenge political, social, and economic structures. Indeed, non-state political violence is as old as human civilisation and stretches back over at least 2,000 years (Law, 2015, 2016). The history of "terrorism" was successfully summarised by David C. Rapoport (2004), to the point that his "four waves"[2] account is now a canon of terrorism studies. Of course, political assassins and zealots can be identified throughout history. In the 1st century AD, for example, a Jewish organisation called the Sicarii violently opposed Rome's annexation and occupation of Judea. Academics often refer to the Sicarii as one of the most extremist and fanatical organisations of the ancient world (Horsely, 1979; Rapoport, 1984; Pedahzur and Perliger, 2011). Some have even argued that they can be called *an ancient forerunner of modern terrorism* (Taylor and Gautron, 2015; Law, 2016). Indeed, their activities and violent principles of resistance and opposition have been mirrored by hundreds, if not thousands, of groups and organisations. And although Schmid and Jongman (2005) might disagree, a similar investigation could be made into the tactics of the 12th-century Order of the Assassins (Rapoport, 1971).

Of course, the term "terrorism" may well have been first used, in Europe at least, by French public officials a few years after the French Revolution (on uses of the term "terreur" at the time, see Jourdan, 2013). Today, the Reign of Terror generally refers to the revolutionary government's efforts not only to kill thousands of opponents but also to create a "climate" of fear across France to avoid civil war and counter foreign invasions (Weinberg, 2009; Hoffman, 2013). In the capital and the provinces, government actors conducted executions and massacres against counter-revolutionary insurgents, reactionary royalist opponents, prostitutes, clergy, and even children by guillotine, firing squads, and mass drownings in the Loire River (Gérard, 1999; Gueniffey, 2000; Tilly, 2004).[3] Most interesting for us might be the use of violence as a means of countering insurgent forces and the populations that supported them. State terrorism, in other words, can be a form of counter-insurgency (see also Stoker's chapter on (counter-) insurgency in this volume).

In typical Eurocentric fashion, examples of 19th-century terrorism are often taken from anarchist and nationalist movements. Here we witness the coldhearted assassinations of Tsars in Saint Petersburg, Empresses in Geneva, Kings in Monza, Presidents in Buffalo, and Archdukes in Sarajevo. Chronicles of terrorism, however, rarely include the history of capital punishment, genocide, or the various forms of intimidation used in European and Asian colonies. Likewise, although the USSR's Great Terror and Nazi Germany's Holocaust, or even Cambodia under the Khmer Rouge, should come to mind when seeking examples of the most significant terrorism in the 20th century (see Primoratz, 2004a; Snyder, 2011), most terrorism historians reference decades of insurgencies in European colonies (see Lefebvre, 2003; Ross, 2007). In fact, for some, anticolonial movements should be seen as the "origins of contemporary terrorism" (Hoffman, 2013). Considering the clearly pejorative connotation of the term terrorism, we must highlight here the significant popularity of wars of national liberation (see Section 5).

During the following six decades, non-state political violence (especially Communist and Islamist non-state violence) soared across the globe but remained sporadic. Al-Qaeda's spectacular attacks on September 11, 2001, and the United States Government's stupendous response (ranging from wars to surveillance to financial sanctions) mark a critical juncture in the history of "terrorism." Such a historiography, of course, depends on one's definition of terrorism.

ACADEMIC DEFINITIONS OF TERRORISM

As much as Rapoport is known for his history of types of terrorism, Schmid and Jongman are known for their survey-based typologies. Although these authors provide a definition of terrorism,[4] their primary finding is that it is virtually impossible to find a common academic definition of terrorism, even when accepting the lowest common denominator (see also Weinberg et al., 2004). Considering these "endless disputes," terrorism might be called a "contested concept" (see Connolly, 1993). The *enfant terrible* of international relations theory, James Der Derian, calls the term terrorism an elusive "catch-all political signifier" (Der Derian, 2005, p. 23).

Concepts have several uses, and since most terrorism research focuses on policy, few people are motivated to create a critical ontology of terrorism that spans continents and centuries. On the contrary, terrorism academics frequently base their conceptualisations on one or two specific incidents. Because certain states or state-like actors are perceived as deserving of greater attention than others, the field of terrorism studies currently focuses almost exclusively on a small number of geographical areas (Weinberg et al., 2004, p. 779). This manuscript, hopefully, will help redress this tendency (for more information on concept stretching, see Collier and Mahon, 1993). The most complex political and ethical issues are typically ignored, even when mental heuristics, shortcuts, and biases are purposefully avoided.

As mentioned, 9/11 marked a critical juncture in terrorism studies, especially in the West. As Dershowitz (2002, p. 7) emphasises:

> The weapons of choice for earlier terrorists were the dagger, the noose, the sword, and the poison elixir. The introduction of the hand-thrown bomb and the pistol, and more recently the machine gun and plastic explosives, enabled terrorists to kill much more efficiently. Now weapons of mass, or "wholesale," destruction allow terrorists to "leverage" their personnel, as proved by the events of September 11, 2001, in which a relatively small number of highly trained individuals armed with primitive box cutters and prepared to give up their own lives were able to use passenger jets as weapons of mass murder.

The point, of course, is that technology and techniques change. Terrorists have been largely successful in adapting to avoid state and non-state counterterrorism measures. What is left are the supposedly immutable essences of terrorism: group nature, target and victim characterisation, and terrorist aims and objectives (see Dershowitz, 2002). But even these characteristics are open to interpretation and based on values and norms that change over time: what is a state, who are acceptable targets of warfare, how does information travel, do the ends ever justify the means, etc. (on the ethics of terrorism, see Primoratz, 2004a).

Consider the notion of "theatre" in warfare, for example. This notion helps determine what is legal and legitimate. With the rise of irregular warfare, however, this concept is becoming increasingly contested, becoming part of the conflicts themselves. Defining the limits of the theatre is part of the war (see Rajkovic, 2019). The question then is whether all is fair in war, and if so, where and when does war end? Where and when does consequentialism cease to apply? Specifically, is it ever legal or legitimate to conduct political violence in times and places of relative peace? To attempt to answer these questions, one could turn to ethics and international humanitarian law, or one could turn to historical anthropology. Some scholars have, in so doing, criticised the idea that a single understanding of "terrorism" is achievable.

Jessica Stern (1999, p. 12) has made the obvious but important (and often forgotten) point that the "definition [of terrorism] inevitably determines the kind of data we collect and analyse, which in turn influences our understanding of trends and our predictions about the future." A blind faith in statistics is necessarily a blind faith in the definitions that founded the data collection endeavour. But data on terrorism is cursed twice, for not only can it suffer from conceptual biases, but it can also suffer from access restrictions, especially in closed states and war zones. Because it is almost impossible to accurately measure the impact of terrorism in closed, poor, and war-torn countries, greater attention is forced to be given to terrorism in rich, open, and peaceful countries (see Asal et al., 2012).

To summarise, terrorism scholars have not hesitated to put forward their own, often idiosyncratic, definitions of terror, terrorists, and terrorism (Tilly, 2004). For all the reasons presented above, the result is a beautiful kaleidoscope of definitions in all shapes and sizes, often tailored to specific purposes and agendas, but with none ruling supreme. In comparison, state definitions are just as diverse, but a slow harmonisation is underway. Depending on your politics, this might not be a felicitous development. Poorly formulated responses to threats, both real and perceived, have themselves come to represent a partial victory for terrorists with an erosion of civil liberties, rights, and freedoms and the alleged principles and values of Western states.

(WESTERN) STATE DEFINITIONS OF TERRORISM

Since most governments try to enforce, or at least pay lip service to, the rule of law, it is only natural that most state legal codes have their own definitions of terrorism, "devised for purpose" (Weinberg, 2009). Although diplomats at the United Nations (UN) find forming a universal legal definition of terrorism difficult, after 9/11 we can notice, in Europe and beyond, a gradual harmonisation of counterterrorism strategies and practises, including via legislation (Young, 2006; Roach, 2011).

According to Acharya (2008, p. 678), "the post-9/11 War on Terror resulted from the long-standing failure of the international community to agree on a definition of terrorism." But definitional consensus does not necessarily lead to cooperation and effectiveness. Universally accepted definitions of genocide, for instance, have failed. Varying definitions of terrorism, rather, allow states and scholars to address non-state violence in different ways. To the degree that lives and liberties are at stake, diversity might be beneficial.

The more realistic conclusion, however, is that most legal definitions of terrorism are sufficiently vague to provide even the most liberal of states with a great deal of discretion. Three Western examples:

- France's Anti-terrorism Act ("Loi n° 86-1020 du 9 septembre 1986") defined acts of terrorism as any deliberate "offense connected with a one-man or collective undertaking, aiming to seriously disturb the public order through intimidation or terror."

- According to the UK's 2000 Terrorism Act (Terrorism Act 2000 (UK), c 11.), terrorism:

  [...] means the use of threat of action where – (a) the action falls within subsection (2), (b) the use of threat is designed to influence the government or to intimidate the public or a section of the public, and (c) the use of threat is made for the purpose of advancing political, religious or ideological cause. (2) Action falls within this subsection if it – (a) involves serious violence against a person, (b) involves serious damage to property, (c) endangers a person's life other than that of the person committing the action, (d) creates a serious risk to health or safety of the public or a section of the public, or (e) is designed to seriously interfere with or seriously to disrupt an electronic system.

  - The definition offered by the US State Department helped to guide US counterterrorism efforts following 9/11. The US Department of State defines terrorism as, "politically motivated violence perpetrated against noncombatant targets by subnational groups or clandestine agents, usually intended to influence an audience" (for more on legal definitions, see; Young 2006; Roach 2011; Hoffman 2013).

The US government illustrates a diverse and seemingly, if intentionally, ambiguous definition likely to afford its various anti-terrorism institutions the legal, political, and military means necessary to address all sorts of threats within and external to the US (see Walter, 1969; Dugard, 1974; Crenshaw, 1983; Gibbs, 1989; Wilkins, 1992; Crenshaw and Pimlott, 1997; Laqueur, 2000; Ganor, 2002; Cronin, 2003; Tilly, 2004; Weinberg et al., 2004; Hoffman, 2006; Schinkel, 2009; Ismayilov, 2010; Nathanson, 2010; Schmid 2011; Richards, 2013; Crenshaw and LaFree, 2016).

Less harshly, we could simply note that different definitions exist because they are written (and applied) in different historical and regional contexts. But with the European Union (EU) Member States having now agreed on a common definition, it is simply not true that finding a common wording between sovereign states, even between those diverse histories and interests, is impossible (see Dumitriu, 2004; Argomaniz, 2008, 2011; Argomaniz et al., 2014).

NON-STATE POLITICAL VIOLENCE

According to Goodall (2013, n.p.), "the possible biases and assumptions inherent in the views and perspectives of those attempting to form definitions are, then, significant and should be explicitly considered." To put this in more general and generous terms, we can say that conceptualisations serve various purposes (see Gerring, 1999). Unlike in everyday speech, where we tend to use words unreflectively, in politics, law, and academia, words are weapons. We wield them consciously, often self-consciously. Oftentimes, scholars and practitioners turn a blind eye to political violence and terrorism. On other occasions, we label individuals and groups "terrorists" prematurely or for ulterior motives. Those who seek a degree of objectivity, then, must proceed with caution.

The most salient characteristic of the term "terrorism," especially in everyday use, is that it refers to *non-state actors,* especially a small number of under-resourced irregular combatants who do not control much or any territory and enjoy little public support. "Terrorists," in ordinary language, are not government officials. They are not soldiers, spies, or police. But if terms such as "non-state" and "irregular" are already at our disposal, and if the term derives from the Reign of Terror in France, then is this common use of the term terrorism to refer to non-state actors not odd, even suspicious? Can we not detect in this particular use the normative insinuation that only state actors may employ violence legally and legitimately?

Some terrorism scholars would argue just this. If the definition of terrorism proffered by English (2009), for example, is taken into consideration, the actions of states operating within their own borders when practising counterterrorism can often be interpreted as terroristic. English (2009, p. 24):

> Terrorism involves heterogeneous violence used or threatened with a political aim; it can involve a variety of acts, of targets, and of actors; it possesses an important psychological dimension, producing terror or fear among a directly threatened group and also a wider implied audience in the hope of maximizing political communication and achievement; it embodies the exerting and implementing of power, and the attempted redressing of power relations; it represents a subspecies of warfare, and as such it can form part of a wider campaign of violent and non-violent attempts at political leverage.

Governments and their forces are regularly accused of either being terrorist actors or sponsors of terrorism. Think, for example, of the World War Two bombings of Coventry, Hamburg, Dresden, Hiroshima, and Nagasaki. Civilians were deliberately targeted. Fear was intended. The objectives were overtly political (Walzer, 2015) (see also Marton's chapter on terror and terrorism in war in this volume). Others might reference the government of Iraq's activities in Kurdistan, Indonesia's actions in East Timor, Idi Amin in Uganda, Pinochet's Chile, or even the threat of nuclear annihilation during the Cold War (Primoratz, 2004a). To this list, we could add particularly gruesome acts committed by de facto states such as Hamas, Hezbollah, and the Taliban (see Yetim and Kasikci's chapter on the al-Qassam Brigades in this volume). When government actors systematically purge, torture, rape, threaten, and have family members "disappear," one can be forgiven for wanting to call this terrorism (on genocide as a form of terrorism, see Taylor, 2002, 2020).

Many scholars argue that, nonetheless, one must distinguish between officially sanctioned acts and non-state acts, if only because causal explanations for such atrocities will differ (Tilly, 2004, p. 11). The causes for totalitarian terrorism under Józef Stalin, Adolf Hitler, or Pol Pot will differ from occasional terrorism of France, Saudi Arabia, or United States officials, which in turn will not have the same causes as terrorism by the National Liberation Front of Corsica, Al-Qaeda, the Ku Klux Klan (KKK), or the Wolverine Watchmen. But such distinctions are not always easy, especially in relation to proxy wars, state sponsors of insurgencies, and covert operations organised by military and intelligence officials (see Lewis and Romaniuk's chapter on conceptualising insurgency in this volume). In 1979, the United States' government labelled Syria's government, for example, state-sponsor of terrorism due to its support of numerous different violent groups. (The country maintained a notorious relationship with Hezbollah, which, confusingly, could very well be classified as a *de facto* state). In 1982, the United States' government designated Cuba a state sponsor of terrorism, accusing it of harbouring fugitives and offering support such as food, housing, and medical supplies to violent non-state actors. In 1993, Sudan was added to the list of state-sponsors of terrorism because of its various activities including harbouring groups inspired by the violent ideology of Al-Qaeda. Iran's Islamic Revolutionary Guard Corps (IRGC) was accused in 2012 of training Taliban militants on "small unit tactics, small arms, explosives, and indirect fire weapons." From a Western perspective, such *listings and sanctioning* are not necessarily controversial, as demonstrated, once again, by the EU's ability to form consensus (see Heupel, 2009).

Surely one reason why policy-oriented terrorism scholars show little interest in totalitarian terror is that such systematic violence is not sufficiently international and fails to cross borders to the point of considerably affecting their governments – note the state of US-based studies of Afghanistan and the Taliban prior to 9/11. Also consider the US State Department's distinction between domestic and international terrorism, and especially terrorism against US interests (Tilly, 2004, p. 7). Another more obvious reason is that it does not pay to bite the hand that feeds you; only a few government executives and legislators are enlightened to the point of funding independent critical studies of their own violent acts. Some parliaments and opposition politicians sponsor detached studies and reports of wars, covert action, and policing, but most terrorism studies funding is of the problem-solving variety. Tilly (2004, p. 6) makes the important point that a wealth of information on state terrorism (and other types of "grim governmental actions") is to be found in reports of human rights violations, notably produced by US embassies but also the EU, the UN, Human Rights Watch, and many others.

The matter of Western innocence, naiveté, and poor historical introspection is a delicate topic that warrants consideration. According to Igor Primoratz's assertion:

> A state that has made use of terrorism, or sponsored it, or condoned it, or supported governments that have done any of the above—in a word, a state which has itself been involved in or with terrorism to any significant degree—lacks the moral standing required for bona fide moral criticism of terrorism (2004b, p. 122).

By focusing on a small section of political violence, terrorism scholars tend to give non-state actors undue importance in the grand scheme of recorded and unrecorded suffering. According to Tristam (2011), discussing non-state violence and not even mentioning state terror is "ignorance by necessity." In reference to US history, we might think of the deliberate killing of non-combatants in the US' many 20th-century wars. Cornel West, instead, ridicules the ingenuity of US leaders, giving special significance to the 9/11 attacks, referring in this context to the US' divisive history of slavery and the sanctioned systematic use of fear to guarantee its perpetuation:

> There is no way to have an honest discussion of terrorism without quickly discovering that "Islamists" are among its most recent and rather selective practitioners, while Westerners have been its more systematic enthusiasts and euphemists. Any reading of Richard Wright, Maya Angelou, James Baldwin, Carter G. Woodson, Frederick Douglass (among other black voices) and, obviously, innumerable slave narratives, clarifies why Cornel West derided the notion that the 9/11 attacks brought terror to "the homeland." Terror – systematic, state-sponsored, genocidal – was the daily bane of black existence until a few decades ago (Tristam, 2011, n.p.).

Examples of slavery-via-terrorism are endless, and many are irrevocably untold. A poignant case study would surely be the regular public rape, torture, and murder of slaves on the plantations of Saint-Domingue (i.e., Haiti). Here can be found a series of intriguing historical and conceptual linkages to be found in the life story of the leader of Haiti's slave rebellion, François-Dominique Toussaint Louverture. As we know, the French Revolution led to the Reign of Terror, but it also triggered the Haitian Revolution against France. Louverture, who was born a slave, later became a free man and even owned his own slaves and plantations. During the insurrection against France, he led and taught guerrilla warfare but also stopped the killing of white prisoners (Bell, 2007, p. 33). In other words, the French Revolution instigated the advent of wars of national liberation and so-called freedom fighters, which even today are associated with terrorism.

WARS OF NATIONAL LIBERATION

As we have seen, defining terrorism as non-state terrorism is controversial, if only because it omits and occults the misdeeds of past and present state actors. From the start, scientific, ethical, and political comparisons of state and non-state forms of political violence are off the research agenda. In their review of definitions found in academic journals dedicated to terrorism studies, Weinberg et al. (2004) argue that "the consensus over the definition of terrorism among academic specialists is not universal but one grounded in the view of Westerners, and Americans in particular." Such a statement is dubious. Clearly, there is no agreement on what constitutes terrorism, and it is unlikely that there ever will be. Moreover, the assertion that academics "have an origin" and therefore can never think beyond their geographic, political, and cultural milieu is tenuous. Clearly, academic definitions can be politically or culturally biased – this is in fact one of the main arguments of this chapter – but this need not lead us to the conclusion that biases cannot be overcome or that where one stands depends wholly on where one sits. Arguably, one of the objectives of a critical ontology of terrorism is to seek to understand whether terrorism is a real and universal phenomenon or merely a rhetorical device meant to reach a political end. Terrorism scholars, moreover, can and often do move across countries and continents. With such a region-based analysis of academics' conceptualisations, we run the risk of essentialisation and prejudice.

The incommensurability of scholars' definitions of terrorism should be demonstrated, not simply asserted. Hoffman's (2013) writings on how to define terrorism are a good example. Clearly, Hoffman writes, like many of his colleagues, from a US perspective, even a US government perspective. Many of his legal examples, for example, are taken from US agencies. Likewise, Hoffman favours a strong distinction between state "terror" and non-state "terrorism." And yet, Hoffman accords much space to debates about definitions of terrorism that took place at the UN, especially in relation to wars of "national liberation," such as in Palestine, for example. Considering this, would it be fair to simply call any definition of terrorism that Hoffman presents the product of "an American view," whatever that might entail? Let us forget, therefore, the purported origin of scholars and focus on the definitions at hand.

The problem remains, however, that by focusing on how non-state actors harm non-combatants, the concept of terrorism aids de jure states and the resource-rich, and this was in effect the crux of the UN debates. It should be possible, however, to remove value judgements from definitions of terrorism, at least in the first instance. Whether it is ever ethical or legal to harm non-combatants or cause fear in a population is another question. From a scientific standpoint, we only need to distinguish terrorism from other forms of political violence. Weinberg et al. (2004) conclude that a consensus definition of terrorism that all can agree on and that applies to a myriad of geographic and historical cases would have to be very abstract, very high on the ladder of abstraction. But is the term terrorism really a lost cause?

"One man's terrorist is another man's freedom fighter" is a common aphorism employed in many instances to remove the stigma of the terrorism label. But the two are not mutually exclusive. Many of those consciously and deliberately fighting for their definition of freedom have publicly harmed and threatened non-combatants. And in this context, in the minds of bystanders at least, the direction of sympathy is the ultimate deciding factor as to how the perpetrators of the political violence are to be judged. The question then, for the parties to the conflict, is how to win the "minds and hearts" of those witnesses. But in this struggle for sympathy, debates over what constitutes terrorism get confused with debates about the legitimacy of the political movement as a whole, such as de-colonialisation or secession. If we seek the sanctuary of estrangement for a moment, which can so easily be obtained by moving back in history, the US' intestine wars (i.e., the so-called revolution and civil war) show that fighting for freedom and the tactics used in this fight are two related but evidently distinct phenomena. In legal terms, we might speak of jus ad bellum and jus in bello (and jus post bello) (on just war theory, see Primoratz, 2004a; Elshtain, 2008; Rengger, 2013; Walzer, 2015).

Explaining terrorism and its glorification requires such ends-means distinctions. Through such distinctions, even pacifists will be able to understand how it can be that those who commit the most cruel and vile acts can be lauded and worshipped. Ends-means distinctions can also help us judge more objectively respected rebels. Think about how the ends/means distinction might help review the life of Nelson Mandela, elected to be the first President of Apartheid-free South Africa and recipient of the Nobel Peace Prize, who argued during his high treason and sabotage trial that the use of bombings was justified as an ultima ratio, i.e., a form of self-defence. By analytically distinguishing the end from the means, we can also empathise with (but not necessarily tolerate or condone) the Sicarii, William Wallace, Theobald Wolfe Tone, or Ernesto "Che" Guevara. Clearly, even when we think the ends fail to justify the means, the type of fighting and the type of freedom sought deserve distinction. Such distinctions are especially important when reviewing wars of national liberation, where both insurgents and counterinsurgents have often deliberately used terrorism, i.e., the public harm of non-combatants, for political ends. And reviewing past wars of national liberation matters today because *trauma and grievance* can be passed on for generations and be used to justify new movements, new wars, and new atrocities, where the innocent will once again often be caught between state terrorism and non-state terrorism (see, for example, Clifford's chapter on the Irish Republican Army in this volume). A fair and dispassionate judgement of massacres and counter-massacres in Algeria and Israel, or Tunisia and Syria, cannot be done without ends/means distinctions (Primoratz, 2004a, p. 123; Lewis, 2015). In as much as setting the historical record straight via proper conceptualisation can be a form of counterterrorism,

The truth is that we can combine the search for a scientific definition of terrorism with a critique of how the term is employed. Rather than simply assume and assert that terrorism is a term employed against the oppressed, we should explore how the term might be of use in characterising additional forms of political violence, such as war crimes and slavery, for example. Just because "terrorism" as a term can be used to political ends does not mean the term is irrevocably politicised.

CONCLUSION: POLITICAL VIOLENCE AS A SIGNAL

If terrorism and wars of national liberation are distinct, then logically, not all freedom fighters employ terrorism, and terrorism can be employed in other types of conflicts. Terrorism is considered a tactic of the weak because terrorism is one of the only options available to a resource-poor party in an armed conflict. Like other types of asymmetric warfare, terrorism involves leverage. By making maximum use of norms and publicity, acts of terrorism can cause a level of intimidation far beyond what might be considered a rational fear. This explains why statistical arguments about the low risks of terrorism (compared to domestic accidents or climate change, for example) often fail to reassure the public (for a review of the so-called bathtub fallacy, see Mueller and Stewart, 2018). But just because terrorism is often a tool of the "weak" fighting the status quo, jealously guarded by de jure states and empires, it does not follow that state actors and the resource-rich have never engaged in terrorism. The truth, rather, is that state actors and their affiliates regularly seek to terrorise via such signals and that the fear caused by totalitarian states is also leveraged (Primoratz, 2004a, p. 116; Tilly, 2004).

From this discussion, it should now be clear that what truly distinguishes terrorism from other forms of political violence is its communicative aspect. As insensitive and dehumanising as it might sound, the killing of civilians, the innocent, non-combatants, and others who were not part of "the game of war" is incidental (in the perpetrators' minds at least), for it is by "cheating," by doing the unthinkable, that the shock value is attained. By definition, to study terrorism is to study the most repulsive and nauseating forms of violence; it is to stare at "monsters" and a moral "abys" at the risk of being desensitised.

With terrorism, the message is in the medium. It is in this sense that we should understand aphorisms such as "terrorism is theatre" or "propaganda of the deed" (see Jenkins 1974; Cowen 2006; Giroux 2016; Livingston 2019). Intimidation is meant to be obtained by operating outside "routine forms" of political struggle (see Tilly, 2004). Indeed, within the kaleidoscope of terrorist definitions, many have focused on threats and violence *as messages to audiences*. Schmid et al. (2005, p. 28) note that terrorism serves as:

> an anxiety-inspiring method of repeated violent action, employed by (semi) clandestine individual, group, or state actors, for idiosyncratic, criminal or political reasons … whereby the direct targets of the violence are not the main targets. The immediate human victims of violence are generally chosen randomly (targets of opportunity) or selectivity (representative or symbolic targets) from a target population, and serve as message generators.

Enders and Sandler (2002, pp. 145–146) describe terrorism as:

> the premeditated use or threat of use of extranormal violence or brutality by subnational groups to obtain a political, religious, or ideological objective through intimidation of a huge audience, usually not directly involved with the policy making that the terrorists seek to influence.

Hoffman (1998, p. 43) argues that terrorism is "the deliberate creation and exploitation of fear through violence or the threat of violence in the pursuit of political change." Stern (2003, p. xx) details the intended targets as something more than "enemies," emphasising that terrorism is "an act or threat of violence against non-combatants, with the objective of intimidating or otherwise influencing an audience or audiences."

The media, consequently, often face ethical dilemmas where they must decide how much attention to give to terrorism and its perpetrators. Waves of terrorism provide the press and other forms of media with spectacular content, drawing attention and thus revenue. Organisations and individuals that employ terrorism, on the other hand, need the press and other media as a means of publicising their attacks, messages, and causes (on signalling via suicide attacks, see Hoffman and McCormick, 2004). Signalling and raising awareness require some sort of platform, some sort of megaphone. Of course, much of these mutual dependencies can be found in other types of violence, such as the often apolitical mass shootings. Some scholars and related NGOs have suggested that journalists "don't name" and "don't show" mass killers, reducing attention and fame and thereby supposedly deterring potential emulators (see Lankford, 2018; Lankford and Madfis, 2018a, 2018b).

More generally, the publicity potential of reporting spectacular political violence has led to a debate about the relationship between terrorism and states with a free press, i.e., liberal democracies (see Drakos and Gofas, 2006; Chenoweth, 2013). What is clear, for now at least, is that the communicative aspect of terrorism is a form of *indirect coercion*. Under this definition, the concept of "collateral damage" takes on a whole new meaning. To commit terrorism is to use innocent victims as mere props in a gruesome intimidatory spectacle.

Notes

1 This chapter is a revised and expanded version of an article previously published under the title, "Tongue-Tied: The Ongoing Debate on Terrorism," in *Hampton Roads International Security Quarterly*, *14*(1), 92–105, 2014.

2 Rapoport (2002) articulates the "four waves" as the "Anarchist Wave" (beginning in the 1880s and continuing for about 40 years), the "Colonial Wave" (from the 1920s until the 1960s), the "New Left Wave" (appearing in the late-1960s until it receded entirely by the 1990s), and the "Religious Wave" (beginning in 1979 and pushing forward to this day).

3 Secher et al. (2011) go so far as to call the killing of thousands from the Vendée region a genocide.

4 "an anxiety-inspiring method of repeated violent action, employed by (semi) clandestine individual, group, or state actors, for idiosyncratic, criminal or political reasons [...] whereby the direct targets of the violence are not the main targets. The immediate human victims of violence are generally chosen randomly (targets of opportunity) or selectively (representative or symbolic targets) from a target population and serve as message generators" (Schmid et al., 2005, p. 28).

References

Acharya, U.D. (2008). War on terror or terror wars: The problem in defining terrorism. Denv. J. Int'l L. and Pol'y, *37*, 653.

Argomaniz, J. (2008). Counter-terrorism policy-making in the EU. PhD Dissertation, School of Politics and International Relations, University of Nottingham.

Argomaniz, J. (2011). The E.U. and counter-terrorism: Politics, polity and policies after 9/11. Routledge.

Argomaniz, J., Bures, O., and Kaunert, C. (2014). A decade of EU counter-terrorism and intelligence: A critical assessment. Intelligence and National Security, 1–16. (Ahead of print)

Asal, I., De la Calle, L., Findley, M., and Young, J. (2012). Killing civilians or holding territory? How to think about terrorism. *International Studies Review*, *14*, 475–497.

Bell, M.S. (2007). Toussaint Louverture: A biography. Pantheon.

Chenoweth, E. (2013). Terrorism and democracy. Annual Review of Political Science, *16*, 355–378.

Coady, C.A. (1985). The morality of terrorism. Philosophy, *60*(231), 47–69.

Coady, C.A. (2004). Terrorism and innocence. The Journal of Ethics, *8*(1), 37–58.

Collier, D. and Mahon, J.E., Jr. (1993). Conceptual "stretching" revisited: Adapting categories in comparative analysis. The American Political Science Review, *87*(4), 845–855. doi:10.2307/2938818

Connolly, W.E. (1993). The terms of political discourse. Princeton University Press.

Cowen, T. (2006). Terrorism as theater: Analysis and policy implications. Public Choice, *128*(1/2): 233–244.

Crenshaw, M. (1983). "Terrorism, legitimacy, and power – the consequences of political violence," US Department of Justice, Office of Justice Programs. ojp.gov/ncjrs/virtual-library/abstracts/terrorism-legitimacy-and-power-consequences-political-violence

Crenshaw, M., and LaFree, G. (2016). *Countering terrorism: No simple solutions*. Washington, DC: Brookings Institution Press.

Crenshaw, M., and Pimlott, J. (1997). International encyclopedia of terrorism. Routledge.

Crimmins, K., and De Vriese, H. (2006). The reason of terror: Philosophical responses to terrorism. Peeters Publishers.

Cronin, A.C. (2003). Behind the curve: Globalization and international terrorism. International Security, *27*(3), 30–58.

Der Derian, J. (2005). Imaging terror: Logos, pathos and ethos. Third World Quarterly, *26*(1), 23–37.

Dershowitz, A.M. (2002). Why terrorism works: Understanding the threat, responding to the challenge. Yale University Press.

Drakos, K. and Gofas, A. (2006). The devil you know but are afraid to face: Underreporting bias and its distorting effects on the study of terrorism. Journal of Conflict Resolution, *50*(5), 714–735.

Dugard, J. (1974). International terrorism: Problems of definition. International Affairs, *50*(1), 67–81.

Dumitriu, E. (2004). The EU's definition of terrorism: The council framework decision on combating terrorism. German Law Journal, *5*(5), 585–602.

Elshtain, J. (2008). Just war against terror: The burden of American power in a violent world. Basic Books.

Enders, W. and Sandler, T. (2002). Patterns of transnational terrorism, 1970–1999: Alternative time-series estimates. International Studies Quarterly, *46*(2), 145–165.

English, R. (2009). *Terrorism: How to respond*. Oxford: Oxford University Press.

Ganor, B. (2002). Defining terrorism: Is one man's terrorist another man's freedom fighter? Police Practice and Research, *3*(4), 287–304.

Gérard, A. (1999). "Par principe d'humanité–": la Terreur et la Vendée. Fayard.

Gerring, J. (1999). What makes a concept good? A criterial framework for understanding concept formation in the social sciences. Polity, *31*(3), 357–393. doi:10.2307/3235246

Gibbs, J.P. (1989). Conceptualization of terrorism. American Sociological Review, *54*(3), 329–340.

Giroux, H.A. (2016). America's addiction to terrorism. New York University Press.

Goodall, C. (2013, June 28). Defining terrorism. E-International Relations. https://www.e-ir.info/2013/07/28/defining-terrorism/

Gueniffey, P. (2000). La politique de la Terreur. Fayard.

Heupel, M. (2009). Multilateral sanctions against terror suspects and the violation of due process standards. International Affairs, *85*(2), 307–321.

Hoffman, B. (1998). Inside terrorism. Columbia University Press.

Hoffman, B. (2006). Inside terrorism. Columbia University Press.

Hoffman, B. (2013). Inside terrorism. Columbia University Press.

Hoffman, B. and McCormick, G.H. (2004). Terrorism, signaling, and suicide attack. Studies in Conflict and Terrorism, *27*(4), 243–281.

Horsely, R.A. (1979). The Sicarii: Ancient Jewish 'terrorists.' The Journal of Religion, 59(4), 435–458.
Ismayilov, M. (2010). Conceptualizing terrorist violence and suicide bombing. Journal of Strategic Security, 3(3), 15–26.
Jenkins, B.M. (1974, April). "Terrorism works – sometimes," Rand Corporation. https://www.ojp.gov/pdffiles1/Photocopy/19510NCJRS.pdf
Jourdan, A. (2013). Les discours de la Terreur à l'èpoque révolutionnaire (1776–1798): Étude comparative sur une notion ambiguë. French Historical Studies, *36*(1), 51–81.
Lankford, A. (2018). Do the media unintentionally make mass killers into celebrities? An assessment of free advertising and earned media value. Celebrity Studies, 9(3), 340–354.
Lankford, A. and Madfis, E. (2018a). Don't name them, don't show them, but report everything else: A pragmatic proposal for denying mass killers the attention they seek and deterring future offenders. American Behavioral Scientist, *62*(2), 260–279.
Lankford, A. and Madfis, E. (2018b). Media coverage of mass killers: Content, consequences, and solutions. American Behavioral Scientist, *62*(2), 151–162.
Laqueur, W. (2000). The new terrorism: Fanaticism and the arms of mass destruction. Oxford University
Law, R.D. (2015). The Routledge history of terrorism. Routledge.
Law, R.D. (2016). Terrorism: A history. John Wiley and Sons.
Lefebvre, S. (2003). Perspectives on Ethno-nationalist/separatist Terrorism. Conflict Studies Research Centre, Royal Military Academy Sandhurst.
Lewis, O. (2015). Conceptualizing counterterrorism. In S.N. Romaniuk and S.T. Webb (Eds.), Insurgency and counterinsurgency in modern war. Taylor and Francis.
Livingston, S. (2019). The terrorism spectacle. Routledge.
Loi n° 86-1020 du 9 septembre 1986. https://www.legifrance.gouv.fr/loda/id/JORFTEXT000000693912/
Mueller, J. and Stewart, M.G. (2018). Terrorism and bathtubs: Comparing and assessing the risks. *Terrorism and Political Violence*, *30*(2), 1–26.
Nathanson, S. (2010). Terrorism and the ethics of war. Cambridge University press.
Nietzsche, F. (2002). Beyond good and evil: Prelude to a philosophy of the future. Cambridge University Press.
Pedahzur, A. and Perliger, A. (2011). Jewish terrorism in Israel. Columbia University Press.
Primoratz, I. (1990). What is terrorism? Journal of Applied Philosophy, 7(2), 129–138.
Primoratz, I. (1997). The morality of terrorism. Journal of Applied Philosophy, *14*(3), 221–233.
Primoratz, I. (2004a). State terrorism and counter-terrorism. In Terrorism (pp. 113–127). Springer.
Primoratz, I. (2004b). *Terrorism: The philosophical issues.* Palgrave-Macmillan.
Primoratz, I. (2015). Terrorism. The Stanford encyclopedia of philosophy. Spring 2015 Edition. http://plato.stanford.edu/archives/spr2015/entries/terrorism/
Rajkovic, N.M. (2019). Performing 'legality' in the theatre of hostilities: Asymmetric conflict, lawfare and the rise of vicarious litigation. San Diego Int'l LJ, *21*, 435.
Rapoport, D.C. (1971). Assassination and terrorism. Canadian Broadcasting Corporation/Societe Radio-Canada.
Rapoport, D.C. (1984). Fear and trembling: Terrorism in three religious traditions. The American Political Science Review, *78*(3), 658–677.
Rapoport, D.C. (2004). The four waves of modern terrorism. In Attacking terrorism: Elements of a grand strategy. Georgetown University Press.
Rengger, N. (2013). Just war and international order: The uncivil condition in world politics. Cambridge University Press.
Richards, A. (2013). Conceptualizing terrorism. Studies in Conflict and Terrorism, 37(3), 213–236.
Roach, K. (2011). The 9/11 effect: Comparative counter-terrorism. Cambridge University Press.
Ross, J.I. (2007). Deconstructing the terrorism – news media relationship. Crime, Media, Culture: An International Journal, *3*(2), 215–225.
Schinkel, W. (2009). On the concept of terrorism. Contemporary Political Theory, *8*(2), 176–198.
Schmid, A. (2011). The Routledge handbook of terrorism research. Routledge.
Schmid, A.P. and Jongman, A.J. (2005). Political terrorism: A new guide to actors, authors, concepts, data bases, theories, and literature, Transaction Publishers.
Schmid, A.P., Jongman, A.J., and Horowitz, I.L. (2005). Political terrorism. Transaction Publishers.
Secher, R., Goldnadel, G.W., Piralian-Simonyan, H., and Courtois, S. (2011). Vendée, du génocide au mémoricide: mécanique d'un crime légal contre l'humanité. Les Editions du Cerf.
Snyder, T. (2011). Bloodlands: Europe between Hitler and Stalin. Random House.
Stern, J. (1999). The ultimate terrorists. Harvard University Press.
Stern, J. (2003). Terror in the name of god: Why religious militants kill. HarperCollins.
Taylor, C.C. (2002). The cultural face of terror in the Rwandan genocide of 1994. In A. L. Hinton (Ed.), Annihilating difference: The anthropology of genocide (pp. 137–178). Online edn, California Scholarship Online, 2012, 24 May.
Taylor, C.C. (2020). Sacrifice as terror: The Rwandan genocide of 1994. Routledge.
Taylor, D. and Gautron, Y. (2015). Pre-modern terrorism: The cases of the Sicarii and the Assassins. In The Routledge history of terrorism (pp. 42–59). Routledge.
Tilly, C. (2004). Terror, terrorism, terrorists. Sociological Theory, *22*(1), 5–13.
Tristam, P. (2011). "What is terrorism? Toward a clear-eyed definition of terrorism – without prejudice." http://middleeast.about.com/od/terrorism/a/what-is-terrorism.htm
Walter, E.V. (1969). Terror and resistance: A study of political violence. Oxford University Press.
Walzer, M. (2015). Just and unjust wars: A moral argument with historical illustrations: Basic Books.
Weinberg, L. (2009). Global terrorism. The Rosen Publishing Group, Inc.
Weinberg, L., Pedahzur, A., and Hirsch-Hoefler, S. (2004). The challenges of conceptualizing terrorism. Terrorism and Political Violence, *16*(4), 777–794.
Wilkins, B.T. (1992). Terrorism and collective responsibility. Routledge.
Young, R. (2006). Defining terrorism: The evolution of terrorism as a legal concept in international law and its influence on definitions in domestic legislation. BC Int'l and Comp. L. Rev., *29*, 23.

6

EPISTEMOLOGICAL FOUNDATIONS OF TERRORISM

Salvin Paul, Sanchita Bhattacharya, and Scott N. Romaniuk

INTRODUCTION AND BACKGROUND

In 1937, the League of Nations established the Convention for the Prevention and Punishment of Terrorism. The League was triggered into action by France after the assassinations of King Alexander I of Yugoslavia and French Foreign Minister Louis Barthou in Marseilles (Pandalai, 2019). The League of Nations Convention in 1937 defined terrorism as "criminal acts directed against a state and intended to create terror in the minds of particular persons, a group of persons, or the general public" (League of Nations, 1937). The convention, however, was not enforced due to the inability of many signatory states to act on the issue of extradition or prosecution.

With the dissolution of the League, the convention, along with the archives of the League of Nations, were transferred to the United Nations in 1946. It was only in September 1972, after 11 members of the Israeli contingent were killed in a terror attack during the Munich Olympics, that the United Nations General Assembly (UNGA) adopted the first UNGA resolution on countering terrorism. That resolution established the Ad Hoc Committee on International Terrorism in 1972, consisting of 35 countries, including India, to carve out a multilateral legal framework for counter-terrorism (Pandalai, 2019). The UNGA Resolution 49/60 subsequently describes terrorism as "criminal acts intended or calculated to provoke a state of terror in the general public, a group of persons, or particular persons for political purposes" (United Nations, 1994).

These acts of terror are considered criminal and unjustifiable, notwithstanding the situations or any form of objective to justify them. The provision further listed the following motives: racial, ideological, ethnic, and religious. Also, the International Convention for the Suppression of Terrorist Bombings (United Nations, 1997) made provisions to the effect that any act "calculated to provoke a state of terror in the general public … or particular persons for political purposes and included acts that jeopardised friendly relations between states and peoples or that threatened the territorial integrity and security of a state" is termed terrorism.

From a broader perspective, terrorism has been defined by the European Union's 2002 Framework Decision on Combating Terrorism as:

> an intentional act which may seriously damage a country or an international organisation, committed with the aim of seriously intimidating a population, unduly compelling a government or an international organisation to perform or abstain from performing any act, seriously destabilising or destroying fundamental political, constitutional, economic, or social structures by means of attacks upon a person's life, attacks upon the physical integrity of a person, kidnapping, hostage-taking, seizure of aircraft or ships, or the manufacture, possession, or transport of weapons or explosives (Alonzo et al., 2006).

EVOLUTION OF THE *ISM*

Terrorism has been practised since ancient times. The official documented beginning, as some believe it, occurred with the killing of Hipparchus, a member of the Greek ruling class, by Aristogeition and Harmodius in 514 BC (Martin, 2011). Others believe it was during the 1st century when the Zealots Sicarii, Jewish terrorists, committed themselves to overthrowing Roman rule in Judea. Also known as dagger men, they would slay their victims during the day in crowded areas for all to see, which created enormous fear among the population and ultimately resulted in a heavily supported rebellion against the Romans (Rapoport, 1984). Terrorism has been prevalent throughout the history of mankind in various forms.

Since 1794, when the term "terrorisme" came into existence during the French Revolution to refer to a policy of more or less arbitrary victimisation of alleged and real political opponents, the understanding of what constitutes "terrorism" has been constantly changing. While the term initially referred to the exercise of punitive and deterrent public violence by the state, current usage tends to associate terrorism mainly,

DOI: 10.4324/9780429426063-8

although not exclusively and sometimes erroneously, with acts of non-state actors only (Alonzo et al., 2006). Meanwhile, terrorism itself began taking on the negative meanings it carries today, helped primarily by the works of those like the British political philosopher Edmund Burke, who propagated the term "terrorism" in English while demonising its French revolutionary practitioners (Burgess, 2015).

The appearance of political ideologies such as Marxism correspondingly created a fertile sense of unrest at the existing order, with terrorism offering a means for change. The Italian revolutionary Carlo Pisacane's theory of the "propaganda of the deed," which recognised the efficacy of terrorism to deliver a message to an audience other than the target and draw attention and sustenance to a cause, symbolised this new form of terrorism (Hoffman, 1988). Anarchist terrorist groups were predominantly captivated by the example set by the Russian populists. Nationalist groups such as those in Ireland and the Balkans implemented terrorism as a means towards their desired ends. As with Europe, terrorism arrived on America's shores before the 20th century (Burgess, 2015).

David Rapoport has delineated four major waves of international terrorism in his seminal work on the history of international terrorism. The first ("anarchist") wave of modern terrorism began in Russia in the 1880s and lasted until the 1920s; the second ("anticolonial") wave began in the 1920s and ended in the 1960s; the third ("new left") wave began in the 1960s and continued through to the 1980s; and the fourth ("religious") wave emerged in 1979 and continues until today (Rapoport, 2004).

As the Cold War intensified in the 1960s, with the world polarised between East and West, a new dynamic developed in transnational terrorism as state-sponsored terrorism exported terrorism to other parts of the world for their own political interests. Iran supported Hezbollah; Libya supported Abu Nidal; and Iraq, Cuba, Sudan, and Algeria provided training camps as well as economic and political support to terrorist groups around the world. Terrorism moved to the Middle East and the Arab-Israeli conflict, with the United States supporting Israel and the Soviet Union supporting various Arab countries (Garrison, 2003).

The 1980s were known as a decade of hostage-taking, with terrorism finding a target in American interests around the world. These incidents included the 1979 Iranian hostage crisis, the bombing of United States embassies, the kidnapping of American citizens, and the bombing of aeroplanes. The last decade of the 20th century provided the most current change in the growth of terrorism. Middle Eastern-based terrorism in the 1960s and 1970s was about gaining publicity for a cause; even in the 1980s, as more American interests were targeted, a terrorist act was generally followed by credit-taking or a warning that future attacks would occur if the United States did not change its policies. The 1990s brought to terrorism the indiscriminate killing of civilians and high mass-casualty counts. According to the FBI, "It does appear that international terrorists will continue to focus on attacks that yield significant destruction and high casualties, thus maximising worldwide media attention and public anxiety" (FBI, 1999).

Terrorism has spread its wings to cover suicide bombings, narco-trafficking, maritime, and airborne crime, and has one eye on weapons of mass destruction. Over a period of time, terror outfits have evolved new techniques and widened their range of operations. More worryingly, a terrorist can no longer be identified by his regional or class background. There is no stereotype. He may have indoctrinated himself or herself on the Internet and may even have taught himself some of the techniques of terrorism (Sood, 2010: 77).

The accomplishment of a nation in maintaining security lies in guaranteeing that there are no visible edges and preventing acts of violence by terrorists and other such groups that can cause collateral damage. The Asia Economic Institute study calculated that the overall loss to the Indian economy in the wake of the 2008 Mumbai terror attacks was about USD 100 billion, arising from the closure of crucial institutions such as the stock exchanges, commodities sector, money markets, trade, and business and commercial establishments. Further, FDI was hit by an estimated USD 20 billion (Bobb, 2015). Such acts of terror and violence have great economic, political, social, and international consequences.

EPISTEMOLOGICAL FOUNDATIONS

Instrumental Approach

In the instrumental approach, the emphasis is on the actions of terrorists. In this approach, an act of terrorism is viewed as a deliberate choice by a terrorist actor in response to external stimuli, where an upsurge in cost or a decrease in reward for terrorist violence will make it less likely (Crenshaw, 2001). Thus, the approach suggests terrorist groups calculate the cost of doing or not doing an action and also the prospect of success in their actions. One of the key questions in all theories is how one can define the "success" of a terrorist organisation. Instrumental theorists suggested that success was defined in terms of achieving the political ends of a given terrorist organisation.

The instrumental approach to terrorism is one of the most developed approaches to the subject in the discipline of political science. It is simple and comprehensible. It is coherent because the intentions of actors are inferred from their behaviour according to logical rules. Also, this approach is intellectually satisfying and provides researchers with a rather easier context for study since information requirements about secretive terrorist organisations are relaxed. It is significantly influenced by conflict studies, so its scope is very broad as it is applied to all types of conflict, irrespective of the identity of the actors. Though this leads to the fragility of the instrumental approach, it cannot clarify how the preferences of the actors are determined since it does not include analyses of the internal workings of terrorist organisations. So, if we assume that actors are identical, we miss the differences in understanding how different terrorist actors act differently (Ozdamar, 2008).

Rational Choice Theory

The instrumental approach emphasises Rational Choice Theory, where terrorists are regarded as rational actors who do a cost-benefit analysis of their actions. It explains that an offender's incentives to engage in criminal acts are determined by the potential cost of action and the anticipated profits. Motivations to commit crime can be an individual's effort to meet common personal needs and involve creating chances for meeting those needs. Individuals are expected to have the capability to weigh the pleasure to be gained against the likely punishment while considering committing illegal behaviour and also have the ability to decide against the act (Williams and Mcshane, 2010). It is also argued that, since terrorism is politically motivated, most or all terrorism campaigns depend on rational political choice. In an attempt to realise benefits or needs, terrorist organisations decide to use acts of terror to oppose a government politically. Thus, terrorist behaviour is rational in the sense that terrorist organisations own internally consistent sets of beliefs, values, and images of the environment (Crenshaw, 1981). Consequently, terrorism is thought to be a "rational choice" for achieving the projected goal.

Organisational Approach

In this approach, the processes are governed by the terrorist organisation's quest for survival and control in a competitive environment where, through a scheme of punishment and incentive, the loyalty of the followers and the maintenance of the establishment are ensured (Crenshaw, 2001). As we analyse more of the examples in this literature, one can observe that great significance is given to the internal dynamics and processes of the organisation. The determinants of political actions or violent policies by terrorist organisations are organisational rather than political or ideological. These organisations are taken as self-sustaining, and they do whatever is essential to survive. The organisation delivers goods to the members to keep them in the organisation. These can be tangible goods or public goods (Olson, 1998). In an organisational approach, short-term rather than long-term goal achievement might work, given that its success depends on external and internal pressures. The advantages of this approach are in understanding the difficulties and differences among and between terrorist organisations and their diverse values, incentive structures, and competitiveness. The disadvantages are that this approach is intricate, incomprehensible, and difficult to undertake given the resource and data constraints (Crenshaw, 2001).

Psychological Approach

In divergence with political scientists and sociologists, who are interested in the political and social contexts of terrorist groups, the relatively few psychologists who study terrorism are mainly interested in the micro-level of the individual terrorist or terrorist group. The psychological approach is concerned with the study of terrorists per se, their recruitment and induction into terrorist groups, their beliefs, personalities, motivations, attitudes, and careers as terrorists (Hudson, 1999).

Syndrome Approach

The syndrome approach assumes terrorism to be a monolithic and meaningful psychological construct with distinguishable traits that allow generalisations in the same manner as a disease with identifiable symptoms. These identifiable traits include behavioural features that differentiate terrorists from non-terrorists and a set of root causes that explain the advent of terrorism. For instance, behavioural traits are said to comprise personality disorders, while the root causes include unemployment, poverty, and political repression (Kruglanski and Fishman, 2006).

The Tool Approach

The tool approach, unlike the syndrome approach, is not a bottom-up approach to the study of terrorism but a top-down approach that makes a conceptual distinction between terrorism (viewed as a means to an end) and terrorists (that can be any social actor). The tool approach sees terrorism as a strategy for achieving objectives that a variety of actors can implement. The psychology that is dealt with here is not one concerned with personal traits or one determined by root causes, but the psychology behind employing certain means. The tool view is to understand why certain groups or actors opt for terrorism as a strategy (Kruglanski and Fishman, 2006). Essentially, this body of knowledge has taught psychologists that a precise method is used when a person considers it to have a high expected value. That is, if a person wants to attain something, he or she is more likely to use a tool or means that are seen as supportive of such achievement. If it is so seen, the tool or means is considered to have high expected utility. Furthermore, a tool is predominantly high in expected utility if the thing the person wants to attain is significant to him or her. Therefore, to the degree that a tool is extremely helpful to the attainment of important goals, it is said to have high psychological utility.

The Radicalisation Model

According to the radicalisation model, people turn to political violence because they have been radicalised. The making of a radical typically unfolds in a multi-step fashion and is strongly influenced by one's surroundings, past experiences, and future prospects. Depending on the specific socio-geographical context, four or five main steps have been identified: pre-radicalisation (at risk), self-identification (susceptible), indoctrination (moderate radical), commitment, and "jihadization" (full radicalization). Radicalisation characteristically occurs through networks of peers and may be enabled through technology in the form of web-based recruitment material or chat rooms. ISIS is a well-known internet-savvy group that uses social media to recruit Western foreign fighters in Syria and Iraq. Marginalised adolescents and young adults, nevertheless, are particularly vulnerable to indoctrination and radicalisation, especially in their formative years (Chuang and Dorsogna, 2015). Imbuing radical thoughts in the minds of young people belonging to an impressionable age actually makes them sympathetic to the cause of a particular individual or a terror organisation and resultantly creates a strong sense of psychological conviction to perpetrate violence towards others.

Sociological Approach

Psychological factors related to the development of a terrorist and the spread of terrorism are often interconnected with sociological factors. The majority of terrorists are not psychotic; psychological as well as sociological factors, when combined together, are the characteristics necessary for the triggering of an individual and the groups they are allied with becoming radicalised and committing terrorist violent actions (Smith, 2013). The sociology of terrorism can be broken down into four broad theories: social learning theory, frustration-aggression theory, relative deprivation theory, and national cultural theory (Victoroff and Krulanski, 2009).

Social Learning Theory

Developed by Albert Bandura, the theory is based on what an individual learns and accepts as appropriate behaviour as a result of what they have witnessed or observed. Individuals imitate their behaviour, thoughts, actions, opinions, and feelings based on what they have grown up learning from their social environment. This theory has been widened to further explain aggressive behaviour, which can be linked to the actions of terrorists (Bandura, 1973). The theory of social learning, which is being heavily exploited by terrorist organisations, is exceptionally powerful. Their ability to control messaging is fundamental to this strategy. One of the astounding consequences of this societal norm is the challenge associated with reteaching generations that are steeped in the ways of terrorism. (Smith, 2013).

Ronald Louis Akers identified four key elements in the study of social learning theory, the first three of which have clear implications for the study of terrorists. First, *differential association* refers to direct social interaction with members of a primary group and less concrete, but no less important, identifications with members of more distal groups, the latter also serving as sources of learning. *Imitation* occurs when an individual copies the behaviour of others, possibly not fully understanding the behaviour's importance, in what ways, or even when it might be rewarding. *Definitions* serve as behavioural guideposts for how we think about certain behaviours as good or bad, rewarding or punishing. The fourth element, *differential reinforcement*, is more complex and exists in both social and nonsocial forms. Such reinforcements are anticipatory or probable in nature, suggesting to the actor whether the conduct guided by those definitions is likely to be rewarded or punished (Akers, 1985).

Frustration-Aggression Theory

The frustration-aggression theory has long been a widespread explanation for terrorism and political violence in general. First conceived in the late 1930s by John Dollard and his colleagues, it argues that aggression occurs when an individual is frustrated. Stated simply, the theory suggests that frustration always leads to aggression and that aggression is always the result of frustration. Terrorism, meanwhile, is an (often unconscious) form of displacement. Frustration with one's goals does seem to play an obvious role in terrorist activity, especially where the political makeup of the state allows no other outlet for "normal" political activity (Wright-Neville and Smith, 2009).

Terrorists are angry over specific issues and feel frustrated because their cause has been exploited by those in power; at the same time, they are recurrently economically marginalised, unemployed, or otherwise unable to attain their desired goals. Thus, the principles of frustration-aggression theory pertinently fit the scenario in most terrorist-torn countries today. Edigin (2010) argues that the frustrating conditions in certain parts of the world that resulted from the denial of access to natural resources coupled with the environmental dilapidation of oil exploration activities generated frustration, which eventually breeds aggression and the attendant attention-seeking through violence. For instance, Mid-Eastern terrorist groups like al-Qaeda are rebelling against Western countries because of the purported US foreign policies against Islamic countries and the adoption of Western culture, which they believe is anti-Islamic and thus deprives them of economic, religious, and political growth. The frustration of not having the same opportunities as other countries has resulted in aggression against the United States and has exacerbated extremists' violent behaviour (Okoye, 2017).

Relative Deprivation Theory

Relative deprivation theory is related to the negative feelings and emotions an individual experiences as a result of not having what others may have. These negative feelings are based on the individual believing they are equal to those that they envy and therefore are permitted all the same perceived welfare. When the individual does not have the same welfare, the individual takes action in order to attain their desired perceptions. This action may take the form of political violence or terrorism, depending on the level of discontentment within the individual. The greater the discontent, which may be the result of the individual's inability to proficiently address the situation, the greater the potential for the individual's frustration level as well as aggression to grow, resulting in violence (Gurr, 1970).

One of the key traits connected to this hypothesis is poverty. The potential for poverty and the population's ability to influence political change as major contributing factors to terrorism have been the subject of extensive research by academics and governments, but more work needs to be done in this area (Victoroff and Krulanski, 2009). The relative deprivation theory and terrorism are both supported by a large body of evidence, however, like all the other ideas put forth, it is unable to explain why people become radicalised. However, it is just one of several elements contributing to the spread of terrorism (Smith, 2013).

Theory of National Culture

The National Cultural Theory of Terrorism was developed as a result of a study by Leonard Weinberg and William Eubank, who noted that cultural differences can be used to help explain differences in terrorism just as they have been used to explain numerous singularities between nations. They emphasised in particular how terrorists differ from one another based on their cultural backgrounds. Like all previous ideas, this one has received criticised to some extent. It has drawn criticism for its inability to clarify boundary challenges and for providing unclear guidance regarding the precise identification of various cultures (Crenshaw, 1981). There is a great deal of criticism of this theory for not covering the complete range of terrorism, much like the other theories. It does, however, confirm one more element that fuels the spread of terrorism and, with additional study, can help advance our understanding of how to combat terrorism (Smith, 2013).

Economic Approach

Theoretical and empirical economic methods are often used to evaluate a multitude of issues related to terrorism. For example, economics and statistics can be used to evaluate the threat posed by a terrorist organisation by measuring the number, frequency, and intensity of these attacks, the number of casualties, the category of weapons most preferred, and the development of the terrorist entity through time series, utility maximisation, game theory, and other statistics-friendly models (Sandler and Enders, 2007).

The economic methodology is mainly well suited to provide insights over and beyond those from a political science approach. Hence, scholars in this approach claim empirical superiority to the definitions, institutional analyses, case studies, and inductive frameworks provided by political science. This explanation can be better elucidated by providing four different arguments from the supporters of this approach. First, they claim that economic analysis can account for strategic interactions among opposing interests. These relationships include terrorist-government or two-targeted country relations in transnational terrorism cases. Secondly, authors from this line of literature suggest that rational choice models can be applied to find out how terrorists are likely to respond to policy-induced changes to their constraints. Thirdly, not only economic methodology but also theories of economics are expected to be valuable in explaining terrorism. Fourth, it is recommended that numerous economic empirical methods be applied to estimate theoretical predictions and policy recommendations. Seeing the advanced and successful methodologies that are used in economics literature is a beneficial option if the researcher's aim is to make predictions and policy recommendations (Ozdamar, 2008).

CONCLUSION

Our interrogation of these approaches provides an illustration of the extent of our knowledge and the limits of human knowledge regarding terrorism. There is now an unprecedented range of actors involved in addressing this phenomenon, which has served many different roles in advancing (though sometimes receding) our (re-)conceptualisation of the nature and gravity of the term "terrorism" and terrorist grievances and, by extension, their causes. Yet, it would be folly to subscribe to the view that none of them have played a role in distorting or hijacking our understanding of the aforesaid. That is, while they may assist in the formulation of effective counter-terror policies, they can, sometimes effortlessly, play a role in shaping and formulating ineffective or counter-productive policies and approaches. Simply put, they can lead to flawed outcomes or overreactions with deleterious effects on society and humanity, possibly undermining society more so than terrorist intentions and actions themselves. It is for this reason that we acknowledge the multitude of approaches that have been crafted as part of a broader effort to build and apply structures that seek to adequately, i.e., dispassionately and objectively, address the physiognomy of terrorism. While none of them offer the so-called silver bullet, they will most certainly continue to serve as important doctrinal structures for addressing this product of and threat to society.

References

Akers, R.L. (1985). *Deviant behavior: A social learning approach*. Belmont: Wadsworth.

Albert Bandura, A. (1973). *Aggression: A social learning analysis*. New York: Prentice Hall.

Alonzo, et al. (2006). Radicalisation processes leading to acts of terrorism. *European Commission*. Retrieved August 20, 2020, from https://www.clingendael.org/sites/default/files/pdfs/20080500_cscp_report_vries.pdf

Bobb, D. (2015). *The fast lane: Economic cost of terror*. Retrieved August 20, 2020, from https://www.financialexpress.com/opinion/the-fast-lane-economic-cost-of-terror/34641/

Burgess, M. (2015). *A brief history of terrorism*. Retrieved August 20, 2020, from https://www.pogo.org/investigation/2015/02/brief-history-of-terrorism/

Chuang, Y.L. and Dorsogna, M. (2015). Mathematical models of radicalization and terrorism. Retrieved August 29, 2020, from https://arxiv.org/pdf/1903.08485.pdf

Crenshaw, M. (1981). The causes of terrorism. *Comparative Politics, 13*(4), 379–399.

Crenshaw, M. (2001). Theories of terrorism: Instrumental and organisational approaches. In D.C. Rapoport (Ed.), *Inside terrorist organizations*. London: Frank Cass.

FBI (1999). *Terrorism in the United States*. Washington, DC: U.S. Department of Justice.

Garrison, A.H. (2003). Terrorism: The nature of its history. *Criminal Justice Studies, 16*(1), 39–52.

Gurr, T.R. (1970). *Why men rebel*. New Jersey: Princeton University Press.

Hoffman, B. (1988). *Inside terrorism*. New York: Columbia University Press.

Hudson, R. (1999). *The sociology and psychology of terrorism: Who becomes a terrorist and why?* Federal Research Division, Library of Congress. Washington, DC: The Division.

Kruglanski, A.W. and Fishman, S. (2006). The psychology of terrorism: "Syndrome" versus "tool" perspectives. *Terrorism and Political Violence. 18*(2), 193–215.

League of Nations (1937). *Convention for the prevention and punishment of terrorism*. Retrieved August 16, 2020, from https://www.wdl.org/en/item/11579/#institution=united-nations-office-geneva-library

Martin, G. (2011). *Essentials of terrorism: Concepts and controversies*. USA: Sage Publication.

Okoye, I.E. (2017). The theoretical and conceptual understanding of terrorism: A content analysis approach. *Journal of Law and Criminal Justice, 5*(1), 36–45.

Olson, M. (1998). *The logic of collective action*. Cambridge: Harvard University Press.

Ozdamar, O. (2008). Theorizing terrorist behavior: Major approaches and their characteristics. *Defence Against Terrorism Review, 1*(2), 89–101.

Pandalai, S. (2019). "India's quest for a global convention on combating terrorism: An overview of regional Responses and recurring challenges." In *Combating Terrorism: Evolving Asian Perspectives*. New Delhi: Pentagon Press.

Rapoport, D.C. (1984). Fear and trembling: Terrorism in three religious traditions. *The American Political Science Review, 78*(3), 669.

Rapoport, D.C. (2004). Four waves of modern terrorism. In A.K. Cronin and J.M. Ludes (Eds.), *Attacking terrorism: Elements of a grand strategy*. Washington, DC: Georgetown University Press.

Ross, J.I. (1993). Structural causes of oppositional political terrorism: Towards a causal model. *Journal of Peace Research, 30*(30), 317–329.

Sandler, T. and Enders, W. (2007). An economic perspective on transnational terrorism. In T. Brück (Ed.), *The economic analysis of terrorism*. Oxon: Routledge.

Smith, M.J. (2013). *Understanding terrorism and contributing factors to development of a terrorist*. Retrieved August 18, 2020, from https://www.cfc.forces.gc.ca/259/290/299/286/smith_j.pdf

Sood, V. (2010). Counter-terrorism: The Indian experience. In *Counter Terrorism in South Asia*. New Delhi: KW Publisher.

United Nations (1994). *Measures to eliminate international terrorism*. Retrieved August 16, 2020, from http://www.un.org/documents/ga/res/49/a49r060.htm

United Nations (1997). *Measures to eliminate international terrorism*. Retrieved August 20, 2020, from http://www.un.org/law/cod/terroris.htm

Victoroff, J. and Krulanski, A. (2009). *Psychology of terrorism*. New York: Psychology Press.

Williams, F.P. and Mcshane M.D. (2010). *Criminological theory*. New Jersey: Pearson Education Inc.

Wright-Neville, D., and Smith, D. (2009). Political rage: Terrorism and the politics of emotion. *Global Change, Peace & Security, 21*(1), 85–98.

7

RELIGION AS A SOURCE OF TERRORISM

Wangchu Lama and Salvin Paul

INTRODUCTION

Terrorism, as it is called today, is not a new trend; it has been in practise since time immemorial and has been transforming its nature and impact with the passing of time. Accordingly, the modes of operation, nature, affiliation, and association of terror groups have not been static since their inception. In the era of globalisation, terrorism has become a rampant menace, and scholars, institutions, and governments grapple with the question of why a person turns to violence to become a terrorist. The causal factors of terrorism, ranging from political to religious, as well as the goals of the terror groups that have been facilitating violent acts at local, national, and international levels, are intensely debated by policymakers as they devise new and often controversial counterterrorism policies to contain terrorism (see Romaniuk, 2021). New forms of terrorism, its repercussions, and growing support among the deprived sections of society are further factored in by modernity, social change, and the adaptation of technology for its dissemination, support, and operations today. Since the 9/11 attack on the World Trade Centre by Al-Qaeda, terrorism has received global attention on the fault lines of clashes of civilisation, demarcating new frontiers on the basis of religion and culture.

Against this backdrop, terrorism has been particularly associated with fringe elements within Islam and has been labelled as perpetrators of terrorism, especially to gain momentum for Islamophobia. Deliberate efforts to tag terrorism within certain religious groups by advertent, politically enabled media pose the question of whether religion became a source of inspiration for terrorists. However, the demonisation of one group of people by another in the name of God is a common tradition in almost all religious histories that have been narrated in the writings and scriptures of religions. Such writings focus primarily on establishing how their gods, saints, prophets, and faithful suffered at the hands of the establishment to justify the violence they engaged in. Remorseless engagement in violence in the name of God as well as hope of heaven or life after death appear to woo religious faithful into terrorism and violence.

The objective of this chapter is to explore and examine whether religions have become a source of inspiration for terrorists and to understand the politics behind this kind of propaganda in contemporary society. The article delves into various features and dimensions of terrorism to examine the factors that shape terrorism and understand how this kind of tactical act has been practised among various groups and religions influenced and inspired by religious dogmas. Finally, the chapter explores counterterrorism measures to analyse how they can be more dangerous and counterproductive in the future. Threats from terrorism have become an alarming global reality, and the efforts by governments and international bodies to combat terrorism may turn futile and counterproductive if a particular religion is accused of or labelled as the source of all terrorism.

TERRORISM

Terrorism is not a new phenomenon, and the earliest record of it can be traced back to the 1st century C.E., when the Zealouts and Sircarii (Jewish) groups were formed to launch terror campaigns against the Roman occupation of Judea (Ghosh, 2018). However, the use of the term "terrorism" was used by Edmund Burke in reference to the Reign of Terror in the French Revolution (Winter, 2017). Since then, terrorism has taken different courses. Earlier, the word terror referred to the conduct of the government against the citizens, where the sovereign ruler instilled fear of God in the minds of the people (Zaia, 2016). Though there is no universally accepted definition of the word "terrorism", debate and contestations among governments and scholars exhibit the gravity of it in society. Some groups legitimise their terror acts as protection of their community, ethnicity, and identity, considering themselves to be revolutionary

DOI: 10.4324/9780429426063-9

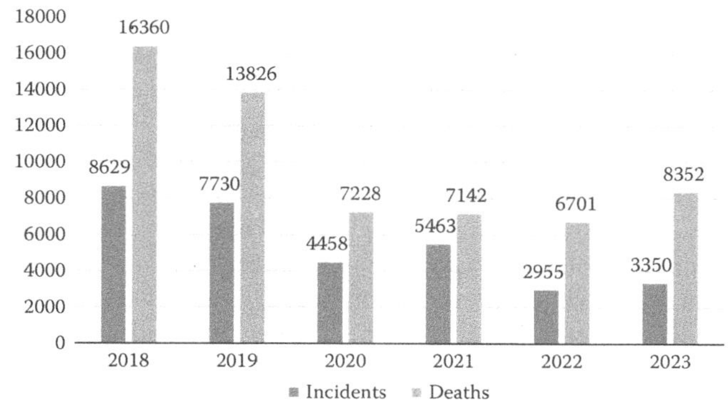

Figure 7.1 Number of Terrorist Attacks Worldwide, 2018–2023.

Institute for Economics & Peace (IEP) (2019, 2020, 2022, 2023, 2024).

fighters against inequality, injustice, and discrimination (UN, n.d.). A layman perceives terrorism as an organised crime carried out by its perpetrators to terrorise the common man to achieve their political goals. Since the 9/11 attack, the term has gained wider political connotations under the rubrics of "war on terror", Islamophobia, counterterrorism policies, etc. It has been theorised by politicians and states as a violent act in order to achieve some kind of political expediency (Stern, 2003). The term terrorism has undoubtedly acquired negative meaning in the contemporary world as it produces a state of terror, panic, and fear psychosis, created by an individual or a group of people (non-state actors) in order to force, coerce, or blackmail the authorities, using violent methods to accept their demands or to attain political, religious, or ideological goals (Reach Out Australia, 2020; Schmid, 2013).

Terrorists, though, have committed violence for a gamut of reasons to draw attention to their cause, which has devastated the lives of innocent people over the years. Since the 9/11 attacks, the number of deaths triggered by terrorism increased significantly in 2014, which were mainly committed by militant groups like Al-Qaeda, Boko Haram, the Taliban, etc. The trend of lone wolves has augmented the threat level (Cheung, 2014; Zewairi et al., 2017). Though the total number of deaths due to terror attacks has declined for the third consecutive term in 2017 since 2014, the number of fatalities remains substantially higher than the previous decade (Figure 7.1).

The major reason behind the decline in death rates is the decline in intensity of violence in the Middle East, but it still remains a global threat as it surged from 18,753 deaths in 2017 to 32,836 in 2018. Its spectacular impact is so alarming that, at certain times, it could overshadow all other global issues such as nuclear proliferation, global warming, pollution, depletion, poverty, etc. Therefore, terrorist attacks are going to become more devastating in the coming days. 71 countries recorded at least one death from terrorism in 2018. Afghanistan had the largest deterioration, recording 7,379 deaths from terrorism, an increase of 59% from the prior year. The impact of terrorism improved in 98 countries, compared to 40 that deteriorated in the past year, but the overall impact of terrorism was still higher in 80 countries when compared to five years ago. Iraq and Somalia experienced the largest fall in deaths from terrorism, owing mainly to less activity from ISIL and Al-Shabaab, respectively. Deaths attributed to ISIL declined by 69%, and attacks declined by 63%. The fall in deaths has been largest in Iraq, Syria, and Nigeria. Bombings and armed assaults have been the most common types of terrorist attacks over the past two decades.

Between 2002 and 2018, South Asia, MENA, and sub-Saharan Africa accounted for 93% of all deaths from terrorism. The largest number was recorded in MENA, with more than 93,700 fatalities (Wilson Center, 2019). South Asia has had the highest impact from terrorism since 2002, while Central America and the Caribbean region have had the lowest impact. Incidents of far-right terrorism have been increasing in the West, particularly in Western Europe, North America, and Oceania (Tarallo, 2020). However, far-right terrorism remains a small fraction of total terrorism worldwide. Even in the West, historically, nationalist or separatist, Islamist, and far-left terrorism have been much more common. Conflict is the primary driver of terrorist activity, and in 2018, 95% of deaths from terrorism occurred in countries where violent conflict was occurring. Insurgent groups use terrorism as a tactic of war and are more likely to target infrastructure, the police, and the state military (Global Terrorism Index, 2019). There have been over 300 suicide attacks involving at least one female since 1985, which have killed 3,071 people. From 2013 to 2018, incidents of female suicide attacks increased from four in 2013 to 22 in 2018. The majority of female suicide attacks in the past five years have been attributed to Boko Haram. Excluding Boko Haram, female suicide deaths have increased by 30% since 2013 and attacks by 200%. Thirteen percent of ISIL foreign recruits were female, with the majority of female recruits joining from the MENA region (Global Terrorism Index, 2019).

FACTORS LEADING TO TERRORISM

The major aphorisms attached to terrorism help in critically understanding the term. One person's terrorist is another person's freedom fighter; extremism in defence of liberty is no vice; it became necessary to destroy the town to save it; one man willing to throw away his life is enough to terrorise a thousand (Martin, 2008). Terrorism is motivated by factors like social, political, economic, and religious factors that need to be monitored carefully so as to combat terrorism from its roots (Sinai, 2005). The destructive capacity of terrorist groups is increasing tremendously as they use the seamless application and wide-ranging effects of modern technology as their medium of operation in the current era. The causal factors of terrorism are examined by structural, psychological, and rational theorists. Structuralists analyse the cultural, environmental, social, political, and economic factors of terrorism. Psychological theory elucidates the reasons why individuals tend to become members of terrorist organisations. The theory of rational choice explains the motive behind individuals opting for terrorist activities based on the deliberation of costs and benefits (Ross, 1993). These factors could shape and influence the process of terrorism and the people involved in it in an overlapping manner in the wake of increasing ethno-nationalist and fundamentally radical movements within and among religious groups.

Clash in Ideology

It is argued that contemporary international terrorism since the 1960s has been driven by two major ideologies, nationalism and religion, and has been effective in polarising the masses (Badey, 2002). A nationalist terrorist confines their activity entirely within the territory that they aim to liberate. Since the 1970s, religion and nationalism have become effective forces, thus being perceived as an alliance in many parts of the world (Delanty and Mahony, 2002). For example, there are a number of violent non-state actors operating in India. The recent surge of Hindu nationalism in the post-2014 election leading to the victory of the current ruling party is quite startling (Zahid, 2017). Such groups are inspired to transform India into a Hindu nation. In this context, violence against minorities along the lines of religion, linguistics, and culture has become rampant by challenging the very ethos and civilisational heritage of Hinduism, posing grave repercussions and polarising society. Moreover, Kashmiri Muslims feel un-Islamic nationalism is against the will of God. Thus, it has been argued that waves of communal violence have paved the way for people belonging to minority groups (especially Muslims) to join Jihadist groups (Zahid, 2017). Civilisation clashes may also result in violence when groups exhibit different identities, like different religions or ethnicities; this may lead to more conflict, either between different groups within a country or between different country groups organised along a civilisation line. The organisations are responsible for inciting violence in the name of God among innocent commoners (Huntington, 1996). Nationalism, coupled with ethnic identity and communal religious sentiments, could play a significant role in attracting people to terrorism.

Socio-Economic Factors

Some scholars suggest that terrorism is rooted in economic deprivation, i.e., in poverty-driven inequality within a country (Botha, 2019). The idea of relative deprivation discerns that violence is generated mostly when there is a discrepancy between what individuals deserve and what they actually get through the economic distribution process. So poor structural economic conditions create frustration among people, which turns into violence. Thus, gross economic deprivation is accepted as leading to more terrorism by inciting frustration and lowering the cost of violence (Richardson, 2011). With respect to the target countries of terrorism, economic success may attract attacks when economic deprivation is assessed globally. However, the correlation between poverty and terror has not been proven as such. Terrorism is said to have been fostered by the process of modernisation. Modernisation encompasses economic change, new forms of communication, new lifestyles, and new ideas. These factors may create grievances associated with socio-economic and demographic stress. For instance, economic growth may be associated with a reconstruction of the labour market, creating grievances among "modernisation losers" who become unemployed due to economic change (Meierrieks and Krieger, 2011). Here, terrorists are able to capitalise on the grievances of modernisation linked to economic dissatisfaction, new forms of alienated living, or other challenges to traditional societal patterns, thus making recruitments, financing, or other forms of support. The global economic order, i.e., globalisation, is also a responsible factor in the growth of terrorism (Global Terrorism Index, 2016). Economic integration, foreign policy, and alliance structure are also likely to play a crucial role in developing grievances and resistance against globalisation. Traditionalist or disenfranchised segments of society may use violence to counter foreign dominance and global modernisation (Bergesan and Lizardo, 2004). Thus, terrorism is justified to combat the impacts of globalisation.

Political Transformation and Instability

Political transformation and instability are also considered factors that cause terrorism, in particular in popular discourse. The main idea is that political change may create political vacuums that terrorist groups can use to push their agendas. Such vacuums are attractive as radical groups are less likely to be challenged by an unstable, thus weak government, making terrorism a less costly venture (Meierrieks and Krieger, 2011). An individual may also find it more attractive to join or support a radical organisation, as it would offer better payments and may provide better facilities to such individuals. Moreover, when the government fails to fulfil the demands of the citizens and turns away from welfare activities and popular policies and schemes, terror organisations will make use of such scenarios and opportunities to attract their activities and recruit dissatisfied citizens. The lack of political freedom can also be one of the myriad causes of terrorism. In this context, those countries that are going through a transition phase from authoritarian to democratic are most likely to face such problems (Abadie, 2004).

FACTORS FACILITATING TERRORIST ACTS

The success and failure of the structure and institutional framework of the non-state actors are primarily determined by their communication strategies to maintain and draw popular support for the cause to which they apply terror activities in society. Communication strategies of terror organisations play a significant role in contemporary society (Klausen, 2014). Globalisation, a multidimensional process that increased the quantum and speed of economic, technological, political, and cultural integration of nations and societies, has been a major facilitator in the surge of terrorism. Be it traditional or modern social media, it has played a crucial role in the functioning of terror groups. Latest reports show that almost 60% of the global population is dependent on social media, accounting for 3.8 billion people (Kemp, 2020). Therefore, cyberspace and the technologies associated with it, especially the Internet, are playing a decisive role in the functioning of terrorists in the present era (Klausen, 2014). The Internet provides a wider canvas for terrorists and extremist groups to expand their cause and get moral support from sympathisers across borders. Weak infrastructural facilities to govern and control the rapid phase of advancement in information and communication technologies by the government apparatus provide a functional advantage in cyberspace for the terrorists, especially to hide their identities, make targets, and base anywhere in the world.

Rapid dissemination and propaganda are advantages of new social media that to a great extent favour terrorists, especially in the promotion of violence, recruitment, training, and financing through the Internet (UNODC, 2012). Terror operations such as attacks, kidnappings, assassinations, and messages, appeals, and talks of the leaders of such groups are easily disseminated through social media by the Jihadist insurgence in Syria and Iraq. Moreover, end-to-end encryption and virtual private network usage in recent times have encouraged widespread operations among radicalised individuals (Harrison, n.d.). The disruptive nature of new technological advancements has become a boon as well as a bane for such terror organisations. Apparently, the scope and features of new technologies such as artificial intelligence and drones can be easily accessed by anyone in the world. Thus, it could be argued that the advancement of technology is arming future terrorists (Cronin, 2020). Terrorists have proven to adapt to technological advancement as soon as it is introduced. In order to make the terror incidents effective, terror groups have exploited technology to stage the attacks. Last year, in 2019, the terrorist made use of Facebook Livestream to stage an attack at a mosque in New Zealand, killing 49 people (BBC, 2019). In 2017, weaponised drones were used by Daesh in Iraq, announcing the establishment of an unmanned aircraft of the Mujahedeen unit (Warrick, 2017). The advancement of technology in terror organisations has been evident from the fact that plane hijacking and the use of small bombs in the past have been replaced by the use of weapons of mass destruction such as nuclear, chemical, and biological weapons, causing widespread damage. Accordingly, today's intensity of terror attacks is evidently worse than in the past. Christian extremists have been consistent in promoting religious motivations for violence through their websites, preaching that Islamic faith is evil. Scholars have also argued that, post-9/11, the media coverage of Muslims and Islam has made the world aware of the religion and its adherents as uncivilised (Morey and Yaqin, 2011). Thus, the media has played a role in inciting hatred against Muslim communities across the world.

RELIGION AND TERRORISM

The most common form of terror in the present time is driven by religious beliefs and communalism. However, terror acts enacted in the name of religion and faith are not something new; they have been prevalent for many decades (McFaul, 2010). The most relevant example that can be cited in history is that of Hindu thugs, who have been engaged in taking innocent lives since the 7th century to please goddess Kali (Hill and Kimney, 2008). Other examples of ancient terrorists that can be referred to are the Muslim assassins who targeted Christian Crusaders in 1090 AD (Brannan, n.d.). The fact that religion is one of the myriad reasons, along with factors like economic deprivation, that motivate acts of terror, cannot be denied. Religion is defined as the ultimate concern that emerges from the deepest levels of human existence and has therefore become a central feature of new terrorism (McFaul, 2010). New terrorism, the most relevant example being Al-Qaeda created by Osama bin Laden, is characterised by asymmetrical tactics, cell-based networks, and the use of high-yield weapons and technologies (Wilkinson, 2003). Religion plays a major role in society and is often considered a synonym for politics in the present era (Odihambo, 2014). Religion has undoubtedly been subjected to political instrumentalisation and has become a means to instigate political violence, which is a fundamental concern for the global community (Sinai, 2005). The period of the late 20th and early 21st centuries witnessed widespread practise of terror acts inspired by religion with global reach. It was not until the 1980s, after the Revolution of 1979 in Iran, that modern religious terrorist groups emerged. Since 1992, thriving religious groups have been witnessed across the globe (Hoffman, 1998).

Religion has been playing a major role in creating hatred towards other religions rather than acting as a catalyst for conflictual situations, and the world has faced sporadic acts of religion-induced terror over the years. It has also been stated that all religions, such as Islam, Judaism, Christianity, and Hinduism, are not about peace alone, nor are they about professing war. Every religion is about having absolute belief in its own supremacy and the right to impose its version of truth upon others (Schafer, 2002). Though there has been a significant rise in religious violence over the past decades (Muggah and Velshi, 2019), it has often been argued that the 1979 Islamic revolution in Iran was one of the major epochs in the emergence of modern religious terrorism, which is considered an offshoot of 20th-century Islamic fundamentalism (Hoffman, 1998–99; Bar, 2004). Also, the Soviet invasion of Afghanistan revived the practise of joining jihad to overthrow corrupt occupiers in a Muslim state as their personal duty (Bar, 2004). Thus, in the current public discourse, religious radicalism is mostly linked to heinous acts of terror and the Islamic religion (Rautio, 2016).

On the occurrence of a terror attack in any part of the world, the media label it as Islamist. The widely used tagline "not all Muslims are terrorists, but all terrorists are Muslims" is repeatedly used by media houses (Kaushal, 2019). However, religious terrorism has not been confined to Iran or Islam alone. Issues such as Islamic extremists perpetrating global jihad, discrimination against Rohingyas in Myanmar, clashes between Christians and Muslims in Africa, and the civil war in Sri Lanka between Hindu and Buddhist Tamils that lasted three decades and caused lakhs of fatalities make evident that religious antagonism is a major source of terrorism in the present world (Muggah and Velshi, 2019). The perpetrators of violent acts in the name of religion are influenced by the misinterpretation of theological understanding (Odihambo, 2014). The Bible of the Judeo-Christian belief system emphasises the complete destruction of enemy nations in the name of faith. Similarly, there are verses in the Bible citing examples of religious communal violence that have had a huge impact on believers today. It must also be noted that religious terrorism does not always mean one faith attacking another. It can also mean clashes between two sects within the same religion, such as between Shia and Sunni Muslims (Finnbogason et al., 2019).

Terrorist attacks on the World Trade Center, aka 9/11, in 2001 not only shook America but most countries across the world. The religious as well as theological response to the 9/11 attack has been quick and constant. Since then, religious violence has been particularly concentrated upon the Islam religion, as the Al-Qaeda group is considered the mastermind behind it (Coady, 2019). Islam has played a major role in changing the world order (Huntington, 1996). The 9/11 attack has brought the religious factor in inciting terrorism to the limelight, though terrorist groups were using religion as a justification for their violent acts way before the 9/11 incident (Farida, 2018; Hodler et al., 2020). Thenceforth, terrorism has continuously manifested itself in the form of Islamic fundamentalism. In the contemporary era, the highlights of the media focus on global patterns of terrorism that are dominated by extremism, especially in the Islamic states (Cordesman, 2017). Moreover, Iran and Iraq have been continuously designated as sponsors of terrorism by the United States (Dannreuther, 2003). The clerics of radical Islamist groups have played a key role in the functioning of terror organisations such as the Brotherhood, Hamas, and Al-Qaeda, motivated by the interpretations in the theological texts of Islam. The radical Islamist interpretations of the Qur'an and other theological texts of Islam, mentioning the confrontations that took place in the 7th century between the two leaders, have been responsible for inciting anti-Semitic feelings among the Islamist movement and terror organisations (Barsky, 2016).

It is said that new Muslim terrorism is a part of the historical legacy of the confrontations among rulers (Counter Extremism Project, n.d.). Al-Qaeda, the epitome of new Muslim terrorism, was formed by bin Laden in 1989. After taking over the Mujahidin al-Arab, he shifted to conflict zones like Kashmir, Mindanao, Tajikistan, Somalia, and others where Muslim communities were supposedly facing hardships. The organisation also focused on overthrowing the corrupt Muslim leaders, as it was considered the personal duty of all Muslims to fight a jihad to liberate the country (Gunaratna, 2003). The popularly known Islamic State of Iraq and Syria (ISIS) targets minority religious groups in the territories that they are ruling, and in Western countries, the targeted groups of ISIS and Al-Qaeda are Christians and Jews (Counter Extremism Project, n.d.). In the year 2018, 3585 people out of 32836 were killed by ISIS worldwide (Statista Research Department, 2019).

Though Semitic religions share a similar civilisational and historical heritage, the contradiction between the Christian and Muslim armies in the First Crusade is believed to have been one of the factors in creating tension between the two religious groups to date. In the year 1099, the Crusaders are believed to have entered Jerusalem to establish Christian sovereignty by killing Muslim masses in the Holy Land (Schafer, 2002). This has, however, strained the relationship between them. In the initial phase of Christianity, there were many rival sects, which are said to have been persecuted by the then rulers (Ehrman, 2005). This has further incited religious violence among different sects within Christianity as well as among other religions. In this context, the relevant example that can be cited is the Gunpowder Treason Plot of 1605 – a failed attempt by a group of Catholic people to explode the Protestant King and the Houses of Parliament, where all the country's laws were legislated (Sharpe, 2018). Christian philosophers have put forward a plethora of ideas to restrict as well as legitimise war. The classic Christian theological understandings of just war, pacifism, the crusade, and holy war have been made clear in the public affirmation. Therefore, the inappropriate mix of religious violence is not confined to any particular religion.

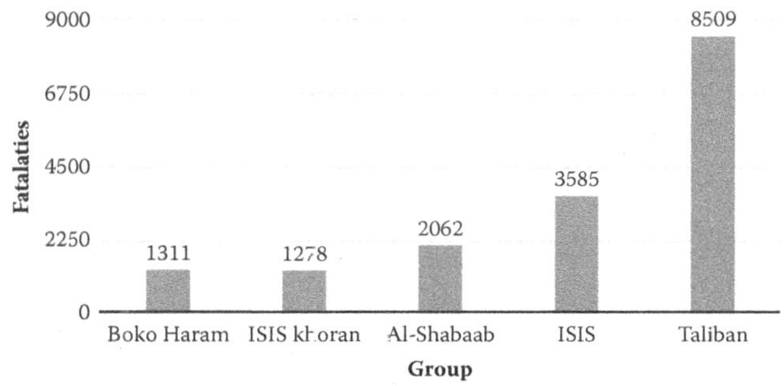

Figure 7.2 Fatality Rates Caused by Different Religious Terror Groups (2018).

Statista Research Department (2018).

Non-violence is central to Buddhist teaching, and the religious texts of Buddhism promote peace and pacifism; however, there have been cases of violent acts executed by Buddhists in the name of religion. Buddhist monks were accused of inducing hatred towards other faiths and ethnic minorities in Sri Lanka (Haviland, 2015). Simultaneously, the 969 Movement, initiated by the Buddhist clan in Myanmar, portrayed itself as a peaceful grassroots movement aiming to promote and protect religion. In reality, the movement was an anti-Muslim campaign started by Buddhist monks, resulting in bloody anti-Muslim riots across the nation (The Observers, 2013). Multiple terror attacks in Sri Lanka's historical churches and hotels in 2019 killed hundreds of people. The Islamic State claimed the attacks were quite overwhelming. The attack came as a shock, as the country had not experienced any incidents of Jihadi violence (Amarsingam, 2019).

Jews and Israel have also been attacked by Al-Qaeda, headed by Osama bin Laden, a couple of times, even before the 9/11 incident. In 2002, Al-Qaeda targeted the El Ghriba synagogue on the Tunisian island, killing 19 people. Subsequently, in the same year, suicide bombings were committed by Al-Qaeda in two Russian hotels (Silber, 2019). However, the 9/11 attack has also brought remarkable changes to the strategic environment. The overthrow of the Taliban regime in Afghanistan, which had been providing a safe haven for Al-Qaeda, was one of the major outcomes of the attack (Wilkinson, 2003). The remarkable changes brought in post-September 11 have been challenged by the number of terror attacks and fatalities that have taken place since the incident. The mortality rate, as indicated by Figure 7.2, makes it evident that even after 17 years, over 50% of deaths are caused by religious terror groups. Moreover, in 2015, 74% of total casualties were caused globally by Islamic groups like Boko Haram, Al-Qaeda, the Taliban, and the Islamic States of Iraq and the Levant (ISIL) (Egger and Magni-Berton, 2019).

Moreover, there are still around 25000 Jihadist fighters in Iraq and Syria belonging to the Islamic states and around 20,000 from Al-Qaeda-linked groups (Hay'at Tahrir al-Sham and Tanzim Hurras al-Din), which is likely to increase terrorist attacks in the near future (CSIS, 2020).

TYPES OF RELIGIOUS TERRORISM

Most religious terrorism in the recent past has been factored in by political or sacred goals. When religious movements are motivated by faith or dogmas of religions, as mentioned earlier, they may get fuelled by nationalism, but the faithful are united by their religious identities. Therefore, insurgents like the Lord Resistance Army under the leadership of Joseph Kony of Uganda used religion as a means of attracting followers. In India, Sikhs of Punjab belonging to various organisations selected terrorism as a means to demand the formation of Khalistan, an independent state for the Sikhs. Government sponsorship and support of terrorism have been rampant. After the monarchy of Shah Muhammed Reza Pahlavi was dethroned, followed by the establishment of the theocratic Islamic Republic of Iran, the country is said to have been the preeminent state to sponsor religious terrorism (Martin, 2008). The US government has listed countries like Iran, Iraq, Sudan, Afghanistan, and many other nations as states sponsoring terrorism.

The terror groups are formed with the political goals of establishing and running the state. Accordingly, terror groups such as Hamas and Hezbollah have been involved in the limited governance of the Gaza Strip since 2007 (Hendy, 2019). Time and again, terrorists have often justified their violent acts on the basis of perceived political unfairness (Lemieux, 2017). Before the establishment of Israel, two paramilitary organisations carried out terror attacks against the British Mandatory Authority and Palestinian Arabs with the aim of creating a Jewish state on both sides of the Jordan River. Sixty terror attacks were carried out within the span of three years (1939–1942), killing more than 100 people (Pedazhur and Perliger, 2009).

Terrorist groups such as Al-Qaeda and ISIS are inspired by their religious interpretations of sacred goals (Lemieux, 2017). The members of terror groups driven by religious belief tend to consider themselves chosen ones in the army of God to fight against their enemies (McTernan, 2003). In the current era of terrorism, it is based on religious fanaticism. All the religions in the world make their followers believe that their existence in the universe is connected to a sacred view, related to the past as well as the future, which brings fulfilment to every being. The ultimate concern of addressing the two major issues involving awareness of mortality and the mystery of life after death makes the diversion of violence more challenging (McFaul, 2010). However, it must be understood that the perpetrators of violence in the name of religion hold their religious beliefs strictly. The fact of the matter is that specific interpretations of their religious scriptures inspire believers to act violently within their theological framework (Brannan, n.d.). The major outcome of their battle against evil (as they would address it) would be the gruesome attack on a huge mass (Burstein, 2017). Therefore, it is evident that the so-called sacred terrorism has failed to be secular practically. Over the past few decades, the sacred goal of religious terrorism has been manifested by the suicide bombings that are taking place on a rampant scale.

COUNTERMEASURES AGAINST TERRORISM

A number of measures have been taken to contain acts of terrorism. According to the World Economic Forum, the most effective ways of combating terrorism are intelligence gathering, strengthening of police forces, and new technological advancement and implementation. Accordingly, NATO (North Atlantic Treaty Organisation), collaborating with various organisations, has been working towards a war against terrorism with the help of technology. NATO's work in countering terrorism emphasises improving awareness of the threat induced by terrorism, developing capabilities to prepare and respond to such attacks, and developing cooperation among nations to combat terror attacks (NATO, 2019). The Organisation for Security and Cooperation in Europe (OSCE) has been contributing to international efforts against terrorism led by the UN, promoting a cooperative and coordinated approach to defy terror acts at national as well as international levels (OSCE, n.d.). The UN has brought international communities together to act against terrorism. Also, an international legal framework has been developed by the UN, enabling its member nations to fight the menace. A total of 16 treaties at an international level with regard to a wide range of issues, such as plane hijacking and nuclear terrorism, have been negotiated at the UN (UN, n.d.).

The Financial Action Task Force, originally established in 1989 with the purpose of countering money laundering, has been given the task of battling against the financing of terrorism since 2001 (Haider, 2020). The use of violence against terrorism has been carried out, like US military action against the Taliban in Afghanistan. Measures such as negotiation have also been used to deal with terrorism. In this context, the best example that can be cited is that of Great Britain's negotiation with the Irish Republican Army and Sinn Fein (the political wing of the Irish Republican Army) (USIP, n.d.). The international community has been fighting the war on terror under the leadership of the US since the 9/11 attack on the World Trade Center (Muni, 2016). The phrase "war on terror" is now synonymous with the US's foreign policy, along with that of many other nations like India (Statista Research Department, 2020). However, it has been argued by many that policies such as the War on Terror have been unfair by focusing on Muslim communities, thus dishonouring them (Francis M.D.M., 2015). Immediately after the 9/11 attack, the UN Security Council passed a new resolution, UNSC 1371, barring links to any group or individual that is linked to the Taliban and Al-Qaeda. To make the world a safer place, religious groups like Quakers have initiated international treaties banning landmines and other weapons of war as a measure towards peace-building and conflict transformation (Muggah and Velshi, 2019). The New Brothers have been putting effort into denouncing terrorism in Muslim as well as Western countries over the past years. The major steps taken in this regard have been movements issuing fatwas by the top clerics, signing petitions, and publicly preaching that evil acts such as suicide bombing are against the teaching of Islam (Vidino, 2010).

Individual states have also made big strides. However, major disparities in their efforts are evident. The developed countries are in a position to spend huge amounts on achieving their national security, while small developing nations struggle to provide even the most basic requirements for countering terrorism. After the 26/11 attack, India has been constantly working towards strengthening its security system and fighting terrorism. India has improved the state's intelligence-gathering mechanism and enhanced inter-agency coordination amongst various agencies through the establishment of multi-agency coordination centres (MAACs) and subsidiary multi-agency coordination centres (SMACCs), which otherwise were lacking in the past. This has reduced the number of terror attacks in urban areas – not completely but to some extent (Desai, 2019). In the era of the Internet of Things, social media sites such as Facebook, Twitter, and YouTube have established a global Internet forum to counter terrorism since 2017 as a partnership initiative with the United Nations (Noor, 2020). Despite the fact that many nations have come up with various strategies to counter terrorism, they show no impact on the terror groups and therefore prove to be ineffective (Muni, 2016). Thus, it can be considered that countering terrorism is quite a task and practically challenging.

CONCLUSION

Terrorism, a tactical method of conflict, has evolved over the years to achieve a sophisticated modus operandi that challenges civilisation, nation-states, societies, etc. across borders in the contemporary era. Though the factors that shape terrorism may vary from case to case, religious faith and its dogmatic fundamentals have inspired terror groups to influence, recruit, and draw sympathy from society. Over the past three decades, terror groups inspired by religion and faith have become dominant actors in creating violence globally. The theological misinterpretations of the religious text are considered to be responsible for the revival of this kind of terrorism. With various other factors such as economic deprivation and political order, it becomes imperative to acknowledge the role of religion in encouraging terror acts at the local, national, and international levels. What has been termed the "new terrorism" that emerged in the 1970s and has been evolving currently to draw new dimensions has undoubtedly inspired or sourced one or more aspects of religion and faith. Instances of terrorism that are influenced by religious dogmas are visible across religions, regions, and countries.

Advancements in technology and social media have played a crucial role in facilitating terror organisations and their acts in every aspect. Such facilities are considered to be responsible for the increased intensity of the threat level of terror attacks today as compared to past centuries. The adaptation of highly advanced weapons by terror groups for their deeds has created a precarious situation worldwide. Thus, to stem the problem of terrorism, an effective body that promotes harmonious institutions and values is needed. High-level intergovernmental organisations, such as the UN, are on the run to curtail the growth of violence. Also, governments at different levels are putting effort into fighting terrorism using myriad measures. Countries are also joining hands for cooperation and counterterrorism at different levels, but if such efforts label one particular religion or faith as a promoter of terrorism through media propaganda or any other means, that can turn out to be more dangerous and counterproductive to inviting more terrorism in the future.

References

Abadie, A. (2004). *Poverty, political freedom, and the roots of terrorism* (pp. 1–15). Harvard University.

Amarsingam, A. (2019). Terrorism on the Teardrop Island: Understanding the Easter 2019 attacks in Sri Lanka. *Combating Terrorism Center at West Point, 12*(5), 1–10

Badey, T.H. (2002). The role of religion in international terrorism. *Sociological Focus, 35*(1), 81–86.

Bar, S. (2004). The religious sources of terrorism. Policy review. Hoover Institution. Retrieved from https://www.hoover.org/research/religious-sources-islamic-terrorism. Accessed on 16/09/2020.

Barsky, Y. (2016). *Terrorist incidents and attacks against Jews and Israelis in the United States 1969–2016*. New York: Community Security Service.

BBC. (2019). Christchurch shootings: 49 dead in New Zealand mosque attacks. Retrieved from https://www.google.co.in/amp/world-asia-47578798. Accessed on 27/09/2020.

Bergesan, A.J. and Lizardo, O. (2004). International terrorism and the world system. *Sociological Theory, 22*(1), 38–52.

Botha, A. and Abdile, M. (2019). Reality versus perception: Toward understanding Boko Haram in Nigeria. *Studies in Conflict & Terrorism, 42*(5), 493–519.

Brannan, D. (n.d.). Religious and theologically motivated terrorism part 1. Center for Homeland Defense and Security. Retrieved from https://www.chds.us/coursefiles/DA3210/lectures/threat_relter_stryln_mod01/script.pdf. Accessed on 20/09/2020.

Burstein, A. (2017). How religious extremism changed the face of terrorism. *Tony Blair Institute for Global Change*. Retrieved from https //institute.global/policy/how-religious-extremism-changed-face-terrorism. Accessed on 30/09/2020.

Cheung, H. (2014). Global terror attack deaths rose sharply in 2013, says report. *BBC News*. Retrieved from https://www.bbc.com/news/world-30086435. Accessed on 18/09/2020.

Coady, T. (2019). Terrorism, war and the problem of "religious violence". *ABC Religion & Ethics*. Retrieved from https://www.abc.net.au/religion/terrorism,-war-and-the-problem-of-religious-violence/11656464. Accessed on 11/09/2020.

Cordesman, A.H. (2017). Islam and the patterns in terrorism and violent extremism. *Center for Strategic & International Studies*. Retrieved from https://csis-website-prod.s3.amazonaws.com/s3fs-public/publication/171017_Report_Islam%20and%20the%20-War_on_Terrorism_.pdf?iI4pb6Py.S_5J9D73QmtXxX5NlXev5bv. Accessed on 10/09/2020.

Counter Extremism Project. (n.d.). Terror targets in the west: Where and why. Retrieved from https://www.counterextremism.com/sites/default/themes/bricktheme/pdfs/CEP_Terror_Targets.pdf. Accessed on 12/09/2020.

Cronin, A.K. (2020). *Power to the people: How open technological innovation is arming tomorrow's terrorists*. Oxford University Press.

CSIS. (2020). The escalating terrorism problem in the United States. Retrieved from https://www.csis.org/analysis/escalating-terrorism-problem-united-states. Accessed on 26/09/2020.

Dannreuther, R. (2003). Radical Islamist state and secular Arab nationalism. In M. Buckley and R. Fawn (Eds.), *Global responses to terrorism: 9/11, Afghanistan and beyond* (pp. 122–133). New York: Routledge.

Delanty, G. and Mahony, P.O. (2002). *Nationalism and social theory: Modernity and the recalcitrance of the nation*. London: Sage Publications.

Desai, D. and Bhatt, P. (2019). Securing India's cities: Remembering 26/11, learning its lessons. *ORF Special Report*. Observer Research Foundation.

Egger, C., and Magni-Berton, R. (2021). The role of Islamist ideology in shaping Muslims believers' attitudes toward terrorism: Evidence from Europe. *Studies in Conflict & Terrorism, 44*(7), 581–604. DOI:10.1080/1057610X.2019.1571696

Ehrman, B.D. (2005). *Lost Christianities: The battles for scripture and the faiths we never knew*. New York: Oxford University Press.

Farida, M. (2018). Adopting religion to meet political goals: The case of Hizbullah. *Journal of Policing, Intelligence and Counter Terrorism, 13*(3), 316–331.

Finnbogason, D., Larsson, G. and Svenson, I. (2019). Is Shia-Sunni violence on the rise? Exploring new data on intra-Muslim Organised Violence 1989–2017. Civil Wars, *21*(1), 25–53.

Francis, M.D.M. (2015). Why the "sacred" is a better resource than "religion" for understanding terrorism. Terrorism and Political Violence, *28*(5). 912–927.

Ghosh, P. (2018). International relations (pp. 264–355). Delhi: PHI Learning Private Limited.

Global Terrorism Index. (2016). Measuring and understanding the impact of terrorism. Sydney: Institute for Economics and Peace.

Global Terrorism Index. (2019). Measuring the impact of terrorism. Sydney: Institute for Economics and Peace.

Gunaratna, R. (2003). *Inside Al Qaeda: Global network of terror*. New York: Berkley Books.

Haider, S. (2020). FATF| On the warpath against terror financing. *The Hindu*. Retrieved from https://www.google.co.in/amp/s/www.thehindu.com/news/international/fatf-on-the-warpath-against-terror-financing/article31934817.ece/amp. Accessed on 30/09/2020

Harrison, S. (n.d.). Evolving tech, evolving terror. Center for Strategic & International Studies, pp. 15, 28–31.

Haviland, C. (2015). The darker side of Buddhism. BBC News. Retrieved from https://www.bbc/news/magazine-32929855. Accessed on 30/09/2020.

Hendy, A. (2019). Debunking the concept of "new terrorism". E-International Relations. Retrieved from https://www.e-ir.info/2019/05/11/debunking-the-concept-of-new-terrorism/. Accessed on 28/09/2020.

Hill, J. and Kimney, A.F. (2008). Sacred violence: Religion and terrorism. Case Western Reserve Journal of International Law, *39*(3), 703–707.

Hodler, R. et al. (2020). Religion and terrorism: Evidence from Ramadan Fasting. Retrieved from https://arxiv.org/pdf/1810.09869.pdf. Accessed on 17/09/2020.

Hoffman, B. (1998–99). Old madness new methods: Revival of religious terrorism begs for broader U.S. policy. RAND Review, pp. 12–17.

Huntington, S.P. (1996). The clash of civilizations? Foreign Affairs, *72*(3), 22–49.

Institute for Economics & Peace (IEP). (2019, November). Global Terrorism Index 2019: Measuring the impact of terrorism, Sydney. https://www.economicsandpeace.org/wp-content/uploads/2023/12/GTI-2019-web.pdf

Institute for Economics & Peace (IEP). (2020, November). Global Terrorism Index 2020: Measuring the impact of terrorism, Sydney. https://www.economicsandpeace.org/wp-content/uploads/2023/12/GTI-2020-web.pdf

Institute for Economics & Peace (IEP). (2022, March). Global Terrorism Index 2022: Measuring the impact of terrorism, Sydney. https://www.economicsandpeace.org/wp-content/uploads/2023/12/GTI-2022-web.pdf

Institute for Economics & Peace (IEP). (2023, March). Global Terrorism Index 2023: Measuring the impact of terrorism, Sydney. https://www.economicsandpeace.org/wp-content/uploads/2023/12/GTI-2023-web.pdf

Institute for Economics & Peace (IEP). (2024, February). Global Terrorism Index 2024: Measuring the impact of terrorism, Sydney. https://www.economicsandpeace.org/wp-content/uploads/2024/02/GTI-2024-web-290224.pdf

Kaushal, N. (2019). Our war against terrorism. *Economic Times*. Retrieved from https://economictimes.indiatimes.com/blogs/et-commentary/our-war-against-errosrism/. Accessed on 30/09/2020.

Kemp, S. (2020). Digital 2020: 3.8 billion people use social media. We Are Social. Retrieved from https://wearesocial.com/blog/2020/01/digital-2020-3-8-billion-people-use-social-media. Accessed on 26/09/2020.

Klausen, J. (2014). Tweeting the Jihad: Social media networks of Western foreign fighters in Syria and Iraq. Studies in Conflict & Terrorism, *38*(1), 1–22.

Lemieux, F. (2017). What is terrorism? What do terrorists want? The Conversation. Retrieved from https://www.google.co.in/amp/s/theconveration.com/amp/what-is-terrorism-what-do-terrorists-want-78228. Accessed on 29/09/2020.

Martin, G. (2008). Essentials of terrorism: Concepts and controversies (pp. 1–14). California: Sage Publications.

McFaul, T.R. (2010). The future of peace & justice in the global village: The role of religion in the twenty-first century. London: Praeger.

McTernan, O. (2003). Violence in the God's name: Religion in an age of conflict. London: Darton, Longman and Todd Ltd.

Meierrieks, D. and Krieger, T. (2011). What causes terrorism? Public Choice, *147*(1–3), 3–27.

Morey, P. and Yaqin, A. (2011). Framing Muslims: Stereotyping and representation after 9/11. Cambridge: Harvard University Press.

Muggah, R. and Velshi, A. (2019). Religious violence is on the rise. What can faith-based communities do about it? World Economic Forum. Retrieved from https://www.weforum.org/agenda/2019/02/how-should-faith-communities-halt-the-rise-in-religious-violence. Accessed on 12/09/2020.

Muni, S.D. (2016). Introduction. In S.D. Muni and V. Chadha (Eds.). Asian strategic review 2016 (p. 1). New Delhi: Institute for Defence Studies & Analyses, Pentagon Press.

NATO. (2019). Countering terrorism. Retrieved from https://www.nato.int/cps/en/natohq/topics_77646.htm. Accessed on 30/09/2020.

Noor, E. (2020). Sharing space: Tech and terrorism. Online Research Foundation. Retrieved from https://www.google.co.in/amp/s/www,orfonline.org/expert-speak/sharing-space-tech-terrorism-60862. Accessed on 28/09/2020.

Odihambo, E.O.S. (2014). Religious fundamentalism and terrorism. Journal of Global Peace and Conflict, *2* (1), 187–205.

OSCE. (n.d.). Countering terrorism. Retrieved from https://www.osce.org/countering-terrorism. Accessed on 30/09/2020.

Pedazhur, A. and Perliger, A. (2009). Jewish terrorism in Israel. Columbia University.

Rautio, P. (2016). Terror in the name of religion? University of Helsinki. Retrieved from https://www.helsinki.fi/en/news/society-economy/terror-in-the-name-of-religion. Accessed on 16/09/2020.

Reach Out Australia. (2020). Understanding terrorism. Retrieved from https://au.reachout.com/articles/understanding-terrorism. Accessed on 10/09/2020.

Richardson, C. (2011). Relative deprivation theory in terrorism: A study of higher education and unemployment as predictors of terrorism. Senior Honors Thesis, Politics Department New York University. https://as.nyu.edu/content/dam/nyu-as/politics/documents/Clare_Richardson_terrorism.pdf

Romaniuk, S. N. (2021). *Under siege: Counterterrorism and civil society in Hungary*. Lanham: Rowman & Littlefield.

Ross, J.I. (1993). Structural causes of oppositional political terrorism: Towards a causal model. *Journal of Peace Research*, *30*(3), 317–329.

Schafer, D. (2002). Islam and terrorism: A humanist view. American Humanist Association: Good without a God.

Retrieved from https://americanhumanist.org/what-is-humanism/islam-terrorism-humanist-view/. Accessed on 17/09/2020.

Schmid, A.P. (Ed.). (2013). The Routledge handbook of terrorism research (pp. 39–98). London: Routledge.

Sharpe, J. (2018). Who was Guy Fawkes, the man behind the mask? *History Magazine*. Retrieved from https://www.nationalgeographic.com/history/magazine/2017/11-12/history-the-explosive-truth-about-guy-fawkes/. Accessed on 17/09/2020.

Silber, M.D. (2019). Terrorist attacks against Jewish in the West (2012–2019): The Atlantic divide between European and American attackers. Combating Terrorism Center at West Point, *12*(5), 30–40.

Sinai, J. (2005). A conceptual framework for resolving terrorism's root causes. In T. Bjorgo (Ed.), Root causes of terrorism, myths, reality and way forward (pp. 215–222). London: Routledge.

Statista Research Department. (2018). Fatality rates caused by different religious terror groups. https://www.statista.com/. Accessed in January 2020.

Statista Research Department. (2019). Retrieved from https://www.statista.com/statistics/202871/number-of-fatalities-by-terrorist-attacks-worldwide/. Accessed on 16/09/2020.

Statista Research Department. (2020). Terrorism – statistics & facts. Retrieved from https://www.statista.com/topics/2267/terrorism. Accessed on 27/09/2020.

Stern, F. (2003). Terror in the name of God. New York: Harper Publications.

Tarallo, M. (2020). Fatalities from terror attacks continue to decrease. ASIS International. Retrieved from https://www.asisonline.org/security-management-magazine/articles/2020/03/fatalities-from-terror-attacks-continue-to-decrease/. Accessed on 08/10/2020.

The Observers. (2013). '969': The three digits that are terrifying Muslims in Burma. Retrieved from https://observers.france24.com/en/20130505-'969'-digits-terrifying-muslims-burma. Accessed on 28/09/2020.

UN. (n.d.). Human Rights, Terrorism and Counter-terrorism: Fact Sheet No. 32. Office of the United Nations High Commissioner for Human Rights. Retrieved from https://www.ohchr.org/documents/publications/factsheet32En.pdf Accessed on 13/09/2020

UN. (n.d.). Securing our future: A decade of counter-terrorism strategies. Retrieved from https://www.un.org/en/chronicle/article/securing-our-future-decade-counter-terrorism-strategies. Accessed on 30/09/2020.

UNODC. (2012). The use of the Internet for terrorist purposes. Retrieved from https://www.unodc.org/documents/frontpage/Use_of_Internet_for_Terrorist_Purposes.pdf. Accessed on 27/09/2020.

USIP. (n.d.). Teaching guide on international terrorism: Definitions, causes and responses. Retrieved from https://www.usip.org/sites/default/files/terrorism.pdf. Accessed on 26/09/2020.

Vidino, L. (2010). The Muslim brotherhood in the West. New York: Columbia University Press.

Warrick, J. (2017). Use of weaponized drones by ISIS spurs terrorism fears. The Washington Post. Retrieved from https://www.washingtonpost.com/world/national-security/use-of-weaponized-drones-by-isis-spurs-terrorism-fears/2017/02/21/9d83d51e-f382-11e6-8d72-263470bf0401_story.html. Accessed on 26/09/2020.

Wilkinson, P. (2003). Implications of 9/11 for the future of terrorism. In M. Buckley and R. Fawn (Eds.), Global responses to terrorism: 9/11, Afghanistan and beyond (pp. 11–36). New York: Routledge.

Wilson Center. (2019). Report: Terrorism on decline in Middle East and North Africa. Retrieved from https://www.wilsoncenter.org/article/report-terrorism-decline-middle-east-and-north-africa. Accessed on 08/10/2020.

Winter, A. (2017). Terrorism (and terrorism studies). In B. Turner et al. (Eds.), Encyclopedia of social theory. Oxford: Wiley-Blackwell.

Zahid, D.F. (2017). The future of terrorism in India. Retrieved from https://cf2r.org/foreign/the-future-of-terrorism-in-india/. Accessed on 16/09/2020.

Zaia, R. (2016). Understanding the factors that lead to terrorism. Policy Options Politiques. Retrieved from https://policyoptions.irpp.org/magazines/october-2016/understanding-the-factors-that-lead-to-terrorism. Accessed on 15/09/2020.

Zewairi, M.A. et al. (2017) Spotting the Islamist radical within: Religious extremists profiling in the United State. Elsevier, *113*, 162–169.

8

CORRELATIONS BETWEEN TERRORISM, EXTREMISM, AND FUNDAMENTALISM

Salvin Paul, Alok Kumar, and Scott N. Romaniuk

INTRODUCTION

Identifying correlations among terrorism, extremism, and fundamentalism has become imperative to devising successful counterterrorism strategies as they mutually constitute each other in one way or another. Adherence to certain fundamental values and dogmas enables people to advocate extreme measures and ideas to lose faith in established institutions and justify terror to achieve their political objectives. This chapter seeks to explore how terrorism, extremism, and fundamentalism relate to each other in contemporary society. When terrorism seeks unlawful use of violence and intimidation to fulfil political, ideological, and religious objectives, extremists advocate extreme measures or ideas, and fundamentalism, which originated in religious contexts and broadened to secular political ideologies, is the rigid and radical interpretation of certain scriptures, values, and dogmas.

Though there are umpteen efforts to understand and explain the complex nature of terrorism, extremism, and fundamentalism, there has yet to be an attempt to explore the correlation among them to understand how they mutually constitute each other, having integral components but being mutually exclusive. A terrorist could be both a fundamentalist and an extremist, whereas it is not always necessary that a fundamentalist and an extremist engage in the use of violence to become a terrorist. Then what activities of extremists and fundamentalists make them terrorists? This chapter will start with a conceptual and historical analysis of terrorism and then examine both extremism and fundamentalism to understand how they correlate with each other and in what situations they do not.

CONCEPTUAL ANALYSIS OF TERRORISM

The impact of terrorism has been widely debated in the first two decades of the twenty-first century among scholars and experts to understand how a person becomes a terrorist, what kind of influence it has on society and the political system, and how it can be resolved. The complex nature of terrorism makes scholars opine on their own unique assumptions that divide them from reaching a consensus on many aspects of terrorism. So societies, institutions, and governments perceive it differently and adopt measures that are shaped by multiple factors and dynamics in society.

Thus, the concept of terrorism is very complex and complicated because it is a contested concept, exists in diverse forms and manifestations, is influenced by different social, religious, economic, and political ideologies and notions, is used by diverse forms of organisations such as state and non-state terrorism for both political and non-political ends, is justified in the context of self-determination and arm resistance against the national and foreign forces (Schmid, 2004), and today they have diversified their mode of operandi beyond borders and are facilitated by advancement in technology, social media, propaganda, and people's sentiments and emotions.

Subjective perceptions of terrorism also vary in time and space. For example, following the statement "one man's terrorist is another man's freedom fighter," the activities of Palestine in the Middle East are defined as "terrorist" by Israel, while many other states define them as legitimate political actions for independence and sovereignty (Scraton, 2002). There are an umpteen number of cases where the existing establishment terms a person a terrorist, and he or she becomes a freedom fighter when that territory attains independence. There appears to be a consensus among scholars in literature that if violence is used to terrorise or target civilians, public infrastructure, and organisations to achieve political, ideological, and religious objectives, then it is called terrorism. Igor Primoratz (1990) states that terrorism is the deliberate use of violence, intimidation, cruelty, and vandalism against innocent people.

Wu Chi, the Chinese philosopher, opines that "one man willing to throw away his like is enough to terrorise a thousand,"

DOI: 10.4324/9780429426063-10

and Professor Boaz Ganor explains that "terrorism is the intentional use of, or threat to use, violence against civilians or civilian targets in order to attain political aims" (Schmid, 2004). But Ganor takes this opportunity to distinguish between the violence of terrorism and violence in other activities, like protests. According to him, (i) activities that do not involve violence or threat should not be included in the definition of terrorism, (ii) activities against civilians that do not have political objectives cannot be said to be terrorist activities. Thus, he differentiated between terrorism and political violence such as guerrilla warfare, civilian rebellion, etc. (Ganor, 2002).

The growing number of terrorist activities across the world enabled the international community, especially the United Nations, to frame 19 international legal instruments to prevent terrorist acts since 1963, including hijacking aircraft, crimes against internationally protected persons and their hostages, unlawful possession, use, transfer, or theft of nuclear material, unlawfully and intentionally seizing or exercising control over a ship by force, threat, or intimidation, plastic explosives, terrorist bombings, financing of terrorism, and nuclear terrorism. For instance, the United Nations "1963 Convention on Offences and Certain Other Acts Committed on Board Aircraft" is considered the first treaty to curb the frequent hijacking of aircraft by terrorist organisations, and it was considered a serious security threat to the world community. It is roughly estimated that around 40 aircraft were hijacked between 1958 and 1967 around the world (Gourdin, 2015). The "1970 Convention for the Suppression of Unlawful Seizure of Aircraft" endorses severe penalties for hijacking aircraft, and Articles 1 and 2 of the Convention state that any person, state, or organisation who attempts to control the aircraft is considered to have committed an unlawful act (United Nations, 1970).

Attacks on diplomatic missions and embassies were common during this period. For example, Count Karl von Spreti was killed by rebel groups in Guatemala in 1970. The rebellions kidnapped him and demanded the release of 25 political prisoners and a ransom of $700,000, but the Guatemalan government refused to negotiate (BBC, 1970). In order to curb such incidents, the UN enacted the 1973 Convention on the Prevention and Punishment of Crimes Against Internationally Protected Persons. Article 2 of the Convention stated that kidnapping, murder, and attempted murder of the Heads of State and Ministers for Foreign Affairs would be considered serious offences (United Nations, 1973). Article 1 of the 1979 International Convention against the Taking of Hostages states that any person who seizes or detains or threatens to kill, injure, or continue to detain another person to compel the third party to release the hostage is considered to be committing a serious offence (United Nations, 1979). Article 5 of the International Convention for the Suppression of Terrorist Bombings, 1997, states that "each state party shall adopt such measures as may be necessary ... under no circumstances justifiable by considerations of a political, philosophical, ideological, racial, ethnic, religious or other similar nature, and are punished by penalties consistent with their grave nature" (United Nations, 1997).

Many of the above-mentioned UN efforts to conceptualise terrorism are unable to answer whether the use of armed force against civilians by the state as well as people's right to resistance against foreign occupation come under the purview of terrorism (Jodhe, 2015). "The Rand Database of World Terrorism Incidents (RDWTI)" is a compilation of terrorist incidents from 1968 to 2009 that focuses mainly on the nature of the act rather than on the identity of perpetrators or the case (RAND, n.d.). In order to address the financing of terror directly or indirectly under the cover of philanthropic activities, the International Convention for the Suppression of Financing of Terrorism was held in 1999. Article 2 of this Convention stated that if any person collects the fund by any means, directly or indirectly, unlawfully, with the intention to kill a civilian, it would be considered a serious offence (United Nations, 1999). Article 2 of the 2005 International Convention for the Suppression of Acts of Nuclear Terrorism states that any person who possesses radioactive material or nuclear instruments and releases or risks the release of radioactive material would be considered to have committed a serious offence (United Nations, 2005).

After the 9/11 attacks, the United Nations Security Council (UNSC) passed a resolution in 2004 that defined "criminal acts, including against civilians, committed with the intent to cause death, serious bodily injury, or the taking of hostages, with the purposes of provoking a state of terror in the general public or in a group of persons or particular persons, intimidate a population, or compel a government or an international organisation to do or abstain from doing any act that contravened terrorism-related conventions and protocols, were not justifiable for any reason – whether of a political, philosophical, ideological, racial, ethnic, or religious nature" (United Nations, 2004). The European Union defines "terrorist acts as intentional acts that, given their nature or context, may seriously damage a country or an international organisation" (Council of the European Union, 2015). Though there are efforts by the UN and other international agencies to prevent terrorism through legal instruments, a lack of consensus still persists at the international level on how to define terrorism, as on the one hand it is associated with moral judgement and emotions, and on the other hand, there are states that are accused of sponsoring and engaging in terrorism.

HISTORICAL DEVELOPMENTS OF TERRORISM

The history of terrorism can be traced back to the Greek classical historian Xenophon (c. 431–c. 350 BCE), who narrated about a strong psychological warfare against enemy populations. The emperors like Tiberius (14–37 CE) and

Caligula (37–41 CE) used various methods of violence, such as capital punishment, banishment, and expropriation of property, to discourage enemies and opposition to their rule (Jenkins, n.d.). Terrorists' traditions in Hinduism, Islam, and Judaism were known as "thugs," "assassins," and "zealots," respectively, and they justified their terror acts in transcendent life after death, which is coterminous with the meaning of the universe (Rapoport, 1984). In the first century, Jewish zealots, one of the four philosophical sects of "Judea," most popular among youths, used violence against the Roman Empire. They imposed religious practises on people, and those who were denied the right to follow them were killed by systematic terror. They announced that we had to gain independence from the Roman Empire. Their religious aims were undividable from their political objectives. Thus, the idea of purity – religious and political – begins to emerge. Jewish zealots were also known as the first organised terrorists in the Middle East region. In the late eleventh century, Islamic sects used terrorism as an instrument to target their enemies and justify the logic of violence. They killed many Muslim dignitaries in order to create military alliances with powerful states, and many Islamic kings used violence as a method to destroy their enemies during the 1200s to 1600s. For example, Jalal-al-Din Hasan used methods of violence to suppress their enemies during 1210–1221 (Chaliand & Blin, 2007). Thugs, who were also known as Phansigars or strangers, used terror acts in the seventh century to rouse public outrage and please Kali, the Hindu goddess of terror and destruction. Though there is no exact estimate for the number of people killed by Thugs terrorists, their impact on the then-Indian economy could be enormous, but their targets were mostly individuals who were travellers and not society or institutions. The Thug terrorism was deeply intertwined with mythologies and traditions associated with Kali, and descendants of Kali were not targets, indicating that it was a cult governed by procedures and rules with the sanction of rulers (Rapoport, 1984).

The French Revolution marked a turning point in the history of terrorism, as the current form of terrorism took shape in this period and the nature of terrorism was widened by "state terrorism" or "modern terrorism" (Chaliand & Blin, 2007). In the modern form of terrorism, a democratic club or a group named "Jacobins" used the method of violence against the enemy of liberty. Their famous slogan was "No liberty for the enemies of liberty" (François Furstenberg, 2007). But there are remarkable differences between the modern terrorism of the French Revolution and the terrorism that is practised among the Jewish zealots and the Islamic Assassins. First of all, terrorism had essentially no religious dimensions until the nineteenth and early twentieth centuries. Secondly, marginalised and frontier groups adopted the methods of violence, but they did not have definite political objectives, though they were often associated with political ideologies such as Marxist, Fascist, Racist, etc. The terrorism of the late nineteenth century was influenced by the romantic traditions that enabled them to engage in mass killings. The nineteenth century, also known as the "violent century," was a time when war became a common phenomenon, engaging the involvement of heads of state, armies, and the entire society. The technological advancement, industrialisation process, and invention of explosive devices factored into increasing the gravity of destruction and facilitated and encouraged the terrorist movement to a great extent (Chaliand & Blin, 2007).

The twentieth century witnessed many revolutions across the world that adopted the method of violence to replace existing or old regimes, for example, the Bolshevik Revolution. The Bolshevik Revolution was ethical, political, and ideological in nature, and the people involved in this revolution worked as a team under one man leadership. The men and women who were part of this revolution were aware of the risk of death. Unlike holy terrorists or religious revolutionaries, the Bolshevik revolutionaries, also known as the Russian Revolution, were atheists, and they sacrificed their lives for the benefit of society to replace the previous regimes. They were not induced to violence by expecting any reward in the next world or a life after death. For example, the members of the revolutionary organisation "Narodnaya Volya" very well knew that their destination was death for the liberation of humankind (Chaliand & Blin, 2007). On June 13, 1881, Sofia Perovskaya, the first woman revolutionary, was executed by the tsarist regime of Russia. It is alleged that Karl Marx did not condemn the execution of Russian attackers. In a letter dated November 11, 1881, he wrote to his daughter Jenny Longuet, "Have you been following the trial of the people who carried out the attack? They are solidly honest people, striking no melodramatic poses, unassuming, realistic, and heroic. Shouting and doing are irreconcilably contradictory" (Chaliand & Blin, 2007).

Lenin applied the method of "state terrorism" to defeat his enemies. He was of the opinion that terrorists' activities were part of a larger military and political strategy. His successor, Joseph Stalin, also continued Lenin's ideology to crush enemies in the same manner in the country. In the early 1930s, Stalin used terror through his "dekulabization" campaign, in which many prosperous peasant families were arrested, deported, and executed during 1929–1932. The Russian model of terrorism is the perfect example of "state terrorism," in which they systematically killed thousands of people with the help of state apparatus such as the police. Thus, the Russian model of revolution had become the "role model" of state terrorism, and many countries, such as China and Cambodia, replicated it (Chaliand & Blin, 2007).

The Second World War marked another turning point in the history of terrorism as it became a method of resistance in the anti-colonial movement. Liberation movements across the world adopted methods of violence such as terrorism and guerrilla warfare, especially in the Korean and Vietnam conflicts, resulting in mass killings. In 1968, Latin American insurgents launched guerrilla tactics, and Palestinians used terrorism as a propagation tactic, which later transitioned to full-scale violence. The Palestine Liberation Organisation (PLO), accused of adopting terrorist activities, hijacked

Egypt's EL Al flight from Rome to Tel Aviv, engaged in killing many political leaders, and was involved in bombings in Europe and America (Chaliand & Blin, 2007).

The year 1979 witnessed the Iranian revolution and the Soviet intervention in Afghanistan, which changed the course of history in the history of terrorism. The Iranian revolution (radical Shiite Islamic revolution) has inspired terrorist organisations such as Hezbollah, Hamas, and Al-Qaeda, cutting across both sects of Islam. In order to oppose the Soviet intervention in Afghanistan, the US funded both Saudi Arabia and Pakistan to train and provide logistical support, weapons, and financial support to the Afghan resistance fighters. "Mujahidin," the defenders of faith, revived their terrorist activities during this period, and Al-Qaeda, which was accused of spreading the world-wide terror network and the 9/11 attack in the US, in fact started their terrorist activities with the support of the US in Afghanistan. The third important turning point started during 1991–1993 when radical Islamic organisations realised that the US was exploiting them as an instrument against the Soviet Union. It was then that they began to develop an independent political-military movement, pursuing its own objectives (Chaliand & Blin, 2007).

During this period, Islamic fundamentalists started "jihad" in Algeria, Kashmir, Chechnya, and Bosnia. In 1993, they attacked the World Trade Centre with a car bomb but could not achieve their targets. But they succeeded in attacking Khobar and Dahran in Saudi Arabia, where around 90 US soldiers lost their lives. Then Osama bin Laden demanded the withdrawal of US forces from Saudi Arabia. From 1994 to 1996, the Taliban was able to lay a strong foundation in Afghanistan as a powerful force and allied themselves with many other terror organisations and governments to carry forward the radical Islamic agenda. In February 1998, Osama bin Laden declared war on "the crusaders and Jews," and the same year, US embassies in East Africa were attacked by Islamic terrorists. The major turning point in terrorism happened with the 9/11 attacks in 2001, and the US declared the "War on Terror" to destroy the infrastructure and the international network of terrorism (Chaliand & Blin, 2007).

There have been international efforts to contain terrorism since 2001, but policymakers have yet to reach a consensus on what measures are more appropriate to contain or counterterrorism. Though the major bone of contention is whether a soft approach or repressive measures are more fruitful for a sustainable counterterrorism strategy, countering violent extremism has become an integral component of counterterrorism strategies in many countries. At the same time, it is alarming to note that extremist groups such as al-Qaida, the Islamic State of Iraq and Syria (ISIS), Boko Haram in Nigeria, and al-Shabaab in Somalia and Kenya continue to hold their ground despite various counterterrorism efforts. Extremism is not only a major source of terrorism but also factors into many other conflicts, causing many causalities, so fostering closer cooperation and collaboration among the security forces, peacebuilders, civil society, and other stakeholders in the fields of conflict management and prevention has become a central element of counterterrorism strategy (Nünlist & Frazer, 2015).

The "UN Plan of Action to Prevent Violent Extremism" that was presented in 2016 acknowledges that only through good governance can the structural causes of violent extremism be addressed, including intolerance, government failure, and political, economic, and social marginalisation. The Organisation for Security and Co-operation in Europe (OSCE), at its Ministerial Council Meeting held in 2001, held the view that extremism, which is the root cause of global terrorism, cannot be countered with military and intelligence alone. Homegrown Islamic radicalisation in Europe has become a major concern with the terrorist attacks in Madrid (2004) and London (2005), and the counterterrorism strategy has started to focus more on the societal conditions that led to individual radicalisation. By 2011, holistic strategies to prevent violent extremism and increase the resilience of societies in the face of terrorism had become integral components of the counterterrorism strategies of many countries.

Violent extremism can be seen in all religions, cutting across cultures and societies, but when it is limited only to addressing Islamophobia, it may become more counterproductive than a resolution. Since there is no unanimity on the definitions of what constitutes terrorism and how it is different from violent extremism, many policymakers grapple with the question of whether both terms can be interchangeably or synonymously used. The term "radicalisation" is often used to describe the process by which an individual becomes a terrorist or a violent extremist by adopting extreme political, social, or religious ideals and aspirations that reject or undermine the status quo or ideas and expressions of freedom of choice. It is a vocal or active opposition to fundamental values, including democracy, the rule of law, individual liberty, and mutual respect and tolerance of different faiths and beliefs. Increasing cases of radicalisation are reported across the world, especially in Europe, even among schoolchildren (Scarcella et al., 2016).

EXTREMISM

The term extremis denotes a sense of being at the margins, boundaries, or edges of any organisation or group that manifests a tenuous link to the relevant normative tradition. Most often, extremism refers to heterodoxy against orthodoxy (Douglas Pratt, 2010). Extremism considers violence a legitimate instrument to achieve their political objectives by engaging in anti-democratic activities to abolish constitutional democracy and the rule of law, openly oppose the concept of human rights and freedom of expression, engage in aggressive and proactive interventions against the established government and political system, and closely promote authoritarian dictatorship and totalitarianism (Bötticher, 2017).

Accordingly, extremism is a deviation from socially accepted norms and is often associated with fundamentalist thoughts and radicalisation. It includes the use of all means that appear to support the aim of extremists to influence and push the mainstream within society to think in that direction. The threats and use of force are considered normal practises that originate from a deep disrespect for the political opponent. Extremists defend their shared values against what *they* consider a deviation from socially and politically accepted norms. Considering themselves the true norm-keepers, they instead consider the mainstream illegitimate and therefore the use of violence justified. Certain times, governments denounce opponents to brand them as extremists, regardless of their own responsibility for an existing social or political conflict (Giessmann, 2013).

In fact, extremism does not always originate from religions alone, as extremist ideological movements with a secular background often seem to share an anti-religious sentiment as well. Extremism typically refers to pre-modern ideologies that intend to justify the case and policy of their followers. Extremist actors are reluctant to opt for democratic political discourses to put their ideologies to the test and often prefer hierarchical and authoritarian political structures. There are no convincing studies to state that fundamentalist thought or radicalisation can become sound platforms for identifying the "ideologies" of terrorism. Generally, terrorist activities are treated as an expression of extremism, but in most cases, they're a reflection of deeds rather than thoughts (Giessmann, 2013).

When we analyse the intentions of terrorism and extremism, they both create fear in society through violent activities to achieve political, ideological, and religious goals. There are a lot of examples in history where multiple political and religious organisations used violence as a method to suppress independent voices or kill their enemies to achieve their goals. For example: (i) Rome fought various wars with the kings of Carthage in 264 BC; Roman Senator Cato the Elder stated that "Carthage must be destroyed." Rome razed Carthage, killing 150,000 residents and forcing survivors to become slaves. Ben Kiernan called it "the first genocide" in history; (ii) a Jewish group also known as the Sicarii was compelled to kill thousands of supporters of the Roman empires for committing suicide at the mountain redoubt of Masada in 73 CE; (iii) in 657 CE, the Kharijites were the sect of Islam that appeared after the death of Muhammad. It denied accepting the authority of Caliph Ali and started a revolt against him. It was the first outbreak of extremism in Islam in which thousands of Muslims lost their lives (McAuliffe, 2001); (iv) during the Second World War, Adolf Hitler systematically killed around six million Jews in various operations in the name of racism (Rummel, 1992); (v) the Klu Klux Klan is an American white supremacy hate group that primarily targets immigrants, Jews, leftists, and homosexual groups to maintain its white supremacy (Wintz, 2009); (vi) after the 1970s, new Islamic extremism has emerged as a major global security challenge. The various organisations, like Al Qaeda and ISIS, have been killing people who are against their ideology (Berger, 2019). These examples clearly show that the objectives of all of them are to create fear in society so that organisations or individuals involved in that can fulfil their political, religious, and other objectives.

The attention given to personal motives and convictions as well as negative experiences of exclusion, rejection, humiliation, injustice, or frustration was a distraction from structural factors that can lead to violent extremism. Studies on "radicalisation" that make an attempt to understand how individuals turn into violent extremists were unable to extrapolate generalisations from the case studies and individual life stories as the motives and ideas that turn individuals into violent extremists are multifaceted and extremely complex. The structural drivers of radicalisation and extremism need to be addressed at the individual, meso, and macro levels by providing human rights, good governance, strengthening the rights of women, and inclusion in the political, economic, and social spheres. Many times, counterterrorism measures are manipulated under the pretext of national security, colour all people from Islam as potential terrorists, fail to promote value-neutral ideas, pay inadequate attention to "counter narratives" of local context, and enforce top-down approaches in communities. Radicalisation and extremism in Switzerland are associated with right-wing, left-wing, and animal rights extremism, as well as a new phenomenon called "foreign fighters" (Nünlist & Frazer, 2015).

A study conducted on "White Extremism" on the last 10 years of extremist attacks from 2011 to 2019, from the Norway attack in 2011 to the late Christchurch attacks in 2019, finds that violence by white extremists has grown in the recent past and that there is an interconnection between later attackers and the earlier attackers who influenced them. They examined attacks perpetrated by anti-immigrant extremists, anti-Muslim extremists, neo-Nazi extremists, right-wing extremists, anti-Semitic extremists, neo-fascists, white extremists, anti-Arab extremists, the Klu Klux Klan, anti-Sikh extremists, and incel extremists. They also examined attacks on migrants and refugees, places of worship and religious figures, and attacks on black people, Hispanic people, and Hindus. The connections between the killers span continents and highlight how the internet and social media have facilitated the spread of white extremist ideology and violence (Cai & Landon, 2019), but terrorist expressions of religion are regarded as fundamentalism, which is evident in Islam, Christianity, Hinduism, Judaism, and almost all religious communities. The upsurge in the fundamentalism of all religions, along with the utilisation of globalised communication, transportation, and related modern technologies, need to be given careful attention to address terrorism (Douglas Pratt, 2010).

FUNDAMENTALISM

When the term *fundamentalism was coined* by Curtis Lee Laws in 1920 in the United States, it had a religious connotation, especially in the Christian context, highlighting the resistance of American Protestant movements to theological liberalism. Later on, researchers and politicians widely used it in the context of religious orthodoxy (Almond et al., 1993). "Though the notion became popular to condemn religious orthodoxy of every kind and be considered equal to religious fanaticism, only in the late twentieth century was the term fundamentalism" broadened to include political discourses such as secular ideologies with strict adherence to their conservative doctrines and values. Currently, most often across the Western political domain, it has been used to refer to non-liberal thoughts in a pejorative and derogatory manner and is associated with variant forms of religious extremism and thus religiously oriented terrorism (Gilling, 1992).

Fundamentalism is the "belief that there is one set of religious teachings that clearly contains the fundamental, basic, intrinsic, essential, and inerrant truth about humanity and deity" (Altemeyer & Hunsberger, 1992, as cited in Hood et al., 2009). Marty and Appleby, in their series on "fundamentalisms" in the early 1990s, explained the extended scope of using the term by arguing that fundamentalism may not exclusively refer to core views of religiosity, but it can be understood as an inherently political, although sometimes clandestine, phenomenon. Though they think fundamentalism is largely religiously inspired, resistance against any kind of modernity with inherent social and ethnic grievances is the root cause of fundamentalist thinking (Marty & Appleby, 1993). The social ethicist Stephan H. Pfurtner (1991) defined "fundamentalism as a flight into radicalism, and it is combined with violence while refusing to accept an adequate perception of reality, of rationality, and of the unfolding freedom for the individual and society" (cited in Schirrmacher et al., 2013).

The followers of all religions almost adopted the method of violence to punish their enemies. They have justified their acts according to religious practises. The term "fundamentalism" was originally used to describe some sects of Christianity that claim "only God," and churches are called "people of God." Initially, terrorism in Christianity is minimal, but when they employ "the just war theory" and see "themselves as God's soldiers" they claim that "God is on their side." And on the basis of these two metaphors, they justified their terrorist activities (Volf, 2008, cited in Hess & Martens, 2008). Those who support Christianity and support the violence cite the events as Jesus driving the moneychanger from the temple with such statements as Jesus dark prophecy: "Do not think that I have come to bring peace on the earth; I have come not to bring peace but a sword" (Mathew, 1984, as cited in Elijah Onyango Standslause Odhiambo, 2014).

Political, academic, and religious elites of the Islamic world are often outraged by Western cultural imperialism vis-à-vis value-based traditions of thought because, to them, the criticism is based on bigotry and double standards in mainstream Western debates about modernity and liberalism. Though orthodoxy and liberal understanding ignite controversies about ideologies, cultures, or religions over change and preservation, a violent confrontation between proponents and opponents of change for the use of violence is neither symbiotic nor empirically proven. Empirically, there is no evidence that orthodoxy would be more prone to the use or threat of violence than liberalism. On the contrary, radical pacifism, which is an important strand of fundamentalist thinking in different social and political contexts, explicitly denounces any use of violence (Giessmann, 2013).

Till Christianity became a state religion in the fourth century, believers in Christianity were pacifists, and since then they have rejected the idea of being pacifists and adopted the "doctrine of just war," and justified the use of military force and violence. In 632 CE, Islam came into existence; since then, it has been spreading across the world, and many Christians have adopted Islam. In the meantime, Islamic leaders captured the holy lands of Christians, and to recover the Holy Land from Islamic rule, Christian crusaders started a series of religious wars during 1100 and 1600 (Crusades in The New Catholic Encyclopaedia, 1966, as cited in Elijah Onyango Standslause Odhiambo, 2014).

Pope Urban II had called the Christian knights and soldiers to join the war. Whoever will fight in this war and sacrifice his life will get the land, glory, spiritual rewards, and a guaranteed place in heaven. The slogan Holy Land Salvation will bring eternal salvation was widely prevalent to induce followers. In July 1099, when Jerusalem was captured, Frankish knights massacred the thousands of Jews, Muslims, and other Christians who opposed the Crusaders. The pope's representative, Arnaud Amaury, stated, "Kill them all, and God will know his own" (Thomas, 2005, cited as Elijah Onyango Standslause Odhiambo, 2014). The popes permitted the atrocities and invasions in the name of God's wishes, and thus their unquestioned faith led to a series of terror campaigns against their enemies.

Judaism believed that Yahvi is the only God, and only God has a covenant in the form of an election. Therefore, the Jews asserted that "their enemies are Yahweh's enemies" which gave rise to "Zionist ideology." They believed that "the Jewish messiah will gather all the Jews in Diaspora in Zion and institute a social order of perfect justice as well as perfect peace in the world" (Weissbrod, 2002, cited as Elijah Onyango Standslause Odhiambo, 2014). They claimed that the land of Israel belongs to the Jews who are living in any part of the world, and they have moral obligations to protect the holy land from enemies (Motyl, 2001). Such religious hostilities are still prevalent in the Middle East and North Africa (MENA) region among Jews,

Christians, and Muslims, constituting the world's most chaotic and violent war zones (Kishi & Theodorou, 2016).

Since 1970, Islamic terrorism has emerged across the globe, and they consider Islam "an ideology and faith, homeland and nationality, creed and state, spirit, and action, book and sword" (Migaux, 2007; cited as Chaliand & Blin, 2007). No Islamic enemy can be tolerated; many organisations, such as Al Qaeda and the Islamic State of Iraq and the Levant (ISIS), are the products of Islamic radicalism. They used religion as a political tool to achieve their non-religious objectives (Rausch, 2015). Osama Bin Laden, the leader of Al Qaeda, adopted the ideas of Abdullah Azzam, who believed that "Islam had been dominated by foreign powers for far too long; this was seen as an opportunity to wage a holy war against the United States, West, Israel, and Muslims who opposed 'jihadist theology'" (White, 2012, cited as Rausch, 2015).

Since the emergence of Al Qaeda, it has conducted various attacks on US forces in various parts of the world. For the killing of the Americans and its allies, the leader of Al-Qaeda issued a "fatwa" in February 1998, stating that "in compliance with God's order, we issue the following fatwa to all Muslims: The ruling to kill the Americans and their allies, civilians and military, is an individual duty for every Muslim who can do it in any country in which it is possible to do it, in order to liberate the Al-Aqsa Mosque and the holy mosque (Mecca) from the grip, and in order for their armies to move out of all the lands of Islam, defeated and unable to threaten any Muslim. This is in accordance with the words of Almighty God, and fight the pagans all together as they fight you all together, and fight them until there is no more tumult or oppression, and there is prevailing justice and faith in God" (Rashid, 2002, cited as Elijah Onyango Standslause Odhiambo, 2014). Thus, Al Qaeda has tried to radicalise Muslims with the help of Islamic dogmas and fundamentals to join the religious campaign and sacrifice themselves for the sake of God. Thus, it is very evident how various religions have used their religious dogmas as fundamentals to promote and induce terror and violence among their faithful to achieve their politico-religious objectives.

CONCLUSION

This chapter has elaborated on the multifaceted and complex relationships that exist among terrorism, extremism, and fundamentalism. Any effort to contain terrorism needs to adopt a holistic strategy that addresses the root causes of radicalisation that culminate in terrorism, such as extremism and fundamentalism. It is beyond doubt that there is a concomitant correlation between terrorism, extremism, and fundamentalism as processes that are mutually exclusive in meaning and concepts. A terrorist can be both an extremist and a fundamentalist because terrorists are greatly inspired by extremist measures and fundamental values, but an extremist need not necessarily be a terrorist because s/he can have extremist ideas without adopting the path of terrorism. On ideological grounds, extremists can follow non-violent political ideas, but a terrorist cannot be non-violent. In the same way, religious fundamentalism that is currently broadened to include political ideologies could be the source or root of terrorism. So fundamentalists could adopt both violent and non-violent means to achieve their goals and even be non-violent sympathisers for the cause of terrorism. Because of the thin demarcation between terrorism, extremism, and fundamentalism, identifying correlations among them would be a complex concern, but successful counter-terrorism strategies could not ignore the mutually constituting factors among them.

References

Altemeyer, B., &Hunsberger, B. E. (1992). Authoritarianism, religious fundamentalism, quest, and prejudice. *International Journal for the Psychology of Religion*, *2*(2), 113–133. DOI:https://doi.org/10.1207/s15327582ijpr0202_5

Almond, G. A., Appleby, R. S., & Emmanuel, S. (1993). *Strong religion: The rise of fundamentalisms around the world*. Chicago: University of Chicago Press.

Berger, J.M. (2019, August 5). A brief history of extremism – From ancient Rome to Al Qaeda. *BBC History*. https://www.historyextra.com/period/roman/extremism-history-examples-explained-definition-facts-prevent-right-wing-religious/

BBC. (1970, April 5). 1970: West German envoy killed by rebels. *BBC*.

Bötticher, A. (2017). Towards academic consensus definitions of radicalism and extremism. *Perspectives on Terrorism*, *11*(4), 73–77.

Cai, W., & Landon, S. (2019, April 3). Attacks by white extremists are growing. So are their connections. *New York Times*.

Council of the European Union. (2015). *The EU list of persons, groups and entities subject to specific measures to combat terrorism*. https://www.consilium.europa.eu/uedocs/cms_data/docs/pressdata/en/jha/138098.pdf

Chaliand, G., & Blin, A. (2007). *The history of terrorism: From Antiquity to al Qaeda*. University of California Press.

Furstenberg, F. (2007, October 28). *Bush's dangerous Liaisons*. The New York Times.

Ganor, B. (2002). Defining terrorism: Is one man's terrorist another man's freedom fighter? *Police Practice and Research*, *3*(4), 287–304. DOI:https://doi.org/10.1080/1561426022000032060

Giessmann, H.J. (n.d.). Fundamentalism, extremism, terrorism. *The Routledge Handbook of International Crime and Justice Studies*. 10.4324/9780203837146.ch23

Giessmann, H.J. (2013). *Fundamentalism, extremism, terrorism from*. The Routledge Handbook of International Crime and Justice Studies Routledge. Accessed on: 31 Oct 2020 https://www.routledgehandbooks.com/doi/10.4324/9780203837146.ch23

Gilling, B., ed. (1992). "Be Ye Separate": Fundamentalism and the New Zealand experience, Red Beach: Colcom Press, xi.

Gourdin, K.N. (2015). *A profile of the global airline industry*. Business Expert Press.

Hess, R.S., & Martens, E.A. (2008). Christianity and violence. In *War in the Bible and terrorism in the twenty-first century* (pp. 1–18). Eisenbrauns.

Hood, R.W.J., Hill, P.C., & Spilka, B. (2009). *The psychology of religion: An empirical approach* (4th ed.). Guilford Press.

Jenkins, J.P. (n.d.). Types of terrorism. In *Encyclopedia Britannica*. Britannica. https://www.britannica.com/topic/terrorism/Types-of-terrorism

Jodie, S. (2015). Terrorism in the eye of the beholder. *The Imperative Quest for a Universally Agreed Definition of Terrorism, Kent Student Law Review, 2*, https://core.ac.uk/download/pdf/228781857.pdf

Kishi, K., & Theodorou, A.E. (2016). *6 facts about religious hostilities in the Middle East and North Africa*. Pew Research Center. https://www.pewresearch.org/fact-tank/2016/07/07/6-facts-about-religious-hostilities-in-the-middle-east-and-north-africa/

Marty, M. E., & Appleby, R. S. (1993). *Fundamentalisms and the state: Remaking polities, economies, and militance*. Chicago: University of Chicago Press.

McAuliffe, J.D. (2001). *Encyclopaedia of the Qur'ān: J-O*. Encyclopaedia of the Qur'ā.

Migaux, P. (2007). The roots of Islamic radicalism. In G. Chaliand (Ed.), *The history of terrorism: From antiquity to Al Qaeda* (pp. 255–313). Berkeley: University of California Press.

Motyl, A.J. (2001). *Encyclopedia of nationalism: Fundamental themes. Leaders, movements, and concepts. Volume 1. Volume 2*. Academic Press.

Nations, U. (1969). *Convention on offences and certain other acts committed on board aircraft* (pp. 222–223). United Nations.

Nünlist, C., & Frazer, O. (2015, December). The concept of countering violent extremism December 2015, CSS Analyses in Security Policy_No. 183.

Odhiambo, E.O.S. (2014). Religious fundamentalism and terrorism. *Journal of Global Peace and Conflict, 2*(1), 187–205.

Pfurtner, S. H. (1991). Fundamentalismus. *Die Flucht ins Rudikale*. Freiburg i. Br.: Herder.

Pratt, D. (2010). Religion and terrorism: Christian fundamentalism and extremism. *Terrorism and Political Violence, 22*(3), 438–456.

Primoratz, I. (1990, October). What is terrorism? *Journal of Applied Philosophy, 7*(2), 129–138. 10.1111/j.1468-5930.1990.tb00261.x

Rapoport, D.C. (1984). Fear and trembling: Terrorism in three religious traditions. *The American Political Science Review, 78*(3), 658–677.

RAND, (n.d.). RAND database of worldwide terrorism incidents, https://www.rand.org/nsrd/projects/terrorism-incidents.html.

Rausch, C.C. (2015). Fundamentalism and terrorism. *Journal of Terrorism Research, 6*(2), 28–35. 10.15664/jtr.1153

Rummel, R.J. (1992). *Democide: Nazi genocide and mass murder*. Transaction Publishers.

Scarcella, A., Page, R., & Furtado, V. (2016). Terrorism, radicalisation, extremism, authoritarianism and fundamentalism: A systematic review of the quality and psychometric properties of assessments. *PLoS One, 11*(12), e0166947. doi:10.1371/journal.pone.0166947

Schirrmacher, T., World Evangelical Alliance, International Institute for Religious Freedom, Seminar, M.B., & Hände, G. (2013). *Fundamentalism: When religion becomes dangerous*. Verlag für Kultur und Wissenschaft (Culture and Science Publication).

Schmid, A. (2004). Terrorism - The definitional problem. *Case Western Reserve Journal of Internal Law, 36*(2), 376–419. https://core.ac.uk/download/pdf/214078705.pdf

Scraton, P. (2002). *Beyond September 11: An anthology of dissent*. Pluto Press (UK).

Thomas, M. (2005). *Crusades: The illustrated history*. Ann Arbor: University of Michigan Press.

United Nations. (1969). *The convention for the suppression of unlawful seizure of aircraft* (12325). https://treaties.un.org/doc/db/Terrorism/Conv2-english.pdf

United Nations. (1970). Convention for the suppression of unlawful seizure of aircraft. https://treaties.un.org/doc/db/Terrorism/Conv2-english.pdf

United Nations. (1973). Convention on the prevention and punishment of crimes against internationally protected persons, including diplomatic agents 1973. https://legal.un.org/ilc/texts/instruments/english/conventions/9_4_1973.pdf

United Nations. (1977). *Prevention and punishment of crimes against internationally protected persons, including diplomatic agents: Convention between the United States of America and other governments, adopted by the General Assembly of the United Nations at New York December 14, 1973 (1035)*. https://legal.un.org/ilc/texts/instruments/english/conventions/9_4_1973.pdf

United Nations. (1979, December 17). International convention against the taking of hostages, New York. https://www.unodc.org/documents/treaties/Special/1979%20International%20Convention%20against%20the%20Taking%20of%20Hostages.pdf

United Nations. (1983). *International convention against the taking hostage (21931)*. https://treaties.un.org/doc/db/terrorism/english-18-5.pdf

United Nations. (1983). *International convention against the taking of hostage (21931)*. https://treaties.un.org/doc/db/terrorism/english-18-5.pdf

United Nation. (1997). International convention for the suppression of terrorist bombings, New York, December 15, 1997. https://treaties.un.org/Pages/ViewDetails.aspx?src=TREATY&mtdsg_no=XVIII-9&chapter=18&clang=_en

United Nations. (1998). *International convention for the suppression of terrorist bombings 11*. https://treaties.un.org/doc/db/terrorism/english-18-9.pdf

United Nations. (1999).*International convention for the suppression of financing of terrorism*. https://treaties.un.org/doc/db/Terrorism/english-18-11.pdf

United Nations. (2004).*Security council acts unanimously to adopt resolution strongly condemning terrorism as one of most serious threats to peace*. https://www.un.org/press/en/2004/sc8214.doc.htm

United Nations. (2005). *International convention for the suppression of acts of nuclear terrorism*.

Volf, M. (2008). Christianity and violence. In R. S. Hess &E. A. Martens (Eds.), *War in the Bible and terrorism in the twenty-first century* (pp. 1–17). Winona Lake: Indiana Eisenbrauns.

Weissbrod, L. (2002). *Israeli identity: In search of a successor to the pioneer, Tsabar and Settler*. London: Frank Cass.

Wintz, C.D. (2009). *Encyclopedia of African American history: 5-volume set*. OUP USA.

9

WARS FOR LIMITED POLITICAL AIMS

Not "Limited War"[1]

Donald Stoker

LIMITED WAR: A DEFINITIONAL MORASS

"Limited War" is hardly a new term. Indeed, Europe in the eighteenth century is sometimes said to have endured "The Age of Limited Wars." The term likely reentered the modern lexicon during the US Senate hearings on the military situation surrounding the 1950–1953 Korean War. In May 1951, General George C. Marshall (then Secretary of Defence), when asked to describe the war in Korea, said: "I would characterize it as a limited war, which I hope will remain limited" (Schwarz, 1967: 95; TIME, 1951, n.p.). But the effort to develop limited war as a type of conflict distinct from itself is more recent and partly a result of the understandable Cold War desire to avoid World War III between the US and the Soviet Union (Osgood, 1969).

Current thinking on the so-called "limited war" has its origins in the work of historian Bernard Brodie for the RAND Corporation in 1952. Brodie notes that he did his first writing on "limited war" at a time when most still believed all wars had to be fought as "total wars." The fact that he suggested something different – limited wars – was, he insists, met with amazement (Brodie 1965).[2] Brodie was "converted" to limited war thinking by the work of British theorist Sir Basil Liddell Hart, of whom he became "a follower," also in 1952. This was probably the result of his reading Liddell Hart's (1947) book, *The Revolution in Warfare*. Brodie noted Liddell Hart's linking the existence of atomic weapons to an "appeal for a return to limited war" (Milevski, 2014; Brodie, 1957: 114). Among other things, the English theorist argued that the area bombing of the Second World War, combined with the development of rockets and pilotless planes, demonstrated that warfare had moved "from a fight to a process of devastation" and that warfare had become so potentially destructive as to make it impossible for major powers to wage war against one another (Liddell Hart, 1947: 36). The end of the US atomic monopoly in 1949 convinced more than one observer that this was indeed the case, but there was also the problem of potential Soviet aggression, particularly by a Soviet client state, as well as the hard reality that wars simply continued to be waged regardless of the risk. Limited war theorising filled what was perceived as a gap.

Brodie wrote an immense amount on limited war, but his seminal work here was *Strategy in the Missile Age* (Brodie, 1959, 1965).[3] His extended definition of limited war bears quoting, as nearly every later writer on the subject draws upon his work:

> What distinguishes limited war from total war? The answer is that limited war involves an important kind and degree of restraint—deliberate restraint. As a rule we do not apply the term "limited war" to conflicts which are limited naturally by the fact that one or both sides lack the capacity to make them total (for example, the colonial war in Algeria). We generally use it to refer to wars in which the United States on the one side and the Soviet Union or Communist China on the other may be involved, perhaps directly but usually through proxies on one or both sides. In such wars the possibility of total or unrestricted conflict is always present as an obvious and immediately available alternative to limited operations. That is why we must emphasize the factor of deliberate restraint.
>
> The restraint must also be massive. One basic restraint always has to be present if the term "limited war" is to have any meaning at all: the strategic bombing of cities with nuclear weapons must be avoided. The minimum restraint is thus already a very great one, particularly in view of the existing traditions of air strategic doctrine with their great emphasis on strategic bombing. (Brodie, 1965: 310–311)

Here, one may see the root of the theoretical issue. In contrast to the equally poorly defined "total war," which has

DOI: 10.4324/9780429426063-11

no meaning because no one can agree on when a war becomes "total," Brodie fails to offer a cogent definition of "limited war" 2016 (Stoker, 2016). He defines limited war in terms of several elements, including the prospect of escalation, the use of nuclear weapons with restraint, and whether or not the US is at war with one of the major communist states.

Political scientist Robert Osgood is the second most important person in the field of limited war studies. Because it is frequently quoted in literature about limited war and exemplifies some of the issues with limited war theory, his expanded definition of limited war from his key 1957 book is also worth repeating in full:

> A limited war is one in which the belligerents restrict the purposes for which they fight to concrete, well-defined objectives that do not demand the utmost military effort of which the belligerents are capable and that can be accommodated in a negotiated settlement. The battle is confined to a local geographical area and directed against selected targets—primarily those of direct military importance. It demands of the belligerents only a fractional commitment of their human and physical resources. It permits their economic, social, and political patterns of existence to continue without serious disruption. (Osgood, 1957: 1–2)

We see here key elements of much-limited war thinking: a limited purpose (or political aim), the level of force is "limited," the bulk of a nation's political, social, and economic forces are not required, the geographical scope is restricted, and what is attacked is constrained.

Osgood elaborates on his definition: "Limited war, however, is not a uniform phenomenon. Such a war can be limited in different ways; it can be limited in some respects and not in others, depending upon its physical characteristics and the perspective of the belligerents. Thus, conceivably, a war can be limited in geographical scope but virtually unlimited in the weapons employed and the targets involved within the area of combat" (Osgood, 1957: 2). Later, he repeats his insistence that limited war requires the "limiting" of the political aims and the means (Osgood, 1957: 238).

All this only clouds the issue by contradicting what he says in regard to the level of means. His definition of limited war provides no firm foundation for analysis because he does not, and indeed cannot, define "means" in a universally applicable manner that provides a basis for analysis. In Osgood's defence, though, he does say the following: "There is one characteristic of overriding importance in distinguishing among wars: the nature of the objectives for which the belligerents fight" (Osgood, 1957: 4). But the other items he heaps onto his definition are not a basis for defining or analysing a so-called limited war; they are factors contributing to the war's nature of infinite variation. They illuminate how the conflict is waged but do not define what it is about. Osgood did not sufficiently apply Occam's Razor and conclude the truth: the political aim sought is *the* defining element and an objective basis for analysis.

A common point raised in efforts to define limited war is the necessity of the non-use of nuclear weapons (Brodie, 1965; Palit, 1966; Singh, 2000). This, though, is not a universal requirement, and as early as 1957, Henry Kissinger was writing about "limited nuclear war" (Kissinger, 1957, 1961). Brodie, among others, also said that there might be limited wars in which nuclear weapons were used (Brodie, 1965; Schelling, 1963). Despite their awesome destructive power, nuclear and atomic weapons are means for pursuing a political aim. They are particularly dangerous means whose use (or potential use) is wrapped in unique political consequences. But they are still a manifestation of a (thus far) nation's means, and one cannot define limited war by the means or base rational analysis on something as subjective as the means.

Other authors attempt to lay out requirements for defining "limited war" by insisting upon restrictions on such factors as the level of violence, the conflict's duration or time, and the geographical boundaries of the theatre of war (Kim, 1994). In 1972, Swedish political scientist Nordal Kerman wrote that a limited war was a conflict in which a nation used only part of its "total military capacity" and where the "capacity for total war must not be affected by the conflict, nor must there be any engagement of the superpowers' home territory." He adds that the war must be confined to "a territorially limited area," and the combatants "must exercise voluntary restraint and have limited and well-defined objectives." Other limitations include the types of weaponry, the geographical area, what can be attacked, the military objectives, "and the nature and number of the combatants involved" (Åkerman, 1972: 16).

Kerman mixes political ends and applied means, repeating the previously discussed error of basing parts of his definition on nebulous factors. He also adds "limitations" to his definition, but these are more accurately described as factors contributing to the nature of the war that governs where and how it will be fought: weapons, geography, the other combatants, and so on. All wars have geographical limits, even the Second World War (in which some countries did not participate). Geographical limits are not part of a usable description of limited war; they are one of the factors contributing to its nature, as are the other so-called "limits" (though it is better to deem them "constraints"). They describe how the war will be waged (or not), but they neither define nor explain what the war is about, which is the cornerstone for analysis.

Low-intensity conflict is also thrown about in discussions of limited war, as are the terms "big war" and "small war" and mentions of guerrilla wars, civil wars, and wars between small states and between big states and small ones. "Big war" is sometimes used to mean a major national war or a so-called "total war." "Small war" is often used with the implication that a limited war must be a "small war" and is another fuzzy, badly defined designator that merely adds to the confusion

(Hampton, 1957). Political scientist Craig Whiteside, a US Army veteran of the Iraq War, gives this tongue-in-cheek definition: "A small war is one in which you're getting shot at, but no one cares" (Stoker, 2019: 33). Well-known nineteenth-century soldier C.E. Callwell defines small wars as conflicts waged by regular forces against irregulars (Callwell, 1996).

The definitions have not improved with the passing decades. A 2010 book noted that "the term limited war implies regular military operations by one nation-state against the regular military force of another nation-state and excludes irregular operations by terrorist organisations [sic] against a state or by other non-state actors like warlords against a state or against other warlords" (Bakshi, 2010: vii–viii). This is only another variation of a definition based on means with the addition of the opponent's doctrinal warfighting methods. All of this demonstrates a potentially fatal problem: if we cannot even clearly define limited war, how can we understand its nature? And if we don't understand what limited war means, *we don't understand what we mean when we describe any war.*

Related to this is an ever-expanding group of buzzwords that describe the means and sometimes the methods of warfighting (generally at the tactical level) and occasionally carry the added, unintended evil of allowing political leaders to not call a war a war: Fourth Generation Warfare, Fifth Generation Warfare, New Wars, Hybrid War, Grey Zone Wars, and the list goes on (Henderson & Singer, 2005). They are generally part of the continuing effort in the political science, international relations, and policy-wonk fields to repackage the old in a new wrapper while failing to understand the difference between peace and war. There are many, many more examples of this, and such terms invariably define war by the means and methods used (Strachan, 2008; Stoker & Whiteside, 2020).

We see in all of this that the various definitions of so-called "limited war" insist upon some or all of the following: limiting the objective or aim (what is meant by this is rarely defined), limiting the means (Osgood, 1957; Chandran, 2005), the prevention of escalation (particularly into the meaningless "total war") (Bakich, 2014), restraints of various types that usually revolve around targeting or the level of violence, non-use of nuclear weapons (usually) (Garnett, 1982; Chandran, 2005), geographic limits (Chandran, 2005), and the awareness of limits on the other side. This is not a basis for analysis; it is a morass.

A BETTER WAY?

Political scientist Robert Osgood insisted on the impossibility of the construction of a functionally limited war theory. "What we are almost certain not to witness," he wrote in 1969, "is the perfection of limited-war conceptions and practise in accordance with some predictable, rational calculus and reliable, universal rules of the game. The conditions and modalities of international conflict are too varied, dynamic, and subjective for limited war to be that determinate. Any search for the strategic equivalent of economic man on the basis of which a grand theory of military behaviour might be erected is bound to be ephemeral and unproductive" (Osgood, 1969: 54).

Osgood was mistaken. Like nearly every writer on limited war, he did not understand the purpose of theory. Carl von Clausewitz gave us the first steps to clarity here: "The primary purpose of any theory is to clarify concepts and ideas that have become confused and entangled" (Clausewitz, 1984: 132). Theory, as Sir Julian Corbett tells us, "can assist a capable man to acquire a broad outlook." Theory should teach us to think, to analyse, to bring a critical but informed eye to the problem at hand, and to consider both its depth and breadth. It also serves to ground us by defining terms, providing a firm foundation for analysis, and teaching us to distinguish between what is important and what is not (Corbett, 1988: 3–7). The results of the theory, Clausewitz insists, "must have been derived from military history, or at least checked against it," thus ensuring "that theory will have to remain realistic. It cannot allow itself to get lost in futile speculation, hairsplitting, and flights of fancy" (Clausewitz, 1984: 144). Most importantly, particularly in any theory addressing warfare, it "is meant to educate the mind of the future commander" (Clausewitz, 1984: 141).

It is imperative to lay a firm, universally applicable groundwork for the analysis because, as noted above, simply put, *we do not know what we mean when we use the term "limited war."* Here are two further broken examples from classic texts on the subject: 1) "Only conflicts which contain the potentiality for becoming total can be described as limited" (Garnett, 1982: 123, 2) "Limited war is a conflict short of general war to achieve specific political objectives, using limited forces and limited force" (McClintock, 1967: 5). Both of these definitions explain limited war in relation to other types of conflict that also lack clear, generally agreed-upon definitions, i.e., "total war" and "general war."

Wars, as Clausewitz wrote, should be analysed based on the political aims sought, not the means employed. Wars are fought for regime change or for something else. Building upon Clausewitz's foundation, Corbett, in his *Some Principles of Maritime Strategy*, gave us the terms "unlimited war" to describe a conflict waged to overthrow the enemy government (an unlimited political aim) and "limited war" for a war fought for something other than regime change (a limited political aim) (Clausewitz, 1984). This provides an ironclad foundation for substantive analysis because examining a war by beginning with the political aims sought by each combatant provides a constant upon which to base any discussion or analysis, as well as a foundation for building a coherent theory in regard to wars in which at least one combatant is pursuing limited political aims. It is important to note that some combatants might be pursuing unlimited aims while others seek limited ones. The applied means certainly help determine the nature of the war being fought, but basing one's analysis or definition upon the means used – or not – lacks universality because it is not concrete and is subjective. Moreover, it helps determine *how* the war is fought, but it is not what the war is about – the political aim – *and this is what matters most because all else flows from here*.

We need to stop building unnecessary, unworkable theoretical castles. Doing so inhibits our ability to understand what is at stake when we go to war. Both Clausewitz and Corbett analysed wars based on the political aims sought by the combatants, whether they were fighting for regime change (an unlimited political aim) or something else (a limited political aim). All wars – civil wars, insurrections, anything – fall under this rubric. The term "total war" should also disappear as a categorical descriptor in serious political, strategic, and historical discussions as it clouds analysis instead of offering clarity.

Notes

1 The following is adapted from: Stoker (2019). *Why America Loses Wars: Limited War and American Strategy From the Korean War to the Present.* Cambridge: Cambridge University Press.

2 Some works incorrectly claim that current limited war thinking is a reaction to John Foster Dulles's 1954 "massive retaliation speech." Åkerman (1972). *On the Doctrine of Limited War*, Lund: Berlingska Boktryckeriet, p. 119. Dulles' speech served as an inspiration for a lot of recent writing on so-called "limited war," but the groundwork came earlier.

3 See references.

References

Åkerman, N. (1972). *On the doctrine of limited war*. Lund: Berlingska Boktryckeriet.

Bakich, S. (2014). *Success and failure in limited war: Information and strategy in the Korean, Vietnam, Persian Gulf, and Iraq wars*. Chicago, IL: University of Chicago Press.

Bakshi, G. (2010). *Limited wars in South Asia: Need for an Indian doctrine*. Delhi: Centre for Land Warfare Studies.

Brodie, B. (1957). More about limited war. *World Politics*, *10*(1), 112–122.

Brodie, B. (1959). *Strategy in the missile age*. Santa Monica, CA: RAND.

Brodie, B. (1965). *Strategy in the missile age*. Princeton, NJ: Princeton University Press.

Callwell, C. (1996). *Small wars: Their principles and practice*. Lincoln, NE: University of Nebraska Press.

Chandran, D. (2005). *Limited war: Revisiting Kargil in the Indo-Pak conflict*. Safdarjung Enclave: India Research Press.

Clausewitz, C. von. (1984). *On War*. M. Howard & P. Paret (Eds. and Trans.). Princeton, NJ: Princeton University Press.

Corbett, J. (1988). *Some principles of maritime strategy*. Annapolis, MD: Naval Institute Press.

Garnett, J. (1982). Limited war In J. Baylis, K. Booth, J. Garnett, & P. Williams (Eds.), *Contemporary strategy: Theories and policies* (pp. 114–131). New York, NY: Holmes & Meier.

Hampton, E. (1957). Unlimited confusion over limited war. *Air University Quarterly Review*, *9*, 28–47.

Henderson, E., & Singer, J. (2005). "New wars" and rumors of "new wars." In P. Diehl (Ed.), *War* (Vol. 1, pp. 398–425). London: Sage Publications.

Kim, A. (1994). A note on Sunzi's art of war and limited war: A modern interpretation. *Korean Journal of Defense Analysis*, *6*(1), 251–252.

Kissinger, H. (1957). *Nuclear weapons and foreign policy*. New York, NY: Harper and Brothers.

Kissinger, H. (1961). Limited war: Conventional or nuclear? *Survival: Global Politics and Strategy*, *3*(1), 2–11.

Liddell Hart, B.H. (1947). *The revolution in warfare*. New Haven, CT: Yale University Press.

Milevski, L. (2014). The modern evolution of grand strategic thought. PhD thesis, University of Reading.

Osgood, R. (1957). *Limited war: The challenge to American strategy*. Chicago, IL: Chicago University Press.

Osgood, R. (1969). The reappraisal of limited war. *The Adelphi Papers*, *9*(54), 41–54.

Palit, D. (1966). *War in the deterrent age*. London: Macdonald.

Schelling, T. (1963). *Strategy of conflict*. Cambridge, MA: Harvard University Press.

Schwarz, U. (1967). *American strategy: A new perspective. The growth of politico-military thinking in the United States*. Garden City, NY: Anchor/Doubleday.

Singh, S. (2000). Indian debate on limited war doctrine. *Strategic Analysis*, *23*(12), 2181–2182.

Stoker, D. (2016). What's in a name II: 'Total War' and other terms that mean nothing. *Infinity Journal*, *5*(3), 21–23.

Stoker, D. (2019). *Why America loses wars: Limited war and American strategy from the Korean war to the present*. Cambridge: Cambridge University Press.

Stoker, D., & Whiteside, C. (2020). Blurred lines: The gray zone and hybrid war: Two failures of American strategic thinking. *Naval War College Review*, *73*(1), https://digital-commons.usnwc.edu/nwc-review?utm_source=digital-commons.usnwc.edu%2Fnwc-review%2Fvol73%2Fiss1%2F4&utm_medium=PDF&utm_campaign=PDFCoverPages.

Strachan, H. (2008). Strategy and the limitation of war. *Survival: Global Politics and Strategy*, *50*(1), 31–54.

TIME. (1951, May 21). The MacArthur hearing: The limited war. https://time.com/archive/6796607/the-macarthur-hearing-the-limited-war/

10

EXAMINING THE ROOTS OF MODERN URBAN TERRORISM

M19 and Shining Path in the Western Hemisphere

Renny Castañeda and Tyler Adams

INTRODUCTION

Contemporary discussions on how to better understand the increasing phenomena of radicalisation and social fragmentation in the western hemisphere have often ignored the origins of the strategy of modern urban terrorism. As such, an expanding level of political penetration by terrorist organisations has escalated to a point where legal frameworks favour terrorist activists at the expense of civil society. These phenomena have also altered the political landscape for radical activism through processes of ideological concealment by radical organisations, some of which can be traced back to the 1970s and 1980s. This chapter aims to explain as such the process of ideological concealment of terrorist organisations, addressing the superior importance of two major groups, the Peruvian "Shining Path," and the Colombian "M-19" terrorist groups, both of which sophisticated the processes of ideological concealment to increasingly penetrate urban settlements in order to demoralise civil society and the state for years. Later on, the chapter aims to transpose how the increasing sophistication of ideological concealment all over the western hemisphere has increasingly been adhered to by most recent terrorist groups, some of which have been able to escalate to positions of power by making use of parallel legal (paralegal) tribunals supported by the state in countries highly affected by terrorist actions directed to exploit urban fear, such as in Colombia.

A substantial part of the theory surrounding security and terrorist studies explains the role of social fragmentation as a tool of radicalisation. As such, radicalisation plays a substantive role in the process of the instrumental use of ideological baggage to increasingly recruit members of a terrorist organisation that often operates outside urban settlements. Over time, however, the increasing displacement of the population to urban settlements caused by terrorist groups, as well as the natural migration of rural populations to more industrialised areas, will demand a criminal strategy to ensure increasing recruitment. Moreover, following the material constraints associated with a more educated population, recruitment processes shift to policies of rural plain force and the implementation of urban ideological concealment, a long-term endeavour directed at increasing levels of social fragmentation.

RADICALISATION AND STATE FRAGMENTATION AS AN IDEOLOGICAL FUNNEL FOR TERRORISM

In a more recent shift on the role of ideology as a device of modern state fragmentation, it has been debated that the phenomenon remains a sociological and political consequence of globalisation. This argument has been defended in studies of global communication, social science, political theory, and international relations theory, stressing the assumption that internal political division derives from the increasing level of global interconnectedness and, thus, the erosion or loss of domestic common values that led to inner detachment from identity or radicalisation. According to these theories, internal fragmentation happens even in states often referred to as modern and sovereign. This means that the consequences derived from the growing levels of interdependence push national identity into a vacuum where other cultures, sources of information, or organisations colonise demoralised populations, increasing their own influence and decreasing the necessary level of domestic identity to make any national political project viable.

This assumption, however, fails to account for how the most recently developed urban settlements and countries,

DOI: 10.4324/9780429426063-12

instead of being a focus of fragmentation, represent a remarkable example of unity, rule of law, and economic progress. Indeed, highly internationalised countries and financial urban HUBs such as Hong Kong, China, the United Arab Emirates, Liechtenstein, Dubai, and others share a common quality of economic development, security, and political stability. In contrast, a substantial portion of countries or regions that have lagged in experiencing processes of trade liberalisation and technological progress will soon or later end up being affected by domestic and international forces that separate the population and aim to profit from radical division. This relevant comparative advantage in ideological discussion and factual reality over globalisation reveals the role of radical ideology in the process of state fragmentation and how long-term processes of indoctrination end up replacing historical divisions by ideological polarisation, such as in Latin America and even contemporary North America.

The most important period to understand the process of violence and state fragmentation in Colombia goes back to the years 1948–1957, when the two major parties translated their hostility into criminal actions directed at the towns and municipalities in the countryside. This period has been commonly known as "The Violence" and was finalised in 1958 with a political agreement between the two main political parties, the "Liberals" and the "Conservatives." Some years later, the processes of international communism's expansion influenced numerous peripheral groups in the country, constituting the main prominent terrorist organisations in the territory. Over time, the so-called "guerrillas" in Colombia became the most important radical organisations against civil society and the government, conforming to institutionalised structures of plain violence to threaten the state with their demands and intimidating and recruiting the underage population in the countryside. Among the biggest guerrillas, one can mention the FARC, the ELN, and the EPL. The territorial actions of these groups, however, remained constant within the periphery and rural territories. It was just by the end of the '70s, with the increasing production of cocaine and marihuana in the Antioquia region (Aguirre & Soto, 2015: 148–169), that a former FARC terrorist, Jaime Bateman, founded the M19th, the single most organised group of urban terrorism in Latin America.

In the case of Peru, the terrorist guerrilla "Shining Path" was officially founded in 1980 with the prominent role of the communist leader Abimael Guzman. Guzmán, a former professor of rhetoric and philosophy in highland Per and later a Chinese-trained Marxist-Leninist-Maoist, gained notoriety during the 1980s and 1990s as the leader behind Shining Path. Guzmán argued that the Soviet Union collapsed because of its inability to sustain puritanical Marxism. He called these failed revolutionaries "revisionists" and "liquidationists." To Guzmán, "revisionists" did grave injustices to Marx, Lenin, and Mao by detouring the world's destiny with revolution. Guzmán was so uncompromising with his rhetoric that he even criticised Mao Tse-tung for being "too soft" during the cultural revolution (Marcus, 1993). The background of Peru shares a similar origin with that of Colombia but is better explained by the regional background of Soviet Union intervention in the continent after the end of the Second World War. This explains why Since the early 1950s, US involvement in the region has been geared towards eradicating Marxist-Leninist philosophy, which has enjoyed fertile popularity among the poverty-stricken classes in those countries. Indeed, some of these policies continued all over the 90th century, when even the most recent organisations were able to consistently fund the military capacity of numerous countries in the region to overtake narcotrafficker subversion in countries like Colombia (Williams, 2008: 49–65). This is because years before the US intervention, Cuba, Nicaragua, Bolivia, Argentina, Mexico, and Perú had all had military alliances with the former Soviet Union, which worked to expand its version of Marxist-Leninist doctrine to the Western Hemisphere.

In both cases, the long-term projects of indoctrination were initiated by bringing neo-Marxist theory to the context and field features of the new territory, adapting the principal thesis of communism to peripheric regions on the verge of political or economic collapse. As such, the communist guerrillas perfected the Soviet strategies by dividing the population into different ethnographic, territorial, and cultural groups. This process was conducted by fitting the theories and main revolutionary subjects of Marxism into propaganda and by recruiting public intellectuals familiar with and acquainted with the international goals of the communist regimes in Cuba and the Soviet Union. Over time, the process of indoctrination of the different radical militias was complemented by the massive recruitment of thousands of minors, substantially increasing their size and their capacity to attack the population. Although during the 1970s, these techniques were able to attract ever-increasing members to the different terrorist groups of the country, it was not until the 1980s, with the rise of the illegal drug trade and the so-called war on drugs (Tambs, 1997: 758), that the terrorist groups multiplied along different regions of the territory, becoming a domestic and international security threat.

THE MEDELLIN CARTEL ALLIANCE WITH THE URBAN TERRORISM OF M19 WAS THE BEGINNING OF LARGE-SCALE URBAN TERROR

The narcoterrorism alliance between the Medellin Cartel, led by Pablo Escobar, and the urban terrorist group M19 goes back to the origins of the M19 and how increasing territorial control pushed forward in Colombia the necessity of marihuana and cocaine crop owners to create private paramilitary groups that became soon the modern terrorist guerrillas such as the M19 and FARC. Indeed, the M19 group was created by militants from the drug trafficking organisation FARC, mainly by the Colombian kidnapper Carlos Pizarro in association with Jaime Bateman. Over the years, Pizarro León Gómez and Bateman led the most accelerated urban kidnapping process of the 1980s at the head of the M19, overcoming the kidnappings of the Medellín Cartel (led by Pablo Escobar) and the Cali Cartel (led by the Orejuela brothers) (Berg, 2010: 97).

The ideological device to make "guerrillas" develop all over Latin America, and especially in Colombia, was boosted by a mixture of Marxist ideology reconfigured and expanded by the regional diplomatic record of communist Cuba, which served as the geographical node of the expansion of the former Soviet Union's influence. Indeed, over time, Cuba became the main centre of operation for numerous Marxist radical organisations that operated in Colombia, becoming the single most important meeting point for terrorist groups such as the M19 (March 19), the FARC (Colombian Revolutionary Army Forces), and the ELN (National Liberation Army).

Among the different terrorist organisations, the M19 rapidly became the main kidnapping group in Latin America on an industrial scale. Over the years, M19 became Pablo Escobar's main ally in urban terrorism, being financed by the drug trafficker to execute the holocaust of the Palace of Justice, where the M19 murdered and burned 11 Magistrates of the Constitutional Court of Colombia as a military retaliation against the occupation of the Colombian military in the Palace (Duncan, 2013: 235).

The terrorist group M19's extortion activity peaked between 1980 and 1985, with former Conservative Party presidential candidate Lvaro Gómez Hurtado standing out among the victims. The information has been compiled for years by Colombian institutions such as the Historical Memory Centre (Gómez et al., 2013), where it is recounted in detail how the M19, much above the Medellin Cartel, became the first terrorist kidnapping organisation in Colombia, long before Pablo Escobar, who later on financially funded the M19, took the decision to create the group "Death to Kidnappers," known in Colombia with the initials MAS (Bialowas, 2007: 194).

The Report of the National Centre for Historical Minorities, "A Kidnapped Society," indicates how the kidnapping became for the M19 the main source of financial and extortion pressure, far exceeding the FARC, the Medellin Cartel, the paramilitaries, the ELN, or the former known terrorist organisation EPL.

"When kidnapping appeared as a phenomenon within Colombian society in the decades of the 1970s and 1980s, an average of 113 cases were reported per year. By this time, the guerrillas had become the main protagonists. In this period, this activity was carried out predominantly by the M-19, which at that historical moment combined political and propaganda motivations with economic ends. Although the number of kidnappings at that time was less than that observed in subsequent decades, the kidnappings of José Raquel Mercado, President of the Confederation of Colombian Workers; Hugo Ferreira Neira, former minister of agriculture; and Álvaro Gómez Hurtado, conservative leader and politician, caused a profound impact on public opinion at the time" (Gómez et al., 2010).

Furthermore, "the M-19 had an essentially urban action, which differentiated it from the other guerrillas. It quickly incurred the crime of kidnapping and maintained it as a line of action until it entered negotiations with the government of President Virgilio Barco, culminating with its demobilisation in 1990. In the beginning of the urban terrorist group (1970–1999), the M19 represented by far along the American continent the main terrorist kidnapper in the hemisphere, being the main author of this crime with 557 kidnappings. The largest number occurred in 1980 and 1985, with 208 and 213, respectively" (Sanchez, 1999: 29).

Additionally, the M19 was logistically and militarily supported by Cuba. This information was later revealed by a recognised former terrorist leader of the group, stating how: "Fidel Castro helped the M19 in many of his" interventions "in Colombia ... and it must even be said that the M19 troops were trained in Cuba, which became a source of separation of the Colombian government with the Cuban government, ending diplomatic relations of both countries" (UNIVISION, 1998).

Textually, the peak of the extortion activity of the terrorist group M19 took place between the years of 1980 and 1985, with among the victims the assassinated unionist José Raquel Mercado, president of the Confederation of Workers of Colombia (CTC), the former presidential candidate of the Party Conservative, Álvaro Gómez Hurtado, Camila Michelsen, and others, among dozens of citizens.

According to the report of the National Centre for Historical Memory, the M19 converted extortion into kidnapping as the main source of financing for military, logistical, and weapons resources. In this type of terrorist activity, the group focused mainly on the commission of kidnappings and urban extortions, with operations mainly in Bogota, Medellín, Zipaquirá (Cundinamarca), and Cali (Serrano, 2003).

As such, the first of the five periods of analysis by the Colombian authorities to track the path of the group begins in 1970 and ends in 1989. During those years, the country experienced a very rapid expansion of violence, leading to the conformation of various self-called "guerrilla organisations," which rapidly entered into bargaining processes and war disputes over the exclusion and dispute of territories with paramilitary groups. "This period represented the beginnings of the kidnapping industry, when this crime was not yet a real threat to the Colombian state or to society in general" (Sanchez, 1999: 29).

It is at this point that the M19 became, over the years, the paramilitary group chosen by the Medellín Cartel, led by Pablo Escobar, to carry out urban terrorism tasks at scales never known in the western hemisphere (Davis, 2014). In addition to profiting from the kidnapping, the organisation also had financial and operational alliances with the Medellín Cartel and retaliation processes with the drug trafficking group known as the "Familia Ochoa Vasquez," which kidnapped one of the clan's women. Over time, the most brutal terrorist leaders of the M19 transformed the guerrilla into a criminal urban organisation. Indeed, most of the foundational figures of the M19 escaped from another well-known terrorist and narcotrafficking group known as the FARC. Over time, the different criminal members of the organisation gathered around the leader, Jaime Bateman, who was the first to understand leverage and apply the practise of kidnapping in its entirety as "Commander in Chief" of the M-19.

"The M-19 refined and reshaped politically the practise of kidnapping, which they used to call the method of 'revolutionary retention', to dimensions unknown to guerrilla groups at the time. Its objectives were political, propagandistic, and economic. Other guerrilla groups quickly adopted this practise, and kidnapping became an uncontrollable epidemic for Colombian authorities in the 1990s. (...) The evidence of infiltration also came to light in the case of the Colombian Jewish community. In 1984, the M-19 and ELN guerrilla groups began kidnapping wealthy businessmen and industrialists from the Jewish community who had purchased insurance policies in their names from English companies. (...) The groups managed to infiltrate the archives with this information through another member of the Jewish community and thus obtained the list of beneficiaries and the sum for which they were insured. Between 1984 and 1989, more than 40 kidnappings occurred, one after another, of insured members of the Jewish community. And in all these cases, the negotiator between the family and the kidnappers was the same man: Victor Sassón" (Sanchez, 1999). These suspicious extortions came to an end after the murder of Sassón, who is believed to have leaked the information to the guerrillas in the first place.

With the increasing military and financial strength of the drug trafficker Pablo Escobar, the M19 became for Escobar the single most useful urban paramilitary group of the Cartel. As such, urban terrorism began to grow throughout the country. At this juncture, different subversive groups, in alliances with drug trafficking organisations, began executing urban sensational terrorist actions to differentiate themselves from other criminal bands and open the possibility of getting different treatment from the authorities. Among the different groups, the brutal methods of the M19, which quickly converted the organisation into the most dangerous kidnapping machine in all of Colombia's history up to that time, achieved the political goal of intimidating the state, asking for a process of amnesty and "negotiation" after years of terror.

Thus, the alliance between the Medellín Cartel, led by Pablo Escobar Gaviria, and the M19 reached its culmination of precision with the joint work of the holocaust of the Palace of Justice, which Escobar valued for the atrocious brutality and coldness that the M19 used when operating in urban areas. Moreover, Escobar's alliances after the enormous subversive growth of the M19 were not limited to the holocaust of the Palace of Justice of Colombia, since even before, it was reported that the M19 mobilised all over the country in the aircraft of the well-known drug trafficker.

Once the murder of union leader Jose Raquel Mercado and the kidnapping in Medellín of Martha Nieves Ochoa (a family member of the Ochoa Mafia) occurred, "a drug war against the guerrilla group began, which almost determined its extinction in Antioquia. Later on, an agreement was reached between both parties, the Medellin Cartel and M19, settling a new era of relations between the two groups" (Rozema, 2009).

Likewise, increasingly, a new set of alliances resulting from Escobar's clandestine meetings with the M19, mainly in Panama, define the future of urban terrorism in Colombia on a scale that surpasses any historical background on the continent. "With the death of the M-19 commander, Jaime Bateman, a meeting with Pablo Escobar in Panama was thwarted," leading to a subsequent meeting in which the M-19 would begin to receive money from this cartel: "Between 1984 and 1985, members of the M-19 leadership met with Pablo Escobar in Medellin, receiving money from that cartel" (Ortiz, 2017).

Additionally, "Iván Marino Ospina, before and after his expulsion as the top commander of the M19, maintained until his death, which occurred in August 1985, a close friendship and unity of action with Pablo Escobar (Vallejo, 2020), and was the only one authorised by the movement to hold meetings with him." As M-19 commander, Ospina agreed with members of the Medellin Cartel that "for every Colombian extradited to the United States, a US citizen in Colombia would be assassinated" (Rubio, 2008).

Finally, during the territorial and urban dominance of the M19, its main objective of subversive dominance was configured in an orchestrated plan with the Medellin Cartel to take over the Palace of Justice in Colombia. The main goal of the brutal attack on the institutions of the country was to burn and disappear the judiciary records of both the Medellin Cartel and the M19. As such, "in mid-1985, members of the M-19 met again with Pablo Escobar, and when Álvaro Fayad succeeded Ospina in the direction of the M-19, the joint actions of both criminal organisations continued." At the time, "John Jairo Velásquez Vásquez, nicknamed 'Popeye,' declared to the Truth Commission that his" boss, "Pablo Escobar, initially paid the M-19 two million dollars for the capture of the Palace of Justice, giving the money directly to Iván Marino Ospina" (Velazquez, 2006).

In this way, the social influence of the drug trafficking cartels of Antioquia and El Valle in Colombia was quickly displaced by the coordinated operations of urban terrorism led by the M19, which over the years gave the group the power to exert pressure over a population terrorised and a government cornered by the group's targeted killings, extortion, and kidnappings.

THE EVOLUTIONARY PATH OF URBAN TERRORIST ACTION AND IDEOLOGY ON THE PERUVIAN SHINING PATH

The process of incorporation of ideological concealment has a fundamental launching scenario with the increasing influence of Marxism as the doctrinarian justification for Latin American subversion. Among the different organisations, and besides the industrial scale of Colombian narcoguerrillas, Peru experienced for many years the increasing impact of the Shining Path terrorist group. The background of the increasing territorial expansion of terrorist groups deals with the political background of the region and the increasing influence of the former Soviet Union to expand the implementation of "revolutionary" action all over the continent. Indeed, during the 1960s, Cuba, Nicaragua, Bolivia, Argentina, Mexico, and Peru all had military alliances with the former Soviet Union, which worked to expand its version of Marxist-Leninist doctrine to the Western Hemisphere (Berrios & Blaiser, 1991).[1] However, even in the face of Marxism-Leninism's popularity among Central and South America's impoverished, most US and Latin American economists agree upon the politically correct need to "democratise" the continent. These policy recommendations were also rooted in South America's potential as a source of raw materials (Cobban, 1992) and the increasing influence of oil in the global economy. During the 1970s, South America possessed natural resources that were in high demand. Petroleum research teams predicted that the upper basins of the continent contained enough crude oil to end US dependence on the Arab-dominated Oil Producing and Exporting Countries (OPEC) (Williams, 1992).[2,3] Lumber from the continent's Amazon forests, while an environmental concern, has the potential to reduce worldwide housing costs (Schneider, 1992). Moreover, during the same period, advances in agrarian technology produced some of the most plentiful crops in South America's farming history (Hockstader, 1992). In addition, deposits of precious metals and diamonds remain impressive despite extensive exploitation by Spain and Britain. Regardless, it was openly acknowledged that South America's inability to maintain stable political institutions hindered her economic development (DiTella, 1990).

Moreover, having historically vacillated from regime to regime since their so-called discovery by European explorers, South American leaders, citizens, and businesspeople yearn for institutional consistency (Peart, 1993; Manning, 1993; Vargas-Llosa, 1992). Having historically vacillated from regime to regime since their so-called discovery by European explorers, South American leaders, citizens, and businesspeople yearn for institutional consistency (Manning, 1993; Vargas-Llosa, 1992). Central to the problem in Peru is the fact that the nation is pitted against itself racially, religiously, and ideologically (Schamis, 1991; Farer, 1991). South American Indians, white and black Hispanics, and immigrants from Japan and China are all constituents of a national populace divided by two opposing belief systems – Incan and Catholic. These social, political, and ultimately economic problems have erupted into a cycle of violence between a peasant-based Maoist revolt and a militia that historically eschews civilian rule. As a result, "some of the worst (human rights) violations in recent years have taken place during civil wars in ... Perú" (Human Rights: Journal, 1993).

Hailed by international comrades as the Peruvian Communist Party (PCP), the Maoist insurgency "Sendero Luminoso," or "Sendero," is better known in the English-speaking world by the direct translation of its name: "Shining Path." Relentless, violent, and uncompromising, Shining Path is directly responsible for approximately 26,500 terrorist-related deaths and more than $26 billion in economic destruction over fourteen years (Marcus, 1993; Brooke, 1993).

On May 18, 1992, at an emergency Executive Council meeting of the Organisation of American States (O.A.S.) in Nassau, Bahamas, Fujimori presented his case. He could not combat the Shining Path in a cocaine-dominated democracy. Perú's drug cartels were financially supporting socialist candidates for office. Consequently, Fujimori announced the temporary abrogation of Per's judiciary, the suspension of parts of the Constitution, and the dismissal of Congress. He justified these actions by stating, "Terrorist groups in Perú are most interested in a return to the old democracy, so that sooner rather than later, they will be able to impose their own leaders" (Fujimori, 1992).

While Fujimori singlehandedly assumed responsibility for the nation, the Revolutionary Front began to intensify its activities. Abimael Guzmán, a former professor of rhetoric and philosophy in highland Perú and later a Chinese-trained Marxist-Leninist-Maoist, gained notoriety during the 1980s and 1990s as the visionary behind Shining Path. Guzmán argued that the Soviet Union collapsed because of its inability to sustain puritanical Marxism. In his book *Shining Path: Terror and Revolution in Perú*, Strong detailed Guzmán's grand design to overthrow the government of Perú:

> Guzmán aims to unite industrial workers, the peasantry, and the petty and middle bourgeoisie (by which he means both its public and private sectors). The driving force of the revolution is the peasantry and the poorest of the urban poor who together form the bulk of the party, the People's Guerrilla Army, and the People's Committees, which are to be the backbone of the People's Republic of New Democracy (Strong, 1993: 84).

While still hailed by dogmatic followers as "The Fourth Sword of Communism," "Punka Inti" (Red Sun), or "Comrade Gonzalo," Guzmán can no longer coordinate his People's Revolution. Strong recounts, "On the night of Saturday, September 12, 1992, Abimael Guzmán was arrested by antiterrorist police in Lima" (Strong 1993: 267). Guzmán's location was determined through extensive monitoring and connections inside the movement. Antiterrorist police confirmed his whereabouts by identifying tubes used for psoriasis medication and Winston cigarette butts in his garbage. Following the capture, Strong predicted, "Guzmán's capture will probably mean that Shining Path will never come to power" (Strong, 1993: 269). In December of 1990, Fujimori vowed to crush Shining Path by August 1995, and in five months he had made considerable progress. That first attempt to control the situation in Peru converted the Shinning Path into the single most sophisticated terrorist group in the country, with the goal of reclaiming the lost territory acquired by Fujimori's administration. As such, it was necessary for the terrorist group to focus on more repeated and more spectacular urban terrorist attacks directed at the population, which were prepared with months of anticipation and finally deployed starting in 1992.

On July 15, more than 35 small bombs detonated in the southern province of Ayacucho. Using the explosions as a diversion tactic, Shining Path robbed a bank, killing six police officers and one civilian in the process (Reuters, 1992). That next morning, another car bomb went off in a middle-class Lima suburb, killing three civilians (Reuters, 1992). In sync with the car bombing, approximately 100 Sendero attacked six different police stations with grenades and automatic machine-gun fire, eliminating ten police officers. Lima's perceptual tranquility was misleading; apparently, the silence was the calm before the storm.

On July 17, Shining Path tossed bombs out of a moving vehicle in an upper-middle-class Lima neighbourhood (Silva, 1992b; Mylrea, 1992). However, the most damaging of these attacks came when two car bombs, a reported total of about 1,320 pounds of dynamite, were discharged. Silva recounted police reports:

> The bombs, the worst in 12 years of political violence in Perú, ripped through two narrow streets, completely demolishing two buildings, one eight stories high. The force of the explosion blew out windows and doors in another 30 buildings, leaving the streets littered with concrete, glass, and bodies of the dead and injured (Silva, 1992b; Press, 1992).

A bomb squad happened upon a third car loaded with dynamite parked one block from the detonated bomb site, disarming it before any damage could occur. Nevertheless, Sendero's notorious red brochures had blown past police forces into onlooking crowds, calling for a renewed assault against "the capitalist oppressors."

Two days later, security forces found an overturned automobile filled with explosives one block away from another police station (United Press, 1992b). The car, which apparently went off the road due to excessive speed, had been abandoned by Shining Path terrorists. Dincoté released no details concerning the amount of explosives found in the vehicle.

In an act of desperation, more than three thousand of Lima's residents gathered at the bomb site for a peace vigil (United Press, 1992a). Holding candles, peace symbols, and white flags, the demonstrators pleaded with Shining Path to stop bombing Lima, asking for an end to the 12-year-old insurgency. A United Press International newswire reported that a Catholic priest urged Peruvians to "pray for peace and hope that Jesus Christ enlightens the souls possessed by the devil" (United Press, 1992b). However, what the citizens of Lima and the priest did not understand was that they were the enemy; their annihilation was part of Shining Path's progression towards a Marxist-Leninist-Maoist-Gonzaloist utopia.

Following the public cry for peace, Shining Path torched a textile plant and gutted seven of Per's regional banks on July 20 (United Press, 1992a). Later that evening, Shining Path also car-bombed Hernando de Soto's Institute for Liberty and Democracy, killing two researchers and a young woman (Mylrea, 1992; Notimex, 1992). The former economic advisor to Fujimori, de Soto, was not inside the building.

Fujimori had planned to go to the Ibero-American Summit in Madrid on July 21 to lure investment initiatives into Perú. However, given Shining Path's recent offensives and announcement of another armed strike on July 22 and 23, Fujimori decided to stay (United Press International, 1992; Coya, 1992; Mylrea, 1992). A press release issued by the president's office noted that Fujimori was not going to the summit because "he needed to remain in Peru to lead the anti-terrorist fight" (United Press International, 1992).

Using de Soto's Institute for Liberty and Democracy as a stepping stone for more symbolically charged terror, Sendero restructured its campaign to include international targets. Making good on their armed strike, Shining Path also set more than forty cars ablaze and bombed three schools on July 22 (Cam, 1992). The guerrillas also promoted their agenda to derail the state through more extreme measures: tricycles rigged with dynamite were left on elementary school playgrounds; mines accompanying Peruvian Communist Party banners and flags planted alongside the highway detonated when state supporters removed them from the ground; rebels dropped grenades into automatic change counters at highway tollbooths; and Senderistas tossed sticks of dynamite into restaurants and supermarkets.

Shining Path expanded their mayhem throughout Lima and her outlying suburbs on July 23 (Silva, 1992a; Star Tribune, 1992). With the government at the whim of Shining Path's invisible attack, Fujimori had only two courses of action: (1) continue his strategy to uproot Sendero selectively while guerrillas were at ease, or (2) unleash the military against the slums in which Shining Path camouflaged itself. Many Peruvians, feeling that they could die just as easily at home as they could at work, decided to go to work anyway (Independent, 1992). "The hell with it all!" said one factory worker. Radio stations began running public service announcements for potential bomb attack victims: "Lie down, open your mouth, and shout when you see the bomb's flash" (Dillon, 1992). For the first time, Peruvians began to wonder whether order existed.

The overarching influence of urban terror led by Shinning Path represented a point of no return for the Peruvian authorities, unable to cope with the multifaceted attack of the terrorist group. It was precisely in this setting that the leading role of the Fujimori administration gained popular support for combating terror with intelligence operations that finally led to the capture of Abimael Guzman. In any case, the level of institutional impact led by the terrorist organisation, as well as the desperation of the administration to control among the attacks the level of expansion and influence of Shinning Path, derived in a period of political crisis, further affected Fujimori's record. Today, however, after decades of terror, Peru has become a political and economic leader in the region, leaving behind the path of ideological concealment and radicalisation endorsed by the Shining Path and rearranging their cultural background far away from the increasing influence of Marxist ideology that dominated the continent all over the 70th decade.

CONCLUSION

The long-term process of social fragmentation led by terrorist organisations operates by instrumentalizing well-known indoctrinatory narratives within the population. Over the past decades, this process has consistently operated in the western hemisphere using Marxist theory, an ideological corpus made public by the end of the 19th century. Through the implementation or reinterpretation of Marxism, radical organisations built up systematically a politically biassed storyline of social events in Latin America, pointing out single cases of power relations as a grand narrative for political action. At the core of every attempt to instrumentalize ideology into a political category, the terrorist fulfils at least three strategic goals: social fragmentation, activism, and terrorist action justification. In all cases, organisations such as terrorist or narcotrafficker organisations profited from the lack of capacity of the population and the government to realise the long-term impact of state fragmentation and long-term processes of indoctrination, much of which is developed by arranging and rearranging radical revolutionary ideology into the marginalised population (Vásquez & Díkaion, 2013). Over time, Marxism became the single most important ideological device for radical subversion all over the western hemisphere, being instrumentalized in terrorist organisations funded and supported by Cuba and later expanding all over the region in Colombia, Mexico, Nicaragua, Venezuela, Peru, and Honduras, among others.

In all cases, ideology served as the main point of intellectual encounter for radicalised members of already fragmented societies unable to cope with the demands of a late industrial process of development, affecting numerous economically disadvantaged countries in the Latin American region. Decades later, cocaine production and cannabis exports boosted the capacity of terrorist organisations to dominate the territory and the institutional landscape in the hemisphere, which later became a scenario of urban warfare led by organisations such as the Medellin Cartel of Pablo Escobar, the M19, and the Shining Path, among others (Mendirichaga, 2016).

This chapter raises attention to the practises, ideological devices, main urban operational actions, and increasing political advantages of two well-recognised terrorist groups, the M19 in Colombia and the Shining Path in Peru. In both cases, Marxist theoretical devices and Cuban subversion practises served as the starting point of events that can be called the genesis of western urban terrorism, directed and imposed over the Latin American population by those same groups. The level of precision of urban operations and the capacity of political destabilisation led by the two terrorist organisations define the before and after of the western hemisphere war on terror, as well as the necessary academic advice for governments and enforcement institutions eager to overcome the current threats of ideology, social fragmentation, and terrorist organisations in the western hemisphere. Moreover, the historical operational data shared in this chapter becomes a substantial tool for security experts eager to understand the sophistication and historical background of new and upcoming radicalised urban organisations, many of which aim to continue profiting from the lack of understanding of contemporary urban subversion.

Notes

1 Utilising low-interest loan guarantees to purchase Soviet arms and ammunition, Latin American nations were able to militarise. United States equipment was not sold to certain nations in the region due to the Hickenlooper and Pelly Amendments barring the nationalisation of US businesses. Europe's arms were expensive and carried heavy interest schedules. Latin America's only option became the Soviet Union. Mechanised equipment further required Soviet support and parts. Hence, a foothold for Soviet assistance was established in the late 1960s and early 1970s.

2 Although several key South American countries, like Venezuela, are already members of OPEC, the untapped petroleum resources could make some of the continent's nations major players inside the organisation or even allow some to claim autonomy.

3 A22; opening one's mouth and yelling tightens the abdominal muscles, creating a natural layer of armour.

References

Aguirre, J., & A. Soto. (2015). Narcoparamilitary, illicit economy and social order in the municipality of Itagüí, Antioquia: Women, children and youth in the complex dynamics of the local. *Boletín de Antropología; Medellín, 30*(50), 148–169.

Associated Press. (1992). At least 18 die in Lima bomb blast: Terrorism: 140 people are injured in attack blamed on leftist Sendero Luminoso rebels. July 18.

Berg, P.D. (2010). Killing Pablo: The hunt for the world's greatest outlaw. *USAF.Air & Space Power Journal; Maxwell AFB, 24*(2), (Summer), 97–98.

Berrios, R., & C. Blaiser. (1991, May 23). Perú and the Soviet Union (1969–1989): Distant partners. *Journal of Latin American Studies, 23*(3), 365–384.

Bialowas, A. (2007). El patrón: vida y muerte de Pablo Escobar. Los archivos privados. *Chasqui; Tempe, 36*(1), (May), 194–196.

Brooke, J. (1993). Perú's leader clears a path with sharp elbows, New York Times 22 Feb: A3.

Cam. (1992). "Shining Path Rebels" newswire report; "Perú Guerrillas Step up Fight" newswire report.

Cobban, H. (1992). Leaving Washington to Search for America's Future, Christian Science Monitor 12 Aug 1993: 19; Hubert L. Valdermo and Fernando G. Fernandini, "Perú Climbs on the Chilean Bandwagon," Benefits and Compensation International 21 (Mar).

Coya, H. (1992). Latin summit Grapples with free enterprise. United Press International 21 July.

Davis, R. (2014). Documentary constructions of Filial memory in Nathaniel Kahn's My Architect and Nicolás Entel's My Father, Pablo Escobar. *Journal of Film and Video; Englewood, 66*(1), (Spring), 52–61.

Dillon, S. (1992). More bombings fuel fear of Peruvian government losing control. Houston Chronicle 24 July.

DiTella, T.S. (1990). *Latin American politics: A theoretical framework*. Austin: University of Texas Press, pp. 83–102.

Duncan, G. (2013). A political approach on Pablo Escobar. *Duncan, Gustavo.Co-herencia; Medellín, 10*(19), (Jul–Dec), 235–262.

Farer, T.J. (1991). Human rights investment in South America: Retrospect and prospect. *Human Rights Quarterly, 13*(Feb 1991), 99–122.

Fujimori, A. (1992). "O.A.S. Address," British Broadcasting Corporation 20 May: newswire.

Gómez, A.N., F. Flórez, A. Soto, & A.M. Van Broeck. (2013). La Catedral y Montecasino: ¿espacios para las memorias ciudadanas y espejos del Estado colombiano? *Gómez, Alba Nelly; Flórez, Franz; Soto, Andrés; Van Broeck, Anne-Marie. Boletín de Antropología; Medellín, 28*(45), 104–129.

Gómez, J.A., J.R. Herrera, & N. Pinilla. (2010). *Informe Final de Comisión de la verdad sobre los hechos del Palacio de Justicia Gómez Gallego, Jorge Aníbal; Herrera Vergara, José Roberto; Pinilla Pinilla, Nilson*. Bogota: Universidad del Rosario.

Hockstader, L. (1992). Europeans, Latins split on price of bananas. Washington Post 1 July 1992: A1; Sandra Evans, "Smithsonian Display Shows Worldwide Appeal of Potatoes," Washington Post 22 Mar: B5.

Human Rights: Journal. (1993). Stated in "Life often grim for Indians, study confirms". *Human Rights: Journal of the Section of Human Rights and Responsibilities, 20*(Dec), 4.

Independent. (1992). Defiant Peruvians ignore strike call. 24 July 1992: 12.

Manning, S. (1993). Can democracy survive? Scholastic Update 125 (12 Feb).

Marcus, D. (1993). What made perú's most feared terrorist change his mind? *Montreal Gazette*, 28 Nov: B5.

Marcus, D.L. (1993). What made perú's most feared terrorist change his mind? *Montreal Gazette*.

Mendirichaga, J.R. (2016). More than silver or lead. *The political power of drug trafficking in Colombia and Mexico. Iconos; Quito, 20*(2), (May 2016), 243–245. 10.17141/iconos.55.2016.1871.

Mylrea, P. (1992). Perú president pulls out of Ibero-American summit after bombs. July 21.

Notimex. (1992). New wave of terrorist attacks in Peruvian capital. Notimex 20 July.

Ortiz, J. (2017). La toma del Palacio de Justicia y el cartel de Medellín. La Campana.

Peart, K. (1993). Filled with hope, fraught with danger. *Scholastic Update 125* (12 Feb), 4–5.

Reuters. (1992). Guerrillas Kill Seven in Perú, Fujimori Launches Militia. Reuters 15 July: newswire report.

Rozema, R. (2009). Jennifer S. Holmes, Sheila Amin Gutiérrez de Piñeres and Kevin M. Curtin, Guns, Drugs and Development in Colombia (Austin: University of Texas Press, 2008), pp. xiv+192, $55.00, hb. *Journal of Latin American Studies, 41*(4), 836–838. 10.1017/s0022216x09990812.

Rubio, M. (2008). Secuestro, narcotráfico y otras audacias del M-19. Hagale hermano. Borrador de Método No. 53. ISSN: 1692-9667 Grupo Transdisciplinario de Investigacion en Ciencias Sociales.

Sanchez, G. (1999). Informe del Centro Nacional de Memoria Historica. Una sociedad Secuestrada.

Schamis, H.E. (1991). Reconceptualizing Latin American authoritarianism in the 70s. *Comparative Politics, 23*(Jan), 201–220.

Schneider, R.M. (1992). Africa, Asia, and Latin America – Amazon conservation in the age of development. *Annals of the American Academy of Political and Social Science, 524*(Nov), 1–11.

Serrano, R.J. (2003, July). Capturing the Cali cartel: Selections from Jaque Mate. *Crime, Law and Social Change; Dordrecht, 40*(1), 43+. 10.1023/A:1024985702002.

Silva. (1992a). Rebel Bombings Rip. newswire report.

Silva, V. (1992b). Rebel bombings rip through downtown Lima, 21 dead. United Press International 17 July.

Star Tribune. (1992). Lima is disrupted as rebels enforces call for strike. Star Tribune 23 July.

Strong, S. (1993). Shining path: Terror and revolution in Peru. Crown; 1st U.S. ed edición.

Tambs, L.A. (1997). Unintended consequences: Illegal drugs and drug policies in nine countries. *The Hispanic American Historical Review; Durham 77*(4), (Nov), 758–759.

United Press. (1992a). Thousands march. United Press International: newswire report.

United Press. (1992b). Thousands march to bomb site to pray for peace. United Press International 19 July: newswire report.

United Press International. (1992). Perú president cancels trip to Ibero-American Summit. 21 July: newswire report.

UNIVISION. (1998). UNIVISION. Archivos. M19. "Fidel Castro ayudó al M19 en muchas de sus operaciones en Colombia. Incluso(...) hay que decirlo, en Cuba se entrenaron tropas del M19(...)," Declaracion a periodistas de cabecilla. Petro Gustavo.

Vallejo, V. (2020). United States Court Of Appeals For The Eleventh Circuit. No. 19-14894. D.C. Docket No. 1:18-cv-23462-RS.

Vargas-Llosa, M. (1992). "Cherish Liberty," Vital Speeches of the Day 58 (1 Oct 1992): 755–9; Reding: 409–15.

Vásquez, T., & H. Díkaion. (2013). Transnational organized crime in Colombia. *Chia, 22*(1), 109–130.

Velazquez, V.J.J. (2006). Revista Semana. Los secretos de Popeye con Pablo Escobar.

Williams, B. (1992). Latin American petroleum sector at crossroads. Oil and Gas Journal 90 (6 July 1992): 43–45; Jimmy Weiskopf, "The Americas: Colombia's Crude Mix of Oil Rights and 'Magic Realism,'" Wall Street Journal 17 Jan: A11.

Williams, M. (2008). The Bush administration, debt relief, and the war on terror: Reforming the international development system as part of the neoconservative project. *S.Social Justice; San Francisco, 35*(3), (2008/2009), 49–65.

11

BLENDING COUNTERINSURGENCY TO DEFEAT HYBRID THREATS

Paul Lushenko, Srinjoy Bose, and Scott N. Romaniuk

INTRODUCTION

The relationship between counterterrorism and counter-insurgency, while not a new subject of inquiry, continues to confound scholars and practitioners. Experts concur that both constitute pervasive practises of irregular warfare, understood as 'warfare *unregulated* by the laws and norms of war' (Ucko & Marks, 2018, 212). Little other agreement exists, and a conceptual consensus continues to evade the literature and military doctrine. On one side of the debate, Daniel Byman conceives the two approaches as mutually constitutive, arguing that 'there is no clear dividing line and, in fact, tremendous overlap exists.' In the same breath, he concedes that 'terrorism and insurgency overlap as concepts, but they are not identical' (2005, 5–6). On the other side of the debate, Douglas Porch contends that counterterrorism and counterinsurgency are not separate categories of warfare as such but differ according to commanders' application of tactics (2013, 318). David Ucko and Thomas Marks intone that these countervailing positions are altogether 'secondary to the implications raised by the distinction,' although the use of military force for counterterrorism and insurgency is often theorised under the banner of separate and distinct 'isms,' if for nothing more than parsimony (Ucko & Marks, 2018, 208; Ucko, 2009). Several factors account for the bifurcation between counterterrorism and counterinsurgency warfare. These include, *inter alia*, the intended purpose of force, force employment methodologies and their effects, the scope of targets, and the anticipated duration of operations.

Counterterrorism is predicated on the lethal application of force, including raids and the so-called 'precision strikes' from unmanned aerial vehicles, also referred to as drones, against a terrorist network's critical requirements. Arguably, international society's campaign to defeat the Islamic State (IS) across Central and South Asia, as well as the Middle East, has codified cyber-attacks against a terrorist network's computer network infrastructure and communications protocols more broadly as a form of counterterrorism. Shane Harris' analysis of the emergence of a 'military-Internet complex' finds that the US military 'now thinks cyber weapons are not so different from missiles, bombs, and bullets' (2014, 59). Forrest B. Hare concurs. 'Precision should by now be the accepted and expected norm in cyberspace as well' (2019, 194).[1] Notwithstanding the exact method, the employment of surgical force is designed to kill or capture combatants and enabling material based on the assumption that their removal will enable a terrorist network's defeat by preventing its attempts to instill fear among a vulnerable population to achieve political objectives.

Counterinsurgency warfare, on the other hand, is designed to redress the normative appeal of insurgents among a milieu of sympathisers and prospective recruits to maintain a pre-existing political order. America's experiences in Afghanistan and Iraq have largely biased the theory and practise of counterinsurgency warfare and encouraged revisionist analyses of the American War of Independence (1775–1783) and subsequent Civil War (1861–1865), as well as the British occupation of Malay to contend with the Malayan National Liberation Army (1948–1966), as sterling examples of a particular brand of counterinsurgency warfare consigned as 'population-centric.' Among the corpus of this rendition, which Gian Gentile explains 'aims to win the hearts and minds of local populations' (2013, 2), John Nagl's book, *Learning to Eat Soup with a Knife: Counterinsurgency Lessons from Malaya and Vietnam* (2005), is the canonical account. As opposed to the appreciably lethal quality of counterterrorism, 'population-centric' counterinsurgency warfare is characterised by restraint or the judicial application of force in support of development projects, governance reforms, and security force assistance. The cumulative effect of these initiatives, ideally pursued in tandem with one another, is to ameliorate social, political, and economic grievances that, if left unaddressed or under-addressed, could incubate additional insurgents and more virulent factions. Critics have admonished this school of thought, however, because it has evidently 'misused history' (Porch, 2013, 332), which is to say, 'finds little support in the historical record' (Gentile, 2013, 5).

DOI: 10.4324/9780429426063-13

Another problem is the intensification of 'hybrid' threats that combine the barbarity of terrorists with the cogitation of insurgents.[2] This development begs important questions regarding the taxonomic separation of counterterrorism and counterinsurgency as well as methods to synthesise the two approaches. Compounding this challenge is the further dichotomisation of how militaries, particularly the US Army, by virtue of its expeditionary deployments since the terrorist attacks of 9/11, exercise counterinsurgency warfare. The caricaturizing of America's approach as merely 'population-centric' distorts complex cultural factors that explain the organisation's actual pursuit of two competing forms of counterinsurgency warfare (Lushenko & Hardy, 2016). While the 'soft' approach is analogous to the prevailing characterisation of America's preference for protecting a population as a verity, the 'hard' approach, sometimes referred to as 'enemy-centric,' conceptualises the population as a means to an end or the killing or capturing of insurgents. Sri Lanka's 'brutal if effective "counter-insurgency" victory' over the Liberation Tigers of Tamil Eelam (LTTE) further evidences this model (Ucko & Marks, 2018, 219). The 'Rajapaksa Model,' named after Sri Lanka's then president, Mahinda Rajapaksa, encouraged wonton tactics to militarily defeat the LTTE, but at the cost of similar attention put towards addressing grievances (Shashikumar, 2009, 111). Contrary to counterterrorism, both the 'soft' and 'hard' approaches incorporate development projects, governance reforms, and security force assistance, although the weight of these tasks relative to lethal operations differs, often drastically. How can the Janus-faced quality of counterinsurgency warfare as practised enable international society to contend with the emergence of transregional hybrid threats epitomised by the IS and its regional affiliates?

We argue that a blended approach to counterinsurgency, or one that combines the forbearance of 'soft' operations with the pertinacious lethality of the 'hard' method, will enable international society to delegitimize hybrid threats pursuant to their defeat. Given that member states of international society and hybrid threats attempt to 'outbid' each other, or deliver consistent, predictable, and adequate services and security more so than the other, a balanced targeting approach that pays equal accord to post-conflict activities stands to erode trust between insurgents, terrorists, and the targeted populations they attempt to manipulate (Ibrahimi & Akbarzadeh, 2019, 3). To be sure, the need to synchronise non-lethal and lethal targeting to manage hybrid threats is well documented (Ucko & Marks, 2018). American military doctrine, for instance, recommends the application of 'informed lethal and non-lethal force to achieve the commander's intent,' an obligation that constitutes the *sine qua non* for success in irregular warfare according to voluminous literature (FM 3–24, 1–38). The problem is not the lack of discussion, however. It is for the lack of doing. It is rare, if not impossible, to identify examples where member states have harmonised 'soft' and 'hard' operations to incentivize peaceful protest while deterring combatants in flashpoints across the globe beset by political violence.

We previously argued that integrating diplomatic and negotiation studies into irregular warfare, particularly a nuanced understanding of spoiling behaviour, could enable member states of international society to overcome the mutual exclusivity of combatants and civilians for the purpose of aligning lethal and non-lethal targeting. An appreciation for spoiling behaviour informs member states how and to what degree combatants influence power structures in the interest of calibrating 'soft' and 'hard' operations (Lushenko & Hardy, 2016). The purpose of this chapter is to promulgate a framework that enables the militaries of member states of international society to operationalise an integrated targeting approach. Unlike other analyses of countering hybrid threats, however, this is not about 'a search for tactical solutions or an escalation of existing techniques: more airpower, more Special Forces operations, the recruitment of local forces en masse' (Johnson, 2018, 144). The blended approach suggested here hinges on a strategic application of 'defeat' and 'stability' mechanisms to enable a consolidation of lethally achieved gains designed to delegitimize hybrid threats towards feasible, suitable, and acceptable security and political outcomes.

The remainder of this chapter proceeds in five parts. The first section, 'Counterinsurgency Models,' positions the practise along the spectrum of conflict and argues it is bookended by two approaches that are often presented as incompatible, although they are fundamentally complementary in their ability to (dis)incentivize combatants. The second section, 'Conceptualising the Defeat of Hybrid Threats,' introduces four defeat mechanisms based on US military doctrine, which is 'the practical expression of theory' (Corum, 1997, 2). These measures, although optimised for interstate conflict, do provide a meaningful framework to condition the application of lethal and non-lethal targeting against hybrid threats, as explored in the following section, 'Defeating Hybrid Threats.' Here, we advance a pathway that encourages commanders to apply lethal options to *dislocate* and *destroy* hybrid threats for the purpose of *isolating* and *disintegrating* them. This sets the conditions for activities designed to consolidate gains. These measures, while prefigured for 'hard' operations, are best achieved through development projects, governance reforms, and security force assistance that ameliorate grievances and are often referred to as 'stability' mechanisms: *influence*, *support*, *control*, and *compel*. The penultimate section applies this approach to IS' affiliate in Central and South Asia: the Islamic State in Khorasan (IS-K). The chapter concludes by enjoining scholars and practitioners to analyse how to incorporate discrete approaches to irregular warfare into a 'range of "ways and means" against hybrid threats,' given their proliferation represents an enduring challenge to the durability of international society (Johnson, 2018, 157).

COUNTERINSURGENCY MODELS

An insurgency consists of an armed struggle whereby antagonists court a population to contest the current political order and institute a putatively more legitimate alternative (FM 3–24, 1–3). On the one hand, insurgents are prepared to resist a state's law enforcement and military efforts to compel conformity with the existing rule of law in perpetuity. The US-led coalition's continued operations against the Taliban in Afghanistan almost twenty years after the invasion testify to this logic. On the other hand, insurgents routinely employ asymmetric tactics, including suicide bombers, that are not existentially threatening in and of themselves. Arguably, it is the aggregation of state resources expended over time to militarily defeat insurgents, typically decoupled from broader political and social reforms, that threatens to engender greater instability.

States have historically pursued one of two approaches to counterinsurgencies: 'hard' and 'soft' counterinsurgency. The fundamental difference between the 'hard' and 'soft' approaches is the importance attached to force in combating insurgents. The 'hard' (variously labelled 'force-based' or 'enemy-centric') approach emphasises the use of military force to defeat an insurgency by undermining its critical requirements, such as its ability to communicate, recruit fighters, finance operations, and promulgate propaganda. Hazelton argues that two factors are critical in this approach: (a) the application of brute force to control civilians and thus reduce the flow of resources to the insurgency; and (b) the application of coercive force to break the insurgency's will and capability to fight (Luttwak, 2007). She cites Edward Luttwak, who notes the successful application of indiscriminate force, including collective punishment and reprisal killings, in successful counterinsurgencies (Ibid., 88). Similarly, Roger Trinquier argues that force is the foundation of counterinsurgency success, and Alexander Downes suggests that under certain conditions, unmitigated violence can defeat an insurgency (Ibid., 87–88). The Syrian counterinsurgency against the Islamist uprising of the early 1980s, as well as the Russian counterinsurgency in Chechnya in the 1990s, employed this brutal strategy to successfully quell rebellion. Other tactics may include killing or capturing insurgents to prevent them from achieving their goal of usurping the government through violent protest (Owen, 2011, 36). The 'Rajapaksa Model' referenced above approximates this lethal approach to counterinsurgency warfare, although US forces in Afghanistan have also employed this method (Lushenko & Hardy, 2016, 110).

Unlike the 'hard' approach that marginalises political and social change required to ameliorate grievances, privileges security force to remove insurgents, and emphasises the role of military control of civilians, the locus of the 'soft' approach, variously labelled 'good governance' or 'population-centric,' is the interrelationship between insurgents, the population, and government. This approach advocates protecting a population from harm and fostering a stable environment to enable development projects and governance reforms to help defeat an insurgency. In this model, 'the main aim is not to kill and capture insurgents but to address the causative factors of violence' (Ucko, 2018, 231). Rather, the objective is to win the politico-strategic battle by establishing positive relations with the population while isolating the insurgent from the support of the population. This method of counterinsurgency warfare emphasises protecting citizens from violence while providing opportunities for host-nation self-sufficiency and is often referred to as 'winning hearts and minds.' The fulcrum that determines the population's support for either insurgents or the government is the weight of citizens' shared perception of legitimacy, defined as generalised and normative support (Bose, 2016, 10–11),[3] in favour of one or the other. Development projects and governance reforms are some of the central ways to arrest popular discontent, and security force assistance is designed to secure peace should insurgents abdicate or reconcile. Hazelton (2013, 80) identifies this prescription as the 'good governance' approach, wherein the counterinsurgent focuses on building a liberal, reformist host-nation government to quell the insurgency.

To be sure, this chastened method of counterinsurgency warfare incorporates lethal force, although it is more selective and often plays a supporting role in non-lethal operations designed to build partnerships with the local populace to legitimise the host government. The Sunni 'awakening' (2005–2008) and US troop 'surge' in Iraq are examples of this approach. A variant of the 'soft' approach is the 'cost-benefit' approach, which eschews trying to win the allegiance of the population purely by introducing good governance reforms and instead emphasises punishing civilians who do not cooperate and providing benefits to those who do. This carrot-and-stick approach 'should prevent insurgents from obtaining resources such as food, shelter, and civilian recruits, while military force should prevent insurgent violence' (Ibid., 88).

CONCEPTUALISING THE DEFEAT OF HYBRID THREATS

This section introduces four defeat mechanisms derived from US military doctrine that can help reconcile 'soft' and 'hard' targeting against hybrid threats. War theorists, particularly those writing during the French Revolution (1789–1799), promulgated ideas of military victory during interstate conflict framed by two central methods of defeat:

attrition and disruption. Antoine-Henri Jomini favoured disruption, which is to say '*offensive* action to *mass forces* against weaker enemy forces at some *decisive point* if the strategy is to lead to victory,' as opposed to the piecemeal destruction of military capabilities over time (Nagl, 2005, emphasis original, 17). The thoughts of Jomini and his contemporaries have become foundational to western approaches to operational art and design. According to US Joint Publication 5–0, *Joint Planning,* operational art is defined as 'the cognitive approach by commands and staffs – supported by their skill, knowledge, experience, creativity, and judgement – to develop strategies, campaigns, and operations to organise and employ military forces by integrating ends, ways, means, and risks' (2017, xxi). Operational design translates the commander's concept of victory into tasks that are synchronised in time, space, and purpose to achieve strategic objectives. Similar to Jomini, Clausewitz emphasised the destruction of opposing forces as integral to success. Because war represented 'a clash of wills' for Clausewitz, however, he also considered a negotiated settlement as a viable alternative (Howard, 2002, 14). This nuanced interpretation encourages a shift away from either/or conceptions of victory towards an appreciation for feasible, suitable, and acceptable outcomes that, in turn, presuppose broader defeat mechanisms arguably more relevant to countering hybrid threats.

Whereas Jomini and other early war theorists favoured a two-dimensional construction of defeat, US military doctrine now aims to incorporate all available ways (methods) and means (resources) to not only *destroy* an adversary's critical capabilities but *dislocate, disintegrate,* and *isolate* them for the purpose of undermining the enemy's centre of gravity. Clausewitz described the centre of gravity as the 'hub of all power and movement, on which everything depends' (1984, 595–596). Others have questioned whether 'Clausewitz's concept hold[s] true for hybrid threats that may not seek decisive battle' (Reilly, 2017, 88). Alternatively, the task of 'COG' analysis may be to identify the enemy's main operational effort, not necessarily the overall fulcrum of its power (Reilly, 2017, 89). Regardless of the exact approach commanders and their staffs favour in deciphering the enemy's source or focus of power, a key component of operational art is to first understand the problem and integrate the defeat mechanisms to solve it (JP 5–0, 2017, III-29). The defeat mechanisms combine more or less lethal methods, bracketed by *destroy* and *isolate*. The former requires the massing of both indirect and direct fire to damage an enemy beyond repair. The latter capitalises on deception and manoeuvre to disorient and fix the enemy within a bounded area for a defined duration. Modulating the two approaches in favour of fire enables *disintegration,* or 'a rapid collapse of the enemy's capabilities or will to fight' (ADRP 3–0, 2017, 2–3). Emphasising manoeuvre over fire explains *dislocation,* which is designed to exploit the enemy's vulnerabilities through positions of advantage.

Notwithstanding its promising usefulness in calibrating 'soft' and 'hard' targeting of hybrid threats, this typology as codified in US military doctrine is problematic for several reasons. First, the defeat mechanisms eschew delegitimizing a hybrid threat as an important objective, instead adopting a strictly materialist definition of defeat. The defeat mechanisms are intended to produce 'physical, temporal, and psychological' effects and not impose reputational costs potentially more relevant to eroding the moral authority of hybrid threats (ADRP 3–0, 2017, 2–3). Yet, hybrid threats project narratives and at times provide public goods such as security and civil services that are purposefully designed to promote their legitimacy at the expense of other antagonists (Ingram, 2015; Ingram, 2016). Writing on the IS, Harmonie Toros and Filippo Diongi note that its 'territorial control, as well as a functioning bureaucracy and economy, were a means to demonstrate to the Western-dominated international society and its regional allies that the IS was a power to be reckoned with, capable of accomplishments in the same sectors in which Western powers and their allies had failed in Iraq and Syria' (2017, 152). Second, to the extent that US military doctrine instructs commanders and planners to apply combinations of defeat mechanisms to achieve 'complementary and reinforcing efforts not attainable with a single mechanism,' this principle is merely descriptive (ADRP 3–0, 2017, 2–3). The doctrine does not prescribe combinations of defeat mechanisms based on representative hybrid threats and operational conditions to enable commanders to optimise their resources in time, space, and purpose.

Thirdly, while US military doctrine encourages the integration of defeat and stability mechanisms to implement a stable, peaceful, and enduring political order after hostilities, this is a culturally unpalatable requirement. It ignores America's military's preference, which is semi-permanent and resistant to change as enumerated by Jack Snyder (1977), Russell Weigley (1977), and Andrew Krepinevich (1986), to maintain warfighting readiness even while recognising that 'early and deliberate combinations of the stability and defeat mechanisms are vital to success' (JP 3–07, 2016, IV-8). The evidence suggests that incorporating stabilisation considerations into operational art and design is often an afterthought and may be more about ensuring a division of labour between those forces designed to fight and those trained to manage development projects, governance reforms, and security force assistance. US Joint Publication 3–07, *Stability*, argues that 'one element of the force can focus on reestablishing security and control while another element can address the immediate humanitarian needs of the populace' (2016, IV–8).

Ironically, this brings us full circle to the bifurcation between 'soft' and 'hard' approaches to countering hybrid threats, the merger of which is at the very least implied within a discussion of defeat and stability mechanisms. A recent investigation of security force assistance in Iraq also finds that such a division is easier said than done based on a misalignment of interests between security providers and recipients, which is often intractable (Biddle et al., 2018, 89–142). Another report by RAND, entitled

Characteristics of Successful U.S. Military Interventions, reaches a similar conclusion. The authors find that 'sending additional ground forces may help to defeat adversaries in combat missions but may have a more contingent effect on success in institution-building in stability operations, where nonmilitary resources and pre-invention planning may be especially vital' (Kavanagh et al., 2019, 354). Notwithstanding quixotic assessments to the contrary, it is surprising that the US Army has inculcated such logic to justify the establishment of Security Force Assistance Brigades designed to advise and assist indigenous security forces as a means to protect the warfighting currency of other units (Griffith, 2017; Cancian, 2019). The next section attempts to rectify these deficiencies by advancing a pathway to synchronise and integrate defeat and stability mechanisms against hybrid threats.

DEFEATING HYBRID THREATS

Although US military doctrine, as an approximation of Western military thinking, reasons that the integrated use of defeat mechanisms is likely to result in 'synergistic and lasting' effects, it does not provide commanders and planners with templates to do so (ADRP 3-0, 2017, 2-3). Equally puzzling is the lack of similar models to guide the integration of stability mechanisms. These offset otherwise 'hard' approaches to materially defeat hybrid threats with 'soft' methods to delegitimize them in social-relational terms. This is an important move to re-establish trust between political officials and citizens that, according to Charles Tilly, 'consists of placing valued outcomes at risk of others' malfeasance, mistakes, or failures' (2005, 12). In this section, we advance a pathway that encourages commanders and staffs to apply lethal options to *dislocate* and *destroy* the critical capabilities of hybrid threats for the purpose of *isolating* and *disintegrating* them prior to pursuing activities that are designed to consolidate gains. These measures, while prefigured for 'hard' operations, are best achieved through 'soft' development projects, governance reforms, and security force assistance. The stability mechanisms aid in redressing grievances by *influencing*, *supporting*, and *controlling* populations, as well as *compelling* insurgents and terrorists to forgo opposition. Yet they are not a panacea. Without effective governance and transparency over time, they are insufficient to overcome all forms of spoiling behaviour as well as the patronage and clientelism that often predate and poison the state-building process in conflict states such as Afghanistan.

Because hybrid threats engage with and operate among vulnerable populations to curry their favour, an essential task for military forces is to first *dislocate* insurgents and terrorists from their sanctuaries (Boyle, 2010, 343). The requirement to dislodge hybrid threats is crucial when considering the non-permissive environments and severely restrictive terrain in which they typically operate. As elucidated below, IS-K has withstood attacks from the US-led coalition on its headquarters in eastern Afghanistan because of the arduous terrain that puts coalition forces at a positional disadvantage by exposing them to hostile fire (Quilty, 2019, 12). The prohibitive areas favouring hybrid threats, ranging from complex megacities to mountainous gradients, beg a key question: exactly how do military forces displace entrenched insurgents and terrorists? The stark reality is that military forces must assume a degree of risk in disrupting strongpoints to compel the movement of hybrid threats. Coalition forces in Afghanistan, Iraq, and elsewhere operate 'by, with, and through' surrogate forces to minimise the risks imposed by engaging hybrid threats. According to Major General James Hecker, Vice Director for Operations at the US Joint Staff, 'surrogate forces [are] designed to achieve U.C. CT [counter-terrorism] objectives at relatively low cost in terms of resources and especially risk to our personnel' (Rempfer, 2019). Indigenous forces externalise the burdens to coalition forces by conducting dangerous clearance operations augmented by enabling capabilities, especially fire, intelligence, logistics, and medical (Krieg & Rickli, 2018, 113). Dislocation of hybrid threats is measured by an increase in the observable signatures of insurgents and terrorists, otherwise content to use secure messaging applications like Telegram or WhatsApp to communicate or move during darkness to obfuscate their location.

By dislocating hybrid threats, military forces create opportunities to remove leaders and fighters through direct and indirect fire, including small arms and mortars. The integration of manoeuvre (*dislocate*) and fire (*destroy*) to impose multiple dilemmas against hybrid threats simultaneously, often referred to as 'combined arms manoeuvre,' usually results in discrete periods to inflict maximum damage against them. Environmental challenges and rules-of-engagement designed to guide military forces in determining when, where, against whom, and how to employ lethal force are further constraining factors (ADP 3-0, 2011, 6; Sagan, 1991, 78). As a case in point, IS-K routinely exploits Afghanistan's permeable border with Pakistan to retrograde from one sanctuary in eastern Afghanistan to another one in Pakistan's Federally Administered Tribal Areas (FATA). The group inundates its painfully obvious formations with women and children to dissuade the coalition's targeting and infiltrates the FATA to consolidate and reorganise. The former commander of US forces in Afghanistan, General (Retired) John Nicholson, cautioned that IS-K 'cannot be defeated while they enjoy external sanctuary and support . . in Pakistan' ('Statement for the Record by General John W. Nicholson, Commander, US Forces in Afghanistan, Before the Senate Armed Services Committee on the Situation in Afghanistan,' 2017). This begs another key question: how do military forces contend with such vulnerabilities?

The use of manoeuvre and tactical and operational deception enables military forces to disorient and fix hybrid threats from advantageous terrains such as hilltops and rooftops. These areas offer unimpeded fields of fire, extended lines of sight, and help limit collateral damage. Military forces can *isolate* hybrid threats by deceiving them through misinformation as well as enveloping them. Military forces purposely supply incorrect information on the time, purpose, and location of their operations through print, communications, and social media to encourage hybrid threats to prepare accordingly. Arrayed in anticipation of blunting an attack from one direction, military forces then exploit the exposed or unprotected flanks of hybrid threats, often converging on them from multiple directions. These tactics force network leaders to make resource and personnel decisions that often result in unavoidable opportunity costs and additional vulnerabilities. Military forces can also fix hybrid threats by disrupting their funding and communications. Only when properly bracketed can a military force rapidly adapt to the critical capabilities of hybrid threats. *Disintegration* is evidenced through the adversary's internal communications, which suggest frustration and suspicion as well as abdication. Such was the case with IS-K's westernmost redoubt in Jowzjan Province. The coalition's pressure, combined with the Taliban's counterattack, compelled IS-K to surrender a useful position that enabled its integration of foreign fighters. Attrition also sets the conditions for military forces to further delegitimize hybrid threats through the application of measures designed to *influence*, *support*, and *control* contestable populations, as well as *compel* insurgents and terrorists to pursue a negotiated settlement. Ideally, military forces will pursue the stability mechanisms in concert with lethal operations and not in sequence, as often happens.

Stability mechanisms help to engender loyalty among populations whose engagement in peaceful political discourse stymies hybrid threats' intent to sow frustration, enmity, and conflict as a means to undermine a government. Development projects such as infrastructure improvements or agricultural initiatives in agrarian societies like Afghanistan are designed to build trust as a prerequisite to altering public opinion in favour of the sitting government (*influence*), enabling wealth accumulation and prosperity among citizens (*support*), and setting the conditions for a sustainable social order (*control*). A challenge has been that coalition forces in Afghanistan, Iraq, and other conflict zones since the terror attacks of 9/11 have conceptualised the employment of development projects as a sort of weapon to help consolidate hard-fought gains against hybrid threats (*Handbook: Commander's Guide to Money as a Weapons System*, 2009, 1). William Maley notes that such initiatives are often fraught and liable to a developing state's limited 'absorptive capacity,' which is a real challenge in Afghanistan given its neopatrimonialism that combines institutionalised governing structures with patronage networks to inform the president's exercise of power (2018, 1004). Development projects are also subject to 'skimming' by hybrid threats, corruption and mismanagement by officially sanctioned contractors, and fragmented aid delivery systems (Maley, 2018, 1008–1011). Hence, development projects require governance reforms to manage corruption to a tolerable degree, or one where the state can provide meaningful benefits to citizens at a greater level than can other antagonists (Goodhand, 2008, 416). As demonstrated in the following pages, security force assistance is foundational to securing the peace, whereby indigenous forces, aided by critical enabling capabilities, use or threaten to use lethal force to *compel* insurgents and terrorists to comply with the rule of law.

DEFEATING THE ISLAMIC STATE IN THE KHORASAN PROVINCE

In 2014, several groups aligned with the Tehrik-i-Taliban Pakistan pledged allegiance to IS and its leader, Abu Bakr al-Baghdadi. According to Antonio Giustozzi, higher salaries were a draw for some defectors. The plans of IS for a world caliphate encouraged most people. They joined IS-K to secure Afghanistan and the so-called 'Khorasan Province' as key components of the caliphate (2018, 24). This area, which Amin Tarzi characterises as 'part myth, part theology, and part geography,' encompasses a swath of Iran, China, Central Asia, India, and Southeast Asia and underpins IS-K's messianic narrative (2019, 123). At the time of its emergence, analysts interpreted IS-K as an ephemeral threat, and some have since argued that Afghanistan 'was not a natural expansion for IS' (MacKenzie & Tassal, 2015; McNally et al., 2016). Yet, the group has resolved to oppose the US-led coalition's counterterrorism operations. While US officials assume a negotiated settlement with the Taliban will enable IS-K's defeat, the group has expanded across Afghanistan at the Taliban's expense (Nordland & Mashal, 2019). In late October 2018, before the coalition seized IS-K's capital in eastern Afghanistan, General Scott Miller, the US commander in Afghanistan, admitted IS-K was 'dangerous.' He added, 'They have external aspirations, they have different capabilities, and they are connected outside of Afghanistan' (Kube, 2018). Amid the loss of its physical caliphate in Iraq and Syria, IS-K arguably represents IS' most viable and lethal regional affiliate and has evolved to represent a significant threat to Afghanistan's security and stability. 'We cannot know just how grave a threat "ISIS-K" could become,' Michael O'Hanlon cautions, and 'nor should we wish to find out' (2019, 2).

The group's *modus operandi* is to emulate the norms and practises of international society while at the same time contesting the very principles from which recognition as a member state is derived, namely the sovereign equality of states and the preservation of human rights (Toros & Diongi, 2017, 157). Therefore, IS-K, similar to IS' other affiliates or *wilayats*, is a hybrid threat that harnesses terror in pursuit of an Islamic governorate based on its guiding ideology, which combines Salafism and Islamism. Amin Saikal explains that this ideology is undergirded by a Wahhabist current that encourages adversarial jihad and biases the group's engagements against the goal of shepherding a puritanical society (2018, 2). Indeed, the exploitation of unclassified documents (Jadoon, 2018, 22), coupled with Giustozzi's field research, suggests that IS-K exercises a 'blitzkrieg' military strategy designed to overwhelm local security forces in areas that are chronically ungoverned and insecure (2018, 42).

To what degree has the coalition synchronised defeat and stability mechanisms in support of a balanced targeting approach that integrates 'hard' (lethal) options to annihilate IS-K's material capabilities with 'soft' (non-lethal) methods to delegitimize the group's appeal, especially among younger adults and intellectuals? From 2015 to early 2017, the coalition attempted to merely *isolate* IS-K, even though officials acknowledged the group was 'operationally emergent in Afghanistan' ("Statement for the Record by General John F. Campbell, Commander, US Forces-Afghanistan, Before the Senate Armed Services Committee on the Situation in Afghanistan," 2015). By May 2017, then-US Secretary of Defence James Mattis had directed the coalition to *destroy* the group (Baron & Weisgerber, 2017). Contextualised against this inflection point, the coalition's conflict with IS-K has unfolded across three phases: (1) January 2015 to January 2017, (2) January 2017 to April 2017, and (3) April 2017 to present. Each is characterised by the coalition's concerted attempt to implement the defeat mechanisms, at times in concert with the stability mechanisms, to eliminate IS-K as a threat to Afghanistan, regional stability, and global security given the group's demonstrated ability to inspire, enable, and direct external attacks (Lushenko et al., 2019, 271–272).

First, following his pledge of allegiance to IS in January 2015, Hafiz Saeed Khan, IS-K's inaugural leader, and his founding cadre infiltrated the Nangarhar Province of eastern Afghanistan for the purpose of executing the group's military strategy (Osman, 2016). Khan weighted the group's combat power against Nangarhar and Kunar Provinces in eastern Afghanistan and Jowzjan Province in western Afghanistan. Nangarhar is the network's headquarters and consists of approximately 2,000 to 3,000 members. Kunar facilitates indoctrination and training and likely hosts 1,000 to 2,000 more members. Jowzjan, until its defeat in mid-2018, served as a reception centre for foreign fighters travelling from Central and South Asia as well as Europe ("IS Group Calls on Muslims to Immigrate to Afghanistan," 2018). It consisted of approximately 1,000 members (Basit et al., 2019, 37). Khan and his successors have pursued this audacious strategy to enable IS-K to encircle Jalalabad City in Nangarhar, as evidenced by attacks against largely 'soft' targets such as checkpoints, government buildings, and election polling sites.

The coalition killed Khan in July 2016 following a drone strike and initiated 'Operation Green Sword' to *dislocate* the group from Nangarhar ('Statement for the Record by General John W. Nicholson, Commander, US Forces, Afghanistan, Before the Senate Armed Services Committee on the Situation in Afghanistan,' 2017). The group consolidated within two districts, Achin and Naziyan, based on the coalition's drone strikes, raids, and clearance operations. This amounted to an 80% reduction of the group's territory (Giustozzi, 2018, 180). Thousands of IS-K members also fled to Pakistan to prevent additional losses and replenish their ranks. The retrograde into Pakistan suggested that IS-K sought to capitalise on the porous Durand Line to regroup, similar to the logic that encouraged the cross-border retreat of al-Qaeda following America's invasion of Afghanistan in 2001. It is also possible that the Pakistan government's 'benign neglect' and/or 'collaboration' explain the sanctuary that IS-K exploited in the FATA. The former results when a state tolerates an extremist group within its borders. The latter presupposes the state's tacit or active support (Tankel, 2016, 562–565). It is likely the group's movement into Pakistan resulted from a combination of these factors, a concept Stephen Tankel dubs 'coopetition.' This explains a state's simultaneous pursuit of toleration, support, and/or targeting of an extremist group based on elastic calculations of its threat and utility (2016, 565–566). The group's relocation to the FATA encouraged the coalition to expand its collaboration and cooperation with Pakistan's military in an attempt to block IS-K's egress.

Second, by the beginning of 2017, IS-K used Afghanistan's formal border with Pakistan to occupy Kunar while integrating Islamic Movement of Uzbekistan defectors to create an enclave in Jowzjan under the leadership of a Taliban defector, Qari Hikmatullah (Nordland & Ghazi, 2018). The coalition capitalised on the dislodgement of IS-K fighters and leaders to *destroy* them through direct and indirect fire. A sterling example is the coalition's employment of the largest non-nuclear bomb ever deployed in combat, the GBU-43, against IS-K in Nangarhar in April 2017. The blast killed hundreds of fighters, destroyed $8 million of IS-K's holdings, and breached the group's defences that protected its headquarters (Giustozzi, 2018, 96). Next, the coalition conducted a raid in Achin that resulted in the death of IS-K's second emir, Abdul Hasib. These lethal operations sowed distrust across IS-K that the coalition stoked through its information operations to *isolate* the group. The heightened suspicion that followed resulted in greater operational security that frustrated IS-K's communications, delayed its disbursement of salaries and weapons to fighters, disrupted its smuggling routes, and stalled offensive operations (*'At Any Price We Will Take The Mines': The Islamic State, The Taliban, and Afghanistan's White Talc Mountains*, 2018).

Afghan forces, advised and assisted by their US patrons, occupied the Achin District Centre at Sra Kala in an attempt to implement the stability mechanisms to consolidate the coalition's lethal gains against IS-K. Their presence was designed to *influence* the population to support the government based on field research that suggests 'local communities are typically keen to engage in initiatives that will prevent their [IS-K] return' (Ingram & Whiteside, 2019). This is a challenging task in southern Afghanistan, however, given the felt absence of political, military, and law enforcement officials based on the austere terrain. Nevertheless, Afghan and US forces established tactical infrastructure, including Observation Post Bravo less than one mile from the GBU-43 blast site, to protect the arrival of previously deracinated Afghan farmers and *support* development projects, including the disbursement of seed corn to kickstart Nangarhar's moribund agricultural sector (Quilty, 2019, 3). Overwatch of a local economic mainstay, the Shedal Bazar, also encouraged the renewal of commercial transactions (Rasmussen, 2017). The deployment of Afghan forces was also envisaged to establish some semblance of stability or *control* over the population, especially because they were prepared to sacrifice themselves to *compel* IS-K's surrender. A recent report finds, for example, that Afghan soldiers die at a rate of 30 to 40 a day, which amounts to 175 a week and over 9,000 in a single year (Basit et al., 2019, 34). The result of the coalition's integration of defeat and stability mechanisms in Nangarhar was IS-K's relocation of its capital further west to Deh Bala District (Quilty, 2019, 12). Notwithstanding this effect, the group expanded its positions in Kunar and Jowzjan, even amid Taliban resistance.

Third, from late 2017, IS-K accelerated its attacks in an attempt to undermine the Afghan parliamentary elections in October 2018, and the coalition shifted towards attempting to *disintegrate* IS-K in Nangarhar through unremitting raids, lethal strikes, and clearance operations. At the same time, the coalition broadened its operations against Jowzjan and capitalised on the Taliban's fortuitous counteroffensive. Following a protracted battle from May to July 2018, US Special Forces, in partnership with Afghan commandos, captured IS-K's capital in southern Nangarhar. Similar to the aftermath of the GBU-43 strike, Afghan Commandos established checkpoints, including Camp Blackbeard 'on a flat, dusty hilltop near the district centre,' delivered humanitarian aid, and initiated developmental projects to erode IS-K's normative appeal by disrupting its ability to provide benefits to local Afghans (Quilty, 2019, 12; Habibzada & Sarwan, 2018). The coalition followed this success by conducting a drone strike that killed the group's third emir, Saad Erhabi, in Achin. Meanwhile, after the death of Qari Hikmatullah due to a drone strike in April 2018, the Taliban counterattacked IS-K in August 2018. The Taliban killed 153 IS-K members, injured 100 more, and captured nearly 135. Over 200 remaining IS-K members surrendered to Afghan forces (Rahim & Nordland, 2018). The loss of Jowzjan demonstrates that while IS-K and the Taliban shared personal and familial ties in Darzab and Qush Tepa Districts, the overall relationship oscillated between conflict and cooperation, the latter of which is often transactional based on a momentary alignment of otherwise competing interests (Ibrahimi & Akbarzadeh, 2019, 4).

These phases indicate that whereas the coalition was intent on simply *isolating* IS-K in 2015, Mattis' guidance in early 2017 encouraged the adoption of an approach designed to *dislocate* leaders and fighters from their sanctuaries through raids and clearance operations for the purpose of *destroying* and *disintegrating* them through lethal strikes. Since 2015, Ibrahimi and Akbarzadeh argue, 'ground and air offensives by the Afghan, US, and NATO forces as well as attacks by the Taliban reduced the capacity of the IS-K to hold and maintain major territories' (2019, 17). The coalition has also removed leader after leader, jeopardising the group's expansionist military strategy. In mid-January 2019, the coalition conducted another raid against IS-K's headquarters in Nangarhar, resulting in the death of Khetab Emir, mastermind of the group's suicide operations ('Senior ISIS Commander Killed in Afghanistan, US Forces Say,' 2019).

Despite losses, IS-K has rebounded and waged attacks across Afghanistan, aided by the coalition's heightened targeting of the Taliban pursuant to a negotiated settlement that affords the Islamic State's regional affiliate greater freedom of ('10 ISIS Fighters Killed Due to Air Attack,' 2019) Since its emergence, IS-K has executed over 200 attacks in Afghanistan alone, resulting in more than 1,500 people killed and almost 3,300 wounded. A recent report issued by the *Afghanistan Analysts Network* also argues that IS-K 'is still not yet gone.' The group 'continues to operate in mountainous areas of the [Nangarhar Province] Spinghhar range, including at least some parts of the Mamand, Pekha, and Bandar valleys.' More disturbingly, IS-K 'is still running its own prison and court systems in parts of the Mamand valley' (Quilty, 2019, 12). At the same time, the group continues to consolidate outside of Afghanistan in Central and South Asia (Lushenko, 2019). Both of these factors suggest that although the coalition has attempted to integrate defeat and stability mechanisms to reconcile lethal and non-lethal targeting against IS-K, more needs to be done, especially to redress the group's ideology.[4]

CONCLUSION: INTERNATIONAL SOCIETY'S APPROACH TO HYBRID THREATS

This chapter has argued that member states of international society should pursue a blended approach to counter hybrid threats that incorporate both terrorist and insurgent tactics. The use of force alone provokes a backlash from the population. Hybrid threats also attempt to garner support from a population by offering more incentives, particularly pay, which can be a real challenge for the government's recruitment of security forces. Incorporating defeat and stability mechanisms derived from US military doctrine can help redress these challenges. Pirnie and O'Connell (2008) also emphasise the importance of applying maximum pressure to specific points across an adversarial network to limit its 'freedom to act and influence.' The value of a balanced approach to countering hybrid threats is evidenced by the coalition's three phases of conflict with IS-K in Afghanistan. The coalition conducted raids and drone strikes to *dislocate* and *destroy* the group's critical requirements for the purpose of *isolating* and *disintegrating* the network. Next, it incorporated development projects, governance reforms, and security force assistance to address grievances. This amounted to the adoption of stability mechanisms designed to *influence*, *support*, and *control* the population, as well as *compel* Islamic State fighters to forgo opposition.

Of course, member states of international society have taken different approaches to dealing with insurgencies and terrorist groups that attempt to approximate the effects of the balanced model proposed here. These approaches include nation-building exercises (such as major development projects and Provincial Reconstruction Teams), the training of indigenous security personnel, the deployment of regional forces (such as the African Union's deployment in Mali), and a broader international response whereby the differing counterinsurgency methodologies and approaches mingle and complement or counter one another based on local cultural, developmental, and political forces. Reconciling 'soft' and 'hard' operations through the use of defeat and stability mechanisms, similar to other force employment options, requires continuous observation, reassessment, and recalibration. The adversary will also adapt. The interplay of actions, reactions, and counteractions is why combating hybrid threats is both an art and a science. *The views expressed in this article are the author's own and do not reflect the official policy or position of the United States Department of the Army, Department of Defense, or Government.*

Notes

1 According to Hare, a precise cyber weapon system consists of four parts, including (1) a platform, (2) an access method, (3) a command and control system, and (4) the software payload (2019, 195).

2 Of course, the definition of 'hybrid' threats and warfare is also contestable. See Johnson.

3 Bose (2016, 10-11) writes, 'By generalised I mean a generalised perception or assumption that the actions of an actor are desirable, proper, or appropriate within some socially constructed system of norms, values, beliefs, and definitions – and not as the attribution of special qualities to an actor, nor to its mere opinions. Therefore, I mean the support for principles and rules, norms and laws, regardless of actor policy and the specificities of time. By normative support I mean a relationship that rests on a principled commitment to a process, is regulated according to understood rules, and confirmed through the expression of consent.'

4 The recent arrest of Abu Obaidullah Mutawakil, a radical cleric in Kabul who recruited fighters for IS-K among his students, is an example of how the coalition can undermine the group's ideological appeal. See 'Kabul imam accused of recruiting hundreds into IS arrested,' 2019.

References

'10 ISIS Fighters Killed Due to Air Attacks.' (2019, February 09). *Bakhtar News*. Retrieved on February 09, 2019 from http://www.bakhtarnews.com.af/eng/security/item/36842-10-isis-fighters-killed-due-to-air-attacks.html.

'At Any Price We Will Take The Mines': The Islamic State, the Taliban and Afghanistan's White Talc Mountains. (2018, June 13). Retrieved on June 13, 2018 from https://www.kpsrl.org/publication/at-any-price-we-will-take-the-mines-the-islamic-state-the-taliban-and-afghanistans-white-talc-mountains.

Basit, A. et al. (2019). "South Asia: Afghanistan, Bangladesh, India, Pakistan, Sri Lanka." In Rohan Gunaratna, Mahfuh Bin Haji Halimi, Muhammad Saiful Alam Shah Bin Sudiman, Nur Aziemah Azman, and Mohammed Sinan Siyech (eds.). *Counter Terrorist Trends and Analyses: Analyst Threat Assessment*, *11*(1), 33–64.

Baron, K., & M. Weisgerber (2017, May 19). New tactics, quicker decisions are helping to 'Annihilate' ISIS, Pentagon says. *Defense One*. Retrieved May 19, 2017 from https://cdn.defenseone.com.

Biddle, S., Macdonald, J., & Baker, R. (2018). Small footprint, small payoff: The military effectiveness of security force assistance. *Journal of Strategic Studies*, *41*(1–2), 89–142.

Bose, S. (2016). Death by a thousand cuts or dance of the seven veils? Legitimacy and generation of authority in Afghanistan's statebuilding enterprise, 2001–2014. PhD Dissertation, The Australian National University, Canberra.

Boyle, M. (2010). Do counterterrorism and counterinsurgency go together? *International Affairs*, *87*(2), 333–353.

Byman, D. (2005). *Going to war with the allies you have: Allies, counterinsurgency, and the war on terrorism*. Carlisle: Strategic Studies Institute.

Cancian, M. (2019). Well-trained partners are more likely to fight. *Army Magazine*, *69*(5), 48–50.

Clausewitz, V. (1984). *On war*. Edited and Translated by M. Howard & P. Paret. Princeton, NJ: Princeton University Press.

Corum, J.S. (1997). *The Luftwaffe: Creating the operational air war, 1918–1940*. Lawrence, KS: University Press of Kansas.

Gentile, C. (2013). *Wrong turn: America's deadly embrace of counterinsurgency*. New York, NY: The New Press.

Giustozzi, A. (2018). *The Islamic State in Khorasan: Afghanistan, Pakistan, and the New Central Asia Jihad*. London: Hurst & Company.

Goodhand, J. (2008). Corruption or consolidating the peace? The drugs economy and post-conflict peacebuilding in Afghanistan. *International Peacekeeping*, *15*(3), 405–423.

Griffith, D. (2017). *Security force assistance brigades: A permanent force for regional engagement and building operational depth*. Fort Leavenworth, KS: U.S. Army Command and General Staff College.

Habibzada, M., & Sarwan, R. (2018, July 09). US, Afghan special forces capture IS De Facto Capital in Afghanistan. *Voa News*. Retrieved from July 09, 2018, from https://www.voanews.com/a/us-afghan-special-forces-islamic-state-de-facto-capital-afghanistan/4476009.html.

Hare, F. (2019). Precision cyber weapon systems: An important component of a responsible national security strategy? *Contemporary Security Policy*, *40*(2), 193–213.

Harris, S. (2014). *@War: The rise of the military-internet complex*. Washington, DC: Eamon Dolan/Houghton Mifflin Harcourt.

Hazelton, J. (2013). The 'hearts and minds' fallacy: Violence, coercion, and success in counterinsurgency. *International Security*, *42*(1), 80–113.

Howard, M. (2002). *Clausewitz: A very short introduction*. Oxford: Oxford University Press.

Ibrahimi, N., & Akbarzadeh, S. (2019). Intra-*jihadist* conflict and cooperation: Islamic State-Khorasan Province and the Taliban in Afghanistan. *Studies in Conflict & Terrorism*, *41*(6), 1–22.

Ingram, H. (2015). The strategic logic of Islamic State information operations. *Australian Journal of International Affairs*, *9*(6), 729–752.

Ingram, H. (2016). An analysis of Islamic State's Dabiq magazine. *Australian Journal of Political Science*, *51*(3), 458–477.

Ingram, H., & Whiteside, C. (2019, February 25, 2019). Do great nations fight endless wars? Against the Islamic State, they might. Retrieved on February 25, 2019 from https://warontherocks.com/2019/02/do-great-nations-fight-endless-wars-against-the-islamic-state-they-might/.

"IS Group Calls on Muslims To Immigrate To Afghanistan." (2018, March 07). *Agence France-Presse*. Retrieved on March 07, 2018 from https://www.dailymail.co.uk/wires/afp/article-5472873/IS-group-calls-Muslims-immigrate-Afghanistan.html.

Jadoon, A. (2018). *Allied & lethal: Islamic State Khorasan's network and organizational capacity in Afghanistan and Pakistan*. West Point, NY: Combating Terrorism Center.

Johnson, R. (2018). Hybrid war and its countermeasures: A critique of the literature. *Small Wars & Insurgencies*, *29*(1), 141–163.

'Kabul imam accused of recruiting hundreds into IS arrested.' (2019, February 09). *1TVnews*. Retrieved February 09, 2019 from http://www.1tvnews.af/en/news/afghanistan/37271-kabul-imam-accused-of-recruiting-hu ndreds-into-is-arrested.

Kavanagh, J. et al. (2019). *Characteristics of successful U.S. military interventions*. Santa Monica, CA: RAND.

Krepinevich, A. (1986). *The army and Vietnam*. Baltimore, MD: John Hopkins University Press.

Krieg, A., & Rickli, J. (2018). Surrogate warfare: The art of war in the 21st century. *Defence Studies*, *18*(2), 113–130.

Kube, C. (2018, October 31). New U.S. commander in Afghanistan says we're going on offense against the Taliban. *NBC News*. Retrieved October 31, 2018 from https://www.nbcnews.com/news/military/new-u-s-commander-afghanistan-says-he-s-going-offense-n926431.

Lushenko, P. (2019, August 13). IS-K: Defeating the new central *and* South Asia Jihad. *Texas National Security Review*. Retrieved on April 12, 2024, from https://tnsr.org/roundtable/book-review-roundtable-a-look-into-the-islamic-state-khorasan/

Lushenko, P., & Hardy, J. (2016). Panjwai: A tale of two COINs in Afghanistan. *Small Wars & Insurgencies*, *27*(1), 106–131.

Lushenko, P., Van Auken, L., & Stebbins, G. (2019). ISIS-K: Deadly nuisance or strategic threat? *Small Wars & Insurgencies*, *30*(2), 265–278.

Luttwak, E. (2007). Dead End: Counterinsurgency warfare as military malpractice. *Harper's Magazine*. https://harpers.org/archive/2007/02/dead-end/

Maley, W. (2018). Institutional design, neopatrimonialism, and the politics of aid in Afghanistan. *Asian Survey*, *58*(6), 995–1015.

MacKenzie, J., & Tassal, A. (2015, January 27). ISIS in Afghanistan is like boogeyman under the bed. *The Week*. Retrieved January 27, 2015 from https://theweek.com/articles/534830/isisin-afghanistan-like-boogeyman-under-bed.

McNally, L. et al. (2016, May 25). The Islamic State in Afghanistan: Examining its threat to stability. *Middle East Institute*. Retrieved May 25, 2016 from https://www.mei.edu/sites/default/files/publications/PF12_McNallyAmiral_ISISAfghan_web.pdf.

Nagl, J. (2005). *Learning to eat soup with a knife: Counterinsurgency lessons from Malaya and Vietnam*. Chicago, IL: University of Chicago Press.

Nordland, R., & Ghazi, Z. (2018, April 09). ISIS leader in Afghanistan is killed in U.S. airstrike. *New York Times*. Retrieved April 09, 2018 from https://www.nytimes.com/201 8/04/09/world/asia/afghanistan-isis-leader.html.

Nordland, R., & Mashal, M. (2019, January 24). U.S. and Taliban make headway in talks for withdrawal from Afghanistan. *New York Times*. Retrieved January 24, 2019 from https://www.nytimes.com/2019/01/24/world/asia/usa-taliban-afghanistan-deal.html.

O'Hanlon, M. (2019). *Afghanistan after Mattis: A revised strategy to focus on counterterrorism and the Afghan security forces*. Washington, DC: The Brookings Institution.

Osman, B. (2016). Decent into Chaos: Why did Nangarhar turn into an IS hub? Afghanistan Analysts Network.

Owen, W. (2011). Killing your way to control. *The British Army Review*, *151*, 34–37.

Pirnie, B.R., & O'Connell, E. (2008). Conducting counterinsurgency operations: Lessons from Iraq (2003–2006). Santa Monica, CA: RAND Corporation. Retrieved December 12, 2019 from https://www.rand.org/pubs/research_briefs/RB9323.html.

Porch, D. (2013). *The origins, development & myth of the new way of war*. Cambridge: Cambridge University Press.

Quilty, A. (2019, February 19). 'Faint lights twinkling against the dark': Reportage from the fight against ISKP in Nangarhar. *Afghanistan Analysts Network*. Retrieved on February 19, 2019 from https://www.afghanistan-analysts.org/faint-lights-twinkling-against-the-dark-reportage-from-the-fight-against-iskp-in-nangrahar/.

Rahim, N., & Nordland, R. (2018, August 01). Taliban surge routs ISIS in Northern Afghanistan. *New York Times*. Retrieved on August 01, 2018 from https://www.nytimes.com/2018/08/01/world/asia/afgh anistan-taliban-isis.html.

Rasmussen, S. (2017, April 17). Devastation and a war that wages on: Visiting the valley hit by the moab attack. *The Guardian*. Retrieved on April 17, 2017 from https://www.theguardian.com/world/2017/apr/17/moab-bomb-site-afghanistan.html.

Reilly, M. (2017). Hybrid threat COG analysis: Taking a fresh look at ISIL. *Joint Forces Quarterly*, *84*(1), 86–92.

Rempfer, K. (2019, February 08). Special operations launches 'secret surrogate' missions in new counter-terrorism strategy. *Military Times*. Retrieved on February 10, 2019 from https://www.militarytimes.com/news/your-army/2019/02/08/fighting-terrorism-may-rely-on-secret-surrogate-forces-going-forward/.

Sagan, S. (1991). Rules of engagement. *Security Studies*, *1*(1), 78–108.

Saikal, A. (2018). How Islamic has the 'Islamic State' been? *Journal of Muslim Minority Affairs*, *38*(2), 1–10.

"Senior ISIS Commander Killed in Afghanistan, US Forces Say." (2019, January 12). *The Jerusalem Post.* Retrieved on January 12, 2019 from https://www.jpost.com/Breaking-News/Senior-ISIS-commander-killed-in-Afghanistan-US-forces-say-577128.

Shashikumar, V.K. (2009). Lessons from Sri Lanka's long war. *Indian Defence Review, 24*(3), 106–112.

Snyder, J.L. (1977). *The Soviet strategic culture: Implications for limited nuclear options.* Santa Monica, CA: RAND.

"Statement for the Record by General John F. Campbell, Commander, U.S. Forces – Afghanistan, Before the Senate Armed Services Committee on the Situation in Afghanistan." (2015, October 06). Retrieved on October 06, 2015 from https://www.armed-services.senate.gov/imo/media/doc/Campbell_10-06-15.pdf.

"Statement for the Record by General John W. Nicholson, Commander, U.S. Forces – Afghanistan, Before the Senate Armed Services Committee on the Situation in Afghanistan." (2017, February 09). Retrieved on February 09, 2017 from https://www.armed-services.senate.gov/imo/media/doc/Nicholson_02-09-17.pdf.

Tankel, S. (2016). Beyond the double game: Lessons from Pakistan's approach to Islamist militancy. *Journal of Strategic Studies, 41*(4), 545–578.

Tarzi, A. (2019). Islamic State-Khurasan province. In F. al-Istrabadi & S. Ganguly (Eds.), *The future of ISIS: Regional and international implications.* Washington, DC: The Brookings Institution.

Tilly, C. (2005). *Trust and rule.* Cambridge: Cambridge University Press.

Toros, H., & Diongi, F. (2017). International society and Islamist non-state actors: The case of the Islamic State organization. In H. Suganami, M. Carr, & A. Humpreys (Eds.), *The anarchical society at 40: Contemporary challenges & prospects* (pp. 145–161). Oxford: Oxford University Press.

Ucko, D. (2009). *The new counterinsurgency era: Transforming the U.S. military for modern wars.*Washington, DC: Georgetown University Press.

Ucko, D., & Marks, T. (2018) Violence in context: Mapping the strategies and operational art of irregular warfare. *Contemporary Security Policy, 39*(2), 206–233.

US Department of the Army. (2011). *Army doctrine publication 3-0: Operations.* Washington DC: Headquarters, Department of the Army.

US Department of the Army. (2017). *Army doctrine reference publication 3-0: Operations.* Washington, DC: Headquarters, Department of the Army.

US Department of the Army. (2009). *Handbook – commander's guide to money as a weapons system.* Fort Leavenworth, KS; Center for Army Lessons.

US Department of the Army. (2014). *FM 3–24 insurgencies and countering insurgencies.* Washington, DC: Headquarters, Department of the Army.

US Department of Defense. (2016). *JP 3-07: Stability.* Washington, DC: Joint Chiefs of Staff.

US Department of Defense. (2016). *JP 5-0: Joint planning.* Washington, DC: Joint Chiefs of Staff.

Weigley, R. (1977). *The American way of war: A history of United States military strategy and policy.* Bloomington, IN: Indiana University Press.

12 THE CRIME-TERROR NEXUS

Tamanna Shah

INTRODUCTION

The crime-terrorism nexus is a theme common in both academic and policy debates, especially with the developments of the global world in the past few decades. In January 2017, the Dutch National Coordinator for Security and Counterterrorism Dick Schoof (Groenendijk & Rosman, 2017) stated that the crime-terror nexus was getting stronger and bolder. In May 2017, the Dutch Minister of Foreign Affairs Bert Koenders (2017) noted that the nexus is "growing," that this is "an alarming development" and that it constitutes "an area we'll need to focus on more in the coming period" (p. 6). The focus on organised crime, illicit trade, and terrorism intensified after 9/11, when terrorist groups such as the Taliban in Afghanistan and Pakistan and the Islamic State (IS) in Iraq and Syria, derived financial profits from participation in illicit activities like the drug trade. The persistence and growth of the illegal activities of the crime-terror nexus has also complicated post-conflict stabilisation and reconstruction efforts in countries like Cambodia or Haiti (Cockayne & Lupel, 2011; Cockayne, 2013; Andreas, 2008).

The overlap between criminality and terrorist or extremist networks emerged in the early 1990s. Traditionally viewed as two separate phenomena: the collapse of the Soviet Union and the subsequent birth of the Information Age blurred the borders between criminal and political violence (Makarenko, 2004, 2009; Shelley, 2002; Hutchinson & O'Malley, 2006; Dishman, 2001, 2005; Ibanez, 2013). However, it was Laqueur (1999) who first acknowledged the "blurred line" between crime and terrorism. The current understanding of the crime-terror nexus is rooted in the "profit-versus-ideology dichotomy" (Ballina, 2011). An organisational analysis reveals that Islamist terrorist groups both engage in alliances with transnational criminal organisations and pursue their criminal enterprises despite ideological commitments. A shift in geopolitics and increasing transnational led to an increase in organisational and operational similarities, while non-state actors adopted illegal ways to achieve their aims. Moreover, after the 11 September 2001 incident, the United States initiated the "war against terror" by freezing assets, blocking informal banking system transactions, and suppressing the financing of terrorist organisations (Mcculloch & Pickering, 2005). Stringer (2011) defines terrorist financing as the raising, storage, and movement of licit or illicit funds for terrorist acts or to sustain the operations of a terrorist organisation.

The conventional view of the nexus between illicit economies and armed conflicts considers theories on "narco-terrorism," the "greed" literature on civil wars, works on the crime-terror nexus, the concept of the "guerre revolutionnaire" and "the cost-benefit analysis of counter-insurgency" (Felbab-Brown, 2019, p. 367). The conventional view recommends governments regulate and curtail the illegal movement of funds and putting an end to the physical resources of the criminal-terror groups (Lindholm & Realuyo, 2013). Putting an end to the funding sources gives rise to "Narco-Terrorism," with an increase in drug trafficking and illicit organised crime to acquire money and material (Dishman, 2001). During the rise of Pablo Escobar and the Columbian drug cartels, narco-terrorism was seen as blurring the lines between crime and terror (Picarelli, 2012). In recent years, scholars have used the term "criminal insurgency" instead of "narco-terrorism" to explain and represent the security threats that states face from criminal organisations (Sullivan, 2012). Several examples of criminal insurgency from around the world account for "in-house criminal capabilities" (Hutchinson & O'Malley, 2007, p. 1095). Since the 1980s, the Hizbullah has invested in South America's illicit narcotics industry; the Taliban depends on Afghanistan's heroin production (Moreau, 2013) and groups like the Irish Republican Army (IRA) have been involved in smuggling counterfeit consumer goods, petrol and cigarettes (Levitt, 2015, 2012). The cooperation between crime and terror is also in part due to international pressure to curb the financing and support of terrorism. Globalisation, too, has a role to play in the convergence of crime and terror.

However, in recent years, scholars have called for a new crime-terror nexus (Basra et al., 2016). The focus is no longer on merging the criminal and terrorist organisations, but rather on their social environment, networks, or

DOI: 10.4324/9780429426063-14

"milieus" (Basra et al., 2016). The crime-terror nexus is complex, and scholars define three main nexus conditions: cooperation, transformation, and convergence (Dishman, 2001, 2005; Makarenko, 2004; Ibanez, 2013). Makarenko (2004) is the pioneer in developing the concept of the "crime-terror continuum" that depicts these main areas. *Cooperation* identifies alliances based on informal transaction-based agreements (i.e., guns for drugs) to coalitions (i.e., coordinating transnational human and drug smuggling routes). On the other end of the continuum is *convergence* or the process by which groups transform into hybrid organisations that retain both criminal and terrorist qualities. For Makarenko (2004), real *transformation* takes place when one group's end aims to evolve entirely to the other end of the crime-terror continuum. However, for Dishman (2001, 2005), transformation occurs the moment groups adopt or develop in-house capabilities for carrying out operations.

Scholars argue for a definite overlap between criminal and terrorist groups, instead of being one or the other, that has consequences for their operations and ways of radicalisation. The relevance of such an approach is visible in the activities of terrorist groups like Daesh (or the Islamic State of Iraq or the Levant, IS, ISIS, or ISIL) in Europe. Nevertheless, there are some fundamental differences between criminal and terrorist organisations. While criminal organisations aim to make money and can escape prosecution, terrorist organisations try to alter or shape the political landscape and face trial. In both of these cases, there is a tremendous impact on society and individuals.

Additionally, some scholars explain the crime-terror nexus according to diverse geographic characteristics. Makarenko (2004) and Ibanez (2013) highlight conditions in Somalia, Africa, Afghanistan, Pakistan, and the Balkans with inadequate border regulations, weak authority, and corruption, which makes them vulnerable to a symbiotic collaboration between criminal and terrorist groups. Makarenko (2012) argues that in these geographic "hotspots," active criminal and terrorist groups "hijack" the social, political, and economic progress of the region.

Some scholars adopt the "methods," not the "motives," of criminal groups to explain the crime-terror nexus (Shelley & Picarelli, 2002). Ballina (2011) concludes that these groups are capable of pursuing two different motives simultaneously: entrepreneurial profit and ideological goals. Aronson (2014) discusses Al-Qaeda in the Islamic Maghreb's (AQIM) strategy of kidnapping for ransom and highlights that the group's motives are "fluid" and continuously shift. Nevertheless, the majority of scholars conclude that the crime-terror nexus is dynamic and opportunistic, and any difference in motives does not mean they do not interact with others. There is definite cooperation between these networks: "these organisations have a professional pragmatism that can and does override ideological differences" (van der Veer, 2019, n.p.). Wang and Wang (2009) assert that the nexus between transnational organised crime and terrorism is increasingly complex, which challenges the security of states at both the national and international levels. Makarenko (2004) argues that despite having distinct identities, the concept of the crime-terror nexus often comes together to attain similar aims and interests.

Points of Divergence for Organised Crime Groups

There is a difference in the interaction between the older criminal groups and terrorist organisations compared to the newly formed crime groups (Shelley, 2005). The older organised criminal groups, such as the Sicilian Mafia, the Russian Mafia, and the Hong Kong Triads, have strong financial support and holdings (Gambetta, 1993; Chu, 2000; Varese, 2001). As a result, the interaction between the state and the traditional longstanding criminal groups is a symbiotic relationship, and hence, they benefit from the post-war arrangements (ibid.). For instance, Chu (2000) observes that the Hong Kong Triads transformed into entrepreneurs to adapt to the changing political and economic situation in the country. The Japanese Yakuza "serves the state" by corrupting the local law enforcement officials and the police for their mutual benefit. In this way, the older organised crime groups can reject outside help from terrorist organisations. The Russian Mafia is another notable example. The Russian Mafia does not ally with terror groups or involve itself in the chemical, biological, radiological, and nuclear defence (CBRN) market (Dishman, 2001). The Russian Mafia has a steady flow of money and makes huge profits from various activities such as debt collection, extortion, and legitimate business (Varese, 2001).

TERRORISM AND CRIMINALITY

The United Nations Convention Against Transnational Organised Crime defines an "organised criminal group" in Article 2 as "a structured group of three or more persons, existing for a period of time and acting in concert with the aim of committing one or more serious crimes or offences [...], in order to obtain, directly or indirectly, a financial or other material benefit" (United Nations, 2004, p. 5). On the other hand, defining terrorism has been controversial from the beginning, and the first proposal for a formal definition of terrorism was submitted in 1937 (Ligeti & Lassalle, 2018). The proposal was to establish an International Court addressing terrorism, with a focus on terrorism as an attack on the state and state officials[1] (Pella, 1950). The international framework has adopted 19 legal instruments to date to prevent terrorist acts in specific areas, such as civil aviation, the taking of hostages, nuclear material, maritime navigation, and so on. Further, in 1996, a draught convention on international terrorism defined terrorism as "when the purpose of the conduct, by its nature or context, is to intimidate a population or to compel a government or an international organisation to do or to abstain from doing any act" (Article 2(1)).

The definition of a terrorist group is controversial as well (Carrapico et al., 2014). A terrorist group not only represents the "identity of the actor" but also the "nature of the act of violence" (Carrapico et al., 2014). The European Union (EU) defines a terrorist group as "a structured group of more than two persons, established over a period of time and acting in concert to commit terrorist offences" (Council of the European Union, 2002, n.p.). Schmid et al. (1988, 2014) provided two academic definitions of terrorism, which were adopted by the United Nations. Scholars agree that there are some key elements central to the definition of terrorism: (a) intentional violence; (b) violence is meant to spread fear not just among the targeted population but also among a wider audience; and (c) political motivation (Schmid & Jongman, 1988; Enders & Sandler, 2012; Hoffman, 2006). Phillips (2015) argues that when it comes to defining terrorist groups, the literature often lacks a thorough discussion of what constitutes a "terrorist group." Jones and Libicki (2008) describe a terrorist group as "a collection of individuals belonging to a non-state entity that uses terrorism to achieve its objectives" (p. 3). Carter offers a similar definition: "A terrorist group is defined as a group that uses terrorist tactics, meaning it deliberately targets civilians in pursuit of political goals" (2012, p. 130).

The 1990s saw a sudden "rise in human smuggling and trafficking by organised crime" (Hutchinson & O'Malley, 2007, p. 1087), primarily because of the lower risks of being detected or prosecuted compared to the drug trade. By the 1990s, the drug trade had been successfully cracked down on by the United States and other countries. As a result of this, large volumes of human cargo were moved from Russia, China, Central Asia, and India by the crime groups, estimated at billions of dollars (Hutchinson & O'Malley, 2007; Shelley & Picarelli, 2002; Levi, 2007). In the guise of human trafficking, terrorist organisations and crime groups mask the movement of their members into other countries. For example, Tamil Tigers smuggle and traffic Sri Lankans, Afghans, and Pakistanis to the Middle East to mask the movement of Al Qaeda operatives (Hutchinson & O'Malley, 2007; Shelley & Picarelli, 2002). This also highlights the highly complicated and extensive operational and organisational bases of terrorist organisations and crime groups. After that, in 2001, the Palermo Convention "called upon all States to recognise the links between transnational organised criminal activities and acts of terrorism."[2] The United Nations Security Council Resolution 1373, Paragraph 7 (28 September 2001), notes that "illicit drugs, money laundering, illegal arms, trafficking, and illegal movement" are the largest sources of income for criminal groups and terrorists (Shelley & Picarelli, 2002). In 2014, the United Nations Security Council adopted Resolution 2195, calling upon states to address the crime-terror nexus as a "threat to international peace and security."

There are also small-scale crimes that fund terrorist activities, such as the manufacture of fake credit cards and credit card fraud by the Tamil Tigers and Al Qaeda. Scholars have also argued that the Madrid bombings in 2004 were a result of terrorists surviving off petty crimes like credit card fraud (Hutchinson & O'Malley, 2007). Members of Abu Sayyaf also resort to kidnapping for ransom to finance their terrorist activities (Sanderson, 2004). The growing cooperation between terrorist organisations and crime groups expands their area of operation, develops revenue streams, and provides logistical support (Shelley & Picarelli, 2007). The crime-terror nexus finds its roots in the transformation of both sides or groups into networked cells that facilitate relationships rather than create a structural bond (Neumann & Salinas, 2017). Such a nexus demonstrates the weakness of the states (Makarenko & Mesquita, 2014) and the independence of these criminal and terrorist groups to function independently of the country and thereby flourish in conflict areas (Shelley, 2014). West Sands Advisory LLP (2012) suggests that the crime-terror nexus takes different forms: alliances with long-term relationships, appropriation, integration to acquire tactical capabilities, or hybridisation, where one type of group transforms into another.

Furthermore, stringent policy reforms limiting terrorist financing have further deprived terrorists of most of their funding, triggering a "turn to crime" (Alda & Sala, 2014, p. 3), making "criminal activity the lifeblood of terrorism" (Makarenko & Mesquita, 2014, p. 138). Shelley (2014) argues that such a transformation has given rise to "business logic in terrorism" (p. 320), where terrorists are compared to white-collar criminals who share a similar logic of maximising profits and advantages in varied conditions. Terrorist organisations and criminal groups share a common desire to establish a transnational presence, which expands their network and makes contact a "force multiplier" (Dishman, 2005; Miklaucic & Brewer, 2013; Farah, 2013). Subsequently, terrorist groups insulated their operations against the clampdown on funding by insourcing the bulk of their financing (Dishman, 2001). Williams (2001, 2008) called this shift "do-it-yourself organised crime," and some called it "the crime-terror nexus" (Makarenko, 2004). ISIS is an example of the crime-terror nexus that recruits members from the criminal underworld (Basra & Neumann, 2016). ISIS engages in various kinds of theft, fraud, and low-level crimes to "micro-finance the Caliphate" (Ranstorp, 2016; Braw, 2015; Warrick & Miller, 2016). Jihadists use their criminal skills to become violent attackers (Basra & Neumann, 2017), morphing into a "gangster jihad" (Rekawek et al., 2017, p. 7). Gangster jihadism is a hybrid version of violence where individuals drift from the criminal world to jihadism. The Irish Republican Army dissident groups and the Kosovo Liberation Army (KLA) are examples of terrorist-criminal hybrids (Makarenko, 2012).

A cutdown on funding by the states compelled terrorists to finance their organisations and attacks through other sources such as information technology and globalisation (Makarenko, 2004; Dishman, 2001, 2005; Picarelli, 2012). Globalisation opened the global market for all and paved the way for increased communication and interactions between criminals and terrorist groups. The crime-terror nexus has adopted technology and is now adept at using modern technologies. Growing dependence on information technology makes transactions easier, and planning becomes more efficient for criminal and terrorist groups. Globalisation, coupled with information and communication technology (ICT), has strengthened the crime-terror nexus over the years. Criminal groups and terrorist organisations mutually benefit from modern technology. Terrorists gain access to new material where deals can be secured online, and this fulfils their ideological needs while the terrorists pay the mafia huge sums of money for the materials.

THE ROLE OF PERSONAL CONNECTIONS

It is important to consider the connection between crime and terror in terms of the personal connections between the members of the two groups. The crime-terror nexus is most substantial on a personal level. In Syria, the role of personal connections is particularly impressive. There is evidence of cooperation between fighters from Hayat Tahrir al-Sham and ISIS operatives (Stewart, 2017). In the planning of an attack, trust plays an important role. Contacts are built with family members or with people who connect with the hardships (Bakker, 2006; Sageman, 2004). The involvement of family members in jihadist terror activities was evident in the Netherlands, where seven people were arrested for planning an attack. Morat M, the half-brother of Abdelkarim el-A., was killed in Aleppo in 2015. His other half-brother, Mohammed, was arrested in Germany in 2013 for trying to travel to Syria to join the jihadist group. He was later convicted in the Netherlands in 2016 (Winters, 2018).

However, Mehra (2016) argues that most people who come to conflict regions are involved in petty crimes, some in serious crimes, and not all of them grew up in relative deprivation. People who left Western countries like the Netherlands to travel to Syria grew up in large or middle-class cities with relatively high crime rates, with youth participating in criminal activities. Social cohesion among these youth was considerably strong, and they shared tight bonds (Kouwenhoven, 2014). "There are several known cases where people who have come to know and trust each other reach out to each other when they need assistance when preparing to commit offences" (van der Veer, 2019, n.p.). Trust is often built into prison; for example, Chérif Kouachi and Amedy Coulibaly. Kouachi and Coulibaly first met at the Fleury-Mérogis prison near Paris in 2007. They formed a bond and built a friendship after spending seven months in the same prison. After that, in January 2015, eight years later, they carried out the Paris attacks, killing 17 people (Basra et al., 2016).

STYLES OF CRIMINAL ORGANISATION

The recent terrorist phenomenon has witnessed the movement of foreign fighters from Europe to Iraq and Syria to fight alongside the Islamic State and other terrorist groups. The difference here is that these individuals have criminal pasts and have adopted the ideology of Salafi-jihadism. This is different from the past, where the Italian mafia and criminal Balkan outfits occasionally bombed or struck against the state, largely because of the obstruction of their criminal activities. This new form of terrorist organisation is "more a confederation of individuals and entities than an organised body of procedures and hierarchies" (Brisard, 2002, p. 2). Hutchinson & O'Malley (2007) argued that there exist "two polar types of criminal activity" (p. 1099): the ephemeral-sporadic and the organised-enduring formations. The ephemeral-sporadic terrorist group requires "specialised skills, an elementary division of labour, few resources, low initial expenditure, and little or no reliance on the existence or establishment of stabilising techniques such as corruption" (Hutchinson & O'Malley, 2007, p. 1099). Such a group has low financial costs for carrying out attacks. For example, in 2000, the *USS Cole* bombing was estimated at around $5,000 compared to the Madrid train bombings, which were estimated at around $10,000 (Brisard, 2002). The monetary requirements are low because the crimes are petty and do not require an elaborate organisational base. Such organisations are also referred to as "profit-for-violence" cells.

Organised-enduring terrorist groups, on the other hand, are more enduring and last over longer periods, thereby having higher financial demands than ephemeral-sporadic terrorist groups. However, since the primary purpose of organised-enduring terrorist groups requires an enduring and regular flow of income, members of the group are "prone to disloyalty when subject to bribery, subversive opportunities to make money, or threats of violence" (Hutchinson & O'Malley, 2007, p. 1101). Such a group also lacks a hierarchical structure with money as the primary motive; trust becomes a problem for these groups. In comparison to the ephemeral-sporadic terrorist groups, the organised-enduring cells are better placed to engage in violence and are well structured. A suitable example is the Liberation Tigers of Tamil Eelam (LTTE), with cells in 38 countries in Europe, North America, and the Middle East, which funds the organisation through a range of criminal activities: extortion, social security fraud, counterfeit currency trading, piracy, human trafficking, gun smuggling, drug trade, and credit card fraud (Williams, 2001). These activities are carried out through well-established "in-house" specialised cells.

Despite differences, there are conflicts where cooperation between the groups is evident. These are situations where the state is weak, where organised crime syndicates control the illegal markets, or when a crime is related to new transnational organised crime groups or terrorist organisations (Hutchinson & O'Malley, 2007). For example, the Peruvian "Shining Path" and the Columbian FARC guerrillas (Schmid, 1996) provide logistics and security support to South American drug cartels to produce and traffic narcotics. The LTTE and the Columbian leftist group M19 engage in similar activities. In all these cases, organised criminal groups use the help of terrorist groups to meet their economic agendas. The new transnational crime groups originate in failing states or post-conflict regions. They tend to make money and achieve their aims through chaos, malfunctioning state administrations, lawlessness, and a conflict-ridden society. As a result of the chaos in society, there has been a drastic increase in criminal activities to establish control and power. In the case of Somalia, the conflict marked the arrival of large transnational organised crime groups to profit from the volatile internal situation. The local clans halt the influx of transnational groups to save the region. Hutchinson and O'Malley (2007) argue that transnational groups and terrorists converge mostly in "Latin America, the Balkans, the Caucasus, regions in West Africa, Afghanistan, and Iraq" (p. 1105).

COUNTERING THE CRIME-TERROR NEXUS

Wannenburg (2003) argues that Al-Qaeda depends on reverse money laundering to fund its military council. The United States adopted a strict policy to combat the financing of terrorism after the September 2001 attacks (Mcculloch & Pickering, 2005; Wannenburg, 2003). The war against terror constituted international and national measures such as the adoption of the UN Security Council Resolution and the International Convention for the Suppression of the Financing of Terrorism (Sheppard, 2002; Hardister, 2003). However, some scholars argue that aggressive anti-terrorism measures tend to interfere with and intrude into the national politics of other countries (Hardister, 2003). The US Center for Defense Information (2002) reportedly froze around 112 million dollars in funds linked to al-Qaeda and other groups. In the 2011 resolution on organised crime, the European Parliament emphasises that "although there is a risk that criminal organisations may cooperate increasingly frequently with terrorist organisations, organised crime should be treated separately from terrorism" (p. 2). The European Union called for a broad strategy to tackle the crime-terror nexus and analyse it not only as the union of crime and terror but also their interactions (West Sands Advisory LLP, 2012). Shelley and Picarelli (2007) proposed seven recommendations for a criminal policy that deals with crime-terror interactions. Orlova and Moore (2004) argued in favour of a "building block approach" instead of an "umbrella approach" that addresses both issues together and on a larger scale. The "building block approach" is based on the "construction of comprehensive legal frameworks to deal with terrorism and organised crime" (Orlova & Moore, 2004, p. 269).

Van der Veer (2019) argues that to counter terrorist networks, "it takes a network to fight a network" (n.p.). Similarly, "'it takes a nexus to counter a nexus': organisations need to be able to overlook their institutional barriers between those working on crime and those working on terrorism to be effective" (van der Veer, 2019, n.p.). However, achieving such synchronicity in countering the crime-terror nexus is not always easy. Practitioners and organisations are not always able to effectively cross the boundaries between crime and terror (Neumann & Basra, 2018). Van der Veer (2019) argues that there exist technical and legal issues where "operational systems that carry data about criminals are often not technically compatible with systems carrying similar data for (potential) extremists or terrorists" (n.p.). There are differences in the systems and software used around the world. Ensuring the validity of the data on international terrorism is complicated. Van der Veer (2019) also highlights the problem of culture in countering the crime-terror nexus. "Investigating a possible terrorist or extremist offence with the intention of preventing it always requires investigation 'before the fact,' whereas regular police investigations usually investigate crimes already committed, hence 'after the fact'" (van der Veer, 2019, n.p.). Cultural investigations demand open minds that can cross over the boundaries between crime and terror.

Scholars also call for good governance as a critical first step towards a comprehensive approach that inoculates the region against supporting the crime-terror nexus. To maintain peace and security, such a strategy requires strong legislation and efficient law enforcement systems. A key task of security agencies is to be able to prevent terrorist and criminal groups from exploiting local dynamics, such as poverty or acts of injustice. But there can be moments when the locals and community members find trust and support in the terrorist and criminal groups operating in the region. This often emanates from sharing mutual religious and historical sentiments in the region (Shah, 2012). The local population welcomes any support gathered in the name of fulfilling mutual aims of self-determination. Therefore, there is a tendency to buy into the community the idea that terrorist or criminal groups are the authority and the source of "good governance" in the region. Communities believe that recognition of advanced cultural and social changes is the first step to achieving social justice (Shah, 2019). Schanzer (in Detmer, 2013) proposes that extremist groups their religio-political agenda by engaging in criminal activities. Schanzer further argues that the primary motive of the radical groups is jihadists "in the name of religion." This reasoning was supported by Stepanova (2005), who proposes that even though attacks are carried out for economic gains, it is "not their dominant raison d'etre." The Salafist-organised follow a similar ideological doctrine, which helps them justify southern crime in the name of religion. Under these circumstances, the state loses the trust of the people and fails to curb the activities of the crime-terror nexus. These dynamics are evident in southern Thailand and terrorist Philippines, where the nexus can grow and persist. Despite the fear experienced by the locals because of criminals and their activities, there is hope that positive social change can happen (Shah, 2013).

Scholars also suggest greater community resilience against criminals and terrorists by establishing strong legal precedents and laws. The state has to ensure effective management and functioning of the local security services to deter citizens from cooperating or collaborating with criminals and terrorists. In addition to these hard approaches, there is a need to keep a check on the flow of illicit financial flows. For example, the Philippines, Malaysia, and Indonesia have joined maritime patrols to counter the growing insecurity in the tri-border region of the Southern Philippines, East Malaysia, and Sulawesi (Quilop, 2018). The three ASEAN member states have jointly collaborated to ensure greater intelligence cooperation to counter the crime-terror nexus.

CONCLUSION

The crime-terror nexus presents itself as a complex phenomenon with serious social, political, and economic consequences. Over the years, scholars have provided ample evidence of the blurring of the lines of distinction between the two groups. The rise of ISIS over the past decade is a notable example of the blurred lines of the crime-terror nexus. ISIS presents an amalgamation of both crime and terror in its use of violence all over the world. Therefore, there is no definite conclusion as to how organised crime and terror intersect or converge. Scholars developed the concept of a crime-terror nexus from 1999 to 2009. The alliance between crime and terror works in several different ways that are presented in this chapter. For some, ideology legitimises the use of violence, and in other cases, personal motives and connections play an essential role in dictating violence. There exist apparent cultural, ideological, political, operational, and practical differences between criminal and political groups. Both groups seek self-transformation at some point. Tactic and strategic alliances between criminal and terrorist groups occur depending on the situation. There are times when their aims and motivations converge, but there are also instances when the relationship is momentary and cannot sustain itself long-term. Makarenko (2002) points out that the nexus has developed because of their "common convergence of causes." Transnational organised crime groups such as the Sicilian Mafia, the Hong Kong Triads, and the Russian Mafia do not cooperate with terror groups because they are financially stable and have useful state contacts.

In contrast, the newly formed criminal actors thrive in chaos and ongoing conflicts (Shelley, 2005). They tend to have a very different attitude towards terrorists. They depend on terrorist groups not just financially but also ideologically. Walter (2015) explains that criminal groups use extremist ideology and create a "market niche" that facilitates the hiring of better recruits.

Ridley (2008) argues that the linkages occur in states that face economic transition or in failing states. Sanderson (2004) asserts that the nexus can prove to be a lethal cocktail, "consisting of one part criminal, one part terrorist, and one part weak or corrupt state, which poses a formidable and increasingly powerful challenge to the US and global interests" (p. 59). Further, it is crucial to keep in mind that there exist several different criminal groups and terrorist organisations, and each of them is distinct from the others. They differ in several aspects: group composition, level of organisation, degree of networking, and so on. To ascertain which group or organisation will engage in what level of violence, it is essential to consider the individual traits, capacities, and needs of these groups and organisations. Much of the current research on terrorism draws on preexisting expertise in organised crime and terror. To increase this breadth of knowledge, there is a need to conduct more ethnographic field research to get deeper insights into the changing dynamics of the nexus.

The growing power of ISIS and other new groups intensifies the need for efficient responses (Stern & Berger, 2015). The state needs to formulate effective and efficient responses to understand and tackle illegal transnational organisations. Countries need to employ strategies and policies that overlap between counterterrorism and anti-crime. Governments and international organisations need to become more responsive and agile in countering the crime-terror nexus. Scholars assert the need for a fully compartmentalised approach: "It takes a nexus to fight a nexus." A synchronised and holistic approach is required to counter the problem of crime and terror.

Notes

1 Convention for the Prevention and Punishment of Terrorism, League of Nations, November 16, 1937.
2 General Assembly resolution 55/25, November 15, 2000, Recital 6.

References

Alda, E., & Sala, J.L. (2014). Links between terrorism, organized crime and crime: The case of the Sahel Region. *International Journal of Security & Development, 3*(1),1–9.

Andreas, P. (2008). *Blue helmets and black markets*. Ithaca, NY: Cornell University Press.

Aronson, S. (2014, April). AQIM's threat to western interests in the Sahel. *Combating Terrorism Center Sentinel, 7*, 6–9.

Bakker, E. (2006). *Jihadi terrorists in Europe, their characteristics and the circumstances in which they joined the Jihad: An exploratory study*. Netherlands Institute of International Relations Clingendael.

Ballina, S. (2011). The crime-terror continuum revisited: A model for the study of hybrid criminal organizations. *Journal of Policing, Intelligence, and Counter Terrorism, 6*, 121–136.

Basra, R., Neumann, P.R., & Brunner, C. (2016). *Criminal pasts, terrorist futures: European jihadists and the new crime-terror nexus*. London: ICSR.

Basra, R., & Neumann, P.R. (2016). Criminal pasts, terrorist futures: European jihadists and the new crime-terror nexus. *Perspectives on Terrorism, 10*(6), 25–40.

Basra, R., & Neumann, P.R. (2017, October). Crime as Jihad: Developments in the crimeterror nexus in Europe. *CTC Sentinel, 10*(9),1–6.

Braw, E. (2015, October 25). Foreign fighters financing. *Foreign Affairs*.

Brisard, J.C. (2002, December 19). Terrorism financing: Roots and trends of Saudi terrorism financing. *Report Prepared for the President of the Security Council*, United Nations.

Carrapico, H., Irrera, D., & Tupman, B. (2014). Transnational organised crime and terrorism: Different peas, same pod? *Global Crime, 15*(3-4), 213–218. 10.1080/17440572.2014.939882

Carter, D.B. (2012). A blessing or a curse? State support for terrorist groups. *International Organization, 66*(1), 129–151.

Chu, Y.K. (2000). *The triads as business*. New York: Routledge.

Cockayne, J. (2013). Chasing shadows: Strategic responses to organized crime in conflict-affected situations. *RUSI Journal, 2*, 10–24.

Cockayne, J., & Lupel, A. eds. (2011). *Peace operations and organized crime: Enemies or allies*. New York: Routledge.

Council of the European Union. (2002). *Council framework decision on combating terrorism*. OJEU L 164/3. Brussels: Publications Office of the European Union.

Detmer, J. (2013, September 12). Syria's jihadists linked to organized crime. *The Daily Beast*. Accessed December 14, 2019. http://www.thedailybeast.com/articles/2013/12/09/syria-s-jihadists-linked-to-organized-crime.html

Dishman, C. (2001). Terrorism, crime, and transformation. *Studies in Conflict & Terrorism, 24*, 43–58.

Dishman, C. (2005). The leaderless nexus: When crime and terror converge. *Studies in Conflict and Terrorism, 28*(3), 237–252.

Enders, W., & Sandler, T. (2012). *The political economy of terrorism*. Cambridge: Cambridge University Press.

Farah, D. (2013). Fixers, superfixers, and shadow facilitators: How networks connect. In J. Brewer & M. Miklaucic (Eds.), *Convergence: Illicit networks and national security in the age of globalization* (pp. 75–96). Washington, DC: NDU Press.

Felbab-Brown, V. (2019, March). The crime–terror nexus and its fallacies, in Erica Chenoweth, and others (eds). *The Oxford handbook of terrorism*, Oxford Handbooks (2019; online edn, Oxford Academic). https://doi.org/10.1093/oxfordhb/9780198732914.013.22

Gambetta, D. (1993). *The Sicilian mafia*. Cambridge: Harvard University Press.

Groenendijk, P., & Rosman, C. (2017, January 28). Terreurbestrijder Schoof: Criminelen helpen jihadisten. *Algemeen Dagblad*. URL (accessed 24 January 2019): http://www.ad.nl/dossiernieuws/terreurbestrijder-schoof-criminelen-helpen-jihadisten~ac5332ba/.

Hardister, A. (2003). Can we buy peace on earth? The price of freezing terrorist assets in a post-September 11 world. *North Carolina Journal of International Law and Commercial Regulation, 28*, 605–661.

Hoffman, B. (2006). *Inside terrorism*. New York: Columbia University Press.

Hutchinson, S., & O'Malley, P. (2006). Actual and potential links between terrorism and criminality. *Trends in Terrorism Series, Integrated Threat Assessment Centre (ITAC), 5*(4), 5–8.

Hutchinson, S., & O'malley, P. (2007). A crime–terror nexus? Thinking on some of the links between terrorism and criminality. *Studies in Conflict Terrorism, 30*(12), 1095–1106.

Ibanez, L.C. (2013). To what extent do global terrorism and organized criminality converge?: General parameters and critical scenarios. *Institute of Forensic Sciences and Security of the Autonomous University of Madrid*, 1–28.

Jones, S.G., & Libicki, M.C. (2008). *How terrorist groups end: Lessons for countering al Qa'ida*. Washington, DC: RAND.

Koenders, B. (2017). Speech by minister Koenders to the plenary meeting of the foreign terrorist fighters working group of the global counterterrorism forum (GCTF), 18 May. URL (accessed 24 December 2019): https://www.rijksoverheid.nl/binaries/rijksoverheid/documenten/toespraken/2017/05/18/toespraak-minister-koenders-tijdens-bijeenkomst-foreign-terrorist-fighter-werkgroep/GCTF+FTF.pdf.

Kouwenhoven, A. (5 July 2014). Het was niet het geloof dat ze dreef, maar afkeer: de Paradijspoortjongeren zijn in het paradijs, hun doel. in *NRC*. https://www.nrc.nl/nieuws/2014/07/05/het-was-niet-het-geloof-dat-ze-dreef-maar-afkeer-1395774-a1132810

Laqueur, W. (1999). *The new terrorism: Fanaticism and the arms of mass destruction*. Cambridge: Oxford University Press on Demand.

Levi, M. (2007). Organized crime and terrorism. In M. Maguire, R. Morgan, & R. Reiner (Eds.) (4th ed.), *The Oxford handbook of criminology*. Cambridge: Oxford University Press.

Levitt, M. (2012, September). Hizbullah narco-trafficking: A growing cross-border threat. *The Washington Institute*.

Levitt, M. (2015, August 27). Want to know what the IRA is now? It's a trust fund. *The Irish News*.

Ligeti, K., & Lassalle, M. (2018, August). The organised crime-terrorism nexus: How to address the issue of ISIS benefitting from lucrative criminal activities? University of Luxembourg Law Working Paper No. 2018-009; University of Luxembourg Law Working Paper No. 2018-009. Available at SSRN: https://ssrn.com/abstract=3230795 or 10.2139/ssrn.3230795

Lindholm, D.C., & Realuyo, C.B. (2013). Threat finance: Critical enabler for illicit networks. In J. Brewer & M. Miklaucic (Eds.), *Convergence: Illicit networks and national security in the age of globalization* (pp. 111–130). Washington, DC: NDU Press.

Makarenko, T. (2002). Crime, terror, and the central Asian drug trade. *Harvard Asia Quarterly, 6*(3), 1–24.

Makarenko, T. (2004). The crime-terror continuum: Tracing the interplay between transnational organised crime and terrorism. *Global Crime, 6*(1), 129–145.

Makarenko, T. (2012). *Europe's crime-terror nexus: Links between terrorist and organised crime groups in the European Union.* European Parliament Directorate-General for Internal Policies, Policy Department C: Citizens' Rights and Constitutional Affairs, Civil Liberties, Justice and Home Affairs.

Makarenko, T. (2009). Terrorist use of organised crime: Operational tool or exacerbating the threat? In F. Allum, F. Longo, D. Irrera, & P. Kostakos (Eds.), *Defining and defying organised crime: Discourse, perceptions, and reality.* Routledge.

Makarenko, T., & Mesquita, M. (2014). Categorising the crime-terror nexus in the European Union. *15 Global Crime*, 259–274.

Mcculloch, J., & Pickering, S. (2005). Suppressing the financing of terrorism: Proliferating state crime, eroding censure and extending neo-colonialism. *British Journal of Criminology, 45*, 470–486.

Mehra, T. (2016). Foreign terrorist fighters: Trends, dynamics and policy responses. *International Centre for Counter-Terrorism (ICCT).*

Miklaucic, M., & Brewer, J. (2013). Introduction. In J. Brewer & M. Miklaucic (Eds.), *Convergence: Illicit networks and national security in the age of globalization* (pp. xiii–xxi). Washington, DC: NDU Press.

Moreau, R. (2013, June 12). The Taliban's new role as Afghanistan's drug mafia. *Newsweek.*

Neumann, P., & Salinas, A. (2017). Preliminary report on terrorism and transnational organized crime.

Neumann, R., & Basra, R. (2018). The crime-terror nexus in the Netherlands. *Crime Terror Nexus.*

Orlova, A.V., & Moore, J.W. (2004). Umbrellas or building blocks: Defining international terrorism and transnational organized crime in international law. *Houston Journal of International Law, 27*, 267.

Pella, V.V. (1950). Towards an international criminal court. *The American Journal of International Law, 44*, 37–68.

Wang, P., & Wang, J. (2009). Transnational crime: Its containment through international cooperation. *Asian Social Science, 5*, 10. DOI:10.5539/ass.v5n11p25

Phillips, B.J. (2015). What is a terrorist group? Conceptual issues and empirical implications. *Terrorism and Political Violence, 27*, 225–242.

Picarelli, J. (2012). Osama bin Corleone? Vito the Jackal? Framing threat convergence through an examination of transnational organized crime and international terrorism. *Terrorism and Political Violence, 24*(2), 183.

Quilop, R.J.G. (2018, March 26). Trilateral cooperation by Indonesia, Malaysia and the Philippines: Temper expectations. *Global Asia.* Available at: https://www.globalasia.org/v13no1/feature/trilateral-

Ranstorp, M. (2016, May 25). Microfinancing the caliphate: How the Islamic State is unlocking the assets of European recruits. *CTC Sentinel.*

Rekawek, K., Matejka, S., Babikova, M., Nagy, T., & Rafay, J. (2017). *From criminals to terrorists and back?* Bratislava: GLOBSEC.

Ridley, N. (2008). Organized crime, money laundering, and terrorism. *Policing, 2*(1), 28–35.

Sageman, M. (2004). *Understanding terror networks.* University of Pennsylvania Press.

Sanderson, T. (2004). Transnational terror and organized crime: Blurring the lines. *SAIS Review, XXIV*(1), 49–61.

Schmid, A. (1996). The links between transnational organized crime and terrorist crimes. *Transnational Organized Crime, 2*, 40–82.

Schmid, A., Albert, J., & Irving, H. (1988). *Political terrorism: A new guide to actors, authors, concepts, databases, theories, and literature.* Amsterdam: Transaction Books.

Schmid, A.P., & Jongman, A. (1988). *Political terrorism: A new guide to actors, authors, concepts, data bases, theories, and literature.* New Brunswick, NJ: Transaction.

Shah, T.M. (2012). Collective memory and narrative: Ethnography of social trauma in Jammu and Kashmir. Master's thesis, Kansas State University, Manhattan, KS.

Shah, T.M. (2013). Chaos and fear: Creativity and hope in an uncertain world. *International Sociology, 28*(5), 513–517.

Shah, T.M. (2019). Social justice and change. In S. Romaniuk, M. Thapa, & P. Marton (Eds.), *The palgrave encyclopedia of global security studies.* Cham: Palgrave Macmillan.

Shelley, L. (2002). The nexus of organized international criminals and terrorism. *International Annals of Criminology, 40*(1-2), 1–6.

Shelley, L. (2005). The unholy trinity: Transnational crime, corruption, and terrorism. *Brown Journal of World Affairs, 11*(2), 101–111.

Shelley, L. (2014). *Dirty entanglements: Corruption, crime, and terrorism.* Cambridge: Cambridge University Press.

Shelley, L., & Picarelli, J.T. (2002). Methods not motives: Implications of the convergence of international organized crime and terrorism. *Police Practice and Research, 3*(4), 305–318.

Shelley, L., & Picarelli, J.T. (2007). Organized crime and terrorism. In J.K. Giraldo & H.A. Trinkunas (Eds.), *Terrorism financing and state responses: A comparative perspective* (pp. 39–55). Redwood City.

Sheppard, H.E. (2002). U.S. actions to freeze assets of terrorism: Manifest and latent implications for Latin America. *American University International Law Review, 17*, 625–639.

Stepanova, E. (2005, December). Illicit drug trafficking and Islamic terrorism as threats to Russian security: The limits of the linkage. *PONARS Policy Memo No. 393, Institute for World Economy and International Relations.*

Stern, J., & Berger, J.M. (2015). *ISIS: The state of terror.* London: HarperCollins Publishers.

Stewart, S. (2017). Can the Islamic State and al Qaeda find common ground? in *Stratfor Worldview.* https://worldview.stratfor.com/article/can-islamic-state-and-al-qaeda-find-common-ground

Stringer, K.D. (2011). Tackling threat finance: A labor for hercules or sisyphus. *Parameters, 41*(1), 101–119.

Sullivan, J. (2012). Criminal insurgency: Narcocultura, social banditry, and information operations. *Small Wars Journal*, 1–13. Sullivan uses Los Zetas of Mexico as an example of a criminal insurgency.

United Nations. (2004). *United nations convention against transnational organised crime.* Vienna: United Nations Office on Drugs and Crime.

US Center for Defense Information. (2002, October 25). Terrorist finances. [Online] Available: www.Cdi.org/terrorism/finance_primer-pr.cfm

Varese, F. (2001). *The Russian mafia*. Oxford University Press.

van der Veer, R. (2019). The crime-terrorism nexus. *Strategic Monitor 2018-2019.* [online] Clingendael.org. Available at: https://www.clingendael.org/pub/2018/strategic-monitor-2018-2019/the-crime-terrorism-nexus/ [Accessed 20 November 2019].

Warrick, J., & Miller, G. (23 March, 2016). New ISIS recruits have deep criminal roots. *Washington Post.*

Wannenburg, G. (2003). Links between organized crime and al-Qaeda. *Spring, 10*(4), 1–14.

Walter, B. (2015, February 3). The strategic incentives for violent extremism. Political Violence at a Glance.

West Sands Advisory LLP. (2012). Europe's crime-terror nexus: Links between terrorist and organised crime groups in the European Union. *Report for the European Parliament.*

Williams, P. (2001). Transnational criminal enterprises, conflict, and instability. In C. Crocker, F.O. Hampson, & P. Aall (Eds.), *Turbulent peace: Challenges of managing international conflict* (pp. 97–112). Washington: US Institute of Peace Press.

Williams, P. (2008). Terrorist financing and organized crime: Nexus, appropriation or transformation? In T. Biersteker & S. Eckert (Eds.), *Countering the financing of terrorism* (pp. 126–149). London: Routledge.

Winters, B. (2018, September 29). Waarom Arnhem een Jihadnest is. *De Gelderlander.* https://www.gelderlander.nl/arnhem/waarom-arnhem-een-jihadnest-is~a93f54e2/?referrer=https%3A%2F%2Fwww.google.com%2F

13

STATE-SPONSORED TERRORISM

Perspectives on Its Practice, Evolution, and Impacts

Gordon Alley-Young

INTRODUCTION

State-sponsored terrorism (SST) occurs when a government, nation, or state provides support, directly or indirectly, actively or passively, to non-state individuals or groups (i.e., proxies) both domestically and abroad who violently coerce, intimidate, suppress, and/or eliminate individuals or groups who are identified as enemies and/or opponents of the state. SST has a long history, while the term was coined relatively recently and has been engaged in by a wide array of governments, nations, and states. While many nations have engaged in behaviours that might be identified as SST, the actual designation of states as terrorist sponsors is, as critics argue, subjective and politicised. This chapter will define the phenomenon as it has been conceptualised by various scholars and historians, discuss how and why SST is perpetuated, identify several governments, nations, and states identified for their engagement with SST, consider how SST might evolve as a relationship dynamic and as a social phenomenon, evaluate attempts to curtail SST, and detail SST's varying impacts. This chapter will conclude by highlighting salient points of the discussion, providing suggestions for future investigations of this phenomenon, and reflecting on the long-term effect of SST.

STATE-SPONSORED TERRORISM: AN OVERVIEW

Fayazi (2017) argues that terrorism, as a term, is both controversial and challenging to define because each definition represents the interests of different stakeholders, which highlights different targets, types of violence, and terroristic purposes. Martin (2017) posits terrorism as perpetuated by governments against their perceived enemies. Fayazi's (2017) definition specifies the targets as non-combatants, the purposes as revenge, intimidation, and influence, and actions that range from bombings to disfigurement. Duncan (2011) distinguishes terrorism from insurgency, where insurgency happens within the context of war between the so-called legitimate combatants, while terrorism involves deliberately attacking civilians. Duncan (2011) notes that when insurgents change tactics to attack civilians, they become terrorists, and their supporters therefore become SST. Byman (2020) considers terrorism in war and insurgency an ambiguous area that makes definitions of SST challenging (i.e., insurgent groups that have engaged in terrorism in the past).

Given the challenges in defining terrorism, there are differing foci of this sponsored terror. Berkowitz (2018) defines state sponsorship as "the deliberate provision of resources and material support to a nondomestic terrorist organization by a government institution" (p. 712). This definition of sponsorship specifies SST as a phenomenon perpetuated by one state against another group or nation outside its borders, while other theorists include domestic terrorism in their conceptual definitions of the term. For instance, Martin (2017) argues that state terrorism can be directed internationally or domestically, depending on the locus of the perceived enemy. Similarly, Saltzman (2020) recognises this dual focus in his conceptualisation of internal state terror (IST). Saltzman (2020, p. 193) argues, "Unlike inter-state 'us' vs. 'them' dynamics focused on outsiders, IST requires producing or intensifying intra-state 'us' vs. 'them' antagonistic dynamics to drive a wedge between people who know each other: neighbours, coworkers, friends, and even family". Jalata (2017) similarly recognises how state terrorism is used domestically to violently eliminate political opposition (i.e., a different national movement, ethnicity, or culture) by destroying its leaders and culture of resistance. Another related concept is government-sponsored mass killing (Uzonyi & Hanania, 2017).

In addition to questions about whether SST is directed externally or internally, questions can be raised about what

DOI: 10.4324/9780429426063-15

sponsorship of terror actually means. For Fayazi (2017), sponsorship is active, intentional, and thus deliberate by way of the state itself or an organisation it designates carrying out the attack, an attack facilitated by state-allocated money, weapons, training, and/or refuge. Others, like Byman (2020), question the validity of grouping states actively supporting terror groups with those states that might better be described as passive supporters. For example, a country like Kenya that lacks the resources to fight Al-Shebaab might be perceived as a passive supporter because its inability to act allows the terror organisation to exist within the country.

Saltzman (2020) cites Alexander Dallin and George Breslauer as coining the term "state terrorism" in 1970 as "the arbitrary use, by organs of political authority, of severe coercion against individuals or groups, the credible threat of such use, or the arbitrary extermination of such individuals or groups" (Dallin and Breslauer cited in Saltzman, 2020, p. 188). Two years later, in 1972, the US Bureau of Counterterrorism coined SST when it noted certain states as state sponsors for repeatedly providing critical support to non-state-terrorist groups (Kirchner, 2014). Historians document terrorism in the first century with the Sicarii, who attacked Roman and Jewish civilians in their fight against Roman rule in Palestine and also during the Reign of Terror of France's revolutionary government, but the use of terrorism as a term meaning a covert group acting violently against society originated in reference to the Anarchist Movement in the mid-to-late 1800s (Duncan, 2011).

HOW AND WHY IS STATE-SPONSORED TERRORISM USED?

During the War of the Second Coalition (1798–1802) on revolutionary France by a collective of monarchies led by Britain, Austria, and Russia, Britain sponsored both Royalist insurgents and terrorists (though they were called conspirators at the time, not terrorists) in France as a low-cost and low-risk alternative to war. Duncan (2011) cites this example to underscore that terrorism is not exclusive to rightist, leftist, nationalist, separatist, and/or religious organisations but is used by many organisations and states so long as it is useful in achieving one's political goals. Drury et al. (2011) concur, noting that states have supported terrorism since the concept's inception to advance their foreign policy goals (e.g., pressure or harass an opponent state or divide their military resources). For some governments, SST is their de facto foreign policy towards certain states, and for others, it is a diplomacy tool to get diplomatic relations reinstated, have sanctions lifted, or improve the political climate, and it does not always result in war (Gal-Or, 1993; Martin, 2017). For example, Pakistan supports groups infiltrating Indian-held Kashmir to pressure India without directly attacking it (i.e., using proxies) (Drury et al., 2011). Similarly, India did not engage Pakistan with its alleged Cold Start doctrine after the SST of the Mumbai terrorist attacks, fearing that a shot across the border would be provocative and escalate tensions (Biswas, 2017). Instead, India warned that if Pakistan initiated another terror attack like those in Mumbai in November 2008, they would support the secessionist movement in the Pakistani province of Balochistan; this is referred to as India's sub-conventional war strategy (Biswas, 2017).

When SST is conducted covertly, it might allow deniability and low risk (i.e., engaging foreign nationals as proxy combatants abroad to create pressure to secure favourable policy outcomes from opponents at the bargaining table) (Martin, 2017). However, the 1990–91 Gulf Crisis demonstrated terrorist diplomacy that was both overt and led to war when Saddam Hussein took around 10,000 foreign nationals from Iraq and Kuwait and held them in strategic military locations to both divide its enemies and prevent coalition attacks (Gal-Or, 1993). When Hussain released the hostages, declaring it a conciliatory gesture meant to avert war while also declaring the presence of Iraqi-loyal terrorist surrogates overseas, neither action prevented a war with the coalition forces (Gal-Or, 1993). SST may be used by both democracies and dictatorships alike to ensure state security and order; however, this is sometimes accomplished with extreme violence (Martin, 2017, p. 4).

SST can be considered in terms of the degree, breadth, and duration of violence and in terms of how complicit the sponsoring state is in the violence. SST can range from a repressive genocide campaign where one ethnic group targets another with oppressive uses of torture where individuals or groups bully, interrogate, shame, and coerce individuals into converting religiously, politically, and/or ideologically (Combs cited in Saltzman, 2020; Iadicola and Shupe cited in Martin, 2017). The threat of violence alone can prompt political change and create or consolidate power for the sponsor (Kirchner, 2014, p. 522). Levels of terrorist sponsorship can vary greatly in reality, even as lists of state sponsors of terror compiled by the US may treat complicity in SST as a singular dimension. For example, Iran has supported Hezbollah with weapons and training, while Syria, Iraq, and Libya have allowed terrorist groups to recruit Palestinian refugees and then used them to attack Jordanian airline pilots (i.e., to derail its peace with Israel) and challenge Yasir Arafat's leadership of the Palestinian movement (Drury et al., 2011; Duncan, 2011). Byman (2005) suggests that such intentional forms of sponsorship should be distinguished from states that inadvertently sponsor terrorism through their failure to act. For example, Thailand not effectively policing its borders allowed terrorists and weapons to cross the border from Malaysia, and Canada's choice not to ban the organisation Liberation Tigers of Tamil Eelam in 2005 despite the United Nations (UN) declaring them a terrorist organisation, even as this failure to ban them allegedly facilitated the organisation being able to extort money from Toronto's large Sri Lankan Tamil community (CBC News, 2005).

STATES IDENTIFIED FOR THEIR ENGAGEMENT IN SST

The US designates Iran, North Korea, Sudan, and Syria as the leading sponsors of terror, while the Obama administration removed Cuba from the state sponsors of terrorism list in 2015 and noted counterterrorism efforts by Sudan in contrast to its history of SST in 2017 (Congressional Research Service, 2018). The US cites Russia's attempts to annex Ukraine by force, a chemical weapons attack in Britain, and violating its nuclear treaties as acts of terrorism, and the US's efforts to call Russia to account for those actions (i.e., expelling 60 diplomats) as evidence of its commitment to fighting terrorism (Pence, 2019). The US identifies Iran as the top sponsor of terrorism worldwide. Byman (2015) argues that Iran's post-revolution reasons for supporting terrorism are undermining and bleeding rivals, projecting power, playing the spoiler (i.e., thwarting Israeli peace negotiations), intimidation (i.e., of those who would ally with the US), deterrence (i.e., of attacks via the potential for violent retaliation), revenge, and preserving options. Pence (2019) reiterated the US position that Iran is the leading world sponsor of terror by supporting groups like Hezbollah and Hamas, supplying missiles, fostering conflict and terrorism in Syria, Yemen, and Europe, and advocating the erasure of the Israeli state. Pence also urged European leaders to support the US in ensuring the effectiveness of sanctions against Iran.

Charges that Iran is the leading worldwide terrorist sponsor have led to criticism of the US for supporting the Muslim Brotherhood in the 1970s in Egypt to fight Marxism and, at various times, Al Qaeda and ISIS, while US ally Saudi Arabia has been criticised for furthering Wahhabism, cited as the key source of radical Islamic extremism (Fayazi, 2017). Also, in the 1970s, it is claimed that the US supported Operation Condor, a pan-Latin American terrorist network including Chile, Argentina, Uruguay, Bolivia, Paraguay, and Brazil (later Peru and Ecuador), meant to prevent Communist subversion (i.e., another Cuba) by sharing tactics, intelligence (i.e., the US helped set up Condortel, an information sharing system between the countries), and providing training (Zanchetta, 2016). In the mid-1980s, senior members of the Reagan administration illegally sold arms to Iran to fund the right-wing Contra rebels who fought against the then-socialist Nicaraguan government. Once the details of this arrangement became public, it was dubbed the Iran-Contra affair or scandal. More recently, cultural critics have argued that the US has a long tradition of terrorising African-Americans, beginning with slavery and evolving into the Prison-Industrial Complex, the practise of private businesses profiting from operating US prisons and also state-run prisons selling inmates' labour, both of which have occurred as the disproportionate imprisonment of African-Americans and the size of the US prison population have increased (Taylor, 2019). While the US has been accused of using labels like *state sponsorship of terror* to advance its political goals, other Western nations have been criticised for not labelling more nations as agents of SST (i.e., Canada) (Byman, 2020).

Iran's Middle East and North African (MENA) regional neighbours, Libya, Syria, and Iraq, have been cited for SST. In the early morning hours of April 5, 1986, Libyan agents, together with German conspirators, bombed La Belle nightclub in Berlin, killing 3 and injuring 230, including 50 US servicemen. Libya, also responsible for the Lockerbie, Scotland, airline bombing, agreed to pay 24 million euros to non-US victims and their families in 2004 in order to normalise relations with Germany (Scheschkewitz & Amies, 2011). In retaliation for the La Belle bombing, the US bombed the Libyan towns of Tripoli and Benghazi (Kirchner, 2014). More recently, President Bashar al-Assad's regime in Syria and Iran have used Hezbollah to fight opposition, while the US has sponsored moderate rebel groups within Syria (Berkowitz, 2018; Fayazi, 2017). Iraq provided shelter to the Abu Nidal Organisation (ANO), a Palestinian militant group that split from the Palestine Liberation Organisation (PLO) in 1974 and thus was implicated in the group's deadly attacks (1970s–1990s) across the West and MENA (Kirchner, 2014). Similarly, the People's Mujahedin of Iran (MEK) sided with Saddam Hussein in the 1980s against the Kurds and Iran, only to switch alliances and sign a ceasefire agreement with the US when coalition forces occupied the country in 2003 (Kirchner, 2014). Also, when Saddam Hussain backed the Syrian Muslim Brotherhood (SMB) in the Islamist uprising against Syria (1976–1982), it strengthened Syrian-Iranian relations and made it hard for Iraq to find Arab State allies in the conflict (Kirchner, 2014).

Far from being a MENA phenomenon, over 50 nations have engaged in SST since 1970 (Berkowitz, 2018). For example, pan-African rebel groups most prone to indiscriminate attacks have external sponsors (e.g., Chad's Union of Forces for Democracy and Development [UFDD], Uganda People's Army [UPA], Lord's Resistance Army [LRA], and Djibouti's Front for the Restoration of Unity and Democracy [FRUD]) (Fortna et al., 2018). Others also rely on natural resources (e.g., Sierra Leone's Revolutionary United Front [RUF], Senegal's Movement of Democratic Forces of Casamance [MFDC], Angola's National Union for the Total Independence of Angola [UNITA], and the Mozambican National Resistance [RENAMO]) (Fortna et al., 2018). Experts note that recent history demonstrates that SST can significantly escalate the conflicts between states more than it has in the past (Gal-Or, 1993; Kirchner, 2014).

THE EVOLUTION OF SST AS A RELATIONSHIP DYNAMIC AND AS A SOCIAL PHENOMENON

There are two dimensions of evolution to be considered when discussing SST. The first is the way in which the sponsor-terrorist relationship can evolve over its duration, and the second is how SST tactics have evolved to keep pace with changes in society and technology. The sponsor-terrorist relationship can evolve in unpredictable ways: sponsorship can lead terrorist groups to lose their identity when the state's wishes take precedence over the group's agenda; states can also play opposing terrorist groups off one another as a control tactic; and states can turn on terrorist groups just as terrorist groups can change their allegiances (Carter, 2012; Byman, 2005; Kirchner, 2014). For example, Pakistan sheltered the Jammu and Kashmir Liberation Front (JKLF) but then allowed India to eliminate the group once it became a security risk (Carter, 2012). Similarly, the MEK switched their support from Saddam Hussain to the US government after coalition forces invaded Iraq in 2003 (Kirchner, 2014). In short, state-terrorist proxy alliances work only as long as both their goals are compatible (Drury et al., 2011).

Martin (2017) argues that SST will continue to endure in the future much as it has in the past, especially in repressive systems, perhaps with enhanced surveillance and communication capabilities (Martin, 2017, p. 6). However, Byman (2020) argues that terrorist groups have not shown a strong propensity towards cyberattacks in repressive systems, perhaps with enhanced surveillance and communication capabilities (Martin, 2017, p. 6). However, Byman (2020) argues that terrorist groups have not shown a strong propensity towards cyberattacks. Some have accused Russia of sponsoring the hacking of international agencies investigating Russia's athletic doping programmes or Iran of being behind the distributed denial-of-service (DDoS) attacks (i.e., disrupting a server or network by overwhelming it with internet traffic) on US banks (Eichensehr, 2020). Conway (2011) distinguishes between cyberterrorism (i.e., websites as targets) and terrorists' use of the Internet (i.e., to facilitate attacks) and argues that the term cyberterrorism is more journalistic hype than reality, as such attacks are labour intensive and lack the desired social impact of other approaches (i.e., attention-grabbing videos, pictures of physical violence). In reality, state-sponsored cyberattacks are often not prosecuted because international laws require varying standards of evidence to accuse a state of a cyberterrorist attack (Eichensehr, 2020).

The term cyberterrorism plays upon people's fear of being dominated by technology together with their fear of random violence (Conway, 2011). Meanwhile, Eid (2014) argues that "terroredia" is a more accurate term to describe terrorists' and the media's codependent relationship whereby terrorist acts and the non-stop coverage of these events satisfy the aims of both the media (i.e., creating newsworthy content) and terrorists (i.e., gaining non-stop coverage). The rise of digital technology and citizen journalism means that many different accounts of various terrorist attacks are made available to the public as well as to those studying terrorism, but at the same time, this allows terrorists to reach wider audiences and thus have a greater degree of influence. Russia has been accused of using social media to promote white power groups in the US and Europe in order to create political instability and cultural division (Byman, 2020). Others argue that some states' use of SST has evolved to include neoliberal globalisation (i.e., removing barriers to business and privatising natural resources), which allows homelands to be annexed and traditional economies to be modernised, which disenfranchises marginalised cultural groups and thereby eliminates political opposition (Jalata, 2017).

ATTEMPTS TO CURTAIL SST

Various approaches have been suggested to prevent states from engaging in SST, including public condemnations, sanctions, threats of attack, reciprocal attacks, and war, with varying opinions as to the effectiveness of any one strategy. Some argue that economic embargoes are not as effective as we might think, despite the potential for a significant decline in the gross domestic product (GDP). Critics argue that more long-term research is needed on sanctions to gauge their true level of effectiveness (Drury et al., 2011). Critics note how embargoes hurt ordinary citizens uninvolved in SST more than social elites and members of government (McFayden, 2009). Others have argued that extreme acts of SST like genocide require greater economic sanctions, including the elimination of military aid and other economic benefits, like suspending all bilateral trading rights (Kopel, 2016).

Others have argued that coordination of responses with partner states is key to ending SST. For example, the US, UK, and France successfully lobbied UN members to impose an air traffic embargo on Libya after airline bombings of US and French airliners (Gal-Or, 1993). Yet Jalata (2017) argues that the UN lacks effective mechanisms to fight SST because those states engaging in crimes against humanity dominate the organisation (Jalata, 2017). Others argue that the solution lies in long-term cooperation between states in terms of information sharing and quick, decisive, and coordinated efforts in response to SST that are well-funded and do not harm civilians (McFayden, 2009). Alternately, others argue for developing a better measurement tool for assessing various criteria of terrorist sponsorship (e.g., during wartime or peacetime, direct or indirect support) that includes a spectrum that would allow better detection of gradual progress made towards the goal of ending state sponsorship (Byman, 2020).

Experts suggest that investment in states that are vulnerable to SST, paired with careful consideration of the outcomes of any course of action, is an effective course of action. This would mean both educating locals in SST recruitment regions about the lasting adverse consequences of terrorist activities (i.e., the loss of potential breadwinners) and having the international community work together to help strengthen weak governments so they can better defend themselves against becoming a locus for SST (McFayden, 2009). While military strikes might quickly address some SST threats (e.g., weakening, disabling, or eliminating Iran's nuclear programme), they might not be worth the long-term consequences (e.g., creating animosity in future generations of Iranians towards the US) (Carter, 2015). Yet it states that neighbouring sponsors of terror are sometimes compelled to retaliate in order to assure the global community that they do not support terrorism, even as such retaliation does little to stop SST or terrorist organisations (McFayden, 2009). Alternately, sometimes a threat of violent action has sufficed, such as when Turkey convinced Syria to stop supporting the Turkish-Kurdish separatist group the Kurdistan Workers Party (PKK), under leader Abdullah Öcalan, in 1998, by convincingly promising them that there would be a swift and painful military response if Syria did not refrain from SST (Carter, 2015).

SOCIAL, POLITICAL, AND ECONOMIC IMPACTS OF SST

SST has lasting social, political, and economic impacts for both the sponsoring states and those states that are targeted. In terms of the social impacts of SST, it is often the most vulnerable groups in society that pay the highest price for SST. Black and brown LGBTQ people, because they are a population already disproportionately impacted by violence and marginalisation in society in general, are especially vulnerable to state-sponsored violence (Lambda Legal, 2020). Women and girls are frequent targets of SST because targeting them with sexual violence allows states to terrorise an enemy into accepting political dominance (Martin, 2017). Sexual violence has lasting psychological effects; children born of sexual violence may serve as reminders of terror, and mass acts of sexual violence desensitise members of the targeted society to rape. Mass acts of sexual violence ultimately destabilise societies from the inside by targeting their building block, the family.

Racial difference, social class, and citizenship status are also wedges that SST seizes upon to tear a society apart. Countries can fight white power and white supremacy movements domestically only to have states such as Russia, with its own extensive history of racial violence, use online resources to fuel racial hatred transnationally and thus destabilise societies (Arsenault & Stabile, 2020; Byman, 2020). Conflicts between neighbouring states can boil over into state-sanctioned terrorism that manifests in the targeting of cultural minorities and undocumented immigrants with violence, family separation, and detention (Schultz, 2018). SST creates social insecurity and fears that make it difficult to help those most in need. For example, international aid agencies are less likely to send workers into regions characterised by actual and potential SST, thus depriving those who are in desperate need of international aid after natural disasters (McFayden, 2009). Without needed post-disaster assistance, society will deteriorate further, and this will leave them increasingly vulnerable to SST as a target or a breeding ground for potential future terrorists.

SST can significantly weaken countries in the process of developing their democratic processes. During Argentina's so-called Process of National Reorganisation (1976–1983), the military dictatorship disappeared a generation of activists, erased memories of them from public consciousness, and cultivated a culture of fear and mistrust (Schindel, 2012). Similarly, Ethiopia, seeking to destroy the Oromo national movement starting in 1992, used terrorism and genocide and transferred land and resources to Tigrayan state elites and their supporters, leaving many remaining Oromo impoverished and marginalised (Jalata, 2017). Ethiopia also passed anti-terrorism laws with the purpose, some argue, of quashing any further political dissent by the Oromo (Jalata, 2017). Argentina is currently doing the difficult work of repairing the damaged social fabric using former clandestine detention sites used in terror to reclaim, heal, and learn from this difficult period in their history. The situation of the Oromo has failed to attract significant internationalist support from countries like the US, which recently signed a security partnership agreement (reaffirmed in 2020) with the Ethiopian government to exchange "logistics, services, and supplies" and plans "for future security cooperation activities designed to meet mutual defence priorities" (Jalata, 2017, p. 100).

SST is an appealing tactic for states because it is less expensive than war and allows them to have coercive power to influence international foreign policy, but the risks include international condemnation, domestic disapproval by political opponents, and reciprocal SST by targeted states (Berkowitz, 2018). The enduring political impacts of SST acts like genocide on target states include counter-killings, power struggles, and waves of terrorism that cause geopolitical destabilisation (Kopel, 2016). Yet the states sponsoring SST can risk their own political stability as well. When states deploy SST domestically against minority groups within a nation (i.e., a nation within a nation), they can help popularise rebel movements and make it harder for the state to maintain peace (Uzonyi & Hanania, 2017). Also, any state using SST to destabilise a foreign government could expect that some of those same foreign states will engage in counter-acts of SST against the initiating state.

As noted previously, many states have participated in SST as an economical alternative to war, spurring political and policy change. However, as noted previously, determining who is deemed a state sponsor of terror is a highly politicised process. The US terror sponsor list fails to name those countries who are too powerful to put on the list (e.g., the UK, China), and also absent are those states that, if they were put on such a list, would create problems for US foreign policy (i.e., Israel, Saudi Arabia) (Byman, 2020). Because the US list of terror sponsors is binary (i.e., you are either a sponsor of terror or not) with no measurements of degree of support, this provides no incentives for states to reduce their levels of support short of stopping state support completely (Byman, 2020). Political incentives for decreasing one's use of SST could include re-establishing diplomatic relations, lifting embargoes, and/or lifting travel restrictions.

The economic costs of SST are borne by states sponsoring terror and their neighbouring states, states targeted by SST, and terror groups. Strong economies are less affected by terrorism than poor economies (Khalid, 2020). Governments must allocate more money to deter terrorism, protect their business interests (e.g., ports for import and export), and ensure consumer and tourist confidence (McFayden, 2009). States sponsoring terror face the potential of economic sanctions that can cause significant declines in their GDP (Drury et al., 2011). Pakistan is a country that has been on both sides of this equation. Pakistan had been previously economically sanctioned for nuclear tests, military coups, and SST, and this made the country a no-go area for foreign investors, but post-9/11, as a neighbour of Afghanistan, Pakistan became a frontline ally state in the war against terror, and sanctions were lifted, debt was cancelled or rescheduled, and foreign aid picked up (Khalid, 2020). The change from a sanctioned nation to a frontline ally saw foreign reserves increase from $700 million to $17 billion within years, the GDP increase from 3.29% to 6.83% in less than a decade, and per capita income increase as investments and exports grow (Khalid, 2020). Yet despite foreign aid received to meet the cost of military operations against terrorism, terrorist activities could not be contained by Pakistan; additionally, despite the economic advantages of being a frontline ally in the war on terror, economic disparity actually increased (Khalid, 2020).

There is a multilayered economic relationship that exists between sponsors of terror, terror groups, and their recruits that variously shapes how SST is enacted. On one hand, foreign sponsorship may free terrorist groups from local accountability somewhat (i.e., they are not answering to local benefactors), but it still leaves them accountable internationally, which could lead to more indiscriminate use of violence as international sponsors might be less well informed about what is happening on the ground when they are at a distance (Fortna et al., 2018). However, terrorist groups relying on local recruits and support might feel the pressure to not alienate this support by indiscriminately targeting civilians (Fortna et al., 2018). Meanwhile, groups funded by local resources (i.e., drugs, jewels) arguably have the least fear of losing international support and the fewest constraints on their use of violence (Fortna et al., 2018).

Survivors of SST and the families of those killed have faced barriers to holding sponsors of terror financially responsible via the courts. In 1996, the US Congress added exceptions under Section 1605 of the 1976 Foreign Sovereign Immunities Act (FSIA) that allowed plaintiffs to sue foreign states for committing or supporting terrorism, as long as they were designated as sponsors of terrorism by the US State Department (Beebe, 2020). Lawsuits have also been filed under the Anti-Terrorism Act (ATA) against banks that are accused of supporting terrorism (Pittman, 2019). To date, these attempts to make terror sponsors financially responsible have not resulted in the payment of damages. Germany did receive a payment of 24 million euros in 2004 from Libya to non-US victims and their families for their role in the La Belle nightclub bombing in 1986, but this was achieved via diplomacy, not the courts, and Libya framed the payment as a humanitarian gesture (Scheschkewitz & Amies, 2011).

CONCLUSION

The debate still focuses on how to define SST, what is included in that definition, and how to effectively measure where states are in their process of supporting or moving away from supporting SST. Meanwhile, the physical, psychological, and socio-cultural damage wrought by SST against the most vulnerable in society is justified as necessary by sponsoring states to create political change or advancing their foreign policy regarding enemy states. While SST is attractive because it is often carried out by non-state proxies, and therefore states can sometimes disclaim ownership, it can have unintended consequences for all those involved. Public condemnation and economic sanctions are the leading responses to SST, but more research needs to be done to gauge their effectiveness. Alternately, others have advocated supporting and developing the governments of nations that are vulnerable to SST organisations seeking shelter. The long-term impacts of SST are considerable and include social dysfunction, disrupting government rule, and the creation of poverty and disadvantage that can make SST an attractive option to societies and individuals, thus creating a cycle of terror that is difficult to interrupt.

For all that is known about SST, there is still much more that we need to explore in terms of expanding conceptualisations of SST, how SST has evolved, and how best to address the devastation caused by SST. The literature suggests that the current understanding of SST needs to be expanded in terms of how we define it and measure or assign sponsorship. Such considerations would be well served to shift the discussion away from excessively focusing on some states while ignoring others to acknowledge the widespread nature of SST. While such a discussion would be politically sensitive, the alternative of not acknowledging some uses of SST while punishing others fosters a sense of bias that could ultimately be used by states that are punished for using SST to justify continuing their practise (i.e., fighting an unfair system).

More investigation needs to be conducted into how digital technology and SST intersect. There is an understanding that digital technology is used as a tool for perpetuating other forms of terror (i.e., informing and training proxies in violent tactics) and as a means of extending the impact of acts of terror (i.e., how the effect of one bombing in one location is magnified through its dissemination across traditional, new, digital, and social forms of media). There is less known about the potential for new, digital, and social forms of media and technology to be used as a means for terrorising others (i.e., in violating privacy, fear-inducing surveillance, blocking, hiding, or damaging access to needed infrastructure and money, subverting individual legitimacy and credibility, and carrying out automated mobile attacks). As digital technology allows identities to be obscured, thus minimising risks to proxies and sponsors, this would seemingly be an attractive option for SST when paired with the capacity for new, digital, and social media to widely publicise such events.

Finally, we need more investigations into the means by which states move forward after SST. We need more case studies of states that have successfully addressed a past history as a sponsor or as a target of SST in order to learn what works and what does not work. Theories that suggest that supporting and helping to build weaker states' defences against SST is an effective strategy are still theoretical until we can study real-world models representing such efforts over the long term. Future scholarship should examine the perspectives of various stakeholders involved in SST, including sponsors (direct and indirect), perpetrators, targets, and those who feel the effects of SST long after it has taken place, in order to learn how we can prevent, and if not prevent, then anticipate, predict, and prepare for, future manifestations of SST.

References

Arsenault, E.G., & Stabile, J. (2020). Confronting Russia's role in transnational white supremacist extremism. *Just Security*. https://www.justsecurity.org/68420/confronting-russias-role-in-transnational-white-supremacist-extremism/

Beebe, M. (2020). Justice for victims of terrorism: Supreme Court Decides Opati v. Republic of Sudan. *International Enforcement Law Reporter*, *36*(6), 238–240.

Berkowitz, J.M. (2018). Delegating terror: Principal-agent based decision making in state sponsorship of terrorism. *International Interactions*, *44*(4), 709–748. https://doi-org.kbcc.ezproxy.cuny.edu/10.1080/03050629.2017.1414811

Biswas, A. (2017). Pakistan's tactical nukes: Relevance and options for India. *Washington Quarterly*, *40*(3), 169–186. https://doi-org.kbcc.ezproxy.cuny.edu/10.1080/0163660X.2017.1370355

Byman, D. (2005). *Deadly connections: States that sponsor terrorism*. Cambridge University Press.

Byman, D. (2015). State sponsor of terror: The global threat of Iran. *The Brookings Institute*. https://www.brookings.edu/wp-content/uploads/2016/06/11-byman-iran-testimony.pdf

Byman, D. (2020). Understanding, and misunderstanding, state sponsorship of terrorism. *Studies in Conflict and Terrorism*. https://www.tandfonline.com/doi/full/10.1080/1057610X.2020.1738682

Carter, D.B. (2012). A blessing or a curse? State support for terrorist groups. *International Organization*, *66*(1), 129–151.

Carter, D.B. (2015). The compellence dilemma: International disputes with violent groups. *International Studies Quarterly*, *59*(3), 461–475. https://doi-org.kbcc.ezproxy.cuny.edu/10.1111/isqu.12192

CBC News. (2005). Tamil tigers illegally fundraising in Toronto: Community member. *Canadian Broadcasting Corporation*. https://www.cbc.ca/news/canada/tamil-tigers-illegally-fundraising-in-toronto-community-member-1.531634

Congressional Research Service. (2018). State sponsors of acts of international terrorism—legislative parameters: In brief. *Congressional Research Service*. https://fas.org/sgp/crs/terror/R43835.pdf

Conway, M. (2011). Privacy and security against cyberterrorism. *Communications of the ACM*, *54*(2), 26–28. https://doi-org.kbcc.ezproxy.cuny.edu/10.1145/1897816.1897829

Drury, A.C., Mohn, J., & Moore, M. (2011). Sanctions and state sponsored terrorism. *University of Missouri at Columbia; APSA 2011 Annual Meeting Paper*. http://papers.ssrn.com/sol3/papers.cfm?abstract_id=1900554

Duncan, K. (2011). A blast from the past: Lessons from a largely forgotten incident of state-sponsored terrorism. *Perspectives on Terrorism*, *5*(1), 3–21. http://www.jstor.com/stable/26298499

Eichensehr, K.E. (2020). The law and politics of cyberattack attribution. *UCLA Law Review*, *67*(3), 520–598.

Eid, M. (2014). *Exchanging terrorism oxygen for media airwaves: The age of terroredia*. IGI Global.

Fayazi, N. (2017). Iran: Is it really the leading state-sponsor of terrorism? *Institute for Global Dialogue*. http://www.jstor.org/stable/resrep17466

Fortna, V.P., Lotito, N.J., & Rubin, M.A. (2018). Don't bite the hand that feeds: Rebel funding sources and the use of terrorism in civil wars. *International Studies Quarterly*, *62*(4), 782–794. https://doi-org.kbcc.ezproxy.cuny.edu/10.1093/isq/sqy038

Gal-Or, N. (1993). State-sponsored terrorism: A mode of diplomacy? *Conflict Quarterly*, *13*(3), 7–23. http://papers.ssrn.com/sol3/papers.cfm?abstract_id=2238833

Jalata, A. (2017). The Oromo movement: The effects of state terrorism and globalization in Oromia and Ethiopia. *Social Justice*, *44*(4), 83–105.

Khalid, A. (2020). Impact of terrorism on the economy of Pakistan. *Pakistan Vision, 21*(1), 404–416.

Kirchner, M. (2014). 'A good investment?' State sponsorship of terrorism as an instrument of Iraqi foreign policy (1979–1991). *Cambridge Review of International Affairs, 27*(3), 521–537. https://doi-org.kbcc.ezproxy.cuny.edu/10.1080/09557571.2013.839629

Kopel, H.K. (2016). The case for sanctioning state sponsors of genocide incitement. *Cornell International Law Journal, 49*(2), 415–468.

Lambda Legal. (2020). Black and brown LGBTQ people particularly vulnerable to state-sponsored violence. *Echo Magazine, 31*(10), 12.

Martin, G. (2017). Types of terrorism. In M. Dawson, D.R. Kisku, P. Gupta, J.K. Sing, & W. Li (Eds.), *Developing next-generation countermeasures for homeland security threat prevention* (pp. 1–16). IGI Global.

McFayden Jr., E. (2009). Global implications of state sponsored terrorism. *Kentucky State University*. http://papers.ssrn.com/sol3/papers.cfm?abstract_id=1528198

Pence, M. (2019). The time has come for our European partners to withdraw from the Iran nuclear deal. *Vital Speeches of the Day, 85*(4), 104–107.

Pittman, E.W. (2019). Your bank may be an international terrorist. *GPSolo, 36*(5), 68–69.

Saltzman, I.Z. (2020). Hurting for solace: Internal state terror, self-injury and the Soviet Union during the interwar period. *Journal of Psychohistory, 47*(3), 188–209.

Scheschkewitz, D., & Amies, N. (2011). Berlin's La Belle nightclub bombing remembered 25 years on. *Deutsche Welle (DW)*. https://www.dw.com/en/berlins-la-belle-nightclub-bombing-remembered-25-years-on/a-14965254

Schindel, E. (2012). 'Now the neighbors lose their fear': Restoring the social network around former sites of terror in Argentina. *International Journal of Transitional Justice, 6*(3), 467–485. https://doi-org.kbcc.ezproxy.cuny.edu/10.1093/ijtj/ijs020

Schultz, H. (2018). Thin edge of barbwire: Pedagogical strategies against borders. *Radical Teacher, 111*, 118–125. https://doi-org.kbcc.ezproxy.cuny.edu/10.5195/RT.2018.464

Taylor, J.R. (2019). A history of tolerance for violence has laid the groundwork for injustice today. *Human Rights, 44*(1), 5–8.

Uzonyi, G., & Hanania, R. (2017). Government-sponsored mass killing and civil war reoccurrence. *International Studies Quarterly, 61*(3), 677–689. https://doi-org.kbcc.ezproxy.cuny.edu/10.1093/isq/sqx050

Zanchetta, B. (2016). Between cold war imperatives and state-sponsored terrorism: The United States and "operation condor". *Studies in Conflict & Terrorism, 39*(12), 1084–1102. https://doi-org.kbcc.ezproxy.cuny.edu/10.1080/1057610X.2016.1159069

14

THE TERROR OF WAR

Ever Present and Always in Error?

Péter Marton

INTRODUCTION

For the purposes of this chapter, terrorism is defined as the use of violence (or the threat thereof) against civilians to create fear in a secondary audience with political aims. War terrorism is the use of violence (or the threat thereof) against people *hors de combat*[1] to create fear in a secondary audience of non-combatants and/or combatants with the purpose of furthering war aims. Based on these definitions, the chapter studies the occurrence of war terrorism in armed (intra-state as well as international) conflicts. Beyond identifying and evaluating a few prominent historical examples of war terrorism without the intention of providing a complete historical overview of the phenomenon, its strategic and ethical implications are discussed, the latter mostly with regard to how the relativisation, in a moral sense, of war motives and war actions should not in fact follow from observing the frequent occurrence of war terrorism in armed conflicts around the world, even as war terrorism itself is generally rightly condemned.

THE MAZE OF VIOLENCE: TERROR IN THE CONTEXT OF CONTEMPORARY ARMED CONFLICT

Consider the following statement, purportedly from a Russian combatant fighting with the Wagner Group, a Russian private military firm, in Syria: "Everyone knows perfectly well that being captured [in this war] means death by torture. I have specialists who remove eyes. They take a spoon and dig around up and down until the eyeballs are just dangling there" (reported in Khazov-Casia & Coalson, 2018). Noteworthy here is how extreme violence is justified through reference to the purported practises of other parties and a *belief* in the need to match what these significant others are doing to create a symmetry of fear (or perhaps to overcome one's own fear).[2]

ISIS (the Islamic State in Iraq and Syria) indeed brought new levels of barbarity to the conflict in Syria in its treatment of captured combatants as well as civilians. To justify their own approach to violence, ISIS ideologues have drawn selectively and instrumentally on religious texts as well as jihadi manuals that have already codified a kind of jihadi canon in this respect, such as "The Management of Savagery"[3] by Abu Bakr Naji (Hassan, 2015a) and "The Jurisprudence of Blood" by Abu Abdullah al-Muhajir (Townsend, 2018; an alternative English title commonly used for this work is "The Theology of Bloodshed": Muir, 2017).

The phrase "deal with them in a way that strikes fear in those behind them" (quoted from ISIS fighters in Hassan, 2015b) could well be regarded as the main guiding principle of ISIS combatants' actions. Regardless of the obvious importance to ISIS of seeking justification for atrocities committed by them specifically through religious texts, it is hard to mistake a kind of cruel and more universal logic of violence behind their tactics. Consider the case of the execution by immolation of downed Jordanian pilot Muath al-Kasasbeh in early 2015, an act that was explained by ISIS in a document with a quote from medieval Sunni Muslim theologian Ibn Taymiyyah, framing the killing as "deterrence" through "exemplary punishment" (Hoover, 2015).

Writing more than a decade before the execution of al-Kasasbeh, Abu Bakr Naji wrote: "the Friend (Abu Bakr) and Ali b. Abi Talib (may God be pleased with them) burned (people) with fire, even though it is odious, because they knew the effect of rough violence in times of need" (Naji, transl. by McCants, 2006: 74). Elsewhere in the same

DOI: 10.4324/9780429426063-16

text, Naji told jihadis that "we need to massacre others and take actions like those that were undertaken against the Banu Qurayza[4] and their like" (p. 75) and that there is a need "to make [our enemies] think one thousand times before attacking us" (p. 72). Thus, ISIS defined waging total war as the norm and hesitation to wage it as a failure to follow what is demanded of the true warrior of jihad.

Over the course of the campaign by multiple coalitions against ISIS, reports emerged of the brutal treatment of ISIS prisoners by Iraqi troops (Meek et al., 2017), by Kurdish forces (Tayler, 2017), and by Russian combatants ("Breaking: Terrifying Footage of Russians …", 2015.[5] Iraqi troops were pictured during the battle of Mosul using the corpses of ISIS combatants killed to demarcate territory under their control (carrying a double deterrent effect as these corpses were not given proper Islamic burial) [Georgy, 2017].

The list of war crimes committed by ISIS is long, and to some, it may seem tempting to regard the abuse of "ISIS prisoners" (people rightly or wrongly accused of having belonged to ISIS) as a consequence of ISIS' own conduct. One ought to keep in mind, however, that ISIS emerged in a region where political regimes regularly intimidate and repress opposition through disappearances and extreme torture. The so-called "Caesar Report," "A Report into the credibility of certain evidence with regard to Torture and Execution of Persons Incarcerated by the current Syrian regime" alone documented the likely deaths of at least 11,000 individuals detained by Syrian regime forces between August 2011 and March 2013 ("A Report into …," 2014). The global jihadi movement gradually radicalised over the decades (since its inception in the 1970s) in a political context where the Assad regime was not unique in this respect. Ironically, ISIS itself took many former members of the similarly merciless Iraqi regime of Saddam Hussein into its ranks (Whiteside, 2017). What we consequently saw in Syria was that an uprising, fuelled partly by grievances over the state's use of terror, ultimately transformed into a brutal war, where terrorising the enemy has come to be regarded as an imperative by most of the combatant parties involved (even as the level of cruelty and the number of victims varied from one party to the other).

The above observations may not come as a surprise concerning the Syrian conflict, notorious for its brutality due to the instant or global availability of sad mementos of its violence in the form of footage accessible on online video-sharing platforms. Less often considered is how terror, understood in this context (the context of armed conflict) as violence against people *hors de combat*[6] with political aims, either as a tactical or as a strategic means to obtain one's objectives, has been put to use in *most* armed conflicts in history, at least by one (or some) of the parties involved, at least occasionally.

To illustrate this with a particularly salient example, an overview of the early period as well as the legacy of strategic aerial bombing and the ideas behind it follows. Although the present study does not aim to provide a full historical overview accounting for all significant cases of war terrorism, there are certain historically grounded reasons for focusing on strategic aerial bombing as a particularly important milestone. That is, up until the 20th century, it took control over territory and population to terrorise non-combatants on a greater scale, beyond individual acts of subversion in the form of assassinations or sabotage. Bloodbaths ensuing the occupation of fortifications in mediaeval siege warfare are salient examples of this. With the advent of modern explosives (including TNT, or trinitrotoluene, whose explosive properties were discovered in 1891) and flight (especially heavier-than-air flight, from 1903), a lethal new combination of capabilities (air-mobile platforms combined with new means of destruction) appeared in warfare, giving rise to the possibility of bombing territories far beyond the area under one's own control.

THE BEGINNINGS OF STRATEGIC AERIAL BOMBING

Strategic aerial bombing began in World War One when German forces carried out attacks against a variety of targets by a variety of means, including the first fixed-wing strategic bombers, the Gothas, and the famous Zeppelin (and other) airships. The fledgling concept of strategic aerial terror bombing was but an element of this on the side of the strategic planners in Germany, while the aim to terrorise was perceived to be the dominant motive by those on the receiving end of these bombings.

Regardless of the actual motives of the attacks, they influenced strategic thinkers regarding the future use of bomber aircraft for a generation to come, from Italy to Japan, resulting in a large number of terror bombings during World War Two and culminating in the use of the atomic bomb by the United States on the Japanese cities of Hiroshima and Nagasaki. Some of the most memorable bombing sorties of World War Two have been attacks either on civilian targets or insufficiently discriminate attacks causing civilian casualties, such as, for example, the bombing of the German city of Dresden. Cruise missiles (the V-1) and ballistic missiles (the V-2) were used by Germany almost exclusively in terror attacks against civilian populations.[7] The post-Cold War period subsequently saw the development of "mutually assured destruction," relying on the assured second strike (retaliation) capability of the main nuclear powers, effectively holding the populations of large cities in the West and in the Soviet Union hostages for the sake of strategic and crisis stability, at least in the minds of many.[8] Parallel to this, armed conflicts since 1945 have frequently featured aerial terror bombings (not necessarily used to, or even hoping for, strategic effect, but used nonetheless).[9]

As mentioned above, airships played the main role in the beginning of this era of aerial bombing. Even though the airship bombings have come to be remembered mostly with reference to attacks against London and purely as a series of terror bombings, it seems that the fog of war and the general impracticality of airships, unequipped with means of precision bombing (which did not exist at the time), have also played into the high number of civilian casualties. For the German Army, "airships' role, especially that of bombing important military and civilian targets in hostile territory but also that of strategic reconnaissance, seemed incapable of being fulfilled during daylight" (Griehl & Dresser, 1990: 81), leading the German General Staff to decide in September 1914 that offensive airship operations were only to take place by night. This not only limited precision in bombing; it also rendered the identification of targets difficult in the first place. A September 1915 combat report explicitly makes mention of how "the first bombs [during this particular attack] were released over Leyton railway station, in order to reduce LZ 74's flying weight rather than because of the interesting nature of the target" (quoted in Griehl & Dresser, 1990: 84).

In another combat report, also from September 1915, but this time from the *Reichskriegsmarine*, the commander accounts of having found London fully illuminated. He then proceeds to describe releasing bombs without specifying the target, concluding that "the explosive effect of the 300 kg bomb must have been quite extensive because a large complex of lights went out." Even here, however, the commander attributes this to "the short time over the target when the weather was clear … [because of which] it was impossible to find single important targets" (quoted in Griehl & Dresser, 1990: 95). The interpretation that bombings of this kind were planned as insufficiently discriminate attacks and then executed as indiscriminate attacks seems to be confirmed by the official number of British casualties, published by *The Times*: a total of 498 civilians and 58 soldiers were killed in aerial attacks in Britain (quoted in Griehl & Dresser, 1990: 115); that is 8.58 civilians per 1 soldier killed, a ratio that could have been much worse had the airship crews only had an interest in attacking civilian targets.

The decision-making background of the case is very interesting. The German *Kaiser* at first took an unwelcoming stance regarding the bombing of England. He, as well as Chancellor Theobald von Bethmann-Hollweg, were looking ahead to the possibility of a peace agreement and were reluctant to escalate (Poolman, 1975: 39). Instead, Navy officers, such as *Konteradmiral* Paul Behncke, the Deputy Chief of the Naval Staff, wanted a piece of this kind of action first and foremost for the Navy's own airships. Behncke expected attacks on "London or the neighbourhood of London" to "cause panic in the population, which may render it doubtful that the war can be continued," promising "material and moral results" (quoted in Robinson, 1971: 78). He showed no particular qualms about causing civilian casualties even as he, too, named specific targets of value (e.g., the Admiralty in London) and warned that buildings of historic value should be spared. Otherwise, he favoured "any means of forcing England to her knees," regarding which he thought that "successful air attacks on London, considering the well-known nervousness of the public, will be a valuable measure" (quoted in Robinson, 1971: 79). Apparently, he eventually found time to try to justify this in terms of the fledgling international humanitarian law of that time by deeming London a "defended place" (given the presence there of military and military-related installations). French aerial attacks' impact on German cities and the Navy's frustration over the lack of a role for its own airships, while the Army was using its assets largely for the war in France, led subsequently to the urging of attacks on England, even by the Chief of the Naval Staff, Hugo von Pohl. His request was approved in January 1915 by the Kaiser with the caveats that "historic buildings and private property will be spared as much as possible" and that London cannot be attacked (Robinson, 1971: 80–82). Factors in the decision included the fear that ongoing British attacks against airship bases and operational losses may eventually leave no Zeppelin that could be used against the enemy's hinterland, and the pressure of all those, including the general public, who thought that the blockade of Germany and the scarcities suffered by the German population demanded counter-action of this kind, taking the war to the British civilian population (Poolman, 1975: 38).

In the following period, German media often framed these attacks as retaliations: "An eye for an eye, a tooth for a tooth, only in this way can we treat with England," declared an article in the *Kölnische Zeitung* on January 21, 2015 (quoted in Robinson, 1971: 87). Enthusiasm was followed at first by concerns about the impact on neutral powers (e.g., the United States) and their condemnation of the raids. Even the Kaiser made a few attempts to impose limitations on airship actions. The competing military branches of the Army and Navy pushed for more aerial attacks, however, and the Kaiser gave his hesitant approval. Ironically, even though the Navy was lobbying for attacks against London from very early on, it was the Army that carried out the first raid against the British capital.

As these attacks were generally perceived as terror attacks by many, the psychological impact was, not surprisingly, very similar to that of actual terror attacks. Many people thought reprisal attacks were necessary. At a public meeting organised at the Cannon Street Hotel that was to call on the British government to formally announce reprisal raids, a member of the public demanded that "the Kaiser be made to realise what it means for his own people to be subjugated … to cold-blooded butchery." Lord Willoughby de Broke similarly wished "to treat [Germany] as they treat us." Major-General Alfred E. Turner wrote in *The Times* that "their [the Germans'] only gospel is brute force, and with brute force they must be met." In the aftermath of the meeting, an article in *The Evening News* declared that "immediate reprisals are the demand of many of our readers ... not because we should compete in murdering harmless civilians, but because they contend the moral effect in Germany would prevent these raids" (all quotes from Barthram, 2008: Ch1).

In at least one case, in Karlsruhe, a reprisal raid *was* carried out; ironically, the German press then demanded "reprisal attacks" itself (Barthram, 2008: Ch1), and the German air campaign against England eventually intensified after this. In the meantime, in a sign of social tensions, London's German population, including many shopkeepers, faced violence, from smaller isolated incidents to rioting (Barthram, 2008: Ch2).

Regardless of how significant the psychological impact of the bombings was, in some ways it was the direct opposite of what the German planners had hoped for: the determination of the civilian population may have even increased, and related British propaganda efforts certainly sought to enhance just this effect – best captured perhaps in the wartime propaganda poster where Germany is described as "Our Friend, the Enemy," with a caption added saying "Ah, here he comes again, my best recruiter," with reference to airships (displayed in Barthram, 2008: Ch1).

From a purely military standpoint, the raids were somewhat more successful, as they drew resources away from the front (e.g., hunter aircraft and ground air defence units). They have also created hesitation in the minds of a generation of future British leaders, affecting their propensity to go to war with the would-be rising challenger, that is, Nazi Germany, in the 1930s. Among other, more important factors, Levy and Ripsman find the significance of the strongly felt need by British leaders to reinforce air defences in explaining why they were not ready to launch a preventive war against Germany before 1939 (Levy & Ripsman, 2007: 55–57). Given that memories of the airship raids were still vivid at the time, this certainly may have reinforced the perceived significance of the German bomber threat, leading Stanley Baldwin to famously utter in the House of Commons in 1932 that "the bomber will always get through" (House of Commons, 1932).

Even more noteworthy, however, is the effect of World War I on strategic thinking about the use of aerial strike capability. The most often quoted thinker in this respect is Italian Giulio Douhet, who was on the one hand merely representative of a trend and on the other hand someone who formulated related ideas with great clarity (hence his influence on many). Douhet concluded on the basis of the incomplete evidence of World War One, i.e., based on a conflict where aerial bombing never played a decisive role, that in the future the ability to attack from the air would be decisive. "Command of the air" is thus absolutely required, implying defeat of the other side's aerial forces to begin with; following this, "the aerial arm" just "makes it easier to act directly against the enemy's national resistance" (1998 [1921]: 282). As he elaborates elsewhere: "To bend the enemy's will, one must put him in intolerable circumstances, and the best way to do that is to attack directly the defenceless population of his cities and great industrial centres" (1998 [1921]: 282). This was especially likely to work, in his view, in the case of advanced nations, which have complex and vulnerable infrastructure: "aerial action intended to break the morale of a nation is bound to be much more effective when its population is dense and civilised" (Douhet, 1998 [1921]: 258).

Douhet is often misrepresented as a heartless thinker and is said to have advocated indiscriminate urban destruction as legitimate warfare. In fact, his thought was informed by various factors that demanded, in his understanding, a turn to aerial warfare not as a desired but rather as an inevitable development, which was to be welcomed if it was to shorten wars. The World War taught him that "a few hardy men with a few bullets and some strings of barbed wire could keep imposing enemy forces at bay for months" and that "insignificant topographical obstacles ... cost rivers of blood and incalculable tonnes of steel before they were conquered foot by foot" (1998 [1921]: 265). Aerial bombing was thus to be welcomed in that "cemeteries would undoubtedly grow larger, but not as large as they became before the peace was signed at Versailles" (1998 [1921]: 282).

Moreover, Douhet's actual strategic concern was the defence of Italy. He was interested in warning of the implications of the aerial superiority of an adversary that could not be stopped from "tormenting" the population even if Italy had command of its maritime environment and an army securing it from a land offensive from the direction of the Alps (1998 [1921]: 275–276). Note that his views of the possible impact of aerial bombardment were informed by his perception of a trend towards the use of "aerochemical weapons,".

This was even before biological weapons programmes, focusing on the weaponization of anthrax in prospective aerial bombings, began in earnest. Notably, Canadian scientist Frederick Banting, whose influence played a key role in the decision of the British government to commence a biological weapons programme, himself was of the opinion that (and this is worth quoting at length):

> In the past, war was confined for the most part to men in uniform, but with increased mechanization of armies and the introduction of air forces ... [it] really amounts to one nation fighting another nation. This being so, it is just as effective to kill or disable ten unarmed workers at home as to put a soldier out of action, and if this can be done with less risk, then it would be advantageous to employ any mode of warfare to accomplish this (quoted in Guillemin, 2006).

To many observers, World War Two proved the validity of their fears for Douhet. The German bombing of towns such as Antwerp, Warsaw, London, or Belgrade and the allied "area" or "saturation" bombing against cities such as Hamburg, Cologne, Berlin, or Dresden, deemed "defended" and thus legitimate military targets, constituted in effect the kind of morale or terror bombing that Douhet envisioned. E.g., even the naming of the bombing of Hamburg as "Operation Gomorrah," with its biblical reference to the destruction of an entire city, seemed to point in this direction. British Prime Minister Winston Churchill himself noted in a memorandum dated March 28, 1945, that after the bombing of Dresden, "the moment has come when the question of the bombing of German cities simply for the sake of increasing the terror ... should be reviewed," to which he later added: "I feel the need for more precise concentration upon military objectives ... behind the immediate battle-zone, rather than on mere acts of terror and wanton destruction, however impressive" (quoted in McKee, 1982: page unknown).

The act of strategic bombing conducted by the warring factions was perceived as a borderline scenario by the strategists, despite the evidence presented above indicating otherwise. Terms such as "industrial targets" and "defended cities" could (especially on a cloudy day, faced with dense air defence fire) cover just about anything that the bombers happened to hit. At the time, international humanitarian law had not yet specified any further how the bombing of an urban area might take place. As Marshal of the Royal Air Force Sir Arthur Harris, the head of the British Bomber Command, summed up: "Attacks on cities, like any other act of war, are intolerable unless they are strategically justified. But they are strategically justified in so far as they tend to shorten the war and to preserve the lives of Allied soldiers." He added: "I do not personally regard the whole of the remaining cities of Germany as worth the bones of one British Grenadier" (letter to Air Marshal Bottomley dated March 28, 1945, quoted in Overy, 2005: 290).

Harris frequently found himself at odds with the British government regarding the dissemination of information pertaining to the bombing campaign's objectives. He insisted that the authentic objectives be disclosed to the public.

> the destruction of German cities, the killing of German workers, and the disruption of civilised life throughout Germany ... the destruction of houses, public utilities, transport and lives, the creation of a refugee problem on an unprecedented scale, and the breakdown of morale both at home and at the battle fronts by fear of extended and intensified bombing (quoted in McKinstry, 2009).

The combatant parties of World War Two often referenced each other's practises as the rationale for the use of strategic bombing. Germany referred to its cruise and ballistic missiles, which it used to indiscriminately target population centres, as V-1 and V-2, respectively, where V stands for "Vergeltungswaffe," i.e., "weapon of retaliation." In the meantime, the British Air Staff concluded in an evaluation of the impact of the German air raid on Coventry that "if [British] Bomber Command could carry out a raid on the Coventry scale every month, the result would be a complete state of panic in the industrialised west of Germany" (quoted in McKinstry, 2009).

There is often an avoidance of the discussion of these issues, with the fear of some being that it may relativise the significance of German crimes during (and also before) World War Two, but this is an ethically ill-founded position to take. To point out some of the most obvious arguments in this regard: the genocide perpetrated by Germany against Jews and other population groups, with a toll far greater than the number of civilian casualties of Allied strategic bombing, never held out the prospect to the victims that they could "capitulate out" from under the threat to their lives, whereas Allied bombing was clearly to stop in the event of German capitulation. Genocide has as its chief purpose the intentional killing of civilians. Allied bombing, in terms of the participants' conception of it, fell somewhere between the "unintended but inevitable" killing of civilians and doing harm to civilians intentionally (but then only as a non-central aim[10]).

The fear of "relativisation" hides the more important question of what is affordable in war, an interactional social process, with a view to what the other side does. How much may the other side's conduct justify moving closer to, or right up to, and at times beyond, the normative boundaries of what is permissible at the time, e.g., by the standards of humanitarian law?

These are haunting questions, especially with the bombing of Hiroshima and Nagasaki in mind – the ultimate closure to World War Two. The "U.S. Strategic Bombing Survey Report" found that "prior to December 31, 1945, and in all probability prior to November 1, 1945, Japan would have surrendered even if the atomic bombs had not been dropped" (Bombing Survey Summary, 1946: 26). Beyond this being speculation, it is safe to note in terms of counterfactual statements that, should the war have continued up to either of the above-mentioned time points, more Japanese and US casualties would have been the result (minus the number of victims in the nuclear bombings). The conventional bombing of Japan was no less lethal (only more resource-intensive) than the nuclear bombings were. Based on the battle of Okinawa, a very large number of land troops would have died in action on the Japanese main islands. In other words, even without a detailed examination of the counterfactual statements cited above, the shortening of the war *may* have resulted in a smaller number of overall deaths. It is the uncertainty of this that makes the second question in the title of this chapter ("always in error?") a haunting puzzle.

Even in the case of the nuclear bombings, the mechanism of effect was, however, not quite what morale bombing advocates would have expected. Douhet's "most direct attack on national resistance" does not seem to have made a mark on the Japanese population overall, as an overwhelming majority "in urban areas other than Hiroshima and Nagasaki" already seems to have[11] doubted if it was possible to win the war, and a near-majority was certain that it could not be won (based on data quoted in: Bombing Survey, 1946: 26–27). The psychological effect of "demoralisation" was found to be localised, restricted largely to the targeted cities themselves. The impact mattered more in the case of decision-makers in the governing cabinet, in subtle ways:

> The bombs did not convince the military that defense of the home islands was impossible, if their behavior in Government councils is adequate testimony. It did permit the Government to say, however, that no army without the weapon [the atomic bomb] could possibly resist an enemy who had it, thus saving "face" for the Army leaders (Bombing Survey, 1946: 28).

In other words, the dropping of the atomic bombs merely reinforced an already existing dynamic in the Japanese cabinet, and it did so not through an effect of demoralisation but through its impact on the assessment of the military prospects by the key actors. The theory that the enemy can be made to "chicken out" of a conflict upon having been hurt wildly enough seems to have proved wrong here again, even as the demonstration of capabilities did matter.

TERROR AS TACTIC AND STRATEGY IN THE CONTEXT OF INSURGENCIES

The first question in the title of the chapter ("ever present?") may be answered with reference to how the leading democratically accountable powers accept limitations regarding warfare and conduct themselves accordingly most of the time. The answer is thus negative. Having said that, a statement that terror is "often present" is merely another side of the same coin in a context where not only democratic powers but also state actors wage war. Intra-state conflicts are the most frequent since World War II compared to any other type of conflict.[12] According to the Uppsala Conflict Database, "non-state" conflicts have outnumbered "state-based" conflicts since 2011,[13] and "internal" conflicts have produced more lethal casualties than "interstate conflicts" in every year since 1976.[14] This matters because adherence to, as well as the monitoring of, compliance with humanitarian law is more complicated in such settings.

The ensuing brief section therefore discusses examples of the most common types of terrorism that manifest in insurgency-like situations, by type of target (combatants and their kith and kin, influencers, cash cows). Insurgency is understood here, for the sake of simplicity, as an armed rebellion against an internationally recognised government. Combat in the context of an insurgency thus takes place typically in the form of smaller surprise engagements whereby insurgent forces seek to inflict casualties on government as well as pro-government forces, and in the form of massive as well as targeted military and security operations by counter-insurgent forces in which they try to identify and, ultimately, capture or kill insurgents. Thinking in terms of types of targets of terror may help isolate relevant incidents from the rest of the combat taking place and identify the exact lines of operation these incidents form part of, from either the insurgents' or the counter-insurgents' perspective.

Targets: Combatants and Their Kith and Kin

In the context of an insurgency, the parties in conflict may seek to terrorise each other directly through the publicised use of violence. The torture and/or execution of prisoners, examined at the beginning of this chapter with reference to the case of the war against ISIS in Iraq and Syria, is but one example in this respect. Even the destruction of property belonging to relatives of terrorism suspects, e.g., as this may be happening in Israel/Palestine (B'Tselem, 2017) or in the North Caucasus within the Russian Federation (HRW, 2015), may belong in this category, as it is apparently intended to carry a deterrent effect with a view to prospective future perpetrators of attacks as well as their communities.

Targets: Influencers

Both insurgents and counter-insurgents may also target key individuals who are not themselves taking part in combat but may be strategically or symbolically relevant to its outcome and are thus influencers speaking or acting in favour of either side (or not speaking or acting in favour of a side that seeks their support). Much discussion about insurgencies centres on the US experience in Vietnam, where the Phoenix Programme (in Vietnamese: *Phung Hoang*) sought to counter Viet Cong influence in villages in ways comparable overall to the brutality of the Viet Cong itself (Moïse, 2005: 317–318).[15] The Taliban-led insurgency in Afghanistan (up to 2021) may be a prominent and therefore valuable contemporary example to shed more light on this dynamic. Key influencers in the Afghan context include, e.g., those speaking to the population from a position of religious authority. Over 300 members of the *ulema*, i.e., Islamic religious scholars, were killed by insurgents in Kandahar province between 2004 and 2017, the insurgents' aim being to deter members of the *ulema* from carrying a pro-government message or one unsupportive of the insurgents' actions (Mashal & Sukhanyar, 2017). Secular influencers, e.g., schoolteachers, have similarly been targeted. In the period between January and August 2013 alone, up to 100 teachers and other education personnel may have been killed by insurgents, according to the Afghan Ministry of Education (Ghanizada, 2013).

Targets: Cash Cows

It is also worth noting the importance, in some contexts, of the role of extortion in financing both terrorism and insurgency-related activities (or the activities of paramilitary forces involved in a counterinsurgency). An example of this may be the Northern Irish context, where to a lesser extent Republican militants and to a greater extent Loyalist forces relied on racketeering as a source of funds (Horgan & Taylor, 1999, 2003 [regarding Republicans]; Silke, 1998, 2000 [regarding Loyalist factions]). The definition of terrorism may apply in the context of extortion given that the message of the racket being required typically reaches beyond those directly targeted, lowering transaction costs for the racketeers (and thus there is a secondary audience to speak of). Kidnapping as a similar and potentially more lethal form of crime may also be a significant source of financing for insurgent groups, as was the case with the Colombian rebel group FARC (in Spanish: *Fuerzas Armadas Revolucionarias de Colombia*), which engaged in a large number of kidnappings up until 2012 (see, e.g., Otis, 2014: 10–11).

To Conclude This Section

It may be pointed out that in specific contexts, other types of targets and, by consequence, other types of insurgents, as well as counter-insurgent use of terror, are conceivable. For instance, the German military regularly countered sabotage and attacks by resistance movements with retaliatory collective punishment against the local civilian populace during WW2 (see, e.g., in the Balkans context, Melson, 2007: 709–711). In the assessment of many observers, forces loyal to the Syrian regime of Bashar al-Assad have systematically engaged, over the course of the Syrian war, in displacing, through terror bombing, the population of rebel-held areas to deprive rebels of a supportive social context and to be able to operate more freely militarily (see this point made, e.g., in Malsin, 2016). Depending on the circumstances, population displacement can considerably burden an enemy force in depth, rendering its movement, logistics, and generally the maintenance of stability behind its lines more complicated. In the meantime, population displacement (e.g., in the case of ethnic cleansing) may be the aim of a combatant party *per se*, to which acts designed to have a terrorising effect can contribute in a major way (as this may have happened most recently in Myanmar to Rohingya Muslims at the hands of the Myanmar military; Kinseth, 2018). Violence against civilians may also serve the aim of disrupting a peace process[16] or deterring would-be defectors from risking a change of sides (see work on "fratricide" by Staniland, 2012). For a final example of yet another type of terror, al-Qaida in Iraq killed a large number of Shi'a and Yezidi Iraqis in the course of the insurgency in Iraq to strengthen the sectarian dividing lines and thus reinforce its image as a defender of the interests of the Sunni population of the country (ICG, 2006: 14–17).

Especially the latter cases (spoiler violence, fratricide, violence seeking status rewards) may show that there is often great complexity in violence employed against civilians: an individual attack may serve multiple different lines of operation at the same time for the employer of such violence.

In summary of the aforesaid, Table 14.1 provides an overview of the types of terror discussed previously.

Table 14.1 Types of Violence Aiming to Terrorise in the Context of Insurgencies

Type of Violence	Primary Target	Secondary Target
Publicised violence against captured combatants and their kith and kin	Combatants and their kith and kin	Combatants specifically, as well as the combatants' social constituency
Assassination of influencers	Individual influencers	The entire group of the type of influencers concerned
Threat of violence against sources of money	Individuals and companies to be "milked"	Similar other money sources
Collectively punitive violence	Randomly selected civilians from a specific locale	The population at large
Indiscriminate application of firepower against a specific locale	A specific locale – an area	All people living in a specific locale
Destruction of settlements, violence against civilians *en masse*	Victims hurt at random in significant numbers	A population to be displaced from their homes
Spoiler violence against civilians in classical terrorism, aiming to cause outrage during peace negotiations	Victims hurt at random	Decision-makers, for whom the audience cost of negotiations and compromise is thereby raised – and their strategic audiences as such
Fratricide: the assassination of people on the (own) side of the combatant party	Potential defectors who are seen as not supportive enough or already about to defect	All potential defectors and those offering wavering support on the side of the combatant party
Violence against civilians in classical terrorism, aiming to be recognised as hurting a specific group other than the combatant party's own constituency	Victims hurt at random from the group being targeted	The combatant party's own constituency (in the hope of gaining their approval); members of other parties' constituencies (to incite from them a response)

Source: Author's compilation.

CONCLUSION

As the chapter argued in this, no doubt, incomplete overview of the historical examples of pure as well as impure forms of war terrorism (i.e., respectively: *indiscriminate* and *insufficiently discriminate* attacks), it is by no means an acceptable form of warfare. Yet at least in some cases discussed here, it may not have been the most evil practise on the part of combatants in a given conflict, and it may have been conducive to bringing hostilities to an end, thus reducing the overall number of conflict dead.

It is also worth noting the evolving nature of norms as well as the role of technological development in how strategic aerial bombing is evaluated today against different standards than during WW1 or even WW2. Having said that, this applies mostly to democratically accountable and militarily advanced powers. Aerial terror bombing remains a tactic seen in some armed conflicts around the world to this day.

Other types of violent actions (assassinations, kidnappings, extortion-related violence, the torture or killing of captured combatants, etc.) similarly and sadly also remain part of the contemporary landscape of armed conflict.

Notes

1 meaning that one is not directly involved in combat. This implies that even uniformed military personnel may be regarded in certain cases as the victims of a terrorist attack (and not merely a surprise attack or violence amounting to a war crime). E.g., the public or publicised execution as well as the torture or humiliation of prisoners of war clearly involve terrorism, too.

2 The actual instrumentality of this (with a view to either of the assumed aims) is, of course, highly questionable.

3 "Management of savagery" by an "administration of savagery" refers here to the kind of organised violence that may be necessary for any social movement to consolidate rule over a land where hitherto existing authority may have weakened or collapsed. If used appropriately, savagery is the bridge to the utopia envisioned by the movement – for Naji, to the order envisioned by Islamists (Naji, transl. by McCants, 2006: 26). In fact, the term "administration of savagery" is used in such a way that it has considerable overlap with terms such as "revolutionary organisation" and "insurgency."

4 Reference to the massacre of the Jewish tribe of Banu Qurayza in the 7th century in the Arabian Peninsula

5 The treatment of suspected ISIS members was in many cases no less extreme than the cruelty ISIS itself has become known for: captives have been beaten and hung from hooks with their hands tied behind their backs for hours on end with regularity, and on at least one occasion a captive person is seen in video footage as his captors break his bones with a sledgehammer.

6 Note that this is inclusive of prisoners of war and other captives.

7 From a military standpoint, the mention of ballistic missiles may be debatable. Given that missiles have their own propulsion system (unlike artillery projectiles) and may even have manoeuvrability to varying degrees (as do, e.g., reprogrammable cruise missiles), they ought to be distinguished from more conventional means of artillery, which, on the other hand, can also be used for indiscriminate fire to terrorise populations.

8 For a source critical of this view, see Yost (2011). He raises doubts as to how much Soviet leaders took "US arguments" about strategic stability into account in their own planning for nuclear war.

9 See, e.g., the use of so-called barrel bombs in Syria, examined in Marton (2017: 34–36).

10 I argue that the aim there may be regarded as non-central precisely with reference to the concept of "terror." The aim was to destroy the will of those not killed by the air raids, never to kill *per se*. It is also important to emphasise that the Allied bombing campaigns were not carried out in ways that maximised civilian casualties. Even in the cases of Dresden and Hamburg, military-related industrial targets *were* considered in the targeting process; arguably, it is noteworthy that there *was* a targeting process as such in the first place.

11 It should be noted that the survey of the attitudes of Japanese members of the public can only be of questionable validity as it was carried out retrospectively.

12 See data at https://www.prio.org/Projects/Extensions/ConflictTrends/Graphs/#List3Tab1. The comparison is with "interstate," "internationalised" and "extrastate" conflicts.

13 where non-state means that no government is involved in the conflict, and state-based means that at least one of the parties involved is a government. See data at: http://ucdp.uu.se/; see the definitions at: https://www.pcr.uu.se/research/ucdp/definitions/.

14 UCDP Battle-Related Deaths Dataset v.5-2014, Uppsala Conflict Data Programme, www.ucdp.uu.se, Uppsala University. Available at https://www.prio.org/Projects/Extensions/ConflictTrends/Graphs/

15 Although, as Moïse points out, "few valid generalisations can be made about the programme; there was too much variation," with a number of different actors involved both from the US and the Republic of Viet Nam (RVN) sides and with local-level commanders working in different environments with different constraints and incentives.

16 Consider here, for example, the attempt by the Real IRA (Real Irish Republican Army) to undermine the Good Friday Agreement of 1997 in the Omagh bombing of 1998 (on this, see e.g. Gray, 2009).

References

"A Report into the credibility of certain evidence with regard to Torture and Execution of Persons Incarcerated by the current Syrian regime" (2014). Prepared for Carter–Ruck and Co. Solicitors of London. 6 St Andrew Street, London, EC4A 3AE. Retrieved from https://www.carter-ruck.com/images/uploads/documents/Syria_Report-January_2014.pdf

Barthram, A. (2008). *How did London civilians respond to the German airship raids of 1915?* BA Thesis. Retrieved from https://www.londonairshipraids1915.co.uk/

"Breaking: Terrifying Footage of Russians Torturing Prisoner with a Sledge Hammer" (2015, June 30). *Funker 530.*

Retrieved from https://www.funker530.com/prisoner-sledge-hammer/

Bombing Survey (1946). *U.S. strategic bombing survey: The effects of the atomic bombings of Hiroshima and Nagasaki*. Retrieved from the Truman Library, at https://www.trumanlibrary.org/whistlestop/study_collections/bomb/large/documents/pdfs/65.pdf

Bombing Survey Summary (1946). *United States strategic bombing survey summary report (pacific war)*. Washington, DC. Retrieved from http://www.anesi.com/ussbs01.htm

B'Tselem (2017, November 11). Home demolition as collective punishment. *B'Tselem*. Retrieved from https://www.btselem.org/punitive_demolitions

Douhet, G. (1998 [1921]). *The command of the air*. Transl. by D. Ferrari. Washington, DC: Air Force History and Museums Program.

Georgy, M. (2017, February 6). Iraqi forces wage psychological war with jihadist corpses. *Reuters*. Retrieved from https://www.reuters.com/article/us-mideast-crisis-mosul-corpses-idUSKBN15L1OT

Ghanizada (2013, August 10). 100 teachers and education officials killed in Afghanistan: MOE. Khaama Press. Retrieved from https://www.khaama.com/100-teachers-and-education-officials-killed-in-afghanistan-moe-2333/

Gray, D. (2009, August 25). The role played by 'spoilers' in peace processes. *E-International Relations*. Retrieved from https://www.e-ir.info/2009/08/25/using-case-studies-of-your-choice-examine-the-role-played-by-%E2%80%98spoilers%E2%80%99-in-peace-processes/

Griehl, M., & Dresser, J. (1990). *Zeppelin! The German airship story*. London: Arms & Armour.

Guillemin, J. (2006). Scientists and the history of biological weapons: A brief historical overview of the development of biological weapons in the twentieth century. *EMBO Reports*, *7*(Spec No), 45–49. 10.1038%2Fsj.embor.7400689

Hassan, H. (2015a, February 8). Isis has reached new depths of depravity. But there is a brutal logic behind it. *The Guardian*. Retrieved from https://www.theguardian.com/world/2015/feb/08/isis-islamic-state-ideology-sharia-syria-iraq-jordan-pilot

Hassan, H. (2015b, January 25). The secret world of Isis training camps – ruled by sacred texts and the sword. *The Guardian*. Retrieved from https://www.theguardian.com/world/2015/jan/25/inside-isis-training-camps

Horgan, J., & Taylor, M. (1999). Playing the 'green card' – financing the provisional IRA: Part 1. *Terrorism and Political Violence*, *11*(2), 1–38.

Horgan, J., & Taylor, M. (2003). Playing the 'green card' – financing the provisional IRA: Part 2. *Terrorism and Political Violence*, *15*(2), 1–60.

Hoover, J. (2015, February 6). How to read the medieval scholar the Islamic State used to justify al-Kasasbeh murder. *The Conversation*. Retrieved from https://theconversation.com/how-to-read-the-medieval-scholar-the-islamic-state-used-to-justify-al-kasasbeh-murder-37293

House of Commons (1932). Transcript. Retrieved from https://api.parliament.uk/historic-hansard/commons/1932/nov/10/international-affairs

HRW (2015, June 18). Invisible War: Russia's abusive response to the Dagestan insurgency. *Human Rights Watch*. Retrieved from https://www.hrw.org/report/2015/06/18/invisible-war/russias-abusive-response-dagestan-insurgency

ICG (2006). The next Iraqi war? Sectarianism and civil conflict. International Crisis Group, *Middle East Report N°52*, 27 February 2006. Retrieved from https://www.crisisgroup.org/middle-east-north-africa/gulf-and-arabian-peninsula/iraq/next-iraqi-war-sectarianism-and-civil-conflict

Khazov-Casia, S., & Coalson, R. (2018, March 14). Russian mercenaries: Vagner commanders describe life inside the 'meat grinder'. *RFE/RL*. Retrieved from https://www.rferl.org/a/russian-mercenaries-vagner-commanders-syria/29100402.html

Kinseth, A.S. (2018, August 25). Did the Myanmar military plan its ethnic cleansing of the Rohingya in advance? *The Washington Post*. Retrieved from https://www.washingtonpost.com/news/democracy-post/wp/2018/08/25/did-the-myanmar-military-plan-its-ethnic-cleansing-of-the-rohingya-in-advance/?noredirect=on&utm_term=.19052e217f64

Levy, J.S., & Ripsman, N.M. (2007). The preventive war that never happened: Britain, France, and the Rise of Germany in the 1930s. *Security Studies*, *16*(1), 32–67.

Malsin, J. (2016, March 4). How Bashar Assad is trying to win the peace in Syria. *Time*. Retrieved from http://time.com/4248050/syria-truce-bashar-assad-strategy/

Marton, P. (2017). Evolution in military affairs in the battlespace of Syria and Iraq. *Corvinus Journal of International Affairs/COJOURN*, *2*(2-3), 30–41.

Mashal, M., & Sukhanyar, J. (2017, May 28). Taliban target: Scholars of Islam. *The New York Times*. Retrieved from https://www.nytimes.com/2017/05/28/world/asia/up-tick-in-killing-of-religious-scholars-as-taliban-look-to-curtail-their-influence.html

McKee, A. (1982). *The devil's tinderbox: Dresden 1945*. London: Souvenir Press.

McKinstry, L. (2009, December17). The revenger's tragedy. *New Statesman*. Retrieved from https://www.newstatesman.com/europe/2009/12/germany-air-bomber-war-bombing

Meek, J.G., Ramos, S., & McLaughlin, E. (2017, July 14). Watchdogs: Iraqi troops beat and execute Mosul prisoners in new videos. *ABC News*. Retrieved from https://abcnews.go.com/International/watchdogs-iraqi-troops-beat-execute-mosul-prisoners-videos/story?id=48645312

Melson, C.D. (2007). German counterinsurgency in the Balkans: The Prinz Eugen division example, 1942–1944. *Journal of Slavic Military Studies*, *20*, 705–737.

Moïse, E.E. (2005). *The A to Z of the Vietnam War*. Lanham, MD: Scarecrow Press.

Muir, J. (2017, October 17). 'Islamic State': Raqqa's loss seals rapid rise and fall. BBC. Retrieved from https://www.bbc.com/news/world-middle-east-35695648

Naji, A.B. (2006). *The management of savagery: The most critical stage through which the Umma Will pass*. Transl. by W. McCants. The John M. Olin Institute for Strategic Studies at Harvard University (US).

Otis, J. (2014). *The FARC and Colombia's illegal drug trade*. Washington, DC: Wilson Center.

Overy, R. (2005). Allied bombing and the destruction of German Cities. In R. Chickering, S. Förster, & B. Greiner (Eds.), *A world at total war: Global conflict and the politics of destruction, 1937–1945* (pp. 277–296). Cambridge: Cambridge University Press & German Historical Institute (in Washington, DC).

Poolman, K. (1975). *Zeppelins over England*. London: White Lion Publishers.

Robinson, D.H. (1971). *The Zeppelin in Combat: A history of the German naval airship division, 1912–1918*. Henley-on-Thames: G.T.Foulis.

Silke, A. (1998). In defense of the realm: Financing loyalist terrorism in Northern Ireland—Part one: Extortion and blackmail. *Studies in Conflict & Terrorism, 23*(2), 107–127.

Silke, A. (2000). Drink, drugs, and Rock'n'Roll: Financing loyalist terrorism in Northern Ireland — Part Two. *Studies in Conflict & Terrorism, 21*(4), 331–361.

Staniland, P. (2012). Between a rock and a hard place: Insurgent fratricide, ethnic defection, and the rise of pro-state paramilitaries. *Journal of Conflict Resolution, 56*(1), 16–40.

Tayler, L. (2017, February 1). The Kurdish Government is Torturing boys. *Foreign Policy*. Retrieved from https://foreignpolicy.com/2017/02/01/the-kurdish-government-is-torturing-boys-islamic-state-krg-asayish/

Townsend, M. (2018, May 13). The core ISIS manual that twisted Islam to legitimise barbarity. *The Guardian*. Retrieved from https://www.theguardian.com/world/2018/may/12/isis-jihadist-manual-analysed-rebutted-by-islamic-scholar

Yost, D.S. (2011). Strategic stability in the Cold War: Lessons for continuing challenges. *IFRI Security Studies Center Proliferation Papers*, Winter 2011. Retrieved from https://www.ifri.org/sites/default/files/atoms/files/pp36yost.pdf

Whiteside, C. (2017). A pedigree of terror: The myth of the Ba'athist influence in the Islamic State movement. *Perspectives on Terrorism, 11*(3). Retrieved from http://www.terrorismanalysts.com/pt/index.php/pot/article/view/605/html

15

FROM NATION-STATE TERRORISM TO MARKET-STATE TERRORISM

Glen M. E. Duerr

INTRODUCTION

In a volume on terrorist insurgencies and violence, an important facet of the conversation is to investigate what the world looks like at present (2019) and how counter-terrorism (CT) methods have changed in recent decades in light of the way the modern world looks. Although most readers will likely have some background on the concept of the nation-state, the idea of the market-state might not be as familiar. According to most scholars, the transition from nation-state to market-state occurred in the late twentieth century, with a greater focus by the state on economic growth and trade and away from the fissiparous nationalism and war-fighting of earlier generations based heavily on a strict national identity. There is some debate on the subject since the transition from nation-state to market-state was a lengthy process. However, the market-state has emerged as a different variety of states, with commerce taking a much more central role in the discussion. National identity is still very important, as it is linked to issues like language and culture, but nearly all major businesses realise the importance of polyglot abilities in order to successfully compete in the world of commerce. Concomitantly, the central ideas of the nation-state have not necessarily eroded; they have been complimented by the importance of the market and economic growth. Put differently, the concept of a market-state still largely overlaps with that of a nation-state, except that less emphasis is placed on identity, such as language and culture, and more on economics and the market. This also means that a state needs some level of power projection in order to help protect its business interests.

Given that this chapter is more conceptual, it diverges from many of the other chapters in this volume and instead seeks to answer four sets of questions related to the concept of the market-state, specifically: 1) What is the market-state, and when did it emerge? 2) How is the market-state different from a nation-state, especially as related to terrorism? 3) What types of counterterrorism (CT) are necessary to protect entities under the market-state, and what provisions are necessary to accomplish this end? 4) What are the impacts of market-state terrorism?

The next section of this chapter addresses the first question on a definition of the market-state and a discussion on its emergence. Following the definition, the next section investigates the second question of why a market-state is different from a nation-state, with a particular emphasis on issues related to terrorism. The third section of the chapter looks at counterterrorism measures from the market-state and identifies three different types of terrorist organisations that typically target commerce and industry within a market-state. Relatedly, the fourth section appraises the direct and indirect impacts of market-state terrorism. This includes a discussion of how some terrorist organisations also seek to fill a gap in society in opposition to the market-state. Finally, this chapter concludes with a reflection on the market-state and CT options against different types of threats.

WHAT IS THE MARKET-STATE, AND WHEN DID IT EMERGE?

In the aftermath of World War II, numerous international organisations like the General Agreement on Tariffs and Trade (GATT) proliferated as a mechanism for building economic internationalism and moving away from mercantilism. By decreasing the barriers to trade, countries were able to expand their economic markets and gain specialisation in certain areas. This was a relatively slow process, but one that was built by lowering tariffs and building bilateral and multilateral trade areas. The most obvious example is what is now the European Union (EU).

Starting with the European Coal and Steel Community (ECSC) with the Treaty of Paris in 1951, the six initial member states (France, West Germany, Italy, Belgium, Luxembourg, and the Netherlands) began pooling coal

DOI: 10.4324/9780429426063-17

and steel resources as a means of using commerce to avoid the pitfalls of hyper-nationalism that led to World War II (Dinan, 2004: 6). The ECSC moved into other areas of policy like atomic energy, agriculture, and fisheries, among others, over the course of the next two decades. The ECSC also became the European Economic Community (EEC) with the ratification of the Treaty of Rome (also known as the Treaty on the Functioning of the European Union) in 1957, which solidified the desire to reduce trade barriers between member states and to develop a larger common economic market (Dinan, 2004).

In North America, Canada and the United States signed the 1965 Auto Pact (formally known as the Canada-United States Automotive Products Agreement), which reduced tariffs primarily on automotive goods between the two countries (Pastor, 2001). It made the Ambassador Bridge crossing between Detroit, Michigan, USA, and Windsor, Ontario, Canada, the most trafficked border crossing in the world since automotive parts began to crisscross the border as companies specialised in various areas of manufacturing. This increased trade between the two countries worked well enough that in 1988, under American President Ronald Reagan and Canadian Prime Minister Brian Mulroney, they signed the Canada-United States Free Trade Agreement (CUSFTA) (Pastor, 2001).

Back in Europe, the EEC was making even more pronounced changes towards the market-state. After several rounds of enlargements, the EEC ballooned from 6 member states to 12 by the late 1980s, with the UK, Ireland, and Denmark joining in 1973; Greece in 1981; and Spain and Portugal in 1986. At the same time, the Cold War that had mired Europe in a seismic clash between capitalism and communism for 45 years (from 1946 to 1991) was beginning to thaw dramatically. Vociferous protests erupted across the Soviet Union in the midst of Premier Mikhail Gorbachev's Perestroika and Glasnost reforms. In Eastern Europe, in the late 1980s, anti-communist protests began to take place from Budapest to Prague, Warsaw to Bucharest, and numerous other cities in between.

In light of this history, the best answer is that the market-state fully emerged in the period from 1989 to 1994, even though the foundation blocks were laid in earlier decades. Although the concept of the market-state had been building since the founding of GATT in 1947, the compilation of events across the world presented the market-state fully on the world stage. In 1989, the Berlin Wall, which was symbolic of the divide between East and West, between communism and capitalism, came down in a very quick succession of events. Prominent countries in Eastern Europe began to hold democratic elections and started the transition to free-market economic systems. The Soviet Union, so long the proprietor of communism, dissolved into 15 different countries, some of which made major attempts to change towards the concept of the market-state. The Treaty of Maastricht formally created the EU out of the EEC with greater connectivity of economies. The EU-12 expanded to the EU-15 in 1995 with the accession of Austria, Sweden, and Finland. In North America, Mexico was added to the CUSFTA to create the North American Free Trade Agreement (NAFTA) in 1994. In South America, the Treaty of Asunción, which created Mercosur/Mercosul (also known as the Southern Common Market), was signed in 1991 between Uruguay, Paraguay, Brazil, and Argentina. In East Africa, the Common Market for Eastern and Southern Africa (COMESA) was signed in 1993 between numerous states. In Southeast Asia, the Association of Southeast Asian Nations (ASEAN) was formally signed in 1992 with six members from across the region.

So, when did the market-state emerge? It had clear beginnings in the post-World War II era, especially with the emergence of GATT. The aforementioned blocs in Western Europe and North America emerged in the 1950s and 1960s, as did other trade areas like the Caribbean Community (Caricom) in the 1970s and the Gulf Cooperation Council (GCC) in the early 1980s. Nevertheless, in the early 1990s, with the creation of the EU, NAFTA, Mercosur, and Comesa, in addition to GATT's reformation as the World Trade Organisation (WTO) in 1995, this cemented the transition around the world from nation-state to market-state.

HOW IS THE MARKET-STATE DIFFERENT FROM A NATION-STATE, ESPECIALLY AS RELATED TO TERRORISM?

A nation-state is an overly generalised term since a nation – with shared ethnic, linguistic, cultural, and/or religious characteristics – overlaps with a state – a political unit comprising a government, population, and defined territory. A state rarely features a homogenous nation, so nation-state often refers to people under a constitution even though they differ on ethnicity, language, culture, and/or religion. Thus, the term nation-state is typically used to include countries, even those with multiple nations.

As noted in the previous section, there is a lot of overlap between the nation-state and the market-state, but with additional emphases on trade and commerce as part of society. Australian academic and diplomat Paul Monk describes:

> A market state, by comparison, is defined by constitutional, economic and strategic adaptation to a world in which the claims of human rights, the reach of weapons of mass destruction, the proliferation of transnational threats to security and well-being, and the emergence of global capital markets that ignore borders, curtailing the power of states to control their

own economies; while the development of telecommunications networks that likewise ignore borders, serves to undermine national languages, customs, cultures and regimes (Monk, 2009).

Law professor Philip Bobbitt argues that the market-state took over from the nation-state at the end of the Cold War as the sixth in a series of constitutional orders. Bobbitt posits these six constitutional orders as follows: 1) princely state (1494–1567), 2) kingly state (1572–1649), 3) territorial state (1651–1776), 4) state nation (1789–1861), 5) nation-state (1870–1989), and 6) market-state (1991–present) (Bobbitt, 2002). Bobbitt argues that the market-state has emerged in the wake of the nation-state. In many ways, Bobbitt's observation is made in the wake of 9/11, when the security features of the nation-state were under attack and the premise of the market-state was to respond to political violence. According to Bobbitt's reviewer, the legal scholar George Martinez, "the nation-state will not be able to satisfy this goal because of a number of current developments in the world. One such development is the realisation that nation-states will no longer be able to protect their citizens or preserve their national cultures" (Bobbitt, 2002: xxii). Instead, the market-state is emerging as an entity to take the nation-state's place. In contrast to the nation-state, the market-state offers to maximise individual opportunities for the people in exchange for power (Bobbitt, 2002: xxvi). Put differently, "the market-state assesses its economic success or failure by its society's ability to secure more and better goods and services, but in contrast to the nation-state, it does not see the state as more than a minimal provider or distributor" (Bobbitt, 2002: 229). In some areas of the world, the market-state is frowned upon because commerce does not uphold "national hono(u)r," which is a key facet of the nation-state. The writer Khaled Ahmed, for example, argues that in South Asia, "the market-state doesn't have national honour as a yardstick but seeks respectability through economic success" (Ahmed, 2010). He argues that the nation-state still has some staying power in the region, even though parts of the rest of the world have adopted the market-state model.

When the Berlin Wall fell in November 1989, it marked the symbolic end of the Cold War standoff between the United States and the Soviet Union, which had lasted since the end of World War II. The American political scientist Francis Fukuyama described it as "the end of history" in that he perceived the best system of governance to be capitalist democracy (Fukuyama, 1989). Fukuyama has largely abandoned this thesis now, given the contemporary challenges to democracy, but, even with the 2008 "Great Recession," some form of capitalism remains the core economic system in the world, with authoritarian states utilising "state-guided capitalism" as a mechanism to increase their national wealth. China is the most prominent example of authoritarian, state-guided capitalism. Thus, the concept of the market-state is one that crosses the boundaries of a definition of the nation-state and the market-state.

Following the earlier discussion, most scholars argue that the market-state emerged primarily in the 1990s following the dissolution of the Soviet Union. There is no exact agreed-upon timeframe given that globalisation has long been a feature of world history but that it accelerated in the post-World War II era. The historian Mark Mazower describes the issue of Americanization in Europe in the 1970s, with the trappings of what could be considered a market-state emerging from the United States but also a concept that spread to Europe by this time period (Mazower, 2009). Monk similarly argues that the rise of the Chinese economy from the 1970s to the present is evidence of the shift from the nation-state to the market-state (Monk, 2009). Thus, most scholars agree that the market-state solidified in the late 1980s and early 1990s, but many also argue that some of the ingredients were already present.

Terrorism and the Market-State

Another facet of the discussion of the market-state's emergence and terrorism against said state is to investigate an academic debate on how terrorism has evolved. Terrorism scholar David Rapoport's work on waves of terrorism forms the foundation of how many scholars look at the world. Rapoport describes four main "waves" of terrorism, starting with an "anarchist" wave in the 1880s that lasted until the emergence of "anti-colonial" terrorism in the 1920s, which continued until the 1960s with the development of "new left" terrorism, until "religious" terrorism, especially Islamist terrorism, grew into a wave in 1979 (Rapoport, 2003: 37). Generally, Rapoport argues that a wave lasts for approximately 40 years and also notes the likelihood of a fifth wave of terrorism in approximately the year 2025 given the usual life cycle of these waves of terrorism (Rapoport, 2003). Market-state terrorism, or some form of economic terrorism, does not yet fit a wave but could fit here in Rapoport's model. However, the concept of new left terrorism in the 1960s has some similarities to terrorism inflicted upon the market-state. New Left terrorism provides some insights into modern terrorism in the market-state, although there are some interesting points. The first wave of terrorism, anarchist terrorism, relied fairly heavily on bank robberies as a means of financing terrorist organisations. New Left terrorism was financed largely through individual donors, so the tactic of bank robberies ironically decreased markedly as connected to terrorism (Rapoport, 2003).

In response to Rapoport's four waves, scholars Tom Parker and Nick Sitter argue that there are four strains of terrorism rather than waves; terrorist methods happen concurrently rather than in systematic waves. These four strains include nationalism, socialism, religious extremism, and social exclusion (Parker & Sitter, 2016: 199). Their second strain, socialist terrorism, utilises a Marxist critique of world affairs, particularly capitalism, as the raison d'etre for terrorist violence (Parker & Sitter, 2016). This is particularly pertinent in a discussion of market-state terrorism because, for decades, radical terrorists, who sometimes use socialism as a justification for their violence, have targeted elements of the economy. Regardless of whether terrorism emerges in waves or strains, the market has long been a target of terrorists and fits a variety of academic models. CT for the market-state thus takes on slightly different dynamics than traditional CT under the nation-state.

Counterterrorism in the Age of the Market-State

What is the difference between counterterrorism in the age of the nation-state versus the age of the market-state? If Bobbitt's time period is used: nation-state (1870–1989), market-state (1991–present), then the big difference is the projection of power overseas. In the era of the nation-state, counterterrorism was more defined as defending the state from terrorists. Although globalisation was significant in the pre-World War I era and then again after the Second World War, most businesses were domestic. There was a dramatic shift, however, with the creation of the GATT, which later became the WTO. With the founding of the WTO, it symbolised the norm of setting up businesses overseas. Thus, with the advancement and proliferation of national businesses, counterterrorism in the market-state era is no longer simply about defending the homeland; it is also about projecting power overseas to protect the interests of the state in foreign territories. This might involve protecting business or trade interests in a range of different countries. Protecting against attacks on the oil reserves within a country, or protecting a well-known multinational company (but also a symbol of Americana) like McDonald's from attacks by various terrorist organisations. Thus, CT in the era of the market-state is much more comprehensive because protecting the market is global. It also means that the world order needs some attention because sea and ocean lanes must be open to trade and commercial activity. Without protection for goods travelling across the world, the foundations of the market-state begin to erode. CT in the era of the market-state, then, requires freedom of navigation as well as special operations forces to protect these ideals. This is a reason why the United States has special operations in over one hundred countries as a means of protecting the market-state and its ability to facilitate global trade. In the aftermath of 9/11, the Authorization of the Use of Military Force (AUMF) gave the President of the United States wide purview to go after the terrorists responsible. Given the global nature of money transfers and the use of illicit drugs to create revenue for terrorist organisations, the AUMF has a significant international reach, which helps to protect the trappings of the market-state.

Moreover, advanced intelligence sharing is necessary to maintain relations between allies. In the market-state system, coordination between allies is an integral part of counterterrorism. For example, in the case of the United States, the leader of the market-state system at present, connections with its "Five Eyes" (FVEY) compatriots are an important component of counterterrorism. FVEY serves as an intelligence alliance across English-speaking countries with the primary goal of notifying one another of threats. Given the propensity of people to cross international borders, tracking would-be terrorists is an important object of shared CT. In the post-9/11 era, the use of FVEY gained greater traction given the movement of people across these societies.

WHAT TYPES OF COUNTERTERRORISM (CT) ARE NECESSARY TO PROTECT ENTITIES UNDER THE MARKET-STATE, AND WHAT PROVISIONS ARE NECESSARY TO ACCOMPLISH THIS END?

In some senses, this section aligns with many other chapters in the volume at this point. In investigating the organisational characteristics and activities of terrorist groups that attack the market-state, the question of CT flows from understanding the characteristics and activities of various groups.

Given the breadth of the subject matter, there are three distinct types of terrorist groups that, for various reasons and objectives, have attacked targets associated with the market-state. The first broad group is Islamist terrorist groups, or at least those that attempt to use the name of Islam to perpetrate atrocities. The most noteworthy include al-Qaeda, ISIS, Boko Haram, al-Shabaab, and Jemaah Islamiyah. In this volume, there are specific chapters discussing all of these terrorist organisations, so a comprehensive overview is not possible here. However, it is worth presenting one terrorist attack by each group that summarises the motivations, tactical innovation, and impact on the market-state.

Al-Qaeda is one of the world's most notorious terrorist groups, and their raison d'être is severalfold, including: defeating the United States, the West, and Israel; enacting a strict form of sharia law; ridding Saudi Arabia of American troops; and fighting against what they view as Shia apostates, among other main goals (Gunaratna, 2002). One mechanism for fighting the West is to target, at times, commercial enterprises. 9/11, for example, saw attacks on landmark sites of the political, military, and economic power of the United States. The attacks on the North and South Towers of the World Trade Centre were symbols of American capitalism and the economic might of the country, linked to the concept of the market-state. Thus, in a sense, al-Qaeda is a terrorist organisation that sometimes attacks economic targets. Of the 2,977 people killed on 9/11, 2,753 were killed at the World Trade Centre, which is still the most horrific terrorist attack in history. Their use of hijacked airliners marked a major innovative change for terrorist groups and also ushered in the era of mass casualty terrorism (Gunaratna, 2002). For ISIS, the November 2015 attack on the city of Paris, which claimed the lives of 130 people, included an attack on a rock concert and numerous restaurants, all elements of economic activity. Their use of larger coordinated cells, armed with different weaponry, harked back to a previous era in the use of guns to conduct terrorism, but built as a tactical innovation the coordination and planning of a sophisticated attack that had a high death toll.

Boko Haram, which means "Western education is forbidden," often targets a range of different locations, especially in northeast Nigeria. Attacks on schools, a tactic of Boko Haram, are linked to the market-state in that public and private monies finance schooling, but also that educated young people are the future of the economic market, so their specific targeting is detrimental to the future of the economy and state. Al-Shabaab is notorious for attacking upscale shopping and tourist spots in Kenya. To provide two examples, the 2013 Westgate shopping mall attack claimed the lives of 71 people, and the attack on the DusitD2 Hotel in Nairobi in January 2019 killed 21 people, which was symbolic of economic advancement in Kenya and a clear connection to the market-state. Al-Shabaab used a mix of gunfire (AK-47s) and explosives and grenades to conduct the attack in coordinated cells of terrorist attackers. Jemaah Islamiyah (JI) is most infamous for its 2002 attack on various tourist destinations in Bali, Indonesia. They also specifically conducted an attack on a McDonald's restaurant in December 2000, which killed three people. Both terrorist attacks are evidence of specific attacks tailored towards the market-state. Finally, Lashkar-e-Taiba (LeT) is the terrorist group responsible for the Mumbai attacks in 2008. Effectively, the attack became a siege on Western investments, hotels, and cafes in the city of Mumbai that lasted for nearly four days. In total, 174 people were killed in an attack designed to target Indian and Western economic locations and, thus, the market-state.

The second group is made up of Marxist-inspired separatist, or ethno-nationalist, groups. To some degree, Euskadi Ta Askatasuna (ETA), the Irish Republican Army (IRA), and the Armée Révolutionnaire Bretonne (ARB) are linked to some form of terrorist attack based against the market-state (Duerr, 2018). When the market-state emerged fully in the early 1990s, all three groups were still very active. Given their ties to "new left" terrorism, the objectives of each group were to create an independent state via some form of armed rebellion against the state. Terrorist attacks by the IRA, ETA, and ARB revolved around numerous military and government targets, but also commercial enterprises that upheld the market-state in Western Europe. After robust policing and CT measures, as well as political agreements, each of the three groups began to lay down their arms. By the end of the decade, the IRA began to decrease attacks in tandem with the Good Friday Agreement, which was signed in 1998 (Sutcliffe & Alchin, 2018). Likewise, ETA announced a definitive end to their terrorist activities in 2011 and then fully disbanded in 2018 (Cartrite, 2018). In contrast, ARB never formally disbanded or signed an agreement with the government. However, the group was only active for a period of time with the emergence of the market-state system from 1998–2000 and rarely conducted attacks. In 2014, the group was responsible for two attacks, none of which claimed any fatalities or injuries (Global Terrorism Database, 2019).

The third group, environmental-based groups, has some differences. The Earth Liberation Front (ELF) and Animal Liberation Front (ALF) do not seek the mass casualties of the aforementioned groups but do conduct terrorist attacks, especially against sites related to commerce. Frequently, ELF targets new housing developments or timber or mining extraction sites in various locations around the world, but especially those connected to the market-state system. In general, ELF and ALF seek to stop the environmental changes in an area rather than specifically target people, yet, as an output of terrorism, innocent people have been injured and even killed as a result of terrorist attacks by the groups.

The concept of eco-terrorism as a means of combating ecological or environmental concerns In general, terrorist violence seeks to cause damage to property and arson but to avoid injuring humans or animals. Of course, with real-life attacks, some people do get hurt, which is one reason for their designation as a terrorist organisation by many. Congressional testimony by FBI Domestic Terrorism Chief James Jarboe helps illustrate the point:

> During the past decade we have witnessed dramatic changes in the nature of the terrorist threat. In the 1990s, right-wing extremism overtook left-wing terrorism as the most dangerous domestic terrorist threat to the country. During the past several years, special interest extremism, as characterized by the Animal Liberation Front (ALF) and the Earth Liberation Front (ELF), has emerged as a serious terrorist threat … . The FBI estimates that the ALF/ELF have committed more than 600 criminal acts in the United States since 1996, resulting in damages in excess of 43 million dollars … . ELF advocates "monkeywrenching," a euphemism for acts of sabotage and property destruction against industries and other entities perceived to be damaging to the natural environment. "Monkeywrenching" includes tree spiking, arson, sabotage of logging or construction equipment, and other types of property destruction … . The most destructive practice of the ALF/ELF is arson. The ALF/ELF members consistently use improvised incendiary devices equipped with crude but effective timing mechanisms. These incendiary

Table 15.1 Summary of the Goals, Attacks, and Outcomes of Market-State Terrorism

	Islamist	Marxist Separatist	Environmentalist
Types of Terrorist Organisations	JI/ISIS/al-Qaeda/Boko Haram/al-Shabaab/LeT	ETA/IRA/ARB	ELF/ALF
Goals	Anti-West; Promotion of a strict form of Islamism	Anti-Capitalist; Support for independence movements	Anti-Capitalist; Environmental impact
Attacks	High-profile, mass casualty	Attacks on restaurants and other places of business	Property damage
Outcomes	Increased use of special ops/ military deployments/CT	Increased intelligence cooperation	Domestic and foreign surveillance

> devices are often constructed based upon instructions found on the ALF/ELF websites. The ALF/ELF criminal incidents often involve pre-activity surveillance and well-planned operations … . The ALF and the ELF have jointly claimed credit for several raids including a November 1997 attack of the Bureau of Land Management wild horse corrals near Burns, Oregon, where arson destroyed the entire complex resulting in damages in excess of four hundred and fifty thousand dollars and the June 1998 arson attack of a U.S. Department of Agriculture Animal Damage Control Building near Olympia, Washington, in which damages exceeded two million dollars. The ELF claimed sole credit for the October 1998, arson of a Vail, Colorado, ski facility in which four ski lifts, a restaurant, a picnic facility and a utility building were destroyed. Damage exceeded $12 million. On 12/27/1998, the ELF claimed responsibility for the arson at the U.S. Forest Industries Office in Medford, Oregon, where damages exceeded five hundred thousand dollars. Other arsons in Oregon, New York, Washington, Michigan, and Indiana have been claimed by the ELF. Recently, the ELF has also claimed attacks on genetically engineered crops and trees. The ELF claims these attacks have totaled close to $40 million in damages (Jarboe, 2002).

As noted in the above section, tactically, terrorist groups attacking the market-state have a wide variety of features. Operationally, there is a wide range of targets with differing modes of conducting attacks. In some cases, the tactic is to damage a location or business in order to enact changes in society. For example, ELF often conducts arson attacks against new home developments. The goal is not to harm anyone but rather to shift the outcome not only in terms of public policy but also those of corporations involved in the development. For some Marxist-based groups, the tactic is similar in that typically the goal is to attack a McDonald's restaurant or similar symbol of capitalism while simultaneously attempting to develop ethno-nationalist claims over a given territory. For some Islamist groups, the central goal is to rid the region of market-state influence, especially the United States. Tactics and operations differ depending on the context, but maximum violence is often the central purpose of conducting terrorist attacks (Table 15.1).

THE IMPACTS OF MARKET-STATE TERRORISM

The direct and indirect effects of terrorist and insurgent groups are examined in this section. Additionally, it looks into the ways in which terrorist organisations have reacted to the notion of the market-state by offering social services and madrassas (schools) to teach children. The effects and motivations of terrorism on the market-state are somewhat similar to those of earlier times or other causes of terrorism. The direct effects are socio-psychological as well as economic and political in nature.

In other ways, there are specific forms of terrorism that seek to impact the market. For example, "green terrorism" purported by environmentalist terrorist groups seeks to deter or halt the construction of new homes in environmentally sensitive lands. The ELF conducts a lot of terrorist attacks, but usually without the overt motive of killing people. Of course, with any violent attack, human beings can be harmed or killed, which is a primary reason why ELF remains designated as a terrorist organisation.

In addition to the aforementioned attacks on the WTC or restaurants in Paris, anti-globalisation, in general, is a major component of market-state terrorism in that it is a force bent on reversing the effects of global trade. The writer Benjamin Barber's 1995 book, *Jihad versus McWorld*, underscores the opposing forces unleashed in an era of globalisation (Barber, 1995). On the one hand, there are strong forces of homogeneity bringing the world together under shared ideas, especially connected to commerce.

Terrorism occurs against economic targets, especially those linked to globalisation and sometimes the United States as a great power. McDonald's, for example, the well-known burger chain, is perhaps an example of an embodiment of the view of the United States abroad. With over

36,000 stores across the world, it has a footprint in 101 countries (Rosenburg, 2018). McDonald's attempts to mesh its Americanized menu with food items from the various countries in which it is located. Dozens of attacks have occurred against McDonald's alone, in part because the golden arches are a symbol of the market-state to terrorists (Rosenburg, 2018).

There are also two major indirect impacts of terrorism on the market-state. First, there is a consumer confidence issue, such that people are less likely to visit a mall or a place of business when there is an expectation that it could be a "soft target." For example, when an ISIS-inspired terrorist, Mahad A. Abdiraham, stabbed two people at the Mall of America in Bloomington, Minnesota, it sent a powerful message against the market-state: that even the everyday conduct of commerce is potentially dangerous. The Mall of America is one of the United States' best-known shopping attractions, and thus a wider socio-psychological impact was felt as a result of the terrorist stabbing.

The second major impact is on the international order. Structured around American power in the aftermath of World War II, the international order is designed to make the world safe for market states. People in market states throughout the world are expected to engage in commerce, especially over international boundaries. High-scale attacks like al-Qaeda's attack on 9/11 or the Paris attack on a set of restaurants in November 2015 are designed to impact commerce and the international order. Even attacks by Somali pirates on the *Maersk Alabama* have an impact on international order.[1] The April 8, 2009, attack on a major American cargo ship changed the nature of security among cargo ships throughout the world. It also created a hole in the international order since a criterion of the order is for goods to move safely and freely across the world. It is impossible to prevent all holes in the international order, but the market-state is juxtaposed on safe and open lanes for commerce, wherein there are penalties for those that conduct terrorist-type attacks.

Finally, it is worth noting how terrorist organisations attempt to create their own parallel market states. Some groups like ISIS, Hezbollah, and LeT have created systems to provide social services to people, including hygiene supplies, access to health care, and schooling in the form of madrassas. During the height of ISIS's power in Syria and Iraq, they attempted to create the rudimentary foundations of a state that sold oil, engaged in commerce, and tried to govern a populace. Hezbollah has significant support in southern Lebanon, mainly because the organisation has found space and support for the predominantly Shia population in the region. LeT is perhaps most notorious for the creation of madrassas that, on the one hand, educate young people while, on the other hand, insisting that said education is based on a strict form of sharia that also professes a violent jihad against what they view as enemies of Islam.

CONCLUSION

Four core questions were posed at the outset of this chapter: 1) What is the market-state, and when did it emerge? 2) How is the market-state different from a nation-state, especially as related to terrorism? 3) What types of counterterrorism (CT) are necessary to protect entities under the market-state, and what provisions are necessary to accomplish this end? 4) What are the impacts of market-state terrorism? This chapter started with a discussion and definition of the market-state and showed the nuances of the transition period in history from nation-state to market-state. Next, this chapter investigated organisations that have conducted terrorist attacks against the market-state. In particular, the rise of other non-state actors and terrorist groups in three broad categories: Islamist, Marxist, and Environmental, has perpetrated different types of attacks on the market-state. The next section on direct and indirect impacts then mirrored the previous section by showing how Islamist, Marxist, and environmental terrorist groups impacted the political, economic, and socio-psychological components of market states.

In some senses, the transition from nation-state to market-state has not changed the nature of terrorism since there are still assassinations, the use of weapons and explosives, and groups that seek various public policy changes. In other ways, the changes have been dramatic. In particular, 9/11 brought the era of mass casualty terrorism, in addition to new and unexpected weapons like hijacked airliners as bombs rather than bargaining chips for negotiation, as was the case in the 1970s in particular. Under Rapoport's waves of terrorism, the fourth wave, religious terrorism, took on new intensity (Rapoport, 2003). Bobbitt's discussion of the emergence of the market-state, for all of the economic successes of the era, has also seen a range of different groups rise to counter the West but also to actively target symbols of economic growth (Bobbitt, 2002).

In terms of CT, terrorism against the market-state requires broad international cooperation to lessen terrorist threats. In the United States, in particular, since it is the leader of the market-state model, the deployment of special ops in approximately one hundred countries is an output of this model, as is increased intelligence cooperation as in FVEY or related intelligence sharing networks. Much of the special ops activity occurs under the purview of the AUMF signed in the aftermath of 9/11 to provide CT support. Since terrorism is such a global concern, the AUMF effectively provides constitutional cover for different methods of fighting terrorism in various corners of the world (GovTrack.us, 2019).

The market-state, post-9/11, required a different method of CT. Given the threats faced, especially by Islamist,

Marxist, and environmental-based organisations, the United States and its allies have used a range of different methods to combat these organisations as well as their impacts, especially coordination through FVEY and the AUMF. The market-state requires a global model of CT in order to protect international commerce, which is pivotal for the market to operate.

Note

1 For a thorough analysis of the pirate problem off the Horn of Africa's coast and the coordinated responses of the European Union (EU) and the North Atlantic Treaty Organisation (NATO) in their extensive reaction measures, see Beseny and Sinkó (2022).

References

Ahmed, K. (2010). Market-state versus nation-state. *The Express Tribune*. September 18, 2010. Accessed on November 15 2018. Available at https://tribune.com.pk/story/51750/market-state-versus-nation-state/

Barber, B. (1995). *Jihad vs. McWorld*. New York, USA: New York, USA: Ballantine Books.

Bobbitt, P. (2002). *The shield of Achilles: War, peace, and the course of history*. New York: Anchor.

Cartrite, B. (2018). Contingent violence: Arana, Franco, and ETA's terrorist actions in the Basque Country. In G. Duerr (Ed.), *Secessionism and terrorism: Bombs, blood, and independence in Europe and Eurasia* (pp. 51–72). London: Routledge.

Dinan, D. (2004). *Europe recast: A history of European Union*. Basingstoke: Palgrave Macmillan.

Duerr, G., ed. (2018). *Secessionism and terrorism: Bombs, blood and independence in Europe and Eurasia*. London: Routledge.

Fukuyama, F. (1989). The end of history? *The National Interest, 16*, 3–18.

Global Terrorism Database. (2019). University of Maryland. Available at: https://www.start.umd.edu/gtd/

GovTrack.us. (2019). S.J.Res. 23 — 107th Congress: Authorization for use of military force. Available at: https://www.govtrack.us/congress/bills/107/sjres23

Gunaratna, R. (2002). *Inside Al Qaeda: Global network of terror*. New York: Columbia University Press.

Jarboe, J. (2002). The threat of eco-terrorism. Testimony of James F. Jarboe, Domestic Terrorism Section Chief, Counterterrorism Division, FBI, before the House Resources Committee, Subcommittee on Forests and Forest Health. Available at: http://www.fbi.gov/congress/congress02/jarboe021202.htm

Mazower, M. (2009). *Dark continent: Europe's twentieth century*. New York: Vintage.

Monk, P. (2009, September). The rise of the market state. *Quadrant Online*. Accessed on December 10, 2018. Available at https://quadrant.org.au/magazine/2009/09/the-rise-of-the-market-state/

Parker, T., & Sitter, N. (2016). The four horsemen of terrorism: It's not waves, it's strains. *Terrorism and Political Violence, 28*(2), 197–216.

Pastor, R. (2001). *Toward a North American Community: Lessons from the old world for the new*. Washington: Institute for International Economics.

Rapoport, D.C. (2003). The four waves of rebel terror and September 11. In C.W. Kegley (Ed.), *The new global terrorism: Characteristics, causes, controls* (pp. 36–52). Upper Saddle River: Prentice-Hall.

Rosenburg, M. (2018). Number of McDonald's restaurants worldwide. (February 11). Thought Co. Available at https://www.thoughtco.com/number-of-mcdonalds-restaurants-worldwide-1435174

Sutcliffe, J., & Alchin, G. (2018). Terrorism from the troubles to Good Friday: The IRA in Northern Ireland and the British Isles. In G. Duerr (Ed.), *Secessionism and terrorism: Bombs, blood, and independence in Europe and Eurasia* (pp. 26–50). London: Routledge.

16

HOMEGROWN TERRORISM

Michael G. Zekulin

INTRODUCTION

There have been several developments in the field of terrorism in the post-9/11 era, which academics and policy-makers continue to unravel and debate today. One of these is the emergence and increase in what has been dubbed "home-grown" terrorism. As with most issues related to terrorism, the concept of homegrown terrorism is contentious and much debated. This chapter intends to deconstruct the phenomenon. It will provide an account of our efforts to understand it, a discussion on how it has changed and evolved over the past several years, and close with introducing some of the larger challenges that Western democratic states will continue to face moving forward.

DEFINING HOMEGROWN TERRORISM

The most logical point of departure is to frame homegrown terrorism in relation to the 9/11 attacks by al-Qaeda. The 2002 arrest of Jose Padilla, a Muslim convert, for plotting to detonate a dirty bomb in Chicago was the first of a series of terrorist plots and attacks in Western democratic states with an interesting twist that soon became a puzzling trend. By the middle of the 2000s, a distinct pattern had emerged: individuals or long-term residents of those very same countries were orchestrating major attacks and foiling plots against Western states. In March 2004, ten backpack bombs exploded on Spain's busiest commuter rail line, five miles outside of Atocha Station in Madrid, killing 192 people and injuring 1500. Those responsible had lived in Spain for many years prior to the attack (Silber & Bhatt, 2007: 24; Zekulin, 2012: 156–167). In July 2005, three bombs detonated in the London underground tube system during the morning commute, and a fourth bomb exploded on a bus shortly after. In total, the explosions killed 56 people, including the bombers, and injured more than 700 others. The four individuals responsible for the attack were either born in Britain or had arrived when they were small children. In 2006, law enforcement agencies in both Toronto, Canada, and Sydney and Melbourne, Australia, disrupted serious plots that would have resulted in wide-spread damage and mass casualties. In the case of the "Toronto 18," all but one were born in Canada or Canadian citizens (Zekulin, 2013). In Australia, two groups, comprised of thirteen individuals in Melbourne and nine individuals in Sydney, were arrested for preparing terrorist attacks. Again, most of the individuals were born and raised in Australia or had arrived early in their lives (Schurmann et al., 2014: 91–96).

These major incidents, among others, set in motion widespread efforts to further investigate this puzzling development and would ultimately lead to the phenomenon labelled "homegrown terrorism." Crone and Harrow are generally credited with coining the term "homegrown" following the London bombing, and their early efforts served as the basis for most of the definitions found in the literature today. They focused on two aspects that, by this point, had become obvious to most observers. They involved individuals plotting or perpetrating attacks who were born and raised in the West or who had a strong attachment to the West, and the individuals (or groups) were acting on their own behalf and not taking direct orders from a group abroad (Crone & Harrow, 2011: 524). Other early accounts reached similar conclusions. Daveed Gartenstein-Ross and Laura Grossman assessed these "homegrown" individuals as those who "either spent a significant portion of their formative years in the West, or their radicalization had a significant connection to the West" (Gartenstein-Ross & Grossman, 2009: 11; Jenkins, 2010: 1). Tomas Precht's definition emphasised "acts of violence against targets primarily, but not always, in Western countries in which the terrorists themselves have been born or raised" (Precht, 2007: 15).

There were, however, some methodological shortcomings with these early definitions. The early efforts appeared to be more descriptive, focusing on what the phenomenon "looked like." To improve the rigour and conceptualisation

DOI: 10.4324/9780429426063-18

of this phenomenon, Crone and Harrow suggested it could be measured by examining degrees of belonging, how one "feels as part of their society," and degrees of autonomy, "how connected the group was to a foreign terrorist group" (Crone & Harrow, 2011: 522). This resulted in a matrix that allowed suspected homegrown incidents to be plotted and categorised. According to this approach, attacks or plots where individuals involved had a high degree of belonging and were autonomous from outside groups would be designated as "homegrown," and those with varying degrees of either would somehow fit on a sliding scale, where close connections to a group or no attachment to a country would not be considered a homegrown incident. This was a welcomed improvement but was unfortunately short-lived. The criticism that emerged focused on how conceptualisations of belonging and autonomy were understood and defined. The inescapable reality was that the terms themselves were subjective and that different people in different states would feel different levels of belonging. Further, there were difficulties in standardising and measuring how people judge their own sense of belonging (Yuval-Davis, 2006: 197–214; Brubaker, 2010: 61–78; Zekulin, 2016: 52–53). Autonomy proved to be equally difficult to conceptualise. Academics wrestled with what connectedness meant. Did communication with a group fulfil this criterion? Did communication need to be frequent, and if so, how many interactions were required? Individuals travelling to training camps abroad were difficult to categorise because some accepted this as tacit evidence of connectivity, while others did not concede this was the sole measure to be considered (Crone & Harrow, 2011; Vidino, 2010; Zekulin, 2016).

Today, those who study this phenomenon continue to wrestle with these questions, although the terminology has slightly changed. Homegrown terrorism is now often discussed or categorised as either "directed," "assisted or facilitated," "enabled," or "inspired." Currently, these distinctions are considered ideal types, and many cases are difficult to categorise accurately. According to the National Counterterrorism Centre, an attack is inspired by a foreign terrorist organisation when an individual or cell carries out the operation on a group's behalf or name but without direct support from that group. At the other end, we have directed attacks. A directed attack occurs when a terrorist group provides support for all or nearly all facets of an attack. Enabled incidents represent a "messy middle," "with varying degrees of support" (Rasmussen, 2017, online; Floris, 2017, online). Nesser et al. (2016: 8–9) focus on the role that ISIS' section for international operations played in a plot or attack. Generally, it refers to how much support, instructions, or directions are given by an actual terrorist group or its affiliated members.

Over time, the definition and conceptualisation of this phenomenon have improved based on two clarifications. First, further observations showed these incidents shared an additional commonality: they were a broader manifestation of the general threat posed by Islamist-inspired terrorism, defined as terrorism perpetrated by individuals, groups, networks, or organisations that evoke a certain interpretation of Islam to justify their action (Europol, 2011: 9). This phenomenon was being driven by groups and individuals inspired by an interpretation of Islamism disseminated by groups, networks, and organisations located and primarily operating in the Middle East and/or Northern Africa (MENA), based on what some have termed the global jihadist narrative. The term global recognises that the underlying narrative and/or message are shared by multiple Islamist groups around the world. While there is no single definition for what constitutes this global jihadist narrative, it revolves around the following set of general premises: first, tension exists between the West and Islam; they are not compatible, and the West hates Islam. Second, the West is continuously at war with Islam; it has been intervening in the Muslim world for its own benefit over the past 1400 years. This explains the link we often see drawn between Western foreign policy and messaging from these groups. Third, it is the duty and divine obligation of every Muslim to fight (Dalgaard-Nielsen, 2010: 798; King & Taylor, 2011: 608; Wilner & Dubouloz, 2010: 42; Zekulin & Anderson, 2016: 184). This set of ideas is felt to be less of a motivating factor for violence towards the West but more succinctly serves as a justification for action. It is perhaps better understood as intertwining an individual's motivations with this rationale, thus providing "permission" to act. The threat Western states were facing was linked to this broader ideology and subsequently could be refined as Islamist-inspired homegrown terrorism (IIHGT).

This refinement helped overcome a second concern: the term homegrown terrorism was somewhat fuzzy; it did not fit easily within our understanding or categorisations of terrorism at the time. Some started to question whether it represented something new or different. Without clarification, homegrown terrorism was a vague term that overlapped with conceptualisations of domestic terrorism, and it needed to be refined further to overcome this ambiguity. In 2007, Sam Mullins (online) presciently predicted that this discussion was likely to occur. He recognised that "Islamist terrorism was a diverse and dynamic phenomenon" and that researchers needed to continue to "capture and understand the progression of its various manifestations." Viewed through this lens, homegrown terrorism arguably represented something different.

A closer examination of the underlying motivations, however, reveals an intriguing finding: the attacks were not motivated by domestic considerations but rather by an ideology, narrative, or agenda promoted by a foreign group. On the surface, it appeared to be nothing more than individuals attacking or plotting against their own states. Breaking down our conceptualisations of domestic terrorism and international terrorism, it is evident that homegrown terrorism contains elements of both and does not fit nicely within either one. Jerome Bjelopera (2013) defines domestic terrorists in the United States as "people who commit crimes within the homeland and draw inspiration from US-based extremist ideologies and movements," while the Federal Bureau of Investigation (FBI)'s definition of domestic terrorism is "Americans attacking Americans based on U.S.-based extremist ideologies" (2009, Online). Wilkinson's view of domestic – or what he termed "internal" – terrorism was that it was characterised as terrorist attacks occurring within one state or province, and that this description was used to specifically differentiate it from international terrorism because it had a domestic agenda, not an international one. It is important to note that until the mid-2000s, the term homegrown terrorism in the United States was reserved for domestic organisations including antigovernment militias, white supremacists, and eco-terrorists. This was done specifically to distinguish them from jihadist terrorist networks because the jihadist cause was always perceived as foreign (Vidino, 2009, online).

On the other hand, terrorism is considered international when more than one country is involved in the attack, including if the nationality of the perpetrator is different from the nationality of the victims; an attack is also considered international if the terrorists are outside their national boundaries or if terrorists of different nationalities act together (Zekulin, 2016: 51). Re-examining the IIHGT that was taking place in Western countries revealed that the plots and attacks were being carried out by citizens or long-term residents of those very same countries, meeting the domestic requirements, but that the motivation or justification for these attacks was an international one first articulated by al-Qaeda in the late 1990s and early 2000s and now by groups like al-Qaeda in the Arabian Peninsula (AQAP) and ISIS today (Zekulin, 2018: 17–37). To date, there are no clear examples where an Islamist-inspired homegrown terrorism plot or attack occurred where targeting the Western government was done to affect what would be considered domestic changes or concessions such as improving living conditions and opportunities or retaliation for negative treatment of Muslims in local communities (Zekulin, 2016: 51). Those perpetrating IIHGT convey their goals through foreign policy objectives such as a cessation of hostilities against Muslims abroad or specific Western interventions or incursions in Muslim countries.

The dichotomy between Islamist-inspired homegrown terrorism and domestic terrorism becomes clear when compared to plots and attacks inspired by right-wing ideology, which are currently on the rise in western states. Incidents inspired by right-wing ideology are also committed by individuals born, raised, and radicalised in the same state where an attack is plotted or conducted. The difference, however, lies in the observation that they are designed to affect domestic policies or goals and are not based on some larger global movement. The nationalist and xenophobic agenda is designed to privilege or protect a local identity or culture from outside incursion, and in each state, the incursion or threat is represented by different groups. In the US, the focus shifts from Muslims to immigrants from Central America or Mexico, while in Europe, it has focused on those arriving from Eastern European states and refugees fleeing the crisis in Syria. While it is possible that this might change in the future, current incidents inspired by right-wing ideology appear domestic or locally focused: they are acting for an ideology or group in their state and not as an arm or branch of a foreign group or for an outcome outside of their locality.

While this exercise may seem to be a case of semantics, it keeps the definitions of domestic terrorism and international terrorism narrow (as narrow as the field itself can succeed) and introduces a distinct conceptualisation of IIHGT, which allows us to account for the unique characteristics this terrorism demonstrates. This is important because the phenomenon continues to change and evolve.

THE EVOLUTION OF HOMEGROWN TERRORISM

Islamist-inspired homegrown terrorism continues to threaten Western democratic states in part because of how it has evolved from its earlier iteration. The first-generation IIHGT plots and attacks in Madrid, London, Toronto, Sydney, and Melbourne shared similar characteristics in that they had 9/11-esque aspirations. These attacks sought to mimic the mass casualties and mass destruction accomplished by al-Qaeda on September 11, 2001. Analysing these earlier efforts in greater detail shows that they were organised by larger groups and were much more sophisticated and ambitious than the IIHGT plots and attacks we started to experience moving into the 2010s. The Madrid attack involved approximately 18 central individuals; it had multiple targets; and the explosives were constructed using industrial-grade explosives (Zekulin, 2012: 100–121). The London attack involved four individuals detonating backpacks in separate locations that contained the highly volatile compound known as HMDT (hexamethylene triperoxide diamine), which they had made themselves. The Toronto 18 had plans to detonate multiple van bombs filled with ammonium nitrate fertiliser-based explosives. A test detonation conducted by experts using one tonne of ammonium nitrate and gasoline created a bomb with the equivalent of 768 kilogrammes of TNT and would have caused "catastrophic damage" to the targets and massive casualties (R. v. Amara, 2010). The Sydney plotters had acquired bomb-making materials and explosives, while the Melbourne group was in the early stages of acquiring their materials. It is unclear what the exact targets were, but floor plans for government buildings were recovered during the arresting raid (Schurmann et al., 2014).

An examination of IIHGT plots and attacks in Australia, Canada, and the US from 9/11 through 2013 revealed that there were a wide range of attacks during this time.

However, in general, the size, sophistication, and ambition of the attacks decreased over time (Zekulin, 2013). This trend has arguably continued, and currently, the most dangerous threat facing Western states is IIHGT conducted by lone actors using everyday objects such as vehicles, knives, and, in countries where they are readily accessible, guns.

Many of these terms, such as scale or sophistication, are arbitrary and subjective. Without agreement on what constitutes a small- or large-scale attack, we can characterise them based on an estimate of the potential size and ambitious nature of the plot as well as the number of individuals affected. An attack to topple a large building, target mass transit, or deploy larger or multiple explosive devices would fall higher on such a scale. The literature does posit a link between group size and the potential lethality of an attack, in part because a larger group is thought to have the ability to secure greater resources (Asal & Rethemeyer, 2008: 437, 439). Traditionally, sophistication has been linked to anything that increases the success or efficiency of the attack, such as knowledge, expertise, or training (Zekulin, 2012), and is based on Teun van Dongen's framework, the Terrorist Attack Complexity Index (van Dongen, 2013). Generally, sophistication makes distinctions between the form or mode an attack might take. For example, plots or attacks involving vehicles, knives, and firearms would be considered less sophisticated and more amateurish than explosives involving the combining of a variety of chemicals with timers or detonators, car bombs, and suicide vests, to name a few.

The questions that arise are as follows: "How do we account for this devolution?" "Was this a purposeful strategy or a matter of necessity?" Considering each possibility indicates that both may be true.

Throughout the 2000s, as the "war on terror" ramped up, it became increasingly difficult for terrorist groups to operate training camps and for individuals from Western states to locate, attend, and return home undetected (Stenersen, 2008: 215–233). Those running such camps acknowledged the "reduced opportunities" and the increased challenges and dangers as the War on Terror began and the United States and its allies actively began locating and destroying or disrupting these camps, which previously operated unabated (Lia, 2008: 520). Accepting the premise that there is a link between sophistication and an individual's knowledge acquisition and training, this might explain why plots and attacks have devolved: simply because the skill level is not there. It also goes to show that acquiring hands-on training makes a significant difference and that publications or online materials, even when they include detailed step-by-step instructions, diagrams, and pictures, are not adequate substitutes. Plotters and attackers may therefore be forced to default to simpler tactics.

It is also possible that there has been a more conscious effort by plotters and attackers to devolve their strategies. Perhaps individuals realised there would be greater psychological effects from a greater number of attacks, even if they were less spectacular. It might also reflect the success of law enforcement and intelligence agencies in disrupting attacks. Throughout the 2000s, these agencies developed significant techniques that allowed them to identify and disrupt plots. These were honed on the larger, more sophisticated efforts. It is logical to infer that as the number of individuals involved in a plot decreases and becomes less sophisticated and ambitious, the more difficult it is for law enforcement and intelligence agencies to be effective. Larger groups require more communication and coordination, which puts them on the radar of those monitoring for such behaviour. Many people having to physically congregate or increase electronic communication create opportunities to be discovered. A more ambitious or sophisticated task requires the acquisition and stockpiling of greater resources and/or quantities of chemicals or other materials, which might increasingly arouse suspicion. These types of devices often need to be developed using trial and error and might require testing to ensure they are operational. Multiple devices and/or multiple targets also require greater coordination, surveillance, and potential test runs to finalise complex plans. All of these increase the likelihood that one or more members of such a group will be detected, jeopardising a plot.

Conversely, less sophisticated plots, such as those using a vehicle or knives, among others, developed by a smaller group or lone actor will develop more covertly, and the opportunities for detection are less likely. Even if an individual plotter "leaks" their intentions online, it is virtually impossible to monitor the online activity of every individual, even if they are previously known to police or intelligence. There are no significant resources to be acquired, combined, or tested. Smaller groups or lone actors using crude or simple tools to conduct attacks are more likely to reach the execution phase of their plot than groups developing larger, more sophisticated attacks. One very concerning development involved the seeming overlap between what would be characterised as a simple, unsophisticated attack leading to mass casualties. On July 4, 2016, during Bastille Day celebrations in France, Mohamed Lahouaiej-Bouhlel drove a heavy cargo truck into the celebrating crowds, killing 87 and injuring over 450. The size and weight of the vehicle employed by the attacker were able to inflict mass casualties compared to the types of vehicle attacks previously witnessed. While there have been some examples of attackers using larger and heavier vehicles since this attack, such as Sayfullo Saipov's 2017 Halloween attack in New York City, this has not yet led to many copycat incidents.

Surveying the landscape of recent IIHGT attacks shows that the lethality of the attacks seems to be a strong indicator of a connection a group had with a terrorist group. The November 2015 terror attacks in Paris were very well organised and coordinated. It involved multiple targets, suicide vests, and automatic weapons, resulting in over 100 deaths and over 400 injuries. The attack was planned and directed by ISIS, and some of the perpetrators had fought with the group in Syria and Iraq before returning to Europe. The same type of connection and lethality were also on display in Brussels approximately four months later. In March 2016, three individuals detonated suicide belts, two at the Brussels airport and one in the metro system. An additional bomb was located at the airport but did not detonate. This attack was also directed by ISIS, and those involved had connections to the cell responsible for the Paris attacks.

There are still many questions about how these attacks will manifest in the future. Will unsophisticated lone-actor attacks remain the predominant *modus operandi*, or will we start seeing more sophisticated attacks once again? In August 2017, two vehicle attacks in Barcelona and Cambrils, Spain, were later tied to a house explosion in Alcanar the previous day. It was later discovered that all of the occurrences were connected to the same gang and that the explosives used in the house explosion were volatile explosives being created for a large-scale, highly complex attack. These individuals were inspired by ISIS but were not directed or assisted by the group, suggesting that some sympathetic to groups such as ISIS might be moving towards large, sophisticated, and more spectacular attacks once again. The reality is that IIHGT will continue to evolve and change. The chess game between individuals and groups seeking to conduct successful attacks and law enforcement and intelligence agencies' efforts to anticipate and prevent them will continue. This reflects some of the larger issues circulating beneath the surface that Western states must ponder moving forward.

FUTURE CHALLENGES OF HOMEGROWN TERRORISM

While IIHGT remains rare, we cannot overlook the fact that, to this point, it has proven to be quite persistent and shows no signs of abating. It is therefore incumbent on us to investigate some additional questions that might help us understand the threat moving forward. To clearly understand this phenomenon, we must determine what is leading some individuals in Western states to adopt these ideas and, in some cases, pursue violence against their own societies. To date, our efforts to explain this have focused on the concept of radicalisation. While there has been some general agreement on several aspects related to radicalisation, there remains much we do not know with a high degree of certainty. For example, there is consensus that radical ideas do not always lead to action and that there is a difference between what has been termed cognitive radicalisation (adopting the ideas) and behavioural radicalisation (acting violently upon them), and it is likely these are two separate processes (McCauley & Moskalenko, 2017: 205–216). It is also recognised to be the outcome of a complex set of factors that differ from individual to individual, at differing rates, and in different circumstances. Essentially, there is no standard process; it is unique to each individual. This helps explain why efforts to identify a profile or personality are unsuccessful.

There is, however, a robust literature (McCauley & Moskalenko, 2008: 415–433; Borum, 2011: 7–36; King & Taylor, 2011: 602–622; Byman & Shapiro, 2014; Weggemans et al., 2014: 100–110; Khosrokhavar, 2016; Coolsaet, 2016; Lindekilde et al., 2016: 858–877; Speckhard, 2016; Borum & Fein, 2016: 248–246; Dawson & Amarasingham, 2017: 191–210; Meleagrou-Hitchens et al., 2018). It emphasises some contributing factors that researchers feel are commonly observed among those who are radicalised. Briefly, it is hypothesised that some individuals are influenced by larger or systemic issues related to social justice or injustice. These might include a sense of anger or frustration at the Western government's intervention in Muslim states or general Western foreign policy towards the Middle East (Dodwell et al., 2016; Meleagrou-Hitchens et al., 2018). Others may be influenced by political events occurring in a specific Muslim state, such as a civil war or atrocities targeting a civilian population with which they can identify. The Syrian civil war provides a poignant example.

Investigating the political, economic, and social conditions within Western states themselves can also provide some explanation. There are indications that some individuals in Western states may be suffering from a lack of integration or a sense of alienation from greater society. This might lead some to feelings of "disconnectedness" from society (Perliger & Milton, 2016: 20) or, as Lindekilde et al. (2016) suggest, a lack of "life embeddedness." Individuals who feel they are not welcome or accepted in their own communities or society can, over time, become frustrated and develop a sense of anger and resentment.

Researchers have also spent considerable time analysing individuals themselves. Because human beings are inherently unique and complex actors, efforts to ascertain and explain individual motivations are very difficult. Nonetheless, the literature has identified several potential factors believed to play a role in radicalisation for some. These include the role that unmet expectations, a sense of disillusionment, or a lack of meaning and purpose in one's life might play in some seeking a new set of ideas that might help explain their predicament. Kruglanski et al. (2017: 69–93) have dubbed this a significance quest. Unable to find direction or meaning in their current lives, they look to find something that will substitute for this empty feeling. Others have suggested it is like "teen angst," a frustration at one's current situation (Coolsaet, 2016: 29). We also recognise the role that camaraderie can play in decision-making. The group dynamic and other socio-psychological processes can have a profound impact on individuals who are seeking belonging. Relationships that individuals establish with others who are like-minded can move a group towards more extreme interpretations of ideas or even violence. There is also a growing body of literature investigating the role that criminality or deviance might play and whether a predisposition to criminality or violence desensitises some individuals, making it easier for them to embrace other violent acts such as terrorism (Byman & Shapiro, 2014: 2). Found predominantly in literature related to Western European homegrown terrorists, ISIS is hypothesised to be substituting as a form of "super-gang," which attracts individuals with criminal backgrounds or tendencies (Coolsaet, 2016). Some also point to adventurism as a contributing factor, but why this influences some and not others remains a mystery. New research hypothesises that at the biochemical level, some individuals might be more inclined to pursue thrill-seeking behaviour, including pursuing a dangerous lifestyle (McGregor et al., 2015: 1–18).

There are several additional ideas that warrant inclusion in this discussion. There is an evolving debate about the role that religion or religious ideology plays in this process. There are those who argue that the "religious" component emphasised by groups such as ISIS is no longer the significant factor it once was (Coolsaet, 2016) and that we need to re-examine the role that religious ideology plays in this process. Others argue that it cannot be discounted as a motivating factor for some individuals (Dawson & Amarasingham, 2017: 191–210), and elements associated with the global jihadist narrative or a religious duty still shape the decisions of many of these individuals. The second relates to the role that mental health plays in this phenomenon. This is a very divisive topic for those engaged in research and analysis on IIHGT. Our efforts to account for the role that mental health plays are currently plagued by a lack of agreement on how mental health should be defined and how it might affect an individual's decision-making. When is the presence of mental health issues a contributing factor, and when is it simply present but a non-factor? There are no easy answers to these questions, and much more multidisciplinary work is needed. Finally, what role does technology play in driving IIHGT? It obviously allows foreign groups to disseminate their ideology to a greater number of people in real time and to reach audiences in Western states. It also allows like-minded people to find each other online, which amplifies closed argument pools or echo chambers, which may contribute to radicalisation. Technology and the forces of globalisation have made the world a much smaller place, and this is affecting identity in ways that we do not yet understand. Policymakers must also wrestle with questions about how technology might help mitigate this threat.

ADDITIONAL THOUGHTS

The challenges posed by IIHGT will unfortunately continue for the foreseeable future. While researchers and policymakers have made some significant progress in understanding this threat, we must remain vigilant and expand our efforts. We must take the lessons we have learned, anticipate how the threat may continue to change, and prepare for what may emerge.

One of the biggest unknowns is how the recent military defeat and subsequent loss of territory will affect ISIS. This is perhaps the first real test to determine the proclivity and popularity of the underlying jihadist narrative. According to analysis, IIHGT has drawn inspiration from AQAP and al-Qaeda, but most recent plots and attacks have been ISIS-inspired (Zekulin, 2018: 17–37). Will IIHGT continue, or will we enter a lull? Will other groups such as al-Qaeda or AQAP re-assert themselves and fill the void? Will we see the emergence of a new group, an ISIS splinter group, or multiple groups, and will any of these groups, existing or emerging, enjoy the same success that ISIS had in reaching individuals in the West? Islamism must be understood more as an ideology or social movement than the goals or agenda of any specific group. It is unknown whether this movement will lose or gain momentum and how it will intersect with larger social, economic, and political forces unfolding around the world today. Populism, emphasising tribalism, is a powerful force leading to increased polarisation and fragmentation within states, society, and communities. When fear and uncertainty increase, more extreme or radical ideologies can offer comfort and answers.

This also requires us to examine and determine what, if any, overlap or relationship exists between Islamist-inspired homegrown terrorism and right-wing-inspired extremism and domestic terrorism. There are clearly some parallels regarding how individuals might become susceptible to messaging or narratives. Are there any concrete lessons or best practises that can be applied from one to the other? With the increasing prevalence of right-wing-inspired extremism and domestic terrorism, will we see an escalation in confrontations between these two groups? Does an attack by an individual or group linked to one ideology increase the likelihood of a retaliation attack and the potential for a tit-for-tat scenario?

By far the most important question we face regarding this phenomenon is how Western states should approach counterterrorism in response to IIHGT. It is a multi-faceted, complex issue, and there are at least three separate yet interrelated parts to this problem that policymakers must consider. The first and most pressing question is how to protect their populations from attacks. Considering how IIHGT has devolved and the real challenges facing law enforcement and intelligence agencies to maintain an upper hand, this involves legislative solutions. There are, however, very real concerns and debates about the best way forward, and they often involve discussions about empowering government agencies and expanding surveillance and detention powers. How these impact or infringe upon individual rights and freedoms, which are a fundamental bedrock of Western democratic states, has become a point of contention. Governments must work openly and transparently to find an appropriate balance between these two positions. The second part of the equation is prevention: how can we address underlying factors that might contribute to some individuals adopting the messaging or narratives espoused by Islamist groups? We must recognise that trying to arrest our way out of this threat is a losing strategy. In the long term, we must work to prevent further generations or cohorts from emerging. It is naive to suggest that we can prevent the emergence of all new potential threats, but the key is to minimise the numbers and keep them manageable so we can deploy existing resources effectively.

When the number of individuals considered to be a potential threat increases, our limited economic and human resources are stretched too thin. One estimate suggests that the cost of monitoring one suspect for an entire year is approximately $8 million. Prevention requires engagement, discussions, and debates on alternative narratives, as well as working with local community actors and individuals who might be vulnerable to these ideas. This must be done collaboratively to avoid demonising or creating the impression of a suspect community. The final part involves discussions about what we do with radicalised individuals once they have been identified, detained, or returned from fighting with an extremist group overseas. There is tremendous debate and disagreement about the effectiveness of deradicalisation programmes and disengagement efforts. Further, there are competing views about the best way to deal with radicalised individuals, often pitting a law enforcement approach against a social justice approach. Law enforcement approaches emphasise arrest and potential incarceration, while a social justice approach offers individuals support, counselling, and incentives to reintegrate within society. The trade-off is that both have obvious drawbacks. Imprisoning radicalised individuals carries the risk that you are providing them access to highly vulnerable individuals who themselves might be susceptible to radicalisation, a point we know all too well as the terrorism literature in the late 2000s identified prisons as potential incubators for radicalisation. Conversely, a social justice approach creates the impression that individuals once deemed a potential threat are being granted a free pass. To date, we have also had limited success measuring whether this approach has been successful or not.

Finally, while coordination and cooperation, especially sharing information, are key to mitigating the threat, there are two problems. Each state must navigate these issues on their own terms because the underlying challenges driving this phenomenon are different from state to state, a reflection of specific domestic factors. Solutions must reflect this reality. This also limits the transfer of successful policies or best practises when they do emerge. Each state must therefore determine its own unique approach to the challenge and threat posed by IIHGT.

References

Asal, V., & Rethemeyer, K. (2008). The nature of the beast: Organizational structures and the lethality of terrorist attacks. *Journal of Politics, 70*(2), 437–449.

Bjelopera, J. (2013). *American Jihadist Terrorism: Combating a complex threat*. Congressional Research Service. 7-5700. www.crs.gov

Borum, R. (2011). Radicalization into violent extremism I: A review of social sciences theories. *Journal of Strategic Security, 4*(4), 7–36.

Borum, R., & Fein, R. (2016). The psychology of foreign fighters. *Studies in Conflict & Terrorism, 40*(3), 248–266.

Brubaker, R. (2010). Migration, membership, and the modern nation-state: Internal and external dimensions of the politics of belonging. *Journal of Interdisciplinary History, XLI*(I), 61–78.

Byman, D., & Shapiro, J. (2014, November). *Be afraid. Be a little afraid: The threat of terrorism from Western foreign fighters in Syria and Iraq*. Brookings Institute, Policy Paper 34.

Coolsaet, R. (2016, March). *Facing the fourth foreign fighter wave: What drives Europeans to Syria and the Islamic State? Insights from the Belgian Case*. The Royal Institute for International Relations-The Egmont Papers.

Crone, M., & Harrow, M. (2011). Homegrown terrorism in the West. *Terrorism and Political Violence, 23*(4), 521–536.

Dalgaard-Nielsen, A. (2010). Violent radicalization in Europe: What we know and what we don't know. *Studies in Conflict and Terrorism, 33*(9), 797–814.

Dawson, L., & Amarasingham, A. (2017). Talking to foreign fighters: Insights into the motivations for Hijrah to Syria and Iraq. *Studies in Conflict & Terrorism, 40*(3), 191–210.

Europol. (2011). *TE-SAT 2010: EU terrorism situation and trend report*. European Police Office.

Federal Bureau of Investigation. (2009). *Domestic terrorism in the post-9/11 Era*. [Online]. Available at http://www.fbi.gov/news/stories/2009/september/domterror_09070

Floris, N. (2017, December 6). Adapting to defend the homeland against the evolving international terrorist threat. Statement before the senate homeland security and government affairs committee, Washington DC. [Online]. Available at www.fbi.gov/news/testimony/adapting-to-defend-the-homeland-against-the-evolving-terrorist-threat

Gartenstein-Ross, D., & Grossman, L. (2009). *Homegrown terrorists in the US and UK: An empirical examination of the radicalization process*. FDD Center for Terrorism Research.

Jenkins, B. (2010). *Would-be warriors: Incidents of jihadist terrorist radicalization in the United States since September 11, 2001*. RAND Corporation.

Khosrokhavar, F. (2016). *Inside jihadism: Understanding jihadi movements worldwide* (2nd Ed.). Routledge.

King, M., & Taylor, D. (2011). The radicalization of homegrown jihadists: A review of theoretical models and social psychological evidence. *Terrorism and Political Violence, 23*(4), 602–622.

Kruglanski, A., Gelfand, M., Bélanger, M., Sheveland, A., Hetiarachchi, M., & Gunaratna, R. (2017). The psychology of radicalization and deradicalization: How significance quest impacts violent extremism. *Political Psychology, 35*, 69–93.

Lia, B. (2008). Doctrines for jihadi terrorist training. *Terrorism and Political Violence, 20*(4), 518–542.

Lindekilde, L., Bertelsen, P., & Stohl, M. (2016). Who goes, why and with what effects: The problem of foreign fighters from Europe. *Small Wars & Insurgencies, 27*(5), 858–877.

McCauley, C., & Moskalenko, S. (2008). Mechanisms of political radicalization: Pathways towards terrorism. *Terrorism and Political Violence*, *20*(3), 415–433.

McCauley, C., & Moskalenko, S. (2017). Understanding political radicalization: The two-pyramids models. *American Psychological Association*, *72*(3), 205–216.

McGregor, I., Hayes, J., & Prentice, M. (2015). Motivation for aggressive religious radicalization: Goal regulation theory and a personality × threat × affordance hypothesis. *Frontiers in Psychology*, *6*, 1–18.

Meleagrou-Hitchens, A., Hughes, S., & Clifford, B. (2018). *The travellers: American jihadists in Syria and Iraq*, Program on Extremism. The George Washington University.

Mullins, S. (2007). Homegrown terrorism: Issues and implications. *Perspectives on Terrorism*, *1*(3). [Online]. Available at http://www.terrorismanalysts.com/pt/index.php/pot/article/view/12/html

Nesser, P., Stenersen, A., & Oftedal, E. (2016). Jihadi terrorism in Europe: The IS effect. *Perspectives on Terrorism*, *10*(6), 3–24.

Perliger, A., & Milton, D. (2016, November). *From cradle to grave: The lifecycle of foreign fighters in Iraq and Syria*. Combating Terrorism Center at West Point.

Precht, T. (2007). Home grown terrorism and Islamist radicalisation in Europe. Denmark: Danish Ministry of Justice.

R. v. Amara. (2010). Ontario Superior Court of Justice. O.J. No. 181 Court File No. 2025/07.

Rasmussen, N. (2017, May 3). Opening remarks at CNAS. [Online]. Available at www.dni.gov/files/NCTC/documetns/news_documents/CNASopeningremarks.pdf

Schurmann, B., Harris-Hogan, S., Zammit, A., & Lentini, P. (2014). Operation Pendennis: A case study of an Australian terrorist plot. *Perspectives in Terrorism*, *8*(4), 91–96.

Silber, M., & Bhatt, A. (2007). *Radicalization in the West: The homegrown threat*. NYPD Intelligence Division. [Online]. Available at https://sethgodin.typepad.com/seths_blog/files/NYPD_Report-Radicalization_in_the_West.pdf

Speckhard, A. (2016). *The lethal cocktail of terrorism: The four necessary ingredients that go into making a terrorist & fifty individual vulnerabilities/motivations that may also play a role*. International Center for the Study of Violent Extremism. [Online]. Available at https://academia.edu.documents/43076517/Speckhard_2016_The_Lethal_Cocktail_of_Terrorism.pdf

Stenersen, A. (2008). The internet: A virtual training camp? *Terrorism and Political Violence*, *20*(2), 215–233.

Van Dongen, T. (2013). The lengths terrorists go to: Perpetrator characteristics and the complexity of jihadist terror attacks in Europe, 2004–2010. *Behavioral Sciences of Terrorism and Political Aggression*, 2, 1–22.

Vidino, L. (2009). *The homegrown terrorist threat to the US homeland*. Real Instituto Elcano. [Online]. Available at http://www.realinstitutoelcano.org/wps/portal/rielcano_eng

Vidino, L. (2010). *Radicalization, linkage and diversity: Current trends in terrorism Europe*. RAND Corporation.

Weggemans, D., Bakker, E., & Grol, P. (2014). Who are they and why do they go? The radicalization and preparatory processes of Dutch jihadist foreign fighters. *Perspectives on Terrorism*, *8*(4), 100–110.

Wilner, A., & Dubouloz, C. (2010). Homegrown terrorism and transformative learning: An interdisciplinary approach to understanding radicalization. *Global Change Peace and Security*, *22*(1), 33–51.

Yuval-Davis, N. (2006). Belonging and the politics of belonging. *Patterns of Prejudice*, *40*(3), 197–214.

Zekulin, M. (2012). *A growing disconnect: Can the contemporary terrorism literature explain domestic homegrown terrorism?* PhD Dissertation. University of Calgary, Calgary, Alberta, Canada.

Zekulin, M. (2013). *Islamic-inspired homegrown terrorism: What we know and what it means moving forward*. Occasional Research Paper #8. Calgary, Calgary Center for Military and Strategic Studies.

Zekulin, M. (2016). Endgames: Improving our understanding of homegrown terrorism. *Studies in Conflict & Terrorism*, *39*(1), 46–66

Zekulin, M., & Anderson, T. (2016). Contemporary terrorism and the true believer. *Behavioral Sciences of Terrorism and Political Aggression*, *8*(3), 177–196.

Zekulin, M. (2018). More than the medium: How the communication literature helps explain ISIS's success in recruiting Westerners. *Journal of Policing, Intelligence and Counter Terrorism*, *13*(1), 17–37.

17

THE RISE IN LONE WOLF ATTACKS

Myth or Reality?

tavis d. jules, Max Crumley-Effinger, and Scott McGallagher

INTRODUCTION

The post-9/11 period brought with it several deeper forms of securitisation (ranging from financialisation to media) as governments sought to reframe the war on terror, combat increases in state-sponsored terrorism, and defeat the rise of global Islamic fundamentalism. While al-Qaeda has been a thorn in the side of Western governments as its affiliates and offshoots seek to carry out global jihadism, with the demise and subsequent banishment of Daesh (Islamic State) in Iraq and Syria under the international coalition and the declaration in March 2019 by the Trump administration that the Caliphate is dead, a void has been created that other extremist groups are seeking to capitalise upon. In today's over-hyped social media culture driven by online platforms and new "disruptive innovations" (Christensen et al., 2011) ranging from end-to-end encryptions, such as Cryptocat, Telegram, Signal, Sicher, WhatsApp, and Wickr; email clients, such as Hushmail, ProtonMail, CounterMail, Mailfence, and Tutanota; encrypted phones, such as BlackPhone, Kitim Phone, and Tor browser, to the Tails operating system (Jules & Barton, 2018), terrorism as we know it is metamorphosing as it no longer relies on outdated *modus operandi*, such as training camps, madrassas, and state sponsorship.

The onset of technological innovation and market fundamentalism in the so-called fourth industrial revolution, or digital age (Schwab, 2016), or "Industry 4.0,"[1] which horizontally integrates the vertical physical, digital, and biological worlds, is changing the nature of terrorism. What was once viewed as the historical orthodoxy of what constitutes violent extremism (encompassing state sponsorship, religious, criminal, ideological, and dissenting forms of terrorism) has become more sophisticated since we no longer make a distinction between homegrown radicalisation and violent international extremists. Thus, we have colloquially come to accept that "one man's terrorist is another man's freedom fighter." However, it is the fear of the "enemies from within," or the so-called "lone wolf attacker," "solo actor," and "leaderless resistance" (Burton, 2007); "freelance terrorism" (Hewitt, 2003); 'individual terrorism" (Robb, 2007; Sageman, 2008); "the super-empowered individual" (Friedman, 1998); "terrorists acting alone" (UNCTED, 2014); and "lone avengers" (Stern, 2004), and their movement beyond battlegrounds of afar to bringing terror home, that is now seen as the greatest threat to state sovereignty, national building, and democratic governance since these individuals are not directly tied to any traditional terrorist group.

While the literature on lone wolves lacks a clear definition (Becker, 2014) and the term itself is contested (Spaaij & Hamm, 2015), in this chapter we define a lone wolf terrorist as one whose "ideologically driven violence, or attempted violence, perpetrated by an individual who plans and executes an attack in the absence of collaboration with other individuals or groups" (Becker, 2014, p. 960) and includes both political and/or financial motivations (Simon, 2016). Leenaars and Reed (2016) have categorised lone wolf offenders as assassins and school shooters, suicide terrorists or "death by cop," copycats (a derivative crime influenced by media), and conventional homicide and murder. In order to include additional cases that ostensibly fall within the bounds of lone wolf terrorism, we expand upon Becker's definition to account for several exceptional cases whose actions drew directly upon some method of organisational support (e.g., Timothy Mcveigh [the 1995 Oklahoma City bombing], Nidal Hasan [the 2009 Fort Hood mass shooting], and the Tsarnaev brothers [the 2013 Boston Marathon bombings]) and who liaise (directly or indirectly) with others to develop strategies and execute an attack. Table 17.1 provides an overview of a selection of attacks used in this chapter.

Perhaps the most troubling contradiction of calling a terrorist attack undertaken by a singular individual a "lone wolf attack" is that once an act has been perpetrated, terrorist organisations and other actors may claim responsibility for this action when they may not have influenced its planning and execution. While the perpetrators of lone wolf

DOI: 10.4324/9780429426063-19

Table 17.1 Selected Lone Wolf and Wolf Pack Attacks in the 20th and 21st Century

Date of Attack (Chronologically)	Place	Perpetrator	Ideological Stance(s)	Brief Synopsis(Collateral and infrastructure damage)
1978–1995	United States (Various locations)	Ted Kaczynski	Anti-government, anarchism; environmental extremism	Between 1978 and 1995, he killed three people and injured 23 others in an attempt to start a revolution by conducting a nationwide bombing campaign targeting people involved with modern technology. Also, he issued a social critique opposing industrialisation and advancing a nature-centred form of anarchism.
August 21–31, 1992	Ruby Ridge, Idaho, United States	Randy Weaver, members of his immediate family, and family friend Kevin Harris	White Nationalism/ Supremacy; Anti-Government	Deaths of Deputy US Marshal W.F. Degan and civilians Samuel Weaver (juvenile) and Vicki Weaver; arrest of participants Randy Weaver and Kevin Harris.
April 19, 1995	Oklahoma City, Oklahoma, United States	Timothy McVeigh	Anti-government, retaliation for Ruby Ridge and Waco Siege	McVeigh and co-conspirators executed a bombing campaign on the Alfred P. Murrah Federal Building in Oklahoma City, killing 168, injuring over 680, and ultimately destroying the building.
November 5, 2009	Fort Hood near Killeen, Texas, United States	Nidal Malik Hasan	Radical Islam	Influenced by the radical Mullah Anwar al-Awaki, Nidal Malik Hasan killed 13 people and wounded thirty when he used a gun in the Soldier Readiness Processing Center at Fort Hood, Texas.
July 22, 2011	Oslo and Utoya, Norway	Anders Behring Breivik	White nationalism/ supremacy, anti-Islam	Breivik's first attack was a car bomb explosion in Oslo, within Regjeringskvartalet, the executive government quarter of Norway. The bomb was placed inside a van next to the tower block housing the office of Prime Minister Jens Stoltenberg. The explosion killed eight people and injured at least 209 others. The second attack occurred at a summer camp on the island of Utøya. The camp was organised by the AUF, the youth division of the ruling Norwegian Labour Party (AP). Breivik opened fire at the participants, killing 69 and injuring at least 110.
December 11, 2010	Stockholm, Sweden	Taimour Abdulwahab al-Abdaly	Islamic extremism, jihad	The first explosion occurred when an Audi 80 Avant automobile exploded. Two people at the site of the explosion were hospitalised with minor injuries. The second explosion occurred, and a man's body, with blast wounds on his abdomen, was discovered nearby. According to a police spokesman, the man blew himself up. According to Aftonbladet, he carried six pipe bombs; only one exploded, killing him.
April 15, 2013	Boston, Massachusetts, United States	Dzhokhar Tsarnaev Tamerlan Tsarnaev	Islamic extremism; retaliation for US wars in Afghanistan and Iraq	With the use of two pressure cooker bombs, the Tsarnaev brothers killed three people and injured roughly 270 others during the 2013 Boston Marathon. Tamerlan died several days later. Due to complications from the incident, Dzhokhar was sentenced to death.

October 2014	Mumbai, India	Anees Ansari	Islamic extremism; ISIS propaganda	Foiled attack: the anti-terror squad uncovered a bombing plot that was targeting American establishments in Mumbai, including a school.
December 1516, 2014	Sydney, Australia	Man Haron Monis	A mix of motivations, eventually seen as motivated by Islamic extremism (treatment of Muslims in Australia)	The Sydney siege led to a 16-hour standoff, after which a gunshot was heard from inside, and police officers from the Tactical Operations Unit stormed the café. Hostage Tori Johnson was killed by Monis, and hostage Katrina Dawson was killed by a police bullet that ricocheted in the subsequent raid. Monis was also killed. Three other hostages and a police officer were injured by police gunfire during the raid.
June 17, 2015	Charleston, South Carolina, United States	Dylann Roof	White supremacy, anti-Black sentiments	Roof murdered nine members of an African Methodist Episcopal Church. He was sentenced to death for all nine counts of murder and terrorism charges.
October 1, 2017	Las Vegas, Nevada, United States	Stephen Paddock	Unknown	Paddock fired upon concertgoers at the Route 91 Harvest Music Festival with assault rifles. Paddock killed 58 and injured 851.
February 2019	Maryland, United States	Christopher Paul Haason	White nationalism/ supremacy	A foiled terror plot was discovered in which Haason targeted US politicians and journalists (especially those who he deemed critical of President Trump). Haason was found with copies of Anders Breivik's manifesto.
February 14, 2019	Pulwama, Kashmir, India	Adil Dar	Anti-India political resentment; affiliations to Jaish-e-Mohammad	Dar carried out a suicide bombing attack on Indian security forces in India-controlled Kashmir. Dar is a Pakistani citizen believed to be a member of Jaish-e-Mohammad, a Pakistani insurgency group.
February 15, 2019	Phoenix, Arizona, United States	Ismail Hamed	Islamic extremism; Pledged allegiance to ISIS, says their propaganda radicalised him	Hamed wanted to speak with a police officer to "deal with them" and to voice his distress over the treatment of Palestinians and Muslims in Arab countries. A Maricopa County Sheriff's deputy arrived on scene, and Hamed began to throw rocks at the officer and brandish a knife. Hamed charged and was shot with non-life-threatening injuries.

Source: Authors' own table.

attacks may have accessed operational (moral or tactical) support and/or read and studied extremist online content, the attack is not always made on behalf of any organisation but may be steeped in the lone wolf's ideological beliefs that are derived from the foundational tenets of the terrorist organisation's message. Therefore, it is often the combination of singular responsibility and the carrying out of an attack, be it by a self-radicalised suicide bomber or former trained fighter, that differentiates lone wolf terrorism from other forms and types of terrorism.

Lone wolf terrorism, in which an individual or small cell not connected to the leadership or hierarchical organisational structure of a terrorist group acts independently to organise and indiscriminately kill individuals deliberately, is not a new phenomenon. We argue that we are witnessing a watershed moment with this form of terrorism given the twin events: (i) the rise and ubiquitous use of the internet to radicalise youth and consolidate the operations of sleeper cells; and (ii) the growth of the so-called "Islamic terrorism" or Islamic extremism defined by the prompting of terrorist sympathisers, or "fanboys" (Ade, 2015). To combat these twin forces, governments are spending billions on domestic counterterrorism measures. Given the ready availability of cheap-to-purchase materials, such as nails and pressure cookers, to build suicide bombs, governments have not been able to plan and monitor individuals effectively. As Alakoc (2017) poignantly asserts, "terrorism is no longer a weapon of the weak but rather a weapon of the determined" (p. 510). Therefore, it is within this vein that lone wolf attacks may be the new frontier in the battle for global terror supremacy as terrorist organisations no longer need to recruit people and individuals with aspirational desires to become suicide bombers have access to numerous platforms, manuals, and materials all with the click of a mouse.

An enduring fundamental component inherent in the idea of "lone wolf terrorism" is the lack of consensus as to what it is. While the literature on lone wolf terrorism (which may go by any number of similar or related monikers) is still growing as perceptions of the threat it constitutes continue to increase, it is still a relatively understudied concept within the broader field of the study of terrorism. Moreover, because several scholarly articles on lone wolf will likely yield as many varied and sometimes competing definitions of the term, it is an ongoing challenge to identify terrorist violence that can be uniformly agreed upon as characteristic of a lone wolf attack. For example, Becker (2014) describes a complete lack of connection between lone wolves and other terrorists or terrorist organisations, while Schurmann et al. (2017) contend that the "loneness" of these actors may be evident only in the execution of the terrorist attack and may entail prior connections with other terrorist actors or groups. This discrepancy, then, highlights the most significant similarity found in the literature on lone wolves: different definitions that lead to an incomparable collection of scholarship on lone wolf actors and events that transpire. Today, the lone wolf perpetrator is not always the radical Islamic jihadist; they may instead hail from a variety of religious or secular backgrounds and financial means. This variance is troubling because it forces scholars and law enforcement officials to exercise a more broad-ranging vigilance that often entails more of a reactive than proactive stance concerning deterring terror. In short, there is no single type of lone wolf perpetrator, no primary ideological predilection, and no precise personal, political, or social drivers. In essence, it can be a combination of several intricate and complex factors that can lead an individual down the path of violent extremism. While the terrorism literature is expansive and has sought to address the distinction between suicide attacks claimed by an organisation and those undertaken by radicalised individuals (Alakoc, 2017) and the socio-demographic profiles and behavioural characteristics of the lone wolf (Gill et al., 2014), these discrepancies and varied perspectives on the features of lone wolf terrorists are explored in detail in the following sections.

In the next section, we outline the historical trajectories that have come to define lone wolf terrorist actions. In doing this, we draw attention to the evolution of lone wolf terrorism, its ideology, and its structures. Next, we discuss the ideological foundations that have driven several lone wolf actions. In the third section, we map the temporal and geographical spaces of lone wolf terrorism by paying attention to the actors, agents, strategies, and tactical manoeuvres. We conclude the chapter by discussing the impact of solo actors and their implications for securitisation in the era of the so-called fourth industrial revolution.

HISTORICAL TRAJECTORIES

In accordance with the working definition above, it should be borne in mind that, while media outlets and national security experts may portray them as a recent phenomenon, lone wolf acts of violence have a strong historical foundation that can be categorised as encompassing four distinct "phases" of terrorism that have arisen since the late 19th century (Post et al., 2014; Rapoport, 2004). The first identifiable phase often cited is that of the anarchist period that arose in Russia in the 1880s during a time of anti-czarist sentiment (Post et al., 2014; Spaaij, 2010). The anti-colonial phase emerged in the 1940s as many former colonies in Africa, the Arab world, and elsewhere engaged in violent tactics to drive out former colonial powers and claim self-dependence (Post et al., 2014). Progressive political movements, such as the "New Left" in the 1950s–1970s, gave way to the third wave of revolutionary ideological violence, which was a generational wave defined, steeped in, and heavily influenced by guerrilla tactics from communist parties in Latin America (Post et al., 2014; Smith et al., 2015). Lastly, the religious wave emerged in the 1980s and 1990s with the strengthening of Christian, Islamic, and Jewish extremist organisations and individuals (Post et al., 2014). These different waves, located as they are with relatively distinct chronological linearity, may perhaps be better understood as "strains" that may be evident simultaneously across the breadth of terrorist activity around the globe (Parker & Sitter, 2016). Although much of the violence that has been analysed is attributed to group plots and cell networks, there are also single-acting radicals who carry out their actions for a different reason. Thus, terrorism scholars have engaged with and critically examined the value of such concise typologies of terrorist activity.

Given the history of individuals fighting against both foreign and domestic states, lone actors have often been viewed as committing what can be argued as ideologically driven acts of violence that were explained as a different form of mental illness. In the aftermath of some attacks (i.e., Michael Zehaf-Bibea's shooting of a Canadian Military Reservist and Martin Couture-Rouleau's hit-and-run of Canadian soldiers), the perpetrator's family has claimed that the offender has had an undiagnosed mental illness. Such defence of lone wolf actions is often contentious, as in several cases these individuals had begun to radicalise, so it is often unclear if their actions were personally or politically motivated. Iviansky (1977, as cited in Pitcavage, 2015) first spoke of "lone wolves" as a protest using a deed carried out through an individual initiative. Outspoken white supremacist Louis Beam, in his essay, *Leaderless Resistance*, was the first American to introduce the future of ideological violence and was a catalyst for the 1992 Ruby Ridge Siege in Ruby Ridge, Idaho, in the United States (Byman, 2017; Spaaij, 2010). Today, we can speak of a new emerging wave of lone wolves fuelled by the globalisation of social media platforms. Lone wolves and extremists can now radicalise and mobilise themselves from anywhere and at any time across the globe, meaning that the "where" of lone wolf terrorism can be anywhere.

There are many types, stripes, and double standards that exist in the framing of lone wolf terrorism (Beydoun, 2018). Of the many kinds of lone wolf terrorists, there is an increasing prevalence of "sleeper cells," especially in Western countries, which utilise advances in communication technology to coordinate attacks. Although these "cells" are defined as groups of two or more members, some cells operate through solo attacks, thus sending counterterrorism experts and law enforcement officials scrambling with the knowledge that even if a cell has been identified, it is even more challenging to track a lone actor. As will be discussed in further detail in the sections to come, some organisations, such as Daesh and al-Qaeda, have taken advantage of the social media revolution of the 21st century and utilised these platforms for their tactics. Organisations such as these realise that radicalised and mobilised jihadists around the globe carrying out homegrown attacks pose a much more malign threat than foot soldiers in their specific localities. This strategy has also puzzled counterterror experts and law enforcement officials, as these organisations will claim responsibility for attacks that were not in any way coordinated by them (e.g., Stephen Paddock [Beydoun, 2018]). Through mapping the historical trajectories and tactics of lone wolf actors throughout the past two centuries, we came across many examples that are highlighted throughout our chapter that conform to our working definition of lone wolf terrorism and add to it. Granted, this is not a comprehensive and exhaustive list of lone wolf attacks within the past two centuries; Table 17.1 presents a baseline approach to the many types and stripes of lone wolf terrorists. Concise summaries of the attacks and backgrounds of the attackers give way to the ideological tenets that motivate lone wolves to attack whom they attack and why.

IDEOLOGICAL TENETS

The ideological impetus for executing a lone wolf terrorist attack can take many forms, but these motivations for proceeding with an assault are seldom straightforward. There is no one-size-fits-all ideological camp for lone actors, and they can fall along a continuum ranging from ardent jihadists subscribing to religious fundamentalism to white supremacists using race as their call to action. Becker (2014) contends that ideologies play a dual role in driving terrorists' actions. Ideology may convince the individual to engage in the act of terror in the first place while simultaneously allowing the terrorist to focus their violence on a target that is representative of what they deem to be the "enemy" (Becker, 2014). The ideology, however, not only drives the attack but also dictates the type of offence and violence in which a terrorist will engage. Capellan (2015), in researching how far-right extremists perpetrate homicides, attests that these terrorists will target multiple victims who are unfamiliar to them, male, and of minority status. Also, ideological as opposed to non-ideological active shooter terrorists differ in that the former will engage unknown targets while the latter may operate from a more revenge-driven fixation (Capellan, 2015).

Thus, a complex matrix of reasons and publicised rationales for attacks are often simplified in the media or official reports, which may obscure the motivations behind these individualised attacks. The conflation of ideological bases for strikes, as well as attempts to create overly simplified typologies of terrorist activities, can obfuscate the complexity inherent in lone wolf attacks. What is most surprising in the literature to date is that the ideological bent of any given lone actor is determined through scholarly and other processes that are only as good as the information available, and acts may be influenced by both endogenous and exogenous factors that are never brought to light (Beydoun, 2018). In other words, while there are clear-cut cases that show a direct relationship between ideology and the actions of an individual perpetrator, in other instances, the evidence may not be as explicit to allow such inferences. Thus, identifying ideological patterns is essential for the scholarly understanding of this contested phenomenon, though, of course, the accuracy and therefore relevance of these findings may be called into question. However, as Becker (2014) argues, this polarisation, as well as unanswered questions, is what makes the threat of lone wolf terrorism so keenly felt.

Terrorism, primarily as it is studied in the United States, is often intricately tied to ideas of the terrorist threat of extremist or fundamentalist Islam. This narrowly defined Western perspective took on new significance with the rise of Daesh and its affiliates in the Middle East and their calls for lone wolves to rise, go out to the streets, and kill men, women, and children in European and American cities (Ade, 2015). One of the earliest propaganda magazines that encouraged lone wolf attacks aimed at British and American youth readers was the online *Inspire* magazine. Al-Qaeda in the Arabian Peninsula (AQAP), which has its headquarters in Yemen, runs *Inspire* magazine, which is a creation of American Samir Khan. In fact, *Inspire*'s first issue, titled *Make a Bomb in the Kitchen of Your Mom*, serves as a blueprint for the actions of would-be loan wolves (e.g., the Tsarnaev brothers). The second edition of *Inspire*, entitled *The Ultimate Mowing Machine*, which appeared on the tenth anniversary of the *USS Cole* attack, aimed to amplify al-Qaeda's message by detailing how the lone *mujahid* (fighter) can use pickup trucks to "mow down the enemies of Allah." In Daesh's first publication of the *Dabiq* magazine (Issues 1–15), which judiciously recounts the ideological tenets of Daesh, it argues that its state-building project has commenced because "the spark has been lit here in Iraq, and its heat will continue to intensify – by Allah's permission – until it burns the crusader armies in Dabiq" (Islamic State, 2014, p. 1). It then calls on youths to

> Therefore, rush O Muslims to your state. Yes, it is your state. Rush, because Syria is not for the Syrians, and Iraq is not for the Iraqis … The State is a state for all Muslims. The land is for the Muslims, all the Muslims. O Muslims everywhere, whoever is capable of performing Hijrah to the Islamic State, then let him do so, because hijrah to the land of Islam is obligatory. (Islamic State, 2014, p. 14)

Inspire, Daesh's *Rumiyah* magazine [Issues 1–13] (*Dabiq*'s replacement), al-Haqiqah,[2] and other glossy, snarky, and slick self-help jihadi magazines act as frontline recruitment tools by delivering a clear and concise message where potential lone wolf terrorists can *read* pearls of wisdom from famous jihadi voices, *learn* how to build bombs and stage attacks, and *view* powerful images and data visualisation. Moreover, such publications may be doubly attractive in that lone wolves know that their actions, if successful, will get a glossy spread in these magazines.

According to Beydoun (2018), the lone wolf culprit's race and religion frequently influence how the media and law enforcement interpret domestic lone wolf incident details. In this vein, Beydoun (2018) further argues that "the recent list of shootings and mass killings [in the United States] involving white non-Muslim and Muslim culprits has revealed a pattern in which the former is generally designated lone wolf killers, and the latter are presumptive lone wolf terrorists" (p. 1217). This illustrates the intricacy and sociopolitical interventions that may occur in the identification of the ideological motivations behind attacks by lone wolf culprits. Furthermore, these concerns again highlight the dissonance and lack of agreement among scholars and law enforcement as to the true definition of lone wolf terrorism.

As has been noted, the stated objectives or impulsions to affect a lone wolf attack may be anything but straightforward. In studying the 2011 attack in Norway by attacker Anders Behring Breivik that killed 77 people, Berntzen and Sandberg (2014) propose that Breivik utilises Christianity as a call to action, but that this is done to "construct a positive common identity," which "primarily serves as a cultural and historical underpinning" (p. 767) for his actions. That is, while seemingly religious, Breivik's lone wolf attack sought to both highlight and prevent perceived threats to Western social values (Berntzen & Sandberg, 2014). Man Haron Monis' (2014) 17-hour siege of a cafe in Sydney, Australia, that killed two and the attacker, is another pertinent example of the challenge of determining actors' ideological underpinnings. Monis claimed during the café siege that he was acting on behalf of Daesh, but significant evidence points to a complete lack of connection between the attacker and the ideological foundations of Daesh. Scott and Shanahan (2018) argue that his supposedly religious lone wolf attack was nothing more than "grievance-fueled violence" (p. 1) because of his multiple run-ins with the law, including a murder charge and sexual assault violations.

Despite the challenges of understanding the ideological propensity of lone wolf terrorists, there are still no clear markers as to what inspires or triggers the solo actor to action. While people, such as Tom Metzger, call on white supremacists to utilise lone wolf methods or a leaderless resistance strategy, in a study with impressive scope, Gill et al. (2014) highlight that a large number (approximately 43%) of terrorist attacks by lone actors in their sample were connected to religious ideologies, something that the authors connect to al-Qaeda's wide-ranging global networks. Furthermore, 34% of the attacks were related to individuals with right-wing ideologies, 18% with single-issue ideological backgrounds (e.g., environmental concerns), and 5% listed as "other" (Gill et al., 2014). The importance of al-Qaeda-related lone wolf violence is reiterated by other scholars, for example in the concern of a "global jihadist movement" (itself a contested and multivariate concept spanning different regions and ideologies and enjoying the support of diverse groups) that is manifest in a significant number of lone wolf terrorist attacks in the Middle East (Carson & Suppenbach, 2016). This points to the salience of the topic of lone wolf terrorism not only in terms of terrorist incidents occurring in Western nations but also in the Middle East and other locations such as Afghanistan (Carson & Suppenbach, 2016). Ideological connections can be difficult to discern, as illustrated by Gill et al. (2014), who suggest that Ted Kaczynski's (i.e., the "Unabomber") actions were built on a "self-made" ideological foundation, while others (Barnett, 2015) argue that the actions of Kaczynski as a solo actor are a form of environmental extremism that is not unique to him (see, for example, the case of Wiebo Arienes Ludwig, the leader of the Trickle Creek Christian Community (Joosse, 2017).

Capellan (2015) provides a valuable voice in the discussion of ideological sources for violent lone wolf attacks. In studying active shooters, Capellan (2015) unearths the complexity of clearly identifying the core ideological tenets of actors and shows that those who hold "extremist values and beliefs" may not be categorised as lone wolf terrorists if the event is not "ideologically motivated" (p. 400). The Global Terrorism Database, in a report on the ideological motivations of terrorist attacks (in general, not focusing on lone wolf terrorism), observes that "classification of terrorist attacks by ideology can be unclear, particularly when perpetrators of attacks identify with more than one ideological group or perspective, which may or may not be relevant to the motivations for the attack itself" (START, 2017, p. 1). Lone wolf terrorist activities can run the gamut of ideological foundations, including violence as a response to and a manifestation of frustrations and anger relating to perceptions of religious, political, and social issues and injustice. That is, the variety of ideological motivations, paired with the lack of communication with others, makes the lone wolf attack that much more pernicious due to the isolation and range of potential targets of these individuals. In short, there is a unique challenge in determining the ideological motivations of lone wolf terrorists, especially in cases in which the attacker dies.

MAPPING THE GEOGRAPHIC AND TEMPORAL SPACES OF LONE WOLF TERRORISM

Realistically, in recent years, when the term "lone wolf" or "single-actor terrorist" comes to mind, many will imagine attacks that have happened in the United States and Western European countries. Despite these acts of terror being the most reported on and widely studied, one must realise that these attacks are not limited to these geographic spaces. The Middle East and North Africa (MENA) region and South Asia account for 42.87% of terrorist activity worldwide; although a heavy presence of organised terror groups exists in these countries, lone actors are still prevalent (Alakoc, 2017). The evolving global terrorist organisations such as Daesh, the Taliban, and al-Qaeda and their affiliates in the MENA region indirectly aid lone wolves through the dissemination of radicalisation material that is readily available on the internet and other social media platforms (Barnes, 2012; Carson & Suppenbach, 2016). Cases of the radicalisation of youth in India in recent years point to how easily accessible radicalisation material is. This is illustrated in the example of the software engineer whose plot to bomb an American school in Mumbai was foiled in 2014 (Ade, 2015). Online radicalisation is also prevalent in industrialised countries, and although the motives may differ from the global Jihad fight, the intentions are the same: attack the target and inflict the most comprehensive possible collateral damage. This is illustrated in the case of Christopher Paul Hasson, a lieutenant in the United States Coast Guard who had read Breivik's manifesto and was arrested and charged in February 2019 for plotting to commit acts of mass terrorism. In addition to stockpiles of illegal drugs and weapons, computer files found suggested that the selection of his intended targets (Democratic members of Congress) was linked to attempting to restore a "white homeland" in the United States.

In recent years, much of the literature on lone wolf attacks in the United States has focused on the rise of active shooter attacks (Becker, 2014; Capellan, 2015). Past attacks, such as the Unabomber, Ted Kaczynski, and the Oklahoma City Bomber Timothy McVeigh, that involved unconventional means of violence have segued into the prevalence of firearm usage. Much of the policy debate in political realms at the state and federal levels in the United States has discussed access to firearms and how to better regulate ownership and purchase of such weapons. Capellan (2015) suggests that many active shooter lone wolf attacks in the United States are highly geographically clustered, often occurring in the Mid-Atlantic, Appalachian Highlands, Southeast, and Pacific Coast, some of which consist of highly populated metropolitan spaces. Although many of these extremists may aim for areas where they can inflict the most damage and cause the most casualties, others strive for specific spaces due to a variety of "revenge" factors (Becker, 2014). Even though lone wolves may be situated in the same or similar geographic spaces, their ideologies and tactics distinguish their presence in the field of terrorism.

Actors and Agents

Just as there are many ways that one may identify who a lone wolf terrorist is, there are just as many ways to distinguish "what" it is that they do that makes them similar or stand out in the crowd. Here we suggest that the actors and agents are defined by their ability to develop, refine, and nurture synced methods that, in many cases, strike a resemblance to the ideologies of extremist organisations. Often, these messages are infused with nationalist sentiment, be it white supremacists' rhetoric about the diminishing role of whites in America or ideas around pushing foreigners off occupied lands in the Middle East. No matter the message or the original intent of a lone wolf, as evidenced below and as Beydoun (2018) suggests, throughout the waves of terrorism, there have been varying stripes and types.

The portrait of the lone actor can be categorised into five distinct types of terrorist activities that share similarities and differences (Beydoun, 2018; Post et al., 2014). Lone soldiers can often be former enlisted members of a terrorist organisation who attack with the consent of the organisation, thus being able to inflict more damage than most lone wolves (Beydoun, 2018). The second, lone vanguards, are extremists who carry out attacks to advance an individual ideology or transgression, such as Ted Kaczynski or Anders Breivik (Beydoun, 2018). Third, loners are lone wolf terrorists who also act upon a particular ideology yet lack the social competence to draw others to their cause (Beydoun, 2018). Fourth, similar to loners, lone followers are often viewed as followers who seize upon an existing ideology and act upon it, though they too are socially incompetent and thus fail to become members of organisations they identify with (Beydoun, 2018). Finally, lone wolf killers are those who fall outside of this typology in that they have no direct ties to terrorism. Lone wolf terrorists are also likely to have a criminal record and to have served jail time (Gill et al., 2014). Barnett (2015) and Berntzen and Sandberg (2014) shine a light in their research on the two lone vanguards, Ted Kaczynski and Anders Breivik, and explain how these men used manifestos to draw support for their cause. Kaczynski used language in his manifesto that would strike an emotional chord with other radical environmentalists by prognosticating a bleak future (Barnett, 2015). Breivik shared many similar sentiments in his manifesto to those of the Anti-Islamic Movement in Norway, yet differed in that he promoted armed resistance and terrorism (Berntzen & Sandberg, 2014). He called for the emancipation of Europe from certain cultural death, believing that Christian European cultures are incongruent with Islam and that terrorism was the only appropriate form of self-defence.

As mentioned previously, with the rise of lone wolf terrorism and the prevalence of stories from Western countries, it is imperative to note that single actors come from varying socio-economic backgrounds. For instance, in India, Ade (2015) reports that most of the radicalised Indian youth are educated, come from middle-class families, and reside in urban and suburban spaces. The source of their ideology and where they channel their resentment manifest in a sense of isolation and disenfranchisement from how the government treats Muslim Indians. Solitary attacks in other Asian countries, many of whom are suspected of formerly being members of a terrorist organisation, act as a symbol of the shifting dynamics of extremist ideologies. Organisations such as al-Qaeda, for example, encourage terrorists to "learn from experience and modify their tactics and targets to exploit perceived vulnerabilities and avoid observed strengths" (Barnes, 2012, p. 1649). It is imperative to point out that although these organisations – Daesh included – may claim to have a stake in the operation of a successful lone wolf attack that has no direct affiliation with them, these groups will distance themselves or deny involvement in foiled or miniscule attacks even if the attacker was radicalised through their material.

In identifying and understanding who these attackers are, the question of "homegrown" vs. foreign national is hotly discussed in terms of national security and immigration policy in many Western countries. In the United States, recent examples of homegrown US-born lone wolf terrorists, such as Dylann Roof (the 2015 Charleston church shooting) and Stephen Paddock (the 2017 Las Vegas shooting), are pitted against diasporas (the Tsarnaev brothers), who have had difficulties relating in their new country (Post et al., 2014). These images of the "other," the authors contend, are propagated by certain media outlets that fix their gaze on a small slice of a much larger picture. Gill et al. (2014) go to great lengths to analyse who the lone wolf terrorists are in the United States and Europe in their examinations of the age, education, and occupations of these terrorists. The study finds that compared to traditional organised terror groups, lone wolf terrorists share a diverse sample of age, as those between 21 and 23 and those over 30 make up over 70% of the sample (Gill et al., 2014). Most of the sample consists of those who attended institutions of higher education but did not complete schooling and are currently unemployed, suggesting an individual who could be described as "disenfranchised" (Gill et al., 2014). All in all, the "who" of this framework must be comprehended through a sociocultural lens to paint a clear picture of the societal factors at play in how lone actors are radicalised.

Strategies and Tactical Manoeuvres

According to Alakoc (2017), suicide missions are especially valuable to lone wolf actors due to their potential lethality. The value of such a one-off approach to terrorism contests one of the standard logics that informs thinking about lone wolf actors as potentially nimbler than a larger terrorist organisation. As Pitcavage (2015) suggests, "one of the rationales used by extremists to promote lone wolf action – that the lone wolf can strike again and again" (p. 1668) – is belied by the fact that multiple instances of lone wolf violence by a lone actor are, in reality, not the norm. For example, Ismail Hamed of Arizona, United States, was arrested on February 14, 2019, by Phoenix police officers on charges of aggravated assault and plotting to commit an act of terror. Phoenix law enforcement responded to a call from

Hamed in which he told the dispatcher that he had pledged allegiance to the Islamic State, had a knife and rocks, and wanted to meet face-to-face with a police officer. "I'd like to do something in protest for the people suffering in Palestine and the Middle East," he told the operator. When the officer arrived and attempted to speak with Hamed, Hamed began throwing rocks at the officer and pulled out his knife, advancing upon the officer. Hamed was shot and taken to the hospital with non-life-threatening injuries. Another significant rationalisation for a lone wolf attack is the relative surprise that may accompany such an attack. In the case of limited or no connections to other terrorist organisations, the lack of communication with other actors and avenues for planning "limits the usefulness of traditional interdiction and surveillance efforts by law enforcement" (Becker, 2014, p. 959). A 2012 study of the threat of lone wolf terrorism in the United States concluded that the solitary nature of such an attack makes it close to impossible to predict or prevent on the one hand, but on the other hand, this same feature means that such attacks are relatively "insignificant" in their impact (Barnes, 2012).

According to Becker (2014), lone wolf attackers are constrained in their tactical options and target selections when making decisions leading up to an attack; in other words, their effectiveness is constrained by their "propensity to strike at the intersection of their ideology and their daily routines" (p. 971). Supporting this line of thinking, many violent lone wolf acts were conducted with firearms, which, according to Pitcavage (2015), evidences the propensity for actors to "stick within their comfort zone" (p. 1669). While explosives are the weapon of choice outside of the United States, in the United States, guns have become the weapon of preference for lone wolves, perhaps due to the legality and ready availability of firearms in the country. Phillips (2011) describes operational methods of decision-making as being related to a rational choice perspective on risk and the level of risk that is deemed appropriate for the individual. Accordingly, "depending on their level of risk aversion (or risk seeking), lone wolves are expected to choose assassination, armed attack, bombing, hostage taking, or unconventional methods" (Phillips, 2011, p. 26). Barnes claims that lone attackers, due to their lack of connections, must rely on themselves and the Internet for training, and that this training deficit ultimately limits the attacker's ability to cause damage. This isolation is, in fact, one of the ways in which Byman (2017) suggests that governments can best limit the abilities of would-be terrorists: by stifling connections to terrorist groups, it is feasible to reduce the impact of terrorist actions.

Impact of Lone Wolf Terrorism

As the threat of lone wolf terrorism shows no signs of dissipating anytime soon, the continued economic, political, and social impacts and outcomes of these attacks must be faced. The social consequences are often the hardest, including effects on the family and friends of the lone wolf actor, who may be interrogated by the security apparatus or law enforcement and then shunned by society. In instances where the lone wolf is using the ideological principles of a known terrorist organisation, the social impact is a bit trickier to assess. On February 14, 2019, in India-administered Kashmir, Adil Dar, an alleged member of the Pakistani-based militant group Jaish-e-Mohammad, carried out a suicide bombing, killing 46 members of Indian security personnel along a highway outside Srinagar. Dar used a vehicle packed with explosives to ram a convoy of 78 buses carrying the security forces. Soon after the attack, Jaish-e-Mohammad released a video of Dar speaking on the ill-treatment of Kashmiri Muslims in India and how he was assigned the task of attacking the militant group. In response, India claims that it has evidence that Pakistan collaborated with Jaish-e-Mohammad in carrying out the attack, even though no evidence has been brought forward. Pakistan states that it is not involved in the attack and that it is willing to cooperate in an investigation with the Indian government.

Politically, lone wolf attacks have pressured governments and intelligence agencies to reevaluate how they identify, track, and counter lone wolf terrorists. In India, intelligence agencies have made the switch to cyberspace intelligence in monitoring suspected terrorists' social media presence (Ade, 2015). As well, there have been calls for community engagement, encouraging leaders in local Muslim communities to denounce radical and extremist behaviours. Law enforcement officials and their conventional tactics of surveillance and deterrence are often ineffective against lone wolves, as these terrorists are less likely to have accomplices and target selection can vary from attacker to attacker (Barnes, 2012; Becker, 2014). Beydoun (2018) touches upon the Countering Violent Extremism (CVE) collaborative that was implemented under the Obama administration in 2011. The purpose of this collaborative was to establish community-based approaches where Muslim informants would report to law enforcement agencies any suspicious behaviour in Muslim communities. Beydoun (2018) suggested these kinds of actions may exacerbate the sense of distrust in Muslim communities of the federal government and a social climate that continues to vilify all Muslims living in the United States.

The surveillance and deterrence of suspected terrorists in the United States tread a fragile line between ethical practises and violations of Fourth Amendment rights. Byman (2017) argues that aside from keeping lone wolves lonely by limiting their contact with other radicals and extremists, law enforcement agencies and intelligence agencies have ramped up efforts to monitor social media activity, financial activity, and the activities of family members. These efforts could stir up debates on ethical standards such as unreasonable searches and seizures in democratic societies. After the Sydney Siege of 2014, the community in Australia experienced, through collective grief, the power of solidarity and strength in knowing that their community would be able to carry on. Mikola et al. (2016) exhibited that in the course of a traumatic event, the city of Sydney was able to set aside the "us" vs. "them" rhetoric and embrace the rhetoric of "us" and inclusiveness. The "productive power" of togetherness and "us" in Sydney showed that the politics of fear would not win out (Mikola et al., 2016). Economic outcomes and impacts of lone wolf terrorism can be analysed through a lens of cost-benefit analysis as governments and intelligence agencies attempt to "bleed dry" lone wolf terrorists.

CONCLUSION

The lone wolf is redefining terrorism globally. There is a false picture of the lone wolf as a foreign, irrational, non-White actor carrying out actions in non-Westphalian contexts and spaces. This image is incorrect as the portrait of lone wolf terrorism is more complex, and today lone wolf attacks span the gamut of actions ranging from actions against Western countries or "the Great Satan" on occupied lands or on lands that they have inhabited unjustly to dissatisfaction with government policies and priorities. Lone-wolf actors are different from people who are active in other forms of political violence. These actors are not motivated by politics alone, and it is often a combination of several things, compounded by personal grievances, that begins the road to radicalisation and late extremism. The act is steeped in complex mixtures of personal, political, and religious (broadly defined) ideologies against the oppressive arm of the dominant elites and the status quo that they maintain. Lone wolf attacks still make up a small percentage of terror attacks compared to organised attacks, yet the rate of single-actor attacks is rising, and governments must react appropriately to these concerns. As we have argued above, new actors and agents using different tactics and strategies to achieve higher political, social, and economic impacts are redefining post-2011 geopolitical terrorism discussions. This is evident in the ten months between July 2016 and April 2017, when there were five vehicle attacks by lone wolves in Nice, New York, Berlin, London, and Stockholm. We are witnessing a structural change in lone wolf terrorism as the extremists have found ways to harness and exploit the significant platforms on the Internet for their benefit while relying on local organisations to provide support.

Moreover, geopolitical strategies are not focused on understanding the root causes of lone wolf terrorism, and often, policy responses have been applied as band-aid solutions to perceived symptoms rather than treating the core causes. Today, social media and digital platforms have changed the very nature of lone wolf terrorism by amplifying the scale and impact of terrorist attacks through imagery, eyewitness accounts, and live video. This makes it difficult for us to predict potential actors and preempt possible targets, given that the process of radicalisation to extremism is never linear or precise. In short, lone wolf attacks, which are different from conventional terrorist attacks, are becoming more common, and this has implications for global and national security.

Since it is hard to predict when or where the next lone wolf will strike and what their defining ideological beliefs are, it also means that global security is often reactive rather than proactive. This is compounded by the fact that emerging technological innovations, such as artificial intelligence, robotics, autonomous vehicles, 3D printing or additive manufacturing, nanotechnology, biotechnology, materials science, energy storage, and quantum computing, provide different venues for the infliction of various forms of terror on unsuspecting individuals. With the rise of the "Internet of Things" (IoT), the movement away from human-to-human or human-to-computer interaction (Ashton, 2009), which creates an "open, global network connecting people, data, and things" through the "use of synergies that are generated by the convergence of consumer, business, and industrial Internet" (Vermesan et al., 2014, p. 9), it will become more and more difficult to discern the acts of an individual from those of a terror cell or significant organisation. In short, the move towards the fourth industrial revolution has the potential to reshape the action of the lone wolf terror attacks in unimaginable ways.

Notes

1 Industry 4.0 was coined in Germany as a way of defining the digitisation of manufacturing and the impact of emerging technologies on automation and data exchange.

2 English-language magazine by pro-al-Qaeda jihadists in Syria

References

Ade, P. (2015). Lone wolf terrorism: How prepared are India's intelligence agencies? *Counter Terrorist Trends and Analyses, 7*(6), 4–11.

Alakoc, B. (2017). Competing to kill: Terrorist organizations versus lone wolf terrorists. *Terrorism and Political Violence, 29*(3), 509–532.

Ashton, K. (2009). That "Internet of Things" thing: In the real world things matter more than ideas. *RFID Journal*. http://www.rfidjournal.com/articles/view?4986

Barnes, B. (2012). Confronting the one-man wolf pack: Adapting law enforcement and prosecution responses to the threat of lone wolf terrorism. *Boston University Law Review, 92*, 1614–1662.

Barnett, B. (2015). 20 years later: A look back at the Unabomber Manifesto. *Perspectives on Terrorism, 9*(6), 60–71.

Becker, M. (2014). Explaining lone wolf target selection in the United States. *Studies in Conflict & Terrorism, 37*(11), 959–978.

Berntzen, L., & Sandberg, S. (2014). The collective nature of lone wolf terrorism: Anders Behring Breivik and the anti-Islamic social movement. *Terrorism and Political Violence, 26*(5), 759–779.

Beydoun, K. (2018). Lone wolf terrorism: Types, stripes, and double standards. *Northwestern University Law Review, 112*(5), 1213–1243.

Burton, F. (2007, May 30). *The challenge of the lone wolf.* Retrieved from https://worldview.stratfor.com/article/challenge-lone-wolf

Byman, D. (2017). How to hunt a lone wolf: Countering terrorists who act on their own. *Foreign Affairs, 96*(2), 96–105.

Capellan, J. (2015). Lone wolf terrorist or deranged shoot? A study of the ideological active shooter events in the United States, 1970–2014. *Studies in Conflict & Terrorism, 38*(6), 395–413.

Carson, J., & Suppenbach, M. (2016). Lone wolf terrorism: The new form of the global jihadist movement? Evidence from Afghanistan (1997–2013). *The Journal of the Middle East and Africa, 7*(4), 441–453.

Christensen, C.M., Horn, M.B., Caldera, L., & Soares, L. (2011). *Disrupting college how disruptive innovation can deliver quality and affordability to postsecondary education.* Washington, D.C.: Innosight Institute, Center for American Progress.

Friedman, T.L. (1998, August 22). *Foreign affairs; Angry, wired and deadly.* Retrieved from https://www.nytimes.com/1998/08/22/opinion/foreign-affairs-angry-wired-and-deadly.html

Gill, P., Horgan, J., & Deckert, P. (2014). Bombing alone: Tracing the motivations and antecedent behaviors of lone-actor terrorists. *Journal of Forensic Sciences, 59*(2), 425–435.

Hewitt, C. (2003). *Understanding terrorism in America: From the Klan to al-Qaeda.* London: Routledge.

Islamic State. (2014). Dabiq: The return of Khilafah (Issue 1). Retrieved from: http://media.clarionproject.org/files/09-2014/isis-isil-islamic-state-magazine-Issue-1-the-return-of-khilafah.pdf

Joosse, P. (2017). Leaderless resistance and the loneliness of lone wolves: Exploring the rhetorical dynamics of lone actor violence. *Terrorism and Political Violence, 29*(1), 52–78.

Jules, T.D., & Barton, T. (2018). *Educational transitions in post-revolutionary spaces: Islam, security and social movements in Tunisia.* London: Bloomsbury Academic.

Leenaars, J., & Reed, A. (2016). *Understanding lone wolves: Towards a theoretical framework for comparative analysis.* The International Centre for Counter-Terrorism (ICCT). The Hague: The Netherlands.

Mikola, M., Colic-Peisker, V., & Dekker, K. (2016). A community of mourners: Collective sentiment, national belonging and the Muslim 'Other' after the 'Sydney Siege'. *Australian Geographer, 47*(3), 325–339. doi:10.1080/00049182.2016.1191135

Parker, T., & Sitter, N. (2016). The four horsemen of terrorism—it's not waves, it's strains. *Terrorism & Political Violence, 28*(2), 197–216.

Phillips, P. (2011). Lone wolf terrorism. *Peace Economics, Peace Science and Public Policy, 17*(1), 1–29.

Pitcavage, M. (2015). Cerberus unleashed: The three faces of the lone wolf terrorist. *American Behavioral Scientist, 59*(13), 1655–1680.

Post, J.M., McGinnis, C., & Moody, K. (2014). The changing face of terrorism in the 21st century: The communications revolution and the virtual community of hatred. *Behavioral Sciences and the Law, 32*, 306–334. doi:10.1002/bsl.2123

Rapoport, D.C. (2004). The four waves of modern terrorism. In A.K. Cronin & J M. Ludes (Eds.), *Attacking terrorism: Elements of a grand strategy* (pp. 46–73). Washington, DC: Georgetown University Press.

Robb, J. (2007). *Brave new war: The next stage of terrorism and the end of globalization.* Hoboken, NJ: Wiley.

Sageman, M. (2008). *Leaderless Jihad: Terror networks in the twenty-first century.* Philadelphia: University of Pennsylvania Press.

Schurmann, B., Lindekilde, L., Malthaner, S., O'Connor, F., Gill, P., & Bouhana, N. (2017). End of the lone wolf: The typology that should not have been. *Studies in Conflict & Terrorism, 42*, 771–778.

Schwab, K. (2016, January 26). *The fourth industrial revolution.* Retrieved from https://www.foreignaffairs.com/articles/2015-12-12/fourth-industrial-revolution

Scott, R., & Shanahan, R. (2018). Man Haron Monis and the Sydney Lindt Café siege – not a terrorist attack. *Psychiatry, Psychology and Law, 25*(6), 1–63.

Simon, J.D. (2016). *Lone wolf terrorism: Understanding the growing threat.* Amherst, NY: Prometheus Books.

Smith, B.L., Gruenewald, J., Roberts, P., & Damphousse, K.R. (2015). The emergence of lone wolf terrorism: Patterns of behavior and implications for intervention. *Terrorism and Counterterrorism Today, 20*, 91–110. doi:10.1108/S1521-613620150000020005

Spaaij, R. (2010). The enigma of lone wolf terrorism: An assessment. *Studies in Conflict & Terrorism, 33*, 854–870. doi:10.1080/1057610X.2010.501426

Spaaij, R., & Hamm, M. (2015). Key issues and research agendas in lone wolf terrorism. *Studies in Conflict & Terrorism, 38*, 167–178.

START. (2017). *Background report: Ideological motivations of terrorism in the United States, 1970–2016.* pp. 1–6. Retrieved from https://www.start.umd.edu/pubs/START_IdeologicalMotivationsOfTerrorismInUS_Nov2017.pdf

Stern, J. (2004). *Terror in the name of God: Why religious militants kill.* New York: Harper Collins.

UNCTED. (2014). *Bringing terrorists to justice: Challenges in the prosecution of terrorists acting alone or in small cells (Rep.).* Retrieved from https://pdfs.semanticscholar.org/8faf/5e3e0120a72f9315b3f3a866a42a4216f07d.pdf

Vermesan, O., Friess, P., Guillemin, P., Sundemaeker, H., Eisenhauer, M., Moessner, K., Arndt, M., Spirito, M., Medagliano, P., Giaffreda, R., Gusmeroli, S., Ladid, L., Serrano, M., Hauswirth, M., & Baldini, G. (2014). Internet of Things strategic research and innovation agenda. In O. Vermesan & P. Friess (Eds.), *Internet of Things: From research and innovation to market deployment* (pp. 7–142). Aalborg, Denmark: River Publishers.

18

NON-STATE ARMED GROUP TRANSITION TO PARTY POLITICS

Mariam Farida

INTRODUCTION

Non-state armed groups (NSAGs) are armed entities operating outside of the control of the state (p. 1) that are willing and able to use illegal armed forces to achieve their goals. Such goals may be political, economic, or ideological in nature and are, in the broadest sense, attempts to influence political outcomes and drive social change outside the boundaries of established institutions of the state. It is the highly political nature of the NSAGs' claims, however, that often makes the resolution of any conflict in which such actors are involved more likely to emerge from political agreements than military defeat (European Union External Action, 2012).

This chapter seeks to examine the elements or factors associated with the successful transition of NSAGs from violent actors to legitimate political entities. A key premise underpinning the examination is that the pressure and/or support for armed groups to disarm, demobilise, and reintegrate into society typically emerges from efforts to protect and sustain the peace that has been achieved. As such, focus is given to three aspects of the transition: the NSAG's willingness to "play by the rules" (i.e., adhere to political processes); the perceived credibility of the NSAG as a political entity as manifested in the extent to which the domestic population accepts its aims and objectives; and how the armed conflict ended.

What is highlighted is that the complexities surrounding the transition of NSAG to a political entity emerge primarily from concerns associated with "legitimising" the group by supporting its entry into the political domain. The contextual factors surrounding the transition, that is, the socio-political setting and the nature of the post-conflict environment, are therefore of critical importance as they will invariably shape the specific security and political agreements that are forged between participating political parties to regulate the post-conflict context (Dudouet et al., 2016).

DEFINING NON-STATE ARMED GROUPS

Non-state armed groups include militias, terrorist organisations, and insurgents (Berti, 2016; Chaudhry, 2013; Clapham, 2010) and are characterised by their "potential to deploy arms for political, economic, and ideological objectives" (European Union External Action, 2012, para. 1). They present an overt challenge to state power and authority because they operate outside of the control of the state and on the basis of their reliance on unconventional and asymmetric violence and force to achieve their objectives (Clapham, 2010; Petrasek, 2000; United Nations, 2006). Indeed, the military, political, and social relevance of NSAGs typically emerges from the "combination of state fragility, conflict, and instability" (Berti, 2016, p. 1). As Chaudhry (2013) explains, states that demonstrate a lack of capacity to maintain security and order or to provide adequate health and welfare services to citizens develop what he refers to as "functional holes that offer opportunities to non-state actors" (p. 169).

The core goals and objectives of NSAGs may be political, economic, and/or ideological in nature, and each entity will generally have at least a minimal level of command, control, and coordination (Chaudhry, 2013; Hofmann, 2006). When considered collectively, NSAGs demonstrate great heterogeneity, manifested in the differences in the extent to which their political objectives are clearly defined, the territory they control, the administrative and command structures under which they operate, their member demographics, and the targets of their armed attacks (Bruderlein, 2000; Chaudhry, 2013; Dudouet et al., 2016; Sindre & Söderström, 2016). Notably, Berti (2016) asserts that a key factor in the ability of NSAGs to transition to legitimate political parties is in fact that their "multi-layered identities and strategies defy simple labelling" (p. 1).

DOI: 10.4324/9780429426063-20

CONCEPTUALISING THE TRANSITION FROM NSAG TO POLITICAL ENTITY

The transition of NSAG to a political party has been conceptualised by Dudouet et al. (2016) as "a continuum of incremental changes, indicating different stages and steps" (p. 7). At one end of the continuum is the renunciation of force by the group and its acceptance of basic political processes. At the other end of the continuum is the full internal democratisation of the group via adjustments to key organisational and programmatic elements and its acceptance of state-based power and governance (Dudouet et al., 2016).

The NSAG's capacity to meet the challenge that adaptation to the settlement presents is also fundamentally dependent upon the character of the NSAG and the degree of its commitment to a political settlement in the post-conflict context (Manning, 2004). According to Rustow (1970), what matters at the beginning of the transition is not the specific values that the leaders hold in the abstract but rather what actions they are willing to take to aid in the transition.

Notwithstanding the potential for nuanced conceptualisations of the "transition" itself, the transition of NSAG into a political party "requires a minimum of legitimisation" (European Union External Action, 2012, p. 4). In this context, legitimacy primarily refers to non-violent participation in political processes at the national or local level (Dudouet et al., 2016). This definition naturally implies the process of engaging with and winning seats in the governing authority (Van Engeland & Rudolph, 2008). Moreover, it implies a reliance "on consent rather than coercion and on authority rather than power or brute force" (p. 169) to achieve party goals and facilitate social change (Chaudhry, 2013).

Rules of the Game

Thus, NSAG transitioning is fundamentally about the "ability" and "willingness" of the NSAG to undertake the adaptation to post-conflict electoral politics, that is, to fully invest themselves "in the formal rules of the game" (Manning, 2004, p. 54), which will determine the transition outcomes. Put more succinctly by Manning (2004), the nature and outcomes of the transition are as much about "the design and enforcement of the game" as they are about "the players themselves" (p. 55). This points to the importance of the institutional engineering required in post-conflict settings to accommodate the transition of NSAGs into political parties – that is, the design of political institutions to address the security concerns of both NSAGs and already established political entities. These institutions can only be as effective as the political actors who operate them (Manning, 2004).

Reducing the "transition" of NSAG to the notion of winning electoral votes can be problematic, however. As Dudouet et al. (2016) point out, such an approach does not assign a suitable focus to an assessment of the shift in "the strategies, behaviour, and preferences" (p. 7) of the NSAG in the context of the transition processes. Indeed, Linz (1978) warns against idealising the "legitimacy" of a government or party based on the number of votes. The author suggests instead that an attribution of democratic legitimacy should be considered little more than the constituents' beliefs "that for that particular country at that particular historical juncture, no other type of regime could assure a more successful pursuit of collective goals" (p. 18).

The stance has clear implications for how one conceptualises the "markers" of genuine transition. Dudouet et al. (2016) have us consider both the behaviours and values of the NSAG, but with greater emphasis on behaviour rather than values at the decision stage. This has long been viewed as a key consideration, with Rustow (1970) declaring, "What matters most is not what values the leaders hold dear in the abstract, but what concrete steps they are willing to take" (p. 357). The "steps" to which these and other authors refer invariably include the DDR of combatants to bring armed forces under legal and civil control, genuine participation in party politics to achieve periodic electoral acknowledgment to retain positions of power, and a political culture that endorses a commitment to democracy.

Notably, if one accepts the premise that the transition of NSAG to a political entity requires "legitimisation", there are considerable implications for how one differentiates NSAGs from terrorist organisations. Terrorist groups have long been linked to processes of political and social change (Crenshaw, 1995). It has been increasingly the case since 9/11 for armed groups to be classified as terrorist organisations by sovereign governments in order to discredit the political claims of these groups "and to legitimise 'zero tolerance' reactions" (European Union External Action, 2012, p. 4). Blindly labelling armed groups as terrorist organisations, however, can adversely impact a government's (or international body's) capacity for mediation and dialogue with the armed group during the transition process. To validate claims that the group is a terrorist organisation and to avoid hindrances to achieving effective mediation and dialogue outcomes, careful consideration must be given to the "structural roots and political causes behind the motivation of non-state armed groups" (European Union External Action, 2012, p. 4).

Armed Groups to Successfully Transition

The list of armed groups to successfully transition to a legitimate political party includes, but is not limited to, the Palestine Liberation Organization (PLO), Hezbollah in Lebanon, the Provisional Irish Republican Army (IRA) in Northern Ireland, Hamas in Palestine, the KLA in Kosovo, and the RUF in Sierra Leone (for further details of the transition, see Berti, 2016; Cronin, 2006; Sindre & Söderström, 2016). Using Lebanese Hezbollah as an example (like Hamas), it operates as an armed organisation, political entity, and social movement organisation that promotes its role as a protector of Lebanon and provider of social services to targeted social groups, primarily Shi'ite communities (Berti, 2016).

Indeed, the capacity of the group to operate as an alternative governance provider to Shi'ite communities via the provision of social services remains significant to the transition process. These efforts to meet the needs of constituents, along with the group's "autonomous, sophisticated, and well-established governance network" (p. 2), contributed to the blurring of the lines of demarcation between state and non-state actors and thus established a political dynamic that both redefined and contested conceptualisations of statehood and sovereignty (Berti, 2016). Moreover, the group's well-developed military apparatus, which had been deployed to great effect as the defender of Lebanon, gave credibility to its integration into the Lebanese political arena (Berti, 2016).

An illustrative case of an NSAG attempting to become mainstream or overground and participate in the governance process is Lashkar-e-Taiba (LeT). Labelled an anti-India group and accused of perpetrating the 2008 Mumbai attacks, the LeT sought to enter mainstream national politics in Pakistan in August 2017 via the launch of the Milli Muslim League (MML) party headed by Saifullah Khalid. Underpinning the attempt to mobilise support for the transition is the domestic humanitarian work of the MML. Specifically, the thousands of volunteers across Pakistan affiliated with the group who provide assistance in the education, disaster, and medical relief sectors Security analysts have raised suspicions, however, of state support for the MML's transition into domestic politics as a way "to cloak the group amid heightening pressure from the international community on Pakistan to crack down on LeT" (Hashim, 2017). Implied in these suspicions is tacit support by the state for the LeT's anti-India stance.

EVALUATING THE PROS AND CONS OF TRANSITION

A diverse range of factors are cited in the literature in support of an NSAG's transition to party politics. Collectively, they point to the potential for outcomes such as bringing an end to armed conflict or violence, promoting compliance by the NSAG to "accepted rules" (i.e., democratic processes), addressing humanitarian concerns, and reducing regional security issues (Dudouet et al., 2016; European Union External Action, 2012; Muriaas et al., 2016). As such, the positive outcomes associated with the transition of NSAG into a political entity are encapsulated in the balance between reducing the risk of political destabilisation in the country or region and acknowledging the political nature of the NSAG claims and their potential social benefits (Berdal & Ucko, 2009; European Union External Action, 2012). Conversely, several factors are cited in the literature as to why caution is required around the provision of support for NSAG to transition to party politics. Paramount among these factors is the need to ensure against the tacit legitimisation of violations of human rights, provide a political environment for the unpredictable use of power, and allow NSAGs to unduly influence the political agenda (Chaudhry, 2013; Dudouet et al., 2016; European Union External Action, 2012).

Supporting NSAGs in Their Transition

In terms of support for the transition of NSAGs, it is worthwhile to consider the international security system and its reliance on a state-centric approach to the prevention and management of conflict. Embedded in this system is the belief that successful security governance in the global context is tied to the "establishment of effective, transparent, and democratically accountable state institutions" (Chaudhry, 2013, p. 181). One might extrapolate from this that transitioning NSAGs into the "formalised" political arena is a way to achieve a more robust alignment between their stated objectives and the institutions of the state.

To elaborate, it may be argued that from the position of the state, the ongoing presence of non-state-sanctioned military personnel, arms, and organised structures in societies embroiled in hostilities presents clear challenges to the established political infrastructures (Berdal & Ucko, 2009). The process of disarmament, demobilisation, and reintegration (DDR) of combatants is therefore regarded as crucial to society's "transition from conflict to normalcy and development" (Berdal & Ucko, 2009, p. 3). Building on this premise, Dudouet et al. (2016) purport that the main drivers for established political entities and institutions engaging with NSAGs in their transition to political legitimacy are "to prevent, manage, and mitigate impacts on human security, international peace, and the deteriorating rule of law affected by their presence and operations" (p. 4). This is what Lyons (2016) refers to as the "demilitarisation of politics" and is well encapsulated in the assertion that facilitating the transition is fundamentally about "bringing armed forces under legal and civil control" (Berdal & Ucko, 2009, p. 7).

Indeed, facilitating the transition of NSAGs can arguably establish a pathway towards raising the group's awareness of and compliance with the "rules of the game" (p. 2) and can increase its awareness of its potential to influence outcomes via negotiation (European Union External Action, 2012). Hence, support for the transition of NSAGs to political parties may emerge from the state's desire to mitigate the security threat and effects of the group's "challenge to the state's monopoly on the use of force" (Berti, 2016, p. 2). Although it is difficult to estimate the total number of armed groups that can successfully transition into the political arena, Högbladh (2012) has suggested that 30 of the 216 peace agreements signed between 1975 and 2011 included provisions to transition the armed group into a political party. Of these, approximately one in three (35.5%) of the armed groups successfully transitioned into a political party (Söderberg & Hatz, 2016).

Notwithstanding that NSAGs use armed force (violence) outside of the "monopoly for violence" held by the state, they also often provide "psychological empowerment for the disempowered, marginalised, and disenfranchised" (Chaudhry, 2013, p. 174). From a constituent perspective, support for the transition of NSAGs to legitimate political entities may be based on the perceived need to address humanitarian and regional security operations (Berti, 2016). These factors are often referred to in the literature as the legitimacy, authority, and capacity gaps of the state (Carment et al., 2014; Ghani & Lockhart, 2008). This is evidenced by armed groups such as Hezbollah and Hamas, for instance, which engage in "multi-layered activities, extending to the social, political, and economic realms" (Berti, 2016, p. 3).

Concerns around the Transition of NSAGs

In terms of the cautions around supporting the transition of NSAG to a political actor, much of the focus is given to the potential for significant adverse impacts on democratic and parliamentary processes. A seat at the governance table affords the group the opportunity to more directly influence the political agenda, potentially elevating the role of violence in the pursuit of political outcomes (European Union External Action, 2012). Established political parties will naturally have concerns about the political prowess of the armed group to transition effectively to a legitimate political actor (Söderström, 2014). That is, questions will be asked as to the capacity of the armed group to contribute to the political landscape with "legitimate political claims and visions" (Sindre & Söderström, 2016, p. 111).

This points to the implications stemming from the strength and extent of the NSAG's support network. It is typically the objective of DDR and security sector reform (SSR) initiatives, for instance, to "try to break such networks and disconnect individuals from each other" (Sindre & Söderström, 2016, p. 112). In turn, the nature of the role played by support countries or organisations in the operations of the armed group seeking political legitimacy can have significant implications for the democratic workings of these parties and the achievement of democratic standards more broadly (Sindre & Söderström, 2016). Moreover, the failure of state institutions to facilitate the transition to the satisfaction of the group and its supporters may result in further violence and the risk of political destabilisation (European Union External Action, 2012).

Cautions around support for the transition of NSAGs to political entities also emerge from concerns about the group's motivation for the transition. As such, it is important to examine the dynamics underpinning the relationship between the group's core objectives and its "capacity" to achieve its objectives. As mentioned above, NSAGs demonstrate clear heterogeneity in terms of their objectives, target groups, strategies and tactics for armed conflict, geographical presence, organisational structures, initiation apparatuses, and relations to the state (Schneckener, 2009; Schlichte, 2009). It is therefore difficult for the state to have a clear understanding of the NSAG's motivation to transition in terms of the group's preferences for the use of arms compared to the use of political processes "to achieve their broader socio-political aspirations" (Dudouet et al., 2016, p. 4).

The transition for some leaders of NSAGs may be about the use of political processes to protect the interests of the group and its voice in political discourse (Dudouet et al., 2016). Alternatively, the transition may be driven by the group's belief in its potential to use political processes to further destabilise the system of governance and so continue to compete with the state (Rosenau, 2001). In such circumstances, the state must assess the extent to which the NSAG has a clear and coherent political agenda, a politically literate membership, and unity between leadership and the rank-and-file participants to ensure a sustainable integration into the political domain (Berdal & Ucko, 2009).

Furthermore, NSAGs and formal political parties are generally viewed as "opposite models of approach to democratic political processes" (European Union External Action, 2012, p. 1). Given the highly political nature of the claims by NSAGs and their desire for conflict as a pathway to "resolution", the inclusion of NSAGs in political processes may be viewed as the tacit legitimisation of violations of human rights by NSAGs in the pursuit of participative politics (European Union External Action, 2012).

FACTORS IMPACTING THE TRANSITION OF NSAG TO A POLITICAL ENTITY

The discussion to this point has acknowledged and briefly explored the complications and implications surrounding the transition of NSAG to a legitimate political actor. In turn, the focus now shifts to the factors most integral to the success of the transition process and the sustainability of its outcomes. In this domain, authors invariably point to the motivation, structure, and leadership of the NSAG; the extent to which there is an inclusive negotiation process; the presence of social and institutional incentives; and the lack of negative externalities to oppose the transition process (e.g., Curtis & de Zeeuw, 2012; European Union External Action, 2012; Taleski, 2011). In addition, the legacy left by the mobilisation of the armed group and the way in which the conflict ended is considered by some authors to be crucial to the transition (e.g., Sindre & Söderström, 2016).

When these factors are considered collectively, it is evident that both predictive factors (i.e., the conditions under which it may reasonably be expected for a successful transition to occur) and intervention factors (i.e., when and how interventions should occur to support the NSAG's political transition) are significant elements underpinning the transition of an NSAG to a political entity (Dudouet et al., 2016). The elements with the greatest potential to help or hinder NSAGs from becoming legitimate political entities are discussed in relation to three broad categories for the purposes of this chapter, reflecting the methodology used by several authors in the field: contextual factors, NSAG characteristics, and public (domestic) perceptions of the social legitimacy of the group. Notably, although it is not within the scope of the discussion in this chapter to examine in depth the role of the international community and/or state sponsors in facilitating the transition of NSAG to a legitimate political entity, several authors provide useful insights into this aspect (see Manning, 2004; Accosta, 2014; Dudouet et al., 2016; Hashim, 2017).

Contextual Factors

The contextual factors regarded as playing an integral role in the successful transition of NSAG to a political entity include the type of conflict in which the group was embroiled and how it was settled, the post-war context, the political provisions in the peace agreements, and the security provisions in the peace agreements. To elaborate, one of the preconditions for successful political transitions of NSAGs identified by Dudouet et al. (2016) is the nature of the conflict in which the NSAG has been involved and how the conflict was settled. In general, conflict settlement may be due to military victory or defeat, regime overthrow, peace agreement, social change, DDR processes, and the like. In turn, the way in which the armed group engages in armed conflict and acknowledges the outcomes of its actions can significantly impact its legacy and capacity for political legitimacy (Lyons, 2016). For instance, Lyons (2016) argues that armed groups that have fought wars over small territories without the support (or only with minimal support) of international groups are more likely to transition to capable political parties than armed groups that have fought over larger areas with significant external support. In addition, Dudouet et al. (2016) assert that an end to conflict via military victory has greater potential to facilitate a transition by the NSAG towards an authoritarian political presence and governance structure.

Thus, the type of armed conflict and the settlement trajectory can have significant implications for the nature of the "transition" process (e.g., electoral processes, power-sharing arrangements, etc.) and the subsequent style of governance demonstrated by the NSAG (Dudouet et al., 2016; Lamb et al., 2015; Lyons, 2016). A political party is established by political actors to achieve stated goals (Aldrich, 1995). As a generalisation, NSAG is unlikely to be incentivised to transition to party politics if it achieves its goals via an armed victory over its adversaries. Conversely, there is a much greater incentive for the NSAG to achieve its goals via transition if it is outmatched or at parity with its adversary (Accosta, 2014). In this context, the incentive is primarily to achieve periodic electoral acknowledgment to retain positions of power (Mainwaring, 1989).

For instance, the NSAG may initiate "self-managed DDR processes" (p. 14) to facilitate its transition to political legitimacy (e.g., Polisario guerrilla front in Western Sahara) in contexts where armed victory or negotiated outcomes are unlikely (Dudouet et al., 2016). Such transition drivers are, in turn, more likely to promote a participatory approach to politics and collaboration towards achieving desired outcomes. Conversely, NSAG's transition to power via force (rather than political processes such as elections) may increase the potential for relatively unstable governance mechanisms due to pressures from newly emerging armed groups seeking to contest the power and governance structures (Dudouet et al., 2016).

Furthermore, the "stabilisation" agreements set in place in the post-conflict context (i.e., the political and security provisions) are crucial to establishing a "foundation on which to build the attitudes, behaviours, and institutions that contribute to lasting peace" (Lamb et al., 2015, p. 8). Such stabilisation agreements underpin the opportunities afforded the NSAG to benefit from its transition to a political entity (Dudouet et al., 2016; Muriaas et al., 2016). Peace arrangements typically include provisions that allow NSAGs to participate in elections or have an active role in governance institutions (Dudouet et al., 2016). Such power-sharing outcomes are regarded as particularly beneficial in divided post-war societies as they help to accommodate different interests and promote an inclusive political system (Hoove & Scholtbach, 2008).

It is important to consider, however, that even though political action is contextual and strategic, determining the extent to which the transition to a political entity is motivated by the pursuit of legitimate political authority rather than self-interest is problematic given that political action also "reflects the ideologies, values, and perceptions" (p. 16) of the political actors (Mainwaring, 1989).

Non-State Armed Group Features

To understand the determinants of NSAG's capacity to meet the challenges that a transition to political legitimacy presents for them, Manning's (2004) assertion that it is fundamentally dependent upon the "political character" of the NSAG and the degree of its commitment to a political settlement in the post-conflict context is important for consideration. As stated by the author, the nature and sustainability of the transition are largely determined by the "ability" and "willingness" of the NSAG to undertake the adaptation to post-conflict electoral politics, that is, to fully invest itself "in the formal rules of the game" (Manning, 2004, p. 54).

Arguably, the features of the NSAG, including its internal structure and cohesion and political motivation and experience, have the greatest potential to impact the nature of its transition to a political entity and the sustainability of its political presence (Cronin, 2006). As Sindre and Söderström (2016) remind us, the origins, organisational structure, political culture, and strategic behaviour of the NSAG all shape the group's capacity to participate in the political arena of the country in which it operates. The combination of organisational structure and political culture, for instance, speaks to the internal cohesion of the NSAG and the extent to which it can ensure compliance by combatants to a command to stop fighting and/or to contain any call to armed action should it emerge (Lamb et al., 2015). Furthermore, as Dudouet et al. (2016) assert, NSAGs with a hierarchical command and control structure, rather than a decentralised network or cell-based approach, and low-level internal cohesion "are more likely to undergo political transitions in a coherent and disciplinary fashion" (p. 10). According to the authors, this is primarily because the leadership within the NSAG can better coordinate the post-war trajectory and transition processes down the chain of command (Dudouet et al., 2016).

Moreover, the NSAG's strategic behaviour in relation to its commitment to political inclusion and better social conditions for citizens and the nature of the support it receives from foreign patrons (if any) to make the transition will impact its capacity to successfully transition to a legitimate political entity (Lamb et al., 2015). NSAGs whose objectives emerge from ideology or an explicit political agenda and who have a genuine interest in participating in the governance of the state are arguably more likely to lead a successful transition into politics in the post-war arena (Muriaas et al., 2016). Of critical importance at the initial stages of transition is the NSAG's ability to generate coherent political discourse and/or clear ideology-driven platforms (Lamb et al., 2015). As such, previous political experience or the existence of an explicit political agenda prior to the cessation of armed conflict – for example, maintaining a political branch during the conflict or delivering parallel governance structures within areas under their control – can emerge as critical success factors for the NSAG's transition to political legitimacy (Dudouet et al., 2016).

Lastly, charismatic leadership is also identified as an important NSAG "feature" in the transition to a political party. This is primarily because of the vital role leadership can play in helping to secure internal support for the legitimacy of the decision to adopt political processes amid scepticism and fear within the NSAG (Dudouet et al., 2016). Examples for consideration include Robert Mugabe's leadership in the transition of Zimbabwe's African National Union-Patriotic Front (ZANU-PF) and Hassan Nasrallah's leadership in the transition of Lebanese Hezbollah. Indeed, it is not unreasonable to assume that "hardliners" or "power seekers" within the NSAG may emerge as sources of tension to protest against the transition. In turn, a charismatic leader is potentially more able to overcome internal fragmentation at the leadership level to ensure a public exhibition of unity and strength towards an effective transition (Van Engeland & Rudolph, 2008). This is exemplified in the transition of the Farabundo Mart National Liberation Front (FMLN) first to a successful opposition party and then to the government in El Salvador in 2009. Confronted with multiple defections by party members and collective splits during the 1990s, the leadership of Jorge Schafik was able "to unify the remaining party members around a cohesive leadership and coherent programme" (Dudouet et al., 2016, p. 11).

Political participation at the local and national levels is characterised by involvement in policymaking and the shaping of public discourse on political agendas (Accosta, 2014). Hence, there are two broad challenges for NSAGs in their transition to political parties via democratisation processes: the capacity of the NSAG to make the necessary "adjustments in inter-elite relations", and the "collective incentive strategies" employed by the NSAG to attract and mobilise a mass following (Manning, 2004). The democratisation of organisational structures implies a shift from a command and control approach, that is, "vertical command structures designed for military struggle" (p. 8), to a pluralistic approach that includes "more horizontal and participatory internal decision-making" (Dudouet et al., 2016, p. 8). Moreover, the democratisation of programmatic elements implies the "recalibration of war-time agendas to the complex reality of post-war politics" (Dudouet et al., 2016, p. 8).

A key indicator of the NSAG's capacity to successfully transition to participatory politics is thus the extent to which it can demonstrate a shift in mentality away from resistance or liberation focus to the implementation of policy and governance agendas (Sindre & Söderström, 2016). That is, the group's willingness to renounce the use of force and to accept the basic rules of political competition emerge as minimal criteria for a successful transformation (Sindre & Söderström, 2016). However, the transition process may not involve a complete shift in ideology or the total renunciation of force (Dudouet et al., 2016). Groups that have successfully transitioned to political entities, such as Lebanese Hezbollah and Palestinian Hamas, illustrate this point, demonstrating how the pursuit of pre-existing ideological objectives via peaceful (political) means can be effectively combined with a determination to retain and use the armed wing of the organisation to achieve stated goals and objectives.

Constituents' Perceptions of Social Legitimacy

The extent to which the domestic population is prepared to accept the goals and/or practises of the NSAG is also integral to the success of the transition. As argued by Accosta (2014), "constituents stand at the centre of organisational survival, and a militant organisation therefore requires constituent support to transition to a political party" (para. 5). In turn, although there is a level of flux to be expected in the composition of constituent support during the transition, with the move potentially attracting new constituents while causing others to withdraw their support, the changing nature of the constituency has significant implications for the transitioning group. Not only must the group convince its core constituents that the transition away from armed force towards party politics is the best way to advance the goals of the group, but it must also demonstrate that it has "not surrendered the cause" (para. 5) in its bid to become a political actor (Accosta, 2014).

Public perceptions of the NSAG's social legitimacy also significantly influence the group's transition to a political entity (Muriaas et al., 2016). Such legitimacy perceptions may be built around the mobilisation of ethno-national communities, religious groups, or a political support base while providing social services, advocating self-determination, and/or endorsing an inclusive political agenda (Dudouet et al., 2016). Yet, whatever its source, evidence shows that NSAGs that offer a genuine representation of the constituency's grievances and interests are more likely to mobilise public support in the political domain in post-conflict contexts (Dudouet et al., 2016).

Further to the question of political capital and the mobilisation of supporters, the extent to which the NSAG engages in identity-based conflicts can be decisive in its transition to party politics. As Sindre and Söderström (2016) explain, the "identity, loyalty, and emotional ties that are forged during armed struggle" (p. 113) prove integral to the armed group's capacity to mobilise individual voters. To clarify, the experience of armed struggle can promote political capital for members of the armed group, as their role and sacrifices in combat can enhance perceptions of their credibility (Sindre & Söderström, 2016). In addition, Cronin (2006) has drawn a connection between NSAG's longevity and the level of "support among the local populace of the same ethnicity for its political or territorial objectives" (p. 13). NSAGs that rely on ideology for their appeal will arguably experience a different set of challenges than those that draw upon ethnic solidarity or material reciprocity to mobilise their supporters (Manning, 2004). Similarly, NSAGs that have relied on external sponsorship will arguably be confronted with different challenges and choices throughout the transition to political legitimacy than NSAGs without such sponsors (Manning, 2004).

Constraints to Transition

Conversely, several constraints are cited in the literature regarding NSAG's capability to transition to a political party. For particular consideration is what Abrahms (2013) refers to as the credibility paradox. While NSAG's transition to a political party implies (at the basic level) an intention to "play by the rules" of participatory politics, the public's perceptions of the NSAG's credibility in this regard are fundamentally shaped by its actions while "not" playing by the rules. This draws attention to the perhaps irreconcilable differences between militant credibility and political party credibility. As stated by Abrahms, the transition of NSAG to party politics must begin by overcoming the credibility problem and external perceptions of the group's past preference for violence. How the credibility paradox for an NSAG is resolved during transition is therefore arguably determined by its commitment to outcome-goal achievement and approach to mobilising popular support (Martin & Perliger, 2012).

In addition, Accosta (2014) asserts two independent but sometimes interrelated transition constraints: the preference for violence demonstrated by the group's base constituency and the credibility deficiencies of the group as highlighted by the adversary. Using Palestinian Fatah as an example, the author posits that the group's willingness to use violence in its resistance to Israel simultaneously established itself as a worthy adversary of Israel while undermining its credibility as a political party willing to commit to negotiations and agreements within the realm of participatory politics (Accosta, 2014).

CONCLUSION

By way of conclusion, it is important to reflect upon how one defines "success" when referring to the transition of NSAG to a political party. While much of the literature broadly defines success in terms of the cessation of violence and fair political participation, Lamb et al. (2015) establish a definition based on the notions of "stability" and "peace". As the authors explain, success defined in terms of "stability" is primarily centred around the "absence of violence" (p. iv) beyond the cause of the cessation of violence. Alternatively, success defined in terms of peace suggests the advancement of significant structural change manifested as the presence of social "institutions and attitudes capable of absorbing conflict" (p. iv).

Implied in this assessment of transition success is the NSAG's "willingness to abandon its capacity to conduct armed activities and demobilise its military apparatus" (p. 8) combined with its active participation in the existing democratic political framework via electoral or power-sharing arrangements (Dudouet et al., 2016). Of course, there are numerous exceptions to this rule. Lebanese Hezbollah, for example, simultaneously operates as an armed militant group and political party. Although the group has participated in elections in Lebanon during the 1990s, 2000s, and most recently in May 2018 with considerable success, it has maintained a connection between militant action and the achievement of core goals, as illustrated in the 2006 Hezbollah-Israel War and its involvement in the Syrian civil war (Berti, 2016).

As with the Nicaraguan Sandinistas, Mozambique RENAMO, and Angolan UNITA, Lebanese Hezbollah maintains its militant origins as central to its identity and exploits this origin as a political entity (Sindre & Söderström, 2016). Perhaps the "success" of NSAG's transition to a political entity is more appropriately evaluated in terms of the extent to which the tension between the legitimisation of the group's previous armed violence and the dilution of the power of the state is accepted by constituents. As such, the successful transition of NSAG to a legitimate political entity is inextricably tied to the motivation of the NSAG, the willingness of established political entities to accommodate the group's transition, and the stated needs and desires of constituents.

References

Abrahms, M. (2013). The credibility paradox: Violence as a double-edged sword in international politics. *International Studies Quarterly, 57*(4), 660–671.

Accosta, B. (2014). The transition of militant organisations to political parties. Political Studies Association. Retrieved 5 July 2018, from https://www.psa.ac.uk/insight-plus/blog/transition-militant-organisations-political-parties.

Aldrich, J.H. (1995). *Why parties?: The origin and transformation of political parties in America.* Chicago, Ill: University of Chicago Press.

Berdal, M., & Ucko, D.H. (2009). The political reintegration of armed groups after war. In M. Berdal & D.H. Ucko (Eds.), *Reintegrating armed groups after conflict: Politics, violence, and transition.* New York, NY: Routledge.

Berti, B. (2016). What's in a name? Re-conceptualizing non-state armed groups in the Middle East. *Palgrave Communications, 2*(1), 1–8.

Bruderlein, C. (2000). The role of non-state actors in building human security. The case of armed groups in intra-state wars. Centre for Humanitarian Dialogue, Geneva.

Carment, D., Langlois-Bertrand, S., & Samy, Y. (2014). Assessing state fragility, with a focus on the Middle East and North Africa region: A 2014 country indicators for foreign policy report. Country Indicators for Foreign Policy.

Chaudhry, R. (2013). Violent non-state actors: Contours, challenges and consequences. *Centre for Land and Warfare Studies (CLAWS)*, 167–187.

Clapham, A. (2010). The rights and responsibilities of armed non-state actors: the legal landscape & issues surrounding engagement. *Geneva academy of international humanitarian law and human rights*, 1–45.

Crenshaw, M. (1995). *Terrorism in context.* University Park: Pennsylvania State University Press.

Cronin, A.K. (2006). How al-Qaida ends: The decline and demise of terrorist groups. *International Security, 31*(1), 7–48.

Curtis, D., & de Zeeuw, J. (2012). Rebel movements and political party development in post-conflict societies: A short literature review. Ralph Bunche Institute for International Studies. http://statesandsecurity.org/_pdfs/CurtisZeeuw.pdf.

Dudouet, V., Planta, K., & Giessmann, H.J. (2016). *The political transformation of armed and banned groups: Lessons learned and implications for international support.* Berghof Foundation.

European Union External Action (2012). Factsheet – EEAS mediation support project – knowledge product: Mediation and dialogue in transitional processes from non-state armed groups to political movements/political parties. Retrieved 6 July 2018, from http://ecdpm.org/wp-content/uploads/2013/11/2011-Transitional-Processes-Non-state-Armed-Groups-Political.pdf.

Ghani, A., & Lockhart, C. (2008). *Fixing failed states: Framework for rebuilding a fractured world.* Oxford, UK: Oxford University Press.

Hashim, A. (2017). 'Pakistani 'terrorist' charity launches political party'. *Al Jazeera* (online news). Retrieved 25 July 2018, from https://www.aljazeera.com/news/2017/08/pakistani-terrorist-charity-launches-political-party-170807155731521.html.

Hofmann, C. (2006). Engaging non-state armed groups in humanitarian action. *International Peacekeeping, 13*(3), 396–409.

Högbladh, S. (2012). Peace agreements 1975–2011: Updating the UCDP peace agreement dataset. In T. Pettersson & L. Themnér (Eds.), *States in armed conflict 2011* (pp. 39–56). Uppsala: Department of Peace and Conflict Research, Uppsala University.

Hoove, L., & Scholtbach, Á. P. (2008). *Democracy and political party assistance in post-conflict societies.* Netherlands Institute for Multi-party Democracy Knowledge Centre, The Hague.

Lamb, R.D., Mixon, K., & Minot, S. (2015). *The uncertain transition from stability to peace.* Washington, DC: Centre for Strategic and International Studies / Rowman and Littlefield.

Linz, J. (1978). *The breakdown of democratic regimes: Crisis, breakdown, and reequilibration.* Baltimore, USA: Johns Hopkins University Press

Lyons, T. (2016). Victorious rebels and post-war politics. *Civil Wars, 18*(2), 1–13.

Mainwaring, S. (1989). *Transitions to democracy and democratic consolidation: Theoretical and comparative issues* (vol. 130). University of Notre Dame, Helen Kellogg Institute for International Studies.

Manning, C. (2004). Armed opposition groups into political parties: comparing Bosnia, Kosovo, and Mozambique. *Studies in Comparative International Development, 39*(1), 54–76.

Martin, S., & Perliger, A. (2012). Turning to and from terror: Deciphering the conditions under which political groups choose violent and nonviolent tactics. *Perspectives on Terrorism, 6*(4/5), 21–45.

Muriaas, R.L., Rakner, L., & Skage, I.A. (2016). Political capital of ruling parties after regime change: Contrasting successful insurgencies to peaceful pro-democracy movements. *Civil Wars, 18*(2), 175–191.

Petrasek, D. (2000). *Ends and means: Human rights approaches to armed groups. International council on human rights policy*. Switzerland: Versoix.

Rosenau, J. (2001). *Along the domestic-foreign frontier: Exploring governance in a turbulent world*. Cambridge, UK: Cambridge University Press.

Rustow, D. (1970). Transitions to democracy. *Comparative Politics 2*, 337–363.

Schlichte, K. (2009). *In the shadow of violence: The politics of armed groups*. Chicago, US: University of Chicago.

Schneckener, U. (2009). Spoilers or governance actors? Engaging armed non-state groups in areas of limited statehood. SFB Governance Working Paper Series No 21, Research Center (SFB) 700, Berlin. Retrieved 3 July 2018, from www.sfb-governance.de/publikationen/working_papers/wp21/SFB-Governance-Working-Paper-21.pdf.

Sindre, G.M., & Söderström, J. (2016). Understanding armed groups and party politics. *Civil Wars, 18*(2), 109–117.

Söderberg K.M., & Hatz, S. (2016). Rebel-to-party transformations in civil war peace processes 1975–2011. *Democratization, 23*, 990–1008.

Söderström, J. (2014). Getting from insurgency to politics. World Politics Review. Retrieved 1 July 2018, from http://www.worldpoliticsreview.com/articles/13863/getting-from-insurgency-topolitics.

Taleski, D. (2011). From bullets to ballots: Guerrilla-to-party transformation in Macedonia. Paper prepared to be presented at the Political Science Departmental Seminar, Central European University. http://web.ceu.hu/polsci/teaching/seminarpapers/Taleski11.pdf.

United Nations (2006). Guidelines on humanitarian negotiations with armed groups. Retrieved 1 July 2018, from http://ochaonline.un.org/humanitariannegotiations/Documents/Guidelines.pdf.

Van Engeland, A., & Rudolph, R.M. (2008). *From terrorism to politics*. London, UK: Ashgate.

19

GOVERNANCE BY SALAFI-JIHADI GROUPS IN THE MIDDLE EAST

Matthew Bamber

INTRODUCTION

Over the past two decades, there has been a substantial rise in the number of Salafi-Jihadi militant groups.[1] Traditionally, Salafi-Jihadi groups have used a mixture of guerrilla and insurgency tactics when engaging in their asymmetric conflicts. Both of these strategies prioritise the need for mobility in the attack. However, in recent years, a number of Salafi-Jihadi groups have abandoned these traditional warfare tactics and instead focused on conquering, holding, and subsequently governing a defined territory. This chapter provides an overview of the motivations behind why Salafi-Jihadist groups choose to pursue a governing strategy. It is followed by an *in-depth case study of Islamic State's governance strategy in Iraq and Syria between 2014 and 2018*, focusing on the advantages and disadvantages of this approach for achieving the stated objectives of this group.

CONTEMPORARY CONCERNS

In comparison to ISIS strikes in the Syrian desert in 2022, ISIS activity in Syria rose in the first quarter of 2023. Although ISIS strikes in northeastern Syria did decline, the group's focus on central Syria is probably to blame. Simply put, ISIS's capacity to continue maintaining support zones in Syria implies that it poses a significant threat to Iraq's hard-won security, particularly given Iraq's failure to effectively eliminate ISIS support zones in rural regions. Government security personnel in the Sahel area are unable to keep militants linked to al Qaeda and the Islamic State in Mali. Despite heightened counterterrorism measures, the Salafi-jihadist group has created new support zones in central Mali (Besenyő & Romaniuk, 2024). These safe havens are probably being used by the organisation to assist attacks on security troops in southern and central Mali.

Security forces are also unlikely to disperse IS-affiliated militants' expanding support networks in northeastern Mali because they place a higher priority on problems in the country's more politically sensitive centre and southern regions. ISIS attack claims in areas under the control of the Syrian Democratic Forces (SDF) decreased in the first quarter of 2023 compared to the same period in 2022, but ISIS is able to compel local communities to support it, so it may not be necessary to carry out attacks as frequently to maintain that support. ISIS doesn't always take credit for its attacks, and it doesn't document non-kinetic behaviour. The first quarter of 2023 may have seen ISIS increase attacks in central Syria while decreasing strikes in northeastern Syria. During the same period, ISIS strikes in the Syrian desert in the centre doubled, while ISIS activity in northeastern Syria declined by half. (Weekly Salafi Jihad Movement Weekly Update, April 27, 2023).

There are between 2,500 and 3,500 ISIS fighters in Syria and Iraq, according to UN estimates (The New York Times, May 15, 2023). According to the Salafi-Jihadi Movement Weekly Update from April 9, 2023, these ISIS warriors have support areas in Syria where they may gather new recruits, train, rest, and prepare for attacks against the military of the regime. Additionally, if the Iraqi Security Forces apply significant pressure to the ISIS cells in western Iraq, they may withdraw to support areas in Syria. In order to prevent ISIS cells from reoccupying rural areas after fleeing ahead of Iraqi offensives, the Iraqi army must first clear and then retain rural territory (al-Kaabi et al., 2023).

DOI: 10.4324/9780429426063-21

WHY DO SALAFI-JIHADI GROUPS CHOOSE TO GOVERN?

Salafi-Jihadism is a religious ideology whose popular usage first emerged in the 1990s. It is a combination of two strands of Islamic belief: salafism and jihadism. Salafists subscribe to the belief that the most authentic Islam is to be found in the lived example of the generations of Muslims (the *salaf*) who lived in the time closest to the Prophet Mohammed, and they attempt to replicate the laws, habits, and customs of the *salaf*. By contrast, jihadists believe that *jihad* (religiously sanctioned warfare) is an individual obligation of all Muslims (Hamid, 2016). Salafi-Jihadists use warfare and violence in order to achieve and impose an Islamic structure that resembles their interpretation of the era of the Prophet Mohammed. The specific tenets of Salafi-Jihadism do not have a common definition, as a broad spectrum of groups, often possessing divergent aims, claim to be Salafi-Jihadists (Hegghammer, 2014, pp. 251–257). In spite of these definitional issues, most contemporary Sunni groups that have been referred to as Islamic terrorists, insurgents, or jihadists describe themselves as Salafi-Jihadists.

The number of Salafi-Jihadist groups has increased dramatically over the past two decades, increasing from just three groups in 1988 to 67 groups by 2018, with the majority of groups located in the Greater Middle East (Jones et al., 2018). Jones ascribes this proliferation to the weakening of governance across the Greater Middle East combined with "the expansion of Salafi-jihadist operatives that have spent time at terrorist training camps, fought on jihadist battlefields, or been released or escaped from prison" (Jones, 2014, p. 26). There has likewise been a concurrent shift in the strategy and tactics pursued by Salafi-Jihadi groups over the past two decades. Salafi-Jihadi militants have traditionally relied on guerrilla and insurgency tactics when engaging their opponents in asymmetric warfare. The goal of Salafi-Jihadi militants was to maintain their mobility so that they could quickly retreat if their adversaries used stronger military force against them. Consequently, the operations of Salafi-Jihadi militants are normally comprised of suicide bomb attacks, improvised explosive devices, ambushes, sniper attacks, and rocket attacks, all of which can be easily achieved by a small team of mobile militants (Hoffman, 2004). In recent years, however, there has been a shift amongst many Salafi-Jihadi groups from prioritising mobility to conquering, holding, and governing a territory and its resident population (Glazzard et al., 2016). This sub-section examines some of the reasons why contemporary Salafi-Jihadi groups in the Middle East have adopted a governance strategy.

Economic Motivation

Like other non-state armed groups (NSAGs) that pursue governance, Salafi-Jihadist groups often decide to conquer and govern territory for its material and economic benefits.[2] The economic advantages of governance are clear when comparing the contrasting financial models of two Salafi-Jihadist groups: al-Qaeda and the Islamic State.

Prior to 2014, al-Qaeda was the most well-financed Salafi-Jihadi group in history. Al Qaeda's strategy does not focus on governing territory, and consequently, it has primarily relied on external sources of funding. Its main revenue stream is through donations that are solicited through an elaborate network of charities, non-governmental organisations, mosques, websites, and individuals (Greenberg et al., 2003). Prior to 9/11, the CIA estimated that al-Qaeda's operational budget was US$30 million, which was almost entirely garnered through fundraising (Roth et al., n.d., p. 19). Due to the worldwide prominence of al-Qaeda in the 2000s and 2010s, much of the counter-terrorism finance operations were based on countering this external model of financing. States enacted national legislation, and new international organisations were created in order to specifically target the fundraising methods of Salafi-Jihadi groups, such as al-Qaeda.[3] In contrast to this external funding approach, Salafi-Jihadi groups that govern territory have the capacity to finance themselves through varied internal revenue streams. These sources of revenue include the exploitation and sale of natural resources within a territory, the taxation of the resident population, agriculture, and human trafficking, among others (FATF, 2015).

Islamic State, when it controlled its Iraqi and Syrian territory between 2014 and 2018, was the most well-financed Salafi-Jihadi group in history and relied overwhelmingly on internal sources of funding that were only achievable by controlling and governing territory. Exact figures for Islamic State's income are difficult to estimate; however, Islamic State's annual revenue in 2015 was approximately between US$1 and US$1.4 billion (Clarke et al., 2017, p. 9). Islamic State's extraction and sale of oil was initially its most significant income source, yielding US $600 million in 2016. However, following effective targeted strikes against Islamic State's oil infrastructure, the taxation of residents became the largest source of income for Islamic State (Centre for the Analysis of Terrorism, 2016; FATF, 2015).

Pursuing a governance strategy thus gives Salafi-Jihadi groups access to a number of potentially lucrative internal revenue streams that are less vulnerable to existing counter-terror financing measures. However, as shown by the concurrent territorial and financial decline of Islamic State in 2017, retaining territory is essential for sustaining the economic advantages of the governance approach.

Legitimacy

Many NSAGs pursue governance in order to gain legitimacy from a specific target audience, such as the international community and states. NSAGs often have the ambition of forming a state or being accepted as the legitimate representative of a population. Therefore, an NSAG often highlights and exhibits its governance in order to prove its governing competence to its target audiences and thus increase its legitimacy. NSAGs that have engaged in governance for legitimacy reasons include the FARC in Colombia, the Tamil Tigers in Sri Lanka, and the Polisario Front in Western Sahara (Schlichte & Schneckener, 2015; Podder, 2017; Terpstra & Frerks, 2017).

Salafi-Jihadi groups similarly aim to gain legitimacy through governance, but crucially, their target audiences often differ from those of NSAGs. Salafi-Jihadists have no interest in joining the Westphalian state system, and consequently, these groups tend not to seek legitimacy from either the international community or states. By contrast, the main target audiences that Salafi-Jihadi groups seek legitimacy from are other Salafi-Jihadi groups, the *ummah* (the Muslim worldwide population), and local sectarian communities.

Pursuing a governance strategy is central to bolstering Salafi-Jihadists claims of legitimacy. Salafi-Jihadi groups that can exhibit their capacity to conquer, hold on to, and govern territory are likely to gain legitimacy and be granted greater authority from other Salafi-Jihadi groups and some parts of the *ummah*. This is partially due to religious reasons (discussed further below), but also because establishing a successful and effective governing regime based on Salafi doctrine is exceptionally rare and thus positively shows the competence, capacity, and authority of that Salafi-Jihadist group.

Islamic State, which established the most extensive governing regime of any contemporary Salafi-Jihadist group between 2014 and 2017, attained legitimacy from its target audiences. It presented the narrative that it had established an effective and fully functioning state, which not only rivalled Western states in terms of capacity but was also organised according to Salafi principles. The legitimacy of Islamic State was confirmed by the fact that at least 41,500 foreign Muslims travelled to Iraq and Syria to join the group (Cook & Vale, 2018) and at least 45 existing Salafi-Jihadist groups pledged their allegiance to Islamic State (Hashim, 2018); this is an unprecedented show of legitimacy for any Salafi-Jihadi group.

Similarly, many Salafi-Jihadi groups exploit fractured sectarian dynamics in order to garner legitimacy from one specific sect of the local population. Often Salafi-Jihadi groups use governance as a legitimising strategy whereby they instill themselves as the sole authority in an area where a state has little control. Often, these sects give legitimacy to the group either through coercion or because the Salafi-Jihadist group actually provides more effective governance than the previous authority in that area.

This pattern has occurred repeatedly in Iraq (since the 2003 invasion) and Syria (since the 2011 revolution), where numerous Salafi-Jihadi groups (most prominently Islamic State) have governed Sunni-majority territory. They have invariably stated that they are the representatives of the local Sunni population and are protecting them against the sectarian attacks of the Iraqi Shia and Syrian Alawi regimes, respectively. Interviews with Iraqis and Syrians who lived under Islamic State control revealed that this was one of the key messages the group used when it entered an area for the first time.[4] Indeed, it was often the case that Islamic State, at least initially, was perceived to have provided greater levels of public security than the regime proceeding them. As such, adopting a governance strategy allows Salafi-Jihadi groups to gain legitimacy from their target audiences of other Salafi-Jihadi groups, the *ummah*, and local sectarian communities.

Religious Obligation

Some Salafi-Jihadi groups view pursuing governance as a religiously ordained obligation, as the conquering and governing of territory is a pre-requisite for establishing an Islamic Caliphate. A caliphate is an Islamic state that is under the stewardship of a caliph and is based upon the model and laws established by the Prophet Mohammed and the *Rashidun* (the four successor caliphs) (Maher, 2016). In the doctrine of many Salafi-Jihadi groups, striving to establish a Caliphate is an individual obligation (*fard al-ayn*) for all Muslims, and once a Caliphate has been declared, it is mandatory for all Muslims to emigrate to the Caliphate in order to defend it (Jones, 2014). Accordingly, some Salafi-Jihadi groups believe that adopting a governance strategy is a necessary stepping stone that must be achieved in order to reach the ultimate objective of establishing a Caliphate. Therefore, for those Salafi-Jihadi groups that aspire to establish a Caliphate, they must pursue a governance strategy.

This is clearly shown when comparing the differing strategies of al-Qaeda and the Islamic State. Al-Qaeda has exerted little effort towards establishing a physical caliphate; its leaders have very rarely mentioned it in their speeches, and they have taken few tangible steps to realise the necessary pre-conditions for declaring a caliphate (Pankhurst, 2013). As a consequence, al-Qaeda has not pursued a governance strategy, as they are not primarily concerned with establishing an Islamic Caliphate. By contrast, Islamic State has been committed to the idea of establishing an Islamic Caliphate since 2006, when they were named Islamic State in Iraq (Bunzel, 2015). This commitment to the Caliphate has been the driving force behind its governance strategy, which it concurrently adopted in 2006.

Intra-Salafi Jihadi Competition

A final factor that has pushed contemporary Middle Eastern Salafi-Jihadi groups to pursue governance is the ongoing rivalry and competition between the two preeminent worldwide Salafi-Jihadi groups: al-Qaeda and the Islamic State. These two groups have been in competition for the legitimacy and material support of the worldwide Jihadi community since slightly prior to al-Qaeda's disavowal of the Islamic State on February 2, 2014. Al-Qaeda made this decision due to the Islamic State's unilateral decision to absorb the al-Qaeda-affiliated Syrian group Jabhat al-Nusra without the permission of al-Qaeda's leadership.

Following the declaration of the Caliphate on June 29, 2014, and the subsequent governance of territory in Iraq and Syria, the Islamic State unequivocally supplanted al-Qaeda as the premier worldwide Salafi-Jihadi group. This was exhibited by the fact that at least 41,500 foreign nationals travelled to Iraq and Syria to join the groups, and at least 45 existing Salafi-Jihadist groups pledged their allegiance to Abu Bakr al-Baghdadi, including many former al-Qaeda-affiliated groups (Cook & Vale, 2018). It appears that much of the worldwide Salafi-Jihadi community wanted to support a Caliphate, and following the declaration, many quickly rescinded their previous pledges of allegiance to al-Qaeda and their leadership.

The subsequent tactical decisions of al-Qaeda reflect the group's realisation of its fall from prominence. It attempted to win back support through a failed emulation of the Islamic State's governance tactics. Following the declaration of the caliphate, al-Qaeda attempted to establish a quasi-caliphate in Afghanistan to challenge the Islamic State's declaration. It re-released a 2001 video of Osama bin Laden swearing allegiance to Mullah Omar (the now-deceased leader of the Afghanistan Taliban) and hailing him as *Amir al-Mu'minin* (Commander of the Faithful, one of the titles given to a Caliph). Al Qaeda also released a newsletter reaffirming that all of al-Qaeda pledged allegiance to Mullah Omar and that it still considers him to be *Amir al-Mu'minin* (Bunzel, 2014). This attempt to position Afghanistan as a new quasi-Caliphate was a failure, as it did not draw any support away from Islamic State or its affiliates supporters. This is in spite of the fact that the Taliban's original governance model, based on an emirate model and without any reference to a caliphate, has successfully endured beyond the caliphate established by Islamic State in Iraq and Syria.

Without establishing a caliphate, Islamic State would not have enjoyed the huge fluxes of human and material capital from the Salafi-Jihadi community that sustained the group between 2014 and 2017. Pursuing a governance strategy thus allowed Islamic State to become the premier worldwide Salafi-Jihadi group at the expense of al-Qaeda.

CASE STUDY OF ISLAMIC STATE GOVERNANCE

This section provides a detailed overview of the Islamic State's governance strategy in Iraq and Syria between 2014 and 2018. It details the historical trajectory of Islamic State's governance strategy, the governing structure it established in Iraq and Syria, and the advantages and disadvantages this brought for the group. The Islamic State case study is relevant for understanding the broader topic of governance by Salafi-Jihadist groups as it governed the most extensive area of territory in the history of contemporary Middle Eastern Salafi-Jihadi groups. Although Islamic State was routed from the overwhelming majority of its territory by the end of 2018, the group's governance struggles illuminate many of the issues, advantages, and limitations that face other Middle Eastern Salafi-Jihadi groups when they adopt a governance strategy.

Historical Trajectory of the Islamic State's Governance Strategy

Prior to 2006, al-Qaeda in Iraq (the name for Islamic State between 2004 and 2006) showed little interest in governance, despite the fact that the group controlled large swathes of Sunni-majority territory during the Iraq war. A limited number of judicial and security institutions were created in a decentralised and haphazard fashion, including a "Religious Police Office" and "Sharia Courts", but there was no governing strategy. Instead, Al Qaeda in Iraq primarily used insurgency tactics targeting multinational forces and the Iraqi Shia population in a campaign of suicide bombings and IED attacks (Napoleoni, 2005; Zelin, 2014).

Al-Qaeda in Iraq changed its name to the Islamic State in Iraq in October 2006. This was more than a mere name change and represented Islamic State's commitment to governing in the territories it controlled. This strategic change was partially at the behest of the central al-Qaeda leadership, which advocated in a series of letters for the Islamic State in Iraq leadership to establish an Islamic state that would attract support from the worldwide Salafi-Jihadi community (Bunzel, 2015). As a result, the Islamic State in Iraq declared a new "state" across the Sunni-majority provinces of Ninavah, Anbar, and Salahaldin, in addition to the Shia-dominated provinces of Babil, Wasit, Diyala, Baghdad, and Kirkuk. In reality, however, the control of Islamic State in Iraq was merely limited to a number of zones in Fallujah, Anbar, Abu Ghraib, al-Karmah, and Dijla that were governed as decentralised independent emirates (Napoleoni, 2014). Islamic State in Iraq had no concerted governing strategy apart from declaring a state; this led to the succinct analysis that Islamic State in Iraq was no more than a "paper state" (Bunzel, 2015). Even this limited paper state was decimated by 2010, when the Islamic State in Iraq was reduced to a few miles of territory in Mosul due to the combined effectiveness of the US surge strategy, the Sahwa movement, and internal Islamic State in Iraq structural problems.

By 2010, Islamic State in Iraq was at its territorial nadir; it was forced to revert to insurgency tactics revolving around two main campaigns: "Breaking the Walls" (freeing members from Iraqi prisons) and "Soldiers' Harvest" (bombing and assassination operations against Iraqi security forces). In spite of this, the period between 2010 and 2014 was essential for the development of the previous Islamic State's governing strategy, as it forced a period of self-reflection about the weaknesses in its previous strategy and led to changes in its governance approach. Internal Islamic State documents reveal that Islamic State in Iraq blamed its governance failures on four major factors: its harsh treatment of and failure to integrate itself with the local civilian population; the division of its members into four specialist units that bred isolation amongst its members; the appointed leaders were often arrogant, refused to fight, and were too far removed from the reality of Islamic State soldiers; and that its financial institutions were unable to cope with the flow of revenue it received and were therefore not able to send money efficiently to the different areas under Islamic State control.[5]

The revival of the Islamic State occurred under the leadership of Abu Bakr al-Baghdadi, who became the leader of the Islamic State in Iraq in May 2010. Al-Baghdadi exploited both the vacuum left by the withdrawal of US forces and the rising Sunni anger against the sectarian actions of Shiite Prime Minister Nouri al-Maliki. Islamic State began re-conquering territory and developed a governing strategy that incorporated the lessons learned from the group's previous failed attempts. In April 2013, al-Baghdadi unilaterally announced that the Islamic State in Iraq was forming with the Syrian group Jabhat al-Nusra to create the Islamic State in Iraq and Syria (ISIS).[6] This decision led to Islamic State's eventual disavowal by Al Qaeda, while Islamic State focused on conquering territory in Syria and began implementing governing structures in Raqqa and Aleppo provinces. In June 2014, Islamic State began a successful new campaign in Iraq's al-Anbar, Ninveah, and Salahadin provinces, seizing control of at least 20 towns, including Mosul and Tikrit. On June 29, Abu Bakr al-Baghdadi announced the changing of the group's name to Islamic State and the establishment of an Islamic Caliphate stretching across the group's Iraqi and Syrian territories (Mohamedou, 2017).

Islamic State Governance Structure

Between 2014 and 2017, the Islamic State embarked on an unprecedented governance project in Syria and Iraq. The group's primary focus was on state-building – establishing governing institutions that would enable the group to create an effective and viable state. At its peak in 2015, Islamic State controlled an area of approximately 90,000 square kilometres and governed the lives of eight million residents under its control. However, Islamic State's governing project was ultimately unsuccessful, as the group had lost almost all of its territory by 2018. This sub-section provides a detailed analysis of the governing institutions and structures that Islamic State established in Syria and Iraq before assessing the various advantages and disadvantages that the adoption of a governing strategy brought the group.

A video published by Islamic State in 2016 reveals the governing structure that the group envisioned implementing in Syria and Iraq.[7] The Islamic State proposed a federal state structure that divided the entirety of Syria and Iraq into 19 provinces (*wilyat)* that were approximately aligned with the previous provinces established by the Syrian and Iraqi states.[8] Documents released by Islamic State reveal that it envisioned a governing structure composed of both federal and provincial level offices. At the federal level, the sovereign head of Islamic State is the "Caliph" who is tasked with upholding religion in the state, preparing the defences of Islamic State and ensuring that all governance is aligned with Sharia law. In these matters, the Caliph is supported by a "Shura Council" composed of clerics. The other main federal body of Islamic State is the "Delegated Committee", which is responsible for communicating and executing orders and overseeing the other three branches of Islamic State: "Provinces", "*Diwans*", *and* "Offices and Committees".

Within each province, the Caliph appoints a governor who is in charge of the running and security of the province but who is ultimately answerable to the federal "Delegated Committee". Islamic State envisioned having 14 *diwans,* which have representative offices in each province. These *diwan* fulfil a similar role to government ministries and cover a specific area of governance: "Judiciary and Ombudsman", "Religious Police", "Mosques and Proselytism", "Religious Taxes", "Military", "Public Security", "Treasury", "Media" "Education", "Health", "Agriculture", "Natural Resources", "War Spoils", and "Public Services".

Alongside the *diwan*, there are six specialised "Committees and Offices" that are under the auspices of the "Delegated Committee" and were created to deal with cross-provincial governance issues: "Research and Studies", "Emigration to the Islamic State", "Public and Tribal Relations", "Affairs of Prisoners and Martyrs", and "Administration of Distant Provinces". Islamic State thus had a clear ambition for the state they wanted to create: a mixture of federal and provincial-level governing institutions that each had a clearly demarcated area of responsibility.

In reality, however, Islamic State was unable to achieve its desired level of capability and efficacy in its governance. Although it divided its territory into 19 provinces, Islamic State only had territorial control in 13 provinces for some time between 2014 and 2018. In addition, the number of diwans that it established varied significantly. In those provinces where Islamic State was in control for longer than one year, such as Ninevah, Raqqa, al-Furat, and al-Khayr, it established a series of diwans covering public services, the judiciary, education, healthcare, the military, and finance. However, in those provinces where it was in control for shorter periods of time, it could only establish basic security institutions.[9] In spite of these governing deficiencies, ISIS still embarked on an ambitious project that stretched across a larger area than any other contemporary Middle Eastern Salafi-Jihadi group. The following two sub-sections detail the advantages and disadvantages that adopting this governance strategy brought to the Islamic State.

Advantages of Governance Strategy for Islamic State

The governance ambitions of Islamic State between 2014 and 2018 brought several advantages for the group that would not have been feasible if it had not adopted a governing strategy. Firstly, Islamic State's governing achievements allowed it to make the claim that it had established an Islamic Caliphate and for this to be accepted by a substantial part of the worldwide Salafi-Jihadi community. The establishment of the Caliphate convinced tens of thousands of foreign Muslims to emigrate to Iraq and Syria, bringing with them a diversity of skills, materials, and monetary resources that significantly helped the Islamic State consolidate the amount of territory under its control. The governing of territory and the creation of state-like governing institutions were central to the Caliphate declaration being accepted by these persons and were a core tenet of the Islamic State's self-narrative. This narrative was propagated through Islamic State's unique use of social media, which the group used to spread messages, videos, and magazines emphasising its purported governance achievements (Winter, 2017). This is shown in Abu Bakr al-Baghdadi's inaugural speech of the Caliphate on July 4, 2014, where he stated: "Rush, O Muslims to your state; it is your state, because Syria is not for Syrians and Iraq is not for Iraqis".[10] If Islamic State had not pursued a governance strategy, it would not have been able to support its claim to have established a Caliphate, which was central to attracting the support of the worldwide Salafi-Jihadi community.

Furthermore, pursuing a governance strategy that led to the creation of an Islamic Caliphate pushed the Islamic State to surpass al-Qaeda as the premier global Salafi-Jihadist group. After Islamic State and al-Qaeda severed ties in 2014, there was a concurrent schism in the worldwide Salafi-Jihadi community over who to support in the divide (Zelin, 2014). The announcement of the Caliphate (although dismissed as false and heretical by al-Qaeda-supporting Salafi-Jihadists) proved to be the ultimate determinant that the Islamic State had overtaken al-Qaeda (Hamming, 2017).

This is evidenced by the unprecedented number of individual Salafi-Jihadists who fled to Iraq and Syria and the number of worldwide Salafi-Jihadis who pledged allegiance to Abu Bakr al-Baghdadi. More than 45 Salafi-Jihadi organisations publicly pledged allegiance to the Islamic State from diverse places such as Nigeria, the Philippines, Uzbekistan, and Mali, amongst many others. Islamic State did not acknowledge the majority of these pledges, although it did turn a number of them into sanctioned Islamic State provinces; these include the Nigerian group Boko Haram, which became the Islamic State in West Africa, and the Egyptian group Ansar Beit al-Maqdis, which subsequently became the Islamic State in the Sinai (Gerges, 2016).

A determining factor in whether Islamic State accepted a pledge of allegiance was that the Salafi-Jihadi group had to likewise be committed to conquering and governing the territory under its rule. An article in Dabiq, an Islamic State-produced digital magazine, listed the criteria that a group had to meet in order to be an official Islamic State province; these include being the sole Salafi-Jihadist group in the area and having a blueprint that has been accepted by the central Islamic State leadership for conquering and governing territory (Gambhir, 2014). Thus, Islamic State was able to create a worldwide network of Salafi-Jihadist groups similarly committed to the concept of governance. This would not have been possible if the Islamic State had not adopted a governing strategy.

The final advantage of the governance strategy for Islamic State is that it successfully indoctrinated an entire generation of Iraqis and Syrians with the notion that establishing an Islamic governing regime is their primary obligation. Islamic State had three years (in some areas of Syria and Iraq) to impose its ideology on the resident population. In interviews with Iraqis and Syrians who lived under Islamic State rule, it appears that children were particularly targeted for indoctrination. Islamic State created a Diwan of Education that completely changed the school curriculum by removing subjects that it viewed as heretical and teaching subjects that instilled and reinforced ISIS's ideology. Accordingly, students were no longer able to learn subjects such as history, sociology, and foreign languages but instead took courses on the Qur'an, Sharia sciences, and weapons. Even though students could still learn math, their new exercise books made them learn to count bombs and calculate how many survivors there would be after a suicide attack (al-Tamimi, 2016). Although Islamic State was territorially defeated in 2018, there is a whole generation of people who have been indoctrinated and will strive again to establish an Islamic state in the same areas. If Islamic State hadn't adopted a governing strategy, they would not have been able to create such a swell of support for their ideology in Iraq and Syria.

Disadvantages of Governance Strategy for Islamic State

In spite of the significant advantages that the governance strategy brought to Islamic State, it was also integral to Islamic State's territorial defeats over the period 2014–2018. Over the course of four years, the intricate governing institutions, apparatus, and systems that Islamic State established were degraded and ultimately abandoned in the face of the combined military operations of the Operation Inherent Resolve coalition partners, Iran, Russia, Turkey, Iraq, and the Syrian regime.

There are several reasons that suggest the Islamic State's governing strategy was a significant contributing factor to its territorial decline. Pursuing such a complex governing strategy required Islamic State to divert significant material and human resources into these civil institutions rather than into military operations. Within weeks of gaining control of Mosul, Islamic State established a series of non-military *diwans*, including public services and education, that attempted to provide the same level of service provision that residents had under the previous regime (Revkin, 2016). This is despite the fact that Islamic State is still engaged in a military campaign to conquer further territory in Anbar and Ninevah provinces. Even when Islamic State faced imminent military defeat, it still devoted significant resources to maintaining the governing institutions it had established. In the days immediately prior to the fall of Aleppo, the Islamic State's governor of Aleppo province wrote a letter to all of the Islamic State's civilian employees under his purview, demanding that they stay in their positions until the Islamic State is victorious or they are killed.[11] This obstinance in Islamic State's commitment to governance meant that it was unable to shift valuable resources to its military operations, which were required to maintain its territory.

Islamic State's governing strategy was also not successful in satisfying the demands of its resident population. Testimony from civilians who lived in Islamic State areas indicates that after an initial period of contentment with Islamic State rule (especially in Iraq), the resident population became exceptionally disaffected. A major aspect of this dissatisfaction was the harsh judicial system of the Islamic State, which it claimed was based on Shariah law.[12] The punishments for breaking these laws include the removal of hands for stealing; the removal of two fingers (plus a fine and prison sentence) for smoking cigarettes; and the execution (by hanging or shooting) for using a mobile phone or laptop. This exceptionally strict form of governance was a contributing factor to the lack of enthusiasm for Islamic State rule. Accordingly, Islamic State had to continually expend efforts on policing its resident population due to their dissatisfaction with the group (Revkin & Kao, 2018). These are resources that were required for Islamic State's military campaigns it was waging to maintain control of its territory.

Due to its hardline Salafi-Jihadi governance style, Islamic State was frequently viewed by the local populace as an enemy occupier rather than a legitimate Iraqi or Syrian military group. Islamic State made the decision to deliberately work to overthrow any competing authorities as soon as it took control of a new region rather than incorporating any local authority structures into its ruling regime. This is demonstrated by how it treats the regional indigenous populations. Forcing existing tribes to pledge allegiance to Abu Bakr al-Baghdadi in a group pledging ceremony whenever Islamic State acquired a new region through either killing them, coopting younger assenting members of a tribe, or killing them (Al-Baalbaky & Mhidi, 2018).

This is in contrast to other Salafi-Jihadi groups in the region, which were perceived by the local population as being more indigenously Syrian or Iraqi. Most notably, Hayat Tahrir al-Sham (previously Jabhat al-Nusra), Islamic State's main Salafi-Jihadi competitor in northern Syria, was perceived as being more Syrian than Islamic State.[13] This is because they successfully integrated existing authority structures into their governance, included local Syrians in their hierarchy, and reached out to the local population. Pursuing a governance strategy for Islamic State ended up alienating the overwhelming majority of its resident population due to the perceived foreign and extreme nature of its governance.[14]

Finally, Islamic State's ambitions for power made it difficult for it to survive. Islamic State was not satisfied with establishing a small number of security and judicial institutions to manage its resident population. Instead, it endeavoured to offer a form of social contract to its residents that replicated the existing relationship between modern nation-states and their citizens (Revkin, 2016). This notion of governance is far beyond the ambitions of any other contemporary Salafi-Jihadist group. Islamic State also attempted to do this in areas that it had only recently gained control of or that were still militarily contested. This governance commitment meant that once Islamic State began to fail territorially in 2016, it could not easily shift resources to its military. It still attempted to maintain these governance institutions even when they were being destroyed beneath them. Accordingly, Islamic State's governance ambitions meant that it was easier to eradicate territorially because it could not devote resources to fighting or simply withdraw from an area, like other Salafi-Jihadi groups.

CONCLUSION

This chapter has detailed the various motivations for why an increasing number of Salafi-Jihadi groups in the Middle East have adopted a governance strategy at the expense of traditional insurgency tactics. Among the primary incentives of Salafi-Jihadi groups are a desire for greater economic strength, an opportunity to gain the legitimacy of the worldwide Salafi-Jihadi community, and the perception that pursuing governance is a necessary precondition for establishing an Islamic Caliphate. A case study of Islamic State's governance strategy highlighted how the group has been committed to pursuing a governance strategy since 2006, which reached its zenith in *2014–2018*. Islamic State attempted to establish an unprecedentedly complex federal governing system across its Iraqi and Syrian provinces that provided for the health, educational, legal, and security needs of its resident population. Although its governing ambitions were ultimately unsuccessful, Islamic State's pursuit of a governing strategy brought a series of distinct advantages and disadvantages for the group that are analytically useful for interpreting the future governing projects of other Salafi-Jihadi groups in the Middle East.

Notes

1 The Greater Middle East here refers to the countries of both the Mashriq and Maghreb regions.
2 For a detailed discussion of the political economy aspects of non-state armed groups, see Weinstein, 2007.
3 Examples of these include the UN Counter-Terrorism Implementation Task Force (created in 2005); the Financial Action Task Force (which adopted its Eight Special Recommendations on Terrorist Financing in October 2001); and the Terrorist Finance Tracking Programme (a joint US-EU programme developed after the September 11, 2001 attacks).
4 Personal interviews conducted by the author between 2018 and 2019 in Iraq, Lebanon, and Turkey with former residents of Islamic State territories.
5 Document available from the Combatting Terrorism Centre at Westpoint: https://ctc.usma.edu/wpcontent/uploads/2013/09/Analysis-of-the-State-of-ISI-Translation.pdf
6 Abu Bakr al-Baghdadi claims to have actually initially created Jabhat al-Nusra by sending a detachment of Islamic State soldiers to Syria in August 2011 under the command of Abu Mohammed al-Jawlani. This version of events was rejected by both Al Qaeda and al-Golani, who rejected the merger.
7 A copy of the video in English is available at: http://jihadology.net/?s=Structure+of+the+Caliphate; A transcript and infographic of the video are available here: http://interactive.achariricenter.org/wp-content/uploads/2016/07/Structure-of-ISIS-Final-1.pdf
8 New provinces created by the Islamic State include al-Khayr, al-Dijlah, and al-Furat.
9 This finding is based on the author's analysis of a database of primary documents released by Islamic State's provincial governing institutions.
10 An English translation of the speech is available here: http://www.gatestoneinstitute.org/documents/baghdadi-caliph.pdf
11 During 2018 interviews in Lebanon, a former Aleppo resident gave the author a copy of this document.
12 This is based on personal interviews conducted by the author between 2018 and 2019 in Iraq, Lebanon, and Turkey with former residents of Islamic State territories.
13 This is based on personal interviews conducted by the author between 2018 and 2019 in Iraq, Lebanon, and Turkey with former residents of Islamic State territories.
14 This is based on personal interviews conducted by the author between 2018 and 2019 in Iraq, Lebanon, and Turkey with former residents of Islamic State territories.

References

al-Baalbaky, R., & Mhidi, A. (2018). *Tribes and the rule of the "Islamic State": The case of the Syrian city of Deir az-Zor*. Issam Fares Institute for Public Policy and International Affairs.

al-Kaabi, A., Knights, M., & Malik, H. (2023). *The Jury al-Sakhar Model: Militias Debate how to carve out a new enclave North of Baghdad. Policy analysis*. Washington D.C.: The Washington Institute.

al-Tamimi, A.J. (2016). A caliphate under strain: The documentary evidence. *CTC Sentinel*, *9*(4), 1–9.

Besenyő, J., & Romaniuk, S. N. (2024, June 7). Mali: comment l'insécurité, l'incertitude et le chaos favorisent le terrorisme. *The Conversation*. https://theconversation.com/mali-comment-linsecurite-lincertitude-et-le-chaos-favorisent-le-terrorisme-230323

Bunzel, C. (2014). *Al-Qaeda's Quasi-Caliph: The recasting of Mullah 'Umar*, Jihadica, July 23.

Bunzel, C. (2015). *From paper state to caliphate: The ideology of the Islamic State*. Brookings Institution.

Centre for the Analysis of Terrorism. (2016). *ISIS financing 2015*. Centre for the Analysis of Terrorism.

Clarke, C., Jackson, K., Johnston, P., Robinson, E., & Shatz, H. (2017). *Financial Futures of the Islamic State of Iraq and the Levant: Findings from a RAND corporation workshop*. RAND Corporation.

Cook, J., & Vale, G. (2018). *From Daesh to 'Diaspora': Tracing the Women and Minors of Islamic State* (p. 76). King's College London: International Centre for the Study of Radicalisation.

FATF. (2015). *Financing of the terrorist organisation Islamic State in Iraq and the Levant (ISIL)*. Financial Action Task Force.

Gambhir, H.K. (2014). *Dabiq: The strategic messaging of the Islamic State*. Institute for the Study of War.

Gerges, F.A. (2016). *ISIS: A history*. Princeton: Princeton University Press.

Glazzard, A., Jesperson, S., Maguire, T., & Winterbotham, E. (2016). *Conflict and Islamist violent extremism (Summary Paper)*. Royal United Services Institute.

Greenberg, M.R., Wechsler, W.F., & Wolosky, L.S. (2003). *Terrorist financing: Report of an independent task force sponsored by the Council on Foreign Relations*. Council on Foreign Relations.

Hamid, S. (2016). *Islamic exceptionalism: How the struggle over Islam is reshaping the world* (First edition). New York, NY: St. Martin's Press.

Hamming, T.R. (2017). The Al Qaeda–Islamic state rivalry: Competition yes, but no competitive escalation. *Terrorism and Political Violence*, *32*(1), 1–18.

Hashim, A. (2018). *The caliphate at war: The ideological, organisational and military innovations of Islamic State*. London: Hurst & Company.

Hegghammer, T. (2014). Jihadi-Salafis or revolutionaries? In R. Meijer (Ed.), *Global salafism* (pp. 245–266). Oxford: Oxford University Press.

Hoffman, B. (2004). *Insurgency and counterinsurgency in Iraq*. Santa Monica: RAND, National Security Research Division.

Jones, S.G. (2014). *A persistent threat: The evolution of Al Qa'ida and other Salafi jihadists*. RAND.

Jones, S., Vallee C., Newlee, D., Harrington, N., Sharb, C., & Byrne, H. (2018). *The evolution of the Salafi-Jihadist threat*. Washington, DC: Center for Strategic and International Studies.

Maher, S. (2016). *Salafi-jihadism: The history of an idea*. Oxford: Oxford University Press.

Mohamedou, M.-M. O. (2017). *A theory of ISIS: Political violence, and the transformation of the global order*. United Kingdom: Pluto Press.

Napoleoni, L. (2005). *Insurgent Iraq: Al Zarqawi and the new generation* (1st North American ed). New York: Seven Stories Press.

Napoleoni, L. (2014). *The Islamist phoenix: The Islamic state and the redrawing of the Middle East*. New York: Seven Stories Press.

Pankhurst, R. (2013). *The inevitable Caliphate? A history of the struggle for global Islamic union, 1924 to present*. London: Hurst & Company.

Podder, S. (2017). Understanding the legitimacy of armed groups: A relational perspective. *Small Wars & Insurgencies*, *28*(4-5), 686–708.

Revkin, M. (2016). *Does the Islamic state have a "Social Contract"? Evidence from Iraq and Syria* (No. Working Paper No.9; pp. 1–37). The Program on Governance and Local Development: University of Gothenburg.

Revkin, M., & Kao, K. (2018). *To punish or to pardon? Reintegrating rebel collaborators after conflict in Iraq* (No. 17). The Program on Governance and Local Development: University of Gothenburg.

Roth, J., Greenburg, D., & Wille, S. (n.d.). *National commission on terrorist attacks upon the United States: Monograph on terrorist financing*. National Commission on Terrorist Attacks Upon the United States.

Schlichte, K., & Schneckener, U. (2015). Armed groups and the politics of legitimacy. *Civil Wars*, *17*(4), 409–424.

Terpstra, N., & Frerks, G. (2017). *Rebel governance and legitimacy: Understanding the impact of rebel legitimation on civilian compliance with the LTTE Rule*. Civil Wars, 1–29.

The New York Times. (May 15, 2023). Salafi-Jihadist Groups Converge.

Weinstein, J.M. (2007). *Inside rebellion: The politics of insurgent violence*. Cambridge; New York: Cambridge University Press.

Winter, C. (2017). *Media Jihad: The Islamic state's doctrine for information Warfare* (p. 28). International Centre for the Study of Radicalisation.

Zelin, A.Y. (2014). *The war between Isis and Al-Qaeda for supremacy of the global jihadist movement* (Research Notes No. 20) (pp. 1–11). Washington Institute for Near East Policy.

20

THE ANATOMY OF TERROR

The Agents and Audiences of Political Terror

Jeroen J. J. Van den Bosch

INTRODUCTION

When encountering the word "terrorism," the average 21st-century reader automatically recalls images of hijacked plane crashes, bomb and knife attacks in European cities, militant Jihadis in the Central Asian mountain passes, and bustling bazaars in the Middle East blown up by suicide bombers. The combination of the surge in media, post-9/11 security doctrines, and the continued ideological clash between liberal democracy and Islamism has blinded many observers to the heterogeneity of terrorism when it comes to its ideological drivers, tactic applications, and evolution throughout human history. The goal of this chapter is not to provide an exhaustive diachronic overview of the phenomenon of terrorism but to reinterpret terror as a political concept and unleash it from its biased political shackles in order to reconnect with earlier explanations of the existing literature and with new insights from related fields, like genocide studies, political regime theory, and the study of sub-state actors.

This chapter is inspired by the Frankfurt School, Critical Terrorism Studies (Jackson et al., 2009), and other works that seek a broader explanation of the uses of terror (Jackson et al., 2010; Koch, 2016). From such a perspective, the current, predominant concept of terrorism is tainted by reductive, narrow political interpretations and biased in favour of normative definitions by elites in Western states, reducing the phenomenon only to the label "violence of which they do not approve." While terrorism studies have been peevishly labelled as "counterinsurgency masquerading as political science" as early as 1988 (Schmid & Jongman, 1988, 182), the basic criticisms of critical theory nonetheless are valid: current definitions of terrorism, claiming to be objective, underpin existing power structures and reproduce the *status quo* in international relations together with its asymmetries of power, wealth, and opportunity (Jackson et al., 2009, 78, 91).

Defining terrorism is a political problem, not a linguistic one (Toscano, 2007, 111). However, keeping in mind the conceptual fatigue clouding the term, my aim is not to reproduce this discussion in full but to use it as a starting point to try something new. For the purpose of this chapter, I propose to drop the narrow interpretation of terrorism as a starting point and just move one rung up the ladder of abstraction by redefining political terror. Then, by decoupling political terror from its perpetrators (agents) as well as intended victims and audiences, my approach unshackles the concept from its usual suspects, sub-state agents, and its usual victims (non-combatants), and allows me to map all empirical links between potential agents of terror and various intended audiences and cover each dyad of interaction separately to compare their repertoires.

MAPPING POLITICAL TERROR

Conceptualising Terror: Back to Basics

Political terror has been defined before (e.g., Wilkinson 1974), but usually in juxtaposition to political terrorism. The former is then considered synonymous with state terror or top-down terrorism, and the latter with bottom-up terrorism, along the lines of the widely accepted definition by Bruce Hoffman (2006) and the current interpretation of the US State Department: "Premeditated, politically motivated violence perpetrated against non-combatant targets by sub-national groups or clandestine agents, usually intended to influence an audience."[1] In both cases, either its agents (perpetrators) and/or its targets (victims) are key defining elements necessary to distinguish it from other forms of violent acts. So, how can we define political terror without relying on its relationship with agents or targets?

 DOI: 10.4324/9780429426063-22

Maybe our first question should be, "What is terror?" And instead of pursuing the etymological origins of *terrere* or *deterrere*, I mean: how is terror understood today in its contemporary Anglo-Saxon context? After browsing the Oxford, Cambridge, and Merriam-Webster dictionaries, terror's most common synonyms are listed as *fear, dread,* and *angst,* and as shown in Figure 20.1, despite the multiple

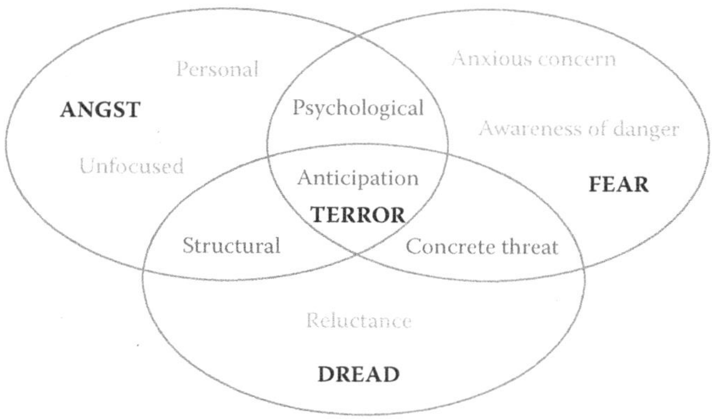

Figure 20.1 Mapping Terror.

Source: Author's compilation.

overlaps in meaning, they all differ on some dimensions. Ignoring the impossible task of ranking all four concepts based on intensity, which is subjective and would require focusing on agents and targets once again, it is clear that *fear* and *dread* share the fact that they are provoked by a concrete threat, unlike *angst,* which is more of a general, unfocused feeling of impending evil. On the other hand, *dread* and *angst* are more structural: Not in the sense that they are caused by a threat that is frequent or repetitive, but because of the acquaintance or familiarity of the subject experiencing the emotion with its cause. *In* this regard, fear is more neutral and can be sudden or related to a previous unfamiliar threat (e.g., fear of the unknown). Other differences are that *dread* is often synonymous with reluctance; *fear* with the awareness of danger; and *angst is* associated with a unique personal psychological state that is partly the cause of the discomfort. As the overlap in Figure 20.1 shows, according to leading dictionaries, *terror* is thus a structural, psychological fear derived from the anticipation of a concrete evil.

This definition of terror can serve as a solid base when constructing a working definition for political terror. In order for an act to be political, it has to have political aims and therefore instrumentalise some form of power to alter the behaviour of a target group. As Wilkinson (1974, 12) noted four decades ago, "outside the pages of science fiction, it is impossible to conceive of an actual political terror that does not resort to extreme violence against the person (in the sense of destructive harm)." Alas, with cyberterrorism, the future is upon us. Despite the difficulties in labelling this specific form of violence, which is very agent-specific and has not claimed a single life up until today, many scholars have concluded that the psychological fear it causes can rival that of traditional terrorism (Gross et al., 2016; 2017).

Since the aim is to account for the power of fear in obtaining political goals regardless of agents and targets, I define "political terror" as "the use of structural fear in anticipation of unexpected acts of premeditated, indiscriminate violence generated from (specific) threats or previous violent acts, as a strategy to alter the behaviour of other groups and achieve political aims."

Before linking this working definition with potential agents and audiences, four remarks: Firstly, the audience's *fear of* indiscriminate violence does not automatically mean that those committing the violence are targeting their victims indiscriminately. The perception of a lack of discrimination helps to spread fear, making terror more effective, for, as Wilkinson (1974, 14) put it, "if no one in particular is a target, no one can be safe." This does not mean that all acts of political terror are indiscriminate. Secondly, by remaining aloof from including agents and targets in the definition, it becomes possible to attribute the use of terror to a variety of agents, some acting in other violent roles like guerrillas or political regimes, but also to others that have been conspicuously absent from the study of the uses of terror, like organised crime networks. Thirdly, my choice of the word *strategy* (instead of tactic) is to underscore the larger endgame of those engaged in intentionally causing terror. But at any time, for various agents, the use of terror can be just one of many ways to obtain political goals. Finally, this working definition is amoral, separating the legality or moral interpretation of the act from the political act itself.

Putting the State Back in and Going Beyond

Before 2007, major works on state terrorism were rare.[2] After the decay or decimation of anti-colonial and Marxist terrorist organisations, terrorism in general abated by the late 1990s before resurging to unprecedented heights. The attacks of 9/11 blended the popular understanding of terrorism with militant Islamism and global Jihadism. In this same shift, Western states and their populations became foremost viewed as defenders against or victims of terror, respectively. The "War on Terror" expanded these labels to other allied states. As these alliances formulated new anti-terror policies, they strengthened their legitimacy by denouncing acts of terrorism as fanatic or illegal, building upon the Western tradition that considers violence legitimate only when it is practised by the state (Chaliand & Blin, 2007, 7). Nonetheless:

> in comparison to the terrorism perpetrated by non-state insurgent groups, the few thousand deaths and injuries caused by "terrorism from below" every year pales into relative insignificance besides the hundreds of thousands of people killed, kidnapped, "disappeared," injured, tortured, raped, abused, intimidated, and threatened by state agents and their proxies in dozens of countries across the globe. (Jackson et al., 2010, 1)

This is why any definition of political terror has to include state agents.

However, it is not enough to stop at that level of analysis. One has to crack open the black box of the state and look at the political regime in charge. There are many sub-classifications of regimes, all with their own merits (Van den Bosch, 2014), but only those typologies that focus on the nature and size of the organisational nexus of regimes will be most helpful to assess their relation to political terror. In addition, the "openness" of their political system as well as the ruling ideology – their comprehensive worldview that legitimises and guides political action by the ruling elite – are key elements that can turn regimes into targets or perpetrators of terror. In this chapter, my basic point of departure will be the typology of Geddes et al. (2014) to classify regimes, differentiating between monarchies, single-party, military, and personalist regimes.

Dyads of Terror: Agents and Targets

My proposed working definition permits me to extend political terror to more than just states (regimes), guerrillas, and traditional "terrorist" organisations. Figure 20.2, therefore, also accounts for criminal organisations, civilian communities, and individuals as agents of political terror. The figure lists the most standard repertoire of interactions between each agent and target. I've opted to highlight those repertoires involving the physical destruction of the targets, although there exist many more non-lethal forms of terror like kidnapping, arson, etc. Keeping all repertoires at the level of first-degree murder makes them more comparable.

The left column in Figure 20.2 lists the agents engaged in political terror; the others label the dyads of interaction encompassing political terror with the respective target. Not all forms of political terror are indiscriminate, although logically, those like total war, civil war, state terror, war crimes, and ethnic clashes do claim the most victims.

<table>
<tr><th rowspan="3">A OF POLITICAL TERROR</th><th colspan="7">TARGETS OF POLITICAL TERROR</th></tr>
<tr><th colspan="2">State actors</th><th colspan="5">Non-state actors</th></tr>
<tr><th>Political Regimes</th><th>Regime Proxies</th><th>Guerrillas</th><th>Terrorist Org.</th><th>Criminal Org.</th><th>Civilian Communities</th><th>Individuals</th></tr>
<tr><td rowspan="3">Political Regimes</td><td colspan="2">War Crimes against Combatants</td><td rowspan="3">Civil War
Counter-insurgency</td><td rowspan="3">Counter-Terrorism</td><td rowspan="3">Crime-prevention
(Drug Raids)</td><td rowspan="4">Democide
Ethnic Cleansing
State Terror</td><td rowspan="4">Political Assassination</td></tr>
<tr><td colspan="2">Terror by State-sponsored Foreign Proxies*</td></tr>
<tr><td colspan="2">Total War
War Atrocities</td></tr>
<tr><td>Regime Proxies</td><td>Partisan war</td><td colspan="2">Proxy War</td><td>State Terror</td><td>Vigilante</td></tr>
<tr><td>Guerrillas</td><td colspan="2">Rebellion/Insurrection</td><td>Warlordism*</td><td rowspan="3">Turf Wars*</td><td>Vigilante</td><td>War Crimes</td><td></td></tr>
<tr><td rowspan="2">Terrorist Organizations</td><td>Regicide
Tyrannicide</td><td></td><td rowspan="2"></td><td rowspan="2"></td><td rowspan="2">Terrorist attacks</td><td rowspan="2"></td></tr>
<tr><td colspan="2">Terrorist attacks</td></tr>
<tr><td rowspan="2">Criminal Organizations</td><td>Political Assassination</td><td rowspan="2"></td><td rowspan="2"></td><td rowspan="2">(Turf Wars)</td><td rowspan="2">(Turf Wars)</td><td rowspan="2">Narco-Terrorism</td><td>(Murder)</td></tr>
<tr><td>Narco-Terrorism</td><td>(Banditry)</td></tr>
<tr><td>Civilian Communities</td><td colspan="2">Riots
Insurrection
Revolution</td><td>Self-defense units</td><td></td><td>(Lynching, people justice)</td><td>Ethnic Clashes
Pogroms
Lynch mobs</td><td>Lynching
(Witch hunts)</td></tr>
<tr><td>Individuals</td><td>Regicide
Tyrannicide</td><td></td><td></td><td></td><td>(Vigilante)</td><td>Lone Wolf attacks</td><td>(Political Assassination)</td></tr>
</table>

© *J. Van den Bosch, 2018.*
Boxes colored in gray denote violent acts with indiscriminate targeting of victims.
(Brackets) denote unclear or doubtful political motivations.
* Often guerrillas and terrorist organizations fight their counterparts as proxies for their foreign sponsors.

Figure 20.2 Mapping Agents and Targets of Political Terror.

Figure 20.2 clearly indicates how selective the narrow, conventional definition of terrorism is *vis-à-vis* political terror. And so, my argument goes as follows: by dismissing the selection bias by linking agents and targets when defining terrorism and instead studying all forms of political terror, we can get a better understanding of the phenomenon in both the narrow and larger sense, both top-down and bottom-up. Below, I will shortly analyse these forms of political terror, provide some examples, place them in historical context, list the possible motivations of the agents, and describe in what way they want to influence their intended audiences.

A CLASH OF STATES: WHEN STATES RESORT TO TERROR ABROAD

In this part below, I will analyse in which instances states use repertoires of terror abroad, either directly or by sponsoring groups using terror. The use of the concept of "*repertoires*" is derived from C. Tilly's theoretical framework on collective claim-making. In his own words:

> Presenting a petition, taking a hostage, or mounting a demonstration constitutes a performance linking at least two actors, a claimant and an object of claims. Innovation occurs incessantly on the small scale, but effective claims depend on a recognizable relation to their setting, to relations between the parties, and to previous uses of the claim-making form.
>
> Performances clump into repertoires of claim-making routines that apply to the same claimant-object pairs (…). The theatrical metaphor calls attention to the clustered, learned, yet improvisational character of people's interactions as they make and receive each other's claims. Claim-making usually more resembles jazz and commedia dell'arte than the ritual reading of scripture. (Tilly, 2006, 35)

Acts of political terror are, of course, the only *performances* under study here, but they are not our object of analysis. This chapter will study the clustered occurrences of these performances between the agent or claimant and their targets (and their larger audiences). The performance (or the act or form of violence) is held constant and always fits the listed definition of political terror, but the resulting repertoires of course vary when linking different dyads, or pairs of agents and targets.

Direct Use of Terror by States Abroad

The first repertoire under scrutiny is the use of political terror abroad. In order to have an "abroad," there have to be polities, borders, and in- and out-groups. Before dismissing thousands of years of human history with an arbitrary starting point, I would like to stress that the primitive world before the advent of states was actually more warlike than the later state societies. Lawrence Keeley found that primitive warfare was much deadlier than that conducted between civilised states because of the greater frequency of combat and the more merciless way it was conducted. "It was efficient in inducing terror by frequently visiting sudden death and mutilating its victims" and only limited by logistics (Keeley 1996, 174–175; Carles Boix, 2015; de Swaan, 2015, 278).

By remaining within the purview of the era of states, I can identify four repertoires of state agents engaging directly in political terror on the territory of other states:

- War crimes (targeting [enemy] combatants and POWs)
- Total War (indiscriminately targeting an opponent's civilians)
- Counter-terrorism or insurgency (that indiscriminately targets civilians)
- Conquerors' Frenzy (war atrocities after occupation, cf. de Swaan, 2015)

The first two take place during military campaigns. During battle, enemy soldiers are either targeted with weapons that are outlawed or they are mistreated and killed after their surrender or capture. In order to count as terror, such actions need to be directed at the opposing military forces (the audience) and aimed to intimidate, break[3] their will to fight, and provoke desertions or mutinies. Most war crimes fall under the Geneva Convention of 1949 and international law, but a recent ruling by the International Criminal Court reframed war crimes to also cover violence against one's own armed forces, including slavery, sexual violence, mistreatment, etc. (McDermott, 2017). In this case, of course, the audience is one's own troops, and terror is an instrument to force them to obey. (See also state terror in Part 3.)

Total war became progressively easier with the rise of modern technology. While during WWI aircraft made their first civilian casualties through bombing, by WWII whole cities were systematically erased for strategic and psychological purposes. The *Blitzkrieg*, the Allied bombings in Germany and Japan, and finally the atom bombs on Hiroshima and Nagasaki were all aimed at inflicting mass fear to break resistance, to manifest the attackers' overwhelming firepower and their unbending determination to accept nothing less than unconditional surrender, as well as for retributive retaliation. The terror of nuclear weapons is so great and so indiscriminate that precisely this fear of mutually assured destruction has kept capable states from using them, therefore limiting the number of known casualties (Chaliand & Blin, 2007, 14–15; de Swaan, 2015, 3–4). Total war has been steadily outlawed since the multilateral Hague Conventions of 1889 and 1907 and the Geneva convention; nonetheless, war atrocities bordering total war have been committed in many instances, often under the guise of counter-insurgency (Vietnam War, Soviet-Afghan War[4]) or during civil wars (Great African War, Sudanese Civil War, Syrian Civil War).[5]

Political terror under the veil of counter-insurgency or counter-terrorism abroad is listed separately because of the covert nature of the operations, the lack of civilian oversight, the larger motivation to prevent future terrorist attacks (and thus save lives), and the influence of states in defining the existing legal framework encompassing counter-terrorism. In essence, we are dealing with war crimes that both discriminate against (unlawful) combatants (e.g., terrorists and mercenaries) and indiscriminately attack civilians located on the territory of the military operations. The former set of discriminatory crimes include abductions, torture, inhumane treatment, and killings of this category of detainees in order to force confessions and solicit information, but can stretch beyond the scope of their target by intimidating other members of their organisation (the audience). The latter set of indiscriminate crimes encompasses raids, the use of hostages, bombings, and disproportional military action during operations that victimise a civilian population in order to punish or discourage them from supporting terrorists or insurgents.

The last form of direct state terror on foreign soil is what Abram de Swaan labelled "conquerors' frenzy," or the use of terror upon a defeated enemy and defenceless population. "The agents are usually regular troops, brutalised by battle, [after] a period of intense fighting with all the anxiety and rage that evoked, while operating in a temporary moral void, where anything can happen" (de Swaan, 2015, 143). Historic examples are rife and date back to pre-biblical times, but some of the more recent deadliest episodes would be the late colonial conquests, like the Dutch subjugation of the Aceh rebellions (1873–1906), the genocide of the Herero and Namaa people in former German South West Africa (1904–1906), or in the Congo Free State by King Leopold II of Belgium (1887–1908). Earlier cases, likewise, of combinations of "germs and steel" are even more glossed over in the history books but not less deadly, like the Zhunghar genocide (1755–1775), in which the Qing Chinese killed between 500,000 and 800,000, or 80% of the Oirat people (Clarke, 2004, 37).

Expulsion, death marches, starvation, massacres – the main goal is the domination of the acquired territories, be it in the form of instrumental settlers' massacres aimed at ethnic cleansing or motivated by ideological purposes like the Nazi mass exterminations behind the Eastern Front. Terror is usually instrumental in getting rid of the conquered peoples in the desired lands, but it can also be retributive, like the Armenian volunteers in the Russian Army that massacred unknown numbers of Turkish Kurds in response to the Armenian genocide (1915–1923[6]). The killers' isolation and their confidence in impunity explain much of the extreme destruction (de Swaan, 2015, 143–148).

In order to count as political terror, all these forms of violence on foreign soil must be linked back to the main agent – the state – and its motivations. And this is easier said than done. One has to rule out that an individual performance of terror was not made by an isolated criminal element without the sanction of the state.[7] Often the state's response after the act is crucial to assess the complicity: "If the state fails to prosecute the [agent] to the full extent of the law and fails to compensate the victims, and if the state attempts to excuse the actions in some way, the state is condoning the [act of terror]" (Jackson et al., 2010, 20–22). Also, the terror must be intentional, either to influence a larger audience or to punish its targets, and is often part of a larger pattern.[8]

For the purpose of being complete, I should include the use of political terror in partisan warfare as a strategy to discourage an enemy state from occupying a territory. Here, terror, mostly assassination, sabotage, and bombings, is more discriminatory insofar as it only targets representatives of the invading state. The use of terror can be tactical since partisans fight from a position of weakness without formal organised structures and with limited means (compared to conventional troops), but it can also be punitive for obvious reasons.

Indirect Use of Terror by States Abroad

When states do not engage enemy states directly, like in the above examples, they can still install terror upon them by providing support to guerrillas or terrorist organisations operating on the territory of other states.[9] While these foreign organisations have their own political aims and agendas, they can be convinced or coerced to serve the interests of a patron. Loyalty is not guaranteed, and this strategy can backfire for the sponsors. The motivations of these organisations will be described in the next parts, but below I would like to present a glimpse into the logic behind sponsoring terror abroad. Sponsorship is understood here as intentional assistance, not passively turning a blind eye (Byman, 2005, 10).

Daniel Byman (2005, 36–50) identifies the following motivations for states to support terror abroad:

- Inadvertently, the primary aims are to support an organisation for its other strategic capabilities (e.g., guerrilla tactics), not for its use of terror, which is an unintended or ignored side effect.
- Strategic aims:
  - Weaken and destabilise a neighbour
  - Project power (to compensate for a lack of state power)
  - Shaping an opposition (to obtain a voice and manipulate opposition forces against a particular regime)
  - Regime change for strategic (and ideological) reasons
- Domestic aims:
  - Aid kin (class, clan, or ethnic groups)
  - Military and operational aid

- Exporting a political system and ideology:
  - International prestige: to support a convergent ideological cause
  - Strategically exporting the regime's state ideology to other states

Of all these motivations, strategic aims are the most common. Terror becomes leverage in negotiations; anti-terror countermeasures will drain enemy resources, but they can also be used as a punishment for the other state's policy choices. Often, states resort to sponsoring terror because they lack the military and economic capabilities to influence target states. A third motivation is to force their influence on an enemy state's political landscape by determining the nature of the opposition against the regime. Such sponsorship comes with strings attached, and the sponsor will try to subordinate "their" opposition organisation. When this fails, they might even decide to support a rival organisation to rein in the actions of the former, which can lead to "turf wars" between terrorist organisations or guerrillas for more influence and thus more sponsorship. (This situation is marked with a "*" in Figure 20.2.)

For example, many Arab states supported the Palestinian cause, but after it became clear that the Palestinian Liberation Organisation (PLO) could not be controlled, Syria forced a split and backed the al-Saiqa faction, led by Abu Musa. Baghdad, in turn, relied on the Abu Nidal Organisation to punish the PLO for refusing to follow suit (Byman, 2005, 40). The same can happen to guerrillas: In Angola, foreign sponsors switched their alliance to more promising guerrillas during the course of the civil war (1975–2002) for purely strategic reasons, almost regardless of their ideological background. Terror in the form of lethal torture, rape, amputations, and impalement was a constant, systemic, indiscriminate, and highly ritualised form of violence against civilians, especially (but not only) by UNITA rebels (Brinkman, 2000).

Other motivations are for domestic reasons, such as providing aid to oppressed kin (ethnic or religious) in a different state. In this case, support reflects well on the sponsor at home (legitimacy) and often significantly raises the capabilities of its beneficiaries. Of course, the motivation, more rarely, can be to obtain military and operational aid without the need for a shared cultural connection; a regime can use a terrorist group to gain a military advantage or other forms of assistance in the state's own struggles in a civil war or against regime dissidents. Byman points to the benefits for Sudan and the Taliban regime of allowing al-Qaida to create training camps on their territories: their own militias received training, and al-Qaida assisted them significantly in their own civil wars (Byman, 2005, 47–50).

Byman (2005, 39) finds that regime change is a less common motivation for states to support terror, but he only compares cases from after the Cold War (1991–2003). When adding up the larger pattern of ideological clashes in world history, the Cold War era yields more examples. Collins (2014) confirms this view, stating that the 1970s and 1980s were the heydays of state-sponsored terror, which then declined into an intermediate (1990–2001) and low (2001–present) phase. But if we zoom out more, there are indicators that the zeniths of political terror correspond with the great ideological clashes of human history.

John Owen (2010, 10–21) identified three long waves of violent regime promotion in world history[10]: between 1520 and 1650, 1770 and 1850, and 1917 and the present day. In all three waves, political ideologies (held by regimes) were causal factors for the violent clashes between states; all waves were accompanied by political terror. For instance, during the first wave (1520–1655), Catholic and Protestant princes proactively intervened in neighbouring polities torn apart by religious civil war to impose their ideologies. From targeted defenestrations of heretic officials to horrible public executions, planned atrocities, and scorched earth tactics, the terror of the first wave escalated in the Thirty Years' War, considered by many scholars to have been the first modern and total war. The religiously-motivated political terror used in this set of wars has often been compared to the short and horrific reign of the Islamic State, but often for the wrong political reasons.

In Owen's second wave (1770–1855), the systematic use of terror driven by political ideology resurfaced when warring European elites tried to impose their republican (non-monarchical), constitutional-monarchical, or absolute-monarchical regimes. It is in this wave that "*la Terreur*" was coined to denote the systemic, indiscriminate violence by the new French Republic against uprisings in order to, ironically, protect the democratic gains of the French Revolution. But, beside this iconic example of state terror, the work of Ken Duncan (2011) provides an interesting account of one of the earliest forms of pure state-sponsored terrorism, encompassing a British plot to support a (failed) regicide on Emperor Napoleon, including offering a safe haven and funding to the French Royalist counter-revolution.

In addition, Duncan also presents one of the first successful historic counter-terrorism campaigns: Napoleon used a combination of military operations in the field to reestablish control over the hotbeds of insurgency and then went about addressing the grievances of elites in exile, allowing them to return and reintegrate in French society. He also tackled the problem of banditry in the countryside, a major grievance of the peasants, and, among other things, restored relations with the Catholic Church to soothe the clergy. Together, these measures were quite successful in draining the pool of recruits for future terrorist networks and insurrections (Duncan, 2011, 16).

The third wave of forcible regime promotions (1917–present) actually started just *after* a long stretch of domestic Russian (Anarchist) terrorism (1878–1908) and isolated surges of regicides in various European countries before World War I. This was an age when radical groups with new ideas clashed with an unbudging imperial status quo. Terrorism (mostly regicide) was the weapon of the oppressed. Only after rapid socio-economic changes and the industrial revolution broke the mould and toppled empires after WWI did new ideologies become state ideologies, pitting various political regimes against each other. Once more, states attempted to force either liberal democracy, communism, or nationalist fascism on other states. In the consolidation phases of these ideological regimes, state terror reached unprecedented heights under Hitler and Stalin.

After WWII, democracy and Marxism became the main three ideological contenders, with both camps containing a superpower and rallying as many newly independent states from former colonies to their cause. The nuclear stand-off had made direct confrontation unfeasible, so the ensuing Cold War and an unstable Third World encouraged both superpowers to support insurgents and terrorists to further their ideological cause or safeguard their reputation. The Iranian revolution of 1979 put a third contender on the map: Islamism. Before, the PLO and other militant Islamist organisations had been co-opted for strategic interests by various Arab states, but Iran was the first Islamist political regime ready to use terror abroad to promote its ideology, followed by Sudan and the Taliban's Afghanistan. The current landscape of Islamist terror is their offspring.

Summarising the indirect way in which states engage in terror abroad, notwithstanding their precise motivations, the decision by states to support foreign groups wielding terror is seldom overtly displayed. The link between principle and agent must be seen as a tradeoff between controlling the agent and the plausible deniability of its actions. The more a state controls a group (changes in funding, more direct links), the more visible the trail between itself and its agent of terror[11] (Byman & Kreps, 2010, 14).

When differentiating between political regimes, democracies stand out because their governments subscribe to human rights, international law, and checks and balances; elites answer to their electorates; and the free press is protected, making it much more difficult to support foreign agents using terror. Closed and centralised political systems make it easier for dictators to resort to terror. Nonetheless, the power of ideas should not be dismissed: democracy in its current form is a relatively young regime type, and earlier forms of democracy did rely on terror. Also, when states are ideologically threatened, like during the Cold War, even democracies do not eschew the use of terror, either directly (total war, counter-terrorism) or indirectly (by co-opting existing terror groups) to achieve their goals.

EXPOSED FEASTS FOR CROWS: WHEN REGIMES OPENLY TERRORISE CIVILIANS AT HOME

State terror in general is not associated with democracies, but "the Troubles" in Northern Ireland or the ongoing situation in Israel clearly show that when faced with terrorism or insurgency at home, even democracies resort to terrifying means to intimidate adversaries and the communities that harbour them. Nonetheless, the nature of such terror is never as lethal or as indiscriminate as under dictatorships, and this has everything to do with the different workings of political regimes.

Political Regimes and State Terrorism

Non-democratic regimes have to rely on force or the threat of force in order to control their populations. After the Cold War, the "winds of change" might have brought elections to many parts of the world, but not necessarily democracy, which I define more broadly, including checks-and-balances, equality, universal suffrage, the rule of law, free and fair elections, and safeguarding political, economic, and civil liberties. In addition, liberal democracy is also an ideology whose ideas must be widely accepted by both its elites and its society. Dictatorships are more heterogeneous because they might lack some or all of the above characteristics necessary to be classified as democracies.[12]

Among dictatorships, some characteristics stand out when it comes to their prevalence of political terror: Firstly, a political ideology that is not based on individual freedom and human rights but is willing to sacrifice human life in order to obtain its goals (Communism, Fascism) Secondly, pure military regimes with no co-optative political institutions (e.g., a *Junta*) might have a predominant military advantage but no means to tie the population to their regime or channel dissent. They rely heavily on their repressive capacity to control their states. Thirdly, the size of the ruling coalition also matters: large coalitions like single-party regimes or multiparty dictatorships can solicit support from more segments of society than military councils or monarchies with closed coalitions. Fourthly, the personalisation of power is a key element in dictatorships as it removes even the most rudimentary checks and balances within the ruling coalition, and therefore such tyrants can implement policy truly unopposed (Bove & Brauner, 2014; C. Davenport, 2007; de Soysa, 2015; Escribà-Folch, 2013; Frantz & Kendall-Taylor, 2014; Geddes et al., 2013). And finally, state capacity matters as well. Vincent Boudreau finds that if the nature of a threat is asymmetrical to the nature of state power, a ruling regime will react more violently to suppress it. Take a strong insular state that has no control over the countryside; its regime will react more violently against nationwide peaceful protests in areas they do not control than, for instance, against violent riots in the capital (Christian Davenport et al., 2005, 47–49).

Hitler, Stalin, and Mao all had strong, centralised states with single-party regimes and comprehensive radical ideologies; in all three cases, power was highly personalised.

Their state of terror was legendary. Then, military regimes in smaller states like Pinochet's Chile or Argentina's *Junta* were also capable of terrorising their populations and killing hundreds of thousands without the guidance of a transformative ideology. But personalist rule in poor and weak states like Idi Amin's Uganda, Suharto's Indonesia, or Said Barre's Somalia likewise contributed to a total of 89 million people (conservative estimates) who died at the hands of their state outside of war during the 20th century (Leitenberg, 2006, 13).

The primary audience of state terror is beyond doubt their citizens, and thus not those who perish or disappear, but their next of kin, neighbours, colleagues, party members, etc. The goal is to terrorise all those affected by the arrest, torture, or murder of the targets, often chosen indiscriminately. The aim is to deter them from engaging in protests against the regime.

State repression, in all its forms, can be classified in various ways. To borrow some categories of Jessica Earl's (2003, 2011) typology, political terror by regimes (against their own civilians) is only a particular type of repression. It is observable, overt, or manifest in order to influence an audience, and it is coerced, involving a direct show and/or use of force. In contrast, other forms of repression are covert or *not intended* to be known to the general public, and they may be indirect, for instance, when a regime channels undesired group behaviour through restrictions (Earl, 2003, 47–48). For instance, during the "Dirty War" in Argentina (1974–1983) and during Pinochet's Chile, it was not uncommon for individuals to be taken by government agents in broad daylight. This made such disappearances both overt and covert forms of repression, intending as much to intimidate an audience as to remove political opponents (Jackson et al., 2010, 22).

In contrast to the fear caused by terrorist attacks, which is greater when it is perceived to be indiscriminate, state terror can have the reverse intent if it merely aims to deter and control. Nonetheless, F. Herreros explains why dictatorships resort to random, indiscriminate violence like mass arrests, deportations, and executions. He found that random political violence against citizens is less costly – instead of gathering evidence, it can be obtained by torture or falsification – and can be effective in deterring groups from mobilising. But only if such arbitrary terror is designed so it does not look random. As soon as the oppressed realise there is no advantage to *not* mobilising (since deference will not protect them), this tactic ceases to be effective (Herreros, 2006; Van den Bosch, 2017a, 2017b, 82).

History has taught us that some states go beyond the use of political terror to control the population in times of contention and regime instability. Even when the populace does not pose a threat and the regime is well-established, some states use terror to rule. A. de Swaan states:

> Under those conditions, repression and extermination are the province of professionals, of specialists in surveillance, intelligence, investigation, interrogation, condemnation, deportation, detention, exploitation, and extermination. Such terror regimes may last for decennia, deporting, detaining, and killing millions, tens of millions of people. (de Swaan, 2015, 139)

It is uncommon that regimes that rule by terror, like Hitler's holocaust, Stalin's purges, and Mao's cultural revolution, could systemise terror without relying on a guiding political ideology. Terror, in this case, can be just a by-product of mass extermination. At times, these regimes utilise terror to break resistance; at other times, they apply more covert means of persecution so as not to alert the targeted groups or interfere with their extermination mission. In the latter case, mass extermination does not meet all the aspects of my working definition of political terror.

State Terrorism and Massacres

Mass extermination and political terror by states may at times overlap with genocide, or more broadly, *democide*. The problem with *genocide* is that it is foremost a legal term (cf. the UN treaty of 1948) and focuses on a fixed group of victims (singled out especially for their race or ethnicity). However, this definition has been framed by states as *not* including the indiscriminate atrocities of colonisation by imperial powers (*ethnocide*, the killing of a culture), the targeting of political opponents (*politicide*), or the extermination of other classes (*classicide*). In addition, in many instances, the "intent to destroy" is hard to demonstrate. Rudolph Rummel's (1994) term of *democide* is more universal, denotes the "murder of a population," includes other victim groups, and presupposes the direct involvement of the state in the preparation and perpetration of the killings (de Swaan, 2015, 85; Provost & Akhavan, 2011; du Preez, 1994, 72).

Peter du Preez's (1994) classification of genocides can be adapted to democides and shows some interesting overlaps with political terror:

- Ideological democide
  - Progressive (e.g., classicides of Stalin, Mao, and Pol Pot)
  - Reactionary (e.g., Hitler's holocaust, the Armenian genocide)
- Pragmatic democide
  - Developmental (e.g., Herero and Namaa ethnocide)
  - Hegemonic (e.g., Biafran genocide (1967–1970), Burundian genocide (1972))
  - Retributive (e.g., Tutsi genocides (1951, 1994) and Hutu genocides (1994, 1996) in Rwanda)
  - Despotic (e.g., North Korea, other politicides)

As I mentioned earlier, terror might be just a side effect of ideological revolutions since the aim is to eliminate chosen groups in society, not terrorise them. The goal is to transform society and purify it by killing. The ideological end goals can either be based on reason and the promise of a new future (progressive) or grounded in faith and the return to an idealised past, like a homogenous nation-state (reactionary). The killing will not stop until these goals are obtained or the regime is overthrown.[13]

Political terror overlaps more often with pragmatic democides. There is no big idea behind the massacres. Killing is a means to achieve a political goal, and so is terror; and therefore, pragmatic democides are often accompanied by political terror. For instance, developmental democides of colonisation or conquest are aimed at destroying and displacing indigenous people, considered inferior. Here the killing stops once the land or resources have been successfully occupied. Terror can be used as a strategy to displace the indigenous people. For instance, Jalata Asafa relates in detail the use of murder, mutilation, child abduction, and systemic rape against Australian Aboriginals and states that these acts of terror are still cloaked by narratives of natural selection (smallpox) or dismissing such violence as to be in line with the "standards of the time" (Asafa, 2016, 73–86).

Somewhat similarly, hegemonic democide is the mass murder of various groups to force the survivors to submit to (state) authority. Once this is achieved, and resistance is broken, the killing stops. Terror also can be an effective way to achieve this goal (du Preez, 1994, 65–73). For example, the Biafran War, after Nigeria's oil-rich southern region seceded in 1967, resulted in war with the federal government, including an economic blockade that created a man-made famine, killing hundreds of thousands of Igbo. However, after Biafra surrendered and was reintegrated, there were no more punitive actions against the region.

Retributive pragmatic democides usually occur in the wake of decolonisation or at the end of a war. An aggrieved group is now in a position of power and abuses this to exert vengeance on a group that has injured or discriminated against them in the past. Terror is a prime instrument for retribution (du Preez, 1994, 70). After the Rwandan Patriotic Army occupied genocide-torn Rwanda in 1994, they unleashed similar waves of terror on those associated with the former Hutu regime, even exterminating refugee camps across the border in Zaire.

The last democide is labelled "despotic" and is pragmatic in its objective to remove enemies of the regime, not only political opposition but also former regime insiders fallen from grace. The goal is subjugation and partly overlaps with hegemonic democides,[14] but here the target is not always a historic outgroup but also recently created outgroups that were excluded from the political system through purges. This is an intended result of power personalisation in dictatorships and the contraction of the ruling coalition around one faction (Roessler, 2011). Such political exclusion often initiates a vicious cycle of exclusion and conflict, with increased defections from aggrieved former regime insiders, and thus the democide is usually self-sustaining, as in many established personalist regimes: North Korea, Saddam's Iraq, Qaddafi's Libya, Idi Amin's Uganda, Bokassa's CAR, etc. In short, since such tyrants do not have any other exit options,[15] personalist regimes rule by terror in order to survive (du Preez, 1994, 76; Van den Bosch, 2017a, 2017b).

An interesting observation by A. de Swaan (2015, 170–190) refers to the "loser's triumph," or when a regime, engaged in democide and facing military defeat, strengthens its genocidal efforts even by deflecting resources from its war effort. The more a regime is ideologically motivated, the more likely it is to pursue its imagined historic destiny and focus on fulfilling its mission, even at the cost of defeat. Examples are: the intensification of the Armenian genocide as the Ottoman empire lost the war; but likewise, the Nazi "Final Solution" for the Jews was pursued "willfully, faithfully, and zealously" despite the rollback of the frontline after 1943; even the Khmer Rouge, faced with impending collapse, remained obsessed with exterminating the "new people" or bourgeoisie of the cities.

Much research needs to be done regarding the role of armed non-state regime proxies in general (Raleigh & Kishi, 2018), let alone their purpose for terrorising civilian populations. As with state-sponsored foreign terror or insurgency groups (see Part 2), autocratic regimes employ paramilitaries, militias, or armed youth movements for various purposes (state control, territorial defence, genocide, ethnic cleansing, etc.) while maintaining plausible deniability[16] as a state to avoid responsibility for atrocities (Mitchell et al., 2014). Many armed groups are sanctioned to use terror to pursue the regime's political objectives, but often some forms of terror are a side effect of their brutality, lack of discipline, or even a tool for building group cohesion in the proxy regime (Cohen & Nordas, 2015). Also, these armed regime proxies have their own agenda and often use terror for criminal purposes, not political goals (Ahram, 2011, 2014; Jentzsch et al., 2015; Staniland, 2015).

A DANCE WITH WAR DOGS: TERRORISTS AND INSURGENCIES

Even though both sub-state actors use political terror, terrorists and insurgents (or guerrillas, rebels, and freedom fighters) are quite distinct: Insurgents aim to control a territory, their logistical base; aim to establish a regular army; wage "war" in platoon- or company-sized units (sometimes even larger) under a command structure; use conventional weapons; usually wear uniforms; and can be internationally recognised if they adhere to the laws of war. Terrorists then operate strictly underground. Their largest known cells number up to 50 people, but most cells count less than ten. Their weaponry includes handguns, assault rifles, homemade bombs, car bombs, and remote-control bombs, but terrorists increasingly improvise their tools of destruction to avoid detection or heighten the sense of fear (e.g. the use of machetes and axes). Terrorism is outlawed both domestically and internationally (Chaliand & Blin, 2007, 24–26).

This part is not aimed at providing an overview or a classification of "terrorist" organisations throughout the ages, but to compare how their use of political terror differs from other agents. The different modus operandi of insurgents and traditional terrorist groups are reflected foremost in their organisational structure and size, but either group can evolve into the other if circumstances allow or force them to adapt. The key difference is an organisational base located in an inhospitable territory, without which sustained insurgency is not possible. The more control and support insurgents have in their region, the less they engage in violence against civilians (Wood, 2010).

Leaving grievances and organisational skills aside (Daly, 2012), insurgents and terrorists alike make claims. These aspirations can be ideological or pragmatic, but tend to be more "nationalist" with insurgents and region-based terrorist groups like the PLO, IRA, Tamil Tigers, or Sendero Luminoso (in contrast to al-Qaida). But even if their claims are pragmatic, the victims of their terror do not have to match their audience (their political opponents). Groups differ very much in their decision to limit the scope of their victims to those in charge (Regicide, Tyrannicide), state representatives (political assassinations), state infrastructure, or civilians. Elements like ideology, cold strategic calculations, tactical errors, and even desperation all contribute to the final decision to apply terror indiscriminately. Terror equals raw intimidation, and the more violent and indiscriminate, the more real the threat.

First, for terrorists and insurgents, terror can be a strategy to seek publicity for their cause and attract more followers. So, targets can be chosen indiscriminately as long as the acts are sensational. Beside this "propaganda by deed," terror is often a provocation that forces targets to act or respond. When states are targeted, they are expected to respond with increased repression, creating grievances and increasing public support for the terrorists, or at least lower popularity for the government. Not acting will make them look weak. So, the third motivation is to demonstrate the inability of a government to enforce the rule of law and protect its citizens. Especially right-wing terrorists use this "strategy of chaos" or "strategy of tension" to increase pressure on "weak" governments to replace them with a strong regime.[17] A final motivation is the strategy of attrition, or to wear out an adversary by draining its resources. If terrorist claims are not vital to the targeted regime and/or its state, such strategies may work, like many of the anti-colonial struggles (Chaliand & Blin, 2007, 33–38). Sometimes, terror is just plain retribution.

Regardless of the strategy at hand, not all states are targeted in the same way. Some recent research found that democracies are more often the target of terrorist attacks because of press freedom (so propaganda reaches its intended audience) and civil liberties, kept in place by checks and balances, limiting the severity of counter-terrorism responses (Chenoweth, 2006). Not all democracies are equally targeted, though (Piazza, 2013). Young democracies are compared with "newly hatched chicks: fragile, untested, and unable to defend themselves." In addition, political groups may not immediately recognise the utility of eschewing armed struggle in favour of nonviolent political engagement in transitional democracies (Eyerman, 1998; Piazza, 2013, 148–250). More research is needed, but ideological contention over the government's agenda-setting during transitions could be an important cause as well.

Likewise, not all dictatorships are targeted equally. Autocratic regimes with lower audience costs[18] – smaller or weaker ruling coalitions unable to remove dictators – are less attractive targets for terrorist attacks. So personalist regimes The reasons are simple: the regime (audience) can barely be influenced; they may be provoked to act accordingly since they care less about their citizens' lives; terrorist's propaganda is limited due to the lack of free press or outright censorship; and such regimes' executives are fairly unrestrained to pursue terrorist organisations merciless, making their work more hazardous (Aksoy et al., 2015; Conrad et al., 2014; Gaibulloev et al., 2017).

Terrorists and insurgents using political terror might not differ much in motivation or selection of their targets, but the respective nature of their organisations makes terrorism *one of many options* for insurgents. They do possess the capacity to engage in other forms of violence. So, terror is a tactical choice. For terrorists, it is their only weapon, and when insurgents are struggling to survive, they are more likely to resort to terror.

SUDDEN GUSTS OF SWORDS: OTHER SUB-NATIONAL AGENTS AND TERROR

In lieu of a conclusion, I would like to highlight some avenues for future research, that so far have gone underexplored when it comes to the study of political terror. As shown in Figure 20.2, criminal organisations, civilian communities, and individuals can also be agents of political terror.

Criminal organisations differ from terrorist organisations that they often do not have political motives, merely economic ones, but this distinction blurs if their organisation encompasses high-level politicians. Similarly, their organisation remains under the radar; is mostly made up of young males; and engages in many similar forms of violence (smuggling, kidnap-for-ransom, murder). And like rebel groups, criminal organisations are location-based and even engage in vigilante "policing" within "their" communities (see "turf wars and vigilante" in Figure 20.2) (Johnston et al., 2016; Mullins & Wither, 2016).

Criminals use terror to intimidate their victims, their neighbourhoods, and other gangs (Turbiville, 2010). Despite the convergence of crime and terror groups, there are occasions when organised crime engages in terror for *political* goals, without uprooting their underground structure. Good examples are the narco-terrorism (targeting anti-drugs law enforcement), or the mafia bombings in Italy in 1992–1993 when the Sicilian Mafia used point-blank assassinations, car bombs near churches, and even indiscriminately blew up part of a highway in order to assassinate Judge Giovanni Falcone. The objective was to intimidate a select category of people working for or with the state, such as judges, jurors, or journalists, through a systematic campaign of assassination, maiming, or kidnapping.

Sometimes civilian-communities resort to terror for political goals. The initiators are integrated into the community, they can be local politicians, gangsters, clerics, but when organising the violence, they do not act in service of the ruling regime; which usually is undergoing some kind of major national crisis. Such acts of terror are usually "mega-pogroms" when local agents concatenate local riots simultaneously in dozens of locations; resulting in a seemingly spontaneously and uncoordinated outburst of communal rage (de Swaan, 2015, 190). For instance, Eamon Murphy analyses the mechanics of local ethnic politics resulting in the violent ethnic (Hindu-Muslim) clashes in the Indian state of Gujarat in 2002, which were instigated in order to win local elections (Jackson et al., 2010, 86–103). Another example would be the ethnic clashes in southern Kyrgyzstan in 2010, in which the expelled regime of ousted president Kurmanbek Bakiyev, used its clan network to unleash havoc in Uzbek ethnic communities in the areas of Osh and Jalalabad. The goal was retribution and to destabilise the interim government of Roza Otunbayeva. In both examples, terror was used to intimidate adversaries, show off power, and manipulate this position of strength with other political actors. The victims were not the audience.

Finally, my definition of political terror also allows to include agents of terror that are individuals and not organisations, permitting extension of the purview to some "lone wolves" with a political agenda, like for example Ted Kaczynski, the Unabomber. From a counterterrorism perspective these agents are difficult to apprehend, since they are self-inspired (not recruited) and self-motivated and have no direct or indirect connections with terrorist groups (Romaniuk et al., 2017, 693).

In these cases, the individual mindset and political convictions of the perpetrator matter, and since few lone wolves survive the attacks they execute, not all cases might be adequately classified. Nonetheless, terrorists like Anders Breivik, who indiscriminately killed 77 people in 2012 in Norway, had a clear audience, a political agenda, and a premeditated plan of terror, despite his mental disorders. In contrast, the political assassination of Dutch politician Pim Fortuyn in 2002 might have been politically motivated and prepared, but the goal was to get rid of the politician, considered a threat to society by Volkert van der Graaf, the assassin, and not intended to influence a wider audience. So only the instrumentalisation of fear for higher political purposes can be considered political terror.

The repertoires described above are neither exhaustive nor complete. Nonetheless, by redefining political terror, I include some new and overlooked agents within the purview of the study of terror. If we narrow down our definition of what constitutes terrorism, we *de facto* remove many interesting avenues for new comparisons and case studies. Indirectly, we ignore the many dyads of terror in which state actors are agents, which happen to be one of the deadliest forms of terror humanity has ever witnessed and will continue to witness if we only see states as victims.

Notes

1 Cf. United States Code, title 22, chapter 38, sec. 2656 f [d].

2 Some notable exceptions are: W.D. Perdue (1989), *Terrorism and the State: A Critique of Domination Through Fear*; M. Selden and A.Y. So (2004), *War and State Terrorism: The United States, Japan, and the Asia-Pacific in the Long Twentieth Century*; C. Menjivar and N. Rodriguez (2005), *When States Kill: Latin America, the U.S., and Technologies of Terror*.

3 For instance, by threatening, no quarter will be given.

4 I am referring to the US bomb raids over Vietnam, Laos, and Cambodia and the systemic abduction of Afghan women by Soviet troops to punish the mujahedeen (Cummins, 2009, 393) as elements of political terror masked as counter-insurgency.

5 It was actually the American Civil War that sparked the tighter regulation of warfare – the Lieber Code.

6 The start and end dates of this genocide are disputed.

7 Nonetheless, the state carries a degree of responsibility for the actions of its representatives (Jackson et al., 2010).

8 For a deeper analysis on how to measure state terror, cf. Mitchell et al. (1986).

9 As shown in Figure 20.2, such support differs from "regime proxies," which, in my understanding, are part of the regime but not an official state actor (e.g., party-linked youth movements, paramilitaries, etc.). Regime proxies are located on the territory of the state controlled by the regime they belong to.

10 Non-violent regime promotions have been even more common but are more difficult to track (Owen, 2010, 10).

11 There is, however, a silver lining to state sponsorship: Most states will not permit their sponsored agents of terror to acquire unconventional capabilities like nuclear, chemical, or biological weaponry out of fear of uncontrolled escalation (Byman & Kreps, 2010, 15).

12 The author realises he contrasts democracies and non-democracies in a dichotomous way, but this has more to do with the current prevalence of liberal democracy as a dominant global political ideology since the end of the Cold War (increasingly challenged since 2010) (Ambrosio, 2008) than with ignoring the historic evidence that dictatorships are our oldest forms of regimes.

13 A very interesting observation by A. de Swaan (2015, 170–190) refers to the "loser's triumph," or when a regime is engaged in democide and facing military defeat, it

strengthens its genocidal efforts even by deflecting resources from its war effort. The more a regime is ideologically motivated, the more likely it is to pursue its imagined historical destiny and focus on fulfilling its mission, even at the cost of defeat. Examples are: the intensification of the Armenian genocide as the Ottoman empire lost the war; but likewise, the Nazi "Final Solution" for the Jews was pursued "willfully, faithfully, and zealously" despite the rollback of the frontline after 1943; even the Khmer Rouge, faced with impending collapse, remained obsessed with exterminating the "new people" or bourgeoisie of the cities.

14 Since the intent is regime survival and control (and not the destruction of a people in whole or in part), this phenomenon clashes with traditional concepts of genocide (Boyle, 2017).

15 For example, kings can abdicate or introduce a constitutional monarchy; military regimes can return to the barracks; single-party regimes can introduce multiparty, free, and fair elections; but personalist leaders either sink or swim with their regime (Escribà-Folch, 2013; Svolik, 2012).

16 Yelena Biberman stresses that some states, like Russia in the 2nd Chechen War, openly endorse the use of nonstate proxies when they are confident that their illicit use of violence will not be challenged. The war, however, is framed as an ongoing counter-terrorism campaign and not like a civil war (like the previous Chechen War) (Koch, 2016, 135–150).

17 For instance, in 1972–1973, the CIA sponsored terror groups in Chile (assassinations, kidnappings) to provoke a coup by the armed forces against Allende's leftist government.

18 Cf. Weeks, 2008; Fjelde, 2010.

References

Ahram, A.I. (2011). Origins and persistence of state-sponsored militias: Path dependent processes in third world military development. *Journal of Strategic Studies, 34*(4), 531–556.

Ahram, A.I. (2014). The role of state-sponsored militias in genocide. *Terrorism and Political Violence, 26*(3), 488–503.

Aksoy, D., Carter, D.B., & Wright, J. (2015). Terrorism and the fate of dictators. *World Politics, 67*(3), 423–468.

Ambrosio, T. (2008). Catching the 'Shanghai Spirit': How the Shanghai cooperation organization promotes authoritarian norms in Central Asia. *Europe-Asia Studies, 60*(8), 1321–1344.

Asafa, J. (2016). *Phases of terrorism in the age of globalization: From Christopher Columbus to Osama bin Laden*. London, New York: Palgrave Macmillan.

Bove, V., & Brauner, J. (2014). The demand for military expenditure in authoritarian regimes. *Birkbeck Working Papers in Economics and Finance 1106*.

Boyle, E.L. (2017). Was Idi Amin's Government a terrorist regime? *Terrorism and Political Violence, 29*(4), 593–609.

Brinkman, I. (2000). Ways of death: Accounts of terror from Angolan Refugees in Namibia. *Africa, 70*(1), 1–24.

Byman, D. (2005). *Deadly connections: States that sponsor terrorism*. UK: Cambridge University Press.

Byman, D., & Kreps, S.E. (2010). Agents of destruction? Applying principal-agent analysis to state-sponsored terrorism. *International Studies Perspectives, 11*(1), 1–18.

Carles Boix. (2015). *Political order and inequality: Their foundations and their consequences for human welfare. Cambridge University Press.*

Chaliand, G., & Blin, A. (2007). *The history of terrorism: From antiquity of Al Qaeda*. Berkeley, Los Angeles, London: University of California Press.

Chenoweth, E. (2006). The Inadvertent Effects of Democracy on Terrorist Group Emergence. In *BCSIA Discussion Paper* (pp. 1–31).

Clarke, M.E. (2004) *In the eye of power: China and Xinjiang from the Qing Conquest to the "New Great Game" for Central Asia, 1759-2004*, doctoral dissertation, Department of International Business & Asian Studies, Griffith University.

Cohen, D.K., & Nordas, R (2015). Do states delegate shameful violence to militias? Patterns of sexual violence in recent armed conflicts. *Journal of Conflict Resolution, 59*(5), 877–898.

Collins, S.D. (2014). State-sponsored terrorism: In decline, yet still a potent threat. *Politics & Policy, 42*(1), 131–159.

Conrad, C.R., Conrad, J., & Young, J.K. (2014). Tyrants and terrorism: Why some autocrats are terrorized while others are not. *International Studies Quarterly, 58*(3), 539–549.

Cummins, J. (2009). *The war chronicles: From flintlocks to machine guns*. Beverly (MA): Fair Winds.

Daly, S.Z. (2012). Organizational legacies of violence: Conditions favoring insurgency onset in Colombia, 1964–1984. *Journal of Peace Research, 49*(3), 473–491.

Davenport, C. (2007). State repression and the Tyrannical peace. *Journal of Peace Research, 44*, 485–504.

Davenport, C., Johston, H., & Mueller, C. (Eds.). (2005). *Repression and mobilization*. Minneapolis, London: University of Minnesota Press.

de Soysa, I. (2015). Oil and the 'new wars': Another look at the resource curse using alternative data. *Development Studies Research, 2*(1), 64–76.

de Swaan, A. (2015). *The killing compartments: The mentality of mass murder*. New Haven, London: Yale University Press.

du Preez, P. (1994). *Genocide: The psychology of mass murder*. London: Boyar.

Duncan, K. (2011). A blast from the past: Lessons from a largely forgotten incident of state-sponsored terrorism. *Perspectives on Terrorism, 5*(1), 3–21.

Earl, J. (2003). Tanks, tear gas, and taxes: Toward a theory of movement repression. *Sociological Theory, 21*(1), 44–68.

Earl, J. (2011). Political repression: Iron fists, velvet gloves, and diffuse control. *Annual Review of Sociology, 37*(1), 261–284.

Escribà-Folch, A. (2013). Repression, political threats, and survival under autocracy. *International Political Science Review, 34*(5), 543–560.

Eyerman, J. (1998) Terrorism and democratic states: Soft targets or accessible systems. *International Interactions, 24*(2):151–170.

Fjelde, H. (2010). Generals, dictators, and kings: Authoritarian regimes and civil conflict, 1973—2004. *Conflict Management and Peace Science, 27*, 195–218.

Frantz, E., & Kendall-Taylor, A. (2014). A dictator's toolkit: Understanding how co-optation affects repression in autocracies. *Journal of Peace Research, 51*(3), 332–346.

Gaibulloev, K., Piazza, J.A., & Sandler, T. (2017). Regime types and terrorism. *International Organization, 71*(3), 491–522.

Geddes, B., Frantz, E., & Wright, J. (2013). New data on autocratic breakdown and regime transitions. Perspectives on Politics, *12*(2), 313–331. https://doi.org/10.1017/S1537592714000851

Geddes, B., Wright, J., & Frantz, E. (2014). Autocratic breakdown and regime transitions: A new data set. *Perspectives on Politics. 12*(1),313–331. DOI:10.1017/S1537592714000851

Gross, M.L., Canetti, D., & Vashdi, D.R. (2016). The psychological effects of cyber terrorism. *Bulletin of the Atomic Scientists, 72*(5), 284–291.

Gross, M.L., Canetti, D., & Vashdi, D.R. (2017). Cyberterrorism: Its effects on psychological well-being, public confidence and political attitudes. *Journal of Cybersecurity*, *3*(1), 49–58.

Herreros, F. (2006). "The Full Weight of the State": The logic of random state-sanctioned violence. *Journal of Peace Research*, *43*(6), 671–689.

Hoffman, B. (2006). *Inside terrorism*. New York: Columbia University Press.

Jackson, R., Murphy, E., & Poynting, S. (Eds.). (2010). *Contemporary state terrorism: Theory and practice*. London, New York: Routledge.

Jackson, R., Smyth, M.B., & Gunning, J. (Eds.). (2009). *Critical terrorism studies: A new research agenda*. London, New York: Routledge.

Jentzsch, C., Kalyvas, S.N., & Schubiger, L.I. (2015). Militias in civil wars. *Journal of Conflict Resolution*, *59*(5), 755–769.

Johnston, P.B., Shapiro, J.N., Shatz, H.J., Jung, D.F., Ryan, P.K., & Wallace, J. (2016). The organizational economics of insurgency and terrorism. In *Foundations of the Islamic state* (pp. 49–66). California, USA: RAND Corporation.

Keeley, L. J. *War before civilization: The myth of the peaceful savage*. Oxford: Oxford University Press, 1996.

Koch, B. (2016). *State terror, state violence: Global perspectives*. Wiesbaden: Springer.

Leitenberg, Milton (2006) Deaths in Wars and Conflicts in the 20th Century, *Occasional Paper, 29,* Peace Studies Program, Cornell University.

McDermott, Y. (2017) "ICC expands definition of war crimes to cover combatants in the same armed forces," The Conversation. (https://theconversation.com/icc-expands-definition-of-war-crimes-to-cover-combatants-in-the-same-armed-forces-71104)

Mitchell, C., Stohl, M., Carleton, D., & Lopez, G. (1986) State terrorism: Issues of concept and measurement, in *Government Violence and Repression: An Agenda for Research*. New York: Greenwood Press: 1–26.

Mitchell, N.J., Carey, S.C., & Butler, C.K. (2014). The impact of pro-government militias on human rights violations. *International Interactions*, *40*(5), 812–836.

Mullins, S., & Wither, J.K. (2016). Terrorism and organized crime. *Terrorism and Organized Crime*, *15*(3), 65–82.

Owen, J.M.I. (2010). *The clash of ideas in world politics. Transnational networks, states, and regime change 1510–2010*. Princeton, New Jersey: Princeton University Press.

Piazza, J.A. (2013). Regime age and terrorism: Are new democracies prone to terrorism? *International Interactions*, *39*(2), 246–263.

Provost, R., & Akhavan, P. (Eds.). (2011). *Confronting genocide*. New York, USA: Springer.

Raleigh, C., & Kishi, R. (2018). Hired guns: Using pro-government militias for political competition. *Terrorism and Political Violence*, *32*(3), 1–22.

Roessler, P. (2011). The enemy within: Personal rule, coups, and civil war in Africa. *World Politics*, *63*(2), 300–346.

Romaniuk, S.N., Francis, G., Irrera, D., & Webb, S. (Eds.). (2017). *The Palgrave handbook of global counterterrorism policy*. London: Palgrave Macmillan.

Rummel, R.J. (1994) *Death by government*. New Brunswick, NJ: Transaction.

Schmid, A., & Jongman A. (1988) *Political terrorism: A new guide to actors, authors, concepts, databases, theories and literature*. Amsterdam: North Holland Publishing Company.

Staniland, P. (2015). Militias, ideology, and the state. *Journal of Conflict Resolution*, *59*(5), 770–793.

Svolik, M.W. (2012). *The politics of authoritarian rule*. Cambridge, New York: Cambridge University Press.

Tilly, C. (2006). *Regimes and repertoires*. Chicago, London: University of Chicago Press.

Toscano, R. (2007). More on defining terror. *World Policy Journal*, *24*(3), 111–112.

Turbiville, G.H. (2010). Firefights, raids, and assassinations: Tactical forms of cartel violence and their underpinnings. *Small Wars and Insurgencies*, *21*(1), 123–144.

Van den Bosch, J. (2014). Mapping political regime typologies. *Przegląd Politologiczny*, *4*, 111–124.

Van den Bosch, J. (2017a). Irreversible regime transitions: The impact of hereditary succession and personalist rule in North Korea. In *The Korean Peninsula unification trajectories: Insights from Poland and Germany* (pp. 47–83). Warsaw.

Van den Bosch, J. (2017b). *Personalist rule in Sub Saharan Africa: The impact of personalism on regime transitions after the Cold War*. Poznan, Poland: Adam Mickiewicz University.

Weeks, J.L. (2008). Autocratic audience costs: Regime type and signaling resolve. *International Organization*, *62*(1), 35–64.

Wilkinson, P. (1974). *Political terrorism*. US: Macmillan Press LTD.

Wood, R.M. (2010). Rebel capability and strategic violence against civilians. *Journal of Peace Research*, *47*(5), 601–614.

21

FRANCHISING TERRORISM AND INSURGENCIES

From Al-Qaeda, ISIS, to Boko Haram

John Sunday Ojo

INTRODUCTION

Over the years, the hierarchical formation and leadership of the trailblazer of international terrorism, al-Qaeda, have followed a centralised organisational configuration (Mendelsohn, 2015). Following the 9/11 attack on the World Trade Centre in New York and the invasion of Iraq, al-Qaeda has instrumentalised a franchise for its global expansion (Fishman, 2008). Providing a franchise network, al-Qaeda's strategic alliance was proclaimed in Syria (2012), Iraq (2004), Saudi Arabia (2003), Somalia (2010), Yemen (2007), and other sub-continents. Specifically, its affiliation with the Islamic State in Iraq and Syria (ISIS), al-Shabab, and most recently with Boko Haram in Nigeria and other regional and local terrorist organisations is well grounded in the literature (Mendelsohn, 2015; Forster, 2011; Azoulay, 2015; Clarke, 2018; Ojo, 2020; McLaughlin, 2010; Jackson, 2006; Romaniuk et al., 2023).

Despite its worthwhile expansive mission, observers around the world have paid diminutive attention to the changing façade in the structural revolution of the organisation. Many observers have considered the decentralisation phenomenon a probable reaction against the global anti-terrorism campaign championed by the United States (Mendelsohn, 2015). The group often relies on its compartments for operational annexation. This expansive consolidation through its franchise has enabled its conglomerates to become fully fledged al-Qaeda members; these include al-Qaeda in the Islamic Maghreb (AQIM), al-Qaeda in the Land of Kinanah (AQLK), which was a former Egyptian Islamic Group, al-Qaeda in Iraq (AQI), and Boko Haram's splinter group, the Islamic State in West Africa (Fishman, 2006).

The franchise strategy has provided an enabling environment for al-Qaeda to promote and build relationships without expending its own resources. The only support for their affiliates revolves around their brand name, ideas, and reputation; this suggests that attacking the global affiliates will be inconsequential and ineffectual on the dexterity of al-Qaeda. Al-Qaeda affiliates often swerve in ideological values and operational arrangements; some of these franchises have not holistically absorbed al-Qaeda's philosophies on global terrorism (Fishman, 2008; Fishman, 2006). Rather than accommodating the broad spectrum of al-Qaeda ideas, the affiliates have blended their local and regional dogmas with al-Qaeda's principles (Baghdadi, 2005). The implication of such ideological synthesis is that it erodes the sanctionable power of the centre, as it was revealed when Bin Laden and Zarqawi directed all of their affiliates to target American interests rather than apostate governments; many of the fighters and affiliates in Algeria, Somalia, Iraq, and Yemen were found pursuing parochial interests. thus eroding the main ideological canons of the parent organisation (Mendelsohn, 2015).

Once al-Qaeda proclaims the formation of a new franchise, it is affirming a political declaration. When the organisation announces that it has a new affiliate in a particular location, it symbolises a significant interest in such a local unit and gives its full support (Mendelsohn, 2015). The group tends to broaden its horizons by employing a dual mechanism: founding its new local affiliates through an "in-house" expansive tactic, which was the same approach that it used to establish its branches in Yemen and Saudi Arabia. Its other approach is to integrate with an existing group, just like how it formed an alliance with the other terrorist groups in Somalia, Algeria, and Iraq.

There are numerous reasons why a terrorist organisation tends to search for affiliates; the rationale behind such adoptions includes opening the possibilities to expand its horizons, which in turn enables them to utilise local resources such as local experts; enhancing the legitimacy of the organisation so that it can be perceived as an international terrorist organisation; and promoting modern techniques in its operational consolidation (Clarke, 2018). The official presence of al-Qaeda in the local units indicates significant solidarity in a strategic or religious sense (Mendelsohn, 2015).

One of the strategies employed by al-Qaeda in 2003 was the creation of a two-level structure consisting of a central

DOI: 10.4324/9780429426063-23

authority and grassroots units that spread across different geographical locations. The central authority was obliged to coordinate ideological sensitisation and orientation and map out a strategy to accomplish their overall political goals. While the grassroots affiliates were autonomous in carrying out their operation. The franchise provided an opportunity for transnational terrorist organisations to pursue their objectives through a chain of command. The group leaders communicated through grassroots channels to encourage other groups to join the mission and support the ideological pursuit of the organisation. Franchising allowed operational flexibility between the central authority and the affiliate groups, unlike the previous model, which encouraged over-centralisation of command and contained a rigid operational structure (Mendelsohn, 2015).

Al-Qaeda's operational strategy has often followed stringent timelines compared to its affiliates, and it has the capacity to implement its long-term goals, which often require several years of planning. The most prominent affiliates are usually vulnerable to operational inaccuracies due to their lack of careful planning (Fishman, 2008). The rationale behind the spreading of al-Qaeda tentacles is founded on creating an Islamic State, which is chiselled in line with the mediaeval caliphate. The restoration of a Sharia mode of governance, which is aimed at incorporating all of the Muslim countries across the world, Importantly, al-Qaeda wants to help shorten the influence of Western nations, especially the United States, in Muslim countries. It considers itself a liberator of Muslim nations that are under foreign occupation, and it wants to implement Sharia law in all of the Muslim countries.

Some of these objectives are sandwiched between the franchise strategy and its mission. The need for solidarity and unity among the numerous Jihadi terrorist groups across the world is part of the core values of the franchise's objectives. The organisation seeks to serve as the vanguard that will provide stimuli to oppressed Muslims and provide adequate resources to its affiliates. As a front-runner in international terrorism, al-Qaeda utilises religious proselytisation, propaganda, online information on bomb-making, and training young people who are willing to join the mission of the group (Mendelsohn, 2011).

However, franchising is not without its implications. In a letter retrieved by the U.S. army in the Bin Laden residence, the late former head of al-Qaeda was concerned about the brand image of the organisation among Muslims, and the indiscriminate killings by its affiliates were considered one of the factors that brought disrepute to the image of al-Qaeda. Due to this, Bin Laden considered changing the name of the group as an alternative strategy in order to gain public sympathy among Muslim communities around the world (Burke, 2011).

It is important to understand the emerging trend in transnational and international jihadist networks and their intersectionality, especially with local insurgencies and terrorist groups. In this chapter, the franchise model presents a valuable insight into the complex terrain of terrorism and insurgencies. Exploring the linkage between al-Qaeda, ISIS, and Boko Haram is important in order to comprehend the general modus operandi of the global jihadist movement. Countering such an expansion has created a mammoth challenge for international security and counter-terrorism experts.

Following this introduction, this chapter begins by explaining the conceptual dialogues between terrorism and insurgencies and continues with an exploration of the different theoretical perspectives of the franchise model in a transnational terrorism context. Then the next section traces the emergence of the use of the franchise model in al-Qaeda, and then the alliance formation between ISIS and Boko Haram has been highlighted. The concluding part of the chapter follows.

RECONCILING TERRORISM AND INSURGENCIES: DEFINITIONAL CONUNDRUMS

Differentiating terrorism from insurgencies has been a laborious task in international security studies. The numerous characters, types, and definitions of terrorism have made such delineation difficult to ascertain. Despite these variations in definitional perspectives, terrorism is commonly considered an act of violence targeted at the civilian population in the pursuit of ideological and political objectives (United Nations, 2008). Over the years, it has been argued that the religious, ideological, and political goals of terrorist organisations have remained the same across the world (Sloan, 1999; Piazza, 2009; Blomberg et al., 2011).

The use of violence against a soft target, such as a civilian population, that is aimed at intimidating and creating fear in order to achieve a political goal is well documented (Beňová et al., 2019; Paraskevas & Arendell, 2007; Abuza, 2003; Nilsson, 2018; Romaniuk, 2021; Romaniuk & Njoku, 2021). In studies of terrorism that were carried out in Germany, the U.S., and Britain, there were three key common components in the legal definitions of terrorism, which were: the intention of creating fear, the use of violence, and political objectives (Merari, 1993).

A terrorist organisation often consists of multilayered structures and chain of command, which includes key planners, bombers, killers, and trainers (Matusitz, 2013). One of the most widely used definitions was provided by Hoffman (2006, p. 43), which encapsulates the contemporary dynamics of global terrorism, according to him:

> Terrorism is ineluctably political in aims and motives, violent—or, equally important, threatens violence,

> designed to have far-reaching psychological repercussions beyond the immediate victim or target, conducted by an organization with an identifiable chain of command or conspiratorial cell structure (whose members wear no uniform or identifying insignia), and perpetrated by a subnational group or non-state entity.

In the search for a globally accepted understanding of the concept, Alex Schmid and Albert Jongman (2017) gathered more than 100 official and academic definitions of the word terrorism and adopted content analysis to assess the main components. The duo observed that the phenomenon of violence appeared in 83.5% of the definitions that were examined; indiscriminate targeting and arbitrariness in 21%; political goals revealed in 65%; neutrals, victimisation of civilians, and noncombatants emerged in 17.5%; and causing fear and terror in 51%. Schmid and Jongman (2017, p. 28) later put forward their definition of terrorism; they defined it as:

> an anxiety-inspiring method of repeated violent action, employed by (semi-) clandestine individual, group, or state actors, for idiosyncratic, criminal, or political reasons, whereby—in contrast to assassination—the direct targets of violence are not the main targets. The immediate human victims of violence are generally chosen randomly (targets of opportunity) or selectively (representative or symbolic targets) from a target population and serve as message generators.

In the view of U.S. Code Congress (1984):

> act of terrorism' means an activity that—(A) involves a violent act or an act dangerous to human life that is a violation of the criminal laws of the United States or any State, or that would be a criminal violation if committed within the jurisdiction of the United States or of any State; and (B) appears to be intended (i) to intimidate or coerce a civilian population, (ii) to influence the policy of a government by intimidation or coercion, or (iii) to affect the conduct of a government by assassination or kidnapping.

Moreover, there are different forms of terrorism, including new-left, religious extremism, anarchism, and anti-colonial (Rapoport, 2001); religious, ethnic, and ideological (Schnabel & Gunaratna, 2006, 2015); and utopian vision (Kaplan, 2007). However, the term insurgency has been widely used in different contexts and has different meanings for different people. The word insurgency has existed since time immemorial. It occurs when something is considered a threat to regional stability. The phenomenon has been dated back to the sixth century B.C., when one of the Chinese military strategists and historians, Sun Tzu, was involved in insurgency and also provided a framework for insurgency. Similar examples include the Roman insurgency against Hannibal, the Russian insurgency against Napoleon, Mao Tse-tung's famous communist insurgency in China, and the Arab insurgency against the Turks (Curtas, 2006).

An insurgency is defined as a political movement with a particular objective. It tends to challenge the existing government or political administration that is in power with the aim of controlling its territory or sharing its political power. Insurgents do not necessarily need to adopt violent mechanisms to achieve their aims. In history, they have often used non-violent methods through political strategy. Insurgent groups are well known for their benevolent role; they may establish schools, food distribution outlets, or essential services for the members of the community. They usually provide such services to show the incompetency of the government in power or the corruption syndrome in the governance system. Insurgents may require the general support of a particular population and equally seek international support to pressurise the government that is in power to succumb to their demands (Siegel, 2009). According to Frisch (2012, p. 2), it is also considered as:

> a non-governmental organization working to affect social and/or political change through violent means against existing power structures and in a way that deliberately challenges the state's monopoly on the legitimate use of violence. It is also important to differentiate insurgencies from organized criminal groups, whose orientation is primarily towards profit-making.

Insurgencies usually depend on external support, which may include permission for transborder movement, especially for the procurement of weapons, strategic planning, and its implementation. A common feature of insurgencies is the control of a particular geographical area and population. This characteristic distinguishes insurgents from terrorist organisations. Unlike a terrorist organisation that usually wants a total overhaul of the existing governance structure with a new replacement, insurgents do not advocate for the creation of a new governing authority (Roper, 2008). For instance, one of the principal objectives of the global jihadist terrorist organisation is to disrupt the existing government structure and build an Islamic state constitutionalised by Sharia law (Gompert & Gordon, 2008).

Insurgents are usually visionary about how society should be organised, and they possess various instruments to achieve such aims. When comparing insurgencies and terrorism, insurgencies are subordinated to or embedded in terrorism. Insurgencies seem to enjoy the relative support of a particular population, whereas terrorist organisations operate on their own without popular backing from the populace (Gompert & Gordon, 2008). Insurgencies differ in their cultural, economic, and social structures; some are considered guerrillas, partisans, or revolutionary movements, while others are pursuing liberation through civil war. Despite the variations in modelling, the end goal of all insurgencies is political control. Insurgencies are usually engaged in illicit trade to raise funds for their operations. Financial gain can be utilised to achieve their primary political goal (Frisch, 2012).

Moreover, both insurgents and terrorists seek domestic and international support and sympathisers. Just about all of the theoretical viewpoints have agreed on this perspective (Kiras, 2007). In order to identify the numerous types of insurgent groups, it is possible to classify them by their pursuits. Insurgencies are usually categorised as either separatist or revolutionary. Whether their political agenda is centred on revolutionising the political regime by overthrowing the government or an anti-migrant movement that often asks foreigners to go back to their home countries (Brooker, 2010),

Separatist insurgencies can be classified in a similar way; they often have an anti-colonial movement that tends to wish to establish an independent state. However, separatist insurgencies cannot only be considered secessionist; some might be agitating for regional autonomy for their ethnic or social group (Brooker, 2010). Other scholars categorised the forms of insurgency as apolitical (Sloan, 1999), people's war, Cuban-style focquismo, urban insurrection (Metz, 1993), liberation, separatist, reform, warlord (Clapham, 1998), economic (Thom, 1999), reactionary, subversive (camouflaged) (Metz, 1995), defensive (Cable, 1993), commercial, and spiritual (Metz, 1993). However, Gompert and Gordon (2008) classified insurgencies as follows:

1. Type 1 – Local: Local-International insurgencies, and Global-Local insurgencies; often categorised as "self-contained" in scope and pursuit. Colombia serves as a good example of such a group.
2. Type 11 – Local – International: The insurgencies that fall under this category often receive external support in terms of funding, propaganda, arms procurement, media coverage, expertise, and foreign fighters. Following the end of World War II, at least, 35% of insurgencies have utilised such external opportunities. Vietnam is a good example of an insurgency that benefitted from external support.
3. Type III – Global - Local: A grassroots insurgent group receiving external support can also transform itself to a regional or global struggle. For instance, in Iraq and Afghanistan, the jihadist strategy is shrouded in between indigenous and foreign movements. When jihadism is employed as a vehicle for insurgency, it cannot be subjugated by a local mechanism. Since World War II, 5% of insurgencies are classified under this trend. With the help of globalisation, they have continued to spread especially in the Muslim countries where incessant proliferation of religious militancy has been sustained. This type of insurgencies usually has a common agenda and is difficult to propitiate by the government due to its transnational arrangement, complexity and global connectivity. Example of such a movement is the persecution of Christians by Muslim militants in countries such as Yemen, Nigeria, Somalia, Pakistan, Algeria, Palestine, Saudi Arabia, Bangladesh, and Indonesia. But these insurgencies are not necessarily Islamic in nature.
4. Type IV - Global Insurgencies: This type of insurgency precedes globalisation; it may consider the state not only its target but also the nation-state. For instance, pre-Bolshevik international communist movements and the anarchist Che Guevara's plan to liberate Latin America from the U.S. influence are good examples of global insurgencies.

It can be argued that all insurgencies possess similar characteristics, whether their grievances are ethnic, economic, religious, or political (Gompert & Gordon, 2008). The differences between insurgencies and terrorism can be explained by considering the nature of their operations, objectives, and social acceptability. The scope and scale of violence differ in their making (Table 21.1). It is rare for terrorism to result in political change, while insurgencies could lead to political transformation by engaging in violent activities (Kiras, 2007).

Table 21.1 Examples of Insurgencies that Commit Acts of Terrorism Tand Examples of Terrorist Groups

Insurgencies That Commit Acts of Terrorism (hold territory)	Terrorist Groups (do not hold territory)
Boko Haram (Nigeria)	ETA
IS (Syria and Iraq)	Baader-Meinhof Gang
FARC (Colombia)	Weather Underground
Al-Shabaab (Somalia)	Armed Forces of National Liberation (FALN)
Taliban (Afghanistan)	Red Brigades
PKK (Turkey)	Aum Shinrikyo
LTTE (Sri Lanka)	Abu Nidal Organization
Naxalites (India)	Abu Sayyaf
Haqqani Network (Afghanistan)	Jemaah Islamiyah
Moro Islamic Liberation Front (MILF) (Philippines)	Japanese Red Army
Shining Path (Peru)	Egyptian Islamic Jihad

Source: Ezrow (2017).

UNDERSTANDING FRANCHISE IN TERRORISM AND INSURGENCIES CONTEXTS

Franchise has emerged recently in terrorism and insurgency milieus; various schools of thought have addressed such extemporaneous emergence, including institutionalism, ideational theory, and realist alliance theories. Of particular relevance is organisational theory as it applies to international organisations and business environments (Shapiro, 2013).

To understand franchises in terrorism and insurgency environments, it is imperative to provide a perfunctory explanation of the phenomenon and its theoretical foundation in business or organisational climates.

A franchise is an agreement between two or more organisations, that is, between the franchisor and the franchisee. The franchisor is considered the parent organisation that has provided a product and service that are for sale. The franchisee is an organisation ready to market the product in a particular environment or location. The franchisor has operational command and control over the behaviour of the franchisee. The franchisor is obliged to provide managerial support to the franchisee. The support may include providing training programmes, mapping out advertising strategies, providing operating manuals, and playing an advisory role.

However, the franchise agreement can be terminated at any point in time (Rubin, 1978). Franchising often provides a structure for a long-term relationship (Byman, 2014). The franchise structure appears to represent a hybrid organisational model and constitutes an embodiment of neoclassical lucidity, which is embedded in economic self-interest (Williamson, 1979). It is expected that the franchise will bring efficiencies due to the expansive nature of the organisation and its membership. The franchisor and the franchisee maintain or share the same trademark, which is the epithet of the bond. The trademark and brand name are shared between the parent organisation and the subsidiaries, which project the conglomerate for future development, which is fundamental to having a competitive advantage (Shapiro, 1983; Klein & Leffer, 1983). The network that is inherent in the franchise relationship can be well-defined as inter-organisational, and the relationship between the different components is enshrined in shared responsibility (Williamson, 1991). Therefore, franchising is classified as a form of solidarity where different units or allies maintain strong ties and reputations within the entire organisational formation (Spinelli & Birley, 1996).

The application of the franchise theory in the context of terrorism and insurgencies is well-defined. Transnational terrorist organisations operate in a similar way, employing similar techniques, such as transnational advocacy networks like human rights and environmental advocacy groups (Asal et al., 2007). For a terrorist organisation to survive, it becomes important to cooperate with one another so that they can achieve their intended goals. They often pursue their agenda by intimidating the general public and the government. They are more likely to seek to develop or acquire chemical, biological, radiological, or nuclear (CBRN) weapons (Asal et al., 2012). Terrorist and insurgent organisations tend to form alliances with organised local structures and sub-groups; these local organisations can be drawn from either ethno-nationalist or Islamic organisations that share similar objectives with them, through which the central goals are propagated (Asal et al., 2016).

It is important to note that religion plays a dominant role in the franchise process. A religious connection is employed as a viable structure to mobilise and seek support from local organisations. Religious similitude can be used to facilitate communication networks and mobilise resources. The existence of a religious pursuit among certain groups is therefore used to foster an alliance among the local groups that share a similar religion that is affiliated with the parent organisation. The transnational terrorist organisations exploit this structure to promote their fellowship and loyalty through a common cause that can be due to religious affinity (Buğday, 2016). Thus, expansion is considered a reasonable tactic for transnational terrorist and insurgent organisations that have spread across many countries. This is done by pursuing a global jihadi agenda and promoting the unification of the brotherhoods (Mendelsohn, 2011).

TOWARDS EXPANSIONISM: AL-QAEDA AND THE ORIGIN OF THE FRANCHISE MODEL

Al-Qaeda is a terrorist organisation that has transformed over time (Farah & Finn, 2003). The group originated from the Mekhtab al-Khidmat (Service Bureau), an organisation founded by Bin Laden and partners to engage in battle with the Soviets in Afghanistan. The organisation has experienced transitory periods, from a hierarchical structure to a venture capital structure and then to a brand structure (Zelinsky & Shubik, 2009). According to Mohamedou (2007, p. 47), Bin Laden founded al-Qaeda as a

> hierarchical system where [Bin Laden] and a deputy … received the advice of a 31-member consultative council (Majlis al Shura) divided into five operational committees: military, religious affairs, financial matters, media and publicity, and logistics.

The rationale behind the transition from a hierarchical formation to a venture capital formation in the late 1990s was that, in order to become more expansive, the intention was to transform itself from a domestic organisation to a global jihadist movement (Sageman 2004). The organisation shifted from the "near enemy" to the "far enemy" (Gerges, 2009). The transition from a "near enemy" to a "far enemy" results in operational complexity for the organisation.

Al-Qaeda depicted its organisational structure during that period as "centralization of decision and decentralization of execution," a situation whereby the targets were determined by the central leadership while planning and strategy to execute the targets were left to the local affiliates that received funding from al-Qaeda. Following this event, al-Qaeda was transformed from a venture capital model to a brand model (Hoffman, 2004). Consequently, al-Qaeda's operational structure metamorphosed from a centralised to a decentralised model linked together through a complex network and cooperation.

> Al Qaeda was no longer a specific organization, but a social movement, consisting of a set of more or less formal organizations, linked in patterns of interaction ranging from the fairly centralized (the East Africa embassy bombings) to the more decentralized (the two millennial plots) and with various degrees of cooperation (the Egyptian Islamic jihad versus the Egyptian Islamic Group, resulting in more or less connected terrorist operations. Participants in the global jihad are not atomized individuals but actors linked to each other through complex webs of direct or mediated exchanges. (Sageman, 2004, p. 137)

Al-Qaeda is considered the foundation of the global jihadist movement that propagates its ideology through a franchise model (Borum and Gelles, 2005). The data publicised by the National Consortium for the Study of Terrorism and Responses to Terrorism (START) Global Terrorism Database (GTD) revealed that only one out of 5,000 attacks that were orchestrated in 2011 by terrorist organisations was credited to al-Qaeda (Central); however, 10 out of the 20 most functional terrorist organisations in the world were linked to al-Qaeda, including al-Shabaab, al-Qaeda in Iraq, Tehrik-i-Taliban Pakistan (TTP), and Al Qaeda in the Arabian Peninsula (AQAP) (Buğday, 2016). An attempt to employ a franchise strategy to launch attacks dates back to the 1980s and 1990s, especially when the organisation was still based in Sudan. During this period, al-Qaeda was enmeshed in a crisis during which some of its active members were looking for more functional jihadist movements somewhere else. The emergence of such a crisis triggered al-Qaeda to proclaim a "blessed jihad" against the U.S., which it later accomplished when it launched attacks on the embassies of the United States in Tanzania and Kenya (Farrall, 2011). The purpose of franchise is well entrenched in al-Qaeda's by-laws, which, according to Lahoud et al. (2012), state that "our relationship with sincere jihadi groups and movements is premised on cooperation [to advance] righteousness and piety."

Terrorist organisations that have often used the franchise model are unpredictable in terms of providing financial resources to their new affiliates; however, some are used to allocating resources intermittently (Zelinsky & Shubik, 2009). The source of al-Qaeda's financial network can be traced to a wide range of recruitment activities that were founded to facilitate the anti-Soviet jihad occupation in Afghanistan. These networks employed businesses and charity organisations on a global scale.

As al-Qaeda metamorphosed into an international terrorist organisation, it developed an organisational structure that accommodated international Muslim charities to conceal the transfer of funds that it needed to sustain its mission as a global jihadist movement. These funds were often used to promote humanitarian missions and facilitate al-Qaeda operations. Some of the activities funded by al-Qaeda include the establishment of new Islamic centres that promote al-Qaeda's principles, especially those campaigning against Western socio-cultural values. These charitable Islamic organisations were used to brainwash and recruit young members into the al-Qaeda terrorist organisation.

Some of these organisations were also employed to encourage donations for logistical, operational, and general attainment of al-Qaeda's goals. According to the 9/11 Commission report, it was believed that the various units were all linked to al-Qaeda funding sources. Islamic charities often source funds from different donors, especially in Saudi Arabia and Gulf countries. It is also argued by Comras (2005, p. 116) in the commission report that:

> the ultimate destination of their donations. ... These financial facilitators also appeared to rely heavily on certain imams at mosques who diverted zakat donations to the facilitators and encouraged support of radical causes.

Al-Qaeda used a franchise network in order to form a global jihad. One of the arguments is whether the al-Qaeda franchise model has succeeded in its mission to globalise Islamic jihadism through its affiliates. Empirical evidence has found that al-Qaeda experienced setbacks in its cooperative model (Byman, 2014). Before his death, Osama bin Laden was concerned about the image of al-Qaeda because of the attacks that caused the deaths of Muslims in Iraq (Agence France-Presse, June 25, 2011). Some of these attacks were carried out by its affiliates, thus deviating from the central goal of the parent organisation, al-Qaeda. The organisation was weakened due to the emergence of splinter groups, for example, ISIS, which will be discussed in the following section.

ISIS: FROM "INTERIOR RING," THE "NEAR ABROAD," TO "FAR ABROAD"

The discourse on the origin and formation of the Islamic State has been virulent. ISIS emerged from al-Qaeda in Iraq following the U.S. invasion. The organisation was championed by Abu Musab al-Zarqawi, a Jordanian jihadist who headed al-Qaeda in Iraq. Al-Zarqawi's plan was to trigger a civil war between the Sunnis and Shiites in order to create a caliphate. Following his death in 2006, his vision for ISIS was consummated in 2014, when ISIS took over northern

Iraq and eastern Syria. The explanation for the reason behind the formation of ISIS from al-Qaeda was centrally due to the divergence of views between Osama bin Laden and Abu Musab al-Zarqawi on whether they should fight the Shiites on the issue of *takfir* or excommunication. The disagreement on the issue led to the emergence of a terrorist organisation known today as ISIS (Hassan, 2008).

The failure to incorporate the Iraqi Sunni community in the decision-making process following the 2003 U.S. invasion of Iraq was considered a major reason for the emergence of the Islamic State in Iraq and Syria (ISIS). Moreover, ISIS tends to destabilise the legitimacy of the incumbent political regime, challenge the government security forces, weaken political institutions, and take control of the political administration of entire communities (Montull, 2016).

The withdrawal of ISIS from al-Qaeda marked a watershed in international terrorism discourse. Thus, it enfeebled the central leadership of the al-Qaeda group that was created by Osama bin Laden (Hubbard, 2014). ISIS was transformed from an insurgent group to a transnational terrorist organisation (Clarke, 2017). ISIS exploited the crises in Iraq and Syria to promote its ideology in the region. The aim of the organisation was to return to the primordial governance model that was employed by the early Muslim caliphs and is embedded in Sharia law (US National Counterterrorism Centre, 2016).

Following the emergence of ISIS and the establishment of the caliphate, a number of local terrorist organisations were encouraged to pledge allegiance to the organisation. The organisation experienced rapid growth and became one of the most highly funded terrorist organisations in the world. Its sources of funding were mainly wealthy donors in Qatar, Kuwait, and the Gulf countries. It was also claimed that the Syrian regime of Bashar al-Assad also contributed to its funding by purchasing oil and gas from ISIS (Montull, 2016).

ISIS has supporters all around the world. It has an estimated 40,000 members from 100 countries. ISIS also extended its tentacles to Europe, which resulted in a series of attacks in the region between 2015 and 2016. Although some of the major attacks were carried out in Syria, Iraq, and neighbouring countries, the European experience regarding the terrorist attacks highlights the proficiency of the organisation to reach Western targets.

Some of the attacks were coordinated or directed by ISIS, while others were carried out by those who were influenced by its ideology. The expansion of ISIS was not only geographically important but also part of a strategic design that facilitated the promotion of its ideology with few resources and risks.

The group was responsible for the hostage-taking in 2015 at a Parisian Kosher supermarket. The November 2015 coordinated attacks on various cafes and nightclubs in Paris that led to the deaths of 130 innocent citizens were carried out by ISIS. Following that, the attack on the airport and subway system that led to the killing of several people in Brussels was coordinated by the Islamic State (Megan, 2019). There are many affiliated insurgent groups around the world, including in West Africa, Afghanistan, Libya, Yemen, Egypt, Somalia, Southeast Asia, Sinai, and the Sahel (BBC, March 23, 2019). The primary objective of ISIS is *baqiya wa tatamadad*, which means expanding (Dabiq Magazine, 2014).

The ISIS operational strategy for global expansion was designed with three fundamental tactics, which were made up of an *interior ring*, a *near abroad*, and a *far abroad*. The interior ring aimed to expand and defend its primary base in Syria and Iraq; the near abroad included the North Africa region and the Greater Middle East. There were Muslim communities in the faraway regions (Gartenstein-Ross, 2016).

ISIS' allegiance to other insurgents and terrorist organisations is based on the principle of *bay'a*, which makes the affiliates subject to the authority of the caliph. The formal acceptance only occurs when the affiliates recognise the authority of the ISIS leadership under al-Baghdadi (Dabiq Magazine, 2014). All the global affiliates are led by trusted individuals who recognise ISIS' leadership (Milton & Al-Ubaydi, 2015). ISIS refers to these affiliates as *Wilayat* or provinces (Mendelsohn, 2016).

ISIS has benefited immensely and is projected to become a global caliphate. Due to the decentralisation of its structural pattern, it has made it difficult for Western intelligence to conduct counter-terrorism operations. Several reports have claimed that approximately forty-three local groups have pledged allegiance to ISIS following the call from Abu Bakr al-Baghdadi for jihadi groups to unite with the organisation (IntelCenter, 2015).

BOKO HARAM: A NEWFOUND AFFILIATE

The word boko haram is derived from the Hausa language, meaning that Western education is forbidden. It is a radical Islamic group initially called "*Jama'atu Ahlus-Sunnah Lidda Awati wal Jihad*," which has based its ideology on the Islamic philosophy that advocates for an Islamic governance model instead of a Western political administration that is claimed to accommodate corruption, social inequality, and social deprivation. The organisation was founded by Mohammed Yusuf in 2002 in Maiduguri, in Borno State, Nigeria. Yusuf was later killed by the Nigerian police while in custody (Ojo et al., 2020).

The death of Yusuf triggered violence between his followers and the Nigerian security forces, claiming and emphasising the role of Nigerian police in the extra-judicial killing of Boko Haram's leader (Ojo, 2020). It is believed that several leaders of Boko Haram fled the country following the killing of Yusuf, the founder of Boko Haram, and re-strategised by seeking support from the al-Qaeda affiliates in the African region. This provided an enabling environment for al-Qaeda's affiliates to support the mission of Boko Haram by providing training, financial support, and operational strategies that included suicide bombings and kidnappings that were alien to Boko Haram's operational techniques. The relationship between Boko Haram and the regional affiliates was evident in various proclamations put forward by the leadership of both organisations. In a statement issued by the interim leadership of Boko Haram following the death of Yusuf in 2009, it stated that "Boko Haram is just a version of al-Qaeda, which we align with and respect. We support Osama bin Laden, and we shall carry out his commands in Nigeria until the country is totally Islamized" (Cook 2018, p. 21).

Since that period, Boko Haram has become an extremely radicalised jihadist group in the northern part of Nigeria. Following the death of Yusuf, Abubakar Shekau took on the mantle of leadership of the organisation (Ojo, 2020). On March 7, 2014, the leader of boko haram, Abubakar Shekau, proclaimed its allegiance to Abu Bakr al-Baghdadi, the self-proclaimed caliph and leader of the Islamic State (ISIS or ISIL, also known as IS). In a video posted by Boko Haram, it stated that "we announce our allegiance to the caliph … and will hear and obey in times of difficulty and prosperity. We call on Muslims everywhere to pledge allegiance to the caliph" (BBC, March 7, 2015).

The acceptance of Shekau into Al-Baghdadi's international terrorist network formalised the relationship between the two terrorist organisations. Boko Haram is affiliated with a number of extremist groups in Morocco, Egypt, Tunisia, Algeria, and Libya, sacrificing its fractional autonomy by declaring ISIS as its supreme authority (Ewi, 2015).

Due to dissatisfaction with the leadership of Boko Haram, headed by Shekau, some of the key leaders in the organisation were disgruntled with Shekau's indiscriminate killings of Muslims in its operational tactics. This resentment led to the fragmentation of the organisation. The main boko haram is currently led by Shekau and its splinter group, the Islamic State in West Africa, led by Abu Musab al-Barnawi (Ojo, 2020).

Following the splitting of the organisation in 2016, the operational base of the Islamic State of West Africa (ISWAP) is confined to north-eastern Nigeria, Chad, Niger, and Cameroon, while Boko Haram operates in the Sambisa Forest, which is a forest in north-eastern Nigeria that can be compared to the geographical size of Belgium. It was estimated that ISWAP has approximately 3,500 militants under the leadership of Abu Musab al-Barnawi, while Boko Haram membership comprises 1,500 militants under the leadership of Abubakr Shekau (Pieri & Zenn, 2016; Zenn, 2017).

In the last few years, the two versions of Boko Haram have attempted to restructure their organisation in an Islamic State pattern. Its transborder organisational structure, which encompasses Niger, Cameroon, and Nigeria, emulates the ISIS operational pattern. Boko Haram was able to achieve its short-term goals due to the failure of the Nigerian military and the corruption that is embedded in it (Ojo et al., 2020). Boko Haram has exploited different political crises in the Sahel, including those in Central Africa (the Central African Republic), North Africa (Libya), and the Sahel (northern Mali), which provided an opportunity for the organisation to form a strong network with non-state actors in the region (Iocchi, 2015).

Boko Haram's expansion cannot be compared with that of the Islamic State (Castells, 1996). However, its organisational structure has followed the hierarchical pattern of al-Qaeda in the Islamic Maghreb (AQIM), and its operational goal is similar to that of ISIS (Pantucci & Jesperson, 2015). Moreover, some of the documents retrieved from Osama bin Laden's residence in Abbottabad, Pakistan, revealed that the Boko Haram leadership had been in touch with al-Qaeda for several months (Burke, 2012). Following such a disclosure, the current leader of Boko Haram, Abubakar Shekau, pronounced solidarity with the al-Qaeda terrorist organisation (Oftedal, 2013). This has linked Boko Haram with the global jihadist movement (Elkaim, 2012).

In a video that was released in July 2014, Shekau made a public pronouncement in support of the ISIS leadership headed by Abu Bakr al-Baghdadi (Milmo & Witherow, 2014; Look, 2020). Equally, the leader of AQIM, Abdelmalek Droukdel, ensured boko haram of adequate support for its operational activities in the quest to defend the rights of the Muslim brotherhood (Elkaim, 2012).

Numerous scholars and international security experts have established a symbiotic relationship between Boko Haram and local and regional terrorist organisations, which could offer mutual benefits for all parties involved (Marret, 2008; Byman, 2012). Boko Haram has benefited immensely from such alliances; such benefits include logistical and financial support, as well as training of the fighters in handling weapons, strategies in guerrilla warfare, and bomb-making.

In the past, boko haram had trained with Al-Shabaab in Somalia, AQIM, Ansar Dine, and MUJAO in Algeria and northern Mali, and insurgent groups in Afghanistan (Pham, 2012). It is evident that the boko haram's expansion into northeastern Nigeria and neighbouring countries such as Niger and Cameroon was a result of its affiliation with ISIS; such credence is linked to the pattern of ISIS operations, which includes a declaration of the Islamic Caliphate, the erection of its flag on the territory captured by the boko haram, the kidnapping of women and young girls, and executions that have been videoed by the organisation (Spangler, 2014; Anyadike, 2015). For instance, in April 2014, ISIS proclaimed the kidnapping of Chibok schoolgirls, which was coordinated by the boko haram (Anyadike, 2015).

As a strong partner of ISIS in Africa, the collaboration provides a congenial ground for Boko Haram's continental or regional expansion, especially in sub-Saharan Africa. The allegiance is capable of providing the opportunity for arms procurement, funding, and recruitment of foreign fighters from different parts of the world. In the Clarion Project (2015) report, it was mentioned that they believed that Boko Haram sent between 80 and 200 fighters to Libya as a measure of solidarity and support for ISIS.

For the Nigerian nation, the collaboration has signalled a danger for the recruitment of more youth into transnational terrorist cartels, meaning that more young Nigerians are able to be recruited, as was demonstrated when Ibrahim Lawal Uwais, the son of the former Chief Justice of Nigeria, Justice Muhammad Lawal Uwais, was caught on his way to join ISIS in Syria (Vanguard Newspaper, 2015). A similar occurrence happened on August 7, 2015, when 24-year-old Imran Kabeer and 25-year-old Sani Jamiliu were apprehended along the India-Pakistan border on their way to Syria to support the ISIS struggle (The Nation, 2015). It was also claimed that five members of Boko Haram were killed in Mosul during a military exercise (Ejiofor, 2015).

Accommodating Boko Haram as one of its affiliates provides a productive ground for ISIS to establish itself in a region decoyed by socio-economic traumatism, political inadequacy, and religious intolerance, which is considered to be hospitable for the recruitment and radicalisation of the unemployed youth.

CONCLUSION

From Southeast Asia, Central Europe, and Eurasia to Africa, Western Europe, and the U.S., al-Qaeda's decentralised approach using the franchise model has become a potent weapon in reaching the global network. Since the 9/11 attack, transnational terrorism operations have continued to increase despite the synergetic efforts of the European Union states, the United States, and their allies to curb the reign of terror at the global level.

The franchise model has been one of the most constructive strategies employed by terrorist organisations for global expansion. Terrorist organisations have shared a similar pattern with business organisations that have sought expansion for survival and promotion of their businesses. Franchising, in terrorist parlance, is an opportunity for survivability, networking, and expansion.

The fundamental aspect of franchising is branding. Affiliate groups are eligible to pursue their local agenda irrespective of the core values or agenda of the parent organisation. Consolidation through alliance formation and solidarity between global terrorist organisations and local militants, insurgents, agitators, or jihadist groups has been the mode of operation in transnational terrorism. There is a possibility that the fragile states could be co-opted into the jihadist franchise arena. Fragile states that are moribund by civil war, face conflicts, and face sectarian crises are considered fertile ground for terrorist expansion.

Regions that have social injustice and corrupt regimes infiltrated them are more susceptible to expansionism. Exploiting such an environment allows terrorist organisations such as ISIS and al-Qaeda to enlarge their bases by coordinating local expertise, promoting innovative ideas, and ensuring their legitimacy, as was evident in the case of Boko Haram in Nigeria. Global terrorist organisations are increasing to fill the lapses of failed states in countries like Syria, Yemen, Libya, Somalia, and Iraq. Unsatisfied groups and individuals are being encouraged to join well-funded jihadist terrorist groups. Refugees and immigrants are also being used in Europe to execute the global terrorist agenda.

In a recent intelligent report by the State of New Jersey Office of Homeland Security and Preparedness (NJOHSP) (June 3, 2020), it stated that:

> international Islamist extremists and terrorist groups continue to publish propaganda about US racial and political tensions and discredit the United States and motivate residents to accept their violent extremism and encourage supporters to conduct terrorist attacks. ISIS have also responded to the racial tensions in the United States by comparing black and Muslim families and insinuating the oppression will spread to the Muslim community in more violent ways. As a result, online supporters suggest Muslim in America arm themselves against law enforcement and looters after online videos have shown rioters attacking individuals of Middle Eastern descent.

Such an environment can be hijacked by global terrorist organisations to promote the interests of the concerned groups. This is able to be achieved by supplying arms and ammunition with encouragement, training, and financial inducement to the concerned local terrorist and insurgent groups. Therefore, governments around the world should take cognisance of the conflict-prone environments that could become a future terrorist-enabling climate for expansionism and transnational terrorist operations.

References

Abuza, Z. (2003). Funding terrorism in Southeast Asia: the financial network of Al Qaeda and Jemaah Islamiya. *Contemporary Southeast Asia*, 169–199.

Agence France-Presse (June 25, 2011). Osama Bin Laden Believed in Image, and Considered Al Qaeda Name Change to Improve 'brand, Al Arabiya News, June 25, 2011.

Anyadike, O. (2015). What does the Boko Haram ISIS alliance mean? *Integrated Regional Information Networks*, March 10, 2015.

Asal, V.H., Park, H.H., Rethemeyer, R.K., & Ackerman, G. (2016). With friends like these … why terrorist organizations ally. *International Public Management Journal, 19*(1), 1–30.

Asal, V., Nussbaum, B., & Harrington, D.W. (2007). Terrorism as transnational advocacy: An organizational and tactical examination. *Studies in Conflict & Terrorism, 30*(1), 15–39.

Asal, V.H., Ackerman, G.A., & Rethemeyer, R.K. (2012). Connections can be toxic: Terrorist organizational factors and the pursuit of CBRN weapons. *Studies in Conflict & Terrorism, 35*(3), 229–254.

Azoulay, R. (2015). *Islamic state franchising.* Clingendael, April 24–25.

Baghdadi, A. (2005). *Why do we fight? How do we fight?* Baghdad, Iraq: Tanzim al-Qa'ida fi Bilad al-Rafidayn (Legal Committee of al-Qa'ida in the Land of Two Rivers).

BBC. (March 23, 2019). IS 'caliphate' defeated but jihadist group remains a threat, March 23, 2019.

BBC. (2015). Nigeria's Boko Haram pledges allegiance to Islamic State, March 7, 2015.

Beňová, P., Hošková-Mayerová, Š., & Navrátil, J. (2019). Terrorist attacks on selected on selected soft targets. *Journal of Security & Sustainability, 8*(3), 453–471.

Blomberg, S.B., Gaibulloev, K., & Sandler, T. (2011). Terrorist group survival: ideology, tactics, and base of operations. *Public Choice, 149*(3-4), 441.

Borum, R., & Gelles, M. (2005). Al-Qaeda's operational evolution: behavioral and organizational perspectives. *Behavioral Sciences & the Law, 23*(4), 467–483.

Brooker, P. (2010). The types and modes of insurgency. In *Modern Stateless Warfare* (pp. 34–49). London: Palgrave Macmillan.

Buğday, A. (2016). Transnational terrorist franchising in sub-Saharan Africa: the effects of religion and natural resources (Doctoral dissertation, Bilkent University).

Burke, J. (2012). Bin Laden files show al-Qaida and Taliban leaders in close contact. !e Guardian, April 29, 2012.

Burke, J. (2011). Bin Laden wanted to change al-Qaida's bloodied name, The Guardian.

Byman, D. (2014). Buddies or burdens? Understanding the Al Qaeda relationship with its affiliate organizations. *Security Studies, 23*(3), 431–470.

Byman, D.L. (2012). *Breaking the bonds between Al-Qa'ida and its affiliate organizations.* Washington, DC: Brookings Institution. https://www.brookings.edu/events/breaking-the-bonds-between-al-qaida-and-its-affiliate-organizations/

Cable, L. (1993). Reinventing the round wheel: Insurgency, counter-insurgency, and peacekeeping post-Cold War. *Small Wars & Insurgencies, 4*(2), 228–262.

Curtas, S.D. (2006). A New Type of Insurgency? A Case Study of the Resistance in Iraq. A Masters thesis submitted to Arts Department of Government and International Affairs College of Arts and Sciences University of South Florida.

Castells, M. (1996). *The rise of the network society. Volume I, The Information Age: Economy. Society and culture.* Oxford: Blackwell.

Clapham, C. (1998). *Introduction: Analysing African insurgencies.* Oxford: James Currey.

Clarion Project. (2015). Boko Haram Sends up to 200 Fighters to Join ISIS in Libya. The Clarion Project, August 26, 2015.

Clarke, C. (2018). Expanding the ISIS Brand. *The National Interest February, 17,* 2018.

Clarke, C.P. (2017). *How ISIS Is Transforming: Why Predictions of Its Demise Are Premature.* Foreign Affairs, 25.

Comras, V. (2005). Al Qaeda Finances and Funding to Affiliated Groups; Strategic Insights, v. 6, issue 1 (January 2005). Strategic Insights, v. 6, issue 1 (January 2005).

Cook, D. (2018). *The Boko Haram Reader: From Nigerian Preachers to the Islamic State.* Oxford University Press.

Dabiq Magazine. (2014). Shariah alone will rule Africa, Issue 8 (2015): 14–16.

Ejiofor, C. (2015) Five Boko Haram Militants Killed in Iraq. Naij, May 13, 2015. Accessed May 22, 2020.

Elkaim, Z. (2012). *Boko Haram: The Rise, Success and Continued Efficacy of The Insurgency in Nigeria.* Herzliya: International Centre for Counter-Terrorism.

Ewi, M. (2015). *What does the Boko Haram-ISIS alliance mean for terrorism in Africa?,* Institute for Security Studies (ISS), March 17, 2015.

Ezrow, N. (2017). *Global politics and violent non-state actors.* New Delhi: Sage.

Farah, D., & Finn, P. (2003). Terrorism, Inc.: Al-Qaida franchises brand of violence to groups across world. *The Washington Post, 21,* A33.

Farrall, L. (2011). How al Qaeda Works: What the Organization's Subsidiaries Say About Its Strength. Foreign Affairs.

Fishman, B. (2008). Using the mistakes of al Qaeda's franchises to undermine its strategies. *The ANNALS of the American Academy of Political and Social Science, 618*(1), 46–54.

Fishman, B. (2006). After Zarqawi: The dilemmas and future of al Qaeda in Iraq. *Washington Quarterly, 29*(4), 19–32.

Forster, B.S. (2011). The global expansion of the Al Qaeda franchise. CMC Senior Theses. Paper 178.

Frisch, E. (2012). Insurgencies are organizations too: organizational structure and the effectiveness of insurgent strategy. *The Peace and Conflict Review, 6*(2012), 1–23.

Gartenstein-Ross, D., Barr, N., Moreng, B., & International Centre for Counter-Terrorism. (2016). *The Islamic State's Global Propaganda Strategy.* The Hague: International Centre for Counter-Terrorism.

Gerges, F.A. (2009). *The far enemy: Why Jihad went global.* Cambridge: Cambridge University Press.

Gompert, D.C., & Gordon IV, J. (2008). *War by Other Means – Building Complete and Balanced Capabilities for Counterinsurgency: RAND Counterinsurgency Study – Final Report.* Rand Corporation.

Gunaratna, R., & Schnabel, A. (2015). The challenge of contemporary insurgencies. In *Wars from within: Understanding and managing insurgent movements* (pp. 3–30).

Hassan, H. (2008) The True Origins of ISIS. The Atlantic, November 30, 2018.

Hoffman, B. (2006). *Inside terrorism* (2nd ed.). New York: Columbia University Press, p. 43.

Hoffman, B. (2004). The changing face of Al Qaeda and the global war on terrorism. *Studies in Conflict and Terrorism, 27*(6), 549–560.

Hubbard, B. (2014). The franchising of Al Qaeda. *New York Times, 25,* 431–470.

Iocchi, A. (2015). Boko Haram Franchise and the war on terror in Nigeria. *Diritto & Questioni Pubbliche, 15,* 203.

IntelCenter (2015, December 15). Islamic State's 43 Global

Affiliates: Interactive World Map. URL: http://www.intelcenter.com/maps/is-affiliates-map.html

Jackson, B.A. (2006). Groups, networks, or movements: A command-and-control-driven approach to classifying terrorist organizations and its application to Al Qaeda. *Studies in Conflict & Terrorism, 29*(3), 241–262.

Kaplan, J. (2007). The fifth wave: The new tribalism?. *Terrorism and Political Violence, 19*(4), 545–570.

Kiras, J.D. (2007). Irregular warfare: Terrorism and insurgency. *Understanding Modern Warfare, 224,* 186–207.

Klein, B., & Leffer, K. (1983). The role of price guaranteeing quality. *Journal of Political Economy*, November: 659–686.

Lahoud, N., Caudill, S., Collins, L., Koehler-Derrick, G., Rassler, D., & Al-Ubaydi, M. (2012). *Letters from Abbottabad: Bin Ladin Sidelined?*. Harmony Program, Combating Terrorism Center at West Point.

Look, A. (2020) Can a Boko Haram ISIS merger work? VOA News, March 10, 2015. Accessed May 22, 2020.

Marret, J.L. (2008). Al-Qaeda in Islamic Maghreb: A "Glocal" Organization. *Studies in Conflict & Terrorism, 31*(6), 541–552.

Matusitz, J. (2013). *Terrorism and communication*. Thousand Oaks, CA: Sage.

McLaughlin, J. (2010). The Al Qaeda Franchise model: An alternative. *Small Wars Journal,* 1–7. https://smallwarsjournal.com/blog/journal/docs-temp/357-mclaughlin.pdf

Mendelsohn, B. (2016). Jihad's civil war. The battle between ISIS and al Qaeda Simmers on. *Foreign Affairs, 16.* https://www.foreignaffairs.com/articles/middle-east/2016-06-16/jihads-civil-war

Mendelsohn, B. (2015). *The al-Qaeda Franchise: The expansion of al-Qaeda and its consequences*. New York: Oxford University Press.

Mendelsohn, B. (2011). Al-Qaeda's franchising strategy. Survival, *53*(3), 29–50.

Megan, S. (2019). The evolution of ISIS: From Rogue state to stateless ideology, New York Times, March 20, 2019.

Merari, A. (1993). Terrorism as a strategy of insurgency. *Terrorism and Political Violence, 5*(4), 213–251. https://doi.org/10.1080/09546559308427227

Metz, S. (1993). *The future of insurgency*. Carlisle, PA: Strategic Studies Institute, US Army War College.

Metz, S. (1995). To insure domestic Tranquillity: Terrorism and the price of global engagement. *Terrorism: National Security Policy and the Home Front, 15,* 65.

Milmo, C., & Witherow, T., (2014). Boko Haram Sets Up African Caliphate with Blessing of Isis," The Independent (London), September 9, 2014.

Milton, D., & Al-Ubaydi, M. (2015). Pledging baya: A benefit or burden to the Islamic State?. CTC Sentinel, *8*(3), 1–6.

Mohamedou, M.M. (2007). *Understanding Al Qaeda: The transformation of war*. Ann Arbor: Pluto Press.

Montull, M. (2016) Franchise terrorism. *BullsEye Magazine*. October 6, 2016.

Nilsson, M. (2018). Hard and soft targets: The lethality of suicide terrorism. *Journal of International Relations and Development, 21*(1), 101–117.

NJOHSP Intelligence Note. (2020). *Violent Islamist extremists promote US Social Tension*. New Jersey Office of Homeland Security and Preparedness, June 3, 2020.

Oftedal, E. (2013). Boko Haram: A transnational phenomenon? (Master's thesis). The Department of Political Science, The University of Oslo.

Ojo, J.S. (2020). Governing "Ungoverned Spaces" in the Foliage of Conspiracy: Toward (Re) ordering Terrorism, from Boko Haram Insurgency, Fulani Militancy to Banditry in Northern Nigeria. *African Security, 13*(1), 77–110.

Ojo, J.S., Lamidi, K.O., Odewale, A.D., Shiyanbade, B., & Ihemeje, G. (2020) Boko Haram insurgency and defense corruption. In Farazmand A. (Ed.), *Global Encyclopedia of Public Administration, Public Policy, and Governance*. Cham: Springer.

Pantucci, R., & Jesperson, S. (2015). *From Boko Haram to Ansaru: The evolution of Nigerian Jihad*. London: Royal United Services Institute.

Paraskevas, A., & Arendell, B. (2007). A strategic framework for terrorism prevention and mitigation in tourism destinations. *Tourism Management, 28*(6), 1560–1573.

Pham, J.P. (2012). *Boko Haram's evolving threat*. Washington, WA: Africa Center for Strategic Studies.

Piazza, J.A. (2009). Is Islamist terrorism more dangerous?: An empirical study of group ideology, organization, and goal structure. *Terrorism and Political Violence, 21*(1), 62–88.

Pieri, Z.P., & Zenn, J. (2016). The Boko Haram paradox: ethnicity, religion, and historical memory in pursuit of a caliphate. *African Security, 9*(1), 66–88.

Rapoport, D.C. (2001). The fourth wave: September 11 in the history of terrorism. *Current History, 100*(650), 419.

Romaniuk, S. N. (2021). Under siege: Counterterrorism and civil society in Hungary. Lanham: Rowman & Littlefield.

Romaniuk, S. N., Fabe, A. P. H. , & Kaunert, C. (Eds.). (2023). Countering terrorist and criminal financing: Theory and practice. New York: CRC Press.

Romaniuk, S. N. , & Njoku, E. T. (2021). Counter-terrorism and civil society: Post-9/11 progress and challenges. Manchester: Manchester University Press.

Roper, J. (2008). Exploring the Links. 147. In (eds) O'Hair, Dan H., Robert Heath, Kevin Ayotte, and Gerald Ledlow. "Terrorism: Communication and rhetorical perspectives.

Rubin, P.H. (1978). The theory of the firm and the structure of the franchise contract. *The Journal of Law and Economics, 21*(1), 223–233.

Sageman, M. (2004) *Understanding terror networks*. Philadelphia, PA: Univer. of Pennsylvania Press.

Shapiro, J.N. (2013). *The terrorist's dilemma: Managing violent covert organizations*. New Jersey: Princeton University Press.

Shapiro, C. (1983). Premiums for high quality products as returns to reputations. *The Quarterly Journal of Economics, 98*(4), 659–679.

Siegel, L.J. (2009). *Essentials of criminal justice* (6th ed.). Mason, OH: Wadsworth Cengage Learning.

Sloan, S. (1999). *The changing face of insurgency in the post-Cold War era: doctrinal and operational implications*. Saving Democracies: US Intervention in Threatened Democratic States, Westport: Praeger, 67–80.

Schmid, A., & Jongman, A. (2017). *Political terrorism: A new guide to actors, authors, concepts, data bases, theories, and literature* (p. 28). New Delhi: Routledge.

Schnabel, A., & Gunaratna, R. (Eds.). (2006). *Understanding and managing insurgent movements*. Singapore: Marshall Cavendish International.

Spangler, T. (2014). ISIS 2.0 in Nigeria. Orange County Register (California), September 21, 2014.

Spinelli, S., & Birley, S. (1996). Toward a theory of conflict in the franchise system. *Journal of Business Venturing, 11*(5), 329–342.

The Nation, (2015). Two ISIS-bound Nigerians arrested in India. The Nation, August 23, 2015. Accessed May 19, 2020.

The US National Counterterrorism Center. (2016). Counterterrorism 2016 Calendar. USA: The US National Counterterrorism Center.

Thom, W.G. (1999). Congo-Zaire's 1996-97 civil war in the context of evolving patterns of military conflict in Africa in the era of independence. *Journal of Conflict Studies*.

United Nations (2008). Human Rights, Terrorism and Counter-terrorism. Office of the United Nations High Commissioner for Human Rights, Fact Sheet No. 32.

U.S. Code Congress Admin. News. (1984). 98th Congress, 2nd Session, v. 2, par. 3077, 98 STAT. (19 October 1984).

Vanguard Newspaper (2015). ISIS: Security men on trail of ex-CJ Uwais' son, March 5, 2015.

Williamson, O.E. (1991). Comparative economic organization: The analysis of discrete structural alternatives. *Administrative Science Quarterly*, 269–296.

Williamson, O.E. (1979). Transaction-cost economics: the governance of contractual relations. *The journal of Law and Economics*, *22*(2), 233–261.

Zelinsky, A., & Shubik, M. (2009). Research note: Terrorist groups as business firms: A new typological framework. *Terrorism and Political Violence*, *21*(2), 327–336.

Zenn, J. (2017). The Al-Qaeda Accelerant in Boko Haram's Rise. CIWAG Case Studies. 3. https://digital-commons.usnwc.edu/ciwag-case-studies/3

22

HIGH-VALUE TARGETING AND INTERNATIONAL SOCIETY'S "WARFARE TRAP"

Paul Lushenko, Srinjoy Bose, and Scott N. Romaniuk

INTRODUCTION

War represents perhaps the most contestable practise shared between member states in international society. On the one hand, Karl von Clausewitz conceptualised war as "an act of force to compel our enemy to do our will" (1827, 127). This reading of war explains the military activities of great powers throughout the 20th century. One need only recount the United States' (US) firebombing campaigns against Japan, including the two atomic attacks against Hiroshima and Nagasaki, and Germany's major cosmopolitan and even non-military centres during the Second World War, as well as its incendiary bombing during the Korean War that followed, to appreciate the logic underpinning an unrestrained application of force. On the other hand, the place of this absolute and idealised interpretation of warfare is dubious given the proliferation of "new" terrorists since 2001. The Islamic State (IS), al-Qaeda (AQ) and its manifold offshoots, and other post-modern terrorist groups and organisations have become increasingly transregional, virulent, and intent on providing their own brand of governance. They also flout international society's common values and institutions, particularly those of human rights and sovereignty. Janina Dill (2014, 140), countermanding a logic that has prevailed among a preponderance of war theorists since at least the 18th century, argues that "[t]he current international legal order rests on a presumption against the use of force as a continuation of politics by other means." Richard Ned Lebow (2010, 225) and other critical theorists similarly contend that contemporary state-based conflict, immaterial of its constitutive and regulative functions and especially when waged unrestrictively, fails to confer status given its destructiveness and collateral damage.

However, war is a durable "social institution whose rules have changed over time" (Finnemore, 1996, 69). The emergence of nuclear weapons following the greatest conflagration of the 20th century expanded the normative prohibitions on the use of force during the Cold War, lest the US and then the Soviet Union exercise the doctrine of mutually assured destruction. This precipitated a concatenation of savage proxy wars between the two superpowers across virtually every continent. The Vietnam War, as well as Moscow's ignominious withdrawal from Afghanistan by 1990, demonstrated the prohibitive costs of sustaining large-scale military formations abroad to conduct nation-building and expeditionary contingency operations. The US' expulsion of Iraq's forces from Kuwait during the Persian Gulf War in 1991 purportedly beckoned a revolution in military affairs by virtue of emerging technologies. The Bush administration's "War on Terrorism" (WOT), initiated immediately after the terrorist attacks of September 11, 2001 (9/11), compounded this latter trend, arguably changing the rules of war once again. Borderless and violent non-state actors have encouraged the pursuit of a calibrated form of force known as "precision strike warfare." This modality connotes a more tailored application of force through drone strikes and raids, but increasingly cyber-attacks, that are anticipated to reduce, if not altogether eliminate, the unintended consequences of conflict, including civilian casualties.

Since 9/11, the US' exercise of this emerging approach to war has outpaced that of other great powers. Washington has proliferated its unmanned aerial vehicle (UAV) fleet, otherwise referred to as drones, heightened the deployment of its special operations forces (SOF), and established the US Cyber Command. Precision strike warfare, in stark contrast to a strategic culture that heretofore encouraged overwhelming firepower to enable the protection of friendly forces at the expense of non-combatants, is now so institutionalised that Byman and Merritt (2018) and Ian Merritt dub it "The New American Way of War." It appeals to US policymakers because it promises to yield minimal monetary and political costs typical of the expeditionary deployment of large military formations that also threaten to elicit accusations of intervention, particularly from post-colonial states beleaguered by terrorism and other forms of political violence. As opposed to the deployment of nearly 5,000 soldiers within a US Army Brigade Combat Team, a SOF unit "will range from a team of half a dozen or so to generally at most a company-size force of about 120 men" (Byman and Merritt, 2018, 88). A Hellfire missile launched from a drone,

DOI: 10.4324/9780429426063-24

although not inexpensive at approximately $110,000 US dollars, further reduces the US' observable signature. A cyberattack putatively maximises security, speed, and surprise, integral to precision warfare, and provides the added benefits of discrimination, deniability, and misattribution. Collectively, these practises are also conceived as economy-of-force responses to terrorism that protect against politically unpalatable friendly casualties while ostensibly retaining the US' lethality amid the emergence of near-peer competitors, namely China and Russia.

Ironically, even this chastened form of warfare has not evolved without criticism. Wali Aslam (2013, 95) argues that the US' "policy of using drone strikes cannot be labelled as a responsible position when measured against the benchmarks of legality, legitimacy, and prudence." It is the derision of practitioners, epitomised by M. Shane Riza, a recently retired US Air Force Colonel, that is most disquieting. Riza (2013, 43) estimates that precision strike warfare threatens a "spectrum of impunity," whereby non-combatants are exposed to greater battlefield dangers than their technologically superior opponents. Contrary to promises of heightened discrimination, precision strike warfare may supplant *jus in bello* principles of discrimination, necessity, and proportionality in favour of a "necroethic" that justifies combatants' right to kill with impunity from a position of relative safety (Chamayou, 2015, 147).[1] This "respatialisation" renders the US' approach to precision strike warfare no different than suicide bombers, according to Hugh Gusterson (2014, 199). Between the two absolute and precision appraisals of war, policymakers and military leaders confront a contradiction. On the one hand, even the Thucydidean logic of "fear, honour, and interest" is seemingly not enough to encourage great powers to overcome the material and ideational costs associated with warfare as conventionally conceived. On the other hand, where military practitioners have attempted to account for the meaningful concerns of contemporary war theorists, as through precision strike warfare, they have encountered similar if not stiffer condemnation.

This chapter presents a pioneering effort to unravel international society's veritable "warfare trap." At first blush, it is possible to conclude that absolute and precision strike warfare are a cause and effect of one another, contributing to international society's confused position. While precision strike warfare does propose a reduction of costs in a variety of ways, it is precisely the limited application of force that may not achieve military and political objectives in the first place, ultimately giving rise to what is known in defence circles as "mission creep." The US military contribution to Combined Joint Task Force-Operation Inherent Resolve, the US-led international coalition to fight against IS in Iraq and Syria, has expanded from an "Expeditionary Targeting Force" of merely 200 special operators to somewhere around 2,200 soldiers drawn from the conventional force in just four years. Even following the coalition's dislocation of IS from its principal strongholds, the Trump administration can be expected to deploy further forces to interdict the group's remaining leaders and has vowed to stay "as long as needed" (Khalid, 2018). Most of the group's leaders have absconded to the Middle Euphrates River Valley. This area, which interlocks and roughly bisects Iraq and Syria, represents the vestiges of IS' declared physical caliphate.

We argue that critics of precision strike warfare have employed a superficial understanding of this nuanced practise that conflates the means – lethal strikes, raids, and cyberattacks – with any number of identified end states, including the disruption, destruction, or defeat of terrorists. Critics have failed to appreciate novel conceptual frameworks governing precision strike warfare that, while employed extensively by the US and its coalition partners, have not penetrated the wider academic discourse on the evolving character of warfare. This is partly a function of anti-intellectualism within Western militaries. No matter how implicit, this condition helps explain the perception that "practitioners too often lack the time or the environment for the kind of considered reflection that best produces introspective analysis and thoughtful guidance" (Dunlap Jr., 2014, 110). Another contributing factor is the lack of an operationally informed evaluation of precision strike warfare since 9/11, especially of the US' practises given its intractable WOT.

The remainder of this chapter unfolds in four parts. To better contextualise the argument, the chapter first provides a fuller account of international society's warfare trap. Next, the chapter differentiates between "old" and "new" terrorism prior to introducing a novel framework employed by the US military that is designed to redress recent incarnations of terror. The evidence shows that commanders employ precision strike warfare to *pressure* a terrorist group in order to harass it; *leverage* central figures such as "middle men" or materiel that enable a terrorist group's critical requirements; and *desynchronise* a terrorist group by capturing or killing key decision-makers and symbolic figureheads to isolate members from each other and disintegrate the group. The chapter then operationalises the framework through a case study of US-led counterterrorism (CT) operations against IS' branch in Central and South Asia. This discussion is informed by insights garnered from the authors' combat experiences, access to unclassified enemy material, and emerging field research. The chapter concludes by presenting a research agenda to help reconcile international society's countervailing positions on warfare.

INTERNATIONAL SOCIETY'S WARFARE TRAP

Although member states may not equally bear the burden of such responsibilities or burdens, the impasse between absolute and precision strike warfare imposes political and moral dilemmas for international society. Arguably, absolute warfare serves as a weak bookend and an ambiguous basis for war as it is understood and practised today. An understanding of sovereignty as a responsibility incumbent on elites to protect citizens, both within and without the contiguous borders of their states, means political authorities must now enhance their ability to precisely engage adversaries while still accommodating some features of absolute warfare (Glanville, 2014, 5). Notably, the maintenance of large military formations is partly designed to deter traditional threats to national security, including intervention and a nuclear strike as a prelude to a wider conflagration. This tenuous balance subjects international society to a slippery slope whereby states are pulled in competing directions, attempting to uphold the virtues of one form of warfare while simultaneously championing another. The result is a glaring yet poorly studied contradiction in the strategic culture of states or interrogative calculations of how, where, when, and why to employ military force.

Normally incontrovertible in absolute warfare, precision strike warfare begs questions of target permissibility. Legal opinions from states that find it challenging to keep up with operations as they actually take place govern this issue. Another octave along this line of inquiry explores the boundaries of war, especially in the case of the ongoing WOT. For practitioners exercising the lethal strikes, raids, and cyberattacks that characterise this conflict, the boundaries are fuzzy. Despite or perhaps because of this ambiguity, there is palpable overlap among the ideas of absolute and precision strike warfare, although it is possible to discern a critical distinction. Whereas precision strike warfare simultaneously refers to the totality of systems and resources required to identify, track, and engage threats and restrains the type and amount of force employed to minimise collateral damage, absolute warfare lacks such restraining logic.

Absolute Warfare

Since 9/11, the omnipresence of warfare has played an outsized role in the maintenance of international order, influencing and often eclipsing the diplomatic resolution of grievances that help engender conflict. According to the current lack of congressional oversight on the US president's "limited" military actions around the world, particularly in Africa, Central Asia, and the Middle East, war now constitutes an axiomatic policy response to signal and correct the transgressions of others. Ironically, Clausewitz referenced the idea of limitlessness when outlining his notion of absolute war, the effects of which stem from a pervasive mobilisation of society – a mobilisation in absolute terms. If the concept of absolute war is to serve as a bookend for the spectrum of conflict, it can hardly be said to provide the kind of stability or outcome associated with the initial idea, namely the unequivocal defeat of an adversary.

Objecting to the treatment of absolute war as an "empirical category" as such, Mary Kaldor (2010, 272) affirms that absolute war remains an "abstract idea, a Kantian type," concerning the "essence of war, its inner nature." Interestingly, Clausewitz (1827, 606) recognised the idealised and perhaps unobtainable nature of absolute war, although historians often characterise the two World Wars as "total" in their means and intent: "[a]s policy becomes more ambitious and vigorous, so will war, and this may reach the point where war attains its absolute form." Thusly, absolute warfare constitutes a routine or structure – a structured routine – that unifies society and encourages immoderation to impose a behavioural change among adversaries. An appreciation of the contemporary threat landscape suggests that absolute warfare is anachronistic, although the US' war on terrorism does reflect some salient features, namely the mobilisation of society cast at war against an assumed existential threat, terrorism.

Precision Strike Warfare

Precision strike warfare, which is also commonly referred to as high-value targeting (HVT), is more reflective of empirical warfare, a "real war" (a term employed by Kaldor (2010)) that diverges from the character and consequences of absolute warfare. The intended effects of HVT are, in a sense, lessened. High-value targeting seeks to temper unintended consequences with the experience of real war. An oft-cited confusion centres on precision, typically thought of as referring to the accuracy of an attack, which actually represents the comprehensiveness of the systems employed to conduct lethal strikes, raids, and cyber-attacks. An application of surgical military force is a function of a system of systems, given the mobilisation of joint and multinational forces as well as emerging technologies. Whereas absolute warfare can be described as total in purpose, involving the use of lethal force, and accommodating a wide range of targets, HVT is conceptualised as inherently limited in purpose and reserved for a narrow scope of targets. It is precisely this misunderstanding that is responsible for the generalisations wielded against the use of HVT. Critics argue that HVT is itself dubious, lacking moral and ethical purchase because, while it is intended to minimise civilian casualties in particular, non-combatants are, at times, incidentally injured or killed (Dershowitz, 2013, 120). Similarly, Audrey Cronin (2013, 44) argues that HVT threatens to substitute means for ends, a factor that prolongs conflict. Selective killing or capturing of terrorists merely neutralises the symptoms but does not eliminate or even treat any of the underlying causes of terrorism.

In spite of these brushstrokes, HVT can occupy a number of positions along the spectrum of conflict, ranging from inter-state conflict to irregular warfare, including CT and counterinsurgency (COIN) operations. Implemented with the intention of leading to select targets and broad engagements, HVT can lead to the opposite. The striking broadness of purpose means that the assumed narrowness of the target selection is arguably antithetical to HVT as intended. This goes well beyond the issue of violating the principles of discrimination and proportionality in the law of armed conflict, which dictate states' adherence to engaging targets directly and with the minimal amount of force necessary to achieve an objective in conflict and war. As elucidated below, a transition from old to new terrorism following 9/11 is largely responsible for international society's movement towards HVT, as informed by America's proliferated use of the practise as a principle policy and CT instrument.

UNPACKING HIGH-VALUE TARGETING

Old and New Terrorism

Since 9/11, which Daniel Shapiro (2018) characterises as an inflection point for the modern terrorism era, scholars and practitioners have attempted to differentiate between old and new terrorism. Although a degree of continuity pervades these archetypes, the scholarly literature problematises them on the basis of four liniments. These include: (i) the purpose and aims of terrorists; (ii) the prosecutors of terrorism; (iii) the organisational structures that undergird terrorist groups; (iv) the production of violence, which refers to the specific instruments and methods employed by terrorist groups. Studying these categories, scholars who identify this continuity argue that not much is really *new* in the research agenda. By measuring changes – or the lack thereof – in a sufficient number of key features of terrorism, they suggest the new wave of terrorism is not qualitatively different from previous waves of terrorism. While they acknowledge that there has been a recognisable evolution in the behaviour of terrorist groups, the strategic goal still remains the same: to compel enemy forces to withdraw and to highlight the symbolic nature of attacks. Writing on the latter, some, like Ariel Merari (1993, 213), highlight that the trope of "expressive terrorism" – in its purest iteration, groups who have little hope of achieving any political object yet commit to terror methodologies regardless – highlights continuity.

Meanwhile, others argue there are a number of key distinguishing features between erstwhile and contemporary forms of terrorism. These analysts identify the indiscriminate nature of intended targets and attacks conducted by terrorists, the religiosity that increasingly explains their motivation[2], their aims and doctrine, their movement towards a horizontal (as opposed to hierarchical) structure, and even the erosion of technical and logistical restraints that previously represented prohibitive entry costs to specialty skills and weapons. Of course, some, including Walter Laqueur (1996), have also abstracted transmutations in the intent and capability of terrorists since the early 20th century. Our analysis adds to this rich body of literature. In some cases, we advance the prevailing analysis given our broad cross-section of experiences simultaneously fighting and studying terrorism since 9/11. While a detailed critique of old and new terrorism is beyond the scope of this chapter, below we interrogate two of these categories in order to better understand the relationship between HVT and international society's warfare trap.

Old terrorism was designed to achieve ethno-nationalistic and ideological agendas. It was therefore bounded territorially and overlapped with the boundaries of sovereign states as well as the interpreted contours of regions and sub-regions. The new terrorism is broader in reach. Terrorist groups now constitute not only non-state but transregional threat networks to the extent that social media and communications protocols, including secure messaging applications, enable their critical requirements and heightened interest in providing governance, security, and other public goods. These are functions that their progenitors were reticent to provide.[3] Highlighting the roles of globalisation and late modernity, these new realities suggest an evolution in terrorism. Take, for example, IS. Although the group's leader, Abu Bakr al-Baghdadi, and his apparatchiks flouted international society's most basic institution, sovereignty, IS harnessed terror to forge a (pariah) state in an attempt to establish an alternative order informed by a comingling of Salafism and Islamism (Saikal, 2018, 7). To be sure, it is difficult to estimate the longevity of this trend. Yet, some notable scholars, including Stephen Walt, enjoin international society to learn to live with IS and its regional affiliates, particularly because member states are not postured to manage the spillage of terrorism across borders other than in extraordinary circumstances or when new terrorists "make a major mistake or are discovered by accident" (Laqueur, 1996, 34).

Globalised communications also allow transregional terrorist groups to enable and direct attacks from sanctuaries in the so-called "fragile" or "failing" states characterised by weak governance, under-addressed grievances, and poor security. The latter condition is often a function of multiple competing security providers, both officially sanctioned by the state and informal, or an absence of security altogether. In fact, myriad terrorist and insurgent groups, epitomised by AQ and the Taliban, operate from veritable safe havens that span the porous border between Afghanistan and Pakistan. The vacuum of security inherent to such safe havens constitutes a cause and effect of these and other groups and largely explains their enduring presence after decades of conflict (Motwani and Bose, 2015, 266). More threatening still, the Internet is responsible for a wave of "lone wolf" terrorists since 2013, recruited and radicalised through social media and inspired to conduct attacks through low-cost but effective means, including knives and vehicles. For IS, these represent "just war tactics" and account for a preponderance of the group's global operations. David Kilcullen (2005, 597) conceptualises such tactics as part and parcel of a "global jihadist movement" wherein new terrorists, in this case IS, exacerbate local grievances and provide the guiding ideology to incite attacks by sympathisers against established political authorities in the interest of husbanding a caliphate.

The production of violence is another important distinction between old and new terrorism. Previous waves of terrorism engaged in selective and discriminatory acts of violence. Bruce Hoffman (1999, 7) points out that organisations targeted "symbolic targets representing the source of their animus" in order to draw attention to themselves and their causes. It is unclear if present-day terrorists subscribe to similar calculations on target selection, namely the expected political dividends of instilling fear among a citizenry and its ruling elite. Arguably, new terrorists employ violence as an end in itself, given their puritanical ideologies, epitomised by IS' "end of times" rationale. Brian Jenkins (2018) makes the provocative argument that terror itself may now constitute ideology. What is clear is that the means of violence employed by new terrorists are comparatively more macabre and indiscriminate. Since the 1990s, terrorist incidents worldwide have declined while the percentage of incidents with fatalities has increased. Increasing lethality, aided by greater access to rudimentary technology and logistics, as epitomised by the improvised explosive device (IED), is often cited as a major evolution in terrorism. If we accept that new terrorism is in fact qualitatively and quantitatively different, have the practises of member states of international society to disrupt, destroy, and defeat transregional terrorist groups fluctuated in kind?

Counterterrorism Challenges in the Contemporary Era

Israel's relentless pursuit of Arab nationalists committed to its destruction, particularly Hezbollah and Hamas, has informed international society's response to seasoned terrorists, which is lethal and intended to kill or capture important figures. Underlining this approach is the assumption that charismatic officials, particularly leaders, are integral to a terrorist group's intent, capability, and longevity. Responses to terrorists today maintain this lethal quality. However, they are increasingly non-lethal and designed to delegitimise the appeal of transregional terrorist groups among sympathisers and potential recruits. Consequently, while CT and HVT as central means are still designed to kill or capture key personalities, the practise is now defined by an equitable application of force across a terrorist group's critical requirements. This approach is predicated on addressing the underlying enablers of terror and not simply its symptoms, including acts of intimidation, oppression, complex attacks, and bombings. On balance, the critical requirements of new terrorists include their ability: (i) to communicate globally; (ii) to generate revenue; (iii) to facilitate lethal aid across borders; (iv) to conduct operations, namely of the martyrdom variety but also from defined, trained, and capable formations; (v) to innovate; and (vi) to produce and disseminate media.

War fatigue and casualty aversion among particularly great powers also mean that contemporary CT is prosecuted indirectly, which is to say through coalitions and surrogates. On the one hand, coalitions pool resources and mitigate risk through a multilateral application of force that is designed to impose multiple dilemmas against transregional terrorist groups simultaneously. As referenced above, an international coalition formed by America and managed by the US Central Command, Combined Joint Task Force-Operation Inherent Resolve, spearheads the campaign to defeat IS. On the other hand, the sponsorship of surrogate forces externalises the burdens associated with the expeditionary deployment of counterterrorist forces. The US-led coalition designed to defeat IS remains equally instructive here. The Peshmerga, or the military forces of an autonomous but stateless Kurdistan straddling the quadripoint shared between Iraq, Iran, Syria, and Turkey, represents perhaps the coalition's most "indispensable" manoeuvre formation and has led the pursuit of IS across parts of Iraq and Syria (Ahmed, 2018).

Unfortunately, multilateral approaches have heretofore resulted from discreet arrangements intermittently established for the myopic purpose of managing threats within a defined area. States ascribe to a pluralistic conception of international society wherein sovereignty constitutes the central legal-rational norm. Contrary to a solidaristic order that adopts consensus-based agreements to "thicken" interstate relations in pursuit of transcendental goals, including global security, a pluralistic order conditions member states for transactional cooperation, namely intelligence sharing (Bellamy, 2005, 283). This practical orientation circumvents integration among states to coordinate political and military responses designed to contain and eventually defeat transregional terrorists. One rare but inchoate example is "Operation Gallant Phoenix." According to the US' top military official, General John Dunford, this is "an intelligence sharing arrangement that started out with eight or so countries and has since expanded to 19 nations who have committed to sharing this intelligence." He added that "Gallant Phoenix allows allied nations not only to share intelligence on the foreign fighter threat but also to get that information back to their law enforcement and homeland security agencies ... in order to deal with this challenge" (Kitfield, 2017). Unfortunately, the *New York Times* reports that as a US military solution to transregional terrorist groups, "Operation Gallant Phoenix" "has caused turf war tensions with the [Central Intelligence Agency] CIA," which is statutorily responsible for sharing intelligence with the US' friends and allies to enable action (Schmitt, 2016). If scholars and practitioners have accounted for broad shifts in terrorism, precisely how does international society, as informed by the US' practises since 9/11, combat new terrorism?

High-Value Targeting[4]

Commanders at all tactical, operational, and strategic levels use the targeting process to apply lethal and non-lethal means against an adversary to achieve the intended effect. Procedurally, the targeting process consists of four steps, including identification of the objective(s), planning, execution, and assessment (Pratzner, 2016, 80). Finite resources, including communications, fires, force protection, intelligence, logistics, and medical support, mean that prioritisation is the *sine qua non* of the targeting process. It is incumbent on commanders to identify priorities, usually communicated as lines of effort pursuant to a broader campaign plan, to enable their staffs to apply limited resources synchronised across time and space against a target to achieve a desired end state. Targeting is therefore both deliberative and iterative, based on measures of performance and effectiveness. The former judged how well a military organisation executed an operation; the latter informed the degree to which the unit achieved its objective(s). As an inherently conceptual process, targeting is also applicable to the range of military operations bookended by capacity building and absolute warfare and coincident with the operational planning phases. According to US military doctrine, operational planning aligns with six phases comprised of the following elements: shape, deter, seize the initiative, dominate, stabilise, and (re)enable civilian authority (2006, IV 26).

High-value targeting transcends these phases and constitutes international society's embryonic approach to addressing transregional terrorists while protecting against collateral damage. This CT practise, which consists of both lethal and non-lethal means, is designed to capture or kill adversarial high-level personnel and essential materiel. It is based on the belief that the removal of key personnel and assets is capable of degrading a terrorist group's capabilities and will inevitably result in its collapse by forcing the group to come to political terms or by creating such disorganisation and chaos that the group cannot operate sufficiently to survive. Defining a target and the intended effect is a matter of debate, however. Decapitation theorists posit that capturing or killing terrorist leaders is the crucial independent variable in the defeat of terrorist groups, with special consideration given to the structure of the group. Appreciation of critical requirements demonstrates that the scope of targets is broader and includes "a selected geographic area, object, capability, person, or organisation" (Ducheine, 2016, 205). Given this logic, commanders focus HVT against high-value and high-payoff targets integral to a terrorist group's critical requirements. High-value targets are personnel or assets required by the enemy for success. Commanders are most interested in capturing or killing high-payoff targets. They represent a prerequisite for the commander to complete his or her mission.

Critics frequently limit the utility of HVT to merely the capturing or killing of high-payoff targets. Just as routinely, they adjudicate the merits of HVT based on the efficiency with which military forces employ lethal and non-lethal means against such targets. The preferred measure of performance for scholars and human rights advocates is collateral damage, primarily civilian casualties. This derives from an estimation that advanced target acquisition systems, collateral damage assessment software, and aerially delivered munitions have all but eliminated unintended consequences. This was the subject of a recent study by Cornell University that resulted in Michael Evangelista's (2014) volume, *The American Way of Bombing: Changing Ethical and Legal Norms, From Flying Fortresses to Drones*, which lambasted the US military's precision warfare approach (Evangelista and Shue, 2014). This and other studies fail to account for both enemy- and friendly-centric anomalies, which are more characteristic of CT than observers appreciate.

The Islamic State and other new terrorists exploit prohibitions against civilian casualties codified in rules of engagement by collocating with women and children to heighten their collateral signature. Charles J. Dunlap, Jr. (2014, 117) also points out that "every legitimate military operation seeks to avoid such losses, yet the fact remains that the law, properly applied, recognises that incidental civilian deaths in connection with an otherwise bona fide attack on a military target are acceptable and often *expected*." This is an unpleasant recrimination, although it does capture an aphorism relating to the nature of war relayed by members of the Israeli Defence Force and intelligence services, lauded by Ronen Bergman as the forebearers of modern-day CT: "[t]he unexpected is the thing that is most expected" (2018, 170). An informed understanding of HVT demonstrates that commanders execute a sophisticated conceptual model that is not reducible to joint and US doctrinal targeting cycles including "F2T2EA" (Find, Fix, Track, Target, Execute, Assess) and "F3EAD" (Find, Fix, Finish, Exploit, Analyse, Disseminate) (Field Manual No. 3–60, 2010, B–1). The model proposed here links a targeting cycle to the targeting methods applied, the intended outcomes of action, and the operational conditions that prescribe or prohibit action. An investigation of US-led CT operations since 9/11 suggests that commanders employ HVT to *pressure*, *leverage*, or *desynchronise* terrorists.

While policymakers, defence intellectuals, and pundits customarily reference pressure, both doctrine and scholarship conspicuously fail to provide a definition. At best, pressure is a platitude. The verb is employed to approximate an intended targeting effect. At worst, pressure is a panacea that represents a seemingly feasible substitute for strategy. Applying pressure involves harassing a terrorist organisation and its members to complicate operations, force errors, and delay communications. It is intended to *disrupt* an adversary by interrupting its operational capacity, tempo, formation, and initiative (Field Manual No. 3–90, 2001, B–16–7). In practise, military forces target multiple critical capabilities, often simultaneously, to desynchronise and confuse a terrorist network's support and operational activities. The pressure method is similar but not analogous to swarming. Also referred to as "whack-a-mole," swarming is a "seemingly amorphous" but deliberate, sustained, and coordinated series of lethal operations intended to disorient the enemy (Arquilla and Ronfeldt, 2001, 1). At the same time, applying pressure enables military forces flexibility to concentrate, surge, or redirect combat power to disrupt a terrorist group piecemeal or holistically. Because the pressure method similarly prioritises targets or casts the widest net across the depth and breadth of a terrorist group, it also increases the probability of capturing or killing consequential terrorists, including financiers and couriers. This approach has the added benefit of generating second-order effects, such as intelligence, that facilitate further operations. It also shapes the battlespace for both military and non-military follow-on operations, often designed to ameliorate grievances and legitimise political authority (Gellman, 2011). Finally, pressure fatigues terrorists by increasing the transaction costs of communication, planning, and operations. This can encourage terrorists to take greater risks and expose themselves by conducting operations to demonstrate resolve and garner support.

Rather than directing action, *leverage* points are assets that enable a terrorist group's activities. They may include individuals with favourable reputations and, therefore, high degrees of social connection. They often facilitate communications, possess niche skills, such as bomb-making, forgery, or media production, are ideological authorities, or facilitate lethal aid, including componentry, money, and supplies. Leverage points may also consist of material that enables and protects terrorists, including ammunition and explosives, communications devices, and sanctuaries. For some analysts, leverage points represent a terrorist group's centre of gravity, or "the hub of all power and movement, on which everything depends" (Meadows, 2008, 145). Network analysis indicates that leverage points are also often associated with task organisation (Davis and Jenkins, 2004, 8). Similar to AQ, IS organises itself across a range of operational and support specialties that require "facilitators, financiers, computer specialists, or bomb-makers" (Frankel, 2011, 27). Commanders attack leverage points to *destroy* a terrorist group's functionality or damage the group "so badly that it cannot perform any function or be restored to a usable condition without being entirely rebuilt" (Field Manual No. 3–90, 2001, B-15). This de-professionalises the network and imposes additional recruitment and training costs that further diminish operational capacity (Wilner, 2010, 312). The impact of such skills shortages on short-term offensive capacity is evidenced by leveraged targeting against the Taliban in the Panjwai District of Kandahar Province in 2012. By killing or capturing explosive handlers faster than Taliban leaders could replace them, the coalition eroded institutional knowledge regarding the whereabouts of IEDs. This resulted in Taliban members being killed or maimed by their own mines and helped reduce enemy activity in the district by 77% (Lushenko and Hardy, 2016, 117).

Desynchronisation, often referred to as decapitation, is the most championed but scrutinised targeting method. It involves capturing or killing visible and symbolic terrorist leaders in order to disintegrate the group and isolate members from each other. The successive removal of terrorist leaders impedes guidance and coherent messaging, which threatens to weaken and delegitimise the group. While replacement leaders are often found, they typically lack the charisma, experience, relationships, and skills of their predecessors. Meanwhile, the loss of leadership disrupts a group's capacity to plan, supply, and stage attacks given the emphasis on defensive measures and poor guidance (Wilner, 2010, 312). Groups that rely on central guidance for autonomous and decentralised cells also suffer setbacks from the targeting of highly visible or influential figures. Interference with a group's key decision-making body can induce power struggles, confuse organisational direction, and encourage infighting. This diverts time and resources from offensive operations to enable a preferred yet contentious line of succession (Wilner, 2007, 5). Such internecine violence can engender competing factions and ultimately fracture a terrorist group, resulting in its demise.

The intent of desynchronising is to both *disrupt* and *destroy* a terrorist group, considering internal confusion impedes and degrades critical capabilities. In certain cases, it may also enable the *defeat* of a terrorist group. Defeat "occurs when an enemy force has temporarily or permanently lost the physical means or the will to fight" and may be induced by a lack of coherent organisational purpose following the capture or killing of an influential leader (Field Manual No. 3–90, 2001, B–15). Bryan Price's (2012, 44) empirical study of leadership decapitation in terrorist groups found that religious organisations were particularly susceptible to leadership targeting, possibly due to the integral role of influential figures in "framing and interpreting organisational goals and strategies." It is important to note that leadership targeting is not utilised as a means to victory in and of itself but should be subordinate to an overall strategy. Yet, the stature and centrality of especially ordained leaders such as Abu Bakr al-Baghdadi mean their removal is capable of at least disrupting terrorist groups.

Although presented discretely, commanders exercise all three HVT methods, often simultaneously and within the same area of operations, against the same or adjacent adversaries. High-value targeting normally entails a high operational tempo in order to exploit the intelligence dividends of previous operations, particularly information on the intent, capability, and structure of terrorist groups gleaned from captured enemy material. This can include communication devices, correspondence, and documents such as ledgers, maps, and plans. Follow-on HVT operations also benefit from "reflections," which are spikes in communication after an operation. Chatter across a terrorist group helps commanders and their staffs identify which individuals are sending and receiving information, the nature of the information, and the group's recourse. Reflections are captured through multiple disciplines: human, imagery, measurement, signature, and signals (intelligence). The exploitation of captured enemy material and reflections is critical to informing measures of effectiveness that justify commanders' decisions to recalibrate HVT. The ability to rapidly transition to another HVT method, pursue an additional method concurrently, or redirect resources towards an altogether different target helps commanders create opportunities and exploit vulnerabilities (Figure 22.1). The chapter now interrogates the US-led coalition's efforts against IS' branch in Central and South Asia to demonstrate how practitioners apply this typology.

ELEMENTS

METHODS	ACTIONS	EFFECTS	OUTCOMES
PRESSURE	High volume and frequency of raids, lethal strikes, and cyber attacks against targets	Harass and Fatigue Shape Battlespace Enable Other Operations	Disrupt
LEVERAGE	Selective targeting of facilitators, highly skilled or highly connected individuals and assets	Deprofessionalize Degrade Functionality Increase Costs	Disrupt Destroy
DESYNCHRONIZE	Targeting of most visible and/or influential figures or leaders	Induce Internal Disharmony Alienate Organization from leaders Deskill and Delegitimize Leaders	Disrupt Destroy Defeat

Figure 22.1 The HVT Model.

Source: Authors' own rendering.

HVT IN PRACTICE – THE ISLAMIC STATE IN THE KHORASAN PROVINCE

On July 15, 2014, multiple groups aligned with the Tehrik-i-Taliban Pakistan (TTP) merged to form the Tehrik-e Khilafat Pakistan (TKP). Approximately 2,000 jihadists from across Pakistan's large population centres combined under the auspices of the "Movement for the Caliphate in Pakistan," or TKP, which constituted the political backbone of the Islamic State in the Khorasan Province (IS-KP) (Giustozzi, 2018, 27). The Islamic State's wider caliphate-building project and the charismatic leadership of Hafiz Saeed Khan incentivised defecting commanders and their fighters to sever ties with the TTP in pursuit of a *Wilayat* (province) *Khorasan*. The Islamic State accepted the TKP's pledge of allegiance on January 10, 2015, and appointed Khan as the IS-KP's inaugural leader. He demonstrated the loyalty and magnetism necessary to galvanise variegated organisations with multiple interests and stakeholders. Abu Muhammed al-Adnani, IS' public relations official in Syria, announced IS-KP's formation on January 26, 2015, after which the founding cadre infiltrated the Spin Ghar mountain range of Nangarhar Province in eastern Afghanistan (Giustozzi, 2018, 31). Through what Borhan Osman (2016) describes as a "campaign of beheadings," Khan and his governing shura forcibly displaced residents not supportive of IS' eschatology. This enabled IS-KP to consolidate its Islamic governorate with the trappings of civil services, including agriculture, education, finance, health, immigration, and judicial departments ("Interview with the Wali of Khurasan," 2016). This is fundamental to IS-KP's intent to secure Afghanistan to legitimise IS' caliphate across the Khorasan Province, which encompasses parts of Iran, China, Central Asia, the Indian Subcontinent, and Southeast Asia.

Successive leaders following Khan's death in July 2016 continue to prosecute an expansionist military strategy pursuant to the group's overarching goal. The strategy entails establishing redoubts across Afghanistan to spread IS-KP's influence through small bands of guerillas that absorb locals and subsume competing groups (Giustozzi, 2018, 42). It is characterised by a decisive effort in Nangarhar Province, a supporting effort in Kunar Province, and, until recently, a shaping effort in Jowzjan Province. Nangarhar constitutes the network's headquarters and enables mission command; Kunar facilitates indoctrination, training, and attacks; and

Jowzjan serves as a principal reception centre for foreign fighters, some fleeing Iraq and Syria but most drawn from Central and South Asia as well as Europe (Johnson, 2016, 2). These efforts are designed to enable the group to encircle Jalalabad City in Nangarhar. This will also provide IS-KP access to a vital artery, the Kabul-Jalalabad highway, which will enable lethal aid smuggled from Pakistan as well as attacks against Kabul City, Afghanistan's capital. To achieve these intermediate objectives, IS-KP pursues guerilla tactics to outmanoeuvre the coalition and avoid decisive engagements. Similarly, the network continues to consolidate its position in Kunar to encourage a hasty deployment of Taliban forces that will create vulnerabilities elsewhere that IS-KP can exploit. If successful, *Wilayat Khorasan* could isolate Jalalabad City and further destabilise eastern Afghanistan.

The group's longevity is a function of this ambitious strategy, and amid IS' losses in Iraq and Syria, *Wilayat Khorasan* is arguably IS' most viable and lethal affiliate. The network continues to broaden its operational reach beyond eastern Afghanistan into areas that are weakly governed and poorly secured, and, although a fraction of its size, even the Taliban cannot expel IS-KP.[5] As a matter of fact, the Taliban did block IS-KP's expansion into Ghor and Zabul Provinces. Yet the group endured and expanded its footprint in Kunar, at the Taliban's expense. While analysts often conflate IS-KP's physical centre of gravity in eastern Afghanistan with the scope of its regional designs, a commitment to supplant militant groups east of Afghanistan explains its efforts to establish new affiliates in South and Southeast Asia. The network has capitalised on territorial and ethnic flashpoints in Bangladesh, India, Myanmar, Pakistan, and Tajikistan to indigenise its agenda among marginalised Muslims and secular populations (Lushenko et al., 2018). Finally, IS-KP is the most lethal extremist group in Afghanistan measured against its intent and capability to inspire, enable, and direct attacks abroad. Unlike local threats such as the Haqqani Network, which wage attacks in Kabul for the purpose of re-establishing an Islamic Emirate under the Taliban's control, IS-KP wields its terror transregionally. In October 2017, the US Justice Department arrested three IS-KP operatives who were in the final throes of executing attacks in New York City ("Acting Manhattan US Attorney Announces The Court's Unsealing of Charges Against Three Men Arrested For Participating In An International Plot To Carry Out Terrorist Attacks In New York City for ISIS In The Summer of 2016"). More recently, IS-KP claimed credit for killing four cyclists in Tajikistan. After running down the cyclists with a vehicle in Dushanbe, five IS members attacked them with knives and firearms (Callimachi, 2018).

These considerations help explain why senior Afghan security officials, while acknowledging that the Taliban represents Afghanistan's existential threat, are concerned that IS-KP is becoming more dangerous (Ferran, 2016). This begs the question of how the coalition has approached IS-KP since 2015. Initially, the coalition attempted to moderate the spectre surrounding IS-KP's rise given competing priorities, namely the coalition's withdrawal from Afghanistan and a rapidly internationalising fight against IS's principle sanctuary in Iraq and Syria. On April 20, 2015, for instance, a Pentagon spokesman prematurely reasoned that "the conditions in Afghanistan are such that ISIL would not be welcome" (Munoz and Harper, 2015). In December 2016, before the evidence indicated that IS-KP constituted more than a fleeting nuisance, the coalition initiated a CT strategy designed to disrupt *Wilayat Khorasan*. In May 2017, the US Secretary of Defence, James Mattis, directed General John Nicholson, then Commander of US and Coalition Forces in Afghanistan, to "annihilate" or defeat IS-KP. This guidance encouraged a heightened operational tempo enabled by enhanced targeting authorities authorised by President Donald Trump's new South Asia policy announced in August 2017 (Baron and Weisgerber, 2017). The twin objectives explicated by Nicholson and Mattis, disrupt and defeat, inform the prevailing methods the coalition adopted to target IS-KP under the banner of "Operation Green Sword."

Since 2015, the coalition has *pressured* IS-KP through unremitting lethal strikes. According to a report published in July 2018, "the number of weapons dropped in the country already surpasses the totals from all years AFCENT [US Air Forces Central Command] has tracked, back to 2013" (Rempfer, 2018). Lethal strikes have been complemented by thousands of clearance operations and raids designed to dislocate the network from its sanctuaries in Nangarhar and Jowzjan. After assuming control of eleven districts in southern Nangarhar in 2016, which amounted to 40% of the province, the coalition's clearance operations forced IS-KP to consolidate and reorganise within two districts – Achin and Naziyan – by late 2017 (Giustozzi, 2018, 180). On July 9, 2018, a multi-phase clearance operation conducted by a combined Afghan and US force also netted the capture of IS-KP's capital in Deh Bala District. According to the ground force commander, Lieutenant Colonel Josh Thiel from the US First Special Forces Group, "ISIS was using this site to prepare and move high-profile attacks on Kabul and Jalalabad." Additionally, "it provided money, finance, and logistics to ISIS, and we've taken that away from them" (Fedschun, 2018). Beyond confusing the group's support and operational activities, the operation killed 170 additional terrorists. This amounts to nearly 10% of IS-KP's estimated end-strength of fighters in Afghanistan, according to the lower membership figure of 2,000. The Taliban's own offensives against IS-KP have incidentally complemented the coalition's operations and presented the group with multiple dilemmas, especially in Kunar, a safe haven for myriad terrorist and insurgency groups given the dense forests and cavernous terrain.

The coalition's *pressure* encouraged IS-KP members to alter their daily routines, and the exploitation of captured enemy material and reflections enabled the coalition to simultaneously *desynchronise* the group. The death of IS-KP's inaugural leader in July 2016 following a lethal strike constituted a prelude for the coalition's attempt to decapitate the network from above while simultaneously disrupting it from below. The former approach resulted from the coalition's intent to exacerbate IS-KP's fundamental challenge, which leadership was central to resolving: reconciling the competing interests of multiple, disparate groups that merged to form *Wilayat Khorasan* (Giustozzi, 2018, 211). A month prior to Mattis' guidance, the coalition employed the largest non-nuclear bomb ever used in combat, the GBU-43, against IS-KP's headquarters. According to Nicholson, this bomb was deployed "to destroy caves and tunnels, which ISIS-K has been using along with extensive belts of IEDs, to thicken their positions against our offensive." "'Right weapon for right target': Top US commander defends use of 'mother of all bombs,'" 2017). Afghan officials stated that the bomb also killed approximately 100 IS-KP members, and an IS-KP source reported it "pulverised" eight million US dollars (Giustozzi, 2018, 96). A month following this singular event, the coalition killed Khan's successor, Sheikh Abdul Hasib, during a raid in Achin. The coalition killed his replacement, Saad Erhabi, formerly IS-KP's leader in Logar Province, nearly a year later following a lethal strike in Nangarhar. His death constituted the removal of *Wilayat Khorasan's* third supreme leader in little over two years.

Similarly, the coalition killed Qari Hikmatullah following a lethal strike in Jowzjan in April 2018. According to the *New York Times*, Qari was admonished by the Taliban for his "extreme savagery" and therefore joined IS-KP, where he roused Jowzjan's Uzbek constituency to join the group, some after splitting from the Islamic Movement of Uzbekistan (Nordland Ghazi, 2018). Afghan and US forces also conducted a clearance operation into IS-KP's sanctuary in Jowzjan, Darzab District, and killed 22 terrorist operatives. While the group quickly identified Habib Rahman as Qari's successor and consolidated and reorganised by occupying houses abandoned by the local population in the vicinity of its new headquarters in Sar Dara District, infighting eroded the group's coherency. Until recently, both the coalition and the Taliban had been reticent to exploit this vulnerability. While preoccupation with IS-KP's headquarters in Deh Bala and logistical constraints hamstrung the coalition, the Taliban failed to recruit fighters and attempted to minimise exposure to lethal strikes during ongoing talks with the coalition pursuant to a negotiated settlement. In August 2018, the Taliban finally counterattacked. The onslaught killed 153 IS-KP members, injured 100 more, and resulted in the capture of nearly 135. Over 200 remaining IS-KP members surrendered to Afghan forces, including Rahman and his deputy, Mufti Nehmatullah. According to him, the surrender of IS-KP's remaining combat power in Jowzjan resulted from fatigue given the coalition's targeting concomitant to the Taliban's counterattack. "We were tired of fighting, and pressure was on us from both sides" (Rahim and Nordland, 2018).

The dividends of the coalition's combined *pressure* and *desynchronisation* approach to targeting IS-KP are palpable. The coalition has killed thousands of fighters, disrupted the group's foreign donations and media operations, isolated members from leaders, and reduced IS-KP's territory in southern Nangarhar. The strategy also capitalised on the Taliban's attacks against IS-KP to enable commanders to reapportion the coalition's limited combat power against emerging challenges elsewhere, including the Taliban's own offensive against district and provincial capitals across Afghanistan. Nonetheless, the longevity of such gains is unclear, and the group continues to resolve. *Wilayat Khorasan* occupies more territory than it did in 2015 and continues to establish redoubts in remote terrain, especially in northern Afghanistan, abetted by the power vacuum imposed by First Vice President Abdul Rashid Dostum's prolonged exile in Turkey following his alleged sodomy of a rival. The group is adept at replenishing combat losses through defectors from other extremist groups and harnesses social media and secure messaging applications to recruit. It has also introduced a "Cubs of the Caliphate" programme to recruit and radicalise children aged six to sixteen. These "child soldiers" are indoctrinated in camps across Kunar and Nangarhar through a regimented pedagogy prescribed by IS' educators. The group's deliberate operationalisation of children is designed to exploit Western legal and moral prohibitions against targeting youth. If not addressed, this practise threatens to institutionalise the enduring recruitment of new, younger, and perhaps more ardent supporters into IS-KP (McCue et al., 2017, 21–26).

The group has capitalised on its talent management to professionalise its attack capability, and its operations tempo now supersedes the Haqqani Network. This is often identified as the most lethal organisation in Afghanistan given its massive car bombs and complex attacks that incorporate suicide bombers (Brown and Rassler, 2013). The biggest threat to Afghanistan's parliamentary and presidential elections is IS-KP, not the Haqqani Network and its parent organisation, the Taliban. The latter are aware that civilian casualties undermine their legitimacy. Despite, or perhaps because of, the collateral damage, IS-KP targets electoral sites heavily trafficked by Afghans based on IS' broader intent to undermine democracies globally. More troublesome is IS-KP's adaptation. The network has capitalised on its increasingly sophisticated attacks within Afghanistan to establish a cadre of facilitators capable of inspiring, enabling, and directing attacks abroad through social media and secure messaging applications. The coalition's emphasis on HVT is therefore problematic because it may not address the group's radical ideology, which enables recruitment and indoctrination, is foundational to its narrative and brand, and legitimises its goal to plant the black flag across the Khorasan. Even considering the imbalance between the coalition's, ergo, the US', lethal and non-lethal CT approaches, however, this assessment oversimplifies the challenge. The surprising resiliency of IS-KP, as noted by a recent United Nations Security Council report, is a function of at least several factors (Umarov, 2018).

First, the coalition has targeted IS-KP's personnel and material discreetly and failed to proactively exploit vulnerabilities associated with the group's critical requirements. A linear approach to *pressure* or *desynchronise* IS-KP has prevented simultaneous operations across the geographic and virtual scope of the group and allowed it to consolidate and reorganise after incurring significant losses. This factor helps explain the coalition's hesitancy in finishing off IS-KP's western enclave in Jowzjan sooner than it could have given its preoccupation with the group's headquarters in Deh Bala.

Second, Afghanistan's government has failed to consolidate gains against IS-KP. Because Afghan forces have not occupied terrain after the coalition has rooted out IS-KP from its principle sanctuaries, the government has not addressed the social, political, and economic grievances that the group hijacked to help establish itself in Nangarhar. For instance, Afghan forces could have exploited the coalition's momentum to eradicate IS-KP in Jowzjan four months earlier than they eventually did. Similarly, Afghan forces could have capitalised on the psychological dividends of the GBU-43 to seize IS-KP's headquarters a year earlier. Notwithstanding Giustozzi's (2018, 48) finding that IS-KP infiltrated Nangarhar "in a haphazard fashion and not as part of any ambitious plan," the recent seizure of IS-KP's capital begs important questions for the coalition's CT strategy as well as Afghan and regional security broadly. Will Afghan forces occupy Deh Bala to help prevent IS-KP's reemergence? Or, is the Afghan government content to enjoy the social media dividends given the anticipated electoral boost, if only temporarily? Regardless, *Wilayat Khorasan* has exploited the Afghan government's neo-patrimonial practises to coopt disillusioned Pashtuns and other ethnic communities to maintain its momentum, suggesting the occupation of terrain is not enough to expunge the group. Just a day after Afghan and US forces expelled IS-KP from Deh Bala, the group attacked a checkpoint in Jalalabad City, killing eight civilians. Three weeks later, the group again attacked Jalalabad City, this time the Department of Refugee Affairs, resulting in 15 civilian deaths (Dempsey, 2018).

Finally, regional states pursue misaligned CT strategies against IS-KP that the group exploits to endure. If IS-KP is a threat to regional security, then its defeat presupposes a regional CT strategy. Unfortunately, Afghanistan is the subject of a "new great game" that subordinates its security to the competing interests of regional and great powers (Goodson, 2015, 248). Suspicion, especially between India and Pakistan as well as America and Russia, has stymied security cooperation. Regional powers have attempted to unilaterally target IS-KP, if not pit multilateral security organisations against each other for their own interests. This has exacerbated interlocking security dilemmas. The coalition must now contend with Russia's statements that it, like Iran and Pakistan, has provided the Taliban lethal aid to reverse IS-KP's momentum. Unlike Iran and Pakistan, Russia is considering unilateral operations against IS-KP that stand to replicate the confused situation in Syria (Gurganus, 2018). Islamabad's inconvertible support for the Taliban has also caused Washington to recalibrate its South Asia policy, resulting in numerous demarches, the suspension of military aid, and scrutiny by financial institutions. In response, Pakistan suggests India's subterfuge is responsible for America's biting measures, and Islamabad has directed its ire towards New Delhi, its existential threat. Meanwhile, Russia has promoted the Shanghai Cooperation Organisation to address IS-KP and eschewed the coalition's use of the Quadrilateral Coordination Group (consisting of Afghanistan, America, China, and Pakistan) (Gurganus, 2018). Managing these tensions is easier said than done. However, IS-KP is a common threat, and shared interest in its defeat may help forge complementary security policies and synchronised targeting across regional states.

THE FUTURE OF WAR IN INTERNATIONAL SOCIETY

Since 9/11, great powers, but especially America, have attempted to manage increasingly transregional and lethal terrorists by proliferating the use of specialised sensors and forces. The construction of specially equipped and trained military formations is designed to enhance precision against terrorists while mitigating the risk of collateral damage, particularly civilian casualties. Some political elites, scholars, and human rights activists have advocated for a solidaristic international society portending enhanced protection for noncombatants and their property, which has encouraged repudiation of any application of force that cannot protect against civilian casualties and other forms of collateral damage. The epithets accompanying the emergence of HVT, including assassinations, intentional slayings, and extrajudicial killings, suggest that the practise lacks as much purchase as does an unrestrained or absolute application of military force propounded by Clausewitz and other theorists of warfare. Consequently, member states confront a "catch-22." A tailored approach to dealing with terrorists through lethal strikes, raids, and cyberattacks does not reconcile the broader tensions inherent in warfare as traditionally conceived, namely a state's application of unremitting force to bend an adversary to its will, even at the expense of civilian casualties. As argued here, international society's warfare trap results from a fundamental misunderstanding of how commanders execute HVT. Contrary to a desultory application of violence, HVT is a conceptual and rigorous practise that enables commanders to *pressure* or disrupt a terrorist group; *leverage* or destroy it by removing critical personnel and requirements; and, in certain instances, *desynchronise* or defeat the group altogether by removing key and symbolic leaders.

The warfare trap explored in this chapter constitutes only one component of a broader research agenda that should inform the direction of terrorism and CT studies. The transregional nature of post-modern terrorists also imposes a collective action imperative among member states of international society. Yet, aside from "Operation Gallant Phoenix," international society has merely explored the policy implications of this new requirement as informed by the United Nations Security Council Counter-Terrorism

Committee and the European Union's [EU] Global Counterterrorism Forum. To the extent international society has attempted to operationalise multilateral arrangements to target terrorists, as in the Combined Joint Task Force-Operation Inherent Resolve designed to defeat IS, they are often ad hoc, episodically formed, and largely symbolic given the US' availing sponsorship. The resiliency of IS and its regional affiliates, including *Wilayat Khorasan*, means CT experts should study the merits of adapting regional and global security forums to fulfil the mandate of enabling member states to move beyond transactional intelligence sharing and towards the systemic integration of personnel and capabilities to proactively pursue terrorist groups across borders. An added benefit of establishing an enduring CT consortium akin to "Operation Gallant Phoenix" is enhanced transparency and governance of HVT akin to the Tallinn Manual (Tallinn Manual on the International Law Applicable to Cyber Warfare, 2013). While non-binding, the Tallinn Manual promulgates rules to reconcile cyberwarfare with the laws of armed conflict. Given competing interests and suspicions among states, this minimalist approach is a useful starting point to help expand the transparency of HVT while standardising the practise pursuant to resolving international society's warfare trap.

The authors want to thank Stephen Tankel and Brian Jenkins for their helpful comments and suggestions on an earlier draft of this chapter.

The views expressed in this article are the author's own and do not reflect the official policy or position of the United States Department of the Army, Department of Defense, or Government.

Notes

1 For an insightful analysis of the concept of "full spectrum" and contemporary conflict, see Shaw (2016).
2 Of course, religious motivations are not *new*. Instead, some observers identify that the difference between past and contemporaneous religiously motivated terrorist groups lies in the aim of attacks and the methods deployed. Whereas past organisations conducted selective attacks and assassinations, contemporaneous organisations indulge in mass slaughter.
3 This is not a new phenomenon. Organisations like Hamas and Hezbollah – ostensibly political groups with military wings that are well-known for carrying out terror attacks – provide both governance and local public goods within their areas of control and authority.
4 This section draws substantially on an article one of the co-authors, Paul Lushenko, published in 2012 on the merits of HVT. See Hardy and Lushenko (2012).
5 The composition, disposition, and strength of IS-KP are debatable. According to unclassified enemy material as well as emerging field research, the number of IS-KP fighters between Afghanistan and Pakistan likely ranges between 2,000 and 5,000 militants. This contingent is probably augmented by a broader support network, whose membership reportedly numbers at least 1,200 (see Giustozzi, 2018, 142).

References

"Acting Manhattan US Attorney Announces the Court's Unsealing of Charges Against Tree Men Arrested For Participating In International Plot To Carry Out Terrorist Attacks In New York City For Isis In The Summer Of 2016." (2016, October 6). US Attorney's Office Southern District of New York. Retrieved October 6, 2016 from https://www.justice.gov/usao-sdny/pr/acting-manhattan-us-attorney-announces-court-s-unsealing-charges-against-three-men.

Arquilla, J., & Ronfeldt, D. (2001). The Advent of Network (Revisited). In J. Arquilla & D. Ronfeldt (Eds.), *The Advent of Netwar (Revisited)* (pp. 1–25). Santa Monica: RAND.

Aslam, W. (2013). *The United States and great power responsibility in international society*. London: Routledge.

Baron, K., & Weisgerber, M. (2017, May 19). New Tactics, Quicker Decisions are Helping to 'Annihilate' ISIS, Pentagon says. *Defense One*. Retrieved May 19, 2017 from https://www.defenseone.com/threats/2017/05/new-tactics-quicker-decisions-are-helping-annihilate-isis-pentagon-says/138024/

Bellamy, A. (2005). Conclusion. In A. Bellamy (Ed.), *International society and its critics* (pp. 283–297). Oxford: Oxford University Press.

Bergman, R. (2018). *Rise up and kill first: The secret history of Israel's targeted assassinations*. New York: Random House.

Brown, V., & Rassler, D. (2013). *Fountainhead of Jihad: The Haqqani Nexus, 1973–2012*. Oxford: Oxford University Press.

Byman, D., & Merritt, I.A. (2018). The new American way of war: Special operations forces in the war on terrorism. *The Washington Quarterly, 41*(2), 79–93.

Callimachi, R. (2018, August 7). A Dream Ended on a Mountain Road: The Cyclists and the ISIS Militants. *New York Times*. Retrieved August 7, 2018 from https://www.nytimes.com/2018/08/07/world/asia/islamic-state-tajikistan-bike-attack.html

Chamayou, G. (2015). *A theory of the drone*. New York: The New Press.

Cronin, A.K. (2013). Why drones fail. *Foreign Affairs, 92*(4), 44–54.

Davis, P., & Jenkins, B. (2004). A system approach to deterring and influencing terrorists. *Conflict Management and Peace Science, 21*(1), 3–15.

Dempsey, M. (2018, August 1). The Islamic state threat hasn't gone away. *Council on Foreign Relations*. Retrieved August 1, 2018 from https://www.cfr.org/article/islamic-state-threat-hasnt-gone-away

Dershowitz, A. (2013). *The case for Israel*. New Jersey: John Wiley & Sons.

Dill, J. (2014). The American way of bombing and International Law: The logic of warfare in tension. In M. Evangelista & H. Shue (Eds.), *The American Way of Bombing: Changing Ethical and Legal Norms, From Flying Fortresses to Drones* (pp. 131–144). Ithaca: Cornell University Press.

Ducheine, P. (2016). Non-Kinetic capabilities: Complementing the kinetic prevalence to targeting. In P.A.L. Ducheine, M.N. Schmitt, & F.P.B. Osinga (Eds.), *Targeting: The challenges of modern warfare* (pp. 202–227). The Hague: Asser Press.

Dunlap Jr., C. (2014). Clever or clueless? Observations about bombing norm debates. In M. Evangelista, & H. Shue (Eds.), *The American way of bombing: Changing ethical and legal norms, from flying fortresses to drones* (pp. 109–130). Ithaca: Cornell University Press.

Evangelista, M., & Shue, H. (Eds.). (2014). *The American way of bombing: Changing ethical and legal norms, from flying fortresses to drones*. Ithaca: Cornell University Press.

Fedschun, T. (2018, July 9). ISIS 'capital' captured in Afghanistan, over 160 fighters killed by US, Afghan troops. *Fox News*. Retrieved July 9, 2018 from https://www.foxnews.com/world/isis-capital-captured-in-afghanistan-over-160-fighters-killed-by-us-afghan-troops

Ferran, L. (2016, June 14). US Designates ISIS Afghan affiliate a Terror group. *ABC News*. Retrieved June 14, 2016 from https://abcnews.go.com/International/us-designates-isis-afghan-affiliate-terror-group/story?id=36289697

Finnemore, M. (1996). *National Interests in International Society*. Ithaca: Cornell University Press.

Field Manual No. 3-60. (2010). *The targeting process*. Washington, DC: Department of the US Army.

Field Manual No. 3-90. (2001). *Combat tactics*. Washington, DC: Department of the US Army.

Frankel, M. (2011). The ABCs of HVT: Key lessons from high value targeting campaigns against insurgents and terrorists. *Studies in Conflict and Terrorism, 34*(1), 17–30.

Gellman, B. (2011, December 15). William McRaven. *Time*. Retrieved December 14, 2011 from http://content.time.com/time/specials/packages/article/0,28804,2101745_2102133_2102330,00.html

Giustozzi, A. (2018). *The Islamic state in Khorasan: Afghanistan, Pakistan, and the New Central Asian Jihad*. London: Hurst & Company.

Glanville, L. (2014). *Sovereignty & the responsibility to protect*. Chicago: Chicago University Press.

Goodson, L. (2015). The US and Afghanistan after 2014. *Asian Survey, 55*(2), 248–272.

Gurganus, J. (2018, January 2018). Russia's Afghanistan strategy: How Moscow is preparing to go it alone. *Majalla Magazine*. Retrieved January 5, 2018 from http://eng.majalla.com/2018/01/article55255133/russias-afghanistan-strategy

Gusterson, H. (2014). Toward an anthropology of drones: Remaking space, time, and valor in Combat. In M. Evangelista and H. Shue (Eds.), *The American Way of Bombing: Changing Ethical and Legal Norms, From Flying Fortresses to Drones* (pp. 191–206). Ithaca: Cornell University Press.

Hardy, J., & Lushenko, P. (2012). The high value of targeting: A conceptual model for using HVT against a networked enemy. *Defence Studies, 12*(3), 413–433.

Hoffman, B. (1999). Terrorism trends and prospects. In I.O. Lesser, B. Hoffman, J. Arquilla, D. Ronfeldt, & M. Zanini (Eds.), *Countering the terrorism challenge* (pp. 7–39). Santa Monica: RAND.

"Interview with the Wali of Khurasan." (2016, January 19). Dabiq. Retrieved January 19, 2016 from https://jihadology.net/2016/01/19/new-issue-of-the-islamic-states-magazine-dabiq-13/

Johnson, C.G. (2016). *The rise and stall of the Islamic state in Afghanistan. United States Institute of peace*. Washington, DC: US Government Printing Office.

Kaldor, M. (2010). Inconclusive wars: Is Clausewitz still relevant in these global times? *Global Policy, 1*(3), 271–281.

Kilcullen, D. (2005). Countering global insurgency. *The Journal of Strategic Studies, 28*(4), 597–617.

Khalid, T. (2018, August 19). "US Forces to Stay in Iraq as Long as Needed: Spokesman. *Reuters*. Retrieved August 19, 2018 from https://www.reuters.com/article/us-mideast-crisis-iraq-usa/u-s-forces-to-stay-in-iraq-as-long-as-needed-spokesman-idUSKBN1L408A

Kitfield, J. (2017, June 16). "CJCS Dunford Talks Turkey, Iran, Afghan Troop Numbers & Daesh," *Breaking Defense*. Retrieved June 16, 2017 from https://breakingdefense.com/2017/06/cjcs-dunford-talks-turkey-iran-afghan-troop-numbers-daesh/

Laqueur, W. (1996). Postmodern terrorism. *Foreign Affairs, 75*(5), 24–36.

Lebow, R.N. (2010). *Why nations fight*. Cambridge: Cambridge University Press.

Lushenko, P. (2018, July 5). Interview with Brian Jenkins.

Lushenko, P. (2018, July 5). Interview with Daniel Shapiro.

Lushenko, P. (2018, July 5). Interview with Qanta Ahmed.

Lushenko, P., & Hardy, J. (2016). Panjwai: A tale of two COINs in Afghanistan. *Small Wars & Insurgencies, 27*(1), 106–131.

Lushenko, P., Van Auken, L., & Stebbins, G. (2018). ISIS-K: Deadly nuisance or strategic threat? *Small Wars & Insurgencies, 29*(6), n.p.

McCue, C., Massengill, J.T., Milbrandt, D., Gaughan, J., & Cumpston, M. (2017). The ISIS long game: A tripartite analysis of youth radicalization and indoctrination. *CTC Sentinel, 10*(8), 21–26.

Meadows, D. (2008). *Thinking in systems: A primer*. White River Junction: Chelsea Green Publishing.

Merari, A. (1993). Terrorism as a strategy of insurgency. *Terrorism and Political Violence, 5*(4), 213–251.

Motwani, N., & Bose, S. (2015). Afghanistan: 'Spoilers' in the regional security context. *Australian Journal of International Affairs, 69*(3), 266–284.

Munoz, C., & Harper, J. (2015, April 20). Intelligence gaps may help Islamic state gain foothold in Afghanistan. *Stars and Stripes*. Retrieved April 20, 2015 from https://www.stripes.com/news/intelligence-gaps-may-help-islamic-state-gain-foothold-in-afghanistan-1.341241

Nordland, R., & Ghazi, Z. (2018, April 9). ISIS Leader in Afghanistan Is Killed in US Airstrike. *The New York Times*. Retrieved April 09, 2018 from https://www.nytimes.com/2018/04/09/world/asia/afghanistan-isis-leader.html

Osman, B. (2016, 27 September). Decent into chaos: Why did Nangarhar turn into an IS Hub? *Afghanistan Analysts Network*. Retrieved September 27, 2016 from https://www.afghanistan-analysts.org/descent-into-chaos-why-did-nangarhar-turn-into-an-is-hub/

Pratzner, P. (2016). *The current targeting process* In P.A.L. Ducheine, M.N. Schmitt, & F.P.B. Osinga (Eds.), *Targeting: The Challenges of Modern Warfare* (pp. 77–97). The Hague: Asser Press.

Price, B. (2012). Targeting top terrorists: How leadership decapitation contributes to counterterrorism. *International Security, 36*(4), 9–46.

Rahim, N., & Nordland, R. (2018, August 1). Taliban Surge Routs ISIS in Northern Afghanistan. *New York Times*. Retrieved August 1, 2018 from https://www.nytimes.com/2018/08/01/world/asia/afghanistan-taliban-isis.html

Rempfer, K. (2018, July 23). US Strikes Continue an Upward Trend in Afghanistan. *AirForce Times*. Retrieved July 23, 2018 from https://www.airforcetimes.com/news/your-air-force/2018/07/23/us-strikes-continue-an-upward-trend-in-afghanistan/

Riza, M.S. (2013). *Killing without heart: Limits on robotic warfare in an age of persistent conflict*. Dulles: Potomac.

Russia Today. (2017, April 14). 'Right Weapon for Fight Target': Top US Commander Defends Use of 'Mother of all Bombs.' Retrieved April 14, 2017 from https://www.rt.com/usa/384767-us-bomb-afghanistan-isis/

Saikal, A. (2018). How Islamic Has the "Islamic State" Been? *Journal of Muslim Minority Affairs*, *38*(2), 143–152.

Schmitt, E. (2016, July 27). US Secures Vast New Trove of Intelligence on ISIS. *New York Times*. Retrieved July 27, 2018 from https://www.nytimes.com/2016/07/28/world/middleeast/us-intelligence-isis.html

Shaw. I. (2016). *Predator empire: Drone warfare and full spectrum dominance*. Minneapolis: University of Minnesota Press.

Tallinn Manual on the International Law Applicable to Cyber Warfare. (2013). Cambridge: Cambridge University Press.

Umarov, K. (2018, January 26). Twenty-First Report of the Analytical Support and Sanctions Monitoring Team Submitted Pursuant to Resolution 2368 (2017) Concerning ISIL (Da'esh), Al-Qaida and Associated Individuals and Entities. United Nations Security Council. Retrieved January 26, 2018 from https://www.un.org/sc/suborg/en/sanctions/1267/monitoring-team/reports

Wilner, A. (2010). Targeting killings in Afghanistan: Measuring coercion and deterrence in counterterrorism and counterinsurgency. *Studies in Conflict and Terrorism*, *33*(4), 307–329.

Wilner, A. (2007). *The best defence is a terrific offense: Four approaches to countering modern terrorism*. Halifax: Atlantic Institute for Market Studies.

23

DISENGAGING FROM ARMED CONFLICT

Cameroon's Disarmament, Demobilisation, and Reintegration of Former Boko Haram Militants and Anglophone Separatists

Ta-Mbi Nkongho and Molua Patrick Ewange

INTRODUCTION

On November 30, 2018, President Paul Biya of Cameroon signed Decree No. 2018/719, creating a disarmament, demobilisation, and reintegration commission charged with the duty of organising, supervising, and managing the disarmament, demobilisation, and reintegration of ex-fighters of the Boko Haram terrorist group in the Far North Region and the armed separatist groups in the Anglophone North-West and South-West Regions under the control of the Prime Minister, Head of Government (Besenyő & Mayer, 2015). Pursuant to this decree, on December 4, 2018, the president signed another decree appointing former and retired Governor Fai Yengo Francis as the national coordinator of the commission, and the Prime Minister also proceeded to appoint regional coordinators of the commission in charge of the Anglophone North-West and South-West Regions and the Far North Region. The purpose and objective of the creation of this commission were to disarm, demobilise, and reintegrate the ex-fighters of Boko Haram and ex-separatist armed fighters for a lasting return of peace and security in the Far North and the North-West and South-West conflict-torn regions of the country.

The nebulous Boko Haram terrorist group, which originated in neighbouring Nigeria, has been operating in the Far North Region of Cameroon since 2011, and it is unanimously considered a terrorist organisation by the Cameroonian government and the international community. Boko Haram has been perpetrating terrorist actions against the population of the Far North Region and other parts of the Grand North area with devastating consequences. On the other hand, the armed separatist groups operating in the English-speaking North-West and South-West Regions since 2017 are an emanation of the Cameroonian government's brutal repression of the Anglophone lawyers, teachers, and University of Buea students' protests in late 2016, which has escalated into a violent armed conflict in the two regions. However, in spite of the above perceptible dichotomy, the two movements pose extraneous security, human rights, and humanitarian challenges to the Cameroonian government and the population of the affected regions at large. It is for these reasons that the Cameroonian government decided to create the disarmament, demobilisation, and reintegration commission as a conflict resolution initiative geared towards pacifying the affected Far North Region and the English-speaking North-West and South-West Regions of the country.

KEY CONCEPTS

Disarmament

Disarmament is the act of reducing, limiting, or abolishing weapons, and it is often taken to mean the total elimination of weapons of mass destruction, such as nuclear arms (UN General Assembly, 2015). Disarmament is the process of reducing or eliminating military forces and weapons through cooperation, treaties, and oversight. Disarmament is usually focused on weapons, but it can include other areas, such as tools and technologies (Prokes, 2018). Most disarmament proposals are based on the assumption that weapons are an important source of conflict, and as a result, the ultimate logic of disarmament points to the total elimination of all weapons (Shaheen, 2016). In the context of this paper, disarmament is the collection, documentation, control, and disposal of small arms, ammunition, explosives, and light and heavy weapons in

DOI: 10.4324/9780429426063-25

the possession of combatants and the civilian population (Adinoyi, 2015: 2).

Disarmament is the first phase of DDR and logically precedes demobilisation and reintegration. However, it is often a long-term process, and one of its major problems is the collection of small weapons and light arms, which are easy to conceal and difficult to account for. Disarmament is important not only for the material improvement of security conditions but also for its psychological impact. There are added psychological benefits when ex-combatants physically disable their own weapons and are led to do so by their commanders immediately upon entering the disarmament site. Additionally, public destruction of weapons is an important tool for sensitising the population and promoting the DDR programme. The process symbolically underscores the transition from military to civilian life (Fusato, 2003).

Nezam and Marc (2009: 3) assert that disarmament often includes the following activities:

- *Information gathering and operational planning*: Information is collected on the size, profile, and deployment of the armed forces and the number, type, and location of their weapons. Information and sensitisation campaigns are also carried out to raise public awareness about the disarmament process.
- *Weapons collection*: Combatants are gathered at pick-up points, moved to weapons collection points or disarmament sites, and disarmed. This process must not be linked to the cash payments provided during reinsertion. Otherwise, the programme may be seen as an arms buy-back scheme, which can lead to increased arms flows to the country.
- *Stockpile management and weapons destruction*: Weapons, ammunition, and explosives are counted, stored, moved, and/or destroyed. Where possible, the United Nations encourages the immediate destruction of all collected weapons. Otherwise, as in Sierra Leone in 2000, they may be used to restart the conflict (Nezam & Marc, 2009: 3). As the first stage of the DDR process, successful disarmament eventually leads to the demobilisation of the disarmed ex-combatants.

Demobilisation

According to Adinoyi (2015: 2), demobilisation is the official, controlled disengagement of active combatants from armed groups and/or armed forces. The first stage of demobilisation engagement involves the processing and placement of combatants in camps otherwise called cantonment sites, encampments, assembly areas, or barracks. The second stage involves support packages geared to aid the demobilised, and this could be referred to as reinsertion (Adinoyi, 2015: 2). Demobilisation includes the dismantling of military units and the transition of ex-combatants from military to civilian life. It includes the assembly of ex-combatants, orientation programmes, and transportation to the communities of destination. These movements of large groups of people should be timed to coincide with phases of civilian life that facilitate reintegration. At the end of a conflict, demobilisation presents the same logistical challenges as programmes of emergency relief and resettlement of displaced persons (Fusato, 2003). Nezam and Marc (2009: 4) state that demobilisation usually consists of the following activities:

- *Registration and documentation*: Eligibility is determined through a screening process; socio-economic data are collected to inform the design of the reintegration assistance; and non-transferable identity documents (numbered, stamped, and with a photo) are given to each ex-combatant.
- *Health screening*: Ex-combatants are screened for chronic illness and/or disability. Voluntary counselling and testing for HIV/AIDS should also be offered. This is important because a combative lifestyle (separation from spouse, opportunities for unprotected sex, tendency to take greater risks) increases the likelihood of contracting HIV/AIDS and other communicable diseases.
- *Pre-discharge orientation*: Information on the DDR process is provided, and the challenges of the transition from military to civilian life (rights and responsibilities) are explained. In Rwanda, inadequate pre-discharge orientation led to unrealistic expectations among ex-combatants.
- *Discharge*. Discharge documents that recognise military involvement, demobilisation, and eligibility for reinsertion and reintegration assistance are given to each ex-combatant (Nezam & Marc, 2009: 4). After the demobilisation process is successfully carried out, the ex-combatants are reintegrated into society to enable them to regain their civilian lives.

Reintegration

Reintegration is the reinstatement of ex-combatants back into society through their acquisition of civilian status and the securing of employment and income opportunities. It is an economic and social process basically at the local government/community level; it is also the prime post-conflict development programme (Adinoyi, 2015: 2–3). After ex-combatants have been demobilised, their effective and sustainable reintegration into civilian life is necessary to prevent a new escalation of the conflict. Reintegration includes the reinsertion of ex-combatants by addressing their most immediate needs to permit them to take charge of their lives (Fusato, 2003). Reintegration is essentially a social and economic process with an open time frame, primarily taking place in communities at the local level. It is part of the general development of a country, a national responsibility, and often necessitates long-term external assistance (UNDDR Resource Centre, 2005).

Nezam and Marc (2009: 5–6) posit that reintegration assistance must be based on a detailed assessment of:

- *Beneficiaries*: A profile of the combatant (age, gender, marital status, dependents, education, health, needs, expectations, and areas of return) is developed before and verified during demobilisation.
- *Areas of return and resettlement*: Based on the profile of combatants, an assessment is made of the economic and social potential of the areas of return (including information on their natural resources, infrastructure, security situation, social capital, and perceptions of and willingness to accept ex-combatants).
- *Reintegration opportunities and services*: A nationwide mapping exercise determines employment opportunities (in existing enterprises, self-employment schemes) and services (education, training, credit, community mobilisation).

Also, this assistance can include the following activities:

- *Information, counselling, and referral*: General information is provided on the reintegration process and the opportunities available to all ex-combatants. Then, specialised counselling is provided to each ex-combatant based on his or her profile. Finally, ex-combatants are referred to support services within the DDR programme (grant mechanisms, for example). They are also referred to as other services such as health, education, training, and jobs.
- *Economic reintegration:* Education and training assistance includes "catch-up" education, vocational training, apprenticeships, and life skills development. This assistance ought to respond to the needs of the labour market, i.e., help ex-combatants find jobs. Livelihood and income generation assistance consists of access to land (where possible), short-term public works, grants for small businesses, business development services, and temporary wage subsidies to businesses that hire ex-combatants.
- *Social reintegration:* Information and sensitisation activities can reduce suspicion and rebuild trust between ex-combatants and the communities that receive them. Religious and/or other community organisations can play a role here. It is important to meet the urgent and specific needs of ex-combatants without turning them into a privileged group, which can create resentment in the receiving community. This means that reintegration assistance should be limited in time and scope and delivered through community-based mechanisms (Nezam & Marc, 2009: 5–6). It should be noted that reinsertion, which is short-term assistance given to ex-combatants to cover their basic needs during demobilisation, is also part of the reintegration process and equally serves to facilitate the long-term reintegration process of ex-combatants.

CONFLICT RESOLUTION

Conflict is the result of a disagreement between actors on the basis of perceived incompatible goals (Conflict Sensitivity Consortium, 2012: 2). Since disagreements and conflicts are inevitable everyday occurrences, their resolution can result in constructive change (Fisher et al., 2000: 6). Conflict resolution is therefore conceptualised as the methods and processes involved in facilitating the peaceful ending of conflict and retribution (Forsyth, 2009). The term broadly refers to efforts to prevent or mitigate violence resulting from intergroup or interstate conflict, as well as efforts to reduce the underlying disagreements (NAP, 2000: 2). It focuses on the deep-rooted causes of conflict, including structural, behavioural, and, above all, attitudinal aspects. Generally speaking, conflict resolution aims to help parties explore, analyse, question, and reframe their positions and interests as a way of transcending conflict. For many, the learning process entailed in resolving a conflict is just as important as the end state it hopes to achieve: the future is not seen as conflict-free but as one where bonds and models exist that conflict parties can use to find further resolutions instead of resorting to violence (Berghof Foundation, 2012: 18). The disarmament, demobilisation, and reintegration (DDR) process is therefore an important conflict resolution technique in post-conflict situations and has been used to resolve several armed conflicts across the world, especially in most internal armed conflicts on the African continent, like the ongoing separatist armed conflict in the Anglophone regions of Cameroon.

According to the UNDDR Resource Centre (2005), the disarmament, demobilisation, and reintegration (DDR) of ex-combatants is a complex process with political, military, security, humanitarian, and socio-economic dimensions. The objective of the DDR process is to contribute to security and stability in post-conflict environments so that recovery and development can begin. It aims to deal with the post-conflict security problem that arises when ex-combatants are left without livelihoods or support networks other than their former comrades during the vital transition period from conflict to peace and development. Through the process of removing arms from the hands of combatants, taking the combatants out of military structures, and helping them to integrate socially and economically into society, DDR seeks to support male and female ex-combatants and men, boys, women, and girls associated with armed forces and groups so that they can become active participants in the peace process (UNDDR Resource Centre, 2005).

Moreover, Fusato (2003) contends that disarmament, demobilisation, and reintegration (DDR) of ex-combatants is therefore a first step in the transition from war to peace by ensuring a safe environment, transferring ex-combatants back to civilian life, and enabling people to earn livelihoods through peaceful means instead of war (Fusato, 2003). The major element of DDR is to institute stability through security reforms and social and developmental programmes. Those programmes ensure the establishment of a functional society by helping combatants and civilians transition from the previous hostile or unstable livelihood or social network into a viable one (Africa Development Bank, 2011: 4–5). This socially and economically integrated combatants and civilians into a long-term peaceful coexistence, induced productivity and development of society, and led to security reforms. However, DDR in itself is not a replacement for ideal development programmes that should exist; rather, it helps in creating a secured environmental ambiance for such programmes to thrive (UNDPO, 2000: 3).

In this regard, Adinoyi (2015: 12) expounds that it is very important for those designing and implementing DDR programmes to link those programmes to the wider sustainable peace efforts, including reforms in the security sector and the development of the socioeconomic frameworks that the targeted national government and its society can use to forestall any relapse into conflict. The DDR process therefore contributes to the broader security sector reforms that create an enabling environment for the advancement of formal education, the development of agriculture, the establishment of small enterprise development such as micro-businesses and other income-generating activities, the initiation of vocational training and apprenticeship programmes, job placements, the promotion of human rights and justice, the integration of fighting forces into national armies, the facilitation of reconciliation, and the building of national unity (Adinoyi, 2015: 12). Accordingly, Nezam and Marc (2009: 8) state that the key ingredients for a successful DDR programme are:

- Political will, including commitment and pragmatism, throughout the process;
- Careful preparation, including participatory methods to profile ex-combatants and assess the economic and social potential of areas of return;
- Transparent and effective institutions, including:
- delivering assistance simply, i.e., minimising transaction costs and corruption and maximising benefits to ex-combatants, and
- coordinating at the central level but decentralising implementation to communities;
- Timely and adequate financing; and
- Integration with ongoing and future humanitarian and development efforts.

Furthermore, Ndikum (2018) argues that disarmament, demobilisation, and reintegration (DDR) most often operate contemporaneously with transitional justice processes in conflict-affected societies. Transitional justice is defined by the United Nations as the full range of processes and mechanisms associated with a society's attempt to come to terms with a legacy of large-scale abuses in order to ensure accountability, serve justice, and achieve reconciliation. It includes judicial and non-judicial mechanisms, primarily individual prosecutions, truth-seeking, reparations, institutional reforms, and vetting. It is applicable in most conflict societies that have undergone dictatorship with unspeakable human rights violations and aim at dealing with the past to chart a way for the future (Ndikum, 2018). Since the end of the Cold War, DDR has been applied as a post-conflict effort to resolve some important internal armed conflicts in Africa, with successful outcomes in most cases.

DDR IN SUB-SAHARAN AFRICA

There exists an abundance of literature on disarmament, demobilisation, and reintegration (DDR) and conflict resolution in post-conflict settings in Africa and across the world. However, the focus of this paper is limited to some selected cases in the Sub-Saharan Africa region.

In his examination of the case of Angola, Adinoyi (2015: 6) asserts that Angola experienced conflict for about four decades, after which the Bicesse Accords of 1991 between the government and the National Union for the Total Independence of Angola (UNITA) came to light. DRR, as contained in the Accord, was to help the combatants from the Popular Armed Forces for the Liberation of Angola (FAPLA), an arm of the Popular Movement for the Liberation of Angola (MPLA) government, and the Armed Forces for the Liberation of Angola (FALA). However, the DRR process was stalled due to the fact that UNITA failed to accept the outcome of the 1992 election, but one of the significant successes of the DRR process was that it was able, to an extent, to demobilise and reintegrate ex-combatants into civilian status. In this case, DDR worked to an extent because the warring parties had a ceasefire and an accord, marking the cessation of hostilities but for the disagreement after the 1992 presidential elections. This Angolan scenario is different from that of Cameroon in that there is neither a ceasefire nor an agreement to end hostilities, which brings the veracity of Cameroon's DDR into question and renders it ineffectual.

Additionally, in the case of Côte d'Ivoire, the country turned into turmoil in 2002 after a failed coup to depose President Laurent Gbagbo, and the Accra I Accord called on all armed groups to cease fighting and engage in a dialogue to bring a peaceful resolution to the crisis. This paved the way for the 2005 agreement between the Ivorian government and Forces Nouvelles to initiate a DDR programme. However, an effective DDR was prevented due to the tension in some provinces and insecurity in the country, although agreement on the implementation of an identification process and pre-cantonment of combatants began in mid-2006. The subsequent Ouagadougou Peace Accord of the fourth of March, 2007, still left low-intensity conflicts, which hindered the objectives of DDR (Adinoyi, 2015: 10). In this scenario, the warring parties had two accords that paved the way for disarmament, unlike in Cameroon, where the government merely ordered the combatants to drop their weapons without any formal or informal accord.

In Sierra Leone, the 1996 and 1999 Peace Accords between the Government of Sierra Leone and the Revolutionary United Front (RUF) brought out the non-hostile environment that made Sierra Leone officially declare that the long decades of civil war were over in 2002. This was also significant as it established a National Commission for Disarmament, Demobilisation, and Reintegration (NCDDR) to manage the DDRP, which aimed to: collect, register, disable, and destroy all conventional weapons and munitions retrieved from combatants during the disarmament period; demobilise approximately 45,000 ex-combatants of the Armed Forces of Sierra Leone, the RUF, and the Civil Defence Forces (CDF); and finally prepare and support ex-combatants for reinsertion and socio-economic reintegration upon discharge from demobilisation centres (Weinstein & Humphreys, 2005). The Sierra Leonean process shows that Cameroon has a long way to go.

In Liberia, the 2003 Comprehensive Peace Agreement (CPA) ushered in processes for disarmament, demobilisation, reintegration, and rehabilitation (DDRR) of all warring parties. In the same year, the UN Security Council established Resolution 1509, mandated not only to support the implementation of the ceasefire agreement but also to develop a DDR Action Plan that would pay particular attention to the needs of child combatants and women. Additionally, at the national level, there was the establishment of the National Commission on Disarmament, Demobilisation, Rehabilitation, and Reintegration (NCDDRR) (KAIPTC/ZIF, 2008). Cameroon's DDR is experiencing hurdles because it has not followed this Liberian model.

Noteworthy is the support provided for the demobilisation and reintegration of former fighters in the Great Lakes region of Central Africa by the Multi-Country Demobilisation and Reintegration Programme (MDRP), which was established in 2002. Over 400,000 former fighters are the focus of the over US$500 million programme, which is being implemented in seven nations: Angola, Burundi, the Central African Republic (CAR), the Democratic Republic of the Congo (DRC), the Republic of the Congo (RoC), Rwanda, and Uganda. The demobilisation, reinsertion, and reintegration of former fighters are assisted with the help of the MDRP, which also provides financial and technical support (Nezam & Marc, 2009: 9), coordination of partner initiatives, and standard procedures (Nezam & Marc, 2009: 9). The approach is failing in Cameroon because the Great Lakes area lacks these carefully thought-out protocols.

Also, in the case of a DDR centre for ex-fighters of a terrorist organisation such as Boko Haram, Issa and Machikou (2019) contend that the challenges of applying competing frameworks for the reintegration of individuals are particularly evident in the management of persons associated with Boko Haram, a group whose origins are as religious as they are economic, sociological, and political. However, Cameroon is the last of the countries in the Lake Chad Basin region to receive voluntary defectors associated with Boko Haram, and the implementation of an approach tailored to the Cameroonian context is ongoing. In Cameroon, a national policy for managing defectors from Boko Haram is beginning to be institutionalised, although efforts remain slow. On October 30, 2017, Midjiyawa Bakary, the Far North Region governor, was the first to set in motion efforts to promote defections, inspired by the experiences of neighbouring countries. That notwithstanding, on November 30, 2018, a Cameroonian presidential decree established the National Disarmament, Demobilisation, and Reintegration Committee for former Boko Haram fighters and armed groups from the North-West Region and the South-West Region (Issa & Machikou, 2019: 1–5). This article hyped praise for a Cameroonian solution to a Cameroonian problem but failed to acknowledge the surge in attacks since the promulgation of the decree without a decisive response. The application of the Cameroonian DDR model to Boko Haram militants and Anglophone separatist fighters is the main focus of this paper, which Issa and Machikou (2019: 1–5) hub solely on Boko Haram in the Far North of Cameroon. The above literature reviewed some selected cases of DDR that could serve as models applicable to other countries, including Cameroon, which presently has not embraced any of the models discussed above.

DDR AS A CONFLICT RESOLUTION TECHNIQUE IN INTERNAL ARMED CONFLICTS IN AFRICA

Africa has experienced quite a number of conflicts, especially intra-state conflicts, since the end of the Cold War (Harbom, 2006: 109). Those conflicts were mostly about power struggles over government control, with the exception of the conflict between Eritrea and Ethiopia, which was an interstate control conflict. The UN has made several efforts through the deployment of multidimensional peace support missions and has also partnered with the African Union on the deployment of hybrid forces. Subsequently, there has been the application of the DRR mechanism in the post-conflict phase in those African countries, such as Côte d'Ivoire, Liberia, and Sierra Leone, that experienced conflict. DDR programmes, as they are known to practitioners, have featured in post-conflict reconstruction from

Afghanistan to Haiti, but the bulk of DDR interventions (24 since 1992) have occurred in Africa. The proliferation of UN peacekeeping operations coincides with an increase in UN-led programmes to disarm and disband warring parties as well as reintegrate ex-combatants into civilian life. The UN adopts a lead role in most single-country DDR programmes in Africa, but various nongovernmental organisations (NGO) and aid groups are also typically involved (Hanson, 2007).

The application of DDR programmes in general and in most internal armed conflicts in Africa always commenced with mediation leading to a peace agreement between the warring factions, which was then accompanied by a ceasefire in order to create the enabling peaceful environment for a successful implementation of the programme. In this light, Fusato (2003) posits that the conditions of security and inclusion must be integrated into a political agreement defining the end of hostilities and the implementation of DDR. Experience has shown that DDR programmes cannot drive a peace process; they can only be implemented in the context of a negotiated settlement, a ceasefire, or a peace agreement. It can reinforce the agreement as a form of security guarantee and a confidence-building measure, but it cannot precede the agreement. Shared political will and a policy of amnesty and reconciliation create the best conditions for the successful implementation of a DDR programme. Specific issues must be directly addressed by the peace process and integrated into the political agreement, including:

- Clear eligibility criteria for participation in the programme;
- Creation of credible and responsible institutions;
- Definition of realistic goals and a timetable for implementation. Political agreements should take into account the practical realities of disarmament and demobilisation in order to set realistic goals that will support the sustainability of the peace accord (Fusato, 2003).

The application of DDR in intra-state conflicts in Angola, the Democratic Republic of the Congo (DRC), Burundi, Liberia, Côte d'Ivoire, Sierra Leone, Sudan, and South Sudan, just to name a few, was preceded by peace agreements by the belligerents, which were followed by ceasefires. For the purpose of this paper, emphasis is laid on the cases of Sierra Leone and Côte d'Ivoire. In this light, Ndikum Ransome Ndikum (2018) states that Sierra Leone, which is considered the "model" and the most cited example when it comes to the success of DDR as replicated in Liberia and Burundi, was well stratified. It came after peace negotiations with a binding agreement at hand that contained formalities on the operationalisation of the DDR and other mechanisms (Ndikum, 2018). In the case of Côte d'Ivoire, which draws certain similarities with the Cameroonian case, Julius Adavize Adinoyi (2015: 10), states that at the national level, there was the creation of the Authority on Disarmament, Demobilisation, and Reintegration (l'Autorité pour le Désarmement, la Démobilisation, and Reintegration, ADDR) in 2012. The authority was tasked with the overall direction of coordination, supervision, and implementation of the actions of disarmament, demobilisation, and reintegration, and most importantly, the socio-economic reintegration of ex-combatants and community rehabilitation in host areas for former combatants. Also, the United Nations Operation in Côte d'Ivoire (UNOCI) had a DDR unit that was in charge of the disarmament, demobilisation, and reintegration of former combatants, and its roles were spelled out in the 1528, 1609, 1765, and 2162 Resolutions of the UN Security Council. The UNOCI had worked to ensure political reforms, which led to the 2010 election. The UNOCI DDR partnered and worked with ADDR on disarmament and demobilisation; reintegration through community reintegration projects; fighting against the proliferation and circulation of light weapons and small arms; and social cohesion projects (Adinoyi, 2015: 10).

It is therefore important to point out that the DDR programmes in the above-cited countries were accompanied by the support of national and international actors who were able to play important roles in the successful implementation of the programmes. In this regard, Nezam and Marc (2009: 7) propound that the national actors, which consist of governments, armed forces and groups, civil society organisations, and national media, have the overall responsibility for the planning and implementation of the programmes while they rely on international actors such as the United Nations system, the World Bank and Regional Development Banks, nongovernmental organisations, and Research and Policy Centres for technical and financial support (Nezam & Marc, 2009: 7). Many DDR specialists expected a similar approach by the Cameroonian government in the creation of its DDR committee for the Far North and the Anglophone Regions, which unfortunately did not follow the mandatory prerequisite steps for a successful DDR programme.

APPLICATION OF DDR TO THE BOKO HARAM TERRORIST CONFLICT IN THE FAR NORTH REGION OF CAMEROON

The Boko Haram terrorist insurgency began its activities in Nigeria in 2009 and extended its lugubrious operations in Niger, Chad, and the Far North Region of Cameroon in 2011, with the objective being to create an Islamic Caliphate in the territories of these countries. In Cameroon, they carried out several terrorist actions in towns and villages in the Far North Region, killing many people. Prominent amongst these is the bomb attack on the

Cameroonian town of Fotokol, which led to the killing of 81 civilians, 6 Cameroonian soldiers, and 13 Chadian soldiers. The heinous and barbaric activities of the Boko Haram terrorist group led to the creation of a military coalition by Nigeria, Cameroon, Chad, and Niger, with the assistance of the United States of America and France, to assist in the fighting, and this led to the systematic waning of their activities. As a result of the reduction of the nuisance capacity of Boko Haram in the Far North Region of Cameroon, President Paul Biya created the disarmament, demobilisation, and reintegration (DDR) committee to disarm, demobilise, and reintegrate the ex-fighters of the group who wanted to return to civilian life. The creation of the committee was followed by the appointments of a national coordinator and a regional coordinator in charge of the Far North Region. Oumar Bichiar was thus appointed as the Regional Coordinator of the Disarmament, Demobilisation, and Reintegration (DDR) Committee for the Far North Region.

Following his appointment as the National Coordinator of the Disarmament, Demobilisation, and Reintegration (NDDR) Commission, Fai Yengo Francis visited the Far North Region in late December 2018 and most especially the Maroua Central Prison, where some Boko Haram ex-fighters are incarcerated, and also selected a cantonment site for ex-combatants. Apart from the abovementioned reconnaissance trip to the Far North Region, nothing has been heard from the commission in terms of ensuring the effective disarmament, demobilisation, and reintegration of ex-Boko Haram fighters. On the contrary, the security situation has remained quite volatile as Boko Haram terrorists have continued to carry out terrorist attacks in the region, resulting in several deaths and injuries. Their activities have extended to the North and Adamaoua Regions, where several people are kidnapped for ransom on a daily basis. By all intents and purposes, it remains to be seen how the creation of a DDR committee to disarm, demobilise, and reintegrate ex-Boko Haram fighters without a prior ceasefire agreement will have a positive impact on a peaceful resolution of the terrorist conflict in the Grand North Regions of Cameroon for a lasting return to peace and security.

It should be noted that following the creation of the DDR committee, Boko Haram attacks have continued to rage in the Far North Region, and an expansion of its activities has been noticed in the North and the Adamawa Regions. *The* Journal du Cameroun (2019) reported that on the night of January 19, 2019, Boko Haram razed 100 houses in the locality of Aschigachia in the Far North Region, leaving seven people injured. This was the second attack in the space of three weeks after the Boko Haram insurgents carried out a similar attack in Kolofata, still in the Far North Region of Cameroon. In another attack, the jihadist group killed at least four people and badly wounded four others in an attack on Kofia, a Cameroonian island on Lake Chad, on April 27, 2019. The attackers also destroyed part of a military post and vandalised shops, while three civilians and one soldier were killed. The jihadist group had stepped up attacks in Cameroon, as earlier in the month of April 2019, they were blamed for an attack that killed eleven civilians in the northern locality of Tcharkamari. That attack was the deadliest one blamed on Boko Haram in recent months, which have seen a surge in violence after a period of calm last year. Still in April 2019, jihadist attacks and a mine blast that hit a military convoy killed at least seven Cameroonian soldiers (Journal du Cameroun, 2019). The attacks have been on the rise, complicated by the withdrawal of the United States' troops and aid assistance worth millions of dollars in 2019 to fight Boko Haram due to human rights' abuses in the Anglophone conflict.

APPLICATION OF DDR TO THE SEPARATIST ARMED CONFLICT IN THE ANGLOPHONE REGIONS OF CAMEROON

The contemporary Anglophone problem, which escalated into an armed conflict, commenced in late 2016 following the Cameroonian government's brutal repression of Anglophone lawyers, teachers, and Buea University students' peaceful protests. The tilting point was on September 22, 2017, and October 1, 2017, when Cameroonian defence and security forces shot several peaceful protesters with live bullets, killing many people and injuring many others. The brutality of the government's reaction quickly transformed the erstwhile peaceful Anglophone political demands for more autonomy into a violent separatist armed conflict in the Anglophone regions. On November 30, 2017, President Paul Biya declared war on the separatists in the Anglophone regions, describing them as terrorists. This led to the creation of several separatist armed groups engaged in guerrilla warfare against the Cameroonian defence and security forces. The armed conflict has had devastating effects in the Anglophone regions, with many civilians killed, several maimed, scores kidnapped, and over 400 villages burned, causing many people to live in deplorable conditions in the bushes and forest, as internally displaced persons, and as refugees in neighbouring Nigeria. It is against the backdrop of these unprecedented security and humanitarian challenges that the government decided to create a disarmament, demobilisation, and reintegration (DDR) committee to disarm, demobilise, and reintegrate the separatist fighters willing to drop their weapons and discontinue hostility.

In light of the above, immediately after his appointment, the National Coordinator of the Commission, Fai Yengo Francis, and his team visited Buea and met with the regional authorities of the restive South-West Region on December 19,

2018, to take stock of the situation on the ground, and thereafter visited the premises of Borstal Institute Buea, which has been selected to serve as the cantonment site for prospective ex-combatants from the South-West Region. Ngonivilin (2018) asserts that the Director of the Institute, Fidelis Njie Ewumbue, introduced the team through the seven workshops of the institution, where those who drop their arms will gain skills. The workshops are woodwork, motto mechanics, welding, building construction, agriculture and livestock, sewing, and fine arts and painting. The team equally inspected dormitories, where all bedding facilities were already installed, bathrooms, and kitchens, which were neatly cleaned to be used by the newcomers. Fai Yengo told the press that all has been put in place to welcome all those who drop their guns in the South-West Region and that the centre can receive 100 to 120 persons. In a working session, he instructed Fonju Njukang Bernard, the South-West Regional Coordinator of the NDDRC, to come up with places B and C to accommodate more people (Ngonivilin, 2018).

It is worth mentioning that Gabsa Nyagha Sixtus and Fonju Njukang Bernard were appointed as Regional Coordinators of the Disarmament, Demobilisation, and Reintegration (DDR) Committee for the English-speaking North-West Region and South-West Region, respectively, by the then Prime Minister and Head of Government, Philemon Yang, to attend to the Anglophone armed separatists who are involved in an armed conflict against the Cameroonian defence and security forces since 2017. Immediately after the appointments, the separatist fighters burned down the residence of the coordinator of the North-West Region, Gabsa Nyagha Sixtus. *The* Journal du Cameroun (2018) asserts that the residence in Balikumbat of Gabsa Nyagha Sixtus, the North-West Coordinator of the Disarmament, Demobilisation, and Reintegration Committee, was set ablaze on December 13, 2018, by unidentified gunmen. The incident came just less than a week after he was appointed by the Prime Minister, Head of Government Philemon Yang, as the Regional Coordinator of the DDR Committee for the North-West Region (Journal du Cameroun, 2018). The burning of the house of the North-West Coordinator was an indicator of the difficult task awaiting the members of the DDR committee.

Furthermore, apart from the decree creating the Cameroonian DDR committee and appointing its coordinators and members, the activities of this committee have been conspicuously absent on the ground, just like other commissions such as the Bilingualism and Multiculturalism Commission and the Emergency Humanitarian Assistance Plan. The armed separatists who rejected the government's DDR initiative have continued to carry out insurgency operations in the Anglophone regions unperturbed. Apart from the regular fighting that has been ongoing since the creation of the DDR, two instances demonstrate that the Anglophone separatist groups have rejected the government's DDR. Three lockdowns in the Anglophone regions attest to this. The first lockdown was from February 4–15, 2019 throughout the entire English-speaking region. This act saw heightened insecurity as both lives and properties were wasted. Socioeconomic activities came to a halt, with businesses losing billions of francs.

The second lockdown began from April 4–14, 2019 and was aimed at frustrating the annual National Festival of Arts and Culture (FESTAC) in the town of Limbe. The lockdown was limited to Fako Division. Though the one-week ceremony still went ahead, the devastating blow was that the fanfare and attendance, which normally witnessed people thronging from other towns, were reduced due to the gun battles between the separatist fighters and the military ignited by the lockdown, especially in the restive town of Buea, the South-West regional capital.

Thirdly, in February 2020, the separatists imposed another lockdown from February 7–14, 2020, in an effort to frustrate the municipal and legislative elections in Cameroon and the February 11 celebration, which is the day Southern Cameroon voted in a UN plebiscite to join French-speaking or East Cameroon. This day was later coined by Ahmadou Ahidjo's administration as "Youth Day" to be celebrated by youths nationwide. Moreover, since the inception of the DDR, the ghost towns on Mondays and other days when Anglophone separatist leaders are taken to court have remained in force. This leads one to conclude that if, after several months of the decree establishing the DDR, the violence in the two regions is on the rise, then the process is failing and not impacting the resolution of the conflict. From the foregoing, several observers have predicted its failure because of outstanding shortcomings observed, most especially in the decree creating the committee, which has rendered its applicability in the Far North and the North-West and South-West Regions unfeasible.

SHORTCOMINGS IN THE APPLICABILITY OF DDR IN THE FAR NORTH REGION AND THE ENGLISH-SPEAKING NORTH-WEST AND SOUTH-WEST REGIONS OF CAMEROON

The decree creating the DDR by the president of Cameroon, which was hailed by the members of the government and some in the diplomatic community in Yaoundé, has not brought down the incidence of violence in the various affected areas. Instead, the violence in the Far North Region has descended to the North and Adamawa Regions, and that in the North-West and South-West Regions is gradually escalating to the Littoral and West Regions, respectively. This increase in violence shows that there are some deficiencies in the application of the DDR in the war-affected regions of Cameroon.

Adinoyi (2015: 1–13) postulates that disarmament, demobilisation, and reintegration (DDR) are critical elements of post-conflict peacebuilding (PCPB). The peace agreement leading up to the ceasefire agreement after the end of conflict situations is not sufficient to prevent a relapse into conflict, and thus there is a need to ensure a long-lasting peace by addressing not only the direct causes of violence but also the structural and cultural causes through reforms. Therefore, it is evident that DRR is important in post-conflict situations to aid security sector reforms, solve issues surrounding female soldiers and dependents, disarmament of combatants, psychosocial aspects of combatants and civilians involved in the conflict, address human rights violations, facilitate economic reintegration processes, and strengthen national capacity in all sectors of the re-built nation. And while DDR mechanisms and their application decrease violence, usher in long-term peace, and increase security through primarily reduced weaponry and violence, there is a need for stronger political willingness and sincerity among warring parties in order to ensure the effectiveness of DDR in preventing the relapse of conflict.

Moreover, Hanson (2007) states that despite the logistical challenges of disarmament, demobilisation, and reintegration, the acquisition of civilian status and sustainable employment and income are considered the most difficult phases of any DDR process. Edward Rackley (2005) states that donors have the mistaken idea that "as soon as you get guns out of their hands, they are suddenly innocuous human beings again, but that is not the case at all." Others argue that reintegration's difficulties push it beyond the scope of any DDR process, and thus this phase should be confined to reinsertion. Because DDR originally focused on short-term disarmament, reintegration is the least developed phase, in some cases confined to vocational training in one or two fields. "You have to provide an economic alternative to living by the gun." But in post-conflict countries, job opportunities are scarce, and sometimes communities are hesitant to employ ex-combatants. Unfortunately, the Cameroonian government's DDR initiative falls short of these important international conventional principles of DDR processes.

In this regard, Ndikum (2018) argues that against the backdrop of conventional international standards and the peculiar case of Cameroon, technical analysis of the DDR beyond doubt evinces another futile attempt to address these conflicts. The decree itself brings to light fundamental shortcomings, which make it only window dressing and yet another misplaced priority, which Ndikum (2018) summarises by the following ten points:

1. To have come out with a DDR law without any dialogue and/or negotiations between the leaders of the various armed groups of Boko Haram and those fighting for the actualisation of the right to self-determination of the people of Southern Cameroons – "Ambazonia" is putting the cart before the horse. DDR is often initiated during ceasefire or immediately after a peace agreement is signed and there has never been any ceasefire, neither have there been any peace agreement arrived at with Boko Haram or pro-independence armed fighters in Anglophone Cameroon to warrant a DDR process.
2. A comprehensive DDR process should have paid attention to vulnerable groups like children, women, disabled, dependents, refugees, and internally displaced persons. The decree failed to address this very important component considering that the emergency humanitarian assistance plan has yielded no visible results thus far.
3. Although disarmament and demobilisation components can contribute to temporary improvements in stability and safety, the decree does not lay down modalities to ensure reintegration, which often occurs within a longer period of time and overlaps with long-term processes of reconciliation, reconstruction, governance reforms, and poverty reduction and economic development. Failure to properly reintegrate combatants can in turn contribute to a cycle of post-conflict crime and violence as ex-combatants transform themselves into violent entrepreneurs.
4. The decree does not make provision for reparation. Reparations provide recognition and acknowledgement of the violations that victims have suffered and reduce resentment of benefits provided to ex-combatants. DDR programs that provide benefits to ex-combatants can cause resentment among civilian populations, particularly in the absence of any reparation programs.
5. Truth and reconciliation commissions are needed, especially in the case of the people of the former Southern Cameroons. DDR has to be designed such that it contributes to national reconciliation. It is only through truth commissions that society can get an even-handed account of the causes and consequences of armed conflicts and they also provide accounts of human rights violations and give a strategy to peace building such as was the case of the truth and reconciliation commission of Sierra Leone.
6. The decree does not address vetting and institutional reform, which are incorporated factors of DDR. Vetting involves excluding from public service persons with serious integrity deficits in order to re-establish civic trust and re-legitimise public institutions. Screening for human rights violators in public institutions and security forces is thus an important component of DDR, which the decree does not address.
7. The composition of the National Commission for Disarmament, Demobilisation, and Reintegration (NCDDR), civic trust, and local ownership is a cause for concern. Shockingly, the composition of the board of the NCDDR, as per the decree is a conglomerate of various government ministers. The Minister of Territorial Administration, the Minister of Defence,

the Delegate General of National Security, and the Secretary of State at the Ministry of Defence in charge of the Gendarmerie are all members of the board. Under conventional DDR processes, these ministers are supposed to be vetted because they play a key role in instigating gross human rights violations as far as these two conflicts are concerned. Such an institution should be manned by civil society leaders, religious and community leaders whom the people trust for it to be successful and not the same people the armed groups are fighting against.

8. In order to promote social reintegration, attention needs to be paid not only to ex-combatants, but also to victims and broader host communities; and to the relationship between ex-combatants on one hand and victims on the other hand. It thus has to be a bottom-up approach and not a top-down approach and with a community-centred reintegration, which breaches the claims and needs of ex-combatants with those of victims and the communities in which they live. Attention must be paid to providing for both individual ex-combatants/victims and receiving communities, which the decree failed to address.
9. The decree makes no provision for amnesties geared towards the transformation of fighters into civilians, which are always part of DDR incentives and processes. There is also no comprehensive and clearly understood selection criteria for an individual's participation in the DDR, neither is there a clearly legal, political and practical security arrangement for those who give up arms and demobilise.
10. The decree is one-sided and it cannot play an important role in limiting violence by disarming a large number of actors and disbanding illegal, dysfunctional and/or bloated military structures. It has not decided on the overall number of combatants to be demobilised and thus the size of the resulting security forces. Also, it has not addressed the issue of who should stay in the formal security sector. It fell short of the security sector reform component, which is crucial in the case of Cameroon in addressing the current conflicts.

Also, in a press conference held on December 29, 2018, in Yaoundé with the objective of making an assessment of the human rights situation of the country, the National President of the National Commission of Human Rights and Freedom (HCHRF), Chemuta Divine Mbanda, stated that the Cameroonian DDR initiative should be applied only after an inclusive dialogue has been initiated between the government and the different stakeholders towards the cessation of hostilities in the conflict-torn Far North Region and the Anglophone regions (Neba, 2017).

However, according to Elvis Teke (2019), the National Coordinator of the National Committee on Disarmament, Demobilisation, and Reintegration (NCDDR) held a working session with officials of the United Nations system on February 12, 2019 in Cameroon. During the meeting, the Regional Coordinator of the North-West Region reported that the three-month-old committee has so far had 12 ex-fighters, including a female, who voluntarily laid down their weapons and are in the camps and receiving psychological assistance from experts, technicians, and religious authorities. The other regional coordinators stated that they are continuously educating and sensitising the public to dispel fear and reassure those in the bushes of the amnesty of the head of state (Teke, 2019). Since then, almost nothing has been heard about the activities of the Cameroonian NDDRC, except the parading of some separatist ex-fighters during the Grand National Dialogue in Yaoundé on September 30 to October 4, 2019 by the government; meanwhile, the conflicts in the Far North and the North-West and South-West Regions are still raging on.

CONCLUSION

The creation of a disarmament, demobilisation, and reintegration (DDR) committee by the Cameroonian government should be taken as laudable effort by the government to resolve the Boko Haram terrorist conflict in the Far North Region and the Anglophone separatist armed conflict in the North-West and South-West Regions of the country. However, the commission could have been effective against ex-Boko Haram fighters because of the nature of the conflict, which is an Islamic terrorist sect that emanated from neighbouring Nigeria and not an internal conflict within the country. Moreover, it is easier to convince recruited Cameroonian Boko Haram fighters from the Far North Region to lay down their arms and go back to normal life without having to broker a ceasefire deal with their hierarchy in Nigeria. On the other hand, the armed separatist fighters of the North-West and South-West Regions are Anglophone Cameroonians fighting against the Cameroonian government's forces and who are motivated by their political quest for the independence of the Anglophone regions. While the DDR plan could work in the Far North Region, regarding its application in the Anglophone regions, applying it without a negotiated ceasefire will be tantamount to putting the cart before the horses, making it just another wasted and futile commission that is condemned to fail.

From the foregoing, it is therefore necessary that the government of Cameroon continue with its campaign to eradicate Boko Haram in the Northern Regions and use the NDDR initiative to disarm, demobilise, and reintegrate Cameroonian citizens who joined the terrorist group and who have manifested their intention to drop their weapons and return to civilian life. In the case of the armed separatist conflict in the North-West and South-West Regions, the government should work with identified credible, trusted, and respected national and international actors to help broker a ceasefire with the armed separatist groups, grant a general amnesty to all the separatists at home and abroad, facilitate the return of internally displaced persons and refugees, initiate an inclusive dialogue and also a justice, peace, and reconciliation process, and finally implement the NDDR on the separatist ex-fighters, while discussion on the root causes of the conflict is accelerated.

The establishment of the DDR to resolve the Anglophone conflict by the government ties with the peacebuilding approach of the New Partnership for African Development (NEPAD). For NEPAD, Africa's peacebuilding approach is an all-encompassing strategy involving (i) restoring security, (ii) managing political transition, (iii) anchoring socioeconomic development, (iv) promoting human rights and justice, and (v) resource mobilisation (NEPAD, 2005). These five dimensions are framed to complement each other in resolving a conflict. The African Union does not see the wisdom of placing these issues in a sequence, for the organisation is against the Western and UN logic that one element is fully needed to be implemented before the commencement of the next phase. At the centre of AU policy is the need to pursue security, development, and peace simultaneously at all times instead of sequencing the various phases. That is why the Cameroonian government, in the midst of the war, will design a humanitarian assistance programme for internally displaced persons (IDPs) while simultaneously creating the DDR. The commission's task of disarming the fighters will provide security, in turn ensuring the return to normalcy and socioeconomic development being pursued with other solutions being implemented.

This approach equally falls in line with Barnett et al. (2007: 49–50), who divided post-conflict peacebuilding into three dimensions: stabilising the post-conflict zone, restoring state institutions, and dealing with social and economic issues. Activities concerning the first phase reinforce post-conflict state stability and discourage former combatants from returning to war (disarmament, demobilisation, and reintegration, or DDR). Second-dimension activities deal with building state capacity to provide public goods and increase the legitimacy of the state. Programmes in the third phase construct a post-conflict society's ability to manage conflicts peacefully and promote socioeconomic development (Barnett et al., 2007: 49–50). While Cameroon's government approach to DDR aims first and foremost at stabilising the state and enhancing its legitimacy, the conflict may not be resolved using the parameters above because the nature of the conflict does not suit such solutions.

References

Adinoyi, J.A. (2015). Importance of disarmament, demobilization and reintegration (DDR) in post-conflict peace building.

Africa Development Bank. (2011). Role of disarmament-reintegration program and post-conflict reconstruction: Some Lessons Learnt (*Africa Development Bank: Fragile States Unit–OFSU*, 2011).

Barnett, M., Kim, H., O'Donnell, M., & Sitea, L. (2007). Peacebuilding: What is in a Name? *Global Governance*, 13.

Berghof Foundation (2012). Berghof glossary on conflict transformation, 20 notions for theory and practice. https://www.berghof-foundation.org

Besenyő, J. & Mayer, Á. (2015). Boko Haram in context: The terrorist organizations's roots in Nigeria's social history. *Defence Against Terrorism Review*, 7(1), 47–58. http://real.mtak.hu/83734/1/04_BokoHaraminContext_TheTerroristOrganizations_RootsinNigeriasSocialHistory_u.pdf

Conflict Sensitivity Consortium (2012). How to Guide to Conflict Sensitivity, Conflict Sensitivity Consortium. https://local.conflictsensitivity.org

Fisher, S., Ludin, J., Smith, R., Williams, S., Williams, S., & Abdi, D.I. (2000). *Working with conflict: Skills and strategies for action*. London: Zed Books.

Forsyth, D.R. (2009). *Group dynamics* 5th ed. Boston: Wadsworth Cengage Learning.

Fusato, M. (2003). Disarmament, demobilization and reintegration (DDR) of ex-combatants: Beyond intractability. In G. Burgess and H. Burgess (Eds.), *Conflict Information Consortium*. Boulder: University of Colorado. https://www.beyongintractability.org/essay/demobilization

Hanson, S. (2007). Disarmament, demobilization, and reintegration (DDR) in Africa. *Council on Foreign Relations*. https://www.cfr.org/publication

Harbom, L.W. (2006). *Patterns of major armed conflicts, 1990–2005*, SIPRI Yearbook, Armaments, Disarmament and International Security, Oxford: Oxford University Press.

Issa, S., & Machikou, N. (2019). Reintegrating former Boko Haram associates: Perspectives from far North Region in Cameroon. *Global Center on Cooperative Security* https://www.jstor.org/stable/resrep20331 Accessed: 10-06-2020 18:53 UTC

Journal du Cameroun. (2018). Cameroon: Residence of Disarmament Committee CoordinatorSet Ablaze.

Journal du Cameroun (2019). Four Dead in Suspected Boko Haram Attacks in Cameroon.

KAIPTC/ZIF. (2008). Post-Conflict Peacebuilding in Liberia: Much Remains to be done, Report on Third Annual KAIPTC / ZIF Seminar Accra, Ghana November 1 – 3, 2007, Center for International Peace Operations – ZIF, Kofi Annan International Peacekeeping Training Centre – KAIPTC.

NAP. (2000). International Conflict Resolution after the Cold War. *The National Academies of Sciences, Engineering and Medicine, Consensus Report Study*. https://www.nap.edu

Ndikum, R.N. (2018, December 13). Opinion: Disarmament Committee, 10 Points why it is Another Misplaced Priority. *Cameroon News Agency*. cameroonnewsagency.com

Neba, S.K. (2017). "National Commission on Human Rights and Freedoms: Authorities Decry Increase in Human Rights Violations in 2016 Report of Activities," Cameroon Radio Television. www.crtv.cm

NEPAD. (2005, June). African Post-Conflict Reconstruction Policy Framework. *Midrand: NEPAL Secretariat*. https://www.securitycouncilreport.org/atf/cf/%7B65BFCF9B-6D27-4E9C-8CD3-CF6E4FF96FF9%7D/SSR%20PCR-PolicyFramework_en[1].pdf

Nezam, T., & Marc, A. (2009, February). Social Development Department, Conflict, Crime and Violence, Disarmament, Demobilization and Reintegration. *Bank for Reconstruction and Development/The World Bank Publication*, No. 119.

Ngonivilin, K. (2018, December 20). The National Coordinator for NDDRC, Fai Yengo says the Centre can Accommodate Between 100–120 Persons while other Plans are in the Offing for more Intakes. *Cameroon Tribune*.

Prokes, C. (2018). What is disarmament? – definition. *Conferences and Meaning, Lesson Transcript*. https://www.study.com

Rackley, A. (2005, August 25). A Big Test for the Whole World.

Shaheen, H. (2016). What is disarmament? *International Relations and South Asian Studies Quora*. https://www.quora.com

Teke, E. (2019). NCDDR Shares Experience with UN System. https://www.crtv.cm

UNDDR Resource Center. (2005). What is DDR?" Secretary General's Note to the General Assembly, A/C.5/59/31, Published in 2005 by the United Nations Disarmament, Demobilization, and Reintegration Center.

UNDPO. (2000). *Disarmament, demobilization and reintegration of ex-combatants in a peacekeeping environment: Principles and guidelines*. New York: Department of Peacekeeping Operations United Nations.

UN General Assembly (2015). Final document of the first special session on disarmament. https://www.un.org

Weinstein, J., & Humphreys, M. (2005). Disentangling the Determinants of Successful Demobilization and Reintegration *Centre for Global Development*, Working Paper No. 69. http://www.cgdev.org/sites/default/files

24

FROM "BLACK WIDOWS" TO "ISIS BRIDES"

Female Recruitment Practices of Islamist Terrorist Networks

Kleanthis Kyriakidis, Renny Castañeda, and Marios P. Efthymiopoulos

INTRODUCTION

This chapter addresses the intersection of "Islamist terrorism" and gender with two specific case studies: the evolution of the "Black Widows" Islamist Chechen female suicide bombers, and the cases of the "ISIS brides". The research highlights the limitations of addressing a correct approach as regards the concept of terrorism since the approach relies on concrete temporal circumstances where one person's terrorist is another person's freedom fighter. As such, the approach explains the difficulties in providing a universally agreed definition, stressing how the biographical and subjective experiences of members of terrorist groups play a substantial role in the motivations for enrolment (Schmid & Jongman, 1988). The concept of "Islamist" terrorism is also highly contested since terror is simply enforced in the name of a religion, and both the causes and the desired end state of terrorism are often political. Finally, the research aims to focus on the role of women, or female recruitment, in terrorist groups. "Terrorism is a highly *gendered* [our own emphasis] phenomenon, producing the figure of the female terrorist that circulates within contemporary Western culture as an object of fascination and heightened concern" (Third, 2014). As such, the cases provided aim to explain the role of gender in terrorist organisations as a pivotal feature of characteristic enrolment, displacing customary approaches to recruitment or the nature of the terrorist group.

In general, a significant portion of academic discussions on this topic have provided assessments regarding the relationship between Islamic women and women's rights (Dalacoura, 2003). Therefore, most scholars agree that the problem is not religion per se but rather its interpretation and reinterpretation by extremists and "jihadists". In this approach, it is common to argue against the claim that since the religion or beliefs show little or no respect for their rights, one should expect to find virtually no women participating in "Islamist" terrorist groups (Kurz, 2007).[1] The evidence, however, shows a different trend in notorious cases such as the "Black Widows" female suicide bombers in Russia and the "ISIS brides", where many women choose to participate in terrorist organisations and take part in seemingly irrational causes and fights.

In the study, we examine the semantics of the two terms that describe our case studies. This is because the term "Black Widows" carries a double connotation. First, it implies that these women lost their husbands in war, most likely in one of the two Chechen wars in which Russia fought against "Islamist terrorists and rebels", as well as with the "Black Widow" spider recognised for its lethality. In contrast with the social and cultural background of Chechen female recruitment practises, the term "ISIS brides" is used in a semi-derogatory manner in the sense that these women are presented as having been tricked or coerced into joining ISIS only to have a "proper" family. As such, it is customary to assume that these women were naive and therefore easily lured into recruitment practises amidst confrontation and social unrest.

"BLACK WIDOWS"

Female terrorism is not something that can be considered a novelty in Russia, as the origin of the activity can date back to the activities of Vera Zasulich, who attempted to assassinate General Fyodor Trepov, the governor of Saint Petersburg, in 1878 to avenge the flogging of a political prisoner (Willcocks, 2008). More than a century later, and more specifically, between 2000 and 2013 (the peak of the phenomenon), 48 predominantly Chechen female suicide bombers staged in Russia a total of 25 attacks that resulted in the deaths of approximately 850 people (Knight & Narozhna, 2005).

DOI: 10.4324/9780429426063-26

The turning point for the mass media and public attention towards the Black Widows was October 2002, during the Dubrovka Theatre hostage crisis in Moscow, when 41 terrorists, including 19 women, held hostage more than 800 people for three days (Stepanova, 2004). A forceful operation by Russian special forces led to the deaths of the majority of the terrorists as well as more than one hundred hostages (Stack, 2011, p. 86).

Ahmed Jamali points out that, "most studies of Chechen female suicide bombers have found that these women have experienced serious personal trauma" (Jamali, 2017). While most young women, orphans or widows, joined the terrorist groups aiming to avenge traumatic experiences in zones of conflict, a lesser fraction found recruitment as a gateway for food, shelter, protection, and employment.[2] However, pushing back against conventional wisdom, Nabi Abdullaev's explanation of the "Black Widows" contends that "suicide terrorism in the largest of the post-Soviet states is an organisational rather than trauma-driven phenomenon" (Abdullaev, 2013). Specifically, he argues that no female suicide attacks took place during the First Chechen War (1994–1996), despite its uncontested viciousness. Instead, the first "Black Widow" appeared in 2000, during the Second Chechen War, which according to Abdullaev, was "far less brutal and indiscriminate than the first" (Speckhard & Akhmedova, 2006).[3] During the Second Chechen War, many "Islamists" came to aid secular Chechen rebels to the point of "Arabization of the Chechen Conflict", where the alleged hijacking of the insurgency was since perceived as a battle of "global jihad" (Gonzalez-Perez, 2008).[4] Moreover, the terms have come to be customarily misused and commonly misunderstood, even by states and their communities that have been the preferred targets of jihadist militant groups and organisations (Qazi, 2020).[5] Caitlin Toto concurs with the aforesaid view, emphasising that "terrorist leader Samil Basayev realised the effectiveness associated with female suicide bombers. These benefits include low degrees of suspicion and high degrees of precision" (Toto, 2015). Furthermore, female terrorists have demonstrated in certain cases that they are able to access their targets with greater ease than their male counterparts, thereby achieving the element of surprise (Cunningham, 2007). Finally, suicide bombing "is inexpensive, cost-effective, media-friendly, and with a built-in intelligent guidance and delivery system, very effective as psychological warfare" (Agara, 2015). Thus, it becomes evident that for a given terrorist group, a combination of female militant operatives and suicide bombing can be considered lethal and cost-effective (Jacques & Taylor, 2009).

As mentioned, the "trauma-driven" cause for enrolment and the leadership decision to use "Black Widows" members have been documented in the process of defining enablers for female participation in radical organisations. In the Chechen conflict, for instance, women have been exposed to war and most likely have experienced the murder, imprisonment, or torture of relatives, increasing ulterior motives for individuals to enrol in battle during violent conflict (Weir, 2003). In other cases, rigid religious indoctrination or tribal reasons can also play a role, endorsing in participants strict codes of honour and beliefs that imply their joining for religious and national motives. According to McGivern (2004), Chechen women have picked up arms in an effort to fight against what they see as cruel and oppressive occupying forces since the collapse of the Soviet Union. Therefore, a woman's participation in a jihadist group or its cause is often not perceived as such in most cases; at the very least, the claim can be made that their desire to fight is driven by a combination of social and political factors.

Anne Speckhard and Khapta Akhmedova compared the data of 26 "Black Widows", showing that only 5 (approximately 25%) of them had been widowed and half of them were single. Among that sample, not a single "Black Widow" was illiterate, and nine of them were either enroled in college or had graduated from college or university (Schweitzer et al., 2006). Their study showed that only two were from poor economic backgrounds, while nine were from upper-middle-class families, and one of them was relatively wealthy. Furthermore, of the 26 "Black Widows" studied, 22 were secular Muslims, and only four considered themselves to be "traditional" Muslims. Nevertheless, almost all had experienced some form of severe trauma, though this could be said of the majority of the Chechen population. Finally, 24 out of 26 "Black Widows" had family members killed or disappeared after arrest, while half of them had more than one family member killed.

Another factor that makes "Black Widows" unique is mass female participation. A study conducted at the University of Chicago comparing female suicide attacks in the Caucasus (2000–2013) and Iraq (highlighted that in the former, women participated in 80% of all recorded terrorist attacks, while in the latter, women played a role in only 8%, while worldwide female participation stands at less than 6% (Pape, 2014). Nevertheless, Caitlin Toto has provided an insightful explanation for this seemingly irrational difference (Toto, 2015). In recent decades, women in the Caucasus republics have increasingly endured social limitations derived from the degraded public order of the region, with a relatively high incidence of problems like polygamy among the Chechen rebels. This social background has affected the behaviour and decisions of women on how to address and deal with grief, being highly defined by their cultural limitations in accessing larger social networks of support. Over time, this vulnerability has increased recruiting in terrorist groups eager to include female participation, although in more traditional roles, such as in organisations like ISIS or Boko Haram (Davis, 2017).

After 2010, a geographical shift in the Balkans regarding the origin of female suicide bombers occurred. Instead of Chechnya, processes of recruitment grow rapidly in Dagestan, where the use of female suicide bombers reflects the tendency of ISIS, differentiating from the practises of "Black Widow" terrorism and resorting to more sensational operations in the region. In "Mass Mediated Terrorism" (Nacos, 2016), Brigitte Nacos explains in detail that "terrorists want a lot of people watching, a lot of people listening, and not a lot of people dead" (Jenkins, 1974). This explained why the idea of the female "Black Widow" was later used to portray a more shocking attraction in the population in comparison with the customary male suicide attack.

The conclusion from the study is that the Chechen female terrorists are usually related to the idea of the "women next door", not relying on exceptional people or "beauty queens". However, they are neither considered easily manipulated, social outcasts, or victims of Chechen men. This portrayal also contradicts published opinions of Russian authorities, who have referred to female members of criminal organisations as drugged, raped, coerced, blackmailed, or tricked into terrorism (Stack, 2011).[6] In consequence, the portraits of Black Widows as persons with no conscience of their actions exclude female responsibility from the activities of criminal organisations. In contrast, the reality appears more problematic, or sociological, based on the individual assumptions of each participant. As Qazi has (2020, p. 30) previously assessed:

> The reasons why women participate in violence will vary, even where common grievances are present, but what motivates women to engage in suicide terrorism is bound to be different for each individual woman … Researchers should not foreclose the possibility that each woman has a strong personal incentive for terror. Hence, no two female terrorists may be alike.

The second conclusion is that female terrorists are no different than male terrorists. As such, female members of terrorist groups also hold subjective motives, doctrinarian motives, or traumatic experiences. This holds true for most of the situations experienced by women, apart from the trauma of rape, often considered a trigger event for female participation. As it has been reported:

> In the absence of rape by soldiers of the other side, the terrorists have taken to raping the women themselves. Rape has become such a fundamental recruiting tool that in February 2009, Samira Ahmed Jassim, known as Um al Mu'emin, Mother of the Faithful, was arrested for having orchestrated the rapes of eighty girls in Baghdad and Diyala province to recruit them as suicide bombers for Ansar al Sunnah, a Sunni group with links to Al Qaeda. Jassim's logic was that once the girls were raped, only an act of martyrdom could eradicate their shame (Bloom, 2011, p. 15).

Finally, we should also underline that the Chechens, or Ingushetians, have a strict honour code ("adat") and are morally bound to seek revenge (Kurz, 2007).[7] This may have influenced a particular trait of community participation: belonging to radical organisations that justify cultural ulterior motives.

"ISIS BRIDES"

The rationale behind the processes of recruitment or participation of women in ISIS, often referred to as "ISIS brides", does not rely on the main idea of the "freedom fight" or personal trauma. ISIS practises differ from Chechen terrorism in that they regularly engage in common human rights violations where women or female children are used for degrading or inhumane treatment (UN, 1948, p. Art. 5). These activities regularly include torture and rape, as well as being enslaved in highly publicised cases, such as those of the Yezidi women. Furthermore, their members are not able to exert, in private or public, freedom of expression, employment, or education, reinforcing social ties that limit any change within the cultural environment (UN, 1948, pp. Art. 19, 23, 26). Finally, the hierarchies also establish differences before the law, distinguishing the members between male and female legal prospects within their own legal jurisdictions. In the case of ISIS, a false interpretation of Islam is consistently considered the driving force behind the decision of these women to join. Nonetheless, it is important to highlight that people who are genuinely religious know that "suicide bombing violates three of the most fundamental truths about the Islamic faith: an opposition to suicide, an opposition to killing civilians, and an opposition to killing other Muslims" (Bloom, 2011, pp. 13–14).

Historically, the Muslim traditional role of the female does not actually forbid their participation in conflicts. Qazi highlights that "early Muslim women in seventh-century Arabia nursed the wounded, protected their homes when men left to fight in the early battles, and in a few well-documented cases, trained and fought valiantly alongside men to ensure the faith's survival" (Qazi, 2020, p. 32). For instance, Nusayba bint Kaab, also known as Umm Umarah, died fighting during the Battle of Uhud (Peresin, 2015).[8] Therefore, if some women see the ISIS "cause" as just, they are justified in participating even in military activities.

In the case of ISIS, empirical research points to the fact that their main role is not to actively participate in war but to socially support it. At the start of the Syrian war, it is believed that more than five hundred Western women (mostly European) travelled to Syria to join ISIS in a case of coordination of social networks beyond the Arab region (Chatterjee, 2016, p. 21). This can be considered unexpected, as the decision of a young European Muslim female to join ISIS is Orientalist, detaching the social origin of the member from their rationale (Gentry, 2011, p. 179). Moreover, this can be a motive for further research, as different tensions between regions rely on the cultural hierarchies between the western and eastern hemispheres, disputing common assumptions that "ISIS brides" are considered entirely oppressed by male family members. In general, it can be considered that Muslim European women can be prone to being disenfranchised, receiving hostility against their religion or their dress code, and later becoming alienated from the community. Hence, there are many that simply wish, as can be assessed, to participate in something bigger, evading an environment where they feel like outcasts (Olivier, 2005, pp. 360–364). Thus, their participation in ISIS can strengthen their religious fervour and ideas of how ISIS implements the "shariah, enforcing processes of social fragmentation that originated decades ago".

Finally, the main roles reserved for women in ISIS are those of wives and mothers to ISIS soldiers. Most recently, this pattern has been shifting to activities such as public relations campaigns and online recruiting of other women for the group (Binetti, 2015). This does not imply that women do not participate in violent acts. In the notorious case of the all-female Al-Khansaa Brigade formed in February 2014, for example, women served duties such as intelligence gathering or prison guards. Amanda Spencer's research provides interesting facts regarding the activities they engage in, accounting for how, besides the roles of wife and mother, 55% are recruiters, 10% are patrol officers (including the Al-Khansaa), 6% are heads of command, 4% are prison guards, and another 4% are overseers (Spencer, 2016, p. 91). We also need to pay attention to a shift towards more fighting roles for women as time passes and ISIS starts to be heavily defeated. In its official publication *Rumiyah*, in July 2017, there was a call to arms for all women (Bont, 2017, p. 13), pointing out that ISIS did not refer only to suicide bombers but also to conventional fighters, as confirmed in January 2018 in an official video released by the terrorist group and entitled "Inside the Khilafah 7" (Winter, 2018, p. 12).

CONCLUSION

Our first observation is that the "ISIS brides" are undoubtedly framed in a more traditional Muslim context than Chechen terrorists. Hence, religion in the latter case is not the predominant reason for joining the "cause" in contrast to "ISIS brides". Moreover, in the case of "Black Widows", potential recruits have often suffered direct historical trauma. As such, Chechen female terrorists can regularly participate in fighting and can be considered fearsome suicide bombers, whereas Western women who join ISIS are mostly reserved for more traditional and supportive roles.

In both cases, gender plays a very important role in the "for and against" propaganda. As it was mentioned, on the one hand, female terrorists can be depicted as "zombies" or "nave brides to be" subjected to coercion. On the other hand, the terrorist groups present them as ideal women or victims of their opponents, resorting to a doctrine that highlights the idea of a "just" cause.

The lack of consensus regarding the driving forces behind the joining of these groups by a female can show that women often justify participation in terrorist activities as their male counterparts do, addressing political, religious, patriotic, socio-economic, or purely personal motivations. Some might argue that the only gender-related motivation could be a false notion of emancipation for women who join a terrorist group, whose activities nonetheless do not influence the overall female role in patriarchal societies (see Romaniuk & Wasylciw, 2010).

Finally, to propose some counter-terrorism policies, we should first state that the abusive or invasive operations of foreign governments can result in the potential raising of a new generation of terrorists (see Romaniuk, 2021). In such cases, the political use of foreign violence can often be instrumentalized for criminal action in territories harmed, resonating with the target population as part of the terrorists' propaganda. This thesis can further be complemented by the assessment as regards terrorist recruiting posed by Mia Bloom, resumed in the "three D's: delegitimize, deglamorize, and demobilise" (Bloom, 2011, p. 19). More specifically, delegitimization can be achieved in the case of female terrorists who have religious motives, since explaining the nature of Islam and the *dicta* of the *Holy Quran* according to the peaceful majority has served other countries to endorse the peaceful nature of the religion, increasing levels of security in the Middle East in countries with almost no presence of terrorism, and *deglamorizing* the "cause".

Finally, it is important to draw attention to the opportunities for demobilisation given to female terrorists. This last suggestion may sound in some aspects limited or utopian, yet numerous demobilisation practises and protocols have been implemented in western territories highly harmed by terrorist violence, such as Colombia, much of which can provide evidence to most effectively implement policies directed to disable female participation in criminal organisations.

Notes

1 There are numerous Islamist terrorist groups in Chechnya, the most prominent, or rather the umbrella term, being "the Army of the Republic of Chechnya-Ichkeria (ARCI)". Kurz & Bartles consider the "Black Widows" a separate "brigade" and also name the following groups: Islamic International Peacekeeping Brigade (IIPB), Riyad US-Saliheyn Martyrs' Brigade, Special Purpose Islamic Regiment (SPIR), Dagestani Shari'ah Jamaat, and Ingush Jama'at Shariat.

2 Among other reasons, female terrorists are forced to join groups through abduction, forced marriages, or by being born and raised within the ranks of the organisation, either because they are orphans or because their mothers were abducted.

3 A case to be noted is the one conducted in June 2000 by Khava Barayeva, who drove a truck loaded with explosives into the Russian military base in Alkhan-Yurt.

4 "Chechnya's separatists received money, men, training, and ideological inspiration from international Islamic organisations,

but they remained as indigenous and largely self-sustained forces motivated more by nationalist rather than Islamic goals", see Chivers (2004).

5 "For believing Muslims, jihad is a living, breathing concept. Muslims strive to embrace good and reject evil. Even for secular, liberal (nonpracticing) Muslims, jihad is a positive term that reflects the inner struggle of one's life" (Qazi, 2020, p. 36).

6 An example can be provided in the case of Zarema Muzhikhoeva, one of the few captured failed female suicide bombers. "Her basic narrative stays fairly consistent. She stated that she was married in her teens and had a child. Her husband died fighting the Russians, and in accordance with Chechen tradition, she and her child became the responsibility of her husband's family. Either desperate to escape servitude to her in-laws or marriage to her brother-in-law, Muzhikhoeva ran away, leaving her child behind. When she could not find work, she borrowed money. When she could not repay her debt, she became a suicide bomber to be absolved of the debt. According to her account, she went to a terrorist camp in the mountains of Chechnya in March 2003, where Arabs taught Chechens Islam and insurgent tactics. She reported having sex with the camp leader and being beaten for dressing inappropriately. She also reported that other women in the camp were raped, beaten, and drugged" (Stack, 2011, p. 88).

7 In Kurz & Bartles, we see most of the rules of "adat": "Murder should be avenged with murder. Only males may avenge; females are only allowed to avenge if there are no males in their family or among their relatives. For the murder of a female, two males should be killed: the murderer and the murderer's family member. The revenge should be directed only at the murderer, not at his family members or close associates. Revenge is not limited in time; it can be realised many years after the murder. The revenge can be averted if respected elders intervene and ask the victim's family to forgive the murderer. Revenge does not mandate that the avenger should kill himself or herself while committing the murder" (Kurz, 2007, p. 534).

8 Some Western female ISIS terrorists "call themselves muhajirat ... It is important to highlight that not all ISIS women, depending on their motivation for making hijra, clearly understand the importance and honourable value of the term in its religious sense, which could offend true believers" (Peresin, 2015, p. 23).

References

Abdullaev, N. (2013, November 8). Russia's 'Black Widows': Organization Behind Sensation, Harvard Belfer Center Paper. https://www.belfercenter.org/publication/russias-black-widows-organization-behind-sensation

Agara, T. (2015). Gendering terrorism: Women, gender, terrorism and suicide bombers. *International Journal of Humanities and Social Science*, 5(6:1), 115–125

Binetti, A. (2015). A new frontier: Human trafficking and ISIS's recruitment of women from the West. Information2 Action. Georgetown Institute for Women, Peace and Security.

Bloom, M. (2011). *Bombshell: Women and terrorism*. Philadelphia: University of Pennsylvania Press

Bont, R. D. (2017, September). Life at ISIS: The roles of Western men, women and children, Institute of Security and Global Affairs, Leiden University. https://www.researchgate.net/publication/320335935_Life_at_ISIS_The_Roles_of_Western_Men_Women_and_Children/link/59de751b0f7e9bcfab2404bf/download

Chatterjee, D. (2016). Gendering ISIS and mapping the role of women. *Contemporary Review of the Middle East*, 3(2), 201–218

Cunningham, K. (2007). Countering female terrorism. *Journal of Studies in Conflict and Terrorism*, *30*(2): 113–129

Dalacoura, K. (2003). *Islam, liberalism and human rights*. London: IB Tauris.

Davis, J. (2017). Women in modern terrorism: From liberation wars to global Jihad and the Islamic State. Lanham: Rowman & Littlefield.

Gentry, C. (2011). The neo-orientalist narratives of women's involvement in Al-Qaeda. In Sjoberg & Gentry (Eds.), *Women, gender and terrorism* (pp. 176–193). Athens: The University of Georgia Press.

Gonzalez-Perez, M. (2008). *Women and terrorism: Female activity in domestic and international terror groups*. New York: Routledge.

Jacques, K., & Taylor, P.J. (2009). Female terrorism: A review. *Terrorism & Political Violence*, *21*(3), 499–515.

Jamali, A. (2017, July 3). Chechen black widows: The lethal female terrorists ever, *Modern Diplomacy* https://moderndiplomacy.eu/2017/07/03/chechen-black-widows-the-lethal-female-terrorists-ever/

Jenkins, B.M. (1974). International terrorism: A new mode of conflict, research paper no. 48, California Seminar on Arms Control and Foreign Policy, Los Angeles: Crescent Publications.

Knight, W.A., & Narozhna, T. (2005). Social contagion and the female face of terror: New trends in the culture of political violence. *Canadian Foreign Policy*, *12*(1), 141–166.

Kurz, R.W. (2007). Chechen suicide bombers. *Journal of Slavic Military Studies*, *20*, 529–547.

McGivern, M. (2004). Slaughter in the school: Terror of the black widows. Chechen women in vanguard of attacks. Daily Record; Glasgow (UK) [Glasgow (UK)] 04 Sep: 8.

Nacos, B. (2016). *Mass-mediated terrorism: The central role of the media in terrorism and counterterrorism*. New York: Rowman & Littlefield.

Olivier, R. (2005). Europe's response to radical Islam. *Current History*, *104*(685), 360–364

Pape, R. (2014). CPOST 2014 Suicide Attack Index. Chicago Project on Security and Terrorism, University of Chicago. https://news.uchicago.edu/story/chicago-project-security-terrorism-creates-first-annual-report-suicide-terrorism

Peresin, A. (2015). Fatal attraction: Western muslimas and ISIS. *Perspectives on Terrorism*, *9*(3), 21–38

Qazi, F. (2020). The Mujahidaat: Tracing the early female warriors of Islam. In L. Sjoberg in L. Sjoberg and C. Gentry (Eds.), *Women, gender and terrorism* (pp. 29–56). Athens: The University of Georgia Press.

Raghavan, S.V., & Balasubramaniyan, V. (2014). Evolving role of women in terror groups: Progression or regression?. *Journal of International Women's Studies*, *15*(2), 197–211.

Romaniuk, S. N. (2021). *Under siege: Counterterrorism and civil society in Hungary*. Lanham: Rowman & Littlefield.

Romaniuk, S. N., & Wasylciw, J. K. (2010). "Gender" includes men too! Recognizing masculinity in security studies and international relations. *Perspectives*, 18(1), 23–39. http://www.jstor.org/stable/23616076

Schmid, P.A., & Jongman, A. (1988). *Political terrorism: A new guide to actors, authors, concepts, data bases, theories and literature*. New Brunswick: Transaction Books.

Schweitzer, Y., Speckhard, A., & Akhmedova, K. (2006). *Black widows: The Chechen female suicide terrorists. Female suicide terrorists*. Tel Aviv: Jaffe Center.

Stack, A. (2011). Zombies versus black widows: Women as propaganda in the chechen conflict. In L. Sjoberg and C. Gentry (Eds.), *Women, gender and terrorism* (pp. 83–95). Athens: The University of Georgia Press.

Stepanova, E. From Dubrovka to Beslan: Who is learning faster?. Institute of World Economy and International Relations. PONARS Policy Memo 347. November 2004.

Speckhard, A. & Akhmedova, K. (2006). Black widows: The Chechen female suicide terrorist. In Y. Schweitzer (Ed.), *Female suicide terrorists* (pp. 1–14). Tel Aviv: Jaffe Center. https://www.researchgate.net/publication/237362743_Black_Widows_The_Chechen_Female_Suicide_Terrorists

Spencer, A. (2016). The hidden face of terrorism: An analysis of the women in Islamic State, *Journal of Strategic Security*, 9(3), 74–98.

Third, A. (2014). *Gender and the political: Deconstructing the female terrorist*. New York: Palgrave MacMillan.

Toto, C. (2015). Behind the veil: A study of Chechen black widows elements, *11*(1). 10.6017/eurj.v11i1.8817

United Nations (UN). (1948). Universal Declaration of Human Rights https://www.un.org/en/universal-declaration-human-rights/

Weir, F. (2003). Chechen women join terror's ranks; Three recent suicide bombings mark a desperately violent trend. The Christian Science Monitor. Boston, Mass. [Boston, Mass]12 June: 1.

Willcocks. (2008). Justice system appears broken. *Daily News*; Prince Rupert, B.C. [Prince Rupert, B.C]26 Nov.

Winter, C. (2018, September). ISIS, women and Jihad: Breaking with convention co-existence, Tony Blair Institute for Global Change, https://institute.global/policy/isis-women-and-jihad-breaking-convention

PART II

CYBER-TERRORISM AND SECURITY

25

CYBER-TERRORISM

A Concept in Flux

Tobias Burgers and Scott N. Romaniuk

INTRODUCTION

In contrast to the remaining sections of this volume that centre on terrorist actors, organisations, and regional terror dynamics, this chapter will adopt a distinct perspective. The examination deals with a notion that is not limited by geographical boundaries and is not affiliated with a singular locality or demographic. The phenomenon occurs globally, without any discernible geographic concentrations. Moreover, the concept extends beyond the realm of corporeal space. A diverse array of terrorist actors, spanning various backgrounds and ideologies, have expressed support for this phenomenon, ranging from ISIS in the Middle East to right-wing extremist groups in the United States. Despite its frequent mention in discussions surrounding terrorism, widespread usage in modern media, and its prevalence in virtually all societies and among the majority of individuals worldwide, the topic remains a subject of extensive debate within academic, security, and societal spheres.

As early as 2012, Peter W. Singer had observed that the subject matter had already garnered a significant amount of scholarly attention, with approximately ten thousand articles having been published on the topic. According to Singer (2012), there were no reported fatalities resulting from cyberattacks. Presently, after a span of seven years, it is highly likely that this inventory has expanded to encompass an additional 10,000 scholarly works. However, despite this escalation, the number of individuals adversely affected by this notion has persisted unchanged. As of the latter part of 2019, there were no recorded fatalities attributed to the aforementioned condition. This prompts an inquiry: what is the rationale behind the extensive literature on a subject that has yielded negligible consequences? Furthermore, the absence of a universally recognised characterisation of this notion adds to its complexity. Conway (2002) suggests that the idea of cyber-terrorism is characterised by its fluidity, variability, and broad applicability.

The present chapter delves into the notion of cyber-terrorism. The objective of this study is to provide a clear definition of cyber-terrorism, distinguish it from other related phenomena, examine its historical usage and misusage, and forecast its potential evolution in the upcoming years. The present study aims to contend that the term "cyber-terrorism" is utilised as a comprehensive and all-encompassing definition, which, according to the authors' perspective, encompasses two distinct concepts. The primary focus of concern pertains to the utilisation of cyber methods by terrorists for the purpose of executing their activities. The utilisation of information and communication technology (ICT) in cyberspace, commonly referred to as the cyber element, functions as a means of communication that facilitates the propagation of terrorist activities, recruitment, and even the execution of terrorist attacks. Additionally, it has the potential to influence individuals to carry out stand-alone attacks. As per the renowned media scholar Torres Soriano (2008), Marshall McLuhan asserted that terrorism is non-existent in the absence of communication. Our assertion is that the aforementioned is a perspective of a terrorist regarding the utilisation of cyber methods for information warfare. By utilising contemporary cyber technologies in the context of twenty-first-century terrorism, it is argued that the notion of cyber-terrorism affords novel avenues of communication and operational strategies for terrorist organisations and their affiliated networks.

TERRORISM THROUGH A NARROW LENS

As we contemplate the future of the limited concept of cyber-terrorism, it is imperative that we do not disregard the possibility of terrorists effectively executing a cyber assault that yields detrimental outcomes in the tangible realm. As

DOI: 10.4324/9780429426063-28

previously stated, it would necessitate a significant amount of resources. It is imperative to consider the potential emergence of state-sponsored cyber-terrorism in the foreseeable future. That is to say, a sovereign state provides backing to terrorist groups outside of its own territory. The employment of terrorist organisations as proxies in cyber conflict may potentially emerge as a novel manifestation of hybrid warfare, wherein nation-states aim to evade accountability and confrontations with their direct opponents. It is important to acknowledge the potential occurrence of a situation wherein proficient and well-equipped cyber agents engage in a digital insurgency with the aim of causing physical harm and destruction. The Hezbollah movement's digital campaigns serve as a noteworthy illustration of cyber proxies. Although their current capabilities are limited and unlikely to result in physical disruption or destruction, it is conceivable that in the future, hackers affiliated with Hezbollah, who have received training from the Iranian government – a prominent actor in offensive cyber operations – could engage in offensive cyber activities.

Terrorism by Digital Means

Cyber-terrorism or terrorism by digital means represents a contemporary technological methodology for a practise that has been in existence for almost 150 years. This iteration of cyber-terrorism involves the utilisation of the digital realm as a conduit for actions that are ultimately aimed at impacting the physical domain through tangible methods. According to Brunst (2008: 34–35), the term "cyber-terrorism" has been defined in a very broad manner. The expanded manifestation of cyber-terrorism, facilitated by the realm of digital technology, has resulted in various assaults and inflicted significant harm on a global scale. In a strict sense, we contend that this manifestation of cyber-terrorism is essentially a pre-existing form of terrorism that predates the advent of the cyber era. The phenomenon of terrorism has undergone alterations and, to a certain degree, has been influenced by the advent of cyberspace. Nonetheless, it still retains its fundamental emphasis on physical space. From a historical perspective, this is not a new phenomenon. Terrorist entities and their networks have endeavoured to incorporate novel and developing technologies into their methods of operation, a practise that dates back to the era of Bakunin.

The second notion pertains to cyber-terrorism and is situated on the opposite end of the spectrum. The approach of this cyber-terrorism form is relatively new when compared to conventional terrorism. Its emergence as a concept has been limited and has only occurred since the proliferation of ICT technologies and the expansion of cyberspace. In this context, cyberspace is not merely a medium for enabling communication and/or activities, but rather the domain in which said activities are executed. That is to say, the focus of operations is on the cyber domain itself rather than using it as a means to achieve other objectives.

This manifestation of cyber-terrorism is strongly associated with the principles of cyber conflict and cyber warfare.[1] This idea of cyber-terrorism is known as the narrowly defined variant, according to Brunst (2008: 34–35). This iteration involves the utilisation of terrorist networks or individual actors who operate independently to cause disruption or destruction of targets via the cyber realm. Primarily, the intended objectives would be situated in the virtual realm, encompassing websites, servers, or other variants of digital data. Given the observed escalation patterns and trends in cyber conflict, it is plausible to anticipate that terrorist entities or individuals may eventually attempt to inflict physical damage on targets via cyberspace. The aforementioned operations bear resemblance to Stuxnet, which is widely regarded as the first digital weapon and was expounded upon by Kim Zetter in her 2015 publication titled Countdown to Zero Day. These operations were characterised by the weaponization of code, a novel approach to cyberattacks. Other notable instances include the 2015 attack on the Ukrainian power grid and the 2018 assault on the Saudi petrochemical plant. In each of the aforementioned incidents, cybernetic systems were employed to impede or obliterate digital infrastructure that governed tangible operations. Verton issued a warning as early as 2003 regarding the potential occurrence of a cyber-terrorist attack in the wake of the commencement of the Global War on Terror (GWOT). Stohl (2007) posited that a discrepancy exists between the apprehensions surrounding such actions and their actual occurrence. In light of Stohl's comments made almost fifteen years ago, it is worth noting that no instances of cyber-terrorism have been reported to date. This raises the question of whether the likelihood of such acts occurring is low.

Given these two distinct definitions of cyber-terrorism, it is understandable that the emerging concept remains fluid and is difficult to define and comprehend. Moreover, as ICT technologies continue to advance, such as the incorporation of new systems – such as the Internet of Things (IoT) into cyberspace, big data, and artificial intelligence (AI) – we can anticipate that the concept of cyber-terrorism will continue to evolve and may remain malleable. Consequently, this chapter is an attempt to clarify the concept as well as a snapshot of the present situation at the end of the second decade of the twenty-first century. The following paragraph will begin with a brief historical overview of how, why, and to what extent terrorist networks and actors became interested in utilising cyber technologies. Then, two distinct cyber-terrorism concepts will be discussed. First, the concept of cyberspace-facilitated terrorism, followed by cyberspace-executed terrorism. A concluding paragraph will discuss how, in the near future, new cyber developments may alter the understanding of the two distinct concepts of cyber-terrorism.

The Roots of Cyber-Terrorism

Barry Collin coined the term cyber-terrorism as the convergence of terrorism and cyberspace sometime between the mid- and late 1980s. Cyber-terrorism is defined by Collin (quoted in White, 1998: 3) as "the intentional abuse of a digital information system, network, or component to support or facilitate a terrorist campaign or action." After Collin's remark, however, the digital sphere remained silent. Not until a decade later did the majority of the ongoing debate on what constitutes cyber-terrorism emerge (Weimann, 2005). Ironically, a significant portion of the historical debate on cyber-terrorism originates from those fearing the outbreak of cyber-terrorism rather than discussing terrorist acts enabled by or through cyber means (Goodman, 2008; White, 1998). As noted by Stohl (2007), there appears to be a significant disparity between the perceived threat and actual events.

Reading a 1998 study conducted by White for the U.S. Army War College gives the impression that a cyber-based terrorist attack is imminent. White (1998: 4) notes, "This threat recognises no boundaries, requires minimal resources to mount an attack, and leaves no human footprint at ground zero." A portion of this fear appears to be related to a more significant overall cyber fear that emerged in the late 1990s and manifested itself in the fear that terrorist organisations could use new technological networks to expand and intensify their operations and potentially launch cyberattacks. Yet, as Embar-Seddon (2002: 1034) notes, "The most destructive forces working against an understanding of the threat of cyber-terrorism are a fear of the unknown and a lack of information, or, worse, too much misinformation." Cyber-terrorism combines two significant contemporary fears: the fear of technology and the fear of terrorism. Both technology and terrorism are subject to considerable uncertainty. Considering that terrorism is predominately based on fear and the manipulation of public opinion, one might question if terrorist organisations, without even engaging in cyber-terrorism, raised fears during this time.

However, terrorist networks were bound to adopt new cyber technologies. As previously stated, this would not be unprecedented: terrorists have long attempted to utilise new technologies. Arquilla and Ronfeldt coined the term "Netwar" in their 1993 article "Cyberwar Is Coming" to describe how terrorist networks, among other possible networks of actors, could attempt to utilise then-emerging cyber technologies. In their 1996 "The Advent of Netwar" report for the RAND cooperation, the authors discussed the terminology in greater detail. In both works, the authors demonstrated how terrorist networks could use cyber technologies to enhance their communications and expand their reach beyond traditional communication channels.

The authors' focus was on how cybertechnologies could establish a new model for operations, specifically netwar. However, it was not a literal interpretation of the terms "net" and "war." Indeed, in their 2001 monograph "Networks and Netwars," the authors noted that netwar was a far cry from operations conducted through cyberspace, which they refer to as "computerised aggression" or "cyber-terrorism" (Arquilla & Ronfeldt, 2001). This definition corresponds to the second definition we posed above. In his description of cyber-terrorism, White (1998) appears to corroborate that, for much of cyber-terrorism's history, it has referred to the incorporation of cyber technologies by terrorist networks and their use as communication tools rather than as weapons.

Furthermore, it has remained this way for much of the intervening decades, probably with the exception of an incident in 2001 in which computers linked to the Al-Qaeda network were seized: Models of dams were discovered on the computers, as well as engineering software that simulated dam collapse (Singer, 2012). However, as far as we can tell, it was a simulation rather than an actual attack. The episode perfectly captures the historical dimension of cyber-terrorism: Terrorist actors and networks expressed a desire to employ cyber methods to create destruction in both the digital and physical domains, but this remained primarily theoretical and never even entered the digital sphere. Terrorists, on the other hand, saw the value in exploiting cyberspace and cybertechnologies to improve, increase, and expand their communication, outreach, and new methods of moving and collecting funds (Stohl, 2007).

Terrorists and terror organisations mirrored much of the 1990s thinking. The emergence and spread of the Internet, together with falling prices to access and use cyber technology, altered the way businesses, governments, and individual actors all operated.[2] There was widespread interest, and probably even hype, in figuring out how the Internet, cyberspace, and cybertechnologies were going to impact the world. Terrorists, rather than engaged in revolutionary new ways of thinking and doing, were part of a larger movement. Terrorists did not become competent at exploiting cyber tools as innovative and highly effective communication tools in unique ways until the turn of the century and the emergence of fundamentalist Islamic terrorism, changing the mode of operation of terrorist groups and operations.

TERRORISM-ENABLED-BY-CYBERSPACE: THE BROAD DEFINITION OF CYBER-TERRORISM

The Centre for Strategic and International Studies (CSIS) had completed its full list of cyber incidents dating back to 2003 and ending with a December 2021 incident involving government-linked hackers from China, Iran, and North Korea, all of whom attempted to access computer networks via the Log4j vulnerability. "China" is named 76 times in its 65-page list of key incidents, "Iran" 122 times, "North Korea" 73 times, and "Russia" 182 times. In practically every case, these countries were mentioned in the context of cyber offensive operations in some way. The explosion of literature in recent years has tended to focus on these countries and groups that may or may not have relations with them.

Framing these states and non-state actors (NSAs) involved in cyber offensive operations, whether state-backed or acting alone, has almost certainly empowered governments and organisations performing tasks in a variety of fields to recognise and internalise these states' identity as cyber-terror states. However, this just defined events in which they may have been involved, sponsored, or have linkages, highlighting governments' proclivity to identify and classify dangers through their (possible and would-be) acts rather than through critical engagement with the notion itself. Indeed, this is not dissimilar to both efforts, or lack thereof, to comprehend conventional terrorist threats, as well as how states become involved with the term terrorism before naming and denouncing them as savage individuals endangering humanity's core values.

In our concise exploration of the definitional gap surrounding cyber-terrorism, we have deliberately refrained from incorporating state-centric assessments and constructions pertaining to the notion, as we strive to adopt a more comprehensive approach. Initially, we present a transient explanation, despite the contradiction with our previously stated objective, as a theoretical starting point.

Cyber-terrorism can be identified as an intentional and politically driven aggressive action or assault directed towards information systems, encompassing the software they employ and the information they contain. As per the definition provided by the Federal Bureau of Investigation (FBI), an attack is considered a terrorist act if it involves the use of violence against noncombatant targets by subnational groups or clandestine agents. According to CSIS, cyber-terrorism refers to the utilisation of computer network tools with the intention of disrupting critical national infrastructures such as energy, transportation, and government operations, or to exert pressure or instill fear in a government or civilian population.

TERRORISM-CONDUCTED-IN-CYBERSPACE: THE NARROW DEFINITION OF CYBER-TERRORISM

Since the discovery of the Al-Qaeda computers with the dam simulation in 2001, the debate over whether cyber-terrorism in its narrow meaning had occurred has continued. Nonetheless, as Brunst (2008: 35–36) points out, the nature of cyberspace and cyberattacks makes it impossible to determine whether cyberattacks occurred and who was responsible. In the logic of cyber security, it may be essential to intrude into a system at times, although it is unclear whether such an attempt was reconnaissance, an attempt to launch an attack, or a genuine attack. As a result, determining whether a terrorist cyberattack occurred has been difficult. Furthermore, even if the attack occurred, as Mayer Lux (2018) points out, it is difficult to determine if it was a cybercrime or an act of cyber-terrorism. In addition, identity in cyberspace is a difficulty. It is difficult to determine who was the initial perpetrator of an attack. There have been a few instances where terrorist actors attempted to take credit for digital strikes while it was unclear at best if they were truly involved. One of the difficulties in recognising cyber-terrorism crimes is that terrorist organisations want to claim responsibility for actions or attacks that were not their own.

Finding an acceptable definition of the act itself in the limited sense should come first, given the myriad of problems that make it difficult to define what exactly qualifies as cyber-terrorism. In this definition, we aim to expand on Dorothy Denning's (2000: n.p.) claims, who made the following assertions:

> Cyber terrorism is the convergence of terrorism and cyberspace. It is generally understood to mean unlawful attacks and threats of attack against computers, networks, and the information stored therein when done to intimidate or coerce a government or its people in furtherance of political or social objectives. Further, to qualify as cyber terrorism, an attack should result in violence against persons or property, or at least cause enough harm to generate fear. Attacks that lead to death or bodily injury, explosions, plane crashes, water contamination, or severe economic loss would be examples. Serious attacks against critical infrastructures could be acts of cyber terrorism, depending on their impact. Attacks that disrupt nonessential services or that are foremost a costly nuisance would not.

Notably, this definition does not include digital terrorist acts such as barring or defacing websites by terrorist organisations as part of the cyber-terrorist arsenal. We believe that this distinction is rational. To comprehend the effect of terrorist acts, one must examine their effect. Graffiti proclaiming the triumph of a terrorist organisation is, if it has any effect at all, primarily an annoyance. Rather, bombings and other physical events that cause damage to people or property are generally considered terrorist acts. Therefore, the online variant of offline graffiti – defacing websites – should not be included in the restricted definition of cyber-terrorism.

Given the current definition of cyber-terrorism, it is possible to assert that instances of cyber-terrorism have not occurred. To date, there is no evidence of any cyberattacks carried out by terrorists that have resulted in tangible harm to individuals or physical assets. To date, there is no evidence to suggest that any terrorist organisation has successfully executed a cyberattack to cause a plane crash or a power plant explosion. The absence of cyber-terrorism incidents can be attributed to their infrequent prevalence and inherent characteristics. In recent times, there has been a notable increase in the occurrence of cyber-attacks that result in harm, whether through disruption or destruction. This phenomenon has gained significant attention in academic circles. Stuxnet, the 2015 Ukrainian power grid incident, and the cyber-attack on a Saudi Arabian petrochemical plant by a Saudi Arabian oil company are all notable examples of cyber-attacks (Kushner, 2013; Perlroth & Krauss, 2018).

However, a common thread among all of these incidents is that they were the outcome of state-sponsored attacks. The aforementioned attacks serve as a manifestation of a phenomenon that appears to contradict the prevailing notion of cyberattacks. Specifically, the implementation of such attacks demands substantial resources. Moreover, a comprehensive comprehension of the functioning of cyber systems, identification of their vulnerabilities, and recognition of potential entry points, among other factors, is imperative. Terrorist groups would require significant personal resources, technical expertise, and a secure location to initiate the planning and execution of such attacks. According to Singer (2012), the majority, if not all, of contemporary terrorist organisations lack the resources to handle such a scenario.

Furthermore, in the event of a change in this equivalence, it remains uncertain whether terrorist organisations' investment in and acquisition of human and technical resources would result in their desired outcome. Brunst (2008) provides an illustration of how investing in said attacks may not yield the intended outcomes. This is supported by evidence presented on pages 43 and 44. Brunst (2008) provides an example of the impact of the W.32 Lovsan worm, which resulted in the temporary disabling of 21 power plants, critical military infrastructure, including Edwards Air Force Base, and power outages affecting 60 million individuals residing in the American and Canadian East Coasts. However, a state of widespread panic, mass casualties, and all-encompassing fear did not ensue within society.

One could posit that terrorists exhibit rational behaviour, particularly in the economic realm, given their limited resources. Therefore, pursuing cyber-terrorism solely for the purpose of causing destruction may not be a cost-effective strategy. The investments required for engaging in cyber-terrorism are substantial, and there are numerous potential risks associated with such activities. For instance, the attack may be detected, and the impact of the attack may be difficult to predict. Therefore, engaging in cyber-terrorism would be illogical. Therefore, the combination of these three factors has resulted in the absence of cyber-terrorism.

Various definitions put forth by governmental bodies, academic institutions, and experts emphasise several crucial aspects, positing primarily a degree of complexity on the part of the cyber-terrorist, as if they were proficient "informational warriors." The attribution of definitions and the subsequent responses by state actors to the threat of cyber-terrorism have contributed to the heightened perception of cyber-terrorists. However, it is worth noting that such individuals are not necessarily the omnipotent digital warriors that they are frequently portrayed as. Moreover, it connotes proficiency in technology, akin to other instruments employed by terrorists. In contrast to the prevailing viewpoint, it is observed that terrorists and terrorist organisations utilise technology as tools, not due to their technical expertise or proficiency in handling such technologies or devices, but rather because the technology serves as a means to an end that ultimately advances their intended objectives, as desired by the terrorists.

Cyber-terrorism is predominantly a virtual phenomenon that exhibits fewer connections to the physical realm than what conventional definitions endeavour to portray. In the fourth instance, criminal activities carried out in the realm of information and as a continuation of information warfare are essentially limited to offences that involve systems that may not necessarily have any connection to the Internet. The concept of cyber-terrorism has undergone a significant expansion, resulting in a parallel issue to that of the overgrowth of the term "terrorism." This phenomenon involves the scrutiny of any act of violence, ranging from assassinations to armed attacks against groups of travellers, as potential instances of terrorism.

CONCLUSION: THE FUTURE OF CYBER-TERRORISM

The potential costs and benefits of cyber-terrorism for terrorists and terrorist groups have led to a significant level of concern among governments, security communities, and citizens, as even the mere possibility of an attack is deemed to be a credible threat. Cyber-terrorism, akin to traditional forms of terrorist threats or other perceived threats, has been depicted as a peril to nation-states and their intricate yet susceptible communication networks and digital framework. In light of the pervasive digitisation of contemporary society, the technologically sophisticated environment in which individuals construct their livelihoods renders them vulnerable to malicious interference by malevolent agents. The conventional forecasting of cyber-terrorist events may have been distorted due to the combination of fear and misunderstandings. To date, there has been no documented occurrence of cyber-terrorism. However, there exists a proliferation of divergent interpretations regarding the potential characteristics of a cyber-terrorism incident. Hence, the probability of cyber-terrorism manifesting as catastrophic events akin to the "9/11" or "Pearl Harbor" incidents is low.

The future of cyber-terrorism will be based on psychological fear as well as the physical impact on critical infrastructure and services. One area of particular concern and a rising threat to development work is terrorists' focused attacks on public health and safety, including healthcare workers in the field (Besenyő et al., 2024), but the challenges to mitigating threats in other areas remain significant. That is, the real impacts on the political, social, and economic aspects of life are powerful interactions that can easily yield intensive psychological fears and impacts capable of delivering circumlocutory effects. Indeed, the term "cyber-terrorism" itself can be cut into its constituent parts, "cyber" and "terrorism," both of which are anxiety-inducing, playing on the natural fears of people when considering unknowns that complement one another. That hype has also been well managed and continuously fed, especially after 9/11. Whereas prior to Al-Qaeda's attacks against the US homeland, less emphasis was placed on cyber-terrorism and the security of the state's cyber dimensions, including its weaknesses and vulnerabilities, the emphasis placed on these issues after 9/11 soared, thus demonstrating the importance of the government and its various security communities in cultivating their own threats.

With that in mind, states, so long as they are increasingly digitising – their citizens and their personal lives included – will always be vulnerable to the nefarious intentions of terrorists who find the cyber element to be attractive as a vulnerability in their enemies or as an instrument with which to facilitate business transactions and other functions on which terrorists and terrorist groups rely. The state is not the only vulnerable entity in this regard; to be sure, every citizen of a given state will present terrorists with their own attractive weak points if they are really interested in exploiting the digital quality of ordinary people and the common household. This reality makes the state's job far more daunting. Knowing that, for example, all approximately 330 million citizens of the US or 447 million citizens of the European Union (EU) – the idea applies to any country and its citizens – are potential cyber-terrorism targets, the state has few immediate options available to prevent terrorists or terrorist groups from inflicting massive damage, be it in a single attack or if we consider the sum of hundreds, if not thousands, of smaller cyberattacks over time.

Although cyberattacks are a frequent occurrence, the notion of a cyber "Pearl Harbour" has been amplified as a significant anxiety in relation to a nation's sensitive military resources, including nuclear weapons, and the crucial infrastructure sectors as identified by CISA. As previously posited, terrorist organisations currently lack the requisite technological resources and expertise to execute cyber attacks on said systems. Given the circumstances, it appears that at present, historical cases of cyberattacks serve as the most reliable point of reference for predicting the nature of cyber-terrorism activities.

Notes

1 The latter term, "cyber warfare," is widely used, albeit disputed, as a definition. In his book *Cyberwar Will Not Take Place*, Thomas Rid makes the case that to be an act of war, an attack needs to be a) political, b) physical, or c) cause physical injury or damage. Yet to date, c) has not taken place. To date, no person has died directly as a result of a cyberattack. As such, in the narrow sense, cyberwar has indeed not taken place. In this chapter, the authors follow Rid's argument. Therefore, we will use the terminology of cyber conflict rather than cyber war. For further information and reference, please refer to Rid.

2 During the mid-1990s, cyber technologies saw a drastic expansion with the advent of browser technology and the proliferation of the World Wide Web (WWW). For a further introduction into the history of the Internet, cyberspace, and its commercialisation, see Leiner et al., 1997, Brief History of the Internet, available at https://www.internetsociety.org/internet/history-internet/brief-history-internet/.

References

Besenyő, J., Márton, K., & Shaffer, R. (2024). Hospital attacks since 9/11: An analysis of terrorism targeting healthcare facilities and workers. *Studies in Conflict & Terrorism, 47*(1), 1–24. 10.1080/1057610X.2021.1937821

Brunst, P. (2008). Use of the internet by terrorists – A threat analysis. In Centre of Excellence – Defence Against Terrorism (Ed.), *Responses to cyber terrorism* (pp. 34–60) NATO Science for Peace and Security Series. Amsterdam: IOS Press.

Conway, M. (2002). What is cyberterrorism? *Current History, 101*(659), 436–442.

Denning, D.E. (2000). Statement of Dorothy E. Denning. https://irp.fas.org/congress/2000_hr/00-05-23denning.htm

Embar-Seddon, A. (2002). Cyberterrorism. *American Behavioral Scientist, 45*(6), 1033–1043. doi:10.1177/0002764202045006007

Goodman, S.E. (2008). Critical information infrastructure protection. In Centre of Excellence – Defence Against Terrorism (Ed.), *Responses to cyber terrorism* (pp. 24–33) NATO Science for Peace and Security Series. Amsterdam: IOS Press.

Kushner, D. (2013, February 23). The real story of stuxnet. Retrieved March 23, 2021, from https://spectrum.ieee.org/telecom/security/the-real-story-of-stuxnet

Mayer Lux, L. (2018). *Revista Chilena De Derecho Y Tecnología, 7*(2), 5. doi:10.5354/0719-2584.2018.51028

Perlroth, N., & Krauss, C. (2018, March 15). A cyberattack in Saudi Arabia had a Deadly Goal. experts fear another try. Retrieved March 23, 2021, from https://www.nytimes.com/2018/03/15/technology/saudi-arabia-hacks-cyberattacks.html

Arquilla, J., & Ronfeldt, D.F. (2001). *Networks and netwars: The future of terror, crime, and militancy*. Santa Monica, CA: Rand Corporation.

Singer, P. (2012, November 1). The cyber terror bogeyman. Retrieved March 23, 2021, from https://www.brookings.edu/articles/the-cyber-terror-bogeyman/

Stohl, M. (2007). Cyber terrorism: A clear and present danger, the sum of all fears, breaking point or patriot games? *Crime, Law and Social Change, 46*(4-5), 223–238. doi:10.1007/s10611-007-9061-9

Torres Soriano, M.R. (2008). Terrorism and the mass media after Al Qaeda: A change of course? *Athena Intelligence Journal*, *3*(1), 1–20.

Weimann, G. (2005). Cyberterrorism: The sum of all fears? *Studies in Conflict & Terrorism*, *28*(2), 129–149. doi:10.1080/10576100590905110

White, K.C. (1998). Cyber-terrorism: Modem mayhem. Carlisle Barracks, Pennsylvania: U.S. Army War College. doi:http://stinet.dtic.mil/cticrev/a345705.pdf

Zetter, K. (2015). *Countdown to zero day: Stuxnet and the launch of the World's First Digital Weapon*. New York: Crown.

26

TURNING TO TERROR ONLINE

Social Media, Recruitment, and Radicalization

Wendell C. Wallace and Scott N. Romaniuk

INTRODUCTION

Due to exponential advances in technology, the reach of terrorists' influence now transcends geographic boundaries and is extremely widespread. Steinbach (2016), in his Statement before the Senate Committee on Homeland Security and Governmental Affairs, Permanent Subcommittee on Investigations, points out that 'as technology advances, so, too, does terrorists' use of technology to communicate – both to inspire and recruit'. In fact, it is no secret that terrorist groups are continuously using the internet to inspire and enlist new members in order to grow their network of terror. This growth of terrorist groups is not limited to those individuals who are recruited and leave their homelands to travel to terrorist hotspots for jihadi purposes (foreign fighters), but also includes residents who are radicalized in their home countries and who remain there to propagate attacks on their home countries (homegrown terrorists).

Therefore, the threat of terrorist attacks can be viewed from a duality of perspectives, namely from: (1) foreign fighters recruited globally to join the Islamic State of Iraq and the Levant (ISIL) and other terror groups, and (2) homegrown violent extremists. However, in spite of their modus operandi (foreign fighters or homegrown terrorists), a common denominator is that many of the newly enlisted individuals were recruited and radicalized by way of social media platforms. What this means is that terrorist recruiters now have direct access to foreign countries like never before, thanks largely to social media. No longer does the recruiter of overseas jihadists need to leave his or her country to establish a physical presence in another country, as social media facilitates a virtual presence that is difficult to detect and counter. According to Weimann (2015), this move from the physical to the online presence represents a shift in the 'oxygen of terrorism' towards the online facilitation of terrorists, terrorist activities, and terrorism.

Contemporary life is facilitated by the increasing use of technology in all facets of our lives and in all facets of society. In fact, just as private citizens and private industries have adapted to modern forms of communication, so too have terrorists and their groups. Undoubtedly, social media is a communication tool that is used by millions of users on a daily basis. Social media is also an important tool for terror groups, as social media can be used to identify potential members of all ages, genders, nationalities, and ethnicities, assess them, and then recruit and radicalize them (Steinbach, 2016). This strategy is all too familiar.

Similar to contemporary business entities, terrorist groups such as Al-Shabaab, al-Qaeda, Boko Haram, ISIS, Moro Islamic Liberation Front, Abu Sayyaf, and Jabhat al-Nusra must recruit new members for growth, expansion, development, and succession planning, as well as to sustain their membership (Besenyő & Sinkó, 2021). However, while contemporary business entities may use legal, open, and unrestricted online platforms to advertise their vacancies, invite applicants and applications, and then conduct interviews in a transparent manner at a fixed location, terrorist groups generally do not have all of those luxuries as their business, that of violence, extremism, and jihad, is illegal (at least to most of us). Therefore, in order to grow their organizations, these terrorist groups use a variety of methods to recruit and radicalize individuals that bear an uncanny resemblance to recruitment by contemporary business organizations; however, there are also distinct differences.

Early recruitment and radicalization efforts by terrorist organizations focused heavily on spreading their doctrine through covert means. For example, radical individuals within the organization would either create sleeper cells in an overseas jurisdiction by funding the travel of local residents to covert training camps in overseas jurisdictions under the guise of vacation and religious training, or the radical individual would covertly travel to various jurisdictions under the guise of vacation or religion to spread their ideology and seek to indoctrinate new members via secret meetings and covert training of likeminded individuals.

DOI: 10.4324/9780429426063-29

However, possibly starting in the late 1980s and early 1990s, but more so in the aftermath of September 11, 2001, terrorist attacks in the USA, recruitment and radicalization efforts by terrorist groups were forced to change and indeed began an evolutionary process as many nation states began increasingly monitoring the activities and movements of the leading functionaries of global terrorist groups, their supporters, financiers, and sympathizers.

Instructively, as the Open Web is increasingly monitored, terrorist groups are again evolving their usage of the Internet and social media for assessment of vulnerable individuals as well as for enlistment, radicalization, and the growth of their terror networks. As laws are developed to control lawful communication on the Internet, other forms of Internet and social media communication have developed and are quickly outpacing these laws. In the face of increasing legislation as well as monitoring aimed at stymying the previous methods of recruitment and radicalization of newer members, terrorist groups were faced with the dilemma of seeking to recruit and indoctrinate susceptible individuals into their fold and responded by partially migrating to the "Deep Web" and the "Dark Web" (Weimann, 2015, 2016) as a means of propaganda, networking, and recruitment with impunity. In fact, it is argued that terrorist groups have migrated away from the open web to the deep and/or dark web (Weimann, 2016), or websites that are not available through regular search engines and have less control and are easier to use for nefarious activities. By using the dark web, terrorist groups now utilize highly paid, highly skilled, and specially trained individuals in ICT to reach out to unsuspecting, disgruntled, and susceptible individuals in order to enlist their services for jihadi purposes. The influx of overseas jihadists may soon be a notion of the past as terrorist groups are using social media to enlist and convert Muslims and non-Muslims into jihadists.

Importantly, social media usage by these terrorist groups means that new members do not have to leave their country of origin for religious indoctrination and training but can remain in their homeland as home-grown terrorists due to social media usage by terrorist groups. In sum, in the contemporary era, terrorist groups are increasingly using the internet to reach across borders into previously unreachable areas and gain access to previously unreachable targets due to the globalization of cyberspace. This effort is aimed at spreading their ideology of violence against non-believers as well as the indoctrination, recruitment, growth, and continuity of their illicit organizations.

DEFINITIONAL CONSIDERATIONS

Before delving into the crux of the chapter, it is important to conceptualize two important and contentious terms, social media and radicalization, so that they are neither esoteric nor mysterious to the readership. Social media is an ever-increasing phenomenon with varied definitions (Davis III et al., 2012). For example, Junco et al. (2011) point out that social media are a collection of Internet websites, services, and practises that support collaboration, community building, participation, and sharing, while for Bryer and Zavattaro (2011, p. 327), "Social media are technologies that facilitate social interaction, make possible collaboration, and enable deliberation across stakeholders." Berthon et al. (2012) also recognize that social media are a series of technological innovations in terms of both hardware and software that facilitate inexpensive content creation, interaction, and interoperability by online users.

Social media is therefore a Web 2.0 development, which is to say that it is founded on the concept of a user-driven, interactive web. In sum, social media generally refers to media technology that is used to enable social interaction and includes blogs, wikis, media (audio, photo, video, and text) sharing tools, networking platforms (including Facebook), and virtual worlds (Bryer & Zavattaro, 2011). The use of social media interfaces through computers and mobile devices has become quite widespread and includes social media interfaces such as Digg, Facebook, MySpace, Friendster, LinkedIn, YouTube, Twitter, and other similar applications (Besenyő & Sinkó, 2021). Though these interfaces serve to enhance our daily lives, they can and are also being used for illicit purposes by terror groups. We employ the term social media to refer to available technologies for social communication, discussion, and interaction among its participants. This interaction can take many forms, but some common types include sharing photos, videos, and posts; commenting on the photos, posts, updates, videos, and links shared by others; and adding public updates to a profile, including information on current activities and even location data.

Despite over a decade of research, there is no generally agreed-upon definition of "radicalization" (Schmid, 2016, p. 7), and like social media, definitions of radicalization vary greatly. For instance, Schmid (2016) points out that radicalization can be viewed: (1) as a process of political socialization towards extremism, (2) as a process of conflict escalation in terms of increased use of illegal methods of political action when confronting an opponent, (3) as a mobilization and recruitment process, masterminded by manipulative political or religious entrepreneurs, and (4) as a conversion process, a life-changing transformation from a more individual-centred personal identity to a new, collective-centred identity which makes the vulnerable individual subservient to the demands of an extremist religious cult while making him or her think of belonging to a superior group of true believers. On the other hand, the Council of the European Union (2002) posits the following: "Radicalisation: Individuals or groups becoming intolerant with regard to basic democratic values like equality and diversity, as well as a rising propensity towards using means of force to reach political goals that negate and/or undermine democracy."

Believing that the multiplicity of definitions of radicalization are either too brief or incomplete, Schmid (2016) proffers a much broader definition of radicalization in the following manner: "an individual or collective (group) process whereby, usually in a situation of political polarization, normal practises of dialogue, compromise, and tolerance between political actors and groups with diverging interests are abandoned by one or both sides in a conflict dyad in favour of a growing commitment to engage in confrontational tactics of conflict-waging. These can include either (a) the use of non-violent pressure and coercion, (b) various forms of political violence other than terrorism, or (c) acts of violent extremism in the form of terrorism and war crimes.

The process is, on the side of rebel factions, generally accompanied by an ideological socialization away from mainstream- or status quo-oriented positions towards more radical or extremist positions involving a dichotomous world view and the acceptance of an alternative focal point of political mobilization outside the dominant political order as the existing system is no longer recognised as appropriate or legitimate" (p. 27). We employ the term radicalization as a process by which an individual or group of individuals increasingly accepts and comes to support the use of undemocratic or violent means, including terrorism and extremist ideologies associated with terrorist groups, in an attempt to reach a specific political and/or ideological objective.

AIMS OF THE STUDY

This chapter explains how terrorist groups and jihadist networks utilize social media for recruitment, radicalization, and growth for the purpose of continuing their terrorist activities. Since 9/11, security officials in almost every nation-state have expressed serious concerns over recruitment, radicalization, the foreign fighter syndrome, and jihadi threats that terrorist groups, now increasingly globalized, are posing to world tranquility. These concerns are real as terrorist groups, particularly ISIS, have intensified their efforts to set up terrorist cells in the global north and south to conduct terrorist attacks in order to demonstrate their continued relevancy. This relevance is premised on a continuous recruitment drive that has as its genesis the contemporaneity of conscription and the indoctrination of susceptible individuals by means that are constantly moving away from physical presence to virtual presence. This chapter presents an overview of the methodologies used by modern terrorist groups to recruit, radicalize, and grow their membership and how their usage of social media serves to facilitate this.

This chapter presents a framework that maps the radicalization and mobilization pathways of susceptible individuals into violent extremism and recognizes that the use of social media by terrorist groups facilitates not only enlistment and indoctrination but also the growth and survival of these groups. This study aims to serve as a foundation for future research and analysis into the enlistment, indoctrination, and growth of terrorist groups and their networks, as well as shed light on possible counter-recruitment and counter-radicalization strategies that may be employed as restraints against terrorist groups usage of social media to recruit and radicalize people into jihadist networks of extremism and violence. Importantly, two primary questions emanate from this research. First, we ask who the terrorists on social media sites are. Second, we ask how terrorists use social media sites.

THEORETICAL FRAMEWORK

Okazaki and Taylor (2013) offer the most comprehensive theoretical foundation that can be used in research on social media. While their framework examined social media usage in the context of international advertising research, it also offered the best rationalization for terrorists' use of social media for their nefarious activities. These three theoretical perspectives (networking capability, image transferability, and personal extensibility) provide strong potential for a better understanding of social media use by terrorists, their supporters, sympathizers, and supporters. This framework is highlighted in Figure 26.1.

Terrorist usage of social media can be understood from the perspective of three principal theoretical foundations, namely: (1) networking capability, (2) image transferability, and (3) personal extensibility. These factors represent the rationale behind social media as well as the benefits that accrue from its usage by terrorist networks. Okazaki and Taylor (2013, p. 59) point out that "the geographical and psychological context refers to an international marketplace consisting of diverse, geographically and emotionally distant locations" that were previously difficult to physically reach; however, these social milieus are now within easy reach due to the advent and exponential advances in the Internet as well as social media.

Networking capability is a relevant theoretical foundation for understanding terrorists' usage of social media for recruitment, radicalization, and growth purposes based on the benefits of Web 2.0 (the second generation of internet-based applications), and this has a lot to do with its

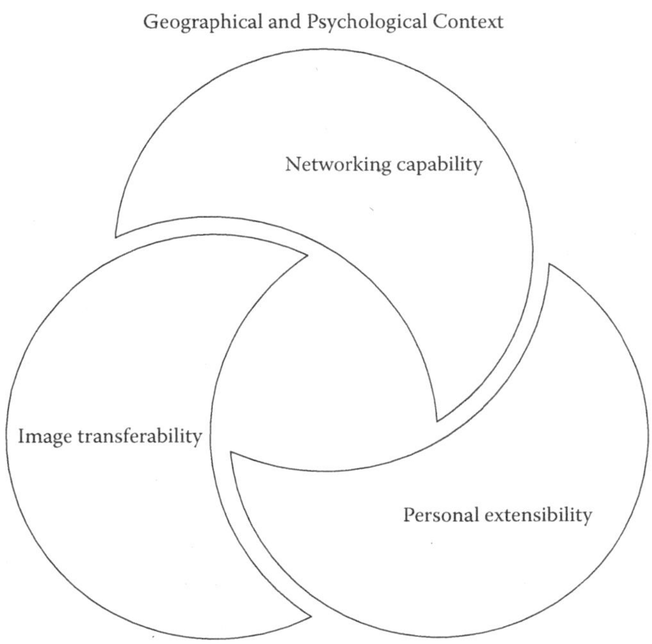

Figure 26.1 Primary Dimensions of Social Media Usage in an International Context.

Source: Okazaki and Taylor (2013). *Authors' re-rendering of Okazaki and Taylor's original illustration.

functionality. For instance, Bell and Loane (2010) point out that potential consumers and real consumers are in control of how information is generated, created, organized, and shared, and social media is therefore high in functionality. For terrorist groups, it is this functionality of social media that affords them networking capability, as "social media cuts across cultures and geographic boundaries and allows groups of individuals who may have never otherwise been able to interact to have communication" (Okazaki & Taylor, 2013, pp. 59–60). Image transferability is the second theoretical perspective that can be utilized to understand terrorists' usage of social media for the enlistment, indoctrination, and growth of their illicit organizations. For terrorist organizations to proffer a brand that is distinctly different from a Western lifestyle as well as unique to the particular organization (different from other terrorist groups), similar to conglomerates, they must construct and brand their own unique image.

In this regard, social media offered an opportunity for terrorist groups to create and market their unique brand of extremist violence, lifestyle, and career, and a plethora of terror-based organizations fully utilized the opportunity, hence their representation on social media. As it relates to personal extensibility, the final theoretical foundation used to explain terrorists' usage of social media for recruitment, radicalization, and growth purposes, personal extensibility (chosen from the perspective of the human mobility theory; Okazaki and Taylor, 2013) is a valid explanation. The focal point of the human mobility theory is that there is an expansion of opportunities for human interaction, rather than improved abilities for movement over greater distances. With this in mind, Parameswaran and Whinston (2007) submit that, due to the design and capacity of Web 2.0, social media differs from traditional media because of its high mobility and capacity for personal extensibility. According to Janelle (1973, p. 11), personal extensibility is "conceptually the reciprocal of time-space convergence."

Janelle (1973), in her seminal work, argues that the rapid advances in communication imply a "shrinking world", with expanding opportunities for personal extensibility. In this light, personal extensibility is a useful explanation for terrorists' usage of social media for their illicit activities. Personal extensibility acknowledges the ability of an individual or individuals to overcome geographical distance and international borders through communication. Therefore, social media offers terror groups the personal extensibility of reaching beyond what would otherwise be considered confined geographical areas in order to radicalize, recruit, and grow their organizations.

SOCIAL MEDIA AS A FACILITATOR OF TERRORISM

Social media usage is a form of "social networking." However, in the modern era, whenever the term "social networking" is utilized, it tends to conjure up thoughts of Facebook and Twitter (Kohlmann, 2011; Besenyő & Sinkó, 2021) and their global usage by technologically savvy people, including terrorists. Instructively, in the era before the existence of the Internet, social networking was conducted via conventional human interaction that took place at schools, marketplaces, religious centres, hotels, motels, sports events, and numerous other nondescript locations.

Without a doubt, the Internet as well as social media are increasingly becoming key components of the daily regimen of many people in the current globalized world. Due to the importance that is placed on social networking and as the traditional press uses photos, videos, and statements from the websites of terrorist groups to sensitize as well as counter-terrorist discourse, the Internet and social media are fast becoming avenues to spread terrorist messages as their images, videos, and posts now find their way into the traditional mass media as well. According to Weimann (2006), what this facilitates is a cheaper alternative to mass printing of newsletters or operating their own radio stations. Therefore, the Internet and the unregulated social media world provide terrorist groups with greater interactivity than traditional media (radio, television, and print) and allow two-way communications – increasing the ability to solicit support, allowing terrorist organizations to deliver direct messages to the specific target audience they are trying to reach, as well as allowing terrorist groups to communicate their message to a global audience instantaneously, anonymously, and without the risks of their censorship (see Weimann, 2006 for support).

Social media usage by ISIS (and other terrorist groups) does not exist in a vacuum, nor was it created in a vacuum; it was a conscious decision made by ISIS forerunner and Jordanian jihadist Abu Musab al-Zarqawi. It was al-Zarqawi who discovered the utility, efficacy, and power of the Internet by uploading videos of his atrocities committed in the name of jihad to the Internet. However, as ISIS grew in strength and numbers (to the chagrin of its rivals, al Qaeda), it attempted to increase its reach and, in so doing, began exploring and exploiting a host of internet platforms. Therefore, social media networks such as Twitter and Facebook, peer-to-peer messaging apps like Telegram and Surespot, and content-sharing systems like JustPaste It saw an increase in usage by ISIS and its supporters and sympathizers (Besenyő & Sinkó, 2021).

To date, ISIS appears to have surpassed all other terrorist groups in terms of social media usage and has broadened its appeal, scope, and reach through its decentralized media operations, which constantly disseminate information aimed at growing its membership through globalized radicalization and enlistment using social media marketing strategies that are often associated with multinational corporations and large conglomerates. Social media marketing (SMM) is a targeted and specialized form of advertising that is effective in creating brand awareness. For terrorist groups, but mostly ISIS, using the SMM approach means utilizing techniques that target social networks and applications to spread their ISIS brand and/or promote their product: extremist violence. In a similar vein to SMM, terrorist organizations utilize social media marketing campaigns that are focused on establishing a social media presence on major platforms and social networking sites (Facebook, Twitter, YouTube, MySpace, LinkedIn), creating shareable content, using catchy advertisements, cultivating dialogue, and offering utopia to those who buy into their product.

SOCIAL MEDIA USAGE BY TERRORIST AND TERRORIST GROUPS

Although most terrorist organizations, their members, and sympathizers make use of social media, the nature and extent of usage vary from organization to organization. While some terrorist groups and their members are heavily represented on the open web and on traditional social media platforms, for example, ISIS and Al-Qaida, other terrorist groups have a distinct preference for the dark web. For instance, contemporary terrorist groups use social media networking sites such as YouTube and Facebook to post their rhetoric, search for new members, upload videos, seek and share advice, raise funds, propagandize, share professional information, send friend requests, upload video clips, portray terrorist territory in a positive light, engage in dialogue with members and critics, plan and launch attacks, publicize the results of attacks, recruit, initiate, share information via electronic bulletin boards, train, and indoctrinate new members (Adkins, 2013; Conway, 2002; Freiburger & Crane, 2008; Kohlmann, 2011; Stern & Berger, 2015; Weimann, 2006). Terrorist groups are also creating websites that are aimed at specific categories of individuals. For example, the website run by Hezbollah features downloadable games for children and two distinct Tamil Tigers (LTTE) websites tailored to a local and international audience (Weimann, 2006) (see Conway, 2002 for support), while Hamas' website presents political cartoons and photomontages depicting the violent deaths of Palestinian children, and the Armed Islamic Group (GIA) has a detailed bomb-making manual on their site (Conway, 2002).

For first-generation terrorist organizations, notably Al-Qaida, social networking was a covert activity that relied on physical presence in far-flung countries, meeting at secretive guesthouses and a few extremist mosques, and fixing training camps at discrete locations (Kohlmann, 2011). However, since 9/11 (the September 11, 2001, terrorist attacks on the United States), terrorist groups have come under intense pressure from global governments, who have successfully conducted air strikes on their 'secret' locations, guesthouses, and physical training camps and who seek to counter their narrative on social media through a variety of mediums. This pressure has caused terrorist groups and their members to seek alternative means of recruitment, radicalization, and training of new inductees and have increasingly turned to social media usage, where they now have an established presence.

According to Kohlmann (2011), as the new generation of Al-Qaida members has come of age in the Internet era, Al-Qaida has spread its online presence and established a tenacious beachhead in cyberspace by organizing a cabal of critical jihadi-oriented online social networking forums. In a similar vein, Al-Qaida members, allies, and supporters heavily populate conventional services like YouTube and Facebook in an effort to remain relevant, spread its insidious message, and recruit, radicalize, and grow their membership. That terrorists conduct recruitment, radicalization, and growth exercises via social media should not be lost on academicians and laypersons, as Chen (2008) submits that the Institute for Security Technology Studies has identified five ways terrorists use the web: propaganda, recruitment and training, fundraising, communication, and targeting. Similarly, Coll and Glasser (2005) and Thomas (2003) submit that terrorist groups are no longer bonded by geographical boundaries; instead, through the Internet, they reach individuals in any location and recruit members from these locations. For terrorist groups on social media, the platforms help to create a new form of public space wherein people can interact without needing to share the same place or have direct physical contact (Ozeren et al., 2018). Further, the terror organization's media messages are used exclusively to shape the perceptions of its target audiences and consolidate their support for their extremist cause (see Ozeren et al., 2018). In other words, terrorist groups are effective agents in cyberspace, and their online rhetoric is a common method that terrorist organizations like ISIS use to both attract and recruit potential members (Ozeren et al., 2018).

Awan (2017) also contributes to the discourse as he points out that ISIS is increasingly present online by way of slick videos, online messages of hate, and even an app that all aim to radicalize and create a new generation of jihadists. Quite notably, in his framework for modelling the radicalization and mobilization pathways into jihadist terrorism, Sinai (2016) points out that terrorist groups frequently employ social media venues, including websites, online magazines, or Twitter and YouTube videos, featuring influential spiritual and jihadist leaders to promote extremist activities on behalf of their cause as well as entice others into becoming fighters on behalf of their co-religionists in a foreign conflict. Indeed, for terror groups, social media has become an important tool in the recruitment of new members and sympathizers (Freiburger & Crane, 2008). The aforementioned position by Freiburger and Crane (2008) is complemented by Alarid (2016), who points out that international terrorist groups use the Internet and social media to radicalise and recruit individuals online and carry out attacks by "people who feel there is "something missing" from their lives [and who] appear to be more susceptible than others" (p. 314). Freiburger and Crane (2008) submit that terrorist organizations can be found on a multiplicity of social media platforms as well as on the Internet. They also offer a typology of efforts by terrorist groups to use the Internet, from the initial recruitment of new converts to final terrorist actions. This is shown in Figure 26.2.

As it relates to the Internet and social media usage, ISIS probably has the most definitive presence of all terror groups. Not only has ISIS cornered the "social media market', they also have autonomous production units that produce glossy photos, in-depth articles, and high-quality videos to disseminate their diatribe. In fact, ISIS has aggressively pursued a technology-based campaign through the Internet and social media that is aimed at radicalization and recruitment and has an extremely wide global reach and appeal. For ISIS, this blend of traditional media platforms and extensive social media campaigns is specifically designed so that the message of radicalization and recruitment is spread quicker than was possible three decades ago and can go viral in a nanosecond (Besenyő & Sinkó, 2021).

It is argued that unlike other terrorist groups, ISIS constructs a broader narrative involving all facets of life, including, but not limited to, a sense of brotherhood, career opportunities, a sense of community, family life, enhanced opportunities, advantageous living conditions, and utopian life in a non-Western manner (Steinbach, 2016). This discourse is created by ISIS for those who openly express symptoms of radicalization; however, it filters down to those who are on the fence as well as those who may not be the least interested, yet it reaches them as they browse the Internet and social media on a daily basis. According to Stern and Berger (2015), 'as part of its quest to terrorize the world, ISIS has mastered an arena no terrorist group had conquered before – the burgeoning world of social media'. In fact, ISIS has been extremely successful at using the internet and social media to recruit disenchanted Muslims, foreign fighters, and non-Muslim Westerners to join their organization. Instructively, Thomas (2003) recognizes that due to a chronic lack of regulation of the Internet as well as social media, terrorist groups present themselves, their organization, and their image in a positive light to potential converts, and that this allows them to convert and radicalize "fence sitters" into jihadists. Further, this process of indoctrination and recruitment facilitates the growth and continuity of these illicit terrorist organizations.

Due to space constraints, this chapter appears to focus on two major terrorist groups (ISIS and al-Qaida) and their

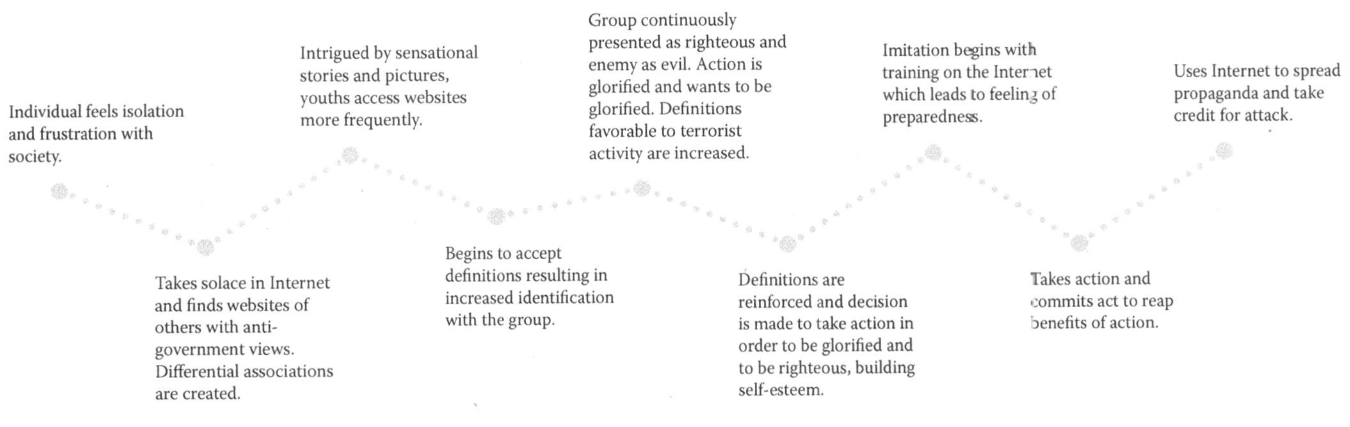

Figure 26.2 Terrorists' Groups Use of the Internet from Initial Recruitment to Final Terrorists' Action

Source: Freiburger and Crane (2008). *Authors' re-rendering of Freiburger and Crane's original illustration.

usage of social media for nefarious activities; however, this should not be construed as implying that these two terror groups are the only ones that make use of social media. In fact, the Armed Islamic Group (GIA), Pakistan Taliban, Hamas, Hezbollah, Mujahedin-e Khalq Organisation, Tamil Tigers, Palestine Islamic Jihad, and a host of other terrorist organizations are prominently featured on social media, and it is no secret that 'there are many websites dedicated to various terrorist groups' (Conway, 2002; Weimann, 2006).

While numerous conspiracy theories abound regarding terrorists' use of social media for nefarious activities, what is certain is that "terrorist organizations and their supporters maintain hundreds of Web sites" (Weimann, 2006). The rationale for this is frighteningly simple: the Internet is largely unregulated by governmental power, anonymous, easily accessible, and lacks geographical limitations (Weimann, 2006). This facilitates social networking and the sending and receiving of a wide array of messages to a variety of borderless audiences. While some of these conversations occur on publicly accessible social networking sites, others take place via private messaging platforms (Steinbach, 2016) that are not easily accessible.

CONCLUSION

This chapter focused on social media usage by terrorist organizations by analysing their forays into cyberspace for recruitment, radicalization, and growth. The analysis shows that a multiplicity of terrorist organizations utilize the Internet and social media for the aforementioned purposes. The analysis also highlighted that for many nation-states in the contemporary era, preventing terrorist attacks is a top priority, as the threat faced by almost every country is persistent and acute. Further, starting in earnest possibly after September 11, 2001, terrorist groups such as the Islamic State (also known as ISIS, ISIL, and Daesh), al-Qaeda, Hamas, Boko Haram, and Hezbollah have established a presence on the Internet and have been making use of social media to recruit, radicalize, and grow their membership. These social media sites include conventional sites such as Facebook, Twitter, LinkedIn, and many others; however, there are also sites such as the far-right social networking site Gab and messaging apps like Kik. The current effort also demonstrates that while terror groups are increasingly making use of social media and the Internet for their illicit activities, the face of contemporary terror groups and their recruitment, indoctrination, and attempts to increase their membership are conducted in a markedly different manner than was done in an earlier era as the available technology affords easier access to a globalized market of vulnerable and/or disenchanted populace while at the same time debunking geographical limitations.

References

Adkins, G. (2013). Utilizing cyber espionage to combat terrorism. Unpublished Master of Science Dissertation. Intelligence and National Security Studies. The University of Texas at El Paso.

Alarid, M. (2016). Recruitment and radicalization: The role of social media and new technology. In M. Hughes & M. Miklaucic (Eds.), *Impunity: Countering illicit power in war and transition* (pp. 313–330). Washington, DC: Peacekeeping and Stability Operations Institute (PKSOI).

Awan, I. (2017). Cyber-extremism: Isis and the power of social media. *Society*, 1–12.

Bell, J., & Loane, S. (2010). New-wave' global firms: Web 2.0 and SME internationalization. *Journal of Marketing Management*, *26*(3/4), 213–229.

Berthon, P.R., Pitt, L.F., Plangger, K., & Shapiro, D. (2012). Marketing meets Web 2.0, Social media, and creative consumers: Implications for international marketing strategy. *Business Horizons*, *55*(3), 261–271.

Besenyő, J., & Sinkó, G. (2021). The social media use of African terrorist organizations: A comparative study of Al-Qaeda in the Islamic Maghreb, Al-Shabaab and Boko Haram. *Insights Into Regional Development*, *3*(3), 66–78. https://jssidoi.org/ird/article/76

Bryer, T., & Zavattaro, S. (2011). Social media and public administration: Theoretical dimensions and introduction to symposium. *Administrative Theory & Praxis*, *33*(3), 325–340.

Chen, H. (2008). Uncovering the dark web: A case study of jihad on the web. *Journal of the American Society for Information Science and Technology*, *59*(8), 1347–1359.

Coll, S., & Glasser, S.G. (2005). Terrorist turn in the Web as base of operations. Washington Post. http://msl1.mit.edu/furdlog/docs/washpost/2005-08-07_washpost_www_weapon_01.pdf

Conway, M. (2002). Reality bytes: Cyberterrorism and terrorist 'use' of the Internet. *First Monday*, *7*(11), 1–17.

Davis III, C.H.F., Deil-Amen, R., Rios-Aguilar, C., & González Canché, M.S. (2012). *Social media and higher education: A literature review and research directions*. Arizona: The University of Arizona and Claremont Graduate University.

Freiburger, T., & Crane, J.S. (2008). A systematic examination of terrorist use of the internet. *International Journal of Cyber Criminology*, *2*(1), 309–319.

Janelle, D.G. (1973). Measuring human extensibility in a shrinking world. *Journal of Geography*, *72*(5), 5–10.

Junco, R., Heiberger, G., & Loken, E. (2011). The effect of Twitter on college student engagement and grades. *Journal of Computer Assisted Learning*, *27*(2), 119–132.

Kohlmann, E.F. (2011). Testimony before the house committee on homeland security. Jihadist use of social media – How to prevent terrorism and preserve innovation. The antisocial network: Countering the use of online social networking technologies by foreign terrorist organizations, December 6, 2011. Cannon House Office Building. Washington, D.C.

Okazaki, S., & Taylor, C.R. (2013). Social media and international advertising: Theoretical challenges and future directions. *International Marketing Review*, *30*(1), 56–71.

Ozeren, S., Hekim, H., Elmas, M.S., & Canbegi, H.I. (2018). An analysis of ISIS propaganda and recruitment activities targeting the Turkish-speaking population. *International Annals of Criminology, 56*, 105–121.

Parameswaran, M., & Whinston, A.B. (2007). Research issues in social computing. *Journal of the Association for Information Systems, 8*(6), 336–350.

Schmid, A.P. (2016). Research on radicalisation topics and themes. *Perspectives on Terrorism, 10*(3), 26–32.

Sinai, J. (2016). Framework for assessing the mobilization of westerners by jihadists in Syria and intervention points for counter-measures. *Perspectives on Terrorism, 10*(3), 45–52.

Steinbach, M. (2016, July 6). ISIL online: Countering terrorist radicalization and recruitment on the internet and social media. Statement before the senate committee on homeland security and governmental affairs, permanent subcommittee on investigations, Washington, DC. https://www.fbi.gov/news/testimony/isil-online-countering-terrorist-radicalization-and-recruitment-on-the-internet-and-social-media-

Stern, J., & Berger, J.M. (2015). *ISIS: The state of terror*. New York, NY: HarperCollins Publishers.

The Council of European Union. (2002). *Council Framework Decision of 13 June 2002 on combating terrorism*. Council Framework Decision 2002/475/JHA.

Thomas, T.L. (2003). Al Qaeda and the internet: The danger of "cyberplanning". *Parameters, 23*(1), 112–123.

Weimann, G. (2006). *Terror on the internet: The new arena, the new challenges*. Washington, DC: US Institute of Peace Press.

Weimann, G. (2015). Terrorist migration to social media. *Georgetown Journal of International Affairs, 16*(1), 180–187.

Weimann, G. (2016). Terrorist migration to the dark web. *Perspectives on Terrorism, 10*(3), 40–44.

27

CYBER COUNTER-TERRORISM

States, Security Services, and Investigations in the Digital Age

Richard McNeil-Willson and Scott N. Romaniuk

INTRODUCTION

The Internet and online spaces have come to play a significant role in discussions over both terrorism and methods to counter it. Recent events have highlighted the role that such online spaces and networks can play in irregular violence. The growth of the Islamic State in Iraq and Syria came with a canon of slick social media videos and online propaganda, aimed at encouraging individuals from throughout the world to pledge support to Da'esh, participate in the state-building process in as-Sham, or to "stay in place" and commit attacks in their home countries.

The role of social media and online spheres has been further underscored by the growth of far-right groups and the way in which platforms have been used to spread information encouraging or enabling violence. The massacre, for instance, of those worshipping at two mosques in Christchurch, New Zealand, in 2019 was live-streamed over social media, with vividly brutal images and the attacker's manifesto easily shared and downloaded during and in the immediate aftermath of the killings. Online elements have been detected in several far-right attacks, such as Charlottesville or Utøya, with the Internet acting as a means by which violent neo-fascist information is created and disseminated. In response, there has been a massive shift in focus by states and security services within counter-terrorism towards cyber investigations.

While cyber-terrorism has become recognised as a significant component of modern-day terrorism, and the online sphere is becoming increasingly relevant in discussions about terrorism and counter-terrorism, more engagement on the problems and limitations of cyber-terrorism, the links between online and offline spheres, and the legal and social ethical implications of Internet-based counterterrorism is required.

Cyber-security and safety doctrines have developed in most countries in recent years, accompanied by a host of research projects, laws, institutions, and mechanisms designed to support cybersecurity and combat the spread of extremist and violent material that could lead to instances of terrorism. However, whilst the use of the Internet has expanded massively by "violent extremist" groups, those engaged in studying them, and policymakers developing a response, there is still limited engagement in understanding and analysing the potential problems and ethical implications of online or cyber-counterterrorism.

Critical terrorism analysis of state practise has highlighted numerous and widespread articulations of authority-led violence, misuse of emergency powers, structural racism, and the use of alarmist discourse employed for populist-style electoral support, whether they are the so-called liberal democracies, hybrid regimes, illiberal governments, or authoritarian states. However, such critical analysis does not seem to have been carried out on the implications of the rapid expansion of counter-terrorism into online spheres. In responding to this gap, this article takes the following questions as its key focus for analysis: What are the limitations and problems with current cyber-terrorism approaches or understandings? Can we identify the impact of limited knowledge about the link between online and offline spheres of terrorism and counter-terrorism? What are the ethical implications of current Internet-based counterterrorism approaches?

In examining these questions, we introduce critical discussions on counterterrorism powers and approaches in the field of online spheres. Each question will be examined in succession by analysing current research projects and drawing on existing research studies. This will be accomplished by providing an overview of the state of online counterterrorism programmes; the exploration of how the Internet is conceptualised in the so-called processes of "radicalisation" and "deradicalisation"; and the specific practical and ethical problems raised by this use and understanding of online spheres.

The term "cyber-terrorism" now encompasses a substantial portion of what is commonly referred to as "terrorism" in the modern era, and discussions and efforts to combat terrorism are increasingly focusing on the digital environment. This

DOI: 10.4324/9780429426063-30

chapter examines the potential problems and ethical implications of cyber-counterterrorism, the connections between the offline and online worlds, and the legal and socio-ethical implications of Internet-based counterterrorism efforts. It aims to fill this gap by bringing critical conversations on counterterrorism authorities and methods into cyberspace.

THE DEVELOPMENT OF CYBER-TERRORISM AND COUNTER-TERRORISM

The potential role of the Internet in terrorism and political violence is vast and growing. Since the rise of Internet messaging and social media, there have been very few violent attacks in the West that have not involved some form of online component. These have ranged from minor engagement with the Internet, such as using online public information for planning attacks or online stores for purchasing items, to more serious, long-term involvement in the online sphere through individuals being deeply embedded in violent online scenes, whereby they have been encouraged to, or encourage others to, perform acts of violence in a real-world setting.

The development of online spheres has offered "interconnectivity, anonymity, cheapness, power enhancement, and new audiences" (Palasinski & Bowman-Grieve, 2017), both for groups and individuals involved in terrorism, as well as counter-terror and counter-extremism organisations. The potential of online spheres in both encouraging and responding to terrorist-style violence was recognised in the early days of the Internet, with far-right and neo-Nazi groups being some of the first organisations to use online messaging. Other violent groups – such as the al Qasam brigade, the military arm of the Palestinian political party HAMAS – were also quick to create early online websites in English, enabling them to better communicate and engage with international audiences, including youth (Hawela, 2020).

Since its early use, the Internet has been largely recognised as changing the way in which terrorism takes place. With more ways to connect to violent networks, attacks have the potential to be more sophisticated in their design. Computer-mediated forms of communication have been described as "ideal for terrorists-as-communicators: they are decentralised, they cannot be subjected to control or restriction, they are not censored, and they allow access to anyone who wants it" (Tsfati & Weimann, 2002: 319). Ideologically speaking, meanwhile, the Internet has meant that it has become easier for those interested in carrying out violence to seek out and engage with others who have similar or overlapping worldviews.

Because of the ease of access to online hate content, more people have become acquainted with previously obscure and potentially dangerous ideologies. The rise of large online platforms and networks, as well as the development of alt-right or alt-light groups (often backed by powerful actors or investors), has arguably played a significant role in shifting the Overton Window – what is seen as acceptable and unacceptable to say in national political discussions – further right than before.

Recently, these have included platforms such as Gab or personal messaging sites including Telegram. Such sites have been used to spread powerful conspiracy theories or ideas, such as the identarian concept of the "Great Replacement," which casts White European ethnic groups as at threat from a global conspiracy, weaving together a powerful concoction of eugenics and racial Darwinism, extreme xenophobia, Islamophobia and Antisemitism. These have been joined by the rise in other hate speech trends, such as the violent misogynism of the "incel" (involuntary celibate) movement, as well as contributing towards a general trend of racism and anti-migrant sentiment evident in right-wing populism.

These trends have led to a host of new cyber responses by authorities, most notably the rise of online counter-extremism approaches or CVE (countering violent extremism). Online responses in the early "War on Terror" were largely characterised by "hard" actions and power configurations, such as the breaking of terror cells or networks through online infiltration. Whilst such cyber counterterrorism is still carried out, the extension of the "War on Terror" in the last decade to include a focus on the role of extremist thoughts and ideas in radicalising individuals towards violence has resulted in a proliferation of the "softer" online approaches that comprise much of current CVE.

The development of online CVE has tended to take one of two forms since its inception in 2014 onward. Firstly, significant CVE work is carried out, encouraging and enabling the removal of content deemed to be "extremist" or encouraging terrorism. Content moderation is largely carried out at the discretion of social media platforms (Citron, 2018; Gillespie, 2018), often in discussion with the government and law enforcement (Brocato, 2015; Brown & Pearson, 2018; Ganesh & Bright, 2020). One of the most significant examples of this is the online disruption of Islamic State-supporting users on social media platforms such as Facebook, Twitter, and Telegram. The increasing removal of material and the blocking of user accounts by tech groups using online algorithms and monitoring has increasingly driven supporters of Islamic State into the darker recesses of the Internet, preventing their engagement with potential sympathisers and recruits. This form of CVE has gradually become inscribed into law, although approaches to disrupting and removing online content have differed both between countries and social media platforms.

The other form of online CVE that has developed, other than open disruption, is that of strategic communication, or "speaking back" to violent groups. Both approaches act to limit audience exposure to extremist narratives and ensure the marginality of extremist views (Ganesh & Bright, 2020). Strategic communication as CVE includes the development of counter-messaging, seen in individual and personal responses and engagement with extreme content; governmental and non-governmental advertising campaigns; the creation of media which counters core violent messaging; and the creation of educational tools or programmes designed to promote critical thinking or non-violence (Bertram, 2016; Beutel et al., 2016; Braddock & Horgan, 2016; Briggs & Feve, 2013; Brown & Marway, 2018; Cherney, 2016; Eerten & Doosje, 2019).

LIMITATIONS OF CURRENT APPROACHES

The development of cyber-counterterrorism and online countering of violent extremism has led to a host of new problems developing; initially, the rise of the Internet and the arrival of the "War on Terror" paradigm in 2001, for instance, led to elaborate concerns about cyber-terrorism that were unfounded and simply have not come to pass.

A significant limitation with countering terrorism and violent counter-extremism online has been the field's lingering definitional issues that have not only not been so far resolved but have been continually muddied with the expansion of the counterterror paradigm to include discussions on "radicalisation" and "violent extremism." With online platforms pushing to detect users who share extremist content early on, the unstable definition of extremism – and thus extremist content – is almost entirely governed by context; different countries, governments, and platforms have developed differing, and sometimes competing, definitions and practical understandings of extremist content. As McNeil-Willson et al. state, "Terms such as radicalism and extremism have a normative, relational and context-specific value: one is judged radical or extremist against culturally specific benchmarks, and this label is dependent on who is doing the labelling" (McNeil-Willson et al., 2019). Because of different limitations and legal standards, it is difficult to determine which content is problematic across borders and platforms.

There has been a serious failure to effectively agree on what is meant by extreme violent content, even in places with significant levels of coordination on security and policy, like the European Union (Hassan et al., 2018). Due to a lack of mutual understanding, this has caused confusion in terms of law enforcement, prosecution, and international collaboration (Jerman-Blažič & Klobuar, 2016: 130). Where there is consensus, governments frequently delegate responses to content linked to terrorism to specific platforms or social media organisations, which reduces effectiveness and supervision. Additionally, there is a perpetual game of cat and mouse going on between terrorist organisations and law enforcement, in which terrorist organisations vary their language, platforms, and discourse to fool algorithms.

The response of social media platforms to some users or groups who might be using their platforms to spread extremist beliefs has also been conflicting, which has spurred discussion among analysts about how to strike a balance between the suppression of violent material and groups and the question of whether driving potentially violent groups into deeper corners of the web is effective. Despite the fact that the platform's decision to ban the majority of Islamic State activity from Telegram in 2019 may have prevented the organisation from engaging in some forms of recruitment and propaganda, it also made it more difficult to keep tabs on the organisation because, in response, its members and supporters scattered across a number of new, more inaccessible websites. Such spaces are more obscure and opaque, potentially giving Islamic State the space and impetus to renew online activities in more hidden spaces of the Internet.

The importance of the Internet's involvement in terrorist-style assaults has also come under intense scrutiny. Mueller and Stewart (2015: 176), for instance, discovered that, based on internal US case studies, "the Internet has not been particularly important to the terrorism enterprise. Although it has been facilitating in some respects, it has scarcely ever been necessary. That is, much of what has taken place could have happened if the Internet had never been invented. The Internet does have special relevance, however, to the counterterrorism enterprise." Furthermore, while the online sphere is only a limited benefit in terrorist actions, online counterterrorism has come with far greater costs to authorities and governments; "the Internet, and the big data complications it makes possible, greatly increase the costs and complications of the counterterrorism quest" (Mueller & Stewart, 2015: 176).

There have also been conflicts concerning the parameters of laws prohibiting hate speech and the contribution of hate speech to terrorist violence. Although offensive, online hate speech and the polarisation it fosters have not been directly linked to terrorist attacks; rather, they have the ability to exacerbate already-existing social divisions. Therefore, just as hate speech is motivated by terrorist actions, so too could extreme speech be motivated by terrorism (Abbas, 2019; McNeil-Willson et al., 2019).

Furthermore, much of the hate content that is currently online is quite subtle or ironic in its character and execution, and boundaries differ between contexts. In Germany, strong hate crime legislation requires the very quick takedown of far-right content by online providers; the centralisation of free speech in US responses, on the other hand, allows for extreme content to go unmoderated. This inconsistency is especially problematic in an online environment that allows users to access data and platforms across national boundaries.

Our incomplete knowledge of the relationship between online and offline domains raises problems with counter-terrorism and counter-extremism as well. Cybersecurity methodologies have generally converged around processes of extremism, trying to target people "susceptible" to particular ideologies and develop "resilience" against violence and polarisation. It is important to emphasise and contest the degree to which such methods are conceptually sound or subscribe to certain problematic versions of the post-2001 security paradigm.

In the early days of the Internet, violent groups, notably those on the far-right, were eager to embrace its possibilities, serving as "pioneers in embracing the newest communication technologies and using them in conjunction with the available media" (Eid, 2010: 2). They have connected the online and physical worlds, using the Internet to "promote terrorist organisation propaganda, connect like-minded extremists, inspire and radicalise terrorist sympathisers, recruit potential terrorists, and plan attacks" (Janbeck & Williams, 2014: 301). However, there have been few studies that investigate the relationships and processes that occur between the online and offline worlds (Hassan et al., 2018). Those who have mostly concentrated on specific cases, such as Drevon (2016), observed that some individuals successfully went to fight in Syria after being exposed to websites supporting extreme Salafist ideology and participating in online debates. While such in-depth investigations are extremely beneficial in understanding local actors, they are not intended to be generalisable.

As a result, there is no clear and substantial evidence to support the claim that the Internet and social media work independently of offline influences. Rather, it appears that online social spaces can only trigger or enhance decision-making for active seekers of extremist online content when combined with offline factors (Hassan et al., 2018: 84), and radicalisation is enabled by the Internet rather than dependent on it (Gill et al., 2015: 35). Adoption of radical beliefs is so frequently a response to offline concerns, and it includes a complicated series of processes and interactions between the online and offline spheres (Scrivens et al., 2020). The fact that so much current research and policy ignores the nuanced relationships between the online and offline spheres makes them problematic. By making online content an independent factor in and of itself, counterterrorism legislation, for instance, has led to the development of cases against individuals after their participation in online extremist materials.

The rise of media-savvy groups like the Islamic State and far-right media activists has led to extensive research into online extremism (Bastug et al., 2020; Binder & Kenyon, 2022; Ebbrecht, 2022; Frissen, 2021; Henschke, 2021; Herath & Whittaker, 2021; Sullivan & Montasari, 2022; Valentini et al., 2020; Winter et al., 2020; Whittaker, 2022; Wolfowicz et al., 2022). Many projects and careers have been built around the analysis of extensive social media content as a component of "online radicalization." However, research investigating extremism has also been found to be guilty of isolating online activity in a way that runs the risk of oversimplifying processes of engagement with violence.

With so much contemporary terrorism research tracking the use of social media or similar platforms by groups such as Islamic State, we ignore the limitations of social media – that it represents only a facet (and an often highly edited one) of individual and group tactics and actions. Focusing on social media content runs the risk of amplifying the message of violent groups and encouraging the acceptance of frequently false online claims with no critical analysis accompanying the message. The argument surrounding groups like Islamic State has been warped because of the obvious overreliance on such data. For example, debates on the legacy of a "Virtual Caliphate" that was to endure after the decline or "downfall" of Da'esh have been entirely false and unsupported.

Current research into online-to-offline radicalisation has currently been identified as failing to properly consider processes (or process tracing) of interaction between different factors, spheres, and networks, and is yet to gain a critical mass for it to appear credible in its conclusions (Hassan et al., 2018: 85). It has also promoted unfounded concepts that overemphasise the means of localised violent groups to use online spheres. Such limitations at the research level have had inevitable knock-on effects on policy, with much counter-terrorism law following a relatively simplistic conceptualisation of causal inference between extremist content, radicalisation, and terroristic violence.

In recent UK counterterrorism laws, from the 2015 "Prevent Duty" to the 2019 Counterterrorism and Border Security Bill, we see increasingly hard-line measures against the access or perceived access of "extremist content". This has included provisions for prosecuting those who may view material over the shoulder of others, despite not being aware of its contents or potential contents, as well as increasing the threshold for prosecution for the number of clicks on extremist or potentially extremist material – from three clicks in 2015 to just one in 2019. Evidence of involvement with extremist content, no matter how minor, has become a basis for prosecution, as part of a growing trend in counter-terrorism legislation to draw a simplistic linear progression between extremism and terrorist violence.

THE ETHICAL IMPLICATIONS OF CURRENT INTERNET-BASED APPROACHES TO COUNTERTERRORISM

Another significant element lacking from the current scholarly debate over cyber counterterrorism policy and programmes is engagement with the specific ethical problems that such practises bring. These range from the use of Internet anonymity by security services to engage in tactics of harassment to more nuanced problems of the replication of problematic notions of extremism.

Security services have used the anonymity of the Internet to engage in entrapment-style tactics against individuals who have sought out extremist platforms. Janbeck and

Williams (2014: 303–304) detail several examples of the FBI creating terrorist-network recruiting websites convincing enough to attract potential terrorists. Potential recruits, some as young as 14, have interacted with security services' websites, gaining both ideological and physical support, such as partial plan development or the provision of money, fake bombs, and even vehicles to suspects. Such provisions by security services to sometimes vulnerable individuals have been used as evidence against suspects arrested under counterterror legislation. Yet, those who have been detained under such tactics have largely been unable to obtain an acquittal using entrapment as a defence (Janbeck & Williams, 2014: 304). The ability to conceal one's identity online, combined with emergency counterterrorism laws that frequently disregard civil and human rights and permit "pre-crime" detention and prosecution, raises serious ethical questions for counterterrorism strategies and has the potential to replicate state authority violence (see Romaniuk & Njoku, 2021; Romaniuk, 2022).

There are also problems with the way that counter-extremism efforts are conducted online. Many organisations compete for government funding or work together with governmental agencies and significant multinational corporations. Large non-governmental organisations have emerged from the development of the CVE sector, often acting as "front groups" for governments as a part of counterterrorism strategies that include strategic communication (Miller & Sabir, 2012: 27; McNeil-Willson, 2020). Such groups have been accused of developing recommendations and programmes in line with problematic counterterror policies, becoming "essential to the efficacy of coercion and the generation of fear" (Miller & Sabir, 2012: 27–28). Online CVE programmes may therefore act to uncritically replicate governmental lines, despite criticism from minority groups or academics concerned about their wider implications.

Due to the presumption that algorithms are exempt from the structural racism of offline state counterterror policies and best practices, online projects may be particularly pertinent in this regard. Therefore, because of their putative ideological neutrality, they constitute an additional potential danger.

References

Abbas, T. (2019). *Islamophobia and radicalisation: A vicious cycle*. London: Hurst.

Bastug, M.F., Douai, A., & Akca, D. (2020). Exploring the "demand side" of online radicalization: Evidence from the Canadian context.*Studies in Conflict & Terrorism*, *43*, 616–637. doi: 10.1080/1057610X.2018.1494409

Bertram, L. (2016). Terrorism, the internet and the social media advantage: Exploring how terrorist organisations exploit aspects of the internet, social media and how these same platforms could be used to counter-violent extremism. *Journal for Deradicalisation*, *7*, 225–252.

Beutel, A., Weine, S., Saeed, A., Mihajlovic, A., Stone, A., Beahrs, J., & Shanfield, S. (2016). Guiding principles for countering and displacing extremist narratives. *Contemporary Voices: St Andrews Journal of International Relations*, *7*, 35–49.

Binder, J.F., & Kenyon, J. (2022). Terrorism and the internet: How dangerous is online radicalization? *Frontiers in Psychology*. *13*, 997390. doi: 10.3389/fpsyg.2022.997390

Braddock, K., & Horgan, J. (2016). Towards a guide for constructing and disseminating counternarratives and reduce support for terrorism. *Studies in Conflict & Terrorism*, *39*, 381–404.

Briggs, R., & Feve, S. (2013). *Review of programmes to counter narratives of violent extremism*. London: Institute for Strategic Dialogue.

Brocato, A. (2015). Tackling terrorists' use of the internet: Propaganda dispersion & the threat of radicalisation. In M.N. Ogun (Ed.), *Terrorist use of cyberspace and cyber terrorism: New challenges and responses*. IOS Press: Amsterdam.

Brown, K., & Pearson, E. (2018). Social media, the online environment and terrorism. In A. Silke (Ed.), *Routledge handbook of terorism and counterterrorism*. London: Routledge.

Brown, K., & Marway, H. (2018). Preventing radicalisation to terrorism and violent extremism: Delivering counter- or alternative narratives. Brussels, Belgium: Radicalisation Awareness Network (RAN).

Cherney, A. (2016). Designing and implementing programmes to tackle radicalisation and violent extremism: Lessons from criminology. *Dynamics of Asymmetric Conflict*, *9*, 82–94.

Citron, D.K. (2018). Extremist speech, compelled conformity and censorship creep. In SSRN Scholarly Paper No. ID 2941880. Rochester NY: Social Science Research Network.

Drevon, J. (2016). Embracing salafi jihadism in Egypt and mobilising in the Syrian jihad. *Middle East Critique*, *25*, 1–16.

Ebbrecht, C.K. (2022). Systematic review: Risk factors and mechanisms of radicalization in lone-actor grievance-fueled violence. *Nordic Psychology*, 1–35. doi: 10.1080/19012276.2022.2074524

Eerten, J.J., & van Doosje, B. (2019). *Challenging extremist views on social media: Developing a counter-messaging response*. Abingdon: Routledge.

Eid, M. (2010). Cyber-terrorism and ethical journalism: A need for rationalism. *International Journal of Technoethics*, *1*, 1–19.

Frissen, T. (2021). Internet, the great radicalizer? Exploring relationships between seeking for online extremist materials and cognitive radicalization in young adults. *Computers in Human Behavior*, *114*, 106549. doi: 10.1016/j.chb.2020.106549

Ganesh, B., & Bright, J. (2020). Countering extremists on social media: Challenges for strategic communication and content moderation. *Policy & Internet*, *12*, 6–19.

Gill, P., Corner, E., Thornton, A., & Conway, M. (2015). What are the roles of the internet in terrorism? Measuring online behaviours of convicted UK terrorists. In *VOX-pol network of excellence*. Dublin: Dublin City University.

Gillespie, T. (2018). *Custodians of the internet: Platforms, content moderation and the hidden decisions that shape social media*. Yale: Yale University Press.

Hassan, G., Brouillette-Alarie, S., Alava, S., Frau-Meigs, D., Lavoie, L., Fetiu, A., Varela, W., Borokhovski, E., Venkatesh, V., Rousseau, C., & Sieckelinck, S. (2018). Exposure to extremist online content could lead to violent radicalisation: A systematic review of empirical evidence. *International Journal of Developmental Science*, *12*, 71–88.

Hawela, H.C. (2020). Collectivindualism and shadow players: Palestinian youth, social media, and hamas's communications strategies. *International Journal of Communication, 14*, 1–23.

Henschke, A. (2021). Terrorism and the internet of things: Cyber-terrorism as an emergent threat. In A. Henschke, A. Reed, S. Robbins and S. Miller (Eds.), *Counter-terrorism, ethics and technology* (pp. 71–87). Cham: Springer.

Herath, C., & Whittaker, J. (2021). Online radicalization: Moving beyond a simple dichotomy. *Terrorism and Political Violence*, 1–22. doi: 10.1080/09546553.2021.1998008

Janbeck, D., & Williams, V. (2014). The role of the internet post-9/11 in terrorism and counterterrorism. *Brown Journal of World Affairs, 20*, 297–308.

Jerman-Blažič, B., & Klobuar, T. (2016). Missing solutions in the fight against cybercrime and cyberterrorism - the new EU research agenda. In *2016 European intelligence and security informatics conference*. Ljubljana, Slovenia: Laboratory for Open Systems and Networks.

McNeil-Willson, R., Gerrand, V., Scrinzi, F., & Triandafyllidou, A. (2019). *Polarisation, violent extremism and resilience in Europe today: An analytical framework for the BRaVE project (concept paper)*. Florence: European University Institute.

McNeil-Willson, R. (2020). Here be dragons: Responding to problems with contemporary research methods in the study of terrorism and political violence. In M. Ronchi, I. Pappe & L. Charles (Eds.), *Researching the Middle East: Cultural, conceptual, theoretical and practical issues*. Edinburgh: Edinburgh University Press.

Miller, D., & Sabir, R.. (2012). Counter-terrorism as counterinsurgency in the UK "war on terror". In S. Poynting & D. Whyte (Eds.), *Counter-terrorism and state political violence*. London and New York: Routledge.

Mueller, J., & Stewart, M.G. (2015). Terrorism, counterterrorism and the Internet: The American cases. *Dynamics of Asymmetric Conflict, 8*, 179–190.

Palasinski, M., & Bowman-Grieve, L. (2017). Tackling cyber-terrorism: Balancing surveillance with counter-communication. *Security Journal, 30*, 556–568.

Romaniuk, S. (2022). *Under siege: Counterterrorism and civil society in Hungary*. Lanham, Maryland: Lexington Books.

Romaniuk, S.N. & Njoku, E.T. (Eds.). (2021). *Counter-terrorism and civil society Post-9/11 progress and challenges*. Manchester: Manchester University Press.

Scrivens, R., Gill, P., & Conway, M. (2020). The role of the internet in facilitating violent extremism and terrorism: Suggestions for progressing research. In T. Holt and A.M. Bossler (Eds.), *The Palgrave handbook of international cybercrime and cyberdeviance*. London: Palgrave Macmillan.

Sullivan, A., & Montasari, R. (2022). The use of the internet and the internet of things in modern terrorism and violent extremism. In R. Montasari, F. Carroll, I. Mitchell, S. Hara and R. Bolton-King (Eds.), *Privacy, security and forensics in the internet of things (IoT)* (pp. 151–165). Cham: Springer.

Tsfati, Y., & G. Weimann. (2002). Terror on the internet. *Studies in Conflict & Terrorism, 25*, 317–332.

Valentini, D., Lorusso, A.M., & Stephan, A. (2020). Onlife extremism: Dynamic integration of digital and physical spaces in radicalization. *Frontiers in Psychology, 11*, 524. doi: 10.3389/fpsyg.2020.00524

Whittaker, J. (2022). Rethinking online radicalization. *Perspectives on Terrorism, 16*, 27–40.

Winter, C., Neumann, P., Meleagrou-Hitchens, A., Ranstorp, M., Vidino, L., & Fürst, J. (2020). Online extremism: Research trends in internet activism, radicalization, and counter-strategies. *International Journal of Conflict and Violence, 14*(2), 1–20. 10.4119/ijcv-3809

Wolfowicz, M., Hasisi, B., & Weisburd, D. (2022). What are the effects of different elements of media on radicalization outcomes? A systematic review. *Campbell Systematic Reviews, 18*, e1244. doi:10.1002/cl2.1244

28

THE IMPORTANCE OF SECURITY AWARENESS IN THE HEALTHCARE SECTOR

Examination of Threat Vectors, Environmental Factors, and Opportunities for Mitigation

János Besenyő and Attila Máté Kovács

INTRODUCTION

In the rapidly evolving global landscape, organisations and agencies from a diverse range of disciplines and industries, as well as state and non-state actors, encounter an abundance of challenges. This extends to the implementation of new technologies to maintain a competitive edge while also ensuring digital security through a cybersecurity policy and strategy that are both ethical and effective (see Romaniuk and Manjikian, 2021). Although technology has improved service delivery and increased safety in the healthcare sector, the risks associated with cyber threats continue to exist in this field. This chapter investigates the security posture of healthcare organisations in relation to the adoption of new technologies, with an emphasis on two critical questions:

1. Can developing organizational and individual knowledge through employee involvement lead to an increased overall security posture?
2. Do regular cybersecurity training and awareness programs for healthcare staff reduce the risk of successful cyberattacks on healthcare organizations?

Indeed, the widespread adoption of technology is transforming various sectors of the economy, ranging from healthcare, education, finance, transportation, and manufacturing. The rise of the Internet and the proliferation of digital devices have enabled businesses to reach new customers, expand their markets, and streamline their operations.

Consequently, the world is becoming a global village (Litan & Rivlin, 2001). Globalization has eliminated the cross-border communication challenges witnessed in the 1990s, facilitating communication across regions. However, cross-border communications have led to challenges that can adversely affect critical sectors such as healthcare. Specifically, adopting technology to ease cross-border challenges poses significant challenges to healthcare providers, the government, and consumers. The continued proliferation of technology in the healthcare sector has created cybersecurity concerns.

Cybersecurity incidents possess the potential to exert a significant impact on the health industry, which encompasses hospitals, clinics, and various healthcare entities. On a global scale, the healthcare industry is experiencing substantial transformations. Hathaliya and Tanwar (2020) highlight the shift within the healthcare industry from a traditional model focusing on the physician to a technology-based model. Integrating cutting-edge technologies in the healthcare sector progressively leads to enhanced precision healthcare, characterized by improved efficiency and effectiveness. Nevertheless, further advancements are imperative in addressing the challenges of cyber hazards (Besenyő et al., 2021). The maintenance of data integrity is contingent upon the criticality of maintaining patient data privacy.

The increasing implementation of digital healthcare systems has led healthcare organizations to rely heavily on legislative frameworks such as the Health Insurance Portability and Accountability Act (HIPAA) or the General Data Protection Regulation (GDPR) to address cybersecurity concerns. However, these organizations remain vulnerable to emerging cyber threats like ransomware despite these measures.

Healthcare organizations must prioritize implementing proactive measures to effectively mitigate, identify, and address cybersecurity threats. Proactive measures may involve implementing effective strategies to combat cybercrime, regularly evaluating potential risks, and providing continuous cybersecurity education to personnel.

From a regional perspective, it is conceivable that cybersecurity and healthcare security will be critical areas for Africa in the future. Many African nations lack sophisticated technological infrastructure to combat cybercrime

DOI: 10.4324/9780429426063-31

threats. In 2017 alone, Kshetri (2019) reported that cybercrime in Africa led to more than US$3.7 billion in losses.

The healthcare sector is rapidly digitizing, leading to increased storage and sharing of electronic health records. The growing interconnectivity between medical devices and cloud storage systems has introduced new avenues for cyber threats (Mansfield-Devine, 2018). Legislative frameworks such as HIPAA and GDPR establish guidelines for safeguarding personal data and ensuring the confidentiality of patient information. However, these frameworks typically lack explicit provisions addressing the ever-changing landscape of security risks.

For instance, HIPAA mandates the protection of protected health information (PHI), ensuring confidentiality and availability. Still, it doesn't delve more into measures against specific cyber threats like ransomware or phishing attacks (Kruse, Frederick, Jacobson, and Monticone, 2017). On the other hand, the GDPR, although broader in terms of data protection, focuses more on the rights of data subjects and transparency than on prescriptive security measures against specific cyberattacks.

Moreover, as indicated by research conducted by the Ponemon Institute, a staggering 90% of healthcare businesses have experienced the detrimental consequences of a cyberattack, with ransomware emerging as a prominent and formidable hazard (Ponemon Institute, 2016). The increasing prevalence of cyber threats within the healthcare industry is a significant concern due to their multifaceted impacts. In addition to compromising the confidentiality of patient data, the deployment of ransomware specifically impairs the provision of healthcare services, posing a direct threat to human life.

LITERATURE REVIEW

Due to the growth in healthcare facilities and innovations, considerable scholarly research has been conducted on cybersecurity threats and their mitigation in the health sector.

Recent studies have shown that the healthcare sector is among the critical infrastructures that have increasingly become targets of cyberattacks, with detrimental consequences for their reputation and financial stability. The consequences of such attacks go beyond the immediate financial losses incurred; they also impact the overall confidence and trust that patients and stakeholders have in the sector's ability to provide safe and secure medical services (Markopoulou & Papakonstantinou, 2021). A comprehensive study was conducted on the difference between critical infrastructure and critical information infrastructure. The researchers also described various cyberattacks in the health sector, such as ransomware, phishing, and DOS attacks, and focused on implementing regulatory standards such as GDPR.

HIPAA is the subject of study by researchers (Brady, 2011; Centers for Disease Control and Prevention, 1996). Brady (2011) focused on why medical centers, despite significant data breaches, fail to comply with the latest HIPAA laws. In a study employing different analysis techniques, such as linear regression and correlation, the researcher notes that adopting support from management, security, cyber security awareness, and security culture was the most significant predictor of security effectiveness.

The COVID-19 epidemic has challenged the cybersecurity level of healthcare information systems, impacting hospitals, pharmaceutical companies, the WHO, and its partners (He et al., 2021). The most crucial goal of the research was to identify the main cybersecurity challenges, current security controls being adopted by the health sector, and areas for improvement. Several significant challenges in cybersecurity were identified. Regarding cybersecurity and risk mitigation, the health sector must adopt concrete solutions and focus on specific areas.

Similar research was conducted on designing, developing, and implanting more secure mechanisms to secure the healthcare industry infrastructure during the COVID-19 pandemic (Baz et al., 2021). Various cybersecurity threats were analyzed in the research by using multiple analytical algorithms, including Fuzzy analytic hierarchy process (F-AHP).

Additionally, Raburu's study (2021) focused on a thorough analysis of hospitals in Nairobi, Kenya. The primary objective of the research was to construct a robust cybersecurity framework explicitly tailored for the health industry. The research targeted a group of hospitals to retrieve various samples of data from people working in the IT departments of these hospitals. Algorithms and techniques like convenience sampling, correlation, and regression analysis were used. This study also focused on cybersecurity awareness among IT staff and medical practitioners to evade and limit the effects of a data breach or cybersecurity incident.

Security researchers interviewed the hospital's IT security and information security management staff, such as the CIO and CISO, to develop a dynamic system model through which the healthcare centers build the required cybersecurity capabilities (Jalali, 2018).

Cybersecurity awareness among users related to the health sector plays a vital role in protecting against various complex cybersecurity data breaches and incidents (Kim, 2017). The research focuses on how organizations related to health care can deal with cybersecurity incidents and what they should know.

Researchers developed an information assurance technique to mitigate the effects of data breaches in the human services sector (Washington, 2022). The research focuses on safeguarding stored data and maintaining confidentiality, integrity, and availability. Proposed methods of preventing data breaches included in the study are analyzing the existing security controls, conducting a security risk analysis, conducting training, keeping the staff well-educated, updating software and patches, and identifying the attack source.

As a part of mitigation techniques for various cybersecurity threats in the health sector, researchers used cybersecurity threat intelligence to identify vulnerabilities in medical equipment (Sills, 2020). The CTI of different medical devices and sources is gathered and augmented, which helps in AI-supported cybersecurity tasks.

A review of recent trends, threats, and mitigation in Australian healthcare organizations is a reference and discussed as a case study (Offner, 2020). The research compares Australian healthcare sector standards with international cybersecurity landscapes, focusing on introducing electronic health records. Various cybersecurity risks associated with using technologies like IoT and cloud computing in the health sector are also being analyzed in the chapter, along with the appropriate mitigation techniques.

The landscape of cybersecurity research and policy frameworks has seen significant transformations in recent decades. According to the findings of Garba and Bade (2021), the earliest endeavors mainly focused on safeguarding computer systems and their respective operating systems. Nevertheless, recent advancements have integrated efforts to mitigate the risks associated with the widespread usage of the Internet. As a result, cybersecurity encompasses several tactics aimed at safeguarding organizations and their valuable resources by identifying potential threats. The objective of threat identification is to detect weaknesses inside an organization's computer systems, such as crucial information (Alese et al., 2014). In addition to discovering dangers, the contemporary notion of cybersecurity encompasses safeguarding and mitigating threats.

A specific aspect of the study is cybersecurity incidents, research, developments, and opportunities in Nigeria as an African example, from a cybersecurity perspective. Although cybersecurity remains critical, numerous African nations lack elaborate technological frameworks to counter cyber threats, leading to significant financial losses (Kshetri, 2019). Nigeria loses $500 million a year due to various kinds of cybercrime (Omogbolagun, 2023).

Research indicates that Nigeria will continue to experience significant financial implications from cybercrime. According to Nnanwube et al. (2019), Nigeria will continue to experience an evolving cybercrime environment as entities invest in new systems and new dimensions take effect. In addition, the increasing implementation of technologies across various economic sectors and a growing unemployed population exacerbate and complicate the fight against cybercrime in the country.

THE IMPORTANCE AND PRACTICAL IMPLEMENTATION OF EDUCATION

Seeing risks and opportunities and being able to cope are two different things. Awareness and education could help with the understanding and safe use of information technology. A study conducted by the Pew Research Center (Smith and Anderson, 2016) found that a significant proportion of Americans have negative perceptions of the impact of technology on their lives. According to the study, about two-thirds of Americans believe that technology has a more negative than positive impact on their privacy. Furthermore, a similar proportion expressed concerns about the potential loss of jobs due to technological advancements.

The following section will list and describe hypothetical incident examples where human factors may have a positive, preventive role. The importance of awareness increases as cybercriminals target the healthcare sector and its workforce. The importance of staff training and awareness cannot be overstated in the context of safeguarding essential information and systems. This is particularly significant given the potentially sensitive nature of patient data and the increasing dependence on digital technology. Healthcare organizations can strengthen their security posture by equipping staff with the knowledge and skills to recognize and respond to potential cyber threats. Key areas of focus in cybersecurity training include phishing and social engineering, password management, secure data handling, physical security, mobile device security, and incident reporting. Reputable organizations and platforms offer tailored cybersecurity awareness training courses to address the unique needs of the healthcare sector. Investing in regular training and awareness programs is essential to protecting sensitive patient data and maintaining trust in healthcare services.

Such fields can be:

- Phishing and social engineering: Training should cover how to recognize phishing emails, social engineering tactics, and the importance of verifying the authenticity of communications before taking any action. Offer simulated phishing exercises to help staff practice identifying and reporting suspicious emails.
- Password management: Educate employees on creating strong, unique passwords and using multi-factor authentication (MFA) wherever possible. Encourage the use of password managers to store and manage credentials securely.
- Secure data handling: Teach staff about properly handling sensitive patient data, including encryption, secure storage, and sharing only with authorized individuals.
- Physical security: Emphasize the importance of protecting physical access to devices and systems, such as by locking workstations, securing portable devices, and being aware of potential shoulder surfing.

- Mobile device security: Train employees on securing their mobile devices, using secure Wi-Fi connections, and avoiding the installation of untrusted apps.
- Incident reporting: Encourage staff to promptly report any suspected security incidents or breaches and provide clear guidelines on how to do so.
- Regularly scheduled updates and refresher workshops: These should be provided to employees to ensure their knowledge and skills remain current on the most recent risks and best practices. These sessions reinforce past learning and enhance overall cybersecurity awareness among staff members.

CYBERSECURITY THREATS AND ATTACKS IN THE HEALTHCARE SECTOR

A multitude of cybersecurity challenges confront the global healthcare industry. Nonetheless, the predominant cyber risks in the healthcare sector encompass malware, ransomware, phishing assaults, and distributed denial of service (DDoS) attacks.

As an illustration, infiltrating malware into computer systems can compromise security measures, facilitating data breaches and identity theft. In the healthcare industry, malware poses a significant threat as it can potentially compromise patient records, putting their safety and confidentiality at risk. Similarly, ransomware can seize hospital data and coerce payment as a condition for its restitution, resulting in substantial interference with medical activities. On the other hand, phishing assaults pertain to the deceptive manipulation of healthcare personnel to obtain confidential information, like login passwords or patient data. The scenario mentioned above has the potential to result in the unlawful retrieval of medical records, thereby creating opportunities for the exploitation of patient information with fraudulent intentions. DDoS assaults are specifically crafted to overwhelm the networks and systems of hospitals, thereby impeding their capacity to deliver medical services to patients. These circumstances may result in the prolongation of medical care, the rescheduling of appointments, and many unfavorable consequences for individuals seeking healthcare.

According to Saheed and Arowolo (2021), the healthcare sector presents distinctive challenges despite the similar vulnerability to threats of other components of a nation's vital infrastructure. The healthcare sector may experience adverse consequences as a result of cyberattacks, in addition to financial ramifications and privacy concerns. Ransomware is a pervasive form of malicious software commonly seen in healthcare facilities due to the potentially life-threatening consequences that may arise from the loss of patient data. The healthcare business has experienced a rise in cyberattacks in recent years, leading to growing concerns regarding cybersecurity within this sector.

Businesses across the healthcare sector remain an attractive focal point for malevolent actors. They become primary targets since healthcare providers possess and manage substantial personal and medical data. The frequency of ransomware attacks in the industry has risen, posing risks to patient safety, data security, and operational continuity. Moreover, insider threats in healthcare enterprises, namely employees and contractors, pose a significant risk due to their authorized access to sensitive data and systems.

A. Interruptions in Critical Medical Services

Cyberattacks against healthcare companies can potentially cause significant disruptions to essential medical services. An illustrative example would be a ransomware assault targeting a hospital's computer system, which might render medical personnel unable to retrieve patient data and provide critical healthcare services. Occasionally, delaying surgical interventions and other medical procedures poses a significant risk to patients' lives. Healthcare organizations may experience considerable financial losses due to the interruption of services, resulting in the need to allocate resources towards restoring normal operations.

B. Information and Privacy Breaches

The possession of a multitude of personal and medical records by healthcare organizations becomes advantageous to individuals with malicious intent, commonly called hackers. Data has been likened to oil in contemporary discourse, emphasizing its significant value. Illicit marketplaces place substantial weight on sensitive information, particularly pertaining to social security numbers, medical histories, and insurance details (Swasey, 2020). Due to data loss, patients are susceptible to various financial crimes, such as identity theft and fraud. Moreover, this practice has the potential to adversely impact the reputation of healthcare organizations and may lead to legal ramifications due to their failure to adequately safeguard patient information.

C. Compromise of Patient Data, Integrity, and Confidentiality

Cyberattacks can lead to a compromise of the hospital network, computers, devices, and data. According to Hübner et al. (2022), cyberattacks on a network system, electronic devices, and information breach confidentiality. Likewise, cyberattacks could compromise, alter, or corrupt the computer system, information, and the entire hospital network, raising integrity challenges. Consequently, cyberattacks can be devastating because hospitals collect and store sensitive information such as medical diagnoses, treatment plans, and test results. Cyberattacks that leak patient information lead to breaches of confidentiality and may cause patients to suffer prejudice and stigma. Also, attacks can alter patient treatment plans, leading to compromised quality of care. Thus, a cyberattack that compromises the triad of patient data, integrity, and confidentiality is devastating.

D. Economic Impact

Research indicates that cyberattacks cause significant financial losses to patients and healthcare providers. Lee (2018) suggests that cyberattacks cost the US healthcare system over US$305 billion in cumulative revenues. A loss of revenues in the region of US$305 billion represents a significant financial loss. In addition, cyberattacks affect patients, and compensating them for losing their personal and medical information would probably be enormous. Compensation for patients occurs when a healthcare facility violates the confidentiality of their medical data or their right to privacy, subjecting the provider to legal consequences such as fines and requests for financial compensation.

Cybersecurity Challenges that the Healthcare Sector Faces

The healthcare sector faces a myriad of challenges, especially cybersecurity concerns. Lee (2018) outlines that IoT built on networks and cloud computing that collects data is a significant source of risk in the healthcare sector. With the advent of technology integration in the healthcare sector, the following are some of the inherent issues:

1. Incidents of unauthorized access and security breaches
2. Intricacies of cybersecurity and information security protocols
3. Safeguarding patient confidentiality and data privacy
4. Vulnerabilities associated with legacy information systems
5. Technological challenges specific to the healthcare industry

Sources of Cybersecurity Risks in Healthcare

1. Malicious or non-malicious insider activities
2. Uninhibited inquisitiveness of staff members
3. Unsanctioned use of IT resources (shadow IT)
4. Inadvertent mistakes leading to data breaches
5. Accidental or unwitting activities causing security concerns

Information breaches can severely affect individuals and organizations, leading to reputational loss, competitive advantage decline, financial loss, and compromise of intellectual and property rights (Safa & Maple, 2016). Consequently, safeguarding information becomes paramount in the healthcare sector, which handles sensitive patient data. Despite the importance of protecting sensitive information, incidences of cyberattacks continue to increase. With the continuous progression of digital technology and the increasing use of advanced technologies like big data, the Internet of Things (IoT), cloud computing, and mobile devices, organizations are seeing a surge in cyberattacks, as reported by those who have implemented these technologies (Sandhu, 2021). However, most cyberattacks occur through the execution of malware with various malicious activities. With malware attacks attributed to ransomware doubling, researchers are keen to understand the primary causes.

Research indicates risks attributed to insider threats, shadow IT, human error, unintentional actions, and drives to satisfy curiosity exacerbate ransomware attacks. Saxena et al. (2020) note that insider threats use legitimate access to gain unauthorized access to information. Insider threats emanate primarily from the organization's employees and authorized subcontractors, who can intentionally or unintentionally provide a gateway to critical information. Authorized access attributed to insider threats can perpetrate fraud, hurting patients and the affected healthcare provider.

Similarly, shadow IT can amplify the risks posed by insider threats. Sometimes known as stealth IT, shadow IT resembles insider threats based on the source and mechanism of attack. Trusted organizational employees perform shadow IT attacks by introducing unsupported software and hardware (Wood, 2021). According to the author, shadow IT attacks occur by circumventing IT security measures applied to approved security technologies. Shadow IT attacks pose risks and can arise at the individual or collective levels (Mallmann et al., 2018). Originally, shadow IT took the form of boxed software that employees bought, including unapproved Microsoft Excel macros (Wood, 2021). However, modern strategies for shadow IT include cloud apps like Dropbox and Google Docs and file sharing across social media platforms like Twitter, Facebook, and WhatsApp WebEx.

Moreover, human errors, unintentional actions, and the drive to satisfy curiosity pose risks to organizational information assets. Safa and Maple (2016) note that human behaviors, whether intentional or unintentional, can lead to data breaches. According to the authors, human errors can lead to data breaches owing to risks attributed to employee poor decision-making, ignorance, technical errors, and skills and policy errors. Human errors ultimately grant unauthorized access to sensitive information and other critical assets to opportunistic cybercriminals. Unlike data breaches that occur through targeted attacks, unintentional actions through inadvertent compromise of security can pose risks to authorized access to confidential data. Involuntary actions occur due to the employee's lack of due diligence, knowledge, and awareness (Leclair & Keeley, 2015). Likewise, the drive to satisfy curiosity can lead employees to click to install malicious software, compromising data security. These risks could lead to unauthorized access to organizations' confidential information and potential damages.

There is a growing concern within the healthcare business over adversarial assaults targeting artificial intelligence (AI) and machine learning (ML) networks. Given that AI and

ML are integral to improving healthcare quality and outcomes and streamlining operations, they have become targets for cybercriminals seeking to interrupt care operations. Besides, introducing healthcare information exchange (HIE) between healthcare providers, carers, patients, and other healthcare stakeholders is challenging (Vest & Gamm, 2020). Although HIE improves data exchange and care outcomes through expedited telemedicine, it also poses risks for cyberattacks. Consequently, researchers outline the need for robust mechanisms to shield HIE against phishing, ransomware, DDoS, and malware attacks (He et al., 2021). Securing the HIE systems remains critical to protecting sensitive information and facilitating the secure transfer of information across different networks.

Since the healthcare system is complex, it consists of different stakeholders. Besides, the healthcare system supports various networks with different types of information recorded or transferred across the networks. As a result, numerous cyberattacks target varying areas in the healthcare system using different types of attacks. The most common types of attacks reported by the healthcare system are ransomware, data breaches, DDoS attacks, and insider threats (He et al., 2021). Ransomware, data breaches, DDoS attacks, and insider threats pose different impacts and disruptions in the healthcare sector.

1. Ransomware

There are three prevalent methods via which ransomware infiltrates systems belonging to victims: the dissemination of phishing emails with malevolent files, the act of users clicking on hazardous links, and the exposure to harmful advertisements, also known as malvertising. The phrase "ransomware" pertains to malevolent software that uses encryption to restrict access to files and immobilize machines, hence demanding a ransom in exchange for restoring access to the affected files. When such an event transpires, it impedes or renders ineffective the essential procedures employed in the field of healthcare. Consequently, cyberattacks compel hospitals to use manual methodologies, which interfere with the pace of recovery and consume a substantial financial allocation that could be useful for diverse enhancements within the healthcare facility.

2. Data Breaches

Research indicates that hospitals might be recording data breaches daily. According to Verizon (2021), when data breaches occur, patients and victims receive incident notifications through email, including free credit for identity monitoring lasting for two years.

The findings in the 2021 Verizon Data Breach Investigations Report (Verizon, 2021) indicate that the healthcare sector is the most targeted, recording a significantly higher frequency of data breaches than any other industry. However, the veracity of this assertion may be subject to certain biases, given the unambiguous and legally enforced reporting protocols established by HIPAA. Regardless, the legislation increases the likelihood of reporting data breaches in the healthcare sector compared to other industries.

Other variables, as previously indicated, contribute to the significant frequency of breaches in the healthcare sector:

- Healthcare data is valuable because individual patent information is in great demand in illegal markets because of its ability to facilitate various criminal actions, such as identity theft, medical billing fraud, and prescription fraud.
- Interconnected systems: Hospitals and healthcare providers often use interconnected systems to provide seamless care to patients. However, this interconnectivity can also increase the attack surface for hackers.
- Legacy systems and a lack of investment in cybersecurity: Many healthcare organizations still use outdated systems that may not have the latest security patches, making them more vulnerable to attacks.
- Human error: Employees in the healthcare sector may unintentionally cause data breaches by accidentally disclosing sensitive information or falling for phishing attacks.

3. DDoS Attacks

Hackers and cybercriminals commonly employ DDoS attacks as a tactic, method, and procedure (TTP) to render a network inoperable. The reliance on network connectivity for healthcare workers is of considerable importance, as it affects their ability to deliver care and use essential resources such as email communication, prescription management, hospital records, and other vital data. Nevertheless, certain distributed denial-of-service assaults may occur opportunistically or inadvertently. For example, some occurrences suggest DDoS attacks aimed at individuals due to social, political, ideological, and economic motivations resulting from circumstances that provoke the cyber threat actors. The motives in question may directly correlate with the DDoS operations or the overall scenario. Healthcare organizations, including hospitals, clinics, and research facilities, are particularly vulnerable to DDoS attacks due to their dependence on real-time access and communication of patient information. These types of organizations encompass research facilities. An illustrative scenario involves a DDoS attack directed at a hospital's network. Such DDoS significantly impedes healthcare practitioners from accessing important hospital systems such as electronic health records, medical imaging, and other vital assets for delivering quick and correct patient treatment.

DDoS attacks can compromise the security of medical data and disrupt the provision of patient treatment. During a DDoS attack, hackers may attempt to breach the safety of the targeted network or exploit the resulting disruption to acquire confidential information illicitly.

4. Insider Threats

The insider threat is arguably the most critical threat facing governments and organizations. According to Saxena et al. (2020), cyberattack mitigation techniques contribute to comprehending insider threats and the associated threat picture. The authors define an insider as someone who exploits or intends to exploit legitimate access to an organization's assets to allow unauthorized access. Insider threats typically occur since trusted employees possess passwords and usernames, which provide a gateway to an organization's information network.

Knowledge of insider threats is critical owing to the confidential data, financial information, and intellectual assets that organizations possess (Saxena et al., 2020). Specifically, understanding insider threats is significant in the healthcare sector, which is the hub of confidential patient information. Insider threats include the theft of patient information and other sensitive data, the compromise of computer networks, the retrieval and sale of vital data to third parties, and other financial frauds. The scale of sensitive data, complexities of medical technologies, and computer networks in hospital settings are the major factors contributing to insider threats within the healthcare industry.

Given the different types and significant impact of cyber threats, the primary question remains: Why is patient information (PHI) more vital than individual data (PII)? Patient data remains valuable, and understanding why healthcare data breaches occur and the types of incidences in the healthcare sector is imperative.

Although hospitals remain the primary targets of cybercriminals, hospitals release little information regarding such attacks. Researchers outline the sensitive nature of data breaches that can attract public attention and cause fear as the main reasons. Cyberattacks such as malware, insider threats, involuntary release of patient data, and negligence that lead to the loss or misplacement of laptops and other electronic components such as USBs and external hard drives facilitate attacks.

Cybercriminals acquire patient data from hospitals and sell it to illicit markets due to its higher demand than standard personal information. The need for patient data in illegal markets motivates cybercriminals to attack hospital databases. Any patient data obtained during hospital attacks provides money to the attackers on the black market. In return, the data buyers employ the information for identity theft and scams.

REPORTED CYBER ATTACKS AND INCIDENCES IN THE HEALTHCARE SECTOR

Studies and daily reports point to rising cases of threats targeting healthcare systems. Abraham et al. (2019) point to a significant increase in security breaches targeting hospitals.

Table 28.1 provides data on high-impact data breaches in the last decade (U.S. Department of Health and Human Services, 2020). The table lists the affected healthcare providers in the order of affected records, also noting the type of the attack and the year when the organizations reported the cyberattacks.

Below are further details of some intrusions affecting the healthcare industry published by the Department of Health and Human Services in 2020 (U.S. Department of Health and Human Services, 2020). The list includes a comprehensive description of the attacks, how they occurred, affected entities, and other reported losses. Each breach reflects the healthcare industry's vulnerabilities and challenges in safeguarding patient information.

1. Tricare (September 2011)

How It Happened:
Tricare fell victim to a physical breach when backup tapes of electronic health records were stolen from a car. The tapes were being transported and not adequately secured, showcasing the importance of physical safeguards and cybersecurity measures.

Impact:
Around five million patients had their information exposed. This breach was significant due to the sheer volume of data lost and the nature of the data, which included a vast amount of sensitive health information.

Damage:
The breach likely led to a significant erosion of trust among Tricare's clientele. Due to the nature of the breach, Tricare had to bolster its cybersecurity measures and physical security protocols. They faced potential legal ramifications and financial costs associated with notifications, investigations, and remediation efforts.

2. Community Health Systems (April–June 2014)

How It Happened:
The hack of Community Health Systems occurred as a result of thieves exploiting a software vulnerability over a period of many months. The cyberattack exploited a vulnerability in the system's security infrastructure, enabling unauthorized individuals to run malicious software and illicitly acquire confidential patient information.

Impact:
The breach significantly impacted many individuals, with around 4.5 million patients affected. The perpetrators were able to obtain sensitive personal information.

Damage:
The aftermath saw Community Health Systems grappling with the dual blow of a tarnished reputation and

Table 28.1 High-Impact Data Breaches in the Last Decade

Organization	Date	Impact (Patients Affected)	Incident Description	Compromised Data
Tricare	Sep-11	5 million	Theft of backup tapes from a car.	Social security numbers, names, addresses, health data, clinical notes, lab tests, prescriptions
Community Health Systems	Jun-14	4.5 million	Exploited software vulnerability.	Names, DOB, Social Security numbers, phone numbers, addresses
UCLA Health	Jul-15	4.5 million	Cyberattack.	Names, DOB, social security numbers, Medicaid, health plan IDs, some medical data
Advocate Health Care	Aug-13	4 million	Theft of unencrypted computers.	Names, addresses, DOB, credit card numbers, health info
Medical Informatics Engineering	Jul-15	3.9 million	Compromised username/ password.	Names, phone numbers, addresses, DOB, social security numbers, lab results, health insurance info
Newkirk Products	Jul-16	3.8 million	Cybercriminals accessed a server.	Primary care info, Medicaid IDs, patient names, DOB, invoice info
Banner Health	Aug-16	3.6 million	Unauthorized access to a private server.	Patient names, addresses, DOB, social security info, appointments
Trinity Health	May-20	3.3 million	Ransomware attack on a third-party vendor.	Full names, addresses, email, DOB, health providers, medical records, lab results, meds, claims, some financial info
OneTouchPoint (OTP)	Jul-22	2.6 million	Files locked and decrypted, third-party involvement.	Names, addresses, DOB, medical records, employee details, service descriptions, diagnosis codes
Shields Healthcare Group	Mar-22	2 million	Unauthorized network access.	Full names, social security numbers, DOB, addresses, provider info, diagnosis, billing info, insurance numbers, medical records
Broward Health	Jan-22	1.3 million	Breach via third-party medical provider.	Names, addresses, DOB, driver's license numbers, insurance info, medical info
Morley Companies	Feb-22	0.5 million	Ransomware attack.	Names, addresses, social security numbers, DOB, client IDs, medical diagnostic/treatment info, health insurance
L'Assurance Maladie	Mar-22	0.5 million	19 accounts compromised.	Names, surnames, DOB, social security numbers, GP details, reimbursement levels
ARcare	Feb-22	0.3 million	Unauthorized system access.	Names, social security numbers, license numbers, DOB, financial info, medical treatment info, prescriptions, diagnosis, health insurance

significant financial losses. Alongside immediate remediation efforts, they likely faced the prospect of regulatory scrutiny, potential lawsuits, and the need for a long-term strategy to ensure such a breach didn't reoccur.

3. UCLA Health (July 2015)

How It Happened:
UCLA Health became the target of a sophisticated cyber-attack that compromised their digital databases. There was unauthorized access to parts of their network that contained personal and medical information.

Impact:
The breach impacted 4.5 million people, exposing various types of data, even particular health-related data, and Medicaid numbers.

Damage:
Apart from the immediate data compromise, UCLA Health faced a significant challenge in regaining the trust of its patients and stakeholders. The breach required them to invest heavily in cybersecurity infrastructure improvements and engage in comprehensive communication campaigns to assure patients of their data's safety. Legal costs, potential penalties, and long-term cybersecurity investments added to the financial burden of the breach.

HEALTHCARE'S DIGITAL SAFEGUARDS: CYBERSECURITY AND PRIVACY REGULATIONS

The healthcare business abides by many cybersecurity rules, which contain the following elements:

- HIPAA establishes specific criteria for maintaining confidentiality and security measures for PHI within the United States. Healthcare organizations must adhere to HIPAA to implement administrative, physical, and technical processes that safeguard personally identifiable health information (PHI) while encompassing privacy, availability, and integrity (HIPAA of 1996; CDC).
- The National Institute of Standards and Technology (NIST) developed a cybersecurity framework that includes numerous rules, benchmarks, and best practices to safeguard information systems within the United States. The Cybersecurity Framework provided by NIST presents a technique focused on managing risks associated with cybersecurity issues.
- The International Organization for Standardization (ISO) provides a range of cybersecurity standards, with one notable example being the ISO 27001 standard, which focuses on establishing and maintaining information security management systems. The establishment, implementation, maintenance, and continual improvement of information security management systems may be achieved by employing the framework delineated in the ISO 27001 standard. The subject under consideration is ISO 27799:2016 (en), a standard that deals with health informatics and especially concentrates on managing information security in the healthcare industry, employing ISO/IEC 27002.
- The European Union Agency for Cybersecurity (ENISA) offers advice and recommendations to the EU in relation to cybersecurity standards, with a particular emphasis on the health sector. The guidelines provided by ENISA cover a wide array of subjects, such as risk management, incident response, and processes for ensuring the security of information systems.
- The Payment Card Industry Data Security Standard (PCI DSS) is a crucial and obligatory protocol for businesses that process credit card transactions. Healthcare organizations that accept card payments must comply with the PCI DSS, notwithstanding its limited relevance to the healthcare industry.

The selection of an appropriate cybersecurity standard for the healthcare industry is contingent upon various factors, including the company's dimensions, intricacy, risk profile, and other pertinent variables. HIPAA is a vital regulatory requirement for healthcare organizations operating within the United States, as it is a mandate in law. The NIST framework provides a customizable and adaptable strategy based on risk assessment, catering to the specific requirements of healthcare organizations. The healthcare industry uses the framework widely. The ISO 27001 standard outlines a comprehensive strategy for managing data security in hospitals with advanced information systems. Healthcare enterprises that are active within the European Union (EU) have the potential to derive advantages from the suggestions provided by ENISA.

HIPAA

HIPAA mandates stringent regulations on managing, disseminating, and securing PHI, granting specific rights to individuals. Ensuring compliance with HIPAA is essential for relevant entities, not just to evade financial penalties but also to maintain the trust and confidence of their patients.

The Privacy and Security Rules constitute the fundamental components of HIPAA. The Privacy Rule regulates the authorized use and dissemination of PHI by entities obligated to adhere to its regulations. The Privacy Rule confers certain rights on individuals concerning their PHI.

Conversely, the Security Rule specifies federal mandates for safeguarding electronic protected health information (ePHI). In accordance with HIPAA regulatory mandates, enterprises falling within its purview must enforce administrative, physical, and technical measures to ensure the confidentiality, accessibility, and reliability of safeguarded PHI. The Security Regulation demands that organizations subject to its provisions do regular risk studies to identify potential security risks and weaknesses and then implement appropriate countermeasures.

From the viewpoint of a healthcare professional, it is crucial to prioritize compliance with HIPAA. Hospitals must develop and execute suitable policies, processes, and security protocols to protect or preserve PHI's confidentiality and integrity. The actions involve implementing appropriate access controls, such as individual user identification and password systems, and providing comprehensive training to staff regarding the regulations outlined in HIPAA and the proper handling of PHI. Additionally, individuals must be well prepared to address instances of HIPAA violations, which can result in severe financial penalties and other punitive measures.

GDPR

The EU implemented the GDPR in May 2018. GDPR is comprehensive and wide-ranging data privacy legislation. The legislation aims to enhance individual privacy rights, harmonize data protection regulations among EU member states, and enhance enterprises' practices concerning collecting, using, and managing personal data. This regulation represents an update to the Data Protection Regulation of 1995.

The primary obligations of organizations according to the GDPR can be summarized as follows:

- Adherence to the expanded interpretation of personal data under the GDPR, which now includes a broader range of information capable of identifying individuals, including but not limited to IP addresses, biometric data, and social media posts.
- Organizations should obtain explicit and unambiguous consent from the respective person to collect, process, or use an individual's data. For organizations to proceed with any action, it is necessary to get clear, well-informed, and freely withdrawable consent at any time.
- The GDPR ensures that individuals are granted specific rights as data subjects, including accessing, rectifying, and erasing their data. Additionally, individuals can transfer data, allowing them to share their data with other entities.
- The GDPR mandates organizations to assess their impact. Data protection impact assessments (DPIAs) seek to evaluate, identify, and mitigate risks that may infringe on individual privacy when processing data.
- Under the GDPR, organizations should inform individuals who may have had their rights and freedoms compromised during a data breach. Additionally, they are required to declare such violations to the relevant supervisory body. Moreover, a declaration of violations should happen within 72 hours of gaining knowledge of any occurrence involving data.
- GDPR necessitates the appointment of data protection officers (DPOs) within enterprises to supervise and guarantee adherence to data protection requirements.
- The GDPR mandates accountability as a crucial component. It requires enterprises to establish appropriate organizational and technical measures to ensure adherence to the regulations and furnish supervisory agencies with evidence of compliance.

According to the GDPR, the non-compliance of an entity may result in a maximum penalty of €20 million or 4% of its annual revenues, whichever is more significant (Fines and Penalties, GDPR).

THE INFLUENCE OF REGULATORY MEASURES ON THE CYBERSECURITY IN HEALTHCARE SECTOR

Legislative acts such as the GDPR and HIPAA influence the development and use of cybersecurity strategies in healthcare enterprises. The regulations mentioned above serve to set regulatory standards on data privacy, security, and breach reporting, with the primary objective of safeguarding sensitive personal and health-related information.

To protect electronic health information, healthcare organizations must implement and maintain administrative, physical, and technical safeguards, as stipulated by HIPAA regulations in the United States (Besenyő & Kovács, 2023).

Within the EU, organizations responsible for administering personal data, including healthcare data, must comply with the GDPR. Data management entails implementing appropriate organizational and technological procedures to ensure the data's safety and security.

The subsequent examination might ascertain the impact of HIPAA and GDPR on cybersecurity measures in the healthcare sector.

The prevalence of cybersecurity threats in healthcare firms is on the rise, mainly attributed to adopting legal frameworks like HIPAA and the GDPR. The GDPR highlights the imperative of safeguarding patient data, emphasizing cybersecurity measures such as encryption keys, access control, and network monitoring.

IMPLEMENTING TECHNOLOGY SAFEGUARDS

Healthcare organizations must implement technical measures per the regulations outlined in HIPAA and the GDPR (Besenyő and Kovács, 2023). Numerous security measures encompass the use of firewalls, data encryption, and the deployment of two-factor authentication. Healthcare institutions have implemented multiple measures to ensure compliance with legal requirements and protect patient information.

Improve Employee Training and Sensitivity

HIPAA and the GDPR require healthcare organizations to provide their employees with comprehensive training and awareness programs regarding the significance of safeguarding data privacy and ensuring security measures. Healthcare organizations have established awareness campaigns and training programs to equip their personnel with cyberattack risks and mitigation strategies.

Compel Providers to Provide Notifications of Data Breaches

Healthcare enterprises are obligated under HIPAA and GDPR to inform the relevant authorities and affected individuals in the event of data breaches. Consequently, healthcare organizations have implemented rules and procedures for breach notification.

Increase Allocation of Funds Towards Cybersecurity Efforts

Healthcare organizations may incur significant costs to adhere to the regulations set forth by HIPAA and the GDPR. Organizations should improve adherence to the main regulations by increasing funds to fight cybersecurity and expanding their workforce through recruitment efforts.

ENHANCING CYBERSECURITY STRATEGIES AND POLICIES TO PROTECT HEALTHCARE DATA

The existing body of research provides empirical evidence that security awareness training helps mitigate cyberattack danger. According to a study by the Ponemon Institute (2020), firms implementing comprehensive security awareness training programs observe a notable decrease in security incidents resulting from employee irresponsibility.

In summary, the study commenced by posing the inquiry: Implementing routine cybersecurity training and awareness initiatives for healthcare personnel can potentially mitigate the likelihood of cybersecurity breaches targeting healthcare institutions. To safeguard sensitive patient data and uphold trust in their services, organizations can effectively achieve this by equipping their workers with the necessary information and tools to recognize and address any threats.

Implementing robust cybersecurity methods and laws is imperative to safeguard health data in contemporary digital healthcare. The increasing frequency, sophistication, and specificity of cyber threats and attacks require effective cybersecurity measures. Cyberattacks on healthcare firms can lead to a range of negative consequences, such as the infringement of patient privacy, financial ramifications, legal and regulatory repercussions, and damage to the company's brand.

Preserving patient confidentiality is a fundamental rationale for adopting and enforcing cybersecurity measures and protocols. Health data include confidential information about an individual's medical history, available treatment alternatives, and personal particulars. Implementing robust cybersecurity measures and protocols is necessary to protect sensitive data from unauthorized access and exposure. The potential consequences of compromising patient privacy are severe, encompassing reputational damage, legal liability, and erosion of public confidence.

Adopting appropriate cybersecurity methods and procedures in the health industry is crucial for preventing data breaches. Healthcare organizations are highly susceptible to cyberattacks because they possess vast amounts of sensitive data. The financial costs of remedying data breaches resulting from cyberattacks on healthcare enterprises can be substantial. At the same time, the negative impact on a company's reputation can last for an extended period of time. The implementation of robust cybersecurity methods and procedures has the potential to mitigate the consequences of data breaches and proactively deter their occurrence.

A LOOK AT THE FUTURE AND FUTURE-PROOF HEALTHCARE CYBERSECURITY STRATEGIES

In implementing cybersecurity objectives and policies within the healthcare sector, it is imperative to prioritize maintaining regulatory compliance. Consequently, healthcare providers are subject to several rules and standards, such as HIPAA. The primary objective is protecting individuals' personal information and guaranteeing and preserving their privacy. Effective cybersecurity methods and practices are essential for maintaining regulatory compliance and mitigating the risk of incurring fines.

The risk of cyberattacks has escalated as healthcare organizations increasingly depend on digital technologies and manage sensitive patient data. Social engineering is a prominent method of attack when attackers manipulate individuals to disclose confidential information or engage in activities that jeopardize their security. Healthcare personnel frequently exhibit a deficiency in their knowledge and expertise when recognizing and addressing such hazards.

Healthcare organizations can address cybersecurity risks by establishing frequent cybersecurity training and awareness initiatives to educate healthcare personnel about potential risks, optimal protocols, and incident reporting. These programs may encompass instruction on the identification of phishing emails, the detection of suspicious activities, the implementation of robust password practices, and the adherence to security protocols.

Moreover, experts recommend that healthcare enterprises engage in a comprehensive risk assessment to ascertain potential risks and vulnerabilities, aiming to develop effective cybersecurity strategies and protocols (Thamer & Alubady, 2021). Subsequently, it is advisable to use technological measures such as access controls, firewalls, and encryption, along with protocols and guidelines for data access, use, and retention. In addition, healthcare enterprises must develop and maintain regular training programs and awareness campaigns to educate staff members on cybersecurity threats and optimal protocols.

In addition to the rationales above, efficient cybersecurity techniques and protocols can effectively mitigate financial losses. Healthcare facilities are susceptible to cybercrime, posing significant financial burdens. A cyberattack has the potential to lead to financial detriment, reputational damage, and substantial legal expenses. However, implementing effective cybersecurity strategies and protocols is critical to preventing losses attributed to cyberattacks.

Given the accelerating digitization of the healthcare sector and the rise of sophisticated cyber threats like ransomware, mere compliance with legislative frameworks like HIPAA or GDPR is insufficient. While these frameworks provide a foundational structure for data protection, there's an imperative need for healthcare organizations to adopt a more proactive and layered approach to cybersecurity. According to organizations like ENISA and NIST, integrating advanced threat intelligence, ongoing employee training, and adopting frameworks specifically designed for current cyber threats will be crucial (Kolias, Kambourakis, Stavrou, & Voas, 2017). The literature and evolving threat landscape highlight the importance of expanding and updating cybersecurity measures in the healthcare sector.

References

Abraham, C., Chatterjee, D., & Sims, R.R. (2019). Muddling through cybersecurity: Insights from the US healthcare industry. *Business Horizons*, *62*(4), 539–548.

Advocate Aurora says 3M patients' health data possibly exposed through tracking technologies. (n.d.). Fierce healthcare. https://www.fiercehealthcare.com/health-tech/advocate-aurora-health-data-breach-revealed-pixels-protected-health-information-3. Accessed: February 24, 2023

Alese, B.K., Thompson, A.F., Owa, K.V., Iyare, O., & Adebayo, O.T. (2014). Analyzing issues of cyber threats in Nigeria. In: Proceedings of the World Congress on Engineering. [online] World Conference on Engineering. London, UK: World Congress on Engineering, pp. 7. Available at: https://www.researchgate.net/publication/271844509_Analysing_Issues_of_Cyber_Threats_in_Nigeria. Accessed: March 1, 2023

Baz, M., Alhakami, H., Agrawal, A., Baz, A., & Ahmad Khan, R. (2021). Impact of COVID-19 pandemic: A cybersecurity perspective. *Intelligent Automation & Soft Computing*, *27*(3), 641–652. 10.32604/iasc.2021.015845

Besenyő, J., Márton, K., & Shaffer, R. (2021). Hospital attacks since 9/11: An analysis of terrorism targeting healthcare facilities and workers. *Studies in Conflict & Terrorism*, 47, 36–59. 10.1080/1057610X.2021.1937821.

Brady, J.W. (2011). Securing health care: assessing factors that affect HIPAA security compliance in academic medical centers. In 2011 44th Hawaii International Conference on System Sciences (HICSS 2011). IEEE. 10.1109/hicss.2011.368

Cost of a data breach 2022. (2022). IBM – Deutschland | IBM. https://www.ibm.com/reports/data-breach. Accessed: February 24, 2023

2022 Data Breach Investigations Report. (2021). Verizon business. https://www.verizon.com/about/news/verizon-2021-data-breach-investigations-report. Accessed: March 1, 2023

Fines/Penalties – General Data Protection Regulation (GDPR). (2016). General Data Protection Regulation (GDPR). https://gdpr-info.eu/issues/fines-penalties/#:~:text=83(4)%20GDPR%20sets%20forth,to%20that%20used%20in%20Art. Accessed: February 24, 2023.

Garba, A., & Bade, A. (2021). The current state of cybersecurity readiness in Nigeria organizations. *International Journal of Multidisciplinary and Current Educational Research*, [online] *3*(1), 154–162. https://www.ijmcer.com/wp-content/uploads/2021/02/IJMCER_U03101540162.pdf. Accessed: March 1, 2023

Health Insurance Portability and Accountability Act of 1996 (HIPAA) | CDC. (1996) Centers for Disease Control and Prevention. https://www.cdc.gov/phlp/publications/topic/hipaa.html. Accessed: March 20, 2023

Health Information Technology (IT). (n.d.). NIST. https://www.nist.gov/healthcare. Accessed: February 24, 2023

Health sector. (2014). ENISA. https://www.enisa.europa.eu/topics/critical-information-infrastructures-and-services/health. Accessed: February 24, 2023

Hathaliya, J.J., & Tanwar, S. (2020). An exhaustive survey on security and privacy issues in healthcare 4.0. *Computer Communications*, *153*, 311–335. 10.1016/j.comcom.2020.02.018.2020.02.018.

He, Y., Aliyu, A., Evans, M., & Luo, C. (2021). Health care cybersecurity challenges and solutions under the climate of COVID-19: Scoping review. *Journal of Medical Internet Research*, *23*(4), Article e21747. 10.2196/21747

ISO 27799:2016(en) Health informatics — Information security management in health using ISO/IEC 27002. (2016). Online Browsing Platform (OBP). https://www.iso.org/obp/ui/#iso:std:iso:27799:ed-2:v1:en. Accessed: February 24, 2023

Jalali, M.S., & Kaiser, J.P. (2018). Cybersecurity in hospitals: A systematic, organizational perspective. *Journal of Medical Internet Research*, *20*(5), e10059.

Kim, Lee JD, BS, CIPP/US, CISSP, FHIMSS Cybersecurity awareness, Nursing Management (Springhouse): (April 2017), *48*(4), 16–19

Kshetri, N. (2019). Cybercrime and cybersecurity in Africa. *Journal of Global Information Technology Management, 22*(2), 77–81.

Litan, R.E., & Rivlin, A.M. (2001). *The globalization of technology: Implications for developing countries*. Brookings Institution Press.

Markopoulou, D., & Papakonstantinou, V. (2021). The regulatory framework for the protection of critical infrastructures against cyber threats: Identifying shortcomings and addressing future challenges: The case of the health sector in particular. *Computer Law & Security Review, 41* (2021), 105502. 10.1016/j.clsr.2020.105502

Nnanwube, E.F., Ani, K.J., & Ojakorotu, V. (2019). Emerging issues around cyber crimes in Nigeria. *Ubuntu: Journal of Conflict Transformation, 1*(1), 55–71.

Notice of Data Security Incident. (n.d.). CommonSpirit Health | Compassionate Care for Our Communities. https://www.commonspirit.org/update/notice-of-data-security-incident. Accessed: February 24, 2023

Notice of Data Security Incident – Shields Health. (n.d.). Shields Health. https://shields.com/notice-of-data-security-incident/. Accessed: February 24, 2023

Offner, K.L., Sitnikova, E., Joiner, K., & MacIntyre, C.R. (2020). Towards understanding cybersecurity capability in Australian healthcare organizations: A systematic review of recent trends, threats, and mitigation. *Intelligence and National Security, 35*(4), 556–585.

Omogbolagun, T. (2023, November 22). Senate laments Nigeria's loss of $500m annually to cybercrime. PUNCH. https://punchng.com/senate-laments-nigerias-loss-of-500m-annually-to-cybercrime/

Ponemon Institute (2020). Cost of insider threats: Global report. https://www.exclusive-networks.com/uk/wp-content/uploads/sites/28/2020/12/UK-VR-Proofpoint-Report-2020-Cost-of-Insider-Threats.pdf. Accessed: March 24, 2023

Raburu, E.E. (2021). A cybersecurity model for the health sector: A case study of hospitals in Nairobi, Kenya (Doctoral dissertation, United States International University-Africa).

Romaniuk, S. N., and Manjikian, M. (Eds.). (2021). *Routledge companion to global cyber-security strategy*. Abingdon: Routledge.

Saheed, Y.K., & Arowolo, M.O. (2021). Efficient cyber attack detection on the internet of medical things-smart environment based on deep recurrent neural network and machine learning algorithms. *IEEE Access, 9*, 161546–161554. 10.1109/access.2021.3128837.

Sills, M., Ranade, P., & Mittal, S. (2020, November). Cybersecurity threat intelligence augmentation and embedding improvement-a healthcare use case. In 2020 IEEE International Conference on Intelligence and Security Informatics (ISI) (pp. 1–6). IEEE.

Smith, A., & Anderson, M. (2016). Americans and cybersecurity. Pew Research Center. https://www.pewresearch.org/internet/2016/01/26/americans-and-cybersecurity/

Swasey, K. (2020). Insufficient healthcare cybersecurity invites ransomware attacks and sale of phi on the dark web. Center for Anticipatory Intelligence Student Research Reports.

Thamer, N., & Alubady, R. (2021). A Survey of ransomware attacks for healthcare systems: Risks, challenges, solutions and opportunity of research. In: 2021 1st Babylon International Conference on Information Technology and Science (BICITS) (pp. 210–216)

US Department of Health & Human Services – Office for Civil Rights. (accessed for 2020 data.). US Department of Health & Human Services – Office for Civil Rights. https://ocrportal.hhs.gov/ocr/breach/breach_report.jsf. Accessed: February 24, 2023.

Washington, C., Yarbrough, P., Parker, S., Islam, R., Patamsetti, V.V., & Abiona, O. (2022). Information assurance technique for mitigation of data breaches in the human service sector. *International Journal of Communications, Network and System Sciences, 15*(2), 15–30.

PART III

CASE STUDIES

Africa

29

JIHAD IN THE HORN OF AFRICA

Somalia's Al-Shabaab Islamist Insurgency

James Okolie-Osemene and Scott N. Romaniuk

INTRODUCTION

Insurgencies have emerged as one of the most serious threats to global security, undermining both internal and cross-border security. The problem is that most Islamist insurgent groups now tend to speak with one voice or establish networks that facilitate the coordination of attacks. Africa is one of the continents that have become flashpoints for new security threats and the growing deployment of state security providers to contain the activities of insurgent groups with a militarisation option that is usually backed by the establishment of Special Forces units or joint task forces (Herbst, 2004). Consequently, the continent's security planners have been preoccupied with defence planning, increasing budgetary allocation for militaries, expansion of armies and mobilisation of troops against rebels and insurgents, security sector reforms, and intelligence-led policing to meet the dynamic challenges of public safety. The Horn of Africa (HoF) is one of the strategic parts of the African continent.

Jihad was historically a tool created by religious movements to compel loyalty, quell resistance, and punish unbelievers. Jihad displays no mercy to perceived adversaries. Usman Dan Fodio, for instance, launched a war against Northern Nigeria's rulers and populace in 1804, accusing them of supporting and maintaining pagan architecture. The successful mission finally paved the way for the founding of the Sokoto Caliphate, which still exists today in modern-day Nigeria and where the Sultan is the Muslim community's highest authority. Jihad is not practised in the same manner it once was in modern-day Africa. Even non-state actors now carry out assaults with a religious motivation, notably extremist groups.

Over the course of fifteen years, Al-Shabaab has demonstrated itself to be the most radicalised and sophisticated militant organisation on the African continent. It possesses the ability to carry out targeted assaults on government officials, security personnel, commercial enterprises, and academic establishments through the use of intelligence-driven tactics, thereby posing a significant threat to both individual and national security. After enduring prolonged periods of insecurity, various groups may choose to employ coping mechanisms in anticipation of a cessation of violence.

RECENT DEVELOPMENTS

The US government and other allies of Somalia, such as Kenya, Djibouti, and Ethiopia, cooperate to deter Al-Shabaab operations in the region. The US ambassador to Somalia, Larry Andre, stated that the Somali government's military operations against al-Shabab have cost the militants one-third of their territory. Since January 2023, the United States has donated weapons to the Somali national forces to support operations against al-Shabab. The US also trains an elite Somali army unit known as Danab, which means "lightning," which has been leading the offensive against al-Shabab. The Somali Ministry of Information stated that 3,000 al-Shabab militants were killed and 3,700 were injured in military operations between August 2022 and January 2023. The government reported that 70 towns have been liberated from al-Shabab (Voice of America, March 28, 2023). Somalia hosted a summit of leaders from several countries in the Horn of Africa to discuss the fight against al-Shabab. The meeting in Mogadishu drew leaders from Kenya's William Ruto, Djibouti's Ismail Omar Guelleh, and Ethiopia's Prime Minister Abiy Ahmed. Somali leader Hassan Sheikh Mohamud and his counterparts discussed implementing a coordinated military offensive against the al-Qaeda-linked group (Al Jazeera, February 1, 2023). Kenyan security forces have killed ten fighters from the Somalia-based al-Shabab group in eastern Kenya. During the course of the operations, the troops also recovered rocket-propelled grenades and

DOI: 10.4324/9780429426063-33

improvised explosive devices in the village of Galmagalla in Garissa County (Al-Jazeera, January 20, 2023).

Al-Shabaab continued to launch terrorist attacks. On January 4, 2023, Al-Shabaab terrorists killed five civilians and set off a bomb when they stormed a government building in Somalia's capital, Mogadishu. The terrorists charged into the block that houses the office of Mogadishu's mayor around noon and engaged in a firefight with security forces (Al Jazeera, January 5, 2023). Fighters from the al-Shabab group stormed a military base in central Somalia that the government had recaptured from them last year, killing seven soldiers, including the base commander. Terrorists rammed the base in the village of Hawadley with a suicide car bomb and then opened fire (Al Jazeera, January 17, 2023).

RELIGION AND CONFLICT IN SOMALIA

The fact that Somalia is a multiethnic society does not mean that religion has not played a role in the evolution of conflict in the country. The large population of Muslims in the Horn of Africa has been linked to the belief that the instability in Somalia now has a religious connection (Omeje, 2007). The armed conflict in Somalia has been explained from different viewpoints. A notable perspective is the sacralization of conflict, which refers to "the process through which religion, or, in most cases, a militant interpretation of it, evolves from being an irrelevant or secondary factor at the onset of a conflict to shaping the views, actions, and aims of one or more of the conflict's key actors" (Vidino et al., 2010, p. 217). From this definition, it is obvious that the instability is religious-centred, having links with a group that uses religious belief as a yardstick to launch attacks in order to enforce strict adherence to its so-called principles that are expected of people.

In the wake of state failure in the 1990s, the armed Islamic Courts sought to provide security and justice to the extent that they recruited young men from the locality to achieve the task of containing aggression by the warlords and later formed the Union of Islamic Courts (UIC), which defeated the warlords in early 2006. Since then, Al-Shabaab has always used religion as an instrument of recruitment by accusing perceived infidels of dividing the country in their bid to form ministates, and this religious perspective disregards the secular (Ingiriis, 2020). This was achieved by the group, which emerged as a faction of the then-UIC in the country, adopting its Islamist ideology as a framework of operation.

ORIGINS AND IDEOLOGY

The origin of Al-Shabaab is traceable to the state failure in Somalia, which is a product of militant Islamism with popular support since 2005 and growing international support, which created a platform for terrorist activities (Hoehne, 2009; Lee, 2011; United States Department of State, 2010). This is also traceable to the clan affiliations that contributed to the fall of Barre's government in 1991, which had earlier proclaimed a socialist state in 1970 that paved the way for close relations with the USSR (Weis, 2011). It was found that in order to achieve the insurgent-terror group's aim to transcend clan and establish an Islamic state with strict implementation of Sharia law, they cooperated with clan and sub-clan elders as well as warlords and their militias (Hoehne, 2009).

Mushtaq (2014b, p. 10) stated that "Somali clans had fought one another for 15 years before the rise of al-Shabaab and the internationalisation of the Somali civil war, to the extent that the politics is dominated by Islamists of different shades." However, the historical antecedent of Al-Shabaab is traceable to the formation of Al-Ittihad Al-Islami (AIAI, called Unity of Islam), a militant Salafi group that climaxed in the 1990s after the collapse of the Siad Barre military regime, which lasted from 1969 to 1991 (Ansel, 2011; Masters & Sergie, 2015). After the period of turbulence, Operation Restore Hope was formed in the early 1990s to restore stability (Mushtaq, 2014a). Al-Shabaab is a product of the factionalisation that greeted the disagreement of rivals during the AIAI conference, when some radical Afghan-trained Somali men stormed out opposing the planned creation of a Salafi political organisation that would have sustained the status quo, leaving the dissidents in a perceived marginalised position with less power and influence (Shinn, 2010).

The group is an extremist group that has an Islamic identity and identifies with groups that have related interests. Most of the members have been trained in accordance with jihadi credentials, such as Adan Hashi Ayro, Mukhtar Robow, and Ahmed Abdi Godani, to the extent that Al-Shabaab is perceived as an individual pragmatic social movement, a political voice in Somalia, and a contestant in the international community with an ideology that threatens other actors (Clos, 2011; Hoehne, 2009; Lee, 2011). Al-Shabaab released a video in 2008 inviting young Muslims to join their campaign (Shinn, 2010). This eventually prepared the ground for their formal recognition and allegiance to the ideology of the same group. According to Cordano (2015, p. 1), "the group that formally pledged allegiance to al-Qaeda in February 2012 professes a quasi-Salafist ideology with a notable Wahhabist inflection." According to the United States Department of State (2010, p. 31), Al-Shabaab consists of a diverse collection of armed clan militias that receive training from typically foreign fighters with ties to al-Qaeda.

Over the years, Al-Shabaab has been operating in tandem with the global jihadist ideology, which prioritises extremism and radicalisation. To advance its ideology, the group endeavours to radicalise people and make them fighters. Radicalisation reflects an increasing involvement and commitment to violent extremism, an increasing receptiveness towards radical ideology, and internalising the beliefs as part of one's social identity (Neo, 2019). The group is usually in the business of indoctrinating fighters into Al-Shabaab martyrdom ideology, taking them through explosives training to identify the on/off switches that are critical for suicide missions (Speckhard and Shajkovci, 2019). The declaration of then-leader Godane in 2009 showed their intention to fight an endless battle for the actualisation of Islamic Shar'ia and implementation in all parts of the world, with the liberation of Jerusalem for Muslims in view, and this is in tandem with the radical Islamist creed of al Qaeda, which instructs a true believer to wage jihad in an effort to create a global place of Islam (Solomon, 2014). It is believed that without violence, this Islamic world cannot become a reality. Therefore, it is not disputable that violence, radicalisation, and indoctrination are the vehicles of the group's ideology.

ORGANISATION AND LEADERSHIP

The insurgent-jihadi group is a highly organised, violent, armed group with operational oversight that is commanded with discipline.

Shura is the top leadership structure, which operates with consensus and is saddled with the responsibility of examining and discussing relevant issues that would promote the development of the organisation, such as strategic decisions, ideological issues, politics, and military affairs (Marchal, 2011). Al-Shabaab is organised in three layers: the top leadership (qiyadah), the foreign fighters (muhajirin), and the local Somali fighters (ansar). With an 85-member executive council, including 42 Somalis and 43 foreigners, the leadership structure shows the group has a commander-in-chief, a deputy leader, a finance department, advisers, directors of training, the recruitment of suicide bombers, an intelligence service, a military and logistics department, and a transport department (Shinn, 2010; Maruf & Joseph, 2018). The group has a structure that guarantees the payment of members' salaries; Al-Shabaab has been able to pay salaries to all its members (Marchal, 2011). There is also a multi-layered governance system, such as sharia courts, missionary propagation (dawa), tax and revenue collection, and the distribution of religious charity (zakat) (Jonsson & Torbjörnsson, 2016).

Strict adherence to Sharia is the priority of the group, which guides their action and direction within the rank and file of the organisation (Ingiriis, 2020). The significance of this sharia legal system is that it prevents members from acting beyond their limits, and they would be punished accordingly without delay. It also offers the group an advantage in the recruitment and indoctrination of new members. The organisation is emboldened by the ability of leaders to go for the best hands and highly committed individuals who subscribe to its ideology, establishing networks that facilitate the desire to mobilise human and material resources for the sustenance of the jihadist agenda.

In terms of leadership, Al-Shabaab has always had easy succession to the extent that the decapitation or downfall of its leaders does not impede the group's campaigns and has little or no limitation on the capacity of the existing fighters to adopt a leader they are loyal to after such counterinsurgency efforts that succeeded in tracking down some of the leaders. The United States has been notorious for adopting a decapitation approach to annihilate Al-Shabaab leaders through consistent attacks. So far, the group has produced radical leaders that changed the social and political affairs of East Africa for decades, with increasing footprints of jihadist members of the group. The year 2008 cannot be forgotten by the group, when a well-planned and launched missile strike by the USA killed then-leader Aden Hashi Ayro, who was succeeded by Ahmed Abdi Godane (Mutanda, 2017). Also, a co-founder of the group, Ibrahim al-Afghani, was killed by an Ahmed Godane-led faction in 2013 (Cordano, 2015). This was part of the internal upheaval that threatened the existence of the group when hostility perception led to friction among some stakeholders in the group.

After the demise of then-leader Ahmed Abdi Godane in a drone strike by the USA in 2014, Ahmed Umar (Abu Ubaidah) became Al-Shabaab leader, and his capacity to manage the affairs of members using tact to sustain the confidence of commanders has stabilised the group, unlike Godane's era between 2012 and 2013, which was characterised by a rivalry that climaxed in the infighting that led to his elimination of rivals (Maruf & Joseph, 2018; Sergie, 2020). The transformation of the group by Godane from a nationalist Islamic insurgency into a transnational Al-Qaeda affiliate capable of administering large parts of southern Somalia laid the foundation for Sheikh Ahmed Umar, who succeeded Godane, as his leadership empowered the group to export violence to Kenya in 2015 and intensify attacks in the Somali capital (Mutanda, 2017). It appears that the leaders have suffered the same fate, having the same pattern of death through lethal violence. The leadership styles of previous and current leaders may have minimised the danger of more splinter factions emerging from the group, though not without threats. Nevertheless, the group has a territorial advantage and the capacity to maintain order within its strongholds to the detriment of the government of Somalia, which is threatened by the activities of the insurgents, who undermine policymakers' security governance efforts.

FOREIGN FIGHTERS

The need to sustain the intensity and firepower of groups, in addition to numerical increases and tactical needs, explains why armed groups opt for foreign fighters. Foreign fighters are different individuals who are involved in the insurgency from outside. The involvement of foreign fighters in the campaign has rather enhanced the sophistication of the group. According to Mendelsohn (2010), the phenomenon of foreign fighters refers to a situation where volunteers leave their homes to get involved in a confrontation occurring in a foreign location, where they may be camped as mercenaries to boost the prospects of the group they support in the asymmetric conflict with the aim of enhancing the lethality of the non-state armed group.

Foreign fighters are divided into three categories: Somalis who were born across the borders in neighbouring countries, like Kenya, and are nationals of the countries; Somalis who were born in Somalia or whose parents were born in Somalia but grew up in diaspora and now carry a foreign passport; and foreigners who have no Somali ethnic connection, with the first and second categories dominating the number in a higher proportion (Shinn, 2010). About 1800 foreign fighters are believed to have been recruited (Solomon, 2014).

The ability to establish recruitment networks and psychologically appeal to or influence the mindsets of target recruits has given the insurgent group an advantage. This has become effective due to the use of charismatic personalities to get people enrolled. In Sweden, the use of Bellevue mosque in Göteborg to recruit fighters through discussions involving leaders from both sides, as well as the use of a youth recreation centre in Rinkeby, which is a suburb of Stockholm, where a Somali cleric, Sheikh Fuad Mohammed Qalaf, leads the way, all explain how the group got volunteers from Sweden to join their campaign of terror (Vidino et al., 2010). Notably, for a group that is locally based with a global mindset, the group was able to utilise the Internet to appeal to people in the UK and USA, including the Somali diaspora in the US and the UK, and those in other African countries to accept their recruitment drive, and this is easier when they are sympathetic to the group (Vidino et al., 2010; Mutanda, 2017). This makes it a transnational terrorist-insurgent organisation that has the capacity to influence and attract interested fighters to volunteer and accept its ideology. With time, foreign fighters are expected to learn the terrain from the local fighters.

Apart from relatives, friends and acquaintances within neighbourhoods have also been instrumental in the radicalisation and recruitment of fighters abroad. An example is the Minneapolis network, which watched videos of extremist activities and established communication with people in Somalia to facilitate their involvement on arrival from the USA (Vidino et al., 2010). This points to the truism that Al-Shabaab does not need to be physically present within some enclaves to penetrate the neighbourhoods and attract recruits as long as the group has the appeal to influence individual decisions using incentives.

MAKING FRIENDS, KEEPING ENEMIES

One of the features of non-state armed groups is their capacity to make friends and identify enemies, creating networks and breaking protocols where necessary. Relations with other militant groups and the opposition have been established.

Friends of the group are those who have similar jihadist objectives that also drive their activities in their localities. For a group that enjoys the endorsement of al Qaeda, which remains one of the most notorious extremist organisations in the world, establishing a formidable group that has al Qaeda's type of insurgent radical group will be an achievement in the Horn of Africa and beyond. During the formation years of Al-Shabaab, four al Qaeda instructors visited Somalia with the aim of training fighters associated with the Islamic Union, AIAI (al Ittihad al Islami), in advanced combat tactics of guerrilla warfare and weapons handling so as to equip them with the needed skills that would position them for confrontation with the United States forces in the Horn of Africa in their bid to establish a formidable Islamic state in Greater Somalia (Vidino et al., 2010). This operation-focused defence preparedness has remained the foundation of the group's operations, and the existence of such a state will eventually remain a potential threat to the entire region as far as security is concerned.

Since the rise of Islamic State, the majority of extremist organisations have worked to forge connections with the Al-Qaeda-affiliated Islamic group in Somalia, transforming it into a global extremist organisation (Speckhard & Shajkovci, 2019). For instance, ISIS claimed responsibility for the bombing in northern Somalia and the gun attacks in February and October 2017 on a hotel in Bosaso, Puntland, which resulted in several fatalities, but the Al-Shabaab leaders refused to acknowledge their loyalty to ISIS (Shay, 2018). The fact that extremist groups are unpredictable and should not be taken seriously, despite some statements to the contrary, is an important argument in this case. Since the Boko Haram group acknowledged Al-Shabaab for having a big part in coordinating training for its jihadist fighters with the objective of duplicating Al-Shabaab's success in Nigeria, the two groups get along well, which renders Nigeria unstable (Solomon, 2012). Al-Shabaab may now spread terror outside of the Horn of Africa because of this. The goal of the jihadi training was to toughen and hone their fighting and planning abilities against the security forces. Due to their financial contributions that help the group's purpose be accomplished, Al-Shabaab has also not taken for granted the substantial assistance of some diaspora stakeholders, particularly the Somalis living in Sweden (Vidino et al., 2010).

In keeping enemies, the group has not overlooked any individual or group that attempts to work against the group's purpose or spy on their activities with the intention of serving as government informants. Such individuals are frequently targeted and apprehended. Making friends and keeping foes as tasks that must not be compromised have been prioritised by the group

AL-SHABAAB'S STRATEGY

Strategic thinking has remained the driver of Al-Shabaab's strategy. Knowing when to execute a plan, identify targets, and adopt strategic withdrawal are some of the ways to make it appear invisible and reduce losses. The group's strategy which can be described as a guerrilla strategy backed by improvised machinery, involves a combination of different tactics, such as strategic withdrawal and avoidance of direct confrontation when clashes escalates, deployment of fighters to storm high-risk areas, the use of grenade and mortar shelling, ambushes, human shields, tank traps, the use of snipers, targeted assassinations using both firearms and explosive devices, hit-and-run attacks and the use of improvised explosive devices (IEDs), and non-suicide vehicle bombs, that affect hotels, military bases and some government institutions (Anzalone, 2018; Hansen, 2011; Jonsson & Torbjörnsson, 2016; Meservey, 2013; Mutanda, 2017; Williams & Bruton, 2014). Escalations of battles forced the group to change terrorism tactics and switch to an insurgency strategy. All these, which point to Al-Shabaab's audacity to use weapons, are done with the intention of overwhelming the security forces, who usually record casualties when taken unawares or attempting to repel such attacks even at so-called highly secured places.

Tactically, Al-Shabaab adopted greatly from the playbooks of the Taliban and al Qaeda to the extent that suicide bombing, which was strange to Somali culture and opposed by the clan system, became a national security threat (Shinn, 2010; Hansen, 2011). To its advantage, military and civilian targets remain the focus, attracting the attention of the group. The jihadi-insurgent group retains significant capabilities to launch a range of attacks targeting both military and soft targets, including major suicide-vehicle bombings inside the most secure areas of the country, such as hotels and government buildings in central Mogadishu (Anzalone, 2018). The soft targets have always been unsuspecting individuals, including women, children, and politicians, who seem to lack security provisions and easily fall victim to the group's military strategy. Knowing the asymmetric nature of the insurgency and counterinsurgency, their security planners usually ensure that they procure weapons that give them a strategic advantage, thereby complicating the enemy's counterinsurgency efforts.

SOCIAL MEDIA

In the 21st century, the media is instrumental to information dissemination in society, and the problem with such media is its unregulated use by individuals and non-state actors, most of whom often use such platforms for illicit purposes, thereby making it somewhat complex for state security providers and the government to track. The internal (within the group) and external (targeting local population) use of social media by the group has all given it an advantage both in recruitment, for numerical increase, and in winning the sympathy, minds, and hearts of the people.

With private telecommunication companies establishing network coverage in many parts of the country and information and communication technology becoming part of Somalia's identity, people have been attracted to the virtual world (Burke, 2018). Social media enables extremist groups to extend their outreach and share information with the public (Neo, 2019). Terrorists have found the Internet to be useful for their goals, which have been categorised into outreach, logistics, and attack, which give them an image-making advantage to the extent that they are not bordered by having multiple social network accounts as long as their campaign is sustained (Mair, 2016; Mutanda, 2017).

Al-Shabaab, as previously mentioned by Mutanda (2017), uses Twitter's wider audience to sway public opinion with the aim of persuading people outside of Somalia that the organisation is more people-oriented and understands the plight of people than governments that work together to quell the insurgency. Social media has been used by Al-Shabaab combatants for psychological warfare, Internet surveillance and networking, radicalising fresh recruits, and maintaining propaganda. Social media was made simple to use by the accessibility of mobile phones and the Internet, which offer connections.

Social media remained one of the weapons of the insurgency by Al-Shabaab, which has an active online presence and uses it for both information dissemination and as a platform for winning the hearts and minds of the local and international audience, as well as expanding its global network beyond the Horn of Africa.

The easy access to social media platforms explains why the group employs Twitter and online videos to initiate recruitment, carry out propaganda to those that are not informed, publicise attacks carried out or claim responsibility, and showcase the tactics that enhance their achievements, although direct messaging through social media has also become a burden on the group's leaders (Cox et al., 2018). They go as far as using social media to issue threats to governments and citizens, warning the public of the consequences of being on the side of government or any act of conspiracy. The Westgate attack orchestrated by Al-Shabaab that killed 67 people and wounded 175, showed the instrumentality of social media during an ongoing operation when it used Twitter to claim responsibility and live-tweeted. While the attack lasted within four days with updates on the hostages while they mocked the security forces for their late response; while the tweets targeted the people and government of Kenya, the media audience, the West, and humanitarian officials (Mair, 2016). This showed the group's notoriety for deploying social networks to gain global attention.

ACTIVITIES

A Nascent Insurgent Group

From its role as the enforcement wing of the Union of Islamic Court's influential faction, when they occupied Mogadishu in 2005, Al-Shabaab had its stay short-lived when Ethiopian forces forced out the Islamic Courts in 2006, but only paved the way for Al-Shabaab to gain control in south-central Somalia and establish a de facto state when Ethiopian forces withdrew in 2009, being able to set up leadership, cross the hurdle of clan divisions by winning popular support, and ensured security provisions (Barnes, 2016; Khalil et al., 2019). The jihadist group grew from a relatively small non-state armed group to a full-fledged regional insurgent group that has forced several states to form a coalition against it. For instance, the invasion of Ethiopian forces during the early years of formation threatened the group. The group took advantage of Ethiopia's withdrawal to establish a strong organisation that has the capacity to withstand external aggression.

Al-Shabaab has operated from the jihadist perspective of conquest, coercively taking over some parts of Somalia after the establishment of the group and recruiting members who were indoctrinated to advance the goals of the founders. This latent phase of the group was the formation years of the organisation, when adequate planning was made using the administrative structure already established to map most parts of the countries, thereby taking people unawares.

As a non-state actor that has struggled to be a relevant voice in the Horn of Africa, Al-Shabaab adopts territoriality as a means of political control for the actualisation of its objectives (Doboš, 2016). The uniqueness of Al-Shabaab is the desire of the group to capture and control the areas captured (Doboš, 2016). From a jihadist perspective, Al-Shabaab became a full-fledged insurgent group that now threatens the stability of the Somali state, with implications for human rights in the Horn of Africa. With the activities of the group in mind, then-United States President Barack Obama tagged Al-Shabaab as a group that distributes death threats and destruction when he visited Ethiopia in 2015 (Horseedmedia, July 27, 2015).

On the Rise

Al-Shabaab violence increased in intensity over a few years as the group became more emboldened in weaponisation, grand strategy, tactics, and operational oversight. With the instrument of suicide bombing, Al-Shabaab has made peace elusive in Somalia, which never witnessed this magnitude of violence prior to the insurgency that has made the state fragile. According to Clos (2011, p. 20), Al-Shabaab is an 'indigenous movement to the sensibilities of Somalia that has committed acts of large-scale violence'. Al-Shabaab eats violence like it's food, as they have a violent appearance and are searching for places to exhibit their restive nature. The group has adopted lethal violence to the extent that it doesn't waste time executing all captured enemies, such as any identified informants working for the government and AMISOM troops in the towns they control. This was the punishment meted out to a 13-year-old teenager called Fatuma after being caught and accused of spying for the Somali armed forces, AMISOM, and Ethiopian military in Dinsor town, southern Somalia (Somalicurrent, July 23, 2014). To them, such a punishment is a jihadist way of responding to offenders without considering their right to life and safety.

With formidable fighters, the use of weapons and numbers remain the strengths of the group. As of 2010, the armed strength of the group ranged from a low of 3,000 to a high of 7,000, having the capacity to mobilise any number for any operation when necessary, with the majority being from Somalia (Shinn, 2010).

The insurgent group has taken advantage of the ungoverned spaces in many parts of Somalia as a result of poor security governance that exposed the weakness of the central government's ability to manage the country's internal affairs. Within five years of its existence, the group had already gained a strategic advantage with the capacity to launch attacks that took it to its peak in 2011, when it captured and held some parts of Mogadishu and Kismayo (Council on Foreign Relations, 2020). This victory was short-lived when coalition forces pushed them out.

Having adequate knowledge of how strategic funding is to the group's success, members usually set up checkpoints within and beyond their strongholds to forcefully collect taxes on farm produce, charcoal exports, other goods, and tolls from road users (Maruf and Joseph, 2018).

With their use of violence, the group has continued to attract audiences across the African continent and beyond, to the extent that there is hardly any political or academic gathering on security where scholars and practitioners do not use Somalia and the group as examples. The killing of both Somali and Kenyan officers, most of whom are yet to come to grips with counterterrorism, by the group is a source of worry to many leaders within and outside Somalia. Those involved in counterterrorism are the Kenyan Army, Somali security forces, and Ethiopian troops, among others. The rising trend of the group's activities prompted the United States to designate it as a terrorist organisation in March 2008 after it became clear of the group's resolve to constitute a security threat to both Somalia and neighbouring countries within the Horn of Africa and beyond.

Apart from banning the use of plastic bags, Al-Shabaab has been helpful to farmers and indigenous businesses within the areas it controls to the extent that many people in those areas regard the group as God-ordained helpers by enhancing their socioeconomic lives after banning non-governmental organisations and the construction of canals, which greatly enhanced food production, making it possible for farmers to record improved yields and multiple harvests, as witnessed in Bulo Mareer town, Lower Shabelle province, where the ban of NGOS was caused by the suspicion the organisations were threatening the group's safety (Mohamed, 2014). Al-Shabaab's massive irrigation reforms, which have been result-oriented and beneficial to the populace, encouraged the people to embrace agriculture to benefit from tax cuts. Such agricultural and social reforms were aimed at generating positive public opinion and winning the people to their side, thereby having the advantage of a better governance style than the Somali government.

Height of Violence

The intensity of violence by the Jihadist group has become so high that security concerns have led various states to decide to support Somalia through stability operations. Violence has become both the weapon and feature of this Somali-based insurgent group, which has caused the deaths of many and murdered unsuspecting citizens and foreigners beyond the country's borders. Insecurity has been a problem in Somalia for more than ten years, and the killings have occurred all over the country. The Amniyat, which is the group's intelligence agency, was able to infiltrate some of the government's security apparatus, thereby making it easier for them to take security agencies unawares (Barnes, 2016). According to Jonsson and Torbjörnsson (2016), the group was responsible for about 860 violent incidents with more than 2000 fatalities in 2014.

The desperation of Al-Shabaab manifests in the group's increasing weaponisation of women and girls, transforming them from soft targets to active combatants. Apart from the young women who voluntarily enrol as members of Al-Shabaab based on different motivations for what they expect to gain materially, the group uses attacks on their emotional intelligence, forcing them or subtly convincing them of the financial and spiritual benefits of joining the campaign. It is difficult for a woman whose husband or lover is emotionally attached to the ideology to decline partaking in the violent group either as a means of avenging attack on loved ones by the security forces. This may have motivated three girls who were arrested trying to cross over to Somalia, from Kenya at a border town in El-Wak in March 2015. Some of them travel into Somalia on bikes at night (Badurdeen, 2018). With the involvement of women as recruiters, it is difficult for recruitees to decline such juicy offers and promises of financial gains.

Council on Foreign Relations reports show that in September 2013, the group killed 67 people in a Nairobi mall; in April 2015, it attacked a university and killed 148 people; and in January 2016, it killed 200 soldiers during an attack on a Kenyan army camp in El Adde. The group also attacked Somalia's ministry offices, killing 15 people, including the minister for labour, in March 2019, executed 18 people in a firing squad, killed 26 people during a gun attack or car bomb, and also bombed a location near Mogadishu airport with 17 fatalities recorded and 28 others wounded, all in July 2019. Of all the attacks by Al-Shabaab, one of the most shocking was the suicide bombing at the office of Mogadishu Mayor Abdirahman Omar Osman on July 25, 2019, during a high-level security meeting, where six people died and the mayor lost his life after one week. Surprisingly, the group claimed it targeted a UN envoy who visited the office (BBC News, 2019; *New York Times*, 2019). From this incident, it is obvious that government officials and other stakeholders need to discourage the announcement of events like such high-level meetings. Some visits involving local and international actors should be unannounced. CFR also reported the attack on the facilities housing the United Nations, European Union, and African Union in March 2020 using mortars, although no casualties were reported.

Days of Wane

Over the years, the group has suffered decline at different points, to the extent that it has had to adopt strategic withdrawal where necessary. This made them withdraw from most towns across the country, just like they did in Mogadishu and Kismayo. However, their withdrawal from some towns was not a sign of weakness as perceived but an opportunity to rethink strategy. During this time, it was no longer easy for the group to collect taxes in Kismayo Port and Mogadishu Bakara Market (Meservey, 2013; Cordano, 2015).

In September 2014, the group was given an opportunity to disarm through an amnesty with an ultimatum for 45 days, but this offer fell on deaf ears when about 30 members defected and surrendered to the Somali national army in Hiran province's frontline, marking the highest since its leader Ahmed Godane died (Somalicurrent, September 19, 2014; Somalicurrent, July 25, 2015; Smith, 2014).

To avert a humanitarian crisis, the AMISOM peacekeepers based in the Galgadud region of central Somalia swiftly conducted a covert operation that ended up routing the Al-Shabaab terrorists that had already planned to cut off the main road linking Dusamareb and El Bur towns, thereby demonstrating an overarching counterterrorism strategy. The 2014 joint security operations caused Al-Shabaab to lose some strongholds. For instance, Operation Eagle liberated eight districts, including Rab Dhuure, Wajid, Xudur,

Bulo Burto, Warsheekh, Qoryooley, Maxaas, and Ceelbuur, as well as Operation Indian Ocean, mainly in Somalia's strategic littoral regions, which also made it possible for them to recover eight towns, including Golweyn, Bulo Marer, Kurtunwarey, Bulo-Gudud, Tayeeglow, Fidow, Jalalaqsi, and the Al-Shabaab strongholds of Baraawe and Cadale (Cordano, 2015, p.2; Ohanesian, 2014).

African Union and Somali government forces successfully launched a joint security operation in the first week of July 2015 in an effort to drive the Al-Shabaab group out of Somalia. On July 22, after taking control of Bardheere in the Gedo region, the group fled the town in large numbers, according to locals and Somali officials (Somali Current, July 22, 2015). Since 2008, the town has had complete authority over the group. Barack Obama, the president of the United States, visited Kenya on July 27, 2015, and during that trip, he advocated for a change in tactics in the war against terrorism in the Horn of Africa, which includes Kenya and Somalia. He contends that while the military and police are powerless to defeat terrorism, community involvement would ensure enough safety. It is now essential to improve coordination of counterterrorism efforts both within Somalia and among states in the Horn of Africa, to strengthen police and intelligence cooperation, and to provide technical assistance to nations lacking the resources and know-how to modernise their counterterrorism tools (Schmid, 2012, p. 77). Al-Shabaab operations were significantly disrupted by the USA's constant deployment of drones, which also led to a rise in the number of external stakeholders since 2016. Given the intelligence value of such repentant persons to the security forces, the defection of some group members is also a blow to Al-Shabaab. Thus, the Salafi jihadist group's days were winding down due to faithful members defecting as well as the loss of strongholds and commanders.

Resurgence of Stroke of Luck?

The insurgent group has greatly benefited strategically over the years as a result of controlling some territories, which has led to the public's perception that they have a psychological advantage because they have used hit-and-run attacks at locations under government control. Despite various security initiatives by the government, the group dispersed and gained control of some parts of the country, as they now consistently attack people with changes in strategy. With the weakness of the government's early warning system, poor response to emergency situations, and inadequate training of counterinsurgents, especially on defence intelligence and military strategy in counterinsurgency, Al-Shabaab gained more ground in influence. They have sustained this by setting up landmines for the government troops and African Union counterparts, like in the incident in the southern Somali town of Marka, about 109 kilometres from Mogadishu, when troops were taken unawares with some 24 civilian casualties recorded (Somalicurrent, July 21, 2015). Troop withdrawals at different points and inadequate resources for the counterinsurgents greatly added value to Al-Shabaab campaigns.

Forest taking and forest holding explain the luck that counts in favour of or against insurgents (Albert, 2017). It is to their advantage when they are able to resist counterinsurgency measures. While most insurgents can capture and control forest areas for a long time, in many instances, security forces struggle to retake and sustain those areas with effective security governance. Al-Shabaab's ability to control forest areas has always counted in favour of the insurgent group, thereby compromising the efforts of the coalition forces. However, holding liberated areas has always been challenging for the security forces.

With their terrain priority, their ability to sustain safe havens instead of always running away, to the extent that there are parts of Somalia where the group has not been pushed out, gives it the freedom to rest, regroup, and plan attacks, thereby using the safe havens to take cover against the counterinsurgents, just like the forests of Lower Jubba remain safe havens and the mountainous Galgala region of Puntland, all of which have functioned as traditional sanctuary for Somali extremists for years due to their inaccessibility to the security forces (Meservey, 2013). Chasing the extremists into their safe havens in forests and caves would portend grave danger for the counterinsurgents. This explains why it is more convenient for the jihadists to conduct training and plan for more operations, knowing that most of the troops involved in counterinsurgency have had little or inadequate training in such combat. The foregoing offers more insight into why the guerrilla tactics of the insurgents can sometimes become a mysterious affair for the security forces.

In addition to the intelligence unit's well-executed surveillance operations on target locations, the group also infiltrates the security forces' ranks and files and other key informants, as they did in El Adde, where some insurgents communicated with 20 Somali troops stationed at the base and launched an attack with ease thanks to the information provided to them by the soldiers (Maruf and Joseph, 2018). Insurgents have benefited from this plot at the expense of counterinsurgency efforts.

AL-SHABAAB'S FUTURE

Al-Shabaab's future is dependent on two factors: the ability of the group to sustain their strategies, making their tactics complex in order to neutralise defence intelligence, and the failure of the coalitions to sustain their funding of the counterinsurgency and logistics supplies.

Lessons from the activities of Al-Shabaab are noteworthy. The group has proven to operate beyond Somali borders and now has the capability of exporting violence to neighbouring countries. The asymmetric nature of the conflict has exposed the weakness of the government and how insurgency can go as far as frustrating coalition efforts when resources are inadequate. It goes a long way towards showcasing the indispensable nature of defence intelligence in counterinsurgency: the enemy should be permanently flushed out of the state.

When counterinsurgents begin to reclaim regions held and administered by the group and preserve state security governance in the successfully freed areas, the future of Al-Shabaab will be fraught with uncertainty, making it difficult for the insurgents to reorganise and launch new operations. Only by persistently neutralising this murderous organisation will this be possible. As the United States expands its presence in the country, Al-Shabaab's future in Somalia and its environs is likely to be chaotic.

One of the greatest achievements of the forces of order would be to block all sources of funding, including forced taxation if possible, to frustrate the insurgent group's war of movement campaign against the government and people of Somalia, because access to funds and fund-raising drives remain critical for the instrument of violence that gives the group a strategic advantage. Apart from preventing the efforts of the group, which revolve around criminality, being able to identify individual donors within and outside Africa and the medium of transfer of the funds would also go a long way to limiting easy access to the funds. All these cannot be achieved without collaboration that goes beyond the security sector's initiatives.

For the insurgent group to have a bright future devoid of any internal threat (from within the areas controlled), it is expected that revolts resisting the zakat payments will be checked and contained. Also, the incidents of drone strikes killing its leaders and commanders need to be checked, and there is a need to possibly design defensive mechanisms to reduce the decapitation that has greatly wreaked havoc on their activities, but this would be difficult if the issue of mobile phone tracking is not addressed.

With the way the insurgency is evolving, it would be difficult to root Al-Shabaab out of the territory of Somalia until the group's safe havens are demolished and the fighters are completely neutralised. Positive change can only come when coalition forces coordinate a fiercer counterinsurgency, capitalising on the extension of the national emergency in an executive order signed by US President Donald Trump in 2019 for the continuation of airstrikes against Al-Shabaab fighters. This will enable them to completely neutralise Al-Shabaab and force repentant members to surrender. Sustained security governance and peacebuilding achievable through the engagement of the defectors would further isolate the insurgent group and make it difficult for the disarmed fighters to remobilise.

References

Al Jazeera. Seven Somali Soldiers killed when Al-Shabaab attacked a Somali Military Base. January 17, 2023.

Al Jazeera. Kenyan security forces kill 10 suspected Al-Shabab fighters. January 20, 2023.

Al Jazeera. At least five killed in bomb, gun attack in Somalia's Mogadishu. March 28, (2023).

Al Jazeera. Somalia hosts regional summit to discuss fighting Al-Shabab. February 1, 2023.

Anzalone, C. (2018). Black banners in Somalia: The state of Al-Shabaab's territorial insurgency and the specter of the Islamic state. *Combating Terrorism Center Sentinel, 11*(3), 14–20.

Badurdeen, F.A. (2018). Women and recruitment in the Al-Shabaab network: Stories of women being recruited by women recruiters in the coastal region of Kenya. *The African Review, 45*(1), 19–48.

Barnes, C. (2016). Somalia's Al-Shabaab down but far from out. International Crisis Group. June 27. https://www.crisisgroup.org/africa/horn-africa/somalia/somalia-s-al-shabaab-down-far-out

Burke, C.J. (2018). The culture of terrorist propaganda in Sub-Saharan Africa: A case study on Al-Shabaab's use of communication technologies in Somalia and Kenya. Master of Arts in Law and Diplomacy Capstone Project. The Fletcher School, Tufts University. https://sites.tufts.edu/hitachi/files/2017/10/Callie_Burke_Capstone.pdf

Cox, K., Marcellino, W., Bellasio, J., Ward, A., Galai, K., Meranto, A.S., & Paoli, G.P. (2018). Social media in Africa: A double-edged sword for security and development. RAND Europe. https://www.rand.org/randeurope/research/projects/social-media-in-africa.html

Cordano, D. (2015). The conflict between Al-Shabaab and the Federal Government of Somalia. Bradbury's Global Risk Partners. January 9. http://www.bradburys.co.uk/wp-content/uploads/2015/01/The-conflict-between-al-Shabaab-and-the-Federal-Government-of-Somalia.pdf

Doboš, B. (2016). Shapeshifter of Somalia: Evolution of the political territoriality of Al-Shabaab. *Small Wars & Insurgencies, 27*(5), 937–957.

Herbst, J. (2004). African militaries and rebellion: The political economy of threat and combat effectiveness. *Journal of Peace Research, 41*(3), 357–369.

Ingiriis, M.H. (2020). The anthropology of Al-Shabaab: The salient factors for the insurgency movement's recruitment project. Small Wars and Insurgencies, *31*(2), 358–380.

Jonsson, M., & Torbjörnsson, D. (2016). Resurgent, Reinvented or Simply Resilient? The Growing Threat of Al-Shabaab in Somalia. Studies in African Security. December https://www.foi.se/download/18.7fd35d7f166c56ebe0bb3bd/1542369060470/Resurgent-Reinvented-or-Simply-Resilient_FOI-Memo-5913.pdf

Khalil, J., Brown, R., Chant, C., Olowo, P., & Wood, N. (2019). Deradicalisation and Disengagement in Somalia evidence from a rehabilitation programme for former members of Al-Shabaab. RUSI Whitehall Report 4-18. Royal United Services Institute for Defence and Security Studies.

Mair, D. (2016). #Westgate: A case study: How Al-Shabaab used Twitter during an ongoing attack. *Studies in Conflict & Terrorism, 40*(1), 24–43.

Marchal, R. (2011). The rise of a Jihadi movement in a country at war: Harakat Al-Shabaab Al Mujaheddin in Somalia. https://www.sciencespo.fr/ceri/sites/sciencespo.fr.ceri/files/art_RM2.pdf

Maruf, H., & Joseph, D. (2018). No end in sight for the Al-Shabaab threat to Somalia. Combating Terrorism Center, *11*, 11: https://ctc.usma.edu/no-end-sight-al-shabaab-threat-somalia/

Mendelsohn, B. (2010). Foreign fighters – Recent trends. In M.P. Noonan (Ed.), *The foreign fighters problems, recent trends and case studies: Selected essays* (pp. 189–202). London, UK: Foreign Policy Research Institute.

Meservey, J. (2013). Al-Shabaab's Somali safe havens: A springboard for terror. *Perspectives on Terrorism, 7*(6), 90–99.

Mohamed, H. (2014). Somalia farmers benefit from Al-Shabaab reforms. Al Jazeera, March 11. https://www.aljazeera.com/indepth/features/2014/03/somali-farmers-benefit-from-al-shabab-reforms-201431053038814400.html?xif=%20-

Mutanda, D. (2017). What makes terrorism tick in Africa? Evidence from Al-Shabaab and boko haram. *Jadavpur Journal of International Relations, 21*(1) 20–40.

Neo, L.S. (2019). An internet-mediated pathway for online radicalisation: RECRO. In Information Resources Management Association (Ed.), *Violent extremism: Breakthroughs in research and practice* (pp. 62–89). USA. PA, USA: IGI Global.

Omeje, K. (2007). The diaspora and domestic insurgencies in Africa. African Sociological Review,*11*(2), 94–107.

Speckhard, A., & Shajkovci, A. (2019). The Jihad in Kenya: Understanding Al-Shabaab recruitment and terrorist activity inside Kenya –in their own words. *African Security*, 1–59.

Shay, S. (2018). *The Islamic terror threat to the horn of Africa.* Washington DC: USA, Institute for Policy and Strategy Publications.

Shinn, D. (2010). Al Shabaab's foreign threat to Somalia. In M.P. Noonan (Ed.), *The foreign fighters problems, recent trends and case studies: Selected essays* (pp. 203–215). London: UK: Foreign Policy Research Institute.

Solomon, H. (2012). Counter-terrorism in Nigeria. *The RUSI Journal 157*(4), 6–11.

Solomon, H. (2014). Somalia's Al Shabaab: Clans vs Islamist nationalism. *South African Journal of International Affairs, 21*(3), 351–366, DOI:10.1080/10220461.2014.967286

Voice of America. Al-Shabab has lost third of its territory, US Ambassador says. March 28, 2023.

Vidino, L., Pantucci, R., & Kohlmann, E. (2010) Bringing global jihad to the horn of Africa: Al Shabaab, western fighters, and the sacralization of the Somali conflict. *African Security, 3*(4), 216–238.

30

THE ROLE OF THE *AMNIYAT* IN AIDING AL-SHABAAB'S LEADERSHIP MOTIVATIONS (SOMALIA)

János Besenyő and Gábor Sinkó

INTRODUCTION

Over the last decade and a half, al-Shabaab has undergone a number of significant organisational and structural changes. While it was only a small group of jihadists at the beginning of the 21st century, it has since become one of the deadliest terrorist organisations in Africa (Institute for Economics and Peace, 2022). The group's early history has been characterised by extremism, since al-Shabaab was on the verge of annihilation in 2006 but then was responsible for controlling large areas in south-central Somalia in 2008. It also managed to overcome fierce infighting and weather a severe internal leadership crisis in the early 2010s. Nothing demonstrates better what a significant security threat al-Shabaab poses than the fact that it has shifted focus to more destructive attacks with higher visibility and its readiness to carry out operations not only locally but regionally as well (Cannon & Iyekekpolo, 2018).

Although motivations could be of different natures, studying them is of paramount importance, as they reveal that al-Shabaab is much more of a political and military organisation than a group indiscriminately abusing civilians, which is a constantly recurring image of them in the media.[1] Despite the fact that the international community has provided help to Somalia diplomatically, financially, politically, and technically (UNSOM and the World Bank, 2017), it cannot be concluded that the war with al-Shabaab is coming to an end. On the contrary, the East African country is increasingly torn apart by a seemingly never-ending war. While the Somali government and its foreign partners are beginning to run out of options, the terrorist group continues to show resilience, adapt to counter-terrorism operations, and remain embedded in Somali society.

The first part of the study is a brief historical overview of al-Shabaab, which helps with understanding the roots of the movement. Following that, the group's leadership motivations are highlighted, and the capacities and capabilities of al-Shabaab's secret service, the Amniyat, are analysed. The conclusion is that it has aided the leadership motivations of the terrorist organisation by performing judicial, administrative, intelligence, and security-related tasks. So far, al-Shabaab has managed to make good use of the Amniyat. If this trend – coupled with the group's ability to provide increased predictability and security, greater internal coherence than its opponents, and its capability to gain local support – continues in the future, we have all the reasons to believe al-Shabaab will not only survive but thrive in the long term.

HISTORICAL ACCOUNT OF AL-SHABAAB

Somalia is one of the most impoverished and undeveloped countries in the world. Over the last couple of decades, several militant groups have tried to assert their dominance in Somalia, taking advantage of the power vacuum left behind after the collapse of the Siad Barre regime in the early 1990s.[2] A Wahhabi Islamist terrorist group, al-Itihaad al-Islamiya (AIAI), had been dreaming about creating an Islamist state in the Horn of Africa since the 1980s, an aspiration also shared by Osama bin Laden. As a result, hoping that the Somali chaos and lawlessness would eventually benefit them, al-Qaeda began providing foreign fighters, training, and financial support to AIAI.[3]

Internal divisions within al-Shabaab brought about a significant change at the beginning of the 2000s. While some of the group's members only intended to form a political coalition, others would have been willing to go further in order to extend Sharia to "Greater Somalia".[4] Realising they were too weak on their own, this latter faction, together with AIAI remnants, joined the Islamic Courts Union (ICU), a legal and political coalition of Sharia courts, which had managed to bring large areas under its

DOI: 10.4324/9780429426063-34

control by late 2006. To understand why the ICU was able to gain public support in a relatively short time, one has to consider their achievements, such as putting an end to infighting between clans and restoring law and order in Somalia.

In response to the expansion of the organisation, a counteroffensive was launched, which was followed by an armed resistance campaign against Ethiopia for its invasion of Somalia.[5] It forced al-Shabaab to improve its effectiveness in guerilla warfare (Menkhaus & Boucek, 2010) and ultra-radicalised the group (Wise, 2011). As a consequence of the invasion and internal disagreements, the ICU dissolved in 2007. With its moderates having fled Somalia and its leaders later becoming members of the Transitional Federal Government (TFG), al-Shabaab became the most influential splinter group, largely because of its ability to rally support after the Ethiopian invasion of Somalia. Presenting itself as a movement with a nationalistic agenda and capable of protecting the locals from foreign aggression was definitely a factor contributing to increased popularity (Committee of Foreign Affairs, 2013).

In the beginning, al-Shabaab received support from the local population and the Somali diaspora. It could take the form of money, but the provision of foreign militants (Marchal, 2011) and intelligence related to the movement of Ethiopian troops[6] proved useful to the group as well. Moreover, high-ranking individuals from the Islamic world also chose to support the insurgency financially (United Nations, 2010, p. 31). While there were only informal ties between al-Shabaab and al-Qaeda before 2012, it is believed that the former took advantage of the latter's public relations and technical expertise in the previous years, too.[7] It might explain how the group was able to become a decisive player in the affairs of the Horn of Africa region in a relatively short time (Kiss et al., 2014). Having forced the TFG, the African Union Mission in Somalia (AMISOM),[8] and the Ethiopian National Defense Force (ENDF) to retreat, the movement had already controlled large areas in south-central Somalia by 2008.

After its initial successes, however, al-Shabaab seemed to lose impetus as the group could not push forward and drive the TFG and AMISOM out of Mogadishu. Besides, since the movement was poorly equipped compared to the African Union (AU) forces, it was continuously defeated by the TFG and AMISOM out of Mogadishu. Not only was al-Shabaab weakened militarily in the coming years, but it also came into conflict with Somali clans, who believed the insurgency was to blame for their losses (Anzalone, 2011). In addition to the increase in civilian casualties, the alienation between the group and the local population was further aggravated by the militants' strict interpretation of Sharia and the growing sense of fear among Somalis (Human Rights Watch, 2011). The United States' designation of al-Shabaab as a terrorist organisation was a huge financial setback for the insurgents, as it was the time when the Somali diaspora decided to drastically reduce its support.

In such a situation, it would have been easy for the group to retain local support; however, the decision of the Emir, Ahmed Abdi Godane, to ban international organisations from delivering foreign food aid to southern Somalia without taxing it led to a sharp decline in the movement's reputation (Menkhaus, 2012). While thousands of people died, the 2011 famine illustrated how al-Shabaab disregarded human life completely. Not much has changed in this regard. As a result of the endless drought, there is now unprecedented starvation in Somalia. Despite the fact that the average yearly income of the terrorist group is about 100 million USD (United Nations, 2022), it remains highly inflexible about collecting taxes. Instead of helping Somalis who live in the territories controlled by the group, al-Shabaab chose to impose higher taxes on them as compensation for lost revenues. Thus, the organisation is indifferent to the economic hardship of the locals, which may lead to clan uprisings and the continuous degradation of al-Shabaab support (Felbab-Brown, 2023).

Having realised that it was simply too costly for them to wage a conventional war with AMISOM, al-Shabaab was forced to withdraw from Mogadishu. Although it may have been considered a victory from the perspective of the international community, the retreat of the terrorist organisation was nothing more than a strategic move, foreshadowing al-Shabaab's return to guerilla operations. Nevertheless, the group suffered financial and strategic losses when the militants lost control over Kismayo and Barawa. These port towns had been responsible for generating substantial revenues for the organisation,[9] and their loss spurred al-Shabaab to look for alternative sources of income, which were eventually found in the taxation of Somali businessmen[10] and clan elders, as well as other criminal activities.[11]

Al-Shabaab also experienced a serious internal leadership problem in the early 2010s. Godane had faced harsh criticism for a number of arguments put out by his opponents.[12] Besides being viewed as a dictator, he was accused of taking no notice of basic principles (e.g., executing "true Muslims") and making mistakes of a strategic nature (e.g., being involved in the struggles against Ahlu Sunna Waljama'a). Disagreements also revolved around power distribution and civilian abuse. The Emir decided to get rid of his opponents brutally and pragmatically as a way of teaching a lesson and purging the terrorist group. Consequently, by 2012, al-Shabaab had become an organisation characterised by compactness and less limitation, which tied in with their idea of shifting to asymmetric warfare with the inclusion of hit-and-run tactics, improvised explosive devices (IEDs), and suicide attacks against the TFG and AMISOM. In the same year, al-Shabaab pledged allegiance to al-Qaeda, presumably to improve the group's image and reputation in the Islamic world.[13] The *bay'ah* appeared to have facilitated al-Shabaab's execution of terrorist attacks in East Africa and put pressure on regional governments to withdraw their forces from Somalia (International Crisis Group, 2018).

However, al-Shabaab was also plagued by symbolic and operational problems at the time (Burns & Baldor, 2014);

the most important of which was the death of Godane in 2014, which gave hope to the international community. It was thought the Emir was a charismatic person with a great ability for strategic planning, and in his absence there would be an emerging power vacuum, paving the way for the fragmentation and possibly disintegration of the terrorist organisation. Nonetheless, Godane's successor, Ahmad Umar, has proved a capable leader who has managed to keep a tight rein on the group, thus keeping it unified on the whole (Klobucista et al., 2021).

Since then, al-Shabaab has been able to improve its capabilities and enhance its capacities both locally and regionally. It is a terrorist group known for its consistency, efficiency, and predictability, especially when it comes to providing security to local Somalis. Despite the fact that the international community has liquidated some of its highest-ranking members and there have been continuous national, bilateral, and multilateral efforts to defeat it, al-Shabaab still holds its ground and controls large territories in west, south, and central Somalia (Anzalone & Warner, 2021). Its secret service, the formidable Amniyat network, has aided the organisation's leadership motivations, facilitating the shift to asymmetric warfare and eventually leading to al-Shabaab's resurgence.

EXPLORING THE CONNECTION BETWEEN LEADERSHIP MOTIVATIONS AND THE AMNIYAT

The motivations of al-Shabaab may show a rather variable trend, considering the group's existence as a whole. In any case, there are two objectives that have been highlighted repeatedly. One of them is opposition to foreign forces inside Somalia, and the other is the implementation of Sharia (Marchal, 2018). Al-Shabaab has a well-defined organisational structure with a number of executive and advisory councils providing assistance to the group in carrying out operations and various specialised departments responsible for military, security, and administrative matters, taxation, justice, propaganda, etc.[14] The resurgence of the organisation, however, may as well be attributed to the efficiency of its independent security bodies, the Hizbah, the Jabhat, and the Amniyat. While the first two play a prominent role in policing and geographical expansion, respectively (Kheyre, 2022), the Amniyat is the *de facto* intelligence wing.

The structure of the Secret Service is similar to that of other intelligence apparatuses. The Amniyat is comprised of approximately 500–1000 operatives and has a central command and a relatively large number of regional commanders. It also has squads responsible for grenade and suicide attacks as well as assassinations. Units that deal with issues ranging from logistics and finance to intelligence collection support the work of the intelligence agency (United Nations, 2013a). It is important for the Amniyat to support the capacity and capability of al-Shabaab to wage an asymmetrical war. Studying the terrorist organisation's arsenal, it can be seen that hand and machine guns are used most frequently, as well as rifles, grenade launchers, and mortar ammunition. Not only does the group spend over 20 million dollars on weapons, but they prefer arms that can be moved freely and quickly, making guerrilla warfare more successful (Hiraal Institute, 2022). In the following, we would like to shed light on how the Amniyat has aided al-Shabaab's leadership motivations.

Al-Shabaab came dangerously close to defeating the ICU when Ethiopian and Western forces invaded Somalia in December 2006. However, the continued presence of foreign troops eventually played into the hands of the terrorists, as they could make opposition to foreigners an integral part of their propaganda. It was a radical but not overly risky approach to take since the idea of Western powers re-colonising African territories appealed strongly to Somali nationalism (Maruf & Joseph, 2018, p. 48). Drawing on deep-seated hostility towards Ethiopians[15] brought the expected results, as al-Shabaab could garner widespread public support and mobilise internally, recruiting thousands of fighters from the local population and the Somali diaspora.

Some of the most talented or best-connected individuals the Amniyat recruits come from the ranks of al-Shabaab; however, the great majority of them hail from the Somali population. The same old method is used, which means they are usually contacted personally after some trustworthy and/or paid informants have run a background check on them (Arango, 1968). The responsibilities of women may range from the provision of food and the conveyance of messages to finding safe shelters for the operatives of the group. Although their number is gradually increasing, the Amniyat are still dominated by young and educated men, sometimes with clan affiliations to prominent al-Shabaab members (United Nations, 2013b, p. 57). Convincing the youth to support them has always been pivotal to the movement's existence. They are the most easily mobilised social stratum and are outraged at how difficult it is to dislodge the elderly from their positions of power, as they would fight tooth and nail to hold on to everything they have amassed. The youth are also dissatisfied with the chiefs, who were promising but then proved unable to end the civil war and create long-term peace.

While it was initially believed that a conventional war against the TFG and AMISOM could be won, the terrorist organisation realised that a shift to asymmetric warfare was inevitable. Since then, the Amniyat have become the most feared, organised, and integral part of al-Shabaab, now primarily engaged in intelligence and counterintelligence. Besides, it functions as an operational body, resorting to targeted assassinations and hit-and-run tactics while carrying out attacks on a small and large scale (Menkhaus, 2014). After the 2010s, roughly coinciding with the terrorist group pledging allegiance to al-Qaeda and Godane's intention to meet the international jihadist agenda, al-Shabaab increased its visibility, and instead of carrying out low-profile attacks, it started conducting deadly operations against the Somali Supreme Court and UN compounds, among others (Sinkó & Besenyő, 2021).

They remained predominantly active within Somalia, but the organisation began to have a regional impact (Bergen et al., 2011), targeting Ugandans watching the 2010 FIFA World Cup Final in Kampala and Kenyans in the Westgate shopping mall in Nairobi and at Garissa University College three and five years later, respectively. All of the above-mentioned attacks can be seen as retaliation for these countries' support for AMISOM and are clearly intended to maximise psychological damage, tying in with the group's desire to inflict harm on civilians in the Horn of Africa (Committee of Foreign Affairs, 2013). The Amniyat supports al-Shabaab's regional aspirations by intimidating, forcibly recruiting, or assassinating businessmen, government officials, Somali journalists, and security agents. Not only is the presence of the secret service threatening to the FGS and AMISOM, but also to international aid organisations and foreign agencies.

Although other Somali groups, such as Hizbul Islam and the Alliance for the Re-liberation of Somalia, had strong nationalistic objectives too, al-Shabaab was the only one to recognise and overcome clan divisions and internal rivalries to have a chance against the TFG and Ethiopian/AMISOM forces. To put an end to its weakening organisational cohesion, al-Shabaab's Emir, Godane, decided to expel and kill foreigners. Following that, taking the Somali clan structure as a basis, he initiated the restructuring of the group, making it non-hierarchical and decentralised. In practise, it meant an increase in the commanders' and subcommanders' responsibilities so that they could now recruit infantrymen and appoint junior officials. Moreover, commanders were allowed to plan and carry out small-scale attacks with their counterparts (Sinkó & Besenyő, 2021).

However, with al-Shabaab being more decentralised, it was crucial to maintain the balance of power and monitor the organisation's commanders, so the dominance and scope of the Amniyat had to be enhanced (Maxwell & Majid, 2016). While the terrorist group itself was then characterised by a higher degree of decentralisation, the leadership was highly centralised, with the Emir enjoying sole control over the secret service. It must be emphasised that al-Shabaab is a movement deeply embedded in Somali society, meaning that they knew exactly how important it was to be involved in clan politics. In fact, the senior leadership of the terrorist group used to act as a mediator in conflicts between clans and sub-clans, which definitely contributed to al-Shabaab's increased acceptance and consolidation of power inside Somalia (Horton, 2017).

Besides their opposition to the presence of foreign troops in the country, the other recurring aim of the group's leadership was the implementation of Sharia. Similar to other Salafi movements, this ambitious goal has accompanied al-Shabaab from the very beginning. Nonetheless, in light of the limited understanding and lack of religious expertise attested by various jihadi groups, it may be reasoned that it has only been symbolic in nature. However, reasserting this objective could be vital for the terrorist organisation to show it is unwilling to make concessions and compromises to others. It is also interesting to see the difference in emphasis. For instance, the implementation of Sharia was high on the agenda when the group needed to retain or regain popular support,[16] but immediately faded into the background when it was necessary to enforce punishments and demonstrate force.

The Amniyat plays a prominent role in the latter, since it not only recruits fighters by force but also intimidates and executes Somali businessmen, journalists, and people working for the government and security agencies. When the terrorist organisation rose to prominence, al-Shabaab made it clear that God's laws were applicable to everyone in the areas they controlled. It included people of power and wealth as well as their own members. The operatives of the intelligence wing had to instill fear in the Somali population by whatever means they deemed necessary. On several occasions, not the targeted individuals themselves but their close friends and relatives were apprehended so that they could be jailed or assassinated (Sinkó & Besenyő, 2021).

There were also defections, especially in times when al-Shabaab was militarily weakened and lost territory or when its members' faith in the organisation's goals wavered as they thought it had crossed certain boundaries. In case they were unsuccessful, the Amniyat either killed or imprisoned the defectors (Hansen, 2013); however, there were situations when the group showed greater flexibility. It was mainly true when it came to the infringement of Sharia or voices critical of the movement, but it seems to have depended on positions and responsibilities. According to a 2022 research report on the experiences of former al-Shabaab members, those accused of the aforementioned crimes were not always detained or executed, especially if they were high-ranking members of the group. There was a person who worked for the Amniyat, but after learning about the organisation's treatment of civilians and that his attitude had changed, he was only punished by being demoted to the Jabhat (Heide-Ottosen et al., 2022).

Tricia Bacon, director of the Policy Anti-Terrorism Hub (PATH) at American University, claims in her 2022 report that "numbers quitting the group [al-Shabaab] are currently low" (Bacon, 2022, p. 94), a claim she defends by combining the absence of order provided by the Somali government with the country's ongoing conflict dynamics. Another reason would be that staying a terrorist group member still carries less risk and expense than defecting, especially if something goes wrong and the person is either kidnapped or killed by the Amniyat. The research of Heide-Ottosen from 2022 indicates that while leaving the organisation is unquestionably extremely risky and fear can be a major barrier to keeping disillusioned soldiers back, it might still be worthwhile to try. Since "certain individuals are allowed to leave freely" (Heide-Ottosen et al., 2022, p. 2), al-Shabaab might let the person go if they are not too deeply ingrained in the terrorist organisation. However, it is still debatable as to who would be willing to risk incurring the wrath of the Amniyat if references to medical conditions or cries for mercy were ignored.

The question may be raised as to why the leadership of al-Shabaab was motivated to call for the implementation of Sharia. Besides the terrorist group's having been able to obtain exclusive control of the religious arena, the legitimacy and practicality of religious law in solving problems are indisputable, which appealed to the Somalis, whether they showed sympathy towards the movement or not. In that sense, the implementation of Sharia is connected to the retention of popular support. Furthermore, al-Shabaab, like other Islamist organisations, genuinely believed force and coercion had to be applied so that the local population could learn and change for the better (Marchal, 2018).

The Amniyat handled all administrative, military, and intelligence-related tasks, but the secret service also oversaw internal justice within the terrorist group. Show trials were held in their designated courts, and prisons were operated with the aim of detaining those who were believed to have been involved in espionage for the TFG or the Federal Government of Somalia (FGS). On top of that, the Amniyat was responsible for monitoring civilian behaviour and was sometimes entrusted with the enforcement of laws and policies. Consequently, the Amniyat played a supervisory role, too, keeping an eye on the group's departments and being in constant dialogue with al-Shabaab to help the leadership achieve their motivations (Sinkó & Besenyő, 2021).

The Secret Service has a fairly wide jurisdiction, so it is able to function outside of al-Shabaab's justice system.[17] This induces fear and puts immense pressure not only on the local population, including clan elders opposing the authority of the terrorist organisation and Somali businessmen unable or unwilling to pay taxes, but on the members of the group as well. The latter are not exempt from the harsh punishments of the Amniyat either, especially if they are rightfully accused of bribery, misconduct, embezzlement, or having spied on or conspired against al-Shabaab. The operatives of the intelligence wing are more respected and better paid than others working for the Hizbah and the Jabhat; however, they are also the ones who need to be the most loyal to the Emir (Maruf & Joseph, 2018, p. 90).

The Amniyat has installed informants across Somalia so that they can be involved in intelligence gathering. A more important achievement of the Secret Service was the infiltration of government offices, the National Intelligence and Security Agency (NISA), and AU headquarters (The New Arab, 2017). Unfortunately, this latter threat is not properly acknowledged, but it demonstrates that the Amniyat is an active player in counterintelligence activities, either on the offensive or defensive front. A former NISA agent argued that the growth in al-Shabaab attacks is "due to the increased level of infiltration by al-Shabaab operatives into our government agencies".[18] It seems the more informants the group has installed in critical locations, the higher the number of attacks carried out against the Somali government. The terrorist organisation has always viewed the FGS as a surrogate, and hence, prevailing over it ties in with leadership motivations too.

CONCLUSION

This study has analysed the nexus of al-Shabaab's leadership motivations and its secret service, the Amniyat. Instead of looking at it exclusively as a terrorist organisation, the military and political nature of the movement and the effective combination of terror and politics must also be emphasised. Another important element that is usually not discussed at length is the group's embeddedness in Somali society. Over the years, al-Shabaab has become an integral part of the security and political arenas in Somalia. It managed to exploit the vulnerabilities of the TFG and FGS through its counterintelligence operations and covert missions, for which the Amniyat was largely responsible.

It is gradually becoming evident that using military force alone won't be sufficient to solve the issue after the Somali government and the rest of the world responded to the threat the group posed. While members of the organisation have been prosecuted and pre-emptive attacks have been launched against al-Shabaab, other avenues must also be explored. The war has been going on for almost two decades, and there are no signs it will end in the near future. The 2022 election of President Hassan Sheikh Mohamud may be a little confidence boost that al-Shabaab will ultimately be defeated; however, it will not be possible as long as the government and its international backers use the same means as the terrorists, namely coercion and violence. A political engagement might be timely with al-Shabaab to see whether it could be a viable alternative to an endless cycle of war (International Crisis Group, 2022).

It is argued that al-Shabaab's leadership motivations have revolved around two recurring themes. The first is the opposition of the group to the presence of foreign troops inside Somalia, and the second is the implementation of Sharia. The former proved useful in recruitment since, from the beginning, the propaganda of the terrorist organisation was built upon antipathy towards Ethiopians. Nevertheless, it was crucial for al-Shabaab to preserve its Somali character and be involved in clan politics as well. While it is mostly regarded as a symbolic weapon, the implementation of Sharia helped the movement seem uncompromising. It was also part of their strategy, since when the group needed to retain or regain popular support, further emphasis was placed on it, but when al-Shabaab became stronger, it allowed the Amniyat to enforce punishments and demonstrate force.

Although the terrorist organisation lost significant territories, the Amniyat is likely to become more formidable in the foreseeable future. The secret service was able to retain its tactical capacities, and in the absence of territorial authority, it needs to be primarily engaged with the survival of the organisation. Even if the Somali government and the international community ultimately succeed in defeating the group, it must be noted that the Amniyat has been established "with the intention of surviving any kind of dissolution" (United Nations, 2013b, p. 7). Somalia has seen the rise and fall of various armed groups over the last three decades. The danger with al-Shabaab is not that there are parts that could potentially survive, but that they could merge into criminal organisations and other entities, wreaking havoc long after its dissolution.

Notes

1 For instance, see Al Jazeera (2022); France24 (2022); and Hassan (2022).
2 For more information on Siad Barre and the establishment of the National Secret Service, which was the predecessor of the National Intelligence and Security Agency, please see Sinkó (2021) and Besenyő (2023).
3 At the beginning of the 21st century, al-Qaeda provided training in Afghanistan to many high-profile al-Shabaab members, including Aden Hashi Farah, Ibrahim Hajji Jamma, and Mukhtar Robow.
4 Somalis were driven by the idea of 'Pan-Somalism', believing that all different territories and clans needed to be unified for the Somali state to possess enough power to become more dominant than the prevailing clan system.
5 Background information on the Ethiopian military intervention in Somalia can be found at Menkhaus (2009).
6 Field interviews conducted in Mogadishu in September-October 2017, In: Ingiriis (2020).
7 See Gartenstein-Ross (2009), for more details on the public relations assistance that al-Qaeda gave to al-Shabaab.
8 The UN Security Council Resolution 2628 has authorised the African Union Peace and Security Council to reconfigure AMISOM and replace it with the African Union Transition Mission in Somalia (ATMIS), with effect from April 1, 2022.
9 It is estimated that al-Shabaab generated 35–50 million dollars a year from port revenues and an additional 30–60 million dollars from "taxes" on businessmen in Somalia. For more details, see Starr (2011).
10 Besides taxation, another important source of income for al-Shabaab is piracy. For more, see Besenyő and Sinkó (2022).
11 As a consequence of the Amniyat's increased capability and its ability to continuously learn from its mistakes, al-Shabaab has since taken a tactical move and started extorting money.
12 Godane's decision to suspend the Shura, which functioned as a forum for settling disputes collectively through mediation, definitely contributed to internal divisions within al-Shabaab.
13 Therefore, pledging allegiance to al-Qaeda did not serve operational purposes; it was meant to solidify ideological links between the organisations and increase the strength of al-Shabaab.
14 Some of these departments include Jugta Ulus (quick reaction force), Mukhabarad (intelligence service), Iclaam and al-Kataib (media offices), Zakawaat (tax collection and taxation), and Mutafajirad (suicide missions unit with two subdivisions: Amaliya Istishhad (suicide bombings) and Amaliya Inquimas (suicide assaults).
15 Following the decision to grant the Ogaden region to Ethiopia in 1948, Somalis repeatedly tried to occupy the territory, which has strategic importance to Somalia both politically and ethnically. The former was crucial in terms of their aspirations to create a greater Somalia, while the latter would have been vital for the reunification of ethnic Somalis.
16 There were other cases when the retention of popular support was not linked to religious motivations. For example, recognising the dependence of al-Shabaab on clan politics, Godane restructured the organisation. As the first part of his two-stage plan, he got rid of foreigners, labelling them 'unnecessary liabilities" so that he could retain support.
17 In cases of spying, the Amniyat was able to circumvent the Sharia courts of the terrorist group. However, if a high-ranking commander was convicted of spying, it was the Shura that dealt with it. Hansen (2013), pp. 84 and 87.
18 Former senior NISA official, interviewed in February 2020, in: Nor Kheyre (2022).

References

Al Jazeera (2022). US military says killed 27 al-Shabab fighters in central Somalia, https://www.aljazeera.com/news/2022/9/21/us-military-says-killed-27-al-shabab-fighters-in-central-somalia (Accessed: February 4, 2023)

Anzalone, C. (2011). Al-Shabab's setbacks in Somalia. *Combating Terrorism Center (CTC) Sentinel*, *4*(10), https://ctc.westpoint.edu/wp-content/uploads/2011/11/CTCSentinel-Vol4Iss107.pdf (Accessed: February 4, 2023)

Anzalone, C. and Warner, J. (2021). Al-Shabaab, Oxford Bibliographies, doi: 10.1093/OBO/9780199743292-0303, https://www.oxfordbibliographies.com/view/document/obo-9780199743292/obo-9780199743292-0303.xml (Accessed: February 4, 2023)

Arango, C.R. (1968). Insurgent counterintelligence. *Studies in Intelligence*, *12*(1), 39–53

Bacon, T. (2022). Inside the minds of Somalia's ascendant insurgents: An identity, mind, emotions and perceptions analysis of al-Shabaab, Program on Extremism, Center for Empathy in International Affairs, the George Washington University, https://extremism.gwu.edu/sites/g/files/zaxdzs2191/f/Al-Shabaab-IMEP_Bacon_March-2022.pdf (Accessed: February 4, 2023)

Bergen, P., Hoffman, B., & Tiedemann, K. (2011). Assessing the jihadist terrorist threat to America and American interests. *Studies in Conflict & Terrorism*, *34*(2), 65–101, doi: 10.1080/1057610X.2011.538830

Besenyő, J. (2023). Somalia: A battlefield of intelligence services. In R. Shaffer (Ed.), *The handbook of African intelligence cultures* (pp. 601–614). Lanham (MD), United States of America: Rowman and Littlefield.

Besenyő, J., & Sinkó, G. (2022). Combating piracy strategically: Analysing the successes and challenges of NATO and EU interventions off the Somali coast. *South African Journal of International Affairs*, *29*(3), doi: 10.1080/10220461.2022.2125064

Burns, R., & Baldor, L.C. (2014). *US Confirms death of Somalia terror group leader*, https://web.archive.org/web/20140906201659/http://www.wsvn.com/story/26458182/pentagon-confirms-death-of-somalia-terror-leader (Accessed: February 4, 2023)

Cannon, B., & Iyekekpolo, W. (2018). Explaining transborder terrorist attacks: The cases of Boko Haram and al-Shabaab. *African Security*, *11*(4), 370–396, doi: 10.1080/19392206.2018.1560970

Committee of Foreign Affairs (2013). Al-Shabaab: How great a threat?, Hearing before the Committee of Foreign Affairs House of Representatives, Serial Number 113-86, https://www.govinfo.gov/content/pkg/CHRG-113hhrg85104/html/CHRG-113hhrg85104.htm (Accessed: February 4, 2023)

Felbab-Brown, V. (2023). Somalia's challenges in 2023, The Brookings Institution, Commentary, https://www.brookings.edu/blog/order-from-chaos/2023/01/27/somalias-challenges-in-2023/ (Accessed: February 4, 2023)

France 24 (2022). Death toll mounts as Somali forces battle to end al-Shabaab hotel siege, https://www.france24.com/en/africa/20220820-several-civilians-killed-in-an-al-shabaab-attack-on-a-hotel-in-somalia (Accessed: February 4, 2023)

Gartenstein-Ross, D. (2009). The strategic challenge of somalia's al-Shabaab. *Middle East Quarterly*, *16*(4), 25–36

Hansen, S.J. (2013). *Al-Shabaab in Somalia: The history and ideology of a militant islamist group, 2005–2012*. London: Hurst Publishers, pp. 208

Hassan, M.O. (2022). Al-Shabab kills 21 in Somalia's Hiran Province, Voice of America English News, https://www.voanews.com/a/al-shabab-attack-somalia/6729854.html (Accessed: February 4, 2023)

Heide-Ottosen, S., Abdi, Y., Nor, A.A., Khalil, J., & Zeuthen, M. (2022). Journeys through extremism: The experiences of former members of al-Shabaab, Research Report, Washington DC, RESOLVE Network, doi: 10.37805/cbags2022.3, https://www.resolvenet.org/system/files/2022-10/SOMALIA_WEB.pdf (Accessed: February 4, 2023

Hiraal Institute (2022). Al shabaab's arsenal: From taxes to terror, GIST Research, https://hiraalinstitute.so/wp-content/uploads/2022/02/Al-Shabaabs-Arsenal-From-Taxes-to-Terror-Web.pdf (Accessed: February 4, 2023)

Horton, M. (2017). Reclaiming lost ground in Somalia: The enduring threat of al-Shabaab. *Terrorism Monitor*, *15*(15), the Jamestown Foundation, https://jamestown.org/program/reclaiming-lost-ground-in-somalia-the-enduring-threat-of-al-shabaab/ (Accessed: February 4, 2023)

Human Rights Watch (2011). Somalia: Al shabaab attack indefensible, https://www.hrw.org/news/2011/10/05/somalia-al-shabaab-attack-indefensible (Accessed: February 4, 2023)

Ingiriis, M.H. (2020). Insurgency and international extraversion in Somalia: The National Intelligence and Security Agency (NISA) and al-Shabaab's amniyat. *African Security Review*, *29*(2), doi: 10.1080/10246029.2020.1740752

Institute for Economics and Peace (2022). Global terrorism index 2022: Measuring the impact of terrorism, Sydney, https://www.economicsandpeace.org/wp-content/uploads/2022/03/GTI-2022-web-09062022.pdf (Accessed: February 4, 2023)

International Crisis Group (2018). Al-Shabaab five years after westgate: Still a menace in East Africa, Report Number 265, https://www.crisisgroup.org/africa/horn-africa/kenya/265-al-shabaab-five-years-after-westgate-still-menace-east-africa (Accessed: February 4, 2023)

International Crisis Group (2022). Considering political engagement with al-Shabaab in Somalia, Crisis Group Africa Report Number 309, https://www.crisisgroup.org/africa/horn-africa/somalia/309-considering-political-engagement-al-shabaab-somalia (Accessed: February 4, 2023)

Kiss, ÁP, Besenyő, J., & Resperger, I.T. (2014). *Szomália: országismertető*. [Somalia: Country Profile] Honvéd Vezérkar, Budapest, http://real.mtak.hu/83745/1/szomalia_imprimatura__boritobelivterkep_u.pdf (Accessed: February 4, 2023)

Klobucista, C., Masters, J., & Sergie, M.A. (2021). Al-Shabab, Backgrounder, Council on Foreign Relations (CFR), https://www.cfr.org/backgrounder/al-shabab (Accessed: February 4, 2023)

Marchal, R. (2011). The rise of a jihadi movement in a country at war: Harakat al-Shabaab al Mujaheddin in Somalia, SciencesPo/ CERI, https://spire.sciencespo.fr/hdl:/2441/5ncvgncesl8n4a0rpg5k3c1j5p/resources/art-rm2-1.pdf (Accessed: February 4, 2023)

Marchal, R. (2018). Motivations and drivers of Al-Shabaab. In M. Keating and W. Matt (Eds.), *War and peace in Somalia: National grievances, local conflict and al-Shabaab* (pp. 309–317). New York: Oxford University Press, doi: 10.1093/oso/9780190947910.003.0027

Maruf, H., & Joseph, D. (2018). *Inside al-Shabaab: The secret history of al-qaeda's most powerful ally*. Bloomington: Indiana University Press, pp. 324, doi: 10.2307/j.ctv6mtfn2

Maxwell, D., & Majid, N. (2016). *Famine in Somalia: Competing imperatives, collecting failures, 2011–2012*, London: Hurst Publishers, pp. 272

Menkhaus, K. (2009). Somalia: They created a desert and called it peace(building). *Review of African Political Economy*, *36*(120), 223–233

Menkhaus, K. (2012). No access: Critical bottlenecks in the 2011 Somali Famine. *Global Food Security*, *1*(1), 29–35, doi: 10.1016/j.gfs.2012.07.004

Menkhaus, K. (2014). Al-Shabab's capabilities post-westgate. *Combating Terrorism Center (CTC) Sentinel*, *7*(2), https://ctc.westpoint.edu/wp-content/uploads/2014/02/CTCSentinel-Vol7Iss2.pdf (Accessed: February 4, 2023)

Menkhaus, K., & Boucek, C. (2010). Terrorism out of Somalia, Carnegie Endowment for International Peace, https://carnegieendowment.org/2010/09/23/terrorism-out-of-somalia/wnc (Accessed: February 4, 2023)

nor Kheyre, Z.A. (2022). The evolution of the Al-Shabaab Jihadist intelligence structure. *Intelligence and National Security*, *32*(7), 1061–1082, doi: 10.1080/02684527.2022.2095599

Sinkó, G. (2021). Different times, same methods: The impact of the National Security Service on the operations of the National Intelligence and Security Agency. *Journal of Central and Eastern European African Studies*, *1*(1-2).

Sinkó, G., & Besenyő, J. (2021). Comparison of the secret service of al-Shabaab, the Amniyat, and the National Intelligence and Security Agency (Somalia). *International*

Journal of Intelligence and CounterIntelligence, pp. 220–240, doi: 10.1080/08850607.2021.1987143

Starr, B. (2011). U.N. Report: Al-Shabaab is raising millions illegally in Somalia, https://edition.cnn.com/2011/WORLD/africa/08/05/somalia.al.shabaab.report/ (Accessed: February 4, 2023)

The New Arab (2017). Car bomb rocks Mogadishu hours after Somalia cabinet announcement, https://english.alaraby.co.uk/english/news/2017/3/21/car-bomb-rocks-mogadishu-hours-after-somalia-cabinet-announcement (Accessed: February 4, 2023)

United Nations (2010). Report of the monitoring group on Somalia pursuant to security council resolution 1853 (2008), p. 31, https://documents-dds-ny.un.org/doc/UNDOC/GEN/N10/246/89/PDF/N1024689.pdf?OpenElement (Accessed: February 4, 2023)

United Nations (2013a). Letter dated 12 July 2013 from the Chair of the Security Council Committee pursuant to resolutions 751 (1992) and 1907 (2009) concerning Somalia and Eritrea addressed to the President of the Security Council, S/2013/413, https://digitallibrary.un.org/record/752852 (Accessed: February 4, 2023)

United Nations (2013b). Report of the monitoring group on Somalia and Eritrea pursuant to security council resolution 2060 (2012): Somalia, p. 57, https://documents-dds-ny.un.org/doc/UNDOC/GEN/N13/361/85/PDF/N1336185.pdf?OpenElement (Accessed: February 4, 2023)

United Nations (2022). Letter dated 11 July 2022 from the Chair of the Security Council Committee pursuant to resolutions 1267 (1999), 1989 (2011) and 2253 (2015) concerning Islamic State in Iraq and the Levant (Da'esh), Al-Qaida and associated individuals, groups, undertakings and entities addressed to the President of the Security Council, S/2022/547, https://www.securitycouncilreport.org/atf/cf/%7B65BFCF9B-6D27-4E9C-8CD3-CF6E4FF96FF9%7D/S%202022%20547.pdf (Accessed: February 4, 2023)

United Nations Assistance Mission in Somalia (UNSOM) and the World Bank (2017). The Somalia security and justice sector public expenditure review, Washington DC, https://www.economicsandpeace.org/wp-content/uploads/2022/03/GTI-2022-web-09062022.pdf (Accessed: February 4, 2023)

Wise, R. (2011). Al Shabaab, case study number 2, *Center for Strategic & International Studies*, https://csis-website-prod.s3.amazonaws.com/s3fs-public/legacy_files/files/publication/110715_Wise_AlShabaab_AQAM%20Futures%20Case%20Study_WEB.pdf (Accessed: February 2, 2023)

31

BOKO HARAM IN NIGERIA

Evolution, Strategy, Impact

Nathaniel D. Danjibo and Scott N. Romaniuk

> *... the Prophet had himself noted that after his death, the umma would split into 73 sects, out of which only one would see salvation ... Many saw their self-chosen sect as the sect that would be saved*
>
> —Mustapha, 2017: 5

INTRODUCTION

Although terrorism is not a recent occurrence, it gained heightened levels of attention after the terrorist attacks on the United States (US) on September 11, 2001. The 9/11 attacks aroused a fresh sense of doubt regarding the influence of religion in the facilitation and intensification of violence. Al-Rasheed and Shterin (2009: xvii) assert that "[i]t was only recently that the link between faith and violence looked like a thing from the past ... The previous generation of scholars of religion predicted the death of faith, but it seems that *dying for faith* is undergoing a revival in the contemporary world." The field of terrorism studies has garnered significant interest across various academic disciplines, encompassing political science, sociology, anthropology, psychology, law, religion, and history. However, similar to many other academic areas, there is a lack of consensus in the conceptualisation and theorisation of the phenomenon of terrorism. According to the assertion made by Frank Jones (cited in Solomon, 2017, p. 4), it was argued that:

> ... despite volumes of books, articles and studies of terrorism, there has been scant investment made in developing a theory of terrorism. Instead, scholars and practitioners devote their effort to writing about the history of terrorism, examining a variety of terrorist movements, discussing the influence of political ideologies and religious beliefs on terrorist motives, dissecting their operational environment, or analyzing the psychological makeup of terrorists. This has resulted in a broken looking glass approach to understanding terrorism whereby each shard casts a portion of the image but not a complete likeness.

Since 2009, Boko Haram (BH), also known as the Nigerian Taliban, Jama'atu Ahlis Sunna Lidda'awati wal-Jihad (JAS), or People Committed to the Prophet's Teachings for Propagation and Jihad, has garnered significant attention in both contemporary literary and academic discussions (Danjibo 2009, 2017). As a result, Nigeria has been struggling to address the widespread violence that BH commits. Following that period, the group's violent activities have resulted in the tragic deaths of more than 32,000 people (UNDP, 2018). The group stands as the most lethal terrorist organisation in the West African region. It was officially recognised as the most perilous and formidable, surpassing even the Islamic State of Iraq and Syria (ISIS) in both 2014 and 2018. Despite the purported efforts of the Nigerian government to significantly weaken the group, the Global Terrorism Index has ranked BH as the third most lethal terrorist organisation globally (Channels Television Report, November 6, 2018). Hence, it is crucial to meticulously record the sequence of occurrences linked to BH in an academic manner while also offering a comprehensive examination of the factors, strategies, and evolutions underlying the group's activities.

RECENT DEVELOPMENTS

Nigeria is host to several armed militant groups, encompassing a range of ideologies and affiliations. These include Fulani extremists and the Islamic State in the Greater Sahara (ISGS), which emerged as a splinter faction from Al Mourabitoun, an al-Qaeda-affiliated militant organisation. Additionally, there are separatist movements such as

DOI: 10.4324/9780429426063-35

the Indigenous People of Biafra (IPOB), as well as various militias, including the Atyap, Tiv, and Jukun militias, with the latter being characterised by limited organisational structure. Furthermore, the Bassa Kwomu, Igburra, Niger Delta, and Koluama Seven Brothers militant/extremist groups are also active within the country. BH is widely recognised as the most formidable and hazardous of the various factions active in Nigeria. BH is a Salafi-jihadist organisation that seeks to establish an Islamic state in Nigeria by replacing the existing secular government with a regime that strictly adheres to Sharia law.

In Hausa, the term "Boko Haram" literally means "Western education is forbidden" (Bertoni et al. 2019). The fact that BH mostly targets Christians and sets churches on fire indicates that it is an organisation opposed to Christianity with an Islamization-focused spiritual goal (Ben-Edet, 2022). Usman Dan Fodio, a jihadist, served as both their source of legitimacy and motivation. They believed that Western democracy had undermined Islamic ideals and that inflicting terror was one way they could win back northern Nigeria for Islam (Pieria & Zennb, 2016).

The group mainly operates within the northeastern region of the country, with a particular focus on the Lake Chad area. Incidents of devastating suicide and armed assaults have been documented in multiple states, namely Borno, Yobe, Bauchi, Kano, Kaduna, Kogi, Plateau, and Adamawa. Additionally, such incidents have also occurred in the Federal Capital Territory (FCT), which encompasses Abuja, the federal capital city. The organisation has also perpetrated lethal assaults in other regions of the country. BH exhibits a significant presence characterised by violent activities in neighbouring nations within the region, namely Chad, Niger, Cameroon, and Mali. BH has exhibited a pattern of indiscriminate targeting, with a notable emphasis on perpetrating violence against Western individuals. Moreover, the group has demonstrated a special inclination towards targeting those who identify as Christians or Muslims, whom they perceive as "infidels." On May 22, 2014, BH was added to the list of individuals and organisations subject to the targeted financial sanctions and arms embargo by the Al-Qaida Sanctions Committee of the Security Council, coinciding with its recognition as the most lethal terrorist organisation globally (United Nations, 2014).

The number of bombings carried out by BH since 2009, which targeted churches, the Nigerian government, the United Nations (UN) headquarters in Abuja, security personnel, and civilians, has increased (Ahmed-Gamgum, 2018). Attacks by BH keep becoming more expert, lethal, and well-planned as time goes by. Between 2016 and 2018, the military was able to restrain their excesses, but towards the end of that year, the BH terrorists came back to life and took control (Ali et al. 2016). According to the Global Coalition to Protect Education from Attack (2018), BH is believed to have displaced 2.2 million people in the Lake Chad region and killed no less than 20,000 people between 2009 and 2019. BH has enlisted men, boys, and young women as warriors, and thousands of them have been kidnapped and may never be freed (Abah, 2021).

Between 2016 and 2017, BH frequently directed its aggression towards villages and military installations. The group perpetrated acts of violence against mosques and engaged in the killing of internally displaced individuals seeking refuge from the intensifying conflicts. BH experienced a notable increase in its attacks and territorial expansion over the course of several years, reaching its peak of violence during the period spanning 2014 and 2015. The indiscriminate use of violence by BH, particularly against Muslims, has resulted in fractures within the group. In 2016, BH underwent a process of fragmentation, resulting in the formation of two distinct factions. Abu Mohammed Abubakar al-Sheikawi, also known as Abubakar Shekau, led the first faction, known as Jama'atu Ahlis Sunna Lidda'adati wal-Jihad, as previously mentioned. Abu Musab al-Barnawi was in charge of the second faction, known as the Islamic State in West Africa (IS-WA).

The group has frequently been depicted as a homogenous entity, and publications rarely make a distinction between its two factions, despite the occurrence of a division. Both militant and extremist organisations pose significant threats and exhibit several similarities, albeit with certain distinctions. JAS, for instance, is widely acknowledged as the more perilous of the two entities, employing more aggressive tactics and organising systematic assaults against Western individuals, especially Christians, as well as Muslims perceived as "infidels" by the group. JAS categorises individuals who do not endorse their cause as direct adversaries and sees them as proponents of the Nigerian government. In contrast, ISIS-WA expresses disapproval of JAS' practice of attacking ordinary Muslims and instead directs its attacks towards Christians. However, it still resorts to violence against those who do not adhere to Sharia law.

The attack methodologies employed by IS-WA exhibit distinct variations compared to their counterparts, characterised by a comparatively lower frequency but a greater magnitude in terms of scale. While JAS is mostly active in the vicinity of the Nigeria-Cameroon border, IS-WA tends to concentrate its activities in close proximity to the Nigeria-Niger border (European Union Agency for Asylum, EUAA, 2021).

HISTORY AND EVOLUTION OF BH

The evolution of BH is attributed to several factors ranging from ideology to poverty, unemployment, underdevelopment, marginalisation, corruption, injustice, and global jihadist expansion (UNDP, 2018). Whatever reasons are adduced for the emergence of BH, it is a form of Islamism or political Islam that "provides Islamists a powerful ideological tool that they can wield to 'purge' Muslim societies of 'impurities' and "accretion," which they see as the reason for Muslim decline" (Ayoob, 2011: 2). Whereas scholars have shown that "Boko Haram emerged in the context of a broader Islamic reform movement in northern Nigeria in the 1990s and subsequently developed from an Islamic insurgency into a full-scale war in 2013" (Cold-Ravnkilde & Plambech, 2015; see Salaam, 2013; Besenyő & Mayer, 2015), others, including the US government, contend that the group first appeared in the early 2000s (Thurston, 2017; Blanchard & Cavigelli, 2018). One common denominator is the fact that it emerged as a fundamentalist sect, challenging not only the existing status quo in Islam but also the very basis of modern state formation, including Westernisation and democracy (Mohammed, 2015). Mohammed Yusuf, who was the founder of BH, was a *Wahabist* who received his early tutelage under Sheikh Jafaru Adam, a renowned *Izala* preacher based in Kano but whose itinerant preaching took him to most parts of the northeast of Nigeria, including Maiduguri.

The organisation known as Izala tul Bidi'a Wa Iqama tul Sunna, which translates to the rejection of innovation and the safeguarding of essential tradition, was initially established by Mallam Suleman. However, it was Sheikh Abubakar Gummi who gained widespread recognition and popularity for this organisation (Mustapha, 2017). This aligns with the teachings and theology of Wahhabism. In general, Wahhabists can be identified as adherents of Salafism, a religious movement that places significant emphasis on strict adherence to orthodox principles. Consequently, they tend to reject the notion of a flexible or evolving interpretation of Islam and its core beliefs, known as aqida. According to Brown (2015) and Thurston (2016), the Salafists hold five core beliefs. These beliefs encompass: i) adherence to Sunni Islam, which entails rejecting Shi'ite practices; ii) a preference for literal interpretations of sacred texts like the Qur'an and Hadith, as opposed to philosophical interpretations; iii) a reliance on direct consultation of the sacred text rather than deference to any particular school of thought; iv) a sense of divine obligation to purify Islam from perceived adulterations; and v) the importance of providing evidence (Hujja) to support their beliefs.

According to Kwabiah (2010), Mohammed ibn Abd-al-Wahhab, a scholar from present-day Saudi Arabia who lived in the 18th century, was the founder of the conservative Sunni Islamic sect known as Wahhabism. This institution, as stated by its founder, advocates for the eradication of purported innovations within the Islamic faith. The rise of Wahhabism throughout the Muslim world can be attributed to the financial support it received from the Persian Gulf oil wealth, which facilitated the establishment and development of mosques, schools, and various other institutions.

The Izala, a Wahabist movement, advocated for the complete repudiation of jurisprudence-based Islam, highlighting the literal or direct replication of Sunna Islam as it was practiced during the lifetime of the Prophet Muhammad. In addition to being revivalists, they also identify as reformists (Charlick, 2007:23).

Mohammed Yusuf allegedly met Sheikh Jafar Adam in Maiduguri during one of his itinerant missions and decided to follow in his footsteps as one of Jafar's most important disciples. They diverged when Mohammed Yusuf developed his doctrine of state condemnation and vehemently rejected the principle that permitted women to receive Western education, in addition to condemning any Muslim who would accept employment in a modern, corrupt state. Sheikh Jafar reportedly warned Yusuf about the dangers of defying state authority and publicly predicted that Yusuf would die like a dog. Khaled Sheikh Jafar was brutally assassinated in his Kano mosque around 5:00 a.m. in April 2007 by assassins who were later identified as Mohammed Yusuf's hitmen.

Other notable Islamic scholars who perished at the hands of the BH sect include Sheikh Bashar Mustapha in 2010, Sheikh Ahmed Abdullahi Bolori in 2011, Sheikh Ibrahim Birkuti in Biu town in June 2011, Sheikh Liman Bana in Ngala in August 2011, and Sheikh Auwal Adam Albani in Zaria in January 2014. These respected Islamic scholars belonged to the Izala sect, which refused to allow Muhammed Yusuf to preach in any of the mosques under their jurisdiction because he did not possess the Saudi certificate that would qualify him to preach in public (Perouse de Montclos, 2017: 29).

Kyari Mohammed's position was that two major phases shaped the evolution of the BH sect. The first was the period of indoctrination and tutelage, while the second was the period of evangelisation, otherwise referred to as the Da'awa. In the first phase, Muhammed Yusuf was influenced by the teachings of Ahmad Ibn Taymiyyah (1268–1328), a 14th-century Islamic scholar who had written extensively about jihad and even interpreted it beyond spiritual self-actualisation through fasting and prayer. Taymiyyah believed that it was a holy obligation for Muslims to go to war against the Mongols to either defend or expand the religion, which was considered a sacred duty for all Muslims living in Mongolia.

To immortalise Ibn Taymiyyah and his teachings, Muhammed Yusuf named the mosque he and his followers worshipped in Markaz Ibn Taymiyyah. According to Mohammed (2015: 9), "Ibn Taymiyya was a puritan Salafi scholar who strove to ensure Islam's adherence to sharia, eradicate alien innovation, and rejuvenate correct Islamic thought and practice." According to Thurston (2016: 5), "Salafis are Sunni Muslims, or even "uber Sunnis," who claim that the earliest Muslims (al-Salaf al-Salih, the pious predecessors) constitute a unified, orthodox, exemplary moral community." There are at least three known Salafi scholars whose unified position is that exegesis (tafsir) and Islamic law should only be derived directly from the Qur'an and the Hadith, devoid of any human interpretations and that innovation should be vehemently rejected. This is a total rejection of rational exegesis. In their chronological order, the scholars are Imam Ibn Hanbal, Imam Ibn Taymiyya, and Imam Muhammad Ibn Abd al-Wahhabi (Thurston, 2016: 35–46; Kassim, 2018). Mohammed Yusuf was emphatic about the Salafi creed when he said:

> We follow the ideology of the Salafists and any fatwa issued by a salafist Islamic scholar, on it we stand. No matter how important an Islamic scholar is, we need to know if he is guided by Salafist principles before we accept such a scholar. We will [only] scholars who preach and follow the Qur'an, the Sunna and the hadith … Every teaching of a scholar must be supported by the writings of salafist scholars (Pieri & Zenn, 2017: 47).

Yusuf could have said this against the backdrop of his fallout with notable Islamic scholars, including his renowned mentor, Sheikh Jafaru Adam, who disagreed with the extremist views propounded by Yusuf and his misguided followers. Later, Abubakar Shekau drew a clear distinction between the Salafists and others whom he classified as infidels when he reiterated, "Either you are with us, I mean real Muslims who are following Salafism or you are with Obama, Francois Hollande, George Bush, and Clinton" (as quoted in Pieri & Zenn, 2017: 46).

> Theologically, Salafis emphasize a literate understanding of the Qur'an and the Sunna (tradition or model) represented by the Prophet Muhammed. Salafis narrowly interpret the Islamic injunction to worship one God, and try to 'purify' other Muslims of alleged deviations in belief and practice (Thurston, 2017: 19).

It is essential to establish a clear differentiation between the evangelical and militant factions of BH. The examination of the transition of BH from proselytism to violent extremism necessitates a foundation in the principles of social justice. In the case of Egypt, for instance, state repression by successive regimes accounted for the emergence of radical jihadist groups responsible for the wave of violence (Anderson, 1997; Kassem, 2004). The arbitrary arrest and widespread indiscriminate extra-judicial killings of both Muhammed Yusuf, the founder, and other top leaders of the sect, including disabled followers, provided the remote justification for the group to embrace violence (Danjibo, 2017).

REJECTION OF SECULARISM AND DEMOCRACY

Muhammed Yusuf's narratives were founded upon four fundamental principles: a) the repudiation of Western education and Westernisation; b) the repudiation of idolatry, encompassing secularism, democracy, and partisan politics; c) the advocacy for modern governments; and d) the reprimand of local ulama who condemned the endeavours of his sect (Mohammed, 2015: 15). Boer (2005: 15–16) underscored the challenge of explicitly differentiating between moderate and fundamentalist Muslims in Nigeria. Both adhere to sharia and reject secularism; the primary distinction is the degree of ferocity with which they pursue their objectives and the risks they are willing to assume. Twelve states in northern Nigeria acceded to Sharia law between 1999 and 2000. This is because "Sharia deals not only with a Muslim's faith, how he prays, when he prays, and where he prays, but with a Muslim's education, health, housing, nutrition, employment, environment, commerce, transportation, and more" (Harnischfeger, 2008: 92). Moreover, the majority of Nigerian Muslims would not tolerate the unbridled expansion of democracy and its "freedoms."

The majority of Nigerian Muslims held the view that democracy not only supplanted the divine authority of Allah but also emerged as an abode of virtue and sanctity. Mohammed Yusuf categorically condemned democracy as a form of apostasy for this reason. To illustrate, he stated:

> Parliamentarians and members of assemblies have combined between (sic) them making themselves gods and ascribing partners to Allah. This is because their mace is their object of worship in various ways such as bowing to it, subjecting themselves to it, loving it and using it as a symbol of shirk (apostasy) as they do not pass any bill or make decisions without it (cited in Mohammed, 2015: 16).

After the bombing incident at St. Theresa's Catholic Church in Madalla, a community near Abuja, on the evening of Christmas Eve in 2011, the former President, Goodluck Jonathan, characterised BH as a "cancer" that necessitated immediate eradication. Abubakar Shekau asserted in his statement that (BH) should not be likened to a cancerous affliction. The individual in question regarded the condition as a manifestation of disbelief and supported his stance by referencing a verse from the Qur'an (2: 191), in which Allah states, "Chaos is worse than killing." Shekau proceeded to strongly denounce democracy and Western education, asserting that they are in direct opposition to the teachings of Allah and the Prophet of Islam:

> Everyone knows democracy is unbelief, and everyone knows the Constitution is unbelief, and everyone knows that there are things that Allah has forbidden in the Qur'an, and that are forbidden in countless hadiths of the Prophet, that are going on in Western schools … (Thurston, 2017: 160).

Despite Yusuf's firm opposition to secularism and democracy, he engaged in negotiations with the administration of

Ali Modu Sherrif during the latter's tenure as the Governor of Borno State. These negotiations resulted in the allocation of significant governmental roles to some of Yusuf's followers. Boi Fugi was appointed as the Commissioner for Religious Affairs; however, he resigned due to a disagreement with Governor Ali Modu Sherrif (Danjibo, 2017). The individual's choice to permit certain members to participate in the administration of Ali Modu Sherrif's government contradicted the directive he imparted to his followers, which said that individuals adhering to the Sunna should refrain from engaging in governmental roles inside contemporary, non-religious nations, as such involvement would contravene the fundamental tenets of sharia law. In order to provide a balanced perspective, it is important to acknowledge that Muhammed Yusuf permitted his adherents to assume governmental roles due to a preexisting agreement with Governor Ali Modu Sherrif, which centred on the comprehensive enforcement of sharia law.

Modu Sherrif made a commitment to fully apply sharia law in the event that Yusuf and his supporters provided their backing. Sheriff emerged victorious in the electoral process and assumed the position of governor of Borno State in 2003. However, he failed to uphold the agreement that had been established between himself and Yusuf. As a consequence, Yusuf instructed his associates to collectively tender their resignations from the incumbent government, thus initiating the onset of a tense dynamic between himself and Ali Modu Sherrif.

THE REJECTION OF WESTERNISATION

One of the core tenets espoused by Mohammed Yusuf was the repudiation of Westernisation, also known as "Boko" in the Hausa language. In relation to personal preference, it is observed that the typical Muslim residing in northern Nigeria tends to favour Islamic education over Western education. This inclination is eloquently depicted in a widely recognised song that resonates throughout the region, even among Muslim students who have received a Western education, as a means of expressing their disinterest in Western educational pursuits. According to Danjibo (2009, 2017), the Hausa song titled "Yan makarantan boko, ba karatu ba salla' sai yawan zagin malam'," which translates as "you, the pupils or students of western schools, do not read (the Quran) and you do not pray; save the constant abuse of a teacher," conveys a message to pupils or students attending Western schools. The song highlights their alleged lack of engagement with religious practices, such as reading the Quran and praying, while emphasising their tendency to subject their teachers to incessant abuse. When Mohammed Yusuf was arrested and interviewed by Nigerian Army personnel, he categorically said, "Yes, it is obviously forbidden." And when asked why he would use products of technology since western education is forbidden, he said, "The knowledge that brings technology is not a derivative of western education; it is from God and so cannot be rejected." According to Thurston (2017: 15):

Mohammed Yusuf's second principle was the rejection of Westernisation, referred to as "Boko" in Hausa. Again, in terms of preference, the average Muslim in northern Nigeria would prefer the Islamic slate to Western education, and this preference was artistically captured by a popular song sung across northern Nigeria even by Muslim students who attended Western schools to show their aversion for western education. The Hausa song *Yan makarantan boko, ba karatu ba salla' sai yawan zagin malam*', which translates as "you, the pupils or students of western schools, do not read (the Quran) and you do not pray; save the constant abuse of a teacher" (Danjibo 2009, 2017). When Mohammed Yusuf was arrested and interviewed by Nigerian Army personnel, he categorically said, "Yes, it is obviously forbidden." And when asked why he would use products of technology since Western education is forbidden, he said, "The knowledge that brings technology is not a derivative of Western education; it is from God and so cannot be rejected." According to Thurston (2017: 15),

> Boko is a tricky word to translate. One false etymology holds that the word is a corruption of the English book. Linguists, however, believe that boko is an indigenous Hausa word. Originally, it meant 'fraud', 'sham' or 'inauthentic'. It could be used as a verb meaning 'doing anything to create an impression that one is better off, or that something is of better quality or larger in amount than it is the case. Boko-boko could mean hoodwinking. During colonial rule in northern Nigeria, this original meaning of boko as 'fraud' was attached to Western-style schooling and to the Romanized script for writing Hausa, known as Hausar Boko. Calling Western-style education boko connotes a feeling that colonial schools could mislead Muslims into accepting false knowledge.

Yusuf's ideological stance, which asserts that Western education is in conflict with the principles of Allah, undermines a pristine system, and enforces values that are inherently contrary to Allah, gained additional support when students from certain tertiary institutions in Borno and Yobe States publicly destroyed their academic certificates, opting instead for the Umma Muhammadiya (community of believers) previously established by Muhammed Yusuf (Danjibo, 2009, 2017). This perspective aligns with the prevailing ideology of the Salafists, who hold the view that the educational framework in its entirety should be discarded in favour of the Salafi method, which draws its principles from the Holy Qur'an and the Hadith, the teachings and practices of the Prophet Muhammad (Thurston, 2016: 7). Following this, a representative from BH expressed in the Vanguard newspaper on August 14, 2009, that:

> Boko Haram does not in any way mean 'Western Education is a sin', as the infidel media continue to portray us. Boko Haram actually means 'Western Civilization' is forbidden. The difference is that while the first gives the impression that we are opposed to formal education coming from the West, that is Europe, which is not true, the second affirms our believe (sic) in the supremacy of Islamic culture (not education), for culture is broader, it includes education but not determined by Western Education. In this case we are talking of Western ways of life which include: constitutional provision as it relates to, for instance, the rights and privileges of women, the idea of homosexualism, lesbianism, sanctions in case of terrible crimes like drug trafficking, rape of infants, multi-party democracy in an overwhelmingly Islamic country like Nigeria, blue films, prostitution, drinking beer and alcohol and many others that are opposed to Islamic civilisation (Onuoha, 2015: 185; Thurston, 2017: 16).

According to Yusuf, the perceived fatal defect in Western education lies in its fundamental principles, which serve as the primary rationale for devout followers of Allah, particularly Muslims, to strongly oppose it. According to Mohammed (2015: 10), "We are ready to debate anyone on this creed. Western education is destructive. We didn't say knowledge is bad, but that the unbelief inside it is more than its usefulness. In the process of becoming educated, you become a mushrik (idolater)." Interestingly, following the seizure of his mosque and school during the uprising in July 2009, it was revealed that two of the classrooms were dedicated to the instruction of mathematics and English (Mustapha, 2017: 80).

FROM DA'AWA TO CONFLICT AND TERRORISM

Da'awa can be compared to the act of preaching and evangelism, namely through proselytization, with the aim of gaining additional converts or attracting individuals who were once Muslims but have strayed from the orthodox doctrines and practices of Islam. Muhammed Yusuf derived inspiration from the jihad led by Sheikh Usman Danfodiyo, which aimed to cleanse the Hausa states of rulers who not only introduced Bidi'a (innovation) but also incorporated elements of African indigenous or ancestral religion into Islam (Kane, 2003). Scholars like Hodgkin (1967), Loimeier (1997), and Mustapha (2017) have extensively discussed the practice known as Takfir, which is considered to be an act of disbelief in Islam. Muhammed Yusuf's pursuit of an unequivocal Islamic state was a determining factor in his selection of the appellation Jama'a til Ahlus Sunna Lid Da'awa khi Wal Jihadi, denoting individuals dedicated to the propagation of orthodox Islam via both proselytization and armed conflict (Danjibo, 2013).

Muhammed Yusuf derived inspiration from the jihad led by Sheikh Usman Danfodiyo, which aimed to cleanse the Hausa states of rulers who not only introduced innovations (known as Bidi'a) but also blended Islam with elements of African indigenous or ancestral religion (Kane, 2003). The practice referred to as Takfir in Islam, or unbelief, is recognised by the puritans (Hodgkin, 1967; Loimeier, 1997; Mustapha, 2017).

Muhammed Yusuf dedicated significant time and resources to propagating his opposition to innovation, employing a framework rooted in the natural Ptolemaic logic. His commitment to this cause was so profound that he even went as far as dismissing scientifically established truths. The individual in question held a disbelief in the spherical nature of the Earth as well as a lack of acceptance of the scientific explanation pertaining to lunar eclipses. He attained a position of influence, garnering a substantial cohort comprised of individuals who were dissatisfied and lacked literacy skills and who had become disillusioned with the shortcomings of the government. The primary objective of the Ahl-us Sunna Wal Jama'a, originally known as the sect, was to establish an Islamic state that strictly adhered to the laws of God (Sharia) and upheld the principles and practices of Prophet Muhammed. This entailed the creation of a caliphate based on the authentic teachings and traditions of the faith. Nevertheless, the amalgamation of Wahabism and Jihad prompted the sect to undergo a name alteration, resulting in the adoption of the title Jama'a til Ahlus Sunna Lid Da'awa tis Wal Jihadi, denoting a group dedicated to the propagation of orthodox Islam by both preaching and armed conflict.

In 2015, almost six years following the demise of Muhammed Yusuf, Abubakar Shekau, his designated successor, altered the sect's name to Wilayat Gharb Ifriqiya, which translates to the Islamic State in West Africa (IS-WA), by pledging loyalty to ISIS, as previously indicated. After the loss of territorial control by the violent extremist group to the Nigerian security forces, the group sought foreign assistance for its jihad. The sect's refusal to accept contemporary states and administrations, particularly those modelled after Western democracy, quickly led to conflicts with state authorities. The cult, by publicly renouncing the legitimacy of the contemporary governing body, demonstrated its reluctance to comply with state regulations, such as the requirement to wear crash helmets. This resistance was particularly evident among its adherents who were engaged in the commercial motorbike industry, commonly referred to as "yan achaba" or "yan kabukabu" in the Hausa language.

The commencement of violence between the BH group and the state became evident in June 2009. After a car accident resulting in the deaths of four individuals belonging to the sect, Operation Flush, the security agency of the state, intercepted a group of sect members who were travelling on motorcycles to perform burial rites for the deceased. The agency proceeded to confront them with their failure to adhere to the mandatory use of helmets. In the aftermath of the confrontations, law enforcement authorities apprehended and held individuals affiliated with the group, concurrently inflicting gunshot wounds on a range of 14 to 17 additional individuals. Muhammed Yusuf perceived this event as the catalyst to assert the sect's readiness to confront both state security agents and all adversaries of Islam in armed conflict. Following the occurrence, Muhammed Yusuf delivered a sermon on a Friday in which he admonished all members of the sect to prepare themselves for potential conflict with the state (Onuoha, 2015).

Between July 26 and August 1, 2009, a significant escalation of violence occurred between members of BH and law enforcement authorities, resulting in the tragic loss of more than 800 lives, which included the unfortunate deaths of 22 police officers (Mustapha, 2017). Due to the inability of the police to effectively manage the issue, the government of Shehu Umaru Yar'Adua made the decision to deploy the Nigerian Army to restore control over the situation. Military personnel apprehended Muhammed Yusuf inside a goat pen belonging to his father-in-law, and after an interrogation process, they transferred him to the custody of law enforcement officials. Several prominent members of the cult, including the individual's father-in-law, were apprehended and transferred into police custody. Several days later, law enforcement authorities conducted extrajudicial killings of Muhammed Yusuf and his adherents, subjecting their remains to public humiliation. This unlawful action exacerbated the ongoing conflict and contributed to the transformation of the sect into a terrorist organisation (Danjibo, 2017).

ORGANISATIONAL STRUCTURE OF BH

During the time when Muhammed Yusuf assumed leadership of the group, BH was reported to possess a centralised command structure, with Mohammed Yusuf serving as its head or sheikh. The gang had not established a formal organisational structure for its operations, relying instead on a network of trusted individuals. Following the demise of Yusuf, Shekau promptly assumed the role of spiritual head and proceeded to restructure the organisation, placing a heightened emphasis on decentralisation. BH employed a decentralised organisational structure consisting of numerous tiny cells strategically dispersed over various regions in northern Nigeria. This approach facilitated efficient decision-making processes and operational techniques. The leaders of the cellular units assembled under the authority of a Shura, or council, with Shekau serving as the principal figure, supported by two prominent deputies (Onuoha, 2015).

Appointing themselves as Amirs (English Emirs), the cell leaders also chose their deputies, who gathered under a smaller shura. Ahmed Salkida, the sole journalist known to have engaged with BH and potentially the exclusive one to have encountered Shekau directly, asserted that "Shekau has groomed men and women in their thousands that even he can no longer keep in line" (as cited in Zenn, 2018: vi). Al-Barnawi, the son of the late Mohammed Yusuf, is the leader of BH, also known as Ansaru or the Islamic State of West African Province (ISWAP). The group demonstrates its commitment to the Islamic State, establishing its global nature. The ISWAP faction under al-Barnawi holds the opinion that Muslims and mosques shouldn't be the focus of jihad, in contrast to the faction under Abubakar Shekau, which commits acts of violence against Muslims and mosques (Danjibo, 2015).

RECRUITMENT STRATEGIES

BH implemented many measures to attract young individuals to join the organisation. The techniques employed encompassed several elements such as ideology, coercion, the issue of young unemployment, poverty, ethnic marginalisation, and the utilisation of criminal gangs (Cole et al. 2017). The group leveraged its substantial following during the Da'awa led by Mohammed Yusuf to transcend various social groups within the societal hierarchy. This allowed them to portray both the group itself and, in certain instances, the Muslim community as victims of persecution perpetrated by the Nigerian state. In pursuit of this objective, the group's leaders would provide instances of the unjustifiable assassination of Muhammed Yusuf and other prominent figures inside the organisation. Additionally, Thurston (2017) provided accounts of the violent incidents that resulted in the loss of Muslim lives in southern Kaduna and Jos. BH benefited from the elevated levels of youth unemployment and poverty in the northeastern region to actively recruit a substantial number of young individuals. The organisation accomplished this by offering assistance to individuals in need, facilitating marriages for its members at no cost, extending low-interest loans to young individuals for the purpose of establishing small-scale enterprises, and utilising coercive tactics. BH also capitalised on the ethnic marginalisation experienced by certain tribes in the north-eastern region, who had previously been marginalised, and strategically selected Emirs from these groups to assume positions of power inside its self-proclaimed caliphate. Additionally, the organisation enlisted individuals with a history of criminal activity and substance abuse, as documented by Danjibo and Aubyn (2017) during their fieldwork.

THE CALIPHATE OF BH AND ITS FUNDING STRATEGY

Following the 2009 clashes and the ensuing death of Mohammed Yusuf, adherents of the religious faction retreated into clandestine operations, employing a period of strategic consolidation to amass resources, restructure their ranks, and expand their membership base. This expansion was facilitated through diverse methods, including the acquisition of individuals through financial incentives, leveraging the prevailing conditions of widespread impoverishment, and exploiting the marginalisation experienced by specific ethnic groups.

The group successfully established territorial dominance over local communities, markets, and border posts in Nigeria, Niger, Cameroon, and Chad. The sect strategically assumed complete authority over the Zambisa forest, which housed a significant training facility known as Camp Zero. Following the unsuccessful coup attempt in April 1990, the General Ibrahim Babangida regime originally established this camp. (Besenyő & Mayer, 2015; Yelwa, 2017). The forest exhibits considerable dimensions surpassing those of multiple European countries while also sharing borders with Cameroon, Chad, Niger, and Nigeria and extending into the Central African Republic. According to Alhaji Sanusi Mudstapha, the district head of Duhu, in a recorded interview, it was revealed that the Zambisa region is home to over 200 farming and fishing villages. This indicates that the forest in this area plays a significant role in supporting the livelihoods and operations of BH (2017 fieldwork).

Unbeknownst to the Nigerian government, the extremist group BH, under the leadership of Abubakar Shekau, was able to establish a caliphate by successfully seizing control of numerous local government areas inside the states of Adamawa, Borno, and Yobe. The conceptualisation of the group posed challenges due to the inclusion of an ethnic dimension, wherein the purpose was defined as the establishment of a Kanuri Caliphate, reflecting the passionate nature of the movement. Pieri and Zenn (2017: 43) wrote a book chapter in which they stated the following:

> To understand Boko Haram and its trajectories—and especially why it has succeeded in winning recruits in specific areas of Borno State and the Lake Chad region—it is also necessary to understand how the relationship between Boko Haram's Kanuri leaders and Kanuri members bind the movement to border-region communities and how its historical narratives and grievances resonate particularly with the Kanuri population. For this reason, this chapter contributes to previous studies of religious and historical aspects of Boko Haram because it is the first one to specifically address the Kanuri aspect of Boko Haram's origins, rise and expansion.

The assertion that BH is a Kanuri movement may face scholarly opposition; however, it is indisputable that not only was its founder, Muhammed Yusuf, a Kanuri from Yobe State, but so are all of its key leaders (including ISWAP's Abubalkar Shekau, his son Al-Barnawi, and the majority of the foot soldiers). During a fieldwork expedition conducted in Adamawa State, it was seen that BH faced significant obstacles in its attempts to infiltrate or seize control of Yola and Jimeta. The Fulani community in these areas, which saw the BH sectarian movement as a direct threat to the established Sokoto Caliphate that Sheikh Usman Danfodiyo founded, was primarily to blame for this. The utilisation of personal interviews provided insights into the mobilisation efforts of the Fulani Emirate in Yola, which aimed to gather Fulani individuals from various regions of West Africa in order to counteract the encroachment of BH into Yola. It can be stated that regardless of the ethnic conflict associated with BH, the primary goal of BH was to restore a pre-colonial Islamic state that existed prior to the establishment of Nigerian borders by British colonialists. This Islamic state aimed to supplant the prevailing Emirate administrative structure of the Sokoto and the Kanem Bonem Caliphates (US Army, 2015: 3).

BH employed various techniques that facilitated the acquisition of funds for the group's activities. Upon establishing its caliphate and acquiring power over many localities, the cult promptly implemented taxation measures on the inhabitants. The group maintained control over the majority of market economies and introduced border crossing fees. It was also significantly reliant on activities such as cattle rustling, bank raids, and involvement in the oil sector beyond the border. At a certain juncture, it assumed authority over the grain, tomato, BH and pepper industries in Chad and the Niger Republic also participated in abductions for monetary gain, exerted pressure on the upper class through threats and force to extort funds, and received financial backing from other terrorist entities (Onyibe, 2016).

Additionally, there exist unverified assertions regarding the group's receipt of financial assistance from sympathetic foreign governments and organisations (fieldwork information, 2017). This corroborates the findings of Fanusie and Entz (2017), who identified several primary sources of funding for BH. These include the abduction of individuals for ransom, levies imposed on local populations, coercive practices to extract funds, pillaging and acquiring resources from conflict zones, illicitly obtaining cash from financial institutions, engaging in bank heists, engaging in illicit trade activities, participating in human trafficking, operating legitimate businesses, engaging in agricultural activities, conducting illegal mining operations, receiving donations from sympathisers, receiving external assistance from terrorist organisations, engaging in cattle rustling, and engaging in automobile theft.

MAJOR ATTACKS BY BH AND JAS

More than 35,000 individuals have been killed as a result of BH's extensive and lethal attacks since the organisation began its insurgency in 2009. BH's initial assault was highly methodical, with security personnel, particularly the police, as its primary target. This could be characterised as a mission of vengeance for the unjust execution of Muhammed Yusuf and BH members. Christian churches and establishments associated with "profanity," such as Western schools and bear parlours, constituted the second target. Muslim clerics, who have unequivocally denounced the group's violent endeavours, constituted the third target (Andekin, 2019). For the sake of brevity, we enumerate the following significant attacks:

- September 7, 2010: BH attacked a prison in Bauchi town, setting free over 720 prisoners, many of whom were members of the sect;
- June 16, 2011: The bombing of the Police Headquarters in Abuja;
- August 26, 2011: The bombing of the UN building;
- November 4, 2011: Over 120 people were killed by the sect's coordinated attacks in Maiduguri and Potiskum;
- April 2014: The kidnapping of over 270 secondary school girls in Chibok, Borno State;
- March 2017: The kidnapping of over 130 secondary school girls in Dapchi, Yobe State;
- October 2018: The killing of over 100 soldiers in Metele, Borno State;
- Over time, the destruction of over 1,500 schools in Adamawa, Borno, and Yobe States;
- Over time, the destruction of over 500 hospitals and clinics in the three abovementioned states (Figures 31.1 and 31.2).

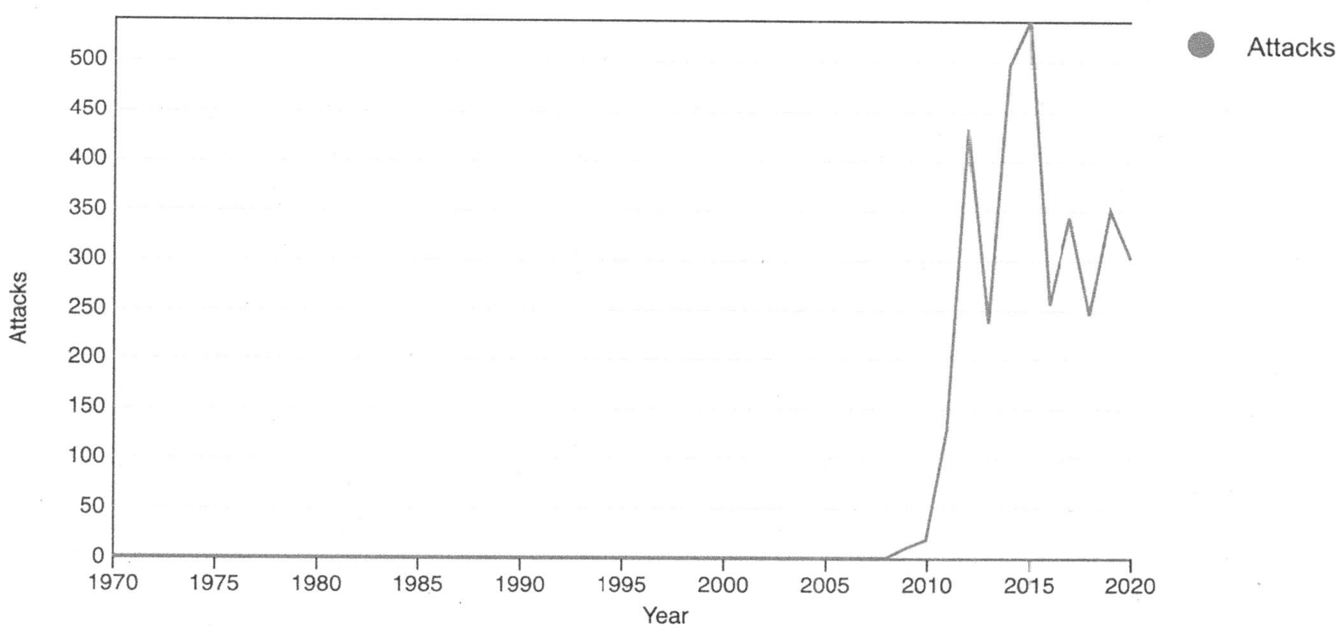

Figure 31.1 BH Attacks.

Source: Global Terrorism Database (GTD) (2024).

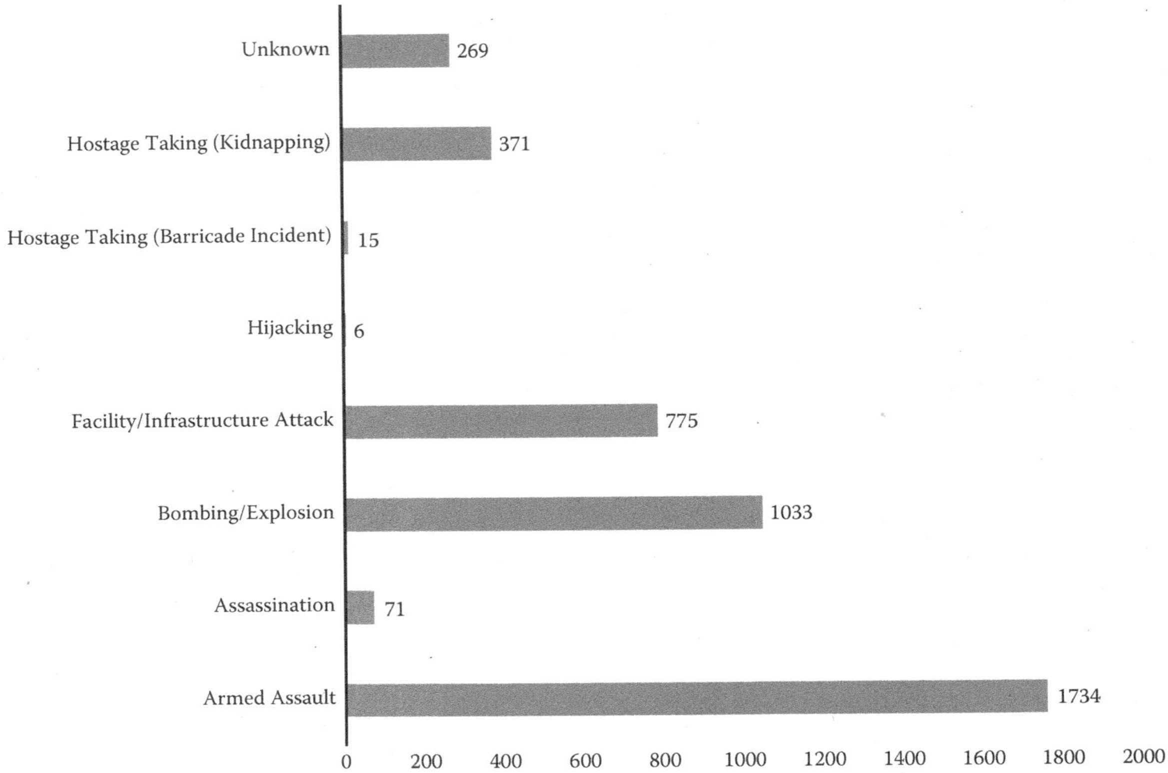

Figure 31.2 Boko Haram Terrorist Attacks.

Source: Global Terrorism Database (GTD) (2024).

IMPACT AND INTENSITY OF BH ATTACKS

In a study by Campbell and Harwood (2018), the Armed Conflict Location and Event Data (ACLED) and the Nigerian Security Tracker (NST) were both used to examine the lethality of BH attacks. The findings indicate that these attacks were highly lethal, to the extent that BH was classified as the most dangerous terrorist organisation globally in 2014:

> From June 2011 through June 2018, the NST documented 2,021 incidents involving Boko Haram, in which 37,530 people were killed, nearly double the conventionally cited estimate of twenty thousand. Over the same period, ACLED identified 3,346 incidents, in which 34,261 people were killed. Both totals reflect deaths of alleged Boko Haram fighters, government forces, and civilians combined. Though ACLED tends toward lower casualty estimates and the NST higher estimates, both identify the same progression: the conflict, beginning in 2012 (sic), escalated quickly and peaked in 2014–2015. Levels of violence declined in 2016, following a major Nigerian military campaign to recover Boko Haram–occupied territory launched in late 2014 that continued through the following year. Troops from Cameroon, Chad, and Niger, as well as some mercenaries, played a major role in this campaign.

The terrorist activities carried out by BH have significant ramifications on several aspects of the social, political, and economic landscape of the Nigerian state. Initially, a considerable number of educational institutions were obliterated, resulting in a substantial population of children being deprived of access to formal education (Favara et al., 2015). Numerous industries, including banking, internet service providers, petrol stations, and markets, experienced complete cessation of operations. The agricultural sector had significant disruptions due to farmers' inability to access their farms, resulting in severe food shortages, hunger, infections, and premature mortality, particularly among the younger population. A number of women have also experienced the loss of their husbands, the absence of children, and psychological distress. In relation to the impact on infrastructure, religious institutions, residential dwellings, transportation structures, electrical facilities, financial institutions, and healthcare facilities have incurred significant damage as a result of terrorist activities perpetrated by BH, as well as the subsequent counter-terrorism measures implemented by the government. Additional consequences of the violence can be attributed to cultural and ecological heritage (Buhari & Soetan, 2018) as well as human security (Amalu, 2015).

According to the Humanitarian Response Plan of February 2018 by the United Nations Children's Fund (UNICEF), a total of 1,400 schools were reported to have been damaged only in Borno State. Additionally, UNICEF (2018: n.p.) mentioned the following in the report:

> Only half of the 755 health facilities in Borno remain functional and nearly 1,400 schools have been damaged or destroyed. Many of these schools are unable to reopen for safety reasons. Over one million children are currently out of school. The protracted crisis has also compromised the physical safety and psychosocial well-being of 2.5 million children in north-east Nigeria, who require immediate assistance. In the three most directly affected states of Adamawa, Borno and Yobe, 7.7 million people require humanitarian assistance.

Practically every hospital, church, and mosque was destroyed by BH, illustrating the extent of the damage BH has caused to soft targets, especially field hospitals and healthcare providers or people who are at risk of being attacked in cities and villages (Besenyő et al., 2021). The scenario led to the emergence of a severe humanitarian crisis, ranking among the most dire globally, as it caused the displacement of more than two million individuals. Based on the findings presented in the 2017 Amnesty International Report, it is evident that a majority exceeding 80% of individuals who have been internally displaced are currently residing within host communities. Conversely, the remaining 20% of these individuals have sought refuge in internally displaced persons (IDP) camps. In an interview conducted with a district head in Adamawa State, it was asserted that members affiliated with the insurgent group BH have reportedly fathered a significant number of offspring, estimated to exceed 20,000. These children, however, have encountered challenges in terms of acceptance and integration into diverse communities. This is why there has been a severe lack of food security and a continuation of the cycle of poverty, along with the resulting drop in economic output and lack of resources. According to the World Bank (2015), it was projected that BH has resulted in a financial loss of US$8.3 billion and infrastructural damage amounting to US$9.2 billion (refer to Magrin & Perouse de Monclos, 2018: 11, note 4).

The adverse consequences of the fatalities of thousands of people and the forced relocation of more than two million individuals had a detrimental effect on the democratic system, which was thus stigmatised by BH. During the 2015 general elections, a significant portion of the population, particularly individuals seeking asylum in the neighbouring nations of Cameroun, Chad, and Niger, as well as those who fled from the northeast to other regions inside the country, experienced disenfranchisement in relation to their voting rights. A significant number of individuals who experienced internal displacement were also unable to exercise their right to vote. The decision to postpone the polls by two weeks was influenced by the increased frequency of attacks by BH and the prevailing state of insecurity. This decision was reached after the recommendations of the National Security Advisor, Col. Sambo Dasuki, and the Service Chiefs. This was because on February 18, 2015, Abubakar Shekau released a video threatening that "this election will not be held even if we are dead." Due to the recent escalation of hostilities and targeted assaults on communities and displaced individuals in the states of Adamawa, Borno, and Yobe by the insurgent group known as BH, a significant number of Nigerian citizens residing in this region will likely face obstacles in exercising their right to vote during the forthcoming elections scheduled for February 2019. The exclusion of a significant portion of the population from participating in the upcoming elections is likely to have profound consequences for democracy, effective governance, and regional and national development. This is due to the increased allocation of resources that would be required to manage the prevailing security concerns within the country.

NIGERIA'S CT STRATEGY AND BH

The Nigerian government has implemented a range of strategies that embrace both hard and soft power tactics, exhibiting a multifaceted approach (Andekin, 2019). According to the Institute for Peace and Conflict Resolution (2017: 161), these strategies are effectively assisting the military in its efforts to restore law, order, and security in the North-East region by using the strategy of winning over the support and trust of the local population. The more rigorous strategies encompassed law enforcement and military interventions. During its early stages, the Nigerian government exhibited a delay in officially recognising BH as a terrorist organisation. Furthermore, the government's response to BH has consistently framed its actions as an internal security operation rather than a full-fledged war. This observation was made during a group discussion at a seminar attended by military and security personnel on November 27, 2018. In addition to the initial suppression of the July 2009 crisis in Maiduguri, the government proceeded to implement a declaration of a state of emergency in 14 local government areas spanning the states of Adamawa, Borno, and Yobe. While this particular strategy achieved certain levels of effectiveness, it also resulted in infringements against the basic rights of individuals, particularly in instances involving military roadblocks and the search of residences belonging to suspected individuals or communities suspected of harbouring such individuals.

The government further implemented a Joint Task Force known as Operation Restore Order, which was later substituted by the construction of a 7th Mechanised Division. This transition shifted the operational strategy from a combined approach to one focused solely on military operations. The establishment of several military operations was deemed necessary in response to the prevailing circumstances. These operations include Operation Boyona, Operation Zaman Lafiya (which aims to promote peaceful co-existence), Operation Lafiya Dole (which seeks to achieve peace through the use of force), Operation Crackdown, Operation Gama Aiki (which aims to accomplish the assigned tasks), the Civilian Joint Task Force (known as the Civilian JTF), and the Multi-National Military Joint Task Force (MNJTF) involving soldiers from Benin Republic, Cameroun, Chad, Niger, and Nigeria (Andekin, 2019). Although these operations have achieved notable successes, such as the recovery of previously controlled territories and the elimination of numerous members of the terrorist group, they have also resulted in a significant disruption of security. Consequently, members of the group have infiltrated the broader society into smaller units, perpetrating attacks on vulnerable targets.

CONTROVERSY OVER US ASSISTANCE

Initially, the US showed a tendency to underestimate the potential of BH to pose a significant danger to its national security. However, this perception was altered following the occurrence of the bombing incident targeting the UN building in Abuja on August 26, 2011. The note left by BH said that the UN building was targeted due to its perceived role as a platform for many forms of global malevolence, specifically a forum for "all global evil." The act was intended to convey a message to the President of the US and other individuals deemed non-believers, or "infidels." There exist a range of opinions regarding the involvement of the US in Nigeria's counterterrorism endeavours. During the tenure of former President Goodluck Jonathan, particularly in the aftermath of the abduction of more than 270 Chibok girls, the US consented to provide technical and logistical assistance. The delegation from the US that came to Nigeria was met with elevated expectations, as there was optimism that their presence would contribute to the successful retrieval of the kidnapped Chibok girls.

Over time, the US was unable to achieve remarkable outcomes, resulting in the team's withdrawal from Nigeria without attaining any significant accomplishments. Furthermore, the US declined to provide weaponry sales to the Nigerian government for the purpose of carrying out military operations against BH. The US implemented a thorough, three-pronged strategy to address and eliminate the threat that BH posed in the nations of the Lake Chad Region after the initial approach proved ineffective. The three key areas encompassed by them were defence, development, and diplomacy. The US has raised concerns about the potential affiliation of BH with al-Qaeda in the Islamic Maghreb (AQIM) and al-Shabaab, which could pose a threat to its national security. According to a report conducted by the United States Institute of Peace (USIP), an examination was conducted on the security conditions prevailing in the Lake Chad Region.

> The United States took special note of BH in 2011 because it was concerned that the group would converge or cooperate with al-Qaeda in the Islamic Maghreb (AQIM) and develop the ambition and capability to threaten US national security. The United States implored Nigeria to remedy poor governance and address corruption and serious abuses by government and security forces which BH leverages to recruit members in northeast Nigeria and in some cases prevented the United States from offering requested security assistance. By 2014, these attempts had failed, so the United States tried a new approach: treating BH as a regional problem and working to convince the LCR countries to cooperate to defeat BH. The 3Ds used bilateral approaches to help these countries fight BH and mitigate its impact, while also organizing regional focused platforms, working groups, programs, exercises, and plans to support cooperation and undermine BH recruitment. The 3Ds delivered humanitarian assistance to internally displaced persons (IDPs), and refugees, supported community resistance to BH, and advised and built the capacity of partner security forces. US support was key to helping LCR countries' forces collaboratively clear and hold territory the size of Belgium (Cole et al., 2017).

During a press conference held in Washington, DC, on February 6, 2020, Mike Pompeo, the Secretary of State of the US, and Jeffery Onyeama, Nigeria's Minister of Foreign Affairs, announced that the US had provided substantial financial support to Nigeria in previous years, amounting to US$450 billion. Additionally, they disclosed that an additional US$46 billion had been allocated by the US to aid Nigeria in addressing the humanitarian needs of displaced individuals. In contrast, Major General Garba Wahab, who has resigned from the Nigerian Army and currently serves as the Director-General of the Nigerian Army Resource Centre, made an appearance on a televised programme on February 7, 2020. During his appearance, he made allegations against various foreign governments, including the US, asserting that they were involved in a comprehensive plot to undermine the stability of Nigeria.

CONCLUSION

BH, initially established as a Salafist organisation, grew to come under the complete scrutiny of the Nigerian government. The faction transitioned from harbouring divisions with the remaining Muslim communities in northern Nigeria to establishing itself as a comprehensive terrorist organisation that garnered international backing. By employing a variety of tactics, BH has caused significant damage to civilian and government security forces, as well as destroyed vital infrastructure, communities, and community assets in northeast Nigeria. The Nigerian government reacted to the group through a combination of soft and hard strategies, including extensive military operations, counter-narratives in the media, and the proclamation of a state of emergency. Additionally, amnesty and de-radicalisation processes were proposed.

Some favourable results have resulted from the implementation of these strategies, including the reestablishment of control over territories that were previously occupied by BH. Despite former President Muhammadu Buhari's persistent assertions to the contrary, BH has persisted in its assaults against security personnel and communities across multiple locations and communities. Being a value-based conflict, it is improbable that the group will be eradicated, as the majority of its members have integrated into mainstream society and presently function as tiny cells.

References

Abah, A. (2021). Exploring the religious motives of Boko Haram terrorism in Nigeria. Dissertation. Walden University.

Al-Rasheed, M., & Shterin, M. (2009). Between death of faith and dying for faith: Reflections on religion, politics, society and violence. In M. Al-Rasheed, & M. Shterin (Eds.). *Dying for faith: Religiously motivated violence in the contemporary world.* (pp. xvii–xxx). London and New York: I.B. Tauris and Co. Ltd.

Ali, Y.M., Musa, B.M., & Fada, K.A. (2016). Implication of Boko Haram insurgency on small and medium enterprises in Borno State, Nigeria: A review. *Saliel Analyst, 4*(1), 96–108.

Amalu, N.S. (2015). Impact of Boko Haram insurgency on human security in Nigeria. *Global Journal of Social Sciences, 14*(4), 35–42.

Amnesty International (2017). Nigeria 2016/2017. https://www.amnesty.org/en/countries/africa/nigeria/report-nigeria/. Retrieved 22 November 2018.

Andekin, A.M. (2019). Dynamics of the Nigerian government conflict management strategies in addressing Boko Haram terrorism, 2009 – 2016. Unpublished Draft PhD Thesis submitted to the Institute for Peace and Strategic Studies, University of Ibadan.

Anderson, L. (1997). Fulfilling prophesies: State policy and Islamist radicalism. In J.L Esposito (Ed.). *Political Islam: Revolution, radicalism or reform?* Boulder, Colorado: Lynne Rienner.

Ayoob, M. (2011). *The many faces of political Islam: Religion and politics in the muslim world.* Ann Arbor: University of Michigan Press.

Bertoni, E., Michele Di Maio, B., Vasco Molini, C., & Roberto, N. (2019). Education is forbidden: The effect of the Boko Haram conflict on education in North-East Nigeria. *Journal of Development Economics, 141*(2), 20–44.

Besenyő, J., & Mayer, Á. (2015). Boko Haram in context: The terrorist organizations's roots in Nigeria's social history. *Defence Against Terrorism Review, 7*(1), 47–58.

Besenyő, J., Márton, K., & Shaffer, R. (2021). Hospital attacks since 9/11: An analysis of terrorism targeting healthcare facilities and workers. *Studies in Conflict & Terrorism, 37,* 1–24. doi:10.1080/1057610X.2021.1937821

Blanchard, L.P., & Cavigelli, K.T. (2018, June 28). Boko Haram and the Islamic State's West Africa Province, Congressional Research Service, Washington, DC.

Boer, J.H. (2005). *Muslims: Why we rejected secularism.* Belleville, Ontario, Canada: Essence Publishing.

Brown, J.A.C. (2015). Is Islam easy to understand or not? Salafis, the democratization of interpretation and the need for the ulema. *Journal of Islamic Studies, 26*(2), 117–144.

Buhari, L.O., & Soetan, O.S. (2018). Integrating the impact of Boko Haram insurgence on the cultural and natural heritage protection in Northern Nigeria. In *International Journal of Humanities and Social Sciences and Education,* 5(10), October, 145–151.

Campbell, J., & Harwood, A. (2018). Boko Haram's deadly attacks, https://www.cfr.org/article/boko-haram's-deadly-impact

Charlick, R.B. (2007). Niger: Islamist identity and the politics of globalization. In W.F.S. Miles (Ed.). *Political Islam in West Africa: State-society relations transformed.* (pp. 19–42). Boulder, Colorado and London: Lynne Rienner Publishers, Inc.

Cold-Ravnkilde, S.M., & Plambech, S. (2015). Boko Haram: From local grievances to violent insurgency. DIIS Report,

No. 2015:21, Danish Institute for International Studies (DIIS), Copenhagen. econstor.eu/bitstream/10419/144733/1/848332970.pdf

Cole, B. Ellen, A.C., Kaster, E., & Sheinbaum, N. (2017). Breaking Boko Haram and ramping up recovery: US engagement in the Lake Chad Region, 2013 to 2016. A Report of the United States Institute for Peace, Washington, DC.

Danjibo, N.D. (2009). Islamic fundamentalism and sectarian violence: 'The Maitatsine' and 'Boko Haram' in Northern Nigeria," IFRA conference on conflict and violence in Nigeria, Zaria, Nigeria. IFRA and Institute of Development Studies, Ahmadu Bello University, Zaria, November 9-11, internal-://Danjibo-1072086017/Danjibo, pdf

Danjibo, N.D. (2017). Islamic fundamentalism and sectarian violence: The 'Maitatsine' and 'Boko Haram' in Northern Nigeria. *Journal of Islamic Sects, 10*(4), Spring, 207–235.

Danjibo N., & Aubyn, F. (2017). Current dynamics and challenges of violent extremism in West Africa. Technical Report Submitted to the West African Network for Peacebuilding (WANEP), Accra, Ghana.

European Union Agency for Asylum. (EUAA). (2021). Boko Haram, including JAS, ISWAP and Ansaru. https://euaa.europa.eu/country-guidance-nigeria-2021/131-boko-haram-including-jas-iswap-and-ansaru

Fanusie, Y.J., & Entz, A. (2017). Boko Haram: Financial assessment, terror finance briefing book by foundation for defense of democracies. https://www.defenddemocracy.org/media-hit/yaya-j-fanusie-terror-finance-briefing-book/.

Favara, M., Appasamy, I., & Marito, H.G. (2015). Nigeria: skills for competitiveness and employability, World Bank 96420 NG June, Washington, DC: The World Bank.

Global Terrorism Database. (GTD). (2024). Boko Haram "Incidents". https://www.start.umd.edu/gtd/search/Results.aspx?search=boko+haram&sa.x=0&sa.y=0

Global Terrorism Database. (GTD). (2024). Boko Haram "Attack Type". https://www.start.umd.edu/gtd/search/Results.aspx?charttype=bar&chart=attack&search=Boko%20Haram&count=100

Harnischfeger, J. (2008). *Democratization and Islamic law: The sharia conflict in Nigeria*. Frankfurt and New York: Campus Verlag.

Hodgkin, T. (1967). The radical tradition in muslim West Africa. In D.P. Little (Ed.). *Essays on Islamic civilization*. Leiden: Brill.

Institute for Peace and Conflict Resolution (2017). *2016 strategic conflict assessment of Nigeria: Consolidated and zonal report*. Abuja: IPCR.

Kane, O. (2003). *Muslim modernity in postcolonial Northern Nigeria: A study of the society for the removal of innovation and reinstatement of tradition*. Leiden: Brill.

Kassim, A. (2018). Bono Haram's internal civil wars: Stealth takfir and jihad as recipes for schism. In J. Zenn (Ed.). *Boko Haram beyond the headlines: Analysis of Africa's enduring insurgency*. Combating Terrorism Centre, Department of Defense, United States Military Academy.

Kassem, M. (2004). *Egyptian politics: The dynamics of authoritarian rule*. Boulder: Lynne Rienner.

Kwabiah, W. (2010). Radical Islam in West Africa and effects on security in the West Africa Sub-Region, A thesis presented to the faculty of the U.S. Army, pp. 1–123.

Loimeier, R. (1997). *Islamic reform and political change in Northern Nigeria*. Evanston, Illinois: Northwestern University Press.

Magrin, G., & Perouse de Monclos, M.-A. (2018). Crisis and development: The Lake Chad Region and Boko Haram. Published by the French Agency for Development (AFD), available at http://edition.afd.fr/

Mohammed, K. (2015). The message and methods of Boko Haram. In M.-A. Perouse de Monclos (Ed.). *Islamism, politics and security and the State in Nigeria*. Leiden: African Studies Centre.

Mustapha, A.-R. (2017). *Sects and social disorder: Muslim identity and conflict in Northern Nigeria*. Abuja: Premium Times Books.

Onuoha, F. (2015). Boko Haram and the evolving salafi jihadist threat in Nigeria, In M.-A. Perouse de Monclos (Ed.). *Islamism, politics and security and the state in Nigeria*. Leiden: African Studies Centre.

Onyibe, M. (2016, May 26). Nigeria, Boko Haram, politics and economies of tomatoes. *TheCable*. https://thecable.ng/heads-roll-fct-board-minister-fires-director-hods/

Pieri, Z.P., & Zenn, J. (2017). The Boko Haram paradox: Ethnicity, religion and historical memory in pursuit of a caliphate. In J.J. Hentz, & H. Solomon (Eds.). *Understanding Boko Haram: Terrorism and insurgency in Africa*. London and New York: Routledge, Taylor and Francis Group.

Pieria, Z.B., & Zennb, J. (2016). The Boko Haram paradox: Ethnicity, religion, and historical memory in pursuit of a caliphate. *African Security, 9*(1), 66–88.

Salaam, A.O. (2013, October). The psychological make-up of 'Muhammad Yusuf'. In I. Mantzikos (Ed.). *Boko Haram: Anatomy of a crisis* (pp. 46–52). Bristol: E-International Relations.

Solomon, H. (2017). Theorizing Boko Haram: Understanding the terrorist threat, In J.J. Henz and H. Solomon (Eds.). *Understanding Boko Haram: Terrorism and insurgency in Africa*. London and New York: Routledge, Taylor and Francis Group.

Thurston, A. (2016). *Salafism in Nigeria: Islam, preaching and politics*. London and Cambridge: International Institute and Cambridge University Press.

Thurston, A. (2017). *Boko Haram: The history of an African jihadist movement*. Princeton and Oxford: Princeton University Press.

United Nations Development Programme (UNDP). (2018). Boko Haram kills 32,570 in eight years, Sunday Punch, October 7.

United Nations Development Programme. (UNDP). (2018). National human development report 2918: Achieving human development in North East Nigeria. Abuja: The UNDP.

United Nations International Children's Emergency Fund (UNICEF). (2018). Humanitarian action for children. https://www.unicef.org/appeals/files/2018-HAC-Nigeria-Revised-August.pdf

United Nations. (2014, May 22). Security council Al-Qaida sanctions committee adds Boko Haram to its sanctions list. Press Release, Security Council, SC11410. https://press.un.org/en/2014/sc11410.doc.htm#:~:text=On%2022%20May%202014%2C%20the,VII%20of%20the%20Charter%20of

Unites States (US) Army. (2015). Threat tactics reports: Boko Haram, TRADOC G-2 ACE Threats Integration, October.

World Bank. (2015). North-East Nigeria recovery and peace building assessment. Washington, DC: World Bank.

Zenn, J. (Ed.) (2018). *Boko Haram beyond the headlines: Analysis of Africa's enduring insurgency*. New York: Combating Terrorism Centre, Department of Defense, United States Military Academy.

32

ANSAR AL-DINE

"Defenders of the Faith" and State Fragility in Mali

William A. Taylor

INTRODUCTION

Ansar al-Dine, known colloquially as "Defenders of the Faith," is a Salafist Islamist violent extremist organisation that has fused Tuareg nationalism with Islamist terrorism and has used it to wage a vicious insurgency in Mali (see Besenyő & Romaniuk, 2024). In doing so, Ansar al-Dine has undermined state institutions in Mali, which previously had proven to be a relatively stable democracy, something unique in the Sahel region. Although decimated by the African and French intervention in Mali in 2013 in response to Ansar al-Dine's incursions, the group has proven extremely resilient, fostering its own splinter groups such as the Macina Liberation Front (FLM). More recently, Ansar al-Dine has joined FLM and al-Qaeda in the Islamic Maghreb (AQIM) to form Jamaat Nosrat al-Islam wal-Mouslimin (JNIM), or the Group to Support Islam and Muslims, a broad al-Qaeda coalition that has threatened Mali and expanded the reach of terrorism from Mali's north to its more populous central and southern areas.

OVERVIEW

The Republic of Mali is a landlocked country in western Africa, covering more than 1.2 million square kilometres; roughly half of this territory is desert, making Mali a comparatively large nation with sprawling ungoverned spaces. Mali is part of the Sahel region, meaning "shore" in Arabic, which is a vast geographical band running from the Red Sea in eastern Africa to the Atlantic Ocean in western Africa and demarcating the transition from the desert in the north to the savanna in the south. Like most nations in the Sahel region, Mali has a low population density. The lone exception is its southern half, including its capital, Bamako, which claims nearly 2.5 million residents and is one of the fastest-growing cities in Africa. Mali is home to a population of almost 18 million people and has a very youthful population: more than two-thirds of Malians are younger than 25 years old. The vast majority, nearly 95%, is Muslim, and the largest ethnic group is the Mande, which comprise approximately half of the population. Mali has numerous ethnic minorities, including the Fulani, Voltaic, Songhai, and Tuareg (Central Intelligence Agency, 2018).

Due to its harsh climate and rugged geography, Mali has porous borders, especially in the north. In addition to this, Mali is one of the world's poorest and least developed countries, ranking 175th out of 188 countries in overall human development (UN Development Programme, 2016). Mali also experiences rampant corruption. Transparency International classified Mali 122nd out of the 180 countries that it tracks, describing it as one of the more corrupt nations in the world (Transparency International, 2017). Mali's main economy involves agriculture and mining, with gold and cotton contributing most of its exports and encompassing the third-largest gold trade on the continent. The nation uses a cash-based economy that makes tracking and preventing illicit commerce difficult. Mali participates in the Economic Community of West African States (ECOWAS) economically, the United Nations and African Union politically, and the Trans-Sahara Counterterrorism Partnership and Security Governance Initiative regarding defence (Central Intelligence Agency, 2018).

In order to comprehend Ansar al-Dine's formation, one must first understand the context of the Tuareg people, who inhabit portions of Algeria, Burkina Faso, Libya, Mali, and Niger and pursue nomadic pastoralism in desert regions throughout the Sahel region. A significant Tuareg minority lives in northern Mali, comprising upward of 10% of the country's population. Since gaining independence from

DOI: 10.4324/9780429426063-36

France on June 20, 1960, however, the central government in Bamako has focused most of its political, economic, and development efforts on the nation's more populated south, generating significant animosity among Tuareg communities that reside in the north. Tuareg rebellions against Mali's government occurred during the 1960s and 1990s, as well as another short-lived uprising in 2006, all seeking either enhanced autonomy or outright independence for Azawad, the name given to Mali's north by the Tuareg (Alesbury, 2013). Stéphane Spet concluded, "Thus, political and economic marginalisation represent the genuine roots of the Tuaregs' claims, whereas religious beliefs and ethnicity have proven only secondary elements that complicate the problem" (Spet 2015, p. 67).

Beginning in 2011, regional dynamics ignited this combustible mix. In early 2011, Libya erupted into conflict, partly in response to the Arab Spring. As a result of the ensuing chaos, the North Atlantic Treaty Organization (NATO) intervened in Libya on March 19, 2011. By August of that same year, National Transitional Council forces had seized Tripoli, and on October 20, 2011, they captured and killed Muammar Gaddafi, Libya's longtime dictatorial ruler (Akanji, 2015). Many Tuareg fighters – by some estimates, 1,000 armed combat veterans – returned afterward from Libya to Mali emboldened with augmented training, battle experience, and heavy weapons (International Coalition for the Responsibility to Protect, 2015). As a result, the overthrow of Gaddafi's authoritarian regime created turbulent waves that crashed throughout the region. Jeremy Keenan explained that "it led to the destabilisation of much of the Sahel, especially Mali" (Keenan, 2016, p. 60).

Once back in Mali, Tuareg leaders formed, in October 2011, the National Movement for the Liberation of Azawad (MNLA), a secular separatist sect for Tuareg independence. By January 2012, a full-fledged Tuareg rebellion had emerged that claimed an independent Azawad as its goal. As a result, Tuareg fighters launched a fierce mutiny against Mali's government. The MNLA led this most recent insurgency and sought independence for Azawad, a territory comprising most of northern Mali. Secular nationalism, however, was not the only dynamic to prey on the increasing weakness of Mali's state institutions.

Terrorism has also wreaked havoc on this nation. The Institute for Economics and Peace ranked Mali as the 25th country in the world most impacted by terrorism (Institute for Economics and Peace, 2017, p. 10). Multiple Islamist violent extremist organisations have operated throughout the Sahel region generally and within Mali specifically, including al-Qaeda in the Islamic Maghreb (AQIM), al-Murabitoun (AMB), the Movement for Unity and Jihad in West Africa (MUJAO), an Islamist terrorist group based in Gao, Mali, and Ansar al-Dine (AAD). Out of this complicated background, Iyad Ag Ghaly formed Ansar al-Dine towards the end of 2011. Ansar al-Dine is a Salafist Islamist terrorist organisation that has primarily manoeuvred in Mali, conducting attacks throughout the northern half of the country and increasingly expanding its assaults into central Mali. Ansar al-Dine has proclaimed two primary objectives: independence for Azawad and the imposition of Sharia law throughout northern Mali. Therefore, Ansar al-Dine has surfaced as a violent extremist organisation that has fused elements of Salafist Islamist terrorism with militant Tuareg separatism.

By the summer of 2012, the international community proved anxious to stop Ansar al-Dine's precipitous onslaughts. The United Nations first prodded the Economic Community of West African States on -Dine's precipitous onslaughts. The United Nations first prodded the Economic Community of West African States on July 5, 2012, to stabilise Mali through UN Security Council Resolution 2085, which authorised the formation of an African-led International Support Mission in Mali (AFISMA) (United Nations, 2012c). In October 2012, the United Nations authorised the use of force through UN Security Council Resolution 2071 (United Nations, 2012b), and on December 20, 2012, the United Nations envisioned ECOWAS intervening in Mali with military force (United Nations, 2012a). Because of repeated delays in AFISMA's training and deployment and swift encroachments by Islamist forces, France intervened in Mali on January 11, 2013, at the explicit request of Dioncounda Traoré, Mali's interim president, because two ominous columns of Islamist fighters approached and threatened Bamako, Mali's capital.

KEY PERSONNEL AND STRUCTURE

Iyad Ag Ghaly led Ansar al-Dine both ideologically and operationally. Colloquially known as the "Lion of the Desert," Ag Ghaly is a well-known Tuareg leader who attempted to seize control of the Tuareg nationalist movement in Mali at the end of 2011 but was unable to do so because of his firm commitment to establish Sharia law throughout Mali. Instead, he formed Ansar al-Dine, an Islamist terrorist group. Ifoghas Tuaregs and Berabiche Arabs comprise Ansar al-Dine's main support base. Ag Ghaly came from a well-known family in the Ifogha tribe and served in Libya as part of Muammar Gaddafi's Islamic Legion, gaining combat experience in Chad. He previously rose to prominence as a Tuareg leader of the rebellion during the 1990s. Throughout the 2000s, he negotiated between AQIM and Mali's government and served as a diplomat from Mali to Saudi Arabia. Ag Ghaly led another brief Tuareg revolt in 2006. Described as "a portly figure, heavily bearded," and labelled as "the strategist," Ag Ghaly is a complex leader, simultaneously known "for his fondness for whisky and music" and for his vehement enactment of Sharia law in territories that his militants controlled (Beaumont, 2012, p. 31). Overall, Ag Ghaly has espoused jihad aimed at implementing Sharia law in Mali while making independence for Azawad a touted but secondary goal. Other important figures in Ansar al-Dine include Sanda Ould Boumana, an Arab from Timbuktu who served as the group's spokesman, and Alghabass Ag Intalla, who represented Ansar al-Dine during negotiations in Burkina Faso in late 2012 prior to defecting from the organisation in early 2013 to found the Islamic Movement of Azawad (MIA). As a result, the group's structure is quite fluid, with various leaders and commanders moving in and out of the organisation as they seek to pursue their own interests and agendas.

Infighting among the erstwhile allies, the MNLA and Ansar al-Dine, burst forth in June and July 2012. These divisions surfaced because of the two groups' distinct aims: MNLA focused on traditional Tuareg claims for autonomy and independence for Azawad, while Ansar al-Dine demanded the application of Sharia law and the establishment of a caliphate in Mali. These competing mandates put the two parties increasingly at odds. By July 2012, Ansar al-Dine had seized control of the insurgency, benefiting from MUJAO's defeat of MNLA forces in Gao and its own rout of MNLA militants in Timbuktu. Roland Marchal documented that Ansar al-Dine "basically dismantled" the MNLA, forcing the secular separatist group to rebrand itself MIA, which renounced violence and advocated compromise with Mali's government (Marchal, 2013, p. 494). Alghabass Ag Intalla, previously an influential leader within Ansar al-Dine, grew disillusioned with the group's malicious tactics and broke from the group to form the MIA. To distinguish himself and his followers from Ansar al-Dine, Ag Intalla and MIA sought to negotiate with Mali's government as an alternative to achieving enhanced autonomy for the Tuareg people (British Broadcasting Corporation, 2013).

ORGANISATIONAL CHARACTERISTICS AND ACTIVITIES

A vast and lucrative illicit trade in cigarettes, drugs, arms, and humans flows through the Sahel region generally and Mali specifically. Criminal activity, especially kidnapping, cocaine, opium, and marijuana, has proven especially profitable for Ansar al-Dine. There are geographical and cultural factors that have contributed to this dynamic. The Sahara Desert and porous borders of most states in this region have made surveillance of trade routes, let alone control of them, quite difficult. Such a situation has redounded "to the full jihadist advantage" (Lounnas, 2013, p. 326) because such groups as Ansar al-Dine and AQIM have leveraged illegal commerce to fund their terrorist activities. As a result, violent extremist organisations in the Sahel region, including Ansar al-Dine, have pursued quasi-commercial smuggling operations. Terje Østebø revealed, "In northern Mali, the intertwining of Islamic militancy and illicit smuggling has produced a complicated mix of incentives" (Østebø, 2012, p. 6).

The leadership of both AQIM and Ansar al-Dine has participated in criminal enterprises, so much so that Mokhtar Belmokhtar, former military commander of AQIM, has earned the moniker of "Mr. Marlboro" due to his money-spinning business in smuggled cigarettes, and some reports have characterised Ag Ghaly as shifting alliances based on financial rather than ideological considerations. In addition, all major Islamist groups in this region, including Ansar al-Dine, AQIM, and MUJAO, have resorted to kidnapping for ransom, often targeting Western aid workers in order to receive large payouts (British Broadcasting Corporation, 2013). Ansar al-Dine, with its close connections to AQIM, has used this market to help finance its terrorist attacks (All Africa, 2018b). In fact, even exertions meant to destroy these terrorist organisations, including Operation SERVAL and the subsequent Operation BARKHANE, have produced unintended consequences for criminal activity in this region. The near-constant presence of unmanned aerial vehicles (UAVs), referred to colloquially as drones, to collect intelligence in an area historically devoid of surveillance has forced smugglers to adapt, reducing the size of their previously large shipments of cocaine transported by caravan into many smaller shipments carried by individuals. This decentralisation of cocaine trafficking has unwittingly allowed Islamist groups, including Ansar al-Dine, to co-opt larger portions of the well-paid exchange and thereby fill their coffers for revitalised terrorist attacks (Keenan, 2016). While difficult to quantify, most estimates have placed the profits from such illicit activity in the millions, if not tens of millions, of dollars (AlArabiya.net, 2013b).

LINKAGES

Since its inception, Ansar al-Dine has maintained close ties with various jihadist groups, including AQIM, and pursued such common goals as the establishment of Sharia law in Mali and throughout the broader Sahel. Abdelmalek Droukdel, emir of AQIM, has coordinated with Iyad Ag Ghaly, founder of Ansar al-Dine, and has considered Ansar al-Dine a branch of his larger organisation. In addition, Ag Ghaly is a cousin of Hamada Ag Hama, a senior AQIM commander. AQIM has provided resources for Ansar al-Dine, including funding, personnel, and weapons. In return, Ansar al-Dine has synchronised its efforts with AQIM. Lounnas observed that AQIM "gained a decisive advantage through their alliance" with Ag Ghaly and Ansar al-Dine, resulting from Ag Ghaly's notoriety as a popular leader in the Tuareg rebellion during the 1990s and Ansar al-Dine's reputation as a homegrown jihadist movement (Lounnas, 2013, p. 327). Some observers characterise Ansar al-Dine's relationship with AQIM as that of a host, similar to the Taliban's role with al-Qaeda in Afghanistan.

In addition to AQIM, Ansar al-Dine maintained an alliance with MUJAO. All three groups, AQIM, Ansar al-Dine, and MUJAO, sought to establish Sharia law in Mali specifically and throughout the Sahel region generally. Between January and April 2012, Ansar al-Dine waged a successful offensive in Mali in coordination with AQIM and MUJAO and seized considerable territory and multiple towns, including Aguelhok, Tessalit, Kidal, Gao, and Timbuktu. Ansar al-Dine was especially ruthless in its operations, executing more than 80 Malian soldiers when it seized the town of Aguelhok. As a practical response to the success of the secular Tuareg nationalist group MNLA, Ansar al-Dine joined forces with it on May 26, 2012. Friction between the two groups increased, however, due to Ansar al-Dine's strict interpretation of Sharia law and its forced imposition on local populations. Ansar al-Dine eventually seized control of the insurgency from the MNLA.

Terrorist groups worldwide have simplified their tactics in recent years. The Institute for Economics & Peace noted, "Since 2014, there has been a shift in tactics towards simpler attacks" (Institute for Economics & Peace, 2017, p. 4). Ansar al-Dine has followed this general trend, employing an array of uncomplicated yet deadly methods, including improvised explosive devices (IEDs), small arms, rockets, and mortars. Several examples prove the point. On October 23, 2013, Ansar al-Dine militants exploded several vehicle suicide bombs at the UN security station in Tessalit, killing seven peacekeepers and civilians. On June 27, 2015, Ansar al-Dine fighters struck a Malian military base located in Nara, killing twelve soldiers and injuring another ten. On December 24, 2015, Ansar al-Dine insurgents assaulted an MNLA stronghold in Talhandak, killing ten rivals and seizing the village. Overall, Ansar al-Dine has targeted UN peacekeepers and Malian military personnel, although it has also displayed ruthlessness against civilians who have resisted its self-imposed rules.

After suffering losses during the African and French interventions in early 2013, Ansar al-Dine spent most of 2014 rebuilding its operational capabilities and returned to the offensive in 2015. Ansar al-Dine perpetrated multiple deadly attacks on UN peacekeepers, focusing on logistics convoys transiting to and from UN bases in Kidal, Gao, and Timbuktu. On February 12, 2016, the group employed suicide bombs and rocket barrages to attack the UN base in Kidal, killing seven Guinean peacekeepers, while on May 18, 2016, the group killed five Chadian peacekeepers in an ambush near Aguelhok (Human Rights Watch, 2018, p. 4). Once on the brink of collapse due to Operation SERVAL, Ansar al-Dine has remained potent and lethal. On November 20, 2015, Ansar al-Dine affiliates attacked the Radisson Hotel, taking 170 hostages and killing twenty of them (All Africa, 2015). On May 29, 2016, Ansar al-Dine ambushed a UN Multidimensional Integrated Stabilization Mission in Mali (MINUSMA) convoy and killed five UN peacekeepers near Sévaré, a town in central Mali (Saudi Press Agency, 2016). Ansar al-Dine assaulted the Malian military compound in Nampala, Mali, on July 16, 2016, killing or kidnapping more than twenty soldiers (Algeria Press Service, 2016).

Ansar al-Dine has proven quite successful in seizing territory, capturing most of northern Mali by the end of 2012. In addition, the group has remained resistant, rebuilding its operational capabilities after intense pressure during the African and French interventions in early 2013. Another feat of Ansar al-Dine has been its ability to foster other violent extremist organisations, including the Macina Liberation Front (FLM). Ag Ghaly trained Amadou Kouffa, FLM's notorious chief, and Ansar al-Dine helped establish FLM in January 2015, primarily as a branch that could spread violence into central Mali, something that Ansar al-Dine had not yet accomplished at that time.

Ansar al-Dine has also had some notable failures. It neglected to capitalise on its alliance with the MNLA and situate itself within the broader context of the Tuareg rebellion, instead rigidly fixating on Sharia law and generating considerable backlash from local populations, many of which protested Ansar al-Dine's brutality against civilians and compulsory application of Sharia law. This misjudgment cost Ansar al-Dine significant momentum and local legitimacy; it also prevented this violent extremist organisation from converting its initial tactical success during the spring of 2012 into sustained long-term gains. This fiasco also allowed Mali's government to broker a separate ceasefire with the MNLA and thereby concentrate the government's entire response on Ansar al-Dine, further weakening the Islamist terrorist group. Stéphane Spet revealed, "Following their agenda, Islamists sidelined the secular MNLA since they had little interest in the idea of a free and secular Azawad and implemented strict Sharia law in the conquered area. The presence of Tuaregs in the coalition meant that the jihadists were losing their main support" (Spet, 2015, pp. 68, 71). As a result, Ansar al-Dine bore the brunt of the African and French interventions, forfeiting its early acquisitions across most of northern Mali.

With regional preparations for intervention moving slowly, the dramatic situation reached a crescendo in January 2013. On January 4 of that year, Omar Hamaha, a senior Ansar al-Dine commander, led 100 vehicles south from Timbuktu towards Mopti, a key town in central Mali, indicating that "the strict observance of Islamic law on all the territory of Azawad (northern Mali) is a non-negotiable imperative" (AlArabiya.net, 2013a, p. 1). This move was part of a larger offensive that Ansar al-Dine launched in early January 2013, culminating when nearly 3,000 Islamist fighters, including many Ansar al-Dine militants, threatened the capital of Bamako. Ansar al-Dine's two rapid advances, one against Mopti and another towards Bamako, signalled the near dissolution of the Malian state.

In response to the crisis in Mali, French forces intervened on January 11, 2013. French leaders launched Operation SERVAL, comprised of approximately 5,000 AFISMA troops and 4,000 French soldiers. Malian and French soldiers quickly seized territory, using a lethal combination of air power and special forces, and secured most of the north within a month. Operation SERVAL succeeded in a quick reversal of militant Islamist incursions and reclaimed most of northern Mali, climaxing in an intense battle in the Ifoghas Mountains during February 2013, where an airstrike killed Abdelhamid Abou Zeid, a senior al-Qaeda commander (AlArabiya.net, 2013b). Operation SERVAL eventually ran from January 11 to July 15, 2014.

In reply, the United Nations designated Ansar al-Dine a terrorist group on March 21, 2013 through its al-Qaeda Sanctions Committee (UPI International Intelligence, 2013). In February of that year, the U.S. Department of State designated Ag Ghaly as an individual involved in terrorism, and on March 21, 2013, it designated Ansar al-Dine as a foreign terrorist organisation. The UN Security Council created MINUSMA on April 25, 2013, by Resolution 2100. In it, the council transferred the mission from AFISMA to MINUSMA, which began on July 1, 2013 and initially comprised 11,200 military personnel and another 1,440 police (UN Security Council, 2013). MINUSMA has replaced Operation SERVAL and has become a difficult and deadly peacekeeping mission. On August 1, 2014, French forces shifted to Operation Barkhane, comprised of approximately 4,000 French soldiers. Operation BARKHANE moved the French base of operations from Mali to Chad and broadened its coverage from Mali to the greater Sahel region, including Mali but also encompassing Burkina Faso, Chad, Mauritania, and Niger (Chivvis, 2016).

MINUSMA has continued to enhance Mali's stability generally and combat Ansar al-Dine specifically and has deployed approximately 12,000 military personnel and another 2,000 police from more than 50 countries. It has proved, however, arduous and deadly: attacks have killed more than 100 UN peacekeepers and wounded another 350 personnel (United Nations, 2018). As a result of these losses, reporters have characterised it as "the world's most dangerous U.N. mission" because it has resulted in more peacekeeper casualties than any other ongoing peacekeeping mission in the world (Sieff, 2017). To bolster regional security, Burkina Faso, Chad, Mali, Mauritania, and Niger created in 2014 the G5 Sahel, which is a coalition to strengthen cooperation among member states on a range of economic and security issues impacting the Sahel region. These gains, however, have been temporary. By the middle of 2014, Islamist forces had begun reasserting control in northern Mali. During 2015 and 2016, Islamist forces expanded their attacks into central Mali.

In March 2017, the three main terrorist groups in Mali joined forces and made substantial expansions. Ansar al-Dine merged with FML and AQIM in Mali to form JNIM, a coalition known as the Group for the Support of Islam and Muslims (All Africa, 2018a). This invigorated alliance first secured additional territory in the north and then gained ground in central Mali, demonstrating a worrisome ability to conduct operations in southern Mali as well. This development was a departure from past precedent, wherein Ansar al-Dine functioned solely in northern Mali. On June 29, 2018, JNIM launched a suicide attack on the military headquarters of the G5 Sahel, killing three soldiers and exhibiting its capacity to mount operations in central Mali (Cape Argus (South Africa), 2018).

IMPACTS

Ansar al-Dine's attacks have resulted in numerous internally displaced persons (IDPs), totalling more than 650,000 IDPs since the outbreak of hostilities in 2012, with approximately 52,000 remaining IDPs as of 2018 (UN High Commissioner for Refugees, 2018). Such displacement has triggered extensive food insecurity. The United Nations has estimated that more than 4.3 million people in Mali have been food insecure and that this number has increased. Much of this shock has been due to the rampant disruption and extensive displacement caused by the attacks of such groups as Ansar al-Dine and JNIM and the consequential and continuing fragility of Mali's government (United Nations, 2018).

Politically, Ansar al-Dine has contributed to conditions that resulted in a coup d'état. From March 21 to 22, 2012, junior officers in the Malian military led by Captain Amadou Sanogo overthrew President Amadou Toumani Touré, known colloquially as President ATT. Two factors drove the takeover: widespread perceptions of corruption within the central government in Bamako and the inability of Mali's military to end the raging insurgency. The resulting coup weakened the government's already feeble response to the revolt and unintentionally allowed militants to gain momentum and strength. These events transformed a stable democracy into a fragile state, at times teetering on the brink of disintegration. The Fund for Peace ranked Mali as one of the "four most critically worsened [states] for the decade," alongside Libya, Syria, and Yemen (Fund for Peace, 2017, p. 11). As a result, the MNLA seized most of northern Mali and declared Azawad an independent state on April 6, 2012 (Arieff, 2013). After ATT's ouster, Dioncounda Traoré became, in April 2012, the interim president of Mali and held elections on July 28. A subsequent run-off election took place two weeks later, on August 11. After winning more than three-quarters of the votes cast, President Ibrahim Boubacar Keïta assumed office on September 4, 2013. Another presidential election occurred on July 29, 2018, which triggered a subsequent runoff election two weeks later on August 12, where Keïta won reelection in a landslide.

Socially, Ansar al-Dine has heightened schisms within Mali through its wanton destruction of age-old shrines in Timbuktu, a longtime trans-Saharan trading outpost and Islamic cultural hub. Timbuktu housed a plethora of important cultural and religious items, stemming from its vaulted historical position. "The city was perhaps the most important centre of learning in sub-Saharan Africa during the 15th and 16th centuries, where scholars of religion, arts, and sciences flourished," Curtis Abraham recorded. "During this time, tens of thousands of manuscripts were commissioned and meticulously executed by African academics" (Abraham, 2012, p. 20). Ansar al-Dine seized control of Timbuktu in June 2012 and destroyed numerous ancient manuscripts and tombs that they deemed apostate. Upon wresting control of the city away from MNLA, Ansar al-Dine militants used pickaxes to destroy several irreplaceable Sufi mausoleum sites, including the tombs of Sidi Alpha Moya, Sidi Mukhtar, and Sidi Mahmoud Ben Amar, the last of which the UN Educational, Scientific, and Cultural Organization (UNESCO) had designated a World Heritage Site. Ansar al-Dine's wilful demolition triggered widespread angst, broad condemnation, and intrepid attempts by residents to safeguard the artefacts. A local imam lamented, "They have raped Timbuktu today. It is a crime" (Agency Tunis Afrique Presse, 2012, p. 1). Irina Bokova, UNESCO's director general, added, "I believe this is a tragedy for all of humanity" (Abraham, 2012, p. 21).

CONCLUSION

In June 2015, Mali's government reached a peace agreement with two armed factions. "Lacklustre implementation," however, prevented such an achievement from eliminating further terrorist activity by Ansar al-Dine (U.S. Department of State, 2017, p. 38). In June 2016, Mali completed a national strategy to combat terrorism. This development illustrated two dynamics: Mali's determinations have represented a fledgling stage in combating violent extremist organisations but have made some progress. As the security situation in Mali deteriorated, the G5 Sahel increased its endeavours in 2017, forming the Force Conjointe du G5 Sahel. The organisation, headquartered in Sévaré, Mali, includes 5,000 soldiers organised into seven battalions and augmented by police and gendarmes. The Africa Centre for Strategic Studies characterised the G5 Sahel as "a focal point for transnational security efforts in the region" (Africa Centre for Strategic Studies, 2018, p. 1). The U.S. Department of State warned, "Continued terrorist activity was widespread in Mali's ungoverned northern region, with limited attacks spreading into central and southern Mali" (U.S. Department of State, 2017, p. 38). This shift in violence into central and southern Mali has signalled that Ansar al-Dine's terrorism has not subsided but rather has spread into areas of Mali that heretofore had remained untouched by it. In response to rampant insecurity, Mali's government has more than doubled its military expenditures, from 1.2% of its gross domestic product (GDP) in 2012 to 2.63% of GDP in 2016 (Central Intelligence Agency, 2018).

Human Rights Watch reported that "several thousand civilians in northern and central Mali were victimized" in a series of more than 400 attacks in 2016 (Human Rights Watch, 2018, p. 1). In August 2017, militants attacked three separate UN bases in northern and central Mali, killing eight peacekeepers (Anadolu Agency, 2017). The threat to Mali remains potent. A diverse range of militant Islamist groups have killed more than 1,100 civilians in the region, causing nearly 400 fatalities in 2017 alone (Africa Center for Strategic Studies, 2018). In 2018, Ansar al-Dine, now operating under the consolidated Islamist alliance of JNIM, has continued to make advances, has demonstrated "increased organizational capacity," and has "created a unified front under one al Qaeda banner" (Africa Center for Strategic Studies, 2017, p. 1). António Guterres, UN secretary-general, reported on "the expansion of violent extremist and criminal groups" and articulated "grave concern" regarding JNIM's ability to engage MINUSMA peacekeepers and Malian soldiers alike, especially in the Mopti and Segou regions (UN Security Council, 2018, pp. 1, 5). On April 14, 2018, a JNIM attack proved especially advanced, using a combination of rockets and car bombs (France 24, 2018). Ansar al-Dine has ultimately undermined Mali's governmental institutions and continues to pose a serious threat to the country's democracy, albeit under shifting circumstances and in different forms.

References

Abraham, C. (2012). Timbuktu's ancient manuscripts under threat. *New African*, *1*(521), 20–24.

Africa Center for Strategic Studies. (2017). Africa's active militant Islamist groups. Retrieved from https://africacenter.org/spotlight/map-africa-militant-islamic-groups-april-2017/.

Africa Center for Strategic Studies. (2018). The G5 Sahel joint force gains traction. Retrieved from https://africacenter.org/spotlight/g5-sahel-joint-force-gains-traction/.

Agency Tunis Afrique Presse. (2012, July 1). Mali Islamists destroy more holy Timbuktu sites, 1.

Akanji, O. (2015). A critical analysis of the security crisis in post-Gaddafi Libya. *Africa Insight*, *45*(2), 11–26.

AlArabiya.net. (2013a, January 4). Al-Qaeda, Ansar Dine seek control over Mali's Mopti, 1.

AlArabiya.net. (2013b, March 3). Al-Qaeda confirms Abou Zeid killed in Mali after France's doubt, 1.

Alesbury, A. (2013). A society in motion: The Tuareg from the pre-colonial era to today. *Nomadic Peoples, 17*(1), 106–125.

Algeria Press Service. (2016, July 20). Algeria strongly condemns attack on military camp in Mali, 1.

All Africa. (2015, November 23). Malians pick up the pieces after hotel attack, 1.

All Africa. (2018a, April 19). Negotiations with jihadists? A radical idea gains currency in Mali, 1.

All Africa. (2018b, July 3). Attack on Sahel counterterror force puts jihadists in focus, 1.

Anadolu Agency. (2017, August 15). Turkey condemns Mali terror attacks, 1.

Arieff, A. (2013). *Crisis in Mali*. Washington, DC: Congressional Research Service.

Beaumont, P. (2012, October 28). Whiskey-loving rebel turned jihadist chief controls Mali's hope of peace. *Observer* (London, England), 31.

Besenyő, J., & Romaniuk, S. N. (2024, June 7). Mali: comment l'insécurité, l'incertitude et le chaos favorisent le terrorisme. *The Conversation*. https://theconversation.com/mali-comment-linsecurite-lincertitude-et-le-chaos-favorisent-le-terrorisme-230323

British Broadcasting Corporation. (2013, March 12). Mali crisis: Key players. Retrieved from https://www.bbc.com/news/world-africa-17582909.

Cape Argus (South Africa). (2018, July 2). Al-Qaeda claims attack on Mali base, 7.

Central Intelligence Agency. (2018). *World factbook*. Retrieved from https://www.cia.gov/library/publications/resources/the-world-factbook/geos/ml.html.

Chivvis, C.S. (2016). *The French War on Al Qa'ida in Africa*. Cambridge: Cambridge University Press.

France 24. (2018, April 15). Mali—Several French soldiers injured in latest Mali Attack, 1.

Fund for Peace. (2017). *Fragile states index 2017*. Retrieved from http://fundforpeace.org/fsi/2017/05/14/fragile-states-index-2017-annual-report/.

Human Rights Watch. (2018, January 18). Mali: Islamist armed group abuses, banditry surge. Retrieved from https://www.hrw.org/news/2017/01/18/mali-islamist-armed-group-abuses-banditry-surge.

Institute for Economics & Peace. (2017). *Global terrorism index 2017*. Retrieved from http://visionofhumanity.org/app/uploads/2017/11/Global-Terrorism-Index-2017.pdf.

International Coalition for the Responsibility to Protect. (2015). Crisis in Mali. Retrieved from http://www.responsiblitytoprotect.org/index.php/crises/crisis-in-mali.

Keenan, J. (2016). How terror came to the Sahel. *New African, 2*(560): 56–61.

Lounnas, D. (2013). The regional fallouts of the French intervention in Mali. *Mediterranean Politics, 18*(2), 325–332.

Marchal, R. (2013). Briefing: Military (mis)adventures in Mali. *African Affairs, 112*(448), 486–497.

Østebø, T. (2012). Islamic militancy in Africa. *Africa Security Brief: A Publication of the Africa Center for Strategic Studies*, (23), 1–8.

Saudi Press Agency. (2016, May 30). Five UN peacekeepers killed in attack in Mali, 1.

Sieff, K. (2017, February 17). The world's most dangerous U.N. mission. *The Washington Post*. Retrieved from https://www.washingtonpost.com/sf/world/2017/02/17/the-worlds-deadliest-u-n-peacekeeping-mission/?utm_term=.ddedbc697161.

Spet, S. (2015). Operation Serval: Analyzing the French strategy against jihadists in Mali. *Air and Space Power Journal—Africa and Francophonie, 6*(4), 66–79.

Transparency International. (2017). Corruption perceptions index 2017. Retrieved from https://www.transparency.org/news/feature/corruption_perceptions_index_2017.

United Nations. (2018). MINUSMA: Fast facts—uniformed personnel. Retrieved from https://minusma.unmissions.org/sites/default/files/fast_facts_march_2018_en.pdf.

UN Development Programme. (2016). Human development report 2016: Human development for everyone. Retrieved from http://hdr.undp.org/sites/default/files/2016_human_development_report.pdf.

UN High Commissioner for Refugees. (2018). Mali situation: Refugees, internally displaced persons and returnees. Retrieved from https://data2.unhcr.org/en/documents/download/64426.

UN Security Council. (2012a). Resolution 2056. Retrieved from http://www.un.org/en/ga/search/view_doc.asp?symbol=S/RES/2056(2012).

UN Security Council. (2012b). Resolution 2071. Retrieved from http://www.un.org/en/ga/search/view_doc.asp?symbol=S/RES/2071(2012).

UN Security Council. (2012c). Resolution 2085. Retrieved from http://www.un.org/en/ga/search/view_doc.asp?symbol=S/RES/2085(2012).

UN Security Council. (2013). Resolution 2100. Retrieved from https://undocs.org/S/RES/2100(2013).

UN Security Council. (2018). Situation in Mali: Report of the secretary-general. Retrieved from https://undocs.org/S/2018/541.

UPI International Intelligence. (2013, March 21). U.N. Sanctions Mali's Ansar Dine, 1.

U.S. Department of State. (2017). *Country reports on terrorism 2016*. Retrieved from https://www.state.gov/documents/organization/272488.pdf.

33

AL-QAEDA IN THE ISLAMIC MAGHREB (AQIM)

tavis d. jules and Scott Romaniuk

INTRODUCTION

Al-Qaeda in the Islamic Maghreb (AQIM),[1] an Algerian Salafi-Jihadist group, is often viewed as an al-Qaeda external force operating out of the Sahel and Sahara. Throughout its history, AQIM evolved from a splinter group *Groupe Salafiste pour la Prédication et le Combat* ([GSPC] the Salafist Group for Preaching and Combat [1998–2006]) which itself fractured from *Groupe Islamique Armé* ([GIA] the Armed Islamic Group [1993–2004]). Although today AQIM is a global organisation with many sleeper cells, its heredity lies in its Islamic-nationalist movement, which is moulded by nationalist struggles. It boasts a cadre of followers on different continents, has countless deaths on its hands, and has a history steeped in the Algerian military coup of 1992 and the ensuing 'Dark Decade,' roughly 1993–1998 that killed more than one hundred thousand individuals. While AQIM began as a local insurgent group, through devotion to a singular message – eradicating foreigners from Algeria or 'to purge the land of the ungodly' (Kepel, 2002, p. 266) – its strong leadership command and control structure aided by geostrategic maneuvering, alignment, and affiliation around domestic homegrown insurgency has today evolved into a recognisable global terrorist threat. AQIM's forefather organisation, GSPC, was significant in shaping domestic terrorism in Algeria where "between 1992 and 1997 some 120,000 people were killed in a terrorist insurgency characterized by staggering cruelty … [as] Fanatical Islamists insurgents pursued a dirty war to topple the state" (Stone, 1997, pp. 1–2).

This chapter discusses and analyses the rise of AQIM. It begins by detailing the historical background and context in which AQIM (originally called GIA) arose and its fight for recognition during the Algerian Civil War. The second section discusses AQIM's metamorphosis from GSPC to its current iteration. Then the chapter analyses the changes that occurred in the organisation's structure as it battled emerging geopolitical and ideological divisions within its ranks. The chapter concludes by situating AQIM within the current political climate besieged by the battle for the title of 'best' global terrorist organisation.

HISTORY AND OVERVIEW

In 1992, the mainstream Muslim party, the *Suni Front Islamique du Salut* (FIS, the Islamic Salvation Army), was heading for political victory. In the country's first democratic elections, the Algerian military cancelled the vote, declared a state of emergency, jailed a majority of its leaders, and banned the party. These events signalled the beginning of *la sale guerre* (the dirty war) and the anti-Islamic insurgency. It was also during this time that GIA (then colloquially called "Harkis" or "Son of Harkis"[2] [Comtat, 2017], designating an enemy from within) emerged as the principal and most aggressive Islamist group fighting the Algerian government. GIA's genesis lay in the insurgence of February 10, 1992, under Mansouri Meliani (alias Salem and ex-Bouyalists)[3] and Mohamed Allel (alias Moh Leveilly),[4] but the organisation was largely developed after their deaths. After Meliani was arrested in September 1992 and sentenced to death in April 1993, Allel took over the embryonic organisation after he had gained notoriety for orchestrating the police ambush in the *Wilaya* (city) of Boumerdes. In 1992, GIA was created by combining Mustafa Bouyali's *Mouvement Islamique Armee* ([MIA] the Islamic Armed Movement) led by General Abdelkader Chebouti[5] and the *Mouvement pour l'état Islamique* ([MEI] the Movement for the Islamic State) founded in 1991. With a newly available position of power following the arrest of Meliani and the death of Allel in August 1992, Abdelhaq Layada (alias Abu Adlane), a former metalworker and Allel's assistant, became the group's *emir* (leader) by uniting several smaller groups fighting in the capital of Algiers. Layada, from the Baraki district of Algiers, became inspired by Islam's teachings during the October 1988 popular uprising and subsequently merged smaller rival networks with different doctrines to create GIA

DOI: 10.4324/9780429426063-37

(Kepel, 2002). GIA was also the most organised and dominant urban terrorist paramilitary group in Algeria and called on its followers to adhere to ardent Islamic principles. In governing GIA, Layada wanted to distinguish the new group from FIS and MIA, which insisted that their members have in-depth Islamic ideological training. Instead, Layada adopted the spiritual philosophy of Omar El-Eulmi, which lacked religious rigour and "resulted in many militant infiltrations and transfers of leadership." Consequently, GIA centred its focus on the re-Islamisation of society and the creation of an Islamic state that sought to impose the strictest Islamic practises. For Layada, the disillusionment of the caliphate in 1924 was a decisive blow to Islam's Community of the Faithful. Under Layada, GIA commenced its signature policy, which consists of indiscriminately purging government officials and civilians working or affiliated with the government. In 1993, shortly before he was arrested in Morocco and extradited to Algeria, Layada declared GIA independent of MIA. Although he was sentenced to death in June 1995 in Algeria, under President Abdelaziz Bouteflika's "Charter for Peace and National Reconciliation," in March 2006, he was released from prison and retired to Baraki.

By 1993, GIA was enlisting upwards of 500 young men per week (Vriens, 2009). Layada was replaced with Mourad Si Ahmed (alias Djafar al-Afghani), a veteran Afghanistan commander who had a primary school education and was *a trabendo* (contraband trader). Ahmed's leadership saw a massive expansion of the group and gained notoriety after he oversaw the first instance of the murder of foreigners when they killed two French surveyors on September 21, 1993. In 1994, GIA declared a caliphate, and the *Front Islamique pour le Djihad* (FIDA, the Islamic Front for Armed Jihad) pledged its loyalty. However, intellectual differences soon led to tense dynamics since the group's leadership now had several prominent ex-FIS personalities. During this time, the GIA gained notoriety for its campaign against foreigners living and working in Algeria. Security forces killed Ahmed at Bouzaréah in 1994.

GIA's history of homegrown insurgency under Cherif Gousmi (alias Abu Abdallah Ahmed) was codified under its motto of "no agreement, no truce, no dialogue" and sums up the group's jihadi practises of vehemently targeting foreigners and *takfirs al-mujtama*[6] (infidel enemies of Islam), including Muslim women (particularly those not wearing the hijab and in professional careers), children, and the elderly (Boeke, 2016; Kepel, 2002; Martinez, 2000). Under Gousmi's brief reign, he proclaimed himself Caliph, established a GIA government with Djamel Zitouni (alias Abou Abd al-Rahmane Amine) as Minister of War, and unified GIA's networks by incorporating the remnants of the FIS. Gousmi established a *Majlis al-Shura* (Consultative Council) and accepted *bayat* (fealty) from several senior commanders who defected from FIS and MIA to GIA; these included Mohammed Said, head of the executive bureau, and Said Makhlouf, author of the "Thesis on Civil Disobedience," which encouraged mass violence (Kepel, 2002). These actions led the German-based FIS executive director, Rabah Kebir, to support the creation of the *Armée Islamique du Salut* (AIS), the Islamic Salvation Army.

Djamel Zitouni, emir from 1994 to 1996, came to power in an armed coup with support from the jihadi Salafi/Djazarist arm of the organisation. He had a francophone secondary school education and made his way through the ranks quickly as a specialist in killing French nationals. During Zitouni's leadership, a series of significant events took place: the 1994 hijacking of Air France *Flight* 8969 in Algeria and the killing of three passengers; the 1995 France bombings that killed eight and injured 157 in the cities of Paris and Lyon, including an attack on a school in Lyon; and the 1996 beheading of seven Tibhirine Algerian monks (Boeke, 2016; Roy & Sfeir, 2007). In January 1995, GIA's leadership executed some 500 supporters and purged all Algerianists (those members who were from the "League for Da'wa and Jihad" and claimed intellectual association with Sheikh Ahmed Sahnoun, the father of the Algerian Islamic movement) and left those who favoured *takfirs al-mujtama* untouched (Roy & Sfeir, 2007). He also published "The Way of God: Elucidations of Salafist Principles on Obligations for Jihad Fighters," which reaffirmed GIA's tactical and ideological position. By the time of his death in Bougara (Blida) in 1996, he had sown seeds of discord across the ranks and exacerbated the differences between the violent GIA and the pro-government FIS.

At the turn of the 21st century, violent fundamentalism continued and deepened under the new regimes. Antar Zouabri (alias Abou Talha), emir from 1996 to 2002, proclaimed, "In our war, there is no neutrality. Except for those who are with us, all others are renegades" (Vriens, 2009, p. 1). Under Zouabri, the 1998 civilian massacre in Algerian villages surrounding *Algiers occurred* (Boeke, 2016; Roy & Sfeir, 2007). Zouabri continued Zitouni's violent strategy of civilian attacks and maintained order by killing rivals. He was backed by Abu Hamza Salafist's orthodoxy, laid out in his manifesto, "The Sharp Sword," which was a doctrine of organised jihad. Ramadan (January–February) 1997 ushered in the deadliest period of the civil war as civilians were slaughtered indiscriminately (Kepel, 2002). By the time of Zouabri's death in Boufarik in February 2002, the ceasefire between the GIA and AIS was unstable.

In sum, from 1993 until its fragmentation in 1998, the GIA orchestrated the murder of some 100,000 civilians. The organisation grew increasingly violent under the leadership of Jamal Zitouni and Antar Zouabri, and this led to the splintering of the group and the creation of GSPC. During its tenure, GIA's core supporters and members, the so-called foreign mujahedin fighters, or "Afghan Algerians," "Afghans," or "elders of Afghanistan," were militants returning home from their jihad stint in Afghanistan's training camps (Boeke, 2016; Younessi, 1995). Over its history, GIA stated that its official duty was to create a caliphate after it overthrew the "apostate" governmental regime, using the "al-Shehada" doctrine and strategy, which condemned "France as the source of all evil" (Roy & Sfeir, 2007, p. 64). In short, it was a "radical ethno-nationalist organisation [that] blended the notion of religious identity as a nationalist cause" (Smith, 2010, p. 64) to secure a Muslim homeland in Algeria. During its tenure, the GIA gained notoriety for its cruelty in that it made no distinction between civilian and security (government and military) targets. Additionally, throughout its history, GIA had nine emirs, lasting on average around eighteen months each, and except for Mourad Si Ahmed, they were all illiterate. GIA first began to inflict its *fatwas* on foreigners in Algeria and subsequently upped its game while gaining international notoriety. The GIA officially ended in 2004.

IDEOLOGY AND NEW LEADERSHIP: THE EMERGENCE OF GPSC

The brutality of GIA's totalitarian leadership, the government's crackdown on its members, and the indiscriminate killing of civilians led to internal dissolution (Cristiani, 2013). From its remnants, Osama bin Laden and al-Qaeda formed a Salafist interpretation of the Qur'an with the sole objective of carrying out jihad against government targets. The 1997 fatwa by Hassan Hattab (alias Abu Hamza) and Zerabib Ahmed (alias Cheikh Ahmed Abou al-Bara) called for an end to the indiscriminate targeting of civilians and the *takfirs al-mujtama* policy, but was, however, ignored. By 1998, disagreements regarding operational tactics and theological differences had led to a splintering within GIA. These ideological differences led Hattab, former GIA commander for Boumerdès, and Ahmed to create GSPC on April 24, 1998, by taking over the networks and phalanges (tightly knit units located in the *Wilayas* of Jijel, Sétif, Batna, El Oued, and Tebessa) of the GIA (Roy & Sfeir, 2007). The transition from GIA to GSPC saw a change in key personnel that shaped the group's outlook and its new version of jihad since Mokhtar Belmokhtar[7] (alias Khaled Abu al-Abbas, the one-eyed commander, or the "Uncatchable" by French intelligence) and the future founder of *Katibat al-Murabitoun*[8] ([AMB] the Masked Men Brigade or Those Who Sign in Blood Brigade) would retain control of the region that encompassed the southern zone.

Moreover, the creation of GSPC initiated a new wave of Algerian ethnonationalism while forging ties with local communities and seeking to integrate into the northern communities (Raleigh & Dowd, 2013; Smith, 2010). The GSPC then became the principal Islamic movement, and anyone working for the Algerian state was viewed as their enemy. Hattab was appointed emir of the group's eastern region, Kabyle, in Algiers and spoke out against the 1995 purge of the Algerians. By 1997, GSPC and AIS (founded in 1994 as the fighting wing of FIS) announced a truce, and other groups, such as al-Bakoun Ala al-Ahd, which spun off from FIS in 1991 and was based in the United Kingdom under the leadership of Kamereddine Kharbane and Boudjemâa Bounoua, pledged allegiance to GSPC and became its logistics and propaganda tool. By September 1998, in addition to battling AIS, GSPC began concentrating its efforts on the toppling of the Algerian government.

In 1999, when the Algerians voted to enact the amnesty programme under the civil concord, GSPC declared that any of its fighters who accepted amnesty would be killed (Boudali, 2017). Also in 1999, GSPC began recruiting from Mali's Tuareg (where Islamic proselytising began in 1995), Arab, and Peul communities to shore up its recruitment and strength. The Tuareg and Arab peoples, who are northerners, self-identify as 'white' and were prominent players in the slave trade. This history eventually led to racial distinction and infighting in AQIM. Since 2001, AQIM (then GSPC) has openly been operating in the Tuareg region and has lucratively financed its activities through a business module of smuggling (drugs, cigarettes, stolen cars, weapons, and people), kidnapping-for-ransom, money-laundering, and other criminal fundraising ventures from foreign donors while providing local employment to youths as informers, drivers, runners, and footsoldiers (Morgan, 2014).

In the early 2000s, the Algerian government began to grant amnesty, and several GSPC fighters took it, leading to internal upheaval. Between 2000 and 2003, GSPC published its monthly magazine *Sada al Qital* (The Echo of Combatants), later renamed *al-Jama'a* (The Group), which was published between 2004 and 2006. Later, between 2012 and 2018, the group, under Adel Seghiri (alias Abu Rawaha al-Qusantini or Hichem Abou Rouaha), would use al-Qaeda's media outlet, *al-Andalus* Media Foundation, and the *Ifriqya el Islamia* terrorist forum, as well as the Twitter account "Africa Muslima," for its recruitment and communication. As GSPC developed militarily, executing guerilla-style attacks and using small arms (mortar, rockets, and improvised explosive devices), political governance structures across the *Wilayas* emerged. GSPC was more disciplined than other organisations and thus less susceptible to internal dysfunction and conflict. This allowed the group to expand its operations and create sleeper cells in Algeria, greater North Africa, and later in Mali. Then, *el-Mithaq* (the charter) *of the* GSPC spelled out its function and structure, which divided the governance of the Political Directorate and the Military Directorate. GSPC then established its killing squads and financed itself through various legal and illegal measures ranging from the acquisition of lands, both residential and commercial, to charitable donations, coercion, and smuggling.

By 2003, the government had hunted down and killed the GIA members who had not joined the GSPC. However, 2003 also signalled a watershed moment in that Amari Saifi (alias Abderrazak El Para), a former Special Forces soldier in the Algerian army, and Abdelhamid Abou Zeid, later head of AQIM's Tariq Ibn Ziyad Brigade, conducted the first significant kidnapping and ransoming operation in North Africa. In late 2003, under Hattab, GSPC pledged an oath of *bayat* to Osama bin Laden and Mullah Mohammed Omar (then supreme commander, spiritual leader of the Taliban, and *de facto* leader of Afghanistan from 1996 to 2001). However, in 2004, Hattab resigned (and was later killed in an anti-terrorist operation), and he was replaced by his second in command, Nabil Sahraoui, until Abdelmalek *Droukdel (alias* Abu Musab Abdel Wadoud*) took over as emir of GSPC in February 2005. Droukdel* was viewed as a counterbalance to Belmokhtar, who was the group's southern commander. Belmokhtar was viewed as a threat given that he spearheaded the "Saharan turn" (Thurston, 2017) in 2003 when he began to establish deep ties (financial and matrimonial) in Mali with the Tuareg and Malian Arabs. By 2005, GSPC had started to train recruits to fight in Iraq while simultaneously having its more experienced fighters train with Hezbollah in Lebanon. Moreover, the group escalated its bombings.

On September 11, 2006, five years after the 9/11 attacks, under the leadership of *Droukdel*, first recognised by Osama bin Laden and Ayman al-Zawahiri (later head of al-Qaeda in 2011 after the death of bin Laden), GSPC announced its complete allegiance[9] to al-Qaeda, al-Qaeda's global jihad fight, and pleaded *bayat* to al-Qaeda's leaders. This meant that GSPC's networks, institutions, and structures were subsumed into al-Qaeda's organisational structure. Droukdel rose through the ranks first as a former commander of the Jerusalem Brigade of the GIA and then as a member of the GSPC's Council of Notables. Under Droukdel's command, from 2004, GSPC took two years to negotiate its merger with al-Qaeda, which argued that GSPC's agenda was too nationalist in its orientation, and al-Qaeda's leaders questioned what the group could bring to the global fight against distant enemies. Now called al-Qaeda in the Islamic Maghreb (AQIM), the group undertook new operations under hybrid governance, in which the directions came directly from the top under the supreme commander. Additionally, the organisation is now supported by the Council of Notables and Shura Council, who then relay instructions to zone commanders and emirs who have discretionary authority over their respective areas (Nessel, 2012; Thurston, 2017). By the time AQIM pledged allegiance to al-Qaeda, it had commanders who controlled four zones, called *katibats:* the central (the urban centres of Algiers, Boumerdes, and Tizi Ouzou), the east (east of Tizi Ouzou to the Tunisian border), the west (Medea province to Morocco), and the south (the Sahara through Niger, Mauritania, and Mali). Under this new structure, commanders and emirs are expected to secure financing, weapons, and recruit while the "headquarters element is free to provide campaign guidance and, where necessary, provide key logistical support for high-priority operations" (Nessel, 2012, p. 31). Moreover, during its tenure, GSPC managed to establish several foreign cells in Europe (Belgium, Spain, Italy, France, and the United Kingdom) and garner support from other global terrorist organisations, primarily al-Qaeda.

THE REGIONALISING OF JIHAD: THE RISE OF AQIM

On January 26, 2007, GSPC merged with al-Qaeda and changed its official name from *Qaidat al-Jihad* (the Islamic Jihad Base) to *Maghreb al Islami* (QJMI), in what the West calls al-Qaeda in the Land of the Islamic Maghreb (AQIM). This name change signalled the deepening of the extra-territorial relations that GSPC had developed with Ayman al-Zawahiri and Mustafa Setmariam Nasar (alias Abu Musab al-Suri) that were negotiated by Belmokhtar. The name change and pledge of allegiance to al-Qaeda were geostrategic manoeuvres to combat declining recruitment and gain strategic support and financing (Boudali, 2017). The affiliation also brought global notoriety and recruits as the group's power and influence were waning in Algeria as it cracked down on terrorist activities. Unlike GIA, which focused on attacking civilian targets, GSPC strategies focused on strictly military targets.

With this change, a new quasi-governance structure was erected at the top with bureaucracies such as the Legal Committee, *Madjliss Echouri* (the Advisory Board), the Council of Notables (like the military or war council), the *Shura* (Consultative) Council (providing religious and legal guidance), along with specialised divisions for military and information and communication. This structure would provide strategic and ideological direction, while local zone commanders would be responsible for their recruitment, finances, and tactical operations. At the local level, AQIM finalised its *katibat* (also called a battalion or brigade) structures that allowed for local and regional zones as well as emirates to have considerable independence (Thurston, 2017). This hands-off approach led to infighting and competition between *katibats*, as well as disparities in resources across the different *katibats*.

The restructuring also saw AQIM's ideological struggle shift from a national one towards a transnational one. Shortly after its name change, Droukdel *sent* GPSC/AQIM fighters to fight alongside al-Zarqawi, leader of al-Qaeda in Iraq (AQI), to confront their common enemy and rid the land of the American occupiers. AQIM's foray into Iraq would signal its entry into the fight for global jihad, and it is during this time that its soldiers would learn and refine the military techniques that would allow them to perform appalling acts of violence against state and non-state actors alike. Droukdel was able to establish legitimacy given the security vacuum that existed across the Sahel region stemming from the ethnic separatist insurrection and government collapse and the vast open swaths of ungoverned land (Thornberry & Levy, 2011).

Once AQIM was rebranded, which represented a dramatic change from its earlier strategy, an upsurge in violence across Algeria began in April 2007 with the killing of 33 people by two suicide car bombs, one of which was at the prime minister's office. Later that year, a UN building and another government construction building were bombed, killing sixty people. Droukdel used an internet video to take responsibility for these bombings and encourage followers to become suicide bombers. In May, Droukdel publicly told regional AQIM commanders to select recruits and potential targets for suicide bombings. By the end of the year, Ayman al-Zawahiri, AQIM's second in command, had called for the cleansing of Spaniards and Frenchmen from Africa's Muslim lands. AQIM also began to employ a new expansion strategy in its southern zone, practically pushing into the Kabylie Mountains and the wastelands of northern Mali towards the Algerian security forces (Nessel, 2012). By 2005, AQIM would target a new extra-Algerian opponent, France, which it saw as standing in its way of creating an Islamic state in Algeria. This new faraway enemy coincided with al-Qaeda's mission to take on Western rather than local targets. This further strategic objective took GSPC back to its GIA roots of attacking France, which it viewed as a "support[er] the apostate Algerian regime" (Boudali, 2017, pp. 2–3).

Disagreement broke out in 2007 between Belmokhtar, then *Katibat* al-Mulathamin (the Veiled Ones) Brigade's commander in the ninth zone, and Abou Zeid, head of kidnappings and commander of the east and southern zones, as to the role that kidnapping-for-ransom played in jihad "since the hostages were generally non-combatants or civilians," and this led to the implementation of "the Islamist agenda in the region" (Guidère, 2014, p. 2) as these tactics drew attention to the movement. This conflict forced Droukdel to clarify the group's jihad practises while cementing its core strategies by outlining that specific tactics, such as ransoming and kidnapping, are legitimate jihad actions that form the core principles of the "Law of War in Islam" (Guidère, 2014). Between 2008 and 2013, AQIM kidnapped thirty-nine Westerners and received $10 million in ransom (Thurston, 2017).

When sixty people lost their lives in bombings in towns outside of Algiers in 2008, the violence AQIM inflicted on civilians only got worse. Between 2008 and 2009, AQIM kidnapped several foreigners across the Sahel (including Mali, Mauritania, and Niger) and held them for ransom until this was paid in 2010. During this time, AQIM's Tariq ibn Ziyad Battalion began training members of the Nigerian jihadist group Boko Haram (aka the Islamic State in West Africa). The fact that France's then-President Nicolas Sarkozy declared war on the organisation after its troops carried out a raid on the Mauritania-Mali border made the year 2010 for AQIM particularly active. AQIM responded to France's statement with a declaration of war against its so-called "far enemy." These pronouncements saw AQIM refocusing its efforts and intensifying the scope and pace of its violent attacks in the Saharan basin. By 2011, violent incidents were frequent, as four successful suicide bombings took place over two months and culminated in an attack upon Algeria's premier military academy, *Académie Militaire Interarmes* (AMIA) at Cherchell, killing eighteen people (Pillar, 2011). Across Algeria, in 2010, AQIM kidnapped for ransom forty-three people and conducted one hundred and ninety-six bombings using suicide attackers and vehicle-borne improvised explosive devices (VBIED), and in 2011, another nineteen people were captured (Thornberry & Levy, 2011). These activities eventually led to the United Nations Security Council, the United States, and the European Union naming AQIM as a terrorist group.

With the onset of the Arabic Awakening, AQIM began to support intra-jihadist struggles by working jointly with the jihadi's group, Ansar al-Sharia, which operated in Libya and Tunisia. Eventually, AQIM would launch a local *katibat*, Uqba ibn Nafi, in Tunisia that ultimately subsumed the members of Ansar al-Sharia in Tunisia (AST). By mid-2011, AQIM suffered an ideological blow when a group of its members from its *Katibat* Mauritanian branch, Hamad al-Khairy[10] and Ahmed el-Tilemsi[11], left to form the *Mouvement pour l'unicité et le jihad en Afrique de l'Ouest* ([MUJAO][12] the Movement for Oneness and Jihad in West Africa). MUJAO's aims were to spread jihad across a more extensive section of West Africa, which was not an area that AQIM was interested in penetrating. Although Algerians had historically predominated AQIM, the splinter was actually the result of ideological jihadism, the role of religion, funding, social strategies, and insurgency tactics (Boas, 2014). An identity steeped in black-African nationalism and racial politics, as opposed to an Algerian-driven or Arab-dominated movement, drove the ideological crisis that AQIM experienced prior to the schism. Since 2013, MUJAO has asserted that it collaborates with AQIM on shared strategic objectives, the Goa incident being one such instance.

The 2012–2013 jihadist occupation of Mali led *Droukdel to expel* Belmokhtar for "fractious behaviour" (Morgan, 2014), stemming from tactical differences (kidnapping, trafficking, and smuggling) and the imposition of Shariah law too quickly in Mali. In December 2012, while maintaining ties to al-Qaeda, Belmokhtar created *Katibat al-Murabitoun* with some of AQIM's best fighters and sought to exhort control in northern Mali. Tuaregs and Arabs, under the guidance of AQIM and backed by Iyad Ag Ghali, drove the Malian army out of the north. Belmokhtar's *katibat* would be responsible for the Tiguentourine gas facility hostage-taking, the twin suicide bombings at the Somair uranium mine, and the army barracks in Agadez.

However, by 2013, elements of the MUJAO, led by Ahmed el Tilems, had combined with other militant groups to establish al-Qaeda in West Africa under the name al-Murabitoun, managed by Mokhtar Belmokhtar, while the remaining MUJAO faction, led by Sultan Ould Badi, operated independently. *Al-Murabitoun* (later relabelled as al-Qaeda in West Africa and pledging allegiance to al-Qaeda's head, Ayman al-Zawahiri) is but one example of how the executive leadership within AQIM has remained chaotic and rife with ideological differences. Moreover, given the group's decentralisation at the local level, it forces commanders and emirs to employ different tactics to remain relevant. For example, Belmokhtar's fight for power was only possible through his marital ties to the northern Malian tribe, the Kounta, which allowed him to cultivate community ties in the Timbuktu region. More importantly, since its rebranding, in addition to MUJAO, AQIM has given rise to some offshoots across the region, including Boko Haram, inclusive of its splinter group in 2014, Vanguards for the Protection of Muslims in Black Africa.[13] [Ansaru] (Aronson, 2014). Boko Haram, under Abubakr Shekau, would pledge *bayat to the Islamic State, eventually becoming its* first (and still only) sub-Saharan African Islamic State *Wilaya*, known as Wilayat West Africa (Warner, 2017). Ansar's occupation of Timbuktu and Gao by MUJAO under AQIM's name was a new height for the organisation, as the offshoot experimented with a different form of bureaucratic administration that sought to provide local services and Islamic rule in place of the government. Mujao, Ansaru, and the occupation of northern Mali were in response to the power vacuum that was created after the Malian government was overthrown in 2012 by the military. While these splinter groups have evolved, they should not be viewed as separate from AQIM but as part of its decentralised and delineated (albeit informal) units that have pledged allegiance to various groups' core leadership and share affinities and loyalties with other global groups.

EVOLVING IN AN ERA OF COMPETITIVE JIHAD

AQIM's ultimate endgame is the replacement of all apostate states and regimes with Sharia states governed by Sharia's core principles and rules. Moreover, AQIM also sought to strengthen its global jihad mission by supplying several groups across the region with weapons, support, and training, including Boko Haram, to carry out its 2001 attack on the United Nations office in Abuja, Nigeria (Aronson, 2014). In 2011, Abu al Hassan Rachid al Bulaydi, head of the Sharia Committee, wrote a booklet entitled "Nasa'ih Wa-tawjihat Shar'iyya li-mujahidi Nijiriy" (Some Religious Advice and Guidelines to the Jihadists of Nigeria), which was released a few years after his death in 2015. This booklet explained AQIM's operational structure and how Droukdel shaped and nurtured the Boko Haram partnership, but it also discussed how it advised other groups on preparing to wage state jihad. Moreover, it sheds light on the financial, training, recruitment, and partnership techniques that AQIM uses. As *Droukdel states, the aim of AQIM is* "to rescue our countries from the tentacles of these criminal regimes that betrayed their religion and their people" (New York Times, 2018, para 30).

When the Islamic State[14] renounced its allegiance to al-Qaeda in June 2014 and set out to proclaim a caliphate, something that was at the heart of al-Qaeda's "General Guidelines for the Work of Jihad" (Holbrook, 2017), Droukdel's leadership of AQIM began to wane as new leaders across the Sahara with different ideologies started fighting for power. AQIM backed al-Qaeda and al-Zawahiri over the Islamic State and clashed with the Islamic State's affiliates in the Sahara. Islamic State's entry into global terrorism led to fractions across its *katibat*. For example, in September 2014, the Islamic State in the Greater Sahara (IS-GS) and Katibat Jund al-Khilafa fi Ard al-Jazaye (Caliphate Soldiers in Algeria) professed allegiance to the Islamic State. Abdulmalik Suleiman Abu Gori (also known as Khaled), the leader of both, is based in northern Algeria. IS-GS's emergence stemmed from ideological differences within Belmokhtar's *al-Murabitoun* between the pro-Islamic State and pro-AQIM factions and the reminiscence of MUJAO. IS-GS's leadership viewed *bayat as an individual's pledge and not one sanctioned by* Belmokhtar. AQIM's leadership declared the Islamic State's caliphate illegitimate while encouraging the creed of "the Islamic Spring," which called for the greater unification of Sunni Muslims. Thus, AQIM, al-Qaeda, and the Islamic State began to compete for recruits, funding, and the accolade of being the best global jihadist group. In light of its internal crisis of leadership, Porter (2011) argues that AQIM's media arm, al-Andalus Foundation, "regularly releases statements claiming responsibility for attacks and employs the vocabulary and symbolism of Salafi-jihadi thought" (p. 5), employing a Salafi-jihadi discourse grounded in the rhetoric of "fitna (disorder), jahiliyya (pre-Islamic ignorance), fasad (corruption), and the importance of fighting for the return of the proper way of life" (p. 7). This has become AQIM's primary recruitment tool to fight the "great Satan" (the West and current and former occupiers of Arab lands) that governs the apostate states through its proxies (police, military, security services, gendarmerie, intelligence apparatuses, judiciary, intelligence, and elites) who aim to secularise the poor (Holbrook, 2017). Its operational tactics consist of false roadblocks, ambushes, bombings, assassinations, and raids on towns or neighbourhoods. By 2014, AQIM had a vast governance structure that extended over several countries in the Middle East, was under the direction of Droukdel, and was supported through decentralised *katibats*. In 2015, after claiming credit for attacks on several foreigners within Mali[15], *al-Murabitoun* merged with AQIM and pledged allegiance to al-Qaeda's core leadership. Under the union and using the name AQIM, both groups were able to tap into each other's resources to undertake raids in Mali, Burkina Faso, and the Ivory Coast in 2015.

Northern Ireland has been in a state of rebellion since the open conflict and uprising of 1963, some three years after independence. During its initial entry into Mali in 2003, AQIM faced local resistance from several ethno-nationalist groups (Raleigh & Dowd, 2013). In 2017, AQIM spearheaded the merging of several local Jihadist groups – AQIM's Sahara division, *al-Murabitoun, the Islamist Tuareg Organisation Ansar al-Dine* ([AAD] the Defenders of the Faith[16]), and *Katibat Front de Libération du Macina* ([FLM] the Macina Liberation Front [led by Amadou Kouffa]) – to create *Jama'at Nusrat al Islam wal Muslimeen* ([JNIM] the Group to Support Islam and Muslims), which is led by the secular and nationalist leader of Ansar al-Dine, Iyad Ag Ghali, who reports to Droukdel. Ag Ghali's complex history spells trouble for AQIM. With the formation of JNIM and the inclusion of the ethnic Tuareg Islamist clans and subclans under Ag Ghali's leadership and the receding of the **National Movement for the Liberation of Azawad's (MNLA) power**, AQIM has entered a racial and political minefield as different Tuareg groups are fighting for different priorities ranging from self-determination to sharia law enclaves to higher social rankings. The northeastern Mali Tuareg are economically, culturally, and historically distinct from the blacks in the south, with whom they are lumped together. For Tuareg, their lineage dates to the prophet Mohamad, and this, they argue, makes them superior to blacks and thus entitled to statehood. The relationship between the Tuareg and AQIM is one that has emerged to protect self-interest and not ideological foundations since Tuareg identity lies not in religion, as it does for AQIM, but in the Tamashek language. As Atallah (2013) argues, Ag Ghali's "ethnic makeup as a Tuareg allows AQIM to operate while he manages the negative Tuareg rhetoric" (p. 75).

Since 2017, with the Libyan instability becoming unsolvable and the demise of the Islamic State's influence and territory across Syria and Iraq, as well as its subsequent banishment to the desolate landscape of *Badiyat al-Sham* (the Syrian Desert), which encompasses some 500,000 square kilometres spanning Southeastern Syria, Northeastern Jordan, Northern Saudi Arabia, and Western Iraq, AQIM has emerged as a regional leader in terrorism. AQIM returned to large-scale terrorism in 2017 with the killing of 77 people and the injuries of dozens more in Gao, Northern Mali. AQIM poses a significant threat to regional stability and America's nationalist agenda under the Trump administration. For too long, America has ignored the rise of Islamic militantism in Africa instead of focusing on and responding to threats of greater Islamisation in the Middle East. This neglect poses a further danger to America's future foreign policy agenda. AQIM has emerged as a regional player by extending its terrorist networks and cells beyond Algeria to northern Africa, Europe, and soon the United States.

AQIM has historically singled out Spain and France as its foremost "far enemies." The aim of AQIM and its various sleeper cells and factions is to attack Western targets (security forces and the military) and undertake violent attacks (kidnappings for ransom and extortion). Since its allegiance to al-Qaeda, AQIM's anti-Western rhetoric has increased as it seeks to create a caliphate through the overthrow of apostate African regimes. In a desperate search for more recruits, AQIM extended its recruitment efforts across the Timbuktu region and into Mauritania (Watch World, 2016). While the AQIM operational centre remains in Algeria, it continues to inflict harm on its enemies and their citizens. AQIM's departure from Algeria was made possible by financing from illegal activities and the killing, kidnapping, and ransoming of civilians. This new strategy of jihad expansionism is both regionally (from Algeria to the Sahara/Sahel to West Africa) and internationally (Europe) steeped in a progressive convergence of interests around global terrorism. With its expansion to the central African region, AQIM is posing a significant threat to groups such as the Lord's Resistance Army (Raleigh & Dowd, 2013). These strategies have enormous consequences for America's security, both foreign and domestic. AQIM, with its hybrid centralised and decentralised Algerian leadership structure, is showing that it is here to play the long game as it continues to morph and adapt to the changing geopolitical circumstances. In short, Algeria should not be treated as a backwater country but as a policy priority in the global fight against terrorism.

CONCLUSION: THE IMPACT OF AQIM ON AMERICAN FOREIGN POLICY

Today, AQIM has substantial Saharan operations across Algeria, Mali, Niger, Libya, Mauritania, and Tunisia. It is responsible for the execution of frequent attacks in North and West Africa. However, the lawlessness of the southern Algerian borders and the ungoverned spaces throughout northern Niger, northern Mali, and eastern Mauritania have been incubators for AQIM's strength in the region as governments have failed to undertake effective counterterrorism measures against the group (Porter, 2011). AQIM's alignment with other groups such as Ansar al-Dine allows it to operate openly in places like Mali and be seen as mainstream rather than an anomaly. With the rise and later banishment of Islamic States, AQIM has also had to crystallise its core mission to secure recruits, as Tunisians and Moroccans accounted for a very significant portion of the foreign fighters making up the ranks of the Islamic State. Since AQIM operates and seeks to govern large swaths of territory as part of its transnational jihadist philosophy, its leadership hierarchy and allegiance are always shifting and coalescing around different groups. Despite this, the mission remains the same: creating Sharia states based on Arabic tribal practises, cultural beliefs, and allegiance to the Prophet Muhammad in the form of *bayat al ridwân* (the Oath of Hudaybiyyah) (Guidere, 2011). In 2018, the Worldwide Threat Assessment report showed that al-Qaeda and Islamic State are active in Algeria, not AQIM (Porter, 2019). 2018 was the first time that Algeria did not directly suffer an attack from AQIM; the organisation was busy undertaking the bulk of its activities in the Sahel region, led by the Algerian national Yahya Abu el Hammam. Moreover, with the creation of JNIM, a large portion of AQIM's leadership is no longer of Algerian descent.

Moreover, AQIM's affiliation with the global al-Qaeda movement is not one that penetrates at the operational level, and it is very similar to other ideological relations that other AQ-affiliates, such as al-Qaeda in Iraq (AQI) and al-Qaeda in the Arabian Peninsula (AQAP), have. In other words, despite being a member of al-Qaeda, AQIM seeks to attack both adversaries that are nearby (in the Sahel and Sahara) and far away (in France, Spain, and the United Kingdom). Thus, AQIM should not be misconstrued as an external force of al-Qaeda but as a "complex and multi-dimensional group that combines a Salafist ideological orientation" and that "pursued strategies of integration in the region based on a sophisticated reading of the local context" (Boas, 2014, pp. 1–2). AQIM has been successful in using jihad websites,[17] blogs,[18] and social media[19] to distribute its communiqués, capitalise upon its jihadist message, recruit, fight its enemies (Islamic and apostate alike), and take credit for the activities of martyrs. More importantly, AQIM has used media propaganda to differentiate itself from other groups while claiming responsibility for terror attacks. These strategic manoeuvres align with AQIM's change in its operational directions in the Sahara/Sahel region, which resulted from changing geo-strategic circumstances across the region, and, as the organisation's actions became quelled in Algeria, it began to expand in other countries. In essence, it is using its strong foundation, stemming from the Algerian Civil War, to project itself as a global terrorist organisation rather than a regional affiliate of the local terrorist branch of historical terror groups such as al-Qaeda.

Instability across the region saw many of AQIM's fighters leave for Libya, Syria, and Iraq. However, the international military offensive against the Islamic State has meant that IS has lost its caliphate status and large cities such as Mosul, Dabiq, and Raqqa, just as it has been banished to the desolate landscape of *Badiyat al-Sham*. The Islamic State's defeat has allowed AQIM to become a dominant force in the region, which holds huge swaths of open land, weak central governments, porous institutions, and unprotected borders that are ripe for exploitation and the enactment of transnational criminal activities. In an age of anti-Islamic rhetoric and calls for more profound adherence to stricter Islamic teachings, AQIM remains a significant global terrorist threat.

Notes

1 Also called Al-Qaeda in the Lands of the Islamic Maghreb (AQLIM).

2 The Algerian political authorities saw Harkis, initially used to describe auxiliaries in the French Army during the Algerian War of Independence from 1954 to 1962, as traitors.

3 The Bouyali Group was composed of former Algerian fighters under the Group for Defence Against the Illicit, founded in 1979. In 1982, it transformed into the Algerian Islamic Armed Movement (MIAA). When its founder, Mustafa Bouyali, died in 1987, the group disbanded, and some of its members reconstituted GIA.

4 The Algerian military killed Leveilly while he was hosting a GIA meeting to coordinate the command of the jihadist forces.

5 MEI became a separate organisation after the purging of the Algerianists and disintegrated in 1993 after Chebouti's death.

6 Under *Takfir al-Mujtama*, both the state and individual are viewed as infidels and subjected to jihad.

7 He was believed to have survived the 2015 US and 2016 French air strikes, and his death had not been confirmed in 2019.

8 Also spelled al-Murabitun, al-Moulathamoun, al-Maulathamun Battalion, al-Mulathameen Brigade, and al-Murabitoun.

9 Under Nabil Sahraoui's leadership, the group pledged allegiance to bin Laden in 2003, and Ayman al-Zawahiri confirmed GSPC's affiliation with al-Qaeda in a video statement released in September 2006 (Boudali, 2017).

10 Aided in the 2008 kidnapping of the Canadian ambassador, Robert Fowler, in Niger.

11 One of the masterminds of the 2011 kidnapping of two French nationals in Niger.

12 Also called the Movement for Unity and Jihad in West Africa (MUJWA), it aims to spread jihad further in West Africa.

13 Also called Al-Qaeda in the Lands Beyond the Sahel.

14 Since 2014, when the name was changed to *Al Dawlah al-Islamiyah* (the Islamic State), which is the current manifestation of *Jama'at al-Tawhid wa-l-Jihad* (2000–2004); *al-Qaeda in the Land of Two Rivers* ([AQI] 2004–2006); *Majlis Shura al-Mujahidin* (2006); *Islamic State of Iraq* (2006–2013); and *Islamic State of Iraq and al-Sham* (2013–2014), under Caliph Abu Bakr al-Baghdadi, the Islamic State has sought to redraw colonial borders to establish a caliphate, a state based on Islamic rules of law, while at the same time attracting foreign fighters. Prior to losing territory in 2017, the Islamic State was defined as a state in physical terms since it held a physical presence, a multi-ethnic army of both foreign and regional Muslims, and several multilayered administrative structures of governments.

15 The Byblos Hotel in Sévaré killed thirteen people, the La Terrasse nightclub in Bamako killed five people, and the Radisson Blue Hotel killed twenty people and took one hundred and seventy hostages.

16 The Malian Tuareg jihadist Salafi Iyad Ag Ghali founded Ansar al-Dine in 2011 with the goal of enforcing Shariah law throughout Mali. Its members include Ifoghas Tuaregs, Berabiche Arabs, and other local ethnic groups. AQIM views Ansar al-Dine as its southern arm in Mali and has

instructed it to act as AQIM's domestic movement in the country.

17 http://www.jihad-algeria.com; http://www.salafiahweb1.tk; http://www.salafia.ne1.net; http://www.jihad-algerie.com; http://www.moon4321.net; http://www.moonnight1234.com; http://www.moonnight9876.com; http://www.qmagreb.org.

18 Such as al-Ekhlas Forum (http://www.al-ekhlaas.net); al-Faloja Forum (http://www.alfalojaweb.info/vb); Jihad Archive (http://www.jarchive.info/index.php); Shumukh al-Islam Forum (https://shamikh1.info); Ansar al-Mujahidin Forum (http://www.as-ansar.com/vb and http://ansar1.info); Atahadi Forum (http://www.atahadi.com/vb; al-Fidaa Forum (https://alfidaa.info); al-Jahad Forum (http://www.aljahad.com) (see Torres-Soriano, 2016).

19 Such as https://twitter.com/Africamuslima; https://twitter.com/Andalus_Media; https://www.facebook.com/africamuslima; https://twitter.com/Andalus_AQMI; https://twitter.com/AfricaMusIlma; https://twitter.com/Al_Andalus https://twitter.com/Africa_Muslima; https://twitter.com/Al; https://twitter.com/Al_Andalus2l; https://twitter.com/Al_Andalus4; https://twitter.com/Afrika_Muslima_Musi

References

Aronson, S.L. (2014, April). AQIM's threat to Western interests in the Sahel. *CTC Sentinel, 7*(4), 6–10.

Atallah, R. (2013). The Tuareg revolt and the Mali coup. *ASPJ Africa & Francophonie.4* (1), 66–79

Boas, M. (2014, April). Guns, money and prayers: AQIM's blueprint for securing control of Northern Mali. *CTC Sentinel, 7*(4), 1–6.

Boeke, S. (2016). Al-Qaeda in the Islamic Maghreb: Terrorism, insurgency, or organized crime? *Small Wars & Insurgencies, 27*(5), 914–936.

Boudali, L.K. (April 2017). The GSPC: Newest franchise in al Qa'ida's global jihad. The North Africa Project. The Combating Terrorism Center, United States Military Academy, West Point.

Comtat, E. (2017). Les disparus civils européens de la guerre d'algérie.processus de construction d'une cause victimairemilitant. *Papeles del CEIC, 1*(166), 1–27.

Cristiani, D. (2013). Focus on leaders? Insights from the Algerian experience. *The Polish Quarterly of International Affairs, 22*(1), 73–80.

Guidere, M. (2011, February). The tribal allegiance system within AQIM. *CTC Sentinel, 4*(2), 9–10.

Holbrook, D. (2017). The spread of its message: Studying the prominence of al Qaida materials in UK terrorism investigations. *Perspectives on Terrorism, 11*(6). Retrieved from http://www.terrorismanalysts.com/pt/index.php/pot/article/view/658/html

Kepel, G. (2002). *Jihad: The trail of political Islam*. Cambridge, MA: Belknap Press of Harvard University Press.

Martinez, L. (2000). *The Algerian civil war, 1990–98*. New York, NY: Columbia University Press.

Morgan, A. (2014). What do the Tuareg want?. Retrieved from https://www.aljazeera.com/indepth/opinion/2014/01/what-do-tuareg-want-20141913923498438.html

Nessel, R.A. (June 2012). *Why failing terrorist groups persist: The case of Al-Qaeda in the Islamic Maghreb*. California: Naval Postgraduate School.

Pillar, P.R. (2011, September). American perceptions of terrorism in the post-9/11 decade. *CTC Sentinel, 4*(9), 1–3.

Porter, G.D. (2011, February). AQIM's objectives in North Africa. *CTC Sentinel, 4*(2), 5–8.

Porter, G.D. (2019, March). AQIM pleads for relevance in Algeria. *CTC Sentinel, 12*(3), 32–36.

Raleigh, C., & Dowd, C. (2013). Governance and conflict in the Sahel's 'ungoverned space'. *Stability: International Journal of Security & Development, 2*(2), 32, 1–17.

Roy, O., & Sfeir, A. (2007). *The Columbia world dictionary of Islamism*. New York, NY: Columbia University Press.

Smith, G.A. (2010). Al-Qaeda in the lands of the Islamic Maghreb. *Journal of Strategic Security, 2*(2), 53–72. DOI: 10.5038/1944-0472.2.2.2

Stone, M. (1997). *The agony of Algeria*. New York: Columbia University Press.

Torres-Soriano, M. (2016). The caliphate is not a tweet away: The social media experience of Al Qaeda in the Islamic Maghreb. *Studies in Conflict & Terrorism, 39*(11), 968–981.

Thornberry, W., & Levy, J. (September 2011). Al-Qaeda in the Islamic Maghreb. *Center for Strategic and International Studies, 4*.

Thurston, A. (October 2017). Al-Qaeda in the Islamic Maghreb (AQIM): An Al-Qaeda affiliate case study. CAN Analysis & Solutions.

Vriens, L. (2009, May 27). Armed Islamic group (Algeria, Islamists). A profile of the Algerian terrorist organization, Armed Islamic Group (GIA). Council on Foreign Relations. Retrieved from https://www.cfr.org/backgrounder/armed-islamic-group-algeria-islamists

Warner, J. (2017). Sub-Saharan Africa's three "new" Islamic state affiliates. *Combating Terrorism Center, 10*, 1. Retrieved from ctc.usma.edu.

Younessi, L'. (1995). Islamisme Algérien: Nébuleuse ou mouvement social? In *Politique étrangère*, n°2—60eannée. pp. 365–376.

34

THE MOVEMENT FOR THE LIBERATION OF AZAWAD IN MALI (MNLA)

Adekunle Toyin Olawunmi

INTRODUCTION AND BACKGROUND

The Sahel is a geopolitical epicentre in and of itself, an unwitting ground zero and staging ground for some of the most radical Islamic forces currently reshaping the international political order. The balance of terror and the political realities of sub-Saharan Africa, especially Malian geopolitics, have become stimulating. Of course, on their own, canons, deep cultural beliefs, and fundamental core values are difficult to unlearn, and when old ways are disturbed, either in Afghanistan, the Middle East, South America, etc., it is a recipe for and often a stimulus that elicits rebellion or armed conflicts.

Events in Mali have transformed into ones of symbiosis and convergence, in which it has become increasingly difficult to draw a meaningful distinction. The activities of terrorists and some privileged states in the illicit trade of natural resources for material benefits frequently reinforce each other, where terrorists engage either directly or indirectly in organised crime activities such as trafficking, smuggling, extortion, and kidnapping for ransom with the tacit approval of some global powers (see Besenyő & Romaniuk, 2024).

Like the Bedouins that are found chiefly around Israel, Jordan, and Syria, Tuaregs are nomads, and this population spreads across a very tough Saharan environment, where they have lived for ages. "The rebellion dates back more than 100 years to the colonisation of the Sahara," said Barbara Worley, an anthropologist at the University of Massachusetts at Boston. The Berlin Conference in 1884 left the Tuaregs divided across Mali, Niger, Libya, and Algeria. It was the artificial boundaries and the introduction of ungainly laws by the French that truly broke up the Tuaregs economic structure and left them bewildered. It is late in the day to dwell on the issues of acts that were inimical to common interests or acts that threatened the safety of the people without cause.

The insurrection in Saharan Africa is not particularly singular; yet such conflicts are often localised and seldom spread very wide until they become irritated by external stimuli. This chapter underscores the profane behaviour of external influencers on domestic political actors in the troubled region – a template that has resulted in civil wars across other African states. Thus, Azawad's and the Tuaregs conduct remains archetypal and foreseeable, and demanding good order and self-restraint from the Tuaregs is incongruous.

The Tuaregs first resisted colonial rule and later defied their inclusion in the postcolonial states. And their wish for an independent state is reminiscence, but also distinct in two specifics. While secessionism is strong enough among the Tuaregs of Mali and Niger to have resulted in armed rebellion in these countries, there has been no formal irredentism; that is, there have been no structural efforts to unite all Tuaregs into one territorial state.

Secondly, the ideal of national independence has never been raised in official negotiations with the states against which the Tuareg fought. From accounts, boundaries are non-existent and inconsequential to Bedouins and the Fulani tribes across West Africa; thus, to make sense of this chapter, it must be well-defined that restraints introduced by France were the watershed and a major cause of conflicts in the Sahel region, as well as the beginning of armed resistance and the formation of the MNLA in northern Mali.

FORMATION OF THE MNLA

The National Movement for the Liberation of Azawad (MNLA) is ethnologically driven, fighting mostly for the rights of Mali's minority Tuareg community. The MNLA, a successor to previous rebel groups, was formed in 2011.

DOI: 10.4324/9780429426063-38

Previously, numerous Malian Tuareg had bolstered Colonel Muammar Gaddafi's army, aiding a struggling Malian government that had been disturbed by the Tuareg's insurgent activities within its borders ("Mali Crisis: Key Players," 2013, p. 1). After Col. Gaddafi was slain in 2011, the Tuaregs returned to Mali, bulging the ranks of the MNLA as it spearheaded an uprising against the Malian army. The Tuareg who were in Libya also brought weapons with them, including surface-to-air missiles.

Though widespread across the Sahel, the Tuaregs are about three million people, and out of these, close to one million Tuareg could be found in Mali alone. After Mali's independence from France in 1960, a series of droughts affected the northern cities of Timbuktu, Kidal, and Gao (Mohanty, 2018). This is one of the country's least developed regions, and the state of Mali failed to assure holistic and inclusive development throughout all regions; the northern half was abandoned by the government and is now crushed under the weight of climate change.

But it is not only this occurrence that provokes the current feud. The Tuareg homeland has the largest energy deposits in Africa. The involvement of international superpowers competing for resources exacerbated their desire for an independent state, separation from Mali, and the right to rule their own land, which they called "Azawad." Expectedly, it was the presence of Western powers that kindled the interest of Al Qaeda in the region. Thus, vested interests from these three fronts arouse passion and threaten the five neighbouring states – a stake that has the potential to elicit a conflict in the Sahara like that of Afghanistan.

The Axis of Evil ideologue is consistent with recent events in the Sahel. As Jihadists were being displaced on other axes, Africa became the next haven. The big picture thus surrounds allies' activities around this mantra; until a few decades ago, the French operated in the Sahelian without much trouble. Afghanistan, Iraq, Libya, and Syria greatly influenced Algeria and northern Mali. The Gulf Wars and subsequent revolutionary ideas in Libya undoubtedly echo the episodes in northern Mali. Inadvertently, these affairs not only expatriated some Mujahedeen from Iraq and the Middle East regions but also magnetised Islamic fighters from Afghanistan, Sudan, and elsewhere into Azawad. In other words, Northern Mali and the Sahel region generally became an alternate and, to a large extent, a rallying point for the mujahedeen. Yet, the internal debates within Al Qaeda's hierarchy about the same historical concerns concerning waning support for the Iraqi and Algerian insurgencies and the failure of Islamist revolutionaries further stimulate the interest of these hardened fighters to engage in Mali.

Prior to his death, the leader of Al Qaeda began to achieve minimally centralised control over the terror organisation's splinter grid. Bin Laden achieved some progress before his death, but this was upturned by the demise of Libyan Gaddafi in 2011. Further on, we shall appreciate why the organisational acumen, determination, and focus of the Malian Tuareg returnees became encumbered.

ACHIEVEMENTS AND FAILURES

The Tuareg fighters of Malian origin had departed Libya with great enthusiasm and hope to bring peace and affluence to the region and revive the dying pastureland, which is their only source of livelihood. The meddling by more radicalised factions with alternate agendas subsequently dashed these expectations.

Ostensibly, the MNLA's alliance with the Islamists collapsed, and Ansar Dine and Mujao drove its forces out of the main northern towns. The MNLA's influence waned after it ran out of money, causing many of its fighters to defect to Ansar Dine and Mujao. Albeit, Tuareg returnees had been part of Gaddafi's mercenary army and returned to northern Mali with sophisticated weaponry; it was an exodus from profusion to despair, having experienced the wealth of Libya, and now suddenly they were back in their home country that was beset with lack, famine, and disease, and most significantly, a lack of central government presence.

Indeed, the Tuaregs ambition was limited to overthrowing government control in the Northern Sector with a view to emancipating their one million population from oppression and enabling Tuaregs to have control of their natural endowment. They equally perceived the central government as a willing tool in the hands of the imperialists in France. These returnees thus formed the MNLA in 2011 as a political-military platform to continue their fight for self-rule. But this seemingly modest ambition to establish a home for Tuaregs failed.

What happened in Mali could be likened to the revolutionary activities that swept through America and resulted in the American Declaration of Independence in 1776 ("Declaration of Independence broadside, July 1776, Jamestown-Yorktown Foundation"). The Second Continental Congress at the time adopted Thomas Jefferson's Declaration of Independence. It was very succinct as to why the British colonies of North America sought independence in July of 1776. What is very remarkable in the American case is the opening preamble, which states categorically that there are certain unalienable rights that governments should never violate. These rights include the right to life, liberty, and the pursuit of happiness. The document went further to decree that when a government fails to protect those rights, it is not only the right but also the duty of the people to overthrow that government. In its place, the people should establish a government that is designed to protect those rights ("Declaration of Independence broadside, July 1776, Jamestown-Yorktown Foundation," 1775).

Pierre Boilley, a professor of contemporary African history at the University of Paris, remarked, "At the beginning, this was essentially a political movement, but with the return of the Tuareg from Libya, it became military as well as political." Colonel Meshkenani Ag Bela of the MNLA, one of the fourth generations in his family to revolt against Mali and its forerunner colonial friends, remarked, "We have a deep-rooted and bitter history; we fought French imperial forces until they left. We never accepted French colonialism or the fact that France gave our land to Mali without our consent. And so, in March 2012, just one year after the formation of the MNLA, the Tuaregs toppled the Malian government forces and declared the independent state of Azawad in what had been northern Mali. Analysts observed that the Tuareg MNLA and Islamist Ansar Dine rebel groups merged and declared northern Mali to be an Islamic state. Ansar Dine begins to impose Islamic law in Timbuktu, and Al-Qaeda in North Africa endorses the deal ("Mali profile – Timeline," 2018, p. 2).

CHALLENGES OF AZAWAD, NORTHERN MALI

One of the reasons adduced by the MNLA while declaring independence on April 6, 2012, was that Mali is an anarchic state (see Figure 34.1), and therefore, they have decided to put in place not only an army capable of securing their territory but also an administrative office capable of forming democratic institutions.

The general idea was the advocacy of a state of cultural, ethnic, tribal, and racial autonomy from the larger group, which is Mali. The competing and self-motivated requirements within the rank of the pugilist and extraterritorial impact are not now obvious.

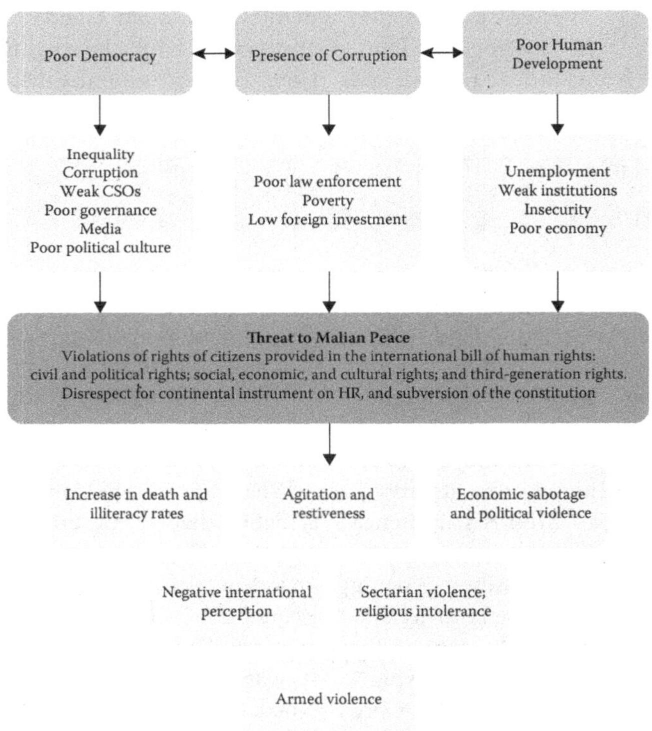

Figure 34.1 Threats to Peace in Northern Mali.

Source: Olawunmi (2019).

SOCIOPOLITICAL TRIGGERS

Ab initio, the MNLA, when compared to Boko Haram (BH) in Nigeria, is differently structured.[1] However, with the infiltration of ISIL into the BH activities in Nigeria, they began assuming a different structure and dimension like Al Shabaab and the MNLA. What is fundamental to the groups is the pervasiveness of violence, which grabbed the world's attention over the course of their operations. Like terrorism in Nigeria, three groups of theories are prominent. These are economic and social integration theories, resource mobilisation theories, and cultural theories.

As shown in Figure 34.1, poor democratic culture, poor leadership, and prevalent human rights abuses in Nigeria further bolster these theories. There are social, political, and economic conditions that feed fundamentalism and intolerance and make ordinary people available for terrorist recruitment. These conditions include poverty and hunger, a lack of access to quality education, unemployment, political manipulation of religion by the elite class, and struggles over control of state resources.

Election malpractices, poor governance, and corruption abate in Mali, too. Society is thus in a state where the majority are disenfranchised and marginalised. Ethnic and religious differences are also a veritable tool in the hands of politicians to settle their scores, leading to further insecurity. The MNLA was out to redress perceived inequalities, restraints, and a lack of responsiveness by their rulers.

Observers were not astonished that Azawad could not succeed as expected, primarily on sociopolitical and economic grounds. But what has arisen from this failure and what the current situation on the ground would become clearer under organisational characteristics and activities in Azawad, the Jama'at Nusra al-Islam wa al-Muslimeen (JNIM, also known as the Group for the Support of Islam and Muslims, or GSIM), that later became a major concern not only in Northern Mali but across the Sahel. Undoubtedly, one of the world's deadliest and most promising among those operating in the semi-arid Sahel region within the Sahara Desert and the south of it

NETWORK OF TERRORIST GROUPS IN AZAWAD

Figure 34.1 depicts the Azawad region as a cauldron of lawlessness and unrest, and it is difficult to give precise clarification to the complex situation that currently surrounds this enclave. Some may see it as a dangerous development, but for the Jihadists, it seems to be a thrilling situation. Northern Mali is a diverse blend of religious fighters, ethnic militias, and secularists.

To make sense of the puzzle, it is expedient to review some of the different groups in Mali and what they want.

There is a core MNLA that would prefer a secular and egalitarian regime. They seem to promote a political system in which the state has substantial and centralised control over social and economic affairs. Within the group, there are the fundamentalists who seemingly do not share this view; this faction could be classified as the Islamists. The Islamist factions within the group wanted to establish Islamic rule with an all-inclusive, ultra-violent, takfirist, and sectarian strategy. It must be stated here that among this group were Jihadists who owed their ideology to the Islamic State, such as al-Qaeda, AQIM, and Mujao ("Al-Qaeda in the Islamic Maghreb: Algerian Challenge or Global Threat," 2009, p. 9).

AZAWAD AND THE UPRISING IN WEST AFRICA

Violence is currently tearing the Sahel apart and spreading across West Africa. But who are the armed groups behind the bloodshed? And where are international actors stationed in the region?" inquired the European Council on Foreign Relations ("Mapping Armed Groups in Mali and the Sahel," 2019). Already, a lot has been said in this Handbook about the AQIM and Ansar al-Din, particularly in Chapters 22 and 23; however, as a primer to deeper analysis, it is significant to highlight that the AQIM is al-Qaeda's North African wing, with roots in Algeria. One of the top commanders is the Algerian Abdelmalek Droukdel, also known as Abu Musab Abdel Wadoud. They consist mostly of foreign fighters, and their focus was to spread Islamic law, liberate Malians from the French colonial legacy, and raise funding through drug trafficking and kidnapping.

Mujao is an AQIM splinter group that formed in mid-2011. The split, essentially, was on the grounds that AQIM's method of jihad was unwieldy and that Arab commanders largely subjugated this cluster. From the beginning, MUJAO had a clearly Sahelian orientation, framing its fight in terms of historical jihads fought in the region in the 19th century and openly promoting recruitment of Sahelian and sub-Saharan Africans. MUJAO controlled Gao during the occupation but still maintained contact with AQIM and Ansar al-Din. The Signed-in-Blood Battalion is essentially an offshoot of AQIM. The group was led by the

Algerian Mokhtar Belmokhtar and had a strong alliance with Ansar Dine and Mujao; he was part of the administration of Gao after Mujao seized it. All these militants follow the Saudi-inspired Wahhabi/Salafi sect of Islam, making them unpopular with most Malian Muslims who belong to the rival Sufi sect.

After the 2011 killing of bin Laden, Zarqawi's Iraq campaign was repeatedly criticised for its sectarian agenda and killing of Muslims (Dillon, 2009). Late AQ's media advisor, American Adam Gadan, was so concerned that AQ's branches were hurting the parent organisation's reputation that he advocated ending links to the organisation's regional appendages (Lahoud et al., 2012, pp. 1–3). Bin Laden lamented the *near-enemy* focus of his affiliates and reproved the emirs of AQIM, AQI, AQAP, and Al Shabaab for their improper execution of his brand of jihad. Meanwhile, in August 2013, MUJAO and its military command under the Gao Arab Ahmed Ould Amer (Ahmed al-Tilemsi, later killed by French forces) joined Mokhtar Belmokhtar's Katibat al-Mulathimeen and Katibat Mouwaqun bi dima ("those who sign in their blood") to form al-Mourabitoun, a reference to the Almoravid empire that burst forth from the Sahara in the mediaeval period and eventually conquered much of north Africa and Spain.

MUJAO split in 2015, with part of the group's fighters becoming the Islamic State in the Greater Sahara under Adnan Abu Walid al-Sahraouian and the rest remaining with al-Mourabitoun and eventually joining Nusrat al-Islam, officially known as Jama'a Nusrat ul-Islam wa al-Muslimin' (JNIM), a militant jihadist organisation in the Maghreb and West Africa formed by the merger of Ansar Al Dine, the Macina Liberation Front, Al-Mourabitoun, and the Saharan branch of Al-Qaeda in the Islamic Maghreb.

One al-Mourabitoun leader was part of JNIM's founding group, Hassan al-Ansari, an Arab fighter from the Tilemsi valley north of Gao. In February 2018, French forces assassinated him along with a few other significant JNIM members close to the Algerian border. Al-Mourabitoun has carried out some of AQIM's and, subsequently, JNIM's larger-scale attacks. The group led by Iyad Ag Ghaly specialises in complex attacks on 'soft' targets, such as the Radisson Blue Hotel in Bamako in November 2015, the Cappuccino Café and HOTEL TK in Ouagadougou in January 2016, and Grand Bassam in Côte d'Ivoire in March 2016. But it has also attacked hardened military bases, such as the attack on the Mécanisme Opérationnel de Coordination (MOC) in Gao in January 2017 that killed dozens of people.

Fittingly, three articles situate recent events in Mali: reason, action, and outcome. The Tuaregs have their reasons for seeking an independent Azawad, but multiple engagements (actions) in Afghanistan, Iraq, Libya, and Syria inflame and obfuscate a hitherto localised civil uprising. The outcome has become evident – tearing West Africa into shreds. Nigeria, though remote, has been destabilised as a corollary of these engagements. Qaddafi's overthrow has forced thousands of his Malian-Tuareg mercenaries back to their home country and given impetus to irredentist and separatist passions. Having failed in prior insurgencies against the central government in Bamako, Tuareg rebels found their capabilities enhanced by the flow of mercenaries and their advanced Qaddafi-era weapons. Again, political freedom and economic opportunities are not widespread in Northern Mali, leading to the upsurge of terrorist activities in Niger, Chad, Nigeria, and other West African states.

INVOLVEMENT IN CRIMINAL ACTIVITY

Besides the relationship between criminals and terrorists and the activities in which they engage, the structure of the MNLA or AQIM and their logistical requirements also warrant further scrutiny. There is no gain in downplaying the notion of a nexus between criminality and terrorism, though it is difficult to concede under certain conditions that terrorists and criminals would cooperate for mutual benefit. Again, there are many factors responsible for this state of affairs. For instance, in the geopolitical environment of the Sahel, poor governance, prolonged marginalisation or persecution by the state (including perceived), and long-standing ethnic or nationalist discord may create opportunities for geographic vulnerabilities. Lack of legitimate opportunities for social advancement, chronic or perceived inequality, and failures of state service delivery could further inflame organised crime (see Figure 34.1).

Though drug trafficking and its use have ensued in Mali long before the emergence of the MNLA or AQIM, the global initiative against transnational organised crime claims that illicit trafficking defines the nature of the Malian crisis and has led to the militarisation of the Sahelian protection economy. Of course, drug cartels in West Africa buy more than real estate, banks, and businesses; they buy elections, candidates, and parties – they buy power (Gberie, 2017). Since the French and United Nations intervention in 2013, counternarcotics policy reform debates in northern Mali have wrongly focused on the theory that jihadists may be in control of the drug trade in Mali and the wider Sahel. Yet this conviction is attributable to the dismal success of counternarcotics and drug use treatment operations in Mali. The Malian government and UN officials within the country seem to be less excited by the premise that jihadists may be controlling the drug trade and consequently making millions of dollars (Gberie, 2018). There is, however, some level of government involvement in the illicit drug trade in Mali.

It is very sticky exonerating government institutions in Mali while drugs are moved brazenly from adjourning states by road and conveyed under escort through the desert to destinations further north towards Europe. For instance, government ministers and senior army and intelligence officers close to President Touré are believed to have been involved in the infamous crash landing of a Boeing 727 in Tarkint (near Gao, in northeast Mali) on November 2, 2009, which had originally come from Venezuela and carried an estimated five to nine tonnes of cocaine (Abderrahmane, 2012). The jet was reported to have first successfully landed on a makeshift airstrip about nine miles from Gao, in an area controlled by Tuareg and Islamist insurgents; it later crashed under suspicious circumstances and was then torched by the traffickers. President Touré described the incident as a threat to Mali's national security but did not call for an official investigation into the matter until three weeks later ("Drugs and Tugs," 2009, p. 19). Thus, romance with drug activities at the highest level of governance emboldened the terrorist organisations in Northern Mali, particularly AQIM, to become deeply involved in drug trafficking activities in the Sahel.

By 2012, MNLA influence had waned, losing territories and influence to AQIM. Consequently, AQIM and its ally, the Islamist group Ansar Ed-Dine, imposed a regime of despotism within the north that included extrajudicial killings, the obliteration of historic monuments in Timbuktu, and the subjugation of women. David Brown, previously the Senior Diplomatic Advisor at the Africa Centre for Strategic Studies, revealed that the illicit drug trade provides tens of millions of dollars, which terrorists then use to finance their operations in the Sahel (Brown, 2013, pp. 1–3).

Wolfram Lacher (Lacher, 2012, p. 5), a North Africa expert at the German Institute for International and Security Affairs in Berlin, contended that the drug trade is just one of a range of illicit activities in which they engage and that the existence of a "drug-terror nexus" in West Africa and the Sahel, on the scale that it has been reported, is misleading. Reiterating that members of the political and business establishment in northern Mali, Niger, and the region's capitals, as well as leaders of supposedly 'secular' armed groups, are complicit. Thus, an emphasis on narco-jihadism, Lacher argues, obscures the role of state actors and corruption in allowing organised crime to take root and grow."

On the other hand, foreign actors are deeply jogging over who takes most of Mali. On a research trip in July 2010 to Mali, the heavy presence of the Chinese was a total surprise. The Americans' presence was visible from the airport, hotels, and everywhere we went, as were the French, the UN, and others. On this occasion, we travelled by road under escort from Bamako to the important northern towns of Mopti and Gao. My team also visited the Manantali Dam in the Kayes region. Analogous to the DRC, Niger, and Nigeria, Mali was comparable to a 'busy restaurant', where foreigners come to eat for free. One could feel the sense of urgency, the whirls, and the disquiet.

Colonel Mustafa Traore, a Malian senior officer, was my responsibility through his course of study at the National Defence College (NDC) in Nigeria, and he was a participant in this 2010 study tour of Mali. Back in Nigeria, in the syndicate room during the report-writing episode, Colonel Traore was asked to give his impression on the most important challenge in Mali. He said, "If France leaves Mali alone, there would be harmony; France is the problem." As the writing team leader, I asked others, "How do we address this challenge proffered by the 'son of the soil' under the sub-paragraph "*strategy*?" Then at the NDC, when you raise a "*challenge*" in your report, it's mandatory to mirror it when you are proposing strategies or solutions to such a problem. The syndicate did not adopt that important contribution by Colonel Mustafa Traore, given that there was no feasible strategy for France to exit Mali. France is aware of the government's and business elites' complicity in the illegal drug trade, but she'd rather politicise the issue.

On one occasion, the concept note France prepared for the UN Security Council debate on drug trafficking and transnational organised crime in December 2013 noted that violence in Mali by criminal networks attempting to control the drug trade "fostered radicalization." Based on the premise that those who become radicalised then participate in the drug trade, the concept note stated, "Cocaine and cannabis trafficking enable extremists to generate income, which in turn finances rebellions" (Report of the Security Council, 2014). Global interests concerning the anti-drug agenda in the Sahel would only align upon reduced complicities among the multinationals operating in Northern Mali and political corruption by the region's governments (*Not Just in Transit Drugs: The State and Society in West Africa*, 2014).

STRATEGIC SHIFTS AND TRAJECTORY IN THE SAHEL

The situation today is different from the crisis that erupted in 2012, when a Tuareg group, the MNLA, allied with Ansar Dine and the Movement for Oneness and Jihad in West Africa (MUJAO) to fight for an independent state in northern Mali. The fronts have since shifted due to external influence. For instance, Ansar Dine, whose full name in Arabic is Harakat Ansar al-Dine, which translates as "movement of defenders of the faith," is seen as a homegrown movement. A renowned former Tuareg rebel leader, Iyad Ag Ghali, whose objective was to impose Islamic law across Mali, led the Ansar Dine. The militant groups that were chased out of the major towns by the French 'Operation Serval' in 2013 dispersed, reorganised, and spread. The first spread of militant groups was from northern Mali to central Mali in early 2015 (under the impetus of the Macina Liberation Front); the second was in late 2016 to western Niger (mainly the Islamic State in the Greater

Sahara (ISGS)) and northern Burkina Faso (Ansarul Islam, a local Burkinabe group with links to Al-Qaeda); the third expansion of militant groups took place in early 2018 to eastern Burkina Faso, where all groups (JNIM, ISGS, and Ansarul Islam) have established bases (Berger, 2019, p. 2). And the fourth wave will potentially see militant groups expand their reach to Côte d'Ivoire, Ghana, Togo, and Benin.

The Jama'at Nusra al-Islam wa al-Muslimeen (JNIM, also known as the Group for the Support of Islam and Muslims, or GSIM) is one of the world's deadliest and most promising terror organisations. The group operates on the fringes of the semi-arid Sahel region south of the Sahara Desert, which is poorly governed. The security situation in the Sahel is, therefore, worsening. The region experienced a massive spike in deadly violence in the first half of 2019 as militant groups continued their expansion southward, now threatening coastal West Africa (Berger, 2019).

SELF-DEFEATING SAHEL STRATEGY

Operation Barkhane

Barkhane is a French-led counter-terrorism initiative that is targeted at two regions: the border area between Mali and Niger, the Liptako, and between Mali and Burkina Faso, the Gourma. Despite this approach by the French, little has been achieved from their kinetic efforts. The French created Barkhane not to foster peace and development but rather to support their advantage over the Northern economy and estate.

MINUSMA

The United Nations Security Council renewed the UN Multidimensional Integrated Stabilisation Mission in Mali (MINUSMA). It launched Operation Oryx to establish a deterrent presence in Bankass, Bandiagara, and Koro districts in recent times, a mandate that is too little, too late. Central Mali has been engulfed in violence since 2015, and it is obvious that the UN forces are no match for the whims of some Security Council Member States, including China, which operates independently of the UN mission in Northern Mali. The legitimacy of MINUSMA was already quite low, as it was incapable of protecting civilians or changing the statutes.

ECOWAS

The regional body has been discussing the potential activation of an ECOWAS standby force, as it did in Liberia and Sierra Leone. While ECOWAS countries take the threat of expansion seriously and want to prevent it from escalating, nothing substantial has been achieved due to the greater goal of foreign interests.

AZAWAD MOVEMENT AND GEOPOLITICS OF MALI

The Azawad movement came to an end in 2013 when the Malian government and the Coordination of Azawad Movements, also known as CMA, signed the Algerian-brokered peace deal. According to the agreement, the CMA will respect the "unity and territorial integrity of Mali." The Malian government agreed to implement a more decentralised system of government, with regional assemblies elected under universal suffrage.

Rather than a single elected assembly, Azawad will have five, one for each of the area's regions, including those of Timbuktu, Gao, Kidal, Taoudeni, and Menaka, with the latter two to be newly created. The agreement also provides for increased representation of the regions of Azawad in Malian state institutions, along with greater economic investment.

However, all of these promises from Mali for greater political autonomy for the Tuaregs in the north have never materialised. As a result, the Malian government failed to develop trust among the Tuaregs.

PERSPECTIVES ON AZAWAD

The issues in northern Mali are not as complex as presented by most writers on the subject. Indeed, authors are most guilty of increasing ambiguity about the narratives not only in Mali but also in the Congo (DRC) and larger Africa. American planners are well aware that their local partners oftentimes fuel the very forces that foster violent extremism and instability through their authoritarian governing styles, said Malik Ibrahim. Malik was quick to note that Mauritania President Mohamed Ould Abdel Aziz pushed his monopolisation of political power when he abolished the country's Senate. Thus, on the one hand, poor governance fuelled by foreign interests is responsible for insecurity in the Sahel.

On the other front, groups that migrated to the region and far beyond have governed Mali interchangeably. And for decades, researchers and authors have played the ostrich about the fundamentals in Mali; this chapter concludes that the time is now to establish a theoretical linkage between human rights protection, justice, and peace in Northern Mali. The capacity of the United States and its European allies to make Mali great again is not in doubt. Germany and Japan were renewed after WWII through the Marshall Plan, which was a joint effort between the United States and Europe, and this was based on the idea that Maoism succeeded only in countries with economic problems, just as terrorism did. Addressing the socio-economic and political causes of the insecurity in the Sahel has taken a hundred years.

Furthermore, the idea of kinetic engagements using proxies, infusing small arms, and establishing weak leaders with a view to stealing resources has become repetitive not only in Africa but across most endowed regions of the world. Pretending to care while impoverishing the poor African population and particularly guaranteeing poverty and ensuring a disaffected population in the Sahel is no doubt a technique that fosters anarchism and produces nihilists. When counter-terrorism experts and writers continue to operationalise the symptoms, the ill-informed machinists in the Sahel may as well be running through quicksand.

To address the security threat, regional security organisations such as ECOWAS could enhance much-needed bilateral exchanges among law enforcement and intelligence agencies. Additionally, the countries implementing the UN global strategy against terrorism should focus considerable attention on the activities of multinationals and drug cartels in the Sahel, not to stop them but to moderate the disquiet.

The threat is on the rise in North Africa and the Sahel, but not yet out of control, said Jean-Pierre Filiu, a professor at the Paris Institute of Political Studies (Sciences Po, Middle East department) and the author of *Apocalypse in Islam* (forthcoming, University of California Press). And this is the right time to conclude and put an end to the duplicity in northern Mali.

Note

1 Besenyő and Mayer (2015) provide a detailed assessment of the origins of Boko Haram in Nigeria's socioeconomic history.

References

Abderrahmane, A. (2012, August 6). Drug Trafficking and the Crisis in Mali." http://www.issafrica.org/iss-today/drug-trafficking-and-the-crisis-in-mail

Al-Qaeda in the Islamic Maghreb: Algerian Challenge or Global Threat? (2009). Carnegie Endowment for International Peace, 9–10. https://carnegieendowment.org/files/al-qaeda_islamic_maghreb.pdf

Berger, F. (2019). West Africa: shifting strategies in the Sahel. IISS, 2. https://www.iiss.org/blogs/analysis/2019/10/csdp-west-africa-sahel

Besenyő, J., & Romaniuk, S. N. (2024, June 7). Mali: comment l'insécurité, l'incertitude et le chaos favorisent le terrorisme. *The Conversation*. https://theconversation.com/mali-comment-linsecurite-lincertitude-et-le-chaos-favorisent-le-terrorisme-230323

Brown, D. (2013). (Rep.). Strategic Studies Institute, US Army War College. www.jstor.org/stable/resrep11261

Declaration of Independence broadside, July 1776, Jamestown-Yorktown Foundation. (1775, April 20). https://www.historyisfun.org/wp-content/uploads/2014/04/RoadtoIndependence.pdf

Dillon, M.R. (2009, September). Wahhabism: Is it a Factor in the Spread of Global Terrorism? https://www.nps.edu/documents/105988371/107571254/DillonWahhabismThesis.pdf/23fc46fb-17a6-41da-83b8-8e312191b5bb

Drugs and Tugs. (2009). Africa Confidential, *50*(24), 19. https://www.africa-confidential.com/article/id/3337/Drugs_and_thugs

Gberie, L. (2017, February 24). State Officials and their Involvement in Drug Trafficking in West Africa -WACD Background Paper No. 51. http://www.globalcommissionondrugs.org/wp-content/uploads/2017/02/State-Officials-and-Drug-Trafficking-2013-12-03.pdf

Gberie, L. (2018, January 5). Crime, Violence, and Politics: Drug Trafficking and Counternarcotics Policies in Mali and Guinea. https://globalinitiative.net/wp-content/uploads/2018/01/Brookings-Crime-Violence-and-Politics-Drug-Trafficking-and-Counternarcotics-Policies-in-Mali-and-Guinea.pdf

Lacher, W. (2012). Organized crime and conflict in the Sahel-Sahara region. *Carnegie Endowment for International Peace*, 5. https://carnegieendowment.org/2012/09/13/organized-crime-and-conflict-in-sahel-sahara-region-pub-49360

Lahoud, N., Caudill, S., & Rassler, D. (2012). Letters from Abbottabad: Bin Ladin sidelined? West Point, United States: Combating Terrorism Center.

Mali Crisis: Key Players. (2013). BBC News, 1. https://www.bbc.com/news/world-africa-17582909

Mali profile – Timeline. (2018). BBC News, 2. https://www.bbc.com/news/world-africa-13881978

Mapping Armed Groups in Mali and the Sahel. (2019, May 21). https://www.ecfr.eu/mena/sahel_mapping/mujao

Mohanty, A. (2018, February 13). Mali Crisis: A Historical Perspective of the Azawad Movement. https://www.geopoliticalmonitor.com/mali-crisis-a-historical-perspective-of-the-azawad-movement/

Not just in transit Drugs, the State and Society in West Africa. (2014, June). http://www.wacommissionondrugs.org/WACD_report_June_2014_english.pdf

Olawunmi, K. (2019, September 25). NIGERIA, GLOBAL PEACE AND HUMAN RIGHTS ISSUES. https://www.academia.edu/36845682/NIGERIA_GLOBAL_PEACE_AND_HUMAN_RIGHTS_ISSUES

Report of the Security Council. (2014, July). https://undocs.org/pdf?symbol=en/a/69/2

35

THE LORD'S RESISTANCE ARMY (LRA) INSURGENCY IN UGANDA

David Andrew Omona and Scott N. Romaniuk

INTRODUCTION

Uganda, a member of the East African community, has endured conflict within its borders for decades. Although there have been conflicts prior to contact with foreign powers, the postcolonial conflicts so far have exceeded what the country could contain within its borders. While the earlier conflicts pitted neighbouring communities against each other over space and power, the colonial and postcolonial conflicts have taken on different shades. During the expansion of British colonial rule, for example, a lot of resistance emerged in different parts. However, once they got hold of the different regions of present-day Uganda, they were able to suppress most of the conflicts. When the British passed the baton of leadership to Ugandans, the country took off in a positive direction. According to Patrick Rubaihayo (2005), soon after independence, the government embarked on transforming Ugandan society from colonial vestiges to a productive and free society. Social services, infrastructure, trade, and commerce were developed following the Uganda Peoples' Congress (UPC) manifesto to fight ignorance, disease, and poverty.

To address this, the independent government, under the leadership of Doctor Apollo Milton Obote, built schools, hospitals, roads, and parastatal bodies. Cooperative societies were set up to promote agricultural production and the marketing of farm produce. Besides, the government developed institutions with competent and effective public service. Pheres Mutiabwa (2010, pp. 29–35) asserts that such a vibrant, independent Uganda made a local artist compose a song in praise of Obote. However, as the glamour of independence was still in the air, the suppressed conflicts during colonial rule sprang up in different parts of the country. Consequently, coups d'états, rebellions, and turmoil characterised much of postcolonial Uganda since some disgruntled power-hungry people felt assuming power by the use of a gun was the only way to go.

Following the above, this chapter looks at one of the enduring conflicts in the history of postcolonial Uganda, the conflict that pitted the Ugandan government against the Lord's Resistant Army/Movement (LRA/M). The LRA/M insurgency began in Northern Uganda in 1988 and spread to other parts of the country, then eventually to Sudan/South Sudan, the Democratic Republic of the Congo (DRC), and the Central African Republic (CAR). One of Africa's most bitter conflicts in recent memory is the one that the LRA is waging under Joseph Kony's leadership, despite the fact that it is currently receiving little attention. Fought with unmerited ferocity, the insurgency devastated northern Uganda and the countries into which its tentacles extended. As we shall see below, characterised by the abduction of children who eventually provide the bulk of its forces, the brutality they saw during training and operations turns them into human rights violators, abductors, and killing machines (Onekalit, 2005, p. 9). Even the military, legal, and peaceful means attempted could not salvage the situation to date.

OVERVIEW OF HOW AND WHY: THE HISTORY OF THE LORD'S RESISTANT ARMY/MOVEMENT

The LRA insurgency is a continuation of insurgent groups that emerged to contest the hold on power by the incumbent government. Even some people go back in locating the LRA rebellion to the colonial period. However, as far as the LRA insurgency is concerned, it emerged after the overthrow of Tito Okello Lutwa by the NRA forces under the leadership of Yuweri Kaguta Museveni (RLP, 2014). The overthrow forced a large

DOI: 10.4324/9780429426063-39

contingent of the UNLA forces, whose bulk came from among the Acholi and Lango, to retreat northward (RLP, 2014). Perhaps fearing a repeat of what the Acholi and Langi suffered after Iddi Amin's coup in 1971, many of the former UNLA forces fled to Sudan with their arms and ammunition, while others decided to demobilise and settle among the local population.

While the initial extension of NRA control to northern Uganda was peaceful, its character was short-lived. The fear of reprisal some former UNLA soldiers had proved right when errant NRA soldiers started to pillage, rape men and women, torture, steal livestock and other properties, destroy infrastructure (RLP, 2014), maim, and kill innocent civilians. In a way of protecting the local population from continuous abuse by the NRA forces, Otema Alimadi and others formed the Uganda People's Defence Movement (UPDM) with a military wing, the Uganda People's Defence Army (UPDA), under the command of Brigadier Odong Latek. After a series of encounters with and the continued NRA brutality on the local population, the Uganda People's Defence Army (UPDA) was joined by the Holy Spirit Mobile Forces and Holy Spirit Movement (HSMF/HSM), led by Alice Auma Lakwena (RLP, 2014), to resist the brutality the government forces were inflicting on the local population. Within a short time, Auma's rebellion gained momentum in northern and eastern Uganda. With such an organised armed force, she was able to march up to Jinja, a few miles from Kampala, the capital city of Uganda. Unfortunately, before crossing the Nile, the HSM rebel was defeated.

After the defeat of Auma's forces in Jinja in 1988 (Westbrook, 2000, sects III, VI), the need to protect the local population from continuous NRA torture ushered in another insurgency under the command of Severino Lukoya Kiberu, Auama's father. Unlike Auma's rebellion, Kiberu's was short-lived and ended when the government forces captured and imprisoned him. Thereafter, the ragtags of Kiberu's and Auma's forces joined another rebel faction under the leadership of Joseph Kony to form the Uganda Peoples Democratic Christian Army (UPDCA) (Omona, 2009, p. 64). After a series of name changes, it eventually settled on the name Lord's Resistance Army (LRA).

Whereas many people think the LRA is an Acholi rebellion, James Alfred Obita (2006), the former secretary for external affairs and mobilisation of the Lord's Resistance Army, said the LRA was not "just an Acholi thing" but rather for the whole of Uganda as laid out in their objectives. Accordingly, these objectives are:

- To fight for the immediate restoration of competitive multi-party democracy in Uganda.
- To see an end to gross violations of human rights and the dignity of Ugandans.
- To ensure the restoration of peace and security in Uganda.
- To ensure unity, sovereignty, and economic prosperity beneficial to all Ugandans.
- To bring an end to the repressive policy of deliberate marginalisation of groups of people who may not agree with the National Resistance Army's ideology (Obita, 1998).

If the above were the objectives for which the LRA is fighting, then what they are doing in the course of their fight is contrary to the objectives set. You cannot say you are fighting to restore democracy, human rights, peace and security, unity, sovereignty, economic prosperity, and eliminate discrimination when you are doing exactly what you claim to be fighting.

JOSEPH KONY: KIDNAPPER, WARLORD, "PROPHET"

Joseph Lony, born on September 18, 1961, is the leader of the Lord's Resistance Army (LRA). While initially purporting to fight against government oppression, the LRA eventually turned against the local population, supposedly to "purify" the Acholi people and turn Uganda into a theocracy. Kony claims to be the spokesperson of God and a spirit medium, and he claims he is visited by 13 spirits, including a Chinese phantom. Ideologically, the LRA is a syncretic mix of mysticism, Acholi nationalism, and Christian fundamentalism. As such, Kony claims his intent is to establish a theocratic state based on the Ten Commandments and local Acholi tradition.

The Ugandan government accused him of ordering the abduction of children, whom he turned into child soldiers and sex slaves. To this extent, about 66,000 children became soldiers, and 2 million people were internally displaced between 1986 and 2009. In 2005, Kony and his deputies were indicted by the International Criminal Court (ICC) for war crimes and crimes against humanity in The Hague, but he evaded capture. Kony has been subject to an Interpol Red Notice at the request of the ICC since 2006. Since the Juba peace talks in 2006, the LRA no longer operates in Uganda. Sources claim that they are in the Democratic Republic of the Congo (DRC), the Central African Republic (CAR), or South Sudan. In 2013, Kony was reported to be in poor health, and Michel Djotodia, president of the CAR, claimed he was negotiating with Kony to surrender.

By April 2017, Kony was still at large, but his armed group was said to have been reduced to approximately 100 soldiers, down from an estimated high of 3,000. As such, both the United States and Uganda suspended the hunt for Kony and the LRA, believing that the LRA was no longer a significant security risk to Uganda (People Pill, n.d.).

THE SPREAD OF THE LRA INSURGENCY BEYOND ACHOLI TERRITORY

Whereas initially the LRA concentrated their operations in northern Uganda's districts of Gulu, Kitgum, and Pader, in 1992 they extended their influence into East Moyo, the present Adjumani District. The attack on Adjumani could have been strategically carried out to divert the attention of the NRA soldiers, who were organised into mobile units to hunt the LRA forces in the Acholi sub-region. In Adjumani, they attacked a United Nations (UN) facility; one could also say the LRA had gone there to collect food and medical supplies for their forces.

In order to frustrate the UPDF efforts from pursuing them, in June 2003, the LRA extended its operations into the Lango and Teso sub-regions. Before that time, Lango sub-regions remained somewhat peaceful, safe from the occasional incursion of Karimojong cattle rustlers on their far flanks. On the part of Teso, he had returned after addressing the Uganda People's Defence Army (UPA) rebellion. At the time of the LRA incursion in Lango and Teso sub-regions, Operation Iron Fist I was at its peak in Acholi sub-region (RLP, 2014). Probably the LRA extended their operation to the Lango and Teso sub-regions in a way to create a buffer zone where they could get food supplies and abduct children who eventually became part of the army.

Whereas in Lango, the LRA entered from various spots given that it borders Acholi sub-region, in Teso sub-region, the LRA entered from Obalanga sub-county in Amuria District. The leader of the Teso operation was Tabuley, the third in command of the LRA rebel force at that time. Those who planned the mission to Teso, among others, included Vincent Otti, Kamdulu Onen, Dominic Ogwen[1], and one called Opio, plus others. On entering Teso, their first two weeks of incursion were peaceful. In an attempt to build trust in the local community, they engaged in playing football with some locals and young children whom they had abducted from other areas. However, the pretence was short-lived, as we shall see later on.

After roaming in Amuria for a while before extending to Soroti town, the LRA tactfully split into smaller units so they could divert the attention of the UPDF in different directions. When the local militia, the Arrow Boys, saw the UPDF were not proactive in attacking the LRA forces, they decided to engage them in fights. Whereas the decision of the local militia to contain the LRA in Teso sub-region was good, it unfortunately gave the LRA a leeway to spread from Amuria to Katakwi, Soroti, and Kaberamaido districts, abducting, looting foodstuffs, and killing whomever they found (JRP, 2012, p. 10). The impressive challenge the UPDF gave to the LRA in Teso sub-region was when they attempted to attack Soroti Flying School. After the UPDF repulsed the LRA attack, the LRA withdrew from the front line (Rice, Sat., Oct. 20, 2007) and moved to their tactical bases in parts of northern Uganda and southern Sudan.

When the Government of Uganda extended Operation Iron Fist into Sudan after seeking permission from the Sudan Government, the LRA exerted its ferocity on the local people. The constant shelling of their location made the LRA leadership tactically extend their desire to talk peace. However, seeing that the peace talks would not yield any results, they decided to extend their base in the DRC's Garamba forest. As we shall see below, after the attacks in the DRC, they spread within and into the Central African Republic. While in these areas, the LRA continued their tactic of abduction, looting, killing, and so forth. As always, they train the abductees to become part of their army; others act as load carriers, and women become sex slaves (Human Rights Watch, 2009).

SOME OF THE ATROCIOUS ATTACKS THE LRA LAUNCHED DURING ITS OPERATIONS

The LRA forces gained wide publicity for their gruesome operations because, right from their inception, they have carried out many attacks in their areas of operations. Among many of the attacks, the following stood out: In March 1994, the LRA set up ambushes and abductions in parts of northern Uganda. On April 20, 1995, the LRA, under the command of Vincent Otti, attacked Atiak Township, killing an estimated 300 people and looting and burning houses. Among those killed were students of Atiak Technical School, soldiers, and civilians (Labeja, 2018). Then, in a four-day operation in January 1997, the LRA killed nearly 400 people in parts of Kitgum.

In March 2002, when the UPDF launched Operation Iron Fist I to flush the LRA from their hideouts, it scattered the LRA into the jungles of both Southern Sudan and Northern Uganda. Given the unfamiliar terrain in southern Sudan, the UPDF's efforts to pursue them swiftly were curtailed, thus aiding the LRA to increase their attacks on the civilian population and military installations, both inside Southern Sudan and Northern Uganda. To prove their discontent with the Khartoum Government for allowing the UPDF to pursue them inside Sudan, in April 2002, the LRA attacked some Sudanese government-controlled villages and military posts near Juba and Sudanese Refugee Camp in Northern

Uganda at a place called Acholi Pii (RLP, 2014). Since Operation Iron Fist stretched the UPDF so much, they failed to protect the local population from the LRA attacks.

In the Teso sub-region, after the local militia provoked them, the LRA started to unleash their wrath on the population, starting on June 15, 2003, in Obalanga. During their first attack, the LRA burned over 115 grass-thatched houses. They also looted 15 shops in the trading centre and abducted several people to carry their booty of rice, maize flour, sugar, biscuits, and sodas to their campsite (JRP, 2012, p. 8). On June 24, 2003, they ambushed a vehicle heading to Obalanga from Soroti and killed scores of people. The majority of the dead in that attack were civilians. As reflected in the Justice and Reconciliation Project's field note (2012), the local population blamed the UPDF for not coming to their aid even though they were informed of the LRA's presence in Obalanga earlier on.

Of all the places in the Teso sub-region, the LRA left a daunting mark in Obalanga, which had about 40,000 people in the Internal Displaced People (IDP) camp. During their operation in Obalanga, the LRA killed over 600 people and abducted over 2000 children. Among those massacred, 265 were buried in a mass grave. In the Wera and Asamuk sub-counties of the Teso sub-region, 133 people were killed, 230 children were abducted, and nine permanent buildings were destroyed (JRP, 2012, p. 11). Unfortunately, instead of protecting the civilian population, the UPDF also resorted to killing, looting, and bombing the local community using helicopter gunships, a mistake for which they have not apologised to date (JRP, 2012, p. 19).

On February 20, 2004, the LRA attacked the Barlonyo Internal Displaced People's (IDP) camp in the Lira district, killing over 200 people, abducting over 206, and burying dozens of huts. Then, on April 29, 2004, under the command of Dominc Ogwen, they attacked the Odek IDP camp in the Lira district, killing 61 people. Then, on May 20, 2004, they attacked Lokodi IDP camp in the Gulu district, killing 40 civilians, injuring 13, abducting 6, and burning over 210 huts. And on June 8, 2004, they attained Adok IDP Camp in Apach district, killing 25 people, abducting 26, and destroying food stocks (International Justice Monitor, nd). More so, on February 5, 2005, the LRA killed 50 people in Abia camp in the Lira district.

The LRA also unleashed ferocity on foreign soil after extending its tentacles to the DRC, CAR, and South Sudan. For example, in January 2006, in a failed UN Special Forces raid codenamed "Operation Rudia" aimed at repulsing LRA deputy leader Vincent Otti from the Democratic Republic of the Congo, eight Guatemalan commandos got killed (Human Rights Watch, 2009, p. 17). Perhaps retaliating against this and other attacks, during Christmas 2008, the LRA brutally killed at least 143 people and abducted 180 during festivities organised by the Roman Catholic Church in Faradje, Democratic Republic of the Congo (Faber, 2017, p. 10). At the same time, the LRA attacked several adjacent communities within the vicinity, thereby murdering 75 people in a church near Dungu, at least 80 in Batande, 48 in Bangadi, and 213 in Gurba. Given the act of brutality, by August 2009, over 320,000 Congolese had been displaced, thus exposing them to famine.

The aforementioned notwithstanding, also in August 2009 in South Sudan, the LRA extended its ferocity on a Catholic church in Ezo on the Feast of the Assumption and crucified the victims. Then, in December 2009, the LRA forces under Dominic Ongwen's command massacred at least 321 civilians and abducted 250 others in a spate of four-day operations in the village and region of Makombo in the DR Congo. More so, in February 2010, the LRA massacred nearly 100 people in Kpanga, around the DRC's border with the Central African Republic and Sudan (Human Rights Watch, 2009, pp. 16–17). The LRA also killed over 1,600 Congolese civilians and abducted over 2,500 by May 2010. Thus, from September 2008 to July 2011, they killed more than 2,300 people, abducted more than 3,000, and displaced over 400,000 across CAR, the DRC, and South Sudan (ICG, April 28, 2010, p. 4). Besides the major attacks, small-scale incursions by the LRA have become part of the daily experience of affected communities to date. Consequently, displacing large numbers of people and worsening an ongoing humanitarian crisis in the affected areas

FACTORS THAT FACILITATED THE PERSISTENCE OF THE INSURGENCY

One may ask, "Why did this conflict continue for this long since Kony and most of the rebel leaders did not undergo prior military training?" According to the Human Rights Peace Centre (HURIPEC) and Liu Institute for Global Security (LIGS), the authoritarian character of governance (HURIPEC, & LI GI, 2003, p. 11) and the militaristic tendencies that reinforced the authoritarian rule (HURIPEC and LIGS, 2005, pp. 62–63) are responsible for dragging the conflict this long. Besides, Andrew Mwenda (2006) asserts Museveni's dislike of Northerners right from the beginning, which could explain this scenario. This, according to him, is reflected in the constant abuse of the former leaders of Uganda from northern Uganda as swine, murderers, terrorists (Mwenda, 2006), thugs, and bandits. This and other related issues add to the reasons for the persistence of the conflict. Furthermore, the Sudan factor and the proliferation of small arms and light weapons were also factors (Omona, 2015, p. 94) that contributed to the resilience and insistence of the LRA to continue the rebellion.

Around that time, the pursuit of the LRA intensified, which forced the LRA to relocate its tactical headquarters to Southern Sudan (presently South Sudan). While in

Sudan, the LRA received overt support from the Sudanese government. This support came as part of the Khartoum government's effort to use the LRA to reduce the strength of the Sudan People's Liberation Army (SPLA), which the Ugandan government was also supporting. From such safe havens in the Sudan, the LRA continued to carry out heinous operations inside Uganda in the Acholi subregion. They looted foodstuffs and medicines and abducted civilians as a way of recruiting to their ranks (RLP, 2014).

KEY PERSONNEL AND STRUCTURE

The key persons in the LRA are Joseph Kony, Otti Langonyi, Charles Opoka, Vincent Otti, Caesar Achellam, Raska Lukwiya, Okot Odhiambo, Dominic Ongwen, Odong Latek, Alphonse Lamola, Nixman Oryanga, Tubuley, etc. The key persons provided leadership to the LRA right from its inception until today. Apart from Joseph Kony, who from the start was the commander-in-chief and the chief ideologue, the rest of the leaders are those who have ever served in different positions at different times (Figure 35.1). Some of the commanders were at certain times demoted due to rumours, or if a person died, some other person replaced him.

Over the years, many people knew the LRA as a ragtag rebel group without any form of organised system; however, looking at the above, the internal hierarchy of the LRA puzzled its opponents. Structurally, the LRA comprises the commander in chief/chairman, second in command/vice chairman, army commander/deputy chairman, army commander, director of operations, division commander, four main brigades, and three battalions under each brigade. All the lower commanders are answerable to the High Command (the "Control Altar"). Hence, all operations directives come from the headquarters.

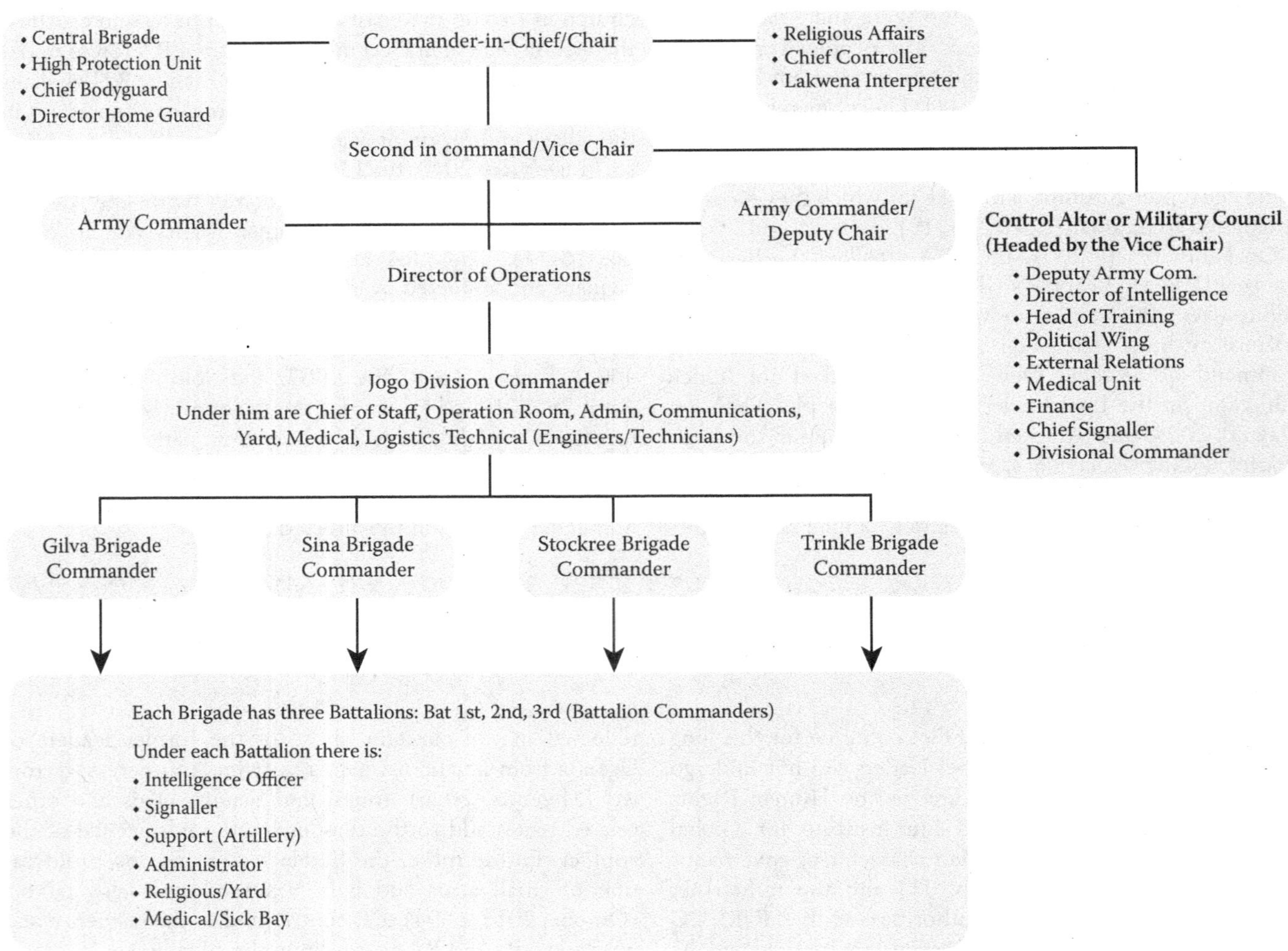

Figure 35.1 The LRA Command Structure.

Source: Authors' illustration

As the LRA forces extended to the DRC and CAR, different discreet units were set up under the direct command of a senior commander. Two such groups operate in the Central African Republic, and one oscillates between the CAR and the DRC. Then eight groups were scattered in the DRC. Each group has between ten and 30 soldiers. At the field level, commanders operate with a certain degree of independence, though with constant updates from the commander in chief. However, as Mareike Schomerus (2007, p. 12) observes, with troops on the move and spread out initially in Sudan and Uganda and now in CAR, DRC, and South Sudan, tracking each group of fighters is a challenge. To the extent that, in mid-2007, the LRA high command also acknowledged for the first time that there might be former LRA groups that no longer answer to it (Schomerus, 2007, p. 12),

ORGANISATIONAL CHARACTERISTICS AND ACTIVITIES: STRUCTURE, CHANGE, AND OPERATIONS

In its operational history, the LRA displayed a mix of rebel, regular army, and cultist groups. As such, many people have failed to understand the LRA insurgent group, thereby making it difficult for the government of Uganda to deal with them both militarily and diplomatically.

Although over the years Ugandan military intelligence sources have impressed on people that the LRA is a weak, ill-equipped, and near-vanquished force, they have chosen camouflage and split into discrete units. Thereby, they scattered in groups of five to ten people across northern and eastern Uganda (before 2006), Southern Sudan/South Sudan, the DRC, and the CAR. Philip Lancaster et al. (2011, p. 19) aptly observe that "the LRA has not necessarily been a homogeneous organisation but rather has been composed of small groups operating at least semi-independently of each other, all reporting to Kony". Whereas such is a strategic move by the leadership, many outsiders wrongly regard that as a form of weakness, thereby making them regard the LRA as a ragtag band of bandits without a coherent strategy. Yet on their part, they resorted to this to avoid a large-scale loss in case they were attacked. Besides, such a small unit helped to diffuse the power base, limit collusion, and facilitate the maximum spread of influence. Through this, the LRA has been able to exert far-flung influence in its operation areas. The tactical small-group operations of the LRA helped them disguise their fighting strength. Consequently, the government of Uganda and its allies have not been able to provide accurate intelligence information as to the exact numbers of the LRA fighters. The intelligence information gathered from top LRA commanders captured or surrendered, like Banya, Ogwen Dominic, Kwoyelo, and so forth, about the strength of the LRA is hard to verify independently. The figures indicate that the LRA has between 100 and 250 fighters, which is not realistic given the virulence the rebels exert and their ability to spread to three countries.

Thomas Kwoyelo, alias Latoni, is a former LRA commander who surrendered to the Uganda People's Defence Forces in 2009. He was enlisted into the Lord's Resistance Army (LRA) under the command of Joseph Kony and rose through the LRA ranks to become a 'colonel'. Kwoyelo led a series of attacks between 1993 and 2005 on the Abera Village and the Pagak and Pablo camps for internally displaced people in what is today the Amuru District. The attacks resulted in the abduction, killing, maiming, and torture of dozens of people, including women and children. In 2011, the Constitutional Court granted Kwoyelo amnesty, but in 2015, the Supreme Court overruled it and held that he could be tried for acts committed outside the "furtherance of the war". The case has been pending before the International Crimes Division, the domestic court with jurisdiction over crimes against humanity and war crimes in Uganda (Trial International, July 6, 2017).

Okot Odhiambo He was a senior leader of the LRA who executed and replaced Vincent Otti. He was the chief of the LRA rebel group that operated from Garamba National Park in the Democratic Republic of the Congo. Odhiambo was one of five people for whom the International Criminal Court (ICC) issued its first-ever arrest warrants in 2005 for alleged war crimes and crimes against humanity. In 2009, he announced his intention to defect from the LRA and return to Uganda if the government would agree not to surrender him to the ICC. However, he was killed in a battle with the UPDF in October 2013. Odhiambo is remembered in LRA circles for three things:

- He is not one of Kony's child soldiers but rather self-enlisted himself during the early days of the LRA.
- He was one of Kony's enforcers who has retained his influence in part because Kony has often relied on him as an enforcer, e.g., he executed Vincent Otti plus his loyalists, and
- He was a link between the LRA and the Sudan government, given his fluency in Arabic. As such, he was part of the LRA Juba peace team (The Resolve, 2013).

To be able to survive and allow for better control and mental conditioning of the fighters, the LRA leadership instilled a sense of secrecy, flexibility, predictability, and adaptability. The secrecy helped eliminate the leak of intelligence information and the disclosure of operational plans to the outside. Whoever was caught faced death by public execution as a retributive measure for the rest (Lancaster et al., 2011, p. 19).

Due to their shift towards a small operation strategy, the LRA became more flexible, making it more difficult for the securities services to find them. The LRA readily collaborated with other belligerent groups and willingly accepted peace negotiations with their foes. For example, they were able to find a way of cooperating with diverse belligerent groups like the West Nile Bank Fronts (WBF), other South Sudanese rebel groups, the Allied Democratic Forces, the Seleka of CAR, and the National Liberation Front (NLF) of Sudan. More so, the LRA is open to talking with the government of Uganda as they use their strength to wreak havoc (Lancaster et al., 2011, p. 20). Many instances were attesting to their strategic participation in peace talks. Other instances where this trick was used were the Betty Oyella Bigombe-initiated peace talks between 1993 and 1994 (O'Kadamire, 2002, pp. 64–73) and the Juba peace talks that started in 2006 and ended in 2008. Immediately after gaining military strength, the LRA abandons talks and shows their presence by wreaking havoc on innocent populations within their reach.

Along with their flexibility, the LRA tactically adapted to changing circumstances. Unlike their initial approach of attacking in a military formation, as time went by, the LRA resorted to hit-and-run tactics and operated in smaller groups. As such, they could easily melt in the jungles when attacked and regroup at an agreed-upon point (Rendezvous, RV). Adaptability to different terrains and weather, be it hilly, bushy, plain, hot, cold, rainy, dry, and so forth, has kept them surviving over the years. Alongside flexibility, in its operation, the LRA has been susceptible to exogenous events. While seen as a closed group, unlike a typical cult, the LRA can be open to outside influence. They listen to the news on the radio, listen to local talks, and respond to whatever is going on, showing their presence (Lancaster et al., 2011, p. 21).

On several occasions, the LRA commanders tried to revive old tactics like not using mobile phones and walkie-talkies by resorting to using messengers and RVs, as in the late 1980s. This is to avoid the use of satellites to locate their whereabouts (Faber, 2017). As noted above, given their number has dwindled greatly, they also resorted to hit-and-run tactics, spitting in small groups, and so forth (Lancaster et al., 2011, p. 21). More so, to avoid enemy forces picking up their communication, they use both simple and complicated coded signals. In most cases, they use Acholi words to derive such codes.

In regards to command and control, Kony tried to show that his power to command is absolute. To the extent he punishes whoever he feels is trying to gunner influence or escape by death, The deaths of some of the top LRA leaders, like Otti Langonyi in 1989, James Opoka in March 2003 (Odong, 2003), Vincent Otti in October 2007 (Maliti, 2017), and scores of others less prominent, have a direct link to such crimes. Whereas there is a possibility for dissent and splits in the LRA ranks, the top leadership ensures that power is centralised. Given that those who have been in the struggle longer could easily cause a splinter in the rebel ranks, the commander in chief of the LRA kept their power in balance by using young and agile members of the group to assume top leadership. To the extent that people say his current chief bodyguard is his own son, Such young people who are now taking command in the rebel ranks are mostly those who were born in the bush or those arrested when they were young and have no sense of where they came from.

Whereas from the start to the peak of the rebellion, the LRA had many fighters, their exact number is currently unknown. While Ugandan government intelligence says they are in the hundreds, some unconfirmed sources say they are over a thousand. Most likely, this could be true because they have kept abducting young people from the DRC, CAR, and South Sudan (Sawyer, 2010). Among other things, in order to disorient and control abductees from DRC, CAR, and South Sudan, they are fitted into a new family and taught to learn Lou as a lingua franca (Kelly et al., 2016; Invisible Children, n.d.).

DYNAMIC WITHIN THE LRA COMMAND STRUCTURE

Given the constant attrition rate, the command structure kept changing from time to time. Notwithstanding, as Lancaster et al. (2011) observe, the LRA has:

- A unified command structure with a capacity for central control of small group independent (or semi-independent) operations through a system that combines strategic guidelines with tactical freedom.
- Charismatic leadership is based on the skilful use of fear, discipline, demonstrated survival skills, and cultural and religious beliefs.
- A demonstrated capacity for analysis and development of attack plans designed for specific purposes such as incapacitating local defences, terrorising local populations, or exploiting boundaries between opposing forces.
- A demonstrated preference for extreme physical violence as well as deliberate psychological operations against civilian targets.
- High off-road mobility on foot. The LRA has been reported as being able to cover up to 50 kilometres per day cross-country.
- The ability to understand the pros and cons of appropriate technologies such as GPS, satellites, and cell phones
- The capacity to understand the vulnerabilities of the above and to adapt accordingly.
- The ability to recruit and train new fighters through a combination of force, psychological conditioning, and effective training.

- The capacity to conduct well-coordinated attacks, sometimes very close to government or UN military installations, and to escape.
- The capacity to operate at night.
- Excellent battlefield and operational discipline.
- The proven capacity to thrive in hostile environments and among people who both hate and fear them.
- A capacity to live off the land indefinitely (Lancaster et al., 2011, p. 41).

Through such means, the LRA has been able to survive to date. In most cases, even though they get arms and ammunition support from their supporters, they would not use it to kill the local population. They instead use clubs so that the gunshots do not attract attention.

THE SOCIAL, POLITICAL, AND ECONOMIC IMPACTS OF THE LRA INSURGENCY

The LRA insurgency left a great deal of impact on the local people, as it did on the states of Uganda, South Sudan, the DRC, and the CAR. The key impacts, among many, of the LRA insurgency were internal displacement, killing and mutilation, a high mortality rate among children, abduction, degeneration of education, lack of access to humanitarian services, and destruction of the economy and infrastructure. Besides, the government spent huge financial resources on paying salaries and allowances for soldiers, buying military hardware, and providing food for the displaced. The insurgency cost the government of Uganda $1.7 billion after 20 years, meaning that during the active periods of the insurgency, the government was spending $85 million annually (GSOPNU, 2006). In other words, the cost of the insurgency was equivalent to Uganda's total annual income from coffee exports. If the government used such funds to deliver services, it could have provided safe and clean drinking water to 3.5 million people per year. Alongside that, the United States provided undisclosed financial, logistical, and diplomatic support to the Ugandan military during the counter-LRA activities (Faber, 2017, p. 10). These all went to waste, given that they did not achieve the intended ends.

The LRA insurgency saw lots of killing and abduction of innocent civilians in Northern Uganda, Sudan, South Sudan, the DRC, and the CAR (Ochola-Onono & Oryem, 2000, p. 1). As a result, many orphans and widows became destitute with no one to take care of them. The porous boundaries between these countries made effective control difficult. Hence, mobile bands of LRA fighters took advantage of this to attack unprotected villages at will. During such attacks, they pillage villages, grab foodstuffs, and abduct people who they turn into sex slaves, porters, and recruits to the rebel ranks. For example, in 2006, UNICEF estimated that the LRA had abducted at least 25,000 children since 1988. Between January and July 2005 alone, the LRA abducted 1,286 Ugandans, 46.4% of whom were children under the age of 15 years. In order to prevent the abductees from escaping, the LRA uses the killings and mutilations of those caught escaping as deterrent measures. This is the same strategy used to terrorise and discourage anyone from reporting their presence to the national security forces.

In the different parts where the insurgent group spread, the civilian population bore the brunt. After the deaths of some men, women and children took care of homes, thus leading to the feminisation of poverty since women became the sole providers for the family. Yet women are not as mobile as men, and they do not have ready access to credit and resources. In regards to children, their conscription into the rebel and government militia ranks imposed a special burden on them. The children became the sole recruits for both the government and the rebel forces. This denied children the opportunity to go to school and receive care from their families. Those who were afraid to join these forces stayed at home or ended up on the streets. Even if some of the children joined the forces willingly or by force, the final analysis is that their physical and mental development has been impaired, thus immersing them in the culture of violence (Omona, 2015, p. 253).

Internal displacement and running into refuge became characteristic of the LRA insurgency. To some extent, the UN Office for the Coordination of Humanitarian Affairs (OCHA) argues, the LRA attacks and the government's counterinsurgency measures have resulted in the displacement of nearly 95% of the Acholi population in three districts of northern Uganda. Consequently, by 2006, the insurgency had forced 1.7 million people to live in more than 200 internally displaced persons (IDP) camps in northern Uganda. The people of the DRC, CAR, and South Sudan are experiencing the same thing this time around, given that the LRA is actively operating in their areas. Whereas the government intended the camps to be for protecting the local population, instead, they became places with the highest mortality rates in the world. For example, the Ugandan Ministry of Health and its partners estimated that about 1,000 people were dying weekly during the first seven months of 2005, largely due to malaria and AIDS.

The LRA and other forces that participated in counterinsurgency exposed a lot of inhuman treatment. The inhuman treatment that was unleashed on the people in such places of abode left bitter memories in the minds of the local population. Common among such inhuman treatments were the rape of women and girls in the presence of their husbands, parents, brothers, and children, and forceful sexual relationships with men – sodomy – in the presence of their family. Furthermore, some UPDF defecated in the water pots or food stuffs of these powerless people as the LRA concentrated on cutting off body parts such as lips, noses, breasts, ears, and arms and wounds left after injury. While recounting such a daunting experience in Pader district in northern Uganda, Omona (2015, p. 255) asserts:

> A certain man, whose dog tried to bark when the LRA were entering his compound, was forced to tie the dog on his back like a child. Then one of the rebels got firewood that had fire on it and started to burn the anus of the dog. Since it was tied on the owners back, the dog thought its owner was the one inflicting this pain on itself. In its desperate attempt to escape, the dog started biting its owner several times at the back of his head, thus leaving him with multiple wounds on his head.

Such suffering made people look forward to an opportune moment to take revenge on the purported criminals.

The conflict also destroyed the social fabric and coping mechanisms of society. Since civilians were direct targets of both the rebels and government forces, people dispersed in different directions for their own security. In the process, it caused the destruction of some of the key cultural values associated with the support provided by the wider family and kinship systems. This thereby exacerbated the division between groups and increased intra-group insecurity and hostility. It also acted to disrupt inter-group economic relations (RLP, 2014).

To add insult to injury, in northern Uganda, the displacement caused men to lose their traditional position of being the breadwinners at home. While in the IDP camps, since women were the ones receiving the relief food and other properties, it caused some to cease respecting their spouses and start to behave contrary to family norms. After the UN stopped providing food rations to families, some women resorted to befriending soldiers in order to survive. This exposed them to sexually transmitted diseases like human immunodeficiency virus (HIV) and acquired immunodeficiency syndrome (AIDS). Since men became powerless, the majority resorted to battering their wives to regain and assert their position as men. Consequently, this led to family breakups during the time in the camps.

Recounting the experience of Northern Uganda, Robert Senath Esuruku (2012) argues the insurgency has reduced the local population into abject poverty, especially after losing their livelihood. Quoting from the Uganda Bureau of Standard and UNDP's statistics, Esuruku (2012, pp. 149–151), about the poverty levels in northern Uganda, states:

> While the national average of Ugandans living in absolute poverty declined from 38.8% in 2002/03 to 31.1% in 2005/6 and to 24.53% in 2009/10, poverty in northern Uganda increased from 2.9 million in 2002/03 to 3.3 million in 2005/ 06 and decreased to 2.9 million in 2009/10. Despite the overall significant reduction in poverty, the northern Uganda regions remained poorer than other regions […]
>
> The human development indices (HDIs) and human poverty indices (HPIs) demonstrate that Northern Uganda is lagging behind the rest of the country in regional and district specific breakdowns. While the national HDI had improved form 0.488 in 2003 to 0.581 in 2006, there were regional imbalances that were skewed against the northern region. The central region, for instance, scored the highest HDI of 0.650, followed by the eastern region with an index of 0.586. The western region registered 0.564 while the northern region brought up the rear with 0.478.
>
> Furthermore, while the national income per capita is estimated at Uganda shillings (UGX) 570,000, the figure for the Northern region stands at a paltry UGX 153,000, which is about 27% of the national average. Although at national level income poverty fell from 56% in 1992 to 31.1% in 2006 and 24.5 in 2009/10, 46.2% of the residents in the northern region have remained poor, […] Although the mean consumption expenditure per adult equivalent has increased from UGX 55,092 in 2006 to 62,545 in 2009/10, the expenditure in the north has remained at UGX 38,988.

The above quote from Esuruku is a real reflection of the poverty level, not only in Northern Uganda but also in the other countries where the LRA insurgency spread. In the case of northern Uganda, this state made some people hailing from northern Uganda think the insurgency was a deliberate ploy by the government to crush their spirit. Due to their level of poverty, many of them have failed to support their families. Instead, some became dependent on food rations from the World Food Programme to the extent that they wanted support even after the end of the LRA insurgency.

Since people got used to receiving food rations, some have failed to adjust to a hard-working life and to fend for themselves. The situation is even worse among those who were born in the IDP camps. The dependency syndrome that developed among the local population caused a number of youths to resort to stealing or roaming around in trading centres without any gainful employment.

The insurgency has also affected harmonious life in the villages. In Gulu, for example, the post-LRA and conflicts caused an arsonist to burn a certain woman and her two daughters in their house near Gulu High School. Relatedly, in Lira, a man confessed to having killed twelve people from the same family due to land conflicts. Besides, the post-traumatic disorder resulting from such incidences has made some people develop mental challenges, thus forcing them to kill their own parents, children, or relatives (Omona, 2015, p. 259).

In the case of northern Uganda, Wade Snow (2009, p. 1) observes that the violent conflicts have greatly contributed to the return rate of the former IPDs to their ancestral land in Gulu as compared to other war-affected districts. This is because some people still fear getting involved in bitter conflicts over land, a common form of conflict during the post-LRA insurgency.

The destruction of properties and infrastructure in Northern Uganda, like roads, for example, led Chris Dolan, at a conference presentation on November 21, 2011, to assert, "The people of Northern Uganda were exposed to structural violence, an event that one lives to remember for the rest of his or her life". Of course, such destruction has also taken place and still takes place in the DRC, CAR, and South Sudan (Omona, 2015, pp. 261–262).

The politicisation of the LRA insurgency led to the negative identification of the Acholi by their neighbours. In the DRC and CAR, whoever speaks Acholi is considered an enemy, yet some of those who speak the language were forced to learn it during their time in abduction. In northern Uganda, for example, during the LRA insurgency, the Acholi were collectively branded rebels. Yet not all of them participated in or supported the LRA rebellion. Such generalisation of a community through stereotype is what leads to failing to look at people as individuals but rather as a community, which is not fair. On May 25, 2003, the negative identity attributed to the Acholi caused a peaceful march in Lira town in protest against the Barlonyo massacre to translate into anti-Acholi sentiments, leading to the killing of five people. The killing of the five people prompted some Acholi youths in Gulu to retaliate against the Langi. Around the same time in Teso, a Member of Parliament urged his people to kill all Acholi who were 18 years old.

In terms of relational cost, the insurgency caused the local people to mistrust and lose confidence in the government of Uganda. The voting pattern in 1997, 2001, 2006, and 2011 The people of northern Uganda's overwhelming vote for the opposition was indicative that they had hoped that things could change for the better if a different government came to power. Besides, the government lost a great number of its human resources due to brutal killings orchestrated by both the LRA and the UPDF (Omona, 2015, pp. 2046–247). More human resources were lost when some citizens opted to run into exile, thus leading to a brain drain. Unfortunately, even when things have changed in the areas where the LRA has operated, some people have decided to remain in exile to avoid being dehumanised and demonised by some people in government. The references made to them as killers, rapists, thugs, and so forth made some feel they were better off staying in exile than returning to their own country, where they were regarded as less human.

The insecurity that ensued during the LRA insurgency led to the wanton destruction of properties by the LRA, UPDF, and other collaborating forces. In the guise of denying the rebel supply, the government of Uganda decided to cram the local people in the IDP camps, where they lived in squalid conditions, a situation that has retarded the economic and social development of people in Northern Uganda. Unfortunately, as Omona (2015, p. 257) argues:

> To contain the situation, a lot of State resources were wasted to support the worthless war [...] Some people were accused of using the insurgency to enrich themselves by diverting the funds meant for the development of the war affected areas for their self-enrichment. Through such, state resources that were meant to do right things ended up being wasted by few individuals. As a result, post conflict reconstruction presents a huge challenge to the government of Uganda. Unless something is done to handle the corrupt officials who squanders monies meant for programs meant to leapfrog the people into better lives after their IDP camp experiences, some people in northern Uganda will continue not to trust the government (Omona, 2015, p. 257).

Indeed, a great deal of money was spent during the active phase of the conflict as soldiers who commanded the operations were given special allowances, and frequent talks were called where people received allowances. If the government had spent all the money on providing social services to the people, their lives could have changed for the better.

In another development, the people who escaped from the LRA abduction have bitter feelings against the government because they did not protect them. One such person said, "The government instead is treating the people who abducted and tortured us better than the way they treat us" (Omona, 2015, pp. 249–250). The echo of such sentiment is indicative that, left to themselves, such people are capable of revenging on others.

ATTEMPTED MEASURES TO ADDRESS THE LRA INSURGENCY

From the onset of the LRA insurgency, the government of Uganda took a realist approach by launching pre-emptive attacks to secure its power base. With assistance from foreign governments, the Ugandan government used military options, peace talks, and legal means to try to contain the LRA insurgency. Of all the strategies devised, the military strategy was the preferred option by the government of Uganda. As an insurgent group that equally launched attacks on the National Resistant Army (NRA), the government of Uganda responded with fire. In 1991, as a measure to counter the LRA, the government of Uganda launched various operations, including Operation North (operation sim-sim), Operation Iron Feast I and II, and Operation Lightening Thunder. Besides, several militia groups sprung up to protect the local population. Among many are the Amuka in Lango, the Arrow boys in Teso and South Sudan, and Local Defence Units (LDUs). Alongside these local defence forces, the NRA continued using mobile forces to guard the people of Northern Uganda.

The government of Uganda launched Operation North in 1991, meant to destroy the LRA, but it did not achieve its goals. Instead, with support from the Sudanese government, the LRA established safe bases in South Sudan. From these bases, they ferociously attacked civilians in northern Uganda. Civilians they suspected to be reporters, and those who formed local defence units, had their ears, lips, and noses cut off. During the attacks, the rebels abducted hundreds of civilians (Rice, Oct. 20, 2007).

Given the devastating effects of the operation north on the local population, a group of local people appealed for peace talks between the government and the LRA. The talks, which Betty Oyella Bigombe promoted, nearly brought about the much-desired peace (Bigombe, 1993, p. 115). Unfortunately, the egocentric leadership in both the government of Uganda and the LRA frustrated the effort towards peace. Consequently, fresh fights ensued between the opposing forces. Some people reasoned that the fact the commanders who were deployed to oversee the operation received special war allowances was the reason for the failure to realise peace because the operation against the LRA became a source of income for the commanders. Nevertheless, given the need for peace, some elders tried to initiate contact with the LRA leadership. This attempt also did not yield any fruit but instead earned the deaths of the champions of the initiative, Mzee Okot-Ogoni and Mzee Rwot Olanya Lagonyi, brother to LRA commander Otti Lagonyi (O'Kadamire, 2002, p. 41).

In the early 1990s, both the Sudanese and Ugandan governments supported insurgent groups to carry out operations in each other's territory, and therefore a proxy war ensued between Khartoum and Kampala. Each party accused the other of destabilising its peace and security. Fortunately, the increased pressure from the international community in the late 1990s forced the Khartoum government to stop overt support for the LRA, though covert support continued through other rebel groups that were loyal to the National Salvation Army (NSA). Subsequently, in 1999, the Sudan and Uganda governments agreed to stop aiding each other's insurgent groups, thus allowing them to renew diplomatic relations. The 9/11 attack further cemented this understanding. When the U.S. State Department listed the LRA as a terrorist group, the Sudanese government tried as much as possible to distance itself from any deals with the LRA. In 2002, as part of an effort to improve its international image, the Sudanese government allowed 10,000 Uganda People's Defence Forces (UPDF) to pursue the LRA inside Southern Sudan. Whereas permission was granted for this operation, it was, however, on condition that the UPDF did not cross the red line, some 100 kilometres north of the Ugandan border along the Juba-Torit road (Human Rights Watch, 20).

To entice the LRA to return home, the government of Uganda came up with the Amnesty Act, which came into force in January 2001. The Amnesty Act provides amnesty for Ugandans involved in acts of a warlike nature in various parts of the country and for other connected purposes (The Amnesty Act, 2001). Though the Act was popularised on local radio stations so that those who cared to head to it would return home and have a soft landing, the grey areas within the Act made it hard for the LRA to come out. To some extent, not all those who were given amnesty were actually those who got involved in the rebellion; also, those who were rescued after abduction were required to seek amnesty. Consequently, the Act lost its major objective.

After failing to manage the LRA insurgency, in December 2003, Ugandan President Yoweri Museveni referred LRA crimes in northern Uganda to the International Criminal Court (ICC) (Human Rights Watch, 2009). After due diligence, on July 8, 2005, the ICC issued warrants against Kony and his top commanders (Mwaniki & Wepundi, 2007, p. 9). The ICC proffered 12 counts of crimes, including crimes against humanity, including murder, enslavement, sexual enslavement, and rape. Furthermore, 21 counts of war crimes were committed, including murder, cruel treatment of civilians, intentionally directing an attack against a civilian population, pillaging, inducing rape, and forced enlistment of children into the rebel ranks. The ICC warrants raised international awareness of the atrocities committed by Kony and the LRA (World Peace Foundation, n.d.). Even after setting up a special chamber in the High Court of Uganda to try some of the crimes within Uganda other than taking those who give themselves out, none of those indicted freely came out, except for Thomas Kwoyelo, who was captured in combat. Hence, this attempt also did not yield any dividends because the trial of Kwoyelo is even more complicated given the ongoing justice versus reconciliation debate (Rugiririza, Nov. 10, 2018).

In May 2006, Kony extended an offer of peace. Subsequently, long negotiations ensued from 2006 to 2008 in Juba, Sudan, between the government of Uganda and the LRA, mediated by the South Sudanese separatist leader Riek Machar. During the talks, "then UN Secretary-General Kofi Annan appointed Joaquim Chissano, former president of Mozambique, as his special envoy for the LRA-affected areas" (Human Rights Watch, 2009, p. 14). The Ugandan government and the LRA signed a truce on August 26, 2006. Under the terms of the agreement, LRA forces would leave Uganda and gather in two assembly areas in Ri-kwangba and the remote Garamba National Park area of the northern Democratic Republic of the Congo that the Ugandan government agreed not to attack. However, the talks ended in failure when Kony later refused to sign the document, instead insisting that the ICC suspend his and his commanders' warrants of arrest (Human Rights Watch, 2009).

In response, on December 13, 2008, Uganda, South Sudan, and the Democratic Republic of the Congo (DRC) launched a joint military operation to break the back of the LRA. The United States provided financial, logistical, and diplomatic support to the Ugandan military during the counter-LRA activities (Faber, 2017, p. 10). While the aerial attacks and raids on the LRA camps in Garamba destroyed the LRA safe haven in the jungle and helped to rescue a few captives, the operation did not yield much. Instead, it facilitated scattering the rebels widely. The rebels retaliated by attacking the Congolese and South Sudanese populations, killing over 1,000 people and abducting others. Unfortunately, the joint military operation ended up costing the local population dearly, given that it displaced thousands of people.

In March 2012, Uganda announced its move to head a new four-nation African Union military force comprising 5,000 soldiers drawn from the DR Congo, Central African Republic, and South Sudan to hunt down Kony and the remnants of the LRA. Although in the same year an intelligence report located the LRA in Djema, Central African Republic, the forces pursuing them withdrew in April 2013 after the overthrow of the government of the Central African Republic by the Séléka Coalition rebels. This gave the LRA leeway to rampage and pillage villages in CAR (People Pill, n.d.).

ATTEMPTS BY THE UNITED STATES GOVERNMENT AND OTHER INTERNATIONAL BODIES

While the U.S. government began supporting the LRA insurgency earlier on, its overt support for the insurgent group came after the September 11 attacks, when it declared the LRA a terrorist group. To this end, on August 28, 2008, the United States Treasury Department placed Kony on its list of "Specially Designated Global Terrorists", a designation that carries financial and other penalties. Following this, in November 2008, U.S. President George W. Bush gave a directive to the United States Africa Command to provide financial and logistical assistance to the Ugandan government to assist the 2008–2009 Operation Lightning Thunder in the Garamba forest of the DRC. While no U.S. troops were directly involved, 17 U.S. advisers and analysts provided intelligence, equipment, and fuel to their Ugandan military counterparts.

Furthermore, in May 2010, U.S. President Barack Obama signed the Lord's Resistance Army Disarmament and Northern Uganda Recovery Act. The legislation aimed at stopping Kony and the LRA passed unanimously in the United States Senate on March 11ern Uganda Recovery Act. The legislation aimed at stopping Kony and the LRA passed unanimously in the United States Senate on March 11. On May 12, 2010, a motion was made to suspend the rules and pass the bill in the House of Representatives. This eventually led President Obama, in November 2010, to deliver a strategy document to Congress, asking for more funding to disarm Kony and the LRA. In October 2011, President Obama authorised the deployment of approximately 100 combat-equipped U.S. troops to central Africa. Their goal is to help regional forces remove Kony and senior LRA leaders from the battlefield. In a letter to Congress, Obama stated: "Although the U.S. forces are combat-equipped, they will only be providing information, advice, and assistance to partner nation forces, and they will not themselves engage LRA forces unless necessary for self-defence" (People Pill, n.d.).

Further still, in 2013, the U.S. State Department offered a $5 million reward to whoever would provide information leading to his capture (Faber, 2017, p. 10). Besides, in 2014, the U.S., under the Obama administration, deployed more personnel and U.S. military aircraft to continue pursuing the insurgent group. Unfortunately, whereas the military operations went alongside large-scale defection campaigns aimed at top LRA commanders, Kony and his commanders are still at large.

Besides the U.S. government, the African Union (AU), the European Union, and the United Nations all supported efforts to end the LRA insurgency. For example, in March 2012, the AU supported the four-nation African Union military force comprising 5,000 soldiers from the DR Congo, Central African Republic, and South Sudan to pursue Kony and LRA remnants (People's Pill, n.d.). Equally, the EU and UN agencies like the United Nations International Children's Emergency Fund (UNICEF) supported trauma counselling, and the UN Security Council also took a proactive stand in sorting out the insurgency. The UN Secretary General, by appointing a special advisor on the LRA affair, closely followed the need to end the LRA insurgency through peaceful means.

Given the elusive nature of the LRA and their continuous attacks, various groups in northern Uganda, the DRC, the CAR, and South Sudan, especially religious and traditional leaders, continue pressing for an idealist approach to peace talks. They argue that a more comprehensive approach is necessary and possible, including a renewed commitment to finding a peaceful solution. However, the general feeling among international policymakers and Ugandan government officials interviewed is that Joseph Kony (leader of the LRA) had his chance to sign, can no longer be trusted, and that military action is the only option left to end the conflict (Hendrickson & Tumutegyereize, 2012, p. 5).

CONCLUSION

To be sure, the LRA has been an active force. From its inception, the leadership used terror, abduction, mutilation, and general cruelty to advance their agenda as well as prove their presence. Whereas over the years different attempts have been made to address the LRA insurgency, including a mix of military means, legal means, and peace talks, the LRA still remains elusive. In the circumstances, deeper efforts are required from all stakeholders to bring peace to the LRA-affected areas and curb human suffering at the hands of the LRA. Since some other people also took advantage of the presence of the LRA to exert pain on the local population, presenting them to trial could also be an incentive for the LRA to know that they are not the only ones meant to face trial but rather all offenders who have committed human rights offences against innocent civilians.

Note

1 Dominic Ongwen was a 10-year-old boy who was walking to school in northern Uganda when the LRA rebel movement (LRA) kidnapped him and turned him into one of its most ruthless commanders. After his abduction in 1990, he rose rapidly in rebel ranks, becoming a major at the age of 18 and a brigadier by his late 20s after winning the confidence of LRA leader Joseph Kony. He earned the reputation of being able to emerge from the bloodiest of battles with few casualties among his fighters. Ongwen had a volatile relationship with Kony, opposing the execution of deputy LRA chief Vincent Otti in 2007 after the two fell out. Ongwen was the only commander who pleaded with Kony to spare Otti's life, a move that weakened his influence within the LRA. However, Kony spared Ongwen from the subsequent purge of Otti loyalists due to Ongwen's value to the LRA, particularly his ability to lead troops on daring missions (Chothia, January 26, 2015).

References

Bigombe, B.O. (1993). Uganda government approach to conflicts in the North and North Eastern Uganda. *Nordic Journal of African Studies, 2*(2), 109–117. http://www.njas.helsinki.fi/pdf-files/vol2num2/bigombe.pdf

Chothia, F. (January 26 2015). Profile: Dominic Ongwen of Uganda's LRA. https://www.bbc.com/news/world-africa-30709581

Esuruku, R.S. (2012). The peace, recovery and development plan for Northern Uganda. In C.M. Okello, et al., (Eds). *Where law meets reality: Forging transitional justice* (pp.144–166). Cape Town, Darker, Nairobi & Orford: Pambozuka Press.

Faber, P. (April 2017). Sources of resilience in the Lord's resistance army. https://www.cna.org/cna_files/pdf/DOP-2017-U-015265-Final.pdf

GSOPNU. (2006). *Counting the cost: Twenty years of war in Northern Uganda*. Gulu: GSCOPNU

Hendrickson, D., & Tumutegyereize, K. (January 2012). Dealing with complexities in peace negotiation: Reflections on the Lord's Resistance Army and the Juba peace talks, Conciliation Resource: Bergdorf Foundation

Human Rights Watch (2009). *The Christmas Massacres: LRA attacks on civilians in Northern Congo*. New York: Human Rights Watch. https://www.hrw.org/sites/default/files/reports/drc0209web_0.pdf

HURIPEC, & LI GI. (2003). *The hidden war: The forgotten people; war in Acholi and its ramifications for peace and security in Uganda*. Kampala: Faculty of Law, Makerere University.

International Crisis Group. (28 April 2010). LRA: A regional strategy beyond killing Kony, Crisis Group Africa Report No.157. https://d2071andvip0wj.cloudfront.net/157-lra-a-regional-strategy-beyond-killing-kony.pdf

Invisible Children (n.d). How do we recognize the LRA? www.invisiblechildren.com

JRP (2012). The day they came: Recounting the LRA's Invasion of Teso Sub-Region through Obalanga Sub-County in 2003, JRP Field Note XIV. http://justiceandreconciliation.com/wp-content/uploads/2012/09/The-Day-the-Came_Obalanga-Erratum-Sept-2012.pdf

Kelly, T.D.J., Branham, L., & Decker, M.R. (2016). Abducted children and youth in Lord's Resistance Army in Northeastern Democratic Republic of Congo (DRC): Mechanism of indoctrination and control. https://conflictandhealth.biomedcetral.com/article/10.1186/s13031-016-0078-5

Labeja, P. (Aug. 30 2018). Atiak to profile 1995 massacre victims. https://ugandaradionetwork.net/story/atiak-to-profile-1995-massacre-victims

Lancaster, P., Lacaille, G., & Cakaj, L. (2011). *Diagnostic study of the Lord's Resistance Army*. Washington DC: World Bank.

Maliti, T. (March 8 2017). Court hears details of last moments of LRA deputy leader Vincent Otti, Trial/Dominic Ogewn. www.ijmonitor.org

Mutiabwa, P. (2010). *Uganda since independence: A history of unfulfilled hopes*. Kampala: Fountain Publishers

Mwaniki, D., & Wepundi, M. (March 28 2007). The Juba Peace Talk- the checkered road to peace for Northern Uganda, Situation Report, Institute for Security Studies. https://www.files.ethz.ch/isn/102067/20070328JUBAPEACETLKS.PDF

Mwenda, A. (2006). Uganda's roadmap to the end of northern region insurgency: Government/ LRA position statement. *The Monitor News Paper 2006*.

O'Kadamire, B. (2002). LRA/Government negotiations 1993–94. In O . Lucima (Ed.),*Protracted conflict, elusive peace to end the violence in Northern Uganda* (pp. 34–41). London: ACCORD. https://rc-services-assets.s3.eu-west-1.amazonaws.com/s3fs-public/Protracted_conflict_elusive_peace_Initiatives_to_end_the_violence_in_northern_Uganda_Accord_Issue_11.pdf

Obita, J. (1998). The official presentation of the Lord's Resistance Movement/Army (LRA/M). A Case for National Reconciliation, Peace, Democracy and Economic Prosperity for All Ugandans. Kacoke Madit. http://everything.explained.today/%2F%5C/Lord%27s_Resistance_Army/

Ochola-Onono, G., & Oryem, A. (2000). The effects of the war in Northern Uganda in education in Gulu District. http://www.km-net.org.uk/conferences/KM98/deo.htm

Odong, J. (March 13th 2003). Opoka confirmed dead. The New Vision. www.newvision.co.ug

Omona, A.D. (2009). Northern Uganda peace process: Why the parties have failed to agree, in *Jesuit Journal of Social Justice in East Africa, issue 01/09* (pp. 64–73). Nairobi: Hekimani.

Omona, A.D. (2015). *Management of intrastate conflicts in Uganda: A case of Northern Uganda*. PhD Thesis, Kenyatta University, Nairobi.

Onekalit, C. (2005). The forgotten crisis: Eighteen years of civil unrest in Northern Uganda. In G. Vasu (Ed.), *Conflict trends*, vol. 2, Durban: ACCORD.

People Pill. (n.d). Joseph Kony. https://peoplepill.com/people/joseph-kony/

Rice, X. (Oct. 20 2007). Background: The Lord's Resistance Army, The Guardian. https://www.theguardian.com/katine/2007/oct/20/about.uganda

RLP. (2014). *Compendium of conflicts in Uganda: Findings of the national reconciliation and transitional justice audit*. Kampala: Refugee Law Project.

Rubaihayo, P. (11th October 2005). Obote the nationalist. *The new vision*. https://www.newvision.co.ug/new_vision/news/1115310/obote-nationalist

Rugiririza, E. (Nov. 10 2018). Uganda faces first test with Kwoyelo LRA trial, justice.net. https://www.justiceinfo.net/en/tribunals/national-tribunals/39463-uganda-faces-first-test-with-kwoyelo-lra-trial.html

Sawyer, I. (August 11 2010). *CAR/DR Congo: LRA conducts massive abduction campaigns*. Washington DC: Human Rights Watch, available from www.hrw.org

Schomerus, M. (2007). *The Lord's Resistance Army in Sudan: A history and overview*. Geneva: Small Arms Survey/Graduate Institute of International Studies.

The Amnesty Act. (2001). https://ulii.org/node/23788

The Resolve. (2013). Hidden in plain sight: Sudan's Harboring of the LRA in the Kafia Kingi Enclave, 2009–2013). https://invisiblechildren.com/wp-content/uploads/2013/04/hidden-in-plain-sight-sudans-support-to-the-lra-april-2013.pdf

Trial International. (July 6 2017). Thomas Kweyelo, available from https://trialinternational.org/latest-post/thomas-kwoyelo/, accessed 9/2/2020

Wade, S. (2009). ARLPI pilot land conflict mitigation project in Lamogi. http://www.arlpi.org

Westbrook, D. (June, 2000). The torment of northern Uganda: A legacy of missed opportunities. *Online Journal of Peace and Conflict Resolution, issue 3.2*. http://www.trinstitute.org/ojpcr/p3_2westbrook.htm

World Peace Foundation. (n.d). AU regional task force against the Lord's resistance army mission. https://sites.tufts.edu/wpf/files/2017/07/Lords-Resistance-Army-Mission.pdf

PART IV

CASE STUDIES

The Americas

36

REVOLUTIONARY ARMED FORCES OF COLOMBIA

People's Army (Fuerzas Armadas Revolucionarias de Colombia – Ejército del Pueblo, FARC-EP)

Diana Flórez and Olivier Lewis

INTRODUCTION

The "Final Agreement to End the Armed Conflict and Build a Stable and Lasting Peace" (FAP), signed between the Colombian Government (GOC) and the biggest and oldest guerrilla group in the state, the Fuerzas Armadas Revolucionarias de Colombia-Ejército del Pueblo (FARC) on November 26, 2016, marked the official end of a five-decade-old armed conflict. Promising to adhere to the rule of law, FARC leaders renounced the use of political violence. In 2017, the FARC's leaders established a new political party, keeping the old acronym but changing the official name to "The Common Alternative Revolutionary Force" (hereafter FARC-PP). GOC officials, for their part, committed to supporting the FARC's reintegration and guaranteeing its participation in politics. Indeed, in 2018, the new party participated in congressional elections for the first time, and meanwhile, the GOC amnestied (and started reintegrating) thousands of FARC fighters, all while establishing, via the FAP, a complex system of transitional justice.

And yet, the FARC-PP has not become a normal political party. In fact, the party's future is increasingly uncertain. Likewise, demobilisation is partial, and the threat of war is constant. Although the GOC is partly responsible for these failures, divisions within the FARC-PP have also hindered its transformation: The FARC was never a homogenous, unitary organisation. It had several units, each with its own functions and goals. As the conflict with the GOC changed, one unit would dominate the others. Today, the FARC has become even less organised. There is no unified organisation. One could even talk of (at least) *three* FARCS (supporters of the FAP, hardliners, and dissident groups). This generates uncertainty and despair among the former FARC guerrillas and FARC civilians.

The rest of this chapter describes in more detail the FARC-PP's challenges. To this end, the chapter contains five sections. Section I covers the historical context of the post-accord period, going from the FARC's origins in the 1960s to the beginning of the formal peace talks in 2012. The bulk of Section II focuses on the peace bargaining process (2012–2016) and the tensions that ran through these negotiations. Section III mostly focuses on the current period and the organisational structure and political agenda of the FARC as a political party (i.e., the FARC-PP). Section IV forms the bulk of the chapter. Here, the chapter explores the FARC-PP's post-agreement vulnerabilities. Section V outlines the preliminary outcomes of the 'transition'. To conclude, the chapter tries to determine whether the FARC-PP is sustainable as a political party and whether this (un)sustainability is a threat to peace in Colombia.

Historical Overview: How and Why the Group Formed

THE IMAGINARY WAR (1964–1982)

The GOC's and the Government of the United States' (USG) coordinated bombing of "peasant self-defence zones" in 1964 gave a reason for the FARC to be founded. Given their rural experience and their Marxist-Leninist dogma, in 1964 the FARC's future leaders produced a manifesto entitled "The Agrarian Programme of the Guerrilleros". Via this pamphlet, they demanded land redistribution and basic rights for peasants. Two years after the bombings (in 1966), under the auspices of the Communist Party of Colombia, the *Fuerzas Armadas Revolucionarias de Colombia* officially emerged. Until the FARC's demobilisation in 2016, agrarian rights remained the main justifications

DOI: 10.4324/9780429426063-41

for armed struggle; programmatic documents, peace negotiation agendas, and the FAP all demonstrate this. But, as in most cases, the enabling factors were numerous and much older than the 1964 bombings. In this instance, the 'structural causes' date back to the agrarian conflicts of 1930. In other words, the FARC's founding is partly the product of the GOC's decades-old persecution of peasants and their political movements (Pécaut, 2008, p. 23).

At first, the FARC vied for isolated areas of little interest to Colombians. Consequently, the FARC was territorially and politically marginal (Guitiérrez Sanín, 2015). Like the other guerrillas that emerged during this period, the FARC's political violence was restricted to a few attacks on 'public forces', and as such, the group did not pose an existential threat to the GOC (Aguilera Peña, 2014, pp. 77–78). The early years of the armed conflict were in fact what Broderick calls "an imaginary war" (2000, p. 156). The guerrillas had few resources and little ability to gain popular support (Pécaut, 2008, pp. 42–43). Nevertheless, in locations long neglected by the government (i.e., the peripheries), the FARC found many willing recruits. Most of the FARC's troops, including its chief commanders, belonged to the farming class (i.e., the peasantry), and the FARC composition remained predominantly rural throughout its existence (Guitiérrez Sanín, 2008; Universidad Nacional de Colombia, 2017).

Arguably, this 'first phase' ended in 1982 with the election of Belisario Betancourt. Contrary to his predecessors, the new president prioritised a negotiated solution to the conflict and recognised several of the insurgents' demands. But the FARC's increasing membership and territorial control (enabled in part by its engagement in the coca economy) also marked a new phase in the organisation's history.

THE SEARCH FOR PEACE IN THE MIDDLE OF WAR (1982–2002)

The early 1980s proved a favourable time for the FARC. The coca 'boom' and the revolutionary atmosphere in Nicaragua and Guatemala contributed to the resurgence and recognition of the guerrilla group that many had considered defeated. In 1982, the FARC devised its ambitious *strategic plan*. This document would frame the FARC's military and political agenda for more than three decades. The plan foresaw the establishment of a unified political structure and an exponential increase in financing, territorial control, and military activity (including the adoption of large-scale attack tactics).[1] With increasing drug trafficking resources, the overthrow of the GOC and the establishment of a provisional government became realistic goals for the FARC (Pécaut, 2008, p. 105). Nevertheless, the FARC's leaders continued to prioritise military means over political ends. This decision would prove to be a strategic mistake for the FARC.

The FARC leadership remained open to dialogue and, in 1984, via the signing of the Uribe Agreement, initiated a peace process. As a result, a new political party, the Patriotic Union (UP), was established to facilitate potential FARC 'reincorporation'. The peace negotiations, however, were not a success. The FARC used the peace negotiations as a means of increasing battlefield victories (Aguilera Peña, 2014, p. 129). And GOC leaders failed to persuade military and political officials to support the process. In fact, with the support of paramilitaries, the GOC conducted irregular warfare (including the use of state terrorism) against the FARC and the UP. As a result, more than 3,000 UP members were killed or 'disappeared' (Dudley, 2008, pp. 143–161).

Over the next 12 years (1986–1998), several rounds of just-as-failed negotiations rendered Colombians rancorous and cynical. They saw the bargaining parties as disingenuous and weak-willed. For their part, the FARC leaders continued to use the negotiations as part of their military strategy but also to gain international recognition and legitimacy. Successive Colombian governments, for their part, shifted their efforts to counternarcotics (especially against the drug cartels) and tolerated (and occasionally enabled) an increase in paramilitary activity.

After the Cold War, guerrilla groups did not disappear. Participation in drug trafficking and thus a need to counter counternarcotics meant both more income and an additional *raison d'être* for the FARC and similar groups (Sánchez Gómez, 2001, pp. 31–32). Through the control of coca cultivation lands and, to a lesser extent, kidnapping and extortion, the FARC's revenues grew. But participation in narcotics and terrorism delegitimized the FARC in the eyes of locals (Aguilera Peña, 2014, p. 150). At the end of the 1990s, the drug/political violence nexus helped the GOC obtain USG financial and military support and led to the bilateral "Plan Colombia" (2000–2008). Paradoxically, while state organisations were preparing for war, the government of Andrés Pastrana (1998–2002) carried out a peace process with the FARC. After three years (1999–2001), the Caguan negotiations ended amid accusations of breaches by the parties (e.g., FARC violations of the demilitarised zone, violations of human rights by both parties and state support of paramilitary forces) (DCP, 2012, p. 11).

By 2002, the FARC had reached what would be the peak of its military significance, being present in 377 of 1,101 Colombian municipalities (Aguilera Peña, 2013, p. 102; 2014, p. 214). Indeed, the next decade would be dramatically different for the FARC due to events both far and near. The September 11th terrorist attacks and the subsequent USG 'War on Terror' led the USG and the GOC to identify the FARC as a terrorist organisation. This characterisation and policy stance occurred just as the GOC's military forces and cooperating paramilitary groups started to gain a military advantage over the FARC's forces, markedly weakening the organisation.

THE POLITICAL-MILITARY DECLINE OF THE FARC (2002–2010)

The failed Caguán process and broken promise to defeat the guerrillas brought Álvaro Uribe Vélez to power in 2002 and 2006. Taking advantage of rising public hostility towards the guerrilla forces, Uribe was ultimately successful in portraying the main guerrilla groups as 'narco-terrorists'. As mentioned, the official denial of an internal war and the use instead of the notion of a "terrorist threat" secured the support of the USG (Pizarro, 2017, pp. 329–330). In this context, the USG-backed GOC ruled out a negotiated end to the conflict and, in its place, waged a costly war against all insurgent groups.

This said, the Uribe government took a different approach with *paramilitary* groups, which had been responsible for most human rights violations in Colombia. From 2002 to 2006, over 30,000 troops demobilised and, in exchange, received extensive legal benefits (Reed, 2010). Meanwhile, the GOC's military forces, with the financial and military support of the USG, substantially reduced the FARC's military capacity, notably by taking control of many of its traditional strongholds and killing several of its top commanders (FIP, 2014, pp. 9–10). This, coupled with the desertion of more than 10,000 FARC troops between 2002 and 2010, reduced the number of FARC combatants by more than half (Aguilera Peña, 2014, p. 217; Group, 2009, p. 2). Accordingly, the FARC's forces were forced to move to the border areas and to change military tactics (from large military attacks and terrorist attacks in large cities to actions that required little military effort) (FIP, 2014, p. 10).

The FARC's increased involvement in drug trafficking meant the group had both a political and profit-oriented character. Although scholars disagree on whether drug trafficking remained a means to finance the armed struggle or had become a goal, the FARC was in all cases quite different from typical paramilitary organisations and criminal enterprises (Guitiérrez Sanín, 2008, pp. 13–14; Sánchez Gómez, 2001, p. 31).

By the end of this period, the FARC was significantly weakened militarily. And yet, its defeat, despite the government's rhetoric, was unlikely in the short term (Aguilera Peña, 2014, p. 221). The FARC's hierarchical and centralised structure, as well as its internal discipline, guaranteed its military resilience (Guitiérrez Sanín, 2008). But most of all, resources obtained from the drug economy allowed the group to resist attacks by government armed forces and paramilitaries and remain in 142 municipalities across Colombia (Aguilera Peña, 2013, p. 102).

Politically, however, the FARC had already been defeated. Although the group never enjoyed great popular acceptance, at this juncture civilian support was at an all-time low. In addition to the 'narcotisation' of the armed conflict, the FARC's violence against politicians and civilians gave rise to growing support for the continuation and intensification of Uribe's military policy (CNMH, 2013, p. 188). Relations between the FARC and civilians in rural areas deteriorated further. The indiscriminate use of anti-personnel mines, bombs, and forced recruitment led to collective movements demanding that the guerrilla group end the armed conflict and respect international human rights and humanitarian law (Aguilera Peña, 2014, pp. 305–320). In 2010, former Uribe administration Defence Minister Juan Manuel Santos was elected to continue a 'hard-line stance' against all insurgent groups.

THE PEACE PROCESS: THE PRIORITISING OF POLITICS (2010–2018)

Oddly, the new Santos government sought to end the war via dialogue. Santos thought the armed conflict was stagnating, meaning that it could continue for years, resulting in high social and economic costs for the state and its citizens (de Boer, Garzón-Vergara, & Bosetti, 2017, p. 8; Santos Calderón, 2018, p. 30). For the FARC, leadership change, the failure of the 1982 Strategic Plan, and a decline in troop numbers, popular support, and territory (see Figure 36.1) all led the guerrilla leaders to enter negotiations (Aguilera Peña, 2014, p. 281).

For two years, secret 'dialogues' were held in Havana, ending in August 2012 with the signing of a detailed negotiation agenda. The five specific topics agreed upon (the end of the conflict, illicit drugs, political participation, rural development, and victims) were the result of the conciliation between the FARC's ambitious historical demands and the GOC's desire to end the conflict (Segura & Mechoulan, 2017, pp. 12–13). The acceptance of a limited agenda, the abandonment of hostage-taking, and the declaration of several unilateral ceasefires were clear signs that the FARC leaders, unlike during previous 'peace processes', were prioritising political aims.

After four years of intense negotiations in Havana, the parties signed the Final Peace Agreement (FPA) in August 2016. The 310-page accord included some timid rural reforms (access to basic services, credits, and limited access to land), political guarantees for the FARC, a complex system of transitional justice, and disarmament, demobilisation, and reintegration. Although the FARC leadership's core demands were not included in the FAP (e.g., land redistribution, reform of the military and of the economic

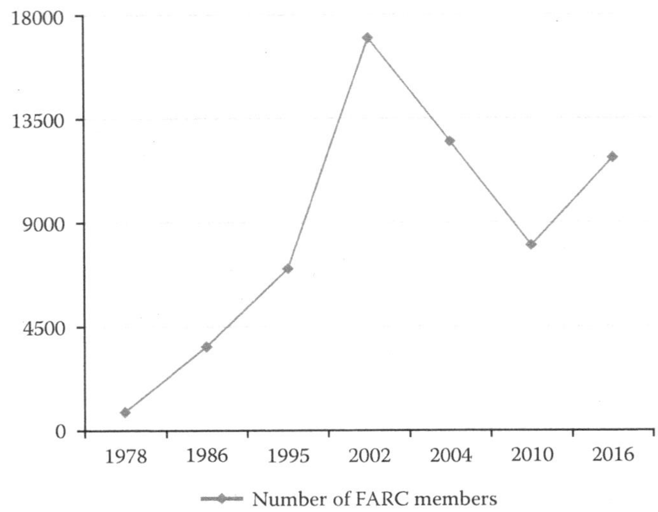

Figure 36.1 Number of FARC Members (1978–2016).

Source: Aguilera Peña, 2013, p. 9.

system, weapons retention), the guerrilla group managed to secure its participation in national politics and the application of 'alternative' penalties (other than jail) for the serious crimes committed throughout the conflict.[2] Unsurprisingly, these points remain contested.

On October 2nd, 2016, the parties agreed to submit the FAP for approval through a plebiscite. After a harsh campaign, the FAP was unexpectedly rejected by a majority of Colombian voters (by a narrow margin of 0.4%), probably due to the concessions made to the FARC (Capone, 2017, p. 128; Matanock & García-Sánchez, 2017; Segura & Mechoulan, 2017). About six weeks later, the parties signed a new agreement, including, according to the GOC, most of the proposals raised by the No campaign. This said, the two main objections Peace, too lenient penalties for FARC criminals and the FARC's participation in politics) were spurned by the parties. As Sergio Jaramillo, the High Commissioner for Peace stated, "trying to impose these conditions would have made it impossible to reach a new peace agreement" (Jaramillo, 2018, p. 56).

With the new FAP signed and ratified (now by the National Congress) in November 2016, the post-conflict stage (post-December 2017) was made official. Today, the benefits of peace include lives saved[3], the FARC's dearmament and disavowal of violence, and modest public investments in conflict zones. But two years after the signing of the new FAP, the accord's sustainability is questioned.

KEY PERSONNEL AND STRUCTURE

The FARC's Governance

Without the legitimacy that the FARC enjoyed in certain areas of Colombia, the armed group would not have been able to operate (Pécaut, 2008, p. 69). Rural and marginalised areas (the homeland of many FARC commanders and soldiers) are where the FARC received the most support. Nevertheless, the FARC's model of government and its relations with rural communities were never uniform or static. These varied from place to place and evolved according to the needs of the insurgent group and the changes in the war's dynamics.

From a historical perspective, the emergence of paramilitary organisations and their expansion into FARC strongholds (from 1995 onward) marked a profound change in the FARC's ways of relating to the civilian population. From here on, "fear and terror" became the rule in most regions (Pécaut, 2008, p. 76). From a more analytical perspective, it is possible to distinguish two types of FARC governance, which in turn were the result of variations in local politics. Thus, it is important to distinguish strategic and historical 'rear-guard zones' from more disputed areas.

Strategic and historic rear-guard zones refer to territories where the FARC established an enduring presence and authority. One could include areas with a pre-existing tradition of communist or liberal values. One could also add areas where, after the 1980s, coca cultivation became the main means of subsistence for farmers and the main source of financing for the FARC. In both types of regions, the FARC did not so much replace the state as take control of lands long abandoned by the state. In these regions, the FARC, in exchange for taxation, provided physical protection, ran a judicial system, policed daily life[4], supported infrastructure works (e.g., roads, schools), and regulated access and mobility (Aguilera Peña, 2014, pp. 156, 338; Provost, 2017, p. 239).

Initially, the guerrilla group sought to establish a 'co-government' with community organisations, supporting the application of local justice mechanisms and the voicing of grievances vis-à-vis the Colombian state (Provost, 2017, pp. 238–239). Within these areas, the FARC's rules on land rights were common, understandable, and accepted by some rural populations. For example, the FARC imposed restrictions on the accumulation of land and supported peasants' *de facto* land occupations (Aguilera Peña, 2014, p. 157; FARC-EP, 1982). But when communities and social organisations demanded autonomy and disengagement from the armed conflict, the FARC intensified its use of violence to silence the dissent (Pécaut, 2008, pp. 71–76). FARC leaders believed that recognising the autonomy claimed by several rural communities would have serious military and economic implications for the FARC, as these communities were key to recruitment, financing, and military mobility (Aguilera Peña, 2014, p. 250).

In contrast, the term 'disputed areas' refers to territories that were part of the post-1982 FARC expansion process. Being in areas where other armed groups normally operate, the insurgent group considered community members as potential informers or supporters of the official Colombian government and non-state groups. Thus, in these regions, the FARC used terrorist tactics to "neutralise" the population (e.g., bomb cylinders, antipersonnel mines, public executions) (Duncan, 2006, pp. 139–140). Here, there was no co-government with local organisations, and the 'guerrilla justice' model was applied with little or no local participation (Aguilera Peña, 2014, p. 25). Because these territories were contested, the loyalty of the population was volatile and depended on the actor who was prevailing.[5]

Regarding the FARC's relations with the local authorities, the same dichotomy applies. In regions where the FARC exerted authority, it did not seek to dismantle the entire state but to "control [local governments] by forcibly intervening in its decisions, capturing it through the appointment of their own members or allies, or both" (Provost, 2017, p. 237). Elsewhere, the insurgent group generally sought to increase territorial control, notably through the eviction of police officers and the systematic murder of state officials (councillors, mayors, and members of the judiciary) (259–262).[6] The FARC's aim was not only to expand its military power but to replace the state and thus seek "the recognition of belligerence by presenting itself as the true power in much of the south of the country" (Aguilera Peña, 2014, p. 266).[7]

The FARC's Organisation

A vertical and closed organisational structure was one of the main reasons the FARC lasted so long (Guitiérrez Sanín, 2008). Since its inception, the insurgent group has operated as an organised army, including military units distributed in marginalised zones far from urban centres. Surprisingly, for more than five decades, the FARC's leaders managed to maintain a clear command line and a strict disciplinary code (Brittain, 2010). The organisation had strict internal regulations that covered all aspects of the combatants' daily lives. Desertion and personal enrichment were severely punished. FARC members did not receive a salary; the organisation covered basic needs.

The FARC's organisational structure was divided into directional, political, and military bodies. The "National Secretariat of the Central Governing Council" (NSC) was the highest coordination unit, made up of seven permanent members. The NSC was responsible for determining the organisation's guidelines as well as being the direct and authorised interlocutor in peace negotiations. The "Central High Command" (CHC) was the next in the chain of command, responsible for choosing the members of the secretariat. The subsequent lower levels included the regional divisions (*bloques*), military fronts (*frentes*), columns, companies, guerrillas, and squads. To receive ideological and political 'training', the insurgents were divided into 12-member cells (i.e., squads).

In September 2017, before more than 1,000 delegates, the new FARC-PP statutes were established. The FARC-PP is composed of demobilised FARC members (now called "militants") who joined the organisation voluntarily. Militants have the right to renounce the party at any time. Following the verticality of its former organisation, the structure of the FARC-PP consists of a series of councils and assemblies ranging from the local to the national, from the "*Comunes*" basic unit (composed of five militants) to the "National Assembly of the *Comunes*" (NAC). The NAC, which replaced the CHC, is the highest instance of FARC-PP leadership and oversees choosing the 15-member "*National Political Council*" (*NPC*). The latter, which replaced the NCS, is the main body responsible for institutional relations and the establishment of internal regulations. The majority of the former FARC's secretariat is in the NPC.

The FARC-PP's Political Agenda

While the FARC-PP leadership has tried to leave behind many of the organisation's original positions, it has also sought to maintain several features. On the one hand, the FARC-PP, as reflected not only in its statutes but also in the FAP, ceded ground on several of its "immovable" demands: not opposing private property, accepting democracy, and recognising responsibility in the war. On the other hand, the FARC-PP's entrance into formal politics has not meant the abandonment of its historical demands: the need to constitute a transitional government, achieve social justice, and reduce inequalities (FARC-PP, 2017).

Thus, the FARC-PP is at a critical point not only due to external factors (change of government, strengthening of non-state armed actors, delays in the fulfilment of the FAP, the murder of more than 100 FARC-PP members) but also due to intrinsic elements. Although the FARC-PP leadership has fulfilled its commitment to abandon armed struggle, its first adverse experience in the legislative elections shows the consequences of having privileged military interests (including obtaining resources) over politics. The decision to maintain the FARC acronym sent a message to the public that there has been no real reflection on past violations and abuses. Meanwhile, at the national level, the FARC-PP is increasingly absent from public agendas, and not only due to changes in the national administration. Although opponents of the FAP continue to use the FARC topic to strengthen their political and economic interests, the everyday problems of millions of Colombians (e.g., crime, corruption, unemployment, and the massive immigration of Venezuelans) now occupy the agenda.

After Armed Conflict: The FARC's Challenges

After having demobilised 13,049 members (including soldiers, militiamen, and prisoners) and handed over more than 8,000 weapons, the new FARC-PP was formed (UNSG, 2019). Within the framework of the FAP, the new party is entitled to ten seats in the National Congress for a period of eight years and can also participate in national and regional elections. And the FARC-PP did indeed present candidates for the 2018 presidential and congressional elections, confirming the decision to participate in democratic politics; n.b., many of the candidates were former FARC leaders (Serrano, 2019). Most Colombians, however, were not ready to forget the FARC's past: its candidates faced violent attacks (which led to the suspension of the FARC-PP's campaign); the FARC-PP only received 0.34% of the votes for Congress (even in FARC 'strongholds'); and the principal opponent of the peace deal, the Uribe-led Democratic Centre (DCP), became the largest party in Congress. This electoral defeat was the beginning of a series of events that have endangered the future of both the FARC-PP and the peace agreement.

The National Level

The FARC-PP's leaders have faced drastic changes in Colombia's political scene. In August 2018, the DCP candidate and a leading voice of the 'No campaign', Ivan Duque, won the presidential elections, notably by promising to reform the most controversial components of the FAP, including the political and legal guarantees granted to FARC members. Although Duque has softened his language against the FAP (due to foreign pressure) (UNSG, 2019, para. 1), the FARC-PP and other opposition parties have denounced a lack of financial support to implement the agreements (e.g., finances are lacking for collective reintegration, transitional justice, and voluntary coca crop replacement programmes) (Herrera Duran, 2019; International Crisis Group, 2018, p. 3).

Conflicts within the FARC are also affecting the implementation of the FAP. Although these tensions are not new (Asmann, 2017; Las2orillas, 2018), the arrest on drug trafficking charges (and a US extradition request) of FARC party leader and designated congressman Zeuxis Pausias "Jesus Santrich" Hernández Solarte has brought the FARC's internal divisions to the fore.[8] In fact, two opposing lines within the party can be observed. While the FARC's political branch, led by Rodrigo 'Timochenko' Londoño Echeverri, former chief commander and party president, made an appeal for calm and stressed the need to comply with the Constitution and the FAP, the FARC's 'hardliners' said that they would not recognise the judicial decision and demanded the immediate release of Santrich (El Tiempo, 2018a). Unsurprisingly, the head of the FARC's peace delegation, Luciano "Iván Márquez" Santrich, and former commanders who belonged to a more radical faction of the FARC are now part of the latter group. As a result, Marquez resigned from his seat in the Senate and went into hiding, notably to avoid a potential US arrest warrant. Other FARC leaders have left their demobilisation zones, and their whereabouts are unknown. Although neither Márquez nor key former commanders have publicly renounced reintegration programmes, their continued criticism of the FAP's implementation and their absence from democratic politics raise concerns about their possible collaboration with violent dissident groups (Clavel, 2018; La Silla Vacía, 2018).

During the negotiations, over 800 FARC members left the organisation. Since the signing of the FAP, this 'splintering" has increased significantly; today, about 1,749 former fighters are in 19 dissident groups (El Tiempo, 2018b). Although many of these former FARC members were associated with the cocaine trade and thus have ties to the business and conflicting allegiances and interests, the departures are also the result of dissatisfaction with the FAP's implementation and the lack of lawful work opportunities for former combatants (Posada, 2018; The New York Times, 2018). Following the FARC's former methods, the splinter groups purchase, manufacture, and traffic drugs, all while seeking to consolidate political and territorial control (International Crisis Group, 2017, pp. 3–4). To do so, they use "low-level' military tactics: bombs, ambushes against security forces, and the assassination of remaining FARC members. These splinter groups do not operate under one line of command, but they do coordinate their actions, especially with regard to political and economic governance (Fundación Ideas para la Paz, 2018a).

The FARC-PP 'on the Ground'

The FARC-PP's challenges are several: FAP implementation delays, electoral failures and low popular support, internal divisions, and the formation of violent dissident groups. These difficulties mean the FARC-PP's future is uncertain. This, in consequence, makes the FARC-PP's 'foot soldiers' and mid-level commanders' despair. Ex-combatants face a series of problems: delayed social integration programmes, little full-time work, and pressure from violent groups (UNSG, 2018a, 2018b, 2019). This strains ex-combatants' reintegration and makes armed group enlistment an attractive alternative. Today, over 55% of lower-ranking FARC-PP members have left the group's territorial areas (El Pais, 2018). Although this does not necessarily mean they abandoned the demobilisation process, neither the GOC nor the FARC-PP knows these persons' whereabouts.

To the extent that FARC-PP leaders and mid- and low-level members are increasingly estranged, the FARC-PP's leadership also bears responsibility for the poor reintegration process (Fundación Ideas para la Paz, 2018b, p. 8). Those on the FARC-PP's lowest rungs argue that while they face threats and murder attempts, their leaders enjoy the benefits of peace. Notable here is the fact that the FAP did not include special treatment for mid-level FARC officials, giving them little incentive to participate in the peace process (Fundación Ideas para la Paz, 2018b, p. 35). In September 2018, for example, six mid-level FARC-PP officers abandoned their reintegration pregame, effectively abandoning the 1,500 former combatants who were under their command (UNSG, 2018b, p. 7).

Before the FAP and the pacification of the FARC, the guerrilla's life was fully regulated, and non-compliance was punished severely (Guitiérrez Sanín, 2008, p. 13). Within the FARC-PP, discipline is harder to maintain. As one FARC-PP senator put it, "it is difficult to exercise that control because we all have permission to move around the national territory … . We are no longer a hierarchical military organisation, but a political organization composed of citizens" (Quintero, 2018).[9] The FARC-PP's 'card-carrying members' are free to leave the organisation.

Still, it is too early to talk of FARC-PP defection *en masse*; most of the demobilised continue to receive a monthly stipend via reintegration programmes and remain committed to the FAP (Semana, 2019; UNSG, 2018a, para. 20). History suggests that mass defections are unlikely. Previous guerrilla demobilisations in Colombia suggest that after beginning their transition to civilian life, former fighters generally try to avoid the hardships of war. The emergence of new violent groups and their significant growth are an omen. If the socio-economic conditions of the regions are not improved and the reintegration process does not offer a sustainable and durable option for former fighters, the level of violence could increase further.

The Ambiguous Role of the USG in the FAP

The USG framed its involvement in the Colombian war first within the war on communism, then the war on drugs, and finally the (global) war on terrorism. In the framework of Plan Colombia (2000–2016), the GOC received more than 10.4 billion USD. With its Marxist-Leninist dogma, its participation in narcotics trafficking, and its killing of non-combatants at various periods, the FARC could have been considered a logical target of these three 'wars'. This said, the GOC also made sure to (re)define the conflict so that it was always in line with the USG's strategic goals. Under 'Plan Colombia', Colombian guerrillas (particularly the FARC) were labelled a 'narco-terrorist' organisation (Leech, 2011, p. 80). Less convincingly, USG officials suggest the FARC was a major 'international' threat, comparable to al-Qaeda (Tate, 2004, p. 73). Under this rationale (and at a great humanitarian cost), the USG helped weaken the FARC and give the GOC a military advantage (Rojas, 2017, p. 40). As such, the USG's participation in the war eventually resulted in the FARC's leaders accepting a peace agreement.

Although the USG played a discreet role in Havana, it did support the peace negotiations (El Pais, 2016; Rojas, 2017, p. 41; Segura & Mechoulan, 2017, p. 25). The USG apparently made concessions, such as not requesting the extradition of certain FARC members for drug trafficking charges, possibly expecting that the FARC would exit the drug business and provide information on the coca trade. The USG's approval in 2017 of a second aid package, called *Paz Colombia*, of 450 million USD also demonstrates the USG's support for the FAP. Although the US leaders continue to emphasise anti-narcotics as a main goal, *Paz Colombia* includes projects designed to strengthen the GOC's presence in historically 'abandoned' areas as well as programmes aimed at assisting war victims (Isacson, 2016).

These projects should not be interpreted as marking a shift in the USG's attitude towards the FARC. The FARC remains on the USG's list of foreign terrorist organisations (FTO), mostly because the FARC-PP has not complied with the FAP (e.g., the FARC-PP's alleged continuation in the drug business).[10] In addition, the US Drug Enforcement Agency's (DEA) involvement in the investigation and arrest of a prominent FARC-PP member on drug trafficking charges (mentioned above) has complicated relations between the GOC and the FARC-PP. The exponential increase in illicit crops, the emergence of FARC dissident groups linked to this business, and the Duque administration's hard line against the FARC-PP all suggest that the USG will maintain its current FARC policy.

A Fragmented Peace

Colombia has hosted not only one of the longest armed conflicts in the Western Hemisphere but also three decades of peace negotiations (Lopez, 2016, p. 22). Due to the diversity of the warring parties and the dynamics of the war, not a single negotiation included all the actors. Between 1982 and 2018, 12 peace processes were carried out, nine of which concluded with peace agreements. While acknowledging the demobilisation of approximately 50,000 combatants that resulted from these negotiations (and thus the incalculable number of lives saved), it is also important that scholars of conflict in Colombia acknowledge that the "fragmented peace" has in fact been a "continuous war" (Sánchez Gómez, 2001, p. 27).

The FAP is a clear example of this. While the FARC's official withdrawal from the armed conflict has helped reduce serious abuses and atrocities, it has also unleashed a series of micro-conflicts. Most notable here is the emergence and strengthening of non-state groups (including FARC-PP dissidents) in territories previously controlled by the FARC. Flaws in the demobilisation process (including the murder of more than 100 former FARC combatants) and uncertainty over the GOC's fulfilment of the FAP have made these guerrilla splinter groups attractive to potential recruits. So, instead of having an organised structure like the FARC, one finds a plethora of autonomous insurgent groups and criminal enterprises, some of which are more radical and violent than the FARC ever was (HRW, 2018). Conscious of the threat that former FARC members face and the difficult situation this creates for them, Duque created a police force in 2019 charged with investigating the murder of former FARC members (Rueda, 2019; Serrano, 2019).

A second consequence of the FARC's pacification has been the breakdown of the FARC's territorial and economic governance (International Crisis Group, 2017, p. 12). In former FARC strongholds, a major reconfiguration of authority is underway, with significant consequences for local inhabitants. Although the GOC has tried to control these regions and thwart the expansion of violent armed groups, the effective and legitimate regulation of force remains divided (Fundación Paz y Reconciliación y CLACSO, 2017, pp. 28–29).

From 2012–2017, violence associated with the FARC *decreased* significantly in several regions, not only regarding homicide rates but also for other crimes such as kidnapping, forced displacement, and the use of anti-personnel mines. This said, in 2018, the national homicide rate increased in comparison to 2017, and in over 160 former-FARC municipalities located in northern Columbia, the number of homicides increased by 30% compared to 2016 (Chaparro, 2019; Fundación Paz y Reconciliación y CLACSO, 2017, Chapter 2).

Global cocaine consumption makes peace less secure. Since 2013, the surface area of Colombian land used for coca bush cultivation has increased, diminishing in the east but increasing in the south (UNODC, 2019, pp. 13–16). In fact, in 2017, the cultivation of coca leaves and the production of cocaine in Colombia reached record highs. These illicit actions generally take place in isolated villages run by corrupt officials far from major cities. Local farmers, consequently, can earn much more money than they would through licit types of farming, but they are also more vulnerable to threats and violence from newly founded criminal enterprises (ibid., pp. 15–16). In these areas, the growth of illicit economies and the ongoing ostracism of the rural population make lasting peace unlikely. In sum, peace is in danger in both the north and south of Colombia.

CONCLUSIONS

This chapter provided a succinct account of the FARC, from its emergence in the 1960s until its demobilisation in 2017. A guerrilla group that in its first years seemed bound to fail, the FARC endured and, in fact, became one of the most influential non-state armed groups worldwide. Two main factors ensured decades of resilience: participation in the cocaine market and internal discipline. On the other hand, this chapter also showed how prioritising military goals over political goals was one of the FARC's biggest blunders. Grave and ongoing violence against civilians, as well as increased participation in drug trafficking, led to a loss of popular support. These activities also gave the GOC a justification to wage war against the guerrilla group and its (alleged) allies. The consequences of this armed conflict were disastrous for both the FARC and civilians in Colombia. While the former was ostensibly weakened, civilians, mainly in rural areas, suffered even more.

During this 'non-international war', several Colombian administrations tried to conduct peace negotiations with the FARC. They all failed. The emergence of pro-government paramilitaries and the FARC's abandonment of its political agenda made compromise impossible. Several years had to pass before the parties to the conflict realised that only negotiation could truly put an end to organised armed conflict. And yet, the peace process, despite all its complications, would not be the FARC-PP's greatest challenge. Assassinated demobilised soldiers, internal divisions and splinter groups, electoral defeat, the peace agreement questioned: the 'post-conflict' phase for the FARC can be characterised as a series of failures.

The question, then, is whether the FARC's failures will lead to the disintegration of the political party and even the failure of *the demobilisation process*. On the one hand, the FARC's demobilisation seems irreversible, if only because many arms, weapons, and other resources have been relinquished. Likewise, some former guerrillas have demobilised and started to live a civilian life. Those who have forged families will hardly remember the hardships of war. Thus, although some demobilised members will continue to join FARC splinter groups and other armed groups, and although small arms and light weapons are easily acquired, the FARC-PP is unlikely to become an armed group again and has little chance of becoming the significant military organisation it once was.

Moreover, the GOC will officially approve the reincorporation process. The political and international costs of undoing this process would be too high. While the Duque administration seems hesitant concerning the peace agreement (in March 2019, Dunque tried, unsuccessfully, to have the transitional justice legal framework changed), the president has reiterated his support for former guerrillas who remain within the framework of legality (Presidencia de la Republica, 2018; Serrano, 2019). But seeing that the GOC has proposed reductions in resources for reintegration programmes, such support may only be symbolic.

The future of the FARC as a political party is even more uncertain. Although internal divisions have ostensibly increased in number and significance, the FARC-PP's greatest weakness remains its lack of popular support. The FARC-PP decision to *maintain its acronym* and to appoint previous leaders (responsible for human rights violations) as members of Congress meant the FARC-PP could not attract new supporters. The fact that FARC members have not served time in jail and, in fact, have started political careers contributes significantly to the party's poor 2018 election results. In 2019, the FARC will seek to participate in the regional elections and form a coalition with other political parties. This is not guaranteed. Other parties, particularly communist parties, are unlikely to bear the political expenses of such a combination. A FARC without armaments and engaged in nonviolent politics was the ideal scenario; such co-option was one of the peace process's key goals. However, given internal conflicts and poor political manoeuvring, this calm conclusion is unlikely to last. Instead, the FARC-PP may cease to exist and be replaced by smaller, more dangerous factions.

Notes

1 Seventh Guerrilla Conference, May 4–8, 1982 During this conference, the FARC adopted the term EP *Ejército del Pueblo* (People´s Army), reflecting their new strategy.

2 The FAP establishes a model of transitional justice in which those who are guilty of crimes under international law voluntarily resort to the Special Jurisdiction for Peace and contribute to the truth and reparation of victims. In return, they receive 'alternative' sentences (between five and eight years).
3 From the beginning of the peace process (August 2012) to November 2017, approximately 3,000 combatant and civilian lives were saved (El Tiempo, 2017).
4 For example, the FARC regulated aspects that went from personal image and sexual conduct to legal and illegal economic activities (Arjona, 2014, p. 1373).
5 For an account that demonstrates the agency of local actors during civil wars and even the manipulation of political organisations by these actors, see Kalyvas (2006).
6 In 2002, for example, police forces were absent in 15% of municipalities, and this was mostly due to the recurrent FARC attacks (Aguilera Peña, 2014, p. 261).
7 Translated by the authors.
8 On May 29, 2019, the Colombian Supreme Court issued an order for Santrich's release, contending that since the former rebel has congressional status, the Supreme Court should hear his case. The leader of the FARC will continue to be investigated for the drug trafficking charges allegedly committed *after* the signing of the peace agreement.
9 Translated by the authors.
10 Beyond the political implications, by keeping the FARC on the terrorist list, all organisations and individuals in the US are forbidden from providing any type of financial assistance to Colombian demobilisation programmes.

References

Aguilera Peña, M. (2013). Las FARC: Auge y quiebre del modelo de guerra. *Análisis Político, 77*(Enero-Abril), 85–111.

Aguilera Peña, M. (2014). *Guerrilla y población civil Trayectoria de las FARC 1949–2013* (Centro de Memoria Histórica, Ed.). Bogotá: Imprenta Nacional de Colombia.

Arjona, A. (2014). Wartime institutions: A research agenda. *Journal of Conflict Resolution, 58*(8), 1360–1389. 10.1177/0022002714547904

Asmann, P. (2017). FARC entrance to Colombia's political arena haunted by Guerrillas' Past. Retrieved August 20, 2012, from insight crime website: https://www.insightcrime.org/news/brief/farc-entrance-colombia-political-arena-haunted-guerrillas-past/

Brittain, J.J. (2010). *Revolutionary social change in Colombia: The origin and direction of the FARC-EP.* 10.2307/j.ctt183p53g

Broderick, W. (2000). *El guerrilero invisible.* Bogotá: Intermedio.

Capone, F. (2017). From the justice and peace law to the revised peace agreement between the Colombian Government and the FARC: Will victim's rights be satisfied at last? *Zeitschrift Für Ausländisches Öffentliches Recht Und Völkerrecht, 77*, 125–160.

Chaparro, M. (2019). Bitter fight for former FARC areas drives surge in Colombia homicides.

Clavel, T. (2018). Is the FARC political experiment dead in the water? Retrieved December 12, 2018, from Insight Crime website: https://www.insightcrime.org/news/analysis/farc-political-experiment-dead/

CNMH. (2013).*¡Basta ya! Colombia: Memorias de guerra y dignidad.* Bogotá.

DCP. (2012). Caguán 10 años: más allá de un proceso de paz-Relatoria de evento. *Documentos Del Departamento De Ciencia Política.* Bogotá: Ediciones Uniandes.

de Boer, J., Garzón-Vergara, J.C., & Bosetti, L. (2017). Criminal agendas and peace negotiations: The case of Colombia. *Crime-Conflict Nexus Series, 6*(April), 1–22.

Dudley, S. (2008). *Armas y Urnas: Historia de un genocidio político.* Bogotá: Planeta.

Duncan, G. (2006). *Los señores de la guerra: de paramilitares, mafiosos y autodefensas en Colombia.* Retrieved from https://books.google.co.uk/books/about/Los_señores_de_la_guerra.html?id=sn5sAAAAMAAJ&redir_esc=y

El Pais. (2016). Estados Unidos apuesta por la paz de Santos.

El Pais. (2018). El 55% de los exguerrilleros de las Farc han abandonado las zonas veredales.

El Tiempo. (2017). *Muertes por conflicto bajaron de casi 3.000 en el 2002 a cero este año.* p. 3A. Retrieved from https://www.eltiempo.com/justicia/conflicto-y-narcotrafico/el-cerac-dice-que-las-muertes-por-el-conflicto-bajaron-en-el-2017-152744

El Tiempo. (2018a). En la Farc preocupa que Márquez dé mensaje distinto al de Timochenko. Retrieved January 3, 2019, from https://www.eltiempo.com/politica/proceso-de-paz/alarma-en-farc-por-mensajes-cruzados-entre-marquez-y-timochenko-por-caso-santrich-208780

El Tiempo. (2018b, December 21). *Los ejércitos ilegales que enfrentará la nueva cúpula militar.*

FARC-EP. (1982). *Ley 001 de Reforma Agraria Revolucionaria.* Retrieved from http://www.cedema.org/ver.php?id=5627

FARC-PP. (2017). *Estatutos de la Fuerza Alternativa Revolucionaria del Común* (pp. 1–16). pp. 1–16. Bogotá.

FIP. (2014). *Seis tesis sobre la evolución reciente del conflicto armado en Colombia.* Bogotá.

Fundación Ideas para la Paz. (2018a). *Las disidencias de las FARC: un problema en auge.* Bogotá.

Fundación Ideas para la Paz. (2018b). *Las Garantías de Seguridad: una mirada desde lo local Informe 31.* Retrieved from http://ideaspaz.org/especiales/garantias-seguridad/documentos/FIP_GarantiasSeguridad_Total_Final.pdf

Fundación Paz y Reconciliación y CLACSO. (2017). *Terminó la guerra, el postconflicto está en riesgo A un año del Acuerdo de Paz.* Retrieved from http://biblioteca.clacso.edu.ar/clacso/se/20171123092706/Termino_la_guerra.pdf

Group, I.C. (2009).*Ending Colombia's FARC conflict: Dealing the right card Latin America Report N°30.* Retrieved from https://d2071andvip0wj.cloudfront.net/30-ending-colombia-s-farc-conflict-dealing-the-right-card.pdf

Guitiérrez Sanín, F. (2008). Telling the difference: Guerrillas and paramilitaries in the Colombian war. *Politics & Society, 36*(1), 3–34. 10.1177/0032329207312181

Guitiérrez Sanín, F. (2015). *¿Una historia simple? Contribución Al Entendimiento Del Conflicto Armado En Colombia. Comisión Histórica Del Conflicto y Sus Víctimas.*, 1–43.

Herrera Duran, N. (2019). Desfinanciación de la paz, visión militarista y menos reparación en el Plan Nacional de Desarrollo. Retrieved February 2, 2019, from El Espectador website: https://colombia2020.elespectador.com/politica/desfinanciacion-de-la-paz-vision-militarista-y-menos-reparacion-en-el-plan-nacional-de

HRW. (2018). *Recycled violence abuses by FARC dissident groups in Tumaco on Colombia's pacific coast.* Retrieved from https://www.hrw.org/report/2018/12/13/recycled-violence/abuses-farc-dissident-groups-tumaco-colombias-pacific-coast

International Crisis Group. (2017). *Colombia' s Armed Groups Battle for the Spoils of Peace.* Brussels.

International Crisis Group. (2018). *Risky Business: The Duque Government's Approach to Peace in Colombia Latin America Report N°67*. Brussels.

Isacson, A. (2016). "Paz Colombia": ¿qué hay de nuevo? Retrieved December 13, 2018, from Razón Pública website: https://www.razonpublica.com/index.php/conflicto-drogas-y-paz-temas-30/9218-paz-colombia-que-hay-de-nuevo

Jaramillo, S. (2018). La posibilidad de la paz. In *Biblioteca del Proceso de Paz con las FARC-EP Tomo I Inicio del Proceso de Paz La Fase Exploratoria y el camino hacia el Acuerdo General 2010–2012* (pp. 35–57). Bogotá: Oficina del Alto Comisionado para la Paz Presidencia de la República.

Kalyvas, S. (2006). *The logic of violence in civil war*. Cambridge:Cambridge University Press.

La Silla Vacía. (2018). La Farc llega golpeada y sin saber de Márquez a su Consejo Nacional.

Las2orillas. (2018). Márquez vs Timochenko: revelaciones de una pelea a muerte. Retrieved January 4, 2019, from https://www.las2orillas.co/marquez-vs-timochenko-revelaciones-de-una-pelea-muerte/

Leech, G. (2011). *The FARC: The longest insurgency*. London and New York: Zed Books.

Lopez, C. (2016). *Adios a las FARC! Y ahora que?* https://doi.org/9789588931395

Matanock, A.M., & García-Sánchez, M. (2017). The Colombian paradox: Peace processes, elite divisions & popular plebiscites. *Daedalus, 146*(4), 152–166. 10.1162/DAED_a_00466

Pécaut, D. (2008).*Las FARC: ¿Una guerrilla sin fin o sin fines?* Bogotá: Grupo Editorial Norma.

Pizarro, E. (2017). *Cambiar el futuro: historia de los procesos de paz en Colombia (1981–2016)*. Bogotá: Penguin Random House.

Posada, J.D. (2018). FARC Dissidents Growing Faster Than Colombia Can Count.

Presidencia de la Republica. (2018). Presidente Duque reitera compromiso de apoyar a desmovilizados en su tránsito hacia la legalidad.

Provost, R. (2017). FARC Justice: Rebel Rule of Law. *UC Irvine L.Rev, 8*(227), 227–274.

Quintero, G. (2018). Excombatientes: un regreso a la vida civil en veremos. Retrieved January 5, 2019, from Semana Rural website: https://semanarural.com/web/articulo/excombatientes-un-regreso-a-la-vida-civil-en-veremos/654

Reed, M. (2010). Justicia transicional bajo fuego: Cinco reflexiones marginales sobre el caso colombiano. In *Transiciones en Contienda: Disyuntivas de la justicia Transicional en colombia desde la experiencia comparada*.

Rojas, D.M. (2017). Estados Unidos en la construcción de la paz en Colombia. *Análisis Político, 91*(Septiembre-Diciembre), 37–52.

Rueda, M. (2019). Despite the peace deal, former FARC fighters face a new war in rural Colombia. Retrieved July 28, 2019, from PRI website: https://www.pri.org/stories/2019-07-18/despite-peace-deal-former-farc-fighters-face-new-war-rural-colombia

Sánchez Gómez, G. (2001). "Introduction problems of violence, prospects for peace." In C. Bergquist, R. Penaranda, & G. Sanchez (Eds.). *Violence in Colombia, 1990–2000: Waging war and negotiating peace*. (p. 300). Washhington DC: SR Books.

Santos Calderón, J.M. (2018). "Una ofrenda para Colombia y el mundo." In Oficina Alto Comisionado para la Paz (Ed.). *Biblioteca del Proceso de Paz con las FARC-EP Tomo I Inicio del Proceso de Paz La Fase Exploratoria y el camino hacia el Acuerdo General 2010–2012*. (pp. 29–34). Bogotá: Presidencia de la República.

Segura, R., & Mechoulan, D. (2017). Made in Havana: How Colombia and the FARC decided to end the war. In *SSRN Electronic Journal*. 10.2139/ssrn.2969332

Semana. (2019, June). *En las regiones no pierden la esperanza de paz*, 9–10.

Serrano, F. (2019). Colombia's uneasy peace.

Tate, W. (2004). Alternatives to war: Colombia's peace processes. *Accord, 14*, 70–73.

The New York Times. (2018). Colombia Struck a Peace Deal With Guerrillas, but Many Return to Arms.

Universidad Nacional de Colombia. (2017). *Caracterización Comunidad FARC-EP Resultados Generales*. Bogotá.

UNODC. (2019). *World Drug Report 2019*. Vienna.

UNSG. (2018a). *Report of the Secretary-General on the United Nations Verification Mission in Colombia S/2018/279*. New York.

UNSG. (2018b). *United Nations Verification Mission in Colombia Report of the Secretary-General S/2018/874*. New York.

UNSG. (2019). *United Nations Verification Mission in Colombia Report of the Secretary-General S/2018/1159*. New York.

37

UNDERSTANDING SENDERO LUMINOSO'S PERUVIAN TERRORISM

Suzette A. Haughton and Scott N. Romaniuk

INTRODUCTION

The Shining Path, or Sendero Luminoso, emerged from the view that democracy has failed many people and that the people must fight to obtain reforms. It was this disillusionment with democracy in Peru that motivated Dr. Abimael Guzmán to lead the charge and establish Shining Path. Shining Path was therefore under the leadership of Dr. Guzmán until his capture and arrest in 1992. For revolutionaries such as Guzmán, the vision of a more egalitarian society based on the philosophy of Marxism, Leninism, and Maoism would accomplish their desired results of a true egalitarian society.

Notwithstanding Dr. Guzmán's initial intent, his movement failed to create an equalitarian system that reflected the views and interests of all Peruvians. Instead, his movement produced reformers who wanted to achieve large-scale societal change through a radicalised and militant posture. Hence, the cause that started out as a fight for justice and democracy transcended into one that used criminal activities and terrorist events in order to achieve its goals. The movement's hard-line position, its association with drug trafficking, and its involvement in terrorist activities in Peru resulted in its categorization as a foreign terrorist organisation (Sullivan, 2009).

The chapter has three broad aims. First, the chapter discusses the genesis of Sendero Luminoso as an organisation domiciled in Peru. Second, it explores Sendero Luminoso's organisational structure and how this led to its success. Finally, it assesses Sendero Luminoso's impacts on the Peruvian state and the governmental efforts used to curb this movement's terrorism.

THE GENESIS OF SENDERO LUMINOSO

The Marxist-Leninist-Maoist model formed the basis for the establishment of Sendero Luminoso's movement, which was steeped in revolutionary notions in Peru. In 1928, Peru's Communist Party (Partido Comunista Peruano) was created. It was established in Moaism, which held the view that peasants should be the centre of societal revolution. The splintering of Partido Comunista Peruvano saw the creation of Partido Communista del Peru (Patria Roja) and Partido Comunista del Peru (Bandera Roja). The Partido Comunista del Peru – Bandera Roja, a creation of Sendero Luminoso, emerged in 1970. It was believed that the Partido Comunista Peruano as well as the Partido Communista del Peru-Patria Roja betrayed the communist class struggle as these parties were not radical enough and were revisionists in their actions and views.

Sendero Luminoso established itself as a Peruvian revolutionary group by supporting Maoism, guerrilla tactics, and violent terrorism. Perhaps the first sign of Sendero Luminoso's terrorism began when the group ordered the assassination of several militants and elected officials from the other communist parties. As the movement evolved, it became one of the most dangerous terrorist groups in Latin America, often carrying out urban terrorist acts in Lima (Alexander and Pluchinsky, 2012).

Sendero Luminoso was located in the Peruvian highland peasant communities of Ayacucho province. McClintock (1984) examined the origins of Sendero Luminoso and found that this rural movement had substantial support among Indian peasant communities in Peru's southern highlands. Its support in these communities was based on the view that a peasant revolutionary regime must replace the Peruvian governmental system. For this reason, Cornell (2005) argued that Sendero Luminoso remains an ideologically motivated group led by intellectuals and university students. Despite this, it is difficult to determine if its involvement in criminality is for the purpose of obtaining capabilities to further its original goals or if such involvement is mainly for criminal aims (Brown, 1999; Makarenko,

DOI: 10.4324/9780429426063-42

2002; Makarenko, 2003; Makarenko, 2004; Cornell, 2005; Osborn, 2007).

Political and economic conditions in the Department of Ayachucho led to the establishment of Sendero Luminoso. The people residing in this department felt that they were politically marginalised by the central government in Lima. Poverty and its associated socio-economic problems were rife in Ayachucho, which was the poorest region of Peru (Stern, 1998). Despite its existing situation and its location, approximately 300 miles away from Lima, the Ayachucho region was integral to Peru's historical development. It was the site of the first pan-Andean empire called the Huari Confederation, and it was the place where the war happened, which resulted in the establishment of the Inca empire. Further, it was at Ayachucho that the final battle for the 1824 Latin American Liberation occurred (McCormick, 2008; Palmer, 1994). The Ayachucho region was therefore a historical zone marked by battle and transformation, and it is not surprising that a revolutionary group such as Sendero Luminoso would be established there.

Laqueur (2017) argued that a guerrilla war with a revolutionary aim is one in which an ethnic minority uses such a war against an existing government of a country with the intent of overthrowing the government and seizing power. Sendero Luminoso used guerrilla operations in remote regions of Peru and was known for assassinating village leaders who failed to defy the state's authority and support the group. It wanted to create an egalitarian utopian society by using guerrilla warfare to destabilise the state in its attempt to gain control. *Sendero Luminoso's* members were mainly Indians who wanted to gain power. Gaining power was an important issue for Indian peasants and Sendero Luminoso's movement since the Indian population was not culturally and economically integrated into Peruvian Hispanic culture. The Indian peasants maintained their own language, customs, and cultural practises and were feared by the large Hispanic population in Peru (Dewitt, 2015).

In addition, there was a highly inequitable land distribution system, which disenfranchised Indians. Successive governments in the 1960s and 1970s were unable to successfully address the unequal land distribution problem in a manner acceptable to the Indian people. The Indians were disenfranchised and located in Peru's central and southern Sierras. Their support for *Sendero Luminoso* allowed them to inappropriately use violence in their attempt to achieve a more just society. Their use of violence was unprecedented and ranked among the most brutal in the Western Hemisphere. The Peruvian state, under the leadership of Belande, was left with little choice but to orchestrate a military offensive against this group. To respond to the violent attacks and deaths, Hernandez and Church (2003) argued that the Peruvian government should establish an emergency response system, conduct emergency residency training programmes, and establish a dedicated trauma centre in Lima.

Dr. Abimael Guzmán is the founding father of the Shining Path, or Sendero Luminoso. He was also popularly known in Peru as Comrade Gonzolo as well as Dr. Puka Inti (Red Sun). As a Peruvian revolutionary, he believed Peruvian governments from as far back as the Spanish conquest lacked legitimacy. In his view, Sendero Luminoso was therefore an insurgency aimed at giving back power to the people through a successful people's war. For Guzmán, this people's war was important to wage against the Peruvian state in order to obtain power for Sendero Luminoso, which, in his view, meant power for the people. Further, Guzmán believed that Sendero Luminoso could generate power through a focused vision geared towards taking control from the state and placing it in Sendero Luminoso. However, as an establishment, Sendero Luminoso had to be projected through an intelligent, motivated, and disciplined organisation, inclusive of the organisation's vision and purposes and reflected in its leaders and supporters.

An important vision of Sendero Luminoso was that the Peruvian state had failed the people, and hence the state should be replaced by Sendero Luminoso. In turn, Sendero Luminoso would maintain its power when it replaced the state by providing a truly Peruvian democracy, one that represented the interests of the people. Replacing the state was central to the mission of Sendero Luminoso because Guzmán felt the state had failed the people. Hence, he wanted to dismantle Peruvian society, including the social, political, economic, and cultural facets of the state. In his view, this was the best way to rid the Peruvian state of foreign domination, which was manifested in the fabric of the entire society. He also believed this would correct the marginalisation of the Indian population, which was pushed to the periphery of society given the foreign dominance of major economic power in Peru.

In this regard, Guzmán aimed to dispel foreign political domination in Peru and replace it with a nationalistic, Indian, and popular democracy. He called for the re-establishment of a Peruvian democracy. To him, the Quechua Indian people formed the first Peruvian socialism. Sendero Luminoso intended to create a bridge between the first true Peruvian democracy and the existing government, as the government, in Guzmán's view, had missed the true meaning of democracy. Hence, Guzmán viewed Sendero Luminoso as forming the third era of democracy but the second true democracy in Peru.

The revolution was the mechanism to be used to achieve Sendero Luminoso's true democracy. Military and verbal revolutions were central to the organisation's mission and to the legitimacy of the regime. Its legitimacy was based on Guzmán's political philosophy of gaining Indian dominance through revolution. As an academic, Guzmán held a PhD in political philosophy and was an authoritative influencer because he was a former university professor in Peru. His connection in Peruvian academic circles was a significant catalyst in the germination of the idea for the establishment of Shining Path, as some top leaders of Sendero Luminoso were formerly under Guzmán's tutelage and were also educated inteligencias (Osborn, 2007).

On October 8, 1997, Sendero Luminoso was labelled a "foreign terrorist organisation." The designation was attached to Sendero Luminoso because, in the 20 years following its inception, it evolved into one of the most ruthless terrorist organisations in Latin America and the Caribbean (The United States Department of State, 2018). Manwaring (1995) identified five stages of Sendero Luminoso's evolution, starting from 1962 to the present. **Phase one,** from 1962 to 1980, was called the organisational stage. This stage laid the foundation for launching Sendero Luminoso. According to Manwaring (1995), there were three features at this stage. The first was the establishment of the movement's doctrine by Dr. Guzmán. The second was the charting of a distinct path for the leadership development of the movement. Third, it involved the formation of relationships with the poor, isolated peasant communities from the highlands surrounding the city of Ayacucho. These relationships proved to be invaluable for Sendero Luminoso as the movement evolved.

Phase two covered the years 1980–1982 and was referred to as the offensive stage of the movement. The victory of Belande in 1980 changed the Peruvian political system from 12 years of military rule to civilian rule. As civilian rule was taking shape, Sendero Luminoso began to attack important symbols of the state. It bombed governmental buildings and private businesses. It also systematically launched attacks on the state's structures and assassinated public figures. These attacks and assassinations were carried out because the leaders of Sendero Luminoso believed that such actions would ultimately lead to the movement's de facto authority in targeted sections of Peru. At times, guerrilla groups use the attack-assassination strategy to force the retreat of legitimate state forces in an attempt to create a vacuum, which is followed by the seizure of the territory and then full control of the area.

Phase three builds on Phase two, but with more extensive and continuous attacks and assassinations. This phase covered the period 1982–1983. In early 1982, Sendero Luminoso attacked the Ayacucho Department prison and released the prisoners. By December 1982, it had launched another attack on the critical infrastructure of the state by destroying high-tension power lines on Lima's electrical grid. This resulted in a blackout in Lima and six other cities in Peru. This phase was also marked by assassinations and death threats against key state personnel and officials in an attempt to cripple the state's institutions. To carry out its threats, Sendero Luminoso has a specific modus operandi, which involves communicating the threat, acting on it, and setting an example through the use of violence to signal to others who oppose or betray the movement that the consequences may be deadly. A zone of liberation is declared once Sendero Luminoso enters an area. This zone of liberation signifies the control Sendero Luminoso has over the area. Thereafter, an informal court system is established where community leaders, administrators, and traitors of the movement are tried before they are shot to death or badly beaten, depending on the severity of their offences. After a trial, a new list is published, sometimes in *El Diario*, Sendero Luminoso's newspaper, for the next round of trials. People on the list often flee out of fear, after which Sendero Luminoso reinforces its control in the community given the absence of the state's community leaders.

Phase four runs from the latter part of 1983 to the present and is referred to as the consolidation of the political and logistic foundations establishing Sendero Luminoso's influence throughout Peru. By 1993, it had a presence in 114 provinces across Peru, including the *Huallaga Valley*, a region located 200 miles northeast of Lima and noted for 60% of the coca bush cultivation, which is used to produce cocaine (McClintock, 1988). There are two implications of Sendero Luminoso's consolidation of its reach in so many provinces. First, it diminished the Peruvian government's legitimate control over the coastal departments and the large cities. Secondly, it gave Sendero Luminoso a strategic advantage from which to launch an occupation of the capital city since it controlled some surrounding provinces around Lima.

Although Peru has five active terrorist organisations, Sendero Luminoso remains the largest and most disruptive to the security of the Peruvian state. It is rooted in an organisational and ideological premise that reflects Andean theology coupled with political Maoist doctrines, which created a large-scale appeal to Andean provincialism. Notably, Sendero Luminoso uses political violence such as murder, arson, and bombings to achieve its goals. McCormick (2008) noted that Sendero Luminoso was unmatched in the manner in which it indiscriminately uses violence as a terrorist organisation, and this has resulted in approximately 10,000 deaths from 12,000 terrorist actions (McCormick, 2008). Likewise, Galdo (2013) has referred to Sendero Luminoso as "one of the world's deadliest terrorist groups" (Galdo, 2013: 792).

In order to be an effective producer of violence, Guzmán had to create a solid organisational structure. The subsequent section discusses the functional structure of Sendero Luminoso.

LEADERSHIP, STRUCTURE, CHANGE, AND OPERATIONS

Leadership and management formed an important part of Sendero Luminoso's philosophy, and Guzmán was a strong, charismatic leader. He hated the Peruvian leadership, which he saw as weak and unable to properly organise society since they did not function as a representation of the people. Guzmán saw himself not only as a revolutionary who was fighting to end the struggles for the Indian community in Peru but also as a global revolutionary fighting for minorities and Indians elsewhere in the world. As originally conceived, Sendero Luminoso's operations were specifically restricted to Peruvian society. However, its philosophy could have widely resonated with Indian communities and minority groups across the entire Latin American and Caribbean region and possibly other regions of the world. To achieve the group's vision, members of Sendero Luminoso were required to pledge allegiance to the organisation and to Guzmán, saying that they would sacrifice their lives for the success of the world revolution.

Succession planning was not a foreign idea for Sendero Luminoso, as Guzmán had a number of trained and trusted leaders who could carry on the cause and legacy of the organisation. The section below discusses the role played by some top-ranking leaders who contributed to the functioning of Sendero Luminoso after Guzmán's demise.

OTHER LEADERS OF SENDERO LUMINOSO

The USA Department of Treasury has classified Sendero Luminoso as a Peruvian criminal narco-terrorist group and has identified some of Sendero Luminoso's top leaders. They are Oscar Ramirez Duran, Victor Quispe Palomino, Jorge Quispe Palomino, and Florindo Eleuterio Flores Hala.

Oscar Ramirez Duran, or Comarade Feliciano, immediately took charge of Sendero Luminoso following Guzmán's capture in 1992. Comrade Feliciano had tertiary-level training, having studied at the Arequipa College of Saint Francis of Assisi in Peru. His leadership of Sendero Luminoso was short-lived, as he was captured seven years later, in 1999, and sentenced to life imprisonment for his contribution to Sendero Luminoso's conflicts in Peru. Since his arrest, he has changed his communist views, lost faith in Guzmán, and testified against Florindo Eleuterio Flores Hala, another top-ranking Sendero Luminoso leader.

Like Comrade Feliciano, Victor Quispe Palomino is another Sendero Luminoso leader. He was widely known as Comrade Jose or Comrade Martin. He studied at the Peruvian state university, Cristobal of Huamanga University, situated in the city of Ayacucho. This university was critical to the formation of Sendero Luminoso, as Guzmán was a professor at the university and a number of the organisation's members studied at this institution. It was therefore at this university that the Maoist ideology to establish Sendero Luminoso germinated and bore fruit.

Apart from Comrade Jose's association with the Peruvian State University, he had a long connection with Sendero Luminoso, as his parents were members. His mother was arrested and his father killed after they participated in Sendero Luminoso's patrols, referred to as *Rondas Campesinas*. Like his parents, Comrade Jose conducted militant Sendero Luminoso's activities, such as the *Lucanamarca massacre*, which resulted in the deaths of 69 Indian peasants (Throssell, 2006). Comrade Jose was also involved in commanding and training Sendero Luminoso's soldiers, some of whom were child soldiers.

Jorge Quispe Palomino, Comrade Jose's brother, was a significant member of the Sendero Luminoso leadership. Both brothers were designated as international terrorists under Executive Order 13224 of the US Department of State, and on June 1, 2015, the US Department of Treasury specifically designated them as drug traffickers under the Foreign Narcotics Kingpin Designation Act (The United States Department of State, 2016). Because Victor and Jorge Quispe Palomino were both considered essential to the terrorist group Sendero Luminoso, the US Department of State offered a substantial USD five million reward for information that would result in their capture. The Palomino brothers are thought to have collaborated on numerous Sendero Luminoso attacks. For instance, Victor Quispe Palomino murdered 69 people, including men, women, and children, in Lucanamarca, Peru, in April 1983, and Jorge Quispe Palomino murdered two Peruvian police officers in the Ayacucho attack in October 2014 (The United States Department of State, 2016).

Florindo Eleuterio Flores-Hala, or Comrade Artemio, was a leader of the Huallaga Valley Sendero Luminoso until his arrest in February 2012. Under his watch, Sendero Luminoso carried out murder, extortion, bribery, and drug trafficking. Sullivan (2009) noted that the leftist Revolutionary Armed Forces of Colombia (FARC) established drug trafficking connections and continued to fund coca cultivation and cocaine production in Peru. The charging of fees for drug traffickers to land aircraft and transport drugs to Colombia on route to the USA was one of the main sources for funding Sendero Luminoso's operations (Cornell, 2005; Kay, 1999; Tarazona-Sevillano and Reuter, 1990; and Palmer, 1992). The other crimes, namely extortion and bribery, were committed in order to supplement Sendero Luminoso's drug trafficking funds. In addition, state officials were murdered, including government personnel and members of the National Police, as they were deemed a threat to Sendero Luminoso's organisation and philosophy (The United States Department of State, 2019). Finally, it is believed that Tarcela Loya Vilchez, or Comrade Olga, led Sendero Luminoso jointly with Victor and Jorge Quispe Palomino. Their terrorist acts were geared towards ousting the legitimate Peruvian government, which they wanted to replace with Sendero Luminoso (The United States Department of State, 2019).

Sendero Luminoso's philosophy was executed through a well-organised structure. The organisation's structure reflected a hybrid of divisional and functional structures. The functional structure grouped the organisation's parts based on their functions. The divisional structure facilitates smaller sections within the wider umbrella organisation and spans a large geographic area. The structure included

Guzmán but was supported by a dedicated set of personnel who were true to Sendero Luminoso's mission. Guzmán established a central machinery, including a revolutionary party, a guerrilla army, and a well-oiled support team to work alongside the party, the army, and the entire organisation.

The organisation was designed internally and externally in a manner to foster its success. Internally, Sendero Luminoso was headed by a National Central Committee. This committee was controlled by key high-ranking officials, including Dr. Guzmán, and was supported by six regional committees. These regional committees were the Northern, Central, Southern, Primary, Eastern, and Metropolitan Committees. Each committee had some level of autonomy, although they were subjected to the regulations and dictates of the National Central Committee. All committees except the Metropolitan Committee comprised varying departments, districts, provinces, zones, sectors, and cells. However, the Metropolitan Committee only included Lima and Callao because of their extensive populations.

Regional Committees were charged with the responsibility of planning, executing, and communicating the activities of Sendero Luminoso in their respective districts and provinces. They were also supposed to plan and execute military operations across the departments, districts, provinces, zones, sectors, and cells. Regional committees had regional commanders who had control over determining when to use force. They made calculations concerning targets, the possibility of success, as well as the location and time to launch an attack. This coordinated approach, in the execution of duties and military planning, increased the efficiency and effectiveness of the daily operations of the Regional Committees.

The coordination between regional committees and the National Central Committee was evidenced by the effective execution of varying annual military celebrations. Some of these operations include military manoeuvres on December 4 in celebration of Dr. Guzmán's birthday and at the Independence Day celebration on July 28 as well as on June 19 to celebrate the lives of the 256 Sendero Luminoso militants who died in the prison uprisings at *El Fronton* and *Lurigancho*.

TRAINING AND ATTACKS

The modus operandi of Sendero Luminoso is to move into a village and establish a revolutionary government and a school. In Sendero Luminoso's philosophy, the reason for reforming the government is to make changes to society. The purpose of the school's establishment is to educate the peasants and equip them with basic literacy and numeracy skills. This education is also used as a basis to transmit Sendero Luminoso's ideologies to the people. At the school, teachers also operate in the capacity of recruiters as they vet students and determine their suitability as potential recruits for membership in Sendero Luminoso (Smith, 1995).

Recruitment is a central part of Sendero Luminoso's strategy. By targeting potential recruits from the school, Sendero Luminoso carefully orchestrates a movement that is hostile to external penetration. Recruits are required to spend 12 months in training designed to support Sendero Luminoso's movement, such as obtaining political indoctrination and conducting propaganda activities. Training and practise of guerrilla strategy are major parts of the school's curriculum for Sendero Luminoso's recruits. This training is further supported by firearms use and the detonation of explosive devices. In addition, recruits obtain physical training, as exercising to maintain fitness is emphasised by the school (Smith, 1995).

After completion of the training, the recruits graduate as full members of Sendero Luminoso and are assigned to terrorist cells within the organisation. These members form Sendero Luminoso's active cadre of terrorist fighters, where they engage in military warfare against government forces, peasants, and other terrorist groups, such as Tupac Amaru collaborators.

Sendero Luminoso does not benefit from external training operations for the training of its recruits. It advocates the principle of self-sufficiency in this regard and hence uses internal training. This strategy was also central to the preservation of the security of the movement, as it prevents impenetrability from outside forces that might aim to infiltrate the group in order to dismantle it.

Ash (1985) refers to Sendero Luminoso as a terrorist revolutionary group that uses terror tactics to generate compliance and crush opponents. People who refuse to align with Sendero Luminoso and who are likely to inform the government about guerrilla activities and plans are at the greatest risk of attack from Sendero Luminoso. In 1983, it was estimated that between 1500 and 2700 Peruvians died and approximately 6,000 disappeared in the Sendero Luminoso-Peruvian Government warfare. It is believed that the dead "senderistas" were people whom Sendero Luminoso surmised to be government sympathisers. The 6,000 "desaparecidoes," or the ones who disappeared, were part of the Sendero Luminoso cadre who took up responsibilities in the group but remained underground to remain off the government watch list (Ash, 1985).

Sendero Luminoso's violent terrorism against the Peruvian state includes bombings, assassinations, and guerrilla attacks. Gupta (2005) has argued that Sendero Luminoso prefers to carry out its violent terrorist acts using bombings, shootings, and kidnappings. Violence was a central fabric of Sendero Luminoso's philosophy and was incorporated as a means to achieve Sendero Luminoso's goals. Sendero Luminoso's fighters were brainwashed into believing that death in combat was justified to achieve the group's mission.

Peru's continuous bloody conflict with Sendero Luminoso began in May 1980 and resulted in the deaths of 70,000 Peruvians. Since the year 2000, however, the death toll resulting from this conflict has significantly diminished. However, from 2002 to 2014, there was a resurgence of Sendero Luminoso's violence directed at the Peruvian state and civilians. In 2013, Sendero Luminoso conducted 50 terrorist attacks in the Apurimac, Ene, and Mantaro River Valleys. In response to these attacks, the Peruvian authorities declared the entire region, including Ayacucho, Cusco, Huancavelica, Huanuco, and Junin, an emergency zone. In October 2014, the Peruvian government claimed that Sendero Luminoso carried out 18 terrorist acts that killed two Peruvian soldiers and two civilians. However, these terrorist acts injured six soldiers, seven civilians, and one police officer. Likewise, in 2015, Sendero Luminoso killed two soldiers and three civilians, injuring seven police officers (Global Security, 2019).

Given its robust organisation and structure, the Peruvian government had to penetrate Sendero Luminoso through the law and special operations as a means of curtailing the group's power and reducing its violent activities against the state's citizens.

COUNTERING SENDERO LUMINOSO'S TERRORISM

A new Peruvian Constitution was ratified in 1993, and this Constitution gave the Peruvian President, Alberto Fujimori, the power to issue decrees having legal force. Prior to this, in 1992, President Fujimori reorganised his government and issued *Decree Law 25475* to stem acts of terrorism. This law provided rules concerning the arrest, detention, investigation, trial, and sentencing of individuals suspected of carrying out terrorist acts (Decree Law No. 25475, 1992). In 2017, Peru's law was amended to forbid public verbal support for terrorism by increasing punishment for those who advocate and sympathise with terrorism. The Peruvian Congress also included a new provision in the law to prevent Peruvians who have either been convicted or who supported terrorism from running for public office.

These anti-terrorism laws created a framework within which those who participated in or sympathised with the terrorist acts committed by Sendero Luminoso could be brought before Peru's military tribunal. Peru's anti-terrorism laws are intended to punish terrorists while simultaneously deterring others from engaging in terrorist activities. Chalk (2017) discusses the criminal justice and military models of counter-terrorism. He argued that Peru adopted highly repressive anti-terrorism measures under Fujimori's leadership of the country in the 1990s. However, despite these anti-terrorism laws, a 2003 Peruvian Constitutional Tribunal found that the terrorism law that convicted Sendero Luminoso fighters and leaders, such as Guzmán, was unconstitutional because the conviction was carried out in a closed military tribunal.

In addition, the Peruvian government embarked on joint police-military operations in Sendero Luminoso's dominated areas of *Apurimac, Ene*, and *Mantaro River Valleys* to apprehend terrorists. In October 2017, a joint police-military operation resulted in the arrest of 13 drug traffickers; two Sendero Luminoso terrorists were killed and eight wounded (US Department of State, 2017). However, Operation Victoria is perhaps the most important law enforcement activity undertaken by the Peruvian state to dismantle Sendero Luminoso by targeting its leadership, primarily Dr. Guzmán.

OPERATION VICTORIA

The violence perpetuated by the Sendero Luminoso's terrorist acts has negatively impacted the social, political, and economic life of the Peruvian State. The 1980s attacks carried out by Shining Path purportedly resulted in 25,000–35,000 deaths and approximately USD 200 billion in material losses. Woy-Hazleton and Hazleton (1994) have noted that in 1990, Sendero Luminoso's guerrilla war resulted in the deaths of 20,000 citizens. They also noted that the government imposed a state of emergency to quell the guerrilla war, which caused restrictions on the movement of the Peruvian population. The heavy financial costs and loss of human life have forced the Peruvian government to embark on a strategy to dismantle the group and capture its main leader, Dr. Guzmán. To this end, in April 1990, police officer Benedicto Jimenez was mandated to establish a secret unit to capture Guzmán. This undertaking became known as Operation Victoria, and despite its limited material resources, which included only one motor vehicle and four radios, it bore fruit in September 1992, when Guzmán was captured. From 1992 to the present, Sendero Luminoso witnessed changes in its top-tier leadership. These changes were in response to increased law enforcement measures, which caused leadership disruptions as Sendero Luminoso leaders were arrested. Hence, after Guzmán's arrest, other leaders, namely Oscar Ramirez Duran, Victor Quispe Palomino, Jorge Quispe Palomino, and Florindo Eleuterio Flores Hala, took charge of commanding and controlling Sendero Luminoso's terrorist activities.

The capture of Guzmán, therefore, did not dismantle the group altogether. By 2015, the Peruvian Defence Minister, Jakke Valakivi, noted that Sendero Luminoso was still in operation, although significantly weakened. Nevertheless, its membership is still strong. The Peruvian Counter-Terrorism Chief, Jose Baella, claimed in 2015 that Sendero Luminoso remains a potent terrorist organisation with 350 members and 80 fighters. This is the case despite the capture of another Shining Path leader, Comrade Artemio, in 2012. The United States Department of State (USDOS) has reported that Sendero Luminoso remains active and continues to carry out terrorist acts. The USDOS has noted that Sendero Luminoso committed 13 terrorist acts in 2015, 20 in 2014, and 49 in 2013. As of 2016, the USDOS estimated that the strength of Sendero Luminoso ranged between 250 and 300 fighters (US Department of State, 2017; Global Security, 2019).

Cornell (2005) argued that the drug trade strengthened Sendero Luminoso's military capability in such a way that it provided a formidable challenge to the stability of the Peruvian State (Cornell, 2005: 757). In addition, the USDOC has reported that the funds used to support the terrorist activities of Sendero Luminoso arise from its involvement in the illicit drug trade. Peru ranks among the three largest global producers of cocaine, with Colombia and Bolivia being the other two (United States Department of State, 2016). The World Drug Report (2018) estimated that Peru's cultivation of the cocoa bush plant, which is processed to produce cocaine, was 34,900 hectares in 2016, 40,300 in 2015, 42,900 in 2014, and 49,800 in 2013 (The World Drug Report, 2018). The large quantities of Peruvian cocaine must be understood against the background of the expansion of cocaine in demand-seeking markets in the USA and Europe. The lucrative yields from the cocaine market provide the financial resources that facilitate Sendero Luminoso's survival. Sendero Luminoso is involved in drug cultivation, distribution, and trafficking and operates in Apurimac, Ene, and the Mantaro River Valley. Its terrorist base is also located in these regions. In 2017, the Peruvian government arrested the Provincial Mayor of Tocache for financing Sendero Luminoso. It was alleged that in 2007, the mayor financed Sendero Luminoso's activities to assassinate a prosecutor and law enforcers who were investigating his connections to drug trafficking (US Department of State, 2017).

CONCLUSION

The founding father of Sendero Luminoso, Dr. Guzmán, aimed to reform Peruvian democracy through a Maoist revolution with widespread support from the Indian peasants in the highlands region of Peru. The use of death threats, assassinations, bombings, and attacks on the state's structure and institutions places Sendero Luminoso among the most violent terrorist groups in Latin America and the Caribbean.

The actions of the Peruvian state to address the challenges posed by Sendero Luminoso were swift and involved the passage of laws coupled with law enforcement operations designed to bring the members of this terrorist organisation before the criminal justice system. A number of terrorist fighters were also killed, and perhaps the state achieved a significant victory when it arrested its founding father and other top leaders in Sendero Luminoso's organisation structure. The Peruvian government's crackdown on Sendero Luminoso weakened this terrorist group by reducing its membership and geographic reach to the Peruvian coca-growing hinterlands. It also resulted in the separation of Sendero Luminoso into two smaller groups, with each group controlling a smaller area and carrying out independent violent attacks on the Peruvian state.

Nevertheless, although substantially weakened, Sendero Luminoso remains active as a terrorist group. It continues to conduct terrorist activities and threaten the stability of the Peruvian state, and it has remained on the USA's watch list of terrorist organisations.

References

Alexander, Y. & Pluchinsky, D. (2012). *Europe's red terrorists: The fighting communist organizations*. New York: Routledge.

Ash, R. (1985). Sendero Luminoso and the Peruvian crisis. *Conflict Quarterly*, *3*(5), 19–31.

Brown, C. (1999). Burma: The political economy of violence. *Disasters*, *23*(3), 234–256.

Chalk, P. (2017). "The response to terrorism as a threat to liberal democracy 1." In A. O'Day (Ed.). *War on Terrorism* (pp. 83–98). New York: Routledge.

Cornell, S.E. (2005). The interaction of narcotics and conflict. *Journal of Peace Research*, *42*(6), 751–760.

Dewitt, C.R. (2015). The rise and development of Sendero Luminoso in Peru, USA Army, US Army War College.

Decree Law No. 25475, art. 12, May 5, 1992, accessed on: http://www.congreso.gob.pe/ntley/Imagenes/Leyes/25475.pdf, retrieved on November 16, 2018.

Galdo, J. (2013). The long-run labour-market consequences of civil war: Evidence from Shining Path in Peru. *Economic Development and Cultural Change*, *61*(4), July, 789–823.

Global Security (2019). Sendero Luminoso, Shining Path (SL), https://www.globalsecurity.org/military/world/para/sendero_luminoso.htm, retrieved on May 15, 2019.

Gupta, D. (2005). "Exploring roots of terrorism." In T. Bjorgo (Ed.). *Root causes of terrorism* (pp. 34–50). New York: Routledge.

Kay, B.H. (1999). Violent opportunities: The rise and fall of "King Coca" and Shining Path. *Journal of Interamerican Studies and World Affairs*, *41*(3), 97–12.

Laqueur, W. (2017). *Guerrilla warfare: A historical and critical study*. New York: Routledge.

Makarenko, T. (2002). Crime, terror, and the Central Asian drug trade. *Harvard Asia Quarterly*, *6*(3) (fas.harvard.edu/-asiactr/haq/ 200203/0203a004.htm).

Makarenko, T. (2003). A model of terrorist- criminal relationships. *Jane's Intelligence Review*, 1 August (http://www.janes.com/jir).

Makarenko, T. (2004). The crime-terror continuum: Tracing the interplay between transnational crime and terrorism. *Global Crime*, *1*(1), 129–145.

Manwaring, M. (1995). The Shining Path beckons. *The Annals of the American Academy of Political and Social Sciences, 541*, 157–166.

McClintock, C. (1988). The war on drugs: The Peruvian case. *Journal of Interamerican Studies and World Affairs, 30*(2-3), 127–142.

McClintock, C. (1984). Why peasants rebel: The case of Peru's Sendero Luminoso. *World Politics, 37*(1), 48–84.

McCormick, G. (2008). The Shining Path and Peruvian terrorism. *Journal of Strategic Studies*, 109–126.

Osborn, R. (2007). On the path of perpetual revolution: From Marx's Millenarianism to Sendero Luminoso.*Totalitarian Movements and Political Religions, 8*(1), 115–135.

Palmer, D.S. (1994). *The Shining Path of Peru*. New York: Palgrave MacMillian.

Palmer, D.S. (1992). Peru, the drug business and Shining Path: Between Scylla and Charybdis. *Journal of Interamerican Studies and World Affairs, 34*(3), 65.

Smith, D. (1995). The training of terrorist organisations, global security, https://www.globalsecurity.org/military/library/report/1995/SDE.htm, retrieved on June 4, 2019.

Stern, S. (1998). "Beyond enigma: An agenda for interpreting Shining Path and Peru, 1980–1995." In S. Stern (Ed.).*Shining and Other Paths: War and Society in Peru, 1980–1995* (pp.1–12). Durham and London: Duke University Press.

Sullivan, M. (2009).*Latin America: Terrorism issues*. Congressional Research Service, Diane Publishing.

Tarazona-Sevillano, G., & Reuter, J. (1990). *Sendero Luminoso and the threat of Narcoterrorism. Washington Papers Series*. New York: Praeger & Center for Strategic and International Studies.

Throssell, L. (2006). Peru: The killings of Lucanamarca. *BBC News*, October 14, http://news.bbc.co.uk/2/hi/americas/6050442.stm, retrieved on June 1, 2019.

The United States Department of State (2019). Narotics rewards program: Bureau of International Narcotics and law enforcement affairs, diplomacy in Action, https://www.state.gov/j/inl/narc/rewards/275737.htm, retrieved on April 30, 2019.

The United States Department of State (2018).*Country Reports on Terrorism 2017 – Foreign Terrorist Organizations: Shining Path*, September 19: https://www.refworld.org/docid/5bcf1f2913.html, retrieved on April 30, 2019.

The United States Department of State (2017). Country report on terrorism 2016 – Chapter 6, Shining Path, accessed on: https://www.ecoi.net/en/document/1404834.html, retrieved on November 11, 2018.

The United States Department of State (2016). State department terrorist designations of Victor Quispe Palomino, Jorge Quispe Palomino and Tarcela Loya Vilchez, Bureau of Counterterrorism and Counter Violent Extremism, November 22, accessed on: https://www.state.gov/j/ct/rls/other/des/266472.htm, retrieved on April 4, 2019.

The World Drug Report (2018). Global overview of drug demand and supply: Latest trends, cross-cutting issues, United Nations Office on Drugs and Crime (UNODC) accessed on: https://www.unodc.org/wdr2018/prelaunch/WDR18_Booklet_2_GLOBAL.pdf, retrieved on November 11, 2018.

Woy-Hazleton, S.a, & Hazleton, W.A. (1994). Shining Path and the Marxist left. *The Shining Path of Peru* (pp. 225–242). New York: Palgrave Macmillan.

38

THE ZAPATISTA ARMY OF NATIONAL LIBERATION'S (EZLN) REVOLUTIONARY STRUGGLE

tavis d. jules and Scott N. Romaniuk

INTRODUCTION

Mexico's Zapatista Army of National Liberation (Ejercito Zapatista de Liberacion Nacional, EZLN), a quasi-armed indigenous guerrilla group named after the revolutionary leader Emiliano Zapata[1], has its roots in Mexican revolutionary ideology. The group gained notoriety in January 1994 as a leftist guerrilla insurgency after the group led an armed uprising across five towns and a city, San Cristóbal de las Casas, in the highlands of Mexico's southernmost state, Chiapas. The indigenous rebellion of a few thousand people was preceded by the 1993 First Declaration of the Lacandón Jungle[2], which declared war against the then government of President Carlos Salinas de Gortari and called for the defeat of the Mexican Federation army. The uprising lasted 12 days and left dozens dead, mostly Zapatistas. The EZLN called for an end to "the genocidal policies that the federal executive imposes on our people" ("Second Declaration," 1994, para 1). The Declaration of the Lacandón Jungle began with the statement "We are a product of 500 years of struggle … But today we say "Ya Basta! (Enough is Enough!)."

On January 1, 1994, the ELZN declared war against the Mexican Army and Executive Branch and seized, with force, the municipal seats of San Cristóbal, Ocosingo, Las Margaritas, and Altamirano. The declaration of war came after the implementation of a regional trading agreement (the North American Free Trade Agreement [NAFTA]), and the indigenous communities felt that such an agreement exhorted more power upon them since "the repression has existed for 500 years for the Indo-Americans … for the Indians, this sort of repression is their daily bread". In short, the EZLN opposed neoliberalism in all of its shapes and forms and "seeks, on a modest scale, to re-enchant the world" (Lowy, 1998, p. 1). This was due to the view of NAFTA as 'economic warfare' and the 'geopolitics of plunder', in that it hastened the dispossession of the indigenous people. However, the 1994 bloody uprising came at a high cost to the EZLN; more than 145 of its members' lives were lost.

The ELZN is the successor of five centuries of defiance to conquest, civilisation, and modernity and has been labelled as the world's first post-communist insurgency or "post-modern revolution" that uses a social netwar[3] strategy (Collier & Collier, 2005; Lowy, 1998). Unlike other Latin American guerrilla groups, the Marxist-Leninist Zapatistas state that their central aim is to bring autonomous control to the indigenous people of Chiapas. Because of the fact that several hundred thousand illegal Central American immigrants running from different wars across the region crossed into Chiapas (Scott, 1994), the Mexican government has long maintained that the EZLN is directed and governed by several foreigners, and therefore their cause is not truly local. Because of this, in the 1990s, the EZLN was dubbed an "ultra-leftist rebel urban terrorists" (Fineman, 1996) organisation. While the EZLN remains a regional powerhouse inside areas of Chiapas, its methods are now carried out through pacifistic means and armed struggle only if necessary. The EZLN demands freedom and democracy for all Mexicans who are oppressed. Today, the ELZN controls 43[4] rebel areas (a mixture of autonomous municipalities and *caracoles* in Chiapas), and state security forces are not allowed in these areas. Education is provided in ELZN-owned and operated schools. Like many Latin American insurgency groups, the EZLN recognised very early on that its political-military strategic tactics allowed it to gain popular sympathies.

Today, the EZLN maintains numerous safehouses in Mexico City and Belize, but the group is active in Chiapas state (Lacandón Jungle, Chiapas Highlands, and along the coast) and has a "security corridor" between Chiapas and the British Commonwealth of Belize. The group is known for its use of black ski masks that hide their appearances as well as their sophisticated use of technology and media to get its message across to the public. In fact, the group places a premium on "publicity media coups," where they relish inviting journalists to conduct interviews in the jungle. The group has also managed to engage non-governmental

DOI: 10.4324/9780429426063-43

organisations, both nationally and internationally, to support their cause and create a vast EZLN network of actors. In fact, given the ELZN's history, Ronfeldt et al. (2008) argue that the ELZN has "generated an information-age prototype of militant social netwar" (p. 1) given its savvy use of media to "arouse a multitude of foreign activists associated with human rights, indigenous rights, and other types of nongovernmental organisations (NGOs)" (p. 3). In what follows, this chapter first provides an overview of the ELZN, followed by a detailed explanation of its key personnel and structure. The next section discusses how the group finances its operations. In the final section, the chapter concludes with some thoughts about the future of the EZLN.

HISTORICAL OVERVIEW

ELZN's heredity lies in the guerrilla-political movement of the National Liberation Forces of the 1960s. The EZLN has a history of collective organising and protesting in the region dating back to the 1970s with the organising of an Indian Congress around the social needs of Catholic parishioners. The movement is a mixture of horizontal and vertical designs and an offspring of the Fuerzas de Liberación Nacional (FLN)[5] and two lesser revolutionary groups, the Unión del Pueblo and the Linea Proletaria faction of Poltica Popular. The Indian Congress was a movement of young leftist militants who were supported by the Catholic Church and self-organised in the 1970s. In the mid-1970s, the group came under attack from ranchers, and, coupled with internal dissent, the movement fractured. In 1983, the EZLN, the political faction of young leftist militants in the region, was born after it splintered away from the Indian Congress. The EZLN was originally founded as a secret army and an armed alternative to the Congress. The EZLN came about during a period when liberation theology was lively across the region and:

> the uprising shook the nation's conscience; put an end to the government's triumphalism; reraised the indigenous question; put the problem of marginalization and poverty … at the top of the country's priorities; and also added, along with other factors, to the pressures for a democratic transition. (Tello, 1995, p. 2019 as cited in Ronfeldt et al., 2008, p. 98)

While a majority of the Indian Congress pursued an economic model of cattle ranching, credit union organising, and coffee planting with the aid of government financing, this political faction rose to prominence after the collapse of world coffee prices bankrupted Indian cooperatives and employment became scarce due to the influence of Guatemalan war refugees (Scott, 1994). The EZLN's message has remained consistent, and it is best summed up in the final speech of Subcomandante Marcos[6], who stated that:

> Against death, we demand life.
> Against silence, we demand the word and respect.
> Against oblivion, memory.
> Against humiliation and contempt, dignity.
> Against oppression, rebellion.
> Against slavery, freedom.
> Against taxation, democracy.
> Against crime, justice (Galeano, 2014, para 17)

The first encounters that the Mexican government had with the EZLN were in late May 1993, when Mexico's Defence Secretariat (*Secretara de la Defensa* [SEDEN]) sent 3000 soldiers into Chiapas on a civic action mission on counter-narcotics activity against guerrillas in Chiapas (Doyle, 2003). In fact, U.S. diplomatic cables from Mexico showed that the Mexican government had no clear counter-insurgency strategy for the EZLN. One of the intelligence forecasts created after the 1993 incursion stated that:

The first encounters that the Mexican government had with the EZLN were in late May 1993, when Mexico's Defence Secretariat (*Secretaría de la Defensa* [SEDEN]) sent 3000 soldiers into Chiapas on a civic action mission on counter-narcotics activity against guerrillas in Chiapas (Doyle, 2003). In fact, U.S. diplomatic cables from Mexico showed that the Mexican government had no clear counterinsurgency strategy for the EZLN. One of the intelligence forecasts created after the 1993 incursion stated that:

> *While the insurgents are not strong enough to face the Mexican army, neither is the army capable of eradicating the rebels in hiding. The government will seek to restrain the army to avoid local complaints of army human rights abuse. A stand-off with recurring violence could frighten foreign investors and embarrass the government, affecting presidential elections in August. The government will beef up security in the region, and could be tempted into repressive tactics.* (as cited in Doyle, 2003, para 17, italics original)

It was the creation of the North American Free Trade Agreement (NAFTA) between the United States, Canada, and Mexico on January 1, 1994[7] that led the group to declare war against the Mexican government in 1994. The 1994 First Declaration of the Lacandón Jungle called attention to the freedoms laid out in the Mexican constitution (particularly Article 39) that were not being given to the indigenous peoples. They also called for Article 27 of the 1917 constitution, which provided for communal property and land reform, to be restored. While the group used NAFTA to declare war, the creation of NAFTA was only one of many motives for waging war against the Mexican government. In fact, "NAFTA has subsequently been the subject of much EZLN criticism because it extended tariff reductions, making it harder for Mexican producers to compete with cheap North American goods" (Shirley, 2001, p. 10). The EZLN went to war against the Mexican government because it felt that "NAFTA will not bring them benefits but 'a death sentence,' and their aim was 'not to usurp power but to exercise it,' sending a forceful reminder that the forgotten indigenous populations are, after all, Mexicans and that they too are entitled to exercise their political and civil rights" (Ponce de León, 2001, p. xxv). The rebellion by the Zapatistas was viewed as starkly different from other rebellions by previous guerrilla groups because armed struggle is the only way left to fight for the most elemental of rights. The Zapatista Army believes that democratisation is not a state endeavour unless the state is forced to do so by society. This kind of thinking was outlined by Subcomandante Marcos[8] on December 2, 1994, who proclaimed in a Declaration:

> We – men and women, whole and free – are conscious that the war that we have declares is a last – but just – resort. For many years, the dictators have been waging an undeclared genocidal war against our people. Therefore, we ask for your decided participation to support this plan by the Mexican people who struggle for work, land, housing, food, health care, education, independence, freedom, democracy, justice, and peace. We declare the war and will not stop fighting until the basic demands of our people have been met, by forming a government for our country that is free and democratic. (as cited in Ponce de León, 2001, p. 15)

The call to arms "caused dozens of deaths in a few days; broke up families; provoked the expulsion of thousands of *indigenas* from their villages; left many poor ranchers without a means of subsistence; increased [the level of] insecurity in the countryside; and led to the militarisation of the *Cañadas*" (Tello, 1995, p. 2019, as cited in Ronfeldt et al., 2008, p. 98). The points of democracy, justice, and peace were reiterated in the Second Declaration of the Lacandón Jungle of June 10, 1994, which condemned militarisation and called for a transition government. This declaration occurred just as the Zapatistas broke off peace talks with the government and were indicted in a kidnapping ring. The second declaration came after increased militarisation and called for Zapatistas to resist threats by the Mexican government against civilian society. In the Third Declaration of the Lacandón Jungle, from December 31, 1994, the EZLN echoed that their struggle is not solely about Chiapas but a national struggle. In January 1996, the Fourth Declaration of the Lacandón Jungle came after the failure of the Mexican government to capture the EZLN in a large-scale military coup. It begins by proclaiming that "the flower of the word will not die" while calling for civic and peaceful organising. However, in February 1996, the San Andres Accords on Indigenous Rights and Culture were signed by the government and the EZLN.

In July 1998, the Fifth Declaration of the Lacandón Jungle was issued after the military crackdown on the EZLN as it sought to expand its autonomous municipalities and called for the reinstatement of peace talks. This declaration was released six months after the Acteal massacre, which killed fifty-five people and was followed by raids on Zapatista bases. The Sixth Declaration of the Lacandón Jungle issued in July 2005 marked the beginning of "La Otra campaña (the Other Campaign)[9] premised upon organising from below. The EZLN sought to expand their base from indigenous peoples to the working class and people on the political left. This declaration claimed that by listening to the Mexican populace, the EZLN would no longer engage in attacks against the Mexican government's military (Sanchez, 2012). However, it reiterated that when (and if) needed, the EZLN would pick up arms again.

MODUS OPERANDI OF THE EZLN

During the first wave of its territorial expansion, the ELZN took over the municipalities of San Cristóbal de las Casas, Ocosingo, Las Margaritas, Altamirano, Chanal, Oxchuc, and Huixtán. In fact, the Zapatistas argue that their principles extend to all the peoples of the world. This has allowed the group to garner support from several non-governmental organisations. As Faramelli (2018) asserts, the ELZN has avoided the "trap of monomania" by "extending and internationalising their scope of critique and action to all oppressed people," given that they have not limited their struggles "only to the reform of the government to include protection of indigenous human rights" (p. 104). The ELZN has found strength and notoriety in having a global message that resonates with people outside of Mexico.

The moulding of the ELZN into its current incarnation is hereditary in several traditions. Guevaraism (Latin American revolutionary Marxism), which combined communist revolutionary thinking with guerrilla warfare, has been influential in shaping the ELZN and Zapatism. Embedded in this thinking are notions of the importance of armed struggle, standing up and fighting against the exploitation of the people by their oppressors, and the emancipation of 'brothers and sisters' from oppression. Another influence, and their namesake, that the ELZN drew upon was that of Emiliano Zapata, the leader of the agrarian revolution in Mexico (with the 'Ejército del Suras,' an army of the masses). From Zapata, the ELZN took the ideas of internationalisation and the fight against "the 'great crime,' against the infamous usurpation of the earth, which, belonging to all, has been monopolised by a few powerful men, supported by the strength of armies and the inequity of laws" (as cited in Lowy, 1998, p. 2). For the ELZN, "land and liberty" are central to their cause (Lowy, 1998). A third influence has been that of liberation theology, taken from Msgr. Samuel Ruiz and his thousands of catechists who, since 1970, have been working to raise consciousness in the indigenous communities (and among the poor) and encouraging them to organise to struggle for their rights and the self-emancipation of the poor. Of course, liberation theology is non-violent, in contrast with EZLN methods. The final influence of Zapatism has been the Mayan culture of the native people of Chiapas and their struggle against "neoliberal modernisation," which is linked to the "magical relation to nature [and] community solidarity" (Lowy, 1998, p. 3). Embedded in this concept are the ideas of the past and the history of pre-capitalist, pre-modern, and pre-Columbian development and their intersection with modernity.

Given its history, the ELZN's *modus operandi* is not always as violent as some other Latin American guerrilla groups. When needed, the ELZN, in standing up to the Mexican government, has at times turned violent, but it has not been the type of brutality that other Latin American guerrilla groups have used to get their message out. In the 1990s, much of the violent methods that the ELZN used were kidnappings, torture, and killings (in 1992, 1993, and 1995),[10] bombings (1994),[11] a dynamite attack (1994),[12] a failed rocket attack[13] and the forceful taking of municipal seats.[14] In January 1995, the ELZN, under Ernesto Zedillo and after months of dialogue, reached an agreement: the Treaties of San Andrés Larráinzar, which granted autonomy, recognition, and rights to indigenous peoples. The treaties were based on five principles that called for respect for the diversity of the indigenous peoples, the conservation of natural resources used by indigenous peoples, the participation of indigenous people in decision-making and public spending, indigenous-driven development, and self-determination within the state. In 1996, the first intercontinental *Encuentro* (gathering),[15] called the Intercontinental Encounter for Humanity and Against Neoliberalism, which brought together workers, campesinos, and intellectuals, along with leaders from the main political parties, was held.

The second aspect of the ELZN's *modus operandi* can be defined as its expansion over three periods: **1994, 2003, and 2019. In 1994, the group emerged and created over 20** autonomous municipalities. In 2003, the group opened five new *caracoles* (formally called Aguascalientes). The third expansion began in 2019, with the addition of new centres beyond the **traditional Zapatismo control zone.** Under the Third Wave, the ELZN broke the current peace agreements and expanded the area under their influence in Chiapas. These three expansions have been at the heart of the group's strategy to gain legitimacy as a political actor rather than being viewed as a terrorist group. With the 2019 territorial expansion of seven new *caracoles* and four new autonomous municipalities (code-named "Samir Flores Vive"[16]), the ELZN remains active but wants to be viewed as being more political. This third wave of territorial expansionism was fuelled by what the ELZN calls "the destructive government policy of community and nature, particularly that of the current self-styled 'Fourth Transformation' government" (as cited in CNN: Expansion, 2019, para 6). By turning away from armed struggle, the group has also been afforded a certain amount of political legitimacy. Unlike their guerrilla brethren in Colombia and Peru, the Zapatistas have extensive backing both from the Mexican left and on the global stage, where they are known as the spearhead of the anti-globalisation movement.

A third aspect of ELZN's *modus operandi* is the way in which it communicates its message both nationally and internationally. The EZLN has strategically mastered the use of communications to disseminate its message in a sophisticated manner. In fact:

> The communiqúes were like a brilliant commentary on Mexican life and the defiant, playful tone struck a nerve throughout the country-and the world-as, one by one, La Jornada, El Financiero (for a short while), and the opposition weekly Proceso circulate the epistles to a wider and wider audience. National and international diffusion was sped along by a press corps that numbered nearly a thousand in the first 23 days of the war. Activists in El Paso were already translating the communiqúes and posting them daily on the web (as cited in Shirley, 2001, pp. 8–9)

The EZLN has used communiqués to clearly and succinctly get their message across, which resonate with the populace because of their simplicity. Moreover, the EZLN seeks to have people relate to their message as a struggle, but frame their struggles as both national and global. The communiqués, the primary Zapatista propaganda campaign, appropriate national symbols and icons (such as Emiliano Zapata and the 1917 constitution) as ways of overcoming "Votán-Zapata"[17] (Mexican nationalism) (Shirley, 2001). Of course, at the heart of the EZLN communiqué has been Subcomandante Marcos' storytelling, fables, and poetry, which drew from indigenous beliefs and fascinated and charmed the Mexican populace. The EZLN's first foray into information warfare was in 1994, a phenomenon that came to be called "Marcosmania," as media coverage of the EZLN eclipsed that of the then-presidential race. Attached to their communiqués was the incorporation of visual tactics to command greater attention. With the aid of the media, the ELZN's communiqué has created "a war of words, images, imagination, and organisation in which the Zapatistas have had surprising success" (Cleaver, 1998, para 3).

In 2005, the Sixth Declaration of the Lacandón Jungle was launched by the EZLN and detailed their history, experience, analysis, and practise. In its analysis, the declaration called attention to issues of the current phase of neoliberal globalisation, a critique of Mexico's political class, and neoliberalism in Mexico. In the conclusion to the declaration, the ELZN laid out what it plans to do to combat neoliberalism in all of its manifestations: develop an anti-capitalist movement at the national level to rescue Mexico from neoliberalism, all while writing a new constitution. The Sixth Declaration's nickname "*La Otra Campaa*" (the Other Campaign)" was a direct reference to the 2006 presidential elections that were being denominated by the then three major political parties **(Partido de Acción Nacional [PAN]; Partido de la Revolución Institucional [PIR]; and Partido Verde Ecologista de México [PVEM]). The launching of the** Sixth Declaration **also saw the call for an international campaign and another** Intercontinental Encuentro of anti-neoliberal groups. The 2007 Intercontinental Encuentro[18] reaffirmed the Declaration for the Indigenous Intercontinental Conference, which stated that "it has been 515 years since the invasion of ancient Indigenous territories and the onslaught of the war of conquest, spoils, and capitalist exploitation" (as cited in Norrell, 2007, para 8). The Sixth Deceleration and the Intercontinental Encuentro drew attention to the fact that neoliberal extremism has evolved as the new war in which the indigenous struggle is now embedded. It was here that Sub-comandante Marcos called for the defence of Mother Earth and the freeing of indigenous peoples from the assault of corporations and governments.

KEY PERSONNEL AND STRUCTURE

The group's hierarchy is structured like a paramilitary with commandants, sub-commandants, lieutenants, sub-lieutenants, mayors, *capitans*, *teniente*, first infantry, mayor infantry, regional head, and so forth. All those of fighting age are called 'compañeros' (like 'companions' or 'comrades'), except for the older members and children who do not fight. The ELZN functions mainly through the radio, the internet, communiqués, the holding of marches and rallies, and the organising of Intercontinental Encuentros. The Mexican government maintains that the EZLN is directed by "important numbers of foreigners" and that the EZLN "is not an Indian movement nor a campesino movement but the acts of a radical group directed by professionals who are tricking or forcing Indians to participate" (Scott, 1994, paras. 2–3). In the early days, the group used pamphlets, especially to distribute among indigenous communities, to get out their message about what the government had been doing to indigenous groups in Mexico since colonisation. On the one hand, the group is viewed as an armed guerilla outfit that is in constant battle with the Mexican state; on the other, it is viewed as just another civil society group fighting for the rights of indigenous peoples. It is within this grey contradiction that the ELZN best functions since it uses both guerilla warfare tactics and pacifist means to achieve its goals.

Rafael Sebastián Guillén Vicente (a.k.a. Sub-comandante Marcos) was a Jesuit-trained graduate with a degree in philosophy from the National Autonomous University of Mexico (UNAM) and did his postgraduate studies at the Sorbonne in Paris and the School of Mexican History and Anthropology. The EZLN was led by Sub-comandante Marcos, who was also the spokesman for the group, until the mid-2000s. He possessed wit, sardonicism, comedic timing, and sophistication that appealed to a broad audience. His messianic speeches have given him the status of a pop star, and he has been dubbed the new Ernesto 'Che' Guevara. Marcos held the public office of Sub-comandante from 1994 to 2014 and served as the translator of the Maya leftist guerrilla rebels' message to the rest of Mexico. It is thought that Marcos taught philosophy at Mexico City's National Autonomous University and moved to Chiapas to work with Indian communities sometime in the early 1980s. Although Marcos governs a group of villages in the southern state of Chiapas, he is thought not to be of indigenous descent. It is unclear if a higher commander exists. As Ponce de León (2001) notes, in one instance, Marcos:

> emerging from the multitude of brown-skinned people, an assigned spokesman proclaims: 'Through me speaks the will of the Zapatista National Liberation Army.' His fair skin and green eyes, which gleam beneath a black ski mark, are as dissonant as the Zapatista's sudden cry in a long, silent night of forgetting. (p. xxv)

The fact that Sub-comandante Marcos is not Indian shows that the ELZN's fight has a broader appeal than merely for the rights of indigenous peoples. In communiques, which are the main source of communication, Sub-comandante Marcos uses storytelling, scholarship, poetry, and humour to connect with and dialogue with people about matters of power and autonomy. As the spokesperson for such a long period, Marcos has been skilful in using his writings to convey the indigenous vision into words that can be understood by the masses. Sub-comandante Marcos was able to use his discourse to break through the white noise of the internet and get his message out. And his main message, under his black ski mask, poncho, and bandolier, was that the local struggles were all connected to the wider struggles and injustices that the EZLN is fighting.

A great deal of speculation has been made about why EZLN members wear black ski masks. Sub-comandante Marcos has stated that the use of black-face ski masks is for anonymity so that the members of the group do not become corrupt. In other words, the black face masks are used to provide "collective leadership" since ELZN members are not praised and there are no heroes or superstars (Clarke & Ross, 2000). In fact, Ponce de León (2001) suggests that

> The mask has a transformative power that allows Marcos to shed the idiosyncrasies of his birth and

> assume a communal identity. This non-self makes it possible for Marcos to become the spokesman for the indigenous communities. He is transparent, and he is iconographic. He hides himself so he can be seen. This paradox will inform all his writing. (p. xxvi)

The ski mask became a powerful symbol for Marcos to show that he was equal to all of the members. However, in 2009, Sub-comandante Marcos vanished after he spoke briefly at the "Digna Rabia" ("Dignified Rage") forum in San Cristobal de las Casas and issued no public communiqués for nineteen months. When Marcos reemerged, he began to plan his retirement, announced in 2014. In his final communiqué, 'Sub-comandante Marcos argues that "this war of resistance is fought day in and day out in the streets of any corner of the five continents, in their countrysides, and in their mountains" ("Between Light and Shade," 2014, para 15).

In 2014, on the twentieth anniversary of the uprising, Sub-comandante Marcos proclaimed that "those who loved and hated Sub-comandante Marcos now know that they hated and loved a hologram. Their love and hatred have been, well, useless, sterile, empty holes" (as cited in Bellani, 2014, para 2), leading some to speculate that he has retired from his leadership position. Just before Sub-comandante Marcos is thought to have retired, in February 2013, the EZLN introduced Compaero Subcomandante Insurgente Moisés as the new spokesman of the movement. Subcomandante Moisés, viewed as a visionary military strategist and organiser, is a native of the Tzetal region and joined the movement in 1983. Prior to becoming Subcomandante Moisés, he served as a major in the 1994 uprising and was a lieutenant colonel during the second wave of territorial expansion, which occurred in 2003.

In 2005, when the Sixth Declaration of the Lacandóna Jungle was launched, Subcomandante Moisés was named "The Intergalactic" and placed in charge of La Intergaláctica, the committee for international affairs with responsibility for communications with national and international civil society. In announcing Subcomandante Moisés, Subcomandante Marcos noted that "He watches over our door, and with his voice are the voices of all of us. We ask you to listen to him, that is, to look at him as we look at ourselves". Subcomandante Moisés is no stranger to the inner workings of the EZLN and was, in fact, present with Subcomandante Marcos in 1995 when the government betrayed Marcos. The literature paints Marco and Moisés as squires. In Subcomandante Moisé's first speech given on June 1, 2014, he reiterated that EZLN's principal obligation is to its communities and that their fight against capitalism is aimed at liberating the indigenous people.

COMMAND STRUCTURE

In delivering his final communiqué, entitled "Between Light and Shade," Sub-comandante Marcos argues that the *"[EZLN] have not hidden the fact that we are an army, with its pyramidal structure, its central command, and its decisions hailing from above to below. We didn't deny who we are in order to ingratiate ourselves with the libertarians or to move with the trends"* (as cited in Hesketh & Morton, 2014, para. 4, italics original). Since its debut with Sub-comandante Marcos, the structure of the Marxist-Leninist EZLN movement has remained a mystery. It remains unclear if there are commanders above the sub-comandante, who is usually the spokesman for the movement. However, under the sub-comandante, there are commanders of the rebellion in the form of the Clandestine Indigenous Revolutionary Committee (CCRI) or the Directing Committee, consisting of all of the major indigenous groups, Tzotziles, Tzeltales, Choles, Tojolabales, Mames, and Zoques, in Chiapa. While some have suggested that the subcommander reports to the CCRI, what is known is that the ELZN structure does not revolve around a singular leader (Solorzano, 2004). The CCRI committee has attributed their name and responsibilities to the fact that they are collectives, who cooperatively make decisions "clandestine[ly] because [they] don't suit the government, rising up in arms this way, organising clandestinely … revolutionary because [they are left with no] other [way] than to rise up in armed struggle to see if this works and gets us a response to our needs'" (Clarke & Ross, 2000, p. 69). The EZLN holds that no commander can hold power in the autonomous municipalities. It is known that the internet has been instrumental in shaping the ELZN, allowing the group to explain and show in detail the plight of the indigenous peoples and their perceived injustices.

Each village selects its own representative, who is tasked with the responsibility of providing information to and from the village. There are also local and regional representatives. As Subcomandante Marcos notes:

> Our leadership is collective … They call this ski mask 'Marcos' here, today, and tomorrow they'll call it 'Pedro' in Margaritas or 'Joshua' in Ocusingo or 'Alfred' in Altamiro. Collective work, democratic thought, the obedience to the will of the majority are all more than traditions in the indigenous zones. They have also been the only possibility for survival, resistance, dignity and rebellion (as cited in Solorzano, 2004, p. 10, italics original)

The leadership structure is modelled after traditional forms of Mayan governance. This command structure is also a response to what is seen as "the domination of Mexican society by the local strongmen and its history of dictators" (Solorzano, 2004, p. 10).

The next governance body is the *caracoles*, which are "centres for political and cultural meetings and exchange between the Zapatista communities and national and international civil society. They are also the headquarters of the Good Government Boards" (Muñoz Ramírez, 2008, p. 13). The *caracoles* are organised regions with governance boards, and in 2019, seven new ones (up from five previous zones) were created under the third wave of the Zapatistas expansion. *Caracoles* are comprised of autonomous municipalities, and decisions are made at assemblies using the principle of *mandar obedeciendo* (rule by obeying) so that sovereignty remains in the community. Given their commitment to a pure form of democracy, the ELZN has Juntas de Buen Gobierno (Good Government Boards) that "provide a living example to the world that it is possible to offer alternative forms of truly participatory democracy" (Muñoz Ramírez, 2008, p. 13). These boards are how villages are organised and are responsible for governing municipalities and communities. Good governance boards also administer autonomous justice. In other words, *caracoles* "**are 'windows to see us inside and for us to see outside,' while the Good Governance Boards 'work through the principles of rotation, the revocation of mandate, and accountability'** and are 'true networks of power below,' in which the municipal councils are articulated" (Zibechi, 2019, para 5).

Of course, the Mexican government has used a two-pronged strategy of negotiating and cracking down on the ELZN. For example, in March 1995, the state unilaterally violated the cease-fire and attacked. In December 1997, the Tzotzil massacre in Chiapas by the Mexican government claimed the lives of 45 members of the Tzotzil indigenous community. ELZN supporters are often harassed by groups linked to the government. However, the Mexican government has maintained its pro-dialogue attitude while also trying to destroy guerrilla forces directly through the use of civic action programmes and propaganda campaigns (Weinberg, 2007; Shirley, 2001).

STRATEGIC COOPERATION AND FINANCING

Like many Latin American guerrilla groups, the EZLN has armed and financed itself through legal and illegal means, but mostly with 'external support.' However, the lack of available information does not allow us to have a complete assessment of the reality in Chiapas. In fact, Subcommandante Marcos and the EZLN have been painted by the government as "not a rebel defender of indigenous rights, but a lawbreaker ... who has enriched himself immensely by illicit activities detected and documented by the government's intelligence organs" (as cited in Weinberg, 2007, para 19). Yet, the EZLN has argued that the government of Mexico is carrying out a "dirty war"[19] against the organisation as it is fought not by the Mexican armed forces but by paramilitaries.

Numerous organisations in various nations around the world have supported the EZLN. Some of these organisations can be found in Western Europe (Germany, Belgium, Denmark, Spain, France, Ireland, and Switzerland), the United States (Arizona, California, Colorado, Illinois, Massachusetts, Michigan, Minnesota, Montana, New Mexico, New York, Oregon, Tennessee, Texas, Virginia, Vermont, Washington, and Wisconsin), Latin America (Brazil and Peru), and Canada (see Executive Intelligence Review, 1995). Several worldwide international organisations, such as Greenpeace, the World Wide Foundation for Nature (WWF), Human Rights Watch, Inter-American Dialogue, and the United Nations High Commission for Refugees, have supported the EZLN as well.

Although both domestic and foreign NGOs have contributed to and supported much of the EZLN's social and political work, the full extent of its funding is still unknown. Some have speculated that this leftist guerrilla movement has stayed away from criminal activity (Ramsey, 2012), while others have argued that its financial support comes from its entanglement with other leftist movements, both local (such as Ejército Popular Revolucionario [EPR][20]) and international actors in the region (Scott, 1994).

During the 1990s, most reports cited that the group was poorly armed, with some AK-47 assault rifles, M14 and G3 rifles, grenades, rocket launchers, and some explosives purchased on the black market. However, the cache of the group's weapons came to light in 1995 when an "arsenal of high-power arms, hand grenades, and explosives" (CIRBC, 2001, para 4) was found. Then-president Ernesto Zedillo ordered the arrest of five EZLN leaders, including Sub-comandante Marcos and Fernando Yañez Muñoz (a.k.a. "Commander Germán"), who was thought to be in charge of the finances and arms purchases. Commander Germán was later arrested with an AK-47 automatic rifle, a 9-millimetre pistol, and 64 bullets in the car. In mid-1995, it was thought that the EZLN was channelling arms from El Salvador (Farabundo Marti National Liberation Front [FMLN]) and Nicaragua (Sandinista National Liberation Front [FSLN]) after a "Mexican and an Italian were arrested in Honduras for attempting to smuggle arms, including rifles, bullets, guns, grenades, a rocket launcher, and grenade launchers, into Chiapas for the Zapatistas" (CIRBC, 2001, para 5). It was thought that El Salvador's FMLN was also responsible for the training of members. Northern Belize and Northwest Guatemala, which are wide open regions, are also thought to be weapons smuggling routes for the EZLN. Since the 1980s, Rigoberta Mench's Guatemalan National Revolutionary Unity (URNG) has maintained cross-border communications with the EZLN through guerrilla groups and Guatemalan refugees living in Chiapas and Tabasco. In a statement in 1994, Guatemala's Interior Minister, Danilo Parinelo, said "most, if not all, of the weapons were to have been smuggled through the Lacandon jungle to the Zapatista National

Liberation Army (EZLN) in Mexico's south-eastern state of Chiapas, having come from Cuba via Nicaragua" (as cited in Davison, 1994, para 2).

It has also been speculated that the EZLN is involved in stealing and pirating to finance its operations. In the 1990s, after the government began to crack down on the EZLN, reports suggested that the organisation was sealing livestock and extorting pesos from local residents to survive (Braley & Taylor, 1998). Moreover, during this period, it is speculated that the EZLN and the Popular Revolutionary Army (EPR) had indirect links, as some of the EPR members may have joined the EZLN in its earlier days. It has also been suggested that some members of the EZLN may have also gone over to the EPR in the early days of the movement (Ronfeldt et al., 2008). Unlike the EZLN, the EPR is known for its violent strategies, and NGOs and the Mexican government shun it.

In addition to smuggling weapons, the EZLN was financed through donations from charitable organisations, such as the Misereor, the German Catholic organisation, and the Coffee Producers' Organisations. It is alleged that Misereor has donated over seven million dollars to finance radio communications equipment. It is said that coffee producers' organisations have contributed a percentage of their coffee exports. Additionally, an international network of NGOs, particularly the International Red Cross, has contributed food, medicine, and material support to the EZLN. In addition to NGOs, the EZLN is believed to receive financial support from two Guatemalan guerrilla/rebel groups, the Ejercito Guerrillero de los Pobres (EGP) and the Comunidads de población en resistencia (CPR), as well as from the clandestine revolutionary workers' party/unions of the poor (Partido de los Pobres, a left-wing political movement and militant group in Mexico) (Doyle, 2003). The Catholic Church also provides significant support to the EZLN.

Another lucrative area of financing for the EZLN has been kidnapping and ransoming. Accusations of kidnapping and ransoming by the group can be traced to one of its founding arms, the Fuerzas de Liberación Nacional, which is known to use these methods to achieve its ends. The EZLN's first kidnapping dates to 1992, when the collective farmer Mariano Encino, from Atamira township, was kidnapped and tortured to death. Then, in 1993, two military officers in San Isidro El Ocotal were kidnapped and tortured. However, Scott (1994) argues that by 1994, the EZLN had amassed around 12 million dollars from the kidnapping and ransom of some 20 ranchers and plantation owners. Fineman (1996) reported that "'there is a high probability" that the rebels were involved in the 1994 kidnapping of Alfredo Harp Helu, a multimillionaire banker released after more than three months in exchange for a reported $30 million ransom" (para 9). In 2010, it was suggested that Subcomandante Marcos was responsible for the kidnapping of the powerful right-wing politician and former presidential candidate Diego Fernandez de Cevallos (aka El Jefe Diego) and that the $50 million USD ransom demand was reduced to $30 million (but $20 million was paid in the end). It is speculated that much of the money received from kidnappings and ransoms was used to finance the purchase of weapons.

Another lucrative endeavour that the EZLN used to finance its operations was drug trafficking. With the rise of the narco-economy in the 1970s and 1980s, Weinberg (2007) points out that "cocaine, heroin, methamphetamine, and marijuana are major NAFTA exports for Mexico, with an annual cross-border drug trade estimated at $20 billion" (para 5). Thus, when NAFTA came into force, plantation owners chose to grow opium and *mota* (marijuana) instead of coffee and beef. However, it has been hard to prove that drug trafficking is part of ELZN's *modus operandi*. In fact, Subcomandante Marcos (2003) asserts that "not only are we not dependent on drug trafficking, but we have fought it since our creation" (Vodovunk, 2003, p. 523). Nevertheless, as far back as 1995, the Mexican government asserted that Chiapas, particularly the border area with Guatemala and Belize, is an important drug-trafficking zone. In citing a former general, Executive Intelligence Review (1995) explained that "there are indications that the cartels count on the support of the EZLN in Chiapas, since the drug lords operate in the armed group's area of influence. The drugs are thrown from small aeroplanes in flight over areas of Chiapas" (para. 57). Other sources have indicated that the drug trade has become intertwined with political struggles and counterinsurgency efforts against neoliberalism. Weinberg (2007) notes that marijuana and, to a lesser extent, opium poppy are grown in Zapatista's autonomous municipalities. EZLN has maintained that drug trafficking is done by other groups (such as the PRIistas)[21] living in the Chiapas region. The government continues to send the army into disloyal *campesino* lands on counternarcotics missions. Interestingly, the U.S. Drug Enforcement Administration has maintained that during the 1990s and 2000s, while the insurgencies in Latin America were using drug trafficking to support their efforts, the EZLN was an exception (Ramsey, 2012; Weinberg, 2007). Around 2010, the Sinaloa Cartel took control of some of the areas that the EZLN generally operates within. With the expansion of cartel territory in the southern area of Mexico, drug trafficking, human trafficking, and disappearances have come to the front door of the Zapatistas.

More recently, the EZLN has turned to the internet to fundraise and make their communiqués and commentary more visible. With the advent of cyberspace as the new social stage for activism, the virtual revolution has begun. As such, the EZLN has begun to use information technology to promote cyberspace campaigns as a way to fund its insurgent revolution. In turning to the internet to raise funds, EZLN began to strengthen its political-military strategy aimed at winning popular sympathies (Shirley, 2001; Solorzano, 2004). The political reach of the EZLN via modern computer networks has led to the weaving of their local revolution into a global phenomenon.

CONCLUSION

Terms such as terrorists, guerrillas, and insurgents are often used interchangeably when labelling organised violent criminal movements. For the EZLN, this is no different. The EZLN is one of three[22] domestically recognised groups by the Mexican government. Since the mid-1990s, the group has been involved in low-intensity gang wars with PRI members. On the one hand, it is labelled locally as an active guerrilla group given its history and use of violence previously; on the other, the group and its leaders claim to be a pacifist group that is fighting for the self-determination of its homeland. The government has maintained that the EZLN is ruled by foreigners. As the ELZN continues to claim that it is no longer a terrorist organisation, it has embarked upon new initiatives, such as Escuelitas Zapatista (Little Zapatista Schools), launched in 2013 and 2014, aimed at keeping the struggle alive. This initiative aims to support autonomous education across its territories by allowing participants to do community collective work part of the day and then study the other part of the day. In fact, in his 2014 retirement speech, Subcomandante Marcos argues that:

> *rather than dedicating ourselves to training guerrillas, soldiers and squadrons, we developed education and health promoters, who went about building the foundations of autonomy that today amaze the world. Instead of constructing barracks, improving our weapons, and building walls and trenches, we built schools, hospitals and health centres; improving our living conditions.* (as cited in Hesketh & Morton, 2014, para 4, italics original)

The EZLN has continued to demand democracy, justice, and land, yet its financing remains contentious, with differing accounts as to how the group finances itself. The accounts range from the group being substantial in its autonomous municipalities to the group running drug rackets and trading in arms. Moreover, the group maintains that it is a civil organisation fighting for the rights of others against the 'bad government' and that the government has been cracking down on the group. Today, the ELZN is highly effective through the support network it has created and is painted as an anti-globalisation grassroots social movement with a certain amount of political legitimacy. While some analysts equate the EZLN as being similar to other narco-insurgent movements across Latin America, others suggest that the EZLN as a movement is unclear and in a different league from other movements in the region. For their part, the Zapatistas continue to state that their *raison d'être* is to promote the rights and protection of the indigenous communities they represent and maintain that while they seek to use pacifistic means to accomplish their goals, when it is deemed necessary, they will revert to an armed struggle. In 2019, the Zapatistas celebrated their 25th anniversary of the movement and made headlines when the group took control of eleven more territories, showing that the group is still very active. Such a drastic move of territorial expansion violated the two-decade-old peace agreement and is a direct challenge to the Mexican government. The EZLN has maintained that it plans on growing exponentially after years of silent work. Moreover, the current Mexican president, Andrés Manuel López Obrador, and his government remain at loggerheads as to the way forward. This impasse stemmed from the 2016 hostilities, when the EZLN completed the idea of launching an indigenous candidature[23] for the Presidency. As we have noted, the Zapatista uprising did not begin in 1994, nor did it come from nowhere; instead, it has its heritage in a history of looting, pillaging, and plundering of the land and the domination and subjection of the natives by nonnatives. Yet, their struggle has remained consistent in advocating and fighting for land reform and dignity for the indigenous peoples while providing protection and basic commodities (health, school, and transportation) to the local communities in which it is active. The group has also made great strides in gender reform. In short, as the group wages its information warfare, it is misinterpreted and misunderstood as either a 'violent terrorist group' or a 'revolutionary organisation.'

Notes

1 Emiliano Zapata, the agrarian revolutionary and commander of the Liberation Army of the South during the Mexican Revolution, is who the EZLN takes its name from. Zapata's name was used in naming the movement because he has been viewed as fighting for similar causes and people throughout his life.
2 The Declaration of the Lacandón Jungle manifesto is now in its sixth iteration as of June 28, 2005.
3 According to Arquilla & Ronfeldt (2001), "netwar refers to an emerging mode of conflict (and crime) at societal levels, short of traditional military warfare, in which the protagonists use network forms of organisation and related doctrines, strategies, and technologies attuned to the information age" (p. 6).
4 Prior to the third wave expansion policy of 2019, the ELZN controlled five *caracoles* (snails) taken in 2003 and 27 autonomous municipalities. However, in 2019, the group broke the peace accords and added 11 territories (seven new *caracoles* and four new municipalities) in Ocosingo, San Cristóbal de las Casas, Chilón, Tila, Amatenango del Valle, Motozintla, and Chicomuselo, for a total of 43 rebel areas.
5 The FLN, which defined its goal as socialism, was created as a reaction to the 1968 massacre of students in Tlatelolco by the Mexican government (Ronfeldt et al., 2008).
6 He also went by the *nom de guerre* of Delegate Zero and Subcomandante Galeano.
7 NAFT broadened the free trade between the U.S. and Canada that had existed since 1989.

8 He also went by the *nom de guerre* of Delegate Zero and Subcomandante Galeano.
9 *La otra campaña* began in 2006 with Subcomandante Marcos going on a national listening tour to hear of the people's struggles while fighting against neoliberalism and capitalism. The ultimate aim of the campaign was to force the Mexican government to rewrite the constitution with protections for indigenous peoples while excluding elements of neoliberal capitalism.
10 These include the 1992 kidnapping, torture, and death of a collective farmer; the 1993 kidnapping, torture, and death of two soldiers; and the 1995 kidnapping, torture, and death of a farmer.
11 In 1994, the Revolutionary Workers' Party-Clandestine Union of the People (Procup) bombed the Plaza Universidad shopping centre in Mexico City.
12 In 1994, the attack on Michoacán and Puebla
13 In 1994, a failed attack on Number One Military Camp in Mexico City
14 In 1994, the taking of San Cristóbal, Ocosingo, Las Margaritas, and Altamirano
15 In addition, the Intercontinental Encuentro was held in 1997.
16 This name was given to memorialise an activist killed on February 20, 2019.
17 Votán is a celebrated figure in Mayan Tzeltales mythology and "represented the heart of the Mayan people and was sent by God to distribute land" (Shirley, 2001, p. 11).
18 was held in the Yaqui community of Vicam in Rio Yaqui, Sonora, from October 11–14, 2007.
19 This is used to describe the techniques such as "secret killings, ambushes, spraying chemicals on their harvests, giving them genetically altered seeds during planting seasons, and buying communities with money or construction materials" (Solorzano, 2004, p. 14) that paramilitaries use.
20 The Popular Revolutionary Army is a leftist guerrilla movement that operates mainly in the Mexican state of Guerrero.
21 PRIistas are people of the Institutional Revolutionary Party (PRI).
22 The other two are the People's Revolutionary Army (Ejército Popular Revolucionario [EPR]), which operates mainly in Guerrero and Oaxaca states, and the Insurgent People (Ejército Revolucionario del Pueblo Insurgente [ERPI]), which is an offshoot of the EPR.
23 María de Jesús Patricio, Marichuy, did not gain the necessary signatures needed to obtain her presidential candidature.

References

Arquilla, J., & Ronfeldt, D. (2001). *Networks and netwars: The future of terror, crime, and militancy*. Santa Monica, CA: Rand Corporation.

Bellani, O. (2014). Subcomandante Marcos announces: "We have decided that as of today, Marcos no longer exists". *America Latina En Movimiento*. Retrieved from https://www.alainet.org/en/active/74959

Braley, G. & Taylor, L. (1998). Mexico Stung as Army Swarms Over Chiapas. *Las Vegas Sun*. Retrieved from https://lasvegassun.com/news/1998/feb/05/mexico-stung-as-army-swarms-over-chiapas/

Canada: Immigration and Refugee Board of Canada, (2001). *Mexico: The ways in which the Zapatista National Liberation Army (EZLN) arms itself and from which sources; whether high-profile politicians have been involved in any arms purchases (1994 to March 2001)*, 12 March 2001, MEX36595.E, Retrieved from: https://www.refworld.org/docid/3df4be6a30.html [accessed 22 January 2020].

Clarke, B., & Ross, C. (2000). *Voice of Fire. Communiqués and Interviews from the Zapatista National Liberation Army*. San Francisco, CA: Freedom Voices.

Cleaver, H. (1998). "The zapatistas and the electronic fabric of struggle." In J. Holloway, & E. Peláez (Eds.). *Zapatista! Reinventing revolution in Mexico*. London: Pluto Press. Retrieved from https://la.utexas.edu/users/hcleaver/zaps.html

CNN: Expansion (2019). The Zapatista army of national liberation assumes control of 11 territories in Mexico; AMLO welcomes you. *CNN Espanol*. Retrieved from https://cnnespanol.cnn.com/2019/08/20/el-ejercito-zapatista-de-liberacion-nacional-asume-el-control-de-11-territorios-en-mexico-amlo-les-da-la-bienvenida/

Collier, G.A., & Collier, J.F. (2005). The Zapatista rebellion in the context of globalization. *The Journal of Peasant Studies, 32*(3-4), 450–460, DOI: 10.1080/03066150500266794

Davison, P. (1994). Arms find triggers new fears of rebel uprising in Mexico. *The Independent*. Retrieved from https://www.independent.co.uk/news/world/arms-find-triggers-new-fears-of-rebel-uprising-in-mexico-1376154.html

Doyle, K. (2003). Rebellion in Chiapas and the Mexican Military. *Proceso*. Retrieved from https://nsarchive2.gwu.edu/NSAEBB/NSAEBB109/

Executive Intelligence Review. (1995, November). EZLN terrorists: A foreign invasion of Mexico. *Executive Intelligence Review, 22*(45), 59–62. Retrieved from https://larouchepub.com/other/1995/2245_ezln.html

Faramelli, A. (2018). *Resistance, revolution and fascism: Zapatismo and assemblage politics*. London and New York: Bloomsbury Academic.

Fineman, M. (1996). Zapatistas break off talks; New rebels linked to Kidnapping. *Los Angeles Times*. Retrieved from https://www.latimes.com/archives/la-xpm-1996-09-04-mn-40515-story.html

Galeano, I. (2014). "Between light and shade". *En Lace Zapatista*. Retrieved from https://enlacezapatista.ezln.org.mx/2014/05/27/between-light-and-shadow/

Hesketh, C., & Morton, A. (2014). Subcomandante Marcos dies, Galeano lives, The Zapatistas Continue. *For the Desk Drawer*. Retrieved from http://adamdavidmorton.com/2014/05/subcomandante-marcos-dies-galeano-lives-the-zapatistas-continue/

Lowy, M. (1998). Sources and resources of Zapatism (J. Pinkham Trans.). *Monthly Review: An Independent Socialist Magazine, 49*(10).

Muñoz Ramírez, G. (2008). *The fire and the word: A history of the Zapatista movement* (L. Carsen, & A. Reyes Arias Trans.). San Francisco, CA: City Lights Books.

Norrell, B. (2007). Zapatistas select Yaqui to host intercontinental summit in Mexico. *The Narco News Bulletin*. Retrieved from https://www.narconews.com/Issue45/article2637.html

Ponce de León, J. (Ed.). (2001). *Our word is our weapon. Selected writings. subcomandante insurgente Marcos*. New York, NY: Seven Stories Press.

Ramsey, G. (2012). How Mexico's Zapatista guerrillas stayed clear of organized crime. *The Christian Science Monitor*. Retrieved from https://www.csmonitor.com/World/Americas/Latin-America-Monitor/2012/0110/How-Mexico-s-Zapatista-guerrillas-stayed-clear-of-organized-crime

Sanchez, W.A. (October 2012). Defining Mexico's Zapatista army of national liberation. *E-International Relations*. Retrieved from https://www.e-ir.info/2012/10/22/defining-mexicos-zapatista-army-of-national-liberation/

Scott, D.C. (1994). Zapatista movement has long history, indigenous roots. *The Christian Science Monitor*. Retrieved from https://www.csmonitor.com/1994/0114/14011.html

Shirley, S. (2001). Zapatista organizing in cyberspace: Winning hearts and minds? Paper presented at the Latin American Studies Association, Washington D.C., September 6–8. Retrieved from http://lasa.international.pitt.edu/lasa2001/shirleysheryl.pdf

Solorzano, M. (2004). *The struggle of the EZLN in modern Mexico*. Retrieved from https://web.stanford.edu/class/e297a/The%20Struggle%20of%20the%20EZLN%20in%20Modern%20Mexico.doc

Vodovunk, Z. (ed). (2003). *Ya Basta! Ten Years of the Zapatista Uprising*. Oakland, CA: AK press.

Weinberg, B. (2007). Drugs, Guerrillas and Politicos in Mexico. *North American Congress of Latin America*. Retrieved from https://nacla.org/article/drugs-guerrillas-and-politicos-mexico

Zibechi, R. (2019). The third expansion of Zapatismo. *Des Informemonos*. Retrieved from https://desinformemonos.org/la-tercera-expansion-del-zapatismo/

39

A HISTORY OF COLOMBIA'S NATIONAL LIBERATION ARMY (ELN)

Jorge Eduardo Delgado

INTRODUCTION

After the historic signing of a peace agreement in late 2016 between the Colombian state and the insurgents of the FARC-EP (*Fuerzas Armadas Revolucionarias-Ejercito del Pueblo*), the National Liberation Army (*Ejército de Liberación Nacional*), better known by its Spanish acronym ELN, took the FARC's place as Latin America's oldest active insurgent group. Since its foundation in the early 1960s, the ELN has been considered Colombia's second-largest left-wing insurgent group, although it usually remained in the shadow of the stronger FARC during the country's more than five decades-long armed conflict. Over the years, the small, localised, and at times marginal ELN has demonstrated its tenacity to survive and adapt to the country's social and security transformations, as well as to the changes in the wider region's geopolitical conditions, in particular after the end of the Cold War. However, the ELN's endurance contrasts with the unsuccessful opportunities it has experienced to consolidate and advance its political goals. The Colombian state's posture towards the ELN has also changed accordingly throughout the years, depending on the level of the threat. Nonetheless, given the bigger challenge posed by other groups like the FARC or narco-terrorist groups like Pablo Escobar's Medellin cartel, historically, the ELN has been merely considered a security nuisance rather than an existential threat to the Colombian state (Porch, 2013, p. 231).

Colombia's 2016 final peace agreement with the FARC-EP, which took more than four years to negotiate, opened a new chapter for the ELN. Currently in the process of being implemented, the peace agreement with the FARC is being politically and financially supported by the international community. Peace with the FARC was expected to pave the way to achieve what Juan Manuel Santos, Colombia's former president and Nobel Peace Prize winner, called a "complete peace", which would bring an end to the country's 50-year-plus conflict with all left-wing insurgent groups (Miroff, 2015). The Santos administration (2010–2018) had hoped that the ELN would also hop on the peace bandwagon and publicly announced the start of peace talks with the group in February 2017 (both parties had actually been engaged in "secret" talks since 2014). Peace talks between the Colombian state and the ELN advanced slowly during 2017 in Quito, Ecuador, with the backing of diverse guarantors, including Cuba, Brazil, Chile, Norway, Sweden, and Germany. But negotiations stalled early in 2018, due to a series of violations of a temporary bilateral ceasefire, increased violence against state forces, continued terrorist attacks, and kidnappings of civilians, but also because of the group's close relationship with the neighbouring authoritarian regime of Nicolas Maduro in Venezuela. The suspension of peace talks in 2018 also showcased internal divisions within the ELN and a lack of command and control by its central leadership. In short, during the peace talks, the ELN did not reveal a common posture towards a negotiated settlement with the Colombian state, nor did it elucidate what it hoped to achieve politically through the peace talks.

As this chapter will discuss, tensions between the group's understanding of the utility of force and the political conduct of their struggle are not new. Internal divisions have been a persistent feature of its behaviour, ultimately affecting the attainment of its goals. The chapter will offer an account of the group's history and evolution and provide answers to its longevity by analysing its politics, organisation, and methods while addressing its strategic strengths and weaknesses.

ORIGINS OF THE ELN

The origins of the Colombian conflict and its notorious Marxist-Leninist guerrilla groups can be traced back to *La Violencia*, an undeclared civil war between the Liberal and Conservative parties that started in 1948. *La Violencia*

DOI: 10.4324/9780429426063-44

raged for more than a decade, making more than 250,000 victims before being resolved by a political compromise. But the power-sharing agreement brokered in 1958 between conservatives and liberals, known as the National Front, quickly spun off new insurgent groups unreconciled to an "elitist" political compromise. In parallel, the expansion of Cold War divisions into Latin America, and in particular Fidel Castro's 1959 triumph in Cuba, also served to embolden the nascent leftist guerrilla groups in Colombia. Local insurgent groups soon adopted new strategic goals aimed at the seizure of political power via the use of force and mustered support from their revolutionary comrades abroad, not only in Havana but also in Moscow and Beijing.

In particular, the Cuban revolution influenced the formation of new local insurgencies following the revolutionary 'foco' theory popularised by Ernesto "Ché" Guevara and French thinker Regis Debray. Followers of 'foquismo' in Colombia, which were to receive overt support from Havana, included the Student-Worker's Movement (*Movimiento Obrero Estudiantil Colombiano*), known as MOEC, founded at the end of 1959, and eventually its offspring, the ELN, founded in 1964 (Rendón, 2014, p. 52). In order to better understand the early evolution of the ELN, one has to look at the rise and fall of the MOEC, as both groups share the same lineage.

The MOEC was founded by a small group of radicalised urban middle-class university students who wanted to create a united Marxist revolutionary front with urban workers and peasants (Gott, 2008, p. 222). Following the 'foco' theory, the front would be led to victory thanks to the action of a rural guerrilla army organised by a student 'vanguard'. The leaders of the group left for Cuba in July 1959, where they received political and military training for six months to plan their scheme. In the end, these students proved to be ineffective. The viability of the MOEC has been in doubt since its inception due to insurmountable ideological divisions between its members, but mainly due to the botched premises of 'foquismo', in particular the view that revolution is an inevitable deed to be led by heroic, bold men. Many original members, disenchanted with the amateur leadership, left the group after a few months and left for Cuba, while others simply ratted out their former comrades. Raul Alameda, a founder of the MOEC, summed up the divisions in the following way after he became disenchanted with the movement: 'Serious men, Marxists that have spent long years of intense struggle without any "revolutionary tourism" [to Cuba], cannot lose time becoming the mistreated nannies of some egotistic and paranoid youngsters [...] These people don't admit to the preparatory stages of insurrection; for them only empirical reality and spontaneity exist.' (Diaz, 2010, p. 104). The MOEC was no match for the also-nascent Colombian intelligence and police services, which were in the process of receiving capacity-building assistance from Washington's US AID-led Public Safety Programme (Delgado, 2016, p. 222). Urban cells were easily infiltrated at an early stage by the Colombian security services. In the rural areas, it was mainly the inherent mistrust of the peasants that facilitated the destruction by the security forces of the *focos* the students of the MOEC attempted to initiate between 1961 and 1962. The MOEC was all but decimated by late 1962 and its surviving leadership found refuge in Cuba.

The failed experience with the MOEC led to a review of revolutionary practise in the country by its surviving members and new recruits from Colombia's universities (Gott, 2008, p. 226). On November 11, 1962, a group of 11 Colombian economics undergraduate students living in Havana, under a Cuban government scholarship, founded the "Brigade for National Liberation" (Rendón, 2014, p. 51). Its leaders, Fabio Vasquez and Victor Medina, with the support of the Cuban government and various MOEC exiles, planned to set up a small "foco" in the eastern Santander province of Colombia, close to the frontier with Venezuela. Santander was carefully chosen as the base for a 'Castroist-inspired insurgency with a genuine chance to subsist and later expand based on that region's unique geographic, social, and economic conditions. First, it was a mountainous region that facilitated guerrilla hit-and-run tactics; second, its rural population who experienced the rage of *La Violencia* and had sided with the left-leaning liberal party during the conflict were not ill-disposed to Marxist revolutionary ideology and were prone to rebel; and thirdly, Colombia's oil-rich city of Barrancabermeja, located in the region's lowland, was not only the heartland of that key national industry from which to extract resources, but mostly it was in the process of experiencing ardent social upheaval by the oil workers' union and students of Santander's Industrial University (UIS), who were all considered to be likely supporters of the insurgency (Pizarro, 2004, p.101). The Brigade for National Liberation arrived in Colombia from Havana on July 14, 1964. It was initially composed of 18 students, and after a short six-month period of organisation, training, and indoctrination of new recruits, they were ready for its baptism of fire under its new name, the National Liberation Army (ELN).

On January 7, 1965, in its first armed action, the group sieged Simacota, a small rural village near Santander, where they killed the four policemen on duty and looted the local bank and pharmacy. The isolated attack was a symbolic event, taking place on the sixth anniversary of the foundation of the MOEC, and was given centre stage by the ELN to publicise its newly minted ideological platform, known since then as the "Simacota Manifesto" (Pizarro, 2004, p. 101).

The ELN's enthusiastic political activism during the late-1960s was a determinant for its expansion, allowing it to increase its recruitment base and move from an estimated 70 members in 1966 up to 270 in 1973, but mostly, it helped increase its visibility and capture the imagination of the population. The context of the country in the period was well described in a CIA intelligence report:

> Colombia one of the two remaining democracies in South America, is beset by economic hardships,

> rampant crime, and guerrilla. These problems weigh heavily in the country's already volatile political arena [...] they have led to an increase in extremist activity, particularly by small leftist groups. They have encouraged strikes in both public and private sectors resulting in demonstrations and violence. The country's long-standing rural terrorism by pro-Moscow, pro-Havana and pro-Peking groups has also increased (CIA, 1976).

Indeed, the popularity of the Cuban revolution among leftist sectors of Latin America, mainly within universities, as well as the ramifications in the region of the rising unpopularity of the US-led intervention in Vietnam, fostered an ambience that helped echo the ELN's discourse. Meanwhile, the FARC and other Marxist-guerrilla groups like the *Ejército Popular de Liberación* (EPL) were going through a "defensive phase," which, following directions from the party lines of Moscow and Beijing, called for the maintenance of a lower political profile to avoid reactions from state forces or even US intervention (Delgado, 2016, p. 89). The ELN's unorthodox Marxist political discourse was also key in attracting an unusual source of support: elements of the Catholic Church, who, as will be discussed in the next section, offered the ELN a unique influence in terms of ideology and organisation. Since the foundation of the ELN in 1965, various radicalised Catholic priests have quickly joined its ranks (US Embassy, 1969). But why would Catholic priests decide to join a Marxist-Leninist insurgency?

Since the early 1960s, sectors of the Catholic Church were becoming vocal in the context of the Church's process of reform known as the Second Ecumenical Council of the Vatican, or Vatican II Council (1962–1965). Certain priests in Latin America pushed towards a more socially oriented stance and promoted the need for the Church to be more politically engaged in questions of economic justice, poverty, and the defence of human rights in the region (Levine, 1981, p. 51). This stance, which was later shunned by the church hierarchy, led to the development of what would be known as liberation theology, which aimed to become an alternative to capitalism by returning the church to its early communitarian principles. Eventually, various priests became radicalised and determined that violence was the only path to achieve social justice, and in that sense, armed struggle was justified to remove oppressive forces (Porch, 2013, p. 231). Soon-to-be guerrilla priests infused the ELN with a high degree of fanaticism that translated into a highly dynamic use of force. The first priest to join the ELN was soon to become the main ideologue of the group, Father Camilo Torres, who, by accepting armed violence as a righteous path to fight oppression, set an example for other socialist-leaning priests who soon convinced themselves of the inevitability of armed revolution in order to achieve social change (Broderick, 1987, p. 35).

Three leftist Spanish priests, Manuel Perez, Domingo Lan, and José Antonio Perez, who travelled to Colombia in the fall of 1968 to attend the Episcopal Conference of Latin America (CELAM) in the context of the Vatican Council II discussions, quickly became foreign fighters. According to the ELN's official history, 48 socialist-leaning priests and students met on a farm on the margins of the CELAM conference, where they drafted a joint declaration known as "Golconda". In this document, they denounced Colombian state violence and repression against the working classes and affirmed the need to begin a revolutionary struggle with the oppressed peoples to achieve a change in the socio-economic structure of Colombia and create a truly socialist society (ELN, 2018). After the signature of the "Golconda" declaration, the three Spanish priests were deported, but they found their way back to the country illegally and took contact with the ELN, which they joined in 1969. In the words of Father Domingo Lan, the decision to join the insurgent group was to "follow the example and thoughts of Camilo", as the ELN professed the "right political line, with honesty resistant to all tests and a faith in the people and the cause for liberation that places the organisation at the vanguard of the fight and in the heart of the exploited masses" (ELN, 2018).

Priests José Perez and Domingo Lan were killed in the early 1970s, when the ELN went through a severe process of decline. From 1970 to 1973, the Colombian military implemented a highly successful counter-insurgency campaign against the second and most powerful "foco" of the ELN, which was composed of the most able military units of the group and which attempted to expand operations into Antioquia, Colombia's second biggest and richest department. The ELN attempted to settle in the surroundings of the village of Anor, in the central Magdalena river delta, but the military had already been forewarned of the ELN's intention after careful intelligence work with the local communities, many of whom distrusted the guerrilla and mounted a highly effective counter-insurgency campaign (Delgado, 2016, p. 274).

In the counterinsurgency campaign known simply as "Operation Anor,", the ELN lost 135 of its estimated 200 members to a well-planned and resourced operation. As the British military attaché reported back to London in 1973, the Colombian armed forces were using various methods of anti-guerrilla tactics, particularly British and French, "including the use of helicopters in conjunction with operations on the ground designed to drive out the guerrillas into a small central area capable of being sealed off and attacked effectively." (British Embassy Bogota, 1973) But apart from the highly effective application of force, the Colombian military considered that the success against the ELN in Operation Anor, which almost annihilated the group, was due to the skilful planning of the phases of the operation. In particular, the initial preparation of the battlefield with well-targeted psychological operations and military-civic action programmes allowed the military to alienate the ELN from the local population and to isolate its military units where they could then be targeted by the army (Villamarin, 1999, p. 214).

However, the ELN recovered from their losses in Anor. The long-standing view for military practitioners studying the Colombian case has been that the Colombian government's leniency towards the surviving members allowed a marginalised ELN to recover forces as its leadership was able to reorganise at the frontier with Venezuela (Vallejo, 2006, p. 160; Valencia, 2013, p. 387). For their part, and as will be discussed in the next section, the ELN believed that they could create revolutionary conditions by taking advantage of the growing oil industry, mobilising the workers, and extorting international companies that settled their businesses in Arauca (Peñate, 1999, p. 72).

STRUCTURE AND IDEOLOGY OF THE ELN

Since its foundation, the ELN's political programme has combined orthodox Marxist-Leninist ideology with self-styled characteristics. At the heart of its programme is the denunciation of Colombia's oligarchic democratic system and a demand for the establishment of a veritable "democratic and popular government". In those lines, the ELN has historically insisted on "the liberation from international monopolies", the "confiscation of imperialist economic interests," and "the nationalisation of the subsoil and its exploitation for the benefit of the people" (ELN, 1965). The ELN's posture regarding Colombia's extractive sector, which since the late 1940s has been the basis of the national economy, has fundamentally been a demand for its nationalisation, a tenet that has defined the group's thinking and overall behaviour in the past five decades in two key ways. First, it has determined the overall structure of the group, in essence by defining its territorial presence along the oil industry's geography, including production, refining, and transit regions, and in particular those along the Magdalena River basin in central Colombia and eastwards in the frontier with Venezuela. Secondly, following this, oil also shaped the group's sphere of influence in specific social sectors, mostly through its encroachment into universities and trade unions in oil-rich areas as an attempt to consolidate through political fronts (Peñate, 1999, p. 71).

The ELN's unorthodox combination of Marxist-Leninist communist ideology with more "down to earth" national issue-based politics, coupled with their attempt to work politically at the local level with social movements both urban and rural, paved the way for the unusual alliance with militant Catholic priests in Colombia and Spain who ascribed to Liberation Theology, as was described in the previous section. One of the chief representatives of liberation theology in Colombia was Father Camilo Torres, a sociologist trained at the Catholic University of Leuven in Belgium who worked as a professor at Colombia's prestigious public National University (Broderick, 1987, p. 32). Father Torres joined the ranks of the ELN in 1965 after declaring that armed revolutionary action was the only way forward to achieve the reform of Colombia's political system (Torres, 1973, p. 97).

Father Torres became one of the chief ideologues of the ELN, having already been in contact while still in civilian life with the group's leaders via diverse university student fronts. Father Torres imbued the armed group with further ideological and practical underpinnings that combined Marxism-Leninism with Christian teachings and have, to date, influenced the group's behaviour and modus operandi. A main influence of Father Torres was in terms of political activism, promoting the development of what he denominated a "plural political apparatus" that could work at the communal level and, in theory, lead to the real democratic participation of diverse social sectors in the revolutionary process (Broderick, 1987, p. 48). This, in practise, has led the ELN to further develop its "entryism" tactics in order to infiltrate diverse organisations of civil society, trade unions, and educational institutions. A second influence can be denominated "revolutionary mysticism", that is, a code of practise in which each guerrilla soldier needs to act as a religious missionary. According to Torres, "mass organisation requires daily and continued work; the working classes demand effective presence and are not to be answered with vain promises or excuses" (Torres, 1973, p. 110). Such a code of conduct has mostly translated into the evolution of diverse populations and social control mechanisms to win over hearts and minds, as well as the selective use of violence in order to prevent the alienation of the local population in which it conducts political work. On the other hand, this sort of fervour has at times instilled its members with a high degree of fanaticism and rendered them ineffective in the long run. In fact, Father Torres' own fervour led him to his death in a failed ambush against a larger Colombian Army unit in 1966. That was his first and only armed combat experience, which he entered with a lack of proper training and which, in the long run, converted him into one of the ELN's first martyrs.

A final influence the ELN received from radical priests was to impact the structure and governance of the group. The ELN soon became a sort of federation, not with a top-down control structure but rather a multi-cephalous organisation with a collective decision-making process. The reason behind such a structure was to replicate the arrangement of the early Catholic Church of the I to III centuries AD, with a "synodal" assembly in which to discuss issues at a strategic level and also to allow local churches to self-govern. In practise, this influence translated into the creation of four key decision-making structures throughout the ELN's history. Since the mid-1960s, the group has been led by a Central Command (COCE) consisting of five commanders, one of whom had the symbolic title of military commander and head of the ELN. The COCE's members are selected by a National Directorate (*Directorio Nacional*) composed of 23 members that also plays an advisory role for the COCE. The first commander of the

COCE up to his expulsion in 1973, as mentioned, was Fabio Vasquez. The COCE was and is still in charge of delineating the group's strategic policy decisions; however, it lacks real operational control of the units at the regional and local levels. Finally, a Central General Staff (Estado Mayor Central), composed of the commanders of the group's armed fronts, is in charge of offering military advice to the COCE and of liaising with the group's armed fronts. Policy and military planning in the ELN are, in essence, parallel processes that sometimes collide.

In terms of political decision-making, the ELN has customarily emphasised the democratic nature of its processes in its attempt to legitimise its activities. Since 1986, in an attempt to strengthen its democratic character, the group has created a National Congress (Congreso Nacional), which, since then, is considered to be the nominal maximum authority of the group. Delegates from all fronts meet every few years to evaluate the plans implemented by the COCE and define the ELN's strategy. Between 1986 and 2015, the ELN clandestinely organised and held five national congresses. Thanks to these outwardly democratic structures, the group's armed war fronts and fronts at the regional and local levels have maintained a high degree of political and operational autonomy in their areas of responsibility. This peculiar multilevel structure has been a fundamental factor that explains the longevity of the ELN, the appeal of its discourse among certain social sectors, and its capacity to adapt its plans of action according to changing circumstances at the political and operational levels. However, such an intricate democratic decision-making process also helps to explain the group's failures at the strategic level, in particular to conduct the armed campaign following a unified policy direction and effective command and control.

Why has the ELN's unique structure and decision-making process been a source of internal tension and affected the group's cohesion up to this date? In essence, the ELN's history is one of divisions and purges. Despite its theoretically democratic structure, individual leaders who have gained ascendancy and attempted to steer the course of the organisation or who have diverged from the COCE have eventually been sidelined, expelled, or even executed. This was the case of Victor Medina, co-founder of the group, and of two other early leaders, all of whom were executed by order of Vasquez in 1968. Medina had been accused by his peers at the COCE of mounting a conspiracy against Vasquez after he had voiced deep criticism for the botched operation in which Father Torres had been killed by the army in 1966. Medina opposed perilous if not irrational operational demands by ELN military commanders, including that of asking guerrillas during their baptism of fire to attempt to obtain at any cost the weapons of soldiers and police killed in ambushes. That demand had cost Father Torres his life, as he was shot at point-blank range by a seriously wounded soldier. Another early case of divergence was that of Jaime Arenas, a student leader who joined the first ranks of the ELN in 1965. He criticised the execution of Medina in 1968 and was then court-martialled and forced to leave the movement. Arenas published in 1971 the book *La Guerrilla por Dentro* (The Guerrilla from Within), which was to become a primer into the behaviour of the early ELN. The 30-year-old Arenas was murdered in cold blood right after the book was published, shot in the back while walking in plain daylight in Bogota's city centre. *La Guerrilla por Dentro* depicts a guerrilla movement deeply affected by internal divisions that, in Arenas' words, failed to fulfil Ché Guevara's promise of the "New Man," or heroic guerrilla. Rather, it had become an organisation overrun by paranoia and internal purges resulting from the regime of terror imposed by the COCE (Arenas, 1971, p. 77).

The internal purges of the ELN also touched its founder and original leader, Fabio Vasquez, who, after the dramatic counter-insurgency campaign of Anori in 1973, became a victim of his own internal control practises, was court-martialled and expelled from the group, and was forced to leave for Cuba, where he still lives in exile. Vasquez's dismissal was part of a conspiracy led by Spaniard Manuel Perez, known by his nom de guerre "Poliarco" or simply "Priest Perez" and a then 14-year-old peasant guerrilla, Nicolas Rodriguez "Gabino", who would become the group's top leaders. Perez and Gabino were strategic in the revival of the ELN after the failure at Anor, transforming the ELN into its present form. Priest Perez became officially the leader of the COCE in 1978 and led the group up to his death from hepatitis in 1998. The leadership of the COCE was then inherited by his protégé "Gabino", who is still the nominal leader of the ELN and has been known to be living in Cuba since the Colombian government initiated peace talks with the group in 2014 (El Heraldo, 2018).

Under the leadership of "Priest Perez", the ELN was not only able to recover from almost total extinction after Operation Anor, when the group lost almost 80% of its armed personnel, but also managed to expand its structure and territorial presence, including into Venezuelan territory. The ELN's expansion into Colombia's eastern border with Venezuela since the late 1970s was enabled by the decision to initiate operations in Arauca, a department of 24,000 km^2 that borders the Orinoco River at the frontier with Venezuela and which has historically been, until this day, under-governed by the Colombian state. Mostly composed of plain lands and tropical jungles with a very low density of peasant population, Arauca became a massive source of income for the Colombian state due to the discovery of new untapped oil reserves. International corporations began to exploit these reserves, and the newly constructed Cao-Limón Coveas pipeline turned into the main artery for the transport of crude oil from the jungles of the Orinoco basin into the Caribbean coast for its final transport to Europe, Asia, and North America. The ELN also began to profit from Arauca's oil wealth, mainly by extorting international oil corporations operating in the department as well as hijacking regional and local administrations' oil royalties received from the Colombian government (Peñate, 1999, p. 54).

In synthesis, the current form of the ELN has consolidated on the oil-rich border between Colombia and Venezuela, thanks to the guidance of the Central Command, which, since the death of Priest Perez, has steered the group until this day. Since 1998, the ELN's key leaders have been Nicolas Rodríguez Bautista alias "Gabino" head of the COCE; Eliecer Herlinto Chamorro Acosta alias "Antonio García" military commander; and Israel Ramírez Pineda alias "Pablo Beltrán," third in command, in charge of political indoctrination and training, and who has led the group's negotiations with the Colombian state on multiple occasions since the mid-1990s (Echandia, 2013, p. 17).

OPERATIONS

The Colombian Ministry of Defence's latest estimate considers that the ELN has exponentially increased its manpower since the effective demobilisation of the FARC in 2016. Whereas earlier figures estimated the strength of the ELN at around 2,000 men by 2000, the most current figures recorded an increase of 1,000 men in the last year, putting its total strength at 4,000. The expansion of the ELN in the context of the peace agreement with the FARC is linked to its encroachment into territories vacated by that group and the recruitment of many of the ex-FARC's rank and file who left the disarmament process during the past year. However, calculating the real strength of the ELN is not a clear-cut task, as its more clandestine modus operandi, networked organisation, and lack of an insurgent army, in the classical sense, make it difficult to account for every member. Moreover, the reliance of the ELN on its support bases and militias for their operations leads to problems in calculating its real strength beyond its more visible war units. Another issue is the evidence of recruitment by the ELN within Venezuela. For example, the Colombian Police recently publicly reported that it had found Venezuelan ID cards on the maimed bodies of ELN operatives killed during botched terrorist operations (El Espectador, 2018). There are also allegations that the group created stand-alone units in that country, which some observers consider a response to a separate new political and armed project by the ELN in support of the defence of the regime of President Nicolas Maduro amid the internal crisis that affects Venezuela (International Crisis Group, 2019, p. 5).

Since the recovery of the ELN from its defeat at Anori in the mid-1970s, its activities have been mainly centred in the Colombian eastern oil-rich departments of Arauca, Santander, and Norte de Santander. At the onset of the 2000s, the group expanded its operations to the southwest of the country, at the frontier with Ecuador, in the departments of Nariño and Putumayo, again because of the development of the oil industry in that part of the country.

In essence, the ELN's assault against the oil industry is based on direct and indirect tactics of confrontation. On the one hand, the ELN's main finance method in these oil-rich areas is to levy local war taxes to allow oil companies to operate and to compel those who do not pay to pay by sabotaging their operations, mainly by kidnapping oil workers for ransom (and in particular foreign executives and engineers). In the 1990s, when it was no longer able to leverage Cold War divisions, the financing mechanisms that the wealthy Colombian petroleum sector offered to the ELN enabled it to secure financing and recruits and to underpin a compelling ideological vision. Since then, the ELN has begun to work more closely with criminal organisations or even engage directly in criminal activities. On the other hand, given the strategic importance of the oil industry for the Colombian state, the ELN's activities impose operational strains on the state's armed forces, which have to focus on the protection of the oil infrastructure, in particular the oil pipelines, which are a target of convenience for the ELN. The need for constant supervision and protection of the oil infrastructure by the Colombian state forces offers an advantage to the group's hit-and-run tactics, wearing down the military through the profuse use of ambushes and minefields.

At the operational level, the latest expansion of the ELN is a result of the leadership of Gustavo Anibal Giraldo Quinchia, alias "Pablito", who is the military commander of the Domingo Lan Front based out of Arauca. It is essentially the core unit of the Eastern War Front, which covers Colombia's eastern departments of Boyacá, Arauca, Casanare, and Norte de Santander. Pablito was recruited in his early teens in 1982 and quickly rose through the ranks, becoming the latest addition to the COCE in 2015 (Verdad Abierta, 2015). The Colombian security forces arrested Pablito in Bogotá in 2008, but he quickly escaped from prison. Since then, he has been considered a "high-value target" not only by Colombian authorities but also by the US, which accuses him of kidnapping American citizens and drug trafficking charges (InSight Crime, 2019). It is considered that "Pablito" has control of over 60% of the ELN's military and financial power, and his influence extends nationally, financially supporting fronts with less armed capacity on the Colombian Pacific coast. The ELN's Eastern War Front, and in particular the Domingo Lain Front, is known to be deeply involved in the illegal drug trade, not only by controlling and taxing coca farmers in the Catatumbo region in Norte de Santander but also by controlling drug routes into Venezuela.

Pablito's Domingo Lain Front has a reputation for being able to carry out special operations outside of his primary area of responsibility, particularly high-impact terrorist attacks in Colombia's major urban areas. A case in point was the January 2019 car bomb attack against the Colombian National Police Academy in central Bogota, in which 20 police cadets were killed. The attack was organised and perpetrated by Pablito's units, allegedly without the knowledge of the ELN's Central Command, and took by surprise the group's peace delegation in Havana (Semana, 2019a). That car bomb attack was Colombia's deadliest terrorist attack in more than a decade and led to the unilateral decision by the incoming Colombian government of President Ivan Duque to put an end to the peace talks taking place in Havana since 2017.

Pablito's political and operational influence also reaches deep into Venezuela, where the Domingo Lain Front has been known to have bases since the 1980s. Since the rise to power of Venezuelan President Nicolas Maduro in April 2013, Pablito's influence has begun to expand across Venezuela, including because of the group's general alignment with the so-called Bolivarian Revolution (La Nación, 2008). As new research by the International Crisis Group has started to reveal, the ELN has become an enforcer for cronies of Nicolas Maduro, particularly to control a booming illegal gold mining business in Venezuela's Amazonian region. In the last two years, Venezuela's "Mining Arc" has become a strategic reserve for the crisis-ridden Venezuelan regime, where the influence of the ELN is manifest (International Crisis Group, 2019, p. ii). The ELN's presence extends up to the Venezuelan frontier with Guyana, 400 miles away from the Colombian border. In October 2018, the group was blamed for the massacre of seven gold miners in that remote region in what are yet unclear circumstances (Ramirez & Parkin-Daniels, 2018). However, that recent event demonstrates the extent of the ELN's presence in Venezuela and its destabilising effects across an already fragile region, all of which deserve more attention from analysts.

The strength of Commander Pablito illustrates the challenges of the ELN's operational autonomy. The power of his front, including its notoriety within Venezuela and its tacit support from the Maduro regime, has allowed him to maintain a hawkish line in the past decade and, in particular, actively resist peace negotiations with the Colombian state that could lead to a unilateral ceasefire of the ELN and an eventual decommissioning of weapons (Semana, 2019b).

CONCLUSION

Colombia's peace agreement with the FARC-EP of September 2016 has brought significant changes to the security landscape of the country. Two years after the signature of the peace agreement, significant parts of the country where the FARC was present are effectively transiting into a "post-conflict" scenario, particularly in terms of the reduction in levels of violence. Yet other areas have actually been experiencing an increase in violence. That increase is in great part due to the reconfiguration of the ELN as a result of the peace with the FARC. Authorities believe that the ELN, in particular its Eastern War Front, took advantage of the FARC's disarmament and demobilisation process to expand their own presence and broker new deals with criminal organisations to improve their rents from illegal economies, including cocaine production, illegal gold mining, and extortion. Future actions by the ELN could potentially undermine the progress made by Colombia in the implementation of its historic 2016 peace agreement.

In this context, and despite exploratory talks since 2014 and a formal peace negotiation that took place in Quito, Ecuador, and then in Havana since January 2017, the ELN continued its military offensive against the state. Ambushes against military and police patrols, extortion, and kidnapping, as well as attacks against oil infrastructure, were part of their day-to-day operations while the talks took place (InSight Crime, 2017). The latest encroachment of the ELN in Venezuela, where it has become a player in the country's political and social crises by strategically supporting the Maduro regime and increasing its armed capacity (International Crisis Group, 2019, p. 5), is definitely another factor that has weakened the group's consensus on the peace talks. The latest divisions are not simply the result of short-term calculations by members of the group but rather reflect structural features and trends that are part of the ELN's long history.

In short, the latest behaviour of the ELN demonstrates that there is a lack of internal consensus within the organisation about a general commitment to peace negotiations. Commanders like Pablito and the cadres of the Eastern War Front in general were known to be reticent about negotiations in the first place. These units are also some of the most active and prosperous ones and have been responsible for most of the ELN's armed activity in the past years. The January 2019 bomb attack against the Colombian Police Academy, the deadliest in a decade, which was conducted by the ELN hardliners, has generated shockwaves both nationally and internationally. It led the Colombian government to unilaterally put an end to the negotiations with the ELN (Maya, 2019). This event also signals yet another chapter of escalation in the unending war between the Colombian state and the small but resilient ELN insurgency.

References

Arenas, J. (1971). *La Guerrilla por Dentro: Análisis del ELN colombiano*. Bogotá: Ediciones Tercer Mundo.

British Embassy Bogota. (1973, February). Colombia internal security. (Guerrilla Activities in Colombia, 1 January 1973 – 31 December 1973, FCO 7/2480). Kew Gardens, United Kingdom: National Archives

Broderick, J. (1987). *Camilo el cura guerrillero*. Bogotá: Ediciones El Labrador.

Central Intelligence Agency. (1976, 26 November). *Colombia: Troubles for President López. Secret intelligence summary. (Colombia and the United States: Political violence, narcotics, and human rights, 1948–2010)*. Digital National Security Archive, George Washington University.

Delgado, J. (2016). *Counter-insurgency in Colombia: the origins and evolution of a military strategic tradition.* (Unpublished doctoral dissertation). Available at: https://kclpure.kcl.ac.uk/portal/en/theses/counterinsurgency-in-colombia(b411b659-7e82-4f30-a7c3-31ff159a866a).html

Díaz, J. (2010). *Movimiento Obrero Estudiantil Campesino y los orígenes de la nueva izquierda en Colombia.* Bogota: Universidad Nacional de Colombia.

ELN. (1965, 7 January). *Manifiesto de Simacota.* [Online]. Available at: http://www.cedema.org/ver.php?id=3703

ELN. (2018, 28 February). *Domingo Laín, Golconda y la CELAM de 1968. ELN Voces.* [Online]. Available at: https://elnvoces.com/domingo-lain-golconda-y-la-celam-de-1968/

Echandía, C. (2013). *Auge y Declive del Ejército de Liberación Nacional (ELN).* Bogota: Fundación Ideas para la paz. [Online]. Available at: http://www.ideaspaz.org/publications/posts/692

El Espectador. (2018, 12 February). Ejército afirma que Eln está "utilizando" venezolanos en atentados. [Online]. Available at: https://www.elespectador.com/noticias/judicial/ejercito-afirma-que-eln-esta-utilizando-venezolanos-en-atentados-articulo-738731

El Heraldo. (2018, 18 November). Duque exige explicaciones a Cuba por alojar a Gabino.*El Heraldo.* [Online]. Available at: https://www.elheraldo.co/colombia/duque-exige-explicaciones-cuba-por-alojar-gabino-quien-habria-viajado-desde-venezuela

Gott, R. (2008). *Guerrilla movements in Latin America.* Oxford: Seagull Books.

Insight Crime. (2017, 31 July). *Despite peace talks, Colombia's ELN Guerrillas Continue Expansion.* [Online]. Available at: https://www.insightcrime.org/news/analysis/despite-peace-talks-colombia-eln-guerrillas-continue-expansion/

Insight Crime. (2019, 3 March). *Gustavo Anibal Giraldo, alias "Pablito".* [Online]. Available at: https://www.insightcrime.org/colombia-organized-crime-news/gustavo-anibal-giraldo-alias-pablito/

International Crisis Group. (2019, February 28). *Gold and grief in Venezuela's Violent South. Latin America Report N°73.* Bogotá/Brussels: ICG. [Online]. Available at: https://www.crisisgroup.org/latin-america-caribbean/andes/venezuela/073-gold-and-grief-venezuelas-violent-south

La Nación. (2008, January 12). Chávez: las FARC 'no son terroristas'. *La Nación (Argentina).* [Online]. Available at: https://www.lanacion.com.ar/el-mundo/chavez-las-farc-no-son-terroristas-nid978386

Levine, D. (1981). *Religion and Politics in Latin America: The Catholic Church in Venezuela and Colombia.* New Jersey: Princeton University Press.

Maya, M. (2019, 25 January). *Enfrentar al Eln sin darle un portazo a la paz. El Tiempo.* [Online]. Available at: https://www.eltiempo.com/justicia/conflicto-y-narcotrafico/la-paz-con-el-eln-despues-de-ataque-con-carro-bomba-columna-319136

Miroff, N. (2015, October 31). Colombia's Juan Manuel Santos sees peace at hand, and threats too. *The Washington Post.* [Online]. Available at: https://www.washingtonpost.com/world/the_americas/colombias-juan-manuel-santos-sees-peace-at-hand-and-threats-too/2015/10/31/c3e8b1a2-7e7b-11e5-bfb6-65300a5ff562_story.html?utm_term=.c92ee77d4cfa

Peñate, A. (1999). "El sendero estratégico del ELN: del idealismo guevarista al clientelismo armado." In M. Deas, & M. Llorente (Eds.), (pp. 53–98). Bogotá: Ediciones Uniandes/CEREC/Editorial Norma.

Pizarro Leongómez, E. (2004). *Una democracia asediada. Balance y perspectivas del conflicto armado en Colombia.* Bogotá: Norma.

Porch, D. (2013). *Counterinsurgency: Exposing the myths of the new way of war.* Cambridge: CUP.

Ramirez, M., & Parkin-Daniels, J. (2018, 30 October). *Colombian rebels blamed for killing spree 400 miles inside Venezuela. The Guardian.* [Online]. Available at: https://www.theguardian.com/global-development/2018/oct/30/venezuelans-say-colombian-rebels-to-blame-for-killing-spree-in-mining-zone

Rendón, J. (2014). "Los del campo", "los de la ciudad". Ideología organizacional, vanguardia revolucionaria campesina y aislamiento político del Ejército de Liberación Nacional 1962–1973. *Análisis Político No.81.* [Online]. Available at: https://revistas.unal.edu.co/index.php/anpol/article/download/45765/47297

Semana. (2019a, 25 January). El atentado en Bogotá es una "acción irrepetible": Pablo Beltrán. *Semana.* [Online]. Available at: https://www.semana.com/nacion/articulo/pablo-beltran-habla-del-rompimiento-de-la-negociacion-de-paz-en-la-habana/599141

Semana. (2019b, 26 January). Pablito el sanguinario. *Semana.* [Online]. Available at: https://www.semana.com/nacion/articulo/pablito-del-eln-comandante-del-frente-domingo-lain-el-sanguinario/599211

Torres, C. (1973). *Revolutionary priest: The complete writings and messages of Camilo Torres.* Harmondsworth: Penguin.

US Embassy Bogotá. (1969, 25 April). *Ferment within Catholic church.* (RG 59 1967-69, Pol3Cons-IA to Pol 12 Col, Box 1989) Record Group 69. College Park, MD: National Archives at College Park

Valencia, A. (2013). *Los presidentes que yo conocí.* Bogotá: Editorial Planeta.

Vallejo, H. (2006). "Operación Anorí: golpe al corazón del ELN." In. G. Martínez, (Ed.). *Hablan los generales* (pp. 145–171). Bogota: Norma

Verdad Abierta. (2015, 9 January). 'Pablito': el fiel de la balanza en el Eln. *Verdad Abierta.* [Online]. Available at: https://verdadabierta.com/alias-pablito-es-el-nuevo-miembro-del-coce-del-eln/

Villamarín, L. (1999). *Condor en el aire.* Bogotá: Tercer Mundo Editores.

40

CAMARENA AS CONTEXT

Mexico, Drug Cartels, and Structures of Insecurity

Matthew Coleman

INTRODUCTION

When Drug Enforcement Administration (DEA) agent Enrique S. "Kiki" Camarena did not show up as scheduled to meet his wife Geneva for lunch on February 7, 1985, she began to worry and notified the proper U.S. authorities aware of his official duties. Her worst fears were later realised. Nearly a month later, a local farmer found his badly bruised and decomposed body wrapped in plastic and lying along a road near the ranch of Manuel Bravo Cervantes, a known small-arms and drug dealer who had died several days before in a raid by Mexican Federal Judicial Police (MFJP) acting on a tip regarding the location of Camarena. Subsequent forensic investigations by the DEA, Federal Bureau of Investigation (FBI), and partnered agencies revealed the bodies of Camarena and his pilot Alfredo Zavala Avelar (also found there) had been removed from another area by the members of the Guadalajara drug cartel and dumped on the Bravo family ranch.

The investigations by the DEA into the death of Camarena found he had been abducted and murdered at the ranch of Miguel ngel Félix Gallardo, where his key associates in the Guadalajara cartel, Rafael Caro Quintero and Ernesto Fonseca Carrillo, had also been complicit. As importantly, Operation Leyanda (the name of the investigation) revealed with time not only the extent of drug cartel organisation and influence in Mexico but also the complicity of its government. The relationship between Mexican drug trafficking organisations (DTOs) and the Government of Mexico (GoM) was far deeper, more active, integrated, and complex than US security officials had estimated (Feess et al., 2017). In fact, the relationship determined the very structures, dynamics, and context shaping the quality of life for modern Mexico and its civil society – the family and private sphere, the third sector of society markedly different from the government and business sectors even though interconnected with them.

The Enrique Camarena case revealed that Mexican DTOs had grown into transregional players able to penetrate deeply into the government of Mexico and control major states and their organisations while shaping security policies. By the mid-1980s, the Guadalajara cartel had grown into one of the world's largest criminal organisations, spanning the borders of Mexico and the region while holding an uncontested position as well as the drug trafficking routes into the United States (Beittel, 2018, p. 8; Haughton & Romaniuk, 2023). But these bare facts of history alone do not uncover the sweeping strategic and structural changes facilitated by the growing drug empire and its effects on civil society.

Geo-political realities involving the interplay of U.S. regional counter-narcotics policy, the Government of Mexico's domestic security practises, and growing Mexican DTO power over drug trafficking to the United States emerged in the period and created enduring relationships to the present. Increased countermeasures from the United States Government (USG) during the administration of President Ronald Reagan on both domestic production and consumption of illegal drugs and on the Columbian cartels shaped the locus and flow of illegal narcotics activities, inadvertently empowering Mexican DTOs and their strategic border with the United States (Lee et al., 2019). The readiness of Mexico's local, state, and federal political and security leaders to work with its expanding drug cartels synergised with the effects of Columbian cartels doing the same with their Mexican counterparts.

Adding to these factors was the skilful leadership of Gallardo, Quintero, and Fonseca, driving key associations, assassinations, network building, and exploitation of assets (such as numerous small airfields and abundant labour) across the political, security, infrastructure, and social domains that structure Mexican life, even when exploited for the development of a sophisticated criminal drug industry. Indeed, Quintero had used "mass corruption" across the political-security domains of Mexico and the region as "a means and method of achieving its goals," the

 DOI: 10.4324/9780429426063-45

U.S. Eastern District of New York Court revealed in 2017 as it listed in detail the vast infrastructure of his organisation (United States v. Quintero, 2017, p. 2). During this time, an associate of the Guadalajara cartel so deftly created transnational facilitation networks for drug trafficking that he earned the alias "El Rapido" (USA v. Guzman Loera, 2018, p. 4). Decades later, he emerged as the leader of the Sinaloa Drug Trafficking Organisation and was better known as Joaquin "El Chapo" Guzman, the most notorious drug trafficker in history.

Although the exact time frames, interactions, and events leading to the dominance of major areas of Mexico by the Guadalajara cartel are sketchy, the outcomes are not. The Mexican DTOs led by the Guadalajara cartel wasted little time in using their strategic gains to seize and reorient areas and states, including the security apparatuses of these states. The state of Jalisco during this period is an example.

In the early 1980s, the drug trafficking organisation later known as the Guadalajara cartel relocated from the Sinaloa state to the city of Guadalajara and took much more than its name. The cartel made a tactical move to this second-largest city in Mexico and centre of Jalisco state for organisational development (sanctuary, consolidation, and coordination) and for the mass cultivation, processing, and shipment of marijuana – in addition to developing the transshipment of Columbian cocaine via this coastal area and others (Feess et al., 2017, p. 50).

The Guadalajara cartel's influence in the state demonstrated not only its complicity but also its cooptation. In addition to the collusion of the governor of the state, the entire police force fell under the cartel's control and became a "private army for narcotraffickers in Guadalajara".

The cartel used the Jalisco State Police for a variety of offensive and defensive activities ranging from assassination to protection and from guarding shipments to performing basic tasks. Juan Vasquez of the *LA Times* (1985) described the situation:

> To judge from the declarations, the state judicial police were virtually at the beck and call of the drug dealers. Officers were frequently summoned to accompany them on trips, to act as bodyguards or simply to wait around in case they were needed at nightclubs and other spots the gangsters frequented. For example, on the day of Camarena's abduction, Torres Lepe said, he was called to the home of Rafael Caro Quintero, reportedly one of the top narcotics dealers in Mexico, and was told only that he was going on a *mandadito*, an errand (Vasquez, 1985).

Although Mexican federal authorities later blamed the Jalisco state police for Camarena's death, the scapegoating did little to address the severe outcomes of cartel influence over state and local police, a security entity lower in rank than its federal counterparts but not lesser in effect on local security.

The consequences of Mexican DTO control of the Jalisco state transcended both a mere increase in the growth of the illegal drug industry presence and the death of Special Agent Camarena. The dominant presence of the Guadalajara cartel had severe consequences for civil society, including the targeted killing of domestic opposition or non-compliance, random killings by cartel leaders, execution of suspected collaborators, and exacerbation of economic downturns for farm labour increasingly burdened by cartel usage of these remote areas (Drug Enforcement Administration Reauthorization for Fiscal Year, 1986, 1985, p. 25). The abduction and killing of Captain Zavala and two Americans killed in Guadalajara by Quintero one evening, mistakenly believed to be DEA agents at a local restaurant, demonstrate the impunity, brazenness, and openness of DTO activities threatening human security in Mexico, a pattern that continues to the present.

During the period, the very term "plata o plomo" (silver or lead) borrowed from violence-ridden Columbia became terminology and practise in Mexico as cartels offered their targets the choice of bribery (the silver) or death (the lead bullet). Also borrowed from Columbia was the tactic of cartel terrorism used against high-ranking political and security officials (DEA Reauthorization for Fiscal Year, 1986, 1985, p. 12).

Indeed, the cooptation of Mexican states by drug cartels was neither episodic nor intrinsic to Jalisco or the Guadalajara cartel. After its dissolution in 1989 and subsequent decentralisation of control, the problem increased over the following decades, as evident in the expansiveness of organisations, levels of drug production, sophistication of movement and distribution, and use of violence to achieve objectives. The divisions of cartel territory after Gallardo's reign coincided with the territories of his lieutenants, their control of key narco-infrastructure, and the political states where the infrastructure existed (Beittel, 2018, p. 1).

Ioan Grillo (2014) aptly summed up the massacre of 43 students at Inguala, Mexico, on September 26, 2014, as a matter of "state capture," a term he uses to describe the cooptation of states and their security apparatus. He notes:

> Why drug cartels want to slaughter students may at first seem inexplicable. But it is a symptom of a systematic process that has been taking place in Mexico for years. Drug cartels are taking over chunks of government apparatus from local police forces to city and state governments. Sometimes, they control the officials; other times, cartel members themselves are the officials. I call it state capture. A student I talked to had a more visceral term for it: narco-politica, or narco-politics (p.8).

The emergent Sonora, Tijuana, Juarez, Sinaloa, and Gulf Cartels suffered inter- and intra-cartel violence, punctuated by periods of narco-peace, in the following decades, but the key infrastructure remained the same. Eduardo Guerrero-Gutierrez noted in 2015 that the current typology of drug trafficking organisations involves designations as *national, regional, toll-collector*, and *cell*. Each designation or characterisation coincides with the enduring areas and operations of the narco-infrastructure: the control of major supply, access, and distribution points (Beittel, 2018, p. 27; see also Knowles, 2008).

Therefore, the vast narco-infrastructure remains intact. Areas such as Tijuana and Juarez remain critical nodes for market access; the Gulf and Pacific Corridors remain vibrant; and the Golden Triangle continues to produce its expanding hectares of poppy fields while Mexico's military exaggerates reports of eradication and furnishes show-piece examples of success, and locals esteem their narco-traffickers as "valientes" (brave ones) (Grillo, 2011; see also The Drug Trade in Mexico and U. Policy Implications, 1995).

Yet, the children of the Golden Triangle often suffer the consequences of this key area of the narco-infrastructure. Anabel Hernandez, in *Narcoland: The Mexican Drug Lords and Their Godfathers* (2010), remarks succinctly:

> [M]inors are put often to work by their parents on the poppy and marijuana harvests. These are kids who become criminals without even realizing it. Many, from the age of seven upwards, die of poisoning by the pesticides used on the plantations. Those who survive into adolescence are already carrying AK-47s, or 'goat's horns' as these weapons are popularly known (p. 2).

The continuity of cartel infrastructure operating holistically and systematically over the decades ensured continuing patterns of violence that supported such durability and growth. An integrated national system of supply routes, cultivation areas, transshipment corridors, market access points, and associated infrastructure of administration, finance, processing, and protection exists no different than similar industry systems in Mexico, such as petroleum or agriculture. The Mexican states of the "Golden Triangle" (Sinaloa, Durango, and Chihuahua), coastal areas of Guerrero, Michoacán (as well as Jalisco), Tamaulipas, border towns, and ports of entry to the United States all serve as modern-day examples of these enduring structures of organised crime and violence operating over large areas of Mexico and its state apparatus (Feuer & Palmer, 2018).

But among these examples, the state of Tamaulipas serves as a case study illustrating the relationship between the narco-infrastructure and violence against Mexico's civil society. The Department of State's Mexico Travel Advisory warns about the state of Tamaulipas:

> Violent crime, such as murder, armed robbery, carjacking, kidnapping, extortion, and sexual assault, is common. Gang activity, including gun battles and blockades, is widespread. Armed criminal groups target public and private passenger buses as well as private automobiles traveling through Tamaulipas, often taking passengers hostage and demanding ransom payments. Federal and state security forces have limited capability to respond to violence in many parts of the state (Mexico Travel Advisory, November 2018, para. 71).

Although the violent rivalry between the Gulf Cartel and Los Zetas Cartel, which lasted from roughly 2010 to 2015, is no longer present in Tamaulipas, violence is still on the rise in 2019 due in large part to factions who are given power by the remaining structures: political, security, financial, judicial, and business. On this crucial transshipment route from Central and South America to the United States, pundits have frequently acknowledged the capabilities of these criminal gangs but not the narco-state's institutional framework (Wilson & Weigend, 2014). Drug trafficking and the attendant violence continue unabated despite the GoM's Plan Tamaulipas, a targeted and regional strategy to break up criminal organisations, block smuggling routes, and reinforce local security institutions.

Corrupt governors of the state included three successive governors, including Tomas Yarrington, who from approximately 1998 to 2013 protected the Gulf Cartel and allowed its "members and associates of the Gulf Cartel to continue their illegal business with little or no interference from police authorities operating in the State of Tamaulipas" (USA v. Yarrington, 2013, p. 6). Members of the state police participated openly with Yarrington, a problem of police corruption that also continues to the present (90 cops dismissed, 2018). Banks, businesses, criminal groups, and other associates constitute structures that link past and present, but with newer types of violence and crime emerging: spillover violence (innocent victims of shoot-outs between rival groups), kidnapping (one-fourth of the national total), extortion, carjacking, and auto theft (Flannery, 2018). Meanwhile, illegal drugs flow through the porous southern and northern borders of Tamaulipas while DTOs exploit this state with the highest number of ports of entry to the United States and the lucrative World Trade Bridge at Laredo-Nuevo Laredo, which is the port for nearly 40% of U.S.-Mexico trade (Wilson & Weigend, 2014, p. 11).

While the Gulf Coast narcotics transit routes remain vibrant in Tamaulipas, much the same can be said about the Pacific corridors of the states of Colima and Michoacán. The results of this unchecked narco-infrastructure are the worst homicide rates in Mexico. In 2017, the United States District Court for the Eastern District of New York noted Sinaloa cartel control of the region:

> Guzman controls corrupt government officials at all levels of Mexico and other foreign governments through bribery. These payments protect shipments as they are transported through Mexico to northern border towns and ensure safe passage of these shipments through border crossings into the United States (USA v. Guzman Loera, 2018, p. 17).

However, the fall of the Sinaloa Cartel after El Chapo's arrest in 2016 has left rival factions and cartels fighting over the prime transshipment route into the United States: the port of Manzanillo, Colima.

Despite the GoM response of major military operations to secure the port (major operations by Mexico's Marines in 2017), the area remains operable for the warring factions while their members benefit from a nearly 100% impunity rate from prosecution (Angel et al., 2019). The corruption of the political, security, and economic sectors of this formerly peaceful state and tourist area of Mexico highlights the enduring relationships of the narco-state that created the humanitarian crisis. Elas Lozano, Mayor of Tecomán, Colima, responded to a question on why such carnage occurs in his town: "the lack of honest politicians. That's the root of it all. Politicians had the choice of deciding between staying on the sidelines or getting involved, and many decided to get involved because there were economic benefits" (Phillips, 2018, para. 28).

Therefore, the growing organisational and operational objectives of Mexican DTOs demanded the protection of political and security officials operating in the states as a critical structure of the drug trafficking industry – a transactional relationship marked by periodic changes due to circumstances and competing economic players but an enduring one nonetheless. The DTO cooptation of supply, cultivation, processing, storage, transshipment, and market access points and areas in Mexico created a national infrastructure well organised and integrated – an outcome served inadequately with designations of "corruption," for corruption as a term does not address the organisation, integration, operation, and durability of this narco-industry. The vastness of the cartel area, structures, capabilities, organisations, activities, and associates mirror the equivalent state structures corrupted towards cartel objectives (Young, 1998, para. 22) – the two systems working symbiotically in a state of mutualism with tendencies to develop competition when federal government power or authority is challenged directly or indirectly (a subject explored later in this paper).

Peter A. Lupsha (1996), "Transnational Organised Crime versus the Nation-State," *Transnational Organised Crime*, Vol. 2, No. 1, theorises the symbiotic relationship between organised crime and the state as a potentially evolutionary process involving three stages: predatory, parasitic, and symbiotic. The development through the stages involves increasing levels of agreement (government and criminal groups), corruption, criminal control of state resources, and complete impunity, creating a collapse of the state's institutions in the final stage. Others have added a bilateral relationship as a variable where the government is not just penetrated by cartels, but the cartels are penetrated by the government (Young, 1998, para. 10). The current state of Mexico's security and civil society indicates entrance into this symbiotic stage where complex and integrated relationships exist and determine the nature of Mexico's local and national security.

The enormous growth of Mexican DTOs from the 1980s to the early 2000s and beyond created yet other consequences affecting public security and governance. The expanding organisations, infrastructure, and area of operations of the cartels correspondingly increased their political power vis-à-vis the central state, upsetting the Government of Mexico's single-party control of drug trafficking and practise of merely taxing small to medium-sized "mafia" families for their illicit activities (Beittel, 2018, p. 8).

The widespread bribery of judges, police, businesses, and politicians at all levels by Mexican DTOs created a politically networked system far more horizontal (broadly local and regional) yet possessing significant vertical or national relationships beyond merely the organisational and operational lines of the ruling Institutional Revolutionary Party (PRI) and their plaza system. The democratisation of Mexican politics and the loosening of PRI control of the state exacerbated the effects. The increased leverage of the cartels allowed them later to assert more independence through violence and predatory economic practises affecting local populations, even when fractured through ineffective counter-narcotics operations by the GoM (USA v. Guzman Loera, 2018, p. 17–18).

Counterarguments to the structural expansion of Mexican DTOs as the causation of enduring violence and insecurity in Mexico and the resulting narco-insurgency rely upon faulty assumptions regarding the non-political objectives of cartels, the patterned areas where their killings occur (as well as the narrow demographic of young males as primary targets), the unsubstantiated determination of socio-economics as the critical security variable, and the alleged government control of most areas of Mexico (Calderon et al., 2018). Far more consideration is required to accurately assess the Mexican DTO threat and transcend ineffective conceptual models.

Critical variables in a threat assessment of the subject necessitate the inclusion of the growing capabilities of cartels and the vulnerability of civil society psychologically, socially, and economically (even when compared to insurgent groups), the latent threats posed by a "narco peace" (areas where cartels dominate and violence decreases), the likelihood and capacity to transition to more violent activities, and the nature of government control (of areas associated with drug trafficking organisations) rather than the mere fact that control is maintained. Utilising threat assessment tools such as CARVER and ISAT can increase both strategic and tactical understanding of these threats (Ulrich, 2010, pp. 40–44; see also Knowles, 2008).

Also, the investigation into Camarena's and Zavala's deaths led to the piecemeal and surprising discovery of the integration of GoM security structures into cartel operations – an issue transcending individuals, isolated departments, and singular events. Specifically, GoM officials were involved in the planning, abduction, torture, death, and cover-up. As importantly, this heinous and complex crime involved surveillance, intelligence, logistics, capture, escape, evasion, freedom of movement, safe haven, and protection – advanced capabilities that could not have occurred without extensive government involvement. Reflecting on the outcomes of the case in 2016, Judge Robert Bonner of the U.S. District Court for the Central District of California, who had presided over the case, noted the complicity of the head of the Mexican

Federal Judicial Police, one of the Federal Security Directorates (DFS), the governor of Jalisco, and the ministerial level of the GoM. Bonner noted not only the complicity but also "the symbiotic relationship that existed between organised crime, major drug trafficking organisations, and the Mexican government" (Feess et al., 2017, pp. 22–23).

The presence of GoM political figures during the life-cycle of the abduction operation – the planning and torture of Camarena as well as the initial cover-up after his death – appeared in emotionally gripping headlines in U.S.-based newspapers. But more importantly, the GoM presence demonstrated the integration of cartel operations with the political and security structures of the Mexican state (McEvoy, 2017, p. 43). See also Poppa, 2000, p. 44. The initial unresponsiveness to USG queries on the agent's death later turned to denial and deception operations. The GoM's assignment of the notoriously corrupt cartel associate Comandante Pavon-Reyes of the MFJP to lead the Mexican investigation of the incident soon demonstrated the collusion. Immediately after Quintero and Fonseca became suspects in the murders and fled to the Guadalajara Airport, the MFJP and DEA confronted the two men. When Pavon-Reyes received a six-figure bribe from Quintero, he departed the airport safely.

The MFJP followed this event with an elaborate hoax to frame the Bravo family for the murder of Camarena, a plot involving an anonymous letter tipping off the location, the exhumed bodies of Camarena and Zaval, and a raid that killed all the members of the Bravo family on-site – an event referenced earlier in this paper. In 1989, the *FBI Bulletin* noted that the whole plan had been contrived by certain Mexican law enforcement officials "in order to obstruct and prematurely conclude the investigation", see Feess et al., 2017, p. 20).

Perhaps even more problematic were the concerted efforts of Mexican officials to destroy and contaminate evidence at the crime scene, delay and obstruct the USG investigation of the site, and only grudgingly and sparingly comply with their counterparts when maximum pressure was applied by the USG. The *FBI Bulletin* recalls the problematic investigation:

> The FBI forensic team was immediately dispatched to Guadalajara; however, they were not allowed to proceed to the residence, located at 881 Lope De Vega, until an MFJP forensic team had processed the residence and had removed all of the obvious evidence. The DEA was also informed that since the abduction of SA Camarena, all of the interior walls had been painted, the entire residence had recently been cleaned, and that a group of MFJP officers were presently occupying, and thereby contaminating, the residence (pp. 3–4).

Other strong indicators of collaboration occurred. Gallardo remained at large well into the late 1980s, when he was apprehended along with a disintegrating network in Sinaloa that had operated openly and with the approval of the governor. Moreover, the Godfather of the Guadalajara cartel remained in control of national operations while he was imprisoned and enjoyed political protection (Vulliamy, 2018).

The investigation into the abduction and killing of Enrique Camarena also demonstrated a complex operation of GoM officials working with Mexican DTOs to protect the drug trafficking infrastructure and to interdict a major counter-narcotics and security operation sponsored by the United States Government (Drug Enforcement Administration Reauthorization for Fiscal Year, 1986, 1985; see also The Drug Trade in Mexico and U.S. Policy Implications, 1995). The coordinated effort of GoM officials to cooperate in the removal of Camarena, the protection and increase of narcotics cultivation areas, and the growth and protection of drug trafficking infrastructure demonstrate the strength of relationships so vital to understanding the complex problems of Mexico's civil society and its security. The financial, emotional, and personal risks invested by the government and cartel associates determine not only the character of the structures but their durability.

Conversely, the mission clarity and operational power the Reagan Administration brought to counter narcotics operations in Latin America during the 1980s struck the Columbian-Florida corridor as well as the drug-producing plantations that plagued the region – and Mexico in particular (McEvoy, 2017, p. 48). The combined Army, Navy, Air Force, Coast Guard, Drug Enforcement Administration, and partner agencies provided intelligence, surveillance, mobility, and offensive capabilities that crippled the Medellin cartel (coupled with domestic security operations of the government of Columbia), degraded other Columbian cartels, and created the pressure that troubled Gallardo, "the Godfather" of the Guadalajara cartel (USA v. Juan Ramon Matta-Lopez, 1995, p.1).

But these potent forces employed by the United States government required human factors in order to be effective: penetration of the dark cartel networks; understanding the presence and tactics of corrupt law enforcement and government officials; and the ability to rapidly assess the changes, movements, and disinformation that characterised cartel operations. Camarena, the agent later called "the Jesus of the DEA" for his heroic sacrifice, possessed the courage, energy, agility, and personality to develop the counter networks forged in the "rowdiest cantinas and grimiest backstreets (Grillo, 2011, location 1180).

Additionally, he was extraordinarily motivated. When his mother tried to talk him out of the mission to serve in Mexico, he replied, "Even if I'm only one person, I can make a difference" (Myall, 2018). The "difference" he made was felt strategically: his tactical synergy created by the identification of corrupt and high-ranking GoM officials, aerial reconnaissance, counter-network operations, and embedded operations with the Mexican military shook the very foundations of the Guadalajara cartel. In fact, his intelligence tips and aerial surveillance led to the largest drug bust of the era, a 2500-acre marijuana plantation called Buffalo Ranch, owned by Quintero (McEvoy, 2017, p. 43). The plantations borne on the exploited agricultural labour of Mexicans earned eight billion dollars a year.

Court records later revealed that Camarena's work had so troubled Gallardo, Quintero, and Fonseca that several meetings were held to plan the abduction of the agent. The court documents also record that Quintero later met and interrogated the battered and moaning agent regarding the names of informants, the ones closest to the leadership circle, and DEA knowledge of the cartel's operations ("Tapes of Agent Slain," 1988).

Particularly troubling was the participation of Mexico's DFS officials (Federal Security Directorate) in both the agent's interrogation and death, as well as their involvement in the wider drug trafficking industry. (The DFS was a major intelligence agency created in 1947 on the eve of the Cold War.) DFS officials (although officially decommissioned in 1985) remained active in drug trafficking before, during, and after the Camarena period. A declassified Department of State report dated March 27, 1990, revealed the corruption, criminal activity, and complicity in Camarena's death:

> Several members of the DFS became heavily involved in drug trafficking and then in the murder of Drug Enforcement Administration Special Agent Enrique Camarena-Salazar … . Despite the DFS involvement with drug trafficking, the [omitted in original] continued having dealings with DFS director [omitted in original] is now believed to have been involved in the murder of special agent Camarena. Mexican authorities have charged [omitted in original] with using his official position to protect drug trafficking. Another EX DFS commander identified as [omitted in original], said to have been working with Mexican drug traffickers, interrogated special agent Camarena the day he was kidnapped. It was furthermore reported that the [omitted in original] became involved in the drug war after it was determined that other United States agencies along with other foreign police could not suppress the flow of narcotics into the United States (Doyle & Franzblau, 2010, pp. 26–27).

Therefore, the removal of Camarena from counter-narcotics operations was a major action by the narco-state against a key actor who had challenged an entire system. The special agent's comparatively low rank in the USG hierarchy did not correlate to low outcomes. His significant successes created strategic losses for the cartels as well as apprehensions of further losses of leadership and infrastructure (McEvoy, 2017, p. 43).

Consequently, the narco-state's protection of the drug trafficking infrastructure entails severe measures and consequences for civil society, including violent crime (40% to 60% of homicides committed by criminal organisations) (Shirk, 2013, p. 4), the paralysis of security organisations serving local communities, and even the crippling of civil society organisations. Mass graves, disappearances, rape, and kidnapping are related issues that have received widespread academic and journalistic coverage. Individuals and institutions have detailed the interaction of cartels, government officials, and security structures.

The University of San Diego's *Justice in Mexico Project* has highlighted two major target groups of Mexican drug trafficking organisations: journalists and mayors. *Drug Violence in Mexico: Data and Analysis Through 2017* (April 2018), it notes: "Mexican journalists were at least three times more likely to be killed (.7 per 1,000) than the general population (.21 per 1,000), and mayors are at least twelve times more likely (2.46 murders per 1,000)" (Calderon et al., 2018, pp. 28–30). The mayoral targets included diverse political parties and sub-categories of mayors (past, present, and emerging candidates). The journalist targets involved individuals working on crime, corruption, and political issues, with the crime reporters being the largest sub-group of targets (78%). These statistics reveal that drug trafficking organisations consider local area control (the role of the mayor) and information security and dominance (the journalists) to be major aims of their organisations and therefore critical factors determining local security.

Among the more important targets of Mexican drug trafficking organisations and one often overlooked as a critical player in civil society is the Roman Catholic Church, with its leadership, priesthood, and extensive organisation reaching throughout Mexico. In distinction from other civil society organisations in Mexico, the Roman Catholic Church holds the advantage of not just urban but rural reach and presence, widespread acceptance across socio-economic divides, doctrinal clarity (creating unity), vast resources, globally and nationally linked platforms, highly trained personnel, and extensive facilities throughout the country, including local parishes that often serve as the only connection and continuous outreach to Mexican communities where DTOs and other criminal groups operate (Seelke, 2015; see also Bergoglio, 2016). However, the widespread targeting of Roman Catholic and lay leadership has effectively crippled the capacity of the Church to hinder cartel operations and foster community security.

On May 24, 1993, Mexican Cardinal Juan Jesus Posadas Ocampo and six associates were brutally murdered at the Guadalajara airport in an apparent professional assassination that the Government of Mexico (GoM) soon thereafter ruled an accidental shooting, a case of mistaken identity among rival cartels. The alleged target, according to the GoM, was Chapo Guzman, the Sinaloa cartel boss, who was a man of thin build and 24 years younger. However, the overweight cleric dressed in his religious garb was not a difficult person to identify, a fact made more believable given the assassins fired 14 rounds from only three feet away from him, leaving powder burns on the dying Cardinal's chin (An End to Impunity, 2006, pp. 1–2). Moreover, days before the attack, the notable cleric had been surveilled as he moved about the streets, his phone had been tapped, and he had demonstrated signs of stress – evidence of deliberate operations rather than accidental.

Cardinal Posadas, who was known as "a fierce critic" of the narco-traffickers and a vocal leader of civil society, not only stood against these criminals but also those who were complicit in their activities, including government authorities who failed to take action against the subsequent violence and terror spreading in Mexico. The Cardinal's advocacy for human rights and security, in addition to his alleged knowledge of drug trafficking and prostitution networks in Mexican society that included officials (An End to Impunity, 2006, p. 13), caused this leader of Mexico's largest civil society network to collide with the expanding lethal networks of Mexican DTOs, with the more powerful network of the two emerging and shaping conditions in which the other would have to accommodate. The subsequent actions of Mexican officials to cover, complicate, and continue the narrative of the crime scene again demonstrate structures that have long shaped the security environment of the country.

Although the tragic death of Cardinal Posadas occurred over 25 years ago, the event remains relevant today as a case study of the conditions affecting Roman Catholics and civil society in modern Mexico. Roman Catholic priests who have opposed the drug cartels, ministered to victims, or become associated with these narco-traffickers have met a violent fate. In the post-Posada era, Roman Catholic leadership in Mexico has not opposed beyond verbal and written statements either the good standing of drug lords in the Church or their lavish gifts to local congregations (Llana, 2009, p. 8). Moreover, Cardinal Norberto Rivera Carrera, head of the Roman Catholic Church of Mexico in 2011, even advocated reframing the drug cartel issue as one of public health rather than crime (Jenkins, 2011, p. 53). The lack of clear policy and practise leaves local clergymen isolated, vulnerable, and victimised, such as the priests of Texcoco, who often face threatening phone calls and visits and an unresponsive local government.

Importantly, the very structures that support and facilitate Mexican drug trafficking organisations grew during the Camarena period, creating enduring challenges for civil society. The areas used for cultivation, movement, storage, transshipment, and distribution expanded, as did the organisations, platforms, facilities, logistics, materiel, and personnel associated with the drug trafficking industry (McEvoy, 2017, p. 43). On May 1, 1985, Acting Administrator of the DEA John C. Lawn admitted during the US Congressional Hearings on Drug Enforcement that despite record numbers of drug eradication metrics, overall production of marijuana in Mexico had increased. The U.S. District Court indictment of Quintero in 2017 revealed a sprawling network of leadership, security personnel, plaza bosses, and transporters "such as boat crews, pilots, truck drivers, etc.," in addition to money launderers and *sicarios* (hitmen), that operated from 1980 to 2017 (United States v. Quintero, 2017, p. 3).

In particular, the vast amount of land in Mexico given over to poppy and marijuana cultivation was a striking feature of Mexico in the late 1980s as well as an indication of GoM protection of the drug industry's infrastructure. Despite large numbers of hectares of marijuana and poppy fields eradicated in the mid-1980s by joint US-Mexico operations, growth of the same occurred amid increasing obstructions of US-sponsored eradication programmes and eventually a complete shutdown of these operations. In 1988, a Government Accountability Office (GAO) report noted the major expansion of cultivation areas:

> The tri-state area of Sinaloa, Durango, and Chihuahua has traditionally been the primary area for opium poppy cultivation. Despite years of eradication efforts to drive growers from the area, reports of fencing, irrigation, and landscaping suggested that fields were prepared for multi-year use. Cultivation extends beyond this area and opium poppy fields have been discovered in about three-fourths of Mexico's states. Marijuana has been found virtually throughout the country (GAO, 1988, p.17).

In addition to the large poppy and marijuana plantations of Mexico, often the targets of eradication programme operations, small farms cultivating illegal crops or supplementing legal agriculture proliferated, causing problems well into the future. The DEA map below illustrates the reorientation of Mexican land area to the illegal narcotics industry as well as the encroachment of drug cartels on Mexico's agricultural sector (GAO, 1988, p. 18). The close relationship between drug cartels and the agricultural sector fostered both oppressive narco-economies and toxic narco-cultures glorifying criminal lifestyles. Scholar James H. McDonald (2005), "The Narcoeconomy and Small-Town, Rural Mexico," *Human Organisation*, notes insightfully the current problems occurring in rural Mexico: inflated land prices, obstruction of GoM programmes to the impoverished, and promotion of the narco-lifestyle as both culture and economic opportunity.

Past and present United States Government reports attributing the expansion of drug trafficking production to conditions in Mexico's economic, geographical, and social spheres, including economic downturns and adaptive farmers countering eradication programmes (GAO, 1988), fail to address the evidence of a vast drug trafficking infrastructure emerging in the Camarena period supported by burgeoning narco-organisational, social, and state structures operating at the local, state, and national levels. Corresponding statements from the USG of record seizures of narcotics, increased funding, training, and partnering with Mexican security organisations, unprecedented pressure from the Government of Mexico, and its alleged comprehensive programme to break the power of narco-traffickers contradict the evidence of the opposite: viable Mexican DTO production, transshipment, protection forces, freedom of movement over large areas of Mexico, market access (border and port control), logistical hubs operating in the open, as well as intact financial and leadership structures (fa failure to prosecute and confiscate assets) (Beittel, 2018, p. 4).

Importantly, the Camarena case revealed that GoM counternarcotics operations and security cooperation with the United States would be marked by a complex security policy of dynamic failure. The GoM's policy of dynamic failure involved obstruction, disinformation, cover, and complicity – all supporting drug cartel organisations – punctuated by apparently contrary and dynamic activities and periods of aggressive countermeasures against drug cartels intentionally falling short of decisive outcomes while maintaining the authority and legitimacy of the government. The defining feature of the policy is the prolonged, patterned, and persistent practise of failing to interdict comprehensively and through integrated operations the structures shaping and driving Mexican DTO growth and capabilities (U.S.-Mexican Security Cooperation, January 23, 2017, p. 25; see also Young, 1998). Moreover, Mexico's security operations have even been protected aggressively, as this paper has demonstrated. Despite the apparent contradiction of practises, the policy of dynamic failure achieves the strategic outcome of allowing the GoM to remain a legitimate and independent member of the international community, engaging in global trade while reaping enormous economic benefits from drug trafficking.

The dynamic failure policy evident in the Camarena era is extraordinarily opaque due to its complexity and acquiescence by the United States government. The rapid juxtaposition of GoM support for and countermeasures to Mexican DTOs, the willingness of the GoM to interdict relatively large numbers of cartel assets, and positive media images of "Mexico's drug war" have added to the public's misunderstanding of the policy and its key objectives. The unwillingness of the United States government to move decisively against one of its most significant political, economic, and social partners is evident in both policy and action (McEvoy, 2017, p. 51) and contributes to the public's misperception of Mexico's security policies and practises. For instance, rather than assessing the specific characteristics of GoM corruption and drug trafficking, a 1988 Government Accounting Office report simply acknowledged the problem, leaving it in the realm of generalisation and ambiguity: "We did not pursue the issue of corruption within the eradication programme. However, numerous INM documents point to corruption as a problem that reduces programme effectiveness" (GAO, 1988, p. 20).

Current U.S. policy recognises the record highs in poppy cultivation in Mexico (White House, 2018) but fails to take a punitive stand and designate Mexico "as [one of the] countries that have failed demonstrably during the previous 12 months to adhere to their obligations under international counternarcotics agreements and to take the measures required by Section 489(a)(1) of the FAA [Foreign Assistance Act of 1961]" (White House, 2018, September 11).

The presidential administration of Donald Trump, however, has taken significant steps to address these shortcomings. The Trump administration's focus on interdicting the "business model" of drug cartels (including production and distribution), as well as consideration of designating DTOs as terrorist entities, could mark a major departure from the failed policies of past United States presidential administrations (Mexico: Evolution of the Mérida Initiative, 2019, p. 2).

Furthermore, civil society organisations in the United States and abroad have inadvertently facilitated the dynamic failure policy of the Government of Mexico by advancing inaccurate indicators of progress in Mexico's drug war. These organisations frequently have relied on GoM declarations, policy shifts, reorganisation of security departments, institutional reform efforts, counter-narcotics campaigns, upticks in counter-narcotics investigations, engagement and mobilisation of the public sector (community engagement), and media images of major seizures, arrests, and killings of the "kingpin strategy" (Human Rights Watch, 2013, 93). Yet, these civil society organisations give little consideration to the structures of the narco-economy and their relationship to the GoM and the human security issues afflicting Mexico. Consequently, key political-business networks of the narco-economy remain intact, resources are misallocated, leadership networks remain viable, public attention is misdirected, and the DTO infrastructure not only survives but also proliferates. As importantly, drug trafficking culture remains attractive to successive generations of Mexicans seeking a better future.

The tragic death of DEA Special Agent Enrique Camarena revealed, through subsequent investigation by the United States Government, far more than a serious crime against an effective counternarcotics operator. The relationship between Mexican drug trafficking organisations and the government of Mexico had been far more involved, integrated, and catalytic to the burgeoning illegal drug industry in Mexico than previously understood by USG officials. The structures of this industry, evident in production areas, facilities, personnel, materiel, organisations, logistics, finances, and supply chains, grew rapidly, becoming determinative of the security of civil society in the 1980s as well as the present. Without a determined, focused, integrated, and continuous targeting and interdiction of the narco-infrastructure by joint US-Mexican security officials, human security in Mexico will continue to be victimised by violent crime related to Mexican DTOs.

References

90 cops dismissed, 100 under investigation in tamaulipas. (2018, October 3). *Mexico News Daily*. https://mexiconewsdaily.com/news/90-cops-dismissed-100-under-investigation-in-tamaulipas/

An end to impunity: investigating the 1993 killing of mexican archbishop juan jesus posadas Ocampo: Hearing Before the Subcommittee on Africa, Global Human Rights. 109th Cong. April 6 2006. https://www.govinfo.gov/content/pkg/CHRG-109hhrg26906/pdf/CHRG-109hhrg26906.pdf

Angel, A., Martinez, P., & Rea, D. (2019, January 2). Solving mexico homicide backlog could take 124 years. *InsightCrime*. https://www.insightcrime.org/news/analysis/solving-mexico-homicide-backlog-could-take-124-years/

Beittel, J.S. (2018, July 3). Mexico: Organized crime and drug trafficking orrganizations. *Congressional Research Service Reports*, 1–29. https://fas.org/sgp/crs/row/R41576.pdf

Bergoglio, J.M. (2016, February 13). Meeting with the bishops of mexico,"mexico city, Mexico. *The Holy See* website. https://w2.vatican.va/content/francesco/en/speeches/2016/february/documents/papa-francesco_20160213_messico-vescovi.html

Calderon, L., Ferreira, R.O., & Shirk, D.A. (2018, April). Drug Violence in Mexico: Data and Analysis Through 2017. *Justice in Mexico*, University of San Diego. https://justiceinmexico.org/wp-content/uploads/2018/04/180411_DrugViolenceinMexico-12mb.pdf

Doyle, K., & Franzblau, J. (2010, March 9). Archival evidence of Mexico's human rights crimes: The case of Aleida Gallangos. *The National Security Archive*. Document 11. pp. 26–27. https://nsarchive2.gwu.edu/NSAEBB/NSAEBB307/doc11.PDF

Drug Enforcement Administration Reauthorizatin For Fiscal Year 1986: Hearing before the Subcomittee on Crime, 99th Cong. Session 1. (May 1, 1985). Washington, D.C. GPO, 1986.

Feess, G., Bonner, R.C., Hoffman, P., & Medrano, M. (2017, February 22). Panel discussion: The enrique "kiki" camarena murder and its aftermath. *Southwestern Law School website*, 17–37. https://www.swlaw.edu/sites/default/files/2017-04/SWT103.pdf

Feuer, A., & Palmer, E. (2018, November 18). Inside el chapo's vast network: What we know after the trial's first week. *New York Times*. https://www.nytimes.com/2018/11/18/nyregion/el-chapo-trial.html

Flannery, N.P. (2018, November 6). Splinter groups of cartel gunmen drive rising violence in tamaulipas, Mexico. *Forbes*. https://www.forbes.com/sites/nathanielparishflannery/2018/11/06/splinter-groups-of-cartel-gunmen-drive-rising-violence-in-tamaulipas-mexico/#5c843071407d

Grillo, I. (2011). El narco: Inside mexico's criminal insurgency [Kindle version]. Retrieved from Amazon.com

Grillo, I. (2014, October 10). Mexico's deadly narco-politics. *International New York Times*, 8.

Haughton, S. A., & Romaniuk, S. N. (2023). Drug trafficking methods along the US southwest border. In S. N. Romaniuk & P. Marton (Eds.), *The Palgrave encyclopedia of global security studies*. Cham: Palgrave Macmillan. https://doi.org/10.1007/978-3-319-74336-3_671-1

Human Rights Watch (2013, February 20). Mexico's disappeared: The enduring cost of a crisis ignored. *Human Rights Watch.org website*, 92–107. https://www.hrw.org/sites/default/files/reports/mexico0213_ForUpload_0_0_0.pdf

Jenkins, P. (2011, March 22). Mexico's crisis of faith. *The Christian Century*, *128*(6), 53.

Knowles, G.J. (2008). Threat analysis: Organized crime and narco-terrorism in northern Mexico. *Military Review*, *88* (1), 73+.

Lee, B., Renwick, D., & Labrador, R.C. (2019, January 24). Mexico's drug war. *Council on Foreign Relations*. https://www.cfr.org/backgrounder/mexicos-drug-war

Llana, S.M.. (2009, October 4). Priests in cross hairs of drug war. *The Christian Science Monitor*, *8*.

Lupsha, P.A. (1996). Transnational organized crime versus the nation-state. *Transnational Organized Crime*, *2*(1), New Mexico, United States.

McDonald, J.H. (2005). The narcoeconomy and small-town, rural Mexico. *Human Organization*, *64*(2), 115+.

McEvoy, A.F. (2017, February 27). The martyrdom and avenging of enrique Camarena-salazar: A review of caselaw and scholarship after thirty years. *Southwestern Journal of International Law*, *23*, 39–72. https://www.swlaw.edu/sites/default/files/2017-04/SWT104.pdf

Mexico: evolution of the mérida initiative, 2007–2019. *Congressional Research Service*. March 11, 2019, 1–2. https://fas.org/sgp/crs/row/IF10578.pdf

Myall, S. (2018, October 18). True story behind netflix's narcos: Mexico – how cop was tortured with cattle prod then murdered after $8bn drug bust. *Mirror*. https://www.mirror.co.uk/news/real-life-stories/true-story-behind-netflixs-narcos-13085457

Phillips, T. (2018, August 9). Can't fight evil with evil': Life in mexico's most murderous town. *The Guardian*. https://www.theguardian.com/world/2018/aug/09/mexico-amlo-war-on-drugs-violence-clean-up

Poppa, T. (2000, July 24). Mexican government is tied to the drug trade. *Insight on the News*, *44*.

Seelke, C.R. (2015, September 8). Pope Francis and selected global issues: Background for papal address to congress. *Congressional Research Service*, 1–18. https://fas.org/sgp/crs/misc/R44184.pdf

Shirk, D. (2013, December 18). The State of Security in Mexico. *The Wilson Center*. Retrieved from https://www.wilsoncenter.org/sites/default/files/security_2013_mexico_shirk.pdf

Tapes of agent slain by captors: 'don't hit me' (1988, August 6), *New York Times*. http://aus.libguides.com/apa/apa-newspaper-web

The Drug Trade in Mexico and U.S. Policy Implictions: Hearing Before the Senate Committee on Foreign Relations, (August 8, 1995) (Testimony of Andrew Reding). https://www.researchgate.net/publication/292148076_Political_corruption_and_drug_trafficking_in_Mexico_Opening_Statement

Ulrich, M. (2010, October). Cutting the Gordian knot: The counterguerrilla's guide to defeating insurgencies and conducting populist centric operations. Counterinsurgency Academy, Kabul, Afghanistan.

United States General Accounting Office. (1988, January 11). Drug control U.S.-Mexico opium poppy and marijuana aerial eradication program, 1–60. https://www.gao.gov/assets/150/146002.pdf

United States of America v. Rafael Caro Quintero. United States District Court of Eastern New York, 2017. https://www.justice.gov/usao-edny/press-release/file/1052231/download

United States of America v. Juan Ramon Matta-Lopez. United States Court of Apeals for the Ninth Circuit, 9th Cir. December 26, 1995. https://law.justia.com/cases/federal/appellate-courts/F3/73/371/557014/

United States of America v. Joaqin Archivaldo Guzman Loera. United States District Court of Eastern New York, 2018. https://dig.abclocal.go.com/wls/documents/El%20Chapo%20Govt.%20support%20of%20part%20sequestered%20jury.pdf

United States of America v. Tomas Yarrington Ruvalcaba. United States District Court Southern District of Texas, Brownsville Division. May 22, 2013. https://www.ice.gov/doclib/news/releases/2013/131202brownsville.pdf

United States Department of State-Bureau of Consular Affairs, Mexico travel advisory. Travel.state.gov. November 18, 2018.

https://travel.state.gov/content/travel/en/traveladvisories/traveladvisories/mexico-travel-advisory.html

U.S. Mexican security cooperation: The merida initiative and beyond. *Congressional Research Service*, 1–33. https://www.everycrsreport.com/files/20170123_R41349_810e7753df6667c77707aaae63b6ecf68eef284f.pdf

Vasquez, J.M. (1985, March 19). Mexican police drug link told: Served as private army for dealers, parpers show. *Los Angeles Times*. http://articles.latimes.com/1985-03-19/news/mn-31679_1_state-police

Vulliamy, Ed. (2018, November 15). Félix Gallardo: The 'bill gates of cocaine' who rules the new Narcos season. *The Guardian*. https://www.theguardian.com/tv-and-radio/2018/nov/15/felix-gallardo-the-bill-gates-of-cocaine-who-rules-the-new-narcos-season

White House. (2018, July 20). New annual data released by white house drug policy office shows record high poppy cultivation and potential heroin production in mexico. *Whitehouse.gov* website. https://www.whitehouse.gov/briefings-statements/new-annual-data-released-white-house-drug-policy-office-shows-record-high-poppy-cultivation-potential-heroin-production-mexico/

White House. (2018, September 11). Presidential memorandum for the secretary of state: Presidential determination on major drug transit or major illicit drug producing countries for fiscal year 2019. *Whitehouse.gov website*. https://www.whitehouse.gov/presidential-actions/presidential-memorandum-secretary-state-12/

Wilson, C., & Weigend, E. (2014, October). *Plan Tamaulipas: A new security strategy for a troubled state*. Wilson Center, Mexico Institute. https://owl.purdue.edu/owl/research_and_citation/apa_style/apa_formatting_and_style_guide/reference_list_articles_in_periodicals.html

Young, S. (1998, April). Mexico: The political economy of narco-corruption in Mexico. *Current History*. http://www.mapinc.org/drugnews/v98/n393/a07.html

PART V

CASE STUDIES

Europe

41

TERRORISTS AS DEFENDERS

The Irish Republican Army

Sarah Clifford

> *We are not the cause of this conflict; we are the victims of it.*
> *We are the product of decades of British tyranny and misrule.*
> (Sinn Féin, 1994)

INTRODUCTION

The *Troubles*, an ethno-nationalist conflict lasting from 1968 to 1996, gripped not only the United Kingdom (UK) but, moreover, garnered worldwide attention. Ireland, one of Britain's many colonialist holdings, had historically undergone a multitude of conflicts aimed at combating its colonialist rulers but had yet to experience anything of comparable magnitude to that of the *Troubles*. The Irish Republican Army's (IRA) emergence, promulgated by the *Troubles*, represented one of the longest-lasting threats to British colonial rule in the 20th century. As such, the IRA was one of the most successful terrorist organisations within Western Europe and still permeates British and Irish societies today. This study aims to tease apart the underlying motivations that led to the IRA's conception, the group's key attacks and political structure, its role in the peacebuilding process, and lastly, whether its purported demise will last with Britain's ensuing break from the European Union (EU).

Before I begin my historical analysis, it is important to note the exclusionary role labelling the *Troubles* as solely an 'ethno-nationalist conflict' entails. By referring to the *Troubles* explicitly as an ethno-nationalist conflict, it becomes easy to overlook the marginalisation and subjugation of communities and groups that did not conform to either the Unionist or Nationalist stereotypical identities. Moreover, it restricts an actor's agency by emphasising only one form of social mobilisation that is acceptable within the conflict (e.g., see Byrne, 2009). Yet, previous literature that is both scholarly and non-scholarly in nature, along with the power-sharing model itself employed in Northern Ireland, reflects a bi-national identity believed to be present on the island. Thus, because my analysis is grounded in research detailing the IRA and because it is beyond the purview of this chapter to discuss the broader social actors and exclusionary practises within the peacebuilding process, I will utilise this language to better understand how the power-sharing model came to be as well as how actors', specifically IRA members, may have viewed themselves within the conflict.

BACKGROUND

The foundation for the eruption of sectarian conflict and the creation of the Irish Republican Army began long before the Troubles in 1968. Great Britain, during its naval supremacy and imperialist world rule, colonised the island in the 16th century (Ellis, 2011). As maltreatment, discrimination, and violence often came hand-in-hand with British colonisation, Ireland soon rebelled. In 1641, the Catholics led a rebellion to protest the vast inequality they faced within society (Farrelly, 2017). The British, mainly Protestant in comparison, massacred the Irish population in retribution. The Irish Catholics, having faced horrific British rule for 100 years, have sought to rule independently from British control ever since. With the rebellion of 1641 failing to gain Irish independence, this event became memorialised within Irish history and folklore, thus becoming a chosen trauma for the Irish people to combat oppression and colonialist rule. The Irish-Catholic people passed down this sense of victimisation and religious commonality through their future generations, creating the basis for sectarian divisions within the country to later ensue (Volkan, 1999).

DOI: 10.4324/9780429426063-47

Easter Rising, 1916

Slowly, over time, growing anti-British animosity culminated in Britain's creation of the Home Rule Bill in 1914. This bill allowed sufficient self-rule, which increased the Irish citizenry's power to govern themselves. Yet, due to the eruption of World War I, Britain soon postponed the Home Rule Bill, once again reducing Ireland to merely a colonialist possession that would only ever be granted independence when the British saw fit. Soon after, with Britain's impending forced conscription laws and wartime rations severely constraining Ireland's access to resources, many Irish Catholics found the war to represent the pinnacle of British occupation. The possibility of conscription, in particular, was a tremendous blow to the Irish nationalist effort. Not only would Irishmen and women be required to fight a war they had not enlisted in, but moreover, they would be required to fight for the King and Crown, an institution responsible for their personal oppression and subjugation. Thus, the war triggered the rebirth of the Irish nationalist movement, exemplified through the Easter Rising of 1916.

The Easter Rising was primarily constructed as a "statement against British rule in Ireland", while taking advantage of Britain's already weakening military force due to World War I (English, 2003, 5). Through funding and arms from the German government, groups from the Irish Republican Brotherhood (IRB), the Irish nationalist militia, the Irish Volunteers, and the Irish Citizen Army (ICA) came together under the leadership of James Connolly to once and for all fight for the end of British colonisation (Ibid.). Through this "insurrectionary gesture against Britain", Patrick Pearse, one of the early leaders of the Irish nationalist cause, declared the independence of the Irish State through the signing of the Irish Proclamation. Pearse stated that:

> [i]n every generation the Irish people have asserted their right to national freedom and sovereignty; six times during the past three hundred years they have asserted it in arms. Standing on that fundamental right and again asserting it in arms in the face of the world, we hereby proclaim the Irish republic as a sovereign independent state. (Ibid., 4)

Although the British crushed the revolt within a week, the Easter Rising and its prominent revolutionaries, who were later executed by British forces, came to significantly define Irish politics and the Irish nationalist struggle. These seven executions "movingly and lastingly haunted political Ireland" through the heroization and memorialization of key figures within the Irish struggle that permeated historical discourses surrounding Irish oppression (Ibid., 6). Of those executed were: Thomas Clarke (1857), Thomas MacDonagh (1878), Patrick Pearse (1879), Joseph Plunkett (1887), Éamonn Ceannt (1881), Seán Mac Diarmada (1884), and James Connolly (1868) (Ibid.).

Not only did the Easter Rising mark a shift within the Irish struggle for independence, but as Irish revolutionary Michael Collins noted:

> the rebellion had marked a departure from a doubly flawed Irish nationalist parliamentary strategy: a strategy wrong both for its suggestion that Ireland was a part of the United Kingdom (rather than an independent nation), and for its implication that the Irish should look not to themselves but to England for improving government or for the gift of freedom. (Ibid., 7)

Moreover, not only did the Irish cause garner a greater amount of attention from both the British government and Irish citizens alike, but it also led to the deepening of "sectarian animosity in Ireland" that drew attention to the Protestant need for greater protection from the Catholic majority on the island (Ibid., 11). With Irish Protestants appalled at the Catholics' "back-stabbing wartime treachery", the Ulster Volunteer Force (UVF) was conceived to resist pressures towards Irish Home Rule (Ibid.). Nationalists then responded with the creation of their own paramilitary group, the Irish Republican Army.

Throughout the next few decades, both the IRA and the UVF's use of force produced relatively mixed and lacklustre results. Although their increase in violence had warranted the signing of the Anglo-Irish Treaty and the creation of the state of Northern Ireland in 1922, what resulted was a Catholic minority in the new region, setting the stage for further British oppression (Brew, 2008). Yet, the Irish Catholic population within Northern Ireland was relatively ambivalent to the IRA's violent tactics, resulting in both paramilitary groups losing traction and popularity within the region until the late 1960s.

Birth of the Provisional IRA (PIRA)

The civil rights movement, emerging in the 1960s as a response to the ongoing civil rights campaign in the United States, sought to further Irish claims towards equal treatment for its Catholic minority in the North. Unsurprisingly, violence from Protestant loyalists, or those loyal to the United Kingdom, erupted in response by attacking a defenceless Catholic community. What resulted was a call for protection, which the Provisionals attempted to fill (England, 2003, 84). The violence of the 1960s, heavily contributed to by the Protestant loyalists, created conditions ripe for not only the creation of the Provisionals but also for popular support to back the movement. What had greatly lacked in the IRA's campaign was public support for their cause, which thus resulted in the IRA being virtually unable to effectively promote Irish independence.

The whole latter half of the 1960s saw increased sectarian violence and Catholic oppression, coupled with the re-establishment of the Ulster Volunteer Force in 1966 and the eruption of police violence in October 1968 in Derry. On January 1, 1969, Catholic marches from Belfast to Derry that were intended to "restart the civil rights movement" were "violently attacked" by loyalist forces. This civil rights movement was promulgated by previous Catholic discrimination in areas such as housing, politics, and employment. The marches were meant as a call to action, not necessarily against the Protestants but more simply against Catholic discrimination and inequality. August 12, 1969, saw the Protestant Apprentice Boys' Parade in Derry that culminated in riots, police brutality, and the first use of tear gas, later known as the Battle of the Bogside. By August 14, the British government had deployed troops to quell the ensuing violence, both officially launching the army's involvement in the North and representing a visible state presence within the region, much to the dismay of many Catholics.

As the death toll in Belfast and particularly the Bogside mounted,

> [m]any Catholics unsurprisingly saw police killings as evidence of the hostility of the northern state towards their community: not only were the police offering inadequate protection, they were, on occasion, the attackers for whom protection was so urgently required. (Ibid., 103)

Therefore, the creation of the Provisionals resulted from the necessity to defend northern Catholics from the ensuing violence they faced. Many members of the IRA had become dismayed with the group's ineffectiveness and the recent loss of power, so they chose to dissent and form a new, more powerful organisation. This is where we see a split between the Provisionals and the later known OIRA, or Original IRA. Yet, the OIRA was relatively ineffective in comparison and disbanded on May 29, 1972 (Ibid., 175).

BLANKET AND NO WASH PROTESTS, HUNGER STRIKES, BOMBINGS, AND SINN FÉIN: UNIQUE FORMS OF RESISTANCE AND THE IRA'S POLITICAL WING

Now that I have given an overview of the history of the IRA and introduced the Provisionals, I want to draw attention to the unique facets and techniques employed by the Provisionals during the Troubles. These include the Blanket and No Wash Protests, the Hunger Strikes, the Bombing of the Brighton Hotel, and the PIRA's political wing, Sinn Féin, which proved monumental in both the peace negotiations and future political contestations that now envelop the North. The first three sections in particular are fascinating as they represent a shift in how the PIRA structured its diverse forms of resistance. Through a Foucauldian lens, one notes how "it is within such a context that the prisoner's mind and body come to form sites of struggle upon which the institutional dynamics of power and resistance are played out" (Wahidin & Powell, 2017, 559). Thus, by focusing on the paramilitary's experiences in prison compared to that of the generic analysis premised on the paramilitary's experiences while outside of the system, this paper attempts to acknowledge the intertwined space between oppression and resistance that prisoners attempted to manipulate to challenge the inherent power dynamic present within all prisons. For this analysis, my paper will rely heavily on that of Azrini Wahidin and Jason Powell (2017), through their coupling of Foucauldian and feminist lenses, to better understand the systems of struggle and resistance present within British prison facilities in the 1980s.

In 1972, Britain granted all of Northern Ireland's political prisoners special-category status. This involved "conditions similar to those enjoyed by internees and which effectively bestowed on them a kind of political status" (England, 2003, 188). The PIRA's approval of this concession is twofold: 1) its soldiers were often released within a short period of time and were often treated well with little abuse; 2) by having its prisoners granted political status, the Provisionals theoretically were also granted political status as an organisation, thus representing Britain's recognition of the organisation and its political goals. Yet, the January 1975 Gardiner Report soon recognised the "sustenance that [the special status] gave to paramilitary organisations" through recognising "the paramilitaries' own depiction of themselves as engaged in a legitimate political struggle" (Ibid., 188–189). Britain now sought to delegitimize the prisoner's goals by criminalising their actions, enraging both the PIRA and the general Catholic populace.

The first form of resistance that ensued to combat this form of political delegitimization was the blanket protest. Kieran Nugent, the first PIRA man for whom the new sentencing took effect, began the protest by refusing to wear clothes. Prisoners, according to each prison's rules, were not allowed to leave their cells until dressed. Nugent was then restricted to his cell for 24 hours a day. According to Richard English:

> [t]he blanket protest embodied IRA prisoners' refusal to accept criminal status, and it led the authorities to respond by removing from prisoners their access to television, radio, reading material (other than the Bible), writing materials and letters, as well as remission on sentences. (Ibid., 191)

Within weeks, other prisoners in H-block (Maze prison near Belfast) had joined the no-wash protest "in response (they said) to prison warders' brutality (bid.). Yet, these so-called "blanketmen", although obviously responding to brutality and the remission of their political status, also fought for a united response against British control. This "solidary culture" grew into the more influential dirty protest" or no wash campaign (O'Hearn, 2009, 491).

No-Wash Protest

The No Wash Protest, unlike the blanket protest, is a site where increasing information about female protesters and their collective roles in resistance is available. Although there is evidence that women played integral roles within the IRA's command structure and fighting capacity – representing 4.9% of all PIRA recruits – little time is spent acknowledging women's roles in resisting British subjugation and rule (Bloom et al., 2012, 63). Not only was women's physical presence within the PIRA oftentimes not acknowledged, but women were also frequently subjected to higher levels of sexual harassment and violence compared to men, another factor continually overlooked by analyses of the PIRA.

To use this unwarranted physical attention to their advantage, women were forced to reinvent their bodies "as actively resisting the power to punish, thus restoring the political potency of political prisoners" (Wahidin & Powell, 2017, 559). Wahidin and Powell further argue that "violence applied to the female body in a visible manner transformed the movement of time across the somatic surfaces of the female political prisoner's body" (Ibid.). Thus, through women utilising their bodies as sites of struggle and oppression, the no-wash protest was utterly transformed into a collective site of resistance by 32 female prisoners.

Women, unlike men within the prison system, were allowed to wear civilian clothes. Importantly, black clothes represented a woman's membership in the PIRA and were often worn after the death of a colleague or in support of other comrades in prisons such as Long Kesh (Ibid., 560). In February 1980, Hugh Delaney, a PIRA volunteer, passed away. Prisoners in Armagh sought to commemorate his death by hosting a parade that included marching in their black uniforms. To the prison officials, the women's parade signalled "not only the women's defiance to the prison regime: it reinforced their political status and collective identity as volunteers or soldiers in the army" (Ibid.). These uniforms, in particular, symbolised an overt threat towards the British political institution and the PIRA's purported legitimacy, which was sustained due to the prisoners' use of the uniforms. Through an attempt to delegitimize the prisoner's cause, the frequency of strip searches, and thus the incorporation and normalisation of sexual assault within the prison system, increased.

The No Wash Protest officially began on February 9, 1980, after prison personnel reportedly confiscated paramilitary clothing and flags from a cell (Ibid., 563). Prison officers moved towards destroying all available pieces of black clothing, coupled with relegating the women to a different wing of the prison – one that deprived them of toilet facilities. In response, women first began throwing the contents of their chamber pots out of the windows, until the prison boarded the windows up. Then, women were relegated to throwing the contents of the pots out onto the landing of the prison whenever a guard opened the door. After that opportunity, too, was deprived by the prison officials, women "resorted to smearing excrement all over the walls of their cells in protest" (Ibid.). Not only did the protest entail a lack of access to toilet facilities, but soon the women elected not to wash their bodies, brush their hair, or brush their teeth. Soon, male prisoners at Long Kesh embarked on a similar protest, with both lasting around a year.

The No Wash protest garnered attention, both civilian and governmental, but with limited success. Much of the public opinion surrounding the protest was met with horror and disgust. Instead of having the general public sympathise with their cause, many civilians found the protesters to be uncivilised, animalistic, and poorly behaved (Ibid., 565). Soon, the protesters moved towards staging the Hunger Protest, a protest that would gain more publicity and popular support but also result in many deaths.

The Hunger Strike

In 1923, the IRA launched its first mass hunger strike, with thousands of IRA prisoners refusing food "with the aim of securing unconditional release from jail" (English, 2003, 37). The strike collapsed within a month. The Provisionals, having witnessed the failure of the first hunger strike, soon discovered that hunger strikes could be much more effective when paired with smaller numbers of prisoners. As the PIRA prisoners, and moreover, the Republican cause, had gained momentum from both the Blanket and No Wash Protests, the PIRA imposed a hunger strike.

On October 10, 1980, the blanket men in H-Block Long Kesh prison issued a joint statement that witnessed the beginning of the strike. It stated:

> [w]e, the republican prisoners of war in H-Block, Long Kesh, demand as of right political recognition and that we be accorded the status of political prisoners. We claim this right as captured combatants in the continuing struggle for national liberation and self determination. We refute most strongly the tag of criminal with which the British have attempted to label us and our struggle, and we point to the divisive partitionist institutions of the six counties as the sole criminal aspect of the present struggle. We wish to make it clear that every channel has now been exhausted and, not wishing to break faith with those from whom we have inherited our principles, we now commit ourselves to a hunger strike. (Dunphy, 1997, 121)

The strike, similar to the former protests, was an attempt to embody the PIRA's causes through personal resistance while placing blame on the British state's lack of acknowledgement of the prisoner's political status. The strike began on October 27, 1980, with three female prisoners from Armagh jail, Mairéad Farrell, Mairéad Nugent, and Mary Doyle, joining the strike on December 1, 1980 (English,

2003, 194). By December 15, 23 more prisoners had joined the strike, with another seven joining on December 16. The first PIRA hunger strike was ordered to cease on December 18, lasting 53 days (Ibid., 195). As the hunger strike had failed to gain British concessions, the PIRA ordered another strike for March 1, 1981.

The second hunger strike, unlike the first, is renowned for being one of the most controversial yet memorialised aspects of the PIRA's strategy to induce concessions from the British. Bobby Sands, the leader of the hunger strike and PIRA member, was the first hunger striker to die, having refused food for 66 days. As more members continued to perish, so too did the Republican resolve to continue the strike, with families intervening to end the strike by October 3, 1981. Bobby Sands' death was particularly monumental for the Republican cause for three reasons: 1) He was the first prisoner to die purely from a form of bodily resistance that was not grounded in acts of violence; 2) Bobby Sands was a Member of Parliament for the Fermanagh and South Tyrone seat (BBC, 1981). After the previous MP, Frank Maguire, had passed suddenly due to a heart attack, Sands ran a controversial campaign from H-Block Prison to win 52% of the vote and stun those in parliament (Ibid.). Sands' victory politically legitimised the PIRA's platform but also later called into question the British' government's lack of involvement in protecting Sands, a member of parliament, from his impending death. 3) After the ten hunger strikers' deaths, Northern Ireland saw an upsurge in both Republican violence and renewed public favour for the PIRA. Although the hunger strike failed to achieve its goals, having gained no concessions from the British government and losing ten innocent lives through its aggressive tactics, the Republican cause gained a renewed sense of nationalist sentiment and hatred towards the British state.

The PIRA, along with the majority of the Irish Catholic populace, held the British accountable for the deaths of its ten soldiers. They viewed the British as malignant and chastised them for their reluctance to react and save the lives of the ten victims. The victims themselves were simply pawns for continued British oppression and therefore were not in charge of their own deaths. Over time, the Hunger Strike came to be remembered as, although a controversial endeavour, one that ignited a fervour within the Republican cause that helped the PIRA continue its war against the British state for another decade.

Bombing of Brighton Hotel

Now that I have detailed examples of the PIRA's physical resistance through the Blanket, No Wash Protests, and Hunger Strikes, I want to move towards briefly discussing a more overt form of resistance that also garnered immense media attention. The Brighton Bombing is one of the most well-known bombings the IRA conducted due to its attempted assassination of Margaret Thatcher, the leader of the Conservative Party and Prime Minister of the United Kingdom at the time. Although this brief section does not mean to take away from the vast other forms of resistance the IRA employed or to overlook the other bombings conducted, such as at Omagh, it serves to showcase the magnitude of the IRA's attacks. Although the Hunger Strike, Blanket, and No Wash Protests displayed the IRA's willingness to dedicate their lives to the cause, these attempts at resistance represented little risk to the UK's government as a whole. This bombing, in comparison, validated the IRA's ability to cause excessive harm to the British but also displayed the lengths to which it was willing to go to obtain its political goal of separation.

Rife with anger from the contested hunger strikes in March 1981, the Republican cause aimed to avenge the deaths of the ten fallen IRA soldiers. As a solution, they looked towards the Conservative Party Conference, held at Brighton's Grand Hotel in October 1984. With Margaret Thatcher representing the focal point for the IRA's disdain towards its British counterparts, the conference posed a unique opportunity to attack Thatcher at her most vulnerable.

On September 14, 1984, a man under the name of Roy Walsh, now known to be Patrick Magee, checked into Brighton's Grand Hotel and left a bomb behind a bathroom panel (Hernon, 2007, 195). The bomb was built to go off 24 days later, during the conference (Ibid.). At 2:54 a.m. on October 12, the bomb exploded. The blast killed five people, injured 31 others, and caused extensive damage to the hotel, collapsing floors and decimating a partial area of the building's façade (Mayer, 2014). Yet Thatcher survived, and so too did the conference, assumedly much to the IRA's dismay. Thatcher moved to use her remaining time at the conference not simply to highlight the tragedy of the bombing and thus give the IRA agency and attention for the attack but to instead stifle any ounce of success that the IRA had hoped to obtain. During her keynote address, Thatcher addressed the bombing by noting that the attack

> was an attempt not only to disrupt and terminate our Conference; it was an attempt to cripple Her Majesty's democratically-elected Government. That is the scale of the outrage in which we have all shared, and the fact that we are gathered here now—shocked, but composed and determined—is a sign not only that this attack has failed, but that all attempts to destroy democracy by terrorism will fail. (Ibid.)

The rhetoric surrounding the attack on the IRA was disastrous. Not only did the campaign fail in killing Thatcher, but it also failed in generating more support for their cause. Yet Magee contended that the Brighton bombing "helped push the Thatcher government towards negotiations with Sinn Féin and the IRA" (Hernon, 2007, 207). Furthermore, Magee asserted that after the bombing, the British finally changed how they viewed the IRA (Ibid.). The IRA now posed a serious threat to the British government and prompted the British to question the extent to which the Republicans would go to promote their cause. Thus, although the bombing may have decreased sentiment towards the IRA, it also helped legitimise the groups' assertion that they were a true army with a true cause that threatened much of Britain's existence on the island of Ireland.

Sinn Féin

Lastly, before discussing the impending peace process and the IRA's involvement in Northern Ireland's consociationalist government, I first wanted to draw attention to another unique aspect of the Republican make-up. In 1917, Sinn Féin, originally a "non-violent, non-republican nationalist party," was recognised and committed itself to an Irish republic" (England, 2003, 15). Following their win in the 1918 election, Sinn Féin created an alternative parliament in Dublin, known as the Dáil Éireann (Ibid.). For Republicans, this was the first legitimate governing body within Ireland.

The body first met on January 21, 1919, where they read out a Declaration of Independence and declared Ireland free from Britain, thus cementing the party's nationalistic goals and future ties to the IRA. Sinn Féin became activated as the IRA's political wing in the 1940s but did not become heavily involved in the PIRA's campaign until the 1980s with the peace process and the election of Gerry Adams as President (Ibid., 75). With members such as Adams and Martin McGuinness having joint membership with both the IRA and Sinn Féin, the group became inherently a political extension of the PIRA. The ability of Sinn Féin to advance the PIRA's goals in a more politically acceptable manner made the PIRA one of the few paramilitary groups in the 20th century to have an active and successful political basis within the government.

Good Friday Agreement

Not only did Sinn Féin help legitimise the IRA's interests, but it also held a key position within the ceasefire negotiations, allowing the IRA to have a voice within the 1998 Good Friday Agreement, unlike most other paramilitary organisations when negotiating a peace settlement.

By 1990, the British government had instigated talks with Sinn Féin's representative, Martin McGuinness, resulting in an IRA ceasefire in December 1990. Yet, this agreement soon fell apart, as did the cessation of political violence. It was not until August 31, 1994, that the IRA issued its own statement, declaring its willingness to stop advancing its goals through the use of political violence and to instead promote its beliefs through its political wing, Sinn Féin. The statement announced that

> [r]ecognising the potential of the current situation and in order to enhance the democratic peace process and underline our definitive commitment to its success the leadership of Óglaigh na hÉireann have decided that as of midnight, Wednesday, 31 August, there will be a complete cessation of military operations. All our units have been instructed accordingly. (England, 2003, 285)

The PIRA's declaration was followed by a hailstorm of media coverage, with the Belfast Telegraph announcing that, "[a]fter 3,168 deaths and twenty-five years of terror, the IRA says … It's Over" (Ibid., 286). The PIRA had argued that, currently, the political climate was not sufficiently favourable to induce a British withdrawal of its troops from the island. Instead, the group believed that it was in their best interest to pursue an agreement that would involve Sinn Féin and then continue advocating for Britain's withdrawal in future negotiations. This did not mean that the Provisionals would lay down their arms while negotiating. In fact, political violence continued into the 2000s, even after the signing of the Good Friday Agreement. Yet, this agreement signified the changing nature of both the PIRA and the British offensive through their willingness to offer concessions to both sides. By September 1997, the UK's Tony Blair government had granted Sinn Féin the ability to participate in the peace negotiations, signalling the Provisionals' long-awaited willingness to negotiate on the government level (Ibid., 296).

April 10, 1998, is a date memorialised within the histories of Northern Ireland, the Republic, and the United Kingdom for its landmark negotiation that culminated in the Good Friday Agreement, alternatively known as the Belfast Agreement. The first agreement of its kind offered "partnership, equality, and mutual respect as the basis of relationships within Northern Ireland, between north and south, and between these islands [of Ireland and Britain]" (Ibid., 297). It discussed the political make-up of the Northern Ireland Assembly but, more importantly, incorporated a consociationalist, or power-sharing, design.

Consociationalism, first defined by Arend Lijphart, is the institutional design of having a government that both represents the main segments of society and the populace proportionately while sharing power between the major groups within the country (1969, 207–225). For Northern Ireland, this meant that there was both a mixture of separation of powers and fusion of powers within the Assembly, resulting in the Assembly being elected separately from the Panel yet fused with the Panel because they both have executive responsibilities. Secondly, both the panel and the assembly would utilise proportional representation for their elections. With the population of Northern Ireland reflecting a ratio of 2:1 Protestants to Catholics (broadly speaking), the Agreement enacted provisions for the minority Catholic group to gain some ruling autonomy within the governing system. In addition, the agreement included both a minority veto right and a panel with special powers that would allow the Catholic community to influence the legislature without needing a majority. Consociationalism, by implementing veto rights, guaranteed the Protestant majority in the legislature while making concessions that favoured the Catholic minority. Ultimately, consociationalism prevented sectarian domination within the government and, subsequently, Catholic oppression. Lastly, consociationalism ensured that the PIRA, or more specifically, Sinn Féin, would always exert influence within the legislature if elected by their Catholic base. This has allowed Sinn Féin to remain powerful to this day, while also giving the Provisionals the political foundation they need if a future conflict arises.

Theoretically, power sharing has been successful in Northern Ireland. Since its implementation, it has seen not only a reduction in sectarian violence and British control over the island but also the creation of a parliament ruled by the people, not by the Queen. Although the power-sharing agreement accomplished its main goal of reducing violence on the island, I argue that the government implemented it too soon within the peace process. Moreover, the power-sharing agreement did not equip Northern Ireland's government with the tools needed to effectively resolve future sectarian disputes, should they arise. For example, shortly after the Good Friday Agreement, the United Kingdom was forced to reimpose Home Rule from 2002–2007, resulting in Northern Ireland once again relinquishing all of its sovereignty to its colonialist controllers, which simply reinvigorated Nationalist disdain for their Unionist counterparts. Northern Ireland was no longer able to make decisions on its behalf, culminating in the loss of any power-sharing and equality between the two religious groups that was originally agreed upon. After years of direct rule, the Nationalists and Unionists in Northern Ireland came together under the St. Andrews agreement in October 2006 to work towards "the restoration of devolution and power sharing in the province" (Owen, 2006). By 2007, Northern Ireland had successfully re-implemented power-sharing, which remained successful until the government's dissolution in 2017.

More recently, Stormont, the Northern Irish Assembly, has been suspended from January 2017 to the present over disagreements between the two main parties, Sinn Féin and the Democratic Unionist Party (DUP) (McDowell, 2018). During the Good Friday Agreement, both Sinn Féin and the DUP agreed to a confederal government. But, after the peace talks had ended, the DUP became disillusioned with its inability to control the legislature and retracted their commitment to back the parliament (McGrattan, 2010, 157). The Unionists agreed, moreover, that the Nationalists gained more from the Agreement, contributing to intensifying the tensions between the Unionists and Nationalists after the signing of the Agreement (Hayes & McAllister, 2013). As a show of force against the DUP's disdain for power-sharing and to protest against its inability to handle the Renewable Heat Incentive, Sinn Féin's leader, Martin McGuinness, resigned from his position in the parliament in January 2017. McGuinness claimed that the incentive had lost approximately 490 million pounds of taxpayer money since its implementation in 2012 (BBC, 2017; Fenton, 2017). With the current use of power-sharing in the parliament, the loss of McGuiness forced first minister Arlene Foster to lose her seat as well, as the two positions are tied together (Page, 2017). Sinn Féin decided not to nominate anyone to fill McGuiness's position in the parliament to dissolve the government, with Stormont's suspension continuing into 2020 (Ibid.). This suspension prompts the question of how effective power sharing has been in promoting long-lasting peace on the island and whether this resignation is simply the first of many to come. This is not to say that consociationalism has not played an integral role in the peace process, as exemplified by the reduced violence within the island, but obviously, the implementation has been flawed since the Good Friday Agreement.

Moreover, the impending future question over the soft border between Northern Ireland and Ireland because of the United Kingdom's break from the European Union has worried many Irish over the potential for the PIRA to begin their violent campaign. Although I cannot answer this question, I can acknowledge the great importance of the current open border between the two countries and also point to the PIRA's ability to renew violence whenever they see fit. Even with the Troubles having ended in 1998 and violence having almost completely stopped, future prospects for the PIRA's renewal appear favourable because of Britain's recent political upheaval with the European Union.

CONCLUSION

In this chapter, I detailed the historical tensions on the island of Ireland that culminated in the Irish Republican Army's creation, the unique tactics and events that served to promote the PIRA's interests, as well as the recent peacebuilding process that saw the paramilitary organisation take an important seat at the negotiating table. The IRA has been unlike any other violent paramilitary group in the 20th century and is one of the most dangerous threats to British governance still remaining today. Although Northern Ireland has remained relatively peaceful since the signing of the Good Friday Agreement, the threat of Brexit and the disastrous suspension of Stormont both showcase the changing political climate on the island, which is ripe for another conflict to occur. With the IRA's still prominent political wing, Sinn Féin, holding a commanding lead over many Catholic votes, the organisation has positioned itself well in both the cultural and governmental makeup of the country to defend Republican interests, if need be, in the future. Thus, displaying that although the IRA may be inactive currently, if an opportunity arises, it has the potential to reignite a violent conflict with huge ramifications for the stability of the island as well as for British rule within the region.

References

BBC. (1981). Hunger striker elected MP. http://news.bbc.co.uk/onthisday/hi/dates/stories/april/10/newsid_2453000/2453183.stm

BBC. (2017, January 10). Martin McGuinness resigns as NI deputy first minister. http://www.bbc.com/news/uk-northern-ireland-38561507

Bloom, M., Gill, P., and Horgan, J. (2012). Tiocfaidh ár Mná: Women in the provisional Irish republican army. *Behavioural Sciences of Terrorism and Political Aggression*, *4*(1), 60–76.

Brew, P. (2008). *The making and remaking of the good friday agreement*. Dublin: The Liffey Press.

Byrne, S. (2009). *Beyond the ethnonational divide: Identity politics and women in Northern Ireland and Israel/Palestine*. Kingston: Queens University. PhD Dissertation.

Dunphy, R. (1997). "The contradictory politics of the official republican movement, 1969-1992." In R. Deutsch (Ed.). *Les Républicanismes Irlandais*. (pp. 117–138). Rennes: Presses Universitaries de Rennes.

Ellis, S. (2011, February 17). Turning Ireland English. BBC. http://www.bbc.co.uk/history/british/tudors/elizabeth_ireland_01.shtml.

England, R. (2003). *Armed struggle: The history of the IRA*. New York: Oxford University Press.

Farrelly, B. (2017). Understanding conflict. Lecture, National University of Ireland Maynooth, Maynooth, the Republic of Ireland, July 6, 2017.

Fenton, S. (2017, January 16). Power-sharing collapses in Northern Ireland, after Sinn Fein refuse to return to Stormont executive. Independent. https://www.independent.co.uk/news/uk/politics/northern-ireland-power-sharing-latest-collapse-end-sinn-fein-refuse-stormont-dup-martin-mcguinness-a7529111.html.

Hayes, B. C., and McAllister, I. (2013). *Conflict to peace: Politics and society in Northern Ireland over half a century*. Manchester: Manchester University Press.

Hernon, I. (2007). *Assassin!: 200 years of British political murder*. London: Pluto Press.

Lijphart, A. (1969). Consociational democracy. *World Politics*, *21*(2), 207–225.

Mayer, C. (2014). How the Brighton bombing 30 years ago portended peace. Time UK. October 10, 2014. https://time.com/3484611/brighton-bombing-thatcher-30-years-1984/.

McDowell, I. (2018, February 5). Stormont deadlock: Need-to-know guide. BBC. https://www.bbc.com/news/uk-northern-ireland-politics-41723268.

McGrattan, C. (2010). *Northern Ireland 1968-2008: The politics of entrenchment*. New York: Palgrave MacMillan.

O'Hearn, D. (2009). Repression and solidary cultures of resistance: Irish political prisoners on protest. *American Journal of Sociology*, *115*(2), 491–526.

Owen, P. (2006, October 17). What is the St. Andrews agreement? The Guardian. https://www.theguardian.com/politics/2006/oct/17/northernireland.devolution1.

Page, C. (2017, January 16). Stormont: All you need to know about NI's latest political crisis. BBC. http://www.bbc.com/news/uk-northern-ireland-38612860.

Sinn Féin. (1994, January 5). Setting the record straight. https://www.sinnfein.ie/files/2009/Settingrecordstraight.pdf

Volkan, V. D. (1999). Post-traumatic states: Beyond individual PTSD in societies ravaged by ethnic conflict. *Canadian Foreign Policy Journal*, *7*(1), 27–38. 10.1080/11926422.1999.9673198.

Wahidin, A., and Powell, J. (2017). "The Irish Conflict" and the experiences of female ex-combatants in the Irish republican army: Power, resistance and subjectivity. *The International Journal of Sociology and Social Policy*, *37*(9/10), 555–571.

42

THE FIGHTING PEOPLE'S REVOLUTIONARY POWERS

Kalliopi Chainoglou

INTRODUCTION

The resurgence of political violence has haunted Greece between 2013 and 2019. The Fighting People's Revolutionary Powers is one of the many urban-guerrilla terrorist organisations that emerged amidst the economic crisis in Greece. The terrorist organisations that have been active during this period present themselves as militant, anti-fascist, and anti-establishment urban-guerrilla collectivities. These new groups, which may display very different forms of structure as well as organisational and operational characteristics between themselves, are engaged in a struggle to claim as much space as they can in the political vacuum that was created in the anarchic spectrum following the dismantling of the infamous "17 November" terrorist organisation. The purpose of this chapter is to outline the history and motivation behind the terrorist attack carried out by the Fighting People's Revolutionary Powers in Greece.

OVERVIEW: HISTORY OF HOW AND WHY THE GROUP OR MOVEMENT FORMED

A catapult of events since 2010 has significantly affected Greek society. The austerity measures and the financial crisis upended the Greek people. Since 2013 and onwards, more and more people have found themselves living beyond the poverty line, and there has been an increase in suicidal rates following the loss of jobs and bankruptcies. The refugee and immigrant flows stranded in Greek territory (even to this day) imposed a heavy burden on the state and Greek society. Data collected from UN agencies reveals how massive the influx has been to a small country like Greece (see Table 42.1, UNHCR, 2023); one has to recall that the thousands of refugees and immigrants were stranded in Greece because many European countries closed their borders and refrained from welcoming refugees on their territories.

Table 42.1 Sea and Land Arrivals into Greece: 2014–2024

Years	Sea Arrivals	Land Arrivals	Dead and Missing
2024 (as of June 30)	18,004	2,743	N/A
2023	41,561	7,160	799
2022	12,758	6,022	434
2021	4,331	4,826	115
2020	9,714	5,982	105
2019	9,714	5,982	71
2018	32,494	18,014	1876
2017	29,718	6,592	56
2016	173,450	3,784	441
2015	856,723	4,907	799
2014	41,038	2,280	405

Source: UNHCR (2024).

Hence, for many years, the Greek economy crashed between the economic and refugee crises. As a consequence, people in Greece, being disappointed and worn out by these events, were exposed to xenophobic and populist claims that were entangled with a distorted narrative of patriotism and the protection of the country from external threats that were posed by the influx of refugees, the lack of support from EU member states that were previously perceived as allies to Greece, or the international organisations that designed and monitored the implementation of the bail-out programmes. Despite the fact that Greek society displayed ample hospitality to refugees and irregular immigrants, there has been a persisting feeling that the Greeks' efforts were not appreciated or acknowledged by their EU counterparts and the EU institutions, while the EU member states refrained from honouring their own commitments to resettling asylum seekers and Turkey systematically hesitated to control the refugee outflow. It should be noted that between 2013 and 2019, there was a profound uprising of populist and extreme-right-wing parties throughout Europe. It was during this time that Greece

DOI: 10.4324/9780429426063-48

became increasingly polarised in the midst of the economic crisis. Hence, the Greek society, much like any other European society, was subjected to claims spreading the blame for the existing economic problems on foreigners, irregular immigrants, and status quo or corrupted/nepotist politicians.

The Fighting People's Revolutionary Powers is a newly-established far-left terrorist organisation that came into existence following the uprising of extreme right-wing movements in Greece. The events that led to the action of this organisation can be traced back to the murder of an anti-fascist rapper, Pavlos Fyssas, in September 2013. The police investigation into the perpetrators of the crime led to the arrest of 69 supporters of the extreme right-wing and elected to the Greek Parliament political party of Golden Dawn. In retaliation for Pavlos Fyssas' murder, two members of the Golden Dawn, Manolis Kapelonis and Giorgos Fountoulis, were killed, and one member of the Golden Dawn, Alexandros Gerondas, was wounded outside the offices of the political party on November 1, 2013. The Fighting People's Revolutionary Forces assumed responsibility for the drive-by shootings as retribution for the fatal stabbing of Pavlos Fyssas in an 18-page proclamation that was originally stored on a USB stick found in Kessariani, Greece.

KEY PERSONNEL AND STRUCTURE

The Fighting People's Revolutionary Powers released two proclamations (manifestos) in 2013 and 2014. Despite the fact that they have been active since 2013, little is known about the leadership, structure, or key personnel of the Fighting People's Revolutionary Powers. With the police unable to thin out the organisation's structure, it looks as if the organisation is divided at best into two branches: the leaders, who set the intellectual and ideological pace upon which the 2013 operation was carried out, and the executive branch, which has carried out the attack. It may be the case that the executive branch has formalised its operation through mercenaries; this may imply that there is no *ad hoc* executive branch. Throughout the years, journalistic sources have occasionally reported that the organisation may have had connections with criminal gangs and especially imprisoned convicts, but the police authorities have not confirmed this. The fact that no other attack has been carried out since 2013 is an indicator that this organisation may not have matured as an urban guerilla organisation.

It is also not known whether the organisation has dissolved; if so, it is not known whether it has happened due to a lack of interest or lack of resources or whether it has been absorbed by any other urban guerilla terrorist organisations. It may also be the case that the organisation may have lost its ideological compass once the Golden Dawn party's trajectory derailed and it failed to win a parliamentary seat in the July 2019 national elections. The collapse of the Golden Dawn has taken place over the past few years as numerous charges were filed against the Golden Dawn's MPs for their participation in a criminal organisation and other charges related to murder and assault.

ORGANISATIONAL CHARACTERISTICS AND ACTIVITIES: STRUCTURE, CHANGE, AND OPERATIONS

The 2013 manifesto, in which the Fighting People's Revolutionary Powers assume responsibility for the two murders, is revealing as to the ideological background of the group. Therein, the actions of the group are described as the "political executions of... the neo-Nazis"; the use of armed pistols was justified in response to the statement of a member of the Golden Dawn (Smith, 2013).

The text of the manifesto heavily references the operation of the extreme-right-wing political party, Golden Dawn. The drafters make lengthy comments on incidents of violence that have allegedly been carried out under the order or with the knowledge of the members of the Golden Dawn against irregular migrants and political opponents, including communist trade unionists in 2013. The despise felt by the drafters of the manifesto against Golden Dawn is evident throughout the text, where they warn that more attacks would follow against their members or supporters:

> The armed attack-response … is the starting point of the people's campaign to send the neo-Nazi scum of Golden Dawn where they belong, the dustbin of history … The revolutionary movement has to proceed with the material destruction of the infrastructure of Golden Dawn and in a coordinated [fashion] attack those who belong to it … their heads should be cracked open with a hammer, their hands cut off, by way of example, with a sickle.
>
> (Smith, 2013)

The whole manifesto, written in prosecutorial form, records the numerous alleged crimes that the Golden Dawn has committed since it came into power and calls for a social revolution against them.

The writing style of the drafters is completely different from any other contemporary active terrorist organisation's writing style. The Fighting People's Revolutionary Powers are producing lengthy manifestos written in a quasi-academic style with references to historical events, contemporary political issues, and knowledge of human rights violations that occurred throughout Greece in the midst of the economic crisis. The text even appears to be edited! The 2013 manifesto seems to have been written by people who belong to the older generation of the anarchist movement. The language they use as well as the plethora of historical references to the execution of alleged fascists during the civil war indicate that the drafters of the manifesto have considerable knowledge of historical events that took place in southern Greece, in particular in the Peloponnesian region. The lack of reference to similar historical events that took place in Macedonia and other parts of Greece rather indicates that the drafter(s) may be from the Attica or Southern Greece region.

The drafters seem to have a soft spot for the hurdles that the Greek population is facing, i.e., by reference to the fact that malnourished children are fading at Greek schools, that the system of public education is deteriorating, that there is a lack of medication due to the austerity cuts in the health sector, or that there is an increase in the number of people who suffer from mental health issues. Furthermore, the drafters echo the concerns of the anti-fascist movement in Greece; they make references to the discriminatory treatment of unemployed people or even irregular immigrants.

The drafters of the manifesto appear to be more than one; in the present writer's opinion, there are differences throughout the text that reveal at least two drafters, possibly one of them being female. The first part of the 2013 manifesto is written in lengthy sentences, while the latter part of the manifesto is written in more sensitised journalistic language with small sentences. The text of the manifesto seems to have been written by people who are older; it lacks the typical passionate and vibrant calls for militant actions or the typical annihilistic statements that younger anarchists would make.

It has also been reported that the Anti-Terrorism Unit of the Greek Police believes that the drafters of the 2013 Manifesto may have had no physical participation in the murder of the two members of the Golden Dawn; instead, there is the belief that the perpetrators of the crime are of younger age who may aspire to the ideology of the organisation without being active members of the organisation, or they may have been mercenaries who were contracted out to carry out the attacks. This seems to be confirmed by the fact that the organisation has not carried out any other attacks since then!

Despite the operational part of the organisation being inactive, the intellectual part of the Fighting People's Revolutionary Powers appears to be active. In 2014, the organisation released its second manifesto without committing a terrorist attack. It is believed that the organisation chose to release a 21-page second manifesto in order to provide answers to the many media outlets and journalists who were covering the murder of the two members of the Golden Dawn. Herein, the manifesto talks the readers through the aspirations of the organisation for the materialisation of a civil conflict or a revolution against the establishment, including the status quo politicians and international organisations, and especially Golden Dawn.

The Fighting People's Revolutionary Powers view themselves as anti-establishment, anti-racist leftists, and socialist militants; at the same time, they have been criticised by some extreme-leftist and anarchist movements as being essentially on the same page with extreme right-wing militants. The second proclamation makes interesting reading as it is not only directed against the Golden Dawn members and supporters, but it is also strongly criticising any other anarchist and anti-establishment movements that dismissed the 2013 murders of the Golden Dawn members as "provocation" that would essentially increase the support of the Greek public in favour of the extreme left-wing party of Syriza or the extreme right-wing party of Golden Dawn. The text also provides a detailed, albeit old-fashioned, analysis of how armed violence can contribute to urban-guerrilla warfare. This second manifesto reveals that there has been much tension between the urban guerilla organisations themselves and that there is, in effect, an unseen civil war taking place between the various anarchic militant movements and the urban guerilla organisations.

It is noteworthy that while the Fighting People's Revolutionary Powers appears to be inactive, there are other urban guerilla terrorist organisations that have emerged around the same time or earlier than 2013, and they are still operative. For example, "Zero Tolerance" ["Mideniki Anohi"] emerged in 2009 and is notorious for the attacks it carries out against the offices of politicians and members of the Parliament. On February 4, 2014, Zero Tolerance placed a bomb at the political office of the Minister of Interior and claimed responsibility for the attack by releasing a three-page proclamation entitled "Concerning Violence". In this manifesto, Zero Tolerance presents its anarchist ideology and applauds the actions of the Fighting People's Revolutionary Powers. This indicates that the Zero Tolerance organisation attempts to engage (possibly as an ally) the Fighting People's Revolutionary Powers in their guerrilla warfare. On November 1, 2019, on the anniversary of the attack that took place in 2013, there was a reported incident at the headquarters of the Golden Dawn. Four explosive mechanisms resulted in setting fire to the offices of the political party. At the time, it was reported that the police suspected the Fighting People's Revolutionary Powers, but the organisation has not assumed responsibility for this attack.

IMPACTS

Capitalising on the impact of the political and economic crisis, the various urban guerilla groups and terrorist organisations flourished during 2013–2019. The uprising of the extreme-right-wing movements and especially Golden Dawn in debt-stricken Greece was matched with the operation of many militant, anti-fascist, urban guerilla groups. The impact of the murder of the two Golden Dawn supporters was immense in social terms. At the time of the attack, there was a highly polarised and torn Greek society that was outraged by the bail-out programmes, the austerity measures, and the massive numbers of refugees and irregular immigrants. The murder of the two members of the Golden Dawn further infuriated the many supporters at the time of the Golden Dawn party. Amid heightened fears of escalating violence, there were numerous public protests organised all over Greece and attended even by non-sympathisers of the Golden Dawn. At the same time, it was observed that there was a considerable increase in the anti-fascist protests that were taking place in memory of Pavlos Fyssas throughout the country. Moreover, the government and the representatives of the political parties strongly condemned the terrorist attack at the time and called for an end to violence. It should be mentioned, though, that the 2013 terrorist attack may have had an indirect impact on the case of the murder of Pavlos Fyssas. While the decision of the Court is still pending, in December 2019, the Attorney General requested the acquittal of the suspects, who are members of the Golden Dawn.

CONCLUSION

Seven years after the terrorist attack, police investigations have stalled. It is noteworthy, however, that a number of sources indicate that other urban guerilla groups have also adopted the Fighting People's Revolutionary Powers' operational strategy. This is a development that has taken place only in the last decade; to put it simply, previously, the urban guerilla groups relied on criminal gangs to get hold of firearms, or they used to be involved in criminal activity themselves, while now the pattern seems to be that the executions of the terrorist acts are contracted out to individuals with recorded criminal activity, acting as mercenaries. Given their long inaction, it is highly unlikely that the Fighting People's Revolutionary Powers will strike again; after all, their existence was primarily justified by the existence of the Golden Dawn. As the latter has collapsed, there is no ideological motivation for the Fighting People's Revolutionary Powers to continue their activities. However, the memory of their 2013 attack is still very much alive within Greek society and the political world, as it is undeniably connected to the ongoing judicial proceedings concerning the murder of the anti-fascist rapper, Pavlos Fyssas.

References

"A veil of mystery covers the attack against the offices of the golden dawn" ['Peplo Mustiriou Kalyptei tin Epithesi Sta Grafeia tis Chrusis Augis'], 1 November 2019, oakke.gr/esoteriki-politiki/item/310-σοσιαλ-ναζιστικό-μανιφέστο-για-απόλυτη-κνίτικη-ηγεμονία-πάνω-στους-αναρχικούς

Marans, Daniel. (2016, March 2). Greece's economy is getting crushed between austerity and the refugee crisis. https://www.huffingtonpost.ca/entry/greece-refugee-crisis-economy_n_56b12f1de4b04f9b57d7b7d4?ri18n=true

OAKKE. (2013, November 4). The proclamation justifying the murder of the neonazi's ['I Prokirixi gia ti dolofonia ton Xrisaugiton'].

Smith, Helena. (2013, November 17). Leftist militants claim Golden Dawn killings as rally honours 1973 uprising. https://www.theguardian.com/world/2013/nov/17/leftist-militants-golden-dawn-killings-rally-uprising

UNHCR. (2024). Operational data portal. Mediterranean situation / Greece. https://data.unhcr.org/en/situations/mediterranean/location/5179

43

CHECHEN TERRORISM

From Modest Nationalist Claims to the Caucasus Emirate

Mary Manjikian

INTRODUCTION

The Chechen region of the North Caucasus is a place that has long been characterised as wild and perhaps ungovernable. Russia, its neighbour, has long sought to bring it under its control through the use of military force, creating violence and conflict between the ethnically Muslim Chechen people and the ethnically Orthodox Christian Russian population. Antipathy between the two groups dates back to the eighteenth century, when Czarist Russia launched incursions into the region, seeking to bring it under Russian control. With the rise of the Soviet Union in 1917, Chechnya (a territory with approximately 1.2 million inhabitants), along with neighbouring areas of the North Caucasus, including Dagestan, were forcibly integrated into the Russian Republic. Many of the leadership positions in society were held by ethnic Russians, and Russian was the language of commerce and education. Resources created and gathered within Chechnya were not kept for the Chechen nation but were frequently exported back to Russia. However, Chechnya retained a nominally separate status as an autonomous republic within Russia.

With the Soviet Union's dissolution in 1991, the fifteen independent republics within the Soviet territory achieved independence. Republics within the South Caucasus, such as Armenia and Azerbaijan, thus become independent states. However, Russia chose to retain control of the autonomous republics within its borders, including those of the North Caucasus Federal District, a territory with a population of ten million that included the territories of Dagestan, Chechnya, Ingushetia, North Ossetia, Kabardino-Balkaria, Karachay Cherkessia, and Stavropol Krai (Lamb, 2005). The Chechen-Ingush Autonomous Republic entity was split into two parts, and Chechnya's leadership (led by Dzhokhar Dudayev) proclaimed the Chechen Republic of Ichkeria in 1991, claiming independence and secession from Russia.

Dzhokhar Dudayev was a former general who had served with the Soviet Air Force. In his position as the first president of the self-declared Chechen Republic of Ichkeria (1991–1996), he headed the nationalist Chechen separatist movement. Dudayev, who led the country through the First Chechen War, was killed in 1996 by Russian airstrikes. His claims on behalf of the republic were avowedly secular and were limited to the cause of Chechen independence, Chechen control over the republic's resources, and sovereignty from Russian control.

Moscow did not recognise this declaration and instead sought to maintain control over the region. As the situation grew increasingly tense, in December 1994, Russia attempted to overthrow the Chechen government and mobilised the Russian Army to take military action against the so-called 'breakaway republic.' In response, thousands of Chechen citizens joined insurgent groups, fighting a guerilla war against Russia's

The ensuing battle between Chechen insurgents and the Russian Army went on for nearly twenty years, until Russia's formal withdrawal from the conflict in 2009. During this time, relations have alternated between outright war and uneasy truces between the groups. Today, many analysts consider the Chechen-Ingush territory neither a clearly legal autonomous republic of Russia nor a failed state. Writing in 2011, Kuchins et al. argued that Russian government's efforts to stabilise the region had failed as it was becoming less integrated with the Russian Federation. Some have compared the region to an unstable frontier zone like the Federally Administered Tribal Area (FATA) in Pakistan on the Afghan border (Kuchins et al., 2011) Others describe it as a de facto state or "a separatist polity … which displays accoutrements of statehood except for international legal status." It is seen as "nominally belonging to a recognised state" but simultaneously declaring its independence from that territory (Florae, 2014) Thus, the standoff between Russia and Chechnya remains uneasy. Russia cannot properly be said to have won the conflict since Chechnya has not been successfully reintegrated into Russia, nor can Chechnya be said to have 'won its independence from Moscow.' The territory itself, as a

DOI: 10.4324/9780429426063-49

somewhat ungoverned frontier zone with an unclear legal status, has proven particularly attractive to terrorist groups from throughout the world, who have brought in foreign fighters from throughout the world to participate in training activities, preparing for terrorist actions in places as diverse as the Middle East, Europe, and North America.

In the nearly thirty years that the conflict has gone on, the initial Chechen insurgent groups involved have changed significantly in their profiles, aims, and ideologies. As is typical with longer-lived terrorist organisations, an initial generation of more moderate members with aims that might have been negotiated and fulfilled has given way to a more radicalised second and third generation, which is increasingly violent and less amenable to negotiation and compromise. As the initial generation has died or moved out of the group, group leaders have turned to other sources of support, including, in the Chechen case, neighbours in Islamic lands bordering Chechnya. Today, Chechen claims for territorial autonomy, sovereignty, and independence have been renounced in a larger, broader drive for the establishment and extension of Sharia law and Islamic fundamentalism throughout the so-called Caucasus Emirate. While native Chechen forces saw the struggle with Russia as one for sovereignty and territorial independence, Islamic fighters saw it as part of a greater narrative of Jihad, or holy war, in which Islamic fighters were seeking to expel foreign invaders or infidels from the Dar el-Islamic, or land of Islam.

As the Chechen terrorist group's goals and strategies changed, the likelihood that there could be a peaceful end to the regional strife by, for example, extracting concessions from Russia became increasingly less likely. At the same time, international public opinion has shifted sharply. From approximately 1991 to 1999, international organisations and international public opinion appeared to support the nationalist claims of Chechen groups, who appeared to be victimised by the unlawful and overwhelmingly brutal show of force carried out by Russia's Army. Today, however, many international observers view these insurgents not as citizens fighting for the cause of national independence but rather as members of a global Islamic fundamentalist movement aimed at establishing a pan-Islamic republic or "caliphate," which would stretch from Saudi Arabia to the Caucasus. Indeed, in the aftermath of the 911 terrorist attack in the United States, Russia's leadership began to speak of an 'arc of terror' that stretched from Central Asia to the Balkans in Eastern Europe, pointing to similarities in structure as well as belief systems shared by a great many terrorist groups, all of which were associated with Wahhabist or Salafist Islamic belief systems (Hill, 2001).

That is, the original insurgents' goals, which included achieving nationalist independence or even the implementation of national cultural strategies such as allowing for the use of two languages or education in the native Chechen language, allowed them to be viewed sympathetically by Western governments outside the region. However, as the groups radicalised, they lost any sympathy they might have garnered for their nationalist agenda. In particular, the actions of Chechen military leader Shamil Basayev and his associate, the Arab fighter Khattab, included several high-profile killings of civilians, including children, in Moscow as well as within the region. The violent tactics and ideology embraced by modern-day Chechen terrorists are more in line with the tactics and strategies of their patrons, groups like AL Qaeda and ISIS, than they are with the aims of a more restrained nationalist movement like the Basque group ETA or those who might agitate for Quebecois nationalist goals within Canada.

THE RUSSIAN RESPONSE

In retrospect, one might argue that Russia missed an opportunity by not moving quickly to solve this conflict in the beginning by negotiating and coming to an agreement with the nationalist insurgents who held more moderate goals. For example, Russia might have come to an agreement that allowed Chechnya a form of limited autonomy or even renounced Russia's territorial claims on the region rather than engaging in a decades-long war that produced upwards of 160,000 casualties and near-total devastation of the region, mainly as the result of successive aerial bombardments of the Chechen capital of Grozny. This campaign has been likened to the Allied bombing of Dresden during World War Two (Radio Free Europe). By late 1996, thousands of Chechens were homeless, and most of Chechnya's roads, hospitals, and educational systems were destroyed. Approximately 15% of Chechnya's agricultural land was strewn with land mines.

However, Russia's leadership took a hard line from the beginning against claims of independence by autonomous regions within Russia for four reasons: First, Russia's leaders feared that allowing any one autonomous region to declare independence could set a dangerous precedent in which Russia's large and expansive territory became increasingly fragmented. In a 2000 interview, Russian President Vladimir Putin stated that "The essence of the situation in the North Caucasus and Chechnya … is the continuation of the collapse of the USSR. If we did not quickly do something to stop it, Russia, as a state in its current form, would cease to exist (Hill, 2013). In that same interview, Putin referred to a situation akin to a 'second Yugoslavia." That is, Chechnya's drive for independence was seen as an 'existential threat' to the survival of Russia. The fear was that a situation might result that paralleled the 'domino effect' in Southeast Asia during the Vietnam War, where one territory after another fell into the North Vietnamese Communist orbit (Notte, 59). That is, Russia's leadership portrayed the threat along its borders as not merely a nationalist rebellion but as part of a broader existential threat to Russia's survival.

Secondly, Russia feared losing access to the resources located within autonomous regions, including the oil resources of Tatarstan and Dagestan and the gas fields of Siberia, as well as the infrastructure that had been developed in economically impoverished regions over the life of the Soviet Union, by pulling resources from the Moscow centre for economic development.

Thirdly, Russia sought to maintain its access to the oil and gas fields of the Caspian Sea as well as its access to a planned pipeline in the region. Losing control of the North Caucasus threatened to destroy these plans. Finally, Russia was also concerned about checking the rise of Turkish political power in the region, as Turkey had traditionally been a political rival with Russia for influence in the Caucasus (Ashour, 2004).

THE FAILURE OF RUSSIAN COUNTERTERRORISM

The Chechen example provides a case study of how a nation's adoption of a harsh counterterrorism strategy can backfire. Russia expected to easily take the territory back in 1994 as the result of a military blitzkrieg. In doing so, it hoped to make an example of Chechnya. Through wearing down the military and psychological support of the separatist movement, Russia hoped to crush this and other separatist movements within its territory. They sought not merely to end the conflict but to utilise disproportionate force to punish the Chechen people for their territorial aspirations. Thus, the two-year-long First Chechen War (1994–1996) saw aerial bombardment and the near-total destruction of the capital of Ingushetia, Grozny. During the 21-month conflict, 70% of Chechnya's housing stock was destroyed, and infrastructure was annihilated. Military conflicts caused upwards of 160,000 casualties, many of them civilians (Aliyev and Souleimanov). As Russian military actions against the region continued, most of Chechnya's roads, educational system, and healthcare system were destroyed. Unemployment approached 80%, and 15% of the territory was covered with landmines. Russia is estimated to have lost approximately 3600 soldiers between 1999 and 2007 as a result of its intervention in the area (Casula, 2015). As the region descended into anarchy, it came to resemble Afghanistan with its rule by regional leaders or warlords and its porous borders, which allowed conflicts to spill over from one region to another. In this way, Chechen nationalist claims became entangled with the conflict in Syria, since fighting in Syria against Assad meant fighting in a proxy war against Russia. (Russia's leader, Putin, had offered troops and military support to the Assad regime as they attempted to keep control of Syria against Islamist fighters.) At the same time, the porous borders allowed for the infiltration of Islamist extremists from Saudi Arabia and elsewhere into Central Asia and Russia proper.

(It should be noted here that the figures regarding the scope of the disaster as well as the responsibilities of both parties in creating casualties are still a matter of academic dispute. Both Russia and Chechnya have been accused of exaggerating the numbers of casualties for public relations purposes, and some Russian academics argue that Russia may even have gone so far as to create terrorist attacks like the Moscow apartment bombing itself to blame Chechnya and the rise in Islamic terrorism as a cover for implementing more draconian measures upon its own people, including the increased use of secret police and surveillance. (Russia may have also exaggerated the threat posed by Chechnya's terrorist movement, particularly during the 2000s, to describe Chechnya as a 'breeding ground for terrorists' to implement preemptive strikes against the region; Gessen, 2020.)

Due to the harshness of the Russian response, the US initially recognised the legitimate grievances of the Chechen people and advocated for a political solution to the conflict. Indeed, Russia's conflation of the Chechen strife with a global terrorist threat never fully resonated with a Western audience and was not accepted as a justification for the actions that Russia carried out. During both the First and Second Russo-Chechen wars, the Council of Europe and the US Holocaust Museum accused Russia of carrying out war crimes and crimes against humanity, including the disproportionate use of force, the conduct of genocide, and the infliction of policies of state terror (Gilligan, 2009) Allegations emerged that Russia was routinely executing civilians who were believed to be aiding Chechen forces, including the family members of those believed to be Chechen rebels. Some of these allegations were difficult to corroborate since Russia routinely restricted press access to the region during the conflicts. The Russian Human Rights Group Memorial alleges that between three thousand and five thousand people disappeared between 1995 and 2005, and mass graves have been identified that are believed to contain the remains of approximately three thousand civilians.

The first Chechen War ended in 1996 with a ceasefire and the signing of a peace treaty with Russia (the Khasar-Yurt Accord). At this time, Russia moved from taking military action against Chechnya to instead seeking to influence Chechnya by intervening in elections and recruiting insiders to serve Moscow's interests. Chechen President Aslan Maskhadov assumed control, with Russia's blessing, in 1997. Maskhadov, a moderate, sought to find a compromise with Islamist forces (led by rebel commander Shamil Basayev), which were becoming increasingly powerful. Thus, he allowed the introduction of Islamic sharia law and the establishment of sharia courts, seeking to tread a fine line between allowing the expression of Islamist sentiments without 'tipping over' into the establishment of an Islamic republic. Under Maskhadov's leadership, one can identify a split within the Chechen separatist movement into two wings: a secular nationalist wing that might have succeeded in creating a rapprochement and concessions from Russia, and a radical Islamic movement that sought to unify Chechnya as part of a broader Islamic movement. This group, led by rebel commander (warlord) Shamil Basayev, saw no path towards rapprochement with Russia as the conflict was viewed through the lens of Jihad.

Many see Russia's 1999 intervention in the region as a response to Maskhadov's inability to contain the Islamic currents circulating through Chechnya (Kramer). Had he been able to maintain control, the conflict and ensuing militancy might not have occurred. Instead, under Maskhadov's rule, the rebel forces of Basayev pursued increasingly militant and broad objectives, in essence seeking to redraw the map of the region by supporting the drive for independence in neighbouring Dagestan. As a result, Russia invaded again in 1999, setting off the Second Russo-Chechen War, which lasted until 2009. During the Second Chechen War (1999–2009), the European Court of Human Rights in Strasbourg identified over one hundred incidents of Russian human rights violations against civilians. It has also found Russia guilty of violating Article 6 of the Human Rights Convention (the right to a fair trial) and Article 10 (the right to freedom of expression) (Bindman, 2013). Maskhadov subsequently went on to serve under Basayev.

Historian Emma Gilligan suggests that Moscow again missed an opportunity for a peaceful solution in 2005 when Moscow's leadership chose to assassinate Maskhadov. She argues that he could have potentially served as a middleman, negotiating a settlement between the two parties, even at this late date. Instead, Maskhadov was replaced by Abdul-Khalim Sadulaev, an ideologue who had worked with Basayev to create the Caucasus Front. Sadulaev died in 2006, but his rise was a symbol of an end to any anticipated conciliatory politics (Gilligan, 2009).

In 2003, Akhmed Kadyrov was elected as Chechnya's president in a contested election that many felt was unconstitutional. After his assassination by rebel forces in 2004, his son, Ramzan Kadyrov, acted as his successor. Chechen rebel forces have targeted Ramzan Kadyrov and his government in multiple incidents, and he has also been accused of human rights abuses and autocratic rule. Kadyrov and his associates have been blacklisted by the United States due to alleged human rights abuses and have been subjected to sanctions through the Magnitsky Act. Religiously, Kadyrov has been supportive of Sunni Islam but in 2016 called upon Russia to outlaw the practise of Salafist Islam in Russia and Chechnya.

Although Kadyrov headed the official government in Chechnya, in the first of many rifts in 2007, Basayev's forces pledged their allegiance to a newly formed Caucasus Emirate, which supported Islamic fundamentalism and the institution of sharia law.

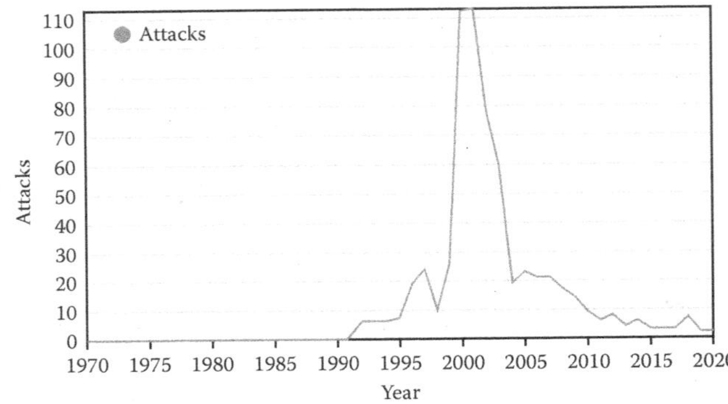

Figure 43.1 Timeline of Terrorist Incidents in Chechnya.

Source: Global Terrorism Database (GTD) (2024).

As Figure 43.1, Timeline of Terrorist Incidents in Chechnya, indicates, terrorist incidents within Chechnya peaked between 2001 and 2004 and declined sharply thereafter, with terrorist incidents in Chechnya itself being relatively minor and uncommon after 2016.

However, despite the sharp decline in terrorist activity within Chechnya after 2004, Russia cannot be said to have quelled the drive for Chechen independence or the activities of Chechen rebel forces. Instead, Chechen terrorism is best understood as a phenomenon that occurred in three waves. In the first wave, from 1991 until 1999, the vast majority of terrorist incidents carried out by Chechen fighters were internal events aimed at Russian forces deployed within the Chechen-Ingush Republic. After 2001, the focus of terrorist activity turned outward, with Chechen fighters taking the fight to Russia itself, carrying out incidents aimed at Russian civilians in Moscow, St. Petersburg, and elsewhere in Russia's own territory. The third and current phase sees Chechen fighters adopting a wider array of causes and deploying Chechen forces abroad in Syria, as well as mobilising members of the Chechen Diaspora to fight on behalf of Muslim causes in Western Europe and North America. Thus, the targets and strategies of the movement have changed, with Russia no longer the primary target of their activities. Analysts like Hughes thus argue that the term "Chechen terrorist" is too broad since it is really only an umbrella term for multiple related groups.

ORGANISATIONAL CHARACTERISTICS AND ACTIVITIES: STRUCTURE, CHANGE, AND OPERATIONS

In retrospect, Russia's harsh counterterrorism approach may be described as singularly ineffective for two reasons: First, from early on, Moscow actively moved to recruit 'insiders' from within the Chechen opposition into its ranks as counterterrorist informants. In some instances, nationalists defected voluntarily to support Russia and its aims, while in other instances, Russian forces kidnapped family members and held them hostage until Chechen fighters agreed to cooperate with Moscow. As the perceived risks of engaging in nationalist terrorism increased for its participants, moderates dropped out of the movement, leaving a membership that increasingly embraced brutal tactics. As a result, most of the moderates within the ranks of the Chechen nationalist opposition were culled, hollowing out the group and leaving only the ideological hardliners. Souleimanov and Aliyev suggest that after 2000, Chechnya's nationalist movement was dominated by Islamists. Thus, it is more correct to suggest that the personnel compromising the Chechen terrorist movement changed rather than that the 'organisation' reoriented its goals. (That is, a second generation came in that was more ideological and radical than its predecessors; Souleimanov & Aliyev, 2020)

Here, we can consider the case of Ahmed Kadyrov, a supporter of Chechnya's first president, Dzhokhar Dudayev. Kadyrov served as Chechnya's Chief Mufti (a position that involves the interpretation of Islamic law and dates back to the Ottoman Empire) throughout the 1990s and during the First Chechen War. Kadyrov is notable because, although he was a supporter of Islamic principles and Chechen nationalist territorial claims, he switched sides, supporting Russia's government and serving as President of the Chechen Republic from 2003 until 2004. Kadyrov abandoned his support for the anti-Russian guerilla movement due to his concern over their overwhelming support and adoption of Wahhabist/Salafist Islam and their movement into the greater Islamic terrorist orbit. That is, he was driven out of the insurgent camp and regarded as a traitor due to the fact that his ideology and goals were seen as too moderate by the movement, which was drifting further and further towards extremism. Kadyrov was assassinated in 2004 by Islamic fighters who viewed him as a traitor (Souleimanov & Aliyev, 2016).

Secondly, in carrying out harsh and punitive measures, Russia did not succeed in pacifying nationalists in the short term, nor did it solve the territorial standoff in the long term. Instead of destroying the opposition through military repression, it merely radicalised them and won them adherents outside their borders. In an analysis of the lifespan of terrorist groups, Phillips suggests that terrorist groups often fade away over the long term as they lose their adherents. However, he notes that terrorist groups that succeed in establishing a long-term profile and presence often find a patron who provides financial and other support, including training and foreign mercenaries who can fight in a conflict (Phillips, 2011).

CHECHNYA SEEKS OUTSIDE PATRONS

The search for outside patronage is particularly likely to occur in autocratic states where it is difficult to establish a strong terrorist infrastructure domestically without outside help (Hausken et al., 2016). Russia's anti-terrorist legislation has long been regarded as some of the most comprehensive and wide-ranging in the world, with an emphasis on the use of computerised surveillance. Under Russia's laws, many entities that possess some knowledge about a planned terrorist activity or about an individual possessing terrorist membership – from computer internet service providers to family members of terrorists – can be held criminally liable and imprisoned if they do not pass on this knowledge to the proper authorities. That is, in situations where there are frequent warrantless searches, extrajudicial executions, and disappearances rather than trials, it is more likely that a group will seek outside training grounds and assistance with activities like money laundering. Both Al Qaeda and later ISIS were thus able to establish a foothold in Chechnya's community by assisting fledgling Chechen separatists in carrying out their activities in a situation where activities were severely restricted and monitored. And in situations where governance is anarchic and infrastructure is lacking, it is not uncommon for civilians to seek the protection of both domestic and international rebel groups that appear able to provide safety and security in the absence of a functioning government (Lyall). Indeed, one can draw parallels between Russia's failed attempts to retain control of the Caucasus and other previous Russian military operations like the Russian invasion of Afghanistan (1979–1989).

Thus, one can see the emergence of structures of cooperation between Chechen rebels and other terrorist groups, like Al Qaeda. These groups have worked together to share resources like financial support and intelligence expertise. Chechen rebels often received training through camps organised by Al Qaeda. At the same time, Al Qaeda and its adherents profited from being able to operate within Chechnya itself, which was becoming increasingly ungoverned (Phillips, 2014). Chechen fighters were also viewed as a resource that could be mobilised by Al Qaeda, as needed, to participate in different conflicts where additional forces were necessary. (Chechens fighting in the Syrian conflict after 2007 were referred to as mujahideen, or foreign fighters, and sometimes as Russian-speaking mujahideen.)

The involvement of outside actors in the region began during the First Chechen War, in 1994–1996, when Chechen fighters were augmented by other Islamic forces. During this conflict, guerilla commander Shamil Basayev, a former Russian Army fighter, rose to prominence. (He would later serve as Chechnya's Prime Minister.) Like many Chechen fighters, he drew upon experience gained through serving in the armed forces of the former Soviet Union. Indeed, it may have been his initial experiences fighting on behalf of Russia in territories like Afghanistan that caused him to feel a kinship with other Muslim states that were fighting against Russian colonial influences in their homelands. In the chaos that accompanied the dissolution of the Soviet Union, Basayev went on to command forces in other regional conflicts, gaining experience and forging contacts with foreign fighters who would later come to the aid of Chechnya.

In 1992, Basayev fought in Azerbaijan in the conflict over the Armenian ethnic enclave of Nagorno-Karabakh, which was seeking independence from Azerbaijan. That same year, he assisted ethnic Abkhazians who were seeking independence from the former Soviet republic of Georgia. In Chechnya's own wars, he was commanding Chechen forces at the first Battle of Grozny (December 1994–February 1995) and is seen as the architect of the 1995 Budyonnovsk Hospital attack. In this attack, which occurred in the Russian border city of Budyonnovsk, a group of approximately 100 Chechen rebels took between 1500 and 1800 people hostage, threatening to kill them if their demands were not met. The standoff was ended when Russia signed a declaration of ceasefire. However, peace talks failed, and the conflict resumed (New York Times).

Basayev went on to fight in efforts to establish an independent republic in neighbouring Dagestan, an event that triggered the second Chechen War in 1999. Working together with Daghestani Salafists led by Bagautdin Magomedov, they hoped to 'liberate' Dagestan, create a rebellion, and topple the pro-Russian government. Dagestan would then be free to join Chechnya as an Islamic republic (Ashour, 2004: 132).

Basayev, who was described as Russia's Bin-Laden and Russia's most wanted terrorist, can thus be described as a foreign fighter or 'mujahideen', whose adherents saw their mission as regional or international in scope, fighting on behalf of an Islamic brotherhood or caliphate whose borders extended beyond Chechnya or even the North Caucasus. Although Chechnya's citizens had been Sunni Muslims prior to the outbreak of the first Chechen War, many citizens and leaders adopted a Wahhabist or Salafi brand of Islam after that date. Some analysts suggest that Salafism had been present in Chechnya prior to the break-up of the Soviet Union, as it was imported by students who had studied abroad in Arab universities. Nonetheless, it was the widespread adoption of Salafi Islam, which rejects a division between the state and religious authorities, that provided the impetus for efforts to establish sharia law and an Islamic Republic in Chechnya after 1999. This tendency was exacerbated after the events of September 11, 2001, when many Chechens began to see their history as inexplicably intertwined with the global struggle between Islam and Christianity and the lands of Islam and the West. After 911, Chechen fighters were enlisted to fight with the Afghan Mujahideen against the Northern Alliance, and as a result, Basayev was able to forge relationships with Pakistan as well. In 2003, Basayev formally adopted the title Emir Abdallah Shamil Abu-Idris.

Throughout the Second Chechen War, Basayev's forces were again supplemented by outside fighters who came to Chechnya to fight on behalf of their 'Muslim brothers.' Today, the relationship between Islamic extremist groups like ISIS and the Chechen terrorist movement can be described as symbiotic. Both groups have provided supplemental fighters to each other's conflicts, and Chechnya has hosted training sites for ISIS and other fighters while profiting from financial and organisational contributions in return.

At the same time that the Chechen insurgents sought patronage from Islamic groups, they also conducted outreach, often online, to the Chechens in diaspora in Europe and North America. These ties came to international attention as a result of the 2013 Boston Marathon bombing. The perpetrators of this event, which killed three spectators and wounded more than 360 others, were the brothers Tamerlan and Dzhokhar Tsarnaev. Both were naturalised Americans from the former Soviet republic of Kyrgyzstan but were ethnically Chechen. Although the event is viewed as an act of Lone Wolf terrorism, the elder brother had travelled to Chechnya in the past, and Russian intelligence had warned American intelligence that he may have received terrorist training in Chechnya (History.com).

The Jamestown Foundation, a think tank tracking terrorism worldwide, estimates that the number of ethnic Chechen refugees from the Chechen Wars residing in Western Europe is about two hundred thousand. In recent years, law enforcement has expressed concerns about the number of these refugees who have been mobilised to travel to Syria to fight against Russia. These refugees have been particularly drawn to the conflict due to the existence of jihadist factions like Jaysh al-Muhajirin wa al-Ansar. This group was originally headed by Abu Omar al-Shishani, an ethnic Chechen from Georgia who fought in the Russo-Georgian War in 2008. Al-Shishani later became a military commander for ISIS (VOA News).

Finally, Chechen insurgents have strengthened ties with other national insurgent groups in neighbouring republics, including the nationalist group Vilayat Dagestan, which came to international prominence as a result of the threats it made against participants in the 2014 Sochi Winter Olympics.

As Phillips notes, a terrorist group is less likely to end with the acquisition of each new ally, particularly when those allies have extensive webs of contacts with other groups. Furthermore,

Clauset and Gleditsch (2012) speak of a 'feedback' loop: as groups continue to survive and gain more expertise, they can grow in prestige and power. In turn, more attacks can lead to more growth, which leads to more attacks.

THE SECOND PHASE OF CHECHEN TERRORISM: BRINGING THE FIGHT TO RUSSIA

Chechen insurgents may be characterised as particularly active during the period from 2002 until 2016. During that time, the majority of their actions were carried out not in Chechnya itself but rather in neighbouring Russian cities as well as in major urban areas like Moscow and St. Petersburg.

That is, by 2002, Russia had succeeded in suppressing much of the domestic opposition in Chechnya. However, rather than concede defeat, Chechen fighters turned the fight outward, launching public terrorist attacks on civilians in Russia's urban areas in particular. They hoped to turn the tide against Russia's fight with Chechnya by creating large-scale public opposition to the deadly conflict from Russian civilians who, it was hoped, would draw parallels with the Afghan conflict and decide that the price of attempting to keep Chechnya within the Russian orbit was simply too high. An attack on Moscow's Dubrovka Theatre in 2002 led to the taking of 900 hostages, including 130 dead. And in 2004, an attack on an elementary school in Beslan, Russia, led to 1,000 adults and children being taken hostage. In a botched rescue attempt by Russia, approximately 300 schoolchildren were killed. Other notable attacks included the 2004 Russian aircraft bombings as well as the 2009 attacks on Russia's transit infrastructure, including the attack on the Nevsky Express train between Moscow and St. Petersburg. In 2010, Chechen insurgents carried out the Moscow metro bombing, and in 2011, an attack at Domodedovo Airport in Moscow led to 37 deaths and 180 injuries.

As noted earlier, the Chechen separatist movement has been characterised by fragmentation and splintering. The 2002 Dubrovka Theatre (Moscow) hostage-taking attack was carried out by two Chechen groups: the SPIR (Special Purpose Islamic Regiment), led by Movsar Barayev, and the RIyadus Salikhin Reconnaissance and Sabotage Battalion of Chechen Martyrs, founded by Shamil Basayev. A third group, the Islamic International Peacekeeping Brigade (IIPB), was commanded jointly by Shamil Basayev and Khattab and Arab Islamists sent by Osama bin Laden to assist in Jihad in Chechnya. Basayev died in 2006. While Russia claims to have killed him, Chechen spokesmen claim that he died in an accident. Upon the deaths of both of its leaders, Arab mujahidin leader Abu al-Walid took over leadership of the group, which consists of approximately four hundred Chechens, Arabs, and other foreign fighters. All three groups were added to the foreign terrorist organisation list compiled by the US State Department in 2003 (Hughes, 2007).

PHASE THREE: THE CAUCASUS EMIRATE AS PART OF THE LARGER ISLAMIC STRUGGLE

If the period of the 2000s was the second stage of the Chechen insurgency, the period since 2013 can be seen as the third. Although by 2003 in particular, Chechen fighters and groups were entangled with other Arab groups and causes, it was not until 2007 that Chechen rebels officially announced their support for the Caucasus Emirate (a coalition of Northern Caucasian movements that advocated for the implementation of sharia law and an Islamic republic in the region) and its leader, Dokka Umarov, President of Ichkeria. In the aftermath of the announcement of the Caucasus Emirate by Umarov, Ichkeria's foreign minister, Akhmed Zakayev, denounced the step out of concern that Chechen fighters would be seen as waging war without clear intentions and goals and could lose domestic and international support (BBC Monitoring Central Asia).

The 2007 announcement can be read as part of a larger Al Qaeda strategy of 'reorienting local groups' and absorbing them into a larger struggle, as well as sending 'foreign fighters' in to augment local troops in places like Chechnya. In allying with AQ, it was common for groups to change their names, as Chechen militants did when they became part of the Caucasus Emirate. Recognising his ties to Al Qaeda, the US offered a five-million-dollar reward for information leading to Umarov's arrest. By 2010, the CE was already seen as in decline, and with Umarov's death in 2014, he was succeeded by Ali Abu Mohammed. This new leader was widely regarded as less charismatic and less skilled at holding the somewhat fragile Caucasus Emirate together.

In this phase, many Chechen rebels have become engaged in the fight against Assad's military forces in Syria, since fighting against Assad is seen as a way of combating Russia, which has supported the Assad regime. While many terrorists may have initially gone to Syria merely in order to receive terrorist training with the hope that they would then return to Chechnya to fight against Russia there, in fact, many rebels found their names on lists of terrorists compiled by Russia and the international community, lessening their ability to travel freely or to return to Chechnya (Nicolson). Today, there are an estimated thirty thousand foreign fighters in Syria, with Chechen and Dagestani fighters numbering approximately eight thousand. Many were initially drawn to the writings and activities of Omar Shishani, an ethnically Chechen military commander who initially fought against Russia in the Russo-Georgian War (2008) (Paraszcuzk, August 17, 2020).

In Syria, these fighters were drawn into Russian-speaking brigades and units operating in Syria. One can identify numerous Russian-speaking emirs, including Muslim Shishani, Salkhuddin Shishani, and Abdul Malik Shishani (the leader of the faction, Ajnad al-Kavkaz). And two Russian-speaking jamaats or brigades – Malhama Tactical and Liwa Muhajireen wal Ansar – play leading roles in teaching military tactics and establishing training centres. In recent years, analysts credit these units with having played a decisive role in conflicts in Aleppo, Idlib, and Latakia.

However, interviews with participants in these conflicts reflect an understanding that Russian-speaking leaders are unlikely to take on central roles within ISIS as a whole. Rather, some ISIS leaders seem to resent the leadership that they have shown in the past and worry about a situation in which fighters who are themselves Russian-speaking or Caucasian may feel more loyal to these leaders than to the movement as a whole (Paraszczuk, n.d.). Here they point to the so-called "Umar Shishani Problem," which occurred when the group Jaysh al-Mujahedeen al-Ansar was split by a rift. Its leader, Umar Shishani, the ISIS military emir for North Syria, chose to support ISIS and its leader, Abu Al-Baghdadi, while some of his followers instead stayed with the Caucasus Emirate faction, choosing not to participate in ISIS infighting. As a result of the rift, Umar Shishani later declared a 'fitnah' against Jabhat al-Nusra. In 2020, another dispute occurred among the Russian-speaking brigades when a group calling itself the Khattab al-Shishani Brigade took credit for attacks in Idlib. Some observers suggested that there was no such brigade and that this was ISIS "public relations" to keep up the inflow of Chechen fighters.

By 2014, the Chechen fighters who were engaged in the conflict in Syria could not be distinguished as a particular group. Rather, their loyalties were divided among a number of competing Al Qaeda and ISIS factions within the region. Formally, CE transferred its support from AL Qaeda to ISIS, establishing an IS Caucasus province in the same year. At that time, many fighters and leaders also took an oath to Abu Bakar Al Baghdadi, IS' leader. However, others chose to leave the CE for other factions or groups operating within Syria. 2015 is thus often given as the official end of the Caucasus Emirate, since most of those remaining were absorbed into other regional movements, including Vilayat Dagestan.

CONCLUSION

In a seminal article written in 2006, analyst Audrey Kurth Cronin (2006) described the myriad ways in which terrorist groups can end. In the article, she lists a number of challenges that groups encounter and the ways in which they might fail to overcome them. What is curious about the lifespan of Chechen terrorism is how well the group has succeeded in overcoming some common challenges. First, we can consider Russia's embrace of the strategy of 'decapitation," or the capture and killing of a leader. Here, the logic suggests that if the main factor holding a group together is a charismatic leader, then in the absence of that leader, the group may fail to sustain itself. However, despite the deaths of numerous Chechen leaders, including Shamil Basayev and later Abu Omar Al-Shishani, the movement has prevailed, sustaining its membership and its goals.

Next, Cronin notes that many terrorist groups may fail to pass on enthusiasm for the cause to a succeeding generation. Thus, supporters can 'age out' of the group and not provide the next generation of fighters. However, one can identify a new generation of Chechen nationalist terrorist insurgents in figures like the Tsarnaev brothers, the architects of the Boston Marathon bombing.

Next, she notes that there may be a diminution of popular support for a group. Here, too, one can identify strong popular support for Chechen nationalist goals, even among those who were not born in 1991, when Chechnya first asserted its independence claims.

However, if Chechnya's terrorist movement appears to be on the decline, one can describe it using Cronin's notion of 'transition'. Gradually, the movement has moved from a domestic, homegrown terrorist group focused on nationalist groups to a small part of a broader coalition of Islamic terrorists. At this point, one can argue that the original group has been absorbed by a larger group, thus losing its distinctive identity. The group has survived, but in a different form.

References

Ashour, O. (2004). Security, Oil and Internal Politics: The causes of the Russo-Chechen conflicts. *Studies in Conflict and Terrorism*, *27*(2), 127–143.

BBC Monitoring Central Asia. Rebel Minister says Caucasus Emirate idea against Chechen statehood. November 2007.

Bindman, E. (2013). Russian, Chechnya and Strasbourg: Russian Official and Press Discourse on the 'Chechen Case' at the European Court of Human Rights. *Europe-Asia Studies*, *65*(10), 1954–1977.

Casula, P. (2015). Between 'Ethnocide' and 'Genocide': Violence and Otherness in the Coverage of the Afghanistan and Chechnya wars. *Nationalities Papers*, *43*(5), 700–718.

Clauset, A. and Gleditsch, Kr. (2012). The Development Dynamics of Terrorist Organizations. *PLOS One*, *7*(11), 1–8.

Cronin, A. (2006). How Al Qaeda Ends: The Decline and Demise of Terrorist Groups. *International Security*, *31*(1), 7–48.

Florae, A. (2014). De Facto States in International Politics (1945-2011): A New Data Set. *International Interactions*, *40*. eprints.gla.ac.uk/118409/7/118409.pdf.

Gessen, M. (2020). *Surviving Autocracy*. Penguin.

Gilligan, E. (2009). *Terror in Chechnya: Russia and the Tragedy of Civilians in War*. Oxford University Press.

Global Terrorism Database (GTD). (2024). Chechnya "Incidents". https://www.start.umd.edu/gtd/search/Results.aspx?search=Chechnya&sa.x=0&sa.y=0

Hausken, K., Banuri, S., Gupta, D. and Abbink, K. (2016). Al Qaeda at the Bar: Coordinating Ideologies and Mercenaries in Terrorist Organizations. *Public Choice, 164*(102), 57–73.

Hill, F. (2001, May 7). West Shouldn't Back Russia's Crackdown on Islamic Terror. Brookings Institution. https://www.brookings.edu/opinion/west-shouldnt-back-russias-crackdown-on-islamic-terror/

Hill, F. (2013, March 25). The Real Reason Putin Supports Assad. Brookings Institute. https://www.brookings.edu/opinions/the-real-reason-putin-supports-assad/

History.com. (No Date). Boston Marathon Bombing. https://www.history.com/topics/21st-century/boston-marathon-bombings

Hughes, J. (2007). The Chechnya Conflict: Freedom Fighters or Terrorists? *Demokratizatsiya, 15*(3), 293–311.

Kramer, J. (2004). The Perils of Counterinsurgency: Russia's War in Chechnya. *International Security, 29*(3), 5–63.

Kuchins, A., Malarkey, M. and Maredonov, S. (2011). *The North Caucasus: Russia's Volatile Frontier*. Center for Strategic and International Studies.

Lamb, Z. (2005). *Instability in Russia's North Caucasus Region.* Council on Foreign Relations.

Lyall, J. (2009). Does Indiscriminate Violence Incite Insurgent Attacks? Evidence from Chechnya. *Journal of Conflict Resolution, 53*(3), 331–362.

New York Times. (1995, June 16). Chechen Rebels Said to Kill Hostages at Russian Hospital. https://www.nytimes.com/1995/06/16/world/chechen-rebels-said-to-kill-hostages-at-russian-hospital.html

Nicolson, D. (2017). Foreign Terrorist Fights from the North Caucasus: Understanding Islamic State Influence in the Region. *Connections Quarterly Journal, 16*(4), 69–88.

Notte, H. (2016). Russia in Chechnya and Syria: Pursuit of Strategic Goals. *Middle East Policy, 23*(1), 59–71.

Paraszczuk, J. (No Date). Syria: Chechen Rift deepens as IS accuses Causes Caucasus Emirate outlet. Chechensinsyria.com/?p=21713

Paraszczuk, J. (2020, August 17). Syrian Amira don't want a repeat of the Umar Shishani Problem – interview with Syrian war veteran Abu Abdullah Al-Kavkazi. Chechensinsyria.com/?p=26404

Phillips, B. (2014). Terrorist Group Cooperation and Longevity. *International Studies Quarterly, 58*(2), 336–347.

Phillips, P. (2011). The life cycle of terrorist organizations. *International advances in Economic Research, 17*, 369–385.

Souleimanov and Aliyev. (2016). Evaluating the Efficacy of Indigenous Forces in Counterinsurgency: Lessons from Chechnya and Dagestan. *Small Wars and Insurgencies, 27*(3), 392–416.

Souleimanov, E. and Aliyev, H. (2020). Ideology and Disengagement: A case study of nationalists and Islamists in Chechnya. *Europe-Asia Studies, 72*(special section), 314–330.

Voice of America News. (No Date). Russia Grievances Push North Caucasus Exiles to Join. https://www.voanews.com/europe/russia-grievances-push-north-caucasus-exiles-join

44

EUSKADI TA ASKATASUNA (ETA)

Nell Bennett

INTRODUCTION

Euskadi Ta Askatasuna (ETA) was a separatist organisation that operated in the Basque region of northern Spain and southern France from the late 1950s until 2011. ETA was a nationalist group that employed terrorist tactics to achieve territorial and political autonomy for the Basque Country. Between 1968 and 2011, ETA was responsible for killing around 840 people and wounding approximately another 2,500 (Whitfield, 2015: 4). ETA emerged out of the Basque nationalist movement, which was based on the ethnic and cultural uniqueness of the Basque people and a rejection of the nation-building policies of the Spanish central government. The nationalist movement gained force after the Spanish Civil War, in particular in response to the repressive regime of General Francisco Franco.

This chapter will examine the rise and fall of ETA. It will discuss its origins in the Basque nationalist movement and the mythology that it used to justify armed struggle. ETA emerged in the late 1950s in response to what its members perceived to be the inability of the Basque Nationalist Party to advance the independence movement (Woodworth, 2001: 35–36). Originally a student movement, ETA soon captured the attention of the Basque people and benefited from widespread popular support. It established a political party in the late 1970s that gave the organisation a means of promoting Basque nationalism and raising funds to finance its operations (Jonsson and Cornell, 2007: 72). ETA also sponsored youth groups, which provided the organisation with potential recruits.

This chapter will also look at ETA's organisation and strategy. ETA used a loose hierarchical structure, which allowed its leaders to communicate the group's objectives to its cells and volunteers. ETA's principal strategy was to provoke the Spanish government into executing repressive countermeasures that enabled them to justify armed rebellion. The chapter will conclude with an analysis of how Spain's transition to democracy, combined with its concerted counterterrorism campaign in collaboration with France, eroded ETA's support base and operational capacities. These factors, in conjunction with a normative shift in public opinion regarding the use of terrorism, put pressure on ETA to enter into negotiations with the Spanish government. After many failed attempts at reaching a resolution to the conflict, ETA finally laid down its arms in 2011.

THE NATIONALIST MOVEMENT

The Basque Country was historically comprised of seven regions in the north of Spain and the south of France. These are Álava, Guipúzcoa and Vizcaya of the current Basque region; the Spanish autonomous community of Navarre; and three French provinces, Basse Navarre, Labourd, and Soule (Whitfield, 2015: 3). The Basque people are culturally and ethnically distinct from those of the surrounding area. While their exact origins are unknown, drawings discovered in the Santimamiñe caves in Guernika suggest that their civilisation may be more than 20,000 years old (Clark, 1979: 10). The unique culture of the Basques is thought to be largely the result of their ability to maintain territorial and political independence over the centuries. This was due to both the inhospitable mountainous terrain of the Basque region and the people's fierce resistance to foreign invasion (Clark, 1979: 11). Indeed, the Basques became known for their ability to ward off intruders, including the Romans, Franks, Visigoths, and Moors (Watson, 1996: 18).

The mythology of an ancient and independent race provided the basis for the modern nationalist movement (Muro, 2005: 576–577). Sabino de Arana y Goiri is considered to be the father of modern Basque separatism. Arana was the author of a volume entitled *Bizcaya por su Independancia*, which laid down the philosophical tenets of the nationalist movement. These included Basque unity under Catholicism, the uniqueness of the Basque race, and the acquisition of autonomy through non-violent political

DOI: 10.4324/9780429426063-50

struggle (Clark, 1979: 44–47). Inspired by the Catalan nationalist movement, Arana founded a political organisation that laid the foundations for the Basque Nationalist Party, the *Partido Nacionalista Vasco* (PNV) (Spencer and Croucher, 2008: 138).

The Basque separatist movement grew in the early twentieth century. Political protests and workers' strikes took place periodically during the early part of the century. By 1918, the nationalist party had achieved such a level of electoral success that it presented the central government with petitions for regional autonomy. These, however, were summarily rejected. The movement suffered a significant setback in 1923 when the government of General Miguel Primo de Rivera issued a decree that illegalised all acts that could be perceived as undermining national unity (Clark, 1979: 49). Regionalism was further suppressed under the dictatorship of General Francisco Franco, and the PNV was forced to become a clandestine organisation.

There are several competing explanations for the rise of the nationalist movement. One prominent theory is that Basque separatism was a response to the rapid industrialisation of the region in the nineteenth century (Watson, 1996: 17–18). The movement originated in the province of Vizcaya, which underwent a rapid transformation from a predominantly rural area to one of the world's top industrial centres (Watson, 1996: 19). It has been argued by scholars, including Juan Dez Medrano (1995), that this change resulted in the disenfranchisement of the pre-industrial Basque elites, who formed the support base for the independence movement.

Another popular explanation is that the movement was a reaction to the heavy-handed nation-building policies of the Spanish government. The expression of Basque identity was prohibited as early as the 1920s (Clark, 1979: 49). This intensified under General Franco, who illegalised a wide variety of typical Basque activities, including hiking, traditional dance and music, and the use of the Basque language, euskera (Hamilton, 2007: 134). Even the most casual use of euskera was punishable by imprisonment (Woodworth, 2001: 34). This gave the Basque people a legitimate sense of grievance and justified the nationalist struggle.

THE RISE OF ETA

The modern Basque terrorist organisation ETA traces its origins to a series of secret study sessions organised by a group of university students in Bilbao in 1952. Its founding members included José Luis Álvarez Emparanza (also known as Txillardegi), Benito del Valle, Julen Madariaga, and José Manuel Aguirre. These students started meeting to discuss the Basque language, but their focus soon shifted to nationalist themes (Woodworth, 2001: 35). This early organisation was known as *Ekin*, which in Basque means 'to do' or 'to make' (Barros, 2003: 402).

Ekin fused with the youth branch of the PNV, forming an alliance that lasted several years. When Ekin split from the PNV in 1958, it took many of the more militant PNV youth with it. A year later, on 31 July, the anniversary of Arana's founding of the PNV, the new group took the name *Euskadi Ta Askatasuna* (Woodworth, 2001: 35). ETA was not created with the intention of becoming a terrorist organisation. Its early activism amounted to little more than petty street vandalism. The group graffitied Basque nationalist slogans on public buildings and staged political and cultural gatherings to advance the nationalist ideology (Hamilton, 2007: 134).

The anti-imperial successes of European colonies in the post-war era had a significant impact on ETA's early members. In particular, they drew inspiration from the anti-colonial movements in Algeria and later in Vietnam (Woodworth, 2001: 36; Zabalo and Saratxo, 2015: 367). The organisation adopted a socialist ideology, in part inspired by Castro's victory in Cuba. Castro's guerrillas demonstrated to the group how violence could be legitimised as a necessary tactic in national liberation movements (Woodworth, 2001: 36; Zabalo and Saratxo, 2015: 367).

ETA also made an important decision to adopt a broad understanding of Basque ethnicity Arana had argued that only ethnic Basques had a legitimate right to populate the Basque homeland. This conception of ethnicity was problematic for ETA principally because they were seeking recruits from the more militant sections of the Basque working class, a substantial proportion of whom were of migrant origin. ETA eschewed the bloodline conception of ethnicity and instead took the view that it was the use of the Basque language and a sense of solidarity with the separatist community that were the chief determinants of Basque identity (Tejerina, 2001: 42). The use of euskera in the 1970s was a costly sign of affiliation with the movement. This was an era in which people were still arrested for speaking Basque (Woodworth, 2001: 34). Also, many Basques, immigrants, second-generation Basques and even Basques who had been raised under Francoist repression, had never learnt this unique and complex language. Accordingly, an individual's ability to identify as Basque was directly related to their willingness to learn euskera and their degree of involvement with the independence movement (Zabalo and Saratxo, 2015: 376).

ORGANISATION AND STRUCTURE

During the 1960s and 1970s, ETA consisted of several hundred activists, many of whom lived in rural and coastal villages in the south of France, near the Spanish border. This position enabled them to engage in operations in Spain and then return to seek refuge in their sanctuary. ETA had no clear organisational structure until it decided to create an Executive Committee in 1962 to facilitate the recruitment of new members (Llera, Mata, and Irvin, 1993: 114). The Executive Committee remained in France, but by 1963 it recognised the need for a formal organisational structure within Spain. ETA then created a sub-structure that encompassed six geographic zones (*herrialdeaks*), each overseen by a leader. The leaders took part in attacks and were also responsible for building the necessary infrastructure for armed resistance (Llera et al., 1993: 114).

By 1967, ETA realised that it required a more complex leadership structure to deal with increased factionalism within the organisation. There were ideological disputes among members and disagreements regarding the legitimacy of armed struggle. To combat these issues ETA established an overarching policy-making committee, *Biltzar Nagusia*, or National Assembly. This was comprised of the Executive Committee and the leaders of the various zones or *herrialdeak*. Below the National Assembly were two subordinate committees, the Small Assembly which was located in France (*Biltzar Txikia*) and the Tactical Executive Committee in Spain, (Llera et al., 1993: 115–116). This provided ETA with a loose hierarchical structure. Volunteers and autonomous cells would operate independently but in accordance with directives of the organisation's leadership.

ETA operatives could be divided into *legales* and *liberados*. *Legales* were ETA operatives who had not yet been identified by police and were therefore able to go about their normal lives while assisting the organisation. Their functions would vary from active participation in terrorist violence to support roles. *Legales* could be *enlaces* who would organise communications, *buzones* or persons who acted as couriers, or intelligence gatherers known as *informativos* (Llera et al., 1993: 124). *Legales*, in many cases, were only loosely affiliated with the ETA. In some instances, they were self-directed volunteers, or what would be labelled today as 'lone wolf terrorists'. *Legales* also included *mugalaris*, whose job it was to assist members in crossing the border between Spain and France without being detected by security personnel. This was a vital function as much of the top leadership lived in France, yet operations were chiefly conducted in Spain. *Mugalaris* were usually smugglers who were very familiar with the terrain and the positions of police along the border area (Rekarte, 2015: 142).

Legales can be contrasted with *liberados*. *Liberados* were operatives who were known to law enforcement and were therefore required to go underground. The *Liberados* typically operated in autonomous commando units. They would select targets in accordance with the leaders' directives and execute operations. They would be paid a stipend to cover living expenses and provided with weapons and explosives (Rekarte, 2015).

The majority of recruits joined in their early twenties and came from rural areas where a high proportion of inhabitants spoke Euskera (Reinares, 2004: 482). The strongest recruitment base for ETA was the province of Guipúzcoa, which supplied nearly half the group's members, despite the fact that it only contributed less than a quarter of the population of the Basque Country. This may be because Guipúzcoa is considered quintessentially Basque. Its lush mountainous geography is readily associated with the historic nation, and it has the highest proportion of native Basque speakers in the region (Reinares, 2004: 479). Around 80% of ETA members were native Basques; however, over time, an increasing number of recruits came from immigrant families (Llera et al., 1993: 125–126).

Herri Batasuna, ETA's political wing, was also helpful. Herri Batasuna was a nationalist political party that was formed in 1978 (Atkins, 2004: 129). It was created in response to what its members considered to be the PNV's weak stance on the nationalist issue, its inability to attract the younger generation of Basque voters, and the PNV's refusal to work with ETA in the pursuit of autonomy (Rueda, 2016: 288). The PNV viewed ETA as a totalitarian Marxist organisation and, from 1964 on, refused to engage in any dialogue with the group (Rueda, 2016: 288).

Another important facet of ETA's organisational structure was its youth movement. In the late 1970s, Herri Batasuna established a youth organisation called Jarrai (Sarabia, 1998: 2). Young people were often recruited by members of ETA, some of whom played active roles in Jarrai. This connection between the youth wing organisation and the terrorist group led Jan Mansvelt Beck to argue that Jarrai constituted a 'transition zone' between casual youth involvement in the nationalist movement and dedication to the separatist cause (Beck, 1999: 110). The connection between ETA and this nationalist youth movement did not go unnoticed by the Spanish government. Jarrai was illegalised in 2005 on the grounds that it was a satellite organisation of ETA and that it provided support for the terrorists' objectives. The Audiencia Nacional held that Jarrai, or as it was later called, Haika or Segi, had used street violence to assist ETA in the execution of its strategy (Hernández, 2006: 96).

ETA'S STRATEGY

ETA's primary strategy was to gain popular support for armed resistance by using violence to provoke the Spanish government into disproportionately punitive responses. The theory behind was first articulated by Federico Sarrailh de Ihartz, writing under the name of Federico Krutwig in the book *Vasconia*. It was later discussed by ETA leader José Luis Zalbide in his 1965 pamphlet entitled *Bases Teòricas de la Guerra Revòluciònaria* and adopted as an official ETA strategy.

ETA's first serious terrorist operation occurred in 1961. It was the attempted derailment of a number of trains carrying Franco supporters to San Sebastian to celebrate the 25th anniversary of Franco's military coup (Barros, 2003: 402). They went to great lengths to ensure that no one would be injured in the incident, and indeed, no one was hurt as the operation was unsuccessful (Murua, 2014: 72). Retaliation from the Spanish government was swift and brutal. More than one hundred Basque citizens were arrested, and many reported being tortured (Woodworth, 2001: 36).

This event set in motion an action-repression-action sequence between ETA and the Spanish government. In 1968, an ETA activist was killed, creating the group's first martyr. ETA responded by killing an officer of the National Police and a member of the Guardia Civil. These acts caused the cycle of violence to escalate (Laitin, 1995: 24). The Franco government laid siege to the Basque region, and a 'state of exception' was instituted, which was akin to martial law (Clark, 1979: 182–183; Laitin, 1995: 24). Habeas corpus was suspended, and people were detained without charge or access to legal representation (Clark, 1979: 170).

In 1969, most of ETA's leadership, who were living in the Spanish Basque Country, were arrested. The Franco regime tried sixteen of them in December 1970 in military tribunal proceedings that became known as the Burgos trial. The trial gave rise to widespread demonstrations and strikes against the government's use of summary military justice. The accused used the trial as a platform to espouse their nationalist ideology. Rather than giving evidence, they made political speeches and sang revolutionary songs. The prosecution had asked for six death sentences, but the tribunal handed down nine. As the defendants included two priests, the Basque clergy protested the trial and gave militant sermons in support of the sixteen accused (Woodworth, 2001: 39). This was highly influential among the predominantly Catholic Basque population and further galvanised the people against the Spanish government.

INTERNAL DIVISIONS

The use of violence to achieve political goals was the subject of recurring controversy among ETA's different factions (Llera et al., 1993: 115). In 1973, ETA planned to kidnap the Navel Minister, Admiral Luis Carrero Blanco (Barros, 2003: 402). However, when Franco made Carrero Blanco Prime Minister in June 1973, the plan changed from kidnapping to assassination. This event was followed by another violent attack in which the militant faction of ETA placed a bomb at a busy Madrid café, killing thirteen people. These two attacks made it clear that ETA had become a terrorist organisation. The result was an internal crisis within the organisation (Soldevilla, 2010: 74).

In 1974, ETA split into two factions: ETA militar (ETA-M), led by José Miguel Beñarán Ordeñana also known as Argala, and ETA politico-militar (ETA-PM) (Woodworth, 2001: 40). ETA-M was a nationalist group that believed in the strict separation of military and political activism. ETA-PM, on the other hand, argued that political and military actions were compatible (Preston, 2005). However, division existed within ETA-PM as well. ETA-PM was comprised of two sections. These were the *Comandos Bereziak* (Special Commandos), who were led by Miguel Angel Apalategui ('Apala'), and the political wing led by Eduardo Moreno Bergareche ('Pertur') (Clark, 1990: 75).

The death of General Franco in 1975 exacerbated these divisions within ETA. In the early part of 1976, the internal factions began to argue over whether ETA should continue with its armed struggle or turn to electoral politics and union organisation. While Pertur saw that a militant strategy within a democratic regime would doom the organisation to failure, Apala continued to plan and execute high-risk terrorist operations. As the disagreement between the two leaders became more intractable, Apala transferred his allegiance to ETA-M (Clark, 1990: 79).

TARGET SELECTION

ETA operations focused mostly on targets that had political symbolic value, such as government agencies, police stations, Guardia Civil outposts, government schools, and the private residences of government officials. They also selected targets they considered to be symbols of oppression and capitalism, including Spanish flags, financial institutions, media stations, and communications installations (Clark, 1979: 166). The bombing of bank branches was particularly popular throughout the 1970s and 1980s.

ETA also used violence to create social change, in particular with regard to workers' rights. The 1972 kidnapping of Lorenzo Zabala Suinaga was an example of this. Zabala was an important shareholder in the company Motorbic and secretary of the board of directors of Precicontrol, two companies that had refused to grant salary increases and the right to collective bargaining to their employees. The conditions for Zabala's release included that the workers fired for striking be reinstated in their former positions and that all employees be given the pay rise they had requested. Once the companies agreed to the conditions Zabala was released (Bruni, 2006: 137–140).

Another target for ETA operatives was persons involved in the drug trade in the Basque Country. ETA encourages its members to kill any known drug dealers operating in the region. In his memoir, former ETA member Iñaki Rekarte wrote about ETA's stance on drugs, saying, 'They were the guardians of purity, those in charge of preventing the Basque youth from being intoxicated by the drugs that abounded in our land. If it were necessary, they were willing to take up arms to finish with that plague.' Indeed, according to Rekarte, within ETA, it was widely believed that the police were involved in spreading drugs among the Basque youth to prevent them from rebelling against the central government (Rekarte, 2015: 32).

THE EFFECTS OF DEMOCRACY

The death of General Franco in 1975 led to a period of political uncertainty within Spain as multiple parties competed for power and influence. In 1978, Spain transitioned from dictatorship to democracy. A new constitution was written that established several autonomous communities, including the Basque Country and Catalonia. This was a substantial reform that provided the Basque Country with increased political, economic, and cultural autonomy (Barros, 2003: 403).

The transition to democracy provided nationalists with the opportunity to consolidate many of the rights that they had been advocating for, such as the right to cultural expression, and to allow their children to be educated in *ikastolas*, which are schools that teach Basque language and history. In spite of this, the highest numbers of ETA casualties were recorded in 1978, which was the year of the referendum to approve the Spanish Constitution; in 1979, the year of the Basque Autonomy Statute; and in 1980, which was the year in which the first regional elections took place in the Basque Country (Llera et al., 1993: 109). It has been reported that between 1978 and 1980, ETA was responsible for around 235 deaths, consisting of approximately 20–25% civilians and 75–80% state officials, including police (De la Calle and Sanchez Cuenca, 2006: 19).

One explanation for this apparent paradox is that the years from 1978 to 1980 were a crucial time in which important power-sharing deals were consolidated. Multiple groups were vying for electoral support and control over the Basque political process. In this new democratic regime, ETA found itself to be but one of a number of interest groups competing for space on the public agenda. Violence provided ETA with a low-cost means of bringing their cause to prominence and monopolising the political debate.

THE DECLINE OF ETA

Many factors contributed to the decline of ETA; however, one of the most salient was the organisation's loss of its sanctuary in France. One of the main reasons that ETA was able to maintain its operations for so many years in spite of brutal state repression was that it was able to keep its organisational headquarters in the French Basque Country. However, this came under attack in the mid-1980s, when France changed its position towards ETA and ceased to tolerate its activities. The French began to collaborate with the Spanish government in joint counterterrorism operations, and by 1992, the two states had managed to arrest the majority of ETA's leadership. While not a fatal blow, this substantially weakened ETA's ability to maintain its armed resistance (Murua, 2017: 95).

It was partly in response to this joint Franco-Spanish operation that ETA began to entertain the idea of seeking a negotiated resolution to its conflict with the Spanish government. ETA's first official negotiation with the Spanish state, known as the *Algiers* process, was short-lived and broke down after only three months. In 1998, the *Lizarra-Garazi* process followed the *Algiers* process. This involved a secret pact between ETA and the moderate Basque nationalist parties. ETA agreed to lay down its arms on the condition that the moderates would take a stronger approach to national building. The ceasefire lasted 15 months. ETA ultimately decided to rearm due to their belief that the moderate nationalists were not doing enough to advance the nationalist cause (Murua, 2017: 95).

Spain's attack on ETA's political wing further weakened the organisation. ETA's political party, Batasuna, was illegalised in 2002. This severely affected ETA's ability to raise money to finance its operations (Jonsson and Cornell, 2007: 72). Perhaps more importantly, it deprived the organisation of political legitimacy. The loss of its political arm placed increased pressure on ETA to reach a negotiated resolution to the conflict. The organisation agreed to another ceasefire in March 2006 during formal negotiations with the Spanish government. However, the truce was terminated by the bombing of the Madrid airport, in which two people were killed. Negotiations were resumed in 2007, but the ceasefire lasted no more than two months.

In October 2011, ETA announced that it was ceasing its terrorist activities. Some scholars have argued that their ultimate decision to abandon this strategy in 2011 was due to a normative shift against terrorist violence. This change in public attitudes is thought to be the result of a number of factors. These include the failed attempts on the lives of Prime Ministerial Candidate Jose Aznar and the popular King Juan Carlos in 1995 and the success of pacifist movements (Barros, 2003: 403).

The attack on the World Trade Center in New York also shifted public perceptions of terrorism. After the events of September 11, 2001, European governments took a tougher stance on terrorism, and Batasuna was included in a list of known terrorist organisations that was approved by the European Union (Murua, 2017: 99). Al Qaeda presented a new kind of terrorism that was radically different from the post-colonial revolutionary movements of the 1960s and 1970s. This further diminished the public's tolerance for political movements that used terrorist tactics (Zabalo and Saratxo, 2015: 371). ETA did not formally disband until early 2018.

COUNTERTERRORISM RESPONSES

The case of ETA is instructive for analysts and policymakers because it shows the results of effective and ineffective counterterrorism strategies. The repressive policies of the Franco regime, which included mass arrests, detentions without charge, states of emergency, and the use of torture, led a substantial proportion of Basques to support the separatist movement and caused many young people to join ETA (Ferret, 2014: 1029). The Spanish government continued to use illegal and even inhumane counter-terrorism tactics after the transition to democracy and thereby weakened and delegitimized the new democratic institutions (Murua, 2014: 96–97). A stark illustration of this was the creation of the Anti-Terrorist Liberation Groups (GAL). The Ministry of the Interior provided funding for GAL, which was in charge of killing and kidnapping ETA members (Tejerina, 2001: 45–46).

The Spanish government gradually shifted its approach from one of indiscriminate repression to targeted assaults on ETA and its affiliates. In the early 1980s, Spain reorganised its security forces to facilitate a more effective counter-terrorism response. In 1981, Spain inaugurated a coordinated counter-terrorism centre called the *Mando Unico de la Lucha Contraterrorista* (MULC). This central command group included representatives from the Interior Ministry, the Guardia Civil, the CSP, and the *Centro Superior de Informacion de la Defensa* (CESID). MULC analysed police intelligence and planned and executed counter-terrorist operations (De Jong, 2016: 336). The creation of dedicated counter-terrorism forces enabled law enforcement to develop targeted strategies to undermine ETA's logistics, propaganda, and recruitment.

An example of Spain's targeted counter-terrorism tactics was the assault on ETA's political party, Batasuna. The government accused the party of collaborating with ETA, and in 1997, the authorities arrested all 23 of its leaders. The detainees were each sentenced to seven years imprisonment. In 2002, the Spanish government sought to pass a law to prohibit political parties that supported terrorism (Atkins, 2004: 129). In 2003, Spain finally succeeded in its efforts to have Batasuna banned. As part of its investigation, the government found that ETA had created a web of businesses and cultural associations that were associated with Batasuna and had the stated objective of furthering Basque culture and language. Many of these organisations received a substantial proportion of their funding from grants from the Spanish state and the EU. The result of this was that for years, Spain and the EU had been unwittingly financing ETA's activities (Jonsson and Cornell, 2007: 72).

Even after it was illegalised, Batasuna still managed to keep its network and political activity intact. In 2007, the Spanish authorities arrested the majority of its leadership, including former Batasuna spokesperson Arnaldo Otegi. This was a serious blow to the organisation, as young, inexperienced members were forced to take over (Murua, 2014: 153). In 2009, after serving his sentence, Otegi, along with another nine members of the radical left, was arrested on the charge of attempting to reconstruct Batasuna under orders from ETA. Otegi and four of the other arrestees ultimately spent more than six years in prison before the European Court of Human Rights ruled that they did not have a fair trial (Naiz, 2018).

Another example of targeted counterterrorism policy was the Spanish and French governments' crackdown on the Basque youth organisation Haika. Haika was born of the union of Jarrai, the youth wing of Herri Batasuna, and its French equivalent, Gazteriak. French and Spanish authorities soon became worried about this new hybrid group, which they believed to be behind the surge in street violence and sabotage, known in Basque as *kale borroka*, which took place in the late 1990s (El Pais, 2001).

On March 6th, 2001, police raided Haika's offices across the region and arrested sixteen of its leaders on the charge of directing its members to commit acts of street violence and sabotage. Judge Baltasar Garzón, who ordered the raids and arrests, claimed that *Kale Borroka* was a part of ETA's grand strategy and that Haika was a subordinate organisation to ETA (El Pais, 2001). In this, they were supported by a document found in a police raid in Bidart, in the French Basque Country, in 1992 that referred to a strategy called XYZ, which consisted of three levels of resistance: political mobilisation, terrorist violence, and *kale borroka* (Ferret, 2014, 1018). The arrests were also significant because weakening ETA's youth movement significantly damaged its recruitment base.

CIVIL SOCIAL MOBILISATION

Another key factor in the decline of ETA was the mobilisation of civil society against political violence. ETA's attacks on prominent Basques led to popular uprisings against the organisation. Peace and victims' rights groups emerged in the 1980s and 1990s to protest terrorist violence and advocate a peaceful solution to the Basque conflict (Whitfield, 2015: 4). Notable among these groups were Gesto por la Paz (Gesture for Peace), Denon Artean (Peace and Reconciliation), Bakea Orain (Peace Now), and Elkarri (Tejerina, 2001: 52–53).

Gesto por la Paz started holding nonviolent demonstrations against terrorist violence in towns and cities all over the Basque Country in 1986, and many of them had local politicians in attendance who were in favour of a compromise. By the mid-1990s, Gesto por la Paz was holding weekly gatherings to protest ETA kidnappings (Murua, 2014: 379). In the 1990s, ETA kidnapped three Basque businessmen and held them for long periods of time until ransom was paid. Gesto por la Paz used the public outrage that these kidnappings generated to create an anti-violence movement that allowed Basques to express their desires for an end to the conflict (Murua, 2014: 51). These protests were often met by crowds of radical Batasuna supporters who had to be held back by police. Clashes between pacifists, radicals, and the police were not uncommon, and in many cases, protestors were hospitalised with severe injuries (El Pais, 1997).

The public activities of such pro-peace advocacy groups stood in sharp contrast to the reluctance of many Basques to speak out against ETA violence. Many Basques have spoken of the culture of silence that existed in the Basque Country while ETA operated. In certain parts of the Basque Country, in particular in smaller towns and villages, residents have reported that they felt unable to freely discuss politics during the conflict (Rodríguez, 2007).

THE IMPACTS OF ARMED RESISTANCE

ETA's operations cast a shadow over the lives of the Basque people for decades. It is estimated that between 1968 and 2011, the group was responsible for killing 840 people, kidnapping 80, and wounding 2,500 (Whitfield, 2015: 4). The conflict touched households across the region, with many families losing members to the movement, either as recruits or victims. The resistance also took a substantial toll on the social fabric of the Basque Country. In certain communities, speaking out against ETA's actions could result in retaliation and social exclusion (Spencer and Croucher, 2008: 148–149). Threats from the ETA forced many outspoken Basques, including writers, journalists, and politicians, into exile (Whitfield, 2015: 4).

A study conducted in 2008 by Anthony T. Spencer and Stephen M. Croucher found that Basques who held unfavourable views of ETA were less likely to express those views to fellow Basques for fear of reprisal or social ostracism. This led to a "spiral of silence" phenomenon in which people felt afraid to express their political preferences (Spencer and Croucher, 2008: 140–141). This would presumably have been most pronounced in areas where support for ETA was strongest, typically small rural communities (Beck, 1999: 119).

The costs of ETA's activities were not only social. They also took a substantial toll on the Basque economy. To finance their activities, ETA engaged in bank robberies and kidnappings and extracted what they referred to as a 'revolutionary tax' on wealthy residents (Murua, 2014: 51). This was part of a much larger campaign. Between 1970 and 1996, ETA is said to have kidnapped 76 people. The targets ranged from successful business people to modest small business owners.

It has been argued that ETA's extortion through the "revolutionary tax" was one of the principal factors responsible for the relative decline of the Basque economy since the transition to democracy. In the 1970s, the Basque Country had the third-highest GDP per capita in Spain. By the 1990s, its position had dropped to that of sixth in the country (Abadie and Gardeazabal, 2003: 113).

CONCLUSION

ETA was a terrorist organisation that used violence to advance the Basque nationalist agenda. ETA was formed in the late 1950s out of its members' frustration with the Basque Nationalist Party's soft stance on Basque nationhood. The group began by rebelling against the Franco regime's prohibitions on Basque cultural expression, and by the late 1960s, it was using violence in the pursuit of its objectives. ETA adopted a deliberate strategy of provoking the Spanish government into disproportionate retaliation in order to set in motion a cycle of action-repression-action. The Spanish state's punitive responses provided ETA with the justification it needed to maintain a campaign of armed resistance.

This chapter has examined the emergence, development, and decline of the ETA. Originally a student movement, ETA grew through the 1960s and 1970s into a sophisticated terrorist organisation. Its operatives were both loose collections of volunteers and organised cells of activists. They were supported by hundreds of ordinary Basque people who sympathised with ETA's objectives. ETA's resistance to Spanish counter-terrorism efforts was facilitated by the unique geography of the Basque Country. Its position between Spain and France allowed the leadership to operate out of the French Basque provinces. There they were able to plan attacks, train new recruits, and provide sanctuary to members who were being pursued by the Spanish police.

The rise and fall of ETA provides a valuable case study for counterterrorism analysts and policymakers. The repressive counterterrorism policies of the Franco regime provided ETA with moral justification for armed resistance. Indiscriminate violence and the use of illegal and illegitimate tactics radicalised many young Basques, who went on to play important roles within the organisation. Spain's shift to targeted, intelligence-based counterterrorism effectively dismantled ETA's operational structure. France's decision to cooperate with the Spanish government in counterterrorism operations severely weakened the organisation and contributed to ETA's willingness to seek a negotiated resolution with the Spanish government. In addition to this, legislative changes under the democratic regime granted a large measure of political autonomy to the Basque region, which eroded ETA's support base. After various failed attempts at reaching an agreement, the group decided to lay down their arms in 2011. ETA formally disbanded in 2018.

References

Abadie, A. and Gardeazabal, J. (2003). The Economic costs of conflict: A case study of the Basque country. *The American Economic Review, 93*(1), 113–132.

Atkins, S. E. (2004). *Encyclopedia of Modern Worldwide Extremists and Extremist Groups*. Westport: Greenwood Press.

Barros, C. P. (2003). An intervention analysis of terrorism: The Spanish ETA case. *Defence and Peace Economics, 14*(6), 401–412.

Beck, J. M. (1999). The continuity of Basque political violence: A geographical perspective on the legitimisation of violence. *GeoJournal, 48*(2), 109–121.

Bruni, L. (2006). *ETA: Historia Política de una Lucha Armada, Part 1*. Tafalla: Txalaparta.

De la Calle, L. and Sánchez-Cuenca, I. (2006). The production of terrorist violence: Analyzing target selection within the IRA and ETA. Estudio Working Paper 2006/230. http://epub.sub.uni-hamburg.de/epub/volltexte/2008/1870/pdf/2006_230.pdf.

Clark, R. P. (1979). *The Basques: The Franco Years and Beyond*. Reno, Nevada: University of Nevada Press.

Clark, R. P. (1990). *Negotiating with ETA: Obstacles to Peace in the Basque Country, 1975-1988*. Reno, Nevada: University of Nevada Press.

El Pais. (2018). ETA releases statement announcing its complete dissolution. *El Pais*. https://elpais.com/elpais/2018/05/03/inenglish/1525349131_830131.html.

El Pais. (2001). Detenida la cúpula de la organización juvenil Haika por su presunta pertenencia a ETA. *El Pais*. https://elpais.com/elpais/2001/03/06/actualidad/983870217_850215.html.

El Pais. (1997). Dos detenidos en un acto pacifista por un intento de agresión. *El Pais*. https://elpais.com/diario/1997/02/24/espana/856738818_850215.html.

Ferret, J. (2014). Young radical nationalists: Prisoners of their own myth? The case of the Kale Borroka in the Spanish Basque country. *Current Sociology, 62*, 1017–1035.

Hamilton, C. (2006). The gender politics of political violence: Women armed activists in ETA. *Feminist Review, 86*, 132–148.

Hernández, A. F. (2006). Jarrai-Haika-Segi: de asociación ilícita a organización terrorist. *Revista Penal, 17*, 95–109.

De Jong, M. (2016). "Spanish Security Forces, Anti-terrorism and the Internal and External Security of Spain, 1959-1992." In R. Beeres, G. Bakx, E. de Waard & S. Rietjens (Eds.). *NL ARMS Netherlands Annual Review of Military Studies 2016*. (pp. 325–350). The Hague: Asser Press.

Jonsson, M. and Cornell, S (2007). Countering terrorist financing: Lessons From Europe. *Georgetown Journal of International Affairs, 8*(1), 69–78.

Laitin, D. D. (1995). National revivals and violence. *European Journal of Sociology, 36*, 3–43.

Llera, F. J., Mata, J. M. and Irvin, C. L. (1993). ETA: From secret army to social movement: The post-Franco schism of the Basque nationalist movement. *Terrorism and Political Violence, 5*(3), 106–134.

Medrano, J. D. (1995). *Divided Nations: Class, Politics, and Nationalism in the Basque Country and Catalonia*. Ithaca and London: Cornell University Press.

Muro, D. (2005). Nationalism and nostalgia: The case of radical Basque nationalism. *Nations and Nationalism, 11*(4), 571–589.

Murua, I. (2014). *The End of ETA (2007–2011): Narratives from the Media and from the Actors*. (Doctoral dissertation). Reno, Nevada: University of Nevada.

Murua, I. (2017). No more bullets for ETA: The loss of internal support as a key factor in the end of the Basque group's campaign. *Critical Studies on Terrorism, 10*(1), 93–114.

Naiz. (2018). Cronología del 'caso Bateragune': condenados por impulsar la solución del conflict. *Naiz*. https://www.naiz.eus/en/actualidad/noticia/20181106/cronologia-del-caso-bateragune-condenados-por-impulsar-la-solucion-del-conflicto.

Preston, P. (2005). *The Triumph of Democracy in Spain*. New York and London: Taylor and Francis.

Reinares, F. (2004). Who are the terrorists? Analyzing changes in sociological profile among members of ETA. *Studies in Conflict & Terrorism, 27*(6), 465–488.

Rekarte, I. (2015). *Lo Difícile es Perdonarse a uno Mismo*. Barcelona: Ediciones Península.

Rodríguez, J. (2007). El silencio de Hernani. *El Pais*. https://elpais.com/diario/2007/07/22/eps/1185084946_850215.html.

Rueda, F. M. (2016). Telesforo Monzón, del Nacionalismo Aranista a Herri Batasuna: Las claves de una evolución. *Revista de Estudios Políticos, 174*, 267–297.

Sarabia, B. (1998). Violencia adolescente. *Revista Cuenta y Razon de Pensamiento Actual, 106*. http://www.cuentayrazon.org/modules.php?op=modload&name=

Publications&file=index&p_op=showcontent&secid=&pnid=1052740202.

Soldevilla, G. F. (2010). El Compañero Ausente y los Aprendices de Brujo: Orígenes de Herri Batasuna (1974–1980) (1). *Revista de Estudios Políticos, 148*, 71–103.

Spencer, A. T. and Croucher, S. M. (2008). Basque nationalism and the spiral of silence: An analysis of public perceptions of ETA in Spain and France. *International Communication Gazette, 70*(2), 137–153.

Tejerina, B. (2001). Protest cycle, political violence and social movements in the Basque country. *Nations and Nationalism, 7*(1), 39–57.

Watson, C. J. (1996). Folklore and Basque nationalism: Language, myth, reality. *Nations and Nationalism, 2*(1), 17–34.

Whitfield, T. (2015). *The Basque Conflict and ETA: The Difficulties of an Ending.* United States Institute of Peace Special Report. https://www.usip.org/publications/2015/12/basque-conflict-and-eta-difficulties-ending.

Woodworth, P. (2001). *Dirty War, Clean Hands: ETA, the GAL and Spanish Democracy.* New Haven and London: Yale University Press.

Zabalo, J. and Saratxo, M. (2015). ETA ceasefire: Armed struggle vs. political practice in Basque nationalism. *Ethnicities, 15*(3), 362–384.

PART VI

CASE STUDIES

Near and Middle East

45

THE KURDISTAN WORKER'S PARTY (PKK)

Origins, History, and Strategic Transformation

Murat Yeşiltaş

INTRODUCTION

The Kurdistan Workers' Party (PKK) is a Kurdish far-left terrorist organisation. It mainly embraces Marxist-Leninist ideology and Maoist guerilla insurgency tactics to achieve its strategic objective in Turkey and the Middle East, particularly across the northern parts of Syria, Iraq, and Iran. The PKK was established by Abdullah Öcalan in 1978 to fight for an independent Kurdish state in predominantly Kurdish-populated areas. Its founder, Öcalan, had fled Turkey in 1979, was expelled from Syria in 1998, and was captured by the Turkish intelligence unit in Kenya via CIA assistance in 1999. The PKK's history can be divided into five strategic periods in terms of the transformation of its strategic objectives, which have been shaped by the developments of internal politics at the national level, the geo-strategic developments at the regional level, and most importantly, the geo-political developments at the international level. It is worth mentioning that the changing regional security complex in the Middle East since the 1970s has had a significant impact on the PKK's strategic transformation as well as on the responses of Turkey and regional countries against this terrorist organisation.

The first period (1970–1984) was the foundational phase for the PKK, in which domestic, regional, and international developments dramatically shaped the organisation's strategy and tactics. The second period (1984–1993) was marked by the structural reformulation of the PKK and its violent strategy against Turkey. The third period (1993–1999) is the post-Cold War era, throughout which the PKK dramatically changed its strategic objectives in Turkey and the region; this period also symbolises the intensification of violence in Turkey since the PKK had intensified its perpetrated war strategy against the Turkish security forces and civilians across the country. This period ended in 1999 with Abdullah Öcalan's capture and the PKK's unilaterally announced ceasefire. The fourth period started in the 2000s, and the PKK initiated a new strategy predominantly shaped by its imprisoned leader, Öcalan. The new period for Öcalan should be articulated in line with the new reality of domestic and regional politics, which he referred to as the "strategic lunge", through which he aimed to reach a strategic autonomy for the PKK in the form of a governing body in southeastern Turkey (Ünal, 2014). The fifth period started following the intensification of the Syrian civil war, especially after ISIS's territorial expansion in Iraq and Syria (Yeşiltaş and Kardaş, 2017). During this period, the PKK initiated a new strategy, which was mainly based on various urban insurgency tactics to achieve its territorial objective in Turkey (Yeşiltaş and Özçelik, 2018). However, due to a lack of military experience in urban warfare, insufficient military capacity to sustain its surge, a lack of popular and external support, and the fight that it carried out against ISIS in Syria, the PKK failed to achieve its strategic objectives via its urban insurgency.

THE HISTORY OF THE PKK: CAUSES AND CONTEXT

The PKK (*Partîya Karkêren Kurdistan*) is an example of an ethnic insurgency using intense terror and Maoist guerilla techniques. It was established in the late 1970s due to a series of national, regional, and international socio-political occurrences in the geopolitical landscape of the Middle East (Özcan N. A., 1999). However, the Kurdish issue and separatist Kurdish nationalism, as the main driving factors behind the emergence of the PKK, have deep historical roots in Turkey (Balcı, 2013). The Kurdish issue as a form of ethnic insurgency first and foremost dates back to the Ottoman Empire, and several Kurdish insurgencies have occurred since the foundation of the Turkish Republic in

DOI: 10.4324/9780429426063-52

1923 (Yavuz, 2007). Some studies claim that Kurdish nationalism is politically and ideologically constructed and that it has been used as an external tool to undermine Turkey's territorial and political unity (Laçiner and Bal, 2004), in which the official narrative regarding the non-existence of Kurds as a distinct nationality has been at the centre, particularly since the late 1990s. Some studies, on the other hand, underline the repressive nation-building state policies that were historically articulated around the discourse of Turkish nationalism with regards to the denial of the existence of Kurdish ethnic and political identity as the main driver behind the long-standing grievances of the PKK in Turkey (Belge, 2011; Yeğen M., The Turkish state discourse and the exclusion of Kurdish identity, 1996). Emerging from among those who have a more radical understanding of the Kurdish question in Turkey, the left-wing Kurdish students in Ankara began to talk of founding a movement in early 1973 (Özcan A. K., 2006), and in 1978, the PKK decided to hold its first party congress and established itself as a secret organisation under the leadership of Abdullah Öcalan (Barkey and Fuller, 1998). He was later captured in Kenya by the Turkish intelligence service with the assistance of the U.S. in 1999 and has been in jail since then. Öcalan spent his early years (1974–1988) most of the time studying the theories of revolutionary political activity and organisation to properly address the solution of the Kurdish issue from a military perspective and in favour of Kurdish nationalism.

The PKK was officially established on November 26–27, 1978, in a village known as Fis near Diyarbakr in Turkey (Güneş, 2013). This was a meeting of about 22 or 23 members (including two female participants) of the group that called themselves 'Apoists,' referring to their leader Apo, also known as Abdullah Öcalan (Marcus, 2009). At this first meeting, Öcalan, Cemil Bayk, and Ahin Dönmez were selected as the central committee of the organisation to determine the main course of the PKK. (Özcan N. A., 1999, p. 42). However, the party and especially Calan himself started the activities in the early 1970s (Saeed, 2014, pp. 116–117). At its first congress meeting, no name was attached to the party because of the political climate in Turkey and Ankara's perception of the Kurdish issue. In the beginning of 1979, publications of the organisation were still signed with the name *Kurdistan Revolutionaries*. The name PKK was given to the organisation only a few months later, in April 1979 (Akkaya and Jongerden, 2011), and its existence was announced soon after that, in July 1979. The party seemed to take its time planning its strategy. The process of group formation had started years ago, as early as 1972–3 (Özcan N. A., 1999), and by the time the PKK was established, the party was already organised throughout the mostly Kurdish-populated areas in the southeastern part of Turkey. Its first objective was to start a communist revolution through guerrilla warfare and establish an independent Kurdish state.

At the national level, the organisation claimed that the PKK was established due to the discriminatory policies of the Turkish state against its own Kurdish population since the establishment of the Turkish Republic (Marcus, 2009). In addition to the discriminatory nation-state policies, devastated socio-economic conditions, social and political prejudices against the Kurdish population living mainly in the eastern parts of the country, as well as the rapid urbanisation due to the dramatic industrialisation process (Yeğen, 2007), were the main driving factors behind the rise of the PKK (Yeğen M., 1996). More importantly, the prohibition on the use of Kurdish in the public sphere and the ban implemented on books published in Kurdish between 1983 and 1991 enabled the PKK to easily mobilise the mostly Kurdish-populated areas in Turkey and gain their consent and support (Olson, 1992). The lack of comprehensive state policies, the underestimation of the Kurdish issue, and the PKK's capacity also contributed to consolidating the PKK's power. The recruitment logic was crucial to deepening the Kurdish issue. The PKK's recruitment strategy specifically targeted the youth, and the families of the recruits were threatened by the PKK with death. Once a member of the family was recruited, families were naturally inclined to support the organisation, and if the recruiter lost his or her life in a clash with the Turkish security forces, an entire family could be converted (Crisis, 1995).

From 1978 to 1984, the PKK initiated a strategy of assassination to eliminate its own Kurdish opposition, including public intellectuals, journalists, and political representatives from the region where the PKK was active, as well as the landlords who allegedly worked for the Turkish state to prevent potential Kurdish insurgencies in Southeastern Turkey (Özcan, 1999). One of the spectacular assassination attempts, in the PKK's initial stage, targeted a member of the parliament from the Justice Party, who was headed by Süleymen Demirel. With these tactics, the PKK made a name for itself and drew attention to the Kurdish issue.

The PKK became the most effective insurgent terrorist group in the southeast (Barkey and Fuller, 1998). The PKK had three strategic objectives in murdering the Kurdish opposition that stood against itself. First, it tried to prove to the local Kurdish population that the PKK is a strong, armed actor with whom they should rebel against the Turkish state. Secondly, it signalled a message to the local people that as long as they remain passive, the PKK will consider them to be on the enemy's side, which means that they will eventually be punished. Thirdly, the PKK directly targeted village guards, particularly those who were armed and employed by the state, to undermine the state's security apparatus in the Kurdish-populated areas (Crisis, 1995, p. 19). By doing so, the PKK became one of the most important representatives of Kurdish identity through the rewriting of Kurdish political subjectivity as a dissident ethnic group (Balcı, 2013).

The most critical turning points for the evolution of the PKK in the early years of the insurgency emerged after the military coup in 1980. Öcalan and his PKK leadership, along with some other small insurgent groups mainly inspired by Marxist-Leninist ideology, had sensed the repercussions of the 1980 coup d'état and fled the country on the eve of the military takeover (Özcan A. K., 2006). But, while the leaders of many Marxist urban underground groups eventually sought refuge in Europe, the PKK and other groups continued preparations for their insurgencies in Syria and Lebanon (Romano, 2006, p. 50; Yeğen M., 1996). The military regime's indiscriminate repression in the southeast and east helped the PKK gain supporters, a large number of whom were in prison in Diyarbakir. Under Syrian tutelage in Lebanon, where the PKK recruits got their first real training, Öcalan and his small group established close links with some of the Palestinian groups as well as the Syrian intelligence (Özcan N. A., 1999). Following the initial stage of the organisation's formation, the PKK launched its first military operation against Turkey in August 1984 after consolidating its rural-based guerilla and insurgency network and structure in the southeast regions (İmset, 1993).

The main external drivers behind the PKK's emergence were the geopolitical developments in the Middle East, specifically the Iran-Iraq war (1980–1988) and the Gulf crisis in 1991, which provided the PKK with significant political and military manoeuvres of action (Özcan, 1999). The onset of the first Iran-Iraq War and eventually the first Gulf crisis provided the PKK with a strategic advantage in its confrontation against Turkey. In the first instance, the Saddam regime in Iraq was forced to reduce its troop concentrations significantly in northern Iraq, creating a power vacuum that granted the PKK freedom of action (Olson, 1992). Similarly, during the much shorter First Gulf War, Iraqi troops were thinned out of Northern Iraq; more importantly, a *de facto* Kurdish autonomous zone mainly controlled by two different Iraqi Kurdish political groups emerged under the protection of the U.S., Britain, and France. Interestingly, the Turkish government followed an active policy to attract U.S. attention to the region during the Gulf crisis, which later became one of the major strategic mistakes for Turkey's foreign and security policy towards the Kurdish issue at the regional level (Aydınlı, 2002). The PKK benefited from the absence of a military presence to impede its activities (Eccarius-Kelly, 2011). On the other hand, the Turkish assumption that the Iraqi regime would be sympathetic to Ankara should it one day regain control of the area was not necessarily true. To impede the PKK's freedom of movement in Northern Iraq, Turkey has mounted numerous cross-border military operations against the organisation in Northern Iraq to prevent the PKK's terrorist infiltration into Turkey's territory (Barkey and Fuller, 1998, s. 23).

At the regional level, Syria also played a crucial role in consolidating the PKK's ideological and material capacities. While Northern Iraq was secure in terms of providing the PKK freedom of action due to its geographical features, Syria constituted one of the most favourable countries for the PKK's recruitment. More importantly, the regional geopolitical dynamics, historical territorial dispute, and water issue between Turkey and Syria motivated Damascus to support the PKK against Turkey in the context of regional politics (Bölükbaşı, 1991). Therefore, Syria always had the closest relations with the PKK, and around 1985, Damascus expanded its relations (Güner, 1997). Firstly, the PKK was allowed to take full control of the Helwe training camp in the Syrian-controlled Bekaa Valley, where PKK militants were trained. This training camp enabled the PKK to mobilise its trained militants to play a key role in the armed operations that took place in Turkey. At the same time, contact between Syria and Öcalan became more frequent. The occupation of Lebanon by Israel provided the PKK with a chance to strengthen its presence in the valley because it could settle in the camps evacuated by Palestinians and acquire arms there. More importantly, the camps have provided the PKK with space to discipline itself organisationally and ideologically. For instance, the PKK organised its second congress meeting there in 1982 (Orhan, 2014). Later, the PKK established the academy of Mahsun Korkmaz, which constituted an important place of political and military formation for the PKK militants until 1992 (İmset, 1993, p. 85). Additionally, Syrian President Hafez al-Assad's younger brother, Cemil Assad, took a particular interest in the PKK and visited its Helwe camp to politically and militarily support the group against Turkey. The PKK's close relations with the Syrian regime provided agency for the PKK militants to move between Turkey, Syria, and Lebanon. Furthermore, Syria was used as a safe haven by the PKK until 1999 to manage its political and military engagements against Turkey. Hence, it is possible to argue that Syria provided strategic leverage and many political opportunities for the organisation, which enabled the PKK to gain freedom of action in the region.

The international political developments that took place between 1970 and 1990 created an important dynamic as well. It is widely accepted that the PKK should be examined within the context of Cold War geopolitical dynamics. In this regard, the Cold War had both direct and indirect effects on the emergence of the PKK. In terms of indirect dynamics, the European student movement should be considered the main political factor, in which left-wing radical student movements influenced the mobilisation process of the Kurdish political movements during the late 1960s. The anti-imperialist and anti-American political ideologies in Turkey during the 1970s also provided an opportunity to take some lessons from other dissident movements across the world and reshaped the Kurdish political movement's political and ideological understanding of the Kurdish issue. When the PKK was established in the late 1970s, its foundational narrative framed U.S. imperialism as the main enemy while the Soviet Union was presented as the organisation's natural ally. More importantly, the founding official documents of the PKK described the U.S.-based international system as imperial and framed the Soviet system as a revolutionary socialist system, one that the Kurdish political movement should adopt (Balcı, 2016). In terms of the direct, the geopolitical competition between the U.S.-led international order and the Soviet-led order also influenced the PKK's initial formulation of its organisational structure, political ideology, and modus operandi against Turkey. The ideological rivalry between the U.S. and the Soviet Union thus dramatically influenced the PKK's ideology.

THE IDEOLOGY OF THE PKK

The PKK cannot be defined by a single, consistent ideology. Rather, it has an ideology, which is an amalgam of different political ideologies, including revolutionary socialism and Kurdish nationalism (Güneş, 2012). It is impossible to describe all of the dramatic ideological shifts in Öcalan's thought across the 40 books that he published over the course of the years (Stansfield and Shareef, 2017). However, it is possible to understand the PKK ideology by looking at how the organisation and Öcalan, address pan-Kurdish nationalism, socio-political and geopolitical developments regarding particular political situations of the Kurds in the region, and interactions among the regional countries and international actors (Bila, 2017). One of the most important fundamental components of the PKK's ideology is the centrality of Abdullah Öcalan as a cult personality (Çağaptay, 2007). However, Öcalan has continually shifted his thought, evolved his pragmatic praxis significantly, and thus dramatically changed the ideology, aims, and practises of the PKK. Initially, Öcalan formed the PKK to fight for Kurdish independence in the form of a state by taking socialist revolutionary ideology at its centre (Güneş, 2012). This period was marked by violent extremism, including guerilla-type terrorism, peaking in 1984 and intensifying in the post-Cold War era. However, Öcalan initiated a strategic shift in terms of framing the PKK's strategy against Turkey in the post-Cold War period and reformulated the entire ideology of the PKK following his capture, which consequently shifted the PKK's entire strategic goal in the process of the Arab uprisings, particularly following the critical developments in Syria.

The PKK simply follows Marxist-Leninist ideology and Maoist guerilla techniques. The first written document to outline the PKK's purpose in the context of Maoist ideology was 1978's "The Road to the Kurdistan Revolution: The Manifesto" and "The Party Programme" (Jongerden and Akkaya, 2012). The organisation, which described itself as Marxist-Leninist, formulated the basis of its ideology during the years of its creation through the commonly accepted ideological source of socialist ideology. Most sources that explain the PKK ideology stem from the "force" and "colony" concepts, which constitute some of the central components within the Marxist-Leninist ideology. These unchanging and undisputed concepts constitute the main axis of the PKK's ideas and actions towards the Turkish state. In line with the Marxist historical understanding, the creation of class societies is explained in the context of a general theoretical reference to the Marxist-Leninist understanding. In addition to this theoretical assumption, as it is articulated within the Marxist literature, the problem is proposed as "How can the existence of exploitation be sustained in class societies?" The answer is illustrated as "through force" (Özcan, 1999). The exploitation that paves the way for force to be used is used both internally and externally. Thus, from the period of slave societies to the period of classless societies until the creation of a socialist state, the exploitation of human societies by external sources as a form of pressure and colonisation was constantly developing (Özcan, 1999, p. 55). Classifying colonisation as internal and external exploitation would be the basis of all ideas and terrible events that were to be experienced. This meant that internal exploiters were "feudal, cooperative, and backwards bourgeois," while the Republic of Turkey constituted the external exploiter.

While this classification identified the "enemies" to combat, history was classified as the struggle of the classes and societies that wanted to be free of these two exploitations. Since the historical necessity of socialism proved the reality that the solution was socialism, the ideological choice was correct. Therefore, "the method to save Kurdistan would be socialism." The organisation that would realise the long-term insurgency war aimed to arrive at the target with a triad organisation, which embodied the following features: A disciplined *party*, an *army* under command, and a *front* establishment that feeds and helps to consolidate its power to achieve determined goals (Özcan, 1999, p. 60). The party is the political establishment that the organisation will create. Hence, the party must, of course, possess certain qualities and play a leadership role.

At the establishment of the party, the hierarchical structure from bottom to top was "Cell, Village Council, Local Committee, Area Committee, Central Committee, and Politburo. The distribution of tasks within the organisational structure enabled the PKK to create propaganda, recruit members, and gain financial support. The system was created so that each higher committee would be responsible for inspecting and controlling those in their purview. The Central Committee, tasked with selecting the four-person Politburo, was also generally responsible for the organisation as a whole. In order for an armed conflict to start, they first needed to "create a militarised" organisational structure. The newly created military organisation would have to be weak and powerless due to the organisation's structure and the circumstances. This is why the PKK had to employ "guerilla" tactics. In the strategic defence period, guerilla warfare was primarily political, not military. It concentrated all its attention on organising the civilians for rebellions, which is defined as the front. The organised civilians would have their own armed forces and fight independently while still aiding the guerillas (Özcan, 1999, p. 70).

The main priority of the front was the process through which the civilians were politically educated during a long-term civil war, after they had been ripped from the Turkish state and then reorganised. The purpose here was to increase the strength of the weak military units via civilian support. In order to acquire public support, the PKK had to propose an end game that would result in victory and make sure that the civilians residing within the range of the PKK's territorial target felt safe (Özcan N. A., 1999). Every liberated area ripped from the government's influence by the PKK would strengthen the organisation while weakening the government. The organised civilians would offer unconditional support to the organisation, and they would engage in either partial or full rebellions once they were fully invested in the organisation. The force that would stem from this phenomenon would then work to isolate the government from civilians through political violence. They would consistently feed the guerilla, and the guerilla would "protect" them.

In the post-Cold War era, the collapse of the Soviet Union caused a quest for a new ideology for the PKK since socialism lost its significance in framing and understanding the Kurdish issue. Therefore, the PKK's ideological configuration went through a radical transformation during the early stages of the post-Cold War. In the post-1999 period, particularly after Ocalan's capture, the PKK had to reformulate its ideological narrative (Marcus, 2009). Calan, after his imprisonment in 1999, adopted some of the fundamental features of Murray Bookchin's (1992) thoughts within his own political model of 'democratic confederalism' (Muhammad, 2018). During their brief correspondence in 2004, Öcalan stated that his 'world view' stands close to Bookchin's, especially in regard to the theory and practise of municipalities in the southern part of Turkey. This was affirmed in the *Declaration of Democratic Confederalism* in Turkey and during the creation of the Kurdistan Communities Union (KCK) in 2005, which called for the implementation of democratic confederalism and a borderless confederation across all four Kurdish regions (Öcalan, 1999). This was extended to northern Syria (also known as Rojova in Kurdish) in 2016, when its three cantons represented the Democratic Federation of Rojava. The Declaration of 2005 marked the formal and practical shift from Marxist-Leninism towards the implementation of Bookchin's social ecology. In theoretical terms, this shift is most clearly articulated in the second volume of calan's Prison Writings (2011), which outlines many of his justifications for these fundamental shifts in ideology; his claims were further elaborated in terms of their political content in the doctrine of Democratic Confederalism (Öcalan A., 2011).

THE ORGANISATIONAL STRUCTURE OF THE PKK

The ideological characteristics of the PKK and its ideological transformation over time have been a determinant factor in shaping its organisational structure. When it was founded, the organisation was composed of some core members led by Abdullah Öcalan. However, the PKK has functioned under a very hierarchical organisational structure, and Öcalan has dominated the PKK leadership since the very beginning. Besides Öcalan, Cemil Bayk has served as one of the other leading people of the organisation, as has Murat Karaylan, who is currently the general spokesperson of the PKK and leads the PKK's armed wing known as the People's Defence Forces (HPG).

Since its establishment, the PKK has gone through several changes in terms of its name (KADEK, KONGRA-GEL, KKK, and KCK), organisational structure, and regional branches, particularly in the period following the capture of Öcalan in 1999. The PKK's functional organisation, until its reformulation in 2005, consisted of a Central Executive Committee controlling a Central Committee whose secretary general was Abdullah Öcalan. During his absolute control of the organisation, Calan ruled the PKK (Posch, 2016). In addition to other sub-committees attached to the central committee, the military and external committees constituted the most functional and important formations within the PKK's organisational structure.

Following the third congress, which was held in 1986, the military sub-committee was renamed the Kurdistan People's Liberation Army (ARGK), and its external operation centre was called the National Liberation Front of Kurdistan (ERNK). While ARGK was responsible for the armed attacks in Turkey, ERNK was responsible for the PKK's political and military propaganda. Following the establishment of KCK in February 2005, the PKK reformulated its organisational structure; KONGRA-GEL (the People's Congress of Kurdistan) started serving as the legislature and presided over KKK, which was the new executive committee consisting of a series of hierarchically formed regional committees. The main strategic rationale behind the new organisational structure was to reformulate the political developments at the regional level and consolidate the Kurdish autonomy or self-governance model by unifying and coordinating the efforts of the regional branches. Regional committees were also formed in Syria, Iraq, and Iran in Kurdish-populated areas (Can and Keskin, 2017). The PKK founded its Syrian branch, the Democratic Union Party (Partiya Yekitiya Demokrat, PYD), in 2003 as a reprisal against the newly emerging political landscape in Syria. The change aimed to form an organisation that would enable the PKK to expand and deepen its social base and consolidate its power over the Kurdish population in Syria.

Following the organisational change, KCK was planned to be a model confederate state on the territories of Turkey, Syria, Iraq, and Iran, which as a whole would represent an independent and united Kurdistan. The PKK has various branches not only in Turkey but also in Iran and many European countries today. While the PKK operates through the Party of Free Life of Kurdistan (PJAK), which has been fighting against the Iranian government since 2004, it has been politically and militarily active in Syria ever since the

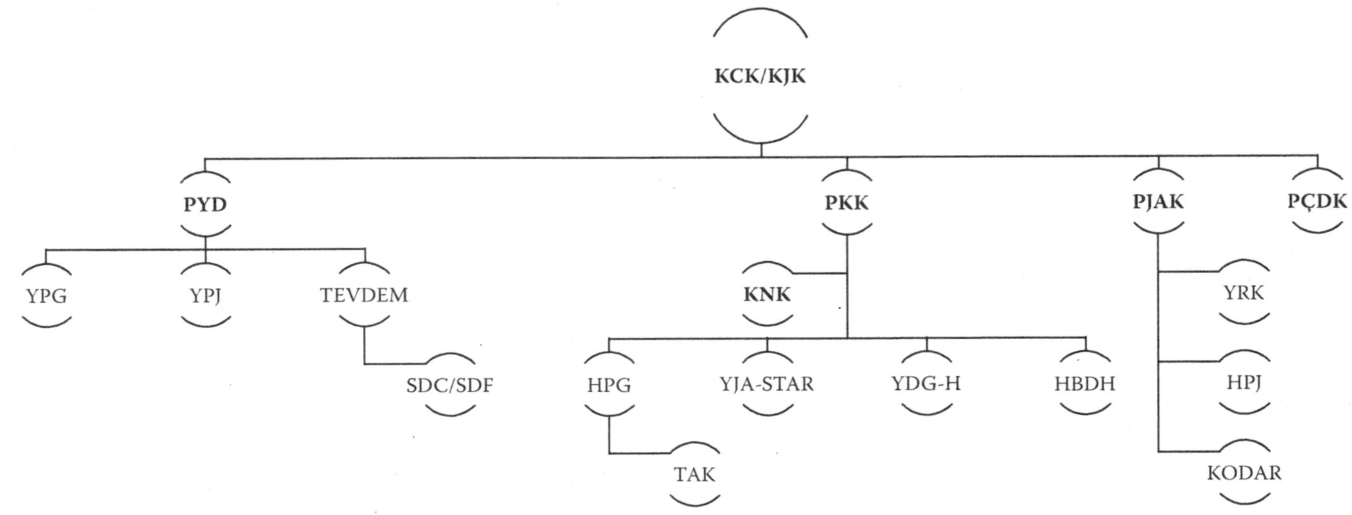

Figure 45.1 Current Organisational Structure of the PKK ***Explanation of abbreviations in the structure:*** **HPG:** The People's Defense Forces, **KCK:** The Kurdistan Communities Union, **KJK:** The female branch of the Kurdistan Communities Union, **KODAR:** The East Kurdistan Democratic and Free Society, **KNK:** The Kurdistan National Congress, **PÇDK:** The Kurdistan Democratic Solution Party; **PJAK:** The Kurdistan Free Life Party; **PKK:** The Kurdistan Workers' Party, **PYD:** The Democratic Union Party, **TAK:** The Kurdistan Freedom Hawks, **YDG-H:** The Patriotic Revolutionary Youth Movement, **YPG:** The People's Protection Units; **YPJ:** The Women's Protection Units; **YPS:** The Civil Protection Units (Karpazlı, 2018).

(Source: Author's own rendering, 2020.)

Arab Spring. The PKK's mobilisation and existence across European countries are more complicated than the cases of Syria, Iraq, and Iran. From the 2000s onward, KNK has become the senior executive committee of the KCK/PKK, responsible for structuring across Europe (Figure 45.1). Holding its place on the agenda with its protests and terrorist attacks in Europe, the PKK has gradually gathered support from European countries and institutions, even though the EU recognises the PKK as a terrorist organisation (Casier, 2010).

THE TRANSFORMATION OF THE PKK'S STRATEGY AND TACTICS

In order to make sense of the PKK's historical transformation since 1978 and understand the changing nature of its strategic objectives, the history of the PKK should be divided into five historical periods. From the very beginning of its organisational and political foundation, the PKK has been involved in different strategic engagements as opposed to its initially determined strategy, ideology, and objective. By taking into consideration the PKK's strategic rationality, the overall process of PKK violence has been subjected to strategic interaction between Turkey and the PKK and the contextual dynamics of regional and international politics. More importantly, the PKK has gradually deviated from its initial strategic objective due to the evolving nature of the socio-political context in Turkey at the domestic level, internal dynamics at the organisational level, and international dynamics at the systemic level. Between 1984 and 1993, in its second term, the PKK exhibited a "Maoist Guerilla" or "politicised guerilla" in its conflict strategy. The successful usage of the "Vietnam Style Guerilla" strategy by the US Army in the Vietnam War initially aimed to gain ascendancy in southeastern Turkey (Aydın and Emrence, 2015). After the government's restoration of authority in the region, they continued this strategy by utilising war of attrition methods along with long-term procedures. The PKK initially embraced a Maoist insurgent strategy aimed at independence in the context of territorial secession. By taking into consideration its overall perception of insurgency, the PKK adopted the "Protracted People's War Strategy" to achieve its strategic goals through several stages (Özcan N. A., 1999).

The First Period: Organisational Foundation and Political Propaganda

In the first period (1973–1984), the PKK focused on its organisational structure to mobilise an effective insurgent movement against the Turkish state. It was a period of preparation to establish the best version of a political and military organisation for the PKK. The lack of a long-term strategy during this period was one of the organisation's most significant concerns. It was mainly a process to consolidate the PKK's power structure in terms of its organisational body and the military and political training of its members. During this period, the PKK mainly conducted its strategy to eliminate its own Kurdish opposition, including public intellectuals, journalists, and political representatives from the region where the PKK was active. When the Kurdish political landscape became more violent and fragmented, the ideological competition over the use of socialism became more pronounced. The tactics promoting violence were decided to be implemented as a main political strategy (Aydın and Emrence, 2015, p. 19). In this period, the PKK also clearly declared its political and strategic objectives as the establishment of an "Independent United Kurdish State" by naming itself a socialist liberation movement (Gürcan, 2012).

Second Period: Strategic Defence and Armed Campaign

The Iraq-Iran War, Syrian presence in Lebanon, and Turkish political and institutional transformation following the coup d'état in 1980 all had an impact on the second stage, which took place between 1984 and 1990. This was the perfect course for the PKK to start its armed campaign to be recognised, domestically, defence and internationally. Contrary to the Maoist strategic organisational aspect, the PKK acted proactively to develop its armed capacity for a large-scale armed campaign. The Gulf War in 1991 and its aftermath provided the PKK with many opportunities to develop its military growth. In this period, the PKK mainly conducted guerilla warfare techniques against the Turkish forces in the rural areas until mid-1993 (Yeşiltaş and Özçelik, 2018).

In this period, the PKK attempted to exterminate the very existence of the Turkish security forces and undermine state authority and sovereignty by attacking mainly military outposts with systemic irregular warfare techniques. During this period, the PKK also conducted intense terror attacks on provisional village guards who were trained, armed, and confronted by the Turkish Armed Forces against the PKK (Ünal, 2014). The PKK also conducted many terrorist attacks against civilians, who were mainly family members of the village guards, due to their support for Turkey's counter-terrorism operations and policies. In the context of strategic change adopted in the fourth congress held in 1991, the PKK shifted to a concept called "hold-control lands," in which it aimed to gradually take control of the Kurdish-populated region as part of its grand strategy. Even though the PKK aimed to initiate its strategic balance and then move to the strategic offence stage, Turkish counter-terrorism activities, mainly based on deterrence, led to more confrontation with the PKK militants on the ground and suppressed the PKK's back-and-forth armed surge during this period (Yeşiltaş and Özçelik, 2018).

The Third Period: Reconciliation and Change in the Violence Level

In the post-1994 period, the PKK changed its sole guerilla warfare technique and started seeking compromise through political activities until 2010. As a result of Turkey's evolving counter-terrorism strategy from the "doctrine of areal control," in which troops were stationed in many rural areas, to the "cordon and search doctrine," especially through conducting large-scale military operations inside and outside of Turkey, the PKK was defeated and had to choose a strategy different from a sole guerilla fight in the first political solution (Ünal, 2014). The large-scale military operations conducted by the Turkish military forces resulted in the PKK's military defeat, but they did not end the violence or undermine the PKK's mobilisation ability in the region. The increasing fragility of the ability to sustain intensive insurgency resulted in the PKK's engagement in a very pragmatic move to resort to different tools. Therefore, the PKK pursued different processes to achieve its overarching strategic objective through the use of violence with different tactics, in which territorial victory was not achievable for the PKK (Aydın and Emrence, 2015).

This new understanding of the conjunctural and structural developments resulted in the PKK strategy adopted to spread conflict and terror attacks to the entire country in order to roll back the military mobilisation in the southeastern region of Turkey (Ünal, 2014). It was mainly based on the strategy of policy change to force Turkey to take non-military measures. During this period, the PKK, in addition to its typical insurgent attacks against strategic military outposts in Kurdish-populated areas, especially rural areas, conducted terror attacks against non-combatant civilians in western cities and public facilities in Turkey. The most important development that caused a strategic shift in the PKK's strategy was the capture of Öcalan in February 1999, as a consequence of Tukey's increasing military threat against Syria, where Öcalan and the PKK leadership took shelter. (Akkaya and Jongerden, 2011). Following Turkey's military threat against Syria, the Syrian government had to deport Öcalan from Syria. Following Öcalan's capture and the political congress held in 2000, the PKK ceased the violence unilaterally and focused on its political activities, mainly in domestic and international political domains. As a pragmatic strategic decision taken in 2000, the PKK began to emphasise the use of political efforts rather than physical violence as the only tool to achieve its strategic objectives.

The Fourth Period: Strategic Reorientation and Political Reconciliation

In the post-Öcalan leadership era, the fourth period, the PKK abolished itself and founded KADEK (Kurdistan Freedom and Democracy Congress) in its 8th Congress in 2002 and KONGRA-GEL (Kurdistan People's Congress) in 2003. The objective of KADEK was to achieve the recognition of Kurds as a distinct ethnic identity in the Turkish Constitution, including particular cultural and linguistic rights, as opposed to the PKK's initial objective of a territorially independent state (Ünal, 2014). With the establishment of the KONGRA-GEL in 2003, following the US's invasion of Iraq, the PKK declared a non-violent political means to reach its objective while maintaining military wings in Turkey and Iraq. In this period, the PKK started to intensify its political network, especially in Europe, to force Turkey into a political solution and, in the meantime, continued to reorganise its armed wing and create HPG (People's Defence Units), which temporarily relocated the PKK fighters in Turkey and Northern Iraq (Tank, 2005).

Regional developments, such as the U.S. invasion of Iraq in 2003, paved the way for the PKK to adopt a new character through the formation of the PYD (Syrian Democratic Forces) in 2003 in Syria and the establishment of the KCK in 2005. More importantly, following its listing as a terrorist organisation by established international organisations such as the EU and NATO and by certain impactful nation-states such as the US, the PKK started to reorganise its existence faction, consolidate its military capacity due to the power vacuum created after the defeat of Saddam in Iraq, and finally deepen group solidarity via reinitiating violence (Ünal, 2014).

After 2005, the PKK melted down within a wider organisational structure. Since then, the PKK has transformed itself through a series of renaming and reshaping processes. By establishing KCK, the PKK introduced its alternative state model in the region for the first time. Following the establishment of the KCK, the process of violent conflict between the PKK and Turkish military forces gained new momentum. In this period, the PKK started to intensify its political activities through its political wing due to Turkey's determination to become an EU member state, which resulted in a new democratic momentum in the Kurdish question (Balcı and Kardaş, 2016). However, at the same time, it also signalled the remobilisation of the PKK fighters in Turkey and Iraq. On the one hand, the PKK strategically aimed to legitimise its founding leader Öcalan as the ultimate decision-maker on the Kurdish issue by declaring a unilateral ceasefire to appease the perception of the PKK among the domestic Turkish audience (Wine, 2015). Through this unilateral ceasefire, the PKK gained recognition as an official actor to negotiate with Turkey and normalise itself among the Kurdish population.

The Fourth Period: Political Reconfiguration and the Peace Process

The fourth period started with the intensification of the peace process attempts in Turkey, particularly after the AK Party (Justice and Development Party) came to power and consolidated its political influence (Balcı and Kardaş, 2016). As a response to the AK Party's peace initiative, in 2010, the PKK initiated a new strategy, which was mainly shaped by its imprisoned founding leader, Öcalan. The objective of the new strategic initiative was to establish an alternative state structure in certain spheres, which mainly consisted of economic, social, political, juridical, and self-defence domains (Ünal, 2014). Due to the declaration of "democratic autonomy", the changing perception of the Kurdish issue in the eyes of the Turkish state, and the loose counter-terrorism practises adopted by Turkey in the region mainly populated by Kurds, the PKK began to dominate the social and political spheres and create de-facto circumstances in the southeastern part of Turkey (Yeşiltaş and Özçelik, 2016). During this period, the PKK conducted attacks through both guerilla and terror techniques. Its primary military unit, called HPG, and other organisations directly affiliated with the PKK (TAK, Kurdistan Liberation Hawks) (Gürcan, 2016) were active in forcing Turkey into a political peace process to achieve the PKK's strategic objectives via intensified civil demonstrations and disobediences through legal and illegal organisations.

This fourth period was described by the PKK as a process framed by 'democratic autonomy' based on the purpose of "securing its existence and ensuring its freedom." It was based on the claim that, against all the odds, they could not achieve a political solution for the Kurdish problem and that they could not achieve strategic success on the basis of the political solution of the Kurdish problem, despite having achieved certain tactical gains (Yeğen M., 2015). KCK was initially perceived by the public as the PKK's urban branch. However, later on, it was seen that beyond this definition, there was an effort to create a much more advanced model of a state system's structure. As a result, public opinion held that with the KCK structure, the PKK's main purpose was to establish a gradually growing and progressive mass movement through urban-centred organisations in line with the organisation's main strategy. Accordingly, the PKK would ensure that social segregation and radicalisation became even more acute (Jiyan, 2016). It is noteworthy that both Öcalan and the KCK explained that if a 'democratic constitutional solution' cannot be achieved, a new 'defensive war' based on insurgency and rebellion will be activated under the name of the 'revolutionary people's war.'

In 2013, the PKK established the Patriotic Revolutionary Youth Movement (YDG-H), later named the Civil Defence Units (YPS), as a new element for urban warfare (YDG-H Analizi, 2016). The changing character of the PKK strategy in this period was that the "young militants" became one of the main elements of the urban conflict. That situation also brought about a change in the nature of the conflict. The PKK's "armed youth movement," YDG-H, was a new phenomenon that emerged in cities and functions as part of the PKK's autonomy strategy towards urban areas (Yeşiltaş and Özçelik, 2016). This strategy has brought about a change in the profile of the terrorists as well as an opportunity for the PKK to materialise a new "autonomy" strategy. The goal of the PKK's autonomous strategy was to stigmatise state sovereignty and security practises as controversial by ensuring that there was a field of conflict in which the masses could engage in the conflict process (Yeşiltaş and Özçelik, 2018, p. 22).

The foundations of the establishment of the YDG-H and the organisation of its units in cities started at the time of the "PKK's Fourth Strategic Struggle Period" in 2012. This was also the year when the group launched the "Revolutionary People's War." In the new struggle period, the organisation, besides "rural guerrillas," aimed to develop "urban guerrillas"

(Yeşiltaş and Özçelik, 2018). One of the new dynamics behind the changing nature of the PKK's strategy was the transformation of regional politics. Within the framework of a new strategy, the PKK felt the need to establish an organisation that would be political in nature and based on "urban force" and, at the same time, would also be capable of using violence by remobilizing its militant structure. It stands out that, in this period, both Öcalan and KCK made statements declaring that "in case a 'democratic constitutional solution' could not be provided, a 'new defensive war' or a 'revolutionary people's war,' by name based on insurrection and rebellion, will step in" (Kalkan, 2011).

The Fifth Period: Urban Insurgency

The fifth period started in 2015. In this process, the PKK initially delegated the use of extremist violence to YDG-H, which consisted of militant youth radicalised within the context of urban warfare in the PKK's newly developed strategy, kept its own militants (HPG) in the background, and assigned a small portion of the HPG as local leaders for the management of YDG-H. As a result, this new process changed the dynamics of conflict between Turkey and the PKK to a great extent when compared with the previous conflict and brought a change to the nature and character of terrorism in general.

The PKK's new strategy had five goals. First, it aimed to expand its sphere of influence from limited rural and mountainous areas to cities, shifting it from a strategy of to one of "neighbourhood/field control" and making its security forces appear pacified. Secondly, it aimed to carry the conflict into society's daily life by forming paramilitary armed forces such as YDG-H and consolidating its armed forces at a maximum level, especially in the areas where the distribution of votes is more homogenous in favour of the HDP. Thirdly, it sought to limit the state by challenging one of its most fundamental functions, namely the monopoly over the legitimate use of force, thus turning itself into the only "legitimate authority" in some regions and cities of the country. Fourthly, it tried to generate victimhood by carrying the conflict into society and, through this method, transformed the idea of "popular resistance" into a point of attraction for society. Finally, it sought to consolidate a practise of sovereignty by ensuring the formation of state-like (semi-state) structures, such as KCK, through courts, ID checks, entrenching, and the normalisation of such practises in society. In this way, the PKK intended to create a "social control" mechanism in which it was the principal power (Yeşiltaş and Özçelik, 2018).

Within the context of the new strategy, which was built upon the PKK's "rural-based urban guerrilla," the PKK, on the one hand, carried out its attacks against the security forces in city centres and intended to position itself as the new "security actor" via its armed elements in the eyes of local people in neighbourhoods, while, on the other hand, it attempted to pose an armed challenge against the state authority in large cities (Kalkan, 2011). In fact, within the context of the organisational structure that constitutes the PKK's military doctrine, the PKK, HPG, and YDG-H formed the parts of the "self-defence" elements: the PKK as the *party*, HPG as the *army*, and YDG-H as the *street force*. In this period, the PKK read all the developments based on a "prolonged political military strategy" aimed at independence (Özcan N. A., 2015). Such a strategy aims at "arousing the people under the cover of guerrilla character." Therefore, the first goal of the new strategy, which formed the backbone of the urban

In the classical political-military Maoist approach, the inferior combatant force in a low-intensity conflict carries the armed struggle from rural areas to cities to create an impact in the latter through the armed struggle against the superior enemy in the rural areas. Mao's "protracted war strategy" was implemented in the 1980s and 1990s by the PKK on the axis of strategic defence, strategic balance, and strategic offence. However, this strategy could not go beyond the defence aspect due to the security dynamics of the period, and the attacks were limited to the gendarmerie stations, mostly in rural areas. Table 45.1

The reasons behind the failure to sustain the PKK's violent urban strategy as part of its long years of popular insurgency are multidimensional. Firstly, as many cases historically show, popular support behind an insurgency movement is the most important dimension of the effectiveness of the insurgency group's short- and long-term strategic goals. In the case of the PKK's surge tactics and strategies regarding public support, it should be underlined that the lack of public support was the main determinant factor behind the PKK's failure. Secondly, as the post-2003 regional security landscape in the context of the U.S. invasion of Iraq demonstrates and the Syrian civil war strongly underlines, the cohesion of the organisational structure and military capacity of the violent non-state armed actors are the most important components of the insurgency movement in enabling the PKK's violent strategy. The PKK's lack of military capacity and its lack of experience in urban warfare played vital roles during the urban conflict between 2015 and 2016 in Turkey. In that context, the role of inexperienced youth militants prevented the PKK from maintaining its urban tactics, and the rapid reaction of the Turkish security forces contained the PKK's ability to extend its violent mobilisation. Thirdly, from the standpoint of the PKK, the Syrian civil war constituted the main driving force behind the failure of urban tactics. The conflict structure in northern Syria, the difficulties in regard to the military mobilisation in two different conflict zones at the same time, and the complex nature of the competitive environment in Syria and Iraq among various violent non-state armed groups weakened the PKK's urban tactics in Turkey. Finally, as many cases show, external support for the insurgents is obviously a decisive factor in determining the outcome of an insurgency. The PKK case shows that during the urban conflict, external support was not an easy task in consolidating the PKK's violent tactics as a full-scale popular insurgency due

Table 45.1 Periods of the PKK's Strategy of Violence

Periods	Time Frame	Strategy	Aim	Tactics
1st Period	1973–1984	Preparation for political and military organisation: Military and political training of its recruits	Gaining political and military domination of the Kurdish political landscape	Political propaganda and assassination of political figures who resist the military strategy
2nd Period	1984–mid-1993	Territorial Change: Armed and guerilla fight	Territorial Secession: Gaining a territorially independent Kurdish state	Terrorist tactics (all types) including guerilla tactics against state officials and civilians
3rd Period	1994–2010	Policy Change: Armed fight and political reconciliation with Turkey	Gaining political autonomy in Turkey's southeastern part	Terrorist tactics (all type) including guerilla tactics against state official and civilian population
4th Period	2010–2015	Policy Change: Peace Process	Establishing a de-facto "democratic autonomy"	Political Propaganda Rural-based guerilla tactics
5th Period	2015–2019	Policy Change: Semi-sovereign administrative governance	Consolidating democratic autonomy.	Urban insurgency

Source: Compiled from author's own work, 2020.

to the fact that Turkey was perceived as a crucial player in many ways by the potential outside supporters, not only in the Middle East but also in the international arena (Yeşiltaş and Özçelik, 2018, pp. 172–173).

THE VIOLENT TACTICS OF THE PKK

The five stages of guerrilla warfare conceptualised in the 1970s by Brian Michael Jenkins are listed as follows: propaganda of violence; organisational growth; guerrilla aggression; mobilisation of the masses; and local uprising (Brain M., 1971). It was seen that between the years 1984 and 1992, the PKK completed the first three stages and tried to move onto the fourth phase, the stage of mass mobilisation. The brochure titled *Theses and Duties on Insurgency Tactics*, which was published in 1992 by Abdullah Öcalan (Orhan, 2016), was accepted as an insurrection manifesto (Özdağ, 2005, p. 66). In those years, through the countermeasures taken by the Turkish security forces, the PKK did not achieve its goal of mobilising the masses and instigating an insurgency. The PKK could not shift from the strategic defence phase to the strategic balance phase referred to by Mao's protracted war concept and, as a result, initiated a dialogue with Turkey by declaring a unilateral ceasefire on March 20, 1993.

The PKK initiated the terrorist campaign in 1984 by using "rural guerrilla" tactics in rural areas, where the political and economic conditions were relatively weak. The PKK also affirmed that, within thirty years, its rural attacks had impacted the people, but the attacks were not sufficient on the main battlefield to gain the full support of the people in the cities. In 2015, to merge rural attacks with urban guerrilla tactics, the PKK differentiated its concept of action. Through this strategic shift, the PKK desired to turn its one-way influence on the people into a two-way relationship with public support. The PKK tried to activate urban warfare in the Nusaybin-Cizre-Sur area, which is a vulnerable and geo-strategically significant region due to the spillover effects of the Syrian crisis. Domestic political developments and foreign security-centred developments also triggered the PKK to take action in favour of this new strategy (Yeşiltaş and Özçelik, 2018).

The PKK looked for reciprocal links between the attack and target variables in order to serve its overall strategy better over time. The PKK employed an aggressive technique, renouncing defensive roles, adapting attack-and-retreat tactics while preserving all available force, and aiming to develop large-scale urban warfare in order to wear out, demoralise, and distract the government forces (Cronin, 2002). Categorically, the violent tactics of the PKK are composed of armed attacks, bombings, assassinations, road blockades, arson attacks, and kidnappings (Yeşiltaş and Özçelik, 2016).

The PKK's first category of violence tactic is *armed attack*. The PKK perpetrated the first armed attack in its history in the form of simultaneous raids in the downtown areas of small districts in 1984. Since then, armed attacks have dominated the PKK's modus operandi. However, contrary to its first armed challenge, the PKK's armed attacks became more rural as the theatre of operations shifted to mountainous areas. The PKK's early weapons included AK-47s, PK machine guns, SVD Dragunov sniper rifles, and RPGs, which were all conducive to mobility and conducting raids and ambushes in mountainous terrain. The ambiguous security environment shaped by the Iraqi invasion in 1991 provided the PKK with mortars in different weapon systems. Unlike the huge volume of raids and ambushes with a large number of rural terrorists within the Turkish territory in the 1990s, until 2012, the rural attacks took on the characteristics of raids and harassing fires with relatively smaller PKK tactical elements (Yeşiltaş and Özçelik, 2018). Especially in the post-Syrian crisis, the PKK improved its military-technical capacity not only in Turkey but also in Syria and Iraq. Armed attacks can be divided into three categories: ambush, raid, and mortar attacks.

The PKK relied on ambush tactics when ground conflict was imminent. The combination of improvised explosive devices (IEDs) and ambushes served the PKK, particularly in rural areas. Military convoys, demining security units on the main roads, and the operation forces in the mountainous regions became the targets of organised ambushes. The PKK also employed raids as their secondary armed attack tactic, and their targets ranged from rural military bases to urban police stations (Yeşiltaş and Özçelik, 2018, p. 60).

The PKK also employed mortar attacks. This system is used by the PKK when attacking security facilities with Russian-made 82 mm and 122 mm mortars from a distance of 1,000–3,500 metres in the mountainous regions. The PKK enjoyed the use of mortars from the PKK's rural strongholds in Turkish territory against the stationary security facilities; from the tactical PKK positions in mountainous Iraqi territory against the Turkish border security bases; and from the PKK/PYD positions in Syria against the Turkish border security posts (Yeşiltaş and Özçelik, 2018). A *harassing fire* is a small arms fire or a long-range mid-calibre anti-aircraft gunfire that is employed to disturb the routine of the Turkish security forces, curtail their movement, threaten them with random losses, and lower morale. The PKK utilises almost every possible weapon type in this category, not only for achieving the objectives mentioned above but also for testing the reaction of the security forces for a future raid. The PKK's use of ATGMs was seen when the YPG elements in Syria began enjoying the U.S. delivery of such systems in 2015 (Suriyegündemi, 2018). Figure 45.2

The PKK also employed assassination as its main tactic. Over the course of the insurgency, the PKK has tried to regain its tactical advantage by intimidating the security personnel of Turkey. The assassinations of the security personnel have been carried out on an individual level as revenge for the losses of armed confrontations. On the other hand, the assassination tactics at the PKK's organisational level are employed to punish the village guards for their support of the security forces. The PKK targeted mostly local figures to discourage them from taking political action locally. Meanwhile, the PKK also aimed to coerce the local people by selectively targeting party members who supported the ruling parties of the Turkish government.

Arson has also proven to be another one of the PKK's chosen tactics. It is mostly carried out against public facilities and buildings in order to spread fear among the desired group of people. The PKK also focuses on

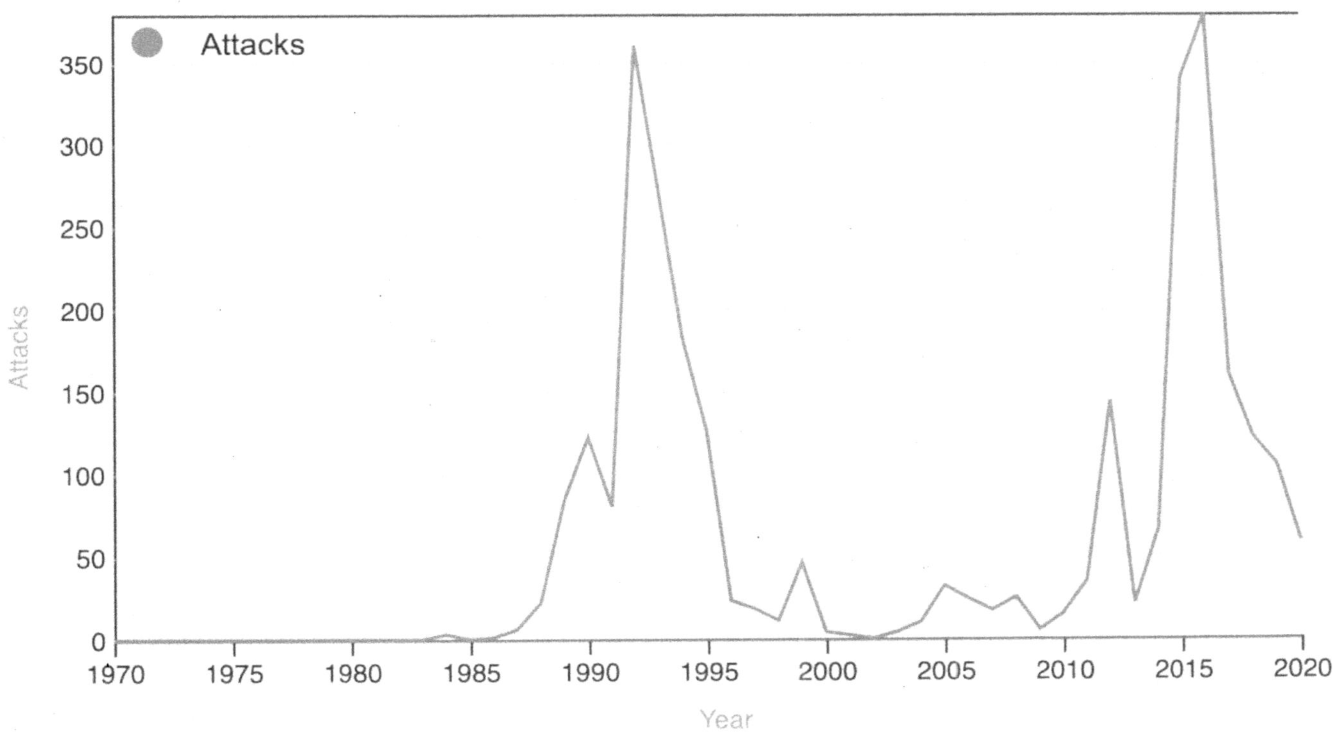

Figure 45.2 PKK Terrorist Activities Over Time.

Source: Global Terrorism Database (GTD) (2024).

intimidating and coercing the desired target group in the area of activity where the arson attacks are carried out. The PKK has three distinguished patterns of utilising arson: (i) the usual arson tactic of setting public buildings on fire: the PKK set school buildings, mosques, and libraries in urban areas on fire; (ii) setting parked vehicles on fire in metropolitan cities in the western part of Turkey; and (iii) setting civilian vehicles on fire, an act committed in relation to road blockade activities, with the help of HPG terrorists in the rural areas of eastern cities (Yeşiltaş and Özçelik, 2018). The third pattern is the most common use of arson and requires tactical organisation similar to ambush attacks on the main roads between major cities in eastern Turkey (Milliyet, 2015).

Bomb attacks: As the technical developments allowed the triggering mechanism to be more sophisticated, the PKK started using IEDs since the 2003 Iraq War in more tactical-oriented operations to kill, destroy, incapacitate, harass, deny mobility, or distract the Turkish security forces. Based on the target selections, IED attacks varied in offensive and defensive objectives. In terms of an offensive term, IED attacks were carried out in the form of roadside implantations. The PKK employed this attack type against the military motor convoys in order to destroy the security forces with maximum casualties. The tactical employment of IEDs by the PKK was seen both in rural and urban security environments. Since the mitigation techniques have varied, the PKK has utilised IED attacks along with other supporting types of attacks. The PKK first adopted the use of car bombs in Turkey in 2012 and, since 2015, has developed its capacity, fostered by foreign support in Syria and Iraq.

Generally conducted as a single attack, a car bomb is the deadliest and preferred by the PKK for several reasons: the desire to cause mass destruction of security workers and civilians; to impose fear on civilians and intimidation on security forces; to disband the security coordination between local people and security forces; and to dominate the international media coverage. The statement "VBIED precisely means "man-made explosive laden on a vehicle" and is conceptualised as the *Vehicle Borne Improvised Explosive Device* (VBIED) (Joint, 2011, p. 391). *SVEST attacks* (suicide vest attacks) have been rarely carried out by the PKK. Yet, to gain leverage, the PKK conducted its SVEST attacks in the same pattern as DAESH. Since the first experience in 1996 in downtown Tunceli, the PKK has forced inactive female terrorists to carry out suicide attacks. However, the implementation of SVEST attacks never occurred in the tactical conflict zone; rather, it was used in areas where civilians and security personnel mingled in city centres. It was TAK (Kurdistan Freedom Falcons) (Gürcan, 2016) that carried out the suicide attack in Bursa, which targeted civilians on April 27, 2016 (BBCTürkçe, 2016).

The PKK also had the practise of kidnapping targeted security personnel, government officials, local political figures, and civilian individuals who were affiliated with government agencies. The objective of the kidnapping is to instill fear among security, political, and local figures and to create a sense of intimidation (Table 45.2).

Table 45.2 Violent Tactics of the PKK

Tactics	Target Selection
Armed attack Ambush Mortar attack Raid Harassing fire ATGM Attack MANPAD Attack	Security personnel Rural military bases and facilities Urban police stations Stationary security facilities Turkish security forces Turkish rotary-wing aircrafts
Assassination	Security personnel Political representative Local civilian figures Village guards and their family members
Arson	Government facilities and public facilities
Bomb attacks (IED) VBIED (SVBIED) SVEST	Turkish security forces Police Government Facilities Civilian individuals
Kidnapping	Security personnel Government officials, Local political figures Civilian individuals

Source: Compiled from author's own work, 2020.

CONCLUSION

Though Turkey has been fighting against the PKK by implementing different counter-terrorism strategies since 1984, the PKK is still one of the strongest insurgent terrorist groups in the Middle East. It also holds on to Syrian territory in the northeastern part of the country via its Syrian branch known as the YPG; it still controls its main headquarters in Qandil Mountain, which is strategically located at the borderline between Turkey, Iraq, and Iran, and continues its military fight mainly against Turkey.

The PKK was born as a product of Cold War socio-political and security developments, transformed its strategy in the post-Cold War security landscape in Turkey and the Middle East, and finally became a hybrid terrorist organisation in the post-Arab Spring. The hybrid nature of the PKK is multidimensional. From a traditional organisational perspective, it seems that the PKK is a classical terrorist organisation that still uses guerilla-type attacks against the Turkish security forces in rural areas. However, the PKK widely operates within public spaces through its political wings in Turkey, Syria, Iraq, Iran, and many other European countries. It is widely recognised as a terrorist organisation, but it consolidates its power through different types of legal civil society organisations, attacks soft targets, controls narco-traffic, and engages in illegal human trafficking and money laundering activities across Europe (Yeşiltaş and Atall, 2019). Different terrorism databases underline that, as a consequence of the conflict between the PKK and Turkey, more than 40,000 people lost their lives. The economic cost of PKK terrorism for Turkey reaches nearly 300 billion U.S. dollars in total.

Over the course of time, the PKK has been transforming its ideology, strategy, tactics, and political objectives. It emerged as a social revolutionary Marxist-Leninist organisation to achieve its political objective by using guerilla tactics, but eventually shifted its determined strategic objective in the post-Cold War era. During the early stages of the post-Cold War, the PKK tried to intensify its war against Turkey but could not alter the balance of power due to a lack of popular support and material capacity, in addition to other regional dynamics.

The Arab Spring, especially the Syrian civil war, created a new regional dynamic for the PKK to achieve its political objective. First, the PKK changed its rural-based guerilla tactics against Turkey by perceiving the urban insurgency backed by rural guerillas as the main tactic to undermine the Turkish state's authority in the region. Secondly, the PKK focused on Syria following the Syrian regime's withdrawal of its troops, mainly from Kurdish-populated areas in northern Syria. The rise of ISIS in the region facilitated the geopolitical expansion of the PKK across northern Syria through its Syrian wing, the YPG, and provided freedom of action for the organisation to mobilise its fighters as well as its discourse on Kurdish nationalism (Yeşiltaş and Kardaş, 2017). In the fight against ISIS, the YPG became one of the most effective ground troops and attracted the attention of the global community.

With the increasing military assistance of the anti-ISIS coalition partner countries, particularly the U.S., the YPG became a dominant actor in northern Syria, and the PKK enjoyed the YPG's hegemony over the region as it increased its military capacity. More importantly, the PKK became one of the strongest agents in the remaking of Kurdish nationalism across the region. However, Turkey's cross-border operations and direct military intervention against the PKK (YPG) in Syria prevented the PKK's territorial expansion in northern Syria and undermined its mobilisation within Turkey. Since then, the PKK has lost its influence within Turkey and has had to retreat from Turkey to its stronghold in northern Iraq.

References

1-02, J. P. (2010). *Dictionary of Military and Associated Terms*. US Department of Defense. (1992).

Akkaya, A., & Jongerden, J. (2011). "The PKK in 2000s: Countinuity thorug break?" In M. Casier, & J. Jongerden (Eds.), *Nationalism and Politics in Turkey: Political Islam, Kemalism and Kurdish Issue* (pp. 143–163). Routledge.

Aydın, A., & Emrence, C. (2015). *Zones of Rebellion: Kurdish Insurgents and the Turkish States*. Ithaca and London: Cornell University Press.

Aydınlı, E. (2002). Between Security and Liberalization: Decoding Turkey's Struggle with the PKK. *Security Dialogue*, *33*(2), 209–225.

Balcı, A. (2013). *The PKK-Kurdistan Workers's Party's Regional Politics: During and after the Cold War*. London: Palgrave McMillan.

Balcı, A. (2016). *The PKK-Kurdistan Working's Party's Regional Politics*. Palgrave.

Balcı, A., & Kardaş, T. (2016). Inter-Societal Security Trilemma in Turkey: Understanding the Failure of the 2009 Kurdish Opening. *Turkish Studies*, *17*(1), 155–180.

Barkey, H. J., & Fuller, G. (1998). *Turkey's Kurdish Question*. The Rowman & Littlefield Publishing Group Inc.

BBC Türkçe. (2016, May 1). *Bursa'daki intihar saldırısını TAK üstlendi*. Retrieved from BBC Türkçe. http://www.bbc.com/turkce/haberler/2016/05/160501_bursa_saldiri_tak

Belge. (2011). State Building and the Limits of Legibility: Kinship Networks and Kurdish Resistance in Turkey. *International Journal of Middle East Studies*, *43*(1), 95–114.

Besenyő, J. (2019). Barry Buzan's Securitizatio Theory and the Case of Iraqi Kurdish Military Action against ISIS in 2014. *Jounral of Security and Sustainability Issues*, *8*(3), 295–306. (2019), http://jssidoi.org/jssi/uploads/papers/31/Besenyo_Barry_Buzans_Securitization_Theory_and_the_case_of_Iraqi_Kurdish_military_action_against_ISIS_in_2014.pdf

Bila, F. (2017). *The Ideological Codes of the PKK*. Doğan Kitap.

Bölükbaşı, S. (1991). Ankara, Damascus, Baghdad, and the Regionalization of Turkey's Kurdish Secessionism. *Journal of South Asian and Middle Eastern Studies*, *14*(4), 15–36.

Brain, M. J. (1971). *Five Stages of Urban Guerrilla Warfare: A Challenge of The 1970s*. RAND Corporation.

Çağaptay, S. (2007). Can the PKK Renounce Violence? Terrorism Resurgent. *Middle East Quarterly, Winter*, 45–52.

Can, A., & Keskin, B. (2017). *The PKK's Branck in Syria: PYD-YPG*. Ankara: SETA Report.

Casier, M. (2010). Designated Terrorists: The Kurdistan Workers' Party and its Struggle to (Re)gain Political Legitimacy. *Mediterranean Politics*, *15*(3), 393–413.

Crisis, N. (1995). The Nature of PKK Terrorism in Turkey. *Studies in Conflict and Terrorism*, *18*, 17–37.

Cronin, I. (2002). *Confronting Fear, A History of Terrorism*. New York: Thunder's Mouth Press.

Eccarius-Kelly, V. (2011). *The Militant Kurds*. Praeger.

Global Terrorism Database (GTD). (2024). PKK "Incidents". https://www.start.umd.edu/gtd/search/Results.aspx?chart=overtime&search=PKK

Güner, S. (1997). The Turkish-Syrian War of Attrition: The Water Dispute. *Journal Studies in Conflict & Terrorism*, *20*(1), 105–116.

Güneş, C. (2012). *The Kurdish National Movement in Turkey: From Protest to Resistance*. London and New York: Routledge.

Güneş, C. (2013). *The Kurdish National Movement in Turkey From Protest to Resistance*. Routledge.

Gürcan, M. (2012). Arming Civilians as a Counterterros Strategy: The Case of the Village Guards System in Turkey. *Dynamics of Asymmetric Conflict: Parthways toward Terrorism and Genocide*, 2–22.

Gürcan, M. (2016). Arming Civilians as a Counterterror Strategy: The Case of the Village Guard System in Turkey. *Dynamics of Asymmetric Conflict: Pathways toward terrorism and genocide*, 1–21.

Gürcan, M. (2016, July). The Profile of Kurdistan Freedom Falcons (TAK). *CTC Centinel*, 24–27.

İmset, İ. (1993). *PKK: Ayrılıkçı Şiddetin 20 Yılı (1973–1992)*. Turkish Daily News Yayınları.

Jiyan. (2016). Retrieved from Jiyan: https://jiyan.us/2015/01/22/kurdistan-devrimcileri-ydg-h-kisa-bir-ydg-h-analizi/

Joint. (2010). *3-07.2 Antiterrorism*. U.S. Joint Chief of Staff.

Joint. (2011). *US of Military and Associated Terms*. Department of Defense Dictionary.

Jongerden, J., & Akkaya, A. (2012). The Kurdistan Workers Party and a New Left in Turkey: Analyis of the Revolutionary Movement in Turkey tgtough the PKK's Memorial Text on Haki Karer. *European Journal of Turkish Studies, 14*.

Jongerden, M. C. (n.d.). *Nationalisms and Politics in Turkey, PART III: Challenging the State*. Routledge.

Kalkan, D. (2011). *Neden Devrimci Halk Savaşı?* Retrieved from http://guncelyorum-canadil.blogspot.com/2011/05/neden-devrimci-halk-savas.html

Kalkan, D. (2011). Retrieved from http://guncelyorum-canadil.blogspot.com/2011/05/neden-devrimci-halk-savas.html

Karpazlı, E. (2018, January 25). *The Many Names of the PKK*. Retrieved from TRT World. https://www.trtworld.com/turkey/the-many-names-of-the-pkk-14598

Laçiner, S., & Bal, İ. (2004). The Ideological and Historical Roots of the Kurdish Movements in Turkey: Ethnicity, Demography, and Politics. *Nationalism and Ethnic Politics, 10*(3), 473–504.

Marcus, A. (2009). *Blood and Belief: The PKK and the Kurdish Fight for Independence*. NYS Press.

Milliyet. (2015, August 14). *"Bitlis'te PKK Yol Kesip Araç Yaktı*. Retrieved from Milliyet. http://www.milliyet.com.tr/bitlis-te-pkk-yol-kesip-arac-yakti-bitlis-yerelhaber-926066/.

Muhammad. (2018). An Unsitable Theorist? Murray Bookchin and the PKK. *Turkish Studies, 19*(5), 799–817.

Öcalan. (1999). *Declaration on the Democratic Solution of the Kurdish Question, trans. Kurdistan Information Centre*. London: Mespotamian Publishers.

Öcalan. (2011). *Prison Writings: The PKK and the Kurdish Question in the 21st Century, trans. Klaus Happel*. London: Transmedia.

Öcalan, A. (2011). *Prison Writings: The PKK and the Kurdish Question in the 21st Century, trans. Klaus Happel*. London: Transmedia.

Olson, R. (1992). The Kurdish Question in the aftermath of the Gulf War: Geopolitical and Geostrategic Changes in the Middle East. *Third World Quarterly, 13*(3), 475–499.

Orhan, M. (2014). Transborder Violence: the PKK in Turkey, Syria and Iraq. *Dynamics of Asymmetric Conflict*.

Orhan, M. (2016). *Political Violence and Kurdis in Turkey: Fragmentation, Mobilization, Representation and Reportoies*. Routledge.

Özcan, A. K. (2006). *Turkey's Kurds: A Theoretical Analysis of the PKK and Abdullah Ocalan*. Routledge.

Özcan, N. A. (1999). *PKK: İdeolojisi, Tarihi ve Yöntemi*. Ankara: AVSAM.

Özcan, N. A. (2015, January 31). *Ökzüs Mutakabat Nereye?* Retrieved from Milliyet. http://www.milliyet.com.tr/oksuz-mutabakat-nereye-/siyaset/ydetay/2095143/default.htm.

Özdağ, Ü. (2005). *Türkiye'de Düşük Yoğunluklu Çatışma ve PKK*. Üç Ok Press.

Posch, W. (2016, 2). *The New PKK Between Extremism, Political Violence, and Strategic Challenges (Part 1)*. Retrieved from oemz-online. https://www.oemz-online.at/display/ENSPACE/The+new+PKK+Part+1

Romano, D. (2006). *The Kurdish Nationalist Movement, Structural conditions and political opportunities*. Cambridge.

Saeed, S. (2014). *The Kurdish National Movement in Turkey: From the PKK to the KCK*. University of Exeter.

Stansfield, G., & Shareef, M. (2017). *The Kurdish Question Revisited, The Kurdistan Workers' Party (PKK): Radical Democracy and The Right to Self Determination beyond the Nation State*. Oxford.

Suriyegündemi. (2018, March 1). *ABD'nin Silahlandırdığı YPG'nin ATGM Saldırıları*. Retrieved from Suriye Gündemi. http://www.suriyegundemi.com/2018/03/01/abdnin-silahlandirdigi-pkk-ypgnin-atgm-saldirilari-21-28-subat-2018/.

Tank, P. (2005). Analysis: The effects of the Iraq War on the Kurdish issue in Turkey. *Journal Conflict, Security & Development, 5*(1), 69–86.

Ünal, M. (2014). Strategist or Pragmatist: A Challenging Look at Ocalan's Retrospective Classification and Definition of PKK's Strategic Periods Between 1973 and 2012. *Terrorism and Political Violence, 24*, 419–448.

Wine, P. (2015). *The PKK: Coming Down from the Mountains*. Zeed Books.

Yavuz. (2007). Five stages of the construction of Kurdish nationalism in Turkey. *Journal Nationalism and Ethnic Politics, 7*(3), 1–24.

YDG-H Analizi. (2016, February 9). Retrieved from Jiyan. https://jiyan.us/2015/01/22/kurdistan-devrimcileri-ydg-h-kisa-bir-ydg-h-analizi/

Yeğen, M. (1996). The Turkish State Discourse and the Exclusion Of Kurdish Identity. *Middle Eastern Studies, 32*(2), 216–229.

Yeğen, M. (2002). *Devlet söyleminde Kürt sorunu*. İstanbul: İletişim.

Yeğen, M. (2007). Turkish Nationalism and the Kurdish Question. *Ethnic and Racial Studies, 30*(1), 119–151.

Yeğen, M. (2015). *Global Turkey in Europe*. The Kurdish Peace Process in Turkey: Genesis, Evolution and Prospects.

Yeşiltaş, M., & at all. (2019). *PKK'nın Avrupa Yapılanması*. İstanbul: SETA.

Yeşiltaş, M., & Kardaş, T. (2017). Rethinking Kurdish GEopolitical Space: The Politics of Image, Insecurity and Gender. *30*(2-3), 256–282.

Yeşiltaş, M., & Özçelik, N. (2016). *Radikalleşme ve PKK Terörünün Yeni Yüzü*. Ankara: SETA Publishing.

Yeşiltaş, M., & Özçelik, N. (2018). *When Strategy Collapses: The PKK Urban Terrorsit Campaing*. Ankara: SETA Publishing.

46

THE SYRIAN MUSLIM BROTHERHOOD (SMB)

Noureddin Mahmoud Zaamout

INTRODUCTION

Since it was created in 1945, the Syrian Muslim Brotherhood (SMB) has played a critical role in Syrian politics. The organisation was created by Mustafa al-Sibai as an offshoot of the Muslim Brotherhood (MB) movement in Egypt but took on a unique character of its own. It started off as an organisation that primarily provided social and community services within existing political institutions but developed into a Jihadi movement that militarily challenged the Syrian state in the 1970s and 1980s. This chapter examines the SMB, analysing its history, development, and ideological transformation. It will be divided into four sections: The first section will discuss this chapter's conceptual framework, drawing on the distinction Asef Bayat articulates between Islamist and post-Islamist ideologies. I will demonstrate in the second and third sections how the SMB was founded on post-Islamist principles but transformed in the 1970s and 1980s to take on a militant Islamist Jihadi agenda. I will show in the fourth and fifth sections how the SMB has tried to rebrand itself as a post-Islamist organisation after being forced into exile since the 1980s. I argue that this re-branding has largely been undermined by the organisation's continued support of Islamist movements in the context of the current Syrian crisis.

CONCEPTUALISING THE SMB: ISLAMISM AND POST-ISLAMISM

Asef Bayat (2013: 4) draws an analytical distinction between Islamist ideologies that seek to create "some kind of an Islamic order—a religious state, Shari'a law, and moral codes in Muslim societies and communities", and post-Islamist ideologies that transcend such Islamist dichotomies. Islamism emerged in a "combative conversation" against the European discourse of modernity (Dabashi, 2012). It has been prompted by the crisis of the post-colonial politics of despair and authoritarianism. It seeks to enforce top-down social, political, and economic systems that derive from specific interpretations of Islamic Shari'a (Bayat, 2013). This should not suggest that all Islamist groups are the same. While they may all ascribe to the same goal of creating an Islamic system of governance, they differ in terms of how they envision their project. In the context of the current Syrian crisis, there are many Islamist groups operating on the ground, driven by competing and conflicting projects (Zaamout, 2017). In contrast to Islamism, post-Islamism is rooted in a "conscious attempt to conceptualise and strategize the rationale and modalities of transcending Islamism in social, political, and intellectual domains" (Bayat, 2013: 8). Yet, in "this sense, post-Islamism is neither anti-Islamic nor un-Islamic nor secular. Rather, it represents an endeavour to fuse religiosity and rights, faith and freedom, Islam and liberty" (2013). While this framework allows for a useful analytical distinction to be drawn between different Islamic ideologies, it seems to suggest that organisations, groups, and parties advocating for political Islam undergo a paradigm shift from reactionary Islamism towards post-Islamism (Pierret, 2013). Thomas Pierret (2013) argues that in the case of Syria, the SMB developed in opposition to this articulation: when the SMB was created, its ideology was clearly rooted in post-Islamist beliefs but moved towards an Islamist trend in the 1970s and 1980s.

THE EARLY YEARS (1945–1969)

The SMB started off as a post-Islamist organisation that sought, in the words of its founder Mustafa al-Sibai, to bring Islamic legislation and the existing political system closer together (Pierret, 2013). Unlike Islamist ideologies that seek to establish an Islamic system of governance, the SMB, during its early years, advanced a reformist agenda by

DOI: 10.4324/9780429426063-53

working within the scope of existing political institutions and structures. It sought to do so through involvement at the grassroot levels, providing social services, as well as participating in democratic parliamentary politics (Ramírez Díaz, 2018).

The founder of the SMB, Mustafa al-Sibai, was born in 1915 in the city of Homs to a middle-class family (Rabil, 2012). He started religious education at a young age, and by the 1930s, he had travelled to Egypt to pursue Islamic studies at al-Azhar University. In Egypt, he befriended Hasan al-Banna, the founder of the MB, and was influenced by his ideas (Rubin, 2010). When he returned to Syria in the early 1940s, he actively sought to unite the different Islamic parties and organisations that operated across the country at that time (Pierret, 2013). In 1945, after years of consultation and discussion with key thinkers, theologians, and figures in Syria, the SMB was formally formed under al-Sibai's leadership. Under his leadership, the SMB pursued "bottom-up Islamisation", providing social, medical, and education services across Syria, primarily in smaller towns and villages (2013). The organisation also sought to spread public awareness and pursue Islamic reform. However, the movement did play a role in parliamentary politics. It created the Islamic National Front Party, which competed in parliamentary politics and was relatively successful. Al-Sibai himself, in addition to his role as a professor at Damascus University, was successfully elected to serve as a Member of Parliament (2013). In 1961, the SMB and its allies "achieved their best electoral result ever by obtaining 8.7% of parliamentary seats" (2013: 325).

In 1949, the SMB issued its formal programme, stressing its commitment to abide by the "limits of the constitution" in order to preserve "the republican system", and "civil rights" (Pierret, 2013; 325). The document stresses that the "people have the right to choose their representatives through free and fair elections and should be recognised as the supreme authority" (2013: 326). This declaration is consistent with al-Sibai's broader discourse on the role the SMB should play in society. More specifically, in his book, *Lessons in the Proselytising of the Muslim Brotherhood*, al-Sibai emphasised that the goals of the SMB are confined to combating the impact of colonialism, putting an end to all forms of injustice against workers and farmers, and reforming and democratising Syria's political system (Al-Dallal, 2006). He adds that the SMB also plays an important grassroots role, providing social services and creating schools, scout camps, and 'fatwa' centres across Syria. Al-Sibai (Al-Dallal, 2006) stresses that the reforms the SMB is calling for are predicated on working through existing political institutions. He writes that "in short, we do not want to overthrow our current laws. We want to bridge the gap between them and theories of Islam that are compatible with the spirit of this era in order to bring them closer together in matters of civil legislation" (2006: 11). The "ideological flexibility of the pre-1963 Syrian Muslim Brothers also manifested itself through their vocal embrace of one of the most fashionable ideologies of that time, that is, socialism" (Pierret, 2013: 325). In his book *The Socialism of Islam (2012)*, al-Sibai (2012) sought to reconcile the relationship between "Islam" and "socialism", demonstrating that Islam is shaped by socialist tendencies. He calls for reforming Syria's economic system in order to mitigate the impact of class struggle and reconcile the relationship between the rich and poor (2012). He critiques both communist and capitalist projects, stressing that, unlike these approaches, Islam presents a balanced and moderate approach that reconciles issues of class politics and capital accumulation.

TOWARDS POLITICAL JIHAD (1970–1982)

In the 1960s and 1970s, a number of key developments took place that radically transformed the political environment in Syria. In 1961, secessionist forces carried out a coup that put an end to Syria's short-lived union with Egypt[1]. (Yassin-Kasseb and Al-Shami, 2016). The post-coup political process was relatively democratic but only lasted for two years. In 1963, in the name of Arab nationalism, the Ba'ath Party ascended to power in a military coup led by a number of officers in the Syrian military, most notably Salah Jadid and Hafez al-Assad (Devlin, 1991). The new regime cracked down on the opposition in hopes of monopolising power. However, after the Arab defeat against Israel in 1967 and the occupation of the Syrian Golan Heights, the West Bank, Gaza, and Sinai, the legitimacy of the Ba'ath party was seriously undermined. As popular unrest grew, in 1970, Hafez al-Assad seized power in a military coup in the name of combating corruption, stagnation, and authoritarianism (Phillips, 2013; Wedeen, 2015). However, Assad's policies were more authoritarian compared to those of all his predecessors since the country gained independence. Determined to cement his control over Syria, Assad centralised power, assigned key positions to trusted loyalists, and expanded the role of the state's oppressive and coercive apparatus. The Ba'ath Party "was transformed and restructured to fit into the authoritarian format of Assad's system, causing it to lose its avant-garde character and become an instrument for generating mass support and political control" (George, 2003: 70). By the mid-1970s, the regime grew increasingly authoritarian; it implemented a complex system of public surveillance and systemically targeted opposition groups (Buchs, 2009). Anyone who spoke against the regime became a target of prosecution. The SMB was targeted by the Hafez al-Assad regime, given that it had been vocal in declaring its opposition to the Ba'athist coups (Lefèvre, 2013). Over the years, tensions grew as the Syrian state began to antagonise Islamists by passing regulations constraining their freedoms as well as purging those who were deemed threats. The SMB began to take on a more active political role, challenging its policies and mandate. Furthermore, Assad's secular discourse garnered suspicion from the SMB, which opposed what they saw as the regime's attempt to draw a systemic separation between religion and politics (Lia, 2016).

As the government crackdown expanded, the SMB found itself in a difficult position, divided between those who were in favour of responding to violence with violence and those who called for peaceful dialogue out of this crisis. By the early to mid-1970s, conservative Islamist thought had begun to gain traction within the ranks of the SMB. Inspired by the work of Sayyid Qutub, emerging voices began to challenge the SMB's founding message, calling for an armed jihad against the Syrian regime (Lia, 2016). Most significantly, in 1975, Marwan Hadid established the Fighting Vanguard, which sought to take on the regime directly through military force. Hadid tried to convince the SMB to support his struggle, but they refused to do so. He accused the organisation of treachery and of aligning with the infidel Allawi regime. He told the SMB elites that "what I really fear is that, if God's servants take on the fight against His enemies, you will sit and watch instead of fighting … by ignoring God's command and abandoning your mujahidin brothers", the SMB would go to hell (Ramírez Díaz, 2018: 52). He described himself as God's agent on earth", stressing that his goal was to establish "the government of Islam" in Syria, insisting that "we will not settle for anything else" (Aljazeera, 2016). He also affirmed that "if the Muslim Brothers cast me out through the door, I will get back inside through the window and pull them into jihad by force" (Lia, 2016). By the late 1970s, Haddid's armed group had successfully attracted many SMB members and began to carry out assassinations against government officials (Ramírez Díaz, 2018: 52–53). The SMB struggled to remain unified, as it was apparent that the younger members of the organisation were shifting towards a jihadi path. Ultimately, the SMB disintegrated into two distinct branches: the first, which was led by Issam al-Attar (1927–), was based in Damascus, and the second, led by Adnan Saad al-Din (1929–2010), was based in Hama and Aleppo. Both branches opposed the regime, but in fundamentally different ways: the first was in favour of peaceful change, while the latter favoured a violent route. Eventually, the conservative Hamas-based branch was able to garner the most support, pushing the SMB towards jihadism (2016).

In 1979, Haddid's Vanguard entered the Artillery School in Aleppo and massacred all Allawi officers. The Syrian regime accused the SMB of carrying out this massacre, an accusation the SMB swiftly denied (Ramírez Díaz, 2018). In retaliation, the regime launched a wide-scale crackdown on the SMB, arresting, torturing, and executing thousands who were suspected of working with the SMB (Lia, 2016). In the same year, the regime of Assad introduced Law 49, which "imposed a death penalty on anyone found to be a member of the SMB" (2016: 551). This paved the way for a series of large-scale massacres throughout the country. Among the most prominent was the Tadmur (Palmyra) prison massacre, where regime forces tortured and killed thousands of prisoners. The regime employed a system of collective violence "involving not only family members of suspects but entire city quarters and towns" (2016: 554).

In 1980, the SMB issued the *Manifesto and Programme of the Islamic Revolution* (Lia, 2016). This was a call for an armed uprising, a jihad, against the regime of Hafez al-Assad. It was the declaration of war the regime needed to justify a large-scale operation against the SMB. By 1981, the SMB and the Islamic Vanguard had started to work closely together in combating the regime (Ramírez Díaz, 2018). At the same time, the instability drove tens of thousands of people across the country to the streets to protest for change. The SMB capitalised on this and tried to steer the uprisings in its direction. The Syrian regime stepped up its offensive in 1982 after it was driven out of the city of Hama by SMB militants (Lefèvre, 2013). Led by Hafez al-Assad's brother, Rifaat al-Assad, the Syrian army deployed 6000–8000 soldiers equipped with over 100 tanks and heavy artillery to take back the city. Hama was besieged and barraged with heavy fire for weeks, which resulted in the deaths of tens of thousands. After a period of prolonged bombardment, regime forces retook the city. The Hama massacre signalled the end of the SMB militancy against the regime. Assad, by the end of 1982, had emerged emboldened and more powerful than at any other time. He successfully drove the SMB members into exile, putting an end to the organisation's 40-year history in Syria. As evident, the SMB abandoned its post-Islamist agenda and sought to take on the regime by force. The goal was to overthrow the regime and establish an Islamic system of governance. This was an exclusionary project, predicated on the demonisation of non-Sunni minorities.

THE SMB IN EXILE (1983–2011)

The experience of exile has had a detrimental impact on the SMB. Scattered all over the world, the organisation was on life support, struggling to envision its post-Hama future. It was plagued with internal disputes and struggles for power (Lefèvre, 2015). It came under heavy criticism from many who saw that the organisation compromised its founding principles by pursuing a violent route and hijacking the 1982 uprisings. By opting for a military route, the SMB gave the regime a reason to engage in a wide-scale, systemic crackdown on opposition. In exile, the SMB tried to reorganise itself, joining a number of anti-government coalitions, such as the National Alliance for the Liberation of Syria, with other exiled political parties and movements. In 1996, Ali Sadreddine al-Bayanouni became the leader of SMB. Hailed as a moderate, Al-Bayanouni sought to revive the party along the principles it was founded upon (Ramírez Díaz, 2018). He engaged in secret negotiations with the regime, demanding the release of all SMB prisoners. He also demanded the regime allow exiled Syrians the right to return home. The regime refused his demands but did release hundreds of prisoners from 1996–2000. In 2004, under Al-Bayanouni's leadership, the SMB published a document titled "The Political Project for Future Syria," outlining the organisation's commitment to the establishment of a plural and democratic Syrian state that respects the rule of law and the separation of power (Syrian Muslim Brotherhood, 2004). It stresses the SMB's commitment to human rights and fair and free elections. It called for a Syrian state that "recognises the equality of all Syrians, regardless of their religion, on the basis of the principles of citizenship" (2004). This was an important document that sought to modernise the SMB and make it more compatible with democratic governance. This was a pragmatic attempt to rebrand the organisation in order to legitimise any possible future involvement in Syrian politics.

THE SMB AND THE CURRENT SYRIAN CRISIS (2011–ONGOING)

The Syrian regime's decades-long violent suppression of the SMB has kept those associated with the SMB outside the country. The organisation, which previously had grassroots links in Syria, was violently purged and systemically uprooted from Syrian society. The Syrian regime remained vocal in its opposition, presenting the SMB through everyday propaganda as dangerous to Syrians and Syria. Since the beginning of the crisis, Assad has quickly moved to accuse the SMB of instigating instability in Syria. The regime refused to acknowledge that a peaceful uprising was occurring and opted to employ violence to suppress dissent (Achcar, 2013; 2016). Assad insisted that Syria was facing a global 'Zionist-Western' conspiracy, carried out by traitorous Arab regimes through their Islamist agents, such as the SMB (Wieland, 2014). Under the pretence of combating terrorism, the regime destroyed cities, towns, and villages, killing hundreds of thousands of innocent civilians. However, as I will demonstrate, the role of the SMB in Syria is far more limited than what the regime claims. As an outsider to Syria, the organisation sought to capitalise on the ongoing crisis by first supporting the peaceful uprisings and later by funding or supporting armed militant groups.

Having been exiled for over 30 years, the SMB did not have popular support or networks in Syria by the time the current crisis broke out in 2011. The Syrian crisis provided the opportunity for the SMB to return to Syria from exile. Hence, the SMB immediately supported the peaceful uprising in the early stages of the crisis and played a critical role in forming the Syrian National Council, a coalition of Syrian opposition groups (Lefèvre, 2015). Around the same time the crisis began, the SMB had a change in leadership. Ali Sadreddine Al-Bayanouni was succeeded by Mohammad Riad al-Shaqfeh, who was a member of the old Conservative Hama branch. Al-Shaqfeh began to push the organisation towards supporting armed militancy in Syria during the latter part of the crisis, when it was clear that Syria had plunged into a geopolitical proxy war. The SMB first supported the Free Syrian Army (FSA). The FSA was created by defectors from the Syrian army in 2011, led by Reid al-Assad and Hussain Harmoosh. The FSA was of course "an umbrella term"; it "was never a unified army, but a collection of militias, some mobile, most local and defensive", unified by the goal of "destroying the regime and establishing a democratic state" (Yassin-Kasseb and Al-Shami, 2016: 382). Initially, such militias confined their activities to protecting protesters from regime violence, but later they began to take on a more offensive form. It is worth mentioning that early army defectors who joined the FSA were not ideologically driven. Their defections came as a response to the regime's policies. The SMB's support for the FSA consisted primarily of financial and military equipment (Oweis, 2012). The SMB also assisted in forming armed units that operated under the umbrella of the FSA (Blanga, 2017).

By late 2012, the FSA as a military opposition began to lose ground, given its failure to act as one unified army. A number of new Islamist groups on the ground soon took its place. The SMB under al-Shaqfeh's leadership tried to expand the SMB's sphere of influence on the ground in Syria by funding and arming Islamist factions (Lefèvre, 2015). By late 2012, the SMB began to take on a more active role on the ground, creating several guerrilla factions under the umbrella of the Revolution Shields Commission and supporting Faylaq al-Sham, a coalition consisting of over a dozen groups that merged together in 2014 (Lefèvre and Yassir, 2014). In 2015, the SMB issued a statement stressing that "defensive jihad is an individual duty for everyone capable of carrying weapons, in light of the outright occupation of our country by the forces of evil" (Ramírez Díaz, 2018: 113). In a recorded statement that was posted on the SMB's website but later taken down, al-Shaqfeh claimed that "the SMB will continue their jihad side by side with the rest of the Syrian people", in order for Syria to return to the time before the Assad regime, when it was "the homeland of every citizen, with no marginalisation or exclusion" (2013).

The SMB has refused to acknowledge its role in supporting armed militancy. More specifically, the organisation's leader, al-Shaqfeh, refuted these allegations, saying, "How can we own any brigades after thirty years in exile" (Ramírez Díaz, 2018: 114). He adds, "Some Islamist brigades contacted us for coordination purposes before their formal announcement, and the reason why they are more prone to the SMB is because we have been unfairly treated and they feel empathy towards us" (2018). However, his comments reveal that the group has been involved in funding different factions operating on the ground, which undermines the organisation's attempt to rebrand itself as a democratic 'post-Islamist' organisation. As Lund (2013) nicely summarises, "while some activity has resumed inside Syria, most of the ageing [SMB] cadre remains on the outside, pleading and scheming for foreign intervention in the hope that it may still be brought to power by the grace of, if not God, then the United States."

Mohammed Hikmat Waleed succeeded al-Shaqfeh as the SMB's leader in 2014. Waleed is the first head of the SMB from the Syrian province of Latakia.[2] Waleed reiterated that the SMB is not to blame for the militarisation of the crisis, insisting that the regime's violence has pushed people towards military means to protect themselves. He emphasised the SMB's continued commitment to oppose the Assad regime and support the struggle of the Syrian people. His approach parallels that of Al-Bayanouni al-Shaqfeh, and the Syrian regime has been able to re-assert its control over large parts of Syria. Many of the rebel groups that were supported by the SMB have been dismantled, and the role of the SMB in Syria is consequently on the decline. Today, the SMB continues to play an active role in the Syrian National Council (SNC), which is a coalition consisting of a variety of opposition groups that oppose the regime of President Assad and was founded in 2011. As the regime tightens its grip on the country, the SMB has supported Turkish military involvement in Syria, a position that has been condemned by Kurdish groups.

CONCLUSION

This chapter has discussed the origins, history, and development of the SMB. The organisation was founded in 1945 by Mustafa al-Sibai as an offshoot of the MB movement in Egypt. Initially, it played a limited role in politics, but considering the crisis of Arab nationalism in the 1960s and 1970s, coupled with the Syrian regime's increasing repressiveness in the 1970s, the SMB began to play a more active political role. In the 1980s, it militarily confronted the regime but was ultimately crushed and forced into exile. In the current crisis (2011–), the SMB has been able to play a greater role in the contemporary crisis through the support of a variety of Islamist organisations operating in the country. This chapter has demonstrated that the SMB has transformed ideologically from post-Islamist to Islamist tendencies. During its early years, the SMB sought to work within the established political system, emphasising its commitment to a democratic and plural Syria. The Syrian regime's violent crackdown on opposition in the 1970s has allowed for the emergence of conservative voices within the SMB, who were successful in steering the organisation towards violent military confrontation with the regime. The post-Islamist principles that were laid down by Sibai were replaced with Islamist ideas that sought to confront the Syrian regime through violence. The SMB's current attempt to rebrand itself as a "post-Islamist" organisation is undermined by its continued support of Islamist movements operating on the ground in the context of the contemporary crisis.

Notes

1 Between 1958 and 1961, Syria and Egypt united, forging the United Arab Republic under the presidency of Gamal Gamal Abdel Nasser.

2 Most of the SMB's leadership over the last four decades was from Aleppo and Hama.

References

Achcar, G. (2013). *The People Want: A Radical Exploration of the Arab Uprising*. Redwood City: Stanford University Press.

Achcar, G. (2016). *Morbid Symptoms: Relapse in the Arab Uprising*. Redwood City: Stanford University Press.

Al-Dallal, A. A. S. I. (2006). *Islamist and Democrats in Syria* [Translated from Arabic]. Cairo: Madbolui Library.

Aljazeera Arabic. (2016, September 9). "I'm God's Agent on Earth" [Translated from Arabic]. *Aljazeera*. Available at: shorturl.at/jopsI

Al-Sibai, M. (2012). *Socialism in Islam* [Translated from Arabic]. Alexandria, Egypt: General Authority for Culture Palaces.

Bayat, A. (2013). "Post-Islamism at Large." In A. Bayat (Ed.), *Post-Islamism: The Many Faces of Political Islam*. (pp. 3–34). New York: Oxford University Press.

Blanga, Y. U. (2017). The Role of the Muslim Brotherhood in the Syrian Civil War. *The Middle East Policy Center*, XXIV.

Buchs, A. (2009). The Resilience of Authoritarian Rule in Syria under Hafez and Bashar Al-Asad. *German Institute of Global and Area Studies* (9).

Dabashi, H. (2012). *The Arab Spring: The End of Post-colonialism*. New York: Zed Books.

Devlin, H. (1991). The Baath Party: Rise and Metamorphosis. *American Historical Review*, *96*(5), 1396–1407.

George, A. (2003). *Syria: Neither Bread nor Freedom*. New York: Zed Books.

Lefèvre, R. (2013, September 27). *Saudi Arabia and the Syrian Brotherhood*. Washington D.C., USA: The Middle East Institute. Available at: http://www.mei.edu/content/saudi-arabia-and-syrian-brotherhood

Lefèvre, R. & Yassir, A. (2014, April 14). *The Sham Legion: Syria's Moderate Islamists*. Beirut, Lebanon: Carnegie Middle East Center. Available at: https://carnegie-mec.org/diwan/55344?lang=en

Lefèvre, R. (2013). *Ashes of Hama: The Muslim Brotherhood in Syria*. New York, USA: Oxford University Press.

Lefèvre, R. (2015). *Islamism Within a Civil War: The Syrian Muslim Brotherhood's Struggle for Survival*. Washington, DC: Brookings Institute. Available at: https://www.brookings.edu/wp-content/uploads/2016/07/Syria_Lefevre-FINALE.pdf

Lia, B. (2016). The Islamist Uprising in Syria, 1976–82: The History and Legacy of a Failed Revolt. *British Journal of Middle Eastern Studies*, *43*(4), 541–559.

Lund, A. (2013, September 24). *The Syrian Brotherhood: On the Sidelines*. Washington D.C., USA: The Middle East Institute. Available at: http://www.mei.edu/content/syrian-brotherhood-sidelines

Oweis, K. Y. (2012, May 6). Syria's Muslim Brotherhood Rise from the Ashes. *Reuters*. Available at: https://www.reuters.com/article/us-syria-brotherhretainhood/syrias-muslim-brotherhood-rise-from-the-ashes-idUSBRE84504R20120506

Phillips, C. (2013). *Everyday Arab Identity: The Daily Reproduction of the Arab World*. Abingdon: Routledge.

Pierret, T. (2013). Syria's Unusual "Islamic Trend." In A. Bayat (Ed.), *Post-Islamism: The Many Faces of Political Islam*. New York: Oxford University Press.

Rabil, R. G. (2012). "The Syrian Muslim Brotherhood." In B. Rubin (Ed.), *The Muslim Brotherhood: The Middle East in Focus*. (pp. 7–18). New York: Palgrave Macmillan.

Ramírez Díaz, N. (2018). *The Muslim Brotherhood in Syria: The Democratic Option of Islamism*. London, UK: Routledge, Taylor & Francis Group.

Rubin, B. (2010). *The Muslim Brotherhood: The Organization and Policies of a Global Islamist Movement*. New York: Palgrave Macmillan.

Syrian Muslim Brotherhood. (2004). "The Political Project for Future Syria." Available at: http://www.ikhwanweb.com/tagBView.php?id=Syrian%20Muslim%20Brotherhood

Wedeen, L. (2015). *Ambiguities of Domination: Politics, Rhetoric, and Symbols in Contemporary Syria*. 2nd Edition. Chicago: University of Chicago Press.

Wieland, C. (2014). "Asad's Decade of Lost Chances." In C. Wieland et al. (Eds.), *The Syrian Uprising*. Scotland, UK: University of St. Andrews Centre for Syrian Studies.

Yassin-Kasseb, R., & Al-Shami, L. (2016). *Burning Country: Syrians in Revolution and War*. London, UK: Pluto Press.

Zaamout, N. M. (2017). "Cosmopolitanism in Retreat? The Crisis of Syrian Identity in Post-Arab Spring." Unpublished master's thesis, University of Alberta, Department of Political Science.

47

HEZBOLLAH

Mariam Farida

INTRODUCTION

The method of conflict used by insurgency groups is ultimately determined by circumstances rather than decision, and they attempt to adopt a range of different strategies of struggle at simultaneously whenever it is practicable. Hezbollah, which was established in 1982 – more than 35 years ago – presents itself as a militant resistance and insurgency organisation, as shown by its ongoing shift towards political representation and legitimacy in Lebanon and growing influence as a key player in regional Middle Eastern relations. However, Hezbollah continues to pose a threat to international interests, including those of the United States, due to its ongoing transformation from a domestic resistance group to a regional non-state actor, its close ties to Iran, and its support for local actors in Iraq, Syria, and Palestine.

CURRENT CHALLENGES

In 2023, Hezbollah encountered setbacks: the UK and US designated a Hezbollah supporter, while Lebanon filed charges against seven of the group's members. The military court in Lebanon has brought charges against seven Hezbollah members for their involvement in an attack that killed a United Nations peacekeeper. On December 14, 2022, a group of Hezbollah fighters opened fire on a UN Interim Force in Lebanon (UNIFIL) vehicle near the hamlet of al-Aqbiya in southern Lebanon, killing Irish Private Sean Rooney, 23, and injuring three other soldiers. The group claimed the man was not one of its members. In order to aid the Lebanese military in expanding its control into the southern part of the country, UN soldiers were stationed along the Israeli border (Al Jazeera, January 5, 2023). The UK has added Nazem Ahmad, a diamond and art trader who backs Hezbollah, to a Treasury sanctions list. With works by Pablo Picasso, Antony Gormley, and Andy Warhol among his collection, Ahmad was charged in the US with money laundering for Hezbollah. The US Treasury had previously placed him on a sanctions list. Ahmad and eight other defendants, including his son and daughter, were accused by the New York court of violating laws by buying and selling works of art and jewellery valued at US$160 million since 2019 (The Guardian, April 18, 2023).

The Iranian Foreign Minister's visit to Lebanon, when he committed Iranian assistance for the building of a Lebanon-wide electrical supply, was a welcome development. Foreign Minister Hossein Amirabdollahian of Iran paid a visit to Lebanon's border with Israel on Friday and endorsed the Lebanese militant Hezbollah group in its conflict with their shared foe, Israel. Amirabdollahian spoke with important figures and offered Tehran's willingness to assist in the construction of power plants in an effort to try to resolve Lebanon's ongoing electrical problem. An economic crisis has resulted from the electrical problem. Three-quarters of Lebanon's 6 million residents, including 1 million Syrian refugees, are now living in poverty as a result of the economic crisis, which broke out in October 2019.

Overview: History of How and Why the Group or Movement Formed

Hezbollah, or the Party of God, emerged as an armed militia to liberate Lebanon's southern regions from Israeli occupation and to improve Shi'ite standing in Lebanon. The Israeli invasion and subsequent occupation of Lebanon in 1982, ostensibly to control members of the Palestine Liberation Organisation (PLO) who had settled in Lebanon and were carrying out attacks against Israel (Norton, 2007), saw Israeli aggression on a grand scale in southern Lebanon, where most of the Shi'ite population resided. In response to the aggression, Iran offered its support to the emerging Shi'ite groups that sought to resist the occupying forces but also recognised the need to establish a well-organised resistance structure. The development of these Islamic groups in Lebanon followed the Islamic revolution in Iran in 1979, where the cooperation between Lebanese Shi'ites and Iran goes back to the 17th century (Norton, 2007,

DOI: 10.4324/9780429426063-54

pp. 475–491). Prior to Imam Ruhollah Khomeini's rise to power in Iran, there were Shi'ite groups already politically active in Lebanon, such as the *Committee of Ulema of the Bekaa*, Islamic Committees, and the Lebanese branch of the Iraqi Shi'ite *Al-Dawa Party* (Al-Agha, 2011, pp. 54–56).

The grounding principles for the creation of Hezbollah were based on resistance against the Israeli occupation and the supremacy of the Supreme Guide (Ayatollah Khomeini at the time) as the descendant of the Prophet and his Imams[1]. As Qassem (2004, pp. 11–40) explained, Shi'ite leaders agreed that Islam would be the guiding principle for this party and that it would follow Khomeini's model of Welayet al-Faqih.

A committee of nine Shi'ite leaders, comprising three senior representatives each from the cells founded in 1982 by the *Committee of Ulema of the Bekaa*, the Islamic Committees, and *Islamic AMAL (Afwaj al-Mouqawma Al-Lubnaniyya)*, was responsible for submitting the proposal to create an organised resistance movement for approval by the Supreme Guide. The creation of that movement came about as a response to the Israeli occupation of southern Lebanon. At this time, there was no single authoritative Shi'ite group, but rather Shi'ite groups and authorities scattered across Lebanon. After receiving the blessing of Ayatollah Khomeini, "the different cells dissolved to form a single federating party that took the name Hezbollah" (Qassem, 2004, p. 32). The party subsequently positioned itself as the only group capable of fighting the ongoing threat to Lebanon posed by Israel and initially did not need to use propaganda to attract members. Given that its target and mission were widely recognised as being to free Lebanese lands from foreign occupation, this was enough to attract large numbers of young Shi'ites to join the organisation. Indeed, recruitment during the 1980s was relatively simple since the country was at war. Nevertheless, Hezbollah's leaders were careful to choose the 'right' people who were driven by their commitment and who had a comprehensive understanding of the mission, in addition to the *Welayet al-Faqih (Mandate of the Jurist) doctrine.*[2]

The Party's dualistic ideology – one nationalistic and the other "transnationally Islamist" – facilitated the emergence of Hezbollah from concurrent transnational, regional, and domestic socio-political dynamics (Dionigi, 2014, p. 97). The complexity of Hezbollah's ideology and identity is articulated in the statement by Levitt (2014): "If you think Hezbollah is a terrorist group only, you are mistaken, and if you think Hezbollah is a resistance group only, you are also mistaken; Hezbollah is all of those; it is a hybrid movement".

Indeed, the emergence of Hezbollah and the unity of its members are tied to the Shi'ite sect (Traboulsi, 2007, pp. 110–130) and the socio-political context of Lebanon during the latter half of the 20th century. Since gaining independence from the French Mandate in 1943, Lebanon has operated within the framework of 'confessionalism', a unique political system that entails a power-sharing arrangement based on religious communities. Yet this attempt at power sharing has not spared the country from civil conflict arising from religious differences combined with economic and political instability. Many Lebanese people endure political and social segregation, and Lebanese Shi'ite communities, particularly those in southern Lebanon and the Bekaa areas, experience great poverty relative to other communities. With the emergence of Hezbollah, Lebanon's Shi'a have sought to reassert themselves, including at the political level.

Indeed, the marginalisation of Shi'ites in Lebanon at this time manifests as social neglect and political underrepresentation (Saad-Ghorayeb, 2002, pp. 35–80). In turn, the Shi'ite community's faith and belief in the guiding mission of Hezbollah were key elements in its capacity to strengthen its position as a legitimate resistance movement and, subsequently, as a legitimate actor in Lebanese politics. As such, the uniqueness of the Party is arguably reflected in its ability to successfully operate across multiple domains, namely, the civilian (*da'wa*) context of social welfare and religious education; as a military-resistance organisation (*jihad*); and as a key player in the Lebanese political system (Azani, 2013, pp. 899–900).

Key Personnel and Structure

Command Structure

The hierarchical structure of Hezbollah reflects a traditional arrangement, namely, a chain of command from top to bottom. Interestingly, McAllister and Schmid (2011) have asserted that hierarchical structure means that Hezbollah is "more adept at providing the social and political goods" (p. 242) associated with success. The decision-making processes, however, remain a controversial and ambiguous aspect of the party's structure. Hamzeh (2004), for example, has asserted that the decision-making authority is divided between the Shura council and other legislative bodies, whereas Al-Agha (2013) has described the role of several executive and legislative bodies in the Party's structure.

Following Hamzeh (2004, pp. 44–79), Hezbollah has two major decision-making bodies: the Shura Council and the Shura al-Qarar. The Secretary-General is in charge of the Shura Council, and the Wali el-Faqih (Supreme Jurist) is responsible for his legitimacy. The Shura Council deals with matters relating to legislation and administration, whereas the Shura al-Qarar deals with matters pertaining to politics. The authority of the two councils is subordinated, however, to the Secretary-General, who has the distinctive and exclusive capacity for taklif shari (religious verdict) (Hamzeh, 2004, pp. 44–79).

Given his role as the head of both legislative bodies, the Secretary-General is thus in a position to guide the development of the Party's hard and soft power capabilities to the extent that it could pursue its goals and objectives more independently (Swanson, 2008, pp. 26–28). Of critical importance to this outcome has been the ability of Nasrallah, as Secretary-General, to facilitate the transition of Hezbollah's primary focus away from a staunchly pan-

Islamic perspective to a more Lebanon-centric perspective (Malthaner, 2011, pp. 97–99).

Moreover, little explanation has been offered to clarify the decision-making process between Hezbollah and Iran. Evidence based on analysis of Hezbollah and leading Shi'ite clerics, particularly Sheikh Qassem, clearly demonstrates that major political decisions, especially on war and peace, remain in the hands of the Wali al-Faqih. However, Hezbollah's actions that led to war with Israel in 2006 do not seem to have been coordinated with Iran. This may imply that the Shura Council, the top legislative body in the party's hierarchical structure, which is under the control of Hezbollah's religious members, exercises a lot of decision-making authority.

Leadership

Sayyid Hassan Nasrallah was appointed Hezbollah Secretary-General in 1992, a position of authority. Nasrallah is referred to as "the central actor" (p. 7) in the Party's decision-making and communication methods by Khatib et al. (2014), with authority that represents a complex interplay between politics and religion. This is demonstrated by his leadership decisions to issue religious orders, deliver religious sermons (like the 10-day Ashoura commemoration), and make political decisions, like the 2008 request for Hezbollah ministers to resign from the Cabinet led by then-Lebanese Prime Minister Fouad Siniora in response to a protest against the creation of the Special Tribunal for Lebanon (Avon and Katchadourian, 2012). Furthermore, Nasrallah leverages his status as a religious figurehead and a Sayyid – a relative of the Prophet – to ensure that his rulings are unassailable (Khatib et al., 2014).

Nasrallah is acknowledged for his astute pragmatism when calculating the manner of the party's involvement in conflicts and its efforts to overcome political obstacles (Khatib, 2013). Indeed, his pragmatism and his potential to appeal to diverse groups have strengthened his prestige as both a political leader and a religious figure (Hamzeh, 2004). It is well documented that the positive impact of Nasrallah's leadership on Hezbollah has been his ability to shape the definition and redefinition of Hezbollah's interests in Lebanon and how they can be achieved successfully (Malthaner, 2011; Swanson, 2008). In turn, this has relied on Nasrallah's acute understanding of Islamic principles and applying religious tools such as ijtihad and taklif shari to drive its resistance efforts from a more nationalistic perspective. Moreover, Hezbollah's shift in orientation towards Lebanon "as its frame of reference" (Malthaner, 2011, p. 89) has in many ways necessitated that Nasrallah adopt a pragmatic approach to his decision-making, that is, a case-based moral interpretation of Shari'a to support the Party's political goals.

Nasrallah is also recognised for his ability to bring members of the Sunni and Shia sects together and to enjoy some support among Christian and secularist groups (Swanson, 2008). However, as stated by Malthaner (2011), "Hezbollah's cardinal reference group was first of all the Shiite community" (p. 98). Nonetheless, the Party's ability, led by Nasrallah, to adapt the concept of Islamic jihad in response to military, societal, and political matters provides it with the ideological flexibility and party mechanism to build political support through its responses to regional and domestic politics (Khashan and Moussawi, 2007, p. 1).

Propaganda

The public appearances of Nasrallah and his use of rhetoric and speech style are considered the backbone of the party's ability to forge its connection with Shi'ites. These public events, or his public addresses more broadly, are used purposefully to deliver ideological propaganda as well as to facilitate the use of religion for political manoeuvring (Khatib, 2014, p. 110).

In addition, Hezbollah's media outlet, Al-Ahd newspaper, operates as a propaganda machine to construct the ideology of 'martyrology'. The concept of martyrdom, argues Saade (2015), is both framed within and augmented by Hezbollah's ideology. Saade's assertion echoes the work conducted by Norton (2007), Hamzeh (2004), Khatib (2013), and Harik (2004), which indicates that Hezbollah's cult of martyrdom has assisted the Party in its propaganda against Israel. This ideology underpins the Party's recruitment programme and political activism and has been instrumental in the Party's resistance against Israel forces, domesticating its political mission, and formulating a "society/culture of resistance" (Harb and Leenders, 2005).

Recruitment

Although Hezbollah's recruitment process is considered a key to its success (Blanford, 2011), an investigation of its recruitment processes is made difficult to some degree due to the secretive nature of the organisation. According to Love (2010, 1–36), Hezbollah's distribution of funds and use of facilities for recruitment were initially influenced by the models of recruitment for guerrilla warfare used by Mao Zedong and Che Guevara. During the 1980s, recruitment was relatively simple for Hezbollah since the country was at war. Nevertheless, Hezbollah leaders were careful to choose the 'right' people who were driven by their commitment and who had a comprehensive understanding of the mission, in addition to the Welayet al-Faqih doctrine.

This may have been true of the Party during its initial stages as a guerrilla movement; however, its emergence as an influential political group in Lebanon has forced Hezbollah to change its model of recruitment to meet the respective challenges (Blanford, 2011). Since the early 1990s, the Party has sought to promote an integrated Shi'ite community through a network of social services (Harb and Leenders, 2005, pp. 173–197). As a result, Lebanese Shi'ites started to join in numbers, and the recruitment process took on a more organised but also more secretive form.

However, it is noteworthy that the party, which formerly relied on voluntary recruiting, now uses social media platforms to promote in order to draw fighters. It gives the Party the means to quickly and effectively disseminate important information, such as the formation of new militia groups, and to quickly and effectively access Shi'ite communities in order to rally fighters for the cause (Smyth, 2015). These two outcomes are what have sparked the shift towards the use of social media for recruitment. Online platforms are also favoured due to their ability to communicate directly with the target audience, the relative anonymity they provide the party low costs and the capacity to quickly clone websites in the event that recruiting activities are interrupted (Smyth, 2015, p. 28).

For instance, Hezbollah's participation in the seemingly endless conflict in Syria has forced it to institute unprecedented efforts to recruit Shi'ites to fight in Syria using social media, advertising posters, and phone calls. According to Smyth (2015), the extent of Hezbollah's human loss compelled the Party to broaden its recruitment network in an effort to promote jihad in Syria for "the protection of Sayyida Zainab shrine" (Smyth, 2015, p. 6). Hence, Hezbollah's use of social media platforms has emerged as a key element in its recruitment programme and its capacity to progress its resistance and political agendas. Assessing the success of Hezbollah's strategy to use social media for recruitment is, of course, difficult given the very limited data available on the outcomes of recruitment drives. However, one possible indication of some success for consideration is that, according to the Immigration and Refugee Board of Canada (2015), the Party appears to have turned around the slowdown in the rate of recruitment that emerged around 2010.

Nasrallah acknowledged in May 2013 the involvement of Hezbollah forces in Syria, thus showing that the party's online recruitment efforts were active. Initially launched by Iran in Iran, the Party's Facebook pages, blogs, messaging, etc. featured the Hezbollah symbol alongside an image of the dome of Sayyida Zainab and the statement, 'Zainab, we are all your Abbas' (Levitt, 2014). Moreover, "Hezbollah's [Shi'ite] open and active recruitment techniques" (p. 30) to help mobilise fighters in Lebanon, Iraq, and Syria include poster designs showing the names of Kataib Hezbollah, Liwa Dhulfiqar, and Lebanese Hezbollah attached to the faces of Afghan Shi'ites. This not only demonstrates that an active recruitment programme is underway for these groups but also points to their links to Iran (Smyth, 2015, p. 30).

Organisational Characteristics and Activities

The Hezbollah-Iran Alliance

Hezbollah officials have had to continuously reject assertions that the party is taking orders from Iran. To safeguard the Party's legitimacy as a resistance group, officials maintain that the Party's decision-making is an internal affair and that Iran is only a friend and an ally (Qassem, 2004). Furthermore, they argue that all political factions in Lebanon are aligned with a foreign country (in reference to the March 14 bloc alignment with America, France, and Saudi Arabia) and that there is nothing wrong with having Iran as a close ally (Fadlallah, 2015).

Nonetheless, Iran is an ally that provides significant financial support, with an annual payment from Iran to Hezbollah of between 100 and 300 billion dollars (Coughlin, 2010; Levitt, 2014). Yet, it is also the case that a wide funding network supports Hezbollah's position and ensures its continuity within Lebanese society. Sources of funding also include *zakat* (Islamic alms) and donations from wealthy Lebanese businessmen and women abroad. Through the funds the party receives, it has established a dynamic social programme and manages a nationwide network of social, educational, and charitable programmes. These efforts, in addition to the long struggle against Israel, have helped Hezbollah gain the support of a wide sector of the Lebanese population, specifically but not exclusively the Muslim Shi'ite sect. Hezbollah has also gained recognition among some segments of society as the strongest political force in the country (Khatib, 2014, pp. 105–111).

Commitment to the Welayet al-Faqih Doctrine

Despite the party's portrayal as a hybrid movement (Ali, 2017; Norton, 2007), its adherence to the Welayet al-Faqih doctrine has an impact on its identity. According to Khashan and Moussawi (2007, p. 9), Hezbollah adopted the Faqih doctrine, in which *Welayet al-Faqih* is mandated to support the installation and empowerment of an Islamic government during the time of occupation. However, Hezbollah officials tend to suggest that even though the Party's ideological commitment is to the Wali, the Party's internal decision-making is strictly separated from the Wali's intervention (Fadlallah, 2015). As such, the Wali becomes essential only in global terms such as war, peace, and foreign policy.

Certainly, the adoption of the *Welayet el-Faqih* doctrine has been tailored by the Party to suit the Lebanese domestic context (Hamzeh, 2004, pp. 44–79). Naim Qassem (2004), a founding member of Hezbollah who was appointed Deputy Secretary-General in 1992, emphasised that the party was a "Lebanese political party in which all leaders, officers, and members are Lebanese" (p. 60). The key implication in Qassem's assertion is that even though Hezbollah recognises the authority of the Faqih in making major political decisions, the "detailed follow-up, resolution of disputes, and daily disposition of political, societal, and cultural matters, including resistance to Israeli occupation, default to the Party's command" (2004, p. 62).

While Hezbollah is in favour of the establishment of a state based on Islam, it is also committed to its integration and the integration of its followers into Lebanese society (Hamzeh, 2004). Moreover, the party leaders and spokespeople have continuously affirmed that Hezbollah has no intention of establishing an Islamic state in Lebanon, even if it remains committed to Islam (Hamzeh, 2004). This concept is recurrently promoted in the party's messaging to maintain public support and to ensure it is not positioned as a threat to national security, as it was in 2008 following the clashes on the street between Hezbollah supporters and the supporters of opposing political parties (discussed below). This incident augmented negative sentiment towards the party, and many political factions framed it as Hezbollah trying to establish an Islamic state in Lebanon (Khatib, 2013). In response, Hezbollah reaffirmed in its 2009 manifesto that its goal was to establish multi-confessional leadership that would guarantee equal participation of all communities in managing the state (Al-Agha, 2011, pp. 50–65).

Impacts

Hezbollah's Evolution as a Legitimate Player in Lebanese Politics

Arguably, the greatest achievement of Hezbollah has been its transition from a resistance movement to a key actor in Lebanese politics, first joining the Lebanese parliament and then the government. Hezbollah initially consolidated its credibility and legitimacy within Lebanese society by maintaining its focus solely on resistance to Israeli occupation and aggression against Lebanon rather than engaging in violent action related to the Lebanese civil war (1975–1990), as AMAL did. Yet, in 1992, the party declared its intention to participate in the Lebanese parliamentary elections. The rationale for this decision was expressed by Qassem (2010, pp. 271–277) as follows:

> It is now imperative to cooperate with other devoted parties in order to complete the necessary steps towards ... the forging of internal peace on the basis of political concord that is furthest as could be from abominable sectarian biases or narrow confessional discriminations.

The 1992 election results were encouraging for Hezbollah, with the party, along with its non-Shi'ite electoral allies, winning 12 parliamentary seats, including eight Shi'ite seats. This equated to about 10% of all parliamentary seats. Hezbollah also won control of two-thirds of important Shi'ite municipalities, including the Beirut suburbs of Burj el-Barajneh and Ghobeyre.[3] Hezbollah's participation in the elections thus resulted in greater engagement in domestic politics by Shi'ite communities after years of exclusion and established its position in the Lebanese political system.

Hezbollah's entry into the Lebanese political system is generally viewed by scholars as evidence that the party was attempting to transition from a resistance group only to a legitimate political actor to consolidate its integration into Lebanese society (Al-Agha, 2011; Bayat, 2010; Harik, 2004; Levitt, 2014; Saad-Ghorayeb, 2002; Saouli, 2011). As Karagiannis (2009, pp. 369–375) suggested, although the initial success of the party was largely due to the ideological indoctrination of Islam and its commitment to *Wali el-Faqih*, its transition to a political party was vital to its continued success. Notably, research conducted on Hezbollah and its internal operations as a developing party (e.g., Harik, 2004) points to the party's use of pragmatism as a political tool to integrate into the Lebanese political system. Indeed, numerous scholars have suggested that Hezbollah's pragmatism (when adopting the infitah-opening/Lebanonization policy) contributed to its success as a resistance-political party and its capacity to mobilise support (Al-Agha, 2006; 2011; 2013; Saad-Ghorayeb, 2002).

However, when commenting on Hezbollah's decision to participate in the Lebanese parliamentary elections in 1992, scholars such as Norton (2007), Harik (2004), and Hamzeh (2004) argued that the Lebanonization of Hezbollah, that is, its transformation into a political party, would eventually see it converted into a conventional Lebanese political party doomed to internal divisiveness (cited in Hoover, 2007, pp. 46–68).

Hezbollah then continued its change of rhetoric as it became more involved in the political process. During the 1996 election campaign, the party issued its programme to achieve justice and equality for all Lebanese people by building a strong, dignified, and prosperous country (Hamzeh, 2004). This would in turn engage all Lebanese in the construction of a country that has equality of opportunity for all people irrespective of class, duties, or political persuasion (cited in Karagiannis, 2009, p. 374).

Social Services for Shi'ites

The withdrawal of Israeli troops from Lebanon in May 2000 was regarded by Hezbollah and, more broadly, the Lebanese people as a decisive victory (Khatib, 2013). At this time, Hezbollah had won its armed struggle against Israel and was now a Lebanese political party with military credibility, a significant arsenal, and highly trained members (Rabil, 2012, pp. 49–64). The party then turned its attention to improving the standing of the Shi'ite community in Lebanon. Its efforts in this regard were primarily directed towards the provision of social services and utilities (e.g., hospital services, education, sports facilities, water, and electricity) not properly delivered by the Lebanese government (Khatib, 2013). This increased the popularity of the party among Shi'ites living in these communities (Khatib, 2013; Saad-Ghorayeb, 2002). Educational and cultural institutions play a key role in Hezbollah's efforts to coordinate the Islamisation process in Lebanon (Deeb, 2006). As discussed by various authors such as Deeb (2006), Harik (2004), and others, the Islamisation process has played a key role in Hezbollah's efforts to mobilise the Shi'ite community in Lebanon.

Several scholars (e.g., Dionigi, 2014; Karagiannis, 2009) also point to the important role that social circumstances (and in Dionigi's case, international factors) have played in Hizbullah's change of politics from the hard-line Islamist discourse in the 1980s to the more pragmatic and nationalistic tone. Indeed, Karagiannis (2009) stated that "Hizballah is a SMO [Social Movement Organisation] since [...] the group has a number of highly committed members and it aims at political change" (p. 369). Both Dionigi (2014) and

Karagiannis (2009) argue that Hezbollah's objectives and efforts to improve the condition of the Shi'ite community have presented it as a social movement organisation in which the movement constitutes two criteria: mobilising supporters for a common cause and developing political objectives that can change the situation for the collective good (Khatib, 2013).

Hezbollah's Changing Fortunes

However, the fortunes of Hezbollah were not all positive at this time. The car-bombing assassination of Rafic Hariri on February 14, 2005, in the Lebanese capital, Beirut, was a major shock to the Lebanese people and a turning point for Hezbollah in particular. From this point on, major strategic factors changed and domestic challenges were introduced. The blame for the attack was generally directed at Syria, Israel, and America. The assassination was followed by several demonstrations calling for justice and revenge and Syria's withdrawal from Lebanon. The demonstrations, along with international pressure, succeeded in the complete withdrawal of Syria from Lebanon in April 2005. Hariri's assassination was followed by the assassinations of other anti-Syrian politicians and activists. As an ally of Syria, these killings increased the pressure on Hezbollah to disarm and further tested the party's popularity in Lebanon as the public's level of trust towards the party started to fall on suspicion of its role in the assassinations.

The party's socio-political standing was somewhat restored by Israel's attack on Lebanon in 2006 (Zisser, 2009, pp. 1–13), with 87% of Lebanese people supporting Hezbollah's response to the Israeli assault (El-Husseini, 2010, p. 808). Consequently, the war with Israel was a major turning point for Hezbollah and its perceived legitimacy as a political party in Lebanon. Israel's aggressive and disproportionate response to the kidnapping of two Israeli border soldiers by Hezbollah shocked the Lebanese people, the government, and Hezbollah, with the 33-day war resulting in the deaths of almost 1,300 civilians and the destruction of major roads, 48 bridges, and the International Airport (Zisser, 2009, pp. 1–13; Norton, 2007, pp. 475–491). The intensity of the Israeli action led Hezbollah to concede that it had miscalculated (Norton, 2007, pp. 475–491), with Nasrallah revealing in an interview with New TV on August 27, 2006, that if Hezbollah had known or anticipated such a response from Israel, they would not have gone ahead with the operation (Norton, 2007, p. 480).

Despite criticism and a lack of support from the Lebanese government, Hezbollah emerged victorious from the war based on the failure of Israel to achieve its main objective, namely, to destroy Hezbollah (Khatib, 2013; Khatib et al., 2014). During the war, Hezbollah was able to limit the ground attacks by Israeli soldiers. Nonetheless, the 2006 war also created further divisions among the Lebanese people. The war ended with a cease-fire agreement in August 2006, under the implementation of Security Council Resolution 1701, which called for the deployment of 15,000 UN soldiers along the border between southern Lebanon and Israel, creating a critical buffer zone.[4] In addition, opponents of Hezbollah continued to question the party's motives, accusing it of being an agent for Syria and Iran whose only purpose was to preserve their interests and establish an Islamic state (Norton, 2007, pp. 475–491).

Notwithstanding that both the 2006 war and the May 7, 2008 conflict weakened popular support for Hezbollah, they did work to secure Hezbollah's position as a major political influence in the Lebanese government. Hezbollah consolidated its power and policies as it was not only presented as a powerful resistance army but had also won one-third of the vote in the Lebanese government. This meant that the party had increased its negotiation position with the government and was increasingly being acknowledged as a political party within the system of government.

Hezbollah and the Syrian War

The nature of Hezbollah's allegiance to Iran and to the wali has been given new focus following the party's intervention in the Syrian war to possibly safeguard Iran's interests in the region (Levitt, 2014). Prior to the Arab Spring in 2011, Hezbollah had established itself as a prominent political party in Lebanon and the region with a plus-one vote following the Doha Accord. For Hezbollah, the objective of power sharing was thus closer than ever (Levitt, 2014). The Syrian war, however, reflected a rivalry for regional control, with the increased role of Turkey and Qatar as supporters of the Syrian opposition meeting Iranian and Russian support for the Assad regime. In turn, Hezbollah's military intervention in the Syrian conflict had "put it at a crossroads" (Khatib, 2013, p. 107). While the Party continued to strengthen its domestic political position, due in no small part to the failings of its political opponents, Hezbollah's intervention in Syria presented new challenges to its capacity "to act in the domestic Lebanese sphere" (Khatib, 2013, p. 105).

Notably, the Party's position on the uprisings in Bahrain, Libya, Tunisia, and Egypt was clear in support of the revolutions, whereas its attitude towards the Syrian uprising was initially ambiguous. The party restricted its political statements to a call for negotiations and reform, yet as the uprisings took an increasingly violent form, Hezbollah changed course. It participated in the fight alongside the Assad regime against militant opposition groups and later fundamentalist groups. To account for these actions, Nasrallah stated in 2012:

> We are fighting alongside our Syrian brothers, alongside the army and the people and the popular resistance in Damascus and Aleppo and Deir Ezzor and Qusayr and Hasakeh and Idlib, [...] we are present today in many places and we will be present in all the places in Syria that this battle requires.
>
> This is not a threat to the resistance in Lebanon or to one sector of the regime in Syria or the government in Iraq or a group in Yemen. This is a danger to everyone. No one should bury their heads in the sand. We invite

everyone in Lebanon and the region to take responsibility and confront this danger and end their silence and hesitation and neutrality (Al Jazeera, 2015).

The party's propaganda campaign has used religion as a central theme to secure its position as a legitimate armed group in the Syrian civil war (Khatib, 2013). Although Hezbollah's position in the Syrian crisis tested the party's standing among its Shi'ite supporters, as mentioned above, the party framed its participation in Syria in the context of protecting the Sayyida Zainab shrine. As Smyth (2015) reminds us, "Given its location in southern Damascus, with the international airport to its east, the shrine's strategic value cannot be overlooked" (p. 4).

Hence, considerable propaganda efforts were made to present Hezbollah's role as protector of the shrine under religious narratives. For instance, the site's prominence in the view of Shi'ite fighters is further evidenced by the shrill, mantra-like chant 'Labayk ya Zainab!' (At your service, O Zainab!), sung regularly at funerals for Lebanese Hezbollah members and Iraqi Shi'ites killed in Syria. Propaganda songs produced by Iraqi Shi'ite organisations and Hezbollah have also featured the slogan" (Smyth, 2015, p. 4). The site's significance was also related to the emergence of pan-Shi'ism in the face of Sunni Jihadist groups such as ISIS.

This intervention has had a number of implications for the Party's loyalty to regional allies, national interests, and its support base (where a number of suicide bombings targeted Dahye, Hezbollah's stronghold, and resulted in numerous human and material losses). A survey of Shi'a communities in Dahye (a suburb in the south of Beirut), South Lebanon, and the Bekaa conducted by ShiaWatch (2015), titled *15 Questions for the Lebanese Shia Community*, in February and March 2015, shows the insecurities of the Shi'ite community following Hezbollah's involvement in the Syrian war. The survey showed that 81.3% thought 'things are moving in the wrong direction' when asked where Lebanon was heading. In the same poll in 2014, this figure was 59%. When asked about their financial situation, 66% indicated that their situation is "worse than it was last year". With respect to the country's economic situation, 86% indicated that it "was worse than it was last year". In another interesting finding, when asked about Hezbollah and the Lebanese army forces, 95.6% answered that there 'should be more cooperation between the Lebanese army and Hezbollah', up from 83% in 2014.

Hezbollah's actions in response to the Syrian Civil War draw the focus towards the Party's relations with surrounding states and political movements and appear to demonstrate that the Party has "other concerns that trump the 'resistance' project" (Szekely, 2016, p. 75). This, according to Szekely (2016), affirms Hezbollah's role as a 'proto-state actor', occupying "a conceptual space somewhere between states and non-state actors" (p. 76). As such, the party has a clear political presence and undertakes actions that support or challenge the elected government's authority or legitimacy but which lack "the authority and recognition afforded to the government" (Szekely, 2016, p. 76).

Hezbollah has clearly gained military, political, and financial benefits from its relationship with Iran, and its political influence in Lebanon (and its access to arms) increased as a result of its alliance with Syria during the Syrian occupation of Lebanon up to 2005 (Szekely, 2016, p. 76). However, even though its alliance with the Assad regime in the Syrian civil war was framed as "necessary to preserve the 'Axis of Resistance' for the fight against Israel" (p. 84), another key objective was arguably to preserve the Assad regime (Szekely, 2016). In turn, this foreign policy approach not only weakened Hezbollah's political position in Lebanon but also contributed to the destabilisation of the country due to the massive influx of nearly 1.2 million Syrian refugees into Lebanon (by the end of 2015), comprising about 25% of the total population (Szekely, 2016, p. 84).

Irrespective of whether Hezbollah's alliance with Syria has weakened its domestic position, the party increasingly regards itself as a regional actor rather than just a resistance group (Guzansky and Berti, 2014). Hezbollah's decision-making in regard to domestic and regional politics has clearly become more influenced by regional issues and not just resistance to Israel. Thus, the point reinforced by Szekely (2016) is that the decision-making and strategic actions performed by the Party to strengthen its legitimacy and survival will increasingly aim to "balance a range of domestic concerns with equally complex issues of foreign policy" (p. 85).

Hezbollah as a Terrorist Organisation

Hezbollah is defined by the West and more recently by the Arab League as an insurgent terrorist organisation with the specific intent to, along with Iran, destabilise the Middle East region (Sabah and Noueihed, 2017). As a generalisation, insurgent terrorism can take three distinct forms: stand-alone terrorist acts; peacetime terrorism manifested primarily as armed propaganda for recruitment and mobilisation; and global terrorism as demonstrated by movements with international ambitions (e.g., Al Qaeda) (McAllister and Schmid, 2011, p. 213).

Associations made in the literature between Hezbollah and insurgent terrorism typically reflect the notion of embedded terrorism, that is, terrorism enmeshed with warfare "as a form of asymmetrical conflict" (McAllister and Schmid, 2011, p. 241). As stated by Jongman (2011), asymmetric conflict perpetrated by insurgent groups manifests as a challenge to 'the monopoly of (legitimate) violence held by states" (p. 342) and generally aims to protect civilian populations from "discriminatory state policies and practises" (p. 343). In such contexts, insurgent (terrorist) groups fight on behalf of oppressed groups through the development of "new protest and action methods to challenge governments" (p. 343), often but not always using violence. Importantly, asymmetric conflict typically relies on networked (and often decentralised) uses of communication, transportation, and weapons technologies to overcome its adversaries and achieve its agenda. This approach is often theorised as providing greater resilience to attack than its hierarchical insurgent counterparts as well as greater adaptability and flexibility to initiate operational changes (McAllister and Schmid, 2011, p. 241).

Some of the attributes of embedded terrorism manifested as asymmetrical conflict are arguably present in the actions of Hezbollah. This has been used by the United States and Israel to label the Party as a violent extremist organisation (Paine, 2017, p. 1) and subsequently to place it on a terrorist watch list. However, as McAllister and Schmid (2011, p. 242) have pointed out, the party is fundamentally a political and hierarchical entity rather than a networked or decentralised organisation. As such, it "must procure social and political goods to maintain organisational salience" (p. 242) and coordinate campaigns of asymmetrical conflict while simultaneously articulating coherent political and social platforms (McAllister and Schmid, 2011).

Certainly, centralised command and control structures make it easier for terrorist organisations to articulate a coherent political platform and coordinate sophisticated terrorist campaigns. Moreover, key elements in what may be regarded as successful terrorist activities often include the provision of social and political goods for constituent communities, such as social welfare outcomes and political victories against the state (McAllister and Schmid, 2011, p. 242). While Hezbollah may reflect these aspects of a terrorist organisation, it is notable that the party is not regarded as a terrorist organisation in Lebanon. Notwithstanding the different perspectives of the party among Shi'ite and Sunni Muslims as a result of their different affiliations in Islam, Hezbollah is generally viewed by the Lebanese people as a legitimate political entity deeply connected to national politics, a legitimate resistance movement, and as necessary to protect and represent them (Dionigi, 2014; Mouzahem, 2017). As stated by Newman (2018), "for Hezbollah, joining party politics led to a decrease in terrorist activity" (p. 2) compared to Hamas, for example, which has demonstrated an albeit slight increase in terrorist activity as a result of joining party politics.

In terms of Hezbollah's ties and alliances with terrorist and insurgency groups, the focus is primarily given to the party's links to Hamas. Like Hezbollah, Hamas has been designated a terrorist organisation by several countries, including the US, Israel, the United Kingdom, the European Union, Australia, Japan, and New Zealand (Counter Extremism Project, 2018). Both Hezbollah and Hamas remain fervent in their calls for the destruction of Israel and in their support for the Palestinian cause (Newman, 2018). Yet Hezbollah faces many challenges moving forward. Hamas and some other Palestinian groups are opposed to Hezbollah's intervention in Syria and have subsequently distanced themselves from the party and its patron, Iran (Newman, 2018). It is unlikely that relations between Hezbollah and Hamas will totally break down, however, given that each party has relatively few allies and that the sectarian fervour in the Middle East appears to be abating. Indeed, the ties between them remain relatively strong based on their shared belief in the need for organised resistance to the threat of invaders, occupiers, and usurpers of their land, namely, Israel and the West (Daoud, 2015).

CONCLUSION

The decision by the Arab League and Gulf Cooperation Council in 2016 to join the US and the European Union in designating Hezbollah as a terrorist group is a further effort to delegitimise the party and its Iranian ally. Although it is argued that the party's attempts to be perceived as a legitimate political party are undermined by its refusal to disarm, its attempts to delegitimise perceptions of it as a terrorist group are primarily manifest in three ways. First, its deployment of military-like strategies and techniques when engaged in armed conflict rather than hit-and-run encounters helps to consolidate the image of a quasi-conventional fighting force (Gross, 2010). Second, the party actively competes in Lebanese political elections on a platform to address domestic rather than regional issues (notwithstanding its decision to act during the Syrian conflict). As such, it continues to deemphasise its original goal to establish a Shi'ite Islamic state in Lebanon and its image as an armed resistance movement, choosing instead to demonstrate a willingness to operate within a democratic framework (Levi, 2016). Third, Hezbollah continues to build an image of its capacity for honest governance and community building via the building and administration of schools and hospitals and the provision of other essential social services to Shi'ite communities in southern Lebanon (Zeidan, 2017).

Moving forward, the future of the party remains inextricably tied to its capacity to take advantage of opportunities to increase its political legitimacy (Newman, 2018). Recent elections in Lebanon saw Hezbollah dominate the outcome in Lebanon's south in particular, with the party and its allies now having the controlling majority in the parliament. In turn, while this presents a platform for Hezbollah to assert popular support for its resistance towards Israel, its military action in Syria, and its alliance with Iran, its support for local actors in Iraq (e.g., Shia insurgents fighting against US soldiers), Syria, and Palestine means the Party remains a threat to the foreign policy interests of the United States.

Notes

1 Many claim that descent from the prophet's bloodline would comprise a certain level of insight. This is important in Shi'ite Islam, where Imams have all claimed direct descent from the prophet. It is the Supreme Guide's duty to set out the plan of action within the Umma (Islamic) nation, and his decisions are binding.
2 Welayet El-Faqih, the rule of the clerics, initiated by Khomeini during the Iranian revolution in 1979, constitutes the recognition of the absolute and supranational political and religious authority of the Supreme Guide, the Wali el-Faqih.
3 These suburbs have major concentrations of Shi'ites and are where significant Hezbollah operations are based.
4 For example, Besenyő (2017) writes about the importance of the so-called buffer zones for territorial protection.

References

Al Jazeera. (2015). Nasrallah: Hezbollah to increase presence in Syria. available at: http://www.aljazeera.com/news/2015/05/nasrallah-hezbollah-increase-presence-syria-150524233716453.html (accessed 2 June 2015).

Al Jazeera. (2023). "Lebanon charges seven over UN peacekeeper Sean Rooney's killing." (January 5, 2023).

Alagha, J. (2006). *The Shifts in Hizbullah's Ideology: Religious Ideology, Political Ideology, and Political Program*. Amsterdam: Amsterdam University Press.

Alagha, J. (2011). *Hizbullah's Documents: From the 1985 Open Letter to the 2009 Manifesto*. Amsterdam: Amsterdam University Press.

Alagha, J. (2011). *Hizbullah's Identity Construction*. Amsterdam: Amsterdam University Press.

Alagha, J. (2013). *Hizbullah's DNA and the Arab Spring*. India: University of Calcutta.

Ali, M. H. (2017). *Nationalism, Transnationalism, and Political Islam: Hizbullah's Institutional Identity*. London UK: Palgrave Macmillan.

Avon, D. & Katchadourian, A. (2012). *Hezbollah: A History of the "Party of God"*. U.S.: Harvard University Press.

Azani, E. (2013). The hybrid terrorist organization: Hezbollah as a case study. *Studies in Conflict & Terrorism*, *36*(11), 899–916.

Bayat, A. (2010). *Life as Politics: How Ordinary People Change the Middle East*. Stanford: Stanford University Press.

Besenyő, J. (2017). Fences and border protection: The question of establishing technical barriers in Europe. *AARMS – Academic and Applied Research in Military and Public Management Science*, *16*(1), 77–87. 10.32565/aarms.2017.1.7.

Blanford, N. (2011). *Warriors of God: Inside Hezbollah's Thirty-Year Struggle Against Israel*. U.S.: Random House Publishing House.

Coughlin, C. (2010). *Khomeini's Ghost*. London: Pan Books.

Counter Extremism Project. (2018). "Hamas". Counter Extremism Project, 2018. Retrieved 22 June 2018, from www.counterextremism.com/threat/hamas.

Daoud, D. (2015). 'Meet the proxies: How Iran spreads its empire through terrorist militias'. The Tower, 2015. accessed 20 June 2018, from www.thetower.org/article/meet-the-proxies-how-iranspreads-its-empire-through-terrorist-militias/.

Deeb, L. (2006). *An Enchanted Modern Gender and Public Piety in Shi'i Lebanon*. London: Princeton University Press.

Dionigi, F. (2014). *Hezbollah, Islamist Politics, and International Society*. U.S.A.: Palgrave Macmillan.

El Husseini, R. (2010). Hezbollah and the axis of refusal: Hamas, Iran and Syria. *Third World Quarterly*, *31*(5), 803–815.

Fadlallah, H. (2015). *Hizbullah and the State in Lebanon: the Vision and the Path*. Lebanon: All Prints Distributors and Publishers s.a.l.

Gross, J. (2010). Talking with terrorists: Terrorist groups and the challenge of legitimization. *Journal of Public & International Affairs*, *21*.

Guzansky, Y. & Berti, B. (2014). Is the new Middle East stuck in its sectarian past? The unspoken dimension of the "Arab Spring". *Orbis*, *57*(1), 135–151.

Hamzeh, N. (2004). *In the Path of Hizbullah*. New York: Syracuse University Press.

Harb, M. & Leenders, R. (2005). Know thy enemy: Hizbullah, 'terrorism' and the politics of perception. *Third World Quarterly*, *26*(1), 173–197.

Harik, J. (2004). *Hezbollah: The Changing Face of Terrorism*. London and New York: I.B. Tauris.

Hoover, J. (2007). Writing the resistance: Recent books on Hizbullah from Lebanese Perspectives. *Theological Review*, *XXVIII*(1), 46–68.

Immigration and Refugee Board of Canada. (2015). 'Responses to information requests'. IRBC. Retrieved 25 July 2018, from https://www.justice.gov/sites/default/files/pages/attachments/2015/09/29/lbn104638.e.pdf.

Jongman, A. J. (2011). "Introduction to the world directory of extremist, terrorist and other organisations associated with guerrilla warfare, political violence, protest, organised crime and cyber-crime." In A. Schmid (Ed.), *The Routledge handbook of terrorism research*. (pp. 341–354). Oxon, UK: Routledge.

Karagiannis, E. (2009). Hizballah as a social movement organization: A framing approach. *Mediterranean Politics*, *14*(3), 365–383.

Khashan, H. & Moussawi, I. (2007). Hizbullah's Jihad concept. *Journal of Religion and Society*, *9*(2007), 1–19.

Khatib, L. (2013). *Image Politics in the Middle East: The Role of the Visual in Political Struggle*. London, New York: I.B. Tauris.

Khatib, L., Matar, D. & Alshaer, A. (2014). *The Hizbullah Phenomenon: Politics and Communication*. Oxford, New York: Oxford University Press.

Levi, R. (2016). Changes in Hezbollah's identity and fundamental worldview. *Strategic Assessment*, *19*(2), 53–66.

Levitt, M. (2014). Hezbollah's Syrian Quagmire. *Prism: A Journal of the Center for Complex Operations*, *5*(1), 100–115.

Love, J. (2010). Hezbollah: Social services as a source of power. *J. Anderson. Florida, Joint Special Operations University*, *10*, 1–50.

Malthaner, S. (2011). *Mobilizing the Faithful: Militant Islamist Groups and their Constituencies*. New York, HY: Campus Verlag.

McAllister, B. & Schmid, A. P. (2011). "Theories of terrorism." In A. Schmid (Ed.), *The Routledge Handbook of Terrorism Research*. (pp. 201–279). Oxon, UK: Routledge.

Mouzahem, H. (2017). Lebanese president provokes outcry with Hezbollah comment. *Al-Monitor*, accessed 20 December 2017, at https://www.al-monitor.com/pulse/originals/2017/03/lebanon-president-defend-hezbollah-weapons.html

Newman, D. (2018). *The Effect of Participation in Party Politics on Terrorist Organizations: A Case Study of Hamas and Hezbollah*. Doctoral dissertation, University of Mississippi.

Norton, R. (2007). *Hezbollah: A Short History*. Princeton and Oxford: Princeton University Press.

Norton, R. (2007). The role of Hezbollah in Lebanese domestic politics. *The International Spectator, 42*(4), 475–491.

Paine, A. (2017). Strategy of the United States of America, 2017. *Daniel Morgan Graduate School of National Security*, 1–19.

Qassem, N. (2010). *Hizbullah*. London: Saqi.

Rabil, R. (2012). Hezbollah: The Islamic association and Lebanese confessional system. *The Levantine Review, 1*(1), 49–67.

Saade, B. (2015). Martyrology and conceptions of time in Hizbullah's writing practices. *International Journal of Middle East Studies, 47*(2015), 723–744.

Saad-Ghorayeb, A. (2002). *Hizbullah: Politics and Religion*. London: Pluto Press.

Sabah, Z. & Noueihed, L. (2017). Arab League condemns Iran, calls Hezbollah a terrorist group. *Bloomberg Politics*, accessed 20 December 2017, at https://www.bloomberg.com/news/articles/2017-11-19/arab-league-labels-lebanon-s-hezbollah-a-terrorist-organization-ja77de7b.

Saouli, A. (2011). Hizbullah in the civilising Process: Anarchy, self-restraint and violence. *Third World Quarterly, 32*(5), 925–942.

ShiaWatch. (2015). Polling Dahyeh: A Hayya bina Project. available at: http://www.shiawatch.com/public/uploads/files/[Polling%20Dahiyeh%20_ShiaWatch33].pdf.pdf

Smyth, P. (2015). The Shiite Jihad in Syria and Its Regional Effects. *The Washington Institute For Near East Policy*, Policy Focus 138. Available at: https://www.washingtoninstitute.org/uploads/Documents/pubs/PolicyFocus138_Smyth-2.pdf

Swanson, N. W. (2008). *Hezbollah's Nasrallah: The "Great Man" of the Levant*. Masters of Arts Thesis in Political Science, Iowa State University.

Szekely, O. (2016). Proto-state realignment and the Arab spring. *Middle East Policy, 23*(1), 75–91.

The Guardian. (April 18, 2023). "UK imposes sanctions on art collector accused of financing Hezbollah."

Traboulsi, F. (2007). *A History of Modern Lebanon*. London: Pluto Press.

Zeidan, D. (2017). Municipal management and service delivery as resilience strategies: Hezbollah's local development politics in South-Lebanon. *Local Politics and Islamist Movements, 37*.

Zisser, E. (2009). "Hizballah in Lebanon: Between Tehran and Beirut, between the Struggle with Israel, and the Struggle for Lebanon." In B. Rubin (Ed.), *Lebanon: Liberation, Conflict, and Crisis*. (pp. 177–193). U.S.: Palgrave McMillan.

48

HEZBOLLAH IN TURKEY

İlim

Nail Elhan and Hikmet Mengüaslan

INTRODUCTION

On January 17, 2000, the Turkish media showed a live broadcast from a villa garden in Beykoz, İstanbul, the most populated city in Turkey. It was an armed conflict between the police and Hezbollah, *İlim*, fighters. After the conflict, the police secured the villa and captured two fighters, Cemal Tutar and Edip Gümüş, alive and one dead, Hüseyin Velioğlu, the leader of the organisation (Seibert, 2011). After the documents were obtained from the villa, archives of Hezbollah, including the plans of the organisation, personal backgrounds of fighters, and videos of killings, were captured. In this process, there have been many operations against the militants and their cell houses. After these operations, the dead bodies of people who were brutally murdered emerged under the gardens, shelters, and grounds of the houses, which horrified the Turkish public. It was clear that the organisation interrogated, tortured, and recorded videos of these actions. The public was closely acquainted with the terror of Hezbollah for the first time (Aydıntaşbaş, 2000, 1). Ambiguities in the propaganda strategies of the organisation and its limited appearances within the public and media have made it a shadowy figure in Turkey. After that, the organisation has been mentioned for its brutal attacks and assassinations, and academic and media contributions discussing the organisation have heavily focused on its instrumentalization of Islam as a generative mechanism of violence.

This chapter examines the emergence of Hezbollah in Turkey, its ideology, organisational strategies, and the periods during which it has evolved from radicalisation to moderation. It will be composed of five parts. In the first part, approaches to analysing *İlim* will be delineated. In the second part, the naming problem of Hezbollah in Turkey will be discussed, and the name of *İlim* will be offered to define the organisation. In the third part, the establishment and ideology of *İlim* will be discussed. In this part, the reasons behind the formation and radicalisation of *İlim* will be explained. In the fourth part, the organisational structure, strategies, and policies of *İlim* will be handled. Its capacity to mobilise people and expand its religious influence will be discussed. The last part will include the trajectory of *İlim* from radicalisation to moderation between the early 1970s and the 2010s. This part will present three periods of the organisation within the context of its trajectory in Turkish political life. The Early Period will deal with the establishment and expansion of the organisation between the early 1970s and 2000, when it put pressure on Islamist circles and the PKK, especially in the Southeastern region of Turkey. The Withdrawal Period will analyse the period between 2000 and the mid-2000s, when the organisation withdrew underground after its last operation with security forces in Diyarbakır on January 24, 2001. In this operation, Hezbollah fighters assassinated the chief of police in Diyarbakır, Gaffar Okkan, along with several other police officers. After that, the organisation went underground until its revival with unarmed mass protests organised by its affiliated groups. In the Period of Moderation, *İlim* operated through social movements and political groups, which resulted in its decision to participate in legal political processes in Turkey with the formation of the Free Cause Party *(Hür Dava Partisi* or HÜDA-PAR)[1] in 2012.

REFLECTING ON APPROACHES TO *İLIM*

Drawing a large amount of scholarly and daily attention, *İlim* has had its part in the conflictual relationship between the Turkish state and the Kurdish movement. It has been transformed into a legal political party, HÜDA-PAR, and left its hardline, militant actions. Unsurprisingly, thus, the organisation's transformation process, its actions, and its

DOI: 10.4324/9780429426063-55

relevance to both the Kurdish insurgency and the Islamist movement in Turkey entailed a wide range of analytical approaches, from state-security-centric to historical and sociological perspectives.

Being informative, the studies analysing *İlim* from a state-security-centric perspective (Bulut and Farac, 1999; Özeren and Yilmaz, 2007; Çitlioğlu, 2001; Çiçek, 2000) define *Ilim* as an Islamist terrorist organisation in the context of the Kurdish problem in Turkey. The fact that *İlim* is a faith-based organisation has led to its handling in the context of Islamist and reactionary movements (Jenkins, 2008; Karmon, 1998; Lapidot, 1996). Lacking a sufficient reflection upon the social, cultural, and religious dimensions of the organisation's origins, evolution, and transformation, state-security-centric contributions are deficient in the evaluation of the organisation. Taking the organisation as an armed and faith-based threat against the security of the state, they lack a sociological and political perspective.

Contributions from historical and sociological perspectives also have deficiencies. Evaluating the trajectory of the organisation, Ruşen Çakır (2016) defines *İlim* as a social and political movement. In his 'semi-academic' study, which has become a reference guide in the field for a long time, Çakır defines *İlim* as an Islamic fundamentalist organisation. He analyses the organisation through his journalistic activities and personal interviews, but he lacks a theoretical perspective and fails to go beyond an informative description. Mehmet Kurt (2017) argues that the literature on *İlim* heavily focuses on violence and points to Islam as a generative, unpredictable, and uncontrollable mechanism of violence. In addition, Taha Akyol (2000, 183) defines the rise of *İlim* as a case of re-tribalization and the rise of a new *asabiyya*. He underlines that *İlim* is an ethnic-tribal organisation and that the ethnic, social, cultural, and religious conditions that created the PKK have also played an important role in the emergence of *İlim* (Akyol, 2000, 201). Within this context, the transformative influence of industrialisation, urbanisation, globalisation, and the import of foreign values are implied as the conditions that created a social reaction. Although these approaches have contributed to explaining the transformation of the organisation, Akyol's and Kurt's works could be improved if the political dimensions and structural factors were integrated into the analysis. In this context, Cuma Çiçek's study provides a useful analysis for understanding the general context, concentrating relations between the Kurds and the state, Europeanisation, and globalisation from a constructivist perspective. Adopting a sociological and political perspective and analysing the politicisation of Kurds in Turkey, Çiçek (2017) points out the influence of nationalist, religious, and economic ideologies as factors that prevented their collective action to build a common identity.

While contributing to the analysis of sociological and political dimensions of *İlim* by focusing on the impact of regional and systemic factors on the relationship between the Turkish political scene and developments pertinent to the Kurdish movement, this study aims to differ from state- and security-centric approaches.

THE NAMING PROBLEM

Hezbollah, an Arabic word meaning the party of God, is composed of two words: *Hezb*, meaning party or faction, and *Allah*, God. The Iranian Revolution in 1979, which overthrew the Shah Regime in Iran, one of the closest allies of the US in the region at the time, served as a model not only for Islamists in Turkey but also for Islamists around the world (Elhan, 2015, 1). In fact, Iran adopted exporting its revolution to other Islamic countries as an official state policy. Tehran-based radical and revolutionary Islamic line, which claims to be universal and developed in this process, is called the "Hezbollahian" way of Islamic thinking. Organisations under the name of Hezbollah have been established, especially in Lebanon, Iraq, and Turkey, or the existing organisations have changed their names to Hezbollah under the influence of the Iranian Revolution. The name Hezbollah became prominent with the emergence of the Lebanese Hezbollah, an Iranian-backed organisation, in Lebanon in the late 1970s and early 1980s (Alagha, 2006, 33).

The first organisation with the name Hezbollah and within the frame of the "Hezbollahian" line was the Kasımpaşa Hezbollah[2], which was established in 1983 and subverted by the operations of the security forces in 1984 (Çakır, 2011, 123; Manaz, 2018). It was reorganised under the name of the Islamic Movement (*İslami Hareket*) in the early 1990s and became popular in the press with the assassinations of intellectuals including Bahriye Üçok, Turan Dursun, and Çetin Emeç.

In addition to the pro-Kurdish and secular PKK, another pro-Kurdish organisation in Southeastern Turkey was *İlim*, an Islamist group in the "Hezbollahian" line established in 1991 that dominated the armed organisations within Islamist circles. In the region, Islamist organisations have taken the names of bookstores that were formed by Islamic circles. As it was an alternative way of political and ideological organising against government pressures, several groups chose clandestine gatherings. *İlim*, which took its name from a bookstore in Diyarbakır, was founded by Hüseyin Velioğlu in the late 1970s (Bagasi, n.d., 35–36).

After the clashes with the PKK and *Menzil*, meaning range[3], another Islamist organisation built around a bookstore circle in Batman, *İlim* was referred to as Hezbollah. In addition to *İlim* and *Menzil*, there were other bookstores established in the southeastern region of Turkey. For instance, the *İkra* and *Selam* bookstores were established in Batman. They were supporters of *İlim*, and united under *İlim* in time. There were also local "Hezbollahian" organisations, such as the Silvan and Nusaybin Hezbollahs, out of *İlim* and *Menzil*. However, these were both scattered and powerless when compared to *İlim* and *Menzil*. *İlim* and *Menzil* had more central and powerful roles in the region that had the support of the public.

The evaluation of Hezbollah, *İlim*, also entails a defining problem. Different perspectives define this radical religious movement in different ways. Due to the use of similar names by several Islamist organisations and the public espousal of the name "Hezbollah" for almost all Iran-inspired armed Islamist groups, a defining problem occurs in the literature of Islamist organisations on the "Hezbollahian" way of thinking in Turkey. In this regard, *İlim*, the most known "Hezbollahian" organisation in Turkey, is defined by several names. First of all, *İlim* was composed of people mainly coming from ethnically Kurdish origins, which causes it to be mentioned as Kurdish Hezbollah (Kurt, 2017; Çiçek, 2017). However, there are studies showing that the organisation includes members from different ethnic origins. Secondly, Hezbollah in Turkey is defined with reference to the Lebanese Hezbollah. However, there are no known links between the Lebanese Hezbollah and the Hezbollah in Turkey (Goerzig, 2010, 100). Therefore, the term "Turkish Hezbollah" is generally used in order to distinguish ideological and territorial differences between the Lebanese Hezbollah and the Hezbollah in Turkey (Kushner, 2003). *İlim* was established in the Southeastern region of Turkey, and it has a Sunni origin. Therefore, it should be interpreted within the Islamic and multi-ethnic structures of Turkey. Thirdly, *İlim*, by its own members, was also called *Cemaat* meaning an Islamic community. In a book written by the organisational management of the organisation, members call themselves *Cemaat* (Bagasi, n.d., 23–24). The name *Cemaat* is used to refer to several Islamist groups in Turkey that are very different from each other in terms of ideological and organisational structures. For instance, the Gülen Movement is also called *Cemaat* in Turkey.

In addition to these, Imset (1992) argues that there are those naming *İlim* as "hezbolcontra" and defining the organisation as a subcontractor of the Turkish and Iranian states because of its brutal attacks against the PKK and rival secular Kurdish movements (Karmon, 1998). As *İlim* entered a conflictual process with the PKK and *Menzil*, there were allegations that the organisation was established by the Turkish state and used against the PKK. Allegedly, the state had aimed to weaken the two opposition organisations by fighting each other. In this regard, Bulut and Faraç (1999, 67–70) claim three points, including ideological, political, and practical-pragmatic, where the interests of the state and *İlim* intersect. It was ideological because the state authorities aimed to fight against leftist movements with the help of religion, and they instrumentalized religion within this context. Since the Kurdish issue was political, it has always been problematic since the foundation of the Turkish Republic, which has been rigid against minorities. Lastly, since the state security forces cooperated with *İlim* against the secessionist Kurdish movements in the region, it was pragmatic. As it can be seen from the figure, the state did not interfere with the organisation and did not make operations in the period between 1992 and 1996, when the organisation fought against the PKK and *Menzil* (Figure 48.1). Hikmet Çiçek (2000, 104–105) provides the number *İlim* members arrested as 2 in 1991, 11 in 1992, 156 in 1993, 485 in 1994, 542 in 1995, 481 in 1996, 644 in 1997, 1106 in 1998, and 1843 in 1999. In the post-1996 period, *İlim* underwent a restructuring process, largely weakening the *Menzil* and establishing dominance in the

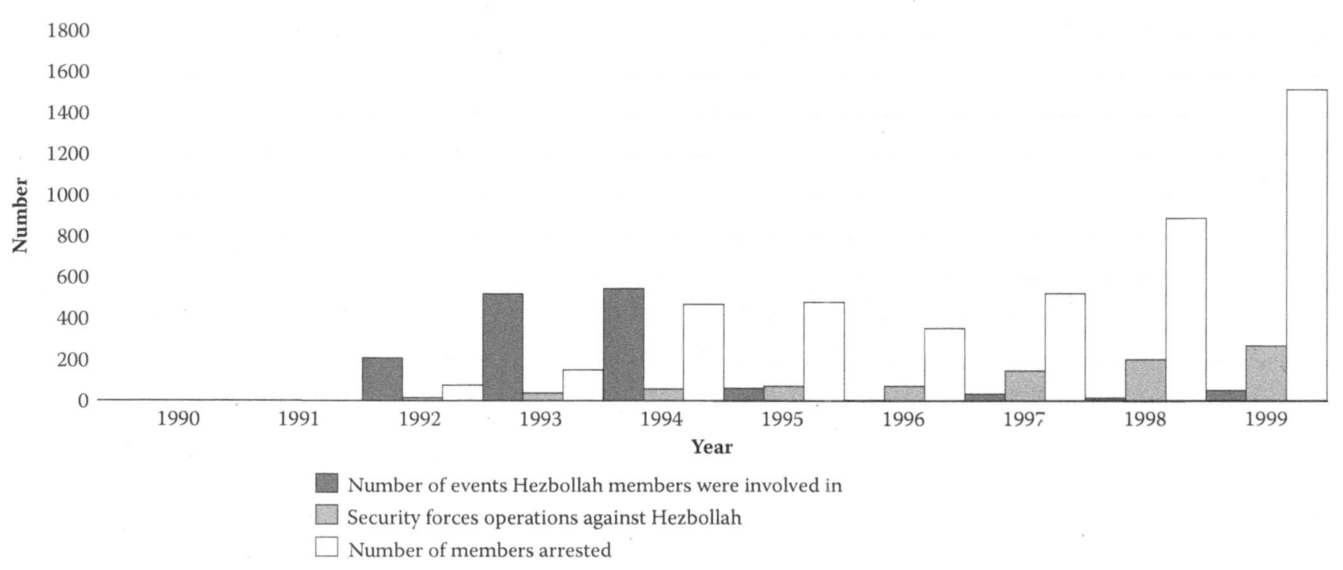

Figure 48.1 Relationship between Hezbollah and the State (1990-1999).

Source: Çakır, R. (2011). *Derin Hizbullah (The Deep Hezbollah)*, Metis Yayınları: İstanbul.

cities against the PKK. According to Ruşen Çakır (2011, 88), although the state did not lead the organisation directly, it overlooked its actions against other anti-state organisations and groups. In this context, it can be said that *İlim* exploited the state in its struggle to establish regional dominance over the PKK and other Islamist groups rather than the state exploiting *İlim*. On the other side, the state stayed silent against *İlim*'s jihadist activities against the PKK in the region in order to weaken the Kurdish movement. With the increase in the state's operations against the organisation, it is obvious that *İlim* has significantly lost its activism. The transformation of the threat and security concept of the Turkish state in the late 1990s also had a serious impact on the policies of *İlim*. The rising numbers of arrested members of *İlim* ~~lim~~ show parallels with the changing security concept of the Turkish state. As the Turkish National Security Council decisions in 1997 stated Islamic reactionism was the primary threat to the national security of the state, operations of security forces against *İlim* also increased.

Moreover, several Islamist groups call the organisation as *hezbolvahset/hezbolzulüm*, which means the party of savagery; *hezbolseytan*, which means the party of the devil, because of its brutal attacks on Islamists due to its strategy of attacking those who do not share its Islamic way of understanding; and *hezbolcontra* due to claims like having close ties with the Turkish intelligence service (Atalar, 2006, 309–313).

Due to their "Hezbollahian" and jihadi understanding of Islam, *İlim* has adopted the name of Hezbollah and carried out its actions under this name. In this context, *İlim* is the organisation called Kurdish Hezbollah, Turkish Hezbollah, or Hezbollah in Turkey. Against this background, *İlim* will be used in order to refer to all of these names in this study, and *İlim* will be analysed as an independent and *sui generis* actor within the context of Turkish political life.

ESTABLISHMENT AND IDEOLOGY OF THE ORGANISATION

There are several claims about the establishment of *İlim*. According to Ruşen Çakır (2011, 58), a well-known journalist studying Islamist organisations in Turkey, *İlim* was established after the military coup in 1980. On the other hand, Mehmet Kurt (2017, 15) claims that the organisation was established prior to the military coup. According to Aslı Elitsoy (2017, 9), there is no written propaganda or claimed responsibility for *İlim*'s actions, and for this reason, the only source to investigate Hizbullah's early stance towards the Kurdish ethnic identity is the book written by Isa Altsoy, under the pseudonym of I. Bagasi, entitled *Kendi Dilinden Hizbullah: Mücadele Tarihinden Kesitler* [*Hizbullah in Its Own Words: Selections From the History of the Struggle*], and the court defences of Hizbullah members. In the book, Bagasi (n.d., 24) points out 1979 as the year that the organisation was formed. According to Bagasi (n.d., 26), the pioneers of the organisation established it throughout the ongoing debates and the vicious cycle in which the Islamist circles were engaged. It was aimed at meeting the aspirations of the Muslims with a new organisation completely original and independent, based on Islamic values, and consisting of the volunteer unity of Muslims who gathered on the basis of sacrifice, loyalty, and Islamic brotherhood. Çakır (2011, 58) argues that Hezbollah in Turkey, *İlim*, was founded at a meeting in which Hüseyin Velioğlu, Molla Mansur Güzelsoy, Fidan Güngör, Ubeydullah Dalar, İhsan Yeşilırmak and Mehmet Ali Bilici attended. It is claimed that only Bilici is alive, and only Güzelsoy's death is a natural death. Others were killed because of intra-organisational disputes. Güngör, who left *İlim* and formed *Menzil*, was kidnapped by *İlim* members and killed in 1995. Dalar was killed after being beaten with sticks by a group of children, and Yeşilırmak was shot. As mentioned above, Velioğlu was killed in an operation organised by the security forces in 2000. Çakır (2011, 58) claims that it was Velioğlu's first armed conflict against the state.

İlim is a late twentieth-century phenomenon and the outcome of a series of socio-historical and political junctures marked by domestic political upheavals and international developments. The emergence of *İlim* is closely related to three factors, including domestic and international components. Firstly, *İlim* is a product of consequences based on Turkey's relationships with Islam and Islamist organisations. "As Turkey was founded on secular and nationalist principles, it was governed by strictly modernist and secularist principles that had always been met with reactions from people who led more traditional and religious lives" (Kurt, 2017, 14). As a reaction, Islamist-oriented political parties have strengthened in Turkey since the early 1950s (Çiçek, 2017, 58–59).

Secondly, *İlim* is a result of Turkey's policies towards ethnic minorities. Turkey has had a security-oriented, rigid policy towards minorities, including the Kurds. As Kurt (2017, 15) suggests, Turkey's modernist and nationalist policies caused similar reactions in the country's predominantly Kurdish region. As a reaction to the policies of the state, several Kurdish armed groups emerged, such as the PKK, which formed in the late 1970s with the ultimate goal of establishing an independent Kurdish state. Akyol (2000, 201) underlines that *İlim* is an ethnic-tribal organisation, and the conditions – ethnic, social, cultural, and religious – that created the PKK played an important role in the emergence of *Ilim*. Parallel to this argument, İsa Bagasi (n.d., 49–51) underlines the impact of the repressive policies of the state on the increasing influence of the *Ilim* in the region.

Thirdly, *İlim* is established under the influence of political Islam. Political Islam is a modern phenomenon dating back to colonialism and the emergence of nation-states. Islamists, who defined Western colonialism as the reason for their backwardness, turned their faces to the era of the Prophet Mohammad and the *Rashidun Caliphate* and presented Islam as a solution. Turning to Islam was believed to be the re-invention of the golden age of Islam. The establishment of an Islamic state and the Islamisation of society were required in order to revive Islam. The radical Islamist movements arose in the 1970s through several factors. In the second half of the twentieth century, there have been three developments leading to the expansion of political Islamist ideology. One is the formation of the Muslim Brotherhood, *Ihkwan*, by Hasan al-Banna in Egypt. It aimed to Islamise societies and topple secular regimes, defined as "*taguti* regimes," which were not governed according to Islamic law. *İlim* activists were familiar with *Ihkwan* ideologues, including Sayyed Qutb and Said Havva, the former of the Syrian Muslim Brotherhood.[4] The other development is the formation of a sharia state in Iran under the leadership of Ayatollah Khomeini after the Iranian Revolution in 1979.

After the revolution, there have been many Islamist movements around the world inspired by the revolution aimed at the realisation of similar regimes (Bulut and Faraç, 1999, 52–53). *İlim* adopted the Islamic model realised by Ayatollah Khomeini and used the Iranian model of popular uprisings (Atalar, 2006, 312). Within this context, mosques were used as centres of struggle. In return for taking Iran as a model, *İlim* was financially and logistically supported by Iran (Bulut, 1997, 397). In addition, Velioğlu and several members of *İlim* visited Iran several times in order to receive ideological and military education (Atalar, 2006, 312). Last is the Green Belt project of the US (Eligür, 2010, 135; Aktürk, 2012, 165). Under the conditions of the Cold War, the US followed a containment policy against the USSR. In this respect, the US supported Islamist organisations in the Middle East and Central Asia.

In order to prevent the Soviets' influence in these regions and constrain communism within the boundaries of the Soviet Republic, the US has given financial and logistical support to Islamists. As a result, Central Asia and the Middle East, including Turkey, have witnessed the strengthening of Islamist movements. The Turkish-Islamic Synthesis became an official state policy during this period, demonstrating the official attitude of the state, especially against leftist movements (Elhan, 2016, 173). Within the Turkish context, one of the most important cultural and religious sources of *İlim* is the *Epistles of Light* written by Said Nursi. *Epistles of Light* has been one of the basic education textbooks for the members of the organisation in every period of the congregational process. The leader of the organisation, Hüseyin Velioğlu, was educated in the *Nur* Schools, inspired by the ideas of Said Nursi (Bagasi, n.d., 225).

İlim was built within this context. It aimed to topple the secular regime in Turkey and build a sharia state based on Islamic law. Its ideology has heavily been influenced by the *Ihkwan* ideologues, Hasan al-Banna and Sayyed Qutb, Ayatollah Khomeini, and Said Nursi. According to Bagasi (n.d., 23–24), Muslims attempted to enter an Islamic struggle in Turkey. However, he claims that it was a fallacy implemented under the control of the regime and within the boundaries it drew. As a result, they have decided to change the strategy of Islamist movements and have initiated an armed struggle against the regime. In the book *Hizbullah in Its Own Words*, written by the leaders of the organisation, *İlim* is claimed to be an independent organisation (Bagasi, n.d., 27). It is alleged that the organisation is not the continuation of any organisation or movement. Instead, it claims that it is the heir of the rich and fertile heritage of all the Islamic movements that lived before and struggled for the domination of Islam.

STRATEGIES AND STRUCTURE OF THE ORGANISATION

The organisation adopted Islam as its primary motivation and an Islamic state as its ultimate objective. In order to realise the establishment of an Islamic state, radical and revolutionary methods were adopted as the most important instruments. The organisation defined the Turkish state and its secular regime as the enemy and the source of oppression. The reason for the existence of the organisation was presented as the struggle against the secular Kemalist regime and its persecutions (Bagasi, n.d., 34). The organisation believed that the regime constantly persecuted Muslim Kurds because of their Islamic and Kurdish identities. Therefore, Mansur Güzelsoy claims that it was necessary to start with a radical solution and a revolutionary method by building a whole new understanding (Güzelsoy, 1966). Within this context, the organisation has a triple-*dawah*, or religious advertising, strategy that includes an invitation to religion, raising awareness among people, the formation of an Islamic community, and jihad. Invitation to religion and raising awareness among people consist of two methods. The secret communication covers the process of raising core cadres. Open communication, on the other hand, covers the efforts of these cadres to go down to the public and expand the base of the organisation. The use of written and visual publications and the adoption of the way of persuasion through direct contact with the people have been the strategies of the organisation in the first process of invitation to religion and raising awareness among people. While the rival organisation, *Menzil*, invested more in the use of written and visual publications, *İlim* preferred the use of its human resources to expand its influence. According to Çitlioğlu (2001, 85), the main reason behind this difference was *Menzil*'s perfection in religious matters.

It is even claimed that *İlim*'s leader, Hüseyin Velioğlu, changed his surname from Durmaz to Velioğlu because of his organisation's religious weaknesses. His surname, Velioğlu, means a person who is the son of a saint (Çitlioğlu, 2001,

78–79). When compared to *Menzil*, *İlim*'s weaknesses in the expansion of its religious and organisational influence led the organisation to act in different ways, declaring jihad against the PKK. In this way, it aimed to gain the appreciation and support of the public. Furthermore, according to *İlim*, most of the organisations and parties that emerged in the context of the Kurdish question in the region were in the Marxist-Leninist line and dealt with the Kurdish question within the framework of illegitimate and non-religious ideologies strange to the values of the people. Since the majority of the people living in the region were Muslims, these ideological approaches were not in the interest of the Kurdish people (Bagasi, n.d., 71–72).

According to Bagasi (n.d., 131), the Turkish state benefited from the *İlim*-PKK dispute in the region. All the negativities and disadvantages of the state before the Hezbollah-PKK conflict turned out to be advantageous in the new situation that emerged after this conflict. The policies of *İlim* and the Turkish State overlapped in the fight against the PKK. Both *İlim* and the state emphasised the PKK's secular ideology as a threat to society. The state also aimed to weaken the PKK by putting emphasis on its foreignness to the public and its non-religious discourse, disrupting the relationship between the organisation and its base in the region. However, the religious messages used by the state and *İlim* against the PKK differed from each other. While the state defined the PKK as a pattern of blasphemy in order to protect the territorial integrity and security of the state, the blasphemy for *Muslims* was the secular regime itself. Consequently, the state has gradually increased its position in the region.

On the other side, *Menzil* worked in secrecy and was opposed to any actions without gaining adequate power. Therefore, it opposed *İlim*'s jihad against the PKK. According to the leader of *Menzil*, Fidan Güngör, fighting against the PKK would lead to the strengthening of the Turkish state (Çitlioğlu, 2001, 105). For this reason, they were in favour of taking an attitude against both the PKK and the state after having adequate infrastructure, staff, and logistics. Along with declaring jihad, the other methods that the organisation followed were 1) armed struggle to safeguard the Islamic way of life and 2) the formation of the *ummah* – the society of Muslims.

Within this context, *Menzil* was considered a greater danger than *İlim* to the state because of its policy of waiting to reach a certain maturity. In this phase, education for the members is provided, and a society composed of Muslims worshipping *Allah* is formed. This phase is defined as equal to the Mecca years of the Prophet Mohammad. Jihad is the last phase before the establishment of the Islamic state. Muslims fight to demolish non-religious institutions aiming at a state that involves Islamicized institutions.

The archives of the organisation obtained after the Beykoz Operation in 2000 showed that there were many members and sympathisers of the organisation.[5] It is claimed that there was broad data about the organisation's structure, plans, members, and strategies in the hands of the security forces (akr, 2011, 186). The organisation recorded any developments related to its activities. For instance, anyone who wanted to be a member of the organisation had to fill out a resume form. This form was composed of questions including birthplace, occupation, the books read by candidate members, their social circles, etc. (Table 48.1, Figure 48.2). It is

Table 48.1 Age Distribution and Occupation of *İlim* Militants

Age Distribution of Militants		Occupations of Militants	
11–14	9%	Free Trader	20%
15–20	14%	Worker	16%
21–24	19%	Student	13%
25–28	21%	Artisan	11%
29–34	17%	Unemployed	6%
35–41	11%	Teacher	6%

Source: (Atalar, 2006). "Hizballah of Turkey: A Pseudo-Threat to the Secular Order?", *Turkish Studies*, 7:2, 307–331.

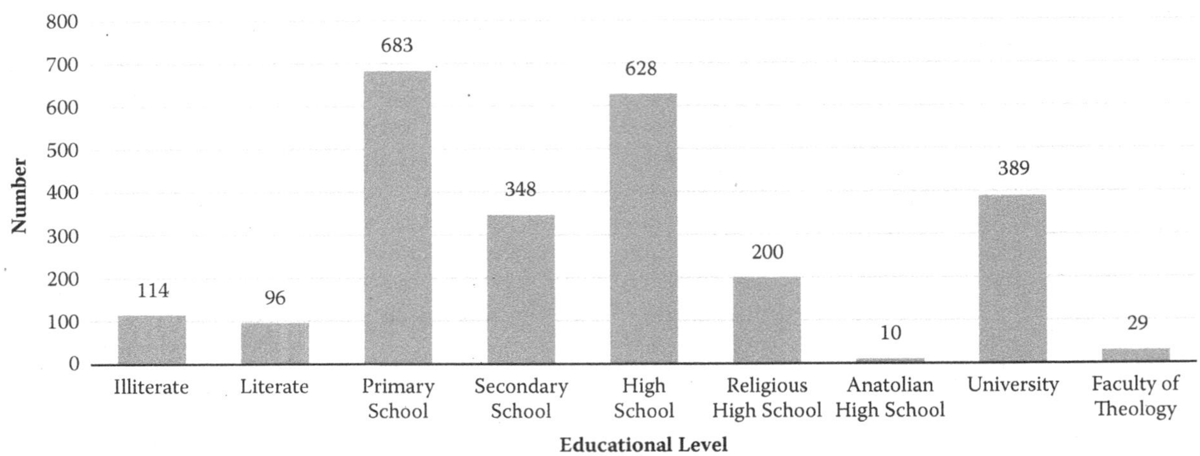

Figure 48.2 Educational Level of *İlim* Militants.

Source: (Atalar, 2006). "Hizballah of Turkey: A Pseudo-Threat to the Secular Order?", *Turkish Studies*, 7:2, 307–331.

obvious that it is a contradiction that an organisation, which gives great importance to secrecy and intelligence, wants a resume form from its members in their own handwriting. However, these resumes were extremely important for the organisation since it controlled the lives of its members through them.

With this information in the resume, the members joining the organisation were completely brought under Hezbollah's control, and this information served as a control mechanism against possible betrayals (Çitlioğlu, 2001, 181). In the 1995 report of the Turkish National Assembly, the organisational structure of *İlim* is claimed to consist of several institutions under the leadership of the guide, Hüseyin Velioğlu (Çakır, 2011, 131). Under the leadership of Velioğlu, the organisation is composed of an archivist, military, political, and financial coordinators, and couriers providing communication between Velioğlu and them. In addition to the top officials of the organisation, there are smaller teams, including regional and provincial operators and couriers. Coordination between all members of the organisation is conducted with such high confidentiality that members of all groups only know the leader but not the other members of the organisation.

IRANIAN REVOLUTION AND RELATIONS WITH IRAN

After its revolution in 1979, Iran aimed to export its revolution and Islamic understanding. Therefore, it became one of the supporters of Islamic movements around the world. As aforementioned, the Islamic movements inspired by the Iranian Revolution and its leader Khomeini, which aimed to establish an Iranian style of sharia governance in their areas of activity, are called, and usually claim to be, "Hezbollahian" movements. Similarly, *İlim* was also referred to as an Iranian Revolution-inspired organisation (Atalar, 2006, 312). When compared to *İlim*, it can be concluded that *Menzil* was more Iran-inspired. According to *Menzil*, the revolutionary ideology of the newly established regime in Iran had to be supported, and its leader, Khomeini, had to be approved as the true leader. Mediating between Shii and Sunni understandings of Islam, *Menzil* aimed to provide a dialogue between the sects. *İlim*, on the other hand, delimited its interest to Iran with the period between 1979 and 1989, the Khomeini era from the revolution to the death of Khomeini. According to *İlim*, Persian nationalism and Shii sectarianism increased in the post-Khomeini period in Iran, which was the reason behind *İlim*'s increasing emphasis on Sunni Islam.

In *Hezbollah in its Own Words*, the organisation clarifies its relations with Iran. The organisation claims that Muslims were subjected to materialist ideologies and cultural imperialism that produced theses such as "religion is an ophium of masses", "Islam's inability to solve economic, political, and social problems in the world" and "Islam's being an old religion completed its role". Therefore, Muslims have moved away from Islam. The Islamic Revolution in Iran emerged against these vicious thoughts and revived Islam, placing it on the world agenda as a divine political order (Bagasi, n.d., 240–241).

> From this point of view, we have shown interest in the revolution from the first day and we have protected the political goals of the revolution and the gains of Ummah. Today, this attitude has not changed, and it continues. This attitude is valid for the leadership of the revolution and the goals it aimed. This attitude and approach cannot be applied to the Iranian state or to the governments acceded. Even if the revolution deviates from its original line and transforms, our view about Imam Khomeini and the revolutionary line will be unchanged. We will always be grateful to Imam Khomeini, his movement and his contributions to the Ummah. (Bagasi, n.d., 242)

Even though the organisation admits its interest in the Khomeini period, it rejects the claims that *İlim* was established with the support of Iran and that its members had military training in Iran. According to the organisation, there were several members that had travelled to Iran for sightseeing or to investigate the revolution on site (Bagasi, n.d., 242-243). Most of these departures were by normal means and carried out with Turkish passports. In this regard, the organisation rejects the idea that the *İlim* fighters had military training in Iran.

PERIODS OF *İIM*: FROM RADICALISM TO MODERATION

İlim underwent a transformation process that resulted in profound changes in its ideology, methods, concepts, and activities (for types and numbers of *İlim*'s activities, see Figures 48.3 and 48.4). The transformation of the ideology of *İlim* was contextually determined through domestic political upheavals and international developments. The rise of secular Kurdish movements such as the PKK and the People's Democratic Party (HDP) influenced the transformation of the organisation. In addition, international developments such as the 9/11 attacks in 2001 and the emergence of global jihadist terrorism influenced the tactics and ideology of the organisation.

These developments, both in domestic and international realms, have affected the nature of *İlim*'s struggle and repositioned the ideological orientation of *Ilim* along with shaping the understanding of threat and enemy. Defining

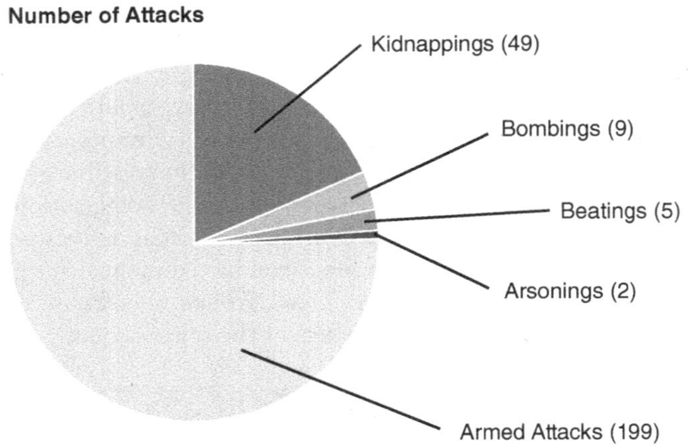

Figure 48.3 *İlim*'s Types of Attacks between 1991 and 2001.

Source: (Yıldırım, 2012). "Hizbullah Terör Örgütünün Şiddet Eylemlerinin Betimsel Analizi (Descriptive Analysis of the Violent Actions of the Hizbullah Terrorist Organization", Unpublished Msc Thesis Submitted to Turkish National Police Academy, Institute of Security Sciences, Ankara, Turkey.

İlim as a social and political movement, Ruşen Çakır divides the organisational and ideological transformation of *İlim* into three periods: the first period includes the foundation and expansion of *İlim* between 1980 and 2000; the second period includes the organisation's withdrawal to the underground between 2001 and 2011. The third period includes the organisation's moderation and involvement in the legal political processes in political life in Turkey after 2011. İsa Bagasi (n.d., 40), on the other hand, claims that the organisation had a two-stage transformation:

> The first one is the period from its foundation in 1979 to 1991, and the second one is the period from 1991 to 2000. In fact, each of these periods has different stages in itself. However, since there are two separate periods with distinctive, vital and important events that have different characteristics, we have deemed it appropriate to divide the two main periods of the *cemaat* into a better understanding of the course of struggle.

In the first period, the organisation compounded its activities throughout the southeast region of Turkey. In order to expand its influence and enhance its support in the region, the organisation spread propaganda in mosques, schools, and trade unions. The year 1991 was considered a turning point for *İlim*. Struggles between the state and *İlim*, and the PKK and *İlim* increased after 1991. Despite the attacks coming from both sides, *İlim* maintained its influence in the region until the Beykoz Operation in 2000. İsa Bagasi concludes his explanations on *İlim* with the Beykoz Operation, without any reference to the post-2000 period. He claims that the organisation continued its actions in Europe during this period.

> The community has a wide potential and sympathetic mass in Europe. There has been no violence in Europe until today. Many of our people, who suffered from the persecution of the Turkish state because of their Islamic or Kurdish identities, took refuge in the European countries. (Bagasi, n.d., 237)

According to Çakır (2011, 65), the early period of *İlim* was full of conflicts with both Islamist and secular groups in the southeastern region of Turkey. In order to dominate politics in the region, Velioğlu decided to confront all other anti-regime movements, regardless of their orientation. In this process, the struggle against the PKK and *Menzil* was quite important. Through its military capabilities, the PKK was the dominant organisation in the region. It was organised in both cities and rural areas. At the end of this period, *İlim* established superiority over the PKK in the cities, destroyed *Menzil*'s logistical capabilities, and dominated the region. Çakır (2011, 185) discusses that the transformation of *İlim* into an underground organisation and the beginning of its second period are symbolised by the assassination of Gaffar Okkan, the Police Chief of Diyarbakr, on January 24, 2001, a

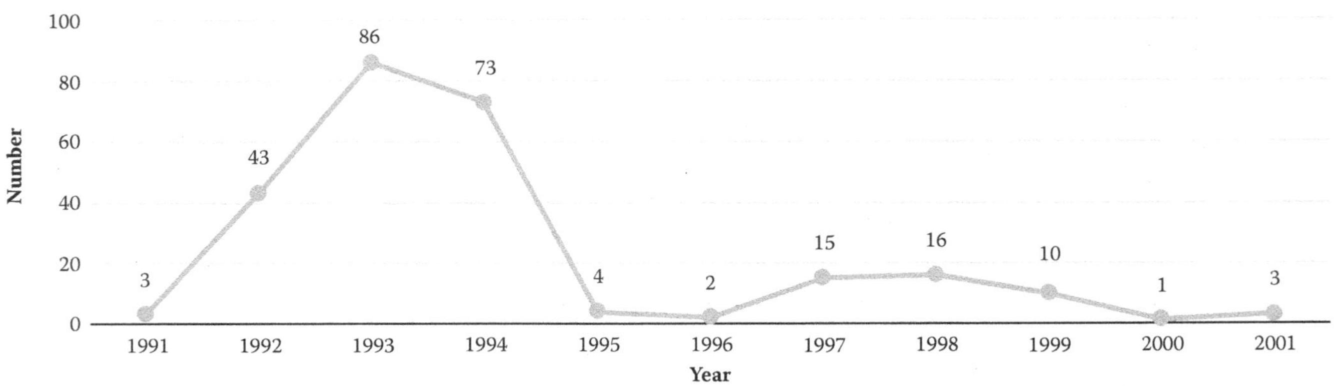

Figure 48.4 *İlim*'s Number of Activities between 1991 and 2001.

Source: (Yıldırım, 2012). "Hizbullah Terör Örgütünün Şiddet Eylemlerinin Betimsel Analizi (Descriptive Analysis of the Violent Actions of the Hizbullah Terrorist Organization", Unpublished Msc Thesis Submitted to Turkish National Police Academy, Institute of Security Sciences, Ankara, Turkey.

year after the Beykoz Operation, where Hüseyin Velioğlu was killed. After the Beykoz operation, the death of Velioğlu and the capture of Cemal Tutar and Edip Gümüş caused a leadership problem within the organisation. Because of Velioğlu's authoritarian attitude and "onemanhood" or bossism, there has been no leading figure within the organisation. Other figures than Velioğlu were claimed to be neither charismatic nor talented (Çakır, 2011, 185). Therefore, the claim of any single authority or leadership may lead to an internal war. For this reason, it was conceivable that *İlim* had to be governed through a *Shura*, the Islamic council. Since the loss of its leadership, or "one man", many expected that *İlim* would undergo a dispersion process and weaken. However, the organisation, which claimed that it could no longer take any action, took a great one and killed the police chief of Diyarbakır in 2001.

Following this, the goals of the organisation have changed. During the first period, the organisation targeted the rival groups, the PKK and *Menzil*, but it did not target the state institutions, state officials, or security forces. However, in the operations held through the documents obtained in the Beykoz Operation, a great number of documents, including plans for attacks on government buildings, maps of the military zones, and routes of security forces, were seized. In addition, there was a wide range of intelligence about the activities of the PKK and the computer codes and passwords of NATO's military establishments. From this point of view, it is clear that the organisation has broadened its range of targets and put the state and international institutions at the top of its list (Çakır, 2011, 198). For example, a map of the US Consulate in Istanbul and sketches of the Turkish National Intelligence Service were confiscated from one of the detained *İlim* militants. Within this context, it was claimed that the organisation collaborated with international jihadist networks, including Al Qaeda. Although there were attack plans by the organisation, none of them were realised due to the operations of the security forces. The assassination of Gaffar Okkan remained the last armed attack on the organisation. Afterward, the organisation ceased operations and went underground until the mid-2000s (Çiçek, 2017, 62). In the third period, it emerged with several legal associations and platforms, such as the Foundation of the Oppressed (*Mustazaf-Der*), the Foundation of Hope (*Umut-Der*) and the Platform of Prophet Lovers. It organised legal demonstrations and formed charitable organisations. When compared with the first period of the organisation, which preferred the armed struggle, the third period of the organisation involves the legal basis, including the activities of non-governmental organisations. *İlim* participated in legal political processes and elections when the *HÜDA-PAR* was founded in 2012. In this context, Çakır (2011, 251) compares it with the Lebanese Hezbollah, which followed a similar line from radicalisation to moderation in the 2000s. Çiçek (2017, 62–63) underlines the transformation of *İlim* from radicalism in the 1980s and 1990s to moderation in the mid-2000s. This is significant in the sense that while the organisation adopted an understanding of the ummah and the establishment of an Islamic state in the earlier years, it embraced a legal position within the boundaries of constitutional order in the moderation period.

THE TODAY AND FUTURE OF *İLIM* AND HÜDA-PAR

With the influence of the Kurdish Initiative of the Turkish state and the civil war in Syria that began in 2011, relations between Kurdish groups and the state transformed from dialogue to conflict. The mutual moderation between Turkey and pro-Kurdish groups evolved into a democratic initiative process that both began in dialogue, which is called the *Solution Process* or *National Unity and Brotherhood Project*, between 2009 and 2010. With the beginning of the civil war in Syria, Turkey has changed its attitude towards the Kurdish issue. Ankara's policies towards the civil war in Syria and Syria's Kurds were framed within the management of its Kurdish conflict. There is increasing tension between the Kurds and Turkey, which is directly related to the increasing influence of Kurdish groups in northern Syria. Turkey interprets developments in Syria's Kurdish regions as a threat to its national security and territorial integrity and is concerned about the spillover effect of the emergence of an autonomous government in Syria, which is able to increase the PKK's power as a regional actor and put more pressure on Turkey on its Kurdish initiative (Lowe and Güneş, 2015; 8).

Due to the end of the "solution process" and the rise of radical Islamist groups in the civil war in Syria, there were intra-community disputes among Kurds in Turkey. On the one hand, the intermediation of the state's initiative towards its Kurdish citizens heavily by secular Kurdish actors increased tensions within Kurdish groups. There have been street fights between HÜDA-PAR and secular groups (Unal, 2016, 113). On the other hand, affiliations between radical Islamist groups, including the Islamic State (ISIS), and the religious Kurds in Turkey increased tensions among Kurds in Turkey. There have been claims that former members of *İlim* and grassroots of the HÜDA-PAR joined ISIS.[6] In this regard, HÜDA-PAR faces the pitfalls of losing popularity among the Kurdish population and comes up against radicalisation and marginalisation.

On the other side, members of *İlim* including Edip Gümüş and Cemal Tutar, arrested after the Beykoz Operation, were released, and they 'disappeared' in 2011. It is claimed that the militants, including high-ranking officials of the organisation, escaped to Iran and Syria (Tahincioğlu, 2011). After that, it is clear that *İlim* will be organised abroad, but returning to the 'golden ages' of Velioğlu has little chance.

CONCLUSION

Arise from domestic and international developments, *İlim* emerged as a local actor in Turkey. Inspired by the revolution in Iran in 1979, it aimed to establish an Islamic state. In this regard, it declared jihad against the state and rival Islamist and secular groups, including the PKK and *Menzil*. However, the death of the leader of the organisation in an armed conflict against the state in the Beykoz Operation in 2000 caused a transformation of the organisation. After that, *İlim* withdrew underground until its re-emergence through non-governmental organisations in the mid-2000s and the formation of *HÜDA-PAR* in 2012. The organisation has begun to perform within a legal process since the Beykoz Operation. While it participates in legal political processes and general-local elections, it is claimed that the armed wing of *İlim* moved its activities to Europe.

Against this background, *İlim* has to be defined at several points. Firstly, although it is known for its brutal attacks, tortures, and assassinations and is defined as a terrorist organisation, *İlim* is a fact that arose from social, cultural, historical, and international developments. It is beyond an organisation that can be destroyed through arms. It has a social base in Turkey and is supported by the Muslim Kurds in general. Secondly, even though there are claims about *İlim*'s relationships with the Turkish and Iranian states, *İlim* is an independent organisation. There are claims defining the organisation as an Iranian agent representing Iranian national interests in Turkey or a Turkish agent founded in order to weaken the secular Kurdish movements. However, the organisation moves through its own dynamics determined by domestic and international developments. As Çakır (2011, 249) argues, *İlim* is a sui generis organisation that has no similarity with any domestic or foreign organisations.

Notes

1 Similar to its meaning in Arabic (Hezbollah), HÜDA-PAR also means the Party of God. The name Hezbollah originates from the Qur'anic verses al-Ma'idah and al-Mujadila.

2 Kasımpaşa is a quarter within the Beyoğlu district of İstanbul.

3 *Menzil* is another Islamist group formed in the Hezbollahian understanding of Islam, and it is a rival of *İlim*. Established in Diyarbakır in 1981, *Menzil* was led by Fidan Güngör and Mansur Güzelsoy. According to *Menzil*, since the regime in Turkey was non-religious, it had to be toppled and an Islamic state had to be established. As a result of rivalry, there were armed conflicts, shootings, kidnappings, and assassinations between *İlim* and *Menzil*. When compared to *İlim*, *Menzil* was composed of more educated people. Although *İlim* was common among people of low income, *Menzil* was more popular among middle-class and high-income groups. After the clashes between the two groups, *İlim* kidnapped the leader of *Menzil*, Fidan Güngör, and killed him. After the death of its leader, *Menzil* broke up, and some of its members joined *İlim*.

4 According to Kürşat Atalar, the Muslim Brotherhood never had any direct relationship with radical Islamist groups, and *İlim* never liked the Brotherhood's branches in the region. For more information, see Kürşat Atalar, "Hizballah of Turkey: A Pseudo-Threat to the Secular Order?", *Turkish Studies*, 7:2, 2006, 307–331.

5 Members of the organisation were heavily from İstanbul and the Southeastern region of Turkey. Some of them were detained after the Beykoz Operation.

6 For instance, Halis Bayancuk, or Abu Hanzala, is claimed to be the leader of ISIS in Turkey. Halis Bayancuk is the son of Haci Bayancuk, who was among the leadership cadres and the emir of the political wing of *İlim*. For more information, see Yayla (2006).

References

Ahmet, S. Y. (2006). Portrait of Turkey's ISIS Leader Halis Bayancuk: Alias Abu Hanzala. Available at: https://www.researchgate.net/publication/309035384_Portrait_of_Turkey's_ISIS_Leader_Halis_Bayancuk_Alias_Abu_Hanzala

Aktürk, Ş. (2012). *Regimes of Ethnicity and Nationhood in Germany, Russia and Turkey*. Cambridge: Cambridge University Press.

Akyol, T. (2000). *Hariciler ve Hizbullah (Kharijites and Heznollah)*. Istanbul: Doğan Kitapçılık A.Ş.

Alagha, J. (2006). *The Shifts in Hezbollah's Ideology: Religious Ideology, Political Ideology and Political Program*. Amsterdam: Amsterdam University Press.

Atalar, K. (2006). Hizballah of Turkey: A Pseudo-Threat to the Secular Order? *Turkish Studies*, *7*(2), 307–331.

Aydıntaşbaş, A. (2000). Murder on the Bosporus. *Middle East Quarterly*, June 2002, 15–22.

Bagasi, İ. (n.d.). Kendi Dilinden Hizbullah ve Mücadele Tarihinden Kesitler (Hizbullah in Its Own Words and Excerpts from the History of Struggle). Available at: http://www.huseynisevda.net

Bulut, F. (1997). *Resmi Belgeler Işığında Ordu ve Din (The Military and the Religion in the Light of Formal Documents)*. Ankara: Doruk Yayıncılık.

Bulut, F. and Faraç, M. (1999). *Kod Adı Hizbullah: Türkiye Hizbullahı'nın Anatomisi (Hezbollah the Code Name: Anatomy of the Hezbollah in Turkey)*. Istanbul: Ozan Yayınları.

Çakır, R. (2011). *Derin Hizbullah (The Deep Hezbollah)*. İstanbul: Metis Yayınları.

Çiçek, C. (2017). *The Kurds of Turkey: National, Religious and Economic Identities*. London: I.B. Tauris.

Çiçek, H. (2000). *Hangi Hizbullah (Which Hezbollah)*. Şti. İstanbul: Analiz Basım Yayın Tasarım Uygulama Ltd.

Çitlioğlu, E. (2001). *Tahran-Ankara Hattında Hizbullah (Hezbollah Between Tehran-Ankara Line)*. Ankara: Ümit Yayıncılık.

Elhan, N. (2015). The Influence of Iranian Revolution in Turkey: Iran-Inspired Islamism. Unpublished Master's Thesis Submitted to Department of Middle East Studies, Middle East Technical University.

Elhan, N. (2016). Money talks: Turkish Islamic synthesis on banknotes of Turkey. *Moment Journal of Cultural Studies*, *3*(1), 171–189.

Eligür, B. (2010). *The Mobilization of Political Islam in Turkey*. Cambridge: Cambridge University Press.

Elitsoy, A. (2017). The Kurdish Hizbullah and its shifting attitude towards Kurdishness and the Kurdish issue in Turkey. *Fritillaria Kurdica: Bulletin of Kurdish Studies*, (17).

Goerzig, C. (2010). *Talking to Terrorists: Concessions and Renunciation of Violence*. London and New York: Routledge.

Güneş, C. (2015). What's Next for Syria's Kurds. *Jadalliya*. Available at: http://www.jadaliyya.com/pages/index/14005/what%E2%80%99s-next-for-syria%E2%80%99s-kurds Date Accessed: 20.01.2019.

Güzelsoy, M. (1966). *İnsan Haklarından İslami Harekete: İlmi ve Siyasi Tahliller (From Human Rights to Islamic Revolution: Scientific and Political Analysis)*. İstanbul: Fıtrat Yayınları.

Imset, I. (1992). *The PKK: A Report on Separatist Violence in Turkey (1973-1992)*. Ankara: Turkish Daily News Publications.

Jenkins, G. (2008). *Political Islam in Turkey: Running West, Heading East*. New York: Palgrave Macmillan.

Karmon, E. (1998). Islamic terrorist activities in Turkey in the 1990s. *Terrorism and Political Violence, 10*(4), 101–121.

Kurt, M. (2017). *Kurdish Hizbullah in Turkey: Islamism, Violence and the State*. London: Pluto Press.

Kushner, H. W. (2003). Turkish Hizballah in *Encylopedia of Terrorism*. New York: SAGE Publications.

Lapidot, A. (1996). Islamic activism in Turkey since the 1980 military takeover. *Terrorism and Political Violence, 8*(2), 62–74.

Lowe, R. and Güneş, C. (2015). *The Impact of the Syrian War on Kurdish Politics Across the Middle East*. Chatham House Report.

Manaz, A. (2018). Türk Hizbullahı (Turkish Hezbollah). Available at: https://www.manaz.net/arastirma/turk-hizbullahi/, Date Accessed: 24.01.2019.

Özeren, S. and Yilmaz, I. (2007). "Counterterrorism in Turkey: Organizational and Operational Structure and Training." In P. C. Kratcoski and K. P. Das (Eds.), *Police Education and Training in Global Society*. (pp. 371–386). New York: Lexington Books.

Seibert, T. (2011). Turkish Hizbollah Men Freed Under New Law. Available at: https://www.thenational.ae/world/europe/turkish-hizbollah-men-freed-under-new-law-1.374121

Tahincioğlu, G. (2011). Hizbullahçılar İran'a mı Kaçtı? (Did Hezbollah Militants Escaped to Iran?). Available at: http://www.milliyet.com.tr/hizbullahcilar-iran-a-mi-kacti–siyaset-1339488/

Unal, M. C. (2016). Is it ripe yet? Resolving Turkey's 30 years of conflict with the PKK. *Turkish Studies, 17*(1), 91–125.

Yayla, S. A. (2006). Portrait of Turkey's ISIS Leader Halis Bayancuk: Alias Abu Hanzala. Available at: https://www.researchgate.net/publication/309035384_Portrait_of_Turkey's_ISIS_Leader_Halis_Bayancuk_Alias_Abu_Hanzala

Yıldırım, I. (2012). Hizbullah Terör Örgütünün Şiddet Eylemlerinin Betimsel Analizi (Descriptive Analysis of the Violent Actions of the Hizbullah Terrorist Organization. Unpublished Msc Thesis Submitted to Turkish National Police Academy, Institute of Security Sciences, Ankara, Turkey.

49

HARAKAT AL-MUKAVVAMA AL-ISLAMIYAH-HAMAS

Filiz Katman

INTRODUCTION

The formation of the Islamic Resistance Movement (Hamas), which emerged from the Muslim Brotherhood, and its development into one of the major players in the Israeli-Palestinian conflict are examined in this chapter, highlighting both continuity and change in the process. Because it adopts a resistance mindset towards achieving objectives quickly, Hamas can be seen as a revisionist organisation. In contrast, the Muslim Brotherhood seeks to achieve societal revolution over time by instituting Islamic values in society. Organisations occasionally select illegal means to accomplish their political objectives. To achieve these ends, violence is used as a tool rather than an appropriate political instrument. In spite of strong criticism by the military wing within the organisation, such groups have recently tended to shift to the lawful sphere of politics, demonstrate their political will for negotiations, and fortify their political branch. In this context, four levels of study are used to examine factors that influence the shift from violence to politics and the politicisation processes: individual, organisational, societal, and international.

The chapter employs the concept of politicisation, which is defined as the reversal of the process from violence to politics, in addition to analysing Hamas through the politicisation of violence lens. In three cases, the concept of politicisation, which denotes a departure from violence, is examined via factor analysis at four levels. An approach that is more rigorous in its analysis of the tendency towards politicisation is to examine each process separately, as opposed to relying on a general model. The framework for analysis is predicated on the following: leadership and generational change at the individual level; divisions within the organisation at the organisational level; a shift in societal perspective regarding the utility of violence versus negotiation at the societal level; and international support for the organisation at the international level. Hamas is continuously politicising violence; therefore, insights gained from the application of these two concepts may be valuable in elucidating and comprehending the process's successful culmination.

CURRENT MILESTONES

The United States (US) levied sanctions on May 20, 2022, against a Hamas finance official, a consortium of financial intermediaries, and enterprises that generated revenue for the Palestinian organisation. The sanctions were imposed on the Hamas Investment Office, which is suspected of possessing assets exceeding $500 million in value. This organisation is associated with enterprises that operate in Algeria, Sudan, Turkey, Saudi Arabia, Sudan, and the United Arab Emirates (UAE). Elizabeth Rosenberg, assistant secretary of the Treasury for terrorist financing and financial crimes (Al Jazeera, May 24, 2022), asserts that Hamas has amassed vast financial resources concealed in its investment portfolio, all the while destabilising Gaza, a region afflicted by dire economic and living conditions.

To address a long-standing conflict between Hamas and Fatah that has caused widespread discontent and eroded public confidence in the Palestinian leadership, the Algerian government launched an ongoing effort in 2023 to find a resolution. The future of the Qassam Brigade, the military component of Hamas that both Fatah and Israel want to see entirely disarmed, is one of the topics up for debate. The two factions engaged in discussions regarding the Palestinian elections and the remuneration of 30,000 Hamas employees stationed in the Gaza Strip. The Palestinian Authority (PA), headed by Fatah, has since been in charge of the occupied West Bank. Hamas, meanwhile, maintains control over the Gaza Strip, which has been under Israeli siege since 2007 (Al Jazeera, October 11, 2022).

On its list of prohibited terrorist organisations, the Australian government has included the whole Palestinian movement, Hamas. Al-Qassam Brigades, the military component of Hamas, had already been named by Australia as a "terror" group in 2003; however, the new designation, which is in effect in April 2022, lists the group, including

DOI: 10.4324/9780429426063-56

its political side. The classification imposes limitations on funding or providing other support to Hamas, and violating these limits will result in a 25-year prison sentence, according to Australian Home Affairs Minister Karen Andrews. Because Britain has designated Hamas as an "Islamist terrorist group" in its entirety, a court in Cairo ruled in 2015 that those who support the movement run the risk of receiving up to 14 years in prison. Israel applauded the deed. The US and EU had taken analogous actions; therefore, this was done in reaction (The Times of Israel, November 26, 2021).

After Operation Al Aqsa Storm, the European Union (EU) declared Hamas as terrorist organisation Izzeddin Al-Qassam Brigades, Hamas' military wing, a terrorist organisation in 'the case brought against the group by a private plaintiff accusing the organisation of involvement in and financing of terrorist attacks inside Egypt and of attacking army and police personnel to destabilise the country' (Amwal Al Ghad, February 1, 2023) and 'further isolating the blockaded rulers of the Gaza Strip once openly welcome' (NBC News, February 28, 2023).

ISLAMIC MOVEMENT IN PALESTINE AND THE BIRTH OF HAMAS[1]

The inception of the Islamic movement in Palestine can be traced back to 1981, when Ihvan established Urat-ul Cihad (Family of Jihad) units in Gaza (Bulut, 2009: 365). With regard to the Muslim Brotherhood's impact in Palestine, the movement's infiltration into Gaza and the West Bank transpires via various international channels. The establishment of the unit in Gaza occurred via Egypt, whereas in the West Bank, it was established via Jordan. The unit in Gaza was established via Jordan owing to the fact that Jordanian citizenship was granted to the inhabitants of the West Bank following the 1948 conflict. In contrast to Nasser, King Hussein legally recognised the organisation, demanded their submission to him, and did not disrupt the equilibrium in reciprocation.

In response, the organisation restricted its endeavours to scholarly and social causes. The sole challenge arose when the organisation employed anti-Western rhetoric to criticise colonialism and non-compliance with Sharia. During the 1980s, individuals who were interested in joining the Ihvan unit in Gaza expressed dissatisfaction with their inability to secure membership in the Palestinian Liberation Organisation (PLO), an organisation comprised of Palestinian refugees residing in Kuwait. Organised under the name Al-Rabıta Islamiye (Islamic Union) at Kuwait University, the PO contained fifteen distinct political organisations (Bulut, 2009: 365). As a consequence, they either established distinct organisations espousing Islamic principles or assumed leadership positions; furthermore, they persisted in establishing Islamic organisations in the United Kingdom (UK) and the US.

This marked the beginning of the path towards a distinct entity from the Muslim Brotherhood. Divergences arose between the Fatah and the Muslim Brotherhood in Palestine with respect to the objectives that ultimately precipitated the establishment of Hamas. As opposed to jihad, the Muslim Brotherhood advocated "social transformation" through the inculcation of Islamic values into society. Fatah, on the other hand, favoured political resistance. Israel entered the fray at this juncture and adopted the policy of providing support to one faction while opposing the other. Yitzhak Segev, the Governor of Gaza for Israel, stated, "[a]s a military government, we allocate the budget provided by the Israeli government to the mosques" (Bayraktar, 2007: 53). The criticism resulting from this support was the allegation that the movement was engaged in a covert partnership with Israel. The Muslim Brotherhood endeavoured to surmount this challenge by invoking the argument that Palestine is the Holy Land, thereby asserting that the establishment of a Palestinian state in that particular region of the territory would amount to an unacceptable recognition of Israel and thus negate the primary reason for the establishment and struggle for an independent Palestine.

A faction of the Muslim Brotherhood identified opportunities for jihadi-armed resistance in Jordan and Kuwait during the 1980s. A covert meeting was convened with the intention of furnishing the Muslim Brotherhood members in Jordan with essential weaponry and equipment, in addition to military instruction. In attendance were representatives from Saudi Arabia, Jordan, Kuwait, Bahrain, Qatar, and Palestinians residing under occupation. The Izzeddin Al-Qassam Brigades emerged from the Palestinian Mujahidin, an organisation with religious motivations, subsequent to the establishment of Hamas (Erdin, 1999: 80). Lecnetu Palestine (Palestinian Committee-Internal Commission), founded in 1983, was an additional significant development. It was the Ottoman Empire's "Bilad al-Sham," an administrative concept that encompassed Palestine, Syria, Lebanon, and Jordan. The Kuwaiti collection of $70,000 for the Palestinian movement was hailed as a significant achievement. Although these advancements serve as precursors to future events, they are not adequate to supplant the PLO with the Muslim Brotherhood (Bulut, 2009: 366–367). Conversely, the Islamic movement's position was bolstered by the PLO's erroneous actions, internal corruption, unfulfilled commitments, and the deterioration of public sentiment; the absence of armed resistance ultimately resulted in the formation of Hamas.

FORMATION OF HAMAS, AIMS, AND STRUCTURE

From the Islamic Association to Hamas

The prevailing conditions in Palestine were conducive to the emergence of a social movement comprised of Islamic factions, which espoused the cause of Palestinian nationalism and called for prompt armed resistance – a principle that the Muslim Brotherhood notably neglected. The Al Mucemma Al Islami-Islam Association was established in 1973 by Sheikh Ahmed Yassin, Abdulaziz Rantisi, and Mahmud Zahar to serve as a coordinating body for all Muslim Brotherhood activities. Later, these three individuals established Hamas.

The gradual expansion of Hamas' sphere of influence was significantly aided by controlling the mosques. The influence of Israel became apparent at this juncture, and in 1979, the Al Mucemma Al Islami-Islam Association was granted a legal activity licence as a social aid organisation. A kindergarten, a clinic, a youth club, a women's activities centre, a zakat committee, and a section dedicated to the education of young females were all affiliated with the association. As an element of Hamas, the upkeep of the family was entrusted to women subsequent to men's enlistment in the resistance. Supportive structures and the provision of essential assistance during periods of need contributed to a rise in public confidence and support. As evidenced by the Intifada, children were considered an integral part of the resistance organisation, and the requisite structures were established in their honour. Printing and donating books featuring anti-Western and religious messages to libraries constituted an activity of the association that furnished the essential framework for children and young individuals during their formative years.

External and internal developments in Palestine significantly influenced the formation of Hamas. In response to the student demonstrations in Egypt that followed the signing of the Camp David Accord with Israel, Egyptian leader Anwar Sadat prohibited Egyptian universities from admitting Palestinian students. This resulted in the establishment of Gaza Islam University, which in the 1980s housed 4,500 students and served as the headquarters of the Palestinian Islamic Movement (Bayraktar,. 2007: 56). The Islamic Revolution of 1979 in Iran fortified Islamic movements in the region's universities, while the Muslim Brotherhood broadened its sphere of influence via the visits of its regional leaders. An additional occurrence beyond Palestine that bolstered the Islamic Movement's sphere of influence was the PLO's withdrawal from Lebanon in 1982.

The only vulnerability of the Muslim Brotherhood at this time was its decision to delay armed resistance. Former members formed the Islamic Resistance, Al-Takfir Vel Hicr, and Tanzim Al Jihad in response to this circumstance. While the Muslim Brotherhood persisted in delaying armed resistance, the Intifada, which ushered in a new era of literature on social resistance, explicitly advocated for the formation of a novel organisational structure among Muslim Brotherhood members in Palestine in order to mobilise. An additional element that contributed to the rift between the Muslim Brotherhood and Hamas was the Muslim Brotherhood's acknowledgement of Arafat as the sole representative of the Palestinian people. Hamas, on the other hand, acknowledged Arafat's representation of the Palestinian people through the PLO, but not independently (Erdin, 1999: 80).

Intifada: From the Beginning of the Resistance to Hamas

In response to the Israeli Defence Forces' (IDF) killing of a young Palestinian man on December 9, 1987, rioting broke out, marking the beginning of the First Palestinian Intifada (1987–93). The impact of increased youth membership was such that Israeli soldiers were compelled to withdraw. This occurrence additionally brought to light the pacifism of the Muslim Brotherhood and incited a gathering of future movement leaders Sheikh Ahmed Yasin, Abdulaziz Rantisi, Ibrahim Al Yazuri, Sheikh Salah Shada, and Issa Al Nashar, who were educators, physicists, chemists, and scientists, to deliberate on the execution of the armed resistance strategy they had been strategizing since the 1980s.

Sheikh Yassin established the organisation's initial armed branch in Gaza in 1982; he was apprehended the following year and received a 14-year prison sentence; he was pardoned along with 1,000 prisoners in 1985, per the prisoner exchange (Bulut, 2009: 347). The impact of the Iranian Islamic Revolution, the resistance efforts in Afghanistan against the Soviet invasion, and the dissatisfaction of the educated youth with the PLO's policies were some of the main drivers behind the establishment of the armed resistance unit. Notwithstanding its capitulation, this unit played a pivotal role in galvanising the disorderly youth in the West Bank and paved the way for the development of an alternative organisation to the PLO.

The imprisonment of Sheikh Yassin played a significant role in garnering support for his Jihazu Palestine (Palestinian Tool), an organisation designed to facilitate communication between Palestinians living abroad and the international community. Notwithstanding the fragmentation of the Islamic Resistance Movement, the Islamic Fight Movement (Harakat Alqital Al'Iislamia), which formed the foundation of the armed structure, transpired in 1986–87. Land allegiances and incarcerated individuals are crucial components in the organisation of armed resistance. The inception of the Intifada was instigated by the foundation of Seraya Al Jihad Al Islami (Islami Jihad Brigades) in 1986 and Palestinians', particularly the youth's, inclination towards Islamic groups in the wake of the Jerusalem incident (Bulut, 2009: 347).

The initial manifesto declared the establishment of the Islamic Resistance Movement (Harakat Al-Mukavvama Al-Islamiyah-Hamas) and concluded deliberations. Conversely, the PLO concurrently established Al-Qiyada Al-Muwhhada and the Unified National Leadership of the Uprising (UNLU); these two organisations served as substitutes for one another. Established with the purpose of coordinating the Intifada, which involved numerous prominent Palestinian organisations, the Front comprised PLO-aligned Fatah, the Palestinian Communist Party, the Public Front, and the Democratic Front. Since 1988, efforts have been made to bridge the administrative and legal void left by Hussein, the King of Jordan, when he declared the separation from the West Bank. The proponents of the PLO declared the formation of the Unified National Leadership of the Uprising (UNLU) through Al-Quds Palestinian Arabic Radio in Tunisia. The Islamic Resistance and Hamas both abstained from membership in the National Unified Leadership Front. As stated by Filiu (2012: 67), although Hamas originated from Palestinian Islamism and utilised it as its primary asset, it was the PLO from the "outside" – and thus the Palestinian diaspora – that ultimately realised the vision of a Palestinian state coexisting with Israel and operating independently.

Aims and Structure

Hamas' stated objective during its formation phase was "the development of a Palestinian state with Islamic values within the territories of Palestine invaded by Israel." Following the 2006 elections, Hamas ceased employing slogans and printed and verbal declarations from its inception, such as "the formation of an Islamic state in the historical Palestinian territories called Islamic Waqif land." Instead, the group adopted the goal of "ending the Israeli invasion." In an interview on January 10, 2007, Halid Meshal, the political bureau chief and foreign relations executive of Hamas, declared, "[a]s a Palestinian, I advocate for a state [based] on the 1967 borders." In doing so, he tacitly acknowledged the existence of an Israeli entity, which Sheikh Yassin categorically rejected with the following statement: "In reality, an Israeli structure or a state in the remaining Palestinian territory is correct." It may be interpreted as an indication of a relaxation in Halid Meshal's strict discourse and rigid stance.

The fundamental components of Hamas' organisational framework comprise the shura, political bureau, and leadership in both Gaza and the West Bank. Decisions rendered in Shura, the primary structure, are implemented by the Political Bureau (Gunning, 2007: 99). With the approval of both the internal and external leadership, the objectives of the organisation are established in accordance with the policies established by Hamas. Political, military, and social entities comprise Hamas' distinctive structure. Organisational structure is classified by Halid Meshal as political activities, military activities, social activities (da'wa), and internal security (Mishal, 2003: 569–589).

Military units abide by the decisions made by the former, with the exception of the autonomy that political units display, particularly when it comes to the interaction between political and military structures. When contemplating the dire conditions endured by the Palestinian people, social aid and relief organisations significantly contribute to eliciting the people's sympathy by providing essentials that the PLO fails to provide. Established in 1991, Izzeddin Al-Qassam Brigades functioned as an official military unit of Hamas and was one of several local initiatives directed by the senior military militia (Mishal, 2000: 64). One argument (Gunning, 2007: 139) concerning relations with the political unit of the organisation is that the military unit has a relatively small number of generals and senior political executives; therefore, the Hamas leaders derive their power from sources other than the military unit's violent capacity.

Following the Palestinian Authority's September 2000 attacks against Israel and the armistice agreement between Israel and the Palestinian Authority in June 2001, confrontations between military units and political leadership materialised. The cessation of hostilities was officially proclaimed by the Izzeddin Al Qassam Brigades on behalf of Hamas. However, Sheikh Yassin, the organisation's founding president (Mishal, 2003: 583), maintained that the ceasefire was unilaterally declared: "Hamas did not declare a ceasefire ... Political unit determines the policies of Hamas, not the military unit ... Military unit is comprised of several groups. There is no single general, but many generals. Thus, we cannot know who declared it."

Hamas began to use Qassam missiles after suicide bombing incidents. The range of the 1,750 homegrown missiles that struck Israel in 2008 was comparable to that of the 281 that struck in 2004; they approached Tel Aviv. Hamas ceased missile launches subsequent to Operation Cast Lead, which in January 2009 resulted in the greatest number of casualties, and advocated for other factions to adopt a comparable strategy. Due to the absence of any missile launches by Hamas during the 34 missile attacks that occurred in 2010, an Israeli Ministry of Foreign Affairs representative asserted that "Hamas is defending Israel" (The Economist, 2010a).

A further example is a declaration made by Hamas concerning their endeavour to halt assaults on Israel (The New York Times, 2010). The pragmatic viewpoint that senior Hamas executioners did not perceive such assaults as serving Palestinian interests accounted for this stance. Hardliners within Hamas and Islamic radicals in other groups were contemplated in the context of the missile attacks; furthermore, these assaults were deemed a retaliatory measure to the January 2010 assassination of Hamas member Mahmud Al-Mabuh in Dubai, which was allegedly carried out by Israeli agents outside of Palestine (The Economist, 2010b). One could argue that Hamas justified its policy decisions throughout the Al-Aqsa intifada and the Gaza War by employing pragmatism and flexibility in framing those decisions in accordance with its long-held beliefs (Wagemakers, 2010: 357).

Sheikh Yassin's religious discourse in Palestine's mosques and prayer rooms during the 1960s and 1970s had a significant impact on the development of Islamic ideology and laid the groundwork for Hamas. In this manner, Ebu Amr (1998: 43–45) emphasised the significance of midday and evening prayers. The authorisation granted to the Islamic Association by Israel in 1979 authorised the use of prayer rooms and mosques to disseminate the concept of armed resistance. The mosques' significance became evident through the populace's mobilisation throughout the Intifada and the subsequent demonstrations. The substantial proliferation of mosques is indicative of the organisation's successful infiltration into society and expansion of its sphere of influence. This structure inevitably resulted in less formal connections and a more relaxed framework. As explained by Mishal (2003: 581):

> Hamas, as a local movement, plays a vital role in the formation of organisational structure and the provision of support to society through friendship and inter-human bonds and interactions instead of hierarchy. Group interaction based on solidarity and horizontal relations, a common past among the participants joining during its formation, influenced more than authoritarian, bureaucratic, and vertical relations and the chain of command.

Gaza Islam University played the most significant role in disseminating the Hamas movement. This university provided Palestinians with the opportunity to earn a tertiary education without having to travel abroad, and student union organisations and students engaged in an exchange of ideas. A number of senior executives at Hamas hold academic degrees from this institution. It played a role in enhancing the organisation's stability. Cemil Hamami, a Palestinian, was instrumental in the establishment and leadership of Hamas in the West Bank in 1988 (Erdin, 1999: 79). Hamas, an organisation that sought to link "religion with politics and social activism," made use of unions and professional organisations.

Social aid from Hamas provided the necessities of Palestinians not met by the Palestinian Authority through religious schools, kindergartens, libraries, sports clubs, and health centres; on the other hand, activities were held in the realisation of the social transformation of the Muslim Brotherhood together with resistance. Such institutions were organised as Islamic Ottoman complexes around the mosques. In terms of health, the Scientific Medicine Union, founded by Hamas in 1997, met one of the vital necessities of public health services that were unmet by the Palestinian Authority. Such structures resemble civil society organisations in terms of functionality, filling the gaps in services (Mishal, 2003: 7). In benefiting from the services of Hamas, the absence of any religious or political limitations allowed Hamas to reach beyond its sympathisers. In this way, support gained by a grassroots organisation through such informal networks was reflected in the number of votes in the January 2006 election and in the surveys.

Numerous Islamic social institutions supported over 275,000 Palestinians in the West Bank and Gaza, according to research conducted at the end of the 1990s (Crisis Group, 2003: 7; Malka, 2005: 39). Hamas administered 65% of primary school education in Gaza in an Islamic manner during the Al-Aqsa Intifada in 2000 (Malka, 2005: 39). This serves as substantiation for the organisation's efficacy and sway in attaining its principal aim, which is to institute an Islamic-oriented societal transformation in Palestine. Destroying Palestinian infrastructure, high unemployment, and poverty all contributed to the Palestinian Authority's detriment during the Second Intifada. As a result, Palestinians were compelled to join social solidarity networks, which bolstered Hamas' support base.

The fact that Hamas considers the struggle for independence an "individual religious duty" (Nüsse, 1998: 72) is crucial for women who are considering participating in the resistance against their spouses' wishes. Article 12 of the Covenant of Hamas (Mideast, 2009), which pertains to strategy and methods, states that "love of nations, resistance to the enemy, and suppressing the enemy are the duties of each man or woman Muslim individually." Hamas was compelled to make way for women as a result of the Palestinian Central Election Committee's quota system, which mandated two female candidates per local structure, and the increase in the quota for chairs in Palestinian legislation. However, as a conservative organisation, Hamas had several restrictions on its organisational perspective regarding women, including the use of roses rather than actual images of female candidates on campaign posters, the refusal to hold mixed election meetings in favour of home meetings with women, and the absence of women from the political leadership to Shura during executions.

Hamas operates under the dual regime of official subordination to a political unit and autonomy in decision-making for its constituent units. Social gatherings are conducted autonomously from military installations. Regarding the operation of the official organisation, Meshal stated:

- Duties are determined through interactions among local members instead of senior executives.
- Decisions are made through interaction among the participants instead of hierarchical authority and control.
- Activities are based on information coming from members at the local level instead of information coming from formal leaders.
- Horizontal communication and consulting among members in different local positions are more common than vertical relations between ruler and ruled.
- Those making activities at the local level dedicate themselves to accomplishing their duties and responsibilities effectively instead of blind loyalty to the leader and obedience (Mishal, 2003: 583).

This administrative framework ensures that information

flows in both directions, from the lowest levels to the highest, and that the policies, activities, and executives in place correspond to the needs and expectations of the lowest levels. These attributes established the foundation for the organisation's triumph in the 2006 elections. The advisory board and the political bureau comprise the senior execution. Prior to the death of Sheikh Yassin, the "external leadership," or leaders residing outside of Palestine, held a more significant position. However, subsequent to that, the "internal leadership," or leaders residing in Palestine, possessed an equal amount of influence.

In contrast to Fatah, one of the assets of Hamas is that its leaders are elected by the general public and grieve in the same locations. An examination of the life narratives of political leaders revealed that their upbringing and residence in refugee camps facilitated their connection with the public, enabled them to identify with the concerns and responses of the populace, and secured their support by formulating solutions to challenges in accordance with their essential requirements. It demonstrates public support for Hamas in contrast to the corruption allegations surrounding Fatah.

Hamas' local leaders maintain traditional and informal relations of solidarity; trust, recognition, and friendship take precedence over hierarchical structures; as a result, the organisation employs persuasion to recruit members and mobilise individuals; and award mechanisms are utilised as opposed to sanctions and punishments (Mishal, 2003: 581). A greater comprehension of these attributes of the structure can be attained by examining organisations with which it has affiliations, including student unions, mosques, and professional organisations.

The organisation's structure is comprised of individuals with advanced degrees. Since the elections of 2006, the average age of the Hamas cabinet has been a mere 49.3 years. With regard to educational attainment, four individuals were recent university graduates from the United States and three individuals were recent graduates from British universities. The young and exceptionally knowledgeable cabinet comprised two professors, eight Ph.D. holders, two surgeons, nine engineers, and four Islamic attorneys. An organisation characterised by its esteemed educational standing engaged in substantive deliberations regarding the means to fulfil the educational requirements of the populace. To solve the problem of keeping children at home rather than sending them to school, they established schools in relatively more secure areas and organised school transportation, as opposed to locating them within Jewish settlements, in order to address security concerns (Doyran, 2006: 98).

In relation to the organisational structure of Hamas, Mishal (2003: 582) posited that horizontal relations and a vertical command chain were essential for mobilising the people. Under this framework, horizontal positions were subordinate to a vertical command chain, wherein directives were issued from the highest level to the lowest, whereas reports were audited by the supervisors and issued from the bottom up. Various responsibilities are categorised vertically in accordance with the organisation's function. The bureaucratic hierarchy encompasses various spheres, including internal security, military operations, political engagements (e.g., protests, demonstrations), and da'wa (Islamisation of the populace). Da'wa is typically conducted in mosques but can also be achieved through religious, athletic, or social activities; recruitment for Hamas membership training is another facet. It is not unusual for the age and social-professional backgrounds of military units to diverge from those of internal and external political leaders, given that Hamas social activists are youthful, educated, militant, charismatic, frequently hail from lower middle class and military organisations, and have close ties to the graduates of Gaza Islam University and colleges in the West Bank and Gaza.

The financial sources and expenditures of Hamas are sufficiently extensive to merit a separate section. In this section, Hamas leaders' and researchers' statements regarding the subject will be disclosed. According to an analysis of Hamas (Council of Foreign Relations, 2009), "90% of Hamas activities were comprised of social, development, cultural, and education activities"; this indicates that a substantial portion of the organisation's budget is allocated to these areas. Israel estimates that between 70 and 90 million dollars of Hamas' budget were allocated to political and social outreach initiatives, including schools, clinics, and welfare organisations, with military operations receiving only 15 to 20% of the budget (Levitt, 2007).

The siege on Gaza, which caused a scarcity of essential supplies, gave rise to a "tunnel economy." This economic strategy is deemed "successful in terms of success in constructing the tunnels, negative psychological impact on Israeli citizens, and limited success in allowing Hamas militants entry to Israel" (Watkins & James, 2016: 84). The argument was made that "Hamas' Economy Ministry had taken control over the tunnel revenues from the Interior Ministry, and receipts were deposited in the single treasury account the Hamas government operates" (Pelham, 2011: 35). Israel sought to deplete Hamas' military forces through tangible means, whereas Hamas pursued a strategy aimed at depleting the Israeli civilian population (Shamir & Hecht, 2014: 81). However, those who were supposed to receive such aid instead held the Palestinian Authority accountable, attributing the situation to the gradual closing of Hamas' bank accounts.

Given that every problem has a corresponding resolution, Hamas resolved this particular one by conserving funds in currency rather than depositing them into bank accounts (Hroub, 2004: 33). Following its triumph in the 2006 elections and subsequent assumption of government in Gaza, Hamas established a monopoly over social assistance through its acquisition of the zakat committee in Gaza (Milton-Edwards, 2008: 1595). According to Sayigh (2010: 1), Hamas achieved success in constructing an operational public administration system by employing a process of trial and error, demonstrating significant adaptability and a noticeable learning curve. During his time in Syria, Meshal played a crucial role as a fundraiser for supporters in the Gulf who funded the clinics and youth organisations. These organisations prevented the attacks in America because they did not want their names to be associated with them (Rees & Hamad, 2004: 45–60).

One form of direct financial assistance to the Palestinians is salary assistance. This aid is particularly designated for the families of suicide bombers and relatives of Palestinian ordinary citizens who perished in the attacks. Zakat (alms) committees fulfil a crucial function in delivering such assistance. There exists a contention that Hamas exercises authority over zakat (alms) committees in Palestine, thereby compromising a substantial revenue stream for Palestinian inhabitants. Hamas' support among the Palestinian people is intricately linked to the redistribution of such revenues. The escalation of external assistance provided to Hamas throughout the Oslo era was also influenced by corruption allegations concerning Fatah.

Hamas made concerted efforts within Muslim social centres in the US and Europe to establish the presence of the Arab and Palestinian societies' movements. Notably, Hamas operated a prominent facility in Dallas, Texas, which served as a hub for publishing, fundraising, and organising events. Hamas disseminated Al-Zaituna through several platforms in North America, including Ila Palestine and the Palestine Monitor. According to Mishal (2003: 581), two sites were established in Springfield, Virginia, in 1991. However, these centres were subsequently shut down in 1993 following the US' designation of Hamas as a terrorist group.

Additionally, it is worth noting that "unfulfilled promises of the short Muslim Brotherhood reign in Egypt and enmity of the military regime in Egypt isolated it regionally and led the Hamas leaders to hold negotiations for mending ties with Iran" with the potential of "internal cohesion leading to a violent outburst against Israel" (Karmon, 2013: 111). According to Dunning (2015: 19), Hamas is perceived as a component of a "religious wave of popular resistance against an established order." Hamas embodies a shift from a focus on reformist and communal approaches to a more politicised emphasis within the Islamic movement. This transition involves a move away from an emphasis on individual spiritual life towards a greater emphasis on activism.

When analysing the events and developments preceding the establishment of Hamas, various factors come into play besides the Muslim Brotherhood. These include the characteristics and inclinations of Hamas leaders, the evolving composition of Palestinian society over time, the structure and performance of other organisations in Palestine, current events, and the policies and initiatives of regional and out-of-region actors. The effects of the changes that have occurred within Hamas since its establishment in 1987 remain comparable. A persistent discourse developed, specifically in response to Hamas' election triumph in 2006, concerning whether Hamas would continue as an actor complying with the rules of a democratic structure or an organisation using illegitimate methods.

GENERATIONAL CHANGE

On an individual level, the ramifications of leadership and membership turnover across generations are critical to Hamas. It has been noted that a shift in leadership has an immediate impact on the propensity for violence or political engagement. The first generation of Hamas represented the organisation's "cause-oriented" ancestors; they exhibited greater zeal, ire, dedication, militancy, and a focus on achieving results. They possess firsthand knowledge of the "good old days" and are capable of drawing parallels between the present and the past. Having personally experienced liberation, they possess a distinct and detailed vision of the day when the "cause" is successfully achieved. They are enthusiastic about achieving it as quickly as possible, given the memories of the past and the freedom that it represents. They are inclined towards resorting to violence and resistance as an immediate resolution. The second generation, conversely, comprises the adherents. They are born into a violent and violent environment, devoid of any conceptions or recollections of freedom. They have suffered losses and violent assaults. They are consequently more inclined to partake in political discourse and negotiation.

Sheikh Ahmed Yassin and Yasser Arafat (in Fatah) are the progenitors of Palestinian resistance and the leaders of the initial generation. Conversely, the second generation encountered liberation during their time spent in the refugee settlements. In contrast to the first generation, which yearns to reclaim the good old days, the second generation is intent on experiencing genuine liberation in the future. Thus, they are more motivated to discover productive solutions, even if they require negotiation. Ismael Haniyeh and Khalid Meshal represent the second generation of leaders.

The notion of refugee introduces an additional attribute to Hamas: a distinction between internal (domestic) and external (exiled) leadership. While external leadership residing outside of Palestine is liberated and shielded from the country's problems, internal (domestic) leadership faces those issues on a daily basis. This situation has an impact on their viewpoint regarding how to advance the cause through negotiation or resistance. Since they are not currently dealing with the difficulties caused by the embargo on Gaza, the external (exiled) leadership continues to maintain its position of resistance. Conversely, internal (domestic) leadership that is confronted with day-to-day challenges and restrictions on personal autonomy exhibits a greater propensity for engaging in political and negotiation processes.

SPLIT AT ORGANISATIONAL LEVEL: MILITARY WING-POLITICAL WING

The organisation has not ruled out a political option in light of the fact that it has chosen an illegitimate route to achieve its political objectives. The organisational structure reflects this division into a military arm and a political wing. However, the military wing has been present since the inception of the organisation, while the political arm has emerged more recently. Bhasin and Carter Hallward (2013: 75) argue that after two decades of active involvement in local and municipal elections, the Reformation and Change Party's establishment as a political party was an obvious progression. Furthermore, "the Hamas leadership of the government has either abandoned its conception of 'resistance' or accepted that its statelet in Gaza is anything like an end point for its ambitions" (Brown, 2012: 4).

The instruments adopted by these organisations vary in accordance with the daily agenda. Every term possesses its own collection of political violence. Every form of violence, from suicide bombings to abductions, is influenced by the specific characteristics of the era. As a weapon, the political wing's presence in the wave of democracy is hardly surprising. Additionally, due to the protracted conflict, this violent organisation has exhibited indications of war fatigue. Nevertheless, this notion may be called into question, especially in light of the recent nefarious assault by Hamas on Israel on October 7, 2023, which was of such magnitude that it earned the moniker "9/11" for Israel.

While setting aside the malevolent assaults that occurred on October 7, the aforementioned crucial issue revolves around the leadership of the organisation: does it consist of the military wing or the political wing? It is essential to consider the power equilibrium between the two wings when attempting to discern a political or violent tendency. When the military wing holds the upper hand, the organisation does not appreciate the endeavours towards negotiations. When the political branch is more powerful than the military wing, negotiations, elections, and politics are prioritised over resistance.

Hamas is divided into a military branch and a political wing within the organisation. There is an observed correlation between the strength of the political faction and the encouragement of negotiations. Furthermore, in the event of fruitful negotiations, the political branch experiences an extra boost. Another characteristic at this juncture is the ability to ascertain the direction of the tendency. Regardless of whether the organisation is hierarchical or cell-based, the dominance of the wing is crucial to the movement. When hierarchical, the wing's dominance exerts a significant influence.

UTILITY OF VIOLENCE VERSUS POLITICS IN PUBLIC SUPPORT

One factor contributing to the utilisation of violence by organisations to achieve their political objectives, or "the cause," is that such organisations either lack the capacity to garner public support or assert that securing public support is impractical; instead, they contend that advancing the cause is an imperative matter. They therefore resort to violence, or "force," as opposed to public relations campaigns, to persuade the public. In doing so, they justify their use of violence. They endeavour to garner public support through acts of violence within a more condensed timeframe, in contrast to political campaigns. Subsequently, an alteration occurs in the association between the organisation and the public. The organisation recognises the critical importance of societal perspective, which is founded upon the notion of the utility of violence. A shift in public opinion regarding the efficacy of violence in pursuit of political objectives has an immediate and direct impact on the propensity for resorting to violent means as opposed to engaging in negotiations.

Hamas, according to one study, asserted accountability for over eighty terrorist attacks that transpired from 1993 to 2008. In the period preceding the 2006 election in Palestine, which spanned from September 2000 to August 2005, 148 suicide bombers executed 1.35 suicide bombings; Hamas was accountable for 39.9% of those attacks (Benmelech & Berrebi, 2007: 223–238). Although both Hamas and the al-Aqsa Martyrs Brigades claimed responsibility for numerous terrorist attacks against Israel, their reactions diverged (Figure 49.1).

Entities within Hamas offer comprehensive public services, including but not limited to healthcare, education, and financial assistance. Consequently, it possesses a robust civil society wing that sustains and generates substantial public support. Furthermore, by maintaining direct channels of communication with Palestinian society, Hamas remains cognizant of the public's needs and viewpoints. In the decision-making process, input from the lowest to the highest levels of the organisation is incorporated, and surveys of the Palestinian people are considered. Ensuring a continuous flow of information and incorporating public needs into the organisation's future decision-making process are imperative for fostering sustainable support. In contrast, the Fatah incident serves as an illustrative example of the detrimental consequences that can arise when an organisation becomes estranged from society.

Conversely, Hamas leaders enjoy an extravagant lifestyle akin to that of average Palestinians; Fatah, on the other

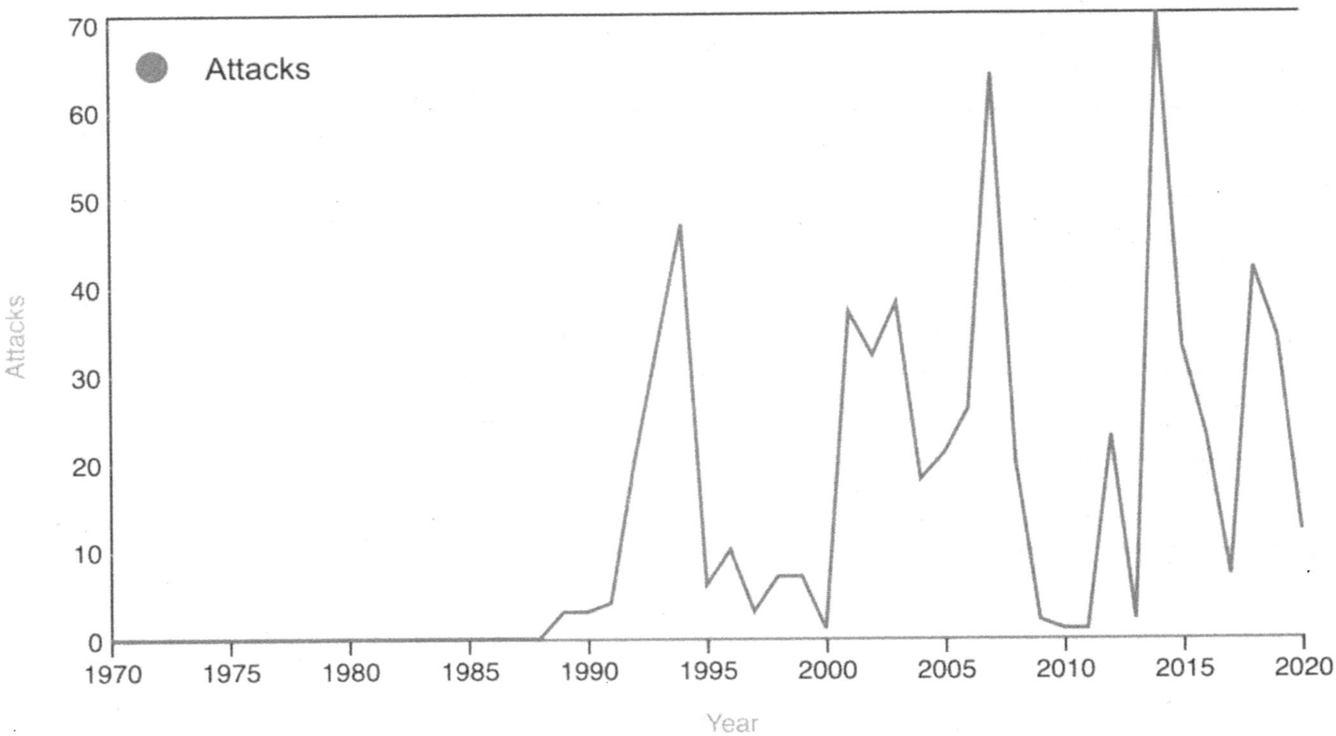

Figure 49.1 Hamas Incidents Perpetrated, 1970–2020.

Global Terrorism Database (GTD) (2024).

hand, is not supported and is harshly criticised for its corruption and extravagant lifestyle. Consequently, surveys indicate that the organisation takes into account public opinion regarding the relative importance of resistance and negotiation in contrast to politics and violence. In instances where the Palestinian people abandon their belief in the efficacy of violence in favour of negotiation as a more fruitful means of attaining the objective, Hamas reciprocally endorses negotiation. Additionally, there is a contention that the provision of ceasefires is constrained by the attributes of a tactical pause (Milton-Edwards, 2017: 212). The establishment of Hamas as the de facto authority of the Gaza Strip, according to Byman (2010: 45), is the greatest impediment to peace between Israel and Palestine. Pastor (2010: 196) supported that argument with criticism for "overstating the difficulty of securing Hamas' agreement to ceasefire and understating the problem of gaining Israel's agreement."

INTERNATIONAL COMMUNITY AS A SUPPORTER OF THE ORGANISATION

In 2013, a warning was made regarding "the ugly truth" (for Israel, the US, and the international community) that "Hamas is winning and it may be too late to reverse that trend" (Byman, 2013: 63).

The international community's support of such groups that employ violence for political purposes is a significant determinant in deciding between resistance and negotiation. In this context, "support" refers to economic, military, or financial assistance for the organisation. Furthermore, the response of the organisation's "enemy" (i.e., the state or government) to constructive measures (such as official declarations endorsing negotiations, truth-telling, and the like) is pivotal in determining whether the organisation will persist in its pursuit of negotiations or revert to violence. A negotiation atmosphere may endure if positive actions taken by the opposing side reciprocate positive actions taken by the violent organisation, as this would strengthen the political branch, also known as the "doves," in the organisation against the "hawks."

In contrast, the absence of constructive actions from the opposing party does not inspire optimism or despondency regarding the necessity of solution-oriented negotiations among the remainder of the organisation. One possible argument is that by offering a ceasefire of approximately five years and initiating negotiations with Hamas, Israel can alleviate the threat posed by Hamas, which demands that the Iranian regime reconsider the cost of maintaining its nuclear programme (Frankel, 2012: 62). Such an offer would require Israel to significantly ease the Israeli blockade of Gaza in exchange for a reduction in Hamas' demands against other militant factions in Gaza. For fear of bolstering Hamas, Israel was averse to a ceasefire (Pastor, 2010: 196).

Permanent cessation of hostilities enhances the efficacy of violent means but ultimately leads to disarmament; in the absence of such an outcome, the organisation's intentions come into doubt. Trusting the opposing side to maintain peace and refrain from reverting to violence reduces feelings of insecurity; consequently violent organisations become more motivated to disengage. The crucial aspect at hand is that if disarmament is stipulated as the principal prerequisite for commencing negotiations with the organisation, it would betray its insecurity and unreliability. Therefore, disarmament represents the final stage in achieving the preconditions for a lasting peace agreement, after which both parties must develop a sense of security and confidence to avoid unexpected outbreaks of violence.

CONCLUSION: KEYS TO SUCCESS IN THE POLITICISATION OF VIOLENCE

The 2006 election victory was a milestone for Hamas because it initially bolstered the political wing's negotiating position. In addition, political participation appeared to mirror the transition from resistance to negotiation in Palestinian society. A political will existed to engage in negotiations, which appeared to be reflected in the temporary ceasefire. Hamas had the political determination to reach a compromise. Furthermore, due to societal disapproval of discord within the Palestinian organisations Fatah and Hamas, Hamas engaged in national unity negotiations with Fatah and adopted a more moderate stance and tone in its official declarations and decisions concerning Israel until October 7, 2023, when it launched Operation Al-Aqsa Storm.

"The Ugly Truth"

Byman (2013: 63) states, "Hamas is winning, and it may be too late to reverse that trend." Ten years after uttering the "ugly truth" (as perceived by the US and Israel), the Israeli-Palestinian conflict escalated once more with Hamas' deadly attack on Israel on October 7. But it was notably dissimilar to its previous attacks in terms of approach, duration, nature, attributes, and domestic and international outcomes: Benjamin Netanyahu declared at the United Nations General Assembly (UNGA) on September 25, 2023, "We will change the Middle East" (Euronews, 2023), that circumstances in Palestine, Israel, and possibly the entire Middle East would never be the same again.

Fifty years after the Yom Kippur War, which commenced on October 6, 1973, an assault was orchestrated on multiple Jewish holidays, including a Sabbath day, this time by Hamas and designated as "Operation Al-Aqsa Storm" (Amaliyyat Tūfān al-Aqṣā). Israel referred to this event as "Black Saturday" and the "Simchat Torah Massacre." It is worth noting that this attack was not orchestrated by a state entity but rather by Hamas. Therefore, with regard to these attributes, it diverges from its predecessors.

In addition, the outset is distinctive: a combination of land, air, and sea assaults, including powered paraglider incursions into the territory, and a rocket barrage of approximately 5,000 rockets directed at Israel. Pre-attacks in the realm of cyberspace are necessary for effective management, given the sophisticated technological infrastructure that underpins Israeli border security. Thus, the assault encompassed land, air, and sea domains and was preceded by a cyber assault that sought to disable the surveillance system. When examining the approaches taken by Hamas in the past, it becomes evident that this is the first instance in which an organisation has used every conventional and modern method against a state. It demonstrates that Hamas has acquired such capability since their last intense confrontation. Given the protracted siege that Gaza has endured over the years, the inquiry pertains to the acquisition of technological capabilities that enable monitoring of tunnels connecting Egypt and Gaza, as well as the provision of aid to Gaza.

In an interview conducted by Haberturk TV on October 14, 2023, Halid Meshal, the leader of the political wing, highlights a notable discrepancy between the political and military wings of the organisation when he says that he hears about operations over television: "Military resistance brigades make plans for the ground. Political decisions are within our authority. What happened on October 7 was related to the ground. We did not know who did it in the beginning; later, we also heard about the details. Then, members of Hamas are invited to a meeting." Conversely, an argument can be made that an internal dispute came to light on October 7. Hamas leaders Ismail Haniyeh and Yahya Sinwar "destroyed" the lower echelons of the terrorist organisation by ordering the attack on October 7, according to a senior Hamas commander: "We don't know in which direction we should go. They destroyed us". Abu Mohammed, the purported commander, stated in a Telegram interview that while the initial objective was to appoint a small number of Israeli soldiers as hostages, Hamas' military commanders abruptly altered the directive to execute the operation on October 7 (The Limited Times, November 10, 2023).

"Something Like This Has Never Happened Before"

According to witness accounts, simultaneous gunfire occurred in dozens of cities and towns: "Militants breached the

Gaza border fence and infiltrated neighbouring settlements in southern Israel." The attack resulted in the fatalities of hundreds of individuals, the injuries sustained by thousands, and the capture of an undetermined number of hostages (Meduza, October 10, 2023).

The Hamas onslaught on Israel that occurred on October 7th has been described as Israel's bloodiest war in nearly 50 years. Following the recent normalisation of relations between Israel and other Arab countries, including Saudi Arabia, there is a contention that a considerable number of Palestinians feel abandoned (Medium, October 15, 2023). The Abrahamic Accords have been subject to debate due to the perception that they provide official acknowledgement from Sunni Arab governments to Israel without necessitating a resolution to the Israeli-Palestinian conflict. Consequently, this leaves the Shiite Muslim nations, specifically Iran, Iraq, and Syria, as the remaining active supporters of Palestinian rights (Oriental Review, November 2, 2023).

It goes further by saying that October 7 was to prevent the Sauds from signing because, if they did, then the entire Palestinian cause would, in effect, have no defenders outside Palestine itself. According to Steven Sahiounie (The Duran, October 29, 2023), an independent Middle Eastern journalist:

> The US has betrayed Egypt again … Sisi knows there is an Israeli plan, condoned and supported by Biden, to remove all Palestinians from Gaza to Egypt, where they will be supported by humanitarian aid, but can never repopulate Gaza again. They will be permanently homeless and stateless refugees.

The leaders of Palestine, Jordan, and Egypt met on October 21 and decided unanimously to reject Netanyahu and Biden's proposal. The foundation of this argument is the assessment that October 7 was "preemptive."

October 7 demonstrates, among other things, that Hamas is not merely an organisation, as the Jerusalem Post (November 11, 2023) refers to it as an "army." Given that the Gaza Strip, which is governed by Hamas, has been subject to a land, sea, and air blockade since 2007, the inquiry pertains to how Hamas manages to operate at its capacity amidst such stringent circumstances. "Tunnel economy" relations with Iran and Hezbollah are an alternative approach, whereas tunnel economy was previously posited as one solution.

Conversely, the primary Israeli criticisms of the first phase of Operation Al-Aqsa Storm, which commenced on October 7, 2023, involve the "underestimation of Hamas by the Israeli army" and the "creation of a system focusing on intentions rather than capabilities." This operation comprised a combination of land, air, and sea assaults, including a rocket barrage consisting of approximately 5,000 rockets directed at Israel, as well as vehicle-borne and powered paraglider incursions into its territory. A cyber operation was conducted beforehand. Furthermore, analysis of the quantity of missiles launched from the Gaza Strip necessitates the inclusion of verified data.

Note

1 This chapter is based on research from the author's PhD thesis, "HAMAS: Bir Terörist Örgütün Siyasal Partileşmesi-Hamas: Political Party Formation of a Terrorist Organisation" (Unpublished PhD Thesis), Turkish Military Academy, Defense Studies Institute, 2010.

References

Al Jazeera. (May 24, 2022). US Sanctions Hamas Official.

Al Jazeera. (October 11, 2022). Palestinian groups Fatah, Hamas meet in Algeria to heal rift.

Amwal Al Ghad. (2023). Egyptian Court declares Hamas' Al-Qassam Brigades a 'Terrorist Group'. February 1, 2015. https://en.amwalalghad.com/egyptian-court-declares-hamas-al-qassam-brigades-a-terrorist-group/

Bayraktar, B. (2007). *Hamas*. İstanbul: Kara Kutu.

Benmelech, E. & Berrebi, C. (2007). Human capital and the productivity of suicide bombers. *Journal of Economic Perspectives, 21*(3), Summer 2007, 223–238. 10.1257/jep.21.3.223

Bhasin, T. & Hallward M.C. (2013). Hamas as a political party: Democratization in the Palestinian territories. *Terrorism and Political Violence, 25*(1), 75–93.

Brown, N.J. (2012). Gaza five years on: Hamas settles in Middle East. June 2012, Washington D.C.: Carnegie Endowment for International Peace. https://carnegieendowment.org/2012/06/11/gaza-five-years-on-hamas-settles-in-pub-48470

Bulut, F. (2009). *İslâmcı Örgütler 2*. İstanbul: Cumhuriyet Kitapları.

Byman, D. (2010). How to handle Hamas: The perils of ignoring Gaza's leadership. *Foreign Affairs, 89*(5), (September/October 2010), 45–62.

Byman, D. (2013). Is Hamas winning?. *The Washington Quarterly, 36*(3), 63–76.

Council on Foreign Relations. (2009). HAMAS. http://www.cfr.org/publication/8968/

Crisis Group. (2003). Islamic social welfare activism in the occupied Palestinian territories: A legitimate target?. Middle East Report, 2 April 2003, No. 13, 62–75.

Doyran, E. (2006). *Bir Direniş Hareketi Olarak Hamas-Hamas as a Resistance Movement (Yayınlanmamış Yüksek Lisans Tezi-Unpublished Graduate Thesis)*. Yildiz Technical University Social Sciences Institute.

Dunning, T. (2015). Islam and resistance: Hamas, ideology and Islamic values in Palestine, Critical Studies on Terrorism. 10.1080/17539153.2015.1042304

Ebu Amr, Z. (1998). *Batı Şeria ve Gazze'de İslâmî Direniş, Hamas ve İslâmî Cihad*. İstanbul: Ekin Yay.

Erdin, M. (1999). *Düşünceleri, Örgüt Yapıları ve Eylemleriyle Hizbullah ve Hamas*. İstanbul: Sarmal Yayınevi.

Euronews. (2023, October 10). 'We will change the Middle East', vows Israeli PM Netanyahu. https://www.euronews.com/2023/10/09/live-death-toll-continues-to-climb-as-israel-pummels-gaza

Filiu, J.P. (2012). The origins of Hamas: Militant legacy or Israeli tool?. *Journal of Palestine Studies, 41*(3), (Spring 2012), 54–70.

Frankel, R.D. (2012). Keeping Hamas and Hezbollah out of war with Iran. *The Washington Quarterly, 35*(4), 53–65.
Global Terrorism Database (GTD). (2024). Hamas "Incidents". https://www.start.umd.edu/gtd/search/Results.aspx?search=Hamas&sa.x=0&sa.y=0
Gunning, J. (2007). *Hamas in politics: Democracy, religion, violence.* London: Hurst Publishers.
Haberturk TV. (October 14, 2023). Hamas'ın siyasi lideri Halid Meşal Habertürk'te, Özel Röportaj. https://www.youtube.com/watch?v=2S1ss3teT7c
Hroub, K. (2004). Hamas after Shaykh Yasin and Rantisi. *Journal of Palestine Studies, 33*(4), 23–33.
Karmon, E. (2013). Hamas in Dire Straits. *Perspectives on Terrorism, 7*(5), October 2013, 111–126.
Levitt, M. (2007). Kingdom of God. http://www.newstatesman.com/books/2007/05/HAMAS-palestinian-israel
Malka, H. (2005). Forcing choices: Testing the transformation of Hamas. *The Washington Quarterly, 28*(4), 37–53.
Medium. (October 15, 2023). Hamas dawn: October 7th, 2023. https://medium.com/lessons-from-history/hamas-dawn-october-7th-2023-b41a6767a3d3
Meduza. (October 10, 2023). Something like this has never happened before. https://meduza.io/en/feature/2023/10/10/something-like-this-has-never-happened-before?ysclid=loucideih431848058
Mideast. (2009). The covenant of the Islamic resistance movement (Hamas). http://www.mideastweb.org/hamas.htm
Milton-Edwards, B. (2008). The ascendance of political Islam: Hamas and consolidation in the Gaza strip. *Third World Quarterly, 29*(8), 1585–1599.
Milton-Edwards, B. (2017). The 'warriors break': Hamas and the limits of ceasefire beyond tactical purpose. *International Peacekeeping, 24*(2), 212–235.
Mishal, S. (2003). The pragmatic dimension of the Palestinian Hamas: A network perspective. *Armed Forces & Society, 29*(4), 569–589.
Mishal, S. & Sela, A. (2000). *The Palestinian hamas: Vision, violence and coexistence.* New York: Columbia University Press.
NBC News. (2023, February 28). Egyptian court declares Hamas a 'terrorist organization'. https://www.nbcnews.com/news/world/egyptian-court-declares-hamas-terrorist-organization-n314801
New York Times. (2010). Gaza: Hamas presses for calm. https://www.nytimes.com/2010/04/03/world/middleeast/03briefs-Gaza.html
Nüsse, A. (1998). *Muslim Palestine: The ideology of Hamas.* Amsterdam: Harwood Academic Publishers.
Oriental Review. (November 2, 2023). How Trump & Biden created this war In The Middle East, and why Hamas attacked Israel on October 7th. https://orientalreview.su/2023/11/02/how-trump-biden-created-this-war-in-the-middle-east-and-why-hamas-attacked-israel-on-october-7th/
Pastor, R. (2010). Talking to Hamas. *Foreign Affairs, 90*(1), (January/February 2011), 196–197.
Pelham, N. (2011). Gaza's tunnel complex. Middle East Report, No 261, Illicit Crossings (Winter 2011), 30–35.
Rees, M. & Hamad, J. (2004). A power play in Hamas. *Time, 163*(18), 45–60.
Reuters. (2007). Q&A with HAMAS leader Khaled Meshal. http://www.reuters.com/article/idUSL1046412720070110
Roy, S. (2000). The transformation of Islamic NGO's in Palestine. Middle East Report, No. 14.
Sayigh, Y. (2010). Hamas rule in Gaza: Three years on. Middle East Brief, No 41 (March 2010), http://ww.brandeis.edu/crown/publications/meb/MEB41.pdf
Shamir, E. & Hecht, E. (2014). Gaza 2014: Israel's attrition vs Hamas' exhaustion. *Parameters, 44*(4), 81–90.
The Duran. (October 29, 2023). The US has betrayed Egypt again. https://theduran.com/the-us-has-betrayed-egypt-again/
The Economist. (2010a). How Israel plays into Hamas's hands. https://www.economist.com/briefing/2010/06/03/how-israel-plays-into-Hamass-hands
The Economist. (2010b). Hamas hangs on. https://www.economist.com/middle-east-and-africa/2010/03/31/Hamas-hangs-on
The Jerusalem Post. (November 11, 2023). General Staff knew Gaza fence couldn't stop a war, but it still underestimated Hamas. https://www.jpost.com/israel-news/defense-news/article-772754
The Limited Times. (November 10, 2023). Hamas internal dispute revealed. https://newsrnd.com/news/2023-11-10-hamas-internal-dispute-revealed–october-7-massacre-was-not-planned.ByXnGEjQp.html
The Times of Israel. (November 26, 2021). UK officially bans Hamas in its entirety as a terrorist group.
Wagemakers, J. (2010). Legitimizing pragmatism: Hamas' framing efforts from militancy to moderation and back?. *Terrorism and Political Violence, 22*(3), 357–377.
Watkins, N.J. & James, A.M. (2016). Digging into Israel: The sophisticated tunneling network of Hamas. *Journal of Strategic Security, 9*(1), 84–103.

50

ISIS

The Dramatic Rise and Decline of an Al-Qaeda Offshoot

Ferdinand Arslanian, Scott N. Romaniuk, and Amparo Pamela Fabe

INTRODUCTION

The rise and fall – or decline – of the Islamic State in Iraq and Syria (ISIS) caught everyone off guard. Its sudden ascent to power in Iraq and Syria, its cinematic display of savagery, and its ability to gather fighters from all over the world horrified the entire world. The shock persisted as it was able to carry out terrorist strikes in the middle of major cities and establish an international network of affiliates. ISIS briefly outperformed all previous al-Qaeda offshoots in building a functional state, managing millions of people, dominating vast areas of land, and enforcing its severe version of Islamic law. By designating its new state as the restoration of the Islamic Caliphate, it accomplished what its mother organisation, al-Qaeda Central, sought. The study of ISIS is a fascinating and exceptional example, from the standpoint of terrorism studies, of a terrorist group that was able to change into a military force that is somewhat conventional and establish an infant state.

This chapter begins by tracing its origins in the interaction between the dynamics of the post-September 11, 2001, global jihadist movement and the dynamics of the post-US invasion of Iraq. Afterward, it addresses the distinct and brief period (April 2013–June 2014) where the organisation metamorphoses from state declaration towards state actualisation. This is followed by a discussion of the structure of ISIS and its leadership and governance, finance, military, and communication strategies. The chapter concludes by discussing the complex network of counter-ISIS operations that led to its demise and the group's lasting political impact.

THE ORIGINS OF ISIS

The genesis of ISIS can be traced back to a series of antecedent insurgent groups that were active in Iraq from 2003 to 2013 (Patel, 2015: 2). The aforementioned statement denotes the manifestation of al-Qaeda's modus operandi subsequent to the September 11 attacks, wherein it aimed to scatter its network beyond Afghanistan and establish a regional al-Qaeda contingent that aligns with the indigenous dynamics of Iraq's political landscape following the US invasion. In this particular context, the emergence of ISIS can be attributed to a gradual process of localisation and "Iraqisation" of the global jihadist movement. This phenomenon occurred as a result of the integration of Iraq's marginalised Arab Sunni community, particularly the younger generation of former officers of Ba'athist Iraq, into the global jihadist movement.

ZARQAWI AND THE AL QAIDA IN IRAQ (AQI)

The Jordanian Ahmad Fadl al-Nazal al-Khalayleh, better known by his alias Abu Musab al-Zarqawi, made the initial connection between the international Jihadist movement and the local Iraqi scene. The initial training facility that Zarqawi managed in Herat, Afghanistan, was intended to recruit soldiers from the Levantine countries. After the US invasion of Afghanistan, Zarqawi relocated to Kurdish Iraq, where the local Jihadist organisation "Ansar al-Islam" kept him in camps. He was able to start Jama'at al-Tawhid wa'l-Jihad (JTWJ) both before and after the US invasion of Iraq thanks to his network of connections (Lister, 2014: 6; Bunzel, 2015: 14). After the US invasion of Iraq in 2003, JTWJ migrated to the "Sunni Triangle" area, which extends north and west of Baghdad, and joined the local Iraqi

DOI: 10.4324/9780429426063-57

resistance there against the US soldiers. Due to its sophisticated military operations, merciless beheading and suicide bombing techniques, and media awareness, JTWJ has been able to distinguish itself from the multitude of other groups involved in Iraq's complex conflict (Gerges, 2016: 65; Plebani, 2014: 5).

In September 2004, Zarqawi pledged allegiance to al-Qaeda and altered the name of his organisation to "al-Qaida in the Land of the Two Rivers" or simply al-Qaeda in Iraq (AQI) (Lister, 2014: 8). This allegiance was, however, "a function of strategic convenience rather than doctrinal agreement" (Fishman, 2006: 21). According to Plebani (2014), "al-Qa'ida needed a charismatic leader on the ground to carry the flag of the group against US forces," whereas "Al-Zarqawi needed Osama bin Laden's blessing to increase his stature within the insurgency and gain more visibility" (p. 6). Eventually, differences came to the forefront. Even al-Qaeda found the excessive brutality, indiscriminate attacks, and mass targeting of Shia civilians by AQI to be counterproductive to the jihadist mission (Lister, 2014: 8; Fishman, 2006: 20).

On the ground, AQI faced a second difficulty: a backlash from local Sunni Arab communities and other insurgency organisations. AQI's undermining of local tribal authorities and stringent application of Islamic law alienated the very communities it claimed to defend, while other insurgent groups blamed AQI for their inability to advance in Baghdad. Overall, AQI was unable to dissuade the Sunni Arab population from progressively participating in the country's political process in 2005, as increasing numbers participated in the Constitution referendum and National Assembly elections (Plebani, 2014: 6–7; Gerges, 2016: 100–101).

THE ESTABLISHMENT OF THE ISLAMIC STATE OF IRAQ (ISI)

To resolve this predicament, AQI sought to heal the rift with the local community by forming the Mujahedeen Shura Council (MSC) in January 2006 by merging with local Jihadist factions and appointing an Iraqi at its top. The MSC was also foreseen to be the nucleus for forming an Islamic government that would better represent the interests of the Sunni Arabs of Iraq. However, Zarqawi would not see his Islamic State come to light, as a few months later he was killed in a US airstrike, and the task was passed over to his successor, Abu Ayyoub al-Masri, Zarqawi's close associate and a former member of the Egyptian Islamic Jihad Group (Bunzel, 2015: 16–17).

The establishment of the Islamic State of Iraq (ISI) was announced in October 2006, after Masri's assumption of power. It emerged because of another organisational merger, this time between the MSM and other like-minded local jihadist groups, and allegiance was given to a former Iraqi police officer, Abu Omar al-Baghdadi, declared "Commander of the Faithful" (Bunzel, 2015: 17). The allegiance to an Iraqi represented a further attempt to localise the Jihadist movement. However, the new state was viewed as a paper state, as by the time of its announcement, the local backlash against the group had reached irreconcilable levels and tribal mobilisation against ISI was already formalised with the creation of local Sahwa (Awakening) councils (Lister, 2014: 9). The US counterinsurgency strategy exploited this rift and supported these councils through money and arms, and, as a result, ISI fighters were pushed out of their strongholds in the Anbar province throughout the year 2007 (Plebani, 2014: 9).

TRANSFORMATION UNDER BAGHDADI

In response, the group relocated to the northern city of Mosul and its surrounding Nineveh plain and underwent a gradual process of restructuring and Iraqisation (Plebani, 2014: 9). The transformation accelerated in 2010 with the assumption of power by Abu Bakr al-Baghdadi, following the assassinations of both Abu Ayoub al-Masri and Abu Umar al-Baghdadi in a US airstrike. The group integrated former Ba'athist officers into its ranks for several reasons. To begin with, the group was in dire need of replacing its cadres, who were either killed or imprisoned (Tønnessen, 2015: 48). Being internally isolated and besieged, and with the tap of foreign fighters flowing from Syria being cut off, the only source of recruitment was to rely on local recruits (Gerges, 2016: 137, 148). Within this context, ISI found in the younger generation of Ba'athist officials an untapped resource of whom their predecessors were too suspicious (Gerges, 2016: 155). This new generation had entered their positions at a time when religious fervour was flourishing owing to 1993 government-led 'Faith Campaign'.

Upon the US occupation of Iraq, those officers contributed to the formation of several insurgent groups with Islamist undertones (Tønnessen, 2015: 54 Patel, 2015: 3). Furthermore, ideological interbreeding between former Ba'athists and Salafi-Jihadists took a unique form in American-led prisons, most notably in the Bucca Camp. In this setting, each group offered the other what it was lacking; ISI was seeking bureaucratic expertise and military discipline, while former Ba'athists found in Salafi-Jihadism a clear ideological orientation (McCoy, 2014). The figure of ISI's new leader, Baghdadi, reflected this Iraqisation process. He was imprisoned in the Bucca Camp. He was a member of a local jihadist group, 'Jama'at al-Jaysh Ahl al-Sunna wal-Jama'a', which played a role in co-founding ISI and was unknown within the global Salafi-Jihadist circles (Gerges, 2016: 132–135; Tønnessen, 2015: 50).

The integration of former Ba'athist officers transformed the group from "a mafia-like network" into a rudimentary form of statehood with a skilled and professional army (Gerges, 2016: 149; Rosiny, 2016: 7). The organisation gradually established "a shadow authority" over the city of Mosul by "carry[ing] out a covert campaign of intimidation targeting military and government officials" and "repeatedly attacking checkpoints and patrols" (Lister, 2014: 18). This "shadow authority" over Mosul enhanced the organisation's financial standing as the city became its primary "source of income" as a "complex extortion network" from the city's businesses was established and the oil smuggling networks from the pre-occupation sanctions era were revived (Lister, 2014: 22).

With ISI restructured, the organisation exploited the latest developments in Iraqi politics. As the US forces were planning a withdrawal, the Shiite-dominated government led by PM Nouri al-Maliki was increasingly monopolising power and harassing Sunni Arab political entities. This included banning many Sunni figures from participating in elections, arresting former Ba'athists, and transferring the responsibility of Sahwa Councils to the Iraqi authorities while putting Sahwa members under investigation, all of which led to a renewed discontent among the Sunni Arab population (Gerges, 2016: 106–115). Within this context, ISIS played a double game with the aim of increasing its dominance over the Sunni Arab population. Learning from its past mistakes, it relied on building networks with the Sunni community rather than relying on coercive methods (e.g., offering higher salaries to Sahwa fighters to join them) (Gerges, 2016: 19; Lister, 2014: 10). At the same time, it undertook a systematic assassination campaign of Sahwa leaders with the aim of severing the community's links with the Sahwa Councils and tribal leaders (Plebani, 2014: 11). This improved "social grounding" led to a "bottom-up revitalization of ISI's operational structure," leading, in turn, to an escalation in its military activities (Lister, 2014: 11).

EXPLOITING THE ARAB SPRING AND THE DECLARATION OF THE ISLAMIC STATE IN IRAQ AND SYRIA

ISI's manipulation of political tensions was not restricted to Iraq's domestic scene but rather transcended to neighbouring Syria, with its uprising growing in violence. Viewing Syria's descent into civil war as a golden opportunity, Baghdadi dispatched his operations chief in Nineveh, Abu Mohammad al-Jowlani, to Syria in August 2011, with the task of forming a military group, Jabhut al-Nusra (JAN), that would join the uprising against the Syrian regime. Avoiding its previous mistakes in Iraq (2005–2007), the new group adopted a 'winning hearts and minds' approach. It coordinated closely with other armed opposition groups, denied having any links to al-Qaida, refrained from implementing harsh Islamic measures, and focused on developing humanitarian and social welfare campaigns. Coupled with its effectiveness in conducting complex military operations, JAN gained prominence within the armed Syrian opposition and popularity among the uprising's popular base (Lister, 2014: 12–13; Cafarella, 2014: 13–16).

Jan's success in Syria was well reflected in ISI's financial standing by attracting donations from international funders and creating a network of illicit activities in Syria. This renewed affluence allowed ISI to further escalate its military activities inside Iraq (Plebani, 2014: 11). By July 2012, the group had launched the "Breaking the Walls" campaign, attacking Iraqi prisons with the aim of freeing its imprisoned members (Lister, 2014: 11–12).

By early 2013, with the fall of the eastern Syrian city of Raqqa in the hands of a JAN-led coalition of armed factions, JAN had gained the upper hand in the country's eastern region, controlling continuous swathes of land along the Euphrates River in proximity to ISI's operational area on the other side of the border (Abuzeid, 2013; Cafarella, 2014: 38; Plebani, 2014: 12). From this strengthened position, Baghdadi took the strategic decision on April 19, 2013, to declare JAN as an ISI subsidiary and announce the two groups' merger into the Islamic State of Syria and Iraq (ISIS) (Plebani, 2014: 12).

FROM STATE DECLARATION TO STATE FORMATION

The Schism within the Global Jihadist Movement

ISIS's April 2013 proclamation had divisive effects on the global jihadist movement. The announcement suggested a horizontal split inside the movement, in contrast to the earlier hostilities between al-Qaeda Central and its offshoot. Jawlani first reacted swiftly to Baghdadi's request to dissolve JAN and join ISIS, recording an audio statement the next day pledging his allegiance to al-Qaeda Central and its leader Ayman al-Zawahiry. Zawahiry personally intervened a month later and issued an order "annul[ing] the Islamic State's incorporation of Syria, ordering the groups to remain separate entities observing separate jurisdictions—Iraq and Syria, respectively" (Bunzel, 2015: 25). ISIS quickly responded, stating "numerous legal and methodological objections" to Zawahiry's order, taking into account the lack of consultation between the parties and how this could strengthen the movement's foes and legitimise existing colonial borders (Bunzel, 2015: 26).

Besides the war of audio releases, the schism in the global jihadist movement was reflected among its scholars as a divide along generational lines came to the fore. Al-Qaeda Central was backed by well-known and elderly scholars such as Abu Muhammad al-Maqdisi, Abu Qutada al-Falistini, and Hani Sibai, whereas ISIS proponents drew from anonymous and younger scholars, including the Bahraini Turki al-Bin'ali, the Jordanian Umar Mahdi Zaydan, and the Mauritanian Abu al-Mundhir al-Shinqiṭi. The main scholarly dispute centres around the nature of the newly declared group. Critics viewed ISIS as nothing more than a battlefield organisation denying its claims to statehood, which ought to adhere to specific steps, while its proponents viewed ISIS as the future Caliphate and, consequently, regard paying allegiance as comprehensive and not restricted to battlefield matters (Bunzel, 2015: 26–27).

The schism was intensified by the escalation of violence on the Syrian ground as clashes intensified between ISIS and JAN, especially as ISIS executed several of JAN's leaders (Hamming, 2017, p. 29). Attempts to contain the situation through calls for settling disputes through independent judicial courts fell on deaf ears as ISIS, viewing itself as a state, regarded itself as above other groups (Bunzel, 2015: 28–29). In February 2014, as clashes escalated towards full-fledged confrontation, Zawahiri released a statement disowning ISIS and thus severing the organisational link between ISIS and al-Qaeda Central (Bunzel, 2015: 29).

Syria: From Precarious Relations with the Armed Opposition to Open War

Despite Jawlani's refusal to dissolve JAN, mass defections towards the newly formed group took place within the ranks of his fighters. This was most nuanced among foreign fighters and fighters located in the city of Raqqa (Ali, 2013; al-Ghali, 2017). Initially, relations between ISIS and the rest of the armed Syrian opposition were best characterised as precarious. ISIS's collaboration with the armed Syrian opposition on several military fronts against the Syrian Army did not refrain the group from initiating limited attacks in areas deemed strategic, such as border towns, as a prelude towards overtaking border-crossing points (Ali, 2013). In Raqqa, the organisation was more explicit in its aggression, as the mass defections towards its ranks facilitated its expansion at the expense of other armed groups, its arrest of civil activists, and levying taxes and imposing its laws on the population (al-Ghali, 2017).

In August 2013, the success of the ISIS-led offensive in capturing the Syrian Army's long-besieged Manegh airbase boosted the group's legitimacy among the Syrian opposition (Nassief, 2014: 28). This allowed ISIS's infiltration of opposition-held areas, beginning with the establishment of da'wa (proselytising) centres, which gradually evolved into military centres (Enjrainy, 2014; al-Ouqdeh, 2015). However, as the groups started to expand, the frequency of their clashes with the armed Syrian opposition began to increase. In the city of Raqqa, the group began to clash with rival factions and managed to oust the 'Ahfad al-Rousoul' faction from the city (al-Ghali, 2017). This was paralleled by the group receiving a series of allegiances from both local tribes and armed factions (Muhammad, 2013). Similarly, in the border town of Azaz, ISIS ousted the 'Northern Storm' faction from the town, using US Senator John McCain's previous visit to the town as evidence of the faction's conspiring against them. Other offensives would follow in Aleppo under the pretext of its campaign against thieves, which involved attacking disreputable armed factions known for their involvement in looting and other clandestine activity (al-Ouqdeh, 2015).

By late 2013, tensions between both sides had escalated, and the descent into full-scale military confrontation was only prevented by the common threat of the Syrian Army (Nassief, 2014: 34–35). The final blow came on January 2, 2014, when a newly formed coalition of armed factions, Jeish al-Mujahideen, declared war on ISIS, as other factions, including JAN, were soon to follow (International Crisis Group, 2014a: 10). Initially, the anti-ISIS coalition was able to make many gains as ISIS fighters were either completely ousted from cities and towns or besieged in their headquarters, as in the city of Raqqa. However, ISIS was soon able to reverse the situation and drive its foes out of Raqqa and other areas in the country's east by manipulating local tribal politics and fighters' sympathies from other jihadist factions, in addition to withdrawing from confrontation lines with the Syrian Army (Caillet, 2014; International Crisis Group, 2014a: 11; Issam, 2014). The withdrawal from confrontational lines with the Syrian Army elevated towards a new relationship of convenience as both sides avoided targeting each other. While ISIS sought to deal with one adversary at a time, the Syrian regime saw in ISIS's ascendancy a means of dissuading its international adversaries from supporting efforts to topple it (International Crisis Group, 2014a: 13).

A second wave of infighting erupted in late February 2014 following ISIS's assassination of Abu-Khaled al-Souri, a prominent jihadist figure, as Jawlani stepped up his threat against ISIS to withdraw from Syria (Jabhat al-nusra tumhilu, 2014). In response, ISIS would make the strategic decision to withdraw from the remaining areas it controlled in the western parts of the country (Latakkia, Idlib, and Azaaz) while consolidating behind "defensible lines" in Raqqa and shifting its focus to the east of the country (International Crisis Group, 2014a: 16). Within this context, it launched the "Deir Ezzour Campaign," aiming at ensuring territorial continuity with Iraq and controlling the region's rich resources of oil, cotton, and wheat (Lister, 2014: 14).

Iraq: From Capturing Fallujah to the Mosul Takeover

Meanwhile in Iraq, the "Breaking of the Walls" campaign was concluded successfully with its groundbreaking July 2013 achievement of attacking the Abu Ghreib prison and freeing hundreds of AQI fighters. This was followed by "the Soldiers' Harvest" campaign, which, in addition to its aim of intimidating the Iraqi Security Force (ISF) soldiers, as its name suggests, marked a more strategic shift towards holding terrain in line with its announcement of establishing a state (Lewis, 2013). Within this context, the group increased its operations in its traditional zones of support inside the Sunni Triangle, especially in Western Anbar, along the Syrian border, as ISIS and ISF increasingly clashed (International Crisis Group, 2014b: 5).

By late December 2013, ISIS had exploited clashes between the government and protestors in the town of Fallujah, in the province of Anbar, to infiltrate the town. Both protesters and armed groups accepted their presence, viewing the group as an asset in their struggle against the central government (International Crisis Group, 2014b: 1). Throughout the first half of 2014, ISIS managed to distract the ISF from recapturing Fallujah by extending the geographic scope of its military operations and opening several military fronts, including the Baghdad Belt, the group of towns surrounding the capital. They also did not hesitate to use their capture of dams to flood nearby areas as a means of halting the ISF's advance (Institute for the Study of War, 2014).

However, the turning point for ISIS in Iraq was realised on June 6, 2014, as ISIS launched an attack on the city of Mosul and managed to capture the city within three days only. Several factors contributed to this abrupt success: the organisation's lengthy shadow presence in the city; its collaboration with other insurgent groups, most notably the former Ba'athist Jeish Rijal al-Tareeqah al-Naqshbandiah (JRTN); the positive reception by the city's disgruntled population; and the ISF's overstretch considering its operations in the Anbar region (Lister, 2014: 18; Lewis et al., 2014; Parker et al., 2014). Within the next few days, the group expanded its control all over the Ninevah Governorate and further south towards Tikrit, Saddam's hometown, and the strategic oil refinery town of Beiji amid the collapse of four divisions of the Iraqi army and the death and capture of thousands of Iraqi soldiers (Lewis et al., 2014). Amid the mass popular mobilisation among the Shiite population in Baghdad and the southern regions, ISIS refrained from advancing further south towards Baghdad and, alternatively, strove to consolidate its hold over the country's north, linking it with its Syrian-held territory (al-Sanjary & Rasheed, 2014; Chivers, 2014).

Declaration of the Caliphate and Internal and External Territorial Consolidation (June–July 2014)

Abu Bakr al-Baghdadi declared the formation of ISIS in April 2013, when he expanded the Islamic State of Iraq (ISI) to include Syria. Through Baghdadi's leadership, ISIS has demonstrated the intent to control territory through military force.

Furthermore, ISIS consolidated its control in Raqqa by detonating multiple vBIeDs (vehicle-borne improvised explosive devices) at the FSA-affiliated Ahfad al-Rasul headquarters building in the Raqqa train station on August 13. This attack ended the presence of the FSA inside Raqqa (Carris & Reynolds, 2014). When ISIS gained full control of Raqqa, they issued new regulations, including bans on smoking and dress requirements for women.

ISIS methodically ensured that the surrounding areas where they governed also fell under their control. For example, ISIS retook towns outside of Raqqa during this period. They seized control over Tal Abyad from Ahrar al-Sham on January 13, and ISIS reportedly executed the remaining Ahrar al-Sham fighters and burned their homes (Prothero, 2014). On January 14, ISIS re-entered Taqba, just west of Raqqa city, after Liwa al-Tawhid fighters agreed to cede the area (Hakkar, 2014). ISIS seized al-Bab in northeastern Aleppo province on the road to the Turkish border (Paraszczuk, 2014). The troop strength for the al-Bab assault was drawn from ISIS fighters who had recently withdrawn from Aleppo city.

By 2014, ISIS had governed Aleppo, Raqqa, Homs, and Deir es-Zour in Syria. In Raqqa and Aleppo, ISIS implemented a whole range of administrative and service-related offices. Such as religious enforcement, adjudication of disputes, infrastructure repair, and humanitarian aid. The ISIS governance system encompasses religious, educational, judicial, infrastructure, and security aspects. In Homs, Damascus, Deir ez-Zour, and Hasaka, ISIS governance activities include Da'wa events, humanitarian aid, and limited infrastructure repair (Carris & Reynolds, 2014).

As a manifestation of its achievements, the organisation released a series of video and audio releases in late June or early July declaring the establishment of the Islamic Caliphate and celebrating "The End of Sykes-Picot" and "Breaking the Borders" between Syria and Iraq. This was followed by the first public appearance of the 'Caliph' Baghdadi in the al-Nouri al-Kabeer Mosque in Mosul (Lister, 2014: 14).

The same territorial consolidation occurred in Syria as ISIS took near full control of Deir Ez-Zour, with the Syrian Army besieged in parts of the provincial city ("Daesh yusaytiru 'ala," 2014). In addition to its military might, its territorial consolidation was attributed to a new wave of allegiances from other armed opposition factions, including JAN, as several cities along the Euphrates River were handed over peacefully ("al-Nusra tubaye' daesh," 2014; "Deir ez-Zour: Daesh," 2014). This period also witnessed the end of its détente with the Syrian regime, with ISIS overrunning its remaining strongpoints surrounding Raqqa, advancing westward to the Syrian Desert, and taking control of the country's main gas fields (Kozak, 2015: 33–34). By summer 2014, ISIS had achieved territorial continuity, a power monopoly, and governance structures that enabled its transformation from a military group into an actual state.

STRUCTURE, STRATEGY AND TACTICS

ISIS can be characterised as a nascent counter state. It is a "counter state" in the sense that it is a "state breaker that can claim new rule and new boundaries after seizing cities across multiple states by force". On the other hand, it is a nascent state in the sense that although it shares "a certain number of characteristics with their modern counterparts", these characteristics have not elevated towards "the same level of sophistication" (European Parliament, 2017: 8).

Organisational Structure

Dating back to the establishment of ISI in 2006, the group's "self-representation" as an actual state implied the existence of a cabinet of ministries assuming social, economic, and security functions as an integral part of its organisational structure (al-Tamimi, 2015: 118). With the reconfiguration of the group as ISIS, its institutional presence assumed "a gradualist approach," beginning with the Da'wa centre acting as a focal point for social outreach towards the locals as it infiltrated areas controlled by other factions, evolving into Islamic courts or military centres, and, in the case of an outright military takeover, designating the town as a province (Wilayah) (al-Tamimi, 2015: 120–121).

With the 2014 declaration of the 'Caliphate', a state-like institutional structure emerged comprising a cabinet-like team of ministries, an administrative structure of Wilayat, and a group of councils. On top of this organisational structure is the Caliph, who acts as a representative of the Prophet Mohammed and thus holds absolute power and acts as "the sole decision-maker in the Islamic State, and his decisions are implemented with no avenue for recourse" (Neriah, 2014). In terms of the administrative structure, the Caliphate has two deputies, both of whom are former Ba'athist officials: one responsible for Syria (originally Abu Ali al-Anbari) and the other responsible for Iraq (originally Abu Muslim al-Turkmani). Each deputy supervises a group of governors in charge of provinces (Wilayat), who, in turn, oversee local councils (Thompson and Shubert, 2015). A cabinet-like team of ministries (Diwan) acts as the executive branch of the state (al-Tamimi, 2015: 123). At the wilayat levels, a similar structure of a ministerial cabinet is replicated, providing them with a wide degree of autonomy (Jefferis, 2016: 243). The group of councils (crucially, the Fighters Assistance Council, Intelligence Council, Legal Council, Leadership Council, and Financial Council) plays more of a supervisory and legislative role, with the Shura Council functioning as the religious monitoring board that ensures all activities in the Caliphate are in accordance with Islamic legislation (Thompson and Shubert, 2015).

Governance and Finance

As ISIS portrayed itself as a state, the question of governance was brought to the fore, rendering it a key factor in determining its success. Herewith, ISIS faced the same "jihadist dilemma", that previous jihadist projects had experienced. This dilemma entailed that while the Jihadist project is pertinent in its ability to govern, jihadists repeatedly fail at the task due to either a domestic backlash or international interference (Lister, 2014: 26; McCants, 2016a: 68–69). Within this context, even though ISIS managed to surpass its predecessors in creating a governance system, it did not evade the "Jihadist Dilemma," as its experience was truncated by international interference.

At the core of ISIS governance is a specific version of a 'social contract' that governs the relationship between the state and its citizens in terms of the duties and rights of each side. In essence, citizens are obliged to display an exclusive allegiance to ISIS and to contribute to the state-building project through taxation or military conscription. In return, citizens receive justice and protection, as well as social services (Revkin, 2016: 9). The exclusive allegiance to the Islamic State implies that Muslims ought to adhere to its strict version of Islamic Sharia Law, which entails enforced personal piety (code of dress, prayer attendance, etc.) and fixed Islamic punishments (hudud) (Lister, 2014: 26; Revkin, 2016: 11). The application of sharia law is buttressed by religious education and public da'wa (proselytising) events and enforced by Islamic courts and religious police (Lister, 2014: 28; Turner, 2015: 219). These enforcement institutions also ensure law and order, personal safety, and the protection of private property.

The Islamic courts investigated the complaints filed by citizens but upheld "the authority to make final and binding decisions without the opportunity for appeal" (Revkin, 2016: 12). As for non-Muslims, ISIS distinguishes between adherents of other Abrahamic religions, most notably Christians, who "are entitled to protection and very limited freedom of worship, but only in exchange for their payment of a special tax known as the jizya" (Revkin, 2016: 11), and adherents to non-monotheistic faiths, most notably the Yezidis, who are deprived of any rights and "could be legitimately enslaved" (Lister, 2014: 27).[1] On the other hand, ISIS places a special emphasis on providing essential services to its citizens, including healthcare, electricity, humanitarian relief, and subsidised bread, among other resources and commodities, and its relative effectiveness in providing such services was a key factor in its popular appeal (Revkin, 2016: 14; Khalaf, 2015).

ISIS' commitment to the administration of the population by providing social services – in addition to its war efforts – entails the necessity of possessing ample and diverse sources of revenue, in the sense that its governance strategy is predicated on its financial strategy, which, contrary to al-Qaida and other terrorist organisations, emphasises financial self-sufficiency and territorial control rather than external resources (donations). These domestic revenues can be divided into two main categories: natural resources and extortion. Revenue from natural resources depends primarily on oil but also includes other minerals (gas and phosphates) and agricultural resources (the sale of cereal crops). Oil sales include sales in the local market, sales to rival Syrian factions, and smuggling abroad to Turkey and Jordan (Center for the Analysis of Terrorism, 2016: 9–14). While revenue from extortion consists mainly of various taxes (religious tax (zakat), state employees, business activities, agriculture production, protection tax for non-Muslims), as well as customs duties on trucks entering ISIS territory, fees and financial penalties, and revenue from predatory and criminal activities such as the resale of confiscated and looted goods, kidnapping and ransom, and antique trading (Center for the Analysis of Terrorism, 2016: 15– A comparison between the years 2014 and 2015 illustrates that the decline of oil revenue from $1bn to $600 million, due to the targeting of the oil industry by counter-ISIS operations, was compensated by the increase in extortion revenue from $360 million to $800 million (Center for the Analysis of Terrorism, 2016: 9, 15).

The final element of the ISIS governance system is the systematic application of violence, which leads to an increase in the cost of non-compliance and the need to support an alternative (Khalaf, 2015). ISIS holds violence as a "religious obligation" and did not hesitate to massacre hundreds of tribe members in cases of disobedience, such as the Shaitat tribe in Syria and the Bu Nimr tribe in Iraq (Rosiny, 2016: 11).

MILITARY STRUCTURE, STRATEGY, AND TACTICS

The transformation of ISIS from a terrorist organisation into a conventional military force represents a "novelty" in military science (Maurer, 2018: 238). The high presence of former Iraqi officers in the ISIS military leadership provided the group with a "high level of military proficiency," making them "qualified to plan and conduct conventional warfare" (Maurer, 2018: 231). However, it was the capturing of weaponry and the absorption of fresh forces through its 2014 territorial expansion that allowed its elevation towards a conventional force (Jasper & Moreland, 2014). By that time, ISIS had "commanded as many as 31,000 fighters" and "possesse[d] a number of weapons systems and vehicles, including tanks, armoured personnel carriers, field artillery, self-propelled howitzers, and multiple rocket launchers, as well as an assortment of anti-tank guided missiles (ATGMs), anti-aircraft guns, and a small number of man-portable air-defense systems" (Lister, 2014: 16–17).

Nonetheless, like its nascent status as a proto-state, its military capabilities fell short of a full-fledged army (e.g., lacking a conventional air force), while its warfare style complied with "hybrid warfare," combining "conventional military capabilities with small unit guerrilla tactics, asymmetric attacks, and highly mobile standoff engagement systems" (Jasper & Moreland, 2014). On the other hand, its counter-state nature, captured in its motto "Remain and Expand", implied "instigat[ing] a broader war to compromise states competing with it for legitimacy". With the counter-ISIS operations taking place, this was translated into a military strategy with three levels of operation: "to defend inside Iraq and Syria; to expand operations regionally; and to disrupt and recruit on a global scale".

In line with its initial strategy to expand, the capture of large urban areas, or provinces, entailed a "multi-stage strategy" (Lister, 2014: 19). It involved a prolonged "preparatory stage" of intelligence collection, infiltration, and targeted killing of local leaders and government officials from one side while utilising the surrounding desert area in a manner that links and manoeuvres between different fronts and cuts off rival supplies from another (Maurer, 2018: 232; Beccaroa, 2018: 213). This prolonged stage facilitated the swift takeover of these areas once the attack took place, as witnessed in Mosul and Der Ez-Zour. Within this context, the resort to terrorist attacks on civilians became more of a "stand-off weapon" used "outside its main theatre of operation" with the aim of "creat[ing] insecurity and project[ing] the power of the group" (Beccaroa, 2018: 212). These terrorist attacks mainly targeted Shia Muslim-dominated areas in Iraq and Alawite Muslim-dominated areas in Syria (Lister, 2014: 18).

In manoeuvring its way in both Syria and Iraq, the organisation's ideological zeal did not deter its pursuit of pragmatic alliances, as discussed earlier. In Syria, the group initially coordinated with the various armed opposition factions against the Syrian Army, only to reach a détente with the latter once it was confronted with an open military confrontation with the former. In addition to military groups, ISIS manipulated tribal politics in its conflict with the armed opposition. Similar tactics were pursued in Iraq as the group situated itself within the armed insurgency in Fallujah against the central government while its takeover of Mosul and Tikrit was facilitated by an alliance with JRTN, among other groups. However, skirmishes soon erupted between ISIS and JRTN, and a year later, the alliance was officially dissolved (University of Stanford, 2015).

In line with its hybrid warfare principles, ISIS "uses existing, common, and basic technology" in innovative ways (Beccaroa, 2018: 214). While its predecessors relied heavily on suicide bombings and suicide vehicle-borne improvised explosive devices (SVBIEDs), ISIS elevated SVBIEDs to a new level with armoured suicide vehicle-borne improvised explosive devices (ASVBIEDs), which, in addition to loading the heavy vehicle with tonnes of explosives, are armoured with steel plates and bulletproof tyres and, thus, allow the vehicle to reach its designated target while breaching adversaries' defence lines through resisting their fire and anti-tank weaponry. ASVBIEDs compensate for the absence of conventional armoured units and are typically used as an "entry weapon" given their dual destructive and psychological impacts that facilitate the subsequent attack from light infantry (Maurer, 2018: 234). As the group went on the defensive with the coalition's aerial bombing, several defensive tactics were contrived. It was reorganised "into smaller tactical units" as its fighters and equipment "melted into the urban landscape" (Jasper & Moreland, 2014). Roads and buildings were saturated with improvised explosive devices (IEDs) that slowed down the pace of enemies' advancement, increased post-retreat casualties, and required time dedicated to demining the retreated areas (Maurer, 2018: 236; Beccaroa, 2018: 218). The strongholds of Raqqa and Mosul were protected through a "complex, multi-layered, circular defence system" that involved trenches, tunnels, and embankments (Maurer, 2018: 236). Finally, ISIS elevated its usage of drones from common surveillance purposes to conducting drone attacks using grenade-size munition and even missiles (Beccaroa, 2018: 216–217).

ISIS' COMMUNICATION STRATEGY: WOOING WOULD-BE HEROES OF THE CALIPHATE

The final aspect to highlight in terms of the organisation's structure and strategy is its communication strategy. In this regard, ISIS employed diverse media sources with the aim of building legitimacy, recruiting fighters, and intimidating enemies. These sources include an official news agency (A'maq), an official radio station (al-Bayan), an official spokesperson (Abu Muhammad al-Adnani), and a multilingual magazine (Dabeq), in addition to high-quality video releases and its intensive use of social media (Pellerin, 2016: 4–7; Neriah, 2014). Setting it apart from other terrorist organisations is its Hollywood-inspired high-quality, catchy, and tailored messaging, as ISIS utilises "an entire stable of spokespeople" and "employ[s] the nationals of the state they are targeting" to convey its message (Zekulin, 2018: 27). ISIS often used Hollywood-style scripts and language and delivered Hollywood-style propaganda messages that were several minutes to several hours long, complete with stylistic production methods and special effects meant to romanticise the self-proclaimed heroism of being an ISIS soldier. The visual and production quality of these long films, which were successful in drawing and seducing would-be heroes of the Caliphate, far surpassed anything previously created by al-Qaeda under Osama bin Laden.

ISIS made efficient and novel use of publications and videos to push its propaganda. For example, the June 5, 2014, issue of Dabiq, ISIS's English-language periodical, featured calls for skilled professionals to immigrate to Syria in addition to fighters (al Furqan Media, July 1, 2014). This sentiment was reflected in an al-Hayat Media release featuring an English-speaking Canadian (al Hayat Media, July 11, 2014). The man, identified as Abu Muslim, said:

> So this is more than just fighting, this means more than just fighting. We need the engineers, we need doctors, we need professionals, we need volunteers, we need fundraising. We need everything. there is a role for everybody … your families will live here in safety, just like how it is back home. We have wide expanses of territory here in Syria, and we can easily find accommodation for you and your families (al-Hayat Media, July 11, 2014).

ISIS's communication strategy – the most enduring act of the Caliphate – covers several themes in relation to its different aims. In building legitimacy and attracting foreign fighters, it seeks to de-legitimise the current world order by highlighting the grievances in the Muslim world and "present[ing] itself as the singular political and religious authority over all Muslims" (Carter Center, 2017: 7) and as the agent of change towards a "new and just political order" (Pellerin, 2016: 11). For this cause, ISIS utilises the prophetic and apocalyptic overtures of the Islamic scripts, including the declaration of the Caliphate itself, which symbolises the "ushering" of "the prophesied new world order" (Dawson, 2017: 3). However, in boosting its legitimacy, ISIS does not restrict itself to scriptural prophecies but depicts the everyday glory of jihadist militancy and tackles the everyday social welfare benefits of living in its controlled areas. On the other hand, the grotesque images of beheadings and executions strive to instill fear in the hearts of their opponents (Carter Center, 2017: 5; Farwell, 2014: 50).

DECLINE OR DOWNFALL? TERRITORIAL AND MILITARY SETBACK, AND COUNTER-ISIS OPS

Although there was a global consensus on viewing the rise of ISIS as an imminent threat, conflicting national interests deterred the establishment of a wide and unified coalition against ISIS (Rosiny, 2016: 12). Counter-ISIS operations materialised in a more fractured manner, consisting mainly of a US-led coalition along with several single country-led operations (Iran, Russia, and Turkey). These different operations coordinated their activities with different local state and non-state actors while arranging ad hoc coordination among each other.

The US-led coalition, named the Combined Joint Task Force-Operation Inherent Resolve (CJTF-OIR), represented the broadest anti-ISIS coalition and was comprised of Western and Arab allies (Tabatabai & Esfandiary, 2017: 456). The US possessed "critical capabilities" that surpassed the rest of the coalition put together (Kagan et al., 2014: 21). Therefore, allies' contributions were confined to participating in air strikes and special forces. The coalition's objective was defined as to "degrade and ultimately destroy ISIS" (Tabatabai & Esfandiary, 2017: 459). This was to be achieved through a strategy that, at its core, combined a "systematic campaign of air strikes against ISIS" while supporting "local 'partner forces' fighting ISIS on the ground" (Patel, 2015: 1). Degrading the group's capabilities implied degrading its military capabilities – through bombing warehouses and factories, stemming the flow of foreign fighters, and assassinating high-level personnel – as well as its financial capabilities – through bombing oil production facilities, oil tankers, and targeting financial accounts and transfers – whereas supporting local partners involved providing training and advisory services, weapons, and humanitarian aid (Tabatabai & Esfandiary, 2017: 457; Patel, 2015: 1; Center for the Analysis of Terrorism, 2016: 10).

The main objective of the early stages of the counter-operations focused on bringing the ISIS impetus to a halt. In Iraq, it involved defending ISIS's advancement towards key cities such as Erbil and Samara and undertaking limited counter-offensives at the periphery of the organisation's territory (Kagan et al., 2014: 16). In Syria, the reversal of the situation was manifested with the Battle of Kobane (Oct. 2014–Feb. 2015), as the US aerial bombing supported the Kurdish PYD paramilitary group in its fight against ISIS, driving them out of town and rendering the group the US's most reliable local partner in Syria ("Battle for Kobane," 2015; Arango & Shmitt, 2015).

The US initiated its airstrikes on August 8, 2014, to stop ISIS's advance towards Erbil, the capital of the Kurdistan Regional Government (KRG), following its takeover of Sinjar Mountain and its atrocities towards its Yezidi population (Pollack, 2014). A month later, the coalition was officially announced, and air strikes were extended to ISIS-held areas inside Syria. The official announcement of the coalition came only after Washington rearranged Iraq's domestic political scene by blocking Maliki's third-term nomination for Prime Minister and forming a relatively more inclusive government headed by Haidar al-Abadi (Miller, 2014; al-Qarawee, 2016: 1; Katzman, 2015: 29).

As for the Iranian-led operations, they predated the coalition's, taking place just after the fall of Mosul. They also involved the provision of logistics, military equipment, and advice to various Iraqi fighting forces (the ISF, the Kurdish Peshmerga, and Shiite paramilitaries); furthermore, Iran did not hesitate to deploy its own forces when the situation was deemed "strategically viable" (Tabatabai & Esfandiary, 2017: 456; Tabatabai & Esfandiary, 2015: 8–9). However, the most significant footprint of Iranian involvement involved the Popular Mobilisation Forces (PMF). Although formed independently from Iran – and because of popular mobilisation in the Iraqi Shiite heartland in light of the collapse of the ISF – the revival of the Shiite paramilitary groups that emerged after the 2003 US invasion of Iraq entailed that the most powerful groups within the PMF had powerful ties with Iran (International Crisis Group, 2018: 3–4).

Russia's counter-ISIS operations were related to its wider involvement in the Syrian civil war, which, beginning in September 2015, took a direct form through providing aerial support to the Syrian Army. Initially, its involvement targeted the other factions of the Syrian armed opposition in the more strategic western parts of the country; however, the February 2016 "Cessation of Hostilities", a truce brokered by international and regional stakeholders, redirected its operations towards ISIS-held areas in the eastern parts of the country (Hanna, 2015; Black & Shaheen, 2016; McDonnell, 2016). Whereas Turkish direct involvement against ISIS materialised in August 2016 because of Turkish fears of the PYD's expansion to control the entire Syria-Turkish Within this context, a Turkish-led invasion, the Euphrates Shield, was launched, capturing ISIS-held territory in the border areas with Syria with the support of several factions of the Syrian armed opposition and US aerial bombing (Shaheen, 2016).

PROGRESS ON THE GROUND AND MAJOR TURNING POINTS

Between 2007 and 2014, US troops and Iraqi tribes killed and imprisoned ISIS core members, which eventually paved the way for the fall of Raqqa and Mosul (Wilson Center and United States Institute of Peace, 2016). US Special Forces provided guidance to the coalition of Kurdish and Arab militias that led the offensive and were successful in liberating Raqqa. US Army Colonel Ryan Dillon, a spokesman for the US-led coalition supporting the campaign against ISIS, explained that "over all, ISIS is losing in every way. We've devastated their networks, targeted them, and eliminated their leaders at all levels. We've degraded their ability to finance their operations, cutting oil revenues by 90%. Their flow of foreign recruits has gone from about fifteen hundred fighters a month down to near zero today (New York Times, October 17, 2017).

Chronicling the Fall of Mosul

ISIS launched its strongest onslaught when it overran Mosul on June 10, 2014, killing 600 Shiites who were prisoners at the Badoush prison at the time of the attack. On June 11, 2014, ISIS operatives seized control of Tikrit. Then, on June 12, 2014, Iran sent troops into Iraq to combat ISIS, assisting Iraqi forces in regaining control of most of Tikrit. Iraq requested that the US carry out airstrikes against ISIS on June 18, 2014. On August 7, 2014, airstrikes against ISIS in Iraq were launched as part of a coalition operation led by the United States called "Operation Inherent Resolve". The alliance entered Syria after a month. In Iraq and Syria, the US had carried out more than 8,000 airstrikes by 2015. ISIS suffered significant losses close to Syria's Turkish border. Ramadi had been retaken by Iraqi forces by December 2015 (Wilson Center, October 28, 2019).

The takeover of the oil refinery town of Beiji in November 2014 represented a turning point in the counter-ISIS operations as the counter-offensives moved further towards ISIS's core areas, cutting the organisation's supply lines ("Iraq troops push," 2014). This was followed by the Peshmerga's cutting of key supply lines to Mosul and the ISF/PMF takeover of the Diyala province and the city of Tikrit in March 2015 ("Iraq forces liberate," 2015; Morris, 2015; Katzman, 2015: 32). In Syria, two different trends emerged during this period. ISIS retreated in the country's northeast, where US-PYD operations were active, while advancing in both government-held and opposition-held areas (Arango & Shmitt, 2015; Enjrainy, 2015; Ayoub, 2015). The ISIS advancement culminated in May 2015 as it gained the upper hand in the Syrian Desert, especially with its takeover of the historically significant desert town of Palmyra. This was paralleled by a counteroffensive in Iraq that captured the city of Ramadi, the capital of Anbar ("Islamic State seizes," 2015).

However, the May 2015 resurge would prove to be short-lived as afterward ISIS experienced continuous retreat, losing Sinjar in the north and retreating from several towns in its stronghold in Anbar, including Ramadi ("Iraq declares Ramadi," 2015; "ISIS pulls out," 2016; "Iraqi forces oust," 2016; Gordon & Callimachi, 2015). In Syria, the February 2016 "Cessation of Hostilities" would allow all warring blocs to focus on ISIS, forcing the group to retreat from several areas. Furthermore, this period witnessed the intensification of the targeted killing of ISIS leaders through airstrikes and the US Delta Commando Forces, including its spokesperson Abu Mohammad al-Adnani and its most prominent foreign commander Omar al-Shishani (Starr, 2016; "Islamic State: Abu," 2016; "Iraq: ISIL says," 2016).

In the second half of 2016, preparations for the battle for the two de facto capitals, Raqqa and Mosul, would begin. These preparations involved deploying additional US military personnel to advise and support the local ground forces ("Nearly 45,000 ISIS," 2016). They also involved discussions and negotiations over which parties should be involved on the battlefield to mitigate residents' sensitivities and regional concerns. The Battle of Mosul was launched in October 2016 and lasted for eight months (June 2017), considering urban warfare-related difficulties. Its forces comprised the ISF, the Kurdish Peshmerga, and a few US advisors, while the PMF was kept outside the city (International Crisis Group, 2018: 14; Copp, 2016). The Battle of Raqqa was launched a month later, in November 2016. Its forces were restricted to the PYD and its junior Arab allies in a coalition termed the Syrian Democratic Forces (SDF), in disregard for Turkish concerns over PYD participation (Babb, 2016; "Syria's U.S.-backed," 2016). It commenced with a long-besieging phase (Nov. 2016–June 2017) that involved advancing in the city's countryside until the city was fully encircled, while the actual fighting in the city lasted until October 2017, when a withdrawal agreement was reached stipulating the safe exit of the remaining fighters from the city (Rai, 2016; Said & Perry, 2017). By the end of 2017, ISIS had lost its territorial hold in Iraq. Meanwhile in Syria, a race between the Russian-supported Syrian Army and the US-supported SDF emerged to inherit the remaining ISIS-held areas along the Euphrates River as ISIS "pivot[ed] away from holding territory to pursuing an all-out insurgency" (Hassan, 2017).

ISIS RESPONSE

As mentioned, the ISIS military developed three levels of operations: "to defend inside Iraq and Syria; to expand operations regionally; and to disrupt and recruit on a global scale". Inside Syria and Iraq, ISIS pursued a change in its military strategy and tactics, as discussed earlier. Nevertheless, these changes failed to reverse its "downward spiral of defeat," as the loss of territory undermined its ability to generate income, forcing them to slash salaries and ration essential materials. This, in turn, led to a decline in the group's credibility and attractiveness to recruit fighters, thus further undermining its territorial hold (Rosiny, 2016: 13).

On the regional and international levels, ISIS resorted to creating state affiliates and launching worldwide terrorist attacks. As early as November 2014, ISIS displayed a series of allegiances to several countries, including Saudi Arabia, Egypt, Algeria, Yemen, and Libya. By early 2016, the list of affiliates had expanded to include affiliates from Afghanistan, Pakistan, the North Caucasus, Tunisia, and Nigeria, among others (Bunzel, 2015: 32; Lister, 2016: 56). These allegiances came from either splinter groups from existing al-Qaida affiliates and local jihadist groups (the Khurasan, Caucasus, and Algeria governorates were the respective splinter groups of the Pakistani Taliban, al-Qa'ida's Caucasus Emirate, and

Al-Qaeda in the Islamic Maghreb) or through the allegiance of the whole group (Boko Haram in Nigeria and Ansar Bait al-Maqdis in Sinai, Egypt) (McCants, 2016b: 21). These affiliates took several forms: statelets that govern a specific territory (Sirte, Libya), insurgencies that control but cannot govern specific territories (Sinai, Egypt), and terrorist organisations that operate clandestinely without holding territory (Algeria Governorate) (McCants, 2016b: 20).

The most prominent ISIS affiliate was in Sirte, Libya, Gadafi's hometown. The group exploited the marginalisation and the resultant security vacuum of the city after Gadafi's fall to gradually establish itself and assume state-like functions (Pack et al., 2017: 26–28). By 2016, ISIS controlled swathes of land stretching 170 km along the Libyan coast (Lister, 2016: 60). The counter-ISIS operation, Bunian al-Marsus, was begun by Misratan militias in mid-2016 as ISIS attacked Mistratan-held territories. With the help of US airstrikes, ISIS's presence was eradicated by late 2016 (Pack et al., 2017: 35–37).

ISIS proceeded to carry out numerous assaults on people in several nations throughout the years, with one of its most prominent strikes being the November 2015 Paris attacks, which were a series of coordinated terrorist attacks in the city's northern neighbourhood, Saint-Denis. The shootings and bomb blasts killed 130 people and injured hundreds more, with more than 100 critically injured. According to French police, the attacks were carried out by three coordinated teams of terrorists. As the search for suspects continued in the days following the attacks, French police conducted hundreds of raids across the country. Raids were also carried out in the Belgian capital of Brussels (CNN, December 9, 2015).

The Islamic State has claimed responsibility for several attacks in Egypt. The first bombing, in Tanta, tore through the inside of St. George Church during its Palm Sunday service, killing at least 27 people and injuring at least 78. The second bombing, in Alexandria, hit Saint Mark's Cathedral, killing 17 people, including three police officers, and injuring 48 (Reuters, April 9, 2017). The Islamic State also claimed responsibility for the attack on a bus filled with Christians. 28 Coptic Christians were killed and dozens more wounded when ISIS attacked them while they were travelling to a monastery in Egypt's Minya province. The Christians were headed to the Saint Samuel Monastery, about 220 kilometres south of the Egyptian capital. Cherif Chekat, a man who had pledged allegiance to ISIS, attacked civilians who were shopping in a public market in Strasbourg on December 11, 2018. The attack on a market resulted in five casualties and about a dozen injuries. A few days later. Chekatt was killed during a shootout with police in Strasbourg (CNN, December 11, 2018).

Between June 2014 (the Declaration of the Caliphate) and February 2018, ISIS-related terrorist attacks amounted to more than 140 attacks in 29 countries and resulted in more than 2000 deaths. These attacks included those that ISIS or one of its affiliates had planned out and funded as well as less sophisticated ones that took their cues from the organisation. Regional attacks mainly targeted Shiite Muslims in Lebanon, Saudi Arabia, Kuwait, and Yemen and foreigners (Western tourists in Tunisia, Russian passenger planes in Egypt, and Coptic Christians in Libya), while ISIS affiliates (Egypt, Russian Caucasus) mainly targeted army and police personnel. Internationally, the most sophisticated attack took place in Paris, France, in November 2015, which involved coordinated attacks in six different locations and killed more than 130 people. Other prominent attacks include the bombing of the Brussels Airport in Belgium (March 2016), the bombing of the Ataturk International Airport in Istanbul, Turkey (June 2016), and the driving of a truck into crowds in Nice, France (July 2016) (Lister et al., 2018). Sadly, the ISIS attacks on civilians continue unabated. In Sri Lanka, several members of an ISIS-affiliated group, the National Thowheed Jamaath, carried out suicide bombings in Catholic churches in Colombo and Negombo during the Easter Masses, resulting in 260 casualties (The Washington Post, April 29, 2019).

THE IMPACT OF ISIS

Fragmentation or Fomentation of the Global Jihadist Movement?

As discussed, the rise of ISIS created a schism within the global jihadist movement as Al Qaeda Central severed its organisational links with its former affiliate. The jihadist schism was not confined to Syria but rather affected the whole global jihadist scene, given that ISIS expanded at the expense of Al Qaeda affiliates (McCants, 2016b: 21). On the other hand, as the spotlight was cast on ISIS, Al Qaeda Central was "quietly rebuilding" itself (Hoffman, 2018). The group expanded into the Indian Subcontinent, solidified its presence in the war-torn countries of Syria, Somalia, and Yemen, and dispersed its leadership away from Afghanistan and Pakistan towards these countries (Hoffman, 2018). Thus, with the collapse of the "Caliphate", the Jihadist movement has become thoroughly divided across the globe, a division that is likely to persist rather than subside given the strategic differences between al-Qaeda Central and its former affiliate (Hassan, 2018: 6–7).

Reshuffling Iraqi Politics

The rise and fall of ISIS had a significant impact on Iraq's domestic politics. Even though it did not change the rules of the game, it managed to reshuffle its cards in terms of both inter- and intra-sectarian contestation of state power. In the case of the former, the Shiites emerged as even more powerful in their control of the central government at the expense of both the Sunni Arabs, devastatingly weakened by the rise and fall of ISIS, and the Kurds, whose interests in preserving influence in Baghdad diminished in favour of consolidating their regional power. This manifested itself in the aftermath of the Kurdish independence referendum as the ISF, aided by the PMF, re-asserted its control over the Kurdish-held city of Kirkuk ("Iraq seizes Kirkuk," 2017).

More profound was the impact of the ISIS episode on the intra-Shiite contestation of power. On the one hand, it empowered the PMF-related parties at the expense of the traditional Shiite parties, as evident from the 2018 parliamentary elections (Ahmed, 2019). On the other hand, the capacity of the Shiite ruling class to rely on identity-based politics as a means of mobilising the masses has been significantly compromised. The 2014 collapse of the security forces exposed the weaknesses and corruptness of the Iraqi regime, which, among other factors, fed into the 2015 protest movement in Shiite-dominated areas. The focus of the protest movement on issues of corruption and poor public services at the time of an existential crisis indicated the emergent role of issue-based politics in Iraqi politics (Mansour, 2017: 11–12).

Shaping the Outcome of the Syrian Civil War

Moving to Syria, the rise and fall of ISIS played a pivotal role in shaping the change in the conflict's balance of power away from the Syrian opposition and in favour of the Syrian regime, in addition to its role in the rise of the Kurdish PYD/YPG. To begin with, the Syrian opposition lost a significant amount of manpower between defections and deaths and lost control of the resource-rich eastern regions of the country during the 2014 conflict with ISIS. Afterward, the Syrian opposition had to deal with ISIS attacks, enclaves within its controlled areas, and sleeping cells. On the other hand, the weakening of the Syrian opposition naturally empowered the Syrian regime, which chose to avoid any confrontation with ISIS during its conflict with the Syrian opposition. Even though the Syrian regime afterward, as in the case of the opposition, suffered from ISIS attacks, the rise of ISIS diverted regime adversaries' attention from its conflict with the regime. Finally, the Battle of Kobane paved the way for a marriage of convenience between the United States and the Kurdish PYD/YPG, rendering the group the US's most reliable ally in its war against ISIS, a key player in the Syrian conflict, and allowing for its territorial expansion beyond Kurdish-populated areas.

CONCLUSION

ISIS, an offshoot of the worldwide jihadist movement, managed, albeit for a limited moment, to accomplish the organisation's aim of establishing an Islamic Caliphate in a significant region of the Islamic World, thirteen years after the attacks of September 11, 2001, and the US "Global War on Terror." ISIS has shown in this short time that it is capable of manoeuvring and manipulating global, regional, and local politics, absorbing various social and political followers and assimilating them into the Caliphate's operational framework, and communicating with, recruiting, and mobilising large numbers of fighters. Consequently, the group's diverse capabilities helped it transition from a terrorist outfit to a quasi-conventional military force and, probably most crucially, into a permanent ideology. As ISIS has remade itself into a terrorist organisation, it will aim to exploit new gaps.

Note

1 For a more in-depth study of the effects of the Arab Spring on the safety and security of Christians, see Besenyő & Gömöri's (2013), "Arab Spring, Christian Fall? The condition of Christian minorities in the Middle East after the Arab Spring"

References

Abuzeid, R. (2013, March 23). How Islamist rebels in Syria are ruling a fallen provincial capital. *Time*. Retrieved from http://world.time.com/2013/03/23/how-islamist-rebels-in-syria-are-ruling-a-fallen-provincial-capital/

Ahmed, R. (January 9, 2019). *A year after the defeat of ISIS in Iraq, what has changed?* Retrieved from the Middle East Institute Website: https://www.mei.edu/publications/year-after-defeat-isis-iraq-what-has-changed.

Ali, A.S. (2013). Bab al-Hawa: min al-ightial al-awwal ila bawader iqtitial bayna al-jabhatayn wa daesh [Bab al-Hawa: From the first assassination to the initial infighting between the two fronts and ISIS]. *al-Manar*. Retrieved from http://archive.almanar.com.lb/article.php?id=671878

Arango, T., & Shmitt, E. (2015, June 29). Turkey uneasy as U.S. support of Syrian Kurds grows. *The New York Times*. Retrieved from http://www.nytimes.com/2015/06/30/world/middleeast/turkey-uneasy-as-us-support-of-syrian-kurds-grows.html

Ayoub, N. (2015, August 10). al-qaryatain: huna hudud daesh [al-Qaryatain: here is the border of ISIL]. *al-Akhbar*. Retrieved from http://al-akhbar.com/node/239600

Babb, C. (2016, October 27). Raqqa fight starting 'soon,' isolation operation to include YPG. *Voice of America*. Retrieved from https://www.voanews.com/a/raqqa-fight-starting-soon-isolation-operation-kurdish-ypg/3567282.html

Battle for Kobane: Key events. (2015, June 25). *BBC*. Retrieved from http://www.bbc.co.uk/news/world-middle-east-29688108

Beccaroa, A. (2018). Modern irregular warfare: The ISIS case study. *Small Wars & Insurgencies, 29*(2), 207–228, 10.1080/09592318.2018.1433469

Besenyő, J. (2019). Barry Buzan's securitization theory and the case of Iraqi Kurdish military action against ISIS in 2014. *Journal of Security and Sustainability Issues*, *8*(3), 295–306. http://jssidoi.org/jssi/uploads/papers/31/Besenyo_Barry_Buzans_Securitization_Theory_and_the_case_of_Iraqi_Kurdish_military_action_against_ISIS_in_2014.pdf

Besenyő, J., & Gömöri, R. (2013). Arab Spring, Christian Fall? The situation of Christian minorities in the Middle East after the Arab Spring. *International Institute for Counter-Terrorism 2013*, *6*(16), 1–20. http://real.mtak.hu/83763/1/Arab_Spring_Christian_Fall_u.pdf

Black, I., & Shaheen, K. (2016, February 12). Partial Syria ceasefire agreed at talks in Munich. *The Guardian*. Retrieved from https://www.theguardian.com/world/2016/feb/12/syria-ceasefire-munich-talks-us-russia

Bunzel, C. (2015). *From paper state to Caliphate: The ideology of the Islamic state*. The Brookings Project on U.S. Relations with the Islamic World, (Analysis Paper No. 19). Retrieved from the Center for Middle East Policy at Brookings https://www.brookings.edu/wp-content/uploads/2016/06/The-ideology-of-the-Islamic-State.pdf

Cafarella, J. (2014). *Jabhat al-Nusra in Syria: An Islamic Emirate for al-Qaeda* (Middle East Security Report No. 25). Retrieved from the Institute for the Study of War Website: https://www.files.ethz.ch/isn/193486/JN%20Final.pdf

Caillet, R. (2014). al-Kawn yuharibu daesh wa la yahzumuha [The universe fights ISIS and does not beat it]. *Al-Akhbar*. Retrieved from https://al-akhbar.com/Opinion/26887.

Carris, C., & Reynolds, S. (2014). *ISIS governance in Syria*. Washington D.C., US: Institute of the Study of War.

Carter Center. (2017). Daesh meta-narratives: From the global Ummah to the hyperlocal. Retrieved from https://www.cartercenter.org/resources/pdfs/peace/conflict_resolution/countering-isis/narratives-report-final-02june2017.pdf

Center for the Analysis of Terrorism. (2016). *ISIS financing in 2015*. Retrieved from https://cat-int.org/wp-content/uploads/2016/06/ISIS-Financing-2015-Report.pdf

Chivers, C.J. (2014, June 21). Answering a cleric's call, Iraqi Shiites take up arms. *The New York Times*. Retrieved from https://www.nytimes.com/2014/06/22/world/middleeast/iraq-militia.html

CNN. (December 9, 2015). "Paris attacks: What happened on the night.".

CNN. (December 11, 2018). "Strasbourg market attacker 'pledged allegiance to ISIS' - source.".

Copp, T. (2016, October 19). Apaches enter fight for Mosul, top US general says. *Stars and Stripes*. Retrieved from https://www.stripes.com/news/apaches-enter-fight-for-mosul-top-us-general-says-1.434876.

Daesh yusaytiru 'ala 95% min muhfazet deir ez-zour [ISIS control 95% of the Govronorate of Deir ez-Zour]. (2014, July 15). al-Arabiya. Retrieved from https://www.alarabiya.net/ar/arab-and-world/syria/2014/07/15/-%D8%AF%D8%A7%D8%B9%D8%B4-%D9%8A%D8%B3%D9%8A%D8%B7%D8%B1-%D8%B9%D9%84%D9%89-95-%D9%85%D9%86-%D9%85%D8%AD%D8%A7%D9%81%D8%B8%D8%A9-%D8%AF%D9%8A%D8%B1-%D8%A7%D9%84%D8%B2%D9%88%D8%B1.html#

Dawson, L.L. (2017). *The failure of prophecy and the future of IS* (Policy brief). Retrieved from International Centre for Counter-Terrorism Website: https://icct.nl/wp-content/uploads/2017/09/ICCT-Dawson-The-Failure-of-Prophecy-and-The-Future-of-ISIS-Sept-2017.pdf

Deir ez-Zour: Daesh yashtaree thawar al-alwiyeh al-jihadiyeh fee al-qouriyeh [Deir ez-Zour: ISIS purchases the revolution of the jihadist brigades in al-Qouriyeh. (2014, July 23). *Taht al-Mijhar*. Retrieved from https://www.almjhar.com/ar-sy/NewsView/7/75798/%D8%AF%D9%8A%D8%B1_%D8%A7%D9%84%D8%B2%D9%88%D8%B1_%D8%AF%D8%A7%D8%B9%D8%B4_%D9%8A%D8%B4%D8%AA%D8%B1%D9%8A_%D8%AB%D9%88%D8%B1%D8%A9_%D8%A7%D9%84%D8%A3%D9%84%D9%88%D9%8A%D8%A9_%D8%A7%D9%84%D8%AC%D9%87%D8%A7%D8%AF%D9%8A%D8%A9_%D9%81%D9%8A_%D8%A7%D9%84%D9%82%D9%88%D8%B1%D9%8A%D8%A9.aspx

Enjrainy, S. (2014, January 6). Jeish al-mujaheedeen vs. dawla al-islam [The army of al-Mujaheedeen vs. the Islamic state]. *al-Akhbar*. Retrieved from https://al-akhbar.com/Syria/24955

Enjrainy, S. (2015, August 28). Daesh yatahadda al-tahaluf: qadeeroun 'ala al-tamadud wa suqut mare' qareeb [ISIL defies the coalition: we are capable of expanding and the fall of Mare' is imminent. *al-Akhbar*. Retrieved from http://al-akhbar.com/node/240960

European Parliament. (2017). *The financing of the 'Islamic State' in Iraq and Syria (ISIS)*. Directorate-General for External Policies, Policy Department. Retrieved from http://www.europarl.europa.eu/RegData/etudes/IDAN/2017/603835/EXPO_IDA(2017)603835_EN.pdf

Farwell, J.P. (2014). The media strategy of ISIS. *Survival*, *56*(6), 49–55. 10.1080/00396338.2014.985436

Fishman, B. (2006). After Zarqawi: The dilemmas and future of Al Qaeda in Iraq. *The Washington Quarterly*, *29*(4), 19–32. 10.1162/wash.2006.29.4.19

al-Furqan Media. Audio message from the Islamic State's AbḤ Bakr al-ḤussaynḤ al-QurayshḤ al-BaghdadḤ: 'Message To the MujahidḤn and the Islamic Ummah In the Month Of Ramadan'," Jihadology, July 1, 2014. http://jihadology.net/2014/07/01/al- furqan-media-presents-a-new-audio-message-from-the-islamic- states-abu-bakr-al-%E1%B8%A5ussayni-al-qurayshi-al-baghdadi- message-to-the-mujahidin-and-the-islamic-ummah-in-the-month-of-rama/.

Gerges, F.A. (2016). *ISIS: A history*. Princeton: Princeton University Press.

al-Ghali, K. (2017). Qissat saqout al-raqqa fe yad daesh [The story of the fall of Raqqa in the hands of ISIS]. *Irfa' Sautak*. Retrieved from https://www.irfaasawtak.com/a/363122.html.

Gordon, M.R., & Callimachi, R. (2015, November 13). Kurdish fighters retake Iraqi city of Sinjar from ISIS. *The New York Times*. Retrieved from https://www.nytimes.com/2015/11/14/world/middleeast/sinjar-iraq-islamic-state.html

Hamming, T.R. (2017). The Al Qaeda–Islamic state rivalry: Competition yes, but no competitive escalation. *Terrorism and Political Violence*. 10.1080/09546553.2017.1342634

al-Hakkar, F. ISIS brings life back to Raqqa, in its own way. al-Akhbar, January 23, 2014, http://english.al-akhbar.com/node/18354.

Hanna, E. (2015, October 9). al-'amiliyyeh al-kubra mistamirrah: Dima' jadidah fee 'urooq al-jeish [The grand operation continues: Fresh blood in the veins of the army]. *al-Akhbar*. Retrieved from http://www.al-akhbar.com/node/243603

Hassan, H. (2017). Insurgents again: The Islamic State's calculated reversion to attrition in the Syria-Iraq border region and beyond. *CTC Sentinel, 10*(11). Retrieved from https://ctc.usma.edu/insurgents-again-the-islamic-states-calculated-reversion-to-attrition-in-the-syria-iraq-border-region-and-beyond/

Hassan, H. (2018). Two houses divided: How conflict in Syria shaped the future of Jihadism. *CTC Sentinel, 11*(9). Retrieved from https://ctc.usma.edu/two-houses-divided-conflict-syria-shaped-future-jihadism/

al-Hayat Media. (July 11, 2014). *Canadian fighter urges Muslims to travel to Syria in Posthumous IS video.* SIte Intelligence Group.

Hoffman, B. (2018, March 6). *al-Qaeda's resurrection.* Retrieved from the Council on Foreign Relations Website: https://www.cfr.org/expert-brief/al-qaedas-resurrection

Institute for the Study of War. (2014). *Warning intelligence update: Escalation in Anbar* (Iraq Update No. 16). Retrieved from http://iswresearch.blogspot.com/2014/04/iraq-update-2014-16-warning.html

International Crisis Group. (2014a). *Rigged cars and barrel bombs: Aleppo and the state of the Syrian War* (Middle East & North Africa Report No. 155). Retrieved from https://d2071andvip0wj.cloudfront.net/rigged-cars-and-barrel-bombs-aleppo-and-the-state-of-the-syrian-war.pdf

International Crisis Group. (2014b). *Iraq: Falluja's Faustian bargain* (Middle East Report No. 150). Retrieved from https://d2071andvip0wj.cloudfront.net/iraq-falluja-s-faustian-bargain.pdf

International Crisis Group. (2018). *Iraq's paramilitary groups: The challenge of rebuilding a functioning state* (Middle East Report No. 188). Retrieved from https://d2071andvip0wj.cloudfront.net/188-iraqs-paramilitary-groups_0.pdf

Iraq declares Ramadi liberated from Islamic State. (2015, December 28). *BBC*. Retrieved from https://www.bbc.com/news/world-middle-east-35188479

Iraq forces 'liberate' Diyala province from IS. (2015, January 26). *Yahoo News*. Retrieved from https://news.yahoo.com/iraq-forces-liberate-diyala-province-jihadists-130947834.html

Iraq seizes Kirkuk from Kurdish forces after independence referendum. (2017, October 16). *ABC*. Retrieved from https://www.abc.net.au/news/2017-10-17/iraqi-forces-seize-kirkuk-from-kurds-in-bold-advance/9056708

Iraq troops 'push Islamic State from oil town of Baiji'. (2014, November 14). *BBC*. Retrieved from https://www.bbc.com/news/world-middle-east-30052714

Iraq: ISIL says Omar al-Shishani killed in air strike. (2016, July 14). *al-Jazeera*. Retrieved from https://www.aljazeera.com/news/2016/07/iraq-isil-omar-al-shishani-killed-air-strike-160713203202458.html

Iraqi forces oust ISIL from key Anbar town. (2016, April 8). *al-Jazeera*. Retrieved from https://www.aljazeera.com/news/2016/04/iraqi-forces-oust-isil-key-anbar-town-160408144126609.html

ISIS pulls out of town in Iraq's Anbar: General. (2016, March 13). *Daily Star*. Retrieved from https://www.dailystar.com.lb/News/Middle-East/2016/Mar-13/341957-isis-pulls-out-of-town-in-iraqs-anbar-general.ashx

Islamic State: Abu Muhammad al-Adnani 'killed in Aleppo'. (2016, August 31). *BBC*. Retrieved from https://www.bbc.com/news/uk-37224570

Islamic State 'seizes key Syria-Iraq border crossing'. (2015, May 22). *BBC*. Retrieved from http://www.bbc.co.uk/news/world-middle-east-32840508

Issam, W. (2014, January 31). Qa'ed jabhat al-nusra lil quds al-araby: muqatilu daesh kanou yunadunana abra ajhezat al-lasilki 'ah 'Ahrar Esh-Sham insahabou wa tarakoukum [The leader of JAN to al-Quds al-Arabi: The fighter of ISIS used to call us over wireless devices 'Ahrar Esh-Sham have retreated and left you']. *al-Quds al-Arabi*. Retrieved from https://www.alquds.co.uk/%d9%82%d8%a7%d8%a6%d8%af-%d8%ac%d8%a8%d9%87%d8%a9-%d8%a7%d9%84%d9%86%d8%b5%d8%b1%d8%a9-%d9%84%d9%80%d8%a7%d9%84%d9%82%d8%af%d8%b3-%d8%a7%d9%84%d8%b9%d8%b1%d8%a8%d9%8a-%d9%85%d9%82%d8%a7%d8%aa/

Jabhat al-nusra tumhilu daesh fee Suriya khamset ayyam lil-sulh aw al-tard [JAN gives ISIS in Syria five days for either reconciliation or eviction]. (2014, February 25). *BBC Arabic*. Retrieved from http://www.bbc.com/arabic/middleeast/2014/02/140225_syria_ultimatum

Jasper, S., & Moreland, S. (2014). The Islamic state is a hybrid threat: Why does that matter? *Small Wars Journal*. Retrieved from https://smallwarsjournal.com/jrnl/art/the-islamic-state-is-a-hybrid-threat-why-does-that-matter?fbclid=IwAR0wN1y5K6ZjsFMYuEoHMYubvmUL-nOhHQYjfuNh9vchjcpppG0UhggKlPg#_edn12

Jefferis, J. (2016). ISIS administrative and territorial organization. In IEMed (Ed.), *Mediterranean yearbook* (pp. 241–244). Retrieved from the European Institute of the Mediterranean Website: https://www.iemed.org/observatori/arees-danalisi/arxius-adjunts/anuari/med.2016/IEMed_MedYearBook2016_ISIS%20Administrative%20Organization_Jeniffer_Jefferis.pdf

Kagan, K., Kagan, F.W., & Lewis J.D. (2014). *A strategy to defeat the Islamic state* (Middle East Security Report No. 23). Retrieved from the Institute for the Study of War Website: http://www.understandingwar.org/sites/default/files/Defeating%20ISIS_0.pdf

Katzman, K. (2015). *Iraq: Politics, security, and U.S. policy* (Congressional Research Service Report No. RS21968). Retrieved from https://www.refworld.org/pdfid/55a4dd1c4.pdf

Khalaf, R. (2015). Beyond arms & beards: Local governance of ISIS in Syria. *Caliphates & Islamic Global Politics, E-IR*. Retrieved from https://www.e-ir.info/2015/01/07/beyond-arms-and-beards-local-governance-of-isis-in-syria/

Kozak, C. (2015). *"An army in all corners": Assad's campaign strategy in Syria* (Middle East Security Report No. 26). Retrieved from The Institute for the Study of War Website: http://www.understandingwar.org/sites/default/files/An%20Army%20in%20All%20Corners%20by%20Chris%20Kozak%201.pdf

Lewis, J. (2013). *Further indications of al-Qaeda's advance in Iraq* (Iraq Update No.39). Retrieved from the Institute for the Study of War Website: http://iswresearch.blogspot.com/2013/11/further-indications-of-al-qaedas.html

Lewis, J., Kagan, K., & Anonymous. (2014). *The ISIS battle plan.* Retrieved from the Institute for the Study of War Website: http://www.understandingwar.org/backgrounder/isis-battle-plan

Lister, C. (2014). *Profiling the Islamic State* (Analysis Paper No. 13). Retrieved from the Brookings Doha Center Website: https://www.brookings.edu/wp-content/uploads/2014/12/en_web_lister.pdf

Lister, C. (2016). Competition among violent Islamist extremists: Combating an unprecedented threat. *The ANNALS of the American Academy of Political and Social Science*, *668*(1), 53–70. 10.1177/0002716216668500

Lister, T., Sanchez, R., Bixler, M., O'Key, S., Hogenmiller, M., & Tawfeeq, M. (2018, February 12). ISIS goes global: 143 attacks in 29 countries have killed 2,043. *CNN*. Retrieved from https://edition.cnn.com/2015/12/17/world/mapping-isis-attacks-around-the-world/index.html

Mansour, R. (2017). *Iraq after the fall of ISIS: The struggle for the state* (Research Paper). Retrieved from the Chatham House Website: https://www.chathamhouse.org/sites/default/files/publications/research/2017-07-04-iraq-after-isis-mansour-final.pdf

Maurer, T. (2018). ISIS's warfare functions: A systematized review of a proto-state's conventional conduct of combat operations. *Small Wars & Insurgencies*, *29*(2), 229–244. 10.1080/09592318.2018.1435238

McCants, W. (2016a). *The ISIS apocalypse: The history, strategy, and doomsday vision of the Islamic state*. New York: St Martin's Press.

McCants, W. (2016b). The polarizing effect of Islamic State aggression on the global jihadist movement. *CTC Sentinel*, *9*(7). Retrieved from https://ctc.usma.edu/the-polarizing-effect-of-islamic-state-aggression-on-the-global-jihadist-movement/

McCoy, T. (2014, November 4). Camp Bucca: The US prison that became the birthplace of Isis. *The Independent*. Retrieved from https://www.independent.co.uk/news/world/middle-east/camp-bucca-the-us-prison-that-became-the-birthplace-of-isis-9838905.html

McDonnell, P. (2016, March 27). March Syrian army's blow to Islamic state presents a paradox for Obama. *Los Angeles Times*. Retrieved from http://www.latimes.com/world/middleeast/

Miller, Z. J. (2014, September 23). U.S. launches air-strike campaign against ISIS in Syria. *Time*. Retrieved from http://time.com/3419906/u-s-launches-airstrike-campaign-against-isis-in-syria/

Morris, L. (January 22, 2015). Kurds say they have ejected Islamic State militants from large area in northern Iraq. *Washington Post*. Retrieved from https://www.washingtonpost.com/world/middle_east/kurds-say-they-have-ejected-islamic-state-from-a-big-area-in-northern-iraq/2015/01/21/ac459372-a1c6-11e4-b146-577832eafcb4_story.html?noredirect=on&utm_term=.968cffb3ee30

Muhammad, N. (2013, December 11). Daesh wal 'asha'er … jadaliyet al-mubaya'ah wal intima' wa rasas al-rifd [ISIS and the tribes … the dialectics of allegiance, belonging and the bullets of rejection]. *Al-Hal*. Retrieved from https://7al.net/2013/12/11/%D8%AF%D8%A7%D8%B9%D8%B4-%D9%88%D8%A7%D9%84%D8%B9%D8%B4%D8%A7%D8%A6%D8%B1-%D8%AC%D8%AF%D9%84%D9%8A%D8%A9-%D8%A7%D9%84%D9%85%D8%A8%D8%A7%D9%8A%D8%B9%D8%A9-%D9%88%D8%A7%D9%84%D8%A7%D9%86%D8%AA%D9%85/

Nassief, I. (2014). *The campaign for Homs and Aleppo: The Assad regime's strategy in 2013* (Middle East Security Report No. 17). Retrieved from the Institute for the Study of War Website: http://www.understandingwar.org/sites/default/files/Nassief-BattleforHomsAleppo-web.pdf

Nearly 45,000 ISIS-linked fighters killed in past 2 years, US military official says. (2016, August 10). *Fox News*. Retrieved from https://www.foxnews.com/world/nearly-45000-isis-linked-fighters-killed-in-past-2-years-us-military-official-says

Neriah, J. (2014). *The structure of the Islamic State (ISIS)*. Retrieved from The Jerusalem Center for Public Affairs Website: http://jcpa.org/structure-of-the-islamic-state/.

New York Times. (October 17, 2017). The ignominious end of the ISIS Caliphate.

al-Nusra tubaye' daesh bi-madinet al-bu kamal al-souriyeh [JAN pledges alleigence to ISIS in the Syrian city of al-Bu Kamal]. (2014, June 25). *Arabi 21*. Retrieved from https://arabi21.com/story/758087/%D8%A7%D9%84%D9%86%D8%B5%D8%B1%D8%A9-%D8%AA%D8%A8%D8%A7%D9%8A%D8%B9-%D8%AF%D8%A7%D8%B9%D8%B4-%D8%A8%D9%85%D8%AF%D9%8A%D9%86%D8%A9-%D8%A7%D9%84%D8%A8%D9%88%D9%83%D9%85%D8%A7%D9%84-%D8%A7%D9%84%D8%B3%D9%88%D8%B1%D9%8A%D8%A9

al-Ouqdeh, A. (2015). Hurub Daesh fee halab wa reefiha [The wars of ISIS in Aleppo and its countryside]. *Orient Net*. Retrieved from https://www.orient-news.net/ar/news_show/90243/حروب-داعش-في-حلب-وريفها-منذ-ب-2013-وحتى-ب-2015

Pack, J., Smith, R., & Mezran, K. (2017). *The origins and evolution of ISIS in Libya*. Retrieved from the Atlantic Council Website: http://www.atlanticcouncil.org/images/publications/The_Origins_and_Evolution_of_ISIS_in_Libya_web_0619.pdf

Paraszczuk, J. Syria: Umar Al-Shishani & Isis Claim advance from al-Bab to manbij, capture Base. from chechnya To Syria Blog, January 20, 2014, http://www.chechensinsyria.com/?p=18077.

Parker, N., Cole, I., & Salman, R. (2014, October 14). Special report - How Mosul fell: An Iraqi general disputes Baghdad's story. *Reuters*. Retrieved from https://www.reuters.com/article/us-mideast-crisis-gharawi-special-report/special-report-how-mosul-fell-an-iraqi-general-disputes-baghdads-story-idUSKCN0I30Z820141014

Patel, D.S. (2015). *ISIS in Iraq: What we get wrong and why 2015 is not 2007* (Middle East Brief No. 87). Retrieved from Brandeis University, Crown Centre for Middle East Studies Website: https://www.brandeis.edu/crown/publications/meb/MEB87.pdf

PBS News Hour. (November 2, 2018). "Christian pilgrims in Egypt ambushed; ISIS claims responsibility.".

Pellerin, C. (2016). *Communicating terror: An analysis of ISIS communication strategy*(Student paper). Kuwait Program at Sciences Po. Kuwait.

Plebani, A. (2014). The unfolding legacy of al-Qa'ida in Iraq: From al-Zarqawi to the new Islamic Caliphate. In A. Plebani (Ed.), *New (and old) patterns of jihadism: al-Qa'ida, the Islamic State and beyond* (pp. 2–25). Milano: Istituto per gli Studi di Politica Internazionale (ISPI).

Pollack, K.M. (2014, August 11). Iraq: Understanding the ISIS offensive against the Kurds [Blog post]. Retrieved from https://www.brookings.edu/blog/markaz/2014/08/11/iraq-understanding-the-isis-offensive-against-the-kurds/

Prothero, M. al Qaida's ISIS takes 2 Syrian cities, executes scores of rivals, McClatchy, January 13, 2014. Retrieved from http://www.mcclatchydc.com/2014/01/13/214335/al-qaidas-isis-takes-2-syrian.html.

al-Qarawee, H.H. (2016). *From Maliki to Abadi: The challenge of being Iraq's Prime Minister* (Middle East Brief No. 100). Retrieved from Brandeis University, Crown Centre for Middle East Studies Website: http://www.brandeis.edu/crown/publications/meb/MEB100.pdf

Rai, M. (2016, November 20). Raqqa will mark Islamic State downfall. *Afghanistan Times*. Retrieved from http://www.afghanistantimes.af/raqqa-will-mark-islamic-state-downfall/

Revkin, M. (2016). *Does the Islamic State have a "Social Contract"? Evidence from Iraq and Syria* (Working Paper No. 9). Retrieved from the Program on Governance and Local Development, University of Gothenburg Website: https://gld.gu.se/media/1133/gld-wp9.pdf

Rosiny, S. (2016). *Brutalisation as a Survival Strategy: How the "Islamic State" is Prolonging Its Doomsday Battle* (Working Papers No.288). Retrieved from German Institute of Global and Area Studies (GIGA) Website: https://www.giga-hamburg.de/en/system/files/publications/wp288_rosiny.pdf

Said, R., & Perry, T. (2017, June 5). U.S.-backed force launches assault on Islamic State's 'capital' in Syria. *Reuters*. Retrieved from https://www.reuters.com/article/us-mideast-crisis-syria-raqqa/u-s-backed-force-launches-assault-on-islamic-states-capital-in-syria-idUSKBN18W29P

al-Sanjary, Z., & Rasheed A. (2014, June 15). Advancing Iraq rebels seize northwest town in heavy battle. *Reuters*. Retrieved from https://www.reuters.com/article/us-iraq-security-idUSKBN0EP0KJ20140615

Shaheen, K. (2016, August 24). Turkey sends tanks into Syria in operation aimed at Isis and Kurds. *The Guardian*. Retrieved from https://www.theguardian.com/world/2016/aug/24/turkey-launches-major-operation-against-isis-in-key-border-town

Starr, B. (2016, February 29). Army's Delta Force begins to target ISIS in Iraq. *CNN*. Retrieved from https://edition.cnn.com/2016/02/29/politics/pentagon-army-target-isis-iraq/index.html

Syrian Observatory for Human Rights facebook post. ISIS release 4 statements to its subjects in 'Wilayat al-Raqqa', January 20, 2014, https://www.facebook.com/syriahroe/posts/477714635670213.

Syria's U.S.-backed SDF says no to Turkish role in Raqqa operation. (2016, November 3). *Reuters*. Retrieved from https://www.reuters.com/article/us-mideast-crisis-syria-raqqa-idUSKBN12Y0V8

Tabatabai, A., & Esfandiary, D. (2015). Iran's ISIS policy. *International Affairs, 91*(1), 1–15. Retrieved from https://www.chathamhouse.org/sites/default/files/field/field_publication_docs/INTA91_1_01_Esfandiary_Tabatabai.pdf

Tabatabai, A., & Esfandiary, D. (2017). Cooperating with Iran to combat ISIS in Iraq. *The Washington Quarterly*, *40*(3), 129–146. 10.1080/0163660X.2017.1370338

al-Tamimi, A. (2015). The evolution in Islamic State administration: The documentary evidence. *Perspectives on Terrorism*, *9*(4), 117–129. Retrieved from http://www.jstor.org/stable/26297420

Thompson, N., & Shubert, A. (2015, January 14). The anatomy of ISIS: How the 'Islamic State' is run, from oil to beheadings. *CNN*. Retreived from https://edition.cnn.com/2014/09/18/world/meast/isis-syria-iraq-hierarchy/index.html

Turner, J. (2015). Strategic differences: Al Qaeda's split with the Islamic State of Iraq and al-Sham. *Small Wars & Insurgencies*, *26*(2), 208–225. 10.1080/09592318.2015.1007563

Tønnessen, T. H. (2015). Heirs of Zarqawi or Saddam? The relationship between al-Qaida in Iraq and the Islamic State. *Perspectives on Terrorism*, *9*(4), 48–60. Retrieved from http://www.jstor.org/stable/26297414

University of Stanford. (2015). Jaysh Rijal al-Tariqa al-Naqshbandia (JRTN). Retrieved from http://web.stanford.edu/group/mappingmilitants/cgi-bin/groups/view/75.

The Washington Post. (April 29, 2019). Sri Lanka's president says intelligence lapse allowed Easter bombings to take place.

Wilson Center. (October 28, 2019). Timeline: The rise, spread and fall of the Islamic State.

Wilson Center and the United States Institute of Peace. (2016). *Jihadi threat: ISIS, Al Qaeda and beyond.* Washington D.C.: Institute of the Study of War.

Zekulin, M.G. (2018). More than the medium: How the communication literature helps explain ISIS's success in recruiting Westerners. *Journal of Policing, Intelligence and Counter Terrorism, 13*(1), 17–37. 10.1080/18335330.2017.1412490

51

HAY'AT TAHRIR AL-SHAM AND JABHAT AL-NUSRA

Serdar Kaya

INTRODUCTION

Hay'at Tahrir al-Sham (HTS), or Levant Liberation Committee, is a jihadist militant group with a Salafi ideology. It is one of the major actors in the Syrian Civil War. It was a product of the merger of five Salafi-leaning organisations on January 28, 2017, but Jabhat Fatah Al-Sham, formerly and more popularly known as Jabhat Al-Nusra, an Al-Qaeda affiliate, was its main predecessor.

The presence of Jabhat al-Nusra in Syria goes back to the beginning of the Syrian Civil War in 2011. Shortly after the outbreak of the war, the Islamic State (IS) in Iraq, also known as Al-Qaeda Iraq at the time, made plans to extend into Syria by exploiting the instability in the country. In August 2011, seven individuals crossed the Syrian border under the orders of Abu Bakr Al-Baghdadi, the leader of the IS, to establish the group's Syrian wing. They were under the leadership of Abu Muhammad Al-Jolani (also known as Ahmed Hussein Al-Shara), a Syrian national who has been associated with Al-Qaeda at least since the US invasion of Iraq in 2003 (Gerges, 2017).

The seven operatives started organising in regions controlled by the Free Syrian Army (FSA) and assembled bands of fighters. They called themselves Jabhat Al-Nusra, or the Victory Front, which was short for the Victory Front for the People of Levant. They began operations on December 23, 2011, with two simultaneous suicide attacks on the Assad regime's security and intelligence buildings in the Kafr Sousa neighbourhood of Damascus, killing 44 and injuring more than 150 (Sinjab, 2011). One month later, on January 23, 2012, the group announced its existence with a video posted to the internet.[1]

Al-Nusra quickly proved to be the most effective actor in the resistance (Ignatius, 2012). It achieved significant victories against the Assad regime and established a presence in Syria's eastern and northern provinces, extending from Idlib to Deir ez-Zor. This success was short-lived, however. The group suffered significant losses after separating from the IS in 2013 and clashing with it afterward.

The separation occurred after IS leader Al-Baghdadi repeatedly urged Jolani to publicly declare his affiliation with the IS. When it became apparent that Jolani was reluctant to make such a declaration, Al-Baghdadi made the announcement himself with an audio recording released on April 3, 2013 (Jihadology, 2013a). In response, Jolani acknowledged Al-Nusra's initial ties to the IS and praised Al-Baghdadi. However, he also declared that his allegiance (*bay'ah*) lay with Ayman Al-Zawahiri, the leader of Al-Qaeda:

> [T]his is a baya'a from the sons of Al-Nusra and its general commander, [and] we renew it to the sheikh Aymen Al-Zawahiri, may Allah preserve him … . [T] he banner of the Front will remain as it is without any change despite our appreciation for the banner of the [Islamic] State and who carries it and who sacrificed his blood from our brothers under its banner (Jihadology, 2013b).

This bold move proved costly for Al-Nusra. First, most of the group's non-Syrian fighters left Syria to join the IS in Iraq, as they were less committed to the Syrian cause than others. Then, the group became a target for the IS when the latter decided to advance into Syria. Despite some losses in the beginning,[2] the IS captured most of eastern Syria by the end of the summer of 2014 and forced Al-Nusra to withdraw to Daraa in the south and Hama in the north.[3]

In the following years, Al-Nusra fought against the Assad regime in northern Syria while occasionally clashing with various opposition forces (Abdulrahim, 2014). Alongside these clashes, the group sought alliances and mergers with them, but few were interested in partnering with an Al-Qaeda affiliate. To overcome this obstacle, Al-Nusra considered severing its formal ties to Al-Qaeda. The group's foreign fighters wished to retain their affiliation with Al-Qaeda, as they were more interested in global jihad. Still, after much deliberation within the group's ranks, Jolani announced the termination of Al-Nusra on July 29, 2016, in a four-minute video, where he also showed his face to the public for the first time.[4] In the video, Jolani also declared the founding of a new group named Jabhat Fatah Al-Sham (Front for the Conquest of the Levant), which he claimed was not affiliated with any external entities. Six

DOI: 10.4324/9780429426063-58

months later, this new group merged with four Salafi-leaning others to form the HTS.[5]

As of early 2019, the HTS is still active. Since the Assad regime gained control of Aleppo in December 2016 (Yan et al., 2016), the HTS now remains largely in the northern city of Idlib and its vicinity. However, the power of the group is in decline due to the advances of the Assad regime and international pressure against armed jihadist groups.

Convictions of Jhabhat al-Nusra Members

German federal prosecutors had indicted four men on suspicion of supporting the Islamist extremist group Jabhat al-Nusra. The German citizen Marius A. allegedly went to Syria in October 2013 and joined al-Nusra. He is understood to have remained a member until March 2014 and took part in fighting at least once. Prosecutors said he also received funds from the group while he was in Turkey. Marius A. was detained last September in Senegal. He was extradited to Germany in May and remains in custody. Three other German nationals, with dual or triple citizenship, were also indicted. They were German-American citizen Maher M., German-Algerian citizen Mohamed S., and German, Spanish, and Moroccan citizen Avid E.G.M. (DW, September 16, 2022)

A Dutch court convicted two Syrian brothers of holding senior roles in the Jabhat al-Nusra extremist group in their home country between 2011 and 2014, the first time Dutch judges have convicted a suspect of leadership in a Syrian extremist organisation. One brother was sentenced to 15 years and nine months, the other to 11 years and nine months. Their identities were not released, in line with Dutch privacy rules. The Dutch court stated in its verdicts that Jabhat al-Nusra carried out attacks targeting the regime of President Bashar Assad. The court said in a statement that the group's attacks also caused civilian casualties and contributed to armed conflict and chaos that drove millions of Syrians to flee the country. Both brothers had been given asylum in the Netherlands (Associated Press, September 20, 2021).

IDEOLOGY AND OBJECTIVES

The ideology of the HTS has two tenets: Salafism and jihadism. Albeit compatible with each other, these tenets are in discrete positions.

Salafism, a conservative school within Sunni Islam, has its roots in the teachings of Muhammad bin Abd Al-Wahhab (1703–1792), a theologian from Central Arabia. Salafism advocates the revival of authentic Islam as practised by Muhammad, the prophet of Islam, and his companions. To achieve that objective, Salafis argue, one must turn to the primary sources of Islam and use them as guides to identify and reject all innovations (*bid'ah*) introduced into the religion after this early era (Meijer, 2009).

Also central to the Salafi theology is a strict monotheism (*tawhid*) that forbids not only idolatry but also any beliefs and practises that involve the intermediary of saints and even the Prophet. Salafis thus react to Shiite and Sufi Muslims, who adhere to saints and visit their shrines and tombs. From the Salafi perspective, such activities constitute *shirk* (ascribing partners to God), which is a violation of the principle of monotheism and a major sin that puts one outside of the religion of Islam. Salafis thus tend to declare those who venerate shrines as unbelievers (*takfir*).

Jihadism is completely different from Salafism in terms of both its content and its relationship to Islam. Unlike Salafism, jihadism is not a school of Islam. It is not even a term in Islamic theology or jurisprudence (*fiqh*). Although the word jihadism is derived from the Quranic term *jihad* (struggle, effort), jihadism is a Western neologism that has been in use only since the Afghani resistance against the Soviet occupation in the 1980s. Whereas *jihad* has both militant and spiritualistic connotations in Islamic terminology (Picken, 2015), jihadism refers to the former. In fact, since the 9/11 attacks in 2001, jihadism has more specifically referred to offensive Islamic militancy, especially against Western targets.

Despite the vast differences between them, Salafism and jihadism are often mentioned together, as most jihadist groups in the world today happen to be Salafis. The reverse is not true, however. Most Salafis are not jihadists. In other words, they do not use violence to impose their religious views on others or to further a political agenda.

The ideological roots of jihadism rather lie with Sayyid Qutb (1906–1966), an influential Egyptian thinker whose formulations on Islam and the West have inspired generations of political Islamists. Qutb likened the Muslims of the twentieth century to those in *jahiliyya*, which, from an Islamic perspective, is the age of ignorance in pre-Islamic Arabia, where people were ignorant of God and lived in foolish ways. By referring to a contemporary *jahiliyya*, Qutb did not necessarily mean that Muslims no longer believed in God. He rather argued that Muslims were so accustomed to the comforts and materialism of modernity that they no longer had any room for spirituality in their lives. He deduced that the West was to blame for such a tremendous change in values, as it was exporting materialism and secularism to the Muslim world and elsewhere (Qutb, 1964).

The solutions Qutb offered to the Muslim world were intellectual awakening and offensive *jihad*. The latter was controversial, but it was still appealing to many at the time for a variety of reasons. First, the wounds of colonialism were fresh, and the West was considered the enemy. Second, the West was providing significant support to the newly-founded state of Israel with little regard for the rights of Palestinian Arabs, further reinforcing the view that the West is an occupying force in Muslim lands. Third, most

Muslim-majority countries had autocratic and secular governments, and their policies often did not reflect the values of their religious societies. These circumstances made it easier for Qutb to make the case that Muslims were under siege and that Islam could set them free.

Qutb's ideas, and more particularly his 1964 book Milestones (*Ma'alim Fi Al-Tariq*), influenced many in Egypt and abroad. The book provided Islamic movements with a framework and laid out objectives: their enemy was Western secularism; their targets were the secular governments in the Muslim world; and their objective was to replace man-made laws with Islamic ones (Osman, 2017).

Eventually, many Islamic movements adopted the objective of establishing an Islamic state in their respective countries. They attached different meanings to the concept, but some form of an Islamic state came to be the cornerstone of almost any Islamic revival project, nonetheless. Even the Mujahideen, whose sole mission was to defeat the Soviets in Afghanistan, developed similar ambitions. Some within the group argued, upon victory, that *jihad* should continue until the establishment of an Islamic state in Afghanistan. In time, some of these ideas evolved into a global understanding of jihad, as represented by Al-Qaeda and its spin-offs such as the IS, Jabhat Al-Nusra, and other Salafi militant groups (Lauzière, 2015).

The ideology of the HTS also falls under this last category, which Gilles Kepel (2002) refers to as Salafi jihadism. This brand of jihadism extends the idea of jihad beyond the borders of the nation-state. Al-Qaeda's distinction between the near enemy and the far enemy demonstrates this more recent change in perspective. With the near enemy, Al-Qaeda refers to the secular governments in Muslim-majority countries and mimics Qutb's offensive idea of *jihad*. The far enemy, however, refers to the West, particularly the United States and others who have a military presence in the Muslim world.

The ideology of the HTS is in a grey area between local and global jihadism, however. On the one hand, Al-Nusra, the major predecessor of the HTS, was an affiliate of first the IS and then Al-Qaeda, which are two of the most notable actors in the short history of global jihad. On the other hand, both Al-Nusra and the HTS refrained from presenting themselves as extensions of a global jihadist network and adopted a national discourse instead, most likely to appeal to the local population in Syria. Although they were open about their Islamist ambitions and even declared their intentions to establish an Islamic emirate (*imara*), this emirate was meant for Syria only, at least in discourse (Lister, 2016a).[6]

The group's idea of Islamic rule is not entirely clear. Nevertheless, Al-Nusra and currently the HTS have somewhat differed from the IS, at least in the way they intend to establish Islamic rule. Following Al-Qaeda, the HTS believes that the Islamization of contemporary Muslim-majority societies is best achieved through a gradual process (Abbas, 2016). They have thus criticised the IS for its widespread and publicised use of cruel punishments that alienate the people under their rule (Joscelyn, 2015). Still, the distinction between the IS and the HTS is not clear-cut. One reason is the Salafi ideology that the two groups share. Like other Salafi groups, the HTS too regards Alawites and Sufis as heretics, and its predecessor has attacked their mosques, shrines, and gatherings on certain occasions.[7] In other words, the HTS is primarily concerned with the loyalty of Syria's Sunni majority and does not always mind alienating others.[8]

Another reason is pragmatism. After the IS's proclamation of the Caliphate in 2014, Al-Nusra found itself in a competition for Islamic legitimacy and credibility. One of the responses of Al-Nusra to this challenge was to establish Dar Al-Qadaa (Judiciaries), a judicial entity that imposed some strict Islamic measures on local civilians. The punishments in this era sometimes went as far as whipping blasphemers, executing prostitutes, and stoning adulterers.[9] Albeit cruel, these punishments were not on par with those of the IS, so imposing them did not stop Al-Nusra and Al-Qaeda from presenting themselves to the domestic and international communities as moderate alternatives.

Overall, Al-Qaeda-leaning groups and the IS have some notable tactical differences despite their ideological similarity. However, these differences tend to converge in certain contexts and become less salient.

ORGANIZATIONAL STRUCTURE

Al-Nusra came into existence as the Syrian wing of the IS and organised under the leadership of Jolani. Alongside Jolani was Majlis Al-Shura (Consultative Council), an executive body composed of twelve senior leaders who advised him and helped make decisions. Both military and religious leaders sat in Majlis Al-Shura. Those in the latter group, and more particularly a chief religious authority (*al-qadi al-a'am*), ensured that the decisions were in line with sharia.[10]

This structure is still in place in the HTS. The changes over the years have rather been in leadership and personnel.[11] For example, Al-Qaeda veterans joined Al-Nusra after the latter joined the former's network in 2013 (Lister, 2016b). Similarly, after the formation of the HTS in January 2017, there were notable additions to the leadership from the ranks of Ahrar Al-Sham, a powerful Islamist group that has been fighting against the Assad regime since the early days of the conflict.[12]

On the local level, the HTS follows a similar method that ensures religious oversight of administrative affairs. Since the Al-Nusra era, each local leader has been accompanied by a religious commissioner (*dabet al-shar'i*). These paired leaders are jointly responsible for all the decisions they make in their jurisdictions.

Activities on the local level extend beyond maintaining order and include the provision of social services as well. Al-Nusra was quick to establish the Administration of

Public Services (Idarat Al-Khidamat Al-Ammah) and the Department of Relief (Qism Al-Ighata) to offer social services. Both institutions are administered on the "national" level, but they delegate powers to local leaders. The former institution provides food, water, gas, electricity, and sanitation services to local communities. The latter distributes humanitarian aid to those impacted by the ongoing conflict. These services help the group gain the support and cooperation of the people it governs (Gartenstein-Ross and Smyth, 2013).

MILITARY ORGANIZATION AND CAPABILITIES

The HTS maintains a small but highly effective paramilitary force, which Al-Nusra started to organise in its early days in a series of platoons (*seraya*) made up of 15 to 25 well-trained fighters. Each platoon was stationed in a small secret cell that remained isolated from others, and fighters often used *kunyas* (*noms de guerre*) for additional security. Platoons had their own commanders, whom the fighters pledged allegiance to, besides Jolani, the general commander. This two-level allegiance system was likely developed to ensure a higher degree of loyalty and obedience (Acun et al., 2017).

Small units of select fighters helped Al-Nusra perform well in asymmetric warfare. In time, the group adapted to changing conditions, and started to maintain battalions of 100 to 200 in certain areas (Benotman and Blake, 2013). Likewise, the group's tactics became more diverse. In the beginning, Al-Nusra's operations against the Assad regime involved suicide attacks, car bombs, kidnappings, and assassinations (Cafarella et al., 2016). Later in 2012, the group became capable of orchestrating more conventional military operations, and wielded more sophisticated weapons, such as drones, and precision-guided armaments (Roggio, 2012).[13] Further, having acquired anti-aircraft weaponry, it declared and successfully maintained a no-fly zone over Aleppo, when in control of the city (Al Jazeera, 2012).

The increase in conventional warfare capabilities did not lead Al-Nusra executives to abandon guerilla tactics, however.[14] The two modes of operation coexisted, and complemented each other. On the one hand, suicide attacks and car bombs targeted the regime's vulnerabilities, and on the other, a well-equipped paramilitary force fended off the attacks of the regime, while also launching offenses (Cafarella et al., 2016).[15]

After the merger, the HTS retained these two modes of operation (Irish et al., 2017). The group did not have any reasons to transition into a more conventional military force, as it failed to expand its territories and has always preferred to keep the number of its fighters small.

ATTACK TYPES AND TARGETS

Bombings and explosions constitute more than two-thirds of the group's attacks. Most suicide attacks also fall under this category, as they involve an explosion almost by definition.[16] Figure 51.1 illustrates the incidents perpetrated and the share

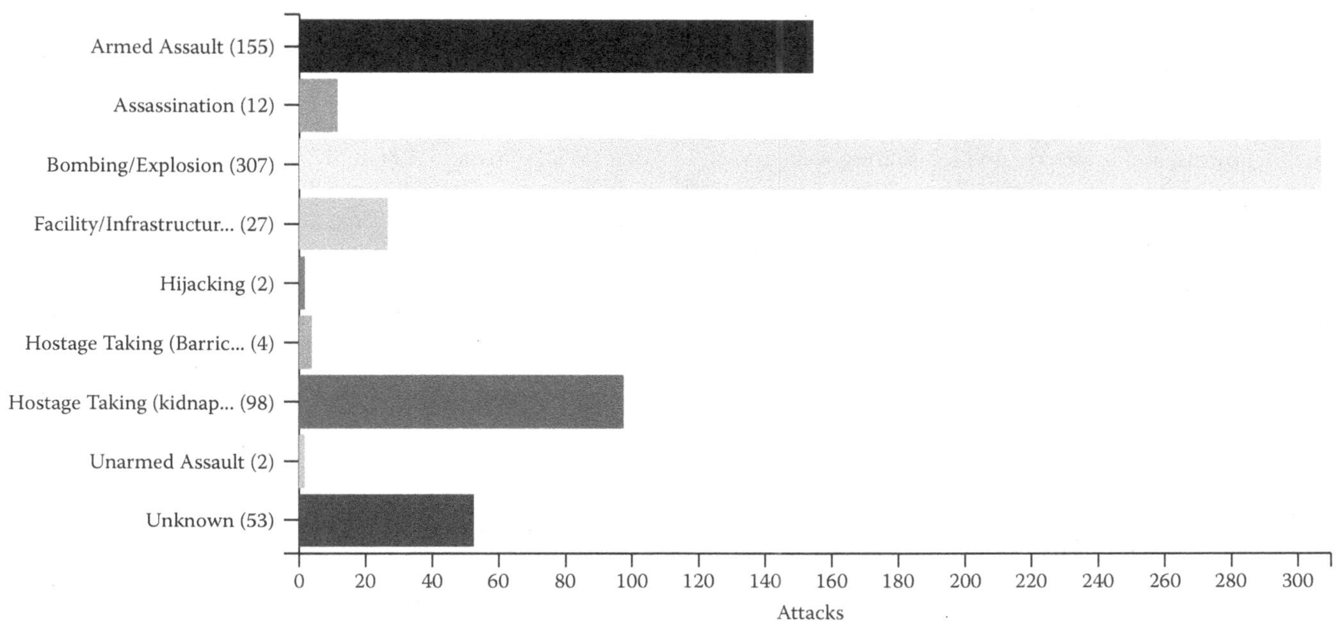

Figure 51.1 Types of Attacks (2012–2020).

Aggregated Data from START (2023). https://www.start.umd.edu/gtd/search/Results.aspx?charttype=bar&chart=attack&search=al%20nusra.

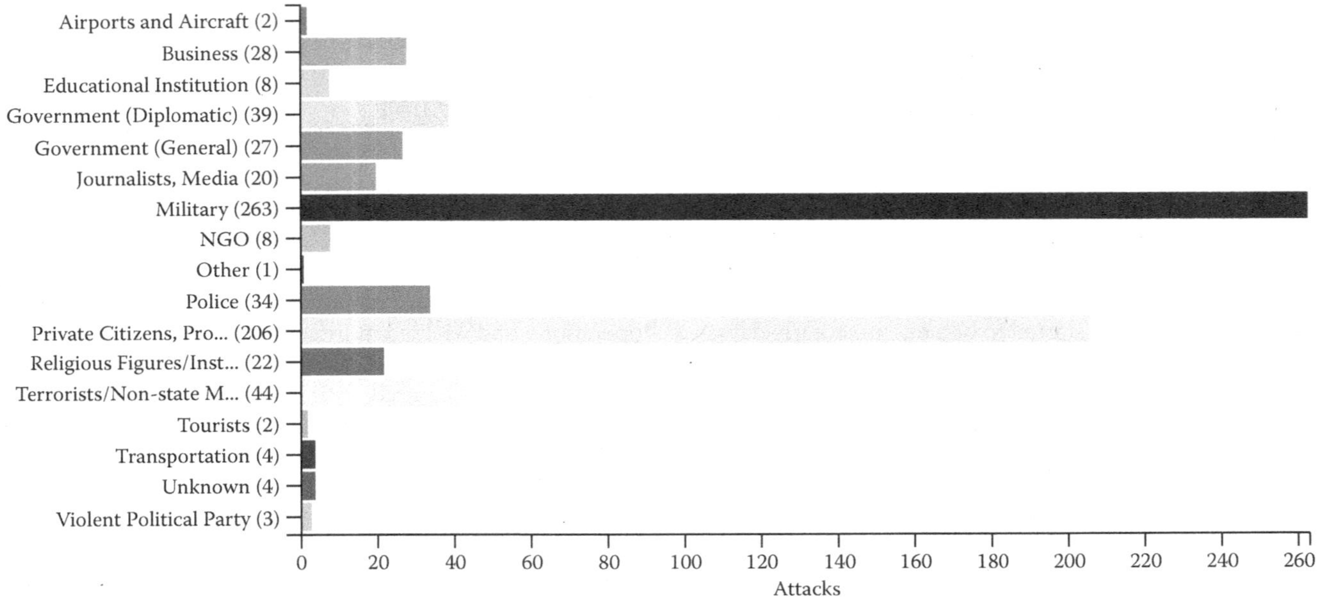

Figure 51.2 Targets of Attacks (2012–2020).

Aggregated Data from START (2023). https://www.start.umd.edu/gtd/search/Results.aspx?charttype=bar&chart=target&search=al%20nusra.

of each attack type while Figure 51.2 demonstrates the plurality of these attacks. They also allow comparisons with the IS and Free Syrian Army and indicate that bombings and explosions are the primary types of attack for all three groups.

OUTREACH

Al-Manara Al-Bayda (the White Minaret) was Al-Nusra's media organisation.[17] It delivered the group's public announcements in audio or video and produced news stories and documentaries on its activities and operations in the field. Some documentaries featured interviews with aspiring suicide bombers, probably to project the dedication of fighters, increase publicity, and facilitate recruitment. The productions of Al-Manara Al-Bayda were posted to social media, jihadist forums, and a variety of video-sharing websites.

Part of Al-Nusra's outreach activities were geared towards the local Syrian population only. The primary institution in that regard was, and under the HTS still is, Maktab Dawa wal Irshad (School of Proselytization and Guidance), which operates under the authority of Dar Al-Qadaa and has the mission of disseminating the group's version of Islam to locals while also distributing humanitarian assistance to those in need (Cafarella et al., 2016). Another such institution is Markaz Duat al Jihad (Center of Invitation to Jihad), founded by the Saudi cleric Abdullah Al-Muhaysini. The Markaz administers many sharia institutes that focus specifically on the religious education of Syrian women and children.[18]

In 2014, during its competition with the IS for Islamic legitimacy, Al-Nusra established Al-Basirah, a second media organisation that was concerned primarily with undermining the religious credibility of the IS and articulating that of Al-Nusra.[19] Relatedly, Al-Risalah magazine commenced in July 2015. It was a digital publication that closely resembled the IS magazine Dabiq, which promoted the group by disseminating news on its activities and glorifying its "martyred" fighters (Kotoulas, 2018). Al-Risalah did not publish any issues after January 2017, as the era of religious competition ended with the decline of the IS in that year.

The media operations of Al-Nusra continue in the same fashion under the HTS. The changes have occurred only in name. Al-Manara Al-Bayda now operates as Iba'a.

RECRUITMENT

Unlike other groups in the Syrian opposition, the HTS always recruits select fighters.[20] A restrictive recruitment policy is a function of the group's mode of operation. The group intends to replace the fighters it lost with the best available, rather than increase the size of its forces.

The HTS recruits primarily from three groups. The first is the Muslim world at large, which it reaches through its network, both in person and via its online communication channels. The second is local Syrians, whose sympathy and support the group tries to gain through the provision of key public services and the imposition of relatively less conservative policies (Hassan, 2014).[21] The third is other opposition groups, whose members have been attracted to the group since the early days of Al-Nusra, as it has always been capable of arming its fighters well (Mahmood and Black, 2013). The religious character of the group also attracts some members of the opposition. As with other Islamic groups, the HTS too benefits from the belief that one will die a shahid (martyr) and go to heaven if one dies while fighting for a religious cause.

Recruits include teenagers, but this policy is not peculiar to the HTS. According to Islam, males reach adulthood in their early teens. Therefore, most jihadist groups do not consider teenagers to be underage. In November 2012, Human Rights Watch documented that Al-Nusra and the IS recruited soldiers as young as 14 and later published its findings in a report, which included interviews with 25 former and current child soldiers who participated in the civil war as fighters or in support roles (HRW, 2014).

Tazqiyya (a voucher from an existing member) is required of all potential recruits. Initially, all recruits receive full-time physical and military training for six to eight weeks, followed by several hours of religious instruction in the evenings (Lister, 2016b). Upon successful completion of the training, each recruit pledges allegiance to Jolani as part of their initiation as new members and starts serving in a platoon (Acun et al., 2017).

CONCLUSION

Al-Nusra started in 2011 as the Syrian extension of the IS, which at the time was part of the Al-Qaeda network. After problems arose between the IS and Al-Qaeda in 2013, the group chose to remain with the latter. Later, in 2017, the group ended its formal ties to Al-Qaeda and terminated itself, but its successors did not go through any changes in ideology. As of early 2019, the HTS is still a typical armed group with a Salafi-jihadist ideology. It has the objective of establishing an emirate in all or part of Syria. On the one hand, this local objective sets the HTS somewhat apart from global jihadist groups, at least in discourse. On the other hand, the HTS has been one of the few Salafi-jihadist groups that have captured territory, successfully defended it against rivals for years, and effectively provided services to people.

The future of the HTS is uncertain, however. While the HTS is still a notable military force, it faces significant threats. It is at war with powerful domestic and international actors. Both Russia and the United States consider the HTS an enemy force, although they are opponents in the Syrian Civil War.[22] Moreover, the Assad regime, supported by Russia, has made significant advances since late 2016 against all of its opponents but the Syrian Democratic Forces.[23] If the Assad regime captures Idlib, which is the only remaining stronghold of the HTS, it will once again gain control of most key areas to the west of the river Euphrates.[24] In short, the current situation is far from a modus vivendi, and the survival prospects of the HTS against the regime forces are low in the long run. If the HTS has one advantage under these circumstances, it is its form of organisation. As a small but elite paramilitary force, the HTS is unlikely to dissolve in the event of losing Idlib. Like the IS since late 2018, it will likely continue primarily as a largely invisible guerilla force.

Notes

1 The video also declared the group's objective of introducing sharia law to Syria (Jihadology, 2012).

2 Joined by Ahrar Al-Sham and some factions of the Islamic Front, Al-Nusra successfully drove the IS out of Raqqa in January 2014 (Barnard and Gladstone, 2014).

3 These events occurred at a time when tensions were rising between Al-Qaeda and the IS, as the latter was acting increasingly as an independent force. The IS eventually seceded from Al-Qaeda towards the end of 2013 and started advancing into Syria in early 2014, targeting both the Syrian opposition and Al-Nusra. For details on the course of events in this period, see Lister (2015).

4 Sitting next to Jolani on his two sides were second-in-command Abu Abdullah Al-Shami (born Abdurrahman Attoun) and veteran jihadist Abu Faraj Al-Masri (born Ahmad Salama Mabruk), both now deceased.

5 Jolani began his announcement by thanking and praising the senior commanders in Al-Qaeda for their support for the people of Syria up until that point (Jihadology, 2016). Although many have taken this opening statement, among other indicators, to mean that the group's separation from Al-Qaeda is likely false and deceptive (Joscelyn, 2016), it is also possible that the group merely intended to remain on friendly terms with Al-Qaeda. Judging by the ideologies of the five groups that formed the HTS six months later, it is safe to say that the group remains the same, at least ideologically.

6 An Islamic emirate was a nationwide project at first. Al-Nusra fighters thus concentrated their initial efforts on overthrowing the Assad regime. After the defeats they suffered in 2014 and afterward, the group found it more realistic to work towards introducing Islamic rule only to parts of Syria.

7 In 2013, Al-Qaeda leader Ayman Zawahiri published a short document titled *General Guidelines for Jihad*, where he advised against fighting non-Sunni sects and specifically indicated that fighters should not attack the religious gatherings or festivals of "deviant sects." Although the Islamic State has its roots in Al-Qaeda, it does not follow these guidelines. Al-Nusra, however, was closer to the official Al-Qaeda policy, as most of its attacks were on military targets and not civilians (Acun et al., 2017). Nevertheless, Al-Nusra committed serious crimes against the Alawite minority in Syria (AFP, 2013). Some of these crimes were to avenge the attacks by the Assad regime and Russia, as Bashar al-Assad belongs to the Alawite minority (Al-Khalidi and Tolba, 2015). Others, however, were

sectarian in nature, and the group offered religious justifications for them. For example, in a video message released on June 3, 2016, Sami Al-Oraydi, the chief religious authority of Al-Nusra, claimed that the Alawites were worse than Jews and Christians and that the land had to be cleansed of them (Heller, 2016). Oraydi supported his arguments with quotes from Islamic scholars Imam Al-Ghazali (1058–1111) and Ibn Taymiyyah (1263–1328). The former figure is a major scholar of Sunni Islam, whereas the latter is revered more specifically by Salafis.

8 Jolani gave his first media interview to Al-Jazeera in December 2013 and affirmed the sectarian aspect of the conflict in his comments (Al Jazeera Arabic, 2013).

9 The videos Al-Nusra released in this era also had a stronger jihadist tone. In June 2015, Al-Nusra released *Heirs of Glory*, a 44-minute video that made references to Ottoman caliphs, with whom the caliphate ended in 1924. The video also featured Osama bin Laden in audio and video and celebrated the 9/11 attacks (Jihadology, 2015a).

10 Consultation is a core Islamic principle mentioned in the Quran. Verses such as "They determine their affairs with consultation among themselves" (Ash-Shura 38) and "[O Prophet!] Consult with [believers] when determining affairs" (Ali Imran 159) emphasise the importance of consultation when making decisions. Jihadist organisations thus tend to have a consultative institution in their organisational structure. How a Shura institution makes decisions or balances the leader varies across organisations, however (Atwan, 2015).

11 Mergers and splits are common among jihadist groups. It is not rare for high- and low-ranking members to switch groups either. Alliances tend to form and break up quickly, and groups that were allies a short while ago often find themselves fighting each other. Further complicating matters is the fact that many jihadist groups are in fact coalitions of various fighter units, which sometimes leave one coalition to join another. The HTS, too, is a coalition, and one of its five original partners, the Nour Al-Din Al-Zenki Movement, decided to leave the HTS after only six months. On February 18, 2018, the movement merged with Ahrar al-Sham to form the Syrian Liberation Front. Another one of the five original partners, the Ansar Al-Din Front, was a coalition of two factions, one of which left the HTS in February 2018.

12 Ahrar Al-Sham was not a part of the merger. It was Abu Jaber Shaykh (born Hashim Al-Shaykh), one of its former leaders, and several other high-ranking members who chose to leave the group to join the HTS. Abu Jaber led Ahrar Al-Sham between September 2014 and September 2015. Upon joining the HTS, he became the first leader of the group and remained in this position for nine months before stepping down to become the head of Majlis Al-Shura. During these first nine months, Jolani served as the military chief of the HTS and has been leading the group again since October 2017.

13 Al-Nusra captured some of these weapons in combat while also procuring them from arms dealers and various groups in the Syrian opposition (Bacchi, 2014).

14 Al-Nusra or the HTS was responsible for 25.1% of all suicide attacks in Syria between 2012 and 2017. Suicide attacks constituted 30.1% of all attacks by the group. 60% of the group's attacks involved bombings or explosions (START, 2018).

15 Al-Nusra also engaged in kidnapping and used it as a way of generating ransom revenue, which, in some cases, was as high as millions of dollars (Callimachi, 2014). Those who were kidnapped included soldiers, writers, reporters, and U.N. peacekeepers (Hubbard, 2014).

16 29.7% of all attacks by the group involve suicide bombers. The figure is 45.8% for bombing and explosion attacks only.

17 Al-Manara Al-Bayda (the White Minaret) is a reference to the Jesus Minaret in the Umayyad Mosque in Damascus. The importance of the minaret derives from an eschatological prophecy attributed to Prophet Muhammad. According to the prophecy, Jesus "will descend at the white minaret on the eastern side of Damascus" near the end of times to lead Muslims (Sahih Muslim 41, 7015). Many in the Muslim world believe in the authenticity of this hadith, despite scholarly claims to the contrary (Nilsson, 2019).

18 In August 2015, the Markaz founded a library in Idlib and named it after Ibn Taymiyyah (Acun et al., 2017).

19 For example, Al-Nusra likened the IS to "the Khawarij" and referred to them as "dogs of hell fire" in the 17-minute Al-Basirah video titled "So the way of the criminals will become clear" (Jihadology, 2015b). Al-Nusra borrowed all three of these references from the primary sources of Islam. First, the title of the video was a reference to a verse in the Quran: "And this is how we detail the verses, so the way of the criminals will become clear" (Cattle, verse 55). Second, the Khawarij are a reactionary group that originated during the First Fitna era (656–661), more than two decades after the death of Muhammad, and came to be rejected by both Sunni and Shiite traditions. Third, likening the IS to the Khawarij and referring to them as "dogs of hell fire" derives from the same source, as Muhammad is reported to have prophetically said, "The Khawarij are the dogs of hell fire" (Ibn Majah, 167).

20 Neither Al-Nusra nor the HTS have ever engaged in mass recruitment. As of October 2018, the HTS is estimated to have between 12,000 and 15,000 fighters (CSIS, 2018). These numbers do not suggest a significant increase in size, as Al-Nusra alone was estimated to have between 6,000 and 10,000 fighters as early as November 2012 (Ignatius, 2012).

21 When dealing with local Syrians, Al-Nusra follows the strategies outlined by the high-profile jihadist author Abu Mus'ab Al-Suri (born Mustafa Setmariam Nasar), who is famous for his 1600-page e-book titled The Global Islamic Resistance Call. Al-Suri (2004) formulated a leaderless form of global jihad waged by lone wolves and small groups of individuals. The book, which the United States Joint Forces Command referred to as a "masterwork" (Lacey, 2008), came to define the principles of global jihad as carried out by Al-Qaeda and its offshoots and led many people to believe that Al-Suri was the "architect of global jihad" (Lia, 2008).

22 In May 2018, more than a year after the formation of the HTS, the U.S. Department of State amended its earlier designation of Al-Nusra as a terrorist organisation to also mention the HTS as an antecedent (USDS, 2018).

23 Syrian Democratic Forces is an alliance of Kurdish, Arab, Turkmen, Syriac, and Chechen militias. The People's Protection Units (YPG), a pro-Kurdish militia, is the primary component of the alliance. The Syrian Democratic Forces have made significant advances against the IS since 2014. As of early 2019, the alliance controls almost all areas to the east of the Euphrates, with the primary exception being the region near Hasakah, which remains an enclave of the Assad regime.

24 The two main exceptions are the Turkish-occupied territory in the northwest and the area surrounding the Tanf border crossing in the south, which is under the control of the Syrian opposition.

References

Abbas, Y. (2016, April 29). Another 'sate' of hate: Al-Nusra's quest to establish an Islamic emirate in the levant. Available at: http://www.hudson.org/research/12454-another-state-of-hate-al-nusra-s-quest-to-establish-an-islamic-emirate-in-the-levant

Abdulrahim, R. (2014, November 28). *Islamic State, rival Al Nusra front each strengthen grip on Syria*. Los Angeles Times. Available at: http://www.latimes.com/world/middleeast/la-fg-syria-nusra-front-20141128-story.html

Acun, C., Keskin, B., & Salaymeh, B. (2017). *Al-Nusra front: From Al-Qaeda to the HTS [El-Kaide'den HTŞ'ye Nusra Cephesi]*. Ankara: SETA.

AFP. (2013, September 15). Syria jihadists claim they killed Homs Alawites. Available at: http://english.alarabiya.net/en/News/2013/09/16/Syria-jihadists-claim-they-killed-Homs-Alawites.html

Al Jazeera Arabic. (2013, December 19). Abu Mohammed Al-Julani. Al-Nusra and the future of Syria [Al-Nusra wa mustakbal Suriya]. Available at: https://www.youtube.com/watch?v=DIr1HoHJlQA

Al Jazeera. (2012, December 23). Syria 'secures chemical weapons stockpile.' Available at: http://www.aljazeera.com/news/middleeast/2012/12/201212221532021654.html

Al-Khalidi, S. & Tolba, A. (2015, October 12). Nusra Front urges attacks on Syria's Alawites to avenge Russian bombings. Reuters. Available at: https://www.reuters.com/article/us-mideast-crisis-nusra/nusra-front-urges-attacks-on-syrias-alawites-to-avenge-russian-bombings-idUSKCN0S625220151013

Al-Suri, Al.-M. (2004). *The global Islamic resistance call* [Da'wat Al-Muqawamah Al-Islamiyyah Al-'alamiyyah].

Associated Press. (September 20, 2021). Dutch court: Syrian brothers guilty of Jabhat al-Nusra roles.

Atwan, A.B. (2015). *Islamic state: The digital caliphate*. Oakland, CA: University of California Press.

Bacchi, U. (2014, November 3). Syria: Al-Nusra jihadists 'capture US TOW anti-tank missiles' from moderate rebels.*International Business Times*. Available at: https://www.ibtimes.co.uk/syria-al-nusra-jihadists-capture-us-weaponry-moderate-rebels-1472864

Barnard, A. & Gladstone, R. (2014, January 6). Rebel infighting spreads to an eastern Syrian city. *The New York Times*. Available at: https://www.nytimes.com/2014/01/07/world/middleeast/rebel-infighting-expands-to-eastern-Syrian-city.html

Benotman, N. & Blake, R. (2013, January 8). *Jabhat Al-Nusra: A strategic briefing*. London: Quilliam Foundation.

Cafarella, J., Gambhir, H. & Zimmerman, K. (2016, February). *Jabhat Al Nusra and ISIS: Sources of strength*. Washington, D.C.: Institute for the Study of War.

Callimachi, R. (2014, August 24). U.S. writer held by Qaeda affiliate in Syria is freed after nearly 2 years. *The New York Times*. Available at: https://www.nytimes.com/2014/08/25/world/middleeast/peter-theo-curtis-held-by-qaeda-affiliate-in-syria-is-freed-after-2-years.html

Center for Strategic and International Studies (CSIS). (2018, October 4). *Hay'at Tahrir Al-Sham*. Washington, D.C.: Center for Strategic and International Studies.

DW. (September 16, 2022). Germany indicts 4 for supporting al-Nusra in Syria.

Gartenstein-Ross, D. & Smyth, P. (2013, August 22). How Syria's jihadists win friends and influence people. *The Atlantic*. Available at: http://www.theatlantic.com/international/archive/2013/08/how-syrias-jihadists-win-friends-and-influence-people/278942/

Gerges, F.A. (2017). *ISIS: A history*. Princeton, NJ: Princeton University Press.

Hassan, H. (2014, March 4). A jihadist blueprint for hearts and minds is gaining traction. *The National*. https://www.thenational.ae/a-jihadist-blueprint-for-hearts-and-minds-is-gaining-traction-1.473058

Heller, S. (2016, June 9). Al-Qaeda speaks the language of Syrian sectarianism. *Radio Free. Europe/Radio Liberty*. Available at: https://www.rferl.org/a/black-flag-syria-islamic-state-al-qaeda-sectarianism-alawites/27788931.html

Hubbard, B. (2014, September 11). Qaeda group has released 45 members of U.N. force. *The New York Times*. Available at: https://www.nytimes.com/2014/09/12/world/middleeast/un-peacekeepers-released-by-captors-in-syria.html

Human Rights Watch (HRW). (2014, June 22). "Maybe we live and maybe we die": Recruitment and use of children by armed groups in Syria. Available at: https://www.hrw.org/sites/default/files/reports/syria0614_crd_ForUpload.pdf

Ibn Majah. Hadith number 157.

Ignatius, D. (2012, November 30). Al-Qaeda affiliate playing larger role in Syria rebellion. Available at: https://www.washingtonpost.com/blogs/post-partisan/post/al-qaeda-affiliate-playing-larger-role-in-syria-rebellion/2012/11/30/203d06f4-3b2e-11e2-9258-ac7c78d5c680_blog.html

Irish, J., Nebehay, S. & Miles, T. (2017, February 24). Bombings, air strikes in Syria rattle Geneva peace talks. *Reuters*. Available at: https://www.reuters.com/article/us-mideast-crisis-syria-idUSKBN16405J

Jihadology. (2012, January 24). Al-Manarah Al-Bayda foundation for media production presents: "Declaration of the support front (Jabhat Al-Nusrah): For the people of Syria from the Mujahidin of Syria in the fields of jihad." Available at: https://jihadology.net/2012/01/24/al-manarah-al-bay%E1%B8%8Da-foundation-for-media-production-presents-for-the-people-of-syria-from-the-mujahidin-of-syria-in-the-fields-of-jihad-jabhah-al-nu%E1%B9%A3rah-the-front-of-victory/

Jihadology. (2013a, April 9). Al-Furqan media presents a new audio message from the Islamic State of Iraq's Shaykh Abu Bakr Al-Ḥussayni Al-Qurayshi Al-Baghdadi: "Announcement of the Islamic state of Iraq and Al-Sham." Available at: https://jihadology.net/2013/04/09/al-furqan-media-presents-a-new-audio-message-from-the-islamic-state-of-iraqs-shaykh-abu-bakr-al-%e1%b8%a5ussayni-al-qurayshi-al-baghdadi-announcement-of-the-islamic-state-of-iraq-an/

Jihadology. (2013b, April 10). Al-Manarah Al-Bayda foundation for media production presents a new audio message from Jabhat Al-Nusrah's Abu Muḥammad Al-Jawlani (Al-Golani): "About the fields of Al-Sham." Available at: https://jihadology.net/2013/04/10/al-manarah-al-bay%e1%b8%8da-foundation-for-media-production-presents-a-new-audio-message-from-jabhat-al-nu%e1%b9%a3rahs-abu-mu%e1%b8%a5ammad-al-jawlani-al-golani-about-the-fields-of-al-sham/

Jihadology. (2015a, June 26). Al-Manarah Al-Bayda foundation for media production presents a new video message from Jabhat Al-Nusrah: "Heirs of Glory." Available at: https://jihadology.net/2015/06/26/al-manarah-al-bay%e1%b8%8da-foundation-for-media-production-presents-a-new-video-message-from-jabhat-al-nu%e1%b9%a3rah-heirs-of-glory/

Jihadology. (2015b, July 18). Al-Basirah foundation for media production presents a new video message from Jabhat Al-Nusrah's Shaykh Abu Khadijah Al-Muhajir: "So the way of the criminals will become clear." Available at: https://jihadology.net/2015/07/18/al-ba%e1%b9%a3irah-foundation-for-media-production-presents-a-new-video-message-from-jabhat-al-nu%e1%b9%a3rahs-shaykh-abu-khadijah-al-muhajir-so-the-way-of-the-criminals-will-become-clear/

Jihadology. (2016, July 28). New video message from Jahbat Fatah Al-Sham's Abu Muhammad Al-Jawlani announcing its formation. Available at: https://jihadology.net/2016/07/28/new-video-message-from-jabhat-fata%e1%b8%a5-al-shams-abu-mu%e1%b8%a5ammad-al-jawlani-announcing-its-formation/

Joscelyn, T. (2016, July 28). Analysis: Al Nusrah Ffront rebrands itself as Jabhat Fath Al Sham. *Long War Journal*. Available at: https://www.longwarjournal.org/archives/2016/07/analysis-al-nusrah-front-rebrands-itself-as-jabhat-fath-al-sham.php

Kepel, G. (2002). *Jihad: The trail of political Islam*. Cambridge, MA: Harvard University Press.

Kotoulas, I.E. (2018). Ideological principles of Jabhat Al-Nusra in Al-Risalah magazine. *Civitas Gentium*, 6(2), 49–60.

Lacey, J.M. (2008). *A terrorist's call to global jihad: Deciphering Abu Musab Al-Suri's Islamic jihad manifesto*. Annapolis, MD: Naval Institute Press.

Lauzière, H. (2015). *The making of salafism: Islamic reform in the twentieth century*. New York: Columbia University Press.

Lia, B. (2008). *Architect of global jihad: The life of Al Qaeda strategist Abu Mus'ab Al-Suri*. New York, NY: Columbia University Press.

Lister, C. (2015). *The Syrian Jihad: Al-Qaeda, the Islamic state and the evolution of an insurgency*. London: Hurst & Company.

Lister, C. (2016a, May 4). Al Qaeda is about to establish an emirate in Northern Syria. *Foreign Policy*. Available at: http://foreignpolicy.com/2016/05/04/al-qaeda-is-about-to-establish-an-emirate-in-northern-syria/

Lister, C. (2016b, July). *Profiling Jabhat Al-Nusra*. Washington, D.C.: Brookings Institution.

Mahmood, M. & Black, I. (2013, May 8). Free Syrian Army rebels defect to Islamist group Jabhat Al-Nusra. *The Guardian*. Available at: https://www.theguardian.com/world/2013/may/08/free-syrian-army-rebels-defect-islamist-group

Meijer, R. (2009). *Global salafism: Islam's new religious movement*. Oxford: Oxford University Press.

National Consortium for the Study of Terrorism and Responses to Terrorism (START). (2018). *Global terrorism database*. Available at: https://www.start.umd.edu/gtd

Nilsson, M. (2019). Jihadiship: From radical behavior to radical beliefs. *Studies in Conflict & Terrorism*. (Forthcoming).

Osman, T. (2017). *Islamism: A history of political Islam from the fall of the Ottoman empire to the rise of ISIS*. New Haven, CT: Yale University Press.

Picken, G. (2015). The 'greater' jihad in classical Islam. In E. Kendall & E. Stein (Eds.), *Twenty-First Century Jihad: Law, Society and* Military Action (pp. 126–138). London and New York: I.B. Tauris.

Qutb, S. (1964). *Milestones [Ma'alim Fi Al-Tariq]*. Createspace Independent Pub.

Roggio, B. (2012, August 4). Al Nusrah front conducts joint operation with free Syrian army. *Long War Journal*. Foundation for the Defense of Democracy, Aug. 4, 2012. Available at: https://www.longwarjournal.org/archives/2012/08/al_nusrah_front_conducts_joint.php

Sahih Muslim. Book 41, Hadith number 7015.

Sinjab, L. (2011, December 23). Syria says twin suicide bombings in Damascus kill 44. *BBC News*. Available at: https://www.bbc.com/news/world-middle-east-16313879

The Quran. Ali Imran, verse 159.

The Quran. Ash-Shura, verse 38.

The Quran. Cattle, verse 55.

United States Department of State (USDS). (2018, May 31). Amendments to the terrorist designations of Al-Nusrah front. Available at: https://www.state.gov/r/pa/prs/ps/2018/05/282880.htm

Yan, H., Grinberg, E. & Basil, Y. (2016, December 23). Syrian regime says it has taken full control of Aleppo. *CNN*. Available at: https://www.cnn.com/2016/12/22/middleeast/syrian-regime-takes-full-control-of-aleppo/index.html

Zawahiri, A. (2013, September). *General guidelines for jihad*.

52

AL-QAEDA IN THE ARABIAN PENINSULA

Rohan Malhotra

The nation that will insist upon drawing a broad line of demarcation between the fighting man and the thinking man is liable to find its fighting done by the fools and its thinking by the cowards.

Sir William F. Butler, Charles George Gordon (1889)

INTRODUCTION

Al-Qaeda in the Arabian Peninsula (AQAP) is the merger of the al-Qaeda branches in Yemen and Saudi Arabia. The goal of AQAP is to topple the governments of Saudi Arabia and Yemen, which act as illegitimate puppets of Western ideologues, and to replace Western influence in the Arabian Peninsula with a puritanical Sunni Islamic caliphate. AQAP propagates al-Qaeda's radical pan-Islamist ideology to express sympathy for the people in the region of the Arabian Peninsula against their rulers. AQAP generally operates in small groups or cells comprised of Yemenis and Saudis, other people of the Arabian Peninsula, and foreigners who have a network of sympathisers across the region. Under the banner of global Jihad, the group has a history of carrying out attacks and violent activities against the Yemeni government and civilians, in particular the Westerners being targeted in Yemen and abroad. According to the report published in 2018 (Dawsari, 2018), the presence of Al-Qaeda has been long maintained in central Yemen, particularly in Marib and al-Bayda provinces, while AQAP has been believed to have a strong presence in the southern part of the country, especially in Abyan and Shabwa provinces. Notably, in many of these southern and central provinces in the state of Yemen, AQAP governs small pockets of territory with sharia (Islamic Law) courts and a heavy presence of armed people. AQAP is one of the few important beneficiaries of Yemen's collapse into civil war. There exists a consensus that AQAP threatens the regional and international security of Yemenis. In a February 2010 edition of AQAP's bimonthly e-magazine *Sada al-Malahim (the echo of epic battles)*, an author named Hamil al-Misk (The Musk Bearer) emphasised that the organisation has now changed its modus operandi from a defensive to an offensive mode of operation, stating that "we bring to our nation the good news that the Mujahidin have passed the stage of defence and repulsion of aggression to the stage where they can take the initiative and attack" (Harris, 2010).

The important factors responsible for Yemen being a haven for jihadi fighters are its civil war being escalated and becoming regionalised, thus helping AQAP and its affiliates thrive in an environment of state collapse, growing sectarianism, shifting alliances, security vacuums, and a burgeoning war economy (International Crisis Group, 2017). Events in the state of Yemen are happening at a rapid pace. The economic and geopolitical crises that have long limited the growth of the state and its stability have attempted to develop a strong centralised stage that now threatens its overall existence. It is thus believed that the instability in the state is in turn the success of AQAP and its affiliates.

To establish an Islamic caliphate at a global level, AQAP has been known to carry out terrorist activities and other violent acts inside Yemen and abroad, notably the failed attempt at the famous Christmas Day bombing of a Northwest Airlines flight to Detroit in 2009 and the 2015 massacre of the *Charlie Hebdo* journalists in Paris, France. The jihadi fighters in Yemen brought a flurry of front-page articles, warning that this fractious Arab state might become the next Afghanistan.

The chapter ahead will unfold the answers to the following questions: whether Al-Qaeda in the Arabian Peninsula (AQAP) could bring about the collapse of the fragile Yemeni government, and how is Yemen becoming the next base for Al-Qaeda to target Western countries and their influence?

DOI: 10.4324/9780429426063-59

AQAP: EVOLUTION, OBJECTIVES, AND STRATEGY

Early Years: The Return from Afghanistan

Al-Qaeda and its affiliates have been active in Yemen since the late 1980s, when thousands of Yemenis who fought the Soviet Union in Afghanistan returned home as mujahidin. Most of these started living a normal civilian life, but a small number who were close aides to Osama bin Laden continued waging jihad. The history of Al-Qaeda and its fighters is tied to both instability in domestic politics and shifting trends in global jihadism. Many analysts believe Tariq al-Fadhli to be the founder of al-Qaeda in Yemen. Al-Fadhli[1] is believed to have worked very closely with Bin Laden in Afghanistan as Arab-Afghans against the Soviets and returned to Yemen to fight the Yemen Socialist Party (YSP), the ruling party of then-southern Yemen. Yemen, at the time, was a relatively young and developing state in which the rules of politics remained under negotiation and the al-Qaeda affiliates found haven in Yemen's tribal regions. Al-Qaeda took advantage of the weak political regime in the state with a brief civil war[2] in 1994, which ended with the defeat of the southern armed forces and the reunification of the state. After this, until mid-2000, al-Qaeda affiliates became one of the most important jihadist strands in Yemen. With their direct ties to Osama Bin Laden and their ability to take advantage of the fragile state of Yemen and its permissive political scenario, the jihadi fighters acquired skills, resources, weaponry, and the capacity to carry out attacks against Western influence that will give them global attention, from the 1998 killings of British and Australian citizens in the Abyan province to the October 2000 bombing of the USS Cole warship near Aden, killing 17 American sailors.

After the 9/11 attacks, countering the jihadi fighters in the Arabian Peninsula and Afghanistan became America's foremost priority, resulting in the crackdown of the mujahidin in Yemen and across the region by killing and detaining several al-Qaeda affiliates by the end of 2005.

2006: Prison Break and Comeback

The morning of February 3, 2006, turned out to be a historic one for the evolution of an offshoot of Bin Laden's terrorist network, Al-Qaeda in the Arabian Peninsula (AQAP), a merger organisation of al-Qaeda branches in Yemen and Saudi Arabia, as 23 prisoners escaped from the prison in Sanaa who were detained for the 2000 USS Cole bombings, including two very close associates of Bin Laden, Nasir al-Wuhayshi[3] and Qasim al-Raymi, each of whom went on to lead AQAP. The deadly comeback of al-Qaeda under the leadership of Nasir al-Wuhayshi in the Arabian Peninsula went on, attacking foreign tourists to establish an international caliphate, and its operatives dispersed throughout Yemen after the prison break. They established their presence in sparsely populated areas of the south-eastern provinces of Abyan, Shabwa, and Hadramout (Roggio, 2009), where later they opened their training camps to carry out the global terror campaign. The al-Qaeda fighters started targeting foreign tourists and Western interests in the form of their lethal suicide bombings, the most significant being the failed simultaneous suicide bombings on oil and gas facilities in Hadramout and Marib in September 2006, two Belgian tourists' killings in Hadramout in January 2008, and a grenade attack on the US embassy in March 2008.

2009: AQAP Formed

In January 2009, after the crackdown of the Saudi government on the al-Qaeda branch located within their territory, the jihadi fighters in the Kingdom of Saudi Arabia were forced to cross the border and land in Yemen. This resulted in the merger of al-Qaeda branches in Yemen and Saudi Arabia, under the leadership of both Yemeni and Saudi founders of al-Qaeda branches, with a focus on expelling Western influence from the Arabian Peninsula and spreading jihad in Israel to liberate Muslim holy sites and brethren in Gaza (Faraj, 2009). Al-Qaeda in the Arabian Peninsula (AQAP) is headquartered in southern and south-eastern Yemen. Following the merger, an inaugural video was released by Nasir al-Wuhayshi in 2009, formally declaring the organisation's intention to avenge its enemies with blood and destruction to focus on a global Salafi-jihadist agenda. According to al-Qaeda's central ideology, the organisation will mobilise its fighters to form four armies that will march from the periphery of the Muslim world to the heart of Palestine: one each from Pakistan and Afghanistan, one from Yemen, and the last from the Levant region (Christian Science Monitor, 2010). AQAP asserted that it would help in forming the army in Yemen, thus working on creating a local and global Sunni Islamic caliphate. AQAP also worked in Yemen against sectarian minorities like the Houthis in northern Yemen, believed to be receiving foreign assistance from Iran and fighting to impose Shia religious law in Yemen.

To showcase its abilities and capabilities, the merger of Yemeni and Saudi fighters started carrying out various terrorist activities, including suicide bombings and large-scale kidnapping and murder of foreigners and people influenced by Western ideology, particularly creating a threat to the United States' integrity and sovereignty. AQAP tapped most of its resources from private Saudi funding and improved its bomb-making skills with the help of Ibrahim al-Assiri, a Saudi national and AQAP's top bomb maker. The first lethal attack carried out by AQAP was an attempted assassination of Saudi Deputy Interior Minister Mohammad Bin Nayef in August 2009. AQAP was aspiring to overthrow both the Saudi and Yemeni regimes to establish an Islamic theocracy. The other lethal failed attempt made by AQAP was when Umar Farouk Abdulmutallab, an AQAP recruit, went on to detonate a bomb concealed in his underwear on a flight headed to Detroit on December 25, 2009, but was stopped by vigilant passengers (Dawsari, 2018). In January 2010, United States President Barack Obama termed AQAP a "foreign terrorist organisation."

2011: Arab Uprising and Expansion of AQAP

In January 2011, a series of anti-government protests took place in Yemen by thousands of youth-led protestors to oust the regime of Ali Abdullah Saleh, the then President of Yemen for the past 30 years. Yemen has long suffered from internal political turmoil that has favoured the jihadi fighters of AQAP to have a strong and centralised presence in the province. AQAP expanded at a very swift pace following the Arab uprising in 2011 and started capturing major cities in Yemen. To carry out its operations effectively, AQAP created a new front and an insurgent force named *Ansar al-Sharia*. The new recruits of Ansar al-Sharia did not have to follow the strict central ideology of al-Qaeda; instead, they were given full liberty to operate with flexibility and should maintain a fair distance from AQAP, as the foremost priority for AQAP was to build trust among the affected Yemeni population with the help of this new front force. Ansar al-Sharia helped AQAP maintain its strong presence in Yemen post-Arab Spring by capturing Zinjibar, the capital of Abyan province, and the nearby city of Ja'ar, thus establishing an Islamic emirate by fighting Saleh's trained security forces funded by the United States (Wenner, 2020).

Ansar al-Sharia started delivering crucial services to the local Yemeni population, including security, electricity, food supplies, water, and other basic needs that the Yemeni government failed to provide. The Sharia courts even resolved several local conflicts that had otherwise been pending for more than a decade in the state courts. But, after a period in 2012, Ansar al-Sharia and its members publicly crucified a man who was accused of spying, and this went against the basic values of the Yemeni population and tribes. Abdul Latif al-Sayed, who went on to lead Ansar al-Sharia, left the frontier force due to these brutal acts of AQAP and its resurgent force, al-Sharia. Later, he joined hands with tribally armed people who went on to capture Zinjibar from al-Sharia in June 2012 with the help of Yemeni security forces. Despite this major setback, AQAP retained its strength and presence and carried out a string of major attacks inside Yemen, the most significant being a suicide bomber killing a senior military commander of Yemeni security forces in June 2013 (Faraj, 2009) and a deadly attack carried out in December 2013 against the Ministry of Defence in Sanaa that resulted in the killing of at least 52 people.

By the end of 2013, AQAP had started creating the same pattern of violent activities in the Arabian Peninsula that it used to do before the Arab Spring. For a time, the jihadi fighters stopped acquiring territories inside Yemen; instead, they focused on more aggressively targeting the Yemeni local population and degrading the capabilities of the Yemeni security forces and their rule of power. The organisation started large-scale kidnappings and assassinations of political leaders, security and intelligence officials, and tribal people who were accused of helping US security forces carry out drone strikes against AQAP. The attacks were more lethal as the organisation started using squad-sized tactical teams for more effectiveness, coupled with a vehicle-borne improvised explosive device (VBIED).

2014: Yemen Civil War: A Great Opportunity for AQAP

Yemen's civil war began in September 2014 after Houthi[4] insurgents stood up against the Sunni government and created an opportunity for AQAP to exploit the security vacuum created by the Yemeni security forces by splitting into pro- and anti-Saleh factions. The cause of the civil war was the capture of Sanaa, the capital and largest city of Yemen, by Houthi insurgents demanding lower fuel prices and a new government. In October 2014, Houthi forces, along with those loyal to Saleh, moved into the central province of al-Bayda, and then in 2015, they captured many provinces like Marib to the north of al-Bayda, Taiz in central Yemen, Aden, Abyan, Lahij, Dhale, and Shabwa in the south (Dawsari, 2018). The simmering unrest in Yemen has helped AQAP to rebuild itself by establishing its first presence in Taiz and Aden, thus helping the organisation to reequip itself through a series of raids it conducted in early 2015 that yielded weaponry to the group from brigade headquarters in southern and eastern Yemen. The local population accepted the presence of AQAP, thus helping AQAP have a strong presence as the country collapsed into a civil war. In January 2015, AQAP fighters captured Hootah in Lahij province and seized the coastal city of Mukalla in Hadramout province, and after three months, they recaptured Zinjibar and Ja'ar provinces as well. At large, as an external actor, AQAP poses a greater threat to the local mechanisms in Yemen (Zelin, 2017).

KEY PERSONNEL AND STRUCTURE OF AQAP: IDEOLOGUE AND MASTERMINDS

AQAP is comprised of Yemenis, Saudis, and foreign fighters who want to fight against Western influence in the Arabian Peninsula. AQAP, as an organisation, is compartmentalised and hierarchical, with a distinct division among its members. The organisation has a political leader that supervises all the administrative and operational capacities and provides an overall direction; a military chief who plans all tactical plans and activities under the supervision of the political leader; a propaganda wing that seeks to engage the new recruits; and, most important, a religious branch that justifies the acts carried out by the group in order to establish an international Islamic caliphate while also offering spiritual guidance to its members and affiliates. The group's fighters are generally veterans of wars in Iraq and Afghanistan and other international recruits who attended religious schools in Yemen.

Leadership

Nasir al-Wuhayshi (2009–June 2015)

Wuhayshi, also known as Abu Basir, was the founder of AQAP in 2009 and a very close aide to Osama bin Laden. He served as the leader of the organisation until June 2015, when he was reportedly killed in a US drone strike in Yemen's Hadramout region. His main intention was to establish an international Islamic caliphate and reduce Western influence in the Arabian Peninsula. In his 2009 opening speech, al-Wuhayshi ended with a prayer that explained the objectives and goals of AQAP:

> O Allah! Bring conquest over the holy mosque and the Haramain (highway from Mecca to Medina) by our hands. O Allah! Give us the honor by establishing the Islamic caliphate with our hands.

Anwar al-Awlaki (2009–2011)

Awlaki was an American and Yemeni citizen and the organisation's chief ideologue who gained prominence among Westerners as a global jihadist using the internet as a medium to spread his religious ideology about Salafism and establishing Sharia law in the Arabian Peninsula and promoting his religious ideas inside the United States. He has been believed to be a very strong religious preacher when it comes to communicating his theological justifications for jihad. He was killed in an American drone strike in southern Yemen in 2011.

Nayif Mohammad Saeed al-Qhatani (2009–April 2010)

He was a senior leader in AQAP who was held responsible for establishing al-Qaeda cells and training camps both in Yemen and Saudi Arabia. Qhatani was a very significant and notable leader, as he was believed to be an important connection between the al-Qaeda branches of both Yemen and Saudi Arabia before the merger. In April 2010, he was killed in a shootout by Saudi security forces.

Said Ali al-Shihri (2009–September 2012)

He was the deputy emir of AQAP and retained that post until he was killed in a military operation in Yemen in September 2012. In 2001, the US forces captured him along the Pakistan-Afghanistan border and detained him for nearly six years at the Guantanamo Bay detention centre. He was an important leader when it came to determining targets, recruiting new members, planning attacks, and providing tactical operational support for carrying out those attacks by AQAP and its affiliates. Shihri was suspected of being involved in the September 2008 attacks on the US embassy and the June 2009 kidnapping of nine Christian missionaries in Yemen.

Qasim al-Raymi (2009–2020)

Raymi, also known as Abu Hurayra, was an active leader since the organisation was formed in 2009 until February 2020, when he was reportedly killed in counterterrorism operations by US security forces. He was among those 23 prisoners who escaped from Sanaa, with Nasir al-Wuhayshi being the second significant member who went on to lead AQAP. Qasim and Wuhayshi were very close aides of Osama Bin Laden, and Qasim took over the leadership of AQAP following the death of Wuhayshi in 2015. The two were responsible for creating a sophisticated propaganda branch for AQAP by making frequent use of audio and video tapes to establish the central ideology of al-Qaeda, i.e., Salafism and Jihad. They also started a bimonthly internet magazine, *Sada al-Malahim (The Echo of Epic Battles)*, to expand their religious propaganda in the Arabian Peninsula. Qasim emerged as one of the most wanted terrorists on a list published by the Saudi Arabian government in 2009; he was also a key suspect in the deadly attack on a convoy of Spanish tourists in July 2007.

Ibrahim Hassan al-Assiri (2009–Reportedly Killed August 2018)

Assiri has been believed to be AQAP's top bomb maker, responsible for making bombs that were used for the attempted assassination of Saudi Deputy Interior Minister Mohammad Bin Nayef and the attempted bombing of the flight to Detroit on Christmas Eve by an underwear bomber. He had also prepared bombs to attack flights in Dubai and the UK in October 2010. In addition to his bomb expertise, he was also an expert in preparing poisons and was well-versed in martial arts. There were several attempts made by US security forces to eliminate him, but he was reportedly killed in a 2017 drone strike when US officials confirmed it in August 2018.

Khalid Batarfi (April 2015–Present)

Batarfi was earlier the top commander for AQAP in Abyan Governorate, Yemen. He is a Saudi national who completed his training in Afghanistan in the 1990s and fought against the US forces with the Taliban in 2001. In 2010, he joined AQAP, and in 2011, Yemeni security forces captured him. He later escaped from the central prison in Mukalla in 2015. He has played a significant role in the propaganda arm of AQAP by calling for and planning attacks against Westerners. He is the current leader of AQAP after the death of Qasim al-Raymi in February 2020.

Organisational Structure: AQAP

AQAP has four main branches: political, military, propaganda, and religious. Every branch has a leader who instigates the sense of spreading jihad in the Arabian Peninsula and is held responsible for directing AQAP's entire programme.

Political Branch

The organisation's leader oversees the political branch, and the same person also oversees the other branches and the entire AQAP programme. The duties involve approving targets, recruiting new members, allocating resources to train new members, and planning attacks.

Military Branch

The military branch plans all of AQAP's suicide missions, kidnappings, and violent attacks. It also takes care of robberies to provide funding to the organisation. Ibrahim al-Assiri was very crucial to the military branch of AQAP, as he was an expert and top bomb maker for the organisation and helped carry out high-profile bombings.

Propaganda Branch

The propaganda branch is one of the most significant branches of AQAP, as it is responsible for attracting new recruits, getting them trained to carry out suicide bombings, and promoting the theological justifications for jihad and Salafism. To establish an international Islamic caliphate, this branch is responsible for its outreach beyond Yemen and Saudi Arabia. AQAP has its own media channel named "al-Malahem," which is the official propaganda arm of AQAP. Al-Malahem is responsible for publishing a bimonthly magazine in Arabic for people in the Arabian Peninsula, and in English, a periodical named Inspire is published to target the Western audience. AQAP also publishes its official newsletter, *"al-Masra."* Al-Masra includes news updates for the entire al-Qaeda network and is very significant in recruiting new members. The current leader of AQAP, Khalid Batarfi, is a well-known spokesperson for the group and has taken over the group's propaganda arm to have global outreach (Counter Extremism Project, 2020).

Religious Branch

The religious branch serves as an extension of the propaganda branch of AQAP. The person responsible has the authority to issue fatwas (religious rulings). The branch is responsible for issuing statements in response to prominent religious clerics across the world to establish an international Islamic caliphate and to advocate AQAP's goals and objectives to justify its violent ideology.

MAJOR ATTACKS CARRIED OUT BY AQAP

AQAP is considered one of the most lethal organisations by US security forces in terms of the attacks carried out by the organisation against Westerners. Some of the deadliest and most lethal attacks carried out by AQAP since 2009 are:

- In March 2009, AQAP claimed responsibility for the killings of four South Korean citizens in the city of Shibam in southeast Yemen by detonating a suicide bomb.
- In June 2009, AQAP kidnapped nine foreign tourists outside the city of Sa'dah and executed three of them, while the presence of others is unknown.
- In August 2009, AQAP attempted to assassinate the Saudi Deputy Interior Minister, Mohammad Bin Nayef, with a suicide bombing, but Nayef survived the attack and the bomber died in the blast.
- In December 2009, AQAP tried to detonate the bomb on a US flight, but the attack was not successful.
- In April 2010, AQAP detonated a suicide bomb in front of the convoy of the British Ambassador.
- In October 2010, AQAP terrorists shot two rocket-propelled grenades at the car of the second-highest-ranking British diplomat in Yemen.
- In February 2012, AQAP targeted Yemeni Republican Guard troops in al-Bayda with a suicide car bombing, leaving 26 dead in the deadly attack.
- On May 21, 2012, AQAP targeted a military parade in Sanaa, killing 96 people and wounding about 300 others in the suicide bomb attack.
- In December 2013, an attack happened at the Defence Military Complex in Sanaa, killing 52 people.
- In January 2014, AQAP attacked the military bases in the town of Rada, a part of central Yemen; reportedly, 10 people were killed in the attack.
- In October 2014, AQAP took responsibility for carrying out back-to-back attacks targeting Houthi rebels, most of them taking place in the town of Rada.
- On January 7, 2015, an attack was carried out at the headquarters of Charlie Hebdo, the French satirical magazine, in Paris, resulting in the killing of 12 people.
- In April 2015, AQAP attacked the central prison in Mukalla and freed some 300 prisoners, including Khalid Batarfi, the current leader of AQAP. Also in January 2015, AQAP seized the coastal city of al-Mukalla in the Hadramout province and the Riyan airport near the city of Mukalla (Center for International Security and Cooperation, 2020).
- On May 11, 2016, AQAP claimed a VBIED attack in northern Hadramout province. The attack wounded General Abdul Rahman, commander of Yemen's military.

- In February 2020, AQAP claimed responsibility for the attack on the US Naval Air Station Pensacola in Florida. The attacker was believed to be a member of the Saudi Air Force. The same year, AQAP attacked Colonel Jamal al-Awlaki, a counter-terrorism specialist of the Yemeni security forces. The attack took place in al-Hamra village in the Abyan governorate.

ORGANISATIONAL CHARACTERISTICS: TIES AND ALLIANCES TO OTHER GROUPS, STRATEGIC SHIFTS OF THE GROUP'S TRAJECTORY AND IDEOLOGUE

Relation with Other Groups

Al-Qaeda in the Arabian Peninsula (AQAP), an offshoot of Bin Laden's core al-Qaeda group, remained loyal to their central ideology of promoting jihad and Salafism across the globe. The AQAP has been committed to the guidelines of Sheikh Ayman al-Zawahiri, the leader of core al-Qaeda. AQAP also supports other al-Qaeda networks and thus poses a threat not only to the Arabian Peninsula but also to the entire world. According to the Somalian government, AQAP not only established its base in Yemen in April 2010, but it also communicated with Hizbul Islam and al-Shabaab in Somalia. AQAP helped al-Shabaab gain monetary assistance to bolster its recruitment capabilities. The AQAP leader, Said Ali al-Shihri, announced that the group will seek to control the Bab el-Mandab Strait, the waterway connecting Yemen, Djibouti, and Eritrea, with the help of Somalian mujahidin to achieve global influence. AQAP has been accused of transferring bomb-making technology from Yemen to Somalia; also, support was given to Syria in terms of technology transfers of explosive materials and designs. In 2011, the US security forces captured Ahmed Warsame, a high-ranking al-Shabaab operative from the outskirts of Yemen, as he was accused of being an important connection between AQAP and al-Shabaab by brokering an agreement between the two where al-Shabaab could directly buy the weaponry from AQAP and its affiliates in Yemen. Also, to fight the Yemeni security forces and the government, al-Shabaab sent its 300 fighters to Yemen to help AQAP (Zelin, 2017).

AQAP and al-Qaeda in the Islamic Maghreb (AQIM) have coordinated in several ways, ranging from planning an attack in Europe to defining strategies against Westerners. AQAP's vision is to transform the local societies into an Islamic caliphate, from Yemen to Mali to Somalia. Since the entrance of Islamic State (IS) in Yemen after the 2014 civil war, AQAP has acted differently to propagate itself as a group that acts as a protector for the local Yemeni tribes against the Saudi and Emirati governments. AQAP started leveraging its status among all local Yemeni communities by showing that it respects Yemeni norms to establish a strong and special relationship with Yemeni tribes.

Tribes and AQAP

Al-Qaeda's leadership has always seen tribes as an important part of Yemen's political system and central to the power and authority in the country. In 1999, a senior al-Qaeda leader, Abu Musab al-Suri, described that Yemen's tribal areas will always provide a haven to the group's central ideologue of establishing sharia courts and an international Islamic caliphate in the region due to their underdevelopment, adherence to the traditional culture, and heavily militarised people, which will help the group establish a strong foothold in the tribal areas. After the formation of AQAP in 2009, al-Wuhayshi announced its support for the local tribes of southern Yemen in their struggle against Yemeni President Ali Abdullah Saleh. The objective was to rule the country and the local population by implementing sharia law. AQAP used poetry as its propaganda to recruit the tribal youth, who are frustrated with the rule of politics, have no good economic opportunities, and have been isolated in their own communities. The AQAP's narrative focused on the humiliation, injustice, underdevelopment, corruption, and destruction of property caused by counterterrorist operations and Houthi attacks (Dawsari, 2018). AQAP's rhetoric helped them tap the resources due to local discontent with the Yemeni government.

The local Yemeni population has helped AQAP in providing a haven for carrying out large-scale recruitment; the high unemployment rates, pervasive poverty, and dwindling supplies of oil and water became significant reasons for tribal people to help AQAP in its objectives and goals (Center for International Security and Cooperation, 2020). AQAP has actively worked with the tribal population by marrying their members with their women and thus providing social and financial assistance to the regions plagued by abject poverty. With social and financial assistance, the group also made use of cultural factors in the form of promoting Arabic in the form of short poems to improve its relationship with the local communities.

Strategic Shift Pertaining to the Groups' Trajectory and Central Ideologue

AQAP is an adaptive organisation, and the group recognised its mistakes in 2011–12 and did not want to repeat them. The mistakes included the formation of a new frontier and insurgent force, Ansar al-Sharia, and then declaring it an emirate, which brought US attention to the force and invited various drone strikes against the group, killing many locals.

Later, al-Sharia went on to implement brutal Sharia law, which alienated the AQAP from the local population.

The group changed its trajectory and its modus operandi in 2015, when it retained al-Sharia as a forward-deployed fighting wing with local groups supporting their goals and objectives. It helped them seize Yemen's third-largest port city, al-Mukalla, in the eastern Hadramout province but operated under the name of a local proxy force named '*Sons of Hadramout*'. The group at large refrained from raising their black flag at the port city. This shift in their trajectory helped them gain the trust of the local population, and it remained even after they lost their territorial gains in April 2016.

AQAP's support for the local tribes does not rest completely on the acceptance of their Salafist ideology; rather, it results from the efforts made by the group to support the tribes and their families in fighting the Houthi-Saleh faction. The Yemen civil war of 2014 completely changed the battlespace; now many Sunni insurgencies are fighting in Yemen. AQAP is providing full support to these insurgencies and has embedded so much in the local population that they now deny AQAP's presence in Yemen.

YEMEN'S HUMANITARIAN CRISIS: IMPACT OF TERRORISTS AND INSURGENT GROUPS IN SOCIAL, POLITICAL, AND ECONOMIC TERMS

Yemen is the Arab world's poorest country, with a poverty rate of more than 50%. In Yemen, approximately 8.4 million people are at risk of starvation, and about 75% of the population needs humanitarian assistance. The situation deteriorated further with the 2018 assault on al-Hudaydah by Saudi-led coalition forces, effectively blocking the main source of food imports in the country. Yemen has always been a haven for terrorist activities and insurgent groups due to its weak political scenario, growing sectarianism, and burgeoning war economy. Following the Houthi rebels' overthrow of the Yemeni government, a blockade and airstrikes by Saudi-led coalition forces intensified Yemen's political and economic difficulties. Due to political and security constraints, the World Bank suspended its operations in the country in 2015.

Yemen has become a fractured state, with several insurgent groups active in the country. While AQAP and its affiliates are firmly under control in the southern and southeastern provinces, Houthi rebel forces control the Northern Province. Due to increased unrest, the Yemeni security forces started withdrawing their soldiers from these areas, thus putting civilian lives in danger. Also, US counterterrorist operations and the air strikes by Saudi-led coalition forces have affected civilian lives on a large scale, killing thousands of them in drone strikes and forcing them into the world's largest humanitarian crisis.

The political transition after the Arab uprising of 2011 was expected to bring some stability to Yemen's political scenario, but President Hadi was not able to tackle the effects of military attacks, food security, corruption, and the loyalty of military officials to Saleh's regime. The country ended up having a civil war in 2014 when Houthi forces took advantage of President Hadi's weakness and seized the Sada province in northern Yemen.

In Sanaa, even international aid and assistance have failed to sustain civilian lives, thus creating a shortage of food, medicines, safe drinking water, and proper sanitation facilities. As of now, more than 18000 air attacks have been carried out in Yemen, with almost one-third of the bombings striking civilian sites (Harris, 2010).

While Yemen continues to suffer one of the deadliest crises of recent times, the insurgent groups also continue waging war with their own agenda of creating a power struggle and acquiring territorial gains in the country.

CONCLUSION

Al-Qaeda in the Arabian Peninsula is a Sunni terrorist organisation with the aim of establishing an international Islamic caliphate and promoting Salafism and jihad across the world. The main objective of the organisation is to follow the ideology of the core al-Qaeda group, target Westerners, and reduce its influence in the Arabian Peninsula. AQAP was formed in 2009 after the Saudi and Yemeni branches of al-Qaeda merged with a central ideologue to target the US and its allies and topple the governments of Yemen and Saudi Arabia.

AQAP's collapse in Yemen is far away until the Yemeni leadership makes some decisive and strong efforts to take hold of their provinces and people and maintain political stability in the country. The counterterrorism operations must include efforts to address the deficiencies of the Yemeni leadership.

The Yemeni tribes' opposition to AQAP will create a more threatening environment for the local Yemeni population, as in the current war scenario, al-Sharia, with the help of tribesmen, is fighting the Houthi rebels with AQAP, creating a tactical arrangement to defeat a common enemy and not a deeper ideological alliance (Dawsari, 2018). The Yemeni tribes can be part of the solution to the counter-terrorism strategies by US and Yemeni security forces to oust the AQAP and its affiliates from the country, but the military action against the AQAP has been harmful to tribesmen as well, resulting in the killing of thousands of Yemeni civilians. The Yemeni government and its instability in dealing with state internal matters have provided an undue advantage to AQAP.

AQAP continues to pose a threat to the Arabian Peninsula and the United States and its allies, and thus US security forces will have to deal with it in a very responsible way. The US government and security forces must adhere to the following policy recommendations to modify their counter-terrorism strategies against AQAP, where the Yemeni tribes also have a significant role to play.

- The US government should work in coalition with the Arab Nations, the UN, and other members of the international community to push the warring parties to agree on a durable political solution to end the war in Yemen. Ongoing conflict simply helps AQAP expand and target its vulnerabilities due to an unstable political scenario. A political settlement with both the northern and southern representatives participating to have a stable political system will end the long-lasting Yemeni conflict, creating more and more Yemeni institutions.
- An effective approach should be to train more security personnel in areas of the southern province where the fighting has stopped. With the help of the Yemeni government, the US security forces, and the local tribesmen should work together to develop security forces that can defeat AQAP and limit their presence. The goal should be to create more effective Yemeni security institutions that can help prevent AQAP and its militants from returning to these areas. More and more civilian participation should be encouraged to focus on improving the social and economic conditions of the region.
- The US security forces should work on reducing the air strikes in regions such as al-Bayda province, where there are ongoing clashes between Houthis and rebels. This creates a narrative for AQAP that Americans are backing Houthi rebels and targeting tribesmen in Yemen.
- The US government and security forces should start rehabilitation programmes for those who have joined AQAP due to political resentment and frustration rather than getting inspired by ideological beliefs about waging jihad. The Yemeni government should try having a dialogue with those who joined the group due to their grievances getting no response from them, which made them susceptible to the group.

Notes

1 "Tariq al-Fadhli is the son of the sultan who, during the British colonisation of South Yemen, ruled the Fadhli Sultanate in part of what is today, Abyan Province. The YSP ruled South Yemen after independence, and Tariq held the party responsible for confiscating his family's land and forcing them into exile in the late 1960s. South Yemen was ruled by a communist regime allied with the Soviet Union until the unification of North and South Yemen in 1990. For more, see International Crisis Group, *Yemen: Coping with Terrorism and Violence in A Fragile State*, January 2003."

2 "The failure to create a single state out of two, along with North Yemen's heavy-handed and corrupt political rule, caused the southerners to reconsider unification, prompting the 1994 civil war. The routing of southern forces (ironically supported by Saudi Arabia) gave a free hand to the north to simply impose conditions of unification. This coerced unification further consolidated the political economy of corruption in Yemen, as southern lands, enterprises and other resources were confiscated and given to northern elites."

3 Notably, he was killed in 2015 in a US drone strike.

4 "The Houthis are Zaydi Shiites, or Zaydiyyah. Shiite Muslims are the minority community in the Islamic world and Zaydis are a minority of Shiites, significantly different in doctrine and beliefs from the Shiites who dominate in Iran, Iraq, and elsewhere." For more read, Bruce Ridel, "Who are Houthis and Why are we at war with them, *The New Geopolitics of the Middle East*, December 18, 2017, https://www.brookings.edu/blog/markaz/2017/12/18/who-are-the-houthis-and-why-are-we-at-war-with-them/.

References

Center for International Security and Cooperation. (2020). *Al-Qaeda in the Arabian peninsula*. California: Freeman Spogli institute for International Studies.

Christian Science Monitor. (2010). *Five key members of Al Qaeda in Yemen*. Retrieved from Christian Science Monitor: https://www.csmonitor.com/World/Middle-East/2010/1102/Five-key-members-of-Al-Qaeda-in-Yemen-AQAP/Nasir-al-Wuhayshi-head-of-AQAP

Counter Extremism Project. (2020). *Al-Qaeda in the Arabian peninsula*. London: Counter Extremism Project.

Dawsari, N.A. (2018). *Foe not friend: Yemeni tribes and Al-Qaeda in Arabian peninsula*. Washington, D.C.: Project on Middle East Democracy.

Faraj, C. (2009, March 16). Al-Qaeda blamed for Yemen attack. Retrieved from CNN: http://edition.cnn.com/2009/WORLD/meast/03/16/yemen.bombing.alqaeda/index.html

Harris, A. (2010, May). *Exploiting grievances: Al-Qaeda in the Arabian peninsula* (p. 26). A Carnegie Paper Series.

International Crisis Group. (2017). *Yemen's al-Qaeda: Expanding the base*. Brussels: International Crisis Group.

Roggio, B. (2009). *Al-Qaeda opens new training camp in Yemen*. Long War Journal.

Wenner, R.B. (2020, April 15). Yemen. Retrieved from Britannica Encyclopedia: https://www.britannica.com/place/Yemen

Zelin, A.Y. (2017). *How al-Qaeda survived drones, uprising and the Islamic state*. Washington, D.C.: The Washington Institute for Near East Policy.

53

ANSAR ALLAH (HOUTHI REBELS)

Júlia Palik

INTRODUCTION

Ansar Allah[1] (Partisans of God), more widely known as the Houthi movement, originates from the Zaydi Shia minority in the northern governorates of Yemen. Ansar Allah began as a theological movement to protest the dilution of Zaydi identity and later transformed into a military resistance movement. Ansar Allah is an insurgent group engaged in a civil war against the internationally recognised government of Yemen and other non-state actors (such as the Southern Transitional Council and al-Qaeda in the Arabian Peninsula) since 2004. Since March 2015, a Saudi-led international coalition has been fighting against Ansar Allah, whom they consider Iranian proxies. As of January 2019, the conflict is still ongoing and is considered by the United Nations (UN) as the "worst humanitarian crisis' (UN OCHA, 2017).[2] The real number of direct conflict deaths is difficult to assess. The UN estimates 10,000, while the Armed Conflict and Location Event Data (ACLED) project reports a substantially higher number: more than 60,000 deaths since January 2016 (ACLED, 2018). This entry provides an overview of the contextual factors that enabled the formation of Ansar Allah, the movement's history, and ideology from the establishment of the Zaydi Imamate up until 2018, its internal and external relations, and its political-military transformation. This section applies a qualitative, single case-study method, where the unit of observation is the rebel group.[3]

CONTEXTUAL DETERMINANTS OF THE FORMATION AND RISE OF ANSAR ALLAH (AGGREGATE-LEVEL)

Yemen is plagued by multiple security challenges, some of which stem from structural factors (e.g., natural resource scarcity, weak state capacity), while others (state repression, corruption, horizontal inequalities) are attributable to the Yemeni political system. Yemen's peculiar socio-political and economic structure is a part of the reason why Ansar Allah has emerged, militarily developed, and been able to challenge the central government. This section provides an overview of the structural variables that enabled Ansar Allah's emergence.

Yemen is in the strategic southwestern corner of the Arabian Peninsula. The present Republic of Yemen was established in 1990 when South Yemen, previously known as the People's Democratic Republic of Yemen (PDR), and North Yemen, the Yemen Arab Republic (YAR), were unified under the leadership of Ali Abdullah Saleh and his General People's Congress (GPC) party.[4] The unification, however, did not lead to the effective integration of the South and North. Rather, the North-Yemen-led unification exacerbated the long-held socio-political grievances of the South and paved the way for the emergence of Ansar Allah. The population of Yemen is approximately 28 million people, with the majority belonging to the Sunni branch of Islam, while approximately 34–45% are Zaydi Shia Muslims, and less than 1% of the population belong to other religious minorities.

Structural characteristics on the aggregate level have important consequences on a rebel group's opportunity to organise. The so-called greed, or opportunity model of civil war (e.g., Collier and Hoeffler, 2004; Fearon and Laitin, 2003) argues that structural conditions that favour insurgency – state weakness, marked by poverty, large male population, and inaccessible terrain– are better predictors of civil war onset than indicators of ethnic and religious diversity or state discrimination against minority religions or languages. Macro-level variables in the case of Yemen clearly favour insurgency: First and foremost, poverty in Yemen has been endemic and has been further increased since the outbreak of the 2014 civil war. According to the World Bank, the country's GDP has shrunk about 50% since 2014. Oil and gas production is operating at about 10% of pre-war capacity and exports have been suspended (World Bank, 2018). According to UNESCO and World Bank data, male secondary enrolment was around 54% in 2008. The

DOI: 10.4324/9780429426063-60

biggest problem remains that there are marked inequalities in access between rural and urban children and between boys and girls across regions. The recruitment base of the Houthis (male residents without secondary education) is higher than in other areas of the country.[5]

The greed model identifies the atypically cheap conflict-specific capital as another factor that increases the propensity for civil war onset. Yemen, as the second most heavily armed nation (Small Arms Survey, 2007), justifies gun ownership not just as a mere tool of defence but as an integral part of masculinity, ceremonies, and tribal gatherings (Palik, 2018: 2). It is commonplace to see young males openly carry AK-47s. Likewise, the jambiya, a curved dagger worn attached to a belt, is routinely carried by men. As Miller notes, "weapons in Yemen are said to be part of the national character and more linked to heritage, tradition, and norms than to violence and killing" (Miller, 2003: 3). Gun culture[6] is most prevalent in rural tribal areas in the northern highlands of Yemen. Saada, for instance, is home to Suq al-Talh, the largest weapons market in the entire country (Salmoni et al., 2010: 31), which operates like a "grocery store" with no or little formal requirement to purchase weapons. The exact number and types of weapons remain challenging to assess, especially since the outbreak of the civil war. Older estimates claimed the number to be between 40 and 60 million. According to Miller and Karp (2003: 172), however, a more realistic number is between six and nine million. This translates to an average of between 33 and 50 guns per 100 people. The influx of arms can also be attributed to the various regional conflicts that have and are occurring, such as the continuous fighting in neighbouring countries like Somalia. Ansar Allah obtains its weapons from the Yemeni black market, corrupt members of the Yemeni military, and more recently, Iran. Yemeni arms markets sell small- and medium-sized arms and heavy weapons as well (Miller, 2003: 10). Weapons have always served political purposes too; the arming of tribal leaders by the central government has been an integral part of the co-optation system, where the Yemeni government would try to tie political favour over rival tribes with loyalty to the state (Al-Dawsari, 2012: 4).

Another structural variable that enables the organisation of insurgency is terrain: forests and mountains provide rebels with haven, and as such, these geographic features favour the conduct of guerilla warfare. Yemen is characterised by a unique dual-governance structure. Historically, the central government possessed only a limited degree of control over the country's peripheral provinces. Water scarcity, the lack of employment opportunities, and harsh weather conditions are all factors that contribute to the semi-autonomous nature of the northern region where Ansar Allah originates. The semi-autonomous nature of the northern region is partly explained by the lack of a road system and necessary infrastructure that could connect the northern provinces to the capital, Sanaa. According to Salmoni et al. (2010: 3), "Perhaps more than any other Arab country, Yemen has a central government that possesses an extremely attenuated degree of control over its peripheries, and the north is the least responsive to Sanaa." In sum, according to the greed model of civil war, Yemen's geographic, economic, and political settings are making the country more prone to civil war.

HISTORICAL BACKGROUND OF ANSAR ALLAH (GROUP LEVEL)

Tribal Relations

Members of Ansar Allah originate from the Zaydi branch of Shia Islam. Zaydis originate from the mountainous northernmost provinces of Saada, al-Jawf, and northern Amran. Although Zaydi Shi'ism (or the so-called "Fivers") is a subsect of Shia Islam, it is doctrinally different from the dominant "Twelver Shiism," which is practised in Iran, Iraq, and Lebanon. In fact, Zaydi religious practises are closer to Sunni Islam (Bonnefoy, 2009: 1). Although the Houthis are not tribesmen, understanding the socio-political context in which they have been historically embedded is necessary. The tribe (*qabilah*) is the central social organising structure of northern Yemen. Politics in the North is dominated by tribal leaders (shaykh), who operate largely independently from the central government (Brandt, 2017: 19–22). Tribes perform important administrative tasks in their areas of control, are responsible for external and internal representation of their tribes and undertake judicial functions. Conflict management and mediation take place according to tribal customary law (*'urf*). Hashid and Bakil are the two largest tribal confederations in northern Yemen.[7] Ansar Allah's tribal relations went through considerable changes due to the political transformations on the national level.

From the Imamate to the Believing Youth (1962–1990)

Ansar Allah was established and led by members of the *sadah* (sing. *sayyid*) social stratum.[8] *Sadah* constitutes a religious elite, claiming to be the descendants of the Prophet through his two grandsons, Husayn and Hasan. The sadah is the leader of secular, religious, and military affairs of the Zaydi community and occupies the position of Imam (Bruck, 2005: 35–40). The Zaydi Imamate was established in northern Yemen in 893 and lasted until the 1962 revolution. The Yemeni sadah trace their descent to the first Zaydi imam, Yahya b. al-Husayn (d. 911), who was invited to Yemen by tribal leaders to mediate an inter-tribal violent conflict according to Sharia (Dresch, 2001: 8). Upon successfully resolving the inter-tribal conflict, Yahya remained in Saada and established the Zaydi state under the Zaydi Hadawi school of law (Brandt, 2017: 21). Zaydis believe that their imam must be both a descendent of Ali and one who makes it his religious duty to oppose and fight unjust and corrupt political rulers (*khurūj*) (King, 2012: 407). The Zaydi imamate and the Sadah leadership were eliminated by the September 26 Revolution of 1962. Egyptian-supported Yemeni army officers overthrew the last imam, Muhammad al-Badr, and the Imamate was replaced by a new political system, the Yemen Arab Republic (YAR), inspired by Gamal Abdel Nasser's political system in Egypt (Bonnefoy, 2009: 1).

The revolution and the ensuing civil war (1962–1970) between the royalist and republican forces marked the beginning of the transformation of the socio-political institution of sadah. The Imamate era's religious and political elite lost political and economic power, and the Sayyid hegemony was substituted by the Shaykhly hegemony. By rewarding shayks with key governmental and military positions, tribal leaders managed to shape Yemeni politics on the national level, which meant a considerable expansion of their influence from their original tribal areas (Clark, 2010: 34). At the same time, in the long run, this national-level integration of shayks negatively affected their tribal ties, as they often moved closer to the capital city of Saana to ensure proximity to the central government and neglected their basic tribal duties (Brandt, 2017: 40). Horizontal inequalities[9] and the ensuing marginalisation of the Zaydi minority can partly be traced back to this post-revolution *elite transformation*. In this new period, Sadah was considered backward and reactionary by other segments of Yemeni society. Brandt (2017: 50–57) characterises the patronage-based post-imamate era as a "big-man game" in which tribal shayks have been co-opted by the central government through their integration into important government and military positions. From the government's perspective, this system served two purposes: to ensure shaykhly loyalty and to expand the state's influence into otherwise remote and hard-to-govern areas. This model constituted the foundations of Saleh's and the northern Hashid tribe's monopolies.

The 1980s saw the expansion of Wahhabi and Salafi religious establishments in northern Yemen. The conversion of many Zaydis to Wahhabism posed an existential threat to the Zaydi community (King, 2012: 406). Both internal and external forces led to the Wahhabi influence. Externally, Saudi Arabia sponsored the Wahhabi infiltration, which was aimed at the gradual transformation of the socio-cultural and religious landscape of northern Yemen. Internally, the "sunnization" of northern Yemen was spearheaded by returning Yemeni guest workers from Saudi Arabia (Bonnefoy, 2010: 16). The aggressive promotion of Wahhabism took both violent and non-violent forms. On the one hand, it entailed the establishment of religious and educational institutions, mosques, and massive social benefit systems. In its violent form, Wahhabi proselytisers have pursued an aggressive anti-Shia policy and denounced the Zaydis as infidels. They attacked Zaydi mosques and vandalised local tombs of the Zaydi religious leaders (Day, 2012: 408; Brandt, 2017: 105). The government also supported these policies since Zaydis were seen as anti-republican forces that had to be neutralised (Phillips, 2008: 43–45).

The prominent al-Houthi family spearheaded a multi-faceted resistance movement in response to this "competitive sectarian environment" (Brandt, 2017: 103) and the resulting economic and political marginalisation of the Zaydis. The first institutionalised manifestation of this resistance movement was the establishment of the Believing Youth (*Shabab al-Moumineen*) organisation in 1990. The Believing Youth (BY) started as a network of educational centres for marginalised northern Yemeni youth. When the BY began to open their summer camps to gradually regain their local influence, they simultaneously began to politicise the Zaydi cause (Freeman, 2009: 1008). This grass-roots-level institution was aimed at re-engaging the Zaydi tribal youth and countering the Wahhabi and Salafi influences in the Zaydi heartland. The BY's summer camps were the Zaydi's response to the Sunni Scientific Institutes. The BY has rapidly gained ground, and by 1994 it had at least 15,000 members (Brandt, 2017: 117; Granzow, 2015: 163). The BY's activities had not received considerable attention from the Yemeni government up until 2003. In fact, the government often supported the BY, which at times has been deemed by Saleh as a useful counterforce against the Sunni Islah party and the excessive Saudi-Wahhabi infiltration in the north (Granzow, 2015: 166).

From Unification to the Saada Wars (1990–2010)

The May 22, 1990, unification of Yemen has replaced the Republic with a multiparty political system. In the post-unification era, Saleh's GPC party continued to rule the North, while the Yemeni Socialist Party (YSP) continued to rule the South. At the same time, the new political era enabled the emergence of new parties, among which the al-Haqq (Party of Truth) and the Islah Party[10] are of particular importance for understanding the emergence of Ansar Allah. The multiparty system opened a window of opportunity for the political representation of Zaydis. The al-Haqq was established in 1990 by al-Houthi and other families as a competitor against the Salafist-supported Islah party.[11] Badr al-Din al-Houthi served as vice president of the party (Brandt, 2017: 119). Hussein al-Houthi, the eldest son of Badr al-Din, won the 1993 election but lost the 1997 election and afterward turned away from politics. After spending the period of 1999–2000 at Khartoum University in Sudan, he returned to Saada and focused on contributing to the work of the BY. (Brandt, 2017: 131). In 2001, the BY was split between the Houthi family and the faction led by Muhammad Izzan and Majd al-Din al-Muayyadi (Brandt, 2017: 132). The group led by Hussein al-Houthi, known as Ashab al-shiar (Followers of the Slogan), constituted the original members of Ansar Allah.

International developments, especially the second intifada and the 9/11 terrorist attacks, resulted in a global geo-political shift in which Yemen gained a strategic role as an ally in the US-led Global War on Terror campaign (Knights, 2018: 17). These developments and the subsequent invasion of Iraq marked a new era for Hussein al-Houthi, who began to raise his opposition against the Yemen-US alliance. Hussein claimed that by cooperating with the US, the GPC leadership had sold out Yemen's sovereignty (Basu, 2015). Hussein al-Houthi has successfully capitalised on the culmination of decades of economic and socio-political marginalisation and the anti-establishment and anti-imperialist sentiments of the northern region. By 2003, Hussein had started to organise anti-American protests across the country and ordered its followers to chant the Houthi's infamous "Allahu akbar, death to America, death to Israel, curse upon the Jews, victory to Islam" slogan after Friday prayers. Hussein also advised his followers to stop paying zakat to the state and instead give it to the Houthis (Day, 2012: 216). His widely visited Friday sermons have attracted authorities' attention, and they began to consider Hussein's political activism as an internal threat to state security (Salmoni et al., 2010: 7). The government claimed that the Houthis were aimed at re-establishing the Imamate and was able to portray the fight against the group as part of the government's counterterrorism efforts (Hammond, 2012).

In June 2004, after a failed attempt by Saleh to find a political compromise with Hussein, the government began its military attack against the Houthis in their mountainous stronghold with the aim of eliminating the leader. Between 2004 and 2010, in the course of six violent rounds of violent conflict known as the Saada wars, the Houthis became irreversibly radicalised (Salmoni et al., 2010: 168–178). In the following six years, the Houthis fought against the forces of General Ali Monsen al-Ahmar. According to Boucek (2010: 1), at the beginning of the war, the Houthis were "protesting the dilution of Zaidi influence and identity". During this period, the Houthis did not seek to remove the government, but they demanded greater political representation and access to development programmes. After the 2004 death of Hussein, he was martyred. This, instead of weakening the Houthis, enabled their further anti-government mobilisation (Brandt, 2017: 167). Upon Hussein's death, his father and later his younger brother, Adbul al-Malik, took charge of the group. According to RAND estimates, casualties ranged from hundreds to more than 20,000 during the Saada wars. In addition, more than 150,000 displaced people were reported, and an estimated 3,000 people have been arrested for supporting the Houthis (Salmoni et al., 2010: 15). The indiscriminate violence by the Yemeni armed forces revoked sympathy for the Houthis and enabled their growth both in terms of manpower and weaponry. Eventually, inter-tribal cleavages came to the fore, and the deployment of tribes external to the Saada region (mostly Hashid) by the government led to a massive enlistment of tribes in favour of the Houthis (Brandt, 2017: 154). The Saada wars ended with a 2010 ceasefire between the government and the Houthis after the Saudi Air Force led a scorched-earth campaign (Reuters, 2010).

From the Yemeni Arab Uprising to the Houthi Takeover

Approximately a year after the end of the Saada wars, in 2011, the Saleh-led GPC announced that it would seek to remove the limit on the number of terms in office for the president. This triggered widespread resistance, as many Yemenis feared that Saleh would retain office for life. At that time, he had already been governing Yemen for 33 years. In early January 2011, the Arab Uprising reached Yemen. The Houthis were among the first to join the country-wide street demonstrations in Sanaa's Change Square (BBC, 2011).

The March 18 indiscriminate violence by the government – approximately 50 protesters were shot and hundreds were wounded – led to the defection of important military factions, most notably the al-Ahmar brothers and General Ali Mohsein[12] (Gaub, 2015: 1). As international pressure mounted over Saleh, he was forced to sign a Gulf Cooperation Council (GCC)-brokered peace deal on November 23, 2011. In exchange for relinquishing his presidential power, the agreement granted immunity to Saleh and his family and allowed him to remain a GPC member. The UN-sponsored transitional plan included three priorities: the drafting of a new constitution before the scheduled February 2014 election based on national dialogue, addressing the issue of transitional justice, unification, and reform of the armed forces (Bellal, 2018: 147). By February 2012, former Vice President Abed Rabbo Mansour Hadi had been elected interim President for a two-year period.

Saleh's November 2011 resignation left a power vacuum, which allowed the rebels to seize Saada, al-Jawf, and Hajjah provinces by May 2012. The GCC agreement failed to address the core grievances of the Yemeni protesters, and it rather re-established the status quo ante. The UN-sponsored National Dialogue Conference (NDC) (March 2013–January 2014) was tasked with reaching national consensus on a new political system for Yemen with the inclusion of all major stakeholders: the Houthis, the Southern Movement, representatives of all political parties, civil society, women, and youth groups. The NDC's tasks were divided into nine thematic areas,[13] one of which was the conflict in Saada. Although the Houthis have rejected the GCC plan, they have participated in the NDC. One of the most important recommendations of the NDC was to reform the federal structure of Yemen by establishing six regions instead of twenty-six. The Houthis and the Southern Movement both rejected this proposal (Bellal, 2018: 148). The Houthis argued that it would reinforce the economic imbalances and leave the northern region without direct access to the sea and natural resources. In June 2014, the Hadi government's decision to cut fuel subsidies prompted a wave of protests. In July 2014, the Houthis seized the province of Omran. The Houthis overran Saana in September with the aid of Saleh supporters, and they placed President Hadi under house arrest (Salmoni et al., 2010: 141). The Houthis took over Hodeidah in October 2014, and the city has been subject to a coalition blockade since 2015.[14] The Houthis put President Hadi under house arrest, disbanded the parliament, and established the Supreme Revolutionary Committee (SRC), under the leadership of Mohammed Ali al-Houthi, in January 2015 following the rejection of the UN-brokered Peace and Nation Partnership Agreement. Later, Hadi escaped to the port city of Aden and then to Riyadh, where he established a government in exile (Gaub, 2015: 3).

From Operation Decisive Storm to the Stockholm Agreement (2015–2018)

On March 26, 2015, Saudi Arabia, Qatar, Kuwait, the United Arab Emirates, Bahrain, Egypt, Morocco, Jordan, Sudan, and Senegal launched Operation Decisive Storm, a military campaign in Yemen against the Houthi movement to restore the rule of the internationally recognised president and to reclaim the Houthi-occupied territories. The coalition is fighting with air and ground forces and receives intelligence, logistical, and military support from countries such as the United States, the United Kingdom, or Germany. As of 2018, the US accounts for more than 60% of major arms sales, followed by the UK (23%), and France (4%) (Dewan, 2018). In April 2015, the United Nations Security Council adopted Resolution 2216, which imposed sanctions on individuals undermining the stability of Yemen and authorised an arms embargo and travel bans against various designated individuals within the Houthi-Saleh forces. Resolution 2216 also demanded that the Houthis withdraw from all territories seized during the conflict and hand over weapons seized from the military during the fighting (UN SC 2216, 2015).

On July 28, 2016, Saleh and the Houthis signed a power-sharing agreement that replaced the Supreme Revolutionary Council with a ten-member Supreme Political Council, with five members nominated by Saleh and five by the Houthis (S/2017/81:20). Two months later, they formed a "national salvation government," dividing ministerial posts.[15] The Ansar Allah-Saleh alliance ended in 2017 after Saleh's assassination by the Houthi rebels after he announced that he was willing to engage in talks with Saudi Arabia if it stopped the aerial bombardment. As of 2018, after two failed peace negotiations (Kuwait 2016 and Geneva 2018), Ansar Allah and representatives of the Yemeni government signed the Stockholm Agreement on December 13, 2018. Parties agreed on a large-scale prisoner exchange, a ceasefire in the port city of Hodeidah, and steps toward resolving the conflict in the city of Taiz (OSESGY, 2018).

KEY PERSONNEL AND STRUCTURE

Hussein al-Houthi, a characteristic "conflict entrepreneur" (Gates, 2001), was the founder of the Houthi insurgency. Following his 2004 assassination, Abdullah Ayed al Ruzami, a former member of the al-Haqq party, led military operations, while Badr al Din (Hussein's father) served as the spiritual and nominal leader of Ansar Allah (Critical Threat, 2010). Abdulmalik al-Houthi, who oversees all major decisions as of January 2019, is Ansar Allah's leader.

According to the 2015 UN Panel of Experts Report, in 2005, Ansar Allah compromised between 1,000 and 3,000 fighters. This number increased to 100,000 and 120,000 by 2010 (S/2015/125:21). During the six rounds of the Saada wars, various northern tribes joined the Houthi insurgency to express tribal solidarity, most notably after the assassination of Hussein al-Houthi, and to gain revenge on government forces after the indiscriminate use of heavy artillery and airstrikes (Knights, 2018: 16).

As of 2018, the Houthis have a political and military wing, yet their organisational structure remains opaque (Counter Extremism Project, 2018). The 2018 UN Panel of Experts Report notes that, despite newly recruited members, Ansar Allah "is at heart a family organisation." This means that the "most trusted commanders are those related to the leader, Abdulmalik al-Houthi" (S/2017/81:20). In 2018, one of the most senior members of the Houthis, Saleh al-Sammad, the "president" of Ansar Allah, was killed by a Saudi airstrike. Al-Sammad was the highest-ranked civilian official in Ansar Allah and second on the coalition's most-wanted list of Houthi leaders. He had been replaced by Mahdi al-Mashat (Aljazeera, 2018). The diplomatic "face" of the Houthis is Mohamed Abdusalam Salah Fletah, who is the lead negotiator (S/2017/81:12). Since 2015, the head of the national security bureau, Abdulrabb Saleh Ahmed Jarban (Abu Taha), has overseen the intelligence services (S/2017/81:10). Annex 4 of the UN Panel of Experts 2018 Report lists the most important Houthi family members and Houthi-affiliated individuals in ministerial positions (S/2017/81: Annex 22–23).

Ansar Allah has developed a public relations strategy and an extensive media presence. In 2007, the movement established an FM radio station, Station 26, and in 2008 it began issuing a newspaper, Al-Haqiqa (The Truth) (Albloshi, 2016: 146). Parallel to developing its own media apparatus, Ansar Allah has also eliminated opposition media outlets in areas under its control (Saana Centre for Strategic Studies, 2018: 23). The current media structure involves a TV channel, Almasirah TV, operating from southern Beirut (Moubayed, 2018), and a website, AlMasirah.net, which has both English and Arabic versions (https://www.almasirah.net/) and features daily updates of (both news, videos, and photographs) Ansar Allah's battlefield successes and the coalitions' human rights violations. Prominent Houthi people also maintain their own social media accounts, including Twitter and Facebook.

ORGANISATIONAL CHARACTERISTICS AND ACTIVITIES: STRUCTURE, CHANGE, AND OPERATION

There is no single Leviathan in Yemen, meaning that no entity has a monopoly on the use of violence. Since 2004, Ansar Allah has gained extensive combat experience and gone through a considerable military transformation. For six years, it waged sporadic guerilla warfare in the mountainous strongholds, but today it can sustain a sophisticated military campaign in urban areas across multiple fronts. This transformation is attributable to Ansar Allah's access to better military equipment, which it gained both from external and internal sources (S/2015/125:22). Ansar Allah has looted and gained access to tanks, artillery, anti-aircraft weapons, and short-range ballistic missiles, as well as to the institutional founding blocks of security, i.e., the defence ministry and intelligence services (Knights, 2018: 17). Externally, albeit to a limited degree, Iranian support facilitated the expansion of Ansar Allah.

Early guerilla tactics consisted of "ambushes with small arms fire, sniping, and mines" (Knights, 2018: 16; citing Salmoni et al., 2010). The six rounds of the Saada wars have significantly contributed to the evolution of military tactics: the Houthis began to conduct terrorist-type operations in the capital, developed their defensive capabilities, and increased the size of their units from 20–30 people to 60–90. By the end of the Saada wars, Ansar Allah was able to defeat an entire government brigade and conduct cross-border attacks against the Saudi forces, eventually prompting the Kingdom to engage in direct combat operations against the Houthis (Knights, 2018: 16). Ansar Allah has not just successfully occupied territories; it has also been able to retain most of the occupied governorates. From 2014 onwards, Ansar Allah has expanded its territory from Sa'ada to Al Jawf, taking over Amran, Sana'a, the strategic port of Hodeidah, Marib, Ibb, and Taiz. Ten years of insurgency and mastering the terrain made Ansar Allah the "strongest armed group in Yemen" (UN S/2015/125:22).

In February 2015, Ansar Allah became the de facto leader of northern Yemen by forcing Hadi to resign and flee the country. From 2015 onward, both UCDP[16] and ACLED[17] coded the Houthis as *state forces* in their datasets. ACLED codes Ansar Allah as "Supreme Political Council (Houthi Forces)," whereas UCDP refers to them as "Government of Yemen." The Saudi-supported forces of Hadi were able to retake five southern governorates, but Taiiz remains under Houthi control (Juneau, 2016: 654). Territorial expansion was achieved through a mixture of violent and non-violent tactics. Non-violent tactics include truce agreements and the cooptation of rival tribes, a strategy that was mastered by former President Saleh (Phillips, 2011: 132) and extensively utilised by Houthi forces. When governorates have been taken over, Houthis then replace state authorities with Houthi loyalist personnel (S/2015/125:23).

Ansar Allah is able to finance its military activities through looting and the imposition of taxes collected from traders, local businesses, and shopping malls (Sanaa Centre, 2018: 23). Since 2016, two central banks have operated in Yemen, one in the Houthi-controlled capital and the other in Aden under the control of the Hadi government. Effective control over the country's monetary institutions provided the Houthis with an important source of economic sustainability. Since 2015, multiple military units have defected to the Houthis. Yet, according to the 2018 Panel of Experts Report, "military units loyal to Ali Abdullah Saleh and those operating under the umbrella of the Houthi leadership continue to remain largely distinct" (S/2017/81:20). Part of Ansar-Allah's post-2015 success is attributable to the extensive use of landmines and improvised explosive devices (IEDs) against the coalition. According to a 2018 report by the Conflict Armament Research Centre, "improved mines, the primary type of landmine contamination in Yemen, are mass-produced by Houthi forces on a scale only previously achieved by Islamic State forces in Iraq and Syria" (CAR, 2018: 29). The biggest problem with such devices is that they will persist long after the conflict is over and can cause significant civilian casualties. Ansar Allah has also developed sophisticated tactics to mitigate the air-power superiority of the coalition forces: Ansar Allah forces move in small groups (3-5 people) who are hardly distinguishable from civilians (Knights, 2018: 17–19). As of 2018, the Saudi-UAE alliance has carried out more than 18,000 raids on Houthi-held areas to reverse their gains (Cumming-Bruce, 2018).

Weapons

Since 2014, Ansar Allah has acquired an impressive stockpile of missiles, rockets, mines, improvised explosive devices (IEDs), and such innovations as drone boats. The government purchased most of the missiles and rockets in the 1990s, primarily from North Korea (Reuters, 2016). The Houthis domestically produce mines and IEDs and obtain them from Yemeni army stockpiles (CAR, 2018: 2). In 2017, Conflict Armament Research (CAR) concluded that the more sophisticated weapon systems, such as the unmanned aerial vehicles (UAVs), were manufactured in Iran and smuggled to the Houthis (CAR, 2017: 3). Since the 2015 Saudi intervention, the Houthis have frequently used ballistic missiles both within and outside Yemen. In November 2017, the Houthis launched a short-range ballistic missile from Amran, which exploded near King Khalid International Airport. As a response, Saudi Arabia closed all of Yemen's air, sea, and land ports, thereby effectively locking out international aid from the country (Reuters, 2017). As the war progressed, Ansar Allah increasingly used missile attacks and deployed unmanned aerial vehicles (UAV) against coalition forces. The initial coalition air strikes failed to destroy the supply of short-range ballistic missiles. The first confirmed short-range ballistic missile launch against Saudi Arabia took place in 2015, and the last reported Scud-C-type attack took place in July 2017. A recent example of the advancement of the weapon system is the Burkan 2-H medium-range ballistic missile, which has been used to attack Riyadh. The UN Panel of Experts found that Burkan 2-H has been produced in Iran (S/2017/81:26). As of October 2018, Saudi military sources reported that the Houthis had fired approximately 200 missiles since 2015 (Middle East Monitor, 2018). According to Knight (2018: 21), "the accumulated balance of evidence strongly suggests that Iran and Lebanese Hezbollah have developed powerful military and technical advisory missions in Yemen since 2014." Using water-borne improvised explosive devices, sea mines, and anti-ship missiles, Ansar Allah has been conducting "maritime hybrid warfare" (Burgers & Romaniuk, 2017) against military and commercial ships in the Red Sea since 2016 (Sharp, 2018: 7). In 2018, Ansar Allah carried out attacks on Saudi oil tankers. One such attack was followed by the temporary suspension of oil shipments through the Bab al Mandab Strait (Al Jazeera, 2018). Since November 2023, the movement has attacked foreign commerce in and around the Red Sea with connections to Israel on numerous occasions with drones, cruise missiles, and ballistic missiles (Romaniuk & Kaunert, 2024).

Although Ansar Allah has successfully expanded its territory, it has done so with extremely high human costs. Human Rights Watch, Amnesty International, and the UN Group of Eminent International and Regional Experts on Yemen have all found evidence that Ansar Allah has perpetrated human rights violations amounting to war crimes (Human Rights Watch, 2018; Amnesty International, 2018; A/HR/39/43). Ansar Allah has recruited child soldiers, conducted arbitrary detentions, torture, and kidnappings, restricted civilian access to humanitarian aid, and violated freedom of expression. Ansar Allah's "failures" stem from the extreme human suffering the group has caused, either directly or indirectly. Gaining civilian support and the necessary political trust in the long run is questionable considering the extensive human rights violations.

ANSAR ALLAH'S RELATIONS WITH OTHER ACTORS

Ansar Allah is involved in both state-based and non-state violence.[18] Yemen's current security landscape is fragmented with shifting loyalties. Ansar Allah is fighting against the Saudi coalition-backed Hadi government and the various UAE-sponsored southern ground forces, most notably the Giant Brigades (al-Amaliqa), the National Resistance Forces, and the Security Belt forces (Saana Centre, 2018). In addition, Ansar Allah is also engaged in a non-state armed conflict against Al-Qaeda in the Arabian Peninsula (AQAP). Since its 2009 formation, AQAP has successfully utilised the evolving security vacuum and has been strengthening its position vis-à-vis the government of Yemen, the coalition forces, the Islamic State, and the Houthis (Kendall, 2018: 18). The AQAP-Ansar Allah relationship is more nuanced than a sectarian-based Sunni AQAP versus Shia Houthi enmity, and it is deeply influenced by tribal relations (International Crisis Group, 2017: 10–12). The first direct confrontation between AQAP and Ansar Allah took place in November 2010, when AQAP members carried out two suicide bombings targeting Ansar Allah members. The AQAP-Ansar Allah violence has mostly been concentrated in the northern al-Jawf province and the southern al-Bayda province (UCDP, 2018).

Iran-Ansar Allah Relations

Iran-Ansar Allah relations are debated and serve multiple political purposes. The Saudi-led coalition (Hameed, 2018), the Saleh (New York Times, 2008), and the Hadi government have all repeatedly accused the Houthis of receiving Iranian funding, training, and military assistance (New York Times, 2015). Observers agree that Iran and its Lebanese ally Hezbollah have aided the Houthis with advice, training, and arms shipments, but the extent of their support is debated. Although Iranian support for the Houthis has increased since 2014, it has remained limited, more reactive than proactive (Juneau, 2016: 656; Zweiri, 2016: 32). Empirical evidence regarding Iranian support is, in fact, scarce. There is no evidence that Iran provided the Houthis with any support prior to the outbreak of war in 2004 (Zweiri, 2016: 31). According to the 2016 UN Panel of Experts Report, Iran has been shipping weapons to the Houthi rebels since at least 2009 (S/2016/73:22–25). The report details various cases in which Iranian fishing vessels attempted to secretly ship hundreds of anti-tank and anti-helicopter rockets to the rebels. The report concluded that Iran was in non-compliance with UNSCR 2216 for failing to prevent the transfer to Houthi forces of Iranian-made short-range ballistic missiles. Iran denies the accusations (The New Arab, 2018). For Iran, Yemen has been a cost-effective way of antagonising Saudi Arabia, and Iranian aid to the Houthis does not match the scale of its involvement in other Middle Eastern conflicts such as Syria, Lebanon, or Iraq.

CONCLUSION

Ansar Allah's rise to power is the result of decades of internal marginalisation, government repression, and external interventions. The Houthi's kin network (in the form of tribal alliances), the group's religious homogeneity (Zaydism), its geographic concentration (in the northernmost governorates), and their previously established network (in the form of the Believing Youth Organisation) provided the social capital essentially for the initial anti-government mobilisation. Ansar Allah's ability to wage a more than decade-long military campaign has proven the group's resilience and depth of reserves. As of January 2019, neither side of the conflict is getting closer to a decisive military victory. Any political solution to the Yemeni civil war will entail some form of political power-sharing agreement with Ansar Allah.

Notes

1 The terms "Ansar Allah," "Houthis," "Houthi rebels," and "Houthi movement" are used interchangeably in this entry.

2 Since 2015, 75% of the population, that is 22 million people, need humanitarian assistance. About 18 million people are food insecure, and 2.9 million children and women are malnourished.

3 Data for this entry has been obtained from primary and secondary sources and interviews with key stakeholders working in Yemen. Interviews have been anonymized and conducted between January 2 and December 19 in Oslo.

4 North and South Yemen went through different historical developments. South Yemen was part of the British Empire from 1839 to 1967, whereas North Yemen has never been under colonial rule.

5 According to Human Rights Watch, in 2014, out of the 725 schools in Saada governorate, 70 were almost completely destroyed, and another 145 were partially destroyed or looted. This means that in the past couple of years, secondary male educational enrolment has drastically decreased, thereby allowing potential students to be involved in the civil war as fighters since they have very few outside options.

6 Ashkenazi (2012:231) defines gun culture as a special characteristic of a society where "guns are fairly common and looked on by some identifiable, normative element of the population as desirable goods in some way."

7 The Al-Ahmar family oversees the Hashid confederation, which also includes the Sanhan tribe of former President Saleh. Bakil leaders are from the Abu Lahoum and Nihm tribes.

8 Although the Houthis family is a Sayyid family, Sayyids and the Houthis are not equal. The Houthis do not represent all Sayyids, and not all Sayyids embrace the Houthi political aspirations.

9 Horizontal inequalities are systematic economic and political inequalities between ethnic, religious, or regional groups. Horizontal inequality differs from vertical inequality. Vertical inequality is a measure of inequality among individuals or households, not groups. The measurement of vertical inequalities is often confined to income or consumption (Stewart, 2008).

10 Hashid tribal shayks have dominated the Sunni Islah party, which governed the nation in coalition with the GPC until 1997. Afterwards, Islah was in opposition. Islah is considered an anti-Houthi force (Schmitz, 2011: 2).

11 The al-Haqq Party still exists in Yemen but has disassociated itself from the Houthis (Yemen Post, 2010).

12 The Al-Ahmar family has been one of the main political challengers to Saleh. The family originates from the Hashid tribal confederation. Abdullah al-Ahmar has been a Saleh supporter, but his sons have gradually distanced themselves from both Saleh and the GPC (Aljazeera, 2011).

13 The nine thematic groups were the following: Southern Issue, Saada Issue, Transitional Justice, State-Building, Good Governance, Military/Security, Special Entities, Rights/Freedoms, and Developments (NDC official website, 2018).

14 Retaking Hodeidah has been a strategic priority for the coalition. The port has been under renewed attack by Emirate-led forces since June. Operation Golden Victory, aimed at recapturing the port from the Houthis, has been described as the "biggest battle of the Yemeni war."

15 The GPC criticised the Houthis for not disbanding the "revolutionary committee," which continued to act as a shadow government, overseeing decision-making within the ministries and thus exercising real power (S/2017/81:20).

16 According to the UCDP, "In 2015, Ansarallah ousted the government led by President Hadi and took control over the capital in January. According to UCDP definitions, Ansarallah was then seen as the government of Yemen."

17 According to ACLED, "ACLED treats the forces allied with both the government of President Hadi and the Houthi-led executive bodies as state forces. It is important to note that the classification does not imply legitimacy but rather acknowledges the fact that there currently exist two distinct governing authorities exercising de facto control over different portions of the Yemeni territory. These include military and paramilitary actors."

18 UCDP hadn't included the rebel group in their dataset up until 2014 "due to the lack of stated incompatibility." The UCDP definitions state that the incompatibility, or conflict issue, can be either concerning government (the type of political system, the replacement of the central government or parts of it, etc.) or territory (secession or autonomy for intrastate conflicts). According to the UCDP, "Ansarallah has persistently claimed that the group does not want to overthrow the sitting government. Instead, the group has stated that it wants the government to end what it perceives as socioeconomic injustices and the government's political discrimination against the group and the Huthi tribe, which does not qualify as an incompatibility according to UCDP criteria. On March 9, 2014, however, the leader of the group, Abd-al-Malik al-Huthi, called on the government to step down."

References

Al-Dawsari, N. (2012, April). *Tribal governance and stability in Yemen*. Washington DC, Carnegie Endowment for International Peace.

Al Jazeera. (2018). Saudi Arabia suspends oil exports through Bab al-Manded, July 26, 2019. Available at: https://www.aljazeera.com/news/2018/07/saudi-arabia-suspends-oilexports- bab-el-mandeb-180725215417388.html

Armed conflict in Yemen in 2017: An increasingly complicated mosaic. In A. Bellal (2018), *The War Report: Armed Conflicts in 2017, The Geneva Academy of International Humanitarian Law and Human Rights* (pp. 144–157).

ACLED, Press Release. (2018). Breaking: Yemen war death toll now exceeds 60,000 according to latest ACLED data. 11.12.2018. Available at: https://www.acleddata.com/wp-content/uploads/2018/12/2018.12_ACLED_Yemen_PressRelease.pdf

ACLED's methodology around coding of the Yemen civil war. (2018). Available at: https://www.acleddata.com/wp-content/uploads/dlm_uploads/2018/10/Coding-of-YemenCivilWar_Final.pdf

Albloshi, H.H. (2016). Ideological roots of the Huthi movement in Yemen. *Journal of Arabian Studies*, *6*(2), 143–162.

Aljazeera. (2011, March 10). For more information on the Yemeni opposition parties and groups: Aljazeera (2011) Who's who in Yemen's opposition? Available at: https://www.aljazeera.com/indepth/spotlight/yemen/2011/02/2011228141453986337.html

Aljazeera. (2018). Saudi Arabia suspends oil exports through Bab al-Manded, July 26, 2019. Available at: https://www.aljazeera.com/news/2018/07/saudi-arabia-suspends-oil-exports-bab-el-mandeb-180725215417388.html

Aljazeera. (2018). What does the death of Saleh al-Sammad mean for Yemen's Houthis? April 25, 2018, Aljazeera. Available at: https://www.aljazeera.com/indepth/features/saleh-al-sammad-yemen-houthis-180424170317613.html https://www.bbc.com/news/world-middle-east-43872482

Basu, T. (2015) Who are the Houthis? The Atlantic, April 9, 2009, Available at: https://www.theatlantic.com/international/archive/2015/04/who-are-yemen-houthis/390111/

BBC. (2011). Change square: The heart of Yemen's creative revolution. Available at: https://www.reuters.com/article/us-yemen-ceasefire/yemen-agrees-to-end-war-with-shiite-rebels-idUSTRE61A4D720100211

Bellal, A. (Ed.). (2018). *The war report: Armed conflicts in 2018*. Geneva: Geneva Academy.

Bonnefoy, L. (2009). Varieties of Islamism in Yemen: The logic of integration under pressure. *Middle East Review of International Affairs*, *13*(1), 1–11.

Bonnefoy, L. (2010) Deconstructing Salafism in Yemen, CTC Sentinel, January 2010 Special Issues, 16–18.

Boucek, C., & Ottaway, M. (Eds.). (2010). *Yemen on the brink*. Washington, DC: Carnegie Endowment for International Peace. https://doi.org/10.2307/j.ctt6wpjfk

Brandt, M. (2017). *Tribes and politics in Yemen: The history of the Houthi conflict*. London: Hurst/Oxford University Press.

Brandt, M. (2018). Twelve years of shifting sands: Conflict mediation in Yemen 2004–2016. *Jemen Report*, *49*(1/2), 104–116.

Bruck, vom G. (2005). *Islam, memory, and morality in Yemen ruling families in transition*. Basingstoke: Palgrave Macmillan.

Burgers, T., & Romaniuk, S. N. (2017, February 16). Hybrid warriors: China's unmanned, guerrilla-style warfare in Asia's littorals. *The Diplomat*. https://thediplomat.com/2017/02/hybrid-warriors-chinas-unmanned-guerilla-style-warfare-in-asias-littorals/

Christopher, B. (2010). War in Saada: From local insurrection to national challenge. In Yemen on the Brink, Carnegie Paper Series, Carnegie Endowment for International Peace, Washington, No. 110, April 2010.

Clark, V. (2010). Yemen: Dancing on the heads of snakes. New Haven: Yale University Press.

Collier, P. (1999). Doing Well Out of War, The World Bank, Paper prepared for Conference on Economic Agendas on Civil Wars, London, April 26–27, 1999.

Collier, P. & Hoeffler, A. (2004). Greed and grievance in civil war. *Oxford Economic Papers*, *56*(4), (Oct 2004), 563–595.

Conflict Armament Research. (2017). *Iranian technology transfers to Yemen, 'Kamikaze' drones used by the Houthis forces to attack coalition missile defence systems*. London: Conflict Armament Research Ltd.

Conflict Armament Research. (2018). *Dispatch from the field: Mines and IEDs employed by Houthi forces on Yemen's west coast*. London: Conflict Armament Research Ltd., September 2018.

Counter Extremism Project. (2018). Houthis profile. Available at: https://www.counterextremism.com/threat/houthis

Cumming-Bruce, N. (2018). War crimes report on Yemen accuses Saudi Arabia and U.A.E. August 28, 2018, The New York Times. Available at: https://www.nytimes.com/2018/08/28/world/middleeast/un-yemen-war-crimes.html

Day, W.S. (2012). *Regionalism and rebellion in Yemen: A troubled national union* (pp. 215–216). Cambridge: Cambridge University Press.

Dewan, A. (2018). These are the countries still selling arms to Saudi Arabia. CNN, November 23, 2018. Available at: https://edition.cnn.com/2018/11/22/middleeast/arms-exports-saudi-arabia-intl/index.html

Dresch, P. (1989). *Tribes, government and history in Yemen*. Oxford.

Dresch, P. (2001). *A history of modern Yemen*. Cambridge: Cambridge University Press.

Fearon, J.D. & Laitin, D.D. (2003). Ethnicity, insurgency, and civil war. *American Political Science Review*, *97*(1), 75–90.

Feierstein, G. (2017). Is there a path out of the Yemen conflict?: Why it matters. *PRISM*, *7*(1), 16–31.

For more information on UCDP coding, see: http://ucdp.uu.se/#/actor/123

Freeman, J. (2009). The al Houthi insurgency in the North of Yemen: An analysis of the Shabab al Moumineen. *Studies in Conflict and Terrorism*, *32*(11), 1008–1019.

Gates, S. (2001). Recruitment and allegiance, the microfoundations of rebellion. *The Journal of Conflict Resolution*, *46*(1), 111–130.

Gaub, F. (2015). Whatever happened to Yemen's army? *European Union Institute for Security Studies*, *9*, 1–4.

Granzow, T. (2015). Violent vs. non-violent struggle: Investigating the impact of frames on movement strategies in Yemen. *Civil Wars*, *17*(2), 161–180.

Hadi, A.R.M. (2015). Yemen's President: The Houthis must be stopped, *New York Times*, 12 April 2015. Available at: https://www.nytimes.com/2015/04/13/opinion/the-west-must-help-save-yemen.html

Hameed, N. (2018). Iran continues to back Houthis, Saudi FM tells OIC. Arab News. Accessed from Arab News. Available at: http://www.arabnews.com/node/1230711/saudi-arabia

Hammond, A. (2012). Houthi rebels seen gaining new influence in Yemen. Reuters. Available at: https://www.reuters.com/article/us-yemen-houthis/houthi-rebels-seen-gaining-new-influence-in-yemen-idUSBRE8920QO20121003

Hugh, N. (2012). Yemen's Office of the Special Envoy of the Secretary-General for Yemen: Full Text of the Stockholm Agreement, December 13, 2018. Available at: https://osesgy.unmissions.org/full-text-stockholm-agreement

Human Rights Watch. (2018). Yemen: Houthi Hostage-Taking: Arbitrary Detention, Torture, Enforced Disappearance Go Unpunished, September 25, 2018. Available at: https://www.hrw.org/news/2018/09/25/yemen-houthi-hostage-taking

Human Rights Watch: Education Under Attack, Yemen Country profile, March 18, 2014. Available at: 2019 https://www.hrw.org/news/2014/03/18/education-under-attack

International Crisis Group. (2017). Yemen's al-Qaeda: Expanding the Base, Middle East Report no. 174, February 2, 2017, Brussels.

Interview with Hasan Zaid, President of the Opposition Parties (JMP), General Secretary of Al-Haq Party. 10 April 2010. Available at: http://www.yemenpost.net/Detail123456789.aspx?ID=100&SubID=1012&MainCat=4

Jones, C. (2011). The tribes that bind: Yemen and the paradox of political violence. *Studies in Conflict and Terrorism, 34*, 902–916.

Juneau, T. (2016). Iran's policy towards the Houthis in Yemen: A limited return on a modest investment. *International Affairs, 92*(3), 647–663. https://doi.org/10.1111/1468-2346.12599

Kendall, E. (2018). *Contemporary Jihadi militancy in Yemen: How is the threat evolving?* Washington: Middle East Institute. July 2018, Policy Paper 2018-7.

King, J.R. (2012). Zaydi revival in a hostile republic: Competing identities, loyalties and visions of state in Republican Yemen. *Arabica, 59*(2012), 404–445.

Knights, M. (2018). The Houthi war machine: From Guerilla war to state capture. *CTC Sentinel, 11*(8), 15–25.

Letter dated 20 February 2015 from the Panel of Experts on Yemen established pursuant to Security Council resolution 2140 (2014) addressed to the President of the Security Council.

Letter dated 22 January 2016 from the Panel of Experts on Yemen - Final report of the Panel of Experts on Yemen established pursuant to Security Council resolution 2140 (2014) (S/2016/73).

Letter dated 27 January 2017 from the Panel of Experts on Yemen addressed to the President of the Security Council, S/2017/81.

Michael, A. (2012). What do the natives know, societal mechanisms for controlling small arms. In O. Greene and N. Marsh (Eds.), *Small arms, crime and conflict global governance and the threat of armed violence* (pp. 230–249). London: Routledge.

Middle East Monitor. (2018). Arab Coalition: 200 ballistic missiles fired by 'Houthis' towards Saudi Arabia, October 2, 2018. Available at: https://www.middleeastmonitor.com/20181002-arab-coalition-200-ballistic-missiles-fired-by-houthis-towards-saudi-arabia/

Miller D. B. (2003, May). Demand, stockpiles, and social controls: Small Arms in Yemen, Small Arms Survey, Occasional Paper Number 09. https://www.smallarmssurvey.org/sites/default/files/resources/SAS-OP09-Yemen.pdf

Miller, D. B., & Karp, A. (2003). Living with weapons: Small Arms in Yemen. *In Small Arms Survey 2003: Develop ment Denied*. Geneva: Oxford University Press/Graduate Institute of International Studies. https://smallarmssurvey.org/resource/small-arms-survey-2003-development-denied

Moubayed, S. (2018, September 9). Houthis' visit to Beirut stirs division and controversy. *The Arab Weekly*. https://thearabweekly.com/houthis-visit-beirut-stirs-division-and-controversy

National Dialogue Conference (NDC) Official website: Available at: http://www.ndc.ye/default.aspx.

OSESGY. (2018, December 23). 'Terrifying' for Yemenis but ultimately a 'year for hope' says UN special envoy. https://osesgy.unmissions.org/2018-%E2%80%98terrifying%E2%80%99-yemenis-ultimately-%E2%80%98year-hope%E2%80%99-says-un-special-envoy

Palik, J. (2017). "Dancing on the heads of snakes": The emergence of the Houthi movement and the role of securitizing subjectivity in Yemen's civil war. *Corvinus Journal of International Affairs*, 2(2-3), 42–56.

Palik, J. (2018). Rebel disarmament, identity and game theory: How Small Arms and Light Weapons (SALW) influences the Yemeni civil war, University of Liverpool, War and Identity in the Balkans and the Middle East Conference, Liverpool.

Phillips, S. (2008). *Yemen's democracy experiment in regional perspective: Patronage and pluralized authoritarianism*. United States: Palgrave Macmillan.

Phillips, S. (2011). *Yemen and the politics of permanent crisis*. United Kingdom: Routledge.

Reuters. (2010). Yemen agrees to end war with Shiite rebels. Available at: https://www.reuters.com/article/us-yemen-ceasefire/yemen-agrees-to-end-war-with-shiite-rebels-idUSTRE61A4D720100211

Reuters. (2016). Houthi missile arsenal holds a key to future Yemen peace, November 22, 2016. Available at: https://www.reuters.com/article/us-yemen-security-missiles-analysis/houthi-missile-arsenal-holds-a-key-to-future-yemen-peace-idUSKBN13H1UU

Reuters. (2017). Saudi-led forces close air, sea and land access to Yemen, November 6, 2017. Available at: https://www.reuters.com/article/us-saudi-missiles-yemen/saudi-led-forces-close-air-sea-and-land-access-to-yemen-idUSKBN1D60I8

Romaniuk, S. N., & Kaunert, C. (2024, January 8). Houthi attacks and military escalation in the Red Sea: What's at stake? *Geopolitical Monitor*. https://www.geopoliticalmonitor.com/houthi-attacks-and-military-escalation-in-the-red-sea-whats-at-stake/

Saana Center. (2018). Starvation, diplomacy and ruthless friends: The Yemen annual review 2018, pp. 34–35. Available at: http://sanaacenter.org/publications/the-yemen-review/6808

Salmoni, B.A., Loidolt, B. & Wells, M. (2010). *Regime and periphery in Northern Yemen: The Huthi phenomenon*. Santa Monica: RAND Corporation.

Schmitz, C. & Burrowes, R.D. (2017). *Historical dictionary of Yemen*, Third Edition. Maryland: Rowman & Littlefield.

Schmitz, C. (2011). Yemen's tribal showdown: Saleh's last ditch attempt to hold onto power, foreign affairs. Accessed 20.12.2018, https://www.foreignaffairs.com/articles/persian-gulf/2011-06-03/yemens-tribal-showdow.

Sharp, J. M. (2018). Yemen: Civil war and regional intervention. Congressional Research Service, Washington D.C. Page-6. https://crsreports.congress.gov/product/pdf/R/R43960/29

Situation of human rights in Yemen, including violations and abuses since September 2014, September 27, 2018. A/HR/39/43. Available at: https://documents-dds-ny.un.org/doc/UNDOC/GEN/G18/252/79/PDF/G1825279.pdf?OpenElement

Small Arms Survey. (2007). Guns and the City, Geneva. Chapter 2, Annexe 4: The largest civilian firearms arsenals for 178 countries. Available at: http://www.smallarmssurvey.org/fileadmin/docs/A-Yearbook/2007/en/Small-Arms-Survey-2007-Chapter-02-annexe-4-EN.pdf

Stewart, F. (Ed.). (2008). *Horizontal inequalities and conflict: Understanding group violence in multiethnic societies*. Basingstoke: Palgrave Macmillan.

The New Arab. (2018). Iran denies Houthi missile deliveries: "We only send them cheesy puffs". April 25, 2018. Available at: https://www.alaraby.co.uk/english/news/2018/4/25/iran-denies-arming-houthis-we-send-them-cheesy-puffs

The New York Times. (28 June 2008). An interview with President Ali Abdullah Saleh. Available at: https://www.nytimes.com/2008/06/28/world/middleeast/28saleh-interview.html

Tribal Confederations. The National. Abu Dhabi Media, Feb 27,.2012. Available at: http://www.thenational.ae/news/world/middle-east/yemens-tribalconfederations

UCDP. (2018). Ansarallah - AQAP. Accessed 18.12.2018, http://ucdp.uu.se/#/nonstate/5545

UCDP: Ansarallah. Available at: http://ucdp.uu.se/#actor/1091

UN OCHA. (2017). Humanitarian needs overview 2018. Available at: https://www.unocha.org/sites/unocha/files/dms/yemen_humanitarian_needs_overview_hno_2018_20171204.pdf

UNSC Res 2216, April 14, 2015, Available at: http://www.securitycouncilreport.org/atf/cf/%7B65BFCF9B-6D27-4E9C-8CD3-CF6E4FF96FF9%7D/s_res_2216.pdf.

Victoria, C. (2010). *Yemen: Dancing on the head of snakes*. New Haven: Yale University Press.

Weir, S. (1997). A clash of fundamentalism: Wahhabism in Yemen, Middle East Research and Information Project, MER 204 – The Arabian Peninsula, Vol. 27, Fall 1997.

Winter, L. (2013). The ansar of Yemen: The Huthis and Al-Qaeda. *Small Wars Journal*, May 1, 2013.

World Bank. (2018). *Yemen economic monitoring brief (English)*. Washington, D.C.: World Bank Group. Available at: http://documents.worldbank.org/curated/en/508301539801659212/Yemen-Economic-Monitoring-Brief

World Bank. Yemen country profile. Available at: http://www.worldbank.org/en/country/yemen/overview

Yemen country profile in: Amnesty International Report 2017/18: The state of the World's Human Rights, February 22, 2018, 400-403. Available at: https://www.amnesty.org/en/documents/pol10/6700/2018/en/

Zimmerman, K., & Harnisch, C. Profile: al Houthi Movement, Critical Threat, January 28, 2010. https://www.criticalthreats.org/analysis/profile-al-houthi-movement#_edne911c19dcc32383c77111b559c98b6bbref

Zweiri, M. (2016). Iran and political dynamism in the Arab world: The case of Yemen. *Domes*, *25*, 4–18. https://doi.org/10.1111/dome.12078

54

MILITARY DIMENSION OF PALESTINIAN RELIGIOUS NATIONALISM

Izz ad-Din al-Qassam Brigades

Mustafa Yetim and Tamer Kaşıkcı

INTRODUCTION

Being one of the most important and effective violent non-state actors (VNSA) in the Middle East Islamic Resistance Movement (Harakat al-Muqawama al-Islamiyya-HAMAS) and its military wing, Izz ad-Din al-Qassam Brigades, is always one of the most discussed and explored topics within the literature. Beyond their local importance over the Palestinian territory, they have also played a partial role over the course of regional developments, as reflected during the Arab Uprising. Such an effective regional and local role is closely associated with its armed struggle against Israel. Therefore, to better understand its lasting impact on the region, one should initially look at its semi-clandestine military structure and strategies. In this context, this study attempts to comprehend the tactics, strategies, transformations, and possible splits within its military wing by initially presenting necessary information about the emergence and organisational-ideational structure of Hamas.

HISTORICAL ROOTS AND ORIGINS OF RELIGIOUS NATIONALISM AND THE EMERGENCE OF HAMAS

Founded in December 1987 in the immediate wake of the emerging Gaza-based first Intifada (uprising) (1987–1991), Hamas radically transformed Palestinian nationalism. Meaning "zeal"[1] in Arabic (Abu-Amr, 1993: 10–11), Hamas challenged Palestinian Liberation Organisation-led (Munazzamat at-Tahrir al-Filastiniyya-PLO) secular Palestinian nationalism and initiated a new guerilla warfare against Israel's invasion of Palestinian territory. Having strong roots in Palestinian Muslim Brotherhood (Al-Ikhwan al-Muslimin-MB) organisations, Hamas declared its charter in August 1988 and turned out to be a critical non-state armed actor (NSAA) in Palestinian politics. Its first charter, titled "Islamic Resistance Movement Charter" (Mithaq Harakat al-Muqawama al-Islamiyya), was a radical and strongly revisionist one, promising the end of "Zionist" occupation and the foundation of an Islamic state over the Palestinian lands. Declaring its commitment to the MB organisation and its principles, it considered the military *jihad* the only and necessary solution to end Israel's occupation. Therefore, its strong adherence to a military-first strategy marked a radical shift within Palestinian-based MB organisations' understanding of their struggle against the "Zionist Entity (*al*-Kiyan al-Sahyuni)" (Maqdsi, 1993: 122–134).

Emerging in 1928 as a Sunni-based religious organisation, MB increasingly extended its influence and power over the Middle East region, including the Palestinians. Accordingly, there appeared to be some MB-affiliated organisations in the region. This shows that religiously oriented military and social organisations in Palestine emerged long before Hamas's foundation. The first MB group was founded in 1946 in Jerusalem, which facilitated the emergence of the Palestinian Islamist party, the Liberation Party (Hizb Tahrir). The second-leading Gaza-based MB group, which was a determinant in Hamas's ideology and structure, was the Islamic Centre (al-Mujamma al-Islami-IC), led by Sheikh Ahmad Yassin and founded in Gaza in 1973 (Knudsen, 2005: 1374–1376). Sheikh Yassin was also the founder and first leader of the Hamas movement until his

DOI: 10.4324/9780429426063-61

assassination in 2004. Along with Sheikh Yassin, there were also six important Palestinian MB figures designing Hamas structure and ideology at the Gaza meeting in 1987. Another assassinated leader of Hamas, Abdul Aziz al-Rantissi, and the first commander of the Izz ad-Din al-Qassam Brigades, Salah Shehada, killed in 2002, were among them (Ashour, 2010: 163).

What was interesting is that Israel initially supported the non-violent Palestinian MB to weaken the PLO-led Palestinian armed struggle against Israel and stoke the fitna (discord) among Palestinian factions. Hence, Israel's policies toward Palestinian domestic issues also indirectly paved the way for the emergence of its formidable "enemy," Hamas (Knudsen, 2005: 1376). Palestine MB preferred Hassan al-Banna's evolutionary approach, who was Egypt-based MB's first and assassinated leader in 1949. As this orientation considered Islamisation of society as the primary objective rather than armed struggle against the enemy, Israel was not largely concerned about these groups' growing influence. Avoiding a general military confrontation with Israel, they focused on social and political activities that could promote the spread of religious values in society. However, after a while, the situation radically reversed, and the PLO struck a deal with Israel and engaged in peace negotiations with it during the 1990s. Unlike the PLO's softening position towards Israel, this time Palestinian MB groups explicitly started their long-term armed struggle following the First Intifada. Before Hamas became MB's combatant arm, MB factions were in fact engaging in some serious and earlier conflicts because of such an evolutionary approach that Israel welcomed. Some MB members advocated and proposed Egypt-based MB's spiritual leader and important figure Sayyid Qutb's militant and revolutionary way in their fight against Israel.

This disagreement led to the first important split among Palestinian MB groups, and Islamic Jihad (al-Jihad al-Islami-IJ) was founded in the early 1980s (Mishal and Sela, 2000: 30–33; Ayhan, 2009: 108–112). Refusing MB's evolutionary approach based on reforming society before military Jihad, IJ prioritised the armed struggle to liberate Palestine and did not deem waiting for the Islamic transformation of society as a necessary condition (Abu-Amr, 1993: 8–10). On the other hand, while it was the first to merge militancy and nationalism, IJ was not the only militant religious group. There were also other MB-affiliated armed organisations fighting Israel. Being the predecessor of Hamas' military wing, Izz ad-Din al-Qassam Brigades, Palestinian Mujahidiyn (al-Mujahidun al-Falastiniyun) was established as an armed wing of MB in Palestine by Sheikh Yassin and Shehada in 1983 (Chehab, 2007: 31). Moreover, when tracing the origins of militant religious nationalism, the Qassamites' ideological orientation and activities in Palestine should also be underlined. Founded by Izz ad-Din al-Qassam (1882–1935), this group also engaged in armed struggle against Britain's (BK) colonial rule in Palestine. Despite the Qassamites' short-lived uprising against BK and the murder of al-Qassam in 1935, this group's anti-colonial stance and especially al-Qassam's personal legacy and struggle constituted the basis of several religiously motivated armed groups, including Hamas (Knudsen, 2005: 1375–1376). In conclusion, militant religious nationalism as a strong anti-colonial ideological force did not come out with Hamas and has a longer and stronger historical-organisational background.

To preserve the historical opportunity to lead the Palestinian people in general and the Gazan people in particular following a civil uprising in Gaza, Gaza-based MB, specifically IC, created Hamas as the last and most effective agent of militant religious nationalism in Palestine. Deciding on the establishment of such an armed organisation was a radical rupture in IC's Islamic understanding since it generally adopted a non-violent path. However, under heavy pressure from pro-revolution members of the IC and an emerging necessity to stand by dispossessed and impoverished Gazans against Israel's atrocities, Sheikh Yassin and other important figures *were bound* to found Hamas. Declaring it a seemingly separate organisation from IC, Sheikh Yassin thought about the possibility of the fall of the Intifada. In the case of a possible fall, Hamas would be discredited by the IC and, thus, any Israel reaction would be prevented (Abu-Amr, 1993: 11). However, completely different developments occurred, and Hamas became the major military and, over time, political force in Palestine, which probably astonished Sheikh Yassin and other IC leading figures. Eventually, Hamas, which was initially designated as a semi-official military wing of IC and a necessary response to the ongoing Gaza uprising, became not only an effective armed resistance movement but also evolved into an essential political force with effective grassroots organisations in Gaza.

THE LEADERSHIP AND CHANGING ORGANISATIONAL-IDEATIONAL STRUCTURE WITHIN HAMAS

As a highly disciplined and simply structured organisation, Hamas has two branches of leadership, identified as inside and outside leadership. Such division within Hamas' organisational structure became more apparent after Sheikh Yassin's and al-Rantissi's assassinations. In this context, outside leadership was led by Head of Political Bureau Khaled Meshaal until his resignation. Inside leadership adopted a new policy identified as "undeclared leadership" following these assassinations, even though it was believed to be directed by Meshaal's deputy and Palestinian former Prime Minister Ismail Haniya (Hroub, 2004: 21–38). In May 2017, Haniya replaced Meshaal, who assumed this post almost 20 years ago, as the new leader of Hamas and head of the political bureau following the Hamas Advisory Council's (Majlis Shura) decision (Gonim, 2017; BBC News). There is a small difference between the inside and outside leadership approaches to Palestine-related issues. External leadership that largely controls the financial and external contacts has been more eager to resort to violent methods to accomplish transnational (ending the occupation) and long-term objectives (formation of an Islamic state) (Knudsen, 2005: 1378). Internal leadership, which is supposed to involve several moderate and pragmatic figures like Haniya, is regarded as more open to possible negotiations with Israel and the PLO and possible participation in Palestinian elections. On the other hand, such differences never threatened Hamas' organisational and ideological unity – cohesion and common policies were generally applied following long discussions (Mishal and Sela, 2000: 134–135; Hroub, 2006: 117–122).

Despite the changing power equilibrium between inside and outside leadership depending on local-regional developments and Sheikh Yassin's assassination, inside leadership has more power and authority in making Hamas's foreign and domestic relations (Chehab, 2007: 121). Indeed, outside leadership was formed as a secondary body to improve relations with the Arab world and increase support for the Hamas-led Palestinian cause. Not only organisationally but also geographically, Hamas has divided local and regional expansion. In this context, its activities are mainly concentrated within three geographical areas, including the West Bank and Gaza inside Palestine and Jordan, Lebanon, and Syria outside Palestine (Hroub, 2006: 118). Although Hamas has such a seemingly less-ordered leadership structure and geographical expansion, it was able to combine al-Banna's reformist approach with Qutb's revolutionary call for Jihad, and thus it overcame the long-term dilemma other militant religious groups faced (Knudsen, 2005: 1378). Therefore, it has neither the global jihad understanding of Qutb-inspired Islamist organisations, nor the non-violent position advocated by al-Banna-oriented groups. To conclude, it confined jihad mainly to the internal-local area to defeat an urgent enemy (Israel) without waiting for the evolutionary transformation of society.

Hamas has developed a simple but effective organisational and ideational structure to materialise its declared purposes. Initially, it had only seven founding members, and then it underwent important changes. Currently, it is assumed that Hamas has three important bodies: political, military, and advisory. The supreme body's Advisory Council is entrusted with monitoring and overseeing the other organs' compliance with the general strategies and policies it has been designing. Headed by Hamas' senior and spiritual leader Sheikh Yasin until his assassination, this body involved the leaders from Gaza and the West Bank, the leadership in exile, and prisoners in Israel. Consequently, it can be stated that it has, to some extent, a fragmented structure. Still, this does not pose a major obstacle to Hamas' active and mobile position over Palestine. The Advisory Council is the final decision-maker and has at least 32 members, who are elected by the members of regional councils (Berti, 2013: 87–88). Another important organ is the Political Bureau (al-Maktab al-Siyasi), whose members are also elected by the Advisory Council. The Political Bureau, composed of 10 to 20 people, has been generally conducting Hamas' daily affairs. This body and the Advisory Council have the ultimate authority to establish some specialised committees that carry out social, economic, cultural, and public relations activities (Hroub, 2006: 118).

Political Bureau exile leader Mehaal was forced to change his location under some local and regional pressures. Located initially in Jordan until 1999, Meshaal, the Political Bureau's leader, moved to Syria and then to Qatar in early 2012 due to the Arab Uprisings' negative impact on relations between Hamas and its former-strongest ally, the Bashar al-Assad regime in Syria. This departure was also the first and most serious split in the "axis of resistance (*jabhat al-muqawama*)" composed of Syria, Iran, Hizbullah, and the only Sunni actor, Hamas. As generally stated, this bloc has a revisionist-revolutionary position on Middle Eastern issues. It means they adopt an anti-western and anti-Zionist orientation in their regional policies. Therefore, Meshaal's departure from Syria generated not only domestic but also regional reflections and implications (Mohns and Bank, 2012: 25–35; Beverly Milton-Edwards, 2013: 60–72). However, currently, there are some Iranian and Hizbullah-led attempts to restore the worsened relations between the two former allies (Cafiero, 2019).

Hamas's third and relatively autonomous body is the Izz ad-Din al-Qassam Brigades. Before the emergence of this military wing in 1992, there were some smaller internal jihad groups collecting intelligence from and conducting their earlier violent actions like "knives war" against the enemy (Berti, 2013: 82). Founded in 1986 by Sheikh Yassin, some small armed groups like the Organisation of Jihad and Dawa (Munazzamat al-Jihad wal-da'wa-Majd) oversaw 1carrying out the "jihad now policy" and armed attacks against "the enemies of Allah". As emphasised earlier, the creation of Islamic Centre-led armed groups was also a radical transformation within its non-violent and evolutionary position towards Israel (Mishal and Sela, 2000: 34–37). It also proves that Islamic Centre leaders decided to establish some military and intelligence battalions before the unexpected Gaza Intifada and the emergence of Hamas. However, these intelligence and military wings amalgamated after the foundation of Hamas' military wing, Izz ad-Din al-Qassam Brigades, whose activities are mainly led and controlled by the Political Bureau (Berti, 2013: 88–89; Knudsen, 2005: 1378).

The Palestinian Islamist armed group Hamas not only changed its organisational structure but also its ideological position over time. The first important change was its participation in municipal and national legislative elections in 2004 and 2006, in which it previously refused to take part

(Berti, 2013: 95–126). Subsequently, Hamas gained a landslide victory, and current Hamas leader Haniya became the Palestine Authority's (PA) Prime Minister. The second and much more essential transformation came on May 1, 2017, with the declaration of the new *Mithaq* by Meshaal in Doha (BBC News, 2017). Despite its unwavering commitment to several ideological pillars, Hamas substantially modified its discourse to reinforce its justifications for the struggle against the "Zionist enemy." Encouraged by states like Qatar and Turkey, Hamas acknowledged the foundation of the Palestinian state on the internationally supported 1967 borders, despite its longstanding emphasis on historical Palestinian borders. Another important change in Mithaq is its alleged divergence from MB. As is known, in its first charter, Hamas declared itself the wing of the MB in Palestine. While it keeps conceding its ideological affinity with this group, there is no hint of its organisational loyalty or allegiance to MB, as strongly highlighted in its first charter.

Defining itself as a Palestinian Islamist resistance movement rather than an arm of MB, Hamas is believed to be trying to amend the strained relations with anti-MB and counter-revolutionary (status quo) states, which are composed of rich Gulf States (except Qatar) and Egypt (Ulutas and Salaymeh, 2017). It also removed heavily criticised and religiously referenced anti-Jewish discourse and, instead, prioritised a more logical anti-Zionist emphasis in its 42-item paper. By avoiding using Quranic verses (Ayat) in its justification of the armed struggle against Israel's occupation, Hamas portrayed a more pragmatic and conciliatory posture without waiving its long-designed purposes. In fact, such transformations and radical changes within its discourse and policies are the results of the changing domestic and, especially, regional landscape. The MB was the most powerful and effective organisation at the beginning of the Arab uprisings. However, it lost its initial power following an anti-MB military coup in Egypt and ensuing attempts by status quo countries to declare MB a "terrorist organisation" (Hedges and Cafiero, 2017 129–151). Already having lost its strongest ally due to its convergence with opposition groups in Syria, Hamas worried about possible regional isolation, which has only one access point to the world through the Egypt-controlled Rafah border. Consequently, considering the anti-MB bloc's concerns, the Qatar-Turkey bloc's modest position, and internal challenges, Hamas is forced to replace its first 36-item, Ayat-based paper with a newly formulated text that is seen as more responsive to shifting realities within the Middle Eastern region (Hroub, 2017: 105–110).

THE FOUNDATION OF THE IZZ AD-DIN AL-QASSAM BRIGADES

Hamas declared the existence of its military wing, named Izz ad-Din al-Qassam Brigades, in 1992. But the official foundation date of the organisation is controversial. In its formal website, the organisation states that it was founded *"in the midst of the Palestinian Intifada (1987–1994)"* and became known as the military wing of Hamas in the middle of 1991. (Ezzedeen Al-Qassam Brigades, Website)

As mentioned earlier, even though Hamas adopted the jihad understanding and was created as a resistance movement, the founders did not establish a direct military organisation. Instead, as underscored before, there were several different armed groups affiliated with Hamas, such as *al-Mujahidun al-Falastiniyun, Abdullah Azzam Brigades,* and *Majd* (Ashour, 2010: 168). Due to the lack of finance and equipment and the fear of drawing attention to the newly established organisation, these groups consciously did not commit important attacks (Hroub, 2000: 243). Moreover, these groups were too weak and not well organised (Ashour, 2010: 168). Later in the process of the first Intifada, the al-Mujahidun group was turned into the Izz ad-Din al-Qassam Brigades. Due to harsh pressure from the Israeli government, Sheikh Yassin was very careful to create a direct link between the newly-born Hamas and those armed groups; therefore, from the beginning, there emerged a political body and a military body seemingly separate from each other (Jefferis, 2016: 109).

The organisation was named after a well-known Syrian warrior. Izz ad-Din al-Qassam was born in 1882 in Syria and got his religious education at Al-Azhar University in Egypt. After university, he returned to Syria and joined the resistance movement against France in the 1920s. Because of French pressure, he had to flee to Palestine. As a *kadi* in the religious court, he became popular. He organised jihadist cells against British rule and Jewish settlers. In 1935, he and his followers were trapped by British forces, and many of them, including al-Qassam, were killed. The killing of al-Qassam, who was known as one of the earliest leaders of the Palestinian resistance, created huge sorrow among the Palestinian people, and his memory became a national resistance symbol (Chehab, 2007: 41). Hamas' leaders deliberately named the organisation after him because al-Qassam represents Islam, nationalism, and resistance, which are Hamas' essentials. Also, by tying themselves to one of the earliest resistance symbols, Hamas tried to demonstrate that they had older roots than the Fatah, which would give them a physiological advantage over their most powerful rival (Jefferis, 2016; p. 108).

The founding leader of the organisation was Sheikh Shehada, who was one of the important founders of Hamas in 1987. Sheikh Shehada, who was born in Gaza in 1952, had joined the Muslim Brothers during his university days in Alexandria. (Ashour, 2010: 170). After the university, he worked in social services both in Egypt and Gaza. While in Gaza, he had ties with Sheikh Yasin and was arrested in 1984 on the accusation of terrorist activities. After two years of imprisonment, he joined the process of establishing Hamas with Sheikh Yassin. In an interview, he narrated those days as follows:

> About the military branch, there was a simple military branch for the Muslim Brotherhood in the Gaza Strip. It was not complex as was the status of the movement back then. My relationship with the military branch was in towards the end of 1983 and till my detention on 26 June 1984. After I came out of prison in 1986, I met Sheikh Ahmad Yassin and we agreed to rebuild the military branch under the name "Al-Mujahidoon Al-Filistiniyoon." This apparatus continued till 1989; while I was imprisoned on 18 August 1988. Afterwards, the military branch developed under the guidance of Allah Almighty then the sincere efforts of Hamas' sons.

Even though Sheikh Sheheda is known as the founder and natural leader of al-Qassam, his days with the organisation were limited since, after 1988, he got arrested again with the accusation of being one of the Hamas leaders and sentenced to 10 years. He got out of prison in 2000, and a few years later, in 2002, he was killed in an Israeli assault. He was accused of commanding the organisation from prison (interview with Shiekh Salah Shehada).

AL-QASSAM STRUCTURE AND THE LEADERSHIP

Al-Qassam Brigades is one of the main power centres, along with the political apparatus within the Hamas structure. (Ashour, 2010: 178). In the first years of Hamas, the military domain and military action were seen as the focus of the organisation. The political domain and actions were only important as much as they helped strengthen military actions. But throughout time, with gaining power and becoming an important player in Palestinian politics, the military domain and action lose their power over the whole organisation. (Hroub, 2000: 243). In several interviews, Sheikh Sheheda explained that the brigades are organised as an army and bond with the political apparatus. Also, he mentioned that the political apparatus only guided the brigades rather than giving direct orders. Moreover, in military issues, the brigades are seen as independent from the political apparatus domain (Interview with Shiekh Salah Shehada).

Even though both political and military domains respected and did not question the leadership of Sheikh Yassin (Jefferis, 2016: 111), there has always been tension within the Hamas structure. For example, even though in their 1988 declaration Hamas stated that they would continue to resist until all of Palestine was liberated, in 1999, with the weakening of Hamas, Sheikh Yassin offered a ten-year *hudna* (ceasefire) in return for Israel's withdrawal to the 1967 borders. After that time, Hamas leadership changed its stance against Israel and accepted its existence. This radical change and Hamas' success in electoral processes enriched Hamas' resistance methods and decreased trust in violent means. For that reason, there emerged a significant divide between the political wing that supports non-violent methods and the two-state solution and the military wing (mainly the al-Qassam Brigades) that insists upon using violent methods and liberating the whole of Palestine from foreign invasion. When looking at its current leader, Mohammed Deif, who has held the post since 2002, According to Israeli resources, Deif, who is on the most wanted list of Israeli security forces, has played a huge role in the development of Qassam rockets and is responsible for the rocket strategy of the organisation (https://www.counterextremism.com/extremists/mohammed-deif). The military council is the main executive organ of the organisation. Along with all kinds of divisions of a regular army, it also consists of scientific, cultural, educational, and counter-terrorism units (Ashour, 2010: 171–179).

AL-QASSAM'S STRATEGIES

As mentioned in Hamas's 1988 Charter, for the organisation, jihad has been the major method of accomplishing its goals. For that reason, from the beginning, the notion of resistance and using force was the rationale behind the existence of the organisation. Throughout the history of Hamas and the al-Qassam Brigades, it has been evident that the violent methods conducted by the organisation have gone through an evolution process. While in the founding years, the organisation waged a "war of knives" with only primitive means such as knives or fake guns, nowadays, after almost 30 years, the organisation has reached the capacity to construct its own rockets. Besides the technological development, the organisation managed to transform itself from a covert, non-permanent, and undisciplined activity cell into an overt, permanent, and disciplined army.

Even though Hamas and its military wing, al-Qassam, never renounced or abandoned violent means, since the beginning of the organisation, they have always been very cautious about the use of these means. First, as mentioned in the 1988 Charter, the primary goal of the organisation is to liberate Palestinian soil. For that reason, the organisation has never attempted an attack outside of Palestine. Secondly, in the first years of the organisation, the members had never committed attacks against civilian targets. Al-Qassam Brigades' main target was always Israel's military personnel. This changed with the Hebron massacre in 1994, when an Israeli soldier killed 29 innocent Palestinians in

Hebron. After that massacre, from time to time, the organisation committed attacks on civilians either directly or indirectly. Another important principle that Hamas and al-Qassam follow is the justification of violent attacks. As a way of gaining domestic and international sympathy, all violent attacks come after violent movements in Israel. The organisation is very cautious about representing its actions not as arbitrary attacks but as retaliation for and revenge for Israeli violence. Also, even though it is a fundamental method for the organisation, the Hamas and al-Qassam leadership do not count on only violent means, and from time to time they argue against giving it up. Lastly, the organisation has a huge struggle against the "terrorist" label given by especially Westerners and tries to demonstrate that their way of armed resistance is suitable to all kinds of laws, both divine and humane (Hroub, 2000: 246–250).

Due to the obstacles in accessing violent means (such as guns and bombs) and recruiting suitable militants, there was almost never an armed attack in the first years of Hamas. For example, in the initial years of the first Intifada, there was massive participation, and protesters, including Hamas members, used only civilian actions such as mass demonstrations, throwing stones, or burning tyres (Hroub, 2000: 242–243). In the first two years of the Intifada, there were only 42 official attacks employed by Hamas members (Jefferis, 2016: 109). The third year of the Intifada was a turning point for Hamas because, with the decrease in massive support for the Intifada, Hamas began to use violent tools to increase the impact of the Intifada. The foundation of the al-Qassam Brigades was effective in that transition. With the help of that permanent armed organisation, violent means became the only method that was used by Hamas, especially between 1992 and 2006 (Hroub, 2000: 242–244).

Al-Qassam forces attempted many attacks during the 1990s. As mentioned before, initially the members of the organisation had problems supplying weapons for their activities. Indeed, they had only fake guns and knives. For that reason, during this period of the "war of knives" (Jefferis, 2016: 108), the first attacks of the organisation were aimed at both killing targets and capturing their weapons. For example, the first targets of the organisation were Yahya Al-Ahwal and Mustapha Al Mashlouh, both of whom were collaborators with the Israelis and well-guarded by them (Chehab, 2007: 43). These attempts made the organisation visible to the Israeli forces and to the Palestinian community. While Israeli forces increased the frequency of their countermeasures against the organisation, such as arresting the top leaders of the organisation, including Sheikh Shehada, the organisation's visibility made it easier to recruit new members and to reach more equipment. In the meantime, despite the harsh pressure from Israeli forces, the organisation managed to enlarge its membership cycle and attack capacity. For example, with the help of some new members, such as Yehia Ayyash, who had engineering education, the organisation was able to produce home-made bombs (Chehab, 2007: 54–57), and that opened the way for suicide bombing, which made the organisation much more dangerous and effective.

Ayyash organised al-Qassam's first suicide bomb attack in 1994, after the Hebron massacre. Raed Zakarneh exploded a bomb near a bus stop and killed eight Israelis by himself (Chehab, 2007: 56). After that, suicide bombing became the most brutal method of the organisation and was used many times throughout its history. However, due to harsh measures taken by both the Israeli government and the Palestine Authority, al-Qassam had to decrease the number of its violent attacks, including suicide bombings, and change its strategies. For example, in an anonymous article in Filistan Al-Muslimah,[2] it was argued that the organisation's groups should organise attacks independently, which gave them the autonomy to act without counselling the central authority (Karmon, 2000: 66–67). For these reasons, towards the end of the 1990s, the organisation's activities decreased significantly.

While the first Intifada caused the creation of the organisation, the second Intifada opened the way for its revival. The collapse of the peace talks between Israel and the Palestinian Authority and Ariel Sharon's visit to the Temple Mount increased hatred among Palestinians, and the Second Intifada began. During the Second Intifada, the organisation engaged in over 700 attacks in four years, much more than since its foundation (Ashour, 2010: 170–171). Al-Qassam's brutal and effective attacks during the Second Intifada made Hamas, in general, the most popular resistance movement among Palestinians. This push opened the way for Hamas' rise in Palestinian politics, and the 2006 election victory was not a big surprise. After rising politically, Hamas became a prominent actor in the Palestinian issue, which created competition with other actors in the region. Since the 1993 Oslo Agreement gave all the responsibilities for violent actions in Palestine to Fatah, the newly born Hamas, as a violent actor, became a natural target for it (Hroub, 2000: 244). The competition between Fatah and Hamas became harsh after the electoral victory of Hamas in 2006, which led to the Gaza War in 2007. Al-Qassam brigades were successful in winning the war and pushing Fatah out of Gaza. (Ashour, 2010: 171).

With the emergence of Hamas as a powerful political actor in Palestinian politics, the al-Qassam Brigades gained a new identity. Especially after the establishment of the first Hamas government, the al-Qassam Brigades, which was known as a militant organisation, became the legal security forces of the current political authority (Jefferis, 2016: 114–115). After that time, the al-Qassam brigades provided all security services, including policing in local areas, border patrol, etc., on the one hand, and continued their resistance activities against the Israeli forces on the other. Meanwhile, the organisation increased its military technology and capacity. In their arsenal, they had rockets sponsored by Iran. Moreover, they could also produce their own rockets, named Qassam rockets. With these rockets, al-Qassam's war with Israeli forces entered a new phase. Rather than committing suicide bombing, which was the main and most effective method of the organisation for a long time, they began to send rockets to the Israeli territories, especially from the Gaza region, which was totally under the control of Hamas. Even though many rockets did not reach their targets successfully for technical reasons (especially the Qassam rockets were not technologically developed enough), "the war of rockets" created a huge fear in the Israeli population and the same level of anger among the Israeli authorities (Jefferis, 2016: 117–120).

CONCLUSION

Hamas and its military wing, al-Qassam, have strong ideological and historical roots that can be traced back to the beginning of the 20th century. Hamas, one of the MB-affiliated groups in Palestine, was founded in 1987 as a tactical response to the ongoing Gaza-based Intifada. However, it became the most influential resistance movement with its extensive social networks and growing military power. Undergoing substantial transformations over time, Hamas also gained political power following its decision to participate in local and national elections in 2005 and 2006. However, its military presence and associated activities have always prompted controversial debates within Palestinian territory. Despite its undisputed importance to the consolidation of Hamas' power over Palestine, al-Qassam's military presence and especially suicide attacks are presented as the main obstacles to both Israel-Palestinian and Hamas-PLO reconciliation negotiations. On the other hand, while Hamas modified and softened its earlier radical approach with its new charter, it never endorsed any deal based on disarmament. Even its political transformation, which resulted in its participation in the elections, did not bring about such a result. From its perspective, its military power and, accordingly, armed resistance will be there until Israel's occupation ends and Palestinian lands are liberated. To conclude, by refusing any call for disarmament, the al-Qassam Brigades have been maintaining their effective violent attacks against Israel and trying to develop and advance their military arsenal.

Notes

1 This term embodies the virtues of the Muslim Brotherhood's (Al-Ikhwan al-Muslimin-MB) slogan: Rights!, Force!, and Freedom!" Zaki Chehab, *Inside Hamas: The Untold Story of Militants, Martyrs, and Spies*, IB Tauris, New York, 2007, p. 23.

2 Filistan Al-Muslimah is known as the monthly periodical magazine of Hamas.

References

Abu-Amr, Z. (1993). Hamas: A historical and political background. *Journal of Palestine Studies, 22*(4), 5–19.

Ashour, O. (2010). Hamas and the prospects of de-radicalization. In K. Mulaj (Ed.), *Violent non-state actors in contemporary world politics* (pp. 157–180). New York: Columbia University Press.

Ayhan, V. (July, 2009). HAMAS: Filistin Direnişinde Politik İslam (Eng. HAMAS: Politic Islam in Palestinian Resistance). *Journal of Middle Eastern Studies, 1*(1), 99–134.

Berti, B. (2013). *Armed political organizations: From conflict to integration*. Baltimore: JHU Press.

Cafiero, G. (2019). Will Iran and Hezbollah Restore the Syria-Hamas Alliance? *Inside Arabia*, 14 February.

Chehab, Z. (2007). *Inside Hamas: The untold story of militants, martyrs and spies*. New York: IB Tauris.

Ezzedeen Al-Qassam Brigades Information Office. Available at: http://www.qassam.ps/.

Gonim, A. (2017). 14 things to know about Hamas' new leader, Ismail Haniya. *TRT World*, 06 May.

"Hamas chooses Ismail Haniya as new leader", BBC News, 6 May 2017. https://www.bbc.com/news/world-middle-east-39830253

Hedges, M.J., & Cafiero, G. (2017). The GCC and the Muslim brotherhood: What does the future hold? *Middle East Policy, 24*(1), 129–153.

"How much of a shift is the new Hamas policy document?" BBC News, 2 May 2017. https://www.bbc.com/news/world-middle-east-39775103

Hroub, K. (2000). *Hamas: Political thought and practice*. Washington, DC: Institute for Palestinian Studies.

Hroub, K. (2004). Hamas after Shaykh Yasin and Rantisi. *Journal of Palestine Studies, 33*(4), 21–38.

Hroub, K. (2006). A 'New HAMAS' through its new documents. *Journal of Palestine Studies, 35*(4), 6–27.

Hroub, K. (2017). A Newer Hamas? The revised charter. *Journal of Palestine Studies, 46*(4), 100–111.

Interview with Shiekh Salah Shehada. Available at: https://www.qassam.ps/specialfile-251-An_Interviews_with_shiekh_Salah_Shehada_2.html).

Jefferis, J. (2016). *Hamas: Terrorism, governance and its future in Middle East politics*. California: Praeger.

Karmon, E. (2000). Hamas terrorism strategy: Operational limitations and political constraints. *Middle East Review of International Affairs, 4*(1), 66–79.

Knudsen, A. (December, 2005). Crescent and sword: The HAMAS enigma. *Third World Quarterly, 26*(8), 1373–1388.

Maqdsi, M. (1993). Charter of the Islamic resistance movement (Hamas) of Palestine. *Journal of Palestine Studies, 22*(4), 122–134.

Milton-Edwards, B. (2013). Hamas and the Arab Spring: Strategic shifts? *Middle East Policy, 20*(3), 60–72.

Mishal, S., & Sela, A. (2000). *The Palestinian Hamas, vision, violence, and coexistence*. New York: Columbia University Press.

Mohns, E., & Bank, A. (2012). Syrian revolt fallout: End of the resistance axis? *Middle East Policy Council, 19*(3), 25–35.

Ulutas, U., & Salaymeh, B. (2017). Hamas'ın Yeni Siyaset Belgesi (Eng. The New Political Document of Hamas). *SETA Perspective, 173*, 1–5.https://setav.org/assets/uploads/2017/05/173_Prspektif.pdf

55

JAISH AL-MAHDI (THE MAHDI ARMY)

Pascal Carlucci

INTRODUCTION

Jaysh al Mahdi (JAM, or Mahdi Army) is an Iraqi militia under the political and religious leadership of Moqtada al Sadr, heir of a Shi'a political dynasty (Cockburn, 2003). The birth and evolution of JAM narrate the story of politics and warfare in Iraq during the post-Saddam period. Its political and spiritual leadership has shown mastery in the use of force during Iraq's US occupation and has used it to maintain a solid footing in domestic power-sharing (Anthony Cordesman, 2008). This chapter aims to analyse this violent political group's key characteristics and outline its essence to understand future developments of both the Moqtada Al Sadr brand of politics and the enduring drivers of political violence by Shi'a groups in Iraq.

The existence of JAM could only have begun and developed in post-Saddam Iraq. Its characteristics are unique to that particular time and space and cannot be replicated elsewhere, even with different undertones. The lifespan and development of this organisation evolve around its leader, and every historical fact is intimately connected to his political ambitions. However, the essence of JAM can lead to interesting reflections on the power of militias, patronage, and power vacuums in conflict societies. This is why JAM's political and military history can be of interest to anyone seeking to understand the Iraqi political system and how the use of force can be honed to great political advantage and power multiplier.

JAM has undergone several internal changes throughout its intermittent history to fit the political objectives of the moment. Recently, it has rebranded itself as a fighting force against ISIL (El Ghobashy & Salim, 2018). However, there is little evidence of the weight of this contribution to military successes in Iraq. Its future lies more in how its leader will interpret local and regional political realities and place this organisation between the fault lines of the Middle East. Moreover, Moqtada al-Sadr has displayed an acute sense of embracing popular instances within the Iraqi populace to build his political profile. No one can verify whether these political positions are genuine or part of a populist strategy to gain consensus within a political system, which has belittled his importance and experience (Rahimi, 2009).

The chapter analyses the historical evolution, the resources, and the characteristics of JAM with careful consideration of how this group has followed the domestic and regional trajectory of Iraqi politics and how it could build, or to some extent, improvise, ways to be influential. The literature and materials consulted provide clear information on this organisation's essence and why certain aspects of its structure and modus operandi remain shrouded in mystery.

OVERVIEW

JAM is a relatively new actor in Iraqi history, emerging clearly from the security vacuum in the days after the start of the US occupation (Bayless, 2012). Since its inception, the evolution of the group has been intimately intertwined with the Iraqi political and security situation. The enduring factor during its 17 years of intermittent existence has been the constant search for space and influence in an extremely delicate, yet violent, political landscape. JAM is a Shi'a political group that has followed a completely different path from other political factions of that same religious group with the aim of carving out an independent foothold in the power dynamics of the country (Thurber, 2014). Therefore, an analysis of the evolution of this violent group contributes to a greater extent to its understanding than a review of ideological and spiritual elements, which have a lesser influence on its operations and organisations than other militant groups. The degree of pragmatism appears to be more similar to that of a criminal organisation than an insurgency. This paragraph analyses the different evolutionary stages with a link to the strategic and tactical imperatives faced by its leader, Moqtada Al Sadr.

Sadiq Al-Sadr (Sadr II) was a significant Shi'a political figure in Iraqi politics during Saddam Hussein's Baathist regime (Taha, 2019). Sadr II became powerful by having a

DOI: 10.4324/9780429426063-62

network of charities and by providing the "oppressed majority" with spiritual and political leadership (Bruno, 2008). His political acuteness came from understanding how to be influential in a dictatorship that was hostile to forms of expression outside of the Baath movement. After the Gulf War, Saqiq Sadr managed to attract poor Shiites from the south of Iraq to Sadr City (Taha, 2019). This area of Baghdad became almost a "ghetto" and an area from which the Sadr family built a future (Welsh, 2004). Given that the Shiite population, especially after the 1991 Iraq War, was prone to rebellion, Saddam Hussein outsourced the control of this disenfranchised urban area to Sadr II (Cockburn, 2003). This approach would prove to be, in later years, a recurring strategy. Sadrism, a form of ideology stemming from this experience, is characterised by a staunch Iraqi nationalism with roots in popular slums rather than mosques and theological universities. According to the literature consulted, there is an absence of a discernible religious message in sadrism. Sadiq Al Sadr was killed in suspicious circumstances in 1999 (Cockburn, 1999). His son, Moqtada, took over his role at a very young age and with an image to build. He was called "Mullah Atari" for his passion for video games (Al Jazeera, 2010).

The Mahdi Army, or Jaysh al Mahdi (JAM), first appeared in the aftermath of the US invasion of Iraq in 2003. Moqtada al-Sadr invited his Shiite followers to join his militia and fight to drive out the Americans from Iraq and establish a Shiite government in the country (Phil Williams & Bisbee, 2014). The spectrum of armed groups in Iraq was extremely complex in the first year of US occupation, but JAM has always been described in official reports and news as "militia" rather than "insurgent" or terrorist. Given the tactics used by the group, which will be analysed in the next paragraph, this is a very fine line. A militia is an armed group that stems from a popular need to fight an enemy in the absence of a standing army (Thurber, 2014; Hughes, 2016). Jam had firm roots in Sadr City, Najaf, and Basra, but with no clear number of fighters. The critical issue of describing JAM as a militia resides in the determination of how voluntarily people in these areas sought their protection rather than government security forces. The Mahdi Army was involved in rackets and intimidation, which raises doubts over its real legitimacy and therefore its status as a "militia." If protection is imposed by violence and intimidation and there is an economic interest, then JAM can be defined as a mafia-style network.

The period between 2004 and 2006 has been characterised by the use of force and the penetration of administrative positions in government. In April 2004, JAM clashed with coalition forces in Najaf, where they managed to take control of that city and Kut. The following month they negotiated a ceasefire, raising, therefore, their political profile (Anthony Cordesman, 2008). The size of the militia, never really confirmed, allowed JAM to gain spaces in Iraq's political spectrum by joining forces with the Dawa Party and other Shiites during the 2005 election won by Nour Al Maliki (van Veen & Grinstead, 2017). Moqtada al-Sadr knew that his support was vital for the Iraqi Union Alliance, and he managed to back candidates, but with the careful approach of never taking any government appointment. This allowed him to take creative political positions without having the responsibility to deliver results. The Mahdi Army was involved in US citizens' kidnappings, which ended after negotiation, and several Iraqi police attacks (CISAC, 2019). The violent activities against government forces displayed a deteriorating relationship between Moqtada al-Sadr and Nour al-Maliki. It also showed how JAM wanted to claim an independent profile from other Shiite groups like Badr (more closely linked with Iran). Given the statistics of attacks against coalition forces during the period 2004–2006 and the actual attacks carried out by JAM, one can see how Moqtada Al Sadr was able to gain political traction with selected violent actions rather than volume (CISAC, 2019). Moreover, his political power tended to derive more from his control over populations than from direct confrontation with coalition forces.

Confronting government forces in Iraq was a way for Moqtada Al-Sadr to prove his leadership and gain political leverage.

2007 was characterised by several attacks against government officials and Iraqi Security Forces (CISAC, 2019). JAM had intensified its activities, mainly as a result of the surge in capabilities at ISF. Militias and legitimate government forces cannot operate side-by-side because, unless there is a political agreement, they compete over legitimacy and consensus over a certain population. Jam could only count in such an unstable environment if it could demonstrate itself to be feared. This is shown by the Madhi Army's willingness to negotiate the release of the people kidnapped, while other violent groups had killed prisoners (Oliver, 2004). A critical aspect of JAM's violence has been its accusation of being a "death squad," launching ethnically inspired attacks against Sunnis (Cerny, 2006). In June 2007, the Mahdi Army launched a series of attacks against Sunnis in Baghdad (CISAC, 2019). The period of the surge was critical for Al-Sadr's militia because it was confronted directly by the ISF. However, damaged by the surge, Moqtada Al Sadr managed to negotiate a ceasefire agreement with the ISF in 2008, reiterating his ability to gain from defeats (Cochrane, 2009). The same year he founded the Mumahidoon, which divided JAM into civilian followers in charge of social care and political activities and the "Special Companies" in charge of military operations (Anthony Cordesman, 2008).

After the ceasefire, Moqtada al-Sadr went on a retreat to Iran, virtually disappearing from mainstream Iraqi politics (Knights, 2011). The withdrawal of US troops from Iraq and the relative consolidation of national authorities left fewer chances for violent actions. Sadr focused on the elections of 2010 to become an essential component of the Iraqi National Alliance (Twfeeq et al., 2010). His relationship with Nour al-Maliki was characterised by periods of cooperation and periods of antagonism. Antagonism ultimately prevailed, despite efforts by Iran to mediate between Shiite leaders.

The rise of ISIS in Syria and ISIL in Iraq gave Moqtada al-Sadr a new chance to orient his militia towards a new political goal that would again place him in a relatively powerful position. The creation of the Popular Mobilisation Force (an auxiliary army created to support the Iraqi government in the fight against ISIL) allowed Moqtada al-Sadr to establish the Peace Companies, which would participate in military operations (EASO, 2019). While his forces were fighting against the Caliphate, Al Sadr managed cleverly to position himself as an interlocutor with Saudi Arabia while not breaking off ties with Iran (Al Arabiya, 2017). This displayed his political acuteness, exploiting the Saudi-Iranian rivalry in his favour and understanding the tendency of Crown Prince Mohammed Bin Salman to make unorthodox decisions. The recent alliance with Iraqi communists further demonstrates the ideological flexibility of Sadrism to continue to build a broader consensus, even with improbable partners.

The evolution of JAM is intimately linked with the recent history of Iraq and with the personality of its leader, Moqtada al-Sadr. Because of this uniqueness, it is difficult to find other armed groups in the world that resemble this militia's abilities. Some similarities with Hizbollah were drawn, but Iraq's recent conflict does not compare with Lebanese politics. From the different phases of its history, one can see how JAM has exploited every political and security phase to its advantage by making sure that its support or "quiteness" was appropriately rewarded. Moqtada al-Sadr has shown the ability to maintain a central role in Shiite politics by establishing relations with Saudi Arabia and maintaining a link with Iran without acting as a proxy. Moreover, compared to others, Al Sadr could claim that his leadership originated during Saddam Hussein's rule, while other political leaders were living abroad. However, the definition of JAM as a militia remains problematic, given its criminal activities and suspicions of ethnically inspired violence.

KEY PERSONNEL AND STRUCTURE

JAM is an Iraqi militia under the political and religious leadership of Moqtada Al Sadr. This violent group draws attention to specific aspects of security governance in failed states and counterinsurgency. Very little is known about its structure compared to other organisations, but a careful examination of the group's history suggests that this ambiguity has been a decisive factor in its leadership's overall strategy. JAM's main asset has been its leader and how he has interpreted this militia's role during different phases of recent Iraqi history. This paragraph analyses the essence of JAM's leadership and will seek to encapsulate its enduring features.

Moqtada Al Sadr has been the leader of JAM since its genesis in 2003. The militia has followed his evolution as a political leader. The first phase as a localised force in Sadr City, Najaf, and Basra originates from the tenets of the Sadrist movement, a populist movement for poor Shiites, and has slowly evolved into a complex organisation that fits Al Sadr's goals (Cochrane, 2009). The strategy of Moqtada al-Sadr has been to use the militia and the support of his supporters to always be at the centre of the political and security landscape. Carl von Clausewitz said that "war is the continuation of policy by other means." Al Sadr was able to clash, retreat, and negotiate to great advantage. The literature consulted does not suggest that his leadership overused force; rather, it suggests the opposite.

Moreover, JAM's operations were always targeted to support his leader's political ambitions, especially prior to the elections. The other Shiite groups always sought to mediate, although reluctantly, with JAM to guarantee their electoral support. For Moqtada Al Sadr, the use of force has always been the guarantee of his political survival rather than his core business. His belief, originating from the early days of sadrism, has been to maximise a certain population's control with his militia to gain political advantages (Thurber, 2014). His militia also created a patronage network that was able to infiltrate Iraqi public institutions (Phil Williams, 2014). Carrying the weight of responsibility for administrative and political roles has never been a priority for Al Sadr. He continues to design strategies that take into consideration the current "Cold War" between Saudi Arabia and Iran by having links with both and therefore expressing the need for an "Iraqi" rather than a "proxy" approach to the political situation.

The structure of JAM has been shrouded in relative mystery since its inception. The militia was mostly comprised of young men, either with no training or military training received in Lebanon. Some of the members were also initially recruited in Saudi Arabia and Kuwait. Recruits believed they would liberate Iraq from the US invasion. The total number of fighters in the militia has different estimates, spanning from 10,000 to 60,000 (CISAC, 2019). This might have been caused by the lack of distinction between followers and members in militant operations. In 2008, when Moqtada Al Sadr created the Mumahidoon (civilian care wing) and the Promised Day Brigades (military wing), this distinction became clearer (Cordesman & Ramos, 2008). This division had created the alibi that JAM was not only a militia but a political force. The military wing was re-branded to join the Popular Mobilisation Force by using the name "Peace Companies" (Al Saraya Al Salam).

The Peace Companies and the Promised Day Brigades have used AK-47 assault rifles, grenades, RPGs, sniper rifles, and light machine guns. These are weapons that can carry out daily security duties and escorts or escalate to armed attacks against armed forces and other rival groups. The militia has used IED (improvised explosive devices), EFP (explosively formed projectile), and IRAM (improvised rocket-assisted mortar) (Cordesman & Ramos, 2008). These devices can be used to strike significant enemy targets and require training and technical skills. It is also an indication that, although the group is not listed as a terrorist organisation in the US or EU, it has used terrorist tactics.

The fluidity in the structure of JAM and the lack of any other leaders than Moqtad Al Sadr demonstrate how this organisation has been moulded around the political objectives of the moment rather than reflecting an ideology or the division of competing orientations. JAM moved from being an urban militia to a full-fledged fighting force against ISIL. It conducted criminal activities and protection rackets as well as high-profile attacks against coalition forces and the ISF. This reflects a great degree of flexibility, which may continue in the future.

ORGANISATIONAL CHARACTERISTICS

JAM has been widely defined as a militia with the characteristics typical of this specific activity. However, this group's variety of activities suggests that this organisation is complex because it follows its leadership direction and adapts to Iraq's political and security context. As previously mentioned, JAM has evolved from being a militia that exploited the security vacuum in the immediate aftermath of the fall of Saddam Hussein into a complex security force able to respond to strategic and tactical challenges quickly. The unifying thread among these characteristics remains leadership.

Unlike other insurgent and terrorist groups, JAM had a very limited geographical scope, limiting its activities only to certain areas of Iraq. This has greatly affected the group's strategic approach, which has never really developed any capabilities to conduct operations or recruitment beyond its borders. As a militia, it has created a force to control urban areas and fight against the ISF and coalition forces. Jam's most famous clashes tend to use force to arrive at a negotiated agreement at the end of hostilities. This was reflected in the attacks carried out in 2004 (CISAC, 2019). During the uprising in April 2004 in Najaf, Kut, Kufa, and Sadr City, JAM attacked and besieged police stations, staged protests, and had sporadic clashes with government forces. The uprising ended in June 2004 with a negotiated agreement between Moqtada Al Sadr and coalition forces, which paved the way for JAM involvement in the 2005 national elections (Cochrane, 2009). Jam uses violence not to seek the enemy's defeat but rather to force him to concede advantageous political deals. This blueprint has been followed in Najaf's battles in 2004, Amarah in 2006, Basra, and the Siege of Sadr City in 2008 (CISAC, 2019). All these big clashes ended with a military defeat of the militia but allowed negotiation with coalition forces, reinforcing its power.

The Mahdi Army has an antagonistic relationship with Al Qaeda and the Islamic State, leading to its deployment as a fighting force among the PMF (Roggio, 2015). The most interesting aspect is its relationship with other Shiite groups like the Dawa Party and the Badr Organisation (van Veen & Grinstead, 2017). Moqtada al-Sadr has used JAM activities to seek respect and consideration from other Shiite political organisations. Jam and Badr have clashed several times in previous years, yet, despite being quite sectarian, the Shiite political archipelago has somehow managed to remain aligned. This could be due to the rise of ISIL, a common enemy. The main difference between JAM and other Shiite groups is their relative autonomy from Iran. While having received training from the IRGC and funds from religious leaders, JAM has conducted a nationalist policy that rejects Iran's proxy.

JAM has conducted criminal activities to consolidate its power over the territory it controls. These activities include protection rackets, robberies, murder, rapes, and kidnappings (Cordesman & Ramos, 2008). This had partially alienated the local consensus. However, the same group demonstrated that it was a service provider to local populations when there were no government institutions in Iraq (Thurber, 2014). Criminal activities include patronage activities connected to elected politicians and members of public institutions.

The territory has been a key resource for JAM, and it has been used with great political astuteness. Sadr City, a poor Shiite neighbourhood in Baghdad, has been the pivot of the group's political and military power. By establishing tight control over this area, Moqtada al-Sadr has been able to leverage political gains. The presence of JAM in Basra had generated concern in Baghdad because it meant that Moqtada Al Sadr was controlling a critical part of the country with access to the Gulf and oil fields (an essential source of economic revenue for the government) (Cordesman & Ramos, 2008).

The mastery of strategy, tactics, opponents, territory, and crime have been defining aspects of JAM in recent history. These aspects contribute to a more flexible definition of JAM, which, in light of these considerations, must be considered something more complex than a simple militia. The capabilities acquired during the protracted period of violent conflict in Iraq give this group the possibility of being an essential piece on the Iraqi chessboard.

IMPACT

JAM has mostly contributed to Shiite politics in Iraq by containing Al Qaeda and ISIL and indirectly creating an alternative political space between Shiites and Sunnis. His nationalist and populist tendencies have resonated with many young Iraqis because, according to them, Al Sadr was a product of the oppression under Saddam Hussein and a frontman in the cause of US troops' withdrawal from Iraq. The impact of Moqtada al-Sadr is, therefore, more political than military. Ultimately, there is no record of a major clash won by his forces. However, he always managed to negotiate favourably in every situation, and, more importantly, no agreement ever included the disarmament of his own forces. JAM has not made Iraq a safer place, nor has it contributed to its political and economic development. Its military contribution to the fight against ISIL remains mostly unaccounted for. The only success of this militia has been contributing to the rise of its leader and his ambitions.

CONCLUSION

Sadrism, an ideology that combined Shiite identity, nationalism, and populism, served as the inspiration for Jaysh Al Mahdi, a Shiite militia. Moqtada Al Sadr, the mastermind of this organisation, has managed to use violent activities not to defeat his stated enemies (US troops, ISF, and rival groups), but to increase his power vis-à-vis other political power brokers who emerged during the post-Saddam era. Al Sadr did not indulge in complex theological concepts, nor did he create a complex political structure. Instead, he concentrated on exploiting widespread feelings and stepping in the gaps left by public institutions that were either missing or inefficient. Jam, although claiming to have a nationalist view of politics, did not have a clear idea of what the future of Iraq had to be. Instead, the only political sophistication was understanding the domestic and regional complexities and the short-term initiatives to stay afloat.

The history of JAM may be unsatisfying for those seeking to understand an ideology or investigate a different form of militant jihadism. Instead, JAM gives an idea of how populist leadership with command over militias can become influential power brokers during the chaos and evolve while maintaining its opportunistic, short-sighted, and violent nature. In the future, peace companies are likely to evolve by following the opportunities given by a troubled region. The lack of a clearly defined political ideology and religious belief will be an advantage for this militia's future. The ability of Moqtada al-Sadr to adapt to changing political circumstances cannot be underestimated.

References

Al Arabiya. (2017). *Muqtada al-Sadr visits Saudi Arabia for the first time in 11 years | Al Arabiya English*. https://english.alarabiya.net/en/News/middle-east/2017/07/30/Muqtada-al-Sadr-in-Saudi-Arabia-for-the-first-time-in-11-years-

Al Jazeera. (2010). *Profile: Muqtada al-Sadr*. https://www.aljazeera.com/news/2010/3/7/profile-muqtada-al-sadr-2

Anthony Cordesman. (2008). *Sadr and the Mahdi Army*. Center for Strategic Studies. https://www.csis.org/analysis/sadr-and-mahdi-army

Bayless, L. (2012). Who is Muqtada al-Sadr? *Studies in Conflict & Terrorism*, *35*(2), 135–155. 10.1080/1057610X.2012.639063

Bruno, G. (2008). *Muqtada al-Sadr*. Council on Foreign Relations. https://www.cfr.org/backgrounder/muqtada-al-sadr

Cerny, J. (2006, June). "Death Squad Operations in Iraq," Conflict Studies Research Center. https://www.files.ethz.ch/isn/28873/06_04_Jun_2.pdf

CISAC. (2019). *Mahdi Army*. Mapping Militant Organizations. https://cisac.fsi.stanford.edu/mappingmilitants/profiles/mahdi-army

Cochrane, M. (2009, January). Iraq Report 12: The fragmentation of the Sadrist Movement. Institute for the Study of War, Washington, DC. https://www.understandingwar.org/sites/default/files/Iraq%20Report%2012%20Sadrist%20Movement%20Fragmentation.pdf

Cockburn, A. (1999). *Saddam's agents 'murdered cleric' |The Independent*. The Independent. https://www.independent.co.uk/news/saddams-agents-murdered-cleric-1073272.html

Cockburn, A. (2003). *Iraq's Oppressed Majority*. Smithsonian Magazine. https://www.smithsonianmag.com/history/iraqs-oppressed-majority-95250996/

Cordesman, A. H. , & Ramos, J. (2008). Sadr and the Mahdi Army: Evolution, capabilities, and a new direction. Center for Strategic and International Studies, Washington, DC. https://www.csis.org/analysis/sadr-and-mahdi-army

EASO. (2019). *Popular Mobilisation Units and Tribal Mobilisation Militias [Text]*. EUROPEAN ASYLUM SUPPORT OFFICE. https://www.easo.europa.eu/country-guidance-iraq/12-popular-mobilisation-units-and-tribal-mobilisation-militias

El-Ghobashy, T., & Salim, M. (2018, July 04). Public enemy or savior an-Iraqi City Could Reveal the True Moqtada Al-Sadr. *Washington Post*. https://www.washingtonpost.com/world/public-enemy-or-savior-an-iraqi-city-could-reveal-the-true-moqtada-al-sadr/2018/06/15/f16d031a-6359-11e8-81ca-bb14593acaa6_story.html

Hughes, G. (2016). Militias in internal warfare: From the colonial era to the contemporary Middle East. *Small Wars & Insurgencies*, *27*(2), 196–225. 10.1080/09592318.2015.1129171

Institute for the Study of War. (n.d.). *Jaysh al-Mahdi*. Institute for the Study of War. Retrieved October 23, 2020, from http://www.understandingwar.org/jaysh-al-mahdi

Knights, M. (2011). *Iran in Iraq: The Role of Muqtada al-Sadr*. https://www.washingtoninstitute.org/policy-analysis/view/iran-in-iraq-the-role-of-muqtada-al-sadr

Oliver. (2004, August 13). *Rebels release UK journalist*. The Guardian. http://www.theguardian.com/world/2004/aug/13/iraq.markoliver

Rahimi, B. (2009). The Rise of Ayatollah Moqtada al-Sadr. *Foreign Policy*. https://foreignpolicy.com/2009/07/27/the-rise-of-ayatollah-moqtada-al-sadr/

Roggio, B. (2015, May 3). *Muqtada al Sadr threatens to "unfreeze the military wing," attack US interests | FDD's Long War Journal*. https://www.longwarjournal.org/archives/2015/05/muqtada-al-sadr-threatens-to-unfreeze-the-military-wing-that-deals-with-the-american-entity.php

Salim, M. (2018). *The truth about Iraq's new kingmaker, Moqtada al-Sadr, is revealed in the city of Samarra—The Washington Post*. The Washington Post. https://www.washingtonpost.com/world/public-enemy-or-savior-an-iraqi-city-could-reveal-the-true-moqtada-al-sadr/2018/06/15/f16d031a-6359-11e8-81ca-bb14593acaa6_story.html

Shia militias in Iraq: Strategic Comments: Vol 23, No 3. (n.d.). Retrieved October 23, 2020, from https://www.tandfonline.com/doi/full/10.1080/13567888.2017.1316086?src=recsys

Taha, A. (2019). Turning ex-combatants into Sadris: Explaining the emergence of the Mahdi Army. *Middle Eastern Studies, 55*(3), 357–373. 10.1080/00263206.2018.1550078

Thurber, C. (2014). Militias as sociopolitical movements: Lessons from Iraq's armed Shia groups. *Small Wars & Insurgencies, 25*(5–6), 900–923. https://doi.org/10.1080/09592318.2014.945633

Twfeeq, M., Bassil, Y., & Jamnoon, M. (2010). *Al-Sadr flexes muscles in Iraqi political jockeying—CNN.com*. https://edition.cnn.com/2010/WORLD/meast/04/01/iraq.politics/index.html

van Veen, E., & Grinstead, N. (2017). *A House Divided: Political relations and coalition-building between Iraq's Shi'a*. 76.

Welsh, M. Y. (2004). *Sadr City: Support from the poor | News | Al Jazeera*. Al Jazeera. https://www.aljazeera.com/news/2004/4/27/sadr-city-support-from-the-poor

Williams, P. (2014). *Chapter 2 Jaish al-Mahdi in Iraq*. PRISM | National Defense University. http://cco.ndu.edu/News/Article/780108/chapter-2-jaish-al-mahdi-in-iraq/

PART VII

CASE STUDIES

Central Asia

56

AL-QAEDA CENTRAL IN AFGHANISTAN AND PAKISTAN

Past, Present, and Future

Abdul Basit

INTRODUCTION

Since the killing of Osama bin Laden in May 2011 and the split of the global jihadist movement in June 2014, al-Qaeda Central (AQC) has struggled to carry out a major terrorist attack in the US or West and has lost several of its leaders in the War on Terror (WOT). Yet, AQC has survived in one form or another in Afghanistan and Pakistan, and it has continued to evolve organisationally and operationally (Stenersen, 2017). Resultantly, the assessments of the group among terrorism scholars and practitioners are divided between those who believe that AQC has been "decimated" and those who think that the group is on a "revival path." Both views are equally compelling and have their merits and demerits.

The predominant view is that AQC is struggling to survive and to keep itself relevant in continuing the cause of global jihadism (Brannen, 2012). AQC leadership suffered losses and organisational setbacks after many US drone attacks and continuing counter-terrorism operations in Pakistan and Afghanistan (Romaniuk & Webb, 2015). This has significantly weakened the terror group (Forster, 2011). Moreover, the strides made against terrorism financing through improved financial regulations and the implementation of anti-money laundering laws have made it difficult for AQC to receive funds from the Middle East. At the same time, the current AQC chief, Ayman Al-Zawahiri, lacks the charisma of his predecessor, and his defensive approach has resulted in the brain drain of seasoned Arab fighters and leaders from Afghanistan and Pakistan towards the Middle East (Riedel, 2015).

CONTEMPORARY DEVELOPMENTS

The Taliban takeover of Kabul and the rest of the country in August and September 2021 was considered an al-Qaeda victory, too. Al-Qaeda provided the Taliban with experienced trainers and advisers, teaching their Afghan allies the use of terrorist tactics, building improvised explosive devices (IEDs), and perpetrating suicide attacks. Being close allies, the Taliban leadership allowed Al-Qaeda to maintain a residual presence in the Pakistani tribal areas and on the Afghan side of the border. Some Al-Qaeda members also remain in the eastern parts of the country and close to Haqqani-controlled territory. After the Taliban victory in August 2021, some al-Qaeda leaders were reported to have moved to Kabul, among them Ayman al-Zawahiri, who was killed in an American drone strike on August 1, 2022.

Al-Qaeda clearly profited from the rise of key allies like Sirajuddin Haqqani to positions of power in the Kabul government. However, it is quite unclear whether the organisation will be able to translate this development into a revival of its terrorist activity abroad. Currently, al-Qaeda lacks recruits from Western countries. (Conrad et al., 2022). By concentrating on the short-term aims and capabilities of IS-K, Bill Roggio, a senior American security analyst, believes that the United States and its allies are missing the long-term threat posed by al-Qaeda. Roggio thinks that al-Qaeda is a greater threat than the Islamic State because it has sufficient patience. Al-Qaeda has a real caliphate-building plan (Foreign Policy, April 11, 2023).

DOI: 10.4324/9780429426063-64

THE VANGUARD OF JIHADISM

The contending view is that AQC is still the vanguard of jihadism in the Af-Pak region. In the face of all the adversities, AQC has proven to be resilient with tremendous regenerative capacity (Fantz, 2013). Further, the proponents of this view uphold that, benefiting from the security vacuum created by the drawdown of US forces from Afghanistan in 2015, AQC has steadily grown in size and expanded its geographical outreach from eastern and north-eastern Afghanistan to southern parts of Afghanistan as well as Karachi, Pakistan (UNSC, 2018). The discovery of al-Qaeda's largest training camp in the Shorabak district of Kandahar, Afghanistan, in 2015 is a case in point (Starr, 2015). In October 2015, the US commander in Afghanistan, John Campbell, noted that "AQC was attempting to rebuild its support networks and planning capabilities against the US homeland and Western interests (McQuaid et al., 2017)". AQC's ability to stay under the radar of intelligence agencies and away from the glare of the media makes it a more dangerous and long-term security threat. Moreover, AQC's alliances and affiliations with the Sunni militant groups in the Af-Pak region have kept it in business (CRS, 2018).

Despite opposing viewpoints concerning the stability of AQC, an evaluation of its organisational evolution and ideological readjustments is needed and also contextualised within the Af-Pak's current geopolitical milieu, its alliances with various Sunni militant groups in the region, and changes taking place in the global jihadist movement, particularly its rivalry with the Islamic State (IS). It has examined why AQC has de-prioritised violent attacks and adopted a localised approach to jihadism. It is flawed to assess AQC's threat vis-à-vis its ability or inability to carry out attacks. Rather, AQC's current status and the threat it poses should be assessed against the short- and long-term goals that it has set for itself and whether it is successful in achieving them or not. A terrorist group's ability to inflict violence is a necessary but not sufficient condition to understand the threat it poses. A nuanced understanding of how terrorism works also enables us to determine why it works. Violence is only one option in the toolkit of a terrorist group. Sometimes, terrorist groups change their cost-benefit calculus if violence is costly and non-violent means give them a better chance of attaining their goals. Particularly when the goal is to survive and lie low, not exercising violence seems like a rational choice. The reality is that AQC is not only an ideological movement acting as the mothership of jihad; rather, it has a distinct and independent organisational structure.

Those risk assessments that focus on particular dimensions of AQC and ignore others lead to a limited understanding of its current capabilities. For instance, Don Rassler argued that, if the analysis is based on the decapitation of AQC leaders, brain drain from the Af-Pak towards the Middle East, and inability to carry out attacks, then we neglect AQC's recruitment drive, its re-orientation from a global to a "glocal" approach, where it has interests both globally and locally, to jihadism, and efforts to reunify the jihadist movement (Rassler, 2017).

As a result, a re-examination of ongoing disputes within AQC about the future of jihadism, particularly in light of IS's failures in Iraq and Syria as well as the group's long-term aims, would provide a more realistic evaluation of its threat. For the time being, survival is more crucial than expansion for AQC, and ideological legitimacy is more important than operational strength.

The scarcity of data and information on AQC's activities in the Af-Pak region and the reclusive nature of the group makes it difficult to assess its organisational makeup and the leadership structure under Zawahiri. But AQC's efforts to reunify the global jihadist movement, its localised recruitment drive, and its enduring alliances with local groups give us an indication of AQC's inner workings.

The analysis has treated AQC and its South Asian franchise, al-Qaeda in the Indian Sub-continent (AQIS), as two linked but separate groups. It has relied on a host of primary and secondary published sources for data collection. The Counter Terrorism Centre's Letters from Abbottabad, online information released by Site Intelligence, the Middle East Media Research Institute (MEMRI), and the James Town Foundation's Terrorism Monitoring Cell have also been consulted. An effort has been made to fill the remaining information gaps through interviews with researchers and Pakistani counter-terrorism officials who have worked on the AQC.

This chapter has four sections. The first section encapsulates AQC's historical background, such as how the group was formed and how it has evolved. The second section outlines AQC's resilience and longevity using the conceptual works of Richard English, Audrey Kurth Cronin, and Susan Olzak. The third section looks at the existing status of the AQC in the Af-Pak region by reflecting on its current approach to jihadism, its key leaders and personnel, its organisational structure, and its alliances with like-minded militant groups. The last section focuses on the implications of AQC's existing status for peace and security in the region and ongoing counter-terrorism efforts.

BACKGROUND

AQC was formed in 1989 after the defeat of the former Soviet Union in the Russo-Afghan jihad. Osama bin Laden and Sheikh Abdullah Azam of the Maktab al-Khidamat (Afghan Services Bureau), which provided travel services to the Arab fighters who participated in the Afghan Jihad, founded al-Qaeda in Peshawar. However, following

Azzam's mysterious murder, Dr. Ayman Al-Zawahiri of the Egyptian Islamic Jihad (EIJ) joined hands with bin Laden (Cruickshank & Bergen, 2011).

Initially, there was an ideological disagreement between bin Laden and Zawahiri on how to approach jihadism, i.e., the "near vs. far enemy" debate (Gerges, 2011). Growing up in Egypt and being part of the underground Islamist struggle against then-Egyptian ruler Anwar Al-Sadat, Zawhiri was keen to focus on the Arab regimes in the Middle East, whom he considered "apostates" and "stooges" of the US (Ibrahim, 2012). Following bin Laden's killing, Zawahiri has reoriented AQC's jihadist approach from the far enemy (globalisation of jihad) to focus on the near enemy (glocalization of jihad). Unlike bin Laden, Zawahiri is more cautious and circumspect in his approach. To him, minimising the damage done to AQC since bin Laden's killing, ensuring survival, grooming future leadership, and strengthening alliances with like-minded Islamist militant groups are more urgent and important goals than carrying out violence (Jones, 2017). Consequently, Zawahiri launched AQC's South Asian affiliate, Al-Qaeda in the Indian Subcontinent (AQIS), in September 2014.

On the contrary, bin Laden was keen to crush the "head of the snake," i.e., the US (far enemy), to neutralise the "near enemy (Hinote et al., 2013)." Bin Laden believed that as long as US support for different regimes in the Middle East continued, it was pointless to target them. He drew his inspiration from the US withdrawals from Vietnam, Lebanon, and Somalia (Gunaratna, 2002).

Initially, bin Laden moved to Sudan with his family and trusted lieutenants, where he was invited by the Sudanese Islamist regime. However, after immense pressure from the Kingdom of Saudi Arabia (KSA), the Sudanese regime asked bin Laden to leave (Astill, 2001). His relocation to Afghanistan coincided with the Afghan Taliban's takeover of Kabul in 1996. This was beneficial for both jihadist organisations. The Taliban received a financial benefactor, while al-Qaeda got a welcoming regime that provided the group with sanctuaries and training centres that it would not have gotten in any other part of the world (CFR, 2009).

In the coming years, AQC's strength grew exponentially under the Taliban regime. The group set up its training camps and sanctuaries, attracting fighters from different parts of the Muslim world (Stenersen, 2017). AQC also strengthened its ties with different jihadist groups in the region, such as Jaish-e-Muhamamd (JeM), Harkat-ull-Jihad al-Islami (HuJI), Harkat-ul-Mujahideen (HuM), and Lashkar-e-Jhangvi (LeJ), among others. In 1998, when bin Laden declared his fatwa (edict) of global jihad against "Jews and Christian Crusaders" in Kabul, the majority of the Af-Pak jihadist groups signed and endorsed it. As a matter of fact, the HuM was one of the groups that arranged transport for local and international journalists from Peshawar to Afghanistan to cover bin Laden's speech. Following bin Laden's fatwa, AQC bombed the US embassies in Kenya and Tanzania in 1998, killing over 200 people (Rassler, 2017).

The US retaliated with cruise missile strikes against AQC's hideouts and training centres in Afghanistan. Notwithstanding large-scale infrastructure damage, bin Laden and his commanders survived the missile strikes (Kessler, 2016). However, US and Saudi pressure increased on the Taliban to expel bin Laden from Afghanistan. Eventually, following the tragic 9/11 attacks, the US launched Operation Enduring Freedom (OEF) in Afghanistan to downgrade, dismantle, and eventually destroy AQC (CNN, 2018).

OEF pushed AQC across the border in Pakistan's tribal regions, particularly in the Waziristan area. Some of the AQC leaders, including bin Laden's family, relocated to the safe houses arranged by Saif Al-Adal in Iran (Lake, 2017). However, Iranian intelligence soon arrested them and moved them to detention centres, where they lived for more than ten years until they were freed in exchange for an Iranian diplomat who was held hostage by al-Qaeda in the Arabian Peninsula (AQAP) in Yemen (Gohel, 2017).

Meanwhile, AQC remnants in Pakistan settled primarily in the Af-Pak tribal region, where a large number of their leaders and operatives were killed or captured in counter-terrorism operations and US drone attacks. Some leaders of AQC hid in Karachi, while a majority resided in Waziristan's Shawal valley and north-eastern Afghanistan's Kunar and Nuristan provinces (CTC, 2012). The biggest blow to AQC came in May 2011 when the US Navy Seals eliminated Osama bin Laden in Abbottabad and took a large cache of computer hard drives into their possession. AQC deputy chief Zawahiri then succeeded bin Laden. Following bin Laden's killing, several senior al-Qaeda leaders, such as Abu Yahya Al-Libi, Atiyya Abdul Rehman, Abu Mustafa Abu al-Yazid, Ilyas Kashmiri, and Sheikh Said al-Masri, were swiftly eliminated by drone strikes. This severely impacted AQC's operational and organisational capabilities (Walsh, 2015).

Another major setback for AQC came in June 2014, when its then-Iraqi affiliate, al-Qaeda in Iraq (AQI), broke away and renamed itself the Islamic State (IS) under Abu Bakr al-Baghdadi. In the following years, AQC was eclipsed by IS as the leader of the global jihadist movement. Compared to IS, AQC came across as a perfunctory, outdated, irrelevant, and struggling jihadist organisation. IS positioned itself as the true heir to bin Laden's cause for a global jihad and questioned the credentials and agenda of AQC and its closest ally, the Afghan Taliban (Williams & Bayman, 2015).

Zawahiri's move to form AQIS in 2014 was an attempt to hold its position as the vanguard of jihadism in South Asia and to reassure its affiliated and associated groups that AQC was still in business (BBC, 2014). Nonetheless, since bin Laden's killing and the emergence of IS, the AQC has struggled to carry out major terrorist attacks in the region or the West, with the exception of the 2015 Charlie Hebdo attack, which was orchestrated by the AQAP (Al-Jazeera, 2015).

RESILIENCE AND LONGEVITY OF AQC

To understand AQC's resilience and re-adaptation to adverse circumstances in the Af-Pak region as well as the current approach to jihadism, developing an understanding of its near-term and long-term aims is essential. As of now, AQC's near-term goal is survival, and its long-term aim is the reunification of the global jihadist movement. This logically raises another question: is AQC successful in securing its short-term and long-term goals? In this regard, the conceptual works of Richard English on how terrorism works, Audrey Cronin on how terrorism ends, and Suzan Olzak on the longevity of terrorist groups are useful.

Terrorist groups persist despite failing to achieve their strategic objectives. They live uneasy lives and face detentions, assassinations, and social stigmatisation, yet they persist. Notwithstanding the obvious hardships and failures associated with terrorism, a deeper understanding of how it works enables a nuanced assessment of why it works. The efficacy of terrorist groups should be measured in relative and not absolute terms. Terrorism is not a zero-sum phenomenon; its incentive structure is so complex and ever-rewarding that terrorist groups can create a win-win situation out of any situation. For example, if a terrorist dies, he becomes a martyr. .On the contrary, if he survives, he is a hero. Bin Laden became a spiritual figurehead for AQC and its associated groups after his killing.

English upholds that terrorism (and by extension, terrorist groups) persists as long as it continues to work for those who use it. Any terrorist group that operates according to a cost-benefit calculation will use policies that are best suited to achieve its immediate and long-term goals (English, 2016). Judging the success of terrorist groups by their ability or inability to achieve their strategic objectives is oversimplistic. Terrorist groups rarely achieve their strategic policy objectives. Moreover, primary goals alone do not explain terrorist actions or success (English, 2016). For instance, Cronin's examination of 450 terrorist groups revealed that 87.1% achieved none of their strategic objectives, 6.4% achieved limited success, 2% achieved a substantial component of their aims, and only 4.4% succeeded in full achievement of their primary goals (Cronin, 2006).

In their life cycles, terrorist groups go through various phases where they adapt to changing circumstances to stay alive and relevant. Even if terrorist groups fail to achieve their primary goals, there can be partial success through secondary strategic aims. Richardson believes that while terrorist groups have struggled to achieve their long-term gains, they have been fairly successful in attaining their near-term aims (Richardson, 2006).

For instance, al Qaeda has not forced the US out of the Arabian Peninsula or compelled it to give up its support for the authoritarian regimes in the Middle East; it has increased the economic, human, and political costs for the US of continuing these policies. Also, the ideological goals and strategic aims of terrorist groups are not fixed; rather, they are flexible and transform with changing circumstances. Crenshaw notes that when survival is at stake, terrorist groups re-interpret their ideologies so that all matters of strategic importance are subordinated to survival (Crenshaw, 2011). Following bin Laden's killing, AQC's recalibration of its jihadist approach by localising its operational strategies and ideological agendas to ensure its survival is consistent with conceptual debates on the longevity of terrorist groups.

Cronin has argued that terrorism never ends, but the campaigns and groups that wage it always do. She outlines six conditions for terrorist groups to end: i) killing of top leaders, ii) compromises by entering into talks, iii) achieving stated goals, iv) implosion and loss of public support; v) outright defeat; and vi) transition from terrorism into other forms of violence (Cronin, 2009).

Despite America's tremendous success against al Qaeda in the Af-Pak region, most of the above-mentioned factors remain unfulfilled. The decapitation of AQC's top leaders through drone strikes was partially successful. The group is survived by Ayman al-Zawahiri and bin Laden's son, Hamza bin Laden. They provide future leadership for the group. Likewise, AQC suffered a partial implosion and internal crisis in June 2014 when some leaders and members of the group joined IS, but the majority of its affiliates and associates remained loyal to it. More importantly, the US-led "War on Terror" weakened AQC in Afghanistan, but it was neither fully defeated nor physically eliminated. The other two conditions mentioned by Cronin – achieving the stated goals or reaching a compromise through negotiations – do not apply in AQC's case. Cronin's last condition about the transition of terrorist groups from one form of violence to another is visible in AQC's organisational evolution, but it was not to give up terrorism but to survive.

Meanwhile, the literature on the lethality and longevity of terrorism grapples with the basic question of how long terrorist groups persist. Olzak maintains that terrorist groups that maintain a clear ideological position are more easily understood, attract supporters, and survive longer compared to those that span multiple and distant ideological categories (Olzak, 2016). Terrorist groups with fluent ideological outlooks are perceived as reliable, which enables them to survive and operate in high-risk environments. On the contrary, terrorist organisations with less clear ideological positions lack legitimacy, and their survival chances are limited (Ibid.). Another factor to consider for AQC's resilience and longevity is its alliances with like-minded groups in Afghanistan and Pakistan. The ability of a terrorist group to enter into alliances with other groups is directly proportional to its longevity and lethality. The greater the number of alliances, the longer the life of a group (Moghadam, 2017).

AQC'S CURRENT OPERATIONAL AND ORGANISATIONAL STRUCTURE

AQC maintains a small but growing footprint in Afghanistan and Pakistan. Though it is survived by its various affiliates in Yemen, Somalia, Syria, the Maghreb, and Mali, the core group is now on a recovery path, benefiting from the worsening security situation in Afghanistan, its deepening ties with the Afghan Taliban, and the battlefield defeats and territorial losses of IS in Iraq and Syria. AQC is trying to leverage IS setbacks in Iraq and Syria to replenish its resources, recruits, and prestige (Thomas, 2018).

Three factors have assisted AQC's rejuvenation in Afghanistan. First, the massive drawdown of US troops from Afghanistan in late 2014 The resulting vacuum and resurgence of the Afghan Taliban have allowed AQC to grow in size and number (Lauren & Weinbaum, 2016). Second, AQC's enduring alliances with the Sunni militant groups in the Af-Pak region have kept it afloat. The longevity and lethality of a terrorist group are directly proportional to its alliances and partnerships with other like-minded groups; the more alliances, the greater the threat. The majority of the South Asian militant groups are still loyal to and allied with AQC. The depth and diversity of AQC's partnerships and alliances with these groups will be discussed in the succeeding section. Third, developments in the Middle East, particularly the civil wars in Syria and Iraq, diverted international attention from those conflicts, allowing AQC to quietly revive (Hoffman, 2017).

Presently, AQC is going through a re-adaptation phase where it is focusing on rebuilding and re-orienting its jihadist approach from global to local jihad by embedding itself with local militant and insurgent organisations in the Af-Pak region (Barr & Ross, 2018). For instance, in the 2018 spring offensive in Afghanistan, al-Qaeda's fighters were fighting alongside the Afghan Taliban to help the latter in its insurgent struggle against the US and Afghan forces. Likewise, in Kashmir, al-Qaeda has grown through a local jihadist group, Ansar Ghazwat-ul-Hind (Ramachandran, 2017). This group comprises a new generation of Kashmiri militants who are introducing Islamism in Kashmir along with nationalist struggles for the right to self-determination. This is more or less similar to the model AQC has adopted in Syria, where it allowed Jabhat Fatah al-Sham to distance itself from the former and operate autonomously to create space for itself in the Syrian landscape and co-exist with other anti-Assad groups. Though Ansar Ghazwat-ul-Hind is neither robust like Jabhat Fatah al-Sham nor do the situations in Kashmir and Syria bear any stark resemblance, the pattern in both cases reveals AQC's approach of localising and re-adapting to environments in different conflict theatres. While AQC has not abandoned its agenda of attacking the US or West, its immediate goal is to survive, and the long-term objective is to reunify the global jihadist movement (Zahid, 2017).

After the discovery of al-Qaeda's largest training camp in Shurabak district of Kandahar province, the estimates of its fighters in Afghanistan were revised from 100 to 300. The more recent US estimates put AQC's numerical strength between 265 and 400 in Afghanistan and Pakistan, while the Afghan estimates suggest that the group has more than 500 members in its ranks in different parts of Afghanistan (Lamothe, 2015). These estimates do not include members of AQC-associated groups such as AQIS and the Turkistan Islamic Party (TIP). If fighters from AQIS and TIP are also included in this figure, then the total number would be around 1,000 to 1,200 fighters.

In December 2018, an Afghan Taliban leader, on the sidelines of US-Taliban talks in the United Arab Emirates (UAE), revealed in an interview with CBS the presence of 2,000 to 3,000 foreign fighters in Afghanistan, including Iraqis, Sudanese, Chechens, Uyghurs, and Turks (Roggio, 2018). This further strengthens the impression that AQC has replenished its ranks and is gradually reviving in Afghanistan (Roggio, 2018). Before this, in September 2018, the Afghan Intelligence, the National Directorate of Security (NDS), following the killing of an al-Qaeda leader, Omar bin Khattab, in the Ghazni province, pointed out that during 2017, in various operations in Ghazni, Paktiya, and Zabdul provinces, as many as 80 al-Qaeda leaders were killed and more than 27 were arrested (UNSC, 2018). Similarly, in December 2016, US officials claimed to have killed or captured 250 AQC operatives (50 leaders and 200 fighters), including the group's commander for north-eastern Afghanistan, Faruq Qahtani.

In Afghanistan, AQC has a notable presence in Badakhshan, Kunar, Nuristan, Nangarhar, Paktika, Paktiya, and Khost provinces. In the south, AQC maintains a presence in Helmand, Kandahar, Urzugan, and Zabul provinces. The Khak-e-Afghan and Day Chopan districts of Zabul are AQC's safe havens, where the group has training centres as well. In Pakistan, AQC has a small footprint in Karachi and small pockets in the erstwhile Federally Administered Tribal Areas (now merged into Khyber Pakhtunkhwa province) and the south-western Balochistan province.

Unlike IS, AQC's approach to violence has always been finely calibrated to reinforce its political message and aims. The core has always been quite careful not to commit excesses that could alienate Muslims and dent its image. A case in point is Zawahiri and bin Laden's message to then-AQI chief Abu Musab al-Zarqawi to refrain from stoking sectarian flames in Iraq. AQC has always insisted on vetting major terrorist plots and discouraged sectarianism (Turner, 2014).

KEY LEADERS AND PERSONALITIES

Given the scarcity of data, it is difficult to accurately outline AQC's organisational structure and leadership hierarchy. AQC's pre-9/11 structure was of a vertical-hierarchical organisation, which transformed into a horizontal-decentralised shape after 9/11, and following bin Laden's killing, it is in cell formations (Weinstein, 2018). Discreet cells are effective for terrorist groups to survive and absorb any setbacks emerging from arrests or killings of their leaders and fighters. Terrorist cell structures are hard to detect and even more difficult to eliminate because these cells are separate and unaware of the activities of other cells. The widespread presence of ungoverned spaces in Afghanistan and Pakistan has also helped AQC's cause lie low and rebuild its operational strength and organisational infrastructure.

Zawahiri is still the overall leader of AQC as well as the chief strategist and ideologue. The current manager is Abd al-Rehman al-Maghrebi, while Abu Mohsin al-Masri is the senior manager (Jones, 2017). Zawahiri defines the policy direction and jihadist strategies and exercises spiritual influence over various al-Qaeda affiliates and associates. According to Newsweek, he is reported to be hiding somewhere in Pakistan (Stein, 2017). Generally, senior AQC leaders (as in the case of bin Laden and the mastermind of the 9/11 attacks, Khalid Sheikh Muhammad) prefer living in the main cities of Pakistan because cities are effective in evading drone attacks.

Zawahiri's current focus is to strengthen the base. He believes that the flame of jihadism will stay alight if the base survives. Zawahiri is overly cautious and does not want further degradation of the existing resources and infrastructure. This is consistent with Crenshaw's argument that when survival is at stake, terrorist groups redefine their objectives to stay alive and relevant. Zawahiri re-oriented bin Laden's goal of attacking the US with the caveat of targeting US nationals and interests in operational areas of AQC affiliates or striking the US homeland and the West through lone-wolf attacks such as the Charlie Hebdo attack in 2015 (Clarke, 2017).

A Saudi national, Abu Akhund, leads AQC in Kunar and Nuristan provinces in Afghanistan. He is a former adviser to bin Laden and replaced Farouq al-Qahtani, who was killed in a US drone attack in 2016. Al-Qahtani managed AQC's operations in north-eastern Afghanistan, along with looking for new sanctuaries for the group. The Egyptian AQC leader Saif al-Adal also assists Zawahiri and is one of his closest deputies. After his release in 2010 from Iran, he has shuttled between Pakistan and Afghanistan. In 2015, Adl negotiated, on Zawahiri's behalf, the tactical split between AQC and Jabhat al-Nusra, now known as Jabhat Fatel al-Sham (Weisfuse, 2016).

Another senior AQC leader and head of the Turkistan Islamic Party (TIP), an ethnic Uyghur militant group, Abdul Haq Turkistani, is also alive. Haq is still residing in Afghanistan and is closely linked with AQC. He became a member of AQC's executive leadership council in 2005 and serves as a liaison between rival Taliban factions. He is also involved in the group's military planning. Recent videos of TIP fighters from Afghanistan's Badakhsan province have shown Uyghur militants fighting alongside the Afghan Taliban in the al-Khandaq offensive (Battle of the Trenches).

Another key AQC leader and new face of the group is bin Laden's charismatic son, Hamza bin Laden. Zawahiri brought Hamza into public view when AQC was struggling to compete with IS and the disclosure of Taliban chief Mullah Muhamamd Omar's death had visibly shaken Af-Pak's jihadist landscape. IS was promoting itself as the true heir of bin Laden's al-Qaeda. At such testing times, promoting Hamza as bin Laden's true successor was a stroke of genius from Zawahiri. This move not only calmed the nerves of the AQC rank-and-file but also reassured the AQ allies that the group was still in business. Hamza emerged on the scene in 2016 with a 21-minute video entitled "We are all Osama." In this video, he threatened to attack the US to avenge his father's killing and portrayed the oppression of Muslims in Afghanistan, Somalia, Syria, Iraq, and Yemen as a direct fallout of US policies (YouTube, 2016).

Hamza, 27, is an articulate speaker and a firebrand orator. He is being promoted at a young age so that he gains acceptability among the jihadist rank-and-file. It cannot be said with certainty, but circumstantial evidence points to his presence in Afghanistan or Pakistan. The letter from Abbottabad indicates that as early as 2010, bin Laden wanted him to move to Afghanistan and take up the position of AQC's spokesman (Soufan, 2017).

After his release from Iran, Hamza never left the region, and he was constantly in touch with bin Laden and his slain brother Khalid bin Laden. In 2011, Hamza was on his way to reunite with his father when he learned about his elimination in Abbottabad. Hamza is serving as AQC's propagandist and has issued several video statements and audio messages repeating his father's message of attacking the US, along with echoing Zawahiri's call for reuniting the global jihadist movement and focusing on "the near enemy" (Stalinsky, 2018).

Hamza, like his father, pledged his oath of allegiance to the Taliban leader, Mullah Haibatullah Akhundzada. This is significant in the sense that other AQC members pledge their allegiance to Zawahiri, who then swear an oath of fealty to the Taliban leader on their behalf. Hamza's direct allegiance indicates his special status and that he is being nurtured for the leadership position (Soufan, 2017).

AQC'S CURRENT APPROACH AND STRATEGY

Currently, AQC and its affiliates are trying to win popular support by focusing on winning the hearts and minds of the people and portraying their brand of jihadism as moderate compared to IS's brutal and indiscriminate approach to jihadism.

Localisation of Jihadist Recruitment and Approach

Since bin Laden's death, a new generation of Pakistani militants has steadily risen in AQC's hierarchy, such as Ilyas Kashmiri, Badr Masnour, Usama Mahmud, and Asim Umar. Prior to this generation, Khalid Sheikh Muhammad, Affia Siddiqui, Amar al-Balouchi, and Ramzi Yousaf were prominent Pakistani nationals who were part of al-Qaeda (Rassler, 2017). In September 2014, AQC's decision to launch its South Asian franchise, AQIS, pointed to its efforts to localise and embed its agendas with local issues involving Muslim grievances and sufferings in the region (Stenersen, 2017). Contrary to the popular perception that AQIS was launched in response to IS's growing popularity and influence in South Asia, the efforts to create a South Asian branch were launched right after the killing of bin Laden. AQC's operational leader in Afghanistan, Mustafa Abu al-Yazid, was working on this much before IS rebelled (Basit, 2014).

The sudden leadership vacuum created by bin Laden's death, the ageing of Zawahiri, who is in his 80s now, and the elimination of several leaders in drone attacks forced AQC to think about its future in Af-Pak, the place of its birth and power bastion. So Yazid was tasked with uniting South Asia's diverse and fractious Sunni militant landscape. AQIS is the fruition of those efforts. The AQIS chief, Asim Umar, was previously associated with HUJI and is quite close to Zawahiri (Joscelyn, 2017). AQIS followed AQC's approach of image rebuilding, focusing on local issues affecting Muslims in the region such as atrocities in Kashmir, discrimination and mistreatment of Muslims in India, the occupation of Afghanistan, and the genocide of the ethnic Rohingya Muslims in Myanmar. Many of these issues have been packaged in the narrative of Ghazwa-e-Hind (The Great Battle of India).

According to Don Rassler, the localisation of AQC in the Af-Pak region is further strengthened by the data on al-Qaeda operatives and leaders' arrests in Karachi, Pakistan, between 2014 and 2017. During these years, of the 102 al-Qaeda operatives arrested, the majority were Pakistani nationals (Rassler, 2017). Farhan Zahid believes that AQC has an elaborate network in major urban centres in Pakistan and that recruitment is vigorously continuing, with the exception that the group has not engaged in any violent activity. This trend gets further validation when one looks at the propaganda literature and videos of the group. The majority of AQC communiqués and videos are in Urdu, Bengali, and Hindi, focusing on the local issues mentioned above.

Alliances with the Afghan Jihadist Groups

In line with its strategy of localisation, AQC is currently helping the Afghan Taliban win the war and force the US out of Afghanistan (SITE Intelligence, 2016). Zawahiri has twice renewed his oath of allegiance to two Taliban chiefs, Akhtar Mansoor and Haibatullah Akhundzada, indicating how closely the two groups are allied (Bacon, 2018). In the al-Khandaq spring offensive, al-Qaeda fighters were spotted fighting alongside the Taliban fighters under their command. The emergence of ISK has further strengthened cooperation between the two entities. After 9/11, the Afghan Taliban distanced themselves from al-Qaeda, always portrayed the group as a nationalist entity focused on Afghanistan, and reiterated their pledge not to allow areas under their control to be used for attacks against any other country. This is one reason why AQC has refrained from engaging in violence.

The Taliban-al-Qaeda nexus was strengthened in 2016 when Mullah Umar's successor, Akhtar Muhammad Mansour, publicly acknowledged Zawahiri's pledge of allegiance to boost his legitimacy and leadership credentials (Reuters, 2016). Following the disclosure of Mullah Umar's death, Mansoor faced fierce opposition within the Taliban movement, including from Omar's son, Mullah Yaqoob, and his brother, Mullah Manan. Zawahiri's pledge of allegiance was of great benefit to Mansoor. However, this was an unequal relationship where the Taliban had the upper hand compared to the past, when AQC dominated all such forms of cooperation (McNally & Weinbaum, 2016).

Likewise, AQC is closely allied with the Haqqani Network, which is part of the Afghan Taliban but maintains its own independent military wing (Rassler & Brown, 2011). The links between AQC and the Haqqanis are as old as the conflict in Afghanistan. In the 1980s, most of the Arab Afghan fighters fought under the veteran Haqqani leader Jalal-ud-Din Haqqani (CFR, 2009). In recent years, the notoriety gained by the Haqqaani Network for launching daring attacks in Kabul and other urban centres of Afghanistan is due to the training imparted by the AQC leader to the Haqqanis. Prior to Operation Zarb-e-Azb, AQC operated in Miranshah, the capital of North Waziristan, under the protection of the Haqqani Network.

AQC and the Haqqaanis have played the role of unifiers and mediators between different warring Pakistani militant factions, particularly the internecine feuds of the Tehrik-e-Taliban Pakistan (TTP) as well as between the Afghanistan-focused Mullah Nazir group and the former. For instance, in

2012, AQC, with the help of the Haqqani Network, formed Shura-e-Muraqba, an anti-US alliance of militant groups, to end infighting in TTP factions and reunite to focus on fighting in Afghanistan. The five-member Shura-e-Muraqba is comprised of the Afghan Taliban, Haqqani Network, TTP, Mullah Nazir Group, and Hafiz Gul Bahadir Group (Feyyaz, 2013).

Similarly, AQC also has close operational links with the Pakistani Taliban. Right after 9/11, most AQC leaders found refuge and safe havens in areas controlled by the Pakistani Taliban (Sharma & Behera, 2014). In fact, AQC was quite instrumental in the formation of TTP after the July 2007 Red Mosque operation. AQC imparted training to TTP cadres and provided them with finances to launch jihad against the Pakistani army (Rassler, 2012). Prior to the formation of TTP's own media wing, Al-Umar Media, most of TTP's videos and propaganda were disseminated by al-Sahaab, AQC's propaganda arm. Following former TTP chief Mullah Fazlullah's killing in a US drone attack in Kunar, Afghanistan, Zawahiri issued a eulogy and condolence statement (SITE Intelligence, 2018). This indicates how closely the two groups are linked.

According to Amir Rana, the majority of the jihadist groups in the Af-Pak region, barring the handful who jumped on the IS bandwagon, are still loyal to AQC and respect the group as the vanguard of jihadism in the region (Rana, 2003). Almost all of them are signatories to bin Laden's fatwa of global jihad against the "Jews and Christian Crusaders." The reorientation of AQC from global to local jihad focused on Kashmir, Afghanistan, and the plight of Muslims in India, Myanmar, and Xingjian, China, will further strengthen these deep and historical ties (SITE Intelligence, 2018). The majority of these groups sprouted from the Afghan Jihad in the 1980s and have shared battlefield experiences and memories, trained in the same training centres, and co-inhabited the same hideouts.

IMPACT

AQC is far from defeated, and if a premature victory is declared in Afghanistan, similar to the one in Syria against IS, then the threat will reconstitute itself. While there is no immediate threat to the US homeland from AQC, nor is the group capable of achieving such operational capability anytime soon, the possibility of AQ-inspired and directed lone-actor attacks in the US and elsewhere cannot be ruled out.

If AQC succeeds in unifying the Sunni militant groups in the region in a post-US Afghanistan, their focus will turn towards conflict pockets within the region that can spark regional tensions, particularly between India and Pakistan. The perpetrator of the 2008 Mumbai attacks, Lashkar-e-Taiba (LeT), is closely linked with AQC. Another Mumbai-like terrorist attack on India emanating from Pakistan would precipitate an India-Pakistani war. So, a possible US hasty withdrawal from Afghanistan and reconstitution of the AQC threat is not just about terrorism but a potential war between two nuclear neighbours.

Another likely implication of AQC's rejuvenation would be the emergence of self-radicalised affiliates in different parts of South Asia who would remotely link themselves with the group and carry out attacks in its name. In recent years, this trend has been witnessed in Pakistan, Indian-administered Kashmir, and Bangladesh. The emergence of Ansar Ghazwat-ul-Hind in Kashmir, Ansar al-Islam in Bangladesh, and Jmaat-ul-Ansar al-Sharia (JAS) in Pakistan are cases in point. These entities were self-initiated and comprised of a few individuals who carried out attacks in the name of AQC in the region. More such affiliates will sprout if AQC is fully rejuvenated in a post-US Afghanistan.

CONCLUSION

AQC is weak, but it is neither defeated nor decimated. The group is well entrenched in Af-Pak's jihadist landscape, and its short-term objective is to survive. Its long-term goal is to re-unite the global jihadist movement. The group seems quite successful in achieving the former goal. It remains to be seen to what extent AQC benefits from the territorial losses and battlefield field defeats of IS in Iraq and Syria and whether they eventually lead to the reunification of the global jihadist movement or not.

In any case, in the face of adverse circumstances, AQC has proven to be resilient, agile, and highly adaptive (Sude, 2015). As shown in the preceding sections, AQC has gradually revived itself by staying underground and focusing on rebuilding and embedding itself with local Islamist militant and jihadist groups instead of trying to carry out attacks against the US or the West (Stenersen, 2016). AQC's ties with the Taliban and the Haqqani Network, particularly after the emergence of the Islamic State of Khurasan (ISK), the IS's formal franchise for Khorasan, have deepened.

The future of AQC would depend on its ideological legitimacy and the resonance of its narrative in the Muslim world. The continued persistence and relevance of Salafi-Jihadism involving Muslim grievances and sufferings in Kashmir, Afghanistan, Yemen, Syria, Somalia, Palestine, the Rakhine states in Myanmar, and Xinjiang in China will keep AQC relevant, and its existence will be strengthened. Looking at the setbacks suffered by IS in the Middle East, it seems that AQC's strategy of patience and gradualism was correct, and now the group seems ready to reap the benefits of its long-term strategy. Notwithstanding criticism, Zawahiri is the most seasoned jihadist leader and ideologue who is reversing AQC's downward spiral.

References

Al-Jazeera. (2015). Al-Qaeda in Yemen claims Charlie Hebdo attack. Retrieved from Al-Jazeera https://www.aljazeera.com/news/middleeast/2015/01/al-qaeda-yemen-charlie-hebdo-paris-attacks-201511410323361511.html.

Al-Shafei, M. (2018). Exclusive: Tehran Sends Hamza Bin Laden to Afghanstan. Retrieved from AShraq Al-Wast https://aawsat.com/english/home/article/1355571/exclusive-tehran-sends-hamza-bin-laden-afghanistan.

Astill, J. (2001). *Osama: The Sudan years*. Retrieved from The Guardian https://www.theguardian.com/world/2001/oct/17/afghanistan.terrorism3.

Bacon, T. (2018). *Deadly Cooperation: The Shifting Ties Between Al-Qaeda and the Taliban*. Retrieved from the War on the Rocks https://warontherocks.com/2018/09/deadly-cooperation-the-shifting-ties-between-al-qaeda-and-the-taliban/.

Barr, N., & Ross, D.G. (2018). How Al-Qaeda works: The Jihadist group's evolving organizational design. *Current Trends in Islamist Ideology, 23*, 66–121. Retrieved from https://s3.amazonaws.com/media.hudson.org/files/publications/CurrentTrends23.pdf.

Basit, A. (2014). Asim Umar—A new kid on the block? *Counter Terrorist Trends and Analyses*, *6*(10), 8–12.

BBC. (2014). AL-Qaeda chief Zawahiri launches al-Qaeda in South Asia. Retrieved from BBC https://www.bbc.com/news/world-asia-29056668.

Brannen, K. (2012). *Panetta: Al Qaeda Decimated*. Retrieved from Politico https://www.politico.com/story/2012/11/panetta-al-qaeda-leadership-decimated-084131.

Brookings Institution. (February 3, 2023). Afghanistan in 2023: Taliban internal power struggles and militancy.

Clarke, C.P. (2017). The moderate face of Al Qaeda. Retrieved from Foreign Affairs https://www.foreignaffairs.com/articles/syria/2017-10-24/moderate-face-al-qaeda.

CNN. (2018). Operation enduring freedom fast facts. Retrieved from CNN https://edition.cnn.com/2013/10/28/world/operation-enduring-freedom-fast-facts/index.html.

Congressional Research Service. (2018). *Al Qaeda and Islamic State affiliated in Afghanistan*. Retrieved from Congressional Research Service https://fas.org/sgp/crs/row/IF10604.pdf

Conrad, G., Koller, S., Doro, H., Nabil, R., Safi, K., Steinberg, G., & Schindler, H. (2022). *The Taliban's take-over in Afghanistan-effects on global terrorism*. Germany: Konrad Adenauer Stiftung.

Council on Foreign Relations. (2009). The al-Qaeda-Taliban Nexus. Council on Foreign Relations. Retrieved from https://www.cfr.org/expert-roundup/al-qaeda-taliban-nexus.

Counter Terrorism Centre. (2012). Letters from Abbottabad: Bin Laden Sidelined? Retrieved from Counter Terrorism Centre https://ctc.usma.edu/app/uploads/2012/05/CTC_LtrsFromAbottabad_WEB_v2.pdf.

Crenshaw, M. (2011). *Explaining terrorism: Causes, process and consequences*. (p. 212). London: Routledge.

Cronin, A.K. (2006). How al-Qaida Ends: The decline and demise of terrorist groups. *International Security*, *31*(1), 7–48.

Cronin, A.K. (2009). *How terrorism ends: Understanding the decline and demise of terrorist campaigns*. New Jersey: Princeton University Press.

Cruickshank, P., & Bergen, P. (2011). Revisiting the early Al Qaeda: An updated account of its formative years. *Studies in Conflict and Terrorism*, *35*(1), 1–36. 10.1080/1057610X.2012.631454.

English, R. (2016). *Does terrorism work?* (pp. 7–8). New York: Oxford University Press.

Fantz, A. (2013). *Still out there and growing—al Qaeda on the rebound, experts say*. Retrieved from CNN https://edition.cnn.com/2013/12/28/world/meast/al-qaeda-growing/index.html.

Feyyaz, M. (2013). Facets of religious violence in Pakistan. *Counter Terrorists Trends and Analyses*, *5*(2), 9–13. Retrieved from https://www.jstor.org/stable/26351124?seq=1#metadata_info_tab_contents.

Forster, B.S. (2011). *The Global Expansion of Al Qaeda Franchise*. CMC Senior Theses, Paper 178. Retrieved from https://scholarship.claremont.edu/cgi/viewcontent.cgi?referer=https://www.google.com/&httpsredir=1&article=1125&context=cmc_theses.

Gerges, F.A. (2011). *The rise and fall of Al-Qaeda*. Washington: Oxford University Press.

Gohel, S.M. (2017). Deciphering Ayman Al-Zawahiri and Al-Qaeda's strategic and ideological imperatives. *Perspectives on Terrorism*, *11*(1), 54–67. Available at: https://eprints.lse.ac.uk/86743/1/Gohel_Deciphering%20Al-Qaeda_2018.pdf.

Gunaratna, R. (2002). *Inside Al-Qaeda: Global terror network*. (p. 18). New York: Columbia University Press.

Hinote et al. (2013). *Cutting off the head of the snake: Applying and assessing leadership attack in military conflict*. Alabama: Air University. Retrieved from https://apps.dtic.mil/dtic/tr/fulltext/u2/a617003.pdf.

Hoffman, B. (2017). A growing terrorist threat on another 9/11. Retrieved from Wall Street Journal https://www.wsj.com/articles/a-growing-terrorist-threat-on-another-9-11-1504888986.

Ibrahim, R. (2012). *Ayman Zawahiri and Egypt: A trip through time*. Retrieved from the Investigative Project on Terrorism https://www.investigativeproject.org/3831/ayman-zawahiri-and-egypt-a-trip-through-time.

Jones, S.G. (2017). Rebuilding the base: How Al-Qaeda could resurge. Retrieved from Rand Corporation https://www.rand.org/content/dam/rand/pubs/testimonies/CT400/CT479/RAND_CT479.pdf.

Jones, S.G. (2017). Will al Qaeda make a comeback? Retrieved from Foreign Affair https://www.foreignaffairs.com/articles/middle-east/2017-08-07/will-al-qaeda-make-comeback.

Joscelyn, T. (2017). Al Qaeda-linked Jihadist in Kashmir criticizes Pakistan Army. Retrieved from Long War Journal https://www.longwarjournal.org/tags/asim-umar.

Kessler, G. (2016). Bill Clinton and the missed opportunities to kill Osama Bin Laden. Retrieved from Washington Post https://www.washingtonpost.com/news/fact-checker/wp/2016/02/16/bill-clinton-and-the-missed-opportunities-to-kill-osama-bin-laden/?noredirect=on&utm_term=.27cb08fa4b16.

Lake, E. (2017). Iran and al-Qaeda: Best of frenemies. Retrieved from Bloomberg https://www.bloomberg.

com/opinion/articles/2017-11-03/iran-and-al-qaeda-best-of-frenemies.

Lamothe, D. (2015). Probably the largest al-Qaeda training camp ever destroyed in Afghanistan. Retrieved from Washington Post https://www.washingtonpost.com/news/checkpoint/wp/2015/10/30/probably-the-largest-al-qaeda-training-camp-ever-destroyed-in-afghanistan/?utm_term=.355b8080900c.

McNally, L., & Weinbaum, M.G. (2016). A resilient Al-Qaeda in Afghanistan and Pakistan. Retrieved from Middle East Institute https://www.mei.edu/sites/default/files/publications/PF18_Weinbaum_AQinAFPAK_web_1.pdf.

McQuaid, J. et al. (2017). Independent assessment of US government efforts against Al-Qaeda. Retrieved from CAN https://www.cna.org/cna_files/pdf/DRM-2017-U-015710-2Rev.pdf.

Moghadam, A. (2017). *Nexus of global Jihad: Understanding cooperation among terrorist actors*. (p. 25). New York: Columbia University Press.

Ohleiser, A. (2014). The State Department Warns of an Evolved and Decentralized Al Qaeda. Retrieved from The Atlantic https://www.theatlantic.com/politics/archive/2014/04/the-state-department-warns-of-an-evolved-decentralized-al-qaeda/361452/.

Olzak, S. (2016). The effect of category spanning on the lethality and longevity of terrorist organizations. *Social Forces*, *95*(2), 559–584.

Ramachandran, S. (2017). Al-Qaeda joins the Kashmir conflict. *Terrorism Monitor*, *15*(22). Retrieved from https://jamestown.org/program/al-qaeda-joins-kashmir-conflict/.

Rana, A. (2003). *Gateway to terrorism*. New Delhi: Minerva Press Limited.

Rassler, D. (2012). *Taliban and All-Qaida: What role the religions plays?* Danish Institute for International Studies. Retrieved from https://www.diis.dk/files/media/publications/import/taliban_and_alqaida_what_role_does_religion_play.pdf.

Rassler, D. (2017). Al-Qaida and the Pakistani Harkat movement: Reflection and questions about the pre-2001 period. *Perspectives on Terrorism*, *11*(6), 38–54. Retrieved from http://www.terrorismanalysts.com/pt/index.php/pot/article/view/655/1304.

Rassler, D. (2017). Al-Qaida in Pakistan: A metric problem? *CTC Sentinel*, *10*(8), 13–20. Retrieved from https://ctc.usma.edu/al-qaida-in-pakistan-a-metric-problem/.

Rassler, D., & Brown, V. (2011). *The Haqqani nexus and evolution of al-Qaida*. West Point, New York: Counter Terrorism Centre (CTC). Retrieved from https://ctc.usma.edu/app/uploads/2011/07/CTC-Haqqani-Report_Rassler-Brown-Final_Web.pdf.

Reuters. (2016). Al Qaeda leader pledges allegiance to new Taliban leader. Retrieved from Reuters https://www.reuters.com/article/us-alqaeda-taliban-idUSKCN0YX04N.

Richardson, L. (2006). *What terrorists want: Understanding the enemy, containing the threat*. (pp. 105–106). New York: Random House Publishing.

Riedel, B. (2015). Where in the world is Al-Qaida's leader? Retrieved from Brookings https://www.brookings.edu/blog/markaz/2015/08/10/where-in-the-world-is-al-qaidas-leader/.

Roggio, B. (2018). Taliban commander admits thousands of foreign fighters are embedded with the group. Retrieved from Long War Journal https://www.longwarjournal.org/archives/2018/12/taliban-commander-admits-thousands-of-foreign-fighters-are-embedded-within-group.php.

Romaniuk, S.N., & Webb, S. (2015). Extraordinary measures: Drone warfare, securitization, and the "War on Terror". *Slovak Journal of Political Sciences*, *15*(3), 221–245. https://sjps.fsvucm.sk/index.php/sjps/article/view/47.

Sajjan, M.G. (2017). Deciphering Ayman Al-Zawahiri and Al-Qaeda's strategic and ideological imperative. *Perspectives on Terrorism*, *11*(1), 54–67.

Sharma, K.S., & Behera, A. (2014). *Militant groups in South Asia*. New Delhi: Pentagon Press, Institute of Defence Studies and Analyses. Retrieved from https://idsa.in/system/files/book/book_militantgroups.pdf.

SITE Intelligence. (2016). Zawahiri calls on fighters to rally around Taliban, reject IS. Retrieved from SITE Intelligence https://news.siteintelgroup.com/Jihadist-News/zawahiri-calls-on-fighters-to-rally-around-afghan-taliban-reject-is.html.

SITE Intelligence. (2018). AQ leader Zawahiri gives eulogy for former TTP leader Fazlullah. Retrieved from SITE Intelligence https://news.siteintelgroup.com/Jihadist-News/aq-leader-zawahiri-gives-eulogy-for-former-ttp-leader-fazlullah.html.

SITE Intelligence. (2018). AQ leader Zawahiri promotes unity among Muslims and rejection of division in video speech. Retrieved from SITE Intelligence https://ent.siteintelgroup.com/Statements/aq-leader-zawahiri-promotes-unity-among-muslims-and-rejection-of-division-in-video-speech.html.

SITE Intelligence. (2018). Pro-AQ group highlights Zawahiri's work on Kashmir in video. Retrieved from SITE Intelligence https://news.siteintelgroup.com/Jihadist-News/pro-aq-group-highlights-zawahiris-words-on-kashmir-in-video.html.

Soufan, A. (2017). Al-Qaida's leader in waiting? *CTC Sentinel*, *10*(8), 1–11.

Stalinsky, S. (2018). A Millennial Bin Laden prepares to takeover Al-Qaeda—And possibly the global Jihadist movement. Retrieved from MEMRI Brief No. 151 https://www.memri.org/reports/millennial-bin-laden-prepares-take-over-al-qaeda---and-possibly-global-jihad-movement.

Starr, B. (2015). *Major al Qaeda camp was unknown to US for month*. Retrieved from CCN https://edition.cnn.com/2015/10/21/politics/al-qaeda-afghanistan-kandahar/index.html.

Stein, J. (2017). Ayman al-Zawahiri: How a CIA drone strike nearly killed the head of Al-Qaeda. Retrieved from Newsweek https://www.newsweek.com/ayman-al-zawahiri-cia-donald-trump-drone-strike-osama-bin-laden-pakistan-587732.

Stenersen, A. (2016). Al-Qaida's comeback in Afghanistan and Pakistan. *CTC Sentinel*, *9*(9), 21–27.

Stenersen, A. (2017). *Al-Qaeda in Afghanistan*. (pp. 96–115). New York: Cambridge University Press.

Stenersen, A. (2017). Thirty years after its foundation—Where is al-Qaida going? *Perspectives on Terrorism*, *11*(6), 5–16. Retrieved from http://www.terrorismanalysts.com/pt/index.php/pot/article/view/653/html.

Sude, B. (2015). Assessing Al-Qaida central's resilience. *CTC Sentinel*, *8*(9), 9–12.

Thomas, C. (2018). Al Qaeda and US policy: Middle East and Africa. Retrieved from Congressional Research Service https://fas.org/sgp/crs/mideast/R43756.pdf.

Turner, J. (2014). Strategic differences: Al Qaeda's split with the Islamic State of Iraq and al-Sham. *Small Wars and Insurgencies*, 26(2), 208–225. Retrieved from 10.1080/09592318.2015.1007563.

United Nations Security Council. (2018). *Letter dated 16 May 2018 from the Chair of the Security Council Committee established pursuant to resolution 1988 (2011) addressed to the President of the Security Council*. New York: United Nations Security Council. Retrieved from https://digitallibrary.un.org/record/1628256.

Walsh, D. (2015). Drone strikes on Al Qaida are said to take toll on leadership in Pakistan. Retrieved from New York Times https://www.nytimes.com/2015/04/25/world/asia/cia-qaeda-drone-strikes-warren-weinstein-giovanni-lo-porto-deaths.html.

Weinstein, F. (2018, May). The decentralization of al Qaeda. Master's Theses. https://digitalcommons.lib.uconn.edu/gs_theses/1196.

Weisfuse, A.R. (2016). The last hope for the al-Qaida old guard? A profile of Saif al Adl. *CTC Sentinel*, 9(3), 24–27.

Williams, J., & Bayman, D.L. (2015). ISIS vs Al Qaeda: Jihadism's civil war. Retrieved from Brookings https://www.brookings.edu/articles/isis-vs-al-qaeda-jihadisms-global-civil-war/.

YouTube. (2016). We are al Osama: Bin Laden's son pledges to continue father's fight. Retrieved from YouTube https://www.youtube.com/watch?v=CkGoKTXRZVM.

Zahid, F. (2017). Waiting for resurgence: Al-Qaeda core in Pakistan. *Counter Terrorists Trends and Analyses*, 9(9), 1–4.

57

AL-QAEDA IN THE INDIAN SUBCONTINENT (AQIS) IN PAKISTAN

Farhan Zahid

INTRODUCTION

The rich jihadi landscape of Pakistan comprises a variety of Islamist terrorist groups. Local, regional, and global Islamist terrorist organisations have been perpetrating acts of terrorism for the last two decades in Pakistan. The landscape has seen the addition of some new globalist Islamist groups. Al-Qaeda in Iraq morphed into a global terrorist franchise called the Islamic State of Iraq and Syria (ISIS), and with the establishment of an Islamic Caliphate, the terrorist entity has opened up regional chapters and embraced local and regional likeminded Islamist terrorist groups. Pakistan was no exception, and a number of Islamist groups pledged allegiance to ISIS's Khurasan Waliyat in the Pakistan-Afghanistan region. The Waliyat-e-Khurasan is one of the 34 governorates of the Islamic State and has been operational since 2014 in Pakistan and Afghanistan.

Two other significant global entries on the Pakistani scene are Al-Qaeda's South Asia Chapter, Al-Qaeda in the Indian Subcontinent (AQIS), and Jamaat Ansar al-Sharia Pakistan. Both are linked to and affiliated with Al-Qaeda Central and act as Al-Qaeda franchises. The establishment of AQIS appeared to be Al-Qaeda Central's response to Islamic State-Central (IS-C) after IS-C launched its local chapter, IS-Khurassan, in July 2014. Al-Qaeda Emir Ayman al-Zawahiri himself appeared in a video introducing Asim Umar, the Zawahiri-nominated Emir of AQIS. In his 55-minute video message, Zawahiri, while celebrating the formation of a new chapter of al-Qaeda, describes AQIS accordingly:

> This entity was not established today, but it is the fruit of a blessed effort for more than two years to gather the mujahideen in the Indian subcontinent into a single entity to be with the main group, Qaedat al-Jihad, from the soldiers of the Islamic Emirate and its triumphant emir, Allah permitting, Emir of the Believers Mullah Muhammad Omar Mujahid (SITE, 2014a).

The Al-Qaeda duo vowed to strike terror in the Indian Subcontinent. Al-Qaeda's rationale was simple: Al-Qaeda just could not allow ISIS to gain ground in the rich jihadi landscape of Pakistan that Al-Qaeda has long been dominating. After the proclamation of the Islamic Caliphate in June 2014, ISIS launched its Khurasan Chapter immediately, keeping in view its goal of gaining ground in Pakistan and Afghanistan. Al-Qaeda even went a step further by including India and Bangladesh in its new set of agendas, apart from not losing any ground to its splinter group, ISIS.

In sum, AQIS is an al-Qaeda project to thwart the IS-K's growing presence in the region, and it is evident that a number of Islamist terrorist organisations (Tehreek-e-Khilafat Pakistan, Jundullah, and the TTP Shahidullah Shahid faction) joined hands with the IS-K operating in Pakistan and based in eastern Afghanistan. Though IS-K did manage to lure in some TTP commanders and militants from sectarian Lashkar-e-Jhangvi and Kashmir-centric Salafi Lashkar-e-Taiba (LeT), overall, few al-Qaeda and other Islamist organisations' militants defected to IS-K. This is perhaps because of the successful strategy of al-Zawahiri for preserving al-Qaeda Central and its associated groups in Pakistan.

A HISTORY OF AQIS'S FORMATION

The Al-Qaeda network in Pakistan is known to be the oldest and strongest. Pakistan is the place where Al-Qaeda was born against the backdrop of the Afghan War (1979–1989) and grew in neighbouring Afghanistan, where it found safe havens during the Afghan Taliban period. AQIS's launch was rather impressive, and the first major operation of AQIS was the attempted hijacking of the Pakistan Navy frigate PNS *Zulfiqar* in September 2014, immediately after the

DOI: 10.4324/9780429426063-65

announcement of AQIS. The perpetrators of the terrorist attack were all radicalised Islamist officers of the Pakistan Navy. The plot did not yield results, and the remaining plotters were arrested by the security forces in Baluchistan province while they were en route to cross the border into neighbouring Afghanistan.

According to details, on September 6, 2014, when National Defence Day was being celebrated across Pakistan, four officers of the Pakistan Navy entered the Pakistan Naval Ships (PNS) Dockyard, located near Karachi harbour, and attempted to take over the warship PNS Zulfiqar. The terrorists planned to hijack the heavily armed destroyer of the Pakistan Navy and then move towards international waters in order to attack US or Indian naval vessels. The carefully planned attack failed miserably. All terrorists (in-service and one retired naval officer of the Pakistan Navy) were subdued and killed by the security forces from the ship, and some who managed to escape were later arrested near Quetta while they were trying to flee to Afghanistan. A week later, on September 11, Al-Qaeda in the Indian Subcontinent (AQIS) Amir Asim Umar claimed responsibility for the attack (Hassan & Houreld, 2014). The attempted hijacking was a mega-terrorist attack, marking the launch of AQIS in the South Asian theatre.

MEDIA AND OUTREACH STRATEGY

Parallel to this development, Al-Qaeda has also inaugurated its new English-language magazine, *Resurgence*. The first issue of Resurgence (released October 2014) primarily focuses on the Indian Subcontinent, with Al-Qaeda Central's official spokesperson Adam Gadahn penning the cover article defining the Al-Qaeda objectives. Gadahn (News Int., Oct. 24, 2014) wrote:

> America considers Islam to be its main enemy and a threat to the foundations of its existence. It has waged an incessant war against Islam and Muslims that has become increasingly overt over the last two decades. It considers itself to be its foremost duty to crush every Islamic movement struggling for the ascendancy of Islam. It is the patron-in-chief of Israel and the real cause of the existence of the oppressive Zionist entity. And last but not the least the United States of America is equally responsible for every single act of oppression carried out against our brethren in Palestine, Syria, Iraq, Yemen, Mali, Burma, Bangladesh, Afghanistan, India, Pakistan as well as the rest of the Islamic world.

With the death of Adam Gadahn in January 2015 in a drone strike in Waziristan, the media and outreach strategy adopted by AQIS appeared to be weakened. It seems that As-Sahab, the primary media wing of Al-Qaeda Central, has now taken over the responsibility of AQIS-related media issues and its publications.

AQIS TARGETS AND ATTACKS

In a separate statement, AQIS' spokesperson, Usama Mehmood, signified the importance of the PNS *Zulfiqar* attack and marvelled at the ferocity of the "mujahideen" who carried out the attack:

> The goal of the PNS Dockyard attack was to take control of two important warships of the PNS Zulfiqar and the PNS Aslat. There were several Mujahid brothers aboard both ships and they were provided with necessary weapons and explosives required for this operation. The first al-Qaeda team was on board PNS Zulfiqar, which departed Karachi on September 3 and was allegedly scheduled to be refueled by USS Supply, which is one of the most important American naval ships after aircraft carriers. While PNS Zulfiqar was to be refueled, some of the Mujahid brothers present on board were to target and destroy the American oil tanker [USS Supply] with the 72 mm anti-aircraft guns on their frigate (News Int., Oct 25, 2014).

Simply put, the AQIS had plans to target the US warships from the hijacked PNS Zulfiqar. The USS Supply, which was part of the naval war games, was the intended target as per the plan.

The establishment of AQIS is the second important strategic decision Zawahiri has taken after the death of former Emir Osama Bin Laden in May 2011. The first one was the appointment of Nasir al-Wuhashi as the Amir of Al-Qaeda in the Arabian Peninsula (AQAP) and upgrading his position to 'General Manager' in Al-Qaeda (Lake, 2013). It appears that Zawahiri is all set to compete with the newly surfaced Jihadi challenger, the Islamic State, a splinter group of Al-Qaeda in Iraq led by Abu Bakr al-Baghdadi, whom Zawahiri has cast out of Al-Qaeda in favour of his favourite Mohammad al-Joulani of the Nusrah Front. The emergence of IS as a competitor to Zawahiri's Jihadi throne seems quite perturbing for him and has compelled him to reorganise his 26-year-old transnational jihadi outfit.

In Bangladesh, Jamiat al Mujahedeen, Ansarullah Bangla Team, and AQIS have perpetrated some isolated acts of terrorism involving lone wolves. The lone wolves inspired by AQIS have claimed and remained involved in murdering secular bloggers, LGBTI activists, and foreigners in terrorist attacks during 2016 and 2017. By 2018, Bangladeshi law enforcement and security forces had been able to disrupt and dismantle planned terrorist attacks and arrest scores of individuals involved in previous terrorist attacks.[1] In India, Zakir Musa is currently leading Ansar al-Ghawa tul Hind (AGH) and has pledged allegiance to al-Zawahiri, which has been duly endorsed by Al-Qaeda Central's Global Islamic Media Front. A US serviceman, Sgt. Leandro Jasso, was killed in November 2018 during a gun battle with AQIS and Afghan Taliban militants in Nimroz province, Afghanistan. The clash showcased the AQIS presence in Afghanistan, and it has become evident that Al-Qaeda militants are embedded in the Afghan Taliban-led insurgency. Despite its presence in Afghanistan and pledge of loyalty to the Afghan Taliban, Al-Qaeda appears not to publicly advertise its presence in Afghanistan.

OBJECTIVES

Zawahiri's primary objective in launching a separate wing amid the presence of al-Qaeda Central in the same region of Pakistan and Afghanistan appears strategic and competitive rather than tactical. It seems he does not want to allow any other global Islamist terrorist organisations to recruit, operate, and establish safe havens in the rich and fertile jihadi landscape of Pakistan. No other country could be richer in Jihadi human resources than Pakistan. Al-Qaeda has been in Pakistan for the last three decades; the organisation was formed and remained in the region (with a sabbatical in Sudan in the early 1990s) and has established relations with local Islamist terrorist organisations, charity groups, and, to some extent, developed links with Islamist political parties. Many al-Qaeda on-the-run high-profile leaders and commanders were arrested from the houses of leaders of Jamaat-e-Islami, a local Islamist party.

Zawahiri appeared with his own hand-picked Emir of AQIS in a video to announce the establishment of this new chapter of al-Qaeda. In his video message, alongside newly-appointed Amir of AQIS Asim Umar and spokesperson Usama Mahmoud, he also stated the objectives of AQIS, which are slightly different from AQ Central's objectives. According to him, the organisation would strive for the establishment of a global caliphate, and its work would start in the Khorasan region, such as Pakistan, India, Afghanistan, Burma, Central Asia, and Bangladesh. As the primary objective is related to terrorist activities in South Asia, he said the imposition of Shaia laws in the region would be another target of the AQIS. Since the organisation is regional, it would work with local Islamist organisations that are fighting against the apostate regimes of Pakistan, India, Burma, and Bangladesh, especially in the regions where Muslims are undersea, such as Kashmir, Arakan, Assam, Gujrat, Ahmadabad, and Bangladesh (SITE, 2014b).

LEADERSHIP, KEY PERSONNEL, AND STRUCTURE

Zawahiri appointed Asim Umar (real name Sana ul Haq) as the Amir of AQIS, who also featured in the same video and stated the salient objectives of AQIS. Umar is a known jihadi ideologue from Pakistan and a former high-ranking leader of Harkat ul Jihad-e-Islami and later Harkat ul Mujahideen (Zahid, 2014). Acknowledged as a skilled propagandist in jihadi circles in Pakistan, Umar has been releasing video statements and press releases for Al-Qaeda and Tehreek-e-Taliban Pakistan (TTP) for the last two years. Umar is also fond of writing books on Dajjal (the Antichrist). His books, such as World War III and Dajjal, Bermuda Triangle and Dajjal, Lashkar of Dajjal: The Black Water in Pakistan, and Friends and Foes of the Messiah, are widely available at jihadi bookstores in Pakistan.

Umar's long association with Al-Qaeda Core is evident from the fact that before being elevated to the position of Amir of AQIS, he served as head of AQ's Sharia committee in Pakistan. After taking charge of AQIS, Umar has reaffirmed his stance by declaring the US his prime enemy and emphasising the need to defeat the US and its allies everywhere. In his message to the Indian youth, he exclaimed, "From the land of Afghanistan, a caravan is heading towards India, not on someone's directive. Not on the basis of some governmental policy. But simply on the basis of abiding by God's command" (CEP, 2014).

Umar, because of his long jihadi career in Afghanistan, Kashmir, and Pakistan, is fluent in Arabic, Urdu, Uzbek, and Pashto. He is not only considered a good orator but also well-versed in Islamic clerical issues. However, little is known about his jihadi credentials as far as jihadi activities are concerned. According to one source in the Karachi police department, he is more of an ideologue than an actual fighter.[2] Umar appears to focus on already ongoing jihadi activities in Indian Kashmir, Assam, Myanmar, and Pakistan. He seems to be galvanising support from Islamist radical youth in order to raise a new cluster of jihadists from the regions experiencing jihadi turbulence. Interestingly, Umar is not a Pakistani by birth, as he joined the jihadi movement in Pakistan at an early age during the Afghan War (1979–1989) period and has since lived in Pakistan and Afghanistan. Now in his mid-40s, Umar received his early education from the notorious Jamia Uloom-ul-Islamia, Karachi, a madrasah noted for its jihadi credentials.

According to senior Pakistani journalist and analyst Hamid Mir, Asim Umar is an Indian national, and he claimed to have met him several times in Afghanistan. Mir also claimed that Asim Umar remained in close contact with Bin Laden until his death in May 2011. Umar is a student of Mufti Nizam ud-Din Shamzia, the former head of Jamia Uloom ul Islamia. Karachi was a widely recognised jihadi cleric, an ardent supporter of the Taliban Movement, and patron of Pakistani Jihadi organisations Harkat-ul Jihad-e-Islami (HuJI), Harkat-ul Mujahideen (HuM), and Jaish-e-Mohammad (JeM). Shamzia issued a fatwa against the US invasion of Afghanistan and called for Jihad against the US, inspiring thousands to reach Afghanistan amid the US invasion in October 2001.

Being a veteran jihadi, Umar has worked with HuM and its forerunner, HuJI, in Afghanistan and Pakistan. HuJI is considered the oldest jihadi group in Pakistan. It emerged in 1983 during the Afghan War (1979–1989). HuJI was led by Qari Saifullah Akhter and Fazal ur-Rehman Khalil. A few years later, in 1987, Khalil parted ways with Akhter and formed his own group, HuM, with a focus on the Islamist insurgency in Indian Kashmir. HuM further splintered into Jaish-e-Mohammad (JeM) after the successful swapping of hijacked Indian airline passengers in 1999 for jailed propagandist of HuM Masoud Azhar in India, along with Ahmed Omar Saeed Shaikh (a British-born, LSE drop-out member of HuM) and Mushtaq Zargar of Al-Badr Mujahedeen.

After the 9/11 attacks and the Pakistani government's decision to become part of the US-led alliance, HuM's new splinter group, HuM-al-Alami, surfaced in Karachi with two consecutive assassination attempts on President General Pervez Musharraf in 2002. In February 1998, HuM organised Bin Laden's press conference in Khost, Afghanistan, where he proclaimed his Fatwa against the US and its allies and also announced the formation of the Islamic Front against Jews and Crusaders.

Umar also studied at Darul Uloom Haqania madrasah, located in Khyber Pakhtunkhawa province of Pakistan and reckoned as a "jihad factory" because of its decades-old practise of sending students to Afghanistan to fight against the Russian and later American forces. With a more than 10,000-strong student body, the madrasah is headed by Sami ul Haq, leader of the Deobandi sect Islamist party Jamiat-e-Ulema Islam. Half of the Afghan Taliban cabinet considered Darul Uloom Haqania their alma mater. (Reuters, 2018) Mullah Omar, the supreme commander of the Afghan Taliban, had reportedly studied at the madrasah. According to senior Pakistani journalist and analyst Hamid Mir, Asim Umar is an Indian national, and he claimed to have met him several times in Afghanistan. In an interview, Hamid Mir stated:

> Asim Umar is an Indian Muslim, that's his only qualification for which he was appointed head of al-Qaeda's South Asia chapter, Yes, I have met Asim Umar … I met him for the first time in 2005, I was visiting Afghanistan. In those days, the Afghan Taliban were in control of Andar district of Ghazni province. I was visiting the tomb of Mahmud Ghaznavi. Somebody there contacted me, it was a taxi driver. He asked me, 'Oh, you come on Geo TV'. I said yes. He said 'Amir sahab wants to meet you'. I asked him who Amir Sahab was. He said, 'Don't worry, don't worry. We will not harm you. We will give you a story' … .in 2007, I met him again in North Waziristan. Then I came to know that he was forced to leave Ghazni province because he had developed differences with some local commander. The local commander had alleged that he was an Indian spy. So the Pakistani Taliban protected him and he came to Pakistani tribal area. Now he is absent. But recently I received a lot of literature written by him, both in English and Urdu. So I had one meeting with him in 2005, and one again in 2007 (Chakraborty, 2014).

Umar appears to be a seasoned jihadi, and his connections with local Islamist terrorist organisations in Pakistan, India, Bangladesh, and Burma would eventually be quite useful for al-Qaeda Central. It is also possible that Umar has been working with al-Qaeda for quite some time but has remained off the radar of the intelligence and security agencies of Pakistan and the US. His contacts and connections would allow AQIS operatives access to and mobility around South Asia's jihadi circles.

ASIM UMAR: A VETERAN JIHADI

Zawahiri's decision to nominate Umar as the head of AQIS is both strategic and tactical. In a way, Zawahiri is trying to regroup the plethora of Pakistani Islamist and jihadist groups under the banner of AQIS. With HuM, HuJI, JeM, and LeJ in despair in Pakistan, the Indian Mujahideen (IM) and Student Islamic Movement of India (SIMI) are indeed looking for a new brand to cover their failures. There is a need to reinvigorate their jihadi activities, and AQIS could provide them with a new setting for renewing their jihadi credentials. The disgruntled Rohingya Muslim community in Myanmar, already tilting towards the Al-Qaeda-linked Itihadul Mujahideen of Arakan (IMA), may slide towards AQIS. The radical Islamist Jamaat-e-Islami in Bangladesh could also provide potential recruits for AQIS. Because of his long affiliation with Islamist terrorist groups active in Indian Kashmir, the primary focus of Umar is expected to be Indian Kashmir, the only Muslim-majority province in India. He reflected on his thoughts in videos released earlier:

> To wave Islam's flag over Srinagar's Lal Chowk … caravans are heading from Afghanistan to liberate India and it is not being done on instructions of any intelligence agency, and not as part of some governmental policy, but simply to abide God's command … (Yasir, 2014).

He further elucidated the cause of Islamist Kashmiri organisations fighting for the freedom of Kashmir from India and eulogised their sacrifices. Umar has repeatedly criticised Pakistani authorities for their failure to support jihad in Indian Kashmir. He denounced the Pakistani state, its intelligence agencies, military, and law enforcement bodies for acting against 'mujahedeen on behalf of 'infidels' (the US and allies). In his July 2013 video titled Why is there no storm in your ocean? Umar elucidated his approach regarding the establishment of a caliphate in accordance with al-Qaeda (Roul, 2013).

AFGHAN TALIBAN CONNECTIONS AND AFFILIATION

In an interesting development, primarily to encounter the growing influence of the Islamic State of Iraq and Syria (ISIS), which recently announced the establishment of a caliphate comprising territories in Iraq and Syria, the AQIS reaffirmed its allegiance to Taliban supreme commander Mullah Mohammad Omar. Omar, the self-proclaimed Emir ul Momineen of the Islamic Emirate of Afghanistan, considers himself the sole Emir (representative) of all Muslims, a claim that Abu Bakr al-Baghdadi has also endeavoured to make. Zawahiri, while announcing AQIS, also deliberated on the Afghan Taliban and eulogised their efforts, calling them the 'soldiers of the Islamic Emirate'. Slain Al-Qaeda chief Osama bin Laden had pledged an oath of allegiance to Mullah Omar during his stay in Taliban-ruled Afghanistan.

> My pledge of allegiance to the Emir of the Believers [Mullah Omar] is the great pledge of allegiance, which is mentioned in the chapters of the Koran and the stories of the Sunnah. Every Muslim should set his mind and heart and pledge allegiance to the Emir of the Believers Mullah Muhammad Omar for this is the great pledge (Joscelyn, 2016).

The oath effectively made Al-Qaeda part of the Afghan Taliban and their short-lived Islamic Emirate of Afghanistan. After the rise of ISIS and the announcement of the Caliphate (Islamic State) by the ISIS leader Abu Bakr al-Baghdadi, the new Al-Qaeda Emir Ayman al-Zawahiri, in a carefully calculated move, reaffirmed its allegiance to Mullah Omar. In a statement issued by Al-Qaeda through its al-Nafir news bulletin,

> The first edition (Al-Nafir) begins by renewing the pledge of allegiance to [the] Emir of the Believers Mullah Muhammad Omar Mujahid, may Allah preserve him, and confirming that al Qaeda and its branches everywhere are soldiers among his soldiers, under his victorious banner to the coming State of the Caliphate (Joscelyn, 2014).

Zawahiri later renewed his pledge of allegiance to Afghan Taliban supreme leaders Mullah Mansour and Mullah Haibatullah in 2015 and 2016, respectively.

A JIHADI IDEOLOGUE AND WARRIOR

Asim Umar is also known for his jihadi credentials as an ideologue, propagandist, and active figure amongst the jihadi forces in Pakistan. His selection by Zawahiri from the available pool of senior jihadis is by no means a coincidence. Umar has worked with almost all major jihadi organisations operating in Pakistan, and he may help Al-Qaeda Core strengthen ties through a possible merger. The immense number of jihadis in Pakistan and the number of attacks during the last 12 years prove the point that Pakistan's huge youth bulge may provide a pool of new potential dedicated jihadis to Al-Qaeda. AQIS may provide a platform to tap the available resources. Umar's connections with Pakistani sectarian outfits and Islamist Kashmiri jihadi organisations would be an asset for Al-Qaeda given its expected resurgence in Pakistan and India.

JIHADI WRITINGS AND OTHER WORKS

Umar, the newly appointed Emir of AQIS, has written a number of conspiracy theory books. Umar writes in Urdu, the national language of Pakistan. His favourite topic is Dajjal (the Antichrist). Despite being part of the Pakistani jihadist network, Umar focuses on cosmic and Manichean issues like the second coming of Christ, Messiah, Armageddon, and Anti-Christ and connects upcoming scenarios with current events like the US invasion of Afghanistan, private security contractor Black Water, or XE, and the Bermuda Triangle. Umar's conspiracy theory books are mainly about Dajjal.

Dajjal Ka Lashkar: Black Water (Army of Anti-Christ: The Black Water)

Umar describes events related to private security company Black Water's (XE) activities in Pakistan and narrates some of his own experiences. In his view, the employment of Black Water in Pakistan and its growing influence at the behest of Pakistani apostate rulers is indeed a Christian-Jewish conspiracy against Pakistan, much bigger than anyone's imaginations. Umar considers Black Water an organisation of religious fanatics spying in Pakistan. Black Water, according to Umar, is working to steal Pakistan's nuclear assets, and it is part of a wider plan for setting conditions right before the arrival of Dajjal. Black Water, as Umar considers it, has managed to create an economic crisis in Pakistan, has already recruited thousands of apostate Pakistanis, and is trying hard to push the Pakistani government to provide them bases and airstrips over Pakistani territory. In the last chapter, Umar lists US military bases in the Indian Ocean and the Middle East (Umar, 2009a).

World War III and Dajjal

Umar links the Third World War with the arrival of Dajjal while describing signs and events before Armageddon. Umar identifies a long list of events, from wars in Bosnia, Chechnya, Pakistan, India, Syria, and Iraq, and even relates the roles of the IMF, World Bank, international media, private firms like Black Water, and multinationals like Nestle, to a 'western plan' to depopulate Muslim countries by launching population control campaigns. (Umar, 2006b).

Friends and foes of the Messiah (Imam Mehdi ke Doost aur Dushman)

Paving the way for another conspiracy theory, Umar links various different conspiracies such as the role of Shia clergy and the collusion of various different Shia sects (Ismailis, Alawis, etc.). Another big sign, according to Umar, is the emancipation of women. Umar lists families such as the Rockefellers, Bush, Agha Khan, and others who have been hatching conspiracies against the Imam (Messiah). In a tacit manner, Umar links the Yemeni people and indirectly Osama Bin Laden in upholding the truth and as friends of the Imam. Umar dedicates the book to Ghazi Abdur Rasheed, leader of radical Islamists killed during the Red Mosque Operation (Operation Silence) in July 2007 in Islamabad (Umar, 2009c).

Bermuda Triangle and Dajjal

Umar describes the Bermuda Triangle and the disappearances of vessels in detail. He narrates eyewitness accounts and then elucidates the links between extraterrestrials and Dajjal with the US government, NASA, the Pentagon, and American scientists in the loop. Umar then comes over to his favourite conspiracy theory: linking Shias, the US government, the European Union, apostate Muslim regimes, Black Water, United Nations' organisations such as WHO, and UNICEF all together in order to side with Dajjal at the end of days. Umar dedicates this book to prisoners at Guantanamo Bay (Umar, 2009d).

ORGANISATIONAL CHARACTERISTICS AND ACTIVITIES: STRUCTURE, CHANGE, AND OPERATIONS

AQIS started its terrorist campaign by assassinating a senior military officer of the Pakistan Army. Brigadier General Zahoor Fazal Qadri was assassinated while saying prayers at a local shrine in his hometown of Sarghoda district in Punjab province on September 6, 2014. The AQIS militants killed Qadri and two others in the attack, while seven other people received injuries. AQIS spokesperson Usama Mahmood claimed responsibility, stating that "the Sargodha attack should be taken as a warning by the slaves of [the United States of] America in the Pakistani Armed Forces to leave the US-backed 'war on terror' or get ready to face the consequences" (Zahid, 2014).

The AQIS's launch was quite impressive, and the first major operation of the AQIS was the attempted hijacking of the Pakistan Navy frigate PNS Zulfiqar in September 2014, immediately after the announcement of the AQIS. The perpetrators of the terrorist attack were all radicalised Islamist officers of the Pakistan Navy. The Navy Cell of AQIS could not successfully execute its grand operation, but the attempt to hijack had indeed showcased AQIS's resolve and ambitions.

Several high-profile leaders of AQIS have been neutralised in the past few years in Pakistan. In 2018, the AQIS could not outperform IS-K as far as terrorist activities are concerned. It suffered some major losses. Some of the most-wanted AQIS terrorists were arrested by CTD Karachi, and the organisation could not manage to strike terror in retaliation.

According to several Pakistani police and security forces officials interviewed for this chapter, the AQIS operates in a cell-based structure, with a number of cells operating in Karachi and other parts of Pakistan. It has connections and bases in Afghanistan with the tacit support of the Afghan Taliban. It has a centralised structure managed by its Emir and a spokesperson responsible for issuing statements and communiqués and seeking intermittent support from Al-Qaeda Central's media wings.[3] It is not clear that Al-Qaeda-linked Jamaat al-Ansar al-Shariah, a terrorist group that perpetrated a number of terrorist attacks in Karachi in 2016–2017, had any links with AQIS. The JAS had pledged allegiance to the Al-Qaeda Emir, dropped their agenda at the site of a terrorist attack, and published a number of communiqués after terrorist attacks against police and workers of the overtly secular political party Muttahida Quami Movement (MQM) in Karachi. It has also come to light that some of the AQIS cells have now defected to IS-K in Pakistan and are now operating from Afghanistan's eastern provinces.[4]

Another AQIS Karachi cell had defected to IS-K and executed the Safoora Goth terrorist attack, massacring 47 Islmaili-Shia community members in May 2015. The arrested militants revealed during investigations that they used to be part of AQIS but later pledged allegiance to Caliph Abu Bakr al-Baghdadi and perpetrated the killing of Shias, MQM workers, and civil society activists in Karachi. Some of the members of the IS-K cell had been arrested after the Safoora attack because of diligent police investigations. Most of the arrested ones turned out to be highly educated, urban, and belonged to affluent families in Karachi.

With a pretty impressive and solid beginning in 2014 and 2015, the AQIS could not continue with its violent spree. In the last two years, i.e., 2017 and 2018, the AQIS could not outperform IS-K as far as terrorist activities are concerned. AQIS has suffered some major losses. The Counter Terrorism Department (CTD) in Karachi has arrested some of the most-wanted AQIS terrorists, and the organisation could not manage to strike terror in retaliation. Most important of all was the arrest of Umar Jalal Chandio, alias Kathio, the Emir of AQIS Sindh. The CTD Karachi arrested him in Karachi's Gulshan-e-Iqbal locality on November 20. Chandio inspired the terrorists involved in the Safoora Goth incident in 2015. Before joining IS-K, Tahir Minhas, alias Sain, remained a member of AQIS and close to Chandio. A total of 47 members of the Ismail-Shia community were shot dead by the IS-K cell militants near Safoora Goth in the suburbs of Karachi. Chandio's wife is also said to be an active member of AQIS (Dawn, 2018). After his arrest, Raja Umar Khattab, in charge of CTD Karachi, revealed in the press conference that:

> Jalal was associated with Al Qaeda's Arab network while Haji Sahib (code name) was active in Karachi and the Wadh area of Balochistan where the group's mainly Baloch youths were involved in kidnapping for ransom, terrorism and attacks on Nato forces' containers (Dawn, 2018).

Another important AQIS commander, Ahsan Mehsud alias Roshan, was arrested in Karachi in March 2018. Mehsud was involved in planning to assassinate secular and anti-Islamist party leaders of the Muthada Quami Movement (MQM) in order to create chaos in the city. He was also considered close to the masterminds of the Safoora Goth incident (Ali, 2018). Apart from operations in Pakistan, where AQIS remained on the back foot, the terror entity has been able to perpetrate acts of terrorism in Afghanistan. It is also said that the AQIS leadership, including its Emir Asim Umar, is based in Afghanistan under Afghan Taliban tutelage. Though some terrorist acts attributed to AQIS have been reported in Afghanistan,

A US serviceman, Sgt. Leandro Jasso, was killed in November 2018 during a gun battle with AQIS and Afghan Taliban militants in Nimroz province, Afghanistan. The clash showcased the AQIS presence in Afghanistan, and it has become evident that Al-Qaeda militants are embedded in the Afghan Taliban-led insurgency. Despite its presence in Afghanistan and pledge of loyalty to the Afghan Taliban, Al-Qaeda appears not to publicly advertise its presence in Afghanistan. (Joscelyn, 2018) Earlier, in 2015, a large training facility (probably the largest ever found) was run and managed by AQIS in Shorabak district of Kandahar province, Afghanistan. The camp was spread over some 30 square miles and was located in the heart of the Afghan Taliban. A senior Al-Qaeda figure, Abu Khalil al-Sudani, was killed in the US airstrike in July 2015 at the same place. According to the US commander, General John F. Campbell, "It's a place where you would probably think you wouldn't have AQ. I would agree with that. This was really AQIS, and probably the largest training camp-type facility that we have seen in 14 years of war." (Joscelyn, 2015).

CAPITALISING ON GHAZWA TUL HIND NARRATIVE

AQIS is cognizant of the fact that the Ghazwa tul Hind narrative could be well utilised during recruitment for AQIS and Dawah practises in South Asia. Zakir Musa, founder of the AQ-affiliated AGH and a former HuM militant active in the Islamist insurgency in Indian Kashmir, is well conversant with the issue. He stated:

> Our struggle is for implementation of Shariah. It is an Islamic struggle ... I am warning them (Hurriyat leaders) not to play their politics. If they again try to become thorns in our path, the first thing we will do is behead you and hang you in Lal Chowk. We will leave the infidels and kill you first (Wire India, 2017).

Radical Islamists and terrorist groups in South Asia have this long tradition of invoking the Ghazwa-e-Hind narrative, i.e., prophesying a great battle against India and bringing Armageddon, as provided in some Hadith (though their traditions are weak). In the same manner, AQIS capitalises on these ancient prophecies, highlighting the concepts of Khurasan, Mahdi (Messiah), the end of times, the surfacing of black banners from Khurasan before the Qayamat (judgement day), and Dajjal (anti-Christ).

These end-of-time concepts and narratives are central to AQIS's building its own version of jihad, though in line with other jihadi groups such as IS. - K. Zawahiri, in his audio message, denounced the governments of Pakistan and Bangladesh for their corrupt and un-Islamic practises and condemned these countries for not having Sharia laws and acting as hired mercenaries (Reed, 2016). The attempted hijacking of PNS Zulfiqar by the Navy Cell of AQIS was another manifestation of its leadership's desire to bring about revolutionary events for the sake of invoking Ghazwa-e-Hind.

THE DEOBANDI INFLUENCE

Al-Qaeda, since its formation in the aftermath of the Afghan War (1979–89), has been a Salafi jihadi organisation. But it could not be termed solely a terrorist movement of Salafis, as many of the Al-Qaeda-linked Islamist terrorist organisations, especially in its birthplace (Pakistan), are Deobandi by virtue of their adherence. Many of the Al-Qaeda-linked Islamist terrorist groups are Deobandi by origin and practise, such as TTP, JeM, LeJ, and others. The Afghan Taliban, the primary backers of Al-Qaeda and its subsidiary AQIS, are staunch Deobandis. Hence, we could safely say that the Deobandi influence on AQIS is immense and is likely to remain. In technical terms, al-Qaeda Central is part of the broader movement of Afghan Taliban because of the repeated pledges of allegiance of Al-Qaeda Emirs to Afghan Taliban Emir al-Momineens, i.e., Bin Laden's pledge of allegiance to Mullah Omar in 1999 and subsequent pledges of allegiance of Zawahiri to Mullah Mansoor and Mullah Haibatullah in 2013 and 2015. Moreover, the current leadership of AQIS is comprised of veteran Deobandi jihadis and ideologues such as Asim Umar.

FACTORS INFLUENCING RESILIENCE

As discussed earlier, the cell-based structure of AQIS is one of the factors influencing its resilience in the subcontinent. One of the renowned Al-Qaeda strategists, Abu Musab al-Suri (Mustafa Set Mariam), has presented the strategy of leaderless Jihad in his book The Global Call for Islamic Resistance, a method inspired by the leaderless resistance of the Christian Fundamentalist Movement. According to Abu Musab, Al-Qaeda cells and members must not coordinate terrorist strikes but instead perpetrate and launch terrorist attacks wherever they are and with whatever means are available at their disposal. Al-Qaeda no longer has the centralised structure that it did prior to the 9/11 attacks. After the US invasion of Afghanistan, Al-Qaeda operated as a network of networks, and after the death of Bin Laden in 2011, the organisation has been working purely on cell-based structures while launching terrorist attacks across the globe and working in tandem with local Islamist terrorist organisations from Indonesia to Nigeria and in the west. The AQIS has also adopted a similar mode in the subcontinent, where it has found a rich jihadi landscape, a plethora of jihadi terrorist groups, educated and urban radicalised youth, and a steady supply of funds from Islamist circles and likeminded Islamist charity organisations. The presence of safe havens in the ungoverned territories of Pakistan and Afghanistan is another factor providing resilience to the sustained growth of AQIS in the subcontinent and Afghanistan.

AQIS CODE OF CONDUCT

In June 2017, the AQIS published its code of conduct for guiding its commanders and rank and file. The code focuses on AQIS's strict obedience to Al-Qaeda's central leadership and its relations with it in following the orders and guidelines of the central leadership. The code describes a number of issues, such as avoiding the killing of non-combatants, preventing its fighters from speaking against Ulemas, waging war against infidel countries, strict obedience to Emir al-Momineen Mullah Haibatullah, fighting beside Afghan Taliban forces, and fighting against the west, Pakistan, India, Bangladesh, and Burma. Concerning Pakistan, the AQIS code is quite specific in identifying targets such as the military, police, intelligence agencies, ministries, launching prison break operations, and kidnappings of security officials and Westerners in the country. The code also signified the importance of launching attacks in India, as this country is an ally of the West and promotes secularism and anti-Islamic ideas. Targets in India include state agencies, the police, the military, Hindu leadership, and all those involved in the 'genocide of Muslims'. In Burma, the AQIS code calls for terrorist strikes against armed Buddhist groups and the military in order to liberate the Arakan region. With all the other targets mentioned earlier, the specific targets in Bangladesh are those individuals involved in blasphemous acts. In a departure from its earlier policy measures, the AQIS designated Shia, Qadyanis, and Ismailis as kafirs but directed its commanders to refrain from attacking them as the AQIS does not want to get involved in peripheral battles unless these communities act against Sunnis in a hostile manner. In other sections of the 20-page document, the AQIS defines areas of operations such as taking prisoners and then exchanging them for imprisoned colleagues or demanding ransom rather than killing them, developing liaisons with other jihadi groups working to achieve the same objectives, advising religious democratic parties despite a difference of opinion on democratic systems of governance, and finally avoiding getting involved in issues related to secondary issues related to denominational matters causing disharmony among Muslims (Joscelyn, 2017).

CONCLUSION

Founded against the backdrop of the Soviet defeat in Afghanistan after a long guerrilla campaign by Afghan Islamists backed by the US, Pakistan, Saudi Arabia, and scores of other countries, Al-Qaeda until recently had not been challenged by any other global Islamist terrorist organisation for reaffirming its jihadi credentials. After the breakaway of Al-Qaeda in Iraq and its rechristening into ISIS, Al-Qaeda Central felt the need to reinvigorate itself. The militant Islamist movement indeed managed to become an umbrella organisation of Islamist terrorist organisations across the world, with branches and affiliates in more than 60 countries. Credited for masterminding and perpetrating some of the biggest ever terrorist attacks in the world and reaching out to Islamist terrorist groups within a span of a quarter century without losing momentum, these are some of the feathers in Al-Qaeda's cap.

The splintering away of Al-Qaeda in Iraq (aka Al-Qaeda in the Land of Two Rivers or Islamic State of Iraq) under the leadership of Abu Bakr al-Baghdadi has indeed challenged Al-Qaeda to keep the throne of jihad. Al-Qaeda badly needed to reinvigorate in order to survive in the jihadi world. The jihadi sympathisers are now expecting much more from Al-Qaeda; otherwise, Al-Qaeda would not be able to lure in younger generations of jihadis. On the other hand, ISIS is in good shape to carve out many of Al-Qaeda's assets. Strategically speaking, Al-Qaeda is on retreat in order to refurbish itself for a long war.

Al-Qaeda's Emir Ayman al-Zawahiri is all set to compete with ISIS. It is expected that with the rich jihadi landscape of Pakistan, where a plethora of jihadi organisations are operating, he may be able to grind his axes and capitalise on the state's existing vulnerabilities. Elevating Asim Umar as Emir of AQIS is a tactical move, keeping in view Umar's experience working with jihadi organisations. It is expected that Umar will also be able to widen the Al-Qaeda network in Pakistan, Bangladesh, Myanmar, and India.

The raison d'être of AQIS is to reinvigorate Al-Qaeda in South Asia and to present a new brand of Al-Qaeda for supporters and sympathisers in India, Pakistan, Myanmar, and Bangladesh. The newly established AQIS would provide an impetus to the moribund existence of Al-Qaeda, especially after the death of former Emir Osama Bin Laden in 2011. The Indian Subcontinent does contain a huge pool of disgruntled Islamist radicals for whom joining IS would be far more difficult than joining hands with already existing Al-Qaeda, only if it provided them with a potent platform to execute terrorist activities.

Notes

1 Personal communication with a senior Bangladesh police officer (Singapore, January 24, 2019).
2 Personal communication with a senior Pakistani police officer (Islamabad, Pakistan, December 10, 2018).
3 Personal communication with a senior Pakistani police officer (Islamabad, Pakistan, December 10, 2018).
4 Personal communication with a senior Pakistani police officer (Islamabad, Pakistan, December 10, 2018).

References

"Al Qaeda threatens jihad on India". https://news.yahoo.com/al-qaeda-threatens-jihad-on-india-090211303.html

Ali, I. (2018, Mar 3). Most wanted AQIS militant said to be close aide of Safoora carnage convicts arrested. *Dawn*. Available at https://www.dawn.com/news/1392746

Chakraborty, N. (2014, Oct 19). Al-Qaeda regional chief an Indian, met him twice: Pakistani journalist Hamid Mir. *Indian Express*. Available at: https://indianexpress.com/article/india/india-others/al-qaeda-regional-chief-an-indian-met-him-twice-pakistani-journalist-hamid-mir/

Dawn. (2018, Nov 20). AQIS 'high profile' militant held in Karachi. Available at: https://www.dawn.com/news/1446665

Hassan, S.R. and Houreld, K. (2014, Oct 1). In attack by al Qaeda, lines blur between Pakistan's military, militants. *Reuters*. Available at: https://www.reuters.com/article/us-pakistan-militants-attacks-insight/in-attack-by-al-qaeda-lines-blur-between-pakistans-military-militants-idUSKCN0HP2MM20141001

Joscelyn, T. (2014, July 21). Al Qaeda renews its oath of allegiance to Taliban leader Mullah Omar. *Long War Journal*. https://www.longwarjournal.org/archives/2014/07/al_qaeda_renews_its.php

Joscelyn, T. (2016, June 11). Ayman al-Zawahiri swears allegiance to the Taliban's new leader. *Long War Journal*. Available at: https://www.longwarjournal.org/archives/2016/06/ayman-al-zawahiri-swears-allegiance-to-the-talibans-new-leader.php

Joscelyn, T. (2015, Oct 31). Al-Qaeda's Kandahar training camp 'probably the largest' in Afghan War. *Long War Journal*. Available at: https://www.longwarjournal.org/archives/2015/10/al-qaedas-kandahar-training-camp-probably-the-largest-in-afghan-war.php

Joscelyn, T. (2017, June 26). AQIS emphasizes allegiance to Ayman al Zawahiri, Taliban in new "code of conduct". *Long War Journal*. https://www.longwarjournal.org/archives/2017/06/aqis-emphasizes-allegiance-to-ayman-al-zawahiri-taliban-in-new-code-of-conduct.php

Joscelyn, T. (2018, Nov 27). US serviceman killed during battle with Al-Qaeda in Afghanistan. *Long War Journal*. Available at: https://www.longwarjournal.org/archives/2018/11/us-service-member-killed-during-battle-with-al-qaeda-in-afghanistan.php

Lake, E. (2013, Aug 9). Meet Al-Qaeda's new General Manager: Nasser al-Wuhayshi. *Daily Beast*. Available at: https://www.thedailybeast.com/meet-al-qaedas-new-general-manager-nasser-al-wuhayshi

News International. (2014, Oct 25). Al-Qaeda unveils future terror plot linking Pakistan. Available at: https://www.thenews.com.pk/archive/print/532669

Personal communication with a senior Bangladesh police officer. (January 24, 2019). Singapore.

Personal communication with a senior Pakistani police officer. (December 10, 2018). Islamabad, Pakistan.

Reed, A. (2016). Al Qaeda in the Indian subcontinent: A new frontline in the Global Jihadist Movement? The International Centre for Counter-Terrorism: The Hague. DOI: 10.19165/2016.2.02

Reuters. (2018, Nov 2). Father of Taliban Mullah Sami ul Haq killed in Pakistan. Available at: https://www.reuters.com/article/us-pakistan-cleric-taliban/father-of-taliban-mullah-sami-ul-haq-killed-in-pakistani-city-deputy-idUSKCN1N71U3

Roul, A. (2013, October 17). Al Qaeda's latest bid to woo India's Muslims. International Security Network. https://www.files.ethz.ch/isn/188268/ISN_170939_en.pdf

SITE. (2014a). Message of Ayman al-Zawahiri, translated by SITE Monitoring Services Group, July 20, 2014.

SITE. (2014b). Message of Dr Ayman al-Zawahiri, translated by SITE Intelligence Group, September 2014.

Umar, A. (2006b). *Teesri Jang -e- Azeem Aur Dajjal*. Bagh, Azad Kashmir: Al-Ghazi Welfare Trust.

Umar, A. (2009c). *Imam Mehdi ke Doost aur Dushman*. Karachi: Al-Hajira Publications.

Umar, A. (2009d). *Bermuda Tikon aur Dajjal*. Karachi: Al-Hajira Publications.

Umar, A.U. (2009a) *Dajjal Ka Lashkar: Black Water*. Islamabad: Jamia Hafsa Urdu Forum.

Wire India. (2017, May 15). With call for 'Islamic Rule', Zakir Musa may have signalled ideological split in Kashmir militancy. https://thewire.in/politics/kashmir-hizbul-mujahideen-hurriyat-zakir-musa

Yasir, S. (2014, June 16). Join global movement for Jihad, al-Qaeda tells Kashmiris in new video. *First Post*. Available at: https://www.firstpost.com/india/join-global-movement-for-jihad-al-qaeda-tells-kashmiris-in-new-video-1572919.html

Zahid, F. (2014, Oct 24). Al-Qaeda's future in Pakistan amid the rise of Islamic State. *Terrorism Monitor, 12*(20), Jamestown Foundation Available at: https://jamestown.org/program/al-qaedas-future-in-pakistan-amid-the-rise-of-islamic-state/

58

THE TALIBAN INSURGENCY IN AFGHANISTAN

Historical Contexts and Contemporary Challenges

Nabil Ouassini and Anwar Ouassini

INTRODUCTION

The war in Afghanistan has become the longest war in American history. In the two decades following the events of September 11, the Afghan Taliban has continued to endure and has signed a 2020 peace deal with the U.S. government under the Trump administration. The contemporary Afghan Taliban is not the same organisation that governed Afghanistan from the mid-1990s through 2001. During the Taliban's five-year rule, the harbouring of terrorist organisations and the implementation of a radical interpretation of Islamic law turned Afghanistan into a pariah state that maintained formal diplomatic relations only with Pakistan, Saudi Arabia, and the United Arab Emirates (UAE). The Taliban's refusal to extradite Usama bin Laden to the United States after the 9/11 attacks led to Operation Enduring Freedom and the overthrow of the Islamic Emirate of Afghanistan.

The international community's authorisation of the International Security Assistance Force (ISAF) to provide security for the newly established Islamic Republic of Afghanistan was a crucial component in the reconstruction of institutions and infrastructure in the war-torn country. However, the Bush Administration's subsequent invasion of Iraq detracted from the efforts in Afghanistan through the diversion of resources. The Taliban regrouped and fought an incessant insurgency against the Afghan government, the Afghan National Security Forces, the U.S.-led coalition, and other factions and groups. The purpose of the following chapter is to provide an overview of the Afghan Taliban, a history of why and how the group was formed, and examine the organisation's ideology, leadership, personnel, alliances, and evolving structure. The chapter will briefly examine the security challenges facing the Taliban regime, which have significant implications for both the Taliban and the future of Afghanistan.

BACKGROUND

The Cold War is a starting point that contextualises how an organisation like the Taliban possesses substantial dominance over large regions of contemporary Afghanistan. On December 27, 1979, the Soviet Union invaded Afghanistan with around 120,000 soldiers to support the military coup by the communist-oriented People's Democratic Party of Afghanistan against the mujahedeen (Islamic freedom fighters) in a war that persisted for nearly a decade. It was during this time that Pakistan, Saudi Arabia, and the United States, through the Central Intelligence Agency (CIA), backed the mujahedeen to thwart Soviet hegemony. The CIA provided intelligence, finances, weapons, ammunition, and other equipment to the mujahedeen in what became known as Operation Cyclone. Along with intelligence agencies in the Muslim world, the CIA actively recruited Muslims to join the religious fight, or *jihad*, against communism. Pakistan's intelligence service, ISI, recruited thousands of Afghan refugees in Pakistani madrasas, and over 35,000 volunteers (including 25,000 Arabs) from different Muslim-majority countries travelled to Afghanistan through Pakistan to frustrate the Soviet invasion (Rashid, 2001).

Many of these recruits trained in camps set up in Pakistan to receive basic combat training combined with centres that propagated pan-Islamic and Wahhabi religious ideology. In one of these camps, Usama Bin Laden, Abdullah Azzam, and other militants would form the terrorist organisation Al Qaeda, or 'the foundation.' By 1986, the tide turned against the Soviets when the United States armed the mujahedeen with anti-aircraft Stinger missiles after extensive deliberation between the CIA, the Reagan Administration, and members of Congress (Kuperman, 1999). After ten years of warfare and around 15,000 dead soldiers, the Soviet Union

DOI: 10.4324/9780429426063-66

finally withdrew from Afghanistan on February 15, 1989, leaving the Afghan people with a failed state and more than a million dead (Rogers, 1992; Grau, 1996). According to Pear (1988), support for the mujahedeen cost American taxpayers $2 billion. In the years that followed, the United States regrettably adopted a negligible role in Afghanistan's post-war plans as the Bush Administration permanently closed the American embassy in Kabul.

The victory of the mujahedeen over the Soviet Union had great ramifications for the Afghan state. Up until Kabul's fall, President Najibullah's Soviet-supported Afghan government kept up the fight against the mujahedeen. Consequently, a coalition of mujahedeen factions came together to form an interim government that rotated the presidency. The rivalry and enmity between militias and ethnic groups proved too strong when President Burhanuddin Rabbani, a member of the Tajik minority, chose to extend his presidential term after it expired. The ensuing civil war between the mujahedeen factions further destroyed Kabul and spread anarchy in the countryside. Militias and various warlords reigned unjustly through murder, extortion, kidnapping, rape, and other forms of violence.

The Afghan Civil War ended when the Afghan Taliban and thousands of foreign mujahedeen took over Kabul. The majority of Taliban members were rural Pashtun students from the traditional madrassas or religious boarding schools in the area, which Saudi Arabia funded and which Pakistani Inter-Services Intelligence (ISI) oversaw. The upper echelons of the Taliban were former mujahedeen who were disillusioned with the warring, corrupt factions. Their declaration to bring stability, law, and order through the imposition of a strict fundamentalist interpretation of Islamic law made the group quite popular among a weary civilian population yearning for stability. In 1996, the Taliban overthrew President Rabbani's government and hung former President Najibullah from a traffic post. During the formation of the Islamic Emirate of Afghanistan, the Taliban were committed to capturing all of Afghanistan and were able to rule over most provinces. The only exception was the northeastern territories under the control of the Northern Alliance, a mixed group of Tajiks, Hazara, Uzbeks, and other non-Pashtun minorities led by a famous member of the mujahedeen, Ahmed Shah Masood.

In their governance of Afghanistan, the Taliban developed an unfavourable reputation on the international stage, with the vast majority of the world's countries refusing to officially recognise the regime. The Taliban implemented an extremist interpretation of Islamic law that subjugated criminals to cruel punishments, public executions, severed limbs, and the stoning of adulterers to death. Women under Taliban rule were banned from working, denied a formal education, and forced to wear the burqa at all times while in public. In 1998, the U.N. Security Council passed two resolutions regarding the Taliban's abusive treatment of women. Movies, music, television, and other forms of popular entertainment were banned, and the creation of the Ministry of the Promotion of Virtue and the Suppression of Vice enforced these strict laws. Furthermore, the Taliban committed other crimes that garnered international attention, the most infamous of which was the destruction of the Buddhas in Bamiyan City. The international community, through the U.N. General Assembly, condemned the Taliban's decision and passed a resolution urging the Taliban to protect and save Afghanistan's cultural heritage.

The close ties to Islamic militants and former mujahedeen were another source of contention between the Islamic Emirate and the international community (Rashid, 1999). Mullah Mohammed Omar, the leader of the Taliban with the title "Commander of the Faithful," had a very close relationship with Usama Bin Laden. Bin Laden would declare war on the Saudi royal family, pro-Western regimes in the Arab world, and the Western states that support them from Afghanistan. Bin Laden and his Al Qaeda operatives organised numerous terrorist attacks, including those in Saudi Arabia, Kenya, Tanzania, and Yemen. Despite the attacks by Bin Laden on these various locations and the affirmed autonomous terrorist cells, the Taliban refused to extradite him, even when the United States retaliated with missile strikes.

The attacks on the World Trade Center by Al Qaeda altered the Taliban's position within Afghanistan. The Taliban controlled approximately 75% of Afghanistan and was close to overrunning the Northern Alliance. Just days before the attacks on 9/11, Al Qaeda operatives successfully assassinated Ahmed Shah Masood in a suicide bombing. The Bush Administration provided an ultimatum to the Taliban: "Deliver to U.S. authorities all the leaders of Al Qaeda that hide in your land" and "Give the U.S. full access to terrorist training camps so we make sure they are no longer operating" (CNN, 2001). The Taliban's refusal initiated Operation Enduring Freedom, with the invasion of the U.S. military and an air campaign that dropped 18,000 bombs. Within months, the Taliban regime was no longer in power, and its leadership went into hiding.

Since the invasion of Afghanistan and the overthrow of the Taliban in 2001, the U.S. has spent $2 trillion on combat, the training of the Afghan military and police, counternarcotics, economic development, and reconstruction programmes (Almukhtar & Nordland, 2019). At the height of the war, there were 100,000 U.S. troops stationed in Afghanistan, with an additional 40,000 from the international coalition. In spite of their disproportionate resources, the Taliban remain resilient in the insurgency. By 2020, the Taliban and the U.S. government had agreed on a peace deal that laid the groundwork for the complete withdrawal of the U.S. military and for future meetings between the Taliban and the central Afghan government. The Taliban have since retaken control of the entire country and established a new government.

The next sections of the chapter will provide detailed insights into the Taliban's ideology, leadership, and strategies so that the reader can better understand how the Afghan Taliban were able to endure in the face of confounding odds.

IDEOLOGY

The Indo-Pakistani traditional madrassa system and a fundamentalist reinterpretation that combines the Deobandi School of Islamic thought, Wahhabi/Salafist jihadism, and Pashtunwali (Pashtun social and cultural norms) facilitate the organisational structure and necessary foot soldiers for the Taliban (Shah, 2017). Historically, the Deobandis were members of a Hanafi Sunni reformist movement that originated during the late nineteenth century in Deoband, India. Although Deobandis fall within a conservative and traditional spectrum of Islamic thought, the Taliban's interpretations are extreme compared to those generally practiced by Deobandis in the Indian subcontinent. The funding of Deobandi madrassas through Saudis and other militant Arabs integrated ultraconservative Wahhabi ideology and Salafist jihadism for the mullahs and talibs/students. According to Hegghammer (2009), Salafist jihadists use violence to overthrow a perceived illegitimate regime, defend the Islamic community, reform the moral behaviour of Muslims, and/or suppress other Islamic sects. The Taliban's link to these religious ideologies and the madrassa system is the foundation for the networks that they actively draw upon for material and symbolic resources.

Ideology reinforces the symbolism of the Taliban as a movement that is legitimately centred on Islamic education. The traditional madrassa system, along with the use of Islam, frames the Taliban in the eyes of the average Afghan and Pakistani recruit as a religious movement fighting for the honour of Islam. This use of religion is critical to the Taliban's mobilisation of resources and recruitment. Furthermore, the use of senior clerics that are recognised by scholars outside of Afghanistan to advise the Taliban's leaders ensures that the movement's actions and goals are within the boundaries of Islamic law, providing the religious legitimacy needed for the movement.

Along with the combination of Deobandi and Wahhabi/Salafist jihadism are the social and cultural norms of the Pashtun people, called Pashtunwali. The Taliban is a predominantly Pashtun movement from both Afghanistan and the refugee camps in Pakistan. In many accounts of the Taliban, the lines between Pashtunwali and Islamic law were blurred. Rashid (2000, p. 112) describes that "Taliban punishments were in fact drawn largely from Pashtunwali rather than the Sharia" and that "Non-Pashtuns saw this as an attempt to impose Kandahari Pashtun laws on the entire country." Pashtunwali was often cited as the reason Mullah Omar refused to hand over Bin Laden to the United States. Cultural codes in Pashtunwali include *melmastia* (hospitality), *nanawatai* (asylum), *badal* (revenge), *tureh* (bravery in times of need), and *sabat* (loyalty) (Zahid, 2013). Although Pashtunwali is a major component of Taliban ideology, the centrality of religion in the Taliban's movement is important to counteract the perception of the Taliban's ethnic and tribal imbalances that favour the Pashtun tribes.

Although the Taliban have made a consistent effort to raise a national Islamic movement representing all the Afghan tribal and ethnic communities, they continue to symbolically represent the Pashtun ethnic community. While there is some diversity in Pashtun representation, the presence of other tribal and ethnic communities, including the Tajiks, Uzbeks, Nuristanis, and Hazara communities, is minimal. The inability of the Taliban to move beyond ethnic and tribal loyalties is one of their foremost organisational problems, as their inability to integrate individuals and communities outside of the Pashtun tribal affiliation undermines their Islamic political frames of a nation united under Islam as opposed to the Pashtunwali and its associated tribal customs and norms.

LEADERSHIP AND PERSONNEL

The development of the Taliban movement has been intricately tied to the personality and biography of Mullah Omar. Since the organisation's founding in the Pashtun-controlled Deobandi madrassahs of the southern Kandahar region of Afghanistan, the Afghan Taliban has had a continuity of leadership roles and structures that remain to the present. The senior figures have always been organised around the Afghan mujahedeen veterans of the Soviet war, the pre-2001 volunteers, and members of the conflict with the Northern Alliance. The majority of the Afghan Taliban and its national leadership, like Mullah Omar, are Pashtun members of the Ghilzai sub-tribe, with others belonging to the Durrani tribe.

In its founding, the title of *Amir al Mumineen*, or Commander of the Faithful, was intended to bestow the ultimate authority on Mullah Omar in most organisational affairs, and thus his decisions are legally binding on membership, internal and external policies, and the Taliban's objectives and goals. The label "*Amir al-Mumineen*" was historically used by Muslim leaders to link their leadership to the Muslim caliphs of the first Islamic century. The title is important for the Taliban's political legitimacy as this collective memory mobilises around Mullah Omar's religious status and struggle against 'anti-Islamic' forces. The *Amir al-Mumineen* designation was essential in the early development of the Taliban, as Mullah Omar was perceived by the public as a leader whose primary interests were in establishing the Taliban's vision of an Islamic state. The practice of veering away from public life only deepened the legend around his personality among his followers as a sincere religious scholar-warrior who sought to implement Islamic law. The central and symbolic role that Mullah Omar played in the establishment of the Taliban movement in the early 1990s was critical to maintaining and sustaining the movement in the post-9/11 context, as he symbolically centralised the resistance against the central Afghan government, the United States, and coalition partners around his identity and vision of an Afghan Islamic Emirate.

The Taliban kept Mullah Omar's death in 2013 a secret for two years. Up until his death in 2016 as a result of a U.S. drone strike, Mullah Akhtar Mansour held the position of the Afghan Taliban's next Amir al-Mumineen. At present, the structure of the Taliban ranks Mawlawi Haibatullah Akhundzada in the *Amir Al Mumineen* position, which he held immediately after the death of Mullah Mansour. Mawlawi Haibatullah has named Mullah Mohammed Yaqoub as his deputy in charge of ideological and religious issues and Sirajuddin Haqqani as his deputy responsible for the insurgency. A top-down framework that consists of the leadership council, various political, military, and administrative commissions, and finally the shadow governors and battlefield commanders follow the hierarchy (Maizland & Laub, 2020). The leadership council, which consists of veteran Taliban members under the direction of Amir and his deputies, is an influential body in the development of policy directives emerging from within the organisation. However, in the context of the insurgency, power rests with the decentralised and relatively independent commissions, which generally construct and implement most of the day-to-day policies regarding governance, politics, and military action under the guidance of the leadership council and the Amir. These regional commissions hold tremendous authority in their localities and often influence the newly formed policy frameworks that shape the overall organisational structure. The regional commissions enable the Taliban's capabilities to address and adapt to any challenges to their power in the locale.

ORGANISATIONAL TIES AND ALLIANCES

One of the fascinating developments surrounding the Taliban's longevity has been the organisation's ability to independently sustain the movement in the Afghan context. Despite a general belief that the Taliban is directly linked with international terrorist organisations like Al Qaeda and ISIS, reality reveals that the Taliban has a complicated relationship with these organisations. Though the Taliban did provide a safe haven for Al Qaeda, the Taliban as a movement never saw itself in cohesion with or in direct support of Al Qaeda. Even before the attacks of 9/11, Mullah Mohammed Rabbani and other members of the Taliban's leadership sought to distance the organisation from Al Qaeda (Van Linschoten & Kuehn, 2011).

The Taliban's ideological frames and accompanying governing structures, for the most part, contradict many of the Islamic fundamentalist transnational terrorist organisations that have sought alignment with the Taliban. This is evident in the Taliban's rhetoric regarding jihad, which rarely focuses outside of the borders of Afghanistan and instead identifies their movement as an Afghan Islamic-national movement. This was apparent post-9/11, when the Taliban not only had strategic and ideological disagreements with Al Qaeda but also began to incrementally disassociate itself from Al Qaeda's vision and religious frames surrounding its tactics and goals vis-à-vis the United States (Van Linschoten & Kuehn, 2011). The Taliban looked inward and sought to protect its organisational presence in Afghanistan, and thus immediately reorganised around the core leadership to rebuild and tactically shift its course to undermine the new Afghan regime and the coalition forces. This deliberate delineation from Al Qaeda has allowed the movement to move beyond the transnational Islamism that was popular in the 1990s to focus internally within the Afghan state in the post-9/11 context.

The contemporary role of international Islamism and the rise of the Islamic State of Khurasan Province (ISKP) are other challenges that the Taliban are presently facing. The current Taliban leadership has opened another military front against the presence and growth of ISIS in Afghanistan with the introduction of a competing Amir or Caliph. Beginning in 2014–2015, the development of the peace rhetoric between the United States and the Taliban's core leadership drove many smaller, independent Taliban factions to switch allegiances to ISIS. According to Basit (2017), ISIS would intentionally recruit existing Taliban members through Pashtu radio interviews, lectures, and songs (nasheeds) that call for members to religiously migrate (make *hijrah*) to their territory and join their campaigns. This has opened up two fronts for the Taliban, who are now fighting against both the Afghan government and coalition forces, as well as ISIS and other composite terrorist groups within their territory. While the threat of ISIS looms large over Afghan society as the Taliban continue peace talks with the United States, many disaffected Taliban, mid-tier leaders, and the rank and file may not agree with the peace provisions that are perceived as contradictory to their ideological, religious, and political aims. The Taliban's internal focus on Afghanistan may undermine its status as a movement that is seeking to establish an Islamic Emirate as it remains silent on conflicts associated with the global Muslim community, which groups like ISIS are vocal about and seek to co-opt. The Taliban's strategic focus on removing ISIS from Afghanistan is as important for the current movement's leadership as the defeat and control of the central Afghan government and coalition forces.

Internationally, the support of the Gulf countries for the Taliban fluctuated based on changing interests, but Pakistan has consistently assisted the Afghan Taliban, directly or indirectly, and is one of the key reasons for the Taliban's longevity. Since the Taliban's founding and its war against the Rabbani government and Shah Masood's Northern Alliance, Pakistan's ISI has provided financial, military, intelligence, and political assistance, with increased support following General Pervez Musharraf's coup (Rashid, 2008). After the 9/11 attacks, Pakistan publicly became a partner in the Bush Administration's War on Terror, but the ISI continued to enact a dual policy of continuing to support the Taliban as an alternative to the Northern Alliance (Waldman, 2010). Officially, the Pakistani government dismisses these accusations and points to the fact that it is fighting its own insurgency against the Pakistani Taliban (Tehrik-e-Pakistan), which is closely associated with the Afghan Taliban (Maizland & Laub, 2020). Meanwhile, throughout its existence, the Afghan Taliban refused to engage in terrorism that targeted Pakistan or Pakistani interests. Pakistan's relationship with the Taliban is one of mutual benefit that centres on the perceived threat from India's close ties to the Afghan government and the contentious idea of a Pashtunistan that would include Pakistan's North West Frontier Province (Hanni & Hegi, 2013).

ORGANISATIONAL STRUCTURE

The rapid growth and success of the Afghan Taliban from the traditional madrassa system into a full-fledged movement reflect the social disorganisation of Afghanistan post-Soviet War. The fractured Afghan state with relentless crime, violence, and death created the conditions that allowed the Taliban to utilise standard military tactics to capture and control nearly all of the country from the North Alliance. With the support of the Pakistani government and some members of the international community, their centralisation of power, even with the implementation of draconian legal prescriptions, produced some international support for their movement's ability to produce a modicum of stability in Afghanistan. This would change in the post-9/11 context as the Taliban were militarily removed from power by the United States and coalition forces by targeting the Amir, the leadership council, members, and supporters with the hope of purging the movement from Afghanistan.

While the coalition campaign did take a heavy toll, the Taliban were flexible enough to shift their tactics and organisational structure to adapt to the new socio-political reality. The leadership went underground while the organisational network became amorphous to conduct a protracted guerrilla war campaign. The loose, decentralised network, while initially disconnected from the centre, still maintained allegiance to Mullah Omar and the Taliban's religious and political objectives. The approach was essential for the long-term success of their campaign against the newly formed central Afghan government and the coalition forces. The pre-9/11 politics of governance shifted to a direct political and military strategy of armed struggle. The shift created networked Taliban factions that function as independent organisations and cells fighting against the coalition forces in the campaign to recapture lost territory. The organisational shift that emerged post-9/11 necessitated new funding sources and a modification in their use of tactics to include the use of IEDs, car bombs, suicide bombers, and other new technologies to foment political and economic instability in the newly formed Afghan state.

The funding campaign to sustain the Taliban's resistance was heavily dependent on the opium trade. There are different estimates of the annual budgets of the Afghan Taliban that range between $500 million and $2 billion (Jackson & Weigand, 2019). Although some of that revenue is generated from taxes, it is the Afghan poppy trade, which makes up 80% of the world's heroin supply, that has been the main funding source for the Afghan Taliban (Na, 2018). The decision was controversial in Taliban political and religious circles, as Mullahs had previously passed edicts that ruled opium cultivation and sale as *haram*, or Islamically prohibited. In pre-9/11 Afghanistan, the Taliban nearly eradicated opium from the territories under their rule. However, after Mullah Omar's government was toppled, the Taliban's leadership council approved jurisprudential opinions regarding the necessity of pursuing the opium trade to sustain their movement's political and military goals. This was initially controversial amongst Islamic scholars in the region who supported the movement; however, it was immediately agreed that the funds generated from opium cultivation produced an economic necessity for which Islamic law could provide legal expediency. The cultivation and sale of opium have allowed the Taliban to link with criminal networks that were solely focused on the drug trade, ransoms, and killings for hire.

One notorious faction that works with the Taliban is the Haqqani network, a criminal enterprise with transnational ties in the North-West Frontier Province of Pakistan (Ali, 2008). The network was founded by Jalaluddin Haqqani and is now led by his son, Sirajuddin Haqqani, the deputy who oversees the Taliban insurgency. The Haqqani network is an integral subgroup within the Taliban that has expanded its access to resources, weapons, and intelligence in the border regions between Pakistan and Afghanistan through established criminal networks. The Haqqanis and other minor clannish organisations persist in various regions of Afghanistan and Pakistan, where they oversee violent criminal operations that provide the Taliban with previously inaccessible resource revenues and networks.

The Taliban's organisational flexibility extends to military strategies and tactics in the fight against U.S., coalition, and Afghan government forces. In a manner reminiscent of the Soviet War, the Taliban resorted to guerilla warfare by hiding in villages while the U.S. and coalition forces relied on capture-and-kill missions. Although successful in arresting and killing leading Taliban officials, the Taliban has been able to steadily replenish new leaders to take over the insurgency. Furthermore, the Taliban leadership has avoided direct engagement and would use illiterate teenage boys recruited from madrassas to fight and exhaust U.S. and coalition forces (Johnson & Mason, 2007). The ensuing collateral damage caused by night raids, airstrikes, drones, and other acts of violence increased recruits for the Taliban as families and tribes would turn to *badal* to avenge the deaths of civilian casualties (see Romaniuk & Webb, 2015). The villagers who continued to collaborate or remain neutral in the conflict would face retaliation from the Taliban. Johnson and Mason (2007) identify several other factors that enabled the permanency of the insurgency, including the lack of cultural understanding by U.S. and coalition soldiers, excessively invasive and violent measures, collateral damage, the absence of the national government throughout the country, the failure of development and reconstruction, and the inability to improve the lives of the common Afghan people. Corruption in the central Afghan government has been one of the top factors that has sustained the Afghan Taliban insurgency (Carroll, 2011). The failure of economic development or any tangible results for the Afghan people has, in the eyes of many Afghans, delegitimised the subsequent governments of Presidents Hamid Karzai and Ashraf Ghani.

THE DOHA DEAL AND TALIBAN 2.0

In 2018, a significant change occurred in Afghanistan's political landscape as the U.S. initiated negotiations with the Taliban. The aim was to withdraw U.S. troops and foster a political agreement between the Taliban and the Afghan Republic. In the two decades of war, the Taliban has remained formidable due to the previously mentioned factors. Under the Trump administration in the U.S., there was a full commitment to end the war between the United States and the Taliban.

The Doha process (the U.S. Taliban Peace Deal in Doha, Qatar), starting in October 2018 and culminating in August 2021, focused on resolving the long-standing conflict between these warring factions. The pivotal moment came with the Doha Agreement, signed in late February 2020 between U.S. Representative Zalmay Khalilzad and the Taliban's Mullah Abdul Ghani Baradar. The agreement focused on four substantial points (U.S. State Department, 2020). The first assurance involved the transformation of the Taliban from a group that supported terrorism against the U.S. and its allies to one seeking political legitimacy within the established Afghan government. The second aspect was the plan for the U.S. and its allies to withdraw from Afghanistan. The United States and its allies had agreed to withdraw all military and civilian personnel within 14 months, reducing their troops to 8,600 in the 135 days following the agreement. Despite this withdrawal, the U.S. committed to continuing to work with the Afghan central government on counterterrorism operations, providing air support for Afghan troops, and training its security forces. The third element was a guarantee from the Taliban to initiate intra-Afghan negotiations with the central government. (The Guardian, 2020). Finally, the Doha deal outlined the conditions for U.S. troop withdrawal and required the Taliban to prevent Afghanistan from being a base for terrorist groups targeting the U.S. and its allies. It also envisioned a political resolution through intra-Afghan negotiations. However, these efforts failed to achieve the intended peace settlement.

A critical flaw in the process was the inadvertent empowerment of the Taliban, elevating their status in the conflict. The Doha deal bolstered the Taliban, allowing them to assert themselves as legitimate contenders for power. Consequently, officials from countries like Russia, China, and Iran began to engage with the Taliban, perceiving them as Afghanistan's future leaders. Capitalising on this recognition, the Taliban rapidly escalated their military campaign, swiftly capturing the provinces of Herat, Qandahar, and Mazar (Sakhi, 2022). Though the marauding advance was hindered by intermittent violence by the rival Islamic State Khurasan province, by mid-August 2021, they had entered Kabul, leading to President Ghani's flight from the country. On August 16, 2021, the Taliban declared the establishment of an Islamic Emirate, effectively dissolving the 20-year-old Islamic Republic of Afghanistan and establishing a totalitarian regime. This marked the end of the previous government and the beginning of Taliban rule (Taliban 2.0) (Sakhi, 2022).

Since August 2021, following the Taliban movement's gain of power, the Taliban leadership has implemented the Sharia system; neither Ashraf Ghani's constitution nor Zahir Shah's were acceptable (Tolo News, October 22, 2022). Furthermore, Hibatullah Akhundzada, the leader of the Taliban-led Islamic Emirate of Afghanistan, ordered in November 2022 that all judges impose hudud (Quran-described) and qisas (retribution: eye-for-eye) punishments, effectively abolishing the Afghan penal code (Jurist, November 14, 2022). Women are excluded in a form of "gender apartheid." They are excluded from work and are no longer allowed to visit public spaces such as restaurants and parks (Teresa Casale, January 20, 2022).

The Taliban's exclusionary Pashtun-centred rule is highly repressive towards any and all forms of opposition. At the national level, it provides few job opportunities, reducing decision-making roles for minorities and those associated with the fallen Afghan Republic. Individual rights have been eviscerated, as has women's access to education and jobs. The public sphere for travel and medical care has been decimated. The General Directorate of Intelligence (GDI) under Sirajuddin "Siraj" Haqqani's Ministry of Interior and the Ministry of the Promotion of Virtue and Prevention of Vice have become strong tools of repression. The prevailing Taliban decision-making has become concentrated in the hands of Amir Haibatullah and his Kandahar-based group. Haibatullah has consistently dismissed input from internationally oriented as well as pragmatic Taliban leaders. He has repeatedly pushed back against criticism from other Islamic countries, organisations, and even conservative scholars. He has defined his version of sharia as the only true interpretation of Hanafi Islam. On December 20, 2022, Haibatullah issued an edict banning women from working for NGOs in Afghanistan. This had dire consequences for U.N. agencies and international NGOs. This is because only female workers can access women and, often, their children. After the ban, all major international NGOs suspended all of their Afghanistan operations, both because their operational capacity was critically hampered and because they hoped the suspension would force the Taliban to reverse the decision. The Taliban changed their mind, and the NGOs restored some of their services. The ban hampered food security for a starving population. Almost half of the Afghan population was projected to be acutely food insecure between November 2022 and March 2023, with 6 million on the brink of famine. Approximately 40 million people have been receiving food packets and cash stipends from the World Food Programme (Felbab-Brown, 2023).

TALIBAN LEADERSHIP

The Taliban leadership consists of the following personalities:

1. Supreme Leader "Amir al-Mu'minin," Hibatullah Akhundzada (Pashtun from Kandahar);
2. Supreme Judge Abdul Hakim Haqqani (Pashtun from Kandahar);
3. Kabul-based Cabinet Directorate: Mullah Hasan Akhund (Pashtun from Kandahar);
4. Mullah Abdul Ghani Baradar (Pashtun from Kandahar);
5. Mullah Abdul Kabir (Pashtun from Baghlan);
6. Abdul Salam Hanafi (Uzbek from Faryab);
7. Director-Generals for Agriculture, Irrigation, and Livestock, Mawlavi Abdul Rahman and Rashid (Uzbek from Faryab);
8. Director General for Borders and Tribal Affairs, Mullah Nurullah Nuri (Pashtun from Zabul); and
9. Director General for Trade, Hajji Nuruddin Azizi (Tajik from Panjsher) (Conrad et al., 2022).

HUMANITARIAN RESPONSE FOR AFGHANISTAN

On December 22, 2021, the United Nations issued Resolution 2615 (2021). This resolution includes a sweeping general exemption from sanctions implementation for humanitarian actors and providers of what the resolution calls "basic human needs." Paragraph 1 of the resolution states:

> humanitarian assistance and other activities that support basic human needs in Afghanistan are not a violation of paragraph 1 (a) of resolution 2255 (2015), and that the processing and payment of funds, other financial assets or economic re- sources, and the provision of goods and services necessary to ensure the timely delivery of such assistance or to support such activities are permit- ted, strongly encourages providers relying on this paragraph to use reasonable efforts to minimize the accrual of any benefits, whether as a result of direct provision or diversion, to individuals or entities designated on the 1988 Sanctions List (United Nations Security Council Resolution, S/RES/2615(2021), 2022).

Since August 2021, Afghanistan under the so-called Taliban Emirate has navigated a labyrinth of threats and challenges, encompassing the Islamic State Khurasan province conflict, egregious violations of women's rights, and intricate internal divisions within the Taliban. The resurgence of ISKP attacks following the Taliban's ascension to power, coupled with the Taliban's anti-Salafist purges, underscores a significant security quagmire. ISKP's ambitions to destabilise the Taliban's governance efforts pose a persistent and formidable challenge (Sayed, 2023). Similarly, over two years into the Taliban's sharia governance, a systematic imposition of repressive policies has drastically curtailed women's rights in Afghanistan. These policies pervasively dictate various aspects of women's lives, from dress codes to education, employment, and freedom of movement. The Taliban's enforcement of stringent restrictions has ignited protests and resistance, showcasing the resilience and defiance of Afghan women and girls against these oppressive measures (UN Women, 2023; Human Rights Office of the High Commissioner, OHCHR, 2023).

FUTURE OF AFGHANISTAN UNDER TALIBAN

Internal rifts have significantly hampered governance since the Taliban took control. Even after two years of interim government, the Islamic Emirate has yet to introduce its official cabinet. The Taliban Emirate's spokesman,

Zabiullah Mujahid, admitted in September 2023 that after the approval of the constitution, some of the issues, such as the establishment of a council and an official cabinet, will be addressed (Tolo News, 2023). Evidently, a dichotomy exists between the Taliban's political faction, which exhibits a more pragmatic approach and is cognizant of both domestic and international dynamics, and its more dominant military wing. This internal power struggle presents an ongoing governance conundrum, particularly in the absence of a unifying external adversary.

The period following August 2021 in Afghanistan has been characterised by a confluence of multifaceted and complex challenges. These include the ongoing strife with the Islamic State, severe infringements on women's rights, and the convoluted internal dynamics within the Taliban. Each of these elements carries profound implications for Afghanistan's security, governance, and human rights landscape, underscoring a period of profound uncertainty and upheaval.

The governance of the Taliban regime in Afghanistan is characterised by a distinct theocratic and centralised model. Sharia law and Pashtunwali traditions serve as the foundation for the government, which concentrates power in the hands of a supreme leader with the support of religious advisors. This approach enforces a strict regime of social and cultural policies. Despite their ability to maintain control, the Taliban's leadership faces significant challenges in establishing a comprehensive governance structure, particularly in the realms of administration, justice, and dispute resolution.

On the international stage, Western countries, most notably the United States, have taken a cautious approach towards the Taliban. They have refrained from granting formal recognition to the regime, withholding the unfreezing of assets, or lifting sanctions. This cautious engagement is predicated on the Taliban's compliance with counterterrorism commitments, with the normalisation of relations contingent upon these factors. The West's stance is emblematic of a broader international hesitancy to fully embrace the Taliban-led government.

Despite these challenges, the Taliban have sought to forge international relationships. They have engaged in high-level diplomatic meetings and endeavoured to build bilateral relations with powerful states like China, Turkey, and Russia. Yet, this engagement has not translated into formal recognition. Countries such as China, Russia, Qatar, and Pakistan maintain an active diplomatic presence through their embassies in Afghanistan but have stopped short of officially recognising the Taliban regime (Weitz, 2022). This delicate balance of engagement without formal recognition reflects the complex geopolitical dynamics at play and the international community's ambivalence towards the Taliban's governance and Afghanistan's future.

References

Ali, I. (2008, March 24). The Haqqani network and cross-border terrorism in Afghanistan. *Terrorism Monitor*, *6*(6). https://jamestown.org/program/the-haqqani-network-and-cross-border-terrorism-in-afghanistan/

Allen, J.R. (2020). The US-Taliban peace deal: A road to nowhere. *Brookings Institution*. https://www.brookings.edu/blog/order-from-chaos/2020/03/05/the-us-taliban-peace-deal-a-road-to-nowhere/

Allen, J.R., & O'Hanlon, M. (2020). Resolving the Ghani-Abdullah impasse in Afghanistan. *Brookings Institution*. https://www.brookings.edu/president/resolving-the-ghani-abdullah-impasse-in-afghanistan/

Almukhtar, S., & Nordland, R. (2019, December 12). What did the U.S. get for $2 Trillion in Afghanistan? *The New York Times*. https://www.nytimes.com/interactive/2019/12/09/world/middleeast/afghanistan-war-cost.html

Basit, A. (2017). I.S. penetration in Afghanistan-Pakistan: Assessment, impact and implications. *Perspectives on Terrorism*, *11*(3), 19–39.

Carroll, K.T. (2011). Afghan corruption-the greatest obstacle to victory in Operation Enduring Freedom. *Georgetown Journal of International Law*, *43*(3), 873–896.

Casale, T. (2022). Afghanistan's gender apartheid: An interview with former Afghan MP Naheed Farid, Mina's List Blog, 20 January 2022, https://www.minaslist.org/blog/afghanistans-gender-apartheid-an-in-terview-with-former-afghan-mp-naheed-farid "lawless society

CNN. (2001). Bush delivers ultimatum. *CNN*. http://edition.cnn.com/2001/WORLD/asiapcf/central/09/20/ret.afghan.bush/

Conrad, G., Koller, S., Doro, H., Nabil, R., Safi, K., Steinberg, G., & Schindler, H. (2022). *The Taliban's take-over in Afghanistan-effects on global terrorism*. Germany: Konrad Adenauer Stiftung.

Derksen, D. (2019). Options for reintegrating Taliban fighters in an Afghan peace process. *United States Institute of Peace*, (444), 1–24.

Felbab-Brown, V. (2023, February 3). *Afghanistan in 2023: Taliban internal power struggles and militancy*. Washington DC: Brookings.

Grau, L.W. (1996). *The bear went over the mountain: Soviet combat tactics in Afghanistan*. Washington D.C.: National Defense University.

Haass, R.N. (2020). How not to leave Afghanistan. *Council of Foreign Relations*. https://www.cfr.org/article/how-not-leave-afghanistan

Hänni, A., & Hegi, L. (2013). The Pakistani godfather: The inter-services intelligence and the Afghan Taliban 1994–2010. *Small Wars Journal*. https://smallwarsjournal.com/jrnl/art/the-pakistani-godfather-the-inter-services-intelligence-and-the-afghan-taliban-1994-2010

Haqqani, S. (2020, February 20). What we, the Taliban, want. *The New York Times*. https://www.nytimes.com/2020/02/20/opinion/taliban-afghanistan-war-haqqani.html

Hegghammer, T. (2009). Jihadi-Salafis or revolutionaries? On religion and politics in the study of militant Islamists. In R. Meijer (Ed.), *Global Salafism: Islam's new religious movement* (pp. 244–266). London: Hurst & Company.

Jackson, A., & Weigand, F. (2019). The Taliban's war for legitimacy in Afghanistan. *Current History*, *118*(807), 143–148.

Johnson, T.H., & Mason, M.C. (2007). Understanding the Taliban and insurgency in Afghanistan. *Orbis*, *51*(1), 71–89.

Jurist News. (2022). Taliban leader: Afghanistan judges must enforce Shariah punishments, 14 November 2022, https://www.jurist.org/news/2022/11/taliban-leader-afghani-stan-judges-must-enforce-shariah-punish- ments/

Kuperman, A.J. (1999). The Stinger missile and US intervention in Afghanistan. *Political Science Quarterly, 114*(2), 219–263.

Maizland, L., & Laub, Z. (2020). The Taliban in Afghanistan. *Council of Foreign Relations*. https://www.cfr.org/backgrounder/taliban-afghanistan.

Mohammad Farshad Daryosh, Efforts Underway to Form New Constitution: Mujahid, Tolo News, 22 October 2022, https://tolonews.com/index.php/afghanistan-180415.

Na, N.W. (2018). Opium production and countering terrorism financing in Afghanistan: Lessons from Thailand's Royal Projects. *Counter Terrorist Trends and Analyses, 10*(2), 1–5.

OHCHR. (2023, March 8). Afghanistan: UN experts say 20 years of progress for women and girls' rights erased since Taliban takeover. https://www.ohchr.org/en/press-releases/2023/03/afghanistan-un-experts-say-20-years-progress-women-and-girls-rights-erased

Pear, R. (1988, April 18). Arming Afghan Guerrillas: A huge effort led by U.S. *The New York Times*. https://www.nytimes.com/1988/04/18/world/arming-afghan-guerrillas-a-huge-effort-led-by-us.html

Rashid, A. (1999, November/December). The Taliban: Exporting extremism. *Foreign Affairs, 78*(6), 22–35.

Rashid, A. (2000). *Taliban: Militant Islam, oil, and fundamentalism in Central Asia*. New Haven: Yale University Press.

Rashid, A. (2001, September 13). Osama Bin Laden: How the US helped midwife a terrorist. *The Center for Public Integrity*. https://publicintegrity.org/accountability/osama-bin-laden-how-the-u-s-helped-midwife-a-terrorist/

Rashid, A. (2008). *Descent into Chaos: The US and the failure of nation building in Pakistan, Afghanistan, and Central Asia*. New York: Penguin.

Romaniuk, S.N., & Webb, S. (2015). Extraordinary measures: Drone warfare, securitization, and the 'War on Terror'. *Slovak Journal of Political Sciences, 15*(3), 221–245. https://sjps.fsvucm.sk/index.php/sjps/article/view/47

Rogers, T. (1992). *The Soviet withdrawal from Afghanistan: Analysis and chronology*. Westport, CT: Greenwood Press.

Sakhi, N. (2022). The Taliban takeover in Afghanistan and security paradox. *Journal of Asian Security and International Affairs, 9*(3), 383–401.

Sayed, C., & Hamming, T.F. (2023, July 7). *The growing threat of the Islamic State in Afghanistan and South Asia*. United States Institute of Peace. https://www.usip.org/publications/2023/06/growing-threat-islamic-state-afghanistan-and-south-asia

Shah, K.M. (2017). The Pashtuns, the Taliban, and America's Longest War. *Asian Survey, 57*(6), 981–1007.

The Guardian. (2020). The U.S. and Taliban sign deal to withdraw American troops. *The Guardian*. https://www.theguardian.com/world/2020/feb/29/us-taliban-sign-peace-agreement-afghanistan-war

Tolo News. (2023, September 17). Two years passed, interim govt yet to be official. https://tolonews.com/afghanistan-185142

U.S. State Department. (2020). *Agreement for bringing peace to Afghanistan*. U.S. State Department. https://www.state.gov/wp-content/uploads/2020/02/Agreement-For-Bringing-Peace-to-Afghanistan-02.29.20.pdf

UN Women. (2023, August 14). In focus: After August – Voices of Afghan women two years after the Taliban takeover. https://www.unwomen.org/en/news-stories/in-focus/2023/08/in-focus-after-august-voices-of-afghan-women-two-years-after-the-taliban-takeover

United Nations General Assembly. (2021). *UN resolution 2451*. New York: UN General Assembly.

United Nations Security Council Resolution, S/RES/2615(2021), January 06, 2022, 1. https://www.un.org/securitycouncil/content/sres2615202

Van Linschoten, A.S., & Kuehn, F. (2011). *Separating the Taliban from Al-Qaeda: The core of success in Afghanistan*. New York University Center on International Cooperation. https://cic.es.its.nyu.edu/sites/default/files/gregg_sep_tal_alqaeda.pdf

Waldman, M. (2010). The sun in the sky: The relationship between Pakistan's ISI and Afghan insurgents. *Crisis States Research Centre, Development Studies Institute, London School of Economics*, (18), 1–28.

Weitz, R. (2022, August 9). *Afghanistan adrift one year after the Taliban takeover*. Middle East Institute. https://www.mei.edu/publications/afghanistan-adrift-one-year-after-taliban-takeover

Zahid, F. (2013, November 30). Understanding Taliban through the Prism of Pashtunwali Code. *Centre Français de Recherche sur le Renseignement*. https://cf2r.org/tribune/understanding-taliban-through-the-prism-of-pashtunwali-code/

59

THE HAQQANI NETWORK

Fatma Yol, Gizem Gönay Akbaş, and Elif Merve Dumankaya

Geography is destiny.
Ibn Khaldun

INTRODUCTION

The world has witnessed the emergence of terrorist organisations embracing Islamic ideology and aiming to make jihad to spread Islam all over the world. However, one group of people who shared a similar ideology and faith differed from the others. The Haqqani Network, which emerged in the 1980s, is one of the most dangerous organisations existing in Afghanistan. Despite its small number of members, who are mainly relatives of Jalaluddin Haqqani, the founder of the network, its terrorising attacks and Islamic ideology have spread among the people of Afghanistan and Pakistan (Romaniuk & Webb, 2015). However, those members are not described as "terrorists", On the contrary, they are believed to play a significant role in politics and peace processes in the region because the Haqqani Network is connected with important actors, such as the Taliban, al-Qaeda, the governments of Afghanistan and Pakistan. Even though they are believed to be jihadists by politicians in Pakistan, they are not targeting international influence.

After the death of Jalaluddin Haqqani, Sirajuddin became the leader of the network and brutalised its actions. The Trump administration halted military aid to the Pakistani government on January 4, 2018, pending more rigorous military action against the organisation. Today, some journalists argue that the Haqqani Network needs to be taken into consideration to regulate a peaceful order in the region, particularly in Afghanistan. However, there is just a little study related to the Haqqani Network. In this study, we approach the Haqqani Network under four main topics: the network's historical background and overview; key personnel and the structure; organisational characteristics and activities; and their impacts on the region and society. This study is a descriptive one that benefits from previous research related to the network. The importance and exclusive features of the Haqqani Network are targeted to demonstrate

HISTORY OF THE FORMATION OF THE HAQQANI NETWORK

When it comes to evaluating the case of Afghanistan, this quote attributed to Ibn Khaldun means a lot. Since the emergence of Rapoport's (2004) fourth wave of modern terrorism in the late 1970s, Afghanistan has not only hosted the most vicious scenes of violence but also become a laboratory of terrorism, its variants, and its tools in particular. Since then, the country has not yet stabilised and has become a geography shaped by various actors. In this respect, Afghanistan requires a much more comprehensive analysis in terms of its domestic structure and external factors.

First of all, it should be emphasised that the emergence of the Haqqani Network is not a coincidence. On the contrary, it has become an expected result of both the domestic and social structure of Afghanistan and the geography in which it is located. Having examined the country's domestic dynamics and structures, it can be stated that Afghanistan has a multi-ethnic society, including several ethnicities as follows: Arab, Baluch, Chahar-Aimak, Hazara, Kirghiz, Pakhtun, Pashai, and Persian. (Grewal, 2013, p. 3) Secondly, in addition to these ethnicities, the fact that the tribes in Afghanistan are very effective both in social life and on a political level complicates making concrete predictions about Afghanistan. Due to the fact that it seems too challenging for Kabul to keep the balance between efforts to grapple with the intense terrorist activities and impositions directed from its domestic and political dynamics; in other words, as the regions and areas in which tribes are active differ from each other, the current situation that

DOI: 10.4324/9780429426063-67

the country has to deal with becomes even more inextricable.

Moving back to the 1970s, when the Haqqani Network was established, with reference to the aforementioned issues, there is no denying that Afghanistan was already affected by the chaotic international conjuncture. Mobilisation, which came to Asia especially due to the decolonisation process, also started among the Afghan tribes. As a result, the interest of both tribes and other groups on the continent began to intensify in Afghanistan (Romaniuk & Webb, 2015, pp. 176–7). This intensified interest emerged both in the economic and political contexts. At this point, the emergence of the Haqqani Network occurred as a reaction to the political atmosphere in the country. Until 1973, Afghanistan had been governed by the monarchy. Mohammad Zahir Shah, the king of that period, was overthrown in 1973 by the initiative of Prime Minister Mohammad Daud Khan, which was not welcomed by the Islamists in the country. As a matter of fact, this turning point was considered one of the most triggering factors that paved the way for the Haqqani Network to find a place in the system (Dressler, 2010, p. 5–7).

The significance of Southeast Afghanistan and Pakistan for the Haqqani Network is worth mentioning. Jalaluddin Haqqani's father, Khwaja Muhammad Khan, and his family are members of the Sultankhel clan of the Zadran tribe. Jalaluddin's father, besides being wealthy, had intensive commercial relations with Pakistan. In addition, Jalaluddin appears to be extremely familiar with this region, as his father, Khwaja Muhammad Khan, sent his sons to Pakistan for religious education (Brown & Rassler, 2013, pp. 28–29). As a result, this background provided Jalaluddin with many opportunities, which will be clarified more in detail. Jalaluddin Haqqani, the founding leader of the Haqqani Network, and his followers strongly opposed the Prime Minister, Mohammad Daud Khan, but supported the royalty. Therefore, they crossed the border to reach Pakistan with the aim of getting organised. In addition to military training, the Haqqani Network received different aid from Pakistan, and this situation continued during the Soviet invasion (Dressler, 2010, p. 7).

During the Soviet invasion, the Haqqani Network built close relations with Pakistan and received a wide range of support from Islamabad, from military equipment to health products. On the other hand, it is noted that they have developed close relations with the ISI and CIA in order to combat the forces of the Soviet Union. After the invasion, the Haqqani Network intensely approached the Taliban to continue its existence (Romaniuk & Webb, 2015, p. 178). Therefore, the Haqqani Network is still an interesting subject for research.

KEY PERSONNEL AND STRUCTURE OF THE HAQQANI NETWORK

The Haqqani Network came into being in the 1970s and was made up of fighters clustered around Jalaluddin Haqqani. The militants of the network were headed by Jalaluddin Haqqani, who was a prominent Taliban commander with a price on his head and a spot on the most sought-after list in the U.S., and his son, Sirajuddin Haqqani. Jalaluddin Haqqani was known to be Taliban supreme leader Mullah Omar's closest deputy and was a mujahideen commander in the 1980s resistance to the Soviet occupation of Afghanistan. He led several successful campaigns against the Soviets. He gained prominence after playing a leading role in the March 1991 defeat of the communist forces of Muhammad Najibullah at Khost (Ali, 2008). After the Soviet withdrawal, Jalaluddin built a cooperative relationship with the Taliban and established close ties with donors from Pakistan and the Gulf. His ability to speak Arabic, raise money, plan attacks, and inspire fighters made him the recipient of an extraordinary amount of CIA and Saudi financing, which was closely monitored by the ISI of Pakistan (Hussain, 2011; Peters, 2012).

After the Taliban's 1995 occupation of Kabul, Jalaluddin Haqqani entered the Taliban movement and ascended to the top tier of regime control. The Taliban were afraid to take him over and tried to incorporate him into their structure of power by making him part of their inner circle (Hussain, 2011). During the Taliban government, he remained a top adviser to Mullah Omar. Prior to the formal foundation of the Haqqani Network, Jalaluddin Haqqani was a leader of the Hizb-i-Islami Executive Committee, one of the region's most militarised anti-Soviet and anti-Daud resistance movements. The network derived its philosophy initially from Hizb-i-Islami. Jalaluddin himself shared the Taliban's conservative outlook; he was a Deobandi (a Sunni Islam movement), but he did not share their political ambition or al-Qaeda's international jihadism (Ali, 2008, p. 2; Dressler). He was ideologically aligned with Al Qaeda, but unlike Al Qaeda, the Haqqani Network's emphasis was more national than worldwide.

Their ideology is highly important for them since Deobandi's interpretation has become their point of view and a milestone for the network. Then one can ask, What is Deobandi? According to Jones (2008), Deobandism is a conservative Islamic orthodoxy following an egalitarian Salafist model and seeking to emulate the Qur'an and Prophet Mohammed's life and times (p. 27). Deobandis claim that they have a divine right and obligation to wage jihad to protect Muslims all over the world. Its philosophy was traced back to the 1860s at the madrassa Dar ul-Ulum in India, but the flourishing of Deobandi madrassas in Pakistan happened in the 1970s. These Deobandi madrassas in Pakistan were called "Haqqaniyya" and were mainly located where Pakhtuns live (Haroon, 2008). Abdul Haq, who was a Sufi Deobandi ideologue, succeeded in attracting a large number of students who were Pakhtun and non-Pakhtun Pakistanis to Haqqaniyya between 1945 and 1978.

As Afghan resistance groups began to patch unity in exile in Iran and Pakistan together, using a language of religious purpose and militancy to organise the country's uprisings and refugee politics into a jihad, Haqqaniyya Madrasa and his Deobandi ideology came to play a significant role in organising the anti-Soviet opposition. Political exiles and armed resistance fighters from among the large number of displaced Pakhtuns, inspired by Haqqaniyya's long-standing popularity in their hometowns, gravitated to Haqqaniyya as a hub for meeting, finding funds, and seeking advice (Haroon, 2008, p. 66).

When Jalaluddin came to the forefront, he immediately created an atmosphere where Pakhtun's highlands were willing to defend their territory and Islamic beliefs (Romaniuk & Webb, 2015, p. 177). He was highly influenced by his research at the Dar al-'UlumHaqqaniyya madrassa. Prior to the Soviet invasion of Afghanistan, a group of Haqqaniyya students stood against it, and Afghan jihad was first initiated in 1973 by Jalaluddin Haqqani (Romaniuk & Webb, 2015). According to Romaniuk and Webb (2015), the threat level raised by Jalaluddin as network chief relates to five key factors. First, as a field commander, he had tremendous experience and political shrewdness as a Mujahedeen leader who established Hizbe-Islami and later Hezb-e-Islami. Second, he was instrumental in consolidating the rebels and establishing groups dedicated to eradicating the region's invading forces (the U.S. and its allies). Third, he was educated by Central Asia's qualified powers, and he acquired close relations with the Central Intelligence Agency (CIA) in previous years and had retained productive relations with Pakistan. Fourth, he was an effective person in Haqqaniyya madrassas and training camps in North Waziristan. Fifth, as Romaniuk and Webb (2015) mention, "Haqqani makes use of religious techniques and radical Islamic principles to influence and fuel Muslims' resolve" (p. 178). These features of him show his talented leadership role in the network until his death.

The patriarchal role of Jalaluddin has put his mark on the network, which owes its durability to his leadership style (Peters, 2012). He was highly successful in organising high-profile and humiliating attacks on the Soviets, which provided him with unrivalled access to clandestine financing and information. Moreover, these attacks, which are written in several magazines, e.g., in Pashto, Urdu, and Arabic, and his religious credentials, have fuelled donations from political supporters. In Yusufzai's words, which are given by Peters, "the Haqqanis have always been very organised and modern in their approach," and "they understand the power of the media and they know it helps them to raise money" (2012, p. 23), Therefore, his fluency in Arabic and use of media provided him with the ability to use religion and anti-Soviet movements, which resulted in gaining donations and funding for the network. Also, Jalaluddin's marriage to an Emirates woman – his second wife – and the historical incorporation of Arab fighters likewise helped ensure his personal ties to the Gulf and the flow of funds from that part of the world during the post-2001 conflict period. Since the fall of the Taliban government in Afghanistan in late 2001, Haqqani has seldom been seen in public (Ali, 2008, p. 2).

However, Jalaluddin Haqqani died in December 2014 (Rosenberg & Mehsud, 2015), and his son, Sirajuddin Haqqani, replaced his leadership. Of course, he is not alone in the network. Key senior leaders of the movement who are known to play a financial role include Sirajuddin Haqqani, Nasuriddin Haqqani, Badruddin Haqqani, Khalil Haqqani, Ibrahim Omari, Jan Baz Zadran, Haji Mali Khan, Fazl Rabbi, Mullah Sangeen Zadran, and Ahmed Jan Wazir. Their personalities and significance are explained by Peters via interviews and phone calls in 2012 for the Combating Terrorism Centre at West Point. These persons, their occupations, and their current situations are provided in Table 59.1.

The Haqqani Network is a fairly small organisation, and the members of it are mostly from Jawaluddin Haqqani's family. According to the report of the Combating Terrorism Centre (2012), the network has almost the same characteristics as the mafia system, in which money moves up and down the command chain in both directions. The network boss may allocate operating funds and wages to the field captains, but those captains with high earnings potential must give a portion of what they collect to their superiors. For Peters (2012), the small and centralised nature of the decision-making process and the distribution network of funds could be a major weakness of the Haqqanis, indicating that killing or capturing key senior figures, particularly those dealing with financial issues and supplies, could dramatically degrade the overall capability of the network. Under the leadership's top tier, the decision-making process had slowly become less centralised. In terms of fundraising and criminal activities, field commanders themselves possess a high degree of autonomy. It is also relevant to point out that Haqqani forces tend to be less motivated by money at the lower ranks than by a combination of religion, prestige, vengeance, and the sense that they are engaging in a significant and grand war (Peters 2012, p. 24).

The network's behaviour in the Afghan war was to serve two main objectives, such as eliminating Western influence and establishing a Taliban regime in Afghanistan. Particularly, it rejects coalition forces dominated by the U.S., the creation of new security services, and the development of new democratic structures (Brown et al., 2013). The role the Haqqani Network played was primarily to impose obedience on its own population. In addition, they were acting to terrorise and deter rival groups (Skorka, 2017). After Sirajuddin Haqqani became the leader of the network, the political aims of the network also changed towards being more militant and aggressive (Brown et al., 2013). Sirajuddin not only filled the void created by his veteran jihadi father's absence, but the Haqqani Network has emerged as the most dangerous and challenging foe for the Afghanistan Coalition forces (Ali, 2008, p. 2). Skorka (2017) argues that the Haqqani Network's recent history demonstrates that it's no longer based purely on fundamentalist religious philosophy or ethnic separatism. Instead, the

Table 59.1 Key Personnel of the Haqqani Network

	Affinity	Occupation	Current Situation
Sirajuddin Haqqani	Jalaluddin's son by his Afghan wife	Manager of network operations, military activities, and the network's business operations with Quetta Shura.	Leader of the Haqqani Network. Chief Executive Officer (CEO). Chair of the Miran Shah Shura.
Nasiruddin Haqqani	Son of Jalaluddin's Afghan wife	Runs the group's financial operations.	Chief Financial Officer. Hasa seat on Miran Shah Shura.
Badruddin Haqqani	Another son of Jalaluddin's Afghan wife	Handling family businesses, high-profile abductees, micromanaging transport, and smuggling operations. Plays a media role.	Chief of Operations (COO). Sits on the Miran Shah Shura, and has a say in business decisions and operations.
Khalil Haqqani	Brother of Jalaluddin.	Fundraiser for the network and military commander. Operates front companies that support network	Vice president in the corporation.
Ibrahim Omari/ Haqqani	Brother of Jalaluddin.	Manager of the real estate holdings in Pakistan and the UAE. Plays role in kidnap-for-ransom operations.	He was detained by the U.S. and Afghan authorities in 2002
Jan Baz Zadran	Not a relative of Jalaluddin	Coordinator of communication. Organised the collection of security payments.	Died in October 2011 during a drone strike
Haji Mali Khan	Married to Jalaluddin's sister	Field commander. Emissary between the Haqqanis and the Pakistani Taliban.	Captured in October 2011 by a joint team of NATO coalition and Afghan security forces
Mullah Sangeen Zadran	Not a relative of Jalaluddin	Operational commander in eastern Afghanistan. "Senior Lieutenant" to Sirajuddin.	Maintains autonomy within the network.
Fazl Rabbi	Not a relative of Jalaluddin	Financial facilitator. Sends suicide bombers, ships illegal narcotics out of Afghanistan	Member of the Taliban's Peshawar financial shura.
Ahmed Jan Wazir	Not a relative of Jalaluddin	Sirajuddin's deputy and advisor. Commander in the province. Provided money and weapons.	Killed in a drone strike in 2013.

Source: Authors' own table based on the information from Peters (2012) "Haqqani Network Financing: The Evolution of an Industry," Combatting Terrorism Center at West Point.

use of power to bring about political change in the modern era, such as to capture territory, revive national emirates, or for relatively fewer concrete reasons, such as helping to create a global Islamic caliphate, is usually the product of a nuanced, strategic combination of motives (Skorka, 2017; CISAC, 2018).

ORGANISATIONAL CHARACTERISTICS AND ACTIVITIES: STRUCTURE, CHANGE, AND OPERATIONS

The Haqqani Network is one of the deadliest terrorist networks in Afghanistan. It operates in North Waziristan, Pakistan, which is close to the eastern border of Afghanistan in the provinces of Paktia, Paktika, and Khost. The Haqqani Network has an advantage due to its geographical location, which is on the eastern border of Afghanistan and the western border of Pakistan, because of the characteristics and history of the region. It also benefits from its tribal connections; therefore, the network has the opportunity to reach resources and exert influence on globalised political violence and regional conflict (Brown & Rassler, 2013). Historically, the group has controlled a power base in the tribal areas of Pakistan (US Department of State, 2018).

When ideological approaches are considered, it is observed that there are certain differences in the religious beliefs of the Taliban and the Haqqani Network. Due to their stance on Islam and tribal political culture, the Haqqanis can be considered conservatives rather than radicals, according to Brown and Rassler (2013). The network follows mainstream Deobandi Islamism apart from Salafi's understandings of jihad, although it is categorised as religious-Sunni-Islamist. For instance, the Haqqani does not aim to seize power in Afghanistan, nor does it follow a revolutionary Islamist world, nor does it declare people following different paths of Islam or other religions as unbelievers. However, Sirajuddin Haqqani, who is Jalaluddin's son and carries out the activities of the group and leads the network, has shifted the group's ideology to a more radical approach, unlike Jalaluddin.

It is clear that the organisation acts mostly as "a local player with local concerns" (Brown & Rassler, 2013) and that its short-term objectives consist of the departure of foreign forces and the emancipation of LoyaPaktia from Afghanistan. Also, the group is the major facilitator of jihadi participants involved in expansive conspiracies and plans that stretch beyond Nonetheless, the global jihad carried out by Al-Qaeda and components of regional jihad in Kashmir have been formed by the safe shelters, networking opportunities, combat experience, resource mobilisation, training, and propaganda support (Brown & Rassler, 2013, p. 237) provided and expedited by the Haqqani Network.

Jalaluddin Haqqani provided financial support for the network through his personal connections. The network also got important assistance from the Gulf region, and Jalaluddin's sons have allegedly travelled to the Gulf on several occasions to get attention and support in the region for their cause and financial aid from their rich supporters outside of Afghanistan. The income of the network generally comes from kidnapping, extortion, smuggling of timber, foreign donors, especially from the Gulf states, and the taxation imposed on the sphere of influence (Dressler, 2010).

The network was "designated as a foreign terrorist organisation on September 19, 2012" (US Department of State, 2018), especially after the attacks on U.S. and Coalition targets in Afghanistan. The designation of the whole organisation as a terrorist organisation paves the way for the U.S. government to point out the global business structure and monitor facilitators of the Haqqani Network. Therefore, designation as a terrorist organisation is expected to deteriorate the fundraising and business activities of the network and consequently reduce their financial power to carry out their terrorist attacks, radicalisation programmes, and foreign fighter training (Dressler, 2012). Besides the group designation, key personnel have also been designated individually. "Haqqani leaders Saidullah Jan, Yahya Haqqani, and Muhammad Omar Zahran, as well as suicide operations chief Qari Abdul Ra'uf (also known as Qari Zakir), and Ibrahim Haqqani, remain either designated for financial sanctions or are on U.S. most-wanted lists" (National Counterterrorism Centre, n.d.).

The support of the United States for the Haqqani Network ended in the early 1990s; however, the Pakistani government has maintained its relationship with the network until now. Due to the fact that the boundary between Afghanistan and Pakistan is the region in which the network exerts influence and the network sides with the Pakistani government, it encourages a clash between the two states. The support of the Pakistani military for the Haqqanis started in the 1970s, at a time when the Pakistani government saw Afghan Islamists as the opponents of a Moscow-led government in Afghanistan and as members of retaliation in the Pakistan-Afghanistan proxy war.

Since India is the major enemy state of Pakistan, Pakistan is dedicated to reducing Indian influence in Afghanistan, and the Haqqanis have proven their willingness to perpetrate violence to this end (Brown & Rassler, 2013). After the invasion of Afghanistan by the United States, an anti-Taliban coalition ran the defence ministry of the Afghan government and was supported by India. Pakistan regarded them as enemies because they were not compatible with Pakistan's interests in the region. Therefore, the powerful structure of the Haqqani Network, which plans to organise attacks on foreign governments in Afghanistan, especially to weaken India's approach, corresponds to the objectives of the Pakistani military.

At the end of 1979, the Soviet invasion of Afghanistan triggered its opponents to find a way to put the Soviets in a difficult position and ensure their withdrawal from Afghanistan. In this case, the Haqqani Network seemed like a strategic partner due to "its advantageous location and well-developed capacity for mobilising the tribes for war, which made them among the most favoured recipients of the massive amounts of military and financial aid that the United States, Saudi Arabia, and several other states poured into Pakistan to counter the Soviet advance." They got a significant amount of financial assistance from Pakistan's Inter-Services Intelligence Directorate (ISI) and Central Intelligence Agency (CIA). As stated by Brown and Rassler (2013), the Haqqanis were provided "at least 12,000 metric tonnes of war material every year during the 1980s conflict with the Soviet Union". Since the withdrawal from Afghanistan, Pakistan has not severed all ties with the Haqqanis and has continued to give support to the Haqqanis for its interests in Afghanistan, which ramifies the relationship between the U.S. and Pakistan.

The relationship between Osama bin Laden, the Al-Qaeda leader, and Jalaluddin Haqqani goes back a long way, until the mid-1980s. Since Osama bin Laden and Abdullah Azzam put up a fight against the Soviet invasion of Afghanistan, the histories of these groups have merged, and they maintained these relationships as long as their activities continued. During the time when al-Qaeda was starting to be formed at the end of the 1980s, the Haqqanis provided al-Qaeda with infrastructure and installations. On the other hand, one thing that needs to be pointed out is that unlike Al-Qaeda, which has revolutionary and global aims, the objectives of the Haqqani Network remain limited within the borders of Afghanistan.

During the times when the ISI and Taliban were in connection and the Taliban was supported by the ISI, the Haqqani Network led by Jalaluddin merged into the Taliban in 1995. There were rumours that the ISI pushed the network to join the organisation because it planned to direct both groups in compliance with Pakistani interests. However, the worldviews of the network and the Taliban did not exactly overlap. "The Taliban wanted to create an Islamic emirate, while Haqqani prefers an Islamic republic." (Gopal, 2009). Their relationship deteriorated after Massoud's Northern Alliance defeated the Taliban in Mazar-e Sharif in 1997; besides, Haqqani stuck with Omar and maintained a power base in Miram Shah (Dressler, 2010).

ATTACKS AND STRATEGIES OF THE HAQQANI NETWORK

The Haqqani Network is seen as the most destructive and complicated insurgency organisation targeting Afghan, U.S., and coalition forces residing in Afghanistan. The network maintained its fight in Afghanistan against the Soviet forces and their Afghan allies through the 1980s (Centre for International Security and Cooperation, n.d.). Since the U.S. invasion of Afghanistan and the withdrawal of Soviet forces, the network has turned its focal point to NATO and U.S. forces. Jalaluddin Haqqani came to the forefront in terms of his military skills and experiences, in addition to his capability of organisation and coordination, because he was very successful in coordinating other tribal families and forces in Loya Paktia alongside controlling his forces within the network.

Considering the 120 attacks carried out by the Haqqani Network, it can be seen that all the attacks targeted Afghanistan (Figure 59.1). Two of them targeted Pakistan; however, one attack is suspected in terms of its uncertainty about whether it was carried out by the network or not because the group did not take any responsibility for the attack. 118 attacks targeted Afghanistan. Although there was a falling tendency in the attacks against Afghanistan from 2010 to 2013, it soared after 2013 but fluctuated afterward.

They mostly carry out organised small-arms attacks, together with suicide attacks, improvised explosive devices (IEDs), and attacks using bomb-laden vehicles (National Counterterrorism Centre, n.d.) (Figures 59.2 and 59.3). Also, the network was in charge of many high-profile attacks in Afghanistan during the Afghan War. In close connection with the Afghan Taliban, it carried out an attack on the Kabul International Hotel in June 2011 and two suicide attacks against the Indian Embassy in Kabul in 2008 and 2009. Also, they instigated attacks on International Security Assistance Force (ISAF) headquarters, the U.S. Embassy, the Afghan National Directorate of Security headquarters, and the Afghan Presidential Palace in Kabul that lasted a whole day. " Both the U.S. and the Kabul

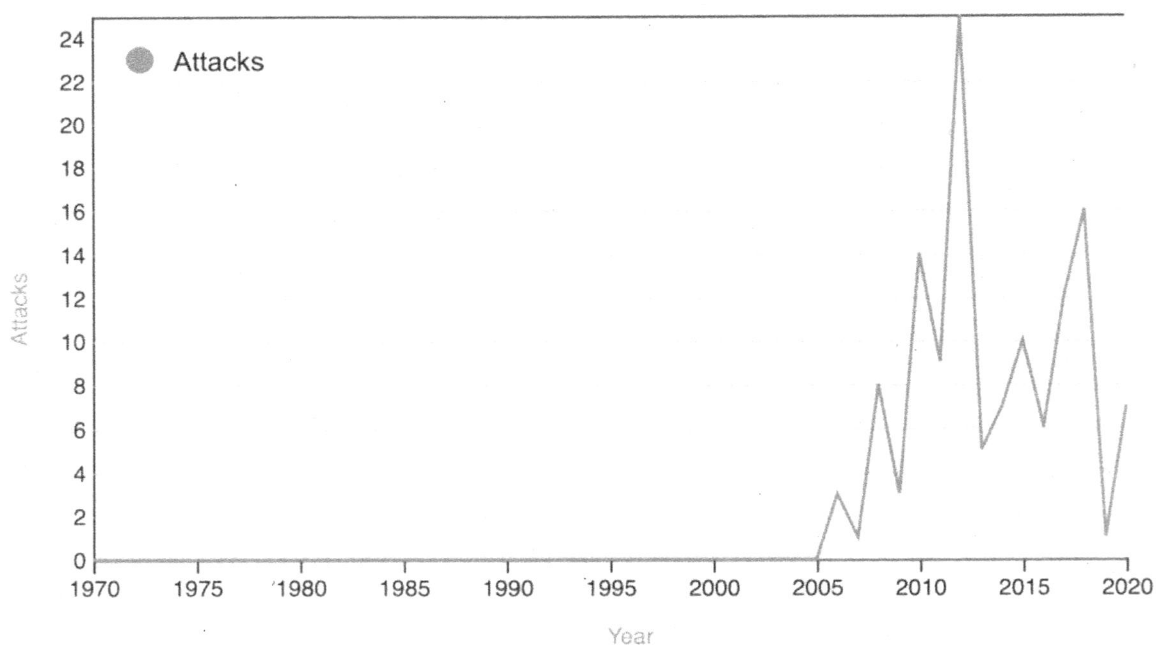

Figure 59.1 Haqqani Incidents in Afghanistan (1970–2020).

Source: Global Terrorism Database (GTD) (2024).

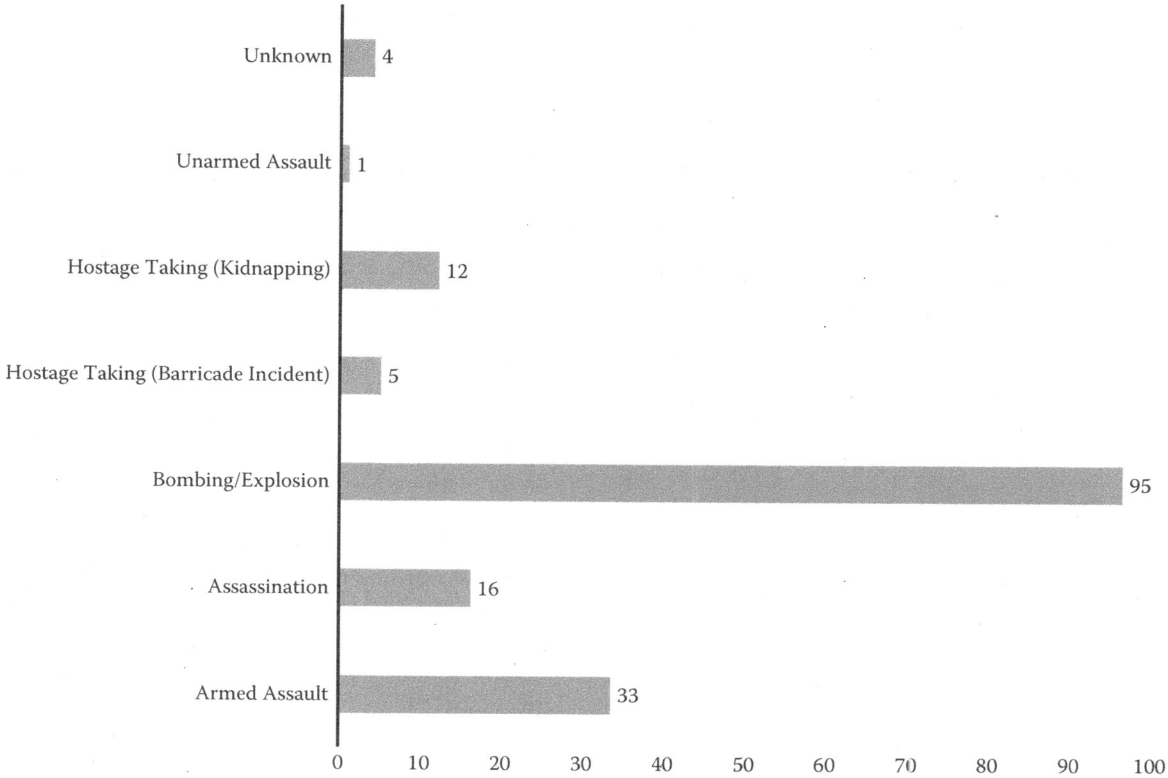

Figure 59.2 Haqqani Incidents by Attack Type (1970-2020).

Source: Global Terrorism Database (GTD) (2024).

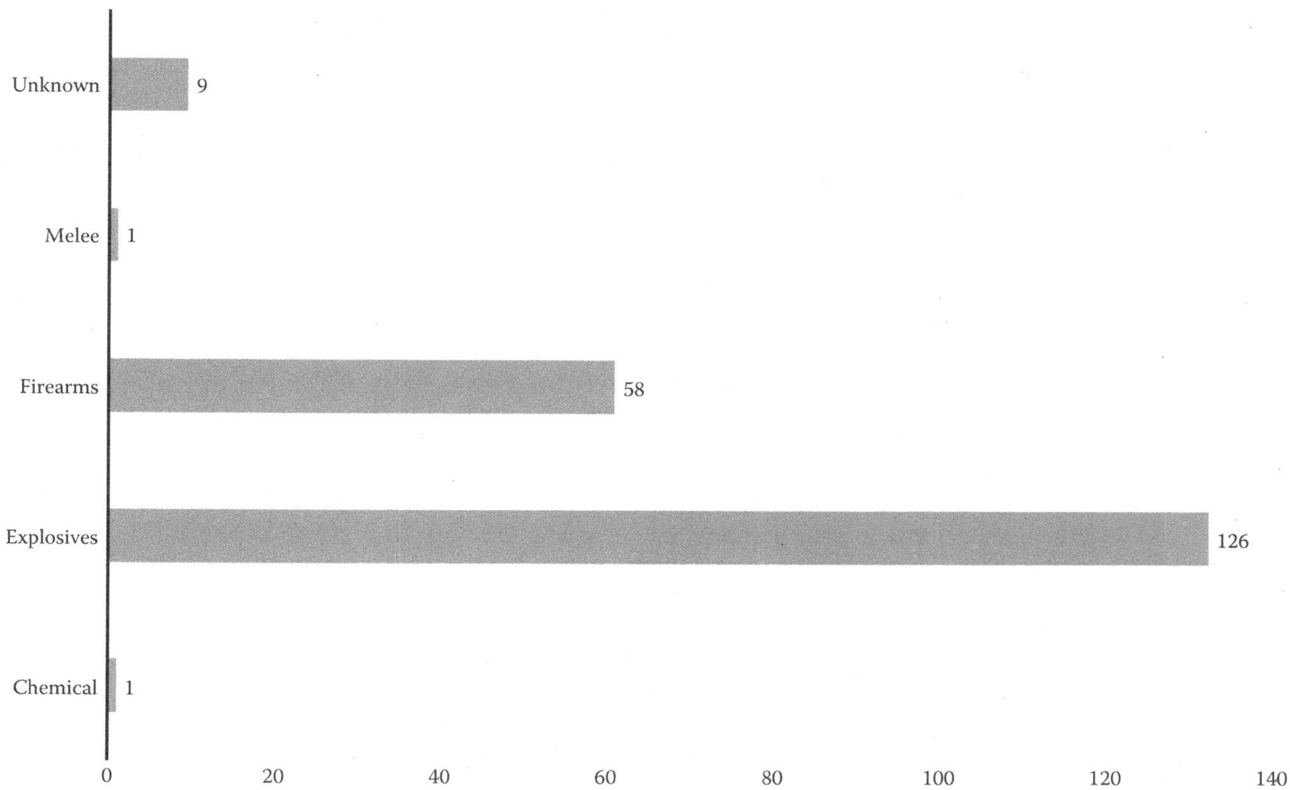

Figure 59.3 Haqqani Incidents by Weapon Type (1970-2020).

Source: Global Terrorism Database (GTD) (2024).

government have repeatedly pointed to the Haqqani network as the organisers of high-publicity terrorist attacks on targets in the capital Kabul." Furthermore, the group participates in several criminal activities ranging from extortion to smuggling in Pakistan and Afghanistan. Yahya Haqqani, who is the brother of Sirajuddin Haqqani, coordinates relationships with other powers in order to improve its tactical goals. It acquires highly advanced technological skills and experience in the fields of remote detonation devices and bomb-making (Center for International Security and Cooperation, n.d.). Also, suicide bombers have a vital place in the Haqqani Network (Dressler, 2010). Due to its significant numbers of foreign militants as a result of its relationships with Uzbekistan, Al-Qaeda, Saudi Arabia, and Chechnya, the network can train and use these people as suicide bombers.

The operational capabilities of the Haqqani Network seemed to have been developed at the end of 2008. It has a large variety of high-value perpetrators, from top al-Qaeda leaders to the Islamic Movement of Uzbekistan, Lashkar-e-Taiba, the Pakistani Taliban, and smaller terrorist organisations carrying out attacks in different parts of the world. Specialised training given by Pakistani militant groups such as Tehrik-i Taliban Pakistan (TTP), Maulvi Nazir, and al-Qaeda led to individual suicide bombings and several multifaceted attacks (Dressler, 2010).

The Haqqani Network's ties with al-Qaeda have always faced serious risks, posed certain problems, and impeded its connections with quite influential and prominent partners like the Pakistani military and the Taliban. In this sense, the annihilation and elimination of the network are crucial to providing both security transformation in Afghanistan and the destruction of groups that exploit Islam for political ends. Today, the Haqqani Network remains important as a lethal threat in Afghanistan. In August 2016, Sirajuddin Haqqani was the elected deputy of Mullah Haibatullah Akhundzada, the newly appointed Afghan Taliban chief (Skorka, 2017). In 2017, the organisation was linked to several high-profile attacks, including a car bombing in Kabul that killed more than 150 people and wounded about 500. The network denied responsibility, but the Afghan government claims responsibility for the party (CISAC, 2018). On January 4, 2018, the Trump administration suspended military aid to the Pakistani government pending more stringent military action against the group (Bloch, 2018).

IMPACTS

Terrorist organisations always have a degree of political, economic, social, and psychological impact on the society in which they live, and typically, at least for some of these areas, other societies beyond their immediate domain. Particularly, the regions where they originated are the most influenced. The Haqqani Network is a relatively small terror group, but it has a considerable effect in its region as well. However, because there is a limited amount of existing data related to this situation, it is not easy to put every impact of it on society forward in this section. The Haqqani Network is a religious-oriented group that follows the ideology of Deobandi. As has already been mentioned in previous sections, the Haqqaniyya Madrassas became one of the basic religious schools for Pakhtuns. Jalaluddin Haqqani was trained in these schools, and the network kept its connection with them in general. Deobandi ideology owes its spread to these madrassas and active participants, who are mainly members of the Haqqani Network. The Haqqani Network's anti-Soviet standing and Islamist behaviour have all been shaped in these schools; thus, supporting them in the region has caused the spread of their ideals in society. Their impact on politics is perhaps the only one studied and negotiated. Therefore, in this section, the Haqqani Network's role in politics will be illustrated.

The most important influence of the Haqqani Network can be argued to be "political." According to Skorka (2019), Haqqani alliances are interpreted as influencing the Afghan political order. They possess a significant political role as they are infiltrating southeastern Afghanistan, reaching up to the northern provinces, and stretching to its western border with Iran. Their connections with al-Qaeda and the Taliban also provide them with advantages in terms of political means. Even when there are counterterrorism operations by Pakistan, Skorka (2019) claims that the attitude of Pakistan towards the Haqqani Network is different from that of other terror groups. For instance, the ISI has not acted to capture the Haqqani Network's most important and influential actors. According to Mullah Omar, interviewed for CFR (2019), "Pakistan is protecting Sirajuddin Haqqani in the hope of continuing jihad by proxy. As the U.S. forces leave Afghanistan, Haqqani will acquire two countries: Pakistan and Afghanistan. Success in Afghanistan will mean our Muslim brothers in the region and around the world have managed to claim back our own rights in our own Islamic country. Sirajuddin understands that." Therefore, one can argue that the Haqqani Network plays a religious role, and such a role is reflected in politics, too.

Vahid Brown and Don Rassier, in their book *Fountainhead of Jihad: Haqqani Nexus, 1973–2012*, state that "the relationship [between the Taliban and Haqqani's] functions as a political alliance built upon similar histories, ideological connections, and a common vision for the future that accommodates each group's regional preferences." In this sense, the release of the leaders of the Haqqani not only shows the closeness of the two parties but also points to the position of the former throughout Afghan politics. Thus, some claim that the Haqqani Network is highly important for the Afghan peace process in the U.S. (Jamal, 2019). Bruce Riedel argued in his book *What We Won: America's Secret War in Afghanistan, 1979–89*, that at one point "the U.S. embassy in Islamabad considered Haqqani[s] the finest and most capable Pashtun commander[s] in the war." In this case, Jamal (2019) argues that if the U.S. wishes to make a deal with the Taliban, then she needs to address the Haqqanis as well. As the U.S. is eager to strike an agreement, it should be anticipated that Islamabad would demand full compromises to suit its defence and political interests. Pakistan has had close ties not only to the Taliban but to the Haqqani network as well.

CONCLUSION

The emergence of the Haqqani Network can be traced back to the Soviet invasion. They had an anti-Soviet stance, so significant intelligence organisations like the CIA of the United States and the ISI of Pakistan supported them. After the withdrawal of the Soviet Union, they shifted their objectives, strategies, and tactics towards the United States and other coalition forces. They started to stand against the U.S. and its values. On the other hand, it does not aim to seize power in Afghanistan, nor does it follow a revolutionary Islamist world, nor does it declare people following different paths of Islam or other religions as unbelievers.

Although the Haqqani Network has not been studied much, it is highly important to study the network to understand the complex structure of Afghanistan. Also, it gives clues about the formation of two lethal terrorist organisations, al-Qaeda and the Taliban. Under Jalaluddin's important leadership, the network is capable of attracting foreign fighters from different parts of the world and maintains not only its financial power but also its radical Islamic ideology. It is also a relatively small organisation. It is one of the deadliest terrorist networks in Afghanistan. Despite not being described as a terrorist organisation, its activities are mainly targeted at private citizens and properties (Figure 59.4). However, the Pakistani government's counterterrorism strategies towards the Haqqani Network are different from those of other terror organisations because

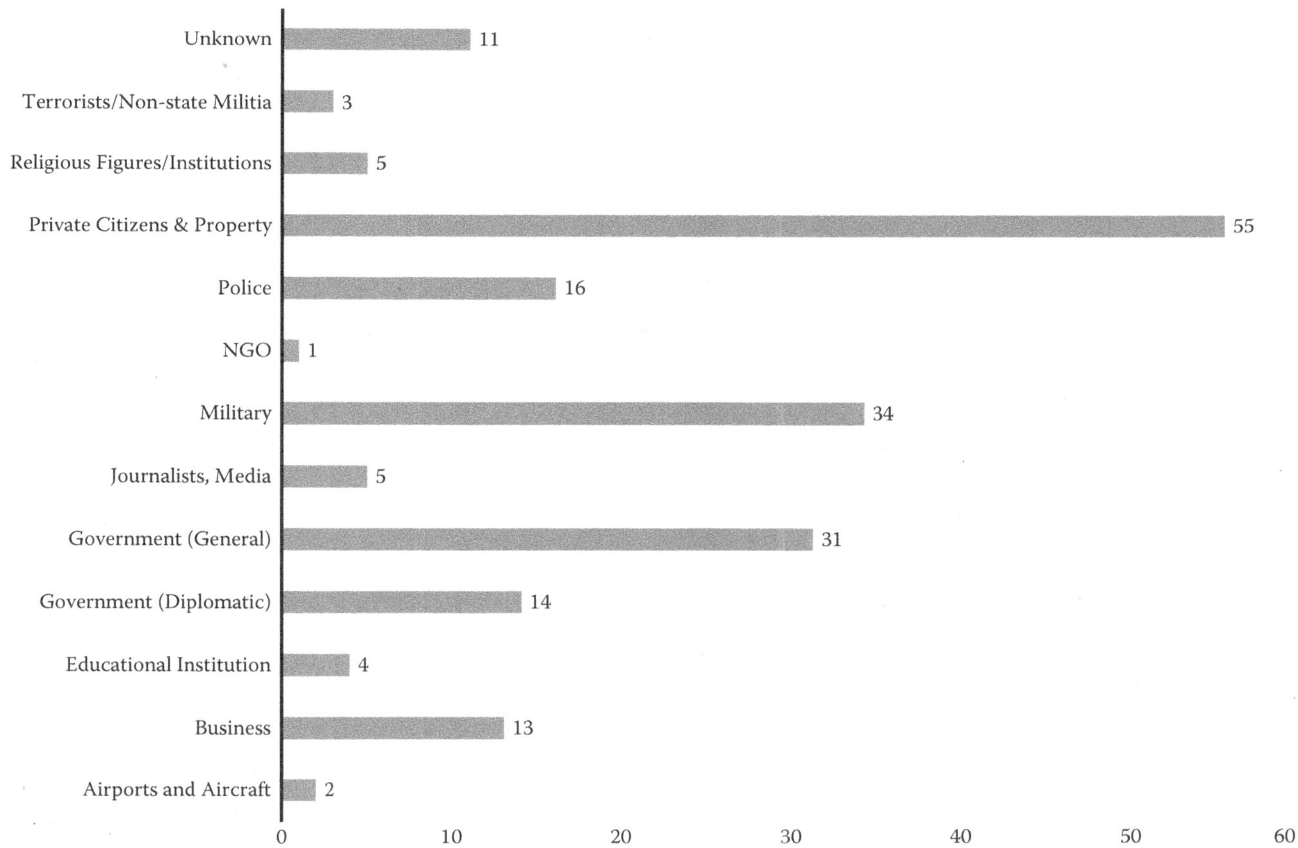

Figure 59.4 Haqqani Incidents by Target Type (1970-2020).

Source: Global Terrorism Database (GTD) (2024).

they do not aim to capture the most important actors of the network. According to this study, one can argue that the main reason for this fact is that the Haqqani Network has a significant role in politics in Pakistan and the peace process in Afghanistan.

References

Ali, I. (2008). The Haqqani network and cross-border terrorism in Afghanistan. *Terrorism Monitor*, 6(6), 1–11.

Bloch, H. (2018, January 4). U.S. suspends most security Assistance to Pakistan. NPR: https://www.npr.org/sections/thetwo-way/2018/01/04/575492300/u-s-suspends-most-security-assistance-to-pakistan

Brown, V., & Rassler, D. (2013). *Fountainhead of Jihad: The Haqqani Nexus 1973–2012*. New York: Oxford University Press.

Center for International Security and Cooperation. (n.d.). Stanford Center for International Security and Cooperation. Retrieved from Haqqani Network at a Glance: https://cisac.fsi.stanford.edu/mappingmilitants/profiles/haqqani-network#_edn2

Dressler, J. (2010). *The Haqqani network from Pakistan to Afghanistan*. Washington: The Institute of the Study of War. Retrieved from January 13, 2020. http://www.understandingwar.org

Dressler, J. (2012). *The Haqqani network: A foreign terrorist organization*. Washington, DC:Institute for the Study of War.

Global Terrorism Database (GTD). (2024). Haqqani network "Attack Type". https://www.start.umd.edu/gtd/search/Results.aspx?charttype=bar&chart=attack&search=Haqqani%20Network

Global Terrorism Database (GTD). (2024). Haqqani network "Incidents". https://www.start.umd.edu/gtd/search/Results.aspx?search=Haqqani+network&sa.x=0&sa.y=0

Global Terrorism Database (GTD). (2024). Haqqani network "Target Type". https://www.start.umd.edu/gtd/search/Results.aspx?charttype=bar&chart=target&search=Haqqani%20Network

Global Terrorism Database (GTD). (2024). Haqqani network "Weapon Type". https://www.start.umd.edu/gtd/search/Results.aspx?charttype=bar&chart=weapon&search=Haqqani%20Network

Gopal, A. (2009, June 1). The most deadly US foe in Afghanistan. The Christian Science Monitor, Access Address: https://www.csmonitor.com/World/Asia-South-Central/2009/0601/p10s01-wosc.html

Grewal, J. (2013). *The Haqqani network*. Leavenworth: Faculty of Us Army Command and General Staff College.

Haroon, S. (2008). The rise of Deobandi Islam in the north-west frontier Province and its implications in Colonial India and Pakistan 1914–1996. *Journal of the Royal Asiatic Society, 18*(1), 47–70.

Hussain, G. (2011, October 12). Who are the Haqqanis? Quilliam, Retrieved from: https://web.archive.org/web/20191225104718/https://www.quilliaminternational.com/who-are-the-haqqanis-3/

Jamal, U. (2019, November 25). Pakistan's Haqqani network increases its profile in Afghan peace talks. The Diplomat. Retrieved from: https://thediplomat.com/2019/11/pakistans-haqqani-network-increases-its-profile-in-afghan-peace-talks/

Jones, S. G. (2008). The rise of Afghanistan's insurgency: State failure and Jihad. *International Security, 32*(4), 7–40.

Mapping Militant Organizations. *Haqqani network*. Stanford University. Last modified July 2018. https://cisac.fsi.stanford.edu/mappingmilitants/profiles/haqqani-network

National Counterterrorism Center. (n.d.). Haqqani network. Retrieved from Counterterrorism Guide: https://www.dni.gov/nctc/groups/haqqani_network.html

Peters, G. (2012, July). Haqqani Network Financing: The evolution of an industry. Harmony Project, Combatting Terrorism Center at West Point. https://ctc.usma.edu/posts/haqqani-network-financing

Rapoport, D. C. (2004). The four waves of modern terrorism. In J. M. içinde (Ed.), *Attacking terrorism: Elements of a grand strategy* (pp. 46–73). Washington: Georgetown University Press.

Romaniuk, S. N., & Webb, S. T. (2015). The Haqqani network threat: Keeping insurgency in the family. In S. N. Romaniuk, & S. T. Webb (Eds.). *Insurgency and counterinsurgency in modern war* (pp. 175–189). New York: Taylor & Francis.

Rosenberg, M., & Mehsud, I. T. (2015, July 31). *Founder of Haqqani network is long dead, Aide Says*. The New York Times. Retrieved from: https://www.nytimes.com/2015/08/01/world/asia/founder-of-haqqani-network-died-nearly-a-year-ago-member-says.html?_r=0

Ruttig, T. (2010, July 1). Talking Haqqani. Retrieved from Afghanistan Analysts Network. https://www.afghanistan-analysts.org/talking-haqqani/

Skorka, M. (2017). Modern terrorist adaptation to Western policy. Unpublished manuscript. Changing Character of War Centre, University of Oxford, Oxford, United Kingdom.

Skorka, M. (2019, August 16). Afghanistan Endgame, Part Two: How Does This War End? Council on Foreign Relations (CFR), Retrieved from: https://www.cfr.org/blog/afghanistan-endgame-part-two-how-does-war-end

US Department of State. (2018, September). *Country reports on terrorism 2017*. United States Department of State Publication. Retrieved on January 13, 2020 https://www.state.gov/wp-content/uploads/2019/04/crt_2017.pdf

60

ISLAMIC MOVEMENT OF UZBEKISTAN (IMU)

Rohan Malhotra

> We live in a regime built on force and lies. In essence, it's the same here in Uzbekistan, except the government here is better at presenting itself to the outside world.
>
> Isa Gambar (Former acting President of Azerbaijan)

INTRODUCTION

The Islamic Movement of Uzbekistan (IMU) is a Salafi-jihadist militant group operating in Central Asia, also known by the name *Harakat ul-Islamiyah* in Arabic. The Islamic Movement of Uzbekistan was officially formed in 1998 in Kabul, Afghanistan, in order to overthrow the Uzbek government under the leadership of Islam Karimov.[1] The existence of the militant group could be traced to the 1990s, and the main aim of the group was to establish the Islamic caliphate in the Fergana Valley[2] region. It all happened under the influence of the Afghan Taliban in order to implement sharia law (Islamic courts) in Uzbekistan and throughout Central Asia. The Islamic Movement of Uzbekistan (IMU) was founded by *Tahir Yuldashev*[3] in the Namangan region of Uzbekistan.

Yuldashev's views were more centralised towards promoting Wahhabism and Salafism, particularly in Central Asia, and his views were shaped by his frequent and extensive travel to Saudi Arabia, Afghanistan, and Pakistan. The idea of initiating a Salafi-jihadist militant group was to establish an Islamic caliphate in Central Asia with the help of al-Qaeda, the Taliban, and al-Jihad in order to spread the radical message throughout the networks of mosques and madrassas in the Fergana Valley region (Fedlholm, 2010). In the initial years since its inception, the group used to carry out its operations extensively in Afghanistan, Tajikistan, and Kyrgyzstan. The Islamic Movement of Uzbekistan (IMU) started recruiting from Central Asia, South Asia, Europe, Africa, China, and the Philippines under the guidance of *Juma Khodjiev Namangani*,[4] the military commander for IMU. Between 1998 and 2001, Namangani went to Afghanistan to carry out extensive recruitment for IMU, and the group started running their offices from Kabul, Kandahar, and Mazar-e-Sharif with the assistance of the Afghan Taliban. It was reported that in these initial years, in order to attract more Islamic fighters to join the movement, Namangani paid between 100 and 500 US dollars per month (Baran, 2006) to the new recruits and to attract men living in those impoverished deserts.

Islamic radicalisation in Central Asia is a result of the Soviet Union's sense of secularism and thus relates to the differing strength of Islam due to external factors involved like foreign proselytising, domestic political and social developments, armed conflicts, and oppressed political systems. In central Asia, the focus is on the Islamic revival and strength of various radical groups, particularly in the Fergana Valley region, which is densely populated and ethically a major Uzbek territory with a political division between Uzbekistan, Kyrgyzstan, and Tajikistan (Baran, 2006). Since years, the Fergana Valley has been a centre for Islamic fervour, thus allowing foreign radicals to establish their presence. Apart from the Fergana Valley, the other centres of Islamic revival and important centres for various radical groups have been Tajikistan and southern Kyrgyzstan. Around the 1980s, the spread of radical Islamic political movements that took place in Tajikistan was the result of the growing interaction between Afghanistan and Tajikistan during the era of the Soviet Union's occupation. Fergana Valley is believed to be the heartland of Central Asia, where 20% of the region's 70 million people live. Many states in the Fergana valley, including Czarist Russia,[5] the Soviet Union, and the independent Central Asian republics, have always sought to limit the role of Islamic tradition in politics and society. However, the two major political transitions that happened in the region – from Czarist rule to Soviet rule in 1917 and from Soviet rule to independence in 1991 – have been the major reasons for the resurgence of many Islamic movements calling for the restoration of Islamic tradition in the politics and society of Central Asia. These movements included primarily the *Basmachis* in 1917 and the Islamic Movement of Uzbekistan (IMU) and other Islamist revival groups in the 1990s (Zenn, 2013).

DOI: 10.4324/9780429426063-68

The Islamic Movement of Uzbekistan, as founded by Tahir Yuldashev and Juma Namangani in 1998, appointed *Zubayr ibn Abdul Raheem* as the spiritual leader of the group. Abdul Raheem declared jihad against the Uzbekistan government in August 1999 and criticised the Karimov government for undermining the ideology of Islam and threatening the various radical groups with pro-western orientations. On the contrary, Islam Karimov, the former President of Uzbekistan, said in 1998 (Baran, 2006):

> We will never admit religious slogans to be used in the struggle for power, or as the pretext for intervention in politics, economy and legislation, because in this we see a serious potential threat to stability and security for the Uzbek state.

The group has conducted several attacks across the region, and the targets included civilians, security forces, and community leaders based in Afghanistan, Pakistan, Uzbekistan, Tajikistan, and Kyrgyzstan. The attacks have been carried out in coordination with the Afghan Taliban, al-Qaeda, and the Tehrik-i-Taliban Pakistan in the form of kidnappings, suicide bombings, and other planned murders of high-profile people who have been influenced by western culture (Counter Extremism Project, 2019). The main sources of funding for IMU have been racketeering, large-scale kidnappings in exchange for ransoms, and collecting foreign donations. At the time of the inception of the group, al-Qaeda was believed to be the major financing partner for the IMU, and the group received a substantial amount of aid from Osama Bin Laden's al-Qaeda network in Afghanistan. The reach of the Islamic Movement of Uzbekistan (IMU) was at a peak between 1999 and 2001.

The first major attack by the group was carried out in August 1999, when Juma Namangani and his fighters abducted the Japanese geologists along with Kyrgyz government officials and military personnel in southern Kyrgyzstan, thus expanding their reach in the region. The group has also been believed to have been involved in carrying out attacks inside the territory of Uzbekistan from their bases in Afghanistan and Tajikistan, including the famous 1999 Tashkent bombings in order to assassinate the then President of Uzbekistan, Islam Karimov (Government of Australia, 2007). In the early months of 2000, Namangani fled to Kabul to establish their training camp under the influence and guidance of the Afghan Taliban. The fighters of the group from the Fergana Valley region also started fleeing to Kabul for their training in order to get trained in terrorism tactics to carry out the objective of establishing the Islamic caliphate in Central Asia, as explained by the co-founder Tahir Yuldashev in his interview he had given in the early months of 2001 (Starr, 2006):

> The goal of IMU activities is the creation of an Islamic State. We declared a jihad in order to create a religious system and government. We want the model of Islam which is nothing like in Afghanistan, Iran, Pakistan or Saudi Arabia.

The chapter will unfold the strategies, aims, and objectives of the group in detail, with a special focus on the ideologue and the masterminds involved.

ISLAMIC MOVEMENT OF UZBEKISTAN: EVOLUTION, OBJECTIVES AND STRATEGY

Early Years: 1989–2001

The Islamic Movement of Uzbekistan (IMU) has been believed to have its origins in the Islamic movement named *Adolat*, meaning justice, which was formed during the Soviet era in the early months of 1990. The Islamic movement Adolat arose out of a faction of a large group called *Islom lashkarlari*, meaning Islamic warriors, which was active in the Namangan region of the Fergana valley as a result of the response to widespread corruption and social injustice by the then Uzbekistan government and the prohibition on carrying out Islamic activities in the country. The Adolat movement has been believed to have been founded by Abdulhakim Qori (a well-known preacher of radical Islam) and supported by other imams and preachers like Obidkhon Qori Nazarov from Tashkent and Umarkhon Domla and Davudkhon Qori from Namangan, who also contributed funds from their mosques, and the movement grew rapidly in the Fergana valley (Mambetaliev, 2010). For the most radical Islamists, the main point of entry to Central Asia was Fergana Valley, and thus, with the Adolat movement, the other small groups active were *Baraka*, meaning blessing, and *Tauba*, meaning repentance, during the period of the early 1990s.

In January 1990, the funding for the Adolat movement started coming from Saudi Arabia; thus, the movement turned out to be more radicalised and influenced by Wahhabism. The movement was then led by Tahir Yuldashev and Juma Namangani, two young men with the objective of establishing an Islamic caliphate in Central Asia. Yuldashev renamed the movement *Islom Adolat*, meaning Islamic justice. In the same year, the movement helped reconstruct many mosques and madrassas in the region with the objective of introducing sharia law (Islamic courts) in Central Asia. Yuldashev started recruiting new men and making them swear *bayat* (an Islamic oath of loyalty) and do extensive patrolling in Namangan initially, thus enforcing the implementation of sharia. In December 1991, the Adolat and its fighters, under the leadership of Yuldashev, occupied the headquarters of the Communist

Party of Uzbekistan (CPU) in Namangan, where the then-President Karimov arrived to address the large population. The demands that were put in front of the government in response to the occupation of CPU headquarters were to immediately establish the Islamic state and implement sharia law in Uzbekistan, to have a separate school or college for boys and girls, and to cease having an orientation towards Turkey. The fighters under Yuldashev started referring to them as mujahidin. Soon after Yuldashev announced himself to be the emir (commander in chief) of the Islamic Adolat, the branches of the Islamic movement rose across the Fergana valley, in Andijon, Margilan, Kuva, Farghona, and Osh in Kyrgyzstan. In early 1992, the government of Uzbekistan banned the Adolat movement and cracked down on its operations. In response to this, Tahir Yuldashev and his fighters fled to Tajikistan and Afghanistan (Starr, 2006).

On the contrary, Juma Namangani, the military commander and support aide for Yuldashev, participated in the Tajik Civil War[6] during the period (1992–97) and remained in Tajikistan only after the end of the civil war in order to start and regain momentum for their Islamic movement in the region. He was believed to be extensively involved in drug trafficking near the Rasht Valley in Tajikistan, and this became one of the most significant funding sources for their movement. Both Juma and Tahir met once again in 1997 in Kabul and together founded a Salafi-jihadist militant group named Islamic Movement of Uzbekistan (IMU) in 1998 under the influence of the Afghan Taliban. The main objective was to overthrow the Uzbek government and establish Islamic law in the region.

Around 1998–99, the IMU started operating from its bases in Tavildara and Rasht Valley in Tajikistan. On February 16, 1999, several bomb blasts occurred in Tashkent, the capital city of Uzbekistan, that resulted in the deaths of 16 people and left around 100 others injured. After these attacks, the Uzbek government planned to crack down on IMU and its bases in Tajikistan due to its involvement in the Tashkent bombings and carried out several air strikes. On August 9, 1999, the IMU and its fighters infiltrated the Batken region of Kyrgyzstan, and its mayor was taken as a hostage among others with the demand of a helicopter to flee to Afghanistan and a ransom of US$ 1 million. In response to this, on August 13, the Kyrgyz government granted safe passage to IMU and its fighters to Afghanistan and also paid a ransom of about US$50,000 in exchange for the release of the hostages (Stein, 2013).

By the year 2001, most of the IMU fighters had fled to northern Afghanistan from the Fergana Valley, where they were being helped by the Taliban, and they had established their training camp in Kabul. It has been believed that Yuldashev took the Islamic oath of loyalty to Mullah Omar, the leader of the Taliban, and pledged their alliance with al-Qaeda. From 1999 to 2001, IMU started recruiting new men under the banner of global jihad with the help of both the Taliban and al-Qaeda. The group also started radio broadcasts in northern Afghanistan with their own publication named *Islom Ummati*, meaning the community of Islam, that were used to radicalise the new recruits and showed the movement's ideology with six main themes, including martyrdom (*shahidlik*), the need for jihad to overthrow the Uzbek government, the oppression of Muslims around the world by Jews and westerners, showing empathy towards Islamic radical groups in Russia and the north Caucasus, particularly Chechnya and Ichkeria, to regain the IMU's roots in Uzbekistan (Zenn, 2013).

A Period of Organisational and Geographical Changes: 2001–2009

After the 9/11 attacks, in late 2001, when the United States security forces invaded Afghanistan, the IMU and its fighters joined the Taliban and al-Qaeda in their fight with US security forces, and that led to the killing of Juma Namangani, the military commander for the IMU. As a result, the group suffered grave losses among its men, and many among them fled to South Waziristan, the Federally Administered Tribal Area (FATA) in Pakistan. Over the next few years, the IMU's focus and ideology completely evolved from being centralised to overthrow the Uzbek government to getting involved with and dependent upon the Pakistani Taliban and al-Qaeda. While in Pakistan, IMU recruited its fighters from various other countries like Tajikistan, Russia, Turkey, Kazakhstan, and China, as well as from their home base of Uzbekistan. The ethnic population of Uzbeks from Uzbekistan became a minority in their own militant group; thus, internal rivalry led to a split in the main group, and a small splinter named Islamic Jihad Union (IJU) was formed in 2003. From 2005 to 2007, the IJU was involved in carrying out a series of suicide bombings in Uzbekistan (Fedlholm, 2010). The IMU shifted its focus to fighting alongside the Pakistani Taliban and al-Qaeda against the North Atlantic Treaty Organization (NATO) forces and the Pakistani allied security forces. The IMU established deep ties to the Islamic extremist Lal Mosque in Islamabad, Pakistan, in 2007, and Yuldashev, declaring himself the emir of the group, said:

> We consider them [Lal Masjid] a part of us before, during and after the siege; their Shaheed are our Shaheed; their prisoners are our prisoners, every member of the Harakat [IMU] will stand up against the terrorist act that took place on Lal Masjid. We will always be a part of these activities.

In response to the siege of the Lal Mosque by Pakistani security forces in 2007, the IMU released two videos showing the execution of Pakistani soldiers by its fighters. Lal Mosque was famous for its militant activism in south Waziristan and Pakistan, including the transport of foreign militants to Afghanistan, large-scale kidnappings in exchange for ransom, and supporting anti-Shia militant groups. Reportedly, in 2009, Tahir Yuldashev was killed in a US drone strike (Counter Extremism Project, 2019).

The IMU in Recent Years: 2009–Present

Yuldashev's death in 2009 has prompted many new-generation leaders to take centre stage within the organisation. After his death, Abu Usman Adil became the emir for IMU; under his leadership, the group expanded its operations in northern and eastern Afghanistan and the Central Asian states. He was also killed in a drone strike in 2012. Thus, by the end of 2012, all the original leadership of IMU had been killed, and the group struggled extensively to maintain its recruitment and organisational ties with Uzbekistan.

Usman Ghazi became the emir after Adil's death in 2012, and the objective and strategic shift could be clearly seen with regard to the subject when the IMU was formed. Now, the objective is more of establishing an Islamic caliphate under the banner of global jihad than overthrowing the Uzbek government and targeting western allies. The group announced its unconditional allegiance to the Islamic State in Iraq and Syria (ISIS) in 2014, in response to which the Taliban demanded that IMU leave Afghanistan in 2015. With this, several jihadi fighters re-affiliated with the Taliban, while Ghazi and others rejected the Taliban, joined hands with ISIS, and remained in Afghanistan. In September 2014, Usman Ghazi issued a statement that, "On behalf of members of our Islamic Movement, I herewith announce to the world that we are siding with the Islamic Caliphate [the Islamic State]."

The IMU, after this statement, focused extensively on carrying out their operations in Pakistan under the support of Tehrik-e-Taliban Pakistan (TTP). The major attacks carried out by IMU fighters included the attack on the Jinnah International Airport in Karachi in 2014, which showed their operational capabilities and ability to strike strategic targets inside Pakistan. Their allegiance to ISIS could provide a platform for them to carry out their operations in Afghanistan and Pakistan, as well as in Central Asia, in coordinated efforts with the IMU. Due to the increased threat to the Afghan Taliban, in 2015 the fighters of the Afghan Taliban launched a military strike against IMU strongholds and killed Ghazi, thus largely wiping out the group (Stein, 2013).

FUNDING, RECRUITMENT, AND TRAINING

Funding

The major source of funding for the Islamic movement in Uzbekistan is fundraising through external sources and getting involved in black market economies. According to the research by the Australian government, the crucial sources of revenue for the movement have been the Uzbek expats in Saudi Arabia, Islamist radical groups in Pakistan, Afghanistan, and Tajikistan, and like-minded Arab foundations and banks. Until 2014, IMU received all its financial support from the Taliban and al-Qaeda; after that, in 2015, the group officially announced its allegiance to ISIS. The IMU was also gaining revenue through its illegal financing activities, such as drug trafficking and racketeering (Counter Extremism Project, 2019).

Recruitment

The initial recruitment policy for the movement revolves around the exploitation of the widespread poverty in the Fergana Valley region. In 1998, when the movement was started, all the fighters came from Uzbekistan, Tajikistan, and Kyrgyzstan and also included Uighurs and Chechens. Between 1998 and 2001, the group ran its recruitment offices from Kabul, Kandahar, and Mazar-e-Sharif in Afghanistan under the influence of the Afghan Taliban. As per the report by the German Federal Office of Criminal Investigation, it has been believed that in 2010, nearly more than 100 fighters joined the movement in the Afghanistan-Pakistan region. However, after most of the fighters that were killed in 2015 while fighting the Taliban were killed, recruitment efforts were significantly lowered as all potential recruits started fleeing to Syria to join coalition forces in order to fight against the Assad regime (Counter Extremism Project, 2019). After officially announcing their allegiance to ISIS, much of their membership consists of men from Africa, Pakistan, Bangladesh, the Philippines, China, Uzbekistan, and Tajikistan that fight along with ISIS (Government of Australia, 2007).

Training

From 1995 until 1998, Tahir Yuldashev lived in Peshawar, Pakistan, and during the initial years of the movement, his fighters were given training in the madrassas under the guidance of the pro-Taliban Jamiat Ulema Islam party. When the movement was officially founded in 1998, the Taliban provided financial aid and helped establish training camps in northern Afghanistan, and from here the attacks were planned and executed against the Uzbekistan and Kyrgyzstan governments. In these Afghan camps, the new recruits have been given training in assembling bombs, operating weaponry, and rigging booby traps (Counter Extremism Project, 2019).

The IMU also trained foreign fighters to carry out suicide bombings and lone-wolf attacks; notably, its trained militants were responsible for the Manhattan attack in October 2017.

KEY PERSONNEL AND STRUCTURE OF IMU: IDEOLOGUES AND MASTERMINDS

The Islamic Movement of Uzbekistan (IMU) was mostly comprised of Uzbeks and was led by the military commander, Juma Namangani, and the spiritual leader and co-founder, Tahir Yuldashev. The IMU has attracted support from a variety of ethnic backgrounds, including Uzbeks, Kyrgyz, Tajiks, Chechens, and Uighurs from western China.

The organisation has a political leader that supervises all the administrative and operational capacities and provides an overall direction; a military chief who plans all tactical plans and activities under the supervision of the political leader; a propaganda wing that seeks to engage the new recruits; and the most important is the religious branch that justifies the acts carried out by the group in order to overthrow the Uzbek government and establish sharia law in the Central Asia region.

Leadership

Juma Namangani (1998–November 2001): Namangani co-founded the IMU in 1998 with Tahir Yuldashev and served as the military chief for the group until 2001. He died in a raid by US security forces in 2001, when the US invaded Afghanistan. He also participated in the Tajik Civil War during the period (1992–97) and remained in Tajikistan only after the end of the civil war in order to start and regain momentum for the Islamic movement in the region.

Tahir Yuldashev (November 2001–August 2009): Tahir co-founded the IMU in 1998 in Kabul and became the first emir of the group. He was a senior commander resisting the US-led Operation Anaconda[7] in Afghanistan in 2002. Yuldashev was killed in a US drone strike in Pakistan. Yuldashev's views were more centralised towards promoting Wahhabism and Salafism, particularly in Central Asia, and his views were shaped by his frequent and extensive travel to Saudi Arabia, Afghanistan, and Pakistan.

Abu Usman Adil (August 2010 to April 29, 2012): Adil was an associate of his predecessor, Yuldashev. Under Adil's leadership, the IMU expanded its operations in northern and eastern Afghanistan and the Central Asian states. He was killed in a US drone strike in 2012 (Center for International Security and Cooperation, 2018).

Usman Ghazi (2012–December 2015): Ghazi was Adil's deputy in the organisation and became the emir after his death in 2012. Ghazi officially announced the group's allegiance to the Islamic State in Iraq and Syria (ISIS) in 2014 and was reportedly killed in December 2015 by Afghan Taliban forces.

The Current Leader of the Group Is Unknown

Organisational Structure: IMU

IMU has been believed to have three main branches, namely political, military, and religious.

Political Branch: The organisation's leader is in charge of the political branch in addition to overseeing all other branches and the entire group. The duties involve approving targets, recruiting new members, allocating resources to train new members, and planning attacks.

Military Branch: The military branch plans all IMU's suicide missions, kidnappings, and violent attacks. It also takes care of robberies and racketeering in order to provide funding to the organisation. Juma Namangani was the crucial military commander for the IMU.

Religious Branch: The religious branch issues statements and videos in order to attract new recruits to the organisation and also to propagate the ideology of Salafism and Jihadism through their media channels, namely the *Jundallah* media wing. In 1998, IMU appointed *Zubayr ibn Abdul Raheem* as the spiritual leader of the group.

Major Attacks Carried out by IMU

IMU is considered one of the most lethal organisations by US security forces in terms of the attacks carried out by the organisation against westerners in the Fergana Valley region, Afghanistan, and Pakistan. The United States (US) has listed IMU as a foreign terrorist organisation since 2000. Prior to October 2001, the group targeted Uzbek civilians and government officials, but after the US-led Operation Enduring Freedom[8] in 2001, the group shifted its focus to battling the US and its allies. Some of the deadliest and most lethal attacks carried out by IMU since 1998 include (Center for International Security and Cooperation, 2018):

- On February 16, 1999, the IMU fighters launched five simultaneous car bombings in Tashkent in an attempt to assassinate former Uzbek President Islam Karimov.
- In August 1999, the IMU fighters kidnapped the mayor and other people from a small town in Kyrgyzstan and demanded a helicopter and US$1 million as a ransom in exchange for the hostages.
- From December 2002 until May 2003, the IMU launched four explosions in the Osh and Bishkek cities of Kyrgyzstan; reportedly, eight people were killed.
- On July 30, 2004, the IMU fighters launched multiple suicide strikes against the embassies of Israel and the US in Tashkent, the capital city of Uzbekistan.
- In June 2007, the IMU allegedly participated in the Red Mosque siege in Islamabad and held about 250 people as hostages while fighting Pakistani security officials.
- On September 19, 2010, the IMU claimed responsibility for ambushing the convoy of Tajiki soldiers in the Rasht Valley in Tajikistan, thus resulting in the killing of 25 soldiers.

- On April 5, 2012, the IMU, along with Pakistan Taliban and TTP militants, attacked the Bannu prison in Pakistan and freed about 384 militants from the jail.
- On June 8, 2014, the IMU, along with the Pakistan Taliban and TTP, attacked the Jinnah International Airport in Karachi; reportedly, all 10 attackers died in the attack.
- In February 2015, the IMU took about 30 Hazara men hostage in Afghanistan. In April, they released a video showing the beheading of one of the hostages.

ORGANISATIONAL CHARACTERISTICS: TIES AND ALLIANCES TO OTHER GROUPS, STRATEGIC SHIFTS PERTAINING TO THE GROUP'S TRAJECTORY AND IDEOLOGUE

Relation with Other Groups

The Islamic Movement of Uzbekistan (IMU) had maintained long-term relationships with several Islamist radical groups. IMU grew out of the Islamic Adolat movement in 1998, founded by Tahir Yuldashev in Kabul, Afghanistan. The IMU was formed to overthrow the Uzbek government and implement sharia law in the Fergana Valley region. IMU maintained long-term relationships with the Afghan Taliban since its formation until 2014, when its last emir, Usman Ghazi, announced its allegiance to ISIS. It has been believed that after the overthrow of the Afghan Taliban regime, IMU maintained close relations with its shadow government in northern Afghanistan (Center for International Security and Cooperation, 2018).

The IMU also maintained good relationships with al-Qaeda. In the late 1990s, Osama bin Laden provided funding to the organisation in order to recruit more men and buy weaponry for its operations in Central Asia. The aid provided IMU with the ability to carry out high-profile attacks in 1999 and 2000. After IMU relocated to South Waziristan, a Federally Administered Tribal Area (FATA) in Pakistan, in 2001, it established training camps under the influence of the Pakistan Taliban. At the same time, IMU has also developed good relations with the al-Qaeda-aligned Haqqani network, as a result of which both groups coordinated several attacks against the western security forces. The Haqqani network helped train IMU fighters, and IMU in return provided them with fighters to launch coordinated attacks. Another close ally of the IMU is the Tehrik-e Taliban Pakistan (TTP). The two groups, in coordination, have launched several attacks against Pakistani security officials. In 2013, IMU and TTP also formed a joint group named Ansar al-Aseer to free TPP members from jails in Pakistan.

In 2015, after the decline of the relationship with the Afghan Taliban, IMU officially announced its allegiance to ISIS. The group started fighting against the government forces in the northern provinces of Afghanistan and Pakistan with the support of the ISIS regional affiliate, the Islamic State-Khorasan Province (IS-KP). In late 2015, the fighters and followers of Usman Ghazi, the last emir of IMU, reportedly fought against the Afghan Taliban in Afghanistan with the support of ISIS fighters and affiliates.

Various other splinter groups formed out of the IMU over the years of its militant activity. *Jamaat Ansarullah*, a Tajik splinter group, was formed in response to the IMU's official declaration to support ISIS and then later reaffirmed its allegiance to the Taliban. *Jundullah*, a militant group based in the Afghan state of Afghanistan, split from the IMU in 2009 after the death of Tahir Yuldashev. Jundullah has similar goals to IMU, and the two groups have been believed to maintain long-term cooperative relations with each other. The Islamic Jihad Group, later renamed the Islamic Jihad Union (IJU), was formed in 2002 after the IMU relocated to Pakistan; the group cooperated with the IMU and the Haqqani Network for its operations in southeast Afghanistan (Center for International Security and Cooperation, 2018).

Strategic Shift Pertaining to the Groups' Trajectory and Central Ideologue

The Islamic Movement of Uzbekistan (IMU) was formed in order to establish the Islamic state in the Fergana Valley region and to overturn the secular and authoritarian regime under the leadership of Islam Karimov. But very soon, the group shifted its goals under the influence of various radical groups. In 2001, under the influence of the Afghan Taliban, the IMU expanded its objectives in order to establish the Islamic caliphate throughout Central Asia. Uzbekistan is part of Turkestan, a collective name for all central Asian feudal[9] states. The IMU's goal is now to establish the Islamic caliphate in Turkestan, stretching from the Caspian Sea to Xinjiang province in China.

In 2015, IMU also officially announced its declaration to associate with ISIS under the banner of global jihad. The IMU suffered an internal split after its association with ISIS, and it's believed that split was due to Usman Ghazi's extensive focus on carrying out operations in Pakistan rather than Central Asia and Afghanistan. As such, the different factions got associated with IMU due to the different motivations involved. The IMU can be best understood as an association of Islamism, drugs, personal vendettas, and terrorism (Starr, 2006).

DIRECT AND INDIRECT IMPACTS OF TERRORIST AND INSURGENT GROUPS IN SOCIAL, POLITICAL, AND ECONOMIC TERMS: THE CASE STUDY OF THE ISLAMIC MOVEMENT OF UZBEKISTAN (IMU) AND THE TAJIKISTAN CIVIL WAR (1992–1997)

The Islamic Movement of Uzbekistan (IMU) is a Salafi-jihadist militant group that was formed in 1998 in order to establish the Islamic caliphate in the Fergana Valley region and to counter the secular and authoritarian regime of the Karimov government. The Fergana Valley region is believed to be one of the poorest regions in Central Asia, consisting of Uzbekistan, Tajikistan, and Kyrgyzstan republics. The governments in these republics have allegedly failed to alleviate poverty and embrace decent economic reforms for the people.

The specific element of concern is the nexus of drugs, crime, and radical Islamists. The close ties between drug dealers and Islamic radicals are undeniable, considering that it all started when IMU was established in 1998. This fusion of crime, drugs, and terrorism can be easily proved in the case of IMU, and thus it affects the young population at large. Rising Afghan opium production in the late 1900s led to an increase in smuggling activities in Central Asia.

Uzbekistan's Fergana valley has been affected by many determined Islamic radical movements, and their presence in the valley became the reason for the oppressive policies of the Karimov government. The Tajikistan civil war broke out in 1992 as anti-government demonstrations led by a coalition of Islamists, nationalists, and western-oriented parties raided the presidential palace. As a result, the Tajikistan economy and government broke down. Reportedly, between 50,000 and 60,000 people were killed during the first year of fighting, and the war was at its peak. According to the United Nations High Commissioner for Refugees (UNHCR) report, some 6 lakh people were internally displaced, and some 80,000 went on to take refuge in Afghanistan.[10] Moreover, many unarmed civilians were murdered in order to make them leave their homes and flee to some other country.

The social costs of the economic collapse, coupled with the large-scale devastation of property due to the war, created hardship for more than half of the country's population. The war also stimulated an increase in violence against women. Central Asia has been the victim of Islamic radicalisation since the 1980s. Radicalisation has often been the cause of the socio-economic crisis and political repression of the state.

IMU has been believed to be strongly involved in drug trafficking from Afghanistan to Osh in Kyrgyzstan; various experts believe that IMU controls about two-thirds of opium entering the Kyrgyz Republic. Therefore, insurgent and radical Islamic groups like IMU are considered diversionary measures to create instability and confuse the military structures with their involvement in more criminal activities rather than fulfilling political goals.

CONCLUSION

The Islamic Movement of Uzbekistan (IMU) has been the longest-lasting militant group in Central Asia. The major prospects of Islamic extremism in Central Asia remain unclear due to the shifting strategic trends of IMU's foremost objective of overthrowing the secular Uzbekistan government under the leadership of Islam Karimov. In spite of political repression, poverty, and foreign proselytising, only a small number of people were influenced by the shifting trends and objectives of the IMU and other splinter groups in Central Asia.

Also, the insurgency along the Afghanistan-Pakistan border has grown again, with western countries showing an inability to deal with the ideological element of the war on terror (Stein, 2013). Various Islamists and radical organisations have shown an ability to cooperate with each other according to geographical demands. The region's governments are failing to meet the basic demands of their population, which fosters an environment in which Islamic radical groups can thrive.

Meanwhile, western influence has seen a tremendous decline over the years in Central Asia, and on the contrary, Russian and Chinese influence is increasing. With this, the Central Asian republics are likely to become more repressive and less reformist in terms of their socio-economic status. The overall environment will create more authoritarian regimes, and it will not improve the economic conditions of the region. And in turn, this will help the Islamists grow stronger.

In 2015, after Usman Ghazi declared his allegiance to ISIS, the Afghan Taliban were forced to retaliate against the IMU in Afghanistan in order to virtually eliminate it. The Uzbek militants in Syria are now ready to take leadership positions in IMU and pose a security threat to Uzbekistan. The governments of the Central Asian republics have to seek alliances with the international community by balancing Russia, China, and the US in order to combat the jihadist influences in Central Asia and the Afghanistan-Pakistan region.

IMU and other radical Islamic groups continue to pose a severe threat to the Central Asia region and Afghanistan. A coordinated mechanism by the governments of the Central Asian republics, along with counterterrorism efforts by the US security forces, the European Union, and NATO forces, is needed to tackle the growing Islamic radicalisation in the Central Asian region. All the stakeholder groups involved have to deal in a responsible way. The following policy recommendations have to be observed by the counter-terrorism forces in order to adjust their counterterrorism policies against Islamic extremism, wherein the governments of the Central Asian republics also have a significant role to play.

1. The links between drug trafficking and Islamic extremism have been proven without a doubt and have been a major source of revenue for groups like IMU. The drug trade in Afghanistan and Central Asia is demand-driven, with the majority of the demand coming from European Union member countries (Starr, 2006). The EU member countries should plan a coordinated effort to provide major financial support to counter-narcotics forces, thus addressing the problem of Islamic extremism at large.
2. The expansion of continental trade across Central Asia is likely to be the single most powerful coordinated mechanism to bring about a positive change in the economic scenario of the region. As roads, pipelines, and electric lines link the region to the great economic centres of Eurasia, the local populations can be believed to move out of situations that breed extremism. The expansion of continental trade and trade routes will in turn open up opportunities at larger levels for the local population, which do not exist at those levels in the present.
3. The US security forces should reconsider their departure from the state of Afghanistan, as this will create a period of instability and could make Uzbekistan vulnerable to terrorist activities. The IMU will be able to exploit this opportunity and could return to its bases in northern Afghanistan in order to target the Fergana Valley region and launch its terror campaign in the region.
4. An effective approach should be to train more security personnel in the northern provinces of Afghanistan. The US and other counterterrorism forces, with the help of the Afghan government and the local people, should work together to develop security forces that can defeat IMU and other radical groups and limit their presence. The goal should be to create more effective Central Asian security institutions that can help prevent IMU and its militants from returning to these areas. More and more civilian participation should be focused on in order to improve the social and economic conditions of the region.
5. The developed economies should focus on educational exchanges between the capital cities and the national elites, which should be extended to the Central Asian provinces, including those now experiencing Islamic radical movements. Significantly, educational transformation will help many young people become sources of future leaders at the regional level. Educational exchange is a productive and cost-effective means of fighting sectarian extremism.

Notes

1 The former President of Uzbekistan.
2 The Fergana Valley stretches across Central Asia across eastern Uzbekistan, southern Kyrgyzstan, and northern Tajikistan, forming a crucial part of the northern Silk Road and thus connecting China to the West.
3 An underground Islamic cleric who operated out of the Otavalihon mosque.
4 Juma was conscripted into the Soviet army in 1987 and fought as an elite paratrooper in the Soviet-Afghan war. For more details, read https://historica.fandom.com/wiki/Juma_Namangani.
5 For more details, refer to https://econfaculty.gmu.edu/bcaplan/museum/czar.htm.
6 "The civil war in Tajikistan broke out less than a year after independence when long-buried clan and political animosity erupted. In August 1992, anti-government demonstrators led by a coalition of Islamic, nationalist, and western-oriented parties raided the presidential palace. Tajikistan President Rahmon Nabyev escaped but was cornered at the airport while trying to flee to Khujand. Nabyev was forced to resign and was replaced by Akbarshah Iskandarov, who led a coalition that included members of the Islamic Renaissance Party (IRP) and secular democratic parties." For more, refer to http://factsanddetails.com/central-asia/Tajikistan/sub8_6a/entry-4858.html#chapter-0.
7 "Operation Anaconda was born out of a plan to trap al Qaeda fighters regrouping in the mountains." For more, refer to https://www.airforcemag.com/article/0902anaconda/.
8 "Operation Enduring Freedom (OEF) was the official name used by the US government for the Global War on Terrorism. On October 7, 2001, in response to the September 11 attacks, President George W. Bush announced that airstrikes targeting Al Qaeda and the Taliban had begun in Afghanistan." For more, refer to https://edition.cnn.com/2013/10/28/world/operation-enduring-freedom-fast-facts/index.html.
9 "Feudal society is a military hierarchy in which a ruler or lord offers mounted fighters a fief (mediaeval beneficium), a unit of land to control, in exchange for military service. The individual who accepted this land became a vassal, and the man who granted the land became known as his liege or his lord." For more, refer to https://web.cn.edu/kwheeler/feudalism.html.
10 For more, refer to the URL: https://www.c-r.org/accord/tajikistan/tajik-civil-war-causes-and-dynamics.

References

Baran, Z. (2006). *Islamic radicalism in central Asia*. Uppsala: Central Asia-Caucasus Institute and Silk Road Studies Program.

Center for International Security and Cooperation. (2018). *Islamic movement of Uzbekistan*. Stanford: Stanford Univeristy.

Counter Extremism Project. (2019). *Islamic movement of Uzbekistan*. London: Counter Extremism Project.

Fedlholm, M. (2010). *From the Fergana valley to Wazristan and beyond*. California: Monterey Institute for International Studies.

Government of Australia. (2007). *Retrieved from house of representatives*. Government of Australia. http://www.aphref.aph.gov.au/house/committee/pjcis/grouped/IMU.pdf

Mambetaliev, A. (2010). *Islam, human rights and security in the post Soviet space*. California: Center for Non- Proliferation Studies.

Starr, S. F. (2006). *Islamic radicalism in Central Asia and the Caucasus: Implications for the EU*. Washington: The Central Asia-Caucasus Institute.

Stein, M. (2013). *The goals of the Islamic movement of Uzbekistan and its impact on Central Asia and the United States*. Washington: Department of Defense, The United States.

Zenn, J. (2013, June 24). On the Eve of 2014: Islamism in Central Asia. *Current Trends in Islamist Ideology*, Hudson Institute (Washington DC), Vol. 15, pp. 67–91.

61

ISLAMIC STATE-KHORASAN PROVINCE (ISKP)

Dominating Jihad in Afghanistan and Pakistan (2015–2022)

Animesh Roul and Scott N. Romaniuk

INTRODUCTION

The declaration of the Islamic State (IS), also infamously known as the Islamic State of Iraq and the Levant (ISIL), and its swift ascent under Abu Bakr al-Baghdadi, the self-declared Caliph, effectively marked a shift in the global jihadist landscape, which was previously dominated by the Al Qaeda franchise. Since then, the IS has sought to establish itself as a global caliphate, expanding its political influence far beyond its local bases in the Levant region, especially Iraq and Syria. In October of that same year, Baghdadi presented a strategy for the growth of IS networks in the South and East during his Ramadan speech. Later, on pro-IS social media, a supposed IS map appeared that clearly showed plans for expanding the territory by creating administrative provinces, or Wilayat. Parts of Central and South Asia, collectively referred to as Khorasan in Islamist terminology and including Pakistan, Afghanistan, regions of Central Asia, and the northern part of India, were included in this bigger concept.

Evidently, ISKhorasan Province (hereafter ISKP or IS Khorasan) has received significant ideological and financial support from the Islamic State, which is centrally based in Iraq and Syria. The IS considered Afghanistan an extension of its caliphate and a stronghold in its quest to unite the Muslim Ummah. Congratulatory messages, media attribution, interviews in official magazines, and communications between the IS central and IS-Khorasan proved the symbiotic ties between the groups (SITE Intelligence, 2015, February 11; SITE Intelligence, 2015, February 20). The ISKP, one of the powerful branches of the Islamic State's Caliphate, was proscribed and sanctioned by the United Nations, the US, and India, among other countries. On May 14, 2019, the UN imposed sanctions on the terror group ISKhorasan Provinvce for its involvement in several attacks in Afghanistan and Pakistan (UNSC, May 2019). Much before that, the United States designated ISKP as a foreign terrorist organisation on January 14, 2016 (US State Department, 2016).

THE EMERGENCE

With the announcement of the Caliphate, the so-called proto-state of the Islamic State of Iraq and Syria (ISIS), which allegedly obliterated modern nation-states and their borders for the entire Muslim Ummah, several Pakistani extremist groups, including those having symbiotic ties with Taliban formations, have extended support to the Islamic State and pledged allegiance to Abu Bakr al-Baghdadi. At the outset, lesser-known extremist groups like Tehreek-e-Khilafat Wa Jihad (Movement for the Caliphate and Jihad, TKJ) and Ansar Al-Dawla Al-Islamiyah Fi Pakistan were the first to declare allegiance to the IS, followed by a faction of the Pakistani Taliban, and sectarian and anti-Shiite militant groups like Jundullah too pledged allegiance to the IS, directly facilitating its physical presence within Pakistan's territory. Many of these groups, which were earlier affiliated with al-Qaeda and loyal to Afghan Taliban leader Mullah Omar, have shifted their support to the IS and Baghdadi-led Caliphate. The broader support base for the IS in Pakistan emerged primarily due to the existing pro-Islamist political and social environment and the infighting between different Taliban factions affiliated with the umbrella group Tehrik-e-Taliban Pakistan (TTP).

Before the actual formalisation, enough effort went into militant consolidations, mostly with returning fighters from Syria and Iraq in eastern Afghanistan and the bordering region of Pakistan (Giustozzi, 2018). Evidence of IS outreach surfaced when at least four Islamic State (ISIS) flags were seized near the Pakistan Ordnance Factory (POF) in Taxila. Also, an IS-linked recruitment drive came to light within Pakistan. IS leaflets and posters in Pashtu and Dari

DOI: 10.4324/9780429426063-69

languages were found in Peshawar and adjoining areas of Khyber Pakhtunkhwa province, with the titles "Salute to ISIS" and "Message to the Islamic Ummah." As early as June 2014, the Islamic State's early footprints were visible in Afghanistan too. Largely ignored by the government forces, intermittent information trickled down about the IS making inroads into Afghanistan, and by early 2015, the IS flags surfaced in Ghazni and Nimroz provinces, following which a large number of Taliban militants switched their allegiance to the IS (Long War Journal, March 2015).

Maulana Abdul Aziz, a powerful radical cleric in Pakistan's Lal Masjid (Red Mosque, Islamabad), was the first to express his support for the IS and al-Baghdadi in July 2014, encouraging hundreds of Taliban militants trained at Lal Masjid towards the Islamic Caliphate (Express Tribune, 2014; Roul, 2015). In October 2014, at least five Taliban commanders who formed the Taliban faction TTP-Jamaat-ul Ahrar (TTP-JA) owed allegiance to the Islamic State. By January 2015, the IS had announced its Khorasan Wilayat (province) with these disgruntled defectors from the TTP and independent militant commanders. The IS-Khorasan province announcement coincided with IS spokesman Abu Muhammad-al-Adnani's audio speech regarding the geographical expansion to the Afghan and Pakistani regions. This famed audio speech was released by the Al-Furqan media wing of the IS on January 26, 2015, titled "Say, Die in Your Rage!" (Adnani, 2015).

In this message, al-Adnani stated that the new IS province would be headed by a former Pakistani Taliban commander, Hafiz Saeed Khan, who had recently fulfilled the necessary conditions to become the governor of the so-called Khorasan province by taking the oath of allegiance to the IS supreme leader, Abu Bakr al-Baghdadi. While urging the militants in Afghanistan and Pakistan to join Saeed Khan in their efforts to come under the banner of the united Caliphate, Adnani chided the crumbling Taliban Emirate in Afghanistan. It soon came to light that many small units of the Taliban and other militant fringe groups in both Afghanistan and Pakistan had pledged their allegiance to the IS and its leader, Abu Bakr al-Baghdadi, and gathered under Hafiz Saeed Khan. The IS Khorasan was then formalised under the leadership of former TTP commander Hafiz Saeed Khan as the first governor of the IS Caliphate's Khorasan province and Abdul Rauf Khadim, another former Taliban commander and Guantanamo Bay detainee, as deputy governor. The IS propaganda materials, e.g., Dabiq (No. 7), mentioned that militants from Nuristan, Kunar, Kandahar, Khost, Ghazni, Wardak, Helmand, Kunduz, Logar, and, of course, Nangarhar, joined the IS bandwagon in Afghanistan, while many others from Bajaur, Orakzai, Kurram, Waziristan, and the Khyber Region of Pakistan came under the ISKP banner.

The IS Khorasan spread its tentacles by making alliances with or co-opting local militant groups and their leaders. In Pakistan, it has garnered the support of sectarian factions such as Lashkar-e-Jhangvi al-Alami, Jundullah, Jamaat-ul-Ahrar, the most powerful faction of the Tehrik-e Taliban (TTP) movement; Mangal Bagh's led Lashkar-e Islam (LeI) group; and Lashkar-e-Khorasan. Late last July (2017), the Taliban movement, TTP in Pakistan, received another setback that boosted the ISKP image in the region when Haji Daud Mehsud (former chief of TTP-Karachi) declared allegiance to Islamic State (Daily Times, July 30, 2017). Earlier, the IS Khorasan too galvanised grassroots militant support, mostly from fringe and lesser-known groups like the Sa'ad bin Abi Waqas Front (Logar, Afghanistan), Tawad al-Jihad (Peshawar), and Ansar al-Mujahideen (Waziristan). In an elaborate interview, Hafiz Saeed Khan (Dabiq, No. 13, 2016) blamed the Taliban for initiating the conflict at the outset, and IS Khorasan was forced to take arms against the Taliban as they have been allied with the Pakistani and Afghan armed forces. This line of argument is perhaps gaining Saeed Khan support from like-minded regional militant formations. Certainly, IS has been exploiting the crumbling edifices of the Taliban-led Islamic Emirate of Afghanistan, especially after the declaration of Mullah Omar's death and coupled with the death of Mullah Mansour in May 2016. This leadership crisis within the Taliban has created an opportunity for IS to rebuild its network in the region. According to an estimate in 2018, the IS-K force consisted of between 2,000 and 5,000 fighters. Another recent US military estimate informed us that there are between 2,000 and 2,500 IS fighters presently active in Afghanistan. Though these figures vary from time to time and from source to source, the IS-K group still has operational bases and training camps in several districts of Kunar Province and possibly in parts of neighbouring Nuristan Province.

In Afghanistan, ISKP's increased influence in the last couple of years rested upon the existing Pakistani militant factions like LeI and factions of the Afghan Taliban movement such as the Mullah Rasool group and the Islamic Movement of Uzbekistan (IMU), which has sworn allegiance to Islamic State in the past. There is also information about IS-K's alliance with the Tajikistan-based Ansarullah militant group, the East Turkestan Islamic Movement, and Harkat-i-Islami Uzbekistan (Tolo News, April 21). Even though these militant alliances remain sketchy across the Durand line (an imaginary border demarcation between Afghanistan and Pakistan), the ISKP has exploited the ever-existing internecine rivalries, using its firepower and co-opting local networks.

VIOLENCE IN AFGHANISTAN

Following the death of Khadim in a drone strike in Helmand in February 2015, then ISKP leader Hafiz Saeed Khan vowed to avenge the death of his deputy and other initial setbacks the group suffered. In a show of force, it perpetrated the first-ever strike in Jalalabad on April 18, killing more than 33 people and injuring over 100 outside a bank where government workers were collecting their salaries (Reuters, 2015). An IS spokesman in Afghanistan claimed responsibility for that anti-government and anti-civilian assault. The IS forces in Afghanistan under Hafiz Saeed Khan have challenged the Taliban's monopoly on waging war and violence for the first time in more than a decade. With fear of losing ground and cadre defections, the Taliban leadership, who have been fighting their own battle within the ranks and file, attempted to fight back the Islamic State's expansion and growing stature, both militarily and ideologically.

Since the April 2015 violence in Jalalabad, the IS-Khorasan has continued to carry out indiscriminate mass fatality attacks from Kabul in Afghanistan to Quetta and Lahore in Pakistan. The most recent violent strike that IS-Khorasan claimed was the deadly Kabul mosque attack on June 2, 2020, that targeted an influential cleric, Mohammad Ayaz Niazi, a well-known imam (prayer leader) of the Wazir Akbar Khan Mosque. Between these two above-mentioned attacks (April 2015–June 2020), ISKP has perpetrated hundreds of deadly sectarian and anti-government offensives in Afghanistan and Pakistan in its five years of existence. From Shia and Sufi congregations and Christian churches to government establishments and security installations in Afghanistan and Pakistan, they remain the target of ISKP's violent campaign.

Pakistan: In Pakistan, the violent footprints of the Islamic State-Khorasan reached primarily Balochistan province. However, Sindh, Punjab, and Khyber Pakhtunkhwa provinces also witnessed ISKP violence. Several mass fatalities proved the group's violent intent and sectarian worldview. To note, ISKP has mostly collaborated with local affiliates such as Jamaat ul Ahrar and the faction of Lashkar e Jhangvi in Pakistan to strike terror. While Balochistan witnessed IS-K violence at regular intervals, the other three provinces have experienced intermittent assaults since the advent of ISKhorasan. The first major attack took place in Karachi (Sind) in May 2015, when ISKP and its affiliate Jundullah militants killed 43 members of the Ismaili Shia community travelling in a bus near the Safoora Chowk area of the port city (Dawn, May 2015; The Independent, May 13, 2015). In 2016, IS-K claimed two major assaults in Balochistan province. On October 24, 2016, IS-K, with its local Al-Alami faction of the Lashkar-i-Jhangvi, carried out a mass shooting at trainee policemen at the Quetta Police Training College. This attack took the lives of 61 cadets. After a couple of weeks, on November 12, ISKP again targeted Shah Noorani Shrine in the Lasbela area of Khuzdar district. This sectarian strike killed over 55 civilians, including women and children (Dawn, November 2016). Pakistan's Punjab province witnessed one of the major incidents of anti-Christian violence in March 2016, when a suicide attack in the famed Gulshan Iqbal theme park killed more than 70 people, mostly children and women belonging to the minority Christian community. Though there was no direct claim of responsibility from the ISKP, a violent Taliban faction and ISKP's close affiliate, Jamaat ul Ahrar (JuA), claimed responsibility for this attack.

IS-Khorasan also claimed several attacks in Pakistan in 2017, starting with an attack on a major Sufi shrine of Lal Shahbaz Qalander in Sehwan (Sindh province) on February 16 that killed at least 88 people and injured over 250 worshippers (Express Tribune, February 2017). Another deadly sectarian strike took place on December 17, 2017, which was attributed to ISKP and allied factions. Two armed militants with suicide vests and assault rifles stormed the Bethel Memorial Methodist Church in Quetta, leaving at least nine Christian worshippers dead and more than 50 seriously wounded (The Nation, December 17). Even though human fatalities were far fewer due to security presence this time, the attack was very much reminiscent of ISKP and JuA's March 2016 Lahore Park bombing.

In 2018, however, IS-K struck multiple times in Pakistan, spreading unprecedented violence across Balochistan province. Among them, the July 2018 attack on an election rally in Mastung killed 149 people and injured more than 300 others in a suicide bombing at the rally. A week later, ISKP struck again in the provincial capital, Quetta, with a suicide bombing, killing 31 people, including five policemen outside a polling station. Pakistan's Khyber Pakhtunkhwa province too faced the wrath of IS-Khorasan, and in November 2018, the group targeted a market in the Shi'ite-dominated area of Kalaya city in Orakzai district. Thirty-two people, mostly from Shia minorities, have died in the explosion (Dawn, November 2018). According to an estimation, there were five major attacks claimed by the IS-Khorasan in Pakistan, taking the lives of 224 people and injuring 301 (Pakistan Security Report, 2018).

In April 2019, ISKP returned to haunt Quetta city, targeting the Hazara Shias at the Hazarganj fruits and vegetable market. It collaborated with Lashkar-e-Jhangvi again to target the monitories in Pakistan. However, for most of late 2019 and early 2020, ISKhorasan's role in Pakistan remained subdued as the group splintered into two dedicated India and Pakistan units in May 2019. With the organisational split, the so-called Islamic State Pakistan Province claimed its first-ever attack on Pakistani soil in May 2019 through IS' global propaganda mouthpiece, Amaq News Agency. IS-Pakistan claimed credit for killing a police officer in Mastung and an anti-Taliban attack in Quetta that week (Gandhara, May 16, 2019). Ironically, Pakistan consistently downplays IS-Khorasan or the newly established IS-Pakistan threats. However, the arrest of Pakistani-origin ISKP chief Abdullah Orakzai in April in Afghanistan and the deaths of four IS-Pakistan terrorists in an operation in Bahawalpur (Punjab, Pakistan) in May 2020 compelled Pakistani authorities to express concerns over the reorganised Islamic State-inspired activities in the country.

Afghanistan: The ISKP remained firm in its core sectarian ideology and charted a similar tactic in Afghanistan as well, turning its gun on minority groups, especially Hazara Shia Muslims and their institutions. Initially, targeted violence was carried out by the ISKP militants in November 2015, when seven Hazaras, including two women and a child, were abducted from the Gilan district of south-eastern Ghazni province, and their dead bodies were recovered from the Khak-e-Afghan district of southern Zabul province. Surprisingly, there was no claim from the IS or its newly founded Wilayat. On July 23, 2016, over 80 people were killed and many more maimed in a brazen suicide attack on the Hazara community in Deh Mazang Square in Kabul, the capital city of Afghanistan. Islamic State has claimed responsibility for the first time, highlighting the group's consolidation and firepower in the country. Abu Omar Khorasani, one of the leading ISKP commanders in Afghanistan, termed the Kabul attack a retribution against the support offered by some Afghan Shia members to the Bashar al-Assad regime in Syria, ostensibly with the help of Iran. Speaking to Reuters, Khorasani threatened further attacks, saying that "unless they (Hazaras') stop going to Syria and stop being slaves of Iran, [we] will definitely continue such attacks."

In late December 2017, an apparent suicide bomb attack on the Shia cultural centre in Kabul left over 40 people dead and many injured (Pajhwok Afghan News, December 28, 2017). The Islamic State's Amaq news agency, claiming responsibility for the attack, argued that the facility is a prominent Shiite centre sponsored by Iranian agencies and used as a recruitment centre for Afghan Shias for the Fatemiyoun Division (part of Hezbollah Afghanistan) engaged in the Syrian civil war against the Islamic State. Earlier in October, IS-Khorasan militants also targeted the Imam Zaman Mosque, a Shiite worshipping place located in the western Dashte-e-Barchi neighbourhood of Kabul. The suicide attack killed nearly 30 Hazara Shias (Khaama Press, October 20, 2017). After a few months of lull, ISKP carried out a couple of suicide bombings targeting Hazara Shia again in Kabul, the capital. On Persian New Year Day (Nowruz) on March 22, 2018, an IS-K bomber killed over 30 people near a Shiite shrine in Kabul (Associated Press, March 22, 2018). The United Nations at that time vehemently condemned the deadly attack, describing it as "reprehensible." Again in August that year, ISKP struck at the Sahib-ul-Zaman Mosque in Khwaja Hassan area in the town of Gardez (Paktia province), killing over 25 people, mostly Shias (Tolo News, August 2018). Besides IS-Khorasan's consistent focus on anti-Shia violence in Afghanistan, it also confronted Taliban forces, targeted government forces, election rallies, educational institutions, and sports centres in and around Khost, Nangarhar, and Kabul provinces in 2018.

In early 2019, IS-Khorasan carried out a few targeted killings of security personnel in Kabul and Jalalabad. However, one major assault to be noted here signified ISKP's anti-Shia campaigns and firepower, despite several setbacks it suffered in terms of mass surrenders and leadership decapitations. The jihadist group once again created mayhem on August 17 when its suicide bomber targeted a wedding hall in a Shia neighbourhood in Kabul, killing 63 people and injuring over 150 of them (Al Arabiya, August 17, 2019).

Following the August strike, concerted efforts were carried out against ISKhorasan in Afghanistan to clip its violent wings. Military offensives in its traditional strongholds in Nangarhar and Kunar provinces have disrupted its command and control structure to some extent. That prompted Afghan President Ashraf Ghani to announce the ISKP's defeat in Afghanistan in November (Ariana News, November 25, 2019). However, the premature celebrations of IS-Khorasan's imminent decimation were short-lived. The group sprang into action with several surprise attacks in the country in March and May 2020, targeting civilians and security forces. On May 12, ISKP's suicide attack at a funeral ceremony in the eastern province of Nangarhar killed at least 32 people and injured more than 60 (Tolo News, May 13). Another purported ISKP suicide assault at a maternity hospital in the Dasht-e-Barchi area of the capital Kabul on May 12 killed at least 24 civilians, including children (Afghanistan Times, May 13). Earlier, in March 2020, ISKP orchestrated a coordinated attack on a Sikh Gurdwara (place of worship) in Kabul's Shor Bazar area, which killed 27 Sikh worshippers. Two Indians were identified as part of this suicide operation: Muhammed Muhsin (a.k.a. Khalid Al-Hindi) and Sajid Kuthirummal, both from India's southernmost Kerala state. Later, IS claimed the attack was to "avenge Muslims in Kashmir" (Express Tribune, March 26).

LEADERSHIP

Since the establishment of ISKP in early 2015, the group has lost at least five leaders, either arrested or killed at the hands of government forces. Surprisingly, these leadership crises have had no significant impact on the group's operations. It is to be noted that while the IS-Khorasan fighters in Afghanistan are a blend of local and foreign fighters, the leaders and masterminds are mostly foreign nationals and particularly of Pakistani origin, with the sole exception of Sheikh Abdul Haseeb Logari of Afghanistan. Since March 2017, joint Afghan and US Force units have launched a dedicated counteroffensive against ISKP to eliminate or displace them from their sanctuaries in Nangarhar and adjacent regions. In its unrelenting offensive and persistent turf war with the rival Taliban, ISKP has lost several top commanders, such as Hafiz Saeed Khan, Saad Emarati, Abdur Rauf Khadim, and Gul Zaman, in the initial years. With the death of Abdul Haseeb Logari in April 2017, ISKP suffered a major setback at a time when the group was seemingly recovering from a leadership vacuum after a series of leadership decapitations. Logari, who was an inspiring Salafi-jihadist ideologue for ISKP, was succeeded by leaders such as Abu Saeed Bajauri, Saad Arhabi

(Abu Sayed Orakzai), and Aslam Farooqi (Abdullah Orakzai), all from Pakistan. Similar to the 2017 situation within ISKhorasan following Logari's death, the group faced a similar leadership crisis once again in April 2020 with the arrest of present chief Aslam Farooqi. However, despite the present leadership vacuum, IS-K succeeded in perpetrating a number of attacks in Kabul and elsewhere in Afghanistan, proving its robust operational capability and resiliency.

FOREIGN FIGHTERS

The involvement of Indian nationals in Kabul's Shor Bazar gurudwara explosion in March 2020 indicated the foreign fighters in ISKP's ranks and file, which have been constantly replenished through volunteers as well as sympathisers who are lured by the Caliphate ideals. In the past, local media reports have informed us about the number of French and Algerian fighters who have joined the ranks of the Islamic State group in northern Afghanistan. The war returnees from Syria and Iraq, including female fighters, have established new bases in the ISKP-controlled districts of Darzab and Qosh Tepa districts of northern Jowzjan province. In 2017, Mohammad Reza Ghafoori, a spokesman for the governor of Jowzjan, told the media that there are "more than 40 foreign Islamic State fighters, mostly Uzbeks […] to recruit locals and train them to become fighters" (Dawn, 2017, December). Local sources also hinted that there were nearly 200 foreign fighters camping near Bibi Mariam village in Darzab (DID Press Agency, 2017).

Besides French and Algerians, fighters from other countries were also present and operating under the command of ISKP. The group released a video in September 2017 titled "The Atmosphere of Eid in Khorasan Province" showing Eid ul-Adha festivities in its territories, underscoring the presence of Indians, Russians, and Tajiks in ISKP's ranks. An approximate six-minute audiovisual message stressed that "all are united in Islam, and our goal is to bring Shariah, the laws of Allah, to all the world."

In his interview in Dabiq No. 13, Hafiz Saeed Khan underscored the importance of foreign fighters in the ranks and file and noted their influx. He said, "The Muslims are making hijrah (religious migration) to the land of Khorasan in multitudes." "We ask Allah to accept their hijrah from them and to support the Khilafah, raise high the word of truth, and vanquish the word of falsehood through them" (Dabiq, No. 13, 2016). Several Indian nationals have also joined IS-K in Afghanistan in 2016. At least 21 people from the southernmost state of Kerala travelled to Afghanistan under the guise of religious migration. Among them, 17 were from Kasaragod and four from Palakkad areas of Kerala, including six women and three children. After ensuing investigations into the missing person cases, it came to light that all these people had travelled to Afghanistan through Iran.

In early February 2020, the UN Security Council's Tenth Report of the Secretary-General on the threat posed by the IS (or Da'esh) to international peace and security noted that Afghan security forces and Taliban fighters have inflicted damage on the ISKP, displacing it from large areas of the Nangarhar province. The report noted that more than 1,400 people surrendered to the Afghan authorities, including dependents of IS-Khorasan fighters. Although most males were Afghan nationals, there were several foreign nationals from Azerbaijan, Canada, France, India, the Maldives, Pakistan, Tajikistan, Turkey, and Uzbekistan. The report also assessed that ISKP has approximately 2,500 fighters in Afghanistan, with about 2,100 of them concentrated in Kunar province (UNSC, February 2020). However, the headcounts are always sketchy, and different sources have different numbers. Local news sources claimed there was a heavy to moderate concentration of fighters from Uzbekistan, Turkey, Russia, and Arab countries too. Alarmingly enough, according to local news reports, about 3,500 Pakistani ISKP fighters are currently fighting the government of Afghanistan and the Taliban in provinces like Nangarhar, Kunar, Nuristan, Laghman, and Badakhshan (Hasht-E Sobh (Dari), May 2020).

CONCLUSION

Within its five years of existence in one of the most difficult terrains of transnational jihad, the ISKP has gained enormous clout in Afghanistan. It has engaged in two frontal turf wars against the Taliban and government forces since its inception and certainly carved a safe haven for itself in eastern Afghanistan, bordering Pakistan. Though the covert state support behind its resilience remains sketchy, it is farfetched to conclude that ISKP is anywhere close to complete decimation in Afghanistan and Pakistan. Arguably, irrespective of mass surrenders, leadership crises, and other military reversals in the last couple of years, the strong pool of foreign fighters and senior commanders from the Pakistan Taliban remains a survival potion for the IS-Khorasan.

References

Abu Muhammed Adnani. (2015). Say: Die in your rage. https://pietervanostaeyen.com/2015/01/26/audio-statement-by-is-spokesman-abu-muhammad-al-adnani-as-shami-say-die-in-your-rage/

Afghanistan Times. (2020, May 13). Kabul hospital attack's death toll rises to 24. http://www.afghanistantimes.af/kabul-hospital-attacks-death-toll-rises-to-24/

Al Arabiya. (2019, August 18). ISIS claims bombing at Kabul wedding that killed 63. https://english.alarabiya.net/en/News/world/2019/08/19/ISIS-claims-bombing-at-Kabul-wedding-that-killed-63

AP News. (2018, March 22). Suicide bomber kills 33 as Afghans celebrate new year. https://apnews.com/1dd475d96e304c94b5f0d4f176b9e878/IS-suicide-bomber-kills-31-as-Afghans-celebrate-new-year

Ariana News. (2019, November 25). Islamic State staggers in Afghanistan, but survives. https://ariananews.co/en/afghanistan/islamic-state-staggers-in-afghanistan-but-survives/

Dabiq. (2016, January). Interview with Wali of Khorasan. (3), 49–54.

Daily Times. (2017, July 31). Senior TTP commander Daud Khan 'switches loyalty' to Daesh. https://dailytimes.com.pk/123065/senior-ttp-commander-daud-khan-switches-loyalty-to-daesh/

Dawn. (2015, May 14). US offers aid to probe Karachi bus attack on Ismaili community. https://www.dawn.com/news/1181950

Dawn. (2016, November 12). At least 52 killed, 102 injured in blast at Khuzdar shrine. https://www.dawn.com/news/1295928

Dawn. (2017, December 12). Afghan forces to launch operation against IS in the north. https://www.dawn.com/news/1376166

Dawn. (2018, November 23). 32 killed, 31 injured in explosion in lower Orakzai district: health official. https://www.dawn.com/news/1447197

DID Press. (2017, December 10). North of Afghanistan; Refuge for French ISIL members. https://www.didpress.com/en/2017/12/10/north-of-afghanistan-refuge-for-french-isil-members/

Express Tribune. (2014, December 15). No regret over supporting IS, says Lal Masjid cleric. https://tribune.com.pk/story/806711/no-regret-over-supporting-is-says-lal-masjid-cleric/

Express Tribune. (2017, February 17). Bloodbath at Sehwan shrine. https://tribune.com.pk/story/1329603/bloodbath-sehwan-shrine/

Express Tribune. (2020, March 26). Gunmen in Afghanistan kill 25 at Sikh complex, Islamic State claims responsibility. https://tribune.com.pk/story/2184479/3-gunmen-afghanistan-kill-25-sikh-complex-islamic-state-claims-responsibility/

Gandhara. (2019, May 16). Islamic State Announces "Pakistan Province". https://gandhara.rferl.org/a/islamic-state-announces-pakistan-province-/29944153.html

Giustozzi, A. (2018). *The Islamic State in Khorasan: Afghanistan, Pakistan and the New Central Asian Jihad*. Oxford University Press.

Hasht-E Sobh. (2020, May 13). Islamic State still a major threat in Afghanistan. https://8am.af/

Khaama Press. (2017, October 20). Over 30 killed as suicide bomber attacks mosque in Kabul city. https://www.khaama.com/over-30-killed-as-suicide-bomber-attacks-mosque-in-kabul-city-03679/

Long War Journal. (2015, March 5). Mapping the emergence of the Islamic State. http://www.longwarjournal.org/archives/2015/03/mapping-the-emergence-of-the-islamic-state-in-afghanistan.php

Pajhwok. (2017, December 28). Cultural centre bombing crime against humanity: Ghani. https://www.pajhwok.com/en/2017/12/28/cultural-centre-bombing-crime-against-humanity-ghani

Pak Institute For Peace Studies. (2019). *Pakistan security report: 2018*, 76.

Reuters. (2015, April 18). Afghan blast kills 33; president blames Islamic State. http://www.reuters.com/article/us-afghanistan-blast-idUSKBN0N904620150418

Reuters. (2016, July 23). Islamic State claims responsibility for Kabul attack, 80 dead. Accessible at http://www.reuters.com/article/us-afghanistan-protests-idUSKCN1030GB

Reuters. (2016, July 26). Afghanistan weighs Islamic State threat after Kabul attack. http://www.reuters.com/article/us-afghanistan-blast-idUSKCN1060Z0.

Roul, A. (2015). Wilayat Khurasan: Islamic State consolidates position in AfPak region terrorism monitor. *13*(7). https://jamestown.org/program/wilayat-khurasan-islamic-state-consolidates-position-in-afpak-region/

SITE Intelligence. (2017, September 6). The atmosphere of Eid in Khorasan Province. https://ent.siteintelgroup.com/Multimedia/english-speaking-is-fighter-in-khorasan-province-video-notes-presence-of-indians-and-russians-in-its-ranks.html.

SITE Intelligence Group. (2015, February 11). IS fighters in Salah al-Din Celebrate Pledge of Khorasan Province in Video, Behead Police Official. https://ent.siteintelgroup.com/Multimedia/is-fighters-in-salah-al-din-celebrate-pledge-of-khorasan-province-in-video-behead-police-official.html.

SITE Intelligence Group. (2015, February 20). IS fighters in Diyala Congratulate "Khorasan Province" for Pledging. https://ent.siteintelgroup.com/Multimedia/is-fighters-in-diyala-congratulate-khorasan-province-for-pledging.html.

The Independent. (2015, May 13). ISIS claims responsibility for Karachi bus attack that killed 43 passengers. https://www.independent.co.uk/news/world/gunmen-open-fire-on-bus-killing-43-passengers-in-pakistan-10245874.html

The Nation. (2017, December 17). ISIS claims responsibility for Quetta church blast. https://nation.com.pk/17-Dec-2017/isis-claims-responsibility

Tolo News. (2018, August 03). Suicide bombers target Mosque In Paktia; 25 Killed. https://tolonews.com/afghanistan/explosion-reported-paktia-casualties-feared

Tolo News. (2020, April 21). Daesh, affiliated groups on rise in Badakhshan: Officials. https://tolonews.com/afghanistan/daesh-affiliated-groups-rise-badakshan-officials

Tolo News. (2020, May 13). Nangarhar funeral bombing death toll rises to 32. https://tolonews.com/afghanistan/nangarhar-funeral-bombing-death-toll-rises-32

UNSC. (2019, May 14). The Islamic State of Iraq and the Levant – Khorasan (ISIL – K). https://www.un.org/securitycouncil/content/islamic-state-iraq-and-levant-khorasan-isil-k

UNSC. (2020, February 04). Tenth report of the Secretary-General on the threat posed by ISIL (Da'esh) to international peace and security and the range of United Nations efforts in support of Member States in countering the threat. pp. 6–7. https://www.securitycouncilreport.org/atf/cf/%7B65BFCF9B-6D27-4E9C-8CD3-CF6E4FF96FF9%7D/s_2020_95.pdf

US State Department. (2016, January 14). Foreign terrorist organization designation of ISIL – Khorasan (ISIL-K). https://2009-2017.state.gov/r/pa/prs/ps/2016/01/251237.htm

62

THE BALOCHISTAN INSURGENCY

Sanchita Bhattacharya

BALOCHISTAN: AN HISTORICAL ACCOUNT

Balochistan has a complex historical background. Tracing the Baloch history is an intricate task, as not much is known about their written history. Some scholars are of the opinion that modern-day Baloch people travelled around three millennia ago from their original abodes in Central Asia and voyaged towards the northwest, the west, and the east, eventually settling in the present location of Balochistan. However, according to Baloch folklore, the people trace their roots back to the city of Aleppo in Syria. They believe the tribes migrated to this region in pre-Christian times. Baloch thought of and thanked the rugged terrain of Balochistan as their shelter through the ages.

Scholastically, the origin of the Baloch people is a conundrum that is much debated among historians and theoreticians due to the dearth of sufficient logical and systematic literature on the topic. However, four dominant theories regarding the origin of the Baloch populace have been offered with varying claims and arguments. First, that they are Arab (Semitic), secondly, that they are Aryans, thirdly, that they are the aboriginal people of Balochistan, and fourthly, that the Baloch as a nation is an admixture of several racial, ethnic, and linguistic groups over a long period of time (Ahmed & Khan, 2017).

The autonomous Confederacy of the Baloch Tribes ranged from the Indus River to the east, modern-day Afghanistan to the north, Iran, and the Persian Gulf to the west and southwest. After enduring various ups and downs during its existence, the Baloch state came to a final end when it gave up its sovereignty to the British Raj in 1839 (Janmahmad, 1989). The most important of the Baloch principalities was Kalat. Within a century, though, the Qajar dynasty established itself in Persia and the British in India, squeezing the Baloch. The British attacked Kalat in 1839 as part of their related invasion of Afghanistan, installing a friendly ruler. In 1854, Kalat became an associated state of the British, and in 1877, the British established the Baluchistan Agency to deal with the Baloch princely states in their Indian Empire and directly rule the northern half of Balochistan, including present-day Quetta (Pillalamarri, 2016).

The erstwhile region's territory was part of present-day Iran, Afghanistan, and Pakistan. The British ceded the western part of the territory, the Sistan-o-Balochistan Province, to Iran; the northern part to Afghanistan (present-day southern portions of Nimroz, Helmand, and Kandahar Provinces); and the remaining part became "British Balochistan." The British portion had four principalities: the Khanate of Kalat along with Kharan, Makran, and Lasbela, which were forced to accede to either India or Pakistan during the partition process. Presently, the Baloch, who are spread in these three countries, want to carve out "Greater Balochistan," uniting the communities of these countries.

The Baloch people living on both sides of the Goldsmid Line, the border between Iran and Pakistan that passes through their ancestral homeland, have long questioned and frequently disregarded it (Kokaislova & Kokaisl, 2012: 50). On June 29, 1947, the *Shahi Jirga* of British Balochistan, along with the elected members of the Quetta municipal body, unanimously passed a resolution to form part of Pakistan (a few non-Muslim members, however, did not take part in the vote). Later on, the three states of Kharan, Makran, and Lasbela called off the mutual suzerainty arrangements and separately acceded to Pakistan in March 1948. In the same month, the Khan of Kalat acceded to Pakistan as well (Pildat Issue Paper, 2012: 13–14).

INITIATION OF THE BALOCH CONFLICT

The understanding of the series of Baloch uprisings since 1948 has had a vital impact on the subsequent formation of various insurgent groups in Balochistan. The present situation in the province has an extensive history of violence and struggle, and its examination helps in better understanding the current scenario.

DOI: 10.4324/9780429426063-70

The accession of Kalat and the signing of the Instrument of Accession by Ahmad Yar Khan resulted in unrest and anti-Pakistan rallies throughout Balochistan. The National Party rejected accession and was behind much of the agitation. Its leaders, Mir Gaus Bakhsh Bizenjo, Mir Abdul Aziz Kurd, and others, were arrested. This first encounter between the Baloch and the forces of the Pakistani state was crucial in shaping nationalist insecurity and fear of repression at the hands of foreigners (Breseeg, 2017). Also, Prince Agha Abdul Karim started a rebellion in the Jhalawan area against his brother Yar Khan's decision in July 1948. Along with Muhammad Rahim, Karim refused to lay down arms, and after a brief skirmish with the well-trained Pakistani army, Agha Abdul Karim and his associates fled to Afghanistan. But in July 1948, Abdul Karim and his party returned to Balochistan. After a minor clash near Harboi with the Pakistani army, the prince, along with more than one hundred of his followers, was arrested. On November 27, 1948, he was tried by a special *Jirga* in Mach Jail and sentenced to 10 years of rigorous imprisonment (Breseeg, 2017). However, the Pakistani establishment allowed Yar Khan to retain his title until the province's termination.

The second Baloch uprising happened in 1958. In reaction to the One Unit Plan, Nauroz Khan and his followers started a guerrilla war against Pakistan. The government responded by bombing villages suspected of harbouring guerrillas and by reinforcing army units (Baluch, 1975). Khan and his followers were arrested, charged with treason, and imprisoned in Hyderabad. A few of his family members were also hanged, and he later died in captivity. After the executions, the government ordered an intensification of military operations. The leadership of the insurgency had now passed into the hands of political activists, who condemned the cruelties of the army against the people (Breseeg, 2017).

The third uprising started in 1962. The General Election of 1962 brought some Baloch nationalists to the front, which the military dictator, Ayub Khan, considered dangerous. During the election, for the first time, several Baloch Sardars were elected. Sardar Khair Bakhsh Murri, Ataullah Mengal, and Ahmad Nawaz Bugti became members of parliament. Unfortunately, they were replaced by some members of the central government, with whom a fresh spate of violence started. Attaullah Mengal was the first to challenge the writ of the government in 1964, and a regular encounter started between the Pakistani forces and the Baloch people. Another reason for the worsening of the situation was the establishment of a military cantonment in Balochistan. The nationalist leaders considered it a colonisation of Balochistan and put up their resistance against it (Rizwan et al., 2014). This triggered another guerrilla movement. The movement is famously known as "*Parari*" (a Balochi word used to illustrate a person or persons whose afflictions cannot be addressed through negotiations). They set up a network of base camps, expanding in the south from the Jhalawan, the Mengal tribal area to the north, and the Murri and Bugti tribes. They eluded large-scale encounters with the army and tried to disperse the forces by ambushing convoys, bombing trains, and conducting raids on military camps (Hashmi, 2015). The rebellion ended after Ayub Khan was replaced by General Yahya Khan in 1969. Yahya Khan ceased the One Unit system on July 1, 1970, and Balochistan was given the status of province for the first time after 23 years (Rizwan et al., 2014).

The fourth uprising took place as Zulfikar Ali Bhutto dismissed the Baloch provincial government and banned the ruling National Awami Party (NAP). Furthermore, he jailed prominent Baloch personalities, including Khair Bakhsh Murri, Ataullah Mengal, and Ghaus Bukhsh Bizenjo. This led to another uprising against the federation (Weaver, 2003). 1973's insurgency was the worst of all. The army and paramilitary forces, which numbered around 80,000 troops, were reinforced by helicopter gunships, armoured vehicles, and mortars to suppress the rebels. On their part, the Baloch could only field some 1,000 guerillas, armed with archaic rifles. However, Bhutto was overthrown before the revolt could be crushed, and the army decided to withdraw forces and accommodate the Baloch leadership. NAP leaders were released, and Mengal retreated to London (Cohen, 2004).

The fifth ongoing insurgency started much later, in 2005, after a hiatus of three decades. The catalyst was the assault on Dr. Shazia Khalid by an army captain in the Pakistan Petroleum Company (PPC) in Sui, Balochistan. The company management, along with the local police, tried to quash the issue, while the central authorities ignored all pleas to intervene. Dr. Khalid was raped at PPC's hospital. However, the government declared the officer innocent, which led to violent clashes between tribesmen and the security forces and an attack on the Sui gas facility. Members of the local Bugti clan saw the incident as a breach of their code of honour, and they attacked the gas field with rockets, mortars, and thousands of AK-47 rounds (Walsh, 2005). The insurgents mainly targeted developmental activities and infrastructure. Gas pipelines, bridges, railway tracks, power transmission lines, telephone exchanges, and military and government installations have been targeted (Bansal, 2006). Meanwhile, differences between Nawab Akbar Bugti and Pervez Musharraf also centred on royalties from natural gas mining in the resource-rich town of Dera Bugti, in northeast Balochistan. Subsequently, the building of military cantonments in Balochistan and the development of Gwadar port by China also became reasons for conflict (Jaaved, 2019). The infamous killing of Bugti in August 2006 further intensified the Baloch insurgency against the Pakistani state. Consequently, the internal dynamics in Balochistan became all the more unsafe for federal unity.

In order to weaken the insurgency movement, the government has initiated the strategy of killing second- and third-tier leaders of the movement. A few such names are Fateh Qumbrani, Abdul Bari Baloch, Mannan Baloch, Zafar Bugti, etc. Another strategy devised by the Pakistani state is offering general amnesty to the insurgents under the Balochistan Peace Programme. According to this programme, a general amnesty was offered to those insurgents who were willing to surrender their arms to the state. Cash rewards were given to enable their rehabilitation and ensure their return to society as lawful citizens. More than 3,000 separatists surrendered between 2015 and 2017 (Nabeel & Asif, 2019).

REASONS FOR INSURGENCY

Rich in largely untapped mineral and energy resources and adjoining the Arabian Sea with access routes to Afghanistan and Iran, Balochistan has chafed against centralised Pakistani control since the end of British rule in 1947. Since then, it has waged a low-level insurgency against the Punjab-dominated Pakistani government that has intermittently resulted in periods of intense armed conflict. Baloch nationalists seek greater autonomy, more control over revenues from Baloch natural resources, greater funds for development, and an end to the extrajudicial killings of Baloch people and human rights violations. Some also call for Balochistan's complete independence from Pakistan (Heinkel & deVillafranca, 2016). The grievances of the common people of Balochistan are varied, and years of neglect and persecution have caused the formation of insurgent groups within the province, trying to put the demands of their people at the crux of the insurgency.

The Baloch people are divided into several tribes and clans and are organised on the lines of the traditional semi-feudal Sardari System (Singh, 2001). The *ethnic diversity* of the province, with ethnic Baloch people being a bare majority, though contested by Pashtuns, adds to its political fragmentation (Pildat Issue Paper, 2012: 10). The province's Pashtun tribes inhabit the north and north-eastern regions; Baloch and Brahvi tribes inhabit the southern ones; and Makranis inhabit the coast. The provincial capital, Quetta, also plays host to a significant Punjabi-speaking community as well as the Hazara, a Persian-speaking community that migrated from Afghanistan in the 19th century. Balochistan's ethnic and linguistic diversity is not unusual in Pakistan, but the competition for limited resources has contributed to violence along ethnic lines (UNDP, 2011: 1). The ethnic Baloch people are therefore extremely vocal about the presence of other ethnicities in their province.

Balochistan has become a province of conflicting realities, being the largest in terms of land area and rich in resources on the one hand and underdeveloped on the other. The state holds an extensive reserve of *natural resources* in terms of gold, copper, uranium, coal, silver, and platinum. In the sense of having a bulk of natural resources while living an economically underdeveloped life, the people of Balochistan have always been distrustful of the role of outsiders in their province, whom they consider the exploiters of their economic activities (Bukhari et al., 2015). Tensions between Baloch nationalists and the Pakistani state became intense when gold was discovered and licences for the extraction of gold and copper at the Duddar lead-zinc project in Lasbela District and the Reko Deq copper-gold projects in Chagai District were issued to French and Australian companies (Wani, 2016). Moreover, about 36% of Pakistan's total gas production occurs here (UNPO, 2014). The Balochistan coast also offers an economic zone potentially rich in oil, gas, and minerals spread over approximately 180,000 square kilometres (Pildat Issue Paper, 2012: 10). But there are problems and grievances associated with Baloch insurgents, who have frequently targeted gas pipelines as a way of demonstrating their disillusionment with the federal government. Nevertheless, Islamabad remains unwilling to negotiate with the Balochs on the very resources that cause the Balochs to remain a nuisance. The Chinese economic incursions into the region with Gwadar and Saindak have made matters worse (Fair, 2012: 6). For example, the Federal Government has excluded Balochs from the Gwadar development process. The project is run entirely by the Federal Government, and it employs few Balochs in the construction of the port, instead relying on Chinese engineers and labourers. Moreover, not only is Balochistan denied the use of its own resources, but the government has historically required Balochistan to sell gas at a lower rate than the other provinces. For example, Balochistan receives a mere $0.29 per thousand cubic feet for its gas. However, the nearby Sindh gets $1.65 and the Punjab gets $2.35 (Fair, 2012).

Water shortages and the deficiency of proper irrigation are another grievance of the Baloch people, which causes droughts for them and also weakens their economic position. The province covers 43% of the land mass of the country, but large parts of the province are dry and face a continuing scarcity of water. Agriculture, comprising field crops and horticultural and vegetable produce, accounts for 42% of the gross domestic product (GDP) of the province. An additional 10% is contributed by livestock activities. In fact, the livestock and crop production sectors are well combined and depend critically on rainfall. Nearly 90% of the land in Balochistan is mostly suitable for grazing and hunting (Bukhari et al., 2015). Also, persistent drought conditions in southern and southwestern areas of Balochistan since 2014 have affected more than 200,000 families due to successive crop failures and significant livestock losses (Nabeel & Asif, 2019). Gross negligence and half-hearted attempts by the government to stem the rot have led to a crisis situation. The government installed a large number of tube wells but did not build any sizable dams. Neither did they take any action against illegal boring for water, which dropped the water table further. In addition to this, the growing population has worsened the problem of water scarcity (Hali, 2018).

Baloch people are of the opinion that Balochistan's population is swollen with large numbers of *Pashtun refugees* from Afghanistan. Already, the northern districts of Killa

Abdullah, Pishin, Harnai, Ziarat, Killa Saifullah, Loralai, Musakhel, Sherani, and Zhob are overwhelmingly dominated by Pashtuns. Also, the census results suggest that the Baloch population has shrunk from 61% to 55.6% in the province over a period of 19 years in 21 districts where the Baloch form a majority (Khan, 2017). According to data from UNHCR, as of March 15, 2020, Balochistan had 23% of the total registered Pashtun refugees (European Asylum Support Office, 2020). The continual presence of refugees in Balochistan is hurting the economy and culture of the province. The government of Balochistan can ill afford to deliver suitable education, healthcare, and employment to its own people; how come it would extend such facilities to the refugees? Against this background, the refugee presence in Balochistan has serious economic implications (Babar, 2017). Also, ethnic Baloch consider the settlement of Pashtuns in their territory a move by the government to demographically dilute the province. Thus, Balochistan Senator Jehanzeb Jamaldini stated on September 8, 2015, that "the government has settled 4 million people in various parts of Balochistan in the past three decades. With broader demographic changes in the province, the government is converting the majority into a minority" (Singh, 2020).

There has also been a *proliferation of state-sponsored radical outfits* in Balochistan. They operate with impunity and function as de facto paramilitary arms of the state. The *Quetta Shura* of the Taliban was also permitted to have its base in Balochistan, where it continued to flourish with the active collusion of the Pakistani military. Pakistan's agencies have unleashed radical Islamist groups such as the Lashkar-e-Jhangvi, Lashkar-e-Taiba, and other non-state actors and collaborators on the Baloch population in their bid to Islamise them. The Baloch people are known to be temperamentally secular and tolerant in their approach to religion (Mir, 2020).

The existence of *military* installations and encampments by the army and paramilitary forces in the state has further alienated the common people. Many Baloch see the army cantonments as part of Pakistan's colonising presence (Fair, 2012). The first deposits of natural gas in the state were discovered in Sui in 1953. But Quetta received its share of gas in 1986 only because the central government decided to extend the gas pipeline because it had decided to station a military garrison in the provincial capital. Pakistan's interest in constructing military garrisons in the three sensitive areas of Sui, Gwadar, and Kohlu has further left the Baloch feeling dispossessed (Grare, 2006). Baloch opposition to military presence cuts across tribal and ethnic divisions, as reflected in the undisputed resolution passed in the Provincial Assembly on September 23, 2003. These cantonments are similar to "parallel governments," functioning autonomously outside the purview of the provincial government. Perceived by locals as instruments of coercion and oppression, the army presence is seen as "pockets of Islamabad" in Balochistan, where political power remains concentrated (Wani, 2016).

The ongoing *CPEC* projects have put Balochistan at the centre of fresh controversies. CPEC has further bolstered Pakistan's resolve to remain in firm control of Balochistan. Yet there is little evidence to suggest that the importance of these projects to Pakistan has had any effect on Pakistan's strategy towards its unruly province and its grievances (Heinkel & deVillafranca, 2016). The insurgents' interest in CPEC is not just as a point of leverage against Islamabad; they also see in CPEC a pattern of outside power exploiting the province (Shams, 2015). In mid-2015, Pakistan's military vowed to crush the insurgency. It amplified military operations in Balochistan, and a protection force for the CPEC Chinese workers was formed. However, sadly, these measures were likely attempted by Islamabad to reassure China about its investment in the province and do not address the fundamental causes of the insurgency (Heinkel & deVillafranca, 2016).

Since the time of Musharraf, the Pakistani establishment has become notorious for its *kill-and-dump policy* in Balochistan. Security forces abduct and kill activists and journalists; their bodies are dumped outside shortly afterward. The Commission of Inquiry on Enforced Disappearances has received 360 cases from Balochistan (Nabeel & Asif, 2019). A few such dead are Jamil Ahmed, working with a daily named Azadi; Sabeen Mahmud; Muhammad Ibrahim Arman Luni; Muhammad Jaan, etc. Armed militants, activists, sympathisers, or any other potential "threat" are detained by security agencies and held incommunicado for weeks or months. Often, those incarcerated are subjected to torture and other inhuman treatment, and the bodies of those killed are dumped on the roadside or at garbage sites. *Pakistan Zindabad* (long live Pakistan) is often carved on many bodies, apparently to teach "anti-national" Balochs a lesson. Many a time, the Pakistani flag is found protruding from the pierced body (Hashmi, 2013). The enforced disappearance of Baloch people has unleashed a reign of terror in the province, where even a simple objection can easily result in abduction and death.

Nevertheless, in 2009, the Pakistani establishment thought to "regulate" the conflict situation in Balochistan in the form of two important policy packages: a) the Aghaz-e-Huqooq-e-Balochistan Package and b) the NFC Award. The Package purported to regulate ethnic conflict in Balochistan by bordering on four important areas: i) constitution-related matters, ii) political-related matters, iii) administrative-related matters, and iv) economic-related matters. The NFC Award addressed one of the major grievances of the smaller provinces of Pakistan: that the financial distribution formula (based on population) should be revised to incorporate their financial needs and that the most populous province (Punjab) is overly privileged as a result of it. Regrettably, all such measures have become the casualties of a stalemate in which both sides are entrenched in a miserable deadlock with the continued killings of the Baloch on the part of the Pakistani state and that of the non-Baloch on the part of the Baloch, which shows no signs of reduction (Siddiqi, 2012).

INSURGENTS

The insurgency has grown from intermittent resistance by a few Baloch leaders and tribes to a much broader, though disjointed, nationalist movement against Balochistan's perceived "Punjabi occupiers," representing the Pakistani establishment and Chinese encroachments. Disparate Baloch groups have differing goals and objectives that encompass multiple, often conflicting end-states, ranging from full independence to greater autonomy to redress of grievances (Lieven, 2011).

Currently, there are at least 22 nationalist groups, including political parties, that are active in Balochistan. According to one estimate, currently, about 55,000 Baloch fighters are belligerent with the Pakistanistan army (Tabassum et al., 2020). The Pakistani government banned five organisations that include: Baloch Liberation Army, the Baloch Republican Army, the Baloch Liberation United Front, the Baloch Mussalah Diffa Tanzim, and the Balochistan Liberation Front.

MAINLY ACTIVE ORGANISATIONS IN THE BALOCH NATIONALIST MOVEMENT

Baloch Liberation Army

The BLA is a Baloch militant organisation, proscribed by the Pakistani government in 2006, that seeks greater autonomy or independence for Balochistan and has been fighting against the Pakistani government to achieve its goals. It was formed in 2000 and aims to create a state of "Greater Balochistan." Numerous accounts also suggest that the group is a resurgence of past insurgent groups, specifically the Independent Balochistan Movement of 1973–1977. It is classified as a terrorist group by Pakistan, the UK, and the US. The major difference between the BLA and the previous phases of the Baloch militancy lies in the fact that the current generation of fighters is mostly educated youth who have made a conscious decision to take on the Pakistani military, which they see as an exploitative arm that is associating with foreign countries to cart away Balochistan's natural resources (Bhattacharjee, 2020). The "Majeed Brigade" is a constituent unit of the group, majorly involved in suicide attacks.

Leadership: Hyrbyair Marri (exiled in the UK) is the leader of BLA. He is the brother of the murdered Baloch leader Balach Marri. The identity of the military commanders of the BLA remains clandestine, as the organisation refuses to announce who conducts the operations locally. Currently, both Mirak Baloch and Jeehand Baloch have been acting as spokespersons for the group.

Cadre strength: The BLA is the most powerful among the various militant organisations operating out of Balochistan. Known to have at least 6,000 cadre (Shukla, 2020).

Area of Influence: The organisation's main area of influence is in the areas populated by the Marri tribe, including Kohlu, Rakni, Barkhan, Maiwand, and mountain ranges adjacent to Much and Lehri in Balochistan.

Linkages: It is suspected that the BLA has a strong footprint in Afghanistan.

Targets and tactics: *The* BLA has been targeting police personnel, non-native Baloch residents, Chinese workers, political leaders, etc. The BLA has used a variety of tactics to achieve its goal of gaining greater regional autonomy. These tactics include the use of car bombs, mortar strikes, rocket strikes, IEDs, landmines, grenades, kidnappings, and small-arms attacks.

Violent Attacks: On June 29, 2020, 11 people were killed when four terrorists attacked the Pakistan Stock Exchange (PSX) on Chundrigar Road in Karachi. Majeed Brigade of the BLA claimed responsibility for the attack.

May 11, 2019: The Zaver Pearl-Continental Hotel in the Gwadar area of Balochistan was targeted, and nine people were killed. At the time of the attack, the hotel had around 70 guests, including 40 Chinese nationals. The BLA's Majeed Brigade claimed this attack as well.

November 23, 2018: BLA insurgents opened fire on the Chinese Consulate in Karachi, which left four people dead.

June 13, 2012: BLA militants claimed a rocket attack and raid on the summer home of Muhammad Ali Jinnah in Ziarat, Balochistan. The Pakistani flag had also been replaced by a BLA flag on the property. One person was killed in the attack.

July 30, 2009: BLA attackers kidnapped 19 Pakistani police personnel in Sui. In addition to the kidnapped personnel, BLA militants also killed one police officer and injured 16.

December 14, 2005: The BLA attacked a federal paramilitary camp in the Kohlu region while then-President Pervez Musharraf was visiting it.

July 22, 2000: The BLA claimed responsibility for a bomb that was placed in a market in Quetta, Balochistan, in which seven people were killed.

Baloch Republican Army

After Akbar Bugti's death in 2006, his Jamhoori Watan Party broke into three factions; one of them, the Baloch Republican Army, is led by his grandson Brahamdagh Bugti (Ali, 2015). The Baloch Republican Army (BRA) is a Baloch nationalist armed militant group that seeks an independent homeland for the Baloch people and is based in Balochistan. The group is involved in terrorist activities against the Pakistani army. BRA's membership is essentially drawn from the Bugti tribe. The main demand of the group is independence for Balochistan. BRA was banned by the Pakistani government on September 8, 2010.

Leadership: Brahamdagh Bugti is the leader of BRA. He had fled to Afghanistan after his grandfather, Nawab Akbar Bugti, was killed in a military operation in Kohlu in 2006. Later, he flew to Switzerland. Beebagr Baloch is the current spokesperson of the group.

Cadre strength: There are approximately 45–50 BRA camps in Balochistan, with 20–25 individuals in each camp (Muhammad, 2014).

Area of influence: The group's area of influence includes Sui, Dera Bugti, Patfeeder Canal adjacent areas, Uch, Naseerabad, and Jaffarabad districts of Balochistan.

Linkages: Since 2018, BRA has been working with the United Baloch Army and Lashkar-e-Balochistan.

Targets and tactics: The BRA has targeted Pakistani security forces and manufacturing infrastructure to try and take back its province's resources for the people of Balochistan. The BRA has also targeted public transportation and threatened to continue to attack civilians if the Pakistani government does not withdraw troops from the region. The group targets Pakistani security forces, Pakistani police, non-Baloch settlers, public buses, railways, communication systems, electricity pylons, gas pipelines, security checkpoints, and civilian offices. The BRA uses car bombs, IEDs, landmines, grenades, small-arms attacks, conventional warfare, unconventional warfare, social media, and nationalist propaganda to attain its goal of creating an independent Balochi state (Stanford University, 2015).

Violent Attacks: April 23, 2015: BRA attacked a Pakistani security forces convoy in Kech, Balochistan, killing eight people.

December 27, 2014: BRA claimed responsibility for an attack against a Frontier Crops convoy, killing nine people.

May 14, 2012: BRA claimed responsibility for two car bombs that went off near Pakistani security forces' vehicles in Quetta, Balochistan, injuring 58 people and killing six others.

October 20, 2007: BRA planted a vehicle-borne IED on a public transportation bus in Dera Bugti, Balochistan, killing eight people.

United Baloch Army

It is an underground armed organisation formed in the year 2000. It emerged as a result of a reported rift between the Marri brothers and the leaders of the BLA. According to a pro-militant web portal, the BLA leadership has accused Mehran Marri and some of his companions of "stealing three million dollars from BLA funds as well as half its weapons stash worth 800 million rupees," with which they then launched the UBA (Ali, 2015). The group was proscribed by the government of Pakistan on March 15, 2013.

Leadership: Mehran Marri founded the UBA. He is the son of Nawab Khair Bakhsh Marri and was appointed the chief of the Marri tribe after his father's death in July 2014 (Shahid, 2014). He is the representative of Balochistan at the United Nations Human Rights Council (UNHRC) and the European Union (EU). Currently, he is based in the UK. On November 9, 2017, the Swiss government put a lifetime ban on Mehran Marri, barring his entry into Switzerland (Shahid, 2017). Mureed Baloch is the current spokesman for the United Baloch Army.

Linkages: Since 2018, UBA has developed linkages with BRA and the lesser-known Lashkar-e-Balochistan for conducting terror operations (Nabeel & Asif, 2019).

Target and tactics: UBA targets Pakistani soldiers, symbols of Pakistani establishments, infrastructure facilities, and also non-Baloch nationals of the state. It is known for attacking civilian settlers from the provinces of Punjab and Khyber Pakhtunkhwa.

Violent Attacks: May 18, 2020: A security convoy of an oil and gas exploration company was targeted by an IED in the Peer-Ghaib area of Bolan district of Balochistan by UBA insurgents.

August 15, 2019: UBA insurgents destroyed a mobile phone tower in the Kech district of Balochistan.

May 29, 2015: UBA insurgents kidnapped and killed passengers of a bus in Balochistan's Mastung area, killing 22, all of them unarmed Pashtun.

April 9, 2014: A bomb blast ripped through an Islamabad market, killing 25 and injuring dozens. UBA claimed responsibility for the attack.

April 8, 2014: UBA insurgents claimed responsibility for the attack on the Jaffar Express in Sibi, Balochistan. The attack claimed the lives of 16 people and wounded 44 others.

Balochistan Liberation Front

The Balochistan Liberation Front (BLF) is an ethno-nationalist separatist organisation with the aim of creating a separate Baloch state. It was founded in 1964 by Juma Khan Marri in Damascus, Syria. Four years after the group's establishment, it joined the Iranian Balochi Revolt. Following the end of the conflict in Iran, the BLF and other Balochi groups turned their attention to inciting an insurgency against the Pakistani state. From 1977 to 2004, the BLF's activities were uncorroborated; however, reports seem to suggest that the group did not disband. In 2004, the group reemerged in the public eye (Stanford University, 2015). The departure of Brahamdagh Bugti from Afghanistan to Switzerland in October 2010 allowed BLF to assume the central role in the Balochistan insurgency, a role that was previously enjoyed by BLA and BRA (Nabeel, 2017). The current leader of the Balochistan Liberation Front (BLF), Nazar, regularly cooperates with nationalist parties within the province of Balochistan to influence political negotiations with the central government over resources. The BLF is the only militant separatist organisation headed by a leader from a non-feudal background. Nazar belongs to a middle-class family from Mashkay in the district of Awaran (Haider, 2010). It was proscribed by the Pakistani government on September 8, 2010.

Leadership: Dr. Allah Nazar Baloch is head of the ethnic Baloch group Balochistan Liberation Front. Baloch is the only leader of a sizeable separatist group who is believed to be waging a guerrilla war from inside Balochistan. He was captured on March 25, 2005, by the Pakistani government and was interrogated and tortured until his release on June 20, 2015. Gwahram Baloch is the current spokesperson of the group.

Cadre strength: Though the exact number of BLF cadres is still unknown, it developed into a plural outfit with members drawn from diverse tribes such as the Mengal, Marri, and Bugti, as well as from the educated middle class. BLF's cadres also include large numbers of Zikris, as members of this sect are concentrated in the Makran belt (Ali, 2015).

Area of Influence: The BLF operates across Balochistan but is primarily concentrated in the coastal Makran belt (PIPS, 2014). The Awaran district of Kalat is also considered to be a stronghold of the BLF (Ali, 2015).

Linkages: Reportedly, BLF has cooperated with both BLA and BRA in the past; this changed, however, after Balach Marri's death, when serious differences emerged between these organisations (Nabeel, 2017).

Target and tactics: The organisation has targeted foreign workers, aid workers, Pakistani security forces, Pakistani political figures, and journalists. The BLF also attacked parts of CPEC projects in Balochistan. BLF uses rocket strikes, IEDs, small-arms attacks, social media, and nationalist press statements to struggle for its goal of an independent Baloch state. BLF fighters stage most of the attacks in the province and have borne the brunt of army operations against the insurgency.

Violent Attacks: July 14, 2020: BLF insurgents ambushed a military convoy in Panjgur district, killing at least three soldiers and injuring eight others.

May 19, 2020: A military convoy was hit by a roadside bomb blast near Quetta, Balochistan, killing six soldiers. The attack was claimed by the BLF.

November 18, 2017: Five bullet-ridden bodies of people from Gujrat district of Punjab were recovered in Turbat district of Balochistan, killed by BLF insurgents.

April 11, 2015: The BLF attacked and killed 20 labourers working on Pakistani government-sponsored dam construction. Nazar claims that the workers were members of the Frontier Works Organisation, which is a Pakistani security force affiliate.

IMPACTS

The activities of the various Baloch insurgent groups have caused a severe law and order problem in the province in terms of maintaining a secure environment. According to partial data compiled by the *South Asia Terrorism Portal* (SATP), during the first 12 days of the year 2020, Pakistan has recorded a total of 22 fatalities (18 civilians, three Security Force (SF) personnel, and one militant) in five incidents of killing (data till January 12, 2020). 18 of these fatalities (17 civilians and one militant) were reported from Balochistan alone (SATP, 2020).

The ethnic divide in the province is also getting worse due to the insurgents' activities, which include attacking and killing non-Baloch Pakistanis. According to the *SATP* database, a total of 229 "outsiders," including 20 in 2019, have been killed in Balochistan since the killing of Nawab Akbar Bugti. Pointedly, most of the Punjabi settler killings were recorded in South Balochistan, which accounts for 156 killings out of the total of 178 (principally in Bolan, Kech, Gwadar, Panjgur, Khuzdar, Sibi, and Lasbela Districts) and 27 in North Balochistan (mostly in Nushki, Quetta, and Mustang Districts). The overwhelming concentration of such killings in the South is because of the presence and dominance of Baloch insurgent groups in this region (Mohanty, 2019).

The ongoing insurgency in Balochistan has critical implications for the CPEC project, as all of the insurgents' groupings are against the Chinese presence in their province. The government of Pakistan is well aware of the need and has taken certain steps to counter the challenge. It is building a Special Protection Unit (SPU) and Armed Division to secure the corridor from any kind of threat (Jaleel & Bibi, 2017). But, in spite of the constant attacks on Chinese workers, the CPEC projects are progressing. Additionally, the insurgent attacks are unable to alter the real issue of Baloch participation in CPEC-related developmental activities.

The prolonged insurgency in the province has resulted in a severe human rights crisis. In the name of curbing the "militants," the Pakistani establishment has, in a way, overtly and covertly orchestrated rampant human rights abuse. The Pakistani state and its security agencies have routinely crushed the human rights of the Baloch people in the name of security and territorial integrity. They are often charged with treason, branded as terrorists, and killed in encounters or picked up by security forces at will, only to be added to the ever-expanding list of missing persons (Mir, 2020). Significantly, the Human Rights Commission of Pakistan (HRCP) admitted to these crimes for the first time in its report, titled "Balochistan Still Neglected." In the report, the Pakistani authorities have been accused of not only killing but also disposing of the bodies of alleged militants, and for years, the bodies of missing Baloch activists have turned up all over the region (Dacre, 2019). Under the pretext of solving the "Baloch Question," the Pakistani establishment has subjugated the ethnic people of Balochistan. Strangely, neither the voice of the Baloch people was restrained nor the insurgency stopped.

The insurgents also eye the economic infrastructure of the Pakistani state, as has been recently seen in the

Karachi Stock Exchange attack (June 2020), in which 11 people were killed. According to partial data compiled by the *SATP*, Baloch groups have claimed at least nine attacks on economic targets in the two provinces of Balochistan (eight) and Sindh (one, the June 29, 2020, attack) of Pakistan since March 2000, when the SATP started compiling data on the conflict in Pakistan. Claiming the June attack BLA spokesperson Jeehand Baloch asserted that the attack was aimed at targeting Pakistan's economy, which is built on 72 years of exploitation of Balochistan and the genocide of Baloch people (Mohanty, 2020).

CONCLUSION

Pakistan as a nation has failed to address the grievances and objections of the Baloch people and has fallen short of administering popular governance in the province. The task is no doubt daunting, and the undoing of tribal structure, facilitation of irrigation, accountability with respect to the utilisation of natural resources, and encouraging political participation of local leaders require an honest and sincere approach from the Pakistani government, which is still a question mark. The movement of the Baloch people is expected to endure because of the strong undercurrent of popular disaffection in the province against the Pakistan state and the continual fervour of the people to fight for liberty, freedom, autonomy, and equal rights.

Balochistan today lies at the node of an evolving economic, political, military, and business strategy that includes global and regional powers, including non-state actors. The call for an independent Baloch state will continue to haunt the Pakistani political landscape until the Baloch nationalists are brought to the negotiating table. The use of force might work in the short term, but only a political solution can bring long-term constancy to the socio-political unity of the Pakistani state and society.

References

Ahmed, M., & Khan, G. (2017). The history of Baloch and Balochistan: A critical appraisal. *South Asian Studies*, *32*(1), 39–52.

Ali, N. S. (2015). *Situationer: Who's who of Baloch insurgency*. Retrieved June 30, 2020, from https://www.dawn.com/news/1185401

Babar, Z. U. D. (2017). *Lingering crisis of Afghan refugees in Balochistan*. Retrieved June 25, 2020, from https://balochistanvoices.com/2017/03/lingering-crisis-afghan-refugees-balochistan/

Baluch, M. A. Y. K. (1975). *Inside Baluchistan: A political autobiography of His Highness Baiglar Baigi, Khan-e-Azam-XIII Mir Ahmad Yar Khan Baluch, Khan-e-Baluch, ex-ruler of Kalat State*. Karachi: Royal Book Co.

Bansal, A. (2006). Balochistan: Continuing violence and its implications. *Strategic Analysis*, *30*(1), 46–63.

Bhattacharjee, K. (2020). *Baloch liberation army | Fighting through generations*. Retrieved July 4, 2020, from https://www.thehindu.com/news/international/baloch-liberation-army-fighting-through-generations/article31990970.ece

Breseeg, T. M. (2017). *Baloch nationalism its origin and development*. Karachi: Royal Book Co.

Bukhari, S. S. H., Roofi, Y., & Bukhari, S. A. (2015). Resolving Balochistan conflict: A human needs approach. *Pakistan Journal of Social Sciences*, *35*(1), 377–389.

Cohen, S. P. (2004). *The idea of Pakistan*. New Delhi: Oxford University Press.

Dacre, J. S. von (2019). *Pakistan confirms human rights abuses in Balochistan*. Retrieved June 18, 2020, from https://www.insideover.com/society/pakistan-confirms-human-rights-abuses-in-balochistan.html

European Asylum Support Office. (2020). *Pakistan situation of Afghan refugees*. Retrieved July 1, 2020, from https://easo.europa.eu/sites/default/files/publications/easo-coi-report-pakistan-situation-afghan-refugees.pdf

Fair, C. C. (2012). *Balochistan*. Retrieved June 30, 2020, from http://home.comcast.net/~christine_fair/pubs/20120208_Testimony_Fair_Balochistan.pdf

Grare, F. (2006, January). *Pakistan: The resurgence of Baluch Nationalism*, Number 65. Washington, DC: Carnegie Endowment for International Peace. http://carnegieendowment. org/files/CP65.Grare.FINAL.pdf.

Haider, N. (2010). *The good doctor*. Retrieved June 20, 2020, from https://www.himalmag.com/the-good-doctor/

Hali, S. M. (2018). *Water scarcity in Balochistan*. Retrieved July 1, 2020, from https://dailytimes.com.pk/250988/250988/

Hashmi, A. (2013). Pakistan's unending battle over Balochistan. Retrieved July 1, 2020, from https://www.aljazeera.com/indepth/features/2013/04/2013415113250391656.html

Hashmi, R. S. (2015). Baloch ethnicity: An analysis of the issue and conflict with state. *JRSP*, *52*(1), 57–84.

Heinkel, J. C., & deVillafranca, R. (2016). Could Pakistan lose Balochistan? Balochistan's insurgency and its implications for Pakistan and the region. *Journal of Strategic Intelligence*, *1*(1), 62–72.

Jaleel, S., & Bibi, N. (2017). Baloch insurgency and its impact on CPEC. Retrieved June 28, 2020, from https://mpra.ub.uni-muenchen.de/90135/1/MPRA_paper_90135.pdf

Janmahmad. (1989). *Essays on Baloch national struggle in Pakistan: Emergence dimensions repercussions*. Quetta: Gosha-e-Adab.

Khan, M. Z. (2017). Number of Balochi-speaking people in Balochistan falls. Retrieved June 30, 2020, from https://www.dawn.com/news/1353899#:~:text=The%20Pashtun%2Dmajority%20districts%20are,1.74m%20reported%20in%201998.

Kokaislova, P., & Kokaisl, P. (2012). Ethnic identity of Baloch people. *Journal of Social and Political Studies*, *13*(3), 45–55.

Lieven, A. (2011). *Pakistan: A hard country*. New York: Public Affairs.

Mir, N. A. (2020). *Abysmal human rights situation in Balochistan*. Retrieved June 20, 2020, from https://idsa.in/idsacomments/abysmal-human-rights-balochistan-nazir-300520

Mohanty, T. R. (2019). *Balochistan: Ethnic Backlash*. Retrieved July 1, 2020, from https://satp.org/south-asia-intelligence-review-Volume-17-No-47

Mohanty, T. R. (2020). *It is unlikely that Baloch Groups will cease their attacks on economic targets in Pakistan*. Retrieved July 10, 2020, from https://www.newageislam.com/radical-islamism-and-jihad/tushar-ranjan-mohanty/it-is-unlikely-that-baloch-groups-will-cease-their-attacks-on-economic-targets-in-pakistan/d/122304

Muhammad, Sh. B. (2014). Dynamics of the nationalist insurgency in the Balochistan province of Pakistan. *Pathways to Peace and Security (Institute of World Economy and International Relations)*, *1*(46), 50–74.

Nabeel, F. (2017). *Factionalism in the Balochistan Insurgency – An overview*. Retrieved July 3, 2020. from https://stratagem.pk/armed-dangerous/factionalism-balochistan-insurgency-overview/

Nabeel, F., & Asif, M. (2019). Pakistan's counter-insurgency campaign in Balochistan: An analysis. *Journal of Contemporary Studies*, *VIII*(1), 52–70.

Pildat Issue Paper. (2012). *Balochistan civil-military relations*. Retrieved June 28, 2020, from http://www.pildat.org/publications/publication/balochistanconflict/IssuePaperBalochistanConflictCMR.pdf.

Pillalamarri, A. (2016). *A brief history of Balochistan*. Retrieved June 28, 2020, from https://thediplomat.com/2016/02/a-brief-history-of-balochistan/

PIPS. (2014). *Pakistan security report*. Retrieved July 10, 2020. From https://www.ecoi.net/en/file/local/1318503/90_1426673478_san-pips-201501-pakistan-security-report-2014.pdf

Rizwan, M., Waqar, M., & Arshad, M. (2014). A wave of contemporary insurgency in Balochistan. *Journal of Humanities and Social Science*, *19*(2), 97–105.

SATP. (2020). *Balochistan: Assessment- 2020*. Retrieved July 10, 2020, from https://satp.org/terrorism-assessment/pakistan-balochistan

Shahid, K. K. (2017). *'Start fearing the Chinese. They will eat your children'*. Retrieved July 10, 2020, from https://asiatimes.com/2017/11/start-fearing-chinese-will-eat-children/

Shahid, S. (2014). Mehran appointed chief of Marri tribe. Retrieved June 20, 2020, from https://www.dawn.com/news/1116704

Shams, S. (2015). *Brahamdagh Bugti: 'China-Pakistan deal usurps Balochistan's resources'*. Retrieved June 30, 2020, from http://www.dw.de/brahamdagh-bugti-china-pakistan-deal-usurps-balochistans-resources/a-18405846?maca=en-rss-en-all-1573-rdf.

Shukla, S. (2020). *Baloch Liberation Army, the insurgent group behind Karachi Stock Exchange attack*. Retrieved July 12, 2020, from, https://theprint.in/world/baloch-liberation-army-the-insurgent-group-behind-karachi-stock-exchange-attack/450960/

Siddiqi, F. H. (2012). Security dynamics in Pakistani Balochistan: Religious activism and ethnic conflict in the war on terror. *Asian Affairs: An American Review*, *39*(3), 157–175.

Singh, P. (2020). *Balochistan separatist movement due to historical, political factors*. Retrieved June 30, 2020, from https://www.sundayguardianlive.com/news/balochistan-separatist-movement-due-historical-political-factors

Stanford University. (2015). Balochistan Liberation Front. Retrieved June 27, 2020, from https://web.stanford.edu/group/mappingmilitants/cgi-bin/groups/view/457

Stanford University. (2015). *Balochistan republican army*. Retrieved June 27, 2020, from https://web.stanford.edu/group/mappingmilitants/cgi-bin/groups/view/571

Tabassum, S., Mustafa, G., & Nawaz Bhatti, M. (2020, March). Issues of national integration in Pakistan with reference to Balochistan. *Pakistan Social Sciences Review*, *4*(1), 204–215.

UNDP. (2011). Report on the Status of Millennium Development Goals Balochistan. Available at: https://www.undp.org/sites/g/files/zskgke326/files/migration/pk/UNDP-PK-MDG-BalochistanReport-2011.pdf

Walsh, D. (2005). *Pakistan's gas fields blaze as rape sparks threat of civil war*. Retrieved June 25, 2020, from https://www.theguardian.com/world/2005/feb/21/pakistan.declanwalsh

Wani, S. A. (2016). The changing dynamics of the Baloch nationalist movement in Pakistan. *Asian Survey*, *56*(5), 807–832.

Weaver, M. A. (2003). *Pakistan: In the shadow of Jihad and Afghanistan*. New Delhi: Viking.

PART VIII

CASE STUDIES

South Asia

63

HIZBUL MUJAHIDEEN (KASHMIR)

S. S. Tabraz

INTRODUCTION

Ever since the Indian subcontinent was partitioned to create India and Pakistan following the British withdrawal in 1947, the two countries have been locked in a territorial dispute over Kashmir with no resolution in sight (Brecher, 1953; Ganguly, 2001; Schofield, 2010). Pakistan, because of its geographical proximity and the fact that, as a Muslim-majority state, Kashmir should have come to it, has used various Islamist militant groups to wage a low-intensity war to force India to concede to its territorial claims (Haqqani, 2005; Hussain, 2005; Jamal, 2009; Evans, 2000). The emergence of militancy in Kashmir coincides with the conclusion of a decade-long "jihad" in Afghanistan when the Soviet Union withdrew from the country in 1989, which left thousands of trained and armed militants affiliated with various radical Islamist ideologies with no cause to fight for (Hussein, 2007). The Pakistani intelligence agency, the Inter-Services Intelligence (ISI), played a vital role in institutionalising the militancy by propping up groups and providing them resources to wage war against India in Kashmir (Roberts, 2008; Fair, 2004; Sirrs, 2017). The Hizbul Mujahideen (HM), or Party of Holy Warriors, is one such outfit that seeks to wrest Kashmir out of India's control in favour of Pakistan.

OVERVIEW

HM is one of the largest and oldest Islamist organisations present in India-restricted Jammu and Kashmir (J&K) (Ministry of Home Affairs, 2017). HM is basically a pro-Pakistani group and has long-standing ties with the Pakistani Islamist party Jamaat-e-Islami (JI). Master Ahsan Dar of Patan in the Baramulla area founded it in 1989, and he led the organisation until Mohammad Yusuf Shah alias Syed Salahuddin took over on November 11, 1991. Mohammad Yusuf Shah remains HM's supreme leader to this day. What gives HM and Syed Salahuddin exceeding leverage in J&K theatre is the fact that it has come to dominate two militant outfits fighting for Kashmir liberation since the 1990s: the Muttahida Jihad Council (MJC) and Shura-e-Jihad (SeJ). These were established by Syed Salahuddin and other Kashmiri militant groups in conjunction with the ISI to devise a common military strategy (Roul, 2014). The MJC comprises some 14 militant groups active in J&K, including Lashkar-e-Taiba (LeT), Jaish-e-Mohammad (JeM), and al-Badr Mujahideen.

The prime objective of HM is the integration of J&K with Pakistan. HM was founded to counter the pro-independence Jammu and Kashmir Liberation Front (JKLF), an outfit in operation since 1977 that had militarily organised itself by the end of the 1980s and subsequently became a dominant force in the Kashmir struggle during the 1990s. Despite its secular agenda and vehement vision of independence for Kashmir, the JKLF was tolerated by the ISI as it lacked a network of its own in Kashmir and hence depended upon the JKLF (SATP, 2014). The failure of the JKLF to remain united for the cause of self-determination led to the emergence of a radical Islamist movement. HM became the face of that movement demanding J&K's accession to Pakistan, and the best way to do it is through increasing Islamisation, the restoration of Sharia (Islamic Law), and Jihad. HM is against those who aspire for independence as a third option and denounces JKLF's position as "childish and highly irresponsible" (Sahani, 2000).

KEY PERSONNEL AND STRUCTURE

HM has its headquarters in the town of Muzaffarabad in PoK and has an estimated strength of 1,500 cadres. According to its institutional setup, HM has a central command under its Emir (Supreme Leader) and commander-in-chief. It also has

DOI: 10.4324/9780429426063-72

district-level and local-level commanders. For better geographical operations, HM has been divided into five divisions: Central (Srinagar); Northern (Kupwara, Bandipora, and Baramulla); Southern (Anantnag and Pulwama); Chenab (Doda and Gool in Udhampur district); and Pir Panjal (Rajouri and Poonch districts) (Fair, 2013). The command structure of HM is highly centralised, with the Emir (aka Syed Salahuddin) at the apex. There are several key personnel in HM who have played an important role in making HM one of the most successful outfits operating in J&K.

PROFILE OF HM LEADERSHIP

Muhammad Ahsan Dar

He is the founder and former head of HM, which he created in 1989. Dar had crossed over to PoK for arms training, and upon his return in 1989, in order to take over the JKLF, he began recruiting youths for jihad (Pandit, 2017). An avid supporter of the idea of Kashmir's accession to Pakistan (Rising Kashmir, 2017), Dar continued to head HM until he was replaced by Syed Salahuddin in 1991. After his expulsion from HM, he formed his own group called "Muslim Mujahideen." However, the group fell apart following his arrest in 1993. He was released in 1999 after seven years of detention and arrested again in 2009. He was released in 2012 and now leads a quiet life despite reports of his disappearance (Baba, 2018).

Syed Salahuddin

With the expulsion of Ahsan Dar from HM in 1991, Yusuf Shah, aka Syed Salahuddin, went on to consolidate his position within the outfit. He became the supreme commander of the outfit, which he continues to head to this day. What gives him immense leverage in the Kashmiri movement is the fact that he also heads the MJC, a body devised to coordinate anti-India jihad among various militant outfits operating in Kashmir. Of late, however, he has been under pressure from multiple corners, wherein he is designated as a "global terrorist" by the US (Department of State, 2017). Moreover, facing increased competition from outfits like LeT and JeM, HM has witnessed a depleting influence in Kashmir-centric operations (Chauhan & Dua, 2018).

Burhan Wani

He was the commander of HM and was active and popular on social media. He was killed in an encounter with Indian security forces in 2016 at the young age of 22, making him a folk hero (Ashiq, 2016). His death embroiled the valley for the rest of 2016, with the magnitude of the unrest not witnessed since 2010 (Gowen, 2016). He represented a new generation of militants in the Kashmir movement who would come from the middle strata of Kashmiri society and not hide their identity to escape the Indian security forces. More on him later in the chapter.

Riyaz Naikoo

He took control of HM after the killing of Sabzar Bhat, who succeeded Burhan Wani, in May 2019 and quickly became its commander-in-chief in Kashmir. He was subsequently listed as a category "A++" militant with Rs 12 lakh (roughly US$15,000) on his head, which made him the most wanted militant in Kashmir (Ahuja, 2018). He introduced several novel methods in the Kashmiri movement, including the gun salute to mark the funeral ceremonies of slain militants and the rather daring method of abducting the family members of police officers with the aim of discouraging locals from being recruited in the state police force (Javaid, 2018). Like Burhan Wani, Naikoo represented a new breed of militants who are not shy of their identity and put across their views in an extremely articulate manner, as is evident in one of his recent interviews (Al Jazeera, 2018). However, his leadership was short-lived, as he was killed in an encounter with security forces in May 2020, just one year after he assumed command of HM.

SOCIAL MEDIA AND INFORMATION DISSEMINATION OF HIZBUL MUJAHIDEEN

HM also runs a media department from Muree in Rawalpindi, Pakistan. It has a news agency, Kashmir Press International, and a research centre, the Kashmir International Centre, which functions from Muzaffarabad in PoK and regularly publishes documents of HM's so-called struggle in Kashmir. Syed Salahuddin and others (like Naikoo) use mainstream media to further their agendas as well. The outfit uses a poster campaign to recruit, fundraise, and do similar activities. It had also established a women's wing, the "Binat-ul-Islam," to convince women to send their youth to join jihad and look after the families of slain militants (Sharma & Behra, 2014).

Hizbul's presence is across all the domains of social media, whether it be Facebook, Twitter, WhatsApp, or YouTube. There is no official HM handle on any of these social media sites; obviously, that would be counterproductive for the terror outfit as they could be easily traced and targeted. A recent report by the Ministry of Home Affairs (MHA) of the Government of India, assessing the misuse and role of social media, clearly highlights how social media, including Facebook, Twitter, YouTube, and WhatsApp, is being used by the terror outfit to instigate people to take to the streets and hold anti-India protests (Early Times, 2016). Most of the time, fake Facebook and Twitter accounts are used to conduct such propaganda operations in which provocative pictures and videos are uploaded. These videos are made viral in order to fan the fire, earn the support of the masses, and incite the youth. It is pertinent to mention that the PhD scholar from Aligarh Muslim University, Mannan Bashir Wani, had joined Hizbul Mujahideen only after watching Facebook posts for a considerable period of time that were provocative in nature (Saaliq, 2018).

Owing to the volatile situation in Kashmir, an exhaustive and classified report was submitted by a senior police officer of the Jammu and Kashmir Police. The PPT presentation of the report, which was shown to the higher officials of the Ministry of Home Affairs, Government of India, stated that the accessibility to social media (in the Kashmir Valley) was 25% in 2010, rose to 30% in 2014, and sharply escalated to 70% in 2015. The glamorisation of guns and violence gets accepted in a small section of young, impressionable minds who consider themselves on the receiving end in the contemporary political scenario (Thakur, 2016).

The National Investigating Agency (NIA), India's premier counterterrorism law enforcement agency, in its exhaustive probe into incidents of unrest in Kashmir, identified the use of social media and messaging apps, particularly WhatsApp, as central to the instigation of unrest. The investigation highlighted the extensive use of "WhatsApp" to mobilise and instruct youth in stone-pelting events against security personnel and cause obstruction in counterterrorism operations. The probe identified almost 79 WhatsApp groups active in spreading messages relating to stone pelting and the venue of the event. These WhatsApp groups play a fundamental role in gathering crowds and imparting instructions regarding the scale and duration of the stone-pelting event in the Kashmir valley. The investigation further identifies 6386 phone numbers to be part of these WhatsApp groups, out of which around 1,000 were found active in Pakistan and Gulf nations, and the remaining 5,386 numbers were found active in various parts of the Valley and neighbouring states. A few of the groups that the NIA found to be active in mobilising violent protests on the streets of Kashmir are, among others, "Valley of Tears," "Pulwama Rebels," "Daftare Surat Auliyan Sophiyan," "Freedom FigHtErz," "Tehreek E Azaadi123," "Mugahideen-a-Islam," and "Al Jahad" (Bhatia, 2017).

It's interesting to note that Burhan Wani has been using social media effectively ever since 2013. It was his social media outreach that made all the difference and catapulted him into the poster boy of insurgency in the Kashmir valley (Majumdar, 2016). He had created a Twitter handle, @Gazi_Burhan2, in October 2012, which was widely used to upload provocative videos and photographs of atrocities allegedly perpetrated by the Indian Security Forces and repeatedly urged the youth of the valley to join the Jihad for the establishment of the Caliphate (Pandit & Singh, 2016).

Burhan Wani exploited social media to his advantage and weaponized it against the Indian establishment and security forces. He was very active on Facebook and also had several websites and Facebook fan pages under his name, like Tral Tiger, HM Tral, Burhan Trali, etc. (Sharma, 2016). These names kept changing in order to avoid detection and maintain some degree of deception. He uploaded a video, communicating and urging the people of Kashmir to establish a Caliphate in the valley, on a fake Facebook account in August 2015. His calls for joining the "Jihad" were coupled with qur'anic verses, fulminating and inflammatory demands for "Azadi," and urging the people in the valley to establish the Nizam-e-Mustafa (God's government) in Kashmir (Rao, 2016). It was in this video that he stated that HM would act against every man in uniform who stands for the Indian Constitution and urged the youth who wished to join HM to keep a track record of all the local police personnel, their movements, and their conduct (Masood, 2016). This message was widely circulated throughout the Valley via WhatsApp and Facebook.

VIOLENT IMPACT OF HM'S SOCIAL MEDIA CAMPAIGN

The impact of these videos and the insinuating message resulted in multiple attacks on the security forces, police personnel, and their families. In one such incident, on July 13, 2016, the mob, which was protesting against the killing of Burhan Wani by the security forces, attacked the wife and daughter of Sub-Inspector Mohammad Ashraf Pal, who was then posted as a duty officer at Sangam police post in Bijbehara area of Anantnag district. The mob brutally assaulted Mohammad Ashraf's wife and daughter before ransacking their home and causing significant damage (Kashmir Times, 2016). The other shocking and barbaric incident took place on June 23, 2017, in which a Deputy Superintendent of Police, Mohammed Ayub Pandith, of Jammu and Kashmir CID (Criminal Investigation Department), was brutally lynched while he was on duty trying to manage the crowd gathered for prayers at Jamia Masjid on Shab-e-Qadr night in Srinagar. It is to be noted that the four men who engaged Ayub Pandith in the initial scuffle and incited the lynching were shouting slogans in support of Zakir Musa, a Hizbul commander, and were present at the mosque to welcome the separatist leader Mirwaiz Umar Farooq (Saha, 2017).

Very recently, the trend of attacking and abducting the family members of local police personnel has gained traction. This left the valley divided between the families and sympathisers of local militants and the families of local police personnel. Slowly, the fault line between the families in the valley seems to be getting wider. In August 2018, 11 people (relatives of the police personnel working in J&K) were abducted from several districts of Kashmir (Mir, 2018). They were subsequently released within 24 hours. But, before their release, a video clip was released by the kidnappers in which the captives were seen begging and urging the chief of the Jammu and Kashmir police, SP Vaid, not to harass the families of militants. Thereafter, Hizbul Mujahideen commander Riyaz Naikoo released an audio in which he warned local policemen of violent repercussions in case any of the militant's family members were harassed, and there would be no second chance for their family members as they would not be released next time (PTI, 2018). In the history of almost three decades of militancy in Kashmir, this is the first time the families of local police personnel have been targeted and used as a bargaining tool. Political analysts and observers fear that these trends might spin out of control, resulting in another dangerous chapter in the Kashmir imbroglio.

ORGANISATIONAL CHARACTERISTICS AND ACTIVITIES

The militancy in J&K since the 1990s has so far claimed 13,976 civilian lives and 5,123 of the security forces' lives (Ministry of Home Affairs, 2017–18: 15). Although, in comparison to other militant outfits like LeT, which masterminded the Mumbai attacks in 2008, HM's theatre of operations has been Kashmir, as have its recruits, who almost all come from the local population (Fair, 2013). However, in recent years, HM appears to have been operating in tandem with other terrorist organisations like LeT and JeM. Several instances and incidents can be examined to decode the nature of cooperation between terror organisations. Very recently, Kashmir's Hizb commander Riyaz Naikoo claimed responsibility for attacking Shri Maharaja Hari Singh Hospital, Srinagar, in February 2018. His intention was to free Laskar terrorist Naveed Jhatt, which he succeeded in doing. Two personnel of the Jammu and Kashmir police were killed by the militants during this attack. Abdullah Ghazanwi, the spokesperson of Lasker-e-Taiba, also acknowledged the fact that all the militant outfits were operating in close coordination with each other and commended the hospital raid, describing it as "historic" in nature (Rashid, 2018).

Secondly, a video surfaced on the internet on January 7, 2018. Terrorists from the two terror groups, HM and LeT, were seen walking together and playing with snow in an area likely to be in north Kashmir. A few weeks later, another video surfaced in which two militants, namely Arif Bashir and Jibran, both from LeT, can be seen entering a room and joining the Hizbul commander. Both of these videos appear to be part of the propaganda strategy of these terrorist organisations. Thirdly, the telephonic conversation that Hizbul commander Burhan Wani had with LeT chief Hafiz Saeed before his encounter with the security forces also exemplifies the fact that both these terror outfits have begun to coordinate and cooperate with each other against India. In the audio tape, Hafiz Saeed extended his support to Burhan Wani by stating, "You people are living in very difficult conditions. But you don't have to worry. Whatever you need, just tell us; we are ready to help. We will be ready for anything; you have to just tell us" (Indian Express, 2016). Wani reciprocated by stating that "we have to go on all-out attacks and shouldn't lose this opportunity. For this, we need ammunition and support from behind. We should work together for this (Hizbul and Lashkar)" (Gupta, 2016).

All these facts clearly outline a marked shift in the strategy of these terror outfits. Earlier, these terror outfits were divided ideologically when it came to the Kashmir issue. But now, these terror outfits are operating in coordination with each other, which is an example of a clever strategy at play. LeT, which mainly comprises Pakistani militants, is exploiting HM's indigenous character and extracting its ground support for launching its fidayeen operations. HM's OGWs (overground workers) are very effective in providing intelligence related to the positioning of the security forces in Jammu and Kashmir, and they serve as guides to terrorists in approaching their target locations because they are well-versed with the local terrain (Parliamentary Committee on Home Affairs, 2018). On the other hand, HM is using the financial and other resources provided by the LeT to gain traction and a stronghold in the valley. The recent resurgence and fusion of HM with other terror outfits in executing its terror attacks has raised the threat level, which was comparatively low earlier.

HM'S RECRUITMENT

HM is applying a multi-pronged strategy for recruiting Kashmiri youth for its terror operations. Its recruitment rates have also risen in recent years. The ground cadres of HM have gained strength, resulting in the frequent execution of terror acts across the valley with the aim of targeting the security forces. Social media is one of the channels through which the majority of HM's recruitment takes place. By posting videos and pictures, it tends to glamorise and valorise militancy.

The grand funerals of the militants also serve as fertile ground for the recruitment of new terror cadres. These funerals are used by the militant leadership to mobilise opinion in their favour and encourage young people to join the terror outfit (Naseem, 2018). These youth are first recruited as OGWs before they are inducted into the ranks. The recruitment and induction of educated youths with university degrees into the ranks of HM is even more sensational yet tragic in nature. 26-year-old Mannan Bashir Wani, a PhD scholar at Aligarh Muslim University, joined HM in January 2018 and was killed in October 2018 (Wani & Sandhu, 2018). Shams ul Haq Mengnoo, who was pursuing a bachelor's degree in Unani medicine in Srinagar and was the younger brother of an IPS officer posted in the North-East, joined the ranks of HM in 2018 and, if one report is to be believed, met the same fate in January 2019 (IANS, 2019). Haroon Abbas Wani, a 29-year-old MBA graduate from Jammu and Kashmir, joined HM in September 2018.

RECENT RISE IN HM'S ACTIVITIES

Since 2011, the various acts of terror (Figure 63.1) executed by HM have substantially increased, as shown in Figure 63.2, as generated by the Global Terrorism Database (GTD 2023).

Also, there has been a sharp spike in the number of youth joining the militancy in Jammu and Kashmir. In 2010, 54 youths joined. The years 2011, 2012, and 2013 saw a slight decline in recruitment, which figured at 23, 21, and 16, respectively. Since 2014, there has been a significant rise in this number. In total, 63 youths joined militancy in 2014, which subsequently reached as high as 66 in 2015 and even higher in 2016, reaching 88. Analysing the data compiled by the J&K's Multi-Agency Centre (MAC), in 2018, the month of June saw 27 youths from the Valley – mainly from the districts of Shopian, Pulwama, Anantnag, and Kulgam in South Kashmir – join militancy. Of the 82 who joined militancy in 2018, 38 joined HM, 18 joined the LeT, and 19 joined the JeM (Singh, 2018). The data (until the end of June) shows that 82 local youths joined the militancy since the beginning of the year; however, the trajectory shifted shortly afterward (SATP, 2018).

Infiltration attempts from across the border have also increased over recent years. The Annual Report 2017–18, published by the Ministry of Home Affairs, Government of India, reflects the rising trends in infiltration attempts from across the border (Ministry of Home Affairs, 2017–18). The reported infiltration attempts and net infiltration in J&K since 2014 are indicated in Figure 63.3.

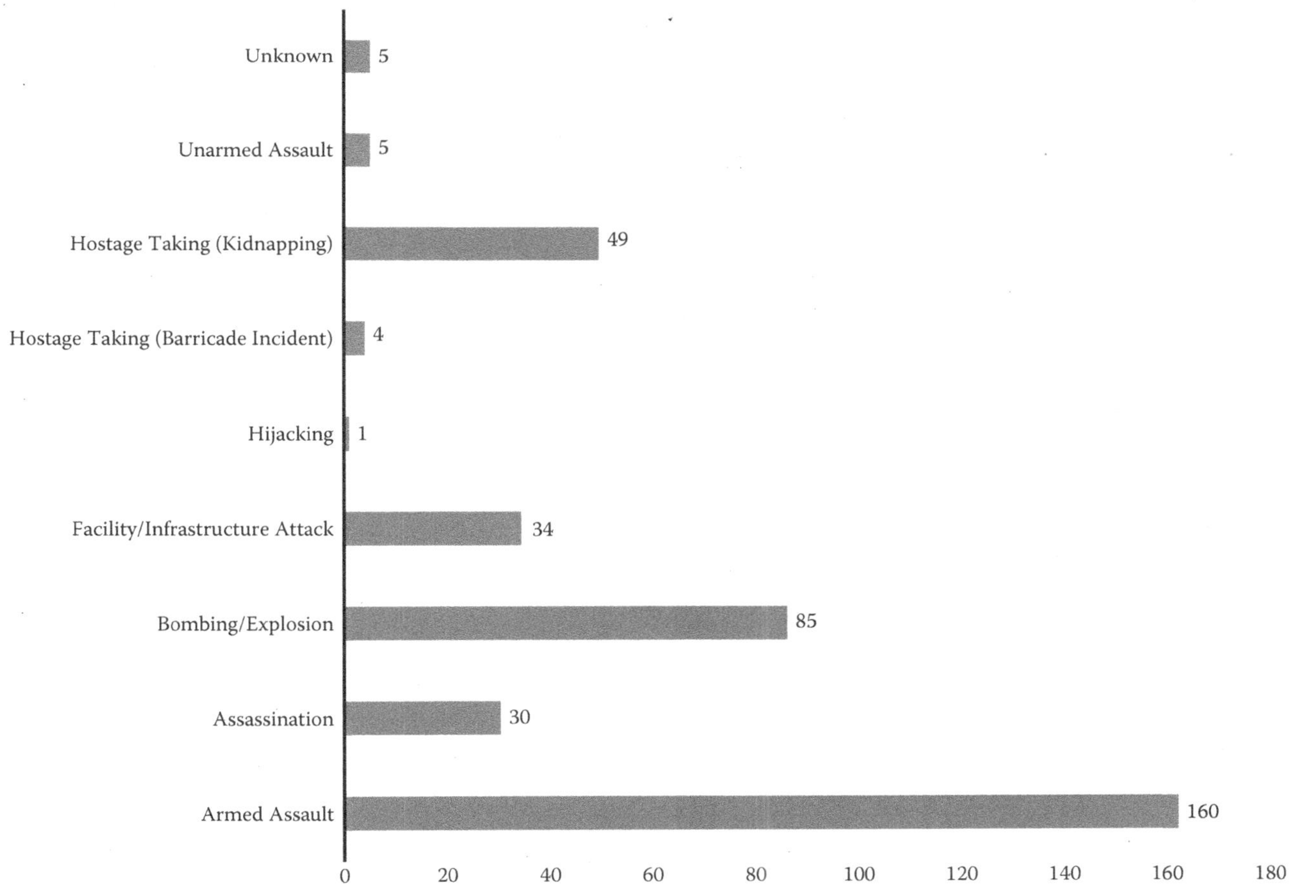

Figure 63.1 HM Attack Type.

Source: Global Terrorism Database (GTD) (2024).

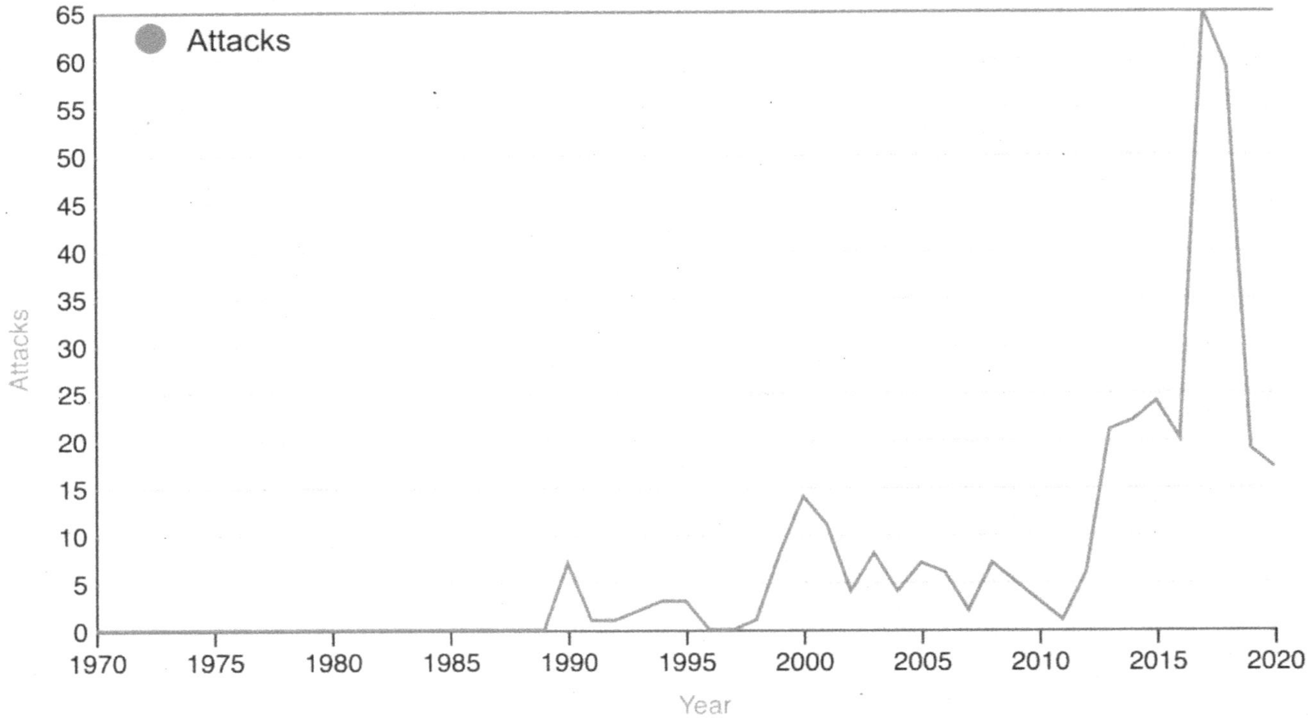

Figure 63.2 Number of Terrorism Incidents Perpetrated by HM, 1970–2020.

Source: Global Terrorism Database (GTD) (2024).

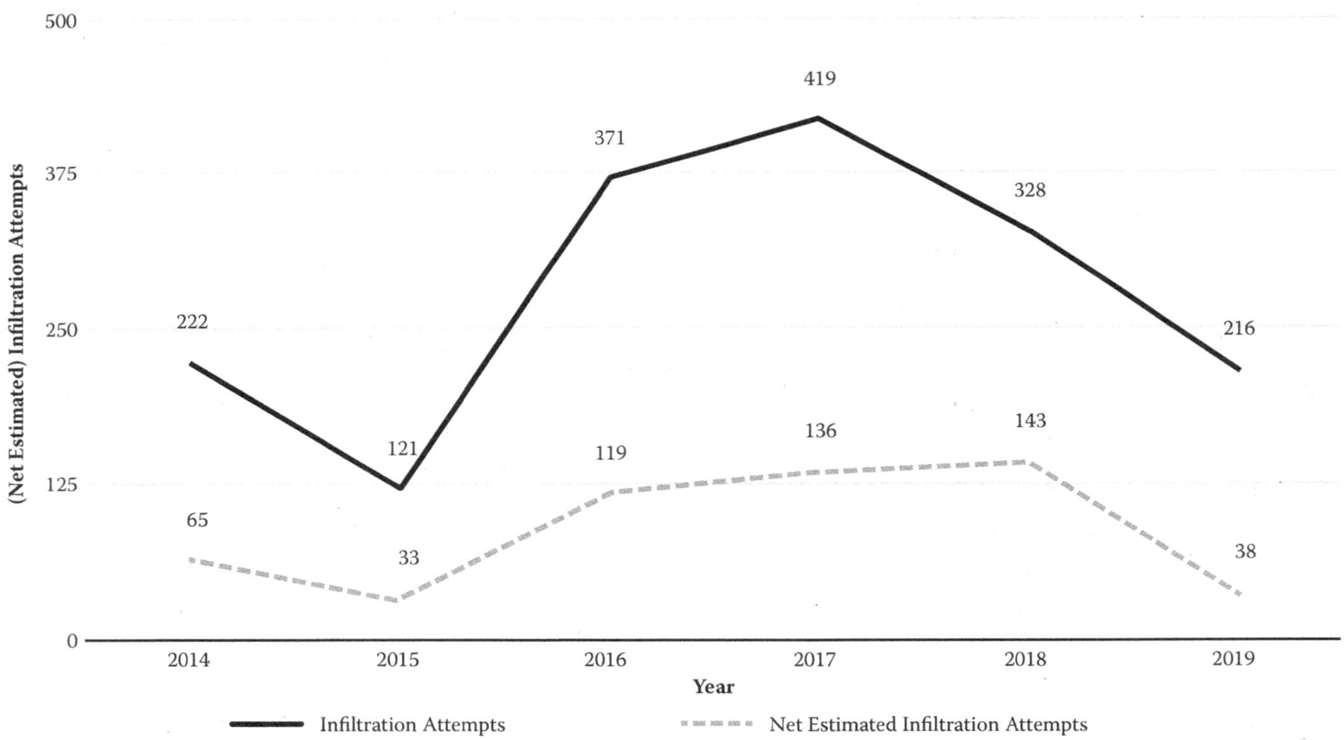

Figure 63.3 Reported and Net Infiltration in J&K, 2014–2019.

Source: Annual Report 2019–2020, Ministry of Home Affairs, Government of India, p. 276.

Taking all the data and statistics into consideration, one can easily conclude that the militancy in the state of Jammu and Kashmir has gained momentum, and HM, owing to its domestic or home-grown nature, is playing a very important role in the recent resurgence of militancy.

IMPACT-PAKISTAN FACTOR

Pakistan and its intelligence agency, ISI, seem to be playing a vital role in shaping Hizbul's strategy. For Pakistan, using Kashmiri youth against India is turning out to be a very cost-effective strategy. Khurram Parvej of the Jammu and Kashmir Coalition of Civil Society says, "It can be considered a success for Pakistani-sponsored terror outfits such as Hizbul and Jaish-e-Mohammad, which had lost their support earlier in the valley as a result of being sidelined by the Pakistani ISI and are now producing suicide bombers" (Sagar, 2018). Just through radicalisation on social media, these terror outfits have succeeded in mobilising youths who are not battle-hardened militants, and therefore, according to Lt Gen H. S. Panag, "ISI does not need a Rs 100-crore (a billion dollar) annual budget to run the insurgency in Kashmir valley" (Sagar, 2018).

By directing and shaping HM through the infiltration of terrorists from LeT and JeM, Pakistan and its ISI are putting out the local faces of newly recruited youths on social media. Thus, on the one hand, it succeeds in projecting the fight for Kashmir as an "indigenous struggle," and on the other hand, it succeeds in using HM and its cadres in Kashmir as mere pawns in their hands. However, by getting HM to expose the identities of its Kashmiri recruits, Pakistan and the ISI have made them vulnerable to action by the Army, CRPF, and J&K police (Jain, 2018). Most of these new recruits of HM are not trained in guerrilla warfare and survival tactics and are thus pushed to death after being pursued by security forces. While the identity of local Kashmiri terror recruits is exposed on social media, which compromises their security and puts their lives in peril, the adequately trained and equipped terrorists from across the border are secretly deployed and trusted with the real terror action in J&K.

However, there is a wider global jihadist perspective, which might become increasingly important in the coming years. This perspective, albeit in a rudimentary form, had always been part of the subcontinent's landscape. It became clear in 2014 when Ayman al-Zawahiri, the leader of Al Qaeda, announced the establishment of what came to be known as Al Qaeda in the Indian Subcontinent (AQIS) (Bruke, 2014). Not to be left far behind was the Islamic State of Iraq and Syria (ISIS), which established Ansar-ut Tawhid fi Bilad al-Hind (loosely translated in English, it means Supporters of Monotheism in the Land of India) around the same time with the similar objective of internationalising jihad (Roul, 2014). While there is rivalry between the two for the leadership, it would be interesting to see how Kashmiri Islamist militant groups, including HM, cultivate their relations with these two and whether it would come to benefit them or simply push them to the margins. These are some of the concerns that would be answered only in the fullness of time.

CONCLUSION

All the incidents and the evidence discussed and analysed in this chapter portray a very threatening picture of HM. It sheds light on the severity of the threat level and the challenging nature of the overall security dynamics prevailing in the Kashmir valley. What has been witnessed in the valley recently is the emergence of a new brand of militants who, unlike the older generation, do not hide their identities. Another manifestation of this new jihad is the rising level of sympathy for the Islamic State in Kashmir (Jadoon, 2018). Although India registered a major victory in August 2017 when the US State Department designated HM as a Foreign Terrorist Organisation (FTO) under Section 219 of the Immigration and Nationality Act and as a Specially Designated Global Terrorist (SDGT) under Section 1(b) of Executive Order 13224 (US Department of State, 2017), the threat posed by HM and other Islamist groups cannot be underestimated. Even if it is agreed that there is a decline in the number of terror incidents, the efficacy of the jihadist narrative in Kashmir is still very potent. What remains unchanged are the general characteristics of Jihad in Kashmir, which revolve around three principles: an exclusive Islamist agenda for the state; expansion of Jihad to other Indian states; and playing the role of spoilers in India-Pakistan peace overtures (D'Souza & Routray, 2016). The radicalisation of Kashmiri youths at the hands of militant outfits controlled and sponsored by Pakistan is dangerous not only for the Kashmiri people and their peaceful growth and development but also very challenging for India's national security.

References

Ahuja, R. (2018, August 31). Who is Riyaz Naikoo, Kashmir's most wanted militant? *The Hindustan Times*. Available at: https://www.hindustantimes.com/india-news/who-is-riyaz-naikoo-kashmir-s-most-wanted-militant/story-Mai4KG2vIFEGSot2vfaFNJ.html.

Al Jazeera. (2018, November 22). Naikoo's interview. *Al Jazeera*. Available at: https://www.aljazeera.com/news/

2018/11/qa-hizbul-mujahideen-leader-surrender-181109111719903.html.

Ashiq, P. (2016, July 8). Burhan Wani, Hizbul poster boy, killed in an encounter. *The Hindu*. Available at: https://www.thehindu.com/news/national/other-states/Burhan-Wani-Hizbul-poster-boy-killed-in-encounter/article14479731.ece.

Baba, A. (2018, May 15). Former HM commander, Ahsan dar not missing. *Rising Kashmir*. Available at: https://www.greaterkashmir.com/news/front-page/former-hm-commander-ahsan-dar-not-missing/285196.html.

Bhatia, V. (2017, September 5). WhatsApp used to gather stone pelters, many admins abroad: NIA. *The Indian Express*. Available at: https://indianexpress.com/article/india/whatsapp-used-to-gather-stone-pelters-many-admins-abroad-nia-4828984/

Brecher, M. (1953). *The struggle for Kashmir*. New York: Oxford University Press.

Bruke, J. (2014, September 4). Al-Qaida Leader Announces Formation of Indian Branch. *The Guardian*. Available at: https://www.theguardian.com/world/2014/sep/04/al-qaida-leader-announces-formation-indian-branch.

Chauhan, N., & Dua, R. (2018, February 16). Lashkar, Jaish Want Hizbul Chief Syed Salahuddin to step down. *The Economic Times*. Available at: https://economictimes.indiatimes.com/news/defence/lashkar-jaish-want-hizbul-chief-syed-salahuddin-to-step-down/articleshow/62942678.cms.

D'Souza, S. M., & Routray, B. P. (2016). Jihad in Kashmir: actors, agendas and expanding benchmarks. *Small Wars & Insurgencies*, *27*(4), 557–577. doi: 10.1080/09592318.2016.1189485

Department of State. (2017, June 26). State department terrorist designation of Mohammad Yusuf Shah AKA Syed Salahuddin. *US Department of State*. Available at: https://www.state.gov/r/pa/prs/ps/2017/06/272168.htm.

Early Times. (2016, July 9). Social media used to fuel trouble in valley: MHA report. *Early Times*. Available on: http://www.earlytimes.in/newsdet.aspx?q=184335

Evans, A. (2000). The Kashmir insurgency: As bad as it gets. *Small Wars and Insurgencies*, *11*(1), 69–81. doi: 10.1080/09592310008423261

Fair, C. C. (2004). Islam and politics in Pakistan. In A. M. Rabasa et al. (Eds.), *The Muslim world after 9/11*. Santa Monica: Rand. Available at: https://www.rand.org/content/dam/rand/pubs/monographs/2004/RAND_MG246.pdf

Fair, C. C. (2013). Insights from a database of Lashkar-e-Taiba and Hizb-ul-Mujahideen militants. *The Journal of Strategic Studies*, *37*(2), 1–32.

Ganguly, S. (2001). *Conflict unending: India-Pakistan tensions since 1947*. New Delhi: Oxford University Press.

Global Terrorism Database (GTD). (2024). Hizbul Mujahideen "Attack Type". https://www.start.umd.edu/gtd/search/Results.aspx?charttype=bar&chart=attack&search=Hizbul%20Mujahideen

Global Terrorism Database (GTD). (2024). Hizbul Mujahideen "Incidents". https://www.start.umd.edu/gtd/search/Results.aspx?search=Hizbul+Mujahideen&sa.x=31&sa.y=17

Gowen, A. (2016, July 11). This violent militant was a folk hero on social media. Now his death has roiled Indian Kashmir. *The Washington Post*. Available at: https://www.washingtonpost.com/news/worldviews/wp/2016/07/11/this-violent-militant-was-a-folk-hero-on-social-media-now-his-death-has-roiled-indian-kashmir/?noredirect=on&utm_term=.6c9e0136a0e4.

Gupta, M. (2016, December 2). Burhan Wani Told Hafiz Saeed: Let's join hands and fight India. *CNN-News18*. Available at: https://www.news18.com/news/india/burhan-wani-told-hafiz-saeed-lets-join-hands-and-fight-india-1318548.html?pk_vid=ab68f606cf5f5aa01538012548899209.

Haqqani, H. (2005). *Pakistan: Between Mosque and military*. Washington, DC: Carnegie Endowment for International Peace.

Hussain, R. (2005). *Pakistan and the emergence of Islamic militancy in Afghanistan*. Burlington: Ashgate.

Hussein, Z. (2007). *Frontline Pakistan: The struggle with militant Islam*. New York: Columbia University Press.

IANS. (2019, January 22). IPS officer's brother among 3 miltants killed in encounter in Kashmir's Shopian district. *News18*. Available at: https://www.news18.com/news/india/ips-officers-brother-among-3-militants-killed-in-encounter-in-kashmirs-shopian-district-2010177.html

Indian Express. (2016, December 2). Burhan Wani allegedly sought help from 26/11 mastermind Hafiz Saeed to defeat the 'enemy'. *The Indian Express*. Available at: https://indianexpress.com/article/india/burhan-wani-allegedly-sought-help-from-2611-mastermind-hafiz-saeed-to-defeat-the-enemy-4407525/.

Jadoon, A. (2018, February 9). An idea or a threat? Islamic State Jammu and Kashmir. *Combating Terrorism Centre (CTC)*. Available at: https://ctc.usma.edu/idea-threat-islamic-state-jammu-kashmir/.

Jain, B. (2018, July 10). In a bid to woo recruits, Hizbul Mujahideen exposes terrorists. *The Times of India*. Available at: https://timesofindia.indiatimes.com/india/in-bid-to-woo-recruits-hizbul-mujahideen-exposes-terrorists/articleshow/64924689.cms.

Jamal, A. (2009). *Shadow war: The untold story of Jihad in Kashmir*. New York: Melville.

Javaid, A. (2018, October 2). How Riyaz Naikoo went from Being a Math Teacher to Hizbul Mujahideen's Chief. *Huffington Post*. Available at: https://www.huffingtonpost.in/2018/10/02/how-riyaz-naikoo-went-from-being-a-math-teacher-to-hizbul-mujahideens-chief_a_23548311/.

Kashmir Times. (2016, July 7). Cop's wife, daughter beaten up by mob. *Kashmir Times*. Available at: http://www.kashmirtimes.com/newsdet.aspx?q=55038.

Majumdar, U. (2016, July 14). Wani, the champ of propaganda by social media. *Outlook*. Available at: https://www.outlookindia.com/website/story/wani-the-champ-of-propaganda-by-social-media/297061

Masood, B. (2016, June 8). Burhan warns of attacks on Sainik colonies. *The Indian Express*. Available at: https://indianexpress.com/article/india/india-news-india/hizbul-mujahideen-burhan-wani-sainik-colonies-attack-threat-2840331/

Ministry of Home Affairs (MHA). (2017). *Banned organisations*. Government of India. Available at: http://mha.nic.in/uniquepage.asp?id_pk=292.

Ministry of Home Affairs (MHA). (2019–20). Annual report of the ministry of home affairs. *Government of India*. https://www.mha.gov.in/sites/default/files/AnnualReport_19_20.pdf

Mir, H. (2018, September 11). Leave Families Alone', Say People In Kashmir, As Police-Militant Tit-For-Tat Kidnappings Rise. *Huffington Post*, Available at: https://www.huffingtonpost.in/2018/09/10/leave-families-alone-say-people-in-kashmir-as-police-militant-tit-for-tat-kidnappings-rise_a_23522369/v

Naseem, I. (2018, July 23). In Jammu and Kashmir, funerals and social media are fertile recruiting grounds for militants. *Firstpost*. Available at: https://www.firstpost.com/india/in-jammu-and-kashmir-funerals-of-militants-and-social-media-are-fertile-recruiting-grounds-for-terrorists-3902087.html.

Pandit, M. S. (2017, August 21). Hizbul wiped out JKLF before dominating valley militancy. *Times of India*. Available at: https://timesofindia.indiatimes.com/india/hizbul-wiped-out-jklf-before-dominating-valley-militancy/articleshow/60150213.cms

Pandit, S. M., & Singh, A. T. (2016, July 9). Tech-savvy face of terror in Kashmir killed in gunfight. *Times of India*. Available at: http://timesofindia.indiatimes.com/city/srinagar/Tech-savvy-face-of-terror-in-Kashmir-killed-in-gunfight/articleshow/53124417.cms

Parliamentary Committee on Home Affairs. (2018, March). Border security: Capacity and institutions. Report No. 203. Available at: http://164.100.47.5/newcommittee/reports/EnglishCommittees/Committee%20on%20Home%20Affairs/203.pdf.

PTI. (2018, September 11). Riyaz Naikoo tells police to back off. Kashmir Reader. Available at: https://kashmirreader.com/2018/09/01/riyaz-naikoo-tells-police-to-back-off/

Rao, P. (2016, July 16). Online radicalisation: The example of Burhan Wani. *IDSA Issue Briefs*. Available at: https://idsa.in/issuebrief/online-radicalisation-burhan-wani_prao_160716

Rashid, T. (2018, February 7). Hizbul claims it freed Lashkar terrorist Naveed Jhatt in Srinagar hospital raid. *Hindustan Times*. Available at: https://www.hindustantimes.com/india-news/hizbul-claims-it-freed-lashkar-terrorist-naveed-jhatt-in-srinagar-hospital-raid/story-71sytLiWRES07HGIGf67GK.html.

Rising Kashmir. (2017, October 7). Pak backed JKLF, HM my creation. *Rising Kashmir*. Available at: http://risingkashmir.com/news/pak-backed-jklf-hm-my-creation.

Roberts, M. J. (2008). Pakistan's inter-services intelligence directorate: A state within a state. *Joint Force Quarterly (JFQ)*, 48. Available at: https://apps.dtic.mil/dtic/tr/fulltext/u2/a517856.pdf.

Roul, A. (2014, April). The 'Pir' of terror in Kashmir's Jihad: A profile of Syed Salahuddin. *Militant Leadership Monitor, 5*(4), 10–12.

Roul, A. (2014, June 13). Ansar-ut Tawhid and the Transnational Jihadist threat to India. *Terrorism Monitor, 12*(12). Available at: https://jamestown.org/program/ansar-ut-tawhid-and-the-transnational-jihadist-threat-to-india/#.V15LYxIau0h.

Saaliq, S. (2018, January 9). PhD Scholar 'Joins' Hizbul Mujahideen months after Facebook Post on 'Harassment' by Soldiers. *New 18*. Available at: https://www.news18.com/news/india/phd-scholar-joins-hizbul-mujahideen-months-after-facebook-post-on-harassment-by-soldiers-1625907.html

Sagar, P. R. (2018, January 21). Home grown trouble. *The Week*. Available at: https://www.theweek.in/theweek/cover/kashmir-local-suicide-attackers.html.

Saha, A. (2017, July 24). Kashmir cop lynched: 20 held for beating Mohammad Ayub Pandith. *Hindustan Times*. Available at: https://www.hindustantimes.com/india-news/kashmir-cop-lynched-20-held-for-beating-mohammad-ayub-pandith-iron-rod-used-to-kill-recovered/story-plqiClEROjoDk6z0kJ7CBO.html

Sahani, S. (2000, July 31). The birth of Hizdul Mujahideen. *redif.com*. Available at: https://www.rediff.com/news/2000/jul/31hizb.htm.

SATP. (2014). Jammu and Kashmir liberation front. *South Asia Terrorism Portal*. Available at: http://www.satp.org/satporgtp/countries/india/states/jandk/terrorist_outfits/jammu_&_kashmir_liberation_front.htm.

SATP. (2018, July 11). Detail of terrorism update: India. *South Asia Terrorism Portal*. Available at: http://www.satp.org/terrorism-update/spike-in-local-militant-recruitment-after-end-of-ramzan-ceasefire-in-jammu-and-kashmir-shows-mac-data.

Schofield, V. (2010). *Kashmir in conflict: India, Pakistan and the unending war*. New York: I. B. Tauris.

Sharma, S. (2016, August 16). Glamour, gadgets and social media: Hizbul Mujahideen hard sells militancy to J&K's youth. *Firstpost*. Available at: https://www.firstpost.com/india/glamour-gadgets-and-social-media-hizbul-mujahideen-hard-sells-militancy-to-jks-youth-2393728.html

Sharma, S. K., & Behra, A. (2014). *Militant groups in South Asia*. New Delhi: IDSA/Pentagon Press.

Singh, S. (2018, July 11). Spike in militant recruitment after end of Valley ceasefire: J&K data. *The Indian Express*. Available at: https://indianexpress.com/article/india/jammu-and-kashmir-militant-hiring-burhan-wani-hizbul-mujahideen-lashkar-e-taiba-terrorist-5254335/.

Sirrs, O. L. (2017). *Pakistan's inter-services intelligence directorate: Covert action and internal operations*. Abingdon: Routledge. (Chapter 12 deals with insurgency in Kashmir and Punjab).

Thakur, S. (2016, July 11). Making of a social media militant. *The Telegraph*. Available at: http://www.earlytimes.in/newsdet.aspx?q=184335

US Department of State. (2017). State department terrorist designation of Hizbul Mujahideen. Available at: https://www.state.gov/r/pa/prs/ps/2017/08/273468.htm.

Wani, A., & Sandhu, K. K. (2018, October 11). PhD scholar-turned-miliatnt Manan Bashir Wani killed in Kupwara encounter. *India Today*. Available at: https://www.indiatoday.in/india/jammu-and-kashmir/story/2-hizbul-mujahideen-militants-gunned-down-in-encounter-in-j-k-s-kupwara-1366450-2018-10-11

64

INDIAN MUJAHEDEEN

Home-grown Jihadist of India

Animesh Roul and Scott N. Romaniuk

INTRODUCTION

India has been facing various forms and waves of Islamist terrorist violence for at least three decades now. Initially restricted to the Kashmir region, the terrorist groups have successfully infiltrated India in due course, mostly from neighbouring countries such as Pakistan and Bangladesh, with the sole objective of fuelling Islamic jihad, perpetrating violence across India, and facilitating the formation of indigenous groups. At least two sets of players are involved in pan-Indian terrorism: one is comprised of Pakistan and Bangladesh-based terror groups like Lashkar-e-Taiba (LeT), Jaish-e-Mohammad (JeM), and Harkat-ul-Jihad Islami (HuJI), and the other is a hybrid, mostly comprising a network of disgruntled and alienated Indian Muslim youths with radical orientations and criminal elements, infamously called the Indian Mujahideen (IM) with rabid anti-India jihadi orientations. With the expansion of terror bases, recruits, and sleeper cells across the country, IM successfully increased its subversive activities between 2007 and 2013, targeting urban centres, strategic infrastructure, and the financial lifelines of the country.

While the exact time of the formation of the IM as a terrorist group is still shrouded in mystery, various interrogation reports of its operatives in the past have corroborated its possible emergence and involvement in terror strikes in India since February 2005, starting from the bombing at the Dasashwadmedha Ghat in Varanasi, Uttar Pradesh (Gupta, 2011; Indian Express, April 2015). Though the Uttar Pradesh police never implicated IM in this first-ever bombing that killed seven people and injured several more, including foreign nationals, shadowy links emerged following the 2008 Batla House encounter incident that took place between IM militants and Delhi police in the National Capital, New Delhi.

In June 2010, the Indian government proscribed the Indian Mujahideen and all its formations and front organisations under the Unlawful Activities (Prevention) Act, 1967 (NDTV, June 2010). IM was designated by the US State Department as a Foreign Terrorist Organisation (FTO) in September 2011 (Reuters, September 2011). The UK also proscribed IM under the Terrorism Act (2000) in the subsequent year (News-18, 2012). The common reason behind the IM's proscription by countries other than India is due to the group's objective of creating an Islamic State through violent jihad in the subcontinent, which is quite similar to the demand to establish a Caliphate of its forerunner, the Student of Islamic Movement of India (SIMI).

PRECURSORS AND IDEOLOGY

The Student Islamic Movement of India

The organisational antecedent of the Indian Mujahedeen is believed to be the Student Islamic Movement of India (SIMI), a radical student organisation in India. SIMI, which is a banned extremist organisation in India, was founded in April 1977 at the University of Aligarh, Uttar Pradesh, as a radical student outfit. The interlinked triad of the ummah, caliphate, and jihad determined SIMI's postures and activities in the country thereafter – the group's logo includes a Quran, an AK-47 assault rifle, and a globe. SIMI started as a united platform for Muslim students and youth in India with the objective of restoring the Caliphate for the unity of the ummah by rejecting the concepts of nationalism, secularism, and democracy. The group's aim was to establish Dar-ul-Islam (the land of Islam) by using violence, if necessary, to convert non-Muslims. SIMI's ideological inspirations were Muslim thinkers who had launched major Islamic movements in the subcontinent, in particular Shah Waliullah, Sayyid Ahmad, Haji Shariat Allah, and the

DOI: 10.4324/9780429426063-73

legendary Sayyid Abu'l-A'la Mawdudi, the founder of Jamaat-e-Islami (JI) (Roul, 2006).

The JI largely believes in Islam-inspired political mobilisation and advocates the establishment of Nizam-e-Mustafa in accordance with Maududi's idea. Maududi advocated the idea of the Nizam-e-Mustafa, or a system, as he perceived it, being ruled the way it was in the time of Prophet Mohammed. He founded Jamaat-e-Islami in 1941 to counter or as an alternative to the Congress Party and Muslim League, two political parties of pre-independence India. However, Maududi's Jamaat was split after the partition of the subcontinent, and thereafter Jamaat-e-Islami Pakistan and Jammat-e-Islami Hind (India) came into existence. For more details on Maududi and JeI, Maududi coined many terminologies to name his idea of government, e.g., "theo-democracy," "divine democratic government," or Nizam-e Mustafa (Ahmed, 2006; Engineer, 1980). SIMI has reiterated these tenets, urging Muslim youths in India to struggle for the revival of Islam in the light of the Quran and Sunnah.

Scholarly investigations traced the militant extremist thinking of SIMI to the impact of the Iranian Revolution of 1979 and the Afghans' jihad against the former Soviet Union in the 1980s (Ahmed, 1997, 2005). The issue of the Babri Mosque demolition in December 1991 provided much-needed fodder for SIMI to fuel popular Muslim sentiments with its anti-Hindu right-wing rhetoric. SIMI subsequently declared Indian secularism to be idolatry and urged Muslims to wage jihad for the establishment of a caliphate. It changed its slogan to "Allah our Lord, Mohammed our Commander, Qur'an our Constitution, Jihad our Path, Shahadat [martyrdom] our Desire," with a mission to revive Islam in India and transform the entire country into an Islamic state (Sikand, October 2001; Ahmed, 2009). SIMI's adoption and vigorous persuasion of the Quran, Jihad, and martyrdom, respectively, branded it as a radical and violent outfit. What started as a student movement became a major radical Islamist movement in due course, with a strong presence in most of the northern and southern states of India.

In the early 1990s, SIMI activists were indoctrinated by Pakistan's Inter-Service Intelligence (ISI) and travelled far and wide to garner support. The outfit convened an Ikhwanul (Muslim Brotherhood) conference in Kanpur city in October 1999, which was attended by around 20,000 people, including Sheikh Yaseen (Hamas), Qazi Hussain Ahmed (JI, Pakistan), and the Imam of the al-Aqsa mosque. In 2001, SIMI again convened a mass conclave in Mumbai, especially for Muslim youths. It was here that SIMI urged fellow Indian Muslims to launch an armed jihad in India with the establishment of an Islamic Caliphate as the goal. SIMI's pro-Taliban stance in the wake of the 9/11 terrorist attacks, anti-U.S. demonstrations in the Indian states of Madhya Pradesh, Uttar Pradesh, Maharashtra, Gujarat, and Rajasthan, and the glorification of Osama bin Laden as the "ultimate jihadi" prompted the Indian government to impose a ban on it (Roul, 2006). After the government proscription, SIMI operated closely with the Hyderabad-based Tehreek Tahaffuz-e-Shair-e-Islam and the radical Islamic vigilante outfit, the Darsgah Jihad-o-Shahadat ("Institute for Holy War and Martyrdom"), which has countrywide centres teaching self-defence training to Muslim youths and aims to make the Quran the constitution of India (MHA (Government of India) 2002). SIMI also operated through the Islamic Youth Front in Kerala and the Tamil Nadu Muslim Munnetra Kazhagam.

SIMI attempted to indoctrinate youths by convincing them to fight for Islam. To accomplish this goal, it used provocative audio and video clippings that selectively depicted the atrocities committed against Muslims from Gujarat to Kashmir and from Bosnia to Afghanistan. Kashmir-centric Pakistani terrorist outfits like Hizbul Mujahedeen, Lashkar-e-Taiba, and Jaish-e-Muhammad have had strong logistical and operational ties with SIMI. In late 2002, Maharashtra police seized as many as 30 compact discs containing speeches of Maulana Masood Azhar, chief of Jaish-e-Muhammad, along with clippings of communal riots in Gujarat, from SIMI offices in Aurangabad. While there was no evidence linking SIMI to al-Qaeda, SIMI leaders were known to have made declarations of support for Osama bin Laden and al-Qaeda in the past. For example, in October 2001, SIMI chief Safdar Nagori stated in Lucknow (Uttar Pradesh) that declaring bin Laden an international terrorist was part of "an evil design of the U.S." (Roul, 2006). This was not a single instance of SIMI's brazen anti-Americanism or support for Al Qaeda. Earlier, in July 1998, SIMI cadres held demonstrations in major cities of India against the presence of U.S. troops in Saudi Arabia, which they called "a sinister plot on the part of the enemies of Islam to desecrate and capture its holiest site." Furthermore, during a special operation, security forces recovered CDs, tapes, books, journals, posters of bin Laden, and documents urging all Muslims to take revenge for the Babri Masjid demolition and to support the secession of Kashmir from India.

With the steady unfolding of SIMI's radical worldview and anti-Indian activities, other Indian-origin local groups with radical extremist orientations simultaneously laid the foundation for the contemporary indigenous terrorist movement in India. The objective of the majority of these organisations was the "need to protect Islam" from the majority Hindu onslaught. During the 1990s, Islamist extremists targeted rival Hindu right-wing groups and started bringing disgruntled Muslims into their fold with some real and perceived Muslim grievances. These groups had links with underworld criminal syndicates and criminal elements with a Jihadist mindset. Most of the groups believed in using violence and subversion to achieve their respective goals. Groups like Al Umma, the Jehad Committee, and Tanzim Islahul Muslimeen were purely Indian in origin and largely funded by Indian Muslims engaged in underground businesses and other criminal elements to protect their interests against Hindu rivals. Others, for example, the Asif Reza Commando Force (ARCF), have somehow maintained links with Pakistan or its powerful intelligence agency, ISI, and with the issue of Kashmir and Muslim liberations. In subsequent years, ARCF and SIMI's violent faction contributed immensely to the creation of the Indian Mujahideen. Intelligence agencies in India have established SIMI and ARCF's involvement in major terrorist strikes in India and exposed how instrumental they were in creating the IM. Even though the affiliation was well known, the most revealing details came to light when one of the leading terrorist masterminds, Sayed Zabiuddin Ansari (a.k.a. Abu Jundal), a Lashkar-e-Taiba (LeT) terrorist, confessed about SIMI's supporting role in many terrorist acts in the country (Asian Age, 2012).

Asif Reza Commando Force (ARCF)

Asif Reza Khan, after whom the ARCF is named, had developed links with Pakistan-based Harkat formations (Harkat-ul-Mujahideen, Harkat-ul-Jihadi Islami, and Harkat ul Ansar), especially with HuJI. He was a resident of Beniapukur, Kolkata (West Bengal), and joined HuJI following the demolition of the Babri Masjid and subsequent rioting across the country. Following his arrest in 1993, he served a five-year jail sentence for criminal activities in Delhi's Tihar Jail, where he met "terrorist kidnappers" Aftab Ansari, Masood Azhar, and Omar Saeed Sheikh, the then two top Harakat operatives who were subsequently released in the Indian Airlines IC-814 hostages-for-prisoners swap deal on December 29, 1999. Asif Reza was arrested again in New Delhi on October 29, 2001, along with a Pakistani accomplice, Arshad Khan. Asif Reza was killed by the Gujarat police during his bid to escape from custody in December 2001 (Times of India, 2002; Indian Express, 2008). This was the time when ARCF was founded in the Malda district of West Bengal, comprising some HuJI-Bangladesh operatives and SIMI cadres. Following his death, his Dubai-based accomplice, Aftab Ansari, and his India-based brother, Amir Reza Khan, took over the reins of ARCF.

In a revenge attack, ARCF perpetrated the attack on the American Centre in Kolkata on January 2, 2002, killing 4 security personnel and injuring 17 others. A Dubai-based senior operative of ARCF, Aftab Ansari, claimed responsibility for this attack. Aftab Ansari was arrested in 2002 and is presently serving jail terms in Kolkata (West Bengal) for the American Centre attack (News 18, 2018). Ansari, who had active links with criminal syndicates in the subcontinent and the Gulf region, operated an extortion and abduction network in India, along with Asif Reza and his brother Amir Reza Khan. He had working ties with Pakistan-based Jaish-e-Muhammad (JeM), Lashkar-e-Taiba, and HuJI operatives in Bangladesh (Rediff, 2002). Ansari and Amir Reza Khan had plotted many criminal acts and were responsible for arms trafficking, including the November 2001 Patan district arms seizure. The National Investigating Agency (NIA) believes Amir Reza Khan is hiding in Pakistan, running international kidnapping and ransom businesses, and reportedly funding IM's activities in India (Times of India, 2012). The NIA has announced a reward of INR 10 lakh (approximately USD $12,000) for his arrest (Indian Express, 2018). The other ARCF operative who closely worked with Ansari is Mohammed Saddik Ishrar Ahmed Shaikh, a staunch SIMI operative. Both Sadiq Ishrar and Amir Reza Khan later became founding members of the Indian Mujahideen (Subrahmanian et al., 2013).

IM: EMERGENCE OF THE JIHADI HYBRID

As stated, before the government ban on the radical SIMI, two major conventions were organised where SIMI's virulent strain was evident with anti-India rhetoric: one in 1999 in Aurangabad, Maharashtra, and a 2001 convention in Mumbai. The leadership made it clear in those conventions that Islam is their nation, not India, and urged the Muslims to take up jihad. Following the proscription and country-wide crackdowns on its offices, the SIMI leadership went underground. The founding leaders of SIMI were Shahid Badar Falah and Safdar Nagori, as the national president and secretary-general, respectively. While Falah was arrested and charged with sedition and communal tension in north India in September 2001, Nagori initially evaded arrest and later became instrumental in bringing a more radical side of SIMI into the limelight before his arrest in 2008 (DNA India, 2016). Preferring armed struggle over peaceful coexistence, Nagori had tried to establish links with Pakistani intelligence operatives, Kashmir militant groups (e.g., LeT and HuJI), the Palestinian group Hamas, and other like-minded organisations beyond India's borders and succeeded in his effort to some extent (India Today, 2001; Pioneer, 2003). Soon, SIMI operatives joined transnational terror groups either as conduits or as local supporters.

Many keen observers of the state of Indian minority issues opined that Indian Muslims may have forgotten the demolition of the Babri mosque, but they are yet to digest two things: the non-implementation of the Sri Krishna Commission report on the excesses allegedly committed by the Mumbai police against the Muslims and the anti-Muslim massacres in Gujarat, including the alleged inaction of the Gujarat Government. Arguably, the major turning point came after the 2002 Gujarat riots, when SIMI's most radical operatives, possibly abetted by external elements, came together to create a new militant offshoot later known as the Indian Mujahideen, which took shape on the above-mentioned premises. IM projects itself as a movement of reprisal terrorism to protest against alleged injustices and excesses against members of the Muslim community. Many of the co-founders of IM were found to be former SIMI and ARCF members during investigations, e.g., Amir Reza Khan, Riyaz, Shahbandri,

Abdul Subhan Qureshi, and Sadiq Ishrar Sheikh. Furthermore, IM's email statements indicate their ties with SIMI when they put forward demands for the release of SIMI cadres under detention or serving jail terms.

The external hands behind the formation of IM cannot be ignored in any discourse on the Jihad movement in India, as the role of Pakistan's ISI and the anti-India Lashkar-e-Taiba combine has surfaced several times during the investigations and interrogations of incarcerated IM operatives. The connection has surfaced on many occasions during interrogations of arrested Indian Mujahideen members and subsequent investigations. For example, IM militant Syed Maqbool said to his interrogators that Pakistan's ISI has provided Yasin and Riyaz Bhatkal Pakistani passports, through which they have been travelling frequently between Karachi and Saudi Arabia, for recruitment and fund-raising for the group. Also, the key connection between LeT and IM has been Zabiuddin Ansari (Abu Jundal), who has provided many incremental pieces of information to Indian investigating agencies. Again, a Pakistani-born militant, Adil (a.k.a. Ajmal), who was arrested with a fake passport, disclosed to his interrogators that in 2009, Abu Jundal trained at least 90 men at Lashkar-e-Taiba's (LeT) Bhawalpur training camp in the Punjab province of Pakistan, many of whom later joined the IM. Hi further said that Jundal showed clips of the 2002 Gujarat riots, the Iraq war, the Afghanistan war, and the USA invasion of Muslim areas to motivate the new recruits to join IM (Hindustan Times, 2008; Indian Express, 2012; New Indian Express, 2013).

The main purpose behind the formation is to localise the Jihadi movement with criminal and militant elements hiding within Pakistan. There is information from Pakistani media sources that ISI's Forward Section 23, which monitored subversive anti-India operations from Pakistan-administered Kashmir (PAK), had been involved in training militants and providing logistics for a proxy war against India. Under duress, primarily from the United States, the ISI reportedly terminated its operations in 2003 by shutting down training camps and operation offices in the region. It supposedly moved its anti-India infrastructure to Karachi to continue its agenda (South Asia Tribune, 2003). Other sources have also claimed that the ISI's Karachi-based 408 Detachment, which oversees terror operations in Maharashtra, Goa, and Gujarat, is behind the whole Karachi Project, which nurtured the Indian Mujahideen (Outlook India, 2008).

After months of speculation on the leadership hierarchy of IM, investigating agencies finally sketched a relatively clear picture of who's who in IM. Earlier, it had been speculated that the group's leader was Abdul Subhan Qureshi (Taqueer), a former SIMI cadre and software engineer by profession. However, it was later concluded that it was in fact Sadiq Israr Sheikh of Azamgarh who was behind the founding of the first home-grown Indian jihadi outfit. Sheikh, a former SIMI member and an electronics engineer by profession, has been identified as the co-founder and leader of the IM. Sheikh is alleged to have contacts with LeT in Pakistan through his brother-in-law, Mujahid Salim (Roul, 2009). The anti-terrorism squad of the Maharashtra police interrogated Sheikh regarding his role in the group's July 2006 serial train blasts in Mumbai. Sheikh has described how the group planted seven cookers filled with explosives on the train before getting off in advance of the blasts. Sheikh's confession also indicated IM's hand in the March 2006 attack on the Sankat Mochan temple in Varanasi. Besides Sadiq Israr, Riyaz Bhatkal Iqbal, Bhatkal, Atif Amin, and Abdul Subhan Qureshi are some of the senior commanders of IM (Gupta, 2011). The most surprising revelation has been the involvement of many IT professionals in IM's activities, including wealthy professionals like Asghar Peerbhoy, Salman Kadar Shaikhand, and Asif Bashiruddin Shaikh, who have played pivotal roles in generating funds for the outfit and planning attacks. Peerbhoy, believed to have headed IM's media wing, reportedly worked for Yahoo.com before being arrested by the Mumbai Anti-Terror Squad in October 2008 (Indian Express, 2009).

JIHADI OPERATIONS IN INDIA

It is open to debate how and when IM's formalisation as a group took place, but it is highly probable that some present cadres of IM had been involved in attacks along with bigger entities like Lashkar-e-Taiba or Harakat ul Jihad Islami (HuJI) within India earlier, though those attacks could not be attributable to IM as an organised entity. While it is difficult to establish the actual date when IM was formalised as a group, the name emerged for the first time when the group claimed responsibility for the serial blasts on court premises in three major cities of the North Indian State of Uttar Pradesh: Varanasi, Faizabad (Ajodhya), and Lucknow on November 23, 2007 (News18, 2007). Subsequently, the police arrested alleged Harkat-ul Jihad Islami (HuJI)-linked operatives Tariq Qazmi, a Unani doctor at Azamgarh, and Khalid Mujahid, a madrasa teacher at Jaunpur, in connection with the blasts at Faizabad and Lucknow courts. Soon after, this hitherto unknown Indian Mujahideen carried out a string of urban terrorist attacks across India in 2008. The IM claimed responsibility for the blasts in Jaipur (Rajasthan) on May 13, 2008; Bengaluru on July 25, 2008; Ahmadabad (Gujarat) on July 26, 2008; Delhi on September 13, 2008; and serial explosions in northeast India's Assam and Tripura states in October 2008. The Assam and Tripura attacks were claimed by the previously unknown Islamic Security Force-Indian Mujahideen (ISF-IM), which appeared to be IM's north-eastern franchise and in all likelihood in active collusion with the Bangladesh-based HuJI (Economic Times, 2008).

A major breakthrough was achieved in unravelling the IM's Jihadi network on September 19, 2008, when police carried out a search and sweep operation in Jamia Nagar, New Delhi, known as the Batla House encounter, which terminated two core Indian Mujahideen leaders, Atif Amin and Muhammad Sajid. Subsequent investigations also unfolded IM's well-entrenched North India module, in and around Delhi and nearby Pilkhuwa and Azamgarh (Uttar Pradesh).

The countrywide serial blasts of 2008 and the aftermath of Lashkar e Taiba's November 26–28 Mumbai operations led to widespread crackdowns and arrests that left IM's pan-Indian network disrupted but for a brief period. The IM raised its ugly head once again after almost 14 long months of hiatus. They succeeded in perpetrating a major attack in the western Indian city of Pune, targeting the popular "German Bakery," frequented by both Indians and foreigners. In total, 17 people were killed and over 50 were injured, including 4 Iranians, 2 Sudanese, 1 Taiwanese, 1 German, and 2 Nepalese nationals (Times of India, 2010). The epicentre of the blast was located in Koregaon Park, near the Osho (Rajneesh cult) Ashram and a Jewish Chabad house. Pune has been a stronghold of IM's media wing under Ashgar Peerbhoy (Rediff, 2008). Also, Lashkar-e-Taiba's David Coleman Headley, who is presently under FBI custody, is believed to have visited the Osho Ashram during his previous visit and provided possible leads on the location. The other interesting fact about the Pune blast, which emerged later during the investigation, was that there was direct collusion between Lashkar-e-Taiba and the Indian Mujahideen. Zabihuddin Ansari (Abu Jundal), who was part of LeT's November 2008 Mumbai operations, revealed that the Pune German Bakery blast conspiracy, though hatched way back in 2008, could not be executed as the LeT leadership in Pakistan wanted otherwise. According to him, the LeT postponed the Pune attack and decided to carry out the 26/11 attacks first. This blast can be considered part of the so-called Karachi Project, where both LeT and IM conspired to Indianize the Jihadi terror movement (Roul, 2010). Shortly after the Pune attack, IM operatives attempted another major attack in Mumbai. However, the Mumbai police's Anti-Terrorism Squad (ATS) foiled it by arresting two IM terrorists identified as Abdul Latif and Riyaz Ali, who were allegedly planning to attack the headquarters of the Indian oil major ONGC, along with the bustling Mangaldas Market and Borivali's Thakkar Mall in Mumbai (NDTV, 2010).

The IM struck again, but with little success, in mid-April of that year (2010), targeting the Chinnaswamy Stadium in Bengaluru. There were two low-intensity explosions outside gate number 12 of the stadium that left nearly eight people injured. Another bomb planted at Gate Number 8 was, however, defused well in time (Deccan Herald, 2010). To avenge the Delhi encounter, the IM launched an attack exactly two years after the Batla House incidents, attacking foreign tourists in Delhi's Jama Masjid locality on September 13, 2010. The group's attempt to detonate a car bomb failed in that area due to a technical snag. In a message, IM indirectly claimed responsibility for the Jama Masjid attacks, blatantly dedicating the attacks to the martyrs of the Batla House events and threatening India against hosting the Commonwealth Games. IM's mail was signed by one Al-Arbi and sent from the email address al.arbi999123@gmail.com. (Mid-Day, 2010).

The holy city of Varanasi (Benaras) in Uttar Pradesh once again became a target of IM's growing anti-India and anti-Hindu anger. On December 7, an explosion occurred at Sheetla Ghat during the spectacular evening prayer ritual, when hundreds of people had gathered to observe the event on the banks of the Ganga River. The bomb blast, although of low intensity, killed a child and injured nearly 30 people. It was largely symbolic. It was an attack directly targeted at Hindu religious sentiment.

IM's biggest strike came in mid-July 2011, when a series of blasts shook India's commercial capital, Mumbai (Maharashtra). The 3 synchronised explosions killed at least 24 people at Dadar's Kabutarkhana, the Opera House, and Zaveri Bazaar. India's intelligence apparatus was caught unaware as IM's operatives managed to strike again in the heart of Mumbai despite the stepped-up security measures that were put in place following the November 2008 Mumbai siege. This time, surprisingly, no terrorist organisation claimed responsibility, perhaps intending to complicate the investigation procedures or to delay follow-up actions by the agencies. For the first time, the Indian government and intelligence agencies refrained from naming any Pakistan-based terror group. However, after a while, Indian government officials emphasised the involvement of a home-grown terror module in the blasts. With the arrests of two IM operatives, Naqi Ahmed and Nadeem Akhtar, from Bihar, Mumbai police unearthed IM's Bihar unit and its links to the mastermind Yasin Bhatkal, who is at this time the chief of the terrorist group in India and still at large. Additionally, further investigations led to a Pakistani angle to the whole episode as a couple of bombers hailed from the neighbouring country (Times of India, 2012).

In 2011, Delhi witnessed a couple of bombing incidents, both targeting the Delhi High Court, one in May and the other in September that year. A relatively smaller explosion that occurred outside Delhi High Court Gate No. 7 on May 25 did not cause any injuries or fatalities. However, the September blast was powerful enough to kill 13 people and injure nearly 80 others (India Today, 2011). The explosion was triggered in the reception area near Gate No. 5 of the Delhi High Court. Two emails followed subsequently, one from the email address "harkatuljihadi2011@gmail.com," claiming that HuJI (Harkat-ul-Jihadi Islami) was responsible for the blast at the Delhi high court. The email said, "Our demand is that Afzal Guru's death sentence should be repealed immediately, as we would target major high courts and the Supreme Court of India" (Times of India, 2010). The other email from email-id "chotoominani5@gmail.com" claimed that the Indian Mujahideen (IM) was behind the blast and that the group would soon attack the city of

Ahmadabad (Gujarat). The sender of the email, identified as Chotoo, denied any HuJI role in the blast. It also threatened to strike at a shopping mall on September 13. The email was traced to Ahmadabad (Times of India, 2011).

In the aftermath of this event, the country (except the Jammu and Kashmir region) experienced a complete lull in terrorist activities, especially by the IM, with a single exception in August 2012. Four low-intensity blasts took place in Pune on August 1 at the bustling Junglee Maharaj Road, injuring only one person. The first blast took place outside the Balgandharva auditorium, the second one outside the popular fast-food joint McDonald's, and the other two blasts were reported near Dena Bank and Garware Chowk in the same vicinity (Hindu, 2012).

One significant terrorist attack by the IM took place in 2013. The February 21 twin blasts in Hyderabad (Andhra Pradesh) killed 17 people and left over 100 others injured. The bombs exploded in the Dilsukhnagar area. Indian Mujahideen was the prime suspect in this case, as investigations found that IM had already surveyed the area in Hyderabad (Times of India, 2013). For this act of terrorism, five senior IM operatives, including IM co-founder Yasin Bhatkal, were awarded the death penalty by a special National Investigating Agency court. This was one of the first cases in which operatives of the IM were convicted (Economic Times, 2018). The other IM signature strike took place that year in early July, targeting the Mahabodhi Temple at Bodh Gaya, where at least ten bombs exploded in the Buddhist Temple complex. The Special National Investigation Agency has arrested five Indian Mujahideen operatives: Imtiaz Ansari, Haider Ali, Mujib Ullah, Omair Siddiqui, and Azharuddin Qureshi (India Today, 2018).

Almost all of the Indian Mujahedeen's email communications contain four important issues that reportedly prompted the IM to carry out acts of revenge against India and its Hindu population: Babri Masjid demolition (1991), Godhra riots (2002), Kashmir issue, and Batla House encounter (2008). There are other issues of concern for the Indian Mujahideen, as its emails suggest, that include the Indian Judiciary, the Muslim Ummah, the English media, etc. (Subrahmanian et al., 2013).

In the very short span of its existence, the Indian Mujahedeen resorted to various means and methods for attacking the Indian state. From multiple coordinated bombings to targeted shootouts, IM used all available local resources to target crowded marketplaces, religious sites, and other civilian targets to maximise the fatalities and at the same time instill fear within the populace. IM operatives were trained to use and manufacture improvised explosive devices from ammonium nitrate and hydrogen peroxide, all locally available on the open market. There were a number of IM training camps held in various forest locations in South India during 2007 and 2008 where the presence of former SIMI cadres and Pakistani-origin nationals was reported. As per available media reports, between April and December 2007, at least six training camps were held at Castle Rock and Dharwad in Karnataka, at Charol near Indore (Madhya Pradesh), and at Nagaman Jungles (Kerala). In early 2008, there was a camp in the Pawagarh jungles near Vadodara (Gujarat).

Undoubtedly, the arrest of IM cadres from different locations demonstrates the geographical spread of the terror network that now spans the length and breadth of India. At certain points in time, the IM as a cohesive group was evidently active in Delhi, Uttar Pradesh, Gujarat, West Bengal, Maharashtra, Karnataka, and Kerala. According to a Mumbai Crime Branch charge sheet, internally, the IM established several subunits to carry out special operations. For example, the Shahabuddin Ghouri Brigade, which was reportedly headed by Amir Raza, is presently inside Pakistan. The other wings were named after Muhammad Ghaznavi (for strikes in Northern India) and the al-Zarqawi brigade (for strikes on VVIPs). IM also had a robust media wing under Mansoor Peerbhoy, which was headquartered in Pune, Maharashtra. Many of IM's top leaders have fled to Pakistan and Middle Eastern countries like the UAE and Saudi Arabia. One case is that of Faish Mehmood, one of the founding members of the Indian Mujahideen, who was deported by the Saudi Arabian government to India. He was investigated for his role in both the Chinnaswamy Stadium blasts in Bengaluru and the Jama Masjid shooting incident. He has reportedly confessed that he was one of the founding members of IM. The charge sheet filed in court names 18 IM suspects, including Riyaz Bhatkal, Iqbal Bhatkal (also known as the Shahbandri brothers), and Yahsin Bhatkal (Ahmed Siddibappa).

IM REMNANTS AND TRANSNATIONAL JIHAD

Though there are no direct operational or logistical linkages between IM and the Islamic State (IS), several fugitive IM militants joined or pledged allegiance to the IS-led Caliphate in 2014. The most important among them were the two brothers, Abdul Qadir Sultan Armar and Safi Armar, who were part of the Indian Mujahideen group and operated under the command of Riyaz and Iqbal Bhatkal. Following the countrywide crackdown on the IM network in 2008, Safi Armar and his elder brother Sultan Armar both fled to the port city of Karachi in Pakistan and established another India-centric militant network called Ansar-ut Tawhid fi Bilad al-Hind (AuT), which pledged its allegiance to the Islamic State and its leader Al Baghdadi (Al Isabah Media, 2014). Mostly comprising militants and criminal fugitives of Indian origin, AuT campaigned and scouted people to participate in the ongoing jihad in both the Syrian and Afghan war theatres through its media arm, Al-Isabah Media. Their role as IM operatives surfaced in mid-2014 when the Anti-Terrorist Squad (ATS) of the Jaipur Police traced their involvement in several attacks in the country. A red-corner notice was issued by Interpol in September 2014 against Safi Armar for criminal conspiracy against the state, raising funds, and recruiting for terrorist acts, among other things (CBI (India) 2014).

In late January 2016, India's elite anti-terrorism agency, the National Investigation Agency (NIA), stumbled upon an unknown extremist network, the Junood al-Khilafa-e-Hind (JKH), known to be sympathetic to the transnational Jihadi group Islamic State (formerly ISIS). With the arrest of nearly 14 suspects in a countrywide search and sweep operation, investigators identified the ringleader as Muhammad Shafi Armar (New Indian Express, January 22). With the revelation, the NIA managed to apprehend JKH's core operatives, such as its leader Amir-e-Hind (India Chief) Mudabbir Sheikh from Maharashtra, and unravel a sinister design, ostensibly at the behest of Shafi Armar, to target vital installations, security personnel, and foreigners in the country as part of the Islamic State's violent campaign in the region. At the time of their respective deaths, both Sultan and Safi Armar, former Indian Mujahideen operatives, acted as IS recruiters. Sultan Armar, also known as Abdur Rahman Nadwi Al Hindi, was reportedly killed while fighting near Kobane on the Syria-Turkey border on March 6, 2015 (One India, 2015). Following the death of his elder brother, Safi Armar took the reins of the AuT and its media unit, attempting to expand its network inside India by pumping money and propaganda of Jihadi materials online to organise Indians under the JKH. Safi was designated a global terrorist by the U.S. State Department in June 2017. However, a few months later, the Islamic State's media agency Amaq claimed Shafi Armar as a suicide bomber in Syria's Raqqa.

On May 19, 2016, an audio-visual message from the Islamic State featured its India brigade purportedly located in the "Homs" province (Wilayat Homs) titled "The Bilad al Hind (Land of India): Between Pain and Hope" (Roul, 2019). The message urged Indian Muslims to travel to Syria (Hijra) and join the Islamic State. The message threatened to wage jihad against India and to take revenge for the atrocities committed against Indian Muslims in Kashmir, for the demolition of Babri Masjid, and for the communal riots in Gujarat and Muzaffarnagar. The video message was, of course, aimed at recruiting more foreign fighters (in this case, India) and showing how volunteers can live in peace and harmony in the Caliphate (Syria and Iraq) while fighting for the cause of all Ah. At least one former Indian Mujahadeen fugitive, Abu Rashid Ahmed, has described how the IM was in trouble following the Battla House encounter and how they were forced to flee India due to security measures. He too explained, "With Allah's grace, we reached Khurasan, fought alongside Mujahideen, and later travelled to Syria to join. He also threatened India with more revenge attacks, boasting about Mumbai serial train blasts, Gujarat, Delhi, and Jaipur serial blasts. He also vowed to fight and attack until polytheism was destroyed in India. His message clearly stated the two immigrations (hijrat) that IM militants have made since 2008: first to Pakistan-Afghanistan (Khurasan) and then to Al Sham (Syria)."

CONCLUSION

For the last several years, more precisely since 2014, the Indian Mujahideen have remained dormant and in disarray. After the arrest of Yasin Bhatkal in August 2013, one of the key leaders of IM, the group is seemingly in hibernating mode. However, despite the arrest of many IM operatives and their revelation that the IM's top leadership is still holed up abroad, it has been suggested that they are looking for an opportune moment to return or find a way to wage jihad against India again, co-opting transnational jihadist groups such as Al Qaeda or Islamic State's regional affiliates. Since anti-India jihadi elements are still alive in neighbouring countries such as Pakistan and Bangladesh, a revival or resurgence of the Indian Mujahideen is not remote.

References

Ahmed, I. (1997, April 01). A new agenda for Muslim radicals. *Times of India*. Retrieved from http://www.hvk.org/1997/0497/0009.html.

Ahmed, I. (2005). Between moderation and radicalization: Transnational interactions of Jamaat-e-Islami of India. *Global Networks*, *5*(3). 10.1111/j.1471-0374.2005.00119.x.

Ahmed, I. (2006). The state in Islamist thought. *ISIM Review*, *18*(Autumn, 2006), 12–13.

Ahmed, I. (2009). *Islamism and democracy in India: The transformation of Jamaat-e-Islami*. Princeton University Press.

Al Isabah Media. (2014). Caliphate & our responsibilities' and announcement of Bayah from Ansar ut Tawheed Fi Bilad Al Hind to Caliph Abu Bakr Al Baghdadi. Retrieved From https://archive.org/details/KhilafataurHumariZimmedariya.

Asian Age. (2012, July 26). SIMI backbone of terror outfits: Abu Jundal. Retrieved from http://archive.asianage.com/india/simi-backbone-terror-outfits-abu-jundal-865.

CBI, India. (2014). Red notice: Mohammad Shafi Armar. Retrieved from http://cbi.nic.in/rnotice/A-7019-9-2014.pdf.

Deccan Herald. (2010, April 17). Blasts force IPL out of Bangalore. Retrieved from https://www.deccanherald.com/content/64501/blasts-force-ipl-bangalore.html.

DNA India. (2016, October 31). Bhopal jailbreak: All you need to know about Students Islamic Movement of India (SIMI). Retrieved from https://www.dnaindia.com/india/report-bhopal-jailbreak-all-you-need-to-know-about-students-islamic-movement-of-india-simi-2269039.

Economic Times. (2008, October 31). ISF-Indian Mujahideen claims responsibility for Assam blasts. Retrieved from https://economictimes.indiatimes.com/news/politics-and-nation/isf-indian-mujahideen-claims-responsibility-for-assam-blasts/articleshow/3659491.cms.

Economic Times. (2018, July 14). Hyderabad blasts: 5 Indian Mujahideen operatives sentenced to death. Retrieved from https://economictimes.indiatimes.com/news/defence/hyderabad-blasts-5-im-operatives-sentenced-to-death/articleshow/56065693.cms?from=mdr.

Engineer, A.A. (1980). *The Islamic state*. Vikas Publication.

Gupta, S. (2011). *Indian Mujahideen: The enemy within*. Hachette India.

Hindustan Times. (2008, September 20). SIMI, IM new faces of Lashkar-e-Taiba. Retrieved from https://www.hindustantimes.com/delhi/simi-im-new-faces-of-lashkar-e-taiba/story-MbiFFg9xmkaCg2HXTuxCYP.html.

India Today. (2001, April 2). Our Madarsas are not nurseries of terror: SIMI leader Safdar Nagori. Retrieved from https://www.indiatoday.in/magazine/interview/story/20010402-our-madarsas-are-not-nurseries-of-terror-simi-leader-safdar-nagori-775397-2001-04-01

India Today. (2011, September 08). Delhi HC blast toll rises to 13 with death of 65-year-old engineer. Retrieved from https://www.indiatoday.in/india/north/story/delhi-high-court-blast-toll-140620-2011-09-08.

India Today. (2012, November 7). Our Madrasas are not nurseries of terror: SIMI leader Safdar Nagori. Retrieved from https://www.indiatoday.in/magazine/interview/story/20010402-our-madarsas-are-not-nurseries-of-terror-simi-leader-safdar-nagori-775397-2001-04-02.

India Today. (2018, June 01). All 5 accused in 2013 Bodh Gaya blasts awarded life imprisonment. Retrieved from https://www.indiatoday.in/india/story/all-5-accused-in-2013-bodh-gaya-blasts-awarded-life-imprisonment-1247673-2018-06-01.

Indian Express. (2008, September 30). Is Indian Mujahideen actually the Asif Reza commando force?. Retrieved from http://archive.indianexpress.com/news/is-indian-mujahideen-actually-the-asif-reza-commando-force-/367590/.

Indian Express. (2009, February 05). Peerbhoy unlikely to be made approver. Retrieved from http://archive.indianexpress.com/news/peerbhoy-unlikely-to-be-made-approver/419504/.

Indian Express. (2012, June 27). Ansari trained 90 at Lashkar camp. Retrieved from https://indianexpress.com/article/news-archive/web/ansari-trained-90-at-lashkar-camp/.

Indian Express. (2015, April 30). 2005 Varanasi blast: Seven years after cops filed closure report, ATS begins fresh probe. Retrieved from, https://indianexpress.com/article/cities/lucknow/2005-varanasi-blast-seven-years-after-cops-filed-closure-report-ats-begins-fresh-probe/.

Indian Express. (2018, January 24). A short history of the Indian Mujahideen. Retrieved from https://indianexpress.com/article/explained/a-short-history-of-the-indian-mujahideen-terror-attacks-abdul-subhan-qureshi-5036679.

MHA (Government of India Notification). (2002, April 08). The unlawful activities (prevention) tribunal, New Delhi order on students Islamic movement of India. Retrieved from https://mha.gov.in/sites/default/files/BanJudgment_09042002.pdf.

Mid Day. (2010, September 20). IM threatens attack on Commonwealth games. https://www.mid-day.com/articles/im-threatens-attack-on-cwg/95525.

NDTV. (2010, June 04). Indian Mujahideen: 35th terrorist organization to face ban. Retrieved from https://www.ndtv.com/india-news/indian-mujahideen-35th-terrorist-organisation-to-face-ban-419936.

NDTV News. (2010, March 14). Terror plot foiled in Mumbai, men with Pak links held. Retrieved from https://www.ndtv.com/india-news/terror-plot-foiled-in-mumbai-men-with-pak-links-held-412702.

New Indian Express. (2013, March 02). Maqbool says recruits streaming into Indian Mujahideen. Retrieved from https://www.newindianexpress.com/states/andhra-pradesh/2013/mar/02/maqbool-says-recruits-streaming-into-indian-mujahideen-454909.html.

New Indian Express. (2016, January 22). Terror crackdown: In countrywide Swoop, NIA picks up 14 youths. Retrieved from http://www.newindianexpress.com/nation/Terror-Crackdown-In-Countrywide-Swoop-NIA-Picks-up-14-Youths/2016/01/22/article3239660.ece.

News 18. (2007, November 23). Indian Mujahideen claims responsibility for UP blasts. Retrieved from https://www.news18.com/news/india/blast-responsibilty-276967.html.

News18. (2008, July 28). Indian Mujahideen cover for international terror groups. Retrieved from https://www.news18.com/videos/india/indian-mujahadeen-293576.html.

News18. (2012, July 6). Indian Mujahideen banned in the UK. Retrieved from https://www.news18.com/news/india/indian-mujahideen-banned-in-the-uk-486096.html.

News18. (2018, August 31). Smartphones, SIM cards seized from underworld Don Aftab Ansari at Kolkata's Alipore Jail. Retrieved from https://www.news18.com/news/india/smartphones-sim-cards-seized-from-underworld-don-aftab-ansari-at-kolkatas-alipore-jail-1863511.html.

NIA. (2012). Activities of Indian Mujahideen, Case No, RC-06/2012/NIA/DLI. Retrieved from https://www.nia.gov.in/case-detail.htm?38

One India. (2015, March 20). Indian ISIS recruits, Armar, Shahnawaz, Tanki reportedly die in Kobane. Retrieved from https://www.oneindia.com/india/indian-isis-recruits-armar-shahnawaz-tanki-reportedly-die-in-kobane-1689918.html.

Outlook India. (2008, July 26). The rise of jihad, revenge of Gujarat. Retrieved from https://www.outlookindia.com/national/the-rise-of-jihad-revenge-of-gujarat-news-238039.

Rediff. (2002, February 15): Ansari admits to taking Lashkar's help. Retrieved from https://www.rediff.com/news/2002/feb/14ansari.htm.

Rediff. (2008 October 07). Indian Mujahideen's media cell busted. Retrieved from https://www.rediff.com/news/2008/oct/06terror.htm.

Reuters. (2011, September 15). U.S. names Indian Mujahideen to terror blacklist. Retrieved from https://www.reuters.com/article/us-india-usa-mujahideen/u-s-names-indian-mujahideen-to-terror-blacklist-idUSTRE78E3CK20110915.

Roul, A. (2006). Students Islamic movement of India: A profile. *Terrorism Monitor*, *4*(7), 8–10.

Roul, A. (2009). India's home-grown Jihadi threat: A profile of the Indian Mujahideen. *Terrorism Monitor*, *7*(4), 9–11. Accessible at https://jamestown.org/wp-content/uploads/2009/03/TM_007_4_03.pdf?x44765.

Roul, A. (2010). Hybrid, homegrown and transnational: The Indian Mujahideen and the Islamist terror matrix. *Terrorism Monitor*, *8*(3), 9–11. Accessible at https://

jamestown.org/wp-content/uploads/2010/01/TM_008_3_04.pdf?x44765.

Roul, A. (2010, April). After Pune, details emerge on the Karachi project and its threat to India. *CTC Sentinel, 3*(4), 6–8. Accessible at https://ctc.usma.edu/app/uploads/2010/08/CTCSentinel-Vol3Iss4-art3.pdf.

Roul, A. (2019). Islamic state-inspired extremist threat looms large in India. *Terrorism Monitor, 17*(3), 5–6. Accessible at https://jamestown.org/wp-content/uploads/2019/02/TM-Feb.-8-2019-Issue-.pdf?x44765.

Shahzad, S.S. (2003, November, 30-December 6). Ceasefire will not hold, with same game, new rules. *South Asia Tribune*, 69. Accessible at https://antisystemic.org/satribune/www.satribune.com/archives/nov30_dec6_03/opinion_saleem.htm.

Sikand, Y. (2001, October 06). Countering fundamentalism: Beyond the banon SIMI. *Economic and Political Weekly, 36*(40), 3803.

Subrahmanian, V.S., Mannes, A., Roul, A., & Raghavan, R.K. (2013). *Indian Mujahideen: Computational analysis and public policy*. Springer.

The Hindu. (2012, August 01). Four low-intensity blasts in Pune; one injured. https://www.thehindu.com/news/national/other-states/four-lowintensity-blasts-in-pune-one-injured/article3713166.ece.

The Pioneer. (2003, July 21). SIMI's Nagori meets Maulana too. Accessible at http://www.hvk.org/2003/0703/166.html.

Times of India. (2002, January 27). Asif Reza Khan: The making of a militant. Retrieved from https://timesofindia.indiatimes.com/india/Asif-Reza-Khan-The-making-of-a-militant/articleshow/453987114.cms.

Times of India. (2010, February 28). German bakery blast toll rises to 17. Retrieved from https://timesofindia.indiatimes.com/city/pune/German-Bakery-blast-toll-rises-to-17/articleshow/5626517.cms.

Times of India. (2011, September 7). HuJI claims responsibility for Delhi high court blast. Retrieved from https://timesofindia.indiatimes.com/india/HuJI-claims-responsibility-for-Delhi-high-court-blast/articleshow/9896388.cms.

Times of India. (2011, September 08). Now, 'Chotoo' of Indian Mujahideen claims responsibility for Delhi terror blast. Retrieved from https://timesofindia.indiatimes.com/india/Now-Chotoo-of-Indian-Mujahideen-claims-responsibility-for-Delhi-terror-blast/articleshow/9911655.cms.

Times of India. (2012, June 05). Pakistan bomber helped 13/7 accused steal vehicles: Police. https://timesofindia.indiatimes.com/city/mumbai/Pakistan-bomber-helped-13/7-accused-steal-vehicles-Police/articleshow/13828914.cms.

Times of India. (2012, November 24). Indian Mujahideen founder Amir Reza Khan still hiding in Pak: NIA. Retrieved from https://timesofindia.indiatimes.com/india/Indian-Mujahideen-founder-Amir-Reza-Khan-still-hiding-in-Pak-NIA/articleshow/17343051.cms.

Times of India. (2013, February 17). Jama Masjid case: Fasih Mahmood charge sheeted. Retrieved from https://timesofindia.indiatimes.com/city/delhi/Jama-Masjid-case-Fasih-Mahmood-chargesheeted/articleshow/18535811.cms.

Times of India. (2013, February 23). Indian Mujahideen hand becomes clearer in Hyderabad blasts. Retrieved from https://timesofindia.indiatimes.com/india/Indian-Mujahideen-hand-becomes-clearer-in-Hyderabad-blasts/articleshow/18635772.cms.

65

THE INDIAN MAOISTS

Naxalbari, Lalgarh, Dantewada, and Beyond

Uddipan Mukherjee

INTRODUCTION

India's .Maoist movement is one of the oldest communist insurgencies in the world. Commencing in the tumultuous 1960s, it paid allegiance to Mao Tse-tung's ideology as well as personality. Nevertheless, the movement witnessed several crests and troughs before emerging in its present avatar, led by the Communist Party of India (Maoist), formed as an outcome of a merger in 2004. This chapter traces the genesis, growth, and spread of the movement and aligns it with the ideology and operational flexibilities adopted by the insurgents over a span of more than five decades. The chapter also focuses on issues like the recruitment methodology of the insurgents and their possible foreign connections. After deliberating on the role of intellectuals in the movement, the chapter projects a possible future trajectory for the insurgency.

ANECDOTE I (OCTOBER 2020: A LEAF FROM PERSONAL EXPERIENCE)

Our grey-coloured sedan was easing its way through the dense traffic of Kolkata, the capital of India's eastern state of West Bengal. I glanced at the person who was in command of our vehicle. A lean young man with bulging eyeballs, appearing to be in his twenties, was manoeuvring the vehicle well.

> "*May I know your name?*"
>
> "*Raju*", came the stern reply after an initial pause. His tone indicated that he was least interested in conversing with me. However, without being discouraged, I continued:
>
> "*Where do you stay?*"
>
> "*In the garage*". He replied promptly.
>
> "*No, I mean where is your native place?*"
>
> "*Lalgarh.*"

Lalgarh saw a Maoist resurrection in West Bengal from November 2008 onward. The grip of the Maoist insurgents, however, ended with the death of their flamboyant leader Mallojula Koteshwara Rao aka Kishenji in 2011:

> "Were *the Maoists were very much active in Lalgarh?*"
>
> "*Yes, they were*", came his sharp reply.
>
> "*Why the Maoists made inroads into Lalgarh?*"
>
> "*The Marxist party's militiamen [read 'harmads'] had turned the lives of the common folk into hell; naturally, the Maoists filled up the political and social space in Lalgarh. It was as simple as that.*"

ANECDOTE II

On January 7, 2011, a few villagers of Netai (a village in Lalgarh) gathered near a house that allegedly had sheltered some "harmads." After some argumentation, the "harmads" started firing indiscriminately at the villagers. According to

DOI: 10.4324/9780429426063-74

the initial media reports, 6 people were killed and close to 15 were injured. Interestingly, the "harmads" were supposed to have been aiding the Village Protection Groups (VPG) so as to thwart the Maoist insurgency in the area.

It has been over a decade now. Still, the events at Lalgarh have not become merely archival. On November 2, 2008, at Shalboni, near Lalgarh, in the West Midnapore district of West Bengal, the convoy of then-state Chief Minister Buddhadeb Bhattacharjee struck a landmine. He was returning from an inspection of the proposed steel plant site of the Jindal Group. Then Union Minister Ram Vilas Paswan was also in the convoy. Both were unhurt.

After the attack on Bhattacharjee's convoy, police from Lalgarh and adjoining areas led a joint operation on November 5, 2008, in the villages of Choto Pelia, Boro Pelia, Bashber, and Kata Pahari, all in the Lalgarh area. There were allegations of alleged police brutalities in Chhoto Pelia village (Sanhati, 2008).

The Maoists could hardly offer amelioration to the Lalgarh adivasis (tribals). In the beginning, the Maoists utilised the Peoples' Committee against Police Atrocities (PCPA) as their frontal organisation, which seemingly had a "tribal" look to it, apparently devoid of any Maoist colour. However, one of the PCPA leaders, Chattradhar Mahato, was arrested on alleged Maoist links. Further, PCPA activists were booked by the Central Bureau of Investigation (CBI) in the wake of the involvement of the Maoists in a train derailment (PTI, 2010).

The Left Front (led by the Marxists) government in West Bengal, at the other end, was pretty much complacent insofar as a Maoist uprising was concerned, mostly because they had been entrenched in the polity of the state for over three decades without facing a substantial challenge. For instance, the lack of a Jehanabad jailbreak (Bhatia, 2005) or the absence of a Nayagarh armoury raid (Routray, 2008) had abetted the confidence of the Marxists. Moreover, they wished to manage the Maoist menace with an innovative plan – by ignoring the Maoists. Thus, when the Union Home Ministry advocated banning the Communist Party of India (Maoist) [CPI-M], the Leftists in West Bengal made an inordinate delay in responding to the "liberation" of Lalgarh by the Maoists.

APPROXIMATELY A DECADE LATER

While ranking India as the fourth-worst terrorism-hit country, the US State Department report described the CPI-M as the world's sixth-deadliest terror organisation (WION, 2019). In its 2018 Country Report on Terrorism, the US State Department blamed the CPI-M for the killing of 311 people in 177 terror incidents (WION, 2019). The US Country Report ranked the CPI-M as the deadliest terror organisation globally after the Taliban (Afghanistan), IS (Islamic State), Al-Shabaab, Boko Haram, and the Communist Party of the Philippines (WION, 2019).

According to the 2018–19 annual report released by India's Ministry of Home Affairs, left-wing extremism (LWE)-related violence underwent a substantial dip. Even the geographical spread of LWE had shrunk. The report states that "there has been a 26.7 percent reduction in violent incidents and a 39.5 percent reduction in LWE-related deaths since end-2013" (MHA, 2019).

NAXALITES: GENESIS, CAUSE, AND IMPACT

After an aborted attempt at a communist insurrection just after India's independence (Bandyopadhyay, 2008), the existing five-decade-long Maoist/communist insurgency began in March 1967 with a sharecropper named Bigul Kisan in the Naxalbari area of the northern part of West Bengal being attacked by armed hooligans of a local wealthy peasant when he had gone to till the land (Banerjee, 2008). A confrontation erupted, as by then the local communists had energised the tribal-peasant bands with the speeches and writings of Charu Mazumdar, the communist ideologue of class annihilation. In fact, the 1960s saw a severe food shortage in India. There was an acute foreign exchange crisis too, exacerbated by the inflated defence expenditures in the wake of the wars with China (in 1962) and Pakistan (in 1965). The Consumer Price Index inflation rate in India was 17% in 1964 and 14% in 1966 (Chatterjee, 2010). As fallout, violent agitations often disturbed the country. Marxist accounts and narratives explained these conflicts and the repressive use of state power as systematic features of Indian democracy (Chatterjee, 2010).

The crux of the problem in 1960s West Bengal was land (Banerjee, 2008). The United Front-Left Front coalition government had pledged to bring about land reforms, a rather contentious issue the communists had been championing since the 1940s. Incidentally, a veteran Marxist peasant leader, Harekrishna Konar, went on to become the minister in charge of land and land revenue. He came out with a policy of distributing surplus land among the landless and also promised to prohibit the eviction of sharecroppers. However, as Banerjee writes, the Marxists were unsure of the modus operandi of recovering the land transferred by landlords under the "benami" (without name) head. Then the Marxist government of West Bengal, facing the allegation of revisionism from within its own quarters and outwardly bound by its pro-poor image, found it hard to manage the issue of land distribution. The legal hassles were also not easy to circumvent.

Since 1967, the Maoist movement in India has seen several ups and downs, bitter internecine showdowns, severe state repressions, splits, mergers, and finally a mega-merger in 2004. But the central theme of the Naxalites [a word derived from Naxalbari] has remained almost the same. They have viewed independent India as a multi-national country and supported the right of "different" nationalities to self-determination, including secession. Moreover, the Naxals have clearly stated that the ruling bourgeoisie is comprador, Indian independence was fake, and India has a semi-colonial and semi-feudal status. Thus, in order to establish a people's government in India, according to the insurgents, Mao Zedong's guerrilla warfare tactics have to be employed, and a protracted armed agrarian revolution is the only feasible solution.

1967 was an eventful year: the death of a student in Berlin in a fracas with the police, which later reached a climax with the rise of the Baader-Meinhoff gang and its series of abductions and high-jackings; the death of Cuban hero Che Guevara in a Bolivian ravine; and finally the commencement of the historic Naxalbari uprising in India. The late 1960s and especially 1966–68 were a period in which modern history boasts of revolutions cutting across regions and continents and a phase when student agitation gained unprecedented ground. Whether it was Berlin, Paris, or Calcutta, intellectual stimulus orchestrated student movements that were highly radicalised in thought and action. Undoubtedly, the zealot philosophers Frantz Fanon, Herbert Marcuse, or Jean-Paul Sartre, to name a few, were responsible for fomenting agitation worldwide!

Fanon passed away due to leukaemia in 1961, but before that, his firebrand writing had created an intellectual ruckus. In "The Wretched of the Earth," Fanon roared: "… this same violence will be vindicated and appropriated when, taking history into their own hands, the colonised swarm into the forbidden cities." Fanon believed, as Peter Reed illuminates, that society had to be transformed and could only be changed through violence. That violence was a personal cathartic – an individual could only find true expression and release in violence (Reed, 1985). The late 1960s were a period of the rise of the "New Left." Marcuse believed that man in Western capitalist society was every bit as enslaved as his counterpart in the totalitarian societies of the Soviet bloc (Reed, 1985). The New Left rejected both western capitalism and Soviet-bred communism.

On March 18, 1967, a peasants' conference was held under the aegis of the CPM's [Communist Party of India – Marxist] Siliguri sub-division in the Darjeeling district of West Bengal. The conference, among other issues, called for the following (Banerjee, 2008):

1. To end the monopoly ownership of land by the landlords.
2. To redistribute land through peasants' committees.
3. To organise and arm the peasants in order to combat the rural reactionaries.

The conference also cautioned the landless to be prepared for a protracted armed struggle. The eviction of Bigul Kisan by a wealthy peasant in spite of a judicial order in his of Kisan acted as the requisite spark for the insurrection. Naxalbari quickly came to enjoy an iconic status among Indian revolutionaries (Guha, 2007). The term "Naxalite" or "Naxal" evoked romanticism at one end of the political spectrum and hatred at the other (Ray, 1987). As Banerjee tells us, Charu Mazumdar was a frail heart patient. However, he emulated the likes of Mao, Guevara, Castro, or perhaps the monstrous Cambodian dictator Pol Pot while unleashing his "Eight Documents" (Mazumdar). He attempted to rationalise the use of violence against the Indian state by positing his "Theory of Annihilation" of class enemies. Mazumdar built the theoretical framework of the movement, which was partly Marxist-Leninist and punctuated with anarchism. Charu Mazumdar, by glorifying violence, inflamed the sentiments of the youth and the subaltern peasants.

The impact of the Naxalite movement was palpable even in the filmography of that period, which brings to the fore strong messages and a portrayal of the existing socio-economic conditions. Oscar-awardee Satyajit Ray's "Pratidwandi" (1970) as a part of his Calcutta Trilogy or Mrinal Sen's much-acclaimed "Calcutta-71" (1971) and "Interview" (1971) depicted the pathos in their unique styles. Bengali novels too rose to the occasion; Magsaysay award winner Mahasweta Devi's 1974 manuscript "Hazaar Churaasir Ma" depicted the turbulent upheaval; it may not be graphically accurate but definitely emotionally piquant. Students from Calcutta's Presidency College and Jadavpur University spilled over into the rural backyards of Bengal to "spread" the revolution – with an apparent Cuban-styled "foco-ism" – without, however, unequivocally accepting the modus operandi. Though the class enemy was not clearly defined, the "annihilation" campaign was on, which was sometimes grotesquely evidenced in the broad daylight murders of subaltern ranks in the police force, often while not on duty and unarmed. Rag-pickers in Calcutta being branded as informers were also not spared the "fasces" in the name of the revolution, or guillotined at the altar of new-found Maoism, which over-enthusiastically claimed "Chairman Mao as Our Chairman," a slogan objected to and refuted by the Chinese leadership.

Alongside the tumultuous demonstration in Calcutta (later Kolkata), the countryside remained the main arena of the movement. Annihilation of usurious landlords through small squad actions – operations that were wrongly termed guerrilla warfare – were carried out with impunity, with the hope that such numerous gory actions would definitely ignite the revolutionary consciousness of the masses. On the contrary, such dissolute actions by the Naxalites only hastened their loss of connectivity with the people and paved the way for their eventual defeat in the first phase of the movement. The party broke up along the pro-mass line and the pro-annihilation line. The chief architect of annihilation theory, Charu Mazumdar, was finally arrested by the Calcutta police on July 16, 1972, and lived barely 12 days thereafter (Banerjee, 2016). Surely, one of the primary reasons for the demise of the movement in its first phase (1967–1972) was the indiscriminate use of violence. Inter-party murders, assassinations of police officials, and torture of the Naxalites (both by the police and the mainstream political party cadres) had created an ambience of fear and the feeling of being in a war zone for the people at large.

The debacle of the Naxalites was due to the lack of armed preparedness and the imperfect development of the People's Liberation Guerrilla Army [PLGA]. Political argumentation was accorded fundamental importance by the ultras, whereas military affairs took a backseat. Kanu Sanyal went to China to learn the art and craft of guerrilla warfare (Lovell, 2019), yet the hastily conducted training was largely inadequate to turn Sanyal and his comrades into competent guerrillas. Sanyal, though he differed ideologically from Mazumdar, wanted to develop mass organisations (frontal or otherwise), while Mazumdar, on the contrary, seems to have favoured the conspiratorial elimination of class enemies. This dichotomy would turn out to be the seeds for the next level of synthesis of the Naxalite/Maoist programme in India. And as Banerjee has described, the movement fizzled away with a "farrango of factions," and gradually the scene, as well as the leadership, rotated outwards from West Bengal to the states of Bihar and Andhra Pradesh. The baton of the race was picked up by two disconnected groups: the Kanhai Chatterjee and Amulya Sen factions, giving rise to the Maoist Communist Centre [MCC] in Bihar, and in Andhra Pradesh, where initially there were three groups led by Nagi Reddy, Chandra Pulla Reddy, and Kondapalli Seetharamayyiah [KS, in short], respectively. In the 1980s, the KS-led People's War [CPI (Marxist-Leninist) (PW)] emerged as the major faction in Andhra Pradesh.

It would be noteworthy to delve into the raison d'etre for the insurrectionary outburst of the Dalits (designated as Scheduled Castes in the Indian Constitution) of West Bengal's neighbour-state Bihar in the late 1960s. Bhatia has worked extensively on this aspect (Bhatia, 2005). Some of the reasons posited by her are as follows:

- Lack of just wages for the village labourers created unrest among them.
- The usurpation (by landlords) of ownership of the village pond was a major contentious matter. Being a source of protein (fish), the disempowerment forced the common villagers to compromise on their diet.
- Lack of proper housing and the presence of criminal gangs (at times in collusion with the landlords) inflamed the rebellious consciousness of the peasants.
- The most important reason, according to Bhatia, however, was the desire to restore *izzat* (dignity or honour) by the Dalit men and women, which was facilitated by the guns supplied by the Maoists.

Bhatia argues that at the village level in Bihar, people joined the Naxalite movement due to their instinctive hatred against injustice. They hardly could be branded as "informed revolutionaries." For the common folk in Bihar's grassroots, the Marxist-Leninist-Maoist literature provided little succour. Once the Naxalite movement could provide the masses with a sense of dignity and pride, and once Yadavs (a social class) got entrenched in the political structure in Bihar (and with the formation of Jharkhand), Naxalite leaders had to seek other gimmicks so as to save their existence and ideology. After all, a protracted guerrilla warfare to usher in a New Democratic Revolution (NDR) in order to replace the incumbent bourgeoisie governmental structure needs considerable patience, which could pose an existential challenge for the economically and socially marginalised subaltern Dalits or adivasis (tribals or Scheduled Tribes). Accordingly, the Maoist leadership periodically pumps "political consciousness" into the cadres through planned acts of violence and terror – be it against the official constabulary, upper caste or class elements, or "informers" – in order to maintain discipline and raise the hopes of the cadres.

FROM NAXALITES TO MAOISTS: GROWTH, SPREAD, OPERATIONS AND PARTY STRUCTURE

Between 1978 and 1985, the Naxalite movement branched out into Andhra Pradesh. It faced heavy state repression during 1985–1990. A phase of resurgence in 1990–92, however, culminated in a ban on the organisation in 1992. On April 22, 1980, the CPI (Marxist-Leninist) (People's War) [CPI (M-L) (PW)] was proclaimed on a formal basis. In the same year, CPI (M-L) (PW) formulated a crucial document called the Guerrilla Zone Perspective (GZP) and attempted to create a guerrilla base in *Dandakaranya* (Venugopal, 2013). Hyderabad-based Tushar Kanti Bhattacharyya was sent by the PW group to form the first squad in Karimnagar district, a tri-junction where the borders of the states of Andhra Pradesh, Maharashtra, and Madhya Pradesh meet (Choudhary, 2012). The GZP was imperative for the insurgents in order to launch guerrilla warfare against the Indian state. Much later, too, the Maoists tried to establish similar guerrilla bases in the Sahayadri mountains (Govind, 2014) and the Malabar (Christy, 2014).

The choice of *Dandakaranya* as a guerrilla base was strategically obvious since it is a geographical area sprawling across Odisha, Madhya Pradesh, Andhra (now also Telangana), and Chhattisgarh. To "create" the bases, KS sent seven teams of seven members each towards the region. Incidentally, one team was led by Ramji, *aka* Mallojula Koteshwar Rao, alias Kishenji (who was eliminated by the police in 2011). The guerrilla zone was to be realised through an undeclared yet implicitly evident foco-theory popularised by Che Guevara, Fidel Castro, Regis Debray, et al.

In his monograph *Guerrilla Warfare*, Che Guevara opines that a nucleus of 30 to 50 men has the potential to spark an insurgency even if the conditions of the rebellion do not appear to exist. A dedicated band of revolutionaries can form a vanguard focus (*foco*) and encourage the rapid growth of guerrilla warfare among the general masses without waiting for the conditions of the insurrection to develop (Dictionary of Revolutionary Marxism, 2020). The "foco," however, does not only radicalise the peasantry, but the peasants in turn serve to politicise the guerrilla fighters in a symbiotic relationship. Guevara asserts that foco-theory discovers Marxism naturally and accords primacy to military actions over political ones.

Did KS and his seven squads (a total of 49 revolutionaries) attempt to create the revolution in *Dandakaranya* through an insurrectional foco? It appears so, at least from a theoretical angle. However, on ground zero, a combination of mass organisations, squad-level operations, and the formation of local militia under the banner of a vanguard party could "create" the guerrilla base over a substantial length of time. In essence, a theoretical merger of Leninism, Maoism, and Guevarism helped create the guerrilla base. In 1991, the CPI (M-L) (PW) leadership baton passed from KS to Ganapathy. Finally, in 2004, the PW merged with the Bihar-Jharkhand-based Maoist Communist Centre (MCC). This indeed provided fresh perspective and energy to the insurgents. The Naxalites now officially began to be called Maoists, and the movement became more organised, hierarchical, and militarised (SATP, 2020). Ganapathy became the general secretary of the CPI-M on October 14, 2004. From the Central Committee to squad/area committees, through state and district formations, the Maoist Party maintained its rigid hierarchy (SATP, 2020). Post-2004, the insurgency, however, reached its peak in the 2010 Dantewada ambush of 75 security personnel (Mukherjee, 2010). The CPI-M was powered by the unity of the Bihar and Andhra groups; in the process, the insurgents accepted the role of a vanguard party (Leninism) and the need for a Protracted People's War (PPW) through guerrilla warfare (Maoism).

Regular ambushes entrapping the security forces at Dantewada (Chattisgarh), Gadchiroli (Maharashtra), or in the Saranda forests (Jharkhand) have shown the capabilities of the Maoists in guerrilla warfare techniques. A thorough knowledge of the topography in *Dandakaranya, along with* winning the "hearts and minds" of the local population, enabled the Maoists to ultimately establish their guerrilla base with the epicentre at the Abujhmaad hills. The lack of governance is a historical factor in these backward yet natural resource-rich regions, and it was the prime reason for the Maoists to intrude into the socio-political space. It is germane to mention that whether pre- or post-independent India, government officials did not have a good reputation in dealing with the tribal population, be it Dandakaranya in the 1980s or post-2000 Lalgarh. The fundamental core nonetheless, from which the Maoists derive their strength, are the cadres of the vanguard party. The party and consequently the movement will move on if cadre recruitment is steady.

RECRUITMENT AND EXTERNAL NETWORKS

Maoists have been reported to have recruited hundreds of cadres from the tea gardens of Barak Valley in the eastern state of Assam. The cadres were then sent to Palamu district in Jharkhand for training (Mukherjee, 2014). Furthermore, Maoists across Chhattisgarh, Odisha, Bihar, and Jharkhand have reportedly "recruited" thousands of children, including girls (in the age group of 10 to 15). They were given basic training to handle weapons (Mukherjee, 2014). The UN Secretary General's annual report informed us that Indian Maoists recruit and indoctrinate children for squad-level formations (Mukherjee, 2014). Such data has been corroborated by authors, commentators, and activists. Arundhati Roy has romanticised the child recruits as part of the Maoist militia (*Walking with the Comrades*), and Gautam Navlakha reported a "considerable number of women" in the People's Liberation Guerrilla Army [PLGA] and in the militia (*Days and Nights in the Heartland of Rebellion*).

Mamidi writes that Maoists try to choose candidates from aboveground sympathisers who are believed to be trustworthy and whose interests are aligned with the group (Mamidi, 2010). Mamidi further asserts that recruiters are likely to run into "bad apples" and that it is quite difficult to distinguish trustworthy candidates from "bad apples." Defection by existing members can cause considerable damage to the Maoists. Kishenji's elimination due to information leaked by the inner party core (turned defectors) is a prime case in this context. In fact, the norm-compliance of aspiring candidates before membership does not guarantee that the candidates do not possess the potential to defect after membership. The case of Shivaji is germane in this regard: a graduate of Regional Engineering College, Warangal Shivaji joined the intelligence branch of the police though he had commenced his insurgent career as a "martyr to be" (Choudhary, 2012). Sumit, who rejected the leisurely comfort of Kolkata and married a tribal girl in *Dandakaranya*, astoundingly turns into a police informer and effects a string of arrests of Maoist cadres and leaders. It is believed that severe beatings by the police are a genuine reason for the change in posture by once dedicated cadres and mid-level Maoist leaders (Choudhary, 2012).

The Maoist insurgency is sustained by the rural base, the guerillas' superior knowledge of local terrain vis-à-vis the security forces, and the rough terrain, which makes it difficult for the security forces to nab the ultras. The Indian Maoists seem to observe very strict regulations while inducting members (Mukherjee, 2014). The norm is that every applicant must be recommended by at least two party members. Moreover, the primary unit recommending the admission of a new member shall secretly investigate the credibility of the applicant. Such membership is called "candidate membership." Also, to put things in a formal perspective, a probationary period exists for every membership. Nonetheless, differential treatment is meted out to categories of candidates belonging to different social backgrounds. For instance, the lower end of Lower Castes [LCs] has only a six-month period of probation. Whereas middle-class peasants, petty bourgeoisie, and urban middle classes [both LCs and Upper Castes (UCs)] have a probation period of one year. Moreover, the upper section of the UCs undergoes a two-year probation (Mukherjee, 2014).

Recruits with expertise in technological fields are preferred. Nevertheless, even if the LC candidate does not possess the requisite skills, his or her chances of being recruited do not go down (Mukherjee, 2014). Another parameter is the physical attribute, which is critical because it manifests its ability to withstand topographical and climatic challenges. One of the biggest impediments to police infiltration into the Naxalite inner circle is the Maoist requirement that aspiring candidates engage in at least a moderate amount of underground crime. For this reason, police find it difficult to plant moles among the Naxalites. Furthermore, the party constitution mandates relinquishing private property as a pre-requisite for joining the group (SATP, 2020). This creates an additional barrier against infiltration by the police. With regard to abdication of private property too, successful LC candidates give up a lesser proportion of their property than successful UC candidates. Giving up one's caste or property and committing underground crimes removes the trust deficit for potential recruits. The Maoists are of the opinion that once someone has committed acts that would not entitle him or her to go back to his or her societal fabric anymore, only that person could be a stable and faithful recruit.

The CPI-M is the major face of LWE in India. Nonetheless, other extremist groups are professing Maoist ideology. On June 13, 2019, officers of the National Investigation Agency (NIA) seized an array of arms and ammunition belonging to the associates of the chairman of the Manipur-based banned group Kangleipak Communist Party (KCP) (Mukherjee, 2019). In fact, instances of terror funding related to the KCP have been noted since 2017 (Mukherjee, 2019).

Is the KCP an isolated group that has more to do with secession from the Indian landmass, or does it have sufficient Maoist leanings and hence linkages with the CPI-M? Furthermore, on the occasion of May Day 2019, a press release by the Maoist Communist Party-Manipur [MCP-Manipur] stated that it will be undertaking a vital role in formulating a general programme for the International Communist Movement. Moreover, 12 Maoist organisations based in Latin America have expressed solidarity in this regard. Communist parties from diverse regions of the globe, extending from Spain to Afghanistan, were in the loop (Mukherjee, 2019). Founded on April 13, 1980, the newly-floated Maoist wing of KCP stated in 2009 that their immediate aim was to carry on NDR in Manipur to establish a communist society through the Protracted People's War (PPW). They also declared their intention to form alliances with other Maoist revolutionary parties. Interestingly, such a network of Maoist outfits extending into the north-east of India opens up the possibility of Chinese interference (Mukherjee, 2011) in the insurgency.

Going back a few years, on July 19, 2016, the NIA submitted a charge sheet before a special court in Delhi that Islamic State (IS) was planning to procure weapons from CPI-M in order to carry out terror strikes (Singh, 2016). Interestingly, on April 27, 2016, India's Minister of State for Home Affairs intimated to the upper house (Rajya Sabha) that there is no nexus between IS and various Maoist groups in the country, even as far as training and seeking weapons are concerned (PTI, 2016).

In this context, it is noteworthy to mention that the Maoists, as guerilla fighters, lead the life of a fish in a sea of people. Any sort of unholy nexus with the anti-national, communal, and terror forces, if established, is sure to tarnish their image as secular, communist revolutionaries. In that scenario, the masses in the rural and tribal heartlands are likely to lose faith in the ultras. With these faux pas, the Maoists would jeopardise their source of existence and nourishment. Furthermore, the Maoists are highly likely to lose the support of urban intellectuals if any such partnership is discovered. Marxism-Leninism-Maoism, the fundamental ideological plank of the insurgents, focuses on class conflict and is antithetical to communal-terror forces.

THE ROLE OF INTELLECTUALS

Is the ongoing LWE in India guided by intellectuals? Do academics, students, writers, journalists, filmmakers, actors, and poets within and without India in any way encourage the insurgency? How is the future trajectory shaping up in the contest between the state, intellectuals, and insurgents? With an octogenarian priest-activist arrested on charges of colluding with the Maoists, the issue of the role of intellectuals in LWE has gained renewed attention (Express, 2020). In the 21st century, a bunch of intellectuals have gained prominence through the media. However, they could be best considered a motley group of professionals. Barring a handful, most are not qualified to be termed "intellectuals." To render an opinion is one thing, but to claim scholastic aptitude in the genre of Voltaire, Rousseau, Sartre, Foucault, or Ranajit Guha is a different game.

The pioneer of subaltern historiography, Ranajit Guha, amazes us as he admits to being a Naxal intellectual inspired by Charu Mazumdar's ideas. Though Guha criticises the weak organisational capability of the Naxals, his penchant for the insurgents is anything but concealed (Guha, 2010).

Guha refers to various kinds of intellectuals: one set of intellectuals who "oppose" the state (to which Guha belongs in this case) and another set that aligns with the state in order to eliminate the former, in a war of ideology. Genuine intellectuals, however, ought to remain neutral and posit an analytical perspective in a dispassionate manner. Moreover, an intellectual cannot be despised simply because her or his viewpoint is congruous with that of the ruling dispensation. It has, however, become quite fashionable for a bulk of the intellectuals in today's India to criticise government policies and programmes. In a sense, criticising the government seems to be a criterion for being qualified to be an intellectual. Rather, India today needs what Gramsci termed "organic intellectuals" – committed to the cause of the people.

Mao Tse-tung attacked intellectuals on a massive scale in his Great Proletariat Cultural Revolution (GPCR). Interestingly, the same man had called for recruiting a large number of intellectuals during the course of the Chinese Revolution (Tse-tung, 1939). Such a posture by Mao, however, can best be described as opportunistic. During the course of the Russian Revolution in 1917, Lenin and Trotsky established a dictatorship of socialist intellectuals (Thacher, 2007) and are alleged to have misled the people about a golden future. Opinions of contemporary scholars and writers have varied regarding the Indian Maoist insurgency. Aruna Roy believes that the adivasis may genuinely protest against maladministration (WSJ, 2009). However, she does not seem to openly subscribe to the view that "Maoist-type insurgency" is the acceptable format of protest. Mahasweta Devi stresses "separating" the tribal-adivasi from the Maoist insurgents (Pro Kerala News, 2010). On the other hand, Arundhati Roy opines that the Maoists have granted the tribal adivasis a semblance of dignity (Roy, 2009). Roy believes that the gun brought in by the Maoists has given the adivasis a weapon for survival. On a similar trajectory, Bela Bhatia agrees that the Naxals empowered the working and oppressed classes of Bihar (Bhatia, 2005). Nonetheless, she feels that the Naxalite leaders are "not interested" in "development," and hence the quality of life in the villages has not improved. Past Naxalite leaders like Kanu Sanyal (Sanyal, 2007) and Azizul Haq (Pandey, 2009) hold the opinion that the present Maoist struggle is a "power struggle" and is using the adivasis as pawns.

Nonetheless, if the urban-bred intellectuals are just "foreigners," then how could they extend their influence? It is difficult to ignore that a governance vacuum did develop in LWE-affected regions. Naturally, the "intellectual foreigner" appeared to the adivasi as the neo-tribal leader of the colonial past. Birsa Munda's chants of "Katong Baba Katong" (O father, kill kill) of 1899 were reflected in the Naxalite slogans (Bhatia, 2005).

In this context, I interviewed (Mazumdar, 2020) Abhijit Mazumdar, Secretary, Darjeeling District Committee, CPI (Marxist-Leninist) Liberation, and the son of Charu Mazumdar. An intellectual by his own right, Mazumdar said that he lauded the erstwhile Naxalbari movement, which, according to him, "could organically address the grass-root ferment towards a revolutionary transformation vis-à-vis the status quo, compromising positions adopted by the revisionist leadership of formal communist parties." Mazumdar further asserted: "I believe that we may refer back to the idea of producing organic intellectuals following Gramsci, which may only be possible through the interface between the rural and urban bases." Being asked what was late Charu Mazumdar's perception of intellectuals, his son was candid enough to refer to his father's ideas about the role of intellectuals, which shaped up "through the debate he [Charu Mazumdar] had with Sushital Roy Choudhury over the issue of demolishing the statues of national icons like Rammohun Roy, Vidyasagar, Tagore, et al." (Mazumdar, 2020). Abhijit Babu lauds public intellectuals like Amartya Sen, Irfan Habib, Romila Thapar, Arundhati Roy, and Ramchandra Guha for having carried on with "the essential dialectical take" of Charu Majumdar.

LOOKING TO THE FUTURE

It has been opined that insurgencies generally end not through military action but due to social, economic, and political change (Connable, 2010). Lt Gen (Retd.) V K Ahluwalia of the Indian army, however, claims (Ahluwalia, 2014) that India's Maoist movement is likely to end when the rebels appreciate the cost factor of continuing the insurgency. Also, according to him, the insurgency would meet its death when the people believed that the government was reasonably effective in addressing their grievances within a suitable time frame (Ahluwalia, 2014). Nonetheless, considering the importance (in the insurgency) of trade in tendu leaves and the incursion of mining activities in tribal regions (Maitreesh Ghatak, 2017), the demise of the insurgency is unlikely to come soon.

From a security perspective, the Maoists are in the strategic defence phase of guerrilla warfare and very likely will continue to do so with more focus on low-end technology like improvised explosive devices. This appears more so after the taking over of leadership in November 2018 by Nambala Keshav Rao, alias Basavaraju, who has a bachelor's degree in technology (Mukherjee, 2019). A basic calculation, of course, would set things straight. As of January 2017, the Central Armed Police Forces (CAPFs) had an actual strength of close to 10,00,000 personnel (BPRD, 2017). On the other hand, the strength of the Maoist guerrilla army varies from 8,500 cadres (PTI, 2014) to an estimated 10,000 to 12,000 cadres and more than 50,000 members of associated wings and militia (Tripathi, 2013). Leaving aside the state police forces, only the CAPFs have an advantage of around a 10:1 personnel ratio vis-à-vis the Maoists. In addition, the modernisation, training, and professional level of the CAPFs and the state police keep them on a much higher pedestal compared to the insurgents, who have still been unable to graduate to the next level of strategic stalemate in guerrilla warfare, and that too in a span of over 50 years since the commencement of the insurgency.

What could be the structure of a perceived Maoist state? Will it be a dictatorship of the proletariat? It could well be a state dominated by the vanguard party bureaucracy, in which the secret police would torture the purported enemies of the state. It may as well be a state in which people are forced to die in labour camps, as was brutally done in Cambodia. Such a future can hardly be popular. Nonetheless, till people-friendly governance completely fills up the political space in India's hinterland, the long war between the state and the Maoists will continue as a low-intensity conflict.

References

Ahluwalia, L.G. (2014, June 05). *Talk by Lt Gen V K Ahluwalia (Retd.) on "Future of the Naxalite Movement"*. Retrieved from MPIDSA: https://idsa.in/event/FutureoftheNaxaliteMovement

Bandyopadhyay, S. (2008). The story of an aborted revolution: Communist insurgency in post-independence West Bengal, 1948–50. *Journal of South Asian Development, 3*(1), 1–32.

Banerjee, R. (2016, July 6). *The week*. Retrieved from The man India loves to forget: https://www.theweek.in/theweek/cover/charu-majumdar-naxalbari.html

Banerjee, S. (2008). *In the wake of Naxalbari*. Sahitya Samsad, 2008, ISBN 978-81-7955-116-5.

Bhatia, B. (2005). Jailbreak and the Maoist movement. *Economic and Political Weekly, 40*(51), 5369–5371.

Bhatia, B. (2005). The Naxalite movement in central Bihar. *Economic and Political Weekly, XL*(15), 1536–1549.

BPRD. (2017). *Data on police organizations*. Bureau of Police Research & Development.

Chatterjee, P. (2010). The state. In N Jayal & P. Mehta (Eds.), *The Oxford companion to politics in India* (p. 5). Oxford University Press.

Choudhary, S. (2012). *Let's call him Vasu*. Penguin. ISBN 9780143067573.

Choudhary, S. (2012). *Let's call him Vasu: With the Maoists in Chhattisgarh*. Penguin India.

Christy, S. (2014, October 2). Maoist presence spreading in Malabar, says intelligence. Retrieved from The New Indian Express: http://www.newindianexpress.com/states/kerala/Maoist-Presence-Spreading-in-Malabar-Says-Intelligence/2014/10/02/article2459013.ece

Connable, B.A. (2010). *How insurgencies end*. RAND Corporation.

Dictionary of Revolutionary Marxism. (2020, November 1). Retrieved from http://www.massline.org/Dictionary/FO.htm

Express, T.I. (2020, October 17). Retrieved from https://indianexpress.com/article/explained/who-is-stan-swamy-6717126/

Govind, B. (2014, October 1). *Maoists plan new war front in Sahyadri*. Retrieved from The Hindu: http://www.thehindu.com/news/national/kerala/maoists-plan-new-war-front-in-sahyadri/article6462926.ece

Guha, R. (2007). *India after Gandhi*. Picador India. ISBN 978-0-330-50554-3.

Guha, R. (2010, February 02). In search of transcendence. (M. Banerjee, Interviewer).

Lovell, J. (2019). *Maoism: A global history*. Penguin Random House.

Maitreesh Ghatak, O.V. (2017, September 30). Economic determinants of the Maoist conflict in India. *Economic and Political Weekly, 52*(39).

Mamidi, P.K. (2010). Signaling and screening for recruitment among the Maoists in India. *Harvard Law School; Nuffield College*.

Mazumdar, A. (2020, January 01). (U. Mukherjee, Interviewer)

Mazumdar, C. (n.d.). *Historic eight documents (1965–1967)*. Retrieved from https://www.marxists.org/reference/archive/mazumdar/index.htm

MHA. (2019). *Annual report*. MHA.

Mukherjee, U. (2010). Book title. In S.A. Bhuyan D (Ed.), *Naxalism: Issues and concerns* (pp. 85–88). Discovery Publishing House.

Mukherjee, U. (2010, April 04). *Newsline*. Retrieved from https://newslinemagazine.com/magazine/the-bad-war/

Mukherjee, U. (2011, December 19). *Centre for land warfare studies*. Retrieved from https://archive.claws.in/744/maoists-north-east-and-china-expanding-net-of-terror-uddipan-mukherjee.html

Mukherjee, U. (2014). Catch them young: Patterns of naxal recruitment. *Institute of Peace and Conflict Studies*.

Mukherjee, U. (2019, May 07). *IEDs and the Maoist insurgency*. Retrieved from MPIDSA: https://idsa.in/idsacomments/ieds-and-maoist-insurgency-umukherjee-070519

Mukherjee, U. (2019, July 8). Retrieved from VIF: https://www.vifindia.org/article/2019/july/08/india-s-lesser-known-yet-dangerous-maoist-groups

Pandey, J.M. (2009, June 19). *Naxal veterans slam Lalgarh misadventure*. Retrieved from TNN: https://timesofindia.indiatimes.com/city/kolkata/Naxal-veterans-slam-Lalgarh-misadventure/articleshow/4673723.cms

Pro Kerala News. (2010, April 07). Retrieved from Mahasweta Devi, Government should talk to Maoistss. http://www.prokerala.com/news/articles/a126638.html

PTI. (2010, May 28). *Times of India*. Retrieved from https://timesofindia.indiatimes.com/india/Maoist-attack-derails-13-coaches-of-Express-train-68-dead/articleshow/5983218.cms

PTI. (2014, July 30). *mint*. Retrieved from https://www.livemint.com/Politics/RHMsouhFl1S2b1HZ9CtdLP/Maoist-groups-strength-is-around-8500-Govt.html

PTI. (2016, April 27). *Times of India*. Retrieved from https://timesofindia.indiatimes.com/india/No-nexus-between-Naxalites-and-Islamic-State-government-says/articleshow/52012080.cms

Ray, R. (1987). *The Naxalites and their ideology*. Oxford. ISBN 0-19-807738-6.

Reed, P. (1985). Latin America: The move to the cities. In J. Pimlott (Ed.), *Guerrilla warfare* (p. 120). Bison Books. ISBN 0 86124 225 4.

Routray, B.P. (2008, February 28). *They came, they saw, they conquered*. Retrieved from Outlook: https://www.outlookindia.com/website/story/they-came-they-saw-they-conquered/236812

Roy, A. (2009, November 09). *Mr Chidambaram's war*. Retrieved from http://www.outlookindia.com/article.aspx?262519

Sanhati. (2008, November). Retrieved from Sanhati: http://sanhati.com/news/1081/

Sanyal, K. (2007, May 25). *Terror can't bring change*. Retrieved from http://www.monstersandcritics.com/news/india/news/article_1309170.php/Terror_can_t_bring_change_Kanu_Sanyal_says

SATP. (2020, November 1). Communist party of India-Maoist (CPI-Maoist) all its formations and front organizations. Retrieved from https://satp.org/terrorist-profile/india/communist-party-of-india-maoist-cpi-maoist-all-its-formations-and-front-organizations

SATP. (2020, November 1). Retrieved from https://www.satp.org/satporgtp/countries/india/terroristoutfits/cpi_m.htm

SATP. (2020, November 1). Retrieved from https://www.satp.org/satporgtp/countries/india/maoist/documents/papers/partyconstitution.htm

Singh, S.K. (2016, July 19). Retrieved from CLAWS: https://www.newindianexpress.com/nation/2016/jul/19/Suspected-ISIS-men-contacted-Maoist-to-procure-weapons-882784.html

Thacher, I.D. (2007). Lenin, Trotsky and the role of the socialist intellectual in politics. *Marxism, Intellectuals and Politics*, 43–67. https://link.springer.com/chapter/10.1057/9780230596351_3.

Tripathi, A.K. (2013). Economics of communist party of India (Maoist). *Journal of Economics & Commerce, 4*(2), 110–115.

Tse-tung, M. (1939, December 1). *Recruit large numbers of intellectuals*. Retrieved from Selected Works of Mao Tse-tung: RECRUIT LARGE NUMBERS OF INTELLECTUALS, December 1, 1939, https://www.marxists.org/reference/archive/mao/selected-works/volume-2/mswv2_22.htm

Venugopal, N. (2013). *Understanding Maoists*. Setu Prakashani.

WION. (2019, November 6). *WION*. Retrieved from https://www.wionews.com/india-news/communist-party-of-india-maoist-sixth-most-dangerous-terrorist-organisation-in-the-world-us-report-260393

WSJ. (2009, November 3). *State will fail if the Army and Air Force are used against the Maoist*. Retrieved from WSJ: https://www.wsj.com/articles/SB125723504437924775

66

THE WAVE OF GLOBAL MAOISM AND THE MAOISTS OF NEPAL

Uddipan Mukherjee

> It's all in vain. We've tried in various ways to change the world; the point is now to interpret it.
>
> (Rancière, 2011)

INTRODUCTION

Historian Eric Hobsbawm doesn't agree that Marx died a failure in 1883 because, by then, his writings had already begun to influence the Russian intellectuals. At the other end, the new radical left movements (of the 1960s) of Europe disliked the amendment brought to Marxism by Lenin – that of the functional concept of a centralised vanguard party that would lead the people in the pursuit of revolution (Hobsbawm, 2011), without the majority of the people being clear what the revolution is all about. The global economic recession as an aftermath of the burst of the American real estate bubble, followed by the public debt crisis in Europe, and then the proliferation of pandemics, are all reflective of global interconnectedness. Nevertheless, a pertinent query in this context is whether these features indicate a discernible signature of decay in the philosophy of the free market and its political acolyte, the Western liberal democracy, or not. If such a thesis holds some ground, then what happens to Francis Fukuyama's now-historical assertion of 1989 (Fukuyama, 1989)?

> What we may be witnessing is not just the end of the Cold War, or the passing of a particular period of post-war history, but the end of history as such: that is, the end point of mankind's ideological evolution and the universalization of Western liberal democracy as the final form of human government.

In simple terms, what Fukuyama intended to convey was that the Hegelian philosophy of history was supreme, overwhelming Marx's thesis on history. Naturally, questions that perturb us at this critical juncture are: in the future, will Western liberal democracy survive as a form of political economy? Will the "other" strand of the ideology of Communism be completely won over by the equations of supply and demand?

GLOBAL MAOISM

Communism as an ideology was certainly not "dead," as Fukuyama intellectually coerced us to believe. Anachronistic regimes, internal contradictions within the liberal-capitalist system, relative economic deprivation, and social inequalities were magnified in the form of reactionary regimes or ultra-left movements, even after 1989, and continued well into the 21st century.

In fact, after the Second World War (WW II), the erstwhile colonies as well as newly found post-colonial states witnessed non-state actor-led insurgencies. There was a surge of Communist insurgencies post-1945, fundamentally due to the success and growth of Marxism, Leninism, and Maoism. The Sino-Soviet diplomatic rift in the late 1950s, followed by Mao Tse-tung's Great Proletariat Cultural Revolution (GPCR) during 1966–76, provided a boost to Maoist insurgencies and movements not only in the Third World but also in Western European countries like France and Norway. Mao's *jixu geming*, or continuous revolution, which began with the GPCR, gave rise to violent perturbations of the existing political establishment (Lovell, 2019). The whole world, along with China, was shaken, somewhat similar to what happened five decades later in 2020, as the whole world went berserk due to the coronavirus emanating from China.

DOI: 10.4324/9780429426063-75

HEGEL, MARX, LENIN, AND MAO

The German philosopher Hegel (1770–1831) enunciated that "idea" was the essence of the universe, i.e., the idea was the force (idealism) behind all historical development. However, Karl Marx (1818–1883) flatly rejected this view and stated that "matter" was the essence of change (materialism). Both of them depended on the Greek concept of dialectics in order to substantiate their philosophies. Dialectics are intellectual debates in which the argument (thesis) and counter-argument (anti-thesis) are juxtaposed to create a synthesis, or the final truth, as neither the thesis nor the anti-thesis is totally immune from untrue elements. The evolved synthesis, however, may not be the absolute truth, and hence it can act as the thesis for further debate! This process of iterative negation goes on until a final synthesis or absolute truth is reached.

The essential difference between Marx and Hegel is that the former proclaimed the philosophy of dialectical materialism instead of the dialectical idealism of the latter. Apart from this, Marx elucidated his concept of historical materialism, which formed the empirical basis of Marxism. According to historical materialism, the social, political, and intellectual relations prevailing at any epoch of historical development are directly proportional to the economic conditions in that period; for instance, the rise of the *Mahajanapads* [second urbanisation in ancient India] in the later part of the Vedic era was due to the strong iron-boosted surplus-agrarian economy (Jha, 2010).

An integral part of historical materialism is class conflict or class struggle – the constant struggle between the dominant and the dependent classes. Starting from the master and the slave to the capitalist (bourgeoisie) and the industrial worker (proletariat), classes as binary opposites keep on forming in different periods of history. Marx and Engels (1820–1895) had full faith in the proletariat. They believed that it would topple capitalism and establish an egalitarian communist society. And that would be the final synthesis, which would not require any further modifications! Marx prescribed the path of dictatorship of the proletariat, i.e., the dictatorship of the industrial workers over the bourgeoisie. The state shall still exist, but it will be a state of the propertyless in order to liquidate "private property." This state will pave the way for a classless society. The communist state shall strive for the highest technological development so as to satisfy the principle: "from each according to his or her ability, to each according to his or her need."

Mao (1893–1976) picked up from the very point where Marx had left. He stated that class struggle does not vanish with the establishment of a communist state but rather takes on new forms! He opined that contradictions must be fought perpetually in order to achieve the goal of communism. Marx and Engels made a distinction between the base and the superstructure. The base is the economic foundation of society, whereas the superstructure comprises institutions, organisations, literature, art, and the like. Normally the base influences the superstructure, but very often it is the other way around too. It was precisely this functional dependence that was shown by Mao. He observed that in the Russian case, a capitalist-type superstructure grew out of a socialist base. Petrified by this, Mao wanted to obliterate the anti-socialist and anti-communist forces from the Chinese superstructure, assuming that the Chinese base was essentially communist. Accordingly, Mao initiated the GPCR to erase the conflict between base and superstructure.

Whereas Marx had denigrated the peasants as "potatoes in a sack" (Lovell, 2019) and Lenin pinned hopes on the industrial worker to lead the revolution, Mao's understanding of the socio-political and economic condition of the Chinese peasantry aided him to devise pragmatic strategies keeping in mind the Chinese scenario. Probably this very astute understanding provided him the confidence to proclaim the famous slogan, "Political power grows out of the barrel of a gun" (Mao Tse-tung, 1938).

Though Mao never moved out of the territorial confines of China and even was not apologetic for not knowing where Brazil was (Lovell, 2019), his ideology of Maoism spread like wildfire, not only within the Chinese landscape but later on in Vietnam, Cambodia, North Korea, the Philippines, India, Latin America, and Nepal, all primarily underdeveloped agrarian economies at the start of their revolutions. Mao's close aide, Kang Sheng, was the mastermind behind exporting the ideology and practise of Maoism to other countries (Lovell, 2019). Instead of concentrating on all aspects of Maoism, it would be pertinent to discuss two major principles of Mao Tse-tung: first, his techniques of revolution, and second, his views on class. Mao was fully convinced that revolution was the only way to emancipate the oppressed classes in China. But his point of concern was the way in which the revolution could be realised. Once he said, "*A revolution is an insurrection, an act of violence by which one class overthrows another*" (Mao Tse-tung, 1927).

This was the central idea of Mao's theory of revolution. Appeal or compromise has no place in his theory. Mao also adopted the techniques of guerrilla warfare to annihilate the enemy in a conspiratorial way. He never indulged in sympathy for the enemy. Mao realised that guerrilla warfare had immense potential for success in the countryside of China. Reliance on this form of warfare was pragmatic, as he knew that the imperialist forces were too powerful to be defeated in a direct tussle. Unlike Marx and Engels, Mao considered that the peasants were the true "proletariat" in China, and they had to lead the struggle in the long run instead of the industrial workers, as their numbers were too few. Also, unlike his predecessors, Mao did not look down upon the petty bourgeoisie, as he felt that this class was amenable to change and could be influenced by the ideas of the revolution. Mao adopted Marxism but modified it according to the needs of China. The popular term "people's war" was coined by Mao. A tactic of revolution that he adopted was to generate compromise whenever he was in trouble and not compromise at all when he was in an advantageous position.

Mao, however, cautioned that since there was no universal principle in any revolution, the techniques and the programme ought to vary from situation to situation and from country to country. If the revolutionaries are glued to any dogmatic method or ideology that is not apposite, then it may lead to disaster. The success of the Chinese revolution had a profound impact on the world, creating a wave of joy amongst the oppressed peoples of South Asia, Africa, and Latin America. Alongside Mao Zedong, personalities like Zhou Enlai, Zhu De, Liu Shaoqi, and Lin Biao began to be venerated.

In connection with Mao's guerrilla warfare, Francis Grice identifies five major themes across Mao's works regarding the military aspects of insurgency. According to Grice, while Mao stated that guerrilla and other irregular forces should play an important role, he recommended that regular forces be used as the primary arm of an insurgency. Grice's analysis shows that Mao believed regular forces should be the main component of an insurgency throughout the entire conflict. Interestingly enough, Mao rarely discussed his three-phase model comprising strategic defence, strategic stalemate, and strategic offence, a concept that is so widely acknowledged by experts in guerrilla warfare (Grice, 2019).

SPREAD OF MAOISM: 1960S ONWARD

The impact of Maoism and the cult of Mao was so intense that in the mid-1960s in India, a frail heart patient named Charu Mazumdar advocated for the students to pick up guns and go to the countryside to foment a rebellion. In the 1980s, in Peru, a philosophy professor named Abumael Guzman ramped up sizable support in order to wage a war against the state. In the mid-1990s, Baburam Bhattarai (after completing his doctoral studies at India's Jawaharlal Nehru University) and his comrade Pushpa Kamal Dahal entrenched themselves among the ethnic Kham Magars in mid-western Nepal so as to declare an armed revolt against the monarchy.

At a different geographical node, a certain physics graduate (a certain senior of this author who later became a faculty member of a premier national institute) in Kolkata's two-hundred-year-old elite Presidency College was ready to give up his studies and immerse himself in Maoist literature. Though his romanticism evaporated soon after as he took his materialistic career much seriously, and like him, many nouveau Maoists of the urban confines of Kolkata, Delhi, Paris, Lima, and Kathmandu must have gone astray, yet the insurgencies encouraged by Maoism and engineered through direct Chinese diplomatic interventions continue to rage on in the 21st century.

The fundamental ideology of Maoism rests on the Protracted People's War (PPW) in order to topple the so-called "reactionary bourgeoisie regime" and consequently usher in a New Democratic Revolution (NDR). Similar movements, launched in Cuba under the Castro-Guevara combo, in Nicaragua under the Sandinistas (Zimmermann, 2000), or in Peru under Guzman, have all done exactly the same: followed the prototype model of the Chinese Revolution of Mao Zedong, though insofar as theoretical attachment is concerned, the Cuban revolution was closer to the Russian model.

If it was "Shampoo" Guzman (Lovell, 2019) leading the insurrection on his "Shining Path" in Peru in the 1980s, the armed conflict between the FARC and the Colombian government had begun in the mid-1960s. There was a temporary lull in violence in Colombia in 1958 when the Liberal Party and the Conservative Party agreed to divide power through an alliance called the National Front. However, the left wing of the Liberal Party, along with the communists influenced by a wave of socialism-influenced revolts across the continent, did not accept this National Front. In the countryside, where inequality was a perennial problem, farmers began revolting against the Bogota-based political elite (Mukherjee, 2016). And it was from this movement that the FARC germinated as a handful of peasants. FARC declared itself independent, forming "The Republic of Marquetalia" in a tiny village on the foot of the Nevada de Huila mountain range. The conflict further escalated in the 1980s, when several leftist rebel groups became active. Drug trafficking revenue was financing weapons across the country (Mukherjee, 2016).

The Maoist insurgency in the Philippines is another case in point. The New People's Army (NPA) strongly believes in Mao's theory of PPW, with the peasantry spearheading the movement. The NPA goes for *agawarmas – the* seizure of weapons through ambushes. *Pangayaw*, or tribal wars, go on with impunity in the insurgency-affected areas. The NPA has lost many of its armed cadres and has an estimated 5,000 fighters (Mukherjee, 2012). The most ruthless and diabolic Maoist insurgency, however, was waged in Cambodia between 1975 and 1979, led by an apparently crackpot high school teacher named Saloth Sar and his deputy Ieng Sary (Lovell, 2019). The Communist Party of Kampuchea, or Khmer Rouge, forcefully evacuated all cities and towns and moved the people to the countryside so as to transform the bourgeoisie society into a communist society in the shortest possible time, causing thousands of deaths in the process.

FORMATION OF THE MAOIST PARTY AND THE BEGINNING OF INSURGENCY IN NEPAL

> I've never been to China, or even to the Chinese embassy myself. I like Mao, China and the Chinese revolution, but I wasn't interested in going there.
>
> Khagendra Sangroula (Lovell, 2019)

The Maoist insurgency in Nepal exhibits the best example of the transformation reflected in Mao's two statements, separated by a decade. In his 1927 world-famous slogan, Mao proclaimed "Political power comes out of the barrel of a gun." Whereas in 1938, he uttered: "The party commands the gun, and the gun must never be allowed to command the party." Similarly, the Nepali Maoists began with a bang of the gun and transformed into a democratic political party at the end of the ten-year-long insurgency.

The Maoists of Nepal certainly inherit the legacy of their communist predecessors. During the 1947 workers' strike at the Biratnagar jute and cloth mills in eastern Nepal, a fledgling communist movement under Man Mohan Adhikari's leadership emerged. Adhikari was a Nepali but a member of the Communist Party of India (Thapa & Sijapati, 2003). Not surprisingly, though, the Communist Party of Nepal (CPN) was founded in the Indian city of Kolkata (then Calcutta) on September 15, 1949, with the help of Indian communists (Lawoti & Pahari, 2015). However, it was Pushpa Lal Shrestha, the erstwhile office secretary of the Nepali National Congress party, who translated the Communist Manifesto (of Marx and Engels) in Nepali and made it public on the foundation day of the CPN (Thapa & Sijapati, 2003a). When the wave of Mao's GPCR hit Nepal and South Asia in general, the radical communist leaders were in exile (Adhikari, 2014). On the eve of the GPCR, not just 16.8% of China's foreign aid flew to Nepal (Lovell, 2019), but also Chinese revolutionary literature and films showcasing Chinese socialism influenced the future Maoists (Adhikari, 2014). However, during 1972–1995, when the Indian Naxals (as the erstwhile followers of Mao were called in popular parlance) were attempting to re-group and re-invigorate after their initial hiccups in 1972 with the death of their leader Charu Mazumdar, the Nepali communist movement spread in a secret manner, battered however with factionalism and frequent splits as Nepal struggled under the autocratic regime of the monarchy (Lawoti & Pahari, 2010).

The CPN-Fourth Congress/Convention in 1974 under Nirmal Lama and Mohan Bikram Singh was held in the Indian city of Banaras (Thapa & Sijapati, 2003). In 1979, Nirmal Lama, the general secretary of the CPN-Fourth Congress/Convention, proposed initiating an armed guerrilla insurrection, and the idea was accepted by the group (Thapa & Sijapati, 2003b).

Interestingly, however, the first documented armed communist rebellion in Nepal (influenced, aided, and abetted by India's Naxalites) took place in May 1971 at Jhapa, a place located in Nepal just across Naxalbari (where India's armed rebellion on Maoist lines originated) on the Indian side (Lawoti & Pahari, 2010). Out of the Jhapa uprising later grew the CPN-Marxist-Leninist (CPN-ML), which had a presence in over 50 districts of Nepal in the 1990s (Thapa & Sijapati, 2003). During the 1980s, many communists in Nepal started to lose faith in the working approach of the CPN, which was viewed as a revisionist party and did not adhere to the core principles of the proletariat revolution to topple the bourgeoisie regime (Adhikari, 2014). Mohan Bikram Singh, with his hardline faction called "Masal," split from the Fourth Congress in 1983 (Adhikari, 2014). However, another split took place in 1985 when Mohan Baidya alias Kiran, disgusted with the dictatorial style of Singh's functioning, carved out the group called "Mas*h*al" (Adhikari, 2014). The radical communists of Nepal were inspired by the Naxalite movement in India and also influenced by the Chinese GPCR (Adhikari, 2014). It is needless to drive home the point that the Indian Naxalites too had accepted "Mao as their chairman." But as the Mas*h*al wing joined the Revolutionary Internationalist Movement (RIM), they were very much energised by Guzman's Shining Path (Adhikari, 2014). In a turn of events, in October 1989, Kiran nominated Pushpa Kamal Dahal, alias Prachanda (the fierce), as his replacement in Mas*h*al (Adhikari, 2014).

Continuing with the culture of splits, mergers, and new formations, the CPN-Unity Centre (CPN-UC) was formed on November 23, 1990. It comprised the CPN-Mas*h*al group led by Prachanda, a breakaway faction of CPN-Mashal led by Dr. Baburam Bhattarai, and the CPN-Fourth Congress led by Nirmal Lama (Lawoti & Pahari, 2010). In 1990, Dahal and Gajurel of the Mas*h*al group had in fact travelled to the Indian state of Bihar and received training in guerrilla warfare from India's erstwhile insurgent group, the Maoist Communist Centre (Adhikari, 2014).

Meanwhile, the CPN-UC started a political front titled United People's Front Nepal (UPFN), headed by Bhattarai, and planned to participate in the elections (Lawoti & Pahari, 2015). Nevertheless, the CPN-UC, in its December 1991 unity congress, passed a resolution to initiate a people's war to usher in NDR in Nepal (Thapa & Sijapati, 2003). However, in May 1994, the CPN-UC split (Thapa & Sijapati, 2003) between the Nirmal Lama group and the faction led by Prachanda, since Lama did not agree to an immediate armed uprising – an occasion reminiscent of the historic split between the Mensheviks and the Bolsheviks. The UPFN also split, with the Bhattarai faction rallying with

Prachanda, and the duo boycotted the 1994 mid-term elections, partly due to the fact that their group was not recognised by the Election Commission of Nepal (Lawoti & Pahari, 2015) and also because armed insurrection was antithetical to electoral politics. Finally, in 1995, the Prachanda-led CPN-UC renamed itself CPN-Maoist [CPN(M)] and decided to begin an armed insurgency (Lawoti & Pahari, 2010).

The insurgency, launched in February 1996 by the Maoists, could have been fuelled by all or a combination of the following fundamental causes (Gates & Roy, 2014):

1. economic grievances of the people over a sustained period of time
2. ethnic tensions among different groups of people
3. political animosity between the ultra-left and the ruling elite
4. an overall struggle of the Nepali people against the Bahun-Chetri-Newari domination in political and cultural life, and of course because of
5. pent-up grievances against the monarchy.

Though overall economic indicators in Nepal showed improvement during the 1990s, Lawoti makes the case that, on closer inspection, poverty, inequality, and relative deprivation were indeed the causal factors for the germination of the uprising in the mid-1990s. He argues that poverty was more widespread in the mountains than in the plains. Moreover, Lawoti brings forth the argument that if properly mobilised by a vanguard party, ethnic groups may support class-based insurgencies, and their support can very well transform the trajectory of the insurgency (Lawoti & Pahari, 2010). In this context, it is to be reiterated that the Nepali Maoist movement started in the Rukum and Rolpa hill areas among the Kham Magar ethnic group.

At the other end of the spectrum, Acharya (2009) finds no evidence that political and economic grievances are linked to the incidence of political violence. However, Nepal, Bohara, and Gawande find strong evidence that greater inequality in Nepalese society gave rise to more killings by the Maoists, i.e., further radicalisation of the movement (Nepal et al., 2011). In fact, absolute poverty, a lack of access to resources, and the failure of political structures to address basic issues made Nepalese society extremely vulnerable to conflict. Furthermore, deep-rooted social cleavages provided fertile ground to escalate the conflict (UKDiss, 2019).

PARTY STRUCTURE AND THE PEOPLE'S ARMY

Nepal's 1990 Jana Andolan (the mass movement), though it ended the three-decade-long coercive party-less Panchayat system and brought forth the multiparty system as an urban movement, was nothing close to the people's war launched by the CPN (M). The PPW by the CPN (M) commenced on February 12, 1996, with barely thirty-six Maoist comrades and only one functioning rifle, the.303 (Adhikari, 2014). But within a short span of time, the movement spread to all parts of Nepal, except for the two districts of Manang and Mustang. Between 1996 and 2006, there was a phenomenal expansion of the Maoists, with their armed forces, or People's Liberation Army (PLA), growing to 30,000 combatants (Ogura, 2008) and having a presence in more than 80% of the territory of Nepal (Lovell, 2019). Though estimates vary, almost 18,000 people lost their lives during the decade-long insurgency (Adhikari, 2014).

The insurgency passed through the strategic defence and strategic stalemate phases and, in 2005, reached the strategic offensive stage. With time, the military capacity of the Maoists also increased. In fact, during the peak period of the insurgency, the PLA was "one of the largest non-state military formations in the world" (Hachhethu, 2008–2009). In CPN (M), the overall control of the party and military remains firmly with the "party headquarters," which in practise means the chairman or general secretary. For the Nepali Maoists, or CPN (M), from 1996 to 2006, the chairman was Prachanda. He had the authority to take all immediate decisions, though these could later be discussed by party committees, which had the power to endorse, revise, or reject them (ICG, 2005). The organisational hierarchy under the chairman comprised the following (ICG, 2005):

1. standing committee
2. politburo
3. central committee
4. divisional commands
5. regional bureaus, sub-regional bureaus
6. district, area, and cell committees.

The Maoist guerrillas operated in about 68 of the 75 districts that comprised Nepal during the period of the insurgency (SATP, 2017). In the districts of Rolpa, Rukum, Jajarkot, Salyan, Pyuthan, and Kalikot in mid-western Nepal, government presence was limited to the district headquarters, and the rest of each district was under Maoist control (SATP, 2017). The politburo of the CPN (M) contained at least 27 members, of whom 10 were alternates. Prachanda was chairman of the politburo's seven-member standing committee, whose other members were (ICG, 2005) Mohan Vaidya (Kiran), Baburam Bhattarai, Ram Bahadur Thapa (Badal), Post Bahadur Bogati (Diwakar), Krishna Bahadur Mahara, and Dev Gurung. The central committee had nearly 100 members and grew as the movement expanded (ICG, 2005). The three divisions – western, special central, or mid-western, and eastern – were defined during the June 2002 central committee's plenary meeting and were granted broad authority. The leader of each command was titled "in-charge" (ICG, 2005). In early 2003, the strength of the CPN-M was reportedly 5,500 combatants, 8,000 militia, 4,500 cadres, 33,000 hard-core followers, and 200,000 sympathisers (SATP, 2017).

Moreover, there was huge female participation in the movement, which, according to one estimate, could have been close to 30% of the total strength (Lovell, 2019).

According to a Jane's Intelligence Review report of October 2001, there were two women in each unit of 35–40 men, and they were used to gather intelligence and act as couriers (SATP, 2017). Furthermore, it has been widely reported that at least 3,500 to 4,500 Nepali children were part of the Maoist fighting forces (HRW, 2007). The CPN (M) recruited children from student political groups. As a matter of fact, several Maoist revolutionary groups in Asia have been accused of recruiting children, for instance, the Khmer Rouge, the Indian Maoists, and the Communist Party of the Philippines (Yazdani, 2015). This trend strongly suggests that Maoist revolutionary groups intend to recruit children into armed groups as combatants, apart from using them as couriers. A considerable number of retired Gorkha soldiers of the British and Indian Army are suspected of having trained the Maoist insurgents (SATP, 2017). Some serving soldiers from the Indian Army on leave in Nepal ran three to four days' training capsules for Maoist guerrillas as a barter in exchange for the donations demanded by the insurgents (Mehta & Lawoti, 2010). Also, the weaponry in the Maoists' possession included AK-47 rifles, self-loading rifles, .303 rifles, country guns, hand grenades, explosives, detonators, mortars, and light machine guns, nearly 85% of which were reportedly looted from the police and Royal Nepal Army (SATP, 2017). All units of the CPN (M) outside Nepal's borders fell under the international department, formerly headed by C. P. Gajurel (Gaurav) and thereafter by Dr. Baburam Bhattarai (ICG, 2005). The international department's responsibilities, among other things, included:

1. Expanding the party organisation
2. Recruiting expatriate Nepalis
3. Establishing international contacts and relations
4. Fundraising
5. Purchase of ammunition and explosives, and
6. Training.

The department initially concentrated on trying to build a base among Nepalis in India. Later on, however, this type of liaison work was expanded to Europe and North America (ICG, 2005). It is alleged that the Maoists of Nepal had well-established linkages with Indian left-wing extremist organisations, primarily with the People's War Group (PWG) of Andhra Pradesh and the Maoist Communist Centre (MCC) of Bihar-Jharkhand. Towards strengthening the collaboration, they began the process of laying a corridor, widely termed the Revolutionary Corridor (RC), extending from Nepal across six Indian states: Bihar, Chhattisgarh, Jharkhand, Andhra Pradesh, Odisha, and Madhya Pradesh. This entire area has been identified in Maoist literature as the Compact Revolutionary Zone (CRZ) (SATP, 2017). Furthermore, it is suspected that the Nepali Maoists received arms training from Sri Lanka's LTTE insurgents. Links between these two groups were possibly facilitated by the PWG of Andhra Pradesh, which had a record of cooperation with the LTTE in arms procurement and training, especially in the use of improvised explosive devices. Interestingly, C. P. Gajurel was arrested at Chennai airport in the Indian state of Tamil Nadu in August 2003 (SATP, 2017).

IDEOLOGY, ACTIVITIES, AND OPERATION

> Prachanda was careerist. With him, it was about personal ambition rather than ideas and ideologies.
>
> Mohan Bikram Singh (Lovell, 2014)

In September 2005, at Chunbang village in Rukum district, the party's central committee confirmed that they were in the third and decisive stage of guerrilla warfare, the strategic offensive phase. Accordingly, they had reorganised their people's army into seven divisions (Adhikari, 2014). Prachanda, however, did not wait, or for that matter, did not possess either the wherewithal or the tenacity to completely win over the rural backyard before capturing the cities. He rather posited a fusion of Mao's rural insurrection and a simultaneous urban insurgency, which was popularised as the "Prachanda Path" (Hachhethu, 2008–2009). Baburam Bhattarai described the "Prachanda Path" as a school of thought that was more than a set of tactics but less than an ideology (ICG, 2005).

The Nepali Maoists, however, started off on a rather modest note in 1996. The organisational hierarchy of the People's Liberation Army (PLA) into division, brigade, battalion, company, platoon, squad, and then militias was a much later development. The first units, which had minimal equipment, were organised into "fighting units" (ladaku dal), "security units" (suraksha dal), and "volunteer units" (swayamsevak dal) (ICG, 2005). The first military actions of the People's War were simultaneous attacks on police posts in three different districts: Rolpa and Rukum in the west, and Sindhuli in the east. The operations led to the successful capture of a limited number of rifles and explosives (Ogura, 2008). According to the then military commander of the Maoists' central region, Sandip, the de facto development of the "people's army" took place after the start of the Nepal government's counterinsurgency Operation Kilo Sierra 2 from May 1998 to April 1999 (ICG, 2005). In 1996, the Maoists had about 200 active cadres. But in 2005, the number of soldiers in their PLA, divided into seven divisions, was reportedly 30,000–35,000. In fact, the PLA was "one of the largest non-state military formations in the world" (Hachhethu, 2008–2009). In August 1998, the central committee meeting (plenum) adopted the slogan of building "base areas" and building up military strength in order to challenge government repression. By the start of 2001, they had effectively defeated a demoralised and weak police force in Nepal (Adhikari, 2014). Knowing full well that they were not capable of fighting with the Royal Nepal Army (RNA), in July 2001, the Maoists reciprocated the government's ceasefire offer and used it to strengthen their military capacity (ICG, 2005).

As the guerrilla army grew in size, the central committee plenary in June 2002 decided to form brigade-level military groupings. In August 2004, these were incorporated into three divisions of three brigades each. The leadership of every fighting unit from company to division level was shared between a military commander and a political commissar, which the Maoists claim ensures political control over the army (ICG, 2005). The commissar ranks higher and is in charge of the party committee formed within each military unit.

In mid-February 2002, two PLA battalions, with approximately 1,200 forces, simultaneously attacked the district headquarters in Mangalsen and the security forces at nearby Sanphebagar airport in the Accham District (Ogura, 2008). Once PLA forces had returned to their base area, the security forces launched an air and land operation against them in an attempt to break up a gathering of PLA forces in eastern Rolpa (Ogura, 2008).

Although intermittent cease-fires began in 2002, fighting continued through 2005, when the CPN (M) finally sought a permanent peace accord by forming a pro-democratic alliance with several other mainstream political parties that wanted to end the Nepalese monarchy. However, Nepal's King Gyanendra lost faith in the reconciliation process and, in February 2005, took complete control of the government by dismissing the parliament. This gave rise to popular protests by opposition political parties. King Gyanendra was forced to reinstate the parliament in April 2006. The United Nations brokered a peace treaty, and the CPN (M)-led insurgency formally came to an end in November 2006 when the Comprehensive Peace Agreement was signed between the Nepali government and the dissident political groups (Gupta, 2020).

Under Prachanda's leadership, the CPN (M) won 220 seats in the April 2008 elections, becoming the single largest party in the 601-member Constituent Assembly. In May 2008, the new assembly voted to declare Nepal a democratic republic, thereby ending the monarchy, and on August 15, Prachanda was elected as the prime minister. Prachanda, however, has been alleged to have been associated with numerous scandals of extravagance and embezzlement (Lovell, 2019).

However, insofar as their military prowess was concerned, the PLA could never defeat the army. In this context, Bhattarai explains (Ogura, 2008):

> From Ghorahi to Arghakhanchi, we carried out mostly successful military actions. But during those periods, the US and Indian governments were providing military assistance to the RNA, supplying them with modern weapons and US army training. The US army also taught the RNA to fortify their barracks, which made it difficult for us to carry out raids. After the Jumla attack, we therefore changed our tactics to drawing the security forces out of their barracks.

CPN(M) believed that the party, PLA, and United Front (tactical alliances with bourgeois political parties and Maoist frontal organisations) were the three weapons for a successful people's revolution (Sharma, 2011). There are two broad aspects to the strategy adopted by the Maoists:

1. To increase their organisational strength and resource capabilities through various means.
2. To expand the area of their control and influence in a gradual but offensive way (Sharma, 2011).

At a plenum of the Central Committee of their party in May/June 2003, CPN (M) adopted a resolution on "the development of democracy in the 21st century." This advanced the concept of working in a multiparty, competitive democratic system within the stipulated constitutional framework (Sharma, 2011). Interestingly, Prachanda put forth two reasons for not attempting to seize state power militarily in 2005, when it seemed within their grasp, but instead turning to negotiate a permanent peace settlement (Sharma, 2011):

1. Given the international balance of forces, the Maoist leadership believed that while they might capture state power, they would not be able to retain it.
2. By abandoning the path of armed struggle for peaceful mass mobilisation, they hoped to achieve a new legitimacy, both domestically and internationally, that would give them greater protection in the long run.

Though the second reason appears to be well thought out and pragmatic, the first one doesn't hold much ground. It was an analytical ruse by Prachanda to cover up the lack of military capabilities of the CPN (M). It was primarily a propaganda tool.

IMPACT OF THE MAOIST INSURGENCY

There is hardly any denying the fact that the Maoist insurgency, along with the Jan Andolans, catapulted Nepal to international media briefings. However, the social, economic, and political strata of the country were deeply affected by the ten-year-long insurgency. Over two centuries of monarchical structures were demolished in the first decade of the 21st century. The Nepal Army had to absorb the Maoist guerrillas in its ranks and file. The Hindu nation turned secular.

B. P. Joshi has carried out a study (Joshi, 2014) of the insurgency by applying the methodology of system dynamics

(SD) within the realm of conflict transformation theory in order to examine the development, management, and cost of conflict in Nepal. The study selected eleven variables with the purpose of describing the dynamism and cost of the insurgency collectively. These variables were classified into four basic categories:

1. Insurgent and security force activity.
2. Public satisfaction.
3. Effect of insurgency on the economy.
4. Cost of the insurgency.

Interestingly, Joshi's study concludes that an armed solution might not be a good answer for any conflict, for that matter. The cost of an armed conflict might always be greater than its benefits. Accordingly, the main effort for the state must be to gain popular support, says Joshi. He, however, opines that it is common sense that the security forces must limit the use of direct actions against the insurgents without having efficient intelligence so as to minimise innocent casualties. Continuous sincere effort must move towards socio-economic and political reform in a post-conflict situation to prevent the country from being trapped in further conflict (Joshi, 2014).

Lawoti and Pahari (2015) argue that the level of participation of indigenous groups in the three insurgencies in Nepal, Peru, and India does explain their varied trajectories. They opine that the support of ethnic groups for class-based insurgencies could transform the nature of the insurgency itself, making it more formidable than a purely class-based insurgency. Majority participation (in the insurgency) of the ethnic communities has possibly turned the Maoist insurrection in Nepal more fruitful vis-à-vis its Indian and Peruvian counterparts. Adhikari (2014), however, talks about the "considerable impact" of the Maoists on the Nepali political fabric. He tells us that Nepal's parliamentary parties started to gather mass support after they signed the 12-point agreement with the Maoists (Adhikari, 2014).

The armed conflict in Nepal has resulted in the deaths of around 18,000 civilians and combatants combined. There was fighting almost every day after November 2001, except during the truce between January and August 2003. Besides the destruction of material goods, the conflict also disrupted the normal lives of the people, causing social and economic losses, most of which were difficult to measure. Socio-cultural impacts (UKDiss, 2019) included displacement of people, human rights violations, and psychological and mental problems in children and women, among other things.

H. B. Jha elaborates on the economic impact of the People's War (Jha, 2013), in which he writes that between 2001 and 2005, the GDP of Nepal declined from 4.8% to as low as 2.6%. Jha cites Upreti to state that private sector investment declined from 15.4% to 12.6% between 1996 and 2004. As a cumulative effect, the rate of economic growth in the country could not increase more than 3.5% in the post-conflict period. The Maoists particularly targeted the state-owned banks. Several banks were looted and robbed. Due to the security issues cropping up because of the decade-long insurgency, a number of banks were forced to withdraw from the remote and rural areas and relocate to the urban areas.

As a result of the conflict, nearly 200,000 people were displaced. Torture and sexual abuse as a consequence of the insurgency were prominent. More than 70% of Nepalese prisoners claim to have been tortured while in custody (Singh, 2004).

FUTURE TRAJECTORY

The CPN (M) joined with other political parties, and in the parliamentary elections held in April 2008, the CPN (M) won the largest share of seats. The Nepalese monarchy was dissolved, and the country was declared a republic.

The CPN (M) merged with the Communist Party of Nepal (Unity Centre-Masal) in January 2009 to become the Unified Communist Party of Nepal (Maoist). In May 2009, Prachanda resigned his post after he failed to remove the chief of the Nepalese armed forces. The UCPN (M) remained a part of the government, however, and was a primary player in the peace talks that led to the November 2011 agreement, which integrated former Maoist rebel fighters into the Nepalese armed forces. In 2016, the party finally merged with ten other Maoist parties and became known as the CPN (Maoist Centre) (Gupta, Britannica). Thereafter, in May 2018, the Dahal-led CPN (Maoist Centre) merged with the moderate CPN (Unified Marxist-Leninist) to form the Nepal Communist Party (NCP), currently the party in Nepal that holds political authority (Bhattarai, 2019).

However, even after this series of violence, bloodletting, and socio-political transformation since 1996, all do not appear to be peaceful in Nepal. A splinter Maoist group, which calls itself the Communist Party of Nepal and is led by Netra Bikram Chand, has been engaging in violent activities with the goal of "completing the revolution" (Bhattarai, 2019), which purportedly was abandoned when the CPN (M) joined democratic politics.

In April 2018, members of Chand's group planted a bomb at the office of the Arun III Hydro Project, which was being developed by an Indian company. The motto was to put across their conservative views on foreign direct investment in Nepal (Adhikari, 2019).

Furthermore, Chand and other dissident Maoists could not accept the policy of integrating Maoist combatants into the Nepal Army. Interestingly, out of the 19,000 Maoist combatants verified by the United Nations Mission in Nepal (UNMIN), only about 6,500 were integrated into the Nepal Army. The rest retired or disappeared (Bhattarai, 2019), which is a matter of serious concern since those cadres can again re-group and ring the bells of a fresh insurgency.

After the fusion of the comparatively radical CPN (Maoist Centre) with the relatively bigger Communist Party of Nepal (Unified Marxist-Leninist) into the Nepal Communist Party in 2018, the CPN (Maoist Centre) was dissolved (Gupta, Britannica). It is a natural fallout that the erstwhile Maoist cadres, a bulk of them, would feel disillusioned and betrayed. In this context, it wouldn't be easy to ignore the finite probability of a fresh round of insurgency in Nepal.

References

Acharya, A. (2009, October). The Maoist insurgency in Nepal and the political economy of violence. In Anup Pahari & Mahendra Lawoti (Eds.), *The Maoist insurgency in Nepal: Revolution in the 21st century*. London: Routledge.

Adhikari, A. (2014). *The bullet and the ballot box: The story of Nepal's Maoist revolution*. London: Verso Books.

Adhikari, G. (2019, April 21). The spectre of a new Maoist conflict in Nepal, Al Jazeera. https://www.aljazeera.com/opinions/2019/4/21/the-spectre-of-a-new-maoist-conflict-in-nepal/?gb=true

Background Paper – Nepal, Australian Government – Refugee Review Tribunal. (2012).

Bhattarai, K.D. (2019, March 13). Are the Maoists rising again in Nepal?. The Diplomat. https://thediplomat.com/2019/03/are-the-maoists-rising-again-in-nepal/. Accessed on 25 March 2021.

Fukuyama, F. (Summer 1989). The end of history?. *The National Interest*, 1. https://tr.uow.edu.au/uow/file/c1e8a018-b551-452a-94c1-f681ed92a4c5/1/fukuyama-1989-1-18.pdf. Accessed on 24 March 2021

Gates, S., & Roy, K. (2014). Unconventional warfare in South Asia. 66–67. ISBN 978–1–4724–0579–1 (epub)

Grice, F. (2019). *The myth of Mao Zedong and modern insurgency*. Palgrave.

Gupta, D. (2020, October 11). Communist party of Nepal (Maoist centre). *Britannica*. https://www.britannica.com/topic/Communist-Party-of-Nepal-Maoist-Centre

Hachhethu, K. (2008–2009). The communist party of Nepal (Maoist): Transformation from an insurgency group to a competitive political party. *European Bulletin of Himalayan Research*, 33–34, 39–71.

Hobsbawm, E. (2011). *How to change the world: Tales of Marx and Marxism*. London: Hachette.

Human Rights Watch. (2007). The Maoists' use of child soldiers in Nepal.

International Crisis Group. (2005, October 27). Nepal's Maoists: Their aims, structure and strategy.

Jha, D.N. (2010). Ancient India in historical outline. New Delhi: Manohar. https://ia800507.us.archive.org/0/items/AncientIndiaInHistoricalOutlineByD.N.Jha/Ancient%20India%20in%20Historical%20Outline%20by%20D.N.Jha.pdf

Jha, H.B. (2013, October 17). Economic impact of People's War in Nepal: A study, Vivekananda International Foundation. https://www.vifindia.org/article/2013/october/17/economic-impact-of-people-s-war-in-nepal-a-study

Joshi, B.P. (2014). *Dynamics and cost of insurgency: The Maoist insurgency in Nepal*. University of Bergen.

Lawoti, M., & Pahari, A.K. (Eds.). (2010). *The Maoist insurgency in Nepal: Revolution in the twenty-first century*. New York: Routledge.

Lawoti, M., & Pahari, A.K. (2015). (Eds.).*The Maoist insurgency in Nepal*, pp. 7–10.

Lovell, J. (2019). *Maoism: A global history*. New York: Penguin Random House.

Mehta, A.K., & Lawoti, M. (2010). Military dimension of the "People's War": Insurgency and counter-insurgency in Nepal. In M. Lawoti & A.K. Pahari (Eds.), *The Maoist insurgency in Nepal: Revolution in the twenty-first century* (pp. 175–194). London and New York: Routledge.

Mukherjee, U. (2016, March 18). Diplomatic courier. https://www.diplomaticourier.com/posts/fragile-peace-in-colombia

Mukherjee, U. (December 17, 2012). India and Philippines: Searching the common contours. *Centre for Land Warfare Studies*. https://archive.claws.in/944/india-and-philippines-searching-the-common-contours-uddipan-mukherjee.html?__cf_chl_jschl_tk__=76e0ce495fe-b91ef8acde549f6985f762ef8cf01-1602422305-0-AW8B7YY-LqwNfx1QxYSS9YfsfT05Di2u_8t-m-3rPvoq_Gdq6NO7-xTZ6EhsHYVDMNI4t0IYbOLNy

Nepal, M., Bohara, A.K., & Gawande, K. (2011, October). More inequality, more killings: The maoist insurgency in Nepal. *American Journal of Political Science*, *55*(4), 886–906.

Ogura, K. (2008). Seeking state power: The communist party of Nepal (Maoist). Berghof Research Center for Constructive Conflict Management.

SATP. (2017, December 31). South Asia terrorism portal, communist party of Nepal – Maoist. https://www.satp.org/satporgtp/countries/nepal/terroristoutfits/index.html

Sharma, P. K. (2011). *Red rebels: Looming fear of maoists*. New Delhi: Surendra publication.

Singh, S. (2004, December 7). Impact of long-term political conflict on population health in Nepal. https://www.ncbi.nlm.nih.gov/pmc/articles/PMC534599/pdf/20041207s00033p1499.pdf

Thapa, D., & Sijapati, B. (2003). *A kingdom under siege: Nepal's Maoist insurgency, 1996 to 2003*. Kathmandu: Printhouse

Tse Tung, M. (1927, March). Report on an investigation of the peasant movement in Hunan. *Selected Works, I*, 28. http://large.stanford.edu/history/kaist/references/marx/mao/c2/

Tse Tung, M. (1938, November 6). Problems of war and strategy. *Selected Works, II*, 224. https://www.marxists.org/reference/archive/mao/works/red-book/ch05.htm

UKDiss. (2019, December 13). Impact of the Maoist insurgency on the Nepalese society. https://ukdiss.com/examples/impact-of-the-maoist-insurgency.php

Yazdani, L. (2015). *Recruitment of child soldiers in Nepal: An analysis of child recruitment in the people's liberation army*. School of Conflict Studies, Faculty of Human Sciences, Saint Paul University and University of Ottawa.

Zimmermann, M. (2000). Sandinista: Carlos Fonseca and the Nicaraguan Revolution. Duke University Press. https://doi.org/10.2307/j.ctv11cw5br

67

LASHKAR-E-TAIBA (LET)

Sameer Patil and Arun Vishwanathan

INTRODUCTION

Lashkar-e-Taiba (LeT, Army of the Pure) is an anti-India terrorist group based in Muridke, near Lahore, in Pakistan's Punjab province. Headed by Hafiz Saeed, the group, under its parent organisation, the Markaz al-Dawa wal-Irshad, began its operations in Afghanistan during the late 1980s. LeT's primary objectives are the liberation of Kashmir from Indian rule, the destruction of India, and the establishment of Islamic rule over the Indian subcontinent.

Since its formation, the group has received preferential treatment and support from the Pakistan Army and the state. It has also served as a proxy for the Army's intelligence wing, the Inter-Services Intelligence (ISI). Fittingly, over the years, LeT has carried out numerous attacks in India, including in Kashmir, targeting the security forces, civilians, and the symbols of the Indian state. On some occasions, these attacks have nearly precipitated a military confrontation between India and Pakistan. The United States designated the group as a foreign terrorist organisation in December 2001, and it was banned in Pakistan a month later. This proscription notwithstanding, the group continued to operate with impunity in Pakistan under the guise of a front organisation called the Jamaat-ud-Dawa (JuD). Global interest in the LeT's activities remained almost nil until the deadly attacks in Mumbai on November 26, 2008.

The carnage in Mumbai was LeT's most significant and high-profile attack. It prompted a crackdown by the Indian security agencies on the group's base in India as well as its extended network in the subcontinent. This action, combined with the sustained United States pressure on Pakistan's "deep state," has sapped the LeT's support in much of India. As a result, today the group is restricted mainly to the Kashmir Valley, where it has also been locked in an intense turf battle with local outfits such as the Hizbul Mujahideen and the local affiliates of al-Qaeda and the Islamic State. In contrast, the group's activities in Pakistan have continued unabated, sometimes under the guise of numerous front organisations. In 2017, LeT also made a political debut by launching a political party, the Milli Muslim League. Most recently, the group has again come to attention for its operations in Afghanistan, the place where its journey began more than three decades ago.

OVERVIEW: HISTORY OF HOW AND WHY THE GROUP OR MOVEMENT FORMED

The genesis of the LeT can be found in the turbulent political conditions of Pakistan in the 1980s. Under the dictatorship of General Zia-ul-Haq, the country was witnessing the rise of Islamic fundamentalism. A devout Muslim, Zia wanted to turn Pakistan into an Islamic nation, termed by analysts as his "Islamization" project, under which he went about systematically enforcing Islamic rules in every sphere of the Pakistani state. It was also a means for Zia to legitimise military rule (Aziz, 2008: 21).

Simultaneously, the conflict in neighbouring Afghanistan had become a full-fledged proxy war between the United States and the Soviet Union after the latter invaded Afghanistan in 1979. Pakistan, too, got involved as a military ally of the United States. In doing so, Zia had two objectives: to stymie the emerging Pashtun nationalist sentiments and expand Pakistan's influence in Afghanistan, and to counter India's conventional military superiority. The two countries then commenced a (not so) covert campaign under which the American Central Intelligence Agency (CIA), along with the ISI, armed and trained the Afghan fighters, known as the *mujahideens* or the holy fighters. These mujahideens stood at the forefront of resistance to the Soviet forces in Afghanistan (Malik, 2008: 170). This effort was matched in equal measure by Saudi Arabia through money and ideology (Johnson & Mason, 2007: 73; Cooley, 2002: 5).

DOI: 10.4324/9780429426063-76

In 1985, JuD was created in Muridke as a small preaching group (Roul, 2015: 23). A year later, it merged into the Markaz al-Dawa wal-Irshad (MDI, Centre for Proselytization and Preaching), created by a group of Islamic scholars to lend support to the mujahideens. According to Bruce Reidel, Osama bin Laden, then a central leader in the Afghan jihad and later the founder of al-Qaeda, played a key role along with the ISI in creating the MDI. Reportedly, Osama donated US $200,000 to set up the group with the ISI's encouragement (Riedel, 2008: 43). The MDI followed the Ahl-e-Hadith school of thought, a relatively smaller Wahhabi group that had existed in Pakistan since the partition of British India in 1947. The infusion of Saudi money helped in the rapid expansion of the Ahl-e-Hadith movement in the 1980s. Yet, as compared to the Deobandi movement (to which most of the other extremist groups adhered), it remained a minor actor (Burke, 2007: 99).

The MDI set up its headquarters in Peshawar, in the then-North-West Frontier Province (now Khyber Pakhtunkhwa). Soon after its formation, it opened its first training camp in Afghanistan's Paktia province, followed by the second camp in Kunar province. It primarily focused on mobilising Pakistani cadres for the Afghan war, though it also helped to manage the flow of Arab volunteers (Tankel, 2011: 20). It worked closely with bin Laden's Maktab-al-Khidmat, al-Qaeda's predecessor, which recruited, trained, and financed the cadres for the Afghan war effort (Sharma & Behera, 2014: 145). The group sent its first batch of 21 cadres to Afghanistan in August 1987. It included Zaki-ur-Rahman Lakhvi, one of the co-founders of the MDI, who later emerged as the senior operational commander of the LeT (Jamal, 2015: 61).

The withdrawal of the Soviet forces from Afghanistan and the subsequent winding-up of the CIA campaign coincided with the outbreak of the armed insurgency in the then-Indian state of Jammu and Kashmir in 1989. This marked the beginning of the MDI's involvement in the Kashmir theatre. Between 1989 and 1992, the first batch of MDI fighters fought along with groups such as the Al Barq and Tehreek ul Mujahideen in the Kashmir Valley (Jamal, 2015: 77).

It was in these circumstances that the MDI set up its armed wing, the Lashkar-e-Taiba, though differences exist among the scholars on its exact year of formation. Tellis (Tellis, 2012: 3) puts it at 1987, Tankel (Tankel, 2011: 4) claims around 1990, while other scholars put the year as 1993 (Jamal, 2015: 24; Macdonald, 2017: 191). According to the South Asia Terrorism Portal (SATP, n.d.), the first presence of the LeT in Kashmir was recorded in 1993, when a group of Pakistani and Afghani fighters infiltrated the Kashmir Valley.

The setting up of the LeT enabled the MDI co-founders to pursue da'wah (religious proselytization) as well as jihad (war against the non-believers). LeT leader Hafiz Saeed, writing about the importance of the two, argued that da'wah and jihad were "equally important and inseparable ... we cannot prefer one over the other" (Ali & Shehzad, 2009: 13). Yasmeen argues that over the years, the narrative of the group has given prominence to jihad as compared to da'wah (Yasmeen, 2017: 19–20). This narrative supported the LeT's mobilisation and recruitment efforts to fight against India. However, since the Kargil crisis of 1999, in which LeT claimed to participate, the narrative has focused equally on jihad as well as da'wah.

Both MDI and LeT have enjoyed extensive support from the Pakistani Army, right from their inception. The Army used the MDI and LeT as proxies to further Pakistan's national interests, first in the Afghan theatre and then in Kashmir and India. Specifically, the LeT's objectives of liberating Kashmir from India's rule and the destruction of India aligned with the goals of the Pakistani Army. Besides, the LeT calls upon the Muslims to help in the establishment of Islamic rule over the Indian subcontinent, which it terms "Ghazwa-e-Hind" (Ali & Shehzad, 2009: 13).

Capitalising on the support from the Army, the MDI and the LeT developed extensive infrastructure in Pakistan and Pakistan-occupied Kashmir (PoK) (Tankel, 2009: 8). By 1994, the group had established a base in the PoK capital, Muzaffarabad, along with recruiting offices throughout Pakistan. It also had the largest number of launch pads along the Line of Control and the India-Pakistan international boundary. It operated six major training camps in Pakistan and the PoK before 2001 (Jamal, 2015: 24).

After al-Qaeda's September 2001 attacks in the United States and Jaish-e-Mohammed's (JeM) attack on the Indian Parliament in December 2001, the terrorist infrastructure in Pakistan came under American and global scrutiny. The United States designated the LeT as a foreign terrorist organisation along with other organisations and also exerted pressure on the Pakistani government to ban the group, which it did in January 2002 (Jamal, 2015: 12).

Post-US designation, the MDI took on the identity of the JuD in December 2001. It quickly became the LeT's front, acting as a charity organisation to offer services such as education, healthcare, and disaster relief in various Pakistani cities. For instance, the JuD played an essential role in the relief work after the October 2005 Kashmir earthquake. Such charity work allowed the group to compensate for the failures of the civilian administration and thereby increase its hold over Pakistani society at the cost of the legitimacy of the Pakistani state. There was a symbiotic relationship between JuD and LeT. By utilising Lashkar's network, JuD's charitable work kept the "Islamists alive and attractive to local communities in Pakistan" (Ali & Shehzad, 2009: 14). Simultaneously, Indian security agencies noted that the JuD's welfare work had enabled the LeT to spread its message and recruit potential cadres.

A similar evolution occurred in the aftermath of the Mumbai attacks, when JuD was listed as a front organisation of the LeT. Again, to evade the intense international scrutiny of its activities and financial sanctions, LeT/JuD propped up multiple organisations, mainly focusing on charity and social work. Chief among these were the

Falah-e-Insaniyat Foundation (FIF, a charity organisation), Tehrik-e-Hurmat-e-Rasool (THR, Movement for Defending the Honour of the Prophet), Tehrik-e-Tahafuz Qibla Awwal (TTQA, the Movement for the Safeguarding of the First Centre of Prayer or the Al Aqsa mosque in Jerusalem), Al-Anfal Trust (used to procure goods from the Persian Gulf), and Idara Khidmat-e Khalq (IKK, a public welfare organisation) (Kapisthalam, 2009). But even as the LeT and JuD mutated under these different names, one thing that remained the same for all these organisations was the leadership and other functionaries. For example, the leader of the FIF, Hafiz Abdur Rauf, was a senior LeT operative (Tanzeem, 2016).

By 2010, FIF and other front organisations had been banned as entities associated with the LeT and JuD. But not much changed for them on the ground. For instance, in August 2016, the FIF, despite the ban, was allowed to set up a camp in Islamabad to collect donations in the name of the "Kashmir Fund" (Hussein, 2016). In addition, new entities emerged, including the Tehreek-e-Azadi-e Kashmir, established in January 2017 to work for Kashmir's freedom from Indian rule (Office of the Spokesperson, 2018).

The preferential treatment and support from the Army and the State for the group have earned LeT the tag of "good terrorist." This tag also gives the Pakistani Army significant leverage as it utilises the group as and when the situation demands it to carry out violence against India.

While the group has carried out terrorist attacks in India and Afghanistan, it has global ambitions. Former US Senator Gary Ackerman, speaking in 2010 at a Congressional hearing on the Lashkar, noted that in the wake of the Mumbai attacks, investigators had uncovered from a Lashkar operative's computer evidence of 320 locations worldwide deemed by the LeT as possible targets for attack. Out of these, only 20 targets were in India (US Congress, 2010). In the 1990s, Lashkar cadres were noted to be involved in fighting in the Tajik civil war as well as Kosovo (Tankel, 2011; Kiessling, 2016: 125). Just like al-Qaeda, the LeT too has an extensive network of operatives worldwide, including in Europe, which provides logistical services. For instance, investigations into the Mumbai attacks revealed a link to a Pakistani father-son duo in Brescia, Italy, who had managed money transfers for the purchase of phone accounts used in the attacks (PTI, 2009).

KEY PERSONNEL AND STRUCTURE

Leadership

Hafiz Saeed is the Amir of the JuD and the head of the LeT. He is a former professor of Arabic and engineering, a description refuted by Jamal, who argues that Saeed taught only Islamic Studies at the University of Engineering and Technology in Lahore (Jamal, 2015: 14). According to Stephen Tankel, while MDI was founded during the time of Afghan jihad, it was never intended to be a militant outfit (Tankel, 2011: 3). It was for this reason that Saeed was chosen over another co-founder, Lakhvi, to lead the MDI, as Saeed was one of the most respected scholars of the Ahl-e-Hadith movement.

For years, Saeed has been the chief ideologue of the LeT, giving out vitriolic statements against India in the annual congregations of the LeT and other rallies across various cities in Pakistan and the PoK. He is a wanted terrorist in India, the United States, and the United Nations. Investigations into the Mumbai attacks have shown him to be the mastermind of the attacks. Subsequently, in December 2008, he was listed as a terrorist under UN Security Council Resolution 1267 (United Nations Security Council, 2008). He carries a bounty of US$10 million (Department of State, n.d.).

Saeed's relatives control important positions within the LeT. Saeed's cousin and brother-in-law, Abdul Rahman Makki, is the Deputy Amir of the LeT and the group's second-in-command. Reportedly, Makki also leads the Departments of Foreign Affairs and Political Affairs (Jamal, 2015: 21; Fair, 2018: 91). He carries a reward of $2 million from the United States. Meanwhile, Saeed's son, Talha, is in charge of LeT's propaganda department and recruitment. The United States designated him in 2012 (Department of Treasury, 2012) (Figure 67.1).

In addition to Saeed, another co-founder of the group and a prominent member is Zafar Iqbal, who heads the finance department (United Nations Security Council, 2020). He also leads the education department, which is charged with putting together the curricula for the schools run by the group. Iqbal, along with Makki, was sentenced to up to five years in a terror financing case by the Lahore anti-terrorism court in June 2020 (Sheikh, 2020).

Another co-founder, Zaki-ur-Rahman Lakhvi, is the senior operational commander of the LeT. Lakhvi is believed to be one of the prominent handlers of the terrorists who carried out the Mumbai attacks (Fair, 2018: 90). He was the only prominent leader of JuD/LeT who was arrested, even if only for his name, in the aftermath of the attacks. Dr. Christine Fair argues that this could also be because Lakhvi is the only leader in the LeT who has resisted the centralised control of the group by Saeed and briefly separated from the group to form his militant group, though he joined back soon after that (Fair, 2018: 90–91).

Hafiz Abdul Salam Bhuttavi is another founder member of the LeT and the group's preeminent scholar. In addition to looking after the group's madrasa network, he is the only leader who has served as the group's acting Amir when Saeed was detained in the past. Bhuttavi was involved in preparing the LeT cadres who carried out the Mumbai attacks (Department of Treasury, 2011).

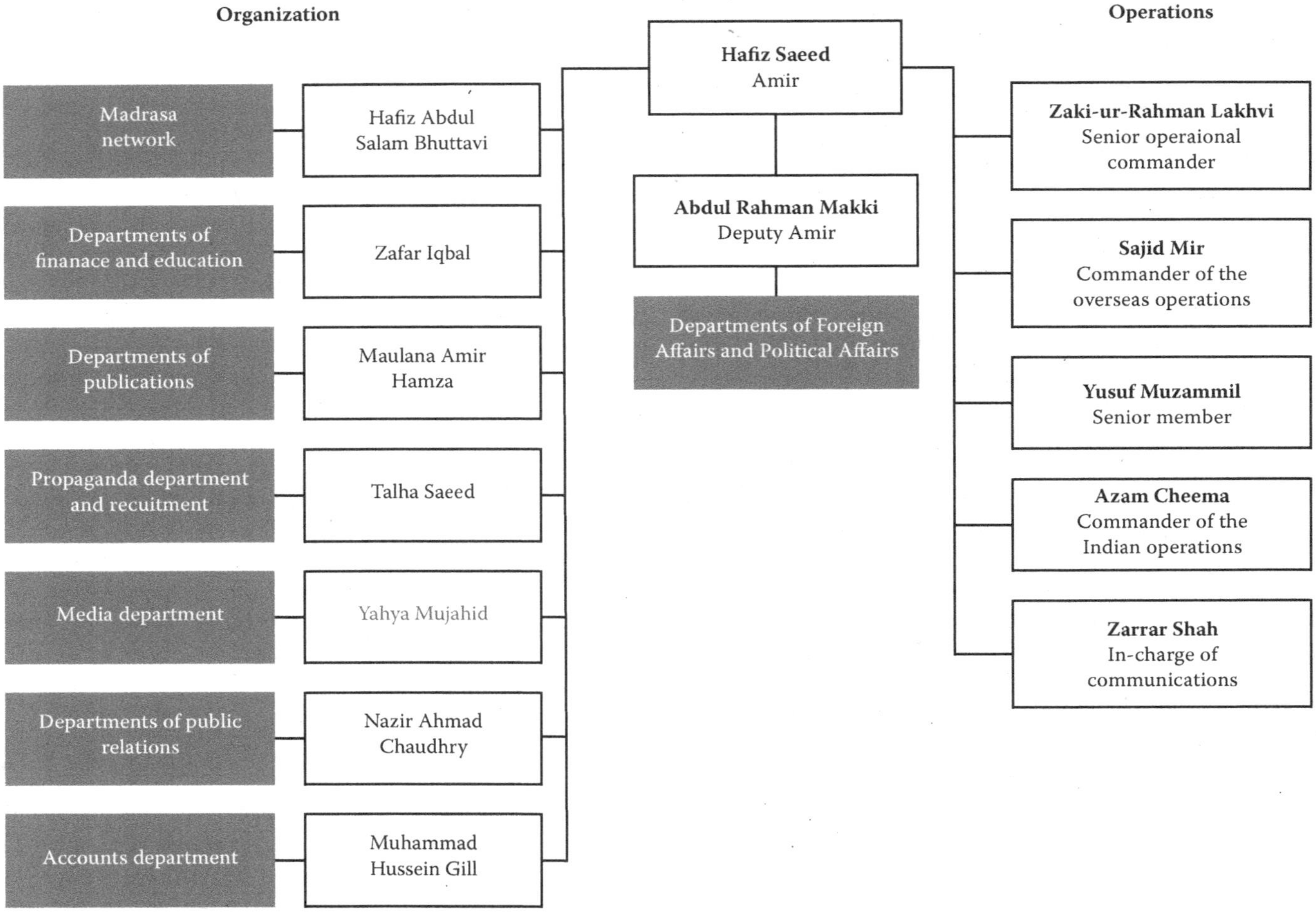

Figure 67.1 Leadership Structure of Lashkar-e-Tayaba.

Compiled by the authors.

Another name that has prominently figured in many news reports is Yahya Mujahid, who heads the group's media department and has served as LeT's spokesman since at least mid-2001 (United Nations Security Council, 2009). Mujahid has claimed responsibility on LeT's behalf for many attacks, including the Mumbai attacks.

Two other figures are worth mentioning. One is Nazir Ahmad Chaudhry, who is part of the central leadership and a close aide to Saeed. The other is Muhammad Hussein Gill, a founder member of the LeT. While Ahmad has handled the group's public relations department in the past, Gill has dealt with matters of finance and also headed the accounts department for several years (Department of Treasury, 2014).

On the operations side of the LeT, a prominent figure is Azam Cheema, who is believed to be the commander of the Indian operations branch and intelligence chief, before which he was the overall chief for the LeT's operations in Bahawalpur. Cheema recruits and trains cadres for terror operations in India and provides training in making bombs and other explosives. The US Treasury designated him in 2011 (Department of Treasury, 2011; Fair, 2018: 92).

Another preeminent member of the LeT is MDI co-founder Maulana Amir Hamza. He heads the department of publications for the group. Also, he serves as editor of several JuD/LeT publications, like its monthly magazine Mujallah ad-Dawah and many other books brought out by the group. Like Cheema, he is also a major recruiter for the group in Iran and Central Asia (Fair, 2018: 93).

From time to time, various other names have emerged who have been in charge of various operations of the LeT. In the immediate aftermath of the Mumbai attacks, many names of LeT operatives came to the forefront. One of them was Sajid Mir, who was noted as the commander of the overseas operations of the LeT. However, it is not clear whether this is a *nom de guerre* or the name of a real individual. Dr. Fair (Fair, 2018: 92) quotes Willie Brigitte (a French terrorist trained in the Lashkar camp in Pakistan) who believes that Mir was a former Pakistani Army officer. What is clear is that he played a critical role in the planning of the attack as the "project" manager and handled David Headley, the American terrorist of Pakistani origin who carried out reconnaissance of the targets for the Mumbai attacks. Mir carries a reward of US $5 million from the United States (Federal Bureau of Investigation, n.d.).

Yusuf Muzammil was another name that emerged during the Mumbai attacks investigations. He was noted as a senior member of the LeT and reportedly served as a control officer in Lahore during the attacks (LeT Stage-Managed Mumbai Strikes: NYT-The New Indian Express, 2008). The other name that came to prominence was Zarrar Shah, identified as the communications manager of the group. It was on Shah's advice that the LeT used a Voice over Internet Protocol (VoIP) call service, enabling the attackers to evade the Indian security agencies' surveillance (Fair, 2018: 91).

After the 2008 attacks, Pakistan arrested several leaders of the LeT, including Lakhvi. The government also put Saeed under house arrest. However, the arrested commanders reportedly led a comfortable life inside the jail. They were allowed to meet their wives, relatives, and the cadres (BBC, 2015). However, as global interest in LeT's activities waned, cases against Saeed were withdrawn, and by June 2009, he was released.

Post-release, Saeed kept a low profile, only to reappear in public life in 2010 by making guest appearances on several TV talk shows (Jamal, 2015: 15). He also continued his fiery speeches at the rallies organised by the LeT/JuD and Difa-e-Pakistan Council, a coalition of conservative parties and extremist groups. In one such gathering in December 2017, he was seen sharing a stage with then-Palestinian Ambassador Walid Abu Ali (Yasin, 2017). The trial against Saeed for his role in the Mumbai attacks, meanwhile, has proceeded at a snail's pace (Ahmad & Laskar, 2019). In February 2020, Saeed was convicted for five and a half years each in two terrorist financing cases by the Lahore anti-terrorism court (Hafiz Saeed Sentenced to 11 Years in Jail, 2020). Scepticism, however, remains about the implementation of the verdict, as it came just before the meeting of the Financial Action Task Force (FATF), the international body that monitors progress on countering terrorist financing.

The kid-glove treatment given to Saeed, Lakhvi, and other terrorist operatives of the LeT after the Mumbai attacks suggests that this crackdown was primarily aimed at parrying the global criticism of Pakistan's terrorist infrastructure rather than a genuine action aimed at dismantling that infrastructure. A case in point was the much-publicised crackdown on the LeT training camps in and around Muzaffarabad after the Mumbai attacks in November 2008. However, days later, a few kilometres away, new training facilities came up like the one in Dulai, using advanced technologies and some cadres practising even deadlier tactics for future attacks (Khan & Petrou, 2009).

Structure

The LeT/JuD has several departments that look after its multiple international and domestic (Pakistani) interests and activities. According to Christine Fair (Fair, 2018: 83–84), the group's internal structure is divided into the following departments:

- Department of Education.
- The Department of Publishing, which is under Dar ul Andlus, the publication arm of the MDI, produces material in Urdu, English, and Arabic.
- Department of Construction of Mosques and Madrassas.
- Department of Ulema and Teachers.
- Department of Preaching and Reform.
- Department of Resources, which raises funds for jihad.
- Martyrs' Department, which looks after the families of fighters who have been killed.
- External Affairs Department.
- Media and Propaganda Department.
- Department of Public Relations.

Besides, the group also has "specialized wings for technology, physicians, women, students, farmers and workers." Not much is known about the leadership of many of these departments. But, given the centralised control that Saeed maintains, it is clear that these departments come under his direct control (Fair, 2018: 83–84).

Most of these departments are located at the group's headquarters in Muridke, which is spread over a spacious 200-acre campus. It also serves as a training and convention centre. Reportedly, the annual conferences in Muridke used to attract as many as 1 million attendees in the late 1990s, indicating LeT's spread in Pakistani society, buttressed by its humanitarian and charity work (Markey, 2013: 100).

Apart from this, the LeT/JuD has offices in all major Pakistani cities, with Fair saying that even in 2000, the group had more than 70 district offices, in addition to several training camps across the country (Fair, 2018: 93). These district offices, training camps, and other offices carry out recruitment and fundraising (SATP, n.d.).

Recruitment and Fundraising

The LeT primarily recruits cadres from central and southern Punjab, making it a Punjabi-dominated group. As a matter of fact, according to Shuja Nawaz, the army recruits heavily in the same area where the LeT recruits (Nawaz, 2010). This makes the economically disadvantaged areas of the central and southern Punjab provinces fertile recruitment pools for the two. So it is natural that the group has had a natural ethnic affinity with the predominantly Punjabi Army (Devasher, 2016: 196).

There is very little information available about the actual funds available to the group. Estimates vary from US $ 100 million (Fair, 2018: 93) to US $ 50 million as estimated by Kambere et al. (2011). There are three major sources of funding for the group. These range from state funding and sponsorship to support received from charity groups and business interests like publication sales and collections of animal hides.

Jyoti Trehan (Trehan, 2002: 210) estimates that about 20% of the funding for terrorist groups like Lashkar comes from Pakistan, both in the form of counterfeit and genuine currency. Ashley Tellis argues that the group's success has been a result of the fact that it receives sustenance and support from the Pakistani Army, especially the ISI

(Tellis, 2010: 2). This was particularly so in the 1990s, as the group focused on Jammu and Kashmir (Tankel, 2011).

While this funding has waned since 2002, it didn't stop completely. In 2012–13, for instance, the Punjab provincial government gave Pakistan Rs. 61.35 million for JuD's training camp and Rs. 350 million for a "Knowledge Park" (Fair, 2018: 97; Sharma & Behera, 2014: 172). Governmental support for the group also takes the form of largesse for its al-Dawah schools across the Punjab province. Therefore, the group continues to receive state patronage, both in terms of funds and the security of its organisations, from the Pakistani state and the military.

The second primary source of funding for the group is through charitable donations from the Persian Gulf, as was brought out in the interrogation of Muhammad Omar Madni, chief of LeT's Nepal operations (Roul, 2009). Moreover, the large Pakistani immigrant population spread across Europe, the United Kingdom, and the Gulf region also supports the group's activities through donations. Britain is one such major source, given the significant presence of the Pakistani diaspora in the country. The group reportedly raised f4 million from Britain alone in 2001. Some of this funding has been funnelled into terrorist activities. For instance, in the case of the foiled 2006 transatlantic bombing plot, funds raised by the charities in British mosques to support the victims of the 2005 Kashmir earthquake were diverted for the attack planning (Clarke, 2010: 25–27). Within Pakistan, the group has donation boxes at major locations such as mosques, and many shopkeepers also add a few rupees to purchases to support the group's activities (Kambere et al., 2011: 12; Fair, 2018: 95).

The third major source of funding for the group comes from its on-ground operations, like *al-Dawa* schools, which number over 127 schools with over 15,000 students (2001 figures) spread across Pakistan. Also, the group has involvement in many businesses, including fish farms, al-Dawah Medical Mission, agricultural tracts, mobile clinics, and ambulance services (SATP, n.d.; Tankel, 2011: 7). Sales of magazines and books brought out by the group's Department of Media and Propagation and its Dar-ul-Andalus Department of Publishing also add substantial, even though unknown, revenue to the group (Fair, 2018: 96). The collection of animal hides and fur during Eid-al-Azha also provides a significant revenue stream for the group (Fair, 2018: 96–97; Kambere et al., 2011: 12–13).

LeT relies on the well-established *hawala* network to move its funds across borders. In July 2006, following the arrest of LeT fundraiser Faizal Sheikh from Mumbai, it was revealed that LeT used the *hawala* network to transfer funds from the Gulf and Pakistan to carry out terror operations in India (2006; Clarke, 2010: 26–27).

ORGANISATIONAL CHARACTERISTICS AND ACTIVITIES: STRUCTURE, CHANGE, AND OPERATIONS

Looking back at the last three decades, three broad phases can be identified in the history of the LeT. The first phase corresponds to its operations in Jammu and Kashmir, while the second phase begins after the group extends operations to the rest of India. The Mumbai attacks and their aftermath mark the third phase of their journey. These phases demonstrate the evolution of LeT's operations, its tactical innovations, the changing nature of ties with peer terrorist groups, and an attempt to adapt to the increasing squeeze on its activities, particularly after the Mumbai attacks.

First Phase: The Early 1990s to 1999

Soon after its entry into Kashmir in 1993, LeT, along with other Pakistan-backed terrorist groups, pushed the violence in the region to an unprecedented level (Burke, 2007: 99, 115). It launched several guerrilla attacks against the Indian security forces, government facilities, the followers of Sufism, and the Hindus and their temples (Joshi, 2019: 189–190; Jamal, 2015: 24, 83).

LeT's signature tactic since its entry in Kashmir has been *fidayeen*, or life-daring attacks (Bose, 2003: 141). But in July 1999, post-Kargil, the LeT formally introduced these operations when its militants ambushed a Border Security Force camp in Baramulla, north Kashmir. The most significant fidayeen attack was in November 1999, when the group attacked the Badamibagh Cantonment of the Indian Army's XV Corps headquarters in Srinagar, killing eight personnel, including a major (Jamal, 2015: 86–87). The success of this tactic was evident from the fact that between August 1999 and January 2000, LeT was able to storm 15 camps of the security forces in the Valley (Swami, 2000).

But throughout this period, LeT's relationship with the local Kashmiri terrorist groups was less than cordial. As a group with a dominant cadre base of Punjabis and Pashtoons at that time, LeT initially spurned joining hands with local groups such as the Hizbul Mujahideen and the Jammu and Kashmir Liberation Front. LeT became part of the United Jihad Council (a conglomerate of Pakistan-based anti-India terrorist groups operating in Kashmir) in 1993 (SATP, n.d.). Nevertheless, the trust gap between the LeT and the Kashmiri groups persisted.

During this phase, LeT also developed links with the transnational organised criminal network of Dawood Ibrahim (also known as the D-company). The D-company had successfully carried out serial blasts in Mumbai in March 1993 and was keen to expand its network. For LeT, this partnership was useful for logistics as the D-company allowed LeT operatives to access its smuggling network, including routes and contacts (Rollins et al., 2010: 15). The proximity between the organised criminal syndicates and their smuggling networks within Pakistan further reinforced these ties.

Second Phase: 2000–2008

Meanwhile, even as it upped the ante for security forces in the Valley, Lashkar looked to expand its operations beyond Jammu and Kashmir. With the blessings of the Pakistan ISI, LeT innovated, adding other methods of attack to its inventory. Its campaign of terrorist violence outside the state began with an attack on labourers in Himachal Pradesh in 1998 (Jamal, 2015: 24). But its major attack in the hinterland came two years later, when its militants stormed the Red Fort in Delhi, killing three army personnel.

The September 2001 attacks did not alter the nature of ties between the LeT and al-Qaeda. Since its formation, the MDI has facilitated the movement of Arab recruits to the war in Afghanistan. As a result, the LeT too had close coordination with al-Qaeda for training, providing hideouts, and moving prominent operatives. This cooperation extended well after the 9/11 attacks. In March 2002, senior al-Qaeda commander Abu Zubaydah was arrested from a LeT safe house in Faisalabad, Punjab province (Burns, 2002). The group also trained western recruits of al-Qaeda as well as al-Qaeda-inspired terrorists, including "shoe bomber" Richard Reid, Willie Brigitte, and members of the Virginia jihad network in the United States (Bohn & Frieden, 2004; Swami, 2009; Anand et al., 2008). This close relationship prompted the former National Security Advisor of India, M. K. Narayanan, to describe LeT as part of the "al-Qaeda compact" (PTI, 2006).

The post-2001 ban on its activities and the increasing influence of the JuD in Pakistan lent even more force to the LeT's campaign of terrorist violence in India. In addition to the Fidayeen attacks, it came to rely on serial bombings to target civilians, as was seen in the case of the pre-Diwali blasts in Delhi in October 2005 and the July 2006 Mumbai suburban train bombings. It also tweaked its tried and tested formula of attacking the security forces by targeting the families of the Indian Army, as was seen in the case of the attack on Kaluchak camp in May 2002 (The Tribune, 2002). The attack added fuel to the already worsening relations between India and Pakistan following the December 2001 Parliament attack.

It was around this time that the LeT began working proactively to create a network of organised sleeper cells in India. Hafiz Saeed had always seen LeT's jihad in Kashmir as a gateway to launch a campaign against India as well as a wider civil war that would "continue until Islam becomes the dominant religion" (Swami, 2008: 309). This led to LeT playing a distinct role in the creation of the Indian Mujahideen (IM), which rose to prominence in 2008 after executing a series of bombings across India. Several IM operatives, including Yasin Bhatkal, Sayed Zabiuddin Ansari, and Mirza Himayat Baig, had been in touch with the Pakistan-based LeT handlers (The Frontline, 2016; Thomas, 2013; The New Indian Express, 2013). According to the Indian security agencies, Ansari was one of the handlers of the LeT terrorists who carried out attacks in the city of Mumbai on November 26, 2008 (Shah, 2018). The creation of the IM also fulfilled a core objective for the Pakistan Army: to showcase the involvement of Indian Muslims in the terrorist act as a manifestation of their discontent with the Indian state while allowing the Pakistan Army to maintain deniability for its support of cross-border terrorism in India. However, with the arrest of one of the terrorists, Ajmal Kasab, this cloak of deniability evaporated into thin air.

LeT also created an extensive network of cadres in India's neighbourhood, particularly in Nepal and Bangladesh, which could be used as jump-off points into Indian territory given the porous borders with these countries.

However, even as the Indian Mujahideen took the lead in violence in the hinterland, in Kashmir, LeT continued its attacks on the security forces and civilians. By this time, LeT had also been able to evolve operational coordination with other terrorist groups at the local level for choosing hideouts and moving cadres. Another visible demonstration of operational coordination was during the infiltration from PoK when joint groups of LeT, JeM, and Al Badr sneaked into the Kashmir Valley.

But the real game-changer for the LeT was the November 2008 Mumbai attacks. The attack was LeT's most complicated operation to date, involving the use of a sea route for ingress into the targeted city, the deployment of small assault teams for simultaneous attacks on multiple targets, and a mixture of different attack tactics, including hostage-taking. It had every imprint of a military operation, right from the reconnaissance of the targets to the execution of the raid by ten terrorists. Termed "swarming attacks" by Jonathan White, other terrorist groups have utilised these tactics in carrying out attacks (White, 2013: 423).

The attacks showed the LeT's ability to think unconventionally and take the Indian security establishment by surprise, particularly in terms of the use of advanced technology. To carry out the attack, the group used Thuraya satellite phones and VoIP calls for communication and Google Earth for navigation, something that had not been seen before in the Indian context (Kahn, 2008). These tools have since become the *sine qua non* for terrorist groups in South Asia.

As a matter of fact, LeT has displayed striking capability in using advanced technologies, just like al-Qaeda. Cadres of the group, with the help of the Pakistan Army, have also shown the ability to customise the use of these communication tools; in 2012, reportedly, LeT had its own version of the Skype VoIP service (Singh, 2012). Simultaneously, security agencies in Kashmir had noted that infiltrating cadres of the LeT and other terrorist groups had been spoofing the location of Thuraya satellite phones to confuse the security forces. Likewise, LeT was one of the first groups to get away from the security agencies' surveillance by teaching its cadres to use the virtual private network (VPN) and also to evade the internet blockade and get on the "deep web" (the Onion Router network) for propaganda and attack planning. Since then, most of the groups operating in Kashmir have followed LeT's lead.

Third Phase: Post-Mumbai Attacks

After the Mumbai attacks, LeT/JuD has faced intense scrutiny of its activities in Pakistan and elsewhere. Noting the severity of the attacks, the United States and the United Nations took several steps to designate the group's front organisations and leadership. India too initiated a crackdown on the group's network in India and neighbouring countries. These steps will be discussed later in the chapter. However, as noted earlier, the group laid low for some months and then resumed its activities with the support of the ISI, which not only made an effort to retain LeT's extensive infrastructure but also expanded the group's ambit.

As seen in the case of the ties with the D-company, the ISI had been attempting to expand LeT's network by linking it with like-minded groups. As part of this, it also attempted to forge a commonality of purpose between the LeT and the Pakistan-based senior Khalistani leadership, which had been fighting with India for a separate homeland for the Sikhs. Accordingly, the LeT established contacts with groups such as the Babbar Khalsa International (BKI), Khalistan Zindabad Force, and the International Sikh Youth Federation to foment violence in India (Khan, 2009; Gupta, 2020). For instance, in 2013, Indian security agencies neutralised a joint plan by LeT and BKI to carry out a car blast in Delhi just before the Diwali festival (Business Standard, 2013).

Similarly, in 2017–18, Indian security agencies noted LeT's attempts to connect with Rohingya Muslim organisations. At the height of the Rohingya refugees' exodus from Myanmar into Bangladesh's Cox's Bazar in 2017–18, FIF, the LeT's front organisation, had been engaged in relief work in the refugee camps in the area. Besides, the LeT had funded and trained cadres of the Rohingya Solidarity Organisation and other extremist groups and also recruited from the camps in Cox's Bazar (Patil, 2018).

In Kashmir, however, the LeT had to play second fiddle in the insurgency as, after the Mumbai attacks, security forces launched an intense crackdown on the activities of the Pakistani groups, including the LeT and JeM. This, combined with the rise of the local insurgency, propped up the fortunes of the local group, Hizbul Mujahideen, bringing it to the forefront of the insurgency. LeT also had to protect its turf from the local affiliates of al-Qaeda (Ansar Ghazwat-ul-Hind) and the Islamic State (Wilayat-e-Hind), which clamoured for space. In 2017, when al-Qaeda announced the formation of the Ansar Ghazwat-ul-Hind, LeT denounced it and blamed India for labelling Kashmir's "freedom struggle" as terrorism by linking it with groups such as al-Qaeda and the Islamic State (Nazir, 2017). Of late, security agencies have noted that their success in weakening the militancy after the Indian government's move to abrogate the region's special status may have forced the groups to join hands together to create a group called "The Resistance Front" to ratchet up the militancy (Shah, 2020; Routray, 2020).

In the last few years, after the JuD appeared on the scene, the LeT has also become involved in political activities through the Difa-e-Pakistan Council (DPC) and is contesting the 2018 national assembly elections.

In October 2011, LeT joined hands with other extremist groups in Pakistan, including the Ahl-e-Sunnat-Wal-Jamaat, Jamat e Islami, and Jamaat Ulema Pakistan, to launch the DPC. The coalition organised rallies in major cities in Pakistan. On its website, the DPC proclaimed to defend Pakistan as "the only ideological nation carved in the name of Islam with our wealth and lives." In its rallies, the DPC demanded severing ties with the United States and rescinding the Most Favoured Nation status granted to India (Sood, 2012). Given the apparent impunity with which the alliance operated and the various extremist leaders, including Saeed, who made an appearance in these rallies, it was widely presumed that it enjoyed the tacit backing of the Pakistan Army (MacDonald, 2012).

Perhaps taking a cue from the DPC, in August 2017, the group announced plans to establish a political party, the Milli Muslim League (MML), to fight the 2018 national elections. The MML's registration as a political party was rejected twice by Pakistan's Election Commission. Yet that did not stop the group from contesting the elections. It put up around 260 candidates – 79 for the National Assembly – under the banner of another party, the Allah-o-Akbar Tehreek, which was already registered with the Election Commission. The MML failed to make a dent in terms of final results. But its ability to find loopholes in the system by fielding known terrorist operatives has reinforced the belief that Pakistani authorities are unwilling to curb or are overlooking the extremist and militant groups' activities.

LeT has also maintained a continued presence in Afghanistan and has supported the Afghan Taliban's military operations, particularly the Haqqani Network (Tellis, 2012: 6–7). It has been involved in attacks against Indian interests in Afghanistan, such as the May 2014 attack on the Indian consulate in Herat (Nelson & Crilly, 2014). Most recently, the Analytical Support and Sanctions Monitoring Team of the United Nations provided details of the LeT activities in Afghanistan in its report. It estimated the group's strength in the country to be around 1000, located in the eastern provinces of Kunar, Nangarhar, and Nuristan and operating under the umbrella of the Afghan Taliban. According to the report, the LeT and JeM facilitate the movement of cadres, who act as advisers, trainers, and specialists in improvised explosive devices (Fitton-Brown, 2020: 20).

Countering the Activities of LeT and Pakistan's Support

As a result of its terror activities and links to groups such as al-Qaeda, LeT/JuD has faced intense global scrutiny of its operations. The group has been banned and designated as a terrorist organisation, notably by India, the United States, the United Nations, and the European Union. To escape these designations and bans, LeT has metamorphosed into various front organisations.

United States

In the aftermath of the September 11, 2001, attacks, the Bush administration of the United States undertook various efforts to choke the flow of funds to terrorist groups. As part of this, LeT was designated as a foreign terrorist organisation (FTO) under Executive Order 13224 on December 20, 2001 (Bush, 2001). The known aliases of the organisation that have been included by the Office of Foreign Assets Control (OFAC) of the US Department of Treasury in the notification as the FTO include the JuD, Al-Anfal Trust, THR, TTQA, FIF, and IKK, among several others. It also includes LeT's political party, MML. As Ambassador Nathan A. Sales, the Coordinator for Counterterrorism at the Department of State, stated in 2018, while announcing the inclusion of MML to the list of aliases for the LeT,

> Today's amendments take aim at Lashkar e-Tayyiba's efforts to circumvent sanctions and deceive the public about its true character. Make no mistake: whatever LeT chooses to call itself, it remains a violent terrorist group. The United States supports all efforts to ensure that LeT does not have a political voice until it gives up violence as a tool of influence (Office of the Spokesperson, 2018).

In addition, the OFAC has also designated 22 individuals linked to the LeT as "Specially Designated Global Terrorists" (Office of Foreign Assets Control (OFAC), US Department of Treasury, 2020). These designations block the assets of the individual or entity in the US. This, in turn, prevents any transfer of funds to the group or entity from any US person. In addition, such designations act as a deterrent to the flow of donations or contributions to such individuals or entities, as well as alerting other governments across the world to American concerns.

United Nations

In addition to the US efforts, the United Nations has also made several efforts to target the LeT. The major resolutions that provide teeth to such action are United Nations Security Council Resolution 1267, which designates individuals who provide material support to terror groups or individuals (United Nations Security Council, 1999).

The other important resolution is UNSC Resolution 1526, passed in 2004, which resulted in the establishment of the UNSC Al Qaeda Sanctions Committee. Under this resolution, LeT and JuD, along with their associated entities, have been designated as terrorist organisations. The Lashkar-e-Taiba was listed as a terrorist organisation with links to al-Qaeda in May 2005. Besides, this committee has listed several top leaders of the LeT as terrorists (United Nations Security Council, 2020, 2018). These include the following:

- Dawood Ibrahim Kaskar, listed on November 3, 2003.
- Mubarak Mushakhas Sanad Mubarak al-Bathali, listed on January 16, 2008.
- Hafiz Muhammad Saeed, listed on December 10, 2008.
- Zaki-Ur-Rehman Lakhvi, listed on December 10, 2008.
- Haji Muhammad Ashraf, listed on December 10, 2008.
- Mahmoud Mohammad Ahmed Bahaziq, listed on December 10, 2008.
- Arif Qasmani, listed on June 29, 2009.
- Mohammed Yahya Mujahid, listed on June 29, 2009.
- Abdul Rahim Ba'aysir, listed on July 19, 2011.
- Hafiz Abdul Salam Bhuttavi, listed on March 14, 2012.
- Zafar Iqbal, listed on March 14, 2012.

In the aftermath of the September 11 attacks, the United Nations Security Council passed Resolution 1373 on September 28, 2001. As this resolution was adopted under Chapter VII of the UN Charter, all member states are obligated to take actions mandated under this resolution, like preventing terror groups from using their territory for training, fundraising, recruiting, and other such activities. Importantly, the resolution considers major terrorist events as a threat to international security, which could prompt a response by the UN or its member states (United Nations Security Council, 2001).

However, as Dr. Fair (Fair, 2018: 199) has pointed out, the United States has done precious little to use the full force of this resolution to force Pakistan to stop terror groups from operating from its soil. In fact, the US has "even actively sought to shield Pakistan from the consequences of its behaviour under UNSC Resolution 1373 … even after the November 2008 terrorist attacks in Mumbai and the subsequent revelations that the attacks had state sponsorship, the United States – along with China – actively shielded Pakistan from any debate over sanctions – much less other more forceful responses – at the United Nations" (Fair, 2018: 198–199).

The lack of American interest in taking any action against Pakistan can also be seen in the fact that not only has the US continued to provide Pakistan with the Coalition Support Fund, but it has diluted the conditions over time. In 2017, the US government did away with the requirement for certification to the US Congress by the Secretary of Defence in coordination with the Secretary of State to the effect that "cooperating with the United States in counterterrorism efforts against the Haqqani network (see, Romaniuk & Webb, 2015), the Quetta Shura Taliban, LeT, JeM, al-Qaeda, and other domestic and foreign terrorist organisations" (US Congress, 2014). Given that UNSC resolutions have designated the LeT along with its main leaders, beginning with Saeed, American behaviour is perplexing, to say the least.

India

India's counterterrorism legislation has been a work in progress. One of the major anti-terrorist laws that India enacted was the Unlawful Activities (Prevention) Act, 2004. The

UAPA of 2004 replaced the earlier Terrorist and Disruptive Activities (Prevention) Act and Prevention of Terrorism Act of 2002. Specifically, after the 2008 attacks, India enlarged the scope of the UAPA. It also passed the National Investigation Agency (NIA) Act 2008, creating a new federal investigative agency, NIA, whose mandate was to investigate and prosecute offences relating to terrorism (Ministry of Home Affairs, n.d.).

In August 2019, another major amendment was passed by the Indian Parliament to the UAPA, wherein it became possible for individuals to also be designated (in addition to entities and groups) as terrorists. On September 4, 2019, by way of a gazette notification, India declared Saeed, Lakhvi, Dawood Ibrahim, and some other terrorist leaders as terrorists under this amended UAPA (Singh, 2019). Moreover, India has worked closely with the local security agencies in Nepal and Bangladesh to dismantle the LeT networks and extradite the involved cadres. In addition, after 2008, India also strengthened the Financial Intelligence Unit-India to deal with cases of money laundering and terrorist financing (FIU-India, n.d.). India also made counterfeiting (fake Indian currency notes) a terrorist act.

IMPACTS

The JuD/LeT's relief work has been seen in many instances, including after the Kashmir earthquake in 2005. Besides, the group offers an expansive network of affordable *al-Dawah* schools and free medical care in *al-Dawah* hospitals. These charity activities are directly linked to the group's growing influence in the country. Moreover, as noted earlier, they act as a base for the recruitment of future members as well as the main source for the group's legitimacy. Especially given the fact that the Pakistani state is unable to provide these services both in terms of quality and access to a large section of society, the group fulfils a vital social need, thereby garnering support and legitimacy and, in turn, weakening the hold and legitimacy of the Pakistani state.

Another impact of the terror activities of the LeT/JuD and other Pakistan-based terrorist groups on the Pakistani state has been the country's greylisting by the FATF. This has been a long process since the Pakistani commitment to curb money laundering and combat terror financing in June 2018. The commitment essentially meant that Pakistan would have to work with the FATF and the Asia Pacific Group to strengthen its anti-money laundering and counterterrorism financing regime, increase risk-based supervision, and pursue domestic and international cooperation to identify cash couriers or *hawala* transfers. However, as the FATF website notes, Pakistan has addressed only 14 of the 27 action items, with varying levels of progress made on the rest of the action plan. As the deadlines for compliance with the action plan neared, Pakistan put up a façade of a crackdown by sentencing Hafiz Saeed and his aides in terror financing-related cases, but that has not helped as the FATF in its June 2020 plenary recommended extension of the greylisting of Pakistan (FATF, 2020). The charade of Pakistani actions is evident by the fact that just a month later, Pakistan restored the bank accounts of Saeed and other senior LeT leaders after requesting the UN Security Council (Syed, 2020).

Importantly, the continued terror activities and anti-India actions by the LeT hinder any normalisation of India-Pakistan relations. In the past, it has been noticed that almost every time some initiative to normalise relations between the two countries has been taken, a terror strike has been carried out by the group, thereby jeopardising any progress and making it difficult for leaders on the Indian side to go ahead with any normalisation of relations, however limited in scope they are.

The support from the Pakistani "deep state," comprising the ISI and the Pakistani Army, for the LeT stems from the fact that the proxy terror groups operating out of Pakistan afford the state the ability to keep carrying out terror activities against India without crossing the nuclear threshold. On the one hand, Pakistan's nuclear weapons prevent an all-out conventional war between the two countries. However, on the other end of the spectrum, Pakistan-based terror groups like the LeT allow the Pakistan Army to continue sub-conventional conflict and terrorist attacks against India with the minimum risk of escalation into a full-scale conventional war, what Dr. Fair calls "jihad under the nuclear umbrella" (Fair, 2014: 227).

CONCLUSION

Daniel Markey (2013) states that if there is any single terrorist organisation in Pakistan most likely to provoke an all-out war with India, it is LeT (Markey, 2013: 52). Given the group's success in carrying out terrorist attacks in India against high-profile targets and using "innovative" means to carry out such strikes, one tends to agree with the above statement.

As a result of its widespread network of businesses and other interests in Pakistan and due to the continued support of the Pakistani Army and the ISI, the group has managed to flourish despite multiple attempts to target it and its leaders. Given the unique relationship shared by the group with the ISI and the Pak Army, such support is likely to continue into the foreseeable future.

References

Ahmad, I., & Laskar, R.H. (2019). Pakistan court stays hearing in Mumbai terror attack case, says witnesses scared. *Hindustan Times*, January 23, 2019. https://www.hindustantimes.com/india-news/pakistan-court-stays-hearing-in-mumbai-terror-attack-case-says-witnesses-scared/story-jotQrWvvNxZayvT5qunk8N.html.

Ali, F., & Shehzad, M. (2009). Lashkar-i-Tayyiba remains committed to jihad. *CTC Sentinel*, *2*(2). https://www.ctc.usma.edu/lashkar-i-tayyiba-remains-committed-to-jihad/.

Anand, G., Rosenberg, M., Gorman, S., & Schmidt, S. (2008). Alleged terrorist group steers young men to fight – WSJ. *Wall Street Journal*, December 8, 2008. https://www.wsj.com/articles/SB122869042642886443.

Aziz, M. (2008). *Military control in Pakistan: The parallel state*. Routledge Advances in South Asian Studies. Abingdon, Oxon, UK: Routledge.

BBC. (2015). Bailed Mumbai suspect Lakhvi's luxury jail time - BBC News. *BBC News*, April 10, 2015. https://www.bbc.com/news/world-asia-31606798.

Bohn, K., & Frieden, T. (2004). 'Virginia Jihad' members found guilty. *CNN*. March 5, 2004. https://edition.cnn.com/2004/US/South/03/04/paintball.terror/.

Bose, S. (2003). *Kashmir: Roots of conflict, paths to peace*. Cambridge, Massachusetts: Harvard University Press.

Burke, J. (2007). *Al-Qaeda: The true story of radical Islam*, 3rd ed. London: Penguin Books.

Burns, J.F. (2002). A nation challenged: The fugitives; in Pakistans interior, a troubling victory in hunt for Al Qaeda. *The New York Times*, April 14, 2002. https://www.nytimes.com/2002/04/14/world/nation-challenged-fugitives-pakistan-s-interior-troubling-victory-hunt-for-al.html.

Bush, G.W. (2001). Executive order 13224. https://www.state.gov/executive-order-13224/.

Business Standard. (2013). Pre-Diwali terror averted, RDX seized from car in Ambala. January 21, 2013. https://www.business-standard.com/article/economy-policy/pre-diwali-terror-averted-rdx-seized-from-car-in-ambala-111101400076_1.html.

Clarke, R. (2010). *Lashkar-I-Taiba: The fallacy of subservient proxies and the future of Islamist terrorism in India*. Letort Papers. Carlisle, Pennsylvania: Strategic Studies Institute, US Army War College. https://publications.armywarcollege.edu/pubs/2058.pdf.

Cooley, J.K. (2002). *Unholy wars: Afghanistan, America and international terrorism*, 3rd ed. London: Pluto Press.

Department of State. (n.d.). Rewards for justice - Wanted for terrorism - Hafiz Saeed. Rewards for Justice. Accessed July 15, 2020. https://rewardsforjustice.net/english/hafiz_saeed.html.

Department of Treasury. (2011). Treasury sanctions Lashkar-e Tayyiba leaders and founders. US Department of Treasury. September 28, 2011. https://www.treasury.gov/press-center/press-releases/Pages/tg1313.aspx.

Department of Treasury. (2014). Treasury sanctions two senior Lashkar-E-Tayyiba network leaders. June 25, 2014. https://home.treasury.gov/news/press-releases/jl2440 .

Department of Treasury. (2012). Treasury designates Lashkar-E Tayyiba leadership. Department of Treasury. August 30, 2012. https://www.treasury.gov/press-center/press-releases/Pages/tg1694.aspx.

Devasher, T. (2016). *Pakistan: Courting the Abyss*. New Delhi: HarperCollins.

Fair, C.C. (2014). *Fighting to the end: The Pakistan Army's way of war*. Oxford: Oxford University Press.

Fair, C.C. (2018). *In their own words: Understanding Lashkar-e-Tayyaba*. New York: Oxford University Press.

Faizal Sheikh Is Key Lashkar-e-Taiba Man: ATS. 2006. Outlook India. July 28, 2006. https://www.outlookindia.com/newswire/story/faizal-sheikh-is-key-lashkar-e-taiba-man-ats/402509.

FATF. (2020). Jurisdictions under increased monitoring. Financial Action Task Force. February 21, 2020. https://www.fatf-gafi.org/publications/high-risk-and-other-monitored-jurisdictions/documents/increased-monitoring-february-2020.html#pakistan.

Federal Bureau of Investigation. (n.d.). SAJID MIR. Person. Federal Bureau of Investigation. Accessed July 15, 2020. https://www.fbi.gov/wanted/wanted_terrorists/sajid-mir.

Fitton-Brown, E. (2020). Eleventh report of the analytical support and sanctions monitoring team submitted pursuant to resolution 2501 (2019) concerning the Taliban and other associated individuals and entities constituting a threat to the peace, stability and security of Afghanistan. Analytical Support and Sanctions Monitoring Team, United Nations. https://www.securitycouncilreport.org/atf/cf/%7B65BFCF9B-6D27-4E9C-8CD3-CF6E4FF96FF9%7D/s_2020_415_e.pdf.

FIU-India. (n.d.). Financial Intelligence Unit - India. Accessed July 16, 2020. https://fiuindia.gov.in/files/About_FIU-IND/About_FIUIND.html.

Gupta, S. (2020). Faces of terror: Why India banned 9 Khalistan-linked terrorists in 5 countries, Hindustan Times. July 04, 2020. https://www hindustantimes.com/india-news/faces-of-terror-why-india-banned-9-khalistan-linked-terrorist-s-in-5-countries/story-aR4fHIdFA3SCe74rAB4mtM.html.

Hafiz Saeed Sentenced to 11 Years in Jail. (2020). The Nation. February 13, 2020. https://nation.com.pk/13-Feb-2020/hafiz-saeed-sentenced-to-11-years-in-jail.

Hussein, D. (2016). Kashmir fund?: Jihadi outfit's charity wing sets up camp to collect donations | The Express Tribune. *The Express Tribune*, August 29, 2016. https://tribune.com.pk/story/1171633/kashmir-fund-jihadi-outfits-charity-wing-sets-camp-collect-donations.

Jamal, A. (2015). *Lashkar-e-Taiba: 1985–2014*. Kautilya Books.

Johnson, T.H., & Mason, M.C. (2007). Understanding the Taliban and insurgency in Afghanistan. *Orbis*, *51*(1), 71–89. 10.1016/j.orbis.2006.10.006.

Joshi, M. (2019). *The lost rebellion: Kashmir in the nineties*. Haryana: Penguin Books Random House India.

Kahn, J. (2008). Mumbai trrorists relied on new technology for attacks. *The New York Times*, December 8, 2008, sec. World. https://www.nytimes.com/2008/12/09/world/asia/09mumbai.html.

Kambere, G., Goh, P.H., Kumar, P., & Msafir, F. (2011). The financing of Lashkar-e-Taiba - Global ECCO. *Combating Terrorism Exchange – CTX*, *1*(1), 6–22.

Kapisthalam, K. (2009). Banned Pakistani terror group re-emerges under new name. FDD's Long War Journal. January 15, 2009. https://www.longwarjournal.org/archives/2009/01/banned_pakistani_ter.php.

Khan, A.R., & Petrou, M. (2009). The extremists who hit Mumbai are poised to strike again - Macleans.Ca. Maclean's. December 2, 2009. https://www.macleans.ca/news/world/the-terror-game/.

Kiessling, H.G. (2016). *Faith, unity, discipline: The ISI of Pakistan*. Harper Collins.

LeT Stage-Managed Mumbai Strikes: NYT- The New Indian Express. 2008. The New Indian Express. December 5, 2008. https://www.newindianexpress.com/nation/2008/dec/05/let-stage-managed-mumbai-strikes-nyt-8409.html.

MacDonald, M. (2012). Difa-e-Pakistan: What we know and do not want to hear. *Reuters Blogs (blog)*. February 16, 2012. http://blogs.reuters.com/pakistan/2012/02/16/difa-e-pakistan-what-we-know-and-do-not-want-to-hear/.

Macdonald, M. (2017). *Defeat is an orphan: How Pakistan lost the great south Asian war*. New Delhi: Random House India.

Malik, I.H. (2008). *The history of Pakistan*. The Modern Nations. Greenwood Press.

Markey, D.S. (2013). *No exit from Pakistan: America's tortured relationship with Islamabad*. New York: Cambridge University Press.

Ministry of Home Affairs, Government of India. (n.d.). Ministry of home affairs, acts & rules. Ministry of Home Affairs. Accessed July 16, 2020. https://www.mha.gov.in/acts?page=1.

Nawaz, S. (2010). Hearing before the sub-committee on the Middle East and South Asia of the committe on foreign affairs, house of representatives, one hundred eleventh congress second session. Government Publishing Office. https://www.govinfo.gov/content/pkg/CHRG-111hhrg55399/html/CHRG-111hhrg55399.htm.

Nazir, A. (2017). Al-Qaeda in Kashmir: Can it gain ground?. South Asian Voices. September 11, 2017. https://southasianvoices.org/al-qaeda-in-kashmir-can-it-gain-ground/.

Nelson, D., & Crilly, R. (2014). Pakistani charity is a terror front which attacked Indian consulate, says US - Telegraph. *The Telegraph*, June 26, 2014. https://www.telegraph.co.uk/news/worldnews/asia/pakistan/10928363/Pakistani-charity-is-a-terror-front-which-attacked-Indian-consulate-says-US.html.

Office of Foreign Assets Control (OFAC), US Department of Treasury. (2020). Complete specially designated nationals list. July 15, 2020. https://www.treasury.gov/ofac/downloads/ctrylst.txt.

Office of the Spokesperson, US Department of State. (2018). Amendments to the terrorist designation of Lashkar E-Tayyiba. US Department of State. April 2, 2018. https://www.state.gov/amendments-to-the-terrorist-designation-of-lashkar-e-tayyiba/.

Patil, S. (2018). The Rohingyas and India's difficult choices. Gateway House. February 8, 2018. https://www.gatewayhouse.in/rohingya-crisis-indias-difficulty/.

PTI. (2006). Al-Qaeda network present in India: NSA. Hindustan Times. August 12, 2006. https://www.hindustantimes.com/india/al-qaeda-network-present-in-india-nsa/story-OUYA4aIbB956wPXs4unEzM.html.

PTI. (2009). Pakistani father-son duo arrested in Italy over Mumbai Attacks. India Today. November 21, 2009. https://www.indiatoday.in/mumbai-terror-strikes/story/pakistani-father-son-duo-held-in-italy-over-mumbai-attacks-61357-2009-11-21.

Riedel, B. (2008). *The search for Al Qaeda: Its leadership, ideology, and future*. Washington DC: Brookings Institution Press.

Rollins, J., Wyler, L.S., & Rosen, S. (2010). International terrorism and transnational crime: Security threats, U.S. policy, and considerations for congress. Congressional Research Service. https://fas.org/sgp/crs/terror/R41004-2010.pdf.

Romaniuk, S.N. & Webb, S. T. (2015). The Haqqani network threat: keeping insurgency in the family. In: S.N. Romaniuk and S.T. Webb (eds.), *Insurgency and counterinsurgency in modern war* (pp. 175–189). New York: Taylor & Francis.

Roul, A. (2009). Lashkar-e-Taiba's financial network targets India from the Gulf states. *Terrorism Monitor*, 7(19), 6–8.

Roul, A. (2015). Jamaat-Ud Daawa: Into the mainstream. *CTC Sentinel*, 8(4), 23–25.

Routray, B.P. (2020). TRF and TMI: Lashkar-e-Toiba's new tools in Kashmir. Policy Brief 34. Mantraya. https://mantraya.org/trf-and-tmi-lashkar-e-toibas-new-tools-in-kashmir/.

SATP. (n.d.). Lashkar-e-Taiba 'Army of the Pure'. South Asia Terrorism Portal. Accessed July 13, 2020. https://www.satp.org/satporgtp/countries/india/states/jandk/terrorist_outfits/lashkar_e_toiba.htm.

Shah, C. (2018). Abu Jundal, the 26/11 Mumbai terror plot's Indian operative. Hindustan Times. November 7, 2018. https://www.hindustantimes.com/mumbai-news/abu-jundal-the-26-11-mumbai-terror-plot-s-indian-operative/story-OOgMoNffEHbNSEwW4vRh8H.html.

Shah, K. (2020). Pakistan using COVID-19 as a cover for crossborder Militancy | ORF. Observer Research Foundation. April 29, 2020. https://www.orfonline.org/expert-speak/pakistan-using-covid19-cover-crossborder-militancy-65377/.

Sharma, S.K., & Behera, A. (2014). *Militant groups in South Asia*. New Delhi: Institute for Defence Studies & Analyses.

Sheikh, W.A. (2020). Four JuD leaders convicted in terror finance case. *Dawn*, June 19, 2020. https://www.dawn.com/news/1564431.

Singh, A.T. (2012). Lashkar's own Skype frazzles Indian intelligence. *The Times of India*, April 30, 2012. https://timesofindia.indiatimes.com/india/Lashkars-own-Skype-frazzles-Indian-intelligence/articleshow/12934037.cms.

Singh, V. (2019). Masood Azhar, Hafiz Saeed, Lakhvi, Dawood Ibrahim declared terrorists under new anti-terror law - The Hindu. *The Hindu*, September 4, 2019. https://www.thehindu.com/news/national/masood-azhar-hafiz-saeed-dawood-ibrahim-declared-terrorists-under-new-anti-terror-law/article29330657.ece.

Sood, V. (2012). Difa-e-Pakistan: The new kid on the block - Indian Defence Review. Indian Defence Review. April 4, 2012. http://www.indiandefencereview.com/news/difa-e-pakistan-the-new-kid-on-the-block/.

Swami, P. (2000). Kashmir after Kandahar. *Frontline*, January 22, 2000. https://frontline.thehindu.com/cover-story/article30253212.ece.

Swami, P. (2008). The well-tempered jihad: The politics and practice of post-2002 Islamist terrorism in India. *Contemporary South Asia*, 16(3), 303–322. 10.1080/09584930802271331.

Swami, P. (2009). U.S. jihadists' stretches through Mumbai to Lahore - The Hindu. *The Hindu*, November 9, 2009. https://www.thehindu.com/news/national/U.S.-jihadistsrsquo-stretches-through-Mumbai-to-Lahore/article16890986.ece.

Syed, A. (2020). Bank accounts of Hafiz Saeed and JuD leaders restored after formal approval from UN sanctions committee. *The News*, July 12, 2020. https://www.thenews.com.pk/print/685681-bank-accounts-of-hafiz-saeed-and-jud-leaders-restored.

Tankel, S. (2009). *Lashkar-e-Taiba: From 9/11 to Mumbai*. Developments in Radicalisation and Political Violence. London: The International Centre for the Study of Radicalisation and Political Violence.

Tankel, S. (2011). Lashkar-e-Taiba: Past operations and futuer prospects. National Security Studies Program Policy Paper. New America Foundation. https://www.newamerica.org/documents/891/lashkar-e-taiba.

Tanzeem, A. (2016). Charity linked to terrorism tries aid delivery to Indian Kashmir | Voice of America – English. VOA News. August 3, 2016. https://www.voanews.com/east-asia-pacific/charity-linked-terrorism-tries-aid-delivery-indian-kashmir.

Tellis, A.J. (2010). Bad company - Lashkar e-Tayyiba and the growing ambition of Islamist militancy in Pakistan. United States House of Representatives, Committee on Foreign Relations, Subcommittee on the Middle East and South Asia and Government Publishing Office. https://carnegieendowment.org/2010/03/11/bad-company-lashkar-e-tayyiba-and-growing-ambition-of-islamist-militancy-in-pakistan-pub-40330.

Tellis, A.J. (2012). The menace that is Lashkar-e-Taiba - Carnegie endowment for international peace. Carnegie Endowment for International Peace. March 13, 2012. https://carnegieendowment.org/2012/03/13/menace-that-is-lashkar-e-taiba-pub-47512.

The Frontline. (2016). The dreaded cell of Jundal – Frontline. January 8, 2016. https://frontline.thehindu.com/cover-story/the-dreaded-cell-of-jundal/article8017729.ece.

The New Indian Express. (2013). Yasin Bhatkal trained by Lashkar in Pakistan- The New Indian Express. September 1, 2013. https://www.newindianexpress.com/nation/2013/sep/01/Yasin-Bhatkal-trained-by-Lashkar-in-Pakistan-512217.html.

The Tribune. (2002). Militants massacre 23 kin of army men. May 14, 2002. https://www.tribuneindia.com/2002/20020515/main1.htm.

Thomas, P. (2013). Mirza Himayat Baig: The man who integrated LeT with Indian Mujahideen.*Hindustan TImes*, April 16, 2013. https://www.hindustantimes.com/mumbai/mirza-himayat-baig-the-man-who-integrated-let-with-indian-mujahideen/story-YX3EMDbjoKlkZaSmeyH13I.html.

Trehan, J. (2002). Terrorism and the funding of terrorism in Kashmir. *Journal of Financial Crime*, 9(3), 201–211. 10.1108/eb026018.

United Nations Security Council. (1999). United Nations security council resolution 1267. http://unscr.com/en/resolutions/1267.

United Nations Security Council. (2001). United Nations security council resolution 1373 - Threats to internal peace and security caused by terrorist acts. United Nations Security Council. September 28, 2001. http://unscr.com/en/resolutions/1373.

United Nations Security Council. (2008). Hafiz Muhammad Saeed. United Nations Security Council. December 10, 2008. https://www.un.org/securitycouncil/sanctions/1267/aq_sanctions_list/summaries/individual/hafiz-muhammad-saeed.

United Nations Security Council. (2009). Mohammed Yahya Mujahid. United Nations Security Council. https://www.un.org/securitycouncil/sanctions/1267/aq_sanctions_list/summaries/individual/mohammed-yahya-mujahid.

United Nations Security Council. (2018). Lashkar-e-Tayyiba. United Nations Security Council. April 17, 2018. https://www.un.org/securitycouncil/sanctions/1267/aq_sanctions_list/summaries/entity/lashkar-e-tayyiba.

United Nations Security Council. (2020). United Nations security council consolidated list. United Nations Security Council. July 14, 2020. https://www.un.org/securitycouncil/content/un-sc-consolidated-list#individuals.

US Congress. (2010). Hearing before the sub-committee on the Middle East and South Asia of the committe on foreign affairs, house of representatives, one hundred eleventh congress second session. Government Publishing Office. https://www.govinfo.gov/content/pkg/CHRG-111hhrg55399/html/CHRG-111hhrg55399.htm.

US Congress. (2014). Consolidated appropriations act, 2014. https://www.govinfo.gov/content/pkg/BILLS-113hr3547enr/pdf/BILLS-113hr3547enr.pdf.

White, J.R. (2013). *Terrorism and homeland security*. Cengage Learning.

Yasin, A. (2017). DPC announces movement for Kashmir, Palestine liberation - Newspaper - DAWN.COM. Dawn. December 30, 2017. https://www.dawn.com/news/1379642/dpc-announces-movement-for-kashmir-palestine-liberation.

Yasmeen, S. (2017). *Jihad and Dawah: Evolving narratives of Lashkar-e-Taiba and Jamat Ud Dawah*. C. Hurst & Co. Publishers Ltd.

68

JAISH-E-MOHAMMAD (THE "ARMY OF MOHAMMED")

Sanchita Bhattacharya

INTRODUCTION AND BACKGROUND

Jaish-e-Mohammad (JeM), also known as the Army of Muhammad, is a Pakistan-based armed militant organisation that seeks to topple and destabilise the Indian government in Jammu and Kashmir by carrying out assaults on Indian security and government targets. The infighting that has driven the Jihadi cause upset Maulana Masood Azhar as well as other Pakistani religious figures. After significant thought and discussion with Islamic elders and scholars, it was determined that Azhar would spearhead the initiative to revive the Jihadi cause by establishing a new group with strong leadership that would prevent the rifts that had developed in other groups (Howenstein, 2008).

The formation of the group can be attributed to Amir (leader) Masood Azhar's notoriety. Masood Azhar, leader of Jaish-e-Mohammed (JeM), began his jihadi career in 1983 with Harkat ul Jihad ul Islami (HuJI), a group of jihadists from Kashmir. He was appointed the 'general secretary' of Harkat ul Mujahedeen (HuM) after the two organisations split in 1987 (Zahid, 2019). Masood Azhar later joined Al Qaeda in fighting US troops in Somalia in 1994 as a member of the HuM. He also helped train Al-Qaeda members in Yemen. Azhar was held in Kote Bhalwal Jail till December 1999 after being arrested by Indian police in December 1999 (Raman, 2001). Using the alias Essa Bin Adam and a Portuguese passport, he was detained in Jammu and Kashmir while on a "mission" (Gunaratna & Iqbal, 2011).

HuM cadres, including his brother Ibrahim Azhar, who had hijacked the IC-814 of Indian Airlines in order to travel to Kandahar, forced Azhar's release in December 1999. Azhar sent articles to the Al Rashid Trust covertly while he was being held, and these articles were then published in their magazine, Zarb-e-Momin. In Pakistan, a number of companies purporting to provide humanitarian aid emerged in the 1980s, allowing Western and Saudi secret services to fund the Mujahideen battling Soviet soldiers. The Al Rashid Trust was one such organisation that was established in Karachi by Pakistan's Inter-Services Intelligence (ISI) and registered as a charitable trust under the Pakistan Income Tax Act. Mufti Rashid Ahmed was its creator (Raman, 2001).

In early 2000, Maulana Masood Azhar announced his official split with HuM and the formation of JeM. It is reported that Maulana Azhar, in addition to a few other religious leaders, was upset with the squabbling that divided the jihadi cause. After much discussion and meetings with Islamic scholars and elders, it was decided that Masood Azhar would lead the effort to revive the jihadi cause by forming a new group under strong leadership that would avoid the rifts that had arisen in other groups. The formation of JeM came with the blessing of the heads of the Majlis-e-Tawan-e-Islami, Darul Ifta-e-Wal-Irshad, and Sheikh-ul-Hadith of Dar-ul-Haqqania Madrasa. Many leaders immediately gave their allegiance to Maulana Azhar as the establishment of JeM took place (Rana, 2004).

Azhar visited Kandahar just before forming the JeM to win the support of the Taliban hierarchy. When the new group was formed, the HuM was astounded and referred to Azhar as "a greedy Indian agent who is out to damage the Kashmiri Jihad." He also gave speeches in a number of Pakistani cities and towns, declaring that his organisation would kill Atal Behari Vajpayee, the former Indian prime minister, whom he referred to as Abu Jahal (one of the main antagonists of the Prophet Mohammad) (Mir, 2009).

OVERVIEW

JeM was founded on January 31, 2000, after Masood Azhar, Mushtaq Ahmed Zargar, and Omar Saeed Sheikh were released by India on December 31, 1999. Since his detention on February 11, 1994, at Khanabal Chowk in Anantnag, Kashmir, he had spent the previous five years in the Kote Bhalwal Prison in Jammu and Kashmir. Indian investigators

DOI: 10.4324/9780429426063-77

claim he told them, "You people will not be able to keep me in custody for long. You don't know how important I am for Pakistan and the ISI. You are underestimating my popularity. The ISI would ensure that I am back in Pakistan." (Mohananey, 2019)

He was one of three terrorists released in exchange for the crew and passengers of the hijacked IC-814, which was flown to Kandahar in Taliban-controlled Afghanistan. After his release, Azhar established the new terrorist organisation JeM and severed ties with HuM. Reportedly, Osama bin Laden, the Taliban, and other extremist organisations supported the formation of JeM. Laden is believed to have also provided financial support to the Jaish (2012) and Australian National Security.

With the substantial support and assistance of ISI, JeM established itself promptly. Azhar was already well-known in Pakistan for his participation in the Afghan Jihad and, more importantly, for his impassioned speeches. The ISI, the Taliban regime in Kabul, and the Al Qaeda leadership provided him with substantial financial and logistical support (Garge and Sahay, 2018). The ISI is rumoured to have taken Azhar on a 'victory tour' across Pakistan to raise funds for JeM. It is believed that the ISI used JeM to wage war in Kashmir and elsewhere.

IDEOLOGY

JeM promotes an anti-Western, anti-Jewish, and anti-Indian pan-Islamic ideology. The ardent personality of Maulana Azhar had a significant impact on the formation of JeM (Howenstein, 2008). According to Azhar, the damage caused by submission and servitude cannot be repaired until Islam is firmly rooted in politics and society (Haqqani, 2002).

In addition, Azhar's jihadist ideology centres around Qital fi Sabeel Allah (armed fighting for Allah's sake), i.e., the killing of kufar and munafiqeen during Jihad (Azhar, 2000). Azhar compares Jihad to other Islamic forms of devotion. He emphasises a vast array of Quranic verses and hadith (prophetic sayings) on the issue of jihad and declares jihad to be a central tenet of the Islamic faith. Jihad, according to Azhar, is an act favoured by God based on the vigour of the mujahid (martyr), the risks involved, the physical and mental exhaustion, and the rewards in this world and the next (Zahid, 2019).

KEY PERSONNEL AND STRUCTURE

Azhar has been involved in a variety of extremist activities. He is a skilled administrator and a shrewd negotiator, in addition to being a prolific jihadist author who has published many volumes. He began his career with the Kashmir insurgency and subsequently shifted between jihadi organisations in Kashmir, Afghanistan, and sectarian killings in Pakistan before joining the Punjabi Taliban forces in the Global War on Terror to aid their Afghan and Pashtun kin (Zahid, 2014). Azhar is for the Deobandi jihadis what Lieutenant General Hameed Gul (the former head of Pakistan's Inter-Services Intelligence, or ISI, who was part of the Afghan Jihad in the 1980s) was for the ISI – an inspirational figure who is well connected in the jihadi world and resolutely believes in Ghazwa-e-Hind and the ultimate crusade against all non-Muslims (Siddiqa, 2019).

Masood Azhar presides over a 12-member Majlis-e-Shura that administers JeM and oversees the organisation's seven departments. The Military Department coordinates the training and deployment of jihadis as well as the identification of their targets. The Department of "Aseerin" (Prisoners) attempts without much success to secure the release of detained mujahideen. The Department of Dawa-o-Irshad coordinates the Tablighi operations of JeM and maintains relationships with the families of "martyred" mujahideen. This latter function is shared with the Department of Martyrs, which compiles lists of martyrs and potential martyrs, updates the families on the status of their kin's martyrdom, provides an assistance stipend after the death of the mujahid, and grants the families special status. This department is also responsible for handling the will of the shahid (martyr) and organising a memorial service. The Department of Amar Bil Ma'aruf-o-Nahi Annal Munkar-Ehtesab (Enforcing Virtue and Preventing Vice and Accountability) ensures that the activities and conduct of the group's members comply with Shariah, and it maintains contact with madrasa leaders in order to recruit students from the schools. JeM also funds a Department of Ehya-e-Sunnah (Revival of Sunnat) that facilitates marriages not only for mujahideen but also for any religious men and women who approach the department. The Department of Broadcast (Media) and Publication, one of the most active components of JeM, maintains media contacts and publishes the organisation's pamphlets and periodicals, including Jaish-e Mohammed (later renamed al Islah) and Shamshir (Rana, 2004).

STRATEGY

JeM's strategy entails collaborating with Indian military forces in armed attacks and recruiting young Kashmiris for the 'liberation' cause. JeM militants are typically deployed in small numbers to launch attacks against Indian forces using sabotage, arson, armed insurgency, and hit-and-run attacks on police and security forces. In addition, they execute suicide attacks against military bases and convoys, killing as many personnel and civilians as possible (Gunaratna & Iqbal, 2011). JeM's primary objective is to seize Kashmir from India and annexe it to Pakistan. It portrays Kashmir as the gateway to all of India. After 'liberating' Kashmir, the group intends to spread jihad throughout the rest of India.

ORGANISATIONAL ACTIVITIES

JeM has continued to operate under the aliases Afzal Guru Squad, Al-Murabitoon, and Tehreek-e-Furq despite being 'officially' banned by Pakistan in 2002. From its headquarters in the city of Bahawalpur in Punjab, Pakistan JeM manages a nationwide network of organisations governed by militant clerics (Ahmad, 2013). The group reportedly built a massive, fortified complex on 6.5 acres in Bahawalpur in 2009, replete with a swimming pool and a horse stable that could be used to train militants.

Jammu and Kashmir is where JeM has launched the vast majority of its attacks against Indian military and police, government buildings, and civilians. According to research by Stanford University (2012), JeM was the first Islamist group to conduct suicide assaults in Kashmir. A local Jaish trainee named Afaq Ahmad Shah, who was only 17 at the time (Ashiq, 2020), slammed an explosives-laden car into the Valley's major Chinar Corps headquarters in Badamibagh in May of 2000, killing four troops. Profiled in the official Jaish publication Zarb-e-Momin, the suicide bomber helped bring JeM into the international jihad league (Jaleel, 2016). According to Stanford University (2012), JeM has carried out suicide assaults on government installations with high levels of security, such as camps, army bases, and public venues, in Kashmir and elsewhere in India.

The 'legal' existence of JeM remained largely unchanged after the attack on the Indian Parliament in December 2001. The State Department of the United States designated them as a foreign terrorist organisation. In a public relations manoeuvre, Pakistani authorities claimed to have apprehended Masood Azhar on December 2, 2001, for his alleged role in the attack. Masood's arrest was a show of force, and a year later, the Lahore High Court determined that it had been illegal. In 2002, then-President Pervez Musharraf banned JeM (Stanford University, 2018).

Although J&K is still a top priority for JeM, some members have pushed the organisation to also target Pakistani government officials and Westerners in the country. On May 26, 2004, terrorists drawn from a number of Pakistani extremist groups, including JeM, detonated two car bombs near the US Consulate in Karachi. They called themselves "Jundullah," a name they adopted after the incident. The same terrorist group was responsible for the June 9, 2004 attack on a heavily armed military convoy carrying Karachi's military commander, which resulted in the deaths of seven people. After receiving information that members of the JeM group Jamaat ul Furkan (JuF) were intending to attack Western interests in Pakistan, the Pakistani government began a crackdown on JuF in August 2006. Two attempts on the life of former President Pervez Musharraf in December 2003 have been linked to JeM members (Australian National Security, 2012).

While Bahawalpur serves as JeM's headquarters, the group also operates out of Peshawar and Muzaffarabad (PoK). It keeps training centres in Afghanistan, Khyber Pakhtunkhwa (Balakot), Punjab (Hazira, Kahuta, Rawalkot, Pallandri, Zaffarwal, Sialkot, etc.), PoK, Doda in Kashmir, and the southern section of the valley. According to Gunaratna and Iqbal (2011), the JeM's Quetta headquarters acts as a hub for foreign fund management and communication between JeM leaders and 'field commanders'.

In addition to their participation in actual acts of terror, JeM also holds gatherings and gives lectures on 'jihadist poems' in a number of different cities throughout Pakistan. These cities' locations demonstrate that JeM has tried to contact people all throughout Pakistan. They are: Faisalabad, Bahawalpur, Sukkur, Gujranwala, Mirpur, Haveli Lakha Okara, Karachi, Peshawar, Swabi, Rawalpindi, Nawabshah, Bannu, Quetta, Mansehra, Tando Allahyar, Kohat, and Sargodha. Common people often attend these meetings, most of which occur once a year, and are provided lessons on how to translate and interpret more than 558 verses on Jihad (Ahmad, 2013).

CADRE RECRUITMENT AND STRENGTH

In an effort to inspire youth to engage in jihad, JeM militants have staged a number of recruitment rallies around Pakistan since the year 2000. In addition to many seasoned Afghan members, the organisation also recruits abroad among Kashmiri and Punjabi emigrants in Britain (Stanford University, 2018). According to a study from March 2019, JeM invests over one million Pakistani rupees, or $10,000 USD, to produce one capable and ready jihadi. Every year, they make 15 to 20 of these. Additionally, JeM recruits from public schools (Siddiqa, 2019). The JeM presently has an estimated 40,000 militants, according to Pakistani security analyst Azaz Syed (Syed, 2019). Initially, Lashkar-e-Jhangvi (LeJ), HuJI, HuM, and Sipah-e-Sahaba Pakistan (SSP) and its militant faction were the main sources of new members for JeM. However, the entry of JeM into Kashmir's jihadist environment heightened rivalry among jihadi groups that were previously present there (Zahid, 2019).

The JeM is thought to have "several hundred members, including 300 to 400 fighters," but the full extent of its command structure is unknown, according to the Australian National Security (Australian National Security, 2012). Due to a failing agricultural system, absentee landowners, little education, and few job possibilities, particularly in the Pakistani state of Punjab, the JeM did reasonably well in recruiting new members (Siddiqa, 2007). Azhar's ferocious sermons, jihadi literature, and speeches have fuelled recruitment and kept the organisation afloat. JeM has been remarkably resilient despite the severe crackdown and increased awareness on a global scale (Zahid, 2019).

ORGANISATIONAL TIES AND ALLIANCES

During the Taliban era, JeM established ties with Al Qaeda. The head cleric of Dar ul Uloom Islamia Binori Town in Karachi and a Deobandi scholar named Mufti Nizamuddin Shamzai gave their approval when JeM was founded. Shamzai's history of connections to the Taliban and Al Qaeda is widely known. The Taliban immediately let JeM's rank and file get instruction at Al Qaeda-run training facilities in Afghanistan once the group was formed (Zahid, 2014). The Taliban let JeM's rank and file get instruction at Al Qaeda-run training facilities in Afghanistan soon after JeM was founded in 2000. Al Qaeda and the JeM collaborated on the capture and murder of Wall Street Journal writer Daniel Pearl in 2002. The terrorist from Al Qaeda, Khalid Sheikh Mohammad, who is suspected of participating in the 9/11 attacks, was also implicated in this occurrence (Zahid, 2019). Sheikh claimed to have murdered Daniel Pearl in 2007. Currently, he is being held in Guantanamo Bay (Bhattacharya, 2020). Osama bin Laden is remembered with affection by JeM members, who assert that he assisted JeM in purchasing some of HuM's infrastructure, such as madrasas, mosques, and training grounds. One of the assets the JeM acquired from the HuM was the Balakot madrasa, which India asserts was bombed on February 26, 2019. After the Pervez Musharraf administration's assault on terrorist organisations following the 9/11 attacks, Azhar spent most of his time at this seminary (Siddiqa, 2019).

JeM has collaborated with Lashkar e-Taiba (LeT) in coordinated operations. It works closely with other Islamic militant organisations operating in Afghanistan, Kashmir, and Pakistan, including HuM, Hizb-ul-Mujahideen (HM), and LeJ.

Politically, JeM is aligned with the prominent fundamentalist Islamic party in Pakistan and Kashmir, the Jamiat-e-Ulema-e-Islam Fazul Rehman faction (JUI-F). Both legitimate commercial interests, such as commodity trading and real estate, and Islamic charitable foundations, such as the Al Rashid Trust, provide funding for JeM (Australian National Security, 2012).

Due to Azhar's relationship with Sipah-e-Sahaba Pakistan (SSP) president Maulana Azam Tariq, the terrorist organisation maintains close ties with the SSP. In the year 2000, Tariq reportedly participated in a "Crush India" rally organised by JeM and declared, "One hundred thousand Sipah-e-Sahaba workers will join Jaish-e-Muhammad to fight the infidels." In October 2000, SSP Chairman Maulana Ziaul Qasmi attended a jihad conference organised by JeM and SSP, where he took the jihad oath from Azhar (Rana, 2004).

Additionally, JeM is a member of the United Jihad Council (UJC). A coalition of 13 to 16 militant groups operating in Kashmir make up the UJC, which receives support from the ISI. In Pakistan, there is concern that if the military-security establishment is unable to prevent Azhar's designation as a terrorist, a host of terrorist organisations will turn their weapons against the Pakistani state and harm Pakistan's interests in Afghanistan. This will exacerbate domestic unrest and worsen Pakistan's security situation (Verma, 2017).

According to a report published on August 28, 2019, by India's Border Security Force (BSF), Jaish-e-Mohammad is also radicalising Rohingya Muslims to further Pakistan's anti-India activities. Maulana Yunus, a member of JeM's Bangladesh unit, reportedly forced four members of the Rohingya community to endure training at a terrorist camp in the Harinmara hills of Bangladesh. There are presently thousands of Rohingya Muslims in Cox's Bazar region, where the JeM is radicalising (Shukla, 2019). In addition, the weekly jihadist publication Al-Qalam contains an article written by Masood Azhar under the pseudonym name Sa'adi. Azhar warns the "oppressive" Myanmar Government to prepare for "the thumping sound of its conquerors' footsteps." He asserts, "The country will soon be devoid of tranquility and peace." In his article titled Betab Burma (Distressed Burma), he urges Muslims of the subcontinent to "act immediately" (Voice of the Nation, 2018).

MAJOR ATTACKS

According to the counter-insurgency cell in Jammu and Kashmir, the Jaish has exhibited two characteristics since its founding by Azhar in 2000. First, its ability to reinvent itself, and second, its use of spectacle attacks to assume centre stage in the Kashmir militancy (Ashiq, 2020) (Figures 68.1–68.3). Major attacks carried out by JeM militants include:

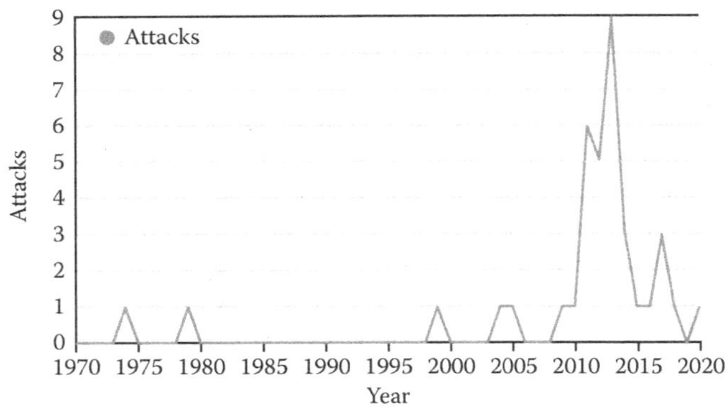

Figure 68.1 Incidents Over Time, 1970–2020.

Source: Global Terrorism Database (GTD) (2024).

- A vehicle carrying explosives collided with a convoy of paramilitary police in Pulwama, Jammu and Kashmir, on February 14, 2019. At least forty individuals were slain in the explosion. The suicide assailant was an agent of JeM.
- 21 persons were killed on September 18, 2016, when four suspected JeM militants attacked an Indian Army brigade headquarters in Uri, Jammu and Kashmir.
- Six heavily armed militants attacked the Pathankot Air Force Station in Punjab, India, on January 2, 2016 with AK-47s and grenades. The attack resulted in a firearms battle that lasted more than 12 hours. According to Indian intelligence, JeM was responsible for the attacks.
- JeM was suspected of murdering National Conference activist Abdul Hafeez Mirza on February 14, 2002. JeM had previously warned individuals in Jammu and Kashmir against participating in the forthcoming electoral process.
- JeM militants attacked the Indian Parliament on December 13, 2001, killing 14 people, including five militants.
- 31 people were killed on October 1, 2001, when a car bomb targeting the State Assembly building in Srinagar, India, was detonated by JeM militants. The militants entered the building and engaged the Indian Security Forces in gunfire.

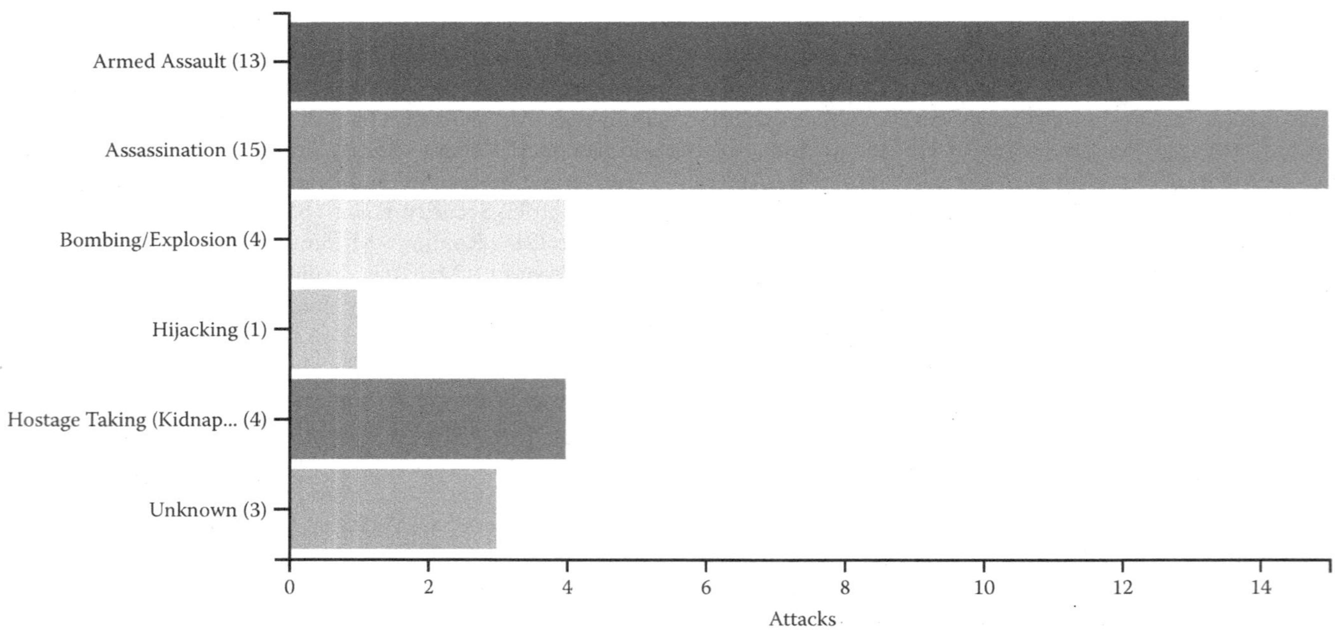

Figure 68.2 Attack Type.

Source: Global Terrorism Database (GTD) (2024).

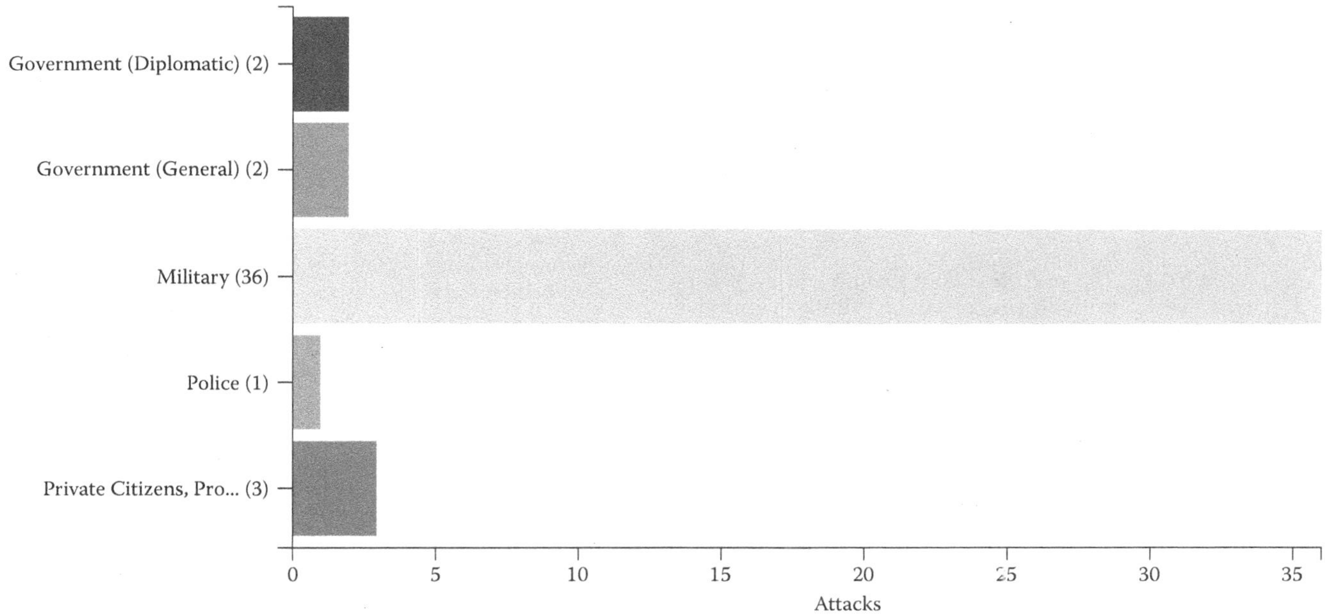

Figure 68.3 Target Type.

Source: Global Terrorism Database (GTD) (2024).

FUNDING

Through hawala and money laundering, substantial financial gains are made through unofficial channels. To avoid asset seizures, funds are withdrawn from bank accounts and invested in lawful businesses, such as commodity trading, real estate, and consumer goods production. Funds are also solicited via donation requests in periodicals and pamphlets, with charitable causes sometimes used to solicit donations (Garge & Sahay, 2018). Al Akhtar, a JeM offshoot, has been designated as an FTO by the US Treasury Department since 2003 and by the United Nations since 2005. It has operated under a variety of names, including the Pakistan Relief Foundation, Pakistani Relief Foundation, Azmat-e-Pakistan Trust, and Azmat Pakistan Trust (Bhattacharya, 2015). In addition, the Al-Rehmat Trust solicited donations of cash and animal hides for Jihad and the care of the dependents of militants slain in Kashmir operations (Ohri, 2017).

CONCLUSION

As there are extremities in JeM with regard to following the strict rule of Jihad and not digressing into inter-sectarian conflict or getting involved in charity and grassroots-level activities, the objective of the militant outfit will not end until the entire world 'converts to Islam'. It has prioritised enhancing its members' comprehension of an Islamic war, which is why its initial training sessions emphasise Jihad proselytization. In the past, jihadi groups selected individuals at random and sent them for military training; however, Jaish has modified this strategy. Before being selected for military training and then combat, candidates must undergo rigorous ideological instruction.

JeM has consistently rebranded and reemerged, demonstrating its tenacity. For example, following the 26/11 Mumbai terrorist assaults, Azhar went into hiding for nearly six years. In January 2014, he reappeared in Muzaffarabad (PoK) and called for the resumption of jihad in Kashmir at a rally. Since then, JeM has become a lethal organisation responsible for significant terrorist attacks in Pathankot, Uri, and Pulwama.

Chinese support for Masood Azhar in the international arena can also be used to assess the significance of the JeM for Pakistan. China refused for many years to remove its technical hold on United Nations Security Council Resolution 1267, which recommends a regime of sanctions against terrorist groups and individuals. As a consequence, India had a difficult time classifying Masood Azhar as a global terrorist. In response to the Pulwama incident, China lifted its hold on Masood Azhar in February 2019, and on May 1, 2019, the United Nations officially designated him as a global terrorist.

As with Hafiz Saeed, however, it is doubtful that Pakistan will bring Azhar to justice. Since his release in 1999, the

Pakistani establishment has ensured that he remains safe, secure, and capable of organising attacks against India without direct involvement. JeM is not an exception to the fact that Pakistani support for terrorist organisations has given them the ability to engage in persistent anti-India rhetoric and cause violent incidents within the country.

References

Ahmad, T. (2013). *The next decade of jihadism in Pakistan*. https://www.hudson.org/research/9884-the-next-decade-of-jihadism-in-pakistan

Ashiq, P. (2020). *Jaish-e-Mohammed | The fountain head of terror*. https://www.thehindu.com/news/national/the-fountainhead-of-terror/article32475263.ece

Australian National Security. (2012). *Terrorist organisations: Jaish-e-Mohammed*. http://www.nationalsecurity.gov.au/Listedterroristorganisations/Pages/JaisheMohammedJeM.aspx

Azhar, M.M. (2000). *Khutbaat-e-Jihad Vol-II*. Bahawalpur: Maktaba Hasan.

Bhattacharya, S. (2020). *Pakistan's fate in FATF once again hangs in balance*. https://southasiamonitor.org/spotlight/pakistans-fate-fatf-once-again-hangs-balance

Bhattacharya, S. (2015). *Terror-financing in Pakistan*. https://spsindia.in/wp-content/uploads/2016/02/SPS-Insight-5-2015.pdf

Garge, R., & Sahay, C.D. (2018). *Rise of Jaish-e-Mohammed in Kashmir valley- An internal security perspective*. https://www.vifindia.org/sites/default/files/rise-of-jaish-e-mohammed-in-kashmir-valley.pdf

Global Terrorism Database (GTD). (2024). Army of Mohammed "Attack Type". https://www.start.umd.edu/gtd/search/Results.aspx?charttype=bar&chart=attack&search=Army%20of%20Mohammed

Global Terrorism Database (GTD). (2024). Army of Mohammed "Incidents". https://www.start.umd.edu/gtd/search/Results.aspx?search=Army+of+Mohammed&sa.x=0&sa.y=0

Global Terrorism Database (GTD). (2024). Army of Mohammed "Target Type". https://www.start.umd.edu/gtd/search/Results.aspx?charttype=bar&chart=target&search=Army%20of%20Mohammed

Gunaratna, R., & Iqbal, K. (2011). *Pakistan terrorism ground zero*. London: Reaktion Books.

Haqqani, H. (2002). The gospel of jihad. *Foreign Policy*, 132, September/October, 72–74.

Howenstein, N. (2008). *The jihadi terrain in Pakistan: An introduction to the Sunni jihadi groups in Pakistan and Kashmir*. https://core.ac.uk/reader/5810

Jaleel, M. (2016). *Explaining the history of Masood Azhar's Jaish-e-Mohammad, the mystery of its reemergence*. http://indianexpress.com/article/explained/in-fact-history-of-masood-azhars-jaish-the-mystery-ofits-re-emergence

Mir, A. (2009).*Talibanisation of Pakistan: From 9/11 to 26/11 and beyond*. New Delhi: Pentagon Press.

Mohananey, A. (2019). *The man who interrogated Masood Azhar recalls the time he sang like a canary*. https://economictimes.indiatimes.com/news/defence/the-man-who-interrogated-masood-azhar-remembers-when-he-sang-like-a-canary/articleshow/68041543.cms

Ohri, R. (2017). *Kashmiri youth visiting Pakistan used as terror conduits: Government agency*. https://economictimes.indiatimes.com/news/defence/kashmiri-youth-visiting-pakistan-used-asterror-conduits-government-agency/articleshow/61620328.cms

Raman, B. (2001). *The Jaish-e-Mohammad (JeM)*. https://www.outlookindia.com/website/story/the-jaish-e-mohammad-jem/214059

Rana, M.R. (2004). *A to Z of jehadi organizations in Pakistan*. Lahore: Mashal Publisher.

Shukla, M. (2019). *Pakistan-based JeM radicalising Rohingya to target India: Border security force*. https://www.dnaindia.com/india/report-pakistan-based-jem-radicalising-rohingya-to-target-india-border-security-force-2785480

Siddiqa, A. (2019). *Jaish-e-Mohammed: Under the hood*. https://thediplomat.com/2019/03/jaish-e-mohammed-under-the-hood/

Siddiqa, A. (2007).*Military Inc.: Inside Pakistan's military economy*. London: Pluto Press.

Stanford University. (2018). *Jaish-e-Mohammad*. https://stanford.app.box.com/s/w0xi3l0jprgduuzl50zkgo5pkq12hsox

Stanford University. (2012). *Jaish-e-Mohammad*. http://web.stanford.edu/group/mappingmilitants/cgi-bin/groups/view/95

Syed, A. (2019). *Kal adum jamaatoon ke khilaf karwai kaisa amal hai*. https://bit.ly/2FV8bbZ

Verma, R. (2017). Pakistan and Jaish- e-Mohammad: An unholy alliance. The Interpreter, July 07, 2017. https://www.lowyinstitute.org/the-interpreter/pakistan-jaish-e-mohammad-unholy-alliance

Voice of the Nation. (2018). *Rohingya Muslims: The terror connection*. https://www.organiser.org/Encyc/2018/4/19/Rohingya-Muslims-the-Terror-Connection.html

Zahid, F. (2019). Profile of Jaish-e-Muhammad and leader Masood Azhar. *Counter Terrorist Trends and Analyses*, *11*(4), 1–5.

Zahid, F. (2014). *Still a force to reckon with: Jaish-e-Mohammad*. https://cf2r.org/foreign/still-a-force-to-reckon-with-jaish-e-mohammad-2/

69

TEHRIK-I-TALIBAN PAKISTAN (TTP)

Zia Ur Rehman

INTRODUCTION

On the first day of 2019, gunmen attacked a Pakistani paramilitary force's training base in Loralai town, in the restive southwestern province of Balochistan, killing a number of security officials. In the same month and same district, militants carried out a suicide attack on January 29 on a district police officer, killing nine people and wounding 21; most of them were policemen. The Tehreek-e-Taliban Pakistan (TTP), or Pakistani Taliban, the country's most fearsome terror outfit, claimed responsibility for both attacks.

After some eleven years of its formation, the TTP is crumbling due to a sustained crackdown by Pakistan's law enforcement and security agencies, the relocation of the terror outfit's headquarters from Pakistan's lawless tribal areas to Afghanistan's neighbouring provinces, the killing of its high-ranking leaders in U.S. drone attacks and capture, and internal rifts mainly because of the arrival of the Islamic State, the middle-eastern militant outfit in the region.

However, despite its weakening and splintering, the TTP still remained the major actor of instability in Pakistan, and two major attacks on Pakistan's law enforcement agencies in January corroborated it. Even in 2018, the TTP and its splinter groups carried out most of the terror attacks in the country, according to various annual security reports. In light of the above-mentioned factors, this chapter reappraises the group's aspirations, capabilities, and significance, highlights some of the challenges it faces, and assesses the group's future direction.

THE HISTORY OF THE TTP

The emergence of the TTP is directly linked with the disintegration of the Taliban's Islamic Emirates in neighbouring Afghanistan since the launch of military operations by the U.S. and its allies one month after the 9/11 attack and the U.S. framing of terrorism as an existential threat under the banner of the "Global War on Terror" (Romaniuk & Webb, 2015). Because of the action, foreign (especially Arab and Central Asian) militants mainly linked with al-Qaeda and other foreign militant outfits fled from the war in Afghanistan and entered Pakistan's' tribal areas, particularly South and North Waziristan districts (Abbas, 2004).

Also, during the Afghan Taliban's reign (1994–2001), the group attracted youth, especially madrassa students, from the tribal areas, particularly South and North Waziristan districts. It was the reason that local commanders and veterans of Afghan jihads living in the two Waziristan provinces welcomed the Taliban and al-Qaeda, especially those fleeing from the U.S.-led Operation Anaconda in the neighbouring province of Paktia in Afghanistan, and provided them shelters in their areas (Yusufzai, 2004). In 2002, the reluctant Pakistani government, under increased pressure from the U.S., sent regular army troops into the two tribal districts to counter the fugitives of the Afghan Taliban and al-Qaeda and their hosts (Khan, 2009).

It made the two Waziristans a new theatre of war. Small skirmishes turned into bloody encounters by the end of 2003. In the beginning, the Pakistani military carried out several operations to dislodge the foreign militants, but after failing in them, it signed several agreements with the local militants and tribal elders in their attempts to achieve peace in the area. Also, taking advantage of differences among the Pakistani militants on a tribal basis, the Pakistani military tried to convince the militants from the Ahmedzai Wazir tribesmen, the traditional rivals of the Mehsud tribe, to take up arms against the foreign militants, especially those belonging to the Islamic Movement of Uzbekistan (IMU). But it also did not work (Khan, 2009).

During this time, Al-Qaeda chalked out a strategy to focus on the two Waziristan districts and inflict its ideology on local militants. Al-Qaeda carried out a few small operations in Pakistan, hoping to neutralise Pakistan's support for the U.S. actions in Afghanistan, but it still did not open a major front in Pakistan. Then, once it had regrouped its forces in the tribal areas, al-Qaeda went back to Afghanistan to support

DOI: 10.4324/9780429426063-78

the Afghan Taliban. In 2007, al-Qaeda briefly returned to Waziristan, not only to regroup but, most importantly this time, to open a war front in Pakistan, whose commitment to the U.S. actions in Afghanistan was now clear (Shahzad, 2011).

As a part of the scheme, Al-Qaeda played an important role in forming the TTP in late 2007 after the former realised that Pakistan's military tried to exploit the differences among militant commanders of various tribes, especially after Nazir's group's efforts to evict the IMU militants and the TTP's Mehsud members from Wana town in South Waziristan (Sherazi, 2012). After forming the TTP and appointing its leadership, the Afghan Taliban's head, Mullah Omar, was declared the newly formed militant outfit's chief patron. But the TTP served as the catalyst to draw the Afghan Taliban away from his influence and carry forward the al-Qaeda agenda in the region (Shahzad, p. 55, 2011). In 2008, Omar repeatedly urged the TTP to shun violence against Pakistan's military, but the TTP paid no attention to him (Shahzad, 2011).

THE FORMATION OF TTP

Until December 2007, a number of Taliban militant groups were operating independently in their respective areas of the then-FATA region and KP province. But after their leaders started networking with each other, the evolution from the smallest independent groups to one mainstream, organised Taliban force started.

It took three days of back and forth, arguments and counterarguments, and some persistent convincing to get the leaders of various Taliban groups to gather under one roof. Participants in the meeting represented groups operating in South Waziristan, North Waziristan, Orakzai, Kurram, Khyber, Mohmand, Bajaur, and Darra Adamkhel tribal regions and the districts of Swat, Buner, Upper Dir, Lower Dir, Bannu, Lakki Marwat, Tank, Peshawar, Dera Ismail Khan, Mardan, and Kohat of KP province. Finally, on December 14, 2007, they met somewhere in South Waziristan, in the tribal belt of Pakistan, and formed the Tehreek-e-Taliban Pakistan (TTP).

Baitullah, 35, from the Mehsud area of South Waziristan, was named the outfit's central chief. Hafiz Gul Bahadur, a commander from North Waziristan, and Maulvi Faqir Muhammad, a militant commander from Bajaur, were his deputies. Also, a 40-member shura (council), representing all the groups, was formed to advise the men on how to run the terror organisation (Dawn, 2009).

The combination of different groups in a coherent organisation infused new strength and vigour, enabling the insurgents to get control of various parts of the country's tribal areas and KP province, where they introduced a parallel governance system by providing justice to people and collecting taxes from them (Akhtar, 2018).

Initially, the TTP was concentrated in South Waziristan and North Waziristan, but by mid-2008, the terror outfit had virtually controlled all seven tribal agencies of the erstwhile tribal belt in Pakistan and expanded its influence to large parts of the Khyber Pakhtunkhwa province, especially the Malakand division. The group was also operating out of Karachi, Pakistan's most populous city and its financial hub, and some pockets of Punjab province. After its formation, the TTP's stated objectives were to enforce Sharia law in the country, fight NATO forces in neighbouring Afghanistan, and most importantly, fight against the Pakistani army's post-9/11 military operations.

Pakistan's interior ministry banned the TTP in August 2008 under the country's anti-terrorism laws for its involvement in terror attacks. Also, in March 2013, the government banned the TTP's various factions, such as the Tehreek-e-Taliban Swat, the Tehreek-e-Taliban Mohmand, the Tehreek-e-Taliban Bajaur, and the Tariq Geedar Group separately (The News, 2015).

KEY LEADERSHIP AND STRUCTURE

Although the TTP is ideologically inspired by the Afghan Taliban, its organisation from the beginning has been fluid and lacks a central command.

With the leadership of the TTP belonging to those who fought in Afghanistan along with the Afghan Taliban, the group emerged as a coalition of Afghan Jihad veterans and students of various religious seminaries across the country belonging to diverse backgrounds, tribes, and ethnicities. With more than two generations of war-hardened inhabitants to draw from, the Taliban recruit experienced fighters who know the terrain and can survive in the harsh environment.

Among them, Pashtuns are known to be in the majority, but the group also absorbed a large number of non-Pashtun cadres of various Jihadi and anti-Shia militant groups, such as the proscribed Lashkar-e-Jhangvi, from the Punjab, Balochistan, and Sindh provinces.

Most of them are young, ranging in age from 16 to 35, with little or no formal education. Within the TTP, there was a significant presence of Central Asian, Arab, and Afghan militants who crossed the border (Sherazi, 2009). There are few reliable estimates of the numerical strength of the TTP. In 2009, the Pakistani military claimed that the strength of the TTP militants, including foreign militants, in South Waziristan was over 10,000 (Walsh, 2009).

Under the leadership of its founding leader Baitullah, whose name appeared in Time magazine's 'Time 100' list of the world's most influential people in 2008, the TTP played a critical role in the upsurge of militancy and extended its network to large swaths of territory in the country's north-western region.

But his August 2009 death in a U.S. drone strike damaged the TTP to a great extent. The group could not choose his successor between Waliur Rehman and Hakeemullah, two top aides of the slain militant commander. However, the TTP's main shura (council) approved the younger Hakeemullah to be the TTP's top leader, and Rahman was appointed as Hakeemullah's deputy. This leadership dispute marked the beginning of a purported rivalry between the two commanders, who belonged to the same tribe but different sub-tribes and experienced a bloody turf war in the port city of Karachi (Rehman, 2013).

After the killing of Hakeemullah in a drone attack on November 1, 2012, in North Wazirsitan, Rahman was made the TTP's new chief. Rehman raised finances for the TTP through a large and influential gang in Karachi that specialised in carrying out bank robberies and kidnappings for ransom (Siddiqui, 2013). He was killed in a drone attack in North Waziristan on May 29, 2013. Reports citing the State Department claimed that

A Hakeemullah supporter gave the drone attack that killed Rahman a tip-off (Express Tribune, 2013).

After the killing of Rehman in a drone attack, the TTP's leadership council, after contentious meetings in November 2013, appointed Maulana Fazlullah, who served as the group's leader in Swat, to lead it. The promotion of Fazlullah ultimately led to a split within the TTP, and the main reason behind it in the beginning was the dominance of Mehsud militants in the organisational structure and policy-making of the TTP. Although Fazlullah's appointment as the TTP's chief signalled a significant shift for the organisation into a group based increasingly on ideology rather than tribal ties, But it did not work (Rehman, 2014).

However, after killing Fazullah in a drone attack in Afghanistan's Kunar province on June 13, 2018, the TTP shura announced Mufti Noor Wali, a commander for the organisation's Mehsud chapter in South Waziristan, as Fazullah's successor. Wali's appointment indicates that the TTP is returning to the Mehsud tribe to serve as the base of its leadership.

RESOURCES

To support their activities in the country, the TTP draws funding from donations (from domestic and international sympathisers), criminal activities, including kidnapping for ransoms and extortions, imposing taxes and robberies, and funds from other international terrorist outfits.

In its 690-page book titled 'Inqilab-e-Mehsud', authored by the TTPs' current chief Mufti Noor Wali and released in December 2017, the outfit admitted that its militants used extortion, kidnappings for ransom, and carrying out assassinations for money to collect funds to support their activities (Samaa, 2018). According to a 2012 media report citing law enforcement officials, only from the three major cities of Karachi, Islamabad, and Rawalpindi had the TTP generated funds of around three billion rupees in the four years through extortions, forced donations, and kidnapping for ransom (The Nation, 2012). Even in some cities, madrassas (religious seminaries) reportedly helped the TTP with the collection of extortion and ransom money by arranging deals between militants and their victims (Such TV, 2014).

Some Taliban groups used unique methods to raise revenue. The Mehsud Taliban, by landline phone from their office in the Miramshah bazaar in North Waziristan, used to call Pashtun traders and affluent people and threaten to target their families if they failed to pay extortion money. In some cases, they even summoned them to appear in the Taliban's courts in Miramshah to resolve disputes (Rehman, 2015). Even so, they imposed a 'donation' of 5,000 Pakistani rupees (about $90) from men who worked as drivers in Gulf nations when they returned to visit their families. Lower-paid overseas labourers who returned for visits were expected to pay 3,000 rupees ($50) (Siddiqui, book).

TIES TO THE AFGHAN TALIBAN AND AL-QAEDA

The TTP is often confused with the Pakistan chapter of the Afghan Taliban, which pursues similar objectives. However, that is not the case, as the TTP, since its formation, has never formed an integral part of the Afghan Taliban organisation and has retained its distinctive identity under various groups despite sharing the ideals of its leaders, who call Omar their *Amir al-Mu'minin* (meaning leader of the faithful).

Most of the TTP leaders and commanders were veterans of Afghan Jihad against the Soviets and served under the command of Afghan Taliban leader Mullah Omar in various parts of Afghanistan. After coming back from Afghanistan, they tried to enforce Taliban-style methods in the North and South Waziristan tribal areas of Pakistan.

On the other hand, the Afghan Taliban do not engage in attacks in Pakistan, and their main focus is on fighting Afghan and international troops in Afghanistan. But they also did not stop the TTP from carrying out attacks in Pakistan because they needed TTP support in Pakistan's tribal region to maintain their sanctuaries and recruit Pashtun tribesmen to fight in Afghanistan. However, in some cases, Omar urged the

TTP to shun violence against Pakistan's military, but the TTP paid no attention to him because of the influence of al-Qaeda.

Al-Qaeda played a key role in the formation of the TTP and gave its cause some legitimacy amid a myriad of transcontinental terrorists with global agendas. Al-Qaeda exerted more influence on the TTP than on the Afghan Taliban. Its main objective in helping form the TTP was to open a war front in Pakistan, whose commitment to the U.S. actions in Afghanistan was now clear (Shahzad, 2011). After forming the TTP and appointing its leadership, the Afghan Taliban's supremo, Mullah Omar, was declared the newly formed militant outfit's chief patron. But the TTP served as the catalyst to draw the Afghan Taliban away from his influence and carry forward the al-Qaeda agenda in the region (Shahzad, p. 55, 2011).

After the start of military operations against the TTP in Pakistan, especially in tribal areas, in 2014, the TTP militants found refuge in Afghanistan's bordering provinces, which are strongholds of the Afghan Taliban (Dawn, 2019). From there, they are regrouping and masterminding their attacks in Pakistan. It is largely believed that the Afghan Taliban have been providing them with sanctuaries and financial support.

THE IS'S ARRIVAL

Since mid-2014, the Islamic State, a Middle Eastern militant group, has also started increasing its influence in Afghanistan and Pakistan and launched its local chapter, called Khorasan, an old name for Afghanistan and surrounding areas (Azami, 2017). Its arrival in the region has made the situation difficult for the TTP and caused splintering in the group because of its ideological appeal, worldwide reputation, and substantial financial resources, which attracted a number of TTP leaders and factions.

The TTP itself has not expressed support for the IS elements in the region, mainly because of the former's alliance with the Afghan Taliban, which has lost a large part of its turf to the IS since 2015. However, a number of TTP commanders, including some top leaders who moved to Afghanistan after the Pakistani military launched an operation in Pakistan's tribal areas, joined the Middle Eastern militant outfit. U.S. military officials believe that around 70% of the IS militants in Afghanistan are Pakistani Taliban who joined IS after being forced out of their country (Iqbal, 2016).

In October 2014, the TTP spokesperson Shahidullah Shahid and other five commanders from various Pakistani districts declared allegiance to the IS's Caliph Abu Bakr al-Baghdadi (Khan, 2014). Later, the TTP Bajaur chapter chief Maulana Abu Bakar and deputy chief Qari Zahid also announced their intention to leave the TTP and join the IS (Khan, 2014).

In January 2015, the IS officially announced Hafiz Saeed Khan, the TTP Orakzai agency's commander, as the outfit's chief for the Khorasan region (Firdous, 2016). In 2017, Haji Daud Khan, the former TTP Karachi chief, also announced his intention to join the IS (Khan, 2017).

Although TTP commanders who defected to the ISI were not key figures, analysts believe that the TTP suffered greatly from their departure because they had influence among Taliban circles and their association with a global terror outfit enhanced their standing in the region (Rafiq, 2014).

CRACKS

The TTP's organisational structure is a loose network of various groups that vary in number and levels of coordination and tribal affiliation, which is why a few commanders and factions have announced their intention to part ways with the central leadership.

Observers argue that tribal divisions are the key factor behind splits among militant factions in Waziristan and elsewhere (Mir, 2015). After the killing of the TTP chief, who was from the Mehsud clan, the TTP's factions in tribal areas were not happy with Fazlullah's leadership. Also, because he was based in Afghanistan, his physical absence damaged the group's running and delayed urgent organisational matters. The internal struggles and widening gaps have divided the TTP into various factions, mainly the Jamaat-ul-Ahrar (JuA), Punjabi Taliban, and Mehsud faction, while Fazlullah continues to lead them from Afghanistan.

Some leaders had shown their disagreement on issues such as attacks on Pakistani authorities and civilians and peace talks with the government.

The JuA, founded in 2014 by TTP commanders from the Mohmand region, is one of the most notable factions to break away from the TTP. The JuA was founded by Omar Khalid Khorasani, an important Taliban commander and a member of the TTP Shura who was not happy with peace talks between the Taliban and the government (Rana, 2014).

However, after one of its key leaders and active spokespersons, Ehsanullah Ehsan, surrendered to the government in April 2017, the JuA too splintered after its commander, Mukarram Khan, created Hizbul Ahrar (Shahid, 2017).

Also, the Asmatullah Muawiya-led TTP Punjab chapter, known as the Punjabi Taliban, announced in September 2014, after reportedly surrendering to the government, the cessation of terror activities in Pakistan and continued to fight in neighbouring Afghanistan (Rehman, 2014). The commanders of the TTP's Mehsud chapter in May 2014 have also abandoned the group (Islam, 2014).

The factionalism has also led to territorial infighting between rival groups. More and more militants are being targeted and killed after being labelled spies by an opposing outfit, further weakening the TTP.

An online booklet titled 'Strategy for the TTP Militants,' released by the group for its members in September 2018, disclosed the new leadership's plans to reconfigure the group for a potential comeback and overcome internal differences. Keeping the cracks within the group, the TTP's manual instructs that a "person, if involved in espionage, can only be killed by an ameer (head) or naib ameer (deputy head)" (Rehman, 2018).

THE CURRENT SITUATION

But starting in 2009, the Pakistan army launched a series of military blitzes to dismantle the network and kill or capture its leaders: in May 2009, Operation Rah-e-Rast in the Swat valley; in June 2009, Operation Rah-e-Nijat in South Waziristan; in September 2013, the operation in Karachi; in June 2014, Operation Zarb-e-Azb in North Waziristan; and then there were the various phases of Operation Khyber in the Khyber Agency between 2014 and 2017.

In early 2014, the TTP's growing influence and terror alarmed the Pakistani political and military elite and generated a strong resolve to confront the terror threat seriously.

Before launching a military operation against the TTP, the government held negotiations with its leaders, and after several rounds of peace talks, a ceasefire was announced. However, the TTP violated the ceasefire by carrying out an attack on Pakistan's busiest airport, Karachi, in June 2014 that killed 36 people, including all 10 attackers. After the attack, the Pakistani public also put pressure on the government to take stern action against the TTP because of its heavy involvement in terrorism in Pakistan. The anti-TTP public mood provided the necessary support for the government to undertake serious military operations against Taliban insurgents.

In retaliation, the Pakistani military launched an operation codenamed 'Zarb-e-Azb' (sharp and cutting strike), carrying out a series of air strikes targeting the TTP's hideouts in the areas, especially North Waziristan, where the outfit's leaders made their headquarters after losing sanctuaries in South Waziristan in the previous operations. However, the severity of the operation came after an attack on a military-run school in Peshawar in December 2014 that killed around 150 schoolchildren and injured more than 200.

During the two years of the operation, the TTP's command and control centres were effectively dismantled in North Waziristan. By April 2016, the Pakistan Army claimed to have successfully restored the writ of the state in the tribal region by destroying 992 terrorist sanctuaries and killing 3500 terrorists. It also claimed that an area of 4,304 kilometres was cleared from militants, 7,500 bomb-making factories were sealed, and 253 tonnes of explosives were seized (Express Tribune, 2016).

While military operations, such as Zarb-e-Azb, have achieved many successes, such as killing a large number of militants and putting such groups on the back foot, there have also been unexpected disadvantages. For instance, in response to the government's military pressure, the TTP is now resolving their differences and carrying out attacks on high-profile targets in Balochistan province.

Though the TTP has suffered huge losses in ongoing military operations, it still remains the major actor in creating instability in the country. In 2018, the group was found involved in 79 terrorist attacks across the country, including 57 in Khyber Pakhtunkhwa province and erstwhile FATA, 18 in Balochistan, 2 in Punjab, and another 2 in Karachi. Combined, these attacks by the TTP claimed 185 lives and left 3336 others injured. In 2017, the group carried out 70 attacks that killed 186 people (Express Tribune, 2019). A close assessment of statistics suggests that the TTP's operational capabilities are still intact, though its outreach has largely shrunk to the tribal districts of the KP province, where it has carried out most terrorist attacks. Still, as cited earlier, the group showed its presence in Balochistan province by conducting 18 terrorist attacks there.

Since the start of 2019, the TTP has carried out three major attacks in Balochistan's Pashtun areas, bordering Afghanistan, and tribal areas (Siddiqi, 2019). On January 1, TTP gunmen wearing suicide vests attacked a residential compound at a paramilitary force's training base in the area, killing security officials in Loralai district. In the same district, on January 29, the group carried out suicide attacks on a district police office in Loralai, killing nine people and wounding 21 – most of them policemen. On March 26, four suspected suicide bombers blew themselves up during a raid conducted by security forces in Loralai.

The group is also desperately struggling to reestablish its network and overcome internal differences. In the booklet 'Strategy for the TTP Militants,' the outfit outlined the group's future plan of action. Written in Urdu, the booklet includes chapters discussing the TTP's overall strategy, internal organisational issues, policies regarding target selection and maal-e-ghanimat (lootings), the use of suicide bombers, and the management of hostages and defectors (Rehman, 2018).

Managing the financial resources has emerged as the biggest challenge for the group, and it is trying to reconnect with financial sources of supply in Karachi, where the group is targeting the outskirts of the city to generate funds.

CONCLUSION

The TTP's birth was a major turning point in the rise of organised insurgency and terrorism within Pakistan. Soon after its formation, it proved to be a lethal and brutal terrorist network. During the last five years (2013), the TTP and its splinter groups were major groups that claimed responsibility for 1,759 fatalities out of a total of 3011. However, the number of fatalities has significantly decreased, from 457 in 2013 to 72 in 2018 (CRSS, 2019).

Years of violence, killing, suicide bombing, loss of lives, and crimes inflicted by the TTP in almost every part of Pakistan urgently called for a comprehensive strategy involving military, political, and institutional solutions.

Since its inception, the group has been loosely administered, immature, and incompetent in achieving its goals, but it has adapted itself to sustain a long-term conflict. Compared to the Afghan Taliban, the TTP has never tried to elaborate on the kind of parallel state structures that have been fundamental to the Afghan Taliban's approach.

Despite being one of the severe internal threats faced by the Pakistani state, the TTP has benefited from the Pakistani state's commitment to proxy warfare in Afghanistan. Pakistan's previous policies were focused only on restricting the space for the TTP to operate rather than denying it completely. It was the reason that the Pakistani military did not kill or arrest any senior militant leaders, making it easier for the TTP to bounce back once government pressure was removed.

However, some eleven years after its founding, the TTP started crumbling. Pakistani military and intelligence-based operations have weakened the terror outfit to a great extent, shattering the Taliban's control and command system and degrading its ability to carry out large-scale attacks. In addition, the group has also long suffered from organisational dysfunction and operational degradation due to both internal and external factors. Statistics compiled by independent security think tanks also suggest that successful crackdowns have resulted in a significant decline in terrorist attacks across Pakistan since 2013, showing the TTP has lost its capabilities to carry out the terror attacks.

On the other side, the killing of all TTP chiefs – from Baitullah to Fazullah – and other important commanders in the drone strikes in both Pakistan and Afghanistan also reiterated the significance of U.S. assistance to Pakistan in countering terrorism. After the killing of Fazullah in a drone strike in Afghanistan, it is believed that increasing cooperation among Pakistan, Afghanistan, and the U.S. may further debilitate the TTP and make it difficult for its top leaders to survive.

But the operations have not been enough to eliminate them, and a number have found safe haven in neighbouring Afghanistan, where the weakened government has been unable to tackle them.

References

Abbas, Z. (2004, September 10). Pakistan's undeclared war. *BBC. [Online]*. Available at http://news.bbc.co.uk/2/hi/south_asia/3645114.stm

Akhtar, S. (2018, December 12). Defeating TTP: An appraisal of Pakistan's counterinsurgency operations. *Pakistan Politico. [Online]*. Available at http://pakistanpolitico.com/defeating-ttp-an-appraisal-of-pakistans-counterinsurgency-operations/

Azami, D. (2017, February 25). IS in Afghanistan: How successful has the group been? *BBC. [Online]*. Available at https://www.bbc.com/news/world-asia-39031000

CRSS. (2019, January 31). Pakistan; remarkable reduction in violence between 2013–2018. *CRSS. [Online]*. Available at https://crss.pk/story/pakistan-remarkable-reduction-in-violence-between-2013-2018/

Dawn. (2009, September 13). Wazirsitan power politics. *Dawn. [Online]*. Available at https://www.dawn.com/news/490334

Dawn. (2019, January 30). TTP sanctuaries. *Dawn. [Online]*. Available at https://www.dawn.com/news/490334/waziristan-power-politics

Express Tribune. (2013, June 2). Wali killed on a tip off by Hakimullah supporter. [Online]. Available at https://tribune.com.pk/story/557769/wali-killed-on-a-tip-off-by-hakimullah-supporter/

Express Tribune. (2016, June 15). 490 soldiers, 3,500 militants killed in Operation Zarb-e-Azb so far: DG ISPR. *Express Tribune. [Online]*. Available at https://tribune.com.pk/story/1123356/1-dg-ispr-addresses-press-conference-afghanistan-pakistan-border-clashes/

Express Tribune. (2019, January 6). 595 martyred in 262 terrorist attacks in 2018. *Express Tribune. [Online]*. Available at https://tribune.com.pk/story/1882804/1-595-martyred-262-terrorist-attacks-2018/

Firdous, I. (2016, August 9). Islamic State's Hafiz Saeed Khan: Short-lived, long felt. *The Friday Times. [Online]*. Available at https://www.thefridaytimes.com/tft/short-lived-long-felt/

Islam, N. (2014, May, 28). Mehsud faction separate from the TTP. *Newsweek Pakistan. [Online]*. Available at http://newsweekpakistan.com/mehsud-faction-separates-from-the-ttp/

Iqbal, A. (2016, August 1). Most IS men in Afghanistan are TTP fighters'. *Dawn. [Online]*. Available at https://www.dawn.com/news/1274558

Khan, I. (September, 2009). Baitullah Mehsud. *Monthly Herald Karachi. (Print)*.

Khan, T. (2014, October 14). Spokesperson, five other leaders declare allegiance to Islamic State. *Express Tribune. [Online]*. Available at https://tribune.com.pk/story/775152/ttp-spokesperson-five-other-leaders-declare-allegiance-to-islamic-state/

Khan, T. (2017, July 31). Senior TTP commander Daud Khan switches loyalty to Daesh. *Daily Times. [Online]*. Available at https://dailytimes.com.pk/123065/senior-ttp-commander-daud-khan-switches-loyalty-to-daesh/

Mir, A. (2015, January 13). Pakistan now has a native Daish Ameer. *The News. [Online]*. Available at https://www.thenews.com.pk/print/18141-pakistan-now-has-a-native-daish-ameer

Rafiq, A. (2014, October 24). Islamic State Defections fracture Pakistan Taliban. *The Diplomat. [Online]*. Available at https://thediplomat.com/2014/10/islamic-state-defections-fracture-pakistan-taliban/

Rana, M. (2014, September 2). Ideological purification: Understanding the TTP split. *Dawn. [Online]*. Available at https://www.dawn.com/news/1129416

Rehman, Z. (2013, November 8). Leaderless Taliban brick over new chief. *The Friday Times. [Online]*. Available at https://www.thefridaytimes.com/tft/leaderless-taliban-bicker-over-new-chief/

Rehman, Z. (2014, September 19). Punjabi Taliban will fight in Afghanistan. *The Friday Times. [Online]*. Available at https://www.thefridaytimes.com/punjabi-taliban-will-fight-in-afghanistan/

Rehman, Z. (2015, July 14). Mehsuds in Karachi no longer in control of Mehsud in Miramshah. *The News. [Online]* Available at https://www.thenews.com.pk/print/51129-mehsuds-in-karachi-no-longer-in-control-of-mehsuds-in-miramshah

Rehman, Z. (2018, October 16). The TTP: Cornered and desperate. *Geo. [Online]*. Available at https://www.geo.tv/latest/214854-the-ttp-cornered-and-desperate

Romaniuk, S. N., & Webb, S. (2015). Extraordinary measures: Drone warfare, securitization, and the 'War on Terror'. *Slovak Journal of Political Sciences, 15*(3), 221–245. https://sjps.fsvucm.sk/index.php/sjps/article/view/47

Samaa. (2018, April 25). TTP member exposes militant outfit's sources of funding in tell-all book. *Samaa. [Online]*. Available at https://www.samaa.tv/news/2018/04/ttp-member-exposes-militant-outfits-sources-of-funding-in-tell-all-book/

Shahid, S. (2017, November 13). Hizbul Ahrar takes birth as internal rifts tear Jamaatul Ahrar apart. *Pakistan Today. [Online]*. Available at https://www.pakistantoday.com.pk/2017/11/13/hizbul-ahrar-takes-birth-as-internal-rifts-tear-jamaatul-ahrar-apart/

Shahzad, S. (2011). *Inside Al-Qaeda and the Taliban: Beyond Bin Laden and 9/11*. Pluto Press.

Sherazi, Z. (September 2009). The Brash young warrior. *Monthly Herald Karachi. [Print]*.

Sherazi, Z. (2012, December 1). Mullah Nazir orders out Mehsud Taliban fighters. *Dawn. [Online]*. Available at https://www.dawn.com/news/768118

Siddiqui, A. (2013, May 29). The potential fallout of a Pakistani militant's death. *Radio Free Europe Free Liberty. [Online]*. Available at https://www.rferl.org/a/pakistan-taliban-rehman-mahsud-death-fallout/25001196.html

Siddiqi, A. (2019, April 10). TTP expands footprint in Balochistan as Quetta Safe City project remains in limbo. *The News. [Online]*. Available at https://www.thenews.com.pk/print/455689-ttp-expands-footprint-in-balochistan-as-quetta-safe-city-project-remains-in-limbo

Such TV. (2014, May 1). Madrassas playing courier for TTP in fund-raising drive. [Online]. Available at https://www.suchtv.pk/pakistan/general/item/11033-madrassas-playing-courier-for-ttp-in-fund-raising-drive.html

The Nation. (2012, September 7). TTP made Rs3b through extortion. *The Nation. [Online]*. Available at https://nation.com.pk/07-Sep-2012/ttp-made-rs3b-through-extortion

The News. (2015, September 4). No change made in list of banned outfits. [Online]. Available at https://www.thenews.com.pk/print/14426-no-change-made-in-list-of-banned-outfits

Walsh, D. (2009, October 17). Pakistan sends 30,000 troops for all-out assault on Taliban. *Guardian. [Online]*. Available at https://www.theguardian.com/world/2009/oct/17/pakistan-sends-troops-against-taliban

Yusufzai, R. (2004, March 4). Waziristan: Bin Laden's hiding place? *BBC. [Online]*. Available at http://news.bbc.co.uk/2/hi/south_asia/3532841.stm

70

THE LIBERATION TIGERS OF TAMIL EELAM (LTTE)

Fathima Azmiya Badurdeen

INTRODUCTION

The Liberation Tigers of Tamil Eelam (LTTE), founded by Velupillai Prabakaran, was a separatist militant organisation based in northern and northeastern Sri Lanka. The organisation waged a secessionist Tamil nationalist insurgency for an independent homeland for Sri Lanka's Tamil minority in northern Sri Lanka, leading to the Sri Lankan civil war from 1983 until 2009. Consequentially, discriminatory policies such as citizenship, national language, and education formed the core grievances for the minority Tamil communities, which culminated in the evolution of the LTTE. The LTTE movement transformed from a guerilla movement to that of a conventional national army, with the military wing of the LTTE headed by Prabakharan. The organisation also had an intelligence wing, a political wing, and an international wing. In May 2009, with the defeat of the LTTE by the Sri Lankan military, an entire terrorist organisation came to a standstill. Nevertheless, the LTTE's ideology was still touted by their supporters and sympathisers in different parts of the country and sections of the diaspora. The context of a "victory's peace" by the Sri Lankan government after militarily defeating the LTTE challenged the reconciliation process between majority and minority identities. Addressing war crimes, human rights abuses, the resettlement of former combatants, and the settlement of land grievances were seen as shaping the conflict transformation processes in the country.

The Eelam[1] War is the name given to the different phases of the armed conflict between the LTTE and the Government of Sri Lanka (GoSL), which had four phases (Eelam War I, II, III, and IV). Eelam I marks the initial phase of tensions between the GoSL and LTTE, which began in the 1970s and reached peaks of violence during 1983–1987. In 1987, the Indo-Sri Lankan Accord was signed, under which the Indian peacekeeping force took control of the north from the Sri Lankan troops. Eelam II commenced after the failed peace talks between the Premadasa government and the LTTE, during which the LTTE massacred more than 600 Sinhalese and Muslims. More than 28,000 Muslims residing in Jaffna were forcibly evicted. Eelam III broke out after the 100-day cease-fire agreement in 1995. This phase marked the military strength of the LTTE as they blew up Sooraya and Ranasuru boats, fired a "Stinger" anti-aircraft missile on a Sri Lankan Air Force AVRO aircraft, and managed to capture key districts in the northeast of Sri Lanka. Eelam IV marked the end of the hostiles after four years of a collapsed ceasefire in 2006 when Sri Lanka Air Force fighter jets bombed LTTE camps in Mavil Aru, Anicut. GoSL made several territorial gains. The LTTE Air Tigers bombed the Katunayake airbase in 2007, which marked the first rebel air attack without external assistance in history. Eelam IV ended on May 18, 2009, when the GoSL gained complete control of the territory. Victory over the LTTE was declared by President Mahinda Rajapakse on May 16, 2009, with the eventual defeat of the LTTE and the killing of LTTE leader Prabakaran by the government forces on May 19, 2009.

RECENT DEVELOPMENTS

As of February 13, 2023, Velupillai Prabhakaran, the LTTE's leader, is still alive and will make an appearance in public, according to Pazha Nedumaran, the leader of the Tamil nationalist organisation. The time has come for the LTTE leader to come out in the open, according to Nedumaran, who said this during a news conference in Thanjavur at Mullivaikkal Mutram in light of the international situation and the Sinhalese demonstrations against Mahinda Rajapaksa. On May 18, 2009, in Mullaivaikkal in the Mullaithivu district, Sri Lankan government troops reported that Prabakaran, the head of the island nation's Tamil minority, had died (Business Today, February 13, 2023). It is difficult to understand what Nedumaran hopes to accomplish by pursuing the claim that Prabhakaran is still alive given that the LTTE, long the most dreaded terrorist group in the world, is effectively gone. All of these

DOI: 10.4324/9780429426063-79

allegations are made despite the Sri Lankan government revealing the body of the murdered leader and announcing that DNA tests were conducted to determine that the victim was, in fact, Prabhakaran. The announcement made by Nedumaran was denied by the Sri Lankan military. In the 2021 assembly elections, the pro-LTTEE political party Naam Tamilar Katchi (NTK) was able to build a support base for itself by obtaining a 6.58% vote share. Most of the NTK's supporters are impressionable children drawn to Seeman's fiery lectures. The NTK does not, however, control a majority in the legislature (Deccan Herald, February 15, 2023).

THE EVOLUTION OF THE SRI LANKAN CIVIL WAR AND THE LTTE MOVEMENT

The continuous political hostility between the majority Sinhalese and the minority Tamils culminated in the evolution of the LTTE, leading to the Sri Lankan civil war. An array of discriminatory policies such as citizenship, national language, and education formed the core grievances for the minority Tamil communities.

Sri Lanka, located in the Indian Ocean, comprises the Sinhalese and the Tamils as the major ethnic groups, representing 67% and 17%, respectively; 7% are Muslims (Moors and Malays); and the rest are Eurasian, Burgher, Veddah, and other communities.[2] Sinhala is spoken by the Sinhalese, and Tamil is spoken by the Tamils and the Moor population. Sinhalese, as an ethnic community, has its roots in the earliest Indo-Aryan settlement around the 5th century BC, with state patronage for Buddhism. Tamils trace their heritage as far back as the 3rd century BC, with various dynasties (Pandya, Pallava, and Chola) from India invading Sinhalese Buddhist kingdoms (Nubin, 2002). Among these invasions, the defeat of Elara (a Tamil king) by a Sinhalese king, Duttugamunu, is cited as an epic tale of victory, evoking ethno-religious sentiments among the Sinhalese (Dharmakirti, 2011).

The British granted Ceylon independence in 1948, and as Ceylon, the island remained a dominion in the British Commonwealth (De Silva, 2005). In 1948, after independence, the controversial Ceylon Citizenship Act was passed, which excluded the Indian Tamil ethnic minority from obtaining citizenship and rendered them stateless (Kanapathipillar, 2009). However, throughout the colonial and independent eras, as in the 1950s, the minority Tamils and majority Sinhalese competed with each other in a peaceful democratic fashion. In 1919, Sinhalese and Tamil political organisations united to form the Ceylon National Congress under Ponnambalam Arunachalam, a Tamil who represented both communities in the national legislative council (Guruge, 2011). Don Stephen Senanayake, the Sinhalese leader of the United National Party (UNP), headed the first independent government in 1947–1952 and was considered impartial on ethnic issues. Nevertheless, there was resentment among the Sinhalese towards Tamil predominance in many professions, specifically the civil service, during the colonial and pre-independence eras, mainly blamed on the British divide-and-rule policies (Wilson, 2000).

The transfer of power after the demise of Senanayake in 1952 to a new platform that pushed forward a Sinhala-only agenda under the Sri Lanka Freedom Party (SLFP) government in 1956 This government under S. W. R. D. Bandaranaike led to the formulation of policies aimed at elevating the prestige of Buddhism and unpopular for the Tamil-speaking Hindu population, leading to the beginning of anti-Tamil rioting in 1958. The "Sinhala Only Act" replaced English with Sinhala as the official language of the country, discriminating against Tamil-speaking minorities and leading some Tamil-speaking civil servants to resign as they were unable to fluently communicate in Sinhala (Wijeyeratne, 2014). The laws led to riots such as the Gal Oya riots in 1956, where hundreds of Tamils were killed, and the relocation of Tamil communities from the Sinhalese-dominated areas to the north, marking the beginning of communal violence (Muscat, 2002). Other forms of discrimination that affected the Tamil community included the state-sponsored colonisation schemes where Sinhalese peasants were given land in traditional Tamil-dominated areas (Muscat, 2002) and the preference given to the Buddhist religion as a state religion under the 1978 Constitution of Sri Lanka (Tambiah, 1992).

During the late 1960s, sprouting Tamil militant movements were evident; among them, five movements were prominent: the Tamil Eelam Liberation Organisation (TELO), the Eelam Revolutionary Organisation of Students (EROS), the Eelam People's Revolutionary Liberation Front (EPRLF), the People's Liberation Organisation of Tamil Eelam (PLOTE), and the LTTE. The Liberation Tigers for Tamil Eelam were founded on May 5, 1976, as the successor to the Tamil New Tigers (TNT) (Bandarage, 2009). LTTE's constitution stated that the members would fight to establish an independent Tamil Eelam, a sovereign and socialist democratic people's government, a socialist mode of production, to abolish all forms of exploitation, particularly the caste system, to uphold the armed revolution struggle as an extension of the political struggle, and to gradually and systematically transform guerilla warfare into a genuine people's war of liberation. (Richards, 2014).

TNT, together with the Tamil Eelam Liberation Organisation (TELO), was involved in several hit-and-run attacks against police, civil administrators, and politicians, including explosions during Prime Minister Sirimavo Bandaranaike's visit to Jaffna in 1974, the assassination of Alfred Duraippah, the Mayor of Jaffna in 1974, and a string of robberies (Wilson, 2000; Wickremasekera, 2016). On

November 27, 1982, the LTTE officially declared war against the GoSL, as it was the day that the LTTE experienced the death of Lieutenant Shankar, killed by Sri Lankan soldiers (Fuglerud, 2011). Many attacks followed, such as in 1983, when the LTTE staged a well-planned attack in Tinnevelli, Jaffna, killing 13 soldiers. In 1984, the LTTE carried out attacks on the Chavakachcheri and Jaffna police stations, blowing up the Yal Devi train, and hijacking a bus that drove from Puttalam to Anuradhapura (Wickremasekera, 2016). In June 1985, five militant groups agreed to a ceasefire with the GoSL, known as the Thimpu Talks, under the patronage of India. The ceasefire did not last, and the fighting continued (Ghosh, 1999).

India's involvement and intervention played a crucial role in the Sri Lankan civil war. Initially, most militant groups received their training from Tamil Nadu, India, which was sympathetic to the Tamil cause (Ciment, 2011). Later, Indian efforts towards peaceful settlements involved India playing a role in negotiations between the GoSL and LTTE under the Indo-Sri Lankan Peace Accord in 1987. The Indian Peacekeeping Force (IPKF), formed under the Indo-Sri Lankan Accord in 1987, was aimed at ending the Sri Lankan civil war. The IPKF's task of disarming the militant groups in Jaffna and forming an interim administrative council was futile, as hostility between the IPKF and LTTE led to a battle, leading to the IPKF's withdrawal in 1990 (Ghosh, 1999). Other efforts towards peaceful settlements involved the Peace Process in 2002, with Norway as the mediator, where an MOU was signed between the two parties for a permanent ceasefire agreement (CFA). The CFA revealed a temporary period of success with the opening up of the A9 highway and commercial air flights between the government-controlled and LTTE-controlled areas. Consequential peace talks began in Thailand, Norway, Germany, and Japan. Peace talks facilitated the agreement on a federal solution, where the LTTE dropped its demand for a separate state and the GoSL agreed to federal solutions. However, in 2003, peace talks broke down and began the emergence of hostility (Salter, 2015).

The major split of the Karuna faction (Col. Karuna, the Eastern Commander of the LTTE, pulled out with 5,000 cadres) from the LTTE, where the GoSL was alleged to have supported the Karuna group, further complicated the existing hostility (Goodhand et al., 2008; Human Rights Watch, 2013). The Karuna group formed the paramilitary group Tamil Makkal Viduthalai Pulikal (TMVP), which later registered as a political party (BBC News, 2009). Efforts for peace talks remained futile in 2004 and 2005. In 2006, the LTTE officially pulled out of the peace talks. The new government in 2006 demanded an abrogation of the ceasefire agreement and emphasised a military solution (Lewer, 2017). The Sri Lankan Monitoring Mission documented 3,830 ceasefire violations by the LTTE and 351 by the security forces (between 2002 and 2007). The GoSL officially pulled out of the Ceasefire Agreement in January 2008 (Wallace, 2017).

KEY PERSONNEL AND STRUCTURE OF THE LTTE

LTTE's structure entailed mainly the military and political wings with varied subgroups. The military wing comprised the intelligence wing, and the political wing was closely associated with the international wing. Vellupillai Prabhakaran, the LTTE's founder, was the chief leader who oversaw all activities of the LTTE as the head of the central governing committee of the LTTE. LTTE members were trained within and outside the country. Some high-level LTTE members were trained in the Middle East by Palestinian groups such as Al Fatah and the Popular Front for the Liberation of Palestine (Hopgood, 2006). In the 1980s, members also underwent training in Tamil Nadu, India. Between 1983 and 1987, the Research and Analysis Wing (RAW), India's external intelligence agency, trained LTTE members, which facilitated the LTTE's takeover of the Jaffna peninsula in 1985 (Ciment, 2011).

THE MILITARY WING

The military wing of the LTTE, headed by Prabakharan, transformed from a guerilla movement to resemble that of a conventional national army. This included various subdivisions led by deputy and special commanders, which included LTTE's ground forces, Sea Tigers, Air Tigers, and LTTE's Intelligence Wing. Since 1999, LTTE has possessed civilian auxiliary units (Eela Padai, Grama Padai, and Thunai Padai) and other units under the ground forces, such as the Jeyanthan infantry brigade, Kittu Artillery Brigade, Victor Anti-Tank and Armoured Unit, Kutti Sri Mortar brigade, Ponnamman mining unit, the women's wing of the Malathi and Sothia brigades, bodyguard brigades (Ratha and Imran Pandian regiments), and elite army brigades reserved for individuals with specialised training, such as the Black Tigers, the Leopard commandos, known as Chiruthaigal, and the Charles Anthony special forces (O'Duffy, 2007; Hashim, 2013; Graeme & Gunaratna, 2004).

In 1991, the Charles Anthony Brigade, a conventional fighting formation of an elite LTTE infantry brigade, comprised troops from the North. The brigade named after Charles Lucas Anthony, the right-hand man of Prabakharan during the LTTE's inception, participated in major combat operations, including Operation Jayasikurui, the Battle of

Kilinochchi, the Second Battle of Elephant Pass, the Battle of Mullaitivu, and Eelam I, II, III, and IV (Richards, 2014). The brigade was completely destroyed during the final days of the Sri Lankan civil war (Reuters, 2009). In 1993, the Jeyanthan brigade was created under Karuna Amman, raising troops from the Eastern Province of Sri Lanka. The brigade was involved in the Battle of Pooneryn, the Battle of Kilinochchi, the Battle of Mullaitivu, Operation Jayasikurui, and the Second Battle of Elephant Pass (Sri Lankan Guardian, 2010).

Since 1995, the LTTE has had artillery units such as the Kittu Artillery Brigade (Tamil Guardian, 2016; Kumar, 2017; Hashim, 2013) procured from raids on the Sri Lankan Army, procured on the black market, or home-made in LTTE factories. This also included mines and mortars used in the Ponnamman Mining Unit. This unit was captured by the Sri Lankan military in the battle of Aanandapuram. Similarly, the Kutti Sri Mortar Brigade was also captured by the Sri Lankan military in the Battle of Aanandapuram (The Sunday Leader, 2012).

The Black Tigers were an elite group that carried out suicide attacks and was comprised of selected members from other cadres of other regiments. The unit emerged with the death of Vasanthan Vallipuran, alias Captain Miller, in 1987 (Hopgood, 2006). Captain Miller was the first Black Tiger to blow himself up when he drove an explosive-laden truck into the Sri Lankan Army camp in Nelliyadi Madya Maha Vidyalaya in Jaffna, leaving 55 dead and halting the Sri Lanka Army's capture of Jaffna (Jayasinghe, 2006). The Black Tiger unit was attached to the TOSIS (Tiger Organisational Security Intelligence Service), which provided the needed intelligence for special operations. Black Tigers played a role in various high-profile assassinations (Tangram, 2018), which included targeting three world leaders: Sri Lankan President Ranasinghe Premadasa in 1993; Rajiv Gandhi, Prime Minister of India, in 1991; and the failed attempt on Chandrika Kumarathunghe in 1999, in which she lost her right eye. The Black Tigers also engaged in conventional warfare and guerrilla attacks. The Black Sea Tigers, established in 1990, were based in the LTTE's naval wing (Fair, 2005). In 2003, it was claimed that there were at least 500 black tigers ready to go into action (312 men and 92 women) and 174 black sea tigers (152 men and 22 women) (Pape, 2005; Hoffman & Maccommick, 2004). Most of their identities remained a secret and would be revealed only after their deaths (Hopgood, 2006). The slain Black Tigers were honoured, and their families were given the status of Maha Viru families (Hassan, 2011). Finally, in terms of ground forces, the LTTE also included an elite Leopard brigade, known as Chiruthaigal, which had a reputation for being a fierce fighting unit (Singer, 2006).

The Sea Tigers, founded in 1984, formed the naval wing of the LTTE. At its inception, the unit was tasked with transporting weapons and fighters back and forth between Tamil Nadu and Northern Sri Lanka and was operated mainly by fishing boats (Murphy, 2010). The unit took on a formalised structure in 1992, with a Sea Tigers fleet of between 2000 and 4000 and well-armed gunboats, oil tankers, ocean-going cargo vessels, and troop carriers (Sridhar, 2008). Sea Tigers were organised into at least 12 subunits: the sea battle regiments, underwater demolition teams, Sea Tiger strike groups, the marine engineering and boat building team, the radar and telecommunications unit, the marine weapons armoury and dump group, the maritime school and academy, the recruiting section, the political, finance, and propaganda section, the reconnaissance team and intelligence section, the welfare section, and the Exclusive Economic Zone Maritime Logistics Support Team. Towards the end of 2008, the Sea Tigers' capabilities were curtailed as the Sri Lankan Army captured their bases (Kumar, 2017; Ariaratnam, 2015).

The Air Tigers were the air wing of the LTTE military wing, with its origins in the late 1980s when guerilla cadres joined flying schools in the United Kingdom and France (Kumar, 2017) and acquired microlights (i.e., ultra-lightweight aircraft) and US-built Robinson R44 helicopters. Airstrips were constructed at the captured Sri Lankan Army base in Mullaitivu, Iranamadu (south of the LTTE's base in Kilinochchi in northern Sri Lanka), and in 2007 in Puthukkudiyiruppu (northern Sri Lanka) (Ariaratnam, 2015). Aircraft and sections of aircraft were smuggled from Indonesia and South Africa via arms smuggling networks such as those in Eretria (Reuters, 2007; Hindustan Times, 2009). However, these aircraft were only identified for the first time in 2007 when the Air Tigers carried out an attack on Katunayake Air Force Base in March 2007. This was followed by more attacks on Sri Lankan military targets, such as the Sri Lanka Air Force headquarters in Colombo (Pape & Feldman, 2010; Braithwaite & D'Costa, 2018).

The women's wing of the LTTE, known as Suthanthiran Paravihal (Freedom Birds), was involved in most sections of the LTTE's military wing. Recruitment of women into the LTTE began in 1979, with the establishment of the first women's training camp in 1984. Women underwent six months of training to gain expertise in combat, strategy, and explosives (Brun, 2008; Jordan & Denov, 2007). Since 1987, LTTE women have engaged in the most prolific female suicide bombing attempts. Women participated alongside men in their activities (Alison, 2003; Maunaguru, 1995), were often sent to the front lines, and were considered more dangerous than men (Alison, 2003). The use of female suicide bombers was an innovative tactic for the LTTE that was later adopted by al-Qaeda and Chechen terrorists. Among the various women-associated terror attempts was the assassination of the Prime Minister of India, Rajiv Gandhi, in 1991. Dhanu, a female black tiger, detonated the explosives strapped to her waist. The assassination was plotted by Lt. Col. Akila, the female deputy chief of the Freedom Birds. Further, in the mid-1980s, during the period of IPKF in the northeast (1987–1990), women also began to engage in intelligence-gathering activities. Women took control of the leadership of military units. Maria Vasanthi Michael, alias Sothia, became the first commander of the women's military unit in 1989 (Murali, 2012).

THE INTELLIGENCE WING

The LTTE's intelligence wing is composed of two units: the Tiger Organisation Security Intelligence (TOSIS) unit and the Military Intelligence unit. The TOSIS was formed in 1983, during the LTTE's fallout with the IPKF (Hamilton & Rimsa, 2007). The unit was headed by Pottu Amman. TOSIS provided the intelligence for the Black Tiger suicide attacks. Some of their main activities included the intelligence and planning of the assassination of the Sri Lankan President, Ranasinghe Premadasa, in 1993, carried out by Janan Master. TOSIS also played a role in identifying RAW agents and spies; an identified case was Gopalswamy Mahendraraja, alias Mahattaya, who leaked secrets to RAW. This led to the dismantling of the entire RAW operation in the north and north-east of Sri Lanka (DeVotta, 2004).

TOSIS functioned as a prime intelligence unit until it was subdivided into the National Intelligence Service and the Military Intelligence Service. The National Intelligence Service, known as Thesiya Pulanaivu, was initially trained by India's RAW in the 1980s until the relationship eroded with the LTTE's assassination of Indian Prime Minister Rajiv Gandhi (Sardeshpande, 1992). The strategic operating structure and tactics were similar to those of the Mossad in the 1980s. The National Intelligence Service was composed of five departments: the collections department for agent handling, which carried out espionage operations; internal security; political and liaison activities; interrogation; and detention. The research and publication department handled communications, press, data banking, and dubbing movies. The Special Operations Division coordinated the assassinations, sabotage, raids, paramilitary operations, psychological warfare projects, propaganda, and deceptive operations with the Black Tigers unit. The LTTE Intelligence Training Centre (known as Pulanaaivu Payitchi Maiyam) was tasked with the following: Recruiting informants and public relations focused on selecting, targeting, building trust, and conducting assessments for new recruits or agents within the communities. There was special training to develop skills and specific techniques in espionage tradecraft such as agent handling, covert communication, counter-interrogation, martial arts, and linguistic skills, depending on the task. Intelligence analysis, assessment, and exploitation meant centralising data and assessment for various needs. Agent handling included the flow of information and the responsibility to make sure that sources were safe and secure (Ariaratnam, 2015).

The military intelligence unit known as Iranuva Pulanaivu Pirivu operated on a smaller scale in contrast to the national intelligence unit, with a focus on gathering military intelligence on the Sri Lankan security forces. However, the unit worked in complement with the National Intelligence Unit as it depended on the training and technological component (Wickremasekera, 2016). Three known departments compose the Military Intelligence Unit: the Collections Department of the Sri Lankan Army (known as Iranuva Thakaval Sekarippu Piruvu). The department was tasked with gathering intelligence on the Sri Lankan Army bases, their strength, weapons, the Army's Order of Battle, brigade commanders, platoon officers, and their deployments. A good example under this department was the information gathering on the Pooneryn Military Complex for two years before the LTTE raided the complex in November 1993 (Independent, 1993; Richards, 2014).

Next, the Collections Department of the Sri Lanka Navy (known as Kadatpadai Thakaval Sekarippu Pirivu) was tasked with gathering intelligence on Sri Lankan naval bases, naval vessels, personnel, and harbours. They coordinated with the Sea Tigers and specially constituted Underwater Demolition Teams (UDT) of the Sea Tigers (Povlock, 2011), known as the Neeradi Neetchal Pirivu, to infiltrate harbours and gather maritime intelligence. Aided by sophisticated technology, they kept an eye on daily naval patrols. The Collections Department of the Sri Lanka Air Force (known as Vaanpadai Thakaval Sekarippu Pirivu) gathered intelligence on Sri Lankan Air Force bases, aircraft, personnel, and helicopters. To gather information, they collaborated with the Sky Tigers of the LTTE. The information gathered was analysed and given to the decision-makers for the execution of specific activities (Ariaratnam, 2015).

THE POLITICAL WING

Civil administrative matters were dealt with under the political wing of the LTTE. The emerging need to administer the merged northeastern territory led to the creation of the Tamil Eelam Secretariat in 1987. With the exit of the IPKF, the LTTE was in control of much of the north-eastern territory, including Jaffna and parts of Wanni. The LTTE restructured its Tamil Eelam secretariat and requested that the GoSL resume service provision in the northeast (Richards, 2014). Service provisions in the fields of health and education by the GoSL existed side by side with the LTTE. The LTTE created district-level political officers to implement directives by the secretariat (Orjuela, 2008). These developments facilitated the LTTE's ability to generate revenue in areas that were under LTTE control, facilitating the development of the Tamil Eelam Economic Development Organisation (TEEDO). TEEDO had many commissions to evaluate areas that needed development after damages incurred during the war, and committees for justice, protection, health, education, etc. were developed accordingly and existed side by side with the GoSL administration (O'Duffy, 2007).

The international secretariat of the LTTE was included in the central governing committee in 1990. Extensive connections with the Tamil diaspora facilitated overseas fundraising and propaganda. Fundraising included voluntary standing orders, where LTTE supporters arranged for their banks to debit a monthly sum, annual general collections, and special collections that targeted Tamils even if they were not pro-LTTE. The Diaspora community also raised money for the LTTE (Byman et al., 2001). LTTE's network of front organisations was extensive and, in 1998, spanned 54 locations in 32 countries (Fair, 2005), of which 12 were considered top-level contributors to LTTE's cause, including Switzerland (The Sunday Leader, 2014). The front organisations of LTTE's international network had various names, such as the Tamil Rehabilitation Organisation, the Tamil Coordinating Committee in France, Germany, Norway, the Netherlands, Australia, South Africa, Sweden, Belgium, and New Zealand, the World Tamil Movement in Canada, the World Tamil Coordinating Committee in Switzerland and the USA, and the British Tamil Association in the United Kingdom. This Swiss LTTE finance unit ran an informal remittance system, known as the Undi system, where a cartel of Tamil jewellery shop owners acted as human couriers, transporting funds to Singapore from Switzerland and then placing them in LTTE holding accounts in Southeast Asia (Byman et al., 2001).

Since 2002, changes have been evident in the International Secretariat. The headquarters of the international secretariat were shifted from Europe to Wanni, Sri Lanka. LTTE's intelligence division created a special unit to oversee intelligence operatives working outside of Wanni and in the international network, including an active Tamil Youth Organisation (TYO) (Kingsbury, 2012; Tangram, 2018; Ariaratnam, 2015).

The Peace Process between the LTTE and GoSL initiated the need for an LTTE Peace Secretariat. The Peace Secretariat supported the LTTE's political wing, facilitating the dissemination of information concerning the peace process to the world. The secretariat was funded by aid from Norway, operated from Kilinochchi, and acted as a counterpart to the Sri Lanka government's Secretariat for Coordinating the Peace Process (SCOPP), established in 2002 (Rupesinghe, 2006).

LTTE had its own communications network that facilitated dissemination of information to the diaspora, feedback to the diaspora on how diaspora funds were utilised, LTTE propaganda, and counter-government-led campaigns (Orjuela, 2008). In 1987, the LTTE started its own TV channel, Nitharsanam ("Reality"), which broadcasted battle footage throughout Jaffna until it was destroyed by the Indian Peacekeeping Force (Vidanage, 2009). In 1990, it was resumed as Thava, which filmed battles and distributed them to the diaspora as propaganda and for financial support. In 2005, the LTTE produced its first satellite channel, the National Television of Tamil Eelam (NTT), where LTTE programmes reached India, parts of Pakistan, Afghanistan, Bangladesh, Nepal, Myanmar, and China. The Paris-based Tamil Television Network (TTN) broadcasted to audiences in Europe and the Middle East. These broadcasts were shut down in May 2007 due to illegally pirating a satellite transponder frequency (Malathy, 2012; Tangram, 2018; Hariharan, 2009), and LTTE programming switched to the Tamil Nadu-based "Makkal" TV network, owned by the pro-LTTE Indian Tamil political party, Pattali Makkal Katchi. However, despite its reach in London and other European cities, it was shut down in 2008 (Asian Tribune, 2008; Dharmawardhane, 2014). Online communication means were used to mobilise support and anonymity among the LTTE, usually maintained by group members or unofficial pro-LTTE sites such as the LTTE Peace Secretariat website, the TEEDO website, eelamweb.com, infoeelam.com, tamilnet.com, tamilcanadian.com, eelam.dk, and tamilnet.net.au.

LTTE ACTIVITIES

The LTTE was condemned on grounds of human rights violations for killing innocent civilians, recruiting child soldiers, and being responsible for the assassinations of political figures and non-military officials (Keenan, 2006). LTTE has attacked non-military targets, which include civilians in commuter trains, buses, places of worship (temples and mosques), and farming villages, resulting in large numbers of deaths (Dissanayake, 2004). Among the major attacks on civilians are the Gonagala massacre (54 dead), the Anuradhapura massacre (146 dead), the Dehiwala train bombing (56 dead), the Palliyagodella massacre (166 dead), the bombing of Sri Lanka's Central Bank (102 dead), and the Kebithigollewa massacre (60 dead). Despite the signing of the ceasefire agreement in 2002, LTTE attacks continued.

LTTE operations involved the transport of large quantities of high explosives using vehicles. Most vehicles were engineered with secret compartments where these explosives were concealed. The largest concentration of explosives ever detected was in a truck loaded with 1,000 kg of C4 that was apprehended at Nikeveratiya while en route to Colombo (Outlook, 2007). Similarly, on June 30, 2007, an explosive-laden vehicle carrying 1,000 kg of C4 explosives was seized at Trincomalee, where explosives were hidden inside a freezer and were set to explode when it was opened (Daily News, 2007). Other explosions occurred via claymore mines set at various points throughout the island, targeting specific individuals or military personnel. There were also synchronised bomb attacks, where explosives were planted at separate locations but programmed to explode simultaneously (IRIN, 2008).

The prolific use of suicide bombers was a major LTTE tactic. They pioneered the use of concealed suicide bomb vests and the tactics of deploying suicide bombers using these prototype vests (Chalk, 2000). Successes included the assassinations of Rajeev Gandhi, Prime Minister of India (1991) (Gopal, 2017), and Sri Lankan President Ranasinghe Premadasa (1993). The LTTE carried out a total of 168 suicide attacks on civilian and military targets between 1980 and 2009. This outnumbered the combined suicide attacks of other terrorist networks (Hezbollah and Hamas) worldwide during this period (Hassan, 2011). Other assassinations committed by the LTTE on political rivals and opponents included: Alfred Duraiappah, mayor of Jaffna (1975); Ranjan Wijeratne, Sri Lankan cabinet minister and former general (1991); Gamini Dissanayake, Sri Lankan presidential candidate (1994); Lakshman Kadirgamar, Sri Lankan foreign minister (2005); Major Gen. Parami Kulatunga, third-highest ranking officer in the Sri Lankan Army (2006); Nadaraja Raviraj, Tamil National Alliance parliamentarian (2006). Other failed attempts included: Chandrika Kumaratunga, President of Sri Lanka (failed attempt in 2006); Lt. Gen. Sarath Fonseka, Sri Lanka army chief of staff (failed attempt in 2006); and Gotabhaya Rajapakse, Secretary of the Sri Lanka defence ministry (failed attempt in 2006). A few other alleged victims of the LTTE who were civilian moderates working towards peace included: Appapillai Amirthalingam, leader of the Tamil United Liberation Front (TULF) (1989); Vettivelu Yogeswaran, TULF politician (1989); Sarojini Yogeswaran, mayor of Jaffna (1998); Pon Sivapalan, mayor of Jaffna (1998); Neelan Thiruchelvam, academic and TULF politician (1999); Kethesh Loganathan, political activist and second chief of the Sri Lanka Peace Secretariat (2006); Selliah Parameswaran Kurukkal, a Hindu priest (2007).

Apart from assassinations, the LTTE was known for its role in ethnic cleansing and executing prisoners of war (POWs). The LTTE was accused of the ethnic cleansing of Muslims and Sinhalese inhabitants from areas under its control (Thiranagama, 2011). Violence was used in the process, which included organised massacres in Sinhala villages that settled in the northeast. The Muslim population of Jaffna was forcibly evicted on two-hour notice in 1990. The LTTE executed POWs despite their declaration to abide by the Geneva Conventions. Executions under the LTTE involved the massacre of 400–600 captured police officers after their surrender to the LTTE in 1990, the execution of 200 soldiers captured during the attack at the Pooneryn army camp, and hundreds of soldiers who surrendered after the Mullaitivu army camp attack (Stedman et al., 2002).

Extortions and other criminal activities facilitated the overall maintenance of the LTTE network. The LTTE relied on the diaspora's networks for financial support. This includes coercing Tamil expatriates to hand over money, directly or indirectly, by threatening the safety of their loved ones who were in areas of LTTE-controlled lands (Tangram, 2018). During raids on the World Tamil Movement in Canada, it was found that the organisation coordinated illegal activities for the LTTE. This was a major way in which the World Tamil Movement controlled the Tamil diaspora in Canada. Some LTTE sympathisers coordinated charities to raise cash for the war using propaganda and lobbied for their cause. The diasporic communities in North America and Europe became lucrative, and money was channelled via personal accounts to the accounts of weapon brokers or KP operatives. In May 2007, two members connected to the LTTE were arrested in Australia for soliciting funds under the pretext of charities for those affected by the Asian Tsunami in 2004, but they were allocating the funds for the Tamil movement (Human Rights Watch, 2006; Parkman & Peeling, 2007).

A sophisticated international network supported LTTE activities via sea piracy, human smuggling, and drug trafficking. Sea piracy involved hijackings of ships and boats and the killing or kidnapping of crew members. Some accusations of piracy involved Irish Mona (1995), Princess Wave (1996), Athena (1997), Misen (1997), Morong Bong (1997), MV Cordiality (1997), Princess Kash (1998), MV Sik Yang (1999), and MV Farah III (2007). In MV Cordiality, the five ship crew members were killed, and in MV Sik Yang, the fate of the crew members remained unknown (Lehr, 2007; Sridhar, 2008). The LTTE profited from the human smuggling of Tamil people to Western countries, for example, Canada. The costs of smuggling ranged from $10,000 to $40,000 for a Sri Lankan Tamil to be smuggled into Canada. Some people who fled from LTTE-controlled areas had to pay for exit visas, and others from wealthy families had to pay extra. Human smuggling also involved passport forgeries and other doctored travel documents. A passport forgery scheme linked to the LTTE was uncovered in Canada (Chalk, 2008). Similarly, the LTTE has been alleged to profit from drug trafficking and drug smuggling activities. In the 1970s, Tamil smugglers, which included a few members of the LTTE, had been carrying heroin from India to Sri Lanka. In 1979, with the advent of the Soviet-Afghan war and the Iranian revolution, the traditional Afghan-Pakistani smuggling routes were disrupted, and the human smuggling networks in Sri Lanka provided new routes for marketing the drugs. Some also started selling drugs in Europe in 1984. Cases were reported from Italy, Switzerland, Poland, and France. In the late 1990s, the LTTE set up their naval base on the island of Twante, off Myanmar, to exploit the heroin trade, where they used their own ships to smuggle heroin to Europe (Cornell, 2009).

The LTTE was involved in arms smuggling to keep up with military operations by smuggling weapons, technologies, and explosives. Most of the smuggling operations fell under the Kumaran Padmanathan (KP) branch. The KP workers remain outside the fighting wing to prevent disclosure and have a minimum connection with the LTTE for security purposes (Bell, 2007). Their role is to deliver shipments to trusted teams under the Sea Tigers. Ocean vessels are owned by private individuals, and some are under the control of the LTTE, who use them to transport legitimate goods and exploit them when the need arises to traffic arms. A known shipping base was Myanmar, and due to diplomatic pressure to leave, the LTTE set up a base on Phuket Island in Thailand (Richardson, 2004).

Finally, experts have drawn many similarities and parallels, showing connections between the LTTE and other terrorist organisations. Deep scrutiny of these links was suspected due to the following: Similarities in modus operandi of attacks by LTTE against Sri Lankan Navy ships and the al-Qaeda attack on the USS Cole (The New York Times, 2003); LTTE providing forged passports to Ramzi Yousef, the man who carried out the first attack against the World Trade Centre in New York in 1993; smuggling of weapons by LTTE using their networks to other terrorist networks and to other LTTE counterparts (Hariharan, 2009); allegations on stolen Norwegian passports and selling them to al-Qaeda for funds to purchase arms (Yass, 2014; Al Jazeera, 2009); Further, security expert Glen Jenvey expressed that al-Qaeda has copied many of the tactics or modus operandi of the LTTE. Jenvey highlighted similarities: the LTTE acted as a trendsetter during that period, other terrorist groups followed, and future groups such as ISIS used them as templates for their terror tactics (Asian Tribune, 2007).

The expert drew his conclusions based on the comparisons of LTTE and Islamist groups using and deploying modern suicide bombing on political, military, and civilian targets; the LTTE attack on the World Trade Centre in Sri Lanka, which was followed by the al-Qaeda attack on the World Trade Centre in New York; and the LTTE's use of women under the women section or brigade being copied by al-Qaeda and Chechen terrorists (Black Widows). The Black Widows played similar roles in suicide bombings. Also, attacks on civilians targeting buses and trains in Sri Lanka are similar to the al-Qaeda attacks on civilian public transport during the July 2005 bombings in London. The LTTE was among the first terrorist groups to use cyber terrorism, which is today perfected by other terrorist networks such as the Islamic State in Syria (ISIS). In 1997, the LTTE engaged in the first recorded use of internet terrorism when an LTTE unit known as the Internet Black Tigers sent the Sri Lankan embassy and consulate networks up to 800 junk emails per day over a period of two weeks. There was also the case of hacking the Sheffield University computer system to email individuals to donate money to a hospital in Colombo (Vidanage, 2009; Michno, 2016).

CONCLUSION

The article highlighted the organisational evolution, structure, and tactics of the LTTE, revealing an organised terrorist network that adopted guerilla warfare tactics. In May 2009, with the death of the leader, Vellupillai Prabakaran, an entire terrorist organisation came to a standstill. However, LTTE ideology was still peddled by their supporters and sympathisers in different parts of the country and sections of the diaspora (Thurairajah, 2017; Kandaudahewa, 2016). The context of a victory's peace by the Sri Lankan government after militarily defeating the LTTE challenged the reconciliation process between majority and minority identities. Amidst positive efforts for reconciliation by the GoSL, many efforts weakened the trust between the majority and the minority groups, such as land grabbing and the loss of livelihoods due to high-security zones by the military in conflict-affected regions, enforced disappearances, the lack of political will for thorough investigations, and the prosecution of war crimes and human rights violations (The Oakland Institute, 2015). Hoglund and Orjuela (2011) expressed in their study that the Sinhalese-dominated political system fails to address power-sharing and minority rights issues, which aggravate minority grievances and amplify the support of the Tamil Diaspora for separatism. However, the government's development plans after 2009, with a major focus on infrastructure and livelihood generation programmes, are seen as long-term solutions towards development in former war-affected regions that would trickle down to the war-affected communities. Nevertheless, discriminatory policies on land belonging to minorities in the HSZs, resettlement of former combatants, and addressing war crimes and human rights abuses would shape the conflict transformation processes in the country (Thiranagama, 2013).

Notes

1 The work Eelam is the native Tamil name for Sri Lanka and has significance in the Tamil nationalist struggle, attributed to the Tamil homeland concept.

2 Data as of the 1971 Census, a period marking the onset of the civil war.

References

Al Jazeera (2009). The history of the Tamil Tigers: Formed in 1975, the group has vowed to carve out a separate Tamil state in Sri Lanka.

Alison, M. (2003). Cogs in the wheels? Women in the liberation tigers of Tamil Eelam. *Civil Wars*, 6(4), 37–54.

Ariaratnam, K. (2015). A typical terrorist cell: The Tiger Organization Security Intelligence Service (TOSIS). https://theofivefile.info/2016/03/18/a-typical-terrorist-cell/

Asian Tribune (2007). Al-Qaeda follows LTTE text book on terror faithfully. Asian Tribune, 12 February 2007. www.asiantribune.com/index.php?q=node/4518

Asian Tribune (2008, June 22). Breaking News: The LTTE TV Tharishanam goes off the air from today onwards. Asian Tribune. http://www.asiantribune.com/node/11890

Bandarage, A. (2009). *The separatist conflict in Sri Lanka: Terrorism, ethnicity, political economy*. London and New York: Routledge.

BBC News (2009, June 29). 'Tamil unit' for Sri Lanka's army, BBC News. http://news.bbc.co.uk/2/hi/south_asia/8124836.stm

Bell, S. (2007). The snow tigers. In Bell, S. (Ed.), *Cold terror: How Canada nurtures and export terrorism around the world*. Mississauga: John Wiley and Sons, Ltd.

Braithwaite, J., & D'Costa, B. (2018). *Cascades of violence, war, crime and peacebuilding across South Asia*. Canberra: ANU Press.

Brun, C. (2008). Birds of freedom: Young people, the LTTE, and representations of gender, nationalism, and governance in Northern Sri Lanka. *Critical Asian Studies, 40*(3), 399–422.

Business Today. (February 13, 2023). LTTE chief Prabhakaran is alive, will emerge in public soon, claims Tamil Nationalist Movement Leader Pazha Nedumaran.

Byman, D., Chalk, P., Hoffman, B., Rosenau, W., & Braman, D. (2001). *Trends in outside support for insurgent movements*. Santa Monica, CA: RAND Corporation.

Chalk, P. (2000, March 17). Liberation Tigers of Tamil Eelam's (LTTE) International Organization and Operations: A Preliminary Analysis, Commentary No.77. A Canadian Security Intelligence Service Publication. https://terroristinformation.wordpress.com/2014/05/17/liberation-tigers-of-tamil-eelams-ltte-international-organization-and-operations-a-preliminary-analysis/

Chalk, P. (2008). The tigers abroad: How the LTTE diaspora supports the conflict in Sri Lanka. *Georgetown Journal of International Affairs*, 9(2), 97–104.

Ciment, J. (2011). *World terrorism: An encyclopedia of political violence from ancient times to the post-9/11 era*. (2nd Ed.). London and New York: Routledge.

Cornell, S.E. (2009). *The interaction of drug smuggling, human trafficking, and terrorism in Jonsson, A. Human Trafficking and Human Security*. London and New York: Routledge.

Daily News (2007, June 30). Forces detect another bomb-laden truck. Daily News. http://archives.dailynews.lk/2007/06/30/sec02.asp

Deccan Herald. (February 15, 2023). What explains Tamil Nadu politics' fascination with LTTE's Prabhakaran?.

De Silva, K.M. (2005). *A history of Sri Lanka*. Colombo: Vijitha Yapa Publications.

DeVotta, N. (2004). *Blowback: Linguistic nationalism, institutional decay, and ethnic conflict in Sri Lanka*. California: Stanford University Press.

Dharmakirti, D.J. (2011). The Saga of Dutugemunu. In J. Holt (Ed.), *The Sri Lanka reader: History, culture, politics*. Durham and London: Duke University Press.

Dharmawardhane, I. (2014). Use of ideology and technology in terrorist warfare in the Sri Lankan conflict. Singapore: Centre for Political Violence and Terrorism Research (ICPVTR) S. Rajaratnam School of International Studies.

Dissanayake, T.D.S.A. (2004). *War or peace in Sri Lanka*. Mumbai: Popular Prakashan Pvt, Ltd.

Fair, C.C. (2005). *Urban battle fields of South Asia: Lessons learned from Sri Lanka, India, and Pakistan*. Arlington, VW: RAND Corporation.

Fuglerud, O. (2011). Aesthetics of martyrdom: The celebration of violent death among the liberation tigers of Tamil Eelam. In Maria Six-Hohenbalken & N. Weiss (Eds.), *Violence expressed: An anthropological approach*. London and New York: Routledge.

Ghosh, P.A. (1999). *Ethnic conflict in Sri Lanka and the role of Indian peace keeping force (IPKF)*. New Delhi: APH Publishing Corporation.

Goodhand, J., Korf, B., & Spencer, J. (2008). *Conflict and peacebuilding in Sri Lanka: Caught in the peace trap?* London and New York: Routledge.

Gopal, N. (2017). *The assassination of Rajiv Gandhi*. India: Random House Publishers.

Graeme, C.S., & Gunaratna, R.S. (2004). *Counterterrorism: A reference book*. California: ABC-CLIO, Inc.

Guruge, A. (2011). *Peace at last in paradise*. Bloomington: Author House.

Hamilton, D., & Rimsa, K. (2007). *Terror threat: International and Homegrown Terrorists and their threat to Canada*. Ontario, Canada: Dundurn Press.

Hariharan, R. (2009). Transnational Tigers: Liberation Tigers of Tamil Eelam's paw across the globe. In J. Saikia & E. Stepanova (Ed.), *Terrorism: Patterns of internationalization*. New Delhi: SAGE Publications India Pvt Ltd, pp. 47–70.

Hashim, A.S. (2013). *When counterinsurgency wins: Sri Lanka's defeat the Tamil Tigers*. Philadelphia: University of Pennsylvania Press.

Hassan, R. (2011). *Life as a weapon: The global rise of suicide bombings*. London and New York: Routledge.

Hindustan Times (2009, September 23). LTTE were set to get new aircraft. Hindustan Times. https://www.hindustantimes.com/world/ltte-were-set-to-get-new-aircraft/story-obBgls2EQUQNLBwlt3U3xK.html

Hoffman, B., & McCormick, G.H. (2004). Terrorism, signaling, and suicide attack. *Studies in Conflict & Terrorism, 27*(4), 243–281. https://doi.org/10.1080/10576100490466498

Höglund, K., & Orjuela, C. (2011). Winning the peace: Conflict prevention after a victor's peace in Sri Lanka. *Contemporary Social Science*, 6(1), 19–37.

Hopgood, S. (2006). Tamil Tigers, 1987–2002. In D. Gambetta (Ed.), *Making sense of suicide missions*. (pp. 43–76). Oxford University Press.

Human Rights Watch (2006). *Funding the Final War: LTTE intimidation and extortion in the Tamil Diaspora*. New York: Human Rights Watch.

Human Rights Watch (2013, March 28). Sri Lanka: Probe into LTTE crimes should start with Karuna: Deputy Minister among senior leaders linked to wartime atrocities. Human Rights Watch. https://www.hrw.org/news/2013/03/28/sri-lanka-probe-ltte-crimes-should-start-karuna

Independent (1993). Tamil Tigers storm key base: Sri Lankan forces suffer their worst defeat in 10 year war with separatists. Friday 12 November 1993, https://www.independent.co.uk/news/world/tamil-tigers-storm-key-base-sri-lankan-forces-suffer-their-worst-defeat-in-10-year-war-with-1503701.html

IRIN. (2008, February 5). Claymore mines used to lethal effect. http://www.irinnews.org/report/76576/sri-lanka-claymore-mines-used-lethal-effect

Jayasinghe, A. (2006). Sri Lanka steps up alert as Tigers honour suicide bombers. Agence France-Presse.

Jeyaraj, D.B.S. (2011, January 28). Ramifications of crackdown on LTTE in Switzerland. DBSJEYARAJ.Com. http://dbsjeyaraj.com/dbsj/archives/1952

Jordan, K., & Denov, M. (2007). Birds of Freedom? Perspectives on female emancipation and Sri Lanka's liberation Tigers of Tamil Eelam. *Journal of International Women's Studies*, 9(1), 42–62.

Kanapathipillar, V. (2009). *Citizenship and statelessness in Sri Lanka: The case of the Tamil estate workers*. London: Anthem Press.

Kandaudahewa, H. (2016). Post war reconstruction and peacebuilding in Sri Lanka: Tamil Diaspora as a decisive factor. https://ssrn.com/abstract=2852969 or 10.2139/ssrn.2852969

Keenan, A. (2006). Building a democratic middle ground: Professional civil society and the politics of human rights in Sri Lanka's peace process. In J. Mertus & J.W. Helsing (Eds.), *Human rights and conflict: Exploring the links between rights, law, and peacebuilding* (pp. 459–508). Washington, D.C: United States Institute of Peace Press.

Kingsbury, D. (2012). *Sri Lanka and the responsibility to protect: Politics, ethnicity and genocide*. London and New York: Routledge.

Kumar, M. (2017). *Thamizh: Is not just a language: The Valour*. New Delhi: EduCreation Publishing.

Lehr, P. (2007). *Violence at Sea: Piracy in the age of global terrorism*. New York and London: Rutledge.

Lewer, N. (2017). Tensions between short term outcomes and long term peacebuilding in post-war Sri Lanka. In V. Rosoux & M. Austey (Ed.), *Negotiating, reconciliation in peacemaking: Quandaries of relationship building* (pp. 277–304). Cham, Switzerland: Springer.

Malathy, N. (2012). *A fleeting moment in my country: The last years of the LTTE de-facto state*. Atlanta: Clarity Press, Inc.

Maunaguru, S. (1995). Gendering Tamil nationalism: The construction of "woman" in projects of protest and control. In Pradeep Jeganathan & Qadri Ismail (Eds.), *Unmaking the nation: The politics of identity and history in modern Sri Lanka* (pp. 158–175). Colombo: Social Scientists' Association.

Michno, M. (2016). Cyberspace: A new 'battlefield', weapon or just a tool? In M. Szkarlat & K. Mojska (Ed.), *New technologies as a factor of international relations*. Newcastle: Cambridge Scholars Publishing.

Murali, S. (2012). *The Prabhakaran Saga: The rise and fall of an eelam warrior*. New Delhi: SAGE Publications India Pvt Ltd.

Murphy, M.N. (2010). Naval support. In T. Rid & T. Keaney (Eds.), *Understanding counterinsurgency warfare: Doctrine, operations, and challenges* (pp. 114–127). Oxon: Routledge.

Nubin, W. (2002). *Sri Lanka: Current issues and historical background*. New York: Nova Science Publishers, Inc.

O'Duffy, B. (2007). LTTE: Liberation Tigers of Tamil Eelam. In M. Heiberg, B. O'Leary, & J. Tirman (Eds.), *Terror, insurgency, and the state: Ending protracted conflicts*. Philadelphia: University of Pennsylvania Press.

Orjuela, C. (2008). *The identity politics of peacebuilding: Civil society in war-torn Sri Lanka*. New Delhi: SAGE Publications India Pvt, Ltd.

Outlook (2007, July 19). Target Colombo. Outlook. https://www.outlookindia.com/website/story/target-colombo/235120

Parkman, T., & Peeling, G. (2007). *Countering terrorist finance: A training handbook for financial services*. Hampshire: Gower Publishing Limited.

Pape, R.A. (2005). *Dying to win: The strategic logic of suicide terrorism*. Crown Publishing Group/Random House.

Pape, R.A., & Feldman, J.K. (2010). *Cutting the fuse: The explosion of global suicide terrorism and how to stop it*. Chicago: University of Chicago Press.

Povlock, P.A. (2011). A Guerilla war at sea: The Sri Lanka civil war. Small Wars Journal. http://smallwarsjournal.com/jrnl/art/a-guerilla-war-at-sea-the-sri-lankan-civil-war

Reuters (2007, March 26). Sri Lanka's Tamil Tigers bomb base in first air raid. Reuters World News. https://www.reuters.com/article/us-srilanka-attack-idUSCOL5577520070326

Reuters (2009, March 9). Sri Lanka fighting surges, 180 rebels die: Army. Reuters. https://www.reuters.com/article/us-srilanka-war/sri-lanka-fighting-surges-180-rebels-die-army-idUSTRE52839020090309

Richards, J. (2014). *An institutional history of the liberation Tigers of Tamil Eelam (LTTE)*. CCDP Working Paper. Geneva: Graduate Institute Geneva and Centre on Conflict, Development and Peacebuilding.

Richardson, M. (2004). *A time bomb for global trade: Maritime related terrorism in the age of weapons of mass destruction*. Singapore: Institute of Southeast Asian Studies.

Rupesinghe, K. (2006). *Negotiating peace in Sri Lanka: Efforts, failures, and lessons*. Colombo: Foundation for Coexistence.

Salter, M. (2015). *To end a civil war: Norway's peace engagement in Sri Lanka*. London: C. Hurst and Co.

Sardeshpande, S.C. (1992). *Assignment Jaffna*. New Delhi: Lancer Publishers.

Singer, P.W. (2006). *Children at war*. California: California University Press.

Sridhar, R. (2008). *Maritime terrorism capabilities of the Sea Tigers of Sri Lanka in Parashar, S. Maritime Counter-Terrorism: A pan-Asian perspective* (pp. 171–183). New Delhi: Pearson Education in South Asia.

Sri Lankan Guardian (2010, May 12). How the LTTE was military defeated: A Soldiers view – Part Nine. http://www.srilankaguardian.org/2010/05/how-ltte-was-military-defeated-soldiers_12.html

Stedman, S.J., Rotchild, D., & Cousens, E.M. (2002). *Ending civil wars: The implementation of peace agreements*. London: Lynne Rienner Publishers.

Tambiah, J.S. (1992). *Buddhism betrayed? Religion, politics, and violence and Sri Lanka*. Chicago and London: The University of Chicago Press.

Tamil Guardian (2016, January 15). Remembering Colonel Kittu. Tamil Guardian. https://www.tamilguardian.com/content/remembering-colonel-kittu

Tangram, D. (2018). *The rise and fall of the Tamil Tigers: How the LTTE terrorists were defeated*. North Carolina: Lulu Press Online.

The New York Times (2003, January 14). Masters of suicide bombing: Tamil Guerillas of Sri Lanka. New York Times. https://www.nytimes.com/2003/01/14/world/masters-of-suicide-bombing-tamil-guerrillas-of-sri-lanka.html

The Oakland Institute (2015). *The long shadow of war: The struggle for justice in postwar Sri Lanka*. Oakland, CA: The Oakland Institute.

The Sunday Leader (2014, October 12). The LTTE Swiss Network. The Sunday Leader. https://www.mfa.gov.lk/ta/5392-the-ltte-swiss-network/

The Sunday Leader (2012, April 8). Anatomy of the LTTE military debacle at Aananthapuran. http://www.thesundayleader.lk/2012/04/08/anatomy-of-the-ltte-military-debacle-at-aananthapuram/comment-page-1/

Thiranagama, S. (2011). *In my mother's house: Civil war in Sri Lanka*. Philadelphia: University of Pennsylvania Press.

Thiranagama, S. (2013). Claiming the state: Postwar reconciliation in Sri Lanka. *Humanity: An International Journal of Human Rights, Humanitarianism, and Development*, *4*(1), 93–116.

Thurairajah, K. (2017). The case of the Sri Lankan Tamil diaspora and homeland: A shared ethnic identity? *Studies in Ethnicity and Nationalism*, *17*(1), 115–132.

Vidanage, H. (2009). Rivalry in cyberspace and virtual contours of a new conflict zone: The Sri Lankan case. In A. Karatzgianni (Ed.), *Cyber conflict and global politics* (pp. 146–161). Oxon: Routledge.

Wallace, M.S. (2017). *Security without weapons: Rethinking violence, non-violent action, and civilian protection*. London and New York: Routledge.

Wickremasekera, C. (2016). *The Tamil separatist war in Sri Lanka*. Oxon: Routledge.

Wilson, J. (2000). *Sri Lanka Tamil nationalism: Its origins and development in the 19th and 20th centuries*. London: Hurst and Company.

Wijeyeratne, R.S. (2014). *Nation, constitutionalism and Buddhism in Sri Lanka*. Oxon: Routledge.

Yass, S. (2014). Sri Lanka and the Tamil Tigers: Conflict and legitimacy. *Military and Strategic Affairs*, *6*(2), 65–82.

71

JAMAAT-UL-MUJAHIDEEN BANGLADESH

Core and Offshoots

Md Nurul Momen

INTRODUCTION

Jamaat-ul-Mujahideen Bangladesh (JMB) is an Islamic militant organisation in Bangladesh. JMB created a terror environment in Bangladesh with deadly serial bomb blasts in 2005 across the country. Following the bomb blasts, the terror outfit suffered a significant setback from the massive crackdown by the counter-terrorism policy and measures of the government, for instance, the extrajudicial killing, sporadic arrests, and subsequent executions of its six top militants in the early hours of March 30, 2007, including its founder Shaikh Abdur Rahman and his second-in-command Siddiqul Islam, alias Bangla Bhai. Remnants of the banned JMB again attempt to regroup and reorganise under different names to advocate their radical Islamic views in the country.

This descriptive chapter examines JMB's ideology, money trails, operational capacity, strategies, and linkages with global terror outfits and evaluates the current counter-terrorism measures in Bangladesh. The study used qualitative content analysis in the writing of this paper, collecting data from media news, books, scholarly articles, official documents, and terrorism reports relating to the scope of the study. Finally, the paper recommends an integrated and comprehensive overhaul of counter-terrorism measures, taking into consideration balancing law enforcement and political consensus in Bangladesh.

NATURE OF TERRORISM AND RELIGIOUS TERRORISM IN BANGLADESH

Because the subject is so contentious, defining terrorism is a difficult undertaking. As a result, there is no single definition of terrorism that is recognised by all; instead, there are numerous conflicting definitions and typologies based on a review of the terrorism literature (Institute for Economics & Peace, 2019; see Romaniuk, 2021). Enders and Sandler (2002, p. 145–146) attempted to operationalise the term as:

> premeditated use or threat of use of extra normal violence or brutality by subnational groups to obtain a political, religious, or ideological objective through intimidation of a huge audience, usually not directly involved with the policy making that the terrorists seek to influence.

However, there are numerous underlying causes for the rise of militancy, and earlier terrorism researchers generally identified three factors as causes for its development and growth: economic, political, and religious factors. Economic factors include extreme poverty, unemployment, and social inequality. She et al. (2020) point out that if economic growth does not make any positive impact on the livelihood of the poor and unequal income and resource distribution persists, this may further generate frustration and discontent among them, thus leading to a growing number of terrorist attacks in society. Although some empirical research produces conflicting findings that poverty is always not connected with terrorism and rich countries generate more terrorism than poor countries (She et al., 2020), political factors are rooted in poor governance, failure of state institutions, despotic government, constant political conflicts of interest among the parties, blocking opponents' freedom of expression and opinions, and the weak capacity of the government in some countries to handle these crises (Matthijs, 2020; She et al., 2020); thus, this may develop terrorism or the fear of terrorism. For religious factors, some scholars have correlated misinterpretations of religion with the emergence of terrorism (Riaz, 2008). Further, religious

DOI: 10.4324/9780429426063-80

terrorism happens due to the behaviour of some extreme interpretations of the religious scriptures and forceful attempts to introduce those faiths and ideologies; thus, self-radicalised people are also observed to join the terror outfits. However, the Quran, as the supreme source of Islam, is inviolate and emphasises peace and harmony in society, and certainly there are no places in the Quran that sanction the murder of innocent bystanders or terrorism (Zaidi, 2008).

Bangladesh faces a terror threat from different militant groups under different Islamic names. These radical groups have basically targeted Western foreigners, secular activists and institutions, religious minorities, and other individuals and/or groups who openly oppose their faith and ideology. Political experts pointed out that, in recent years, these groups, especially the new JMB, appear to be connected to global terror outfits, although their transnational network is largely rooted in domestic political dynamics (International Crisis Group, 2018).

Religious terrorism in Bangladesh is a complex issue to understand since no single theoretical explanation can be applied to identify its emergence and development. For instance, Riaz (2008) identifies several causes for the rise of religiously motivated terrorism in Bangladesh, most notably the complexity of local, regional, and international incidents and their dynamics. The author added that Islamist terrorism occurs due to the failure of political institutions, and the current political instability has generated a crisis of militancy and further worsened the situation in the country (Riaz, 2008). On the other hand, Datta (2007) relates the growth of religiously fuelled terrorism in Bangladesh to the role of madrassa (religious school) education, although these findings can be nullified by looking at the profile of the Holey Artisan attackers in July 2016, which shows that militants are now recruited from secular educational institutions (Momen, 2020).

Since the 1990s, there have been several Islamic militancy organisations operating in Bangladesh, and the government has already outlawed their activities, notably HuJI-B, JMB, Hizb-ut-Tahrir, Ansarullah Bangla Team, or Ansar al Islam, and New JMB. Although identifying terrorist organisations and their members in Bangladesh is not an easy task because of the lack of authentic data and the constant and rapid name-changing approach adopted by the terror outfits, it is quoted in the media that approximately 20 terrorist groups are now operating; on the other hand, security forces claim the number reported by the press should be much smaller, namely 12 (EFSAS, 2019). Despite their similar ideological terrorism, these groups widely vary in their respective goals, attack methods, organisational composition, and so on.

ORIGIN OF RELIGIOUS TERRORISM AND RADICALISATION IN BANGLADESH: THREAT FROM AFGHAN WAR RETURNEES

Bangladesh is located in South Asia and is one of the most densely populated countries and the third-largest Muslim-majority nation in the world (Rahman, 2016). However, the question is how Islamist militancy started in Bangladesh; it is observed that returnees from the Afghan war are the carriers of the jihadi terror strain, which is now a threat to a traditionally moderate and peaceful Muslim country. Data retrieved from the Global Terrorism Database, which is organised and maintained by the National Consortium for the Study of Terrorism and Responses to Terrorism (START), indicated that around 944 terrorist incidents have been reported in the time period between 2000 and 2015. Further, the majority of the attacks remain unidentified perpetrators, which are mainly blamed on opposition political parties in order to serve the regime's interests, although 114 attacks were specifically committed by verifiable radical Islamic terror groups (EFSAS, 2019). The International Crisis Group (2018) explores that Islamic militancy in Bangladesh started to breed in the 1980s, when around 3,000 people from Bangladesh reportedly joined the anti-Soviet war in Afghanistan. Bashar (2019) also echoed the same findings that terrorism led by radical Islamists was brought into Bangladesh in the early 1990s when the fighters from the Soviet-Afghan War returned and desired to turn the country into a state ruled by their radical interpretation of Islam (Bashar, 2019).

As already stated, there are many radical Islamic groups operating in Bangladesh. There are some commonalities among the terror outfits that consider themselves defenders of Islam. All these groups declare war against Western secular ideas and mainly target those individuals or groups who like to oppose or insult their ideological zeal.

JMB was created in 1998 under the leadership of Shaykh Maulana Abdur Rahman, whose aim was to assume power and introduce radical Islamic ideology through military struggles, while the Jagrata Muslim Janata Bangladesh (JMJB) is an offshoot of JMB, founded in 2003 with the same faith and ideology. Both JMB and JMJB as terror outfits overlap in their structure and personnel; JMB members become members of JMJB. Further, JMJB basically worked in the northeastern regions that had been the stronghold of extreme left-wing movements for decades (International Crisis Group, 2018). It is important to note that during the rule of the Bangladesh Nationalist Party (BNP) government (2001–2006), they initially refused to take stern action against the JMJB due to their alliance government with other Islamic political parties and the limited capacity of local security forces (International Crisis Group, 2018).

The growth and development of radical Islam are intertwined with the faith and ideology of JMB's founder, Sheikh Abdur Rahman. Having analysed the profile of Rahman, it shows how he gradually shifted his faith and ideology from piety to militant acts (International Crisis Group, 2010; Momen, 2020). During the united Pakistan, Rahman joined Islami Chattra Sangha (Islamic Student Association), the student wing of the Jamaat-i-Islami (JeI) (Riaz, 2008; Momen, 2020), which acted as resistance to Bangladesh's independence to promote unity for a radical Islamic Pakistan. That was recognised as a legacy factor for the recent growth of radicalisation and militant acts led by JMB (Riaz, 2008).

About the structure and personnel, the Majlish-e-Shura (council) is the supreme decision-making body of JMB, and this body is composed of seven members. Bangla Bhai and Abdur Rahman were the members of the Shura, and the other members were Ataur Rahman Sunny, Hafez Mahmud, Abdul Awal, Salahuddin Salehin, and Khaled Saifullah (Momen, 2020). The structure of the organisation is designed in three tiers, such as *'Ehsar'* (full-time members and the higher echelons) who are experienced with extensive militant training, *'Gayeri Ehsar'* (part-time members), and the third tier addresses those who indirectly support their faith and ideology (Prakash, 2011; Momen, 2020); however, there is no authentic information regarding the total members of JMB. In March 2007, six top JMB leaders, including the group's founder Abdur Rahman and his deputy leader, Siddiqul Islam alias Bangla Bhai, were hanged in two different jails, as were the four other JMB members from *Majlish-e-Shura* Abdul Awal, Khaled Saifullah, Ataur Rahman Sunny, and Iftekhar Hasan Al-Mamun (Momen, 2020).

Bangladesh first experienced religiously fueled terror attacks on August 17, 2005, when JMB, a homegrown, Bangladesh-based terror outfit, managed to blast 459 serial bombs in 63 of the country's 64 districts with the objective of creating a terror environment to push for the adoption of certain forms of radical Islam (EFSAS, 2019). Bangladesh, being the image of a liberal Muslim country in the world, terrorism, or the fear of terrorism caused by Islamic radicalisation and terrorist attacks, has gained major global attention since the JMB's nationwide serial bomb blasts in 2005 (Rahman, 2016). However, the exact number of JMB members might not be ascertained because the terror outfit changes its recruitment strategy from time to time. JMB made a multitude of risky choices with their operatives; however, the group mainly targeted and threatened secular political parties, cultural groups and their locations, intellectuals, diplomats, NGO offices, and religious places of minorities (Rahman, 2016).

Since its establishment in 1998, JMB has changed its operational strategy and recruitment focus at different times, but through its recent resurgence, JMB still continues to indoctrinate for the establishment of radical Islam and targets and attacks those who disagree with their interpretation of Islam. Thus, the new JMB targets individuals such as Bangladeshi secular bloggers and minority communities, attacking non-Muslim worship places as well as prominent leaders of these communities. On the other hand, some of the attacks made by new JMB members are claimed by ISIS, but the government of Bangladesh has always denied the presence of any international terror outfits. Since 2015, the new JMB has increased its operational strength beyond its earlier strongholds in the north and southwest regions of the country and even conducted major attacks in the Holey Artisan on the night of July 1, 2016, leaving 20 people dead, most of them foreigners (International Crisis Group, 2018).

DOMESTIC AND INTERNATIONAL TERROR NETWORKS

In recent years, the terms "militancy," "terrorism," and "JMB" have often been used synonymously, and these terms are not new in Bangladesh. There are some other words, such as "radical," "extremist," "militant," and "terrorist," that are also used interchangeably (Abuza, 2003). However, the rise of Islamist militancy and terrorism in Southeast Asia, South Asia, the Middle East, and Africa was linked to various historical and politico-religious factors, including the direct and indirect presence of al-Qaeda and domestic militant groups (Abuza, 2003). It is worthy of noting that between 2002 and 2018, South Asia, MENA, and sub-Saharan Africa were recorded for 93% of all deaths arising out of different forms of terrorism, and among the terrorist attacks, the largest number was reported in the MENA region, with more than 93,700 causalities (Institute for Economics & Peace, 2019).

EFSAS (2019) reports that two transnational Islamist terrorist groups, the Islamic State (IS) and Al-Qaeda in the Indian Subcontinent (AQIS), have become increasingly active and announced their presence in Bangladeshi territory. Mostofa and Doyle (2019) relate the current status of terrorism in Bangladesh to global terror outfits. It is noteworthy that since the 1990s, these regions have experienced violent acts by regional terror outfits and witnessed the rapid emergence of Islamist militancy with the goal of establishing a radical Islamic state. It is noteworthy that there is some evidence of developing linkages between JMB and the Islamic State (IS) as a global terror outfit. For instance, on August 9, 2019, just a day after security forces captured five pro-IS militants in Dhaka, the IS uploaded a video message in Bangla through the Amaq news agency that claimed that their war on establishing radical Islam would be continued until the achievement of their faith and ideology. The video also urged followers in Bangladesh to target and attack some groups of people, including secular political leaders, members of the parliament, and law enforcement agencies (Bashar, 2019).

Political commentators and terrorism specialists have highlighted the fact that the IS terrorist group has already attracted a significant amount of attention from young people (Phillips, 2016; Shanthie, 2017). Further, the Syrian conflict brought about a new emergence of Islamist militancy. Interestingly, at least 50 citizens from Bangladesh participated in the Syrian war and joined under the leadership of IS, which fought against the regime of President Asad (Sultan, 2019). It is also reported that more than a hundred young people of Bangladeshi descent have also travelled to Syria (Sultan, 2019), but there is no reliable information on whether these people are directly involved in the Syrian war.

OPERATIONAL CAPACITY AND MONEY TRAIL

360 civilians and 33 members of the security services were among the 393 people who died as a result of terrorist acts and incidents between 2005 and July 2016, according to a report by the South Asian Terrorism Portal (SATP) (BIPSS, 2017; Momen, 2020). Bangladesh has a high score on the Global Terrorism Index (GTI), which is a measure of terrorism, making it one of the subcontinent's areas with rising Islamic militancy, though the score has decreased since 2018. According to the index, for measuring and understanding the impact of terrorism, Bangladesh experienced a medium level of terrorism, which ranked 25 among the total 163 countries with a score of 5.697 out of 10, but in 2017, the country scored 6.181, which placed it at 21 (Institute for Economics & Peace, 2018; Momen, 2020). Bangladesh continued to decline in terrorist attacks and incidents and recorded only 31 terrorist incidents and seven casualties in 2018, which accounted for 70% less in terms of death casualties than the prior year. It is also reported that only five terrorist organisations were attributed to perpetrating terrorist attacks in 2017, while there were no attacks in 2018 (Institute for Economics & Peace, 2019).

After the 9/11 attacks, terrorism experts attempted to explore financing for terrorist organisations, which gained a lot of attention in terrorism studies. In recent years, much progress has been made in identifying the methods and sources by which different terrorist organisations raise and transfer funds for their activities (Phillips, 2016). However, terrorism financing can be perpetrated by individuals, groups, or even states. JMB collects money from multiple sources, especially militants' families, who contribute a considerable amount of their assets for operational costs, to support operatives, and to procure weapons. Further, Zakat (a type of obligatory almsgiving for the poor) was one of the major sources of income for the earlier generation of JMB, which is still tapped by JMB (International Crisis Group, 2018). Further, JMB has also been reported to use *Hundi* or *Hawala*, an informal and illegal money transfer system (EFSAS, 2019).

EXPLORING THE TARGETS AND TACTICS OF THE NEW JMB

Due to the deadliest single terrorist attack on July 1, 2016, the international media attributed Bangladesh's customarily peaceful coexistence society as the future of terror in the South Asia region (Kugelman & Ahmad, 2017; Momen, 2020). With five 'neo-JMB', a pro-IS JMB faction deadly attacked the Holey Artisan Bakery, a very famous restaurant in Dhaka for foreigners, which ended with the death of 20 hostages, 18 of whom were foreigners (EFSAS, 2019; Momen, 2020). Before the Holey Artisan attack in 2016, terrorism experts indicated that poverty-driven areas (southern and northern districts) and vulnerable young population groups (unemployed youths among refugee camps, madrassa students, and poor people) were associated with the growth of religious extremism, radicalisation, and militancy (BEI, 2015; Momen, 2020). There is now concern for the young people who become engaged in militancy and terrorism led by JMB.

Since the 2016 Holey Artisan attack, security forces have also begun using the new name "neo-Jamaat-ul Mujahideen" (JMB), a pro-IS JMB faction. Independent terrorism analysis has shown that law enforcement agencies use this term to hide the presence of IS in Bangladesh. While JMB's current Amir, Salahuddin, denied the allegation of international linkages with IS, he acknowledged that some of JMB's members had joined IS (International Crisis Group, 2018).

Despite the Holey Artisan attack claimed by the IS, the Awami League-led government of Bangladesh has continuously denied the presence of Islamic State (ISIS) on its territory; rather, it is attributed to the *'neo-JMB', an* indigenous terror faction in the country, although the activities of the *'neo-JMB'* appear to follow the same principles of ISIS's ideology (EFSAS, 2019). The "neo-JMB," an offshoot of JMB, was believed to be guided by a Canadian-Bangladeshi citizen, Tamim Chowdhury, until he died in an extrajudicial killing in August 2016 (International Crisis Group, 2018; EFSAS, 2019).

Each unit of the New JMB is geographically divided, and a regional commander oversees and instructs operatives in each unit (International Crisis Group, 2018). However, several regional commanders were killed in different parts of the country through extrajudicial killings. Thus, the structure and personnel that Chowdhury headed in the new JMB appear to have been fractioned, and while law enforcement agencies assume that the group might have been fractioned into smaller or sub-groups operating in the country sporadically, for now they are only able to conduct minor or low-intensity attacks (International Crisis Group, 2018).

An offshoot of the banned terrorist group JMB, it first came to light on May 22, 2016, when a professor in the

Department of English at the University of Rajshahi was hacked to death for his call for atheism. In the same year, these new JMB militants also killed some non-Muslim people because of their disbelief in Islam and for insulting the Prophet (PBUH). Having analysed their targets of ideological terrorism, this shows that the new JMB aims to achieve political control by eliminating any kind of anti-Islamic opinions and views.

However, the profile of recent arrestees shows that the militants are male, young, educated, and from middle-class and affluent backgrounds (Riaz, 2016). Hence, youth radicalisation has been seen as a major concern for Bangladesh ever since the Holey Artisan attack on July 1, 2016. The government of Bangladesh now needs to think about how radicalised youth can pose a threat to a peaceful society, as it has observed significant changes in the recruitment of militants. In the beginning, JMB as a terror outfit targeted the poor and illiterate and the students of madrasas (religious schools), but now the focus has shifted to indoctrinate youths from secular higher education institutions from affluent backgrounds to simultaneously target rural and urban youth (Kumar, 2019).

Bashar (2019) finds that the new JMB, as IS followers, recruits both madrassa (religious schools) students and youth from secular educational institutions with no prior experience or record in militant activities. According to the author, quoting from Bangladesh's Counter-Terrorism and Transnational Crime Unit, 82% of the captured militants were recruited through online networking. In recent years, there has been a significant decline in online recruitment as the designated sites for online networks are being blocked by the government. But still, informal relationships on the internet with people of the same faith and ideology are exchanged with prospective followers (Bashar, 2019). To counter terrorism, different actions have been taken to eliminate the structure of the new JMB. Despite the relative success of the security forces, some sporadic minor attacks to create panic and fear of terrorism are being conducted by new JMB militants, which have also been claimed by IS through its official media outlets (Bashar, 2019).

CONTESTING COUNTER-TERRORISM POLICY MEASURES

Immediately after the Holey Artisan attack in 2016, the then government started to adopt massive crackdown measures against the new JMB terrorists and ended with approximately 11,000 suspected terrorists in 2016 (EFSAS, 2019). The 'Neo JMB' lost much of its operational capacity and networking after the extrajudicial killings of its chief commander, Tamim Ahmed Chowdhury, and many other key leaders in counter-terrorism operations by the security forces following the Holy Artisan attack in 2016. Khan (2020) finds that the terror outfit 'Neo JMB' might have declared its new chief and brought about changes in the top leadership as the IS-inspired terror group is trying to get back on its feet by regrouping its structure. Having searched many reports and encrypted channels, Khan (2020) finds that the new chief is declared to be Abul Abbas Al-Bangali Hafizullah, who is of Bangladeshi origin and is now staying abroad.

For countering terrorism, it is also important to observe the latest terrorist attacks and developments in South Asia, for instance, the declaration of an IS wilayah (province) in India and Pakistan in May 2019 and the very unexpected Easter Sunday bombing in Sri Lanka in April 2019 (Bashar, 2019). At the very outset, it is also required to know about the radicalisation process, whereby an individual accepts terrorist violence (Ferguson & Binks, 2015; Routray, 2017) that poses a threat to society and states. Although Bangladesh has seen a decline in terrorist incidents and attacks since 2017, it is likely that new JMB as well as IS followers may emerge and launch further strikes. Bashar (2019) stresses that the recent trend of terrorism led by the new JMB relates to the growing focus on international linkages with militant activities in South Asia.

The government has adopted different legal measures to stop terrorist financing, which is important for the survival of the terror group. The Anti-Terrorism Act was passed in 2009, which empowered Bangladesh Bank to freeze any accounts maintaining terror financing and their activities. Further, the Money Laundering Prevention Act of 2012 and the necessary amendments to the Anti-Terrorism Act in 2013 included more lists of terrorist financing cases and broadened the issues and areas of legal action (International Crisis Group, 2018). Apart from that, the Mutual Legal Assistance Act was passed in 2012, which aimed to enhance international cooperation, and the country also became a member of the Asia Pacific Group on Money Laundering in July 2013 (International Crisis Group, 2018).

There are, in general, two approaches to combating terrorism. The first approach refers to a hard approach or zero tolerance for terrorism, which is regarded as offensive measures because this approach involves the necessary military actions taken to fully eliminate terrorism, while the other approach adopts conciliatory measures as a counter-terrorism strategy for encountering terrorism (Malvesti, 2002), which is considered defensive measures against terrorism (Sandler, 2005) to get broader societal responses. However, the use of soft power alongside a proactive response from law enforcement agencies is believed to reduce the risks to individuals' lives and property from terror incidents (Sederberg, 1995).

It is stressed that educational institutions and mass media can contribute to a reduction of youth radicalisation through militant activities. Especially religious educational institutions may provide an authentic interpretation of religious testimony, and they may also urge and indoctrinate youth about the destructive aspects of radicalisation in Islam and why any form of extremism or militancy should never be encouraged or provoke activities that can lead to radicalisation. Further, in the weekly prayer on Friday, imams (religious preachers) must clarify that Islam never allows any form of violent activity. Due to security sensitivity, mass media should always broadcast correct reporting and authentic news and create awareness in society through political commentary and analysis. The media should never cover any form of fake news that serves the support base of terrorists.

Fatalities arising from militant activities and the fear of terrorism may have significant negative impacts on the economy. Militant incidents and acts are believed to have effects on investment decisions, primarily by changing economic behaviour and diverting resources away from productive activities. It is further argued that if terrorism and the fear of violent incidents prevail, this may also create significant welfare losses due to low productivity in the economy and distort expenditure, which eventually affects the price of necessary items (Institute for Economics & Peace, 2019). Keeping these issues in mind, the government of Bangladesh, from time to time, publicly underestimates JMB's threat of terrorism, as any negative image of the high level of terrorism may generate fear and anxiety among peaceful foreign direct investors and international trade partners (Bashar, 2019).

Since the growth of militant activities and terrorism, the current government has always denied the international presence of IS and the military nexus between the new JMB and IS, and the government has continued to blame opposition political parties for promoting terrorist activities. According to them, the opposition Jamat-e-Islami Bangladesh (JIB) and its student wing, Islami Chatra Shibir (ICS), were responsible for all the militant attacks against the Awami League (AL) government between 1996 and 2001. This kind of political polarisation has significantly contributed to the growth of militant activity. Further, the marginalisation of the BNP through politically fueled corruption allegations and the trials of its top leaders also deteriorates the condition (International Crisis Group, 2018; EFSAS, 2019). EFSAS (2019) further points out that it is evidently clear about political marginalisation since the main political rival of the Awami League government and chairperson of the BNP, Khaleda Zia, was convicted for five years in the Zia Orphanage Trust case on February 8, 2018. In another case of Zia Charitable Trust corruption, on October 30, 2018, Khaleda Zia was sentenced to an additional seven years in prison (EFSAS, 2019).

The BNP government (2001–2006) also initially denied the presence of militancy and blamed the opposition political party, AL, for its terrorist propaganda. But due to international concerns and pressures, the government shifted its position from denial to acceptance of terrorism when the 2005 series of countrywide bomb blasts occurred (Rahman, 2016). It is highlighted that the exercise of political blaming between the two rival major political parties has continued to create a favourable environment for the growth of terrorism. Hence, it needs to comprehensively address the root causes of terrorism, and the political commitment, whatever their political ideology and thoughts, should not politicise the issue of terrorism (Momen, 2020). It is also important for political parties to become tolerant, and instead of blaming each other, they need to explore the underlying causes of terrorism and address this issue effectively (Rahman, 2016).

Having analysed the operational capacity and weapons recovered from JMB members from the earlier generation, they basically used light weapons and explosives, which could not create many fatalities. But in the Holey Artisan attack in Dhaka in 2016, new JMB members carried heavy weapons and improvised explosive devices (IEDs) as well (Rana, 2018; Momen, 2020). After the attack, it was stressed that the new JMB might have illegally acquired weapons and explosives from other terror outfits in neighbouring countries, which reached them either by sea or border. Roul (2018) highlighted that illegal cross-border movement in the border areas is found to be responsible for the procurement of weapons and explosives, which both governments need to address effectively. It is further added that the northeastern region of India, especially Assam and West Bengal, has the second-largest Muslim population, which might have supported the new JMB to hide and search for money, weapons, and personnel (Roul, 2018; Momen, 2020).

CONCLUSION

This paper has attempted to understand the organisation, tactics, and terror financing of JMB for the establishment of its objectives and the development of linkages with other terrorist groups. In recent years, despite the counter-terrorism efforts by the security forces in Bangladesh, the New JMB, as followers of IS ideology, remains a key threat and fear of terrorism to peace and security. Although it is widely believed that the operational strength and capacity of the terror outfit have significantly reduced, the web of informal relations and future operational capacity need to be monitored periodically, and law enforcement agencies must remain watchful of their activities. Further, political polarisation may act as an enabling environment for the growth and development of new JMBs. It is also to be noted that the government needs to avoid heavily applying indiscriminate and unlawful force (Momen, 2014); rather, it needs to have broad strategies and measures to improve access to justice and strengthen the capacity of counter-terrorism units. Finally, simply cracking down on militants is not an easy task; rather, the government should adopt a comprehensive approach, especially political consensus on how to encounter terrorism; otherwise, the country might potentially become a future source of religiously fueled terrorism.

References

Abuza, Z. (2003). *Militant Islam in Southeast Asia: Crucible of terror*. Boulder, CO: Lynne Rienner Publishers.

Bashar, I. (2019). *Islamic State ideology continues to resonate in Bangladesh*. (pp. 1–7). Washington: Middle East Institute, September 3, 2019, https://www.researchgate.net/publication/335600592

BEI (Bangladesh Enterprise Institute). (2015). *The role of education in countering radicalization in Bangladesh*. Dhaka: Bangladesh Enterprise Institute. Retrieved June 8, 2019 from http://bei-bd.org/wp-content/uploads/2015/05/The-role-of-education-in-countering-radicalization.pdf

BIPSS (2017). Local drivers and dynamics of youth radicalisation in Bangladesh. Published by Bangladesh Institute of Peace and Security Studies (BIPSS): Dhaka, pages. 78

Datta, S. (2007). Islamic militancy in Bangladesh: The threat from within. *South Asia: Journal of South Asian Studies*, *30*(1), 145–170. DOI: 10.1080/00856400701264084

D'Souza, S.M. (2017). Countering Insurgencies, terrorism and violent extremism in South Asia. *Small Wars & Insurgencies*, *28*(1), 1–11, DOI: 10.1080/09592318.2016.1266163

EFSAS (2019). The rise of political Islam and Islamist terrorism in Bangladesh. European Foundation for South Asian Studies (EFSAS), October 2019, Amsterdam Available at https://www.efsas.org/publications/study-papers/the-rise-of-political-islam-and-islamist-terrorism-in-bangladesh/

Enders, W., & Sandler, T. (2002). Patterns of transnational terrorism, 1970–1999: Alternative time-series estimates. *International Studies Quarterly*, *46*(2), 145–165. DOI: 10.1111/1468-2478.00227

Ferguson, N., & Binks, E. (2015). Understanding radicalization and engagement in terrorism through religious conversion motifs. *Journal of Strategic Security*, *8*(1), 16–26. DOI: 10.5038/1944-0472.8.1.1430

Institute for Economics & Peace (2019). Global Terrorism Index 2019: Measuring the impact of terrorism. Sydney, November 2019. Available from: http://visionofhumanity.org/reports.

Institute for Economics & Peace (2018). Global Terrorism Index 2018: Measuring the impact of terrorism. Sydney, November 2018. Available from: http://visionofhumanity.org/reports

International Crisis Group (2010). *The threat from Jamaat-ul Mujahideen Bangladesh*. Asia ReportNumber187, March 1, 2010, pp. 1–34. Brussels, Belgium: International Crisis Group.

International Crisis Group. (2018). *Countering Jihadist Militancy in Bangladesh*. Asia Report Number 295, February 28, 2018, pp. 1–34. Brussels, Belgium: International Crisis Group.

Khan, M.J. (2020). Neo JMB' rising again? Daily Star, September 29, 2020.

Kugelman, M., & Ahmad, A. (2017). Why extremism is on the rise in Bangladesh. *Foreign Affairs*, July 27, 2017. https://www.foreignaffairs.com/articles/asia/2017-07-27/why-extremism-rise-bangladesh (accessed on October 10, 2020).

Kumar, N. (2019). Rise of Islamic terror in Bangladesh and impact on Northeast India. Section IV Regional Neighbourhood, Centre for Land Warfare Studies. https://www.researchgate.net/publication/331732569

Malvesti, L.M. (2002). Bombing bin Laden: Assessing the effectiveness of air strikes as a counter-terrorism strategy. *The Fletcher Forum of World Affairs*, *26*(1), 17–29.

Matthijs, B. (2020). Kinder, gentler, safer? A re-examination of the relationship between consensus democracy and domestic terrorism. *Studies in Conflict & Terrorism*, *43*(10), 886–903, DOI: 10.1080/1057610X.2018.1507312

Momen, M.N. (2020). Jamaat-ul-Mujahideen Bangladesh: Analysis of organizational design and activities. *Dynamics of Asymmetric Conflict*, *13*(3), 245–257, DOI: 10.1080/17467586.2020.1821072

Momen, M.N. (2014). Access to justice: Assumptions and reality checks in Bangladesh. *International Journal of Public Law and Policy (IJPLAP)*, *4*(2), 161–168, DOI: 10.1504/IJPLAP.2014.060082

Mostofa, S.M., & Doyle, N.J. (2019). Profiles of Islamist militants in Bangladesh. *Perspectives on Terrorism (A Journal of the Terrorism Research Institute)*, *13*(5), 111–128.

Phillips, P.J. (2016). *The economics of terrorism*. Abingdon, UK: Routledge.

Prakash, V. (2011). Bangladesh and terrorism within, will secular polity ever emerge? In V. Prakash (Ed.), *Encyclopedia of terrorism in the world* (Vol. 2). Delhi: Kalpaz Publications.

Rahman, M.A. (2016). The forms and ecologies of Islamist militancy and terrorism in Bangladesh. *Journal of Deradicalization*, Summer 2016, No. 7, pp. 68–106. https://journals.sfu.ca/jd/index.php/jd/article/view/58Rahman

Riaz, A. (2008). *Islamist militancy in Bangladesh: A complex web*. NY: Routledge.

Riaz, A. (2016). Who are the Bangladeshi 'Islamist Militants?' *Perspectives on Terrorism*, *10*(1). Retrieved June 20, 2019, from http://www.terrorismanalysts.com/pt/index.php/pot/article/view/485/html

Rana, M.S. (February 2018). The Dhaka attack: Lessons for Bangladesh. *IOSR Journal of Humanities and Social Science (IOSR-JHSS)*, *23*(2), 16–24.

Romaniuk, S. N. (2021). *Under siege: Counterterrorism and civil society in Hungary*. Lanham: Rowman & Littlefield.

Roul, A. (2018). Fugitive Bangladeshi militants bring Jamaat ul Mujahideen to India. *Terrorism Monitor, 16*(13), June 29, 2018.

Routray, B.P. (March, 2017). *Bangladesh 2017: Resurgence of radicalism. Trends, threats, projections*. (No. 17, pp. 1–8). Bengaluru-560 012, India: International Strategic and Security Studies Programme, National Institute of Advanced Studies (NIAS) Strategic Forecast, Indian Institute of Science Campus.

Sandler, T. (2005). Collective versus unilateral responses to terrorism. *Public Choice*, *124*(1-2), 75–93.

Sederberg, P.C. (1995). Conciliation as counter-terrorist strategy. *Journal of Peace Research*, 295–312. DOI: 10.1177/0022343395032003004

She, S., Wang, Q., & Weimann-Saks, D. (2020). Correlation factors influencing terrorist attacks: political, social or economic? A study of terrorist events in 49 "Belt and Road" countries. *Quality and Quantity*, *54*, 125–146 DOI: 10.1007/s11135-019-00946-x

Sultan, T. (2019). Bangladeshi militants who traveled to Syria are the major concern. *Prothom Alo*, July 1, 2019, https://bit.ly/2Yx9N6Q

Zaidi, S.M.A. (2008). The fundamentalist distortion of Islamic message. *Athena Intelligence Journal*, *3*(4), 59–75.

72

THE UNITED LIBERATION FRONT OF ASSAM (ULFA)

Piyali Basu

INTRODUCTION

Since India's independence, armed extremism has become a subject of serious concern in Northeast India in the form of insurgencies that broke out in undivided Assam, leading to the formation of present-day Nagaland, Mizoram, and Meghalaya. Located in the strategic northeastern corner of India, Assam is part of a region that shares a sensitive frontier with China in the north, Myanmar in the east, Bangladesh in the southwest, and Bhutan in the northwest. The strategic importance of Northeast India can be determined from the fact that it shares a 4,500 km-long international border with four South Asian neighbours but is connected to the Indian mainland by only a meagre 22 km-long land corridor passing through Siliguri in the eastern state of West Bengal, described as the "Chicken's Neck." Assam and the entire Northeastern region of India are believed to be crisscrossed with ethnically variant sections of people, different not only from the rest of the country but also among themselves. The tensions that arise from this ethnic diversity are due to the fact that the people of Assam have begun to objectify themselves based on the idea of ethnicity. Turbulence in India's Northeast is therefore caused not just by armed separatist groups representing different ethnic communities fighting for autonomy against the central or regional governments but also by the recurring battles for territorial supremacy among the different ethnic groups themselves.

Extremism in Northeast India has drawn the attention of a large number of scholars like Tilottama Misra, A. K. Baruah, Udayon Misra, S. K. Chaube, Amalendu Misra, Sanjib Baruah, J. B. Bhattacharjee, Hiren Gohain, Samir Kumar Das, Sanjoy Hazarika, Dinesh Kotwal, Kiranshankar Maitra, B. Pakem, M. S. Prabhakara, B. G. Verghese, and others, many of whom support the "Colonial Hinterland Theory", as a cause for its rise. T. Misra (1980: 1357–1364) shows that Assam has become a colonial hinterland, which became a major thesis of many extremist groups in the Northeast as there has been systematic exploitation of the rich resources of Assam before 1947 by the colonial rulers and since then by the Indian State and Indian capitalists who have continued the colonial tradition. This thesis was further developed by A. K. Baruah, who argued, as its cause, the opposition of educated elites in Assam towards the immigrants from mainland India with a big brotherly attitude towards local inhabitants (Baruah, 1984: 322–28). Chaube regards underdevelopment and relative deprivation syndrome as the major factors contributing to a sense of alienation and ultimately leading to insurgency (Chaube, 1997: 29–30). S. K. Das puts forward the United Liberation Front of Assam's (ULFA) argument that India has only replaced the colonial rule of Great Britain in Assam (Das, 1994:29–30). Udayon Misra credits ULFA with being the first insurgent outfit in the Northeast that focused effectively on the colonial thesis (Misra, 2000: 157).

HISTORICAL BACKGROUND OF ULFA

Assam, due to its abundance of resources and fertile land, has been a favourite destination, particularly for migrant peasants. In the wake of Partition, large-scale migration in the region due to the incessant immigration of the Bengali middle class started being perceived by the natives as a threat to the ecological and demographic balance of the region, sparking off ethnic and communal riots and threatening the democratic setup of the state (Das, 1993: 165–175). This led a section of the educated elite of Assam to opt to secede from the Indian nation as the only way to save Assamese nationality. The Asamiya Samrakhini Sabha and Asom Deka Dal submitted a memorandum to Jawaharlal Nehru, then Prime Minister of the country, for the secession of Assam from India, which stated, "For years we have been standing face to face with extinction as a people ... As a means of saving the Assamese race from extinction, a considerable section of the intelligentsia has even expressed their minds in favour of the secession of Assam from India." A memorandum by Asom Deka Dal read, "The only alternative that we can think of is that we

DOI: 10.4324/9780429426063-81

should get separated from India as Burma had done" (Guha, 1977: 316). It was during the initial years of consolidation of Assamese nationalism in the 1920s and 1930s that the idea of "Swadhin Assam" (independent Assam) began to fire the imagination of a section of the middle class. Incidentally, ULFA ideologues claim to take inspiration from this period.

IDEOLOGUES OF ULFA

Parag Das, a social activist and writer, provided the ideological foundation for independent Assam. Through his writings as editor of *Budhbar*, the weekly that acted as a front for the outfit, and a magazine called *Aagan*, he also expressed his dream of an independent Assam. Writers and cultural activists like Nibaran Bora and Suresh Phukan also influenced the thought process of ULFA by trying to create awareness about illegal immigrants. The six-year-long Assam movement (1979–1985) was directed towards detecting, disenfranchising, and deporting the foreigners settled in Assam. The intense police and army atrocities during the Assam movement, particularly during 1983–1985, led a section of its leadership and ideologues to embrace a more militant course and a unified struggle against "New Delhi". Precursors of ULFA in the form of organisations were the Brachin National Liberation Army (BNLA) and the Assam Peoples' Liberation Army (APLA).

FORMATION OF ULFA AND ITS AGENDA

ULFA was formed on April 7, 1979, with seven members: Buddheswar Gogoi, Suren Dihingia, Someswar Gogoi, Bhimkanta Borgohain, Bhupen Borgohain, Ponaram Baruah, and Pradip Gogoi, most of whom belong to the Muttock region of upper Assam (Mahanta, 2013b). It was decided that Rajib Rajknowar would frame the constitution of the organisation, keeping "Unity, Revolution, and Liberation" as the chief motto. The name "United Liberation Front of Assam", or ULFA, was proposed by Pradip Gogoi. The founders had convinced themselves that Assam was never a part of India. The Indian Independence Act of 1947 joined it artificially with India through a narrow strip of land, the Siliguri Corridor. Their professed aim was the liberation of Assam from "Indian Colonial rule" and the setting up of an independent sovereign state, through armed struggle if necessary. According to a ULFA publication, "to create an exploitation-free society, our next step must be a national war of liberation. We have no alternative to armed revolution" (Prakash, 2008: 31, 188). Eight more members were added to the organisation towards the end of 1979. In 1980, ULFA was essentially divided into two wings: political and military. The Central General Council was designed to look after political activities. In the first meeting of the Central Council, a Military Council was formed.

ULFA surfaced in the public arena after 1983, when it joined hands with the All-Assam Students' Union (AASU) and All-Assam Gana Sangram Parishad (AAGSP) in enforcing the boycott of polls in 1983 till the names of the illegally settled 'foreigners' were struck off from the electoral rolls. Most of ULFA's cadres were drawn from the ranks of AASU (Misra, 2000: 134). The Asom Gana Parishad (AGP) regime that came to power in 1985 as a legatee of the Assam movement was reportedly "hand in glove" with ULFA (Das, 1998). Significantly, a founding member and the first Chair of ULFA, Bhadreshwar Gohain, went on to serve as the Deputy Speaker of the State Legislative Assembly after being elected on an AGP ticket (Hazarika, 1995: 169–175). However, a series of scandals, charges of corruption, nepotism, and dissension within the ranks of the ruling AGP, coupled with a deterioration in the law and order situation, led to the imposition of Presidents' Rule on November 28, 1990. 1990 marks a watershed, for it was in this year that ULFA was declared illegal. An army operation, the first of its kind, codenamed "Operation Bajrang", was launched against it, and ULFA was invited by the Government of India (GOI) to join the peace talks.

In 1991, when the second military operation, "Operation Rhino 1", was in full swing, the GOI and ULFA were reportedly engaged in dialogue. Raju Baruah, the then chief of ULFA's Nalbari unit, observed that the question of compromise with the treacherous state or its representatives is absurd. On the other hand, there were reports that five ULFA leaders under the leadership of Arabinda Rajkhowa acquiesced to the Constitution and signed what Parag Kumar Das termed "a treaty of compromise" with the Government of India (GOI) (Budhbar, January 22, 1992, cited in Das, 2012: 8, 9). In 1992, immediately after the military operation 'Operation Rhino 2' was over, a section of the ULFA leadership was involved in peace talks, which however broke off when one of its delegations led by Arabinda Rajkhowa decided to withdraw due to "the pressure from his uncompromising commander-in-chief, Paresh Barua" who expressed his "dissatisfaction" with the "unconditional surrender of arms" and "one-sided acquiescence to the Constitution of India". Joint operations, codenamed "On Golden Bird", were launched by the Indian and Burmese armies in April and May 1995. 52 ULFA and PLA cadres were arrested and 45 killed (Prakash, 2008: 208).

A radical shift in the outfit's agenda was evident in a statement made in July 1992, when ULFA stated that "East Bengal migrants are considered Assamese. Without this exploited lot, ULFA cannot be successful. They are our real well-wishers, better than the Indians earning at the cost of the Assamese people". In the same publication, ULFA went on to define the term *"Bidekhi"* (foreigner). "Those who do not regard this state as their own ... are not ready to sacrifice their lives for the sake of his country, are aliens, *bidekhis* for us" (South Asia Terrorism Portal, "ULFA, The Revolution Comes Full Circle"). ULFA has defined the concept of the "Assamese" (Axomiya) as "a people of all communities, a mixture of people who are determined to work for the all-around progress of Assam". In this description, the immigrants from Bangladesh are considered "an indispensable part" of the revised notion of Axomiya (South Asia Terrorism Portal, "Assam Insurgency and the Disintegration of Civil Society"). This somersault has certainly negated the very basis of ULFA's existence and brought it into direct conflict with AASU, which believed that ULFA's extortion and murders had destabilised the situation in Assam (Hazarika, 1995: 233). This shift, analogous to the vote-bank politics practised by established political parties in India, was aimed at neutralising the erosion in the traditional support base of ULFA in Assamese society and widening its base among the immigrant community, which was numerically significant (Hindu, 1992).

A five-member team consisting of Golap Baruah (General Secretary), Robin Neog (Chief Instructor), Kalpajyoti Neogi (Foreign Secretary), Siddhartha Phukan (Convenor, Publicity Cell), and Sobhan Saikia (Member) signed a "Letter of Intent" (*Pratisruti Patra*) on January 12, 1992, as a step towards holding talks with the Government of India (GOI). A section of surrendered ULFA cadres, popularly known as SULFA, expressed their willingness to enter some form of peace negotiations with the GOI, surrendering arms at their disposal. In exchange, they requested that the government stop military operations and arrest its cadres, withdraw the Armed Forces Special Powers Act, and expedite the proceedings against all those who were held in police custody. To ensure cooperation between the security forces fighting the insurgents and the intelligence agencies, a "unified command structure" was set up by the Government of India (GOI) in 1997. On January 3, 1999, Assam Chief Minister Prafulla Kumar Mahanta announced the extension of the "safe passage" offer till January 17 after 257 militants opted for the same. "Operation All Clear" started on December 15, 2003. Between 2003 and 2004, 312 terrorists have been eliminated, 930 have been apprehended, and 1356 weapons have been recovered. More importantly, 3457 militants have surrendered, having realised the futility of continuing their armed struggle. As a result, both the National Democratic Front of Bodoland and the United Liberation Front of Assam (ULFA) have been greatly marginalised (Indian Ministry of Defence, Annual Report 2003–2004:30).

On November 16, 2004, Indira Goswami, one of the highly respected Asomiya litterateurs, met the then Prime Minister Manmohan Singh and handed over a memorandum drafted in consultation with the academics from Delhi University. The Prime Minister agreed to invite ULFA for talks, provided violence was shunned. In early 2005, Goswami again met the Prime Minister, requesting the start of a dialogue between ULFA leaders and the government. An 11-member "People's Consultative Group" (PCG), consisting mainly of well-known civil society activists, was set up by ULFA to conduct negotiations with the government. This is the first time that ULFA has inducted members of civil society into the peace process. However, the process was jeopardised abruptly when both sides got involved in an armed engagement in the Dibru-Saikhowa forests of upper Assam. Despite the resumption of army operations on September 24, 2006, and the PCG backing out of talks, the government continued holding peace dialogues, and in early January 2007, the Prime Minister offered "safe passage" to ULFA leaders, should they come for direct negotiations (Das, 2012: 9, 10). The inner schisms within ULFA were becoming increasingly evident when its 28th Battalion made the offer of peace talks in 2007. This is the first time that one of ULFA's fragments has offered peace. An eight-member ULFA delegation led by its chairman, Arabinda Rajkhowa, met the Home Minister and Home Secretary in February 2011 with the aim of exploring the viability of protecting the sovereignty of the people of Assam within the Indian Constitution (Deb, 2011: 20).

FACTORS THAT FAVOURED ULFA

Analysts considered that ULFA had emerged as a mindset in Assam. ULFA succeeded in voicing the issue of Assamese alienation from the Indian mainstream in a manner that created a substantial support base not only among the common people but also produced 'sympathy' among bureaucrats, police, intelligentsia, and politicians, strengthened by ULFA's social activities, including the campaign against social evils such as corruption, prostitution, molestation of women, drunkenness, private tuitions, drug trade, and the like, contributing to the popular "legitimacy" of the group. Since the people at large shared the sentiment that India was exploiting Assam, ULFA got away with the bank robberies and the murders (Hindu, March 9, 1990). ULFA held sway over the media as well. A number of newspapers in Assam produced each ULFA press release verbatim. In the early 1990s, the weekly *Budhbar* acted as a front for the outfit, in which ULFA's "publicity secretary" answered queries and explained the organisation's policies in almost every issue. *Budhbar*, which is no longer in circulation, was the only daily that not only dared to discuss the activities of ULFA but also opposed its terrorist activities and even supported its social welfare activities (Sharma, 2002: 68). From November 25–26, 1991, two journalists, Rajib Bora of the *Sentinel* and Manjit Mahanta of *Ajir Asom*, were arrested for their links with ULFA (Hindu, March 9, 1990).

ORGANISATIONAL STRUCTURE AND POWERS

ULFA's membership comprises local and central Apart from convincing the local people to join ULFA, local members are engaged in wall painting, the distribution of propaganda literature, and making lodging arrangements for central members who visit their place. Central members generally remained underground as they organised action squads (Chandra, 2004). During its initial years, ULFA had primary units, mouza, or sub-divisional units, zila, or district units, and the central committee. Later, in 1985–86, the General Headquarters (GHQ) was formed to look into military issues and the Central Headquarters (CHQ) to look into political activities. When the military pressure became more intense, a mobile headquarters (MHQ) was created in 1993. The United Liberation Force of Assam, the military wing of ULFA, was formed in 1995 under Article 1 of ULFA's constitution.

ULFA had clearly partitioned its political and military wings. Paresh Barua headed the "military wing" as the outfit's "commander-in-chief", and Raju Baruah was the "Deputy Commander-in-Chief". Arabinda Rajkhowa was the Chairman of the "political wing", Pradip Gogoi was the "Vice Chairman", Anup Chetia was the "General Secretary", Sashadhar Choudhury was the Foreign Secretary, Chitraban Hazarika was the Finance Secretary, Mithinga Daimary was the "Central Publicity Secretary", Bolin Das was the "Assistant Secretary", and Pranati Deka was the "Cultural Secretary". A military wing of ULFA, the Sanjukta Mukti Fouj (SMF), was formed on March 16, 1996. SMF had three full-fledged battalions: the 7th, 28th, and 709th. The organisation also has a women's wing known as Nari Bahini, who are generally trained in medical services, to secure the release of the arrested ULFA leaders by mobilising people's support and collecting information necessary for the organisation through spying and other means (South Asia Terrorism Portal, "Major Incidents of Terrorist Violence in Assam", 1990–2017).

AIMS, OBJECTIVES AND ACTIVITIES OF ULFA

The propagated aims and objectives of ULFA include:

1. Achievement of the liberation of Assam from the Indian state and building an independent, sovereign Assamese state; represent not only the Assamese but the struggling repressed people irrespective of race, gender, and ethnicity, encompassing a wider identity;
2. Adopt a method of armed struggle for self-defence to deal with the various problems confronting them, most importantly, their national identity problem;
3. Persistent struggle against the colonial government, which they believed had exploited the natural resources of the state and continues to do so, perpetrating economic backwardness (ULFA Pamphlet, 1985).

With these set objectives, ULFA was involved with "individual killing" who they thought were enemies of Assam. During the initial phase, ULFA got people's support due to its "Robin Hood image" and anti-foreigner stance (Mishra, 2004). ULFA's military members took up arms training and bank robberies while the political members took to social reform activities like punishing businessmen dealing with alcohol, banning sex-related cinema, women and child trafficking, and undertaking developmental activities like road construction, protection of dams during flood, and irrigation. They ran parallel government and also started agricultural firms based on cooperatives in several districts of Assam. However, gradually its Robin Hood image began to deteriorate because, in the name of punishment, ULFA committed atrocities on innocent people and amassed money by unfair means. To repair the dented self-image and to arouse the morale of their cadres, the UFLA leadership, discarding their ideology and ideals, launched vicious attacks on the minorities to divide the Asamese towards the last quarter of 2000. (Prakash, 2008: 208).

TRAJECTORY OF VIOLENCE

The modus operandi of ULFA included propaganda aimed at embarrassing the elected government, extortion, intimidation and abduction for ransom, detonating explosive devices causing the death of innocent people and creating a fear psychosis (Saikia, 2001: 120). The activities of ULFA included organising political killings and lootings, claiming responsibility for murdering Utsavananda Goswami of Congress (I) for his alleged involvement in the riots at Gohpur in 1983 and again in 1989. Similarly, it claimed responsibility for killing an IAS officer at Jorhat in 1983. ULFA also started a big extortionist racket, demanding protection money from tea gardens and big companies such as Tata Tea, Macleod Russell, McNeil Major and Unilever, and refusing to comply with demands meant assassination. According to the Amnesty International Report published in London, 1996, ULFA held two government officials as hostages for ransom until April 1994. Hemram Keet, a sales tax commissioner, had been held for 11 months. In May 1994, ULFA released three traders held since October 1994; a fourth seized at the same time had died in captivity. The Report noted torture of detainees, including beatings with *lathis* (canes), suspension by the wrists or ankles, electric shocks and rape, to extract information (Amnesty International Report 1996: 175). ULFA developed an armed force of about 15,000 fighters, all armed with weapons bought in Burma. ULFA's military wing chief, Paresh Barua, admitted that he had received Rs 30 lakh (3 million) from the Chief Minister's Fund in 1986 (Bhaumik, 2009: 120).

The outbreak of clashes between the Bodos and the Santhals added another deadly dimension to the conflicts already raging in Assam. Over 300 people died in the Bodo-Santhals clashes of May 1996, which carried on for over two weeks and rendered 200,000 people homeless. During 1998, 499 people were killed in 635 incidents. However, coordinated action by security forces led to the surrender of 334 ULFA and 51 Bodo insurgents. Apart from sporadic incidents of violence, the worst was on October 30, 2008, when serial blasts in Assam claimed at least 66 lives while more than 350 others were injured. Again, on July 6 and 19, 2012, four minority community people were killed while on July 20, 2012; four ex-Boro Liberation Tigers cadres were shot dead. The year 2013 witnessed the arrest of 341 militants, the surrender of 2,055, in addition to 534 militants arrested in 2012 and 407 in 2011. Clashes between two tribes in northern Assam in early January 2014 left 16 people dead and more than 3,000 people from the Karbi and Rengma Naga tribes evacuated their homes and took shelter in relief camps opened by the government (Basu, 2017: 154).

According to Tehelka magazine reports, the Maoists have come to an understanding with ULFA commander-in-chief, Paresh Barua, who provided the Maoists with Chinese grenades and firearms. The report also says that Naga insurgents are training a group of new Maoist recruits in Myanmar (Choudhury, 2013). The twin objectives pursued in the region by the Maoists have been using the Northeast as a transit route to ferry arms and other ammunition from China and the extremists also had a geographical expansion strategy in the region. In October 2008, the Maoists issued a joint statement with the Manipur-based People's Liberation Army (PLA) reiterating their commitment to "consolidate the mutual understanding and friendship" and pledged to "overthrow the common enemy". The PLA assisted the Maoists in procuring Chinese arms and equipment via Myanmar. The nexus between ULFA and the Maoists became apparent in 2010 when ULFA Chief Paresh Baruah congratulated the Maoists for carrying out successful strikes on the security forces in Chhattisgarh's Dantewada. Again, in 2011, after senior Maoist leader Kishenji was killed in West Bengal, ULFA extended its sympathy. In May 2012, Baruah extended complete moral support towards the killing of four Maoist cadres in Assam, reiterating that despite different ideologies, they shared a common quest. A database of 150 active Maoist cadres in Assam was created by Assam Police. Chief Minister Tarun Gogoi asserted close links between the terrorist groups, ULFA, NSCN-IM or PLA with the Maoists. In December 2012, Union Rural Development Minister, Jairam Ramesh declared that the upper Assam districts of Dibrugarh and Tinsukia should be included in the list of Left-Wing Extremism-affected districts (Routray, 2013).

Like ULFA, the National Socialist Council of Nagaland-Isak and Muivah (NSCN-IM), which emerged as the most powerful Naga militant group, began aggressively to support insurgents beyond Nagaland by helping them obtain funds, arms, training, and cross-border sanctuaries. Both ULFA and the NSCN-IM have been able to substantially increase the territory over which the police and military must deploy, diluting the Indian government's security presence in the region. NSCN-IM has, in fact, been even more successful than the Assamese insurgents in promoting the proliferation of small rebellions. In 2006, it was estimated that there were about 50 active insurgencies in the Northeast (Cline, 2006). Northeast Indian militants engaged in myriad rivalries sustained by intense competition for land and employment and the system of community-based reservations used to allocate scarce resources. A more important factor is the weakness and corruption of formal political institutions. Many of the small insurgent groups flourished by partnering with weak local governments through extortion, partisan clashes, and criminality. Politicians in Assam, Nagaland, Manipur, and West Bengal are routinely coerced or bribed by insurgents who deploy militants to intimidate voters and rivals (Hazarika, 2003; Mukherjee, 2008).

EFFORTS BY THE GOVERNMENT AND PEACE INITIATIVES BY CIVIL SOCIETY

To contain terrorism in Assam, the Government of India (GOI) passed the Illegal Activities (Restriction) Act 1976 and banned a number of terrorist organisations including ULFA and National Democratic Front of Bodoland (NDFB) in Assam. Armed Forces (Special powers) Act 1958 (amended in 1972) was imposed in Assam along with other laws such as the Disturbed Areas Act, 1950, Unlawful Activities (Preventive) Act, 1967, National Security Act, 1980, Terrorists and Disruptive Activities Act, 1987 and Prevention of Terrorist Activities Act, 2002 (see Romaniuk & Njoku, 2021). The GOI also planned to provide a 100% grant for the expenditure on the modernisation of the Assam police force, including arms and ammunition, vehicles and communication equipment due to its pitiable condition and the inadequate funds of the state government to improve it. Surrender of militants and the rehabilitation of the Surrendered United Liberation Front of Assam (SULFA) through professional training of their interests and employment opportunities were offered and petty criminal cases filed against them were withdrawn. Construction of Border Roads and Fencing along the Bangladesh border joined with Assam, Meghalaya, Tripura and Mizoram was started by GOI, aimed at restricting the entry of Bangladesh infiltrators. ULFA has been accused by the GOI of maintaining links with the Inter-Services Intelligence (ISI) of Pakistan and waging a proxy war on their behalf against India and also emphasised opening up the peace process and thereby bringing peace, stability and development (Chandra 2004).

Rehabilitation of Surrendered United Liberation Front of Assam (SULFA)

Regarding rehabilitation of the SULFA, two 'surrender schemes' have been devised in Assam, the first in 1992 and the second in 1998. Chief Minister Hiteshwar Saikia launched the "100% Special Margin Money Scheme" on June 1, 1992, under which each SULFA cadre was given Rs 2.5 lakh cash [approximately US$3,483 in March 2019 and Rs 1.5 lakh soft loan[approximately US$2,089 in March 2019], which was never returned. They were also allowed to retain their weapons. The enormity of this must be understood against the backdrop of the fact that in 1993–94, 40.9% of Assam's population was below the poverty line. 813 SULFA men were given government employment and a self-employment program was created by the State government including piggery, fishery, poultry and dairy farming. According to an observer, "while initially some Surrendered United Liberation Front of Assam (SULFA) were given jobs in Border Security Force (BSF), Central Reserve Police Force (CRPF), and Railways, the State government later realized that this could be self-defeating leading to a perception that joining militancy was a good launching pad for joining government service" (South Asia Terrorism Portal, "SULFA Terror by another Name").

Failure of the scheme led to another surrender scheme launched by the Prafulla Kumar Mahanta government with the backing of the Centre in August 1998. The new scheme had the projected objective to "wean away the misguided youth and hardcore militants and not to provide soft bank loans to the surrendered terrorists to start businesses." Officially, the surrender scheme sought the "rehabilitation" of the militants in legitimate professions and vocations of their own liking. However, with the exception of a few prominent leaders, the majority of the SULFA simply continued with their previous activities like extortion, intimidation, crimes of extreme violence and terrorisation of wide sections of the population. According to Gill (2000), these "surrender policies" in Assam have been outrageous both in their conception and their consequences as they displayed greater concern among our political establishment for the welfare of the terrorists than for the security and welfare of the common people. Again, in the run-up to the Legislative Assembly Elections of May 2001, an intense debate was generated regarding the alleged nexus between factions of the SULFA, on the one hand, and the ruling AGP and the Congress-I, on the other. Several SULFA leaders had sought Congress-I and AGP tickets for these elections (Saikia, 2001:105–125).

Civil Society Initiatives

The first civil society initiative in Assam towards a peace process with ULFA was taken by the All Assam Democratic Citizen's Association (AADCA), established in the year 1990. It was a platform comprising intellectuals from all sections of the society. On December 16, 1990, the AADCA organised a state-level convention in Guwahati, where a resolution was taken against the continuation of the Disturbed Areas Act and AFSPA. The convention also decided to set up a five-member committee to mediate the negotiation between ULFA and GOI, urging ULFA to abjure violence. However, ULFA rejected the mediatory offer of the convention as it did not consider the AADCA as an impartial organisation (Mahanta, 2013a). Another major initiative for peace effort was taken by Asom Jatiyatabadi Yuva Chatra Parishad (AJYCF) in December 2000. The first national convention on the issue of ULFA-GOI talk was organised by AJYCP on September 20 and 21, 2004, attended by more than 120 organisations. The convention urged to tackle the ULFA issue through political means instead of excessive reliance on military means and blamed GOI for not paying heed to the demands of the people of Assam through dialogue. In March 2005, a National Convention was organised by the People's Committee for Peace Initiative in Assam (PCPIA), attended by more than 45 organisations as well as prominent personalities of the state.

The People's Consultative Group (PCG) held three rounds of talks with GOI in New Delhi in 2006. However, on September 27, 2006, the PCG decided to pull out from the peace process alleging a lack of sincerity on the part of the GOI on the issue of peace talks with ULFA. On March 19, 2007, a Citizen Peace Forum was constituted and on March 22, 2007, another national convention on the ULFA issue was held at the Machkhowa ITA complex where nearly 2500 people attended. On December 28, 2007, top ULFA leaders and Directorate General of Forces Intelligence (DGFI) officials of Bangladesh met in Dhaka and an operational task was charted out to create serious disruptions in Assam and in Siliguri to divert Indian attention from the election impasse in Bangladesh. The central leadership was criticised for 'selling out to fundamentalist forces and being under the influence and control of ISI in Pakistan and DGFI of Bangladesh.' A conglomeration of 12 non-Congress political parties initiated an effort to bring together intellectuals, journalists and NGOs for a citizen's meeting on February 24, 2007, for a durable peace in Assam. The Peace and

Conflict Studies of the Department of Political Science, Guwahati University, conducted several Round Table Dialogues on the issue, 'In Search of Peace' on December 3, 2008. This was the first time that various armed groups, student groups, political parties, intellectuals and journalists came together under one platform to discuss the issues of peace and justice. The dialogue emphasised the primary responsibility of the state towards taking the peace initiatives (Choudhury, 2015: 150–152). On April 24, 2010, a major initiative was undertaken by Assam Jatiya Mahasabha when more than 130 civil society organisations, and intellectuals across the state gathered at ITA Machkhowa to chalk out modalities for GOI and ULFA talk. The draft resolution of the convention made a plea that both the government and ULFA should shun violence (Das, 2012: 11). Inaugurating the meeting, chief convener and noted intellectual of the state, Professor Hiren Gohain said: "... both the ULFA and the government have shown positive gesture for peace talks, but a sense of mistrust pulls them back" (Gohain, 2011: 125).

ULFA'S DECLINE

The decline of ULFA refers to its growing inability to pursue the cause that once formed part of its revolutionary political agenda. ULFA failed to take up the pressing issues like corruption, unemployment and illiteracy, among many others, confronting the people of Assam, in its obsession with sovereignty and fight against the government, ending up to be yet another emotionally-driven misplaced revolutionary movement. It failed to provide any alternative to the existing state system. Though ULFA claimed to fight a war on behalf of the people, in reality, they failed to attract the common masses, as revealed in the frequent hacking to death of rebels by the public, who faced continuous harassment and extortion. Support to Pakistan during the Kargil war, support to Bangladeshi immigrants, indiscriminate killings, including Russian Engineer Sergei Gritsenko, ONGC engineer, T. S. Raju, activist Sanjay Ghosh, among a hundred others, had nothing to do with its propagated aim of emancipating the people of Assam from the shackles of exploitation and discrimination. ULFA's reportedly indiscriminate and random use of violence is believed to be responsible for its allegedly 'terrorist' transformation and ushering in a 'gun culture' in Assam. However, during the early 1990s, ULFA took notice of the public criticisms leveled against it and felt it necessary to respond to them. *Budhbar* would carry a column on public opinion (*janmat*) through which the Publicity Secretary of ULFA was in regular correspondence with the reading public. Again, the activities undertaken by the *Jatiya Unnayan Bahini*, one of ULFA's over-ground organisations, were geared towards the objective of being in constant touch with the people at large and making them self-reliant (South Asia Terrorism Portal "Assam Insurgency and the Disintegration of Civil Society")

According to Misra (2000: 140), "... right from the beginning the ULFA was organised as a militaristic organisation where the political wing occupied a subsidiary status, resulting in erosion of 'inner-party democracy". The fight for ULFA is gradually losing its importance in terms of values and ideologies as the violence it takes resort to is often deployed in order to settle "personal scores". Jaideep Saikia has "put on record" that "the lion's share of the ULFA coffer is being operated without the knowledge of the organisation's cadres" (Saikia, 2001: 32–34). This is reflected in the reportedly lavish lifestyles of ULFA's top leadership which made it evident that the top leadership has been successful in monopolising its control over arms and finance, the two key resources of an insurgent organisation, thus alienating the public support and sympathy that it had hitherto enjoyed. Saikia also accused ULFA of having subordinated its ideology to what he calls, "operational requirements". The shift in ULFA's stance on the question of immigrants from Bangladesh in 1992 reflects the organisation's move to secure safe hideouts in a foreign country from the Indian security forces, exposing its political and ideological bankruptcy. In Saikia's (2001: 19) words, the dream of a "*Swadhin Asom*" (Independent Assam) may soon turn into a nightmare of a "*Brihat Bangla*" (Greater Bengal), if ULFA continues its hobnobbing with external espionage agencies.

RESURGENCE OF ULFA (I)

After a prolonged Counterinsurgency (COIN) campaign, ULFA entered into peace talks with the Government of India (GOI) in 2011. During the peace talks the group saw a split in the organisation in the form of an Anti-Talk faction, the ATF led by Paresh Baruah, the Commander-in-Chief (C-in-C) of ULFA and the Pro-Talk Faction (PTF), led by Arabinda Rajkhowa, the Chairman of the group. The Paresh Baruah-led-faction was named ULFA (Independent) in April 2013 which has shown a resurgence to upsurge attacks on army personnel, civilians, including a series of "improvised explosive device" (IED), explosions that took place on Republic Day that year. ULFA (I) has been successful in gaining its strength after the organisational split and is currently armed with nearly 300 cadres, operating at the inter-state border areas along Nagaland and Arunachal Pradesh (Karmakar, 2017). The period of dormancy of the hardline faction of ULFA could be seen from 2011 to 2015 after which the organisation showed signs of resurgence through fresh attacks (Sharma & Singh, 2017). In ULFA (I) related violence in 2016, there have been casualties of six civilians and three security forces personnel, including a kidnapping (South Asia Terrorism Portal "Assam Assessment"). The outfit also continued killing civilians and harassing the population through extortion in the name of protection money or business tax from the business houses (Goswami, 2015).

In an exclusive interview with *The Week*, Baruah opined that popular support is not enough to bring about a revolution. There is a need for continuous international support and trust from other countries and civil organisations. Exemplifying his argument, Baruah opined that the success of LTTE (Liberation Tigers of Tamil Eelam)is due to the international support it enjoyed. This, according to him, is the rationale behind their formation of the United National Liberation Front of Western (UNLFW) South East Asia in 2015, as an umbrella organisation of banned insurgent groups. Its major members are the National Socialist Council of Nagaland (Khaplang) NSCN (K), the National Democratic Front of Boroland, the People's Revolutionary Party of Kangleipak, the Kangleipak Communist Party and the Kamtapur Liberation Organisation. According to him, the front has two clear-cut objectives. First, to build an alliance of militant organisations to effectively take on the Indian Army and second, to "internationalize" the struggles for sovereignty in the north-east. Propagating their decade-long struggle, they are reaching out to countries and international bodies like the United Nations, to boost opinion in their favour. The UNLFW has tied up with another deadly terror network, the Coordination Committee. Better known as CorCom, it operates mainly in Manipur, while its leaders live in Myanmar- CorCom has six militant outfits as members and has links to the Maoists in Jharkhand and Chhattisgarh. The tie-up between UNLFW and CorCom helped them to emerge as the largest terror alliance in South Asia. The militants are allegedly trying to raise funds through kidnapping and extortion. Incidents like the abduction of a tea estate manager in Namsai district in Arunachal Pradesh demanding huge ransom on November 10, 2018, allegedly by ULFA (I), is a case in point. According to the police, Namsai is dominated by ULFA (I) and the National Democratic Front of Boroland (Songbijit), another UNFLW constituent.

The pro-talk faction of ULFA has conveyed its strong opposition to government interlocutor A. B. Mathur and threatened to derail the peace accord with the Centre if the Modi government goes ahead with the Citizenship (Amendment) Bill, 2016. The bill, for making minority communities such as Hindus, Sikhs, Buddhists, Jains, Parsis and Christians from Afghanistan, Bangladesh and Pakistan eligible for applying for Indian citizenship, is referred to a Joint Parliamentary Committee of both Houses, under the chairmanship of Satyapal Singh for examination. ULFA suspects the bill, if passed, would reduce the indigenous people in Assam to a minority. On July 30, 2018, Assam scripted history with the publication of the final draft of the much anticipated National Register of Citizens (NRC). Chief Minister Sarbananda Sonowal expressed his confidence that NRC, which has become the instrument to safeguard the interest of greater Assamese society, would be able to create a positive atmosphere and it will also pave the way for realising the hopes and aspirations of the genuine Indian citizens. In a press statement, ULFA(I) expressing its happiness over the publication of the final draft NRC declared its willingness to extend cooperation in preparation for the final NRC. (Das & Pathak, 2018)

CONCLUSION

On October 13, 2018, two days before the Durga Puja celebrations, an explosion in Guwahati's Pan Bazaar area, injured four people. Paresh Baruah telephoned a local television channel and claimed that ULFA(I) had set off the explosion to oppose India's attempt "to settle Bengali immigrants in Assam" through the revision of the National Register of Citizens. Barely three weeks later, on November 2, 2018, six militants rode into Bisonimukh village in Tinsukia district and each of them seized a Bengali-speaking villager, made them kneel down, and fired. This time, the police announced ULFA (I)'s role in the attack. According to intelligence agencies, the killings were not by a single terror outfit, but by a "terror consortium", The United Liberation Front of Western Southeast Asia (UNLFW). Baruah in an interview with *The Week* revealed their grand plan to infuse fresh blood into UNLFW leadership with an aim to fight the Indian Army as a unit, the new National Socialist Council of Nagaland (Khaplang), NSCN (K) chief, Yung Aung, a postgraduate in political science, is only 45 who joined the Naga rebellion in 1998. With Aung at the helm of the NSCN (K), Baruah is now the de facto head of the UNLFW.

It is indeed surprising that ULFA is now heavily recruiting people. In August 2018, Pankaj Pratim Dutta, vice president of the All Assam Students Union (AASU) in Golaghat district, left his home to join ULFA (I). In October 2018, he posted on social media a video of himself holding a Kalashnikov rifle. ULFA (I) has asked various student organisations to join it. According to intelligence officers, around 150 youths from Assam, Arunachal Pradesh and Nagaland have joined ULFA(I) Karishma Mech, a Class of ten students from Jagun village in Tinsukia, joined ULFA (I) in October 2018. According to police sources, at least seven girls from adjoining areas, who were reported to be missing, had followed suit. In November 2018, Paresh Baruah's nephew Munna Baruah, an electrical engineer at Indian Oil Corporation in Dibrugarh, and several of his friends joined ULFA (I). In 2018 alone, ULFA (I) and its associates have carried out 16 attacks in the northeast, five of them in Assam alone. Baruah reiterated that the government, both at the Centre and in the state, must not underestimate them as they are growing in leaps and bounds.

Addressing the question of whether a resurgence of ULFA is in the offing is not easy. That ULFA had to rope in school children to trigger the blasts in Tinsukia speaks a lot about its current conditions. It suffers from low motivation among the cadres and also the absence of a single experienced commander in Myanmar, says freelance journalist Rajeev Bhattacharya, probably the only journalist to have access to the group's base in Myanmar's Sagaing Division, the account of which he has documented in the book, *Rendezvous with Rebels: Journey to Meet India's Most Wanted Men* (Bhattacharya, 2015). However, the group still continues to have support in pockets of Tinsukia, Dibrugarh and Sivasagar districts. With disenchantment and uncertainty in the air, a full-fledged resurgence, may be far-fetched but it is important to understand that the strength of ULFA is also contingent upon several external factors, perhaps the most important being the political leadership in India's neighbouring countries, particularly Bangladesh, where the group has largely operated in the last two decades. Resurgence of militancy in Assam may be a possibility if a Bangladesh Nationalist Party government comes to power in Bangladesh in the next elections. There could also be trouble if there is an attempt to evict the illegal Bangladesh settlers in Assam. The Sonowal government does not have the autonomy to be responsive, through its course of action, to the constituencies it mobilised during the elections. It is imperative for New Delhi to expedite the peace process with ULFA and bring it to a logical conclusion at the earliest.

References

Baruah, A.K. (1984). Elites in a colonial hinterland. In B.L. Abbi (Ed.), *North-East region: Problems and prospects of development*. Chandigarh: Centre for Research in Rural and Industrial Development.

Basu, K. (2017). The Boroland agitation and ethnic violence in Assam. *EPRA International Journal of Economic and Business Review*, *5*(12), December.

Bhattacharya, R. (2015). Birth of UNLFWSEA: Internal dynamics and implications for India's North-East. *Journal of Defense Studies*, *9*(4), 95–110.

Bhaumik, S. (2009). *Troubled Periphery: Crisis of India's North-East*. New Delhi: Sage.

Chandra, B. (2004). *Terrorism and separation in North-East India*. Delhi: Kalpaz Publications.

Chaube, S.K. (1997). Insurgency in Northeast India: A heretical view. In B. Pakem (Ed.), *Insurgency in North East India*. New Delhi: Omsons.

Choudhury, M.H. (2015). A study on ULFA and its socio-political impact on Assam with special reference to Kamrup District a thesis submitted to Guwahati University in partial fulfillment for the requirement of the Degree of Doctor of Philosophy in Political Science.

Choudhury, R. (2013). How ULFA's strongholds are falling to the reds'. *Tehelka Magazine*, *10*(30), 27 July, web source: http://www.tehelka.com/how-ulfa-strongholds-are-falling-to-the-reds/-), accessed on 18.7.2018.

Cline, L.E. (2006). The Insurgency Environment in Northeast India. web source: 10.1080/09592310600562894, accessed on 23.7.2018.

Das, M., & Pathak, A. (2018). Assam: AASU, ULFA welcome publication of final draft of NRC, web source: https://nenow.in/north-east-news/assam-aasu-ulfa-welcome-publication-final-draft-nrc.html

Das, S.K. (1993). Immigration and agricultural modernization: The case of Assam (1979–83). *Socialist Perspective*, *20*(3–4), December 1992 – March 1993.

Das, S.K. (1994). *ULFA: United Liberation Front of Assam: A political analysis*. Delhi: Ajanta Publications.

Das, S.K. (1998). *Regionalism in power: The case of Asom Gana Parishad 1985–1990*. New Delhi: Omsons.

Das, S.K. (2012). *Peace by governance or governing peace? A case study of the United Liberation Front of Assam (ULFA)*. Mahanirban Calcutta Research Group.

Deb, S. (2011). ULFA peace talks: All that glitters might not be gold. *Eastern Panorama*, *XIX*(3), March.

Gill, K.P.S. (2000). Uncertain wisdom of policy makers. *Pioneer*, New Delhi, December 9.

Gohain, H. (2011). *Jatiya Bibhrantir Nirasan, (in Assamese)*. Guwahati: Santi Prakasan.

Goswami, N. (2015). *Indian National Security and counter insurgency: The use of force vs. non-violent response*. New York: Routledge.

Guha, A. (1977). *Planter Raj to Swaraj: Freedom struggle and electoral politics in Assam 1826–1947*. Delhi: ICHR.

Hazarika, S. (1995). *Strangers of the mist: Tales of war and peace from India's Northeast*. New Delhi: Penguin.

Hazarika, S. (2003). Ethnic conflict and civil society in the Northeast. *The Little Magazine* New Delhi, 3, *5*(6), March.

Hindu (1990). *Rebels acquiring legitimacy*, March 9, https://www.thehindu.com.

Hindu (1991). *Press under freedom in Assam*, December 28, https://www.thehindu.com.

Hindu (1992). *ULFA's links with Bangladesh*, September 8, https:// www.thehindu.com.

Indian Ministry of Defense, Annual Report 2003–2004.

Karmakar, S. (2017). Paresh ahead in mantle race – Khaplang death spawns new equations. *The Telegraph*, June 11.

Mahanta, N.G. (2013a). *Confronting the state: ULFA's quest for sovereignty*. India: Sage Publications.

Mahanta, N.G. (2013b). Politics of space and violence in Bodoland. *Economic and Political Weekly*, *48*(23), June.

Mishra, R.C. (2004). *Terrorism: Implication of tactics and technology*. Delhi: Author press.

Misra, T. (1980). Assam: A colonial hinterland. *Economic and Political Weekly*, *15*(32), 1357–1359+1361–1364. August.

Misra, U. (2000). *The periphery strikes back, challenges to the Nation-State in Assam and Nagaland*. Shimla: Indian Institute of Advanced Study, RashtrapatiNivas.

Mukherjee J.R. (2008). An insider's experience. In S. Chakma (Ed)., *India Human Rights Report, 2008*. New Delhi: Asian Center for Human Rights.

Prakash, V. (2008). *A gathering storm: Terrorism in India's North-East*. New Delhi: Gyan Publishing House.

Report, Amnesty International (1996). London: Amnesty International Publications.

Romaniuk, S. N. , & Njoku, E. T. (2021). *Counter-terrorism and civil society: Post-9/11 progress and challenges*. Manchester: Manchester University Press.

Routray Bibhu Prasad (2013). Naxal violence: Expanding into India's North-East? web source: http://www.ipcs.org/comm_select.php?articleNo=3795), accessed on 18.7.2018.

Saikia, J. (2001a). Allies in the closet: Over-ground linkages and terrorism in Assam. *Faultlines, 8*, April.

Saikia, J. (2001b). Revolutionaries or Warlords-ULFA's organizational profile. *Faultlines, 9*, 105–129, July.

Saikia, J. (2001c). *Contours: Essays on Security and Strategy*. Guwahati: Sagittarius.

Sharma, I., & Singh, N.M. (2017). Resurgence of ULFA (I) in Assam: Implications for Internal Security. *32*(3) July-September, web source: http://www.indiandefencereview.com/spotlights/resurgence-of-ulfa-i-in-assam-implications-for-internal-security/, accessed on 23.05.2018.

Sharma, S. (2002). *Socio-political condition of Assam today and role of media in this regard: A Study*, web source: http://www.prembhatiatrust.com/sangeeta.pdf, accessed on 20.05.2018.

South Asia Terrorism Portal. Major incidents of terrorist violence in Assam, 1990–2017, web source: http://www.satp.org/satporgtp/countries/india/states/assam/data_sheets/majorincidents.htm, accessed on 19.05. 18.

South Asia Terrorism Portal, Bibhu Prasad Ruotray. ULFA, The Revolution comes Full Circle. web source: HYPERLINK "http://www.satp org/satporgtp/publication/faultlines/volume13/article5.htmaccessed%20on%2019.05.%2018" http://www.satp.org/satporgtp/publication/faultlines/volume13/Article6.htm HYPERLINK "http://www.satp.org/satporgtp/publication/faultlines/volume13/article5.htmaccessed%20on%2019.05.%2018"accessed on 19.05. 18.

South Asia Terrorism Portal. Das, S.K.. Assam Insurgency and the Disintegration of Civil Society. web source: http://www.satp.org/satporgtp/publication/faultlines/volume13/article5.htmaccessed on 19.05. 18.

South Asia Terrorism Portal. Assam Assessment. web source: http://www.satp.org/satporgtp/countries/india/states/assam/index.html accessed on 19.05. 2018.

South Asia Terrorism Portal. SULFA Terror by another Name, web source: http://www.satp.org/satporgtp/publication/faultlines/volume9/article1.htm, accessed on 03.07.2018.

Ulfar Raijor Uchurat Nibedon (In Asamese), a pamphlet of ULFA, 1985.

PART IX

CASE STUDIES

Southeast Asia and the Indo-Pacific

73

TIBETAN RESISTANCE AND INSURGENCY

Francis Grice and Alexandra J. Macintire

CONTEXT AND HISTORY

Tibet, which lies to the southwest of China, is acknowledged by the international community as being within the PRC's territorial jurisdiction. However, since the Chinese Communists invaded their country in 1950, the Tibetan people have persistently rejected this label. Their fight is comparable to other separatist movements around the world, such as Islamic and Communist insurgencies, but differs due to its Buddhist roots and emphasis on nonviolent resistance.

According to the Chinese government, Tibet consists of 2.9 million people and 460,000 square miles that make up the Tibetan Autonomous Region (TAR) (Lee, 2012). Yet, Tibet was historically comprised of three provinces – U-Tsang, Kham, and Amdo – only parts of which sit inside the TAR (Lee, 2012). A further 410,000 square miles and 3.1 million Tibetans exist in those Tibetan areas outside of the TAR, a fact that the Chinese Government itself partially acknowledges through its designation of Tibetan Autonomous Prefectures in the neighbouring provinces of Qinghai, Sichuan, Gansu, and Yunnan (Lee, 2012). This chapter focuses on the resistance of all Tibetans against the Chinese occupation, so it will adopt the more expansive definition of Tibet as being historical Tibet rather than just the TAR.

The Cause

The struggle for Tibet is founded on an intense conflict between divergent perspectives about who should rule the territory. The Chinese government believes that Tibet is historically an inalienable part of China and, as a result, China cannot attain its full former glory if Tibet is allowed to secede. Beyond this, China has multiple strategic rationales for holding onto Tibet, including that it serves as a buffer zone and strategic outpost on the India-China border. Letting go of the territory would not only deprive China of this benefit but could also hand the advantage over to India or Western rivals such as the United States and Britain, both of whom have used Tibet as a backdoor into China in the past (Hartnett, 2013, p. 290). It further offers China the pretext to maintain its claim to the contested territory of Arunachal Pradesh, which was historically part of Tibet, as well as control of the largest source of freshwater outside of the Arctic and Antarctica and other crucial natural resources in the region, which are increasingly vital for China's population needs (Lehmann & Ninkovic, 2013; India-China Border Dispute, 2015). Finally, it stands as a gateway between China and Central Asia and a vital stepping stone in China's One Road, One Belt initiative (Cheung, 2016).

Many Tibetans desire independence, however. They assert that Tibet was historically its own state and was never voluntarily a part of China, meaning that the occupation of their land in 1950 represented an invasion rather than a liberation. As Dr. Lobsang Sangay, President of the Central Tibetan Administration, recently commented: "As per the treaty signed in 821, it clearly says that Tibetans will be happy in the great land of Tibet and the Chinese will be happy in the China signed by the representative of the Chinese emperor" (Choesang, 2018). This feeds into a national identity that remembers a past in which they had their own language, currency, religion, and taxation system. Seven decades of PRC repression, cultural erosion, and natural resource exploitation have further fortified their dedication towards independence.

The gulf between these two positions helps to explain why the struggle has lasted so long. Tibetan resisters have faced repeated setbacks at the hands of the Chinese security forces, yet their resolute commitment to achieving independence has caused them to regroup after each defeat and await another opportunity. Similarly, the Chinese government has been caught on the back foot by unexpected outbursts of defiance multiple times, yet their determination to hold onto the territory has meant that they have always endured temporary losses while calling in reinforcements to restore order. Neither side is willing to back down or compromise.

Since 1987, a third group under the Dalai Lama has tried to stake out a "middle way" to bring about peaceful reconciliation between the two sides. This would involve accepting Chinese sovereignty over Tibet while also providing greater autonomy for its people. This group does not

DOI: 10.4324/9780429426063-83

disagree that Tibet has a right to be independent per se, but rather has tempered their beliefs on independence with a pragmatism that holds that removing China from Tibet represents an all but impossible task. Rather than being seen as a reasonable compromise, however, the middle way has been condemned as insincere and duplicitous by the Chinese government, defeatist, and a betrayal of the cause by pro-independence Tibetans.

Early Years

Despite its current status as a province in the PRC, Tibet has its own rich history that helps to explain why its population has proved so resolute in struggling against Chinese rule. An early high point was the emergence of the Tibetan Empire under the Yarlung Kings, who oversaw a cultural, linguistic, legal, and economic golden age that is still celebrated by Tibetans today. It was during this era that Buddhism was first introduced into Tibet (Pinfold, 1991, p. xx). This period saw some of the earliest historical tensions between Tibet and China, ironically with Tibet as the aggressor that raided and seized territory from China's ailing Tang Dynasty (Pinfold, 1991, p. xvi).

The Mongols, under Genghis Khan, conquered the Tibetan Empire in the 13th century. It retained its own religious hierarchy, however, as the Mongol Chieftain Altan Khan granted the title of the first Dalai Lama and the "spiritual authority" of Tibet to an indigenous Tibetan (Pinfold, 1991, p. xv). As Mongol power receded, temporal authority was restored, culminating in the fifth Dalai Lama regaining full civil and spiritual sovereignty over Tibet, which sparked the establishment of a theocratic political system that lasted until the mid-20th century (Pinfold, 1991, p. xvii). These early events positioned the Dalai Lama at the heart of Tibet's historical traditions, religion, and culture, which helps to explain why he remains such an inspirational figure for the Tibetan resistance today.

At the end of the 17th century, following a series of conflicts, the newly installed Qing Dynasty invaded Tibet, ostensibly to throw out the Mongols and re-install a Tibetan ruler, but with the real motivation of establishing a protectorate over a territory of vital strategic interest (Goldstein, 1997, p. 14). From this point on, the Qing came to view Tibet as necessary for the success of their dynasty, which defined the Sino-Tibetan relationship and formed one of several keystones in China's argument that Tibet is historically an integral part of China. The British subsequently challenged this dominion through its colony in India, but its eventual acquiescence further cemented the Qing Empire's belief that Tibet was part of China and established a precedent for international recognition of Chinese domination (Goldstein, 1997, p. 28).

Following the collapse of the Qing Empire in 1911, Chinese troops abandoned Tibet, leading to de facto independence for nearly 40 years (Goldstein, 1997, p. 37). This was cut short when the Chinese Communists, fresh from their victory over the Guomindang in mainland China, invaded in 1950. This caused particular resentment among the Tibetan people because the Communists had previously pledged to respect Tibetan self-determination. This invasion was partly for revenge because the Communists had been harassed by Tibetan tribesmen when they traversed through Tibet during the Long March of 1934–1935 (Spence, 1990, p. 408).

The Dalai Lama looked abroad for assistance, but little was forthcoming. Britain and India declined for fear of creating friction with China, and they justified this by claiming Tibet's status had been unclear to the international community (Pinfold, 1991, p. xx). The United Nations also took no action, and even the remaining Guomindang, licking their wounds in Taiwan, agreed with the PRC claim (Pinfold, 1991, p. xx). The United States alone showed some concern, but it did not become meaningfully involved until later. Out of options, the Dalai Lama signed the "Seventeen-Point Agreement for the Peaceful Liberation of Tibet" on May 23rd, 1951. Despite language promising that Tibet would retain its own religion, culture, and political system, the agreement formally ceded Tibet's sovereignty to China (Melvyn & Rimpoche, 1989).

Post-Occupation

The Chinese government immediately enacted policies that changed Tibetan society, including introducing currency and building roads, which reinforced the physical and political connections between Tibet and China. As the occupation continued, the government began taking away food and property, forcing the Tibetans to work on land they no longer owned and bringing famine into the region (Barton, 2003, p. 33). These harsh conditions led the Tibetan people to protest using non-violent means, with little success. The PRC continued seizing land and apportioning it to Han Chinese migrants, all in the name of "socialism", while also removing privately owned guns (Barton, 2003, p. 38). This further angered the population and led the previously peaceful protests to transition into a militant insurgency in 1956. Following some early successes, the guerrilla movement spread throughout Tibet, eventually reaching Lhasa in the centre (Barton, 2003, p. 41). As the revolt continued, the United States shifted from supplying limited aid to undertaking a major CIA operation, entitled Operation St. Cruz. This trained the Tibetans in guerrilla warfare and provided ammunition and supplies (Liu, 1999, p. 34).

Concerned by the threat, the Chinese government decided in 1959 to pacify the insurgency using more forceful measures. To this end, they invited the Dalai Lama to attend a "theatrical performance at the Chinese military camp" (Barton, 2003, p. 46). This was interpreted by the Tibetan people as an attempt to intimidate their spiritual and political leader, and so thousands of Tibetans surrounded his palace in Lhasa to protect his possible abduction (Latson, 2015). The rebels then declared independence and began mobilising to fight against the Chinese, while the Dalai Lama acceded to the urgings of his chief advisor to flee, leaving behind thousands of Tibetan insurgents to be killed or deported by a resurgent PRC (Latson, 2015). This insurrection led the Chinese government to adopt an even more totalitarian and abusive stance towards Tibet, which set the tone for much of the animosity between the two sides in the decades ahead. It also helped to establish the complex relationship between the United States and Tibet that endures today.

After the 1959 revolt, the PRC intensified its suppression, ignoring two United Nations resolutions condemning its actions (UN General Assembly, 1961; 1965). This included a new round of "democratic reforms" that further stripped Tibetans of their private lands and currency while also closing or destroying Buddhist monasteries (Barton, 2003, p. 53). The PRC further constructed labour camps and forced the Tibetans to build railways, cut down forests, and harvest other raw materials. This cruelty continued and worsened until, spurred on by the political and economic liberalisations of mainland China under Deng Xiaoping, a new wave of protests erupted during the late 1980s. Unlike in the 1950s, however, this outburst was hampered by internal fractures, with some participants striving for unequivocal independence and others seeking greater autonomy instead. This division was caused in part by several decades of occupation and socialisation by the Chinese Communists, which had left their mark on the perspectives of the Tibetan people. Equally importantly, the Dalai Lama had recently embraced the cause of autonomy because he believed that independence had become unrealistic and he hoped one day to go home (Pinfold, 1991, p. xxii). Some Tibetans accepted his change as pragmatically necessary, but others felt betrayed and refused to rally behind it.

The new upswelling of resistance began on September 27, 1987, when a group of Tibetan monks demonstrated in Lhasa for Tibetan independence. Arrests quickly followed, leading to further protests, and, on October 1, thousands of protestors clashed with police outside a police station, leaving about 300 injured (Barton, 2003, p. 90). Further protests broke out over the subsequent months, leading the PRC to vow to crush the resistance with "force and brutal punishment" and a campaign of "merciless repression" (Barton, 2003, p. 91). Overt dissidence was again temporarily pacified, and for the next two decades, the Tibetan people continued to live in poverty, with only limited and state-controlled education, under the watchful eye of the Chinese security apparatus. Han settlers continued to migrate into the territory at the behest of the Chinese government, settling predominantly in Lhasa, which caused fear and resentment among the indigenous population.

The year 2008 brought a fresh opportunity for the Tibetan struggle. With the first-ever Chinese Olympics to be held in Beijing that year, a number of monks saw a chance to expose the world to their plight. Preparations were made, and on March 10, 2008, the anniversary of the 1959 revolt, around 200 monks tried to march through the streets of Lhasa with banned Tibetan flags. After the monks were beaten by Chinese security forces, thousands of Tibetans rioted, killing 22 Han Chinese and burning and looting Han shops, offices, and homes. The People's Liberation Army (PLA) used lethal force against the rioters, killing over 100 people, but this only fuelled the fire, and further riots erupted in eastern Tibet (Smith, 2010). By the end of the year, 344 protests had broken out across Tibet, but all were ruthlessly crushed.

These events galvanised the international community to pressure the PRC to negotiate directly with the Dalai Lama, but the Chinese government responded with angry refutations about Tibet being an internal Chinese affair. Instead, it intensified its crackdown, including arresting, torturing, and killing hundreds of Tibetans, instigating re-education programmes, and propagating pro-China and Communist propaganda, all with the goal of suppressing any further resistance and dismantling the concept of Tibetan nationhood (Crowem, 2013). The protests themselves were quashed, but resentment and aspirations of independence have lingered on among the Tibetan population, despite the best efforts of the Chinese to snuff them out altogether.

ORGANISATIONAL STRUCTURES AND ACTIVITIES

In recent years, resistance in Tibet has shifted towards smaller displays of non-violent protest. This is partially because the Dalai Lama teaches that Buddhism and non-violence are inseparable, and his revered status in the Tibetan community – even amongst those who disagree with his views on autonomy over independence – means that his messages have a profound effect on the resistance movement. It is also partially because the Tibetan resistance movement has tried and failed to achieve any meaningful results with other forms of resistance, such as guerrilla warfare and mass protests, as discussed above. Moreover, the pervasiveness of China's pacification campaigns in Tibet has made it increasingly difficult and dangerous for local dissenters to assemble to organise a violent campaign or coordinate widespread demonstrations, which leaves small-scale non-violent actions as their only viable option. The main groups that struggle against Chinese rule are the monasteries and their communities in Tibet itself, the Central Tibetan Administration (CTA) in northwest India, and the global movements to free Tibet.

Monasteries

Prior to 1950, the monasteries in Tibet were hubs of political administration, education, money lending, and dispute arbitration (Tibet's "Intolerable" Monasteries, 2016, p. 4). Today, they serve as springboards for anti-Chinese political activity in the territory, yet they are unable to coordinate with one another to present a united front.

Instead, individual monasteries act independently as launching points for acts of defiance (Tibet's "Intolerable" Monasteries, 2016, pp. 2–3). This lack of a unified front has happened, in part, because Buddhism in Tibet is split between four main sects: the Nyingmapa, the Kagyupa, the Sakyapa, and the Gelugpa, each of which has its own monasteries. While there are similarities across these offshoots, there is also considerable tension. These divisions are deliberately acerbated by the Chinese government to undermine the resistance by supporting some factions against others (Ranade, 2017, p. 4; Lague et al., 2015).

Even within the individual monasteries, there is some confusion and tension regarding the instigation, coordination, and implementation of acts of resistance. This is in part because Tibetan monasteries are not monolithic institutions and have their own internal schisms over religious doctrine, outside interactions, whether defying the Chinese is justified within Buddhism or not, and whether the Dalai Lama was right to abandon independence as a goal (Hopkins, 2001, pp. 260–268; Watts, 2012). This is compounded by the placement of Chinese officials into the monastic hierarchies, along with the subversion of the younger monks through educational indoctrination (China Forces Young Tibetan Monks Out of Monastery, 2018). This has undercut trust between monks, and, consequently, acts of resistance are increasingly planned and carried out alone, with support from sympathetic colleagues coming only after the fact.

One of the most prominent forms of resistance since 2008 has been self-immolations by monks and other Tibetans. Since February 2009, at least 153 people in Tibet have self-immolated themselves, 122 of whom died as a result ("Self-Immolations by Tibetans", 2012). Although these immolations could be viewed as acts of despair, most scholars believe they represent a form of altruistic sacrifice in which the perpetrators lay down their lives to protest Chinese rule for the benefit of the community (Carrico, 2015). The Dalai Lama himself noted that the self-immolations were a non-violent substitution for violent resistance such as suicide bombings (Flynn, 2018). The number of self-immolations annually peaked at 86 in 2012 but has since plummeted, with just three carried out in 2016 and six in 2017 (Self-Immolation Fact Sheet, 2022). Solo protests, involving single monks walking through Tibetan townships and villages while clamouring for the long life of the Dalai Lama, human rights, and freedom for Tibet, are increasingly replacing it as the dominant form of protest (Haas, 2015; Tibet's "Intolerable" Monasteries, 2016, p. 10). Other types of suicide protest have materialised as well, such as the attempted self-killing in 2013 of a Tibetan woman who drove her motorbike into a wall while demanding the cessation of Chinese aggression and interference towards its monasteries and villages (Tibet's "Intolerable" Monasteries, 2016, p. 47).

There have been no region-wide protests since 2008, but there have been local demonstrations against specific Chinese government actions. For example, a demonstration of roughly 5,000 Tibetans erupted in Driru County in 2013 to oppose the exploitation of the sacred Naglha Dzamba Mountain (Thousands of Tibetans Protest Against Mine, 2013). Similarly, in May 2015, approximately 1,000 Tibetans gathered at Nyitso Monastery to protest the detention of local people and monks who had been arrested for trying to prevent the Chinese authorities from confiscating the burning body of a self-immolating monk (Tibet's "Intolerable" Monasteries, 2016, pp. 35–36). Other forms of non-violent resistance have also been used, including refusing to work, hunger strikes, and denying government access to wanted protestors. For example, following the self-immolation of a monk from Kirti Monastery in 2011, over 1,400 monks and other Tibetans sat outside the monastery in order to impede Chinese security forces from entering and apprehending the still-living monk, who died the next day (Tibet's "Intolerable" Monasteries, 2016, p. 28). A hunger strike in solidarity with the monk also occurred at a nearby school soon afterward (Ngaba Students Protest Crackdown, 2011). Similarly, in 2012, after Chinese police arrested a monk in his house for solo protesting, a crowd of Tibetans surrounded the house to prevent his removal into custody. They only dispersed when the police fired into the crowd, killing one person, which led to 10,000 people from the surrounding areas arriving to protest the detention and death (At Least One Shot Dead in Ngaba Protest, 2012, p. 6).

Staged defiance of oppressive Chinese laws represents another form of non-violent resistance. In particular, the celebration of the Dalai Lama's birthday, outlawed by the Chinese government, has been carried out by Tibetans in their own homes and, periodically, in larger group gatherings. In 2011, for example, several thousand Tibetans travelled to the sacred Machen Pomra Mountain to commemorate the day, defying recently passed laws banning this activity. The mountain was occupied in advance by Chinese security forces, but the protestors ignored them and conducted their festivities anyway (Tibet's "Intolerable" Monasteries, 2016, p. 37). Similarly, in 2013, residents of Mowa in Driru County refused to fly Chinese flags from their houses and instead threw them into a river. The Chinese government deployed thousands of troops to force their compliance, but the villagers fought back, and 40 of them were arrested. Even then, they maintained a solid front, and 800 villagers marched upon the county office to demand that the detainees be freed (Tibetans Clash with Police over Chinese Flag Campaign, 2013).

Monasteries have also worked to oppose Chinese efforts to destroy and replace Tibetan culture and identity with pan-Chinese versions. This has included providing schooling in the Tibetan language, providing educational counterpoints to pro-Chinese propaganda in schools, offering religious services, and sharing Tibetan culture and traditions (Tibet's "Intolerable" Monasteries, 2016, pp. 4–5). They have further defied much of the information blackout imposed by the Chinese government by finding ways to bypass China's Great Firewall in order to transmit descriptions, photographs, and videos of Chinese transgressions to the outside world (Tibet's "Intolerable" Monasteries, 2016, p. 2).

Shadow Government

The Central Tibetan Administration (CTA) is a shadow government-in-exile that challenges the Chinese provincial government in Tibet. Formed by the Dalai Lama soon after he fled to India, it is located today in Dharamshala, Himachal Pradesh. This territory was chosen because of its proximity to Tibet, similar topography, preexisting cultural and economic ties, and the fact that it was already home to several groups of Buddhists (Chauhan, 2012, p. 158). The CTA is not recognised as the legal government of Tibet by any country, and even its Indian hosts recognise PRC sovereignty over Tibet. Yet it has secured financial support from many external powers. The United States, for example, has funded many of the organisation's activities, including annual contributions of $1.735 million each year between 1964 and 1968, a U.S. Aid Grant of $23 million in 2016, and a $17 million dollar package that was approved by Congress in March 2018 (Huang, 2018).

The CTA is intended to operate as a democratic government for the approximately 150,000 Tibetans outside of Tibet, most of whom reside in India (120,000), Nepal (20,000), and the United States (10,000). It has an elected parliament of 44 members to represent the traditional territories of Tibet, four schools of Buddhism and two schools of Bon, and those Tibetans living in Europe and the United States (McKissick, 2015). The parliament is headed by a Speaker and Deputy Speaker, along with a seven-member Cabinet known as the Kashag, who address religion and culture, home affairs, education, finance, security, information and international relations, and health (McKissick, 2015; Tsekyi, 2016, p. 51). The parliament meets twice annually for 10–15 days, outside of which the responsibilities of government are conducted by an 11-member Standing Committee (McKissick, 2015). The CTA raises funds primarily via contributions from foreign governments and a "voluntary tax" on Tibetan expats that varies by region (Deng, 2017, p. 18).

The very existence of the CTA signals defiance against the Chinese rule of Tibet. By purporting to exist as the real government of Tibet, in contrast to the illegitimate Chinese regime, the CTA disputes the Chinese government's claim that it possesses the right to rule over Tibet and its people. The CTA functions, therefore, as an icon of resistance that offers hope to Tibetans living in occupied Tibet and offers them an alternative institution to the Chinese provincial government towards which they can extend their loyalty. Beyond this, the CTA seeks a better future for Tibet, either by securing its independence or by bringing about increased political, cultural, and religious autonomy (Chauhan, 2012, p. 160). It also aims to maintain and promote the historical customs and traditions of the Tibetan people, including by supporting projects and organisations that share Tibetan art, music, literature, philosophy, and history with Tibetan exiles and the global community. This represents a concerted effort to deny the Chinese government the ability to extinguish the idea of a Tibetan identity and replace it with a pan-Chinese one (Chauhan, 2012, p. 160).

The Dalai Lama and the CTA regularly implore the Chinese government to enter into meaningful talks, but the only Chinese response to date has been to reject the legitimacy of the Dalai Lama and his followers. The openness to negotiation of the CTA and the obstinacy of the Chinese in response have been influential in painting them in a positive light and the Chinese in a negative one to the international community. The CTA also works to rally the international community to support its cause through lobbying the politicians and diplomats of different countries and international organisations. This is done to encourage foreign powers to pressure the Chinese government into making greater concessions to the Tibetan people, including obtaining the same rights and protections as Han Chinese, as well as ensuring guarantees of protection for the Tibetan language, environment, and genuine autonomy (Dalai Lama, 2012). This has been at least somewhat successful, with states passing over 80 resolutions condemning the Chinese occupation in international, regional, and national venues such as the European Parliament, the Australian Senate, and the United States Congress (Chauhan, 2012, p. 160). The issue has even been raised and debated in the United Nations, although China's position as a permanent member of the Security Council has stymied any real movement there (Chauhan, 2012, p. 160).

Global Tibet Movement

Pro-Tibetan organisations from all over the world also carry the torch of Tibetan resistance. The exact number is unknown, but the CTA recognises 318 Tibetan Support Groups and Tibetan Associations, while Tibet Online claims that there are 380 such organisations ("Global Tibet Movement", 2018; Tibet Online, 2016). These groups are distributed disproportionately heavily in "the West", with 271 of the 318 organisations listed by the CTA, for example, being headquartered there, including 176 in Europe, 53 in North America, 25 in Australia and New Zealand, and 19 in Japan and Taiwan ("Global Tibet Movement", 2018). Most of these movements are non-governmental organisations in individual states or transnational institutions with offices in multiple countries. They range from large organisations with formal hierarchies, mission statements, and paid employees, such as the Tibet Fund, to smaller organisations with informally defined goals and volunteer staff. These organisations operate mostly independently of one another, but rivalry is rare, and some efforts have been made to coordinate their efforts. Most prominently, the International Tibet Network (ITN) was founded in 2000 specifically for this purpose and now claims to have a membership of 180 organisations. As ITN itself notes, however, many differences of belief and purpose exist between their members, such as whether they believe that the goal for Tibet should be independence or greater autonomy.

Although their ability to directly affect events in Tibet is limited, the various global Tibetan groups try to aid the Tibetan people and limit the harm that the Chinese government can do to them and their homes. This includes promoting human rights, civil liberties, and religious freedoms; combating Chinese propaganda about Tibet; raising awareness about the actions of the Chinese government; promoting environmental conservation; supporting the continuation of the American and European arms embargo against China; and keeping knowledge about the Tibetan language and culture alive ("Global Tibet Movement", 2018). To this end, they generate publicity about the plight of the Tibetans and the actions of the Chinese government; initiate legal action in national and international courts against China and those states that abet or turn a blind eye to their activities; help to create and refine legislation in the United Nations, regional organisations, and national legislatures; pressure governments and multinational corporations to cease collaborations with China that detriment the Tibetan people; lobby the Chinese government to cease its malpractices in Tibet and to engage in constructive negotiations about the future of Tibet; and supply educational services and materials to raise awareness about the Tibetan way of life ("Global Tibet Movement", 2018).

One example of an active Tibetan support group is the Washington, D.C.-based International Campaign for Tibet (ICT). As noted in its 2018 tax return, ICT spent $2.5 million on services for Tibetans in 2017, including $410,000 on programmes to educate and train members of the Tibetan community in leadership, advocacy, communications, and diplomacy; $260,000 on campaigns for the release of Tibetan political prisoners, promotion of human rights in Tibet, and religious freedom; $900,000 on building public awareness about issues in Tibet, $45,000 to support its offices in Europe and India, $165,000 on campaigns and programmes to help protect of the Tibetan plateau ecosystem, including opposing unchecked Chinese migration and wanton extraction of natural resources; $285,000 on outreach to state governments, regional organisations, and the United Nations; $540,000 on communication activities, and $75,000 on cultivating greater understanding about Tibetan issues amongst the Chinese people (Internal Revenue Service, 2018).

CHINESE PACIFICATION AND DELEGITIMIZATION

The PRC has responded to the Tibetan resistance with a comprehensive pacification strategy. This has included the deployment of armed force, with the PLA, the People's Armed Police (PAP), local police forces, and armed Han mobs all being used at various points to attack and intimidate Tibetan resisters and their supporters (Grice, 2015, pp. 204–206). It has also involved the use of wide-scale propaganda, "patriotic education" in schools, the destruction or cooption of Tibetan religious institutions, the importation of loyal Han citizens, information warfare, and international diplomacy to try to cut off Tibet from the outside world (Grice, 2015, pp. 206–213). The human and social impact of China's pacification efforts has been colossal, with over 1.2 million Tibetan people killed and 99% of Tibet's monasteries, temples, and shrines looted or destroyed since 1949 (Lortie, 2018).

The intensity and character of Chinese pacification have varied according to events. Against the Tibetan guerrilla insurgency of the 1950s and 1960s, for example, the Chinese government acted aggressively to put down the revolt using mobile warfare supported by artillery and planes against the insurgents and any villages or monasteries that supported them (Smith, 1996, p. 421). It also imposed martial law, closed or destroyed numerous monasteries, and subjected the population to torture and labour camps (Powers, 2007, p. 205). During the Great Leap Forward and the Cultural Revolution, the Chinese Communists tried to grind the idea of an independent Tibetan identity into extinction and replace it with Communist values through mass violence, pervasive propaganda, and social indoctrination. Following Mao's death in 1976, efforts to pacify the region were initially relaxed, but in response to the protests of the late 1980s, a new campaign of "merciless repression" and propaganda was launched. These efforts were heightened further after the September 11 attacks in the United States as a precautionary measure and escalated again in the aftermath of the 2008 protests (Crowem, 2013, p. 1121). Most recently, in response to the rise of self-immolations, the Chinese government has again increased its pacification and propaganda measures, including tracking which monks might try to self-immolate so they can preemptively intervene (Crowem, 2013, pp. 1121–1127).

As part of its efforts to delegitimize the Tibetan resistance, the Chinese government has repeatedly rebranded much of the resistance it has faced. For example, the Dalai Lama has stated that he left Tibet in 1959 because of increased Chinese military action, but the Chinese claim that he and his fellow Tibetans fled following a failed armed uprising ("China Calls Dalai Lama a 'Separatist", 2017). He is also dubbed a "dangerous separatist", while those who commit suicide or other forms of non-violent resistance are labelled as "terrorists", "criminals," and "outcasts" (Crowem, 2013, pp. 1124–1125). They have further sought to reject outside interference by emphasising that Tibet is an internal Chinese sovereign affair and denouncing foreign leaders who meet with the Dalai Lama ("China urges the U.S. not to interfere," 2016; Patranobis, 2017).

CULTURE WAR

The Sino-Tibetan struggle is not merely a clash between resistors and the government but also a conflict between cultures, religions, and ideologies. On the Chinese side, while its constitution allows for religious freedom, the formal creed of the country is atheism, and religion is still viewed as something that should be grudgingly tolerated at best and actively combated as a tool of imperialist and feudal oppression at worst. Indeed, Chinese rhetoric about the invasion of Tibet still depicts it as a benevolent act intended to liberate the Tibetan people from living in a "feudal backwater" under the thrall of Buddhism (Hartnett, 2013). Moreover, because the Chinese government fears religion for being a potential alternative ideology and source of loyalty, religion is heavily regulated, individuals can be persecuted for their religious practises, and religious groups such as the Tibetan Buddhists, Uyghur Muslims, and Falun Gong are all suppressed (Albert, 2018). It is difficult to know how much the PRC believes its own rhetoric about liberating Tibet from religious tyranny, but they likely feel that their suspicions have been confirmed by the fact that much of the opposition to their rule originates in Tibet's monasteries.

The threat that Chinese rule poses to the political, civil, and religious rights of Tibetans makes their struggle even more difficult. Chinese efforts to undermine the resistance by attacking its Buddhist institutions further serve to heighten their fear about the extermination of their religion, causing many to become yet more wedded to resistance. Buddhism also affects their struggles through its embrace of nonviolence over violence as a tool for change, which constrains the options available to Tibetan resisters. Other clashes of culture influence the nature of the struggle as well. The Chinese fixation on material goods and prosperity, for example, contrasts with traditional Buddhist beliefs on the need for austerity. Similarly, the Chinese government promotes a supranational Chinese identity for its people and Mandarin as a universal language. This contrasts with the Tibetan belief that their nation and language are and should remain separate.

OUTCOMES

Despite their efforts, the Tibetan resistance has made no real headway towards driving the Chinese out of Tibet. If anything, the PRC is more firmly embedded today than ever, with Han immigrants spread across the territory, an extensive security grid and information monitoring systems stretched all over the region, the embedment of Han officials in the region's Buddhist monasteries, and an ever-lengthening occupation that means very few Tibetans can remember a Tibet that was not ruled by China (Grice, 2015, pp. 204–215). Nor do the prospects look any better for the foreseeable future: small acts of self-violence such as self-immolations are unlikely to shift the Chinese political and security apparatus, especially given that the guerrilla warfare of the 1950s–60s and the mass protests of the 1980s–2000s failed to make even a dent.

There are a number of reasons for this failure. One is that the imbalance of power is vast, with many tens of thousands of Chinese military personnel, paramilitary forces, and police facing much smaller numbers of active Tibetan resisters. Moreover, because the Chinese government views Tibet as an inalienable part of China and a vital strategic asset, they possess the "infinite political will" needed to hold onto the territory, regardless of any financial, human, or political costs (Blanchard, 2013). A third is that, while nonviolent protest has delivered some successes in other parts of the world, such as in India in the 1920s–1940s and Egypt in the recent Arab Spring Uprising, it is a methodology that is difficult to leverage against a truly determined adversary such as the PRC. Finally, Chinese pacification measures go beyond simple military oppression to include educational and political indoctrination, widespread secret policing, infiltration of cultural and religious institutions, electronic surveillance, and censorship. Overcoming this behemoth would be a titanic task that, at least for now, is beyond the abilities of the Tibetan resistance.

Even though the odds of success for the Tibetan resisters are minute, their activities tie up considerable Chinese resources, with large contingents of PLA and PAP forces needing to be kept in the area in order to keep the area pacified. At present, China has at least three mechanised brigades, a reserve forces brigade, a PAP division, and six garrisons, for an estimated total of 44,000 troops with accompanying tanks, artillery, and aircraft permanently stationed in the TAR, along with an unknown number of PAP and regular police, although it should be noted that the military serves the dual purpose of keeping the region pacified and deterring potential Indian aggression over the border (Wortzel, 2015, p. 240; Moore, 2013). During times of strife in the past, the Chinese government has deployed substantially greater amounts of personnel and equipment. Equally importantly, the resistance keeps hope alive for the Tibetan people by illustrating that there is still a will to defy Chinese rule, which reduces the potential for true assimilation of the Tibetan people into the greater "Chinese" identity promoted by the Chinese government. It further signals the defiance of the Tibetan people towards the occupying Chinese forces and the world more broadly, demonstrating that the population has not accepted its lot and remains fundamentally discontent with their situation.

The ongoing resistance further contributes to Chinese fears of separatism within its borders, which has ripple effects on its foreign policy. For example, China abstained from its usual stance of voting in Russia's favour at the UN when voting on Ukraine in the UN Security Council sessions in 2014 because they were afraid of setting a pro-separatist precedent that might influence Tibet (and Xinjiang) back home. Similarly, China's co-creation and involvement in the Shanghai Cooperation Organisation are heavily driven by a desire to pressure the neighbouring states that comprise its members into returning any Tibetan (and Uyghur) dissidents who seek refuge with them back to China.

The actions of the Tibetan resistance and China's corresponding repression also influence how the international community views and interacts with China. Despite the longstanding recognition of Tibet as an inseparable part of China by most world leaders, many of them – particularly in the West – have condemned the harshness of China's pacification policies in Tibet and encouraged a peaceful solution. Following the crackdown launched by the Chinese against the 2008 Tibetan Uprisings, for example, numerous leaders and legislatures in the United States, the United Kingdom, France, Australia, and elsewhere called for the Chinese Government to exercise constraint and to negotiate with the Dalai Lama for a lasting solution, even alluding to potentially boycotting the Olympics if conditions did not improve (Tethong, 2008). Of course, not everyone condemned China, with traditional allies and sympathetic states such as Russia, Pakistan, North Korea, and Venezuela expressing support for China's sovereign right to suppress the uprising and restore order free from external interference (Faulconbridge, 2008; Protests in Tibet condemned, 2008; Kim, 2008).

CONCLUSION

After nearly seventy years of occupation, Tibet remains an unresolved conflict between two resolute actors, neither of whom possesses either the ability to defeat the other entirely or a willingness to back down. Rather than using guerrilla warfare, terrorism, and other forms of violence like many other insurgent groups, Tibetan resisters in Tibet and abroad today rely predominantly on non-violent protests to oppose the Chinese government. This has failed so far to meaningfully threaten PRC rule, but it has also proved difficult for the Chinese government to completely and permanently defeat.

Ultimately, as long as a kindling of defiance remains, there remains the potential for the Tibetan people to someday regain their independence if circumstances change and the possibility of forcefully ejecting the Chinese from Tibet or convincing them to go peacefully becomes viable. Yet if the Chinese government can somehow extinguish that flickering flame of resistance and replace the Tibetan identity with a pan-Chinese version, then the Tibetan national dream may still die and be forgotten.

References

Albert, E. (2018, October 11). Religion in China. *Council on Foreign Relations*. Retrieved from https://www.cfr.org/backgrounder/religion-china

At Least One Shot Dead in Ngaba Protest. (2012). *Tibetan review: The monthly magazine on all aspects of Tibet, 47*(1/2), 6.

Barton, P.J. (2003). *Tibet and China: History, insurgency, and beyond*. Calhoun: The NPS Institutional Archive.

Blanchard, B. (2013). China says Tibet policy 'correct,' no turning back. *Reuters*. Retrieved from https://www.reuters.com/article/us-china-tibet/china-says-tibet-policy-correct-no-turning-back-idUSBRE99L04N20131022

Carrico, K. (2015, August). Tibetan Buddhist self-immolation. *Oxford Handbooks Online*. Retrieved from http://www.oxfordhandbooks.com/view/10.1093/oxfordhb/9780199935420.001.0001/oxfordhb-9780199935420-e-22

Cheung, J. (2016, May 27). China's Chengdu-Lhasa railway: Tibet and 'one belt, one road'. *The Diplomat*. Retrieved from https://thediplomat.com/2016/05/chinas-chengdu-lhasa-railway-tibet-and-one-belt-one-road/

China calls Dalai Lama a 'Separatist', says he Fled after Failed Armed Rebellion. (2017, April 8). *Hindustan Times*. Retrieved from https://www.hindustantimes.com/world-news/china-calls-dalai-lama-a-separatist-says-he-fled-after-failed-armed-rebellion/story-zDQ7oFcG4D7UFNdblP3DlK.html

China Forces Young Tibetan Monks out of Monastery into Government-run Schools as Part of Drive to Replace Monastic Education with Political Propaganda. (2018, July 12). *International Campaign for Tibet*. Retrieved from https://www.savetibet.org/china-forces-young-tibetan-monks-out-of-monastery-into-government-run-schools-as-part-of-drive-to-replace-monastic-education-with-political-propaganda/

China Urges U.S. not to Interfere in Domestic Affairs on Tibet Issues. (2016, June 16). *Xinhua*. Retrieved from http://www.xinhuanet.com//english/2016-06/16/c_135442608.htm

Choesang, Y. (2018, Janurary 21). Any country who says Tibet is part of China is wrong. Retrieved from http://www.thetibetpost.com/en/outlook/interviews-and-recap/5885-any-country-who-says-tibet-is-part-of-china-is-wrong-tibetan-president

Crowem, D.M. (2013). *The 'Tibet question': Tibetan Chines and western perspectives*. Nationalities Papers. Retrieved from https://www.tandfonline.com/doi/abs/10.1080/00905992.2013.801946

Dalai Lama. (2012, April 22). His holiness bestows Yamantaka initiations and talks about peace in troubled times. *His Holiness The 14th Dalai Lama of Tibet*. Retrieved from https://www.dalailama.com/news/2012/his-holiness-bestows-yamantaka-initiations-and-talks-about-peace-in-troubled-times.

Deng, D. (2017). Not just based on land": A study on the ethnic Tibetan community in Toronto (MA Thesis). Retrieved from Western Graduate and Postdoctoral Studies Electronic Thesis and Dissertation Repository. (4970).

Faulconbridge, G. (2008, March 17). Russia wants China to curtail "unlawful" acts in Tibet. *Reuters*. Retrieved from https://www.reuters.com/article/us-china-tibet-russia-idUSL1712670020080317

Flynn, J. (2018, March 17). Self-immolation for Tibet: Why the Dalai Lama's silence is costing lives. *Brown Political Review*. Retrieved from http://www.brownpoliticalreview.org/2018/03/self-immolation-tibet-dalai-lamas-silence-costing-lives/

Fulford, R. (2017, March 24). In China, a jealous state begins to clamp down on the lives of its faithful. *The National Post*. Retrieved from https://nationalpost.com/opinion/robert-fulford-in-china-a-jealous-state-begins-to-clamp-down-on-the-lives-of-its-faithful

"Global Tibet Movement." (2018). *Central Tibetan administration*. Retrieved from https://tibet.net/about-tibet/worldwide-tibet-movement/#code0slide1;

Goldstein, M.C., & Rimpoche, G. (1989). *A history of modern Tibet, 1913–1951: the demise of the Lamaist state*. Berkeley: University of California Press.

Goldstein, M.C. (1997). *The snow lion and the dragon: China, Tibet, and the Dalai Lama*. Berkeley: University of California Press.

Grice, F. (2015). From David to Goliath: Chinese pacification and counterinsurgency operations in modern wars. In S.N. Romaniuk & S.T. Webb (Eds.), *Insurgency and counterinsurgency in modern war*. (pp. 203–218). Boca Raton, FL: CRC Press.

Haas, B. (2015, December 22). Tibetan self-immolations replaced by solo demonstrations?. *Tibet Sun*. Retrieved from https://www.tibetsun.com/features/2015/12/22/tibetan-self-immolations-replaced-by-solo-demonstrations

Hartnett, S.J. (2013). "Tibet is burning": Competing rhetorics of liberation, occupation, resistance, and paralysis on the roof of the world. *Quarterly Journal of Speech*, *99*(3), 283–316.

Hopkins, J. (2001). Tibetan monastic colleges: Rationality versus the demands of allegiance. In T. Dodin & H. Raether (Eds.), *Imagining Tibet – Perceptions, projections, and fantasies*. (pp. 257–268). Boston: Wisdom Publications.

Huang, P. (2018, March 25). US congress affirms support for Tibet with $17 million in aid to exiled government and Tibetans worldwide. *The Epoch Times*. Retrieved from https://www.theepochtimes.com/us-congress-affirms-support-for-tibet-with-17-million-in-aid-to-exiled-government-and-tibetans-worldwide_2475193.html.

India-China Border Dispute: Li and Modi Seek Resolution. (2015, 15 May). *BBC News*. Retrieved from https://www.bbc.com/news/world-asia-china-32747667

Internal Revenue Service. (2018). *Form 990: Return of organization exempt from income tax: International campaign for Tibet*. Retrieved from https://www.savetibet.org/2017-annual-financial-report/

Kim, J. (2008, March 19). North Korea denounces Tibet riots. *Reuters*. Retrieved from https://www.reuters.com/article/us-korea-north-tibet-idUSSEO33573520080320

Lague, D., Mooney, P., & Kang Lim, B. (2015, December 21). The politics of Tibet's poisonous religious divide. *Reuters*. Retrieved from https://www.reuters.com/article/china-dalailama-divide-idINKBN0U41X120151221

Latson, J. (2015, March 17). *How and why the Dalai Lama left Tibet*. Retrieved from http://time.com/3742242/dalai-lama-1959/

Lee, J. (2012). Tibet. *The land of the snows*. Retrieved from https://www.thelandofsnows.com/tibet/

Lehmann, J., & Ninkovic, N. (2013, July 11). Tibet and 21st century water wars. *The Globalist*. Retrieved from https://www.theglobalist.com/tibet-and-21st-century-water-wars/

Lortie, M. (2018). China ramps up heavy military presence in Tibet for Tibetan uprising day. *Tibet Post International*. Retrieved from http://www.thetibetpost.com/en/news/tibet/6044-china-ramps-up-heavy-military-presence-in-tibet-for-tibetan-uprising-day

Liu, M., Clifton, T., Roberts, P., & Laird, T. (1999). A secret war on the roof of the world. *Newsweek*. Retrieved from https://www.newsweek.com/secret-war-roof-world-165592

Map: Tibetan Self-Immolations from 2009–2017. *International campaign for Tibet*. Retrieved from https://www.savetibet.org/resources/fact-sheets/self-immolations-by-tibetans/map-tibetan-self-immolations-from-2009-2013/

McKissick, E. (2015, August 11). How the central Tibetan administration works. *Contact Magazine*. Retrieved from http://www.contactmagazine.net/election-2016/how-the-central-tibetan-administration-works/

Moore, M. (2013, May 21). Chinese troops suffering post-traumatic stress disorder in Tibet. *The Telegraph*. Retrieved from https://www.telegraph.co.uk/news/worldnews/asia/tibet/10071121/Chinese-troops-suffering-post-traumatic-stress-disorder-in-Tibet.html

Ngaba Students Protest Crackdown, Authorities Respond; New Information on Deaths of Tibetans who Tried to Protect Monks. (2011, May 9). *International campaign for Tibet*. Retrieved from https://www.savetibet.org/ngaba-students-protest-crackdown-authorities-respond-new-information-on-deaths-of-tibetans-who-tried-to-protect-monks/

Patranobis, S. (2017, October 21). *Hindustan Times*. Retrieved from https://www.hindustantimes.com/world-news/china-says-no-excuses-for-foreign-officials-meeting-dalai-lama/story-KXCfhwXZTxibcE4cAO5F4M.html

Pinfold, J. (1991). *Tibet (world bibliography series)*. Santa Barbara, CA: ABC-Clio.

Powers, J. (2007). *Introduction to Tibetan Buddhism*. Ithaca: Snow Lion.

Protests in Tibet condemned. (2008, March 19). *Dawn*. Retrieved from https://www.dawn.com/news/294428/protests-in-tibet-condemned

Ranade, J. (2017, May 28). *Buddhism: A new frontier in the China-India rivalry*. New Delhi, India: Carnegie India.

Self-Immolation Fact Sheet: Tibetans have self-immolated in Tibet and China since 2009, Save Tibet, April 6, 2022. https://savetibet.org/tibetan-self-immolations/

Self-immolations by Tibetans. (2018, March 7). *International campaign for Tibet*. Retrieved from https://www.savetibet.org/resources/fact-sheets/self-immolations-by-tibetans/

Smith, Jr., W.W. (2010). *Tibet's last stand? The Tibetan uprising of 2008 and China's response*. Plymouth, UK: Rowman & Littlefield Publishers.

Smith Jr., W.W. (1996). *Tibetan nation: A history of Tibetan nationalism and sino-Tibetan relations*. Boulder: Westview.

Spence, J. (1990). *The search for modern China*, D. *The search for modern China*. London: W. W. Norton & Company.

Tethong, W. (2008, June 22). The 2008 uprising and the olympics. *Tibetan Review*. Retrieved from http://www.tibetanreview.net/the-2008-uprising-and-the-olympics/

Thousands of Tibetans Protest Against Mine. (2013, May 28). *Radio free Asia*. https://www.rfa.org/english/news/tibet/mine-05282013170400.html

Tibet Online (2016). *Tibet Online*. Retrieved from http://www.tibet.org/index.html

Tibetans Clash with Police over Chinese Flag Campaign. (2013, October 2). *Radio free Europe*. Retrieved from https://www.rfa.org/english/news/tibet/clash-10022013162635.html

Tibet's "Intolerable" Monasteries. (2016). London: Tibet Watch.

Tsekyi, T. (2016). An empirical study on socioeconomic status of Tibetans in Karnataka (Doctoral Thesis). Retrieved from The Shodhganga@INFLIBNET Centre. (http://hdl.handle.net/10603/136994)

United Nations General Assembly (1961, 20 December). *UN general assembly resolution 1723 (XVI) of 1961*. Retrieved from https://www.tibetpolicy.eu/un-general-assembly-resolution-1723-xvi-of-1961/

United Nations General Assembly (1965, 20 December). *UN general assembly resolution 2079 (XX) of 1965*. Retrieved from https://www.tibetpolicy.eu/un-general-assembly-resolution-2079-xx-of-1965/

Watts, J. (2012, February 12). Tibetan acts of self-immolation rise amid the battle for hearts and minds. *The Guardian*. Retrieved from https://www.theguardian.com/world/2012/feb/12/tibets-acts-self-immolation-china

Wortzel, L.M. (2015). PLA contingency planning and the case of India. In A. Scobell, A.S. Ding, P.C. Saunders, & S.W. Harold (Eds.), *The People's Liberation Army and contingency planning in China*. (pp. 225–250). Washington DC: National University Press.

74

BETWEEN CRIMINALITY AND TERRORIST VIOLENCE

The Abu Sayyaf Group in the Philippines

Anwar Ouassini and Nabil Ouassini

INTRODUCTION

One of the most notoriously violent Islamic terrorist movements of the recent past has been the Abu Sayyaf Group (ASG). The organisation arose at the height of the global Islamic fundamentalist movement of the late eighties and early nineties, utilising brutal terrorist violence and crude criminal tactics (Banlaoi, 2010). The ASG was founded by Islamist activists seeking to establish an independent "Islamic state" in the Southern Philippines to address the historical grievances of the Bangsamoro Muslim people. The group today is a loose, networked criminal organisation that does not possess any succinct ideology or movement goals (Ugarte & Turner, 2011). This facilitates Abu Sayyaf's amorphous organisational structure to continue its criminal violence under the guise of Islamic mobilisation, making members and leaders wealthy while actively destabilising and undermining regional political settlements (Kalicharan, 2019).

This chapter will first explore the historical development of the Abu Sayyaf and track its evolution from the early 1990s to the present. It will then examine Abu Sayyaf's ideological frameworks and their links to Jihadist Islamic movements like Al Qaeda and ISIS. The paper will then discuss the organisational structure of Abu Sayyaf to reveal how its fragmentation sustains its mobilisation and presence in the Southern Philippines. Finally, we will end the paper by addressing Abu Sayyaf's continued impact on the peace process in the Philippines, its newly formulated ties to ISIS, and the ever-evolving nature of Islamic mobilisation in the Philippines.

CONTEXT

To understand the historical emergence of the Abu Sayyaf Group, one must contextualise its rise and evolution in the political instability, economic disenfranchisement, and incessant discrimination experienced by the Bangsamoro Muslim peoples of the Southern Philippines (Banlaoi, 2010). The unwillingness of the central government in Manilla to grant the Bangsamoro communities' greater autonomy and control over their resources and political destinies post-independence has allowed the ongoing insurgencies to last until the present (International Crisis Group, 2019). The first movement to encapsulate the Moro independence struggle was the Moro National Liberation Front (MNLF). Since its founding in the seventies, this organisation has embodied the Bangsamoro resistance against the central government in both political and military frameworks to become the main representative body striving for full Bangsamoro independence (Banlaoi, 2010; Atkinson, 2012).

In 1987, the MNLF signed a peace treaty with the central government that included partial autonomy for the regions in the south, which were renamed the Autonomous Region of Muslim Mindanao on August 1, 1989 (Banlaoi, 2010; Ugarte & Turner, 2011). The mainstreaming of the MNLF introduced another more radical player in the struggle for independence, the Moro Islamic Liberation Front (MILF) (Banlaoi, 2010; Ugarte & Turner, 2011). The would-be leaders of the MILF splintered from the MNLF in 1977 as they refused to accept the MNLF-GRPH Tripoli Agreement of 1976, in which the MNLF agreed to accept semi-autonomous status (Ugarte & Turner, 2011). In 1984, the former members of the MNLF established the MILF and continued their armed struggle against the state until 2014, when they signed the Comprehensive Agreement on the Bangsamoro. This agreement established full autonomy for the Bangsamoro peoples of the South. While nearly all of the major resistance movements have accepted the peace agreement, one of the notable players in the Bangsamoro region that is still actively mobilising against the state is the Abu Sayyaf Group.

DOI: 10.4324/9780429426063-84

HISTORY OF ABU SAYYAF

The historical rise of Abu Sayyaf has mirrored the global eruption of jihadist organisations in the post-Afghan Jihad against the Soviet Union. The US-Saudi alliance encouraged thousands of Muslims to participate in the Afghan jihad, producing a generation of individuals radicalised under the Jihadist-Wahhabi ideologies of Saudi-Najdi clerical circles. One of the thousands of recruits who heeded the call for Jihad in Afghanistan was Abdurajak Abubakar Janjalani (Banlaoi, 2006; Abuza, 2008; Banlaoi, 2010; Ugarte & Turner, 2011). A Bangsamoro Muslim scholar is said to have joined the Afghan Jihad with several infamous foreign fighters, including Usama Bin Laden and Abdullah Azzam. The inspired "victory" of the Jihadist movements in Afghanistan against the Soviet Union was seen by Abdurajak Janjalani and other Filipino Jihadists as central to not only achieving Muslim independence in the Southern Philippines but also a divine mandate to establish an Islamic state (Abuza, 2008; Banlaoi, 2010; Ugarte & Turner, 2011). Before joining the Afghan Jihad, Abdurajak Janjalani was an affiliated member of the MNLF and later the MILF. However, Abdurajak's radicalisation as a result of the Afghan Jihad and the subsequent global shift towards Islamic political and military resistance encouraged his religious networks to splinter from the MILF and create the Al Harakatul Islamiyya, or Islamic Movement. The goal of Abdurajak's movement was to implement the divine mandate of Jihad (active warfare) against what was framed as the "non-Muslim" occupation force in Manila (Banlaoi, 2006).

While the organisation did not have the same support as the MNLF and MILF, members that did join the Abu Sayyaf movement were disillusioned and dissatisfied with the political and economic compromises regarding Bangsamoro independence vis-à-vis Manila (Banlaoi, 2010). The Islamic movement's violent and obscure tactics led the Philippine military to label the actions and claims of the movement as "Abu Sayyaf" (Father of the Swordsman), which was the jihadi nickname of its founder (Atkinson, 2012). Abdurajak used this pen name when addressing followers or delivering sermons in local mosques and would later begin using the "Abu Sayyaf" label to reframe the Islamic movement organisation (Al Harakatul Islamiyya) (Banlaoi, 2010; Atkinson, 2012; Ugarte & Turner, 2011, p. 411). The calculated rebranding of the movement facilitated the recruitment of new members but also provided a lens into its evolving ideology. The meteoric rise of Abdurajak and the Abu Sayyaf was initially due to the movement's connections to Al Qaeda (Banlaoi, 2006; Abuza, 2008; Banlaoi, 2010; Ugarte & Turner, 2011). In linking with known Al Qaeda associates, Abdurajak and Abu Sayyaf gained access to its vast networks and resources in the Arab Gulf. This was important for their mobilisation as they attacked strategic targets, including government and military installations, churches, and political opponents. However, this had a minimal impact on geopolitical processes due to Abu Sayyaf's insufficient access to military hardware, poor operational capacity, and the US-Philippines active targeting of Al Qaeda in East Asia after the failed Bojinka Plot to kill Pope John Paul II, blow up American airliners, and crash a plane into CIA headquarters (Ilardi, 2009).

The removal of Al Qaeda from the Southern Philippines forced Abu Sayyaf to shift tactics towards illicit criminal activities to secure the necessary resources to sustain their movement. The ASG's criminal ventures included robbing banks and kidnapping and ransoming Western tourists and Catholic citizens living in the South (Banlaoi, 2006; Abuza, 2008; Banlaoi, 2010; Ugarte & Turner, 2011). The organised criminal actions became even more entrenched once the leader, Abdurajak, died in 1998 (Banlaoi, 2010). Following his death, the ASG was no longer confined to a succinct Islamist ideology that purported to create a utopian Islamic state. Consequently, the jihadist ideological frameworks no longer played a central role in the decision-making processes of individual factions as they pursued criminal ventures to fund their activities and brute violence to instill fear (Ugarte, 2008; Banlaoi, 2010; Ugarte & Turner, 2011). This generated tremendous tensions among the Islamic organisations in the region, and in particular the MILF, as they labelled Abu Sayyaf's tactics and methods as un-Islamic. The ASG's recruitment strategies also reflected the shift towards criminality as it marketed would-be recruits' access to the underground market and cash as opposed to the creation of an Islamic state (Ugarte, 2008). This attracted local neighbourhood gangsters and illicit criminal networks from Muslim villages across the South to continue their criminal operations under the banner of the ASG (Banlaoi, 2006; Abuza, 2008; Ugarte, 2008; Banlaoi, 2010; Ugarte & Turner, 2011). These criminal factions in the post-Abdurajak era further fragmented the Abu Sayyaf as they did not cooperate nor act as one cohesive unit; as Wadi describes the Abu Sayyaf, "it has no organisational structure. It is merely a jamaat, a loose, almost chaotic grouping of disenchanted Muslim youth" (Wadi, 2003, p. 16; Ugarte & Turner, 2011).

In the post-911 context, the new leader of ASG, Abubakar's brother Khadafy Janjalani, began to reorient the movement towards the general mission and objectives of Al Qaeda in the region (Banlaoi, 2010; Ugarte & Turner, 2011). He actively worked to disassociate the organisation from the label of Abu Sayyaf by reviving the original title, the Islamic Movement. This was his attempt at re-Islamicizing the goals and identity of the organisation while inferring that the Abu Sayyaf label was imposed by the Philippine military and the CIA. Moreover, this was done to reorient the movement away from its criminal identity and legitimise it as an Islamic movement with links to Al Qaeda (Banlaoi, 2006; Abuza, 2008; Atkinson, 2012). The declaration produced renewed attention from the US War on Terror, as it deployed its troops to the Philippines to actively assist in their operations against the MILF and the ASG (Atkinson, 2012; Hammerberg & Faber, 2017). The increased attention raised the international profile of Abu Sayyaf as they successfully executed several attacks in the Philippines targeting Westerners, including American citizens. This culminated in one of the largest terrorist attacks in the history of the Philippines as the ASG bombed a superferry in Manila Bay in 2004, killing 116 people (Banlaoi, 2010; Ugarte & Turner, 2011). In response to the expansion and increasing reach of Abu Sayyaf, the United States directed a counter-terrorism campaign to undermine the capacity and presence of Abu Sayyaf in the Philippines and the broader region. The US-led operations limited Abu Sayyaf's access to international donors and funding, severed ties with known Al Qaeda associates, and conducted military operations with the Philippines to capture or kill leaders of Abu Sayyaf (Hammerberg & Faber, 2017). The impact of this campaign splintered the organisation into several factions with differing affiliations across the region (Ugarte, 2008; Banlaoi, 2010; Ugarte & Turner, 2011). In response, in 2006, the Philippine government waged another operation called the Oplan Ultimatum, a counterterrorism offensive designed to destroy the multiple factions affiliated with the Abu Sayyaf. This offensive led to the deaths of Khadafy Janjalani and several other leaders throughout the southern Philippines.

This was a critical juncture for the Abu Sayyaf, as they lacked critical resources and community support and were actively targeted by rival groups and the political structure. In June 2008, a leaderless ASG shifted tactics again to focus on kidnapping for ransom to raise funds and create revenue sources for local gangs, who were encouraged to join the fledgling factions of Abu Sayyaf. This period led to some of their most brutal campaigns, including the kidnapping and ransoming of journalists, workers of the International Red Cross, foreign tourists, and residents. These criminal recruitment campaigns attracted many street youths to the organisation, utilising their "skills of conniving with ordinary criminals' groups in their operational areas to mount kidnapping and other criminal activities" (Banlaoi, 2010 p. 19). This has only reinforced the common perception that Abu Sayyaf field commanders and their associated members are no more than street bandits whose objectives are to make money.

While some ASG commanders remained ideologically inclined towards Abdurajak's vision of an Islamic State, the vast majority utilised the Abu Sayyaf label to raise personal funds and address political and economic issues in their localities. In one published declaration, an array of Abu Sayyaf faction commanders proclaimed in their demands to the government the banning of large fishing boats to protect local fishermen, the prevention of international vessels from fishing in their local waters, a return to barter trading in Sulu, and the repatriation of three Abu Sayyaf convicted terrorists from the United States (Ugarte & Turner, 2011 p. 407). The confusing demands have nothing to do with the establishment of an independent Islamic state, as Janjalani envisioned, but more to do with local economic issues. This led the former President of the Philippines, Gloria Arroyo, to state, "The Abu Sayyaf does not know what it wants. It does not know where it wants to go or how to articulate the problem of Muslims in Mindanao well beyond what has already been articulated by other Muslim rebel groups. It is therefore wrong for the government to assume that it is dealing with a cohesive organisation with set doctrines, rules or solid leadership" (Ugarte & Turner, 2011 p. 408). Thus, the state actively challenged the ASG's religious claims as an Islamic organisation while reinforcing the common perception that the ASG is a criminal cartel.

Beginning in 2014, Isnilon Hapilon, a leading member of the ASG's Basilon faction, pledged allegiance to Abu Bakr al-Baghdadi and ISIS (Ressa, 2014; Kalicharan, 2019). This marriage between Abu Sayyaf and ISIS reflected geopolitical developments in the global Jihadist movement's action but also the ASG's lack of ideological and organisational cohesiveness (Kusuma, 2018; Kalicharan, 2019). Hence, some factions remained under the banner of Abu Sayyaf, while others self-identified as ISIS in the Philippines (Hart, 2019). In August 2016, Abu Sayyaf militants embarked on one of their biggest attacks on the island of Jolo, killing fifteen Philippine military personnel and prompting a new military campaign. In 2017, the first self-proclaimed ASG-ISIS suicide bombing attacks were conducted on military personnel, killing five Philippine soldiers in the city of Marawi (Samuel, 2016; Kalicharan, 2019). This attack would be part of a larger effort to capture provincial territory for ASG-ISIS in the city of Marawi. The ASG-ISIS defeat in the battle of Marawi resulted in the deaths of hundreds of fighters, including Isnilon Hapilon (Kusuma, 2018; Hart, 2019). While the ASG-ISIS factions would conduct another major terrorist operation in January 2019 (Gomez, 2019a), with the bombing of a cathedral in Jolo, killing twenty civilians and injuring hundreds, their ability to mobilise and gain a foothold in the South has been severely undermined. This is a result of several factors, including the mainstreaming of Islamic-nationalist organisations like the MILF and MNLF.

This undermines Abu Sayyaf's rhetoric of fighting on behalf of Islam and Muslims by challenging their legitimacy in the region. Second, the defeat of ISIS in Syria and Iraq and the subsequent death of Al Baghdadi dispute the rhetoric around the perceived power of the Islamic state, ultimately weakening their frames. Third, the regional and international support from the United States, Indonesia, Malaysia, and Vietnam has hampered their capabilities in the region to fundraise, recruit, or have any access to regional safe-havens. Finally, President Duterte's positive relations with the Bangsamoro Muslim community and the southern provinces, in general, have challenged the ASG-ISIS rhetoric surrounding political and religious discrimination at the hands of the state.

ABU SAYYAF'S LEADERSHIP AND IDEOLOGIES

Abu Sayyaf surfaced at a time when the MNLF and the MILF were perceived as deficient in their approaches to achieving Bangsamoro independence. Through his religious training across parts of the Arab world, Abdurajak Abubakr Janjalani presented an Islamic extremist option to the struggle. It was during these formative years that Abdurajak established Abu Sayyaf as an ideological alternative to all the other Moro political organisations, with the explicit goal of establishing an independent state in the southern Philippines that adheres to Islamic law in its literal and strictest form (Ugarte, 2008; Banlaoi, 2010; Ugarte & Turner, 2011). During Abdurajak's tenure as the leader of Abu Sayyaf, the group professed Wahhabi ideologies that were similar to those of Islamic extremist groups that were aligned with Al Qaeda and Abdullah Azzam's theory of the necessity of global jihad. Usama Bin Laden had a personal relationship with Abdurajak and made sure to spiritually, financially, and strategically support the group's activities in the Philippines (Abuza, 2008). Ramzi Yousef was sent by Al Qaeda, for example, to provide training in explosives before the first World Trade Centre bombing. In Al Qaeda's worldview, Abu Sayyaf participated in the struggle of global jihad, uplifting the Moros to fight oppression while seeking justice through armed resistance (Atkinson, 2012).

The conditions in the southern Philippines were ripe for Abdurajak and Al Qaeda's ideology. The MNLF and the MILF frustrated the locals in their protracted struggle for independence. The Mindanao regions experience massive social disorganisation and are the poorest regions in the Philippines and South Asia (International Crisis Group, 2019). The lack of opportunities, investment, and marginalisation of those living in the region is largely blamed on the government. Residents perceive the central government as the source of their grievances because of their historical status as a Muslim minority in a Catholic-majority state (Banlaoi, 2006; International Crisis Group, 2019). The usual heavy-handed military approach exercised by the central government created legitimate objections, especially regarding the violation of the local population's human rights. It was under these conditions, along with weak governance and a lack of penetration by police forces into many areas in the south, that resistance groups were able to spread, function, and train largely without any interruption (International Crisis Group, 2019). Abdurajak introduced a deadly alternative to the status quo as a religious leader who studied transnational jihadist ideology abroad.

The ideology that Abdurajak imported into the southern Philippines was centred on Al Qaeda's goal of inspiring Muslims to violently fight against all those that are identified as the enemies of Islam and Muslims. Through this paradigm, Al Qaeda has been successful in mobilising regions of the Muslim world that experience suffering and disenfranchisement from their governments by placing the blame for their misfortunes on the Western world and their respective un-Islamic or illegitimate governments. Al Qaeda's ideological movement rallies these populations towards jihad against their professed enemies (Gunaratna, 2002). In each nation, whether in a predominantly Muslim or non-Muslim country, Al Qaeda calls for the overthrow of the government and the establishment of an "egalitarian" Islamic society, with Sharia as the ultimate law of the land (Gunaratna, 2002). The senior members of Al Qaeda lead this ideology and call for militant jihadism as the only reliable way to revolutionise societies and ensure that their fundamentalist systems will survive (Gunaratna, 2002). As a militant jihadist group, martyrdom is at the centre of its ideology. Members must be willing to sacrifice their lives for this cause, with the crucial conviction that they will be rewarded in the afterlife for their efforts. The mantra for many of the groups associated with Al Qaeda is that in their versions of jihad, one is either victorious in their actions or achieves martyrdom (Gunaratna, 2002).

Abdurajak's knowledge of Islam and his assent to Al Qaeda's goals and strategies helped introduce ideological proclamations that he compiled and called the "Four Basic Truths." According to Banlaoi, the first presents Abu Sayyaf as an intermediary between MNLF and MILF rather than a new faction; the second is the establishment of a pure and peaceful Islamic government; the third truth is the recognition that war and violence will continue until oppression and injustices against the Moro people no longer exist; and finally, "war disturbs peace only for the attainment of the true and real objective of humanity – the establishment of justice and righteousness for all under the law of the noble Quran and the purified Sunnah" (2006, p. 26) Furthermore, the hierarchy of Abu Sayyaf included a centralised leadership that was supported by a Majlis Ash-Shura, or Islamic council, that provided religious legitimacy and justifications for the terrorism that was unleashed in the region. The concept of the majlis comes from early Islamic history, when the majlis, or council of Islamic scholars and elders, elected and advised the first four caliphs. Before his death, Abdurajak provided lessons that criticised Islamic scholars' traditional and classical orientations in the Philippines and called for the adoption of the more fundamentalist and ultra-conservative Wahhabi strand of Islam in the region (Banlaoi, 2006). The recruitment of loyal religious leaders was central to his strategy for expanding the group's extremist ideology in the region.

Before his brother Khadaffy became the next leader of Abu Sayyaf, the ideology and goals became ambiguous and unclear (Banlaoi, 2006). Members of the terrorist group scattered throughout the region and became significantly decentralised. The numerous factions relied on criminality and became known for theft, robberies, raids, assassinations, and kidnapping for ransom operations that primarily targeted foreigners. Rather than the ideology set by Abdurajak, Abu Sayyaf's members competed for money and other financial purposes (Banlaoi, 2006; Hart, 2019). Hammerberg and Faber (2017) emphasise that Abdurajak's death left Abu Sayyaf with no ideological leader to develop the theological reasoning for their fighting, and therefore the group focused on survival and resolved to meet its financial needs through crime over any lofty ideals, religious convictions, or jihadist dogma. It was only in the years after the events of September 11th, when Khadaffy consolidated power from the factions, that the Wahhabi ideology became the centre of the organisation once more, as he openly declared that Abu Sayyaf was an organisation with goals and alliances that were closely linked to Al Qaeda (Hammerberg & Faber, 2017). By 2004, the ideological reorientation would mobilise new attacks, including the deadliest attack in Philippine history, the Superferry 14 bombing, which killed 116 people. By 2007, the US and Philippine armed forces had killed many senior members of Abu Sayyaf, including Khadaffy, which had left the group once again in ideological confusion and disarray.

Currently, the group is fragmented between a variety of local factions. In the rise and fall of ISIS, there is a concern that the terrorist group might reorganise in the Philippines and provide Abu Sayyaf with the ideological conformity for which it is yearning (Beech & Gutierrez, 2019). Although ISIS and Al Qaeda's ideologies are quite similar, ISIS has been more successful in achieving its goals of establishing an actual state on the Iraq/Syria border with control over territory, resources, a significant population, and governance through an ISIS interpretation of Islam. An alliance between ISIS and Abu Sayyaf would have great implications for the southern Philippines. Rather than a conflict with the United States and the West, ISIS's ideological policies are more focused on establishing states or territories that pledge their allegiance to the Caliph. For Abu Sayyaf, an ISIS alliance would provide the ideological and strategic blueprints for establishing a state with an impressive spectrum of resources in social media, recruitment, and terrorist activities. In a study on ISIS's influence over Abu Sayyaf from mid-2014 to the present, Kalicharan (2019) found that there were significant changes in the group's ideology, attacks and target types, and inner group dynamics. The Basilan Abu Sayyaf faction had openly pledged allegiance to ISIS (Ressa, 2014) when its leader, Isnilon Totoni Hapilon, tried to establish an ISIS caliphate in the southern Philippines. He was eventually killed after President Duterte declared martial law and conducted military operations in Marawi City. Meanwhile, the Sulu-based faction continues to utilise terrorism for financial goals and purposes (Hammerberg & Faber 2017). There are reports that, with close to 100 fighters comprised of both Filipinos and foreigners, Hatib Hajan Sawadjaan has become the new leader of ISIS in the Philippines (Gomez, 2019). Raddulan Sahiron is the current leader of the Sulu-based faction, having taken command after Khadaffy's death. The State Department is offering a $1 million reward for information leading to his arrest, and he is one of the FBI's most wanted terrorists (FBI, 2020).

ORGANISATIONAL STRUCTURE AND CHARACTERISTICS

Since ASG's founding, the terrorist group has transitioned from a well-organised, disciplined hierarchical structure led by Abudrajak to a factionalized, heterogeneous group of Islamic extremists with diverging interests (De Castro, 2010). Abdurajak's death impeded the group's ideological development, thus causing Abu Sayyaf to pursue financial and criminal benefits rather than a fundamentalist Islamic state and fragmenting members into sub-groups (Samuel, 2016). The structure of semi-autonomous groups grants the leader of each unit command over small or high-impact operations and the formation of newer sub-groups (De Castro, 2010). It is this decentralised structure that enabled Abu Sayyaf to continuously subsist as a terrorist organisation despite its frequent engagements against the Philippines, the United States, and other international allies (Banlaoi, 2010).

The organisational structure of Abu Sayyaf operates in the rural areas of the Sulu archipelago, the Basilan province, and sections of western Mindanao. Before the creation of Abu Sayyaf, the largest armed group was the MILF, followed by the MNLF. Many members of these two organisations have defected to ASG in the past 30 years. However, there are new splinter groups like the Bangsamoro Islamic Freedom Fighters (BIFF) and the Maute Group (MG). These groups reject the MILF's efforts in peace talks with the government and have either aligned themselves with pro-ASG-ISIS elements or even pledged full allegiance to ISIS. Abu Sayyaf itself consists of two main branches, with smaller factions of local commanders in Sulu and Basilan. The Sulu branch of Abu Sayyaf has developed a reputation for being a predominantly criminal organisation that has periodically carried out violent attacks and bombings. Although the same can be said about the Basilan branch of Abu Sayyaf. this splinter group has been more ideological and closely aligned with international terror groups such as ISIS. Overall, the Sulu archipelago, Basilan Province, and Mindanao are the areas most affected by Abu Sayyaf and its expression of crime and terrorism. The rest of the Philippines has experienced vastly lower levels of terrorism from Abu Sayyaf.

One of Abu Sayyaf's most distinct characteristics is its alliances with and fusion with the region's criminal elements. For its survival, ASG and all its factions are driven by their financial gains more than any other organisational or ideological cause (Dominguez, 2014). Gerdes et al. (2014) describe Abu Sayyaf as a collection of bandits that are creating fear and insecurity through crime. The group is renowned for kidnapping and extortion but also uses terrorism and variegated forms of violence against government forces and civilians. Throughout the 1990s, ASG was funded through Al Qaeda's illicit charities based in Saudi Arabia until they were eventually disconnected in the late 1990s with the death of Abdurajak. Abu Sayyaf primarily generates money from kidnapping-for-ransom schemes that target foreigners and occasionally locals. The terrorist organisation coerces locals to support them and even extorts money through taxes (Banlaoi, 2010). The group's criminal activities are also a source of recruitment for fighters. Many of the recruits are drawn to Abu Sayyaf because of its opportunities to attain wealth and status in a region of the Philippines that is economically and socially deprived. The criminal component of the Abu Sayyaf has been the group's main source of funding outside of donors from the Middle East. The Philippine military has recently claimed that ISIS has funnelled millions of dollars to Abu Sayyaf, particularly after the Marawi City siege (Gomez, 2017).

Part of Abu Sayyaf's strategy is its financial, ideological, and logistical support from other jihadist organisations. According to Banlaoi (2006), Abu Sayyaf has been actively linked to Al Qaeda, Hezbollah, Jamaat al-Islami, Hizbul Mujahideen, al-Gama'a al-Islamiyya, the Islamic Liberation Front, and in recent years, ISIS, amongst others (Banlaoi, 2006). Many of these international terrorist organisations provide training in military operations, bomb-making, and guerilla warfare, even though they hold differing ideological persuasions. Members of Indonesia's Jamaat al-Islami that masterminded the 2002 Bali attacks trained Abu Sayyaf in bomb-making, and recently, Abu Sayyaf has adopted suicide bombing as a strategy. In June of 2017, two suicide bombers, the first in the Philippines, killed five Philippine soldiers in Jolo (Gomez, 2019b; Hart, 2019).

MAJOR ATTACKS AND SECURITY INTERVENTIONS

Abu Sayyaf is responsible for over thirty years of terrorist kidnappings and attacks in the southern Philippines. The first recorded attack occurred on a Christian missionary ship in 1991. The attack, orchestrated by Abdurajak, killed two missionaries and wounded 40, and transpired when the organisation was first named Abu Sayyaf. One of the major incidents ensued when members of Abu Sayyaf, in the summer of 2001, kidnapped tourists and villagers from resorts and villages in the south. The kidnappings made international headlines, with President Gloria Macapagal-Arroyo declaring that the Philippine military would declare an all-out war on the terrorist organisation. Abu Sayyaf murdered and beheaded many of the captives, including Guillermo Sobero, one of three Americans held by the terrorist organisation at the time. In 2003, Abu Sayyaf bombed the Davao International Airport, killing 22 people and wounding 170. The deadliest terrorist attack in the history of the Philippines occurred a year later on the Superferry 14, which killed 116 people. Throughout the years, Abu Sayyaf kidnapped hundreds of foreigners, government officials, and locals, clashing numerous times with the Philippine military in the process. In 2017, the region experienced one of its most violent years with the fight in Marawi City against the military. The Marawi incident witnessed ISIS influence over the Abu Sayyaf and the unification of Mindanao's three largest ethnic groups (the Maguindanao, Maranao, and Tausug) in the fight against military forces, which resulted in more deaths per incident than those witnessed in the past seven years (International Crisis Group, 2019). In 2019, Abu Sayyaf and ISIS claimed responsibility for the bombing of Our Lady of Mount Carmel Cathedral, which killed 23 people and wounded 100. The Philippine government then revealed that an Indonesian couple carried out the attack. Since 2016, over 150,000 people have died in the conflicts in the Muslim regions of Mindanao over the past fifty years (Barron et al., 2016).

Security intervention for the past decades has relied heavily on the use of Philippine military strength to eliminate Abu Sayyaf and movements in the region that have called for Moro independence. Many of Abu Sayyaf's leaders, ideologues, and senior commanders were killed. Nevertheless, the group has endured. Lately, the Philippine government has formed a special Muslim military unit as a way of gaining local community support but with the intent of continuing the consistent and forceful counterterrorism cycle (Kusuma, 2018). The characteristics and factors described above call for a comprehensive approach to anti-terrorism rather than a conventional one. Banlaoi (2018) argues that the current programmes that exist in the Philippines could be effective if only they were funded, implemented, managed, monitored, and assessed routinely. The Programme Management Centre of the Philippine Anti-Terrorism Council (ATC) is a framework that could fully address the various threats of terrorism made by Abu Sayyaf. In particular, Banlaoi (2018) identifies Philippine politics as directly influencing the funding and support for the programmes of national terrorism prevention, capacity building, operational readiness assessment, compliance monitoring, and legal and international affairs. Furthermore, the Philippine government can implement the United Nations Global Counterterrorism Strategy (2018) in a comprehensive and innovative way against Abu Sayyaf. The strategy consists of four points that will force the government to (1) address the conditions that spread terrorism, (2) take specific measures to prevent and combat terrorism, (3) build the states' capacity and strengthen the UN role in the conflict, and (4) respect the human rights of citizens and ensure the rule of law.

CONCLUSION

The future of Abu Sayyaf will rest on the ability of Manila and the leaders of the Bangsamoro people to deliver the necessary social, political, and economic reforms in the region (International Crisis Group, 2019). The historical development of the Abu Sayyaf, along with its ideology and organisational structure, has revealed its ability to adapt to local, regional, and international developments, from the Afghan Jihad to the emergence of Al Qaeda to the recent rise and fall of ISIS (Banlaoi, 2006). The success of the autonomy plan, granting "Muslim self-rule," will determine the future mobilisation potential of Abu Sayyaf in the Philippines (International Crisis Group, 2019). The sustained mobilisation of the ASG has been achieved through its amorphous structure and the absence of ideological cohesiveness, which allows Abu Sayyaf to remain fragmented and designed around criminal-monetary ventures while engaging with Islamic politics and identity when beneficial (Banlaoi, 2006; Abuza, 2008; Ugarte, 2008; Banlaoi, 2010; Ugarte & Turner, 2011). This may also be their downfall, as the greatest threat to Abu Sayyaf is the delegitimization campaign conducted by local, regional, and international Islamic scholars, organisations, and movements. This has greatly influenced their standing with local inhabitants, Bangsamoro Islamic activists (MNLF and MILF), and the state, which has bolstered the narrative that the ASG are un-Islamic, non-religious criminals. Nevertheless, as a terrorist-criminal enterprise, Abu Sayyaf's future will depend on Manila and the Bangsamoro elites to ensure social, political, and economic development in the South (International Crisis Group, 2019). Without significant reforms, Abu Sayyaf and its multiple expressions will continue to live another day (United Nations, 2018; FBI, 2020).

References

Abuza, Z. (2008). The demise of the Abu Sayyaf group in the southern Philippines. *CTC Sentinel, 1*(7). Retrieved from: https://ctc.usma.edu/posts/the-demise-of-the-abu-sayyaf-group-in-the-southern-philippines

Atkinson, G. (2012). ASG: The father of the swordsman. American Security Project. Retrieved from: https://www.americansecurityproject.org/wp-content/uploads/2012/03/Abu-Sayyaf-The-Father-of-the-Swordsman.pdf

Banlaoi, R.C. (2006). The Abu Sayyaf group: From mere banditry to genuine terrorism. *Southeast Asian Affairs*, 247–262.

Banlaoi, R.C. (2010). The sources of Abu Sayyaf's resilience in the southern Philippines. *CTC Sentinel, 3*(5). Retrieved from: https://ctc.westpoint.edu/the-sources-of-the-abu-sayyafs-resilience-in-the-southern-philippines/

Banlaoi, R.C. (2018). The lamitan bombing and terrorist threat in the Philippines. *Counter Terrorist Trends and Analyses, 10*(9), 1–5.

Barron, P. Engvall, A., & Morel, A. (2016). Understanding violence in Southeast Asia the contribution of violent incidents monitoring systems. Asia Foundation. Retrieved from: http://asiafoundation.org/wp-content/uploads/2016/10/UnderstandingViolenceinSEAsia.pdf

Beech, H., & Gutierrez, J. (March 9, 2019). How ISIS is rising in the Philippines as it dwindles in the middle East. New York Times. Retrieved from: https://www.nytimes.com/2019/03/09/world/asia/isis-philippines-jolo.html

De Castro, R.C. (2010). Abstract of counter-insurgency in the Philippines and the global war on terror. Examining the dynamics of the twenty-first century long wars. European Journal of East Asian Studies, 9, 135–160.

Dominguez, G. (September 25, 2014). Abu Sayyaf 'seeking global attention' with hostage kill threat. Deutsche Welle. Retrieved from: http://www.dw.com/en/abu-sayyaf-seeking-global-attention-with-hostage-kill-threat/a-17954921

Federal Bureau of Investigation (2020). Most wanted terrorist: Raddulan Sahiron. Retrieved from: https://www.fbi.gov/wanted/wanted_terrorists/raddulan-sahiron

Gerdes, L.M., Ringler, K., & Autin, B. (2014). Assessing the Abu Sayyaf Group's strategic and learning capacities. Studies in Conflict & Terrorism, 37(3), 267–293.

Gomez, J. (October 24, 2017). AP interview: Philippine military chief says IS funded siege. Associated Press. Retrieved from: https://www.apnews.com/0dde0525561f424d860d445fa691ec5e.

Gomez, J. (February 21, 2019). Amid loss of leaders, unknown militant rises in Philippines. Associated Press. Retrieved from: https://www.apnews.com/730b6ee409364975817a82ad9f15d90c.

Gomez, J. (July 2, 2019). Philippines: 1 known Filipino suicide attacker identified. Associated Press. Retrieved from: https://www.apnews com/2df091f681254512824864fe62ab4130.

Gunaratna, R. (2002). *Inside Al Qaeda: Global network of terror*. New York: Columbia University Press.

Hart, M. (July 22, 2019). Abu Sayyaf is bringing more of ISIS' brutal tactics to the Philippines. World Politics Review. Retrieved from: https://www.worldpoliticsreview.com/articles/28054/abu-sayyaf-is-bringing-more-of-isis-brutal-tactics-to-the-philippines

Hammerberg, P., & Faber, P.G. (2017). Abu Sayyaf group: An Al Qaeda associate case study. *CAN Analysis and Solutions*, 1–25.

Ilardi, G.J. (2009). The 9/11 attacks—A study of Al Qaeda's use of intelligence and counterintelligence. *Studies in Conflict and Terrorism, 32*(3), 171–187.

International Crisis Group. (2019). The Philippines: Militancy and the new Bangsamoro. ICG: Report 301. Retrieved from: https://www.crisisgroup.org/asia/south-east-asia/philippines/301-philippines-militancy-and-new-bangsamoro

Kalicharan, V.S. (2019). An evaluation of the Islamic state's influence over the Abu Sayyaf. Perspectives on Terrorism, *13* (5), 90–101.

Kusuma, B.M.A. (2018). Transnational Islam, regional terrorism, and military power The rise of muslim special unit in the Philippines armed force. *Journal of Southeast Asian Human Rights, 2*(2), 471–487.

Ressa, M.A. (August 4, 2014) Senior Abu Sayyaf leader swears oath to ISIS. Rappler. Retrieved from http://www.rappler.com/nation/65199-abu-sayyaf-leader-oath-isis

Samuel, T.K. (2016). Radicalisation in southeast Asia a selected case study of daesh in Indonesia, Malaysia and the Philippines. Southeast Asia Regional Centre for Counter Terrorism (SEARCCT). Retrieved from: https://www.unodc.org/documents/southeastasiaandpacific/Publications/2016/Radicalisation_SEA_2016.pdf.

Ugarte, E., & Turner, M. (2011). What is the 'Abu Sayyaf'? How labels shape reality. *The Pacific Review*, *24*(4), 397–420.

Ugarte, E.F. (2008). The phenomenon of kidnapping in the southern Philippines: An overview. *South East Asia Research*, *16*(3), 293–341.

United Nations (2018). UN Global counterterrorism strategy. Retrieved from: https://www.un.org/counterterrorism/un-global-counter-terrorism-strategy

Wadi, J.M. (2003). They've come this far. Newsbreak, January-June, pp. 16–19.

75

THE EVOLUTION OF THE MORO ISLAMIC LIBERATION FRONT

From Armed Conflict Actor to Peace Agreement Signatory with the Philippines

Amparo Pamela Fabe and Scott N. Romaniuk

INTRODUCTION

The Moro conflict involves a dynamic and complex web of actors that continuously evolves and changes over time. The major Moro separatist groups are the Moro National Liberation Front (MNLF), which had previously been the key negotiating partner in all earlier peace settlements from the 1970s through the 1990s, and its splinter group, the Moro Islamic Liberation Front (MILF). The Moro Islamic Liberation Front (MILF) was formed when the Maguindanaoans and Maranaws broke away when the Government of the Republic of the Philippines brokered peace with Chairman Nur Misuari's Moro National Liberation Front (MNLF) (Villanueva & Aguilar, 2000).

The MNLF had split along ethnic lines and given rise to an important mutation of the Bangsamoro secessionist movement. Misuari's bulwark of support had come from the Tausugs in the Moro-populated areas of Lanao del Norte, Basilan, Sulu, Zamboanga, Tawi-Tawi, and Palawan. His chief rival for control of the MNLF by the mid-1970s was an Islamic scholar named Salamat Hashim. Hashim's support base is in Maguindanao, Lanao del Sur, Lanao del Norte, and Zamboanga provinces. Hashim harshly criticised Misuari for treading far from "the Islamic basis" and towards "Marxist-Maoist orientations". According to Hashim, the MNLF became an organisation that seemed to answer only to Misuari (Kamlian, 2003).

THE FORMATION OF MILF

In a personal letter to Amadhou Karim Kaye, then secretary general of the Organization of Islamic Countries (OIC), Salamat Hashim demanded the removal of Misuari from the MNLF leadership, as he argued that the MNLF leadership was tending towards a Marxist-Maoist orientation. Instead of showing harmonised and collective leadership, Hashim said, the Central Committee had evolved into a mysterious, exclusive, secretive, and monolithic body whose policies and plans, decisions, and dispositions – political, financial, and/or strategic – had transformed to become an exclusive domain of Misuari. The internal acrimony led to the establishment of two wings within the MNLF: the Misuari wing and the Hashim wing (Kamlian, 2003).

After his unsuccessful attempt to oust MNLF Chairman Nur Misuari in 1976, Hashim Salamat quit his position as MNLF vice chairman and brought with him fifty-seven senior leaders. Hashim chafed at the fact that the OIC had formally acknowledged Misuari's MNLF as the legitimate organisational representative of the Bangsamoro people. Hashim formally established the Moro Islamic Liberation Front (MILF) in Jeddah in 1984 as an alternative standard for the Moros. MILF sought to emphasise its Islamic credentials, and its armed wing, the Bangsamoro Islamic Army, grew from six thousand in the early 1990s to fifteen thousand by the end of the decade (Abinales, 2004).

DOI: 10.4324/9780429426063-85

MILF IDEOLOGY

MILF ideology centres on the propagation of *dakwah* (proselytization) and *tarbiyah* (education). The organisation was focused on building the theological and political basis for an independent Bangsamoro Islamic State. MILF supervised and opened several hundred Islamic schools, or *madaris* in its areas of operation. The organisation also established regular *ulama* summits in the Dakwah Centre in Sultan Kudarat, Maguindanao. MILF also appointed spiritual guides to every Bangsamoro Islamic Armed Forces unit to ensure, *inter alia*, that religious prohibitions on drinking and smoking were enforced. The organisation established the establishment of an Islamic court that handled the finer interpretations of Islamic *fiqh* (jurisprudence) (Liow, 2006). Hashim completed his studies at the Al-Azhar University in Cairo, and he is well-versed with the key Islamist ideologues, Sayyid Qutb of Egypt and Maulana Mawdudi of Pakistan (Banlaoi, 2011).

MILF sent its fighters during the Soviet occupation of Afghanistan in the 1980s in order to fight against the invaders and undergo military training. This experience strongly reinforced Hashim's Islamist beliefs (Abuza, 2003). In brief, MILF, under Hashim, sought nothing less than an Islamized Bangsamoro State in the Mindanao region, to be achieved by both *dakwah* and *jihad*. However, despite MILF's Islamization agenda with Hashim and foreign affairs head Abu Zahir as clerics, other senior leaders like the current MILF Amir Al-Hajj Murad Ebrahim (Hashim Salamat died in July 2003), Information Head Mohagher Iqbal, and Vice Chairman for Internal Affairs Abdul Azia Mimbintas were not. The rank-and-file members of MILF consisted of ordinary Maguindanaons, Maranaons, and Tausugs, who were primarily a mixture of "mainly folk Islam with some elements of scholarly Islam." (Abinales, 2011).

MILF then declared its non-recognition of the 1996 MNLF accord with the Government of the Republic of the Philippines, organised mass demonstrations in Cotabato City in 1996 to protest against Misuari's acceptance of mere autonomy rather than complete independence, and engaged in fierce combat with the Philippine Army that left more than a hundred dead and generated thousands of refugees. This hostile posture prompted Ramos's successor, President Joseph Estrada, to launch an all-out campaign against MILF from April to July 2000, overrunning the main MILF camp complex in Abubakar in the process. When Estrada's successor, President Gloria Macapagal-Arroyo, adopted in the early 2000s a dual strategy of limited tactical AFP operations combined with peace talks, the negotiations between MILF and the Government of the Republic of the Philippines commenced.

MILF agreed to commence peace talks with government representatives, but Hashim granted MILF's local commanders enough flexibility to determine when to engage Philippine security forces. This organisation adopted an "armed but open-to-negotiation movement," sought the help of politicians in its areas of operations as a "buffer between itself and the national state," and resulted in funding coming in to reconstruct war-torn Mindanao.

MILF'S FOUR POINT PROGRAM

MILF's armed component came to be known as the Bangsamoro Islamic Auxiliary Force (BIAF). Initially, MILF had to contend with military defeats in the 1970s, when conventional warfare was the norm, and focused on accumulating strength by organising mass bases in Mindanao. By 1986, in its bid to be a participant as a co-equal of the MNLF, which was then talking peace with the Aquino administration, it mounted a series of military offensives with a big show of force. Starting from its lake-river-estuary base in Central Mindanao, MILF leadership moved to the mountainous areas of the same region in 1983. The implementation of their four-point, 20-year programme needed mountainous base areas. MILF leadership concentrated in the forested boundaries of Maguindanao (now Shariff Kabunsuan), Lanao del Sur, and Bukidnon to strengthen and fortify their central mass base. MILF leaders, including Al Haj Murad, Ghazzali Jaafar, Mohagher Iqbal, Udstadz Castro, and Udstadz Ubak, implemented agricultural projects.

MILF's first 20-year, four-point programme included the following: dawa'h (or political and ideological strengthening through Islam), organisational building, military strengthening, and self-reliance. It also built the Abdurahman Bedis Military Academy in the heart of Camp Abubakar, its central base. Organisation building included establishing committees from barangay to district levels for political matters and corresponding structures for judicial matters. Barangay Reconciliation Committees and District Shari'ah Courts made up MILF structures. These were implemented in Camp Abubakar.

THE MILITARY STRENGTH OF MILF

MILF forces were divided into regulars and reserves. The reserves were formed after a series of military training exercises. They are called back for additional training or whenever there is mass mobilisation, for example, during the all-out war in 2000. MILF manufactured ordnance such as the rocket-propelled grenade (RPG). MILF also built an Islamic school with a public grade school to a high school system inside Camp Abubakar. A local university that is based in Cotabato City offered undergraduate and graduate courses for MILF officers.

Moro entrepreneurs engaged in business inside a small commercial complex inside the camp with eateries, stores, drugstores, and hardware serving the staff of MILF leaders, trainees, students, and visitors. With executive, legislative, and judicial structures in place, a virtual shadow government was functioning in MILF-controlled territories with a central base in Camp Abubakar.

In December 1990, MILF launched a propaganda campaign to gain the support of social sectors that are highly influential in shaping public opinion: the church, mass media, academia, traditional politicians, and the NGO community. Camp Abubakar was opened to visitors so that they could see the MILF programme of a micro-Islamic state. In 1997, the Ulama-Professional League launched the Bangsamoro People's Consultative Assembly at Crossing Simuay Sultan Kudarat Sharip Kabunsuan. The assembly reportedly drew about a million people, comprising Moro and non-Moro indigenous groups, from all over Mindanao and Sulu.

The Ramos administration initiated peace negotiations with MILF. The peace negotiations started after the signing of the GRP-MNLF Final Peace Accord and the many years of low-intensity military offensives in MILF base areas in Central Mindanao, Basilan, Lanao, and Zamboanga. The Ramos administration wanted to tap the overseas development assistance (ODA) funds that all the international agencies had promised to the Philippine government once MILF signed a final peace agreement. These peace initiatives eventually led to the signing of the Agreement for General Cessation of Hostilities on June 21, 1997. This agreement was closely followed by the Official Declaration of Intent for the holding of formal peace talks on October 27, 1998, under the Estrada administration. The government then recognised MILF areas of operation where the agreement would be enforced. Approximately eight out of the 47 declared MILF areas were recognised as "camps" by the Government of the Republic of the Philippines in the official agreements that were signed during the Ramos administration.

President Joseph E. Estrada, who succeeded President Ramos, declared an all-out war against MILF in the second quarter of 2000, thus ending the first round of talks with the rebel group. The Estrada government reportedly spent around PhP7.5 billion for three months of bombing and ground assaults, mainly targeting Camp Abubakar.

The successor of President Estrada, President Gloria M. Arroyo, resumed formal negotiations with MILF, resulting in the signing of the Agreement of Peace in Tripoli, Libya, in June 2002. The agreement identified three areas of concern: security, rehabilitation and development, and ancestral domain. During that time, the two panels signed agreements and laid down the implementing guidelines for the first two talking points. The second round got stalled in the first quarter of 2003 when the Arroyo administration launched an all-out war against MILF forces in Buliok Complex. In March 2004, before the resumption of the formal talks, a Malaysian-led International Monitoring Team (IMT) tasked with monitoring the observation of the ceasefire agreement between the two parties was put in place. In April 2005, the formal talks on the ancestral domain continued, only to be stalled again in the last quarter of 2006.

MILF was open to other options for the resolution of the Bangsamoro struggle aside from the creation of a separate and independent state. It is open to the options of being a commonwealth state, a federal set-up, or a member of an association of free states. In 2008, peace talks were at a snail's pace following the resignation of Silvestre Afable, Jr., as head of the GRP panel, with government negotiators appearing bent on pursuing the ancestral domain within so-called "constitutional processes." The foreign members of the ceasefire monitoring council have withdrawn one after the other. The monitoring council was set to terminate its task in August 2008 (Abreu, 2008).

COMPREHENSIVE AGREEMENT ON THE BANGSAMORO

On March 27, 2014, the Government of the Republic of the Philippines and MILF finally signed the Comprehensive Agreement on Bangsamoro, the basis for a new Bangsamoro Basic Law (BBL) to underpin an autonomous Bangsamoro political entity to replace the ARMM. The draught BBL was submitted to the Philippine Congress on September 10, 2014.

While conflict actors, government mediators, and stakeholders in ongoing peace negotiations are fully aware that the implementation of most of the terms they have agreed to will not begin until a final agreement has been signed, scholars have tended to analyse peace agreements falling within a larger negotiation sequence as having immediate peace-promoting effects upon being signed. From a stakeholders' perspective, the signing of a Comprehensive Peace Agreement represents the culmination of all previous negotiations and agreed-upon terms, marking the commencement of a large-scale process in which the collection of mutually acceptable terms to the underlying conflict issues is in the process of being evaluated (Joshi, 2017).

THE BANGSAMORO ORGANIC LAW

President Rodrigo Duterte signed the Bangsamoro Organic Law (BOL) or Republic Act 1104 on July 26, 2018. The law, which repealed Republic Act 6734, which established the autonomous region in Muslim Mindanao, provides for enhanced autonomy for the Moro region in the southern Philippines. The Bangsamoro Organic Law is expected to address some of the principal grievances that underlie the decades-long conflict in the Philippines' southern region of Mindanao. Among the key features of the law is the replacement of the Autonomous Region in Muslim Mindanao, or ARMM, with a new autonomous region, namely, the Bangsamoro Autonomous Region in Muslim Mindanao (BARMM).

The BARMM covers more core territories compared to the ARMM. The BARMM covers the provinces of Maguindanao, Tawi-Tawi, Basilan, and Lanao del Sur, including the cities of Marawi and Lamitan. The BOL, as provided for in Article XV, Section 3a, provides that the five provinces and the cities of Marawi and Lamitan shall vote as one geographical area. The BARMM includes the following: 1) the six towns in Lanao del Norte and 39 barangays in six North Cotabato towns that voted yes for inclusion in the supposed "expanded" ARMM in the 2001 plebiscite; and 2) all other areas of the local government units contiguous with the ARMM that had petitioned, as provided by law, for inclusion in the BARMM. Twenty barangays from four municipalities of North Cotabato have been granted inclusion in the BARMM: those of Barangays Libungan Torreta, Upper Pangankalan, Datu Mantil, and Simsiman in Pigcawayan; Pagangan in Aleosan; Langogan, Pebpoloan, Kibayao, Kotulaan, and Tupig in Carmen; and Rajahmuda, Barungis, Gli-gli, Nalapaan, Palicupan, Nunguan, Manaulanan, Bulol, Bualan, and Nabundas in Pikit.

Furthermore, under Article 5 of the law, the Bangsamoro Government enjoys greater autonomy over budgeting, administration of justice, resources and revenues, civil services, culture and language, customary law, indigenous people's rights, ancestral domain, and natural resources. The implementation of the BOL may curtail the further spread and influence of jihadism from pro-ISIS groups and may prevent the splintering of the separatist groups into various factions (Ximenes, 2018). Under the provisions of the BOL, there will be a 75–25 sharing of revenues in favour of the Bangsamoro, an automatic allocation of the annual block grant for the Bangsamoro equivalent to 5% of the net national internal revenue, and cases involving Muslims will be tried in Sharia courts. As a result of the full implementation of the BOL, the 30,000 members of MILF's Bangsamoro Army will be deactivated. These combatants could either be integrated into the Armed Forces of the Philippines and the Philippine National Police or become part of the planned Bangsamoro Peacekeeping Force. The National Plebiscite Board of Canvassers affirmed that the majority of voters from the BARMM voted in favour of the measure, thus ratifying the Bangsamoro Organic Law. According to then-Presidential Spokesperson Salvador Panel, the sovereign voice of the participating voters in the plebiscite has spoken, ushering a ray of hope to that war-weary, poverty-stricken, long-neglected, and much heralded promised land of the fifties.

Maja Kocijancic, Spokesperson for Foreign Affairs and Security Policy, stated that the passage of the BOL "represents an opportunity for the Filipino people to embrace peace and stability after decades of strife" (European External Action Service, 2018). The EU remains a staunch supporter of the Mindanao Peace Process and is prepared to support the implementation of the Bangsamoro Organic Law. The BOL provides for the establishment of the Bangsamoro Transition Authority, which will oversee its interim government. All the stakeholders joined hands in unity and harmony to craft an autonomous government that will be responsive to the needs of the Bangsamoro people and other citizens within the jurisdiction of BARMM.

INTERGOVERNMENTAL RELATIONS AND THE BANGSAMORO ADMINISTRATIVE REGION FOR MUSLIM MINDANAO

The Bangsamoro Organic Law (BOL) was ratified in a plebiscite on January 21, 2019. President Duterte appointed the officials constituting the Bangsamoro Transition Authority (BTA). Under the BOL, the BTA has a dual function: it is a transitional government and a Bangsamoro parliamentary government. The BTA oversees the transition from the previous Organic Act to the BOL. As a parliamentary government, it is authorised to carry out its mission as the government of the autonomous region, which will be engaged in service delivery. A key challenge is that a parliamentary type of government, where the executive and legislative functions are joined in one governmental body, is being implemented for the first time in a sub-national government under the Philippine Presidential System of government. It is important to note that the defunct ARMM was a presidential-type administration with a strong executive under a directly elected regional governor. In the BARMM, the Members of Parliament will elect a Chief Minister as head of the government of the day. Moreover, a system of proportional representation to elect half of an 80-member parliament is also going to be tried for the first time in the country. These reforms in the governmental body and electoral system are supposed to make the autonomous region more democratic, responsive, and accountable to the people by encouraging party-based democracy in a region where warlords and strongmen politicians have held sway for decades. This phenomenon, while equally prevalent in the political dynasties of other Philippine regions, is seen as a state failure to integrate the majority Muslim provinces of Mindanao.

The national government has the daunting task of funding the BARMM while exercising the oversight powers of the president over the autonomous region. The main funding will be in the form of a block grant amounting to P63 billion upwards of P70 billion, as a special development fund is included for post-conflict reconstruction. The BTA will pass an appropriation law to allocate the block grant, which strictly follows national government budgetary laws, rules, guidelines, and procedures, including disbursements and accountability. The Block Grant makes the BARMM more fiscally autonomous than its predecessor, the ARMM, which had a budget that was programmed by the national government. The BTA restructured the BARMM bureaucracy into new offices as the old ARMM bureaucracy was gradually phased out. This entails creating new offices and institutions while hiring new personnel, as the employees of the previous ARMM were given separation benefits. Hence, under the BOL, the BTA is supposed to legislate laws and codes for the new structure of the BARMM government. All these tasks, which are supposed to be in place by next year, cannot be done by the BTA alone. Policies have to be made regarding the transition, in which the national government and its officials are the principal decision-makers.

Under the BOL, there is no equivalent oversight committee composed of the Office of the President, cabinet officials, legislators from Congress, and ARMM regional officials created by the previous Organic Act to administer the change process and coordinate different agencies, tiers, and levels of government. Instead, the BOL created an Intergovernmental Relations Body. To wit: Art. VI, Section 2. Intergovernmental Relations Mechanism. There is hereby created a National Government-Bangsamoro Government Intergovernmental Relations Body, hereinafter referred to as the "Intergovernmental Relations Body," to coordinate and resolve issues on intergovernmental relations through regular consultation and continuing negotiation in a non-adversarial manner. This IGR body is supposed to be a formal body with representatives from the national government and the regional government. The IGR Body acts as the clearinghouse to sort out issues regarding the transition and the BOL implementation. But the IGR Body is not only for the transition period; rather, it is supposed to be the main formal interface for cooperation and coordination between the two levels of government.

The IGR Body has been constituted by the national government. The BTA established its IGR committee. The Philippine Department of Finance likewise set up an inter-agency technical working group to interface with the BARMM government, particularly its budget and finance ministries. The BARMM obtained a significant share from the Internal Revenue Allotment (IRA) and funds for special development. The national funding is intended to fast-track the region's economic progress and peace efforts. The BTA distributed funds to LGUs that were not receiving regular IRAs from the central government (Bangsamoro Information Office, 2019). Initial meetings of the TWG with the relevant BARMM agencies have taken place. Aside from the IGR Body, the national government can also utilise as an implementation mechanism the powers of general supervision over autonomous regions of the President to see to it that laws are faithfully executed.

The general supervision of the President over autonomous regions has been delegated to the DILG during the administration of then-President Gloria Arroyo, and that is why the DILG announced recently that it will exercise judicious supervision and will prepare a roadmap for the transition in governance from ARMM to BARMM. It is expected that these mechanisms, particularly the IGR Body of the national government, will be in place to help and guide the transition from ARMM to BARMM, as it is expected that next year will be the start of new structures in BARMM being in place.

GRIEVANCES AGAINST MILF

The formation of the BARMM under the leadership of MILF marks the transition of the rebel group from an armed insurgency into a political party. The grievances against MILF's old guard are highly relevant. MILF is the target of grievances held by alienated youths who consider them to have betrayed the Moro cause and collaborated closely with national politicians. The Bangsamoro Islamic Freedom Fighters and the Islamic State East Asia, or the Omar Maute Group, are disaffected splinter groups from the MILF. The father of the two Maute leaders, the late Cayamora Maute, was a member of MILF. The extent of fragmented Moro allegiances at the level of the family constitutes a major challenge to Moro leaders, given an environment where individuals hold and adhere to multiple affiliations. The different extremist groups have fuzzy borders, and their membership can change very quickly. Some families are fragmented to the extent that the parents might be aligned with MILF or MNLF, while the children support BIFF. Thus, any sense of setback or betrayal in the peace process could serve as a new grievance that fuels splintering among rebel groups and violent extremism.

BARMM Chief Minister Murad Ebrahim has been remiss in addressing new forms of grievance in the region. The first form of grievance against the BARMM is the appointment of former MILF commanders like Abdullah Makapaar, or "Commander Bravo," who was named a Member of Parliament of the Bangsamoro Transition Authority. As an MILF rebel, Commander Bravo had killed police and military officers. Despite committing these heinous crimes, he has not been brought to court to account for them. Currently, he is a government official with the BARMM.

The second grievance is that the block grant for the BARMM has focused on benefiting Muslim communities to the detriment of the minority groups who are living in the BARMM and are composed of Christians, Catholics, and Indigenous Peoples.

The third grievance is the unhappy group of rogue MILF and rogue MNLF commanders who are excluded from partaking in the economic and social benefits of the BARMM. These unhappy MNLF and MILF fighters turn to violence themselves. For example, on September 13, 2013, 180 fighters from the Misuari faction, led by the late Habier Malik, took over the city of Zamboanga as a protest against the government's peace agreement with the MILF, from which they felt excluded and which ultimately led to the creation of the BARMM. By the time the military regained control after 19 days, 300 people were dead and hundreds of thousands of residents were displaced.

The fourth grievance is that several Muslim communities have not benefited from the economic and social dividends that were given to the BARMM. These Muslim groups include the Tausugs, the Marinas, and the Yakan Indigenous Peoples. Several proclaim allegiance to ISIS; most also profess to fight for Moro independence.

The fifth form of grievance is that the MILF never renounced its ties with a terrorist organisation, the Jemaah Islamiyah (JI), with which they had a decade-long alliance from 1994 to 2005. Given the series of terrorist attacks the MILF and JI launched against many communities in Mindanao, only a few MILF members have been brought to court to render an account of their crimes against civilians. The MILF leadership has not offered any form of compensation for the lives they have killed and the livelihoods that have been lost as a consequence of their violent actions. For example, 44 officers of the Philippine National Police Special Action Force (SAF) were killed by MILF rebels and lawless individuals when they entered the bailiwick of the MILF to arrest wanted international terrorist Zulfikli bin Hir, alias "Marwan," and Basit Osman in the Municipality of Mamasapano, Maguindanao, on January 25, 2017. Zulfikli bin Hir was killed during the early morning operation, which was called "Oplan Exodus."

However, the operation resulted in the deaths of 44 personnel, 18 MILF terrorists, and seven civilians (Philippine News Agency, January 25, 2022). In 2017, former Philippine President Rodrigo Duterte signed Presidential Proclamation No. 164 on February 21, declaring January 25 of every year as a day of national remembrance for the heroic sacrifice of the 44 SAF commandos who died during the Mamasapano clash (Rappler, 2017). The proclamation reads, "I ask all our countrymen to remember the heroism of the SAF 44 and recall the daily sacrifices of our uniformed personnel for the sake of the continued peace and security of our nation." (Philippine Star, January 26, 2023). According to Philippine Senator Grace Poe, "the members of the MILF, BIFF, and other armed groups murdered and robbed the 44 PNP SAF commandos" (Mendez, 2015).

The sixth grievance is that the BARMM, despite the BOL, still accounts for the largest number of private armed groups (PAGS) in the country. A positive development is that the National Task Force for the Disbandment of Private Armed Groups (NTF-DPAGs) has successfully disbanded 14 PAGs operating in the BARMM and Region 12. Former Department of Interior and Local Government (DILG) Secretary Eduardo Año, NTF-DPAGs chairman, stated that the DILG applied a whole-of-government and a whole-of-nation approach in combating PAGs. The national government's programme on the disbandment of these PAGS is being carried out through the security component of the normalisation track under the Comprehensive Agreement on the Bangsamoro (CAB) signed between the Government of the Philippines (GPH) and the Moro Islamic Liberation Front (MILF) in 2014 (Philippine News Agency, April 21, 2022).

The sixth grievance is that the Muslim communities remain poor, and therefore, they are vulnerable to constant ISIS recruitment. For instance, the Marawi Siege in Lanao del Sur province in 2017 represented the emergence of a pro-ISIS alliance that united fighters from Mindanao's three largest ethnic groups, the Tausug, Maranao, and Maguindanao, with foreign terrorist fighters from the surrounding Southeast Asian countries. Since the Philippine armed forces ousted the militants in October 2017, ISIS-linked groups have been under heavy military pressure in Mindanao, as well as the provinces of Basilan and Sulu, where loosely organised factions of the Abu Sayyaf Group maintain their control and territory. Despite this pressure, groups that pledged fealty to ISIS have staged several damaging bombings over the past year and continue fighting the security forces (International Crisis Group, 2019).

An important development for the BTA is that it has set up mechanisms to resolve intra-ethnic conflicts or clan feuds that have been affecting the peace of the Moro Region for decades. In 2019 alone, 146 clan feuds were recorded in the BARMM, which resulted in 107 deaths. To address the problem, the BTA, through its Ministry of Public Order and

Safety, has been conducting consultative dialogues in the different provinces of the region. The BARMM is seeking the assistance of various non-governmental organisations (NGOs), cause-oriented groups, security forces, and local government executives to facilitate several reconciliations between warring clans (Dy, 2022). The young, violent extremists such as those of the Maute Group cast the ageing leadership of MILF as traitors to the Muslim cause who have collaborated with the infidel occupier, the government from Manila. The renewed challenge of the so-called "Moro convergence," which pertains to the unity among different factions and ethnic groups in Muslim Mindanao, has been a priority for the Bangsamoro Transition Commission and the Office of the Presidential Peace Advisor (Temby, 2019).

It is also important to point out that the ISIS recruiters are thoroughly well-positioned to channel growing discontent over Marawi into support for their own agenda, especially if they are able to tap into terrorism funding from foreign sources (Fabe, 2019). A strong need for community-based reintegration and rehabilitation programmes targeting former ISIS-inspired militants and at-risk youth in Lanao del Sur province who are susceptible to pro-ISIS, anti-government, and a host of grievance narratives had to be addressed. The longer at-risk youth remain displaced from their homes, the greater the risk of their being recruited by militant and terrorist groups (Temby, 2019).

In addition, the Mindanao region has become fertile ground for the emergence of violent extremist pro-Islamic State (ISIS) groups, thus causing some serious violent actors who are against any form of peace efforts. Cooperation from the MILF is very critical to the Philippines' fight against extremist militant groups such as the Abu Sayyaf Group (ASG), the Bangsamoro Islamic Freedom Fighters (BIFF), and the Maute Group. These three groups were the key players in last year's Battle of Marawi, which left more than a thousand dead, hundreds of thousands displaced, and the city of Marawi in ruins (Franco, 2018).

CONCLUSION

The transition of MILF from an armed conflict actor or rebel group to a peace agreement signatory should be viewed with guarded optimism. The leadership of the MILF, which also assumed leadership of the BARMM, should exert tremendous efforts to maintain peace in the midst of the challenges presented by the presence of terrorist organisations and violent extremist groups. The BARMM is funded by an annual block grant from the national government and takes control of key sectors in the new territory, including the administration of justice, based on local, national, and Islamic law for Muslim Filipinos. It is imperative that BARMM Chief Minister Ahod Ibrahim be cognizant of the new forms of grievances that are increasing. Failure to address this new list of grievances will lead to the emergence of violence and conflict in different communities.

Although there are mixed opinions among the Filipinos, with 62% of the Mindanao residents opposed to the Bangsamoro Organic Law, the relative willingness of the MILF to work with the government on the peace process is an imperative milestone achievement that should be nurtured sustainably. As the Philippine Government strongly commits to the BOL, the peace and stability that Filipinos wish to see in Mindanao will hopefully be achieved. The conflict in Mindanao has transitioned away from one of the powerful terrorist groups that have the ability to control territory towards one of a decentralised terrorist network composed of small, autonomous groups and cells that are more likely to engage in tactics such as suicide bombing (Franco, 2018). As the MILF insurgency subsides and the BARMM assumes leadership, there is hope that the path to peace is viable.

References

Abinales, P. (2004). American military presence in the southern Philippines: A Comparative Historical Overview (Honolulu: East-West Center Working Paper 7, October 2004), 3.

Abinales, P. (2011). *Orthodoxy and history in the Muslim-Mindanao narrative*. Honolulu: University of Hawai'i Press.

Abreu, L. (2008). 40 Years of Revolutionary Struggles. In B. Tuazon (Eds.), *The Moro reader*. Manila: CENPEG.

Abuza, Z. (2003). *Militant Islam in Southeast Asia: Crucible of terror*. Boulder and London: Lynne Rienner.

Bangsamoro Information Office. (2019, December 26). Bangsamoro Government made significant strides in governance. Available at https://bangsamoro.gov.ph/news/latest-news/2019-bangsamoro-government-made-significant-strides-in-governance/

Banlaoi, R. (2011). Bangsamoroism and the Nexus of Identity Politics and Violent Extremism in the Southern Philippines, paper presented at the International Workshop on "The Impact of Identity Politics on Violent Extremism," organized by the Centre of Excellence for National Security of the S. Rajaratnam School of International Studies, Nanyang Technological University, and the Global Futures Forum, Singapore, October 23–25, 2011.

Dy, V. (2022). *Clan politics: A critical role in resolving muslim conflict in the Philippines*. Masteral Thesis. Monterey, California, US: Naval Postgraduate School.

European External Action Service. (2018, July 27). Statement by the spokesperson on the signing of the Bangsamoro Organic Law in the Philippines. https://eeas.europa.eu/delegations/guatemala/48899/statement-spokesperson-signing-bangsamoro-organic-law-philippines_en

Fabe, A.P. (2019). The financial mosaic of violence. In M. Llasos and M.A. Chungalao (Eds), *Perspectives on terrorism in the Philippine context*. Quezon City, Philippines: UP Institute of International Legal Studies.

Franco, J. (2018).Preventing other "marawis" in the southern Philippines. *Asia & the Pacific Policy Studies*, *5*(2), 362–369.

International Crisis Group. (2019, June 27). The Philippines: Militancy and the new Bangsamoro. *Asia Report* (301). https://www.crisisgroup.org/asia/south-east-asia/philippines/301-philippines-militancy-and-new-bangsamoro

Joshi, M., and Quinn, J.M. (2017). Implementing the peace: The aggregate implementation of the comprehensive peace agreements and peace duration after intrastate armed conflict. *British Journal of Political Science*, *47*(4), 869–892.

Kamlian, J. (2003). Ethnic and religious conflict in Southern Philippines: A discourse on self determination, political autonomy and conflict resolution, Lecture at Emory University, November 4, 200.

Liow, J. (2006). *Muslim resistance in Southern Thailand and Southern Philippines: Religion, ideology and politics*. (pp. 8–9). Washington, DC: East-West Center, 2006).

Mendez, C. (2015, March 26). Poe stands by report SAF troops murdered. *The Philippine Star* (Online). Available at https://www.philstar.com/headlines/2015/03/26/1437594/poe-stands-report-saf-troops-murdered

Office of the President. *Government of the Republic of the Philippines*. Proclamation Number 164. Manila: Malacanang Palace.

Philippine Star. Palace: SAF 44's sacrifice won't be forgotten. January 26, 2023.

Philippine News Agency. Bicol police remembers bravery, heroism of SAF 44. January 25, 2022.

Philippine News Agency. 15 private armed groups in Mindanao neutralized: OPAPRU. April 21, 2022.

Philippine Senate. Report on the Mamasapano tragedy. Manila: Office of the Philippine Senate.

Rappler (2017, Feb 26). Duterte declares Jan 25 "Day of National Remembrance" for SAF 44. Available at https://lawphil.net/executive/proc/proc2017/pdf/proc_164_2017.pdf

Temby, Q. (2019). Cells, factions and suicide operatives: The fragmentation of militant Islamism in the Philippines post-Marawi. *Contemporary Southeast Asia*, *41*(1), 114–137.

Villanueva, C., and Aguilar, G. (2000). *The reintegration of the Moro National Liberation Front in Mindanao: Mini case study*. Centre for International Cooperation and Security. University of Bradford.

Ximenes, F.B. (2018). Bringing peace to the Philippines' troubled South: The Bangsamoro organic law. The Diplomat (Oct 2, 2018).

76

LEAVING A WAKE OF DEATH AND DESTRUCTION

The Communist Party of the Philippines-New People's Army, and the National Democratic Front

Amparo Pamela Fabe and Joan Andrea Toledo

INTRODUCTION AND BACKGROUND

The Anti-Terrorism Council, the highest governing body on counterterrorism in the Philippines, has designated the Communist Party of the Philippines-New People's Army-National Democratic Front (CPP-NPA-NDF) as a terrorist organisation as provided by the Anti-Terrorism Act of 2020 (Anti-Terrorism Act, 2020). The government, with the assistance of its defence allies such as the United States, Japan, Israel, and Australia, has invested heavily in education, local economies, public works, and social welfare programmes to address counterterrorism, particularly the communist terrorists (Fridovich & Krawchuk, 2007).

The communist terrorists remain a credible threat to national security. They had established 14 Regional Operational Commands (ROC): five operate in Luzon and Mindanao, while four operate in the Visayas. Each of the ROCs is composed of five to seven guerilla fronts with two platoons each. Each platoon has three squads of seven personnel. Each of these fronts covers at least one congressional district composed of three to five municipalities. The total strength of the communist terrorists is placed at 12,000; On average, 12 villages from each of the five municipalities are part of the guerrilla front. The terrorists are being supported by mass base (MB) elements, organised masses (OM), and contacts in terms of food, shelter, and other logistical requirements. The communist terrorists launch an average of five offensive actions a month directed at Armed Forces of the Philippines (AFP) detachments, vital installations, and other significant targets (Parlade, 2006). The communist terrorists in the three main island groups of the Philippines have different tasks. Those in Luzon serve as the link between the CPP-NPA and other provinces and house the national organisations. Those in the Visayas facilitate the movement of CPP-NPA cadres from Luzon to Mindanao and provide sanctuaries. Those in Mindanao provide material resources, such as money, from the revolutionary taxation (Yuson, 2021).

The CPP-NPA-NDF is responsible for over 50,000 military, police, and civilian deaths. Yet in their official publications, they boast of ambushing and killing the Republic's military and police. Even its "chairman emeritus," Jose Ma. Sison, publicly asked the NPA two years ago to kill at least one soldier a day (*The Manila Times*, November 17, 2020). Other credible sources, such as the publications of many communist terrorists and their surviving victims, point to over a million war casualties that have never been investigated. As with the Soviets' predilection for poisons, communist terrorists in the Philippines surreptitiously poison countless targets using arsenic, cyanide, and insecticides such as thiodan. The United States, European Union, Australia, Canada, and New Zealand (Center of Defense Information, 2001; US State Department, 2001) The United Nations has also designated the CPP-NPA-NDF as a foreign terrorist organisation through several UN Security Council Resolutions (United Nations Security Council Resolutions 1267/1989 and 2253/1988).

The Philippine National Police (PNP) has disclosed information about the existence of 86 mass graves all over the country, which were the result of the killings done by communist terrorists. Some communist terrorist surrenderers have played an integral role in leading the PNP to uncover more mass graves. For example, the Philippine National Police (PNP) Region 13 discovered mass graves in Lawan-Lawan in Las Nieves, Agusan del Norte, that are attributed to the New People's Army (UNTV News, November 1, 2018). The Armed Forces of the Philippines discovered the remains of the victims of the Inopacan massacre perpetrated by the New People's Army (NPA) in the 1980s (Philippine News Agency, September 1, 2021). Several mass graves were dug in Tarlac, Bukidnon, and Cagayan de Oro by the Philippine military. The military officers discovered 20 bodies that had been killed by communist terrorists. The victims' family members expressed their willingness to stand as witnesses as

DOI: 10.4324/9780429426063-86

the government files charges against the communist terrorists who are responsible for the killings (Philippine Star, May 15, 2006). The Philippine military discovered three dozen bodies that were killed by the communists in Inopacan, Leyte, in 1988. The uncovered human remains showed signs of torture, gunshots, and stabbings. The military conducted forensic tests, and they expected to find that their identities would match those of several dozen leftist activists who had disappeared since 1987 (The Christian Science Monitor, June 9, 1989).

TERRORIST ATTACKS

Communist terrorists have launched several terrorist attacks in the Philippines, such as arson, rape, and kidnapping for ransom. The communists have launched arson attacks against private businesses. They have set fire to three cement mixers, a compactor, a grader, and a dump truck (GMA News, March 1, 2019). For example, the communist terrorists burned four pieces of heavy equipment worth PhP 10 million in the province of Quezon (Philippine Daily Inquirer, February 10, 2019). The communist terrorists have raped young people, including their members. Former CPP-NPA-NDF terrorist Arian Jane Ramos, alias Ka Marikit, stated that sexual harassment, abuse, and rape among women are happening inside the camps of the communist terrorists. Ramos was the former secretary of the NPA Guerrilla Front (GF) 55, Southern Mindanao Regional Command, and former chairperson of Gabriela Youth, University of the Philippines-Mindanao (Philippine News Agency, March 16, 2022). The Army's 901st Infantry Brigade confirmed that Police Staff Sergeant Restie Dandan was killed by communists after 18 days in captivity. Dandan was kidnapped on July 31, 2020, in Barangay San Isidro, Municipality of Sison (Philippine News Agency, 2020). Senior police officer Reil Morgado of the Santiago Municipal Police Station died fighting off communist terrorists who tried to kidnap him in Agusan del Norte (Inquirer.net, December 14, 2018).

The communists killed soldiers, policemen, government intelligence agents, government informants, rebel returnees, members of civilian volunteer organisations, barangay tanod (watchmen), local officials, and party members suspected of pilfering party funds. These killings are part of special tactical operations against individuals whom they consider to be counter-revolutionaries. Communists attacked the Municipality of Ayungon police station, killing police officers Relebert Beronio, Raffy Callo, Roel Cabellon, and Marquino de Leon on July 18, 2019. The terrorists also looted their victims' firearms, valuables, and motorcycles (CNN Philippines, July 19, 2019). Communists ambushed a police officer in Sagada, Benguet Province. He was on his way to give aid to the local community (CNN Philippines, January 19, 2023). The communists have killed innocent civilians. The communist terrorists were responsible for the killing of Nolven and Kieth Absalon, former UAAP football juniors most valuable players, and the wounding of a minor in Masbate City (Rappler, June 8, 2021). Kieth, who was tapped by the Philippine National Police for their Sports Against Terrorism Programme and had represented the country in international football tournaments, encouraged the Masbate youth to engage in sports development and to apply for sports scholarships to fund their college studies instead of joining the communist terrorist group.

The communist terrorists have carried out killings of civilians who reported them to authorities. Communists killed Rodel Nobles on August 7, 2022, for reporting them to the Army. They also killed Benjamin Javoc, a local official of Calatrava, Negros Occidental, on August 26, 2022. The terrorists killed Rene Estrebillo on August 12, 2022, for informing the military about their attempts to harass the local population (Human Rights Watch, November 21, 2022).

The communist terrorists have committed multiple human rights violations, thus violating international human rights conventions. The Geneva Convention of 1949 prohibits murder, mutilation, torture, cruel, humiliating, and degrading treatment, the taking of hostages, and an unfair trial. It requires that the wounded, sick, and shipwrecked be collected and cared for (Geneva Convention, 1949).

The members of the National Task Force to End Local Communist Armed Conflict (NTF-ELCAC) have exposed the violations committed by the CPP-NPA-NDF. Senior police officer Jonard Requina of the Malimono Police Station shared that the communists had destroyed a prawn farm in Surigao del Norte after they failed to receive extortion money from the owners. Alfredo Antojado, a local government official, relayed the brutal killing of civilians and the burning of equipment by a private construction company in the municipality of Lanuza, Surigao del Sur. George Banzon, a Philippine Army general, emphasised that the primary motive of the communist terrorist group is to instill fear among the civilian population before they conduct extortion activities and start the destruction of privately owned properties in Surigao del Sur province. The evil acts and deeds of these communists showed that they are heartless.

TERRORISM FINANCING

The communist terrorists conduct fundraising activities through extortion and threats to private businesses. The National Intelligence Coordinating Agency (NICA) revealed that the communist terrorists are extorting millions of pesos from politicians who wish to campaign and win in local areas. They also harass the local population (Philippine News Agency, October 11, 2021). According to the Philippine Army's Third Infantry Division, the communist terrorists are pocketing more than PhP1 million (USD25,000) monthly from regular extortion activities (Daily Guardian, September 15, 2022). The collection of revolutionary taxes by communist terrorists has long hurt the business sector in the country, according to former Philippine Secretary of National Defense Delfin Lorenza. The government received several reports and complaints from business groups in Mindanao about the extortion activities of the communist terrorists (Anadolu Agency, 2017).

Government efforts to stem terrorism financing have resulted in a court conviction against a communist terrorist. Angeline Magdua, cashier of the Rural Missionaries of the Philippines (RMP), was convicted of 55 counts of violating Section 7 of the terrorism financing law, which penalises being an accessory to the crime of terrorist financing. The RMP is a non-government organisation composed of priests and laypersons who obtained donations from abroad to finance the operations of the Communist Party of the Philippines and the New People's Army. The Philippine Department of Justice stated that this is the first conviction under Republic Act 10168, or the Terrorism Financing Prevention and Suppression Act of 2012 (Philippine Star, March 28, 2023).

GOVERNMENT EFFORTS

The Philippine government exerted considerable efforts to address the violence and social harm that were caused by communist terrorists. On December 4, 2018, former President Rodrigo Duterte signed Executive Order No. 70, Series of 2018, "institutionalizing the Whole of Nation approach to attaining inclusive and sustainable peace, creating a national task force to end local communist armed conflict, and directing the adoption of a national peace framework." The National Task Force to End Local Communist Armed Conflict (NTF-ELCAC) was created to orchestrate and ensure that the whole-of-nation approach is effectively implemented. It is composed of representatives from various national government agencies, such as the DILG and Department of Social Welfare and Development (DSWD), and two representatives from the private sector who are appointed by the president for a one-year term. Former President Rodrigo Duterte launched the National Task Force to End Local Communist Armed Conflict (Executive Order, 2018). The whole-of-nation approach by NTF-ELCAC could be the most effective counter-terrorism programme, as evidenced by the continuous and consistent reduction of the influence and strength of communists. Moreover, government agencies are tasked with serving as the lead convenors in instituting, improving, and integrating the delivery of government services that address the root causes of terrorism.

The NTF-ELCAC has implemented successful projects to promote equity among the local population and prevent the recruitment of residents as communist terrorists. The NTF-ELCAC has constructed 136 farm-to-market roads in the whole country. The Western Visayas NTF-ELCAC task force reported that 314 livelihood projects are fully funded. The task force intensified its information drive, such as counter-youth infiltration, to neutralise and overwhelm communist terrorism group propaganda in Candoni, Hinobaan, Ilog, Cauayan, Kabankalan, and Sipalay City in Negros Occidental. The Ilocos Sur NTF ELCAC task force has given various financial, food, and non-food assistance, including skills training such as training on meat and camote processing. The regional task forces continually strengthen inter-agency collaboration, tackle environmental protection, and apply the participatory approach. The Central Visayas NTF-ELCAC task force reported that the Retooled Community Support Programme has successfully identified targets for basic services and strengthened local government empowerment, leading to greater public awareness and expanded infrastructure and resource management (Philippine News Agency, January 19, 2023).

Parallel to these initiatives, the Armed Forces of the Philippines implemented the Community Support Programme, which increases intra-governmental collaboration, an enhanced partnership with civil society, and the creation of a national task force to help consolidate the diverse efforts of multiple national agencies, local government units, and civil society to improve security, good governance, and economic conditions and opportunities. The AFP hopes to harness nationalist sentiment and rally the support of civil society (The Center for International Human Rights, 2020). The armed forces have collaborated with diverse sectors of society by working on respect for human rights, community engagements, and strategic communications with other stakeholders.

The AFP's Community Support Programme operations have also been effective in identifying community issues that need to be resolved. The government had implemented a National Internal Security Plan, which has the components of peace and order: security; political, legal, and diplomatic response; socio-economic and psychosocial development; and informational dissemination (Executive Order, 2001). This plan basically taps all government agencies – military, civilian, and diplomatic – to promote good governance and public confidence in the government, alleviate poverty, and provide the people with a secure environment that is conducive to human development.

CONCLUSION

The CPP-NPA-NDF terrorist group remains the primary threat to national security. To counter this security threat, the Philippine government consistently carries out multi-pronged intervention programmes and projects through a well-crafted national security plan that sustains operations against the terrorists and their raison d'etre. The NTF-ELCAC has so far been successful in promoting economic development and implementing health and environmental projects in *barangays* (local villages) all over the country. The AFP and the PNP, the government security sector, have been receiving the necessary collaboration and convergence that they need with the national government agencies, the private sector organisations, the non-profit organisations, the local government units, and civil society organisations.

The government policy has a wider reach that goes beyond counterterrorism programmes by achieving these paramount objectives: (1) ensure good governance by fighting corruption and promoting transparency and public accountability, (2) accelerate programmes to reduce poverty and promote respect for human rights and the right to development, and (3) apply the left- and right-hand efforts to address terrorism with the help of improved intelligence efforts. Interagency collaboration is greatly emphasised in this strategy to ensure the effective delivery of public services. The government also needs to satisfy the requirements of justice in the face of terrorism. Given the magnitude of the number of victims of communist terrorists over the past years and up to the present, the government has to carry out serious efforts to bring communist terrorists who are responsible for arson attacks, rape, kidnapping for ransom, murder of civilians, local chief executives, law enforcement officials, and mass murders to justice.

References

Anadolu Agency. Philippines: NPA collects P1.2B in extortion activities. September 26, 2017.

CNN Philippines. Police officer killed in class with NPA in Sagada. January 19, 2023.

CNN Philippines. Four policemen killed. July 19, 2019.

Daily Guardian. Rebels earning P1 million a month through extortion. September 15, 2022.

Executive Order Number 21. (2001). *National internal security plan*. Manila, Philippines: Office of the President.

Executive Order No. 70. (2018). The president of the philippines. Available at, https://www.officialgazette.gov.ph/2018/12/04/executive-order-no-70-s-2018/

Fabe, A.P. (2021). Countering the financing of terrorism and financial technology: Assessing Philippine risks and evaluating responses. *National Security Review*, *I*(2), 36–39.

Fridovich, D., and Krawchuk, F.T. (1st Quarter 2007). Winning in the Pacific: The special operations forces indirect approach. *Joint Force Quarterly (JFQ) Forum*, Issue 44, 26–27.

GMA news. NPAs set fire to Cagayan road-building project. March 1, 2019.

Human Rights Watch. Rebels execute 3 after sham trials. November 21, 2022.

Inquirer.net. Cop dies fighting off NPA kidnap try in Agusan del Norte. December 14, 2018.

Parlade, A. G. (2006). An analysis of the Communist insurgency in the Philippines. Master's Thesis, U.S. Army Command and General Staff College. Ft. Leavenworth, Kansas. https://apps.dtic.mil/sti/tr/pdf/ADA463770.pdf

Philippine Daily Inquirer. NPA terrorists burn equipment of the Kaliwa Dam Project. February 10, 2019.

Philippine Congress. (2020). *Anti-terrorism act of 2020*. Quezon City, Philippines: Congressional Laws.

Philippine News Agency. No halt to NTF-ELCAC projects despite leadership transition. January 19, 2023.

Philippine News Agency. Honor victims by denouncing the NPA brutality: Army Exec. September 3, 2021.

Philippine News Agency. Surigao Norte cop abducted, slain by NPA: Army says. August 19, 2020.

Philippine News Agency. CPP-NPA-NDF rake in millions from poll extortions. October 11, 2021.

Philippine News Agency. Sexual abuse, rape rampant inside CPP-NPA-NDF: Ex-cadre. March 16, 2022.

Philippine Star. Graves of CPP-NPA purge victims uncovered. May 15, 2006.

Philippine Star. NGO cashier convicted of terrorist financing for NPA. March 28, 2023.

Rappler. CPP-NPA takes responsibility for killing of labor leader, UAAP football player in Masbate. June 8, 2021.

The Christian Science Monitor. Human rights abuse pinned on communists. June 9, 1989. UNTV News. " PNP Checks on NPA Mass Grave in Agusan del Norte." November 1, 1988.

The Geneva Conventions of 1949 and their Additional Protocols, ICRC, Geneva. Available at https://www.icrc.org/en/doc/war-and-law/treaties-customary-law/geneva-conventions/overview-geneva-conventions.htm

The Manila Times. (2020, November17). Not an enemy? CPP-NPA killed 50,000 Filipinos — and continues to kill. *The Manila Times*. Available at https://www.manilatimes.net/2020/11/27/opinion/columnists/topanalysis/not-an-enemy-cpp-npa-killed-50000-filipinos-and-continues-to-kill/801807

The Center for International Human Rights. (2020). *The closing of civic space in the Philippines*. New York, NY: John Jay College of Criminal Justice, 5.

Protocol Additional to the Geneva Conventions of 12 August 1949, and relating to the Protection of Victims of International Armed Conflicts (Protocol I), 8 June 1977 available online in full text at www.icrc.org/ihl.nsf/7c4d08d9b287a42141256739003e636b/f6c8b9fee14a77fdc125641e0052b0 79, 2005-12-01.

UN General Assembly. (1989). *United Nations security council resolutions 1267*. New York: UN General Assembly.

UN General Assembly. (1988). *United Nations security council resolutions 2253*. New York: UN General Assembly.

Yuson, M. (2021). *An assessment of Philippine counterinsurgency strategies: Why has communist insurgency continued to exist in the Philippines?* Masteral Thesis. California: US Naval Postgraduate School.

77

ETHNIC DIVIDE AND ARMED INSURGENT GROUPS IN MYANMAR

Biplab Debnath

INTRODUCTION

Myanmar, home to 135 national races, is one of the most ethnically diverse nations in Asia. The ethnic groups mostly fall under eight designated categories: Kachin, Kayah, Kayin, Chin, Mon, Bamar, Rakhine, and Shan (Cline, 2009). The Bamar, most commonly known as the Burman, are the majority ethnic group, comprising 69% of the population, while one-third of the population are ethnic minorities, which include Shan (8.5%), Kayin (6.2%), Rakhine (4.5%), Mon (2.4%), Chin (2.2%), Kachin (1.4%), and Kayah (0.4%) (Thawnghmung & Furnari, 2019). While the Burmans are concentrated in the central plains and Irrawaddy delta region, the minority ethnic groups dwell in the resource-rich peripheral mountainous region bordering Thailand, China, India, and Bangladesh. Even within the broader ethnic group, one can witness a great deal of heterogeneity in terms of language, dialects, and religious affiliations. For instance, Shans are a combination of 33 different ethnic groups speaking four different languages; among Karens, 30% are Christians, 10% are animists, and the rest are Buddhists; and of the eight million people of Mon descent, only one million speak Mon while the rest speak Burmese as their primary language (Cline, 2009).

The roots of the ethnic divide in Myanmar and the consequent assertion of 'minority' rights through numerous ethnic armed organisations (EAO) have a long history. The geographic isolation of the ethnic minorities dwelling in the mountainous terrain meant that they mostly remained unaffected by the political power and control of whatever semblance of state was administering the plains. Neither the ethnic groups themselves nor the rulers, both pre-colonial and colonial, made any attempt to assimilate the frontiers and the plains. Over the years, the hill people were like runaways from the state-making process in the lowlands, cultivating agricultural and social practises designed to purposely evade state power and maintaining their distinct identity to largely dissociate themselves from the majority Burmans in the plains (Dukalskis, 2015).

The colonial period (1886–1947) further accentuated the ethnic divide between the Burmans and the rest. The British policy of dividing Myanmar into 'Ministerial Burma' and 'frontier areas', effectively keeping the latter away from the administrative influence of the former, meant that the frontier areas rarely came under central control. During the Second World War, distraught by their marginalisation in jobs and economic activities that were dominated by Englishmen and Indians during colonial rule, the Barman sided with Japan while ethnic minority groups such as Karen, Shan, Kachin, and Chin supported Great Britain under the latter's assurance of independent statehood in the post-colonial political structure. Frequent conflicts ensued between the Burmese army, trying to suppress the calls for separation, and minority communities, especially the Karen, throughout the 1930s and early 1940s, which led to numerous deaths, displacement, and destruction of villages in Karen territory (Kipgen, 2015).

The challenge of bringing together a diverse set of independently governing ethnic groupings with ill-defined boundaries under a single political unit was realised after the end of British rule, a challenge that persists to this day. At the end of British rule, which left the Burman in charge of Myanmar, a working agreement was sought in 1947 at Panglong between General Aung San, the premier of the British Crown Colony of Burma, and major ethnic groups such as Kachin, Shan, and Chin to establish a Union of Burma that provided substantial autonomy to ethnic groups and even succession rights after ten years. However, the absence of Karen, Mon, and Arakanese groups in the conference and the lack of uniformity in the rights promised to different ethnic groups led to frequent inter-ethnic clashes. Ang Sung's demise, just months after the Panglong conference, halted the reconciliation process as his successor, U Nu, the first Prime Minister of independent Burma, could not sustain the momentum going forward. The constitution of 1947, formulated by the Burmese regime in a considerable rush to realise the reality of irresolvable ethnic differences, did not reflect much of the spirit agreed to at Panglong and, as expected, was rejected by many ethnic groups.

DOI: 10.4324/9780429426063-87

The minority ethnic groups accused the Burman leaders of not fulfilling the promise made at Panglong, and a growing sense of neglect and discrimination led them to take up arms to demand their rights (O'Hara & Selling, 2012). This marked the beginning of an unending civil war as numerous minority ethnic groups, with their independent armed organisations, waged a war not only against the Burman-dominated government but also among themselves. The ensuing instability and the lack of central control were ripe for General Ne Win to seize power by overthrowing the Union Parliament of U Nu through a *coup d'etat* in 1962 that the general justified as an attempt to save Burma from disintegration (O'Hara & Selling, 2012). A series of policies by Ne Win – an integrated Burmese Union project through an official religion and language for the entire country, regulation of civil liberties and ethnic expression, rejection of frontier autonomy, etc. – further distanced the minority ethnic groups from the government, thereby intensifying the former's armed resistance against the Tatmadaw. Factors such as an intense nationalisation campaign that involved the suppression of minority language and culture, discrimination against non-Buddhists in jobs and education, and the destruction of their places of worship shaped the negative attitude of ethnic minority groups as they took up arms to protect their land and identity against the ruling junta.

ETHNIC ARMED ORGANISATIONS IN MYANMAR

The civil war in post-independent Myanmar has revolved around three groups: the government of Myanmar, the Communist Party of Burma (CPB), and minority ethnic groups along with their political and military wings, the latter termed the Ethnic Armed Organisation (EAO). While the objectives of the CPB and the EAOs vary – the former is an ideologically well-organised group aspiring for a wholesale regime change based on communist ideas, while the latter aims to protect their people's identity, culture, and territories in the frontier areas – their activities often overlap with each other. While some EAOs have aligned with and many have opposed the CPB, the latter has also recruited heavily from a few insurgent groups, which has the advantage of providing training and experience for those opposing the government (Cline, 2009). While the CPB and EAOs posed a significant internal security threat to the government, clashes within and among minority ethnic groups, as well as those between many EAOs and the CPB, brought to the fore the complexity of the ethnic dynamics in Myanmar.

Since independence, around 40 ethnic groups have taken up arms against the government in Myanmar (Thawnghmung & Furnari, 2019). They vary in size, with some large groups such as the Kachin Independence Army (KIA), Karen National Liberation Army (KNLA), and United Wa State Party (UWSA) possessing troops ranging from 5,000 to 25,000, while there are smaller ones with only a few recruits. Over the years, new insurgent groups have emerged; many older ones became weaker and surrendered to the government; a few groups splintered from their parent organisation to form a new one; many formed alliances with other EAOs on a common agenda; and a few joined the government in an armed conflict with their fellow EAOs. The EAOs also altered their objectives and strategies vis-à-vis the government depending on their capabilities and circumstances. Starting with a demand for full independence, a majority of the ethnic groups subsequently adjusted their political objectives to ask for limited autonomy within a federal structure. While many ethnic groups agreed to a ceasefire agreement with the government and joined the peace process, some refused to do so, while others broke off the ceasefire agreement to resume armed conflict against the government.

Given the multitude of ethnic armed groups in Myanmar, the chapter, while avoiding an individual analysis of all, selected four major ones for in-depth analysis: the Karen National Liberation Army, the Kachin Independence Army, the United Wa State Army, and the Shan State Army (South). The four EAOs are the most influential insurgent group representing the interests of their ethnic community, belong to different time periods, have a few differing objectives, have different equations with other EAOs and the Tatmadaw, and as a result, have evolved on different trajectories from each other. More importantly, on causes of formation, grievances, structure, organisational strategies, alliances, and relations with the government, etc., these four groups reflect the dynamics of insurgency across the country.

KAREN NATIONAL LIBERATION ARMY (KNLA)

The Karen National Liberation Army (KNLA) is the armed wing of the Karen National Union (KNU), the political organisation formed in 1947 to represent the interests of the Karen ethnic group, and is the oldest ethnic armed organisation involved in the longest-running civil war in Myanmar (Romaniuk, 2015). The roots of KNU's formation can be traced to the ethnic conflicts between the Karen and the Burmese that date back to the pre-independence period. During colonial rule, the suppression of the Burmese rebellion against the Britishers by the British Army, which comprised around 38% of Karens, created considerable animosity and violence between the two communities throughout the 1930s and 1940s (Dukalskis, 2015; Kipgen, 2015). However, the real source of Karen discontent lay in what they believed was an unfulfilled promise of an independent Karen state in Great Britain as a reward to the ethnic group for fighting alongside their colonial masters during the Second World War. Instead, the Karen found themselves the victims of atrocities committed by the post-colonial Burmese government dominated by the Barmans. Karen's discontent with the Panglong conference and the subsequent constitution of 1947; the arrest of Karen leaders, especially Smith Dun, the commander-in-chief of the armed force of Myanmar, to be replaced by a Bamar nationalist, Ne Win; and the armed offensive by the Tatmadaw in the Karen areas led the ethnic group to initiate a prolonged armed resistance against the government forces since 1949.

While the KNU served as the political platform of the Karen movement, it had two successive military branches: the Karen National Defence Organisation (KNDO), formed by the KNU in 1947, undertook armed resistance until 1949, following which the Karen National Liberation Army (KNLA) was made the official military wing. The KNLA was once the strongest of all ethnic armed groups, boasting a powerful army of 20,000 soldiers during its peak in the 1980s, but its military strength has declined significantly in recent times (Cline, 2009). In the initial stages, KNU controlled a large portion of territory in northern Burma, including Mandalay, the Instein town on the outskirts of Rangoon, and a significant portion of territory along the border with Thailand (Dukalskis, 2015). The KNLA started with the objective of setting up an independent Karen state, encompassing the present-day territories of Kayin and Kayah in outer Myanmar. KNLA's political wing, the KNU, established a political and administrative structure in the Karen state with ministries for education, health, and agriculture, a military and police apparatus, and a taxation system, besides promoting Karen cultural values and traditions (O'Hara & Selling, 2012).

Since 1949, the KNLA has engaged in a violent armed conflict with the Burmese army in one of the longest-running civil wars in the country. They conducted military operations mostly with small arms, mainly AK-47s and other assault rifles, though getting access to these weapons in recent times has been difficult for the group (O'Hara & Selling, 2012). KNLA is also known to use landmines as a deterrent to army encroachment, even though in many cases, civilians end up being the victims of the strategy. The group is also infamous for recruiting child soldiers, a policy that generates considerable grievance among the local populace and repudiation in the international community.

Over the years, the KNLA/KNU has received considerable international support, especially from the Western world. Confronted with long-running discrimination, military assault, human rights violations, and displacement at the hands of the military junta, the Karen community is viewed with considerable sympathy, which in turn generates international support for the armed organisation. The preponderance of Christians in KNU likely led to its greater visibility among foreign supporters, especially financial donors (Cline, 2009). A large proportion of the Karen Diaspora community also stands up for the goals of the KNLA and provides economic assistance for the armed group. As far as nation-states are concerned, KNLA's relations with Thailand, a traditional supporter of the group, have transformed in recent times. From turning a blind eye to the cross-border smuggling of weapons in Karen areas, Thai support for the group has waned in recent years on account of the country's attempt to engage with Myanmar in a range of development and cross-border connectivity projects. In fact, in support of the Myanmar government's military offensive in Karen State, the Thai government has also ordered the KNU to leave all Thai territory (O'Hara & Selling, 2012).

In a notable development that considerably weakened the KNLA, a group of Buddhist soldiers and officers, complaining about marginalisation on religious lines by the majority of Christians, split from the KNU in 1994 to form the Democratic Karen Buddhist Organization (DKBO) along with its military arm, the Democratic Karen Buddhist Army (DKBA), with a strength of around 6,000 troops. The splinter group, unlike the KNU, not only entered into a working alliance with the Myanmar government in return for military and financial assistance but also joined hands with the Myanmar army in the government's counter-insurgency operations against the KNLA. The DKBO fractured further after becoming a part of the Border Guards Force (BGF), a scheme initiated by the State Peace and Development Council (SPDC) government in Myanmar in 2009 wherein all the armed insurgent groups have to transform themselves into border guards forces and serve under the command of the Burmese army. In 2010, Bo Nat Khann Mway, in opposition to the BGF, led around 1500 personnel and splintered from the DKBO to form the Democratic Karen Benevolent Army, Brigade 5 (DKBA-5) and resumed armed struggle against the Tatmadaw (Sharma, 2014).

Relentless counter-insurgency campaigns by the Burmese military government against the KNLA since 1949, in an unending civil war lasting six decades, have resulted in thousands of deaths, over a million refugees and internally displaced people, and poverty and underdevelopment in the Karen areas (Thawnghmung & Furnari, 2019). Since Burma's independence, the KNLA has been among the primary targets of the government's counter-insurgency strategy, for which the majority of the armed forces, numbering around 135,000 personnel in 1964, were mobilised (Kuppuswamy, 2013). Under Ne Win, the army employed the *Pya Ley Pya*, or "four cuts" policy, an adaptation of the British strategy during the Malayan Emergency, of cutting off the insurgents from their key inputs: funding, food, intelligence, and recruits (Abrahamain, 2017). As a component of the 'four cuts' strategy, the army used villages as a line of defence, established a "people's militia" with villagers who were forced to fight on the government side as porters and guards, recruited child soldiers, deployed landmines, and used locals as human minesweepers where they were forced to walk ahead of the military units in suspected landmine areas (Cline, 2009). The military junta also received military assistance from China and looked to China to combat the KNLA.

While 'fours cuts' did pay dividends for the government militarily as well as in shrinking the revenue generation of the KNLA, the strategy did have its pitfalls, the most notable being the sense of resentment it generated among the locals, which in turn metamorphosed into sympathy for the armed group (Kipgen, 2015). Militarily, the army's ruthless counter-insurgency efforts did erode the KNLA's territorial control, as the insurgents had to recede to what is termed "hiding villages" across the borders, from where the group employed hit-and-run tactics in a desperate attempt to protect and administer the pockets that are still in their control (Dukalskis, 2015). Since its split in 1994, the KNLA has also been fighting on two fronts: against the Tatmadaw on the one hand and the DKBA, which enjoyed the support of the Myanmar army, on the other. The ceasefire agreements initiated by the government with EAOs since the 1990s did not help non-ceasefire groups like the KNU and KNLA, as the military, now with relatively fewer groups to deal with, could channel the military campaign against the KNLA (Thawnghmung & Furnari, 2019). The fall of Manerplaw in 1995, the headquarters of the KNLA as well as home to thousands of pro-democracy activists fighting against the military junta, was a significant blow to the Karen armed resistance.

KNLA's diminished influence, as a result of the government's military offensive as well as due to internal factions, compelled the group to engage in ceasefire talks with the Myanmar government since the mid-1990s, a move that it has avoided for almost 50 years. From 1995 to 2012, representatives from the KNU and the Myanmar government met multiple times to work out a ceasefire, only for the negotiations to break down due to a lack of any substantial common ground. One major hiatus was the government's condition for the insurgent group to denounce violence as a precondition to entering into a political dialogue, a demand that was outrightly rejected by the KNLA (Kipgen, 2015). Each breakdown of ceasefire talks led to a resumption of armed hostilities between the KNLA and the Burmese army, either unaided or in collaboration with the DKBA, resulting in a mass exodus of refugees across the borders of Thailand. In fact, the KNLA-Tatmadaw conflict has induced one of the least reported refugee crises, with about 100,000 refugees living in rudimentary camps across the Myanmar-Thailand border (Routray, 2013).

In 2011, the KNU joined ten other ethnic insurgent groups in establishing the United Nationalities Federal Council (UNFC), an alliance of armed ethnic groups created to have a united front in the ceasefire negotiations with the government, only to leave the alliance a few months later to negotiate in 2012 a bilateral ceasefire agreement with the Union Solidarity and Development (USDP) led government (Thawnghmung & Furnari, 2019). Subsequently, KNU signed the Nationwide Ceasefire Agreement (NCA) in 2015, a long-term peace initiative by the Myanmar government to end armed hostilities and set off a peace process through union-level ceasefire agreements with ethnic armed organisations (EAOs). In a notable transformation from its formative years, the KNU is not just a signatory to the NCA but also a leading member, driving many other ethnic insurgent groups into the NCA process. However, while the ceasefire agreement and the NCA are positive developments, a lasting political solution may still have a long way to go. Long-standing distrust between the KNU/KNLA and the Myanmar government has disrupted the peace process numerous times. Despite KNU's status as an NCA signatory, clashes between the Burmese Army and the KNLA have continued unabated, with the insurgent group accusing the government forces of violating the ceasefire. One prominent bone of contention is the road construction project by the Tatmadaw in the KNLA-controlled Ler Mu Plaw area of Hpapun district, where armed conflict between the insurgent group and government forces has led to the displacement of more than 2,400 villagers (Nyein, 2018). After a temporary halt, the renewal of construction activities has led to over 50 clashes in the first few months of 2020 (Network Media Group, 2020). The renewal of conflict is a reflection of the fact that durable peace in Myanmar has to go beyond mere ceasefire agreements and address the genuine grievances of the insurgent groups.

KACHIN INDEPENDENCE ARMY

The Kachin Independence Army (KIA), the armed wing of the Kachin Independence Organization (KIO), is the most prominent ethnic armed insurgent group in the Kachin region. The formation of KIA is rooted in a similar set of grievances, as was evident in the case of the Karens. With a population of approximately 1.5 million (Kipgen, 2015), the Kachins, like the Karens, formed a significant part of the British army and hoped for an independent Kachin state as a reward for their service. The Kachin also resented the discrimination meted out by the Burmese majority, stifling the minority ethnic group's identity, culture, and autonomy. However, unlike the Karen, the Kachin leaders signed the Panglong Agreement in 1947, which provided for the formation of the Kachin state. The Kachin leaders remained in the agreement for a decade, despite the lack of any substantial progress towards their goal of independence, after which they were compelled to change their position. Preferential treatment by the state to the majority Burman, U Nu's decision to introduce Buddhism as a state religion, and the transfer of three Kachin villages to China in 1960 under the China-Myanmar border agreement prompted the Kachin to initiate an organised armed resistance against the military junta. Two former soldiers of the Burmese Army, Lamung Tu Jai and Lama La Ring, along with Zaw Seng, a former Karen National Defense Organization (KNDO) agent, formed the KIO in 1960. Subsequently, on February 5, 1960, KIA, as the military wing, was formed under the command of Zau Say. This marked the beginning of an organised armed resistance movement against the Tatmadaw with the primary goal of an independent Kachin state.

Since its formation, the KIA has expanded significantly to now consist of approximately 10,000 troops with another 10,000 civilian reserves operating in eight brigades across the Kachin and Northern Shan states (Myanmar Peace Monitor, n.d.). KIA's ammunition mostly includes AK-47s and homemade rifles such as the KA-078 as well as landmines, which the group uses in guerilla warfare against the Tatmadaw. The insurgent group consistently recruits child soldiers, currently numbering around 1,000, mainly by tweaking the system of "national service," which requires compulsory military and non-military service for everyone between the ages of 18 and 60, including children below the age of 18 in the first batch of recruits (Child Soldiers International, 2015). Within its territory, the KIA maintains an elaborate system of administration that includes a police department, educational institutes, a fire brigade, an immigration department, and hospitals, among other bureaucratic machinery. Revenue mainly comes from exploiting natural resources such as gold, jade, and timber, along with taxes from a lucrative cross-border trade with China, with which KIA maintains strong business and commercial links (Sharma, 2014). Such earnings have enabled the insurgent group not just to create and maintain a powerful army but also to develop trade centres in several cities along the Sino-Myanmar border (Myanmar Peace Monitor, n.d.).

After a few rounds of failed talks in 1963 and 1980, resulting in more than two decades of armed conflict between the KIA and the Burmese army, a ceasefire agreement was concluded in 1994 between the insurgent group and the then-ruling State Peace and Development Council (SLORC) military junta. KIA's decision to sign a ceasefire agreement can be attributed to a number of factors. Firstly, the KIA, instead of having a consistent and coherent ideology, was rather pragmatic and flexible in assessing the strengths and weaknesses of its own as well as those of its friends and foes (O'Hara & Selling, 2012; Dukalskis, 2015). Such pragmatism is apparent in KIA's objectives as well as in its relations with other actors, especially the Communist Party of Burma (CPB). After the breakdown of the 1963 peace talks over KIA's unwavering demand for an independent Kachinland, KIA subsequently decided on a more moderate political goal of an autonomous state as part of the federal union. Similarly, after fighting against the communist forces since 1976, the KIA shifted towards a pro-communist stance to develop an alliance with the CPB that was strong enough for the insurgent group to receive arms from China through the CPB's trading networks (O'Hara & Selling, 2012). Secondly, KIA has geopolitical limitations over the territory it controls. The KIA-controlled territory is not a solid chunk of land but a patchy network of rural areas with overlapping control among multiple actors, including the KIA, the Burmese state, and other Kachin groups like the New Democratic Army-Kachin (NDA-K) (O'Hara & Selling, 2012). Moreover, Kachin administration is more decentralised as compared to other insurgent groups with the presence of a vibrant civil society, meaning that the insurgent group may not directly administer the areas that it militarily controlled (O'Hara & Selling, 2012; Dukalskis, 2015). Worse still, KIA lost a substantial amount of territory due to numerous counter-insurgency operations by the Burmese Army, resulting in thousands of internally displaced people being forced to move from the highlands to low-lying plains (Kipgen, 2015). From 1988 to 1992, Burmese counter-insurgency operations forcefully relocated up to 100,000 Kachins (O'Hara & Selling, 2012). In fact, the negotiation of the ceasefire agreement preceded a military offensive by the Tatmadaw that seized most of the jade mines in Kachin state. In such circumstances, the ceasefire agreement was a pragmatic political decision to at least retain the territory that was still under control.

Though the ceasefire agreement put a halt to armed conflict between the KIA and Tatmadaw, the government strategically utilised the agreement to almost triple its armed presence in the Kachin state and steadily limit the KIA's mobility through land confiscation, forced labour, and other human rights abuses (Cline, 2009; Kipgen, 2015). As a result, despite the ceasefire agreement, tensions between the contending parties prevailed as KIA resisted the military mobilisation of the Burmese armed forces. The declining capability of the KIA to unilaterally challenge the government forces also led the insurgent group to join the UNFC in 2011 and the Northern Alliance in 2016. As expected, the truce between the KIA and the Myanmar government was short-lived, as by 2010, irreconcilable differences between the two led to the resumption of armed conflict. KIA's opposition to the Border Guards Force, classification of KIA as an 'insurgent' rather than a 'ceasefire' group in 2010 by a state-run newspaper, restrictions on China-KIA border trade by the military junta, and Kachin opposition against the proposed Myitsone Dam project, which can destroy a dozen Karen villages displacing thousands of locals, are some of the reasons for the breakdown of the ceasefire agreement (O'Hara & Selling, 2012). In 2012, the Burmese military launched a full-scale attack on the KIA using heavy artillery such as helicopters, gunships, and aircraft to bomb KIA positions (Ganesan, 2015). The ensuing conflict, besides leaving heavy casualties on both sides, resulted in 90,000 internally displaced people – 30,000 in government-controlled areas and 60,000 taking refuge in Kachin State (Routray, 2013). Following a ceasefire by the Union Solidarity and Development Party (USDP)-led central government in 2013, two rounds of peace talks were held in February and March 2013 hosted by China, which, on its part, was keen to resolve the situation peacefully as the country's Yunan province bordering the KIA region was affected by shelling in the 2012 conflict (Ganesan, 2015). While the peace talks led to a preliminary ceasefire in May 2013, bitter historical experiences and mistrust between the two parties did not lead to a lasting solution. It was evident in the shelling of KIA's cadet training school in November 2014 by the military, killing 23 trainees (Ferrie, 2014), the attack by KIA, as a part of the Northern Alliance, on Muse township along the China-Myanmar border in 2016 (Gilani, 2020), and more recently on a military college in Nawnghkio township in August 2019 (Aung, 2019). Incidentally, 2018 has witnessed the worst outbreak of violence in decades between the Tatmadaw and the KIA in the townships of Sumprabum, Waingmav, and Tanai, where Tatmadew shelled KIA positions and engaged in a series of human rights abuses like disproportionate attacks, extra-judicial killings, enforced displacements, torture, and rape, thereby adding to the 120,000 internally displaced persons living in the squid camps of Kachin (Hart, 2018). Currently, KIO remains a non-signatory to the NCA process, and persistent armed conflict with the government forces presents the most pressing challenge to a durable political solution in Myanmar.

THE UNITED WA STATE ARMY

Formed in 1989, the United Wa State Army (UWSA) is among the more recent ethnic armed organisations in Myanmar. UWSA represents the interests of the Wa people, an ethnic group residing in northern Myanmar along the China-Myanmar border. For centuries, the Wa people have succeeded in avoiding direct central leadership, including British control during the colonial period, not just due to their settlement in unbidden geographic terrain at the frontiers but also because of a perception of the Wa people as wild, uncivilised, and a violent group adverse to outsiders. After Burma's independence, the ethnic group came under the influence of the Communist Party of Burma (CPB), as the latter recruited a large number of Wa people and supplied them with modern weaponry. In fact, many of the rank-and-file soldiers of the CPB until 1989 were Wa, even though the leadership was largely Burman (Dukalskis, 2015). The influx of communist forces in the Wa region, where they developed military bases, dragged the ethnic group into a military conflict with the government (O'Hara & Selling, 2012). However, while the Wa people were adverse and distrustful towards the central leadership in Burma, their dislike for the CPB was to no lesser degree. Many in the Wa community believed the communist insurgency to be a 'sham revolt' that cheated on the Wa region and its people (Dukalskis, 2015). This perception was because the Burman-controlled CPB made little effort to develop physical infrastructure and administrative capacity in the Wa region, especially in the rural areas, and provide their people with a viable economic avenue (O'Hara & Selling, 2012; Dukalskis, 2015). Thus, in 1989, when the CPB was on the verge of disintegration, the Wa soldiers took over the party head-quarters, arrested their leaders, took control of their weapons, and subsequently formed the United Wa State Party (UWSP) and its armed wing, the United Wa State Army (UWSA) (Dukalskis, 2015).

With a strength of around 30,000 active military personnel (Kai, 2016), the UWSA is one of the largest and most powerful ethnic armed organisations in Myanmar. It has a total of eight divisions: five along the Myanmar-Thailand border and three along Myanmar's border with China. The UWSA operates in the area termed "special region 2" with a population of around 600,000 people, mostly ethnic Wa, where the armed group has established a system of administration that includes health services, education, agriculture, treasury, and external relations (O'Hara & Selling, 2012). They are reported to possess a sophisticated stockpile of weapons that includes light and heavy machine guns, rocket-propelled grenades, mortars, the QBZ-95 assault rifle, CS/LS06 9 mm sub-machine guns, M-99 12.7 mm anti-materiel rifles, the FN-6 man-portable air defence system (MANPADS), HJ-8 Red Arrow wire-guided anti-tank missiles, 107 mm surface-to-surface free-flight missiles, armoured personnel carriers (APC), MIL-MI-17 helicopters armed with TY-90 air-to-air missiles, etc. (Davis, 2019). UWSA also has its own arms production units that develop a line of AK-47s (Weng, 2008), an activity that acts as a supplementary income source to trafficking drugs. However, most of UWSA's weapons come from China, a country that also imparts training to the group's members and provides technical capability building in arms production. The USWA maintains a close connection with Chinese arms trading networks, with the group often acting as a middleman between Chinese arms manufacturers and insurgent groups in northeast India (O'Hara & Selling, 2012). The UWSA has also gained notoriety for the recruitment of child soldiers. In fact, among all the ethnic armed groups in Myanmar, UWSA is alleged to be the biggest recruiter of child soldiers, with 2000 of them under the age of 18 and 600–800 recruits less than 15 years of age (Heppner, 2002). UWSA, however, denies the allegations, pointing out that the children are orphans to whom the group imparts education and livelihood training rather than recruiting them as child soldiers (Han, 2019).

UWSA's military standing is, however, primarily attributed to the income it generates through the production and trafficking of drugs. While most insurgent groups in Myanmar are engaged in the drug business, the level of concession provided to the UWSA by the government of Myanmar is not extended to any other group, which enables the UWSA to expand its drug trade logistics without any government interference. Consequently, the UWSA has attained the status of a major drug supplier to China, Laos, Thailand, and the Northeast region of India. With a ban on poppy cultivation under the government's strict anti-drug policy since 2000, the UWSA has managed to diversify its business to become a global player in synthetic drugs (O'Hara & Selling, 2012). In fact, in 2008, the U.S. labelled UWSA as the largest and most powerful drug trafficking organisation in Southeast Asia and a major producer of synthetic drugs, including methamphetamine (O'Hara & Selling, 2012). The inextricable link between drugs and politics in Myanmar has also put the government in a quandary. While the government is keen to get hold of the insurgent areas, the lack of alternative economic opportunities other than the drug trade makes the government's ban on drugs have the effect of inviting the displeasure of the local population. However, in recent times, the UWSA has been trying to clean up its image as a drug hub to attract foreign investment in the Wa territory by assisting the government in the latter's anti-drug initiative. UWSA has caught and handed over drugs and suspected drug traffickers a number of times, as it did in May 2020 by handing over 351 million illegal stimulant pills to the Tatmadev military (Mon, 2020).

Unlike many other ethnic armed organisations in Myanmar, UWSA never sought complete independence as their political goal. What they aim is to break free from the Shan state and create an autonomous Wa state directly under the responsibility of the central government (O'Hara & Selling, 2012). In 2009, UWSA declared its territory as the 'Wa State Government Special Administrative Region', a status which the Myanmar government refuses to recognise. The 2008 constitution, by contrast, refers to the Wa territory as 'Wa Administered Division', excluding many UWSA claimed territories, especially Mong Pawk and Hato areas which the armed group claims to be managing for more than three decades (O'Hara & Selling, 2012).

UWSA's disagreement with the Myanmar government on territoriality does not prevent the ethnic group from enjoying a level of nexus with the government that no other group does. The UWSA agreed to a ceasefire agreement with the government in 1989, within months of its formation. The agreement enabled UWSA to administer its territory, effectively maintain its army, and expand its lucrative trade in drugs and small arms without any government interference. The fact that the SLORC/SDPC troops had to obtain permission to enter the UWSA-administered territory reflects the level of administrative freedom and control that the armed group enjoys. In return, besides refraining from its demand for complete independence, the UWSA acts like the government's private army, conducting joint military action not just against government-opposed ethnic groups but also against other states such as Thailand. In 1996, the UWSA helped the Burmese military fight Shan insurgents, which led to the surrender of drug lord Klun Sa and his Mong Tai Army (Sharma, 2014). Both have also clashed with the Thai troops, with Thailand harbouring a long-standing suspicion of the UWSA because of its communist linkages and blaming the ethnic group for being a major source of drugs flowing into Thailand (O'Hara & Selling, 2012).

While UWSA's links with the Myanmar government are crucial, an external actor vital for the group's sustenance is China. As a breakaway faction of the CPB, the UWSA inherited the past linkages that the CPB enjoyed with China, and currently, the latter is a friend that the UWSA cannot afford to lose (O'Hara & Selling, 2012). For UWSA, China is an essential source of military capability and economic revenue. Besides, opening up the Wa border areas with China is not just lucrative from a business point of view but also symbolically crucial in asserting a self-sufficient, autonomous Wa state (O'Hara & Selling, 2012). China also has considerable influence on USWA's relations with other EAOs as well as the group's approach to the peace process.

On the other hand, UWSA has threaded its relations with the Myanmar government with caution. Currently, a beneficial working alliance with the Myanmar government holds UWSA back from engaging in other agreements, including the ongoing NCA process. While UWSA did not outright reject the BGF proposal, it opposes being under the command of the Tatmadaw and hence refuses to disarm (O'Hara & Selling, 2012). Pressure from the Myanmar government on the EAOs to accede to the BGF and military assaults against some non-conforming groups prompted the UWSA to form alliances with the KIA, National Democratic Alliance Army, SSN-N, and New Moon Party (O'Hara & Selling, 2012). At the same time, UWSA refrains from assisting armed groups facing military action by the Tatmadaw lest UWSA forfeit the current equations with the government besides pressure from China not to develop connections with groups opposing the government (O'Hara & Selling, 2012). Creating complications in the current peace process, the UWSA has neither become a part of the UNFC nor the NCA. Instead, the armed group has taken the lead among many NCA non-signatories in proposing an alternate route to the peacekeeping process (Thawnghmung & Furnari, 2019). For instance, at the Pangong summit in 2015, the UWSA proposed several changes to the draught ceasefire agreement that the National Ceasefire Coordination Team (NCCT) had earlier agreed to (Ganesan, 2015) and insisted that the EAOs enter into a political dialogue with the government on genuine autonomy without being signatories to the NCA (Thawnghmung & Furnari, 2019), a line of thinking that complements the armed group's renewed demands in recent times for a separate Wa state. The Myanmar government, given UWSA's links with China and apprehensive of the influence that UWSA's presence at the NCA process might have on other EAOs, has not insisted on USWA joining the NCA. UWSA's complex equations with the government, other EAOs, and external actors like China create a distinct level of complexity for a viable all-inclusive peace process in Myanmar.

THE SHAN STATE ARMY, SOUTH

The Shan State Army-South (SSA-S) is the largest armed group in the Shan state, representing the interests of the Shan community. While the ethnic group's fight for identity and independence against the majority Burmans dates back to the pre-independence era, the SSA-S is the most contemporary of all groups discussed here and is engaged in an armed conflict against the military junta. The SAA-S was formed in 1996 as a breakaway faction from the Mong Tai Army (MTA), under the leadership of Lieutenant General Yawd Serk, after he refused to follow the path of the MTA, which, following a prolonged period of fighting the Tatmadaw, laid down their arms and surrendered in 1995.

From approximately 1000 soldiers during the time of its formation, the SSA-S has grown in strength to now consist of around 7,000 soldiers under the control of village heads and emerged as a prominent anti-government armed group in Myanmar (Dukalskis, 2015). SSA-S primarily operates along the Thai-Myanmar border, where it has established five bases, with Loi Tai as the largest base, one of which also serves as the headquarters of the insurgent group. While SSA-S maintains some administrative units in Loi Tai, such as schools and training centres for the new recruits, the group's overall administrative territory is relatively small and non-contiguous, as in the case of Loi Tai itself, which cannot be accessed without passing through Thai territory (Dukalskis, 2015). In 2000, SSA-S formed its political wing, the Restoration Council of Shan State (RCSS), with seven central executive committees under the chairmanship of Yawd Serk. Since an initial demand for independence in 2011, SSA-S has sought autonomy within a federal Burma. However, small Shan groups do on occasion continue to call for independence, as Shan state exiles did in 2005, but without much effect.

A considerable number of the recruits made by the SSA-S are children, teenagers, and orphans. In a communication to Human Rights Watch, the SSA-S admitted to the conscription of teenagers with a minimum age of 16 until 2011, after which the group modified the policy to stop recruiting people below 18 years of age (Facts & Details, n.d.). SSA-S also admitted to a programme called *nang harn*, "meaning brave girls," under which basic rudimentary training, including weapons training, is provided for teenage girls so that they are not used in combat roles (Ibid.). However, allegations of the recruitment of child soldiers are regularly made by the Burmese government against SAA-S. Human Rights Watch, while stating that the SSA-S does not use child soldiers widely, nevertheless prescribes close monitoring of the insurgent group given the increased pace of recruitment, thereby not completely ruling out the possibility (Ibid.).

The SSA-S carried out raids in the southern Shan state and is linked with other organs of Shan nationalism, including other Shan ceasefire groups, the Shan Nationalities League for Democracy (SNLD), and civil society groups based in Thailand (Dukalskis, 2015). In 2005, the SSA-S formed a working alliance with the Shan State National Army (SSNA), another group from the MTA, which eventually led to the merger of the SSNA with the SSA-S for the common cause of the independence of the Shan state. In 2008, RCSS, along with the Lahu Democratic Union (LDU), Pa-O National Liberation Organization (PNLO), Tai Coordination Committee, and Wa National Organization (WNO), formed the Shan State Congress. The SSA-S is also a member of the parallel ethnic alliance, the National Democratic Front (NDF), and a full member of the UNFC (Sharma, 2014).

For two decades, the SSA-S has engaged in armed conflicts not just against the Tatmadaw but also with the Wa Army, a rival ethnic group allied to the military junta. The clashes have led to numerous casualties on both sides, including villages, and the forced evacuation of thousands of local villagers to refugee camps in Thailand. Between 1996 and 1998, around 1,000 villages in central Shan state were shut down, forcing around 300,000 people to take shelter in the so-called 'strategic helmets', with their original abodes converted to 'free-fire zones' by the military from where they could pursue insurgents without locals getting in the way (Facts & Details, n.d.). While there are reports of severe human rights abuses, including rape, mass killing, and forced labour by the Tatmadaw, the SSA-S is accused of seizing government outposts and capturing and killing Myanmar soldiers. Insurgent activities have also flared up tensions between Myanmar and Thailand, which shares a border with the Shan area, with Myanmar accusing the Thai government of supporting Shan rebels (Facts & Details, n.d.).

In 2011, the SSA-S agreed to a ceasefire agreement with the USDP-led government while receding from its earlier demand for complete independence to now demanding autonomy within a federal Burma. The diminishing strength and influence of the insurgent group over a decentralised territory, lack of coherent ideology, and short life span of the group without a long history of mistrust and failed arguments with the government were some of the factors behind the willingness of SSA-S to a ceasefire agreement (Dukalskis, 2015). The group signed an 11-point agreement with the government that provides for joint coordination on several issues such as township administration, the security of SAA-S leaders, demarcation of the area of control, the opening of liaison offices, the business activities of SSA-S, combating drug trafficking, and overall regional development. The SSA-S/RCSS also agreed to and signed the NCA in 2015, leading to the removal of the group from the government blacklist (Ganesan, 2015).

While a welcome development, the inclusion of the SSA-S at the negotiating table of the peace process did not lead to a complete cessation of hostilities, as armed hostilities, both inter-ethnic and between the SSA-S and the Tatmadaw, continue to disrupt a durable ceasefire. The animosity between the SSA-S and the government has been growing due to Tatmadew's continued forced withdrawal of Shan insurgents from bases with rich economic incentives. Within three years of the ceasefire agreement, around 100 clashes between the Tatmadaw and the SSA-S were reported, including a government attack in 2013 on a base at Nam Kham township, displacing around 1000 villages, and an army shell attack in 2014 at Shan villages, leading to the evacuation of 180 villagers (Facts & Details, n.d.). After signing the NCA, the RCSS/SSA-S increased its presence in the northern Shan state, which led to inter-ethnic clashes with the Ta'ang National Liberation Army (TNLA), which has joined the Shan State Army-North (SSN-N) to fight the SSA-S ("Understanding Inter-Ethnic Conflict in Myanmar", 2018). In 2018, much of the fighting between the SSA-S and the TNLA was due to recourse wars that occurred in and around the resource-rich Namtu Township ("Understanding Inter-Ethnic Conflict in Myanmar", 2018). Even in recent times, conflicts between government forces and SSA-S have resulted in growing political instability and human rights violations. Even with the declaration of a unilateral ceasefire in May 2020 by the NLD-led government in Myanmar to focus on the COVID-19 pandemic, clashes occurred between the army and the SSA-S that led to the displacement of 500 villages in Kyaukme (Quadrini, 2020). Such political instability in Shan State presents the most serious challenge to the current peace process in Myanmar.

CONCLUSION

The conflict between the government and ethnically armed insurgent groups has been a perennial feature in Myanmar since independence. However, the trajectory of insurgency in Myanmar did undergo many changes that could be explained by the transformations in EAO's capacity, objectives, and relationship dynamics with the government and other ethnic groups. One noticeable feature is the declining capacity of the many EAOs to mount as big a unilateral military challenge to the Tatmadaw as they once could. There is evidence of wariness among many insurgent groups. With a third or fourth generation of recruits and being cornered by the government's stringent counter-insurgency measures, the groups are essentially fighting a defensive war to protect whatever remaining territory they control. Besides this, internal factions leading to splinter groups, a reduction in revenue generation, inter-ethnic conflicts due to overlapping territorial claims, and a lack of a common strategy have further weakened the capacity of the insurgent groups to mount a unified armed challenge against the government forces.

Despite this, complete government control over insurgent activities has yet to happen. While many small insurgent groups, as well as large ones with reduced capabilities, have agreed to a ceasefire agreement, many have declined to negotiate such an agreement and continue to engage in armed hostility against the government. Worse still, many signatories to the ceasefire have abandoned the negotiations and resumed conflict. The end result is that the NCA has failed in its primary objective of maintaining peace between the Tatmadaw and the EAOs. The distrust of the minority ethnic groups against the majority Barman runs deep, which prevents the EAOs from surrendering their arms.

This is a primary challenge confronting the current NLD-led government of Myanmar. While Suu Kyi has pointed out the ongoing peace process as the government's top priority and initiated the 21st Century Panglong Conference in 2016, bringing the representatives of the EAOs to the negotiating table, the disagreements are strong enough to prevent a viable political solution. Issues such as self-determination, the federal army, and succession continue to evade a final solution. Worse still, armed conflict between the Tatmadaw and insurgent groups in Shan, Kachin, and Karen states continues unabated due to a lack of trust between the contending parties. While the future trajectory of the peace process is still unclear, one can be sure that peace cannot prevail without an inclusive ceasefire process that genuinely addresses the grievances of the ethnic minorities.

References

Abrahamain, A. (2017, 4 September). The Tatmadaw returns to the 'four cuts' doctrine. *Lowy Institute*. Retrieved from https://www.lowyinstitute.org/the-interpreter/tadmadaw-ominous-return-four-cuts-doctrine

Aung, T.T. (2019, 15 August). Myanmar insurgents attack elite military college, other targets; 15 killed. *Reuters*. Retrieved from https://in.reuters.com/article/myanmarinsurgency/myanmar-insurgents-attack-elite-military-college-other-targets-15-killed-idINKCN1V50ER

Boh Ze Kai, B.Z. (2016, 27 January). Narco diplomacy: Foreign policy of the United Wa state army. *Mantraya*. Retrieved from https://mantraya.org/narco-diplomacy-foreign-policy-of-the-united-wa-state-army/

Child Soldiers International. (2015). *A dangerous refuge ongoing child recruitment by the Kachin independence army*. Retrieved from https://resourcecentre.savethechildren.net/node/9339/pdf/childsoldiersinternationalkiareportfinaltoupload online9367343.pdf

Cline, L. (2009). Insurgency in amber: Ethnic opposition groups in Myanmar. *Small Wars & Insurgencies*, *20*(3), 574–591, 10.1080/09592310903027215

Davis, A. (2019, 9 April). It's party time for Myanmar's largest armed ethnic faction. *Asia Times*. Retrieved from https://asiatimes.com/2019/04/anthony-davis-wa-story/

Dukalskis, A. (2015). Why do some insurgent groups agree to cease-fires while others do not? A within-case analysis of Burma/Myanmar, 1948–2011. *Studies in Conflict & Terrorism*, *38*(10), 841–863. 10.1080/1057610X.2015.1056631

Facts and Details. (n.d.). *Shan state army, Shan political groups and the Shan insurgency*. Retrieved 14 September, 2020, from http://factsanddetails.com/southeast-asia/Myanmar/sub5_5k/entry-3063.html

Ferrie, J. (2014, 20 November). Myanmar Kachin rebels say 23 cadets killed by army shell. *Reuters*. Retrieved from https://in.reuters.com/article/myanmar-kachin-casualties-idINKCN0J40IY20141120

Ganesan, N. (2015). Ethnic insurgency and nationwide ceasefire agreement in Myanmar. *Asian Journal of Peacebuilding, 3*(2), 273–286. http://hdl.handle.net/10371/94820

Han, N.B. (2019, 3 April). Tatmadaw discharges young soldiers. *Myanmar Times*. Retrieved from https://www.mmtimes.com/news/tatmadaw-discharges-young-soldiers.html

Hart, M. (2018, 24 May). Myanmar's ethnic conflicts have multiple fronts, and high barriers to peace. *World Politics Review*. Retrieved from https://www.worldpoliticsreview.com/articles/24782/myanmar-s-ethnic-conflicts-have-multiple-fronts-and-high-barriers-to-peace

Heppner, K. (2002). My gun was tall as me: Child soldiers in Burma. *Human Rights Watch*. Retrieved from https://www.hrw.org/reports/2002/burma/Burma0902.pdf.

Iftikhar Gilani, I. (2020, 25 August). Analysis - Myanmar 2 faces: Embrace insurgents, ostracize Rohingya. *Anadolu Agency*. Retrieved from https://www.aa.com.tr/en/analysis/analysis-myanmar-2-faces-embrace-insurgents-ostracize-rohingya/1952789

Kipgen, N. (2015). Ethnicity in Myanmar and its importance to the success of democracy. *Ethnopolitics, 14*(1), 19–31, 10.1080/17449057.2014.926610

Kuppuswamy, C.S. (2013). Challenging the reconciliation process: Myanmar's ethnic divide and conflicts. Retrieved from http://www.jstor.com/stable/resrep09130

Mon, S.L. (2020, 22 May). UWSA turns over millions of pills to Tatmadaw. *Myanmar Times*. Retrieved from https://www.mmtimes.com/news/uwsa-turns-over-millions-pills-tatmadaw.html

Myanmar Peace Monitor. (n.d.). *Kachin independence organization*. Retrieved 23 August 2020, from https://www.mmpeacemonitor.org/1529

Network Media Group (2020, 2 April). First months of 2020 see dozens of clashes between Burma Army, KNU. Retrieved from https://www.bnionline.net/en/news/first-months-2020-see-dozens-clashes-between-burma-army-

Nyein, N. (2018, 17 May). Tatmadaw agrees to halt contentious road project in Karen state. *The Irrawaddy*. Retrieved from https://www.irrawaddy.com/news/burma/tatmadaw-agrees-halt-contentious-road-project-karen-state.html

O'Hara, C., & Selling, N. (2012). *Myanmar's ethnic insurgents: UWSA, KNU and KIO*. Singapore: Institute for Security and Development Policy.

Quadrini, M. (2020, 1 August). Myanmar's ceasefire falls apart in Shan state. *The Diplomat*. Retrieved from https://thediplomat.com/2020/08/myanmars-ceasefire-falls-apart-in-shan-state/

Romaniuk, S. N. (2015). The "father-to-son" WarBurma's Karen nationalist insurgency. InS. N. Romaniuk &T. S. Webb (Eds.), *Insurgency and counterinsurgency in modern war* (pp. 219.–243). Boca Raton: CRC Press.

Routray, B.P. (2013). *Myanmar's national reconciliation an audit of insurgencies and ceasefires an audit of insurgencies and ceasefires*. Retrieved from http://www.ipcs.org/issue_briefs/issue_brief_pdf/SR138-Myanmar-Bibhu.pdf

Sharma, S.J. (2014). Ethnicity and insurgency in Myanmar. *World Affairs: The Journal of Internal Issues, 18*(3), 150–168. https://www.jstor.org/stable/10.2307/48505114

Thawnghmung, A.M., & Furnari, A. (2019). Anti-state armed groups in Myanmar: Origins, evolution and implications. In B. Schreer, & A.T.H. Tan (Eds.), *Terrorism and insurgency in Asia a contemporary examination of terrorist and separatist movements*. (pp. 133–146). Vanderbilt Avenue, New York: Routledge.

Understanding Inter-Ethnic Conflict in Myanmar. (2018, 28 September). The armed conflict location & event data project. Retrieved from https://acleddata.com/2018/09/28/understanding-inter-ethnic-conflict-in-myanmar/

Weng, L. (2008, 16 December). AK-47s—Made in WA state. *The Irrawaddy*. Retrieved from https://www2.irrawaddy.com/article.php?art_id=14804

78

ARAKAN ROHINGYA SALVATION ARMY

Spearheading Myanmar's Islamic Insurgency

Scott N. Romaniuk and Animesh Roul

INTRODUCTION

Myanmar's (formerly Burma's) restive Rakhine State, which was formerly known as Arakan, is facing a violent Muslim insurgency mostly restricted to the three districts of Maungdaw, Buthidaung, and Rathedaung. The prevalent mistrust and hatred between majority Buddhists and the Muslim minority escalated substantially in Rakhine, resulting in infrequent rioting, arson, and widespread unrest between 2012 and 2013, which gave birth to an insurgency under the garb of defending the rights, dignity, and lives of Rohingyas in Myanmar. The insurgency and plight of the Rohingya Muslims due to massive government-backed counter-insurgency measures have been drawing the attention of transnational jihadi groups in support of the Rohingya Muslim community. This insurgency, relatively new in the region, is spearheaded by the Arakan Rohingya Salvation Army (ARSA), headed by Attaullah with the nom de guerre Abu Amar al Joonuni. Even though the insurgency is still in its nascent stage and is mostly subdued and less violent at the moment, frequent clashes with the Myanmar military and counter-insurgency operations in 2017 and 2018 triggered a large-scale migration of local Muslims to neighbouring Bangladesh. This chapter explores the emergence of ARSA as a violent insurgent group and examines the situations behind the rise and consolidation of ARSA in the guise of defending the Rohingya people in Myanmar.

THE MILITARY JUNTA SEIZES POWER

Myanmar has been the target of widespread civil disobedience since the Tatmadaw's February 1, 2022, coup d'état. The Tatmadaw instigated a humanitarian predicament that resulted in the migration of numerous ethnic Rohingyas to the adjacent country of Bangladesh. During the course of the conflict, the ARSA experienced a decline. As an illustration, the quantity of ARSA assaults that were reported in Myanmar experienced a decline from 70 in 2017 to a mere one in 2018. The employment of improvised explosive device (IED) attacks by the Arakan Rohingya Salvation Army (ARSA) has exhibited a decline. Since 2018, the ARSA has been able to execute only five. Since the year 2019, the Arakan Rohingya Salvation Army (ARSA) has engaged in a total of 19 minor armed conflicts with the security forces of Myanmar. The magnitude of these assaults cannot be equated to the "human wave" tactics observed in 2016 and 2017, as the strength of ARSA's troops presently varies from minor factions to platoon-level units. The group's assaults have predominantly been restricted to the hilly topography that extends along the boundary between Myanmar and Bangladesh. The Tatmadaw's resources were reportedly stretched; however, ARSA was unable to take advantage of this situation by initiating any fresh offensives (The Diplomat, January 24, 2022).

RELIGIOUS TENSIONS

Myanmar refuses to recognise its estimated 800,000 Rohingya Muslims as an ethnic group and has denied them citizenship rights. The Rohingyas are considered "outsiders" and illegal immigrants from Bangladesh. In the initial years, militant groups sympathetic to the Rohingya cause from Pakistan, Bangladesh, Indonesia, India, and Afghanistan called for a campaign against the growing Buddhist "969" nationalist movement in Myanmar, spearheaded by radical

DOI: 10.4324/9780429426063-88

Buddhist monk Ashan Wirathu. The Buddhist nationalists maintain that the movement's purpose is to restrict the spread of Islam in predominantly Buddhist countries (Roul, 2013; Ware and Laoutides, 2018). The Buddhist nationalists under Wirathu and the organisation Ma Ba Tha (loosely translated as the Patriotic Association of Myanmar) aim to restrict the spread of Islam and fight to protect the country's Buddhist identity. Arguably, Ma Ba Tha (which morphed into the Buddha Dhamma Prahita Foundation) and Wirathu's messages are often directed against Rohingyas to disenfranchise them further (Frontier Myanmar, June 2016). Wirathu and his followers have been accused of inciting violence through religious hate speeches laced with heavy anti-Islamic rhetoric. Even though anti-Rohingya sentiments remain high in Buddhist-majority Myanmar, the government banned Wirathu to clip the wings of nationalist Buddhists. Ostensibly with the government's nod, the Ma Ha Na (or the State Sangha Maha Nayaka Committee), the highest government-appointed Buddhist clergy, banned Wirathu from delivering sermons across the country for one year, starting from March 10, 2017 (Al Jazeera, March 2017). It was also reported that Wirathu visited the Rohingya-dominated Rakhine districts, subsequently raising communal tensions in the area. However, as of October 2019, Wirathu was declared a fugitive with an arrest warrant against him for his hate-preaching sermons against the Rohingyas and other minority Muslims that had stoked religious tensions in the country. He also faces charges under the country's sedition law for contempt towards the government (Irrawaddy, October 31, 2019).

ARSA: BIRTH OF AN INSURGENCY

Myanmar's government declared ARSA a terrorist organisation following the deadly coordinated attacks on its security installations on August 25, 2017. It declared that ARSA is a threat to national security, and any violence perpetrated by its members would be considered a criminal offence under Myanmar's Penal Code or the 2014 Counter-Terrorism Law.

The factors that led to the emergence and rise of ARSA as a violent insurgent group date back to the intercommunal violent events of June 2012, when three Muslim youths brutally killed a Buddhist woman in the Rakhine village of Kyauknimaw, which triggered Buddhists in the locality to take the law into their own hands. Ten Muslims were killed in a revenge attack in Taunggoke. These two violent events triggered waves of anti-Muslim violence from Buddhist vigilante groups in the region. According to official Rakhine State government estimates, 98 people died and 123 others were injured from both communities in the aftermath. In addition, thousands of people, mostly Muslim ethnic Bengali Rohingyas, were displaced by subsequent violent incidents. Once again, in September 2013, a wave of violent sectarian clashes erupted, resulting in the deaths of five Muslims around the city of Thandwe. The violence left nearly a hundred members of the community injured and displaced. It was triggered by a Buddhist mob marking the peak of Buddhist nationalism in Myanmar, which had already created a sense of mistrust and antagonism between the two communities.

ATTAULLAH, SPEARHEADING THE INSURGENCY

Soon afterward, the propaganda machinery of the Rohingya militant group, which refers to itself as Harakah al-Yaqin (Faith Movement, HaY), became active. Graphic details of the conflict surfaced on video and message-sharing virtual platforms. One such early video release featured HaY's leader Attaullah (Abu Ammar Junooni) declaring jihad against Myanmar and urging Rohingya Muslims to come out and join the jihad. Speaking in a Bengali-Arabic-laced local dialect, HaY leader Abu Ammar Junooni has issued several statements and propaganda videos highlighting the plights of Rohingya Bengalis and the military excesses of the Myanmar government on the community. The statements mention jihad and Islam, ostensibly aimed at inviting fellow radicalised Rohingyas, mostly settled in the Middle Eastern countries of India, Bangladesh, and Pakistan, to join the surge against the Myanmar government.

Undoubtedly, the protagonist of many militant videos flooding the Internet since October 2016 is Attaullah, a Rohingya Bengali Muslim in his mid-forties (age: 45). Born in Karachi, Pakistan, Attaullah's (also Hafiz Tohar's) parents stayed as refugees and later shifted to Mecca in Saudi Arabia. He reportedly received his early education at an Islamic seminary in Mecca. It is apparent from the video messages that he is quite well-versed in Arabic, Urdu, and the Bengali-laced Arakanese dialect. According to available information, he travelled to Pakistan in 2012 from Saudi Arabia after the Rakhine State sectarian violence between Buddhist Rakhine and Rohingya Muslims and underwent militant training under the Taliban group. He sneaked into Myanmar through Bangladesh, where he was registered as a refugee. Along with nearly 20 followers from Saudi Arabia and Pakistan with Rohingya origins, Attaullah entered northern Rakhine sometime in 2015, as per available sources, and started mobilising local villagers for an organised uprising against Myanmar's atrocities. Attaullah and his associates have reportedly trained 25 to 30 operatives in modern guerrilla tactics (Dhaka Tribune, January 10). Attaullah perhaps stayed at Kyaukpyinseik village in Maungdaw Township for some time before going underground with his armed followers. Observers have identified a few militant members from the videos who escaped from refugee camps in Nayapara and Kutabaloun in Bangladesh.

Although the video clips circulated by the group (now removed from YouTube) suggested the indigenous character of the ongoing jihad, Hafiz Tohar's direct appeal for support, both in terms of foot soldiers and weapons, is clearly targeted at urging transnational Rohingyas or sympathetic Islamist groups. A couple of successive video messages surfaced in mid-October 2016 urging international as well as local Rohingya support and invoking Islam. In one of his messages, Attaullah said, "If you (Rohingyas worldwide) want to save the honor of mothers and sisters of Arakan, if you want to save all the masjid and madrasha of Arakan from destruction, [...] take part in this great jihad with us." He also urged Islamic scholars around the world to issue fatwas for Jihad in Rakhine State. This call is aimed at gaining religious legitimacy for the ongoing armed campaign. So far, the group has not targeted civilians; rather, their target remains the police force and Myanmar's Army (known as Tatmadaw). In another video message, Attaullah vows to continue the "Jihad in Arakan," similar to the ongoing Gazwa-e Hind, the religious pretext to wage jihad against India by Al Qaeda and Pakistan-based militant formations.

Various investigations undertaken by organisations such as the International Crisis Group (ISG) and media investigations, especially by the Bangladesh-based Dhaka Tribune (DT), revealed and corroborated some aspects of the government's claim on AMM or HaY's emergence and international links and how the newly emerged group under the leadership of Attaullah has the backing of a section of the radicalised Rohingya diaspora based in Saudi Arabia, Pakistan, and Bangladesh (International Crisis Group, December 2016). As per the ISG report, the group was established after the June–October 2012 rioting and sectarian violence. The report specifically pointed out HaY's connection with a committee of Rohingya migrants based in Mecca, Saudi Arabia, and beyond. The report also underscores Attaullah and his band of militants' training under the supervision of Rohingya Jihadi veterans trained in Pakistan or Afghanistan'. In subsequent messages, ARSA refuted previous media reports and interviews, especially with DT, on its official Twitter account (Twitter/ARSA Official, April 2017).

Violence Under the Faith Movement, 2016

Sporadic armed attacks against Myanmar's border posts in support of minority Rohingya Muslims became routine affairs. Several attacks against border police were reported in Rakhine State's Maungdaw area between February and May 2014 (The Irrawaddy, May 2014). No organised insurgent group claimed responsibility for any of the violence that affected the Rakhine district. After a few years of lull, organised violence erupted in Rakhine starting on October 9, 2016, when armed Rohingya militants targeted Myanmar's Border Guard Police (BGP) posts in Maungdaw area. This single event witnessed the deaths of nine border policemen and as many attackers in the ensuing gun battles, while the militants decamped with a large number of arms and ammunition from BGP headquarters in Maungdaw town. A similar ambush attack on October 11 left four more policemen dead in the locality. Again, violence erupted on November 12–13, 2016, when armed militants launched a surprise attack on a military convoy during a clearance operation in Ma Yinn Taung village in Maungdaw town. Two security personnel, including a senior army officer, died in the ambush, while several suspected militants were killed. The Rohingya militants also decamped with a huge cache of arms and ammunition from BGP headquarters in Maungdaw. The government's initial estimation showed that militants took possession of at least 51 weapons of various makes and over ten thousand rounds of assorted ammunition (International Crisis Group, December 2016). A relatively new group called Harakah al-Yaqin (HaY-Arakan Faith Movement) claimed responsibility for the October and November 2016 attacks on the border posts (AFP/Frontier Myanmar, November 13, 2016).

Interviews with members of HaY revealed that this group was actually responsible for the series of attacks on Myanmar Border Guard Police outposts. In an 18-minute YouTube video statement released following the attack, Ata Ullah defended the assault, blaming the Myanmar army for inciting the violence. He said, "For over 75 years there have been various crimes and atrocities committed against the Rohingya ... that's why we carried out the October 9, 2016, attack – to send a message that if the violence is not stopped, we have the right to defend ourselves" (Al Jazeera, September 13, 2017).

In one of the interviews with the DT, the commanders of HaY denied being a terrorist group as portrayed by the Myanmar government and said that they would rather be called a "revolutionary group waging a movement against the oppression of Rohingya Muslims by the Myanmar government." (Dhaka Tribune, January 2017) HaY's propaganda suggests that they are seeking religious (Islamic) legitimacy for their organised violence through fatwas from senior clerics in Saudi Arabia and elsewhere. This would help this fringe group unite scattered Rohingya militants on one platform.

Subsequent interrogations of the captured HaY's members have also brought the inner working style of the group to light, especially about the plots and details of its core members. Besides Attaullah, who reportedly attended a six-month Taliban training course in Pakistan and frequented Myanmar from a village near Teknaf in Bangladesh to organise an armed insurgency, another prominent member was Kalis, a Pakistani who attended militant training there before coming to Bangladesh and then moving to Nakhuya village in Myanmar. Other members have been identified as Ibrahim, Aza, and Ayatullah, who spent some time in the Kutabaloun refugee camp in Bangladesh (President Office, Myanmar, October 2016). Some other members identified by the government agencies were Abdul Rahman, Munet,

Kapiktulah, and Akis, who have previously attended militant training under the Rohingya Solidarity Organisation (RSO).

Subsequently, Myanmar government investigations blamed a lesser-known Aqa-Mul Mujahidin (AMM – communities of fighters) group. The investigations based on statements of the arrested militants and militant videos in circulation around that time also pointed towards an operational link between AMM and Pakistani and Bangladeshi-based Rohingya Islamists, especially having past ties with the RSO and Harkat-ul-Jihad-al-Islami Arakan (HuJI-A), the two largest militant formations concerning the Rohingya crisis (Crisis Group, December 2016). Though it was not very clear at the outset if AMM was just another name for the Harakah al-Yaqin, which took responsibilities, media reports at that time suggested that these two could be the same group with different nomenclature or that HaY could be a front for AMM. Subsequent government-backed counter-insurgency operations in the area witnessed an escalation of armed clashes that claimed the lives of nearly 70 suspected Rohingya militants and 17 security force personnel.

ARSA and Violence Rerun, 2017–2018

The Rohingya militants under the HaY banner carried out random low-scale strikes in January and February 2017 as well, mostly in Norula and Aung Zaya localities in Maungdaw (Eleven Myanmar, March 2017). The Myanmar military and border police beefed up security measures at sensitive border outposts in the area, mostly in Ngakhuya, Kyainchaung, and Sabaekone localities, amid renewed fears of major militant raids targeting government infrastructure, including communication lines (Eleven Myanmar, March 2017). In March 2017, preceding the massive coordinated HaY attacks on Myanmar security outposts in Rakhine in August of that year, the group morphed into a more organised version, reinventing itself as the Arakan Rohingya Salvation Army (ARSA). It joined the social media outlet Twitter to announce ARSA's arrival (@https://twitter.com/arsa_official @ARSA_Official1), duly mentioning that it was formerly called Faith Movement or Harakah Al Yaqeen. With that announcement, it went official and claimed that it was fighting for the liberation of persecuted Rohingyas (Twitter, March 2017).

On August 25, 2017, ARSA launched one of its major armed raids against Myanmar's security force, targeting around 30 police posts and one army base in Maung Nu, Gu Dar Pyin and Koe Tan Kauk, Kyauk Pan Du and Myin Hlut, and Mee Chaung Zay (the Burmese names of the villages) in Buthidaung, Rathedaung, and Maungdaw districts (Human Rights Council, September 2018). These surprise coordinated attacks continued for the next three days in different places. The ARSA attacks triggered a massive military offensive and search and sweep (clearance) operation by the Myanmar military in the affected districts until early September 2017. The Myanmar government estimated 376 Rohingya militants and 13 security force personnel dead between August 25 and September 5, 2017. The government forces also sieged 15 assorted arms, 97 rounds of ammunition, 30 packs of gunpowder, and 67 homemade mines from ARSA militants.

In the aftermath of the clearance operation, a refugee crisis erupted in Rakhine State as the mass exodus of Rohingyas to neighbouring Bangladesh triggered a humanitarian emergency. The Rohingya civilians were clearly escaping military excesses in the epicentres of the conflict. In the face of a massive military crackdown, ARSA declared a month-long ceasefire on September 10, 2017, claiming that it would allow access to humanitarian agencies to assess and respond to the humanitarian crisis (Mizzima/AFP, September 11, 2017; ARSA, Twitter, September 9, 2017.) According to subsequent ARSA statements, the August 2017 attacks were in response to atrocities and oppression against Rohingyas by the military (Tatmadaw) and police, including 'arbitrary arrests and interrogations, extortion, increasing restrictions on freedom of movement, and disappearances.'

Observers opined that with limited or non-existent military capability, ARSA may have triggered the conflict to solicit military action and to draw international attention to the Rohingya's sufferings. However, it is difficult to assess the real intentions of ARSA amid the August-September 2017 surge in violence in western Myanmar that resulted in a massive humanitarian crisis.

After the 2017 violence, ARSA militants have intermittently carried out violent acts in 2018 and 2019. For example, in early January 2018, ARSA claimed responsibility for an ambush on a military convoy in northern Maungdaw. (See ARSA Statement, ARSA/PR/23/2018, on January 7, 2018.)

Beyond its direct confrontation with Myanmar security forces, ARSA was accused of intimidating and attacking Rohingya civilians, mostly forcing them to join the insurgency against Myanmar government forces, and for being informants for Myanmar security forces (Fortify Rights, July 2018). It also targets other minority populations, such as Hindus, for siding with the Buddhist majority. Amnesty International's report of May 22, 2018, documented this massacre, which was blamed squarely on ARSA. The report cited Hindu women witnesses who alleged they were abducted by ARSA fighters and forced to convert to Islam (Daily Star, May 2018; Amnesty International, May 22, 2018). Myanmar authorities in September 2017 recovered 45 dead bodies near Kha Maung Seik and accused the ARSA of carrying out the killings. AI also documented a separate killing of six Hindus by ARSA fighters on August 26 near the town of Maungdaw. In early August 2017, ARSA militants also killed six members of Mro, a Buddhist ethnic minority, in the Mayu mountain range near the town of Maungdaw in western Myanmar (The Irrawaddy, August 2017). ARSA denied any responsibility for these killings through press statements and publications (Twitter Statement, May 28, 2018) and (Reviving the Courageous Hearts, February 2019).

ANATOMY OF THE ARSA INSURGENCY

Initially, with the announcement of the new name, ARSA issued several statements mentioning its objectives to defend Rohingya rights. One of its earliest press statements, released on Twitter, said its "objective is to defend, salvage, and protect the innocent Rohingya indigenous native ethnic community of Arakan State with our best capacities as we have the legitimate right under international law to defend ourselves in line with the principle of self-defence. In doing so, our defensive attacks have been aimed only at the Burmese terrorist government and its terrorist military regime in accordance with international norms and principles until our demands are filled."

By changing the name, HaY and its leaders perhaps attempted to reinvent the group as a legitimate force representing all Rohingyas and their struggle for liberation, distancing themselves from accusations of religiously motivated insurgency and suspected transnational Islamist linkages. It mentioned in one of its press statements that "ARSA does not have stated religious motivations but has a seemingly secular ideology with a strong Muslim identity." (Twitter, ARSA Press Release No. 2, May 30, 2017). It clarified on many occasions through its audio-visual releases that the prime target remains the Myanmar armed forces, or "Tatmadaw," and it does not target civilians or members of other ethnic groups.

Frequently, through its press releases, ARSA portrayed itself as an ethno-nationalist movement and sometimes as an armed resistance movement, often refuting being branded as Islamist jihadis. It also stipulated its area of operation as "its ancestral homeland, 'Arakan' (Rakhine) in Myanmar.' ARSA reiterated through its press releases that 'it will never transcend beyond the homeland." It listed 20 demands in its first press release, comprising political, economic, social, and cultural rights for Rohingyas (ARSA, PR-1, March 29, 2017).

Though little information is available about the organisational and operational structures of ARSA, government and independent investigations have revealed that ARSA is restructured into political and military wings like an insurgency group. While the military wing is governed by the Supreme Council (Shura) with a small group of commanders at the helm headed by the Commander-in-Chief Ata Ullah, the political wing has a five-member body living outside Myanmar. The original locations of this five-member team are not known, but they are authorised to represent the organisation and are in charge of the political and media strategy of the ARSA, including issuing public statements, press releases through the official Twitter handle, and publications, including the booklet titled "Reviving the Courageous Hearts: A Report By Arakan Rohingya Salvation Army" (Issue.com, February 03, 2019). The 69-page booklet deals with the history of Rohingya, their resistance movements, alleged genocide, and the emergence of ARSA, among other things concerning Rohingya rights. ARSA officially designated Abdullah as its spokesperson.

The total number of members of ARSA is not known. However, various available estimates suggest that ARSA has a small dedicated member base with a larger over-the-ground support base or support system (volunteers and informers) within its operational zone, mostly composed of Rohingya villagers in three Rohingya-dominated Rakhine districts. Despite ARSA's rise as an armed insurgency movement against Myanmar's powerful military and police, logistically, it lacks sophisticated weapons or military-grade explosives to carry out large-scale and deadly attacks. However, it is amply evident that ARSA's guerrilla war tactic has surprised Myanmar's security apparatus on many occasions with limited firepower. The armoury is said to comprise several looted assault rifles and small arms. Most videos have depicted ARSA fighters with knives, machetes, and even sticks. Even though it receives financial support from the Rohingya diaspora, the shortage of arms and ammunition is visible on the ground and in the scale of damage it has inflicted on Myanmar's security during attacks.

As far as the training and indoctrination of ARSA leaders are concerned, investigation reports more or less indicated well-entrenched Pakistani and Bangladeshi links to this latest militant resurgence. Information also suggested that AMM has its origins in the HUJI-A under the patronage of Abdus Qadoos Burmi, the Pakistan-based HUJI-A leader who works closely with militant groups there that are sympathetic to the Rohingya's cause. Many Pakistan-based militant groups intermittently organise fund-raising and manpower mobilisation campaigns under the banner of the Difa-e-Arakan conference in Pakistan. Neighbouring Bangladesh, on the other hand, was cautious about the militant spillover through its porous borders but could not help but restrict the militant movement taking place mostly under the guise of refugee movements or undergoing arms and religious training with local armed groups in the remote hill tracts of Chittagong or Cox Bazar area.

RESISTING CALL FOR JIHAD?

Although ARSA denies having any links with transnational Islamist terrorist organisations such as Al-Qaeda or Islamic State, these groups have sought public support for the Rohingya cause. While it appears that groups like Al Qaeda have always extended unsolicited support for the plight of the Muslim Ummah, ARSA leaders have explicitly rejected any linkages with them through their press releases. In a statement released on September 14, 2017, ARSA said it had "no links with al-Qaeda, the Islamic State of Iraq and the Levant (ISIS), Lashkar-e-Taiba, or any other transnational terrorist group" (ARSA, Statement, ARSA/PR/12/2017, September 14, 2017).

However, the ARSA-led insurgency has undoubtedly appealed to the international jihadists who have rallied behind the cause of Rohingyas, who have suffered at the hands of the Buddhist majority in Myanmar. Statements and sympathy messages have poured in from Al Qaeda and IS that have sparked fears of Rohingyas being co-opted and radicalised further. Alarmingly, the conflict has featured in every piece of Jihadi propaganda around the world in the last couple of years. Words of support have come from Al-Qaeda, which has warned the Myanmar government and army against the plight of millions of Rohingya Muslims. It said in a statement: "The savage treatment meted out to our Muslim brothers ... shall not pass without punishment. The government of Myanmar shall be made to taste what our Muslim brothers have tasted."

Al Qaeda's South Asian branch (AQIS) also threatened to avenge the persecution of Rohingyas in Myanmar. Al-Qaeda's Arabian Peninsula branch, known as AQAP, also issued a similar call for attacks against Myanmar authorities. Its statement said, "We call upon all mujahidin brothers in Bangladesh, India, Pakistan, and the Philippines to set out for Burma to help their Muslim brothers and to make the necessary preparations – training and the like – to resist this oppression." Similarly, the Islamic State (ISIS)'s propaganda magazine Dabiq (Issue 14), fomenting anti-Buddhist sentiment, has documented how it planned to target Myanmar "once it reached the capability to do so" and after "bringing an end to [...] the apostate Bengali regime" in neighbouring Bangladesh. The Islamic State already influenced a bombing plot at the Myanmar Embassy in Jakarta in late November 2016. The conspiracy hatched by IS-affiliated Jemaah Ansar Daulah to avenge Rohingya atrocities was foiled by local police then (Roul, A. 2017).

In many ARSA statements, Attaullah calls upon Rohingya Muslims "to take up arms against government forces to liberate people from oppression perpetrated by all successive Myanmar regimes." He and a few of his commanders have successfully mobilised this armed insurgency since late last year, but so far they have refrained from giving the fight any religious colour. After declaring a ceasefire in mid-September, Attaullah made it clear that he or his group is not getting any support from Jihadi groups such as Al Qaeda or Lashkar-e-Taiba. This could be a calculated posturing to highlight the Rohingya cause worldwide as an indigenous ethnic conflict, and this is the reason why ARSA was adopted as a new name, replacing the earlier Islamist-centric name of HaY. The group at present fights for ethnic identity rather than a separate homeland struggle based on Sharia or Islamic laws. But given the sporadic use of Allah or Islam in many of the videos of ARSA and the background and training of Attaullah and others in Pakistan or Saudi Arabia, it would not be far-fetched to speculate on the chances of complete Islamisation of this nascent Rohingya insurgency in the future. It has the potential to snowball into a major armed movement against Myanmar if the refugee crisis and the atrocities against Rohingya people continue unabated.

CONCLUSIONS

Arguably, following an overtly active two years, ARSA became quiet for some time but renewed low-scale fighting again in 2019 against the government troops. A cursory look at recent press releases suggests that ARSA is rigorously working on a public relations campaign to win the hearts and minds of Rohingyas as well as sympathetic governments (Bangladesh and Malaysia, for instance) across the world. Atrocities against Rohingya civilians committed after August 25, 2017 operations, often termed Myanmar's campaign of "ethnic cleansing," have captured global attention too. But that does not help ARSA's public image. There are international investigative reports (such as Amnesty International's) that expose and blame ARSA for mindless terrorist violence against the government forces and Hindu and Christian minorities in Myanmar's Rakhine state. To regain its stature as a legitimate insurgency movement representing all Rohingyas, the ARSA put out a two-part message on social media in February 2020. In one message, the ARSA commander Suhaib attempted to portray a secular face of ARSA by saying that whatever ARSA is doing is for the "betterment of all Rohingyas irrespective of their faiths (Hindu, Muslims, and Christians), and their struggle is against Myanmar's (Burmese) genocidal military." It also calls for unity among the Rohingya refugees to stand against Myanmar (Twitter, February 11). With dwindling cadre strength, ARSA is struggling to make an impact at the moment and is perhaps resorting to a hibernation strategy to survive the military offensives and mobilise Rohingya support further to resurge in the future.

References

Al Jazeera (2017, March 12). Wirathu silenced by Myanmar's top Buddhist body. Retrieved from http://www.aljazeera.com/news/2017/03/wirathu-silenced-myanmar-top-buddhist-body-170311141258664.html.

Al Jazeera (2017, September 13). ARSA: Who are the Arakan Rohingya Salvation Army? Retrieved from https://www.aljazeera.com/news/2017/09/myanmar-arakan-rohingya-salvation-army-170912060700394.html.

Amnesty International (2018, May 22). Myanmar: New evidence reveals Rohingya armed group massacred scores in Rakhine State. Accessible at https://www.amnesty.org/en/latest/news/2018/05/myanmar-new-evidence-reveals-rohingya-armed-group-massacred-scores-in-rakhine-state/.

Arakan Rohingya Salvation Army (2019, February 03). Reviving the courageous hearts. Accessible at https://issuu.com/arsapublisher/docs/report_1_final_2.

Daily Star (2018, May 23). Rohingya insurgents killed Hindu villagers in Myanmar violence: Amnesty. https://www.thedailystar.net/rohingya-crisis/rohingya-insurgents-killed-hindu-villagers-myanmar-violence-amnesty-refugee-crisis-1580257.

Dhaka Tribune (2017, January 10). We will fight until the last drop of blood. Retrieved from http://www.dhakatribune.com/bangladesh/2017/01/10/will-fight-last-drop-blood/.

Eleven Myanmar (2017, March 12). Security tightened in Maungdaw. Retrieved from http://elevenmyanmar.com/local/8270.

Fortify Rights (2018, July). They gave them long swords. Retrieved from http://www.fortifyrights.org/downloads/Fortify_Rights_Long_Swords_July_2018.pdf.

Frontier Myanmar (2016, June 06). Ma Ba Tha monks regroup after political change. Retrieved from https://frontiermyanmar.net/en/ma-ba-tha-monks-regroup-after-political-change.

Frontier Myanmar (2016, November 13). Eight killed in surge of Rakhine violence: Tatmadaw. Retrieved from http://frontiermyanmar.net/en/news/8-killed-surge-violence-rakhine-tatmadaw.

Human Rights Council (2018, September 17). Report of the detailed findings of the Independent Commission of Fact Finding Mission on Myanmar by Human Rights Council. Accessible at https://www.icoe-myanmar.org/documents.

ICG. (2016). Myanmar: A new muslim insurgency in Rakhine state. Asia Report Number 283, December 15, 2016. https://www.crisisgroup.org/asia/south-east-asia/myanmar/283-myanmar-new-muslim-insurgency-rakhine-state.

Johnston, T., & Neelakantan, A. (2016, December 15). Myanmar: A new muslim insurgency in Rakhine State. *Crisis Group Report*. No. 283. Accessible at https://www.crisisgroup.org/asia/south-east-asia/myanmar/283-myanmar-new-muslim-insurgency-rakhine-state.

Mizzima (2017, September 11). ARSA declare one-month ceasefire: Twitter statement. Retrieved from http://www.mizzima.com/news-domestic/arsa-declare-one-month-ceasefire-twitter-statement/.

President Office, Myanmar (2016, October 13). Press release regarding the attacks on the Border Guard Police posts in Maungdaw Township. Accessible at http://www.president-office.gov.mm/en/?q=briefing-room/statements-and-releases/2016/10/15/id-6678.

Reuters (2016, November 15). Myanmar army says 86 killed in fighting in northwest. Retrieved from http://in.reuters.com/article/myanmar-rohingya-idINKBN13A11N.

Roul, A. (2013, October 17). Militant Islam meets militant Buddhism in Myanmar. *Terrorism Monitor, 11*(19), Accessible at https://jamestown.org/program/militant-islam-meets-militant-buddhism-in-myanmar/.

Roul, A. (2017, March 10). Myanmar's Muslim insurgency gaining prominence with jihadist groups. *Terrorism Monitor, 15*(5), Accessible at https://jamestown.org/program/myanmars-muslim-insurgency-gaining-prominence-jihadist-groups/.

The Diplomat. ARSA after the Myanmar coup: Between a rock and a hard place. January 24, 2022.

The Global New Light of Myanmar (2017, August 31). Members of the Mro ethnic tribe killed in a terrorist attack by ARSA; thousands continue to flee to Sittwe and border. https://www.globalnewlightofmyanmar.com/seven-more-civilians-killed-in-rakhine/.

The Irrawaddy (2014, May 19). Four police killed in attack on Burma-Bangladesh border. Retrieved from http://www.irrawaddy.com/news/burma/four-police-killed-attack-burma-bangladesh-border.html.

The Irrawaddy. (2017, August 3). Six bodies with gunshot, machete wounds found in Maungdaw. https://www.irrawaddy.com/news/burma/six-bodies-gunshot-machete-wounds-found-maungdaw.html.

The Irrawaddy (2019, October 31). Myanmar court freezes bank accounts of fugitive monk U Wirathu. Retrieved from https://www.irrawaddy.com/news/burma/myanmar-court-freezes-bank-accounts-fugitive-monk-u-wirathu.html.

Twitter (2017, April 09). ARSA_Offcial: Denial of Dhaka Tribune Interview. Accessible at https://twitter.com/ARSA_Official/status/851079906658091008.

Twitter (2017, March 29). Statement of Arakan Rohingya Salvation Army. ARSA/PR/01/2017. Available at http://www.rohingyablogger.com/2017/03/statement-of-arakan-rohingya-salvation.html.

Twitter (2017, May 30). Salvation Army officially refutes accusations of committing 'Killings or any forms of Terrorism against Civilians. ARSA/PR/02/2017. Accessible at https://twitter.com/ARSA_Official/status/869458081737916417/photo/1.

Twitter (2017, September 10). Declaration of humanitarian pause: Cessation of offensive military operations in Arakan state for humanitarian access. ARSA/PR/10/2017. Retrieved from https://twitter.com/arsa_official/status/906570961985658880?lang=en.

Twitter (2017, September 14). ARSA statement on humanitarian pause and allegations of links with transnational terror groups. ARSA/PR/12/2017, Accessible at https://twitter.com/ARSA_Official/status/908218055125172224.

Twitter (2020, February 11). Unity message for Rohingya (Part-1 and 2). Accessible at https://twitter.com/ARSA_Official/status/1227230898178801667.

Ware, A., & Laoutides, C. (2018). *Myanmar's 'Rohingya' conflict* (pp. 53–54). London: Oxford University Press.

You Tube (2016, November 20). Faith movement message. Retrieved from http://web.archive.org/web/20170415024930/https://www.youtube.com/watch?v=eEHhcSwaRNM.

You Tube (2016, October 12). Islamic terrorist asked Rohingya to join them for Jihad. Retrieved from http://web.archive.org/web/20170415023127/https://www.youtube.com/watch?v=SqTqCzLVeSs.

79

ISLAMIC INSURGENCY IN SOUTHERN THAILAND

The Mara Patani and Barisan Revolusi Nasional (BRN)

Animesh Roul and Scott N. Romaniuk

INTRODUCTION

Thailand's southernmost provinces have been troubled by an ethno-nationalist insurgency spearheaded by Islamic insurgents representing the minority Malay-Muslim communities since January 2004. Three Muslim-majority southern provinces, Yala, Pattani, and Narathiwat, are worst affected by this long-standing insurgency in this Buddhist-majority kingdom. These three provinces were part of an independent Malay Muslim sultanate before being annexed by Thailand in the early 1900s. A few other neighbouring provinces, such as Songkhla and Satun, bordering Malaysia, have also experienced intermittent tensions in the last several years. Armed separatism, which was actually started in the 1970s in Southern Thailand mostly with outside support (e.g., Thai Patani Diaspora and Middle Eastern countries), was subdued in the 1990s due to Thailand's holistic counterinsurgency strategy and amnesty programme Tai Rom Yen, locally known as "Pleasant South" or "South Under Cool Shade" (Bunbongkarn, 1987; Low & Pathan, 2010). What started by the Malay Muslims as a loosely organised ethno-nationalist insurgency aimed at achieving independence in the 1960s gradually turned into a demand for greater autonomy within Thailand. The insurgent groups have been fighting with varied objectives in this long-standing ethnic identity-based insurgency. This chapter aims to explore the deadly course of this 16-year-long violent insurgency and examine the major groups and factions of this long-standing insurgency. While documenting four major violent incidents that somehow demonstrate the dynamics of the ongoing conflict, the chapter will also briefly argue how it remains aloof from the transnational Jihadist movements.

VIOLENCE RE-RUN

In southern Thailand, the Malayan-speaking Muslim populace thinks the majority Buddhist Thai state has been ignoring them and feels alienated. The simmering discontent that was again growing in the early 2000s within the Malay-Muslim community in these three provinces came to the surface on January 4, 2004, with an audacious raid on a military base in Narathiwat. However, the factors for the reemergence of violent insurgencies in the region notwithstanding, this raid and subsequent violence marked the beginning of a new phase of conflict in southern Thailand. On that fateful day, a large number of Islamic insurgents launched a surprise raid on the 4th Development Battalion headquarters at the KNR (Kromluang Naradhiwas Rajanagarindra) military camp in Cho Airong district in Narathiwat province. The insurgents decamped with over 400 guns, including M16 and AK47 rifles, along with other firearms and explosives from the armoury. Four Royal Thai Army soldiers, apparently Buddhists, were killed during the raid. It is believed that those stolen arms and ammunition have been used against government forces ever since. The raid on the armoury was preceded by coordinated arson attacks targeting schools in Narathiwat and Yala provinces later that day. Peace parleys (i.e., Dialogue-1) were attempted with the mediation of neighbouring Malaysia in February 2013 between Thailand's National Security Council and the powerful Barisan Revolusi Nasional Melayu Patani (or BRN). But with continuing violence in the South, the talks derailed (Bangkok Post, 2013).

Since the Constitution was revoked after the May 2014 coup, the military-backed (Junta) National Council for Peace and Order (NCPO) has brought martial law, restructured the administrative structures in southern Thailand, and stepped up counter-insurgency measures. The NCPO's action largely stifled the militant movements and significantly quelled the overall violence, though not completely. Violent incidents and deaths have declined gradually since 2014, coinciding

DOI: 10.4324/9780429426063-89

with the peace parleys and reconciliation efforts (i.e., dialogue 2: Happiness Process) between Thailand's National Security Council and five insurgent groups that were represented under a conglomerate called MARA Patani (Majlis Syura Patani or Patani Consultative Council). After this process also failed to reach any settlement, Mara Patani was replaced by BRN again in 2020. Despite these unofficial dialogues facilitated by neighbouring Malaysia, violence persisted, but on a limited scale, for the last several years. However, since the so-called peace-dialogue process hits roadblocks every now and then, the fear of a violence rerun looms large on South Thailand's horizon. The latest November 2019 Lam Phaya violence largely vindicated that fear or speculation about a violence rerun in the "Deep South." After sixteen long years since the present wave of violence started, the situation remains grim and unresolved, with no lasting solutions in sight. An estimated 7,085 people have been killed and approximately 13,233 have been injured since then. The total number of violent incidents stands at just over a whopping 20,500 (Bangkok Post, 2020).

INSURGENT GROUPS IN THE DEEP SOUTH

There are a number of active and dormant insurgent groups and factions operating in southern Thailand, or Thailand's 'Deep South.' They are Barisan Revolusi Nasional (BRN), Barisan Revolusi Nasional-Coordinate (BRN-C), Gerakan Mujahidin Islam Patani (GMIP), Barisan Islam Pembebasan Patani (BIPP, or Islamic Liberation Front of Patani), Patani United Liberation Organisation (PULO), and New PULO, and last but not least, Barisan Bersatu Mujahideen Patani (BBMP). Besides liberating the old Pattani kingdom, these groups have varied agendas or objectives, ranging from separatist demands based on Malay Islamic identity to sovereignty and complete independence. Largely, the decades-long conflict is an ethno-religious one that has been waged by ethnic Malay Muslims against Thai government forces.

Irrespective of these many groups and their respective agendas, two major formations are active and dominating the conflict landscape at present. They are Barisan Revolusi Nasional (BRN) and Majlis Syura Patani (also 'Mara Patani'), a militant conglomerate comprising several members from BRN (BRN Action Group), three factions of the PULO (PULO-P4, PULO-dspp, and PULO-mkp), and independent entities such as BIPP and GMIP. While the powerful BRN is presently engaged in a Malaysian-sponsored dialogue with the Thai government since late January 2020, the Mara Patani umbrella group has been negotiating with Thai authorities to resolve the conflict since mid-2015 but withdrew from the process in early February 2019 (Bangkok Post, August 2015; Bangkok Post, February 2019; The Star, January 2020). The latest round of dialogue has been held in Kuala Lumpur, facilitated again by neighbouring Malaysia, where most of the insurgent leadership has taken refuge for a long time. To note, BRN pulled out of an earlier peace dialogue process in 2014. BRN's return to the dialogue process is seen as a positive step towards the resolution of conflict.

Although South Thailand's Islamic groups primarily target Thai government forces, including the military and police, civilians always bear the brunt of violence and are often targeted for revenge. As of now, two major militant formations dominate the Islamic militancy landscape in South Thailand: the Mara Patani militant conglomerate and the Barisan Revolusi Nasional (BRN), one of the longest-standing and by far the strongest militant networks in South Thailand. A brief profile of the major groups operating and dominating the South Thai insurgency movement

The Mara Patani (Majlis Syura Patani or Patani Consultative Council)

Mara Patani, or Patani Consultative Council, came into existence in May 2015 after six militant groups merged and entered into a dialogue with the Thai government. The larger goal of Mara Patani was to serve as a consultative platform for all stakeholders, including Pattani liberation movements, civil society groups, and NGOs, and to find a just, comprehensive, and sustainable political solution (Abuza, 2015). The Consultative Council idea was initially conceived by senior members of BRN, which remains the most powerful and violent entity among all the South Thai militant groups. Previously conceived as Majlis Amanah Rakyat Patani and later formalised as Mara Patani with all pro-dialogue groups and factions In June 2015, one of the PULO factions backed out of the Mara Patani's founding agreement, leaving five groups in this conglomerate (Deep South Watch, 2015). These Islamic formations, part of the Mara Patani, have weakened over the years due to a dismantled network, strong counter-insurgency efforts by the Thai government, and also because many of their leaders are living in exile in Malaysia. With less firepower and manpower, the Mara Patani conglomerate is considered less powerful than the BRN and lacks control over the larger insurgency.

Barisan Revolusi Nasional

(BRN, National Revolutionary Front): With an objective to establish an independent Islamic State and to promote Malay nationalism, BRN emerged on South Thailand's conflict landscape in the early 1960s. By far the largest, strongest, and most violent armed group in South Thailand, BRN was established by Ustad Haji Abdul Karim Hassan as an opposition to the education reform programme instituted by the Royal Thai government. With high operational secrecy coupled with guerilla tactics, BRN has turned out to be a major headache for the Thai security establishment since 2004. Ever since, the BRN has remained powerful and dictates the terms of negotiation. The vast majority of the current generation of Patani Malay militants (locally known as *juwae* or *perjuang (freedom fighters))* falls under the command of the BRN. The fighters are organised in small cells and scattered throughout the Malay-speaking regions in the Deep South (Askew & Helbardt, 2012). BRN's support base is comprised of hundreds of Islamic madrassas (Ponoh or Pondok), students, and teachers in the Malay-speaking region of South Thailand. One of its violent factions, BRN-Coordinate, caused much of the violence that plagued South Thailand. Though BRN was involved in a short-lived dialogue process in 2013, it stayed out of the Mara Patani-led negotiations, though some of its senior members were independently involved in the process until it derailed in 2019 over several issues, including implementing a safety zone in the Deep South. In a statement in April 2017, BRN announced that it was willing to negotiate directly with the Thai government, and in early 2020, BRN officially entered into a dialogue process with Thai authorities.

Pattani United Liberation Organisation

Presently splintered and weakened, Pattani United Liberation Organisation (PULO) factions have become a part of the larger Mara Patani conglomerate. However, the original PULO was formed in 1968 and dominated the insurgency scene in the 1970s and 1980s as the most powerful and violent group. It was established by Tengku Bira Kotanila (Kabir Abdul Rahman), an Islamic scholar with educational and spiritual links to Saudi Arabia and India. According to its present website, PULO's goal is to resist the Thai-Buddhist actions aimed at exterminating Islam and Muslims. However, historically, PULO wanted to establish an Islamic State by liberating the Malay Muslim provinces of South Thailand. In due course, the movement was splintered into various subgroups, such as New PULO, Pulo-P4, Pulo-DSPP, and Pulo-MKP. By the early 1990s, the New PULO emerged under Arrong Moo-reng (Muhamad Bin Muhammad) and Hajji Abdul Rohman Bazo as a dissident faction of the original PULO. At present, most of the surviving leadership of PULO is mainly operating from exile in Middle Eastern and European countries (e.g., Saudi Arabia and Sweden).

Gerakan Mujahideen Islam Patani (GMIP)

Returnees from the Afghanistan-Soviet war founded the Gerakan Mujahidin Islam Pattani (GMIP) in 1995 with the goal of establishing an independent Islamic state. With its Afghan jihad lineage, it was suspected that the group had ties with transnational jihadist entities. Its leaders, such as Cheku Mae Abdul Rahman (Abbas bin Ahmad) and Nasoreee Saesang (Haji Wae), moved away from the overtly political parent group GMP (Gerakan Mujahideen Patani) and strived for an independent Islamic state in south Thailand under the banner of GMIP. The GMIP, along with other groups, was responsible for a number of small attacks from mid-1997 to early-1998.

Other than these four violent groups, there were several small groups and umbrella formations that are still operating, though on a limited scale, for example, BERSATU (the United Front for the Independence of Patani), Permuda, the BNPP (the National Front for the Liberation of Pattani), Runda Kumpulan Kecil (RKK), and Jemaah Salafi (Abuza, 2006; Crisis Group, May 2005).

Barisan Islam Pembebasan Patani (BIPP)

Being part of Mara Pattani, the BIPP (also known as the Islamic Front for the Liberation of Patani) was engaged in the dialogue process. The present incarnation of BIPP has a link with the old Barisan Nasional Pembebasan Patani (BNPP), founded by Tengku Abdul Jalal Nasare in the late 1950s in Kelantan, Malaysia. The BNPP, one of the pioneer armed separatist groups, aimed at establishing an Islamic State in South Thailand. However, it changed its name to BIPP in the mid-1980s and became dormant until 2002 (Rubin, 2010).

MAJOR VIOLENT INCIDENTS

It is imperative to examine the past violent incidents that have rocked South Thailand for the last 16 years, primarily to understand the dynamics of power play in the conflict and, more importantly, as turning points in the ongoing insurgency. Even though militant violence and counterinsurgency operations went hand in hand on a regular basis between 2004 and 2020, at least five major incidents in the aftermath of the early January 2004 armed raid in Narathiwat are worth examining here. These events largely intensified the insurgency.

The Krue Se Mosque Raid, April 2004

While martial law in south Thailand was in place, militants launched synchronised attacks on eleven police posts and army checkpoints across Pattani, Yala, and Songkhla on April 28, 2004. The ensuing confrontations with Thai security forces ended in a bloody showdown at the Krue Se Mosque in Pattani when the Thai army stormed the mosque and killed 37 people held up inside the mosque (Human Rights Watch, 2006). This armed battle ended with the deaths of over 100 militants and five security personnel. Several reports mentioned events inside the Krue Se mosque, where militants belonging to a radical religious group called Hikmat Allah Abadan or Abadae (Brotherhood of the Eternal Judgement of God) were reportedly engaged in mystical religious prayer services to become 'invincible and invisible'. The group was led by a religious teacher by the name of Ismail Yaralong, also known as Ustaz Soh.

Booklets and leaflets found at the epicentre of the conflict, especially a 34-page booklet titled "Berjihad di Patani," called for a separate Patani state and for the extermination of people of different religious faiths. It certainly propounded intolerance and violence in the name of Islam and Jihad. The booklet also suggested the formation of a constitutional state of Patani based on the Sunni-Shafi'i school of law (Sugunnasil, 2006; Pathan Don, 2017). The Krue Se mosque incident spurred a discourse in Thailand and beyond regarding the methods being used to quell the insurgency and drew a great deal of criticism from the Thai government and army.

The Tak Bai Incident, October 2004

Another horrifying incident took place in the same year when a demonstration turned tragic, with deaths and destruction outside a police station in the Tak Bai district of Narathiwat in October 2004. Seven people were killed when soldiers and police moved against the demonstrators, mostly Muslim civilians accused of helping militants, and some 78 died of suffocation after they were piled into Army trucks to be transported to a military camp (Benar News, 2015; The Star, 2019). The then-Thaskin Shinawatra government was criticised again for excessive use of force, negligence, and gross human rights violations. This tragic event made its way into the militant narrative to reinforce the prevalent notion of atrocities against Muslims and mistreatment at the hands of government forces. This event triggered subsequent revenge attacks on the Buddhist populace in the province. One such incident occurred in early November 2010, when a senior Buddhist deputy police chief was found beheaded in the Sukhirin district of Narathiwat province. A leaflet there described the killing as retaliation for the deaths at Tak Bai (The Independent, 2004).

In 2006, Prime Minister Surayud Chulanont officially apologised for the Tak Bai incident and other atrocities committed by the Thai state against the Patani people. Surayud, a former Army general, attempted to reconnect with senior militant leaders, especially from PULO and BRN, and was ready to offer them roles in larger reconciliation efforts and dialogue with younger generations of militants. Surayud's outreach effort failed as Barisan Revolusi Nasional-Coordinate (BRN-C), the most active insurgent group, rejected any type of negotiation, including the possibility of granting autonomy.

Despite these positive government overtures, the following years witnessed a spike in the number of attacks in Yala and Narathiwat provinces. The militants unleashed indiscriminate attacks targeting Thai security forces and civilians, mostly Buddhists. Even pro-government Muslims were targeted for collaborating with government agencies. Decapitations, abductions, and shootings became routine. The most audacious and brutal were the April 27 (2009) coordinated attacks to mark the fifth anniversary of the Krue-Se mosque incident (Al Jazeera, 2009).

Revenge attacks on Thai government officials and civilians (mostly Buddhists) increased following the May 29 (2009) Songkhla provincial court verdict that cleared the Thai military of any responsibility for the October 2004 Tak Bai incident. The court noted that the Thai authorities were acting under an emergency law (ABC News, 2009).

Al-Furquan Mosque Massacre, June 2009

While the Muslim insurgency continued unabated in South Thailand, the Malay Muslims faced another major violence at the hands of government forces on June 8, 2009, when gunmen opened fire at worshippers performing the evening prayer at Al-Furquan mosque in Joh Ai Rong district, Narathiwat. At least ten people, including the chief priest of the mosque, died in the shootout, and several others were injured (International Commission Of Jurists, 2009; CNN, 2009). The killings created a global outrage, and both Thai and Malayan Muslims in Thailand heavily criticised the then-prime minister Abhisit Vejjajiva's administration for serious rights violations in the southern border provinces.

The following weeks of mosque massacres witnessed an escalation in violence against non-Muslims, especially Buddhist monks, teachers, and rubber plantation workers in the province and elsewhere in South Thailand. Within a week of the incident, an estimated 13 people were killed, and leaflets found at the crime scene read, "You kill our innocents, so we kill your people" (ABC News, 2009; Hindustan Times, 2009). There were also notes that these targeted killings were revenge for the Al Furuqan mosque assault (Herald Banner, June 2009).

Battle of Bacho, February 2013

The so-called "Battle of Bacho," as it is known in the annals of South Thailand's violent history, occurred when around 16 Islamic militants purported to be members of a hitherto unknown "Pattani Army" were killed during a raid. The insurgent attack on a Thai military base was rebuffed (Bangkok Post, February 14, 2013). This incident took place at a Marine Corps base in the Bacho district of Narathiwat province and was considered to be the deadliest for Islamic militants in the last several years. The slain militants were considered martyrs by the local Muslim populace. The Bacho incident triggered nearly 30 reprisal attacks by Muslim militants in the subsequent week in Pattani (Space War, February 2013).

Lam Phaya Raid, November 2019

Thai militants unleashed a deadly attack in Yala, killing 15 people on November 5, 2019 The deadly attack was led by suspected BRN insurgents against a village defence unit in Tambon Lam Phaya village in Muang district, Yala province. This incident raised the fear of a militant resurgence in South Thailand once again after years of dormancy while the dialogue process was lingering (Bangkok Post, 2019). This latest attack was considered a signal from BRN to come to the negotiating table with the Thai government and also a signal to convey Thai authorities that BRN is still powerful enough to inflict damage and renew the insurgency at will. Expectedly, BRN has now entered into a dialogue process with Thai authorities that started in the Malaysian capital Kuala Lumpur in January 2020 in another effort to resolve the long-standing conflict (BenarNews, January 2020).

ELUDING A GLOBAL JIHAD TRAP?

There are some legitimate concerns about possible linkages between South Thailand's militant insurgents and transnational jihadist groups or Islamist ideology. As of now, there is no evidence that South Thailand's insurgency is influenced by or has any operational, ideological, or logistical links with any regional (e.g., Jemaah Islamiyah of Indonesia) or global jihadist movements (such as Al Qaeda or Islamic State). A detailed examination by the International Crisis Group of the vexed conflict suggests that the insurgency and violence are nationalistic and identity-oriented rather than manifestations of global jihad (Crisis Group, November 2017; Crisis Group, May 2005).

Nevertheless, there are instances where Thai militant groups resorted to Islam, concepts like Caliphate (Islamic State) or Dar-us-Salam, and several Qur'anic injunctions to legitimise violence, giving the whole insurgency a religious war or conflict (against Thai Buddhist occupation) narrative. The concerns are not baseless, either. Various unsubstantiated reports about Al Qaeda's or Islamic State's inroads into South Thailand have caused panic and concerns within the security establishments in the region in the past. Also, Thai Muslim diaspora or students studying abroad voicing support for the Islamic revolution or the notion of an Islamic State are not uncommon either. For instance, on September 24, 2019, a Thai student from Yala province was arrested in Cairo, Egypt, following the circulation of an online video clip that showed him voicing support for an "Islamic revolution" in an interview. According to the reports, photos allegedly linked to the Islamic State (IS) had also been discovered on his mobile phone (Nation Thailand, October 2019). However, the concerns about any jihadi traction notwithstanding, he returned to Thailand through government interventions.

Back in 2006, Wan Kadir Che Wan, leader of Bersatu, claimed that the Jemaah Islamiyah (JI) terrorist network of Indonesia was helping Thailand's militant groups (Irrawaddy, November 22, 2006). Though proved to be unfounded, several media reports in the last few years have alleged that foreign fighters of Islamic State in Syria and Iraq had attempted to exploit the situations in southern Thailand, but most of these reports turned out to be false and unsubstantiated. For example, reports about IS fighters visiting a religious school in Sungai Kolok district in Narathiwat province in late 2015 or news about several IS militants entering Thailand to attack Russian interests remain uncorroborated (Thai Tribune, 2016; Vice News, 2015). Similar reports surfaced in January 2018 about a Pakistani national identified as Muhammad Iqbal, who was arrested in the Phasi Charoen district of the capital city of Bangkok. Iqbal was accused of producing fake passports for Islamic State operatives and transnational criminals to arrive in Thailand (Bangkok Post, 2017). Similarly, a Thai student held in custody in Egypt on suspicion of links to Islamic State, later released and returned to his family in the southern Thai province of Yala in October 2019 (Thai PBS World, 2019). Irrespective of the veracity of past news reports about Jihadi inroads, these kinds of reports are still pouring in every now and then as fear of a transnational Jihadi outreach looms large over southern Thailand's militant movements. Ironically, Thailand's unique localised Islamist insurgency has not transformed into a jihadist struggle yet.

While the long-standing conflict remains unresolved with both parties (the government and Islamic insurgent groups) unwavering in their respective demands, all hopes lie in the ongoing round of peace talks. As the dialogue process moves on, the apprehensions of possible exploitation of South Thailand's conflict by transnationals or their regional affiliates will still remain a headache for Thailand and the region.

References

ABC News. (2009, June 15). Rubber tapper beheaded in Thailand. https://www.abc.net.au/news/2009-06-15/rubber-tapper-beheaded-in-thailand/1714258.

Abuza, Z. (2015, September 7). No peace soon in Thailand's Deep South. *New Mandala*. https://www.newmandala.org/no-peace-soon-in-thailands-deep-south/.

Abuza, Z. (2006). A breakdown of Southern Thailand's insurgent groups. *Terrorism Monitor*, *4*(17). https://jamestown.org/program/a-breakdown-of-southern-thailands-insurgent-groups/.

Al Jazeera. (2009, April 28). Deadly attacks sweep south Thailand. https://www.aljazeera.com/news/asia-pacific/2009/04/200942853538748606.html.

Bangkok Post. (2013, April 29). BRN YouTube clip threatens talks. http://www.bangkokpost.com/news/local/347469/brn-demands-hard-to-believe.

Bangkok Post. (2013, February 14). Death zone awaited unsuspecting raiders. https://www.bangkokpost.com/thailand/general/335785/death-zone-awaited-unsuspecting-raiders.

Bangkok Post. (2015, August 28). Mara Patani 'evidence of progress' in peace process. https://www.bangkokpost.com/thailand/general/672804/mara-patani-evidence-of-progress-in-peace-process.

Bangkok Post. (2017, January 17). Pakistani was Islamic State forger, Prawit says. https://www.bangkokpost.com/archive/pakistani-was-islamic-state-forger-prawit-says/1396926.

Bangkok Post. (2019, February 04). Southern peace talks put off until poll. https://www.bangkokpost.com/thailand/general/1622962/southern-peace-talks-put-off-until-poll.

Bangkok Post. (2019, November 06). Insurgents attack security checkpoint in Yala, 15 killed. https://www.bangkokpost.com/thailand/general/1788474/insurgents-attack-securitycheckpoint-in-yala-15-killed.

Bangkok Post. (2020, January 12). No end in sight for carnage in deep South, despite peace talks. https://www.bangkokpost.com/thailand/special-reports/1833574/no-end-in-sight-for-carnage-in-deep-south-despite-peace-talks#cxrecs_s.

Benar News. (2015, October 22). Victims Cannot Forget Tak Bai Tragedy in Thailand. https://www.benarnews.org/english/news/thai/Tak-Bai-10222015155832.html.

Benar News. (2020, January 21). Thai Peace Negotiator Meets with BRN Rebel Delegates in Malaysia. https://www.benarnews.org/english/news/malaysian/peace-talks-01212020154917.html.

Banner, H. (2009, June 22). Noon Monday- Thailand attacks raise threat of sectarian war. https://www.heraldbanner.com/news/noon-monday–thailand-attacks-raise-threat-of-sectarian-war/article_cf5b6a60-0d75-536a-87d9-14a0a2932ef7.html.

Bunbongkarn, S. (1987). The military in Thai politics, 1981-86. Institute of Southeast Asian Studies, pp. 20–21.

CNN. (2009). Shooting at Thai mosque kills 10, police say, CNN, 8 June 2009. https://edition.cnn.com/2009/WORLD/asiapcf/06/08/thailand.mosque.shooting/index.html.

Crisis Group. (2005, May 18). Southern Thailand: Insurgency, Not Jihad, (No. 98). https://www.crisisgroup.org/asia/south-east-asia/thailand/southern-thailand-insurgency-not-jihad.

Deep South Watch. (2015, June 06). What is Mara Patani? https://www.deepsouthwatch.org/node/7211.

Hindustan Times. (2009, June 16). Female teacher killed in Thai south: police. https://www.hindustantimes.com/world/female-teacher-killed-in-thai-south-police/story-YxqHCgQPNsUK3hLUiiP7aM.html.

Human Rights Watch. (2006, April 28). Thailand: Investigate Krue Se Mosque raid no justice two years after deadly clashes in South. https://www.hrw.org/news/2006/04/28/thailand-investigate-krue-se-mosque-raid.

International Commission Of Jurists. (2009, June 10). Thailand: ICJ condemns Killing of at least 10 worshipers in the Alfurquan Mosque. http://www.refworld.org/pdfid/4a51e8d22.pdf.

International Crisis Group. (2005, May 18). Southern Thailand: Insurgency, Not Jihad, Asia Report No. 98. https://www.crisisgroup.org/asia/south-east-asia/thailand/southern-thailand-insurgency-not-jihad.

International Crisis Group. (2017, November 08). Jihadism in Southern Thailand: A Phantom Menace, Asia Report No. 291. https://www.crisisgroup.org/asia/south-east-asia/thailand/291-jihadism-southern-thailand-phantom-menace.

Irrawaddy. (2006, November 22). Al-Qaida-linked Terror Group infiltrates Thai South. https://www2.irrawaddy.com/article.php?art_id=6354.

Liow, J.C., & Pathan, D. (2010). *Confronting ghosts: Thailand's Shapeless Southern Insurgency*, Paper No 30, Lowy Institute for International Policy.

Marc, A., & Helbardt, S. (2012). Becoming Patani Warriors: Individuals and the insurgent collective in Southern Thailand. *Studies in Conflict & Terrorism*, *35*(11), 779–809. http://www.tandfonline.com/doi/abs/10.1080/1057610X.2012.720239?src=recsys&journalCode=uter20.

Nation Thailand. (2019, October 7). Thai student accused of supporting IS is back home. https://www.nationthailand.com/news/30377156.

Pathan, D. (2017). *Thailand, world Islamic Almanac*. American Foreign Policy Council.

Rubin, B.M. (Ed.). (2010). *Guide to Islamist movements* (Vol. II). M.E. Sharpe.

Space War. (2013, February 25). Thai Muslim insurgents launch attacks. https://www.spacewar.com/reports/Thai_Muslim_insurgents_launch_attacks_999.html.

Sugunnasil, W. (2006). Islam, radicalism, and violence in Southern Thailand: Berjihad Patani and the 28 April 2004 attacks. *Critical Asian Studies*, *38*(1), 119–144. https://www.tandfonline.com/doi/full/10.1080/14672710600556494

Thai PBS World. (2019, October 7). Thai student with suspected IS link released by Egypt. https://www.thaipbsworld.com/thai-student-with-suspected-is-link-released-by-egypt/.

Thai Tribune. (2016, January 23). ISIS may have tried to make alliance in Thailand's South. http://thaitribune.org/contents/detail/297?content_id=17249&rand=1453476369.

The Independent. (2004, November 03). Buddhist chief beheaded in revenge for Muslim deaths. http://www.independent.co.uk/news/world/asia/buddhist-chief-beheaded-in-revenge-for-muslim-deaths-5350491.html.

The Star. (2019, October 26). Muslims in Thai south mark 15 years since 'Tak Bai. https://www.thestar.com.my/news/regional/2019/10/26/muslims-in-thai-south-mark-15-years-since-tak-bai-massacre.

The Star. (2020, January 21). Thai officials resume peace dialogue with main southern insurgents. https://www.thestar.com.my/news/regional/2020/01/21/thai-officials-resume-peace-dialogue-with-main-southern-insurgents.

VICE News. (2015, December 4). Syrians linked to Islamic State travelled to Thailand to attack Russian interests. https://news.vice.com/article/syrians-linked-to-islamic-state-traveled-to-thailand-to-attack-russian-interests.

80

JEMA'AH ISLAMIYAH IN INDONESIA

Embracing Violence as a Methodology

Scott N. Romaniuk and Amparo Pamela Fabe

INTRODUCTION

Islamist militancy is an integral part of Malaysia's political tapestry. Mohd Mizan Aslam documents the presence of up to thirteen radical groups, with their common aim of shaping some form of 'Islamic state' through means of force. The presence of Abdullah Sungkar and Abu Bakar Ba'asyhir, the founders of JI, in Malaysia fostered the development of this group. The goal of establishing an Islamic state in Indonesia (Darul Islam) remained the main agenda of JI (Temby, 2010). As part of its vision of an "Islamic state" that encompasses Malaysia and the regions beyond, the JI called for a meeting of its members in Kampung Serting Ulu, Jempol Negeri, and Negeri Sembilan in 1993 (Aslam, 2009).

The JI convened the Rabitatul Mujahidin in 1999 after a meeting in Kuala Lumpur in 2000, which was supported by representatives from KMM (Malaysia), the Moro Islamic Liberation Front (Philippines), JI Singapore Cell (Singapore), the Patani Islamic Liberation Front and Wa-Ka-Rae (Thailand), Gerakan Aceh Merdeka and Sulawesi Muslims Organisation (Indonesia), and Rohingya Solidarity Organisation (Myanmar) to foster discussions on the establishment of an Islamic caliphate in Southeast Asia (Ministry of Home Affairs Singapore, 2003). Nicholas Chan (2019) highlighted the factors that are responsible for JI's stable and enduring presence in Malaysia. One, the JI helped in the militarisation of local and regional recruits through the provision of military training to its recruits in the states of Selangor, Negeri Sembilan, Johor Bahru, and Perak. Two, the JI introduced its armed struggle into Malaysia through appeals for Muslim solidarity beyond nation-state boundaries. Three, the JI established the Luqmanul Hakiem Islamic School (LHIS) in Ulu Tiram, Johor, which served as an Islamic learning centre as well as a recruitment and ideological indoctrination venue for its Darul Islam struggles.

The JI maintains close relationships with other terrorist organisations. The JI's top operatives, Hambali and Abu Jibril, had such a strong influence on the Kumpulan Mujahidin Malaysia (KMM) membership that one of its groups, the K3M group led by the Malaysian terrorist Zulfilki bin Hir, alias "Marwan", took orders from Indonesian JI leaders (Abuza, 2003). The K3M is the only faction in KMM that has been involved in multiple violent operations. It was the K3M connection that led to JI's downfall in Malaysia. With Hambali as JI's leader, the Malaysian police officers realised that the global jihadism of al-Qaeda, including its terrorism financing, had reached Southeast Asia (Abdullah, 2009).

KINSHIP

The Jemaah Islamiyah (JI) manifesto, entitled *Pedoman Umum Perjuangan al-Jama'ah al-Islamiyah* (General Guide for the Struggle of al-Jama'ah al-Islamiyah), has its own charter, operational guidelines, and strategic programmes (Pavlova, 2006). The JI is a well-organised hierarchical organisation with deep roots in Indonesia. Through the implementation of methodical terrorist attacks on the symbols of opulence and moral decadence of the capitalist West, such as luxury hotels, bars, and pubs, the JI wants to establish a pan-Islamic state by means of spreading violence and fear among communities. The JI reinforces strong familial relationships and marriage ties. A strong sense of belonging – a comforting sense of being part of a large family – strengthens the personal bonds of the members to the entire organisation. This strong sense of belonging helps the JI expand to Malaysia and the Philippines through the deployment of new foreign recruits. The JI keeps their illegal activities exclusively within the family circle, thus safeguarding the secrecy of their operations at all times. Loyalty to the JI is similar to loyalty to the family; hence, the member's allegiance to the JI is certainly rock solid. The families and family members are expected to provide the unconditional

DOI: 10.4324/9780429426063-90

support and protection needed by these terrorists whenever they need to conduct high-risk operations. There have been several occasions where family members of JI terrorists have willingly put themselves at risk in order to keep their kin safe from law enforcement officials and military officers. It seems that this close symbiotic relationship among the members makes JI formidable as a terrorist organisation.

ONLINE PRESENCE OF JI

Convicted terrorists from Jemaah Islamiyah (JI) have attested to using the Internet in one way or another during their operations, from sending messages to one another to looking for extremist *fatwas* online as a way to justify their actions. More often than not, more traditional elements – blood relations and marriage ties – remain the key to individual religious radicalisation and political violence in JI (Osman, 2010). Sageman (2004) notes the significance of the emotional attachment of group members to one another, the perceived social benefits of remaining in the group, and "one-upmanship" as part of the radicalisation process towards violence. A strong factor of JI is the organising of kin to help carry out suicide bombing attacks in Southeast Asia (Magouirk & Atran, 2008). For example, the October 2002 Bali bombings featured a family of brothers who carried out the attacks. Ali Ghufron, a.k.a. Mukhlas, and Amrozi were brothers. Both were executed in November 2008. Ali Imron, the third brother, is serving a life sentence in a Jakarta detention centre. Kinship within JI is also extended through marriage ties. The JI elders would play matchmaker for the younger members by fixing them up with their sisters, daughters, or other female relatives, or those of their peers (Ismail, 2005).

AN ISLAMIC SOCIETY

The JI members subscribe to living by Islamic laws and principles in small groups of *usroh*, a term that literally means family. In each *usroh*, every man within the network is *an ikhwan* ("brother" in Arabic). This adoption of an Arabic term reveals a great sense of camaraderie, and this brotherhood sets them apart from the other Muslims in society. Further, this greatly limited brotherhood is reinforced by its members' unique in-group language and appearance. The jihadists speak Arabic, possess their own group-speak, sport beards, and don "jihadist" garb that usually consists of a baggy top and a matching pair of pants that ends above the ankles (Jacob, 2020). This assumed fraternity simply means that the JI can have a tactical alliance with other terrorist groups. The Indonesian police, taking the lead from its elite counter-terrorism force, Detachment 88, seem to have taken lessons from this. Accordingly, the families of captured or killed JI terrorist militants often receive assistance from the governing authorities, in part to help keep the affected families on their feet, especially if the person captured or killed was a breadwinner, and in part to show that they have not been ostracised or discriminated against for the actions of one member (Jacob, 2020).

RADICAL MADRASSAHS

The radical madrassahs are useful for Jemaah Islamiyah (JI) in Southeast Asia, both for the overall JI network and for their individual attack networks. These radical madrassah networks serve multiple purposes, namely for ideological indoctrination, focal point creation, and leadership training (Magouirk & Atran, 2008). The JI employs a wide network of radical pesantren (Islamic boarding schools) to garner support, expand its membership base, and facilitate communication among its members. The most prominent pesantren in this network include Ba'asyir's Al-Mukmin pesantren (known as Ngruki) in Solo, Central Java, and the Dar Us-Syahadsih pesantren in Boyolali, Central Java. The Hidaystoillah pesantren in East Kalimantan are members of this network (Hastings, 2008).

VIOLENCE AS A METHODOLOGY

The Jemaah Islamiyah's (JI) founders are Abdullah Sungkar and Abu Bakar Ba'asyir, an Indonesian cleric who was in self-imposed exile in Malaysia. These founders were formerly members of the Darul Islam movement (Temby, 2010). The Darul Islam (DI) movement was filled with local militias that helped the indigenous authority fight the colonialists (Bruinessen, 2002). The Darul Islam sent batches of men to train with the Mujahideen along the Afghanistan-Pakistan border. The Indonesians, Malaysians, and Filipinos received military training and studied the

Salafi-Jihadism of Abdullah Yusuf Azzam (Sumpter & Franco, 2022). When Pakistan finally eradicated the camps in the early 1990s, training moved to the southern Philippines. The Afghan experience was highly significant for DI participants, strengthening their interpretations of *jihad* and developing an internationalist perspective as the men met militants from the Middle East and South Asia. This visible sense of transnational solidarity, combined with heightening tensions and differences between the DI's core leadership in Indonesia and the exiles in Malaysia regarding the concept of an Islamic state and how best to achieve it, led Sungkar and Ba'asyir to break away, establishing JI on January 1, 1993 (Bruinessen, 2002).

On January 1, 1993, the JI sought to establish an Islamic state in Indonesia by utilising violence as their main instrument (Pavlova, 2006). The JI network carried out these successive attacks: a.) the bombing of the Jakarta Stock Exchange on September 13, 2000; b.) the bombing of churches on Christmas Eve of 2000; c.) the bombing of the Australian Embassy in Indonesia on September 9, 2004; d.) a coordinated bombing attack in Bali on October 1, 2005; and e.) the twin explosions at Jakarta's JW Marriot and Ritz Carlton hotels on July 17, 2009. Their willingness to attack both domestic and foreign targets, including military targets and civilians, encompasses JI's identification of legitimate targets. Furthermore, the JI's choice of targets valuably reinforces that violence is always central to their mission to create an Islamic state. The JI has established internal funding via contributions from its members, syphoning off charity donations from corporate entities and wealthy individuals. For example, the financing for the Bali bombing attacks was facilitated through robbery and direct transfers via Hambali, who then had strong links to al-Qaeda.

BREAKAWAY FROM THE DARUL ISLAM MOVEMENT

After splitting from the Darul Islam (DI), a movement started in West Java between 1947 and 1948 by Sekarmaji Marjan (SM) Kartosuwiryo, Sungkar and Ba'asyir established the network. The objective of the DI was to liberate Indonesia from colonial rule and to replace the Republic led by President Sukarno with the *Negara Islam Indonesia* (NII), the Islamic State of Indonesia (Kippe, 2010). In 1985, Sungkar and Ba'asyir met with Abdul Rasul Sayyaf, a prominent Afghan *mujahidin* commander, during their trip to Peshawar, Pakistan. Working with the Palestinian ideologue Abdullah Azzam, Sayyaf had begun running training camps for foreigners willing to join the mujahidin in their fight against the Soviet Union. The two Indonesians maximised this opportunity to offer military training and achieve combat experience for the DI members so that they could continue their armed struggle against the Indonesian government. By 1986, the first cohort of DI cadres had arrived in Pakistan (Kippe, 2010). Approximately 10 separate groups of DI members, consisting of between 10 and 59 individuals per group, trained in Pakistan and Afghanistan from 1985 to 1991. The participants included approximately more than 200 Indonesians, including Imam Samudra, Huda bin Abdul Haq, alias "Ali Ghufron," and his brother, Ali Amrozi bin Haji Nurhasyim, who was the mastermind of the Bali bombings (Jacob, 2020).

SUNGKAR'S IDEOLOGY

Sungkar defines Muslim leaders who failed to implement *shari'*a and Islamic governance structures as '*murtad*'. He thinks that these government leaders have failed in their duty as Muslims to guide their people and ensure their physical and spiritual well-being. For example, in one sermon, Sungkar asks his listeners the rhetorical question of whether '[Suharto and his cabinet] understand *shari'a*?' or if they are 'ignorant about *shari'a*.' He responds that the distinction does not matter since '[in] either case, he is not implementing it' (Jacob, 2020).

Furthermore, Sungkar claimed that 'all legal decisions belong to God alone' and that 'worshipping God means obeying God's law'. Sungkar also strongly reinforced the notion that the only way for a leader to be legitimate, which is to be accepted by Muslims and be a practising Muslim himself, is through the implementation of *shari'a*. In subsequent sermons, he claimed that 'your leaders are actually Allah, the prophets, and the believers … those who do not submit to Allah's law are not believers', thus again excommunicating the Muslims that made up the government of Indonesia (Jacob, 2020).

Sungkar further enjoined all of his followers to be 'hostile' to the government for its failure to implement Islamic law. He expounded that the government may collapse 'unless they have the full support of Muslims'. By claiming that the government's leadership had committed a serious sin, Sungkar justified going against a Muslim regime (Jacob, 2020). Sungkar's interpretation of *takfir* emphasised the necessity of *jihad* against the government, highlighting the concept's supportive role in the structure of the group's ideology (Jacob, 2020). In the same sermon, Sungkar also condemned Muslims who supported the government, referring to them as 'fools' and 'hypocrites' for 'choosing infidel leaders' (Jacob, 2020). He exhorted that Muslims can be judged and excommunicated for any aspect of their thoughts or deeds. This specific understanding of *takfir* gave Sungkar and the DI greater scope to judge and condemn potential enemies. Sungkar's sermons also showed that he believed that minority Muslim sects were heretical and worthy of censure. In one sermon, he spent nearly 45 minutes discussing the apparent dangers of Shia ideology, claiming that its main goal is to undermine Sunni Islam (Jacob, 2020).

In one sermon, Sungkar cautioned listeners against engaging in any of the interfaith 'reconciliation' efforts (Jacob, 2020). This particular stance will shut down ways in which the DI members can co-exist peacefully with, or tolerate the presence of, non-Muslim groups in their present society (Jacob, 2020). Moreover, Sungkar encouraged the building of community among Muslims, strengthening their commitment to their faith while simultaneously withdrawing from non-Islamic practises and society. His support for the *al-walā' wa-l-barā'* served as a useful instrument to assist in the building of communal solidarity for the achievement of *hākimiyya*. Sungkar's use of *al-walā' wa-l-barā'* ensured that supporters were constantly affirming their faith by continuously rejecting and distancing themselves from the un-Islamic concepts, practises, and people in society (Jacob, 2020). This concept was an exceptional instrument for garnering support for his movement and ensuring that a pure form of Islam was adhered to by the members (Jacob, 2020).

Sungkar made use of *al-walā' wa-l-barā'* as a tool of in-group control that reinforced his followers' understanding of the world. This concept served as a powerful mobilising force, encouraging DI members to better their practise of their faith and support each other in this pursuit (Jacob, 2020). Sungkar added this concept to the group's ideological framework, widening its coverage to encompass personal beliefs and actions during a time when members were not actively engaged in armed conflict against the state. Sungkar made Islam the only legitimate basis of a Muslim's relationship with others inside and outside the faith, drawing heavily on the interpretations of Ibn Taymiyya and Wahab (Jacob, 2020).

Due to Sungkar's strong influence, the Muslims established stronger bonds amongst themselves and subsequently distanced themselves from situations or from people who were un-Islamic. This loyalty to Muslims and disavowal of the non-Muslim world would reduce the spheres in which Muslims could exist in a state of ambiguity with non-Muslims or with un-Islamic ideas and practices. This once again helped to ensure a cohesive and loyal movement but also fostered a polarised climate, in which DI supporters could not possibly accept or exist in a non-Islamic polity. Therefore, the major themes that run through Sungkar's sermons with regard to *al-walā' wa-l-barā'* can be divided into two groups; one, the requirement to actively resist the un-Islamic Indonesian Republic, and two, the serious obligation to support fellow Muslims by observing Islam correctly (Jacob, 2020).

TRAINING IN SOUTHERN PHILIPPINES

A Saudi funding shortage in 1995 forced Sungkar to relocate the Afghan training camps to the southern Philippines. The new location also featured an Indonesian community, which has the capacity to provide a reliable support structure to new recruits. In 1996, Mukhlis, an "Afghan alumnus" and a commander of the Philippine Moro Islamic Liberation Front (MILF), established a JI cell within the MILF main base at Camp Abu Bakr. The MILF and JI operated on the principle of reciprocity. This new training location empowered JI to have immediate access to weapons and explosives. It also provided all JI members with actual and live combat experience through their involvement as participants in the Mindanao conflict (Golburt, 2004). The JI's military preparation since 2012 has been comprehensive and exhaustive. It encompasses the construction of underground bunkers that are used to store weapons and ammunition. These bunkers offer refuge to militants who launch attacks. These also serve as the setting for home-made weapon factories. These locations serve as training grounds for cadres prior to deployment to Syria. (Arianti and Levenia, 2020). The JI and Abu Sayyaf Group (ASG) in Southeast Asia launched daring and bloody attacks within their own territories (Arianti, 2021).

The JI conducted five major terrorist assaults in Indonesia. The 2002 Bali nightclub bombings that JI members carried out killed 200 people, of whom 88 were Australian tourists. This attack was followed by well-executed attacks orchestrated against Western hotels and embassies between 2003 and 2005. There was a gap in attacks until 2009. However, JI revealed its strength when it attacked two U.S. hotel chains in Jakarta. JI continued its attacks on Catholic churches and priests. The JI provoked the inter-communal strife between Muslims and Christians in Sulawesi.

JI PRESENCE IN THE PHILIPPINES AND INDONESIA

JI operates in the Philippines, primarily in the Bangsamoro Autonomous Region of Muslim Mindanao (BARMM) through its linkages with the Abu Sayyaf Group (ASG). Violence in Mindanao is related to the shadow economy. These "shadow economies" led to the proliferation of illegal firearms, kidnapping for ransom crimes, the exchange of informal land markets, illicit cross-border trade, informal credit provision, and the distribution and sale of illegal drugs. The JI is one of the founders of this shadow economy (Schoofs and de Lara, 2014). The Philippine Government's passage of the Bangsamoro Organic Law in 2018 has placed the responsibility of dealing with this shadow economy on the leaders of the BARMM. The BARMM established a regional police unit that monitors and addresses the JI security threat.

In Indonesia, the Hilal al-Ahmar Society (HASI) has sent medical supplies, food, and personnel to communities. The UN Security Council designated the HASI as a terrorist organisation on March 13, 2015, pursuant to paragraphs two and four of UN Security Council Resolution (UNSCR) 2161 (2014) as being associated with Al-Qaida for "participating in the financing, planning, facilitating, preparing, or perpetrating of acts or activities by, in conjunction with, under the name of, on behalf of, or in support of", "recruiting for," and "otherwise supporting acts or activities of Jemaah Islamiyah." The JI continues to abuse charitable giving to raise and use funds to support violent acts and to provide funds for logistical requirements. The JI is responsible for numerous acts of terrorism, including the Bali bombing in 2002, which killed over 200 people from 27 countries. The HASI has supported the recruitment and travel of JI foreign terrorist fighters to Syria. The JI members were sent for military training in Syria and joined the Foreign Terrorist Fighters (FTF) there. The HASI supported the travel of JI officials, including senior JI leader Bambang Sukirno and JI operative Angga Dimas Pershada, to Syria. JI used HASI to raise funds by organising several fundraisers in Indonesia that raised tens of thousands of dollars. The JI officials encouraged followers to provide material support for the fighting in Syria. The HASI works with the Al-Nusrah Front for the People of the Levant (UNSCR 2161, 2014).

ORGANISATIONAL RESILIENCE

Para Wijayanto, who had been JI's emir (military commander) since 2009, had carefully revived JI's hierarchy through the erection of functional divisions. For example, Para instructed that each division have well-delineated areas of responsibility. Division leaders had to consistently synchronise their tasks with other divisions so as to avoid conflict as they worked in the communities. The specific divisions of JI consisted of the following aspects: *dakwah* (religious outreach); education (Forum Komunikasi Pondok Pesantren (FKPP), i.e., overseeing JI's Islamic boarding pesantren (schools); *tahjiz* (logistics); and *Al Amnu wal Istikhbaro* (ALWI) (Security and Intelligence) (Arianti, 2021). In 2016, Para further expanded JI's functional structure. Examples of these units include *Koordinasi dan Sinkronisasi (KOSIN)*, which means coordination and synchronisation. The formation of KOSIN reflects the JI's consolidation efforts through the role of mediation by the leaders in the event of the emergence of any form of internal conflict among the JI members (Arianti, 2021).

The *Tamkin* strategy stably reinforces the *Dakwah* core of JI by building up a sufficient base of support. This strategy is in addition to jihad work. The *tamkin siyasi* (political consolidation) aims to cultivate the sympathy of Indonesian Muslims by winning their hearts and minds. The JI programmes of *dakwah* through *dauroh* (sermons/religious study sessions) and pesantren (Islamic boarding schools) introduced the *naqib* (leader) programme. The aim of the *naqib* programme is to court community leaders' sympathy for the JI cause (Arianti, 2021). The *tamkin siyasi* justifies JI's active involvement in political mass protests, such as the massive rallies they launched against then Jakarta governor Basuki Tjahaja Purnama in 2016, which required collaborating and working with other like-minded Islamist groups (Hwang, 2019).

The JI leaders implemented TASTOS as a response to the arrest of multiple JI leaders and personnel after the 2002 Bali bombings. The TASTOS was approved by the JI leadership when Zarkasih assumed the *amir* position from 2005 to 2007. TASTOS identified eight security problems and their respective solutions. The TASTOS offers guidelines for JI personnel to conduct their activities safely and successfully evade arrest by law enforcement officials. One of them was the implementation of *selter*, an abbreviation of the term *sel terputus* (disconnected cells), that defines the communication chain within and across the JI's entire organisational set-up. A key element was that personnel at different hierarchical levels and divisions should not be in direct contact with one another. In addition, the JI's accountability mechanism, which included punishment and reward mechanisms, can be regarded as contributing factors that kept the JI largely unified during Para's tenure. Members are faithful to the group's guidelines and leaders' instructions. Consequently, the members were disciplined if they violated the established rules. Similarly, the members receive rewards for excellent work (Arianti, 2021).

JI HIERARCHICAL STRUCTURE

The first structure was a territorial-based model. It consisted of four regions: *Mantiqi* I (covering Singapore, Malaysia, and Southern Thailand); *Mantiqi* II (most parts of Indonesia); *Mantiqi* III [Sulawesi Island of Indonesia, East Malaysia (Sabah), and the Southern Philippines]; and *Mantiqi* IV (Papua and Australia) (Arianti, 2021). Even if the JI members do not launch an attack for a long period of time, they can still work with the large pool of trained cadres that exists outside the JI organisation with the aim of undertaking more acts of violence and terrorism (International Crisis Group, 2002).

It was in response to the multiple JI terrorist attacks that the Indonesian Government created a special police counter-terrorism force, the *Detasemen Khusus* 88, or Densus 88, which will apply the Intelligence-Led Policing (ILP) framework. The ILP contributes to the prevention and reduction of serious crime, including terrorism, organised crime, and transnational organised crime. The core framework of ILP is proactive in nature: it offers a collaborative approach to law enforcement based on information sharing and police accountability, enhanced by intelligence operations (Paripurna, 2017).. The Densus 88 has either captured or killed the group's most notorious members, such as Riduan Isamuddin, a.k.a. Hambali; the Bali bombers and their accomplices; and bomb expert Azahari Husin. The JI was responsible for the first J.W. Marriott Hotel bombing of 2003, the Australian Embassy bombing of 2004, and the second wave of Bali bombings of 2005. Due to the massive size of JI's membership, Detachment 88 continued to arrest those involved in the Tamkin Askari project. This means that JI's non-violent divisions such as dakwah and education (which oversee tasks such as sending preachers across Indonesia to build a local support base and running JI pesantren, respectively) remain intact and can persist with their recruitment activities (Sheikh, 2019). In addition, Densus 88 officers recognise that kinship has an impact on the overall success of their counter-terrorism efforts. By extending financial aid and other forms of aid to the families of JI members, the government helps reduce the JI members' possible resentment of the authorities to a low level, ultimately preventing the radicalisation of a younger generation of violent extremists.

RECURRING THREATS FROM JI TERRORISTS: DONATION BOXES, SLEEPER CELLS AND HARBOURING OF FUGITIVES

The JI continues to show its considerable presence in Indonesia by distributing donation boxes to grocery stores, funding terrorist sleeper cells, and harbouring terrorist fugitives. The Indonesian National Police revealed that the JI has deployed charity boxes at minimarkets in several regions throughout Indonesia to trick unsuspecting shoppers into giving money that would fund the group's terror activities. The police uncovered the funding operation after questioning 24 Jamaah Islamiyah members who were arrested from October to November 2020 (Jakarta Globe, December 2, 2020).

During the first quarter of 2023, the Indonesian National Police carried out a massive manhunt to find the remaining members of JI. The police arrested five JI terrorists during raids in Central Sulawesi, where they seized documents, knives, telescopes, and guns. The National Police spokesman, Inspector General Dedi Prasetyo, warned that the counterterrorism squad, Detachment 88, possesses a database of active JI sympathisers. The Indonesian law enforcement authorities stated that the JI continues to pose latent threats to national security. Police Brigadier General Ahmad Ramadhan described the current state of JI as "sleeping terror cells," which often operate under affiliate groups to disguise their numerous activities in collecting funding from the public and acquiring weapons from various suppliers (Jakarta Globe, March 27, 2023).

Indonesia's counterterrorism police, Densus 88, continues to implement comprehensive anti-terror operations against JI terrorists. On April 11, 2023, the police fatally shot two JI members, known only by their initials, BA and ZK, during a raid in Lampung, a province at the southern tip of Sumatra Island. A police officer was seriously injured in the shootout, and he was hospitalised. The police raid was part of a broader nationwide crackdown on JI, following reliable tips that the terrorist group is currently recruiting and training new members. The shadowy network is blamed for attacks in the Philippines and Indonesia, including the 2002 bombings on the Indonesian resort island of Bali that killed 202 people, mostly foreign tourists. The two men were also accused of harbouring Zulkarnaen, the JI military commander who eluded capture for 18 years. Zulkarnaen was sentenced to 15 years in prison last year after being found guilty of hiding information about the 2002 Bali bombings from authorities. The men also harboured another JI fugitive, bombmaker Upik Lawanga, who eluded capture for 16 years. Lawanga was sentenced to life in prison in 2022 for making the bombs that were used in a 2005 market attack in Poso that killed 22 people, mostly Christians. The police also arrested four JI members and seized an M-16 rifle, several handmade guns, and machetes in a separate raid in Lampung on April 12, 2023 (APSN/Associated Press, 2023).

CONCLUSION

The Jemaah Islamiyah (JI) is a well-organised and hierarchical terrorist organisation. The JI had visionary leaders who drafted a clear manifesto, established effective operational guidelines, and maintained regional cooperation with other terrorist organisations such as the Moro Islamic Liberation Front and the Al-Nusrah Front for the People of the Levant. Moreover, the JI leaders implemented a well-thought-out strategy of violence that inflicted the greatest possible social harm, primarily to Indonesia and to the surrounding countries such as Malaysia and the Philippines, which led to programmes. Its success in inflicting violence in Southeast Asia can be attributed to the strong kinship networks and marriage ties among its members. It was one of the founders of JI, Sungkar, who cemented his ideological framework within the organisation. The JI's Para Wirayanto improved the effectiveness of the JI by means of a well-thought-out structure and supporting layers of structure that can operate independently as lone wolf terrorists. Since the JI terrorists operate independently of each other, they are able to avoid detection and monitoring by law enforcement authorities in the region. Current trends in JI reflect its push for sustainability and viability by focusing on accessing terrorism funding through donation boxes, the spread of "sleeper terrorist cells," and the harbouring of terrorist fugitives who are either members or non-members of JI. Moreover, the JI invests in its strong affiliates among the terrorist organisations in Malaysia and the Philippines, subsequently spreading its methodology of violence more efficiently and effectively.

References

Abuza, Z. (2003). Funding terrorism in Southeast Asia: The financial network of Al Qaeda and Jemaah Islamiyah. *National Bureau of Research Analysis, 14*(5), 8.

Abdullah, K. (2009). Kumpulan Mujahidin Malaysia (KMM) and Jemaah Islamiyah (JI): The links. *Journal of Policing, Intelligence and Counter Terrorism, 4*(1), 43.

APSN/Associated Press. (2023, April 13). Indonesia police kill 2 suspected Jemaah Islamiyah militants. Available at https://www.asia-pacific-solidarity.net/news/2023-04-13/indonesia-police-kill-2-suspected-jemaah-islamiyah-militants.html

Arianti, V. (June 2021). Jemaah Islamiyah's hierarchical structure Jemaah Islamiyah's hierarchical structure: Security implications for Indonesia. *Counter Terrorist Trends and Analyses*, June 2021, *13*(3), 15–21. Stable URL: https://www.jstor.org/stable/10.2307/27040262.

Arianti, V., & Levenia, U. (November 2, 2020). Jemaah Islamiyah on the Brink of Splintering. *Indonesia at Melbourne*, URL: https://indonesiaatmelbourne.unimelb.edu.au/jemaah-islamiyah-on-the-brink-of-splintering

Aslam, M.M. (2009). A critical study of Kumpulan Militant Malaysia, its wider connections in the region and the Implications of Radical Islam for the Stability of Southeast Asia. unpublished PhD thesis, Victoria University of Wellington, pp. 104–105.

Bruinessen, M.V. (2002). Genealogies of Islamic Radicalism in post-Suharto Indonesia. *South East Asia Research, 10*(2), 117–154. Group Asia Report no. 92.

Chan, N. (2019, January). From Jemaah Islamiyah to Islamic state in Malaysia. In Mona Kanwal Sheikh (Ed.), *Global Jihad in Southeast Asia* (pp. 59–79). Copenhagen: Danish Institute of International Studies. https://pure.diis.dk/ws/files/3071520/DIIS_Book_Global_jihad_in_Southeast_Asia_2019_final.pdf

Golburt, Y. (2004). An in-depth look at the Jemaah Islamiyah network. *al Nakhlah online Journa*, Article 2.

Hastings, J. (2008). Geography, globalization, and terrorism: The plots of Jemaah Islamiyah. *Security Studies, 17*(3), 505–530.

Hwang, J. (2019). Dakwah before Jihad: Understanding the behaviour of Jemaah Islamiyah. *Contemporary Southeast Asia, 41*(1), 14–34.

International Crisis Group (ICG). (11 December 2002). Asia Report No. 43, Indonesia Backgrounder: How the Jemaah Islamiyah Terrorist Network Operates, last accessed 14 July 2022. Available from http://www.crisisweb.org//library/documents/report_archive/A400845_11122002.pdf.

Ismail, N. H. (2005). Familial kinship among Islamists. Bridging without Prejudice Blog. Available at http://noorhudaismail.blogspot.com/2005/11/familial-kinship-among-islamists.html

Jacob, J. (September 2020). From Kartosuwiryo to Sungkar: The evolution of Indonesia's Darul Islam movement, 1928–1993. Department of International History of the London School of Economics and Political Science for the degree of Doctor of Philosophy, London.

Jakarta Globe. (March 27, 2023). Terror Threats from Jemaah Islamiyah Remain Potent: Police.

Jakarta Globe. (December 2, 2020). Jemaah Islamiyah Uses Charity Boxes to Collect Fund for Terror Activities.

Kippe, G. (2010). *Jemaah Islamiyah: Reevaluating the most dangerous terrorist threat in Southeast Asia*. Masteral Thesis. Monterey, California, US: Naval Postgraduate School.

Magouirk, J., & Atran, S. (2008). Jemaah Islamiyah's Radical Madrassah networks. *Dynamics of Asymmetric Conflict, 1*(1), 25–41, DOI: 10.1080/17467580802016130

Ministry of Home Affairs Singapore. (2003). The Jemaah Islamiyah arrests and the threat of terrorism (White Paper). Available at https://www.mha.gov.sg/docs/librariesprovider3/default-document-library/ji-white-paper_english0eb936fc72de4ab1a0da64c798905535.pdf

Osman, S. (June 1, 2010). Jemaah Islamiyah: Of Kin and Kin. *Journal of Current Southeast Asian Affairs*.

Pavlova, E. (2006). From counter-society to counter-state: Jemaah Islamiyah. *IDSS Working Paper No. 117*.

Paripurna, A. (2017). *The use of intelligence in Indonesian counter terrorism policing*. Unpublished Dissertation. University of Washington.

Sumpter, C., & Franco, J. (15 Sep 2022). Islamist Militancy in Indonesia and the Philippines: Domestic lineage and sporadic foreign influence. *Perspective*. Available at URL: https://icct.nl/publication/islamist-militancy-in-indonesia-and-the-philippines-domestic-lineage-and-sporadic-foreign-influence/.

Sageman, M. (2004). *Understanding terror networks*. Philadelphia: University of Pennsylvania Press.

Sungkar, A. U Abdullah Sungkar 12. undated, *Internet Archive*, https://archive.org/details/audio_abdullah_sungkar/U_Abdullah_Sungkar_12.mp3, accessed: 26 January 2020.

Sungkar, A. U Abdullah Sungkar 16. undated, *Internet Archive*, https://archive.org/details/audio_abdullah_sungkar/U_Abdullah_Sungkar_16.mp3, accessed: 13 February 2020.

Schoofs, S., & Lara, Jr., F. (2014). Mindanao's shadow economies. Minimizing risks, maximizing peace dividends. *Policy Brief*. International Alert, Australian Aid.

Sheikh, M. (2019). *Global Jihad in Southeast Asia: Examining the expansion of the Islamic State and al-Qaeda*. Denmark: Danish Institute for International Studies.

Temby, Q. (2010). Imagining an Islamic State in Indonesia: From Darul Islam to Jemaah Islamiyah. *Indonesia, 1*(89), 1–36.

Voice of America. (April 23, 2023). Indonesia Police Kill 2 Suspected Jemaah Islamiyah Militants.

81

FROM REBELS TO TERRORISTS

The Future of the Maoist Insurgency in the Philippines

Dennis F. Quilala

INTRODUCTION

On December 5, 2017, Philippine President Rodrigo Duterte declared the Communist Party of the Philippines (CPP) and its armed group, the New People's Army (NPA), as terrorist organisations under Proclamation Number 374. This was a stark contrast to Duterte's declaration of a unilateral ceasefire against the CPP/NPA during his State of the Nation Address (SONA) on July 25, 2016. According to Duterte, the declaration of a unilateral ceasefire with the CPP/NPA is aimed at providing an enabling environment that will be conducive to the resumption of peace talks with the rebels. While four rounds of peace talks were held, Duterte ordered the termination of the peace negotiations with the CPP/NPA through Proclamation Number 360 on November 23, 2017. Duterte claims that the CPP/NPA was not committed to genuine and meaningful peace negotiations. He accused the CPP/NPA of engaging in violent acts against innocent people while negotiating with the government.

Government policies on the CPP/NPA vary across and within the different administrations. Like the previous administrations, the CPP/NPA and the Philippine government would hold peace negotiations, which would end with a suspension or termination of peace talks. However, Duterte's position on the CPP/NPA is different from the previous administrations because not only did he terminate the peace negotiations with the CPP/NPA, he also declared them terrorists. Moreover, he attempted to proscribe the CPP/NPA as terrorists using the *Human Security Act*. It will be the first group to be proscribed as such when approved by a Philippine Regional Trial Court.

This chapter explores the 50-year history of the armed struggle the CPP/NPA has waged against the Philippine government, arguably the longest-running Maoist insurgency in the world (Santos, 2010). It will chart its growth and decline, its resilience, and the government's responses to its armed struggle. However, the main contribution of the chapter is to document the Duterte administration's attempt to tag the CPP/NPA as a terrorist organisation and its implications for achieving peace and security in the Philippines.

HISTORICAL BACKDROP AND OVERVIEW

Using the Uppsala Conflict Database (1989–2016), it can be observed that there has been an increase in the reported armed clashes between the Philippine government and the CPP/NPA in the Benigno S. Aquino administration (2011–2016). This is the highest in the post-martial law period. This is interesting data because, according to the Armed Forces of the Philippines (Task Force Balik Loob, n.d.), the number of NPA personnel has gone down to less than 5,000 since 2011 and to less than 4,000 in 2018. There were more than 25,000 NPA insurgents in 1987 (Task Force Balik Loob, n.d.). Moreover, since 2001, when the continued decrease in NPA personnel was observed, there have been more armed clashes between the two parties compared to the mid-1990s. The reported increase in armed clashes despite the estimated decrease in NPA personnel makes the CPP/NPA an important armed group to study (Figure 81.1). Moreover, with the signing of the peace agreements by the Philippine government with the different Muslim rebel groups in the Philippines, the CPP/NPA is the only remaining internal security threat from a rebel group in the country.

The formation of the CPP/NPA is a combination of internal dynamics within an old communist party and the social ills that the CPP/NPA wants to resolve through armed struggle. The CPP was founded by Jose Maria Sison in 1968. Sison is the chief ideologue of the CPP/NPA. He used the name Amado Guerrero in writing the *Philippine Society and*

DOI: 10.4324/9780429426063-91

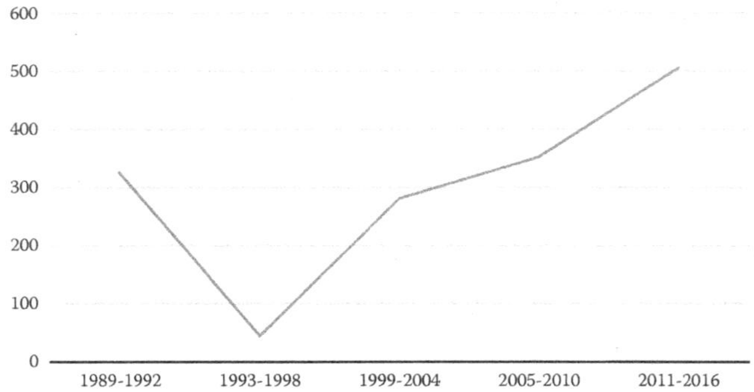

Figure 81.1 Number of Reported Armed Clashes between the Philippines Government and the CPP/NPA.

(Source: Uppsala Conflict Database, 1989–2016.)

Revolution, which is the "bible" of the communists in the Philippines. The CPP was a product of a Sison-led faction's split from the old Partido Komunista ng Pilipinas (PKP) (in English, this can be translated to the Communist Party of the Philippines as well) in 1967. The split might have been a generational conflict between the old cadres of the PKP and the young new cadres from the University of the Philippines (Nemenzo, 1982). The new cadres wanted a "truthful and critical" review of the history of the party. The young cadres led by Sison believed that this review of party history would allow the party to learn from its failures and rebuild. The idea was not amenable to the old cadres because it would reflect badly on them as decision-makers of the failing party. The faction was expelled from the PKP.

The CPP accused the PKP's leaders, the Lava brothers and Luis Taruc, of being counterrevolutionary revisionists. From their perspective, the founding of the CPP is a reestablishment of the party rather than the establishment of a new one (Guerrero, 2006). In 1967, the CPP also declared its four internationalist duties: to go against United States imperialism and its local reactionary allies; to go against revisionism and opportunism; to forge alliances with Marxist-Leninist parties; and to commit to an international united front (CPP, 1967). The CPP is envisioned to be made up of Filipino proletariats, who comprise the leading class of the Philippine Revolution. The CPP is "the most advanced embodiment and the principal instrument of the revolutionary leadership" and "the concentrated expression of the ideological, political, and organisational strength of the proletariat as a leading class" (Guerrero, 2006).

Sison and Bernabe Buscayno established the NPA in 1969. Buscayno was a member of the armed component of the PKP and, like Sison, was disillusioned with the way the communist movement was handled by the old cadres of the PKP. Buscayno wanted an agrarian revolution that would improve the lives of the farmers in the central part of Luzon (Jones, 1989). The NPA is tasked with "waging armed struggle, conducting agrarian revolution, and building revolutionary base areas" (Guerrero, 2006). According to the NPA, it will be made up mostly of peasants.

In the analysis of the CPP/NPA, the Philippines is a semifeudal and semi-colonial society. As a semi-colonial society, the Philippines is not fully independent from the United States. It continues to suffer from the imperialism of the United States. Officials of the Philippine government may be elected by the Filipinos, but its policies are still influenced by its former coloniser. Guerrero (2006) contends that "before and after the grant of nominal independence, US imperialism made sure that it would continue to control the Philippine economy, politics, culture, military, and foreign relations." Much of the criticism of the CPP/NPA of the government comes from how intimate the governmental relations are between the Philippines and the United States. Before the Philippine Senate voted against the United States military bases presence in the Philippines, the CPP/NPA used the fact that the Philippines hosted the United States military as proof of the Philippines' illusory independence. Today, the CPP/NPA criticises the Visiting Forces Agreement, which allows the continuous presence of United States military personnel in the Philippines. More than the strong United States-Philippine relations, the CPP/NPA also argues that the relations favour the United States more than the Philippines. The relationship is not between equal sovereign states.

According to the CPP/NPA, the Philippines is semifeudal because of the dominance of landlords and United States capitalists in its economy. The relationship between the local feudal lords and the American capitalists is "interactive and symbiotic" (Guerrero, 2006). Moreover, Guerrero (2006) argues that the United States has protected feudalism and the landlords "to perpetuate the poverty of the broad masses of the people, subjugate the most numerous class, which is the peasantry, and manipulate local backwardness for the purpose of having cheap labour and cheap raw materials from the country." The Philippine economy is not self-sufficient, as it relies on and produces for United States capitalism. There is also no intention to make the Philippine economy self-sufficient. The United States will benefit more from this condition than the Filipinos. The United States exports its surplus capital and products to the Philippines while exploiting cheap labour and raw materials from the Philippines. The CPP/NPA believes that an agrarian revolution is necessary to break this condition in the Philippine economy.

The CPP/NPA is waging an armed struggle because of the three basic problems of Philippine society: imperialism, feudalism, and bureaucratic capitalism (Guerrero, 2006). Using Lenin, Guerrero (2006) explains that imperialism is the last stage or the advanced stage of monopoly capitalism with the following features: "1) the concentration of production and capital has developed to such a high stage that it has created monopolies which plays a decisive role in economic life; 2) the merging of bank capital with industrial capital, and the creation on the basis of this 'finance capital,' of a financial oligarchy; 3) the export of capital as distinguished from the export of commodities acquires exceptional importance; 4) the formation of international monopoly capitalist combines which share the world among themselves; and 5) the territorial division of the whole world among the biggest capitalist powers is completed." Guerrero (2006) argues that the United States was in this last stage of capitalism when it decided to colonise the Philippines and the other Spanish colonies. In order to prevent the problems brought about by overproduction, it is important for the United States to find new markets for its products. The Philippines is one of those new markets for the United States.

The imperial hold of the United States in the Philippines continued even after the granting of Philippine independence in 1946. Guerrero (2006) explains that this was through the unequal treaties signed by the Philippine government with the United States that included the Laurel-Langley Agreement, the US-RP (Republic of the Philippines) Military Bases Agreement, the US-RP Military Assistance Pact, the Economic and Technical Cooperation Agreement, the US-RP Mutual Defence Pact, the Manila Pact, and the Agricultural Commodities Agreement. He also argues that the United States has influence not only politically but also in terms of culture, education, and the economy.

Guerrero (2006) explains that while United States imperialism dominates the Philippine economy, feudalism continues to exist. In this mode of production, he explains that the land is owned by a few landlords, while many peasants work for the landlords on those lands. The landlords earn money by demanding rent from the peasants. The landlords can protect their interests because their economic power extends to the political realm. He opines that in this relationship, the peasants are oppressed because they are often left with very little after they pay the rent to the landlords. The peasants are "further subjected to such feudal practises as usury, compulsory menial service, and various forms of tribute" (Guerrero, 2006). Spain, he says, is the one that allowed for the entrenchment of feudalism in the Philippines through the encomienda system and the compulsory cultivation of crops. The encomienda system is the royal grant of large tracts of land to individuals or groups. Spain colonised the Philippines for more than three hundred years.

Bureaucratic capitalism refers to the system in which government officials who represent the interests of the ruling classes in the Philippines and who are cooperative with the United States support the exploitation of the masses. Guerrero (2006) calls the bureaucrat capitalists "local traitors" who, through elections and their political parties, provide the people with an illusion of democracy. He argues that the bureaucrats' share of the exploitation of the people is the amount wasted through graft and corruption.

The founders of the CPP/NPA wanted to rebuild an ailing PKP, which resulted in their expulsion from the old communist party. They did not cower and instead "rebuilt" the party without the support of the old cadres. In rebuilding the party, they would do away with the revisionist and opportunist tendencies of the old cadres. According to Nemenzo (1982), this was the first time that an expelled faction fought back against the PKP, accused the old cadres of revisionism, and claimed to be the true guardians of Marxism. Moreover, in the eyes of its chief ideologue, the CPP/NPA is necessary to resolve the problems of imperialism, feudalism, and bureaucratic capitalism in the Philippines. These problems have benefited the few and left the majority of poor Filipinos oppressed and exploited. With the armed struggle waged by the CPP/NPA, the Philippines will be able to have a self-sufficient economy free of external interference and influence from landlords and "local traitors". Through a revolution, the Filipinos will truly be liberated.

There are alternative explanations for why armed groups are organised in the Philippines. In 1992, former Philippine President Fidel V. Ramos constituted the National Unification Commission (NUC) to formulate a plan for the conduct of a comprehensive peace process. The NUC conducted consultations at the national and local levels of government with different sectors and with the different armed groups in the Philippines, including the CPP/NPA. One of the outputs of the NUC report was an enumeration of the different root causes of the armed conflicts in the Philippines. The root causes of armed conflict in the Philippines are:

- Massive and abject poverty and economic inequity, particularly in the distribution of wealth and control over the resource base for livelihood,
- Poor governance, including a lack of basic social services, absenteeism of elected local officials, corruption and inefficiency in government bureaucracy, and poor implementation of laws, including those that should protect the environment,
- Injustice, abuse of those in authority and power, violation of human rights, inequity, corruption, and delays in the administration of justice
- Structural inequities in our political system, including control by an elite minority, traditional politicians, and political dynasties, and enforcement of such control through private armies.
- Exploitation and marginalisation of Indigenous Cultural Communities, including lack of respect and recognition of ancestral domain and indigenous legal and political systems (OPAPP, 2006)

The NUC report on the root causes of armed conflict in the Philippines is more comprehensive than how the CPP/NPA views the rationale of its own formation. There are commonalities like inequity, corruption, and the presence of an elite minority. However, the methodology used by the NUC makes its report more inclusive in terms of the views that were included in its consultations. It did not only account for the view of the CPP/NPA as a rebel group but also that of other stakeholders.

STRUCTURE AND STRATEGIES

The CPP, as a leading political party of the proletariat, sees itself as the successor of the Philippine Revolution that began with the revolution waged by the Filipinos against Spain in 1896 (Guerrero, 2006). It is leading a national-democratic revolution against imperialism, feudalism, and bureaucratic capitalism. According to Guerrero, the revolution is national because it seeks to fight for true national sovereignty, and it is democratic because it is for the great majority of the Filipino people. From a few of Sison's trained followers, the CPP claims to have grown to tens of thousands of cadres and members (Sison, 2018) on its 50th anniversary. It is also a national movement as compared to a movement based only in Central Luzon before.

The CPP has a function when it comes to the advancement of an ideology. It is the main instrument with which Marxism, Leninism, and Maoism will be applied to the socio-economic conditions of the Philippines. The influence of Marxist and Leninist ideas can be seen in the CPP/NPA's analysis of Philippine society and the means by which the Philippines will be carried through to a socialist society and eventually to a communist society. The CPP therefore has an important role in using ideology to lead the movement and the revolution. The importance placed by the party on the peasantry and its role in the national democratic revolution are the main contributions of Maoism to the movement.

The NPA is the armed component of the revolution. It started with 50 men with only 35 weapons (Jones, 1989) and reached more than 25,000 in the late 1980s. Although the government estimates their number to be less than 4,000 today, Sison (2018) claims that they operate in 73 of the 81 provinces of the Philippines and in 110 guerrilla fronts. While it is tasked with waging the armed struggle, its importance can be seen in organising and mobilising communities.

The other main component of the revolutionary movement led by the CPP is the national united front through the National Democratic Front (NDF). The NDF was established in 1974 as an effort to bring together different factions of the Philippine Leftist movement. The NDF is also tasked to ensure the alliance between the proletariats and the peasantry, and eventually the petty bourgeoisie. According to the NDF website, the twelve points of the NDF programme are:

- "unite the people for the overthrow of the semi-colonial and semifeudal system through a people's war and for the completion of the national democratic revolution";
- "establish a People's Democratic Republic and a democratic coalition government";
- "build the people's army and a people's defense system";
- "uphold and promote the people's democratic rights";
- "terminate all unequal relations with the United States and other foreign entities";
- "implement genuine agrarian reform, promote agricultural cooperation, raise rural production and employment through modernization of agriculture and rural industrialization and ensure agricultural sustainability";
- "break the US-big comprador-landlord dominance over the economy, carry out national industrialization and build an independent and self-reliant economy";
- "adopt a comprehensive and progressive social policy";
- "promote a national and progressive people's culture";
- "uphold the rights of the Bangsa Moro and the Cordillera peoples and other indigenous peoples to self-determination and democracy";
- "advance the revolutionary emancipation of women in all spheres"; and
- "adopt an active, independent and peaceful foreign policy".

Sison (2018) claims that with the NDF, the CPP could mobilise millions of people. He attributes the fall of former Philippine president Ferdinand E. Marcos and former Philippine president Joseph E. Estrada to the mobilisation of the NDF. One of the prominent leaders of the NDF is Horacio Morales, a former official of the Marcos administration.

The CPP/NPA is aware of the problem of compromising ideals when alliances are forged. According to Guerrero (2006), in uniting efforts with other groups, "the correct policy is to unite with it only to the extent that it supports the revolution at a given time and at the same time to criticise it appropriately for its vacillations or tendency to betray the revolution". Nemenzo (1982) observed that the NDF remains a real united front since it is still made up of mostly CPP-led mass organisations. He further argued that it would be difficult for other organisations to have meaningful participation (Nemenzo, 1982) and influence in such conditions. Today, the NDF is also tasked with handling peace negotiations with the Philippine government. Currently, the NDF has 18 member organisations, including the CPP and the NPA, and could be found in the 70 provinces of the Philippines, according to its website.

Aside from the CPP, NPA, and NDF, it is also important to know that the revolutionary movement has its supporters and sympathisers. Sison (2018) also mentions people's militias and the self-defence units of mass organisations that assist the NPA in its work. These are rich sources of cadres and personnel for the CPP/NPA. Moreover, the recruitment of members from schools and universities continues. The Philippine military estimates that the NPA has been decreasing in numbers, but the revolutionary movement is not limited to the NPA alone. The strength, therefore, of the movement is not just in its armed component.

Guerrero (2006) enumerated the five main tasks in the waging of the people's democratic revolution, namely: 1) tasks in the political field; 2) tasks in the military field; 3) tasks in the economic field; 4) tasks in the cultural field; and 5) tasks in the field of foreign relations. The main goal of these tasks is to do away with imperialism, feudalism, and bureaucratic capitalism. In the political field, the government that is controlled by the ruling classes must be overthrown and replaced by a dictatorship of all revolutionary classes under the leadership of the proletariat. In the future, there will be people's congresses at all levels of government with elected people's representatives. This could already be implemented on a revolutionary basis. In the military field, the NPA is tasked with taking political power and destroying all the armed forces of the enemies of the revolution. It should be led by the CPP, and its forms include a regular mobile force, a people's guerrilla, and a people's militia. It is also tasked with creating revolutionary bases and guerrilla zones. It is from there that the cities will be encircled and, through a protracted war, seize political power. In the economic field, members are encouraged to live simply and follow the principle of self-reliance. When the revolution is successful, the state will take over the means of production, and land will be given to the peasants. In the cultural field, the idea of national democracy and a national, scientific, and mass culture will be taught at all levels of a free educational system. In the field of international relations, the Philippines will pursue relations with other states if they recognise the sovereignty of the Philippines. There will be special relations established with other socialist states and revolutionary movements.

There have been challenges to the NPA's ability to perform its military tasks. The NPA relies on seizing weapons from the armed forces of the Philippine government. "To build up the NPA armoury, platoons and squads of the guerrilla army seized guns from government forces during raids and ambushes, and its 'sparrow' teams undertook *agaw armas* operations, grabbing guns from isolated soldiers or policemen, often killing or wounding them" (Quimpo, 2014). This would not be enough to wage a national, protracted people's war. Guerrero (2006) is aware of the importance of weapons when he borrows Mao's idea that political power grows from the barrel of a gun. Quimpo (2014) also talked about the foiled attempts of the CPP/NPA on two occasions to acquire weapons from abroad. Without the necessary weapons, it would be difficult for the CPP/NPA in the immediate future to seize power from the government. This is particularly true today when the Philippine military continues to modernise, gets training and hardware support from foreign states, including the United States, and can focus its offensives on the NPA after the signing of the peace agreement with the Moro Islamic Liberation Front in 2014.

Another issue in the NPA's military task is the early adoption of Mao's idea of establishing revolutionary bases. The NPA is tasked with establishing base areas from which they could encircle the cities. According to Nemenzo (1982), the NPA established its version of the Chinese Communist Party's Yenan in the northern part of Luzon. However, this was overtaken by the Philippine military in its campaign during the martial law period. This paved the way for the indigenisation of the concept of people's war (Nemenzo, 1982) by applying the general idea of people's war to an archipelago. Instead of one base, the revolutionary movement has many bases. The bases are supposed to be self-sufficient and politically autonomous (Nemenzo, 1982). Moreover, they continue to observe centralised leadership, where general policies are crafted by central leaders, and decentralised operations, where regional party organs have autonomy in their areas of operations (Nemenzo, 1982).

The main strategy of waging a protracted people's war is also questioned. The protracted war by the CPP/NPA has remained in the first stage of strategic defence for already five decades. At this point, it takes considerably more time to get to the stage of a strategic stalemate and a strategic offensive. Quimpo (2014) discussed some of the possible strategies considered by those in the CPP/NPA.

> In internal CPP-NPA discussions and debates, a number of cadres at the national and regional levels raised questions about the Maoist protracted people's war strategy, and advocated for shifts or adjustments in the revolutionary movement's strategic framework. Some cadres called for a shift to the Vietnamese version of protracted people's war, which had veered away from the 'primacy of armed struggle' doctrine and emphasized that both armed (or military) and political struggles were fundamental and decisive. Vietnamese people's war had also moved away from the 'encircling the cities from the countryside' framework that put primacy on rural struggle, and had called for waging revolutionary struggle in three strategic areas – hill forests, plains and cities. Other CPP-NPA cadres proposed Sandinista-style 'insurrectional strategy', which put principal emphasis on transforming the open mass movement into an insurrectional movement, with guerrilla forces playing only a supportive and secondary role. (Quimpo, 2014)

The CPP rejected these alternatives (Quimpo, 2014). In a five-decade armed struggle, these discussions and debates may not only be venues for expressing one's opinion about strategy but also cause some frustration for some who have been engaged in the movement and who know that there are other possible effective means to achieve their goals.

The NPA is weak when it comes to its military capabilities. It will remain so unless the NPA acquires the necessary weapons for it to advance into a strategic stalemate and a strategic offensive. However, the NPA is not only a military organisation but also a political organisation. Its strength is in its ability to organise people. The members of the NPA would organise areas and provide political education until they became stable areas for the NPA. In the observation of Jones (1989), "the NPA has become a significant national movement not so much by terror and killing, although these tactics are selectively employed, but by the painstaking forging of bonds with an impoverished, landless peasantry that has been ignored by a succession of governments. The rebel movement has expanded its base by addressing a number of key issues that the government has either been unwilling or unable to resolve. Agrarian reform, social services, rudimentary health care, law enforcement, justice, and other local services are being provided in an effective, if sometimes brutal, fashion by rebels." These activities of the NPA not only provide the revolutionary movement with a base from which it can conduct its activities, but they also allow for the creation of relationships that may be difficult to break. Jones (1989) has put it more eloquently when he writes, "The rebels are weaving themselves into the fabric of Philippine society, stitching together thousands of relationships and arrangements that are slowly neutralising members of the traditional economic and political elite." With these political activities of the NPA, the communities become part of the whole structure of the revolutionary movement.

GOVERNMENT RESPONSES AND DUTERTE

The Philippine government can be observed to have used both military and peacemaking approaches in resolving the protracted war waged by the CPP/NPA. In fact, this is what the government has been doing with other internal security threats (Delos Reyes et al., 2015). Delos Reyes et al. further argue that the different administrations would emphasise one more than the other, depending on the group and the priorities of the administration. In the case of the CPP/NPA, it can be observed that for the five administrations before Duterte, both approaches have been used. It would usually start with the conduct of peace negotiations but end up with the use of the military approach. The past five administrations have failed to end the communist insurgency through peace negotiations because they would usually be suspended or through the military approach, although the military has reported a continued decrease in the armed component of the insurgency. What is not clear, however, is whether the military approach is also effective in decreasing the supporters and sympathisers of the CPP/NPA.

In the inaugural State of the Nation address of Duterte in 2016, he promised the Filipino people that he would work for "permanent and lasting" peace. In the same speech, he declared a unilateral ceasefire with the CPP/NPA to show his sincerity and go back to the negotiating tables. The government peace panel was formed, and exploratory and formal talks were held. On November 23, 2017, through Proclamation No. 360, Duterte ordered the Office of the Presidential Adviser on the Peace Process and the Government Peace Panel for Talks with the CPP, NPA, and NDF to cancel all peace talks and meetings with the CPP, NPA, and NDF. Duterte accused the CPP, NPA, and NDF of insincerity and a lack of commitment to the peace process. The proclamation states that the CPP, NPA, and NDF continued to use violence against the lives and properties of civilians. Prior to these, there have been reports of NPA attacks against government forces, including the Presidential Security Group in Cotabato (Mendez, 2017). The cancellation and sometimes suspension of peace negotiations can also be observed in previous administrations. The reasons vary, but what is common is that in most cases, advancing the peace negotiations to discuss substantial issues is prevented by accusations of insecurity on both sides.

The difference in Duterte's approach is his declaration of the CPP/NPA as a terrorist organisation. Using the *Terrorism Financing Prevention and Suppression Act of 2012*, Duterte designated the CPP/NPA as a terrorist organisation. Part of Duterte's reason for designating the CPP/NPA as such is that it has already been designated as a foreign terrorist organisation by the United States since 2002. The designation is important so that the *Terrorism Financing Prevention and Suppression Act* may be applied to the CPP/NPA. However, there are limitations to this designation by the president. According to the Human Security Act of 2007, only a Philippine Regional Trial Court could designate an organisation or an individual as a terrorist group or a terrorist. Where Duterte's designation may allow the government to prevent and suppress the finances directed to or coming from the CPP/NPA, the designation may not be useful in the application of the *Human Security Act* against the CPP/NPA without the decision of a Philippine Regional Trial Court. The declaration has not prevented the military from using it against the CPP/NPA. In some of the online posts of the military, the group is called the communist terrorist group, or CTG. This is a branding issue that may affect the reputation of the CPP/NPA.

The Philippine Department of Justice has submitted a petition to the Regional Trial Court Branch 19 asking for the designation of the CPP/NPA as a terrorist organisation. The case is being pursued by Senior Assistant Prosecutor Peter Ong, who cited 12 incidents of terrorist acts committed by the CPP/NPA during the Duterte administration. Among those who have been named in the second amended petition are Jose Maria Sison, who is based in the Netherlands, and Antonio Cabanatan, who is the secretary of the Mindanao Commission. The original petition received a lot of criticism because of the listing of individuals whom the Department of Justice may have included allegedly only out of suspicion rather than based on solid evidence. From a list of more than 600 names, the petition is down to two names. If the DOJ petition is approved by the Regional Trial Court, the full force of the *Human Security Act*, which includes surveillance, can be used against the CPP/NPA.

The government has also been accused of red-tagging individuals and legal groups. One example is the red-tagging by Presidential Communications Operations Office

Undersecretary Lorraine Badoy of IBON, a think tank, in a news programme. Badoy accused the think tank of being a front organisation of the CPP/NPA (Madarang, 2020). On February 10, 2020, IBON filed an administrative complaint against Badoy and other government officials in the Office of the Ombudsman.

The Duterte administration is also taking a whole-of-nation approach against the CPP/NPA. In Executive Order 70, the Duterte administration considers the CPP/NPA armed struggle as not only a military concern but, more importantly, as a product of social, economic, and historical problems. The whole-of-nation approach would not only include a military approach against the CPP/NPA but also a harmonisation of government programmes in conflict-affected areas. A National Task Force to End Local Communist Armed Conflict was created and is headed by Duterte. Under this national task force are regional task forces, which have designated cabinet secretaries who will link the regions to the president. Provincial and municipal task forces are also created to harmonise all government programmes within their jurisdictions. The harmonisation of national and local government programmes is expected to address the root cause of the armed conflict. The national government, through the Department of Interior and Local Government, has been mobilising local governments to provide the services that are needed by communities. Partly, this is a response to the political organising that the NPA has been doing in the communities.

The Duterte administration also centralised the reintegration efforts for rebels who would surrender to the government. Duterte created Task Force *Balik-Loob* (literally return inside or Task Force Return Back to the Fold of the Law) that not only remunerates the surrender of weapons but also customises the government services required by each former rebel. This means that some would receive education packages, skills-training packages, livelihood packages, housing, or whatever else they need to live normal lives. The programme is also not only for members of the NPA but also for supporters or sympathisers who may need government assistance.

THE FUTURE OF THE MAOIST INSURGENCY IN THE PHILIPPINES

The strength of the CPP/NPA is not in the military capability of its organisation. It has failed several times to acquire the weapons necessary for it to move from a strategic defensive to a strategic stalemate. The *agaw armas* would not be enough to allow it to seize power anytime soon. However, it has created a network of supporters through its organising and political education activities. Like Jones' observation, the CPP/NPA has become an intrinsic part of some of the communities in the Philippines. They are influential in many sectors because their personnel have penetrated them. Moving forward, there might be a need to reconsider some of its strategies if it wants to further develop its military capability. The delay in its promise of revolution may cause frustration among its ranks.

The efforts of the government to use both peaceful and military means to end the armed conflict have failed. The CPP/NPA has endured and still exists after more than 50 years. If its members continue to be significant in the lives of the communities in the Philippines, it can be expected that the CPP/NPA will survive whatever effort the government plans to stop it. The Duterte administration has introduced new ways to end the communist armed conflict. If the Regional Trial Court allows the proscription of the CPP/NPA as a terrorist group, it might face a considerable challenge from a government that would be allowed to conduct surveillance and therefore acquire information that would be damaging to the movement and its members. Without the protection of anonymity, supporters, sympathisers, and funders might be discouraged from supporting the movement. If the government also becomes successful in harmonising its programmes and if they provide what the CPP/NPA are providing in the communities, then the movement may become irrelevant to its supporters in the communities.

References

Administrative Order Number 10, s. 2018

Communist Party of the Philippines (1967). Firm May Day Statement by Philippine Communists. In *People's Voice* (May 10).

delos Reyes, A., Hernandez, C., & Quilala, D. (2015). Counterterrorism and Conflict Resolution in the Philippines. Project contracted by the Japan-ASEAN Integration Fund.

Department of Peace and Conflict Research. *Uppsala Conflict Data Program (1989–2016)*.

Executive Order 70, s. 2018.

Guerrero, A. (2006). *Philippine society and revolution* (5th ed). Philippines: Aklat ng Bayan, Inc.

Human Security Act of 2007, Republic Act No. 9372, 2007

Jones, G. (1989). *Red revolution: Inside the Philippine Guerrilla movement*. Boulder: Westview Press.

Madarang, C. (2020). PCOO's Lorraine Badoy tried to red-tag a think tank on a show. Here's what happened next. In *Interaksyon.com* January 29. Retrieved from https://www.interaksyon.com/trends-spotlights/2020/01/29/160970/lorraine-badoy-ibon-foundation-the-chiefs/.

Mendez, C. (2017). NPAs ambush PSG convoy in Cotabato. In *Philstar.com* July 19. Retrieved from https://www.philstar.com/headlines/2017/07/19/1727838/npas-ambush-psg-convoy-cotabato.

National Democratic Front of the Philippines website. www.ndfp.org

Nemenzo, F. (1982). *Rectification Process in the Philippine Communist Movement: A Revised Version of a Paper prepared for the seminar-workshop on "Armed Communism in Southeast Asia*. Institute of Southeast Asian Studies Singapore.

Office of the Presidential Adviser on the Peace Process (OPAPP) (2006). *Milestones: Policy Journey to Peace*. Philippines: OPAPP.

Proclamation number 360, s. 2017

Proclamation number 374, s. 2017

Quimpo, N. (2014). Revolutionary taxation' and the logistical and strategic dilemmas of the Maoist Insurgency in the Philippines. *Journal of Asian Security and International Affairs, I* (3), 263–287.

Santos, P.V. (2010). The communist front: Protracted people's war and counter-insurgency in the Philippines (Overview). In S. Santos, and P.V. Santos (Eds). *Primed and Purposeful: Armed Groups and Human Security Efforts in the Philippines*. Switzerland: Small Arms Survey.

Sison, J.M. (2018). *Great achievements of the CPP in 50 years of waging revolution*. August 22. Retrieved from https://josemariasison.org/great-achievements-of-the-cpp-in-50-years-of-waging-revolution/.

State of the Nation Address 2016

Task Force Balik-Loob (n.d.). *Enhanced Comprehensive Local Integration Program*. [Powerpoint slides].

Terrorism Financing Prevention and Suppression Act of 2012. Republic Act 10168. 2012

INDEX

Note: Italicized and bold page numbers refer to figures and tables. Page numbers followed by "n" refer to notes.